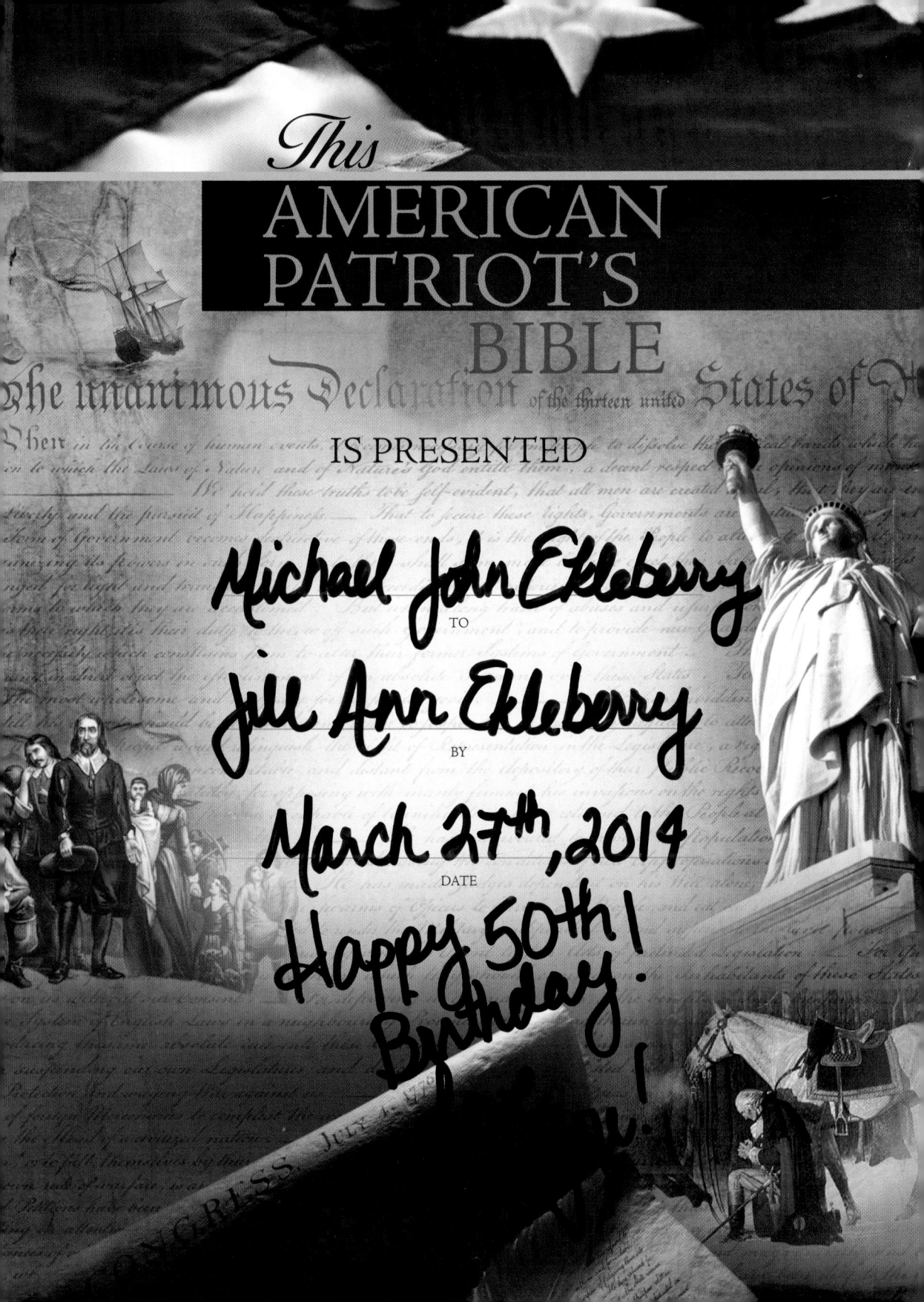

This

AMERICAN
PATRIOT'S

BIBLE

IS PRESENTED

Michael John Ekleberry

TO

Jill Ann Ekleberry

BY

March 27th, 2014

DATE

Happy 50th!
Birthday!

THIS CERTIFIES THAT

_____

and

_____

Were United in

HOLY
MATRIMONY

On the day of _____

in the Year of Our Lord _____

At _____

_____

By _____

Witness _____

Witness _____

HUSBAND'S FAMILY

GRANDFATHER

Date Born

Brothers & Sisters

GRANDMOTHER

Date Born

Brothers & Sisters

GRANDFATHER

Date Born

Brothers & Sisters

GRANDMOTHER

Date Born

Brothers & Sisters

FATHER

Date Born

Place

Brothers & Sisters

MOTHER

Date Born

Place

Brothers & Sisters

NAME

Date Born

Place

Brothers & Sisters

Our FAMILY RECORDS

WIFE'S FAMILY

GRANDFATHER

Date Born

Brothers & Sisters

GRANDMOTHER

Date Born

Brothers & Sisters

GRANDFATHER

Date Born

Brothers & Sisters

GRANDMOTHER

Date Born

Brothers & Sisters

FATHER

Date Born

Place

Brothers & Sisters

MOTHER

Date Born

Place

Brothers & Sisters

NAME

Date Born

Place

Brothers & Sisters

Our CHILDREN

NAME

Date Born

Place

Weight & Height

Hair & Eye Color

NAME

Date Born

Place

Weight & Height

Hair & Eye Color

NAME

Date Born

Place

Weight & Height

Hair & Eye Color

NAME

Date Born

Place

Weight & Height

Hair & Eye Color

NAME

Date Born

Place

Weight & Height

Hair & Eye Color

NAME

Date Born

Place

Weight & Height

Hair & Eye Color

Our FAMILY RECORDS

Our GRANDCHILDREN

NAME

Date Born

Place

Mother

Father

NAME

Date Born

Place

Mother

Father

NAME

Date Born

Place

Mother

Father

NAME

Date Born

Place

Mother

Father

NAME

Date Born

Place

Mother

Father

NAME

Date Born

Place

Mother

Father

NAME

Date Born

Place

Mother

Father

NAME

Date Born

Place

Mother

Father

NAME

Date Born

Place

Mother

Father

Church RECORD

Record significant church events in your family's history

FATHER'S PARENTS

_____

_____

_____

_____

MOTHER'S PARENTS

_____

_____

_____

_____

FATHER

_____

_____

_____

_____

MOTHER

_____

_____

_____

_____

OUR CHILDREN

_____

_____

_____

_____

OUR GRANDCHILDREN

_____

_____

_____

_____

Special FAMILY HISTORY

Record significant events in your family's history

ANCESTORS *of* INTEREST

Record immigrants, pioneers, and others who helped build our nation

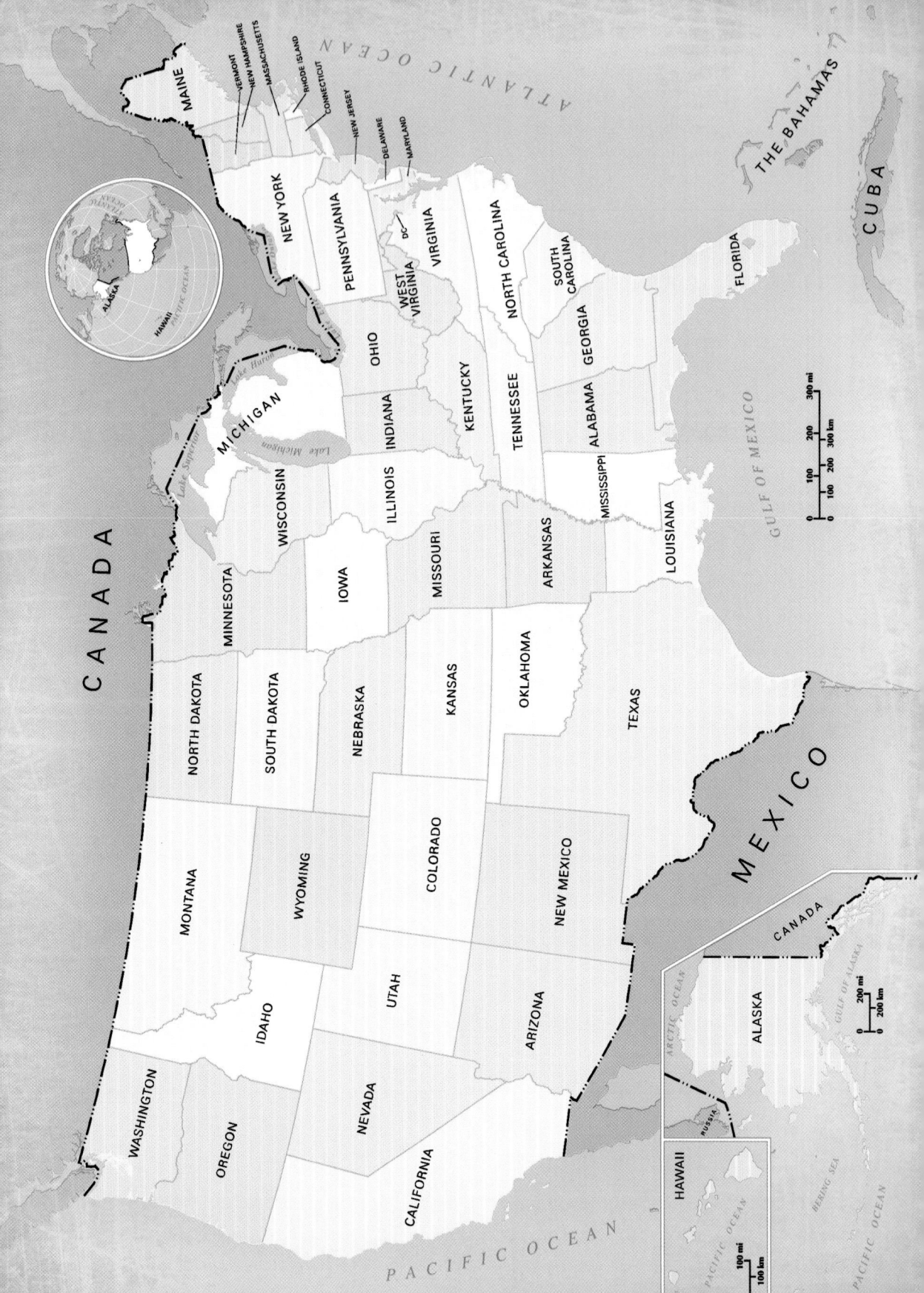

The FIFTY STATES

Order	State	Admitted	Order	State	Admitted
1st	Delaware	Dec. 7, 1787	27th	Florida	March 3, 1845
2nd	Pennsylvania	Dec. 12, 1787	28th	Texas	Dec. 29, 1845
3rd	New Jersey	Dec. 18, 1787	29th	Iowa	Dec. 28, 1846
4th	Georgia	Jan. 2, 1788	30th	Wisconsin	May 29, 1848
5th	Connecticut	Jan. 9, 1788	31st	California	Sept. 9, 1850
6th	Massachusetts	Feb. 6, 1788	32nd	Minnesota	May 11, 1858
7th	Maryland	April 28, 1788	33rd	Oregon	Feb. 14, 1859
8th	South Carolina	May 23, 1788	34th	Kansas	Jan. 29, 1861
9th	New Hampshire	June 21, 1788	35th	West Virginia	June 20, 1863
10th	Virginia	June 25, 1788	36th	Nevada	Oct. 31, 1864
11th	New York	July 26, 1788	37th	Nebraska	March 1, 1867
12th	North Carolina	Nov. 21, 1789	38th	Colorado	Aug. 1, 1876
13th	Rhode Island	May 29, 1790	39th or 40th	North Dakota	Nov. 2, 1889
14th	Vermont	March 4, 1791	39th or 40th	South Dakota	Nov. 2, 1889
15th	Kentucky	June 1, 1792	41st	Montana	Nov. 8, 1889
16th	Tennessee	June 1, 1796	42nd	Washington	Nov. 11, 1889
17th	Ohio	March 1, 1803	43rd	Idaho	July 3, 1890
18th	Louisiana	April 30, 1812	44th	Wyoming	July 10, 1890
19th	Indiana	Dec. 11, 1816	45th	Utah	Jan. 4, 1896
20th	Mississippi	Dec. 10, 1817	46th	Oklahoma	Nov. 16, 1907
21st	Illinois	Dec. 3, 1818	47th	New Mexico	Jan. 6, 1912
22nd	Alabama	Dec. 14, 1819	48th	Arizona	Feb. 14, 1912
23rd	Maine	March 15, 1820	49th	Alaska	Jan. 3, 1959
24th	Missouri	Aug. 10, 1821	50th	Hawaii	Aug. 21, 1959
25th	Arkansas	June 15, 1836			
26th	Michigan	Jan. 26., 1837			

MILITARY *and* PUBLIC SERVICE

NAME

Dates of Service

Call of action

NAME

Dates of Service

Call of action

NAME

Dates of Service

Call of action

NAME

Dates of Service

Call of action

NAME

Dates of Service

Call of action

NAME

Dates of Service

Call of action

NAME

Dates of Service

Call of action

DEATHS of FAMILY MEMBERS

NAME

Dates   Place

NAME

Dates   Place

NAME

Dates   Place

NAME

Dates   Place

NAME

Dates   Place

NAME

Dates   Place

NAME

Dates   Place

NAME

Dates   Place

NAME

Dates   Place

NAME

Dates   Place

NAME

Dates   Place

NAME

Dates   Place

NAME

Dates   Place

NAME

Dates   Place

NAME

Dates   Place

NAME

Dates   Place

NAME

Dates   Place

NAME

Dates   Place

THE SEVEN PRINCIPLES *of the* JUDEO-CHRISTIAN ETHIC

WHEN OUR NATION'S FOUNDING FATHERS gave us documents such as the Declaration of Independence, the Constitution, the Bill of Rights, and others, they had to lean upon a common understanding of law, government, social order, and morality. That understanding sprang from the common acceptance of what has come to be known as the Judeo-Christian Ethic, which is the system of the moral and social values that originates in the Old and New Testaments of the Word of God.

Whether each of the Founding Fathers was a Christian is not the issue. Their writings, their statements, and their votes evidence the fact that the majority of them embraced these great principles as the basis for a civilized nation.

Principle #1 – The Dignity *of* Human Life

The Scriptures emphatically teach the great importance of the respect and preservation of human life. In the Declaration of Independence our nation's Founding Fathers wrote that everyone has "unalienable rights," and that among these rights are "life, liberty, and the pursuit of happiness." We Americans not only believe this for *our* land, but also we send our brave military men and women around the world to defend the rights of those who are threatened.

"You shall not murder."

—Exodus 20:13

"You shall love your neighbor as yourself."

—Matthew 22:39

If people and nations do not grant ultimate respect and protection to both the born and the unborn, all other professed morals and values are meaningless. The dignity of human life is not just a principle of the Bible—it is the first principle of any civilized society.

John Hancock
President of the Second Continental Congress
Signer of the Declaration of Independence

Principle #2 – The Traditional Monogamous Family

Our society has been based upon the belief that the biblical view of traditional marriage and family is the backbone of a healthy social order. Since the joining together of Adam and Eve, marriage has been recognized as a holy union between one man and one woman, and out of that union comes children—born into a home with a father and a mother to love them, nurture them, and teach them how to become healthy, productive, and responsible citizens.

And Adam said: "This is now bone of my bones and flesh of my flesh; she shall be called Woman, because she was taken out of Man." Therefore a man shall leave his father and mother and be joined to his wife, and they shall become one flesh.

—Genesis 2:23, 24

The plan of God, nature, and common sense is a man and a woman producing children within the institution of marriage. When that plan is lost, "marriage" and "family" become meaningless, and a nation and its people will follow the road to ruin. World history has proven it over and again. Preserving the traditional family is vital to the future of any great nation.

Principle #3 – A National Work Ethic

Ingrained deep within the American spirit is the willingness and the desire to give an honest day's work for an honest day's pay. This independent spirit has no desire to simply exist on handouts from government or to depend on the generosity of others. It is this same independent spirit that has allowed America to create the greatest and strongest economy in the history of the world.

Americans have had their challenges. The Great Depression of the 1930's knocked us to our knees, but it did not beat us. Together, Americans helped one another and lifted our nation back to its economic might. The powers of the world look at our nation and ask where that spirit of honest labor came from and where this work ethic originated. It came from the men and women who lived before us. Those generations were raised to believe in this third principle of honest work, which is found throughout the Word of God.

For even when we were with you, we commanded you this: If anyone will not work, neither shall he eat.

—2 Thessalonians 3:10

Principle #4 – The Right *to a* God-Centered Education

We see in Proverbs 1:7 that "the fear of the LORD is the beginning of knowledge." How can one understand the creation without first knowing its Creator? The answer is that one cannot.

Our Forefathers certainly understood this. For example, did you know that most of America's

> *And you, fathers, do not provoke your children to wrath, but bring them up in the training and admonition of the Lord.*
>
> —Ephesians 6:4

oldest universities such as Harvard, Yale, Princeton, and Dartmouth were founded by Christian preachers or churches? Harvard University, founded in 1636, adopted "Rules and Precepts" which stated: "Let every Student be plainly instructed, and earnestly pressed to consider well, the main end of his life and studies is, to know God and Jesus Christ which is eternal life." Harvard's original seal has upon it these words: "Truth for Christ and the Church."

The early children's textbook *The New England Primer* taught the ABC's by having children memorize: "A—In Adam's fall, we sinned all. B—Heaven to find, the Bible mind." Today's youth are tomorrow's America. There is truth in the statement attributed to George Washington: "Reason and experience both forbid us to expect that national morality can prevail to the exclusion of religious principle.... It is impossible to rightly govern the world without God and the Bible."

Principle # 5 – The Abrahamic Covenant

> *Now the LORD had said to Abram: "Get out of your country, from your family and from your father's house, to a land that I will show you. I will make you a great nation; I will bless you and make your name great; and you shall be a blessing. I will bless those who bless you, and I will curse him who curses you; and in you all the families of the earth shall be blessed."*
>
> —Genesis 12:1–3

A covenant is a decision involving two individuals or groups stating that they will keep a promise or fulfill an agreement between them. The Book of Genesis records the story of God making a covenant with Abraham. The basis of that covenant was that if Abraham would follow God, obeying His laws and commandments, God would bless Abraham with generations of children that would outnumber the stars in the heavens (Gen. 15:5). Abraham believed God, obeyed his Word, and God rewarded him with many descendants, a nation of people now known as Israel.

This principle of the Abrahamic covenant states that if a person or a nation obeys God, observing the moral truths found in the Bible, that person or nation will be blessed. If they disobey, they will bring punishment upon themselves. For most of our nation's history, Americans have accepted the belief that good deeds produce good

results and that people who were "God-fearing" in language and in lifestyle would be blessed by Him. That belief has been proven to be true time and again. The writer of Proverbs tells it plainly, "Righteousness exalts a nation, but sin is a reproach to any people" (14:34).

> *Therefore know that only those who are of faith are sons of Abraham.*
> —Galatians 3:7

Principle #6 –Common Decency

Simply put, this is the belief that a decent nation is made up of decent people. That nation, when faced with any trying or difficult situation, will do the decent, right, and honest thing. And for the most part, that has been the record of our national history. For example, Americans have given their lives in wars on foreign soil so that others might experience freedom. Americans have worked to feed the world's poor, to clothe the naked, and to aid the hurting. Americans have opened their arms to many of the world's oppressed and given them safe haven.

Engraved on a bronze plaque on the base of the Statue of Liberty are these words from the poem "The New Colossus" by Emma Lazarus: "Give me your tired, your poor, your huddled masses yearning to breathe free, the wretched refuse of your teeming shore. Send these, the homeless, tempest-tost to me; I lift my lamp beside the golden door!" A world-renowned symbol of freedom, this statue stands to remind us all that America has indeed been, and continues to be today, a nation of common decency.

> *"You shall love your neighbor as yourself."*
> —Matthew 22:39

Principle #7 –Our Personal Accountability *to* God

Perhaps the greatest restraint against acts of evil toward others is the knowledge that every person and nation will one day give an account for their actions to Almighty God. Certainly the Bible tells us that we are responsible for our actions and we must be accountable for what we do or don't do. It also teaches that there is a penalty for doing wrong and a blessing when we do that which is right, noble, and just.

> *And as it is appointed for men to die once, but after this the judgment.*
> —Hebrews 9:27

The great American statesman Daniel Webster was once asked, "What is the most sobering thought that ever entered your mind?" He quickly responded, "My personal accountability to God." Webster knew that he would one day stand before God in eternity and give an account for his actions. The same applies to every man, woman, and nation.

A CALL *to* ACTION

URING SOME OF THE DARK-EST DAYS of the Civil War, President Abraham Lincoln reminded his fellow Americans that "we have been the recipients of the choicest bounties of heaven." To be born in a land of freedom, to live in a nation founded as "One Nation Under God" by those who served the one, true God of the Bible, is both a tremendous privilege and a great responsibility.

While we have much to admire and love and be thankful for in being able to call America our home, our nation is rapidly drifting from its biblical foundations. Our freedom to serve God and to promote the gospel in our land is disintegrating. We are engaged in a great spiritual battle that threatens our country, our families, and our lives. Only God's intervention will return America to solid footing and restore a moral nation that righteousness will exalt.

As believers in Jesus, we have His call to be "salt" and "light" to the world (Matt. 5:13–16). We must take seriously our responsibility to put God first, not only in our homes but also in our national affairs.

Here is a clear and honorable pathway that any generation of Americans can use to protect that which is right and change that which is wrong within our great nation:

PRAY. Our Founding Fathers knew the power and purpose of prayer. From our nation's beginning through times of war and tragedy, we have been called to pray that the hand of Almighty God might show forth His mercy and intervene with His grace toward America. Today is no different. Second Chronicles 7:14 instructs us: "... if My people who are called by My name will humble themselves, and pray and seek My face, and turn from their wicked ways, then I will hear from heaven, and will for forgive their sin and heal their land."

PROCESS. Within the God-given wisdom of our founding documents, we have been granted clear and certain processes for bringing about change concerning things that we perceive as wrong for our land. From the local municipality to the halls of Congress and the White House, imbedded in the laws and governmental processes of America are pathways for nonviolent moral, social, and political change. But first they must be learned and understood before they can be properly applied.

PARTICIPATE. Participating within the process for change is the ultimate key to its success. It is futile to gripe and complain about what one considers "wrong" or "unjust" in our land and not participate in the process of changing it for the better. The Scriptures are clear on this matter, "... to him who knows to do good and does not do it, to him it is sin" (James 4:17).

PERSEVERE. When fighting for the right, we must never cease until we prevail. The battle is not always won by the strongest, the smartest, or the most elite, but ultimately it comes to those who persist and persevere. When soon-to-be President George Washington led his troops into battle during the Revolutionary War, he lost most of those battles, but through perseverance he ultimately won the war. As a result, we won our independence from the British and became a free people. Our Lord taught us that when we put our hands to the plow of a righteous cause, we are never to look back, but to persevere and prevail (Luke 9:62).

All the resources of the Almighty God and His Word are available to us. He rules in the affairs of men, and nothing is too hard for Him. He is the sovereign King of the universe, with all power and authority, and He is compassionate, gracious, and ready to extend His love and mercy to us.

Let us bend our knees and humble our hearts and pray. Let us be willing to be used of God to help turn this great nation back to Him. Let us stand in the gap and make our lives to be salt and light in our families and neighborhoods and workplaces. God wants to come and bless us, to forgive our sins and heal our nation.

We the People

insure domestic Tranquility, provide for the common defence

and our Posterity, Ad ordain and establish this Constitution

Article

Section. 1. All legislative Powers herein granted shall be

of Representatives.

Section. 2. The House of Representatives shall be composed

in each State shall have the Qualifications requisite for Electors of the

No Person shall be a Representative who shall not have

and who shall not, when elected, be an Inhabitant of that State in wh

Representatives and direct Taxes shall be apportioned among

Numbers, which shall be determined by adding to the whole Number

not taxed, three fifths of all other Persons. The actual Enumeration

and within every subsequent Term of Ten Years, in such Manner as

The

AMERICAN
PATRIOT'S
BIBLE

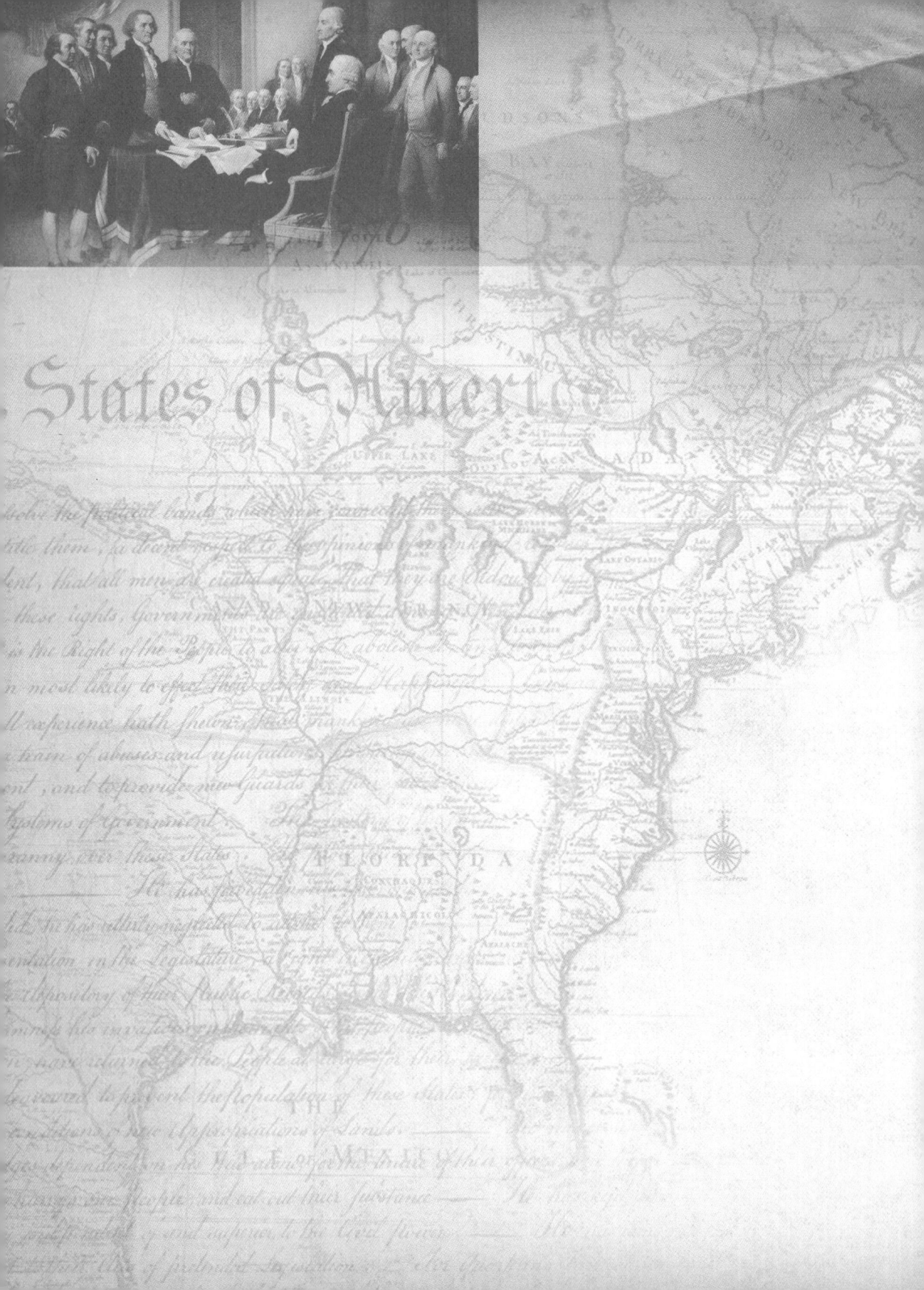

The

AMERICAN
PATRIOT'S
BIBLE

The Word of God and the Shaping of America

DR. RICHARD G. LEE | General Editor

THOMAS NELSON
Since 1798

NASHVILLE   DALLAS   MEXICO CITY   RÍO DE JANEIRO

www.ThomasNelson.com

The
AMERICAN PATRIOT'S BIBLE

FULL COLOR FEATURES

CONTENTS

INTRODUCTION

Blessed is the nation
whose God is the LORD. . . .
PSALM 33:12

*T*HE MEETING of the Second Continental Congress in May 1776 was
well underway in Philadelphia when a tall
44-year-old Virginian, Richard Henry Lee,
stood before his peers and called for the
Continental Congress to pass a resolution
declaring their separation from British rule.
This declaration would state that the American colonies would no longer be subject to
King George III and his oppressive acts of
taxation and intimidation. Yes, to those
present it seemed to be a noble action by
Lee, but little did any of the delegates realize that their actions would soon change
the course of world history.

Congress did not vote that day but enlisted Lee's fellow Virginian, Thomas Jefferson,
to draft a Declaration of Independence for
their consideration. Finally, after much
debate and several revisions, on July 4,
1776, 56 brave patriots adopted the Declaration of Independence to form a new
nation that was to become known as the
United States of America—a nation dedicated to a new and somewhat radical
proposition that all men were created
equal and endowed by their Creator with
certain inalienable rights, such as life, liberty, and the pursuit of happiness.

This new experiment of personal liberty
and human rights through representative
government was uncommon, if not
unheard of for its day. Ultimately, at great
cost, the colonies won their freedom in
1783, and the American experiment was
underway.

Naturally, many questions had to be
answered for the new nation to survive.
How would she acquire and preserve her
freedom from the British and other powers
who would seek to impose their wills upon

her? If independence was achieved, upon
what principles of law and government
would her constitution be formed? Through
what lens of understanding would she view
the world outside her own people? These
questions and many more faced these
Founding Fathers.

Fortunately, for them and for us, the
source for these answers had already been
adopted and its principles interwoven into
the charters of the 13 original colonies.
That source is the book you hold in your
hands today, the Holy Bible. It is the book
that bound colonial American society
together from Maine to Georgia.

Our seventh President, Andrew Jackson,
said concerning the Bible, *"That book, sir, is
the Rock upon which our republic rests."* Not
only was that the opinion of President Jackson, but also the sentiment of countless
Americans. On the whole, Americans are a
people who love the Bible and the God of
the Bible. There is no book more powerful
than the Bible to shape the morals and values of men and nations to be right and
noble and just. It has proven itself over and
over again in the formation and continuance of the greatest nation in history, the
United States of America.

While other nations have built their governments upon the shaky foundations of
communism, socialism, and countless
other anti-God philosophies, only to see
those foundations crumble, America stands
without equal as a beacon of hope and
freedom in a hurting world. Our Founding
Fathers delivered to us a system of government that has enjoyed unprecedented success: we are now the world's longest
ongoing constitutional republic. Well over
two hundred years under one form of government is an accomplishment unknown
among contemporary nations.

Within this special edition of *The American Patriot's Bible*, you will find a great volume of both information and inspiration
revealing the "strong cord" of the Bible's

influence that runs through the colorful fabric of our nation's past and present.

Joining with the sacred text are stories of American heroes, quotations from many of America's greatest thinkers, and beautiful illustrations that present the rich heritage and tremendous future of our nation. If you love America and the Scriptures, you will treasure this Bible.

Much effort has gone into the verification of the quotes and stories included so that the reader can be assured of the validity of that which is recorded herein. To handle the Word of God in any manner is to do so with great care and respect, and that has been done by all who have been involved in this project. May God bless the truth within these pages, and may God continue to bless America!

Dr. Richard G. Lee
There's Hope America

The notes and articles display Characteristics of the American Patriot, which can be found listed in the Subject Index starting on p. 1457.

LEADERSHIP

Then I proclaimed a fast . . . that we might humble ourselves before our God. . . .

EZRA 8:21

COURAGE

. . . and they did not love their lives to the death.

REVELATION 12:11

THIS MEMORIAL IS IN MEMORY OF THE BRAVE MEN AND WOMEN WHO GAVE THEIR LIVES TO SAVE SO MANY OTHERS

HOPE
But the path of

The Whole Hope
William Henry

T H A N K S

Deepest appreciation and gratitude to the following individuals who gave of their time and talents to bring this Bible to print:

At Thomas Nelson Publishers: Blake Aldridge, Jack Countryman, Wayne Hastings, Audrey Kidd, Maegan Roper, Bob Sanford, and Bob Sennett.

At Koechel Peterson & Associates: David Abeler, David Bohon, Andy Kaupang, David Koechel, Bridget Lindquist, Dana Long, Terry McDowell, John Peterson, Ryan Schmidt, Duff Smith, Lisa VonDeLinde, and Lance Wubbels.

Each and every one is a true American Patriot.

Preface
to the New King James Version®

The purpose of this most recent revision of the King James Version is in harmony with the purpose of the original King James scholars: "Not to make a new translation . . . but to make a good one better." The New King James Version is a continuation of the labors of the King James translators, unlocking for today's readers the spiritual treasures found especially in the Authorized Version of the Holy Bible.

While seeking to maintain the excellent *form* of the traditional English Bible, special care has also been taken to preserve the work of *precision* which is the legacy of the King James translators.

Where new translation has been necessary, the most complete representation of the original has been rendered by considering the definition and usage of the Hebrew, Aramaic, and Greek words in their contexts. This translation principle, known as *complete equivalence,* seeks to preserve accurately all of the information in the text while presenting it in good literary form.

In addition to accuracy, the translators have also sought to maintain those lyrical and devotional qualities that are so highly regarded in the King James Version. The thought flow and selection of phrases from the King James Version have been preserved wherever possible without sacrificing clarity.

The format of the New King James Version is designed to enhance the vividness, devotional quality, and usefulness of the Bible. Words or phrases in italics indicate expressions in the original language that require clarification by additional English words, as was done in the King James Version. Oblique type in the New Testament indicates a quotation from the Old Testament. Poetry is structured as verse to reflect the form and beauty of the passage in the original language. The covenant name of God was usually translated from the Hebrew as LORD or GOD, using capital letters as shown, as in the King James Version. This convention is also maintained in the New King James Version when the Old Testament is quoted in the New.

The Hebrew text used for the Old Testament is the 1967/1977 Stuttgart edition of the *Biblia Hebraica,* with frequent comparisons to the Bomberg edition of 1524-25. Ancient versions and the Dead Sea Scrolls were consulted, but the Hebrew is followed wherever possible. Significant variations, explanations, and alternate renderings are mentioned in footnotes.

The Greek text used for the New Testament is the one that was followed by the King James translators: the traditional text of the Greek-speaking churches, called the Received Text or Textus Receptus, first published in 1516. Footnotes indicate significant variants from the Textus Receptus as found in two other editions of the Greek New Testament:

(1) NU-Text: These variations generally represent the Alexandrian or Egyptian text type as found in the critical text published in the twenty-sixth edition of the Nestle-Aland Greek New Testament (N) and in the United Bible Societies' third edition (U).

(2) M-Text: These variations represent readings found in the text of the first edition of *The Greek New Testament According to the Majority Text,* which follows the consensus of the majority of surviving New Testament manuscripts.

The textual notes in the New King James Version make no evaluation, but objectively present the facts about variant readings.

THE OLD TESTAMENT

GENESIS

Author: Moses

When Written: Around 1440 B.C.

Theme: Beginnings

Key Verses: Genesis 12:2, 3—"I will make you a great nation; I will bless you and make your name great; and you shall be a blessing. I will bless those who bless you, and I will curse him who curses you; and in you all the families of the earth shall be blessed."

Key Chapter: Genesis 15—This chapter emphasizes the specific promises of the Abrahamic covenant—a covenant that is central to all Scripture. God promises to 1) give His people a great land; 2) make them a great nation; and 3) pour out a great blessing over them.

Foundations are crucial to the success of any venture, from building a house to building a nation. When the Founding Fathers set about to establish the bedrock that would define America's greatness, they went right to the source, declaring that all human beings are "endowed by their Creator with certain unalienable Rights. . . ."

Genesis contains the foundational truth that God is the source and beginning of all things and our only hope for the peace, happiness, and true liberty we all crave. In this "book of beginnings," we witness God's creation of heaven and earth through His Word, the beginnings of man's rebellion and sin, and God's calling of a covenant people through which He would bring salvation to all the peoples of the earth through His one and only Son.

GENESIS

The History of Creation

1 In the beginning God created the heavens and the earth. [2]The earth was without form, and void; and darkness *was*[a] on the face of the deep. And the Spirit of God was hovering over the face of the waters.

[3]Then God said, "Let there be light"; and there was light. [4]And God saw the light, that *it was* good; and God divided the light from the darkness. [5]God called the light Day, and the darkness He called Night. So the evening and the morning were the first day.

[6]Then God said, "Let there be a firmament in the midst of the waters, and let it divide the waters from the waters." [7]Thus God made the firmament, and divided the waters which *were* under the firmament from the waters which *were* above the firmament; and it was so. [8]And God called the firmament Heaven. So the evening and the morning were the second day.

[9]Then God said, "Let the waters under the heavens be gathered together into one place, and let the dry *land* appear"; and it was so. [10]And God called the dry *land* Earth, and the gathering together of the waters He called Seas. And God saw that *it was* good.

[11]Then God said, "Let the earth bring forth grass, the herb *that* yields seed, *and* the fruit tree *that* yields fruit according to its kind, whose seed *is* in itself, on the earth"; and it was so. [12]And the earth brought forth grass, the herb *that* yields seed according to its kind, and the tree *that* yields fruit, whose seed *is* in itself according to its kind. And God saw that *it was* good. [13]So the evening and the morning were the third day.

[14]Then God said, "Let there be lights in the firmament of the heavens to divide the day from the night; and let them be for signs and seasons, and for days and years; [15]and let them be for lights in the firmament of the heavens to give light on the earth"; and it was so. [16]Then God made two great lights: the greater light to rule the day, and the lesser light to rule the night. *He made* the stars also. [17]God set them in the firmament of the heavens to give light on the earth, [18]and to rule over the day and over the night, and to divide the light from the darkness. And God saw that *it was* good. [19]So the evening and the morning were the fourth day.

[20]Then God said, "Let the waters abound with an abundance of living creatures, and let birds fly above the earth across the face of the firmament of the heavens." [21]So God created great sea creatures and every living thing that moves, with which the waters abounded, according to their kind, and every winged bird according to its kind. And God saw that *it was* good. [22]And God blessed them, saying, "Be fruitful and multiply, and fill the waters in the seas, and let birds multiply on the earth." [23]So the evening and the morning were the fifth day.

[24]Then God said, "Let the earth bring forth the living creature according to its kind: cattle and creeping thing and beast of the earth, *each* according to its kind"; and it was so. [25]And God made the beast of the earth according to its kind, cattle according to its kind, and everything that creeps on the earth according to its kind. And God saw that *it was* good.

[26]Then God said, "Let Us make man in Our image, according to Our likeness; let them have dominion over the fish of the sea, over the birds of the air, and over the cattle, over all[a] the earth and over every creeping thing that creeps on the earth." [27]So God created man in His *own* image; in the image of God He created him; male and female He created them. [28]Then God blessed them, and God said to them, "Be fruitful and multiply; fill the earth and subdue it; have dominion over the fish of

---

1:2 [a]Words in italic type have been added for clarity. They are not found in the original Hebrew or Aramaic. **1:26** [a]Syriac reads *all the wild animals of.*

In the BEGINNING GOD. . . .

Apollo 8, the first manned mission to circle the Moon, entered lunar orbit on Christmas Eve, December 24, 1968. That evening, the three astronauts—Frank Borman, Jim Lovell, and William Anders—did a live television broadcast during the ninth lunar orbit, in which they showed pictures of the Earth and Moon seen from Apollo 8. At the time, the broadcast was the most watched TV program ever.

About six weeks before launch, a NASA official had called Borman and said, "We figure more people will be listening to your voice than that of any man in history. So we want you to say something appropriate." Appropriately, the Apollo 8 team ended the broadcast taking turns reading from the book of Genesis.

William Anders: "We are now approaching lunar sunrise and, for all the people back on Earth, the crew of Apollo 8 has a message that we would like to send to you. 'In the beginning God created the heavens and the earth. And the earth was without form, and void; and darkness was upon the face of the deep. And the Spirit of God moved upon the face of the waters. And God said, Let there be light: and there was light. And God saw the light, that it was good: and God divided the light from the darkness.'"

Jim Lovell: " 'And God called the light Day, and the darkness he called Night. And the evening and the morning were the first day. And God said, Let there be a firmament in the midst of the waters, and let it divide the waters from the waters. And God made the firmament, and divided the waters which were under the firmament from the waters which were above the firmament: and it was so. And God called the firmament Heaven. And the evening and the morning were the second day.'"

Frank Borman: " 'And God said, Let the waters under the heavens be gathered together unto one place, and let the dry land appear: and it was so. And God called the dry land Earth; and the gathering together of the waters called he Seas: and God saw that it was good.' And from the crew of Apollo 8, we close with good night, good luck, a Merry Christmas—and God bless all of you, all of you on the good Earth."

the sea, over the birds of the air, and over every living thing that moves on the earth."

²⁹And God said, "See, I have given you every herb *that* yields seed which *is* on the face of all the earth, and every tree whose fruit yields seed; to you it shall be for food. ³⁰Also, to every beast of the earth, to every bird of the air, and to everything that creeps on the earth, in which *there is* life, *I have given* every green herb for food"; and it was so. ³¹Then God saw everything that He had made, and indeed *it was* very good. So the evening and the morning were the sixth day.

2 Thus the heavens and the earth, and all the host of them, were finished. ²And on the seventh day God ended His work which He had done, and He rested on the seventh day from all His work which He had done. ³Then God blessed the seventh day and sanctified it, because in it He rested from all His work which God had created and made.

⁴This *is* the history^a of the heavens and the earth when they were created, in the day that the LORD God made the earth and the heavens, ⁵before any plant of the field was in the earth and before any herb of the field had grown. For the LORD God had not caused it to rain on the earth, and *there was* no man to till the ground; ⁶but a mist went up from the earth and watered the whole face of the ground.

⁷And the LORD God formed man *of* the dust of the ground, and breathed into his nostrils the breath of life; and man became a living being.

Life in God's Garden

⁸The LORD God planted a garden eastward in Eden, and there He put the man whom He had formed. ⁹And out of the ground the LORD God made every tree grow that is pleasant to the sight and good for food. The tree of life *was* also in the midst of the garden, and the tree of the knowledge of good and evil.

¹⁰Now a river went out of Eden to water the garden, and from there it parted and became four riverheads. ¹¹The name of the first *is* Pishon; it *is* the one which skirts the whole land of Havilah, where *there is* gold. ¹²And the gold of that land *is* good. Bdellium and the onyx stone *are* there. ¹³The name of the second river *is* Gihon; it *is* the one which goes around the whole land of Cush. ¹⁴The name of the third river *is* Hiddekel;^{a} it *is* the one which goes toward the east of Assyria. The fourth river *is* the Euphrates.

¹⁵Then the LORD God took the man and put him in the garden of Eden to tend and keep it. ¹⁶And the LORD God commanded the man, saying, "Of every tree of the garden you may freely eat; ¹⁷but of the tree of the knowledge of good and evil you shall not eat, for in the day that you eat of it you shall surely die."

¹⁸And the LORD God said, "*It is* not good that man should be alone; I will make him a helper comparable to him." ¹⁹Out of the ground the LORD God formed every beast of the field and every bird of the air, and brought *them* to Adam to see what he would call them. And whatever Adam called each living creature, that *was* its name. ²⁰So Adam gave names to all cattle, to the birds of the air, and to every beast of the field. But for Adam there was not found a helper comparable to him.

²¹And the LORD God caused a deep sleep to fall on Adam, and he slept; and He took one of his ribs, and closed up the flesh in its place. ²²Then the rib which the LORD God had taken from man He made into a woman, and He brought her to the man.

²³And Adam said:

> "This *is* now bone of my bones
> And flesh of my flesh;
> She shall be called Woman,
> Because she was taken out of Man."

²⁴Therefore a man shall leave his father and mother and be joined to his wife, and they shall become one flesh.

²⁵And they were both naked, the man and his wife, and were not ashamed.

2:4 ^{a}Hebrew *toledoth,* literally *generations*
2:14 ^{a}Or *Tigris*

The Temptation and Fall of Man

3 Now the serpent was more cunning than any beast of the field which the LORD God had made. And he said to the woman, "Has God indeed said, 'You shall not eat of every tree of the garden'?"

²And the woman said to the serpent, "We may eat the fruit of the trees of the garden; ³but of the fruit of the tree which *is* in the midst of the garden, God has said, 'You shall not eat it, nor shall you touch it, lest you die.'"

⁴Then the serpent said to the woman, "You will not surely die. ⁵For God knows that in the day you eat of it your eyes will be opened, and you will be like God, knowing good and evil."

⁶So when the woman saw that the tree *was* good for food, that it *was* pleasant to the eyes, and a tree desirable to make *one* wise, she took of its fruit and ate. She also gave to her husband with her, and he ate. ⁷Then the eyes of both of them were opened, and they knew that they *were* naked; and they sewed fig leaves together and made themselves coverings.

⁸And they heard the sound of the LORD God walking in the garden in the cool of the day, and Adam and his wife hid themselves from the presence of the LORD God among the trees of the garden.

⁹Then the LORD God called to Adam and said to him, "Where *are* you?"

¹⁰So he said, "I heard Your voice in the garden, and I was afraid because I was naked; and I hid myself."

¹¹And He said, "Who told you that you *were* naked? Have you eaten from the tree of which I commanded you that you should not eat?"

¹²Then the man said, "The woman whom You gave *to be* with me, she gave me of the tree, and I ate."

¹³And the LORD God said to the woman, "What *is* this you have done?"

The woman said, "The serpent deceived me, and I ate."

¹⁴So the LORD God said to the serpent:

"Because you have done this,
　You *are* cursed more than all cattle,

And more than every beast of the
　field;
On your belly you shall go,
And you shall eat dust
All the days of your life.
15　And I will put enmity
Between you and the woman,
And between your seed and her
　Seed;
He shall bruise your head,
And you shall bruise His heel."

¹⁶To the woman He said:

"I will greatly multiply your sorrow
　and your conception;
In pain you shall bring forth
　children;
Your desire *shall be* for your husband,
And he shall rule over you."

¹⁷Then to Adam He said, "Because you have heeded the voice of your wife, and have eaten from the tree of which I commanded you, saying, 'You shall not eat of it':

"Cursed *is* the ground for your sake;
　In toil you shall eat *of* it
　All the days of your life.
18　Both thorns and thistles it shall bring
　　forth for you,
And you shall eat the herb of the
　field.
19　In the sweat of your face you shall eat
　　bread
Till you return to the ground,
For out of it you were taken;
For dust you *are*,
And to dust you shall return."

²⁰And Adam called his wife's name Eve, because she was the mother of all living.

²¹Also for Adam and his wife the LORD God made tunics of skin, and clothed them.

²²Then the LORD God said, "Behold, the man has become like one of Us, to know good and evil. And now, lest he put out his hand and take also of the tree of life, and eat, and live forever"— ²³therefore the LORD God sent him out of the garden of Eden to till the ground from which he was

"THE BATTLE HYMN OF THE REPUBLIC"

JULIA WARD HOWE

In November 1861, after a visit to a Union Army camp, Julia Ward Howe wrote the poem that came to be called "The Battle Hymn of the Republic." It became the best-known Civil War song of the Union Army as well as a well-loved American patriotic anthem.

Mine eyes have seen the glory of the coming of the Lord:
He is trampling out the vintage where the grapes of wrath are stored;
He hath loosed the fateful lightning of His terrible swift sword:
His truth is marching on.

I have seen Him in the watch-fires of a hundred circling camps,
They have builded Him an altar in the evening dews and damps;
I can read His righteous sentence by the dim and flaring lamps:
His day is marching on.

I have read a fiery gospel writ in burnished rows of steel:
"As ye deal with my contemners, so with you my grace shall deal;
Let the Hero, born of woman, crush the serpent with His heel,
Since God is marching on."

He has sounded forth the trumpet that shall never call retreat;
He is sifting out the hearts of men before His judgment-seat:
Oh, be swift, my soul, to answer Him! be jubilant, my feet!
Our God is marching on.

In the beauty of the lilies Christ was born across the sea,
With a glory in His bosom that transfigures you and me:
As He died to make men holy, let us die to make men free,
While God is marching on.

taken. [24]So He drove out the man; and He placed cherubim at the east of the garden of Eden, and a flaming sword which turned every way, to guard the way to the tree of life.

Cain Murders Abel

4 Now Adam knew Eve his wife, and she conceived and bore Cain, and said, "I have acquired a man from the LORD." [2]Then she bore again, this time his brother Abel. Now Abel was a keeper of sheep, but Cain was a tiller of the ground. [3]And in the process of time it came to pass that Cain brought an offering of the fruit of the ground to the LORD. [4]Abel also brought of the firstborn of his flock and of their fat. And the LORD respected Abel and his offering, [5]but He did not respect Cain and his offering. And Cain was very angry, and his countenance fell.

[6]So the LORD said to Cain, "Why are you angry? And why has your countenance fallen? [7]If you do well, will you not be accepted? And if you do not do well, sin lies at the door. And its desire *is* for you, but you should rule over it."

[8]Now Cain talked with Abel his brother;[a] and it came to pass, when they were in the field, that Cain rose up against Abel his brother and killed him.

[9]Then the LORD said to Cain, "Where *is* Abel your brother?"

He said, "I do not know. *Am* I my brother's keeper?"

[10]And He said, "What have you done? The voice of your brother's blood cries out to Me from the ground. [11]So now you *are* cursed from the earth, which has opened its mouth to receive your brother's blood from your hand. [12]When you till the ground, it shall no longer yield its strength to you. A fugitive and a vagabond you shall be on the earth."

[13]And Cain said to the LORD, "My punishment *is* greater than I can bear! [14]Surely You have driven me out this day from the face of the ground; I shall be hidden from Your face; I shall be a fugitive and a vagabond on the earth, and it will happen *that* anyone who finds me will kill me."

[15]And the LORD said to him, "Therefore,[a] whoever kills Cain, vengeance shall be taken on him sevenfold." And the LORD set a mark on Cain, lest anyone finding him should kill him.

The Family of Cain

[16]Then Cain went out from the presence of the LORD and dwelt in the land of Nod on the east of Eden. [17]And Cain knew his wife, and she conceived and bore Enoch. And he built a city, and called the name of the city after the name of his son—Enoch. [18]To Enoch was born Irad; and Irad begot Mehujael, and Mehujael begot Methushael, and Methushael begot Lamech.

[19]Then Lamech took for himself two wives: the name of one *was* Adah, and the name of the second *was* Zillah. [20]And Adah bore Jabal. He was the father of those who dwell in tents and have livestock. [21]His brother's name *was* Jubal. He was the father of all those who play the harp and flute. [22]And as for Zillah, she also bore Tubal-Cain, an instructor of every craftsman in bronze and iron. And the sister of Tubal-Cain *was* Naamah.

[23]Then Lamech said to his wives:

> "Adah and Zillah, hear my voice;
>   Wives of Lamech, listen to my speech!
> For I have killed a man for wounding me,
>   Even a young man for hurting me.
> [24] If Cain shall be avenged sevenfold,
>   Then Lamech seventy-sevenfold."

A New Son

[25]And Adam knew his wife again, and she bore a son and named him Seth, "For God has appointed another seed for me instead of Abel, whom Cain killed." [26]And as for Seth, to him also a son was born; and he named him Enosh.[a] Then *men* began to call on the name of the LORD.

4:8 [a]Samaritan Pentateuch, Septuagint, Syriac, and Vulgate add *"Let us go out to the field."*
4:15 [a]Following Masoretic Text and Targum; Septuagint, Syriac, and Vulgate read *Not so.*
4:26 [a]Greek *Enos*

The Family of Adam

5 This is the book of the genealogy of Adam. In the day that God created man, He made him in the likeness of God. ²He created them male and female, and blessed them and called them Mankind in the day they were created. ³And Adam lived one hundred and thirty years, and begot *a son* in his own likeness, after his image, and named him Seth. ⁴After he begot Seth, the days of Adam were eight hundred years; and he had sons and daughters. ⁵So all the days that Adam lived were nine hundred and thirty years; and he died.

⁶Seth lived one hundred and five years, and begot Enosh. ⁷After he begot Enosh, Seth lived eight hundred and seven years, and had sons and daughters. ⁸So all the days of Seth were nine hundred and twelve years; and he died.

⁹Enosh lived ninety years, and begot Cainan.ᵃ ¹⁰After he begot Cainan, Enosh lived eight hundred and fifteen years, and had sons and daughters. ¹¹So all the days of Enosh were nine hundred and five years; and he died.

¹²Cainan lived seventy years, and begot Mahalalel. ¹³After he begot Mahalalel, Cainan lived eight hundred and forty years, and had sons and daughters. ¹⁴So all the days of Cainan were nine hundred and ten years; and he died.

¹⁵Mahalalel lived sixty-five years, and begot Jared. ¹⁶After he begot Jared, Mahalalel lived eight hundred and thirty years, and had sons and daughters. ¹⁷So all the days of Mahalalel were eight hundred and ninety-five years; and he died.

¹⁸Jared lived one hundred and sixty-two years, and begot Enoch. ¹⁹After he begot Enoch, Jared lived eight hundred years, and had sons and daughters. ²⁰So all the days of Jared were nine hundred and sixty-two years; and he died.

²¹Enoch lived sixty-five years, and begot Methuselah. ²²After he begot Methuselah, Enoch walked with God three hundred years, and had sons and daughters. ²³So all the days of Enoch were three hundred and sixty-five years. ²⁴And Enoch walked with God; and he *was* not, for God took him.

²⁵Methuselah lived one hundred and eighty-seven years, and begot Lamech. ²⁶After he begot Lamech, Methuselah lived seven hundred and eighty-two years, and had sons and daughters. ²⁷So all the days of Methuselah were nine hundred and sixty-nine years; and he died.

²⁸Lamech lived one hundred and eighty-two years, and had a son. ²⁹And he called his name Noah, saying, "This *one* will comfort us concerning our work and the toil of our hands, because of the ground which the Lord has cursed." ³⁰After he begot Noah, Lamech lived five hundred and ninety-five years, and had sons and daughters. ³¹So all the days of Lamech were seven hundred and seventy-seven years; and he died.

³²And Noah was five hundred years old, and Noah begot Shem, Ham, and Japheth.

The Wickedness and Judgment of Man

6 Now it came to pass, when men began to multiply on the face of the earth, and daughters were born to them, ²that the sons of God saw the daughters of men, that they *were* beautiful; and they took wives for themselves of all whom they chose.

³And the Lord said, "My Spirit shall not striveᵃ with man forever, for he *is* indeed flesh; yet his days shall be one hundred and twenty years." ⁴There were giants on the earth in those days, and also afterward, when the sons of God came in to the daughters of men and they bore *children* to them. Those *were* the mighty men who *were* of old, men of renown.

⁵Then the Lordᵃ saw that the wickedness of man *was* great in the earth, and *that* every intent of the thoughts of his heart *was* only evil continually. ⁶And the Lord was sorry that He had made man on the earth, and He was grieved in His heart. ⁷So the Lord said, "I will destroy man whom I have created from the face of the earth, both man and beast, creeping thing and

---

5:9 ᵃHebrew *Qenan*   **6:3** ᵃSeptuagint, Syriac, Targum, and Vulgate read *abide.*   **6:5** ᵃFollowing Masoretic Text and Targum; Vulgate reads *God;* Septuagint reads Lord *God.*

birds of the air, for I am sorry that I have made them." ⁸But Noah found grace in the eyes of the LORD.

Noah Pleases God

⁹This is the genealogy of Noah. Noah was a just man, perfect in his generations. Noah walked with God. ¹⁰And Noah begot three sons: Shem, Ham, and Japheth.

¹¹The earth also was corrupt before God, and the earth was filled with violence. ¹²So God looked upon the earth, and indeed it was corrupt; for all flesh had corrupted their way on the earth.

The Ark Prepared

¹³And God said to Noah, "The end of all flesh has come before Me, for the earth is filled with violence through them; and behold, I will destroy them with the earth. ¹⁴Make yourself an ark of gopherwood; make rooms in the ark, and cover it inside and outside with pitch. ¹⁵And this is how you shall make it: The length of the ark *shall be* three hundred cubits, its width fifty cubits, and its height thirty cubits. ¹⁶You shall make a window for the ark, and you shall finish it to a cubit from above; and set the door of the ark in its side. You shall make it *with* lower, second, and third *decks*. ¹⁷And behold, I Myself am bringing floodwaters on the earth, to destroy from under heaven all flesh in which *is* the breath of life; everything that *is* on the earth shall die. ¹⁸But I will establish My covenant with you; and you shall go into the ark—you, your sons, your wife, and your sons' wives with you. ¹⁹And of every living thing of all flesh you shall bring two of every *sort* into the ark, to keep *them* alive with you; they shall be male and female. ²⁰Of the birds after their kind, of animals after their kind, and of every creeping thing of the earth after its kind, two of every *kind* will come to you to keep *them* alive. ²¹And you shall take for yourself of all food that is eaten, and you shall gather *it* to yourself; and it shall be food for you and for them."

²²Thus Noah did; according to all that God commanded him, so he did.

The Great Flood

7 Then the LORD said to Noah, "Come into the ark, you and all your household, because I have seen *that* you *are* righteous before Me in this generation. ²You shall take with you seven each of every clean animal, a male and his female; two each of animals that *are* unclean, a male and his female; ³also seven each of birds of the air, male and female, to keep the species alive on the face of all the earth. ⁴For after seven more days I will cause it to rain on the earth forty days and forty nights, and I will destroy from the face of the earth all living things that I have made." ⁵And Noah did according to all that the LORD commanded him. ⁶Noah *was* six hundred years old when the floodwaters were on the earth.

⁷So Noah, with his sons, his wife, and his sons' wives, went into the ark because of the waters of the flood. ⁸Of clean animals, of animals that *are* unclean, of birds, and of everything that creeps on the earth, ⁹two by two they went into the ark to Noah, male and female, as God had commanded Noah. ¹⁰And it came to pass after seven days that the waters of the flood were on the earth. ¹¹In the six hundredth year of Noah's life, in the second month, the seventeenth day of the month, on that day all the fountains of the great deep were broken up, and the windows of heaven were opened. ¹²And the rain was on the earth forty days and forty nights.

¹³On the very same day Noah and Noah's sons, Shem, Ham, and Japheth, and Noah's wife and the three wives of his sons with them, entered the ark— ¹⁴they and every beast after its kind, all cattle after their kind, every creeping thing that creeps on the earth after its kind, and every bird after its kind, every bird of every sort. ¹⁵And they went into the ark to Noah, two by two, of all flesh in which *is* the breath of life. ¹⁶So those that entered, male and female of all flesh, went in as God had commanded him; and the LORD shut him in.

¹⁷Now the flood was on the earth forty days. The waters increased and lifted up the ark, and it rose high above the earth.

18The waters prevailed and greatly increased on the earth, and the ark moved about on the surface of the waters. 19And the waters prevailed exceedingly on the earth, and all the high hills under the whole heaven were covered. 20The waters prevailed fifteen cubits upward, and the mountains were covered. 21And all flesh died that moved on the earth: birds and cattle and beasts and every creeping thing that creeps on the earth, and every man. 22All in whose nostrils *was* the breath of the spirita of life, all that *was* on the dry *land,* died. 23So He destroyed all living things which were on the face of the ground: both man and cattle, creeping thing and bird of the air. They were destroyed from the earth. Only Noah and those who *were* with him in the ark remained *alive.* 24And the waters prevailed on the earth one hundred and fifty days.

Noah's Deliverance

8 Then God remembered Noah, and every living thing, and all the animals that *were* with him in the ark. And God made a wind to pass over the earth, and the waters subsided. 2The fountains of the deep and the windows of heaven were also stopped, and the rain from heaven was restrained. 3And the waters receded continually from the earth. At the end of the hundred and fifty days the waters decreased. 4Then the ark rested in the seventh month, the seventeenth day of the month, on the mountains of Ararat. 5And the waters decreased continually until the tenth month. In the tenth *month,* on the first *day* of the month, the tops of the mountains were seen.

6So it came to pass, at the end of forty days, that Noah opened the window of the ark which he had made. 7Then he sent out a raven, which kept going to and fro until the waters had dried up from the earth. 8He also sent out from himself a dove, to see if the waters had receded from the face of the ground. 9But the dove found no resting place for the sole of her foot, and she returned into the ark to him, for the waters *were* on the face of the whole earth. So he put out his hand and took her, and drew her into the ark to himself. 10And he waited yet another seven days, and again he sent the dove out from the ark. 11Then the dove came to him in the evening, and behold, a freshly plucked olive leaf *was* in her mouth; and Noah knew that the waters had receded from the earth. 12So he waited yet another seven days and sent out the dove, which did not return again to him anymore.

13And it came to pass in the six hundred and first year, in the first *month,* the first *day* of the month, that the waters were dried up from the earth; and Noah removed the covering of the ark and looked, and indeed the surface of the ground was dry. 14And in the second month, on the twenty-seventh day of the month, the earth was dried.

15Then God spoke to Noah, saying, 16"Go out of the ark, you and your wife, and your sons and your sons' wives with you. 17Bring out with you every living thing of all flesh that *is* with you: birds and cattle and every creeping thing that creeps on the earth, so that they may abound on the earth, and be fruitful and multiply on the earth." 18So Noah went out, and his sons and his wife and his sons' wives with him. 19Every animal, every creeping thing, every bird, *and* whatever creeps on the earth, according to their families, went out of the ark.

God's Covenant with Creation

20Then Noah built an altar to the LORD, and took of every clean animal and of every clean bird, and offered burnt offerings on the altar. 21And the LORD smelled a soothing aroma. Then the LORD said in His heart, "I will never again curse the ground for man's sake, although the imagination of man's heart *is* evil from his youth; nor will I again destroy every living thing as I have done.

22 "While the earth remains,
   Seedtime and harvest,
   Cold and heat,
   Winter and summer,
   And day and night
   Shall not cease."

7:22 aSeptuagint and Vulgate omit *of the spirit.*

9 So God blessed Noah and his sons, and said to them: "Be fruitful and multiply, and fill the earth.ª ²And the fear of you and the dread of you shall be on every beast of the earth, on every bird of the air, on all that move *on* the earth, and on all the fish of the sea. They are given into your hand. ³Every moving thing that lives shall be food for you. I have given you all things, even as the green herbs. ⁴But you shall not eat flesh with its life, *that is,* its blood. ⁵Surely for your lifeblood I will demand *a reckoning;* from the hand of every beast I will require it, and from the hand of man. From the hand of every man's brother I will require the life of man.

6   "Whoever sheds man's blood,
       By man his blood shall be shed;
       For in the image of God
       He made man.
7   And as for you, be fruitful and
           multiply;
       Bring forth abundantly in the earth
       And multiply in it."

⁸Then God spoke to Noah and to his sons with him, saying: ⁹"And as for Me, behold, I establish My covenant with you and with your descendantsª after you, ¹⁰and with every living creature that *is* with you: the birds, the cattle, and every beast of the earth with you, of all that go out of the ark, every beast of the earth. ¹¹Thus I establish My covenant with you: Never again shall all flesh be cut off by the waters of the flood; never again shall there be a flood to destroy the earth." ¹²And God said: "This *is* the sign of the covenant which I make between Me and you, and every living creature that *is* with you, for perpetual generations: ¹³I set My rainbow in the cloud, and it shall be for the sign of the covenant between Me and the earth. ¹⁴It shall be, when I bring a cloud over the earth, that the rainbow shall be seen in the cloud; ¹⁵and I will remember My covenant which *is* between Me and you and every living creature of all flesh; the waters shall never again become a flood to destroy all flesh. ¹⁶The rainbow shall be in the cloud, and I will look on it to remember the everlasting covenant between God and every living creature of all flesh that *is* on the earth." ¹⁷And God said to Noah, "This *is* the sign of the covenant which I have established between Me and all flesh that *is* on the earth."

Noah and His Sons

¹⁸Now the sons of Noah who went out of the ark were Shem, Ham, and Japheth. And Ham *was* the father of Canaan. ¹⁹These three *were* the sons of Noah, and from these the whole earth was populated.

²⁰And Noah began *to be* a farmer, and he planted a vineyard. ²¹Then he drank of the wine and was drunk, and became uncovered in his tent. ²²And Ham, the father of Canaan, saw the nakedness of his father, and told his two brothers outside. ²³But Shem and Japheth took a garment, laid *it* on both their shoulders, and went backward and covered the nakedness of their father. Their faces *were* turned away, and they did not see their father's nakedness.

²⁴So Noah awoke from his wine, and knew what his younger son had done to him. ²⁵Then he said:

   "Cursed *be* Canaan;
       A servant of servants
       He shall be to his brethren."

²⁶And he said:

   "Blessed *be* the LORD,
       The God of Shem,
       And may Canaan be his servant.
27   May God enlarge Japheth,
       And may he dwell in the tents of
           Shem;
       And may Canaan be his servant."

²⁸And Noah lived after the flood three hundred and fifty years. ²⁹So all the days of Noah were nine hundred and fifty years; and he died.

9:1 ªCompare Genesis 1:28   **9:9** ªLiterally *seed*

Nations Descended from Noah

10 Now this *is* the genealogy of the sons of Noah: Shem, Ham, and Japheth. And sons were born to them after the flood.

²The sons of Japheth *were* Gomer, Magog, Madai, Javan, Tubal, Meshech, and Tiras. ³The sons of Gomer *were* Ashkenaz, Riphath,ᵃ and Togarmah. ⁴The sons of Javan *were* Elishah, Tarshish, Kittim, and Dodanim.ᵃ ⁵From these the coastland *peoples* of the Gentiles were separated into their lands, everyone according to his language, according to their families, into their nations.

⁶The sons of Ham *were* Cush, Mizraim, Put,ᵃ and Canaan. ⁷The sons of Cush *were* Seba, Havilah, Sabtah, Raamah, and Sabtechah; and the sons of Raamah *were* Sheba and Dedan.

⁸Cush begot Nimrod; he began to be a mighty one on the earth. ⁹He was a mighty hunter before the Lᴏʀᴅ; therefore it is said, "Like Nimrod the mighty hunter before the Lᴏʀᴅ." ¹⁰And the beginning of his kingdom was Babel, Erech, Accad, and Calneh, in the land of Shinar. ¹¹From that land he went to Assyria and built Nineveh, Rehoboth Ir, Calah, ¹²and Resen between Nineveh and Calah (that *is* the principal city).

¹³Mizraim begot Ludim, Anamim, Lehabim, Naphtuhim, ¹⁴Pathrusim, and Casluhim (from whom came the Philistines and Caphtorim).

¹⁵Canaan begot Sidon his firstborn, and Heth; ¹⁶the Jebusite, the Amorite, and the Girgashite; ¹⁷the Hivite, the Arkite, and the Sinite; ¹⁸the Arvadite, the Zemarite, and the Hamathite. Afterward the families of the Canaanites were dispersed. ¹⁹And the border of the Canaanites was from Sidon as you go toward Gerar, as far as Gaza; then as you go toward Sodom, Gomorrah, Admah, and Zeboiim, as far as Lasha. ²⁰These *were* the sons of Ham, according to their families, according to their languages, in their lands *and* in their nations.

²¹And *children* were born also to Shem, the father of all the children of Eber, the brother of Japheth the elder. ²²The sons of Shem *were* Elam, Asshur, Arphaxad, Lud, and Aram. ²³The sons of Aram *were* Uz, Hul, Gether, and Mash.ᵃ ²⁴Arphaxad begot Salah,ᵃ and Salah begot Eber. ²⁵To Eber were born two sons: the name of one *was* Peleg, for in his days the earth was divided; and his brother's name *was* Joktan. ²⁶Joktan begot Almodad, Sheleph, Hazarmaveth, Jerah, ²⁷Hadoram, Uzal, Diklah, ²⁸Obal,ᵃ Abimael, Sheba, ²⁹Ophir, Havilah, and Jobab. All these *were* the sons of Joktan. ³⁰And their dwelling place was from Mesha as you go toward Sephar, the mountain of the east. ³¹These *were* the sons of Shem, according to their families, according to their languages, in their lands, according to their nations.

³²These *were* the families of the sons of Noah, according to their generations, in their nations; and from these the nations were divided on the earth after the flood.

The Tower of Babel

11 Now the whole earth had one language and one speech. ²And it came to pass, as they journeyed from the east, that they found a plain in the land of Shinar, and they dwelt there. ³Then they said to one another, "Come, let us make bricks and bake *them* thoroughly." They had brick for stone, and they had asphalt for mortar. ⁴And they said, "Come, let us build ourselves a city, and a tower whose top *is* in the heavens; let us make a name for ourselves, lest we be scattered abroad over the face of the whole earth."

⁵But the Lᴏʀᴅ came down to see the city and the tower which the sons of men had built. ⁶And the Lᴏʀᴅ said, "Indeed the people *are* one and they all have one language, and this is what they begin to do; now nothing that they propose to do will be withheld from them. ⁷Come, let Us go down and there confuse their language, that they may not understand one another's speech." ⁸So the Lᴏʀᴅ scattered them

---

10:3 ᵃSpelled *Diphath* in 1 Chronicles 1:6
10:4 ᵃSpelled *Rodanim* in Samaritan Pentateuch and 1 Chronicles 1:7   **10:6** ᵃOr *Phut*   **10:23** ᵃCalled *Meshech* in Septuagint and 1 Chronicles 1:17
10:24 ᵃFollowing Masoretic Text, Vulgate, and Targum; Septuagint reads *Arphaxad begot Cainan, and Cainan begot Salah* (compare Luke 3:35, 36).
10:28 ᵃSpelled *Ebal* in 1 Chronicles 1:22

abroad from there over the face of all the earth, and they ceased building the city. [9]Therefore its name is called Babel, because there the LORD confused the language of all the earth; and from there the LORD scattered them abroad over the face of all the earth.

Shem's Descendants

[10]This *is* the genealogy of Shem: Shem *was* one hundred years old, and begot Arphaxad two years after the flood. [11]After he begot Arphaxad, Shem lived five hundred years, and begot sons and daughters.

[12]Arphaxad lived thirty-five years, and begot Salah. [13]After he begot Salah, Arphaxad lived four hundred and three years, and begot sons and daughters.

[14]Salah lived thirty years, and begot Eber. [15]After he begot Eber, Salah lived four hundred and three years, and begot sons and daughters.

[16]Eber lived thirty-four years, and begot Peleg. [17]After he begot Peleg, Eber lived four hundred and thirty years, and begot sons and daughters.

[18]Peleg lived thirty years, and begot Reu. [19]After he begot Reu, Peleg lived two hundred and nine years, and begot sons and daughters.

[20]Reu lived thirty-two years, and begot Serug. [21]After he begot Serug, Reu lived two hundred and seven years, and begot sons and daughters.

[22]Serug lived thirty years, and begot Nahor. [23]After he begot Nahor, Serug lived two hundred years, and begot sons and daughters.

[24]Nahor lived twenty-nine years, and begot Terah. [25]After he begot Terah, Nahor lived one hundred and nineteen years, and begot sons and daughters.

[26]Now Terah lived seventy years, and begot Abram, Nahor, and Haran.

Terah's Descendants

[27]This *is* the genealogy of Terah: Terah begot Abram, Nahor, and Haran. Haran begot Lot. [28]And Haran died before his father Terah in his native land, in Ur of the Chaldeans. [29]Then Abram and Nahor took wives: the name of Abram's wife *was* Sarai, and the name of Nahor's wife, Milcah, the daughter of Haran the father of Milcah and the father of Iscah. [30]But Sarai was barren; she had no child.

[31]And Terah took his son Abram and his grandson Lot, the son of Haran, and his daughter-in-law Sarai, his son Abram's wife, and they went out with them from Ur of the Chaldeans to go to the land of Canaan; and they came to Haran and dwelt there. [32]So the days of Terah were two hundred and five years, and Terah died in Haran.

Promises to Abram

12 Now the LORD had said to Abram:

"Get out of your country,
From your family
And from your father's house,
To a land that I will show you.

2　I will make you a great nation;
I will bless you
And make your name great;
And you shall be a blessing.

3　I will bless those who bless you,
And I will curse him who curses you;
And in you all the families of the
　earth shall be blessed."

[4]So Abram departed as the LORD had spoken to him, and Lot went with him. And Abram *was* seventy-five years old when he departed from Haran. [5]Then Abram took Sarai his wife and Lot his brother's son, and all their possessions that they had gathered, and the people whom they had acquired in Haran, and they departed to go to the land of Canaan. So they came to the land of Canaan. [6]Abram passed through the land to the place of Shechem, as far as the terebinth tree of Moreh.[a] And the Canaanites *were* then in the land.

[7]Then the LORD appeared to Abram and said, "To your descendants I will give this land." And there he built an altar to the LORD, who had appeared to him. [8]And he moved from there to the mountain east of Bethel, and he pitched his tent *with* Bethel

---

12:6 [a]Hebrew *Alon Moreh*

on the west and Ai on the east; there he built an altar to the LORD and called on the name of the LORD. ⁹So Abram journeyed, going on still toward the South.ᵃ

Abram in Egypt

¹⁰Now there was a famine in the land, and Abram went down to Egypt to dwell there, for the famine *was* severe in the land. ¹¹And it came to pass, when he was close to entering Egypt, that he said to Sarai his wife, "Indeed I know that you *are* a woman of beautiful countenance. ¹²Therefore it will happen, when the Egyptians see you, that they will say, 'This *is* his wife'; and they will kill me, but they will let you live. ¹³Please say you *are* my sister, that it may be well with me for your sake, and that Iᵃ may live because of you."

¹⁴So it was, when Abram came into Egypt, that the Egyptians saw the woman, that she *was* very beautiful. ¹⁵The princes of Pharaoh also saw her and commended her to Pharaoh. And the woman was taken to Pharaoh's house. ¹⁶He treated Abram well for her sake. He had sheep, oxen, male donkeys, male and female servants, female donkeys, and camels.

¹⁷But the LORD plagued Pharaoh and his house with great plagues because of Sarai, Abram's wife. ¹⁸And Pharaoh called Abram and said, "What *is* this you have done to me? Why did you not tell me that she *was* your wife? ¹⁹Why did you say, 'She *is* my sister'? I might have taken her as my wife. Now therefore, here is your wife; take *her* and go your way." ²⁰So Pharaoh commanded *his* men concerning him; and they sent him away, with his wife and all that he had.

Abram Inherits Canaan

13 Then Abram went up from Egypt, he and his wife and all that he had, and Lot with him, to the South.ᵃ ²Abram *was* very rich in livestock, in silver, and in gold. ³And he went on his journey from the South as far as Bethel, to the place where his tent had been at the beginning, between Bethel and Ai, ⁴to the place of the altar which he had made there at first. And there Abram called on the name of the LORD.

⁵Lot also, who went with Abram, had flocks and herds and tents. ⁶Now the land was not able to support them, that they might dwell together, for their possessions were so great that they could not dwell together. ⁷And there was strife between the herdsmen of Abram's livestock and the herdsmen of Lot's livestock. The Canaanites and the Perizzites then dwelt in the land.

⁸So Abram said to Lot, "Please let there be no strife between you and me, and between my herdsmen and your herdsmen; for we *are* brethren. ⁹*Is* not the whole land before you? Please separate from me. If *you take* the left, then I will go to the right; or, if *you go* to the right, then I will go to the left."

¹⁰And Lot lifted his eyes and saw all the plain of Jordan, that it *was* well watered everywhere (before the LORD destroyed Sodom and Gomorrah) like the garden of the LORD, like the land of Egypt as you go toward Zoar. ¹¹Then Lot chose for himself all the plain of Jordan, and Lot journeyed east. And they separated from each other. ¹²Abram dwelt in the land of Canaan, and Lot dwelt in the cities of the plain and pitched *his* tent even as far as Sodom. ¹³But the men of Sodom *were* exceedingly wicked and sinful against the LORD.

¹⁴And the LORD said to Abram, after Lot had separated from him: "Lift your eyes now and look from the place where you are—northward, southward, eastward, and westward; ¹⁵for all the land which you see I give to you and your descendantsᵃ forever. ¹⁶And I will make your descendants as the dust of the earth; so that if a man could number the dust of the earth, *then* your descendants also could be numbered. ¹⁷Arise, walk in the land through its length and its width, for I give it to you."

¹⁸Then Abram moved *his* tent, and went and dwelt by the terebinth trees of Mamre,ᵃ which *are* in Hebron, and built an altar there to the LORD.

12:9 ᵃHebrew *Negev*   **12:13** ᵃLiterally *my soul*
13:1 ᵃHebrew *Negev*   **13:15** ᵃLiterally *seed,*
and so throughout the book   **13:18** ᵃHebrew *Alon Mamre*

Lot's Captivity and Rescue

14 And it came to pass in the days of Amraphel king of Shinar, Arioch king of Ellasar, Chedorlaomer king of Elam, and Tidal king of nations,ᵃ ²that they made war with Bera king of Sodom, Birsha king of Gomorrah, Shinab king of Admah, Shemeber king of Zeboiim, and the king of Bela (that is, Zoar). ³All these joined together in the Valley of Siddim (that is, the Salt Sea). ⁴Twelve years they served Chedorlaomer, and in the thirteenth year they rebelled.

⁵In the fourteenth year Chedorlaomer and the kings that *were* with him came and attacked the Rephaim in Ashteroth Karnaim, the Zuzim in Ham, the Emim in Shaveh Kiriathaim, ⁶and the Horites in their mountain of Seir, as far as El Paran, which *is* by the wilderness. ⁷Then they turned back and came to En Mishpat (that *is,* Kadesh), and attacked all the country of the Amalekites, and also the Amorites who dwelt in Hazezon Tamar.

⁸And the king of Sodom, the king of Gomorrah, the king of Admah, the king of Zeboiim, and the king of Bela (that *is,* Zoar) went out and joined together in battle in the Valley of Siddim ⁹against Chedorlaomer king of Elam, Tidal king of nations,ᵃ Amraphel king of Shinar, and Arioch king of Ellasar—four kings against five. ¹⁰Now the Valley of Siddim *was full of* asphalt pits; and the kings of Sodom and Gomorrah fled; *some* fell there, and the remainder fled to the mountains. ¹¹Then they took all the goods of Sodom and Gomorrah, and all their provisions, and went their way. ¹²They also took Lot, Abram's brother's son who dwelt in Sodom, and his goods, and departed.

¹³Then one who had escaped came and told Abram the Hebrew, for he dwelt by the terebinth trees of Mamreᵃ the Amorite, brother of Eshcol and brother of Aner; and they *were* allies with Abram. ¹⁴Now when Abram heard that his brother was taken captive, he armed his three hundred and eighteen trained *servants* who were born in his own house, and went in pursuit as far as Dan. ¹⁵He divided his forces against them by night, and he and his servants attacked them and pursued them as far as Hobah, which *is* north of Damascus. ¹⁶So he brought back all the goods, and also brought back his brother Lot and his goods, as well as the women and the people.

¹⁷And the king of Sodom went out to meet him at the Valley of Shaveh (that *is,* the King's Valley), after his return from the defeat of Chedorlaomer and the kings who *were* with him.

Abram and Melchizedek

¹⁸Then Melchizedek king of Salem brought out bread and wine; he *was* the priest of God Most High. ¹⁹And he blessed him and said:

"Blessed be Abram of God Most
   High,
   Possessor of heaven and earth;
20   And blessed be God Most High,
   Who has delivered your enemies
      into your hand."

And he gave him a tithe of all.

²¹Now the king of Sodom said to Abram, "Give me the persons, and take the goods for yourself."

²²But Abram said to the king of Sodom, "I have raised my hand to the LORD, God Most High, the Possessor of heaven and earth, ²³that I *will take* nothing, from a thread to a sandal strap, and that I will not take anything that *is* yours, lest you should say, 'I have made Abram rich'— ²⁴except only what the young men have eaten, and the portion of the men who went with me: Aner, Eshcol, and Mamre; let them take their portion."

God's Covenant with Abram

15 After these things the word of the LORD came to Abram in a vision, saying, "Do not be afraid, Abram. I *am* your shield, your exceedingly great reward."

²But Abram said, "Lord GOD, what will You give me, seeing I go childless, and the heir of my house *is* Eliezer of Damascus?"

14:1 ᵃHebrew *goyim*   **14:9** ᵃHebrew *goyim*
14:13 ᵃHebrew *Alon Mamre*

THE RIGHT TO KEEP AND BEAR ARMS

GEORGE MASON

Now when Abram heard that his brother was taken captive, he armed his three hundred and eighteen trained servants. . . .

GENESIS 14:14

The Second Amendment to the U.S. Constitution reads: "A well-regulated militia being necessary to the security of a free State, the right of the People to keep and bear arms shall not be infringed."

Having fled persecution in Great Britain, the Puritans had laws requiring every family to own a gun, to carry it in public places, and to train children in the use of firearms. In 1619, the colony of Virginia had statutes that required everyone to bear arms. Connecticut law in 1650 required every man above the age of sixteen to possess "a good musket or other gun, fit for service."

The early laws of America are very clear about this. The people were responsible for their own defense and freedoms and needed to be prepared to fight. Thomas Jefferson said, "The strongest reason for the people to retain the right to bear arms is, as a last resort, to protect themselves against tyranny in government." At that time, there was no concept of a professional army, created and paid to defend the colonies. George Mason, called the father of the Bill of Rights, said, "What is the militia? It is the whole people. To disarm the people is the best and most effectual way to enslave them."

With the approach of the American Revolution, the natural rights philosophers had established the foundation for self-defense. Every man's life, they said, belongs to God, and to allow one's life to be taken because one failed to defend it was wrong. This natural law to the right of self-defense was also applied to the duty to protect one's family, community, and national liberties. For the colonists, at the heart of their religion was liberty, a sacred gift from God.

For the most part, the colonial churches, particularly New England's Congregational congregations, believed that to revolt against tyrants, such as King George, was to obey God. It may have had its roots in the Old Testament accounts of Israel's wars for freedom, but it became a powerful fire that impassioned the citizenry. And it remains a belief that continues to influence Americans' views about the right to bear arms today.

³Then Abram said, "Look, You have given me no offspring; indeed one born in my house is my heir!"

⁴And behold, the word of the LORD *came* to him, saying, "This one shall not be your heir, but one who will come from your own body shall be your heir." ⁵Then He brought him outside and said, "Look now toward heaven, and count the stars if you are able to number them." And He said to him, "So shall your descendants be."

⁶And he believed in the LORD, and He accounted it to him for righteousness.

⁷Then He said to him, "I *am* the LORD, who brought you out of Ur of the Chaldeans, to give you this land to inherit it."

⁸And he said, "Lord GOD, how shall I know that I will inherit it?"

⁹So He said to him, "Bring Me a three-year-old heifer, a three-year-old female goat, a three-year-old ram, a turtledove, and a young pigeon." ¹⁰Then he brought all these to Him and cut them in two, down the middle, and placed each piece opposite the other; but he did not cut the birds in two. ¹¹And when the vultures came down on the carcasses, Abram drove them away.

¹²Now when the sun was going down, a deep sleep fell upon Abram; and behold, horror *and* great darkness fell upon him. ¹³Then He said to Abram: "Know certainly that your descendants will be strangers in a land *that is* not theirs, and will serve them, and they will afflict them four hundred years. ¹⁴And also the nation whom they serve I will judge; afterward they shall come out with great possessions. ¹⁵Now as for you, you shall go to your fathers in peace; you shall be buried at a good old age. ¹⁶But in the fourth generation they shall return here, for the iniquity of the Amorites *is* not yet complete."

¹⁷And it came to pass, when the sun went down and it was dark, that behold, there appeared a smoking oven and a burning torch that passed between those pieces. ¹⁸On the same day the LORD made a covenant with Abram, saying:

"To your descendants I have given this land, from the river of Egypt to the great river, the River Euphrates— ¹⁹the Kenites, the Kenezzites, the Kadmonites, ²⁰the Hittites, the Perizzites, the Rephaim, ²¹the Amorites, the Canaanites, the Girgashites, and the Jebusites."

Hagar and Ishmael

16 Now Sarai, Abram's wife, had borne him no *children*. And she had an Egyptian maidservant whose name was Hagar. ²So Sarai said to Abram, "See now, the LORD has restrained me from bearing *children*. Please, go in to my maid; perhaps I shall obtain children by her." And Abram heeded the voice of Sarai. ³Then Sarai, Abram's wife, took Hagar her maid, the Egyptian, and gave her to her husband Abram to be his wife, after Abram had dwelt ten years in the land of Canaan. ⁴So he went in to Hagar, and she conceived. And when she saw that she had conceived, her mistress became despised in her eyes.

⁵Then Sarai said to Abram, "My wrong *be* upon you! I gave my maid into your embrace; and when she saw that she had conceived, I became despised in her eyes. The LORD judge between you and me."

⁶So Abram said to Sarai, "Indeed your maid *is* in your hand; do to her as you please." And when Sarai dealt harshly with her, she fled from her presence.

⁷Now the Angel of the LORD found her by a spring of water in the wilderness, by the spring on the way to Shur. ⁸And He said, "Hagar, Sarai's maid, where have you come from, and where are you going?"

She said, "I am fleeing from the presence of my mistress Sarai."

⁹The Angel of the LORD said to her, "Return to your mistress, and submit yourself under her hand." ¹⁰Then the Angel of the LORD said to her, "I will multiply your descendants exceedingly, so that they shall not be counted for multitude." ¹¹And the Angel of the LORD said to her:

"Behold, you *are* with child,
And you shall bear a son.
You shall call his name Ishmael,
Because the LORD has heard your
    affliction.
¹² He shall be a wild man;

PROTECTOR

*"... his hand shall
be against every man,
and every man's hand
against him."*

GENESIS 16:12

THE BARBARY PIRATES

The Barbary pirates were Muslim pirates who operated from modern-day Morocco, Algeria, Tunisia, and Libya, from the time of the Crusades until the early nineteenth century. They often made raids on European coastal towns to capture Christian slaves to sell at slave markets in places such as Algeria and Morocco. It is estimated that from the sixteenth to the nineteenth century, pirates captured 1 million to 1.25 million Europeans as slaves. France, England, and Spain each lost thousands of ships in these attacks, and long stretches of coast in Spain and Italy were almost completely abandoned by their inhabitants.

In 1783, the United States won its freedom from the British monarchy, which had been paying tribute money to the pirates, and in 1784 the first American ship was seized by pirates from Morocco. Two more ships were seized in 1785 by Algeria. In 1786, Thomas Jefferson and John Adams, then the ambassadors to France and Britain respectively, met with the Libyan ambassador to Britain, Sidi Adja, asking why his government was hostile to American ships. The ambassador's response, which was reported to the Continental Congress, stated that it was their right "to plunder and enslave."

After some serious debate over what to do, the United States chose to fight the pirates of Barbary rather than pay tribute, as did all the other nations who traded in the Mediterranean Sea. The decision was bold, and the United States Navy was born in March 1794. Six frigates were authorized, and this new military presence helped lead to the two Barbary Wars along the North African coast: the First Barbary War from 1801 to 1805 and the Second Barbary War in 1815. Naval victories in 1815 ended tribute payments by the U.S., although some European nations continued annual payments until the 1830s.

The tiny United States Navy broke a pattern of international blackmail and terrorism dating back more than one hundred and fifty years. The actions of the United States Marine Corps in these wars led to the line "to the shores of Tripoli" in the opening of the Marine Hymn. Due to the hazards of boarding hostile ships, Marines' uniforms had a leather high collar to protect against cutlass slashes. This led to the nickname *Leatherneck* for U.S. Marines.

His hand *shall be* against every man,
And every man's hand against him.
And he shall dwell in the presence of
    all his brethren."

[13]Then she called the name of the LORD who spoke to her, You-Are-the-God-Who-Sees; for she said, "Have I also here seen Him who sees me?" [14]Therefore the well was called Beer Lahai Roi;ᵃ observe, *it is* between Kadesh and Bered.

[15]So Hagar bore Abram a son; and Abram named his son, whom Hagar bore, Ishmael. [16]Abram *was* eighty-six years old when Hagar bore Ishmael to Abram.

The Sign of the Covenant

17 When Abram was ninety-nine years old, the LORD appeared to Abram and said to him, "I *am* Almighty God; walk before Me and be blameless. [2]And I will make My covenant between Me and you, and will multiply you exceedingly." [3]Then Abram fell on his face, and God talked with him, saying: [4]"As for Me, behold, My covenant is with you, and you shall be a father of many nations. [5]No longer shall your name be called Abram, but your name shall be Abraham; for I have made you a father of many nations. [6]I will make you exceedingly fruitful; and I will make nations of you, and kings shall come from you. [7]And I will establish My covenant between Me and you and your descendants after you in their generations, for an everlasting covenant, to be God to you and your descendants after you. [8]Also I give to you and your descendants after you the land in which you are a stranger, all the land of Canaan, as an everlasting possession; and I will be their God."

[9]And God said to Abraham: "As for you, you shall keep My covenant, you and your descendants after you throughout their generations. [10]This *is* My covenant which you shall keep, between Me and you and your descendants after you: Every male child among you shall be circumcised; [11]and you shall be circumcised in the flesh of your foreskins, and it shall be a sign of the covenant between Me and you. [12]He who is eight days old among you shall be circumcised, every male child in your generations, he who is born in your house or bought with money from any foreigner who is not your descendant. [13]He who is born in your house and he who is bought with your money must be circumcised, and My covenant shall be in your flesh for an everlasting covenant. [14]And the uncircumcised male child, who is not circumcised in the flesh of his foreskin, that person shall be cut off from his people; he has broken My covenant."

[15]Then God said to Abraham, "As for Sarai your wife, you shall not call her name Sarai, but Sarah *shall be* her name. [16]And I will bless her and also give you a son by her; then I will bless her, and she shall be *a mother of* nations; kings of peoples shall be from her."

[17]Then Abraham fell on his face and laughed, and said in his heart, "Shall *a child* be born to a man who is one hundred years old? And shall Sarah, who is ninety years old, bear *a child?*" [18]And Abraham said to God, "Oh, that Ishmael might live before You!"

[19]Then God said: "No, Sarah your wife shall bear you a son, and you shall call his name Isaac; I will establish My covenant with him for an everlasting covenant, *and* with his descendants after him. [20]And as for Ishmael, I have heard you. Behold, I have blessed him, and will make him fruitful, and will multiply him exceedingly. He shall beget twelve princes, and I will make him a great nation. [21]But My covenant I will establish with Isaac, whom Sarah shall bear to you at this set time next year." [22]Then He finished talking with him, and God went up from Abraham.

[23]So Abraham took Ishmael his son, all who were born in his house and all who were bought with his money, every male among the men of Abraham's house, and circumcised the flesh of their foreskins that very same day, as God had said to him. [24]Abraham *was* ninety-nine years old when he was circumcised in the flesh of his foreskin. [25]And Ishmael his son *was* thirteen

---

16:14 ᵃLiterally *Well of the One Who Lives and Sees Me*

years old when he was circumcised in the flesh of his foreskin. [26]That very same day Abraham was circumcised, and his son Ishmael; [27]and all the men of his house, born in the house or bought with money from a foreigner, were circumcised with him.

The Son of Promise

18 Then the Lord appeared to him by the terebinth trees of Mamre,[a] as he was sitting in the tent door in the heat of the day. [2]So he lifted his eyes and looked, and behold, three men were standing by him; and when he saw *them,* he ran from the tent door to meet them, and bowed himself to the ground, [3]and said, "My Lord, if I have now found favor in Your sight, do not pass on by Your servant. [4]Please let a little water be brought, and wash your feet, and rest yourselves under the tree. [5]And I will bring a morsel of bread, that you may refresh your hearts. After that you may pass by, inasmuch as you have come to your servant."

They said, "Do as you have said."

[6]So Abraham hurried into the tent to Sarah and said, "Quickly, make ready three measures of fine meal; knead *it* and make cakes." [7]And Abraham ran to the herd, took a tender and good calf, gave *it* to a young man, and he hastened to prepare it. [8]So he took butter and milk and the calf which he had prepared, and set *it* before them; and he stood by them under the tree as they ate.

[9]Then they said to him, "Where *is* Sarah your wife?"

So he said, "Here, in the tent."

[10]And He said, "I will certainly return to you according to the time of life, and behold, Sarah your wife shall have a son."

(Sarah was listening in the tent door which *was* behind him.) [11]Now Abraham and Sarah were old, well advanced in age; *and* Sarah had passed the age of childbearing.[a] [12]Therefore Sarah laughed within herself, saying, "After I have grown old, shall I have pleasure, my lord being old also?"

[13]And the Lord said to Abraham, "Why did Sarah laugh, saying, 'Shall I surely bear *a child,* since I am old?' [14]Is anything too hard for the Lord? At the appointed time I will return to you, according to the time of life, and Sarah shall have a son."

[15]But Sarah denied *it,* saying, "I did not laugh," for she was afraid.

And He said, "No, but you did laugh!"

Abraham Intercedes for Sodom

[16]Then the men rose from there and looked toward Sodom, and Abraham went with them to send them on the way. [17]And the Lord said, "Shall I hide from Abraham what I am doing, [18]since Abraham shall surely become a great and mighty nation, and all the nations of the earth shall be blessed in him? [19]For I have known him, in order that he may command his children and his household after him, that they keep the way of the Lord, to do righteousness and justice, that the Lord may bring to Abraham what He has spoken to him." [20]And the Lord said, "Because the outcry against Sodom and Gomorrah is great, and because their sin is very grave, [21]I will go down now and see whether they have done altogether according to the outcry against it that has come to Me; and if not, I will know."

[22]Then the men turned away from there and went toward Sodom, but Abraham still stood before the Lord. [23]And Abraham came near and said, "Would You also destroy the righteous with the wicked? [24]Suppose there were fifty righteous within the city; would You also destroy the place and not spare *it* for the fifty righteous that were in it? [25]Far be it from You to do such a thing as this, to slay the righteous with the wicked, so that the righteous should be as the wicked; far be it from You! Shall not the Judge of all the earth do right?"

[26]So the Lord said, "If I find in Sodom fifty righteous within the city, then I will spare all the place for their sakes."

[27]Then Abraham answered and said, "Indeed now, I who *am but* dust and ashes have taken it upon myself to speak to the Lord: [28]Suppose there were five less than

---

18:1 [a]Hebrew *Alon Mamre*　　　**18:11** [a]Literally *the manner of women had ceased to be with Sarah*

the fifty righteous; would You destroy all of the city for *lack of* five?"

So He said, "If I find there forty-five, I will not destroy *it*."

29And he spoke to Him yet again and said, "Suppose there should be forty found there?"

So He said, "I will not do *it* for the sake of forty."

30Then he said, "Let not the Lord be angry, and I will speak: Suppose thirty should be found there?"

So He said, "I will not do *it* if I find thirty there."

31And he said, "Indeed now, I have taken it upon myself to speak to the Lord: Suppose twenty should be found there?"

So He said, "I will not destroy *it* for the sake of twenty."

32Then he said, "Let not the Lord be angry, and I will speak but once more: Suppose ten should be found there?"

And He said, "I will not destroy *it* for the sake of ten." 33So the LORD went His way as soon as He had finished speaking with Abraham; and Abraham returned to his place.

Sodom's Depravity

19Now the two angels came to Sodom in the evening, and Lot was sitting in the gate of Sodom. When Lot saw *them,* he rose to meet them, and he bowed himself with his face toward the ground. 2And he said, "Here now, my lords, please turn in to your servant's house and spend the night, and wash your feet; then you may rise early and go on your way."

And they said, "No, but we will spend the night in the open square."

3But he insisted strongly; so they turned in to him and entered his house. Then he made them a feast, and baked unleavened bread, and they ate.

4Now before they lay down, the men of the city, the men of Sodom, both old and young, all the people from every quarter, surrounded the house. 5And they called to Lot and said to him, "Where are the men who came to you tonight? Bring them out to us that we may know them *carnally.*"

6So Lot went out to them through the doorway, shut the door behind him, 7and said, "Please, my brethren, do not do so wickedly! 8See now, I have two daughters who have not known a man; please, let me bring them out to you, and you may do to them as you wish; only do nothing to these men, since this is the reason they have come under the shadow of my roof."

9And they said, "Stand back!" Then they said, "This one came in to stay *here,* and he keeps acting as a judge; now we will deal worse with you than with them." So they pressed hard against the man Lot, and came near to break down the door. 10But the men reached out their hands and pulled Lot into the house with them, and shut the door. 11And they struck the men who *were* at the doorway of the house with blindness, both small and great, so that they became weary *trying* to find the door.

Sodom and Gomorrah Destroyed

12Then the men said to Lot, "Have you anyone else here? Son-in-law, your sons, your daughters, and whomever you have in the city—take *them* out of this place! 13For we will destroy this place, because the outcry against them has grown great before the face of the LORD, and the LORD has sent us to destroy it."

14So Lot went out and spoke to his sons-in-law, who had married his daughters, and said, "Get up, get out of this place; for the LORD will destroy this city!" But to his sons-in-law he seemed to be joking.

15When the morning dawned, the angels urged Lot to hurry, saying, "Arise, take your wife and your two daughters who are here, lest you be consumed in the punishment of the city." 16And while he lingered, the men took hold of his hand, his wife's hand, and the hands of his two daughters, the LORD being merciful to him, and they brought him out and set him outside the city. 17So it came to pass, when they had brought them outside, that he[a] said, "Escape for your life! Do not look behind you nor stay anywhere in the plain. Escape to the mountains, lest you be destroyed."

19:17 aSeptuagint, Syriac, and Vulgate read *they.*

18Then Lot said to them, "Please, no, my lords! 19Indeed now, your servant has found favor in your sight, and you have increased your mercy which you have shown me by saving my life; but I cannot escape to the mountains, lest some evil overtake me and I die. 20See now, this city *is* near *enough* to flee to, and it *is* a little one; please let me escape there (*is* it not a little one?) and my soul shall live."

21And he said to him, "See, I have favored you concerning this thing also, in that I will not overthrow this city for which you have spoken. 22Hurry, escape there. For I cannot do anything until you arrive there."

Therefore the name of the city was called Zoar.

23The sun had risen upon the earth when Lot entered Zoar. 24Then the LORD rained brimstone and fire on Sodom and Gomorrah, from the LORD out of the heavens. 25So He overthrew those cities, all the plain, all the inhabitants of the cities, and what grew on the ground.

26But his wife looked back behind him, and she became a pillar of salt.

27And Abraham went early in the morning to the place where he had stood before the LORD. 28Then he looked toward Sodom and Gomorrah, and toward all the land of the plain; and he saw, and behold, the smoke of the land which went up like the smoke of a furnace. 29And it came to pass, when God destroyed the cities of the plain, that God remembered Abraham, and sent Lot out of the midst of the overthrow, when He overthrew the cities in which Lot had dwelt.

The Descendants of Lot

30Then Lot went up out of Zoar and dwelt in the mountains, and his two daughters were with him; for he was afraid to dwell in Zoar. And he and his two daughters dwelt in a cave. 31Now the firstborn said to the younger, "Our father *is* old, and *there is* no man on the earth to come in to us as is the custom of all the earth. 32Come, let us make our father drink wine, and we will lie with him, that we may preserve the lineage of our father." 33So they made their father drink wine that night. And the firstborn went in and lay with her father, and he did not know when she lay down or when she arose.

34It happened on the next day that the firstborn said to the younger, "Indeed I lay with my father last night; let us make him drink wine tonight also, and you go in *and* lie with him, that we may preserve the lineage of our father." 35Then they made their father drink wine that night also. And the younger arose and lay with him, and he did not know when she lay down or when she arose.

36Thus both the daughters of Lot were with child by their father. 37The firstborn bore a son and called his name Moab; he *is* the father of the Moabites to this day. 38And the younger, she also bore a son and called his name Ben-Ammi; he *is* the father of the people of Ammon to this day.

Abraham and Abimelech

20 And Abraham journeyed from there to the South, and dwelt between Kadesh and Shur, and stayed in Gerar. 2Now Abraham said of Sarah his wife, "She *is* my sister." And Abimelech king of Gerar sent and took Sarah.

3But God came to Abimelech in a dream by night, and said to him, "Indeed you *are* a dead man because of the woman whom you have taken, for she *is* a man's wife."

4But Abimelech had not come near her; and he said, "Lord, will You slay a righteous nation also? 5Did he not say to me, 'She *is* my sister'? And she, even she herself said, 'He *is* my brother.' In the integrity of my heart and innocence of my hands I have done this."

6And God said to him in a dream, "Yes, I know that you did this in the integrity of your heart. For I also withheld you from sinning against Me; therefore I did not let you touch her. 7Now therefore, restore the man's wife; for he *is* a prophet, and he will pray for you and you shall live. But if you do not restore *her,* know that you shall surely die, you and all who *are* yours."

8So Abimelech rose early in the morning, called all his servants, and told all

these things in their hearing; and the men were very much afraid. ⁹And Abimelech called Abraham and said to him, "What have you done to us? How have I offended you, that you have brought on me and on my kingdom a great sin? You have done deeds to me that ought not to be done." ¹⁰Then Abimelech said to Abraham, "What did you have in view, that you have done this thing?"

¹¹And Abraham said, "Because I thought, surely the fear of God is not in this place; and they will kill me on account of my wife. ¹²But indeed she is truly my sister. She is the daughter of my father, but not the daughter of my mother; and she became my wife. ¹³And it came to pass, when God caused me to wander from my father's house, that I said to her, 'This is your kindness that you should do for me: in every place, wherever we go, say of me, "He is my brother." ' "

¹⁴Then Abimelech took sheep, oxen, and male and female servants, and gave them to Abraham; and he restored Sarah his wife to him. ¹⁵And Abimelech said, "See, my land is before you; dwell where it pleases you." ¹⁶Then to Sarah he said, "Behold, I have given your brother a thousand pieces of silver; indeed this vindicates youᵃ before all who are with you and before everybody." Thus she was rebuked.

¹⁷So Abraham prayed to God; and God healed Abimelech, his wife, and his female servants. Then they bore children; ¹⁸for the LORD had closed up all the wombs of the house of Abimelech because of Sarah, Abraham's wife.

Isaac Is Born

21 And the LORD visited Sarah as He had said, and the LORD did for Sarah as He had spoken. ²For Sarah conceived and bore Abraham a son in his old age, at the set time of which God had spoken to him. ³And Abraham called the name of his son who was born to him—whom Sarah bore to him—Isaac. ⁴Then Abraham circumcised his son Isaac when he was eight days old, as God had commanded him. ⁵Now Abraham was one hundred years old when his son Isaac was born to him. ⁶And Sarah said, "God has made me laugh, and all who hear will laugh with me." ⁷She also said, "Who would have said to Abraham that Sarah would nurse children? For I have borne him a son in his old age."

Hagar and Ishmael Depart

⁸So the child grew and was weaned. And Abraham made a great feast on the same day that Isaac was weaned.

⁹And Sarah saw the son of Hagar the Egyptian, whom she had borne to Abraham, scoffing. ¹⁰Therefore she said to Abraham, "Cast out this bondwoman and her son; for the son of this bondwoman shall not be heir with my son, namely with Isaac." ¹¹And the matter was very displeasing in Abraham's sight because of his son.

¹²But God said to Abraham, "Do not let it be displeasing in your sight because of the lad or because of your bondwoman. Whatever Sarah has said to you, listen to her voice; for in Isaac your seed shall be called. ¹³Yet I will also make a nation of the son of the bondwoman, because he is your seed."

¹⁴So Abraham rose early in the morning, and took bread and a skin of water; and putting it on her shoulder, he gave it and the boy to Hagar, and sent her away. Then she departed and wandered in the Wilderness of Beersheba. ¹⁵And the water in the skin was used up, and she placed the boy under one of the shrubs. ¹⁶Then she went and sat down across from him at a distance of about a bowshot; for she said to herself, "Let me not see the death of the boy." So she sat opposite him, and lifted her voice and wept.

¹⁷And God heard the voice of the lad. Then the angel of God called to Hagar out of heaven, and said to her, "What ails you, Hagar? Fear not, for God has heard the voice of the lad where he is. ¹⁸Arise, lift up the lad and hold him with your hand, for I will make him a great nation."

¹⁹Then God opened her eyes, and she saw a well of water. And she went and filled the skin with water, and gave the lad a drink. ²⁰So God was with the lad; and he

---

20:16 ᵃLiterally it is a covering of the eyes for you

grew and dwelt in the wilderness, and became an archer. [21]He dwelt in the Wilderness of Paran; and his mother took a wife for him from the land of Egypt.

A Covenant with Abimelech

[22]And it came to pass at that time that Abimelech and Phichol, the commander of his army, spoke to Abraham, saying, "God *is* with you in all that you do. [23]Now therefore, swear to me by God that you will not deal falsely with me, with my offspring, or with my posterity; but that according to the kindness that I have done to you, you will do to me and to the land in which you have dwelt."

[24]And Abraham said, "I will swear."

[25]Then Abraham rebuked Abimelech because of a well of water which Abimelech's servants had seized. [26]And Abimelech said, "I do not know who has done this thing; you did not tell me, nor had I heard *of it* until today." [27]So Abraham took sheep and oxen and gave them to Abimelech, and the two of them made a covenant. [28]And Abraham set seven ewe lambs of the flock by themselves.

[29]Then Abimelech asked Abraham, "What *is the meaning of* these seven ewe lambs which you have set by themselves?"

[30]And he said, "You will take *these* seven ewe lambs from my hand, that they may be my witness that I have dug this well." [31]Therefore he called that place Beersheba,[a] because the two of them swore an oath there.

[32]Thus they made a covenant at Beersheba. So Abimelech rose with Phichol, the commander of his army, and they returned to the land of the Philistines. [33]Then *Abraham* planted a tamarisk tree in Beersheba, and there called on the name of the LORD, the Everlasting God. [34]And Abraham stayed in the land of the Philistines many days.

Abraham's Faith Confirmed

22 Now it came to pass after these things that God tested Abraham, and said to him, "Abraham!"

And he said, "Here I am."

[2]Then He said, "Take now your son, your only *son* Isaac, whom you love, and go to the land of Moriah, and offer him there as a burnt offering on one of the mountains of which I shall tell you."

[3]So Abraham rose early in the morning and saddled his donkey, and took two of his young men with him, and Isaac his son; and he split the wood for the burnt offering, and arose and went to the place of which God had told him. [4]Then on the third day Abraham lifted his eyes and saw the place afar off. [5]And Abraham said to his young men, "Stay here with the donkey; the lad[a] and I will go yonder and worship, and we will come back to you."

[6]So Abraham took the wood of the burnt offering and laid *it* on Isaac his son; and he took the fire in his hand, and a knife, and the two of them went together. [7]But Isaac spoke to Abraham his father and said, "My father!"

And he said, "Here I am, my son."

Then he said, "Look, the fire and the wood, but where *is* the lamb for a burnt offering?"

[8]And Abraham said, "My son, God will provide for Himself the lamb for a burnt offering." So the two of them went together.

[9]Then they came to the place of which God had told him. And Abraham built an altar there and placed the wood in order; and he bound Isaac his son and laid him on the altar, upon the wood. [10]And Abraham stretched out his hand and took the knife to slay his son.

[11]But the Angel of the LORD called to him from heaven and said, "Abraham, Abraham!"

So he said, "Here I am."

[12]And He said, "Do not lay your hand on the lad, or do anything to him; for now I know that you fear God, since you have not withheld your son, your only *son,* from Me."

[13]Then Abraham lifted his eyes and looked, and there behind *him was* a ram caught in a thicket by its horns. So Abraham went and took the ram, and offered it

---

21:31 [a]Literally *Well of the Oath* or *Well of the Seven*
22:5 [a]Or *young man*

up for a burnt offering instead of his son. ¹⁴And Abraham called the name of the place, The-LORD-Will-Provide;^a as it is said *to* this day, "In the Mount of the LORD it shall be provided."

¹⁵Then the Angel of the LORD called to Abraham a second time out of heaven, ¹⁶and said: "By Myself I have sworn, says the LORD, because you have done this thing, and have not withheld your son, your only *son*— ¹⁷blessing I will bless you, and multiplying I will multiply your descendants as the stars of the heaven and as the sand which *is* on the seashore; and your descendants shall possess the gate of their enemies. ¹⁸In your seed all the nations of the earth shall be blessed, because you have obeyed My voice." ¹⁹So Abraham returned to his young men, and they rose and went together to Beersheba; and Abraham dwelt at Beersheba.

The Family of Nahor

²⁰Now it came to pass after these things that it was told Abraham, saying, "Indeed Milcah also has borne children to your brother Nahor: ²¹Huz his firstborn, Buz his brother, Kemuel the father of Aram, ²²Chesed, Hazo, Pildash, Jidlaph, and Bethuel." ²³And Bethuel begot Rebekah.^a These eight Milcah bore to Nahor, Abraham's brother. ²⁴His concubine, whose name was Reumah, also bore Tebah, Gaham, Thahash, and Maachah.

Sarah's Death and Burial

23 Sarah lived one hundred and twenty-seven years; *these were* the years of the life of Sarah. ²So Sarah died in Kirjath Arba (that *is,* Hebron) in the land of Canaan, and Abraham came to mourn for Sarah and to weep for her.

³Then Abraham stood up from before his dead, and spoke to the sons of Heth, saying, ⁴"I *am* a foreigner and a visitor among you. Give me property for a burial place among you, that I may bury my dead out of my sight."

⁵And the sons of Heth answered Abraham, saying to him, ⁶"Hear us, my lord: You *are* a mighty prince among us; bury your dead in the choicest of our burial places. None of us will withhold from you his burial place, that you may bury your dead."

⁷Then Abraham stood up and bowed himself to the people of the land, the sons of Heth. ⁸And he spoke with them, saying, "If it is your wish that I bury my dead out of my sight, hear me, and meet with Ephron the son of Zohar for me, ⁹that he may give me the cave of Machpelah which he has, which *is* at the end of his field. Let him give it to me at the full price, as property for a burial place among you."

¹⁰Now Ephron dwelt among the sons of Heth; and Ephron the Hittite answered Abraham in the presence of the sons of Heth, all who entered at the gate of his city, saying, ¹¹"No, my lord, hear me: I give you the field and the cave that *is* in it; I give it to you in the presence of the sons of my people. I give it to you. Bury your dead!"

¹²Then Abraham bowed himself down before the people of the land; ¹³and he spoke to Ephron in the hearing of the people of the land, saying, "If you *will give it,* please hear me. I will give you money for the field; take *it* from me and I will bury my dead there."

¹⁴And Ephron answered Abraham, saying to him, ¹⁵"My lord, listen to me; the land *is worth* four hundred shekels of silver. What *is* that between you and me? So bury your dead." ¹⁶And Abraham listened to Ephron; and Abraham weighed out the silver for Ephron which he had named in the hearing of the sons of Heth, four hundred shekels of silver, currency of the merchants.

¹⁷So the field of Ephron which *was* in Machpelah, which *was* before Mamre, the field and the cave which *was* in it, and all the trees that *were* in the field, which *were* within all the surrounding borders, were deeded ¹⁸to Abraham as a possession in the presence of the sons of Heth, before all who went in at the gate of his city.

¹⁹And after this, Abraham buried Sarah his wife in the cave of the field of Machpelah, before Mamre (that *is,* Hebron) in

---

22:14 ^aHebrew *YHWH Yireh*   **22:23** ^aSpelled *Rebecca* in Romans 9:10

the land of Canaan. 20So the field and the cave that *is* in it were deeded to Abraham by the sons of Heth as property for a burial place.

A Bride for Isaac

24 Now Abraham was old, well advanced in age; and the LORD had blessed Abraham in all things. 2So Abraham said to the oldest servant of his house, who ruled over all that he had, "Please, put your hand under my thigh, 3and I will make you swear by the LORD, the God of heaven and the God of the earth, that you will not take a wife for my son from the daughters of the Canaanites, among whom I dwell; 4but you shall go to my country and to my family, and take a wife for my son Isaac."

5And the servant said to him, "Perhaps the woman will not be willing to follow me to this land. Must I take your son back to the land from which you came?"

6But Abraham said to him, "Beware that you do not take my son back there. 7The LORD God of heaven, who took me from my father's house and from the land of my family, and who spoke to me and swore to me, saying, 'To your descendantsª I give this land,' He will send His angel before you, and you shall take a wife for my son from there. 8And if the woman is not willing to follow you, then you will be released from this oath; only do not take my son back there." 9So the servant put his hand under the thigh of Abraham his master, and swore to him concerning this matter.

10Then the servant took ten of his master's camels and departed, for all his master's goods *were in* his hand. And he arose and went to Mesopotamia, to the city of Nahor. 11And he made his camels kneel down outside the city by a well of water at evening time, the time when women go out to draw *water.* 12Then he said, "O LORD God of my master Abraham, please give me success this day, and show kindness to my master Abraham. 13Behold, *here* I stand by the well of water, and the daughters of the men of the city are coming out to draw water. 14Now let it be that the young woman to

whom I say, 'Please let down your pitcher that I may drink,' and she says, 'Drink, and I will also give your camels a drink'—*let* her *be the one* You have appointed for Your servant Isaac. And by this I will know that You have shown kindness to my master."

15And it happened, before he had finished speaking, that behold, Rebekah, who was born to Bethuel, son of Milcah, the wife of Nahor, Abraham's brother, came out with her pitcher on her shoulder. 16Now the young woman *was* very beautiful to behold, a virgin; no man had known her. And she went down to the well, filled her pitcher, and came up. 17And the servant ran to meet her and said, "Please let me drink a little water from your pitcher."

18So she said, "Drink, my lord." Then she quickly let her pitcher down to her hand, and gave him a drink. 19And when she had finished giving him a drink, she said, "I will draw *water* for your camels also, until they have finished drinking." 20Then she quickly emptied her pitcher into the trough, ran back to the well to draw *water,* and drew for all his camels. 21And the man, wondering at her, remained silent so as to know whether the LORD had made his journey prosperous or not.

22So it was, when the camels had finished drinking, that the man took a golden nose ring weighing half a shekel, and two bracelets for her wrists weighing ten *shekels* of gold, 23and said, "Whose daughter *are* you? Tell me, please, is there room *in* your father's house for us to lodge?"

24So she said to him, "I *am* the daughter of Bethuel, Milcah's son, whom she bore to Nahor." 25Moreover she said to him, "We have both straw and feed enough, and room to lodge."

26Then the man bowed down his head and worshiped the LORD. 27And he said, "Blessed *be* the LORD God of my master Abraham, who has not forsaken His mercy and His truth toward my master. As for me, being on the way, the LORD led me to the house of my master's brethren." 28So the young woman ran and told her mother's household these things.

24:7 ªLiterally *seed*

²⁹Now Rebekah had a brother whose name *was* Laban, and Laban ran out to the man by the well. ³⁰So it came to pass, when he saw the nose ring, and the bracelets on his sister's wrists, and when he heard the words of his sister Rebekah, saying, "Thus the man spoke to me," that he went to the man. And there he stood by the camels at the well. ³¹And he said, "Come in, O blessed of the LORD! Why do you stand outside? For I have prepared the house, and a place for the camels."

³²Then the man came to the house. And he unloaded the camels, and provided straw and feed for the camels, and water to wash his feet and the feet of the men who *were* with him. ³³*Food* was set before him to eat, but he said, "I will not eat until I have told about my errand."

And he said, "Speak on."

³⁴So he said, "I *am* Abraham's servant. ³⁵The LORD has blessed my master greatly, and he has become great; and He has given him flocks and herds, silver and gold, male and female servants, and camels and donkeys. ³⁶And Sarah my master's wife bore a son to my master when she was old; and to him he has given all that he has. ³⁷Now my master made me swear, saying, 'You shall not take a wife for my son from the daughters of the Canaanites, in whose land I dwell; ³⁸but you shall go to my father's house and to my family, and take a wife for my son.' ³⁹And I said to my master, 'Perhaps the woman will not follow me.' ⁴⁰But he said to me, 'The LORD, before whom I walk, will send His angel with you and prosper your way; and you shall take a wife for my son from my family and from my father's house. ⁴¹You will be clear from this oath when you arrive among my family; for if they will not give *her* to you, then you will be released from my oath.'

⁴²"And this day I came to the well and said, 'O LORD God of my master Abraham, if You will now prosper the way in which I go, ⁴³behold, I stand by the well of water; and it shall come to pass that when the virgin comes out to draw *water,* and I say to her, "Please give me a little water from your pitcher to drink," ⁴⁴and she says to

me, "Drink, and I will draw for your camels also,"—*let* her *be* the woman whom the LORD has appointed for my master's son.'

⁴⁵"But before I had finished speaking in my heart, there was Rebekah, coming out with her pitcher on her shoulder; and she went down to the well and drew *water.* And I said to her, 'Please let me drink.' ⁴⁶And she made haste and let her pitcher down from her *shoulder,* and said, 'Drink, and I will give your camels a drink also.' So I drank, and she gave the camels a drink also. ⁴⁷Then I asked her, and said, 'Whose daughter *are* you?' And she said, 'The daughter of Bethuel, Nahor's son, whom Milcah bore to him.' So I put the nose ring on her nose and the bracelets on her wrists. ⁴⁸And I bowed my head and worshiped the LORD, and blessed the LORD God of my master Abraham, who had led me in the way of truth to take the daughter of my master's brother for his son. ⁴⁹Now if you will deal kindly and truly with my master, tell me. And if not, tell me, that I may turn to the right hand or to the left."

⁵⁰Then Laban and Bethuel answered and said, "The thing comes from the LORD; we cannot speak to you either bad or good. ⁵¹Here *is* Rebekah before you; take *her* and go, and let her be your master's son's wife, as the LORD has spoken."

⁵²And it came to pass, when Abraham's servant heard their words, that he worshiped the LORD, *bowing himself* to the earth. ⁵³Then the servant brought out jewelry of silver, jewelry of gold, and clothing, and gave *them* to Rebekah. He also gave precious things to her brother and to her mother.

⁵⁴And he and the men who *were* with him ate and drank and stayed all night. Then they arose in the morning, and he said, "Send me away to my master."

⁵⁵But her brother and her mother said, "Let the young woman stay with us *a few* days, at least ten; after that she may go."

⁵⁶And he said to them, "Do not hinder me, since the LORD has prospered my way; send me away so that I may go to my master."

⁵⁷So they said, "We will call the young woman and ask her personally." ⁵⁸Then

they called Rebekah and said to her, "Will you go with this man?"

And she said, "I will go."

⁵⁹So they sent away Rebekah their sister and her nurse, and Abraham's servant and his men. ⁶⁰And they blessed Rebekah and said to her:

"Our sister, *may* you *become*
The mother of thousands of ten
　　thousands;
And may your descendants possess
The gates of those who hate them."

⁶¹Then Rebekah and her maids arose, and they rode on the camels and followed the man. So the servant took Rebekah and departed.

⁶²Now Isaac came from the way of Beer Lahai Roi, for he dwelt in the South. ⁶³And Isaac went out to meditate in the field in the evening; and he lifted his eyes and looked, and there, the camels *were* coming. ⁶⁴Then Rebekah lifted her eyes, and when she saw Isaac she dismounted from her camel; ⁶⁵for she had said to the servant, "Who *is* this man walking in the field to meet us?"

The servant said, "It *is* my master." So she took a veil and covered herself.

⁶⁶And the servant told Isaac all the things that he had done. ⁶⁷Then Isaac brought her into his mother Sarah's tent; and he took Rebekah and she became his wife, and he loved her. So Isaac was comforted after his mother's *death.*

Abraham and Keturah

25 Abraham again took a wife, and her name *was* Keturah. ²And she bore him Zimran, Jokshan, Medan, Midian, Ishbak, and Shuah. ³Jokshan begot Sheba and Dedan. And the sons of Dedan were Asshurim, Letushim, and Leummim. ⁴And the sons of Midian *were* Ephah, Epher, Hanoch, Abidah, and Eldaah. All these *were* the children of Keturah.

⁵And Abraham gave all that he had to Isaac. ⁶But Abraham gave gifts to the sons of the concubines which Abraham had; and while he was still living he sent them

eastward, away from Isaac his son, to the country of the east.

Abraham's Death and Burial

⁷This *is* the sum of the years of Abraham's life which he lived: one hundred and seventy-five years. ⁸Then Abraham breathed his last and died in a good old age, an old man and full *of years,* and was gathered to his people. ⁹And his sons Isaac and Ishmael buried him in the cave of Machpelah, which *is* before Mamre, in the field of Ephron the son of Zohar the Hittite, ¹⁰the field which Abraham purchased from the sons of Heth. There Abraham was buried, and Sarah his wife. ¹¹And it came to pass, after the death of Abraham, that God blessed his son Isaac. And Isaac dwelt at Beer Lahai Roi.

The Families of Ishmael and Isaac

¹²Now this *is* the genealogy of Ishmael, Abraham's son, whom Hagar the Egyptian, Sarah's maidservant, bore to Abraham. ¹³And these *were* the names of the sons of Ishmael, by their names, according to their generations: The firstborn of Ishmael, Nebajoth; then Kedar, Adbeel, Mibsam, ¹⁴Mishma, Dumah, Massa, ¹⁵Hadar,ᵃ Tema, Jetur, Naphish, and Kedemah. ¹⁶These *were* the sons of Ishmael and these *were* their names, by their towns and their settlements, twelve princes according to their nations. ¹⁷These *were* the years of the life of Ishmael: one hundred and thirty-seven years; and he breathed his last and died, and was gathered to his people. ¹⁸(They dwelt from Havilah as far as Shur, which *is* east of Egypt as you go toward Assyria.) He died in the presence of all his brethren.

¹⁹This *is* the genealogy of Isaac, Abraham's son. Abraham begot Isaac. ²⁰Isaac was forty years old when he took Rebekah as wife, the daughter of Bethuel the Syrian of Padan Aram, the sister of Laban the Syrian. ²¹Now Isaac pleaded with the LORD for his wife, because she *was* barren; and the LORD granted his plea, and Rebekah his wife conceived. ²²But the children struggled together within her; and she said, "If *all is*

25:15 ᵃMasoretic Text reads *Hadad.*

well, why *am I like* this?" So she went to inquire of the LORD.

²³And the LORD said to her:

"Two nations *are* in your womb,
 Two peoples shall be separated
  from your body;
 One people shall be stronger than
  the other,
 And the older shall serve the
  younger."

²⁴So when her days were fulfilled *for her* to give birth, indeed *there were* twins in her womb. ²⁵And the first came out red. *He was* like a hairy garment all over; so they called his name Esau.ᵃ ²⁶Afterward his brother came out, and his hand took hold of Esau's heel; so his name was called Jacob.ᵃ Isaac *was* sixty years old when she bore them.

²⁷So the boys grew. And Esau was a skillful hunter, a man of the field; but Jacob was a mild man, dwelling in tents. ²⁸And Isaac loved Esau because he ate *of his* game, but Rebekah loved Jacob.

Esau Sells His Birthright

²⁹Now Jacob cooked a stew; and Esau came in from the field, and he *was* weary. ³⁰And Esau said to Jacob, "Please feed me with that same red *stew,* for I *am* weary." Therefore his name was called Edom.ᵃ

³¹But Jacob said, "Sell me your birthright as of this day."

³²And Esau said, "Look, I *am* about to die; so what *is* this birthright to me?"

³³Then Jacob said, "Swear to me as of this day."

So he swore to him, and sold his birthright to Jacob. ³⁴And Jacob gave Esau bread and stew of lentils; then he ate and drank, arose, and went his way. Thus Esau despised *his* birthright.

Isaac and Abimelech

26 There was a famine in the land, besides the first famine that was in the days of Abraham. And Isaac went to Abimelech king of the Philistines, in Gerar.

²Then the LORD appeared to him and said: "Do not go down to Egypt; live in the land of which I shall tell you. ³Dwell in this land, and I will be with you and bless you; for to you and your descendants I give all these lands, and I will perform the oath which I swore to Abraham your father. ⁴And I will make your descendants multiply as the stars of heaven; I will give to your descendants all these lands; and in your seed all the nations of the earth shall be blessed; ⁵because Abraham obeyed My voice and kept My charge, My commandments, My statutes, and My laws."

⁶So Isaac dwelt in Gerar. ⁷And the men of the place asked about his wife. And he said, "She *is* my sister"; for he was afraid to say, "*She is* my wife," *because he thought,* "lest the men of the place kill me for Rebekah, because she *is* beautiful to behold." ⁸Now it came to pass, when he had been there a long time, that Abimelech king of the Philistines looked through a window, and saw, and there was Isaac, showing endearment to Rebekah his wife. ⁹Then Abimelech called Isaac and said, "Quite obviously she *is* your wife; so how could you say, 'She *is* my sister'?"

Isaac said to him, "Because I said, 'Lest I die on account of her.'"

¹⁰And Abimelech said, "What *is* this you have done to us? One of the people might soon have lain with your wife, and you would have brought guilt on us." ¹¹So Abimelech charged all *his* people, saying, "He who touches this man or his wife shall surely be put to death."

¹²Then Isaac sowed in that land, and reaped in the same year a hundredfold; and the LORD blessed him. ¹³The man began to prosper, and continued prospering until he became very prosperous; ¹⁴for he had possessions of flocks and possessions of herds and a great number of servants. So the Philistines envied him. ¹⁵Now the Philistines had stopped up all the wells which his father's servants had dug in the days of Abraham his father, and they had filled them with earth. ¹⁶And Abimelech said to Isaac, "Go away from us, for you are much mightier than we."

25:25 ᵃLiterally *Hairy*   **25:26** ᵃLiterally *Supplanter*
25:30 ᵃLiterally *Red*

¹⁷Then Isaac departed from there and pitched his tent in the Valley of Gerar, and dwelt there. ¹⁸And Isaac dug again the wells of water which they had dug in the days of Abraham his father, for the Philistines had stopped them up after the death of Abraham. He called them by the names which his father had called them.

¹⁹Also Isaac's servants dug in the valley, and found a well of running water there. ²⁰But the herdsmen of Gerar quarreled with Isaac's herdsmen, saying, "The water *is* ours." So he called the name of the well Esek,ᵃ because they quarreled with him. ²¹Then they dug another well, and they quarreled over that *one* also. So he called its name Sitnah.ᵃ ²²And he moved from there and dug another well, and they did not quarrel over it. So he called its name Rehoboth,ᵃ because he said, "For now the LORD has made room for us, and we shall be fruitful in the land."

²³Then he went up from there to Beersheba. ²⁴And the LORD appeared to him the same night and said, "I *am* the God of your father Abraham; do not fear, for I *am* with you. I will bless you and multiply your descendants for My servant Abraham's sake." ²⁵So he built an altar there and called on the name of the LORD, and he pitched his tent there; and there Isaac's servants dug a well.

²⁶Then Abimelech came to him from Gerar with Ahuzzath, one of his friends, and Phichol the commander of his army. ²⁷And Isaac said to them, "Why have you come to me, since you hate me and have sent me away from you?"

²⁸But they said, "We have certainly seen that the LORD is with you. So we said, 'Let there now be an oath between us, between you and us; and let us make a covenant with you, ²⁹that you will do us no harm, since we have not touched you, and since we have done nothing to you but good and have sent you away in peace. You *are* now the blessed of the LORD.'"

³⁰So he made them a feast, and they ate and drank. ³¹Then they arose early in the morning and swore an oath with one another; and Isaac sent them away, and they departed from him in peace.

³²It came to pass the same day that Isaac's servants came and told him about the well which they had dug, and said to him, "We have found water." ³³So he called it Shebah.ᵃ Therefore the name of the city *is* Beershebaᵇ to this day.

³⁴When Esau was forty years old, he took as wives Judith the daughter of Beeri the Hittite, and Basemath the daughter of Elon the Hittite. ³⁵And they were a grief of mind to Isaac and Rebekah.

Isaac Blesses Jacob

27 Now it came to pass, when Isaac was old and his eyes were so dim that he could not see, that he called Esau his older son and said to him, "My son."

And he answered him, "Here I am."

²Then he said, "Behold now, I am old. I do not know the day of my death. ³Now therefore, please take your weapons, your quiver and your bow, and go out to the field and hunt game for me. ⁴And make me savory food, such as I love, and bring *it* to me that I may eat, that my soul may bless you before I die."

⁵Now Rebekah was listening when Isaac spoke to Esau his son. And Esau went to the field to hunt game and to bring *it*. ⁶So Rebekah spoke to Jacob her son, saying, "Indeed I heard your father speak to Esau your brother, saying, ⁷'Bring me game and make savory food for me, that I may eat it and bless you in the presence of the LORD before my death.' ⁸Now therefore, my son, obey my voice according to what I command you. ⁹Go now to the flock and bring me from there two choice kids of the goats, and I will make savory food from them for your father, such as he loves. ¹⁰Then you shall take *it* to your father, that he may eat *it*, and that he may bless you before his death."

¹¹And Jacob said to Rebekah his mother, "Look, Esau my brother *is* a hairy man, and I *am* a smooth-*skinned* man. ¹²Perhaps my father will feel me, and I shall seem to be a deceiver to him; and I shall bring a curse on myself and not a blessing."

26:20 ᵃLiterally *Quarrel*   **26:21** ᵃLiterally *Enmity*
26:22 ᵃLiterally *Spaciousness*   **26:33** ᵃLiterally *Oath* or *Seven* ᵇLiterally *Well of the Oath* or *Well of the Seven*

¹³But his mother said to him, "*Let* your curse *be* on me, my son; only obey my voice, and go, get *them* for me." ¹⁴And he went and got *them* and brought *them* to his mother, and his mother made savory food, such as his father loved. ¹⁵Then Rebekah took the choice clothes of her elder son Esau, which *were* with her in the house, and put them on Jacob her younger son. ¹⁶And she put the skins of the kids of the goats on his hands and on the smooth part of his neck. ¹⁷Then she gave the savory food and the bread, which she had prepared, into the hand of her son Jacob.

¹⁸So he went to his father and said, "My father."

And he said, "Here I am. Who *are* you, my son?"

¹⁹Jacob said to his father, "I *am* Esau your firstborn; I have done just as you told me; please arise, sit and eat of my game, that your soul may bless me."

²⁰But Isaac said to his son, "How *is it* that you have found *it* so quickly, my son?"

And he said, "Because the LORD your God brought *it* to me."

²¹Isaac said to Jacob, "Please come near, that I may feel you, my son, whether you *are* really my son Esau or not." ²²So Jacob went near to Isaac his father, and he felt him and said, "The voice *is* Jacob's voice, but the hands *are* the hands of Esau." ²³And he did not recognize him, because his hands were hairy like his brother Esau's hands; so he blessed him.

²⁴Then he said, "*Are* you really my son Esau?"

He said, "I *am*."

²⁵He said, "Bring *it* near to me, and I will eat of my son's game, so that my soul may bless you." So he brought *it* near to him, and he ate; and he brought him wine, and he drank. ²⁶Then his father Isaac said to him, "Come near now and kiss me, my son." ²⁷And he came near and kissed him; and he smelled the smell of his clothing, and blessed him and said:

"Surely, the smell of my son
Is like the smell of a field
Which the LORD has blessed.

28 Therefore may God give you
Of the dew of heaven,
Of the fatness of the earth,
And plenty of grain and wine.
29 Let peoples serve you,
And nations bow down to you.
Be master over your brethren,
And let your mother's sons bow down
   to you.
Cursed *be* everyone who curses you,
And blessed *be* those who bless you!"

Esau's Lost Hope

³⁰Now it happened, as soon as Isaac had finished blessing Jacob, and Jacob had scarcely gone out from the presence of Isaac his father, that Esau his brother came in from his hunting. ³¹He also had made savory food, and brought it to his father, and said to his father, "Let my father arise and eat of his son's game, that your soul may bless me."

³²And his father Isaac said to him, "Who *are* you?"

So he said, "I *am* your son, your first-born, Esau."

³³Then Isaac trembled exceedingly, and said, "Who? Where *is* the one who hunted game and brought *it* to me? I ate all *of it* before you came, and I have blessed him— *and* indeed he shall be blessed."

³⁴When Esau heard the words of his father, he cried with an exceedingly great and bitter cry, and said to his father, "Bless me—me also, O my father!"

³⁵But he said, "Your brother came with deceit and has taken away your blessing."

³⁶And *Esau* said, "Is he not rightly named Jacob? For he has supplanted me these two times. He took away my birthright, and now look, he has taken away my blessing!" And he said, "Have you not reserved a blessing for me?"

³⁷Then Isaac answered and said to Esau, "Indeed I have made him your master, and all his brethren I have given to him as servants; with grain and wine I have sustained him. What shall I do now for you, my son?"

³⁸And Esau said to his father, "Have you only one blessing, my father? Bless me—

me also, O my father!" And Esau lifted up his voice and wept.

³⁹Then Isaac his father answered and said to him:

"Behold, your dwelling shall be of the
　fatness of the earth,
And of the dew of heaven from above.
⁴⁰　By your sword you shall live,
And you shall serve your brother;
And it shall come to pass, when you
　become restless,
That you shall break his yoke from
　your neck."

Jacob Escapes from Esau

⁴¹So Esau hated Jacob because of the blessing with which his father blessed him, and Esau said in his heart, "The days of mourning for my father are at hand; then I will kill my brother Jacob."

⁴²And the words of Esau her older son were told to Rebekah. So she sent and called Jacob her younger son, and said to him, "Surely your brother Esau comforts himself concerning you *by intending* to kill you. ⁴³Now therefore, my son, obey my voice: arise, flee to my brother Laban in Haran. ⁴⁴And stay with him a few days, until your brother's fury turns away, ⁴⁵until your brother's anger turns away from you, and he forgets what you have done to him; then I will send and bring you from there. Why should I be bereaved also of you both in one day?"

⁴⁶And Rebekah said to Isaac, "I am weary of my life because of the daughters of Heth; if Jacob takes a wife of the daughters of Heth, like these *who are* the daughters of the land, what good will my life be to me?"

28 Then Isaac called Jacob and blessed him, and charged him, and said to him: "You shall not take a wife from the daughters of Canaan. ²Arise, go to Padan Aram, to the house of Bethuel your mother's father; and take yourself a wife from there of the daughters of Laban your mother's brother.

³　"May God Almighty bless you,
And make you fruitful and multiply
　you,
That you may be an assembly
　of peoples;
⁴　And give you the blessing of
　Abraham,
To you and your descendants
　with you,
That you may inherit the land
In which you are a stranger,
Which God gave to Abraham."

⁵So Isaac sent Jacob away, and he went to Padan Aram, to Laban the son of Bethuel the Syrian, the brother of Rebekah, the mother of Jacob and Esau.

Esau Marries Mahalath

⁶Esau saw that Isaac had blessed Jacob and sent him away to Padan Aram to take himself a wife from there, *and that* as he blessed him he gave him a charge, saying, "You shall not take a wife from the daughters of Canaan," ⁷and that Jacob had obeyed his father and his mother and had gone to Padan Aram. ⁸Also Esau saw that the daughters of Canaan did not please his father Isaac. ⁹So Esau went to Ishmael and took Mahalath the daughter of Ishmael, Abraham's son, the sister of Nebajoth, to be his wife in addition to the wives he had.

Jacob's Vow at Bethel

¹⁰Now Jacob went out from Beersheba and went toward Haran. ¹¹So he came to a certain place and stayed there all night, because the sun had set. And he took one of the stones of that place and put it at his head, and he lay down in that place to sleep. ¹²Then he dreamed, and behold, a ladder *was* set up on the earth, and its top reached to heaven; and there the angels of God were ascending and descending on it. ¹³And behold, the LORD stood above it and said: "I *am* the LORD God of Abraham your father and the God of Isaac; the land on which you lie I will give to you and your descendants. ¹⁴Also your descendants shall be as the dust of the earth; you shall spread abroad to the west and the east, to the north and the south; and in you and in your seed all the families of the earth shall be blessed. ¹⁵Behold, I *am* with you and will

keep you wherever you go, and will bring you back to this land; for I will not leave you until I have done what I have spoken to you."

¹⁶Then Jacob awoke from his sleep and said, "Surely the LORD is in this place, and I did not know *it*." ¹⁷And he was afraid and said, "How awesome *is* this place! This *is* none other than the house of God, and this *is* the gate of heaven!"

¹⁸Then Jacob rose early in the morning, and took the stone that he had put at his head, set it up as a pillar, and poured oil on top of it. ¹⁹And he called the name of that place Bethel;ᵃ but the name of that city had been Luz previously. ²⁰Then Jacob made a vow, saying, "If God will be with me, and keep me in this way that I am going, and give me bread to eat and clothing to put on, ²¹so that I come back to my father's house in peace, then the LORD shall be my God. ²²And this stone which I have set as a pillar shall be God's house, and of all that You give me I will surely give a tenth to You."

Jacob Meets Rachel

29 So Jacob went on his journey and came to the land of the people of the East. ²And he looked, and saw a well in the field; and behold, there *were* three flocks of sheep lying by it; for out of that well they watered the flocks. A large stone *was* on the well's mouth. ³Now all the flocks would be gathered there; and they would roll the stone from the well's mouth, water the sheep, and put the stone back in its place on the well's mouth.

⁴And Jacob said to them, "My brethren, where *are* you from?"

And they said, "We *are* from Haran."

⁵Then he said to them, "Do you know Laban the son of Nahor?"

And they said, "We know him."

⁶So he said to them, "Is he well?"

And they said, "*He is* well. And look, his daughter Rachel is coming with the sheep."

⁷Then he said, "Look, *it is* still high day; *it is* not time for the cattle to be gathered together. Water the sheep, and go and feed *them*."

⁸But they said, "We cannot until all the flocks are gathered together, and they have rolled the stone from the well's mouth; then we water the sheep."

⁹Now while he was still speaking with them, Rachel came with her father's sheep, for she was a shepherdess. ¹⁰And it came to pass, when Jacob saw Rachel the daughter of Laban his mother's brother, and the sheep of Laban his mother's brother, that Jacob went near and rolled the stone from the well's mouth, and watered the flock of Laban his mother's brother. ¹¹Then Jacob kissed Rachel, and lifted up his voice and wept. ¹²And Jacob told Rachel that he *was* her father's relative and that he *was* Rebekah's son. So she ran and told her father.

¹³Then it came to pass, when Laban heard the report about Jacob his sister's son, that he ran to meet him, and embraced him and kissed him, and brought him to his house. So he told Laban all these things. ¹⁴And Laban said to him, "Surely you *are* my bone and my flesh." And he stayed with him for a month.

Jacob Marries Leah and Rachel

¹⁵Then Laban said to Jacob, "Because you *are* my relative, should you therefore serve me for nothing? Tell me, what *should* your wages *be?*" ¹⁶Now Laban had two daughters: the name of the elder *was* Leah, and the name of the younger *was* Rachel. ¹⁷Leah's eyes *were* delicate, but Rachel was beautiful of form and appearance.

¹⁸Now Jacob loved Rachel; so he said, "I will serve you seven years for Rachel your younger daughter."

¹⁹And Laban said, "*It is* better that I give her to you than that I should give her to another man. Stay with me." ²⁰So Jacob served seven years for Rachel, and they seemed *only* a few days to him because of the love he had for her.

²¹Then Jacob said to Laban, "Give *me* my wife, for my days are fulfilled, that I may go in to her." ²²And Laban gathered together all the men of the place and made a feast. ²³Now it came to pass in the evening,

---

28:19 ᵃLiterally *House of God*

that he took Leah his daughter and brought her to Jacob; and he went in to her. [24]And Laban gave his maid Zilpah to his daughter Leah *as* a maid. [25]So it came to pass in the morning, that behold, it *was* Leah. And he said to Laban, "What is this you have done to me? Was it not for Rachel that I served you? Why then have you deceived me?"

[26]And Laban said, "It must not be done so in our country, to give the younger before the firstborn. [27]Fulfill her week, and we will give you this one also for the service which you will serve with me still another seven years."

[28]Then Jacob did so and fulfilled her week. So he gave him his daughter Rachel as wife also. [29]And Laban gave his maid Bilhah to his daughter Rachel as a maid. [30]Then *Jacob* also went in to Rachel, and he also loved Rachel more than Leah. And he served with Laban still another seven years.

The Children of Jacob

[31]When the LORD saw that Leah *was* unloved, He opened her womb; but Rachel *was* barren. [32]So Leah conceived and bore a son, and she called his name Reuben;[a] for she said, "The LORD has surely looked on my affliction. Now therefore, my husband will love me." [33]Then she conceived again and bore a son, and said, "Because the LORD has heard that I *am* unloved, He has therefore given me this *son* also." And she called his name Simeon.[a] [34]She conceived again and bore a son, and said, "Now this time my husband will become attached to me, because I have borne him three sons." Therefore his name was called Levi.[a] [35]And she conceived again and bore a son, and said, "Now I will praise the LORD." Therefore she called his name Judah.[a] Then she stopped bearing.

30 Now when Rachel saw that she bore Jacob no children, Rachel envied her sister, and said to Jacob, "Give me children, or else I die!"

[2]And Jacob's anger was aroused against Rachel, and he said, "*Am* I in the place of God, who has withheld from you the fruit of the womb?"

[3]So she said, "Here is my maid Bilhah; go in to her, and she will bear *a child* on my knees, that I also may have children by her." [4]Then she gave him Bilhah her maid as wife, and Jacob went in to her. [5]And Bilhah conceived and bore Jacob a son. [6]Then Rachel said, "God has judged my case; and He has also heard my voice and given me a son." Therefore she called his name Dan.[a] [7]And Rachel's maid Bilhah conceived again and bore Jacob a second son. [8]Then Rachel said, "With great wrestlings I have wrestled with my sister, *and* indeed I have prevailed." So she called his name Naphtali.[a]

[9]When Leah saw that she had stopped bearing, she took Zilpah her maid and gave her to Jacob as wife. [10]And Leah's maid Zilpah bore Jacob a son. [11]Then Leah said, "A troop comes!"[a] So she called his name Gad.[b] [12]And Leah's maid Zilpah bore Jacob a second son. [13]Then Leah said, "I am happy, for the daughters will call me blessed." So she called his name Asher.[a]

[14]Now Reuben went in the days of wheat harvest and found mandrakes in the field, and brought them to his mother Leah. Then Rachel said to Leah, "Please give me *some* of your son's mandrakes."

[15]But she said to her, "*Is it* a small matter that you have taken away my husband? Would you take away my son's mandrakes also?"

And Rachel said, "Therefore he will lie with you tonight for your son's mandrakes."

[16]When Jacob came out of the field in the evening, Leah went out to meet him and said, "You must come in to me, for I have surely hired you with my son's mandrakes." And he lay with her that night.

[17]And God listened to Leah, and she conceived and bore Jacob a fifth son. [18]Leah said, "God has given me my wages, because I have given my maid to my husband." So she called his name Issachar.[a] [19]Then Leah conceived again and bore

---

29:32 [a]Literally *See, a Son*   **29:33** [a]Literally *Heard*
29:34 [a]Literally *Attached*   **29:35** [a]Literally *Praise*
30:6 [a]Literally *Judge*   **30:8** [a]Literally *My Wrestling*
30:11 [a]Following Qere, Syriac, and Targum; Kethib, Septuagint, and Vulgate read *in fortune.* [b]Literally *Troop* or *Fortune*   **30:13** [a]Literally *Happy*
30:18 [a]Literally *Wages*

Jacob a sixth son. ²⁰And Leah said, "God has endowed me *with* a good endowment; now my husband will dwell with me, because I have borne him six sons." So she called his name Zebulun.ᵃ ²¹Afterward she bore a daughter, and called her name Dinah.

²²Then God remembered Rachel, and God listened to her and opened her womb. ²³And she conceived and bore a son, and said, "God has taken away my reproach." ²⁴So she called his name Joseph,ᵃ and said, "The LORD shall add to me another son."

Jacob's Agreement with Laban

²⁵And it came to pass, when Rachel had borne Joseph, that Jacob said to Laban, "Send me away, that I may go to my own place and to my country. ²⁶Give *me* my wives and my children for whom I have served you, and let me go; for you know my service which I have done for you."

²⁷And Laban said to him, "Please *stay,* if I have found favor in your eyes, *for* I have learned by experience that the LORD has blessed me for your sake." ²⁸Then he said, "Name me your wages, and I will give *it.*"

²⁹So *Jacob* said to him, "You know how I have served you and how your livestock has been with me. ³⁰For what you had before I *came was* little, and it has increased to a great amount; the LORD has blessed you since my coming. And now, when shall I also provide for my own house?"

³¹So he said, "What shall I give you?"

And Jacob said, "You shall not give me anything. If you will do this thing for me, I will again feed and keep your flocks: ³²Let me pass through all your flock today, removing from there all the speckled and spotted sheep, and all the brown ones among the lambs, and the spotted and speckled among the goats; and *these* shall be my wages. ³³So my righteousness will answer for me in time to come, when the subject of my wages comes before you: every one that *is* not speckled and spotted among the goats, and brown among the lambs, will be considered stolen, if *it is* with me."

³⁴And Laban said, "Oh, that it were according to your word!" ³⁵So he removed that day the male goats that were speckled and spotted, all the female goats that were speckled and spotted, every one that had *some* white in it, and all the brown ones among the lambs, and gave *them* into the hand of his sons. ³⁶Then he put three days' journey between himself and Jacob, and Jacob fed the rest of Laban's flocks.

³⁷Now Jacob took for himself rods of green poplar and of the almond and chestnut trees, peeled white strips in them, and exposed the white which *was* in the rods. ³⁸And the rods which he had peeled, he set before the flocks in the gutters, in the watering troughs where the flocks came to drink, so that they should conceive when they came to drink. ³⁹So the flocks conceived before the rods, and the flocks brought forth streaked, speckled, and spotted. ⁴⁰Then Jacob separated the lambs, and made the flocks face toward the streaked and all the brown in the flock of Laban; but he put his own flocks by themselves and did not put them with Laban's flock.

⁴¹And it came to pass, whenever the stronger livestock conceived, that Jacob placed the rods before the eyes of the livestock in the gutters, that they might conceive among the rods. ⁴²But when the flocks were feeble, he did not put *them* in; so the feebler were Laban's and the stronger Jacob's. ⁴³Thus the man became exceedingly prosperous, and had large flocks, female and male servants, and camels and donkeys.

Jacob Flees from Laban

31 Now *Jacob* heard the words of Laban's sons, saying, "Jacob has taken away all that was our father's, and from what was our father's he has acquired all this wealth." ²And Jacob saw the countenance of Laban, and indeed it *was* not *favorable* toward him as before. ³Then the LORD said to Jacob, "Return to the land of your fathers and to your family, and I will be with you."

⁴So Jacob sent and called Rachel and Leah to the field, to his flock, ⁵and said to them, "I see your father's countenance,

---

30:20 ᵃLiterally *Dwelling*   **30:24** ᵃLiterally *He Will Add*

that it *is* not *favorable* toward me as before; but the God of my father has been with me. 6And you know that with all my might I have served your father. 7Yet your father has deceived me and changed my wages ten times, but God did not allow him to hurt me. 8If he said thus: 'The speckled shall be your wages,' then all the flocks bore speckled. And if he said thus: 'The streaked shall be your wages,' then all the flocks bore streaked. 9So God has taken away the livestock of your father and given *them* to me.

10"And it happened, at the time when the flocks conceived, that I lifted my eyes and saw in a dream, and behold, the rams which leaped upon the flocks *were* streaked, speckled, and gray-spotted. 11Then the Angel of God spoke to me in a dream, saying, 'Jacob.' And I said, 'Here I am.' 12And He said, 'Lift your eyes now and see, all the rams which leap on the flocks *are* streaked, speckled, and gray-spotted; for I have seen all that Laban is doing to you. 13I *am* the God of Bethel, where you anointed the pillar *and* where you made a vow to Me. Now arise, get out of this land, and return to the land of your family.' "

14Then Rachel and Leah answered and said to him, "Is there still any portion or inheritance for us in our father's house? 15Are we not considered strangers by him? For he has sold us, and also completely consumed our money. 16For all these riches which God has taken from our father are *really* ours and our children's; now then, whatever God has said to you, do it."

17Then Jacob rose and set his sons and his wives on camels. 18And he carried away all his livestock and all his possessions which he had gained, his acquired livestock which he had gained in Padan Aram, to go to his father Isaac in the land of Canaan. 19Now Laban had gone to shear his sheep, and Rachel had stolen the household idols that were her father's. 20And Jacob stole away, unknown to Laban the Syrian, in that he did not tell him that he intended to flee. 21So he fled with all that he had. He arose and crossed the river, and headed toward the mountains of Gilead.

Laban Pursues Jacob

22And Laban was told on the third day that Jacob had fled. 23Then he took his brethren with him and pursued him for seven days' journey, and he overtook him in the mountains of Gilead. 24But God had come to Laban the Syrian in a dream by night, and said to him, "Be careful that you speak to Jacob neither good nor bad."

25So Laban overtook Jacob. Now Jacob had pitched his tent in the mountains, and Laban with his brethren pitched in the mountains of Gilead.

26And Laban said to Jacob: "What have you done, that you have stolen away unknown to me, and carried away my daughters like captives *taken* with the sword? 27Why did you flee away secretly, and steal away from me, and not tell me; for I might have sent you away with joy and songs, with timbrel and harp? 28And you did not allow me to kiss my sons and my daughters. Now you have done foolishly in *so* doing. 29It is in my power to do you harm, but the God of your father spoke to me last night, saying, 'Be careful that you speak to Jacob neither good nor bad.' 30And now you have surely gone because you greatly long for your father's house, *but* why did you steal my gods?"

31Then Jacob answered and said to Laban, "Because I was afraid, for I said, 'Perhaps you would take your daughters from me by force.' 32With whomever you find your gods, do not let him live. In the presence of our brethren, identify what I have of yours and take *it* with you." For Jacob did not know that Rachel had stolen them.

33And Laban went into Jacob's tent, into Leah's tent, and into the two maids' tents, but he did not find *them*. Then he went out of Leah's tent and entered Rachel's tent. 34Now Rachel had taken the household idols, put them in the camel's saddle, and sat on them. And Laban searched all about the tent but did not find *them*. 35And she said to her father, "Let it not displease my lord that I cannot rise before you, for the manner of women *is* with me." And he searched but did not find the household idols.

³⁶Then Jacob was angry and rebuked Laban, and Jacob answered and said to Laban: "What *is* my trespass? What *is* my sin, that you have so hotly pursued me? ³⁷Although you have searched all my things, what part of your household things have you found? Set *it* here before my brethren and your brethren, that they may judge between us both! ³⁸These twenty years I *have been* with you; your ewes and your female goats have not miscarried their young, and I have not eaten the rams of your flock. ³⁹That which was torn *by beasts* I did not bring to you; I bore the loss of it. You required it from my hand, *whether* stolen by day or stolen by night. ⁴⁰*There* I was! In the day the drought consumed me, and the frost by night, and my sleep departed from my eyes. ⁴¹Thus I have been in your house twenty years; I served you fourteen years for your two daughters, and six years for your flock, and you have changed my wages ten times. ⁴²Unless the God of my father, the God of Abraham and the Fear of Isaac, had been with me, surely now you would have sent me away empty-handed. God has seen my affliction and the labor of my hands, and rebuked *you* last night."

Laban's Covenant with Jacob

⁴³And Laban answered and said to Jacob, "*These* daughters *are* my daughters, and *these* children *are* my children, and *this* flock *is* my flock; all that you see *is* mine. But what can I do this day to these my daughters or to their children whom they have borne? ⁴⁴Now therefore, come, let us make a covenant, you and I, and let it be a witness between you and me." ⁴⁵So Jacob took a stone and set it up *as a* pillar. ⁴⁶Then Jacob said to his brethren, "Gather stones." And they took stones and made a heap, and they ate there on the heap. ⁴⁷Laban called it Jegar Sahadutha,ᵃ but Jacob called it Galeed.ᵇ ⁴⁸And Laban said, "This heap *is* a witness between you and me this day." Therefore its name was called Galeed, ⁴⁹also Mizpah,ᵃ because he said, "May the Lord watch between you and me when we are absent one from another. ⁵⁰If you afflict my daughters, or if you take *other* wives besides my daughters, *although* no man *is* with us—see, God *is* witness between you and me!"

⁵¹Then Laban said to Jacob, "Here is this heap and here is *this* pillar, which I have placed between you and me. ⁵²This heap *is* a witness, and *this* pillar *is* a witness, that I will not pass beyond this heap to you, and you will not pass beyond this heap and this pillar to me, for harm. ⁵³The God of Abraham, the God of Nahor, and the God of their father judge between us." And Jacob swore by the Fear of his father Isaac. ⁵⁴Then Jacob offered a sacrifice on the mountain, and called his brethren to eat bread. And they ate bread and stayed all night on the mountain. ⁵⁵And early in the morning Laban arose, and kissed his sons and daughters and blessed them. Then Laban departed and returned to his place.

Esau Comes to Meet Jacob

32 So Jacob went on his way, and the angels of God met him. ²When Jacob saw them, he said, "This *is* God's camp." And he called the name of that place Mahanaim.ᵃ

³Then Jacob sent messengers before him to Esau his brother in the land of Seir, the country of Edom. ⁴And he commanded them, saying, "Speak thus to my lord Esau, 'Thus your servant Jacob says: "I have dwelt with Laban and stayed there until now. ⁵I have oxen, donkeys, flocks, and male and female servants; and I have sent to tell my lord, that I may find favor in your sight."'"

⁶Then the messengers returned to Jacob, saying, "We came to your brother Esau, and he also is coming to meet you, and four hundred men *are* with him." ⁷So Jacob was greatly afraid and distressed; and he divided the people that *were* with him, and the flocks and herds and camels, into two companies. ⁸And he said, "If Esau comes to the one company and attacks it, then the other company which is left will escape."

31:47 ᵃLiterally, in Aramaic, *Heap of Witness*
ᵇLiterally, in Hebrew, *Heap of Witness*
31:49 ᵃLiterally *Watch*   **32:2** ᵃLiterally *Double Camp*

⁹Then Jacob said, "O God of my father Abraham and God of my father Isaac, the LORD who said to me, 'Return to your country and to your family, and I will deal well with you': ¹⁰I am not worthy of the least of all the mercies and of all the truth which You have shown Your servant; for I crossed over this Jordan with my staff, and now I have become two companies. ¹¹Deliver me, I pray, from the hand of my brother, from the hand of Esau; for I fear him, lest he come and attack me *and* the mother with the children. ¹²For You said, 'I will surely treat you well, and make your descendants as the sand of the sea, which cannot be numbered for multitude.'"

¹³So he lodged there that same night, and took what came to his hand as a present for Esau his brother: ¹⁴two hundred female goats and twenty male goats, two hundred ewes and twenty rams, ¹⁵thirty milk camels with their colts, forty cows and ten bulls, twenty female donkeys and ten foals. ¹⁶Then he delivered *them* to the hand of his servants, every drove by itself, and said to his servants, "Pass over before me, and put some distance between successive droves." ¹⁷And he commanded the first one, saying, "When Esau my brother meets you and asks you, saying, 'To whom do you belong, and where are you going? Whose *are* these in front of you?' ¹⁸then you shall say, 'They *are* your servant Jacob's. It *is* a present sent to my lord Esau; and behold, he also *is* behind us.'" ¹⁹So he commanded the second, the third, and all who followed the droves, saying, "In this manner you shall speak to Esau when you find him; ²⁰and also say, 'Behold, your servant Jacob *is* behind us.'" For he said, "I will appease him with the present that goes before me, and afterward I will see his face; perhaps he will accept me." ²¹So the present went on over before him, but he himself lodged that night in the camp.

Wrestling with God

²²And he arose that night and took his two wives, his two female servants, and his eleven sons, and crossed over the ford of Jabbok. ²³He took them, sent them over the brook, and sent over what he had. ²⁴Then Jacob was left alone; and a Man wrestled with him until the breaking of day. ²⁵Now when He saw that He did not prevail against him, He touched the socket of his hip; and the socket of Jacob's hip was out of joint as He wrestled with him. ²⁶And He said, "Let Me go, for the day breaks."

But he said, "I will not let You go unless You bless me!"

²⁷So He said to him, "What *is* your name?"

He said, "Jacob."

²⁸And He said, "Your name shall no longer be called Jacob, but Israel;ᵃ for you have struggled with God and with men, and have prevailed."

²⁹Then Jacob asked, saying, "Tell *me* Your name, I pray."

And He said, "Why *is* it *that* you ask about My name?" And He blessed him there.

³⁰So Jacob called the name of the place Peniel:ᵃ "For I have seen God face to face, and my life is preserved." ³¹Just as he crossed over Penuelᵃ the sun rose on him, and he limped on his hip. ³²Therefore to this day the children of Israel do not eat the muscle that shrank, which *is* on the hip socket, because He touched the socket of Jacob's hip in the muscle that shrank.

Jacob and Esau Meet

33 Now Jacob lifted his eyes and looked, and there, Esau was coming, and with him were four hundred men. So he divided the children among Leah, Rachel, and the two maidservants. ²And he put the maidservants and their children in front, Leah and her children behind, and Rachel and Joseph last. ³Then he crossed over before them and bowed himself to the ground seven times, until he came near to his brother.

⁴But Esau ran to meet him, and embraced him, and fell on his neck and kissed him, and they wept. ⁵And he lifted his eyes and saw the women and children, and said, "Who *are* these with you?"

32:28 ᵃLiterally *Prince with God*   **32:30** ᵃLiterally *Face of God*   **32:31** ᵃSame as *Peniel*, verse 30

So he said, "The children whom God has graciously given your servant." [6]Then the maidservants came near, they and their children, and bowed down. [7]And Leah also came near with her children, and they bowed down. Afterward Joseph and Rachel came near, and they bowed down.

[8]Then Esau said, "What *do* you *mean by* all this company which I met?"

And he said, "*These are* to find favor in the sight of my lord."

[9]But Esau said, "I have enough, my brother; keep what you have for yourself."

[10]And Jacob said, "No, please, if I have now found favor in your sight, then receive my present from my hand, inasmuch as I have seen your face as though I had seen the face of God, and you were pleased with me. [11]Please, take my blessing that is brought to you, because God has dealt graciously with me, and because I have enough." So he urged him, and he took *it*.

[12]Then Esau said, "Let us take our journey; let us go, and I will go before you."

[13]But Jacob said to him, "My lord knows that the children *are* weak, and the flocks and herds which are nursing *are* with me. And if the men should drive them hard one day, all the flock will die. [14]Please let my lord go on ahead before his servant. I will lead on slowly at a pace which the livestock that go before me, and the children, are able to endure, until I come to my lord in Seir."

[15]And Esau said, "Now let me leave with you *some* of the people who *are* with me."

But he said, "What need is there? Let me find favor in the sight of my lord." [16]So Esau returned that day on his way to Seir. [17]And Jacob journeyed to Succoth, built himself a house, and made booths for his livestock. Therefore the name of the place is called Succoth.[a]

Jacob Comes to Canaan

[18]Then Jacob came safely to the city of Shechem, which *is* in the land of Canaan, when he came from Padan Aram; and he pitched his tent before the city. [19]And he bought the parcel of land, where he had pitched his tent, from the children of Hamor, Shechem's father, for one hundred pieces of money. [20]Then he erected an altar there and called it El Elohe Israel.[a]

The Dinah Incident

34 Now Dinah the daughter of Leah, whom she had borne to Jacob, went out to see the daughters of the land. [2]And when Shechem the son of Hamor the Hivite, prince of the country, saw her, he took her and lay with her, and violated her. [3]His soul was strongly attracted to Dinah the daughter of Jacob, and he loved the young woman and spoke kindly to the young woman. [4]So Shechem spoke to his father Hamor, saying, "Get me this young woman as a wife."

[5]And Jacob heard that he had defiled Dinah his daughter. Now his sons were with his livestock in the field; so Jacob held his peace until they came. [6]Then Hamor the father of Shechem went out to Jacob to speak with him. [7]And the sons of Jacob came in from the field when they heard *it;* and the men were grieved and very angry, because he had done a disgraceful thing in Israel by lying with Jacob's daughter, a thing which ought not to be done. [8]But Hamor spoke with them, saying, "The soul of my son Shechem longs for your daughter. Please give her to him as a wife. [9]And make marriages with us; give your daughters to us, and take our daughters to yourselves. [10]So you shall dwell with us, and the land shall be before you. Dwell and trade in it, and acquire possessions for yourselves in it."

[11]Then Shechem said to her father and her brothers, "Let me find favor in your eyes, and whatever you say to me I will give. [12]Ask me ever so much dowry and gift, and I will give according to what you say to me; but give me the young woman as a wife."

[13]But the sons of Jacob answered Shechem and Hamor his father, and spoke deceitfully, because he had defiled Dinah their sister. [14]And they said to them, "We cannot do this thing, to give our sister to one who is uncircumcised, for that *would be* a reproach to us. [15]But on this *condition* we

---

33:17 [a]Literally *Booths*   **33:20** [a]Literally *God, the God of Israel*

40

will consent to you: If you will become as we *are,* if every male of you is circumcised, [16]then we will give our daughters to you, and we will take your daughters to us; and we will dwell with you, and we will become one people. [17]But if you will not heed us and be circumcised, then we will take our daughter and be gone."

[18]And their words pleased Hamor and Shechem, Hamor's son. [19]So the young man did not delay to do the thing, because he delighted in Jacob's daughter. He *was* more honorable than all the household of his father.

[20]And Hamor and Shechem his son came to the gate of their city, and spoke with the men of their city, saying: [21]"These men *are* at peace with us. Therefore let them dwell in the land and trade in it. For indeed the land *is* large enough for them. Let us take their daughters to us as wives, and let us give them our daughters. [22]Only on this *condition* will the men consent to dwell with us, to be one people: if every male among us is circumcised as they *are* circumcised. [23]*Will* not their livestock, their property, and every animal of theirs *be* ours? Only let us consent to them, and they will dwell with us." [24]And all who went out of the gate of his city heeded Hamor and Shechem his son; every male was circumcised, all who went out of the gate of his city.

[25]Now it came to pass on the third day, when they were in pain, that two of the sons of Jacob, Simeon and Levi, Dinah's brothers, each took his sword and came boldly upon the city and killed all the males. [26]And they killed Hamor and Shechem his son with the edge of the sword, and took Dinah from Shechem's house, and went out. [27]The sons of Jacob came upon the slain, and plundered the city, because their sister had been defiled. [28]They took their sheep, their oxen, and their donkeys, what *was* in the city and what *was* in the field, [29]and all their wealth. All their little ones and their wives they took captive; and they plundered even all that *was* in the houses.

[30]Then Jacob said to Simeon and Levi, "You have troubled me by making me obnoxious among the inhabitants of the land, among the Canaanites and the Perizzites; and since I *am* few in number, they will gather themselves together against me and kill me. I shall be destroyed, my household and I."

[31]But they said, "Should he treat our sister like a harlot?"

Jacob's Return to Bethel

35 Then God said to Jacob, "Arise, go up to Bethel and dwell there; and make an altar there to God, who appeared to you when you fled from the face of Esau your brother."

[2]And Jacob said to his household and to all who *were* with him, "Put away the foreign gods that *are* among you, purify yourselves, and change your garments. [3]Then let us arise and go up to Bethel; and I will make an altar there to God, who answered me in the day of my distress and has been with me in the way which I have gone." [4]So they gave Jacob all the foreign gods which *were* in their hands, and the earrings which *were* in their ears; and Jacob hid them under the terebinth tree which *was* by Shechem.

[5]And they journeyed, and the terror of God was upon the cities that *were* all around them, and they did not pursue the sons of Jacob. [6]So Jacob came to Luz (that *is,* Bethel), which *is* in the land of Canaan, he and all the people who *were* with him. [7]And he built an altar there and called the place El Bethel,[a] because there God appeared to him when he fled from the face of his brother.

[8]Now Deborah, Rebekah's nurse, died, and she was buried below Bethel under the terebinth tree. So the name of it was called Allon Bachuth.[a]

[9]Then God appeared to Jacob again, when he came from Padan Aram, and blessed him. [10]And God said to him, "Your name *is* Jacob; your name shall not be called Jacob anymore, but Israel shall be your name." So He called his name Israel. [11]Also God said to him: "I *am* God Almighty. Be fruitful and multiply; a nation and a

---

35:7 [a]Literally *God of the House of God*
35:8 [a]Literally *Terebinth of Weeping*

company of nations shall proceed from you, and kings shall come from your body. [12]The land which I gave Abraham and Isaac I give to you; and to your descendants after you I give this land." [13]Then God went up from him in the place where He talked with him. [14]So Jacob set up a pillar in the place where He talked with him, a pillar of stone; and he poured a drink offering on it, and he poured oil on it. [15]And Jacob called the name of the place where God spoke with him, Bethel.

Death of Rachel

[16]Then they journeyed from Bethel. And when there was but a little distance to go to Ephrath, Rachel labored *in childbirth,* and she had hard labor. [17]Now it came to pass, when she was in hard labor, that the midwife said to her, "Do not fear; you will have this son also." [18]And so it was, as her soul was departing (for she died), that she called his name Ben-Oni;[a] but his father called him Benjamin.[b] [19]So Rachel died and was buried on the way to Ephrath (that *is,* Bethlehem). [20]And Jacob set a pillar on her grave, which *is* the pillar of Rachel's grave to this day.

[21]Then Israel journeyed and pitched his tent beyond the tower of Eder. [22]And it happened, when Israel dwelt in that land, that Reuben went and lay with Bilhah his father's concubine; and Israel heard *about it.*

Jacob's Twelve Sons

Now the sons of Jacob were twelve: [23]the sons of Leah *were* Reuben, Jacob's firstborn, and Simeon, Levi, Judah, Issachar, and Zebulun; [24]the sons of Rachel *were* Joseph and Benjamin; [25]the sons of Bilhah, Rachel's maidservant, *were* Dan and Naphtali; [26]and the sons of Zilpah, Leah's maidservant, *were* Gad and Asher. These *were* the sons of Jacob who were born to him in Padan Aram.

Death of Isaac

[27]Then Jacob came to his father Isaac at Mamre, or Kirjath Arba[a] (that *is,* Hebron), where Abraham and Isaac had dwelt. [28]Now the days of Isaac were one hundred and eighty years. [29]So Isaac breathed his last and died, and was gathered to his people, *being* old and full of days. And his sons Esau and Jacob buried him.

The Family of Esau

36 Now this *is* the genealogy of Esau, who is Edom. [2]Esau took his wives from the daughters of Canaan: Adah the daughter of Elon the Hittite; Aholibamah the daughter of Anah, the daughter of Zibeon the Hivite; [3]and Basemath, Ishmael's daughter, sister of Nebajoth. [4]Now Adah bore Eliphaz to Esau, and Basemath bore Reuel. [5]And Aholibamah bore Jeush, Jaalam, and Korah. These *were* the sons of Esau who were born to him in the land of Canaan.

[6]Then Esau took his wives, his sons, his daughters, and all the persons of his household, his cattle and all his animals, and all his goods which he had gained in the land of Canaan, and went to a country away from the presence of his brother Jacob. [7]For their possessions were too great for them to dwell together, and the land where they were strangers could not support them because of their livestock. [8]So Esau dwelt in Mount Seir. Esau *is* Edom.

[9]And this *is* the genealogy of Esau the father of the Edomites in Mount Seir. [10]These *were* the names of Esau's sons: Eliphaz the son of Adah the wife of Esau, and Reuel the son of Basemath the wife of Esau. [11]And the sons of Eliphaz were Teman, Omar, Zepho,[a] Gatam, and Kenaz.

[12]Now Timna was the concubine of Eliphaz, Esau's son, and she bore Amalek to Eliphaz. These *were* the sons of Adah, Esau's wife.

[13]These *were* the sons of Reuel: Nahath, Zerah, Shammah, and Mizzah. These were the sons of Basemath, Esau's wife.

[14]These were the sons of Aholibamah, Esau's wife, the daughter of Anah, the daughter of Zibeon. And she bore to Esau: Jeush, Jaalam, and Korah.

35:18 [a]Literally *Son of My Sorrow* [b]Literally *Son of the Right Hand*   **35:27** [a]Literally *Town of Arba*   **36:11** [a]Spelled *Zephi* in 1 Chronicles 1:36

The Chiefs of Edom

15These *were* the chiefs of the sons of Esau. The sons of Eliphaz, the firstborn *son* of Esau, were Chief Teman, Chief Omar, Chief Zepho, Chief Kenaz, 16Chief Korah,ª Chief Gatam, *and* Chief Amalek. These *were* the chiefs of Eliphaz in the land of Edom. They *were* the sons of Adah.

17These *were* the sons of Reuel, Esau's son: Chief Nahath, Chief Zerah, Chief Shammah, and Chief Mizzah. These *were* the chiefs of Reuel in the land of Edom. These *were* the sons of Basemath, Esau's wife.

18And these *were* the sons of Aholibamah, Esau's wife: Chief Jeush, Chief Jaalam, and Chief Korah. These *were* the chiefs *who descended* from Aholibamah, Esau's wife, the daughter of Anah. 19These *were* the sons of Esau, who is Edom, and these *were* their chiefs.

The Sons of Seir

20These *were* the sons of Seir the Horite who inhabited the land: Lotan, Shobal, Zibeon, Anah, 21Dishon, Ezer, and Dishan. These *were* the chiefs of the Horites, the sons of Seir, in the land of Edom. 22And the sons of Lotan were Hori and Hemam.ª Lotan's sister *was* Timna. 23These *were* the sons of Shobal: Alvan,ª Manahath, Ebal, Shepho,ᵇ and Onam. 24These *were* the sons of Zibeon: both Ajah and Anah. This *was the* Anah who found the waterª in the wilderness as he pastured the donkeys of his father Zibeon. 25These *were* the children of Anah: Dishon and Aholibamah the daughter of Anah. 26These *were* the sons of Dishon:ª Hemdan,ᵇ Eshban, Ithran, and Cheran. 27These *were* the sons of Ezer: Bilhan, Zaavan, and Akan.ª 28These *were* the sons of Dishan: Uz and Aran.

29These *were* the chiefs of the Horites: Chief Lotan, Chief Shobal, Chief Zibeon, Chief Anah, 30Chief Dishon, Chief Ezer, and Chief Dishan. These *were* the chiefs of the Horites, according to their chiefs in the land of Seir.

The Kings of Edom

31Now these *were* the kings who reigned in the land of Edom before any king reigned over the children of Israel: 32Bela the son of Beor reigned in Edom, and the name of his city *was* Dinhabah. 33And when Bela died, Jobab the son of Zerah of Bozrah reigned in his place. 34When Jobab died, Husham of the land of the Temanites reigned in his place. 35And when Husham died, Hadad the son of Bedad, who attacked Midian in the field of Moab, reigned in his place. And the name of his city *was* Avith. 36When Hadad died, Samlah of Masrekah reigned in his place. 37And when Samlah died, Saul of Rehoboth-*by*-the-River reigned in his place. 38When Saul died, Baal-Hanan the son of Achbor reigned in his place. 39And when Baal-Hanan the son of Achbor died, Hadarª reigned in his place; and the name of his city *was* Pau.ᵇ His wife's name *was* Mehetabel, the daughter of Matred, the daughter of Mezahab.

The Chiefs of Esau

40And these *were* the names of the chiefs of Esau, according to their families and their places, by their names: Chief Timnah, Chief Alvah,ª Chief Jetheth, 41Chief Aholibamah, Chief Elah, Chief Pinon, 42Chief Kenaz, Chief Teman, Chief Mibzar, 43Chief Magdiel, and Chief Iram. These *were* the chiefs of Edom, according to their dwelling places in the land of their possession. Esau *was* the father of the Edomites.

Joseph Dreams of Greatness

37 Now Jacob dwelt in the land where his father was a stranger, in the land of Canaan. 2This *is* the history of Jacob.

Joseph, *being* seventeen years old, was feeding the flock with his brothers. And the lad *was* with the sons of Bilhah and the sons

---

36:16 ªSamaritan Pentateuch omits *Chief Korah*.
36:22 ªSpelled *Homam* in 1 Chronicles 1:39
36:23 ªSpelled *Alian* in 1 Chronicles 1:40 ᵇSpelled *Shephi* in 1 Chronicles 1:40 **36:24** ªFollowing Masoretic Text and Vulgate (*hot springs*); Septuagint reads *Jamin;* Targum reads *mighty men;* Talmud interprets as *mules.* **36:26** ªHebrew *Dishan* ᵇSpelled *Hamran* in 1 Chronicles 1:41
36:27 ªSpelled *Jaakan* in 1 Chronicles 1:42
36:39 ªSpelled *Hadad* in Samaritan Pentateuch, Syriac, and 1 Chronicles 1:50 ᵇSpelled *Pai* in 1 Chronicles 1:50 **36:40** ªSpelled *Aliah* in 1 Chronicles 1:51

of Zilpah, his father's wives; and Joseph brought a bad report of them to his father.

³Now Israel loved Joseph more than all his children, because he *was* the son of his old age. Also he made him a tunic of *many* colors. ⁴But when his brothers saw that their father loved him more than all his brothers, they hated him and could not speak peaceably to him.

⁵Now Joseph had a dream, and he told *it* to his brothers; and they hated him even more. ⁶So he said to them, "Please hear this dream which I have dreamed: ⁷There we were, binding sheaves in the field. Then behold, my sheaf arose and also stood upright; and indeed your sheaves stood all around and bowed down to my sheaf."

⁸And his brothers said to him, "Shall you indeed reign over us? Or shall you indeed have dominion over us?" So they hated him even more for his dreams and for his words.

⁹Then he dreamed still another dream and told it to his brothers, and said, "Look, I have dreamed another dream. And this time, the sun, the moon, and the eleven stars bowed down to me."

¹⁰So he told *it* to his father and his brothers; and his father rebuked him and said to him, "What *is* this dream that you have dreamed? Shall your mother and I and your brothers indeed come to bow down to the earth before you?" ¹¹And his brothers envied him, but his father kept the matter *in mind.*

Joseph Sold by His Brothers

¹²Then his brothers went to feed their father's flock in Shechem. ¹³And Israel said to Joseph, "Are not your brothers feeding *the flock* in Shechem? Come, I will send you to them."

So he said to him, "Here I am."

¹⁴Then he said to him, "Please go and see if it is well with your brothers and well with the flocks, and bring back word to me." So he sent him out of the Valley of Hebron, and he went to Shechem.

¹⁵Now a certain man found him, and there he was, wandering in the field. And the man asked him, saying, "What are you seeking?"

¹⁶So he said, "I am seeking my brothers. Please tell me where they are feeding *their* flocks."

¹⁷And the man said, "They have departed from here, for I heard them say, 'Let us go to Dothan.'" So Joseph went after his brothers and found them in Dothan.

¹⁸Now when they saw him afar off, even before he came near them, they conspired against him to kill him. ¹⁹Then they said to one another, "Look, this dreamer is coming! ²⁰Come therefore, let us now kill him and cast him into some pit; and we shall say, 'Some wild beast has devoured him.' We shall see what will become of his dreams!"

²¹But Reuben heard *it,* and he delivered him out of their hands, and said, "Let us not kill him." ²²And Reuben said to them, "Shed no blood, *but* cast him into this pit which *is* in the wilderness, and do not lay a hand on him"—that he might deliver him out of their hands, and bring him back to his father.

²³So it came to pass, when Joseph had come to his brothers, that they stripped Joseph *of* his tunic, the tunic of *many* colors that *was* on him. ²⁴Then they took him and cast him into a pit. And the pit *was* empty; *there was* no water in it.

²⁵And they sat down to eat a meal. Then they lifted their eyes and looked, and there was a company of Ishmaelites, coming from Gilead with their camels, bearing spices, balm, and myrrh, on their way to carry *them* down to Egypt. ²⁶So Judah said to his brothers, "What profit *is there* if we kill our brother and conceal his blood? ²⁷Come and let us sell him to the Ishmaelites, and let not our hand be upon him, for he *is* our brother *and* our flesh." And his brothers listened. ²⁸Then Midianite traders passed by; so *the brothers* pulled Joseph up and lifted him out of the pit, and sold him to the Ishmaelites for twenty *shekels* of silver. And they took Joseph to Egypt.

²⁹Then Reuben returned to the pit, and indeed Joseph *was* not in the pit; and he tore his clothes. ³⁰And he returned to his brothers and said, "The lad *is* no *more;* and I, where shall I go?"

³¹So they took Joseph's tunic, killed a kid of the goats, and dipped the tunic in the blood. ³²Then they sent the tunic of *many* colors, and they brought *it* to their father and said, "We have found this. Do you know whether it *is* your son's tunic or not?"

³³And he recognized it and said, "*It is* my son's tunic. A wild beast has devoured him. Without doubt Joseph is torn to pieces." ³⁴Then Jacob tore his clothes, put sackcloth on his waist, and mourned for his son many days. ³⁵And all his sons and all his daughters arose to comfort him; but he refused to be comforted, and he said, "For I shall go down into the grave to my son in mourning." Thus his father wept for him.

³⁶Now the Midianitesᵃ had sold him in Egypt to Potiphar, an officer of Pharaoh *and* captain of the guard.

FREEDOM

. . . and sold [Joseph] to the Ishmaelites for twenty shekels of silver.   GENESIS 37:28

Taking Liberty for Granted

Dick Cheney, the 46th vice president of the United States, stated:

> *It is easy to take liberty for granted, when you have never had it taken from you.*

Judah and Tamar

38 It came to pass at that time that Judah departed from his brothers, and visited a certain Adullamite whose name *was* Hirah. ²And Judah saw there a daughter of a certain Canaanite whose name *was* Shua, and he married her and went in to her. ³So she conceived and bore a son, and he called his name Er. ⁴She conceived again and bore a son, and she called his name Onan. ⁵And she conceived yet again and bore a son, and called his name Shelah. He was at Chezib when she bore him.

⁶Then Judah took a wife for Er his firstborn, and her name *was* Tamar. ⁷But Er, Judah's firstborn, was wicked in the sight of the LORD, and the LORD killed him. ⁸And Judah said to Onan, "Go in to your brother's wife and marry her, and raise up an heir to your brother." ⁹But Onan knew that the heir would not be his; and it came to pass, when he went in to his brother's wife, that he emitted on the ground, lest he should give an heir to his brother. ¹⁰And the thing which he did displeased the LORD; therefore He killed him also.

¹¹Then Judah said to Tamar his daughter-in-law, "Remain a widow in your father's house till my son Shelah is grown." For he said, "Lest he also die like his brothers." And Tamar went and dwelt in her father's house.

¹²Now in the process of time the daughter of Shua, Judah's wife, died; and Judah was comforted, and went up to his sheepshearers at Timnah, he and his friend Hirah the Adullamite. ¹³And it was told Tamar, saying, "Look, your father-in-law is going up to Timnah to shear his sheep." ¹⁴So she took off her widow's garments, covered *herself* with a veil and wrapped herself, and sat in an open place which *was* on the way to Timnah; for she saw that Shelah was grown, and she was not given to him as a wife. ¹⁵When Judah saw her, he thought she *was* a harlot, because she had covered her face. ¹⁶Then he turned to her by the way, and said, "Please let me come in to you"; for he did not know that she *was* his daughter-in-law.

So she said, "What will you give me, that you may come in to me?"

¹⁷And he said, "I will send a young goat from the flock."

So she said, "Will you give *me* a pledge till you send *it*?"

¹⁸Then he said, "What pledge shall I give you?"

So she said, "Your signet and cord, and your staff that *is* in your hand." Then he gave *them* to her, and went in to her, and she conceived by him. ¹⁹So she arose and went away, and laid aside her veil and put on the garments of her widowhood.

²⁰And Judah sent the young goat by the hand of his friend the Adullamite, to receive *his* pledge from the woman's hand, but he did not find her. ²¹Then he asked the men of that place, saying, "Where is the harlot who *was* openly by the roadside?"

37:36 ᵃMasoretic Text reads *Medanites*.

And they said, "There was no harlot in this *place.*"

²²So he returned to Judah and said, "I cannot find her. Also, the men of the place said there was no harlot in this *place.*"

²³Then Judah said, "Let her take *them* for herself, lest we be shamed; for I sent this young goat and you have not found her."

²⁴And it came to pass, about three months after, that Judah was told, saying, "Tamar your daughter-in-law has played the harlot; furthermore she *is* with child by harlotry."

So Judah said, "Bring her out and let her be burned!"

²⁵When she *was* brought out, she sent to her father-in-law, saying, "By the man to whom these belong, I *am* with child." And she said, "Please determine whose these are—the signet and cord, and staff."

²⁶So Judah acknowledged *them* and said, "She has been more righteous than I, because I did not give her to Shelah my son." And he never knew her again.

²⁷Now it came to pass, at the time for giving birth, that behold, twins *were* in her womb. ²⁸And so it was, when she was giving birth, that *the one* put out *his* hand; and the midwife took a scarlet *thread* and bound it on his hand, saying, "This one came out first." ²⁹Then it happened, as he drew back his hand, that his brother came out unexpectedly; and she said, "How did you break through? *This* breach *be* upon you!" Therefore his name was called Perez.ᵃ ³⁰Afterward his brother came out who had the scarlet *thread* on his hand. And his name was called Zerah.

Joseph a Slave in Egypt

39 Now Joseph had been taken down to Egypt. And Potiphar, an officer of Pharaoh, captain of the guard, an Egyptian, bought him from the Ishmaelites who had taken him down there. ²The LORD was with Joseph, and he was a successful man; and he was in the house of his master the Egyptian. ³And his master saw that the LORD *was* with him and that the LORD made all he did to prosper in his hand. ⁴So Joseph found favor in his sight, and served him.

Then he made him overseer of his house, and all *that* he had he put under his authority. ⁵So it was, from the time *that* he had made him overseer of his house and all that he had, that the LORD blessed the Egyptian's house for Joseph's sake; and the blessing of the LORD was on all that he had in the house and in the field. ⁶Thus he left all that he had in Joseph's hand, and he did not know what he had except for the bread which he ate.

Now Joseph was handsome in form and appearance.

⁷And it came to pass after these things that his master's wife cast longing eyes on Joseph, and she said, "Lie with me."

⁸But he refused and said to his master's wife, "Look, my master does not know what *is* with me in the house, and he has committed all that he has to my hand. ⁹*There is* no one greater in this house than I, nor has he kept back anything from me but you, because you *are* his wife. How then can I do this great wickedness, and sin against God?"

¹⁰So it was, as she spoke to Joseph day by day, that he did not heed her, to lie with her *or* to be with her.

¹¹But it happened about this time, when Joseph went into the house to do his work, and none of the men of the house *was* inside, ¹²that she caught him by his garment, saying, "Lie with me." But he left his garment in her hand, and fled and ran outside. ¹³And so it was, when she saw that he had left his garment in her hand and fled outside, ¹⁴that she called to the men of her house and spoke to them, saying, "See, he has brought in to us a Hebrew to mock us. He came in to me to lie with me, and I cried out with a loud voice. ¹⁵And it happened, when he heard that I lifted my voice and cried out, that he left his garment with me, and fled and went outside."

¹⁶So she kept his garment with her until his master came home. ¹⁷Then she spoke to him with words like these, saying, "The Hebrew servant whom you brought to us came in to me to mock me; ¹⁸so it happened, as I lifted my voice and cried out,

---

38:29 ᵃLiterally *Breach* or *Breakthrough*

that he left his garment with me and fled outside."

¹⁹So it was, when his master heard the words which his wife spoke to him, saying, "Your servant did to me after this manner," that his anger was aroused. ²⁰Then Joseph's master took him and put him into the prison, a place where the king's prisoners *were* confined. And he was there in the prison. ²¹But the LORD was with Joseph and showed him mercy, and He gave him favor in the sight of the keeper of the prison. ²²And the keeper of the prison committed to Joseph's hand all the prisoners who *were* in the prison; whatever they did there, it was his doing. ²³The keeper of the prison did not look into anything *that was* under *Joseph's* authority,ᵃ because the LORD was with him; and whatever he did, the LORD made *it* prosper.

The Prisoners' Dreams

40 It came to pass after these things *that* the butler and the baker of the king of Egypt offended their lord, the king of Egypt. ²And Pharaoh was angry with his two officers, the chief butler and the chief baker. ³So he put them in custody in the house of the captain of the guard, in the prison, the place where Joseph *was* confined. ⁴And the captain of the guard charged Joseph with them, and he served them; so they were in custody for a while.

⁵Then the butler and the baker of the king of Egypt, who *were* confined in the prison, had a dream, both of them, each man's dream in one night *and* each man's dream with its *own* interpretation. ⁶And Joseph came in to them in the morning and looked at them, and saw that they *were* sad. ⁷So he asked Pharaoh's officers who *were* with him in the custody of his lord's house, saying, "Why do you look *so* sad today?"

⁸And they said to him, "We each have had a dream, and *there is* no interpreter of it."

So Joseph said to them, "Do not interpretations belong to God? Tell *them* to me, please."

⁹Then the chief butler told his dream to Joseph, and said to him, "Behold, in my dream a vine *was* before me, ¹⁰and in the vine *were* three branches; it *was* as though it budded, its blossoms shot forth, and its clusters brought forth ripe grapes. ¹¹Then Pharaoh's cup *was* in my hand; and I took the grapes and pressed them into Pharaoh's cup, and placed the cup in Pharaoh's hand."

¹²And Joseph said to him, "This *is* the interpretation of it: The three branches *are* three days. ¹³Now within three days Pharaoh will lift up your head and restore you to your place, and you will put Pharaoh's cup in his hand according to the former manner, when you were his butler. ¹⁴But remember me when it is well with you, and please show kindness to me; make mention of me to Pharaoh, and get me out of this house. ¹⁵For indeed I was stolen away from the land of the Hebrews; and also I have done nothing here that they should put me into the dungeon."

¹⁶When the chief baker saw that the interpretation was good, he said to Joseph, "I also *was* in my dream, and there *were* three white baskets on my head. ¹⁷In the uppermost basket *were* all kinds of baked goods for Pharaoh, and the birds ate them out of the basket on my head."

¹⁸So Joseph answered and said, "This *is* the interpretation of it: The three baskets *are* three days. ¹⁹Within three days Pharaoh will lift off your head from you and hang you on a tree; and the birds will eat your flesh from you."

²⁰Now it came to pass on the third day, *which was* Pharaoh's birthday, that he made a feast for all his servants; and he lifted up the head of the chief butler and of the chief baker among his servants. ²¹Then he restored the chief butler to his butlership again, and he placed the cup in Pharaoh's hand. ²²But he hanged the chief baker, as Joseph had interpreted to them. ²³Yet the chief butler did not remember Joseph, but forgot him.

Pharaoh's Dreams

41 Then it came to pass, at the end of two full years, that Pharaoh had a dream; and behold, he stood by the river.

39:23 ᵃLiterally *his hand*

²Suddenly there came up out of the river seven cows, fine looking and fat; and they fed in the meadow. ³Then behold, seven other cows came up after them out of the river, ugly and gaunt, and stood by the *other* cows on the bank of the river. ⁴And the ugly and gaunt cows ate up the seven fine looking and fat cows. So Pharaoh awoke. ⁵He slept and dreamed a second time; and suddenly seven heads of grain came up on one stalk, plump and good. ⁶Then behold, seven thin heads, blighted by the east wind, sprang up after them. ⁷And the seven thin heads devoured the seven plump and full heads. So Pharaoh awoke, and indeed, *it was* a dream. ⁸Now it came to pass in the morning that his spirit was troubled, and he sent and called for all the magicians of Egypt and all its wise men. And Pharaoh told them his dreams, but *there was* no one who could interpret them for Pharaoh.

⁹Then the chief butler spoke to Pharaoh, saying: "I remember my faults this day. ¹⁰When Pharaoh was angry with his servants, and put me in custody in the house of the captain of the guard, *both* me and the chief baker, ¹¹we each had a dream in one night, he and I. Each of us dreamed according to the interpretation of his *own* dream. ¹²Now there *was* a young Hebrew man with us there, a servant of the captain of the guard. And we told him, and he interpreted our dreams for us; to each man he interpreted according to his *own* dream. ¹³And it came to pass, just as he interpreted for us, so it happened. He restored me to my office, and he hanged him."

¹⁴Then Pharaoh sent and called Joseph, and they brought him quickly out of the dungeon; and he shaved, changed his clothing, and came to Pharaoh. ¹⁵And Pharaoh said to Joseph, "I have had a dream, and *there is* no one who can interpret it. But I have heard it said of you *that* you can understand a dream, to interpret it."

¹⁶So Joseph answered Pharaoh, saying, "*It is* not in me; God will give Pharaoh an answer of peace."

¹⁷Then Pharaoh said to Joseph: "Behold, in my dream I stood on the bank of the river. ¹⁸Suddenly seven cows came up out of the river, fine looking and fat; and they fed in the meadow. ¹⁹Then behold, seven other cows came up after them, poor and very ugly and gaunt, such ugliness as I have never seen in all the land of Egypt. ²⁰And the gaunt and ugly cows ate up the first seven, the fat cows. ²¹When they had eaten them up, no one would have known that they had eaten them, for they *were* just as ugly as at the beginning. So I awoke. ²²Also I saw in my dream, and suddenly seven heads came up on one stalk, full and good. ²³Then behold, seven heads, withered, thin, *and* blighted by the east wind, sprang up after them. ²⁴And the thin heads devoured the seven good heads. So I told *this* to the magicians, but *there was* no one who could explain *it* to me."

²⁵Then Joseph said to Pharaoh, "The dreams of Pharaoh *are* one; God has shown Pharaoh what He *is* about to do: ²⁶The seven good cows *are* seven years, and the seven good heads *are* seven years; the dreams *are* one. ²⁷And the seven thin and ugly cows which came up after them *are* seven years, and the seven empty heads blighted by the east wind are seven years of famine. ²⁸This *is* the thing which I have spoken to Pharaoh. God has shown Pharaoh what He *is* about to do. ²⁹Indeed seven years of great plenty will come throughout all the land of Egypt; ³⁰but after them seven years of famine will arise, and all the plenty will be forgotten in the land of Egypt; and the famine will deplete the land. ³¹So the plenty will not be known in the land because of the famine following, for it *will be* very severe. ³²And the dream was repeated to Pharaoh twice because the thing *is* established by God, and God will shortly bring it to pass.

³³"Now therefore, let Pharaoh select a discerning and wise man, and set him over the land of Egypt. ³⁴Let Pharaoh do *this*, and let him appoint officers over the land, to collect one-fifth *of the produce* of the land of Egypt in the seven plentiful years. ³⁵And let them gather all the food of those good years that are coming, and store up grain under the authority of Pharaoh, and

let them keep food in the cities. ³⁶Then that food shall be as a reserve for the land for the seven years of famine which shall be in the land of Egypt, that the land may not perish during the famine."

Joseph's Rise to Power

³⁷So the advice was good in the eyes of Pharaoh and in the eyes of all his servants. ³⁸And Pharaoh said to his servants, "Can we find *such a one* as this, a man in whom *is* the Spirit of God?"

³⁹Then Pharaoh said to Joseph, "Inasmuch as God has shown you all this, *there is* no one as discerning and wise as you. ⁴⁰You shall be over my house, and all my people shall be ruled according to your word; only in regard to the throne will I be greater than you." ⁴¹And Pharaoh said to Joseph, "See, I have set you over all the land of Egypt."

⁴²Then Pharaoh took his signet ring off his hand and put it on Joseph's hand; and he clothed him in garments of fine linen and put a gold chain around his neck. ⁴³And he had him ride in the second chariot which he had; and they cried out before him, "Bow the knee!" So he set him over all the land of Egypt. ⁴⁴Pharaoh also said to Joseph, "I *am* Pharaoh, and without your consent no man may lift his hand or foot in all the land of Egypt." ⁴⁵And Pharaoh called Joseph's name Zaphnath-Paaneah. And he gave him as a wife Asenath, the daughter of Poti-Pherah priest of On. So Joseph went out over *all* the land of Egypt.

⁴⁶Joseph was thirty years old when he stood before Pharaoh king of Egypt. And Joseph went out from the presence of Pharaoh, and went throughout all the land of Egypt. ⁴⁷Now in the seven plentiful years the ground brought forth abundantly. ⁴⁸So he gathered up all the food of the seven years which were in the land of Egypt, and laid up the food in the cities; he laid up in every city the food of the fields which surrounded them. ⁴⁹Joseph gathered very much grain, as the sand of the sea, until he stopped counting, for *it was* immeasurable.

⁵⁰And to Joseph were born two sons before the years of famine came, whom Asenath, the daughter of Poti-Pherah priest of On, bore to him. ⁵¹Joseph called the name of the firstborn Manasseh:ᵃ "For God has made me forget all my toil and all my father's house." ⁵²And the name of the second he called Ephraim:ᵃ "For God has caused me to be fruitful in the land of my affliction."

⁵³Then the seven years of plenty which were in the land of Egypt ended, ⁵⁴and the seven years of famine began to come, as Joseph had said. The famine was in all lands, but in all the land of Egypt there was bread. ⁵⁵So when all the land of Egypt was famished, the people cried to Pharaoh for bread. Then Pharaoh said to all the Egyptians, "Go to Joseph; whatever he says to you, do." ⁵⁶The famine was over all the face of the earth, and Joseph opened all the storehousesᵃ and sold to the Egyptians. And the famine became severe in the land of Egypt. ⁵⁷So all countries came to Joseph in Egypt to buy *grain,* because the famine was severe in all lands.

Joseph's Brothers Go to Egypt

42 When Jacob saw that there was grain in Egypt, Jacob said to his sons, "Why do you look at one another?" ²And he said, "Indeed I have heard that there is grain in Egypt; go down to that place and buy for us there, that we may live and not die."

³So Joseph's ten brothers went down to buy grain in Egypt. ⁴But Jacob did not send Joseph's brother Benjamin with his brothers, for he said, "Lest some calamity befall him." ⁵And the sons of Israel went to buy *grain* among those who journeyed, for the famine was in the land of Canaan.

⁶Now Joseph *was* governor over the land; and it was he who sold to all the people of the land. And Joseph's brothers came and bowed down before him with *their* faces to the earth. ⁷Joseph saw his brothers and recognized them, but he acted as a stranger to them and spoke roughly to them. Then he said to them, "Where do you come from?"

And they said, "From the land of Canaan to buy food."

41:51 ᵃLiterally *Making Forgetful*   **41:52** ᵃLiterally *Fruitfulness*   **41:56** ᵃLiterally *all that was in them*

⁸So Joseph recognized his brothers, but they did not recognize him. ⁹Then Joseph remembered the dreams which he had dreamed about them, and said to them, "You *are* spies! You have come to see the nakedness of the land!"

¹⁰And they said to him, "No, my lord, but your servants have come to buy food. ¹¹We *are* all one man's sons; we *are* honest *men;* your servants are not spies."

¹²But he said to them, "No, but you have come to see the nakedness of the land."

¹³And they said, "Your servants *are* twelve brothers, the sons of one man in the land of Canaan; and in fact, the youngest *is* with our father today, and one *is* no more."

¹⁴But Joseph said to them, "It *is* as I spoke to you, saying, 'You *are* spies!' ¹⁵In this *manner* you shall be tested: By the life of Pharaoh, you shall not leave this place unless your youngest brother comes here. ¹⁶Send one of you, and let him bring your brother; and you shall be kept in prison, that your words may be tested to see whether *there is* any truth in you; or else, by the life of Pharaoh, surely you *are* spies!" ¹⁷So he put them all together in prison three days.

¹⁸Then Joseph said to them the third day, "Do this and live, *for* I fear God: ¹⁹If you *are* honest *men,* let one of your brothers be confined to your prison house; but you, go and carry grain for the famine of your houses. ²⁰And bring your youngest brother to me; so your words will be verified, and you shall not die."

And they did so. ²¹Then they said to one another, "We *are* truly guilty concerning our brother, for we saw the anguish of his soul when he pleaded with us, and we would not hear; therefore this distress has come upon us."

²²And Reuben answered them, saying, "Did I not speak to you, saying, 'Do not sin against the boy'; and you would not listen? Therefore behold, his blood is now required of us." ²³But they did not know that Joseph understood *them,* for he spoke to them through an interpreter. ²⁴And he turned himself away from them and wept. Then he returned to them again, and talked with them. And he took Simeon from them and bound him before their eyes.

The Brothers Return to Canaan

²⁵Then Joseph gave a command to fill their sacks with grain, to restore every man's money to his sack, and to give them provisions for the journey. Thus he did for them. ²⁶So they loaded their donkeys with the grain and departed from there. ²⁷But as one *of them* opened his sack to give his donkey feed at the encampment, he saw his money; and there it was, in the mouth of his sack. ²⁸So he said to his brothers, "My money has been restored, and there it is, in my sack!" Then their hearts failed *them* and they were afraid, saying to one another, "What *is* this *that* God has done to us?"

²⁹Then they went to Jacob their father in the land of Canaan and told him all that had happened to them, saying: ³⁰"The man *who is* lord of the land spoke roughly to us, and took us for spies of the country. ³¹But we said to him, 'We *are* honest *men;* we are not spies. ³²We *are* twelve brothers, sons of our father; one *is* no *more,* and the youngest *is* with our father this day in the land of Canaan.' ³³Then the man, the lord of the country, said to us, 'By this I will know that you *are* honest *men:* Leave one of your brothers *here* with me, take *food for* the famine of your households, and be gone. ³⁴And bring your youngest brother to me; so I shall know that you *are* not spies, but *that* you *are* honest *men.* I will grant your brother to you, and you may trade in the land.'"

³⁵Then it happened as they emptied their sacks, that surprisingly each man's bundle of money *was* in his sack; and when they and their father saw the bundles of money, they were afraid. ³⁶And Jacob their father said to them, "You have bereaved me: Joseph is no *more,* Simeon is no *more,* and you want to take Benjamin. All these things are against me."

³⁷Then Reuben spoke to his father, saying, "Kill my two sons if I do not bring him *back* to you; put him in my hands, and I will bring him back to you."

[38]But he said, "My son shall not go down with you, for his brother is dead, and he is left alone. If any calamity should befall him along the way in which you go, then you would bring down my gray hair with sorrow to the grave."

Joseph's Brothers Return with Benjamin

43 Now the famine *was* severe in the land. [2]And it came to pass, when they had eaten up the grain which they had brought from Egypt, that their father said to them, "Go back, buy us a little food." [3]But Judah spoke to him, saying, "The man solemnly warned us, saying, 'You shall not see my face unless your brother *is* with you.' [4]If you send our brother with us, we will go down and buy you food. [5]But if you will not send *him,* we will not go down; for the man said to us, 'You shall not see my face unless your brother *is* with you.' " [6]And Israel said, "Why did you deal *so* wrongfully with me *as* to tell the man whether you had still *another* brother?" [7]But they said, "The man asked us pointedly about ourselves and our family, saying, '*Is* your father still alive? Have you *another* brother?' And we told him according to these words. Could we possibly have known that he would say, 'Bring your brother down'?" [8]Then Judah said to Israel his father, "Send the lad with me, and we will arise and go, that we may live and not die, both we and you *and* also our little ones. [9]I myself will be surety for him; from my hand you shall require him. If I do not bring him *back* to you and set him before you, then let me bear the blame forever. [10]For if we had not lingered, surely by now we would have returned this second time." [11]And their father Israel said to them, "If *it must be* so, then do this: Take some of the best fruits of the land in your vessels and carry down a present for the man—a little balm and a little honey, spices and myrrh, pistachio nuts and almonds. [12]Take double money in your hand, and take back in your hand the money that was returned in the mouth of your sacks; perhaps it was an oversight. [13]Take your brother also, and arise, go back to the man. [14]And may God Almighty give you mercy before the man, that he may release your other brother and Benjamin. If I am bereaved, I am bereaved!"

[15]So the men took that present and Benjamin, and they took double money in their hand, and arose and went down to Egypt; and they stood before Joseph. [16]When Joseph saw Benjamin with them, he said to the steward of his house, "Take *these* men to my home, and slaughter an animal and make ready; for *these* men will dine with me at noon." [17]Then the man did as Joseph ordered, and the man brought the men into Joseph's house.

[18]Now the men were afraid because they were brought into Joseph's house; and they said, "*It is* because of the money, which was returned in our sacks the first time, that we are brought in, so that he may make a case against us and seize us, to take us as slaves with our donkeys."

[19]When they drew near to the steward of Joseph's house, they talked with him at the door of the house, [20]and said, "O sir, we indeed came down the first time to buy food; [21]but it happened, when we came to the encampment, that we opened our sacks, and there, *each* man's money *was* in the mouth of his sack, our money in full weight; so we have brought it back in our hand. [22]And we have brought down other money in our hands to buy food. We do not know who put our money in our sacks." [23]But he said, "Peace *be* with you, do not be afraid. Your God and the God of your father has given you treasure in your sacks; I had your money." Then he brought Simeon out to them.

[24]So the man brought the men into Joseph's house and gave *them* water, and they washed their feet; and he gave their donkeys feed. [25]Then they made the present ready for Joseph's coming at noon, for they heard that they would eat bread there.

[26]And when Joseph came home, they brought him the present which *was* in their hand into the house, and bowed down before him to the earth. [27]Then he asked them about *their* well-being, and said, "*Is*

your father well, the old man of whom you spoke? *Is* he still alive?"

²⁸And they answered, "Your servant our father *is* in good health; he *is* still alive." And they bowed their heads down and prostrated themselves.

²⁹Then he lifted his eyes and saw his brother Benjamin, his mother's son, and said, "*Is* this your younger brother of whom you spoke to me?" And he said, "God be gracious to you, my son." ³⁰Now his heart yearned for his brother; so Joseph made haste and sought *somewhere* to weep. And he went into *his* chamber and wept there. ³¹Then he washed his face and came out; and he restrained himself, and said, "Serve the bread."

³²So they set him a place by himself, and them by themselves, and the Egyptians who ate with him by themselves; because the Egyptians could not eat food with the Hebrews, for that *is* an abomination to the Egyptians. ³³And they sat before him, the firstborn according to his birthright and the youngest according to his youth; and the men looked in astonishment at one another. ³⁴Then he took servings to them from before him, but Benjamin's serving was five times as much as any of theirs. So they drank and were merry with him.

Joseph's Cup

44 And he commanded the steward of his house, saying, "Fill the men's sacks with food, as much as they can carry, and put each man's money in the mouth of his sack. ²Also put my cup, the silver cup, in the mouth of the sack of the youngest, and his grain money." So he did according to the word that Joseph had spoken. ³As soon as the morning dawned, the men were sent away, they and their donkeys. ⁴When they had gone out of the city, *and* were not *yet* far off, Joseph said to his steward, "Get up, follow the men; and when you overtake them, say to them, 'Why have you repaid evil for good? ⁵*Is* not this *the one* from which my lord drinks, and with which he indeed practices divination? You have done evil in so doing.' "

⁶So he overtook them, and he spoke to them these same words. ⁷And they said to

him, "Why does my lord say these words? Far be it from us that your servants should do such a thing. ⁸Look, we brought back to you from the land of Canaan the money which we found in the mouth of our sacks. How then could we steal silver or gold from your lord's house? ⁹With whomever of your servants it is found, let him die, and we also will be my lord's slaves."

¹⁰And he said, "Now also *let* it *be* according to your words; he with whom it is found shall be my slave, and you shall be blameless." ¹¹Then each man speedily let down his sack to the ground, and each opened his sack. ¹²So he searched. He began with the oldest and left off with the youngest; and the cup was found in Benjamin's sack. ¹³Then they tore their clothes, and each man loaded his donkey and returned to the city.

¹⁴So Judah and his brothers came to Joseph's house, and he *was* still there; and they fell before him on the ground. ¹⁵And Joseph said to them, "What deed *is* this you have done? Did you not know that such a man as I can certainly practice divination?"

¹⁶Then Judah said, "What shall we say to my lord? What shall we speak? Or how shall we clear ourselves? God has found out the iniquity of your servants; here we are, my lord's slaves, both we and *he* also with whom the cup was found."

¹⁷But he said, "Far be it from me that I should do so; the man in whose hand the cup was found, he shall be my slave. And as for you, go up in peace to your father."

Judah Intercedes for Benjamin

¹⁸Then Judah came near to him and said: "O my lord, please let your servant speak a word in my lord's hearing, and do not let your anger burn against your servant; for you *are* even like Pharaoh. ¹⁹My lord asked his servants, saying, 'Have you a father or a brother?' ²⁰And we said to my lord, 'We have a father, an old man, and a child of *his* old age, *who is* young; his brother is dead, and he alone is left of his mother's children, and his father loves him.' ²¹Then you said to your servants, 'Bring him down to me, that I may set my eyes on him.' ²²And

we said to my lord, 'The lad cannot leave his father, for *if* he should leave his father, *his father* would die.' ²³But you said to your servants, 'Unless your youngest brother comes down with you, you shall see my face no more.'

²⁴"So it was, when we went up to your servant my father, that we told him the words of my lord. ²⁵And our father said, 'Go back *and* buy us a little food.' ²⁶But we said, 'We cannot go down; if our youngest brother is with us, then we will go down; for we may not see the man's face unless our youngest brother *is* with us.' ²⁷Then your servant my father said to us, 'You know that my wife bore me two sons; ²⁸and the one went out from me, and I said, "Surely he is torn to pieces"; and I have not seen him since. ²⁹But if you take this one also from me, and calamity befalls him, you shall bring down my gray hair with sorrow to the grave.'

³⁰"Now therefore, when I come to your servant my father, and the lad *is* not with us, since his life is bound up in the lad's life, ³¹it will happen, when he sees that the lad *is* not *with us,* that he will die. So your servants will bring down the gray hair of your servant our father with sorrow to the grave. ³²For your servant became surety for the lad to my father, saying, 'If I do not bring him *back* to you, then I shall bear the blame before my father forever.' ³³Now therefore, please let your servant remain instead of the lad as a slave to my lord, and let the lad go up with his brothers. ³⁴For how shall I go up to my father if the lad *is* not with me, lest perhaps I see the evil that would come upon my father?"

Joseph Revealed to His Brothers

45 Then Joseph could not restrain himself before all those who stood by him, and he cried out, "Make everyone go out from me!" So no one stood with him while Joseph made himself known to his brothers. ²And he wept aloud, and the Egyptians and the house of Pharaoh heard *it.*

³Then Joseph said to his brothers, "I *am* Joseph; does my father still live?" But his brothers could not answer him, for they were dismayed in his presence. ⁴And Joseph said to his brothers, "Please come near to me." So they came near. Then he said: "I *am* Joseph your brother, whom you sold into Egypt. ⁵But now, do not therefore be grieved or angry with yourselves because you sold me here; for God sent me before you to preserve life. ⁶For these two years the famine *has been* in the land, and *there are* still five years in which *there will be* neither plowing nor harvesting. ⁷And God sent me before you to preserve a posterity for you in the earth, and to save your lives by a great deliverance. ⁸So now *it was* not you *who* sent me here, but God; and He has made me a father to Pharaoh, and lord of all his house, and a ruler throughout all the land of Egypt.

⁹"Hurry and go up to my father, and say to him, 'Thus says your son Joseph: "God has made me lord of all Egypt; come down to me, do not tarry. ¹⁰You shall dwell in the land of Goshen, and you shall be near to me, you and your children, your children's children, your flocks and your herds, and all that you have. ¹¹There I will provide for you, lest you and your household, and all that you have, come to poverty; for *there are* still five years of famine."'

¹²"And behold, your eyes and the eyes of my brother Benjamin see that *it is* my mouth that speaks to you. ¹³So you shall tell my father of all my glory in Egypt, and of all that you have seen; and you shall hurry and bring my father down here."

¹⁴Then he fell on his brother Benjamin's neck and wept, and Benjamin wept on his neck. ¹⁵Moreover he kissed all his brothers and wept over them, and after that his brothers talked with him.

¹⁶Now the report of it was heard in Pharaoh's house, saying, "Joseph's brothers have come." So it pleased Pharaoh and his servants well. ¹⁷And Pharaoh said to Joseph, "Say to your brothers, 'Do this: Load your animals and depart; go to the land of Canaan. ¹⁸Bring your father and your households and come to me; I will give you the best of the land of Egypt, and you will eat the fat of the land. ¹⁹Now you are commanded—do this: Take carts out of the

land of Egypt for your little ones and your wives; bring your father and come. ²⁰Also do not be concerned about your goods, for the best of all the land of Egypt *is* yours.'"

²¹Then the sons of Israel did so; and Joseph gave them carts, according to the command of Pharaoh, and he gave them provisions for the journey. ²²He gave to all of them, to each man, changes of garments; but to Benjamin he gave three hundred *pieces* of silver and five changes of garments. ²³And he sent to his father these *things:* ten donkeys loaded with the good things of Egypt, and ten female donkeys loaded with grain, bread, and food for his father for the journey. ²⁴So he sent his brothers away, and they departed; and he said to them, "See that you do not become troubled along the way."

²⁵Then they went up out of Egypt, and came to the land of Canaan to Jacob their father. ²⁶And they told him, saying, "Joseph *is* still alive, and he *is* governor over all the land of Egypt." And Jacob's heart stood still, because he did not believe them. ²⁷But when they told him all the words which Joseph had said to them, and when he saw the carts which Joseph had sent to carry him, the spirit of Jacob their father revived. ²⁸Then Israel said, "*It is* enough. Joseph my son *is* still alive. I will go and see him before I die."

FAITH

". . . for God sent me before you to preserve life."

GENESIS 45:5

God-Made Rights of God-Made Man

Clarence Manion, dean of the Notre Dame College of Law (1941–1952), stated concerning the Declaration of Independence:

> *Look closely at these self-evident truths, these imperishable articles of American faith upon which all our government is firmly based. First and foremost is the existence of God. Next comes the truth that all men are equal in the sight of God. Third is the fact of God's great gift of unalienable rights to every person on earth. Then follows the true and single purpose of all American government, namely, to preserve and protect these God-made rights of God-made man.*

Jacob's Journey to Egypt

46 So Israel took his journey with all that he had, and came to Beersheba, and offered sacrifices to the God of his father Isaac. ²Then God spoke to Israel in the visions of the night, and said, "Jacob, Jacob!"

And he said, "Here I am."

³So He said, "I *am* God, the God of your father; do not fear to go down to Egypt, for I will make of you a great nation there. ⁴I will go down with you to Egypt, and I will also surely bring you up *again;* and Joseph will put his hand on your eyes."

⁵Then Jacob arose from Beersheba; and the sons of Israel carried their father Jacob, their little ones, and their wives, in the carts which Pharaoh had sent to carry him. ⁶So they took their livestock and their goods, which they had acquired in the land of Canaan, and went to Egypt, Jacob and all his descendants with him. ⁷His sons and his sons' sons, his daughters and his sons' daughters, and all his descendants he brought with him to Egypt.

⁸Now these *were* the names of the children of Israel, Jacob and his sons, who went to Egypt: Reuben *was* Jacob's firstborn. ⁹The sons of Reuben *were* Hanoch, Pallu, Hezron, and Carmi. ¹⁰The sons of Simeon *were* Jemuel,ᵃ Jamin, Ohad, Jachin,ᵇ Zohar,ᶜ and Shaul, the son of a Canaanite woman. ¹¹The sons of Levi *were* Gershon, Kohath, and Merari. ¹²The sons of Judah *were* Er, Onan, Shelah, Perez, and Zerah (but Er and Onan died in the land of Canaan). The sons of Perez were Hezron and Hamul. ¹³The sons of Issachar *were* Tola, Puvah,ᵃ Job,ᵇ and Shimron. ¹⁴The sons of Zebulun *were* Sered, Elon, and Jahleel. ¹⁵These *were* the sons of Leah, whom she bore to Jacob in Padan Aram, with his daughter Dinah. All the persons, his sons and his daughters, *were* thirty-three.

¹⁶The sons of Gad *were* Ziphion,ᵃ Haggi, Shuni, Ezbon,ᵇ Eri, Arodi,ᶜ and Areli. ¹⁷The

---

46:10 ᵃSpelled *Nemuel* in 1 Chronicles 4:24 ᵇCalled *Jarib* in 1 Chronicles 4:24 ᶜCalled *Zerah* in 1 Chronicles 4:24 **46:13** ᵃSpelled *Puah* in 1 Chronicles 7:1 ᵇSame as *Jashub* in Numbers 26:24 and 1 Chronicles 7:1 **46:16** ᵃSpelled *Zephon* in Samaritan Pentateuch, Septuagint, and Numbers 26:15 ᵇCalled *Ozni* in Numbers 26:16 ᶜSpelled *Arod* in Numbers 26:17

sons of Asher *were* Jimnah, Ishuah, Isui, Beriah, and Serah, their sister. And the sons of Beriah *were* Heber and Malchiel. 18These *were* the sons of Zilpah, whom Laban gave to Leah his daughter; and these she bore to Jacob: sixteen persons.

19The sons of Rachel, Jacob's wife, *were* Joseph and Benjamin. 20And to Joseph in the land of Egypt were born Manasseh and Ephraim, whom Asenath, the daughter of Poti-Pherah priest of On, bore to him. 21The sons of Benjamin *were* Belah, Becher, Ashbel, Gera, Naaman, Ehi, Rosh, Muppim, Huppim,a and Ard. 22These *were* the sons of Rachel, who were born to Jacob: fourteen persons in all.

23The son of Dan *was* Hushim.a 24The sons of Naphtali *were* Jahzeel,a Guni, Jezer, and Shillem.b 25These *were* the sons of Bilhah, whom Laban gave to Rachel his daughter, and she bore these to Jacob: seven persons in all.

26All the persons who went with Jacob to Egypt, who came from his body, besides Jacob's sons' wives, *were* sixty-six persons in all. 27And the sons of Joseph who were born to him in Egypt *were* two persons. All the persons of the house of Jacob who went to Egypt were seventy.

Jacob Settles in Goshen

28Then he sent Judah before him to Joseph, to point out before him *the way* to Goshen. And they came to the land of Goshen. 29So Joseph made ready his chariot and went up to Goshen to meet his father Israel; and he presented himself to him, and fell on his neck and wept on his neck a good while.

30And Israel said to Joseph, "Now let me die, since I have seen your face, because you *are* still alive."

31Then Joseph said to his brothers and to his father's household, "I will go up and tell Pharaoh, and say to him, 'My brothers and those of my father's house, who *were* in the land of Canaan, have come to me. 32And the men *are* shepherds, for their occupation has been to feed livestock; and they have brought their flocks, their herds, and all that they have.' 33So it shall be,

when Pharaoh calls you and says, 'What is your occupation?' 34that you shall say, 'Your servants' occupation has been with livestock from our youth even till now, both we *and* also our fathers,' that you may dwell in the land of Goshen; for every shepherd *is* an abomination to the Egyptians."

47 Then Joseph went and told Pharaoh, and said, "My father and my brothers, their flocks and their herds and all that they possess, have come from the land of Canaan; and indeed they *are* in the land of Goshen." 2And he took five men from among his brothers and presented them to Pharaoh. 3Then Pharaoh said to his brothers, "What *is* your occupation?"

And they said to Pharaoh, "Your servants *are* shepherds, both we *and* also our fathers." 4And they said to Pharaoh, "We have come to dwell in the land, because your servants have no pasture for their flocks, for the famine *is* severe in the land of Canaan. Now therefore, please let your servants dwell in the land of Goshen."

5Then Pharaoh spoke to Joseph, saying, "Your father and your brothers have come to you. 6The land of Egypt *is* before you. Have your father and brothers dwell in the best of the land; let them dwell in the land of Goshen. And if you know *any* competent men among them, then make them chief herdsmen over my livestock."

7Then Joseph brought in his father Jacob and set him before Pharaoh; and Jacob blessed Pharaoh. 8Pharaoh said to Jacob, "How old *are* you?"

9And Jacob said to Pharaoh, "The days of the years of my pilgrimage *are* one hundred and thirty years; few and evil have been the days of the years of my life, and they have not attained to the days of the years of the life of my fathers in the days of their pilgrimage." 10So Jacob blessed Pharaoh, and went out from before Pharaoh.

11And Joseph situated his father and his brothers, and gave them a possession in the land of Egypt, in the best of the land,

---

46:21 aCalled *Hupham* in Numbers 26:39
46:23 aCalled *Shuham* in Numbers 26:42
46:24 aSpelled *Jahziel* in 1 Chronicles 7:13 bSpelled *Shallum* in 1 Chronicles 7:13

in the land of Rameses, as Pharaoh had commanded. ¹²Then Joseph provided his father, his brothers, and all his father's household with bread, according to the number in *their* families.

Joseph Deals with the Famine

¹³Now *there was* no bread in all the land; for the famine *was* very severe, so that the land of Egypt and the land of Canaan languished because of the famine. ¹⁴And Joseph gathered up all the money that was found in the land of Egypt and in the land of Canaan, for the grain which they bought; and Joseph brought the money into Pharaoh's house.

¹⁵So when the money failed in the land of Egypt and in the land of Canaan, all the Egyptians came to Joseph and said, "Give us bread, for why should we die in your presence? For the money has failed."

¹⁶Then Joseph said, "Give your livestock, and I will give you *bread* for your livestock, if the money is gone." ¹⁷So they brought their livestock to Joseph, and Joseph gave them bread *in exchange* for the horses, the flocks, the cattle of the herds, and for the donkeys. Thus he fed them with bread *in exchange* for all their livestock that year.

¹⁸When that year had ended, they came to him the next year and said to him, "We will not hide from my lord that our money is gone; my lord also has our herds of livestock. There is nothing left in the sight of my lord but our bodies and our lands. ¹⁹Why should we die before your eyes, both we and our land? Buy us and our land for bread, and we and our land will be servants of Pharaoh; give *us* seed, that we may live and not die, that the land may not be desolate."

²⁰Then Joseph bought all the land of Egypt for Pharaoh; for every man of the Egyptians sold his field, because the famine was severe upon them. So the land became Pharaoh's. ²¹And as for the people, he moved them into the cities,ᵃ from *one* end of the borders of Egypt to the *other* end. ²²Only the land of the priests he did not buy; for the priests had rations *allotted to them* by Pharaoh, and they ate their rations

which Pharaoh gave them; therefore they did not sell their lands.

²³Then Joseph said to the people, "Indeed I have bought you and your land this day for Pharaoh. Look, *here is* seed for you, and you shall sow the land. ²⁴And it shall come to pass in the harvest that you shall give one-fifth to Pharaoh. Four-fifths shall be your own, as seed for the field and for your food, for those of your households and as food for your little ones."

²⁵So they said, "You have saved our lives; let us find favor in the sight of my lord, and we will be Pharaoh's servants." ²⁶And Joseph made it a law over the land of Egypt to this day, *that* Pharaoh should have one-fifth, except for the land of the priests only, *which* did not become Pharaoh's.

Joseph's Vow to Jacob

²⁷So Israel dwelt in the land of Egypt, in the country of Goshen; and they had possessions there and grew and multiplied exceedingly. ²⁸And Jacob lived in the land of Egypt seventeen years. So the length of Jacob's life was one hundred and forty-seven years. ²⁹When the time drew near that Israel must die, he called his son Joseph and said to him, "Now if I have found favor in your sight, please put your hand under my thigh, and deal kindly and truly with me. Please do not bury me in Egypt, ³⁰but let me lie with my fathers; you shall carry me out of Egypt and bury me in their burial place."

And he said, "I will do as you have said."

³¹Then he said, "Swear to me." And he swore to him. So Israel bowed himself on the head of the bed.

Jacob Blesses Joseph's Sons

48 Now it came to pass after these things that Joseph was told, "Indeed your father *is* sick"; and he took with him his two sons, Manasseh and Ephraim. ²And Jacob was told, "Look, your son Joseph is coming to you"; and Israel strengthened

---

47:21 ᵃFollowing Masoretic Text and Targum; Samaritan Pentateuch, Septuagint, and Vulgate read *made the people virtual slaves.*

himself and sat up on the bed. ³Then Jacob said to Joseph: "God Almighty appeared to me at Luz in the land of Canaan and blessed me, ⁴and said to me, 'Behold, I will make you fruitful and multiply you, and I will make of you a multitude of people, and give this land to your descendants after you *as* an everlasting possession.' ⁵And now your two sons, Ephraim and Manasseh, who were born to you in the land of Egypt before I came to you in Egypt, *are* mine; as Reuben and Simeon, they shall be mine. ⁶Your offspring whom you beget after them shall be yours; they will be called by the name of their brothers in their inheritance. ⁷But as for me, when I came from Padan, Rachel died beside me in the land of Canaan on the way, when *there was* but a little distance to go to Ephrath; and I buried her there on the way to Ephrath (that is, Bethlehem)."

⁸Then Israel saw Joseph's sons, and said, "Who *are* these?"

⁹Joseph said to his father, "They *are* my sons, whom God has given me in this *place.*"

And he said, "Please bring them to me, and I will bless them." ¹⁰Now the eyes of Israel were dim with age, *so that* he could not see. Then Joseph brought them near him, and he kissed them and embraced them. ¹¹And Israel said to Joseph, "I had not thought to see your face; but in fact, God has also shown me your offspring!"

¹²So Joseph brought them from beside his knees, and he bowed down with his face to the earth. ¹³And Joseph took them both, Ephraim with his right hand toward Israel's left hand, and Manasseh with his left hand toward Israel's right hand, and brought *them* near him. ¹⁴Then Israel stretched out his right hand and laid *it* on Ephraim's head, who *was* the younger, and his left hand on Manasseh's head, guiding his hands knowingly, for Manasseh *was* the firstborn. ¹⁵And he blessed Joseph, and said:

"God, before whom my fathers
    Abraham and Isaac walked,
The God who has fed me all my
    life long to this day,

¹⁶ The Angel who has redeemed me
        from all evil,
    Bless the lads;
    Let my name be named upon them,
    And the name of my fathers Abraham
        and Isaac;
    And let them grow into a multitude
        in the midst of the earth."

¹⁷Now when Joseph saw that his father laid his right hand on the head of Ephraim, it displeased him; so he took hold of his father's hand to remove it from Ephraim's head to Manasseh's head. ¹⁸And Joseph said to his father, "Not so, my father, for this *one is* the firstborn; put your right hand on his head."

¹⁹But his father refused and said, "I know, my son, I know. He also shall become a people, and he also shall be great; but truly his younger brother shall be greater than he, and his descendants shall become a multitude of nations."

²⁰So he blessed them that day, saying, "By you Israel will bless, saying, 'May God make you as Ephraim and as Manasseh!'" And thus he set Ephraim before Manasseh.

²¹Then Israel said to Joseph, "Behold, I am dying, but God will be with you and bring you back to the land of your fathers. ²²Moreover I have given to you one portion above your brothers, which I took from the hand of the Amorite with my sword and my bow."

Jacob's Last Words to His Sons

49 And Jacob called his sons and said, "Gather together, that I may tell you what shall befall you in the last days:

2 "Gather together and hear, you sons
        of Jacob,
    And listen to Israel your father.

3 "Reuben, you are my firstborn,
    My might and the beginning of my
        strength,
    The excellency of dignity and the
        excellency of power.
4 Unstable as water, you shall not excel,
    Because you went up to your father's
        bed;

Then you defiled *it*—
He went up to my couch.

5 "Simeon and Levi *are* brothers;
  Instruments of cruelty *are in* their
    dwelling place.
6 Let not my soul enter their council;
  Let not my honor be united to their
    assembly;
  For in their anger they slew a man,
  And in their self-will they hamstrung
    an ox.
7 Cursed *be* their anger, for *it is* fierce;
  And their wrath, for it is cruel!
  I will divide them in Jacob
  And scatter them in Israel.

8 "Judah, you *are he* whom your
    brothers shall praise;
  Your hand *shall be* on the neck
    of your enemies;
  Your father's children shall bow
    down before you.
9 Judah *is* a lion's whelp;
  From the prey, my son, you have
    gone up.
  He bows down, he lies down as a lion;
  And as a lion, who shall rouse him?
10 The scepter shall not depart from
    Judah,
  Nor a lawgiver from between his feet,
  Until Shiloh comes;
  And to Him *shall be* the obedience
    of the people.
11 Binding his donkey to the vine,
  And his donkey's colt to the choice
    vine,
  He washed his garments in wine,
  And his clothes in the blood of
    grapes.
12 His eyes *are* darker than wine,
  And his teeth whiter than milk.

George Washington placed his hand on Genesis 49:13 as he took the presidential oath of office in 1789.

---

13 "Zebulun shall dwell by the haven of
    the sea;
  He *shall become* a haven for ships,
  And his border shall adjoin Sidon.

14 "Issachar is a strong donkey,
  Lying down between two burdens;
15 He saw that rest *was* good,
  And that the land *was* pleasant;
  He bowed his shoulder to bear *a*
    burden,
  And became a band of slaves.

16 "Dan shall judge his people
  As one of the tribes of Israel.
17 Dan shall be a serpent by the way,
  A viper by the path,
  That bites the horse's heels
  So that its rider shall fall backward.
18 I have waited for your salvation,
  O LORD!

19 "Gad, a troop shall tramp upon him,
  But he shall triumph at last.

20 "Bread from Asher *shall be* rich,
  And he shall yield royal dainties.

21 "Naphtali *is* a deer let loose;
  He uses beautiful words.

22 "Joseph *is* a fruitful bough,
  A fruitful bough by a well;
  His branches run over the wall.
23 The archers have bitterly grieved him,
  Shot *at him* and hated him.
24 But his bow remained in strength,
  And the arms of his hands were made
    strong
  By the hands of the Mighty *God* of
    Jacob
  (From there *is* the Shepherd, the Stone
    of Israel),
25 By the God of your father who will
    help you,
  And by the Almighty who will bless
    you
  With blessings of heaven above,
  Blessings of the deep that lies beneath,
  Blessings of the breasts and of the
    womb.
26 The blessings of your father
  Have excelled the blessings of my
    ancestors,
  Up to the utmost bound of the
    everlasting hills.

They shall be on the head of Joseph,
And on the crown of the head of him
who was separate from his brothers.

27 "Benjamin is a ravenous wolf;
In the morning he shall devour the
prey,
And at night he shall divide the spoil."

28All these *are* the twelve tribes of Israel, and this *is* what their father spoke to them. And he blessed them; he blessed each one according to his own blessing.

Jacob's Death and Burial

29Then he charged them and said to them: "I am to be gathered to my people; bury me with my fathers in the cave that *is* in the field of Ephron the Hittite, 30in the cave that *is* in the field of Machpelah, which *is* before Mamre in the land of Canaan, which Abraham bought with the field of Ephron the Hittite as a possession for a burial place. 31There they buried Abraham and Sarah his wife, there they buried Isaac and Rebekah his wife, and there I buried Leah. 32The field and the cave that *is* there *were* purchased from the sons of Heth." 33And when Jacob had finished commanding his sons, he drew his feet up into the bed and breathed his last, and was gathered to his people.

50 Then Joseph fell on his father's face and wept over him, and kissed him. 2And Joseph commanded his servants the physicians to embalm his father. So the physicians embalmed Israel. 3Forty days were required for him, for such are the days required for those who are embalmed; and the Egyptians mourned for him seventy days.

4Now when the days of his mourning were past, Joseph spoke to the household of Pharaoh, saying, "If now I have found favor in your eyes, please speak in the hearing of Pharaoh, saying, 5'My father made me swear, saying, "Behold, I am dying; in my grave which I dug for myself in the land of Canaan, there you shall bury me." Now therefore, please let me go up and bury my father, and I will come back.' "

6And Pharaoh said, "Go up and bury your father, as he made you swear."

7So Joseph went up to bury his father; and with him went up all the servants of Pharaoh, the elders of his house, and all the elders of the land of Egypt, 8as well as all the house of Joseph, his brothers, and his father's house. Only their little ones, their flocks, and their herds they left in the land of Goshen. 9And there went up with him both chariots and horsemen, and it was a very great gathering.

10Then they came to the threshing floor of Atad, which *is* beyond the Jordan, and they mourned there with a great and very solemn lamentation. He observed seven days of mourning for his father. 11And when the inhabitants of the land, the Canaanites, saw the mourning at the threshing floor of Atad, they said, "This *is* a deep mourning of the Egyptians." Therefore its name was called Abel Mizraim,[a] which *is* beyond the Jordan.

12So his sons did for him just as he had commanded them. 13For his sons carried him to the land of Canaan, and buried him in the cave of the field of Machpelah, before Mamre, which Abraham bought with the field from Ephron the Hittite as property for a burial place. 14And after he had buried his father, Joseph returned to Egypt, he and his brothers and all who went up with him to bury his father.

Joseph Reassures His Brothers

15When Joseph's brothers saw that their father was dead, they said, "Perhaps Joseph will hate us, and may actually repay us for all the evil which we did to him." 16So they sent *messengers* to Joseph, saying, "Before your father died he commanded, saying, 17'Thus you shall say to Joseph: "I beg you, please forgive the trespass of your brothers and their sin; for they did evil to you."' Now, please, forgive the trespass of the servants of the God of your father." And Joseph wept when they spoke to him.

18Then his brothers also went and fell down before his face, and they said, "Behold, we *are* your servants."

50:11 ªLiterally *Mourning of Egypt*

¹⁹Joseph said to them, "Do not be afraid, for *am* I in the place of God? ²⁰But as for you, you meant evil against me; *but* God meant it for good, in order to bring it about as *it is* this day, to save many people alive. ²¹Now therefore, do not be afraid; I will provide for you and your little ones." And he comforted them and spoke kindly to them.

Death of Joseph

²²So Joseph dwelt in Egypt, he and his father's household. And Joseph lived one hundred and ten years. ²³Joseph saw Ephraim's children to the third *generation.* The children of Machir, the son of Manasseh, were also brought up on Joseph's knees.

²⁴And Joseph said to his brethren, "I am dying; but God will surely visit you, and bring you out of this land to the land of which He swore to Abraham, to Isaac, and to Jacob." ²⁵Then Joseph took an oath from the children of Israel, saying, "God will surely visit you, and you shall carry up my bones from here." ²⁶So Joseph died, *being* one hundred and ten years old; and they embalmed him, and he was put in a coffin in Egypt.

EXODUS

Author: Moses

When Written: Around 1400 B.C.

Theme: Deliverance

Key Verses: Exodus 14:13, 14—"And Moses said to the people, 'Do not be afraid. Stand still, and see the salvation of the LORD, which He will accomplish for you today. For the Egyptians whom you see today, you shall see again no more forever. The LORD will fight for you, and you shall hold your peace.'"

Key Chapters: Exodus 12–14—God's powerful deliverance of Israel through the blood and through His power is dramatically depicted in these chapters.

On December 17, 1620, a small group of Pilgrims who had left England in search of greater freedom to worship God dropped anchor of the *Mayflower* at Plymouth Harbor in what is now Massachusetts. These were some of the very first individuals and families in whose soul beat the heart of what we now call the "American spirit."

Their flight from oppression mirrored a much earlier Exodus, when God led the children of Israel out of the bondage and oppression of Egypt and into a land that He had promised their forefather Abraham. The Book of Exodus recounts how through His mercy—and through the "blood of the Lamb"—God delivered His people, placed them at the door of liberty, and promised them great success through obedience to His Word and will.

EXODUS

Israel's Suffering in Egypt

1 Now these *are* the names of the children of Israel who came to Egypt; each man and his household came with Jacob: ²Reuben, Simeon, Levi, and Judah; ³Issachar, Zebulun, and Benjamin; ⁴Dan, Naphtali, Gad, and Asher. ⁵All those who were descendants[a] of Jacob were seventy[b] persons (for Joseph was in Egypt *already*). ⁶And Joseph died, all his brothers, and all that generation. ⁷But the children of Israel were fruitful and increased abundantly, multiplied and grew exceedingly mighty; and the land was filled with them.

⁸Now there arose a new king over Egypt, who did not know Joseph. ⁹And he said to his people, "Look, the people of the children of Israel *are* more and mightier than we; ¹⁰come, let us deal shrewdly with them, lest they multiply, and it happen, in the event of war, that they also join our enemies and fight against us, and *so* go up out of the land." ¹¹Therefore they set taskmasters over them to afflict them with their burdens. And they built for Pharaoh supply cities, Pithom and Raamses. ¹²But the more they afflicted them, the more they multiplied and grew. And they were in dread of the children of Israel. ¹³So the Egyptians made the children of Israel serve with rigor. ¹⁴And they made their lives bitter with hard bondage—in mortar, in brick, and in all manner of service in the field. All their service in which they made them serve *was* with rigor.

¹⁵Then the king of Egypt spoke to the Hebrew midwives, of whom the name of one *was* Shiphrah and the name of the other Puah; ¹⁶and he said, "When you do the duties of a midwife for the Hebrew women, and see *them* on the birthstools, if it *is* a son, then you shall kill him; but if it *is* a daughter, then she shall live." ¹⁷But the midwives feared God, and did not do as the king of Egypt commanded them, but saved the male children alive. ¹⁸So the king of Egypt called for the midwives and said to them, "Why have you done this thing, and saved the male children alive?"

¹⁹And the midwives said to Pharaoh, "Because the Hebrew women *are* not like the Egyptian women; for they *are* lively and give birth before the midwives come to them."

²⁰Therefore God dealt well with the midwives, and the people multiplied and grew very mighty. ²¹And so it was, because the midwives feared God, that He provided households for them.

²²So Pharaoh commanded all his people, saying, "Every son who is born[a] you shall cast into the river, and every daughter you shall save alive."

Moses Is Born

2 And a man of the house of Levi went and took *as wife* a daughter of Levi. ²So the woman conceived and bore a son. And when she saw that he *was* a beautiful *child,* she hid him three months. ³But when she could no longer hide him, she took an ark of bulrushes for him, daubed it with asphalt and pitch, put the child in it, and laid *it* in the reeds by the river's bank. ⁴And his sister stood afar off, to know what would be done to him.

⁵Then the daughter of Pharaoh came down to bathe at the river. And her maidens walked along the riverside; and when she saw the ark among the reeds, she sent her maid to get it. ⁶And when she opened *it,* she saw the child, and behold, the baby wept. So she had compassion on him, and said, "This is one of the Hebrews' children."

⁷Then his sister said to Pharaoh's daughter, "Shall I go and call a nurse for you from the Hebrew women, that she may nurse the child for you?"

1:5 [a]Literally *who came from the loins of* [b]Dead Sea Scrolls and Septuagint read *seventy-five* (compare Acts 7:14). **1:22** [a]Samaritan Pentateuch, Septuagint, and Targum add *to the Hebrews.*

[8]And Pharaoh's daughter said to her, "Go." So the maiden went and called the child's mother. [9]Then Pharaoh's daughter said to her, "Take this child away and nurse him for me, and I will give *you* your wages." So the woman took the child and nursed him. [10]And the child grew, and she brought him to Pharaoh's daughter, and he became her son. So she called his name Moses,[a] saying, "Because I drew him out of the water."

Moses Flees to Midian

[11]Now it came to pass in those days, when Moses was grown, that he went out to his brethren and looked at their burdens. And he saw an Egyptian beating a Hebrew, one of his brethren. [12]So he looked this way and that way, and when he saw no one, he killed the Egyptian and hid him in the sand. [13]And when he went out the second day, behold, two Hebrew men were fighting, and he said to the one who did the wrong, "Why are you striking your companion?"

[14]Then he said, "Who made you a prince and a judge over us? Do you intend to kill me as you killed the Egyptian?"

So Moses feared and said, "Surely this thing is known!" [15]When Pharaoh heard of this matter, he sought to kill Moses. But Moses fled from the face of Pharaoh and dwelt in the land of Midian; and he sat down by a well.

[16]Now the priest of Midian had seven daughters. And they came and drew water, and they filled the troughs to water their father's flock. [17]Then the shepherds came and drove them away; but Moses stood up and helped them, and watered their flock.

[18]When they came to Reuel their father, he said, "How *is it that* you have come so soon today?"

[19]And they said, "An Egyptian delivered us from the hand of the shepherds, and he also drew enough water for us and watered the flock."

[20]So he said to his daughters, "And where *is* he? Why *is* it *that* you have left the man? Call him, that he may eat bread."

[21]Then Moses was content to live with the man, and he gave Zipporah his daughter to Moses. [22]And she bore *him* a son. He called his name Gershom,[a] for he said, "I have been a stranger in a foreign land."

[23]Now it happened in the process of time that the king of Egypt died. Then the children of Israel groaned because of the bondage, and they cried out; and their cry came up to God because of the bondage. [24]So God heard their groaning, and God remembered His covenant with Abraham, with Isaac, and with Jacob. [25]And God looked upon the children of Israel, and God acknowledged *them.*

Moses at the Burning Bush

3 Now Moses was tending the flock of Jethro his father-in-law, the priest of Midian. And he led the flock to the back of the desert, and came to Horeb, the mountain of God. [2]And the Angel of the LORD appeared to him in a flame of fire from the midst of a bush. So he looked, and behold, the bush was burning with fire, but the bush *was* not consumed. [3]Then Moses said, "I will now turn aside and see this great sight, why the bush does not burn."

[4]So when the LORD saw that he turned aside to look, God called to him from the midst of the bush and said, "Moses, Moses!"

And he said, "Here I am."

[5]Then He said, "Do not draw near this place. Take your sandals off your feet, for the place where you stand *is* holy ground." [6]Moreover He said, "I *am* the God of your father—the God of Abraham, the God of Isaac, and the God of Jacob." And Moses hid his face, for he was afraid to look upon God.

[7]And the LORD said: "I have surely seen the oppression of My people who *are* in Egypt, and have heard their cry because of their taskmasters, for I know their sorrows. [8]So I have come down to deliver them out of the hand of the Egyptians, and to bring them up from that land to a good and large land, to a land flowing with milk and honey, to the place of the Canaanites and the Hittites and the Amorites and the Perizzites and the Hivites and the Jebusites.

2:10 [a]Literally *Drawn Out*   **2:22** [a]Literally *Stranger There*

⁹Now therefore, behold, the cry of the children of Israel has come to Me, and I have also seen the oppression with which the Egyptians oppress them. ¹⁰Come now, therefore, and I will send you to Pharaoh that you may bring My people, the children of Israel, out of Egypt."

¹¹But Moses said to God, "Who *am* I that I should go to Pharaoh, and that I should bring the children of Israel out of Egypt?"

¹²So He said, "I will certainly be with you. And this *shall be* a sign to you that I have sent you: When you have brought the people out of Egypt, you shall serve God on this mountain."

¹³Then Moses said to God, "Indeed, *when* I come to the children of Israel and say to them, 'The God of your fathers has sent me to you,' and they say to me, 'What *is* His name?' what shall I say to them?"

¹⁴And God said to Moses, "I AM WHO I AM." And He said, "Thus you shall say to the children of Israel, 'I AM has sent me to you.'" ¹⁵Moreover God said to Moses, "Thus you shall say to the children of Israel: 'The LORD God of your fathers, the God of Abraham, the God of Isaac, and the God of Jacob, has sent me to you. This *is* My name forever, and this *is* My memorial to all generations.' ¹⁶Go and gather the elders of Israel together, and say to them, 'The LORD God of your fathers, the God of Abraham, of Isaac, and of Jacob, appeared to me, saying, "I have surely visited you and *seen* what is done to you in Egypt; ¹⁷and I have said I will bring you up out of the affliction of Egypt to the land of the Canaanites and the Hittites and the Amorites and the Perizzites and the Hivites and the Jebusites, to a land flowing with milk and honey."'

¹⁸Then they will heed your voice; and you shall come, you and the elders of Israel, to the king of Egypt; and you shall say to him, 'The LORD God of the Hebrews has met with us; and now, please, let us go three days' journey into the wilderness, that we may sacrifice to the LORD our God.' ¹⁹But I am sure that the king of Egypt will not let you go, no, not even by a mighty hand. ²⁰So I will stretch out My hand and strike Egypt with all My wonders which I will do in its midst; and after that he will let you go. ²¹And I will give this people favor in the sight of the Egyptians; and it shall be, when you go, that you shall not go empty-handed. ²²But every woman shall ask of her neighbor, namely, of her who dwells near her house, articles of silver, articles of gold, and clothing; and you shall put *them* on your sons and on your daughters. So you shall plunder the Egyptians."

Miraculous Signs for Pharaoh

4 Then Moses answered and said, "But suppose they will not believe me or listen to my voice; suppose they say, 'The LORD has not appeared to you.'"

²So the LORD said to him, "What *is* that in your hand?"

He said, "A rod."

³And He said, "Cast it on the ground." So he cast it on the ground, and it became a serpent; and Moses fled from it. ⁴Then the LORD said to Moses, "Reach out your hand and take *it* by the tail" (and he reached out his hand and caught it, and it became a rod in his hand), ⁵"that they may believe that the LORD God of their fathers, the God of Abraham, the God of Isaac, and the God of Jacob, has appeared to you."

⁶Furthermore the LORD said to him, "Now put your hand in your bosom." And he put his hand in his bosom, and when he took it out, behold, his hand *was* leprous, like snow. ⁷And He said, "Put your hand in your bosom again." So he put his hand in his bosom again, and drew it out of his bosom, and behold, it was restored like his *other* flesh. ⁸"Then it will be, if they do not believe you, nor heed the message of the first sign, that they may believe the message of the latter sign. ⁹And it shall be, if they do not believe even these two signs, or listen to your voice, that you shall take water from the river[a] and pour *it* on the dry *land*. The water which you take from the river will become blood on the dry *land*."

¹⁰Then Moses said to the LORD, "O my Lord, I *am* not eloquent, neither before nor since You have spoken to Your servant; but I *am* slow of speech and slow of tongue."

4:9 [a]That is, the Nile

GEORGE WASHINGTON, THE "AMERICAN MOSES"

GEORGE WASHINGTON

"First in war, first in peace, and first in the hearts of his countrymen," said Major General Henry Lee about George Washington, after his death. He was surely that and more. Emerging as the most significant leader in the founding of the United States, he was the essential man, the American Moses, the Father of the Country. At the three major crossroads in the establishment of the nation, he led our troops to victory in the Revolutionary War, he superintended the Constitutional Convention, and he was unanimously elected as the first president.

How, one wonders, is it possible for so much greatness to be embodied in one man? After all, he was surrounded by a host of other courageous leaders, brilliant thinkers, passionate orators, and gifted writers—Franklin, Jefferson, Patrick Henry, Mason, John and Samuel Adams, Hamilton, Madison—almost all of whom were far better educated than he. Yet Washington always led the way.

While much has often been made of his physical stature (he stood six feet two inches when the average man stood five feet seven inches, and he weighed two hundred pounds), or his courage, charisma, energy, vision, calm demeanor, or wealth, it was his high moral character that most historical sources commonly cite as the reason for his emergence as the supreme leader. Combine his sterling character and his genius in the area of leadership, and here was a man who could be trusted implicitly to lead over a long period of time and in the course of extraordinary difficulties.

Abigail Adams, wife of John Adams, the second president of the United States, said about Washington: "He was . . . possessed of power, possessed of an extensive influence, but he never used it but for the benefit of his country. . . . If you look through the whole tenor of his life, history will not produce to us a parallel."

Thomas Jefferson wrote of Washington: "His integrity was most pure, his justice the most inflexible I have ever known. No motives . . . of friendship or hatred being able to bias his decision. He was, indeed, in every sense of the word, a wise, a good, and a great man. It may truly be said that never did nature and fortune combine more perfectly to make a man great, and to place him in the same constellation with whatever worthies have merited from man an everlasting remembrance."

[11]So the LORD said to him, "Who has made man's mouth? Or who makes the mute, the deaf, the seeing, or the blind? *Have* not I, the LORD? [12]Now therefore, go, and I will be with your mouth and teach you what you shall say."

[13]But he said, "O my Lord, please send by the hand of whomever *else* You may send."

[14]So the anger of the LORD was kindled against Moses, and He said: "Is not Aaron the Levite your brother? I know that he can speak well. And look, he is also coming out to meet you. When he sees you, he will be glad in his heart. [15]Now you shall speak to him and put the words in his mouth. And I will be with your mouth and with his mouth, and I will teach you what you shall do. [16]So he shall be your spokesman to the people. And he himself shall be as a mouth for you, and you shall be to him as God. [17]And you shall take this rod in your hand, with which you shall do the signs."

Moses Goes to Egypt

[18]So Moses went and returned to Jethro his father-in-law, and said to him, "Please let me go and return to my brethren who *are* in Egypt, and see whether they are still alive."

And Jethro said to Moses, "Go in peace."

[19]Now the LORD said to Moses in Midian, "Go, return to Egypt; for all the men who sought your life are dead." [20]Then Moses took his wife and his sons and set them on a donkey, and he returned to the land of Egypt. And Moses took the rod of God in his hand.

[21]And the LORD said to Moses, "When you go back to Egypt, see that you do all those wonders before Pharaoh which I have put in your hand. But I will harden his heart, so that he will not let the people go. [22]Then you shall say to Pharaoh, 'Thus says the LORD: "Israel *is* My son, My first-born. [23]So I say to you, let My son go that he may serve Me. But if you refuse to let him go, indeed I will kill your son, your firstborn." '"

[24]And it came to pass on the way, at the encampment, that the LORD met him and sought to kill him. [25]Then Zipporah took a sharp stone and cut off the foreskin of her son and cast *it* at *Moses'*[a] feet, and said, "Surely you *are* a husband of blood to me!" [26]So He let him go. Then she said, "*You are* a husband of blood!"—because of the circumcision.

[27]And the LORD said to Aaron, "Go into the wilderness to meet Moses." So he went and met him on the mountain of God, and kissed him. [28]So Moses told Aaron all the words of the LORD who had sent him, and all the signs which He had commanded him. [29]Then Moses and Aaron went and gathered together all the elders of the children of Israel. [30]And Aaron spoke all the words which the LORD had spoken to Moses. Then he did the signs in the sight of the people. [31]So the people believed; and when they heard that the LORD had visited the children of Israel and that He had looked on their affliction, then they bowed their heads and worshiped.

First Encounter with Pharaoh

5 Afterward Moses and Aaron went in and told Pharaoh, "Thus says the LORD God of Israel: 'Let My people go, that they may hold a feast to Me in the wilderness.'"

[2]And Pharaoh said, "Who *is* the LORD, that I should obey His voice to let Israel go? I do not know the LORD, nor will I let Israel go."

[3]So they said, "The God of the Hebrews has met with us. Please, let us go three days' journey into the desert and sacrifice to the LORD our God, lest He fall upon us with pestilence or with the sword."

[4]Then the king of Egypt said to them, "Moses and Aaron, why do you take the people from their work? Get *back* to your labor." [5]And Pharaoh said, "Look, the people of the land *are* many now, and you make them rest from their labor!"

[6]So the same day Pharaoh commanded the taskmasters of the people and their officers, saying, [7]"You shall no longer give the people straw to make brick as before. Let them go and gather straw for themselves. [8]And you shall lay on them the

---

4:25 [a]Literally *his*

quota of bricks which they made before. You shall not reduce it. For they are idle; therefore they cry out, saying, 'Let us go *and* sacrifice to our God.' ⁹Let more work be laid on the men, that they may labor in it, and let them not regard false words."

¹⁰And the taskmasters of the people and their officers went out and spoke to the people, saying, "Thus says Pharaoh: 'I will not give you straw. ¹¹Go, get yourselves straw where you can find it; yet none of your work will be reduced.' " ¹²So the people were scattered abroad throughout all the land of Egypt to gather stubble instead of straw. ¹³And the taskmasters forced *them* to hurry, saying, "Fulfill your work, *your* daily quota, as when there was straw." ¹⁴Also the officers of the children of Israel, whom Pharaoh's taskmasters had set over them, were beaten *and* were asked, "Why have you not fulfilled your task in making brick both yesterday and today, as before?"

¹⁵Then the officers of the children of Israel came and cried out to Pharaoh, saying, "Why are you dealing thus with your servants? ¹⁶There is no straw given to your servants, and they say to us, 'Make brick!' And indeed your servants *are* beaten, but the fault *is* in your *own* people."

¹⁷But he said, "You *are* idle! Idle! Therefore you say, 'Let us go *and* sacrifice to the LORD.' ¹⁸Therefore go now *and* work; for no straw shall be given you, yet you shall deliver the quota of bricks." ¹⁹And the officers of the children of Israel saw *that* they *were* in trouble after it was said, "You shall not reduce *any* bricks from your daily quota."

²⁰Then, as they came out from Pharaoh, they met Moses and Aaron who stood there to meet them. ²¹And they said to them, "Let the LORD look on you and judge, because you have made us abhorrent in the sight of Pharaoh and in the sight of his servants, to put a sword in their hand to kill us."

Israel's Deliverance Assured

²²So Moses returned to the LORD and said, "Lord, why have You brought trouble on this people? Why *is* it You have sent me? ²³For since I came to Pharaoh to speak in Your name, he has done evil to this people; neither have You delivered Your people at all."

6 Then the LORD said to Moses, "Now you shall see what I will do to Pharaoh. For with a strong hand he will let them go, and with a strong hand he will drive them out of his land."

²And God spoke to Moses and said to him: "I *am* the LORD. ³I appeared to Abraham, to Isaac, and to Jacob, as God Almighty, but *by* My name LORDᵃ I was not known to them. ⁴I have also established My covenant with them, to give them the land of Canaan, the land of their pilgrimage, in which they were strangers. ⁵And I have also heard the groaning of the children of Israel whom the Egyptians keep in bondage, and I have remembered My covenant. ⁶Therefore say to the children of Israel: 'I *am* the LORD; I will bring you out from under the burdens of the Egyptians, I will rescue you from their bondage, and I will redeem you with an outstretched arm and with great judgments. ⁷I will take you as My people, and I will be your God. Then you shall know that I *am* the LORD your God who brings you out from under the burdens of the Egyptians. ⁸And I will bring you into the land which I swore to give to Abraham, Isaac, and Jacob; and I will give it to you *as* a heritage: I *am* the LORD.' " ⁹So Moses spoke thus to the children of Israel; but they did not heed Moses, because of anguish of spirit and cruel bondage.

¹⁰And the LORD spoke to Moses, saying, ¹¹"Go in, tell Pharaoh king of Egypt to let the children of Israel go out of his land."

¹²And Moses spoke before the LORD, saying, "The children of Israel have not heeded me. How then shall Pharaoh heed me, for I *am* of uncircumcised lips?"

¹³Then the LORD spoke to Moses and Aaron, and gave them a command for the children of Israel and for Pharaoh king of Egypt, to bring the children of Israel out of the land of Egypt.

The Family of Moses and Aaron

¹⁴These *are* the heads of their fathers' houses: The sons of Reuben, the firstborn

---

6:3 ᵃHebrew *YHWH*, traditionally *Jehovah*

of Israel, *were* Hanoch, Pallu, Hezron, and Carmi. These are the families of Reuben. [15]And the sons of Simeon *were* Jemuel,[a] Jamin, Ohad, Jachin, Zohar, and Shaul the son of a Canaanite woman. These *are* the families of Simeon. [16]These *are* the names of the sons of Levi according to their generations: Gershon, Kohath, and Merari. And the years of the life of Levi *were* one hundred and thirty-seven. [17]The sons of Gershon *were* Libni and Shimi according to their families. [18]And the sons of Kohath *were* Amram, Izhar, Hebron, and Uzziel. And the years of the life of Kohath *were* one hundred and thirty-three. [19]The sons of Merari *were* Mahli and Mushi. These *are* the families of Levi according to their generations.

[20]Now Amram took for himself Jochebed, his father's sister, as wife; and she bore him Aaron and Moses. And the years of the life of Amram *were* one hundred and thirty-seven. [21]The sons of Izhar *were* Korah, Nepheg, and Zichri. [22]And the sons of Uzziel *were* Mishael, Elzaphan, and Zithri. [23]Aaron took to himself Elisheba, daughter of Amminadab, sister of Nahshon, as wife; and she bore him Nadab, Abihu, Eleazar, and Ithamar. [24]And the sons of Korah *were* Assir, Elkanah, and Abiasaph. These are the families of the Korahites. [25]Eleazar, Aaron's son, took for himself one of the daughters of Putiel as wife; and she bore him Phinehas. These *are* the heads of the fathers' houses of the Levites according to their families.

[26]These *are the same* Aaron and Moses to whom the Lord said, "Bring out the children of Israel from the land of Egypt according to their armies." [27]These *are* the ones who spoke to Pharaoh king of Egypt, to bring out the children of Israel from Egypt. These *are the same* Moses and Aaron.

Aaron Is Moses' Spokesman

[28]And it came to pass, on the day the Lord spoke to Moses in the land of Egypt, [29]that the Lord spoke to Moses, saying, "I *am* the Lord. Speak to Pharaoh king of Egypt all that I say to you."

[30]But Moses said before the Lord, "Behold, I *am* of uncircumcised lips, and how shall Pharaoh heed me?"

7 So the Lord said to Moses: "See, I have made you *as* God to Pharaoh, and Aaron your brother shall be your prophet. [2]You shall speak all that I command you. And Aaron your brother shall tell Pharaoh to send the children of Israel out of his land. [3]And I will harden Pharaoh's heart, and multiply My signs and My wonders in the land of Egypt. [4]But Pharaoh will not heed you, so that I may lay My hand on Egypt and bring My armies *and* My people, the children of Israel, out of the land of Egypt by great judgments. [5]And the Egyptians shall know that I *am* the Lord, when I stretch out My hand on Egypt and bring out the children of Israel from among them."

[6]Then Moses and Aaron did *so;* just as the Lord commanded them, so they did. [7]And Moses *was* eighty years old and Aaron eighty-three years old when they spoke to Pharaoh.

Aaron's Miraculous Rod

[8]Then the Lord spoke to Moses and Aaron, saying, [9]"When Pharaoh speaks to you, saying, 'Show a miracle for yourselves,' then you shall say to Aaron, 'Take your rod and cast *it* before Pharaoh, *and* let it become a serpent.'" [10]So Moses and Aaron went in to Pharaoh, and they did so, just as the Lord commanded. And Aaron cast down his rod before Pharaoh and before his servants, and it became a serpent. [11]But Pharaoh also called the wise men and the sorcerers; so the magicians of Egypt, they also did in like manner with their enchantments. [12]For every man threw down his rod, and they became serpents. But Aaron's rod swallowed up their rods. [13]And Pharaoh's heart grew hard, and he did not heed them, as the Lord had said.

The First Plague: Waters Become Blood

[14]So the Lord said to Moses: "Pharaoh's heart *is* hard; he refuses to let the people

---

6:15 [a]Spelled *Nemuel* in Numbers 26:12

go. ¹⁵Go to Pharaoh in the morning, when he goes out to the water, and you shall stand by the river's bank to meet him; and the rod which was turned to a serpent you shall take in your hand. ¹⁶And you shall say to him, 'The Lord God of the Hebrews has sent me to you, saying, "Let My people go, that they may serve Me in the wilderness"; but indeed, until now you would not hear! ¹⁷Thus says the Lord: "By this you shall know that I *am* the Lord. Behold, I will strike the waters which *are* in the river with the rod that *is* in my hand, and they shall be turned to blood. ¹⁸And the fish that *are* in the river shall die, the river shall stink, and the Egyptians will loathe to drink the water of the river." ' "

¹⁹Then the Lord spoke to Moses, "Say to Aaron, 'Take your rod and stretch out your hand over the waters of Egypt, over their streams, over their rivers, over their ponds, and over all their pools of water, that they may become blood. And there shall be blood throughout all the land of Egypt, both in *buckets of* wood and *pitchers of* stone.' " ²⁰And Moses and Aaron did so, just as the Lord commanded. So he lifted up the rod and struck the waters that *were* in the river, in the sight of Pharaoh and in the sight of his servants. And all the waters that *were* in the river were turned to blood. ²¹The fish that *were* in the river died, the river stank, and the Egyptians could not drink the water of the river. So there was blood throughout all the land of Egypt.

²²Then the magicians of Egypt did so with their enchantments; and Pharaoh's heart grew hard, and he did not heed them, as the Lord had said. ²³And Pharaoh turned and went into his house. Neither was his heart moved by this. ²⁴So all the Egyptians dug all around the river for water to drink, because they could not drink the water of the river. ²⁵And seven days passed after the Lord had struck the river.

The Second Plague: Frogs

8 And the Lord spoke to Moses, "Go to Pharaoh and say to him, 'Thus says the Lord: "Let My people go, that they may serve Me. ²But if you refuse to let *them* go, behold, I will smite all your territory with frogs. ³So the river shall bring forth frogs abundantly, which shall go up and come into your house, into your bedroom, on your bed, into the houses of your servants, on your people, into your ovens, and into your kneading bowls. ⁴And the frogs shall come up on you, on your people, and on all your servants." ' "

⁵Then the Lord spoke to Moses, "Say to Aaron, 'Stretch out your hand with your rod over the streams, over the rivers, and over the ponds, and cause frogs to come up on the land of Egypt.' " ⁶So Aaron stretched out his hand over the waters of Egypt, and the frogs came up and covered the land of Egypt. ⁷And the magicians did so with their enchantments, and brought up frogs on the land of Egypt.

⁸Then Pharaoh called for Moses and Aaron, and said, "Entreat the Lord that He may take away the frogs from me and from my people; and I will let the people go, that they may sacrifice to the Lord."

⁹And Moses said to Pharaoh, "Accept the honor of saying when I shall intercede for you, for your servants, and for your people, to destroy the frogs from you and your houses, *that* they may remain in the river only."

¹⁰So he said, "Tomorrow." And he said, "*Let it be* according to your word, that you may know that *there is* no one like the Lord our God. ¹¹And the frogs shall depart from you, from your houses, from your servants, and from your people. They shall remain in the river only."

¹²Then Moses and Aaron went out from Pharaoh. And Moses cried out to the Lord concerning the frogs which He had brought against Pharaoh. ¹³So the Lord did according to the word of Moses. And the frogs died out of the houses, out of the courtyards, and out of the fields. ¹⁴They gathered them together in heaps, and the land stank. ¹⁵But when Pharaoh saw that there was relief, he hardened his heart and did not heed them, as the Lord had said.

The Third Plague: Lice

¹⁶So the Lord said to Moses, "Say to Aaron, 'Stretch out your rod, and strike the

dust of the land, so that it may become lice throughout all the land of Egypt.'" [17]And they did so. For Aaron stretched out his hand with his rod and struck the dust of the earth, and it became lice on man and beast. All the dust of the land became lice throughout all the land of Egypt.

[18]Now the magicians so worked with their enchantments to bring forth lice, but they could not. So there were lice on man and beast. [19]Then the magicians said to Pharaoh, "This *is* the finger of God." But Pharaoh's heart grew hard, and he did not heed them, just as the Lord had said.

The Fourth Plague: Flies

[20]And the Lord said to Moses, "Rise early in the morning and stand before Pharaoh as he comes out to the water. Then say to him, 'Thus says the Lord: "Let My people go, that they may serve Me. [21]Or else, if you will not let My people go, behold, I will send swarms *of flies* on you and your servants, on your people and into your houses. The houses of the Egyptians shall be full of swarms *of flies,* and also the ground on which they *stand.* [22]And in that day I will set apart the land of Goshen, in which My people dwell, that no swarms *of flies* shall be there, in order that you may know that I *am* the Lord in the midst of the land. [23]I will make a difference[a] between My people and your people. Tomorrow this sign shall be."'" [24]And the Lord did so. Thick swarms *of flies* came into the house of Pharaoh, *into* his servants' houses, and into all the land of Egypt. The land was corrupted because of the swarms *of flies.*

[25]Then Pharaoh called for Moses and Aaron, and said, "Go, sacrifice to your God in the land."

[26]And Moses said, "It is not right to do so, for we would be sacrificing the abomination of the Egyptians to the Lord our God. If we sacrifice the abomination of the Egyptians before their eyes, then will they not stone us? [27]We will go three days' journey into the wilderness and sacrifice to the Lord our God as He will command us."

[28]So Pharaoh said, "I will let you go, that you may sacrifice to the Lord your God in the wilderness; only you shall not go very far away. Intercede for me."

[29]Then Moses said, "Indeed I am going out from you, and I will entreat the Lord, that the swarms *of flies* may depart tomorrow from Pharaoh, from his servants, and from his people. But let Pharaoh not deal deceitfully anymore in not letting the people go to sacrifice to the Lord."

[30]So Moses went out from Pharaoh and entreated the Lord. [31]And the Lord did according to the word of Moses; He removed the swarms *of flies* from Pharaoh, from his servants, and from his people. Not one remained. [32]But Pharaoh hardened his heart at this time also; neither would he let the people go.

The Fifth Plague: Livestock Diseased

9 Then the Lord said to Moses, "Go in to Pharaoh and tell him, 'Thus says the Lord God of the Hebrews: "Let My people go, that they may serve Me. [2]For if you refuse to let *them* go, and still hold them, [3]behold, the hand of the Lord will be on your cattle in the field, on the horses, on the donkeys, on the camels, on the oxen, and on the sheep—a very severe pestilence. [4]And the Lord will make a difference between the livestock of Israel and the livestock of Egypt. So nothing shall die of all *that* belongs to the children of Israel."'" [5]Then the Lord appointed a set time, saying, "Tomorrow the Lord will do this thing in the land."

[6]So the Lord did this thing on the next day, and all the livestock of Egypt died; but of the livestock of the children of Israel, not one died. [7]Then Pharaoh sent, and indeed, not even one of the livestock of the Israelites was dead. But the heart of Pharaoh became hard, and he did not let the people go.

The Sixth Plague: Boils

[8]So the Lord said to Moses and Aaron, "Take for yourselves handfuls of ashes from a furnace, and let Moses scatter it toward the heavens in the sight of Pharaoh. [9]And it will become fine dust in all the land of

---

8:23 [a]Literally *set a ransom* (compare Exodus 9:4 and 11:7)

Egypt, and it will cause boils that break out in sores on man and beast throughout all the land of Egypt." [10]Then they took ashes from the furnace and stood before Pharaoh, and Moses scattered *them* toward heaven. And *they* caused boils that break out in sores on man and beast. [11]And the magicians could not stand before Moses because of the boils, for the boils were on the magicians and on all the Egyptians. [12]But the Lord hardened the heart of Pharaoh; and he did not heed them, just as the Lord had spoken to Moses.

The Seventh Plague: Hail

[13]Then the Lord said to Moses, "Rise early in the morning and stand before Pharaoh, and say to him, 'Thus says the Lord God of the Hebrews: "Let My people go, that they may serve Me, [14]for at this time I will send all My plagues to your very heart, and on your servants and on your people, that you may know that *there is* none like Me in all the earth. [15]Now if I had stretched out My hand and struck you and your people with pestilence, then you would have been cut off from the earth. [16]But indeed for this *purpose* I have raised you up, that I may show My power *in* you, and that My name may be declared in all the earth. [17]As yet you exalt yourself against My people in that you will not let them go. [18]Behold, tomorrow about this time I will cause very heavy hail to rain down, such as has not been in Egypt since its founding until now. [19]Therefore send now *and* gather your livestock and all that you have in the field, for the hail shall come down on every man and every animal which is found in the field and is not brought home; and they shall die." ' "

[20]He who feared the word of the Lord among the servants of Pharaoh made his servants and his livestock flee to the houses. [21]But he who did not regard the word of the Lord left his servants and his livestock in the field.

[22]Then the Lord said to Moses, "Stretch out your hand toward heaven, that there may be hail in all the land of Egypt—on man, on beast, and on every herb of the field, throughout the land of Egypt." [23]And Moses stretched out his rod toward heaven; and the Lord sent thunder and hail, and fire darted to the ground. And the Lord rained hail on the land of Egypt. [24]So there was hail, and fire mingled with the hail, so very heavy that there was none like it in all the land of Egypt since it became a nation. [25]And the hail struck throughout the whole land of Egypt, all that *was* in the field, both man and beast; and the hail struck every herb of the field and broke every tree of the field. [26]Only in the land of Goshen, where the children of Israel *were,* there was no hail.

[27]And Pharaoh sent and called for Moses and Aaron, and said to them, "I have sinned this time. The Lord *is* righteous, and my people and I *are* wicked. [28]Entreat the Lord, that there may be no *more* mighty thundering and hail, for *it is* enough. I will let you go, and you shall stay no longer."

[29]So Moses said to him, "As soon as I have gone out of the city, I will spread out my hands to the Lord; the thunder will cease, and there will be no more hail, that you may know that the earth *is* the Lord's. [30]But as for you and your servants, I know that you will not yet fear the Lord God."

[31]Now the flax and the barley were struck, for the barley *was* in the head and the flax *was* in bud. [32]But the wheat and the spelt were not struck, for they *are* late crops. [33]So Moses went out of the city from Pharaoh and spread out his hands to the Lord; then the thunder and the hail ceased, and the rain was not poured on the earth. [34]And when Pharaoh saw that the rain, the hail, and the thunder had ceased, he sinned yet more; and he hardened his heart, he and his servants. [35]So the heart of Pharaoh was hard; neither would he let the children of Israel go, as the Lord had spoken by Moses.

The Eighth Plague: Locusts

10 Now the Lord said to Moses, "Go in to Pharaoh; for I have hardened his heart and the hearts of his servants, that I may show these signs of Mine before him, [2]and that you may tell in the hearing of

your son and your son's son the mighty things I have done in Egypt, and My signs which I have done among them, that you may know that I *am* the LORD."

³So Moses and Aaron came in to Pharaoh and said to him, "Thus says the LORD God of the Hebrews: 'How long will you refuse to humble yourself before Me? Let My people go, that they may serve Me. ⁴Or else, if you refuse to let My people go, behold, tomorrow I will bring locusts into your territory. ⁵And they shall cover the face of the earth, so that no one will be able to see the earth; and they shall eat the residue of what is left, which remains to you from the hail, and they shall eat every tree which grows up for you out of the field. ⁶They shall fill your houses, the houses of all your servants, and the houses of all the Egyptians—which neither your fathers nor your fathers' fathers have seen, since the day that they were on the earth to this day.'" And he turned and went out from Pharaoh.

⁷Then Pharaoh's servants said to him, "How long shall this man be a snare to us? Let the men go, that they may serve the LORD their God. Do you not yet know that Egypt is destroyed?"

⁸So Moses and Aaron were brought again to Pharaoh, and he said to them, "Go, serve the LORD your God. Who *are* the ones that are going?"

⁹And Moses said, "We will go with our young and our old; with our sons and our daughters, with our flocks and our herds we will go, for we must hold a feast to the LORD."

¹⁰Then he said to them, "The LORD had better be with you when I let you and your little ones go! Beware, for evil is ahead of you. ¹¹Not so! Go now, you *who are* men, and serve the LORD, for that is what you desired." And they were driven out from Pharaoh's presence.

¹²Then the LORD said to Moses, "Stretch out your hand over the land of Egypt for the locusts, that they may come upon the land of Egypt, and eat every herb of the land—all that the hail has left." ¹³So Moses stretched out his rod over the land of Egypt,

and the LORD brought an east wind on the land all that day and all *that* night. When it was morning, the east wind brought the locusts. ¹⁴And the locusts went up over all the land of Egypt and rested on all the territory of Egypt. *They were* very severe; previously there had been no such locusts as they, nor shall there be such after them. ¹⁵For they covered the face of the whole earth, so that the land was darkened; and they ate every herb of the land and all the fruit of the trees which the hail had left. So there remained nothing green on the trees or on the plants of the field throughout all the land of Egypt.

¹⁶Then Pharaoh called for Moses and Aaron in haste, and said, "I have sinned against the LORD your God and against you. ¹⁷Now therefore, please forgive my sin only this once, and entreat the LORD your God, that He may take away from me this death only." ¹⁸So he went out from Pharaoh and entreated the LORD. ¹⁹And the LORD turned a very strong west wind, which took the locusts away and blew them into the Red Sea. There remained not one locust in all the territory of Egypt. ²⁰But the LORD hardened Pharaoh's heart, and he did not let the children of Israel go.

The Ninth Plague: Darkness

²¹Then the LORD said to Moses, "Stretch out your hand toward heaven, that there may be darkness over the land of Egypt, darkness *which* may even be felt." ²²So Moses stretched out his hand toward heaven, and there was thick darkness in all the land of Egypt three days. ²³They did not see one another; nor did anyone rise from his place for three days. But all the children of Israel had light in their dwellings.

²⁴Then Pharaoh called to Moses and said, "Go, serve the LORD; only let your flocks and your herds be kept back. Let your little ones also go with you."

²⁵But Moses said, "You must also give us sacrifices and burnt offerings, that we may sacrifice to the LORD our God. ²⁶Our livestock also shall go with us; not a hoof shall be left behind. For we must take some of them to serve the LORD our God, and even

we do not know with what we must serve the LORD until we arrive there."

²⁷But the LORD hardened Pharaoh's heart, and he would not let them go. ²⁸Then Pharaoh said to him, "Get away from me! Take heed to yourself and see my face no more! For in the day you see my face you shall die!"

²⁹So Moses said, "You have spoken well. I will never see your face again."

Death of the Firstborn Announced

11 And the LORD said to Moses, "I will bring one more plague on Pharaoh and on Egypt. Afterward he will let you go from here. When he lets *you* go, he will surely drive you out of here altogether. ²Speak now in the hearing of the people, and let every man ask from his neighbor and every woman from her neighbor, articles of silver and articles of gold." ³And the LORD gave the people favor in the sight of the Egyptians. Moreover the man Moses *was* very great in the land of Egypt, in the sight of Pharaoh's servants and in the sight of the people.

⁴Then Moses said, "Thus says the LORD: 'About midnight I will go out into the midst of Egypt; ⁵and all the firstborn in the land of Egypt shall die, from the firstborn of Pharaoh who sits on his throne, even to the firstborn of the female servant who *is* behind the handmill, and all the firstborn of the animals. ⁶Then there shall be a great cry throughout all the land of Egypt, such as was not like it *before,* nor shall be like it again. ⁷But against none of the children of Israel shall a dog move its tongue, against man or beast, that you may know that the LORD does make a difference between the Egyptians and Israel.' ⁸And all these your servants shall come down to me and bow down to me, saying, 'Get out, and all the people who follow you!' After that I will go out." Then he went out from Pharaoh in great anger.

⁹But the LORD said to Moses, "Pharaoh will not heed you, so that My wonders may be multiplied in the land of Egypt." ¹⁰So Moses and Aaron did all these wonders before Pharaoh; and the LORD hardened Pharaoh's heart, and he did not let the children of Israel go out of his land.

The Passover Instituted

12 Now the LORD spoke to Moses and Aaron in the land of Egypt, saying, ²"This month *shall be* your beginning of months; it *shall be* the first month of the year to you. ³Speak to all the congregation of Israel, saying: 'On the tenth of this month every man shall take for himself a lamb, according to the house of *his* father, a lamb for a household. ⁴And if the household is too small for the lamb, let him and his neighbor next to his house take *it* according to the number of the persons; according to each man's need you shall make your count for the lamb. ⁵Your lamb shall be without blemish, a male of the first year. You may take *it* from the sheep or from the goats. ⁶Now you shall keep it until the fourteenth day of the same month. Then the whole assembly of the congregation of Israel shall kill it at twilight. ⁷And they shall take *some* of the blood and put *it* on the two doorposts and on the lintel of the houses where they eat it. ⁸Then they shall eat the flesh on that night; roasted in fire, with unleavened bread *and* with bitter *herbs* they shall eat it. ⁹Do not eat it raw, nor boiled at all with water, but roasted in fire—its head with its legs and its entrails. ¹⁰You shall let none of it remain until morning, and what remains of it until morning you shall burn with fire. ¹¹And thus you shall eat it: *with* a belt on your waist, your sandals on your feet, and your staff in your hand. So you shall eat it in haste. It *is* the LORD's Passover.

¹²'For I will pass through the land of Egypt on that night, and will strike all the firstborn in the land of Egypt, both man and beast; and against all the gods of Egypt I will execute judgment: I *am* the LORD. ¹³Now the blood shall be a sign for you on the houses where you *are.* And when I see the blood, I will pass over you; and the plague shall not be on you to destroy *you* when I strike the land of Egypt.

¹⁴'So this day shall be to you a memorial; and you shall keep it as a feast to the

LORD throughout your generations. You shall keep it as a feast by an everlasting ordinance. ¹⁵Seven days you shall eat unleavened bread. On the first day you shall remove leaven from your houses. For whoever eats leavened bread from the first day until the seventh day, that person shall be cut off from Israel. ¹⁶On the first day *there shall be* a holy convocation, and on the seventh day there shall be a holy convocation for you. No manner of work shall be done on them; but *that* which everyone must eat—that only may be prepared by you. ¹⁷So you shall observe *the Feast of* Unleavened Bread, for on this same day I will have brought your armies out of the land of Egypt. Therefore you shall observe this day throughout your generations as an everlasting ordinance. ¹⁸In the first *month,* on the fourteenth day of the month at evening, you shall eat unleavened bread, until the twenty-first day of the month at evening. ¹⁹For seven days no leaven shall be found in your houses, since whoever eats what is leavened, that same person shall be cut off from the congregation of Israel, whether *he is* a stranger or a native of the land. ²⁰You shall eat nothing leavened; in all your dwellings you shall eat unleavened bread.'"

²¹Then Moses called for all the elders of Israel and said to them, "Pick out and take lambs for yourselves according to your families, and kill the Passover *lamb.* ²²And you shall take a bunch of hyssop, dip *it* in the blood that *is* in the basin, and strike the lintel and the two doorposts with the blood that *is* in the basin. And none of you shall go out of the door of his house until morning. ²³For the LORD will pass through to strike the Egyptians; and when He sees the blood on the lintel and on the two doorposts, the LORD will pass over the door and not allow the destroyer to come into your houses to strike *you.* ²⁴And you shall observe this thing as an ordinance for you and your sons forever. ²⁵It will come to pass when you come to the land which the LORD will give you, just as He promised, that you shall keep this service. ²⁶And it shall be, when your children say to you, 'What

do you mean by this service?' ²⁷that you shall say, 'It *is* the Passover sacrifice of the LORD, who passed over the houses of the children of Israel in Egypt when He struck the Egyptians and delivered our households.'" So the people bowed their heads and worshiped. ²⁸Then the children of Israel went away and did *so;* just as the LORD had commanded Moses and Aaron, so they did.

SERVICE
"So this day shall be to you a memorial. . . ."
EXODUS 12:14

What We Can Do for Our Country
In honor of the veterans of the Civil War, Supreme Court Justice Oliver Wendell Holmes Jr., who had been wounded three times during the war, said in a Memorial Day Address in 1884:

It is now the moment when by common consent we pause to become conscious of our national life and to rejoice in it, to recall what our country has done for each of us, and to ask ourselves what we can do for our country in return.

The Tenth Plague: Death of the Firstborn

²⁹And it came to pass at midnight that the LORD struck all the firstborn in the land of Egypt, from the firstborn of Pharaoh who sat on his throne to the firstborn of the captive who *was* in the dungeon, and all the firstborn of livestock. ³⁰So Pharaoh rose in the night, he, all his servants, and all the Egyptians; and there was a great cry in Egypt, for *there was* not a house where *there was* not one dead.

The Exodus

³¹Then he called for Moses and Aaron by night, and said, "Rise, go out from among my people, both you and the children of Israel. And go, serve the LORD as you have said. ³²Also take your flocks and your herds, as you have said, and be gone; and bless me also." ³³And the Egyptians urged the people, that they might send them out of the land in haste. For they said, "We *shall* all *be* dead." ³⁴So the people took their dough

before it was leavened, having their kneading bowls bound up in their clothes on their shoulders. [35]Now the children of Israel had done according to the word of Moses, and they had asked from the Egyptians articles of silver, articles of gold, and clothing. [36]And the LORD had given the people favor in the sight of the Egyptians, so that they granted them *what they requested.* Thus they plundered the Egyptians.

[37]Then the children of Israel journeyed from Rameses to Succoth, about six hundred thousand men on foot, besides children. [38]A mixed multitude went up with them also, and flocks and herds—a great deal of livestock. [39]And they baked unleavened cakes of the dough which they had brought out of Egypt; for it was not leavened, because they were driven out of Egypt and could not wait, nor had they prepared provisions for themselves.

[40]Now the sojourn of the children of Israel who lived in Egypt[a] *was* four hundred and thirty years. [41]And it came to pass at the end of the four hundred and thirty years—on that very same day—it came to pass that all the armies of the LORD went out from the land of Egypt. [42]It *is* a night of solemn observance to the LORD for bringing them out of the land of Egypt. This *is* that night of the LORD, a solemn observance for all the children of Israel throughout their generations.

Passover Regulations

[43]And the LORD said to Moses and Aaron, "This *is* the ordinance of the Passover: No foreigner shall eat it. [44]But every man's servant who is bought for money, when you have circumcised him, then he may eat it. [45]A sojourner and a hired servant shall not eat it. [46]In one house it shall be eaten; you shall not carry any of the flesh outside the house, nor shall you break one of its bones. [47]All the congregation of Israel shall keep it. [48]And when a stranger dwells with you *and wants* to keep the Passover to the LORD, let all his males be circumcised, and then let him come near and keep it; and he shall be as a native of the land. For no uncircumcised person shall eat it. [49]One law

shall be for the native-born and for the stranger who dwells among you."

[50]Thus all the children of Israel did; as the LORD commanded Moses and Aaron, so they did. [51]And it came to pass, on that very same day, that the LORD brought the children of Israel out of the land of Egypt according to their armies.

The Firstborn Consecrated

13 Then the LORD spoke to Moses, saying, [2]"Consecrate to Me all the firstborn, whatever opens the womb among the children of Israel, *both* of man and beast; it is Mine."

The Feast of Unleavened Bread

[3]And Moses said to the people: "Remember this day in which you went out of Egypt, out of the house of bondage; for by strength of hand the LORD brought you out of this *place.* No leavened bread shall be eaten. [4]On this day you are going out, in the month Abib. [5]And it shall be, when the LORD brings you into the land of the Canaanites and the Hittites and the Amorites and the Hivites and the Jebusites, which He swore to your fathers to give you, a land flowing with milk and honey, that you shall keep this service in this month. [6]Seven days you shall eat unleavened bread, and on the seventh day *there shall be* a feast to the LORD. [7]Unleavened bread shall be eaten seven days. And no leavened bread shall be seen among you, nor shall leaven be seen among you in all your quarters. [8]And you shall tell your son in that day, saying, '*This is done* because of what the LORD did for me when I came up from Egypt.' [9]It shall be as a sign to you on your hand and as a memorial between your eyes, that the LORD's law may be in your mouth; for with a strong hand the LORD has brought you out of Egypt. [10]You shall therefore keep this ordinance in its season from year to year.

The Law of the Firstborn

[11]"And it shall be, when the LORD brings you into the land of the Canaanites, as He

---

12:40 [a]Samaritan Pentateuch and Septuagint read *Egypt and Canaan.*

swore to you and your fathers, and gives it to you, [12]that you shall set apart to the LORD all that open the womb, that is, every firstborn that comes from an animal which you have; the males *shall be* the LORD's. [13]But every firstborn of a donkey you shall redeem with a lamb; and if you will not redeem *it*, then you shall break its neck. And all the firstborn of man among your sons you shall redeem. [14]So it shall be, when your son asks you in time to come, saying, 'What *is* this?' that you shall say to him, 'By strength of hand the LORD brought us out of Egypt, out of the house of bondage. [15]And it came to pass, when Pharaoh was stubborn about letting us go, that the LORD killed all the firstborn in the land of Egypt, both the firstborn of man and the firstborn of beast. Therefore I sacrifice to the LORD all males that open the womb, but all the firstborn of my sons I redeem.' [16]It shall be as a sign on your hand and as frontlets between your eyes, for by strength of hand the LORD brought us out of Egypt.'"

The Wilderness Way

[17]Then it came to pass, when Pharaoh had let the people go, that God did not lead them *by* way of the land of the Philistines, although that *was* near; for God said, "Lest perhaps the people change their minds when they see war, and return to Egypt." [18]So God led the people around *by* way of the wilderness of the Red Sea. And the children of Israel went up in orderly ranks out of the land of Egypt.

[19]And Moses took the bones of Joseph with him, for he had placed the children of Israel under solemn oath, saying, "God will surely visit you, and you shall carry up my bones from here with you."[a]

[20]So they took their journey from Succoth and camped in Etham at the edge of the wilderness. [21]And the LORD went before them by day in a pillar of cloud to lead the way, and by night in a pillar of fire to give them light, so as to go by day and night. [22]He did not take away the pillar of cloud by day or the pillar of fire by night *from* before the people.

The Red Sea Crossing

14 Now the LORD spoke to Moses, saying: [2]"Speak to the children of Israel, that they turn and camp before Pi Hahiroth, between Migdol and the sea, opposite Baal Zephon; you shall camp before it by the sea. [3]For Pharaoh will say of the children of Israel, 'They *are* bewildered by the land; the wilderness has closed them in.' [4]Then I will harden Pharaoh's heart, so that he will pursue them; and I will gain honor over Pharaoh and over all his army, that the Egyptians may know that I *am* the LORD." And they did so.

[5]Now it was told the king of Egypt that the people had fled, and the heart of Pharaoh and his servants was turned against the people; and they said, "Why have we done this, that we have let Israel go from serving us?" [6]So he made ready his chariot and took his people with him. [7]Also, he took six hundred choice chariots, and all the chariots of Egypt with captains over every one of them. [8]And the LORD hardened the heart of Pharaoh king of Egypt, and he pursued the children of Israel; and the children of Israel went out with boldness. [9]So the Egyptians pursued them, all the horses *and* chariots of Pharaoh, his horsemen and his army, and overtook them camping by the sea beside Pi Hahiroth, before Baal Zephon.

[10]And when Pharaoh drew near, the children of Israel lifted their eyes, and behold, the Egyptians marched after them. So they were very afraid, and the children of Israel cried out to the LORD. [11]Then they said to Moses, "Because *there were* no graves in Egypt, have you taken us away to die in the wilderness? Why have you so dealt with us, to bring us up out of Egypt? [12]*Is* this not the word that we told you in Egypt, saying, 'Let us alone that we may serve the Egyptians'? For *it would have been* better for us to serve the Egyptians than that we should die in the wilderness."

[13]And Moses said to the people, "Do not be afraid. Stand still, and see the salvation of the LORD, which He will accomplish for you today. For the Egyptians whom you see

13:19 [a]Genesis 50:25

today, you shall see again no more forever. [14]The LORD will fight for you, and you shall hold your peace."

[15]And the LORD said to Moses, "Why do you cry to Me? Tell the children of Israel to go forward. [16]But lift up your rod, and stretch out your hand over the sea and divide it. And the children of Israel shall go on dry *ground* through the midst of the sea. [17]And I indeed will harden the hearts of the Egyptians, and they shall follow them. So I will gain honor over Pharaoh and over all his army, his chariots, and his horsemen. [18]Then the Egyptians shall know that I *am* the LORD, when I have gained honor for Myself over Pharaoh, his chariots, and his horsemen."

[19]And the Angel of God, who went before the camp of Israel, moved and went behind them; and the pillar of cloud went from before them and stood behind them. [20]So it came between the camp of the Egyptians and the camp of Israel. Thus it was a cloud and darkness *to the one,* and it gave light by night *to the other,* so that the one did not come near the other all that night. [21]Then Moses stretched out his hand over the sea; and the LORD caused the sea to go *back* by a strong east wind all that night, and made the sea into dry *land,* and the waters were divided. [22]So the children of Israel went into the midst of the sea on the dry *ground,* and the waters *were* a wall to them on their right hand and on their left. [23]And the Egyptians pursued and went after them into the midst of the sea, all Pharaoh's horses, his chariots, and his horsemen. [24]Now it came to pass, in the morning watch, that the LORD looked down upon the army of the Egyptians through the pillar of fire and cloud, and He troubled the army of the Egyptians. [25]And He took off[a] their chariot wheels, so that they drove them with difficulty; and the Egyptians said, "Let us flee from the face of Israel, for the LORD fights for them against the Egyptians."

[26]Then the LORD said to Moses, "Stretch out your hand over the sea, that the waters may come back upon the Egyptians, on their chariots, and on their horsemen." [27]And Moses stretched out his hand over the sea; and when the morning appeared, the sea returned to its full depth, while the Egyptians were fleeing into it. So the LORD overthrew the Egyptians in the midst of the sea. [28]Then the waters returned and covered the chariots, the horsemen, *and* all the army of Pharaoh that came into the sea after them. Not so much as one of them remained. [29]But the children of Israel had walked on dry *land* in the midst of the sea, and the waters *were* a wall to them on their right hand and on their left.

[30]So the LORD saved Israel that day out of the hand of the Egyptians, and Israel saw the Egyptians dead on the seashore. [31]Thus Israel saw the great work which the LORD had done in Egypt; so the people feared the LORD, and believed the LORD and His servant Moses.

The Song of Moses

15 Then Moses and the children of Israel sang this song to the LORD, and spoke, saying:

> "I will sing to the LORD,
> For He has triumphed gloriously!
> The horse and its rider
> He has thrown into the sea!
> 2 The LORD *is* my strength and song,
> And He has become my salvation;
> He *is* my God, and I will praise Him;
> My father's God, and I will exalt Him.
> 3 The LORD *is* a man of war;
> The LORD *is* His name.
> 4 Pharaoh's chariots and his army He
>   has cast into the sea;
> His chosen captains also are drowned
>   in the Red Sea.
> 5 The depths have covered them;
> They sank to the bottom like a stone.
>
> 6 "Your right hand, O LORD, has become
>   glorious in power;
> Your right hand, O LORD, has dashed
>   the enemy in pieces.
> 7 And in the greatness of Your excellence
> You have overthrown those who rose
>   against You;

14:25 [a]Samaritan Pentateuch, Septuagint, and Syriac read *bound.*

You sent forth Your wrath;
It consumed them like stubble.
8 And with the blast of Your nostrils
The waters were gathered together;
The floods stood upright like a heap;
The depths congealed in the heart
of the sea.
9 The enemy said, 'I will pursue,
I will overtake,
I will divide the spoil;
My desire shall be satisfied on them.
I will draw my sword,
My hand shall destroy them.'
10 You blew with Your wind,
The sea covered them;
They sank like lead in the mighty
waters.

11 "Who *is* like You, O Lord, among the
gods?
Who *is* like You, glorious in holiness,
Fearful in praises, doing wonders?
12 You stretched out Your right hand;
The earth swallowed them.
13 You in Your mercy have led forth
The people whom You have redeemed;
You have guided *them* in Your strength
To Your holy habitation.

14 "The people will hear *and* be afraid;
Sorrow will take hold of the
inhabitants of Philistia.
15 Then the chiefs of Edom will be
dismayed;
The mighty men of Moab,
Trembling will take hold of them;
All the inhabitants of Canaan will
melt away.
16 Fear and dread will fall on them;
By the greatness of Your arm
They will be *as* still as a stone,
Till Your people pass over, O Lord,
Till the people pass over
Whom You have purchased.
17 You will bring them in and plant them
In the mountain of Your inheritance,
In the place, O Lord, *which* You have
made
For Your own dwelling,
The sanctuary, O Lord, *which* Your
hands have established.

18 "The Lord shall reign forever and ever."

19For the horses of Pharaoh went with his chariots and his horsemen into the sea, and the Lord brought back the waters of the sea upon them. But the children of Israel went on dry *land* in the midst of the sea.

The Song of Miriam

20Then Miriam the prophetess, the sister of Aaron, took the timbrel in her hand; and all the women went out after her with timbrels and with dances. 21And Miriam answered them:

"Sing to the Lord,
For He has triumphed gloriously!
The horse and its rider
He has thrown into the sea!"

Bitter Waters Made Sweet

22So Moses brought Israel from the Red Sea; then they went out into the Wilderness of Shur. And they went three days in the wilderness and found no water. 23Now when they came to Marah, they could not drink the waters of Marah, for they *were* bitter. Therefore the name of it was called Marah.ᵃ 24And the people complained against Moses, saying, "What shall we drink?" 25So he cried out to the Lord, and the Lord showed him a tree. When he cast *it* into the waters, the waters were made sweet.

There He made a statute and an ordinance for them, and there He tested them, 26and said, "If you diligently heed the voice of the Lord your God and do what is right in His sight, give ear to His commandments and keep all His statutes, I will put none of the diseases on you which I have brought on the Egyptians. For I *am* the Lord who heals you."

27Then they came to Elim, where there *were* twelve wells of water and seventy palm trees; so they camped there by the waters.

Bread from Heaven

16 And they journeyed from Elim, and all the congregation of the children of Israel came to the Wilderness of Sin,

15:23 ᵃLiterally *Bitter*

"EMANCIPATE! ENFRANCHISE! EDUCATE!"

HENRY HIGHLAND GARNET

"You in Your mercy have led forth the people whom You have redeemed. . . ."

EXODUS 15:13

The ratification of the Thirteenth Amendment on December 18, 1865, completed legislation to abolish slavery, which had begun with the Emancipation Proclamation issued by President Abraham Lincoln in 1863. At Lincoln's request, Presbyterian minister Henry Highland Garnet was asked to deliver a sermon in the House of Representatives to commemorate the event on February 12, 1865.

For the first time in the history of the Republic, a black American spoke in the Capitol, and he delivered these powerful words:

Augustine, Constantine, Ignatius, Polycarp, Maximus, and the most illustrious lights of the ancient church denounced the sin of slaveholding. Thomas Jefferson said—at a period of his life when his judgment was matured and his experience was ripe— "There is preparing, I hope, under the auspices of heaven, a way for a total emancipation." The sainted Washington said, near the close of his mortal career and when the light of eternity was beaming upon him, "It is among my first wishes to see some plan adopted by which slavery in this country shall be abolished by law. I know of but one way by which this can be done, and that is by legislative action; and so far as my vote can go, it shall not be wanting." Patrick Henry said, "We should transmit to posterity our abhorrence of slavery." So also thought [this] Congress. . . .

Let the verdict of death which has been brought in against slavery by Congress be affirmed and executed by the people. Let the gigantic monster perish. Yes, perish now, and perish forever! . . . Let slavery die. It has had a long and fair trial; God Himself has pleaded against it. Its death warrant is signed by God and man. Do not commute its sentence. Give it no respite, but let it be ignominiously executed.

Honorable Senators and Representatives! Illustrious rulers of this great nation! I cannot refrain this day from invoking upon you, in God's name, the blessings of millions who were ready to perish but to whom a new and better life has been opened by your humanity, justice, and patriotism. You have said, "Let the Constitution of the country be so amended that slavery and involuntary servitude shall no longer exist in the United States, except in punishment for a crime." Surely, an act so sublime could not escape Divine notice; and doubtless, the deed has been recorded in the archives of Heaven! . . . Favored men—and honored of God as His instruments—speedily finish the work which He has given you to do. Emancipate! Enfranchise! Educate! and give the blessings of the Gospel to every American citizen!

which is between Elim and Sinai, on the fifteenth day of the second month after they departed from the land of Egypt. [2]Then the whole congregation of the children of Israel complained against Moses and Aaron in the wilderness. [3]And the children of Israel said to them, "Oh, that we had died by the hand of the Lord in the land of Egypt, when we sat by the pots of meat *and* when we ate bread to the full! For you have brought us out into this wilderness to kill this whole assembly with hunger."

[4]Then the Lord said to Moses, "Behold, I will rain bread from heaven for you. And the people shall go out and gather a certain quota every day, that I may test them, whether they will walk in My law or not. [5]And it shall be on the sixth day that they shall prepare what they bring in, and it shall be twice as much as they gather daily."

[6]Then Moses and Aaron said to all the children of Israel, "At evening you shall know that the Lord has brought you out of the land of Egypt. [7]And in the morning you shall see the glory of the Lord; for He hears your complaints against the Lord. But what *are* we, that you complain against us?" [8]Also Moses said, "*This shall be seen* when the Lord gives you meat to eat in the evening, and in the morning bread to the full; for the Lord hears your complaints which you make against Him. And what *are* we? Your complaints *are* not against us but against the Lord."

[9]Then Moses spoke to Aaron, "Say to all the congregation of the children of Israel, 'Come near before the Lord, for He has heard your complaints.' " [10]Now it came to pass, as Aaron spoke to the whole congregation of the children of Israel, that they looked toward the wilderness, and behold, the glory of the Lord appeared in the cloud.

[11]And the Lord spoke to Moses, saying, [12]"I have heard the complaints of the children of Israel. Speak to them, saying, 'At twilight you shall eat meat, and in the morning you shall be filled with bread. And you shall know that I *am* the Lord your God.' "

[13]So it was that quails came up at evening and covered the camp, and in the morning the dew lay all around the camp. [14]And when the layer of dew lifted, there, on the surface of the wilderness, was a small round substance, *as* fine as frost on the ground. [15]So when the children of Israel saw *it,* they said to one another, "What is it?" For they did not know what it *was.*

And Moses said to them, "This *is* the bread which the Lord has given you to eat. [16]This is the thing which the Lord has commanded: 'Let every man gather it according to each one's need, one omer for each person, *according to the* number of persons; let every man take for *those* who *are* in his tent.' "

[17]Then the children of Israel did so and gathered, some more, some less. [18]So when they measured *it* by omers, he who gathered much had nothing left over, and he who gathered little had no lack. Every man had gathered according to each one's need. [19]And Moses said, "Let no one leave any of it till morning." [20]Notwithstanding they did not heed Moses. But some of them left part of it until morning, and it bred worms and stank. And Moses was angry with them. [21]So they gathered it every morning, every man according to his need. And when the sun became hot, it melted.

[22]And so it was, on the sixth day, *that* they gathered twice as much bread, two omers for each one. And all the rulers of the congregation came and told Moses. [23]Then he said to them, "This *is what* the Lord has said: 'Tomorrow *is* a Sabbath rest, a holy Sabbath to the Lord. Bake what you will bake *today,* and boil what you will boil; and lay up for yourselves all that remains, to be kept until morning.' " [24]So they laid it up till morning, as Moses commanded; and it did not stink, nor were there any worms in it. [25]Then Moses said, "Eat that today, for today *is* a Sabbath to the Lord; today you will not find it in the field. [26]Six days you shall gather it, but on the seventh day, the Sabbath, there will be none."

[27]Now it happened *that some* of the people went out on the seventh day to gather, but they found none. [28]And the Lord said

to Moses, "How long do you refuse to keep My commandments and My laws? ²⁹See! For the LORD has given you the Sabbath; therefore He gives you on the sixth day bread for two days. Let every man remain in his place; let no man go out of his place on the seventh day." ³⁰So the people rested on the seventh day.

³¹And the house of Israel called its name Manna.ᵃ And it *was* like white coriander seed, and the taste of it *was* like wafers *made* with honey.

³²Then Moses said, "This *is* the thing which the LORD has commanded: 'Fill an omer with it, to be kept for your generations, that they may see the bread with which I fed you in the wilderness, when I brought you out of the land of Egypt.'" ³³And Moses said to Aaron, "Take a pot and put an omer of manna in it, and lay it up before the LORD, to be kept for your generations." ³⁴As the LORD commanded Moses, so Aaron laid it up before the Testimony, to be kept. ³⁵And the children of Israel ate manna forty years, until they came to an inhabited land; they ate manna until they came to the border of the land of Canaan. ³⁶Now an omer *is* one-tenth of an ephah.

Water from the Rock

17 Then all the congregation of the children of Israel set out on their journey from the Wilderness of Sin, according to the commandment of the LORD, and camped in Rephidim; but *there was* no water for the people to drink. ²Therefore the people contended with Moses, and said, "Give us water, that we may drink."

So Moses said to them, "Why do you contend with me? Why do you tempt the LORD?"

³And the people thirsted there for water, and the people complained against Moses, and said, "Why *is* it you have brought us up out of Egypt, to kill us and our children and our livestock with thirst?"

⁴So Moses cried out to the LORD, saying, "What shall I do with this people? They are almost ready to stone me!"

⁵And the LORD said to Moses, "Go on before the people, and take with you some of the elders of Israel. Also take in your hand your rod with which you struck the river, and go. ⁶Behold, I will stand before you there on the rock in Horeb; and you shall strike the rock, and water will come out of it, that the people may drink."

And Moses did so in the sight of the elders of Israel. ⁷So he called the name of the place Massahᵃ and Meribah,ᵇ because of the contention of the children of Israel, and because they tempted the LORD, saying, "Is the LORD among us or not?"

Victory over the Amalekites

⁸Now Amalek came and fought with Israel in Rephidim. ⁹And Moses said to Joshua, "Choose us some men and go out, fight with Amalek. Tomorrow I will stand on the top of the hill with the rod of God in my hand." ¹⁰So Joshua did as Moses said to him, and fought with Amalek. And Moses, Aaron, and Hur went up to the top of the hill. ¹¹And so it was, when Moses held up his hand, that Israel prevailed; and when he let down his hand, Amalek prevailed. ¹²But Moses' hands *became* heavy; so they took a stone and put *it* under him, and he sat on it. And Aaron and Hur supported his hands, one on one side, and the other on the other side; and his hands were steady until the going down of the sun. ¹³So Joshua defeated Amalek and his people with the edge of the sword.

¹⁴Then the LORD said to Moses, "Write this *for* a memorial in the book and recount *it* in the hearing of Joshua, that I will utterly blot out the remembrance of Amalek from under heaven." ¹⁵And Moses built an altar and called its name, The-LORD-Is-My-Banner;ᵃ ¹⁶for he said, "Because the LORD has sworn: the LORD *will have* war with Amalek from generation to generation."

Jethro's Advice

18 And Jethro, the priest of Midian, Moses' father-in-law, heard of all that God had done for Moses and for Israel His people—that the LORD had brought Israel out of Egypt. ²Then Jethro, Moses'

16:31 ᵃLiterally *What?* (compare Exodus 16:15)
17:7 ᵃLiterally *Tempted* ᵇLiterally *Contention*
17:15 ᵃHebrew *YHWH Nissi*

father-in-law, took Zipporah, Moses' wife, after he had sent her back, ³with her two sons, of whom the name of one *was* Gershom (for he said, "I have been a stranger in a foreign land")ᵃ ⁴and the name of the other *was* Eliezerᵃ (for *he said,* "The God of my father *was* my help, and delivered me from the sword of Pharaoh"); ⁵and Jethro, Moses' father-in-law, came with his sons and his wife to Moses in the wilderness, where he was encamped at the mountain of God. ⁶Now he had said to Moses, "I, your father-in-law Jethro, am coming to you with your wife and her two sons with her."

⁷So Moses went out to meet his father-in-law, bowed down, and kissed him. And they asked each other about *their* well-being, and they went into the tent. ⁸And Moses told his father-in-law all that the LORD had done to Pharaoh and to the Egyptians for Israel's sake, all the hardship that had come upon them on the way, and *how* the LORD had delivered them. ⁹Then Jethro rejoiced for all the good which the LORD had done for Israel, whom He had delivered out of the hand of the Egyptians. ¹⁰And Jethro said, "Blessed *be* the LORD, who has delivered you out of the hand of the Egyptians and out of the hand of Pharaoh, *and* who has delivered the people from under the hand of the Egyptians. ¹¹Now I know that the LORD *is* greater than all the gods; for in the very thing in which they behaved proudly, *He was* above them." ¹²Then Jethro, Moses' father-in-law, tookᵃ a burnt offering and *other* sacrifices *to offer* to God. And Aaron came with all the elders of Israel to eat bread with Moses' father-in-law before God.

¹³And so it was, on the next day, that Moses sat to judge the people; and the people stood before Moses from morning until evening. ¹⁴So when Moses' father-in-law saw all that he did for the people, he said, "What *is* this thing that you are doing for the people? Why do you alone sit, and all the people stand before you from morning until evening?"

¹⁵And Moses said to his father-in-law, "Because the people come to me to inquire of God. ¹⁶When they have a difficulty, they

INTEGRITY
"... able men, such as fear God. ..."

EXODUS 18:21

Character Matters
Noah Webster, known as the "Father of American Scholarship and Education" and author of the famous *Webster's Dictionary*, stated:

> In selecting men for office, let principle be your guide. Regard not the particular sect [party] of the candidate—look to his character. ... It is alleged by men of loose principles or defective views of the subject that religion and morality are not necessary or important qualifications for political stations. But the Scriptures teach a different doctrine. They direct that rulers should be men "who rule in the fear of God, able men, such as fear God, men of truth, hating covetousness."

come to me, and I judge between one and another; and I make known the statutes of God and His laws."

¹⁷So Moses' father-in-law said to him, "The thing that you do *is* not good. ¹⁸Both you and these people who *are* with you will surely wear yourselves out. For this thing *is* too much for you; you are not able to perform it by yourself. ¹⁹Listen now to my voice; I will give you counsel, and God will be with you: Stand before God for the people, so that you may bring the difficulties to God. ²⁰And you shall teach them the statutes and the laws, and show them the way in which they must walk and the work they must do. ²¹Moreover you shall select from all the people able men, such as fear God, men of truth, hating covetousness; and place *such* over them *to be* rulers of thousands, rulers of hundreds, rulers of fifties, and rulers of tens. ²²And let them judge the people at all times. Then it will be *that* every great matter they shall bring to you, but every small matter they themselves shall judge. So it will be easier for you, for they will bear *the burden* with you. ²³If you do this thing, and God *so* commands you,

---

18:3 ᵃCompare Exodus 2:22   **18:4** ᵃLiterally *My God Is Help*   **18:12** ᵃFollowing Masoretic Text and Septuagint; Syriac, Targum, and Vulgate read *offered.*

then you will be able to endure, and all this people will also go to their place in peace."

²⁴So Moses heeded the voice of his father-in-law and did all that he had said. ²⁵And Moses chose able men out of all Israel, and made them heads over the people: rulers of thousands, rulers of hundreds, rulers of fifties, and rulers of tens. ²⁶So they judged the people at all times; the hard cases they brought to Moses, but they judged every small case themselves.

²⁷Then Moses let his father-in-law depart, and he went his way to his own land.

Israel at Mount Sinai

19 In the third month after the children of Israel had gone out of the land of Egypt, on the same day, they came *to* the Wilderness of Sinai. ²For they had departed from Rephidim, had come *to* the Wilderness of Sinai, and camped in the wilderness. So Israel camped there before the mountain.

³And Moses went up to God, and the Lord called to him from the mountain, saying, "Thus you shall say to the house of Jacob, and tell the children of Israel: ⁴'You have seen what I did to the Egyptians, and *how* I bore you on eagles' wings and brought you to Myself. ⁵Now therefore, if you will indeed obey My voice and keep My covenant, then you shall be a special treasure to Me above all people; for all the earth *is* Mine. ⁶And you shall be to Me a kingdom of priests and a holy nation.' These *are* the words which you shall speak to the children of Israel."

⁷So Moses came and called for the elders of the people, and laid before them all these words which the Lord commanded him. ⁸Then all the people answered together and said, "All that the Lord has spoken we will do." So Moses brought back the words of the people to the Lord. ⁹And the Lord said to Moses, "Behold, I come to you in the thick cloud, that the people may hear when I speak with you, and believe you forever."

So Moses told the words of the people to the Lord.

¹⁰Then the Lord said to Moses, "Go to the people and consecrate them today and tomorrow, and let them wash their clothes. ¹¹And let them be ready for the third day. For on the third day the Lord will come down upon Mount Sinai in the sight of all the people. ¹²You shall set bounds for the people all around, saying, 'Take heed to yourselves *that* you do *not* go up to the mountain or touch its base. Whoever touches the mountain shall surely be put to death. ¹³Not a hand shall touch him, but he shall surely be stoned or shot *with an arrow;* whether man or beast, he shall not live.' When the trumpet sounds long, they shall come near the mountain."

¹⁴So Moses went down from the mountain to the people and sanctified the people, and they washed their clothes. ¹⁵And he said to the people, "Be ready for the third day; do not come near *your* wives."

¹⁶Then it came to pass on the third day, in the morning, that there were thunderings and lightnings, and a thick cloud on the mountain; and the sound of the trumpet was very loud, so that all the people who *were* in the camp trembled. ¹⁷And Moses brought the people out of the camp to meet with God, and they stood at the foot of the mountain. ¹⁸Now Mount Sinai *was* completely in smoke, because the Lord descended upon it in fire. Its smoke ascended like the smoke of a furnace, and the whole mountain[a] quaked greatly. ¹⁹And when the blast of the trumpet sounded long and became louder and louder, Moses spoke, and God answered him by voice. ²⁰Then the Lord came down upon Mount Sinai, on the top of the mountain. And the Lord called Moses to the top of the mountain, and Moses went up.

²¹And the Lord said to Moses, "Go down and warn the people, lest they break through to gaze at the Lord, and many of them perish. ²²Also let the priests who come near the Lord consecrate themselves, lest the Lord break out against them."

²³But Moses said to the Lord, "The people cannot come up to Mount Sinai; for You warned us, saying, 'Set bounds around the mountain and consecrate it.'"

19:18 ᵃSeptuagint reads *all the people.*

²⁴Then the LORD said to him, "Away! Get down and then come up, you and Aaron with you. But do not let the priests and the people break through to come up to the LORD, lest He break out against them." ²⁵So Moses went down to the people and spoke to them.

The Ten Commandments

20 And God spoke all these words, saying:

² "I *am* the LORD your God, who brought you out of the land of Egypt, out of the house of bondage.

> **Harry S. Truman** placed his hand on Matthew 5:3–11 and Exodus 20:3–17 as he took the presidential oath of office in 1949.

³ "You shall have no other gods before Me.
⁴ "You shall not make for yourself a carved image—any likeness *of anything* that *is* in heaven above, or that *is* in the earth beneath, or that *is* in the water under the earth; ⁵you shall not bow down to them nor serve them. For I, the LORD your God, *am* a jealous God, visiting the iniquity of the fathers upon the children to the third and fourth *generations* of those who hate Me, ⁶but showing mercy to thousands, to those who love Me and keep My commandments.
⁷ "You shall not take the name of the LORD your God in vain, for the LORD will not hold *him* guiltless who takes His name in vain.
⁸ "Remember the Sabbath day, to keep it holy. ⁹Six days you shall labor and do all your work, ¹⁰but the seventh day *is* the Sabbath of the LORD your God. *In it* you shall do no work: you, nor your son, nor your daughter, nor your male servant, nor your female servant, nor your cattle, nor your stranger who *is* within your gates. ¹¹For *in* six days the LORD made the heavens and the earth, the sea, and all that *is* in them, and rested the seventh day. Therefore the LORD blessed the Sabbath day and hallowed it.
¹² "Honor your father and your mother, that your days may be long upon the land which the LORD your God is giving you.
¹³ "You shall not murder.
¹⁴ "You shall not commit adultery.
¹⁵ "You shall not steal.
¹⁶ "You shall not bear false witness against your neighbor.
¹⁷ "You shall not covet your neighbor's house; you shall not covet your neighbor's wife, nor his male servant, nor his female servant, nor his ox, nor his donkey, nor anything that *is* your neighbor's."

HONOR
"Remember the Sabbath day, to keep it holy."
EXODUS 20:8

A Church for Each Parish
In 1665, the Legislature of New York Colony enacted:

> Whereas, the public worship of God is much discredited for want of painful [serious] and able ministers to instruct the people in the true religion, it is ordered that a church shall be built in each parish, capable of holding two hundred persons; that ministers of every church shall preach every Sunday, and pray for the king, queen, the Duke of York, and the royal family; and to marry persons after legal publication of license. . . .

> Sunday is not to be profaned by traveling, by laborers, or vicious persons. . . . Church wardens to report twice a year all misdemeanors, such as swearing, profaneness, Sabbath-breaking, drunkenness, fornication, adultery, and all such abominable sins.

The People Afraid of God's Presence
¹⁸Now all the people witnessed the thunderings, the lightning flashes, the sound of the trumpet, and the mountain smoking; and when the people saw *it,* they trembled and stood afar off. ¹⁹Then they said to Moses, "You speak with us, and we will hear; but let not God speak with us, lest we die."

20And Moses said to the people, "Do not fear; for God has come to test you, and that His fear may be before you, so that you may not sin." 21So the people stood afar off, but Moses drew near the thick darkness where God *was*.

The Law of the Altar

22Then the LORD said to Moses, "Thus you shall say to the children of Israel: 'You have seen that I have talked with you from heaven. 23You shall not make *anything to be* with Me—gods of silver or gods of gold you shall not make for yourselves. 24An altar of earth you shall make for Me, and you shall sacrifice on it your burnt offerings and your peace offerings, your sheep and your oxen. In every place where I record My name I will come to you, and I will bless you. 25And if you make Me an altar of stone, you shall not build it of hewn stone; for if you use your tool on it, you have profaned it. 26Nor shall you go up by steps to My altar, that your nakedness may not be exposed on it.'

The Law Concerning Servants

21 "Now these *are* the judgments which you shall set before them: 2If you buy a Hebrew servant, he shall serve six years; and in the seventh he shall go out free and pay nothing. 3If he comes in by himself, he shall go out by himself; if he *comes in* married, then his wife shall go out with him. 4If his master has given him a wife, and she has borne him sons or daughters, the wife and her children shall be her master's, and he shall go out by himself. 5But if the servant plainly says, 'I love my master, my wife, and my children; I will not go out free,' 6then his master shall bring him to the judges. He shall also bring him to the door, or to the doorpost, and his master shall pierce his ear with an awl; and he shall serve him forever.

7"And if a man sells his daughter to be a female slave, she shall not go out as the male slaves do. 8If she does not please her master, who has betrothed her to himself, then he shall let her be redeemed. He shall have no right to sell her to a foreign people, since he has dealt deceitfully with her. 9And if he has betrothed her to his son, he shall deal with her according to the custom of daughters. 10If he takes another *wife,* he shall not diminish her food, her clothing, and her marriage rights. 11And if he does not do these three for her, then she shall go out free, without *paying* money.

The Law Concerning Violence

12"He who strikes a man so that he dies shall surely be put to death. 13However, if he did not lie in wait, but God delivered *him* into his hand, then I will appoint for you a place where he may flee.

14"But if a man acts with premeditation against his neighbor, to kill him by treachery, you shall take him from My altar, that he may die.

15"And he who strikes his father or his mother shall surely be put to death.

16"He who kidnaps a man and sells him, or if he is found in his hand, shall surely be put to death.

17"And he who curses his father or his mother shall surely be put to death.

18"If men contend with each other, and one strikes the other with a stone or with *his* fist, and he does not die but is confined to *his* bed, 19if he rises again and walks about outside with his staff, then he who struck *him* shall be acquitted. He shall only pay *for* the loss of his time, and shall provide *for him* to be thoroughly healed.

20"And if a man beats his male or female servant with a rod, so that he dies under his hand, he shall surely be punished. 21Notwithstanding, if he remains alive a day or two, he shall not be punished; for he *is* his property.

22"If men fight, and hurt a woman with child, so that she gives birth prematurely, yet no harm follows, he shall surely be punished accordingly as the woman's husband imposes on him; and he shall pay as the judges *determine*. 23But if *any* harm follows, then you shall give life for life, 24eye for eye, tooth for tooth, hand for hand, foot for foot, 25burn for burn, wound for wound, stripe for stripe.

26"If a man strikes the eye of his male or female servant, and destroys it, he shall let

him go free for the sake of his eye. ²⁷And if he knocks out the tooth of his male or female servant, he shall let him go free for the sake of his tooth.

Animal Control Laws

²⁸"If an ox gores a man or a woman to death, then the ox shall surely be stoned, and its flesh shall not be eaten; but the owner of the ox *shall be* acquitted. ²⁹But if the ox tended to thrust with its horn in times past, and it has been made known to his owner, and he has not kept it confined, so that it has killed a man or a woman, the ox shall be stoned and its owner also shall be put to death. ³⁰If there is imposed on him a sum of money, then he shall pay to redeem his life, whatever is imposed on him. ³¹Whether it has gored a son or gored a daughter, according to this judgment it shall be done to him. ³²If the ox gores a male or female servant, he shall give to their master thirty shekels of silver, and the ox shall be stoned.

³³"And if a man opens a pit, or if a man digs a pit and does not cover it, and an ox or a donkey falls in it, ³⁴the owner of the pit shall make *it* good; he shall give money to their owner, but the dead *animal* shall be his.

³⁵"If one man's ox hurts another's, so that it dies, then they shall sell the live ox and divide the money from it; and the dead *ox* they shall also divide. ³⁶Or if it was known that the ox tended to thrust in time past, and its owner has not kept it confined, he shall surely pay ox for ox, and the dead animal shall be his own.

Responsibility for Property

22"If a man steals an ox or a sheep, and slaughters it or sells it, he shall restore five oxen for an ox and four sheep for a sheep. ²If the thief is found breaking in, and he is struck so that he dies, *there shall be* no guilt for his bloodshed. ³If the sun has risen on him, *there shall be* guilt for his bloodshed. He should make full restitution; if he has nothing, then he shall be sold for his theft. ⁴If the theft is certainly found alive in his hand, whether it is an ox or donkey or sheep, he shall restore double.

⁵"If a man causes a field or vineyard to be grazed, and lets loose his animal, and it feeds in another man's field, he shall make restitution from the best of his own field and the best of his own vineyard.

⁶"If fire breaks out and catches in thorns, so that stacked grain, standing grain, or the field is consumed, he who kindled the fire shall surely make restitution.

⁷"If a man delivers to his neighbor money or articles to keep, and it is stolen out of the man's house, if the thief is found, he shall pay double. ⁸If the thief is not found, then the master of the house shall be brought to the judges *to see* whether he has put his hand into his neighbor's goods.

⁹"For any kind of trespass, *whether it concerns* an ox, a donkey, a sheep, or clothing, *or* for any kind of lost thing which *another* claims to be his, the cause of both parties shall come before the judges; *and* whomever the judges condemn shall pay double to his neighbor. ¹⁰If a man delivers to his neighbor a donkey, an ox, a sheep, or any animal to keep, and it dies, is hurt, or driven away, no one seeing *it*, ¹¹then an oath of the Lord shall be between them both, that he has not put his hand into his neighbor's goods; and the owner of it shall accept *that,* and he shall not make *it* good. ¹²But if, in fact, it is stolen from him, he shall make restitution to the owner of it. ¹³If it is torn to pieces *by a beast, then* he shall bring it as evidence, *and* he shall not make good what was torn.

¹⁴"And if a man borrows *anything* from his neighbor, and it becomes injured or dies, the owner of it not *being* with it, he shall surely make *it* good. ¹⁵If its owner *was* with it, he shall not make *it* good; if it *was* hired, it came for its hire.

Moral and Ceremonial Principles

¹⁶"If a man entices a virgin who is not betrothed, and lies with her, he shall surely pay the bride-price for her *to be* his wife. ¹⁷If her father utterly refuses to give her to him, he shall pay money according to the bride-price of virgins.

¹⁸"You shall not permit a sorceress to live.

¹⁹"Whoever lies with an animal shall surely be put to death.

²⁰"He who sacrifices to *any* god, except to the LORD only, he shall be utterly destroyed.

²¹"You shall neither mistreat a stranger nor oppress him, for you were strangers in the land of Egypt.

²²"You shall not afflict any widow or fatherless child. ²³If you afflict them in any way, *and* they cry at all to Me, I will surely hear their cry; ²⁴and My wrath will become hot, and I will kill you with the sword; your wives shall be widows, and your children fatherless.

²⁵"If you lend money to *any of* My people *who are* poor among you, you shall not be like a moneylender to him; you shall not charge him interest. ²⁶If you ever take your neighbor's garment as a pledge, you shall return it to him before the sun goes down. ²⁷For that *is* his only covering, it *is* his garment for his skin. What will he sleep in? And it will be that when he cries to Me, I will hear, for I *am* gracious.

²⁸"You shall not revile God, nor curse a ruler of your people.

²⁹"You shall not delay *to offer* the first of your ripe produce and your juices. The firstborn of your sons you shall give to Me. ³⁰Likewise you shall do with your oxen *and* your sheep. It shall be with its mother seven days; on the eighth day you shall give it to Me.

³¹"And you shall be holy men to Me: you shall not eat meat torn *by beasts* in the field; you shall throw it to the dogs.

Justice for All

23 "You shall not circulate a false report. Do not put your hand with the wicked to be an unrighteous witness. ²You shall not follow a crowd to do evil; nor shall you testify in a dispute so as to turn aside after many to pervert *justice.* ³You shall not show partiality to a poor man in his dispute.

⁴"If you meet your enemy's ox or his donkey going astray, you shall surely bring it back to him again. ⁵If you see the donkey of one who hates you lying under its burden, and you would refrain from helping it, you shall surely help him with it.

⁶"You shall not pervert the judgment of your poor in his dispute. ⁷Keep yourself far from a false matter; do not kill the innocent and righteous. For I will not justify the wicked. ⁸And you shall take no bribe, for a bribe blinds the discerning and perverts the words of the righteous.

⁹"Also you shall not oppress a stranger, for you know the heart of a stranger, because you were strangers in the land of Egypt.

The Law of Sabbaths

¹⁰"Six years you shall sow your land and gather in its produce, ¹¹but the seventh *year* you shall let it rest and lie fallow, that the poor of your people may eat; and what they leave, the beasts of the field may eat. In like manner you shall do with your vineyard *and* your olive grove. ¹²Six days you shall do your work, and on the seventh day you shall rest, that your ox and your donkey may rest, and the son of your female servant and the stranger may be refreshed.

¹³"And in all that I have said to you, be circumspect and make no mention of the name of other gods, nor let it be heard from your mouth.

Three Annual Feasts

¹⁴"Three times you shall keep a feast to Me in the year: ¹⁵You shall keep the Feast of Unleavened Bread (you shall eat unleavened bread seven days, as I commanded you, at the time appointed in the month of Abib, for in it you came out of Egypt; none shall appear before Me empty); ¹⁶and the Feast of Harvest, the firstfruits of your labors which you have sown in the field; and the Feast of Ingathering at the end of the year, when you have gathered in *the fruit of* your labors from the field.

¹⁷"Three times in the year all your males shall appear before the Lord GOD.ᵃ

¹⁸"You shall not offer the blood of My sacrifice with leavened bread; nor shall the fat of My sacrifice remain until morning. ¹⁹The first of the firstfruits of your land you shall bring into the house of the LORD your God. You shall not boil a young goat in its mother's milk.

23:17 ᵃHebrew *YHWH,* usually translated LORD

The Angel and the Promises

20"Behold, I send an Angel before you to keep you in the way and to bring you into the place which I have prepared. 21Beware of Him and obey His voice; do not provoke Him, for He will not pardon your transgressions; for My name *is* in Him. 22But if you indeed obey His voice and do all that I speak, then I will be an enemy to your enemies and an adversary to your adversaries. 23For My Angel will go before you and bring you in to the Amorites and the Hittites and the Perizzites and the Canaanites and the Hivites and the Jebusites; and I will cut them off. 24You shall not bow down to their gods, nor serve them, nor do according to their works; but you shall utterly overthrow them and completely break down their *sacred* pillars.

25"So you shall serve the LORD your God, and He will bless your bread and your water. And I will take sickness away from the midst of you. 26No one shall suffer miscarriage or be barren in your land; I will fulfill the number of your days.

27"I will send My fear before you, I will cause confusion among all the people to whom you come, and will make all your enemies turn *their* backs to you. 28And I will send hornets before you, which shall drive out the Hivite, the Canaanite, and the Hittite from before you. 29I will not drive them out from before you in one year, lest the land become desolate and the beasts of the field become too numerous for you. 30Little by little I will drive them out from before you, until you have increased, and you inherit the land. 31And I will set your bounds from the Red Sea to the sea, Philistia, and from the desert to the River.ᵃ For I will deliver the inhabitants of the land into your hand, and you shall drive them out before you. 32You shall make no covenant with them, nor with their gods. 33They shall not dwell in your land, lest they make you sin against Me. For if you serve their gods, it will surely be a snare to you."

Israel Affirms the Covenant

24 Now He said to Moses, "Come up to the LORD, you and Aaron, Nadab and Abihu, and seventy of the elders of Israel, and worship from afar. 2And Moses alone shall come near the LORD, but they shall not come near; nor shall the people go up with him."

3So Moses came and told the people all the words of the LORD and all the judgments. And all the people answered with one voice and said, "All the words which the LORD has said we will do." 4And Moses wrote all the words of the LORD. And he rose early in the morning, and built an altar at the foot of the mountain, and twelve pillars according to the twelve tribes of Israel. 5Then he sent young men of the children of Israel, who offered burnt offerings and sacrificed peace offerings of oxen to the LORD. 6And Moses took half the blood and put *it* in basins, and half the blood he sprinkled on the altar. 7Then he took the Book of the Covenant and read in the hearing of the people. And they said, "All that the LORD has said we will do, and be obedient." 8And Moses took the blood, sprinkled *it* on the people, and said, "This is the blood of the covenant which the LORD has made with you according to all these words."

On the Mountain with God

9Then Moses went up, also Aaron, Nadab, and Abihu, and seventy of the elders of Israel, 10and they saw the God of Israel. And *there was* under His feet as it were a paved work of sapphire stone, and it was like the very heavens in *its* clarity. 11But on the nobles of the children of Israel He did not lay His hand. So they saw God, and they ate and drank.

12Then the LORD said to Moses, "Come up to Me on the mountain and be there; and I will give you tablets of stone, and the law and commandments which I have written, that you may teach them."

13So Moses arose with his assistant Joshua, and Moses went up to the mountain of God. 14And he said to the elders, "Wait here for us until we come back to you. Indeed, Aaron and Hur *are* with you. If any man has a difficulty, let him go to them."

23:31 ᵃHebrew *Nahar*, the Euphrates

¹⁵Then Moses went up into the mountain, and a cloud covered the mountain.

¹⁶Now the glory of the LORD rested on Mount Sinai, and the cloud covered it six days. And on the seventh day He called to Moses out of the midst of the cloud. ¹⁷The sight of the glory of the LORD *was* like a consuming fire on the top of the mountain in the eyes of the children of Israel. ¹⁸So Moses went into the midst of the cloud and went up into the mountain. And Moses was on the mountain forty days and forty nights.

Offerings for the Sanctuary

25 Then the LORD spoke to Moses, saying: ²"Speak to the children of Israel, that they bring Me an offering. From everyone who gives it willingly with his heart you shall take My offering. ³And this *is* the offering which you shall take from them: gold, silver, and bronze; ⁴blue, purple, and scarlet *thread,* fine linen, and goats' *hair;* ⁵ram skins dyed red, badger skins, and acacia wood; ⁶oil for the light, and spices for the anointing oil and for the sweet incense; ⁷onyx stones, and stones to be set in the ephod and in the breastplate. ⁸And let them make Me a sanctuary, that I may dwell among them. ⁹According to all that I show you, *that is,* the pattern of the tabernacle and the pattern of all its furnishings, just so you shall make *it.*

The Ark of the Testimony

¹⁰"And they shall make an ark of acacia wood; two and a half cubits *shall be* its length, a cubit and a half its width, and a cubit and a half its height. ¹¹And you shall overlay it with pure gold, inside and out you shall overlay it, and shall make on it a molding of gold all around. ¹²You shall cast four rings of gold for it, and put *them* in its four corners; two rings *shall be* on one side, and two rings on the other side. ¹³And you shall make poles *of* acacia wood, and overlay them with gold. ¹⁴You shall put the poles into the rings on the sides of the ark, that the ark may be carried by them. ¹⁵The poles shall be in the rings of the ark; they shall not be taken from it. ¹⁶And you shall

put into the ark the Testimony which I will give you.

¹⁷"You shall make a mercy seat of pure gold; two and a half cubits *shall be* its length and a cubit and a half its width. ¹⁸And you shall make two cherubim of gold; of hammered work you shall make them at the two ends of the mercy seat. ¹⁹Make one cherub at one end, and the other cherub at the other end; you shall make the cherubim at the two ends of it *of one piece* with the mercy seat. ²⁰And the cherubim shall stretch out *their* wings above, covering the mercy seat with their wings, and they shall face one another; the faces of the cherubim *shall be* toward the mercy seat. ²¹You shall put the mercy seat on top of the ark, and in the ark you shall put the Testimony that I will give you. ²²And there I will meet with you, and I will speak with you from above the mercy seat, from between the two cherubim which *are* on the ark of the Testimony, about everything which I will give you in commandment to the children of Israel.

DEVOTION
"And there I will meet with you. . . ."
EXODUS 25:22

Reverence for the Word
William Cullen Bryant (1794–1878), known as the "Father of American Poets" and long-time editor of the *New York Evening Post,* wrote about the Bible:

> *The sacredness of the Bible awes me, and I approach it with the same sort of reverential feeling that an ancient Hebrew might be supposed to feel who was about to touch the ark of God with unhallowed hands.*

The Table for the Showbread

²³"You shall also make a table of acacia wood; two cubits *shall be* its length, a cubit its width, and a cubit and a half its height. ²⁴And you shall overlay it with pure gold, and make a molding of gold all around. ²⁵You shall make for it a frame of a handbreadth all around, and you shall make a gold molding for the frame all around. ²⁶And you shall make for it four rings of

gold, and put the rings on the four corners that *are* at its four legs. ²⁷The rings shall be close to the frame, as holders for the poles to bear the table. ²⁸And you shall make the poles of acacia wood, and overlay them with gold, that the table may be carried with them. ²⁹You shall make its dishes, its pans, its pitchers, and its bowls for pouring. You shall make them of pure gold. ³⁰And you shall set the showbread on the table before Me always.

The Gold Lampstand

³¹"You shall also make a lampstand of pure gold; the lampstand shall be of hammered work. Its shaft, its branches, its bowls, its *ornamental* knobs, and flowers shall be *of one piece.* ³²And six branches shall come out of its sides: three branches of the lampstand out of one side, and three branches of the lampstand out of the other side. ³³Three bowls *shall be* made like almond *blossoms* on one branch, *with* an *ornamental* knob and a flower, and three bowls made like almond *blossoms* on the other branch, *with* an *ornamental* knob and a flower—and so for the six branches that come out of the lampstand. ³⁴On the lampstand itself four bowls *shall be* made like almond *blossoms, each with* its *ornamental* knob and flower. ³⁵And *there shall be* a knob under the *first* two branches of the same, a knob under the *second* two branches of the same, and a knob under the *third* two branches of the same, according to the six branches that extend from the lampstand. ³⁶Their knobs and their branches *shall be of one piece;* all of it *shall be* one hammered piece of pure gold. ³⁷You shall make seven lamps for it, and they shall arrange its lamps so that they give light in front of it. ³⁸And its wick-trimmers and their trays *shall be* of pure gold. ³⁹It shall be made of a talent of pure gold, with all these utensils. ⁴⁰And see to it that you make *them* according to the pattern which was shown you on the mountain.

The Tabernacle

26 "Moreover you shall make the tabernacle *with* ten curtains *of* fine woven linen and blue, purple, and scarlet *thread;*

with artistic designs of cherubim you shall weave them. ²The length of each curtain *shall be* twenty-eight cubits, and the width of each curtain four cubits. And every one of the curtains shall have the same measurements. ³Five curtains shall be coupled to one another, and *the other* five curtains *shall be* coupled to one another. ⁴And you shall make loops of blue *yarn* on the edge of the curtain on the selvedge of *one* set, and likewise you shall do on the outer edge of *the other* curtain of the second set. ⁵Fifty loops you shall make in the one curtain, and fifty loops you shall make on the edge of the curtain that *is* on the end of the second set, that the loops may be clasped to one another. ⁶And you shall make fifty clasps of gold, and couple the curtains together with the clasps, so that it may be one tabernacle.

⁷"You shall also make curtains of goats' *hair,* to be a tent over the tabernacle. You shall make eleven curtains. ⁸The length of each curtain *shall be* thirty cubits, and the width of each curtain four cubits; and the eleven curtains shall all have the same measurements. ⁹And you shall couple five curtains by themselves and six curtains by themselves, and you shall double over the sixth curtain at the forefront of the tent. ¹⁰You shall make fifty loops on the edge of the curtain that is outermost in *one* set, and fifty loops on the edge of the curtain of the second set. ¹¹And you shall make fifty bronze clasps, put the clasps into the loops, and couple the tent together, that it may be one. ¹²The remnant that remains of the curtains of the tent, the half curtain that remains, shall hang over the back of the tabernacle. ¹³And a cubit on one side and a cubit on the other side, of what remains of the length of the curtains of the tent, shall hang over the sides of the tabernacle, on this side and on that side, to cover it.

¹⁴"You shall also make a covering of ram skins dyed red for the tent, and a covering of badger skins above that.

¹⁵"And for the tabernacle you shall make the boards of acacia wood, standing upright. ¹⁶Ten cubits *shall be* the length of a board, and a cubit and a half *shall be* the

width of each board. [17]Two tenons *shall be* in each board for binding one to another. Thus you shall make for all the boards of the tabernacle. [18]And you shall make the boards for the tabernacle, twenty boards for the south side. [19]You shall make forty sockets of silver under the twenty boards: two sockets under each of the boards for its two tenons. [20]And for the second side of the tabernacle, the north side, *there shall be* twenty boards [21]and their forty sockets of silver: two sockets under each of the boards. [22]For the far side of the tabernacle, westward, you shall make six boards. [23]And you shall also make two boards for the two back corners of the tabernacle. [24]They shall be coupled together at the bottom and they shall be coupled together at the top by one ring. Thus it shall be for both of them. They shall be for the two corners. [25]So there shall be eight boards with their sockets of silver— sixteen sockets—two sockets under each of the boards.

[26]"And you shall make bars of acacia wood: five for the boards on one side of the tabernacle, [27]five bars for the boards on the other side of the tabernacle, and five bars for the boards of the side of the tabernacle, for the far side westward. [28]The middle bar shall pass through the midst of the boards from end to end. [29]You shall overlay the boards with gold, make their rings of gold *as* holders for the bars, and overlay the bars with gold. [30]And you shall raise up the tabernacle according to its pattern which you were shown on the mountain.

[31]"You shall make a veil woven of blue, purple, and scarlet *thread,* and fine woven linen. It shall be woven with an artistic design of cherubim. [32]You shall hang it upon the four pillars of acacia *wood* overlaid with gold. Their hooks *shall be* gold, upon four sockets of silver. [33]And you shall hang the veil from the clasps. Then you shall bring the ark of the Testimony in there, behind the veil. The veil shall be a divider for you between the holy *place* and the Most Holy. [34]You shall put the mercy seat upon the ark of the Testimony in the Most Holy. [35]You shall set the table outside the veil, and the lampstand across from the table on the side of the tabernacle toward the south; and you shall put the table on the north side.

[36]"You shall make a screen for the door of the tabernacle, *woven of* blue, purple, and scarlet *thread,* and fine woven linen, made by a weaver. [37]And you shall make for the screen five pillars of acacia *wood,* and overlay them with gold; their hooks *shall be* gold, and you shall cast five sockets of bronze for them.

The Altar of Burnt Offering

27 "You shall make an altar of acacia wood, five cubits long and five cubits wide—the altar shall be square—and its height *shall be* three cubits. [2]You shall make its horns on its four corners; its horns shall be of one piece with it. And you shall overlay it with bronze. [3]Also you shall make its pans to receive its ashes, and its shovels and its basins and its forks and its firepans; you shall make all its utensils of bronze. [4]You shall make a grate for it, a network of bronze; and on the network you shall make four bronze rings at its four corners. [5]You shall put it under the rim of the altar beneath, that the network may be midway up the altar. [6]And you shall make poles for the altar, poles of acacia wood, and overlay them with bronze. [7]The poles shall be put in the rings, and the poles shall be on the two sides of the altar to bear it. [8]You shall make it hollow with boards; as it was shown you on the mountain, so shall they make *it.*

The Court of the Tabernacle

[9]"You shall also make the court of the tabernacle. For the south side *there shall be* hangings for the court *made of* fine woven linen, one hundred cubits long for one side. [10]And its twenty pillars and their twenty sockets *shall be* bronze. The hooks of the pillars and their bands *shall be* silver. [11]Likewise along the length of the north side *there shall be* hangings one hundred *cubits* long, with its twenty pillars and their twenty sockets of bronze, and the hooks of the pillars and their bands of silver. [12]"And along the width of the court on the west side *shall be* hangings of fifty cubits,

with their ten pillars and their ten sockets. ¹³The width of the court on the east side *shall be* fifty cubits. ¹⁴The hangings on *one* side *of the gate shall be* fifteen cubits, *with* their three pillars and their three sockets. ¹⁵And on the other side *shall be* hangings of fifteen *cubits, with* their three pillars and their three sockets.

¹⁶"For the gate of the court *there shall be* a screen twenty cubits long, *woven of* blue, purple, and scarlet *thread,* and fine woven linen, made by a weaver. It *shall have* four pillars and four sockets. ¹⁷All the pillars around the court shall have bands of silver; their hooks *shall be* of silver and their sockets of bronze. ¹⁸The length of the court *shall be* one hundred cubits, the width fifty throughout, and the height five cubits, *made of* fine woven linen, and its sockets of bronze. ¹⁹All the utensils of the tabernacle for all its service, all its pegs, and all the pegs of the court, *shall be* of bronze.

The Care of the Lampstand

²⁰"And you shall command the children of Israel that they bring you pure oil of pressed olives for the light, to cause the lamp to burn continually. ²¹In the tabernacle of meeting, outside the veil which *is* before the Testimony, Aaron and his sons shall tend it from evening until morning before the Lord. *It shall be* a statute forever to their generations on behalf of the children of Israel.

Garments for the Priesthood

28 "Now take Aaron your brother, and his sons with him, from among the children of Israel, that he may minister to Me as priest, Aaron *and* Aaron's sons: Nadab, Abihu, Eleazar, and Ithamar. ²And you shall make holy garments for Aaron your brother, for glory and for beauty. ³So you shall speak to all *who are* gifted artisans, whom I have filled with the spirit of wisdom, that they may make Aaron's garments, to consecrate him, that he may minister to Me as priest. ⁴And these *are* the garments which they shall make: a breastplate, an ephod,^a a robe, a skillfully woven tunic, a turban, and a sash. So they shall make holy garments for Aaron your brother and his sons, that he may minister to Me as priest.

The Ephod

⁵"They shall take the gold, blue, purple, and scarlet *thread,* and the fine linen, ⁶and they shall make the ephod of gold, blue, purple, *and* scarlet *thread,* and fine woven linen, artistically worked. ⁷It shall have two shoulder straps joined at its two edges, and *so* it shall be joined together. ⁸And the intricately woven band of the ephod, which *is* on it, shall be of the same workmanship, *made of* gold, blue, purple, and scarlet *thread,* and fine woven linen.

⁹"Then you shall take two onyx stones and engrave on them the names of the sons of Israel: ¹⁰six of their names on one stone and six names on the other stone, in order of their birth. ¹¹With the work of an engraver in stone, *like* the engravings of a signet, you shall engrave the two stones with the names of the sons of Israel. You shall set them in settings of gold. ¹²And you shall put the two stones on the shoulders of the ephod *as* memorial stones for the sons of Israel. So Aaron shall bear their names before the Lord on his two shoulders as a memorial. ¹³You shall also make settings of gold, ¹⁴and you shall make two chains of pure gold like braided cords, and fasten the braided chains to the settings.

The Breastplate

¹⁵"You shall make the breastplate of judgment. Artistically woven according to the workmanship of the ephod you shall make it: of gold, blue, purple, and scarlet *thread,* and fine woven linen, you shall make it. ¹⁶It shall be doubled into a square: a span *shall be* its length, and a span *shall be* its width. ¹⁷And you shall put settings of stones in it, four rows of stones: *The first* row *shall be* a sardius, a topaz, and an emerald; *this shall be* the first row; ¹⁸the second row *shall be* a turquoise, a sapphire, and a diamond; ¹⁹the third row, a jacinth, an agate, and an amethyst; ²⁰and the fourth row, a beryl, an onyx, and a jasper. They shall be

---

28:4 ^aThat is, an ornamented vest

set in gold settings. ²¹And the stones shall have the names of the sons of Israel, twelve according to their names, *like* the engravings of a signet, each one with its own name; they shall be according to the twelve tribes.

²²"You shall make chains for the breastplate at the end, like braided cords of pure gold. ²³And you shall make two rings of gold for the breastplate, and put the two rings on the two ends of the breastplate. ²⁴Then you shall put the two braided *chains* of gold in the two rings which are on the ends of the breastplate; ²⁵and the *other* two ends of the two braided *chains* you shall fasten to the two settings, and put them on the shoulder straps of the ephod in the front.

²⁶"You shall make two rings of gold, and put them on the two ends of the breastplate, on the edge of it, which is on the inner side of the ephod. ²⁷And two *other* rings of gold you shall make, and put them on the two shoulder straps, underneath the ephod toward its front, right at the seam above the intricately woven band of the ephod. ²⁸They shall bind the breastplate by means of its rings to the rings of the ephod, using a blue cord, so that it is above the intricately woven band of the ephod, and so that the breastplate does not come loose from the ephod.

²⁹"So Aaron shall bear the names of the sons of Israel on the breastplate of judgment over his heart, when he goes into the holy *place,* as a memorial before the Lord continually. ³⁰And you shall put in the breastplate of judgment the Urim and the Thummim,^a and they shall be over Aaron's heart when he goes in before the Lord. So Aaron shall bear the judgment of the children of Israel over his heart before the Lord continually.

Other Priestly Garments

³¹"You shall make the robe of the ephod all of blue. ³²There shall be an opening for his head in the middle of it; it shall have a woven binding all around its opening, like the opening in a coat of mail, so that it does not tear. ³³And upon its hem you shall make pomegranates of blue, purple, and scarlet, all around its hem, and bells of gold between them all around: ³⁴a golden bell and a pomegranate, a golden bell and a pomegranate, upon the hem of the robe all around. ³⁵And it shall be upon Aaron when he ministers, and its sound will be heard when he goes into the holy *place* before the Lord and when he comes out, that he may not die.

³⁶"You shall also make a plate of pure gold and engrave on it, *like* the engraving of a signet:

HOLINESS TO THE LORD.

³⁷And you shall put it on a blue cord, that it may be on the turban; it shall be on the front of the turban. ³⁸So it shall be on Aaron's forehead, that Aaron may bear the iniquity of the holy things which the children of Israel hallow in all their holy gifts; and it shall always be on his forehead, that they may be accepted before the Lord.

³⁹"You shall skillfully weave the tunic of fine linen *thread,* you shall make the turban of fine linen, and you shall make the sash of woven work.

⁴⁰"For Aaron's sons you shall make tunics, and you shall make sashes for them. And you shall make hats for them, for glory and beauty. ⁴¹So you shall put them on Aaron your brother and on his sons with him. You shall anoint them, consecrate them, and sanctify them, that they may minister to Me as priests. ⁴²And you shall make for them linen trousers to cover their nakedness; they shall reach from the waist to the thighs. ⁴³They shall be on Aaron and on his sons when they come into the tabernacle of meeting, or when they come near the altar to minister in the holy *place,* that they do not incur iniquity and die. *It shall be* a statute forever to him and his descendants after him.

Aaron and His Sons Consecrated

29 "And this is what you shall do to them to hallow them for ministering to Me as priests: Take one young bull and two rams without blemish, ²and unleavened

---

28:30 ^aLiterally *the Lights and the Perfections* (compare Leviticus 8:8)

bread, unleavened cakes mixed with oil, and unleavened wafers anointed with oil (you shall make them of wheat flour). ³You shall put them in one basket and bring them in the basket, with the bull and the two rams.

⁴"And Aaron and his sons you shall bring to the door of the tabernacle of meeting, and you shall wash them with water. ⁵Then you shall take the garments, put the tunic on Aaron, and the robe of the ephod, the ephod, and the breastplate, and gird him with the intricately woven band of the ephod. ⁶You shall put the turban on his head, and put the holy crown on the turban. ⁷And you shall take the anointing oil, pour *it* on his head, and anoint him. ⁸Then you shall bring his sons and put tunics on them. ⁹And you shall gird them with sashes, Aaron and his sons, and put the hats on them. The priesthood shall be theirs for a perpetual statute. So you shall consecrate Aaron and his sons.

¹⁰"You shall also have the bull brought before the tabernacle of meeting, and Aaron and his sons shall put their hands on the head of the bull. ¹¹Then you shall kill the bull before the LORD, *by* the door of the tabernacle of meeting. ¹²You shall take *some* of the blood of the bull and put *it* on the horns of the altar with your finger, and pour all the blood beside the base of the altar. ¹³And you shall take all the fat that covers the entrails, the fatty lobe *attached* to the liver, and the two kidneys and the fat that *is* on them, and burn *them* on the altar. ¹⁴But the flesh of the bull, with its skin and its offal, you shall burn with fire outside the camp. It *is* a sin offering.

¹⁵"You shall also take one ram, and Aaron and his sons shall put their hands on the head of the ram; ¹⁶and you shall kill the ram, and you shall take its blood and sprinkle *it* all around on the altar. ¹⁷Then you shall cut the ram in pieces, wash its entrails and its legs, and put *them* with its pieces and with its head. ¹⁸And you shall burn the whole ram on the altar. It *is* a burnt offering to the LORD; it *is* a sweet aroma, an offering made by fire to the LORD.

¹⁹"You shall also take the other ram, and Aaron and his sons shall put their hands on the head of the ram. ²⁰Then you shall kill the ram, and take some of its blood and put *it* on the tip of the right ear of Aaron and on the tip of the right ear of his sons, on the thumb of their right hand and on the big toe of their right foot, and sprinkle the blood all around on the altar. ²¹And you shall take some of the blood that is on the altar, and some of the anointing oil, and sprinkle *it* on Aaron and on his garments, on his sons and on the garments of his sons with him; and he and his garments shall be hallowed, and his sons and his sons' garments with him.

²²"Also you shall take the fat of the ram, the fat tail, the fat that covers the entrails, the fatty lobe *attached to* the liver, the two kidneys and the fat on them, the right thigh (for it *is* a ram of consecration), ²³one loaf of bread, one cake *made with* oil, and one wafer from the basket of the unleavened bread that *is* before the LORD; ²⁴and you shall put all these in the hands of Aaron and in the hands of his sons, and you shall wave them *as* a wave offering before the LORD. ²⁵You shall receive them back from their hands and burn *them* on the altar as a burnt offering, as a sweet aroma before the LORD. It *is* an offering made by fire to the LORD.

²⁶"Then you shall take the breast of the ram of Aaron's consecration and wave it *as* a wave offering before the LORD; and it shall be your portion. ²⁷And from the ram of the consecration you shall consecrate the breast of the wave offering which is waved, and the thigh of the heave offering which is raised, of *that* which *is* for Aaron and of *that* which is for his sons. ²⁸It shall be from the children of Israel *for* Aaron and his sons by a statute forever. For it is a heave offering; it shall be a heave offering from the children of Israel from the sacrifices of their peace offerings, *that is,* their heave offering to the LORD.

²⁹"And the holy garments of Aaron shall be his sons' after him, to be anointed in them and to be consecrated in them. ³⁰That son who becomes priest in his place shall

put them on for seven days, when he enters the tabernacle of meeting to minister in the holy *place.*

31"And you shall take the ram of the consecration and boil its flesh in the holy place. 32Then Aaron and his sons shall eat the flesh of the ram, and the bread that *is* in the basket, *by* the door of the tabernacle of meeting. 33They shall eat those things with which the atonement was made, to consecrate *and* to sanctify them; but an outsider shall not eat *them,* because they *are* holy. 34And if any of the flesh of the consecration offerings, or of the bread, remains until the morning, then you shall burn the remainder with fire. It shall not be eaten, because it *is* holy.

35"Thus you shall do to Aaron and his sons, according to all that I have commanded you. Seven days you shall consecrate them. 36And you shall offer a bull every day *as* a sin offering for atonement. You shall cleanse the altar when you make atonement for it, and you shall anoint it to sanctify it. 37Seven days you shall make atonement for the altar and sanctify it. And the altar shall be most holy. Whatever touches the altar must be holy.ᵃ

The Daily Offerings

38"Now this *is* what you shall offer on the altar: two lambs of the first year, day by day continually. 39One lamb you shall offer in the morning, and the other lamb you shall offer at twilight. 40With the one lamb shall be one-tenth *of an ephah* of flour mixed with one-fourth of a hin of pressed oil, and one-fourth of a hin of wine *as* a drink offering. 41And the other lamb you shall offer at twilight; and you shall offer with it the grain offering and the drink offering, as in the morning, for a sweet aroma, an offering made by fire to the Lord. 42*This shall be* a continual burnt offering throughout your generations *at* the door of the tabernacle of meeting before the Lord, where I will meet you to speak with you. 43And there I will meet with the children of Israel, and *the* tabernacle shall be sanctified by My glory. 44So I will consecrate the tabernacle of meeting and the altar. I will also consecrate both Aaron and his sons to minister to Me as priests. 45I will dwell among the children of Israel and will be their God. 46And they shall know that I *am* the Lord their God, who brought them up out of the land of Egypt, that I may dwell among them. I *am* the Lord their God.

The Altar of Incense

30 "You shall make an altar to burn incense on; you shall make it of acacia wood. 2A cubit *shall be* its length and a cubit its width—it shall be square—and two cubits *shall be* its height. Its horns *shall be* of one piece with it. 3And you shall overlay its top, its sides all around, and its horns with pure gold; and you shall make for it a molding of gold all around. 4Two gold rings you shall make for it, under the molding on both its sides. You shall place *them* on its two sides, and they will be holders for the poles with which to bear it. 5You shall make the poles of acacia wood, and overlay them with gold. 6And you shall put it before the veil that *is* before the ark of the Testimony, before the mercy seat that *is* over the Testimony, where I will meet with you.

7"Aaron shall burn on it sweet incense every morning; when he tends the lamps, he shall burn incense on it. 8And when Aaron lights the lamps at twilight, he shall burn incense on it, a perpetual incense before the Lord throughout your generations. 9You shall not offer strange incense on it, or a burnt offering, or a grain offering; nor shall you pour a drink offering on it. 10And Aaron shall make atonement upon its horns once a year with the blood of the sin offering of atonement; once a year he shall make atonement upon it throughout your generations. It *is* most holy to the Lord."

The Ransom Money

11Then the Lord spoke to Moses, saying: 12"When you take the census of the children of Israel for their number, then every man shall give a ransom for himself to the Lord, when you number them, that there

---

29:37 ᵃCompare Numbers 4:15 and Haggai 2:11–13

may be no plague among them when *you* number them. ¹³This is what everyone among those who are numbered shall give: half a shekel according to the shekel of the sanctuary (a shekel *is* twenty gerahs). The half-shekel *shall be* an offering to the LORD. ¹⁴Everyone included among those who are numbered, from twenty years old and above, shall give an offering to the LORD. ¹⁵The rich shall not give more and the poor shall not give less than half a shekel, when *you* give an offering to the LORD, to make atonement for yourselves. ¹⁶And you shall take the atonement money of the children of Israel, and shall appoint it for the service of the tabernacle of meeting, that it may be a memorial for the children of Israel before the LORD, to make atonement for yourselves."

The Bronze Laver

¹⁷Then the LORD spoke to Moses, saying: ¹⁸"You shall also make a laver of bronze, with its base also of bronze, for washing. You shall put it between the tabernacle of meeting and the altar. And you shall put water in it, ¹⁹for Aaron and his sons shall wash their hands and their feet in water from it. ²⁰When they go into the tabernacle of meeting, or when they come near the altar to minister, to burn an offering made by fire to the LORD, they shall wash with water, lest they die. ²¹So they shall wash their hands and their feet, lest they die. And it shall be a statute forever to them— to him and his descendants throughout their generations."

The Holy Anointing Oil

²²Moreover the LORD spoke to Moses, saying: ²³"Also take for yourself quality spices—five hundred *shekels* of liquid myrrh, half as much sweet-smelling cinnamon (two hundred and fifty *shekels*), two hundred and fifty *shekels* of sweet-smelling cane, ²⁴five hundred *shekels* of cassia, according to the shekel of the sanctuary, and a hin of olive oil. ²⁵And you shall make from these a holy anointing oil, an ointment compounded according to the art of the perfumer. It shall be a holy anointing oil. ²⁶With it you shall anoint the tabernacle of meeting and the ark of the Testimony; ²⁷the table and all its utensils, the lampstand and its utensils, and the altar of incense; ²⁸the altar of burnt offering with all its utensils, and the laver and its base. ²⁹You shall consecrate them, that they may be most holy; whatever touches them must be holy.ᵃ ³⁰And you shall anoint Aaron and his sons, and consecrate them, that *they* may minister to Me as priests.

³¹"And you shall speak to the children of Israel, saying: 'This shall be a holy anointing oil to Me throughout your generations. ³²It shall not be poured on man's flesh; nor shall you make *any other* like it, according to its composition. It *is* holy, *and* it shall be holy to you. ³³Whoever compounds *any* like it, or whoever puts *any* of it on an outsider, shall be cut off from his people.'"

The Incense

³⁴And the LORD said to Moses: "Take sweet spices, stacte and onycha and galbanum, and pure frankincense with *these* sweet spices; there shall be equal amounts of each. ³⁵You shall make of these an incense, a compound according to the art of the perfumer, salted, pure, *and* holy. ³⁶And you shall beat *some* of it very fine, and put some of it before the Testimony in the tabernacle of meeting where I will meet with you. It shall be most holy to you. ³⁷But *as for* the incense which you shall make, you shall not make any for yourselves, according to its composition. It shall be to you holy for the LORD. ³⁸Whoever makes *any* like it, to smell it, he shall be cut off from his people."

Artisans for Building the Tabernacle

31 Then the LORD spoke to Moses, saying: ²"See, I have called by name Bezalel the son of Uri, the son of Hur, of the tribe of Judah. ³And I have filled him with the Spirit of God, in wisdom, in understanding, in knowledge, and in all *manner of* workmanship, ⁴to design artistic works, to work in gold, in silver, in bronze, ⁵in cutting jewels for setting, in carving wood, and to work in all *manner of* workmanship.

30:29 ᵃCompare Numbers 4:15 and Haggai 2:11–13

6"And I, indeed I, have appointed with him Aholiab the son of Ahisamach, of the tribe of Dan; and I have put wisdom in the hearts of all the gifted artisans, that they may make all that I have commanded you: 7the tabernacle of meeting, the ark of the Testimony and the mercy seat that *is* on it, and all the furniture of the tabernacle— 8the table and its utensils, the pure *gold* lampstand with all its utensils, the altar of incense, 9the altar of burnt offering with all its utensils, and the laver and its base— 10the garments of ministry,ᵃ the holy garments for Aaron the priest and the garments of his sons, to minister as priests, 11and the anointing oil and sweet incense for the holy *place*. According to all that I have commanded you they shall do."

The Sabbath Law

12And the LORD spoke to Moses, saying, 13"Speak also to the children of Israel, saying: 'Surely My Sabbaths you shall keep, for it *is* a sign between Me and you throughout your generations, that *you* may know that I *am* the LORD who sanctifies you. 14You shall keep the Sabbath, therefore, for *it is* holy to you. Everyone who profanes it shall surely be put to death; for whoever does *any* work on it, that person shall be cut off from among his people. 15Work shall be done for six days, but the seventh *is* the Sabbath of rest, holy to the LORD. Whoever does *any* work on the Sabbath day, he shall surely be put to death. 16Therefore the children of Israel shall keep the Sabbath, to observe the Sabbath throughout their generations *as* a perpetual covenant. 17It *is* a sign between Me and the children of Israel forever; for *in* six days the LORD made the heavens and the earth, and on the seventh day He rested and was refreshed.'"

18And when He had made an end of speaking with him on Mount Sinai, He gave Moses two tablets of the Testimony, tablets of stone, written with the finger of God.

The Gold Calf

32 Now when the people saw that Moses delayed coming down from the mountain, the people gathered together to Aaron, and said to him, "Come, make us gods that shall go before us; for *as for* this Moses, the man who brought us up out of the land of Egypt, we do not know what has become of him."

2And Aaron said to them, "Break off the golden earrings which *are* in the ears of your wives, your sons, and your daughters, and bring *them* to me." 3So all the people broke off the golden earrings which *were* in their ears, and brought *them* to Aaron. 4And he received *the gold* from their hand, and he fashioned it with an engraving tool, and made a molded calf.

Then they said, "This *is* your god, O Israel, that brought you out of the land of Egypt!" 5So when Aaron saw *it,* he built an altar before it. And Aaron made a proclamation and said, "Tomorrow *is* a feast to the LORD." 6Then they rose early on the next day, offered burnt offerings, and brought peace offerings; and the people sat down to eat and drink, and rose up to play.

7And the LORD said to Moses, "Go, get down! For your people whom you brought out of the land of Egypt have corrupted *themselves.* 8They have turned aside quickly out of the way which I commanded them. They have made themselves a molded calf, and worshiped it and sacrificed to it, and said, 'This *is* your god, O Israel, that brought you out of the land of Egypt!'" 9And the LORD said to Moses, "I have seen this people, and indeed it *is* a stiff-necked people! 10Now therefore, let Me alone, that My wrath may burn hot against them and I may consume them. And I will make of you a great nation."

11Then Moses pleaded with the LORD his God, and said: "LORD, why does Your wrath burn hot against Your people whom You have brought out of the land of Egypt with great power and with a mighty hand? 12Why should the Egyptians speak, and say, 'He brought them out to harm them, to kill them in the mountains, and to consume them from the face of the earth'? Turn from Your fierce wrath, and relent from this harm to Your people. 13Remember Abraham, Isaac, and Israel, Your servants,

---

31:10 ᵃOr *woven garments*

to whom You swore by Your own self, and said to them, 'I will multiply your descendants as the stars of heaven; and all this land that I have spoken of I give to your descendants, and they shall inherit it forever.' "[a] [14]So the LORD relented from the harm which He said He would do to His people.

[15]And Moses turned and went down from the mountain, and the two tablets of the Testimony were in his hand. The tablets were written on both sides; on the one side and on the other they were written. [16]Now the tablets were the work of God, and the writing was the writing of God engraved on the tablets.

[17]And when Joshua heard the noise of the people as they shouted, he said to Moses, "There is a noise of war in the camp." [18]But he said:

"It is not the noise of the shout
   of victory,
 Nor the noise of the cry of defeat,
 But the sound of singing I hear."

[19]So it was, as soon as he came near the camp, that he saw the calf and the dancing. So Moses' anger became hot, and he cast the tablets out of his hands and broke them at the foot of the mountain. [20]Then he took the calf which they had made, burned it in the fire, and ground it to powder; and he scattered it on the water and made the children of Israel drink it. [21]And Moses said to Aaron, "What did this people do to you that you have brought so great a sin upon them?"

[22]So Aaron said, "Do not let the anger of my lord become hot. You know the people, that they are set on evil. [23]For they said to me, 'Make us gods that shall go before us; as for this Moses, the man who brought us out of the land of Egypt, we do not know what has become of him.' [24]And I said to them, 'Whoever has any gold, let them break it off.' So they gave it to me, and I cast it into the fire, and this calf came out."

[25]Now when Moses saw that the people were unrestrained (for Aaron had not restrained them, to their shame among their enemies), [26]then Moses stood in the entrance of the camp, and said, "Whoever is on the LORD's side—come to me!" And all the sons of Levi gathered themselves together to

---

32:13 [a]Genesis 13:15 and 22:17

MORAL STRENGTH

"Whoever is on the LORD's side—come to me!"

EXODUS 32:26

Wernher von Braun

SCIENCE AND THE BIBLE

Known as "The Father of the American Space Program," Wernher von Braun (1912–1977) was the director of NASA. He was sometimes said to be the preeminent rocket scientist of the twentieth century, and he stated:

In this age of space flight, when we use the modern tools of science to advance into new regions of human activity, the Bible—this grandiose, stirring history of the gradual revelation and unfolding of the moral law—remains in every way an up-to-date book.

Our knowledge and use of the laws of nature that enable us to fly to the moon also enable us to destroy our home planet with the atom bomb. Science itself does not address the question whether we should use the power at our disposal for good or for evil.

The guidelines of what we ought to do are furnished in the moral law of God. It is no longer enough that we pray that God may be with us on our side. We must learn to pray that we may be on God's side.

him. [27]And he said to them, "Thus says the LORD God of Israel: 'Let every man put his sword on his side, and go in and out from entrance to entrance throughout the camp, and let every man kill his brother, every man his companion, and every man his neighbor.'" [28]So the sons of Levi did according to the word of Moses. And about three thousand men of the people fell that day. [29]Then Moses said, "Consecrate yourselves today to the LORD, that He may bestow on you a blessing this day, for every man has opposed his son and his brother."

[30]Now it came to pass on the next day that Moses said to the people, "You have committed a great sin. So now I will go up to the LORD; perhaps I can make atonement for your sin." [31]Then Moses returned to the LORD and said, "Oh, these people have committed a great sin, and have made for themselves a god of gold! [32]Yet now, if You will forgive their sin—but if not, I pray, blot me out of Your book which You have written."

[33]And the LORD said to Moses, "Whoever has sinned against Me, I will blot him out of My book. [34]Now therefore, go, lead the people to *the place* of which I have spoken to you. Behold, My Angel shall go before you. Nevertheless, in the day when I visit for punishment, I will visit punishment upon them for their sin."

[35]So the LORD plagued the people because of what they did with the calf which Aaron made.

The Command to Leave Sinai

33 Then the LORD said to Moses, "Depart *and* go up from here, you and the people whom you have brought out of the land of Egypt, to the land of which I swore to Abraham, Isaac, and Jacob, saying, 'To your descendants I will give it.' [2]And I will send *My* Angel before you, and I will drive out the Canaanite and the Amorite and the Hittite and the Perizzite and the Hivite and the Jebusite. [3]*Go up* to a land flowing with milk and honey; for I will not go up in your midst, lest I consume you on the way, for you *are* a stiff-necked people."

[4]And when the people heard this bad news, they mourned, and no one put on his ornaments. [5]For the LORD had said to Moses, "Say to the children of Israel, 'You *are* a stiff-necked people. I could come up into your midst in one moment and consume you. Now therefore, take off your ornaments, that I may know what to do to you.'" [6]So the children of Israel stripped themselves of their ornaments by Mount Horeb.

Moses Meets with the LORD

[7]Moses took his tent and pitched it outside the camp, far from the camp, and called it the tabernacle of meeting. And it came to pass *that* everyone who sought the LORD went out to the tabernacle of meeting which *was* outside the camp. [8]So it was, whenever Moses went out to the tabernacle, *that* all the people rose, and each man stood *at* his tent door and watched Moses until he had gone into the tabernacle. [9]And it came to pass, when Moses entered the tabernacle, that the pillar of cloud descended and stood *at* the door of the tabernacle, and *the* LORD talked with Moses. [10]All the people saw the pillar of cloud standing *at* the tabernacle door, and all the people rose and worshiped, each man *in* his tent door. [11]So the LORD spoke to Moses face to face, as a man speaks to his friend. And he would return to the camp, but his servant Joshua the son of Nun, a young man, did not depart from the tabernacle.

The Promise of God's Presence

[12]Then Moses said to the LORD, "See, You say to me, 'Bring up this people.' But You have not let me know whom You will send with me. Yet You have said, 'I know you by name, and you have also found grace in My sight.' [13]Now therefore, I pray, if I have found grace in Your sight, show me now Your way, that I may know You and that I may find grace in Your sight. And consider that this nation *is* Your people."

[14]And He said, "My Presence will go *with you,* and I will give you rest."

[15]Then he said to Him, "If Your Presence does not go *with us,* do not bring us up from here. [16]For how then will it be known that Your people and I have found grace in

Your sight, except You go with us? So we shall be separate, Your people and I, from all the people who *are* upon the face of the earth."

[17]So the LORD said to Moses, "I will also do this thing that you have spoken; for you have found grace in My sight, and I know you by name."

[18]And he said, "Please, show me Your glory."

[19]Then He said, "I will make all My goodness pass before you, and I will proclaim the name of the LORD before you. I will be gracious to whom I will be gracious, and I will have compassion on whom I will have compassion." [20]But He said, "You cannot see My face; for no man shall see Me, and live." [21]And the LORD said, "Here is a place by Me, and you shall stand on the rock. [22]So it shall be, while My glory passes by, that I will put you in the cleft of the rock, and will cover you with My hand while I pass by. [23]Then I will take away My hand, and you shall see My back; but My face shall not be seen."

Moses Makes New Tablets

34 And the LORD said to Moses, "Cut two tablets of stone like the first *ones,* and I will write on *these* tablets the words that were on the first tablets which you broke. [2]So be ready in the morning, and come up in the morning to Mount Sinai, and present yourself to Me there on the top of the mountain. [3]And no man shall come up with you, and let no man be seen throughout all the mountain; let neither flocks nor herds feed before that mountain."

[4]So he cut two tablets of stone like the first *ones.* Then Moses rose early in the morning and went up Mount Sinai, as the LORD had commanded him; and he took in his hand the two tablets of stone.

[5]Now the LORD descended in the cloud and stood with him there, and proclaimed the name of the LORD. [6]And the LORD passed before him and proclaimed, "The LORD, the LORD God, merciful and gracious, longsuffering, and abounding in goodness and truth, [7]keeping mercy for thousands,

forgiving iniquity and transgression and sin, by no means clearing *the guilty,* visiting the iniquity of the fathers upon the children and the children's children to the third and the fourth generation."

[8]So Moses made haste and bowed his head toward the earth, and worshiped. [9]Then he said, "If now I have found grace in Your sight, O Lord, let my Lord, I pray, go among us, even though we *are* a stiff-necked people; and pardon our iniquity and our sin, and take us as Your inheritance."

The Covenant Renewed

[10]And He said: "Behold, I make a covenant. Before all your people I will do marvels such as have not been done in all the earth, nor in any nation; and all the people among whom you *are* shall see the work of the LORD. For it *is* an awesome thing that I will do with you. [11]Observe what I command you this day. Behold, I am driving out from before you the Amorite and the Canaanite and the Hittite and the Perizzite and the Hivite and the Jebusite. [12]Take heed to yourself, lest you make a covenant with the inhabitants of the land where you are going, lest it be a snare in your midst. [13]But you shall destroy their altars, break their *sacred* pillars, and cut down their wooden images [14](for you shall worship no other god, for the LORD, whose name *is* Jealous, *is* a jealous God), [15]lest you make a covenant with the inhabitants of the land, and they play the harlot with their gods and make sacrifice to their gods, and *one of them* invites you and you eat of his sacrifice, [16]and you take of his daughters for your sons, and his daughters play the harlot with their gods and make your sons play the harlot with their gods.

[17]"You shall make no molded gods for yourselves.

[18]"The Feast of Unleavened Bread you shall keep. Seven days you shall eat unleavened bread, as I commanded you, in the appointed time of the month of Abib; for in the month of Abib you came out from Egypt.

[19]"All that open the womb *are* Mine, and every male firstborn among your livestock,

whether ox or sheep. ²⁰But the firstborn of a donkey you shall redeem with a lamb. And if you will not redeem *him,* then you shall break his neck. All the firstborn of your sons you shall redeem.

"And none shall appear before Me empty-handed.

²¹"Six days you shall work, but on the seventh day you shall rest; in plowing time and in harvest you shall rest.

²²"And you shall observe the Feast of Weeks, of the firstfruits of wheat harvest, and the Feast of Ingathering at the year's end.

²³"Three times in the year all your men shall appear before the Lord, the LORD God of Israel. ²⁴For I will cast out the nations before you and enlarge your borders; neither will any man covet your land when you go up to appear before the LORD your God three times in the year.

²⁵"You shall not offer the blood of My sacrifice with leaven, nor shall the sacrifice of the Feast of the Passover be left until morning.

²⁶"The first of the firstfruits of your land you shall bring to the house of the LORD your God. You shall not boil a young goat in its mother's milk."

²⁷Then the LORD said to Moses, "Write these words, for according to the tenor of these words I have made a covenant with you and with Israel." ²⁸So he was there with the LORD forty days and forty nights; he neither ate bread nor drank water. And He wrote on the tablets the words of the covenant, the Ten Commandments.ᵃ

The Shining Face of Moses

²⁹Now it was so, when Moses came down from Mount Sinai (and the two tablets of the Testimony *were* in Moses' hand when he came down from the mountain), that Moses did not know that the skin of his face shone while he talked with Him. ³⁰So when Aaron and all the children of Israel saw Moses, behold, the skin of his face shone, and they were afraid to come near him. ³¹Then Moses called to them, and Aaron and all the rulers of the congregation returned to him; and Moses talked with them. ³²Afterward all the children of

Israel came near, and he gave them as commandments all that the LORD had spoken with him on Mount Sinai. ³³And when Moses had finished speaking with them, he put a veil on his face. ³⁴But whenever Moses went in before the LORD to speak with Him, he would take the veil off until he came out; and he would come out and speak to the children of Israel whatever he had been commanded. ³⁵And whenever the children of Israel saw the face of Moses, that the skin of Moses' face shone, then Moses would put the veil on his face again, until he went in to speak with Him.

Sabbath Regulations

35 Then Moses gathered all the congregation of the children of Israel together, and said to them, "These *are* the words which the LORD has commanded *you* to do: ²Work shall be done for six days, but the seventh day shall be a holy day for you, a Sabbath of rest to the LORD. Whoever does any work on it shall be put to death. ³You shall kindle no fire throughout your dwellings on the Sabbath day."

Offerings for the Tabernacle

⁴And Moses spoke to all the congregation of the children of Israel, saying, "This *is* the thing which the LORD commanded, saying: ⁵'Take from among you an offering to the LORD. Whoever *is* of a willing heart, let him bring it as an offering to the LORD: gold, silver, and bronze; ⁶blue, purple, and scarlet *thread,* fine linen, and goats' *hair;* ⁷ram skins dyed red, badger skins, and acacia wood; ⁸oil for the light, and spices for the anointing oil and for the sweet incense; ⁹onyx stones, and stones to be set in the ephod and in the breastplate.

Articles of the Tabernacle

¹⁰'All *who are* gifted artisans among you shall come and make all that the LORD has commanded: ¹¹the tabernacle, its tent, its covering, its clasps, its boards, its bars, its pillars, and its sockets; ¹²the ark and its poles, *with* the mercy seat, and the veil of the covering; ¹³the table and its poles, all its

---

34:28 ᵃLiterally *Ten Words*

utensils, and the showbread; ¹⁴also the lampstand for the light, its utensils, its lamps, and the oil for the light; ¹⁵the incense altar, its poles, the anointing oil, the sweet incense, and the screen for the door at the entrance of the tabernacle; ¹⁶the altar of burnt offering with its bronze grating, its poles, all its utensils, *and* the laver and its base; ¹⁷the hangings of the court, its pillars, their sockets, and the screen for the gate of the court; ¹⁸the pegs of the tabernacle, the pegs of the court, and their cords; ¹⁹the garments of ministry,ᵃ for ministering in the holy *place*—the holy garments for Aaron the priest and the garments of his sons, to minister as priests.' "

The Tabernacle Offerings Presented

²⁰And all the congregation of the children of Israel departed from the presence of Moses. ²¹Then everyone came whose heart was stirred, and everyone whose spirit was willing, *and* they brought the Lᴏʀᴅ's offering for the work of the tabernacle of meeting, for all its service, and for the holy garments. ²²They came, both men and women, as many as had a willing heart, *and* brought earrings and nose rings, rings and necklaces, all jewelry of gold, that is, every man who *made* an offering of gold to the Lᴏʀᴅ. ²³And every man, with whom was found blue, purple, and scarlet *thread,* fine linen, goats' *hair,* red skins of rams, and badger skins, brought *them.* ²⁴Everyone who offered an offering of silver or bronze brought the Lᴏʀᴅ's offering. And everyone with whom was found acacia wood for any work of the service, brought *it.* ²⁵All the women *who were* gifted artisans spun yarn with their hands, and brought what they had spun, of blue, purple, *and* scarlet, and fine linen. ²⁶And all the women whose hearts stirred with wisdom spun yarn of goats' *hair.* ²⁷The rulers brought onyx stones, and the stones to be set in the ephod and in the breastplate, ²⁸and spices and oil for the light, for the anointing oil, and for the sweet incense. ²⁹The children of Israel brought a freewill offering to the Lᴏʀᴅ, all the men and women whose hearts were willing to bring *material* for all

kinds of work which the Lᴏʀᴅ, by the hand of Moses, had commanded to be done.

The Artisans Called by God

³⁰And Moses said to the children of Israel, "See, the Lᴏʀᴅ has called by name Bezalel the son of Uri, the son of Hur, of the tribe of Judah; ³¹and He has filled him with the Spirit of God, in wisdom and understanding, in knowledge and all manner of workmanship, ³²to design artistic works, to work in gold and silver and bronze, ³³in cutting jewels for setting, in carving wood, and to work in all manner of artistic workmanship.

³⁴"And He has put in his heart the ability to teach, *in* him and Aholiab the son of Ahisamach, of the tribe of Dan. ³⁵He has filled them with skill to do all manner of work of the engraver and the designer and the tapestry maker, in blue, purple, and scarlet *thread,* and fine linen, and of the weaver—those who do every work and those who design artistic works.

36 "And Bezalel and Aholiab, and every gifted artisan in whom the Lᴏʀᴅ has put wisdom and understanding, to know how to do all manner of work for the service of the sanctuary, shall do according to all that the Lᴏʀᴅ has commanded."

The People Give More than Enough

²Then Moses called Bezalel and Aholiab, and every gifted artisan in whose heart the Lᴏʀᴅ had put wisdom, everyone whose heart was stirred, to come and do the work. ³And they received from Moses all the offering which the children of Israel had brought for the work of the service of making the sanctuary. So they continued bringing to him freewill offerings every morning. ⁴Then all the craftsmen who were doing all the work of the sanctuary came, each from the work he was doing, ⁵and they spoke to Moses, saying, "The people bring much more than enough for the service of the work which the Lᴏʀᴅ commanded *us* to do."

⁶So Moses gave a commandment, and they caused it to be proclaimed throughout the camp, saying, "Let neither man nor woman do any more work for the offering

---

35:19 ᵃOr *woven garments*

of the sanctuary." And the people were restrained from bringing, ⁷for the material they had was sufficient for all the work to be done—indeed too much.

Building the Tabernacle

⁸Then all the gifted artisans among them who worked on the tabernacle made ten curtains woven of fine linen, and of blue, purple, and scarlet *thread; with* artistic designs of cherubim they made them. ⁹The length of each curtain *was* twenty-eight cubits, and the width of each curtain four cubits; the curtains *were* all the same size. ¹⁰And he coupled five curtains to one another, and *the other* five curtains he coupled to one another. ¹¹He made loops of blue *yarn* on the edge of the curtain on the selvedge of one set; likewise he did on the outer edge of *the other* curtain of the second set. ¹²Fifty loops he made on one curtain, and fifty loops he made on the edge of the curtain on the end of the second set; the loops held one *curtain* to another. ¹³And he made fifty clasps of gold, and coupled the curtains to one another with the clasps, that it might be one tabernacle.

¹⁴He made curtains of goats' *hair* for the tent over the tabernacle; he made eleven curtains. ¹⁵The length of each curtain *was* thirty cubits, and the width of each curtain four cubits; the eleven curtains *were* the same size. ¹⁶He coupled five curtains by themselves and six curtains by themselves. ¹⁷And he made fifty loops on the edge of the curtain that is outermost in one set, and fifty loops he made on the edge of the curtain of the second set. ¹⁸He also made fifty bronze clasps to couple the tent together, that it might be one. ¹⁹Then he made a covering for the tent of ram skins dyed red, and a covering of badger skins above *that*.

²⁰For the tabernacle he made boards of acacia wood, standing upright. ²¹The length of each board *was* ten cubits, and the width of each board a cubit and a half. ²²Each board had two tenons for binding one to another. Thus he made for all the boards of the tabernacle. ²³And he made boards for the tabernacle, twenty boards for the south side. ²⁴Forty sockets of silver he made to go under the twenty boards: two sockets under each of the boards for its two tenons. ²⁵And for the other side of the tabernacle,

EQUIPPER

"He has filled them with skill to do all manner of work of the . . . tapestry maker. . . ."

EXODUS 35:35

Harriet Powers

HARRIET POWERS

Harriet Powers (1837–1910) was an African-American slave folk artist and quilt maker from rural Georgia. While only two of her quilts have survived, Bible Quilt 1886 and Bible Quilt 1898, they are nationally recognized as masterworks of American folk art. Her panel-storied quilts used traditional appliqué techniques and piecework to record local legends, Bible stories, and astronomical events. Considered among the finest examples of nineteenth-century Southern quilting, her work is on display at the National Museum of American History in Washington, D.C., and the Museum of Fine Arts in Boston, Massachusetts.

Her quilts demonstrate both African and African-American influences and consist of numerous pictorial squares, with each panel depicting a biblical story or celestial phenomenon. Scenes such as Adam and Eve naming the animals in the Garden of Eden, Cain killing his brother Abel, and the baptism of Christ are observed. Her art is powerful, vivid, and clearly tells a story. It is thought that Powers could neither read nor write, but she knew the Bible stories from singing Negro spirituals and from church sermons.

the north side, he made twenty boards
26and their forty sockets of silver: two sockets under each of the boards. 27For the west
side of the tabernacle he made six boards.
28He also made two boards for the two back
corners of the tabernacle. 29And they were
coupled at the bottom and coupled together
at the top by one ring. Thus he made both
of them for the two corners. 30So there were
eight boards and their sockets—sixteen
sockets of silver—two sockets under each of
the boards.

31And he made bars of acacia wood: five
for the boards on one side of the tabernacle,
32five bars for the boards on the other side of
the tabernacle, and five bars for the boards
of the tabernacle on the far side westward.
33And he made the middle bar to pass
through the boards from one end to the
other. 34He overlaid the boards with gold,
made their rings of gold *to be* holders for
the bars, and overlaid the bars with gold.

35And he made a veil of blue, purple,
and scarlet *thread,* and fine woven linen; it
was worked *with* an artistic design of
cherubim. 36He made for it four pillars of
acacia *wood,* and overlaid them with gold,
with their hooks of gold; and he cast four
sockets of silver for them.

37He also made a screen for the tabernacle door, of blue, purple, and scarlet *thread,*
and fine woven linen, made by a weaver,
38and its five pillars with their hooks. And
he overlaid their capitals and their rings
with gold, but their five sockets *were* bronze.

Making the Ark of the Testimony

37 Then Bezalel made the ark of acacia
wood; two and a half cubits *was* its
length, a cubit and a half its width, and a
cubit and a half its height. 2He overlaid it
with pure gold inside and outside, and
made a molding of gold all around it. 3And
he cast for it four rings of gold *to be set* in
its four corners: two rings on one side, and
two rings on the other side of it. 4He made
poles of acacia wood, and overlaid them
with gold. 5And he put the poles into the
rings at the sides of the ark, to bear the ark.
6He also made the mercy seat of pure gold;
two and a half cubits *was* its length and a

cubit and a half its width. 7He made two
cherubim of beaten gold; he made them of
one piece at the two ends of the mercy seat:
8one cherub at one end on this side, and the
other cherub at the *other* end on that side.
He made the cherubim at the two ends *of
one piece* with the mercy seat. 9The cherubim spread out *their* wings above, *and*
covered the mercy seat with their wings.
They faced one another; the faces of the
cherubim were toward the mercy seat.

Making the Table for the Showbread

10He made the table of acacia wood; two
cubits *was* its length, a cubit its width, and a
cubit and a half its height. 11And he overlaid
it with pure gold, and made a molding of
gold all around it. 12Also he made a frame
of a handbreadth all around it, and made a
molding of gold for the frame all around it.
13And he cast for it four rings of gold, and
put the rings on the four corners that *were*
at its four legs. 14The rings were close to the
frame, as holders for the poles to bear the
table. 15And he made the poles of acacia
wood to bear the table, and overlaid them
with gold. 16He made of pure gold the utensils which were on the table: its dishes, its
cups, its bowls, and its pitchers for pouring.

Making the Gold Lampstand

17He also made the lampstand of pure
gold; of hammered work he made the lampstand. Its shaft, its branches, its bowls, its
ornamental knobs, and its flowers were of
the same piece. 18And six branches came
out of its sides: three branches of the lampstand out of one side, and three branches
of the lampstand out of the other side.
19There were three bowls made like almond
blossoms on one branch, with an *ornamental* knob and a flower, and three bowls
made like almond *blossoms* on the other
branch, with an *ornamental* knob and a
flower—and so for the six branches coming out of the lampstand. 20And on the
lampstand itself *were* four bowls made like
almond *blossoms, each with* its *ornamental*
knob and flower. 21*There was* a knob under
the *first* two branches of the same, a knob
under the *second* two branches of the same,

and a knob under the *third* two branches of the same, according to the six branches extending from it. 22Their knobs and their branches were of one piece; all of it *was* one hammered piece of pure gold. 23And he made its seven lamps, its wick-trimmers, and its trays of pure gold. 24Of a talent of pure gold he made it, with all its utensils.

Making the Altar of Incense

25He made the incense altar of acacia wood. Its length *was* a cubit and its width a cubit—*it was* square—and two cubits *was* its height. Its horns were *of one piece* with it. 26And he overlaid it with pure gold: its top, its sides all around, and its horns. He also made for it a molding of gold all around it. 27He made two rings of gold for it under its molding, by its two corners on both sides, as holders for the poles with which to bear it. 28And he made the poles of acacia wood, and overlaid them with gold.

Making the Anointing Oil and the Incense

29He also made the holy anointing oil and the pure incense of sweet spices, according to the work of the perfumer.

Making the Altar of Burnt Offering

38 He made the altar of burnt offering of acacia wood; five cubits *was* its length and five cubits its width—*it was* square—and its height *was* three cubits. 2He made its horns on its four corners; the horns were *of one piece* with it. And he overlaid it with bronze. 3He made all the utensils for the altar: the pans, the shovels, the basins, the forks, and the firepans; all its utensils he made of bronze. 4And he made a grate of bronze network for the altar, under its rim, midway from the bottom. 5He cast four rings for the four corners of the bronze grating, *as* holders for the poles. 6And he made the poles of acacia wood, and overlaid them with bronze. 7Then he put the poles into the rings on the sides of the altar, with which to bear it. He made the altar hollow with boards.

Making the Bronze Laver

8He made the laver of bronze and its base of bronze, from the bronze mirrors of the serving women who assembled at the door of the tabernacle of meeting.

Making the Court of the Tabernacle

9Then he made the court on the south side; the hangings of the court *were of* fine woven linen, one hundred cubits long. 10There *were* twenty pillars for them, with twenty bronze sockets. The hooks of the pillars and their bands *were* silver. 11On the north side *the hangings were* one hundred cubits *long,* with twenty pillars and their twenty bronze sockets. The hooks of the pillars and their bands *were* silver. 12And on the west side *there were* hangings of fifty cubits, with ten pillars and their ten sockets. The hooks of the pillars and their bands *were* silver. 13For the east side *the hangings were* fifty cubits. 14The hangings of one side *of the gate were* fifteen cubits *long, with* their three pillars and their three sockets, 15and the same for the other side of the court gate; on this side and that *were* hangings of fifteen cubits, *with* their three pillars and their three sockets. 16All the hangings of the court all around *were of* fine woven linen. 17The sockets for the pillars *were* bronze, the hooks of the pillars and their bands *were* silver, and the overlay of their capitals *was* silver; and all the pillars of the court had bands of silver. 18The screen for the gate of the court *was* woven of blue, purple, and scarlet *thread,* and of fine woven linen. The length *was* twenty cubits, and the height along its width *was* five cubits, corresponding to the hangings of the court. 19And *there were* four pillars *with* their four sockets of bronze; their hooks *were* silver, and the overlay of their capitals and their bands *was* silver. 20All the pegs of the tabernacle, and of the court all around, *were* bronze.

Materials of the Tabernacle

21This is the inventory of the tabernacle, the tabernacle of the Testimony, which was counted according to the commandment of Moses, for the service of the Levites, by the hand of Ithamar, son of Aaron the priest. 22Bezalel the son of Uri, the son of Hur, of the tribe of Judah, made all that the LORD

had commanded Moses. [23]And with him *was* Aholiab the son of Ahisamach, of the tribe of Dan, an engraver and designer, a weaver of blue, purple, and scarlet *thread,* and of fine linen.

[24]All the gold that was used in all the work of the holy *place,* that is, the gold of the offering, was twenty-nine talents and seven hundred and thirty shekels, according to the shekel of the sanctuary. [25]And the silver from those who were numbered of the congregation *was* one hundred talents and one thousand seven hundred and seventy-five shekels, according to the shekel of the sanctuary: [26]a bekah for each man (*that is,* half a shekel, according to the shekel of the sanctuary), for everyone included in the numbering from twenty years old and above, for six hundred and three thousand, five hundred and fifty *men.* [27]And from the hundred talents of silver were cast the sockets of the sanctuary and the bases of the veil: one hundred sockets from the hundred talents, one talent for each socket. [28]Then from the one thousand seven hundred and seventy-five *shekels* he made hooks for the pillars, overlaid their capitals, and made bands for them.

[29]The offering of bronze *was* seventy talents and two thousand four hundred shekels. [30]And with it he made the sockets for the door of the tabernacle of meeting, the bronze altar, the bronze grating for it, and all the utensils for the altar, [31]the sockets for the court all around, the bases for the court gate, all the pegs for the tabernacle, and all the pegs for the court all around.

Making the Garments of the Priesthood

39 Of the blue, purple, and scarlet *thread* they made garments of ministry,[a] for ministering in the holy *place,* and made the holy garments for Aaron, as the LORD had commanded Moses.

Making the Ephod

[2]He made the ephod of gold, blue, purple, and scarlet *thread,* and of fine woven linen. [3]And they beat the gold into thin sheets and cut *it into* threads, to work *it in with* the blue, purple, and scarlet *thread,* and the fine linen, *into* artistic designs. [4]They made shoulder straps for it to couple *it* together; it was coupled together at its two edges. [5]And the intricately woven band of his ephod that *was* on it *was* of the same workmanship, *woven of* gold, blue, purple, and scarlet *thread,* and *of* fine woven linen, as the LORD had commanded Moses.

[6]And they set onyx stones, enclosed in settings of gold; they were engraved, as signets are engraved, with the names of the sons of Israel. [7]He put them on the shoulders of the ephod *as* memorial stones for the sons of Israel, as the LORD had commanded Moses.

Making the Breastplate

[8]And he made the breastplate, artistically woven like the workmanship of the ephod, of gold, blue, purple, and scarlet *thread,* and of fine woven linen. [9]They made the breastplate square by doubling it; a span *was* its length and a span its width when doubled. [10]And they set in it four rows of stones: a row with a sardius, a topaz, and an emerald *was* the first row; [11]the second row, a turquoise, a sapphire, and a diamond; [12]the third row, a jacinth, an agate, and an amethyst; [13]the fourth row, a beryl, an onyx, and a jasper. *They were* enclosed in settings of gold in their mountings. [14]*There were* twelve stones according to the names of the sons of Israel: according to their names, *engraved like* a signet, each one with its own name according to the twelve tribes.

[15]And they made chains for the breastplate at the ends, like braided cords of pure gold. [16]They also made two settings of gold and two gold rings, and put the two rings on the two ends of the breastplate. [17]And they put the two braided *chains* of gold in the two rings on the ends of the breastplate. [18]The two ends of the two braided *chains* they fastened in the two settings, and put them on the shoulder straps of the ephod in the front. [19]And they made two rings of gold and put *them* on the two ends of the breastplate, on the edge of it, which *was* on the inward side of the ephod. [20]They made

39:1 [a]*Or woven garments*

two *other* gold rings and put them on the two shoulder straps, underneath the ephod toward its front, right at the seam above the intricately woven band of the ephod. ²¹And they bound the breastplate by means of its rings to the rings of the ephod with a blue cord, so that it would be above the intricately woven band of the ephod, and that the breastplate would not come loose from the ephod, as the Lord had commanded Moses.

Making the Other Priestly Garments

²²He made the robe of the ephod of woven work, all of blue. ²³And *there was* an opening in the middle of the robe, like the opening in a coat of mail, *with* a woven binding all around the opening, so that it would not tear. ²⁴They made on the hem of the robe pomegranates of blue, purple, and scarlet, and of fine woven *linen.* ²⁵And they made bells of pure gold, and put the bells between the pomegranates on the hem of the robe all around between the pomegranates: ²⁶a bell and a pomegranate, a bell and a pomegranate, all around the hem of the robe to minister in, as the Lord had commanded Moses.

²⁷They made tunics, artistically woven of fine linen, for Aaron and his sons, ²⁸a turban of fine linen, exquisite hats of fine linen, short trousers of fine woven linen, ²⁹and a sash of fine woven linen with blue, purple, and scarlet *thread,* made by a weaver, as the Lord had commanded Moses.

³⁰Then they made the plate of the holy crown of pure gold, and wrote on it an inscription *like* the engraving of a signet:

HOLINESS TO THE LORD.

³¹And they tied to it a blue cord, to fasten *it* above on the turban, as the Lord had commanded Moses.

The Work Completed

³²Thus all the work of the tabernacle of the tent of meeting was finished. And the children of Israel did according to all that the Lord had commanded Moses; so they did. ³³And they brought the tabernacle to Moses, the tent and all its furnishings: its clasps, its boards, its bars, its pillars, and

its sockets; ³⁴the covering of ram skins dyed red, the covering of badger skins, and the veil of the covering; ³⁵the ark of the Testimony with its poles, and the mercy seat; ³⁶the table, all its utensils, and the showbread; ³⁷the pure *gold* lampstand with its lamps (the lamps set in order), all its utensils, and the oil for light; ³⁸the gold altar, the anointing oil, and the sweet incense; the screen for the tabernacle door; ³⁹the bronze altar, its grate of bronze, its poles, and all its utensils; the laver with its base; ⁴⁰the hangings of the court, its pillars and its sockets, the screen for the court gate, its cords, and its pegs; all the utensils for the service of the tabernacle, for the tent of meeting; ⁴¹and the garments of ministry,ᵃ to minister in the holy *place:* the holy garments for Aaron the priest, and his sons' garments, to minister as priests.

⁴²According to all that the Lord had commanded Moses, so the children of Israel did all the work. ⁴³Then Moses looked over all the work, and indeed they had done it; as the Lord had commanded, just so they had done it. And Moses blessed them.

The Tabernacle Erected and Arranged

40 Then the Lord spoke to Moses, saying: ²"On the first day of the first month you shall set up the tabernacle of the tent of meeting. ³You shall put in it the ark of the Testimony, and partition off the ark with the veil. ⁴You shall bring in the table and arrange the things that are to be set in order on it; and you shall bring in the lampstand and light its lamps. ⁵You shall also set the altar of gold for the incense before the ark of the Testimony, and put up the screen for the door of the tabernacle. ⁶Then you shall set the altar of the burnt offering before the door of the tabernacle of the tent of meeting. ⁷And you shall set the laver between the tabernacle of meeting and the altar, and put water in it. ⁸You shall set up the court all around, and hang up the screen at the court gate.

⁹"And you shall take the anointing oil, and anoint the tabernacle and all that *is* in it; and you shall hallow it and all its

---

39:41 ᵃOr *woven garments*

utensils, and it shall be holy. ¹⁰You shall anoint the altar of the burnt offering and all its utensils, and consecrate the altar. The altar shall be most holy. ¹¹And you shall anoint the laver and its base, and consecrate it.

¹²"Then you shall bring Aaron and his sons to the door of the tabernacle of meeting and wash them with water. ¹³You shall put the holy garments on Aaron, and anoint him and consecrate him, that he may minister to Me as priest. ¹⁴And you shall bring his sons and clothe them with tunics. ¹⁵You shall anoint them, as you anointed their father, that they may minister to Me as priests; for their anointing shall surely be an everlasting priesthood throughout their generations."

¹⁶Thus Moses did; according to all that the Lord had commanded him, so he did.

¹⁷And it came to pass in the first month of the second year, on the first *day* of the month, *that* the tabernacle was raised up. ¹⁸So Moses raised up the tabernacle, fastened its sockets, set up its boards, put in its bars, and raised up its pillars. ¹⁹And he spread out the tent over the tabernacle and put the covering of the tent on top of it, as the Lord had commanded Moses. ²⁰He took the Testimony and put *it* into the ark, inserted the poles through the rings of the ark, and put the mercy seat on top of the ark. ²¹And he brought the ark into the tabernacle, hung up the veil of the covering, and partitioned off the ark of the Testimony, as the Lord had commanded Moses.

²²He put the table in the tabernacle of meeting, on the north side of the tabernacle, outside the veil; ²³and he set the bread in order upon it before the Lord, as the Lord had commanded Moses. ²⁴He put the lampstand in the tabernacle of meeting,

across from the table, on the south side of the tabernacle; ²⁵and he lit the lamps before the Lord, as the Lord had commanded Moses. ²⁶He put the gold altar in the tabernacle of meeting in front of the veil; ²⁷and he burned sweet incense on it, as the Lord had commanded Moses. ²⁸He hung up the screen *at* the door of the tabernacle. ²⁹And he put the altar of burnt offering *before* the door of the tabernacle of the tent of meeting, and offered upon it the burnt offering and the grain offering, as the Lord had commanded Moses. ³⁰He set the laver between the tabernacle of meeting and the altar, and put water there for washing; ³¹and Moses, Aaron, and his sons would wash their hands and their feet *with water* from it. ³²Whenever they went into the tabernacle of meeting, and when they came near the altar, they washed, as the Lord had commanded Moses. ³³And he raised up the court all around the tabernacle and the altar, and hung up the screen of the court gate. So Moses finished the work.

The Cloud and the Glory

³⁴Then the cloud covered the tabernacle of meeting, and the glory of the Lord filled the tabernacle. ³⁵And Moses was not able to enter the tabernacle of meeting, because the cloud rested above it, and the glory of the Lord filled the tabernacle. ³⁶Whenever the cloud was taken up from above the tabernacle, the children of Israel would go onward in all their journeys. ³⁷But if the cloud was not taken up, then they did not journey till the day that it was taken up. ³⁸For the cloud of the Lord *was* above the tabernacle by day, and fire was over it by night, in the sight of all the house of Israel, throughout all their journeys.

LEVITICUS

Author: Moses

When Written: Around 1440 B.C.

Theme: Holiness

Key Verse: Leviticus 20:26—"And you shall be holy to Me, for I the LORD am holy, and have separated you from the peoples, that you should be Mine."

Key Chapter: Leviticus 16—The Day of Atonement, explained in this chapter, was the most important day in the Hebrew calendar. It was the one and only day when the high priest could enter the Holy of Holies to make atonement for the sins of the people.

When America's Founders wrapped up the Constitutional Convention in Philadelphia on September 18, 1787, they knew they had hammered out a system of government far different from any that then existed throughout the world. It was a government based on the "Laws of Nature and of Nature's God" rather than on the arbitrary and unjust rule of man.

God created humans to lead upright and orderly lives, but through the fall we lost the God-given ability to choose consistently between right and wrong. The Book of Leviticus reflects God's plan to lead humanity back to righteousness, initially through a set of righteous laws, and effectively through the righteousness of His only Son, Jesus Christ.

LEVITICUS

The Burnt Offering

1 Now the LORD called to Moses, and spoke to him from the tabernacle of meeting, saying, ²"Speak to the children of Israel, and say to them: 'When any one of you brings an offering to the LORD, you shall bring your offering of the livestock—of the herd and of the flock.

³'If his offering *is* a burnt sacrifice of the herd, let him offer a male without blemish; he shall offer it of his own free will at the door of the tabernacle of meeting before the LORD. ⁴Then he shall put his hand on the head of the burnt offering, and it will be accepted on his behalf to make atonement for him. ⁵He shall kill the bull before the LORD; and the priests, Aaron's sons, shall bring the blood and sprinkle the blood all around on the altar that *is by* the door of the tabernacle of meeting. ⁶And he shall skin the burnt offering and cut it into its pieces. ⁷The sons of Aaron the priest shall put fire on the altar, and lay the wood in order on the fire. ⁸Then the priests, Aaron's sons, shall lay the parts, the head, and the fat in order on the wood that *is* on the fire upon the altar; ⁹but he shall wash its entrails and its legs with water. And the priest shall burn all on the altar as a burnt sacrifice, an offering made by fire, a sweet aroma to the LORD.

¹⁰'If his offering *is* of the flocks—of the sheep or of the goats—as a burnt sacrifice, he shall bring a male without blemish. ¹¹He shall kill it on the north side of the altar before the LORD; and the priests, Aaron's sons, shall sprinkle its blood all around on the altar. ¹²And he shall cut it into its pieces, with its head and its fat; and the priest shall lay them in order on the wood that *is* on the fire upon the altar; ¹³but he shall wash the entrails and the legs with water. Then the priest shall bring *it* all and burn *it* on the altar; it *is* a burnt sacrifice, an offering made by fire, a sweet aroma to the LORD.

¹⁴'And if the burnt sacrifice of his offering to the LORD *is* of birds, then he shall bring his offering of turtledoves or young pigeons. ¹⁵The priest shall bring it to the altar, wring off its head, and burn *it* on the altar; its blood shall be drained out at the side of the altar. ¹⁶And he shall remove its crop with its feathers and cast it beside the altar on the east side, into the place for ashes. ¹⁷Then he shall split it at its wings, *but* shall not divide *it* completely; and the priest shall burn it on the altar, on the wood that *is* on the fire. It *is* a burnt sacrifice, an offering made by fire, a sweet aroma to the LORD.

The Grain Offering

2 'When anyone offers a grain offering to the LORD, his offering shall be *of* fine flour. And he shall pour oil on it, and put frankincense on it. ²He shall bring it to Aaron's sons, the priests, one of whom shall take from it his handful of fine flour and oil with all the frankincense. And the priest shall burn *it as* a memorial on the altar, an offering made by fire, a sweet aroma to the LORD. ³The rest of the grain offering *shall be* Aaron's and his sons'. *It is* most holy of the offerings to the LORD made by fire.

⁴'And if you bring as an offering a grain offering baked in the oven, *it shall be* unleavened cakes of fine flour mixed with oil, or unleavened wafers anointed with oil. ⁵But if your offering *is* a grain offering *baked* in a pan, *it shall be of* fine flour, unleavened, mixed with oil. ⁶You shall break it in pieces and pour oil on it; it *is* a grain offering.

⁷'If your offering *is* a grain offering *baked* in a covered pan, it shall be made *of* fine flour with oil. ⁸You shall bring the grain offering that is made of these things to the LORD. And when it is presented to the priest, he shall bring it to the altar. ⁹Then the priest shall take from the grain offering a memorial portion, and burn *it* on the altar. *It is* an offering made by fire, a sweet aroma to the LORD. ¹⁰And what is left of the grain

offering *shall be* Aaron's and his sons'. *It is* most holy of the offerings to the LORD made by fire.

¹¹'No grain offering which you bring to the LORD shall be made with leaven, for you shall burn no leaven nor any honey in any offering to the LORD made by fire. ¹²As for the offering of the firstfruits, you shall offer them to the LORD, but they shall not be burned on the altar for a sweet aroma. ¹³And every offering of your grain offering you shall season with salt; you shall not allow the salt of the covenant of your God to be lacking from your grain offering. With all your offerings you shall offer salt.

¹⁴'If you offer a grain offering of your firstfruits to the LORD, you shall offer for the grain offering of your firstfruits green heads of grain roasted on the fire, grain beaten from full heads. ¹⁵And you shall put oil on it, and lay frankincense on it. It *is* a grain offering. ¹⁶Then the priest shall burn the memorial portion: *part* of its beaten grain and *part* of its oil, with all the frankincense, as an offering made by fire to the LORD.

The Peace Offering

3 'When his offering *is* a sacrifice of a peace offering, if he offers *it* of the herd, whether male or female, he shall offer it without blemish before the LORD. ²And he shall lay his hand on the head of his offering, and kill it *at* the door of the tabernacle of meeting; and Aaron's sons, the priests, shall sprinkle the blood all around on the altar. ³Then he shall offer from the sacrifice of the peace offering an offering made by fire to the LORD. The fat that covers the entrails and all the fat that *is* on the entrails, ⁴the two kidneys and the fat that *is* on them by the flanks, and the fatty lobe *attached* to the liver above the kidneys, he shall remove; ⁵and Aaron's sons shall burn it on the altar upon the burnt sacrifice, which *is* on the wood that *is* on the fire, *as* an offering made by fire, a sweet aroma to the LORD.

⁶'If his offering as a sacrifice of a peace offering to the LORD *is* of the flock, *whether* male or female, he shall offer it without blemish. ⁷If he offers a lamb as his offering, then he shall offer it before the LORD. ⁸And he shall lay his hand on the head of his offering, and kill it before the tabernacle of meeting; and Aaron's sons shall sprinkle its blood all around on the altar.

⁹'Then he shall offer from the sacrifice of the peace offering, as an offering made by fire to the LORD, its fat *and* the whole fat tail which he shall remove close to the backbone. And the fat that covers the entrails and all the fat that *is* on the entrails, ¹⁰the two kidneys and the fat that *is* on them by the flanks, and the fatty lobe *attached* to the liver above the kidneys, he shall remove; ¹¹and the priest shall burn *them* on the altar *as* food, an offering made by fire to the LORD.

¹²'And if his offering *is* a goat, then he shall offer it before the LORD. ¹³He shall lay his hand on its head and kill it before the tabernacle of meeting; and the sons of Aaron shall sprinkle its blood all around on the altar. ¹⁴Then he shall offer from it his offering, as an offering made by fire to the LORD. The fat that covers the entrails and all the fat that *is* on the entrails, ¹⁵the two kidneys and the fat that *is* on them by the flanks, and the fatty lobe *attached* to the liver above the kidneys, he shall remove; ¹⁶and the priest shall burn them on the altar *as* food, an offering made by fire for a sweet aroma; all the fat *is* the LORD's.

¹⁷'*This shall be* a perpetual statute throughout your generations in all your dwellings: you shall eat neither fat nor blood.' "

The Sin Offering

4 Now the LORD spoke to Moses, saying, ²"Speak to the children of Israel, saying: 'If a person sins unintentionally against any of the commandments of the LORD *in anything* which ought not to be done, and does any of them, ³if the anointed priest sins, bringing guilt on the people, then let him offer to the LORD for his sin which he has sinned a young bull without blemish as a sin offering. ⁴He shall bring the bull to the door of the tabernacle of meeting before the LORD, lay his hand on the bull's head, and kill the bull before the LORD. ⁵Then the anointed priest shall take some

of the bull's blood and bring it to the tabernacle of meeting. ⁶The priest shall dip his finger in the blood and sprinkle some of the blood seven times before the Lord, in front of the veil of the sanctuary. ⁷And the priest shall put some of the blood on the horns of the altar of sweet incense before the Lord, which is in the tabernacle of meeting; and he shall pour the remaining blood of the bull at the base of the altar of the burnt offering, which is at the door of the tabernacle of meeting. ⁸He shall take from it all the fat of the bull as the sin offering. The fat that covers the entrails and all the fat which is on the entrails, ⁹the two kidneys and the fat that is on them by the flanks, and the fatty lobe attached to the liver above the kidneys, he shall remove, ¹⁰as it was taken from the bull of the sacrifice of the peace offering; and the priest shall burn them on the altar of the burnt offering. ¹¹But the bull's hide and all its flesh, with its head and legs, its entrails and offal— ¹²the whole bull he shall carry outside the camp to a clean place, where the ashes are poured out, and burn it on wood with fire; where the ashes are poured out it shall be burned.

¹³'Now if the whole congregation of Israel sins unintentionally, and the thing is hidden from the eyes of the assembly, and they have done something against any of the commandments of the Lord in anything which should not be done, and are guilty; ¹⁴when the sin which they have committed becomes known, then the assembly shall offer a young bull for the sin, and bring it before the tabernacle of meeting. ¹⁵And the elders of the congregation shall lay their hands on the head of the bull before the Lord. Then the bull shall be killed before the Lord. ¹⁶The anointed priest shall bring some of the bull's blood to the tabernacle of meeting. ¹⁷Then the priest shall dip his finger in the blood and sprinkle it seven times before the Lord, in front of the veil. ¹⁸And he shall put some of the blood on the horns of the altar which is before the Lord, which is in the tabernacle of meeting; and he shall pour the remaining blood at the base of the altar of burnt offering, which is

at the door of the tabernacle of meeting. ¹⁹He shall take all the fat from it and burn it on the altar. ²⁰And he shall do with the bull as he did with the bull as a sin offering; thus he shall do with it. So the priest shall make atonement for them, and it shall be forgiven them. ²¹Then he shall carry the bull outside the camp, and burn it as he burned the first bull. It is a sin offering for the assembly.

²²'When a ruler has sinned, and done something unintentionally against any of the commandments of the Lord his God in anything which should not be done, and is guilty, ²³or if his sin which he has committed comes to his knowledge, he shall bring as his offering a kid of the goats, a male without blemish. ²⁴And he shall lay his hand on the head of the goat, and kill it at the place where they kill the burnt offering before the Lord. It is a sin offering. ²⁵The priest shall take some of the blood of the sin offering with his finger, put it on the horns of the altar of burnt offering, and pour its blood at the base of the altar of burnt offering. ²⁶And he shall burn all its fat on the altar, like the fat of the sacrifice of the peace offering. So the priest shall make atonement for him concerning his sin, and it shall be forgiven him.

²⁷'If anyone of the common people sins unintentionally by doing something against any of the commandments of the Lord in anything which ought not to be done, and is guilty, ²⁸or if his sin which he has committed comes to his knowledge, then he shall bring as his offering a kid of the goats, a female without blemish, for his sin which he has committed. ²⁹And he shall lay his hand on the head of the sin offering, and kill the sin offering at the place of the burnt offering. ³⁰Then the priest shall take some of its blood with his finger, put it on the horns of the altar of burnt offering, and pour all the remaining blood at the base of the altar. ³¹He shall remove all its fat, as fat is removed from the sacrifice of the peace offering; and the priest shall burn it on the altar for a sweet aroma to the Lord. So the priest shall make atonement for him, and it shall be forgiven him.

32'If he brings a lamb as his sin offering, he shall bring a female without blemish. 33Then he shall lay his hand on the head of the sin offering, and kill it as a sin offering at the place where they kill the burnt offering. 34The priest shall take *some* of the blood of the sin offering with his finger, put *it* on the horns of the altar of burnt offering, and pour all *the remaining* blood at the base of the altar. 35He shall remove all its fat, as the fat of the lamb is removed from the sacrifice of the peace offering. Then the priest shall burn it on the altar, according to the offerings made by fire to the LORD. So the priest shall make atonement for his sin that he has committed, and it shall be forgiven him.

The Trespass Offering

5 'If a person sins in hearing the utterance of an oath, and *is* a witness, whether he has seen or known *of the matter*—if he does not tell *it*, he bears guilt.

2'Or if a person touches any unclean thing, whether *it is* the carcass of an unclean beast, or the carcass of unclean livestock, or the carcass of unclean creeping things, and he is unaware of it, he also shall be unclean and guilty. 3Or if he touches human uncleanness—whatever uncleanness with which a man may be defiled, and he is unaware of it—when he realizes *it,* then he shall be guilty.

4'Or if a person swears, speaking thoughtlessly with *his* lips to do evil or to do good, whatever *it is* that a man may pronounce by an oath, and he is unaware of it—when he realizes *it,* then he shall be guilty in any of these *matters.*

5'And it shall be, when he is guilty in any of these *matters,* that he shall confess that he has sinned in that *thing;* 6and he shall bring his trespass offering to the LORD for his sin which he has committed, a female from the flock, a lamb or a kid of the goats as a sin offering. So the priest shall make atonement for him concerning his sin.

7'If he is not able to bring a lamb, then he shall bring to the LORD, for his trespass which he has committed, two turtledoves or two young pigeons: one as a sin offering and the other as a burnt offering. 8And he shall bring them to the priest, who shall offer *that* which *is* for the sin offering first, and wring off its head from its neck, but shall not divide *it* completely. 9Then he shall sprinkle *some* of the blood of the sin offering on the side of the altar, and the rest of the blood shall be drained out at the base of the altar. It *is* a sin offering. 10And he shall offer the second *as* a burnt offering according to the prescribed manner. So the priest shall make atonement on his behalf for his sin which he has committed, and it shall be forgiven him.

11'But if he is not able to bring two turtledoves or two young pigeons, then he who sinned shall bring for his offering one-tenth of an ephah of fine flour as a sin offering. He shall put no oil on it, nor shall he put frankincense on it, for it *is* a sin offering. 12Then he shall bring it to the priest, and the priest shall take his handful of it as a memorial portion, and burn *it* on the altar according to the offerings made by fire to the LORD. It *is* a sin offering. 13The priest shall make atonement for him, for his sin that he has committed in any of these matters; and it shall be forgiven him. *The rest shall be the priest's as a grain offering.'"*

Offerings with Restitution

14Then the LORD spoke to Moses, saying: 15"If a person commits a trespass, and sins unintentionally in regard to the holy things of the LORD, then he shall bring to the LORD as his trespass offering a ram without blemish from the flocks, with your valuation in shekels of silver according to the shekel of the sanctuary, as a trespass offering. 16And he shall make restitution for the harm that he has done in regard to the holy thing, and shall add one-fifth to it and give it to the priest. So the priest shall make atonement for him with the ram of the trespass offering, and it shall be forgiven him.

17"If a person sins, and commits any of these things which are forbidden to be done by the commandments of the LORD, though he does not know *it,* yet he is guilty and shall bear his iniquity. 18And he shall

bring to the priest a ram without blemish from the flock, with your valuation, as a trespass offering. So the priest shall make atonement for him regarding his ignorance in which he erred and did not know *it,* and it shall be forgiven him. ¹⁹It is a trespass offering; he has certainly trespassed against the LORD."

6 And the LORD spoke to Moses, saying: ²"If a person sins and commits a trespass against the LORD by lying to his neighbor about what was delivered to him for safekeeping, or about a pledge, or about a robbery, or if he has extorted from his neighbor, ³or if he has found what was lost and lies concerning it, and swears falsely— in any one of these things that a man may do in which he sins: ⁴then it shall be, because he has sinned and is guilty, that he shall restore what he has stolen, or the thing which he has extorted, or what was delivered to him for safekeeping, or the lost thing which he found, ⁵or all that about which he has sworn falsely. He shall restore its full value, add one-fifth more to it, *and* give it to whomever it belongs, on the day of his trespass offering. ⁶And he shall bring his trespass offering to the LORD, a ram without blemish from the flock, with your valuation, as a trespass offering, to the priest. ⁷So the priest shall make atonement for him before the LORD, and he shall be forgiven for any one of these things that he may have done in which he trespasses."

The Law of the Burnt Offering

⁸Then the LORD spoke to Moses, saying, ⁹"Command Aaron and his sons, saying, 'This *is* the law of the burnt offering: The burnt offering *shall be* on the hearth upon the altar all night until morning, and the fire of the altar shall be kept burning on it. ¹⁰And the priest shall put on his linen garment, and his linen trousers he shall put on his body, and take up the ashes of the burnt offering which the fire has consumed on the altar, and he shall put them beside the altar. ¹¹Then he shall take off his garments, put on other garments, and carry the ashes outside the camp to a clean place. ¹²And the fire on the altar shall be kept burning on it; it shall not be put out. And the priest shall burn wood on it every morning, and lay the burnt offering in order on it; and he shall burn on it the fat of the peace offerings. ¹³A fire shall always be burning on the altar; it shall never go out.

The Law of the Grain Offering

¹⁴'This *is* the law of the grain offering: The sons of Aaron shall offer it on the altar before the LORD. ¹⁵He shall take from it his handful of the fine flour of the grain offering, with its oil, and all the frankincense which *is* on the grain offering, and shall burn *it* on the altar *for* a sweet aroma, as a memorial to the LORD. ¹⁶And the remainder of it Aaron and his sons shall eat; with unleavened bread it shall be eaten in a holy place; in the court of the tabernacle of meeting they shall eat it. ¹⁷It shall not be baked with leaven. I have given it *as* their portion of My offerings made by fire; it *is* most holy, like the sin offering and the trespass offering. ¹⁸All the males among the children of Aaron may eat it. *It shall be* a statute forever in your generations concerning the offerings made by fire to the LORD. Everyone who touches them must be holy.' "[a]

¹⁹And the LORD spoke to Moses, saying, ²⁰"This *is* the offering of Aaron and his sons, which they shall offer to the LORD, *beginning* on the day when he is anointed: one-tenth of an ephah of fine flour as a daily grain offering, half of it in the morning and half of it at night. ²¹It shall be made in a pan with oil. *When it is* mixed, you shall bring it in. The baked pieces of the grain offering you shall offer *for* a sweet aroma to the LORD. ²²The priest from among his sons, who is anointed in his place, shall offer it. *It is* a statute forever to the LORD. It shall be wholly burned. ²³For every grain offering for the priest shall be wholly burned. It shall not be eaten."

The Law of the Sin Offering

²⁴Also the LORD spoke to Moses, saying, ²⁵"Speak to Aaron and to his sons, saying, 'This *is* the law of the sin offering: In the

---

6:18 ᵃCompare Numbers 4:15 and Haggai 2:11–13

place where the burnt offering is killed, the sin offering shall be killed before the LORD. It *is* most holy. 26The priest who offers it for sin shall eat it. In a holy place it shall be eaten, in the court of the tabernacle of meeting. 27Everyone who touches its flesh must be holy.a And when its blood is sprinkled on any garment, you shall wash that on which it was sprinkled, in a holy place. 28But the earthen vessel in which it is boiled shall be broken. And if it is boiled in a bronze pot, it shall be both scoured and rinsed in water. 29All the males among the priests may eat it. It *is* most holy. 30But no sin offering from which *any* of the blood is brought into the tabernacle of meeting, to make atonement in the holy *place,*a shall be eaten. It shall be burned in the fire.

The Law of the Trespass Offering

7 'Likewise this *is* the law of the trespass offering (it *is* most holy): 2In the place where they kill the burnt offering they shall kill the trespass offering. And its blood he shall sprinkle all around on the altar. 3And he shall offer from it all its fat. The fat tail and the fat that covers the entrails, 4the two kidneys and the fat that *is* on them by the flanks, and the fatty lobe *attached* to the liver above the kidneys, he shall remove; 5and the priest shall burn them on the altar *as* an offering made by fire to the LORD. It *is* a trespass offering. 6Every male among the priests may eat it. It shall be eaten in a holy place. It *is* most holy. 7The trespass offering *is* like the sin offering; *there is* one law for them both: the priest who makes atonement with it shall have *it.* 8And the priest who offers anyone's burnt offering, that priest shall have for himself the skin of the burnt offering which he has offered. 9Also every grain offering that is baked in the oven and all that is prepared in the covered pan, or in a pan, shall be the priest's who offers it. 10Every grain offering, *whether* mixed with oil or dry, shall belong to all the sons of Aaron, to one *as much* as the other.

The Law of Peace Offerings

11'This *is* the law of the sacrifice of peace offerings which he shall offer to the LORD:

12If he offers it for a thanksgiving, then he shall offer, with the sacrifice of thanksgiving, unleavened cakes mixed with oil, unleavened wafers anointed with oil, or cakes of blended flour mixed with oil. 13Besides the cakes, *as* his offering he shall offer leavened bread with the sacrifice of thanksgiving of his peace offering. 14And from it he shall offer one cake from each offering *as* a heave offering to the LORD. It shall belong to the priest who sprinkles the blood of the peace offering.

15'The flesh of the sacrifice of his peace offering for thanksgiving shall be eaten the same day it is offered. He shall not leave any of it until morning. 16But if the sacrifice of his offering *is* a vow or a voluntary offering, it shall be eaten the same day that he offers his sacrifice; but on the next day the remainder of it also may be eaten; 17the remainder of the flesh of the sacrifice on the third day must be burned with fire. 18And if *any* of the flesh of the sacrifice of his peace offering is eaten at all on the third day, it shall not be accepted, nor shall it be imputed to him; it shall be an abomination *to* him who offers it, and the person who eats of it shall bear guilt.

19'The flesh that touches any unclean thing shall not be eaten. It shall be burned with fire. And as for the *clean* flesh, all who are clean may eat of it. 20But the person who eats the flesh of the sacrifice of the peace offering that *belongs* to the LORD, while he is unclean, that person shall be cut off from his people. 21Moreover the person who touches any unclean thing, *such as* human uncleanness, *an* unclean animal, or any abominable unclean thing,a and who eats the flesh of the sacrifice of the peace offering that *belongs* to the LORD, that person shall be cut off from his people.'"

Fat and Blood May Not Be Eaten

22And the LORD spoke to Moses, saying, 23"Speak to the children of Israel, saying:

6:27 aCompare Numbers 4:15 and Haggai 2:11–13
6:30 aThe Most Holy Place when capitalized
7:21 aFollowing Masoretic Text, Septuagint, and Vulgate; Samaritan Pentateuch, Syriac, and Targum read *swarming thing* (compare 5:2).

'You shall not eat any fat, of ox or sheep or goat. ²⁴And the fat of an animal that dies *naturally,* and the fat of what is torn by wild beasts, may be used in any other way; but you shall by no means eat it. ²⁵For whoever eats the fat of the animal of which men offer an offering made by fire to the LORD, the person who eats *it* shall be cut off from his people. ²⁶Moreover you shall not eat any blood in any of your dwellings, *whether* of bird or beast. ²⁷Whoever eats any blood, that person shall be cut off from his people.' "

The Portion of Aaron and His Sons

²⁸Then the LORD spoke to Moses, saying, ²⁹"Speak to the children of Israel, saying: 'He who offers the sacrifice of his peace offering to the LORD shall bring his offering to the LORD from the sacrifice of his peace offering. ³⁰His own hands shall bring the offerings made by fire to the LORD. The fat with the breast he shall bring, that the breast may be waved *as* a wave offering before the LORD. ³¹And the priest shall burn the fat on the altar, but the breast shall be Aaron's and his sons'. ³²Also the right thigh you shall give to the priest *as* a heave offering from the sacrifices of your peace offerings. ³³He among the sons of Aaron, who offers the blood of the peace offering and the fat, shall have the right thigh for *his* part. ³⁴For the breast of the wave offering and the thigh of the heave offering I have taken from the children of Israel, from the sacrifices of their peace offerings, and I have given them to Aaron the priest and to his sons from the children of Israel by a statute forever.' "

³⁵This *is* the consecrated portion for Aaron and his sons, from the offerings made by fire to the LORD, on the day when *Moses* presented them to minister to the LORD as priests. ³⁶The LORD commanded this to be given to them by the children of Israel, on the day that He anointed them, *by* a statute forever throughout their generations.

³⁷This *is* the law of the burnt offering, the grain offering, the sin offering, the trespass offering, the consecrations, and the sacrifice of the peace offering, ³⁸which the LORD commanded Moses on Mount Sinai, on the day when He commanded the children of Israel to offer their offerings to the LORD in the Wilderness of Sinai.

Aaron and His Sons Consecrated

8 And the LORD spoke to Moses, saying: ²"Take Aaron and his sons with him, and the garments, the anointing oil, a bull as the sin offering, two rams, and a basket of unleavened bread; ³and gather all the congregation together at the door of the tabernacle of meeting."

⁴So Moses did as the LORD commanded him. And the congregation was gathered together at the door of the tabernacle of meeting. ⁵And Moses said to the congregation, "This *is* what the LORD commanded to be done."

⁶Then Moses brought Aaron and his sons and washed them with water. ⁷And he put the tunic on him, girded him with the sash, clothed him with the robe, and put the ephod on him; and he girded him with the intricately woven band of the ephod, and with it tied *the ephod* on him. ⁸Then he put the breastplate on him, and he put the Urim and the Thummim^a in the breastplate. ⁹And he put the turban on his head. Also on the turban, on its front, he put the golden plate, the holy crown, as the LORD had commanded Moses.

¹⁰Also Moses took the anointing oil, and anointed the tabernacle and all that *was* in it, and consecrated them. ¹¹He sprinkled some of it on the altar seven times, anointed the altar and all its utensils, and the laver and its base, to consecrate them. ¹²And he poured some of the anointing oil on Aaron's head and anointed him, to consecrate him.

¹³Then Moses brought Aaron's sons and put tunics on them, girded them with sashes, and put hats on them, as the LORD had commanded Moses.

¹⁴And he brought the bull for the sin offering. Then Aaron and his sons laid their hands on the head of the bull for the sin offering, ¹⁵and Moses killed *it.* Then he took the blood, and put *some* on the horns of

---

8:8 ^aLiterally *the Lights and the Perfections* (compare Exodus 28:30)

the altar all around with his finger, and purified the altar. And he poured the blood at the base of the altar, and consecrated it, to make atonement for it. [16]Then he took all the fat that *was* on the entrails, the fatty lobe *attached to* the liver, and the two kidneys with their fat, and Moses burned *them* on the altar. [17]But the bull, its hide, its flesh, and its offal, he burned with fire outside the camp, as the LORD had commanded Moses.

[18]Then he brought the ram as the burnt offering. And Aaron and his sons laid their hands on the head of the ram, [19]and Moses killed *it.* Then he sprinkled the blood all around on the altar. [20]And he cut the ram into pieces; and Moses burned the head, the pieces, and the fat. [21]Then he washed the entrails and the legs in water. And Moses burned the whole ram on the altar. It *was* a burnt sacrifice for a sweet aroma, an offering made by fire to the LORD, as the LORD had commanded Moses.

[22]And he brought the second ram, the ram of consecration. Then Aaron and his sons laid their hands on the head of the ram, [23]and Moses killed *it.* Also he took *some* of its blood and put it on the tip of Aaron's right ear, on the thumb of his right hand, and on the big toe of his right foot. [24]Then he brought Aaron's sons. And Moses put *some* of the blood on the tips of their right ears, on the thumbs of their right hands, and on the big toes of their right feet. And Moses sprinkled the blood all around on the altar. [25]Then he took the fat and the fat tail, all the fat that *was* on the entrails, the fatty lobe *attached to* the liver, the two kidneys and their fat, and the right thigh; [26]and from the basket of unleavened bread that was before the LORD he took one unleavened cake, a cake of bread *anointed with* oil, and one wafer, and put *them* on the fat and on the right thigh; [27]and he put all *these* in Aaron's hands and in his sons' hands, and waved them *as* a wave offering before the LORD. [28]Then Moses took them from their hands and burned *them* on the altar, on the burnt offering. They *were* consecration offerings for a sweet aroma. That *was* an offering made by fire to the LORD.

[29]And Moses took the breast and waved it *as* a wave offering before the LORD. It was Moses' part of the ram of consecration, as the LORD had commanded Moses.

[30]Then Moses took some of the anointing oil and some of the blood which *was* on the altar, and sprinkled *it* on Aaron, on his garments, on his sons, and on the garments of his sons with him; and he consecrated Aaron, his garments, his sons, and the garments of his sons with him.

[31]And Moses said to Aaron and his sons, "Boil the flesh *at* the door of the tabernacle of meeting, and eat it there with the bread that *is* in the basket of consecration offerings, as I commanded, saying, 'Aaron and his sons shall eat it.' [32]What remains of the flesh and of the bread you shall burn with fire. [33]And you shall not go outside the door of the tabernacle of meeting *for* seven days, until the days of your consecration are ended. For seven days he shall consecrate you. [34]As he has done this day, *so* the LORD has commanded to do, to make atonement for you. [35]Therefore you shall stay *at* the door of the tabernacle of meeting day and night for seven days, and keep the charge of the LORD, so that you may not die; for so I have been commanded." [36]So Aaron and his sons did all the things that the LORD had commanded by the hand of Moses.

The Priestly Ministry Begins

9 It came to pass on the eighth day that Moses called Aaron and his sons and the elders of Israel. [2]And he said to Aaron, "Take for yourself a young bull as a sin offering and a ram as a burnt offering, without blemish, and offer *them* before the LORD. [3]And to the children of Israel you shall speak, saying, 'Take a kid of the goats as a sin offering, and a calf and a lamb, *both* of the first year, without blemish, as a burnt offering, [4]also a bull and a ram as peace offerings, to sacrifice before the LORD, and a grain offering mixed with oil; for today the LORD will appear to you.' "

[5]So they brought what Moses commanded before the tabernacle of meeting. And all the congregation drew near and stood

before the LORD. 6Then Moses said, "This *is* the thing which the LORD commanded you to do, and the glory of the LORD will appear to you." 7And Moses said to Aaron, "Go to the altar, offer your sin offering and your burnt offering, and make atonement for yourself and for the people. Offer the offering of the people, and make atonement for them, as the LORD commanded."

8Aaron therefore went to the altar and killed the calf of the sin offering, which *was* for himself. 9Then the sons of Aaron brought the blood to him. And he dipped his finger in the blood, put *it* on the horns of the altar, and poured the blood at the base of the altar. 10But the fat, the kidneys, and the fatty lobe from the liver of the sin offering he burned on the altar, as the LORD had commanded Moses. 11The flesh and the hide he burned with fire outside the camp.

12And he killed the burnt offering; and Aaron's sons presented to him the blood, which he sprinkled all around on the altar. 13Then they presented the burnt offering to him, with its pieces and head, and he burned *them* on the altar. 14And he washed the entrails and the legs, and burned *them* with the burnt offering on the altar.

15Then he brought the people's offering, and took the goat, which *was* the sin offering for the people, and killed it and offered it for sin, like the first one. 16And he brought the burnt offering and offered it according to the prescribed manner. 17Then he brought the grain offering, took a handful of it, and burned *it* on the altar, besides the burnt sacrifice of the morning.

18He also killed the bull and the ram *as* sacrifices of peace offerings, which *were* for the people. And Aaron's sons presented to him the blood, which he sprinkled all around on the altar, 19and the fat from the bull and the ram—the fatty tail, what covers *the entrails* and the kidneys, and the fatty lobe *attached to* the liver; 20and they put the fat on the breasts. Then he burned the fat on the altar; 21but the breasts and the right thigh Aaron waved *as* a wave offering before the LORD, as Moses had commanded.

22Then Aaron lifted his hand toward the people, blessed them, and came down from offering the sin offering, the burnt offering, and peace offerings. 23And Moses and Aaron went into the tabernacle of meeting, and came out and blessed the people. Then the glory of the LORD appeared to all the people, 24and fire came out from before the LORD and consumed the burnt offering and the fat on the altar. When all the people saw *it,* they shouted and fell on their faces.

The Profane Fire of Nadab and Abihu

10 Then Nadab and Abihu, the sons of Aaron, each took his censer and put fire in it, put incense on it, and offered profane fire before the LORD, which He had not commanded them. 2So fire went out from the LORD and devoured them, and they died before the LORD. 3And Moses said to Aaron, "This is what the LORD spoke, saying:

'By those who come near Me
   I must be regarded as holy;
And before all the people
   I must be glorified.'"

So Aaron held his peace.

4Then Moses called Mishael and Elzaphan, the sons of Uzziel the uncle of Aaron, and said to them, "Come near, carry your brethren from before the sanctuary out of the camp." 5So they went near and carried them by their tunics out of the camp, as Moses had said.

6And Moses said to Aaron, and to Eleazar and Ithamar, his sons, "Do not uncover your heads nor tear your clothes, lest you die, and wrath come upon all the people. But let your brethren, the whole house of Israel, bewail the burning which the LORD has kindled. 7You shall not go out from the door of the tabernacle of meeting, lest you die, for the anointing oil of the LORD *is* upon you." And they did according to the word of Moses.

Conduct Prescribed for Priests

8Then the LORD spoke to Aaron, saying: 9"Do not drink wine or intoxicating drink, you, nor your sons with you, when you go

NOAH WEBSTER AND EDUCATION

NOAH WEBSTER

Noah Webster, who has been called the "Father of American Scholarship and Education," was the great American lexicographer who gave us the very first *American Dictionary of the English Language*. To do so, he learned 26 languages in order to supplement the documentation of the etymology of the words. In that dictionary, Webster defined *education* as:

> *The bringing up, as of a child; instruction; formation of manners. Education comprehends all that series of instruction and discipline which is intended to enlighten the understanding, correct the temper, and form the manners and habits of youth, and fit them for usefulness in their future stations. To give children a good education in manners, arts, and science is important; to give them a religious education is indispensable; and an immense responsibility rests on parents and guardians who neglect these duties.*

Webster believed a well-educated citizenry was essential to the preservation of freedom. "Information is fatal to despotism," he wrote, and part of his life was spent in the writing and publishing of textbooks to be used in local schools and in homes that would convey the rudiments of spelling and grammar, as well as provide both moral formation and civic education. He wrote:

> *An attempt to conduct the affairs of a free government with wisdom and impartiality, and to preserve the just rights of all classes of citizens, without the guidance of Divine precepts, will certainly end in disappointment. God is the supreme moral Governor of the world He has made, and as He Himself governs with perfect rectitude, He requires His rational creatures to govern themselves in like manner. If men will not submit to be controlled by His laws, He will punish them by the evils resulting from their own disobedience. . . .*
>
> *Any system of education, therefore, which limits instruction to the arts and sciences and rejects the aids of religion in forming the characters of citizens, is essentially defective. . . .*
>
> *In my view, the Christian religion is the most important and one of the first things in which all children, under a free government ought to be instructed. . . . No truth is more evident to my mind than that the Christian religion must be the basis of any government intended to secure the rights and privileges of a free people.*

As one of America's Founders, he knew that an education devoid of religious training was defective.

into the tabernacle of meeting, lest you die. *It shall be* a statute forever throughout your generations, [10]that you may distinguish between holy and unholy, and between unclean and clean, [11]and that you may teach the children of Israel all the statutes which the LORD has spoken to them by the hand of Moses."

[12]And Moses spoke to Aaron, and to Eleazar and Ithamar, his sons who were left: "Take the grain offering that remains of the offerings made by fire to the LORD, and eat it without leaven beside the altar; for it *is* most holy. [13]You shall eat it in a holy place, because it *is* your due and your sons' due, of the sacrifices made by fire to the LORD; for so I have been commanded. [14]The breast of the wave offering and the thigh of the heave offering you shall eat in a clean place, you, your sons, and your daughters with you; for *they are* your due and your sons' due, *which* are given from the sacrifices of peace offerings of the children of Israel. [15]The thigh of the heave offering and the breast of the wave offering they shall bring with the offerings of fat made by fire, to offer *as* a wave offering before the LORD. And it shall be yours and your sons' with you, by a statute forever, as the LORD has commanded."

[16]Then Moses made careful inquiry about the goat of the sin offering, and there it was—burned up. And he was angry with Eleazar and Ithamar, the sons of Aaron *who were* left, saying, [17]"Why have you not eaten the sin offering in a holy place, since it *is* most holy, and *God* has given it to you to bear the guilt of the congregation, to make atonement for them before the LORD? [18]See! Its blood was not brought inside the holy *place;*[a] indeed you should have eaten it in a holy *place,* as I commanded."

[19]And Aaron said to Moses, "Look, this day they have offered their sin offering and their burnt offering before the LORD, and such things have befallen me! *If* I had eaten the sin offering today, would it have been accepted in the sight of the LORD?" [20]So when Moses heard *that,* he was content.

Foods Permitted and Forbidden

11 Now the LORD spoke to Moses and Aaron, saying to them, [2]"Speak to the children of Israel, saying, 'These *are* the animals which you may eat among all the animals that *are* on the earth: [3]Among the animals, whatever divides the hoof, having cloven hooves *and* chewing the cud—that you may eat. [4]Nevertheless these you shall not eat among those that chew the cud or those that have cloven hooves: the camel, because it chews the cud but does not have cloven hooves, is unclean to you; [5]the rock hyrax, because it chews the cud but does not have cloven hooves, *is* unclean to you; [6]the hare, because it chews the cud but does not have cloven hooves, *is* unclean to you; [7]and the swine, though it divides the hoof, having cloven hooves, yet does not chew the cud, *is* unclean to you. [8]Their flesh you shall not eat, and their carcasses you shall not touch. They *are* unclean to you.

[9]'These you may eat of all that *are* in the water: whatever in the water has fins and scales, whether in the seas or in the rivers—that you may eat. [10]But all in the seas or in the rivers that do not have fins and scales, all that move in the water or any living thing which *is* in the water, they *are* an abomination to you. [11]They shall be an abomination to you; you shall not eat their flesh, but you shall regard their carcasses as an abomination. [12]Whatever in the water does not have fins or scales—that *shall be* an abomination to you.

[13]'And these you shall regard as an abomination among the birds; they shall not be eaten, they *are* an abomination: the eagle, the vulture, the buzzard, [14]the kite, and the falcon after its kind; [15]every raven after its kind, [16]the ostrich, the short-eared owl, the sea gull, and the hawk after its kind; [17]the little owl, the fisher owl, and the screech owl; [18]the white owl, the jackdaw, and the carrion vulture; [19]the stork, the heron after its kind, the hoopoe, and the bat.

[20]'All flying insects that creep on *all* fours *shall be* an abomination to you. [21]Yet these you may eat of every flying insect that creeps

---

10:18 [a]The Most Holy Place when capitalized

on *all* fours: those which have jointed legs above their feet with which to leap on the earth. [22]These you may eat: the locust after its kind, the destroying locust after its kind, the cricket after its kind, and the grasshopper after its kind. [23]But all *other* flying insects which have four feet *shall be* an abomination to you.

Unclean Animals

[24]'By these you shall become unclean; whoever touches the carcass of any of them shall be unclean until evening; [25]whoever carries part of the carcass of any of them shall wash his clothes and be unclean until evening: [26]*The carcass* of any animal which divides the foot, but is not cloven-hoofed or does not chew the cud, *is* unclean to you. Everyone who touches it shall be unclean. [27]And whatever goes on its paws, among all kinds of animals that go on *all* fours, those *are* unclean to you. Whoever touches any such carcass shall be unclean until evening. [28]Whoever carries *any such* carcass shall wash his clothes and be unclean until evening. It *is* unclean to you.

[29]'These also *shall be* unclean to you among the creeping things that creep on the earth: the mole, the mouse, and the large lizard after its kind; [30]the gecko, the monitor lizard, the sand reptile, the sand lizard, and the chameleon. [31]These *are* unclean to you among all that creep. Whoever touches them when they are dead shall be unclean until evening. [32]Anything on which *any* of them falls, when they are dead shall be unclean, whether *it is* any item of wood or clothing or skin or sack, whatever item *it is,* in which *any* work is done, it must be put in water. And it shall be unclean until evening; then it shall be clean. [33]Any earthen vessel into which *any* of them falls you shall break; and whatever *is* in it shall be unclean: [34]in such a vessel, any edible food upon which water falls becomes unclean, and any drink that may be drunk from it becomes unclean. [35]And everything on which *a part* of *any such* carcass falls shall be unclean; *whether it is* an oven or cooking stove, it shall be broken down; *for they are* unclean, and shall be

unclean to you. [36]Nevertheless a spring or a cistern, *in which there is* plenty of water, shall be clean, but whatever touches any such carcass becomes unclean. [37]And if a part of *any such* carcass falls on any planting seed which is to be sown, it *remains* clean. [38]But if water is put on the seed, and if *a part* of *any such* carcass falls on it, it *becomes* unclean to you.

[39]'And if any animal which you may eat dies, he who touches its carcass shall be unclean until evening. [40]He who eats of its carcass shall wash his clothes and be unclean until evening. He also who carries its carcass shall wash his clothes and be unclean until evening.

[41]'And every creeping thing that creeps on the earth *shall be* an abomination. It shall not be eaten. [42]Whatever crawls on its belly, whatever goes on *all* fours, or whatever has many feet among all creeping things that creep on the earth—these you shall not eat, for they *are* an abomination. [43]You shall not make yourselves abominable with any creeping thing that creeps; nor shall you make yourselves unclean with them, lest you be defiled by them. [44]For I *am* the Lord your God. You shall therefore consecrate yourselves, and you shall be holy; for I *am* holy. Neither shall you defile yourselves with any creeping thing that creeps on the earth. [45]For I *am* the Lord who brings you up out of the land of Egypt, to be your God. You shall therefore be holy, for I *am* holy.

[46]'This *is* the law of the animals and the birds and every living creature that moves in the waters, and of every creature that creeps on the earth, [47]to distinguish between the unclean and the clean, and between the animal that may be eaten and the animal that may not be eaten.'"

The Ritual After Childbirth

12 Then the Lord spoke to Moses, saying, [2]"Speak to the children of Israel, saying: 'If a woman has conceived, and borne a male child, then she shall be unclean seven days; as in the days of her customary impurity she shall be unclean. [3]And on the eighth day the flesh of his foreskin shall be

circumcised. ⁴She shall then continue in the blood of *her* purification thirty-three days. She shall not touch any hallowed thing, nor come into the sanctuary until the days of her purification are fulfilled.

⁵'But if she bears a female child, then she shall be unclean two weeks, as in her customary impurity, and she shall continue in the blood of *her* purification sixty-six days.

⁶'When the days of her purification are fulfilled, whether for a son or a daughter, she shall bring to the priest a lamb of the first year as a burnt offering, and a young pigeon or a turtledove as a sin offering, to the door of the tabernacle of meeting. ⁷Then he shall offer it before the Lord, and make atonement for her. And she shall be clean from the flow of her blood. This *is* the law for her who has borne a male or a female.

⁸'And if she is not able to bring a lamb, then she may bring two turtledoves or two young pigeons—one as a burnt offering and the other as a sin offering. So the priest shall make atonement for her, and she will be clean.' "

The Law Concerning Leprosy

13 And the Lord spoke to Moses and Aaron, saying: ²"When a man has on the skin of his body a swelling, a scab, or a bright spot, and it becomes on the skin of his body *like* a leprousᵃ sore, then he shall be brought to Aaron the priest or to one of his sons the priests. ³The priest shall examine the sore on the skin of the body; and if the hair on the sore has turned white, and the sore appears *to be* deeper than the skin of his body, it *is* a leprous sore. Then the priest shall examine him, and pronounce him unclean. ⁴But if the bright spot *is* white on the skin of his body, and does not appear *to be* deeper than the skin, and its hair has not turned white, then the priest shall isolate *the one who has* the sore seven days. ⁵And the priest shall examine him on the seventh day; and indeed *if* the sore appears to be as it was, *and* the sore has not spread on the skin, then the priest shall isolate him another seven days. ⁶Then the priest shall examine him again on the seventh day; and indeed *if* the sore has faded, *and* the sore has not spread on the skin, then the priest shall pronounce him clean; it *is only* a scab, and he shall wash his clothes and be clean. ⁷But if the scab should at all spread over the skin, after he has been seen by the priest for his cleansing, he shall be seen by the priest again. ⁸And *if* the priest sees that the scab has indeed spread on the skin, then the priest shall pronounce him unclean. It *is* leprosy.

⁹"When the leprous sore is on a person, then he shall be brought to the priest. ¹⁰And the priest shall examine *him;* and indeed *if* the swelling on the skin *is* white, and it has turned the hair white, and *there is* a spot of raw flesh in the swelling, ¹¹it *is* an old leprosy on the skin of his body. The priest shall pronounce him unclean, and shall not isolate him, for he *is* unclean.

¹²"And if leprosy breaks out all over the skin, and the leprosy covers all the skin of *the one who has* the sore, from his head to his foot, wherever the priest looks, ¹³then the priest shall consider; and indeed *if* the leprosy has covered all his body, he shall pronounce *him* clean *who has* the sore. It has all turned white. He *is* clean. ¹⁴But when raw flesh appears on him, he shall be unclean. ¹⁵And the priest shall examine the raw flesh and pronounce him to be unclean; *for* the raw flesh *is* unclean. It *is* leprosy. ¹⁶Or if the raw flesh changes and turns white again, he shall come to the priest. ¹⁷And the priest shall examine him; and indeed *if* the sore has turned white, then the priest shall pronounce *him* clean *who has* the sore. He *is* clean.

¹⁸"If the body develops a boil in the skin, and it is healed, ¹⁹and in the place of the boil there comes a white swelling or a bright spot, reddish-white, then it shall be shown to the priest; ²⁰and *if,* when the priest sees it, it indeed appears deeper than the skin, and its hair has turned white, the priest shall pronounce him unclean. It *is* a leprous sore which has broken out of the boil. ²¹But if the priest examines it, and indeed *there are* no white hairs in it, and it

---

13:2 ᵃHebrew *saraath,* disfiguring skin diseases, including leprosy, and so in verses 2–46 and 14:1–32

is not deeper than the skin, but has faded, then the priest shall isolate him seven days; [22]and if it should at all spread over the skin, then the priest shall pronounce him unclean. It *is* a leprous sore. [23]But if the bright spot stays in one place, *and* has not spread, it *is* the scar of the boil; and the priest shall pronounce him clean.

[24]"Or if the body receives a burn on its skin by fire, and the raw *flesh* of the burn becomes a bright spot, reddish-white or white, [25]then the priest shall examine it; and indeed *if* the hair of the bright spot has turned white, and it appears deeper than the skin, it *is* leprosy broken out in the burn. Therefore the priest shall pronounce him unclean. It *is* a leprous sore. [26]But if the priest examines it, and indeed *there are* no white hairs in the bright spot, and it *is* not deeper than the skin, but has faded, then the priest shall isolate him seven days. [27]And the priest shall examine him on the seventh day. If it has at all spread over the skin, then the priest shall pronounce him unclean. It *is* a leprous sore. [28]But if the bright spot stays in one place, *and* has not spread on the skin, but has faded, it *is* a swelling from the burn. The priest shall pronounce him clean, for it *is* the scar from the burn.

[29]"If a man or woman has a sore on the head or the beard, [30]then the priest shall examine the sore; and indeed if it appears deeper than the skin, *and there is* in it thin yellow hair, then the priest shall pronounce him unclean. It *is* a scaly leprosy of the head or beard. [31]But if the priest examines the scaly sore, and indeed it does not appear deeper than the skin, and *there is* no black hair in it, then the priest shall isolate *the one who has* the scale seven days. [32]And on the seventh day the priest shall examine the sore; and indeed *if* the scale has not spread, and there is no yellow hair in it, and the scale does not appear deeper than the skin, [33]he shall shave himself, but the scale he shall not shave. And the priest shall isolate *the one who has* the scale another seven days. [34]On the seventh day the priest shall examine the scale; and indeed *if* the scale has not spread over the skin, and does not appear deeper than the skin, then the priest shall pronounce him clean. He shall wash his clothes and be clean. [35]But if the scale should at all spread over the skin after his cleansing, [36]then the priest shall examine him; and indeed *if* the scale has spread over the skin, the priest need not seek for yellow hair. He *is* unclean. [37]But if the scale appears to be at a standstill, and there is black hair grown up in it, the scale has healed. He *is* clean, and the priest shall pronounce him clean.

[38]"If a man or a woman has bright spots on the skin of the body, *specifically* white bright spots, [39]then the priest shall look; and indeed *if* the bright spots on the skin of the body *are* dull white, it *is* a white spot *that* grows on the skin. He *is* clean.

[40]"As for the man whose hair has fallen from his head, he *is* bald, *but* he *is* clean. [41]He whose hair has fallen from his forehead, he *is* bald on the forehead, *but* he *is* clean. [42]And if there is on the bald head or bald forehead a reddish-white sore, it *is* leprosy breaking out on his bald head or his bald forehead. [43]Then the priest shall examine it; and indeed *if* the swelling of the sore *is* reddish-white on his bald head or on his bald forehead, as the appearance of leprosy on the skin of the body, [44]he is a leprous man. He *is* unclean. The priest shall surely pronounce him unclean; his sore *is* on his head.

[45]"Now the leper on whom the sore *is,* his clothes shall be torn and his head bare; and he shall cover his mustache, and cry, 'Unclean! Unclean!' [46]He shall be unclean. All the days he has the sore he shall be unclean. He *is* unclean, and he shall dwell alone; his dwelling *shall be* outside the camp.

The Law Concerning Leprous Garments

[47]"Also, if a garment has a leprous plague[a] in it, *whether it is* a woolen garment or a linen garment, [48]whether *it is* in the warp or woof of linen or wool, whether in leather or in anything made of leather, [49]and if the plague is greenish or reddish in

---

13:47 [a]A mold, fungus, or similar infestation, and so in verses 47–59

the garment or in the leather, whether in the warp or in the woof, or in anything made of leather, it *is* a leprous plague and shall be shown to the priest. ⁵⁰The priest shall examine the plague and isolate *that which has* the plague seven days. ⁵¹And he shall examine the plague on the seventh day. If the plague has spread in the garment, either in the warp or in the woof, in the leather *or* in anything made of leather, the plague *is* an active leprosy. It *is* unclean. ⁵²He shall therefore burn that garment in which is the plague, whether warp or woof, in wool or in linen, or anything of leather, for it *is* an active leprosy; *the garment* shall be burned in the fire.

⁵³"But if the priest examines *it,* and indeed the plague has not spread in the garment, either in the warp or in the woof, or in anything made of leather, ⁵⁴then the priest shall command that they wash *the thing* in which *is* the plague; and he shall isolate it another seven days. ⁵⁵Then the priest shall examine the plague after it has been washed; and indeed if the plague has not changed its color, though the plague has not spread, it *is* unclean, and you shall burn it in the fire; it continues eating away, *whether* the damage *is* outside or inside. ⁵⁶If the priest examines *it,* and indeed the plague has faded after washing it, then he shall tear it out of the garment, whether out of the warp or out of the woof, or out of the leather. ⁵⁷But if it appears again in the garment, either in the warp or in the woof, or in anything made of leather, it *is* a spreading *plague;* you shall burn with fire that in which is the plague. ⁵⁸And if you wash the garment, either warp or woof, or whatever is made of leather, if the plague has disappeared from it, then it shall be washed a second time, and shall be clean.

⁵⁹"This *is* the law of the leprous plague in a garment of wool or linen, either in the warp or woof, or in anything made of leather, to pronounce it clean or to pronounce it unclean."

The Ritual for Cleansing Healed Lepers

14 Then the LORD spoke to Moses, saying, ²"This shall be the law of the leper for the day of his cleansing: He shall be brought to the priest. ³And the priest shall go out of the camp, and the priest shall examine *him;* and indeed, *if* the leprosy is healed in the leper, ⁴then the priest shall command to take for him who is to be cleansed two living *and* clean birds, cedar wood, scarlet, and hyssop. ⁵And the priest shall command that one of the birds be killed in an earthen vessel over running water. ⁶As for the living bird, he shall take it, the cedar wood and the scarlet and the hyssop, and dip them and the living bird in the blood of the bird *that was* killed over the running water. ⁷And he shall sprinkle it seven times on him who is to be cleansed from the leprosy, and shall pronounce him clean, and shall let the living bird loose in the open field. ⁸He who is to be cleansed shall wash his clothes, shave off all his hair, and wash himself in water, that he may be clean. After that he shall come into the camp, and shall stay outside his tent seven days. ⁹But on the seventh day he shall shave all the hair off his head and his beard and his eyebrows—all his hair he shall shave off. He shall wash his clothes and wash his body in water, and he shall be clean.

¹⁰"And on the eighth day he shall take two male lambs without blemish, one ewe lamb of the first year without blemish, three-tenths *of an ephah* of fine flour mixed with oil as a grain offering, and one log of oil. ¹¹Then the priest who makes *him* clean shall present the man who is to be made clean, and those things, before the LORD, *at* the door of the tabernacle of meeting. ¹²And the priest shall take one male lamb and offer it as a trespass offering, and the log of oil, and wave them *as* a wave offering before the LORD. ¹³Then he shall kill the lamb in the place where he kills the sin offering and the burnt offering, in a holy place; for as the sin offering *is* the priest's, so *is* the trespass offering. It *is* most holy. ¹⁴The priest shall take *some* of the blood of the trespass offering, and the priest shall put *it* on the tip of the right ear of him who is to be cleansed, on the thumb of his right hand, and on the big toe of his right foot. ¹⁵And the priest shall take *some* of the log

of oil, and pour *it* into the palm of his own left hand. [16]Then the priest shall dip his right finger in the oil that *is* in his left hand, and shall sprinkle some of the oil with his finger seven times before the LORD. [17]And of the rest of the oil in his hand, the priest shall put *some* on the tip of the right ear of him who is to be cleansed, on the thumb of his right hand, and on the big toe of his right foot, on the blood of the trespass offering. [18]The rest of the oil that *is* in the priest's hand he shall put on the head of him who is to be cleansed. So the priest shall make atonement for him before the LORD.

[19]"Then the priest shall offer the sin offering, and make atonement for him who is to be cleansed from his uncleanness. Afterward he shall kill the burnt offering. [20]And the priest shall offer the burnt offering and the grain offering on the altar. So the priest shall make atonement for him, and he shall be clean.

[21]"But if he *is* poor and cannot afford it, then he shall take one male lamb *as* a trespass offering to be waved, to make atonement for him, one-tenth *of an ephah* of fine flour mixed with oil as a grain offering, a log of oil, [22]and two turtledoves or two young pigeons, such as he is able to afford: one shall be a sin offering and the other a burnt offering. [23]He shall bring them to the priest on the eighth day for his cleansing, to the door of the tabernacle of meeting, before the LORD. [24]And the priest shall take the lamb of the trespass offering and the log of oil, and the priest shall wave them *as* a wave offering before the LORD. [25]Then he shall kill the lamb of the trespass offering, and the priest shall take *some* of the blood of the trespass offering and put *it* on the tip of the right ear of him who is to be cleansed, on the thumb of his right hand, and on the big toe of his right foot. [26]And the priest shall pour some of the oil into the palm of his own left hand. [27]Then the priest shall sprinkle with his right finger *some* of the oil that *is* in his left hand seven times before the LORD. [28]And the priest shall put *some* of the oil that *is* in his hand on the tip of the right ear of him who is to be cleansed, on the thumb of the right hand, and on the big toe of his right foot, on the place of the blood of the trespass offering. [29]The rest of the oil that *is* in the priest's hand he shall put on the head of him who is to be cleansed, to make atonement for him before the LORD. [30]And he shall offer one of the turtledoves or young pigeons, such as he can afford— [31]such as he is able to afford, the one *as* a sin offering and the other *as* a burnt offering, with the grain offering. So the priest shall make atonement for him who is to be cleansed before the LORD. [32]This *is* the law *for one* who had a leprous sore, who cannot afford the usual cleansing."

The Law Concerning Leprous Houses

[33]And the LORD spoke to Moses and Aaron, saying: [34]"When you have come into the land of Canaan, which I give you as a possession, and I put the leprous plague[a] in a house in the land of your possession, [35]and he who owns the house comes and tells the priest, saying, 'It seems to me that *there is* some plague in the house,' [36]then the priest shall command that they empty the house, before the priest goes *into it* to examine the plague, that all that *is* in the house may not be made unclean; and afterward the priest shall go in to examine the house. [37]And he shall examine the plague; and indeed *if* the plague *is* on the walls of the house with ingrained streaks, greenish or reddish, which appear to be deep in the wall, [38]then the priest shall go out of the house, to the door of the house, and shut up the house seven days. [39]And the priest shall come again on the seventh day and look; and indeed *if* the plague has spread on the walls of the house, [40]then the priest shall command that they take away the stones in which *is* the plague, and they shall cast them into an unclean place outside the city. [41]And he shall cause the house to be scraped inside, all around, and the dust that they scrape off they shall pour out in an unclean place outside the city. [42]Then they shall take other stones and put

---

14:34 [a]Decomposition by mildew, mold, dry rot, etc., and so in verses 34–53

them in the place of *those* stones, and he shall take other mortar and plaster the house.

⁴³"Now if the plague comes back and breaks out in the house, after he has taken away the stones, after he has scraped the house, and after it is plastered, ⁴⁴then the priest shall come and look; and indeed *if* the plague has spread in the house, it *is* an active leprosy in the house. It *is* unclean. ⁴⁵And he shall break down the house, its stones, its timber, and all the plaster of the house, and he shall carry *them* outside the city to an unclean place. ⁴⁶Moreover he who goes into the house at all while it is shut up shall be unclean until evening. ⁴⁷And he who lies down in the house shall wash his clothes, and he who eats in the house shall wash his clothes.

⁴⁸"But if the priest comes in and examines *it,* and indeed the plague has not spread in the house after the house was plastered, then the priest shall pronounce the house clean, because the plague is healed. ⁴⁹And he shall take, to cleanse the house, two birds, cedar wood, scarlet, and hyssop. ⁵⁰Then he shall kill one of the birds in an earthen vessel over running water; ⁵¹and he shall take the cedar wood, the hyssop, the scarlet, and the living bird, and dip them in the blood of the slain bird and in the running water, and sprinkle the house seven times. ⁵²And he shall cleanse the house with the blood of the bird and the running water and the living bird, with the cedar wood, the hyssop, and the scarlet. ⁵³Then he shall let the living bird loose outside the city in the open field, and make atonement for the house, and it shall be clean.

⁵⁴"This *is* the law for any leprous sore and scale, ⁵⁵for the leprosy of a garment and of a house, ⁵⁶for a swelling and a scab and a bright spot, ⁵⁷to teach when *it is* unclean and when *it is* clean. This *is* the law of leprosy."

The Law Concerning Bodily Discharges

15 And the LORD spoke to Moses and Aaron, saying, ²"Speak to the children of Israel, and say to them: 'When any man has a discharge from his body, his discharge *is* unclean. ³And this shall be his uncleanness in regard to his discharge—whether his body runs with his discharge, or his body is stopped up by his discharge, it *is* his uncleanness. ⁴Every bed is unclean on which he who has the discharge lies, and everything on which he sits shall be unclean. ⁵And whoever touches his bed shall wash his clothes and bathe in water, and be unclean until evening. ⁶He who sits on anything on which he who has the discharge sat shall wash his clothes and bathe in water, and be unclean until evening. ⁷And he who touches the body of him who has the discharge shall wash his clothes and bathe in water, and be unclean until evening. ⁸If he who has the discharge spits on him who is clean, then he shall wash his clothes and bathe in water, and be unclean until evening. ⁹Any saddle on which he who has the discharge rides shall be unclean. ¹⁰Whoever touches anything that was under him shall be unclean until evening. He who carries *any of* those things shall wash his clothes and bathe in water, and be unclean until evening. ¹¹And whomever the one who has the discharge touches, and has not rinsed his hands in water, he shall wash his clothes and bathe in water, and be unclean until evening. ¹²The vessel of earth that he who has the discharge touches shall be broken, and every vessel of wood shall be rinsed in water.

¹³'And when he who has a discharge is cleansed of his discharge, then he shall count for himself seven days for his cleansing, wash his clothes, and bathe his body in running water; then he shall be clean. ¹⁴On the eighth day he shall take for himself two turtledoves or two young pigeons, and come before the LORD, to the door of the tabernacle of meeting, and give them to the priest. ¹⁵Then the priest shall offer them, the one *as* a sin offering and the other *as* a burnt offering. So the priest shall make atonement for him before the LORD because of his discharge.

¹⁶'If any man has an emission of semen, then he shall wash all his body in water, and be unclean until evening. ¹⁷And any

garment and any leather on which there is semen, it shall be washed with water, and be unclean until evening. [18]Also, when a woman lies with a man, and *there is* an emission of semen, they shall bathe in water, and be unclean until evening.

[19]If a woman has a discharge, *and* the discharge from her body is blood, she shall be set apart seven days; and whoever touches her shall be unclean until evening. [20]Everything that she lies on during her impurity shall be unclean; also everything that she sits on shall be unclean. [21]Whoever touches her bed shall wash his clothes and bathe in water, and be unclean until evening. [22]And whoever touches anything that she sat on shall wash his clothes and bathe in water, and be unclean until evening. [23]If *anything* is on *her* bed or on anything on which she sits, when he touches it, he shall be unclean until evening. [24]And if any man lies with her at all, so that her impurity is on him, he shall be unclean seven days; and every bed on which he lies shall be unclean.

[25]If a woman has a discharge of blood for many days, other than at the time of her *customary* impurity, or if it runs beyond her *usual time of* impurity, all the days of her unclean discharge shall be as the days of her *customary* impurity. She *shall be* unclean. [26]Every bed on which she lies all the days of her discharge shall be to her as the bed of her impurity; and whatever she sits on shall be unclean, as the uncleanness of her impurity. [27]Whoever touches those things shall be unclean; he shall wash his clothes and bathe in water, and be unclean until evening. [28]But if she is cleansed of her discharge, then she shall count for herself seven days, and after that she shall be clean. [29]And on the eighth day she shall take for herself two turtledoves or two young pigeons, and bring them to the priest, to the door of the tabernacle of meeting. [30]Then the priest shall offer the one *as* a sin offering and the other *as* a burnt offering, and the priest shall make atonement for her before the LORD for the discharge of her uncleanness.

[31]Thus you shall separate the children of Israel from their uncleanness, lest they die in their uncleanness when they defile My tabernacle that *is* among them. [32]This *is* the law for one who has a discharge, and *for him* who emits semen and is unclean thereby, [33]and for her who is indisposed because of her *customary* impurity, and for one who has a discharge, either man or woman, and for him who lies with her who is unclean.'"

The Day of Atonement

16 Now the LORD spoke to Moses after the death of the two sons of Aaron, when they offered *profane fire* before the LORD, and died; [2]and the LORD said to Moses: "Tell Aaron your brother not to come at *just* any time into the Holy *Place* inside the veil, before the mercy seat which *is* on the ark, lest he die; for I will appear in the cloud above the mercy seat.

[3]"Thus Aaron shall come into the Holy *Place:* with *the blood of* a young bull as a sin offering, and *of* a ram as a burnt offering. [4]He shall put the holy linen tunic and the linen trousers on his body; he shall be girded with a linen sash, and with the linen turban he shall be attired. These *are* holy garments. Therefore he shall wash his body in water, and put them on. [5]And he shall take from the congregation of the children of Israel two kids of the goats as a sin offering, and one ram as a burnt offering.

[6]"Aaron shall offer the bull as a sin offering, which *is* for himself, and make atonement for himself and for his house. [7]He shall take the two goats and present them before the LORD *at* the door of the tabernacle of meeting. [8]Then Aaron shall cast lots for the two goats: one lot for the LORD and the other lot for the scapegoat. [9]And Aaron shall bring the goat on which the LORD's lot fell, and offer it *as* a sin offering. [10]But the goat on which the lot fell to be the scapegoat shall be presented alive before the LORD, to make atonement upon it, *and* to let it go as the scapegoat into the wilderness.

[11]"And Aaron shall bring the bull of the sin offering, which is for himself, and make atonement for himself and for his house, and shall kill the bull as the sin offering which *is* for himself. [12]Then he shall take a

censer full of burning coals of fire from the altar before the Lord, with his hands full of sweet incense beaten fine, and bring *it* inside the veil. ¹³And he shall put the incense on the fire before the Lord, that the cloud of incense may cover the mercy seat that *is* on the Testimony, lest he die. ¹⁴He shall take some of the blood of the bull and sprinkle *it* with his finger on the mercy seat on the east *side;* and before the mercy seat he shall sprinkle some of the blood with his finger seven times.

¹⁵"Then he shall kill the goat of the sin offering, which *is* for the people, bring its blood inside the veil, do with that blood as he did with the blood of the bull, and sprinkle it on the mercy seat and before the mercy seat. ¹⁶So he shall make atonement for the Holy *Place,* because of the uncleanness of the children of Israel, and because of their transgressions, for all their sins; and so he shall do for the tabernacle of meeting which remains among them in the midst of their uncleanness. ¹⁷There shall be no man in the tabernacle of meeting when he goes in to make atonement in the Holy *Place,* until he comes out, that he may make atonement for himself, for his household, and for all the assembly of Israel. ¹⁸And he shall go out to the altar that *is* before the Lord, and make atonement for it, and shall take some of the blood of the bull and some of the blood of the goat, and put it on the horns of the altar all around. ¹⁹Then he shall sprinkle some of the blood on it with his finger seven times, cleanse it, and consecrate it from the uncleanness of the children of Israel.

²⁰"And when he has made an end of atoning for the Holy *Place,* the tabernacle of meeting, and the altar, he shall bring the live goat. ²¹Aaron shall lay both his hands on the head of the live goat, confess over it all the iniquities of the children of Israel, and all their transgressions, concerning all their sins, putting them on the head of the goat, and shall send *it* away into the wilderness by the hand of a suitable man. ²²The goat shall bear on itself all their iniquities to an uninhabited land; and he shall release the goat in the wilderness.

²³"Then Aaron shall come into the tabernacle of meeting, shall take off the linen garments which he put on when he went into the Holy *Place,* and shall leave them there. ²⁴And he shall wash his body with water in a holy place, put on his garments, come out and offer his burnt offering and the burnt offering of the people, and make atonement for himself and for the people. ²⁵The fat of the sin offering he shall burn on the altar. ²⁶And he who released the goat as the scapegoat shall wash his clothes and bathe his body in water, and afterward he may come into the camp. ²⁷The bull *for* the sin offering and the goat *for* the sin offering, whose blood was brought in to make atonement in the Holy *Place,* shall be carried outside the camp. And they shall burn in the fire their skins, their flesh, and their offal. ²⁸Then he who burns them shall wash his clothes and bathe his body in water, and afterward he may come into the camp.

²⁹"*This* shall be a statute forever for you: In the seventh month, on the tenth *day* of the month, you shall afflict your souls, and do no work at all, *whether* a native of your own country or a stranger who dwells among you. ³⁰For on that day *the priest* shall make atonement for you, to cleanse you, *that* you may be clean from all your sins before the Lord. ³¹It *is* a sabbath of solemn rest for you, and you shall afflict your souls. *It is* a statute forever. ³²And the priest, who is anointed and consecrated to minister as priest in his father's place, shall make atonement, and put on the linen clothes, the holy garments; ³³then he shall make atonement for the Holy Sanctuary,ᵃ and he shall make atonement for the tabernacle of meeting and for the altar, and he shall make atonement for the priests and for all the people of the assembly. ³⁴This shall be an everlasting statute for you, to make atonement for the children of Israel, for all their sins, once a year." And he did as the Lord commanded Moses.

The Sanctity of Blood

17 And the Lord spoke to Moses, saying, ²"Speak to Aaron, to his sons, and to

16:33 ᵃThat is, the Most Holy Place

all the children of Israel, and say to them, 'This *is* the thing which the LORD has commanded, saying: [3]"Whatever man of the house of Israel who kills an ox or lamb or goat in the camp, or who kills *it* outside the camp, [4]and does not bring it to the door of the tabernacle of meeting to offer an offering to the LORD before the tabernacle of the LORD, the guilt of bloodshed shall be imputed to that man. He has shed blood; and that man shall be cut off from among his people, [5]to the end that the children of Israel may bring their sacrifices which they offer in the open field, that they may bring them to the LORD at the door of the tabernacle of meeting, to the priest, and offer them *as* peace offerings to the LORD. [6]And the priest shall sprinkle the blood on the altar of the LORD *at* the door of the tabernacle of meeting, and burn the fat for a sweet aroma to the LORD. [7]They shall no more offer their sacrifices to demons, after whom they have played the harlot. This shall be a statute forever for them throughout their generations."'

[8]"Also you shall say to them: 'Whatever man of the house of Israel, or of the strangers who dwell among you, who offers a burnt offering or sacrifice, [9]and does not bring it to the door of the tabernacle of meeting, to offer it to the LORD, that man shall be cut off from among his people.

[10]'And whatever man of the house of Israel, or of the strangers who dwell among you, who eats any blood, I will set My face against that person who eats blood, and will cut him off from among his people. [11]For the life of the flesh *is* in the blood, and I have given it to you upon the altar to make atonement for your souls; for it *is* the blood *that* makes atonement for the soul.' [12]Therefore I said to the children of Israel, 'No one among you shall eat blood, nor shall any stranger who dwells among you eat blood.'

[13]"Whatever man of the children of Israel, or of the strangers who dwell among you, who hunts and catches any animal or bird that may be eaten, he shall pour out its blood and cover it with dust; [14]for *it is* the life of all flesh. Its blood sustains its life.

Therefore I said to the children of Israel, 'You shall not eat the blood of any flesh, for the life of all flesh is its blood. Whoever eats it shall be cut off.'

[15]"And every person who eats what died *naturally* or what was torn *by beasts, whether he is* a native of your own country or a stranger, he shall both wash his clothes and bathe in water, and be unclean until evening. Then he shall be clean. [16]But if he does not wash *them* or bathe his body, then he shall bear his guilt."

Laws of Sexual Morality

18 Then the LORD spoke to Moses, saying, [2]"Speak to the children of Israel, and say to them: 'I am the LORD your God. [3]According to the doings of the land of Egypt, where you dwelt, you shall not do; and according to the doings of the land of Canaan, where I am bringing you, you shall not do; nor shall you walk in their ordinances. [4]You shall observe My judgments and keep My ordinances, to walk in them: I *am* the LORD your God. [5]You shall therefore keep My statutes and My judgments, which if a man does, he shall live by them: I *am* the LORD.

[6]'None of you shall approach anyone who is near of kin to him, to uncover his nakedness: I *am* the LORD. [7]The nakedness of your father or the nakedness of your mother you shall not uncover. She *is* your mother; you shall not uncover her nakedness. [8]The nakedness of your father's wife you shall not uncover; it *is* your father's nakedness. [9]The nakedness of your sister, the daughter of your father, or the daughter of your mother, *whether* born at home or elsewhere, their nakedness you shall not uncover. [10]The nakedness of your son's daughter or your daughter's daughter, their nakedness you shall not uncover; for theirs *is* your own nakedness. [11]The nakedness of your father's wife's daughter, begotten by your father—she *is* your sister—you shall not uncover her nakedness. [12]You shall not uncover the nakedness of your father's sister; she *is* near of kin to your father. [13]You shall not uncover the nakedness of your mother's sister, for she *is* near of kin to

your mother. ¹⁴You shall not uncover the nakedness of your father's brother. You shall not approach his wife; she *is* your aunt. ¹⁵You shall not uncover the nakedness of your daughter-in-law—she *is* your son's wife—you shall not uncover her nakedness. ¹⁶You shall not uncover the nakedness of your brother's wife; it *is* your brother's nakedness. ¹⁷You shall not uncover the nakedness of a woman and her daughter, nor shall you take her son's daughter or her daughter's daughter, to uncover her nakedness. They *are* near of kin to her. It *is* wickedness. ¹⁸Nor shall you take a woman as a rival to her sister, to uncover her nakedness while the other is alive.

¹⁹'Also you shall not approach a woman to uncover her nakedness as long as she is in her *customary* impurity. ²⁰Moreover you shall not lie carnally with your neighbor's wife, to defile yourself with her. ²¹And you shall not let any of your descendants pass through *the fire* to Molech, nor shall you profane the name of your God: I *am* the LORD. ²²You shall not lie with a male as with a woman. It *is* an abomination. ²³Nor shall you mate with any animal, to defile yourself with it. Nor shall any woman stand before an animal to mate with it. It *is* perversion.

²⁴'Do not defile yourselves with any of these things; for by all these the nations are defiled, which I am casting out before you. ²⁵For the land is defiled; therefore I visit the punishment of its iniquity upon it, and the land vomits out its inhabitants. ²⁶You shall therefore keep My statutes and My judgments, and shall not commit *any* of these abominations, *either* any of your own nation or any stranger who dwells among you ²⁷(for all these abominations the men of the land have done, who *were* before you, and thus the land is defiled), ²⁸lest the land vomit you out also when you defile it, as it vomited out the nations that *were* before you. ²⁹For whoever commits any of these abominations, the persons who commit *them* shall be cut off from among their people.

³⁰'Therefore you shall keep My ordinance, so that *you* do not commit *any* of these abominable customs which were committed before you, and that you do not defile yourselves by them: I *am* the LORD your God.' "

Moral and Ceremonial Laws

19 And the LORD spoke to Moses, saying, ²"Speak to all the congregation of the children of Israel, and say to them: 'You shall be holy, for I the LORD your God *am* holy.

³'Every one of you shall revere his mother and his father, and keep My Sabbaths: I *am* the LORD your God.

⁴'Do not turn to idols, nor make for yourselves molded gods: I *am* the LORD your God.

⁵'And if you offer a sacrifice of a peace offering to the LORD, you shall offer it of your own free will. ⁶It shall be eaten the same day you offer *it,* and on the next day. And if any remains until the third day, it shall be burned in the fire. ⁷And if it is eaten at all on the third day, it *is* an abomination. It shall not be accepted. ⁸Therefore *everyone* who eats it shall bear his iniquity, because he has profaned the hallowed *offering* of the LORD; and that person shall be cut off from his people.

⁹'When you reap the harvest of your land, you shall not wholly reap the corners of your field, nor shall you gather the gleanings of your harvest. ¹⁰And you shall not glean your vineyard, nor shall you gather *every* grape of your vineyard; you shall leave them for the poor and the stranger: I *am* the LORD your God.

¹¹'You shall not steal, nor deal falsely, nor lie to one another. ¹²And you shall not swear by My name falsely, nor shall you profane the name of your God: I *am* the LORD.

¹³'You shall not cheat your neighbor, nor rob *him.* The wages of him who is hired shall not remain with you all night until morning. ¹⁴You shall not curse the deaf, nor put a stumbling block before the blind, but shall fear your God: I *am* the LORD.

¹⁵'You shall do no injustice in judgment. You shall not be partial to the poor, nor honor the person of the mighty. In righteousness you shall judge your neighbor.

¹⁶You shall not go about *as* a talebearer among your people; nor shall you take a stand against the life of your neighbor: I *am* the LORD.

¹⁷'You shall not hate your brother in your heart. You shall surely rebuke your neighbor, and not bear sin because of him. ¹⁸You shall not take vengeance, nor bear any grudge against the children of your people, but you shall love your neighbor as yourself: I *am* the LORD.

¹⁹'You shall keep My statutes. You shall not let your livestock breed with another kind. You shall not sow your field with mixed seed. Nor shall a garment of mixed linen and wool come upon you.

²⁰'Whoever lies carnally with a woman who *is* betrothed to a man as a concubine, and who has not at all been redeemed nor given her freedom, for this there shall be scourging; *but* they shall not be put to death, because she was not free. ²¹And he shall bring his trespass offering to the LORD, to the door of the tabernacle of meeting, a ram as a trespass offering. ²²The priest shall make atonement for him with the ram of the trespass offering before the LORD for his sin which he has committed. And the sin which he has committed shall be forgiven him.

²³'When you come into the land, and have planted all kinds of trees for food, then you shall count their fruit as uncircumcised. Three years it shall be as uncircumcised to you. *It* shall not be eaten. ²⁴But in the fourth year all its fruit shall be holy, a praise to the LORD. ²⁵And in the fifth year you may eat its fruit, that it may yield to you its increase: I *am* the LORD your God.

²⁶'You shall not eat *anything* with the blood, nor shall you practice divination or soothsaying. ²⁷You shall not shave around the sides of your head, nor shall you disfigure the edges of your beard. ²⁸You shall not make any cuttings in your flesh for the dead, nor tattoo any marks on you: I *am* the LORD.

²⁹'Do not prostitute your daughter, to cause her to be a harlot, lest the land fall into harlotry, and the land become full of wickedness.

³⁰'You shall keep My Sabbaths and reverence My sanctuary: I *am* the LORD.

³¹'Give no regard to mediums and familiar spirits; do not seek after them, to be defiled by them: I *am* the LORD your God.

³²'You shall rise before the gray headed and honor the presence of an old man, and fear your God: I *am* the LORD.

³³'And if a stranger dwells with you in your land, you shall not mistreat him. ³⁴The stranger who dwells among you shall be to you as one born among you, and you shall love him as yourself; for you were strangers in the land of Egypt: I *am* the LORD your God.

³⁵'You shall do no injustice in judgment, in measurement of length, weight, or volume. ³⁶You shall have honest scales, honest weights, an honest ephah, and an honest hin: I *am* the LORD your God, who brought you out of the land of Egypt.

³⁷'Therefore you shall observe all My statutes and all My judgments, and perform them: I *am* the LORD.' "

Penalties for Breaking the Law

20 Then the LORD spoke to Moses, saying, ²"Again, you shall say to the children of Israel: 'Whoever of the children of Israel, or of the strangers who dwell in Israel, who gives *any* of his descendants to Molech, he shall surely be put to death. The people of the land shall stone him with stones. ³I will set My face against that man, and will cut him off from his people, because he has given *some* of his descendants to Molech, to defile My sanctuary and profane My holy name. ⁴And if the people of the land should in any way hide their eyes from the man, when he gives *some* of his descendants to Molech, and they do not kill him, ⁵then I will set My face against that man and against his family; and I will cut him off from his people, and all who prostitute themselves with him to commit harlotry with Molech.

⁶'And the person who turns to mediums and familiar spirits, to prostitute himself with them, I will set My face against that person and cut him off from his people. ⁷Consecrate yourselves therefore, and be

holy, for I *am* the LORD your God. [8]And you shall keep My statutes, and perform them: I *am* the LORD who sanctifies you.

[9]'For everyone who curses his father or his mother shall surely be put to death. He has cursed his father or his mother. His blood *shall be* upon him.

[10]'The man who commits adultery with *another* man's wife, *he* who commits adultery with his neighbor's wife, the adulterer and the adulteress, shall surely be put to death. [11]The man who lies with his father's wife has uncovered his father's nakedness; both of them shall surely be put to death. Their blood *shall be* upon them. [12]If a man lies with his daughter-in-law, both of them shall surely be put to death. They have committed perversion. Their blood *shall be* upon them. [13]If a man lies with a male as he lies with a woman, both of them have committed an abomination. They shall surely be put to death. Their blood *shall be* upon them. [14]If a man marries a woman and her mother, it *is* wickedness. They shall be burned with fire, both he and they, that there may be no wickedness among you. [15]If a man mates with an animal, he shall surely be put to death, and you shall kill the animal. [16]If a woman approaches any animal and mates with it, you shall kill the woman and the animal. They shall surely be put to death. Their blood *is* upon them.

[17]'If a man takes his sister, his father's daughter or his mother's daughter, and sees her nakedness and she sees his nakedness, it *is* a wicked thing. And they shall be cut off in the sight of their people. He has uncovered his sister's nakedness. He shall bear his guilt. [18]If a man lies with a woman during her sickness and uncovers her nakedness, he has exposed her flow, and she has uncovered the flow of her blood. Both of them shall be cut off from their people.

[19]'You shall not uncover the nakedness of your mother's sister nor of your father's sister, for that would uncover his near of kin. They shall bear their guilt. [20]If a man lies with his uncle's wife, he has uncovered his uncle's nakedness. They shall bear their sin; they shall die childless. [21]If a man takes his brother's wife, it *is* an unclean thing. He has uncovered his brother's nakedness. They shall be childless.

[22]'You shall therefore keep all My statutes and all My judgments, and perform them, that the land where I am bringing you to dwell may not vomit you out. [23]And you shall not walk in the statutes of the nation which I am casting out before you; for they commit all these things, and therefore I abhor them. [24]But I have said to you, "You shall inherit their land, and I will give it to you to possess, a land flowing with milk and honey." I *am* the LORD your God, who has separated you from the peoples. [25]You shall therefore distinguish between clean animals and unclean, between unclean birds and clean, and you shall not make yourselves abominable by beast or by bird, or by any kind of living thing that creeps on the ground, which I have separated from you as unclean. [26]And you shall be holy to Me, for I the LORD *am* holy, and have separated you from the peoples, that you should be Mine.

[27]'A man or a woman who is a medium, or who has familiar spirits, shall surely be put to death; they shall stone them with stones. Their blood *shall be* upon them.'"

Regulations for Conduct of Priests

21 And the LORD said to Moses, "Speak to the priests, the sons of Aaron, and say to them: 'None shall defile himself for the dead among his people, [2]except for his relatives who are nearest to him: his mother, his father, his son, his daughter, and his brother; [3]also his virgin sister who is near to him, who has had no husband, for her he may defile himself. [4]*Otherwise* he shall not defile himself, *being* a chief man among his people, to profane himself.

[5]'They shall not make any bald *place* on their heads, nor shall they shave the edges of their beards nor make any cuttings in their flesh. [6]They shall be holy to their God and not profane the name of their God, for they offer the offerings of the LORD made by fire, *and* the bread of their God; therefore they shall be holy. [7]They shall not take a wife *who is* a harlot or a defiled woman,

nor shall they take a woman divorced from her husband; for *the priest*[a] is holy to his God. [8]Therefore you shall consecrate him, for he offers the bread of your God. He shall be holy to you, for I the Lord, who sanctify you, *am* holy. [9]The daughter of any priest, if she profanes herself by playing the harlot, she profanes her father. She shall be burned with fire.

[10]*He who is* the high priest among his brethren, on whose head the anointing oil was poured and who is consecrated to wear the garments, shall not uncover his head nor tear his clothes; [11]nor shall he go near any dead body, nor defile himself for his father or his mother; [12]nor shall he go out of the sanctuary, nor profane the sanctuary of his God; for the consecration of the anointing oil of his God *is* upon him: I *am* the Lord. [13]And he shall take a wife in her virginity. [14]A widow or a divorced woman or a defiled woman *or a* harlot— these he shall not marry; but he shall take a virgin of his own people as wife. [15]Nor shall he profane his posterity among his people, for I the Lord sanctify him.'"

[16]And the Lord spoke to Moses, saying, [17]"Speak to Aaron, saying: 'No man of your descendants in *succeeding* generations, who has *any* defect, may approach to offer the bread of his God. [18]For any man who has a defect shall not approach: a man blind or lame, who has a marred *face* or any *limb* too long, [19]a man who has a broken foot or broken hand, [20]or is a hunchback or a dwarf, or *a man* who has a defect in his eye, or eczema or scab, or is a eunuch. [21]No man of the descendants of Aaron the priest, who has a defect, shall come near to offer the offerings made by fire to the Lord. He has a defect; he shall not come near to offer the bread of his God. [22]He may eat the bread of his God, *both* the most holy and the holy; [23]only he shall not go near the veil or approach the altar, because he has a defect, lest he profane My sanctuaries; for I the Lord sanctify them.'"

[24]And Moses told *it* to Aaron and his sons, and to all the children of Israel.

22 Then the Lord spoke to Moses, saying, [2]"Speak to Aaron and his sons,

that they separate themselves from the holy things of the children of Israel, and that they do not profane My holy name *by* what they dedicate to Me: I *am* the Lord. [3]Say to them: 'Whoever of all your descendants throughout your generations, who goes near the holy things which the children of Israel dedicate to the Lord, while he has uncleanness upon him, that person shall be cut off from My presence: I *am* the Lord.

[4]'Whatever man of the descendants of Aaron, who *is* a leper or has a discharge, shall not eat the holy offerings until he is clean. And whoever touches anything made unclean *by* a corpse, or a man who has had an emission of semen, [5]or whoever touches any creeping thing by which he would be made unclean, or any person by whom he would become unclean, whatever his uncleanness may be— [6]the person who has touched any such thing shall be unclean until evening, and shall not eat the holy *offerings* unless he washes his body with water. [7]And when the sun goes down he shall be clean; and afterward he may eat the holy *offerings,* because it *is* his food. [8]Whatever dies *naturally* or is torn *by beasts* he shall not eat, to defile himself with it: I *am* the Lord.

[9]'They shall therefore keep My ordinance, lest they bear sin for it and die thereby, if they profane it: I the Lord sanctify them.

[10]'No outsider shall eat the holy *offering;* one who dwells with the priest, or a hired servant, shall not eat the holy thing. [11]But if the priest buys a person with his money, he may eat it; and one who is born in his house may eat his food. [12]If the priest's daughter is married to an outsider, she may not eat of the holy offerings. [13]But if the priest's daughter is a widow or divorced, and has no child, and has returned to her father's house as in her youth, she may eat her father's food; but no outsider shall eat it.

[14]'And if a man eats the holy *offering* unintentionally, then he shall restore a holy *offering* to the priest, and add one-fifth to it. [15]They shall not profane the holy *offerings* of the children of Israel, which they offer to the Lord, [16]or allow them to bear the

---

21:7 [a]Literally *he*

guilt of trespass when they eat their holy *offerings;* for I the LORD sanctify them.' "

Offerings Accepted and Not Accepted

[17]And the LORD spoke to Moses, saying, [18]"Speak to Aaron and his sons, and to all the children of Israel, and say to them: 'Whatever man of the house of Israel, or of the strangers in Israel, who offers his sacrifice for any of his vows or for any of his freewill offerings, which they offer to the LORD as a burnt offering— [19]*you shall offer* of your own free will a male without blemish from the cattle, from the sheep, or from the goats. [20]Whatever has a defect, you shall not offer, for it shall not be acceptable on your behalf. [21]And whoever offers a sacrifice of a peace offering to the LORD, to fulfill *his* vow, or a freewill offering from the cattle or the sheep, it must be perfect to be accepted; there shall be no defect in it. [22]Those *that are* blind or broken or maimed, or have an ulcer or eczema or scabs, you shall not offer to the LORD, nor make an offering by fire of them on the altar to the LORD. [23]Either a bull or a lamb that has any limb too long or too short you may offer *as* a freewill offering, but for a vow it shall not be accepted.

[24]'You shall not offer to the LORD what is bruised or crushed, or torn or cut; nor shall you make *any offering of them* in your land. [25]Nor from a foreigner's hand shall you offer any of these as the bread of your God, because their corruption *is* in them, *and* defects *are* in them. They shall not be accepted on your behalf.' "

[26]And the LORD spoke to Moses, saying: [27]"When a bull or a sheep or a goat is born, it shall be seven days with its mother; and from the eighth day and thereafter it shall be accepted as an offering made by fire to the LORD. [28]*Whether it is* a cow or ewe, do not kill both her and her young on the same day. [29]And when you offer a sacrifice of thanksgiving to the LORD, offer *it* of your own free will. [30]On the same day it shall be eaten; you shall leave none of it until morning: I *am* the LORD.

[31]"Therefore you shall keep My commandments, and perform them: I *am* the LORD. [32]You shall not profane My holy name, but I will be hallowed among the children of Israel. I *am* the LORD who sanctifies you, [33]who brought you out of the land of Egypt, to be your God: I *am* the LORD."

Feasts of the LORD

23 And the LORD spoke to Moses, saying, [2]"Speak to the children of Israel, and say to them: 'The feasts of the LORD, which you shall proclaim *to be* holy convocations, these *are* My feasts.

The Sabbath

[3]'Six days shall work be done, but the seventh day *is* a Sabbath of solemn rest, a holy convocation. You shall do no work *on it;* it *is* the Sabbath of the LORD in all your dwellings.

The Passover and Unleavened Bread

[4]'These *are* the feasts of the LORD, holy convocations which you shall proclaim at their appointed times. [5]On the fourteenth *day* of the first month at twilight *is* the LORD's Passover. [6]And on the fifteenth day of the same month *is* the Feast of Unleavened Bread to the LORD; seven days you must eat unleavened bread. [7]On the first day you shall have a holy convocation; you shall do no customary work on it. [8]But you shall offer an offering made by fire to the LORD for seven days. The seventh day *shall be* a holy convocation; you shall do no customary work *on it.*' "

The Feast of Firstfruits

[9]And the LORD spoke to Moses, saying, [10]"Speak to the children of Israel, and say to them: 'When you come into the land which I give to you, and reap its harvest, then you shall bring a sheaf of the firstfruits of your harvest to the priest. [11]He shall wave the sheaf before the LORD, to be accepted on your behalf; on the day after the Sabbath the priest shall wave it. [12]And you shall offer on that day, when you wave the sheaf, a male lamb of the first year, without blemish, as a burnt offering to the LORD. [13]Its grain offering *shall be* two-tenths *of an ephah* of fine flour mixed with oil, an offering

made by fire to the LORD, for a sweet aroma; and its drink offering *shall be* of wine, one-fourth of a hin. [14]You shall eat neither bread nor parched grain nor fresh grain until the same day that you have brought an offering to your God; *it shall be* a statute forever throughout your generations in all your dwellings.

The Feast of Weeks

[15]'And you shall count for yourselves from the day after the Sabbath, from the day that you brought the sheaf of the wave offering: seven Sabbaths shall be completed. [16]Count fifty days to the day after the seventh Sabbath; then you shall offer a new grain offering to the LORD. [17]You shall bring from your dwellings two wave *loaves* of two-tenths *of an ephah*. They shall be of fine flour; they shall be baked with leaven. *They are* the firstfruits to the LORD. [18]And you shall offer with the bread seven lambs of the first year, without blemish, one young bull, and two rams. They shall be *as* a burnt offering to the LORD, with their grain offering and their drink offerings, an offering made by fire for a sweet aroma to the LORD. [19]Then you shall sacrifice one kid of the goats as a sin offering, and two male lambs of the first year as a sacrifice of a peace offering. [20]The priest shall wave them with the bread of the firstfruits *as a* wave offering before the LORD, with the two lambs. They shall be holy to the LORD for the priest. [21]And you shall proclaim on the same day *that* it is a holy convocation to you. You shall do no customary work *on it. It shall be* a statute forever in all your dwellings throughout your generations.

[22]'When you reap the harvest of your land, you shall not wholly reap the corners of your field when you reap, nor shall you gather any gleaning from your harvest. You shall leave them for the poor and for the stranger: I *am* the LORD your God.'"

The Feast of Trumpets

[23]Then the LORD spoke to Moses, saying, [24]"Speak to the children of Israel, saying: 'In the seventh month, on the first *day* of the month, you shall have a sabbath-*rest*,

a memorial of blowing of trumpets, a holy convocation. [25]You shall do no customary work *on it;* and you shall offer an offering made by fire to the LORD.'"

The Day of Atonement

[26]And the LORD spoke to Moses, saying: [27]"Also the tenth *day* of this seventh month *shall be* the Day of Atonement. It shall be a holy convocation for you; you shall afflict your souls, and offer an offering made by fire to the LORD. [28]And you shall do no work on that same day, for it *is* the Day of Atonement, to make atonement for you before the LORD your God. [29]For any person who is not afflicted *in soul* on that same day shall be cut off from his people. [30]And any person who does any work on that same day, that person I will destroy from among his people. [31]You shall do no manner of work; *it shall be* a statute forever throughout your generations in all your dwellings. [32]It *shall be* to you a sabbath of *solemn* rest, and you shall afflict your souls; on the ninth *day* of the month at evening, from evening to evening, you shall celebrate your sabbath."

The Feast of Tabernacles

[33]Then the LORD spoke to Moses, saying, [34]"Speak to the children of Israel, saying: 'The fifteenth day of this seventh month *shall be* the Feast of Tabernacles *for* seven days to the LORD. [35]On the first day *there shall be* a holy convocation. You shall do no customary work *on it.* [36]*For* seven days you shall offer an offering made by fire to the LORD. On the eighth day you shall have a holy convocation, and you shall offer an offering made by fire to the LORD. It *is* a sacred assembly, *and* you shall do no customary work *on it.*

[37]'These *are* the feasts of the LORD which you shall proclaim *to be* holy convocations, to offer an offering made by fire to the LORD, a burnt offering and a grain offering, a sacrifice and drink offerings, everything on its day— [38]besides the Sabbaths of the LORD, besides your gifts, besides all your vows, and besides all your freewill offerings which you give to the LORD.

PUBLIC SCHOOLS AND RELIGIOUS INSTRUCTION

SUPREME COURT
OF THE UNITED STATES

*"These are the feasts
of the LORD which you
shall proclaim to be
holy convocations. . . ."*

LEVITICUS 23:37

In the 1952 case of *Zorach v. Clauson*, the Supreme Court upheld the position that New York City permits its public schools to release students during school hours to go to religious centers for religious instruction or devotional exercises:

The First Amendment, however, does not say that in every respect there shall be a separation of Church and State. Rather, it studiously defines the manner, the specific ways, in which there shall be no concert or union or dependency one on the other. That is the common sense of the matter. Otherwise the state and religion would be aliens to each other—hostile, suspicious, and even unfriendly. . . .

Municipalities would not be permitted to render police or fire protection to religious groups. Policemen who helped parishioners into their places of worship would violate the Constitution. Prayers in our legislative halls; the appeals to the Almighty in the messages of the Chief Executive; the proclamation making Thanksgiving Day a holiday; "so help me God" in our courtroom oaths—these and all other references to the Almighty that run through our laws, our public rituals, our ceremonies, would be flouting the First Amendment.

A fastidious atheist or agnostic could even object to the supplication with which the Court opens each session: "God save the United States and this Honorable Court."

We are a religious people and our institutions presuppose a Supreme Being. . . .

When the state encourages religious instruction or cooperates with religious authorities by adjusting the schedule of public events to sectarian needs, it follows the best of our traditions. For it then respects the religious nature of our people and accommodates the public service to their spiritual needs. To hold that it may not would be to find in the Constitution a requirement that the government show a callous indifference to religious groups. That would be preferring those who believe in no religion over those who do believe. . . .

We find no constitutional requirement makes it necessary for government to be hostile to religion and to throw its weight against the efforts to widen the scope of religious influence. The government must remain neutral when it comes to competition between sects. . . . We cannot read into the Bill of Rights such a philosophy of hostility to religion.

39'Also on the fifteenth day of the seventh month, when you have gathered in the fruit of the land, you shall keep the feast of the LORD *for* seven days; on the first day *there shall be* a sabbath-*rest,* and on the eighth day a sabbath-*rest.* 40And you shall take for yourselves on the first day the fruit of beautiful trees, branches of palm trees, the boughs of leafy trees, and willows of the brook; and you shall rejoice before the LORD your God for seven days. 41You shall keep it as a feast to the LORD for seven days in the year. *It shall be* a statute forever in your generations. You shall celebrate it in the seventh month. 42You shall dwell in booths for seven days. All who are native Israelites shall dwell in booths, 43that your generations may know that I made the children of Israel dwell in booths when I brought them out of the land of Egypt: I *am* the LORD your God.'"

44So Moses declared to the children of Israel the feasts of the LORD.

Care of the Tabernacle Lamps

24 Then the LORD spoke to Moses, saying: 2"Command the children of Israel that they bring to you pure oil of pressed olives for the light, to make the lamps burn continually. 3Outside the veil of the Testimony, in the tabernacle of meeting, Aaron shall be in charge of it from evening until morning before the LORD continually; *it shall be* a statute forever in your generations. 4He shall be in charge of the lamps on the pure *gold* lampstand before the LORD continually.

The Bread of the Tabernacle

5"And you shall take fine flour and bake twelve cakes with it. Two-tenths *of an ephah* shall be in each cake. 6You shall set them in two rows, six in a row, on the pure *gold* table before the LORD. 7And you shall put pure frankincense on *each* row, that it may be on the bread for a memorial, an offering made by fire to the LORD. 8Every Sabbath he shall set it in order before the LORD continually, *being taken* from the children of Israel by an everlasting covenant. 9And it shall be for Aaron and his sons, and they shall eat it in a holy place; for it *is* most holy to him from the offerings of the LORD made by fire, by a perpetual statute."

The Penalty for Blasphemy

10Now the son of an Israelite woman, whose father *was* an Egyptian, went out among the children of Israel; and this Israelite *woman's* son and a man of Israel fought each other in the camp. 11And the Israelite woman's son blasphemed the name *of the* LORD and cursed; and so they brought him to Moses. (His mother's name *was* Shelomith the daughter of Dibri, of the tribe of Dan.) 12Then they put him in custody, that the mind of the LORD might be shown to them.

13And the LORD spoke to Moses, saying, 14"Take outside the camp him who has cursed; then let all who heard *him* lay their hands on his head, and let all the congregation stone him. 15"Then you shall speak to the children of Israel, saying: 'Whoever curses his God shall bear his sin. 16And whoever blasphemes the name of the LORD shall surely be put to death. All the congregation shall certainly stone him, the stranger as well as him who is born in the land. When he blasphemes the name *of the* LORD, he shall be put to death.

17'Whoever kills any man shall surely be put to death. 18Whoever kills an animal shall make it good, animal for animal. 19'If a man causes disfigurement of his neighbor, as he has done, so shall it be done to him— 20fracture for fracture, eye for eye, tooth for tooth; as he has caused disfigurement of a man, so shall it be done to him. 21And whoever kills an animal shall restore it; but whoever kills a man shall be put to death. 22You shall have the same law for the stranger and for one from your own country; for I *am* the LORD your God.'"

23Then Moses spoke to the children of Israel; and they took outside the camp him who had cursed, and stoned him with stones. So the children of Israel did as the LORD commanded Moses.

The Sabbath of the Seventh Year

25 And the LORD spoke to Moses on Mount Sinai, saying, 2"Speak to the

children of Israel, and say to them: 'When you come into the land which I give you, then the land shall keep a sabbath to the LORD. ³Six years you shall sow your field, and six years you shall prune your vineyard, and gather its fruit; ⁴but in the seventh year there shall be a sabbath of solemn rest for the land, a sabbath to the LORD. You shall neither sow your field nor prune your vineyard. ⁵What grows of its own accord of your harvest you shall not reap, nor gather the grapes of your untended vine, *for* it is a year of rest for the land. ⁶And the sabbath *produce* of the land shall be food for you: for you, your male and female servants, your hired man, and the stranger who dwells with you, ⁷for your livestock and the beasts that *are* in your land—all its produce shall be for food.

The Year of Jubilee

8'And you shall count seven sabbaths of years for yourself, seven times seven years; and the time of the seven sabbaths of years shall be to you forty-nine years. ⁹Then you shall cause the trumpet of the Jubilee to sound on the tenth *day* of the seventh month; on the Day of Atonement you shall make the trumpet to sound throughout all your land. ¹⁰And you shall consecrate the fiftieth year, and proclaim liberty throughout *all* the land to all its inhabitants. It shall be a Jubilee for you; and each of you shall return to his possession, and each of you shall return to his family. ¹¹That fiftieth year shall be a Jubilee to you; in it you shall neither sow nor reap what grows of its own accord, nor gather *the grapes* of your untended vine. ¹²For it *is* the Jubilee; it shall be holy to you; you shall eat its produce from the field.

13'In this Year of Jubilee, each of you shall return to his possession. ¹⁴And if you sell anything to your neighbor or buy from your neighbor's hand, you shall not oppress one another. ¹⁵According to the number of years after the Jubilee you shall buy from your neighbor, and according to the number of years of crops he shall sell to you. ¹⁶According to the multitude of years you

---

FREEDOM

". . . proclaim liberty throughout all the land. . . ."

LEVITICUS 25:10

The Liberty Bell

THE LIBERTY BELL

The Pennsylvania Assembly ordered the bell in 1751 to commemorate the golden anniversary of William Penn's 1701 Charter of Privileges, Pennsylvania's original Constitution, which speaks of the rights and freedoms valued by people the world over. As the bell was created, the biblical quotation "Proclaim liberty throughout all the land unto all the inhabitants thereof" was particularly apt. For the line in the Bible immediately preceding "proclaim liberty" is, "And ye shall hallow the 50th year." What better way to pay homage to Penn and hallow the fiftieth year than with a bell proclaiming liberty?

The Liberty Bell gained iconic importance when abolitionists in their efforts to put an end to slavery throughout America adopted it as a symbol of emancipation and liberty in 1837.

Related to a popular fictional story written in 1747, tradition says that on July 8, 1776, the Liberty Bell rang out from the tower of Independence Hall, summoning the citizens of Philadelphia to hear the first public reading of the Declaration of Independence. The truth is that the steeple was in bad condition, and historians today highly doubt this account. However, its association with the Declaration of Independence became fixed in the collective mythology.

shall increase its price, and according to the fewer number of years you shall diminish its price; for he sells to you *according* to the number *of the years* of the crops. [17]Therefore you shall not oppress one another, but you shall fear your God; for I *am* the LORD your God.

Provisions for the Seventh Year

[18]'So you shall observe My statutes and keep My judgments, and perform them; and you will dwell in the land in safety. [19]Then the land will yield its fruit, and you will eat your fill, and dwell there in safety. [20]'And if you say, "What shall we eat in the seventh year, since we shall not sow nor gather in our produce?" [21]Then I will command My blessing on you in the sixth year, and it will bring forth produce enough for three years. [22]And you shall sow in the eighth year, and eat old produce until the ninth year; until its produce comes in, you shall eat *of* the old *harvest.*

Redemption of Property

[23]'The land shall not be sold permanently, for the land *is* Mine; for you *are* strangers and sojourners with Me. [24]And in all the land of your possession you shall grant redemption of the land.

[25]'If one of your brethren becomes poor, and has sold *some* of his possession, and if his redeeming relative comes to redeem it, then he may redeem what his brother sold. [26]Or if the man has no one to redeem it, but he himself becomes able to redeem it, [27]then let him count the years since its sale, and restore the remainder to the man to whom he sold it, that he may return to his possession. [28]But if he is not able to have *it* restored to himself, then what was sold shall remain in the hand of him who bought it until the Year of Jubilee; and in the Jubilee it shall be released, and he shall return to his possession.

[29]'If a man sells a house in a walled city, then he may redeem it within a whole year after it is sold; *within* a full year he may redeem it. [30]But if it is not redeemed within the space of a full year, then the house in the walled city shall belong permanently to him who bought it, throughout his generations. It shall not be released in the Jubilee. [31]However the houses of villages which have no wall around them shall be counted as the fields of the country. They may be redeemed, and they shall be released in the Jubilee. [32]Nevertheless the cities of the Levites, *and* the houses in the cities of their possession, the Levites may redeem at any time. [33]And if a man purchases a house from the Levites, then the house that was sold in the city of his possession shall be released in the Jubilee; for the houses in the cities of the Levites *are* their possession among the children of Israel. [34]But the field of the common-land of their cities may not be sold, for it *is* their perpetual possession.

Lending to the Poor

[35]'If one of your brethren becomes poor, and falls into poverty among you, then you shall help him, like a stranger or a sojourner, that he may live with you. [36]Take no usury or interest from him; but fear your God, that your brother may live with you. [37]You shall not lend him your money for usury, nor lend him your food at a profit. [38]I *am* the LORD your God, who brought you out of the land of Egypt, to give you the land of Canaan *and* to be your God.

The Law Concerning Slavery

[39]'And if *one of* your brethren *who dwells* by you becomes poor, and sells himself to you, you shall not compel him to serve as a slave. [40]As a hired servant *and* a sojourner he shall be with you, *and* shall serve you until the Year of Jubilee. [41]And *then* he shall depart from you—he and his children with him—and shall return to his own family. He shall return to the possession of his fathers. [42]For they *are* My servants, whom I brought out of the land of Egypt; they shall not be sold as slaves. [43]You shall not rule over him with rigor, but you shall fear your God. [44]And as for your male and female slaves whom you may have—from the nations that are around you, from them you may buy male and female slaves. [45]Moreover you may buy the children of

the strangers who dwell among you, and their families who are with you, which they beget in your land; and they shall become your property. ⁴⁶And you may take them as an inheritance for your children after you, to inherit *them as* a possession; they shall be your permanent slaves. But regarding your brethren, the children of Israel, you shall not rule over one another with rigor.

⁴⁷'Now if a sojourner or stranger close to you becomes rich, and *one of* your brethren *who dwells* by him becomes poor, and sells himself to the stranger *or* sojourner close to you, or to a member of the stranger's family, ⁴⁸after he is sold he may be redeemed again. One of his brothers may redeem him; ⁴⁹or his uncle or his uncle's son may redeem him; or *anyone* who is near of kin to him in his family may redeem him; or if he is able he may redeem himself. ⁵⁰Thus he shall reckon with him who bought him: The price of his release shall be according to the number of years, from the year that he was sold to him until the Year of Jubilee; *it shall be* according to the time of a hired servant for him. ⁵¹If *there are* still many years *remaining,* according to them he shall repay the price of his redemption from the money with which he was bought. ⁵²And if there remain but a few years until the Year of Jubilee, then he shall reckon with him, *and* according to his years he shall repay him the price of his redemption. ⁵³He shall be with him as a yearly hired servant, and he shall not rule with rigor over him in your sight. ⁵⁴And if he is not redeemed in these *years,* then he shall be released in the Year of Jubilee—he and his children with him. ⁵⁵For the children of Israel *are* servants to Me; they *are* My servants whom I brought out of the land of Egypt: I *am* the LORD your God.

Promise of Blessing and Retribution

26 'You shall not make idols for yourselves;
neither a carved image nor a *sacred* pillar shall you rear up for yourselves;
nor shall you set up an engraved stone in your land, to bow down to it;
for I *am* the LORD your God.

² You shall keep My Sabbaths and reverence My sanctuary:
I *am* the LORD.

³ 'If you walk in My statutes and keep My commandments, and perform them,
⁴ then I will give you rain in its season, the land shall yield its produce, and the trees of the field shall yield their fruit.
⁵ Your threshing shall last till the time of vintage, and the vintage shall last till the time of sowing;
you shall eat your bread to the full, and dwell in your land safely.
⁶ I will give peace in the land, and you shall lie down, and none will make *you* afraid;
I will rid the land of evil beasts, and the sword will not go through your land.
⁷ You will chase your enemies, and they shall fall by the sword before you.
⁸ Five of you shall chase a hundred, and a hundred of you shall put ten thousand to flight;
your enemies shall fall by the sword before you.

⁹ 'For I will look on you favorably and make you fruitful, multiply you and confirm My covenant with you.
¹⁰ You shall eat the old harvest, and clear out the old because of the new.
¹¹ I will set My tabernacle among you, and My soul shall not abhor you.
¹² I will walk among you and be your God, and you shall be My people.
¹³ I *am* the LORD your God, who brought you out of the land of Egypt, that *you* should not be their slaves;
I have broken the bands of your yoke and made you walk upright.

¹⁴ 'But if you do not obey Me, and do not observe all these commandments,
¹⁵ and if you despise My statutes, or if your soul abhors My judgments, so that you do not perform all My commandments, *but* break My covenant,

16 I also will do this to you:
I will even appoint terror over you,
wasting disease and fever which shall
consume the eyes and cause sorrow
of heart.
And you shall sow your seed in vain,
for your enemies shall eat it.

17 I will set My face against you, and you
shall be defeated by your enemies.
Those who hate you shall reign over
you, and you shall flee when no one
pursues you.

18 'And after all this, if you do not obey Me,
then I will punish you seven times
more for your sins.

19 I will break the pride of your power;
I will make your heavens like iron and
your earth like bronze.

20 And your strength shall be spent in
vain;
for your land shall not yield its produce,
nor shall the trees of the land yield
their fruit.

21 'Then, if you walk contrary to Me, and
are not willing to obey Me, I will bring
on you seven times more plagues,
according to your sins.

22 I will also send wild beasts among you,
which shall rob you of your children,
destroy your livestock, and make you
few in number;
and your highways shall be desolate.

23 'And if by these things you are not
reformed by Me, but walk contrary to
Me,

24 then I also will walk contrary to you,
and I will punish you yet seven times
for your sins.

25 And I will bring a sword against you
that will execute the vengeance of
the covenant;
when you are gathered together within
your cities I will send pestilence
among you;
and you shall be delivered into the
hand of the enemy.

26 When I have cut off your supply of
bread, ten women shall bake your
bread in one oven, and they shall
bring back your bread by weight, and
you shall eat and not be satisfied.

27 'And after all this, if you do not obey
Me, but walk contrary to Me,

28 then I also will walk contrary to you in
fury;
and I, even I, will chastise you seven
times for your sins.

29 You shall eat the flesh of your sons, and
you shall eat the flesh of your
daughters.

30 I will destroy your high places, cut
down your incense altars, and cast
your carcasses on the lifeless forms of
your idols;
and My soul shall abhor you.

31 I will lay your cities waste and bring
your sanctuaries to desolation, and I
will not smell the fragrance of your
sweet aromas.

32 I will bring the land to desolation, and
your enemies who dwell in it shall be
astonished at it.

33 I will scatter you among the nations
and draw out a sword after you;
your land shall be desolate and your
cities waste.

34 Then the land shall enjoy its sabbaths
as long as it lies desolate and you *are*
in your enemies' land;
then the land shall rest and enjoy its
sabbaths.

35 As long as *it* lies desolate it shall rest—
for the time it did not rest on your
sabbaths when you dwelt in it.

36 'And as for those of you who are left, I
will send faintness into their hearts
in the lands of their enemies;
the sound of a shaken leaf shall cause
them to flee;
they shall flee as though fleeing from a
sword, and they shall fall when no
one pursues.

37 They shall stumble over one another,
as it were before a sword, when no
one pursues;
and you shall have no *power* to stand
before your enemies.

38 You shall perish among the nations,
    and the land of your enemies shall
    eat you up.
39 And those of you who are left shall
    waste away in their iniquity in your
    enemies' lands;
    also in their fathers' iniquities, which
    are with them, they shall waste away.

40 'But if they confess their iniquity and the
    iniquity of their fathers, with their
    unfaithfulness in which they were
    unfaithful to Me, and that they also
    have walked contrary to Me,
41 and that I also have walked contrary to
    them and have brought them into
    the land of their enemies;
    if their uncircumcised hearts are hum-
    bled, and they accept their guilt—
42 then I will remember My covenant with
    Jacob, and My covenant with Isaac
    and My covenant with Abraham I
    will remember;
    I will remember the land.
43 The land also shall be left empty by
    them, and will enjoy its sabbaths
    while it lies desolate without them;
    they will accept their guilt, because they
    despised My judgments and because
    their soul abhorred My statutes.
44 Yet for all that, when they are in the
    land of their enemies, I will not cast
    them away, nor shall I abhor them,
    to utterly destroy them and break My
    covenant with them;
    for I am the LORD their God.
45 But for their sake I will remember the
    covenant of their ancestors, whom I
    brought out of the land of Egypt in
    the sight of the nations, that I might
    be their God:
    I am the LORD.' "

46These are the statutes and judgments
and laws which the LORD made between
Himself and the children of Israel on
Mount Sinai by the hand of Moses.

Redeeming Persons and Property Dedicated to God

27 Now the LORD spoke to Moses, saying,
2"Speak to the children of Israel, and
say to them: 'When a man consecrates by
a vow certain persons to the LORD, according
to your valuation, 3if your valuation is of a
male from twenty years old up to sixty years
old, then your valuation shall be fifty
shekels of silver, according to the shekel of
the sanctuary. 4If it is a female, then your
valuation shall be thirty shekels; 5and if
from five years old up to twenty years old,
then your valuation for a male shall be
twenty shekels, and for a female ten shekels;
6and if from a month old up to five years
old, then your valuation for a male shall be
five shekels of silver, and for a female your
valuation shall be three shekels of silver;
7and if from sixty years old and above, if it
is a male, then your valuation shall be fifteen shekels, and for a female ten shekels.

8'But if he is too poor to pay your valuation, then he shall present himself before
the priest, and the priest shall set a value
for him; according to the ability of him who
vowed, the priest shall value him.

9'If it is an animal that men may bring
as an offering to the LORD, all that anyone
gives to the LORD shall be holy. 10He shall
not substitute it or exchange it, good for bad
or bad for good; and if he at all exchanges
animal for animal, then both it and the
one exchanged for it shall be holy. 11If it is
an unclean animal which they do not offer
as a sacrifice to the LORD, then he shall
present the animal before the priest; 12and
the priest shall set a value for it, whether it
is good or bad; as you, the priest, value it, so
it shall be. 13But if he wants at all to redeem
it, then he must add one-fifth to your valuation.

14'And when a man dedicates his house
to be holy to the LORD, then the priest shall
set a value for it, whether it is good or bad;
as the priest values it, so it shall stand. 15If
he who dedicated it wants to redeem his
house, then he must add one-fifth of the
money of your valuation to it, and it shall
be his.

16'If a man dedicates to the LORD part of
a field of his possession, then your valuation shall be according to the seed for it. A
homer of barley seed shall be valued at fifty
shekels of silver. 17If he dedicates his field

from the Year of Jubilee, according to your valuation it shall stand. [18]But if he dedicates his field after the Jubilee, then the priest shall reckon to him the money due according to the years that remain till the Year of Jubilee, and it shall be deducted from your valuation. [19]And if he who dedicates the field ever wishes to redeem it, then he must add one-fifth of the money of your valuation to it, and it shall belong to him. [20]But if he does not want to redeem the field, or if he has sold the field to another man, it shall not be redeemed anymore; [21]but the field, when it is released in the Jubilee, shall be holy to the LORD, as a devoted field; it shall be the possession of the priest.

[22]'And if a man dedicates to the LORD a field which he has bought, which is not the field of his possession, [23]then the priest shall reckon to him the worth of your valuation, up to the Year of Jubilee, and he shall give your valuation on that day as a holy offering to the LORD. [24]In the Year of Jubilee the field shall return to him from whom it was bought, to the one who owned the land as a possession. [25]And all your valuations shall be according to the shekel of the sanctuary: twenty gerahs to the shekel.

[26]'But the firstborn of the animals, which should be the LORD's firstborn, no man shall dedicate; whether it is an ox or sheep, it is the LORD's. [27]And if it is an unclean animal, then he shall redeem it according to your valuation, and shall add one-fifth to it; or if it is not redeemed, then it shall be sold according to your valuation.

[28]'Nevertheless no devoted offering that a man may devote to the LORD of all that he has, both man and beast, or the field of his possession, shall be sold or redeemed; every devoted offering is most holy to the LORD. [29]No person under the ban, who may become doomed to destruction among men, shall be redeemed, but shall surely be put to death. [30]And all the tithe of the land, whether of the seed of the land or of the fruit of the tree, is the LORD's. It is holy to the LORD. [31]If a man wants at all to redeem any of his tithes, he shall add one-fifth to it. [32]And concerning the tithe of the herd or the flock, of whatever passes under the rod, the tenth one shall be holy to the LORD. [33]He shall not inquire whether it is good or bad, nor shall he exchange it; and if he exchanges it at all, then both it and the one exchanged for it shall be holy; it shall not be redeemed.'"

[34]These are the commandments which the LORD commanded Moses for the children of Israel on Mount Sinai.

NUMBERS

Author: Moses

When Written: Around 1400 B.C.

Theme: Wanderings

Key Verses: Numbers 14:22, 23—". . . because all these men who have seen My glory and the signs which I did in Egypt and in the wilderness, and have put Me to the test now these ten times, and have not heeded My voice, they certainly shall not see the land of which I swore to their fathers, nor shall any of those who rejected Me see it."

Key Chapter: Numbers 14—This chapter represents a critical turning point for Israel as the people choose to reject God by refusing to go up and conquer the Promised Land.

America's rich history is filled with accounts of men and women who left the comfort and familiarity of their homes and families in search of greater freedom and opportunity. With hearts set on adventure, these early pioneers braved hardships and hazards to claim their personal "promised land." It was a life that required courage, determination, and faith in God.

Similarly, the Book of Numbers recounts one of the greatest adventures in history, as God prepares His people to conquer the land of "milk and honey" that He had promised them throughout previous generations. Before they can succeed, however, they must deal with the fear and doubt that grip them. God requires that those called by His Name put their faith in Him alone. Numbers shows the process by which He brings His people to that place of trust and leads them into blessing.

NUMBERS

The First Census of Israel

1 Now the LORD spoke to Moses in the Wilderness of Sinai, in the tabernacle of meeting, on the first *day* of the second month, in the second year after they had come out of the land of Egypt, saying: ²"Take a census of all the congregation of the children of Israel, by their families, by their fathers' houses, according to the number of names, every male individually, ³from twenty years old and above—all who *are able to* go to war in Israel. You and Aaron shall number them by their armies. ⁴And with you there shall be a man from every tribe, each one the head of his father's house.

⁵"These are the names of the men who shall stand with you: from Reuben, Elizur the son of Shedeur; ⁶from Simeon, Shelumiel the son of Zurishaddai; ⁷from Judah, Nahshon the son of Amminadab; ⁸from Issachar, Nethanel the son of Zuar; ⁹from Zebulun, Eliab the son of Helon; ¹⁰from the sons of Joseph: from Ephraim, Elishama the son of Ammihud; from Manasseh, Gamaliel the son of Pedahzur; ¹¹from Benjamin, Abidan the son of Gideoni; ¹²from Dan, Ahiezer the son of Ammishaddai; ¹³from Asher, Pagiel the son of Ocran; ¹⁴from Gad, Eliasaph the son of Deuel;ᵃ ¹⁵from Naphtali, Ahira the son of Enan." ¹⁶These *were* chosen from the congregation, leaders of their fathers' tribes, heads of the divisions in Israel.

¹⁷Then Moses and Aaron took these men who had been mentioned by name, ¹⁸and they assembled all the congregation together on the first *day* of the second month; and they recited their ancestry by families, by their fathers' houses, according to the number of names, from twenty years old and above, each one individually. ¹⁹As the LORD commanded Moses, so he numbered them in the Wilderness of Sinai.

²⁰Now the children of Reuben, Israel's oldest son, their genealogies by their families, by their fathers' house, according to the number of names, every male individually, from twenty years old and above, all who *were able to* go to war: ²¹those who were numbered of the tribe of Reuben *were* forty-six thousand five hundred.

²²From the children of Simeon, their genealogies by their families, by their fathers' house, of those who were numbered, according to the number of names, every male individually, from twenty years old and above, all who *were able to* go to war: ²³those who were numbered of the tribe of Simeon *were* fifty-nine thousand three hundred.

²⁴From the children of Gad, their genealogies by their families, by their fathers' house, according to the number of names, from twenty years old and above, all who *were able to* go to war: ²⁵those who were numbered of the tribe of Gad *were* forty-five thousand six hundred and fifty.

²⁶From the children of Judah, their genealogies by their families, by their fathers' house, according to the number of names, from twenty years old and above, all who *were able to* go to war: ²⁷those who were numbered of the tribe of Judah *were* seventy-four thousand six hundred.

²⁸From the children of Issachar, their genealogies by their families, by their fathers' house, according to the number of names, from twenty years old and above, all who *were able to* go to war: ²⁹those who were numbered of the tribe of Issachar *were* fifty-four thousand four hundred.

³⁰From the children of Zebulun, their genealogies by their families, by their fathers' house, according to the number of names, from twenty years old and above, all who *were able to* go to war: ³¹those who

---

1:14 ᵃSpelled *Reuel* in 2:14

were numbered of the tribe of Zebulun *were* fifty-seven thousand four hundred.

32From the sons of Joseph, the children of Ephraim, their genealogies by their families, by their fathers' house, according to the number of names, from twenty years old and above, all who *were able to* go to war: 33those who were numbered of the tribe of Ephraim *were* forty thousand five hundred.

34From the children of Manasseh, their genealogies by their families, by their fathers' house, according to the number of names, from twenty years old and above, all who *were able to* go to war: 35those who were numbered of the tribe of Manasseh *were* thirty-two thousand two hundred.

36From the children of Benjamin, their genealogies by their families, by their fathers' house, according to the number of names, from twenty years old and above, all who *were able to* go to war: 37those who were numbered of the tribe of Benjamin *were* thirty-five thousand four hundred.

38From the children of Dan, their genealogies by their families, by their fathers' house, according to the number of names, from twenty years old and above, all who *were able to* go to war: 39those who were numbered of the tribe of Dan *were* sixty-two thousand seven hundred.

40From the children of Asher, their genealogies by their families, by their fathers' house, according to the number of names, from twenty years old and above, all who *were able to* go to war: 41those who were numbered of the tribe of Asher *were* forty-one thousand five hundred.

42From the children of Naphtali, their genealogies by their families, by their fathers' house, according to the number of names, from twenty years old and above, all who *were able to* go to war: 43those who were numbered of the tribe of Naphtali *were* fifty-three thousand four hundred.

44These are the ones who were numbered, whom Moses and Aaron numbered, with the leaders of Israel, twelve men, each one representing his father's house. 45So all who were numbered of the children of Israel, by their fathers' houses, from twenty years old and above, all who *were able to*

go to war in Israel— 46all who were numbered were six hundred and three thousand five hundred and fifty.

47But the Levites were not numbered among them by their fathers' tribe; 48for the LORD had spoken to Moses, saying: 49"Only the tribe of Levi you shall not number, nor take a census of them among the children of Israel; 50but you shall appoint the Levites over the tabernacle of the Testimony, over all its furnishings, and over all things that belong to it; they shall carry the tabernacle and all its furnishings; they shall attend to it and camp around the tabernacle. 51And when the tabernacle is to go forward, the Levites shall take it down; and when the tabernacle is to be set up, the Levites shall set it up. The outsider who comes near shall be put to death. 52The children of Israel shall pitch their tents, everyone by his own camp, everyone by his own standard, according to their armies; 53but the Levites shall camp around the tabernacle of the Testimony, that there may be no wrath on the congregation of the children of Israel; and the Levites shall keep charge of the tabernacle of the Testimony."

54Thus the children of Israel did; according to all that the LORD commanded Moses, so they did.

The Tribes and Leaders by Armies

2 And the LORD spoke to Moses and Aaron, saying: 2"Everyone of the children of Israel shall camp by his own standard, beside the emblems of his father's house; they shall camp some distance from the tabernacle of meeting. 3On the east side, toward the rising of the sun, those of the standard of the forces with Judah shall camp according to their armies; and Nahshon the son of Amminadab *shall be* the leader of the children of Judah." 4And his army was numbered at seventy-four thousand six hundred.

5"Those who camp next to him *shall be* the tribe of Issachar, and Nethanel the son of Zuar *shall be* the leader of the children of Issachar." 6And his army was numbered at fifty-four thousand four hundred.

7"Then *comes* the tribe of Zebulun, and Eliab the son of Helon *shall be* the leader of the children of Zebulun." 8And his army was numbered at fifty-seven thousand four hundred. 9"All who were numbered according to their armies of the forces with Judah, one hundred and eighty-six thousand four hundred—these shall break camp first.

10"On the south side *shall be* the standard of the forces with Reuben according to their armies, and the leader of the children of Reuben *shall be* Elizur the son of Shedeur." 11And his army was numbered at forty-six thousand five hundred.

12"Those who camp next to him *shall be* the tribe of Simeon, and the leader of the children of Simeon *shall be* Shelumiel the son of Zurishaddai." 13And his army was numbered at fifty-nine thousand three hundred.

14"Then *comes* the tribe of Gad, and the leader of the children of Gad *shall be* Eliasaph the son of Reuel."ᵃ 15And his army was numbered at forty-five thousand six hundred and fifty. 16"All who were numbered according to their armies of the forces with Reuben, one hundred and fifty-one thousand four hundred and fifty—they shall be the second to break camp.

17"And the tabernacle of meeting shall move out with the camp of the Levites in the middle of the camps; as they camp, so they shall move out, everyone in his place, by their standards.

18"On the west side *shall be* the standard of the forces with Ephraim according to their armies, and the leader of the children of Ephraim *shall be* Elishama the son of Ammihud." 19And his army was numbered at forty thousand five hundred.

20"Next to him *comes* the tribe of Manasseh, and the leader of the children of Manasseh *shall be* Gamaliel the son of Pedahzur." 21And his army was numbered at thirty-two thousand two hundred.

22"Then *comes* the tribe of Benjamin, and the leader of the children of Benjamin *shall be* Abidan the son of Gideoni." 23And his army was numbered at thirty-five thousand four hundred. 24"All who were numbered according to their armies of the forces with Ephraim, one hundred and eight thousand one hundred—they shall be the third to break camp.

25"The standard of the forces with Dan *shall be* on the north side according to their armies, and the leader of the children of Dan *shall be* Ahiezer the son of Ammishaddai." 26And his army was numbered at sixty-two thousand seven hundred.

27"Those who camp next to him *shall be* the tribe of Asher, and the leader of the children of Asher *shall be* Pagiel the son of Ocran." 28And his army was numbered at forty-one thousand five hundred.

29"Then *comes* the tribe of Naphtali, and the leader of the children of Naphtali *shall be* Ahira the son of Enan." 30And his army was numbered at fifty-three thousand four hundred. 31"All who were numbered of the forces with Dan, one hundred and fifty-seven thousand six hundred—they shall break camp last, with their standards."

32These *are* the ones who were numbered of the children of Israel by their fathers' houses. All who were numbered according to their armies of the forces *were* six hundred and three thousand five hundred and fifty. 33But the Levites were not numbered among the children of Israel, just as the LORD commanded Moses.

34Thus the children of Israel did according to all that the LORD commanded Moses; so they camped by their standards and so they broke camp, each one by his family, according to their fathers' houses.

The Sons of Aaron

3 Now these *are* the records of Aaron and Moses when the LORD spoke with Moses on Mount Sinai. 2And these *are* the names of the sons of Aaron: Nadab, the firstborn, and Abihu, Eleazar, and Ithamar. 3These *are* the names of the sons of Aaron, the anointed priests, whom he consecrated to minister as priests. 4Nadab and Abihu had died before the LORD when they offered profane fire before the LORD in the Wilderness of Sinai; and they had no children. So Eleazar and Ithamar ministered as priests in the presence of Aaron their father.

2:14 ᵃSpelled *Deuel* in 1:14 and 7:42

The Levites Serve in the Tabernacle

⁵And the LORD spoke to Moses, saying: ⁶"Bring the tribe of Levi near, and present them before Aaron the priest, that they may serve him. ⁷And they shall attend to his needs and the needs of the whole congregation before the tabernacle of meeting, to do the work of the tabernacle. ⁸Also they shall attend to all the furnishings of the tabernacle of meeting, and to the needs of the children of Israel, to do the work of the tabernacle. ⁹And you shall give the Levites to Aaron and his sons; they *are* given entirely to him[a] from among the children of Israel. ¹⁰So you shall appoint Aaron and his sons, and they shall attend to their priesthood; but the outsider who comes near shall be put to death."

¹¹Then the LORD spoke to Moses, saying: ¹²"Now behold, I Myself have taken the Levites from among the children of Israel instead of every firstborn who opens the womb among the children of Israel. Therefore the Levites shall be Mine, ¹³because all the firstborn *are* Mine. On the day that I struck all the firstborn in the land of Egypt, I sanctified to Myself all the firstborn in Israel, both man and beast. They shall be Mine: I *am* the LORD."

Census of the Levites Commanded

¹⁴Then the LORD spoke to Moses in the Wilderness of Sinai, saying: ¹⁵"Number the children of Levi by their fathers' houses, by their families; you shall number every male from a month old and above."

¹⁶So Moses numbered them according to the word of the LORD, as he was commanded. ¹⁷These were the sons of Levi by their names: Gershon, Kohath, and Merari. ¹⁸And these *are* the names of the sons of Gershon by their families: Libni and Shimei. ¹⁹And the sons of Kohath by their families: Amram, Izehar, Hebron, and Uzziel. ²⁰And the sons of Merari by their families: Mahli and Mushi. These *are* the families of the Levites by their fathers' houses.

²¹From Gershon *came* the family of the Libnites and the family of the Shimites; these *were* the families of the Gershonites. ²²Those who were numbered, according to the number of all the males from a month old and above—of those who were numbered *there were* seven thousand five hundred. ²³The families of the Gershonites were to camp behind the tabernacle westward. ²⁴And the leader of the father's house of the Gershonites *was* Eliasaph the son of Lael. ²⁵The duties of the children of Gershon in the tabernacle of meeting *included* the tabernacle, the tent with its covering, the screen for the door of the tabernacle of meeting, ²⁶the screen for the door of the court, the hangings of the court which *are* around the tabernacle and the altar, and their cords, according to all the work relating to them.

²⁷From Kohath *came* the family of the Amramites, the family of the Izharites, the family of the Hebronites, and the family of the Uzzielites; these *were* the families of the Kohathites. ²⁸According to the number of all the males, from a month old and above, *there were* eight thousand six[a] hundred keeping charge of the sanctuary. ²⁹The families of the children of Kohath were to camp on the south side of the tabernacle. ³⁰And the leader of the fathers' house of the families of the Kohathites *was* Elizaphan the son of Uzziel. ³¹Their duty *included* the ark, the table, the lampstand, the altars, the utensils of the sanctuary with which they ministered, the screen, and all the work relating to them.

³²And Eleazar the son of Aaron the priest *was to be* chief over the leaders of the Levites, *with* oversight of those who kept charge of the sanctuary.

³³From Merari *came* the family of the Mahlites and the family of the Mushites; these *were* the families of Merari. ³⁴And those who were numbered, according to the number of all the males from a month old and above, *were* six thousand two hundred. ³⁵The leader of the fathers' house of the families of Merari *was* Zuriel the son of Abihail. These *were* to camp on the north side of the tabernacle. ³⁶And the appointed duty of the children of Merari *included* the boards of the tabernacle, its bars, its pillars,

---

3:9 [a]Samaritan Pentateuch and Septuagint read *Me*.
3:28 [a]Some manuscripts of the Septuagint read *three*.

its sockets, its utensils, all the work relating to them, [37]and the pillars of the court all around, with their sockets, their pegs, and their cords.

[38]Moreover those who were to camp before the tabernacle on the east, before the tabernacle of meeting, *were* Moses, Aaron, and his sons, keeping charge of the sanctuary, to meet the needs of the children of Israel; but the outsider who came near was to be put to death. [39]All who were numbered of the Levites, whom Moses and Aaron numbered at the commandment of the LORD, by their families, all the males from a month old and above, *were* twenty-two thousand.

Levites Dedicated Instead of the Firstborn

[40]Then the LORD said to Moses: "Number all the firstborn males of the children of Israel from a month old and above, and take the number of their names. [41]And you shall take the Levites for Me—I *am* the LORD—instead of all the firstborn among the children of Israel, and the livestock of the Levites instead of all the firstborn among the livestock of the children of Israel." [42]So Moses numbered all the firstborn among the children of Israel, as the LORD commanded him. [43]And all the firstborn males, according to the number of names from a month old and above, of those who were numbered of them, were twenty-two thousand two hundred and seventy-three.

[44]Then the LORD spoke to Moses, saying: [45]"Take the Levites instead of all the firstborn among the children of Israel, and the livestock of the Levites instead of their livestock. The Levites shall be Mine: I *am* the LORD. [46]And for the redemption of the two hundred and seventy-three of the firstborn of the children of Israel, who are more than the number of the Levites, [47]you shall take five shekels for each one individually; you shall take *them* in the currency of the shekel of the sanctuary, the shekel of twenty gerahs. [48]And you shall give the money, with which the excess number of them is redeemed, to Aaron and his sons."

[49]So Moses took the redemption money from those who were over and above those who were redeemed by the Levites. [50]From the firstborn of the children of Israel he took the money, one thousand three hundred and sixty-five *shekels,* according to the shekel of the sanctuary. [51]And Moses gave their redemption money to Aaron and his sons, according to the word of the LORD, as the LORD commanded Moses.

Duties of the Sons of Kohath

4 Then the LORD spoke to Moses and Aaron, saying: [2]"Take a census of the sons of Kohath from among the children of Levi, by their families, by their fathers' house, [3]from thirty years old and above, even to fifty years old, all who enter the service to do the work in the tabernacle of meeting.

[4]"This *is* the service of the sons of Kohath in the tabernacle of meeting, *relating to* the most holy things: [5]When the camp prepares to journey, Aaron and his sons shall come, and they shall take down the covering veil and cover the ark of the Testimony with it. [6]Then they shall put on it a covering of badger skins, and spread over *that* a cloth entirely of blue; and they shall insert its poles.

[7]"On the table of showbread they shall spread a blue cloth, and put on it the dishes, the pans, the bowls, and the pitchers for pouring; and the showbread[a] shall be on it. [8]They shall spread over them a scarlet cloth, and cover the same with a covering of badger skins; and they shall insert its poles. [9]And they shall take a blue cloth and cover the lampstand of the light, with its lamps, its wick-trimmers, its trays, and all its oil vessels, with which they service it. [10]Then they shall put it with all its utensils in a covering of badger skins, and put *it* on a carrying beam.

[11]"Over the golden altar they shall spread a blue cloth, and cover it with a covering of badger skins; and they shall insert its poles. [12]Then they shall take all the utensils of service with which they minister in the sanctuary, put *them* in a blue cloth, cover them with a covering of badger skins, and put *them* on a carrying

---

4:7 [a]Literally *the continual bread*

beam. [13]Also they shall take away the ashes from the altar, and spread a purple cloth over it. [14]They shall put on it all its implements with which they minister there—the firepans, the forks, the shovels, the basins, and all the utensils of the altar—and they shall spread on it a covering of badger skins, and insert its poles. [15]And when Aaron and his sons have finished covering the sanctuary and all the furnishings of the sanctuary, when the camp is set to go, then the sons of Kohath shall come to carry *them;* but they shall not touch any holy thing, lest they die.

"These *are* the things in the tabernacle of meeting which the sons of Kohath are to carry.

[16]"The appointed duty of Eleazar the son of Aaron the priest *is* the oil for the light, the sweet incense, the daily grain offering, the anointing oil, the oversight of all the tabernacle, of all that *is* in it, with the sanctuary and its furnishings."

[17]Then the Lord spoke to Moses and Aaron, saying: [18]"Do not cut off the tribe of the families of the Kohathites from among the Levites; [19]but do this in regard to them, that they may live and not die when they approach the most holy things: Aaron and his sons shall go in and appoint each of them to his service and his task. [20]But they shall not go in to watch while the holy things are being covered, lest they die."

Duties of the Sons of Gershon

[21]Then the Lord spoke to Moses, saying: [22]"Also take a census of the sons of Gershon, by their fathers' house, by their families. [23]From thirty years old and above, even to fifty years old, you shall number them, all who enter to perform the service, to do the work in the tabernacle of meeting. [24]This *is* the service of the families of the Gershonites, in serving and carrying: [25]They shall carry the curtains of the tabernacle and the tabernacle of meeting *with* its covering, the covering of badger skins that *is* on it, the screen for the door of the tabernacle of meeting, [26]the screen for the door of the gate of the court, the hangings of the court which *are* around the tabernacle and

altar, and their cords, all the furnishings for their service and all that is made for these things: so shall they serve.

[27]"Aaron and his sons shall assign all the service of the sons of the Gershonites, all their tasks and all their service. And you shall appoint to them all their tasks as their duty. [28]This *is* the service of the families of the sons of Gershon in the tabernacle of meeting. And their duties *shall be* under the authority[a] of Ithamar the son of Aaron the priest.

Duties of the Sons of Merari

[29]"*As for* the sons of Merari, you shall number them by their families and by their fathers' house. [30]From thirty years old and above, even to fifty years old, you shall number them, everyone who enters the service to do the work of the tabernacle of meeting. [31]And this *is* what they must carry as all their service for the tabernacle of meeting: the boards of the tabernacle, its bars, its pillars, its sockets, [32]and the pillars around the court with their sockets, pegs, and cords, with all their furnishings and all their service; and you shall assign *to each man* by name the items he must carry. [33]This *is* the service of the families of the sons of Merari, as all their service for the tabernacle of meeting, under the authority[a] of Ithamar the son of Aaron the priest."

Census of the Levites

[34]And Moses, Aaron, and the leaders of the congregation numbered the sons of the Kohathites by their families and by their fathers' house, [35]from thirty years old and above, even to fifty years old, everyone who entered the service for work in the tabernacle of meeting; [36]and those who were numbered by their families were two thousand seven hundred and fifty. [37]These *were* the ones who were numbered of the families of the Kohathites, all who might serve in the tabernacle of meeting, whom Moses and Aaron numbered according to the commandment of the Lord by the hand of Moses.

4:28 [a]Literally *hand*   **4:33** [a]Literally *hand*

³⁸And those who were numbered of the sons of Gershon, by their families and by their fathers' house, ³⁹from thirty years old and above, even to fifty years old, everyone who entered the service for work in the tabernacle of meeting— ⁴⁰those who were numbered by their families, by their fathers' house, were two thousand six hundred and thirty. ⁴¹These *are* the ones who were numbered of the families of the sons of Gershon, of all who might serve in the tabernacle of meeting, whom Moses and Aaron numbered according to the commandment of the LORD.

⁴²Those of the families of the sons of Merari who were numbered, by their families, by their fathers' house, ⁴³from thirty years old and above, even to fifty years old, everyone who entered the service for work in the tabernacle of meeting— ⁴⁴those who were numbered by their families were three thousand two hundred. ⁴⁵These *are* the ones who were numbered of the families of the sons of Merari, whom Moses and Aaron numbered according to the word of the LORD by the hand of Moses.

⁴⁶All who were numbered of the Levites, whom Moses, Aaron, and the leaders of Israel numbered, by their families and by their fathers' houses, ⁴⁷from thirty years old and above, even to fifty years old, everyone who came to do the work of service and the work of bearing burdens in the tabernacle of meeting— ⁴⁸those who were numbered were eight thousand five hundred and eighty. ⁴⁹According to the commandment of the LORD they were numbered by the hand of Moses, each according to his service and according to his task; thus were they numbered by him, as the LORD commanded Moses.

Ceremonially Unclean Persons Isolated

5 And the LORD spoke to Moses, saying: ²"Command the children of Israel that they put out of the camp every leper, everyone who has a discharge, and whoever becomes defiled by a corpse. ³You shall put out both male and female; you shall put them outside the camp, that they may not defile their camps in the midst of which I dwell." ⁴And the children of Israel did so, and put them outside the camp; as the LORD spoke to Moses, so the children of Israel did.

Confession and Restitution

⁵Then the LORD spoke to Moses, saying, ⁶"Speak to the children of Israel: 'When a man or woman commits any sin that men commit in unfaithfulness against the LORD, and that person is guilty, ⁷then he shall confess the sin which he has committed. He shall make restitution for his trespass in full, plus one-fifth of it, and give *it* to the one he has wronged. ⁸But if the man has no relative to whom restitution may be made for the wrong, the restitution for the wrong *must go* to the LORD for the priest, in addition to the ram of the atonement with which atonement is made for him. ⁹Every offering of all the holy things of the children of Israel, which they bring to the priest, shall be his. ¹⁰And every man's holy things shall be his; whatever any man gives the priest shall be his.' "

Concerning Unfaithful Wives

¹¹And the LORD spoke to Moses, saying, ¹²"Speak to the children of Israel, and say to them: 'If any man's wife goes astray and behaves unfaithfully toward him, ¹³and a man lies with her carnally, and it is hidden from the eyes of her husband, and it is concealed that she has defiled herself, and *there was* no witness against her, nor was she caught— ¹⁴if the spirit of jealousy comes upon him and he becomes jealous of his wife, who has defiled herself; or if the spirit of jealousy comes upon him and he becomes jealous of his wife, although she has not defiled herself— ¹⁵then the man shall bring his wife to the priest. He shall bring the offering required for her, one-tenth of an ephah of barley meal; he shall pour no oil on it and put no frankincense on it, because it *is* a grain offering of jealousy, an offering for remembering, for bringing iniquity to remembrance.

¹⁶'And the priest shall bring her near, and set her before the LORD. ¹⁷The priest

shall take holy water in an earthen vessel, and take some of the dust that is on the floor of the tabernacle and put *it* into the water. ¹⁸Then the priest shall stand the woman before the LORD, uncover the woman's head, and put the offering for remembering in her hands, which *is* the grain offering of jealousy. And the priest shall have in his hand the bitter water that brings a curse. ¹⁹And the priest shall put her under oath, and say to the woman, "If no man has lain with you, and if you have not gone astray to uncleanness *while* under your husband's *authority,* be free from this bitter water that brings a curse. ²⁰But if you have gone astray *while* under your husband's *authority,* and if you have defiled yourself and some man other than your husband has lain with you"— ²¹then the priest shall put the woman under the oath of the curse, and he shall say to the woman—"the LORD make you a curse and an oath among your people, when the LORD makes your thigh rot and your belly swell; ²²and may this water that causes the curse go into your stomach, and make *your* belly swell and *your* thigh rot."

Then the woman shall say, "Amen, so be it."

²³'Then the priest shall write these curses in a book, and he shall scrape *them* off into the bitter water. ²⁴And he shall make the woman drink the bitter water that brings a curse, and the water that brings the curse shall enter her *to become* bitter. ²⁵Then the priest shall take the grain offering of jealousy from the woman's hand, shall wave the offering before the LORD, and bring it to the altar; ²⁶and the priest shall take a handful of the offering, as its memorial portion, burn *it* on the altar, and afterward make the woman drink the water. ²⁷When he has made her drink the water, then it shall be, if she has defiled herself and behaved unfaithfully toward her husband, that the water that brings a curse will enter her *and become* bitter, and her belly will swell, her thigh will rot, and the woman will become a curse among her people. ²⁸But if the woman has not defiled herself, and is clean, then she shall be free and may conceive children.

²⁹'This *is* the law of jealousy, when a wife, *while* under her husband's *authority,* goes astray and defiles herself, ³⁰or when the spirit of jealousy comes upon a man, and he becomes jealous of his wife; then he shall stand the woman before the LORD, and the priest shall execute all this law upon her. ³¹Then the man shall be free from iniquity, but that woman shall bear her guilt.'"

The Law of the Nazirite

6 Then the LORD spoke to Moses, saying, ²"Speak to the children of Israel, and say to them: 'When either a man or woman consecrates an offering to take the vow of a Nazirite, to separate himself to the LORD, ³he shall separate himself from wine and *similar* drink; he shall drink neither vinegar made from wine nor vinegar made from *similar* drink; neither shall he drink any grape juice, nor eat fresh grapes or raisins. ⁴All the days of his separation he shall eat nothing that is produced by the grapevine, from seed to skin.

⁵'All the days of the vow of his separation no razor shall come upon his head; until the days are fulfilled for which he separated himself to the LORD, he shall be holy. *Then* he shall let the locks of the hair of his head grow. ⁶All the days that he separates himself to the LORD he shall not go near a dead body. ⁷He shall not make himself unclean even for his father or his mother, for his brother or his sister, when they die, because his separation to God *is* on his head. ⁸All the days of his separation he shall be holy to the LORD.

⁹'And if anyone dies very suddenly beside him, and he defiles his consecrated head, then he shall shave his head on the day of his cleansing; on the seventh day he shall shave it. ¹⁰Then on the eighth day he shall bring two turtledoves or two young pigeons to the priest, to the door of the tabernacle of meeting; ¹¹and the priest shall offer one as a sin offering and *the* other as a burnt offering, and make atonement for him, because he sinned in regard to the corpse; and he shall sanctify his head that same day. ¹²He shall consecrate to the LORD

the days of his separation, and bring a male lamb in its first year as a trespass offering; but the former days shall be lost, because his separation was defiled.

13'Now this *is* the law of the Nazirite: When the days of his separation are fulfilled, he shall be brought to the door of the tabernacle of meeting. 14And he shall present his offering to the LORD: one male lamb in its first year without blemish as a burnt offering, one ewe lamb in its first year without blemish as a sin offering, one ram without blemish as a peace offering, 15a basket of unleavened bread, cakes of fine flour mixed with oil, unleavened wafers anointed with oil, and their grain offering with their drink offerings.

16'Then the priest shall bring *them* before the LORD and offer his sin offering and his burnt offering; 17and he shall offer the ram as a sacrifice of a peace offering to the LORD, with the basket of unleavened bread; the priest shall also offer its grain offering and its drink offering. 18Then the Nazirite shall shave his consecrated head *at* the door of the tabernacle of meeting, and shall take the hair from his consecrated head and put *it* on the fire which is under the sacrifice of the peace offering.

19'And the priest shall take the boiled shoulder of the ram, one unleavened cake from the basket, and one unleavened wafer, and put *them* upon the hands of the Nazirite after he has shaved his consecrated *hair,* 20and the priest shall wave them as a wave offering before the LORD; they *are* holy for the priest, together with the breast of the wave offering and the thigh of the heave offering. After that the Nazirite may drink wine.'

21"This is the law of the Nazirite who vows to the LORD the offering for his separation, and besides that, whatever else his hand is able to provide; according to the vow which he takes, so he must do according to the law of his separation."

The Priestly Blessing

22And the LORD spoke to Moses, saying: 23"Speak to Aaron and his sons, saying, 'This is the way you shall bless the children of Israel. Say to them:

24 "The LORD bless you and keep you;
25   The LORD make His face shine upon
      you,
   And be gracious to you;
26   The LORD lift up His countenance
      upon you,
   And give you peace." '

27"So they shall put My name on the children of Israel, and I will bless them."

Offerings of the Leaders

7 Now it came to pass, when Moses had finished setting up the tabernacle, that he anointed it and consecrated it and all its furnishings, and the altar and all its utensils; so he anointed them and consecrated them. 2Then the leaders of Israel, the heads of their fathers' houses, who *were* the leaders of the tribes and over those who were numbered, made an offering. 3And they brought their offering before the LORD, six covered carts and twelve oxen, a cart for *every* two of the leaders, and for each one an ox; and they presented them before the tabernacle.

4Then the LORD spoke to Moses, saying, 5"Accept *these* from them, that they may be used in doing the work of the tabernacle of meeting; and you shall give them to the Levites, *to* every man according to his service." 6So Moses took the carts and the oxen, and gave them to the Levites. 7Two carts and four oxen he gave to the sons of Gershon, according to their service; 8and four carts and eight oxen he gave to the sons of Merari, according to their service, under the authority[a] of Ithamar the son of Aaron the priest. 9But to the sons of Kohath he gave none, because theirs *was* the service of the holy things, *which* they carried on their shoulders.

10Now the leaders offered the dedication *offering* for the altar when it was anointed; so the leaders offered their offering before the altar. 11For the LORD said to Moses, "They shall offer their offering, one leader each day, for the dedication of the altar."

12And the one who offered his offering on the first day *was* Nahshon the son of

---

7:8 [a]Literally *hand*

Amminadab, from the tribe of Judah. [13]His offering *was* one silver platter, the weight of which *was* one hundred and thirty *shekels,* and one silver bowl of seventy shekels, according to the shekel of the sanctuary, both of them full of fine flour mixed with oil as a grain offering; [14]one gold pan of ten *shekels,* full of incense; [15]one young bull, one ram, and one male lamb in its first year, as a burnt offering; [16]one kid of the goats as a sin offering; [17]and for the sacrifice of peace offerings: two oxen, five rams, five male goats, and five male lambs in their first year. This *was* the offering of Nahshon the son of Amminadab.

[18]On the second day Nethanel the son of Zuar, leader of Issachar, presented *an offering.* [19]*For* his offering he offered one silver platter, the weight of which *was* one hundred and thirty *shekels,* and one silver bowl of seventy shekels, according to the shekel of the sanctuary, both of them full of fine flour mixed with oil as a grain offering; [20]one gold pan of ten *shekels,* full of incense; [21]one young bull, one ram, and one male lamb in its first year, as a burnt offering; [22]one kid of the goats as a sin offering; [23]and as the sacrifice of peace offerings: two oxen, five rams, five male goats, and five male lambs in their first year. This *was* the offering of Nethanel the son of Zuar.

[24]On the third day Eliab the son of Helon, leader of the children of Zebulun, *presented an offering.* [25]His offering *was* one silver platter, the weight of which *was* one hundred and thirty *shekels,* and one silver bowl of seventy shekels, according to the shekel of the sanctuary, both of them full of fine flour mixed with oil as a grain offering; [26]one gold pan of ten *shekels,* full of incense; [27]one young bull, one ram, and one male lamb in its first year, as a burnt offering; [28]one kid of the goats as a sin offering; [29]and for the sacrifice of peace offerings: two oxen, five rams, five male goats, and five male lambs in their first year. This *was* the offering of Eliab the son of Helon.

[30]On the fourth day Elizur the son of Shedeur, leader of the children of Reuben, *presented an offering.* [31]His offering *was* one silver platter, the weight of which *was* one

hundred and thirty *shekels,* and one silver bowl of seventy shekels, according to the shekel of the sanctuary, both of them full of fine flour mixed with oil as a grain offering; [32]one gold pan of ten *shekels,* full of incense; [33]one young bull, one ram, and one male lamb in its first year, as a burnt offering; [34]one kid of the goats as a sin offering; [35]and as the sacrifice of peace offerings: two oxen, five rams, five male goats, and five male lambs in their first year. This *was* the offering of Elizur the son of Shedeur.

[36]On the fifth day Shelumiel the son of Zurishaddai, leader of the children of Simeon, *presented an offering.* [37]His offering *was* one silver platter, the weight of which *was* one hundred and thirty *shekels,* and one silver bowl of seventy shekels, according to the shekel of the sanctuary, both of them full of fine flour mixed with oil as a grain offering; [38]one gold pan of ten *shekels,* full of incense; [39]one young bull, one ram, and one male lamb in its first year, as a burnt offering; [40]one kid of the goats as a sin offering; [41]and as the sacrifice of peace offerings: two oxen, five rams, five male goats, and five male lambs in their first year. This *was* the offering of Shelumiel the son of Zurishaddai.

[42]On the sixth day Eliasaph the son of Deuel,[a] leader of the children of Gad, *presented an offering.* [43]His offering *was* one silver platter, the weight of which *was* one hundred and thirty *shekels,* and one silver bowl of seventy shekels, according to the shekel of the sanctuary, both of them full of fine flour mixed with oil as a grain offering; [44]one gold pan of ten *shekels,* full of incense; [45]one young bull, one ram, and one male lamb in its first year, as a burnt offering; [46]one kid of the goats as a sin offering; [47]and as the sacrifice of peace offerings: two oxen, five rams, five male goats, and five male lambs in their first year. This *was* the offering of Eliasaph the son of Deuel.

[48]On the seventh day Elishama the son of Ammihud, leader of the children of Ephraim, *presented an offering.* [49]His offering *was* one silver platter, the weight of which

---

7:42 [a]Spelled *Reuel* in 2:14

was one hundred and thirty *shekels,* and one silver bowl of seventy shekels, according to the shekel of the sanctuary, both of them full of fine flour mixed with oil as a grain offering; ⁵⁰one gold pan of ten *shekels,* full of incense; ⁵¹one young bull, one ram, and one male lamb in its first year, as a burnt offering; ⁵²one kid of the goats as a sin offering; ⁵³and as the sacrifice of peace offerings: two oxen, five rams, five male goats, and five male lambs in their first year. This *was* the offering of Elishama the son of Ammihud.

⁵⁴On the eighth day Gamaliel the son of Pedahzur, leader of the children of Manasseh, *presented an offering.* ⁵⁵His offering *was* one silver platter, the weight of which *was* one hundred and thirty *shekels,* and one silver bowl of seventy shekels, according to the shekel of the sanctuary, both of them full of fine flour mixed with oil as a grain offering; ⁵⁶one gold pan of ten *shekels,* full of incense; ⁵⁷one young bull, one ram, and one male lamb in its first year, as a burnt offering; ⁵⁸one kid of the goats as a sin offering; ⁵⁹and as the sacrifice of peace offerings: two oxen, five rams, five male goats, and five male lambs in their first year. This *was* the offering of Gamaliel the son of Pedahzur.

⁶⁰On the ninth day Abidan the son of Gideoni, leader of the children of Benjamin, *presented an offering.* ⁶¹His offering *was* one silver platter, the weight of which *was* one hundred and thirty *shekels,* and one silver bowl of seventy shekels, according to the shekel of the sanctuary, both of them full of fine flour mixed with oil as a grain offering; ⁶²one gold pan of ten *shekels,* full of incense; ⁶³one young bull, one ram, and one male lamb in its first year, as a burnt offering; ⁶⁴one kid of the goats as a sin offering; ⁶⁵and as the sacrifice of peace offerings: two oxen, five rams, five male goats, and five male lambs in their first year. This *was* the offering of Abidan the son of Gideoni.

⁶⁶On the tenth day Ahiezer the son of Ammishaddai, leader of the children of Dan, *presented an offering.* ⁶⁷His offering *was* one silver platter, the weight of which

was one hundred and thirty *shekels,* and one silver bowl of seventy shekels, according to the shekel of the sanctuary, both of them full of fine flour mixed with oil as a grain offering; ⁶⁸one gold pan of ten *shekels,* full of incense; ⁶⁹one young bull, one ram, and one male lamb in its first year, as a burnt offering; ⁷⁰one kid of the goats as a sin offering; ⁷¹and as the sacrifice of peace offerings: two oxen, five rams, five male goats, and five male lambs in their first year. This *was* the offering of Ahiezer the son of Ammishaddai.

⁷²On the eleventh day Pagiel the son of Ocran, leader of the children of Asher, *presented an offering.* ⁷³His offering *was* one silver platter, the weight of which *was* one hundred and thirty *shekels,* and one silver bowl of seventy shekels, according to the shekel of the sanctuary, both of them full of fine flour mixed with oil as a grain offering; ⁷⁴one gold pan of ten *shekels,* full of incense; ⁷⁵one young bull, one ram, and one male lamb in its first year, as a burnt offering; ⁷⁶one kid of the goats as a sin offering; ⁷⁷and as the sacrifice of peace offerings: two oxen, five rams, five male goats, and five male lambs in their first year. This *was* the offering of Pagiel the son of Ocran.

⁷⁸On the twelfth day Ahira the son of Enan, leader of the children of Naphtali, *presented an offering.* ⁷⁹His offering *was* one silver platter, the weight of which *was* one hundred and thirty *shekels,* and one silver bowl of seventy shekels, according to the shekel of the sanctuary, both of them full of fine flour mixed with oil as a grain offering; ⁸⁰one gold pan of ten *shekels,* full of incense; ⁸¹one young bull, one ram, and one male lamb in its first year, as a burnt offering; ⁸²one kid of the goats as a sin offering; ⁸³and as the sacrifice of peace offerings: two oxen, five rams, five male goats, and five male lambs in their first year. This *was* the offering of Ahira the son of Enan.

⁸⁴This *was* the dedication *offering* for the altar from the leaders of Israel, when it was anointed: twelve silver platters, twelve silver bowls, and twelve gold pans. ⁸⁵Each silver platter *weighed* one hundred and thirty *shekels* and each bowl seventy *shekels.* All

the silver of the vessels *weighed* two thousand four hundred *shekels,* according to the shekel of the sanctuary. 86The twelve gold pans full of incense *weighed* ten *shekels* apiece, according to the shekel of the sanctuary; all the gold of the pans *weighed* one hundred and twenty *shekels.* 87All the oxen for the burnt offering *were* twelve young bulls, the rams twelve, the male lambs in their first year twelve, with their grain offering, and the kids of the goats as a sin offering twelve. 88And all the oxen for the sacrifice of peace offerings were twenty-four bulls, the rams sixty, the male goats sixty, and the lambs in their first year sixty. This *was* the dedication *offering* for the altar after it was anointed.

89Now when Moses went into the tabernacle of meeting to speak with Him, he heard the voice of One speaking to him from above the mercy seat that *was* on the ark of the Testimony, from between the two cherubim; thus He spoke to him.

Arrangement of the Lamps

8 And the LORD spoke to Moses, saying: 2"Speak to Aaron, and say to him, 'When you arrange the lamps, the seven lamps shall give light in front of the lampstand.'" 3And Aaron did so; he arranged the lamps to face toward the front of the lampstand, as the LORD commanded Moses. 4Now this workmanship of the lampstand *was* hammered gold; from its shaft to its flowers it *was* hammered work. According to the pattern which the LORD had shown Moses, so he made the lampstand.

Cleansing and Dedication of the Levites

5Then the LORD spoke to Moses, saying: 6"Take the Levites from among the children of Israel and cleanse them *ceremonially.* 7Thus you shall do to them to cleanse them: Sprinkle water of purification on them, and let them shave all their body, and let them wash their clothes, and *so* make themselves clean. 8Then let them take a young bull with its grain offering of fine flour mixed with oil, and you shall take another young bull as a sin offering.

9And you shall bring the Levites before the tabernacle of meeting, and you shall gather together the whole congregation of the children of Israel. 10So you shall bring the Levites before the LORD, and the children of Israel shall lay their hands on the Levites; 11and Aaron shall offer the Levites before the LORD *like* a wave offering from the children of Israel, that they may perform the work of the LORD. 12Then the Levites shall lay their hands on the heads of the young bulls, and you shall offer one as a sin offering and the other as a burnt offering to the LORD, to make atonement for the Levites.

13"And you shall stand the Levites before Aaron and his sons, and then offer them *like* a wave offering to the LORD. 14Thus you shall separate the Levites from among the children of Israel, and the Levites shall be Mine. 15After that the Levites shall go in to service the tabernacle of meeting. So you shall cleanse them and offer them *like* a wave offering. 16For they *are* wholly given to Me from among the children of Israel; I have taken them for Myself instead of all who open the womb, the firstborn of all the children of Israel. 17For all the firstborn among the children of Israel *are* Mine, *both* man and beast; on the day that I struck all the firstborn in the land of Egypt I sanctified them to Myself. 18I have taken the Levites instead of all the firstborn of the children of Israel. 19And I have given the Levites as a gift to Aaron and his sons from among the children of Israel, to do the work for the children of Israel in the tabernacle of meeting, and to make atonement for the children of Israel, that there be no plague among the children of Israel when the children of Israel come near the sanctuary."

20Thus Moses and Aaron and all the congregation of the children of Israel did to the Levites; according to all that the LORD commanded Moses concerning the Levites, so the children of Israel did to them. 21And the Levites purified themselves and washed their clothes; then Aaron presented them *like* a wave offering before the LORD, and Aaron made atonement for them to cleanse them. 22After that the Levites went in to do their work in the tabernacle of

meeting before Aaron and his sons; as the Lord commanded Moses concerning the Levites, so they did to them.

23Then the Lord spoke to Moses, saying, 24"This *is* what *pertains* to the Levites: From twenty-five years old and above one may enter to perform service in the work of the tabernacle of meeting; 25and at the age of fifty years they must cease performing this work, and shall work no more. 26They may minister with their brethren in the tabernacle of meeting, to attend to needs, but they *themselves* shall do no work. Thus you shall do to the Levites regarding their duties."

The Second Passover

9 Now the Lord spoke to Moses in the Wilderness of Sinai, in the first month of the second year after they had come out of the land of Egypt, saying: 2"Let the children of Israel keep the Passover at its appointed time. 3On the fourteenth day of this month, at twilight, you shall keep it at its appointed time. According to all its rites and ceremonies you shall keep it." 4So Moses told the children of Israel that they should keep the Passover. 5And they kept the Passover on the fourteenth day of the first month, at twilight, in the Wilderness of Sinai; according to all that the Lord commanded Moses, so the children of Israel did.

6Now there were *certain* men who were defiled by a human corpse, so that they could not keep the Passover on that day; and they came before Moses and Aaron that day. 7And those men said to him, "We *became* defiled by a human corpse. Why are we kept from presenting the offering of the Lord at its appointed time among the children of Israel?"

8And Moses said to them, "Stand still, that I may hear what the Lord will command concerning you."

9Then the Lord spoke to Moses, saying, 10"Speak to the children of Israel, saying: 'If anyone of you or your posterity is unclean because of a corpse, or *is* far away on a journey, he may still keep the Lord's Passover. 11On the fourteenth day of the second month, at twilight, they may keep it. They shall eat it with unleavened bread

and bitter herbs. 12They shall leave none of it until morning, nor break one of its bones. According to all the ordinances of the Passover they shall keep it. 13But the man who *is* clean and is not on a journey, and ceases to keep the Passover, that same person shall be cut off from among his people, because he did not bring the offering of the Lord at its appointed time; that man shall bear his sin.

14'And if a stranger dwells among you, and would keep the Lord's Passover, he must do so according to the rite of the Passover and according to its ceremony; you shall have one ordinance, both for the stranger and the native of the land.'"

The Cloud and the Fire

15Now on the day that the tabernacle was raised up, the cloud covered the tabernacle, the tent of the Testimony; from evening until morning it was above the tabernacle like the appearance of fire. 16So it was always: the cloud covered it *by day,* and the appearance of fire by night. 17Whenever the cloud was taken up from above the tabernacle, after that the children of Israel would journey; and in the place where the cloud settled, there the children of Israel would pitch their tents. 18At the command of the Lord the children of Israel would journey, and at the command of the Lord they would camp; as long as the cloud stayed above the tabernacle they remained encamped. 19Even when the cloud continued long, many days above the tabernacle, the children of Israel kept the charge of the Lord and did not journey. 20So it was, when the cloud was above the tabernacle a few days: according to the command of the Lord they would remain encamped, and according to the command of the Lord they would journey. 21So it was, when the cloud remained only from evening until morning: when the cloud was taken up in the morning, then they would journey; whether by day or by night, whenever the cloud was taken up, they would journey. 22*Whether it was* two days, a month, or a year that the cloud remained above the tabernacle, the children of Israel would remain encamped

and not journey; but when it was taken up, they would journey. ²³At the command of the LORD they remained encamped, and at the command of the LORD they journeyed; they kept the charge of the LORD, at the command of the LORD by the hand of Moses.

Two Silver Trumpets

10 And the LORD spoke to Moses, saying: ²"Make two silver trumpets for yourself; you shall make them of hammered work; you shall use them for calling the congregation and for directing the movement of the camps. ³When they blow both of them, all the congregation shall gather before you at the door of the tabernacle of meeting. ⁴But if they blow *only* one, then the leaders, the heads of the divisions of Israel, shall gather to you. ⁵When you sound the advance, the camps that lie on the east side shall then begin their journey. ⁶When you sound the advance the second time, then the camps that lie on the south side shall begin their journey; they shall sound the call for them to begin their journeys. ⁷And when the assembly is to be gathered together, you shall blow, but not sound the advance. ⁸The sons of Aaron, the priests, shall blow the trumpets; and these shall be to you as an ordinance forever throughout your generations.

⁹"When you go to war in your land against the enemy who oppresses you, then you shall sound an alarm with the trumpets, and you will be remembered before the LORD your God, and you will be saved from your enemies. ¹⁰Also in the day of your gladness, in your appointed feasts, and at the beginning of your months, you shall blow the trumpets over your burnt offerings and over the sacrifices of your peace offerings; and they shall be a memorial for you before your God: I *am* the LORD your God."

Departure from Sinai

¹¹Now it came to pass on the twentieth *day* of the second month, in the second year, that the cloud was taken up from above the tabernacle of the Testimony. ¹²And the children of Israel set out from the Wilderness of Sinai on their journeys; then the cloud settled down in the Wilderness of Paran. ¹³So they started out for the first time according to the command of the LORD by the hand of Moses.

¹⁴The standard of the camp of the children of Judah set out first according to their armies; over their army was Nahshon the son of Amminadab. ¹⁵Over the army of the tribe of the children of Issachar *was* Nethanel the son of Zuar. ¹⁶And over the army of the tribe of the children of Zebulun *was* Eliab the son of Helon.

¹⁷Then the tabernacle was taken down; and the sons of Gershon and the sons of Merari set out, carrying the tabernacle.

¹⁸And the standard of the camp of Reuben set out according to their armies; over their army *was* Elizur the son of Shedeur. ¹⁹Over the army of the tribe of the children of Simeon *was* Shelumiel the son of Zurishaddai. ²⁰And over the army of the tribe of the children of Gad *was* Eliasaph the son of Deuel.

²¹Then the Kohathites set out, carrying the holy things. (The tabernacle would be prepared for their arrival.)

²²And the standard of the camp of the children of Ephraim set out according to their armies; over their army *was* Elishama the son of Ammihud. ²³Over the army of the tribe of the children of Manasseh *was* Gamaliel the son of Pedahzur. ²⁴And over the army of the tribe of the children of Benjamin *was* Abidan the son of Gideoni.

²⁵Then the standard of the camp of the children of Dan (the rear guard of all the camps) set out according to their armies; over their army *was* Ahiezer the son of Ammishaddai. ²⁶Over the army of the tribe of the children of Asher *was* Pagiel the son of Ocran. ²⁷And over the army of the tribe of the children of Naphtali *was* Ahira the son of Enan.

²⁸Thus *was* the order of march of the children of Israel, according to their armies, when they began their journey.

²⁹Now Moses said to Hobab the son of Reuel[a] the Midianite, Moses' father-in-law,

10:29 ᵃSeptuagint reads *Raguel* (compare Exodus 2:18).

"We are setting out for the place of which the LORD said, 'I will give it to you.' Come with us, and we will treat you well; for the LORD has promised good things to Israel."

³⁰And he said to him, "I will not go, but I will depart to my *own* land and to my relatives."

³¹So *Moses* said, "Please do not leave, inasmuch as you know how we are to camp in the wilderness, and you can be our eyes. ³²And it shall be, if you go with us—indeed it shall be—that whatever good the LORD will do to us, the same we will do to you."

³³So they departed from the mountain of the LORD on a journey of three days; and the ark of the covenant of the LORD went before them for the three days' journey, to search out a resting place for them. ³⁴And the cloud of the LORD *was* above them by day when they went out from the camp.

³⁵So it was, whenever the ark set out, that Moses said:

"Rise up, O LORD!
Let Your enemies be scattered,
And let those who hate You flee before
You."

³⁶And when it rested, he said:

"Return, O LORD,
To the many thousands of Israel."

The People Complain

11 Now *when* the people complained, it displeased the LORD; for the LORD heard *it,* and His anger was aroused. So the fire of the LORD burned among them, and consumed *some* in the outskirts of the camp. ²Then the people cried out to Moses, and when Moses prayed to the LORD, the fire was quenched. ³So he called the name of the place Taberah,ᵃ because the fire of the LORD had burned among them.

11:3 ᵃLiterally *Burning*

PROTECTOR

". . . as a guardian carries a nursing child. . . ."

NUMBERS 11:12

Andrew Jackson

ETERNAL VIGILANCE

In his Farewell Address in 1837, President Andrew Jackson stated:

But you must remember, my fellow citizens, that eternal vigilance by the people is the price of liberty, and that you must pay the price if you wish to secure the blessing.

You have no longer any cause to fear danger from abroad; your strength and power are well known throughout the civilized world, as well as the high and gallant bearing of your sons. It is from within, among yourselves—from cupidity, from corruption, from disappointed ambition and inordinate thirst for power—that factions will be formed and liberty endangered. It is against such designs, whatever disguise the actors may assume, that you have especially to guard yourselves. You have the highest of human trusts committed to your care. Providence has showered on this favored land blessings without number, and has chosen you as the guardians of freedom, to preserve it for the benefit of the human race. May He who holds in His hands the destinies of nations make you worthy of the favors He has bestowed and enable you, with pure hearts and pure hands and sleepless vigilance, to guard and defend to the end of time the great charge He has committed to your keeping.

4Now the mixed multitude who were among them yielded to intense craving; so the children of Israel also wept again and said: "Who will give us meat to eat? 5We remember the fish which we ate freely in Egypt, the cucumbers, the melons, the leeks, the onions, and the garlic; 6but now our whole being *is* dried up; *there is* nothing at all except this manna *before* our eyes!"

7Now the manna *was* like coriander seed, and its color like the color of bdellium. 8The people went about and gathered *it,* ground *it* on millstones or beat *it* in the mortar, cooked *it* in pans, and made cakes of it; and its taste was like the taste of pastry prepared with oil. 9And when the dew fell on the camp in the night, the manna fell on it.

10Then Moses heard the people weeping throughout their families, everyone at the door of his tent; and the anger of the Lord was greatly aroused; Moses also was displeased. 11So Moses said to the Lord, "Why have You afflicted Your servant? And why have I not found favor in Your sight, that You have laid the burden of all these people on me? 12Did I conceive all these people? Did I beget them, that You should say to me, 'Carry them in your bosom, as a guardian carries a nursing child,' to the land which You swore to their fathers? 13Where am I to get meat to give to all these people? For they weep all over me, saying, 'Give us meat, that we may eat.' 14I am not able to bear all these people alone, because the burden *is* too heavy for me. 15If You treat me like this, please kill me here and now—if I have found favor in Your sight—and do not let me see my wretchedness!"

The Seventy Elders

16So the Lord said to Moses: "Gather to Me seventy men of the elders of Israel, whom you know to be the elders of the people and officers over them; bring them to the tabernacle of meeting, that they may stand there with you. 17Then I will come down and talk with you there. I will take of the Spirit that *is* upon you and will put *the same* upon them; and they shall bear the burden of the people with you, that you

may not bear *it* yourself alone. 18Then you shall say to the people, 'Consecrate yourselves for tomorrow, and you shall eat meat; for you have wept in the hearing of the Lord, saying, "Who will give us meat to eat? For *it was* well with us in Egypt." Therefore the Lord will give you meat, and you shall eat. 19You shall eat, not one day, nor two days, nor five days, nor ten days, nor twenty days, 20but *for* a whole month, until it comes out of your nostrils and becomes loathsome to you, because you have despised the Lord who is among you, and have wept before Him, saying, "Why did we ever come up out of Egypt?"'"

21And Moses said, "The people whom I *am* among *are* six hundred thousand men on foot; yet You have said, 'I will give them meat, that they may eat *for* a whole month.' 22Shall flocks and herds be slaughtered for them, to provide enough for them? Or shall all the fish of the sea be gathered together for them, to provide enough for them?"

23And the Lord said to Moses, "Has the Lord's arm been shortened? Now you shall see whether what I say will happen to you or not."

24So Moses went out and told the people the words of the Lord, and he gathered the seventy men of the elders of the people and placed them around the tabernacle. 25Then the Lord came down in the cloud, and spoke to him, and took of the Spirit that *was* upon him, and placed *the same* upon the seventy elders; and it happened, when the Spirit rested upon them, that they prophesied, although they never did *so* again.ᵃ

26But two men had remained in the camp: the name of one *was* Eldad, and the name of the other Medad. And the Spirit rested upon them. Now they *were* among those listed, but who had not gone out to the tabernacle; yet they prophesied in the camp. 27And a young man ran and told Moses, and said, "Eldad and Medad are prophesying in the camp." 28So Joshua the son of Nun, Moses' assistant, *one* of his choice men, answered and said, "Moses my lord, forbid them!"

11:25 ᵃTargum and Vulgate read *did not cease.*

²⁹Then Moses said to him, "Are you zealous for my sake? Oh, that all the LORD's people were prophets *and* that the LORD would put His Spirit upon them!" ³⁰And Moses returned to the camp, he and the elders of Israel.

The LORD Sends Quail

³¹Now a wind went out from the LORD, and it brought quail from the sea and left *them* fluttering near the camp, about a day's journey on this side and about a day's journey on the other side, all around the camp, and about two cubits above the surface of the ground. ³²And the people stayed up all that day, all night, and all the next day, and gathered the quail (he who gathered least gathered ten homers); and they spread *them* out for themselves all around the camp. ³³But while the meat *was* still between their teeth, before it was chewed, the wrath of the LORD was aroused against the people, and the LORD struck the people with a very great plague. ³⁴So he called the name of that place Kibroth Hattaavah,ᵃ because there they buried the people who had yielded to craving.

HONOR

". . . [Moses] is faithful in all My house."

NUMBERS 12:7

The Purest Patriotism

Stephen Grover Cleveland, who served as both the 22nd and 24th President of the United States, stated:

> All must admit that the reception of the teachings of Christ results in the purest patriotism, in the most scrupulous fidelity to public trust, and in the best type of citizenship.

> Those who manage the affairs of government are by this means reminded that the law of God demands that they should be courageously true to the interests of the people, and that the Ruler of the universe will require of them a strict account of their stewardship.

> The teachings of both human and Divine law thus merging into one word, duty, form the only union of church and state that a civil and religious government can recognize.

---

³⁵From Kibroth Hattaavah the people moved to Hazeroth, and camped at Hazeroth.

Dissension of Aaron and Miriam

12 Then Miriam and Aaron spoke against Moses because of the Ethiopian woman whom he had married; for he had married an Ethiopian woman. ²So they said, "Has the LORD indeed spoken only through Moses? Has He not spoken through us also?" And the LORD heard *it.* ³(Now the man Moses *was* very humble, more than all men who *were* on the face of the earth.)

⁴Suddenly the LORD said to Moses, Aaron, and Miriam, "Come out, you three, to the tabernacle of meeting!" So the three came out. ⁵Then the LORD came down in the pillar of cloud and stood *in* the door of the tabernacle, and called Aaron and Miriam. And they both went forward. ⁶Then He said,

> "Hear now My words:
> If there is a prophet among you,
> *I,* the LORD, make Myself known to
>   him in a vision;
> I speak to him in a dream.
> ⁷ Not so with My servant Moses;
> He *is* faithful in all My house.
> ⁸ I speak with him face to face,
> Even plainly, and not in dark sayings;
> And he sees the form of the LORD.
> Why then were you not afraid
> To speak against My servant Moses?"

⁹So the anger of the LORD was aroused against them, and He departed. ¹⁰And when the cloud departed from above the tabernacle, suddenly Miriam *became* leprous, as *white as* snow. Then Aaron turned toward Miriam, and there she was, a leper. ¹¹So Aaron said to Moses, "Oh, my lord! Please do not lay *this* sin on us, in which we have done foolishly and in which we have sinned. ¹²Please do not let her be as one dead, whose flesh is half consumed when he comes out of his mother's womb!"

¹³So Moses cried out to the LORD, saying, "Please heal her, O God, I pray!"

¹⁴Then the LORD said to Moses, "If her father had but spit in her face, would she

---

11:34 ᵃLiterally *Graves of Craving*

not be shamed seven days? Let her be shut out of the camp seven days, and afterward she may be received *again*." ¹⁵So Miriam was shut out of the camp seven days, and the people did not journey till Miriam was brought in *again*. ¹⁶And afterward the people moved from Hazeroth and camped in the Wilderness of Paran.

Spies Sent into Canaan

13 And the Lord spoke to Moses, saying, ²"Send men to spy out the land of Canaan, which I am giving to the children of Israel; from each tribe of their fathers you shall send a man, every one a leader among them."

³So Moses sent them from the Wilderness of Paran according to the command of the Lord, all of them men who *were* heads of the children of Israel. ⁴Now these *were* their names: from the tribe of Reuben, Shammua the son of Zaccur; ⁵from the tribe of Simeon, Shaphat the son of Hori; ⁶from the tribe of Judah, Caleb the son of Jephunneh; ⁷from the tribe of Issachar, Igal the son of Joseph; ⁸from the tribe of Ephraim, Hoshea^a the son of Nun; ⁹from the tribe of Benjamin, Palti the son of Raphu; ¹⁰from the tribe of Zebulun, Gaddiel the son of Sodi; ¹¹from the tribe of Joseph, *that is,* from the tribe of Manasseh, Gaddi the son of Susi; ¹²from the tribe of Dan, Ammiel the son of Gemalli; ¹³from the tribe of Asher, Sethur the son of Michael; ¹⁴from the tribe of Naphtali, Nahbi the son of Vophsi; ¹⁵from the tribe of Gad, Geuel the son of Machi.

¹⁶These *are* the names of the men whom Moses sent to spy out the land. And Moses called Hoshea^a the son of Nun, Joshua.

¹⁷Then Moses sent them to spy out the land of Canaan, and said to them, "Go up this *way* into the South, and go up to the mountains, ¹⁸and see what the land is like: whether the people who dwell in it *are* strong or weak, few or many; ¹⁹whether the land they dwell in *is* good or bad; whether the cities they inhabit *are* like camps or strongholds; ²⁰whether the land *is* rich or poor; and whether there are forests there or not. Be of good courage.

And bring some of the fruit of the land." Now the time *was* the season of the first ripe grapes.

²¹So they went up and spied out the land from the Wilderness of Zin as far as Rehob, near the entrance of Hamath. ²²And they went up through the South and came to Hebron; Ahiman, Sheshai, and Talmai, the descendants of Anak, *were* there. (Now Hebron was built seven years before Zoan in Egypt.) ²³Then they came to the Valley of Eshcol, and there cut down a branch with one cluster of grapes; they carried it between two of them on a pole. *They* also *brought* some of the pomegranates and figs. ²⁴The place was called the Valley of Eshcol,^a because of the cluster which the men of Israel cut down there. ²⁵And they returned from spying out the land after forty days.

²⁶Now they departed and came back to Moses and Aaron and all the congregation of the children of Israel in the Wilderness of Paran, at Kadesh; they brought back word to them and to all the congregation, and showed them the fruit of the land. ²⁷Then they told him, and said: "We went to the land where you sent us. It truly flows with milk and honey, and this *is* its fruit. ²⁸Nevertheless the people who dwell in the land *are* strong; the cities *are* fortified *and* very large; moreover we saw the descendants of Anak there. ²⁹The Amalekites dwell in the land of the South; the Hittites, the Jebusites, and the Amorites dwell in the mountains; and the Canaanites dwell by the sea and along the banks of the Jordan."

³⁰Then Caleb quieted the people before Moses, and said, "Let us go up at once and take possession, for we are well able to overcome it."

³¹But the men who had gone up with him said, "We are not able to go up against the people, for they *are* stronger than we." ³²And they gave the children of Israel a bad report of the land which they had spied out, saying, "The land through which we have gone as spies *is* a land that

---

13:8 ^aSeptuagint and Vulgate read *Oshea.*
13:16 ^aSeptuagint and Vulgate read *Oshea.*
13:24 ^aLiterally *Cluster*

devours its inhabitants, and all the people whom we saw in it *are* men of *great* stature. [33]There we saw the giants[a] (the descendants of Anak came from the giants); and we were like grasshoppers in our own sight, and so we were in their sight."

Israel Refuses to Enter Canaan

14 So all the congregation lifted up their voices and cried, and the people wept that night. [2]And all the children of Israel complained against Moses and Aaron, and the whole congregation said to them, "If only we had died in the land of Egypt! Or if only we had died in this wilderness! [3]Why has the LORD brought us to this land to fall by the sword, that our wives and children should become victims? Would it not be better for us to return to Egypt?" [4]So they said to one another, "Let us select a leader and return to Egypt."

[5]Then Moses and Aaron fell on their faces before all the assembly of the congregation of the children of Israel.

[6]But Joshua the son of Nun and Caleb the son of Jephunneh, *who were* among those who had spied out the land, tore their clothes; [7]and they spoke to all the congregation of the children of Israel, saying: "The land we passed through to spy out *is* an exceedingly good land. [8]If the LORD delights in us, then He will bring us into this land and give it to us, 'a land which flows with milk and honey.'[a] [9]Only do not rebel against the LORD, nor fear the people of the land, for they *are* our bread; their protection has departed from them, and the LORD *is* with us. Do not fear them."

[10]And all the congregation said to stone them with stones. Now the glory of the LORD appeared in the tabernacle of meeting before all the children of Israel.

Moses Intercedes for the People

[11]Then the LORD said to Moses: "How long will these people reject Me? And how long will they not believe Me, with all the signs which I have performed among them? [12]I will strike them with the pestilence and disinherit them, and I will make of you a nation greater and mightier than they."

[13]And Moses said to the LORD: "Then the Egyptians will hear *it,* for by Your might You brought these people up from among them, [14]and they will tell *it* to the inhabitants of this land. They have heard that You, LORD, *are* among these people; that You, LORD, are seen face to face and Your cloud stands above them, and You go before them in a pillar of cloud by day and in a pillar of fire by night. [15]Now *if* You kill these people as one man, then the nations which have heard of Your fame will speak, saying, [16]'Because the LORD was not able to bring this people to the land which He swore to give them, therefore He killed them in the wilderness.' [17]And now, I pray, let the power of my Lord be great, just as You have spoken, saying, [18]'The LORD is longsuffering and abundant in mercy, forgiving iniquity and transgression; but He by no means clears *the guilty,* visiting the iniquity of the fathers on the children to the third and fourth *generation.'*[a] [19]Pardon the iniquity of this people, I pray, according to the greatness of Your mercy, just as You have forgiven this people, from Egypt even until now."

[20]Then the LORD said: "I have pardoned, according to your word; [21]but truly, as I live, all the earth shall be filled with the glory of the LORD— [22]because all these men who have seen My glory and the signs which I did in Egypt and in the wilderness, and have put Me to the test now these ten times, and have not heeded My voice, [23]they certainly shall not see the land of which I swore to their fathers, nor shall any of those who rejected Me see it. [24]But My servant Caleb, because he has a different spirit in him and has followed Me fully, I will bring into the land where he went, and his descendants shall inherit it. [25]Now the Amalekites and the Canaanites dwell in the valley; tomorrow turn and move out into the wilderness by the Way of the Red Sea."

Death Sentence on the Rebels

[26]And the LORD spoke to Moses and Aaron, saying, [27]"How long *shall I bear with*

13:33 [a]Hebrew *nephilim*   14:8 [a]Exodus 3:8
14:18 [a]Exodus 34:6, 7

this evil congregation who complain against Me? I have heard the complaints which the children of Israel make against Me. ²⁸Say to them, 'As I live,' says the Lord, 'just as you have spoken in My hearing, so I will do to you: ²⁹The carcasses of you who have complained against Me shall fall in this wilderness, all of you who were numbered, according to your entire number, from twenty years old and above. ³⁰Except for Caleb the son of Jephunneh and Joshua the son of Nun, you shall by no means enter the land which I swore I would make you dwell in. ³¹But your little ones, whom you said would be victims, I will bring in, and they shall know the land which you have despised. ³²But *as for* you, your carcasses shall fall in this wilderness. ³³And your sons shall be shepherds in the wilderness forty years, and bear the brunt of your infidelity, until your carcasses are consumed in the wilderness. ³⁴According to the number of the days in which you spied out the land, forty days, for each day you shall bear your guilt one year, *namely* forty years, and you shall know My rejection. ³⁵I the Lord have spoken this. I will surely do so to all this evil congregation who are gathered together against Me. In this wilderness they shall be consumed, and there they shall die.' "

³⁶Now the men whom Moses sent to spy out the land, who returned and made all the congregation complain against him by bringing a bad report of the land, ³⁷those very men who brought the evil report about the land, died by the plague before the Lord. ³⁸But Joshua the son of Nun and Caleb the son of Jephunneh remained alive, of the men who went to spy out the land.

A Futile Invasion Attempt

³⁹Then Moses told these words to all the children of Israel, and the people mourned greatly. ⁴⁰And they rose early in the morning and went up to the top of the mountain, saying, "Here we are, and we will go up to the place which the Lord has promised, for we have sinned!"

⁴¹And Moses said, "Now why do you transgress the command of the Lord? For this will not succeed. ⁴²Do not go up, lest you be defeated by your enemies, for the Lord *is* not among you. ⁴³For the Amalekites and the Canaanites *are* there before you, and you shall fall by the sword; because you have turned away from the Lord, the Lord will not be with you."

⁴⁴But they presumed to go up to the mountaintop. Nevertheless, neither the ark of the covenant of the Lord nor Moses departed from the camp. ⁴⁵Then the Amalekites and the Canaanites who dwelt in that mountain came down and attacked them, and drove them back as far as Hormah.

Laws of Grain and Drink Offerings

15And the Lord spoke to Moses, saying, ²"Speak to the children of Israel, and say to them: 'When you have come into the land you are to inhabit, which I am giving to you, ³and you make an offering by fire to the Lord, a burnt offering or a sacrifice, to fulfill a vow or as a freewill offering or in your appointed feasts, to make a sweet aroma to the Lord, from the herd or the flock, ⁴then he who presents his offering to the Lord shall bring a grain offering of one-tenth *of an ephah* of fine flour mixed with one-fourth of a hin of oil; ⁵and one-fourth of a hin of wine as a drink offering you shall prepare with the burnt offering or the sacrifice, for each lamb. ⁶Or for a ram you shall prepare as a grain offering two-tenths *of an ephah* of fine flour mixed with one-third of a hin of oil; ⁷and as a drink offering you shall offer one-third of a hin of wine as a sweet aroma to the Lord. ⁸And when you prepare a young bull as a burnt offering, or as a sacrifice to fulfill a vow, or as a peace offering to the Lord, ⁹then shall be offered with the young bull a grain offering of three-tenths *of an ephah* of fine flour mixed with half a hin of oil; ¹⁰and you shall bring as the drink offering half a hin of wine as an offering made by fire, a sweet aroma to the Lord.

¹¹'Thus it shall be done for each young bull, for each ram, or for each lamb or young goat. ¹²According to the number that you prepare, so you shall do with

everyone according to their number. ¹³All who are native-born shall do these things in this manner, in presenting an offering made by fire, a sweet aroma to the Lord. ¹⁴And if a stranger dwells with you, or whoever *is* among you throughout your generations, and would present an offering made by fire, a sweet aroma to the Lord, just as you do, so shall he do. ¹⁵One ordinance *shall be* for you of the assembly and for the stranger who dwells *with you*, an ordinance forever throughout your generations; as you are, so shall the stranger be before the Lord. ¹⁶One law and one custom shall be for you and for the stranger who dwells with you.'"ᵃ

¹⁷Again the Lord spoke to Moses, saying, ¹⁸"Speak to the children of Israel, and say to them: 'When you come into the land to which I bring you, ¹⁹then it will be, when you eat of the bread of the land, that you shall offer up a heave offering to the Lord. ²⁰You shall offer up a cake of the first of your ground meal *as* a heave offering; as a heave offering of the threshing floor, so shall you offer it up. ²¹Of the first of your ground meal you shall give to the Lord a heave offering throughout your generations.

Laws Concerning Unintentional Sin

²²'If you sin unintentionally, and do not observe all these commandments which the Lord has spoken to Moses— ²³all that the Lord has commanded you by the hand of Moses, from the day the Lord gave commandment and onward throughout your generations— ²⁴then it will be, if it is unintentionally committed, without the knowledge of the congregation, that the whole congregation shall offer one young bull as a burnt offering, as a sweet aroma to the Lord, with its grain offering and its drink offering, according to the ordinance, and one kid of the goats as a sin offering. ²⁵So the priest shall make atonement for the whole congregation of the children of Israel, and it shall be forgiven them, for it was unintentional; they shall bring their offering, an offering made by fire to the Lord, and their sin offering before the Lord, for their unintended sin. ²⁶It shall be forgiven the whole congregation of the children of Israel and the stranger who dwells among them, because all the people *did it* unintentionally.

²⁷'And if a person sins unintentionally, then he shall bring a female goat in its first year as a sin offering. ²⁸So the priest shall make atonement for the person who sins unintentionally, when he sins unintentionally before the Lord, to make atonement for him; and it shall be forgiven him. ²⁹You shall have one law for him who sins unintentionally, *for* him who is native-born among the children of Israel and for the stranger who dwells among them.

Law Concerning Presumptuous Sin

³⁰'But the person who does *anything* presumptuously, *whether he is* native-born or a stranger, that one brings reproach on the Lord, and he shall be cut off from among his people. ³¹Because he has despised the word of the Lord, and has broken His commandment, that person shall be completely cut off; his guilt *shall be* upon him.'"

Penalty for Violating the Sabbath

³²Now while the children of Israel were in the wilderness, they found a man gathering sticks on the Sabbath day. ³³And those who found him gathering sticks brought him to Moses and Aaron, and to all the congregation. ³⁴They put him under guard, because it had not been explained what should be done to him.

³⁵Then the Lord said to Moses, "The man must surely be put to death; all the congregation shall stone him with stones outside the camp." ³⁶So, as the Lord commanded Moses, all the congregation brought him outside the camp and stoned him with stones, and he died.

Tassels on Garments

³⁷Again the Lord spoke to Moses, saying, ³⁸"Speak to the children of Israel: Tell them to make tassels on the corners of their garments throughout their generations, and to put a blue thread in the tassels of the corners. ³⁹And you shall have the tassel,

---

15:16 ᵃCompare Exodus 12:49

that you may look upon it and remember all the commandments of the LORD and do them, and that you *may* not follow the harlotry to which your own heart and your own eyes are inclined, ⁴⁰and that you may remember and do all My commandments, and be holy for your God. ⁴¹I *am* the LORD your God, who brought you out of the land of Egypt, to be your God: I *am* the LORD your God."

Rebellion Against Moses and Aaron

16 Now Korah the son of Izhar, the son of Kohath, the son of Levi, with Dathan and Abiram the sons of Eliab, and On the son of Peleth, sons of Reuben, took *men;* ²and they rose up before Moses with some of the children of Israel, two hundred and fifty leaders of the congregation, representatives of the congregation, men of renown. ³They gathered together against Moses and Aaron, and said to them, "*You take* too much upon yourselves, for all the congregation *is* holy, every one of them, and the LORD *is* among them. Why then do you exalt yourselves above the assembly of the LORD?"

⁴So when Moses heard *it,* he fell on his face; ⁵and he spoke to Korah and all his company, saying, "Tomorrow morning the LORD will show who *is* His and *who is* holy, and will cause *him* to come near to Him. That one whom He chooses He will cause to come near to Him. ⁶Do this: Take censers, Korah and all your company; ⁷put fire in them and put incense in them before the LORD tomorrow, and it shall be *that* the man whom the LORD chooses *is* the holy one. *You take* too much upon yourselves, you sons of Levi!"

⁸Then Moses said to Korah, "Hear now, you sons of Levi: ⁹*Is it* a small thing to you that the God of Israel has separated you from the congregation of Israel, to bring you near to Himself, to do the work of the tabernacle of the LORD, and to stand before the congregation to serve them; ¹⁰and that He has brought you near *to Himself,* you and all your brethren, the sons of Levi, with you? And are you seeking the priesthood also? ¹¹Therefore you and all your company *are* gathered together against the LORD. And what *is* Aaron that you complain against him?"

¹²And Moses sent to call Dathan and Abiram the sons of Eliab, but they said, "We will not come up! ¹³*Is it* a small thing that you have brought us up out of a land flowing with milk and honey, to kill us in the wilderness, that you should keep acting like a prince over us? ¹⁴Moreover you have not brought us into a land flowing with milk and honey, nor given us inheritance of fields and vineyards. Will you put out the eyes of these men? We will not come up!"

¹⁵Then Moses was very angry, and said to the LORD, "Do not respect their offering. I have not taken one donkey from them, nor have I hurt one of them."

¹⁶And Moses said to Korah, "Tomorrow, you and all your company be present before the LORD—you and they, as well as Aaron. ¹⁷Let each take his censer and put incense in it, and each of you bring his censer before the LORD, two hundred and fifty censers; both you and Aaron, each *with* his censer." ¹⁸So every man took his censer, put fire in it, laid incense on it, and stood at the door of the tabernacle of meeting with Moses and Aaron. ¹⁹And Korah gathered all the congregation against them at the door of the tabernacle of meeting. Then the glory of the LORD appeared to all the congregation.

²⁰And the LORD spoke to Moses and Aaron, saying, ²¹"Separate yourselves from among this congregation, that I may consume them in a moment."

²²Then they fell on their faces, and said, "O God, the God of the spirits of all flesh, shall one man sin, and You be angry with all the congregation?"

²³So the LORD spoke to Moses, saying, ²⁴"Speak to the congregation, saying, 'Get away from the tents of Korah, Dathan, and Abiram.'"

²⁵Then Moses rose and went to Dathan and Abiram, and the elders of Israel followed him. ²⁶And he spoke to the congregation, saying, "Depart now from the tents of these wicked men! Touch nothing of theirs, lest you be consumed in all their sins." ²⁷So they got away from around the

tents of Korah, Dathan, and Abiram; and Dathan and Abiram came out and stood at the door of their tents, with their wives, their sons, and their little children.

28And Moses said: "By this you shall know that the LORD has sent me to do all these works, for *I have* not *done them* of my own will. 29If these men die naturally like all men, or if they are visited by the common fate of all men, *then* the LORD has not sent me. 30But if the LORD creates a new thing, and the earth opens its mouth and swallows them up with all that belongs to them, and they go down alive into the pit, then you will understand that these men have rejected the LORD."

31Now it came to pass, as he finished speaking all these words, that the ground split apart under them, 32and the earth opened its mouth and swallowed them up, with their households and all the men with Korah, with all *their* goods. 33So they and all those with them went down alive into the pit; the earth closed over them, and they perished from among the assembly. 34Then all Israel who *were* around them fled at their cry, for they said, "Lest the earth swallow us up *also!*"

PRAYER
. . . and the glory of the LORD appeared.

NUMBERS 16:42

Covered with His Providence
In his 1805 Inaugural Address, President Thomas Jefferson stated:

> *I shall need, too, the favor of that Being in whose hands we are, who led our forefathers, as Israel of old, from their native land and planted them in a country flowing with all the necessities and comforts of life, who has covered our infancy with His Providence and our riper years with His wisdom and power, and to whose goodness I ask you to join with me in supplications that He will so enlighten the minds of your servants, guide their councils and prosper their measures, that whatever they do shall result in your good, and shall secure to you the peace, friendship, and approbation of all nations.*

35And a fire came out from the LORD and consumed the two hundred and fifty men who were offering incense.

36Then the LORD spoke to Moses, saying: 37"Tell Eleazar, the son of Aaron the priest, to pick up the censers out of the blaze, for they are holy, and scatter the fire some distance away. 38The censers of these men who sinned against their own souls, let them be made into hammered plates as a covering for the altar. Because they presented them before the LORD, therefore they are holy; and they shall be a sign to the children of Israel." 39So Eleazar the priest took the bronze censers, which those who were burned up had presented, and they were hammered out as a covering on the altar, 40*to be* a memorial to the children of Israel that no outsider, who *is* not a descendant of Aaron, should come near to offer incense before the LORD, that he might not become like Korah and his companions, just as the LORD had said to him through Moses.

Complaints of the People

41On the next day all the congregation of the children of Israel complained against Moses and Aaron, saying, "You have killed the people of the LORD." 42Now it happened, when the congregation had gathered against Moses and Aaron, that they turned toward the tabernacle of meeting; and suddenly the cloud covered it, and the glory of the LORD appeared. 43Then Moses and Aaron came before the tabernacle of meeting.

44And the LORD spoke to Moses, saying, 45"Get away from among this congregation, that I may consume them in a moment."

And they fell on their faces.

46So Moses said to Aaron, "Take a censer and put fire in it from the altar, put incense *on it,* and take it quickly to the congregation and make atonement for them; for wrath has gone out from the LORD. The plague has begun." 47Then Aaron took *it* as Moses commanded, and ran into the midst of the assembly; and already the plague had begun among the people. So

he put in the incense and made atonement for the people. ⁴⁸And he stood between the dead and the living; so the plague was stopped. ⁴⁹Now those who died in the plague were fourteen thousand seven hundred, besides those who died in the Korah incident. ⁵⁰So Aaron returned to Moses at the door of the tabernacle of meeting, for the plague had stopped.

The Budding of Aaron's Rod

17 And the LORD spoke to Moses, saying: ²"Speak to the children of Israel, and get from them a rod from each father's house, all their leaders according to their fathers' houses—twelve rods. Write each man's name on his rod. ³And you shall write Aaron's name on the rod of Levi. For there shall be one rod for the head of *each* father's house. ⁴Then you shall place them in the tabernacle of meeting before the Testimony, where I meet with you. ⁵And it shall be *that* the rod of the man whom I choose will blossom; thus I will rid Myself of the complaints of the children of Israel, which they make against you."

⁶So Moses spoke to the children of Israel, and each of their leaders gave him a rod apiece, for each leader according to their fathers' houses, twelve rods; and the rod of Aaron *was* among their rods. ⁷And Moses placed the rods before the LORD in the tabernacle of witness.

⁸Now it came to pass on the next day that Moses went into the tabernacle of witness, and behold, the rod of Aaron, of the house of Levi, had sprouted and put forth buds, had produced blossoms and yielded ripe almonds. ⁹Then Moses brought out all the rods from before the LORD to all the children of Israel; and they looked, and each man took his rod. ¹⁰And the LORD said to Moses, "Bring Aaron's rod back before the Testimony, to be kept as a sign against the rebels, that you may put their complaints away from Me, lest they die." ¹¹Thus did Moses; just as the LORD had commanded him, so he did.

¹²So the children of Israel spoke to Moses, saying, "Surely we die, we perish, we all perish! ¹³Whoever even comes near the tabernacle of the LORD must die. Shall we all utterly die?"

Duties of Priests and Levites

18 Then the LORD said to Aaron: "You and your sons and your father's house with you shall bear the iniquity *related to* the sanctuary, and you and your sons with you shall bear the iniquity *associated with* your priesthood. ²Also bring with you your brethren of the tribe of Levi, the tribe of your father, that they may be joined with you and serve you while you and your sons *are* with you before the tabernacle of witness. ³They shall attend to your needs and all the needs of the tabernacle; but they shall not come near the articles of the sanctuary and the altar, lest they die—they and you also. ⁴They shall be joined with you and attend to the needs of the tabernacle of meeting, for all the work of the tabernacle; but an outsider shall not come near you. ⁵And you shall attend to the duties of the sanctuary and the duties of the altar, that there *may* be no more wrath on the children of Israel. ⁶Behold, I Myself have taken your brethren the Levites from among the children of Israel; *they are* a gift to you, given by the LORD, to do the work of the tabernacle of meeting. ⁷Therefore you and your sons with you shall attend to your priesthood for everything at the altar and behind the veil; and you shall serve. I give your priesthood *to you* as a gift for service, but the outsider who comes near shall be put to death."

Offerings for Support of the Priests

⁸And the LORD spoke to Aaron: "Here, I Myself have also given you charge of My heave offerings, all the holy gifts of the children of Israel; I have given them as a portion to you and your sons, as an ordinance forever. ⁹This shall be yours of the most holy things *reserved* from the fire: every offering of theirs, every grain offering and every sin offering and every trespass offering which they render to Me, *shall be* most holy for you and your sons. ¹⁰In a most holy *place* you shall eat it; every male shall eat it. It shall be holy to you.

[11]"This also *is* yours: the heave offering of their gift, with all the wave offerings of the children of Israel; I have given them to you, and your sons and daughters with you, as an ordinance forever. Everyone who is clean in your house may eat it.

[12]"All the best of the oil, all the best of the new wine and the grain, their firstfruits which they offer to the LORD, I have given them to you. [13]Whatever first ripe fruit is in their land, which they bring to the LORD, shall be yours. Everyone who is clean in your house may eat it.

[14]"Every devoted thing in Israel shall be yours.

[15]"Everything that first opens the womb of all flesh, which they bring to the LORD, whether man or beast, shall be yours; nevertheless the firstborn of man you shall surely redeem, and the firstborn of unclean animals you shall redeem. [16]And those redeemed of the devoted things you shall redeem when one month old, according to your valuation, for five shekels of silver, according to the shekel of the sanctuary, which *is* twenty gerahs. [17]But the firstborn of a cow, the firstborn of a sheep, or the firstborn of a goat you shall not redeem; they *are* holy. You shall sprinkle their blood on the altar, and burn their fat *as* an offering made by fire for a sweet aroma to the LORD. [18]And their flesh shall be yours, just as the wave breast and the right thigh are yours.

[19]"All the heave offerings of the holy things, which the children of Israel offer to the LORD, I have given to you and your sons and daughters with you as an ordinance forever; it *is* a covenant of salt forever before the LORD with you and your descendants with you."

[20]Then the LORD said to Aaron: "You shall have no inheritance in their land, nor shall you have any portion among them; I *am* your portion and your inheritance among the children of Israel.

Tithes for Support of the Levites

[21]"Behold, I have given the children of Levi all the tithes in Israel as an inheritance in return for the work which they perform, the work of the tabernacle of meeting. [22]Hereafter the children of Israel shall not come near the tabernacle of meeting, lest they bear sin and die. [23]But the Levites shall perform the work of the tabernacle of meeting, and they shall bear their iniquity; *it shall be* a statute forever, throughout your generations, that among the children of Israel they shall have no inheritance. [24]For the tithes of the children of Israel, which they offer up *as* a heave offering to the LORD, I have given to the Levites as an inheritance; therefore I have said to them, 'Among the children of Israel they shall have no inheritance.'"

The Tithe of the Levites

[25]Then the LORD spoke to Moses, saying, [26]"Speak thus to the Levites, and say to them: 'When you take from the children of Israel the tithes which I have given you from them as your inheritance, then you shall offer up a heave offering of it to the LORD, a tenth of the tithe. [27]And your heave offering shall be reckoned to you as though *it were* the grain of the threshing floor and as the fullness of the winepress. [28]Thus you shall also offer a heave offering to the LORD from all your tithes which you receive from the children of Israel, and you shall give the LORD's heave offering from it to Aaron the priest. [29]Of all your gifts you shall offer up every heave offering due to the LORD, from all the best of them, the consecrated part of them.' [30]Therefore you shall say to them: 'When you have lifted up the best of it, then *the rest* shall be accounted to the Levites as the produce of the threshing floor and as the produce of the winepress. [31]You may eat it in any place, you and your households, for it *is* your reward for your work in the tabernacle of meeting. [32]And you shall bear no sin because of it, when you have lifted up the best of it. But you shall not profane the holy gifts of the children of Israel, lest you die.'"

Laws of Purification

19 Now the LORD spoke to Moses and Aaron, saying, [2]"This *is* the ordinance of the law which the LORD has commanded,

saying: 'Speak to the children of Israel, that they bring you a red heifer without blemish, in which there *is* no defect *and* on which a yoke has never come. ³You shall give it to Eleazar the priest, that he may take it outside the camp, and it shall be slaughtered before him; ⁴and Eleazar the priest shall take some of its blood with his finger, and sprinkle some of its blood seven times directly in front of the tabernacle of meeting. ⁵Then the heifer shall be burned in his sight: its hide, its flesh, its blood, and its offal shall be burned. ⁶And the priest shall take cedar wood and hyssop and scarlet, and cast *them* into the midst of the fire burning the heifer. ⁷Then the priest shall wash his clothes, he shall bathe in water, and afterward he shall come into the camp; the priest shall be unclean until evening. ⁸And the one who burns it shall wash his clothes in water, bathe in water, and shall be unclean until evening. ⁹Then a man *who is* clean shall gather up the ashes of the heifer, and store *them* outside the camp in a clean place; and they shall be kept for the congregation of the children of Israel for the water of purification;ᵃ it *is* for purifying from sin. ¹⁰And the one who gathers the ashes of the heifer shall wash his clothes, and be unclean until evening. It shall be a statute forever to the children of Israel and to the stranger who dwells among them.

¹¹'He who touches the dead body of anyone shall be unclean seven days. ¹²He shall purify himself with the water on the third day and on the seventh day; *then* he will be clean. But if he does not purify himself on the third day and on the seventh day, he will not be clean. ¹³Whoever touches the body of anyone who has died, and does not purify himself, defiles the tabernacle of the LORD. That person shall be cut off from Israel. He shall be unclean, because the water of purification was not sprinkled on him; his uncleanness *is* still on him.

¹⁴'This *is* the law when a man dies in a tent: All who come into the tent and all who *are* in the tent shall be unclean seven days; ¹⁵and every open vessel, which has no cover fastened on it, *is* unclean. ¹⁶Whoever in the open field touches one who is slain by a sword or who has died, or a bone of a man, or a grave, shall be unclean seven days.

¹⁷'And for an unclean *person* they shall take some of the ashes of the heifer burnt for purification from sin, and running water shall be put on them in a vessel. ¹⁸A clean person shall take hyssop and dip *it* in the water, sprinkle *it* on the tent, on all the vessels, on the persons who were there, or on the one who touched a bone, the slain, the dead, or a grave. ¹⁹The clean *person* shall sprinkle the unclean on the third day and on the seventh day; and on the seventh day he shall purify himself, wash his clothes, and bathe in water; and at evening he shall be clean.

²⁰'But the man who is unclean and does not purify himself, that person shall be cut off from among the assembly, because he has defiled the sanctuary of the LORD. The water of purification has not been sprinkled on him; he *is* unclean. ²¹It shall be a perpetual statute for them. He who sprinkles the water of purification shall wash his clothes; and he who touches the water of purification shall be unclean until evening. ²²Whatever the unclean *person* touches shall be unclean; and the person who touches *it* shall be unclean until evening.'"

Moses' Error at Kadesh

20 Then the children of Israel, the whole congregation, came into the Wilderness of Zin in the first month, and the people stayed in Kadesh; and Miriam died there and was buried there.

²Now there was no water for the congregation; so they gathered together against Moses and Aaron. ³And the people contended with Moses and spoke, saying: "If only we had died when our brethren died before the LORD! ⁴Why have you brought up the assembly of the LORD into this wilderness, that we and our animals should die here? ⁵And why have you made us come up out of Egypt, to bring us to this evil place? It *is* not a place of grain or figs or vines or pomegranates; nor *is* there any

19:9 ᵃLiterally *impurity*

water to drink." 6So Moses and Aaron went from the presence of the assembly to the door of the tabernacle of meeting, and they fell on their faces. And the glory of the LORD appeared to them.

7Then the LORD spoke to Moses, saying, 8"Take the rod; you and your brother Aaron gather the congregation together. Speak to the rock before their eyes, and it will yield its water; thus you shall bring water for them out of the rock, and give drink to the congregation and their animals." 9So Moses took the rod from before the LORD as He commanded him.

10And Moses and Aaron gathered the assembly together before the rock; and he said to them, "Hear now, you rebels! Must we bring water for you out of this rock?" 11Then Moses lifted his hand and struck the rock twice with his rod; and water came out abundantly, and the congregation and their animals drank.

12Then the LORD spoke to Moses and Aaron, "Because you did not believe Me, to hallow Me in the eyes of the children of Israel, therefore you shall not bring this assembly into the land which I have given them."

13This *was* the water of Meribah,a because the children of Israel contended with the LORD, and He was hallowed among them.

Passage Through Edom Refused

14Now Moses sent messengers from Kadesh to the king of Edom. "Thus says your brother Israel: 'You know all the hardship that has befallen us, 15how our fathers went down to Egypt, and we dwelt in Egypt a long time, and the Egyptians afflicted us and our fathers. 16When we cried out to the LORD, He heard our voice and sent the Angel and brought us up out of Egypt; now here we are in Kadesh, a city on the edge of your border. 17Please let us pass through your country. We will not pass through fields or vineyards, nor will we drink water from wells; we will go along the King's Highway; we will not turn aside to the right hand or to the left until we have passed through your territory.' "

18Then Edom said to him, "You shall not pass through my *land,* lest I come out against you with the sword."

19So the children of Israel said to him, "We will go by the Highway, and if I or my livestock drink any of your water, then I will pay for it; let me only pass through on foot, nothing *more.*"

20Then he said, "You shall not pass through." So Edom came out against them with many men and with a strong hand. 21Thus Edom refused to give Israel passage through his territory; so Israel turned away from him.

Death of Aaron

22Now the children of Israel, the whole congregation, journeyed from Kadesh and came to Mount Hor. 23And the LORD spoke to Moses and Aaron in Mount Hor by the border of the land of Edom, saying: 24"Aaron shall be gathered to his people, for he shall not enter the land which I have given to the children of Israel, because you rebelled against My word at the water of Meribah. 25Take Aaron and Eleazar his son, and bring them up to Mount Hor; 26and strip Aaron of his garments and put them on Eleazar his son; for Aaron shall be gathered *to his people* and die there." 27So Moses did just as the LORD commanded, and they went up to Mount Hor in the sight of all the congregation. 28Moses stripped Aaron of his garments and put them on Eleazar his son; and Aaron died there on the top of the mountain. Then Moses and Eleazar came down from the mountain. 29Now when all the congregation saw that Aaron was dead, all the house of Israel mourned for Aaron thirty days.

Canaanites Defeated at Hormah

21 The king of Arad, the Canaanite, who dwelt in the South, heard that Israel was coming on the road to Atharim. Then he fought against Israel and took *some* of them prisoners. 2So Israel made a vow to the LORD, and said, "If You will indeed deliver this people into my hand, then I will utterly destroy their cities." 3And the LORD

20:13 aLiterally *Contention*

listened to the voice of Israel and delivered up the Canaanites, and they utterly destroyed them and their cities. So the name of that place was called Hormah.[a]

The Bronze Serpent

4Then they journeyed from Mount Hor by the Way of the Red Sea, to go around the land of Edom; and the soul of the people became very discouraged on the way. 5And the people spoke against God and against Moses: "Why have you brought us up out of Egypt to die in the wilderness? For *there is* no food and no water, and our soul loathes this worthless bread." 6So the LORD sent fiery serpents among the people, and they bit the people; and many of the people of Israel died.

7Therefore the people came to Moses, and said, "We have sinned, for we have spoken against the LORD and against you; pray to the LORD that He take away the serpents from us." So Moses prayed for the people.

8Then the LORD said to Moses, "Make a fiery *serpent,* and set it on a pole; and it shall be that everyone who is bitten, when he looks at it, shall live." 9So Moses made a bronze serpent, and put it on a pole; and so it was, if a serpent had bitten anyone, when he looked at the bronze serpent, he lived.

PRAYER
So Moses prayed for the people.

NUMBERS 21:7

Chaplains for the United States Congress

On May 1, 1789, the United States Congress elected the Reverend William Linn, a Dutch Reformed minister from New York City, to be the first chaplain of the U.S. House of Representatives, appropriating five hundred dollars from the federal treasury to pay his salary. During the period when Congress first met in the new capitol of Washington, D.C., the House and Senate chaplains regularly led Christian services every Sunday in the House Chamber. In 1860, Rabbi Morris Jacob Raphall was the first Jewish clergyman invited to open a House session with prayer. Both the House and the Senate have continued to regularly open every session with prayer.

From Mount Hor to Moab

10Now the children of Israel moved on and camped in Oboth. 11And they journeyed from Oboth and camped at Ije Abarim, in the wilderness which *is* east of Moab, toward the sunrise. 12From there they moved and camped in the Valley of Zered. 13From there they moved and camped on the other side of the Arnon, which *is* in the wilderness that extends from the border of the Amorites; for the Arnon *is* the border of Moab, between Moab and the Amorites. 14Therefore it is said in the Book of the Wars of the LORD:

> "Waheb in Suphah,[a]
> The brooks of the Arnon,
> 15   And the slope of the brooks
> That reaches to the dwelling of Ar,
> And lies on the border of Moab."

16From there *they went* to Beer, which *is* the well where the LORD said to Moses, "Gather the people together, and I will give them water." 17Then Israel sang this song:

> "Spring up, O well!
> All of you sing to it—
> 18   The well the leaders sank,
> Dug by the nation's nobles,
> By the lawgiver, with their staves."

And from the wilderness *they went* to Mattanah, 19from Mattanah to Nahaliel, from Nahaliel to Bamoth, 20and from Bamoth, *in* the valley that *is* in the country of Moab, to the top of Pisgah which looks down on the wasteland.[a]

King Sihon Defeated

21Then Israel sent messengers to Sihon king of the Amorites, saying, 22"Let me pass through your land. We will not turn aside into fields or vineyards; we will not drink water from wells. We will go by the King's Highway until we have passed through your territory." 23But Sihon would not allow Israel to pass through his territory. So Sihon

---

21:3 [a]Literally *Utter Destruction*   **21:14** [a]Ancient unknown places; Vulgate reads *What He did in the Red Sea.*   **21:20** [a]Hebrew *Jeshimon*

gathered all his people together and went out against Israel in the wilderness, and he came to Jahaz and fought against Israel. [24]Then Israel defeated him with the edge of the sword, and took possession of his land from the Arnon to the Jabbok, as far as the people of Ammon; for the border of the people of Ammon *was* fortified. [25]So Israel took all these cities, and Israel dwelt in all the cities of the Amorites, in Heshbon and in all its villages. [26]For Heshbon *was* the city of Sihon king of the Amorites, who had fought against the former king of Moab, and had taken all his land from his hand as far as the Arnon. [27]Therefore those who speak in proverbs say:

"Come to Heshbon, let it be built;
    Let the city of Sihon be repaired.

[28] "For fire went out from Heshbon,
    A flame from the city of Sihon;
    It consumed Ar of Moab,
    The lords of the heights of the Arnon.
[29]   Woe to you, Moab!
    You have perished, O people of
        Chemosh!
    He has given his sons as fugitives,
    And his daughters into captivity,
    To Sihon king of the Amorites.

[30] "But we have shot at them;
    Heshbon has perished as far as Dibon.
    Then we laid waste as far as Nophah,
    Which *reaches* to Medeba."

[31]Thus Israel dwelt in the land of the Amorites. [32]Then Moses sent to spy out Jazer; and they took its villages and drove out the Amorites who *were* there.

King Og Defeated

[33]And they turned and went up by the way to Bashan. So Og king of Bashan went out against them, he and all his people, to battle at Edrei. [34]Then the LORD said to Moses, "Do not fear him, for I have delivered him into your hand, with all his people and his land; and you shall do to him as you did to Sihon king of the Amorites, who dwelt at Heshbon." [35]So they defeated him, his sons, and all his people, until there was no survivor left him; and they took possession of his land.

Balak Sends for Balaam

22 Then the children of Israel moved, and camped in the plains of Moab on the side of the Jordan *across from* Jericho. [2]Now Balak the son of Zippor saw all that Israel had done to the Amorites. [3]And Moab was exceedingly afraid of the people because they *were* many, and Moab was sick with dread because of the children of Israel. [4]So Moab said to the elders of Midian, "Now this company will lick up everything around us, as an ox licks up the grass of the field." And Balak the son of Zippor *was* king of the Moabites at that time. [5]Then he sent messengers to Balaam the son of Beor at Pethor, which *is* near the River[a] in the land of the sons of his people,[b] to call him, saying: "Look, a people has come from Egypt. See, they cover the face of the earth, and are settling next to me! [6]Therefore please come at once, curse this people for me, for they *are* too mighty for me. Perhaps I shall be able to defeat them and drive them out of the land, for I know that he whom you bless *is* blessed, and he whom you curse is cursed."

[7]So the elders of Moab and the elders of Midian departed with the diviner's fee in their hand, and they came to Balaam and spoke to him the words of Balak. [8]And he said to them, "Lodge here tonight, and I will bring back word to you, as the LORD speaks to me." So the princes of Moab stayed with Balaam.

[9]Then God came to Balaam and said, "Who *are* these men with you?" [10]So Balaam said to God, "Balak the son of Zippor, king of Moab, has sent to me, *saying*, [11]'Look, a people has come out of Egypt, and they cover the face of the earth. Come now, curse them for me; perhaps I shall be able to overpower them and drive them out.'" [12]And God said to Balaam, "You shall not go with them; you shall not curse the people, for they *are* blessed."

22:5 [a]That is, the Euphrates [b]Or *the people of Amau*

¹³So Balaam rose in the morning and said to the princes of Balak, "Go back to your land, for the LORD has refused to give me permission to go with you."

¹⁴And the princes of Moab rose and went to Balak, and said, "Balaam refuses to come with us."

¹⁵Then Balak again sent princes, more numerous and more honorable than they. ¹⁶And they came to Balaam and said to him, "Thus says Balak the son of Zippor: 'Please let nothing hinder you from coming to me; ¹⁷for I will certainly honor you greatly, and I will do whatever you say to me. Therefore please come, curse this people for me.' "

¹⁸Then Balaam answered and said to the servants of Balak, "Though Balak were to give me his house full of silver and gold, I could not go beyond the word of the LORD my God, to do less or more. ¹⁹Now therefore, please, you also stay here tonight, that I may know what more the LORD will say to me."

²⁰And God came to Balaam at night and said to him, "If the men come to call you, rise *and* go with them; but only the word which I speak to you—that you shall do." ²¹So Balaam rose in the morning, saddled his donkey, and went with the princes of Moab.

Balaam, the Donkey, and the Angel

²²Then God's anger was aroused because he went, and the Angel of the LORD took His stand in the way as an adversary against him. And he was riding on his donkey, and his two servants *were* with him. ²³Now the donkey saw the Angel of the LORD standing in the way with His drawn sword in His hand, and the donkey turned aside out of the way and went into the field. So Balaam struck the donkey to turn her back onto the road. ²⁴Then the Angel of the LORD stood in a narrow path between the vineyards, *with* a wall on this side and a wall on that side. ²⁵And when the donkey saw the Angel of the LORD, she pushed herself against the wall and crushed Balaam's foot against the wall; so he struck her again. ²⁶Then the Angel of the LORD went further, and stood in a narrow place where there *was* no way to turn either to the right hand or to the left. ²⁷And when the donkey saw the Angel of the LORD, she lay down under Balaam; so Balaam's anger was aroused, and he struck the donkey with his staff.

²⁸Then the LORD opened the mouth of the donkey, and she said to Balaam, "What have I done to you, that you have struck me these three times?"

²⁹And Balaam said to the donkey, "Because you have abused me. I wish there were a sword in my hand, for now I would kill you!"

³⁰So the donkey said to Balaam, "*Am* I not your donkey on which you have ridden, ever since *I became* yours, to this day? Was I ever disposed to do this to you?"

And he said, "No."

³¹Then the LORD opened Balaam's eyes, and he saw the Angel of the LORD standing in the way with His drawn sword in His hand; and he bowed his head and fell flat on his face. ³²And the Angel of the LORD said to him, "Why have you struck your donkey these three times? Behold, I have come out to stand against you, because *your* way is perverse before Me. ³³The donkey saw Me and turned aside from Me these three times. If she had not turned aside from Me, surely I would also have killed you by now, and let her live."

³⁴And Balaam said to the Angel of the LORD, "I have sinned, for I did not know You stood in the way against me. Now therefore, if it displeases You, I will turn back."

³⁵Then the Angel of the LORD said to Balaam, "Go with the men, but only the word that I speak to you, that you shall speak." So Balaam went with the princes of Balak.

³⁶Now when Balak heard that Balaam was coming, he went out to meet him at the city of Moab, which *is* on the border at the Arnon, the boundary of the territory. ³⁷Then Balak said to Balaam, "Did I not earnestly send to you, calling for you? Why did you not come to me? Am I not able to honor you?"

³⁸And Balaam said to Balak, "Look, I have come to you! Now, have I any power

at all to say anything? The word that God puts in my mouth, that I must speak." ³⁹So Balaam went with Balak, and they came to Kirjath Huzoth. ⁴⁰Then Balak offered oxen and sheep, and he sent *some* to Balaam and to the princes who *were* with him.

Balaam's First Prophecy

⁴¹So it was, the next day, that Balak took Balaam and brought him up to the high places of Baal, that from there he might observe the extent of the people.

23 Then Balaam said to Balak, "Build seven altars for me here, and prepare for me here seven bulls and seven rams."

²And Balak did just as Balaam had spoken, and Balak and Balaam offered a bull and a ram on *each* altar. ³Then Balaam said to Balak, "Stand by your burnt offering, and I will go; perhaps the LORD will come to meet me, and whatever He shows me I will tell you." So he went to a desolate height. ⁴And God met Balaam, and he said to Him, "I have prepared the seven altars, and I have offered on *each* altar a bull and a ram."

⁵Then the LORD put a word in Balaam's mouth, and said, "Return to Balak, and thus you shall speak." ⁶So he returned to him, and there he was, standing by his burnt offering, he and all the princes of Moab.

⁷And he took up his oracle and said:

"Balak the king of Moab has brought me from Aram,
From the mountains of the east.
'Come, curse Jacob for me,
And come, denounce Israel!'

8 "How shall I curse whom God has not cursed?
And how shall I denounce *whom* the LORD has not denounced?
9 For from the top of the rocks I see him,

SAMUEL MORSE

Samuel Morse (1791–1872), an accomplished artist by profession, was captivated with the notion that electricity could be used to transmit messages instantly. He worked for years to become the creator of a single wire telegraph system, and co-inventor, with Alfred Vail, of the Morse Code, with letters represented by dots and dashes, to convey the telegraph message. His invention in the 1830s revolutionized and changed forever the realm of communications.

Although Morse had a patent, it took him years of failures and poverty before he was able to secure financial backing to implement his project. About those years, he said, "The only gleam of hope . . . is from confidence in God. When I look upward it calms any apprehension for the future, and I seem to hear a voice saying: 'If I clothe the lilies of the field, shall I not also clothe you?' Here is my strong confidence, and I will wait patiently for the direction of Providence."

In 1843, Congress finally awarded Morse $30,000 to construct a telegraphic line between Baltimore and Washington. By Friday May 24, 1844, the lines were ready, and the words of the first official message were sent: "What hath God wrought!" selected from Numbers 23:23, in recognition that it was God who had inspired and sustained Morse throughout.

And from the hills I behold him;
There! A people dwelling alone,
Not reckoning itself among the
    nations.

10 "Who can count the dust[a] of Jacob,
Or number one-fourth of Israel?
Let me die the death of the righteous,
And let my end be like his!"

¹¹Then Balak said to Balaam, "What have you done to me? I took you to curse my enemies, and look, you have blessed *them* bountifully!"

¹²So he answered and said, "Must I not take heed to speak what the LORD has put in my mouth?"

Balaam's Second Prophecy

¹³Then Balak said to him, "Please come with me to another place from which you may see them; you shall see only the outer part of them, and shall not see them all; curse them for me from there." ¹⁴So he brought him to the field of Zophim, to the top of Pisgah, and built seven altars, and offered a bull and a ram on *each* altar.

¹⁵And he said to Balak, "Stand here by your burnt offering while I meet[a] the LORD over there."

¹⁶Then the LORD met Balaam, and put a word in his mouth, and said, "Go back to Balak, and thus you shall speak." ¹⁷So he came to him, and there he was, standing by his burnt offering, and the princes of Moab were with him. And Balak said to him, "What has the LORD spoken?"

¹⁸Then he took up his oracle and said:

"Rise up, Balak, and hear!
Listen to me, son of Zippor!

19 "God *is* not a man, that He should lie,
Nor a son of man, that He should
    repent.
Has He said, and will He not do?
Or has He spoken, and will He not
    make it good?

20 Behold, I have received *a command* to
    bless;
He has blessed, and I cannot reverse it.

21 "He has not observed iniquity in
    Jacob,
Nor has He seen wickedness in Israel.
The LORD his God *is* with him,
And the shout of a King *is* among
    them.

22 God brings them out of Egypt;
He has strength like a wild ox.

23 "For *there is* no sorcery against Jacob,
Nor any divination against Israel.
It now must be said of Jacob
And of Israel, 'Oh, what God has
    done!'

24 Look, a people rises like a lioness,
And lifts itself up like a lion;
It shall not lie down until it devours
    the prey,
And drinks the blood of the slain."

²⁵Then Balak said to Balaam, "Neither curse them at all, nor bless them at all!"

²⁶So Balaam answered and said to Balak, "Did I not tell you, saying, 'All that the LORD speaks, that I must do'?"

Balaam's Third Prophecy

²⁷Then Balak said to Balaam, "Please come, I will take you to another place; perhaps it will please God that you may curse them for me from there." ²⁸So Balak took Balaam to the top of Peor, that overlooks the wasteland.[a] ²⁹Then Balaam said to Balak, "Build for me here seven altars, and prepare for me here seven bulls and seven rams." ³⁰And Balak did as Balaam had said, and offered a bull and a ram on *every* altar.

24 Now when Balaam saw that it pleased the LORD to bless Israel, he did not go as at other times, to seek to use sorcery, but he set his face toward the wilderness. ²And Balaam raised his eyes, and saw Israel encamped according to their tribes; and the Spirit of God came upon him. ³Then he took up his oracle and said:

23:10 [a]Or *dust cloud*   **23:15** [a]Following Masoretic Text, Targum, and Vulgate; Syriac reads *call;* Septuagint reads *go and ask God.*   **23:28** [a]Hebrew *Jeshimon*

"The utterance of Balaam the son of Beor,
The utterance of the man whose eyes
    are opened,
4 The utterance of him who hears the
    words of God,
Who sees the vision of the Almighty,
Who falls down, with eyes wide open:

5 "How lovely are your tents, O Jacob!
    Your dwellings, O Israel!
6 Like valleys that stretch out,
    Like gardens by the riverside,
    Like aloes planted by the LORD,
    Like cedars beside the waters.
7 He shall pour water from his buckets,
    And his seed *shall be* in many waters.

"His king shall be higher than Agag,
    And his kingdom shall be exalted.

8 "God brings him out of Egypt;
    He has strength like a wild ox;
    He shall consume the nations, his
      enemies;
    He shall break their bones
    And pierce *them* with his arrows.
9 'He bows down, he lies down as a lion;
    And as a lion, who shall rouse him?'[a]

"Blessed *is* he who blesses you,
    And cursed *is* he who curses you."

10Then Balak's anger was aroused against Balaam, and he struck his hands together; and Balak said to Balaam, "I called you to curse my enemies, and look, you have bountifully blessed *them* these three times! 11Now therefore, flee to your place. I said I would greatly honor you, but in fact, the LORD has kept you back from honor." 12So Balaam said to Balak, "Did I not also speak to your messengers whom you sent to me, saying, 13'If Balak were to give me his house full of silver and gold, I could not go beyond the word of the LORD, to do good or bad of my own will. What the LORD says, that I must speak'? 14And now, indeed, I am going to my people. Come, I will advise you what this people will do to your people in the latter days."

Balaam's Fourth Prophecy

15So he took up his oracle and said:

"The utterance of Balaam the son of
    Beor,
    And the utterance of the man whose
      eyes are opened;
16 The utterance of him who hears the
    words of God,
    And has the knowledge of the Most
      High,
    Who sees the vision of the Almighty,
    Who falls down, with eyes wide open:

17 "I see Him, but not now;
    I behold Him, but not near;
    A Star shall come out of Jacob;
    A Scepter shall rise out of Israel,
    And batter the brow of Moab,
    And destroy all the sons of tumult.[a]

18 "And Edom shall be a possession;
    Seir also, his enemies, shall be a
      possession,
    While Israel does valiantly.
19 Out of Jacob One shall have
      dominion,
    And destroy the remains of the city."

20Then he looked on Amalek, and he took up his oracle and said:

"Amalek *was* first among the nations,
    But *shall be* last until he perishes."

21Then he looked on the Kenites, and he took up his oracle and said:

"Firm is your dwelling place,
    And your nest is set in the rock;
22 Nevertheless Kain shall be burned.
    How long until Asshur carries you
      away captive?"

23Then he took up his oracle and said:

"Alas! Who shall live when God does
    this?

24:9 [a]Genesis 49:9   **24:17** [a]Hebrew *Sheth* (compare Jeremiah 48:45)

24 But ships *shall come* from the coasts of
    Cyprus,ᵃ
And they shall afflict Asshur and
    afflict Eber,
And so shall *Amalek*,ᵇ until he
    perishes."

²⁵So Balaam rose and departed and returned to his place; Balak also went his way.

Israel's Harlotry in Moab

25 Now Israel remained in Acacia Grove,ᵃ and the people began to commit harlotry with the women of Moab. ²They invited the people to the sacrifices of their gods, and the people ate and bowed down to their gods. ³So Israel was joined to Baal of Peor, and the anger of the LORD was aroused against Israel.

⁴Then the LORD said to Moses, "Take all the leaders of the people and hang the offenders before the LORD, out in the sun, that the fierce anger of the LORD may turn away from Israel."

⁵So Moses said to the judges of Israel, "Every one of you kill his men who were joined to Baal of Peor."

⁶And indeed, one of the children of Israel came and presented to his brethren a Midianite woman in the sight of Moses and in the sight of all the congregation of the children of Israel, who *were* weeping at the door of the tabernacle of meeting. ⁷Now when Phinehas the son of Eleazar, the son of Aaron the priest, saw *it,* he rose from among the congregation and took a javelin in his hand; ⁸and he went after the man of Israel into the tent and thrust both of them through, the man of Israel, and the woman through her body. So the plague was stopped among the children of Israel. ⁹And those who died in the plague were twenty-four thousand.

¹⁰Then the LORD spoke to Moses, saying: ¹¹"Phinehas the son of Eleazar, the son of Aaron the priest, has turned back My wrath from the children of Israel, because he was zealous with My zeal among them, so that I did not consume the children of Israel in My zeal. ¹²Therefore say, 'Behold, I give to him

My covenant of peace; ¹³and it shall be to him and his descendants after him a covenant of an everlasting priesthood, because he was zealous for his God, and made atonement for the children of Israel.'"

¹⁴Now the name of the Israelite who was killed, who was killed with the Midianite woman, *was* Zimri the son of Salu, a leader of a father's house among the Simeonites. ¹⁵And the name of the Midianite woman who was killed *was* Cozbi the daughter of Zur; he *was* head of the people of a father's house in Midian.

¹⁶Then the LORD spoke to Moses, saying: ¹⁷"Harass the Midianites, and attack them; ¹⁸for they harassed you with their schemes by which they seduced you in the matter of Peor and in the matter of Cozbi, the daughter of a leader of Midian, their sister, who was killed in the day of the plague because of Peor."

The Second Census of Israel

26 And it came to pass, after the plague, that the LORD spoke to Moses and Eleazar the son of Aaron the priest, saying: ²"Take a census of all the congregation of the children of Israel from twenty years old and above, by their fathers' houses, all who are able to go to war in Israel." ³So Moses and Eleazar the priest spoke with them in the plains of Moab by the Jordan, *across from* Jericho, saying: ⁴"*Take a census of the people* from twenty years old and above, just as the LORD commanded Moses and the children of Israel who came out of the land of Egypt."

⁵Reuben *was* the firstborn of Israel. The children of Reuben *were:* of Hanoch, the family of the Hanochites; *of* Pallu, the family of the Palluites; ⁶*of* Hezron, the family of the Hezronites; *of* Carmi, the family of the Carmites. ⁷These *are* the families of the Reubenites: those who were numbered of them were forty-three thousand seven hundred and thirty. ⁸And the son of Pallu *was* Eliab. ⁹The sons of Eliab *were* Nemuel, Dathan, and Abiram. These *are* the Dathan and Abiram, representatives of the

---

24:24 ᵃHebrew *Kittim* ᵇLiterally *he* or *that one*
25:1 ᵃHebrew *Shittim*

congregation, who contended against Moses and Aaron in the company of Korah, when they contended against the LORD; [10]and the earth opened its mouth and swallowed them up together with Korah when that company died, when the fire devoured two hundred and fifty men; and they became a sign. [11]Nevertheless the children of Korah did not die.

[12]The sons of Simeon according to their families *were:* of Nemuel,[a] the family of the Nemuelites; *of* Jamin, the family of the Jaminites; *of* Jachin,[b] the family of the Jachinites; [13]*of* Zerah,[a] the family of the Zarhites; *of* Shaul, the family of the Shaulites. [14]These *are* the families of the Simeonites: twenty-two thousand two hundred.

[15]The sons of Gad according to their families *were:* of Zephon,[a] the family of the Zephonites; *of* Haggi, the family of the Haggites; *of* Shuni, the family of the Shunites; [16]*of* Ozni,[a] the family of the Oznites; *of* Eri, the family of the Erites; [17]*of* Arod,[a] the family of the Arodites; *of* Areli, the family of the Arelites. [18]These *are* the families of the sons of Gad according to those who were numbered of them: forty thousand five hundred.

[19]The sons of Judah *were* Er and Onan; and Er and Onan died in the land of Canaan. [20]And the sons of Judah according to their families were: *of* Shelah, the family of the Shelanites; *of* Perez, the family of the Parzites; *of* Zerah, the family of the Zarhites. [21]And the sons of Perez were: *of* Hezron, the family of the Hezronites; *of* Hamul, the family of the Hamulites. [22]These *are* the families of Judah according to those who were numbered of them: seventy-six thousand five hundred.

[23]The sons of Issachar according to their families *were: of* Tola, the family of the Tolaites; *of* Puah,[a] the family of the Punites;[b] [24]of Jashub, the family of the Jashubites; of Shimron, the family of the Shimronites. [25]These *are* the families of Issachar according to those who were numbered of them: sixty-four thousand three hundred.

[26]The sons of Zebulun according to their families *were:* of Sered, the family of the Sardites; of Elon, the family of the Elonites; of Jahleel, the family of the Jahleelites.

[27]These *are* the families of the Zebulunites according to those who were numbered of them: sixty thousand five hundred.

[28]The sons of Joseph according to their families, by Manasseh and Ephraim, *were:* [29]The sons of Manasseh: of Machir, the family of the Machirites; and Machir begot Gilead; of Gilead, the family of the Gileadites. [30]These *are* the sons of Gilead: *of* Jeezer,[a] the family of the Jeezerites; of Helek, the family of the Helekites; [31]*of* Asriel, the family of the Asrielites; *of* Shechem, the family of the Shechemites; [32]*of* Shemida, the family of the Shemidaites; *of* Hepher, the family of the Hepherites. [33]Now Zelophehad the son of Hepher had no sons, but daughters; and the names of the daughters of Zelophehad *were* Mahlah, Noah, Hoglah, Milcah, and Tirzah. [34]These *are* the families of Manasseh; and those who were numbered of them *were* fifty-two thousand seven hundred.

[35]These *are* the sons of Ephraim according to their families: of Shuthelah, the family of the Shuthalhites; of Becher,[a] the family of the Bachrites; of Tahan, the family of the Tahanites. [36]And these *are* the sons of Shuthelah: of Eran, the family of the Eranites. [37]These *are* the families of the sons of Ephraim according to those who were numbered of them: thirty-two thousand five hundred.

These *are* the sons of Joseph according to their families.

[38]The sons of Benjamin according to their families were: of Bela, the family of the Belaites; of Ashbel, the family of the Ashbelites; of Ahiram, the family of the Ahiramites; [39]of Shupham,[a] the family of the

---

26:12 [a]Spelled *Jemuel* in Genesis 46:10 and Exodus 6:15 [b]Called *Jarib* in 1 Chronicles 4:24
26:13 [a]Called *Zohar* in Genesis 46:10
26:15 [a]Called *Ziphion* in Genesis 46:16
26:16 [a]Called *Ezbon* in Genesis 46:16
26:17 [a]Spelled *Arodi* in Samaritan Pentateuch, Syriac, and Genesis 46:16   **26:23** [a]Hebrew *Puvah* (compare Genesis 46:13 and 1 Chronicles 7:1); Samaritan Pentateuch, Septuagint, Syriac, and Vulgate read *Puah.* [b]Samaritan Pentateuch, Septuagint, Syriac, and Vulgate read *Puaites.*   **26:30** [a]Called *Abiezer* in Joshua 17:2   **26:35** [a]Called *Bered* in 1 Chronicles 7:20   **26:39** [a]Masoretic Text reads *Shephupham,* spelled *Shephuphan* in 1 Chronicles 8:5.

Shuphamites; of Hupham,[b] the family of the Huphamites. 40And the sons of Bela were Ard[a] and Naaman: *of Ard,* the family of the Ardites; of Naaman, the family of the Naamites. 41These *are* the sons of Benjamin according to their families; and those who were numbered of them *were* forty-five thousand six hundred.

42These *are* the sons of Dan according to their families: of Shuham,[a] the family of the Shuhamites. These *are* the families of Dan according to their families. 43All the families of the Shuhamites, according to those who were numbered of them, *were* sixty-four thousand four hundred.

44The sons of Asher according to their families *were:* of Jimna, the family of the Jimnites; of Jesui, the family of the Jesuites; of Beriah, the family of the Beriites. 45Of the sons of Beriah: of Heber, the family of the Heberites; of Malchiel, the family of the Malchielites. 46And the name of the daughter of Asher *was* Serah. 47These *are* the families of the sons of Asher according to those who were numbered of them: fifty-three thousand four hundred.

48The sons of Naphtali according to their families *were:* of Jahzeel,[a] the family of the Jahzeelites; of Guni, the family of the Gunites; 49of Jezer, the family of the Jezerites; of Shillem, the family of the Shillemites. 50These *are* the families of Naphtali according to their families; and those who were numbered of them *were* forty-five thousand four hundred.

51These *are* those who were numbered of the children of Israel: six hundred and one thousand seven hundred and thirty.

52Then the LORD spoke to Moses, saying: 53"To these the land shall be divided as an inheritance, according to the number of names. 54To a large *tribe* you shall give a larger inheritance, and to a small *tribe* you shall give a smaller inheritance. Each shall be given its inheritance according to those who were numbered of them. 55But the land shall be divided by lot; they shall inherit according to the names of the tribes of their fathers. 56According to the lot their inheritance shall be divided between the larger and the smaller."

57And these *are* those who were numbered of the Levites according to their families: of Gershon, the family of the Gershonites; of Kohath, the family of the Kohathites; of Merari, the family of the Merarites. 58These *are* the families of the Levites: the family of the Libnites, the family of the Hebronites, the family of the Mahlites, the family of the Mushites, and the family of the Korathites. And Kohath begot Amram. 59The name of Amram's wife *was* Jochebed the daughter of Levi, who was born to Levi in Egypt; and to Amram she bore Aaron and Moses and their sister Miriam. 60To Aaron were born Nadab and Abihu, Eleazar and Ithamar. 61And Nadab and Abihu died when they offered profane fire before the LORD.

62Now those who were numbered of them were twenty-three thousand, every male from a month old and above; for they were not numbered among the other children of Israel, because there was no inheritance given to them among the children of Israel.

63These *are* those who were numbered by Moses and Eleazar the priest, who numbered the children of Israel in the plains of Moab by the Jordan, *across from* Jericho. 64But among these there was not a man of those who were numbered by Moses and Aaron the priest when they numbered the children of Israel in the Wilderness of Sinai. 65For the LORD had said of them, "They shall surely die in the wilderness." So there was not left a man of them, except Caleb the son of Jephunneh and Joshua the son of Nun.

Inheritance Laws

27 Then came the daughters of Zelophehad the son of Hepher, the son of Gilead, the son of Machir, the son of Manasseh, from the families of Manasseh the son of Joseph; and these *were* the names of his daughters: Mahlah, Noah, Hoglah, Milcah, and Tirzah. 2And they stood before

---

26:39 [b]Called *Huppim* in Genesis 46:21
26:40 [a]Called *Addar* in 1 Chronicles 8:3
26:42 [a]Called *Hushim* in Genesis 46:23
26:48 [a]Spelled *Jahziel* in 1 Chronicles 7:13

Moses, before Eleazar the priest, and before the leaders and all the congregation, *by* the doorway of the tabernacle of meeting, saying: 3"Our father died in the wilderness; but he was not in the company of those who gathered together against the LORD, in company with Korah, but he died in his own sin; and he had no sons. 4Why should the name of our father be removed from among his family because he had no son? Give us a possession among our father's brothers."

5So Moses brought their case before the LORD.

6And the LORD spoke to Moses, saying: 7"The daughters of Zelophehad speak *what is* right; you shall surely give them a possession of inheritance among their father's brothers, and cause the inheritance of their father to pass to them. 8And you shall speak to the children of Israel, saying: 'If a man dies and has no son, then you shall cause his inheritance to pass to his daughter. 9If he has no daughter, then you shall give his inheritance to his brothers. 10If he has no brothers, then you shall give his inheritance to his father's brothers. 11And if his father has no brothers, then you shall give his inheritance to the relative closest to him in his family, and he shall possess it.'" And it shall be to the children of Israel a statute of judgment, just as the LORD commanded Moses.

Joshua the Next Leader of Israel

12Now the LORD said to Moses: "Go up into this Mount Abarim, and see the land which I have given to the children of Israel. 13And when you have seen it, you also shall be gathered to your people, as Aaron your brother was gathered. 14For in the Wilderness of Zin, during the strife of the congregation, you rebelled against My command to hallow Me at the waters before their eyes." (These *are* the waters of Meribah, at Kadesh in the Wilderness of Zin.)

15Then Moses spoke to the LORD, saying: 16"Let the LORD, the God of the spirits of all flesh, set a man over the congregation, 17who may go out before them and go in before them, who may lead them out and bring them in, that the congregation of the LORD may not be like sheep which have no shepherd."

18And the LORD said to Moses: "Take Joshua the son of Nun with you, a man in whom *is* the Spirit, and lay your hand on him; 19set him before Eleazar the priest and before all the congregation, and inaugurate him in their sight. 20And you shall give *some* of your authority to him, that all the congregation of the children of Israel may be obedient. 21He shall stand before Eleazar the priest, who shall inquire before the LORD for him by the judgment of the Urim. At his word they shall go out, and at his word they shall come in, he and all the children of Israel with him—all the congregation."

22So Moses did as the LORD commanded him. He took Joshua and set him before Eleazar the priest and before all the congregation. 23And he laid his hands on him and inaugurated him, just as the LORD commanded by the hand of Moses.

Daily Offerings

28 Now the LORD spoke to Moses, saying, 2"Command the children of Israel, and say to them, 'My offering, My food for My offerings made by fire as a sweet aroma to Me, you shall be careful to offer to Me at their appointed time.'

3"And you shall say to them, 'This *is* the offering made by fire which you shall offer to the LORD: two male lambs in their first year without blemish, day by day, as a regular burnt offering. 4The one lamb you shall offer in the morning, the other lamb you shall offer in the evening, 5and one-tenth of an ephah of fine flour as a grain offering mixed with one-fourth of a hin of pressed oil. 6*It is* a regular burnt offering which was ordained at Mount Sinai for a sweet aroma, an offering made by fire to the LORD. 7And its drink offering *shall be* one-fourth of a hin for each lamb; in a holy *place* you shall pour out the drink to the LORD as an offering. 8The other lamb you shall offer in the evening; as the morning grain offering and its drink offering, you shall offer *it* as an offering made by fire, a sweet aroma to the LORD.

IT IS IMPOSSIBLE
TO RIGHTLY GOVERN THE WORLD
without
GOD AND THE BIBLE.

Attributed to George Washington, 1st President

THE BIBLE
AND
AMERICAN PRESIDENTS

A NATION IS MADE GREAT by its people and its values, particularly by its leaders and the values they embrace. It has been said that a nation rises and falls on its leadership. Throughout the Bible, when ancient Israel had a king who reverenced God and held the Word of God in high esteem, the nation prospered. When they had a bad king, life within the nation was full of misery.

American history is vividly clear that a faith in God and a reverence for the Bible provided the basis for the founding of our nation. That same reverence for God by many of our presidents has had a profound impact on the greatness of our nation. One fact is undeniable: the Bible has been one of the greatest influences on America's presidents.

The first and almost the only book deserving of universal attention is the Bible. I speak as a man of the world…and I say to you, "Search the Scriptures."

John Quincy Adams, Sixth President

In regard for this Great Book, I have this to say,
it is the best gift God has given to man.

ALL THE GOOD SAVIOR GAVE TO THE WORLD
WAS COMMUNICATED THROUGH THIS BOOK.

ABRAHAM LINCOLN | 16TH PRESIDENT

THAT BOOK, SIR,
IS THE ROCK
ON WHICH OUR
REPUBLIC RESTS.

ANDREW JACKSON
7th President

The Bible is the one supreme source of revelation of the meaning of life,
the nature of God, and spiritual nature and needs of men.
It is the only guide of life which really leads the spirit in the way
of peace and salvation. America was born a Christian nation.
America was born to exemplify that devotion to the elements of righteousness
which are derived from the revelations of Holy Scripture.

Woodrow Wilson | 28TH PRESIDENT

The strength of our country is the strength of its religious convictions.
The foundations of our society and our government rest so much
on the teachings of the Bible that it would be difficult
to support them if faith in these teachings would cease to be
practically universal in our country.

Calvin Coolidge | 30TH PRESIDENT

We cannot read the history of our rise and development as a nation
without reckoning with the place the Bible has occupied
in shaping the advances of the Republic.
Where we have been the truest and most consistent in obeying its precepts,
we have attained the greatest measure of contentment and prosperity.

Franklin Roosevelt | 32ND PRESIDENT

The fundamental basis of this nation's laws was given to Moses on the Mount.
The fundamental basis of our Bill of Rights comes from the teachings
we get from Exodus and Saint Matthew, from Isaiah and Saint Paul. . . .
If we don't have a proper fundamental moral background,
we will finally end up with a totalitarian government
which does not believe in rights for anybody except the State!

Harry Truman | 33RD PRESIDENT

I–3

HOLD FAST TO THE BIBLE AS THE SHEET ANCHOR OF YOUR LIBERTIES. WRITE ITS PRECEPTS IN YOUR HEARTS, AND PRACTICE THEM IN YOUR LIVES. TO THE INFLUENCE OF THIS BOOK ARE WE INDEBTED FOR ALL THE PROGRESS MADE IN TRUE CIVILIZATION, AND TO THIS WE MUST LOOK AS OUR GUIDE IN THE FUTURE. RIGHTEOUSNESS EXALTETH A NATION, BUT SIN IS A REPROACH TO ANY PEOPLE. | ULYSSES S. GRANT, 18th President

If you take out of your statutes, your constitution, your family life all that is taken from the Sacred Book, what would there be left to bind society together?
Benjamin Harrison | 23RD PRESIDENT

Inside the Bible's pages lie all the answers to all of the problems man has ever known. . . . It is my firm belief that the enduring values presented in its pages have a great meaning for each of us and for our nation. The Bible can touch our hearts, order our minds, and refresh our souls.

Ronald Reagan, 40th President

Sabbath Offerings

9'And on the Sabbath day two lambs in their first year, without blemish, and two-tenths *of an ephah* of fine flour as a grain offering, mixed with oil, with its drink offering— 10*this is* the burnt offering for every Sabbath, besides the regular burnt offering with its drink offering.

Monthly Offerings

11'At the beginnings of your months you shall present a burnt offering to the LORD: two young bulls, one ram, and seven lambs in their first year, without blemish; 12three-tenths *of an ephah* of fine flour as a grain offering, mixed with oil, for each bull; two-tenths *of an ephah* of fine flour as a grain offering, mixed with oil, for the one ram; 13and one-tenth *of an ephah* of fine flour, mixed with oil, as a grain offering for each lamb, as a burnt offering of sweet aroma, an offering made by fire to the LORD. 14Their drink offering shall be half a hin of wine for a bull, one-third of a hin for a ram, and one-fourth of a hin for a lamb; this *is* the burnt offering for each month throughout the months of the year. 15Also one kid of the goats as a sin offering to the LORD shall be offered, besides the regular burnt offering and its drink offering.

Offerings at Passover

16'On the fourteenth day of the first month *is* the Passover of the LORD. 17And on the fifteenth day of this month *is* the feast; unleavened bread shall be eaten for seven days. 18On the first day *you shall have* a holy convocation. You shall do no customary work. 19And you shall present an offering made by fire as a burnt offering to the LORD: two young bulls, one ram, and seven lambs in their first year. Be sure they are without blemish. 20Their grain offering shall be of fine flour mixed with oil: three-tenths *of an ephah* you shall offer for a bull, and two-tenths for a ram; 21you shall offer one-tenth *of an ephah* for each of the seven lambs; 22also one goat *as* a sin offering, to make atonement for you. 23You shall offer these besides the burnt offering of the morning, which *is* for a regular burnt offering.

24In this manner you shall offer the food of the offering made by fire daily for seven days, as a sweet aroma to the LORD; it shall be offered besides the regular burnt offering and its drink offering. 25And on the seventh day you shall have a holy convocation. You shall do no customary work.

Offerings at the Feast of Weeks

26'Also on the day of the firstfruits, when you bring a new grain offering to the LORD at your *Feast of* Weeks, you shall have a holy convocation. You shall do no customary work. 27You shall present a burnt offering as a sweet aroma to the LORD: two young bulls, one ram, and seven lambs in their first year, 28with their grain offering of fine flour mixed with oil: three-tenths *of an ephah* for each bull, two-tenths for the one ram, 29and one-tenth for each of the seven lambs; 30*also* one kid of the goats, to make atonement for you. 31Be sure they are without blemish. You shall present *them* with their drink offerings, besides the regular burnt offering with its grain offering.

Offerings at the Feast of Trumpets

29 'And in the seventh month, on the first *day* of the month, you shall have a holy convocation. You shall do no customary work. For you it is a day of blowing the trumpets. 2You shall offer a burnt offering as a sweet aroma to the LORD: one young bull, one ram, *and* seven lambs in their first year, without blemish. 3Their grain offering *shall be* fine flour mixed with oil: three-tenths *of an ephah* for the bull, two-tenths for the ram, 4and one-tenth for each of the seven lambs; 5also one kid of the goats *as* a sin offering, to make atonement for you; 6besides the burnt offering with its grain offering for the New Moon, the regular burnt offering with its grain offering, and their drink offerings, according to their ordinance, as a sweet aroma, an offering made by fire to the LORD.

Offerings on the Day of Atonement

7'On the tenth *day* of this seventh month you shall have a holy convocation. You shall afflict your souls; you shall not do

any work. 8You shall present a burnt offering to the LORD *as* a sweet aroma: one young bull, one ram, *and* seven lambs in their first year. Be sure they are without blemish. 9Their grain offering *shall be of* fine flour mixed with oil: three-tenths *of an ephah* for the bull, two-tenths for the one ram, 10and one-tenth for each of the seven lambs; 11also one kid of the goats *as* a sin offering, besides the sin offering for atonement, the regular burnt offering with its grain offering, and their drink offerings.

Offerings at the Feast of Tabernacles

12'On the fifteenth day of the seventh month you shall have a holy convocation. You shall do no customary work, and you shall keep a feast to the LORD seven days. 13You shall present a burnt offering, an offering made by fire as a sweet aroma to the LORD: thirteen young bulls, two rams, *and* fourteen lambs in their first year. They shall be without blemish. 14Their grain offering *shall be of* fine flour mixed with oil: three-tenths *of an ephah* for each of the thirteen bulls, two-tenths for each of the two rams, 15and one-tenth for each of the fourteen lambs; 16also one kid of the goats *as* a sin offering, besides the regular burnt offering, its grain offering, and its drink offering.

17'On the second day *present* twelve young bulls, two rams, fourteen lambs in their first year without blemish, 18and their grain offering and their drink offerings for the bulls, for the rams, and for the lambs, by their number, according to the ordinance; 19also one kid of the goats *as* a sin offering, besides the regular burnt offering with its grain offering, and their drink offerings.

20'On the third day *present* eleven bulls, two rams, fourteen lambs in their first year without blemish, 21and their grain offering and their drink offerings for the bulls, for the rams, and for the lambs, by their number, according to the ordinance; 22also one goat *as* a sin offering, besides the regular burnt offering, its grain offering, and its drink offering.

23'On the fourth day *present* ten bulls, two rams, *and* fourteen lambs in their first year, without blemish, 24and their grain offering and their drink offerings for the bulls, for the rams, and for the lambs, by their number, according to the ordinance; 25also one kid of the goats *as* a sin offering, besides the regular burnt offering, its grain offering, and its drink offering.

26'On the fifth day *present* nine bulls, two rams, *and* fourteen lambs in their first year without blemish, 27and their grain offering and their drink offerings for the bulls, for the rams, and for the lambs, by their number, according to the ordinance; 28also one goat *as* a sin offering, besides the regular burnt offering, its grain offering, and its drink offering.

29'On the sixth day *present* eight bulls, two rams, *and* fourteen lambs in their first year without blemish, 30and their grain offering and their drink offerings for the bulls, for the rams, and for the lambs, by their number, according to the ordinance; 31also one goat *as* a sin offering, besides the regular burnt offering, its grain offering, and its drink offering.

32'On the seventh day *present* seven bulls, two rams, *and* fourteen lambs in their first year without blemish, 33and their grain offering and their drink offerings for the bulls, for the rams, and for the lambs, by their number, according to the ordinance; 34also one goat *as* a sin offering, besides the regular burnt offering, its grain offering, and its drink offering.

35'On the eighth day you shall have a sacred assembly. You shall do no customary work. 36You shall present a burnt offering, an offering made by fire as a sweet aroma to the LORD: one bull, one ram, seven lambs in their first year without blemish, 37and their grain offering and their drink offerings for the bull, for the ram, and for the lambs, by their number, according to the ordinance; 38also one goat *as* a sin offering, besides the regular burnt offering, its grain offering, and its drink offering.

39'These you shall present to the LORD at your appointed feasts (besides your vowed offerings and your freewill offerings) as your burnt offerings and your grain offerings, as your drink offerings and your peace offerings.'"

⁴⁰So Moses told the children of Israel everything, just as the LORD commanded Moses.

The Law Concerning Vows

30 Then Moses spoke to the heads of the tribes concerning the children of Israel, saying, "This *is* the thing which the LORD has commanded: ²If a man makes a vow to the LORD, or swears an oath to bind himself by some agreement, he shall not break his word; he shall do according to all that proceeds out of his mouth.

³"Or if a woman makes a vow to the LORD, and binds *herself* by some agreement while in her father's house in her youth, ⁴and her father hears her vow and the agreement by which she has bound herself, and her father holds his peace, then all her vows shall stand, and every agreement with which she has bound herself

shall stand. ⁵But if her father overrules her on the day that he hears, then none of her vows nor her agreements by which she has bound herself shall stand; and the LORD will release her, because her father overruled her.

⁶"If indeed she takes a husband, while bound by her vows or by a rash utterance from her lips by which she bound herself, ⁷and her husband hears *it,* and makes no response to her on the day that he hears, then her vows shall stand, and her agreements by which she bound herself shall stand. ⁸But if her husband overrules her on the day that he hears *it,* he shall make void her vow which she took and what she uttered with her lips, by which she bound herself, and the LORD will release her.

⁹"Also any vow of a widow or a divorced woman, by which she has bound herself, shall stand against her.

MORAL STRENGTH

"If a man . . . swears an oath to bind himself by some agreement, he shall not break his word. . . ."

NUMBERS 30:2

George Washington

RELIGION AND MORALITY

In his Farewell Address in 1796, President George Washington put his finger on the importance of preserving a freedom of religion within a society:

> Of all the dispositions and habits which lead to political prosperity, religion and morality are indispensable supports. In vain would that man claim the tribute of patriotism who should labor to subvert these great pillars of human happiness—these firmest props of the duties of men and citizens. The mere politician, equally with the pious man, ought to respect and to cherish them. A volume could not trace all their connections with private and public felicity. Let it simply be asked, "Where is the security for property, for reputation, for life, if the sense of religious obligation desert the oaths which are the instruments of investigation in courts of justice?" And let us with caution indulge the supposition that morality can be maintained without religion. Whatever may be conceded to the influence of refined education on minds of peculiar structure, reason and experience both forbid us to expect that national morality can prevail in exclusion of religious principle.
>
> It is substantially true that virtue or morality is a necessary spring of popular government. The rule indeed extends with more or less force to every species of free government. Who that is a sincere friend to it can look with indifference upon attempts to shake the foundation of the fabric?

10"If she vowed in her husband's house, or bound herself by an agreement with an oath, 11and her husband heard *it,* and made no response to her *and* did not overrule her, then all her vows shall stand, and every agreement by which she bound herself shall stand. 12But if her husband truly made them void on the day he heard *them,* then whatever proceeded from her lips concerning her vows or concerning the agreement binding her, it shall not stand; her husband has made them void, and the LORD will release her. 13Every vow and every binding oath to afflict her soul, her husband may confirm it, or her husband may make it void. 14Now if her husband makes no response whatever to her from day to day, then he confirms all her vows or all the agreements that bind her; he confirms them, because he made no response to her on the day that he heard *them.* 15But if he does make them void after he has heard *them,* then he shall bear her guilt."

16These *are* the statutes which the LORD commanded Moses, between a man and his wife, and between a father and his daughter in her youth in her father's house.

Vengeance on the Midianites

31 And the LORD spoke to Moses, saying: 2"Take vengeance on the Midianites for the children of Israel. Afterward you shall be gathered to your people."

3So Moses spoke to the people, saying, "Arm some of yourselves for war, and let them go against the Midianites to take vengeance for the LORD on Midian. 4A thousand from each tribe of all the tribes of Israel you shall send to the war."

5So there were recruited from the divisions of Israel one thousand from *each* tribe, twelve thousand armed for war. 6Then Moses sent them to the war, one thousand from *each* tribe; he sent them to the war with Phinehas the son of Eleazar the priest, with the holy articles and the signal trumpets in his hand. 7And they warred against the Midianites, just as the LORD commanded Moses, and they killed all the males. 8They killed the kings of Midian with *the rest of* those who were

killed—Evi, Rekem, Zur, Hur, and Reba, the five kings of Midian. Balaam the son of Beor they also killed with the sword.

9And the children of Israel took the women of Midian captive, with their little ones, and took as spoil all their cattle, all their flocks, and all their goods. 10They also burned with fire all the cities where they dwelt, and all their forts. 11And they took all the spoil and all the booty—of man and beast.

Return from the War

12Then they brought the captives, the booty, and the spoil to Moses, to Eleazar the priest, and to the congregation of the children of Israel, to the camp in the plains of Moab by the Jordan, *across from* Jericho. 13And Moses, Eleazar the priest, and all the leaders of the congregation, went to meet them outside the camp. 14But Moses was angry with the officers of the army, *with* the captains over thousands and captains over hundreds, who had come from the battle.

15And Moses said to them: "Have you kept all the women alive? 16Look, these *women* caused the children of Israel, through the counsel of Balaam, to trespass against the LORD in the incident of Peor, and there was a plague among the congregation of the LORD. 17Now therefore, kill every male among the little ones, and kill every woman who has known a man intimately. 18But keep alive for yourselves all the young girls who have not known a man intimately. 19And as for you, remain outside the camp seven days; whoever has killed any person, and whoever has touched any slain, purify yourselves and your captives on the third day and on the seventh day. 20Purify every garment, everything made of leather, everything woven of goats' *hair,* and everything made of wood."

21Then Eleazar the priest said to the men of war who had gone to the battle, "This *is* the ordinance of the law which the LORD commanded Moses: 22Only the gold, the silver, the bronze, the iron, the tin, and the lead, 23everything that can endure fire, you shall put through the fire, and it shall be clean; and it shall be purified with the

water of purification. But all that cannot endure fire you shall put through water. [24]And you shall wash your clothes on the seventh day and be clean, and afterward you may come into the camp."

Division of the Plunder

[25]Now the LORD spoke to Moses, saying: [26]"Count up the plunder that was taken—of man and beast—you and Eleazar the priest and the chief fathers of the congregation; [27]and divide the plunder into two parts, between those who took part in the war, who went out to battle, and all the congregation. [28]And levy a tribute for the LORD on the men of war who went out to battle: one of every five hundred of the persons, the cattle, the donkeys, and the sheep; [29]take *it* from their half, and give *it* to Eleazar the priest as a heave offering to the LORD. [30]And from the children of Israel's half you shall take one of every fifty, drawn from the persons, the cattle, the donkeys, and the sheep, from all the livestock, and give them to the Levites who keep charge of the tabernacle of the LORD." [31]So Moses and Eleazar the priest did as the LORD commanded Moses.

[32]The booty remaining from the plunder, which the men of war had taken, was six hundred and seventy-five thousand sheep, [33]seventy-two thousand cattle, [34]sixty-one thousand donkeys, [35]and thirty-two thousand persons in all, of women who had not known a man intimately. [36]And the half, the portion for those who had gone out to war, was in number three hundred and thirty-seven thousand five hundred sheep; [37]and the LORD's tribute of the sheep was six hundred and seventy-five. [38]The cattle *were* thirty-six thousand, of which the LORD's tribute *was* seventy-two. [39]The donkeys *were* thirty thousand five hundred, of which the LORD's tribute *was* sixty-one. [40]The persons *were* sixteen thousand, of which the LORD's tribute *was* thirty-two persons. [41]So Moses gave the tribute *which was* the LORD's heave offering to Eleazar the priest, as the LORD commanded Moses.

[42]And from the children of Israel's half, which Moses separated from the men who fought— [43]now the half belonging to the congregation was three hundred and thirty-seven thousand five hundred sheep, [44]thirty-six thousand cattle, [45]thirty thousand five hundred donkeys, [46]and sixteen thousand persons— [47]and from the children of Israel's half Moses took one of every fifty, drawn from man and beast, and gave them to the Levites, who kept charge of the tabernacle of the LORD, as the LORD commanded Moses.

[48]Then the officers who *were* over thousands of the army, the captains of thousands and captains of hundreds, came near to Moses; [49]and they said to Moses, "Your servants have taken a count of the men of war who *are* under our command, and not a man of us is missing. [50]Therefore we have brought an offering for the LORD, what every man found of ornaments of gold: armlets and bracelets and signet rings and earrings and necklaces, to make atonement for ourselves before the LORD." [51]So Moses and Eleazar the priest received the gold from them, all the fashioned ornaments. [52]And all the gold of the offering that they offered to the LORD, from the captains of thousands and captains of hundreds, was sixteen thousand seven hundred and fifty shekels. [53](The men of war had taken spoil, every man for himself.) [54]And Moses and Eleazar the priest received the gold from the captains of thousands and of hundreds, and brought it into the tabernacle of meeting as a memorial for the children of Israel before the LORD.

The Tribes Settling East of the Jordan

32 Now the children of Reuben and the children of Gad had a very great multitude of livestock; and when they saw the land of Jazer and the land of Gilead, that indeed the region *was* a place for livestock, [2]the children of Gad and the children of Reuben came and spoke to Moses, to Eleazar the priest, and to the leaders of the congregation, saying, [3]"Ataroth, Dibon, Jazer, Nimrah, Heshbon, Elealeh, Shebam, Nebo, and Beon, [4]the country which the LORD defeated before the congregation of Israel, *is* a land for livestock, and your servants have livestock." [5]Therefore they said, "If we have

found favor in your sight, let this land be given to your servants as a possession. Do not take us over the Jordan."

⁶And Moses said to the children of Gad and to the children of Reuben: "Shall your brethren go to war while you sit here? ⁷Now why will you discourage the heart of the children of Israel from going over into the land which the LORD has given them? ⁸Thus your fathers did when I sent them away from Kadesh Barnea to see the land. ⁹For when they went up to the Valley of Eshcol and saw the land, they discouraged the heart of the children of Israel, so that they did not go into the land which the LORD had given them. ¹⁰So the LORD's anger was aroused on that day, and He swore an oath, saying, ¹¹'Surely none of the men who came up from Egypt, from twenty years old and above, shall see the land of which I swore to Abraham, Isaac, and Jacob, because they have not wholly followed Me, ¹²except Caleb the son of Jephunneh, the Kenizzite, and Joshua the son of Nun, for they have wholly followed the LORD.' ¹³So the LORD's anger was aroused against Israel, and He made them wander in the wilderness forty years, until all the generation that had done evil in the sight of the LORD was gone. ¹⁴And look! You have risen in your fathers' place, a brood of sinful men, to increase still more the fierce anger of the LORD against Israel. ¹⁵For if you turn away from following Him, He will once again leave them in the wilderness, and you will destroy all these people."

¹⁶Then they came near to him and said: "We will build sheepfolds here for our livestock, and cities for our little ones, ¹⁷but we ourselves will be armed, ready *to go* before the children of Israel until we have brought them to their place; and our little ones will dwell in the fortified cities because of the inhabitants of the land. ¹⁸We will not return to our homes until every one of the children of Israel has received his inheritance. ¹⁹For we will not inherit with them on the other side of the Jordan and beyond, because our inheritance has fallen to us on this eastern side of the Jordan."

²⁰Then Moses said to them: "If you do this thing, if you arm yourselves before the LORD for the war, ²¹and all your armed men cross over the Jordan before the LORD until He has driven out His enemies from before Him, ²²and the land is subdued before the LORD, then afterward you may return and be blameless before the LORD and before Israel; and this land shall be your possession before the LORD. ²³But if you do not do so, then take note, you have sinned against the LORD; and be sure your sin will find you out. ²⁴Build cities for your little ones and folds for your sheep, and do what has proceeded out of your mouth."

²⁵And the children of Gad and the children of Reuben spoke to Moses, saying: "Your servants will do as my lord commands. ²⁶Our little ones, our wives, our flocks, and all our livestock will be there in the cities of Gilead; ²⁷but your servants will cross over, every man armed for war, before the LORD to battle, just as my lord says."

²⁸So Moses gave command concerning them to Eleazar the priest, to Joshua the son of Nun, and to the chief fathers of the tribes of the children of Israel. ²⁹And Moses said to them: "If the children of Gad and the children of Reuben cross over the Jordan with you, every man armed for battle before the LORD, and the land is subdued before you, then you shall give them the land of Gilead as a possession. ³⁰But if they do not cross over armed with you, they shall have possessions among you in the land of Canaan."

³¹Then the children of Gad and the children of Reuben answered, saying: "As the LORD has said to your servants, so we will do. ³²We will cross over armed before the LORD into the land of Canaan, but the possession of our inheritance *shall remain* with us on this side of the Jordan."

³³So Moses gave to the children of Gad, to the children of Reuben, and to half the tribe of Manasseh the son of Joseph, the kingdom of Sihon king of the Amorites and the kingdom of Og king of Bashan, the land with its cities within the borders, the cities of the surrounding country. ³⁴And the children of Gad built Dibon and Ataroth and Aroer, ³⁵Atroth and Shophan and Jazer and Jogbehah, ³⁶Beth Nimrah and Beth Haran,

fortified cities, and folds for sheep. [37]And the children of Reuben built Heshbon and Elealeh and Kirjathaim, [38]Nebo and Baal Meon (*their* names being changed) and Shibmah; and they gave *other* names to the cities which they built.

[39]And the children of Machir the son of Manasseh went to Gilead and took it, and dispossessed the Amorites who *were* in it. [40]So Moses gave Gilead to Machir the son of Manasseh, and he dwelt in it. [41]Also Jair the son of Manasseh went and took its small towns, and called them Havoth Jair.[a] [42]Then Nobah went and took Kenath and its villages, and he called it Nobah, after his own name.

Israel's Journey from Egypt Reviewed

33 These *are* the journeys of the children of Israel, who went out of the land of Egypt by their armies under the hand of Moses and Aaron. [2]Now Moses wrote down the starting points of their journeys at the command of the LORD. And these *are* their journeys according to their starting points:

[3]They departed from Rameses in the first month, on the fifteenth day of the first month; on the day after the Passover the children of Israel went out with boldness in the sight of all the Egyptians. [4]For the Egyptians were burying all *their* firstborn, whom the LORD had killed among them. Also on their gods the LORD had executed judgments.

[5]Then the children of Israel moved from Rameses and camped at Succoth. [6]They departed from Succoth and camped at Etham, which *is* on the edge of the wilderness. [7]They moved from Etham and turned back to Pi Hahiroth, which *is* east of Baal Zephon; and they camped near Migdol. [8]They departed from before Hahiroth[a] and passed through the midst of the sea into the wilderness, went three days' journey in the Wilderness of Etham, and camped at Marah. [9]They moved from Marah and came to Elim. At Elim *were* twelve springs of water and seventy palm trees; so they camped there.

[10]They moved from Elim and camped by the Red Sea. [11]They moved from the Red Sea and camped in the Wilderness of Sin. [12]They journeyed from the Wilderness of Sin and camped at Dophkah. [13]They departed from Dophkah and camped at Alush. [14]They moved from Alush and camped at Rephidim, where there was no water for the people to drink.

[15]They departed from Rephidim and camped in the Wilderness of Sinai. [16]They moved from the Wilderness of Sinai and camped at Kibroth Hattaavah. [17]They departed from Kibroth Hattaavah and camped at Hazeroth. [18]They departed from Hazeroth and camped at Rithmah. [19]They departed from Rithmah and camped at Rimmon Perez. [20]They departed from Rimmon Perez and camped at Libnah. [21]They moved from Libnah and camped at Rissah. [22]They journeyed from Rissah and camped at Kehelathah. [23]They went from Kehelathah and camped at Mount Shepher. [24]They moved from Mount Shepher and camped at Haradah. [25]They moved from Haradah and camped at Makheloth. [26]They moved from Makheloth and camped at Tahath. [27]They departed from Tahath and camped at Terah. [28]They moved from Terah and camped at Mithkah. [29]They went from Mithkah and camped at Hashmonah. [30]They departed from Hashmonah and camped at Moseroth. [31]They departed from Moseroth and camped at Bene Jaakan. [32]They moved from Bene Jaakan and camped at Hor Hagidgad. [33]They went from Hor Hagidgad and camped at Jotbathah. [34]They moved from Jotbathah and camped at Abronah. [35]They departed from Abronah and camped at Ezion Geber. [36]They moved from Ezion Geber and camped in the Wilderness of Zin, which *is* Kadesh. [37]They moved from Kadesh and camped at Mount Hor, on the boundary of the land of Edom.

[38]Then Aaron the priest went up to Mount Hor at the command of the LORD, and died there in the fortieth year after the children of Israel had come out of the land

---

32:41 [a]Literally *Towns of Jair*   **33:8** [a]Many Hebrew manuscripts, Samaritan Pentateuch, Syriac, Targum, and Vulgate read *from Pi Hahiroth* (compare verse 7).

of Egypt, on the first *day* of the fifth month. ³⁹Aaron *was* one hundred and twenty-three years old when he died on Mount Hor.

⁴⁰Now the king of Arad, the Canaanite, who dwelt in the South in the land of Canaan, heard of the coming of the children of Israel.

⁴¹So they departed from Mount Hor and camped at Zalmonah. ⁴²They departed from Zalmonah and camped at Punon. ⁴³They departed from Punon and camped at Oboth. ⁴⁴They departed from Oboth and camped at Ije Abarim, at the border of Moab. ⁴⁵They departed from Ijimᵃ and camped at Dibon Gad. ⁴⁶They moved from Dibon Gad and camped at Almon Diblathaim. ⁴⁷They moved from Almon Diblathaim and camped in the mountains of Abarim, before Nebo. ⁴⁸They departed from the mountains of Abarim and camped in the plains of Moab by the Jordan, *across from* Jericho. ⁴⁹They camped by the Jordan, from Beth Jesimoth as far as the Abel Acacia Groveᵃ in the plains of Moab.

Instructions for the Conquest of Canaan

⁵⁰Now the Lord spoke to Moses in the plains of Moab by the Jordan, *across from* Jericho, saying, ⁵¹"Speak to the children of Israel, and say to them: 'When you have crossed the Jordan into the land of Canaan, ⁵²then you shall drive out all the inhabitants of the land from before you, destroy all their engraved stones, destroy all their molded images, and demolish all their high places; ⁵³you shall dispossess *the inhabitants of* the land and dwell in it, for I have given you the land to possess. ⁵⁴And you shall divide the land by lot as an inheritance among your families; to the larger you shall give a larger inheritance, and to the smaller you shall give a smaller inheritance; there everyone's *inheritance* shall be whatever falls to him by lot. You shall inherit according to the tribes of your fathers. ⁵⁵But if you do not drive out the inhabitants of the land from before you, then it shall be that those whom you let remain *shall be* irritants in your eyes and thorns in your sides, and they shall harass you in the land where you dwell. ⁵⁶More-

over it shall be *that* I will do to you as I thought to do to them.'"

The Appointed Boundaries of Canaan

34 Then the Lord spoke to Moses, saying, ²"Command the children of Israel, and say to them: 'When you come into the land of Canaan, this *is* the land that shall fall to you as an inheritance— the land of Canaan to its boundaries. ³Your southern border shall be from the Wilderness of Zin along the border of Edom; then your southern border shall extend eastward to the end of the Salt Sea; ⁴your border shall turn from the southern side of the Ascent of Akrabbim, continue to Zin, and be on the south of Kadesh Barnea; then it shall go on to Hazar Addar, and continue to Azmon; ⁵the border shall turn from Azmon to the Brook of Egypt, and it shall end at the Sea.

⁶'As for the western border, you shall have the Great Sea for a border; this shall be your western border.

⁷'And this shall be your northern border: From the Great Sea you shall mark out your *border* line to Mount Hor; ⁸from Mount Hor you shall mark out *your border* to the entrance of Hamath; then the direction of the border shall be toward Zedad; ⁹the border shall proceed to Ziphron, and it shall end at Hazar Enan. This shall be your northern border.

¹⁰'You shall mark out your eastern border from Hazar Enan to Shepham; ¹¹the border shall go down from Shepham to Riblah on the east side of Ain; the border shall go down and reach to the eastern side of the Sea of Chinnereth; ¹²the border shall go down along the Jordan, and it shall end at the Salt Sea. This shall be your land with its surrounding boundaries.'"

¹³Then Moses commanded the children of Israel, saying: "This *is* the land which you shall inherit by lot, which the Lord has commanded to give to the nine tribes and to the half-tribe. ¹⁴For the tribe of the children of Reuben according to the house of their fathers, and the tribe of the children

---

33:45 ᵃSame as *Ije Abarim,* verse 44
33:49 ᵃHebrew *Abel Shittim*

of Gad according to the house of their fathers, have received *their inheritance;* and the half-tribe of Manasseh has received its inheritance. ¹⁵The two tribes and the half-tribe have received their inheritance on this side of the Jordan, *across from* Jericho eastward, toward the sunrise."

The Leaders Appointed to Divide the Land

¹⁶And the LORD spoke to Moses, saying, ¹⁷"These *are* the names of the men who shall divide the land among you as an inheritance: Eleazar the priest and Joshua the son of Nun. ¹⁸And you shall take one leader of every tribe to divide the land for the inheritance. ¹⁹These *are* the names of the men: from the tribe of Judah, Caleb the son of Jephunneh; ²⁰from the tribe of the children of Simeon, Shemuel the son of Ammihud; ²¹from the tribe of Benjamin, Elidad the son of Chislon; ²²a leader from the tribe of the children of Dan, Bukki the son of Jogli; ²³from the sons of Joseph: a leader from the tribe of the children of Manasseh, Hanniel the son of Ephod, ²⁴and a leader from the tribe of the children of Ephraim, Kemuel the son of Shiphtan; ²⁵a leader from the tribe of the children of Zebulun, Elizaphan the son of Parnach; ²⁶a leader from the tribe of the children of Issachar, Paltiel the son of Azzan; ²⁷a leader from the tribe of the children of Asher, Ahihud the son of Shelomi; ²⁸and a leader from the tribe of the children of Naphtali, Pedahel the son of Ammihud."

²⁹These *are* the ones the LORD commanded to divide the inheritance among the children of Israel in the land of Canaan.

Cities for the Levites

35 And the LORD spoke to Moses in the plains of Moab by the Jordan *across from* Jericho, saying: ²"Command the children of Israel that they give the Levites cities to dwell in from the inheritance of their possession, and you shall *also* give the Levites common-land around the cities. ³They shall have the cities to dwell in; and their common-land shall be for their cattle, for their herds, and for all their animals. ⁴The common-land of the cities which you will give the Levites *shall extend* from the wall of the city outward a thousand cubits all around. ⁵And you shall measure outside the city on the east side two thousand cubits, on the south side two thousand cubits, on the west side two thousand cubits, and on the north side two thousand cubits. The city *shall be* in the middle. This shall belong to them as common-land for the cities. ⁶"Now among the cities which you will give to the Levites *you shall appoint* six cities of refuge, to which a manslayer may flee. And to these you shall add forty-two cities. ⁷So all the cities you will give to the Levites *shall be* forty-eight; these *you shall give* with their common-land. ⁸And the cities which you will give *shall be* from the possession of the children of Israel; from the larger *tribe* you shall give many, from the smaller you shall give few. Each shall give some of its cities to the Levites, in proportion to the inheritance that each receives."

Cities of Refuge

⁹Then the LORD spoke to Moses, saying, ¹⁰"Speak to the children of Israel, and say to them: 'When you cross the Jordan into the land of Canaan, ¹¹then you shall appoint cities to be cities of refuge for you, that the manslayer who kills any person accidentally may flee there. ¹²They shall be cities of refuge for you from the avenger, that the manslayer may not die until he stands before the congregation in judgment. ¹³And of the cities which you give, you shall have six cities of refuge. ¹⁴You shall appoint three cities on this side of the Jordan, and three cities you shall appoint in the land of Canaan, *which* will be cities of refuge. ¹⁵These six cities shall be for refuge for the children of Israel, for the stranger, and for the sojourner among them, that anyone who kills a person accidentally may flee there.

¹⁶'But if he strikes him with an iron implement, so that he dies, he *is* a murderer; the murderer shall surely be put to death. ¹⁷And if he strikes him with a stone in the hand, by which one could die, and he does die, he *is* a murderer; the murderer shall surely be put to death. ¹⁸Or *if* he strikes him with a wooden hand weapon, by which

one could die, and he does die, he *is* a murderer; the murderer shall surely be put to death. [19]The avenger of blood himself shall put the murderer to death; when he meets him, he shall put him to death. [20]If he pushes him out of hatred or, while lying in wait, hurls something at him so that he dies, [21]or in enmity he strikes him with his hand so that he dies, the one who struck *him* shall surely be put to death. He *is* a murderer. The avenger of blood shall put the murderer to death when he meets him.

[22]'However, if he pushes him suddenly without enmity, or throws anything at him without lying in wait, [23]or uses a stone, by which a man could die, throwing *it* at him without seeing *him,* so that he dies, while he was not his enemy or seeking his harm, [24]then the congregation shall judge between the manslayer and the avenger of blood according to these judgments. [25]So the congregation shall deliver the manslayer from the hand of the avenger of blood, and the congregation shall return him to the city of refuge where he had fled, and he shall remain there until the death of the high priest who was anointed with the holy oil. [26]But if the manslayer at any time goes outside the limits of the city of refuge where he fled, [27]and the avenger of blood finds him outside the limits of his city of refuge, and the avenger of blood kills the manslayer, he shall not be guilty of blood, [28]because he should have remained in his city of refuge until the death of the high priest. But after the death of the high priest the manslayer may return to the land of his possession.

[29]'And these *things* shall be a statute of judgment to you throughout your generations in all your dwellings. [30]Whoever kills a person, the murderer shall be put to death on the testimony of witnesses; but one witness is not *sufficient* testimony against a person for the death *penalty.* [31]Moreover you shall take no ransom for the life of a murderer who *is* guilty of death, but he shall surely be put to death. [32]And you shall take no ransom for him who has fled to his city of refuge, that he may return to dwell in the land before the death of the priest. [33]So you shall not pollute the land where you *are;* for blood defiles the land, and no atonement can be made for the land, for the blood that is shed on it, except by the blood of him who shed it. [34]Therefore do not defile the land which you inhabit, in the midst of which I dwell; for I the LORD dwell among the children of Israel.' "

Marriage of Female Heirs

36 Now the chief fathers of the families of the children of Gilead the son of Machir, the son of Manasseh, of the families of the sons of Joseph, came near and spoke before Moses and before the leaders, the chief fathers of the children of Israel. [2]And they said: "The LORD commanded my lord *Moses* to give the land as an inheritance by lot to the children of Israel, and my lord was commanded by the LORD to give the inheritance of our brother Zelophehad to his daughters. [3]Now if they are married to any of the sons of the *other* tribes of the children of Israel, then their inheritance will be taken from the inheritance of our fathers, and it will be added to the inheritance of the tribe into which they marry; so it will be taken from the lot of our inheritance. [4]And when the Jubilee of the children of Israel comes, then their inheritance will be added to the inheritance of the tribe into which they marry; so their inheritance will be taken away from the inheritance of the tribe of our fathers."

[5]Then Moses commanded the children of Israel according to the word of the LORD, saying: "What the tribe of the sons of Joseph speaks is right. [6]This *is* what the LORD commands concerning the daughters of Zelophehad, saying, 'Let them marry whom they think best, but they may marry only within the family of their father's tribe.' [7]So the inheritance of the children of Israel shall not change hands from tribe to tribe, for every one of the children of Israel shall keep the inheritance of the tribe of his fathers. [8]And every daughter who possesses an inheritance in any tribe of the children of Israel shall be the wife of one of the family of her father's tribe, so that the children of Israel each may possess the

inheritance of his fathers. ⁹Thus no inheritance shall change hands from *one* tribe to another, but every tribe of the children of Israel shall keep its own inheritance."

¹⁰Just as the LORD commanded Moses, so did the daughters of Zelophehad; ¹¹for Mahlah, Tirzah, Hoglah, Milcah, and Noah, the daughters of Zelophehad, were married to the sons of their father's brothers.

¹²They were married into the families of the children of Manasseh the son of Joseph, and their inheritance remained in the tribe of their father's family.

¹³These *are* the commandments and the judgments which the LORD commanded the children of Israel by the hand of Moses in the plains of Moab by the Jordan, *across from* Jericho.

DEUTERONOMY

Author: Moses

When Written: Around 1400 B.C.

Theme: Covenant

Key Verses: Deuteronomy 30:19, 20—"I call heaven and earth as witnesses today against you, that I have set before you life and death, blessing and cursing; therefore choose life, that both you and your descendants may live; that you may love the LORD your God, that you may obey His voice, and that you may cling to Him, for He is your life and the length of your days; and that you may dwell in the land which the LORD swore to your fathers, to Abraham, Isaac, and Jacob, to give them."

Key Chapter: Deuteronomy 28—In this chapter, Moses declares to the people of Israel the blessings that will follow them if they take heed to obey God, and the curses they can expect if they do not.

As God's people Israel prepared to enter the land of Canaan after their nearly 40-year sojourn in the desert, Moses took the opportunity to remind them of God's faithfulness, as well as their obligation to live as a holy and righteous people "chosen" by God.

Deuteronomy means a "repeating of the law" and demonstrates how crucial it is for God's people to keep His Word always on their hearts, minds, and lips, so that they will be positioned for blessing in all their endeavors.

As "one nation under God," America has traditionally placed a high priority on faithfulness to God's Word. It is a priority that each generation must pass on to the next, so that we will continue to be "the land of the free and the home of the brave."

DEUTERONOMY

The Previous Command to Enter Canaan

1 These *are* the words which Moses spoke to all Israel on this side of the Jordan in the wilderness, in the plain[a] opposite Suph,[b] between Paran, Tophel, Laban, Hazeroth, and Dizahab. [2]*It is* eleven days' *journey* from Horeb by way of Mount Seir to Kadesh Barnea. [3]Now it came to pass in the fortieth year, in the eleventh month, on the first *day* of the month, *that* Moses spoke to the children of Israel according to all that the LORD had given him as commandments to them, [4]after he had killed Sihon king of the Amorites, who dwelt in Heshbon, and Og king of Bashan, who dwelt at Ashtaroth in[a] Edrei.

[5]On this side of the Jordan in the land of Moab, Moses began to explain this law, saying, [6]"The LORD our God spoke to us in Horeb, saying: 'You have dwelt long enough at this mountain. [7]Turn and take your journey, and go to the mountains of the Amorites, to all the neighboring *places* in the plain,[a] in the mountains and in the lowland, in the South and on the seacoast, to the land of the Canaanites and to Lebanon, as far as the great river, the River Euphrates. [8]See, I have set the land before you; go in and possess the land which the LORD swore to your fathers—to Abraham, Isaac, and Jacob—to give to them and their descendants after them.'

Tribal Leaders Appointed

[9]"And I spoke to you at that time, saying: 'I alone am not able to bear you. [10]The LORD your God has multiplied you, and here you *are* today, as the stars of heaven in multitude. [11]May the LORD God of your fathers make you a thousand times more numerous than you are, and bless you as He has promised you! [12]How can I alone bear your problems and your burdens and your complaints? [13]Choose wise, understanding, and knowledgeable men from among your tribes, and I will make them heads over you.' [14]And you answered me and said, 'The thing which you have told *us* to do *is* good.' [15]So I took the heads of your tribes, wise and knowledgeable men, and made them heads over you, leaders of thousands, leaders of hundreds, leaders of fifties, leaders of tens, and officers for your tribes.

[16]"Then I commanded your judges at that time, saying, 'Hear *the cases* between your brethren, and judge righteously between a man and his brother or the stranger who is with him. [17]You shall not show partiality in judgment; you shall hear the small as well as the great; you shall not be afraid in any man's presence, for the judgment *is* God's. The case that is too hard for you, bring to me, and I will hear it.' [18]And I commanded you at that time all the things which you should do.

Israel's Refusal to Enter the Land

[19]"So we departed from Horeb, and went through all that great and terrible wilderness which you saw on the way to the mountains of the Amorites, as the LORD our God had commanded us. Then we came to Kadesh Barnea. [20]And I said to you, 'You have come to the mountains of the Amorites, which the LORD our God is giving us. [21]Look, the LORD your God has set the land before you; go up *and* possess *it,* as the LORD God of your fathers has spoken to you; do not fear or be discouraged.'

[22]"And every one of you came near to me and said, 'Let us send men before us, and let them search out the land for us, and bring back word to us of the way by which we should go up, and of the cities into which we shall come.'

[23]"The plan pleased me well; so I took twelve of your men, one man from *each*

1:1 [a]Hebrew *arabah* [b]One manuscript of the Septuagint, also Targum and Vulgate, read *Red Sea.* **1:4** [a]Septuagint, Syriac, and Vulgate read *and* (compare Joshua 12:4). **1:7** [a]Hebrew *arabah*

tribe. [24]And they departed and went up into the mountains, and came to the Valley of Eshcol, and spied it out. [25]They also took *some* of the fruit of the land in their hands and brought *it* down to us; and they brought back word to us, saying, 'It is a good land which the LORD our God is giving us.'

[26]"Nevertheless you would not go up, but rebelled against the command of the LORD your God; [27]and you complained in your tents, and said, 'Because the LORD hates us, He has brought us out of the land of Egypt to deliver us into the hand of the Amorites, to destroy us. [28]Where can we go up? Our brethren have discouraged our hearts, saying, "The people *are* greater and taller than we; the cities *are* great and fortified up to heaven; moreover we have seen the sons of the Anakim there."'

[29]"Then I said to you, 'Do not be terrified, or afraid of them. [30]The LORD your God, who goes before you, He will fight for you, according to all He did for you in Egypt before your eyes, [31]and in the wilderness where you saw how the LORD your God carried you, as a man carries his son, in all the way that you went until you came to this place.' [32]Yet, for all that, you did not believe the LORD your God, [33]who went in the way before you to search out a place for you to pitch your tents, to show you the way you should go, in the fire by night and in the cloud by day.

The Penalty for Israel's Rebellion

[34]"And the LORD heard the sound of your words, and was angry, and took an oath, saying, [35]'Surely not one of these men of this evil generation shall see that good land of which I swore to give to your fathers, [36]except Caleb the son of Jephunneh; he shall see it, and to him and his children I am giving the land on which he walked, because he wholly followed the LORD.' [37]The LORD was also angry with me for your sakes, saying, 'Even you shall not go in there. [38]Joshua the son of Nun, who stands before you, he shall go in there. Encourage him, for he shall cause Israel to inherit it.

[39]'Moreover your little ones and your children, who you say will be victims, who today have no knowledge of good and evil, they shall go in there; to them I will give it, and they shall possess it. [40]But *as for* you, turn and take your journey into the wilderness by the Way of the Red Sea.'

[41]"Then you answered and said to me, 'We have sinned against the LORD; we will go up and fight, just as the LORD our God commanded us.' And when everyone of you had girded on his weapons of war, you were ready to go up into the mountain.

[42]"And the LORD said to me, 'Tell them, "Do not go up nor fight, for I *am* not among you; lest you be defeated before your enemies."' [43]So I spoke to you; yet you would not listen, but rebelled against the command of the LORD, and presumptuously went up into the mountain. [44]And the Amorites who dwelt in that mountain came out against you and chased you as bees do, and drove you back from Seir to Hormah. [45]Then you returned and wept before the LORD, but the LORD would not listen to your voice nor give ear to you.

[46]"So you remained in Kadesh many days, according to the days that you spent *there.*

The Desert Years

2 "Then we turned and journeyed into the wilderness of the Way of the Red Sea, as the LORD spoke to me, and we skirted Mount Seir for many days.

[2]"And the LORD spoke to me, saying: [3]'You have skirted this mountain long enough; turn northward. [4]And command the people, saying, "You *are about to* pass through the territory of your brethren, the descendants of Esau, who live in Seir; and they will be afraid of you. Therefore watch yourselves carefully. [5]Do not meddle with them, for I will not give you *any* of their land, no, not so much as one footstep, because I have given Mount Seir to Esau *as* a possession. [6]You shall buy food from them with money, that you may eat; and you shall also buy water from them with money, that you may drink.

[7]"For the LORD your God has blessed you in all the work of your hand. He knows

your trudging through this great wilderness. These forty years the LORD your God *has been* with you; you have lacked nothing.' "

8"And when we passed beyond our brethren, the descendants of Esau who dwell in Seir, away from the road of the plain, away from Elath and Ezion Geber, we turned and passed by way of the Wilderness of Moab. 9Then the LORD said to me, 'Do not harass Moab, nor contend with them in battle, for I will not give you *any* of their land *as* a possession, because I have given Ar to the descendants of Lot *as* a possession.' "

10(The Emim had dwelt there in times past, a people as great and numerous and tall as the Anakim. 11They were also regarded as giants,ᵃ like the Anakim, but the Moabites call them Emim. 12The Horites formerly dwelt in Seir, but the descendants of Esau dispossessed them and destroyed them from before them, and dwelt in their place, just as Israel did to the land of their possession which the LORD gave them.)

13"'Now rise and cross over the Valley of the Zered.' So we crossed over the Valley of the Zered. 14And the time we took to come from Kadesh Barnea until we crossed over the Valley of the Zered *was* thirty-eight years, until all the generation of the men of war was consumed from the midst of the camp, just as the LORD had sworn to them. 15For indeed the hand of the LORD was against them, to destroy them from the midst of the camp until they were consumed.

16"So it was, when all the men of war had finally perished from among the people, 17that the LORD spoke to me, saying: 18'This day you are to cross over at Ar, the boundary of Moab. 19And *when* you come near the people of Ammon, do not harass them or meddle with them, for I will not give you *any* of the land of the people of Ammon *as* a possession, because I have given it to the descendants of Lot *as* a possession.' "

20(That was also regarded as a land of giants;ᵃ giants formerly dwelt there. But the Ammonites call them Zamzummim, 21a people as great and numerous and tall as the Anakim. But the LORD destroyed them before them, and they dispossessed them and dwelt in their place, 22just as He had done for the descendants of Esau, who dwelt in Seir, when He destroyed the Horites from before them. They dispossessed them and dwelt in their place, even to this day. 23And the Avim, who dwelt in villages as far as Gaza—the Caphtorim, who came from Caphtor, destroyed them and dwelt in their place.)

24"'Rise, take your journey, and cross over the River Arnon. Look, I have given into your hand Sihon the Amorite, king of Heshbon, and his land. Begin to possess *it,* and engage him in battle. 25This day I will begin to put the dread and fear of you upon the nations under the whole heaven, who shall hear the report of you, and shall tremble and be in anguish because of you.'

King Sihon Defeated

26"And I sent messengers from the Wilderness of Kedemoth to Sihon king of Heshbon, with words of peace, saying, 27'Let me pass through your land; I will keep strictly to the road, and I will turn neither to the right nor to the left. 28You shall sell me food for money, that I may eat, and give me water for money, that I may drink; only let me pass through on foot, 29just as the descendants of Esau who dwell in Seir and the Moabites who dwell in Ar did for me, until I cross the Jordan to the land which the LORD our God is giving us.'

30"But Sihon king of Heshbon would not let us pass through, for the LORD your God hardened his spirit and made his heart obstinate, that He might deliver him into your hand, as *it is* this day.

31"And the LORD said to me, 'See, I have begun to give Sihon and his land over to you. Begin to possess *it,* that you may inherit his land.' 32Then Sihon and all his people came out against us to fight at Jahaz. 33And the LORD our God delivered him over to us; so we defeated him, his sons, and all his people. 34We took all his cities at that time, and we utterly destroyed the men, women, and little ones of every city; we left none remaining. 35We took only the livestock as plunder for ourselves,

---

2:11 ᵃHebrew *rephaim*   **2:20** ᵃHebrew *rephaim*

with the spoil of the cities which we took. [36]From Aroer, which *is* on the bank of the River Arnon, and *from* the city that *is* in the ravine, as far as Gilead, there was not one city too strong for us; the LORD our God delivered all to us. [37]Only you did not go near the land of the people of Ammon—anywhere along the River Jabbok, or to the cities of the mountains, or wherever the LORD our God had forbidden us.

King Og Defeated

3 "Then we turned and went up the road to Bashan; and Og king of Bashan came out against us, he and all his people, to battle at Edrei. [2]And the LORD said to me, 'Do not fear him, for I have delivered him and all his people and his land into your hand; you shall do to him as you did to Sihon king of the Amorites, who dwelt at Heshbon.'

[3]"So the LORD our God also delivered into our hands Og king of Bashan, with all his people, and we attacked him until he had no survivors remaining. [4]And we took all his cities at that time; there was not a city which we did not take from them: sixty cities, all the region of Argob, the kingdom of Og in Bashan. [5]All these cities *were* fortified with high walls, gates, and bars, besides a great many rural towns. [6]And we utterly destroyed them, as we did to Sihon king of Heshbon, utterly destroying the men, women, and children of every city. [7]But all the livestock and the spoil of the cities we took as booty for ourselves.

[8]"And at that time we took the land from the hand of the two kings of the Amorites who *were* on this side of the Jordan, from the River Arnon to Mount Hermon [9](the Sidonians call Hermon Sirion, and the Amorites call it Senir), [10]all the cities of the plain, all Gilead, and all Bashan, as far as Salcah and Edrei, cities of the kingdom of Og in Bashan.

[11]"For only Og king of Bashan remained of the remnant of the giants.[a] Indeed his bedstead *was* an iron bedstead. (*Is* it not in Rabbah of the people of Ammon?) Nine cubits *is* its length and four cubits its width, according to the standard cubit.

The Land East of the Jordan Divided

[12]"And this land, *which* we possessed at that time, from Aroer, which *is* by the River Arnon, and half the mountains of Gilead and its cities, I gave to the Reubenites and the Gadites. [13]The rest of Gilead, and all Bashan, the kingdom of Og, I gave to half the tribe of Manasseh. (All the region of Argob, with all Bashan, was called the land of the giants.[a] [14]Jair the son of Manasseh took all the region of Argob, as far as the border of the Geshurites and the Maachathites, and called Bashan after his own name, Havoth Jair,[a] to this day.)

[15]"Also I gave Gilead to Machir. [16]And to the Reubenites and the Gadites I gave from Gilead as far as the River Arnon, the middle of the river as *the* border, as far as the River Jabbok, the border of the people of Ammon; [17]the plain also, with the Jordan as *the* border, from Chinnereth as far as the east side of the Sea of the Arabah (the Salt Sea), below the slopes of Pisgah.

[18]"Then I commanded you at that time, saying: 'The LORD your God has given you this land to possess. All you men of valor shall cross over armed before your brethren, the children of Israel. [19]But your wives, your little ones, and your livestock (I know that you have much livestock) shall stay in your cities which I have given you, [20]until the LORD has given rest to your brethren as to you, and they also possess the land which the LORD your God is giving them beyond the Jordan. Then each of you may return to his possession which I have given you.'

[21]"And I commanded Joshua at that time, saying, 'Your eyes have seen all that the LORD your God has done to these two kings; so will the LORD do to all the kingdoms through which you pass. [22]You must not fear them, for the LORD your God Himself fights for you.'

Moses Forbidden to Enter the Land

[23]"Then I pleaded with the LORD at that time, saying: [24]'O Lord GOD, You have begun to show Your servant Your greatness

---

3:11 [a]Hebrew *rephaim*   **3:13** [a]Hebrew *rephaim*
3:14 [a]Literally *Towns of Jair*

and Your mighty hand, for what god *is there* in heaven or on earth who can do *anything* like Your works and Your mighty *deeds?* [25]I pray, let me cross over and see the good land beyond the Jordan, those pleasant mountains, and Lebanon.'

[26]"But the LORD was angry with me on your account, and would not listen to me. So the LORD said to me: 'Enough of that! Speak no more to Me of this matter. [27]Go up to the top of Pisgah, and lift your eyes toward the west, the north, the south, and the east; behold *it* with your eyes, for you shall not cross over this Jordan. [28]But command Joshua, and encourage him and strengthen him; for he shall go over before this people, and he shall cause them to inherit the land which you will see.'

[29]"So we stayed in the valley opposite Beth Peor.

Moses Commands Obedience

4 "Now, O Israel, listen to the statutes and the judgments which I teach you to observe, that you may live, and go in and possess the land which the LORD God of your fathers is giving you. [2]You shall not add to the word which I command you, nor take from it, that you may keep the commandments of the LORD your God which I command you. [3]Your eyes have seen what the LORD did at Baal Peor; for the LORD your God has destroyed from among you all the men who followed Baal of Peor. [4]But you who held fast to the LORD your God *are* alive today, every one of you.

[5]"Surely I have taught you statutes and judgments, just as the LORD my God commanded me, that you should act according *to them* in the land which you go to possess. [6]Therefore be careful to observe *them;* for this *is* your wisdom and your understanding in the sight of the peoples who will hear all these statutes, and say, 'Surely this great nation *is* a wise and understanding people.'

[7]"For what great nation *is there* that has God *so* near to it, as the LORD our God *is* to us, for whatever *reason* we may call upon Him? [8]And what great nation *is there* that has *such* statutes and righteous judgments as are in all this law which I set before you

this day? [9]Only take heed to yourself, and diligently keep yourself, lest you forget the things your eyes have seen, and lest they depart from your heart all the days of your life. And teach them to your children and your grandchildren, [10]*especially concerning* the day you stood before the LORD your God in Horeb, when the LORD said to me, 'Gather the people to Me, and I will let them hear My words, that they may learn to fear Me all the days they live on the earth, and *that* they may teach their children.'

[11]"Then you came near and stood at the foot of the mountain, and the mountain burned with fire to the midst of heaven, with darkness, cloud, and thick darkness. [12]And the LORD spoke to you out of the midst of the fire. You heard the sound of the words, but saw no form; *you* only *heard* a voice. [13]So He declared to you His covenant which He commanded you to perform, the Ten Commandments; and He wrote them on two tablets of stone. [14]And the LORD commanded me at that time to teach you statutes and judgments, that you might observe them in the land which you cross over to possess.

Beware of Idolatry

[15]"Take careful heed to yourselves, for you saw no form when the LORD spoke to you at Horeb out of the midst of the fire, [16]lest you act corruptly and make for yourselves a carved image in the form of any figure: the likeness of male or female, [17]the likeness of any animal that *is* on the earth or the likeness of any winged bird that flies in the air, [18]the likeness of anything that creeps on the ground or the likeness of any fish that *is* in the water beneath the earth. [19]And *take heed,* lest you lift your eyes to heaven, and *when* you see the sun, the moon, and the stars, all the host of heaven, you feel driven to worship them and serve them, which the LORD your God has given to all the peoples under the whole heaven as a heritage. [20]But the LORD has taken you and brought you out of the iron furnace, out of Egypt, to be His people, an inheritance, as you are this day. [21]Furthermore the LORD was angry with me for your sakes, and swore that I would not cross

over the Jordan, and that I would not enter the good land which the LORD your God is giving you as an inheritance. ²²But I must die in this land, I must not cross over the Jordan; but you shall cross over and possess that good land. ²³Take heed to yourselves, lest you forget the covenant of the LORD your God which He made with you, and make for yourselves a carved image in the form of anything which the LORD your God has forbidden you. ²⁴For the LORD your God *is* a consuming fire, a jealous God.

²⁵"When you beget children and grandchildren and have grown old in the land, and act corruptly and make a carved image in the form of anything, and do evil in the sight of the LORD your God to provoke Him to anger, ²⁶I call heaven and earth to witness against you this day, that you will soon utterly perish from the land which you cross over the Jordan to possess; you will not prolong *your* days in it, but will be utterly destroyed. ²⁷And the LORD will scatter you among the peoples, and you will be left few in number among the nations where the LORD will drive you. ²⁸And there you will serve gods, the work of men's hands, wood and stone, which neither see nor hear nor eat nor smell. ²⁹But from there you will seek the LORD your God, and you will find *Him* if you seek Him with all your heart and with all your soul. ³⁰When you are in distress, and all these things come upon you in the latter days, when you turn to the LORD your God and obey His voice ³¹(for the LORD your God *is a* merciful God), He will not forsake you nor destroy you, nor forget the covenant of your fathers which He swore to them.

³²"For ask now concerning the days that are past, which were before you, since the day that God created man on the earth, and *ask* from one end of heaven to the other, whether *any* great *thing* like this has happened, or *anything* like it has been heard. ³³Did *any* people *ever* hear the voice of God speaking out of the midst of the fire, as you have heard, and live? ³⁴Or did God *ever* try to go *and* take for Himself a nation from the midst of *another* nation, by trials, by signs, by wonders, by war, by a mighty hand and an outstretched arm, and by

great terrors, according to all that the LORD your God did for you in Egypt before your eyes? ³⁵To you it was shown, that you might know that the LORD Himself *is* God; *there is* none other besides Him. ³⁶Out of heaven He let you hear His voice, that He might instruct you; on earth He showed you His great fire, and you heard His words out of the midst of the fire. ³⁷And because He loved your fathers, therefore He chose their descendants after them; and He brought you out of Egypt with His Presence, with His mighty power, ³⁸driving out from before you nations greater and mightier than you, to bring you in, to give you their land *as* an inheritance, as *it is* this day. ³⁹Therefore know this day, and consider *it* in your heart, that the LORD Himself *is* God in heaven above and on the earth beneath; *there is* no other. ⁴⁰You shall therefore keep His statutes and His commandments which I command you today, that it may go well with you and with your children after you, and that you may prolong *your* days in the land which the LORD your God is giving you for all time."

Cities of Refuge East of the Jordan

⁴¹Then Moses set apart three cities on this side of the Jordan, toward the rising of the sun, ⁴²that the manslayer might flee there, who kills his neighbor unintentionally, without having hated him in time past, and that by fleeing to one of these cities he might live: ⁴³Bezer in the wilderness on the plateau for the Reubenites, Ramoth in Gilead for the Gadites, and Golan in Bashan for the Manassites.

Introduction to God's Law

⁴⁴Now this *is* the law which Moses set before the children of Israel. ⁴⁵These *are* the testimonies, the statutes, and the judgments which Moses spoke to the children of Israel after they came out of Egypt, ⁴⁶on this side of the Jordan, in the valley opposite Beth Peor, in the land of Sihon king of the Amorites, who dwelt at Heshbon, whom Moses and the children of Israel defeated after they came out of Egypt. ⁴⁷And they took possession of his land and the land of Og king of Bashan, two kings

THE CONSTITUTION OF THE UNITED STATES

DETAIL FROM *SIGNING*
OF THE CONSTITUTION

The Constitution of the United States has been the supreme law of the nation since it was adopted on September 17, 1787, by the Constitutional Convention in Philadelphia, Pennsylvania. George Washington was chosen to serve as president of the convention by the 55 delegates, who represented 12 states. The delegates drafted the document and sent it to Congress for approval. It was then sent to the states for ratification in the name of "the People." All 13 states had ratified the Constitution by May 29, 1790. The First U.S. Congress also ratified ten amendments, which became known as the Bill of Rights. Seventeen more amendments have been added since. It is the oldest federal constitution of any existing nation and occupies the central place in United States law and political culture.

The Constitution provides the framework for the organization of the United States government, outlining the three main branches of the government. The legislative branch is embodied in the bicameral Congress. The executive branch is headed by the President. The judicial branch is headed by the Supreme Court. The Constitution carefully outlines the limits of delegated powers each branch may exercise. It also reserves numerous rights for the individual states, and thus establishes the United States' federal system of government.

Our Founders wrote "We the people of the United States" in the preamble to the Constitution, designating that the power to govern belongs to the people who have created the government to protect their rights and promote their welfare. The preamble established the fact that the federal government has no authority outside of the limited powers given to the three government branches that follow in the preamble, as amended. It is imperative, therefore, that we know those specific delegated powers.

Much has been made of the Constitution's silence on the subject of God or any Christian designation. The consensus of the Framers was that religious matters were best left to the individual citizens and their respective state governments, and relationships between religion and civil government were already defined in most state constitutions in the founding era. For the federal government to enter into matters regarding religion would have been to encroach upon or usurp state jurisdiction.

of the Amorites, who *were* on this side of the Jordan, toward the rising of the sun, [48]from Aroer, which *is* on the bank of the River Arnon, even to Mount Sion[a] (that is, Hermon), [49]and all the plain on the east side of the Jordan as far as the Sea of the Arabah, below the slopes of Pisgah.

The Ten Commandments Reviewed

5 And Moses called all Israel, and said to them: "Hear, O Israel, the statutes and judgments which I speak in your hearing today, that you may learn them and be careful to observe them. [2]The LORD our God made a covenant with us in Horeb. [3]The LORD did not make this covenant with our fathers, but with us, those who *are* here today, all of us who *are* alive. [4]The LORD talked with you face to face on the mountain from the midst of the fire. [5]I stood between the LORD and you at that time, to declare to you the word of the LORD; for you were afraid because of the fire, and you did not go up the mountain. *He* said:

[6] 'I *am* the LORD your God who brought you out of the land of Egypt, out of the house of bondage.

[7] 'You shall have no other gods before Me.

[8] 'You shall not make for yourself a carved image—any likeness *of anything* that *is* in heaven above, or that *is* in the earth beneath, or that *is* in the water under the earth; [9]you shall not bow down to them nor serve them. For I, the LORD your God, *am* a jealous God, visiting the iniquity of the fathers upon the children to the third and fourth *generations* of those who hate Me, [10]but showing mercy to thousands, to those who love Me and keep My commandments.

[11] 'You shall not take the name of the LORD your God in vain, for the LORD will not hold *him* guiltless who takes His name in vain.

[12] 'Observe the Sabbath day, to keep it holy, as the LORD your God commanded you. [13]Six days you shall labor and do all your work, [14]but the seventh day *is* the Sabbath of the LORD your God. *In it* you shall do no work: you, nor your son, nor your daughter, nor your male servant, nor your female servant, nor your ox, nor your donkey, nor any of your cattle, nor your stranger who *is* within your gates, that your male servant and your female servant may rest as well as you. [15]And remember that you were a slave in the land of Egypt, and the LORD your God brought you out from there by a mighty hand and by an outstretched arm; therefore the LORD your God commanded you to keep the Sabbath day.

[16] 'Honor your father and your mother, as the LORD your God has commanded you, that your days may be long, and that it may be well with you in the land which the LORD your God is giving you.

[17] 'You shall not murder.

[18] 'You shall not commit adultery.

[19] 'You shall not steal.

[20] 'You shall not bear false witness against your neighbor.

[21] 'You shall not covet your neighbor's wife; and you shall not desire your neighbor's house, his field, his male servant, his female servant, his ox, his donkey, or anything that *is* your neighbor's.'

[22]"These words the LORD spoke to all your assembly, in the mountain from the midst of the fire, the cloud, and the thick darkness, with a loud voice; and He added no more. And He wrote them on two tablets of stone and gave them to me.

The People Afraid of God's Presence

[23]"So it was, when you heard the voice from the midst of the darkness, while the mountain was burning with fire, that you came near to me, all the heads of your tribes and your elders. [24]And you said: 'Surely the LORD our God has shown us His glory and His greatness, and we have heard His voice from the midst of the fire. We have seen this day that God speaks with man; yet he *still* lives. [25]Now therefore, why should we die? For this great fire will consume us; if

---

4:48 [a]Syriac reads *Sirion* (compare 3:9).

we hear the voice of the LORD our God anymore, then we shall die. 26For who *is there* of all flesh who has heard the voice of the living God speaking from the midst of the fire, as we *have,* and lived? 27You go near and hear all that the LORD our God may say, and tell us all that the LORD our God says to you, and we will hear and do *it.*'

28"Then the LORD heard the voice of your words when you spoke to me, and the LORD said to me: 'I have heard the voice of the words of this people which they have spoken to you. They are right *in* all that they have spoken. 29Oh, that they had such a heart in them that they would fear Me and always keep all My commandments, that it might be well with them and with their children forever! 30Go and say to them, "Return to your tents." 31But as for you, stand here by Me, and I will speak to you all the commandments, the statutes, and the judgments which you shall teach them, that they may observe *them* in the land which I am giving them to possess.'

32"Therefore you shall be careful to do as the LORD your God has commanded you; you shall not turn aside to the right hand or to the left. 33You shall walk in all the ways which the LORD your God has commanded you, that you may live and *that it may be* well with you, and *that* you may prolong *your* days in the land which you shall possess.

The Greatest Commandment

6 "Now this *is* the commandment, *and these are* the statutes and judgments which the LORD your God has commanded to teach you, that you may observe *them* in the land which you are crossing over to possess, 2that you may fear the LORD your God, to keep all His statutes

---

James Wilson

MORAL STRENGTH

"You shall teach them diligently to your children. . . ."
DEUTERONOMY 6:7

THE NORTHWEST ORDINANCE

On July 13, 1787, the Continental Congress passed the "Northwest Ordinance," which declared that the United States intended to settle the region north of the Ohio River and east of the Mississippi River. It set up the method by which new states would be admitted to the Union, giving them the same rights and powers as the established states, including the freedom of religion. Interestingly, it also stated the importance that Congress attached to religion: "Religion, morality, and knowledge being necessary to good government and the happiness of mankind, schools and the means of education shall forever be encouraged."

While the exact meaning of this sentence is still hotly debated, it is certainly positive legislation regarding religion and morality. James Wilson, one of only six Founders to have signed both the Declaration of Independence and the Constitution, pronounced in his law lectures at the University of Pennsylvania: "Far from being rivals or enemies, religion and law are twin sisters, friends, and mutual assistants." Not surprisingly, throughout American history up until the middle years of the twentieth century, government looked positively on both religion and morality. Various states worked out particular arrangements reflecting their particular circumstances, but in each case, religious freedom was respected while religion was looked upon as part of the common good, a "seedbed of virtue" contributing to American society.

and His commandments which I command you, you and your son and your grandson, all the days of your life, and that your days may be prolonged. ³Therefore hear, O Israel, and be careful to observe *it,* that it may be well with you, and that you may multiply greatly as the LORD God of your fathers has promised you—'a land flowing with milk and honey.'ᵃ

⁴"Hear, O Israel: The LORD our God, the LORD *is* one!ᵃ ⁵You shall love the LORD your God with all your heart, with all your soul, and with all your strength.

⁶"And these words which I command you today shall be in your heart. ⁷You shall teach them diligently to your children, and shall talk of them when you sit in your house, when you walk by the way, when you lie down, and when you rise up. ⁸You shall bind them as a sign on your hand, and they shall be as frontlets between your eyes. ⁹You shall write them on the doorposts of your house and on your gates.

Caution Against Disobedience

¹⁰"So it shall be, when the LORD your God brings you into the land of which He swore to your fathers, to Abraham, Isaac, and Jacob, to give you large and beautiful cities which you did not build, ¹¹houses full of all good things, which you did not fill, hewn-out wells which you did not dig, vineyards and olive trees which you did not plant—when you have eaten and are full— ¹²*then* beware, lest you forget the LORD who brought you out of the land of Egypt, from the house of bondage. ¹³You shall fear the LORD your God and serve Him, and shall take oaths in His name. ¹⁴You shall not go after other gods, the gods of the peoples who *are* all around you ¹⁵(for the LORD your God *is* a jealous God among you), lest the anger of the LORD your God be aroused against you and destroy you from the face of the earth.

¹⁶"You shall not tempt the LORD your God as you tempted *Him* in Massah. ¹⁷You shall diligently keep the commandments of the LORD your God, His testimonies, and His statutes which He has commanded you. ¹⁸And you shall do *what is* right and good in the sight of the LORD, that it may be well with you, and that you may go in and possess the good land of which the LORD swore to your fathers, ¹⁹to cast out all your enemies from before you, as the LORD has spoken.

²⁰"When your son asks you in time to come, saying, 'What *is the meaning of* the testimonies, the statutes, and the judgments which the LORD our God has commanded you?' ²¹then you shall say to your son: 'We were slaves of Pharaoh in Egypt, and the LORD brought us out of Egypt with a mighty hand; ²²and the LORD showed signs and wonders before our eyes, great and severe, against Egypt, Pharaoh, and all his household. ²³Then He brought us out from there, that He might bring us in, to give us the land of which He swore to our fathers. ²⁴And the LORD commanded us to observe all these statutes, to fear the LORD our God, for our good always, that He might preserve us alive, as *it is* this day. ²⁵Then it will be righteousness for us, if we are careful to observe all these commandments before the LORD our God, as He has commanded us.'

A Chosen People

7 "When the LORD your God brings you into the land which you go to possess, and has cast out many nations before you, the Hittites and the Girgashites and the Amorites and the Canaanites and the Perizzites and the Hivites and the Jebusites, seven nations greater and mightier than you, ²and when the LORD your God delivers them over to you, you shall conquer them *and* utterly destroy them. You shall make no covenant with them nor show mercy to them. ³Nor shall you make marriages with them. You shall not give your daughter to their son, nor take their daughter for your son. ⁴For they will turn your sons away from following Me, to serve other gods; so the anger of the LORD will be aroused against you and destroy you suddenly. ⁵But thus you shall deal with them: you shall destroy their altars, and break down their *sacred* pillars, and cut down their wooden images,ᵃ and burn their carved images with fire.

6:3 ᵃExodus 3:8 **6:4** ᵃOr *The LORD is our God, the LORD alone* (that is, the only one) **7:5** ᵃHebrew *Asherim,* Canaanite deities

6"For you *are* a holy people to the LORD your God; the LORD your God has chosen you to be a people for Himself, a special treasure above all the peoples on the face of the earth. 7The LORD did not set His love on you nor choose you because you were more in number than any other people, for you were the least of all peoples; 8but because the LORD loves you, and because He would keep the oath which He swore to your fathers, the LORD has brought you out with a mighty hand, and redeemed you from the house of bondage, from the hand of Pharaoh king of Egypt.

9"Therefore know that the LORD your God, He *is* God, the faithful God who keeps covenant and mercy for a thousand generations with those who love Him and keep His commandments; 10and He repays those who hate Him to their face, to destroy them. He will not be slack with him who hates Him; He will repay him to his face. 11Therefore you shall keep the commandment, the statutes, and the judgments which I command you today, to observe them.

Blessings of Obedience

12"Then it shall come to pass, because you listen to these judgments, and keep and do them, that the LORD your God will keep with you the covenant and the mercy which He swore to your fathers. 13And He will love you and bless you and multiply you; He will also bless the fruit of your womb and the fruit of your land, your grain and your new wine and your oil, the increase of your cattle and the offspring of your flock, in the land of which He swore to your fathers to give you. 14You shall be blessed above all peoples; there shall not be a male or female barren among you or among your livestock. 15And the LORD will take away from you all sickness, and will afflict you with none of the terrible diseases of Egypt which you have known, but will lay *them* on all those who hate you. 16Also you shall destroy all the peoples whom the LORD your God delivers over to you; your eye shall have no pity on them; nor shall you serve their gods, for that *will be* a snare to you.

17"If you should say in your heart, 'These nations are greater than I; how can I dispossess them?'— 18you shall not be afraid of them, *but* you shall remember well what the LORD your God did to Pharaoh and to all Egypt: 19the great trials which your eyes saw, the signs and the wonders, the mighty hand and the outstretched arm, by which the LORD your God brought you out. So shall the LORD your God do to all the peoples of whom you are afraid. 20Moreover the LORD your God will send the hornet among them until those who are left, who hide themselves from you, are destroyed. 21You shall not be terrified of them; for the LORD your God, the great and awesome God, *is* among you. 22And the LORD your God will drive out those nations before you little by little; you will be unable to destroy them at once, lest the beasts of the field become *too* numerous for you. 23But the LORD your God will deliver them over to you, and will inflict defeat upon them until they are destroyed. 24And He will deliver their kings into your hand, and you will destroy their name from under heaven; no one shall be able to stand against you until you have destroyed them. 25You shall burn the carved images of their gods with fire; you shall not covet the silver or gold *that is* on them, nor take *it* for yourselves, lest you be snared by it; for it *is* an abomination to the LORD your God. 26Nor shall you bring an abomination into your house, lest you be doomed to destruction like it. You shall utterly detest it and utterly abhor it, for it *is* an accursed thing.

Remember the LORD Your God

8 "Every commandment which I command you today you must be careful to observe, that you may live and multiply, and go in and possess the land of which the LORD swore to your fathers. 2And you shall remember that the LORD your God led you all the way these forty years in the wilderness, to humble you *and* test you, to know what *was* in your heart, whether you would keep His commandments or not. 3So He humbled you, allowed you to hunger, and fed you with manna which you did not know nor did your fathers know, that

He might make you know that man shall not live by bread alone; but man lives by every *word* that proceeds from the mouth of the Lord. ⁴Your garments did not wear out on you, nor did your foot swell these forty years. ⁵You should know in your heart that as a man chastens his son, *so* the Lord your God chastens you.

⁶"Therefore you shall keep the commandments of the Lord your God, to walk in His ways and to fear Him. ⁷For the Lord your God is bringing you into a good land, a land of brooks of water, of fountains and springs, that flow out of valleys and hills; ⁸a land of wheat and barley, of vines and fig trees and pomegranates, a land of olive oil and honey; ⁹a land in which you will eat bread without scarcity, in which you will lack nothing; a land whose stones *are* iron and out of whose hills you can dig copper. ¹⁰When you have eaten and are full, then you shall bless the Lord your God for the good land which He has given you.

¹¹"Beware that you do not forget the Lord your God by not keeping His commandments, His judgments, and His statutes which I command you today, ¹²lest—*when* you have eaten and are full, and have built beautiful houses and dwell *in them;* ¹³and *when* your herds and your flocks multiply, and your silver and your gold are multiplied, and all that you have is multiplied; ¹⁴when your heart is lifted up, and you forget the Lord your God who brought you out of the land of Egypt, from the house of bondage; ¹⁵who led you through that great and terrible wilderness, *in which were* fiery serpents and scorpions and thirsty land where there was no water; who brought water for you out of the flinty rock; ¹⁶who fed you in the wilderness with manna, which your fathers did not know, that He might humble you and that He might test you, to do you good in the end— ¹⁷then you say in your heart, 'My power and the might of my hand have gained me this wealth.'

¹⁸"And you shall remember the Lord your God, for *it is* He who gives you power to get wealth, that He may establish His covenant which He swore to your fathers, as *it is* this day. ¹⁹Then it shall be, if you by any means forget the Lord your God, and follow other gods, and serve them and worship them, I testify against you this day that you shall surely perish. ²⁰As the nations which the Lord destroys before you, so you shall perish, because you would not be obedient to the voice of the Lord your God.

Israel's Rebellions Reviewed

9 "Hear, O Israel: You *are* to cross over the Jordan today, and go in to dispossess nations greater and mightier than yourself, cities great and fortified up to heaven, ²a people great and tall, the descendants of the Anakim, whom you know, and *of whom* you heard *it said,* 'Who can stand before the descendants of Anak?' ³Therefore understand today that the Lord your God *is* He who goes over before you *as a* consuming fire. He will destroy them and bring them down before you; so you shall drive them out and destroy them quickly, as the Lord has said to you.

⁴"Do not think in your heart, after the Lord your God has cast them out before you, saying, 'Because of my righteousness the Lord has brought me in to possess this land'; but *it is* because of the wickedness of these nations *that* the Lord is driving them out from before you. ⁵*It is* not because of your righteousness or the uprightness of your heart *that* you go in to possess their land, but because of the wickedness of these nations *that* the Lord your God drives them out from before you, and that He may fulfill the word which the Lord swore to your fathers, to Abraham, Isaac, and Jacob. ⁶Therefore understand that the Lord your God is not giving you this good land to possess because of your righteousness, for you *are* a stiff-necked people.

⁷"Remember! Do not forget how you provoked the Lord your God to wrath in the wilderness. From the day that you departed from the land of Egypt until you came to this place, you have been rebellious against the Lord. ⁸Also in Horeb you provoked the Lord to wrath, so that the Lord was angry *enough* with you to have destroyed you. ⁹When I went up into the

mountain to receive the tablets of stone, the tablets of the covenant which the LORD made with you, then I stayed on the mountain forty days and forty nights. I neither ate bread nor drank water. ¹⁰Then the LORD delivered to me two tablets of stone written with the finger of God, and on them *were* all the words which the LORD had spoken to you on the mountain from the midst of the fire in the day of the assembly. ¹¹And it came to pass, at the end of forty days and forty nights, *that* the LORD gave me the two tablets of stone, the tablets of the covenant.

¹²"Then the LORD said to me, 'Arise, go down quickly from here, for your people whom you brought out of Egypt have acted corruptly; they have quickly turned aside from the way which I commanded them; they have made themselves a molded image.'

FAITH

"... written with the finger of God. ..."

DEUTERONOMY 9:10

The Finger of God

Alexander Hamilton (1755–1804) was a Founding Father, one of America's first Constitutional lawyers, and wrote 51 of the 85 *Federalist Papers*. After the Constitutional Convention of 1787, Hamilton stated:

For my own part, I sincerely esteem it a system which without the finger of God, never could have been suggested and agreed upon by such a diversity of interests.

---

¹³"Furthermore the LORD spoke to me, saying, 'I have seen this people, and indeed they are a stiff-necked people. ¹⁴Let Me alone, that I may destroy them and blot out their name from under heaven; and I will make of you a nation mightier and greater than they.'

¹⁵"So I turned and came down from the mountain, and the mountain burned with fire; and the two tablets of the covenant *were* in my two hands. ¹⁶And I looked, and behold, you had sinned against the LORD your God—had made for yourselves a molded calf! You had turned aside quickly from the way which the LORD had commanded you. ¹⁷Then I took the two tablets and threw them out of my two hands and broke them before your eyes. ¹⁸And I fell down before the LORD, as at the first, forty days and forty nights; I neither ate bread nor drank water, because of all your sin which you committed in doing wickedly in the sight of the LORD, to provoke Him to anger. ¹⁹For I was afraid of the anger and hot displeasure with which the LORD was angry with you, to destroy you. But the LORD listened to me at that time also. ²⁰And the LORD was very angry with Aaron *and* would have destroyed him; so I prayed for Aaron also at the same time. ²¹Then I took your sin, the calf which you had made, and burned it with fire and crushed it *and* ground *it* very small, until it was as fine as dust; and I threw its dust into the brook that descended from the mountain.

²²"Also at Taberah and Massah and Kibroth Hattaavah you provoked the LORD to wrath. ²³Likewise, when the LORD sent you from Kadesh Barnea, saying, 'Go up and possess the land which I have given you,' then you rebelled against the commandment of the LORD your God, and you did not believe Him nor obey His voice. ²⁴You have been rebellious against the LORD from the day that I knew you.

²⁵"Thus I prostrated myself before the LORD; forty days and forty nights I kept prostrating myself, because the LORD had said He would destroy you. ²⁶Therefore I prayed to the LORD, and said: 'O Lord GOD, do not destroy Your people and Your inheritance whom You have redeemed through Your greatness, whom You have brought out of Egypt with a mighty hand. ²⁷Remember Your servants, Abraham, Isaac, and Jacob; do not look on the stubbornness of this people, or on their wickedness or their sin, ²⁸lest the land from which You brought us should say, "Because the LORD was not able to bring them to the land which He promised them, and because He hated them, He has brought them out to kill them in the wilderness." ²⁹Yet they *are* Your people and Your inheritance, whom You brought out by Your mighty power and by Your outstretched arm.'

The Second Pair of Tablets

10 "At that time the LORD said to me, 'Hew for yourself two tablets of stone like the first, and come up to Me on the mountain and make yourself an ark of wood. ²And I will write on the tablets the words that were on the first tablets, which you broke; and you shall put them in the ark.'

³"So I made an ark of acacia wood, hewed two tablets of stone like the first, and went up the mountain, having the two tablets in my hand. ⁴And He wrote on the tablets according to the first writing, the Ten Commandments, which the LORD had spoken to you in the mountain from the midst of the fire in the day of the assembly; and the LORD gave them to me. ⁵Then I turned and came down from the mountain, and put the tablets in the ark which I had made; and there they are, just as the LORD commanded me."

⁶(Now the children of Israel journeyed from the wells of Bene Jaakan to Moserah, where Aaron died, and where he was buried; and Eleazar his son ministered as priest in his stead. ⁷From there they journeyed to Gudgodah, and from Gudgodah to Jotbathah, a land of rivers of water. ⁸At that time the LORD separated the tribe of Levi to bear the ark of the covenant of the LORD, to stand before the LORD to minister to Him and to bless in His name, to this day. ⁹Therefore Levi has no portion nor inheritance with his brethren; the LORD *is* his inheritance, just as the LORD your God promised him.)

¹⁰"As at the first time, I stayed in the mountain forty days and forty nights; the LORD also heard me at that time, *and* the LORD chose not to destroy you. ¹¹Then the LORD said to me, 'Arise, begin *your* journey before the people, that they may go in and possess the land which I swore to their fathers to give them.'

SERVICE

"... to serve the LORD your God with all your heart...."

DEUTERONOMY 10:12

William Samuel Johnson

PURPOSE OF A PUBLIC EDUCATION

William Samuel Johnson (1727–1819), president of Columbia University (formerly King's College), said to the first graduating class after the Revolutionary War:

> You have ... received a public education, the purpose whereof hath been to qualify you the better to serve your Creator and your country. ... Your first great duties ... are those you owe to Heaven, to your Creator and Redeemer. Let these be ever present to your minds and exemplified in your lives and conduct.
>
> Imprint deep upon your minds the principles of piety toward God, and a reverence and fear of His holy name. The fear of God is the beginning of wisdom, and its consummation is everlasting felicity. ... Remember, too, that you are the redeemed of the Lord, that you are bought with a price, even the inestimable price of the precious blood of the Son of God. Adore Jehovah, therefore, as your God and your Judge. Love, fear, and serve Him as your Creator, Redeemer, and Sanctifier. Acquaint yourselves with Him in His Word and holy ordinances.
>
> Make Him your friend and protector and your felicity is secured both here and hereafter. And with respect to particular duties to Him, it is your happiness that you are well assured that he best serves his Maker, who does most good to his country and to mankind.

The Essence of the Law

12"And now, Israel, what does the LORD your God require of you, but to fear the LORD your God, to walk in all His ways and to love Him, to serve the LORD your God with all your heart and with all your soul, 13and to keep the commandments of the LORD and His statutes which I command you today for your good? 14Indeed heaven and the highest heavens belong to the LORD your God, *also* the earth with all that *is* in it. 15The LORD delighted only in your fathers, to love them; and He chose their descendants after them, you above all peoples, as *it is* this day. 16Therefore circumcise the foreskin of your heart, and be stiff-necked no longer. 17For the LORD your God *is* God of gods and Lord of lords, the great God, mighty and awesome, who shows no partiality nor takes a bribe. 18He administers justice for the fatherless and the widow, and loves the stranger, giving him food and clothing. 19Therefore love the stranger, for you were strangers in the land of Egypt. 20You shall fear the LORD your God; you shall serve Him, and to Him you shall hold fast, and take oaths in His name. 21He *is* your praise, and He *is* your God, who has done for you these great and awesome things which your eyes have seen. 22Your fathers went down to Egypt with seventy persons, and now the LORD your God has made you as the stars of heaven in multitude.

Love and Obedience Rewarded

11 "Therefore you shall love the LORD your God, and keep His charge, His statutes, His judgments, and His commandments always. 2Know today that I do not *speak* with your children, who have not known and who have not seen the chastening of the LORD your God, His greatness and His mighty hand and His outstretched arm— 3His signs and His acts which He did in the midst of Egypt, to Pharaoh king of Egypt, and to all his land; 4what He did to the army of Egypt, to their horses and their chariots: how He made the waters of the Red Sea overflow them as they pursued you, and *how* the LORD has destroyed them to this day; 5what He did for you in the wilderness until you came to this place;

6and what He did to Dathan and Abiram the sons of Eliab, the son of Reuben: how the earth opened its mouth and swallowed them up, their households, their tents, and all the substance that *was* in their possession, in the midst of all Israel— 7but your eyes have seen every great act of the LORD which He did.

8"Therefore you shall keep every commandment which I command you today, that you may be strong, and go in and possess the land which you cross over to possess, 9and that you may prolong *your* days in the land which the LORD swore to give your fathers, to them and their descendants, 'a land flowing with milk and honey.'ª 10For the land which you go to possess *is* not like the land of Egypt from which you have come, where you sowed your seed and watered *it* by foot, as a vegetable garden; 11but the land which you cross over to possess *is* a land of hills and valleys, which drinks water from the rain of heaven, 12a land for which the LORD your God cares; the eyes of the LORD your God *are* always on it, from the beginning of the year to the very end of the year.

13'And it shall be that if you earnestly obey My commandments which I command you today, to love the LORD your God and serve Him with all your heart and with all your soul, 14then Iª will give *you* the rain for your land in its season, the early rain and the latter rain, that you may gather in your grain, your new wine, and your oil. 15And I will send grass in your fields for your livestock, that you may eat and be filled.' 16Take heed to yourselves, lest your heart be deceived, and you turn aside and serve other gods and worship them, 17lest the LORD's anger be aroused against you, and He shut up the heavens so that there be no rain, and the land yield no produce, and you perish quickly from the good land which the LORD is giving you.

18"Therefore you shall lay up these words of mine in your heart and in your soul,

---

11:9 ªExodus 3:8   **11:14** ªFollowing Masoretic Text and Targum; Samaritan Pentateuch, Septuagint, and Vulgate read *He.*

and bind them as a sign on your hand, and they shall be as frontlets between your eyes. ¹⁹You shall teach them to your children, speaking of them when you sit in your house, when you walk by the way, when you lie down, and when you rise up. ²⁰And you shall write them on the doorposts of your house and on your gates, ²¹that your days and the days of your children may be multiplied in the land of which the LORD swore to your fathers to give them, like the days of the heavens above the earth.

²²"For if you carefully keep all these commandments which I command you to do—to love the LORD your God, to walk in all His ways, and to hold fast to Him— ²³then the LORD will drive out all these nations from before you, and you will dispossess greater and mightier nations than yourselves. ²⁴Every place on which the sole of your foot treads shall be yours: from the wilderness and Lebanon, from the river, the River Euphrates, even to the Western Sea,ª shall be your territory. ²⁵No man shall be able to stand against you; the LORD your God will put the dread of you and the fear of you upon all the land where you tread, just as He has said to you.

²⁶"Behold, I set before you today a blessing and a curse: ²⁷the blessing, if you obey the commandments of the LORD your God which I command you today; ²⁸and the curse, if you do not obey the commandments of the LORD your God, but turn aside from the way which I command you today, to go after other gods which you have not known. ²⁹Now it shall be, when the LORD your God has brought you into the land which you go to possess, that you shall put the blessing on Mount Gerizim and the curse on Mount Ebal. ³⁰Are they not on the other side of the Jordan, toward the setting sun, in the land of the Canaanites who dwell in the plain opposite Gilgal, beside the terebinth trees of Moreh? ³¹For you will cross over the Jordan and go in to possess the land which the LORD your God is giving you, and you will possess it and dwell in it. ³²And you shall be careful to observe all the statutes and judgments which I set before you today.

A Prescribed Place of Worship

12 "These *are* the statutes and judgments which you shall be careful to observe in the land which the LORD God of your fathers is giving you to possess, all the days that you live on the earth. ²You shall utterly destroy all the places where the nations which you shall dispossess served their gods, on the high mountains and on the hills and under every green tree. ³And you shall destroy their altars, break their *sacred* pillars, and burn their wooden images with fire; you shall cut down the carved images of their gods and destroy their names from that place. ⁴You shall not worship the LORD your God *with* such *things*.

⁵"But you shall seek the place where the LORD your God chooses, out of all your tribes, to put His name for His dwelling place; and there you shall go. ⁶There you shall take your burnt offerings, your sacrifices, your tithes, the heave offerings of your hand, your vowed offerings, your freewill offerings, and the firstborn of your herds and flocks. ⁷And there you shall eat before the LORD your God, and you shall rejoice in all to which you have put your hand, you and your households, in which the LORD your God has blessed you.

⁸"You shall not at all do as we are doing here today—every man doing whatever *is* right in his own eyes— ⁹for as yet you have not come to the rest and the inheritance which the LORD your God is giving you. ¹⁰But *when* you cross over the Jordan and dwell in the land which the LORD your God is giving you to inherit, and He gives you rest from all your enemies round about, so that you dwell in safety, ¹¹then there will be the place where the LORD your God chooses to make His name abide. There you shall bring all that I command you: your burnt offerings, your sacrifices, your tithes, the heave offerings of your hand, and all your choice offerings which you vow to the LORD. ¹²And you shall rejoice before the LORD your God, you and your sons and your daughters, your male and female servants, and the Levite who *is*

within your gates, since he has no portion nor inheritance with you. [13]Take heed to yourself that you do not offer your burnt offerings in every place that you see; [14]but in the place which the LORD chooses, in one of your tribes, there you shall offer your burnt offerings, and there you shall do all that I command you.

[15]"However, you may slaughter and eat meat within all your gates, whatever your heart desires, according to the blessing of the LORD your God which He has given you; the unclean and the clean may eat of it, of the gazelle and the deer alike. [16]Only you shall not eat the blood; you shall pour it on the earth like water. [17]You may not eat within your gates the tithe of your grain or your new wine or your oil, of the firstborn of your herd or your flock, of any of your offerings which you vow, of your freewill offerings, or of the heave offering of your hand. [18]But you must eat them before the LORD your God in the place which the LORD your God chooses, you and your son and your daughter, your male servant and your female servant, and the Levite who *is* within your gates; and you shall rejoice before the LORD your God in all to which you put your hands. [19]Take heed to yourself that you do not forsake the Levite as long as you live in your land.

[20]"When the LORD your God enlarges your border as He has promised you, and you say, 'Let me eat meat,' because you long to eat meat, you may eat as much meat as your heart desires. [21]If the place where the LORD your God chooses to put His name is too far from you, then you may slaughter from your herd and from your flock which the LORD has given you, just as I have commanded you, and you may eat within your gates as much as your heart desires. [22]Just as the gazelle and the deer are eaten, so you may eat them; the unclean and the clean alike may eat them. [23]Only be sure that you do not eat the blood, for the blood *is* the life; you may not eat the life with the meat. [24]You shall not eat it; you shall pour it on the earth like water. [25]You shall not eat it, that it may go well with you and your children after you, when you do *what is* right in the sight of

the LORD. [26]Only the holy things which you have, and your vowed offerings, you shall take and go to the place which the LORD chooses. [27]And you shall offer your burnt offerings, the meat and the blood, on the altar of the LORD your God; and the blood of your sacrifices shall be poured out on the altar of the LORD your God, and you shall eat the meat. [28]Observe and obey all these words which I command you, that it may go well with you and your children after you forever, when you do *what is* good and right in the sight of the LORD your God.

Beware of False Gods

[29]"When the LORD your God cuts off from before you the nations which you go to dispossess, and you displace them and dwell in their land, [30]take heed to yourself that you are not ensnared to follow them, after they are destroyed from before you, and that you do not inquire after their gods, saying, 'How did these nations serve their gods? I also will do likewise.' [31]You shall not worship the LORD your God in that way; for every abomination to the LORD which He hates they have done to their gods; for they burn even their sons and daughters in the fire to their gods.

[32]"Whatever I command you, be careful to observe it; you shall not add to it nor take away from it.

Punishment of Apostates

13 "If there arises among you a prophet or a dreamer of dreams, and he gives you a sign or a wonder, [2]and the sign or the wonder comes to pass, of which he spoke to you, saying, 'Let us go after other gods'—which you have not known—'and let us serve them,' [3]you shall not listen to the words of that prophet or that dreamer of dreams, for the LORD your God is testing you to know whether you love the LORD your God with all your heart and with all your soul. [4]You shall walk after the LORD your God and fear Him, and keep His commandments and obey His voice; you shall serve Him and hold fast to Him. [5]But that prophet or that dreamer of dreams shall be put to death, because he has spoken in order to turn *you* away from the LORD your

God, who brought you out of the land of Egypt and redeemed you from the house of bondage, to entice you from the way in which the LORD your God commanded you to walk. So you shall put away the evil from your midst.

6"If your brother, the son of your mother, your son or your daughter, the wife of your bosom, or your friend who is as your own soul, secretly entices you, saying, 'Let us go and serve other gods,' which you have not known, neither you nor your fathers, 7of the gods of the people which *are* all around you, near to you or far off from you, from *one* end of the earth to the *other* end of the earth, 8you shall not consent to him or listen to him, nor shall your eye pity him, nor shall you spare him or conceal him; 9but you shall surely kill him; your hand shall be first against him to put him to death, and afterward the hand of all the people. 10And you shall stone him with stones until he dies, because he sought to entice you away from the LORD your God, who brought you out of the land of Egypt, from the house of bondage. 11So all Israel shall hear and fear, and not again do such wickedness as this among you.

12"If you hear someone in one of your cities, which the LORD your God gives you to dwell in, saying, 13'Corrupt men have gone out from among you and enticed the inhabitants of their city, saying, "Let us go and serve other gods"'—which you have not known— 14then you shall inquire, search out, and ask diligently. And *if it is* indeed true *and* certain *that* such an abomination was committed among you, 15you shall surely strike the inhabitants of that city with the edge of the sword, utterly destroying it, all that is in it and its livestock—with the edge of the sword. 16And you shall gather all its plunder into the middle of the street, and completely burn with fire the city and all its plunder, for the LORD your God. It shall be a heap forever; it shall not be built again. 17So none of the accursed things shall remain in your hand, that the LORD may turn from the fierceness of His anger and show you mercy, have compassion on you and multiply you, just as He swore to your fathers, 18because you

have listened to the voice of the LORD your God, to keep all His commandments which I command you today, to do *what is* right in the eyes of the LORD your God.

Improper Mourning

14 "You *are* the children of the LORD your God; you shall not cut yourselves nor shave the front of your head for the dead. 2For you *are* a holy people to the LORD your God, and the LORD has chosen you to be a people for Himself, a special treasure above all the peoples who *are* on the face of the earth.

Clean and Unclean Meat

3"You shall not eat any detestable thing. 4These *are* the animals which you may eat: the ox, the sheep, the goat, 5the deer, the gazelle, the roe deer, the wild goat, the mountain goat,ᵃ the antelope, and the mountain sheep. 6And you may eat every animal with cloven hooves, having the hoof split into two parts, *and that* chews the cud, among the animals. 7Nevertheless, of those that chew the cud or have cloven hooves, you shall not eat, *such as* these: the camel, the hare, and the rock hyrax; for they chew the cud but do not have cloven hooves; they *are* unclean for you. 8Also the swine is unclean for you, because it has cloven hooves, yet *does* not *chew* the cud; you shall not eat their flesh or touch their dead carcasses.

9"These you may eat of all that *are* in the waters: you may eat all that have fins and scales. 10And whatever does not have fins and scales you shall not eat; it *is* unclean for you.

11"All clean birds you may eat. 12But these you shall not eat: the eagle, the vulture, the buzzard, 13the red kite, the falcon, and the kite after their kinds; 14every raven after its kind; 15the ostrich, the short-eared owl, the sea gull, and the hawk after their kinds; 16the little owl, the screech owl, the white owl, 17the jackdaw, the carrion vulture, the fisher owl, 18the stork, the heron after its kind, and the hoopoe and the bat.

14:5 ᵃOr *addax*

¹⁹"Also every creeping thing that flies is unclean for you; they shall not be eaten.

²⁰"You may eat all clean birds.

²¹"You shall not eat anything that dies *of itself;* you may give it to the alien who *is* within your gates, that he may eat it, or you may sell it to a foreigner; for you *are a* holy people to the LORD your God.

"You shall not boil a young goat in its mother's milk.

Tithing Principles

²²"You shall truly tithe all the increase of your grain that the field produces year by year. ²³And you shall eat before the LORD your God, in the place where He chooses to make His name abide, the tithe of your grain and your new wine and your oil, of the firstborn of your herds and your flocks, that you may learn to fear the LORD your God always. ²⁴But if the journey is too long for you, so that you are not able to carry *the tithe, or* if the place where the LORD your God chooses to put His name is too far from you, when the LORD your God has blessed you, ²⁵then you shall exchange *it* for money, take the money in your hand, and go to the place which the LORD your God chooses. ²⁶And you shall spend that money for whatever your heart desires: for oxen or sheep, for wine or similar drink, for whatever your heart desires; you shall eat there before the LORD your God, and you shall rejoice, you and your household. ²⁷You shall not forsake the Levite who *is* within your gates, for he has no part nor inheritance with you.

²⁸"At the end of *every* third year you shall bring out the tithe of your produce of that year and store *it* up within your gates. ²⁹And the Levite, because he has no portion nor inheritance with you, and the stranger and the fatherless and the widow who *are* within your gates, may come and eat and be satisfied, that the LORD your God may bless you in all the work of your hand which you do.

PRAYER

"For the LORD your God will bless you just as He promised you. . . ."

DEUTERONOMY 15:6

Irving Berlin

"GOD BLESS AMERICA"

Born in a poor Russian Jewish ghetto, Irving Berlin immigrated to America with his parents when he was five, settling in New York's Lower East Side. He became one of the most prolific American songwriters in history. "God Bless America" is an American patriotic song he originally wrote in 1918 and revised in 1938, as war and the Nazis were threatening Europe. It takes the form of a prayer for God's blessing and peace for the nation. Singer Kate Smith introduced the revised "God Bless America" during her radio broadcast on Armistice Day 1938, and the song was an immediate sensation. It is considered an unofficial national anthem of the United States.

While the storm clouds gather far across the sea,
Let us swear allegiance to a land that's free,
Let us all be grateful for a land so fair,
As we raise our voices in a solemn prayer.

God bless America, land that I love
Stand beside her and guide her
Through the night with the light from above
From the mountains, to the prairies,
to the ocean white with foam
God bless America, my home sweet home.

Debts Canceled Every Seven Years

15 "At the end of *every* seven years you shall grant a release *of debts.* ²And this *is* the form of the release: Every creditor who has lent *anything* to his neighbor shall release *it;* he shall not require *it* of his neighbor or his brother, because it is called the LORD's release. ³Of a foreigner you may require *it;* but you shall give up your claim to what is owed by your brother, ⁴except when there may be no poor among you; for the LORD will greatly bless you in the land which the LORD your God is giving you to possess *as* an inheritance— ⁵only if you carefully obey the voice of the LORD your God, to observe with care all these commandments which I command you today. ⁶For the LORD your God will bless you just as He promised you; you shall lend to many nations, but you shall not borrow; you shall reign over many nations, but they shall not reign over you.

Generosity to the Poor

⁷"If there is among you a poor man of your brethren, within any of the gates in your land which the LORD your God is giving you, you shall not harden your heart nor shut your hand from your poor brother, ⁸but you shall open your hand wide to him and willingly lend him sufficient for his need, whatever he needs. ⁹Beware lest there be a wicked thought in your heart, saying, 'The seventh year, the year of release, is at hand,' and your eye be evil against your poor brother and you give him nothing, and he cry out to the LORD against you, and it become sin among you. ¹⁰You shall surely give to him, and your heart should not be grieved when you give to him, because for this thing the LORD your God will bless you in all your works and in all to which you put your hand. ¹¹For the poor will never cease from the land; therefore I command you, saying, 'You shall open your hand wide to your brother, to your poor and your needy, in your land.'

The Law Concerning Bondservants

¹²"If your brother, a Hebrew man, or a Hebrew woman, is sold to you and serves you six years, then in the seventh year you shall let him go free from you. ¹³And when you send him away free from you, you shall not let him go away empty-handed; ¹⁴you shall supply him liberally from your flock, from your threshing floor, and from your winepress. *From what* the LORD your God has blessed you with, you shall give to him. ¹⁵You shall remember that you were a slave in the land of Egypt, and the LORD your God redeemed you; therefore I command you this thing today. ¹⁶And if it happens that he says to you, 'I will not go away from you,' because he loves you and your house, since he prospers with you, ¹⁷then you shall take an awl and thrust *it* through his ear to the door, and he shall be your servant forever. Also to your female servant you shall do likewise. ¹⁸It shall not seem hard to you when you send him away free from you; for he has been worth a double hired servant in serving you six years. Then the LORD your God will bless you in all that you do.

The Law Concerning Firstborn Animals

¹⁹"All the firstborn males that come from your herd and your flock you shall sanctify to the LORD your God; you shall do no work with the firstborn of your herd, nor shear the firstborn of your flock. ²⁰You and your household shall eat *it* before the LORD your God year by year in the place which the LORD chooses. ²¹But if there is a defect in it, *if it is* lame or blind *or has* any serious defect, you shall not sacrifice it to the LORD your God. ²²You may eat it within your gates; the unclean and the clean *person* alike *may eat it,* as *if it were* a gazelle or a deer. ²³Only you shall not eat its blood; you shall pour it on the ground like water.

The Passover Reviewed

16 "Observe the month of Abib, and keep the Passover to the LORD your God, for in the month of Abib the LORD your God brought you out of Egypt by night. ²Therefore you shall sacrifice the Passover to the LORD your God, from the flock and the herd, in the place where the LORD chooses to put His name. ³You shall eat no leavened bread with it; seven days you shall eat unleavened bread with it, *that is,*

the bread of affliction (for you came out of the land of Egypt in haste), that you may remember the day in which you came out of the land of Egypt all the days of your life. [4]And no leaven shall be seen among you in all your territory for seven days, nor shall *any* of the meat which you sacrifice the first day at twilight remain overnight until morning.

[5]"You may not sacrifice the Passover within any of your gates which the Lord your God gives you; [6]but at the place where the Lord your God chooses to make His name abide, there you shall sacrifice the Passover at twilight, at the going down of the sun, at the time you came out of Egypt. [7]And you shall roast and eat *it* in the place which the Lord your God chooses, and in the morning you shall turn and go to your tents. [8]Six days you shall eat unleavened bread, and on the seventh day there *shall be* a sacred assembly to the Lord your God. You shall do no work *on it.*

The Feast of Weeks Reviewed

[9]"You shall count seven weeks for yourself; begin to count the seven weeks from *the time* you begin *to put* the sickle to the grain. [10]Then you shall keep the Feast of Weeks to the Lord your God with the tribute of a freewill offering from your hand, which you shall give as the Lord your God blesses you. [11]You shall rejoice before the Lord your God, you and your son and your daughter, your male servant and your female servant, the Levite who *is* within your gates, the stranger and the fatherless and the widow who *are* among you, at the place where the Lord your God chooses to make His name abide. [12]And you shall remember that you were a slave in Egypt, and you shall be careful to observe these statutes.

The Feast of Tabernacles Reviewed

[13]"You shall observe the Feast of Tabernacles seven days, when you have gathered from your threshing floor and from your winepress. [14]And you shall rejoice in your feast, you and your son and your daughter, your male servant and your female servant and the Levite, the stranger

and the fatherless and the widow, who *are* within your gates. [15]Seven days you shall keep a sacred feast to the Lord your God in the place which the Lord chooses, because the Lord your God will bless you in all your produce and in all the work of your hands, so that you surely rejoice.

[16]"Three times a year all your males shall appear before the Lord your God in the place which He chooses: at the Feast of Unleavened Bread, at the Feast of Weeks, and at the Feast of Tabernacles; and they shall not appear before the Lord empty-handed. [17]Every man *shall give* as he is able, according to the blessing of the Lord your God which He has given you.

Justice Must Be Administered

[18]"You shall appoint judges and officers in all your gates, which the Lord your God gives you, according to your tribes, and they shall judge the people with just judgment. [19]You shall not pervert justice; you shall not show partiality, nor take a bribe, for a bribe blinds the eyes of the wise and twists the words of the righteous. [20]You shall follow what is altogether just, that you may live and inherit the land which the Lord your God is giving you.

[21]"You shall not plant for yourself any tree, as a wooden image, near the altar which you build for yourself to the Lord your God. [22]You shall not set up a *sacred* pillar, which the Lord your God hates.

17 "You shall not sacrifice to the Lord your God a bull or sheep which has any blemish *or* defect, for that *is* an abomination to the Lord your God.

[2]"If there is found among you, within any of your gates which the Lord your God gives you, a man or a woman who has been wicked in the sight of the Lord your God, in transgressing His covenant, [3]who has gone and served other gods and worshiped them, either the sun or moon or any of the host of heaven, which I have not commanded, [4]and it is told you, and you hear *of it,* then you shall inquire diligently. And if *it is* indeed true *and* certain that such an abomination has been committed in Israel, [5]then you shall bring out to your gates that man or woman who has committed that wicked

thing, and shall stone to death that man or woman with stones. 6Whoever is deserving of death shall be put to death on the testimony of two or three witnesses; he shall not be put to death on the testimony of one witness. 7The hands of the witnesses shall be the first against him to put him to death, and afterward the hands of all the people. So you shall put away the evil from among you.

8"If a matter arises which is too hard for you to judge, between degrees of guilt for bloodshed, between one judgment or another, or between one punishment or another, matters of controversy within your gates, then you shall arise and go up to the place which the LORD your God chooses. 9And you shall come to the priests, the Levites, and to the judge *there* in those days, and inquire *of them;* they shall pronounce upon you the sentence of judgment. 10You shall do according to the sentence which they pronounce upon you in that place which the LORD chooses. And you shall be careful to do according to all that they order you. 11According to the sentence of the law in which they instruct you, according to the judgment which they tell you, you shall do; you shall not turn aside *to* the right hand or *to* the left from the sentence which they pronounce upon you. 12Now the man who acts presumptuously and will not heed the priest who stands to minister there before the LORD your God, or the judge, that man shall die. So you shall put away the evil from Israel. 13And all the people shall hear and fear, and no longer act presumptuously.

Principles Governing Kings

14"When you come to the land which the LORD your God is giving you, and possess it and dwell in it, and say, 'I will set a king over me like all the nations that *are* around me,' 15you shall surely set a king over you whom the LORD your God chooses; *one* from among your brethren you shall set as king over you; you may not set a foreigner over you, who *is* not your brother. 16But he shall not multiply horses for himself, nor cause the people to return to Egypt to multiply horses, for the LORD has said to

you, 'You shall not return that way again.' 17Neither shall he multiply wives for himself, lest his heart turn away; nor shall he greatly multiply silver and gold for himself.

18"Also it shall be, when he sits on the throne of his kingdom, that he shall write for himself a copy of this law in a book, from *the one* before the priests, the Levites. 19And it shall be with him, and he shall read it all the days of his life, that he may learn to fear the LORD his God and be careful to observe all the words of this law and these statutes, 20that his heart may not be lifted above his brethren, that he may not turn aside from the commandment *to* the right hand or *to* the left, and that he may prolong *his* days in his kingdom, he and his children in the midst of Israel.

The Portion of the Priests and Levites

18 "The priests, the Levites—all the tribe of Levi—shall have no part nor inheritance with Israel; they shall eat the offerings of the LORD made by fire, and His portion. 2Therefore they shall have no inheritance among their brethren; the LORD is their inheritance, as He said to them.

3"And this shall be the priest's due from the people, from those who offer a sacrifice, whether *it is* bull or sheep: they shall give to the priest the shoulder, the cheeks, and the stomach. 4The firstfruits of your grain and your new wine and your oil, and the first of the fleece of your sheep, you shall give him. 5For the LORD your God has chosen him out of all your tribes to stand to minister in the name of the LORD, him and his sons forever.

6"So if a Levite comes from any of your gates, from where he dwells among all Israel, and comes with all the desire of his mind to the place which the LORD chooses, 7then he may serve in the name of the LORD his God as all his brethren the Levites *do,* who stand there before the LORD. 8They shall have equal portions to eat, besides what comes from the sale of his inheritance.

Avoid Wicked Customs

9"When you come into the land which the LORD your God is giving you, you shall not learn to follow the abominations of

those nations. ¹⁰There shall not be found among you *anyone* who makes his son or his daughter pass through the fire, *or one* who practices witchcraft, *or* a soothsayer, or one who interprets omens, or a sorcerer, ¹¹or one who conjures spells, or a medium, or a spiritist, or one who calls up the dead. ¹²For all who do these things *are* an abomination to the Lord, and because of these abominations the Lord your God drives them out from before you. ¹³You shall be blameless before the Lord your God. ¹⁴For these nations which you will dispossess listened to soothsayers and diviners; but as for you, the Lord your God has not appointed such for you.

A New Prophet Like Moses

¹⁵"The Lord your God will raise up for you a Prophet like me from your midst, from your brethren. Him you shall hear, ¹⁶according to all you desired of the Lord your God in Horeb in the day of the assembly, saying, 'Let me not hear again the voice of the Lord my God, nor let me see this great fire anymore, lest I die.'

¹⁷"And the Lord said to me: 'What they have spoken is good. ¹⁸I will raise up for them a Prophet like you from among their brethren, and will put My words in His mouth, and He shall speak to them all that I command Him. ¹⁹And it shall be *that* whoever will not hear My words, which He speaks in My name, I will require *it* of him. ²⁰But the prophet who presumes to speak a word in My name, which I have not commanded him to speak, or who speaks in the name of other gods, that prophet shall die.' ²¹And if you say in your heart, 'How shall we know the word which the Lord has not spoken?'— ²²when a prophet speaks in the name of the Lord, if the thing does not happen or come to pass, that *is* the thing which the Lord has not spoken; the prophet has spoken it presumptuously; you shall not be afraid of him.

Three Cities of Refuge

19 "When the Lord your God has cut off the nations whose land the Lord your God is giving you, and you dispossess them and dwell in their cities and in their houses, ²you shall separate three cities for yourself in the midst of your land which the Lord your God is giving you to possess. ³You shall prepare roads for yourself, and divide into three parts the territory of your land which the Lord your God is giving you to inherit, that any manslayer may flee there.

⁴"And this *is* the case of the manslayer who flees there, that he may live: Whoever kills his neighbor unintentionally, not having hated him in time past— ⁵as when *a man* goes to the woods with his neighbor to cut timber, and his hand swings a stroke with the ax to cut down the tree, and the head slips from the handle and strikes his neighbor so that he dies—he shall flee to one of these cities and live; ⁶lest the avenger of blood, while his anger is hot, pursue the manslayer and overtake him, because the way is long, and kill him, though he *was* not deserving of death, since he had not hated the victim in time past. ⁷Therefore I command you, saying, 'You shall separate three cities for yourself.'

⁸"Now if the Lord your God enlarges your territory, as He swore to your fathers, and gives you the land which He promised to give to your fathers, ⁹and if you keep all these commandments and do them, which I command you today, to love the Lord your God and to walk always in His ways, then you shall add three more cities for yourself besides these three, ¹⁰lest innocent blood be shed in the midst of your land which the Lord your God is giving you *as* an inheritance, and *thus* guilt of bloodshed be upon you.

¹¹"But if anyone hates his neighbor, lies in wait for him, rises against him and strikes him mortally, so that he dies, and he flees to one of these cities, ¹²then the elders of his city shall send and bring him from there, and deliver him over to the hand of the avenger of blood, that he may die. ¹³Your eye shall not pity him, but you shall put away *the guilt of* innocent blood from Israel, that it may go well with you.

Property Boundaries

¹⁴"You shall not remove your neighbor's landmark, which the men of old have set,

in your inheritance which you will inherit in the land that the Lord your God is giving you to possess.

The Law Concerning Witnesses

15"One witness shall not rise against a man concerning any iniquity or any sin that he commits; by the mouth of two or three witnesses the matter shall be established. 16If a false witness rises against any man to testify against him of wrongdoing, 17then both men in the controversy shall stand before the Lord, before the priests and the judges who serve in those days. 18And the judges shall make careful inquiry, and indeed, *if* the witness *is* a false witness, who has testified falsely against his brother, 19then you shall do to him as he thought to have done to his brother; so you shall put away the evil from among you. 20And those who remain shall hear and fear, and hereafter they shall not again commit such evil among you. 21Your eye shall not pity: life *shall be* for life, eye for eye, tooth for tooth, hand for hand, foot for foot.

Principles Governing Warfare

20 "When you go out to battle against your enemies, and see horses and chariots *and* people more numerous than you, do not be afraid of them; for the Lord your God *is* with you, who brought you up from the land of Egypt. 2So it shall be, when you are on the verge of battle, that the priest shall approach and speak to the people. 3And he shall say to them, 'Hear, O Israel: Today you are on the verge of battle with your enemies. Do not let your heart faint, do not be afraid, and do not tremble or be terrified because of them; 4for the Lord your God *is* He who goes with you, to fight for you against your enemies, to save you.'

5"Then the officers shall speak to the people, saying: 'What man *is there* who has built a new house and has not dedicated it? Let him go and return to his house, lest he die in the battle and another man dedicate it. 6Also what man *is there* who has planted a vineyard and has not eaten of it? Let him go and return to his house, lest he die in the battle and another man eat of it. 7And what man *is there* who is betrothed to a woman and has not married her? Let him go and return to his house, lest he die in the battle and another man marry her.'

8"The officers shall speak further to the people, and say, 'What man *is there who is* fearful and fainthearted? Let him go and return to his house, lest the heart of his brethren faint[a] like his heart.' 9And so it shall be, when the officers have finished speaking to the people, that they shall make captains of the armies to lead the people.

10"When you go near a city to fight against it, then proclaim an offer of peace to it. 11And it shall be that if they accept your offer of peace, and open to you, then all the people *who are* found in it shall be placed under tribute to you, and serve you. 12Now if *the city* will not make peace with you, but war against you, then you shall besiege it. 13And when the Lord your God delivers it into your hands, you shall strike every male in it with the edge of the sword. 14But the women, the little ones, the livestock, and all that is in the city, all its spoil, you shall plunder for yourself; and you shall eat the enemies' plunder which the Lord your God gives you. 15Thus you shall do to all the cities *which are* very far from you, which *are* not of the cities of these nations.

16"But of the cities of these peoples which the Lord your God gives you *as* an inheritance, you shall let nothing that breathes remain alive, 17but you shall utterly destroy them: the Hittite and the Amorite and the Canaanite and the Perizzite and the Hivite and the Jebusite, just as the Lord your God has commanded you, 18lest they teach you to do according to all their abominations which they have done for their gods, and you sin against the Lord your God.

19"When you besiege a city for a long time, while making war against it to take it, you shall not destroy its trees by wielding an ax against them; if you can eat of them,

---

20:8 [a]Following Masoretic Text and Targum; Samaritan Pentateuch, Septuagint, Syriac, and Vulgate read *lest he make his brother's heart faint.*

THE CONNECTION BETWEEN RELIGION AND DEMOCRACY

FRANKLIN D. ROOSEVELT

The following excerpt from Franklin D. Roosevelt's State of the Union to Congress in 1939 underscores how, until recent years, America's leadership understood the vital connection between religion and democracy. With Hitler on the move in Europe, President Roosevelt said:

Storms from abroad directly challenge three institutions indispensable to Americans, now as always. The first is religion. It is the source of the other two—democracy and international good faith.

Religion, by teaching man his relationship to God, gives the individual a sense of his own dignity and teaches him to respect himself by respecting his neighbors.

Democracy, the practice of self-government, is a covenant among free men to respect the rights and liberties of their fellows.

International good faith, a sister of democracy, springs from the will of civilized nations of men to respect the rights and liberties of other nations of men.

In a modern civilization, all three—religion, democracy, and international good faith—complement and support each other.

Where freedom of religion has been attacked, the attack has come from sources opposed to democracy. Where democracy has been overthrown, the spirit of free worship has disappeared. And where religion and democracy have vanished, good faith and reason in international affairs have given way to strident ambition and brute force.

An ordering of society which relegates religion, democracy, and good faith among nations to the background can find no place within it for the ideals of the Prince of Peace. The United States rejects such an ordering and retains its ancient faith.

There comes a time in the affairs of men when they must prepare to defend, not their homes alone, but the tenets of faith and humanity on which their churches, their governments, and their very civilization are founded. The defense of religion, of democracy, and of good faith among nations is all the same fight. To save one we must now make up our minds to save all.

do not cut them down to use in the siege, for the tree of the field *is* man's *food.* ²⁰Only the trees which you know *are* not trees for food you may destroy and cut down, to build siegeworks against the city that makes war with you, until it is subdued.

The Law Concerning Unsolved Murder

21 "If *anyone* is found slain, lying in the field in the land which the Lord your God is giving you to possess, *and* it is not known who killed him, ²then your elders and your judges shall go out and measure *the distance* from the slain man to the surrounding cities. ³And it shall be *that* the elders of the city nearest to the slain man will take a heifer which has not been worked *and* which has not pulled with a yoke. ⁴The elders of that city shall bring the heifer down to a valley with flowing water, which is neither plowed nor sown, and they shall break the heifer's neck there in the valley. ⁵Then the priests, the sons of Levi, shall come near, for the Lord your God has chosen them to minister to Him and to bless in the name of the Lord; by their word every controversy and every assault shall be *settled.* ⁶And all the elders of that city nearest to the slain *man* shall wash their hands over the heifer whose neck was broken in the valley. ⁷Then they shall answer and say, 'Our hands have not shed this blood, nor have our eyes seen *it.* ⁸Provide atonement, O Lord, for Your people Israel, whom You have redeemed, and do not lay innocent blood to the charge of Your people Israel.' And atonement shall be provided on their behalf for the blood. ⁹So you shall put away the *guilt of* innocent blood from among you when you do *what is* right in the sight of the Lord.

Female Captives

¹⁰"When you go out to war against your enemies, and the Lord your God delivers them into your hand, and you take them captive, ¹¹and you see among the captives a beautiful woman, and desire her and would take her for your wife, ¹²then you shall bring her home to your house, and she shall shave her head and trim her nails. ¹³She shall put off the clothes of her captivity, remain in your house, and mourn her father and her mother a full month; after that you may go in to her and be her husband, and she shall be your wife. ¹⁴And it shall be, if you have no delight in her, then you shall set her free, but you certainly shall not sell her for money; you shall not treat her brutally, because you have humbled her.

Firstborn Inheritance Rights

¹⁵"If a man has two wives, one loved and the other unloved, and they have borne him children, *both* the loved and the unloved, and if the firstborn son is of her who is unloved, ¹⁶then it shall be, on the day he bequeaths his possessions to his sons, *that* he must not bestow firstborn status on the son of the loved wife in preference to the son of the unloved, the *true* firstborn. ¹⁷But he shall acknowledge the son of the unloved wife *as* the firstborn by giving him a double portion of all that he has, for he *is* the beginning of his strength; the right of the firstborn *is* his.

The Rebellious Son

¹⁸"If a man has a stubborn and rebellious son who will not obey the voice of his father or the voice of his mother, and *who,* when they have chastened him, will not heed them, ¹⁹then his father and his mother shall take hold of him and bring him out to the elders of his city, to the gate of his city. ²⁰And they shall say to the elders of his city, 'This son of ours is stubborn and rebellious; he will not obey our voice; he is a glutton and a drunkard.' ²¹Then all the men of his city shall stone him to death with stones; so you shall put away the evil from among you, and all Israel shall hear and fear.

Miscellaneous Laws

²²"If a man has committed a sin deserving of death, and he is put to death, and you hang him on a tree, ²³his body shall not remain overnight on the tree, but you shall surely bury him that day, so that you do not defile the land which the Lord your God is giving you *as* an inheritance; for he who is hanged *is* accursed of God.

22 "You shall not see your brother's ox or his sheep going astray, and hide yourself from them; you shall certainly bring them back to your brother. ²And if your brother *is* not near you, or if you do not know him, then you shall bring it to your own house, and it shall remain with you until your brother seeks it; then you shall restore it to him. ³You shall do the same with his donkey, and so shall you do with his garment; with any lost thing of your brother's, which he has lost and you have found, you shall do likewise; you must not hide yourself.

⁴"You shall not see your brother's donkey or his ox fall down along the road, and hide yourself from them; you shall surely help him lift *them* up again.

⁵"A woman shall not wear anything that pertains to a man, nor shall a man put on a woman's garment, for all who do so *are* an abomination to the LORD your God.

⁶"If a bird's nest happens to be before you along the way, in any tree or on the ground, with young ones or eggs, with the mother sitting on the young or on the eggs, you shall not take the mother with the young; ⁷you shall surely let the mother go, and take the young for yourself, that it may be well with you and *that* you may prolong *your* days.

⁸"When you build a new house, then you shall make a parapet for your roof, that you may not bring guilt of bloodshed on your household if anyone falls from it.

⁹"You shall not sow your vineyard with different kinds of seed, lest the yield of the seed which you have sown and the fruit of your vineyard be defiled.

¹⁰"You shall not plow with an ox and a donkey together.

¹¹"You shall not wear a garment of different sorts, *such as* wool and linen mixed together.

¹²"You shall make tassels on the four corners of the clothing with which you cover *yourself.*

Laws of Sexual Morality

¹³"If any man takes a wife, and goes in to her, and detests her, ¹⁴and charges her with shameful conduct, and brings a bad name on her, and says, 'I took this woman, and when I came to her I found she *was* not a virgin,' ¹⁵then the father and mother of the young woman shall take and bring out *the evidence of* the young woman's virginity to the elders of the city at the gate. ¹⁶And the young woman's father shall say to the elders, 'I gave my daughter to this man as wife, and he detests her. ¹⁷Now he has charged her with shameful conduct, saying, "I found your daughter *was* not a virgin," and yet these *are the evidences of* my daughter's virginity.' And they shall spread the cloth before the elders of the city. ¹⁸Then the elders of that city shall take that man and punish him; ¹⁹and they shall fine him one hundred *shekels* of silver and give *them* to the father of the young woman, because he has brought a bad name on a virgin of Israel. And she shall be his wife; he cannot divorce her all his days.

²⁰"But if the thing is true, *and evidences of* virginity are not found for the young woman, ²¹then they shall bring out the young woman to the door of her father's house, and the men of her city shall stone her to death with stones, because she has done a disgraceful thing in Israel, to play the harlot in her father's house. So you shall put away the evil from among you.

²²"If a man is found lying with a woman married to a husband, then both of them shall die—the man that lay with the woman, and the woman; so you shall put away the evil from Israel.

²³"If a young woman *who is* a virgin is betrothed to a husband, and a man finds her in the city and lies with her, ²⁴then you shall bring them both out to the gate of that city, and you shall stone them to death with stones, the young woman because she did not cry out in the city, and the man because he humbled his neighbor's wife; so you shall put away the evil from among you.

²⁵"But if a man finds a betrothed young woman in the countryside, and the man forces her and lies with her, then only the man who lay with her shall die. ²⁶But you shall do nothing to the young woman; *there is* in the young woman no sin *deserving of*

death, for just as when a man rises against his neighbor and kills him, even so *is* this matter. ²⁷For he found her in the countryside, *and* the betrothed young woman cried out, but *there was* no one to save her.

²⁸"If a man finds a young woman *who is* a virgin, who is not betrothed, and he seizes her and lies with her, and they are found out, ²⁹then the man who lay with her shall give to the young woman's father fifty *shekels* of silver, and she shall be his wife because he has humbled her; he shall not be permitted to divorce her all his days.

³⁰"A man shall not take his father's wife, nor uncover his father's bed.

Those Excluded from the Congregation

23 "He who is emasculated by crushing or mutilation shall not enter the assembly of the LORD.

²"One of illegitimate birth shall not enter the assembly of the LORD; even to the tenth generation none of his *descendants* shall enter the assembly of the LORD.

³"An Ammonite or Moabite shall not enter the assembly of the LORD; even to the tenth generation none of his *descendants* shall enter the assembly of the LORD forever, ⁴because they did not meet you with bread and water on the road when you came out of Egypt, and because they hired against you Balaam the son of Beor from Pethor of Mesopotamia,^a to curse you. ⁵Nevertheless the LORD your God would not listen to Balaam, but the LORD your God turned the curse into a blessing for you, because the LORD your God loves you. ⁶You shall not seek their peace nor their prosperity all your days forever.

⁷"You shall not abhor an Edomite, for he *is* your brother. You shall not abhor an Egyptian, because you were an alien in his land. ⁸The children of the third generation born to them may enter the assembly of the LORD.

Cleanliness of the Campsite

⁹"When the army goes out against your enemies, then keep yourself from every wicked thing. ¹⁰If there is any man among you who becomes unclean by some occurrence in the night, then he shall go outside the camp; he shall not come inside the camp. ¹¹But it shall be, when evening comes, that he shall wash with water; and when the sun sets, he may come into the camp.

¹²"Also you shall have a place outside the camp, where you may go out; ¹³and you shall have an implement among your equipment, and when you sit down outside, you shall dig with it and turn and cover your refuse. ¹⁴For the LORD your God walks in the midst of your camp, to deliver you and give your enemies over to you; therefore your camp shall be holy, that He may see no unclean thing among you, and turn away from you.

Miscellaneous Laws

¹⁵"You shall not give back to his master the slave who has escaped from his master to you. ¹⁶He may dwell with you in your midst, in the place which he chooses within one of your gates, where it seems best to him; you shall not oppress him.

¹⁷"There shall be no *ritual* harlot^a of the daughters of Israel, or a perverted^b one of the sons of Israel. ¹⁸You shall not bring the wages of a harlot or the price of a dog to the house of the LORD your God for any vowed offering, for both of these *are* an abomination to the LORD your God.

¹⁹"You shall not charge interest to your brother—interest on money *or* food *or* anything that is lent out at interest. ²⁰To a foreigner you may charge interest, but to your brother you shall not charge interest, that the LORD your God may bless you in all to which you set your hand in the land which you are entering to possess.

²¹"When you make a vow to the LORD your God, you shall not delay to pay it; for the LORD your God will surely require it of you, and it would be sin to you. ²²But if you abstain from vowing, it shall not be sin to you. ²³That which has gone from your lips you shall keep and perform, for you voluntarily vowed to the LORD your God what you have promised with your mouth.

23:4 ^aHebrew *Aram Naharaim*   **23:17** ^aHebrew *qedeshah,* feminine of *qadesh* (see note b)   ^bHebrew *qadesh,* that is, one practicing sodomy and prostitution in religious rituals

²⁴"When you come into your neighbor's vineyard, you may eat your fill of grapes at your pleasure, but you shall not put *any* in your container. ²⁵When you come into your neighbor's standing grain, you may pluck the heads with your hand, but you shall not use a sickle on your neighbor's standing grain.

Law Concerning Divorce

24 "When a man takes a wife and marries her, and it happens that she finds no favor in his eyes because he has found some uncleanness in her, and he writes her a certificate of divorce, puts *it* in her hand, and sends her out of his house, ²when she has departed from his house, and goes and becomes another man's *wife,* ³*if* the latter husband detests her and writes her a certificate of divorce, puts *it* in her hand, and sends her out of his house, or if the latter husband dies who took her as his wife, ⁴*then* her former husband who divorced her must not take her back to be his wife after she has been defiled; for that *is* an abomination before the LORD, and you shall not bring sin on the land which the LORD your God is giving you *as* an inheritance.

Miscellaneous Laws

⁵"When a man has taken a new wife, he shall not go out to war or be charged with any business; he shall be free at home one year, and bring happiness to his wife whom he has taken.

⁶"No man shall take the lower or the upper millstone in pledge, for he takes *one's* living in pledge.

⁷"If a man is found kidnapping any of his brethren of the children of Israel, and mistreats him or sells him, then that kidnapper shall die; and you shall put away the evil from among you.

⁸"Take heed in an outbreak of leprosy, that you carefully observe and do according to all that the priests, the Levites, shall teach you; just as I commanded them, *so* you shall be careful to do. ⁹Remember what the LORD your God did to Miriam on the way when you came out of Egypt!

¹⁰"When you lend your brother anything, you shall not go into his house to get his pledge. ¹¹You shall stand outside, and the man to whom you lend shall bring the pledge out to you. ¹²And if the man *is* poor, you shall not keep his pledge overnight. ¹³You shall in any case return the pledge to him again when the sun goes down, that he may sleep in his own garment and bless you; and it shall be righteousness to you before the LORD your God.

¹⁴"You shall not oppress a hired servant *who is* poor and needy, *whether* one of your brethren or one of the aliens who *is* in your land within your gates. ¹⁵Each day you shall give *him* his wages, and not let the sun go down on it, for he *is* poor and has set his heart on it; lest he cry out against you to the LORD, and it be sin to you.

¹⁶"Fathers shall not be put to death for *their* children, nor shall children be put to death for *their* fathers; a person shall be put to death for his own sin.

¹⁷"You shall not pervert justice due the stranger or the fatherless, nor take a widow's garment as a pledge. ¹⁸But you shall remember that you were a slave in Egypt, and the LORD your God redeemed you from there; therefore I command you to do this thing.

¹⁹"When you reap your harvest in your field, and forget a sheaf in the field, you shall not go back to get it; it shall be for the stranger, the fatherless, and the widow, that the LORD your God may bless you in all the work of your hands. ²⁰When you beat your olive trees, you shall not go over the boughs again; it shall be for the stranger, the fatherless, and the widow. ²¹When you gather the grapes of your vineyard, you shall not glean *it* afterward; it shall be for the stranger, the fatherless, and the widow. ²²And you shall remember that you were a slave in the land of Egypt; therefore I command you to do this thing.

25 "If there is a dispute between men, and they come to court, that *the judges* may judge them, and they justify the righteous and condemn the wicked, ²then it shall be, if the wicked man deserves to be beaten, that the judge will cause him to lie down and be beaten in his presence, according to his guilt, with a certain number of blows. ³Forty blows he may

give him *and* no more, lest he should exceed this and beat him with many blows above these, and your brother be humiliated in your sight.

4"You shall not muzzle an ox while it treads out *the grain.*

Marriage Duty of the Surviving Brother

5"If brothers dwell together, and one of them dies and has no son, the widow of the dead man shall not be *married* to a stranger outside *the family;* her husband's brother shall go in to her, take her as his wife, and perform the duty of a husband's brother to her. 6And it shall be *that* the firstborn son which she bears will succeed to the name of his dead brother, that his name may not be blotted out of Israel. 7But if the man does not want to take his brother's wife, then let his brother's wife go up to the gate to the elders, and say, 'My husband's brother refuses to raise up a name to his brother in Israel; he will not perform the duty of my husband's brother.' 8Then the elders of his city shall call him and speak to him. But *if* he stands firm and says, 'I do not want to take her,' 9then his brother's wife shall come to him in the presence of the elders, remove his sandal from his foot, spit in his face, and answer and say, 'So shall it be done to the man who will not build up his brother's house.' 10And his name shall be called in Israel, 'The house of him who had his sandal removed.'

Miscellaneous Laws

11"If *two* men fight together, and the wife of one draws near to rescue her husband from the hand of the one attacking him, and puts out her hand and seizes him by the genitals, 12then you shall cut off her hand; your eye shall not pity *her.*

13"You shall not have in your bag differing weights, a heavy and a light. 14You shall not have in your house differing measures, a large and a small. 15You shall have a perfect and just weight, a perfect and just measure, that your days may be lengthened in the land which the LORD your God is giving you. 16For all who do such things, all who behave unrighteously, *are* an abomination to the LORD your God.

Destroy the Amalekites

17"Remember what Amalek did to you on the way as you were coming out of Egypt, 18how he met you on the way and attacked your rear ranks, all the stragglers at your rear, when you *were* tired and weary; and he did not fear God. 19Therefore it shall be, when the LORD your God has given you rest from your enemies all around, in the land which the LORD your God is giving you to possess *as* an inheritance, *that* you will blot out the remembrance of Amalek from under heaven. You shall not forget.

Offerings of Firstfruits and Tithes

26 "And it shall be, when you come into the land which the LORD your God is giving you *as* an inheritance, and you possess it and dwell in it, 2that you shall take some of the first of all the produce of the ground, which you shall bring from your land that the LORD your God is giving you, and put *it* in a basket and go to the place where the LORD your God chooses to make His name abide. 3And you shall go to the one who is priest in those days, and say to him, 'I declare today to the LORD youra God that I have come to the country which the LORD swore to our fathers to give us.'

4"Then the priest shall take the basket out of your hand and set it down before the altar of the LORD your God. 5And you shall answer and say before the LORD your God: 'My father *was* a Syrian,a about to perish, and he went down to Egypt and dwelt there, few in number; and there he became a nation, great, mighty, and populous. 6But the Egyptians mistreated us, afflicted us, and laid hard bondage on us. 7Then we cried out to the LORD God of our fathers, and the LORD heard our voice and looked on our affliction and our labor and our oppression. 8So the LORD brought us out of Egypt with a mighty hand and with an outstretched arm, with great terror and with signs and wonders. 9He has brought us to this place and has given us this land, "a land flowing with milk and honey";a 10and now, behold,

---

I have brought the firstfruits of the land which you, O LORD, have given me.'

"Then you shall set it before the LORD your God, and worship before the LORD your God. [11]So you shall rejoice in every good *thing* which the LORD your God has given to you and your house, you and the Levite and the stranger who *is* among you.

[12]"When you have finished laying aside all the tithe of your increase in the third year—the year of tithing—and have given *it* to the Levite, the stranger, the fatherless, and the widow, so that they may eat within your gates and be filled, [13]then you shall say before the LORD your God: 'I have removed the holy *tithe* from *my* house, and also have given them to the Levite, the stranger, the fatherless, and the widow, according to all Your commandments which You have commanded me; I have not transgressed Your commandments, nor have I forgotten *them*. [14]I have not eaten any of it when in mourning, nor have I removed *any* of it for an unclean *use,* nor given *any* of it for the dead. I have obeyed the voice of the LORD my God, and have done according to all that You have commanded me. [15]Look down from Your holy habitation, from heaven, and bless Your people Israel and the land which You have given us, just as You swore to our fathers, "a land flowing with milk and honey." '[a]

A Special People of God

[16]"This day the LORD your God commands you to observe these statutes and judgments; therefore you shall be careful to observe them with all your heart and with all your soul. [17]Today you have proclaimed the LORD to be your God, and that you will walk in His ways and keep His statutes, His commandments, and His judgments, and that you will obey His voice. [18]Also today the LORD has proclaimed you to be His special people, just as He promised you, that *you* should keep all His commandments, [19]and that He will set you high above all nations which He has made, in praise, in name, and in honor, and that you may be a holy people to the LORD your God, just as He has spoken."

The Law Inscribed on Stones

27 Now Moses, with the elders of Israel, commanded the people, saying: "Keep all the commandments which I command you today. [2]And it shall be, on the day when you cross over the Jordan to the land which the LORD your God is giving you, that you shall set up for yourselves large stones, and whitewash them with lime. [3]You shall write on them all the words of this law, when you have crossed over, that you may enter the land which the LORD your God is giving you, 'a land flowing with milk and honey,'[a] just as the LORD God of your fathers promised you. [4]Therefore it shall be, when you have crossed over the Jordan, *that* on Mount Ebal you shall set up these stones, which I command you today, and you shall whitewash them with lime. [5]And there you shall build an altar to the LORD your God, an altar of stones; you shall not use an iron *tool* on them. [6]You shall build with whole stones the altar of the LORD your God, and offer burnt offerings on it to the LORD your God. [7]You shall offer peace offerings, and shall eat there, and rejoice before the LORD your God. [8]And you shall write very plainly on the stones all the words of this law."

[9]Then Moses and the priests, the Levites, spoke to all Israel, saying, "Take heed and listen, O Israel: This day you have become the people of the LORD your God. [10]Therefore you shall obey the voice of the LORD your God, and observe His commandments and His statutes which I command you today."

Curses Pronounced from Mount Ebal

[11]And Moses commanded the people on the same day, saying, [12]"These shall stand on Mount Gerizim to bless the people, when you have crossed over the Jordan: Simeon, Levi, Judah, Issachar, Joseph, and Benjamin; [13]and these shall stand on Mount Ebal to curse: Reuben, Gad, Asher, Zebulun, Dan, and Naphtali.

[14]"And the Levites shall speak with a loud voice and say to all the men of Israel:

26:15 [a]Exodus 3:8　　　**27:3** [a]Exodus 3:8

¹⁵'Cursed *is* the one who makes a carved or molded image, an abomination to the Lord, the work of the hands of the craftsman, and sets *it* up in secret.'

"And all the people shall answer and say, 'Amen!'

¹⁶'Cursed *is* the one who treats his father or his mother with contempt.'

"And all the people shall say, 'Amen!'

¹⁷'Cursed *is* the one who moves his neighbor's landmark.'

"And all the people shall say, 'Amen!'

¹⁸'Cursed *is* the one who makes the blind to wander off the road.'

"And all the people shall say, 'Amen!'

¹⁹'Cursed *is* the one who perverts the justice due the stranger, the fatherless, and widow.'

"And all the people shall say, 'Amen!'

²⁰'Cursed *is* the one who lies with his father's wife, because he has uncovered his father's bed.'

"And all the people shall say, 'Amen!'

²¹'Cursed *is* the one who lies with any kind of animal.'

"And all the people shall say, 'Amen!'

²²'Cursed *is* the one who lies with his sister, the daughter of his father or the daughter of his mother.'

"And all the people shall say, 'Amen!'

²³'Cursed *is* the one who lies with his mother-in-law.'

"And all the people shall say, 'Amen!'

²⁴'Cursed *is* the one who attacks his neighbor secretly.'

"And all the people shall say, 'Amen!'

²⁵'Cursed *is* the one who takes a bribe to slay an innocent person.'

"And all the people shall say, 'Amen!'

²⁶'Cursed *is* the one who does not confirm *all* the words of this law by observing them.'

"And all the people shall say, 'Amen!'"

Blessings on Obedience

28 "Now it shall come to pass, if you diligently obey the voice of the Lord your God, to observe carefully all His commandments which I command you today, that the Lord your God will set you high above all nations of the earth. ²And all these blessings shall come upon you and overtake you, because you obey the voice of the Lord your God:

³"Blessed *shall* you *be* in the city, and blessed *shall* you *be* in the country.

⁴"Blessed *shall be* the fruit of your body, the produce of your ground and the increase of your herds, the increase of your cattle and the offspring of your flocks.

⁵"Blessed *shall be* your basket and your kneading bowl.

⁶"Blessed *shall* you *be* when you come in, and blessed *shall* you *be* when you go out.

⁷"The Lord will cause your enemies who rise against you to be defeated before your face; they shall come out against you one way and flee before you seven ways.

⁸"The Lord will command the blessing on you in your storehouses and in all to which you set your hand, and He will bless you in the land which the Lord your God is giving you.

⁹"The Lord will establish you as a holy people to Himself, just as He has sworn to you, if you keep the commandments of the Lord your God and walk in His ways. ¹⁰Then all peoples of the earth shall see that you are called by the name of the Lord, and they shall be afraid of you. ¹¹And the Lord will grant you plenty of goods, in the fruit of your body, in the increase of your livestock, and in the produce of your ground, in the land of which the Lord swore to your fathers to give you. ¹²The Lord will open to you His good treasure, the heavens, to give the rain to your land in its season, and to bless all the work of your hand. You shall lend to many nations, but you shall not borrow. ¹³And the Lord will make you the head and not the tail; you shall be above only, and not be beneath, if you heed the commandments of the Lord your God, which I command you today, and are careful to observe *them.* ¹⁴So you shall not turn aside from any of the words which I command you this day, *to* the right or the left, to go after other gods to serve them.

Curses on Disobedience

¹⁵"But it shall come to pass, if you do not obey the voice of the Lord your God, to observe carefully all His commandments

and His statutes which I command you today, that all these curses will come upon you and overtake you:

16"Cursed *shall* you *be* in the city, and cursed *shall* you *be* in the country.

17"Cursed *shall be* your basket and your kneading bowl.

18"Cursed *shall be* the fruit of your body and the produce of your land, the increase of your cattle and the offspring of your flocks.

19"Cursed *shall* you *be* when you come in, and cursed *shall* you *be* when you go out.

20"The LORD will send on you cursing, confusion, and rebuke in all that you set your hand to do, until you are destroyed and until you perish quickly, because of the wickedness of your doings in which you have forsaken Me. 21The LORD will make the plague cling to you until He has consumed you from the land which you are going to possess. 22The LORD will strike you with consumption, with fever, with inflammation, with severe burning fever, with the sword, with scorching, and with mildew; they shall pursue you until you perish. 23And your heavens which *are* over your head shall be bronze, and the earth which is under you *shall be* iron. 24The LORD will change the rain of your land to powder and dust; from the heaven it shall come down on you until you are destroyed.

25"The LORD will cause you to be defeated before your enemies; you shall go out one way against them and flee seven ways before them; and you shall become troublesome to all the kingdoms of the earth. 26Your carcasses shall be food for all the birds of the air and the beasts of the earth, and no one shall frighten *them* away. 27The LORD will strike you with the boils of Egypt, with tumors, with the scab, and with the itch, from which you cannot be healed. 28The LORD will strike you with madness and blindness and confusion of heart. 29And you shall grope at noonday, as a blind man gropes in darkness; you shall not prosper in your ways; you shall be only oppressed and plundered continually, and no one shall save *you.*

30"You shall betroth a wife, but another man shall lie with her; you shall build a house, but you shall not dwell in it; you shall plant a vineyard, but shall not gather its grapes. 31Your ox *shall be* slaughtered before your eyes, but you shall not eat of it; your donkey *shall be* violently taken away from before you, and shall not be restored to you; your sheep *shall be* given to your enemies, and you shall have no one to rescue *them.* 32Your sons and your daughters *shall be* given to another people, and your eyes shall look and fail *with longing* for them all day long; and *there shall be* no strength in your hand. 33A nation whom you have not known shall eat the fruit of your land and the produce of your labor, and you shall be only oppressed and crushed continually. 34So you shall be driven mad because of the sight which your eyes see. 35The LORD will strike you in the knees and on the legs with severe boils which cannot be healed, and from the sole of your foot to the top of your head.

36"The LORD will bring you and the king whom you set over you to a nation which neither you nor your fathers have known, and there you shall serve other gods—wood and stone. 37And you shall become an astonishment, a proverb, and a byword among all nations where the LORD will drive you.

38"You shall carry much seed out to the field but gather little in, for the locust shall consume it. 39You shall plant vineyards and tend *them,* but you shall neither drink *of* the wine nor gather the *grapes;* for the worms shall eat them. 40You shall have olive trees throughout all your territory, but you shall not anoint *yourself* with the oil; for your olives shall drop off. 41You shall beget sons and daughters, but they shall not be yours; for they shall go into captivity. 42Locusts shall consume all your trees and the produce of your land.

43"The alien who *is* among you shall rise higher and higher above you, and you shall come down lower and lower. 44He shall lend to you, but you shall not lend to him; he shall be the head, and you shall be the tail.

45"Moreover all these curses shall come upon you and pursue and overtake you, until you are destroyed, because you did

not obey the voice of the LORD your God, to keep His commandments and His statutes which He commanded you. ⁴⁶And they shall be upon you for a sign and a wonder, and on your descendants forever.

⁴⁷"Because you did not serve the LORD your God with joy and gladness of heart, for the abundance of everything, ⁴⁸therefore you shall serve your enemies, whom the LORD will send against you, in hunger, in thirst, in nakedness, and in need of everything; and He will put a yoke of iron on your neck until He has destroyed you. ⁴⁹The LORD will bring a nation against you from afar, from the end of the earth, *as swift* as the eagle flies, a nation whose language you will not understand, ⁵⁰a nation of fierce countenance, which does not respect the elderly nor show favor to the young. ⁵¹And they shall eat the increase of your livestock and the produce of your land, until you are destroyed; they shall not leave you grain or new wine or oil, *or* the increase of your cattle or the offspring of your flocks, until they have destroyed you.

⁵²"They shall besiege you at all your gates until your high and fortified walls, in which you trust, come down throughout all your land; and they shall besiege you at all your gates throughout all your land which the LORD your God has given you. ⁵³You shall eat the fruit of your own body, the flesh of your sons and your daughters whom the LORD your God has given you, in the siege and desperate straits in which your enemy shall distress you. ⁵⁴The sensitive and very refined man among you will be hostile toward his brother, toward the wife of his bosom, and toward the rest of his children whom he leaves behind, ⁵⁵so that he will not give any of them the flesh of his children whom he will eat, because he has nothing left in the siege and desperate straits in which your enemy shall distress you at all your gates. ⁵⁶The tender and delicate woman among you, who would not venture to set the sole of her foot on the ground because of her delicateness and sensitivity, will refuseᵃ to the husband of her bosom, and to her son and her daughter, ⁵⁷her placenta which comes out from between her feet and her children

whom she bears; for she will eat them secretly for lack of everything in the siege and desperate straits in which your enemy shall distress you at all your gates.

⁵⁸"If you do not carefully observe all the words of this law that are written in this book, that you may fear this glorious and awesome name, THE LORD YOUR GOD, ⁵⁹then the LORD will bring upon you and your descendants extraordinary plagues—great and prolonged plagues—and serious and prolonged sicknesses. ⁶⁰Moreover He will bring back on you all the diseases of Egypt, of which you were afraid, and they shall cling to you. ⁶¹Also every sickness and every plague, which *is* not written in this Book of the Law, will the LORD bring upon you until you are destroyed. ⁶²You shall be left few in number, whereas you were as the stars of heaven in multitude, because you would not obey the voice of the LORD your God. ⁶³And it shall be, *that* just as the LORD rejoiced over you to do you good and multiply you, so the LORD will rejoice over you to destroy you and bring you to nothing; and you shall be plucked from off the land which you go to possess.

⁶⁴"Then the LORD will scatter you among all peoples, from one end of the earth to the other, and there you shall serve other gods, which neither you nor your fathers have known—wood and stone. ⁶⁵And among those nations you shall find no rest, nor shall the sole of your foot have a resting place; but there the LORD will give you a trembling heart, failing eyes, and anguish of soul. ⁶⁶Your life shall hang in doubt before you; you shall fear day and night, and have no assurance of life. ⁶⁷In the morning you shall say, 'Oh, that it were evening!' And at evening you shall say, 'Oh, that it were morning!' because of the fear which terrifies your heart, and because of the sight which your eyes see.

⁶⁸"And the LORD will take you back to Egypt in ships, by the way of which I said to you, 'You shall never see it again.' And there you shall be offered for sale to your enemies as male and female slaves, but no one will buy *you.*"

28:56 ᵃLiterally *her eye shall be evil toward*

The Covenant Renewed in Moab

29 These *are* the words of the covenant which the Lord commanded Moses to make with the children of Israel in the land of Moab, besides the covenant which He made with them in Horeb.

[2]Now Moses called all Israel and said to them: "You have seen all that the Lord did before your eyes in the land of Egypt, to Pharaoh and to all his servants and to all his land— [3]the great trials which your eyes have seen, the signs, and those great wonders. [4]Yet the Lord has not given you a heart to perceive and eyes to see and ears to hear, to this *very* day. [5]And I have led you forty years in the wilderness. Your clothes have not worn out on you, and your sandals have not worn out on your feet. [6]You have not eaten bread, nor have you drunk wine or *similar* drink, that you may know that I *am* the Lord your God. [7]And when you came to this place, Sihon king of Heshbon and Og king of Bashan came out against us to battle, and we conquered them. [8]We took their land and gave it as an inheritance to the Reubenites, to the Gadites, and to half the tribe of Manasseh. [9]Therefore keep the words of this covenant, and do them, that you may prosper in all that you do.

[10]"All of you stand today before the Lord your God: your leaders and your tribes and your elders and your officers, all the men of Israel, [11]your little ones and your wives—also the stranger who *is* in your camp, from the one who cuts your wood to the one who draws your water— [12]that you may enter into covenant with the Lord your God, and into His oath, which the Lord your God makes with you today, [13]that He may establish you today as a people for Himself, and *that* He may be God to you, just as He has spoken to you, and just as He has sworn to your fathers, to Abraham, Isaac, and Jacob.

[14]"I make this covenant and this oath, not with you alone, [15]but with *him* who stands here with us today before the Lord our God, as well as with *him* who *is* not here with us today [16](for you know that we dwelt in the land of Egypt and that we came through the nations which you passed by, [17]and you saw their abominations and their idols which *were* among them—wood and stone and silver and gold); [18]so that there may not be among you man or woman or family or tribe, whose heart turns away today from the Lord our God, to go *and* serve the gods of these nations, and that there may not be among you a root bearing bitterness or wormwood; [19]and so it may not happen, when he hears the words of this curse, that he blesses himself in his heart, saying, 'I shall have peace, even though I follow the dictates[a] of my heart'—as though the drunkard could be included with the sober.

[20]"The Lord would not spare him; for then the anger of the Lord and His jealousy would burn against that man, and every curse that is written in this book would settle on him, and the Lord would blot out his name from under heaven. [21]And the Lord would separate him from all the tribes of Israel for adversity, according to all the curses of the covenant that are written in this Book of the Law, [22]so that the coming generation of your children who rise up after you, and the foreigner who comes from a far land, would say, when they see the plagues of that land and the sicknesses which the Lord has laid on it:

[23]'The whole land *is* brimstone, salt, and burning; it is not sown, nor does it bear, nor does any grass grow there, like the overthrow of Sodom and Gomorrah, Admah, and Zeboiim, which the Lord overthrew in His anger and His wrath.' [24]All nations would say, 'Why has the Lord done so to this land? What does the heat of this great anger mean?' [25]Then *people* would say: 'Because they have forsaken the covenant of the Lord God of their fathers, which He made with them when He brought them out of the land of Egypt; [26]for they went and served other gods and worshiped them, gods that they did not know and that He had not given to them. [27]Then the anger of the Lord was aroused against this land, to bring on it every curse

---

29:19 [a]Or *stubbornness*

that is written in this book. [28]And the LORD uprooted them from their land in anger, in wrath, and in great indignation, and cast them into another land, as *it is* this day.'

[29]"The secret *things belong* to the LORD our God, but those *things which are* revealed *belong* to us and to our children forever, that *we* may do all the words of this law.

The Blessing of Returning to God

30 "Now it shall come to pass, when all these things come upon you, the blessing and the curse which I have set before you, and you call *them* to mind among all the nations where the LORD your God drives you, [2]and you return to the LORD your God and obey His voice, according to all that I command you today, you and your children, with all your heart and with all your soul, [3]that the LORD your God will bring you back from captivity, and have compassion on you, and gather you again from all the nations where the LORD your God has scattered you. [4]If *any* of you are driven out to the farthest *parts* under heaven, from there the LORD your God will gather you, and from there He will bring you. [5]Then the LORD your God will bring you to the land which your fathers possessed, and you shall possess it. He will prosper you and multiply you more than your fathers. [6]And the LORD your God will circumcise your heart and the heart of your descendants, to love the LORD your God with all your heart and with all your soul, that you may live.

[7]"Also the LORD your God will put all these curses on your enemies and on those who hate you, who persecuted you. [8]And you will again obey the voice of the LORD and do all His commandments which I command you today. [9]The LORD your God will make you abound in all the work of your hand, in the fruit of your body, in the increase of your livestock, and in the produce of your land for good. For the LORD will again rejoice over you for good as He rejoiced over your fathers, [10]if you obey the voice of the LORD your God, to keep His commandments and His statutes which are written in this Book of the Law, *and* if

you turn to the LORD your God with all your heart and with all your soul.

The Choice of Life or Death

[11]"For this commandment which I command you today *is* not *too* mysterious for you, nor *is* it far off. [12]It *is* not in heaven, that you should say, 'Who will ascend into heaven for us and bring it to us, that we may hear it and do it?' [13]Nor *is* it beyond the sea, that you should say, 'Who will go over the sea for us and bring it to us, that we may hear it and do it?' [14]But the word *is* very near you, in your mouth and in your heart, that you may do it.

[15]"See, I have set before you today life and good, death and evil, [16]in that I command you today to love the LORD your God, to walk in His ways, and to keep His commandments, His statutes, and His judgments, that you may live and multiply; and the LORD your God will bless you in the land which you go to possess. [17]But if your heart turns away so that you do not hear, and are drawn away, and worship other gods and serve them, [18]I announce to you today that you shall surely perish; you shall not prolong *your* days in the land which you cross over the Jordan to go in and possess. [19]I call heaven and earth as witnesses today against you, *that* I have set before you life and death, blessing and cursing; therefore choose life, that both you and your descendants may live; [20]that you may love the LORD your God, that you may obey His voice, and that you may cling to Him, for He *is* your life and the length of your days; and that you may dwell in the land which the LORD swore to your fathers, to Abraham, Isaac, and Jacob, to give them."

Joshua the New Leader of Israel

31 Then Moses went and spoke these words to all Israel. [2]And he said to them: "I *am* one hundred and twenty years old today. I can no longer go out and come in. Also the LORD has said to me, 'You shall not cross over this Jordan.' [3]The LORD your God Himself crosses over before you; He will destroy these nations from before you, and you shall dispossess them. Joshua

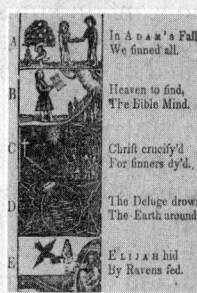

". . . teach it to the children of Israel; put it in their mouths. . . ."

DEUTERONOMY 31:19

THE NEW ENGLAND PRIMER

The New England Primer was first published between 1688 and 1690 by Benjamin Harris of Boston. It was the first reading primer designed for the American colonies and became the most successful educational textbook published in the early days of U.S. history. The 90-page work contained religious maxims, woodcuts, alphabetical assistants, catechisms, and moral lessons. Many of its selections were drawn from the King James Bible.

The following selection reflects the primer's blend of alphabetical and biblical instruction.

A   In ADAM'S Fall
We sinned all.

B   Heaven to find,
The BIBLE Mind.

C   CHRIST crucify'd
For sinners dy'd.

D   The DELUGE drown'd
The Earth around.

E   ELIJAH hid
By Ravens fed.

F   The judgment made
FELIX afraid.

G   As runs the GLASS,
Our Life doth pass.

H   My Book and HEART
Must never part.

J   JOB feels the Rod,
Yet blesses God.

K   Proud KORAH'S troop
Was swallowed up.

L   LOT fled to *Zoar*
Saw fiery Shower
On *Sodom* pour.

M   MOSES was he
Who *Israel's* Host
Led thro' the Sea.

N   NOAH did view
The old world & new.

O   Young OBADIAS,
David, Josias
All were pious.

P   PETER deny'd
His Lord and cry'd.

Q   QUEEN Esther sues
And saves the Jews.

R   Young pious RUTH,
Left all for Truth.

S   Young SAM'L dear
The Lord did fear.

T   Young TIMOTHY
Learnt sin to flee.

V   VASHTI for Pride,
Was set aside.

W   WHALES in the Sea.
God's Voice obey.

X   XERXES did die
And so must I.

Y   While YOUTH do chear
Death may be near.

Z   ZACCHEUS he
Did climb the Tree
Our Lord to see.

himself crosses over before you, just as the LORD has said. [4]And the LORD will do to them as He did to Sihon and Og, the kings of the Amorites and their land, when He destroyed them. [5]The LORD will give them over to you, that you may do to them according to every commandment which I have commanded you. [6]Be strong and of good courage, do not fear nor be afraid of them; for the LORD your God, He *is* the One who goes with you. He will not leave you nor forsake you."

[7]Then Moses called Joshua and said to him in the sight of all Israel, "Be strong and of good courage, for you must go with this people to the land which the LORD has sworn to their fathers to give them, and you shall cause them to inherit it. [8]And the LORD, He *is* the One who goes before you. He will be with you, He will not leave you nor forsake you; do not fear nor be dismayed."

The Law to Be Read Every Seven Years

[9]So Moses wrote this law and delivered it to the priests, the sons of Levi, who bore the ark of the covenant of the LORD, and to all the elders of Israel. [10]And Moses commanded them, saying: "At the end of *every* seven years, at the appointed time in the year of release, at the Feast of Tabernacles, [11]when all Israel comes to appear before the LORD your God in the place which He chooses, you shall read this law before all Israel in their hearing. [12]Gather the people together, men and women and little ones, and the stranger who *is* within your gates, that they may hear and that they may learn to fear the LORD your God and carefully observe all the words of this law, [13]and *that* their children, who have not known it, may hear and learn to fear the LORD your God as long as you live in the land which you cross the Jordan to possess."

Prediction of Israel's Rebellion

[14]Then the LORD said to Moses, "Behold, the days approach when you must die; call Joshua, and present yourselves in the tabernacle of meeting, that I may inaugurate him."

So Moses and Joshua went and presented themselves in the tabernacle of meeting. [15]Now the LORD appeared at the tabernacle in a pillar of cloud, and the pillar of cloud stood above the door of the tabernacle.

[16]And the LORD said to Moses: "Behold, you will rest with your fathers; and this people will rise and play the harlot with the gods of the foreigners of the land, where they go *to be* among them, and they will forsake Me and break My covenant which I have made with them. [17]Then My anger shall be aroused against them in that day, and I will forsake them, and I will hide My face from them, and they shall be devoured. And many evils and troubles shall befall them, so that they will say in that day, 'Have not these evils come upon us because our God *is* not among us?' [18]And I will surely hide My face in that day because of all the evil which they have done, in that they have turned to other gods.

[19]"Now therefore, write down this song for yourselves, and teach it to the children of Israel; put it in their mouths, that this song may be a witness for Me against the children of Israel. [20]When I have brought them to the land flowing with milk and honey, of which I swore to their fathers, and they have eaten and filled themselves and grown fat, then they will turn to other gods and serve them; and they will provoke Me and break My covenant. [21]Then it shall be, when many evils and troubles have come upon them, that this song will testify against them as a witness; for it will not be forgotten in the mouths of their descendants, for I know the inclination of their behavior today, even before I have brought them to the land of which I swore *to give them*."

[22]Therefore Moses wrote this song the same day, and taught it to the children of Israel. [23]Then He inaugurated Joshua the son of Nun, and said, "Be strong and of good courage; for you shall bring the children of Israel into the land of which I swore to them, and I will be with you."

[24]So it was, when Moses had completed writing the words of this law in a book, when they were finished, [25]that Moses commanded the Levites, who bore the ark of the covenant of the LORD, saying: [26]"Take

this Book of the Law, and put it beside the ark of the covenant of the LORD your God, that it may be there as a witness against you; 27for I know your rebellion and your stiff neck. *If* today, while I am yet alive with you, you have been rebellious against the LORD, then how much more after my death? 28Gather to me all the elders of your tribes, and your officers, that I may speak these words in their hearing and call heaven and earth to witness against them. 29For I know that after my death you will become utterly corrupt, and turn aside from the way which I have commanded you. And evil will befall you in the latter days, because you will do evil in the sight of the LORD, to provoke Him to anger through the work of your hands."

The Song of Moses

30Then Moses spoke in the hearing of all the assembly of Israel the words of this song until they were ended:

32 "Give ear, O heavens, and I will speak;
And hear, O earth, the words of my mouth.
2 Let my teaching drop as the rain,
My speech distill as the dew,
As raindrops on the tender herb,
And as showers on the grass.
3 For I proclaim the name of the LORD:
Ascribe greatness to our God.
4 *He is* the Rock, His work *is* perfect;
For all His ways *are* justice,
A God of truth and without injustice;
Righteous and upright *is* He.

5 "They have corrupted themselves;
They are not His children,
Because of their blemish:
A perverse and crooked generation.
6 Do you thus deal with the LORD,
O foolish and unwise people?
Is He not your Father, *who* bought you?
Has He not made you and established you?

7 "Remember the days of old,
Consider the years of many generations.
Ask your father, and he will show you;
Your elders, and they will tell you:
8 When the Most High divided their inheritance to the nations,
When He separated the sons of Adam,
He set the boundaries of the peoples
According to the number of the children of Israel.
9 For the LORD's portion *is* His people;
Jacob *is* the place of His inheritance.

10 "He found him in a desert land
And in the wasteland, a howling wilderness;
He encircled him, He instructed him,
He kept him as the apple of His eye.
11 As an eagle stirs up its nest,
Hovers over its young,
Spreading out its wings, taking them up,
Carrying them on its wings,
12 *So* the LORD alone led him,
And *there was* no foreign god with him.

13 "He made him ride in the heights of the earth,
That he might eat the produce of the fields;
He made him draw honey from the rock,
And oil from the flinty rock;
14 Curds from the cattle, and milk of the flock,
With fat of lambs;
And rams of the breed of Bashan, and goats,
With the choicest wheat;
And you drank wine, the blood of the grapes.

15 "But Jeshurun grew fat and kicked;
You grew fat, you grew thick,
You are obese!
Then he forsook God *who* made him,
And scornfully esteemed the Rock of his salvation.
16 They provoked Him to jealousy with foreign *gods;*
With abominations they provoked Him to anger.
17 They sacrificed to demons, not to God,

To gods they did not know,
To new *gods,* new arrivals
That your fathers did not fear.
18 Of the Rock *who* begot you, you are
   unmindful,
   And have forgotten the God who
   fathered you.

19 "And when the LORD saw *it,* He spurned
   them,
   Because of the provocation of His sons
   and His daughters.
20 And He said: 'I will hide My face from
   them,
   I will see what their end *will be,*
   For they *are* a perverse generation,
   Children in whom *is* no faith.
21 They have provoked Me to jealousy by
   what is not God;
   They have moved Me to anger by
   their foolish idols.
   But I will provoke them to jealousy by
   those who are not a nation;
   I will move them to anger by a foolish
   nation.
22 For a fire is kindled in My anger,
   And shall burn to the lowest hell;
   It shall consume the earth with her
   increase,
   And set on fire the foundations of the
   mountains.

23 'I will heap disasters on them;
   I will spend My arrows on them.
24 *They shall be* wasted with hunger,
   Devoured by pestilence and bitter
   destruction;
   I will also send against them the teeth
   of beasts,
   With the poison of serpents of the
   dust.
25 The sword shall destroy outside;
   There shall be terror within
   For the young man and virgin,
   The nursing child with the man of
   gray hairs.
26 I would have said, "I will dash them
   in pieces,
   I will make the memory of them to
   cease from among men,"
27 Had I not feared the wrath of the
   enemy,

Lest their adversaries should
   misunderstand,
Lest they should say, "Our hand *is*
   high;
And it is not the LORD who has done
   all this." '

28 "For they *are* a nation void of counsel,
   Nor *is there any* understanding in
   them.
29 Oh, that they were wise, *that* they
   understood this,
   That they would consider their latter
   end!
30 How could one chase a thousand,
   And two put ten thousand to flight,
   Unless their Rock had sold them,
   And the LORD had surrendered them?
31 For their rock *is* not like our Rock,
   Even our enemies themselves *being*
   judges.
32 For their vine *is* of the vine of Sodom
   And of the fields of Gomorrah;
   Their grapes *are* grapes of gall,
   Their clusters *are* bitter.
33 Their wine *is* the poison of serpents,
   And the cruel venom of cobras.

34 '*Is* this not laid up in store with Me,
   Sealed up among My treasures?
35 Vengeance is Mine, and recompense;
   Their foot shall slip in *due* time;
   For the day of their calamity *is* at hand,
   And the things to come hasten upon
   them.'

36 "For the LORD will judge His people
   And have compassion on His servants,
   When He sees that *their* power is gone,
   And *there is* no one *remaining,* bond or
   free.
37 He will say: 'Where *are* their gods,
   The rock in which they sought refuge?
38 Who ate the fat of their sacrifices,
   And drank the wine of their drink
   offering?
   Let them rise and help you,
   And be your refuge.

39 'Now see that I, *even* I, *am* He,
   And *there is* no God besides Me;
   I kill and I make alive;

I wound and I heal;
Nor *is there any* who can deliver from
    My hand.
40 For I raise My hand to heaven,
    And say, "*As* I live forever,
41 If I whet My glittering sword,
    And My hand takes hold on
        judgment,
    I will render vengeance to My
        enemies,
    And repay those who hate Me.
42 I will make My arrows drunk with
        blood,
    And My sword shall devour flesh,
    With the blood of the slain and the
        captives,
    From the heads of the leaders of the
        enemy." '

43 "Rejoice, O Gentiles, *with* His people;ᵃ
    For He will avenge the blood of His
        servants,
    And render vengeance to His
        adversaries;
    He will provide atonement for His
        land *and* His people."

⁴⁴So Moses came with Joshuaᵃ the son of
Nun and spoke all the words of this song in
the hearing of the people. ⁴⁵Moses finished
speaking all these words to all Israel, ⁴⁶and
he said to them: "Set your hearts on all the
words which I testify among you today,
which you shall command your children
to be careful to observe—all the words of
this law. ⁴⁷For it *is* not a futile thing for you,
because it *is* your life, and by this word you
shall prolong *your* days in the land which
you cross over the Jordan to possess."

Moses to Die on Mount Nebo

⁴⁸Then the LORD spoke to Moses that very
same day, saying: ⁴⁹"Go up this mountain
of the Abarim, Mount Nebo, which *is* in
the land of Moab, across from Jericho; view
the land of Canaan, which I give to the
children of Israel as a possession; ⁵⁰and die
on the mountain which you ascend, and
be gathered to your people, just as Aaron
your brother died on Mount Hor and was
gathered to his people; ⁵¹because you trespassed against Me among the children of

Israel at the waters of Meribah Kadesh, in
the Wilderness of Zin, because you did not
hallow Me in the midst of the children of
Israel. ⁵²Yet you shall see the land before *you,*
though you shall not go there, into the land
which I am giving to the children of Israel."

Moses' Final Blessing on Israel

33 Now this *is* the blessing with which
Moses the man of God blessed the
children of Israel before his death. ²And he
said:

    "The LORD came from Sinai,
        And dawned on them from Seir;
    He shone forth from Mount Paran,
        And He came with ten thousands of
            saints;
    From His right hand
    Came a fiery law for them.
3   Yes, He loves the people;
    All His saints *are* in Your hand;
    They sit down at Your feet;
    Everyone receives Your words.
4   Moses commanded a law for us,
    A heritage of the congregation of
        Jacob.
5   And He was King in Jeshurun,
    When the leaders of the people were
        gathered,
    All the tribes of Israel together.

6   "Let Reuben live, and not die,
    Nor let his men be few."

⁷And this he said of Judah:

    "Hear, LORD, the voice of Judah,
    And bring him to his people;
    Let his hands be sufficient for him,
    And may You be a help against his
        enemies."

⁸And of Levi he said:

    "*Let* Your Thummim and Your Urim *be*
        with Your holy one,

32:43 ᵃA Dead Sea Scroll fragment adds *And let all the
gods (angels) worship Him* (compare Septuagint and
Hebrews 1:6).   **32:44** ᵃHebrew *Hoshea* (compare
Numbers 13:8, 16)

Whom You tested at Massah,
And with whom You contended at the
    waters of Meribah,
9 Who says of his father and mother,
    'I have not seen them';
    Nor did he acknowledge his brothers,
    Or know his own children;
    For they have observed Your word
    And kept Your covenant.
10 They shall teach Jacob Your
    judgments,
    And Israel Your law.
    They shall put incense before You,
    And a whole burnt sacrifice on Your
    altar.
11 Bless his substance, LORD,
    And accept the work of his hands;
    Strike the loins of those who rise
    against him,
    And of those who hate him, that they
    rise not again."

12Of Benjamin he said:

"The beloved of the LORD shall dwell in
    safety by Him,
Who shelters him all the day long;
And he shall dwell between His
    shoulders."

13And of Joseph he said:

"Blessed of the LORD *is* his land,
With the precious things of heaven,
    with the dew,
And the deep lying beneath,
14 With the precious fruits of the sun,
    With the precious produce of the
    months,
15 With the best things of the ancient
    mountains,
    With the precious things of the
    everlasting hills,
16 With the precious things of the earth
    and its fullness,
    And the favor of Him who dwelt in
    the bush.
    Let *the blessing* come 'on the head of
    Joseph,
    And on the crown of the head of him
    who was separate from his
    brothers.'[a]

17 His glory *is like* a firstborn bull,
    And his horns *like* the horns of the
    wild ox;
    Together with them
    He shall push the peoples
    To the ends of the earth;
    They *are* the ten thousands of
    Ephraim,
    And they *are* the thousands of
    Manasseh."

18And of Zebulun he said:

"Rejoice, Zebulun, in your going out,
And Issachar in your tents!
19 They shall call the peoples *to* the
    mountain;
    There they shall offer sacrifices of
    righteousness;
    For they shall partake *of* the
    abundance of the seas
    And *of* treasures hidden in the sand."

20And of Gad he said:

"Blessed *is* he who enlarges Gad;
He dwells as a lion,
And tears the arm and the crown of
    his head.
21 He provided the first *part* for himself,
    Because a lawgiver's portion was
    reserved there.
    He came *with* the heads of the people;
    He administered the justice of the
    LORD,
    And His judgments with Israel."

22And of Dan he said:

"Dan *is* a lion's whelp;
He shall leap from Bashan."

23And of Naphtali he said:

"O Naphtali, satisfied with favor,
And full of the blessing of the LORD,
Possess the west and the south."

24And of Asher he said:

33:16 [a]Genesis 49:26

"Asher *is* most blessed of sons;
Let him be favored by his brothers,
And let him dip his foot in oil.
25 Your sandals *shall be* iron and bronze;
As your days, *so shall* your strength *be.*

26 "*There is* no one like the God of
Jeshurun,
Who rides the heavens to help you,
And in His excellency on the clouds.
27 The eternal God *is your* refuge,
And underneath *are* the everlasting
arms;
He will thrust out the enemy from
before you,
And will say, 'Destroy!'
28 Then Israel shall dwell in safety,
The fountain of Jacob alone,
In a land of grain and new wine;
His heavens shall also drop dew.
29 Happy *are* you, O Israel!
Who *is* like you, a people saved by the
Lord,
The shield of your help
And the sword of your majesty!
Your enemies shall submit to you,
And you shall tread down their high
places."

Moses Dies on Mount Nebo

34 Then Moses went up from the plains of Moab to Mount Nebo, to the top of Pisgah, which is across from Jericho. And the Lord showed him all the land of Gilead as far as Dan, 2all Naphtali and the land of Ephraim and Manasseh, all the land of Judah as far as the Western Sea,ᵃ 3the South, and the plain of the Valley of Jericho, the city of palm trees, as far as Zoar. 4Then the Lord said to him, "This *is* the land of which I swore to give Abraham, Isaac, and Jacob, saying, 'I will give it to your descendants.' I have caused you to see *it* with your eyes, but you shall not cross over there."

5So Moses the servant of the Lord died there in the land of Moab, according to the word of the Lord. 6And He buried him in a valley in the land of Moab, opposite Beth Peor; but no one knows his grave to this day. 7Moses *was* one hundred and twenty years old when he died. His eyes were not dim nor his natural vigor diminished. 8And the children of Israel wept for Moses in the plains of Moab thirty days. So the days of weeping *and* mourning for Moses ended.

9Now Joshua the son of Nun was full of the spirit of wisdom, for Moses had laid his hands on him; so the children of Israel heeded him, and did as the Lord had commanded Moses.

10But since then there has not arisen in Israel a prophet like Moses, whom the Lord knew face to face, 11in all the signs and wonders which the Lord sent him to do in the land of Egypt, before Pharaoh, before all his servants, and in all his land, 12and by all that mighty power and all the great terror which Moses performed in the sight of all Israel.

34:2 ᵃThat is, the Mediterranean

JOSHUA

Author: Uncertain

When Written: 1400–1375 B.C.

Theme: Conquest

Key Verse: Joshua 1:8—"This Book of the Law shall not depart from your mouth, but you shall meditate in it day and night, that you may observe to do according to all that is written in it. For then you will make your way prosperous, and then you will have good success."

Key Chapter: Joshua 24—Before his death and in preparation for a major transition of leadership, Joshua reviews God's fulfillment of His promises and challenges the people to renew their commitment to the covenant, which is the foundation for their success both personally and as a nation.

Horace Greeley, one of America's leading nineteenth-century newspaper editors, reminded his fellow citizens what many of the Founding Fathers of the previous generation had emphasized, that "liberty cannot be established without morality, nor morality without faith." Indeed, as the children of Israel began their conquest of Canaan, their leader Joshua reminded them that their success depended upon God's Word being in their hearts and minds and upon their lips.

From individual, to family, to nation, each of us must, as Joshua challenges his fellow Israelites (24:15), make the choice to serve the Lord. Such a choice is foundational to the moral and spiritual resolve that will give us success in all we set out to accomplish.

JOSHUA

God's Commission to Joshua

1 After the death of Moses the servant of the LORD, it came to pass that the LORD spoke to Joshua the son of Nun, Moses' assistant, saying: [2]"Moses My servant is dead. Now therefore, arise, go over this Jordan, you and all this people, to the land which I am giving to them—the children of Israel. [3]Every place that the sole of your foot will tread upon I have given you, as I said to Moses. [4]From the wilderness and this Lebanon as far as the great river, the River Euphrates, all the land of the Hittites, and to the Great Sea toward the going down of the sun, shall be your territory. [5]No man shall *be able to* stand before you all the days of your life; as I was with Moses, *so* I will be with you. I will not leave you nor forsake you. [6]Be strong and of good courage, for to this people you shall divide as an inheritance the land which I swore to their fathers to give them. [7]Only be strong and very courageous, that you may observe to do according to all the law which Moses My servant commanded you; do not turn from it to the right hand or to the left, that you may prosper wherever you go. [8]This Book of the Law shall not depart from your mouth, but you shall meditate in it day and night, that you may observe to do according to all that is written in it. For then you will make your way prosperous, and then you will have good success. [9]Have I not commanded you? Be strong and of good courage; do not be afraid, nor be dismayed, for the LORD your God *is* with you wherever you go."

The Order to Cross the Jordan

[10]Then Joshua commanded the officers of the people, saying, [11]"Pass through the camp and command the people, saying, 'Prepare provisions for yourselves, for within three days you will cross over this Jordan, to go in to possess the land which the LORD your God is giving you to possess.' "

[12]And to the Reubenites, the Gadites, and half the tribe of Manasseh Joshua spoke, saying, [13]"Remember the word which Moses the servant of the LORD commanded you, saying, 'The LORD your God is giving you rest and is giving you this land.' [14]Your wives, your little ones, and your livestock shall remain in the land which Moses gave you on this side of the Jordan. But you shall pass before your brethren armed, all your mighty men of valor, and help them, [15]until the LORD has given your brethren rest, as He *gave* you, and they also have taken possession of the land which the LORD your God is giving them. Then you shall return to the land of your possession and enjoy it, which Moses the LORD's servant gave you on this side of the Jordan toward the sunrise."

[16]So they answered Joshua, saying, "All that you command us we will do, and wherever you send us we will go. [17]Just as we heeded Moses in all things, so we will heed you. Only the LORD your God be with you, as He was with Moses. [18]Whoever rebels against your command and does not heed your words, in all that you command him, shall be put to death. Only be strong and of good courage."

Rahab Hides the Spies

2 Now Joshua the son of Nun sent out two men from Acacia Grove[a] to spy secretly, saying, "Go, view the land, especially Jericho."

So they went, and came to the house of a harlot named Rahab, and lodged there. [2]And it was told the king of Jericho, saying, "Behold, men have come here tonight from the children of Israel to search out the country."

[3]So the king of Jericho sent to Rahab, saying, "Bring out the men who have come to you, who have entered your house, for

---

2:1 [a]Hebrew *Shittim*

they have come to search out all the country."

4Then the woman took the two men and hid them. So she said, "Yes, the men came to me, but I did not know where they *were* from. 5And it happened as the gate was being shut, when it was dark, that the men went out. Where the men went I do not know; pursue them quickly, for you may overtake them." 6(But she had brought them up to the roof and hidden them with the stalks of flax, which she had laid in order on the roof.) 7Then the men pursued them by the road to the Jordan, to the fords. And as soon as those who pursued them had gone out, they shut the gate.

8Now before they lay down, she came up to them on the roof, 9and said to the men:

"I know that the LORD has given you the land, that the terror of you has fallen on us, and that all the inhabitants of the land are fainthearted because of you. 10For we have heard how the LORD dried up the water of the Red Sea for you when you came out of Egypt, and what you did to the two kings of the Amorites who *were* on the other side of the Jordan, Sihon and Og, whom you utterly destroyed. 11And as soon as we heard *these things,* our hearts melted; neither did there remain any more courage in anyone because of you, for the LORD your God, He *is* God in heaven above and on earth beneath. 12Now therefore, I beg you, swear to me by the LORD, since I have shown you kindness, that you also will show kindness to my father's house, and give me a true

PROTECTOR

"Be strong and of good courage; do not be afraid. . . ."

JOSHUA 1:9

Arlington National Cemetary

SHIELD OF STRENGTH

Captain Russell Rippetoe was a member of the Alpha Company, Third Battalion, 75th Ranger Regiment, serving in Operation Iraqi Freedom in March 2003. Previously, while serving in Afghanistan, Rippetoe saw men die for the first time; and it brought a renewal to his Christian faith and a new passion for the Bible, which he carried in his backpack. On the chain around his neck, he wore a "Shield of Strength," a one-by-two-inch emblem that displays a U.S. flag on one side and the words from Joshua 1:9 on the other. In his combat diary dated March 27, Rippetoe had written: "Think about what Mom and I talked about: all things happening for a reason, and God knows the reason."

On April 3, 2003, Alpha Company was manning a nighttime checkpoint near the Hadithah Dam in western Iraq when a vehicle approached. Suddenly, a woman jumped out and cried, "I'm hungry. I need food and water!" Protecting his men, Rippetoe gave the order to "hold back" as he moved toward the woman to see how he could help. When she hesitated, the driver detonated a car bomb that killed Captain Rippetoe, Sergeant Nino Livaudais, and Specialist Ryan Long, and wounded others.

Rippetoe believed the ancient words given to Joshua: ". . . the Lord your God is with you wherever you go." That he died trying to help someone else came as no surprise to those who knew him. He became the first casualty of the Iraq conflict to be buried at Arlington National Cemetery, the hallowed ground that is memorial to more than 250,000 American soldiers spanning back to the Revolutionary War.

token, 13and spare my father, my mother, my brothers, my sisters, and all that they have, and deliver our lives from death."

14So the men answered her, "Our lives for yours, if none of you tell this business of ours. And it shall be, when the Lord has given us the land, that we will deal kindly and truly with you."

15Then she let them down by a rope through the window, for her house *was* on the city wall; she dwelt on the wall. 16And she said to them, "Get to the mountain, lest the pursuers meet you. Hide there three days, until the pursuers have returned. Afterward you may go your way."

17So the men said to her: "We *will be* blameless of this oath of yours which you have made us swear, 18unless, *when* we come into the land, you bind this line of scarlet cord in the window through which you let us down, and unless you bring your father, your mother, your brothers, and all your father's household to your own home. 19So it shall be *that* whoever goes outside the doors of your house into the street, his blood *shall be* on his own head, and we *will be* guiltless. And whoever is with you in the house, his blood *shall be* on our head if a hand is laid on him. 20And if you tell this business of ours, then we will be free from your oath which you made us swear."

21Then she said, "According to your words, so *be* it." And she sent them away, and they departed. And she bound the scarlet cord in the window.

22They departed and went to the mountain, and stayed there three days until the pursuers returned. The pursuers sought *them* all along the way, but did not find *them.* 23So the two men returned, descended from the mountain, and crossed over; and they came to Joshua the son of Nun, and told him all that had befallen them. 24And they said to Joshua, "Truly the Lord has delivered all the land into our hands, for indeed all the inhabitants of the country are fainthearted because of us."

Israel Crosses the Jordan

3 Then Joshua rose early in the morning; and they set out from Acacia Grove[a] and came to the Jordan, he and all the children of Israel, and lodged there before they crossed over. 2So it was, after three days, that the officers went through the camp; 3and they commanded the people, saying, "When you see the ark of the covenant of the Lord your God, and the priests, the Levites, bearing it, then you shall set out from your place and go after it. 4Yet there shall be a space between you and it, about two thousand cubits by measure. Do not come near it, that you may know the way by which you must go, for you have not passed *this* way before."

5And Joshua said to the people, "Sanctify yourselves, for tomorrow the Lord will do wonders among you." 6Then Joshua spoke to the priests, saying, "Take up the ark of the covenant and cross over before the people."

So they took up the ark of the covenant and went before the people.

7And the Lord said to Joshua, "This day I will begin to exalt you in the sight of all Israel, that they may know that, as I was with Moses, *so* I will be with you. 8You shall command the priests who bear the ark of the covenant, saying, 'When you have come to the edge of the water of the Jordan, you shall stand in the Jordan.'"

9So Joshua said to the children of Israel, "Come here, and hear the words of the Lord your God." 10And Joshua said, "By this you shall know that the living God *is* among you, and *that* He will without fail drive out from before you the Canaanites and the Hittites and the Hivites and the Perizzites and the Girgashites and the Amorites and the Jebusites: 11Behold, the ark of the covenant of the Lord of all the earth is crossing over before you into the Jordan. 12Now therefore, take for yourselves twelve men from the tribes of Israel, one man from every tribe. 13And it shall come to pass, as soon as the soles of the feet of the priests who bear the ark of the Lord, the Lord of all the earth, shall rest in the waters of the Jordan, *that* the waters of the Jordan shall be cut off, the waters that come down from upstream, and they shall stand as a heap."

14So it was, when the people set out from their camp to cross over the Jordan, with

3:1 aHebrew *Shittim*

the priests bearing the ark of the covenant before the people, [15]and as those who bore the ark came to the Jordan, and the feet of the priests who bore the ark dipped in the edge of the water (for the Jordan overflows all its banks during the whole time of harvest), [16]that the waters which came down from upstream stood *still, and* rose in a heap very far away at Adam, the city that *is* beside Zaretan. So the waters that went down into the Sea of the Arabah, the Salt Sea, failed, *and* were cut off; and the people crossed over opposite Jericho. [17]Then the priests who bore the ark of the covenant of the Lord stood firm on dry ground in the midst of the Jordan; and all Israel crossed over on dry ground, until all the people had crossed completely over the Jordan.

The Memorial Stones

4 And it came to pass, when all the people had completely crossed over the Jordan, that the Lord spoke to Joshua, saying: [2]"Take for yourselves twelve men from the people, one man from every tribe, [3]and command them, saying, 'Take for yourselves twelve stones from here, out of the midst of the Jordan, from the place where the priests' feet stood firm. You shall carry them over with you and leave them in the lodging place where you lodge tonight.'"

[4]Then Joshua called the twelve men whom he had appointed from the children of Israel, one man from every tribe; [5]and Joshua said to them: "Cross over before the ark of the Lord your God into the midst of the Jordan, and each one of you take up a stone on his shoulder, according to the number of the tribes of the children of Israel, [6]that this may be a sign among you when your children ask in time to come, saying, 'What do these stones *mean* to you?' [7]Then you shall answer them that the waters of the Jordan were cut off before the ark of the covenant of the Lord; when it crossed over the Jordan, the waters of the Jordan were cut off. And these stones shall be for a memorial to the children of Israel forever."

[8]And the children of Israel did so, just as Joshua commanded, and took up twelve stones from the midst of the Jordan, as the Lord had spoken to Joshua, according to the number of the tribes of the children of Israel, and carried them over with them to the place where they lodged, and laid them down there. [9]Then Joshua set up twelve stones in the midst of the Jordan, in the place where the feet of the priests who bore the ark of the covenant stood; and they are there to this day.

[10]So the priests who bore the ark stood in the midst of the Jordan until everything was finished that the Lord had commanded Joshua to speak to the people, according to all that Moses had commanded Joshua; and the people hurried and crossed over. [11]Then it came to pass, when all the people had completely crossed over, that the ark of the Lord and the priests crossed over in the presence of the people. [12]And the men of Reuben, the men of Gad, and half the tribe of Manasseh crossed over armed before the children of Israel, as Moses had spoken to them. [13]About forty thousand prepared for war crossed over before the Lord for battle, to the plains of Jericho. [14]On that day the Lord exalted Joshua in the sight of all Israel; and they feared him, as they had feared Moses, all the days of his life.

[15]Then the Lord spoke to Joshua, saying, [16]"Command the priests who bear the ark of the Testimony to come up from the Jordan." [17]Joshua therefore commanded the priests, saying, "Come up from the Jordan." [18]And it came to pass, when the priests who bore the ark of the covenant of the Lord had come from the midst of the Jordan, *and* the soles of the priests' feet touched the dry land, that the waters of the Jordan returned to their place and overflowed all its banks as before.

[19]Now the people came up from the Jordan on the tenth *day* of the first month, and they camped in Gilgal on the east border of Jericho. [20]And those twelve stones which they took out of the Jordan, Joshua set up in Gilgal. [21]Then he spoke to the children of Israel, saying: "When your children ask their fathers in time to come, saying, 'What *are* these stones?' [22]then you shall let your children know, saying, 'Israel crossed over this Jordan on dry land'; [23]for the Lord your God dried up the waters of the Jordan before you until you had

crossed over, as the LORD your God did to the Red Sea, which He dried up before us until we had crossed over, ²⁴that all the peoples of the earth may know the hand of the LORD, that it *is* mighty, that you may fear the LORD your God forever."

The Second Generation Circumcised

5 So it was, when all the kings of the Amorites who *were* on the west side of the Jordan, and all the kings of the Canaanites who *were* by the sea, heard that the LORD had dried up the waters of the Jordan from before the children of Israel until we^a had crossed over, that their heart melted; and there was no spirit in them any longer because of the children of Israel.

²At that time the LORD said to Joshua, "Make flint knives for yourself, and circumcise the sons of Israel again the second time." ³So Joshua made flint knives for himself, and circumcised the sons of Israel at the hill of the foreskins.^a ⁴And this *is* the reason why Joshua circumcised them: All the people who came out of Egypt *who were* males, all the men of war, had died in the wilderness on the way, after they had come out of Egypt. ⁵For all the people who came out had been circumcised, but all the people born in the wilderness, on the way as they came out of Egypt, had not been circumcised. ⁶For the children of Israel walked forty years in the wilderness, till all the people *who were* men of war, who came out of Egypt, were consumed, because they did not obey the voice of the LORD—to whom the LORD swore that He would not show them the land which the LORD had sworn to their fathers that He would give us, "a land flowing with milk and honey."^a ⁷Then Joshua circumcised their sons *whom* He raised up in their place; for they were uncircumcised, because they had not been circumcised on the way.

⁸So it was, when they had finished circumcising all the people, that they stayed in their places in the camp till they were healed. ⁹Then the LORD said to Joshua, "This day I have rolled away the reproach of Egypt from you." Therefore the name of the place is called Gilgal^a to this day.

¹⁰Now the children of Israel camped in Gilgal, and kept the Passover on the fourteenth day of the month at twilight on the plains of Jericho. ¹¹And they ate of the produce of the land on the day after the Passover, unleavened bread and parched grain, on the very same day. ¹²Then the manna ceased on the day after they had eaten the produce of the land; and the children of Israel no longer had manna, but they ate the food of the land of Canaan that year.

The Commander of the Army of the LORD

¹³And it came to pass, when Joshua was by Jericho, that he lifted his eyes and looked, and behold, a Man stood opposite him with His sword drawn in His hand. And Joshua went to Him and said to Him, "*Are* You for us or for our adversaries?"

¹⁴So He said, "No, but *as* Commander of the army of the LORD I have now come."

And Joshua fell on his face to the earth and worshiped, and said to Him, "What does my Lord say to His servant?"

¹⁵Then the Commander of the LORD's army said to Joshua, "Take your sandal off your foot, for the place where you stand *is* holy." And Joshua did so.

The Destruction of Jericho

6 Now Jericho was securely shut up because of the children of Israel; none went out, and none came in. ²And the LORD said to Joshua: "See! I have given Jericho into your hand, its king, *and* the mighty men of valor. ³You shall march around the city, all *you* men of war; you shall go all around the city once. This you shall do six days. ⁴And seven priests shall bear seven trumpets of rams' horns before the ark. But the seventh day you shall march around the city seven times, and the priests shall blow the trumpets. ⁵It shall come to pass, when they make a long *blast* with the ram's horn, *and* when you hear the sound of the trumpet, that all the people shall shout

---

5:1 ^aFollowing Kethib; Qere, some Hebrew manuscripts and editions, Septuagint, Syriac, Targum, and Vulgate read *they.*   **5:3** ^aHebrew *Gibeath Haaraloth*   **5:6** ^aExodus 3:8   **5:9** ^aLiterally *Rolling*

WOMEN in the CIVIL WAR

COURAGE

*. . . she hid the messengers
whom Joshua sent
to spy out Jericho. . . .*

JOSHUA 6:25

During the Civil War, hundreds of women served as frontline nurses, spies, saboteurs, and in the infantry, cavalry, and artillery for both the Union and Confederate armies. From all walks of life and for numerous reasons, many took on male disguises and often remained undiscovered until they were either wounded or killed, enduring hardships and dangers and serving with distinction.

Sarah Rosetta Wakeman, called Rosetta, was a poor farm girl who cut her hair and joined the 153rd Regiment of New York State Volunteers. Enlisting under the name "Lyons Wakeman" on August 30, 1862, she sent most of her army pay home to keep the family farm going. Her regiment first performed guard duty in Alexandria, Virginia, and then they marched 700 miles to join General Banks' Red River campaign in Louisiana in February 1864. The Unionists repelled a Confederate attack, but soon had to retreat.

Near the end of the campaign, Rosetta was stricken with dysentery and died in the Marine Hospital of New Orleans on June 19, 1864. Her identity remained undiscovered for more than a century until her letters home surfaced. She had left behind a ring, which was engraved with her regiment and name on it. She is buried in Louisiana in a grave marked by a headstone that reads simply: "4006 Lyons Wakeman, N.Y."

In her letters home, Rosetta wrote of the battlefield and the pride she felt at being a good soldier, but she also expressed her strong religious faith as well as her strong desire to be financially independent and buy a farm of her own after the war. In one letter she wrote: "I don't feel afraid to go [into battle]. I don't believe there are any Rebel bullets made for me yet. . . . But if it is God's will for me to fall in the field of battle, it is my will to go and never return home."

Rose Rooney joined the Confederate Army, openly signing on as a female enlistee to serve as cook and laundress for the Crescent Blues Volunteers at New Orleans in 1861. Her unit eventually became Company K of the 15th Louisiana Infantry and went to Virginia. At the First Battle of Bull Run, she is reported to have run through a field of heavy fire to tear down a rail fence, allowing a battery of Confederate artillery to stop a Union charge. She served through the end of the war.

with a great shout; then the wall of the city will fall down flat. And the people shall go up every man straight before him."

6Then Joshua the son of Nun called the priests and said to them, "Take up the ark of the covenant, and let seven priests bear seven trumpets of rams' horns before the ark of the Lord." 7And he said to the people, "Proceed, and march around the city, and let him who is armed advance before the ark of the Lord."

8So it was, when Joshua had spoken to the people, that the seven priests bearing the seven trumpets of rams' horns before the Lord advanced and blew the trumpets, and the ark of the covenant of the Lord followed them. 9The armed men went before the priests who blew the trumpets, and the rear guard came after the ark, while *the priests* continued blowing the trumpets. 10Now Joshua had commanded the people, saying, "You shall not shout or make any noise with your voice, nor shall a word proceed out of your mouth, until the day I say to you, 'Shout!' Then you shall shout." 11So he had the ark of the Lord circle the city, going around *it* once. Then they came into the camp and lodged in the camp.

12And Joshua rose early in the morning, and the priests took up the ark of the Lord. 13Then seven priests bearing seven trumpets of rams' horns before the ark of the Lord went on continually and blew with the trumpets. And the armed men went before them. But the rear guard came after the ark of the Lord, while *the priests* continued blowing the trumpets. 14And the second day they marched around the city once and returned to the camp. So they did six days.

15But it came to pass on the seventh day that they rose early, about the dawning of the day, and marched around the city seven times in the same manner. On that day only they marched around the city seven times. 16And the seventh time it happened, when the priests blew the trumpets, that Joshua said to the people: "Shout, for the Lord has given you the city! 17Now the city shall be doomed by the Lord to destruction, it and all who *are* in it. Only Rahab the harlot shall live, she and all who *are* with her in the house, because she hid the

messengers that we sent. 18And you, by all means abstain from the accursed things, lest you become accursed when you take of the accursed things, and make the camp of Israel a curse, and trouble it. 19But all the silver and gold, and vessels of bronze and iron, *are* consecrated to the Lord; they shall come into the treasury of the Lord."

20So the people shouted when *the priests* blew the trumpets. And it happened when the people heard the sound of the trumpet, and the people shouted with a great shout, that the wall fell down flat. Then the people went up into the city, every man straight before him, and they took the city. 21And they utterly destroyed all that *was* in the city, both man and woman, young and old, ox and sheep and donkey, with the edge of the sword.

22But Joshua had said to the two men who had spied out the country, "Go into the harlot's house, and from there bring out the woman and all that she has, as you swore to her." 23And the young men who had been spies went in and brought out Rahab, her father, her mother, her brothers, and all that she had. So they brought out all her relatives and left them outside the camp of Israel. 24But they burned the city and all that *was* in it with fire. Only the silver and gold, and the vessels of bronze and iron, they put into the treasury of the house of the Lord. 25And Joshua spared Rahab the harlot, her father's household, and all that she had. So she dwells in Israel to this day, because she hid the messengers whom Joshua sent to spy out Jericho.

26Then Joshua charged *them* at that time, saying, "Cursed *be* the man before the Lord who rises up and builds this city Jericho; he shall lay its foundation with his firstborn, and with his youngest he shall set up its gates."

27So the Lord was with Joshua, and his fame spread throughout all the country.

Defeat at Ai

7 But the children of Israel committed a trespass regarding the accursed things, for Achan the son of Carmi, the son of

Zabdi,ª the son of Zerah, of the tribe of Judah, took of the accursed things; so the anger of the LORD burned against the children of Israel.

²Now Joshua sent men from Jericho to Ai, which *is* beside Beth Aven, on the east side of Bethel, and spoke to them, saying, "Go up and spy out the country." So the men went up and spied out Ai. ³And they returned to Joshua and said to him, "Do not let all the people go up, but let about two or three thousand men go up and attack Ai. Do not weary all the people there, for *the people of Ai are* few." ⁴So about three thousand men went up there from the people, but they fled before the men of Ai. ⁵And the men of Ai struck down about thirty-six men, for they chased them *from* before the gate as far as Shebarim, and struck them down on the descent; therefore the hearts of the people melted and became like water.

⁶Then Joshua tore his clothes, and fell to the earth on his face before the ark of the LORD until evening, he and the elders of Israel; and they put dust on their heads. ⁷And Joshua said, "Alas, Lord GOD, why have You brought this people over the Jordan at all—to deliver us into the hand of the Amorites, to destroy us? Oh, that we had been content, and dwelt on the other side of the Jordan! ⁸O Lord, what shall I say when Israel turns its back before its enemies? ⁹For the Canaanites and all the inhabitants of the land will hear *it,* and surround us, and cut off our name from the earth. Then what will You do for Your great name?"

The Sin of Achan

¹⁰So the LORD said to Joshua: "Get up! Why do you lie thus on your face? ¹¹Israel has sinned, and they have also transgressed My covenant which I commanded them. For they have even taken some of the accursed things, and have both stolen and deceived; and they have also put *it* among their own stuff. ¹²Therefore the children of Israel could not stand before their enemies, *but* turned *their* backs before their enemies, because they have become doomed to destruction. Neither will I be with you anymore, unless you destroy the accursed from among you. ¹³Get up, sanctify the people, and say,

'Sanctify yourselves for tomorrow, because thus says the LORD God of Israel: "*There is* an accursed thing in your midst, O Israel; you cannot stand before your enemies until you take away the accursed thing from among you." ¹⁴In the morning therefore you shall be brought according to your tribes. And it shall be *that* the tribe which the LORD takes shall come according to families; and the family which the LORD takes shall come by households; and the household which the LORD takes shall come man by man. ¹⁵Then it shall be *that* he who is taken with the accursed thing shall be burned with fire, he and all that he has, because he has transgressed the covenant of the LORD, and because he has done a disgraceful thing in Israel.' "

MORAL STRENGTH

"Therefore the children of Israel could not stand before their enemies. . . ."   JOSHUA 7:12

The Loss of Virtue

Samuel Adams, the great American patriot accused by King George III of being "the chief rabble-rouser" of American independence, wrote in a letter to James Warren in 1779:

> *A general dissolution of principles and manners will more surely overthrow the liberties of America than the whole force of the common enemy. While the people are virtuous they cannot be subdued; but when once they lose their virtue, they will be ready to surrender their liberties to the first external or internal invader. How necessary then is it for those who are determined to transmit the blessings of liberty as a fair inheritance to posterity, to associate on public principles in support of public virtue.*

---

¹⁶So Joshua rose early in the morning and brought Israel by their tribes, and the tribe of Judah was taken. ¹⁷He brought the clan of Judah, and he took the family of the Zarhites; and he brought the family of the Zarhites man by man, and Zabdi was taken. ¹⁸Then he brought his household man by man, and Achan the son of Carmi,

---

7:1 ªCalled *Zimri* in 1 Chronicles 2:6

CHRISTIANITY IN COLONIAL AMERICA

*B*EGINNING EARLY IN THE seventeenth century, settlers from Spain, France, Sweden, Holland, and England claimed land and formed colonies along the eastern coast of North America, and the struggle for control of this land continued for well over a hundred years. By the time the Declaration of Independence was signed in 1776, there were thirteen fully operational American colonies with independent governments and constitutions.

The first permanent settlement was the English colony at Jamestown, in 1607, in what is now Virginia. Similar to the other colonial charters, the First Charter of Virginia emphasized the Christian character of their purpose: "We, greatly commending, and graciously accepting of, their desires for the furtherance of so noble a work, which may, by the providence of Almighty God, hereafter tend to the glory of His Divine Majesty, in propagating of Christian religion to such people, as yet live in darkness and miserable ignorance of the true knowledge and worship of God."

IN 1620, THE PILGRIMS FOLLOWED and set up a colony at Plymouth, in what is now Massachusetts. The purpose of the Pilgrims was to establish a political commonwealth governed by biblical standards. The Mayflower Compact, their initial governing document, clearly stated that what they had undertaken was for "the glory of God and the advancement of the Christian faith." William Bradford, the second governor of Plymouth, said, "[The colonists] cherished a great hope and inward zeal of laying good foundations . . . for the propagations and advance of the Gospel of the kingdom of Christ in the remote parts of the world."

In June 1630, Governor John Winthrop landed in Massachusetts Bay with 700 people in 11 ships, thus beginning the Great Migration, which lasted sixteen years and saw more than 20,000 Puritans sail for New England. The Puritans so believed that this New World would be a place to escape the corruptions in their own church-state homeland, they called their Massachusetts Bay Colony a "Zion in wilderness" and "a city upon a hill."

Winthrop also organized the first American experiment in federation in 1643, the New England Confederation, stating that the aim of the colonists of New Plymouth, New Haven, Massachusetts, and Connecticut was "to advance the kingdom of our Lord Jesus Christ, and to enjoy the liberties of the gospel thereof in purities and peace."

IN 1638, A COLONY WAS ESTABLISHED in New Haven, in what is now Connecticut, by the Reverend John Davenport and Theophilus Eaton. A year later, the Fundamental Orders of Connecticut, often called the world's first written constitution, was adopted. It reads in part: "For as much as it hath pleased Almighty God by the wise disposition of His Divine Providence so to order and dispose of things that we the inhabitants and residents…; and well knowing where a people are gathered together the Word of God requires that to maintain the peace and union of such a people there should be an orderly and decent government established according to God, to order and dispose of the affairs of the people at all seasons as occasion shall require."

Other English colonies sprang up all along the Atlantic coast, from Maine in the north to Georgia in the south. Swedish and Dutch colonies took shape in and around what is now New York. As more and more people arrived in the New World, more and more disputes arose over territory. Many wars were fought in the 1600s and 1700s. Eventually, the two countries with the largest presence were England and France.

The two nations fought for control of North America in the French and Indian War (1754–1763). England won the war and took control of Canada, as well as keeping control of all the English colonies. By this time, the thirteen English colonies were Massachusetts, New Hampshire, Connecticut, Rhode Island, New York, New Jersey, Pennsylvania, Maryland, Delaware, Virginia, North Carolina, South Carolina, and Georgia.

WHEN THESE COLONIAL SETTLERS arrived in America, the influence of the Bible on their lives came with them. For many, their Christian faith was as much a part of who they were as their brave spirit, and it touched all they touched. This stands out boldly as one sees the goal of government based on Scripture being affirmed over and over by individual colonies, such as in the Rhode Island Charter of 1683, which begins: "We submit our person, lives, and estates unto our Lord Jesus Christ, the King of kings and Lord of lords, and to all those perfect and most absolute laws of His given us in His Holy Word."

From the first colony at Jamestown to the Pennsylvania Charter of Privileges granted to William Penn in 1701, where "all persons who . . . profess to believe in Jesus Christ, the Savior of the world, shall be capable . . . to serve this government in any capacity, both legislatively and executively," the Bible was used as the rule of life in the colonies. Every evidence indicates the profound effect God's Word had on the early Americans.

> *"We submit our person, lives, and estates unto our Lord Jesus Christ, the King of kings and Lord of lords, and to all those perfect and most absolute laws of His given us in His Holy Word."*
>
> RHODE ISLAND CHARTER OF 1683

the son of Zabdi, the son of Zerah, of the tribe of Judah, was taken.

¹⁹Now Joshua said to Achan, "My son, I beg you, give glory to the LORD God of Israel, and make confession to Him, and tell me now what you have done; do not hide *it* from me."

²⁰And Achan answered Joshua and said, "Indeed I have sinned against the LORD God of Israel, and this is what I have done: ²¹When I saw among the spoils a beautiful Babylonian garment, two hundred shekels of silver, and a wedge of gold weighing fifty shekels, I coveted them and took them. And there they are, hidden in the earth in the midst of my tent, with the silver under it."

²²So Joshua sent messengers, and they ran to the tent; and there it was, hidden in his tent, with the silver under it. ²³And they took them from the midst of the tent, brought them to Joshua and to all the children of Israel, and laid them out before the LORD. ²⁴Then Joshua, and all Israel with him, took Achan the son of Zerah, the silver, the garment, the wedge of gold, his sons, his daughters, his oxen, his donkeys, his sheep, his tent, and all that he had, and they brought them to the Valley of Achor. ²⁵And Joshua said, "Why have you troubled us? The LORD will trouble you this day." So all Israel stoned him with stones; and they burned them with fire after they had stoned them with stones.

²⁶Then they raised over him a great heap of stones, still there to this day. So the LORD turned from the fierceness of His anger. Therefore the name of that place has been called the Valley of Achor^a to this day.

The Fall of Ai

8 Now the LORD said to Joshua: "Do not be afraid, nor be dismayed; take all the people of war with you, and arise, go up to Ai. See, I have given into your hand the king of Ai, his people, his city, and his land. ²And you shall do to Ai and its king as you did to Jericho and its king. Only its spoil and its cattle you shall take as booty for yourselves. Lay an ambush for the city behind it."

³So Joshua arose, and all the people of war, to go up against Ai; and Joshua chose thirty thousand mighty men of valor and sent them away by night. ⁴And he commanded them, saying: "Behold, you shall lie in ambush against the city, behind the city. Do not go very far from the city, but all of you be ready. ⁵Then I and all the people who *are* with me will approach the city; and it will come about, when they come out against us as at the first, that we shall flee before them. ⁶For they will come out after us till we have drawn them from the city, for they will say, '*They are* fleeing before us as at the first.' Therefore we will flee before them. ⁷Then you shall rise from the ambush and seize the city, for the LORD your God will deliver it into your hand. ⁸And it will be, when you have taken the city, *that* you shall set the city on fire. According to the commandment of the LORD you shall do. See, I have commanded you."

⁹Joshua therefore sent them out; and they went to lie in ambush, and stayed between Bethel and Ai, on the west side of Ai; but Joshua lodged that night among the people. ¹⁰Then Joshua rose up early in the morning and mustered the people, and went up, he and the elders of Israel, before the people to Ai. ¹¹And all the people of war who *were* with him went up and drew near; and they came before the city and camped on the north side of Ai. Now a valley *lay* between them and Ai. ¹²So he took about five thousand men and set them in ambush between Bethel and Ai, on the west side of the city. ¹³And when they had set the people, all the army that *was* on the north of the city, and its rear guard on the west of the city, Joshua went that night into the midst of the valley.

¹⁴Now it happened, when the king of Ai saw *it,* that the men of the city hurried and rose early and went out against Israel to battle, he and all his people, at an appointed place before the plain. But he did not know that *there was* an ambush against him behind the city. ¹⁵And Joshua and all Israel made as if they were beaten before them, and fled by the way of the wilderness. ¹⁶So all the people who *were* in Ai were called together to pursue them. And they pursued Joshua and were drawn

7:26 ^aLiterally *Trouble*

away from the city. [17]There was not a man left in Ai or Bethel who did not go out after Israel. So they left the city open and pursued Israel.

[18]Then the LORD said to Joshua, "Stretch out the spear that *is* in your hand toward Ai, for I will give it into your hand." And Joshua stretched out the spear that *was* in his hand toward the city. [19]So *those in* ambush arose quickly out of their place; they ran as soon as he had stretched out his hand, and they entered the city and took it, and hurried to set the city on fire. [20]And when the men of Ai looked behind them, they saw, and behold, the smoke of the city ascended to heaven. So they had no power to flee this way or that way, and the people who had fled to the wilderness turned back on the pursuers. [21]Now when Joshua and all Israel saw that the ambush had taken the city and that the smoke of the city ascended, they turned back and struck down the men of Ai. [22]Then the others came out of the city against them; so they were *caught* in the midst of Israel, some on this side and some on that side. And they struck them down, so that they let none of them remain or escape. [23]But the king of Ai they took alive, and brought him to Joshua.

[24]And it came to pass when Israel had made an end of slaying all the inhabitants of Ai in the field, in the wilderness where they pursued them, and when they all had fallen by the edge of the sword until they were consumed, that all the Israelites returned to Ai and struck it with the edge of the sword. [25]So it was *that* all who fell that day, both men and women, *were* twelve thousand—all the people of Ai. [26]For Joshua did not draw back his hand, with which he stretched out the spear, until he had utterly destroyed all the inhabitants of Ai. [27]Only the livestock and the spoil of that city Israel took as booty for themselves, according to the word of the LORD which He had commanded Joshua. [28]So Joshua burned Ai and made it a heap forever, a desolation to this day. [29]And the king of Ai he hanged on a tree until evening. And as soon as the sun was down, Joshua commanded that they should take his corpse down from the tree, cast it at the entrance of the gate of the city, and raise over it a great heap of stones *that remains* to this day.

Joshua Renews the Covenant

[30]Now Joshua built an altar to the LORD God of Israel in Mount Ebal, [31]as Moses the servant of the LORD had commanded the children of Israel, as it is written in the Book of the Law of Moses: "an altar of whole stones over which no man has wielded an iron *tool.*"[a] And they offered on it burnt offerings to the LORD, and sacrificed peace offerings. [32]And there, in the presence of the children of Israel, he wrote on the stones a copy of the law of Moses, which he had written. [33]Then all Israel, with their elders and officers and judges, stood on either side of the ark before the priests, the Levites, who bore the ark of the covenant of the LORD, the stranger as well as he who was born among them. Half of them *were* in front of Mount Gerizim and half of them in front of Mount Ebal, as Moses the servant of the LORD had commanded before, that they should bless the people of Israel. [34]And afterward he read all the words of the law, the blessings and the cursings, according to all that is written in the Book of the Law. [35]There was not a word of all that Moses had commanded which Joshua did not read before all the assembly of Israel, with the women, the little ones, and the strangers who were living among them.

The Treaty with the Gibeonites

9 And it came to pass when all the kings who *were* on this side of the Jordan, in the hills and in the lowland and in all the coasts of the Great Sea toward Lebanon—the Hittite, the Amorite, the Canaanite, the Perizzite, the Hivite, and the Jebusite—heard *about it,* [2]that they gathered together to fight with Joshua and Israel with one accord.

[3]But when the inhabitants of Gibeon heard what Joshua had done to Jericho and Ai, [4]they worked craftily, and went and pretended to be ambassadors. And

---

8:31 [a]Deuteronomy 27:5, 6

they took old sacks on their donkeys, old wineskins torn and mended, 5old and patched sandals on their feet, and old garments on themselves; and all the bread of their provision was dry *and* moldy. 6And they went to Joshua, to the camp at Gilgal, and said to him and to the men of Israel, "We have come from a far country; now therefore, make a covenant with us."

7Then the men of Israel said to the Hivites, "Perhaps you dwell among us; so how can we make a covenant with you?"

8But they said to Joshua, "We *are* your servants."

And Joshua said to them, "Who *are* you, and where do you come from?"

9So they said to him: "From a very far country your servants have come, because of the name of the LORD your God; for we have heard of His fame, and all that He did in Egypt, 10and all that He did to the two kings of the Amorites who *were* beyond the Jordan—to Sihon king of Heshbon, and Og king of Bashan, who was at Ashtaroth. 11Therefore our elders and all the inhabitants of our country spoke to us, saying, 'Take provisions with you for the journey, and go to meet them, and say to them, "We *are* your servants; now therefore, make a covenant with us."' 12This bread of ours we took hot *for* our provision from our houses on the day we departed to come to you. But now look, it is dry and moldy. 13And these wineskins which we filled *were* new, and see, they are torn; and these our garments and our sandals have become old because of the very long journey."

14Then the men of Israel took some of their provisions; but they did not ask counsel of the LORD. 15So Joshua made peace with them, and made a covenant with them to let them live; and the rulers of the congregation swore to them.

16And it happened at the end of three days, after they had made a covenant with them, that they heard that they *were* their neighbors who dwelt near them. 17Then the children of Israel journeyed and came to their cities on the third day. Now their cities *were* Gibeon, Chephirah, Beeroth, and Kirjath Jearim. 18But the children of Israel did not attack them, because the rulers of the congregation had sworn to them by the LORD God of Israel. And all the congregation complained against the rulers.

19Then all the rulers said to all the congregation, "We have sworn to them by the LORD God of Israel; now therefore, we may not touch them. 20This we will do to them: We will let them live, lest wrath be upon us because of the oath which we swore to them." 21And the rulers said to them, "Let them live, but let them be woodcutters and water carriers for all the congregation, as the rulers had promised them."

22Then Joshua called for them, and he spoke to them, saying, "Why have you deceived us, saying, 'We *are* very far from you,' when you dwell near us? 23Now therefore, you *are* cursed, and none of you shall be freed from being slaves—woodcutters and water carriers for the house of my God."

24So they answered Joshua and said, "Because your servants were clearly told that the LORD your God commanded His servant Moses to give you all the land, and to destroy all the inhabitants of the land from before you; therefore we were very much afraid for our lives because of you, and have done this thing. 25And now, here we are, in your hands; do with us as it seems good and right to do to us." 26So he did to them, and delivered them out of the hand of the children of Israel, so that they did not kill them. 27And that day Joshua made them woodcutters and water carriers for the congregation and for the altar of the LORD, in the place which He would choose, even to this day.

The Sun Stands Still

10 Now it came to pass when Adoni-Zedek king of Jerusalem heard how Joshua had taken Ai and had utterly destroyed it—as he had done to Jericho and its king, so he had done to Ai and its king—and how the inhabitants of Gibeon had made peace with Israel and were among them, 2that they feared greatly, because Gibeon *was* a great city, like one of the royal cities, and because it *was* greater than Ai, and all its men *were* mighty. 3Therefore Adoni-Zedek king of Jerusalem sent to Hoham king of Hebron, Piram king

of Jarmuth, Japhia king of Lachish, and Debir king of Eglon, saying, [4]"Come up to me and help me, that we may attack Gibeon, for it has made peace with Joshua and with the children of Israel." [5]Therefore the five kings of the Amorites, the king of Jerusalem, the king of Hebron, the king of Jarmuth, the king of Lachish, *and* the king of Eglon, gathered together and went up, they and all their armies, and camped before Gibeon and made war against it.

[6]And the men of Gibeon sent to Joshua at the camp at Gilgal, saying, "Do not forsake your servants; come up to us quickly, save us and help us, for all the kings of the Amorites who dwell in the mountains have gathered together against us."

[7]So Joshua ascended from Gilgal, he and all the people of war with him, and all the mighty men of valor. [8]And the LORD said to Joshua, "Do not fear them, for I have delivered them into your hand; not a man of them shall stand before you." [9]Joshua therefore came upon them suddenly, having marched all night from Gilgal. [10]So the LORD routed them before Israel, killed them with a great slaughter at Gibeon, chased them along the road that goes to Beth Horon, and struck them down as far as Azekah and Makkedah. [11]And it happened, as they fled before Israel *and* were on the descent of Beth Horon, that the LORD cast down large hailstones from heaven on them as far as Azekah, and they died. *There were* more who died from the hailstones than the children of Israel killed with the sword.

[12]Then Joshua spoke to the LORD in the day when the LORD delivered up the Amorites before the children of Israel, and he said in the sight of Israel:

"Sun, stand still over Gibeon;
     And Moon, in the Valley of Aijalon."
[13]   So the sun stood still,
     And the moon stopped,
     Till the people had revenge
     Upon their enemies.

Is this not written in the Book of Jasher? So the sun stood still in the midst of heaven, and did not hasten to go *down* for about a whole day. [14]And there has been no day

like that, before it or after it, that the LORD heeded the voice of a man; for the LORD fought for Israel.

[15]Then Joshua returned, and all Israel with him, to the camp at Gilgal.

The Amorite Kings Executed

[16]But these five kings had fled and hidden themselves in a cave at Makkedah. [17]And it was told Joshua, saying, "The five kings have been found hidden in the cave at Makkedah."

[18]So Joshua said, "Roll large stones against the mouth of the cave, and set men by it to guard them. [19]And do not stay *there* yourselves, *but* pursue your enemies, and attack their rear *guard*. Do not allow them to enter their cities, for the LORD your God has delivered them into your hand." [20]Then it happened, while Joshua and the children of Israel made an end of slaying them with a very great slaughter, till they had finished, that those who escaped entered fortified cities. [21]And all the people returned to the camp, to Joshua at Makkedah, in peace.

No one moved his tongue against any of the children of Israel.

[22]Then Joshua said, "Open the mouth of the cave, and bring out those five kings to me from the cave." [23]And they did so, and brought out those five kings to him from the cave: the king of Jerusalem, the king of Hebron, the king of Jarmuth, the king of Lachish, *and* the king of Eglon.

[24]So it was, when they brought out those kings to Joshua, that Joshua called for all the men of Israel, and said to the captains of the men of war who went with him, "Come near, put your feet on the necks of these kings." And they drew near and put their feet on their necks. [25]Then Joshua said to them, "Do not be afraid, nor be dismayed; be strong and of good courage, for thus the LORD will do to all your enemies against whom you fight." [26]And afterward Joshua struck them and killed them, and hanged them on five trees; and they were hanging on the trees until evening. [27]So it was at the time of the going down of the sun *that* Joshua commanded, and they took them down from the trees, cast them

into the cave where they had been hidden, and laid large stones against the cave's mouth, *which remain* until this very day.

Conquest of the Southland

²⁸On that day Joshua took Makkedah, and struck it and its king with the edge of the sword. He utterly destroyed them[a]—all the people who *were* in it. He let none remain. He also did to the king of Makkedah as he had done to the king of Jericho.

²⁹Then Joshua passed from Makkedah, and all Israel with him, to Libnah; and they fought against Libnah. ³⁰And the LORD also delivered it and its king into the hand of Israel; he struck it and all the people who *were* in it with the edge of the sword. He let none remain in it, but did to its king as he had done to the king of Jericho.

³¹Then Joshua passed from Libnah, and all Israel with him, to Lachish; and they encamped against it and fought against it. ³²And the LORD delivered Lachish into the hand of Israel, who took it on the second day, and struck it and all the people who *were* in it with the edge of the sword, according to all that he had done to Libnah. ³³Then Horam king of Gezer came up to help Lachish; and Joshua struck him and his people, until he left him none remaining.

³⁴From Lachish Joshua passed to Eglon, and all Israel with him; and they encamped against it and fought against it. ³⁵They took it on that day and struck it with the edge of the sword; all the people who *were* in it he utterly destroyed that day, according to all that he had done to Lachish.

³⁶So Joshua went up from Eglon, and all Israel with him, to Hebron; and they fought against it. ³⁷And they took it and struck it with the edge of the sword—its king, all its cities, and all the people who *were* in it; he left none remaining, according to all that he had done to Eglon, but utterly destroyed it and all the people who *were* in it.

³⁸Then Joshua returned, and all Israel with him, to Debir; and they fought against it. ³⁹And he took it and its king and all its cities; they struck them with the edge of the sword and utterly destroyed all the people who *were* in it. He left none remaining; as he had done to Hebron, so he did to Debir and its king, as he had done also to Libnah and its king.

⁴⁰So Joshua conquered all the land: the mountain country and the South[a] and the lowland and the wilderness slopes, and all their kings; he left none remaining, but utterly destroyed all that breathed, as the LORD God of Israel had commanded. ⁴¹And Joshua conquered them from Kadesh Barnea as far as Gaza, and all the country of Goshen, even as far as Gibeon. ⁴²All these kings and their land Joshua took at one time, because the LORD God of Israel fought for Israel. ⁴³Then Joshua returned, and all Israel with him, to the camp at Gilgal.

The Northern Conquest

11 And it came to pass, when Jabin king of Hazor heard *these things*, that he sent to Jobab king of Madon, to the king of Shimron, to the king of Achshaph, ²and to the kings who *were* from the north, in the mountains, in the plain south of Chinneroth, in the lowland, and in the heights of Dor on the west, ³to the Canaanites in the east and in the west, the Amorite, the Hittite, the Perizzite, the Jebusite in the mountains, and the Hivite below Hermon in the land of Mizpah. ⁴So they went out, they and all their armies with them, *as* many people *as* the sand that *is* on the seashore in multitude, with very many horses and chariots. ⁵And when all these kings had met together, they came and camped together at the waters of Merom to fight against Israel.

⁶But the LORD said to Joshua, "Do not be afraid because of them, for tomorrow about this time I will deliver all of them slain before Israel. You shall hamstring their horses and burn their chariots with fire." ⁷So Joshua and all the people of war with him came against them suddenly by the waters of Merom, and they attacked them. ⁸And the LORD delivered them into the hand of Israel, who defeated them and

---

10:28 [a]Following Masoretic Text and most authorities; many Hebrew manuscripts, some manuscripts of the Septuagint, and some manuscripts of the Targum read *it.*   **10:40** [a]Hebrew *Negev,* and so throughout this book

chased them to Greater Sidon, to the Brook Misrephoth,ᵃ and to the Valley of Mizpah eastward; they attacked them until they left none of them remaining. ⁹So Joshua did to them as the LORD had told him: he hamstrung their horses and burned their chariots with fire.

¹⁰Joshua turned back at that time and took Hazor, and struck its king with the sword; for Hazor was formerly the head of all those kingdoms. ¹¹And they struck all the people who *were* in it with the edge of the sword, utterly destroying *them*. There was none left breathing. Then he burned Hazor with fire.

¹²So all the cities of those kings, and all their kings, Joshua took and struck with the edge of the sword. He utterly destroyed them, as Moses the servant of the LORD had commanded. ¹³But *as for* the cities that stood on their mounds,ᵃ Israel burned none of them, except Hazor only, *which* Joshua burned. ¹⁴And all the spoil of these cities and the livestock, the children of Israel took as booty for themselves; but they struck every man with the edge of the sword until they had destroyed them, and they left none breathing. ¹⁵As the LORD had commanded Moses his servant, so Moses commanded Joshua, and so Joshua did. He left nothing undone of all that the LORD had commanded Moses.

Summary of Joshua's Conquests

¹⁶Thus Joshua took all this land: the mountain country, all the South, all the land of Goshen, the lowland, and the Jordan plainᵃ—the mountains of Israel and its lowlands, ¹⁷from Mount Halak and the ascent to Seir, even as far as Baal Gad in the Valley of Lebanon below Mount Hermon. He captured all their kings, and struck them down and killed them. ¹⁸Joshua made war a long time with all those kings. ¹⁹There was not a city that made peace with the children of Israel, except the Hivites, the inhabitants of Gibeon. All *the others* they took in battle. ²⁰For it was of the LORD to harden their hearts, that they should come against Israel in battle, that He might utterly destroy them, *and* that they might receive no mercy, but that He might destroy them, as the LORD had commanded Moses.

²¹And at that time Joshua came and cut off the Anakim from the mountains: from Hebron, from Debir, from Anab, from all the mountains of Judah, and from all the mountains of Israel; Joshua utterly destroyed them with their cities. ²²None of the Anakim were left in the land of the children of Israel; they remained only in Gaza, in Gath, and in Ashdod.

²³So Joshua took the whole land, according to all that the LORD had said to Moses; and Joshua gave it as an inheritance to Israel according to their divisions by their tribes. Then the land rested from war.

The Kings Conquered by Moses

12 These *are* the kings of the land whom the children of Israel defeated, and whose land they possessed on the other side of the Jordan toward the rising of the sun, from the River Arnon to Mount Hermon, and all the eastern Jordan plain: ²*One king was* Sihon king of the Amorites, who dwelt in Heshbon *and* ruled half of Gilead, from Aroer, which is on the bank of the River Arnon, from the middle of that river, even as far as the River Jabbok, *which is* the border of the Ammonites, ³and the eastern Jordan plain from the Sea of Chinneroth as far as the Sea of the Arabah (the Salt Sea), the road to Beth Jeshimoth, and southward below the slopes of Pisgah. ⁴*The other king was* Og king of Bashan and his territory, *who was* of the remnant of the giants, who dwelt at Ashtaroth and at Edrei, ⁵and reigned over Mount Hermon, over Salcah, over all Bashan, as far as the border of the Geshurites and the Maachathites, and over half of Gilead *to* the border of Sihon king of Heshbon.

⁶These Moses the servant of the LORD and the children of Israel had conquered; and Moses the servant of the LORD had given it *as* a possession to the Reubenites, the Gadites, and half the tribe of Manasseh.

11:8 ᵃHebrew *Misrephoth Maim* a heap of successive city ruins   **11:13** ᵃHebrew *tel,* a heap of successive city ruins   **11:16** ᵃHebrew *arabah*

The Kings Conquered by Joshua

7And these *are* the kings of the country which Joshua and the children of Israel conquered on this side of the Jordan, on the west, from Baal Gad in the Valley of Lebanon as far as Mount Halak and the ascent to Seir, which Joshua gave to the tribes of Israel *as* a possession according to their divisions, 8in the mountain country, in the lowlands, in the *Jordan* plain, in the slopes, in the wilderness, and in the South—the Hittites, the Amorites, the Canaanites, the Perizzites, the Hivites, and the Jebusites: 9the king of Jericho, one; the king of Ai, which *is* beside Bethel, one; 10the king of Jerusalem, one; the king of Hebron, one; 11the king of Jarmuth, one; the king of Lachish, one; 12the king of Eglon, one; the king of Gezer, one; 13the king of Debir, one; the king of Geder, one; 14the king of Hormah, one; the king of Arad, one; 15the king of Libnah, one; the king of Adullam, one; 16the king of Makkedah, one; the king of Bethel, one; 17the king of Tappuah, one; the king of Hepher, one; 18the king of Aphek, one; the king of Lasharon, one; 19the king of Madon, one; the king of Hazor, one; 20the king of Shimron Meron, one; the king of Achshaph, one; 21the king of Taanach, one; the king of Megiddo, one; 22the king of Kedesh, one; the king of Jokneam in Carmel, one; 23the king of Dor in the heights of Dor, one; the king of the people of Gilgal, one; 24the king of Tirzah, one—all the kings, thirty-one.

Remaining Land to Be Conquered

13 Now Joshua was old, advanced in years. And the LORD said to him: "You are old, advanced in years, and there remains very much land yet to be possessed. 2This is the land that yet remains: all the territory of the Philistines and all *that of* the Geshurites, 3from Sihor, which *is* east of Egypt, as far as the border of Ekron northward (*which* is counted as Canaanite); the five lords of the Philistines—the Gazites, the Ashdodites, the Ashkelonites, the Gittites, and the Ekronites; also the Avites; 4from the south, all the land of the Canaanites, and Mearah that belongs to the Sidonians as far as Aphek, to the border of the Amorites; 5the land of the Gebalites,a and all Lebanon, toward the sunrise, from Baal Gad below Mount Hermon as far as the entrance to Hamath; 6all the inhabitants of the mountains from Lebanon as far as the Brook Misrephoth,a *and* all the Sidonians—them I will drive out from before the children of Israel; only divide it by lot to Israel as an inheritance, as I have commanded you. 7Now therefore, divide this land as an inheritance to the nine tribes and half the tribe of Manasseh."

The Land Divided East of the Jordan

8With the other half-tribe the Reubenites and the Gadites received their inheritance, which Moses had given them, beyond the Jordan eastward, as Moses the servant of the LORD had given them: 9from Aroer which *is* on the bank of the River Arnon, and the town that *is* in the midst of the ravine, and all the plain of Medeba as far as Dibon; 10all the cities of Sihon king of the Amorites, who reigned in Heshbon, as far as the border of the children of Ammon; 11Gilead, and the border of the Geshurites and Maachathites, all Mount Hermon, and all Bashan as far as Salcah; 12all the kingdom of Og in Bashan, who reigned in Ashtaroth and Edrei, who remained of the remnant of the giants; for Moses had defeated and cast out these. 13Nevertheless the children of Israel did not drive out the Geshurites or the Maachathites, but the Geshurites and the Maachathites dwell among the Israelites until this day.

14Only to the tribe of Levi he had given no inheritance; the sacrifices of the LORD God of Israel made by fire *are* their inheritance, as He said to them.

The Land of Reuben

15And Moses had given to the tribe of the children of Reuben *an inheritance* according to their families. 16Their territory was from Aroer, which *is* on the bank of the River Arnon, and the city that *is* in the midst of the ravine, and all the plain by

---

13:5 aOr *Giblites*   **13:6** aHebrew *Misrephoth Maim*

Medeba; [17]Heshbon and all its cities that *are* in the plain: Dibon, Bamoth Baal, Beth Baal Meon, [18]Jahaza, Kedemoth, Mephaath, [19]Kirjathaim, Sibmah, Zereth Shahar on the mountain of the valley, [20]Beth Peor, the slopes of Pisgah, and Beth Jeshimoth— [21]all the cities of the plain and all the kingdom of Sihon king of the Amorites, who reigned in Heshbon, whom Moses had struck with the princes of Midian: Evi, Rekem, Zur, Hur, and Reba, who *were* princes of Sihon dwelling in the country. [22]The children of Israel also killed with the sword Balaam the son of Beor, the soothsayer, among those who were killed by them. [23]And the border of the children of Reuben was the bank of the Jordan. This *was* the inheritance of the children of Reuben according to their families, the cities and their villages.

The Land of Gad

[24]Moses also had given *an inheritance* to the tribe of Gad, to the children of Gad according to their families. [25]Their territory was Jazer, and all the cities of Gilead, and half the land of the Ammonites as far as Aroer, which *is* before Rabbah, [26]and from Heshbon to Ramath Mizpah and Betonim, and from Mahanaim to the border of Debir, [27]and in the valley Beth Haram, Beth Nimrah, Succoth, and Zaphon, the rest of the kingdom of Sihon king of Heshbon, with the Jordan as *its* border, as far as the edge of the Sea of Chinnereth, on the other side of the Jordan eastward. [28]This *is* the inheritance of the children of Gad according to their families, the cities and their villages.

Half the Tribe of Manasseh (East)

[29]Moses also had given *an inheritance* to half the tribe of Manasseh; it was for half the tribe of the children of Manasseh according to their families: [30]Their territory was from Mahanaim, all Bashan, all the kingdom of Og king of Bashan, and all the towns of Jair which are in Bashan, sixty cities; [31]half of Gilead, and Ashtaroth and Edrei, cities of the kingdom of Og in Bashan, *were* for the children of Machir the son of Manasseh, for half of the children of Machir according to their families.

[32]These *are the areas* which Moses had distributed as an inheritance in the plains of Moab on the other side of the Jordan, by Jericho eastward. [33]But to the tribe of Levi Moses had given no inheritance; the Lord God of Israel *was* their inheritance, as He had said to them.

The Land Divided West of the Jordan

14 These *are the areas* which the children of Israel inherited in the land of Canaan, which Eleazar the priest, Joshua the son of Nun, and the heads of the fathers of the tribes of the children of Israel distributed as an inheritance to them. [2]Their inheritance *was* by lot, as the Lord had commanded by the hand of Moses, for the nine tribes and the half-tribe. [3]For Moses had given the inheritance of the two tribes and the half-tribe on the other side of the Jordan; but to the Levites he had given no inheritance among them. [4]For the children of Joseph were two tribes: Manasseh and Ephraim. And they gave no part to the Levites in the land, except cities to dwell *in*, with their common-lands for their livestock and their property. [5]As the Lord had commanded Moses, so the children of Israel did; and they divided the land.

Caleb Inherits Hebron

[6]Then the children of Judah came to Joshua in Gilgal. And Caleb the son of Jephunneh the Kenizzite said to him: "You know the word which the Lord said to Moses the man of God concerning you and me in Kadesh Barnea. [7]I *was* forty years old when Moses the servant of the Lord sent me from Kadesh Barnea to spy out the land, and I brought back word to him as *it was* in my heart. [8]Nevertheless my brethren who went up with me made the heart of the people melt, but I wholly followed the Lord my God. [9]So Moses swore on that day, saying, 'Surely the land where your foot has trodden shall be your inheritance and your children's forever, because you have wholly followed the Lord my God.' [10]And now, behold, the Lord has kept me alive, as He said, these forty-five years, ever since the Lord spoke this word to Moses while Israel wandered in the wilderness; and now,

here I am this day, eighty-five years old. ¹¹As yet I *am as* strong this day as on the day that Moses sent me; just as my strength *was* then, so now *is* my strength for war, both for going out and for coming in. ¹²Now therefore, give me this mountain of which the Lord spoke in that day; for you heard in that day how the Anakim *were* there, and *that* the cities *were* great *and* fortified. It may be that the Lord *will be* with me, and I shall be able to drive them out as the Lord said."

¹³And Joshua blessed him, and gave Hebron to Caleb the son of Jephunneh as an inheritance. ¹⁴Hebron therefore became the inheritance of Caleb the son of Jephunneh the Kenizzite to this day, because he wholly followed the Lord God of Israel. ¹⁵And the name of Hebron formerly was Kirjath Arba (*Arba was* the greatest man among the Anakim).

Then the land had rest from war.

The Land of Judah

15 So *this* was the lot of the tribe of the children of Judah according to their families:

The border of Edom at the Wilderness of Zin southward *was* the extreme southern boundary. ²And their southern border began at the shore of the Salt Sea, from the bay that faces southward. ³Then it went out to the southern side of the Ascent of Akrabbim, passed along to Zin, ascended on the south side of Kadesh Barnea, passed along to Hezron, went up to Adar, and went around to Karkaa. ⁴*From there* it passed toward Azmon and went out to the Brook of Egypt; and the border ended at the sea. This shall be your southern border.

⁵The east border *was* the Salt Sea as far as the mouth of the Jordan.

And the border on the northern quarter *began* at the bay of the sea at the mouth of the Jordan. ⁶The border went up to Beth Hoglah and passed north of Beth Arabah; and the border went up to the stone of Bohan the son of Reuben. ⁷Then the border went up toward Debir from the Valley of Achor, and it turned northward toward Gilgal, which *is* before the Ascent of Adummim, which *is* on the south side of the

valley. The border continued toward the waters of En Shemesh and ended at En Rogel. ⁸And the border went up by the Valley of the Son of Hinnom to the southern slope of the Jebusite *city* (which *is* Jerusalem). The border went up to the top of the mountain that *lies* before the Valley of Hinnom westward, which *is* at the end of the Valley of Rephaimᵃ northward. ⁹Then the border went around from the top of the hill to the fountain of the water of Nephtoah, and extended to the cities of Mount Ephron. And the border went around to Baalah (which *is* Kirjath Jearim). ¹⁰Then the border turned westward from Baalah to Mount Seir, passed along to the side of Mount Jearim on the north (which *is* Chesalon), went down to Beth Shemesh, and passed on to Timnah. ¹¹And the border went out to the side of Ekron northward. Then the border went around to Shicron, passed along to Mount Baalah, and extended to Jabneel; and the border ended at the sea.

¹²The west border *was* the coastline of the Great Sea. This *is* the boundary of the children of Judah all around according to their families.

Caleb Occupies Hebron and Debir

¹³Now to Caleb the son of Jephunneh he gave a share among the children of Judah, according to the commandment of the Lord to Joshua, *namely,* Kirjath Arba, which *is* Hebron (*Arba was* the father of Anak). ¹⁴Caleb drove out the three sons of Anak from there: Sheshai, Ahiman, and Talmai, the children of Anak. ¹⁵Then he went up from there to the inhabitants of Debir (formerly the name of Debir *was* Kirjath Sepher).

¹⁶And Caleb said, "He who attacks Kirjath Sepher and takes it, to him I will give Achsah my daughter as wife." ¹⁷So Othniel the son of Kenaz, the brother of Caleb, took it; and he gave him Achsah his daughter as wife. ¹⁸Now it was so, when she came *to him,* that she persuaded him to ask her father for a field. So she dismounted from *her* donkey, and Caleb said to her, "What do you wish?" ¹⁹She answered, "Give me a

---

15:8 ᵃLiterally *Giants*

blessing; since you have given me land in the South, give me also springs of water." So he gave her the upper springs and the lower springs.

The Cities of Judah

20This *was* the inheritance of the tribe of the children of Judah according to their families:

21The cities at the limits of the tribe of the children of Judah, toward the border of Edom in the South, were Kabzeel, Eder, Jagur, 22Kinah, Dimonah, Adadah, 23Kedesh, Hazor, Ithnan, 24Ziph, Telem, Bealoth, 25Hazor, Hadattah, Kerioth, Hezron (which *is* Hazor), 26Amam, Shema, Moladah, 27Hazar Gaddah, Heshmon, Beth Pelet, 28Hazar Shual, Beersheba, Bizjothjah, 29Baalah, Ijim, Ezem, 30Eltolad, Chesil, Hormah, 31Ziklag, Madmannah, Sansannah, 32Lebaoth, Shilhim, Ain, and Rimmon: all the cities *are* twenty-nine, with their villages.

33In the lowland: Eshtaol, Zorah, Ashnah, 34Zanoah, En Gannim, Tappuah, Enam, 35Jarmuth, Adullam, Socoh, Azekah, 36Sharaim, Adithaim, Gederah, and Gederothaim: fourteen cities with their villages; 37Zenan, Hadashah, Migdal Gad, 38Dilean, Mizpah, Joktheel, 39Lachish, Bozkath, Eglon, 40Cabbon, Lahmas,a Kithlish, 41Gederoth, Beth Dagon, Naamah, and Makkedah: sixteen cities with their villages; 42Libnah, Ether, Ashan, 43Jiphtah, Ashnah, Nezib, 44Keilah, Achzib, and Mareshah: nine cities with their villages; 45Ekron, with its towns and villages; 46from Ekron to the sea, all that *lay* near Ashdod, with their villages; 47Ashdod with its towns and villages, Gaza with its towns and villages—as far as the Brook of Egypt and the Great Sea with *its* coastline.

48And in the mountain country: Shamir, Jattir, Sochoh, 49Dannah, Kirjath Sannah (which *is* Debir), 50Anab, Eshtemoh, Anim, 51Goshen, Holon, and Giloh: eleven cities with their villages; 52Arab, Dumah, Eshean, 53Janum, Beth Tappuah, Aphekah, 54Humtah, Kirjath Arba (which *is* Hebron), and Zior: nine cities with their villages; 55Maon, Carmel, Ziph, Juttah, 56Jezreel, Jokdeam, Zanoah, 57Kain, Gibeah, and Timnah: ten cities with their villages; 58Halhul, Beth Zur, Gedor, 59Maarath, Beth Anoth, and Eltekon: six cities with their villages; 60Kirjath Baal (which *is* Kirjath Jearim) and Rabbah: two cities with their villages.

61In the wilderness: Beth Arabah, Middin, Secacah, 62Nibshan, the City of Salt, and En Gedi: six cities with their villages.

63As for the Jebusites, the inhabitants of Jerusalem, the children of Judah could not drive them out; but the Jebusites dwell with the children of Judah at Jerusalem to this day.

Ephraim and West Manasseh

16 The lot fell to the children of Joseph from the Jordan, by Jericho, to the waters of Jericho on the east, to the wilderness that goes up from Jericho through the mountains to Bethel, 2then went out from Bethel to Luz,a passed along to the border of the Archites at Ataroth, 3and went down westward to the boundary of the Japhletites, as far as the boundary of Lower Beth Horon to Gezer; and it ended at the sea.

4So the children of Joseph, Manasseh and Ephraim, took their inheritance.

The Land of Ephraim

5The border of the children of Ephraim, according to their families, was *thus:* The border of their inheritance on the east side was Ataroth Addar as far as Upper Beth Horon.

6And the border went out toward the sea on the north side of Michmethath; then the border went around eastward to Taanath Shiloh, and passed by it on the east of Janohah. 7Then it went down from Janohah to Ataroth and Naarah,a reached to Jericho, and came out at the Jordan.

8The border went out from Tappuah westward to the Brook Kanah, and it ended at the sea. This *was* the inheritance of the tribe of the children of Ephraim according to their families. 9The separate cities for the children of Ephraim *were* among the inheritance of the children of Manasseh, all the cities with their villages.

15:40 aOr *Lahmam*   **16:2** aSeptuagint reads *Bethel* (that is, Luz).   **16:7** aOr *Naaran* (compare 1 Chronicles 7:28)

¹⁰And they did not drive out the Canaanites who dwelt in Gezer; but the Canaanites dwell among the Ephraimites to this day and have become forced laborers.

The Other Half-Tribe of Manasseh (West)

17 There was also a lot for the tribe of Manasseh, for he *was* the firstborn of Joseph: *namely* for Machir the firstborn of Manasseh, the father of Gilead, because he was a man of war; therefore he was given Gilead and Bashan. ²And there was *a lot* for the rest of the children of Manasseh according to their families: for the children of Abiezer,ᵃ the children of Helek, the children of Asriel, the children of Shechem, the children of Hepher, and the children of Shemida; these *were* the male children of Manasseh the son of Joseph according to their families.

³But Zelophehad the son of Hepher, the son of Gilead, the son of Machir, the son of Manasseh, had no sons, but only daughters. And these *are* the names of his daughters: Mahlah, Noah, Hoglah, Milcah, and Tirzah. ⁴And they came near before Eleazar the priest, before Joshua the son of Nun, and before the rulers, saying, "The LORD commanded Moses to give us an inheritance among our brothers." Therefore, according to the commandment of the LORD, he gave them an inheritance among their father's brothers. ⁵Ten shares fell to Manasseh, besides the land of Gilead and Bashan, which *were* on the other side of the Jordan, ⁶because the daughters of Manasseh received an inheritance among his sons; and the rest of Manasseh's sons had the land of Gilead.

⁷And the territory of Manasseh was from Asher to Michmethath, that *lies* east of Shechem; and the border went along south to the inhabitants of En Tappuah. ⁸Manasseh had the land of Tappuah, but Tappuah on the border of Manasseh *belonged* to the children of Ephraim. ⁹And the border descended to the Brook Kanah, southward to the brook. These cities of Ephraim *are* among the cities of Manasseh. The border of Manasseh *was* on the north side of the brook; and it ended at the sea.

¹⁰Southward *it was* Ephraim's, northward *it was* Manasseh's, and the sea was its border. Manasseh's territory was adjoining Asher on the north and Issachar on the east. ¹¹And in Issachar and in Asher, Manasseh had Beth Shean and its towns, Ibleam and its towns, the inhabitants of Dor and its towns, the inhabitants of En Dor and its towns, the inhabitants of Taanach and its towns, and the inhabitants of Megiddo and its towns—three hilly regions. ¹²Yet the children of Manasseh could not drive out *the inhabitants of* those cities, but the Canaanites were determined to dwell in that land. ¹³And it happened, when the children of Israel grew strong, that they put the Canaanites to forced labor, but did not utterly drive them out.

More Land for Ephraim and Manasseh

¹⁴Then the children of Joseph spoke to Joshua, saying, "Why have you given us *only* one lot and one share to inherit, since we *are* a great people, inasmuch as the LORD has blessed us until now?"

¹⁵So Joshua answered them, "If you *are* a great people, *then* go up to the forest *country* and clear a place for yourself there in the land of the Perizzites and the giants, since the mountains of Ephraim are too confined for you."

¹⁶But the children of Joseph said, "The mountain country is not enough for us; and all the Canaanites who dwell in the land of the valley have chariots of iron, *both those* who *are* of Beth Shean and its towns and *those* who *are* of the Valley of Jezreel."

¹⁷And Joshua spoke to the house of Joseph—to Ephraim and Manasseh—saying, "You *are* a great people and have great power; you shall not have *only* one lot, ¹⁸but the mountain country shall be yours. Although it *is* wooded, you shall cut it down, and its farthest extent shall be yours; for you shall drive out the Canaanites, though they have iron chariots *and* are strong."

The Remainder of the Land Divided

18 Now the whole congregation of the children of Israel assembled together

---

17:2 ᵃCalled *Jeezer* in Numbers 26:30

at Shiloh, and set up the tabernacle of meeting there. And the land was subdued before them. ²But there remained among the children of Israel seven tribes which had not yet received their inheritance.

CIVIL DUTY

"Pick out from among you three men for each tribe. . . ."
JOSHUA 18:4

Voting

Since the founding of our nation, voting has been considered one of the core responsibilities of citizenship. The "Father of the American Revolution" and signer of the Declaration of Independence, Samuel Adams, said of voting in 1781:

> Let each citizen remember at the moment he is offering his vote that he is not making a present or a compliment to please an individual—or at least that he ought not so to do; but that he is executing one of the most solemn trusts in human society for which he is accountable to God and his country.

---

³Then Joshua said to the children of Israel: "How long will you neglect to go and possess the land which the LORD God of your fathers has given you? ⁴Pick out from among you three men for *each* tribe, and I will send them; they shall rise and go through the land, survey it according to their inheritance, and come *back* to me. ⁵And they shall divide it into seven parts. Judah shall remain in their territory on the south, and the house of Joseph shall remain in their territory on the north. ⁶You shall therefore survey the land in seven parts and bring *the survey* here to me, that I may cast lots for you here before the LORD our God. ⁷But the Levites have no part among you, for the priesthood of the LORD *is* their inheritance. And Gad, Reuben, and half the tribe of Manasseh have received their inheritance beyond the Jordan on the east, which Moses the servant of the LORD gave them."

⁸Then the men arose to go away; and Joshua charged those who went to survey the land, saying, "Go, walk through the land, survey it, and come back to me, that I may cast lots for you here before the LORD in Shiloh." ⁹So the men went, passed through the land, and wrote the survey in a book in seven parts by cities; and they came to Joshua at the camp in Shiloh. ¹⁰Then Joshua cast lots for them in Shiloh before the LORD, and there Joshua divided the land to the children of Israel according to their divisions.

The Land of Benjamin

¹¹Now the lot of the tribe of the children of Benjamin came up according to their families, and the territory of their lot came out between the children of Judah and the children of Joseph. ¹²Their border on the north side began at the Jordan, and the border went up to the side of Jericho on the north, and went up through the mountains westward; it ended at the Wilderness of Beth Aven. ¹³The border went over from there toward Luz, to the side of Luz (which *is* Bethel) southward; and the border descended to Ataroth Addar, near the hill that *lies* on the south side of Lower Beth Horon.

¹⁴Then the border extended around the west side to the south, from the hill that *lies* before Beth Horon southward; and it ended at Kirjath Baal (which *is* Kirjath Jearim), a city of the children of Judah. This *was* the west side.

¹⁵The south side *began* at the end of Kirjath Jearim, and the border extended on the west and went out to the spring of the waters of Nephtoah. ¹⁶Then the border came down to the end of the mountain that *lies* before the Valley of the Son of Hinnom, which *is* in the Valley of the Rephaim[a] on the north, descended to the Valley of Hinnom, to the side of the Jebusite *city* on the south, and descended to En Rogel. ¹⁷And it went around from the north, went out to En Shemesh, and extended toward Geliloth, which is before the Ascent of Adummim, and descended to the stone of Bohan the son of Reuben. ¹⁸Then it passed along toward the north side of Arabah,[a] and went down to Arabah. ¹⁹And the border passed along to the north side of Beth Hoglah; then the border ended at the north bay at the Salt Sea, at the south end of the Jordan. This *was* the southern boundary.

18:16 ªLiterally *Giants*   **18:18** ªOr *Beth Arabah* (compare 15:6 and 18:22)

20The Jordan was its border on the east side. This *was* the inheritance of the children of Benjamin, according to its boundaries all around, according to their families.

21Now the cities of the tribe of the children of Benjamin, according to their families, were Jericho, Beth Hoglah, Emek Keziz, 22Beth Arabah, Zemaraim, Bethel, 23Avim, Parah, Ophrah, 24Chephar Haammoni, Ophni, and Gaba: twelve cities with their villages; 25Gibeon, Ramah, Beeroth, 26Mizpah, Chephirah, Mozah, 27Rekem, Irpeel, Taralah, 28Zelah, Eleph, Jebus (which *is* Jerusalem), Gibeath, *and* Kirjath: fourteen cities with their villages. This was the inheritance of the children of Benjamin according to their families.

Simeon's Inheritance with Judah

19 The second lot came out for Simeon, for the tribe of the children of Simeon according to their families. And their inheritance was within the inheritance of the children of Judah. 2They had in their inheritance Beersheba (Sheba), Moladah, 3Hazar Shual, Balah, Ezem, 4Eltolad, Bethul, Hormah, 5Ziklag, Beth Marcaboth, Hazar Susah, 6Beth Lebaoth, and Sharuhen: thirteen cities and their villages; 7Ain, Rimmon, Ether, and Ashan: four cities and their villages; 8and all the villages that *were* all around these cities as far as Baalath Beer, Ramah of the South. This *was* the inheritance of the tribe of the children of Simeon according to their families.

9The inheritance of the children of Simeon *was included* in the share of the children of Judah, for the share of the children of Judah was too much for them. Therefore the children of Simeon had *their* inheritance within the inheritance of that people.

The Land of Zebulun

10The third lot came out for the children of Zebulun according to their families, and the border of their inheritance was as far as Sarid. 11Their border went toward the west and to Maralah, went to Dabbasheth, and extended along the brook that is east of Jokneam. 12Then from Sarid it went eastward toward the sunrise along the border of Chisloth Tabor, and went out toward

Daberath, bypassing Japhia. 13And from there it passed along on the east of Gath Hepher, toward Eth Kazin, and extended to Rimmon, which borders on Neah. 14Then the border went around it on the north side of Hannathon, and it ended in the Valley of Jiphthah El. 15Included were Kattath, Nahallal, Shimron, Idalah, and Bethlehem: twelve cities with their villages. 16This *was* the inheritance of the children of Zebulun according to their families, these cities with their villages.

The Land of Issachar

17The fourth lot came out to Issachar, for the children of Issachar according to their families. 18And their territory went to Jezreel, and *included* Chesulloth, Shunem, 19Haphraim, Shion, Anaharath, 20Rabbith, Kishion, Abez, 21Remeth, En Gannim, En Haddah, and Beth Pazzez. 22And the border reached to Tabor, Shahazimah, and Beth Shemesh; their border ended at the Jordan: sixteen cities with their villages. 23This *was* the inheritance of the tribe of the children of Issachar according to their families, the cities and their villages.

The Land of Asher

24The fifth lot came out for the tribe of the children of Asher according to their families. 25And their territory included Helkath, Hali, Beten, Achshaph, 26Alammelech, Amad, and Mishal; it reached to Mount Carmel westward, along *the Brook* Shihor Libnath. 27It turned toward the sunrise to Beth Dagon; and it reached to Zebulun and to the Valley of Jiphthah El, then northward beyond Beth Emek and Neiel, bypassing Cabul *which was* on the left, 28including Ebron,ᵃ Rehob, Hammon, and Kanah, as far as Greater Sidon. 29And the border turned to Ramah and to the fortified city of Tyre; then the border turned to Hosah, and ended at the sea by the region of Achzib. 30Also Ummah, Aphek, and Rehob *were included:* twenty-two cities with their villages. 31This *was* the inheritance of the tribe

---

19:28 ᵃFollowing Masoretic Text, Targum, and Vulgate; a few Hebrew manuscripts read *Abdon* (compare 21:30 and 1 Chronicles 6:74).

of the children of Asher according to their families, these cities with their villages.

The Land of Naphtali

³²The sixth lot came out to the children of Naphtali, for the children of Naphtali according to their families. ³³And their border began at Heleph, enclosing the territory from the terebinth tree in Zaanannim, Adami Nekeb, and Jabneel, as far as Lakkum; it ended at the Jordan. ³⁴From Heleph the border extended westward to Aznoth Tabor, and went out from there toward Hukkok; it adjoined Zebulun on the south side and Asher on the west side, and ended at Judah by the Jordan toward the sunrise. ³⁵And the fortified cities *are* Ziddim, Zer, Hammath, Rakkath, Chinnereth, ³⁶Adamah, Ramah, Hazor, ³⁷Kedesh, Edrei, En Hazor, ³⁸Iron, Migdal El, Horem, Beth Anath, and Beth Shemesh: nineteen cities with their villages. ³⁹This *was* the inheritance of the tribe of the children of Naphtali according to their families, the cities and their villages.

The Land of Dan

⁴⁰The seventh lot came out for the tribe of the children of Dan according to their families. ⁴¹And the territory of their inheritance was Zorah, Eshtaol, Ir Shemesh, ⁴²Shaalabbin, Aijalon, Jethlah, ⁴³Elon, Timnah, Ekron, ⁴⁴Eltekeh, Gibbethon, Baalath, ⁴⁵Jehud, Bene Berak, Gath Rimmon, ⁴⁶Me Jarkon, and Rakkon, with the region near Joppa. ⁴⁷And the border of the children of Dan went beyond these, because the children of Dan went up to fight against Leshem and took it; and they struck it with the edge of the sword, took possession of it, and dwelt in it. They called Leshem, Dan, after the name of Dan their father. ⁴⁸This *is* the inheritance of the tribe of the children of Dan according to their families, these cities with their villages.

Joshua's Inheritance

⁴⁹When they had made an end of dividing the land as an inheritance according to their borders, the children of Israel gave an inheritance among them to Joshua the son of Nun. ⁵⁰According to the word of the LORD they gave him the city which he asked for, Timnath Serah in the mountains of Ephraim; and he built the city and dwelt in it.

⁵¹These *were* the inheritances which Eleazar the priest, Joshua the son of Nun, and the heads of the fathers of the tribes of the children of Israel divided as an inheritance by lot in Shiloh before the LORD, at the door of the tabernacle of meeting. So they made an end of dividing the country.

The Cities of Refuge

20 The LORD also spoke to Joshua, saying, ²"Speak to the children of Israel, saying: 'Appoint for yourselves cities of refuge, of which I spoke to you through Moses, ³that the slayer who kills a person accidentally *or* unintentionally may flee there; and they shall be your refuge from the avenger of blood. ⁴And when he flees to one of those cities, and stands at the entrance of the gate of the city, and declares his case in the hearing of the elders of that city, they shall take him into the city as one of them, and give him a place, that he may dwell among them. ⁵Then if the avenger of blood pursues him, they shall not deliver the slayer into his hand, because he struck his neighbor unintentionally, but did not hate him beforehand. ⁶And he shall dwell in that city until he stands before the congregation for judgment, *and* until the death of the one who is high priest in those days. Then the slayer may return and come to his own city and his own house, to the city from which he fled.' "

⁷So they appointed Kedesh in Galilee, in the mountains of Naphtali, Shechem in the mountains of Ephraim, and Kirjath Arba (which *is* Hebron) in the mountains of Judah. ⁸And on the other side of the Jordan, by Jericho eastward, they assigned Bezer in the wilderness on the plain, from the tribe of Reuben, Ramoth in Gilead, from the tribe of Gad, and Golan in Bashan, from the tribe of Manasseh. ⁹These were the cities appointed for all the children of Israel and for the stranger who dwelt among them, that whoever killed a person accidentally might flee there, and not die by the hand of the avenger of blood until he stood before the congregation.

Cities of the Levites

21 Then the heads of the fathers' *houses* of the Levites came near to Eleazar the priest, to Joshua the son of Nun, and to the heads of the fathers' *houses* of the tribes of the children of Israel. ²And they spoke to them at Shiloh in the land of Canaan, saying, "The LORD commanded through Moses to give us cities to dwell in, with their common-lands for our livestock." ³So the children of Israel gave to the Levites from their inheritance, at the commandment of the LORD, these cities and their common-lands:

⁴Now the lot came out for the families of the Kohathites. And the children of Aaron the priest, *who were* of the Levites, had thirteen cities by lot from the tribe of Judah, from the tribe of Simeon, and from the tribe of Benjamin. ⁵The rest of the children of Kohath had ten cities by lot from the families of the tribe of Ephraim, from the tribe of Dan, and from the half-tribe of Manasseh.

⁶And the children of Gershon had thirteen cities by lot from the families of the tribe of Issachar, from the tribe of Asher, from the tribe of Naphtali, and from the half-tribe of Manasseh in Bashan.

⁷The children of Merari according to their families had twelve cities from the tribe of Reuben, from the tribe of Gad, and from the tribe of Zebulun.

⁸And the children of Israel gave these cities with their common-lands by lot to the Levites, as the LORD had commanded by the hand of Moses.

⁹So they gave from the tribe of the children of Judah and from the tribe of the children of Simeon these cities which are designated by name, ¹⁰which were for the children of Aaron, one of the families of the Kohathites, *who were* of the children of Levi; for the lot was theirs first. ¹¹And they gave them Kirjath Arba (*Arba was* the father of Anak), which *is* Hebron, in the mountains of Judah, with the common-land surrounding it. ¹²But the fields of the city and its villages they gave to Caleb the son of Jephunneh as his possession.

¹³Thus to the children of Aaron the priest they gave Hebron with its common-land (a city of refuge for the slayer), Libnah with its common-land, ¹⁴Jattir with its common-land, Eshtemoa with its common-land, ¹⁵Holon with its common-land, Debir with its common-land, ¹⁶Ain with its common-land, Juttah with its common-land, and Beth Shemesh with its common-land: nine cities from those two tribes; ¹⁷and from the tribe of Benjamin, Gibeon with its common-land, Geba with its common-land, ¹⁸Anathoth with its common-land, and Almon with its common-land: four cities. ¹⁹All the cities of the children of Aaron, the priests, *were* thirteen cities with their common-lands.

²⁰And the families of the children of Kohath, the Levites, the rest of the children of Kohath, even they had the cities of their lot from the tribe of Ephraim. ²¹For they gave them Shechem with its common-land in the mountains of Ephraim (a city of refuge for the slayer), Gezer with its common-land, ²²Kibzaim with its common-land, and Beth Horon with its common-land: four cities; ²³and from the tribe of Dan, Eltekeh with its common-land, Gibbethon with its common-land, ²⁴Aijalon with its common-land, *and* Gath Rimmon with its common-land: four cities; ²⁵and from the half-tribe of Manasseh, Tanach with its common-land and Gath Rimmon with its common-land: two cities. ²⁶All the ten cities with their common-lands were for the rest of the families of the children of Kohath.

²⁷Also to the children of Gershon, of the families of the Levites, from the *other* half-tribe of Manasseh, *they gave* Golan in Bashan with its common-land (a city of refuge for the slayer), and Be Eshterah with its common-land: two cities; ²⁸and from the tribe of Issachar, Kishion with its common-land, Daberath with its common-land, ²⁹Jarmuth with its common-land, *and* En Gannim with its common-land: four cities; ³⁰and from the tribe of Asher, Mishal with its common-land, Abdon with its common-land, ³¹Helkath with its common-land, and Rehob with its common-land: four cities; ³²and from the tribe of Naphtali, Kedesh in Galilee with its common-land (a city of refuge for the slayer), Hammoth Dor with its common-land, and Kartan with its

common-land: three cities. ³³All the cities of the Gershonites according to their families *were* thirteen cities with their common-lands.

³⁴And to the families of the children of Merari, the rest of the Levites, from the tribe of Zebulun, Jokneam with its common-land, Kartah with its common-land, ³⁵Dimnah with its common-land, *and* Nahalal with its common-land: four cities; ³⁶and from the tribe of Reuben, Bezer with its common-land, Jahaz with its common-land, ³⁷Kedemoth with its common-land, and Mephaath with its common-land: four cities;ᵃ ³⁸and from the tribe of Gad, Ramoth in Gilead with its common-land (a city of refuge for the slayer), Mahanaim with its common-land, ³⁹Heshbon with its common-land, *and* Jazer with its common-land: four cities in all. ⁴⁰So all the cities for the children of Merari according to their families, the rest of the families of the Levites, were *by* their lot twelve cities.

⁴¹All the cities of the Levites within the possession of the children of Israel *were* forty-eight cities with their common-lands. ⁴²Every one of these cities had its common-land surrounding it; thus *were* all these cities.

The Promise Fulfilled

⁴³So the LORD gave to Israel all the land of which He had sworn to give to their fathers, and they took possession of it and dwelt in it. ⁴⁴The LORD gave them rest all around, according to all that He had sworn to their fathers. And not a man of all their enemies stood against them; the LORD delivered all their enemies into their hand. ⁴⁵Not a word failed of any good thing which the LORD had spoken to the house of Israel. All came to pass.

Eastern Tribes Return to Their Lands

22 Then Joshua called the Reubenites, the Gadites, and half the tribe of Manasseh, ²and said to them: "You have kept all that Moses the servant of the LORD commanded you, and have obeyed my voice in all that I commanded you. ³You have not left your brethren these many days, up to this day, but have kept the charge of the commandment of the LORD your God. ⁴And now the LORD your God has given rest to your brethren, as He promised them; now therefore, return and go to your tents *and* to the land of your possession, which Moses the servant of the LORD gave you on the other side of the Jordan. ⁵But take careful heed to do the commandment and the law which Moses the servant of the LORD commanded you, to love the LORD your God, to walk in all His ways, to keep His commandments, to hold fast to Him, and to serve Him with all your heart and with all your soul." ⁶So Joshua blessed them and sent them away, and they went to their tents.

⁷Now to half the tribe of Manasseh Moses had given a possession in Bashan, but to the *other* half of it Joshua gave *a possession* among their brethren on this side of the Jordan, westward. And indeed, when Joshua sent them away to their tents, he blessed them, ⁸and spoke to them, saying, "Return with much riches to your tents, with very much livestock, with silver, with gold, with bronze, with iron, and with very much clothing. Divide the spoil of your enemies with your brethren."

⁹So the children of Reuben, the children of Gad, and half the tribe of Manasseh returned, and departed from the children of Israel at Shiloh, which *is* in the land of Canaan, to go to the country of Gilead, to the land of their possession, which they had obtained according to the word of the LORD by the hand of Moses.

An Altar by the Jordan

¹⁰And when they came to the region of the Jordan which *is* in the land of Canaan, the children of Reuben, the children of Gad, and half the tribe of Manasseh built an altar there by the Jordan—a great, impressive altar. ¹¹Now the children of Israel heard *someone* say, "Behold, the children of Reuben, the children of Gad, and half the tribe of Manasseh have built an altar on the frontier of the land of Canaan, in the

21:37 ᵃFollowing Septuagint and Vulgate (compare 1 Chronicles 6:78, 79); Masoretic Text, Bomberg, and Targum omit verses 36 and 37.

region of the Jordan—on the children of Israel's side." [12]And when the children of Israel heard *of it,* the whole congregation of the children of Israel gathered together at Shiloh to go to war against them.

[13]Then the children of Israel sent Phinehas the son of Eleazar the priest to the children of Reuben, to the children of Gad, and to half the tribe of Manasseh, into the land of Gilead, [14]and with him ten rulers, one ruler each from the chief house of every tribe of Israel; and each one *was* the head of the house of his father among the divisions[a] of Israel. [15]Then they came to the children of Reuben, to the children of Gad, and to half the tribe of Manasseh, to the land of Gilead, and they spoke with them, saying, [16]"Thus says the whole congregation of the LORD: 'What treachery *is* this that you have committed against the God of Israel, to turn away this day from following the LORD, in that you have built for yourselves an altar, that you might rebel this day against the LORD? [17]*Is* the iniquity of Peor not enough for us, from which we are not cleansed till this day, although there was a plague in the congregation of the LORD, [18]but that you must turn away this day from following the LORD? And it shall be, if you rebel today against the LORD, that tomorrow He will be angry with the whole congregation of Israel. [19]Nevertheless, if the land of your possession *is* unclean, *then* cross over to the land of the possession of the LORD, where the LORD's tabernacle stands, and take possession among us; but do not rebel against the LORD, nor rebel against us, by building yourselves an altar besides the altar of the LORD our God. [20]Did not Achan the son of Zerah commit a trespass in the accursed thing, and wrath fell on all the congregation of Israel? And that man did not perish alone in his iniquity.'"

[21]Then the children of Reuben, the children of Gad, and half the tribe of Manasseh answered and said to the heads of the divisions[a] of Israel: [22]"The LORD God of gods, the LORD God of gods, He knows, and let Israel itself know—if *it is* in rebellion, or if in treachery against the LORD, do not save us this day. [23]If we have built ourselves an altar to turn from following the LORD, or if to offer on it burnt offerings or grain offerings, or if to offer peace offerings on it, let the LORD Himself require *an account.* [24]But in fact we have done it for fear, for a reason, saying, 'In time to come your descendants may speak to our descendants, saying, "What have you to do with the LORD God of Israel? [25]For the LORD has made the Jordan a border between you and us, *you* children of Reuben and children of Gad. You have no part in the LORD." So your descendants would make our descendants cease fearing the LORD.' [26]Therefore we said, 'Let us now prepare to build ourselves an altar, not for burnt offering nor for sacrifice, [27]but *that* it *may be* a witness between you and us and our generations after us, that we may perform the service of the LORD before Him with our burnt offerings, with our sacrifices, and with our peace offerings; that your descendants may not say to our descendants in time to come, "You have no part in the LORD."' [28]Therefore we said that it will be, when they say *this* to us or to our generations in time to come, that we may say, 'Here is the replica of the altar of the LORD which our fathers made, though not for burnt offerings nor for sacrifices; but it *is* a witness between you and us.' [29]Far be it from us that we should rebel against the LORD, and turn from following the LORD this day, to build an altar for burnt offerings, for grain offerings, or for sacrifices, besides the altar of the LORD our God which *is* before His tabernacle."

[30]Now when Phinehas the priest and the rulers of the congregation, the heads of the divisions[a] of Israel who *were* with him, heard the words that the children of Reuben, the children of Gad, and the children of Manasseh spoke, it pleased them. [31]Then Phinehas the son of Eleazar the priest said to the children of Reuben, the children of Gad, and the children of Manasseh, "This day we perceive that the LORD *is* among us, because you have not committed this treachery against the LORD. Now you have delivered the children of Israel out of the hand of the LORD."

22:14 [a]Literally *thousands*   **22:21** [a]Literally *thousands*   **22:30** [a]Literally *thousands*

³²And Phinehas the son of Eleazar the priest, and the rulers, returned from the children of Reuben and the children of Gad, from the land of Gilead to the land of Canaan, to the children of Israel, and brought back word to them. ³³So the thing pleased the children of Israel, and the children of Israel blessed God; they spoke no more of going against them in battle, to destroy the land where the children of Reuben and Gad dwelt.

³⁴The children of Reuben and the children of Gadᵃ called the altar, *Witness,* "For *it is* a witness between us that the LORD *is* God."

Joshua's Farewell Address

23Now it came to pass, a long time after the LORD had given rest to Israel from all their enemies round about, that Joshua was old, advanced in age. ²And Joshua called for all Israel, for their elders, for their heads, for their judges, and for their officers, and said to them:

"I am old, advanced in age. ³You have seen all that the LORD your God has done to all these nations because of you, for the LORD your God *is* He who has fought for you. ⁴See, I have divided to you by lot these nations that remain, to be an inheritance for your tribes, from the Jordan, with all the nations that I have cut off, as far as the Great Sea westward. ⁵And the LORD your God will expel them from before you and drive them out of your sight. So you shall possess their land, as the LORD your God promised you. ⁶Therefore be very courageous to keep and to do all that is written in the Book of the Law of Moses, lest you turn aside from it to the right hand or to the left, ⁷*and* lest you go among these nations, these who remain among you. You shall not make mention of the name of their gods, nor cause *anyone* to swear *by them;* you shall not serve them nor bow down to them, ⁸but you shall hold fast to the LORD your God, as you have done to this day. ⁹For the LORD has driven out from before you great and strong nations; but *as for* you, no one has been able to stand against you to this day. ¹⁰One man of you shall chase a thousand, for the LORD your God *is* He who fights for you, as He promised you. ¹¹Therefore take

careful heed to yourselves, that you love the LORD your God. ¹²Or else, if indeed you do go back, and cling to the remnant of these nations—these that remain among you—and make marriages with them, and go in to them and they to you, ¹³know for certain that the LORD your God will no longer drive out these nations from before you. But they shall be snares and traps to you, and scourges on your sides and thorns in your eyes, until you perish from this good land which the LORD your God has given you.

¹⁴"Behold, this day I *am* going the way of all the earth. And you know in all your hearts and in all your souls that not one thing has failed of all the good things which the LORD your God spoke concerning you. All have come to pass for you; not one word of them has failed. ¹⁵Therefore it shall come to pass, that as all the good things have come upon you which the LORD your God promised you, so the LORD will bring upon you all harmful things, until He has destroyed you from this good land which the LORD your God has given you. ¹⁶When you have transgressed the covenant of the LORD your God, which He commanded you, and have gone and served other gods, and bowed down to them, then the anger of the LORD will burn against you, and you shall perish quickly from the good land which He has given you."

The Covenant at Shechem

24Then Joshua gathered all the tribes of Israel to Shechem and called for the elders of Israel, for their heads, for their judges, and for their officers; and they presented themselves before God. ²And Joshua said to all the people, "Thus says the LORD God of Israel: 'Your fathers, *including* Terah, the father of Abraham and the father of Nahor, dwelt on the other side of the Riverᵃ in old times; and they served other gods. ³Then I took your father Abraham from the other side of the River, led him throughout all the land of Canaan, and multiplied his descendants and gave him Isaac. ⁴To Isaac

---

22:34 ᵃSeptuagint adds *and half the tribe of Manasseh.*
24:2 ᵃHebrew *Nahar,* the Euphrates, and so in verses 3, 14, and 15

"...ASK NOT...."

Called the most memorable speech of any twentieth-century politician, President John F. Kennedy spoke these inspirational words to an American citizenry that was torn by fears of war in his 1961 Inaugural Address:

... The world is very different now. For man holds in his mortal hands the power to abolish all forms of human poverty and all forms of human life. And yet the same revolutionary beliefs for which our forebears fought are still at issue around the globe—the belief that the rights of man come not from the generosity of the state, but from the hand of God.

We dare not forget today that we are the heirs of that first revolution. Let the word go forth from this time and place, to friend and foe alike, that the torch has been passed to a new generation of Americans, born in this century, tempered by war, disciplined by a hard and bitter peace, proud of our ancient heritage and unwilling to witness or permit the slow undoing of those human rights to which this nation has always been committed, and to which we are committed today at home and around the world.

Let every nation know, whether it wishes us well or ill, that we shall pay any price, bear any burden, meet any hardship, support any friend, oppose any foe, to assure the survival and the success of liberty. ...

In the long history of the world, only a few generations have been granted the role of defending freedom in its hour of maximum danger. I do not shrink from this responsibility—I welcome it. I do not believe that any of us would exchange places with any other people or any other generation. The energy, the faith, the devotion which we bring to this endeavor will light our country and all who serve it—and the glow from that fire can truly light the world.

And so, my fellow Americans: ask not what your country can do for you—ask what you can do for your country. ...

Finally, ... with a good conscience our only sure reward, with history the final judge of our deeds, let us go forth to lead the land we love, asking His blessing and His help, but knowing that here on earth God's work must truly be our own.

I gave Jacob and Esau. To Esau I gave the mountains of Seir to possess, but Jacob and his children went down to Egypt. [5]Also I sent Moses and Aaron, and I plagued Egypt, according to what I did among them. Afterward I brought you out.

[6]'Then I brought your fathers out of Egypt, and you came to the sea; and the Egyptians pursued your fathers with chariots and horsemen to the Red Sea. [7]So they cried out to the LORD; and He put darkness between you and the Egyptians, brought the sea upon them, and covered them. And your eyes saw what I did in Egypt. Then you dwelt in the wilderness a long time. [8]And I brought you into the land of the Amorites, who dwelt on the other side of the Jordan, and they fought with you. But I gave them into your hand, that you might possess their land, and I destroyed them from before you. [9]Then Balak the son of Zippor, king of Moab, arose to make war against Israel, and sent and called Balaam the son of Beor to curse you. [10]But I would not listen to Balaam; therefore he continued to bless you. So I delivered you out of his hand. [11]Then you went over the Jordan and came to Jericho. And the men of Jericho fought against you—also the Amorites, the Perizzites, the Canaanites, the Hittites, the Girgashites, the Hivites, and the Jebusites. But I delivered them into your hand. [12]I sent the hornet before you which drove them out from before you, also the two kings of the Amorites, but not with your sword or with your bow. [13]I have given you a land for which you did not labor, and cities which you did not build, and you dwell in them; you eat of the vineyards and olive groves which you did not plant.'

[14]"Now therefore, fear the LORD, serve Him in sincerity and in truth, and put away the gods which your fathers served on the other side of the River and in Egypt. Serve the LORD! [15]And if it seems evil to you to serve the LORD, choose for yourselves this day whom you will serve, whether the gods which your fathers served that were on the other side of the River, or the gods of the Amorites, in whose land you dwell. But as for me and my house, we will serve the LORD."

[16]So the people answered and said: "Far be it from us that we should forsake the LORD to serve other gods; [17]for the LORD our God is He who brought us and our fathers up out of the land of Egypt, from the house of bondage, who did those great signs in our sight, and preserved us in all the way that we went and among all the people through whom we passed. [18]And the LORD drove out from before us all the people, including the Amorites who dwelt in the land. We also will serve the LORD, for He is our God."

[19]But Joshua said to the people, "You cannot serve the LORD, for He is a holy God. He is a jealous God; He will not forgive your transgressions nor your sins. [20]If you forsake the LORD and serve foreign gods, then He will turn and do you harm and consume you, after He has done you good."

[21]And the people said to Joshua, "No, but we will serve the LORD!"

[22]So Joshua said to the people, "You are witnesses against yourselves that you have chosen the LORD for yourselves, to serve Him."

And they said, "We are witnesses!"

[23]"Now therefore," he said, "put away the foreign gods which are among you, and incline your heart to the LORD God of Israel."

[24]And the people said to Joshua, "The LORD our God we will serve, and His voice we will obey!"

[25]So Joshua made a covenant with the people that day, and made for them a statute and an ordinance in Shechem. [26]Then Joshua wrote these words in the Book of the Law of God. And he took a large stone, and set it up there under the oak that was by the sanctuary of the LORD. [27]And Joshua said to all the people, "Behold, this stone shall be a witness to us, for it has heard all the words of the LORD which He spoke to us. It shall therefore be a witness to you, lest you deny your God." [28]So Joshua let the people depart, each to his own inheritance.

Death of Joshua and Eleazar

[29]Now it came to pass after these things that Joshua the son of Nun, the servant of the LORD, died, being one hundred and ten years old. [30]And they buried him within the

border of his inheritance at Timnath Serah, which *is* in the mountains of Ephraim, on the north side of Mount Gaash.

[31]Israel served the LORD all the days of Joshua, and all the days of the elders who outlived Joshua, who had known all the works of the LORD which He had done for Israel.

[32]The bones of Joseph, which the children of Israel had brought up out of Egypt, they buried at Shechem, in the plot of ground which Jacob had bought from the sons of Hamor the father of Shechem for one hundred pieces of silver, and which had become an inheritance of the children of Joseph.

[33]And Eleazar the son of Aaron died. They buried him in a hill *belonging to* Phinehas his son, which was given to him in the mountains of Ephraim.

JUDGES

Author: Unknown

When Written: 1050–1000 B.C.

Theme: Deliverance

Key Verse: Judges 21:25—In those days there was no king in Israel; everyone did what was right in his own eyes.

Key Chapter: Judges 2—The second chapter of Judges demonstrates the cycle of behavior that would define the spiritual path of Israel after the death of Joshua and his generation. The people would drift from godliness to apostasy; they would ultimately cry out to God for deliverance, which He would send through a series of judges.

U.S. Supreme Court Justice Clarence Thomas recalls that as he was growing up, his grandfather taught him some important foundational lessons about the connection between personal responsibility and liberty. "What my grandfather believed was that people have their responsibilities, and that if they are left alone to fulfill their responsibilities, that is freedom," noted Justice Thomas. "Honesty and responsibility, those are the things he taught." He added that in today's society, there is not enough emphasis on the responsibilities of all Americans to live in such a way that will maintain and protect the foundations of freedom. "Too many conversations today have to do with rights and wants," he said. "There is not enough talk about responsibilities and duties."

The Book of Judges offers a graphic demonstration of the consequences of such self-seeking behavior among the citizens of a nation—and of the need for personal and collective humility, repentance, and steadfast faith in God to turn a nation back to righteousness.

JUDGES

The Continuing Conquest of Canaan

1 Now after the death of Joshua it came to pass that the children of Israel asked the LORD, saying, "Who shall be first to go up for us against the Canaanites to fight against them?"

2 And the LORD said, "Judah shall go up. Indeed I have delivered the land into his hand."

3 So Judah said to Simeon his brother, "Come up with me to my allotted territory, that we may fight against the Canaanites; and I will likewise go with you to your allotted territory." And Simeon went with him. 4 Then Judah went up, and the LORD delivered the Canaanites and the Perizzites into their hand; and they killed ten thousand men at Bezek. 5 And they found Adoni-Bezek in Bezek, and fought against him; and they defeated the Canaanites and the Perizzites. 6 Then Adoni-Bezek fled, and they pursued him and caught him and cut off his thumbs and big toes. 7 And Adoni-Bezek said, "Seventy kings with their thumbs and big toes cut off used to gather *scraps* under my table; as I have done, so God has repaid me." Then they brought him to Jerusalem, and there he died.

8 Now the children of Judah fought against Jerusalem and took it; they struck it with the edge of the sword and set the city on fire. 9 And afterward the children of Judah went down to fight against the Canaanites who dwelt in the mountains, in the South,[a] and in the lowland. 10 Then Judah went against the Canaanites who dwelt in Hebron. (Now the name of Hebron *was* formerly Kirjath Arba.) And they killed Sheshai, Ahiman, and Talmai.

11 From there they went against the inhabitants of Debir. (The name of Debir *was* formerly Kirjath Sepher.) 12 Then Caleb said, "Whoever attacks Kirjath Sepher and takes it, to him I will give my daughter Achsah as wife." 13 And Othniel the son of Kenaz, Caleb's younger brother, took it; so he gave him his daughter Achsah as wife. 14 Now it happened, when she came *to him,* that she urged him[a] to ask her father for a field. And she dismounted from *her* donkey, and Caleb said to her, "What do you wish?" 15 So she said to him, "Give me a blessing; since you have given me land in the South, give me also springs of water."

And Caleb gave her the upper springs and the lower springs.

16 Now the children of the Kenite, Moses' father-in-law, went up from the City of Palms with the children of Judah into the Wilderness of Judah, which *lies* in the South *near* Arad; and they went and dwelt among the people. 17 And Judah went with his brother Simeon, and they attacked the Canaanites who inhabited Zephath, and utterly destroyed it. So the name of the city was called Hormah. 18 Also Judah took Gaza with its territory, Ashkelon with its territory, and Ekron with its territory. 19 So the LORD was with Judah. And they drove out the mountaineers, but they could not drive out the inhabitants of the lowland, because they had chariots of iron. 20 And they gave Hebron to Caleb, as Moses had said. Then he expelled from there the three sons of Anak. 21 But the children of Benjamin did not drive out the Jebusites who inhabited Jerusalem; so the Jebusites dwell with the children of Benjamin in Jerusalem to this day.

22 And the house of Joseph also went up against Bethel, and the LORD *was* with them. 23 So the house of Joseph sent men to spy out Bethel. (The name of the city *was* formerly Luz.) 24 And when the spies saw a man coming out of the city, they said to him, "Please show us the entrance to the city, and we will show you mercy." 25 So he showed them the entrance to the city, and they struck the city with the edge of the

---

1:9 [a]Hebrew *Negev,* and so throughout this book
1:14 [a]Septuagint and Vulgate read *he urged her.*

sword; but they let the man and all his family go. ²⁶And the man went to the land of the Hittites, built a city, and called its name Luz, which *is* its name to this day.

Incomplete Conquest of the Land

²⁷However, Manasseh did not drive out *the inhabitants of* Beth Shean and its villages, or Taanach and its villages, or the inhabitants of Dor and its villages, or the inhabitants of Ibleam and its villages, or the inhabitants of Megiddo and its villages; for the Canaanites were determined to dwell in that land. ²⁸And it came to pass, when Israel was strong, that they put the Canaanites under tribute, but did not completely drive them out.

²⁹Nor did Ephraim drive out the Canaanites who dwelt in Gezer; so the Canaanites dwelt in Gezer among them.

³⁰Nor did Zebulun drive out the inhabitants of Kitron or the inhabitants of Nahalol; so the Canaanites dwelt among them, and were put under tribute.

³¹Nor did Asher drive out the inhabitants of Acco or the inhabitants of Sidon, or of Ahlab, Achzib, Helbah, Aphik, or Rehob. ³²So the Asherites dwelt among the Canaanites, the inhabitants of the land; for they did not drive them out.

³³Nor did Naphtali drive out the inhabitants of Beth Shemesh or the inhabitants of Beth Anath; but they dwelt among the Canaanites, the inhabitants of the land. Nevertheless the inhabitants of Beth Shemesh and Beth Anath were put under tribute to them.

³⁴And the Amorites forced the children of Dan into the mountains, for they would not allow them to come down to the valley; ³⁵and the Amorites were determined to dwell in Mount Heres, in Aijalon, and in Shaalbim;ᵃ yet when the strength of the house of Joseph became greater, they were put under tribute.

³⁶Now the boundary of the Amorites *was* from the Ascent of Akrabbim, from Sela, and upward.

Israel's Disobedience

2 Then the Angel of the LORD came up from Gilgal to Bochim, and said: "I led you up from Egypt and brought you to the land of which I swore to your fathers; and I said, 'I will never break My covenant with you. ²And you shall make no covenant with the inhabitants of this land; you shall tear down their altars.' But you have not obeyed My voice. Why have you done this? ³Therefore I also said, 'I will not drive them out before you; but they shall be *thorns* in your side,ᵃ and their gods shall be a snare to you.'" ⁴So it was, when the Angel of the LORD spoke these words to all the children of Israel, that the people lifted up their voices and wept.

⁵Then they called the name of that place Bochim;ᵃ and they sacrificed there to the LORD. ⁶And when Joshua had dismissed the people, the children of Israel went each to his own inheritance to possess the land.

Death of Joshua

⁷So the people served the LORD all the days of Joshua, and all the days of the elders who outlived Joshua, who had seen all the great works of the LORD which He had done for Israel. ⁸Now Joshua the son of Nun, the servant of the LORD, died *when he was* one hundred and ten years old. ⁹And they buried him within the border of his inheritance at Timnath Heres, in the mountains of Ephraim, on the north side of Mount Gaash. ¹⁰When all that generation had been gathered to their fathers, another generation arose after them who did not know the LORD nor the work which He had done for Israel.

Israel's Unfaithfulness

¹¹Then the children of Israel did evil in the sight of the LORD, and served the Baals; ¹²and they forsook the LORD God of their fathers, who had brought them out of the land of Egypt; and they followed other gods from *among* the gods of the people who *were* all around them, and they bowed down to them; and they provoked the LORD to anger. ¹³They forsook the LORD and served Baal and the Ashtoreths.ᵃ ¹⁴And the anger of the

---

1:35 ᵃSpelled *Shaalabbin* in Joshua 19:42
2:3 ᵃSeptuagint, Targum, and Vulgate read *enemies to you.*   **2:5** ᵃLiterally *Weeping*   **2:13** ᵃCanaanite goddesses

LORD was hot against Israel. So He delivered them into the hands of plunderers who despoiled them; and He sold them into the hands of their enemies all around, so that they could no longer stand before their enemies. [15]Wherever they went out, the hand of the LORD was against them for calamity, as the LORD had said, and as the LORD had sworn to them. And they were greatly distressed.

[16]Nevertheless, the LORD raised up judges who delivered them out of the hand of those who plundered them. [17]Yet they would not listen to their judges, but they played the harlot with other gods, and bowed down to them. They turned quickly from the way in which their fathers walked, in obeying the commandments of the LORD; they did not do so. [18]And when the LORD raised up judges for them, the LORD was with the judge and delivered them out of the hand of their enemies all the days of the judge; for the LORD was moved to pity by their groaning because of those who oppressed them and harassed them. [19]And it came to pass, when the judge was dead, that they reverted and behaved more corruptly than their fathers, by following other gods, to serve them and bow down to them. They did not cease from their own doings nor from their stubborn way.

[20]Then the anger of the LORD was hot against Israel; and He said, "Because this nation has transgressed My covenant which I commanded their fathers, and has not heeded My voice, [21]I also will no longer drive out before them any of the nations which Joshua left when he died, [22]so that through them I may test Israel, whether they will keep the ways of the LORD, to walk in them as their fathers kept *them,* or not." [23]Therefore the LORD left those nations, without driving them out immediately; nor did He deliver them into the hand of Joshua.

The Nations Remaining in the Land

3 Now these *are* the nations which the LORD left, that He might test Israel by them, *that is,* all who had not known any of the wars in Canaan [2](*this was* only so that the generations of the children of Israel might be taught to know war, at least those who had not formerly known it), [3]*namely,* five lords of the Philistines, all the Canaanites, the Sidonians, and the Hivites who dwelt in Mount Lebanon, from Mount Baal Hermon to the entrance of Hamath. [4]And they were *left, that He might* test Israel by them, to know whether they would obey the commandments of the LORD, which He had commanded their fathers by the hand of Moses.

[5]Thus the children of Israel dwelt among the Canaanites, the Hittites, the Amorites, the Perizzites, the Hivites, and the Jebusites. [6]And they took their daughters to be their wives, and gave their daughters to their sons; and they served their gods.

Othniel

[7]So the children of Israel did evil in the sight of the LORD. They forgot the LORD their God, and served the Baals and Asherahs.[a] [8]Therefore the anger of the LORD was hot against Israel, and He sold them into the hand of Cushan-Rishathaim king of Mesopotamia; and the children of Israel served Cushan-Rishathaim eight years. [9]When the children of Israel cried out to the LORD, the LORD raised up a deliverer for the children of Israel, who delivered them: Othniel the son of Kenaz, Caleb's younger brother. [10]The Spirit of the LORD came upon him, and he judged Israel. He went out to war, and the LORD delivered Cushan-Rishathaim king of Mesopotamia into his hand; and his hand prevailed over Cushan-Rishathaim. [11]So the land had rest for forty years. Then Othniel the son of Kenaz died.

Ehud

[12]And the children of Israel again did evil in the sight of the LORD. So the LORD strengthened Eglon king of Moab against Israel, because they had done evil in the sight of the LORD. [13]Then he gathered to himself the people of Ammon and Amalek, went and defeated Israel, and took possession of the City of Palms. [14]So the children of Israel served Eglon king of Moab eighteen years.

3:7 [a]Name or symbol for Canaanite goddesses

¹⁵But when the children of Israel cried out to the Lord, the Lord raised up a deliverer for them: Ehud the son of Gera, the Benjamite, a left-handed man. By him the children of Israel sent tribute to Eglon king of Moab. ¹⁶Now Ehud made himself a dagger (it was double-edged and a cubit in length) and fastened it under his clothes on his right thigh. ¹⁷So he brought the tribute to Eglon king of Moab. (Now Eglon *was* a very fat man.) ¹⁸And when he had finished presenting the tribute, he sent away the people who had carried the tribute. ¹⁹But he himself turned back from the stone images that *were* at Gilgal, and said, "I have a secret message for you, O king."

He said, "Keep silence!" And all who attended him went out from him.

²⁰So Ehud came to him (now he was sitting upstairs in his cool private chamber). Then Ehud said, "I have a message from God for you." So he arose from *his* seat. ²¹Then Ehud reached with his left hand, took the dagger from his right thigh, and thrust it into his belly. ²²Even the hilt went in after the blade, and the fat closed over the blade, for he did not draw the dagger out of his belly; and his entrails came out. ²³Then Ehud went out through the porch and shut the doors of the upper room behind him and locked them.

²⁴When he had gone out, *Eglon's*ᵃ servants came to look, and *to their* surprise, the doors of the upper room were locked. So they said, "He is probably attending to his needs in the cool chamber." ²⁵So they waited till they were embarrassed, and still he had not opened the doors of the upper room. Therefore they took the key and opened *them*. And there was their master, fallen dead on the floor.

²⁶But Ehud had escaped while they delayed, and passed beyond the stone images and escaped to Seirah. ²⁷And it happened, when he arrived, that he blew the trumpet in the mountains of Ephraim, and the children of Israel went down with him from the mountains; and he led them. ²⁸Then he said to them, "Follow *me,* for the Lord has delivered your enemies the Moabites into your hand." So they went down after him, seized the fords of the Jordan leading to Moab, and did not allow anyone to cross over. ²⁹And at that time they killed about ten thousand men of Moab, all stout men of valor; not a man escaped. ³⁰So Moab was subdued that day under the hand of Israel. And the land had rest for eighty years.

Shamgar

³¹After him was Shamgar the son of Anath, who killed six hundred men of the Philistines with an ox goad; and he also delivered Israel.

Deborah

4 When Ehud was dead, the children of Israel again did evil in the sight of the Lord. ²So the Lord sold them into the hand of Jabin king of Canaan, who reigned in Hazor. The commander of his army *was* Sisera, who dwelt in Harosheth Hagoyim. ³And the children of Israel cried out to the Lord; for Jabin had nine hundred chariots of iron, and for twenty years he had harshly oppressed the children of Israel.

⁴Now Deborah, a prophetess, the wife of Lapidoth, was judging Israel at that time. ⁵And she would sit under the palm tree of Deborah between Ramah and Bethel in the mountains of Ephraim. And the children of Israel came up to her for judgment. ⁶Then she sent and called for Barak the son of Abinoam from Kedesh in Naphtali, and said to him, "Has not the Lord God of Israel commanded, 'Go and deploy *troops* at Mount Tabor; take with you ten thousand men of the sons of Naphtali and of the sons of Zebulun; ⁷and against you I will deploy Sisera, the commander of Jabin's army, with his chariots and his multitude at the River Kishon; and I will deliver him into your hand'?"

⁸And Barak said to her, "If you will go with me, then I will go; but if you will not go with me, I will not go!"

⁹So she said, "I will surely go with you; nevertheless there will be no glory for you in the journey you are taking, for the Lord will sell Sisera into the hand of a woman." Then Deborah arose and went with Barak

---

3:24 ᵃLiterally *his*

to Kedesh. [10]And Barak called Zebulun and Naphtali to Kedesh; he went up with ten thousand men under his command,[a] and Deborah went up with him.

[11]Now Heber the Kenite, of the children of Hobab the father-in-law of Moses, had separated himself from the Kenites and pitched his tent near the terebinth tree at Zaanaim, which *is* beside Kedesh.

[12]And they reported to Sisera that Barak the son of Abinoam had gone up to Mount Tabor. [13]So Sisera gathered together all his chariots, nine hundred chariots of iron, and all the people who *were* with him, from Harosheth Hagoyim to the River Kishon.

[14]Then Deborah said to Barak, "Up! For this *is* the day in which the LORD has delivered Sisera into your hand. Has not the LORD gone out before you?" So Barak went down from Mount Tabor with ten thousand men following him. [15]And the LORD routed Sisera and all *his* chariots and all *his* army with the edge of the sword before Barak; and Sisera alighted from *his* chariot and fled away on foot. [16]But Barak pursued the chariots and the army as far as Harosheth Hagoyim, and all the army of Sisera fell by the edge of the sword; not a man was left.

[17]However, Sisera had fled away on foot to the tent of Jael, the wife of Heber the Kenite; for *there was* peace between Jabin king of Hazor and the house of Heber the Kenite. [18]And Jael went out to meet Sisera, and said to him, "Turn aside, my lord, turn aside to me; do not fear." And when he had turned aside with her into the tent, she covered him with a blanket.

[19]Then he said to her, "Please give me a little water to drink, for I am thirsty." So she opened a jug of milk, gave him a drink, and covered him. [20]And he said to her, "Stand at the door of the tent, and if any man comes and inquires of you, and says, 'Is there any man here?' you shall say, 'No.'"

[21]Then Jael, Heber's wife, took a tent peg and took a hammer in her hand, and went softly to him and drove the peg into his temple, and it went down into the ground; for he was fast asleep and weary. So he died. [22]And then, as Barak pursued Sisera, Jael came out to meet him, and said to him, "Come, I will show you the man whom you seek." And when he went into her *tent,* there lay Sisera, dead with the peg in his temple.

[23]So on that day God subdued Jabin king of Canaan in the presence of the children of Israel. [24]And the hand of the children of Israel grew stronger and stronger against Jabin king of Canaan, until they had destroyed Jabin king of Canaan.

The Song of Deborah

5 Then Deborah and Barak the son of Abinoam sang on that day, saying:

2 "When leaders lead in Israel,
　　When the people willingly offer
　　　　themselves,
　　Bless the LORD!

3 "Hear, O kings! Give ear, O princes!
　　I, *even* I, will sing to the LORD;
　　I will sing praise to the LORD God
　　　　of Israel.

4 "LORD, when You went out from Seir,
　　When You marched from the field
　　　　of Edom,
　　The earth trembled and the heavens
　　　　poured,
　　The clouds also poured water;
5 　The mountains gushed before the
　　　　LORD,
　　This Sinai, before the LORD God of
　　　　Israel.

6 "In the days of Shamgar, son of Anath,
　　In the days of Jael,
　　The highways were deserted,
　　And the travelers walked along the
　　　　byways.
7 　Village life ceased, it ceased in Israel,
　　Until I, Deborah, arose,
　　Arose a mother in Israel.
8 　They chose new gods;
　　Then *there was* war in the gates;
　　Not a shield or spear was seen among
　　　　forty thousand in Israel.
9 　My heart *is* with the rulers of Israel
　　Who offered themselves willingly
　　　　with the people.
　　Bless the LORD!

4:10 [a]Literally *at his feet*

WOMEN in the REVOLUTIONARY WAR

COURAGE

It was not unusual to see women on the battlefield during the Revolutionary War, particularly as camp followers, who mostly came from poor families that were reduced to homelessness without their husband's income. Camp followers would perform the army's mundane but vital chores of cooking, doing laundry and mending, carrying water, loading weapons, and nursing the wounded. Though not in uniform, these women shared soldiers' hardships, including inadequate housing and little compensation.

Margaret Corbin, for instance, followed her husband, John, when he joined the Continental Army in 1776. During the Battle of Fort Washington in 1776, an artillery bombardment fatally wounded John, who manned one of the two cannons. Seeing him dead, she took his place, firing the cannon until she also was severely wounded. Three years later, she became the first woman in the United States to receive a pension from Congress.

Deborah Sampson Gannett was the first known American woman to impersonate a man in order to join the army and take part in combat. She fought in several skirmishes and took musket balls in her thigh and a huge cut on her forehead from a bullet. Her secret was discovered after she came down with a malignant fever. After the war, Sampson requested equal payment for her service and received a pension that matched that of the men who fought.

Women also served as spies during the Revolutionary War, alerting American troops to enemy movement, carrying messages and contraband. For instance, Ann Simpson Davis was handpicked by General Washington to carry messages to his generals while the army was in eastern Pennsylvania. Davis was an accomplished horsewoman and slipped through areas occupied by the British army unnoticed. She carried secret orders in sacks of grain and sometimes in her clothing to various mills around Philadelphia and Bucks Country. Davis received a letter of commendation for her services from General Washington.

10 "Speak, you who ride on white donkeys,
    Who sit in judges' attire,
    And who walk along the road.
11 Far from the noise of the archers,
      among the watering places,
    There they shall recount the righteous
      acts of the LORD,
    The righteous acts *for* His villagers in
      Israel;
    Then the people of the LORD shall go
      down to the gates.

12 "Awake, awake, Deborah!
    Awake, awake, sing a song!
    Arise, Barak, and lead your captives
      away,
    O son of Abinoam!

13 "Then the survivors came down, the
      people against the nobles;
    The LORD came down for me against
      the mighty.
14 From Ephraim *were* those whose roots
      were in Amalek.
    After you, Benjamin, with your peoples,
    From Machir rulers came down,
    And from Zebulun those who bear
      the recruiter's staff.
15 And the princes of Issachar[a] *were*
      with Deborah;
    As Issachar, so *was* Barak
    Sent into the valley under his
      command;[b]
    Among the divisions of Reuben
    There were great resolves of heart.
16 Why did you sit among the sheepfolds,
    To hear the pipings for the flocks?
    The divisions of Reuben have great
      searchings of heart.
17 Gilead stayed beyond the Jordan,
    And why did Dan remain on ships?[a]
    Asher continued at the seashore,
    And stayed by his inlets.
18 Zebulun *is* a people *who* jeopardized
      their lives to the point of death,
    Naphtali also, on the heights of the
      battlefield.

19 "The kings came *and* fought,
    Then the kings of Canaan fought
    In Taanach, by the waters of Megiddo;
    They took no spoils of silver.

20 They fought from the heavens;
    The stars from their courses fought
      against Sisera.
21 The torrent of Kishon swept them away,
    That ancient torrent, the torrent of
      Kishon.
    O my soul, march on in strength!
22 Then the horses' hooves pounded,
    The galloping, galloping of his steeds.
23 'Curse Meroz,' said the angel[a] of the
      LORD,
    'Curse its inhabitants bitterly,
    Because they did not come to the help
      of the LORD,
    To the help of the LORD against the
      mighty.'

24 "Most blessed among women is Jael,
    The wife of Heber the Kenite;
    Blessed is she among women in tents.
25 He asked for water, she gave milk;
    She brought out cream in a lordly bowl.
26 She stretched her hand to the tent peg,
    Her right hand to the workmen's
      hammer;
    She pounded Sisera, she pierced his
      head,
    She split and struck through his temple.
27 At her feet he sank, he fell, he lay still;
    At her feet he sank, he fell;
    Where he sank, there he fell dead.

28 "The mother of Sisera looked through
      the window,
    And cried out through the lattice,
    'Why is his chariot *so* long in coming?
    Why tarries the clatter of his chariots?'
29 Her wisest ladies answered her,
    Yes, she answered herself,
30 'Are they not finding and dividing the
      spoil:
    To every man a girl *or* two;
    For Sisera, plunder of dyed garments,
    Plunder of garments embroidered and
      dyed,
    Two pieces of dyed embroidery for the
      neck of the looter?'

5:15 [a]Following Septuagint, Syriac, Targum, and Vulgate; Masoretic Text reads *And my princes in Issachar.* [b]Literally *at his feet*   **5:17** [a]Or *at ease*
5:23 [a]Or *Angel*

31 "Thus let all Your enemies perish,
　　O LORD!
　But *let* those who love Him *be* like
　　the sun
　When it comes out in full strength."

So the land had rest for forty years.

Midianites Oppress Israel

6 Then the children of Israel did evil in
the sight of the LORD. So the LORD delivered them into the hand of Midian for
seven years, 2and the hand of Midian prevailed against Israel. Because of the Midianites, the children of Israel made for
themselves the dens, the caves, and the
strongholds which *are* in the mountains.
3So it was, whenever Israel had sown, Midianites would come up; also Amalekites
and the people of the East would come up
against them. 4Then they would encamp
against them and destroy the produce of
the earth as far as Gaza, and leave no sustenance for Israel, neither sheep nor ox nor
donkey. 5For they would come up with
their livestock and their tents, coming in as
numerous as locusts; both they and their
camels were without number; and they
would enter the land to destroy it. 6So
Israel was greatly impoverished because of
the Midianites, and the children of Israel
cried out to the LORD.

7And it came to pass, when the children
of Israel cried out to the LORD because of
the Midianites, 8that the LORD sent a
prophet to the children of Israel, who said
to them, "Thus says the LORD God of Israel:
'I brought you up from Egypt and brought
you out of the house of bondage; 9and I
delivered you out of the hand of the Egyptians and out of the hand of all who
oppressed you, and drove them out before
you and gave you their land. 10Also I said
to you, "I *am* the LORD your God; do not fear
the gods of the Amorites, in whose land you
dwell." But you have not obeyed My voice.'"

Gideon

11Now the Angel of the LORD came and
sat under the terebinth tree which *was* in
Ophrah, which *belonged* to Joash the
Abiezrite, while his son Gideon threshed

wheat in the winepress, in order to hide *it*
from the Midianites. 12And the Angel of the
LORD appeared to him, and said to him,
"The LORD *is* with you, you mighty man of
valor!"

13Gideon said to Him, "O my lord,ᵃ if the
LORD is with us, why then has all this happened to us? And where *are* all His miracles
which our fathers told us about, saying,
'Did not the LORD bring us up from Egypt?'
But now the LORD has forsaken us and delivered us into the hands of the Midianites."

14Then the LORD turned to him and said,
"Go in this might of yours, and you shall
save Israel from the hand of the Midianites. Have I not sent you?"

15So he said to Him, "O my Lord,ᵃ how
can I save Israel? Indeed my clan *is* the
weakest in Manasseh, and I *am* the least in
my father's house."

16And the LORD said to him, "Surely I will
be with you, and you shall defeat the Midianites as one man."

17Then he said to Him, "If now I have
found favor in Your sight, then show me a
sign that it is You who talk with me. 18Do
not depart from here, I pray, until I come
to You and bring out my offering and set *it*
before You."

And He said, "I will wait until you come
back."

19So Gideon went in and prepared a
young goat, and unleavened bread from
an ephah of flour. The meat he put in a
basket, and he put the broth in a pot; and
he brought *them* out to Him under the terebinth tree and presented *them*. 20The Angel
of God said to him, "Take the meat and the
unleavened bread and lay *them* on this rock,
and pour out the broth." And he did so.

21Then the Angel of the LORD put out the
end of the staff that *was* in His hand, and
touched the meat and the unleavened
bread; and fire rose out of the rock and
consumed the meat and the unleavened
bread. And the Angel of the LORD departed
out of his sight.

22Now Gideon perceived that He *was* the
Angel of the LORD. So Gideon said, "Alas, O

6:13 ᵃHebrew *adoni,* used of man　　**6:15** ᵃHebrew
Adonai, used of God

Lord GOD! For I have seen the Angel of the LORD face to face."

23Then the LORD said to him, "Peace *be* with you; do not fear, you shall not die." 24So Gideon built an altar there to the LORD, and called it The-LORD-*Is*-Peace.ª To this day it *is* still in Ophrah of the Abiezrites.

25Now it came to pass the same night that the LORD said to him, "Take your father's young bull, the second bull of seven years old, and tear down the altar of Baal that your father has, and cut down the wooden imageª that *is* beside it; 26and build an altar to the LORD your God on top of this rock in the proper arrangement, and take the second bull and offer a burnt sacrifice with the wood of the image which you shall cut down." 27So Gideon took ten men from among his servants and did as the LORD had said to him. But because he feared his father's household and the men of the city too much to do *it* by day, he did *it* by night.

Gideon Destroys the Altar of Baal

28And when the men of the city arose early in the morning, there was the altar of Baal, torn down; and the wooden image that *was* beside it was cut down, and the second bull was being offered on the altar *which had been* built. 29So they said to one another, "Who has done this thing?" And when they had inquired and asked, they said, "Gideon the son of Joash has done this thing." 30Then the men of the city said to Joash, "Bring out your son, that he may die, because he has torn down the altar of Baal, and because he has cut down the wooden image that *was* beside it."

31But Joash said to all who stood against him, "Would you plead for Baal? Would you save him? Let the one who would plead for him be put to death by morning! If he *is* a

---

6:24 ªHebrew *YHWH Shalom*   **6:25** ªHebrew *Asherah,* a Canaanite goddess

---

COURAGE

"The LORD is with you, you mighty man of valor!"

JUDGES 6:12

Francis Marion, left,
and a British officer

FRANCIS MARION, THE "SWAMP FOX"

Francis Marion (1732–1795) was a brigadier general in the South Carolina Militia during the American Revolutionary War. He became known as the "Swamp Fox" because he set up his base of operations in a swamp. "Marion's Brigade" was a volunteer force that could assemble at a moment's notice, hit British and Loyalist units and garrisons, and then disappear into the swamps. He is considered one of the fathers of modern guerrilla warfare.

While the British occupied most of the southern colonies, large-scale resistance was impossible. Marion and his patriot unit was a powerful force in the south, as Nathanael Greene later wrote in praise: "Surrounded on every side with a superior force, hunted from every quarter with veteran troops, you have found means to elude their attempts and keep alive the expiring hopes of an oppressed militia."

After the war, Marion served in the state senate of South Carolina for several terms. He stated: "Who can doubt that God created us to be happy, and thereto made us to love one another? It is plainly written as the Gospel. The heart is sometimes so embittered that nothing but Divine love can sweeten it, so enraged that devotion can only becalm it, and so broken down that it takes all the forces of heavenly hope to raise it. In short, the religion of Jesus Christ is the only sure and controlling power over sin."

god, let him plead for himself, because his altar has been torn down!" [32]Therefore on that day he called him Jerubbaal,[a] saying, "Let Baal plead against him, because he has torn down his altar."

[33]Then all the Midianites and Amalekites, the people of the East, gathered together; and they crossed over and encamped in the Valley of Jezreel. [34]But the Spirit of the LORD came upon Gideon; then he blew the trumpet, and the Abiezrites gathered behind him. [35]And he sent messengers throughout all Manasseh, who also gathered behind him. He also sent messengers to Asher, Zebulun, and Naphtali; and they came up to meet them.

The Sign of the Fleece

[36]So Gideon said to God, "If You will save Israel by my hand as You have said— [37]look, I shall put a fleece of wool on the threshing floor; if there is dew on the fleece only, and *it is* dry on all the ground, then I shall know that You will save Israel by my hand, as You have said." [38]And it was so. When he rose early the next morning and squeezed the fleece together, he wrung the dew out of the fleece, a bowlful of water. [39]Then Gideon said to God, "Do not be angry with me, but let me speak just once more: Let me test, I pray, just once more with the fleece; let it now be dry only on the fleece, but on all the ground let there be dew." [40]And God did so that night. It was dry on the fleece only, but there was dew on all the ground.

Gideon's Valiant Three Hundred

7 Then Jerubbaal (that *is,* Gideon) and all the people who *were* with him rose early and encamped beside the well of Harod, so that the camp of the Midianites was on the north side of them by the hill of Moreh in the valley.

[2]And the LORD said to Gideon, "The people who *are* with you *are* too many for Me to give the Midianites into their hands, lest Israel claim glory for itself against Me, saying, 'My own hand has saved me.' [3]Now therefore, proclaim in the hearing of the people, saying, 'Whoever *is* fearful and afraid, let him turn and depart at once from Mount Gilead.'" And twenty-two thousand of the people returned, and ten thousand remained.

[4]But the LORD said to Gideon, "The people *are* still *too* many; bring them down to the water, and I will test them for you there. Then it will be, *that* of whom I say to you, 'This one shall go with you,' the same shall go with you; and of whomever I say to you, 'This one shall not go with you,' the same shall not go." [5]So he brought the people down to the water. And the LORD said to Gideon, "Everyone who laps from the water with his tongue, as a dog laps, you shall set apart by himself; likewise everyone who gets down on his knees to drink." [6]And the number of those who lapped, *putting* their hand to their mouth, was three hundred men; but all the rest of the people got down on their knees to drink water. [7]Then the LORD said to Gideon, "By the three hundred men who lapped I will save you, and deliver the Midianites into your hand. Let all the *other* people go, every man to his place." [8]So the people took provisions and their trumpets in their hands. And he sent away all *the rest of* Israel, every man to his tent, and retained those three hundred men. Now the camp of Midian was below him in the valley.

[9]It happened on the same night that the LORD said to him, "Arise, go down against the camp, for I have delivered it into your hand. [10]But if you are afraid to go down, go down to the camp with Purah your servant, [11]and you shall hear what they say; and afterward your hands shall be strengthened to go down against the camp." Then he went down with Purah his servant to the outpost of the armed men who *were* in the camp. [12]Now the Midianites and Amalekites, all the people of the East, were lying in the valley as numerous as locusts; and their camels *were* without number, as the sand by the seashore in multitude.

[13]And when Gideon had come, there was a man telling a dream to his companion. He said, "I have had a dream: *To my* surprise, a loaf of barley bread tumbled into the camp of Midian; it came to a tent and struck it so that it fell and overturned, and the tent collapsed."

6:32 [a]Literally *Let Baal Plead*

¹⁴Then his companion answered and said, "This *is* nothing else but the sword of Gideon the son of Joash, a man of Israel! Into his hand God has delivered Midian and the whole camp."

¹⁵And so it was, when Gideon heard the telling of the dream and its interpretation, that he worshiped. He returned to the camp of Israel, and said, "Arise, for the Lord has delivered the camp of Midian into your hand." ¹⁶Then he divided the three hundred men *into* three companies, and he put a trumpet into every man's hand, with empty pitchers, and torches inside the pitchers. ¹⁷And he said to them, "Look at me and do likewise; watch, and when I come to the edge of the camp you shall do as I do: ¹⁸When I blow the trumpet, I and all who *are* with me, then you also blow the trumpets on every side of the whole camp, and say, '*The sword of* the Lord and of Gideon!'"

¹⁹So Gideon and the hundred men who *were* with him came to the outpost of the camp at the beginning of the middle watch, just as they had posted the watch; and they blew the trumpets and broke the pitchers that *were* in their hands. ²⁰Then the three companies blew the trumpets and broke the pitchers—they held the torches in their left hands and the trumpets in their right hands for blowing—and they cried, "The sword of the Lord and of Gideon!" ²¹And every man stood in his place all around the camp; and the whole army ran and cried out and fled. ²²When the three hundred blew the trumpets, the Lord set every man's sword against his companion throughout the whole camp; and the army fled to Beth Acacia,ᵃ toward Zererah, as far as the border of Abel Meholah, by Tabbath.

²³And the men of Israel gathered together from Naphtali, Asher, and all Manasseh, and pursued the Midianites.

²⁴Then Gideon sent messengers throughout all the mountains of Ephraim, saying, "Come down against the Midianites, and seize from them the watering places as far as Beth Barah and the Jordan." Then all the men of Ephraim gathered together and seized the watering places as far as Beth Barah and the Jordan. ²⁵And they captured two princes of the Midianites, Oreb and Zeeb. They killed Oreb at the rock of Oreb, and Zeeb they killed at the winepress of Zeeb. They pursued Midian and brought the heads of Oreb and Zeeb to Gideon on the other side of the Jordan.

Gideon Subdues the Midianites

8 Now the men of Ephraim said to him, "Why have you done this to us by not calling us when you went to fight with the Midianites?" And they reprimanded him sharply.

²So he said to them, "What have I done now in comparison with you? *Is* not the gleaning *of the grapes* of Ephraim better than the vintage of Abiezer? ³God has delivered into your hands the princes of Midian, Oreb and Zeeb. And what was I able to do in comparison with you?" Then their anger toward him subsided when he said that.

⁴When Gideon came to the Jordan, he and the three hundred men who *were* with him crossed over, exhausted but still in pursuit. ⁵Then he said to the men of Succoth, "Please give loaves of bread to the people who follow me, for they are exhausted, and I am pursuing Zebah and Zalmunna, kings of Midian."

⁶And the leaders of Succoth said, "*Are* the hands of Zebah and Zalmunna now in your hand, that we should give bread to your army?"

⁷So Gideon said, "For this cause, when the Lord has delivered Zebah and Zalmunna into my hand, then I will tear your flesh with the thorns of the wilderness and with briers!" ⁸Then he went up from there to Penuel and spoke to them in the same way. And the men of Penuel answered him as the men of Succoth had answered. ⁹So he also spoke to the men of Penuel, saying, "When I come back in peace, I will tear down this tower!"

¹⁰Now Zebah and Zalmunna *were* at Karkor, and their armies with them, about fifteen thousand, all who were left of all the army of the people of the East; for one hundred and twenty thousand men who drew the sword had fallen. ¹¹Then Gideon went up by the road of those who dwell in

---

7:22 ᵃHebrew *Beth Shittah*

tents on the east of Nobah and Jogbehah; and he attacked the army while the camp felt secure. ¹²When Zebah and Zalmunna fled, he pursued them; and he took the two kings of Midian, Zebah and Zalmunna, and routed the whole army.

¹³Then Gideon the son of Joash returned from battle, from the Ascent of Heres. ¹⁴And he caught a young man of the men of Succoth and interrogated him; and he wrote down for him the leaders of Succoth and its elders, seventy-seven men. ¹⁵Then he came to the men of Succoth and said, "Here are Zebah and Zalmunna, about whom you ridiculed me, saying, '*Are* the hands of Zebah and Zalmunna now in your hand, that we should give bread to your weary men?'" ¹⁶And he took the elders of the city, and thorns of the wilderness and briers, and with them he taught the men of Succoth. ¹⁷Then he tore down the tower of Penuel and killed the men of the city.

¹⁸And he said to Zebah and Zalmunna, "What kind of men *were they* whom you killed at Tabor?"

So they answered, "As you *are,* so *were* they; each one resembled the son of a king."

¹⁹Then he said, "They *were* my brothers, the sons of my mother. *As* the LORD lives, if you had let them live, I would not kill you." ²⁰And he said to Jether his firstborn, "Rise, kill them!" But the youth would not draw his sword; for he was afraid, because he *was* still a youth.

²¹So Zebah and Zalmunna said, "Rise yourself, and kill us; for as a man *is, so is* his strength." So Gideon arose and killed Zebah and Zalmunna, and took the crescent ornaments that *were* on their camels' necks.

Gideon's Ephod

²²Then the men of Israel said to Gideon, "Rule over us, both you and your son, and your grandson also; for you have delivered us from the hand of Midian."

²³But Gideon said to them, "I will not rule over you, nor shall my son rule over you; the LORD shall rule over you." ²⁴Then Gideon said to them, "I would like to make a request of you, that each of you would give me the earrings from his plunder." For they had golden earrings, because they *were* Ishmaelites.

²⁵So they answered, "We will gladly give *them.*" And they spread out a garment, and each man threw into it the earrings from his plunder. ²⁶Now the weight of the gold earrings that he requested was one thousand seven hundred *shekels* of gold, besides the crescent ornaments, pendants, and purple robes which *were* on the kings of Midian, and besides the chains that *were* around their camels' necks. ²⁷Then Gideon made it into an ephod and set it up in his city, Ophrah. And all Israel played the harlot with it there. It became a snare to Gideon and to his house.

²⁸Thus Midian was subdued before the children of Israel, so that they lifted their heads no more. And the country was quiet for forty years in the days of Gideon.

Death of Gideon

²⁹Then Jerubbaal the son of Joash went and dwelt in his own house. ³⁰Gideon had seventy sons who were his own offspring, for he had many wives. ³¹And his concubine who *was* in Shechem also bore him a son, whose name he called Abimelech. ³²Now Gideon the son of Joash died at a good old age, and was buried in the tomb of Joash his father, in Ophrah of the Abiezrites.

³³So it was, as soon as Gideon was dead, that the children of Israel again played the harlot with the Baals, and made Baal-Berith their god. ³⁴Thus the children of Israel did not remember the LORD their God, who had delivered them from the hands of all their enemies on every side; ³⁵nor did they show kindness to the house of Jerubbaal (Gideon) in accordance with the good he had done for Israel.

Abimelech's Conspiracy

9 Then Abimelech the son of Jerubbaal went to Shechem, to his mother's brothers, and spoke with them and with all the family of the house of his mother's father, saying, ²"Please speak in the hearing of all the men of Shechem: 'Which is better for you, that all seventy of the sons of Jerubbaal reign over you, or that one reign over

you?' Remember that I *am* your own flesh and bone."

3And his mother's brothers spoke all these words concerning him in the hearing of all the men of Shechem; and their heart was inclined to follow Abimelech, for they said, "He is our brother." 4So they gave him seventy *shekels* of silver from the temple of Baal-Berith, with which Abimelech hired worthless and reckless men; and they followed him. 5Then he went to his father's house at Ophrah and killed his brothers, the seventy sons of Jerubbaal, on one stone. But Jotham the youngest son of Jerubbaal was left, because he hid himself. 6And all the men of Shechem gathered together, all of Beth Millo, and they went and made Abimelech king beside the terebinth tree at the pillar that *was* in Shechem.

The Parable of the Trees

7Now when they told Jotham, he went and stood on top of Mount Gerizim, and lifted his voice and cried out. And he said to them:

"Listen to me, you men of Shechem,
  That God may listen to you!

8 "The trees once went forth to anoint
    a king over them.
  And they said to the olive tree,
  'Reign over us!'
9 But the olive tree said to them,
  'Should I cease giving my oil,
  With which they honor God and
    men,
  And go to sway over trees?'

10 "Then the trees said to the fig tree,
  'You come *and* reign over us!'
11 But the fig tree said to them,
  'Should I cease my sweetness and
    my good fruit,
  And go to sway over trees?'

12 "Then the trees said to the vine,
  'You come *and* reign over us!'
13 But the vine said to them,
  'Should I cease my new wine,
  Which cheers *both* God and men,
  And go to sway over trees?'

14 "Then all the trees said to the bramble,
  'You come *and* reign over us!'
15 And the bramble said to the trees,
  'If in truth you anoint me as king
    over you,
  Then come *and* take shelter in my
    shade;
  But if not, let fire come out of the
    bramble
  And devour the cedars of Lebanon!'

16"Now therefore, if you have acted in truth and sincerity in making Abimelech king, and if you have dealt well with Jerubbaal and his house, and have done to him as he deserves— 17for my father fought for you, risked his life, and delivered you out of the hand of Midian; 18but you have risen up against my father's house this day, and killed his seventy sons on one stone, and made Abimelech, the son of his female servant, king over the men of Shechem, because he is your brother— 19if then you have acted in truth and sincerity with Jerubbaal and with his house this day, *then* rejoice in Abimelech, and let him also rejoice in you. 20But if not, let fire come from Abimelech and devour the men of Shechem and Beth Millo; and let fire come from the men of Shechem and from Beth Millo and devour Abimelech!" 21And Jotham ran away and fled; and he went to Beer and dwelt there, for fear of Abimelech his brother.

Downfall of Abimelech

22After Abimelech had reigned over Israel three years, 23God sent a spirit of ill will between Abimelech and the men of Shechem; and the men of Shechem dealt treacherously with Abimelech, 24that the crime *done* to the seventy sons of Jerubbaal might be settled and their blood be laid on Abimelech their brother, who killed them, and on the men of Shechem, who aided him in the killing of his brothers. 25And the men of Shechem set men in ambush against him on the tops of the mountains, and they robbed all who passed by them along that way; and it was told Abimelech. 26Now Gaal the son of Ebed came with his brothers and went over to Shechem; and the men of Shechem put their confidence

in him. ²⁷So they went out into the fields, and gathered *grapes* from their vineyards and trod *them,* and made merry. And they went into the house of their god, and ate and drank, and cursed Abimelech. ²⁸Then Gaal the son of Ebed said, "Who *is* Abimelech, and who *is* Shechem, that we should serve him? *Is he* not the son of Jerubbaal, and *is not* Zebul his officer? Serve the men of Hamor the father of Shechem; but why should we serve him? ²⁹If only this people were under my authority!ᵃ Then I would remove Abimelech." So heᵇ said to Abimelech, "Increase your army and come out!"

³⁰When Zebul, the ruler of the city, heard the words of Gaal the son of Ebed, his anger was aroused. ³¹And he sent messengers to Abimelech secretly, saying, "Take note! Gaal the son of Ebed and his brothers have come to Shechem; and here they are, fortifying the city against you. ³²Now therefore, get up by night, you and the people who *are* with you, and lie in wait in the field. ³³And it shall be, as soon as the sun is up in the morning, *that* you shall rise early and rush upon the city; and *when* he and the people who are with him come out against you, you may then do to them as you find opportunity."

³⁴So Abimelech and all the people who *were* with him rose by night, and lay in wait against Shechem in four companies. ³⁵When Gaal the son of Ebed went out and stood in the entrance to the city gate, Abimelech and the people who *were* with him rose from lying in wait. ³⁶And when Gaal saw the people, he said to Zebul, "Look, people are coming down from the tops of the mountains!"

But Zebul said to him, "You see the shadows of the mountains as *if they were* men."

³⁷So Gaal spoke again and said, "See, people are coming down from the center of the land, and another company is coming from the Diviners'ᵃ Terebinth Tree."

³⁸Then Zebul said to him, "Where indeed *is* your mouth now, with which you said, 'Who is Abimelech, that we should serve him?' *Are* not these the people whom you despised? Go out, if you will, and fight with them now."

³⁹So Gaal went out, leading the men of Shechem, and fought with Abimelech.

⁴⁰And Abimelech chased him, and he fled from him; and many fell wounded, to the *very* entrance of the gate. ⁴¹Then Abimelech dwelt at Arumah, and Zebul drove out Gaal and his brothers, so that they would not dwell in Shechem.

⁴²And it came about on the next day that the people went out into the field, and they told Abimelech. ⁴³So he took his people, divided them into three companies, and lay in wait in the field. And he looked, and there were the people, coming out of the city; and he rose against them and attacked them. ⁴⁴Then Abimelech and the company that *was* with him rushed forward and stood at the entrance of the gate of the city; and the *other* two companies rushed upon all who *were* in the fields and killed them. ⁴⁵So Abimelech fought against the city all that day; he took the city and killed the people who *were* in it; and he demolished the city and sowed it with salt.

⁴⁶Now when all the men of the tower of Shechem had heard *that,* they entered the stronghold of the temple of the god Berith. ⁴⁷And it was told Abimelech that all the men of the tower of Shechem were gathered together. ⁴⁸Then Abimelech went up to Mount Zalmon, he and all the people who *were* with him. And Abimelech took an ax in his hand and cut down a bough from the trees, and took it and laid *it* on his shoulder; then he said to the people who were with him, "What you have seen me do, make haste *and* do as I *have done.*" ⁴⁹So each of the people likewise cut down his own bough and followed Abimelech, put *them* against the stronghold, and set the stronghold on fire above them, so that all the people of the tower of Shechem died, about a thousand men and women.

⁵⁰Then Abimelech went to Thebez, and he encamped against Thebez and took it. ⁵¹But there was a strong tower in the city, and all the men and women—all the people of the city—fled there and shut themselves in; then they went up to the top of the tower. ⁵²So Abimelech came as far as the

---

9:29 ᵃLiterally *hand* ᵇFollowing Masoretic Text and Targum; Dead Sea Scrolls read *they;* Septuagint reads *I.*
9:37 ᵃHebrew *Meonenim*

tower and fought against it; and he drew near the door of the tower to burn it with fire. [53]But a certain woman dropped an upper millstone on Abimelech's head and crushed his skull. [54]Then he called quickly to the young man, his armorbearer, and said to him, "Draw your sword and kill me, lest men say of me, 'A woman killed him.'" So his young man thrust him through, and he died. [55]And when the men of Israel saw that Abimelech was dead, they departed, every man to his place.

[56]Thus God repaid the wickedness of Abimelech, which he had done to his father by killing his seventy brothers. [57]And all the evil of the men of Shechem God returned on their own heads, and on them came the curse of Jotham the son of Jerubbaal.

Tola

10 After Abimelech there arose to save Israel Tola the son of Puah, the son of Dodo, a man of Issachar; and he dwelt in Shamir in the mountains of Ephraim. [2]He judged Israel twenty-three years; and he died and was buried in Shamir.

Jair

[3]After him arose Jair, a Gileadite; and he judged Israel twenty-two years. [4]Now he had thirty sons who rode on thirty donkeys; they also had thirty towns, which are called "Havoth Jair"[a] to this day, which are in the land of Gilead. [5]And Jair died and was buried in Camon.

Israel Oppressed Again

[6]Then the children of Israel again did evil in the sight of the LORD, and served the Baals and the Ashtoreths, the gods of Syria, the gods of Sidon, the gods of Moab, the gods of the people of Ammon, and the gods of the Philistines; and they forsook the LORD and did not serve Him. [7]So the anger of the LORD was hot against Israel; and He sold them into the hands of the Philistines and into the hands of the people of Ammon. [8]From that year they harassed and oppressed the children of Israel for eighteen years—all the children of Israel who were on the other side of the Jordan in the land of the Amorites, in Gilead. [9]Moreover the people of Ammon crossed over the Jordan to fight against Judah also, against Benjamin, and against the house of Ephraim, so that Israel was severely distressed.

[10]And the children of Israel cried out to the LORD, saying, "We have sinned against You, because we have both forsaken our God and served the Baals!"

[11]So the LORD said to the children of Israel, "Did I not deliver you from the Egyptians and from the Amorites and from the people of Ammon and from the Philistines? [12]Also the Sidonians and Amalekites and Maonites[a] oppressed you; and you cried out to Me, and I delivered you from their hand. [13]Yet you have forsaken Me and served other gods. Therefore I will deliver you no more. [14]Go and cry out to the gods which you have chosen; let them deliver you in your time of distress."

[15]And the children of Israel said to the LORD, "We have sinned! Do to us whatever seems best to You; only deliver us this day, we pray." [16]So they put away the foreign gods from among them and served the LORD. And His soul could no longer endure the misery of Israel.

[17]Then the people of Ammon gathered together and encamped in Gilead. And the children of Israel assembled together and encamped in Mizpah. [18]And the people, the leaders of Gilead, said to one another, "Who is the man who will begin the fight against the people of Ammon? He shall be head over all the inhabitants of Gilead."

Jephthah

11 Now Jephthah the Gileadite was a mighty man of valor, but he was the son of a harlot; and Gilead begot Jephthah. [2]Gilead's wife bore sons; and when his wife's sons grew up, they drove Jephthah out, and said to him, "You shall have no inheritance in our father's house, for you are the son of another woman." [3]Then Jephthah fled from his brothers and dwelt in the land of Tob; and worthless men banded together with Jephthah and went out raiding with him.

10:4 [a]Literally Towns of Jair (compare Numbers 32:41 and Deuteronomy 3:14)   **10:12** [a]Some Septuagint manuscripts read Midianites.

⁴It came to pass after a time that the people of Ammon made war against Israel. ⁵And so it was, when the people of Ammon made war against Israel, that the elders of Gilead went to get Jephthah from the land of Tob. ⁶Then they said to Jephthah, "Come and be our commander, that we may fight against the people of Ammon."

⁷So Jephthah said to the elders of Gilead, "Did you not hate me, and expel me from my father's house? Why have you come to me now when you are in distress?"

⁸And the elders of Gilead said to Jephthah, "That is why we have turned again to you now, that you may go with us and fight against the people of Ammon, and be our head over all the inhabitants of Gilead."

⁹So Jephthah said to the elders of Gilead, "If you take me back home to fight against the people of Ammon, and the LORD delivers them to me, shall I be your head?"

¹⁰And the elders of Gilead said to Jephthah, "The LORD will be a witness between us, if we do not do according to your words." ¹¹Then Jephthah went with the elders of Gilead, and the people made him head and commander over them; and Jephthah spoke all his words before the LORD in Mizpah.

¹²Now Jephthah sent messengers to the king of the people of Ammon, saying, "What do you have against me, that you have come to fight against me in my land?"

¹³And the king of the people of Ammon answered the messengers of Jephthah, "Because Israel took away my land when they came up out of Egypt, from the Arnon as far as the Jabbok, and to the Jordan. Now therefore, restore those *lands* peaceably."

¹⁴So Jephthah again sent messengers to the king of the people of Ammon, ¹⁵and said to him, "Thus says Jephthah: 'Israel did not take away the land of Moab, nor the land of the people of Ammon; ¹⁶for when Israel came up from Egypt, they walked through the wilderness as far as the Red Sea and came to Kadesh. ¹⁷Then Israel sent messengers to the king of Edom, saying, "Please let me pass through your land." But the king

of Edom would not heed. And in like manner they sent to the king of Moab, but he would not *consent*. So Israel remained in Kadesh. ¹⁸And they went along through the wilderness and bypassed the land of Edom and the land of Moab, came to the east side of the land of Moab, and encamped on the other side of the Arnon. But they did not enter the border of Moab, for the Arnon *was* the border of Moab. ¹⁹Then Israel sent messengers to Sihon king of the Amorites, king of Heshbon; and Israel said to him, "Please let us pass through your land into our place." ²⁰But Sihon did not trust Israel to pass through his territory. So Sihon gathered all his people together, encamped in Jahaz, and fought against Israel. ²¹And the LORD God of Israel delivered Sihon and all his people into the hand of Israel, and they defeated them. Thus Israel gained possession of all the land of the Amorites, who inhabited that country. ²²They took possession of all the territory of the Amorites, from the Arnon to the Jabbok and from the wilderness to the Jordan.

²³'And now the LORD God of Israel has dispossessed the Amorites from before His people Israel; should you then possess it? ²⁴Will you not possess whatever Chemosh your god gives you to possess? So whatever the LORD our God takes possession of before us, we will possess. ²⁵And now, *are* you any better than Balak the son of Zippor, king of Moab? Did he ever strive against Israel? Did he ever fight against them? ²⁶While Israel dwelt in Heshbon and its villages, in Aroer and its villages, and in all the cities along the banks of the Arnon, for three hundred years, why did you not recover *them* within that time? ²⁷Therefore I have not sinned against you, but you wronged me by fighting against me. May the LORD, the Judge, render judgment this day between the children of Israel and the people of Ammon.' " ²⁸However, the king of the people of Ammon did not heed the words which Jephthah sent him.

Jephthah's Vow and Victory

²⁹Then the Spirit of the LORD came upon Jephthah, and he passed through Gilead and Manasseh, and passed through Mizpah

of Gilead; and from Mizpah of Gilead he advanced *toward* the people of Ammon. ³⁰And Jephthah made a vow to the LORD, and said, "If You will indeed deliver the people of Ammon into my hands, ³¹then it will be that whatever comes out of the doors of my house to meet me, when I return in peace from the people of Ammon, shall surely be the LORD's, and I will offer it up as a burnt offering."

³²So Jephthah advanced toward the people of Ammon to fight against them, and the LORD delivered them into his hands. ³³And he defeated them from Aroer as far as Minnith—twenty cities—and to Abel Keramim,ᵃ with a very great slaughter. Thus the people of Ammon were subdued before the children of Israel.

Jephthah's Daughter

³⁴When Jephthah came to his house at Mizpah, there was his daughter, coming out to meet him with timbrels and dancing; and she *was his* only child. Besides her he had neither son nor daughter. ³⁵And it came to pass, when he saw her, that he tore his clothes, and said, "Alas, my daughter! You have brought me very low! You are among those who trouble me! For I have given my word to the LORD, and I cannot go back on it."

³⁶So she said to him, "My father, *if* you have given your word to the LORD, do to me according to what has gone out of your mouth, because the LORD has avenged you of your enemies, the people of Ammon." ³⁷Then she said to her father, "Let this thing be done for me: let me alone for two months, that I may go and wander on the mountains and bewail my virginity, my friends and I."

³⁸So he said, "Go." And he sent her away *for* two months; and she went with her friends, and bewailed her virginity on the mountains. ³⁹And it was so at the end of two months that she returned to her father, and he carried out his vow with her which he had vowed. She knew no man.

And it became a custom in Israel ⁴⁰*that* the daughters of Israel went four days each year to lament the daughter of Jephthah the Gileadite.

Jephthah's Conflict with Ephraim

12 Then the men of Ephraim gathered together, crossed over toward Zaphon, and said to Jephthah, "Why did you cross over to fight against the people of Ammon, and did not call us to go with you? We will burn your house down on you with fire!"

²And Jephthah said to them, "My people and I were in a great struggle with the people of Ammon; and when I called you, you did not deliver me out of their hands. ³So when I saw that you would not deliver *me*, I took my life in my hands and crossed over against the people of Ammon; and the LORD delivered them into my hand. Why then have you come up to me this day to fight against me?" ⁴Now Jephthah gathered together all the men of Gilead and fought against Ephraim. And the men of Gilead defeated Ephraim, because they said, "You Gileadites *are* fugitives of Ephraim among the Ephraimites *and* among the Manassites." ⁵The Gileadites seized the fords of the Jordan before the Ephraimites *arrived*. And when *any* Ephraimite who escaped said, "Let me cross over," the men of Gilead would say to him, "*Are* you an Ephraimite?" If he said, "No," ⁶then they would say to him, "Then say, 'Shibboleth'!" And he would say, "Sibboleth," for he could not pronounce *it* right. Then they would take him and kill him at the fords of the Jordan. There fell at that time forty-two thousand Ephraimites.

⁷And Jephthah judged Israel six years. Then Jephthah the Gileadite died and was buried among the cities of Gilead.

Ibzan, Elon, and Abdon

⁸After him, Ibzan of Bethlehem judged Israel. ⁹He had thirty sons. And he gave away thirty daughters in marriage, and brought in thirty daughters from elsewhere for his sons. He judged Israel seven years. ¹⁰Then Ibzan died and was buried at Bethlehem.

¹¹After him, Elon the Zebulunite judged Israel. He judged Israel ten years. ¹²And Elon the Zebulunite died and was buried at Aijalon in the country of Zebulun.

11:33 ᵃLiterally *Plain of Vineyards*

13After him, Abdon the son of Hillel the Pirathonite judged Israel. 14He had forty sons and thirty grandsons, who rode on seventy young donkeys. He judged Israel eight years. 15Then Abdon the son of Hillel the Pirathonite died and was buried in Pirathon in the land of Ephraim, in the mountains of the Amalekites.

The Birth of Samson

13 Again the children of Israel did evil in the sight of the LORD, and the LORD delivered them into the hand of the Philistines for forty years.

2Now there was a certain man from Zorah, of the family of the Danites, whose name *was* Manoah; and his wife *was* barren and had no children. 3And the Angel of the LORD appeared to the woman and said to her, "Indeed now, you are barren and have borne no children, but you shall conceive and bear a son. 4Now therefore, please be careful not to drink wine or *similar* drink, and not to eat anything unclean. 5For behold, you shall conceive and bear a son. And no razor shall come upon his head, for the child shall be a Nazirite to God from the womb; and he shall begin to deliver Israel out of the hand of the Philistines."

6So the woman came and told her husband, saying, "A Man of God came to me, and His countenance *was* like the countenance of the Angel of God, very awesome; but I did not ask Him where He *was* from, and He did not tell me His name. 7And He said to me, 'Behold, you shall conceive and bear a son. Now drink no wine or *similar* drink, nor eat anything unclean, for the child shall be a Nazirite to God from the womb to the day of his death.' "

8Then Manoah prayed to the LORD, and said, "O my Lord, please let the Man of God whom You sent come to us again and teach us what we shall do for the child who will be born."

9And God listened to the voice of Manoah, and the Angel of God came to the woman again as she was sitting in the field; but Manoah her husband *was* not with her. 10Then the woman ran in haste and told her husband, and said to him,

"Look, the Man who came to me the *other* day has just now appeared to me!"

11So Manoah arose and followed his wife. When he came to the Man, he said to Him, "Are You the Man who spoke to this woman?"

And He said, "I *am.*"

12Manoah said, "Now let Your words come *to pass!* What will be the boy's rule of life, and his work?"

13So the Angel of the LORD said to Manoah, "Of all that I said to the woman let her be careful. 14She may not eat anything that comes from the vine, nor may she drink wine or *similar* drink, nor eat anything unclean. All that I commanded her let her observe."

15Then Manoah said to the Angel of the LORD, "Please let us detain You, and we will prepare a young goat for You."

16And the Angel of the LORD said to Manoah, "Though you detain Me, I will not eat your food. But if you offer a burnt offering, you must offer it to the LORD." (For Manoah did not know He *was* the Angel of the LORD.)

17Then Manoah said to the Angel of the LORD, "What *is* Your name, that when Your words come *to pass* we may honor You?"

18And the Angel of the LORD said to him, "Why do you ask My name, seeing it *is* wonderful?"

19So Manoah took the young goat with the grain offering, and offered it upon the rock to the LORD. And He did a wondrous thing while Manoah and his wife looked on— 20it happened as the flame went up toward heaven from the altar—the Angel of the LORD ascended in the flame of the altar! When Manoah and his wife saw *this,* they fell on their faces to the ground. 21When the Angel of the LORD appeared no more to Manoah and his wife, then Manoah knew that He *was* the Angel of the LORD.

22And Manoah said to his wife, "We shall surely die, because we have seen God!"

23But his wife said to him, "If the LORD had desired to kill us, He would not have accepted a burnt offering and a grain offering from our hands, nor would He have shown us all these *things,* nor would He have told us *such things* as these at this time."

²⁴So the woman bore a son and called his name Samson; and the child grew, and the LORD blessed him. ²⁵And the Spirit of the LORD began to move upon him at Mahaneh Danᵃ between Zorah and Eshtaol.

Samson's Philistine Wife

14 Now Samson went down to Timnah, and saw a woman in Timnah of the daughters of the Philistines. ²So he went up and told his father and mother, saying, "I have seen a woman in Timnah of the daughters of the Philistines; now therefore, get her for me as a wife."

³Then his father and mother said to him, "*Is there* no woman among the daughters of your brethren, or among all my people, that you must go and get a wife from the uncircumcised Philistines?"

And Samson said to his father, "Get her for me, for she pleases me well."

⁴But his father and mother did not know that it was of the LORD—that He was seeking an occasion to move against the Philistines. For at that time the Philistines had dominion over Israel.

⁵So Samson went down to Timnah with his father and mother, and came to the vineyards of Timnah.

Now *to his* surprise, a young lion *came* roaring against him. ⁶And the Spirit of the LORD came mightily upon him, and he tore the lion apart as one would have torn apart a young goat, though *he had* nothing in his hand. But he did not tell his father or his mother what he had done.

⁷Then he went down and talked with the woman; and she pleased Samson well. ⁸After some time, when he returned to get her, he turned aside to see the carcass of the lion. And behold, a swarm of bees and honey *were* in the carcass of the lion. ⁹He took some of it in his hands and went along, eating. When he came to his father and mother, he gave *some* to them, and they also ate. But he did not tell them that he had taken the honey out of the carcass of the lion.

¹⁰So his father went down to the woman. And Samson gave a feast there, for young men used to do so. ¹¹And it happened, when they saw him, that they brought thirty companions to be with him.

¹²Then Samson said to them, "Let me pose a riddle to you. If you can correctly solve and explain it to me within the seven days of the feast, then I will give you thirty linen garments and thirty changes of clothing. ¹³But if you cannot explain *it* to me, then you shall give me thirty linen garments and thirty changes of clothing."

And they said to him, "Pose your riddle, that we may hear it."

¹⁴So he said to them:

"Out of the eater came something to
    eat,
  And out of the strong came something
    sweet."

Now for three days they could not explain the riddle.

¹⁵But it came to pass on the seventhᵃ day that they said to Samson's wife, "Entice your husband, that he may explain the riddle to us, or else we will burn you and your father's house with fire. Have you invited us in order to take what is ours? *Is that* not *so?*"

¹⁶Then Samson's wife wept on him, and said, "You only hate me! You do not love me! You have posed a riddle to the sons of my people, but you have not explained *it* to me."

And he said to her, "Look, I have not explained *it* to my father or my mother; so should I explain *it* to you?" ¹⁷Now she had wept on him the seven days while their feast lasted. And it happened on the seventh day that he told her, because she pressed him so much. Then she explained the riddle to the sons of her people. ¹⁸So the men of the city said to him on the seventh day before the sun went down:

"What *is* sweeter than honey?
  And what *is* stronger than a lion?"

And he said to them:

"If you had not plowed with my heifer,
  You would not have solved my riddle!"

13:25 ᵃLiterally *Camp of Dan* (compare 18:12)
14:15 ᵃFollowing Masoretic Text, Targum, and Vulgate; Septuagint and Syriac read *fourth.*

[19] Then the Spirit of the LORD came upon him mightily, and he went down to Ashkelon and killed thirty of their men, took their apparel, and gave the changes *of clothing* to those who had explained the riddle. So his anger was aroused, and he went back up to his father's house. [20] And Samson's wife was *given* to his companion, who had been his best man.

Samson Defeats the Philistines

15 After a while, in the time of wheat harvest, it happened that Samson visited his wife with a young goat. And he said, "Let me go in to my wife, into *her* room." But her father would not permit him to go in.

[2] Her father said, "I really thought that you thoroughly hated her; therefore I gave her to your companion. *Is* not her younger sister better than she? Please, take her instead."

[3] And Samson said to them, "This time I shall be blameless regarding the Philistines if I harm them!" [4] Then Samson went and caught three hundred foxes; and he took torches, turned *the foxes* tail to tail, and put a torch between each pair of tails. [5] When he had set the torches on fire, he let *the foxes* go into the standing grain of the Philistines, and burned up both the shocks and the standing grain, as well as the vineyards *and* olive groves.

[6] Then the Philistines said, "Who has done this?"

And they answered, "Samson, the son-in-law of the Timnite, because he has taken his wife and given her to his companion." So the Philistines came up and burned her and her father with fire.

[7] Samson said to them, "Since you would do a thing like this, I will surely take revenge on you, and after that I will cease." [8] So he attacked them hip and thigh with a great slaughter; then he went down and dwelt in the cleft of the rock of Etam.

[9] Now the Philistines went up, encamped in Judah, and deployed themselves against Lehi. [10] And the men of Judah said, "Why have you come up against us?"

So they answered, "We have come up to arrest Samson, to do to him as he has done to us."

[11] Then three thousand men of Judah went down to the cleft of the rock of Etam, and said to Samson, "Do you not know that the Philistines rule over us? What *is* this you have done to us?"

And he said to them, "As they did to me, so I have done to them."

[12] But they said to him, "We have come down to arrest you, that we may deliver you into the hand of the Philistines."

Then Samson said to them, "Swear to me that you will not kill me yourselves."

[13] So they spoke to him, saying, "No, but we will tie you securely and deliver you into their hand; but we will surely not kill you." And they bound him with two new ropes and brought him up from the rock.

[14] When he came to Lehi, the Philistines came shouting against him. Then the Spirit of the LORD came mightily upon him; and the ropes that *were* on his arms became like flax that is burned with fire, and his bonds broke loose from his hands. [15] He found a fresh jawbone of a donkey, reached out his hand and took it, and killed a thousand men with it. [16] Then Samson said:

"With the jawbone of a donkey,
  Heaps upon heaps,
With the jawbone of a donkey
  I have slain a thousand men!"

[17] And so it was, when he had finished speaking, that he threw the jawbone from his hand, and called that place Ramath Lehi.[a]

[18] Then he became very thirsty; so he cried out to the LORD and said, "You have given this great deliverance by the hand of Your servant; and now shall I die of thirst and fall into the hand of the uncircumcised?" [19] So God split the hollow place that *is* in Lehi,[a] and water came out, and he drank; and his spirit returned, and he revived. Therefore he called its name En Hakkore,[b] which is in Lehi to this day. [20] And he judged Israel twenty years in the days of the Philistines.

15:17 [a]Literally *Jawbone Height*   **15:19** [a]Literally *Jawbone* (compare verse 14) [b]Literally *Spring of the Caller*

Samson and Delilah

16 Now Samson went to Gaza and saw a harlot there, and went in to her. [2]*When the Gazites were told,* "Samson has come here!" they surrounded *the place* and lay in wait for him all night at the gate of the city. They were quiet all night, saying, "In the morning, when it is daylight, we will kill him." [3]And Samson lay *low* till midnight; then he arose at midnight, took hold of the doors of the gate of the city and the two gateposts, pulled them up, bar and all, put *them* on his shoulders, and carried them to the top of the hill that faces Hebron.

[4]Afterward it happened that he loved a woman in the Valley of Sorek, whose name *was* Delilah. [5]And the lords of the Philistines came up to her and said to her, "Entice him, and find out where his great strength *lies,* and by what *means* we may overpower him, that we may bind him to afflict him; and every one of us will give you eleven hundred *pieces* of silver."

[6]So Delilah said to Samson, "Please tell me where your great strength *lies,* and with what you may be bound to afflict you."

[7]And Samson said to her, "If they bind me with seven fresh bowstrings, not yet dried, then I shall become weak, and be like any *other* man."

[8]So the lords of the Philistines brought up to her seven fresh bowstrings, not yet dried, and she bound him with them. [9]Now *men were* lying in wait, staying with her in the room. And she said to him, "The Philistines *are* upon you, Samson!" But he broke the bowstrings as a strand of yarn breaks when it touches fire. So the secret of his strength was not known.

[10]Then Delilah said to Samson, "Look, you have mocked me and told me lies. Now, please tell me what you may be bound with."

[11]So he said to her, "If they bind me securely with new ropes that have never been used, then I shall become weak, and be like any *other* man."

[12]Therefore Delilah took new ropes and bound him with them, and said to him, "The Philistines *are* upon you, Samson!" And *men were* lying in wait, staying in the room. But he broke them off his arms like a thread.

[13]Delilah said to Samson, "Until now you have mocked me and told me lies. Tell me what you may be bound with."

And he said to her, "If you weave the seven locks of my head into the web of the loom"—

[14]So she wove *it* tightly with the batten of the loom, and said to him, "The Philistines *are* upon you, Samson!" But he awoke from his sleep, and pulled out the batten and the web from the loom.

[15]Then she said to him, "How can you say, 'I love you,' when your heart *is* not with me? You have mocked me these three times, and have not told me where your great strength *lies.*" [16]And it came to pass, when she pestered him daily with her words and pressed him, *so* that his soul was vexed to death, [17]that he told her all his heart, and said to her, "No razor has ever come upon my head, for I *have been* a Nazirite to God from my mother's womb. If I am shaven, then my strength will leave me, and I shall become weak, and be like any *other* man."

[18]When Delilah saw that he had told her all his heart, she sent and called for the lords of the Philistines, saying, "Come up once more, for he has told me all his heart." So the lords of the Philistines came up to her and brought the money in their hand. [19]Then she lulled him to sleep on her knees, and called for a man and had him shave off the seven locks of his head. Then she began to torment him,[a] and his strength left him. [20]And she said, "The Philistines *are* upon you, Samson!" So he awoke from his sleep, and said, "I will go out as before, at other times, and shake myself free!" But he did not know that the Lord had departed from him.

[21]Then the Philistines took him and put out his eyes, and brought him down to Gaza. They bound him with bronze fetters, and he became a grinder in the prison. [22]However, the hair of his head began to grow again after it had been shaven.

16:19 [a]Following Masoretic Text, Targum, and Vulgate; Septuagint reads *he began to be weak.*

Samson Dies with the Philistines

23Now the lords of the Philistines gathered together to offer a great sacrifice to Dagon their god, and to rejoice. And they said:

"Our god has delivered into our hands
  Samson our enemy!"

24When the people saw him, they praised their god; for they said:

"Our god has delivered into our hands
    our enemy,
  The destroyer of our land,
  And the one who multiplied our dead."

25So it happened, when their hearts were merry, that they said, "Call for Samson, that he may perform for us." So they called for Samson from the prison, and he performed for them. And they stationed him between the pillars. 26Then Samson said to the lad who held him by the hand, "Let me feel the pillars which support the temple, so that I can lean on them." 27Now the temple was full of men and women. All the lords of the Philistines *were* there—about three thousand men and women on the roof watching while Samson performed. 28Then Samson called to the LORD, saying, "O Lord GOD, remember me, I pray! Strengthen me, I pray, just this once, O God, that I may with one *blow* take vengeance on the Philistines for my two eyes!" 29And Samson took hold of the two middle pillars which supported the temple, and he braced himself against them, one on his right and the other on his left. 30Then Samson said, "Let me die with the Philistines!" And he pushed with *all his* might, and the temple fell on the lords and all the people who *were* in it. So the dead that he killed at his death were more than he had killed in his life.

31And his brothers and all his father's household came down and took him, and brought *him* up and buried him between Zorah and Eshtaol in the tomb of his father Manoah. He had judged Israel twenty years.

Micah's Idolatry

17Now there was a man from the mountains of Ephraim, whose name *was* Micah. 2And he said to his mother, "The eleven hundred *shekels* of silver that were taken from you, and on which you put a curse, even saying it in my ears—here *is* the silver with me; I took it."

And his mother said, "*May you be* blessed by the LORD, my son!" 3So when he had returned the eleven hundred *shekels* of silver to his mother, his mother said, "I had wholly dedicated the silver from my hand to the LORD for my son, to make a carved image and a molded image; now therefore, I will return it to you." 4Thus he returned the silver to his mother. Then his mother took two hundred *shekels* of silver and gave them to the silversmith, and he made it into a carved image and a molded image; and they were in the house of Micah.

5The man Micah had a shrine, and made an ephod and household idols;a and he consecrated one of his sons, who became his priest. 6In those days *there was* no king in Israel; everyone did *what was* right in his own eyes.

7Now there was a young man from Bethlehem in Judah, of the family of Judah; he *was* a Levite, and was staying there. 8The man departed from the city of Bethlehem in Judah to stay wherever he could find *a place*. Then he came to the mountains of Ephraim, to the house of Micah, as he journeyed. 9And Micah said to him, "Where do you come from?"

So he said to him, "I *am* a Levite from Bethlehem in Judah, and I am on my way to find *a place* to stay."

10Micah said to him, "Dwell with me, and be a father and a priest to me, and I will give you ten *shekels* of silver per year, a suit of clothes, and your sustenance." So the Levite went in. 11Then the Levite was content to dwell with the man; and the young man became like one of his sons to him. 12So Micah consecrated the Levite, and the young man became his priest, and lived in the house of Micah. 13Then Micah said,

---

17:5 aHebrew *teraphim*

"Now I know that the LORD will be good to me, since I have a Levite as priest!"

The Danites Adopt Micah's Idolatry

18 In those days *there was* no king in Israel. And in those days the tribe of the Danites was seeking an inheritance for itself to dwell in; for until that day *their* inheritance among the tribes of Israel had not fallen to them. [2]So the children of Dan sent five men of their family from their territory, men of valor from Zorah and Eshtaol, to spy out the land and search it. They said to them, "Go, search the land." So they went to the mountains of Ephraim, to the house of Micah, and lodged there. [3]While they *were* at the house of Micah, they recognized the voice of the young Levite. They turned aside and said to him, "Who brought you here? What are you doing in this *place?* What do you have here?"

[4]He said to them, "Thus and so Micah did for me. He has hired me, and I have become his priest."

[5]So they said to him, "Please inquire of God, that we may know whether the journey on which we go will be prosperous."

[6]And the priest said to them, "Go in peace. The presence of the LORD *be* with you on your way."

[7]So the five men departed and went to Laish. They saw the people who *were* there, how they dwelt safely, in the manner of the Sidonians, quiet and secure. *There were* no rulers in the land who might put *them* to shame for anything. They *were* far from the Sidonians, and they had no ties with anyone.[a]

[8]Then *the spies* came back to their brethren at Zorah and Eshtaol, and their brethren said to them, "What *is* your *report?*"

[9]So they said, "Arise, let us go up against them. For we have seen the land, and indeed it *is* very good. *Would* you *do* nothing? Do not hesitate to go, *and* enter to possess the land. [10]When you go, you will come to a secure people and a large land. For God has given it into your hands, a place where *there is* no lack of anything that *is* on the earth."

[11]And six hundred men of the family of the Danites went from there, from Zorah and Eshtaol, armed with weapons of war. [12]Then they went up and encamped in Kirjath Jearim in Judah. (Therefore they call that place Mahaneh Dan[a] to this day. There *it is,* west of Kirjath Jearim.) [13]And they passed from there to the mountains of Ephraim, and came to the house of Micah.

[14]Then the five men who had gone to spy out the country of Laish answered and said to their brethren, "Do you know that there are in these houses an ephod, household idols, a carved image, and a molded image? Now therefore, consider what you should do." [15]So they turned aside there, and came to the house of the young Levite man—to the house of Micah—and greeted him. [16]The six hundred men armed with their weapons of war, who *were* of the children of Dan, stood by the entrance of the gate. [17]Then the five men who had gone to spy out the land went up. Entering there, they took the carved image, the ephod, the household idols, and the molded image. The priest stood at the entrance of the gate with the six hundred men *who were* armed with weapons of war.

[18]When these went into Micah's house and took the carved image, the ephod, the household idols, and the molded image, the priest said to them, "What are you doing?"

[19]And they said to him, "Be quiet, put your hand over your mouth, and come with us; be a father and a priest to us. *Is it* better for you to be a priest to the household of one man, or that you be a priest to a tribe and a family in Israel?" [20]So the priest's heart was glad; and he took the ephod, the household idols, and the carved image, and took his place among the people.

[21]Then they turned and departed, and put the little ones, the livestock, and the goods in front of them. [22]When they were a good way from the house of Micah, the men who *were* in the houses near Micah's house gathered together and overtook the children of Dan. [23]And they called out to the children of Dan. So they turned around

---

18:7 [a]Following Masoretic Text, Targum, and Vulgate; Septuagint reads *with Syria.* **18:12** [a]Literally *Camp of Dan*

and said to Micah, "What ails you, that you have gathered such a company?"

24So he said, "You have taken away my gods which I made, and the priest, and you have gone away. Now what more do I have? How can you say to me, 'What ails you?' "

25And the children of Dan said to him, "Do not let your voice be heard among us, lest angry men fall upon you, and you lose your life, with the lives of your household!" 26Then the children of Dan went their way. And when Micah saw that they *were* too strong for him, he turned and went back to his house.

Danites Settle in Laish

27So they took *the things* Micah had made, and the priest who had belonged to him, and went to Laish, to a people quiet and secure; and they struck them with the edge of the sword and burned the city with fire. 28*There was* no deliverer, because it *was* far from Sidon, and they had no ties with anyone. It was in the valley that belongs to Beth Rehob. So they rebuilt the city and dwelt there. 29And they called the name of the city Dan, after the name of Dan their father, who was born to Israel. However, the name of the city formerly *was* Laish.

30Then the children of Dan set up for themselves the carved image; and Jonathan the son of Gershom, the son of Manasseh,a and his sons were priests to the tribe of Dan until the day of the captivity of the land. 31So they set up for themselves Micah's carved image which he made, all the time that the house of God was in Shiloh.

The Levite's Concubine

19 And it came to pass in those days, when *there was* no king in Israel, that there was a certain Levite staying in the remote mountains of Ephraim. He took for himself a concubine from Bethlehem in Judah. 2But his concubine played the harlot against him, and went away from him to her father's house at Bethlehem in Judah, and was there four whole months. 3Then her husband arose and went after her, to speak kindly to her *and* bring her back, having his servant and a couple of donkeys with him. So she brought him into her father's house; and when the father of the young woman saw him, he was glad to meet him. 4Now his father-in-law, the young woman's father, detained him; and he stayed with him three days. So they ate and drank and lodged there.

5Then it came to pass on the fourth day that they arose early in the morning, and he stood to depart; but the young woman's father said to his son-in-law, "Refresh your heart with a morsel of bread, and afterward go your way."

6So they sat down, and the two of them ate and drank together. Then the young woman's father said to the man, "Please be content to stay all night, and let your heart be merry." 7And when the man stood to depart, his father-in-law urged him; so he lodged there again. 8Then he arose early in the morning on the fifth day to depart, but the young woman's father said, "Please refresh your heart." So they delayed until afternoon; and both of them ate.

9And when the man stood to depart—he and his concubine and his servant—his father-in-law, the young woman's father, said to him, "Look, the day is now drawing toward evening; please spend the night. See, the day is coming to an end; lodge here, that your heart may be merry. Tomorrow go your way early, so that you may get home."

10However, the man was not willing to spend that night; so he rose and departed, and came opposite Jebus (that *is,* Jerusalem). With him were the two saddled donkeys; his concubine *was* also with him. 11They *were* near Jebus, and the day was far spent; and the servant said to his master, "Come, please, and let us turn aside into this city of the Jebusites and lodge in it."

12But his master said to him, "We will not turn aside here into a city of foreigners, who *are* not of the children of Israel; we will go on to Gibeah." 13So he said to his servant, "Come, let us draw near to one of these places, and spend the night in Gibeah or in Ramah." 14And they passed by and went their way; and the sun went down on

---

18:30 aSeptuagint and Vulgate read *Moses.*

them near Gibeah, which belongs to Benjamin. ¹⁵They turned aside there to go in to lodge in Gibeah. And when he went in, he sat down in the open square of the city, for no one would take them into *his* house to spend the night.

¹⁶Just then an old man came in from his work in the field at evening, who also *was* from the mountains of Ephraim; he was staying in Gibeah, whereas the men of the place *were* Benjamites. ¹⁷And when he raised his eyes, he saw the traveler in the open square of the city; and the old man said, "Where are you going, and where do you come from?"

¹⁸So he said to him, "We *are* passing from Bethlehem in Judah toward the remote mountains of Ephraim; I *am* from there. I went to Bethlehem in Judah; *now* I am going to the house of the LORD. But there *is* no one who will take me into his house, ¹⁹although we have both straw and fodder for our donkeys, and bread and wine for myself, for your female servant, and for the young man *who is* with your servant; *there is* no lack of anything."

²⁰And the old man said, "Peace *be* with you! However, *let* all your needs *be* my responsibility; only do not spend the night in the open square." ²¹So he brought him into his house, and gave fodder to the donkeys. And they washed their feet, and ate and drank.

Gibeah's Crime

²²As they were enjoying themselves, suddenly certain men of the city, perverted men,^a surrounded the house *and* beat on the door. They spoke to the master of the house, the old man, saying, "Bring out the man who came to your house, that we may know him *carnally!*"

²³But the man, the master of the house, went out to them and said to them, "No, my brethren! I beg you, do not act *so* wickedly! Seeing this man has come into my house, do not commit this outrage. ²⁴Look, *here is* my virgin daughter and *the man's*^a concubine; let me bring them out now. Humble them, and do with them as you please; but to this man do not do such a vile thing!" ²⁵But the men would not heed

him. So the man took his concubine and brought *her* out to them. And they knew her and abused her all night until morning; and when the day began to break, they let her go.

²⁶Then the woman came as the day was dawning, and fell down at the door of the man's house where her master *was,* till it was light.

²⁷When her master arose in the morning, and opened the doors of the house and went out to go his way, there was his concubine, fallen *at* the door of the house with her hands on the threshold. ²⁸And he said to her, "Get up and let us be going." But there was no answer. So the man lifted her onto the donkey; and the man got up and went to his place.

²⁹When he entered his house he took a knife, laid hold of his concubine, and divided her into twelve pieces, limb by limb,^a and sent her throughout all the territory of Israel. ³⁰And so it was that all who saw it said, "No such deed has been done or seen from the day that the children of Israel came up from the land of Egypt until this day. Consider it, confer, and speak up!"

Israel's War with the Benjamites

¹20 So all the children of Israel came out, from Dan to Beersheba, as well as from the land of Gilead, and the congregation gathered together as one man before the LORD at Mizpah. ²And the leaders of all the people, all the tribes of Israel, presented themselves in the assembly of the people of God, four hundred thousand foot soldiers who drew the sword. ³(Now the children of Benjamin heard that the children of Israel had gone up to Mizpah.)

Then the children of Israel said, "Tell *us,* how did this wicked deed happen?"

⁴So the Levite, the husband of the woman who was murdered, answered and said, "My concubine and I went into Gibeah, which belongs to Benjamin, to spend the night. ⁵And the men of Gibeah rose against me, and surrounded the house at night because of me. They intended to kill me,

---

19:22 ^aLiterally *sons of Belial*   **19:24** ^aLiterally *his*
19:29 ^aLiterally *with her bones*

but instead they ravished my concubine so that she died. ⁶So I took hold of my concubine, cut her in pieces, and sent her throughout all the territory of the inheritance of Israel, because they committed lewdness and outrage in Israel. ⁷Look! All of you *are* children of Israel; give your advice and counsel here and now!"

⁸So all the people arose as one man, saying, "None *of us* will go to his tent, nor will any turn back to his house; ⁹but now this *is* the thing which we will do to Gibeah: *We will go up* against it by lot. ¹⁰We will take ten men out of *every* hundred throughout all the tribes of Israel, a hundred out of *every* thousand, and a thousand out of *every* ten thousand, to make provisions for the people, that when they come to Gibeah in Benjamin, they may repay all the vileness that they have done in Israel." ¹¹So all the men of Israel were gathered against the city, united together as one man.

¹²Then the tribes of Israel sent men through all the tribe of Benjamin, saying, "What *is* this wickedness that has occurred among you? ¹³Now therefore, deliver up the men, the perverted menᵃ who *are* in Gibeah, that we may put them to death and remove the evil from Israel!" But the children of Benjamin would not listen to the voice of their brethren, the children of Israel. ¹⁴Instead, the children of Benjamin gathered together from their cities to Gibeah, to go to battle against the children of Israel. ¹⁵And from their cities at that time the children of Benjamin numbered twenty-six thousand men who drew the sword, besides the inhabitants of Gibeah,

---

20:13 ᵃLiterally *sons of Belial*

DEFENDER

*. . . united together
as one man.*

JUDGES 20:11

George W. Bush

THE FOUNDATION OF AMERICA

On September 11, 2001, in his address to the American people, President George Bush stated:

> The pictures of airplanes flying into buildings, fires burning, huge structures collapsing, have filled us with disbelief, terrible sadness, and a quiet, unyielding anger. These acts of mass murder were intended to frighten our nation into chaos and retreat. But they have failed; our country is strong.
>
> A great people has been moved to defend a great nation. Terrorist attacks can shake the foundations of our biggest buildings, but they cannot touch the foundation of America. These acts shattered steel, but they cannot dent the steel of American resolve.
>
> America was targeted for attack because we're the brightest beacon for freedom and opportunity in the world. And no one will keep that light from shining.
>
> Today, our nation saw evil, the very worst of human nature. And we responded with the best of America— with the daring of our rescue workers, with the caring for strangers and neighbors who came to give blood and help in any way they could.
>
> This is a day when all Americans from every walk of life unite in our resolve for justice and peace. America has stood down enemies before, and we will do so this time. None of us will ever forget this day. Yet, we go forward to defend freedom and all that is good and just in our world.

who numbered seven hundred select men. [16]Among all this people *were* seven hundred select men *who were* left-handed; every one could sling a stone at a hair's *breadth* and not miss. [17]Now besides Benjamin, the men of Israel numbered four hundred thousand men who drew the sword; all of these *were* men of war.

[18]Then the children of Israel arose and went up to the house of God[a] to inquire of God. They said, "Which of us shall go up first to battle against the children of Benjamin?"

The Lord said, "Judah first!"

[19]So the children of Israel rose in the morning and encamped against Gibeah. [20]And the men of Israel went out to battle against Benjamin, and the men of Israel put themselves in battle array to fight against them at Gibeah. [21]Then the children of Benjamin came out of Gibeah, and on that day cut down to the ground twenty-two thousand men of the Israelites. [22]And the people, that is, the men of Israel, encouraged themselves and again formed the battle line at the place where they had put themselves in array on the first day. [23]Then the children of Israel went up and wept before the Lord until evening, and asked counsel of the Lord, saying, "Shall I again draw near for battle against the children of my brother Benjamin?"

And the Lord said, "Go up against him."

[24]So the children of Israel approached the children of Benjamin on the second day. [25]And Benjamin went out against them from Gibeah on the second day, and cut down to the ground eighteen thousand more of the children of Israel; all these drew the sword.

[26]Then all the children of Israel, that is, all the people, went up and came to the house of God[a] and wept. They sat there before the Lord and fasted that day until evening; and they offered burnt offerings and peace offerings before the Lord. [27]So the children of Israel inquired of the Lord (the ark of the covenant of God *was* there in those days, [28]and Phinehas the son of Eleazar, the son of Aaron, stood before it in those days), saying, "Shall I yet again go out to battle against the children of my brother Benjamin, or shall I cease?"

And the Lord said, "Go up, for tomorrow I will deliver them into your hand."

[29]Then Israel set men in ambush all around Gibeah. [30]And the children of Israel went up against the children of Benjamin on the third day, and put themselves in battle array against Gibeah as at the other times. [31]So the children of Benjamin went out against the people, *and* were drawn away from the city. They began to strike down *and* kill some of the people, as at the other times, in the highways (one of which goes up to Bethel and the other to Gibeah) and in the field, about thirty men of Israel. [32]And the children of Benjamin said, "They *are* defeated before us, as at first."

But the children of Israel said, "Let us flee and draw them away from the city to the highways." [33]So all the men of Israel rose from their place and put themselves in battle array at Baal Tamar. Then Israel's men in ambush burst forth from their position in the plain of Geba. [34]And ten thousand select men from all Israel came against Gibeah, and the battle was fierce. But *the Benjamites*[a] did not know that disaster *was* upon them. [35]The Lord defeated Benjamin before Israel. And the children of Israel destroyed that day twenty-five thousand one hundred Benjamites; all these drew the sword.

[36]So the children of Benjamin saw that they were defeated. The men of Israel had given ground to the Benjamites, because they relied on the men in ambush whom they had set against Gibeah. [37]And the men in ambush quickly rushed upon Gibeah; the men in ambush spread out and struck the whole city with the edge of the sword. [38]Now the appointed signal between the men of Israel and the men in ambush was that they would make a great cloud of smoke rise up from the city, [39]whereupon the men of Israel would turn in battle. Now Benjamin had begun to strike *and* kill about thirty of the men of Israel. For they said, "Surely they are defeated before us, as *in* the first battle." [40]But when the cloud began

---

20:18 [a]Or *Bethel*   **20:26** [a]Or *Bethel*
20:34 [a]Literally *they*

to rise from the city in a column of smoke, the Benjamites looked behind them, and there was the whole city going up *in smoke* to heaven. ⁴¹And when the men of Israel turned back, the men of Benjamin panicked, for they saw that disaster had come upon them. ⁴²Therefore they turned *their backs* before the men of Israel in the direction of the wilderness; but the battle overtook them, and whoever *came* out of the cities they destroyed in their midst. ⁴³They surrounded the Benjamites, chased them, *and* easily trampled them down as far as the front of Gibeah toward the east. ⁴⁴And eighteen thousand men of Benjamin fell; all these *were* men of valor. ⁴⁵Then theyᵃ turned and fled toward the wilderness to the rock of Rimmon; and they cut down five thousand of them on the highways. Then they pursued them relentlessly up to Gidom, and killed two thousand of them. ⁴⁶So all who fell of Benjamin that day were twenty-five thousand men who drew the sword; all these *were* men of valor.

⁴⁷But six hundred men turned and fled toward the wilderness to the rock of Rimmon, and they stayed at the rock of Rimmon for four months. ⁴⁸And the men of Israel turned back against the children of Benjamin, and struck them down with the edge of the sword—from *every* city, men and beasts, all who were found. They also set fire to all the cities they came to.

Wives Provided for the Benjamites

21 Now the men of Israel had sworn an oath at Mizpah, saying, "None of us shall give his daughter to Benjamin as a wife." ²Then the people came to the house of God,ᵃ and remained there before God till evening. They lifted up their voices and wept bitterly, ³and said, "O LORD God of Israel, why has this come to pass in Israel, that today there should be one tribe *missing* in Israel?"

⁴So it was, on the next morning, that the people rose early and built an altar there, and offered burnt offerings and peace offerings. ⁵The children of Israel said, "Who *is there* among all the tribes of Israel who did not come up with the assembly to the LORD?" For they had made a great oath concerning anyone who had not come up to the LORD at Mizpah, saying, "He shall surely be put to death." ⁶And the children of Israel grieved for Benjamin their brother, and said, "One tribe is cut off from Israel today. ⁷What shall we do for wives for those who remain, seeing we have sworn by the LORD that we will not give them our daughters as wives?"

⁸And they said, "What one *is there* from the tribes of Israel who did not come up to Mizpah to the LORD?" And, in fact, no one had come to the camp from Jabesh Gilead to the assembly. ⁹For when the people were counted, indeed, not one of the inhabitants of Jabesh Gilead *was* there. ¹⁰So the congregation sent out there twelve thousand of their most valiant men, and commanded them, saying, "Go and strike the inhabitants of Jabesh Gilead with the edge of the sword, including the women and children. ¹¹And this *is* the thing that you shall do: You shall utterly destroy every male, and every woman who has known a man intimately." ¹²So they found among the inhabitants of Jabesh Gilead four hundred young virgins who had not known a man intimately; and they brought them to the camp at Shiloh, which is in the land of Canaan.

¹³Then the whole congregation sent *word* to the children of Benjamin who *were* at the rock of Rimmon, and announced peace to them. ¹⁴So Benjamin came back at that time, and they gave them the women whom they had saved alive of the women of Jabesh Gilead; and yet they had not found enough for them.

¹⁵And the people grieved for Benjamin, because the LORD had made a void in the tribes of Israel.

¹⁶Then the elders of the congregation said, "What shall we do for wives for those who remain, since the women of Benjamin have been destroyed?" ¹⁷And they said, "*There must be* an inheritance for the survivors of Benjamin, that a tribe may not be destroyed from Israel. ¹⁸However, we cannot give them wives from our daughters, for the children of Israel have sworn an oath, saying, 'Cursed *be* the one who gives

---

20:45 ᵃSeptuagint reads *the rest.*   **21:2** ᵃOr *Bethel*

a wife to Benjamin.'" [19]Then they said, "In fact, *there is* a yearly feast of the LORD in Shiloh, which *is* north of Bethel, on the east side of the highway that goes up from Bethel to Shechem, and south of Lebonah."

[20]Therefore they instructed the children of Benjamin, saying, "Go, lie in wait in the vineyards, [21]and watch; and just when the daughters of Shiloh come out to perform their dances, then come out from the vineyards, and every man catch a wife for himself from the daughters of Shiloh; then go to the land of Benjamin. [22]Then it shall be, when their fathers or their brothers come to us to complain, that we will say to them, 'Be kind to them for our sakes, because we did not take a wife for any of them in the war; for *it is* not *as though* you have given the *women* to them at this time, making yourselves guilty of your oath.'"

[23]And the children of Benjamin did so; they took enough wives for their number from those who danced, whom they caught. Then they went and returned to their inheritance, and they rebuilt the cities and dwelt in them. [24]So the children of Israel departed from there at that time, every man to his tribe and family; they went out from there, every man to his inheritance.

[25]In those days *there was* no king in Israel; everyone did *what was* right in his own eyes.

RUTH

Author: Unknown

When Written: 1050–500 B.C.

Theme: Redemption

Key verse: Ruth 1:16—"Entreat me not to leave you, or to turn back from following after you; for wherever you go, I will go; and wherever you lodge, I will lodge; your people shall be my people, and your God, my God."

Key Chapter: Ruth 4—In this short chapter, Ruth moves from widowhood and poverty to marriage and wealth, demonstrating how God works all things according to the counsel of His will to bring redemption to His people. The key is faith and patience in His perfect provision.

Like Ruth of the Old Testament, women of steadfast loyalty and faith have been key to America's strength. One such woman was Ruth Bell Graham, wife of America's beloved twentieth-century spiritual leader Dr. Billy Graham. Throughout their life together, Dr. Graham often emphasized how vital his wife was to his own success, noting that "my work through the years would have been impossible without her encouragement and support."

For her own part, Mrs. Graham's quiet commitment to her God and to her family reflected the determination of her biblical namesake to follow the God of Israel. Mrs. Graham once explained, "I must faithfully, patiently, lovingly, and happily do my part— then quietly wait for God to do His." That same faithfulness was what led the widowed and desolate Ruth to become the wife of Boaz and a part of the lineage of Jesus Christ.

RUTH

Elimelech's Family Goes to Moab

1 Now it came to pass, in the days when the judges ruled, that there was a famine in the land. And a certain man of Bethlehem, Judah, went to dwell in the country of Moab, he and his wife and his two sons. ²The name of the man *was* Elimelech, the name of his wife *was* Naomi, and the names of his two sons *were* Mahlon and Chilion— Ephrathites of Bethlehem, Judah. And they went to the country of Moab and remained there. ³Then Elimelech, Naomi's husband, died; and she was left, and her two sons. ⁴Now they took wives of the women of Moab: the name of the one *was* Orpah, and the name of the other Ruth. And they dwelt there about ten years. ⁵Then both Mahlon and Chilion also died; so the woman survived her two sons and her husband.

Naomi Returns with Ruth

⁶Then she arose with her daughters-in-law that she might return from the country of Moab, for she had heard in the country of Moab that the LORD had visited His people by giving them bread. ⁷Therefore she went out from the place where she was, and her two daughters-in-law with her; and they went on the way to return to the land of Judah. ⁸And Naomi said to her two daughters-in-law, "Go, return each to her mother's house. The LORD deal kindly with you, as you have dealt with the dead and with me. ⁹The LORD grant that you may find rest, each in the house of her husband."

So she kissed them, and they lifted up their voices and wept. ¹⁰And they said to her, "Surely we will return with you to your people."

¹¹But Naomi said, "Turn back, my daughters; why will you go with me? *Are* there still sons in my womb, that they may be your husbands? ¹²Turn back, my daughters, go—for I am too old to have a husband. If I should say I have hope, *if* I should have a husband tonight and should also bear sons, ¹³would you wait for them till they were grown? Would you restrain yourselves from having husbands? No, my daughters; for it grieves me very much for your sakes that the hand of the LORD has gone out against me!"

¹⁴Then they lifted up their voices and wept again; and Orpah kissed her mother-in-law, but Ruth clung to her.

¹⁵And she said, "Look, your sister-in-law has gone back to her people and to her gods; return after your sister-in-law."

¹⁶But Ruth said:

"Entreat me not to leave you,
Or to turn back from following after you;
For wherever you go, I will go;
And wherever you lodge, I will lodge;
Your people *shall be* my people,
And your God, my God.
17 Where you die, I will die,
And there will I be buried.
The LORD do so to me, and more also,
If *anything but* death parts you and me."

¹⁸When she saw that she was determined to go with her, she stopped speaking to her.

¹⁹Now the two of them went until they came to Bethlehem. And it happened, when they had come to Bethlehem, that all the city was excited because of them; and the women said, "*Is* this Naomi?"

²⁰But she said to them, "Do not call me Naomi;ᵃ call me Mara,ᵇ for the Almighty has dealt very bitterly with me. ²¹I went out full, and the LORD has brought me home again empty. Why do you call me Naomi, since the LORD has testified against me, and the Almighty has afflicted me?"

²²So Naomi returned, and Ruth the Moabitess her daughter-in-law with her, who returned from the country of Moab.

1:20 ᵃLiterally *Pleasant* ᵇLiterally *Bitter*

The PLEDGE of ALLEGIANCE

DWIGHT D. EISENHOWER

Every morning across the United States of America, over 60 million teachers and students recite The Pledge of Allegiance. Congress sessions open with the recitation of the Pledge, and it is recited at many public events:

> *I pledge allegiance to the Flag*
> *of the United States of America,*
> *and to the Republic for which it stands:*
> *one Nation under God, indivisible,*
> *With Liberty and Justice for all.*

The Pledge of Allegiance to the United States flag was first created in 1892 as a celebratory remark used throughout public schools in celebration of the 400th anniversary of Columbus discovering the New World. Since then, it has become a national oath of loyalty to the country, a motto of unity, and a defense of the American way of life. It should be recited by standing at attention facing the flag with the right hand over the heart. When not in uniform, men should remove any non-religious headdress with their right hand and hold it at the left shoulder, the hand being over the heart. Persons in uniform should remain silent, face the flag, and stand at the position of attention.

The Pledge of Allegiance was recited daily by children in schools across America and gained heightened popularity among adults during the patriotic fervor created by World War II. It was an unofficial pledge until June 22, 1942, when the United States Congress included the Pledge to the Flag in the United States Flag Code (Title 36). This was the first official sanction given to the words that had been recited each day by children for almost 50 years. One year after receiving this official sanction, the U.S. Supreme Court ruled that schoolchildren could not be forced to recite the Pledge as part of their daily routine. In 1945, the Pledge to the Flag received its official title as: The Pledge of Allegiance.

In 1954, President Dwight D. Eisenhower approved the words "under God" in the Pledge in order to differentiate the United States from the officially atheist Soviet Union. As he authorized this change he said: "In this way we are reaffirming the transcendence of religious faith in America's heritage and future; in this way we shall constantly strengthen those spiritual weapons which forever will be our country's most powerful resource in peace and war."

Now they came to Bethlehem at the beginning of barley harvest.

Ruth Meets Boaz

2 There was a relative of Naomi's husband, a man of great wealth, of the family of Elimelech. His name *was* Boaz. [2]So Ruth the Moabitess said to Naomi, "Please let me go to the field, and glean heads of grain after *him* in whose sight I may find favor."

And she said to her, "Go, my daughter." [3]Then she left, and went and gleaned in the field after the reapers. And she happened to come to the part of the field *belonging* to Boaz, who *was* of the family of Elimelech.

[4]Now behold, Boaz came from Bethlehem, and said to the reapers, "The LORD *be* with you!"

And they answered him, "The LORD bless you!"

[5]Then Boaz said to his servant who was in charge of the reapers, "Whose young woman *is* this?"

[6]So the servant who was in charge of the reapers answered and said, "It *is* the young Moabite woman who came back with Naomi from the country of Moab. [7]And she said, 'Please let me glean and gather after the reapers among the sheaves.' So she came and has continued from morning until now, though she rested a little in the house."

[8]Then Boaz said to Ruth, "You will listen, my daughter, will you not? Do not go to glean in another field, nor go from here, but stay close by my young women. [9]*Let* your eyes *be* on the field which they reap, and go after them. Have I not commanded the young men not to touch you? And when you are thirsty, go to the vessels and drink from what the young men have drawn."

[10]So she fell on her face, bowed down to the ground, and said to him, "Why have I found favor in your eyes, that you should take notice of me, since I *am* a foreigner?"

[11]And Boaz answered and said to her, "It has been fully reported to me, all that you have done for your mother-in-law since the death of your husband, and *how* you have left your father and your mother and the land of your birth, and have come to a people whom you did not know before. [12]The LORD repay your work, and a full reward be given you by the LORD God of Israel, under whose wings you have come for refuge."

[13]Then she said, "Let me find favor in your sight, my lord; for you have comforted me, and have spoken kindly to your maidservant, though I am not like one of your maidservants."

[14]Now Boaz said to her at mealtime, "Come here, and eat of the bread, and dip your piece of bread in the vinegar." So she sat beside the reapers, and he passed parched *grain* to her; and she ate and was satisfied, and kept some back. [15]And when she rose up to glean, Boaz commanded his young men, saying, "Let her glean even among the sheaves, and do not reproach her. [16]Also let *grain* from the bundles fall purposely for her; leave *it* that she may glean, and do not rebuke her."

[17]So she gleaned in the field until evening, and beat out what she had gleaned, and it was about an ephah of barley. [18]Then she took *it* up and went into the city, and her mother-in-law saw what she had gleaned. So she brought out and gave to her what she had kept back after she had been satisfied.

[19]And her mother-in-law said to her, "Where have you gleaned today? And where did you work? Blessed be the one who took notice of you."

So she told her mother-in-law with whom she had worked, and said, "The man's name with whom I worked today *is* Boaz."

[20]Then Naomi said to her daughter-in-law, "Blessed *be* he of the LORD, who has not forsaken His kindness to the living and the dead!" And Naomi said to her, "This man *is* a relation of ours, one of our close relatives."

[21]Ruth the Moabitess said, "He also said to me, 'You shall stay close by my young men until they have finished all my harvest.' "

[22]And Naomi said to Ruth her daughter-in-law, "*It is* good, my daughter, that you go out with his young women, and that people do not meet you in any other field."

²³So she stayed close by the young women of Boaz, to glean until the end of barley harvest and wheat harvest; and she dwelt with her mother-in-law.

Ruth's Redemption Assured

3 Then Naomi her mother-in-law said to her, "My daughter, shall I not seek security for you, that it may be well with you? ²Now Boaz, whose young women you were with, *is he* not our relative? In fact, he is winnowing barley tonight at the threshing floor. ³Therefore wash yourself and anoint yourself, put on your *best* garment and go down to the threshing floor; *but* do not make yourself known to the man until he has finished eating and drinking. ⁴Then it shall be, when he lies down, that you shall notice the place where he lies; and you shall go in, uncover his feet, and lie down; and he will tell you what you should do."

⁵And she said to her, "All that you say to me I will do."

⁶So she went down to the threshing floor and did according to all that her mother-in-law instructed her. ⁷And after Boaz had eaten and drunk, and his heart was cheerful, he went to lie down at the end of the heap of grain; and she came softly, uncovered his feet, and lay down.

⁸Now it happened at midnight that the man was startled, and turned himself; and there, a woman was lying at his feet. ⁹And he said, "Who *are* you?"

So she answered, "I *am* Ruth, your maidservant. Take your maidservant under your wing,ª for you are a close relative."

¹⁰Then he said, "Blessed *are* you of the LORD, my daughter! For you have shown more kindness at the end than at the beginning, in that you did not go after young men, whether poor or rich. ¹¹And now, my daughter, do not fear. I will do for you all that you request, for all the people of my town know that you *are* a virtuous woman. ¹²Now it is true that I *am* a close relative; however, there is a relative closer than I. ¹³Stay this night, and in the morning it shall be *that* if he will perform the duty of a close relative for you—good; let him do it. But if he does not want to perform the duty for you, then I will perform the duty

for you, *as* the LORD lives! Lie down until morning."

¹⁴So she lay at his feet until morning, and she arose before one could recognize another. Then he said, "Do not let it be known that the woman came to the threshing floor." ¹⁵Also he said, "Bring the shawl that *is* on you and hold it." And when she held it, he measured six *ephahs* of barley, and laid *it* on her. Then sheª went into the city.

¹⁶When she came to her mother-in-law, she said, "Is that you, my daughter?"

Then she told her all that the man had done for her. ¹⁷And she said, "These six *ephahs* of barley he gave me; for he said to me, 'Do not go empty-handed to your mother-in-law.' "

¹⁸Then she said, "Sit still, my daughter, until you know how the matter will turn out; for the man will not rest until he has concluded the matter this day."

Boaz Redeems Ruth

4 Now Boaz went up to the gate and sat down there; and behold, the close relative of whom Boaz had spoken came by. So Boaz said, "Come aside, friend,ª sit down here." So he came aside and sat down. ²And he took ten men of the elders of the city, and said, "Sit down here." So they sat down. ³Then he said to the close relative, "Naomi, who has come back from the country of Moab, sold the piece of land which *belonged* to our brother Elimelech. ⁴And I thought to inform you, saying, 'Buy *it* back in the presence of the inhabitants and the elders of my people. If you will redeem *it,* redeem *it;* but if youª will not redeem *it, then* tell me, that I may know; for *there is* no one but you to redeem *it,* and I *am* next after you.' "

And he said, "I will redeem *it.*"

⁵Then Boaz said, "On the day you buy the field from the hand of Naomi, you must also buy *it* from Ruth the Moabitess, the wife

---

3:9 ªOr *Spread the corner of your garment over your maidservant*   **3:15** ªMany Hebrew manuscripts, Syriac, and Vulgate read *she;* Masoretic Text, Septuagint, and Targum read *he.*   **4:1** ªHebrew *peloni almoni;* literally *so and so*   **4:4** ªFollowing many Hebrew manuscripts, Septuagint, Syriac, Targum, and Vulgate; Masoretic Text reads *he.*

of the dead, to perpetuate[a] the name of the dead through his inheritance."

⁶And the close relative said, "I cannot redeem *it* for myself, lest I ruin my own inheritance. You redeem my right of redemption for yourself, for I cannot redeem *it.*"

⁷Now this *was the custom* in former times in Israel concerning redeeming and exchanging, to confirm anything: one man took off his sandal and gave *it* to the other, and this *was* a confirmation in Israel.

⁸Therefore the close relative said to Boaz, "Buy *it* for yourself." So he took off his sandal. ⁹And Boaz said to the elders and all the people, "You *are* witnesses this day that I have bought all that was Elimelech's, and all that *was* Chilion's and Mahlon's, from the hand of Naomi. ¹⁰Moreover, Ruth the Moabitess, the widow of Mahlon, I have acquired as my wife, to perpetuate the name of the dead through his inheritance, that the name of the dead may not be cut off from among his brethren and from his position at the gate.[a] You *are* witnesses this day."

¹¹And all the people who *were* at the gate, and the elders, said, "*We are* witnesses. The LORD make the woman who is coming to your house like Rachel and Leah, the two who built the house of Israel; and may you prosper in Ephrathah and be famous in Bethlehem. ¹²May your house be like the house of Perez, whom Tamar bore to Judah, because of the offspring which the LORD will give you from this young woman."

Descendants of Boaz and Ruth

¹³So Boaz took Ruth and she became his wife; and when he went in to her, the LORD gave her conception, and she bore a son. ¹⁴Then the women said to Naomi, "Blessed *be* the LORD, who has not left you this day without a close relative; and may his name be famous in Israel! ¹⁵And may he be to you a restorer of life and a nourisher of your old age; for your daughter-in-law, who loves you, who is better to you than seven sons, has borne him." ¹⁶Then Naomi took the child and laid him on her bosom, and became a nurse to him. ¹⁷Also the neighbor women gave him a name, saying, "There is a son born to Naomi." And they called his name Obed. He *is* the father of Jesse, the father of David.

¹⁸Now this *is* the genealogy of Perez: Perez begot Hezron; ¹⁹Hezron begot Ram, and Ram begot Amminadab; ²⁰Amminadab begot Nahshon, and Nahshon begot Salmon;[a] ²¹Salmon begot Boaz, and Boaz begot Obed; ²²Obed begot Jesse, and Jesse begot David.

4:5 [a]Literally *raise up*   **4:10** [a]Probably his civic office   **4:20** [a]Hebrew *Salmah*

1 SAMUEL

Author: Uncertain

When Written: 931–722 B.C.

Theme: Transition

Key Verse: 1 Samuel 15:22—"Has the LORD as great delight in burnt offerings and sacrifices, as in obeying the voice of the LORD? Behold, to obey is better than sacrifice, and to heed than the fat of rams."

Key Chapter: 1 Samuel 15—This pivotal chapter in the history of Israel records the tragic transition of the nation's leadership from the faithless and unbelieving Saul to King David, a man after God's own heart. Verse 23 records the consequences that Saul's sinfulness brought, as Samuel declares, "Because you have rejected the word of the LORD, He also has rejected you from being king."

First Samuel offers us a contrast between two very different national leaders: Saul, who relied on his own abilities and reason to make crucial decisions about God's people; and David, who chose a path of humility and faith in God. As long as King David chose righteousness, God's blessing followed the nation of Judah.

Similarly, as America entered the dark days of the Civil War, President Abraham Lincoln realized the need for the nation to turn its heart to God. After the Union Army's defeat at the Battle of Bull Run, President Lincoln called the American people to a time of repentance, prayer, and fasting, so that "the united prayer of the nation may ascend to the throne of grace and bring down plentiful blessings upon our country."

God's heart is turned to such humility.

1 SAMUEL

The Family of Elkanah

1 Now there was a certain man of Ramathaim Zophim, of the mountains of Ephraim, and his name *was* Elkanah the son of Jeroham, the son of Elihu,[a] the son of Tohu,[b] the son of Zuph, an Ephraimite. [2]And he had two wives: the name of one *was* Hannah, and the name of the other Peninnah. Peninnah had children, but Hannah had no children. [3]This man went up from his city yearly to worship and sacrifice to the LORD of hosts in Shiloh. Also the two sons of Eli, Hophni and Phinehas, the priests of the LORD, *were* there. [4]And whenever the time came for Elkanah to make an offering, he would give portions to Peninnah his wife and to all her sons and daughters. [5]But to Hannah he would give a double portion, for he loved Hannah, although the LORD had closed her womb. [6]And her rival also provoked her severely, to make her miserable, because the LORD had closed her womb. [7]So it was, year by year, when she went up to the house of the LORD, that she provoked her; therefore she wept and did not eat.

Hannah's Vow

[8]Then Elkanah her husband said to her, "Hannah, why do you weep? Why do you not eat? And why is your heart grieved? *Am* I not better to you than ten sons?"

[9]So Hannah arose after they had finished eating and drinking in Shiloh. Now Eli the priest was sitting on the seat by the doorpost of the tabernacle[a] of the LORD. [10]And she *was* in bitterness of soul, and prayed to the LORD and wept in anguish. [11]Then she made a vow and said, "O LORD of hosts, if You will indeed look on the affliction of Your maidservant and remember me, and not forget Your maidservant, but will give Your maidservant a male child, then I will give him to the LORD all the days of his life, and no razor shall come upon his head."

[12]And it happened, as she continued praying before the LORD, that Eli watched her mouth. [13]Now Hannah spoke in her heart; only her lips moved, but her voice was not heard. Therefore Eli thought she was drunk. [14]So Eli said to her, "How long will you be drunk? Put your wine away from you!"

[15]But Hannah answered and said, "No, my lord, I *am* a woman of sorrowful spirit. I have drunk neither wine nor intoxicating drink, but have poured out my soul before the LORD. [16]Do not consider your maidservant a wicked woman,[a] for out of the abundance of my complaint and grief I have spoken until now."

[17]Then Eli answered and said, "Go in peace, and the God of Israel grant your petition which you have asked of Him."

[18]And she said, "Let your maidservant find favor in your sight." So the woman went her way and ate, and her face was no longer *sad*.

Samuel Is Born and Dedicated

[19]Then they rose early in the morning and worshiped before the LORD, and returned and came to their house at Ramah. And Elkanah knew Hannah his wife, and the LORD remembered her. [20]So it came to pass in the process of time that Hannah conceived and bore a son, and called his name Samuel,[a] *saying*, "Because I have asked for him from the LORD."

[21]Now the man Elkanah and all his house went up to offer to the LORD the yearly sacrifice and his vow. [22]But Hannah did not go up, for she said to her husband, "*Not* until the child is weaned; then I will take him, that he may appear before the LORD and remain there forever."

[23]So Elkanah her husband said to her, "Do what seems best to you; wait until you have weaned him. Only let the LORD establish

---

1:1 [a]Spelled *Eliel* in 1 Chronicles 6:34 [b]Spelled *Toah* in 1 Chronicles 6:34 **1:9** [a]Hebrew *heykal*, palace or temple **1:16** [a]Literally *daughter of Belial* **1:20** [a]Literally *Heard by God*

His[a] word." Then the woman stayed and nursed her son until she had weaned him.

24Now when she had weaned him, she took him up with her, with three bulls,[a] one ephah of flour, and a skin of wine, and brought him to the house of the Lord in Shiloh. And the child *was* young. 25Then they slaughtered a bull, and brought the child to Eli. 26And she said, "O my lord! As your soul lives, my lord, I *am* the woman who stood by you here, praying to the Lord. 27For this child I prayed, and the Lord has granted me my petition which I asked of Him. 28Therefore I also have lent him to the Lord; as long as he lives he shall be lent to the Lord." So they worshiped the Lord there.

Hannah's Prayer

2 And Hannah prayed and said:

"My heart rejoices in the Lord;
　My horn[a] is exalted in the Lord.
I smile at my enemies,
Because I rejoice in Your salvation.

2　"No one is holy like the Lord,
　For *there is* none besides You,
　Nor *is there* any rock like our God.

3　"Talk no more so very proudly;
　Let no arrogance come from your
　　mouth,
　For the Lord *is* the God of knowledge;
　And by Him actions are weighed.

4　"The bows of the mighty men *are*
　　broken,
　And those who stumbled are girded
　　with strength.
5　*Those who were* full have hired
　　themselves out for bread,
　And the hungry have ceased *to hunger.*
　Even the barren has borne seven,
　And she who has many children has
　　become feeble.

6　"The Lord kills and makes alive;
　He brings down to the grave and
　　brings up.
7　The Lord makes poor and makes rich;
　He brings low and lifts up.

8　He raises the poor from the dust
　And lifts the beggar from the ash heap,
　To set *them* among princes
　And make them inherit the throne
　　of glory.

"For the pillars of the earth *are* the Lord's,
　And He has set the world upon them.
9　He will guard the feet of His saints,
　But the wicked shall be silent in
　　darkness.

"For by strength no man shall prevail.
10　The adversaries of the Lord shall be
　　broken in pieces;
　From heaven He will thunder against
　　them.
　The Lord will judge the ends of the
　　earth.

"He will give strength to His king,
　And exalt the horn of His anointed."

11Then Elkanah went to his house at Ramah. But the child ministered to the Lord before Eli the priest.

The Wicked Sons of Eli

12Now the sons of Eli *were* corrupt;[a] they did not know the Lord. 13And the priests' custom with the people *was that* when any man offered a sacrifice, the priest's servant would come with a three-pronged flesh-hook in his hand while the meat was boiling. 14Then he would thrust *it* into the pan, or kettle, or caldron, or pot; and the priest would take for himself all that the flesh-hook brought up. So they did in Shiloh to all the Israelites who came there. 15Also, before they burned the fat, the priest's servant would come and say to the man who sacrificed, "Give meat for roasting to the priest, for he will not take boiled meat from you, but raw."

16And *if* the man said to him, "They should really burn the fat first; *then* you may take *as much* as your heart desires," he

---

1:23 [a]Following Masoretic Text, Targum, and Vulgate; Dead Sea Scrolls, Septuagint, and Syriac read *your.*
1:24 [a]Dead Sea Scrolls, Septuagint, and Syriac read *a three-year-old bull.*　　**2:1** [a]That is, strength
2:12 [a]Literally *sons of Belial*

would then answer him, "*No,* but you must give *it* now; and if not, I will take *it* by force."

¹⁷Therefore the sin of the young men was very great before the LORD, for men abhorred the offering of the LORD.

Samuel's Childhood Ministry

¹⁸But Samuel ministered before the LORD, *even as* a child, wearing a linen ephod. ¹⁹Moreover his mother used to make him a little robe, and bring *it* to him year by year when she came up with her husband to offer the yearly sacrifice. ²⁰And Eli would bless Elkanah and his wife, and say, "The LORD give you descendants from this woman for the loan that was given to the LORD." Then they would go to their own home.

²¹And the LORD visited Hannah, so that she conceived and bore three sons and two daughters. Meanwhile the child Samuel grew before the LORD.

Prophecy Against Eli's Household

²²Now Eli was very old; and he heard everything his sons did to all Israel,^a and how they lay with the women who assembled at the door of the tabernacle of meeting. ²³So he said to them, "Why do you do such things? For I hear of your evil dealings from all the people. ²⁴No, my sons! For *it is* not a good report that I hear. You make the LORD's people transgress. ²⁵If one man sins against another, God will judge him. But if a man sins against the LORD, who will intercede for him?" Nevertheless they did not heed the voice of their father, because the LORD desired to kill them.

²⁶And the child Samuel grew in stature, and in favor both with the LORD and men.

²⁷Then a man of God came to Eli and said to him, "Thus says the LORD: 'Did I not clearly reveal Myself to the house of your father when they were in Egypt in Pharaoh's house? ²⁸Did I not choose him out of all the tribes of Israel *to be* My priest, to offer upon My altar, to burn incense, and to wear an ephod before Me? And did I not give to the house of your father all the offerings of the children of Israel made by fire? ²⁹Why do you kick at My sacrifice and My offering which I have commanded *in My* dwelling place, and honor your sons more than Me,

to make yourselves fat with the best of all the offerings of Israel My people?' ³⁰Therefore the LORD God of Israel says: 'I said indeed *that* your house and the house of your father would walk before Me forever.' But now the LORD says: 'Far be it from Me; for those who honor Me I will honor, and those who despise Me shall be lightly esteemed. ³¹Behold, the days are coming that I will cut off your arm and the arm of your father's house, so that there will not be an old man in your house. ³²And you will see an enemy *in My* dwelling place, *despite* all the good which God does for Israel. And there shall not be an old man in your house forever. ³³But any of your men *whom* I do not cut off from My altar shall consume your eyes and grieve your heart. And all the descendants of your house shall die in the flower of their age. ³⁴Now this *shall be* a sign to you that will come upon your two sons, on Hophni and Phinehas: in one day they shall die, both of them. ³⁵Then I will raise up for Myself a faithful priest *who* shall do according to what *is* in My heart and in My mind. I will build him a sure house, and he shall walk before My anointed forever. ³⁶And it shall come to pass that everyone who is left in your house will come *and* bow down to him for a piece of silver and a morsel of bread, and say, "Please, put me in one of the priestly positions, that I may eat a piece of bread." ' "

Samuel's First Prophecy

3 Now the boy Samuel ministered to the LORD before Eli. And the word of the LORD was rare in those days; *there was* no widespread revelation. ²And it came to pass at that time, while Eli *was* lying down in his place, and when his eyes had begun to grow so dim that he could not see, ³and before the lamp of God went out in the tabernacle^a of the LORD where the ark of God *was,* and while Samuel was lying down, ⁴that the LORD called Samuel. And he answered, "Here I am!" ⁵So he ran to Eli and said, "Here I am, for you called me."

2:22 ^aFollowing Masoretic Text, Targum, and Vulgate; Dead Sea Scrolls and Septuagint omit the rest of this verse.   **3:3** ^aHebrew *heykal,* palace or temple

HONOR

". . . for those who honor me I will honor. . . ."

1 SAMUEL 2:30

"UNDER GOD"

On July 2, 1776, as the Continental Congress was meeting in Philadelphia to declare independence, Commander-in-Chief George Washington was gathering his troops on Long Island to meet the British in battle in and around New York City. He wrote in the General Orders to his men that day these memorable words, which declare that we, as a nation, serve under God:

The time is now near at hand which must probably determine whether Americans are to be freemen or slaves; whether they are to have any property they can call their own; whether their houses and farms are to be pillaged and destroyed, and they consigned to a state of wretchedness from which no human efforts will probably deliver them. The fate of unborn millions will now depend, under God, on the courage and conduct of this army. Our cruel and unrelenting enemy leaves us no choice but a brave resistance, or the most abject submission; this is all we can expect.

We have therefore to resolve to conquer or die: Our own country's honor, all call upon us for a vigorous and manly exertion, and if we now shamefully fail, we shall become infamous to the whole world.

Let us therefore rely upon the goodness of the cause, and the aid of the supreme Being, in whose hands victory is, to animate and encourage us to great and noble actions. The eyes of all our countrymen are now upon us, and we shall have their blessings and praises, if happily we are the instruments of saving them from the tyranny meditated against them. Let us therefore animate and encourage each other and show the whole world that a freeman contending for liberty on his own ground is superior to any slavish mercenary on earth.

And he said, "I did not call; lie down again." And he went and lay down.

[6]Then the LORD called yet again, "Samuel!"

So Samuel arose and went to Eli, and said, "Here I am, for you called me." He answered, "I did not call, my son; lie down again." [7](Now Samuel did not yet know the LORD, nor was the word of the LORD yet revealed to him.)

[8]And the LORD called Samuel again the third time. So he arose and went to Eli, and said, "Here I am, for you did call me."

Then Eli perceived that the LORD had called the boy. [9]Therefore Eli said to Samuel, "Go, lie down; and it shall be, if He calls you, that you must say, 'Speak, LORD, for Your servant hears.'" So Samuel went and lay down in his place.

[10]Now the LORD came and stood and called as at other times, "Samuel! Samuel!"

And Samuel answered, "Speak, for Your servant hears."

[11]Then the LORD said to Samuel: "Behold, I will do something in Israel at which both ears of everyone who hears it will tingle. [12]In that day I will perform against Eli all that I have spoken concerning his house, from beginning to end. [13]For I have told him that I will judge his house forever for the iniquity which he knows, because his sons made themselves vile, and he did not restrain them. [14]And therefore I have sworn to the house of Eli that the iniquity of Eli's house shall not be atoned for by sacrifice or offering forever."

[15]So Samuel lay down until morning,[a] and opened the doors of the house of the LORD. And Samuel was afraid to tell Eli the vision. [16]Then Eli called Samuel and said, "Samuel, my son!"

He answered, "Here I am."

[17]And he said, "What is the word that the LORD spoke to you? Please do not hide it from me. God do so to you, and more also, if you hide anything from me of all the things that He said to you." [18]Then Samuel told him everything, and hid nothing from him. And he said, "It is the LORD. Let Him do what seems good to Him."

[19]So Samuel grew, and the LORD was with him and let none of his words fall to the ground. [20]And all Israel from Dan to Beersheba knew that Samuel had been established as a prophet of the LORD. [21]Then the LORD appeared again in Shiloh. For the LORD revealed Himself to Samuel in Shiloh by the word of the LORD.

4 And the word of Samuel came to all Israel.[a]

The Ark of God Captured

Now Israel went out to battle against the Philistines, and encamped beside Ebenezer; and the Philistines encamped in Aphek. [2]Then the Philistines put themselves in battle array against Israel. And when they joined battle, Israel was defeated by the Philistines, who killed about four thousand men of the army in the field. [3]And when the people had come into the camp, the elders of Israel said, "Why has the LORD defeated us today before the Philistines? Let us bring the ark of the covenant of the LORD from Shiloh to us, that when it comes among us it may save us from the hand of our enemies." [4]So the people sent to Shiloh, that they might bring from there the ark of the covenant of the LORD of hosts, who dwells between the cherubim. And the two sons of Eli, Hophni and Phinehas, were there with the ark of the covenant of God.

[5]And when the ark of the covenant of the LORD came into the camp, all Israel shouted so loudly that the earth shook. [6]Now when the Philistines heard the noise of the shout, they said, "What does the sound of this great shout in the camp of the Hebrews mean?" Then they understood that the ark of the LORD had come into the camp. [7]So the Philistines were afraid, for they said, "God has come into the camp!" And they said, "Woe to us! For such a thing has never happened before. [8]Woe to us! Who will deliver us from the hand of these mighty gods? These are the gods who struck the Egyptians with all the plagues in the wilderness. [9]Be strong and conduct

3:15 [a]Following Masoretic Text, Targum, and Vulgate; Septuagint adds *and he arose in the morning.*
4:1 [a]Following Masoretic Text and Targum; Septuagint and Vulgate add *And it came to pass in those days that the Philistines gathered themselves together to fight;* Septuagint adds further *against Israel.*

yourselves like men, you Philistines, that you do not become servants of the Hebrews, as they have been to you. Conduct yourselves like men, and fight!"

[10]So the Philistines fought, and Israel was defeated, and every man fled to his tent. There was a very great slaughter, and there fell of Israel thirty thousand foot soldiers. [11]Also the ark of God was captured; and the two sons of Eli, Hophni and Phinehas, died.

Death of Eli

[12]Then a man of Benjamin ran from the battle line the same day, and came to Shiloh with his clothes torn and dirt on his head. [13]Now when he came, there was Eli, sitting on a seat by the wayside watching,[a] for his heart trembled for the ark of God. And when the man came into the city and told *it,* all the city cried out. [14]When Eli heard the noise of the outcry, he said, "What *does* the sound of this tumult *mean?*" And the man came quickly and told Eli. [15]Eli was ninety-eight years old, and his eyes were so dim that he could not see.

[16]Then the man said to Eli, "I *am* he who came from the battle. And I fled today from the battle line."

And he said, "What happened, my son?"

[17]So the messenger answered and said, "Israel has fled before the Philistines, and there has been a great slaughter among the people. Also your two sons, Hophni and Phinehas, are dead; and the ark of God has been captured."

[18]Then it happened, when he made mention of the ark of God, that Eli fell off the seat backward by the side of the gate; and his neck was broken and he died, for the man was old and heavy. And he had judged Israel forty years.

Ichabod

[19]Now his daughter-in-law, Phinehas' wife, was with child, *due* to be delivered; and when she heard the news that the ark of God was captured, and that her father-in-law and her husband were dead, she bowed herself and gave birth, for her labor pains came upon her. [20]And about the time of her death the women who stood by her said to her, "Do not fear, for you have

borne a son." But she did not answer, nor did she regard *it.* [21]Then she named the child Ichabod,[a] saying, "The glory has departed from Israel!" because the ark of God had been captured and because of her father-in-law and her husband. [22]And she said, "The glory has departed from Israel, for the ark of God has been captured."

HONOR
"The glory has departed from Israel!"

1 SAMUEL 4:21

A Nation's Flag

Henry Ward Beecher, a prominent nineteenth-century Congregationalist clergyman and social reformer, stated:

> A thoughtful mind, when it sees a nation's flag, sees not the flag only, but the nation itself; and whatever may be its symbols, its insignia, he reads chiefly in the flag the government, the principles, the truths, the history which belongs to the nation that sets it forth.

The Philistines and the Ark

5 Then the Philistines took the ark of God and brought it from Ebenezer to Ashdod. [2]When the Philistines took the ark of God, they brought it into the house of Dagon[a] and set it by Dagon. [3]And when the people of Ashdod arose early in the morning, there was Dagon, fallen on its face to the earth before the ark of the LORD. So they took Dagon and set it in its place again. [4]And when they arose early the next morning, there was Dagon, fallen on its face to the ground before the ark of the LORD. The head of Dagon and both the palms of its hands *were* broken off on the threshold; only Dagon's *torso*[a] was left of it. [5]Therefore neither the priests of Dagon nor any who come into Dagon's house tread on the threshold of Dagon in Ashdod to this day.

[6]But the hand of the LORD was heavy on the people of Ashdod, and He ravaged them

---

4:13 [a]Following Masoretic Text and Vulgate; Septuagint reads *beside the gate watching the road.*
4:21 [a]Literally *Inglorious*   **5:2** [a]A Philistine idol
5:4 [a]Following Septuagint, Syriac, Targum, and Vulgate; Masoretic Text reads *Dagon.*

SAMUEL ADAMS

JOHN ADAMS

JOHN HANCOCK

FAITH
OF THE
FOUNDERS

WHILE MUCH HAS BEEN WRITTEN in recent years to try to dismiss the fact that America was founded upon the biblical principles of Judeo-Christianity, all the revisionism in the world cannot change the facts. Anyone who examines the original writings, personal correspondence, biographies, and public statements of the individuals who were instrumental in the founding of America will find an abundance of quotations showing the profound extent to which their thinking and lives were influenced by a Christian worldview.

That is not to say that all of the Founding Fathers were Christians. Clearly, they were not. But the point is that even those who were not Christians were deeply influenced by the principles of Christianity— a mind-set that helped to shape their political ideals. It is possible to be so distracted with whether Benjamin Franklin or Thomas Jefferson ever put their personal faith in Jesus Christ that one misses the fact that the Founders almost all *thought* from a biblical perspective, whether they believed or not.

My only hope of salvation is in the infinite, transcendent love of God manifested to the world by the death of His Son upon the cross. Nothing but His blood will wash away my sins. I rely exclusively upon it. Come, Lord Jesus! Come quickly!

BENJAMIN RUSH,
Signer of the Declaration of Independence

WE RECOGNIZE NO SOVEREIGN BUT GOD, AND NO KING BUT JESUS!

JOHN HANCOCK and JOHN ADAMS

The general principles upon which the Fathers achieved independence were the general principles of Christianity. . . . I will avow that I believed and now believe that those general principles of Christianity are as eternal and immutable as the existence and attributes of God.

JOHN ADAMS,
Second President

He who made all men hath made the truths necessary to human happiness obvious to all. . . . Our forefathers opened the Bible to all.

SAMUEL ADAMS,
Signer of the
Declaration of
Independence

CLEARLY, THERE WAS A PREDOMINANT Christian consensus in colonial America that shaped the Founders' thinking and their writing of the founding documents and laws, resulting in the republic we have today. The Declaration of Independence identified the source of all authority and rights as "Their Creator," and then accentuated that individual human rights were God-given, not man-made. Thus, there would be no king or established religion to stand in the way of human liberty or dignity—uniquely Judeo-Christian ideals.

While most historians do not limit the "Founding Fathers" to the 55 delegates to the Constitutional Convention, this core group of men represents the religious sentiments of those who shaped the political foundations of our nation. As a matter of public record, the delegates included 28 Episcopalians, 8 Presbyterians, 7 Congregationalists, 2 Lutherans, 2 Dutch Reformed, 2 Methodists, 2 Roman Catholics, 1 unknown, and 3 deists (those who believe in an impersonal God who gave the world its initial impetus but then left it to run its course). A full 93 percent of its members were members of Christian churches, and all were deeply influenced by a biblical view of mankind and government.

Even a brief study of the Founders' last wills and testaments provides convincing declarations of the strong religious beliefs among so many of them. Add to that their personal writings concerning their faith in Christ, plus their leadership roles in establishing and guiding numerous Bible societies, plus their service in active ministries, and the evidence is overwhelming.

We the People

insure domestic Tranquility, provide for the common defence Peace and establish the Constitution

Here is a small sample of the convictions of some of the Founders:

It cannot be emphasized too clearly and too often that this nation was founded, not by religionists, but by Christians; not on religion, but on the gospel of Jesus Christ.

Attributed to Patrick Henry | GOVERNOR OF VIRGINIA

Principally and first of all, I give and recommend my soul into the hands of God that gave it: and my body I recommend to the earth . . . nothing doubting but at the general resurrection I shall receive the same again by the mercy and power of God.

John Hancock | SIGNER OF THE DECLARATION OF INDEPENDENCE

Providence has given to our people the choice of their rulers, and it is the duty, as well as the privilege and interest of our Christian nation, to select and prefer Christians for their rulers.

John Jay | FIRST CHIEF JUSTICE OF THE SUPREME COURT

. . . to the supreme head of the universe—to that great and tremendous Jehovah—Who created the universal frame of nature, worlds, and systems in number infinite . . . To this awfully sublime Being do I resign my spirit with unlimited confidence of His mercy and protection.

Henry Knox | REVOLUTIONARY WAR GENERAL

Without morals a republic cannot subsist any length of time; they therefore who are decrying the Christian religion, whose morality is so sublime and pure . . . are undermining the solid foundation of morals, the best security for the duration of free governments.

Charles Carroll | SIGNER OF THE DECLARATION OF INDEPENDENCE

and struck them with tumors,[a] *both* Ashdod and its territory. [7]And when the men of Ashdod saw how *it was,* they said, "The ark of the God of Israel must not remain with us, for His hand is harsh toward us and Dagon our god." [8]Therefore they sent and gathered to themselves all the lords of the Philistines, and said, "What shall we do with the ark of the God of Israel?"

And they answered, "Let the ark of the God of Israel be carried away to Gath." So they carried the ark of the God of Israel away. [9]So it was, after they had carried it away, that the hand of the LORD was against the city with a very great destruction; and He struck the men of the city, both small and great, and tumors broke out on them. [10]Therefore they sent the ark of God to Ekron. So it was, as the ark of God came to Ekron, that the Ekronites cried out, saying, "They have brought the ark of the God of Israel to us, to kill us and our people!" [11]So they sent and gathered together all the lords of the Philistines, and said, "Send away the ark of the God of Israel, and let it go back to its own place, so that it does not kill us and our people." For there was a deadly destruction throughout all the city; the hand of God was very heavy there. [12]And the men who did not die were stricken with the tumors, and the cry of the city went up to heaven.

The Ark Returned to Israel

6 Now the ark of the LORD was in the country of the Philistines seven months. [2]And the Philistines called for the priests and the diviners, saying, "What shall we do with the ark of the LORD? Tell us how we should send it to its place."

[3]So they said, "If you send away the ark of the God of Israel, do not send it empty; but by all means return *it* to Him *with* a trespass offering. Then you will be healed, and it will be known to you why His hand is not removed from you."

[4]Then they said, "What *is* the trespass offering which we shall return to Him?"

They answered, "Five golden tumors and five golden rats, *according to* the number of the lords of the Philistines. For the same plague *was* on all of you and on your lords. [5]Therefore you shall make images of your tumors and images of your rats that ravage the land, and you shall give glory to the God of Israel; perhaps He will lighten His hand from you, from your gods, and from your land. [6]Why then do you harden your hearts as the Egyptians and Pharaoh hardened their hearts? When He did mighty things among them, did they not let the people go, that they might depart? [7]Now therefore, make a new cart, take two milk cows which have never been yoked, and hitch the cows to the cart; and take their calves home, away from them. [8]Then take the ark of the LORD and set it on the cart; and put the articles of gold which you are returning to Him *as* a trespass offering in a chest by its side. Then send it away, and let it go. [9]And watch: if it goes up the road to its own territory, to Beth Shemesh, *then* He has done us this great evil. But if not, then we shall know that *it is* not His hand *that* struck us—it happened to us by chance."

[10]Then the men did so; they took two milk cows and hitched them to the cart, and shut up their calves at home. [11]And they set the ark of the LORD on the cart, and the chest with the gold rats and the images of their tumors. [12]Then the cows headed straight for the road to Beth Shemesh, *and* went along the highway, lowing as they went, and did not turn aside to the right hand or the left. And the lords of the Philistines went after them to the border of Beth Shemesh.

[13]Now *the people of* Beth Shemesh *were* reaping their wheat harvest in the valley; and they lifted their eyes and saw the ark, and rejoiced to see *it.* [14]Then the cart came into the field of Joshua of Beth Shemesh, and stood there; a large stone *was* there. So they split the wood of the cart and offered the cows as a burnt offering to the LORD. [15]The Levites took down the ark of the LORD and the chest that *was* with it, in which *were* the articles of gold, and put *them* on the large stone. Then the men of Beth Shemesh offered burnt offerings and made sacrifices the same day to the LORD. [16]So when the five lords of the Philistines had seen *it,* they returned to Ekron the same day.

5:6 [a]Probably bubonic plague. Septuagint and Vulgate add here *And in the midst of their land rats sprang up, and there was a great death panic in the city.*

¹⁷These *are* the golden tumors which the Philistines returned *as* a trespass offering to the LORD: one for Ashdod, one for Gaza, one for Ashkelon, one for Gath, one for Ekron; ¹⁸and the golden rats, *according to* the number of all the cities of the Philistines *belonging* to the five lords, *both* fortified cities and country villages, even as far as the large *stone of* Abel on which they set the ark of the LORD, *which stone remains* to this day in the field of Joshua of Beth Shemesh. ¹⁹Then He struck the men of Beth Shemesh, because they had looked into the ark of the LORD. He struck fifty thousand and seventy menᵃ of the people, and the people lamented because the LORD had struck the people with a great slaughter.

The Ark at Kirjath Jearim

²⁰And the men of Beth Shemesh said, "Who is able to stand before this holy LORD God? And to whom shall it go up from us?" ²¹So they sent messengers to the inhabitants of Kirjath Jearim, saying, "The Philistines have brought back the ark of the LORD; come down *and* take it up with you."

7 Then the men of Kirjath Jearim came and took the ark of the LORD, and brought it into the house of Abinadab on the hill, and consecrated Eleazar his son to keep the ark of the LORD.

Samuel Judges Israel

²So it was that the ark remained in Kirjath Jearim a long time; it was there twenty years. And all the house of Israel lamented after the LORD. ³Then Samuel spoke to all the house of Israel, saying, "If you return to the LORD with all your hearts, *then* put away the foreign gods and the Ashtorethsᵃ from among you, and prepare your hearts for the LORD, and serve Him only; and He will deliver you from the hand of the Philistines." ⁴So the children of Israel put away the Baals and the Ashtoreths,ᵃ and served the LORD only.

⁵And Samuel said, "Gather all Israel to Mizpah, and I will pray to the LORD for you." ⁶So they gathered together at Mizpah, drew water, and poured *it* out before the LORD. And they fasted that day, and said there, "We have sinned against the LORD."

And Samuel judged the children of Israel at Mizpah.

⁷Now when the Philistines heard that the children of Israel had gathered together at Mizpah, the lords of the Philistines went up against Israel. And when the children of Israel heard *of it,* they were afraid of the Philistines. ⁸So the children of Israel said to Samuel, "Do not cease to cry out to the LORD our God for us, that He may save us from the hand of the Philistines."

⁹And Samuel took a suckling lamb and offered *it as* a whole burnt offering to the LORD. Then Samuel cried out to the LORD for Israel, and the LORD answered him. ¹⁰Now as Samuel was offering up the burnt offering, the Philistines drew near to battle against Israel. But the LORD thundered with a loud thunder upon the Philistines that day, and so confused them that they were overcome before Israel. ¹¹And the men of Israel went out of Mizpah and pursued the Philistines, and drove them back as far as below Beth Car. ¹²Then Samuel took a stone and set *it* up between Mizpah and Shen, and called its name Ebenezer,ᵃ saying, "Thus far the LORD has helped us."

¹³So the Philistines were subdued, and they did not come anymore into the territory of Israel. And the hand of the LORD was against the Philistines all the days of Samuel. ¹⁴Then the cities which the Philistines had taken from Israel were restored to Israel, from Ekron to Gath; and Israel recovered its territory from the hands of the Philistines. Also there was peace between Israel and the Amorites.

¹⁵And Samuel judged Israel all the days of his life. ¹⁶He went from year to year on a circuit to Bethel, Gilgal, and Mizpah, and judged Israel in all those places. ¹⁷But he always returned to Ramah, for his home *was* there. There he judged Israel, and there he built an altar to the LORD.

Israel Demands a King

8 Now it came to pass when Samuel was old that he made his sons judges over

---

6:19 ᵃOr *He struck seventy men of the people and fifty oxen of a man*   **7:3** ᵃCanaanite goddesses   **7:4** ᵃCanaanite goddesses   **7:12** ᵃLiterally *Stone of Help*

Israel. ²The name of his firstborn was Joel, and the name of his second, Abijah; *they were* judges in Beersheba. ³But his sons did not walk in his ways; they turned aside after dishonest gain, took bribes, and perverted justice.

⁴Then all the elders of Israel gathered together and came to Samuel at Ramah, ⁵and said to him, "Look, you are old, and your sons do not walk in your ways. Now make us a king to judge us like all the nations."

⁶But the thing displeased Samuel when they said, "Give us a king to judge us." So Samuel prayed to the LORD. ⁷And the LORD said to Samuel, "Heed the voice of the people in all that they say to you; for they have not rejected you, but they have rejected Me, that I should not reign over them. ⁸According to all the works which they have done since the day that I brought them up out of Egypt, even to this day—with which they have forsaken Me and served other gods—so they are doing to you also. ⁹Now therefore, heed their voice. However, you shall solemnly forewarn them, and show them the behavior of the king who will reign over them."

¹⁰So Samuel told all the words of the LORD to the people who asked him for a king. ¹¹And he said, "This will be the behavior of the king who will reign over you: He will take your sons and appoint *them* for his own chariots and *to be* his horsemen, and *some* will run before his chariots. ¹²He will appoint captains over his thousands and captains over his fifties, *will set some* to plow his ground and reap his harvest, and *some* to make his weapons of war and equipment for his chariots. ¹³He will take your daughters *to be* perfumers, cooks, and bakers. ¹⁴And he will take the best of your fields, your vineyards, and your olive groves, and give *them* to his servants. ¹⁵He will take a tenth of your grain and your vintage, and give it to his officers and servants. ¹⁶And he will take your male servants, your female servants, your finest young men,ᵃ and your donkeys, and put *them* to his work. ¹⁷He will take a tenth of your sheep. And you will be his servants. ¹⁸And you will cry out in that day because of your king whom you have chosen for yourselves, and the LORD will not hear you in that day."

¹⁹Nevertheless the people refused to obey the voice of Samuel; and they said, "No, but we will have a king over us, ²⁰that we also may be like all the nations, and that our king may judge us and go out before us and fight our battles."

²¹And Samuel heard all the words of the people, and he repeated them in the hearing of the LORD. ²²So the LORD said to Samuel, "Heed their voice, and make them a king."

And Samuel said to the men of Israel, "Every man go to his city."

PROTECTOR
"And you will be his servants."

1 SAMUEL 8:17

The History of Liberty
In 1912, the 28th president of the United States, Woodrow Wilson, who was also a distinguished historian and a profound student of government, stated:

> The history of liberty is the history of resistance. The history of liberty is a history of the limitation of governmental power, not the increase of it. When we resist the concentration of power, we are resisting the powers of death. Concentration of power precedes the destruction of human liberties.

Saul Chosen to Be King

9 There was a man of Benjamin whose name *was* Kish the son of Abiel, the son of Zeror, the son of Bechorath, the son of Aphiah, a Benjamite, a mighty man of power. ²And he had a choice and handsome son whose name *was* Saul. *There was* not a more handsome person than he among the children of Israel. From his shoulders upward *he was* taller than any of the people.

³Now the donkeys of Kish, Saul's father, were lost. And Kish said to his son Saul, "Please take one of the servants with you, and arise, go and look for the donkeys."

8:16 ᵃSeptuagint reads *cattle*.

⁴So he passed through the mountains of Ephraim and through the land of Shalisha, but they did not find *them.* Then they passed through the land of Shaalim, and *they were* not *there.* Then he passed through the land of the Benjamites, but they did not find *them.*

⁵When they had come to the land of Zuph, Saul said to his servant who *was* with him, "Come, let us return, lest my father cease *caring* about the donkeys and become worried about us."

⁶And he said to him, "Look now, *there is* in this city a man of God, and *he is* an honorable man; all that he says surely comes to pass. So let us go there; perhaps he can show us the way that we should go."

⁷Then Saul said to his servant, "But look, *if* we go, what shall we bring the man? For the bread in our vessels is all gone, and *there is* no present to bring to the man of God. What do we have?"

⁸And the servant answered Saul again and said, "Look, I have here at hand one-fourth of a shekel of silver. I will give *that* to the man of God, to tell us our way."

⁹(Formerly in Israel, when a man went to inquire of God, he spoke thus: "Come, let us go to the seer"; for *he who is* now *called* a prophet was formerly called a seer.)

¹⁰Then Saul said to his servant, "Well said; come, let us go." So they went to the city where the man of God *was.*

¹¹As they went up the hill to the city, they met some young women going out to draw water, and said to them, "Is the seer here?"

¹²And they answered them and said, "Yes, there he is, just ahead of you. Hurry now; for today he came to this city, because there is a sacrifice of the people today on the high place. ¹³As soon as you come into the city, you will surely find him before he goes up to the high place to eat. For the people will not eat until he comes, because he must bless the sacrifice; afterward those who are invited will eat. Now therefore, go up, for about this time you will find him." ¹⁴So they went up to the city. As they were coming into the city, there was Samuel, coming out toward them on his way up to the high place.

¹⁵Now the LORD had told Samuel in his ear the day before Saul came, saying,

¹⁶"Tomorrow about this time I will send you a man from the land of Benjamin, and you shall anoint him commander over My people Israel, that he may save My people from the hand of the Philistines; for I have looked upon My people, because their cry has come to Me."

¹⁷So when Samuel saw Saul, the LORD said to him, "There he is, the man of whom I spoke to you. This one shall reign over My people." ¹⁸Then Saul drew near to Samuel in the gate, and said, "Please tell me, where *is* the seer's house?"

¹⁹Samuel answered Saul and said, "I *am* the seer. Go up before me to the high place, for you shall eat with me today; and tomorrow I will let you go and will tell you all that *is* in your heart. ²⁰But as for your donkeys that were lost three days ago, do not be anxious about them, for they have been found. And on whom *is* all the desire of Israel? *Is it* not on you and on all your father's house?"

²¹And Saul answered and said, "*Am* I not a Benjamite, of the smallest of the tribes of Israel, and my family the least of all the families of the tribeª of Benjamin? Why then do you speak like this to me?"

²²Now Samuel took Saul and his servant and brought them into the hall, and had them sit in the place of honor among those who were invited; there *were* about thirty persons. ²³And Samuel said to the cook, "Bring the portion which I gave you, of which I said to you, 'Set it apart.'" ²⁴So the cook took up the thigh with its upper part and set *it* before Saul. And *Samuel* said, "Here it is, what was kept back. *It* was set apart for you. Eat; for until this time it has been kept for you, since I said I invited the people." So Saul ate with Samuel that day.

²⁵When they had come down from the high place into the city, *Samuel* spoke with Saul on the top of the house.ª ²⁶They arose early; and it was about the dawning of the day that Samuel called to Saul on the top of the house, saying, "Get up, that I may send you on your way." And Saul arose,

---

9:21 ªLiterally *tribes*   9:25 ªFollowing Masoretic Text and Targum; Septuagint omits *He spoke with Saul on the top of the house;* Septuagint and Vulgate add *And he prepared a bed for Saul on the top of the house, and he slept.*

and both of them went outside, he and Samuel.

Saul Anointed King

27As they were going down to the outskirts of the city, Samuel said to Saul, "Tell the servant to go on ahead of us." And he went on. "But you stand here awhile, that I may announce to you the word of God."

10 Then Samuel took a flask of oil and poured *it* on his head, and kissed him and said: "*Is it* not because the LORD has anointed you commander over His inheritance?ª 2When you have departed from me today, you will find two men by Rachel's tomb in the territory of Benjamin at Zelzah; and they will say to you, 'The donkeys which you went to look for have been found. And now your father has ceased caring about the donkeys and is worrying about you, saying, "What shall I do about my son?"' 3Then you shall go on forward from there and come to the terebinth tree of Tabor. There three men going up to God at Bethel will meet you, one carrying three young goats, another carrying three loaves of bread, and another carrying a skin of wine. 4And they will greet you and give you two *loaves* of bread, which you shall receive from their hands. 5After that you shall come to the hill of God where the Philistine garrison *is.* And it will happen, when you have come there to the city, that you will meet a group of prophets coming down from the high place with a stringed instrument, a tambourine, a flute, and a harp before them; and they will be prophesying. 6Then the Spirit of the LORD will come upon you, and you will prophesy with them and be turned into another man. 7And let it be, when these signs come to you, *that* you do as the occasion demands; for God *is* with you. 8You shall go down before me to Gilgal; and surely I will come down to you to offer burnt offerings *and* make sacrifices of peace offerings. Seven days you shall wait, till I come to you and show you what you should do."

9So it was, when he had turned his back to go from Samuel, that God gave him another heart; and all those signs came to pass that day. 10When they came there to the hill, there was a group of prophets to meet him; then the Spirit of God came upon him, and he prophesied among them. 11And it happened, when all who knew him formerly saw that he indeed prophesied among the prophets, that the people said to one another, "What *is* this *that* has come upon the son of Kish? *Is* Saul also among the prophets?" 12Then a man from there answered and said, "But who *is* their father?" Therefore it became a proverb: "*Is* Saul also among the prophets?" 13And when he had finished prophesying, he went to the high place.

14Then Saul's uncle said to him and his servant, "Where did you go?"

So he said, "To look for the donkeys. When we saw that *they were* nowhere *to be found,* we went to Samuel."

15And Saul's uncle said, "Tell me, please, what Samuel said to you."

16So Saul said to his uncle, "He told us plainly that the donkeys had been found." But about the matter of the kingdom, he did not tell him what Samuel had said.

Saul Proclaimed King

17Then Samuel called the people together to the LORD at Mizpah, 18and said to the children of Israel, "Thus says the LORD God of Israel: 'I brought up Israel out of Egypt, and delivered you from the hand of the Egyptians *and* from the hand of all kingdoms and from those who oppressed you.' 19But you have today rejected your God, who Himself saved you from all your adversities and your tribulations; and you have said to Him, 'No, set a king over us!' Now therefore, present yourselves before the LORD by your tribes and by your clans."ª

20And when Samuel had caused all the tribes of Israel to come near, the tribe of Benjamin was chosen. 21When he had caused the tribe of Benjamin to come near by their families, the family of Matri was chosen.

10:1 ªFollowing Masoretic Text, Targum, and Vulgate; Septuagint reads *His people Israel; and you shall rule the people of the Lord;* Septuagint and Vulgate add *And you shall deliver His people from the hands of their enemies all around them. And this shall be a sign to you, that God has anointed you to be a prince.*   **10:19** ªLiterally *thousands*

And Saul the son of Kish was chosen. But when they sought him, he could not be found. [22]Therefore they inquired of the LORD further, "Has the man come here yet?"

And the LORD answered, "There he is, hidden among the equipment."

[23]So they ran and brought him from there; and when he stood among the people, he was taller than any of the people from his shoulders upward. [24]And Samuel said to all the people, "Do you see him whom the LORD has chosen, that *there is* no one like him among all the people?"

So all the people shouted and said, "Long live the king!"

[25]Then Samuel explained to the people the behavior of royalty, and wrote *it* in a book and laid *it* up before the LORD. And Samuel sent all the people away, every man to his house. [26]And Saul also went home to Gibeah; and valiant *men* went with him, whose hearts God had touched. [27]But some rebels said, "How can this man save us?" So they despised him, and brought him no presents. But he held his peace.

Saul Saves Jabesh Gilead

11 Then Nahash the Ammonite came up and encamped against Jabesh Gilead; and all the men of Jabesh said to Nahash, "Make a covenant with us, and we will serve you."

[2]And Nahash the Ammonite answered them, "On this *condition* I will make *a covenant* with you, that I may put out all your right eyes, and bring reproach on all Israel."

[3]Then the elders of Jabesh said to him, "Hold off for seven days, that we may send messengers to all the territory of Israel. And then, if *there is* no one to save us, we will come out to you."

[4]So the messengers came to Gibeah of Saul and told the news in the hearing of the people. And all the people lifted up their voices and wept. [5]Now there was Saul, coming behind the herd from the field; and Saul said, "What *troubles* the people, that they weep?" And they told him the words of the men of Jabesh. [6]Then the Spirit of God came upon Saul when he heard this news, and his anger was greatly aroused. [7]So he took a yoke of oxen and cut them in pieces, and sent *them* throughout all the territory of Israel by the hands of messengers, saying, "Whoever does not go out with Saul and Samuel to battle, so it shall be done to his oxen."

And the fear of the LORD fell on the people, and they came out with one consent. [8]When he numbered them in Bezek, the children of Israel were three hundred thousand, and the men of Judah thirty thousand. [9]And they said to the messengers who came, "Thus you shall say to the men of Jabesh Gilead: 'Tomorrow, by *the time* the sun is hot, you shall have help.'" Then the messengers came and reported *it* to the men of Jabesh, and they were glad. [10]Therefore the men of Jabesh said, "Tomorrow we will come out to you, and you may do with us whatever seems good to you."

[11]So it was, on the next day, that Saul put the people in three companies; and they came into the midst of the camp in the morning watch, and killed Ammonites until the heat of the day. And it happened that those who survived were scattered, so that no two of them were left together.

[12]Then the people said to Samuel, "Who *is* he who said, 'Shall Saul reign over us?' Bring the men, that we may put them to death."

[13]But Saul said, "Not a man shall be put to death this day, for today the LORD has accomplished salvation in Israel."

[14]Then Samuel said to the people, "Come, let us go to Gilgal and renew the kingdom there." [15]So all the people went to Gilgal, and there they made Saul king before the LORD in Gilgal. There they made sacrifices of peace offerings before the LORD, and there Saul and all the men of Israel rejoiced greatly.

Samuel's Address at Saul's Coronation

12 Now Samuel said to all Israel: "Indeed I have heeded your voice in all that you said to me, and have made a king over you. [2]And now here is the king, walking before you; and I am old and grayheaded, and look, my sons *are* with you. I have walked before you from my childhood to this day. [3]Here I am. Witness against me

before the LORD and before His anointed: Whose ox have I taken, or whose donkey have I taken, or whom have I cheated? Whom have I oppressed, or from whose hand have I received *any* bribe with which to blind my eyes? I will restore *it* to you."

4And they said, "You have not cheated us or oppressed us, nor have you taken anything from any man's hand."

5Then he said to them, "The LORD *is* witness against you, and His anointed *is* witness this day, that you have not found anything in my hand."

And they answered, "*He is* witness."

6Then Samuel said to the people, "*It is* the LORD who raised up Moses and Aaron, and who brought your fathers up from the land of Egypt. 7Now therefore, stand still, that I may reason with you before the LORD concerning all the righteous acts of the LORD which He did to you and your fathers: 8When Jacob had gone into Egypt,a and your fathers cried out to the LORD, then the LORD sent Moses and Aaron, who brought your fathers out of Egypt and made them dwell in this place. 9And when they forgot the LORD their God, He sold them into the hand of Sisera, commander of the army of Hazor, into the hand of the Philistines, and into the hand of the king of Moab; and they fought against them. 10Then they cried out to the LORD, and said, 'We have sinned, because we have forsaken the LORD and served the Baals and Ashtoreths;a but now deliver us from the hand of our enemies, and we will serve You.' 11And the LORD sent Jerubbaal,a Bedan,b Jephthah, and Samuel,c and delivered you out of the hand of your enemies on every side; and you dwelt in safety. 12And when you saw that Nahash king of the Ammonites came against you, you said to me, 'No, but a king shall reign over us,' when the LORD your God *was* your king.

13"Now therefore, here is the king whom you have chosen *and* whom you have desired. And take note, the LORD has set a king over you. 14If you fear the LORD and serve Him and obey His voice, and do not rebel against the commandment of the LORD, then both you and the king who reigns over you will continue following the LORD your God. 15However, if you do not

obey the voice of the LORD, but rebel against the commandment of the LORD, then the hand of the LORD will be against you, as *it was* against your fathers.

16"Now therefore, stand and see this great thing which the LORD will do before your eyes: 17*Is* today not the wheat harvest? I will call to the LORD, and He will send thunder and rain, that you may perceive and see that your wickedness *is* great, which you have done in the sight of the LORD, in asking a king for yourselves."

18So Samuel called to the LORD, and the LORD sent thunder and rain that day; and all the people greatly feared the LORD and Samuel.

19And all the people said to Samuel, "Pray for your servants to the LORD your God, that we may not die; for we have added to all our sins the evil of asking a king for ourselves."

20Then Samuel said to the people, "Do not fear. You have done all this wickedness; yet do not turn aside from following the LORD, but serve the LORD with all your heart. 21And do not turn aside; for *then you would go* after empty things which cannot profit or deliver, for they *are* nothing. 22For the LORD will not forsake His people, for His great name's sake, because it has pleased the LORD to make you His people. 23Moreover, as for me, far be it from me that I should sin against the LORD in ceasing to pray for you; but I will teach you the good and the right way. 24Only fear the LORD, and serve Him in truth with all your heart; for consider what great things He has done for you. 25But if you still do wickedly, you shall be swept away, both you and your king."

Saul's Unlawful Sacrifice

13 Saul reigned one year; and when he had reigned two years over Israel,a 2Saul chose for himself three thousand *men* of Israel. Two thousand were with Saul in

---

12:8 aFollowing Masoretic Text, Targum, and Vulgate; Septuagint adds *and the Egyptians afflicted them.*
12:10 aCanaanite goddesses   **12:11** aSyriac reads *Deborah;* Targum reads *Gideon.* bSeptuagint and Syriac read *Barak;* Targum reads *Simson.* cSyriac reads *Simson.*
13:1 aThe Hebrew is difficult (compare 2 Samuel 5:4; 2 Kings 14:2; see also 2 Samuel 2:10; Acts 13:21).

THE PRIVILEGE AND RESPONSIBILITY FOR VOTING

BENJAMIN RUSH

CIVIL DUTY

"... here is the king whom you have chosen and whom you have desired...."

1 SAMUEL 12:13

Benjamin Rush, one of America's Founding Fathers, said, "Every citizen of a republic . . . must watch for the state as if its liberties depended upon his vigilance alone." The most basic democratic participation of citizenry is voting. When we vote, we help determine who will lead the nation, make the laws, and protect our liberties. Unfortunately, the church and people of faith often vote at an alarmingly low rate. When people of faith fail to vote, is it any wonder that policies are enacted that are contrary to believers' core values?

Not participating in the civic and political arenas not only violates historical precedent but ignores what America's leaders have always taught. For example:

> If America is to survive, we must elect more God-centered men and women to public office—individuals who will seek Divine guidance in the affairs of state.
>
> BILLY GRAHAM

> The time has come that Christians must vote for honest men and take consistent ground in politics. . . . God cannot sustain this free and blessed country which we love and pray for unless the Church will take right ground. . . . It seems sometimes as if the foundations of the nation are becoming rotten, and Christians seem to act as if they think God does not see what they do in politics.
>
> CHARLES FINNEY

> Now, more than ever before, the people are responsible for the character of their Congress. If that body be ignorant, reckless, and corrupt, it is because the people tolerate ignorance, recklessness, and corruption. If it be intelligent, brave, and pure, it is because the people demand these high qualities to represent them in the national legislature.
>
> PRESIDENT JAMES A. GARFIELD

> . . . God commands you to choose for rulers, just men who will rule in the fear of God. The preservation of a republican government depends on the faithful discharge of this duty; if the citizens neglect their duty and place unprincipled men in office, the government will soon be corrupted; laws will be made, not for the public good, so much as for selfish or local purposes; corrupt or incompetent men will be appointed to execute the laws; the public revenues will be squandered on unworthy men; and the rights of the citizens will be violated or disregarded.
>
> NOAH WEBSTER

Michmash and in the mountains of Bethel, and a thousand were with Jonathan in Gibeah of Benjamin. The rest of the people he sent away, every man to his tent.

[3]And Jonathan attacked the garrison of the Philistines that *was* in Geba, and the Philistines heard *of it.* Then Saul blew the trumpet throughout all the land, saying, "Let the Hebrews hear!" [4]Now all Israel heard it said *that* Saul had attacked a garrison of the Philistines, and *that* Israel had also become an abomination to the Philistines. And the people were called together to Saul at Gilgal.

[5]Then the Philistines gathered together to fight with Israel, thirty[a] thousand chariots and six thousand horsemen, and people as the sand which *is* on the seashore in multitude. And they came up and encamped in Michmash, to the east of Beth Aven. [6]When the men of Israel saw that they were in danger (for the people were distressed), then the people hid in caves, in thickets, in rocks, in holes, and in pits. [7]And *some of* the Hebrews crossed over the Jordan to the land of Gad and Gilead.

As for Saul, he *was* still in Gilgal, and all the people followed him trembling. [8]Then he waited seven days, according to the time set by Samuel. But Samuel did not come to Gilgal; and the people were scattered from him. [9]So Saul said, "Bring a burnt offering and peace offerings here to me." And he offered the burnt offering. [10]Now it happened, as soon as he had finished presenting the burnt offering, that Samuel came; and Saul went out to meet him, that he might greet him.

[11]And Samuel said, "What have you done?"

Saul said, "When I saw that the people were scattered from me, and *that* you did not come within the days appointed, and *that* the Philistines gathered together at Michmash, [12]then I said, 'The Philistines will now come down on me at Gilgal, and I have not made supplication to the LORD.' Therefore I felt compelled, and offered a burnt offering."

[13]And Samuel said to Saul, "You have done foolishly. You have not kept the commandment of the LORD your God, which

He commanded you. For now the LORD would have established your kingdom over Israel forever. [14]But now your kingdom shall not continue. The LORD has sought for Himself a man after His own heart, and the LORD has commanded him *to be* commander over His people, because you have not kept what the LORD commanded you."

[15]Then Samuel arose and went up from Gilgal to Gibeah of Benjamin.[a] And Saul numbered the people present with him, about six hundred men.

DEFENDER

"But now your kingdom shall not continue."

1 SAMUEL 13:14

When Kings Un-King Themselves

Jonathan Mayhew (1720–1766), a Congregational minister and distinguished Dudlein Lecturer at Harvard in 1765, reflected on the colonists' feelings toward King George III's hated Stamp Act:

> *The king is as much bound by his oath not to infringe the legal rights of the people, as the people are bound to yield subjection to him. From whence it follows that as soon as the prince sets himself above the law, he loses the king in the tyrant. He does, to all intents and purposes, un-king himself.*

No Weapons for the Army

[16]Saul, Jonathan his son, and the people present with them remained in Gibeah of Benjamin. But the Philistines encamped in Michmash. [17]Then raiders came out of the camp of the Philistines in three companies. One company turned onto the road to Ophrah, to the land of Shual, [18]another company turned to the road *to* Beth Horon, and another company turned *to* the road of the border that overlooks the Valley of Zeboim toward the wilderness.

[19]Now there was no blacksmith to be found throughout all the land of Israel, for

---

13:5 [a]Following Masoretic Text, Septuagint, Targum, and Vulgate; Syriac and some manuscripts of the Septuagint read *three.* **13:15** [a]Following Masoretic Text and Targum; Septuagint and Vulgate add *And the rest of the people went up after Saul to meet the people who fought against them, going from Gilgal to Gibeah in the hill of Benjamin.*

the Philistines said, "Lest the Hebrews make swords or spears." ²⁰But all the Israelites would go down to the Philistines to sharpen each man's plowshare, his mattock, his ax, and his sickle; ²¹and the charge for a sharpening was a pim[a] for the plowshares, the mattocks, the forks, and the axes, and to set the points of the goads. ²²So it came about, on the day of battle, that there was neither sword nor spear found in the hand of any of the people who *were* with Saul and Jonathan. But they were found with Saul and Jonathan his son.

²³And the garrison of the Philistines went out to the pass of Michmash.

Jonathan Defeats the Philistines

14 Now it happened one day that Jonathan the son of Saul said to the young man who bore his armor, "Come, let us go over to the Philistines' garrison that *is* on the other side." But he did not tell his father. ²And Saul was sitting in the outskirts of Gibeah under a pomegranate tree which *is* in Migron. The people who *were* with him *were* about six hundred men. ³Ahijah the son of Ahitub, Ichabod's brother, the son of Phinehas, the son of Eli, the LORD's priest in Shiloh, was wearing an ephod. But the people did not know that Jonathan had gone.

⁴Between the passes, by which Jonathan sought to go over to the Philistines' garrison, *there was* a sharp rock on one side and a sharp rock on the other side. And the name of one *was* Bozez, and the name of the other Seneh. ⁵The front of one faced northward opposite Michmash, and the other southward opposite Gibeah.

⁶Then Jonathan said to the young man who bore his armor, "Come, let us go over to the garrison of these uncircumcised; it may be that the LORD will work for us. For nothing restrains the LORD from saving by many or by few."

⁷So his armorbearer said to him, "Do all that is in your heart. Go then; here I am with you, according to your heart."

⁸Then Jonathan said, "Very well, let us cross over to *these* men, and we will show ourselves to them. ⁹If they say thus to us, 'Wait until we come to you,' then we will stand still in our place and not go up to them. ¹⁰But if they say thus, 'Come up to us,' then we will go up. For the LORD has delivered them into our hand, and this *will be* a sign to us."

¹¹So both of them showed themselves to the garrison of the Philistines. And the Philistines said, "Look, the Hebrews are coming out of the holes where they have hidden." ¹²Then the men of the garrison called to Jonathan and his armorbearer, and said, "Come up to us, and we will show you something."

Jonathan said to his armorbearer, "Come up after me, for the LORD has delivered them into the hand of Israel." ¹³And Jonathan climbed up on his hands and knees with his armorbearer after him; and they fell before Jonathan. And as he came after him, his armorbearer killed them. ¹⁴That first slaughter which Jonathan and his armorbearer made was about twenty men within about half an acre of land.[a]

¹⁵And there was trembling in the camp, in the field, and among all the people. The garrison and the raiders also trembled; and the earth quaked, so that it was a very great trembling. ¹⁶Now the watchmen of Saul in Gibeah of Benjamin looked, and *there* was the multitude, melting away; and they went here and there. ¹⁷Then Saul said to the people who *were* with him, "Now call the roll and see who has gone from us." And when they had called the roll, surprisingly, Jonathan and his armorbearer *were* not *there*. ¹⁸And Saul said to Ahijah, "Bring the ark[a] of God here" (for at that time the ark[b] of God was with the children of Israel). ¹⁹Now it happened, while Saul talked to the priest, that the noise which *was* in the camp of the Philistines continued to increase; so Saul said to the priest, "Withdraw your hand." ²⁰Then Saul and all the people who *were* with him assembled, and they went to the battle; and indeed every man's sword was against his neighbor, *and there was* very great confusion. ²¹Moreover the Hebrews

---

13:21 [a]About two-thirds shekel weight
14:14 [a]Literally *half the area plowed by a yoke* (of oxen in a day)   **14:18** [a]Following Masoretic Text, Targum, and Vulgate; Septuagint reads *ephod.*
[b]Following Masoretic Text, Targum, and Vulgate; Septuagint reads *ephod.*

who were with the Philistines before that time, who went up with them into the camp *from the* surrounding *country,* they also joined the Israelites who *were* with Saul and Jonathan. ²²Likewise all the men of Israel who had hidden in the mountains of Ephraim, *when* they heard that the Philistines fled, they also followed hard after them in the battle. ²³So the Lord saved Israel that day, and the battle shifted to Beth Aven.

Saul's Rash Oath

²⁴And the men of Israel were distressed that day, for Saul had placed the people under oath, saying, "Cursed *is* the man who eats *any* food until evening, before I have taken vengeance on my enemies." So none of the people tasted food. ²⁵Now all *the people* of the land came to a forest; and there was honey on the ground. ²⁶And when the people had come into the woods, there was the honey, dripping; but no one put his hand to his mouth, for the people feared the oath. ²⁷But Jonathan had not heard his father charge the people with the oath; therefore he stretched out the end of the rod that *was* in his hand and dipped it in a honeycomb, and put his hand to his mouth; and his countenance brightened. ²⁸Then one of the people said, "Your father strictly charged the people with an oath, saying, 'Cursed *is* the man who eats food this day.'" And the people were faint.

²⁹But Jonathan said, "My father has troubled the land. Look now, how my countenance has brightened because I tasted a little of this honey. ³⁰How much better if the people had eaten freely today of the spoil of their enemies which they found! For now would there not have been a much greater slaughter among the Philistines?"

³¹Now they had driven back the Philistines that day from Michmash to Aijalon. So the people were very faint. ³²And the people rushed on the spoil, and took sheep, oxen, and calves, and slaughtered *them* on the ground; and the people ate *them* with the blood. ³³Then they told Saul, saying, "Look, the people are sinning against the Lord by eating with the blood!"

So he said, "You have dealt treacherously; roll a large stone to me this day." ³⁴Then

Saul said, "Disperse yourselves among the people, and say to them, 'Bring me here every man's ox and every man's sheep, slaughter *them* here, and eat; and do not sin against the Lord by eating with the blood.'" So every one of the people brought his ox with him that night, and slaughtered *it* there. ³⁵Then Saul built an altar to the Lord. This was the first altar that he built to the Lord.

³⁶Now Saul said, "Let us go down after the Philistines by night, and plunder them until the morning light; and let us not leave a man of them."

And they said, "Do whatever seems good to you."

Then the priest said, "Let us draw near to God here."

³⁷So Saul asked counsel of God, "Shall I go down after the Philistines? Will You deliver them into the hand of Israel?" But He did not answer him that day. ³⁸And Saul said, "Come over here, all you chiefs of the people, and know and see what this sin was today. ³⁹For *as* the Lord lives, who saves Israel, though it be in Jonathan my son, he shall surely die." But not a man among all the people answered him. ⁴⁰Then he said to all Israel, "You be on one side, and my son Jonathan and I will be on the other side."

And the people said to Saul, "Do what seems good to you."

⁴¹Therefore Saul said to the Lord God of Israel, "Give a perfect *lot.*"[a] So Saul and Jonathan were taken, but the people escaped. ⁴²And Saul said, "Cast *lots* between my son Jonathan and me." So Jonathan was taken. ⁴³Then Saul said to Jonathan, "Tell me what you have done."

And Jonathan told him, and said, "I only tasted a little honey with the end of the rod that *was* in my hand. So now I must die!"

⁴⁴Saul answered, "God do so and more also; for you shall surely die, Jonathan."

⁴⁵But the people said to Saul, "Shall Jonathan die, who has accomplished this great deliverance in Israel? Certainly not!

14:41 ᵃFollowing Masoretic Text and Targum; Septuagint and Vulgate read *Why do You not answer Your servant today? If the injustice is with me or Jonathan my son, O Lord God of Israel, give proof; and if You say it is with Your people Israel, give holiness.*

As the Lord lives, not one hair of his head shall fall to the ground, for he has worked with God this day." So the people rescued Jonathan, and he did not die.

⁴⁶Then Saul returned from pursuing the Philistines, and the Philistines went to their own place.

Saul's Continuing Wars

⁴⁷So Saul established his sovereignty over Israel, and fought against all his enemies on every side, against Moab, against the people of Ammon, against Edom, against the kings of Zobah, and against the Philistines. Wherever he turned, he harassed *them.*ᵃ ⁴⁸And he gathered an army and attacked the Amalekites, and delivered Israel from the hands of those who plundered them.

⁴⁹The sons of Saul were Jonathan, Jishui,ᵃ and Malchishua. And the names of his two daughters *were these:* the name of the first-born Merab, and the name of the younger Michal. ⁵⁰The name of Saul's wife *was* Ahinoam the daughter of Ahimaaz. And the name of the commander of his army *was* Abner the son of Ner, Saul's uncle. ⁵¹Kish *was* the father of Saul, and Ner the father of Abner *was* the son of Abiel.

⁵²Now there was fierce war with the Philistines all the days of Saul. And when Saul saw any strong man or any valiant man, he took him for himself.

Saul Spares King Agag

15 Samuel also said to Saul, "The Lord sent me to anoint you king over His people, over Israel. Now therefore, heed the voice of the words of the Lord. ²Thus says the Lord of hosts: 'I will punish Amalek *for* what he did to Israel, how he ambushed him on the way when he came up from Egypt. ³Now go and attack Amalek, and utterly destroy all that they have, and do not spare them. But kill both man and woman, infant and nursing child, ox and sheep, camel and donkey.' "

⁴So Saul gathered the people together and numbered them in Telaim, two hundred thousand foot soldiers and ten thousand men of Judah. ⁵And Saul came to a city of Amalek, and lay in wait in the valley.

⁶Then Saul said to the Kenites, "Go, depart, get down from among the Amalekites, lest I destroy you with them. For you showed kindness to all the children of Israel when they came up out of Egypt." So the Kenites departed from among the Amalekites. ⁷And Saul attacked the Amalekites, from Havilah all the way to Shur, which is east of Egypt. ⁸He also took Agag king of the Amalekites alive, and utterly destroyed all the people with the edge of the sword. ⁹But Saul and the people spared Agag and the best of the sheep, the oxen, the fatlings, the lambs, and all *that was* good, and were unwilling to utterly destroy them. But everything despised and worthless, that they utterly destroyed.

Saul Rejected as King

¹⁰Now the word of the Lord came to Samuel, saying, ¹¹"I greatly regret that I have set up Saul *as* king, for he has turned back from following Me, and has not performed My commandments." And it grieved Samuel, and he cried out to the Lord all night. ¹²So when Samuel rose early in the morning to meet Saul, it was told Samuel, saying, "Saul went to Carmel, and indeed, he set up a monument for himself; and he has gone on around, passed by, and gone down to Gilgal." ¹³Then Samuel went to Saul, and Saul said to him, "Blessed *are* you of the Lord! I have performed the commandment of the Lord."

¹⁴But Samuel said, "What then *is* this bleating of the sheep in my ears, and the lowing of the oxen which I hear?"

¹⁵And Saul said, "They have brought them from the Amalekites; for the people spared the best of the sheep and the oxen, to sacrifice to the Lord your God; and the rest we have utterly destroyed."

¹⁶Then Samuel said to Saul, "Be quiet! And I will tell you what the Lord said to me last night."

And he said to him, "Speak on."

¹⁷So Samuel said, "When you *were* little in your own eyes, *were* you not head of the tribes of Israel? And did not the Lord anoint

---

14:47 ᵃSeptuagint and Vulgate read *prospered.*
14:49 ᵃCalled *Abinadab* in 1 Chronicles 8:33 and 9:39

you king over Israel? [18]Now the LORD sent you on a mission, and said, 'Go, and utterly destroy the sinners, the Amalekites, and fight against them until they are consumed.' [19]Why then did you not obey the voice of the LORD? Why did you swoop down on the spoil, and do evil in the sight of the LORD?"

[20]And Saul said to Samuel, "But I have obeyed the voice of the LORD, and gone on the mission on which the LORD sent me, and brought back Agag king of Amalek; I have utterly destroyed the Amalekites. [21]But the people took of the plunder, sheep and oxen, the best of the things which should have been utterly destroyed, to sacrifice to the LORD your God in Gilgal."

[22]So Samuel said:

"Has the LORD *as great* delight in burnt
    offerings and sacrifices,
As in obeying the voice of the LORD?
Behold, to obey is better than sacrifice,
And to heed than the fat of rams.
[23] For rebellion *is as* the sin of witchcraft,
And stubbornness *is as* iniquity and
    idolatry.
Because you have rejected the word
    of the LORD,
He also has rejected you from *being*
    king."

[24]Then Saul said to Samuel, "I have sinned, for I have transgressed the commandment of the LORD and your words, because I feared the people and obeyed their voice. [25]Now therefore, please pardon my sin, and return with me, that I may worship the LORD."

[26]But Samuel said to Saul, "I will not return with you, for you have rejected the word of the LORD, and the LORD has rejected you from being king over Israel." [27]And as Samuel turned around to go away, *Saul* seized the edge of his robe, and it tore. [28]So Samuel said to him, "The LORD has torn the kingdom of Israel from you today, and has given it to a neighbor of yours, *who is* better than you. [29]And also the Strength of Israel will not lie nor relent. For He *is* not a man, that He should relent."

[30]Then he said, "I have sinned; *yet* honor me now, please, before the elders of my people and before Israel, and return with me, that I may worship the LORD your God." [31]So Samuel turned back after Saul, and Saul worshiped the LORD.

[32]Then Samuel said, "Bring Agag king of the Amalekites here to me." So Agag came to him cautiously.

And Agag said, "Surely the bitterness of death is past."

[33]But Samuel said, "As your sword has made women childless, so shall your mother be childless among women." And Samuel hacked Agag in pieces before the LORD in Gilgal.

[34]Then Samuel went to Ramah, and Saul went up to his house at Gibeah of Saul. [35]And Samuel went no more to see Saul until the day of his death. Nevertheless Samuel mourned for Saul, and the LORD regretted that He had made Saul king over Israel.

David Anointed King

16 Now the LORD said to Samuel, "How long will you mourn for Saul, seeing I have rejected him from reigning over Israel? Fill your horn with oil, and go; I am sending you to Jesse the Bethlehemite. For I have provided Myself a king among his sons."

[2]And Samuel said, "How can I go? If Saul hears *it,* he will kill me."

But the LORD said, "Take a heifer with you, and say, 'I have come to sacrifice to the LORD.' [3]Then invite Jesse to the sacrifice, and I will show you what you shall do; you shall anoint for Me the one I name to you."

[4]So Samuel did what the LORD said, and went to Bethlehem. And the elders of the town trembled at his coming, and said, "Do you come peaceably?"

[5]And he said, "Peaceably; I have come to sacrifice to the LORD. Sanctify yourselves, and come with me to the sacrifice." Then he consecrated Jesse and his sons, and invited them to the sacrifice.

[6]So it was, when they came, that he looked at Eliab and said, "Surely the LORD's anointed *is* before Him!"

⁷But the LORD said to Samuel, "Do not look at his appearance or at his physical stature, because I have refused him. For *the LORD does* not *see* as man sees;ª for man looks at the outward appearance, but the LORD looks at the heart."

⁸So Jesse called Abinadab, and made him pass before Samuel. And he said, "Neither has the LORD chosen this one." ⁹Then Jesse made Shammah pass by. And he said, "Neither has the LORD chosen this one." ¹⁰Thus Jesse made seven of his sons pass before Samuel. And Samuel said to Jesse, "The LORD has not chosen these." ¹¹And Samuel said to Jesse, "Are all the young men here?" Then he said, "There remains yet the youngest, and there he is, keeping the sheep."

And Samuel said to Jesse, "Send and bring him. For we will not sit downª till he comes here." ¹²So he sent and brought him in. Now he *was* ruddy, with bright eyes, and good-looking. And the LORD said, "Arise, anoint him; for this *is* the one!" ¹³Then Samuel took the horn of oil and anointed him in the midst of his brothers; and the Spirit of the LORD came upon David from that day forward. So Samuel arose and went to Ramah.

A Distressing Spirit Troubles Saul

¹⁴But the Spirit of the LORD departed from Saul, and a distressing spirit from the LORD troubled him. ¹⁵And Saul's servants said to him, "Surely, a distressing spirit from God is troubling you. ¹⁶Let our master now command your servants, *who are* before you, to seek out a man *who is* a skillful player on the harp. And it shall be that he will play it with his hand when the distressing spirit from God is upon you, and you shall be well." ¹⁷So Saul said to his servants, "Provide me now a man who can play well, and bring *him* to me." ¹⁸Then one of the servants answered and said, "Look, I have seen a son of Jesse the Bethlehemite, *who is* skillful in playing, a mighty man of valor, a man of war, prudent in speech, and a handsome person; and the LORD *is* with him." ¹⁹Therefore Saul sent messengers to Jesse, and said, "Send me your son David, who *is*

with the sheep." ²⁰And Jesse took a donkey *loaded with* bread, a skin of wine, and a young goat, and sent *them* by his son David to Saul. ²¹So David came to Saul and stood before him. And he loved him greatly, and he became his armorbearer. ²²Then Saul sent to Jesse, saying, "Please let David stand before me, for he has found favor in my sight." ²³And so it was, whenever the spirit from God was upon Saul, that David would take a harp and play *it* with his hand. Then Saul would become refreshed and well, and the distressing spirit would depart from him.

David and Goliath

17 Now the Philistines gathered their armies together to battle, and were gathered at Sochoh, which *belongs* to Judah; they encamped between Sochoh and Azekah, in Ephes Dammim. ²And Saul and the men of Israel were gathered together, and they encamped in the Valley of Elah, and drew up in battle array against the Philistines. ³The Philistines stood on a mountain on one side, and Israel stood on a mountain on the other side, with a valley between them.

⁴And a champion went out from the camp of the Philistines, named Goliath, from Gath, whose height *was* six cubits and a span. ⁵He had a bronze helmet on his head, and he *was* armed with a coat of mail, and the weight of the coat *was* five thousand shekels of bronze. ⁶And *he had* bronze armor on his legs and a bronze javelin between his shoulders. ⁷Now the staff of his spear *was* like a weaver's beam, and his iron spearhead *weighed* six hundred shekels; and a shield-bearer went before him. ⁸Then he stood and cried out to the armies of Israel, and said to them, "Why have you come out to line up for battle? *Am* I not a Philistine, and you the servants of Saul? Choose a man for yourselves, and let him come down to me. ⁹If he is able to fight with me and

---

16:7 ªSeptuagint reads *For God does not see as man sees;* Targum reads *It is not by the appearance of a man;* Vulgate reads *Nor do I judge according to the looks of a man.* **16:11** ªFollowing Septuagint and Vulgate; Masoretic Text reads *turn around;* Targum and Syriac read *turn away.*

kill me, then we will be your servants. But if I prevail against him and kill him, then you shall be our servants and serve us." ¹⁰And the Philistine said, "I defy the armies of Israel this day; give me a man, that we may fight together." ¹¹When Saul and all Israel heard these words of the Philistine, they were dismayed and greatly afraid.

¹²Now David *was* the son of that Ephrathite of Bethlehem Judah, whose name *was* Jesse, and who had eight sons. And the man was old, advanced *in years,* in the days of Saul. ¹³The three oldest sons of Jesse had gone to follow Saul to the battle. The names of his three sons who went to the battle *were* Eliab the firstborn, next to him Abinadab, and the third Shammah. ¹⁴David *was* the youngest. And the three oldest followed Saul. ¹⁵But David occasionally went and returned from Saul to feed his father's sheep at Bethlehem.

¹⁶And the Philistine drew near and presented himself forty days, morning and evening.

¹⁷Then Jesse said to his son David, "Take now for your brothers an ephah of this dried *grain* and these ten loaves, and run to your brothers at the camp. ¹⁸And carry these ten cheeses to the captain of *their* thousand, and see how your brothers fare, and bring back news of them." ¹⁹Now Saul and they and all the men of Israel *were* in the Valley of Elah, fighting with the Philistines.

²⁰So David rose early in the morning, left the sheep with a keeper, and took *the things* and went as Jesse had commanded him. And he came to the camp as the army was going out to the fight and shouting for the battle. ²¹For Israel and the Philistines had drawn up in battle array, army against army. ²²And David left his supplies in the hand of the supply keeper, ran to the army, and came and greeted his brothers. ²³Then as he talked with them, there was the champion, the Philistine of Gath, Goliath by name, coming up from the armies of the Philistines; and he spoke according to the same words. So David heard *them.* ²⁴And all the men of Israel, when they saw the man, fled from him and were dreadfully afraid. ²⁵So the men of Israel said, "Have you seen this man who has come

up? Surely he has come up to defy Israel; and it shall be *that* the man who kills him the king will enrich with great riches, will give him his daughter, and give his father's house exemption *from taxes* in Israel."

²⁶Then David spoke to the men who stood by him, saying, "What shall be done for the man who kills this Philistine and takes away the reproach from Israel? For who *is* this uncircumcised Philistine, that he should defy the armies of the living God?"

²⁷And the people answered him in this manner, saying, "So shall it be done for the man who kills him."

²⁸Now Eliab his oldest brother heard when he spoke to the men; and Eliab's anger was aroused against David, and he said, "Why did you come down here? And with whom have you left those few sheep in the wilderness? I know your pride and the insolence of your heart, for you have come down to see the battle."

²⁹And David said, "What have I done now? *Is there* not a cause?" ³⁰Then he turned from him toward another and said the same thing; and these people answered him as the first ones *did.*

³¹Now when the words which David spoke were heard, they reported *them* to Saul; and he sent for him. ³²Then David said to Saul, "Let no man's heart fail because of him; your servant will go and fight with this Philistine."

³³And Saul said to David, "You are not able to go against this Philistine to fight with him; for you *are* a youth, and he a man of war from his youth."

³⁴But David said to Saul, "Your servant used to keep his father's sheep, and when a lion or a bear came and took a lamb out of the flock, ³⁵I went out after it and struck it, and delivered *the lamb* from its mouth; and when it arose against me, I caught *it* by its beard, and struck and killed it. ³⁶Your servant has killed both lion and bear; and this uncircumcised Philistine will be like one of them, seeing he has defied the armies of the living God." ³⁷Moreover David said, "The LORD, who delivered me from the paw of the lion and from the paw of the bear, He will deliver me from the hand of this Philistine."

And Saul said to David, "Go, and the LORD be with you!"

38So Saul clothed David with his armor, and he put a bronze helmet on his head; he also clothed him with a coat of mail. 39David fastened his sword to his armor and tried to walk, for he had not tested *them*. And David said to Saul, "I cannot walk with these, for I have not tested *them*." So David took them off.

40Then he took his staff in his hand; and he chose for himself five smooth stones from the brook, and put them in a shepherd's bag, in a pouch which he had, and his sling was in his hand. And he drew near to the Philistine. 41So the Philistine came, and began drawing near to David, and the man who bore the shield *went* before him. 42And when the Philistine looked about and saw David, he disdained him; for he was *only* a youth, ruddy and good-looking. 43So the Philistine said to David, "*Am* I a dog, that you come to me with sticks?" And the Philistine cursed David by his gods. 44And the Philistine said to David, "Come to me, and I will give your flesh to the birds of the air and the beasts of the field!"

45Then David said to the Philistine, "You come to me with a sword, with a spear, and with a javelin. But I come to you in the name of the LORD of hosts, the God of the armies of Israel, whom you have defied. 46This day the LORD will deliver you into my hand, and I will strike you and take your head from you. And this day I will give the carcasses of the camp of the Philistines to the birds of the air and the wild beasts of the earth, that all the earth may know that there is a God in Israel. 47Then all this assembly shall know that the LORD does not save with sword and spear; for the battle *is* the LORD's, and He will give you into our hands."

48So it was, when the Philistine arose and came and drew near to meet David, that David hurried and ran toward the army to meet the Philistine. 49Then David put his hand in his bag and took out a stone; and he slung *it* and struck the Philistine in his forehead, so that the stone sank into his forehead, and he fell on his face to the earth. 50So David prevailed over the Philistine with a sling and a stone, and struck the Philistine and killed him. But *there was* no sword in the hand of David. 51Therefore David ran and stood over the Philistine, took his sword and drew it out of its sheath and killed him, and cut off his head with it.

And when the Philistines saw that their champion was dead, they fled. 52Now the men of Israel and Judah arose and shouted, and pursued the Philistines as far as the entrance of the valleyᵃ and to the gates of Ekron. And the wounded of the Philistines fell along the road to Shaaraim, even as far as Gath and Ekron. 53Then the children of Israel returned from chasing the Philistines, and they plundered their tents. 54And David took the head of the Philistine and brought it to Jerusalem, but he put his armor in his tent.

55When Saul saw David going out against the Philistine, he said to Abner, the commander of the army, "Abner, whose son *is* this youth?"

And Abner said, "As your soul lives, O king, I do not know."

56So the king said, "Inquire whose son this young man *is*."

57Then, as David returned from the slaughter of the Philistine, Abner took him and brought him before Saul with the head of the Philistine in his hand. 58And Saul said to him, "Whose son *are* you, young man?"

So David answered, "*I am* the son of your servant Jesse the Bethlehemite."

Saul Resents David

18 Now when he had finished speaking to Saul, the soul of Jonathan was knit to the soul of David, and Jonathan loved him as his own soul. 2Saul took him that day, and would not let him go home to his father's house anymore. 3Then Jonathan and David made a covenant, because he loved him as his own soul. 4And Jonathan took off the robe that *was* on him and gave it to David, with his armor, even to his sword and his bow and his belt.

5So David went out wherever Saul sent him, *and* behaved wisely. And Saul set him

---

17:52 ᵃFollowing Masoretic Text, Syriac, Targum, and Vulgate; Septuagint reads *Gath*.

over the men of war, and he was accepted in the sight of all the people and also in the sight of Saul's servants. ⁶Now it had happened as they were coming *home,* when David was returning from the slaughter of the Philistine, that the women had come out of all the cities of Israel, singing and dancing, to meet King Saul, with tambourines, with joy, and with musical instruments. ⁷So the women sang as they danced, and said:

"Saul has slain his thousands,
  And David his ten thousands."

⁸Then Saul was very angry, and the saying displeased him; and he said, "They have ascribed to David ten thousands, and to me they have ascribed *only* thousands. Now *what* more can he have but the kingdom?" ⁹So Saul eyed David from that day forward.

¹⁰And it happened on the next day that the distressing spirit from God came upon Saul, and he prophesied inside the house. So David played *music* with his hand, as at other times; but *there was* a spear in Saul's hand. ¹¹And Saul cast the spear, for he said, "I will pin David to the wall!" But David escaped his presence twice.

¹²Now Saul was afraid of David, because the LORD was with him, but had departed from Saul. ¹³Therefore Saul removed him from his presence, and made him his captain over a thousand; and he went out and came in before the people. ¹⁴And David behaved wisely in all his ways, and the LORD *was* with him. ¹⁵Therefore, when Saul saw that he behaved very wisely, he was afraid of him. ¹⁶But all Israel and Judah loved David, because he went out and came in before them.

David Marries Michal

¹⁷Then Saul said to David, "Here is my older daughter Merab; I will give her to you as a wife. Only be valiant for me, and fight the LORD's battles." For Saul thought, "Let my hand not be against him, but let the hand of the Philistines be against him." ¹⁸So David said to Saul, "Who *am* I, and what *is* my life *or* my father's family in Israel, that I should be son-in-law to the king?" ¹⁹But it happened at the time when Merab, Saul's daughter, should have been given to David, that she was given to Adriel the Meholathite as a wife.

²⁰Now Michal, Saul's daughter, loved David. And they told Saul, and the thing pleased him. ²¹So Saul said, "I will give her to him, that she may be a snare to him, and that the hand of the Philistines may be against him." Therefore Saul said to David a second time, "You shall be my son-in-law today."

²²And Saul commanded his servants, "Communicate with David secretly, and say, 'Look, the king has delight in you, and all his servants love you. Now therefore, become the king's son-in-law.' "

²³So Saul's servants spoke those words in the hearing of David. And David said, "Does it seem to you *a* light *thing* to be a king's son-in-law, seeing I *am* a poor and lightly esteemed man?" ²⁴And the servants of Saul told him, saying, "In this manner David spoke."

²⁵Then Saul said, "Thus you shall say to David: 'The king does not desire any dowry but one hundred foreskins of the Philistines, to take vengeance on the king's enemies.' " But Saul thought to make David fall by the hand of the Philistines. ²⁶So when his servants told David these words, it pleased David well to become the king's son-in-law. Now the days had not expired; ²⁷therefore David arose and went, he and his men, and killed two hundred men of the Philistines. And David brought their foreskins, and they gave them in full count to the king, that he might become the king's son-in-law. Then Saul gave him Michal his daughter as a wife.

²⁸Thus Saul saw and knew that the LORD *was* with David, and *that* Michal, Saul's daughter, loved him; ²⁹and Saul was still more afraid of David. So Saul became David's enemy continually. ³⁰Then the princes of the Philistines went out *to war.* And so it was, whenever they went out, *that* David behaved more wisely than all the servants of Saul, so that his name became highly esteemed.

Saul Persecutes David

19 Now Saul spoke to Jonathan his son and to all his servants, that they

should kill David; but Jonathan, Saul's son, delighted greatly in David. ²So Jonathan told David, saying, "My father Saul seeks to kill you. Therefore please be on your guard until morning, and stay in a secret *place* and hide. ³And I will go out and stand beside my father in the field where you *are,* and I will speak with my father about you. Then what I observe, I will tell you."

⁴Thus Jonathan spoke well of David to Saul his father, and said to him, "Let not the king sin against his servant, against David, because he has not sinned against you, and because his works *have been* very good toward you. ⁵For he took his life in his hands and killed the Philistine, and the LORD brought about a great deliverance for all Israel. You saw *it* and rejoiced. Why then will you sin against innocent blood, to kill David without a cause?"

⁶So Saul heeded the voice of Jonathan, and Saul swore, "*As* the LORD lives, he shall not be killed." ⁷Then Jonathan called David, and Jonathan told him all these things. So Jonathan brought David to Saul, and he was in his presence as in times past.

⁸And there was war again; and David went out and fought with the Philistines, and struck them with a mighty blow, and they fled from him.

⁹Now the distressing spirit from the LORD came upon Saul as he sat in his house with his spear in his hand. And David was playing *music* with *his* hand. ¹⁰Then Saul sought to pin David to the wall with the spear, but he slipped away from Saul's presence; and he drove the spear into the wall. So David fled and escaped that night.

¹¹Saul also sent messengers to David's house to watch him and to kill him in the morning. And Michal, David's wife, told him, saying, "If you do not save your life tonight, tomorrow you will be killed." ¹²So Michal let David down through a window. And he went and fled and escaped. ¹³And Michal took an image and laid *it* in the bed, put a cover of goats' *hair* for his head, and covered *it* with clothes. ¹⁴So when Saul sent messengers to take David, she said, "He *is* sick."

¹⁵Then Saul sent the messengers *back* to see David, saying, "Bring him up to me in the bed, that I may kill him." ¹⁶And when the messengers had come in, there was the image in the bed, with a cover of goats' *hair* for his head. ¹⁷Then Saul said to Michal, "Why have you deceived me like this, and sent my enemy away, so that he has escaped?"

And Michal answered Saul, "He said to me, 'Let me go! Why should I kill you?'"

¹⁸So David fled and escaped, and went to Samuel at Ramah, and told him all that Saul had done to him. And he and Samuel went and stayed in Naioth. ¹⁹Now it was told Saul, saying, "Take note, David *is* at Naioth in Ramah!" ²⁰Then Saul sent messengers to take David. And when they saw the group of prophets prophesying, and Samuel standing *as* leader over them, the Spirit of God came upon the messengers of Saul, and they also prophesied. ²¹And when Saul was told, he sent other messengers, and they prophesied likewise. Then Saul sent messengers again the third time, and they prophesied also. ²²Then he also went to Ramah, and came to the great well that *is* at Sechu. So he asked, and said, "Where *are* Samuel and David?"

And *someone* said, "Indeed *they are* at Naioth in Ramah." ²³So he went there to Naioth in Ramah. Then the Spirit of God was upon him also, and he went on and prophesied until he came to Naioth in Ramah. ²⁴And he also stripped off his clothes and prophesied before Samuel in like manner, and lay down naked all that day and all that night. Therefore they say, "*Is* Saul also among the prophets?"[a]

Jonathan's Loyalty to David

20 Then David fled from Naioth in Ramah, and went and said to Jonathan, "What have I done? What *is* my iniquity, and what *is* my sin before your father, that he seeks my life?"

²So Jonathan said to him, "By no means! You shall not die! Indeed, my father will do nothing either great or small without first telling me. And why should my father hide this thing from me? It *is* not *so!*"

³Then David took an oath again, and said, "Your father certainly knows that I

19:24 ᵃCompare 1 Samuel 10:12

have found favor in your eyes, and he has said, 'Do not let Jonathan know this, lest he be grieved.' But truly, *as* the Lord lives and *as* your soul lives, *there is* but a step between me and death."

⁴So Jonathan said to David, "Whatever you yourself desire, I will do *it* for you."

⁵And David said to Jonathan, "Indeed tomorrow *is* the New Moon, and I should not fail to sit with the king to eat. But let me *go*, that I may hide in the field until the third *day* at evening. ⁶If your father misses me at all, then say, 'David earnestly asked *permission* of me that he might run over to Bethlehem, his city, for *there is* a yearly sacrifice there for all the family.' ⁷If he says thus: '*It is* well,' your servant will be safe. But if he is very angry, be sure that evil is determined by him. ⁸Therefore you shall deal kindly with your servant, for you have brought your servant into a covenant of the Lord with you. Nevertheless, if there is iniquity in me, kill me yourself, for why should you bring me to your father?"

⁹But Jonathan said, "Far be it from you! For if I knew certainly that evil was determined by my father to come upon you, then would I not tell you?"

¹⁰Then David said to Jonathan, "Who will tell me, or what *if* your father answers you roughly?"

¹¹And Jonathan said to David, "Come, let us go out into the field." So both of them went out into the field. ¹²Then Jonathan said to David: "The Lord God of Israel *is witness!* When I have sounded out my father sometime tomorrow, *or* the third *day*, and indeed *there is* good toward David, and I do not send to you and tell you, ¹³may the Lord do so and much more to Jonathan. But if it pleases my father *to do* you evil, then I will report it to you and send you away, that you may go in safety. And the Lord be with you as He has been with my father. ¹⁴And you shall not only show me the kindness of the Lord while I still live, that I may not die; ¹⁵but you shall not cut off your kindness from my house forever, no, not when the Lord has cut off every one of the enemies of David from the face of the earth." ¹⁶So Jonathan made *a covenant* with the house of David, *saying,*

"Let the Lord require *it* at the hand of David's enemies."

¹⁷Now Jonathan again caused David to vow, because he loved him; for he loved him as he loved his own soul. ¹⁸Then Jonathan said to David, "Tomorrow *is* the New Moon; and you will be missed, because your seat will be empty. ¹⁹And *when* you have stayed three days, go down quickly and come to the place where you hid on the day of the deed; and remain by the stone Ezel. ²⁰Then I will shoot three arrows to the side, as though I shot at a target; ²¹and there I will send a lad, *saying,* 'Go, find the arrows.' If I expressly say to the lad, 'Look, the arrows *are* on this side of you; get them and come'—then, as the Lord lives, *there is* safety for you and no harm. ²²But if I say thus to the young man, 'Look, the arrows *are* beyond you'—go your way, for the Lord has sent you away. ²³And as for the matter which you and I have spoken of, indeed the Lord *be* between you and me forever."

²⁴Then David hid in the field. And when the New Moon had come, the king sat down to eat the feast. ²⁵Now the king sat on his seat, as at other times, on a seat by the wall. And Jonathan arose,ᵃ and Abner sat by Saul's side, but David's place was empty. ²⁶Nevertheless Saul did not say anything that day, for he thought, "Something has happened to him; he *is* unclean, surely he *is* unclean." ²⁷And it happened the next day, the second *day* of the month, that David's place was empty. And Saul said to Jonathan his son, "Why has the son of Jesse not come to eat, either yesterday or today?"

²⁸So Jonathan answered Saul, "David earnestly asked *permission* of me *to go* to Bethlehem. ²⁹And he said, 'Please let me go, for our family has a sacrifice in the city, and my brother has commanded me *to be there.* And now, if I have found favor in your eyes, please let me get away and see my brothers.' Therefore he has not come to the king's table."

³⁰Then Saul's anger was aroused against Jonathan, and he said to him, "You son of a perverse, rebellious *woman!* Do I not

---

20:25 ᵃFollowing Masoretic Text, Syriac, Targum, and Vulgate; Septuagint reads *he sat across from Jonathan.*

know that you have chosen the son of Jesse to your own shame and to the shame of your mother's nakedness? ³¹For as long as the son of Jesse lives on the earth, you shall not be established, nor your kingdom. Now therefore, send and bring him to me, for he shall surely die."

³²And Jonathan answered Saul his father, and said to him, "Why should he be killed? What has he done?" ³³Then Saul cast a spear at him to kill him, by which Jonathan knew that it was determined by his father to kill David.

³⁴So Jonathan arose from the table in fierce anger, and ate no food the second day of the month, for he was grieved for David, because his father had treated him shamefully.

³⁵And so it was, in the morning, that Jonathan went out into the field at the time appointed with David, and a little lad was with him. ³⁶Then he said to his lad, "Now run, find the arrows which I shoot." As the lad ran, he shot an arrow beyond him. ³⁷When the lad had come to the place where the arrow was which Jonathan had shot, Jonathan cried out after the lad and said, "Is not the arrow beyond you?" ³⁸And Jonathan cried out after the lad, "Make haste, hurry, do not delay!" So Jonathan's lad gathered up the arrows and came back to his master. ³⁹But the lad did not know anything. Only Jonathan and David knew of the matter. ⁴⁰Then Jonathan gave his weapons to his lad, and said to him, "Go, carry them to the city."

⁴¹As soon as the lad had gone, David arose from a place toward the south, fell on his face to the ground, and bowed down three times. And they kissed one another; and they wept together, but David more so. ⁴²Then Jonathan said to David, "Go in peace, since we have both sworn in the name of the Lord, saying, 'May the Lord be between you and me, and between your descendants and my descendants, forever.'" So he arose and departed, and Jonathan went into the city.

David and the Holy Bread

21 Now David came to Nob, to Ahimelech the priest. And Ahimelech was afraid when he met David, and said to him, "Why are you alone, and no one is with you?"

²So David said to Ahimelech the priest, "The king has ordered me on some business, and said to me, 'Do not let anyone know anything about the business on which I send you, or what I have commanded you.' And I have directed my young men to such and such a place. ³Now therefore, what have you on hand? Give me five loaves of bread in my hand, or whatever can be found."

⁴And the priest answered David and said, "There is no common bread on hand; but there is holy bread, if the young men have at least kept themselves from women."

⁵Then David answered the priest, and said to him, "Truly, women have been kept from us about three days since I came out. And the vessels of the young men are holy, and the bread is in effect common, even though it was consecrated in the vessel this day."

⁶So the priest gave him holy bread; for there was no bread there but the show-bread which had been taken from before the Lord, in order to put hot bread in its place on the day when it was taken away.

⁷Now a certain man of the servants of Saul was there that day, detained before the Lord. And his name was Doeg, an Edomite, the chief of the herdsmen who belonged to Saul.

⁸And David said to Ahimelech, "Is there not here on hand a spear or a sword? For I have brought neither my sword nor my weapons with me, because the king's business required haste."

⁹So the priest said, "The sword of Goliath the Philistine, whom you killed in the Valley of Elah, there it is, wrapped in a cloth behind the ephod. If you will take that, take it. For there is no other except that one here."

And David said, "There is none like it; give it to me."

David Flees to Gath

¹⁰Then David arose and fled that day from before Saul, and went to Achish the king of Gath. ¹¹And the servants of Achish said to him, "Is this not David the king of the land? Did they not sing of him to one another in dances, saying:

'Saul has slain his thousands,
And David his ten thousands'?"ᵃ

¹²Now David took these words to heart, and was very much afraid of Achish the king of Gath. ¹³So he changed his behavior before them, pretended madness in their hands, scratched on the doors of the gate, and let his saliva fall down on his beard. ¹⁴Then Achish said to his servants, "Look, you see the man is insane. Why have you brought him to me? ¹⁵Have I need of madmen, that you have brought this *fellow* to play the madman in my presence? Shall this *fellow* come into my house?"

David's Four Hundred Men

22 David therefore departed from there and escaped to the cave of Adullam. So when his brothers and all his father's house heard *it,* they went down there to him. ²And everyone *who was* in distress, everyone who *was* in debt, and everyone *who was* discontented gathered to him. So he became captain over them. And there were about four hundred men with him.

³Then David went from there to Mizpah of Moab; and he said to the king of Moab, "Please let my father and mother come here with you, till I know what God will do for me." ⁴So he brought them before the king of Moab, and they dwelt with him all the time that David was in the stronghold.

⁵Now the prophet Gad said to David, "Do not stay in the stronghold; depart, and go to the land of Judah." So David departed and went into the forest of Hereth.

Saul Murders the Priests

⁶When Saul heard that David and the men who *were* with him had been discovered—now Saul was staying in Gibeah under a tamarisk tree in Ramah, with his spear in his hand, and all his servants standing about him— ⁷then Saul said to his servants who stood about him, "Hear now, you Benjamites! Will the son of Jesse give every one of you fields and vineyards, *and* make you all captains of thousands and captains of hundreds? ⁸All of you have conspired against me, and *there is* no one who reveals to me that my son has made a

covenant with the son of Jesse; and *there is* not one of you who is sorry for me or reveals to me that my son has stirred up my servant against me, to lie in wait, as *it is* this day."

⁹Then answered Doeg the Edomite, who was set over the servants of Saul, and said, "I saw the son of Jesse going to Nob, to Ahimelech the son of Ahitub. ¹⁰And he inquired of the LORD for him, gave him provisions, and gave him the sword of Goliath the Philistine."

¹¹So the king sent to call Ahimelech the priest, the son of Ahitub, and all his father's house, the priests who *were* in Nob. And they all came to the king. ¹²And Saul said, "Hear now, son of Ahitub!"

He answered, "Here I am, my lord."

¹³Then Saul said to him, "Why have you conspired against me, you and the son of Jesse, in that you have given him bread and a sword, and have inquired of God for him, that he should rise against me, to lie in wait, as it is this day?"

¹⁴So Ahimelech answered the king and said, "And who among all your servants *is* as faithful as David, who is the king's son-in-law, who goes at your bidding, and is honorable in your house? ¹⁵Did I then begin to inquire of God for him? Far be it from me! Let not the king impute anything to his servant, *or* to any in the house of my father. For your servant knew nothing of all this, little or much."

¹⁶And the king said, "You shall surely die, Ahimelech, you and all your father's house!" ¹⁷Then the king said to the guards who stood about him, "Turn and kill the priests of the LORD, because their hand also *is* with David, and because they knew when he fled and did not tell it to me." But the servants of the king would not lift their hands to strike the priests of the LORD. ¹⁸And the king said to Doeg, "You turn and kill the priests!" So Doeg the Edomite turned and struck the priests, and killed on that day eighty-five men who wore a linen ephod. ¹⁹Also Nob, the city of the priests, he struck with the edge of the sword, both men and women, children and nursing

---

21:11 ᵃCompare 1 Samuel 18:7

infants, oxen and donkeys and sheep—with the edge of the sword.

20Now one of the sons of Ahimelech the son of Ahitub, named Abiathar, escaped and fled after David. 21And Abiathar told David that Saul had killed the LORD's priests. 22So David said to Abiathar, "I knew that day, when Doeg the Edomite *was* there, that he would surely tell Saul. I have caused *the death* of all the persons of your father's house. 23Stay with me; do not fear. For he who seeks my life seeks your life, but with me you *shall be* safe."

David Saves the City of Keilah

23 Then they told David, saying, "Look, the Philistines are fighting against Keilah, and they are robbing the threshing floors."

2Therefore David inquired of the LORD, saying, "Shall I go and attack these Philistines?"

And the LORD said to David, "Go and attack the Philistines, and save Keilah."

3But David's men said to him, "Look, we are afraid here in Judah. How much more then if we go to Keilah against the armies of the Philistines?" 4Then David inquired of the LORD once again.

And the LORD answered him and said, "Arise, go down to Keilah. For I will deliver the Philistines into your hand." 5And David and his men went to Keilah and fought with the Philistines, struck them with a mighty blow, and took away their livestock. So David saved the inhabitants of Keilah.

6Now it happened, when Abiathar the son of Ahimelech fled to David at Keilah, *that* he went down *with* an ephod in his hand.

7And Saul was told that David had gone to Keilah. So Saul said, "God has delivered him into my hand, for he has shut himself in by entering a town that has gates and bars." 8Then Saul called all the people together for war, to go down to Keilah to besiege David and his men.

9When David knew that Saul plotted evil against him, he said to Abiathar the priest, "Bring the ephod here." 10Then David said, "O LORD God of Israel, Your servant has certainly heard that Saul seeks to come to Keilah to destroy the city for my sake.

11Will the men of Keilah deliver me into his hand? Will Saul come down, as Your servant has heard? O LORD God of Israel, I pray, tell Your servant."

And the LORD said, "He will come down."

12Then David said, "Will the men of Keilah deliver me and my men into the hand of Saul?"

And the LORD said, "They will deliver *you*."

13So David and his men, about six hundred, arose and departed from Keilah and went wherever they could go. Then it was told Saul that David had escaped from Keilah; so he halted the expedition.

David in Wilderness Strongholds

14And David stayed in strongholds in the wilderness, and remained in the mountains in the Wilderness of Ziph. Saul sought him every day, but God did not deliver him into his hand. 15So David saw that Saul had come out to seek his life. And David *was* in the Wilderness of Ziph in a forest.ᵃ 16Then Jonathan, Saul's son, arose and went to David in the woods and strengthened his hand in God. 17And he said to him, "Do not fear, for the hand of Saul my father shall not find you. You shall be king over Israel, and I shall be next to you. Even my father Saul knows that." 18So the two of them made a covenant before the LORD. And David stayed in the woods, and Jonathan went to his own house.

19Then the Ziphites came up to Saul at Gibeah, saying, "Is David not hiding with us in strongholds in the woods, in the hill of Hachilah, which *is* on the south of Jeshimon? 20Now therefore, O king, come down according to all the desire of your soul to come down; and our part *shall be* to deliver him into the king's hand."

21And Saul said, "Blessed *are* you of the LORD, for you have compassion on me. 22Please go and find out for sure, and see the place where his hideout is, *and* who has seen him there. For I am told he is very crafty. 23See therefore, and take knowledge of all the lurking places where he hides; and come back to me with certainty, and I will go with you. And it shall be, if he is in

23:15 ᵃOr *in Horesh*

the land, that I will search for him throughout all the clans[a] of Judah."

²⁴So they arose and went to Ziph before Saul. But David and his men *were* in the Wilderness of Maon, in the plain on the south of Jeshimon. ²⁵When Saul and his men went to seek *him,* they told David. Therefore he went down to the rock, and stayed in the Wilderness of Maon. And when Saul heard *that,* he pursued David in the Wilderness of Maon. ²⁶Then Saul went on one side of the mountain, and David and his men on the other side of the mountain. So David made haste to get away from Saul, for Saul and his men were encircling David and his men to take them.

²⁷But a messenger came to Saul, saying, "Hurry and come, for the Philistines have invaded the land!" ²⁸Therefore Saul returned from pursuing David, and went against the Philistines; so they called that place the Rock of Escape.[a] ²⁹Then David went up from there and dwelt in strongholds at En Gedi.

David Spares Saul

24 Now it happened, when Saul had returned from following the Philistines, that it was told him, saying, "Take note! David *is* in the Wilderness of En Gedi." ²Then Saul took three thousand chosen men from all Israel, and went to seek David and his men on the Rocks of the Wild Goats. ³So he came to the sheepfolds by the road, where there *was* a cave; and Saul went in to attend to his needs. (David and his men were staying in the recesses of the cave.) ⁴Then the men of David said to him, "This is the day of which the LORD said to you, 'Behold, I will deliver your enemy into your hand, that you may do to him as it seems good to you.'" And David arose and secretly cut off a corner of Saul's robe. ⁵Now it happened afterward that David's heart troubled him because he had cut Saul's robe. ⁶And he said to his men, "The LORD forbid that I should do this thing to my master, the LORD's anointed, to stretch out my hand against him, seeing he *is* the anointed of the LORD." ⁷So David restrained his servants with *these* words, and did not allow them to rise against Saul. And Saul got up from the cave and went on *his* way.

⁸David also arose afterward, went out of the cave, and called out to Saul, saying, "My lord the king!" And when Saul looked behind him, David stooped with his face to the earth, and bowed down. ⁹And David said to Saul: "Why do you listen to the words of men who say, 'Indeed David seeks your harm'? ¹⁰Look, this day your eyes have seen that the LORD delivered you today into my hand in the cave, and *someone* urged *me* to kill you. But *my eye* spared you, and I said, 'I will not stretch out my hand against my lord, for he *is* the LORD's anointed.' ¹¹Moreover, my father, see! Yes, see the corner of your robe in my hand! For in that I cut off the corner of your robe, and did not kill you, know and see that *there is* neither evil nor rebellion in my hand, and I have not sinned against you. Yet you hunt my life to take it. ¹²Let the LORD judge between you and me, and let the LORD avenge me on you. But my hand shall not be against you. ¹³As the proverb of the ancients says, 'Wickedness proceeds from the wicked.' But my hand shall not be against you. ¹⁴After whom has the king of Israel come out? Whom do you pursue? A dead dog? A flea? ¹⁵Therefore let the LORD be judge, and judge between you and me, and see and plead my case, and deliver me out of your hand."

¹⁶So it was, when David had finished speaking these words to Saul, that Saul said, "*Is* this your voice, my son David?" And Saul lifted up his voice and wept. ¹⁷Then he said to David: "You *are* more righteous than I; for you have rewarded me with good, whereas I have rewarded you with evil. ¹⁸And you have shown this day how you have dealt well with me; for when the LORD delivered me into your hand, you did not kill me. ¹⁹For if a man finds his enemy, will he let him get away safely? Therefore may the LORD reward you with good for what you have done to me this day. ²⁰And now I know indeed that you shall surely be king, and that the kingdom of Israel shall be established in your hand. ²¹Therefore swear now to me by the LORD that you will not cut off my descendants

---

23:23 ªLiterally *thousands*   **23:28** ªHebrew *Sela Hammahlekoth*

after me, and that you will not destroy my name from my father's house."

²²So David swore to Saul. And Saul went home, but David and his men went up to the stronghold.

Death of Samuel

25 Then Samuel died; and the Israelites gathered together and lamented for him, and buried him at his home in Ramah. And David arose and went down to the Wilderness of Paran.ᵃ

David and the Wife of Nabal

²Now *there was* a man in Maon whose business *was* in Carmel, and the man *was* very rich. He had three thousand sheep and a thousand goats. And he was shearing his sheep in Carmel. ³The name of the man *was* Nabal, and the name of his wife Abigail. And *she was* a woman of good understanding and beautiful appearance; but the man *was* harsh and evil in *his* doings. He *was of the house of* Caleb.

⁴When David heard in the wilderness that Nabal was shearing his sheep, ⁵David sent ten young men; and David said to the young men, "Go up to Carmel, go to Nabal, and greet him in my name. ⁶And thus you shall say to him who lives *in prosperity:* 'Peace *be* to you, peace to your house, and peace to all that you have! ⁷Now I have heard that you have shearers. Your shepherds were with us, and we did not hurt them, nor was there anything missing from them all the while they were in Carmel. ⁸Ask your young men, and they will tell you. Therefore let *my* young men find favor in your eyes, for we come on a feast day. Please give whatever comes to your hand to your servants and to your son David.'"

⁹So when David's young men came, they spoke to Nabal according to all these words in the name of David, and waited.

¹⁰Then Nabal answered David's servants, and said, "Who *is* David, and who *is* the son of Jesse? There are many servants nowadays who break away each one from his master. ¹¹Shall I then take my bread and my water and my meat that I have killed for my shearers, and give *it* to men when I do not know where they *are* from?"

¹²So David's young men turned on their heels and went back; and they came and told him all these words. ¹³Then David said to his men, "Every man gird on his sword." So every man girded on his sword, and David also girded on his sword. And about four hundred men went with David, and two hundred stayed with the supplies.

¹⁴Now one of the young men told Abigail, Nabal's wife, saying, "Look, David sent messengers from the wilderness to greet our master; and he reviled them. ¹⁵But the men *were* very good to us, and we were not hurt, nor did we miss anything as long as we accompanied them, when we were in the fields. ¹⁶They were a wall to us both by night and day, all the time we were with them keeping the sheep. ¹⁷Now therefore, know and consider what you will do, for harm is determined against our master and against all his household. For he *is such* a scoundrelᵃ that *one* cannot speak to him."

¹⁸Then Abigail made haste and took two hundred *loaves* of bread, two skins of wine, five sheep already dressed, five seahs of roasted *grain,* one hundred clusters of raisins, and two hundred cakes of figs, and loaded *them* on donkeys. ¹⁹And she said to her servants, "Go on before me; see, I am coming after you." But she did not tell her husband Nabal.

²⁰So it was, *as* she rode on the donkey, that she went down under cover of the hill; and there were David and his men, coming down toward her, and she met them. ²¹Now David had said, "Surely in vain I have protected all that this *fellow* has in the wilderness, so that nothing was missed of all that *belongs* to him. And he has repaid me evil for good. ²²May God do so, and more also, to the enemies of David, if I leave one male of all who *belong* to him by morning light."

²³Now when Abigail saw David, she dismounted quickly from the donkey, fell on her face before David, and bowed down to the ground. ²⁴So she fell at his feet and said: "On me, my lord, *on* me *let* this iniquity *be!* And please let your maidservant speak in

---

25:1 ᵃFollowing Masoretic Text, Syriac, Targum, and Vulgate; Septuagint reads *Maon.* **25:17** ᵃLiterally *son of Belial*

your ears, and hear the words of your maidservant. ²⁵Please, let not my lord regard this scoundrel Nabal. For as his name *is,* so *is* he: Nabalᵃ *is* his name, and folly *is* with him! But I, your maidservant, did not see the young men of my lord whom you sent. ²⁶Now therefore, my lord, *as* the LORD lives and *as* your soul lives, since the LORD has held you back from coming to bloodshed and from avenging yourself with your own hand, now then, let your enemies and those who seek harm for my lord be as Nabal. ²⁷And now this present which your maidservant has brought to my lord, let it be given to the young men who follow my lord. ²⁸Please forgive the trespass of your maidservant. For the LORD will certainly make for my lord an enduring house, because my lord fights the battles of the LORD, and evil is not found in you throughout your days. ²⁹Yet a man has risen to pursue you and seek your life, but the life of my lord shall be bound in the bundle of the living with the LORD your God; and the lives of your enemies He shall sling out, *as from* the pocket of a sling. ³⁰And it shall come to pass, when the LORD has done for my lord according to all the good that He has spoken concerning you, and has appointed you ruler over Israel, ³¹that this will be no grief to you, nor offense of heart to my lord, either that you have shed blood without cause, or that my lord has avenged himself. But when the LORD has dealt well with my lord, then remember your maidservant."

³²Then David said to Abigail: "Blessed *is* the LORD God of Israel, who sent you this day to meet me! ³³And blessed *is* your advice and blessed *are* you, because you have kept me this day from coming to bloodshed and from avenging myself with my own hand. ³⁴For indeed, *as* the LORD God of Israel lives, who has kept me back from hurting you, unless you had hurried and come to meet me, surely by morning light no males would have been left to Nabal!" ³⁵So David received from her hand what she had brought him, and said to her, "Go up in peace to your house. See, I have heeded your voice and respected your person."

³⁶Now Abigail went to Nabal, and there he was, holding a feast in his house, like the feast of a king. And Nabal's heart *was* merry within him, for he *was* very drunk; therefore she told him nothing, little or much, until morning light. ³⁷So it was, in the morning, when the wine had gone from Nabal, and his wife had told him these things, that his heart died within him, and he became *like* a stone. ³⁸Then it happened, *after* about ten days, that the LORD struck Nabal, and he died.

³⁹So when David heard that Nabal was dead, he said, "Blessed *be* the LORD, who has pleaded the cause of my reproach from the hand of Nabal, and has kept His servant from evil! For the LORD has returned the wickedness of Nabal on his own head."

And David sent and proposed to Abigail, to take her as his wife. ⁴⁰When the servants of David had come to Abigail at Carmel, they spoke to her saying, "David sent us to you, to ask you to become his wife."

⁴¹Then she arose, bowed her face to the earth, and said, "Here is your maidservant, a servant to wash the feet of the servants of my lord." ⁴²So Abigail rose in haste and rode on a donkey, attended by five of her maidens; and she followed the messengers of David, and became his wife. ⁴³David also took Ahinoam of Jezreel, and so both of them were his wives.

⁴⁴But Saul had given Michal his daughter, David's wife, to Paltiᵃ the son of Laish, who *was* from Gallim.

David Spares Saul a Second Time

26 Now the Ziphites came to Saul at Gibeah, saying, "Is David not hiding in the hill of Hachilah, opposite Jeshimon?" ²Then Saul arose and went down to the Wilderness of Ziph, having three thousand chosen men of Israel with him, to seek David in the Wilderness of Ziph. ³And Saul encamped in the hill of Hachilah, which *is* opposite Jeshimon, by the road. But David stayed in the wilderness, and he saw that Saul came after him into the wilderness. ⁴David therefore sent out spies, and understood that Saul had indeed come.

25:25 ᵃLiterally *Fool*   **25:44** ᵃSpelled *Paltiel* in 2 Samuel 3:15

⁵So David arose and came to the place where Saul had encamped. And David saw the place where Saul lay, and Abner the son of Ner, the commander of his army. Now Saul lay within the camp, with the people encamped all around him. ⁶Then David answered, and said to Ahimelech the Hittite and to Abishai the son of Zeruiah, brother of Joab, saying, "Who will go down with me to Saul in the camp?"

And Abishai said, "I will go down with you."

⁷So David and Abishai came to the people by night; and there Saul lay sleeping within the camp, with his spear stuck in the ground by his head. And Abner and the people lay all around him. ⁸Then Abishai said to David, "God has delivered your enemy into your hand this day. Now therefore, please, let me strike him at once with the spear, right to the earth; and I will not *have to strike* him a second time!"

⁹But David said to Abishai, "Do not destroy him; for who can stretch out his hand against the LORD's anointed, and be guiltless?" ¹⁰David said furthermore, "*As* the LORD lives, the LORD shall strike him, or his day shall come to die, or he shall go out to battle and perish. ¹¹The LORD forbid that I should stretch out my hand against the LORD's anointed. But please, take now the spear and the jug of water that *are* by his head, and let us go." ¹²So David took the spear and the jug of water *by* Saul's head, and they got away; and no man saw or knew *it* or awoke. For they *were* all asleep, because a deep sleep from the LORD had fallen on them.

¹³Now David went over to the other side, and stood on the top of a hill afar off, a great distance *being* between them. ¹⁴And David called out to the people and to Abner the son of Ner, saying, "Do you not answer, Abner?"

Then Abner answered and said, "Who *are* you, calling out to the king?"

¹⁵So David said to Abner, "*Are* you not a man? And who *is* like you in Israel? Why then have you not guarded your lord the king? For one of the people came in to destroy your lord the king. ¹⁶This thing that you have done *is* not good. *As* the LORD lives, you deserve to die, because you have not

guarded your master, the LORD's anointed. And now see where the king's spear *is,* and the jug of water that *was* by his head."

¹⁷Then Saul knew David's voice, and said, "*Is* that your voice, my son David?"

David said, "*It is* my voice, my lord, O king." ¹⁸And he said, "Why does my lord thus pursue his servant? For what have I done, or what evil *is* in my hand? ¹⁹Now therefore, please, let my lord the king hear the words of his servant: If the LORD has stirred you up against me, let Him accept an offering. But if *it is* the children of men, *may* they *be* cursed before the LORD, for they have driven me out this day from sharing in the inheritance of the LORD, saying, 'Go, serve other gods.' ²⁰So now, do not let my blood fall to the earth before the face of the LORD. For the king of Israel has come out to seek a flea, as when one hunts a partridge in the mountains."

²¹Then Saul said, "I have sinned. Return, my son David. For I will harm you no more, because my life was precious in your eyes this day. Indeed I have played the fool and erred exceedingly."

²²And David answered and said, "Here is the king's spear. Let one of the young men come over and get it. ²³May the LORD repay every man *for* his righteousness and his faithfulness; for the LORD delivered you into *my* hand today, but I would not stretch out my hand against the LORD's anointed. ²⁴And indeed, as your life was valued much this day in my eyes, so let my life be valued much in the eyes of the LORD, and let Him deliver me out of all tribulation."

²⁵Then Saul said to David, "*May* you *be* blessed, my son David! You shall both do great things and also still prevail."

So David went on his way, and Saul returned to his place.

David Allied with the Philistines

27 And David said in his heart, "Now I shall perish someday by the hand of Saul. *There is* nothing better for me than that I should speedily escape to the land of the Philistines; and Saul will despair of me, to seek me anymore in any part of Israel. So I shall escape out of his hand." ²Then David arose and went over with the six

hundred men who *were* with him to Achish the son of Maoch, king of Gath. ³So David dwelt with Achish at Gath, he and his men, each man with his household, *and* David with his two wives, Ahinoam the Jezreelitess, and Abigail the Carmelitess, Nabal's widow. ⁴And it was told Saul that David had fled to Gath; so he sought him no more.

⁵Then David said to Achish, "If I have now found favor in your eyes, let them give me a place in some town in the country, that I may dwell there. For why should your servant dwell in the royal city with you?" ⁶So Achish gave him Ziklag that day. Therefore Ziklag has belonged to the kings of Judah to this day. ⁷Now the time that David dwelt in the country of the Philistines was one full year and four months.

⁸And David and his men went up and raided the Geshurites, the Girzites,ᵃ and the Amalekites. For those *nations* were the inhabitants of the land from of old, as you go to Shur, even as far as the land of Egypt. ⁹Whenever David attacked the land, he left neither man nor woman alive, but took away the sheep, the oxen, the donkeys, the camels, and the apparel, and returned and came to Achish. ¹⁰Then Achish would say, "Where have you made a raid today?" And David would say, "Against the southern *area* of Judah, or against the southern *area* of the Jerahmeelites, or against the southern *area* of the Kenites." ¹¹David would save neither man nor woman alive, to bring *news* to Gath, saying, "Lest they should inform on us, saying, 'Thus David did.'" And thus *was* his behavior all the time he dwelt in the country of the Philistines. ¹²So Achish believed David, saying, "He has made his people Israel utterly abhor him; therefore he will be my servant forever."

28 Now it happened in those days that the Philistines gathered their armies together for war, to fight with Israel. And Achish said to David, "You assuredly know that you will go out with me to battle, you and your men."

²So David said to Achish, "Surely you know what your servant can do."

And Achish said to David, "Therefore I will make you one of my chief guardians forever."

Saul Consults a Medium

³Now Samuel had died, and all Israel had lamented for him and buried him in Ramah, in his own city. And Saul had put the mediums and the spiritists out of the land.

⁴Then the Philistines gathered together, and came and encamped at Shunem. So Saul gathered all Israel together, and they encamped at Gilboa. ⁵When Saul saw the army of the Philistines, he was afraid, and his heart trembled greatly. ⁶And when Saul inquired of the LORD, the LORD did not answer him, either by dreams or by Urim or by the prophets.

⁷Then Saul said to his servants, "Find me a woman who is a medium, that I may go to her and inquire of her."

And his servants said to him, "In fact, *there is* a woman who is a medium at En Dor."

⁸So Saul disguised himself and put on other clothes, and he went, and two men with him; and they came to the woman by night. And he said, "Please conduct a séance for me, and bring up for me the one I shall name to you."

⁹Then the woman said to him, "Look, you know what Saul has done, how he has cut off the mediums and the spiritists from the land. Why then do you lay a snare for my life, to cause me to die?"

¹⁰And Saul swore to her by the LORD, saying, "*As* the LORD lives, no punishment shall come upon you for this thing."

¹¹Then the woman said, "Whom shall I bring up for you?"

And he said, "Bring up Samuel for me."

¹²When the woman saw Samuel, she cried out with a loud voice. And the woman spoke to Saul, saying, "Why have you deceived me? For you *are* Saul!"

¹³And the king said to her, "Do not be afraid. What did you see?"

And the woman said to Saul, "I saw a spiritᵃ ascending out of the earth."

¹⁴So he said to her, "What *is* his form?"

And she said, "An old man is coming up, and he *is* covered with a mantle." And

---

27:8 ᵃOr *Gezrites*   **28:13** ᵃHebrew *elohim*

Saul perceived that it *was* Samuel, and he stooped with *his* face to the ground and bowed down.

¹⁵Now Samuel said to Saul, "Why have you disturbed me by bringing me up?"

And Saul answered, "I am deeply distressed; for the Philistines make war against me, and God has departed from me and does not answer me anymore, neither by prophets nor by dreams. Therefore I have called you, that you may reveal to me what I should do."

¹⁶Then Samuel said: "So why do you ask me, seeing the LORD has departed from you and has become your enemy? ¹⁷And the LORD has done for Himself^a as He spoke by me. For the LORD has torn the kingdom out of your hand and given it to your neighbor, David. ¹⁸Because you did not obey the voice of the LORD nor execute His fierce wrath upon Amalek, therefore the LORD has done this thing to you this day. ¹⁹Moreover the LORD will also deliver Israel with you into the hand of the Philistines. And tomorrow you and your sons *will be* with me. The LORD will also deliver the army of Israel into the hand of the Philistines."

²⁰Immediately Saul fell full length on the ground, and was dreadfully afraid because of the words of Samuel. And there was no strength in him, for he had eaten no food all day or all night.

²¹And the woman came to Saul and saw that he was severely troubled, and said to him, "Look, your maidservant has obeyed your voice, and I have put my life in my hands and heeded the words which you spoke to me. ²²Now therefore, please, heed also the voice of your maidservant, and let me set a piece of bread before you; and eat, that you may have strength when you go on *your* way."

²³But he refused and said, "I will not eat."

So his servants, together with the woman, urged him; and he heeded their voice. Then he arose from the ground and sat on the bed. ²⁴Now the woman had a fatted calf in the house, and she hastened to kill it. And she took flour and kneaded *it,* and baked unleavened bread from it. ²⁵So she brought *it* before Saul and his servants, and they ate. Then they rose and went away that night.

The Philistines Reject David

29 Then the Philistines gathered together all their armies at Aphek, and the Israelites encamped by a fountain which *is* in Jezreel. ²And the lords of the Philistines passed in review by hundreds and by thousands, but David and his men passed in review at the rear with Achish. ³Then the princes of the Philistines said, "What *are* these Hebrews *doing here?*"

And Achish said to the princes of the Philistines, "*Is* this not David, the servant of Saul king of Israel, who has been with me these days, or these years? And to this day I have found no fault in him since he defected *to me.*"

⁴But the princes of the Philistines were angry with him; so the princes of the Philistines said to him, "Make this fellow return, that he may go back to the place which you have appointed for him, and do not let him go down with us to battle, lest in the battle he become our adversary. For with what could he reconcile himself to his master, if not with the heads of these men? ⁵*Is* this not David, of whom they sang to one another in dances, saying:

> 'Saul has slain his thousands,
> And David his ten thousands'?"^a

⁶Then Achish called David and said to him, "Surely, *as* the LORD lives, you have been upright, and your going out and your coming in with me in the army *is* good in my sight. For to this day I have not found evil in you since the day of your coming to me. Nevertheless the lords do not favor you. ⁷Therefore return now, and go in peace, that you may not displease the lords of the Philistines."

⁸So David said to Achish, "But what have I done? And to this day what have you found in your servant as long as I have been with you, that I may not go and fight against the enemies of my lord the king?"

⁹Then Achish answered and said to David, "I know that you *are* as good in my sight as an angel of God; nevertheless the

---

28:17 ^aOr *him,* that is, David   **29:5** ^aCompare 1 Samuel 18:7

princes of the Philistines have said, 'He shall not go up with us to the battle.' [10]Now therefore, rise early in the morning with your master's servants who have come with you.[a] And as soon as you are up early in the morning and have light, depart."

[11]So David and his men rose early to depart in the morning, to return to the land of the Philistines. And the Philistines went up to Jezreel.

David's Conflict with the Amalekites

30 Now it happened, when David and his men came to Ziklag, on the third day, that the Amalekites had invaded the South and Ziklag, attacked Ziklag and burned it with fire, [2]and had taken captive the women and those who *were* there, from small to great; they did not kill anyone, but carried *them* away and went their way. [3]So David and his men came to the city, and there it was, burned with fire; and their wives, their sons, and their daughters had been taken captive. [4]Then David and the people who *were* with him lifted up their voices and wept, until they had no more power to weep. [5]And David's two wives, Ahinoam the Jezreelitess, and Abigail the widow of Nabal the Carmelite, had been taken captive. [6]Now David was greatly distressed, for the people spoke of stoning him, because the soul of all the people was grieved, every man for his sons and his daughters. But David strengthened himself in the LORD his God.

[7]Then David said to Abiathar the priest, Ahimelech's son, "Please bring the ephod here to me." And Abiathar brought the ephod to David. [8]So David inquired of the LORD, saying, "Shall I pursue this troop? Shall I overtake them?"

And He answered him, "Pursue, for you shall surely overtake *them* and without fail recover *all*."

[9]So David went, he and the six hundred men who *were* with him, and came to the Brook Besor, where those stayed who were left behind. [10]But David pursued, he and four hundred men; for two hundred stayed *behind,* who were so weary that they could not cross the Brook Besor.

[11]Then they found an Egyptian in the field, and brought him to David; and they gave him bread and he ate, and they let him drink water. [12]And they gave him a piece of a cake of figs and two clusters of raisins. So when he had eaten, his strength came back to him; for he had eaten no bread nor drunk water for three days and three nights. [13]Then David said to him, "To whom do you *belong,* and where *are* you from?"

And he said, "I *am* a young man from Egypt, servant of an Amalekite; and my master left me behind, because three days ago I fell sick. [14]We made an invasion of the southern *area* of the Cherethites, in the *territory* which *belongs* to Judah, and of the southern *area* of Caleb; and we burned Ziklag with fire."

[15]And David said to him, "Can you take me down to this troop?"

So he said, "Swear to me by God that you will neither kill me nor deliver me into the hands of my master, and I will take you down to this troop."

[16]And when he had brought him down, there they were, spread out over all the land, eating and drinking and dancing, because of all the great spoil which they had taken from the land of the Philistines and from the land of Judah. [17]Then David attacked them from twilight until the evening of the next day. Not a man of them escaped, except four hundred young men who rode on camels and fled. [18]So David recovered all that the Amalekites had carried away, and David rescued his two wives. [19]And nothing of theirs was lacking, either small or great, sons or daughters, spoil or anything which they had taken from them; David recovered all. [20]Then David took all the flocks and herds they had driven before those *other* livestock, and said, "This *is* David's spoil."

[21]Now David came to the two hundred men who had been so weary that they could not follow David, whom they also

---

29:10 [a]Following Masoretic Text, Targum, and Vulgate; Septuagint adds *and go to the place which I have selected for you there; and set no bothersome word in your heart, for you are good before me. And rise on your way.*

had made to stay at the Brook Besor. So they went out to meet David and to meet the people who *were* with him. And when David came near the people, he greeted them. ²²Then all the wicked and worthless men[a] of those who went with David answered and said, "Because they did not go with us, we will not give them *any* of the spoil that we have recovered, except for every man's wife and children, that they may lead *them* away and depart."

²³But David said, "My brethren, you shall not do so with what the Lord has given us, who has preserved us and delivered into our hand the troop that came against us. ²⁴For who will heed you in this matter? But as his part *is* who goes down to the battle, so *shall* his part *be* who stays by the supplies; they shall share alike." ²⁵So it was, from that day forward; he made it a statute and an ordinance for Israel to this day.

²⁶Now when David came to Ziklag, he sent *some* of the spoil to the elders of Judah, to his friends, saying, "Here is a present for you from the spoil of the enemies of the Lord"— ²⁷to *those* who *were* in Bethel, *those* who *were* in Ramoth of the South, *those* who *were* in Jattir, ²⁸*those* who *were* in Aroer, *those* who *were* in Siphmoth, *those* who *were* in Eshtemoa, ²⁹*those* who *were* in Rachal, *those* who *were* in the cities of the Jerahmeelites, *those* who *were* in the cities of the Kenites, ³⁰*those* who *were* in Hormah, *those* who *were* in Chorashan,[a] *those* who *were* in Athach, ³¹*those* who *were* in Hebron, and to all the places where David himself and his men were accustomed to rove.

The Tragic End of Saul and His Sons

31 Now the Philistines fought against Israel; and the men of Israel fled from before the Philistines, and fell slain on Mount Gilboa. ²Then the Philistines followed hard after Saul and his sons. And the Philistines killed Jonathan, Abinadab, and Malchishua, Saul's sons. ³The battle became fierce against Saul. The archers hit him, and he was severely wounded by the archers.

⁴Then Saul said to his armorbearer, "Draw your sword, and thrust me through with it, lest these uncircumcised men come and thrust me through and abuse me."

But his armorbearer would not, for he was greatly afraid. Therefore Saul took a sword and fell on it. ⁵And when his armorbearer saw that Saul was dead, he also fell on his sword, and died with him. ⁶So Saul, his three sons, his armorbearer, and all his men died together that same day.

⁷And when the men of Israel who *were* on the other side of the valley, and *those* who *were* on the other side of the Jordan, saw that the men of Israel had fled and that Saul and his sons were dead, they forsook the cities and fled; and the Philistines came and dwelt in them. ⁸So it happened the next day, when the Philistines came to strip the slain, that they found Saul and his three sons fallen on Mount Gilboa. ⁹And they cut off his head and stripped off his armor, and sent *word* throughout the land of the Philistines, to proclaim *it in* the temple of their idols and among the people. ¹⁰Then they put his armor in the temple of the Ashtoreths, and they fastened his body to the wall of Beth Shan.[a]

¹¹Now when the inhabitants of Jabesh Gilead heard what the Philistines had done to Saul, ¹²all the valiant men arose and traveled all night, and took the body of Saul and the bodies of his sons from the wall of Beth Shan; and they came to Jabesh and burned them there. ¹³Then they took their bones and buried *them* under the tamarisk tree at Jabesh, and fasted seven days.

30:22 [a]Literally *men of Belial*   **30:30** [a]Or *Borashan*
31:10 [a]Spelled *Beth Shean* in Joshua 17:11 and elsewhere

2 SAMUEL

Author: Unknown, possibly Abiathar the Priest

When Written: 931–722 B.C.

Theme: Kingship of David, Forerunner of the Messiah

Key Verses: 2 Samuel 22:21, 22—"The LORD rewarded me according to my righteousness; according to the cleanness of my hands He has recompensed me. For I have kept the ways of the LORD, and have not wickedly departed from my God."

Key Chapter: 2 Samuel 11—All of the abundant blessings enjoyed by David's family and kingdom are quickly removed when God chastises David for his sin with Bathsheba. This episode demonstrates how intricately the affairs of a nation are tied to the spiritual and moral conditions of its leaders.

Just as choices made by King David dramatically impacted the plight of his people, similarly, choices made by our own national leaders can and do determine whether we will suffer or be blessed as a nation. America's Founding Fathers took this truth very seriously. John Adams, second president of the United States, wrote that America's tradition of liberty "is productive of everything which is great and excellent among men. But its principles are as easily destroyed as human nature is corrupted. . . ." Noting that effective government can only be built upon a moral foundation, Adams concluded, "Private and public virtue is the only foundation of Republics."

The Report of Saul's Death

1 Now it came to pass after the death of Saul, when David had returned from the slaughter of the Amalekites, and David had stayed two days in Ziklag, ²on the third day, behold, it happened that a man came from Saul's camp with his clothes torn and dust on his head. So it was, when he came to David, that he fell to the ground and prostrated himself.

³And David said to him, "Where have you come from?"

So he said to him, "I have escaped from the camp of Israel."

⁴Then David said to him, "How did the matter go? Please tell me."

And he answered, "The people have fled from the battle, many of the people are fallen and dead, and Saul and Jonathan his son are dead also."

⁵So David said to the young man who told him, "How do you know that Saul and Jonathan his son are dead?"

⁶Then the young man who told him said, "As I happened by chance *to be* on Mount Gilboa, there was Saul, leaning on his spear; and indeed the chariots and horsemen followed hard after him. ⁷Now when he looked behind him, he saw me and called to me. And I answered, 'Here I am.' ⁸And he said to me, 'Who *are* you?' So I answered him, 'I *am* an Amalekite.' ⁹He said to me again, 'Please stand over me and kill me, for anguish has come upon me, but my life still *remains* in me.' ¹⁰So I stood over him and killed him, because I was sure that he could not live after he had fallen. And I took the crown that *was* on his head and the bracelet that *was* on his arm, and have brought them here to my lord."

¹¹Therefore David took hold of his own clothes and tore them, and *so did* all the men who *were* with him. ¹²And they mourned and wept and fasted until evening for Saul and for Jonathan his son, for the people of the LORD and for the house of Israel, because they had fallen by the sword.

¹³Then David said to the young man who told him, "Where *are* you from?"

And he answered, "I *am* the son of an alien, an Amalekite."

¹⁴So David said to him, "How was it you were not afraid to put forth your hand to destroy the LORD's anointed?" ¹⁵Then David called one of the young men and said, "Go near, *and* execute him!" And he struck him so that he died. ¹⁶So David said to him, "Your blood *is* on your own head, for your own mouth has testified against you, saying, 'I have killed the LORD's anointed.'"

The Song of the Bow

¹⁷Then David lamented with this lamentation over Saul and over Jonathan his son, ¹⁸and he told *them* to teach the children of Judah *the Song of* the Bow; indeed *it is* written in the Book of Jasher:

19 "The beauty of Israel is slain on your
        high places!
    How the mighty have fallen!
20 Tell *it* not in Gath,
    Proclaim *it* not in the streets of
        Ashkelon—
    Lest the daughters of the Philistines
        rejoice,
    Lest the daughters of the
        uncircumcised triumph.

21 "O mountains of Gilboa,
    Let there be no dew nor rain upon you,
    Nor fields of offerings.
    For the shield of the mighty is cast
        away there!
    The shield of Saul, not anointed with
        oil.
22 From the blood of the slain,
    From the fat of the mighty,
    The bow of Jonathan did not turn
        back,

And the sword of Saul did not return
empty.

23 "Saul and Jonathan *were* beloved and
pleasant in their lives,
And in their death they were not
divided;
They were swifter than eagles,
They were stronger than lions.

24 "O daughters of Israel, weep over Saul,
Who clothed you in scarlet, with
luxury;
Who put ornaments of gold on your
apparel.

25 "How the mighty have fallen in the
midst of the battle!
Jonathan *was* slain in your high places.
26 I am distressed for you, my brother
Jonathan;
You have been very pleasant to me;
Your love to me was wonderful,
Surpassing the love of women.

27 "How the mighty have fallen,
And the weapons of war perished!"

David Anointed King of Judah

2 It happened after this that David inquired of the LORD, saying, "Shall I go
up to any of the cities of Judah?"
And the LORD said to him, "Go up."
David said, "Where shall I go up?"
And He said, "To Hebron."
2So David went up there, and his two
wives also, Ahinoam the Jezreelitess, and
Abigail the widow of Nabal the Carmelite.
3And David brought up the men who *were*
with him, every man with his household.
So they dwelt in the cities of Hebron.
4Then the men of Judah came, and there
they anointed David king over the house
of Judah. And they told David, saying,
"The men of Jabesh Gilead *were the ones*
who buried Saul." 5So David sent messengers to the men of Jabesh Gilead, and said
to them, "You *are* blessed of the LORD, for
you have shown this kindness to your lord,

HONOR

*"How the mighty have fallen
in the midst of the battle!"*

2 SAMUEL 1:25

Douglas MacArthur

DUTY—HONOR—COUNTRY

In his farewell speech to Corps of Cadets at West Point, General Douglas MacArthur gave a moving tribute to the ideals
that inspire the great American soldier. For as long as other
Americans serve their country courageously and honorably,
his words will live on. The following excerpt from May 1962
is one small paragraph of his famous speech:

Duty—Honor—Country.

*The code which those words perpetuate embraces the
highest moral laws and will stand the test of any ethics
or philosophies ever promulgated for the uplift of mankind. Its requirements are for the things that are right,
and its restraints are from the things that are wrong. The
soldier, above all other men, is required to practice the
greatest act of religious training—sacrifice. In battle and
in the face of danger and death, he discloses those divine
attributes which his Maker gave when He created man in
His own image. No physical courage and no brute instinct
can take the place of the Divine help which alone can
sustain him. However horrible the incidents of war may be,
the soldier who is called upon to offer and to give his life
for his country is the noblest development of mankind.*

to Saul, and have buried him. [6]And now may the LORD show kindness and truth to you. I also will repay you this kindness, because you have done this thing. [7]Now therefore, let your hands be strengthened, and be valiant; for your master Saul is dead, and also the house of Judah has anointed me king over them."

Ishbosheth Made King of Israel

[8]But Abner the son of Ner, commander of Saul's army, took Ishbosheth[a] the son of Saul and brought him over to Mahanaim; [9]and he made him king over Gilead, over the Ashurites, over Jezreel, over Ephraim, over Benjamin, and over all Israel. [10]Ishbosheth, Saul's son, *was* forty years old when he began to reign over Israel, and he reigned two years. Only the house of Judah followed David. [11]And the time that David was king in Hebron over the house of Judah was seven years and six months.

Israel and Judah at War

[12]Now Abner the son of Ner, and the servants of Ishbosheth the son of Saul, went out from Mahanaim to Gibeon. [13]And Joab the son of Zeruiah, and the servants of David, went out and met them by the pool of Gibeon. So they sat down, one on one side of the pool and the other on the other side of the pool. [14]Then Abner said to Joab, "Let the young men now arise and compete before us."

And Joab said, "Let them arise."

[15]So they arose and went over by number, twelve from Benjamin, *followers* of Ishbosheth the son of Saul, and twelve from the servants of David. [16]And each one grasped his opponent by the head and *thrust* his sword in his opponent's side; so they fell down together. Therefore that place was called the Field of Sharp Swords,[a] which *is* in Gibeon. [17]So there was a very fierce battle that day, and Abner and the men of Israel were beaten before the servants of David.

[18]Now the three sons of Zeruiah were there: Joab and Abishai and Asahel. And Asahel *was as* fleet of foot as a wild gazelle. [19]So Asahel pursued Abner, and in going he did not turn to the right hand or to the left from following Abner.

[20]Then Abner looked behind him and said, "*Are* you Asahel?"

He answered, "I *am*."

[21]And Abner said to him, "Turn aside to your right hand or to your left, and lay hold on one of the young men and take his armor for yourself." But Asahel would not turn aside from following him. [22]So Abner said again to Asahel, "Turn aside from following me. Why should I strike you to the ground? How then could I face your brother Joab?" [23]However, he refused to turn aside. Therefore Abner struck him in the stomach with the blunt end of the spear, so that the spear came out of his back; and he fell down there and died on the spot. So it was *that* as many as came to the place where Asahel fell down and died, stood still.

[24]Joab and Abishai also pursued Abner. And the sun was going down when they came to the hill of Ammah, which *is* before Giah by the road to the Wilderness of Gibeon. [25]Now the children of Benjamin gathered together behind Abner and became a unit, and took their stand on top of a hill. [26]Then Abner called to Joab and said, "Shall the sword devour forever? Do you not know that it will be bitter in the latter end? How long will it be then until you tell the people to return from pursuing their brethren?"

[27]And Joab said, "*As* God lives, unless you had spoken, surely then by morning all the people would have given up pursuing their brethren." [28]So Joab blew a trumpet; and all the people stood still and did not pursue Israel anymore, nor did they fight anymore. [29]Then Abner and his men went on all that night through the plain, crossed over the Jordan, and went through all Bithron; and they came to Mahanaim.

[30]So Joab returned from pursuing Abner. And when he had gathered all the people together, there were missing of David's servants nineteen men and Asahel. [31]But the servants of David had struck down, of Benjamin and Abner's men, three hundred

---

2:8 [a]Called *Esh-Baal* in 1 Chronicles 8:33 and 9:39
2:16 [a]Hebrew *Helkath Hazzurim*

and sixty men who died. ³²Then they took up Asahel and buried him in his father's tomb, which *was in* Bethlehem. And Joab and his men went all night, and they came to Hebron at daybreak.

3 Now there was a long war between the house of Saul and the house of David. But David grew stronger and stronger, and the house of Saul grew weaker and weaker.

Sons of David

²Sons were born to David in Hebron: His firstborn was Amnon by Ahinoam the Jezreelitess; ³his second, Chileab, by Abigail the widow of Nabal the Carmelite; the third, Absalom the son of Maacah, the daughter of Talmai, king of Geshur; ⁴the fourth, Adonijah the son of Haggith; the fifth, Shephatiah the son of Abital; ⁵and the sixth, Ithream, by David's wife Eglah. These were born to David in Hebron.

Abner Joins Forces with David

⁶Now it was so, while there was war between the house of Saul and the house of David, that Abner was strengthening *his hold* on the house of Saul. ⁷And Saul had a concubine, whose name *was* Rizpah, the daughter of Aiah. So *Ishbosheth* said to Abner, "Why have you gone in to my father's concubine?"

⁸Then Abner became very angry at the words of Ishbosheth, and said, "*Am* I a dog's head that belongs to Judah? Today I show loyalty to the house of Saul your father, to his brothers, and to his friends, and have not delivered you into the hand of David; and you charge me today with a fault concerning this woman? ⁹May God do so to Abner, and more also, if I do not do for David as the LORD has sworn to him— ¹⁰to transfer the kingdom from the house of Saul, and set up the throne of David over Israel and over Judah, from Dan to Beersheba." ¹¹And he could not answer Abner another word, because he feared him.

¹²Then Abner sent messengers on his behalf to David, saying, "Whose *is* the land?" saying *also,* "Make your covenant with me, and indeed my hand *shall be* with you to bring all Israel to you."

¹³And *David* said, "Good, I will make a covenant with you. But one thing I require of you: you shall not see my face unless you first bring Michal, Saul's daughter, when you come to see my face." ¹⁴So David sent messengers to Ishbosheth, Saul's son, saying, "Give *me* my wife Michal, whom I betrothed to myself for a hundred foreskins of the Philistines." ¹⁵And Ishbosheth sent and took her from *her* husband, from Paltielᵃ the son of Laish. ¹⁶Then her husband went along with her to Bahurim, weeping behind her. So Abner said to him, "Go, return!" And he returned.

¹⁷Now Abner had communicated with the elders of Israel, saying, "In time past you were seeking for David *to be* king over you. ¹⁸Now then, do *it!* For the LORD has spoken of David, saying, 'By the hand of My servant David, Iᵃ will save My people Israel from the hand of the Philistines and the hand of all their enemies.'" ¹⁹And Abner also spoke in the hearing of Benjamin. Then Abner also went to speak in the hearing of David in Hebron all that seemed good to Israel and the whole house of Benjamin.

²⁰So Abner and twenty men with him came to David at Hebron. And David made a feast for Abner and the men who *were* with him. ²¹Then Abner said to David, "I will arise and go, and gather all Israel to my lord the king, that they may make a covenant with you, and that you may reign over all that your heart desires." So David sent Abner away, and he went in peace.

Joab Murders Abner

²²At that moment the servants of David and Joab came from a raid and brought much spoil with them. But Abner *was* not with David in Hebron, for he had sent him away, and he had gone in peace. ²³When Joab and all the troops that *were* with him had come, they told Joab, saying, "Abner the son of Ner came to the king, and he sent him away, and he has gone in peace." ²⁴Then Joab came to the king and said,

---

3:15 ᵃSpelled *Palti* in 1 Samuel 25:44
3:18 ᵃFollowing many Hebrew manuscripts, Septuagint, Syriac, and Targum; Masoretic Text reads he.

"What have you done? Look, Abner came to you; why *is* it *that* you sent him away, and he has already gone? ²⁵Surely you realize that Abner the son of Ner came to deceive you, to know your going out and your coming in, and to know all that you are doing."

²⁶And when Joab had gone from David's presence, he sent messengers after Abner, who brought him back from the well of Sirah. But David did not know *it.* ²⁷Now when Abner had returned to Hebron, Joab took him aside in the gate to speak with him privately, and there stabbed him in the stomach, so that he died for the blood of Asahel his brother.

²⁸Afterward, when David heard *it,* he said, "My kingdom and I *are* guiltless before the LORD forever of the blood of Abner the son of Ner. ²⁹Let it rest on the head of Joab and on all his father's house; and let there never fail to be in the house of Joab one who has a discharge or is a leper, who leans on a staff or falls by the sword, or who lacks bread." ³⁰So Joab and Abishai his brother killed Abner, because he had killed their brother Asahel at Gibeon in the battle.

David's Mourning for Abner

³¹Then David said to Joab and to all the people who were with him, "Tear your clothes, gird yourselves with sackcloth, and mourn for Abner." And King David followed the coffin. ³²So they buried Abner in Hebron; and the king lifted up his voice and wept at the grave of Abner, and all the people wept. ³³And the king sang *a lament* over Abner and said:

"Should Abner die as a fool dies?
³⁴   Your hands were not bound
     Nor your feet put into fetters;
     As a man falls before wicked men,
        so you fell."

Then all the people wept over him again.

³⁵And when all the people came to persuade David to eat food while it was still day, David took an oath, saying, "God do so to me, and more also, if I taste bread or anything else till the sun goes down!" ³⁶Now all the people took note *of it,* and it pleased them, since whatever the king did pleased all the people. ³⁷For all the people and all Israel understood that day that it had not been the king's *intent* to kill Abner the son of Ner. ³⁸Then the king said to his servants, "Do you not know that a prince and a great man has fallen this day in Israel? ³⁹And I *am* weak today, though anointed king; and these men, the sons of Zeruiah, *are* too harsh for me. The LORD shall repay the evildoer according to his wickedness."

Ishbosheth Is Murdered

4When Saul's son[a] heard that Abner had died in Hebron, he lost heart, and all Israel was troubled. ²Now Saul's son *had* two men *who were* captains of troops. The name of one *was* Baanah and the name of the other Rechab, the sons of Rimmon the Beerothite, of the children of Benjamin. (For Beeroth also was *part* of Benjamin, ³because the Beerothites fled to Gittaim and have been sojourners there until this day.)

⁴Jonathan, Saul's son, had a son *who was* lame in *his* feet. He was five years old when the news about Saul and Jonathan came from Jezreel; and his nurse took him up and fled. And it happened, as she made haste to flee, that he fell and became lame. His name *was* Mephibosheth.[a]

⁵Then the sons of Rimmon the Beerothite, Rechab and Baanah, set out and came at about the heat of the day to the house of Ishbosheth, who was lying on his bed at noon. ⁶And they came there, all the way into the house, *as though* to get wheat, and they stabbed him in the stomach. Then Rechab and Baanah his brother escaped. ⁷For when they came into the house, he was lying on his bed in his bedroom; then they struck him and killed him, beheaded him and took his head, and were all night escaping through the plain. ⁸And they brought the head of Ishbosheth to David at Hebron, and said to the king, "Here is the head of Ishbosheth, the son of Saul your enemy, who sought your life; and the LORD has avenged my lord the king this day of Saul and his descendants."

4:1 ᵃThat is, Ishbosheth   **4:4** ᵃCalled *Merib-Baal* in 1 Chronicles 8:34 and 9:40

[9]But David answered Rechab and Baanah his brother, the sons of Rimmon the Beerothite, and said to them, "*As* the LORD lives, who has redeemed my life from all adversity, [10]when someone told me, saying, 'Look, Saul is dead,' thinking to have brought good news, I arrested him and had him executed in Ziklag—the one who *thought* I would give him a reward for *his* news. [11]How much more, when wicked men have killed a righteous person in his own house on his bed? Therefore, shall I not now require his blood at your hand and remove you from the earth?" [12]So David commanded his young men, and they executed them, cut off their hands and feet, and hanged *them* by the pool in Hebron. But they took the head of Ishbosheth and buried *it* in the tomb of Abner in Hebron.

David Reigns over All Israel

5 Then all the tribes of Israel came to David at Hebron and spoke, saying, "Indeed we *are* your bone and your flesh. [2]Also, in time past, when Saul was king over us, you were the one who led Israel out and brought them in; and the LORD said to you, 'You shall shepherd My people Israel, and be ruler over Israel.'" [3]Therefore all the elders of Israel came to the king at Hebron, and King David made a covenant with them at Hebron before the LORD. And they anointed David king over Israel. [4]David *was* thirty years old when he began to reign, *and* he reigned forty years. [5]In Hebron he reigned over Judah seven years and six months, and in Jerusalem he reigned thirty-three years over all Israel and Judah.

The Conquest of Jerusalem

[6]And the king and his men went to Jerusalem against the Jebusites, the inhabitants of the land, who spoke to David, saying, "You shall not come in here; but the blind and the lame will repel you," thinking, "David cannot come in here." [7]Nevertheless David took the stronghold of Zion (that *is,* the City of David). [8]Now David said on that day, "Whoever climbs up by way of the water shaft and defeats the Jebusites (the lame and the blind, *who are* hated by David's soul), he

shall be chief and captain."[a] Therefore they say, "The blind and the lame shall not come into the house."

[9]Then David dwelt in the stronghold, and called it the City of David. And David built all around from the Millo[a] and inward. [10]So David went on and became great, and the LORD God of hosts *was* with him.

[11]Then Hiram king of Tyre sent messengers to David, and cedar trees, and carpenters and masons. And they built David a house. [12]So David knew that the LORD had established him as king over Israel, and that He had exalted His kingdom for the sake of His people Israel.

[13]And David took more concubines and wives from Jerusalem, after he had come from Hebron. Also more sons and daughters were born to David. [14]Now these *are* the names of those who were born to him in Jerusalem: Shammua,[a] Shobab, Nathan, Solomon, [15]Ibhar, Elishua,[a] Nepheg, Japhia, [16]Elishama, Eliada, and Eliphelet.

5:8 [a]Compare 1 Chronicles 11:6   **5:9** [a]Literally *The Landfill*   **5:14** [a]Spelled *Shimea* in 1 Chronicles 3:5   **5:15** [a]Spelled *Elishama* in 1 Chronicles 3:6

The Philistines Defeated

17Now when the Philistines heard that they had anointed David king over Israel, all the Philistines went up to search for David. And David heard *of it* and went down to the stronghold. 18The Philistines also went and deployed themselves in the Valley of Rephaim. 19So David inquired of the LORD, saying, "Shall I go up against the Philistines? Will You deliver them into my hand?"

And the LORD said to David, "Go up, for I will doubtless deliver the Philistines into your hand."

20So David went to Baal Perazim, and David defeated them there; and he said, "The LORD has broken through my enemies before me, like a breakthrough of water." Therefore he called the name of that place Baal Perazim.a 21And they left their images there, and David and his men carried them away.

22Then the Philistines went up once again and deployed themselves in the Valley of Rephaim. 23Therefore David inquired of the LORD, and He said, "You shall not go up; circle around behind them, and come upon them in front of the mulberry trees. 24And it shall be, when you hear the sound of marching in the tops of the mulberry trees, then you shall advance quickly. For then the LORD will go out before you to strike the camp of the Philistines." 25And David did so, as the LORD commanded him; and he drove back the Philistines from Gebaa as far as Gezer.

The Ark Brought to Jerusalem

6 Again David gathered all *the* choice *men* of Israel, thirty thousand. 2And David arose and went with all the people who *were* with him from Baale Judah to bring up from there the ark of God, whose name is called by the Name,a the LORD of Hosts, who dwells *between* the cherubim. 3So they set the ark of God on a new cart, and brought it out of the house of Abinadab, which *was* on the hill; and Uzzah and Ahio, the sons of Abinadab, drove the new cart.a 4And they brought it out of the house of Abinadab, which *was* on the hill, accompanying the ark of God; and Ahio went before the ark. 5Then David and all

the house of Israel played *music* before the LORD on all kinds of *instruments of* fir wood, on harps, on stringed instruments, on tambourines, on sistrums, and on cymbals.

6And when they came to Nachon's threshing floor, Uzzah put out *his hand* to the ark of God and took hold of it, for the oxen stumbled. 7Then the anger of the LORD was aroused against Uzzah, and God struck him there for *his* error; and he died there by the ark of God. 8And David became angry because of the LORD's outbreak against Uzzah; and he called the name of the place Perez Uzzaha to this day.

9David was afraid of the LORD that day; and he said, "How can the ark of the LORD come to me?" 10So David would not move the ark of the LORD with him into the City of David; but David took it aside into the house of Obed-Edom the Gittite. 11The ark of the LORD remained in the house of Obed-Edom the Gittite three months. And the LORD blessed Obed-Edom and all his household.

12Now it was told King David, saying, "The LORD has blessed the house of Obed-Edom and all that *belongs* to him, because of the ark of God." So David went and brought up the ark of God from the house of Obed-Edom to the City of David with gladness. 13And so it was, when those bearing the ark of the LORD had gone six paces, that he sacrificed oxen and fatted sheep. 14Then David danced before the LORD with all *his* might; and David *was* wearing a linen ephod. 15So David and all the house of Israel brought up the ark of the LORD with shouting and with the sound of the trumpet.

16Now as the ark of the LORD came into the City of David, Michal, Saul's daughter, looked through a window and saw King David leaping and whirling before the LORD; and she despised him in her heart. 17So they brought the ark of the LORD, and set it in its place in the midst of the tabernacle

---

5:20 aLiterally *Master of Breakthroughs*
5:25 aFollowing Masoretic Text, Targum, and Vulgate; Septuagint reads *Gibeon*.
6:2 aSeptuagint, Targum, and Vulgate omit *by the Name;* many Hebrew manuscripts and Syriac read *there.* **6:3** aSeptuagint adds *with the ark.*
6:8 aLiterally *Outburst Against Uzzah*

that David had erected for it. Then David offered burnt offerings and peace offerings before the LORD. ¹⁸And when David had finished offering burnt offerings and peace offerings, he blessed the people in the name of the LORD of hosts. ¹⁹Then he distributed among all the people, among the whole multitude of Israel, both the women and the men, to everyone a loaf of bread, a piece *of meat,* and a cake of raisins. So all the people departed, everyone to his house.

²⁰Then David returned to bless his household. And Michal the daughter of Saul came out to meet David, and said, "How glorious was the king of Israel today, uncovering himself today in the eyes of the maids of his servants, as one of the base fellows shamelessly uncovers himself!"

²¹So David said to Michal, "*It was* before the LORD, who chose me instead of your father and all his house, to appoint me ruler over the people of the LORD, over Israel. Therefore I will play *music* before the LORD. ²²And I will be even more undignified than this, and will be humble in my own sight. But as for the maidservants of whom you have spoken, by them I will be held in honor."

²³Therefore Michal the daughter of Saul had no children to the day of her death.

God's Covenant with David

7 Now it came to pass when the king was dwelling in his house, and the LORD had given him rest from all his enemies all around, ²that the king said to Nathan the prophet, "See now, I dwell in a house of cedar, but the ark of God dwells inside tent curtains."

³Then Nathan said to the king, "Go, do all that *is* in your heart, for the LORD *is* with you."

⁴But it happened that night that the word of the LORD came to Nathan, saying, ⁵"Go and tell My servant David, 'Thus says the LORD: "Would you build a house for Me to dwell in? ⁶For I have not dwelt in a house since the time that I brought the children of Israel up from Egypt, even to this day, but have moved about in a tent and in a tabernacle. ⁷Wherever I have moved about with all the children of Israel, have I ever

spoken a word to anyone from the tribes of Israel, whom I commanded to shepherd My people Israel, saying, 'Why have you not built Me a house of cedar?'"' ⁸Now therefore, thus shall you say to My servant David, 'Thus says the LORD of hosts: "I took you from the sheepfold, from following the sheep, to be ruler over My people, over Israel. ⁹And I have been with you wherever you have gone, and have cut off all your enemies from before you, and have made you a great name, like the name of the great men who *are* on the earth. ¹⁰Moreover I will appoint a place for My people Israel, and will plant them, that they may dwell in a place of their own and move no more; nor shall the sons of wickedness oppress them anymore, as previously, ¹¹since the time that I commanded judges *to be* over My people Israel, and have caused you to rest from all your enemies. Also the LORD tells you that He will make you a house.ᵃ

¹²"When your days are fulfilled and you rest with your fathers, I will set up your seed after you, who will come from your body, and I will establish his kingdom. ¹³He shall build a house for My name, and I will establish the throne of his kingdom forever. ¹⁴I will be his Father, and he shall be My son. If he commits iniquity, I will chasten him with the rod of men and with the blows of the sons of men. ¹⁵But My mercy shall not depart from him, as I took *it* from Saul, whom I removed from before you. ¹⁶And your house and your kingdom shall be established forever before you.ᵃ Your throne shall be established forever."'"

¹⁷According to all these words and according to all this vision, so Nathan spoke to David.

David's Thanksgiving to God

¹⁸Then King David went in and sat before the LORD; and he said: "Who *am* I, O Lord GOD? And what is my house, that You have brought me this far? ¹⁹And yet this was a small thing in Your sight, O Lord GOD; and You have also spoken of Your servant's house for a great while to come. *Is* this the

---

7:11 ᵃThat is, a royal dynasty   **7:16** ᵃSeptuagint reads *Me.*

manner of man, O Lord God? [20]Now what more can David say to You? For You, Lord God, know Your servant. [21]For Your word's sake, and according to Your own heart, You have done all these great things, to make Your servant know *them*. [22]Therefore You are great, O Lord God.[a] For *there is* none like You, nor *is there any* God besides You, according to all that we have heard with our ears. [23]And who *is* like Your people, like Israel, the one nation on the earth whom God went to redeem for Himself as a people, to make for Himself a name—and to do for Yourself great and awesome deeds for Your land—before Your people whom You redeemed for Yourself from Egypt, the nations, and their gods? [24]For You have made Your people Israel Your very own people forever; and You, Lord, have become their God.

[25]"Now, O Lord God, the word which You have spoken concerning Your servant and concerning his house, establish *it* forever and do as You have said. [26]So let Your name be magnified forever, saying, 'The Lord of hosts *is* the God over Israel.' And let the house of Your servant David be established before You. [27]For You, O Lord of hosts, God of Israel, have revealed *this* to Your servant, saying, 'I will build you a house.' Therefore Your servant has found it in his heart to pray this prayer to You.

[28]"And now, O Lord God, You are God, and Your words are true, and You have promised this goodness to Your servant. [29]Now therefore, let it please You to bless the house of Your servant, that it may continue before You forever; for You, O Lord God, have spoken *it,* and with Your blessing let the house of Your servant be blessed forever."

David's Further Conquests

8 After this it came to pass that David attacked the Philistines and subdued them. And David took Metheg Ammah from the hand of the Philistines.

[2]Then he defeated Moab. Forcing them down to the ground, he measured them off with a line. With two lines he measured off those to be put to death, and with one full line those to be kept alive. So the Moabites became David's servants, *and* brought tribute.

[3]David also defeated Hadadezer the son of Rehob, king of Zobah, as he went to recover his territory at the River Euphrates. [4]David took from him one thousand *chariots,* seven hundred[a] horsemen, and twenty thousand foot soldiers. Also David hamstrung all the chariot *horses,* except that he spared *enough* of them for one hundred chariots.

[5]When the Syrians of Damascus came to help Hadadezer king of Zobah, David killed twenty-two thousand of the Syrians. [6]Then David put garrisons in Syria of Damascus; and the Syrians became David's servants, *and* brought tribute. So the Lord preserved David wherever he went. [7]And David took the shields of gold that had belonged to the servants of Hadadezer, and brought them to Jerusalem. [8]Also from Betah[a] and from Berothai, cities of Hadadezer, King David took a large amount of bronze.

[9]When Toi[a] king of Hamath heard that David had defeated all the army of Hadadezer, [10]then Toi sent Joram[a] his son to King David, to greet him and bless him, because he had fought against Hadadezer and defeated him (for Hadadezer had been at war with Toi); and *Joram* brought with him articles of silver, articles of gold, and articles of bronze. [11]King David also dedicated these to the Lord, along with the silver and gold that he had dedicated from all the nations which he had subdued—[12]from Syria,[a] from Moab, from the people of Ammon, from the Philistines, from Amalek, and from the spoil of Hadadezer the son of Rehob, king of Zobah.

[13]And David made *himself* a name when he returned from killing eighteen thousand Syrians[a] in the Valley of Salt. [14]He also put garrisons in Edom; throughout all Edom he put garrisons, and all the Edomites became David's servants. And the Lord preserved David wherever he went.

7:22 [a]Targum and Syriac read *O Lord God.*
8:4 [a]Or *seven thousand* (compare 1 Chronicles 18:4)
8:8 [a]Spelled *Tibhath* in 1 Chronicles 18:8
8:9 [a]Spelled *Tou* in 1 Chronicles 18:9
8:10 [a]Spelled *Hadoram* in 1 Chronicles 18:10
8:12 [a]Septuagint, Syriac, and some Hebrew manuscripts read *Edom.*   **8:13** [a]Septuagint, Syriac, and some Hebrew manuscripts read *Edomites* (compare 1 Chronicles 18:12).

David's Administration

[15]So David reigned over all Israel; and David administered judgment and justice to all his people. [16]Joab the son of Zeruiah *was* over the army; Jehoshaphat the son of Ahilud *was* recorder; [17]Zadok the son of Ahitub and Ahimelech the son of Abiathar *were* the priests; Seraiah[a] *was* the scribe; [18]Benaiah the son of Jehoiada *was over* both the Cherethites and the Pelethites; and David's sons were chief ministers.

David's Kindness to Mephibosheth

9Now David said, "Is there still anyone who is left of the house of Saul, that I may show him kindness for Jonathan's sake?"

[2]And *there was* a servant of the house of Saul whose name *was* Ziba. So when they had called him to David, the king said to him, "*Are* you Ziba?"

He said, "At your service!"

[3]Then the king said, "*Is* there not still someone of the house of Saul, to whom I may show the kindness of God?"

And Ziba said to the king, "There is still a son of Jonathan *who is* lame in *his* feet."

[4]So the king said to him, "Where *is* he?"

And Ziba said to the king, "Indeed he *is* in the house of Machir the son of Ammiel, in Lo Debar."

[5]Then King David sent and brought him out of the house of Machir the son of Ammiel, from Lo Debar.

[6]Now when Mephibosheth the son of Jonathan, the son of Saul, had come to David, he fell on his face and prostrated himself. Then David said, "Mephibosheth?"

And he answered, "Here is your servant!"

[7]So David said to him, "Do not fear, for I will surely show you kindness for Jonathan your father's sake, and will restore to you all the land of Saul your grandfather; and you shall eat bread at my table continually."

[8]Then he bowed himself, and said, "What *is* your servant, that you should look upon such a dead dog as I?"

[9]And the king called to Ziba, Saul's servant, and said to him, "I have given to your master's son all that belonged to Saul and to all his house. [10]You therefore, and your sons and your servants, shall work the land for him, and you shall bring in *the harvest,* that your master's son may have food to eat. But Mephibosheth your master's son shall eat bread at my table always." Now Ziba had fifteen sons and twenty servants.

[11]Then Ziba said to the king, "According to all that my lord the king has commanded his servant, so will your servant do."

"As for Mephibosheth," *said the king,* "he shall eat at my table[a] like one of the king's sons." [12]Mephibosheth had a young son whose name *was* Micha. And all who dwelt in the house of Ziba *were* servants of Mephibosheth. [13]So Mephibosheth dwelt in Jerusalem, for he ate continually at the king's table. And he was lame in both his feet.

The Ammonites and Syrians Defeated

10It happened after this that the king of the people of Ammon died, and Hanun his son reigned in his place. [2]Then David said, "I will show kindness to Hanun the son of Nahash, as his father showed kindness to me."

So David sent by the hand of his servants to comfort him concerning his father. And David's servants came into the land of the people of Ammon. [3]And the princes of the people of Ammon said to Hanun their lord, "Do you think that David really honors your father because he has sent comforters to you? Has David not *rather* sent his servants to you to search the city, to spy it out, and to overthrow it?"

[4]Therefore Hanun took David's servants, shaved off half of their beards, cut off their garments in the middle, at their buttocks, and sent them away. [5]When they told David, he sent to meet them, because the men were greatly ashamed. And the king said, "Wait at Jericho until your beards have grown, and *then* return."

[6]When the people of Ammon saw that they had made themselves repulsive to David, the people of Ammon sent and hired the Syrians of Beth Rehob and the Syrians of Zoba, twenty thousand foot soldiers; and

---

8:17 [a]Spelled *Shavsha* in 1 Chronicles 18:16
9:11 [a]Septuagint reads *David's table.*

from the king of Maacah one thousand men, and from Ish-Tob twelve thousand men. [7]Now when David heard *of it,* he sent Joab and all the army of the mighty men. [8]Then the people of Ammon came out and put themselves in battle array at the entrance of the gate. And the Syrians of Zoba, Beth Rehob, Ish-Tob, and Maacah *were* by themselves in the field.

[9]When Joab saw that the battle line was against him before and behind, he chose some of Israel's best and put *them* in battle array against the Syrians. [10]And the rest of the people he put under the command of Abishai his brother, that he might set *them* in battle array against the people of Ammon. [11]Then he said, "If the Syrians are too strong for me, then you shall help me; but if the people of Ammon are too strong for you, then I will come and help you. [12]Be of good courage, and let us be strong for our people and for the cities of our God. And may the LORD do *what is* good in His sight."

[13]So Joab and the people who *were* with him drew near for the battle against the Syrians, and they fled before him. [14]When the people of Ammon saw that the Syrians were fleeing, they also fled before Abishai, and entered the city. So Joab returned from the people of Ammon and went to Jerusalem.

[15]When the Syrians saw that they had been defeated by Israel, they gathered together. [16]Then Hadadezer[a] sent and brought out the Syrians who *were* beyond the River,[b] and they came to Helam. And Shobach the commander of Hadadezer's army *went* before them. [17]When it was told David, he gathered all Israel, crossed over the Jordan, and came to Helam. And the Syrians set themselves in battle array against David and fought with him. [18]Then the Syrians fled before Israel; and David killed seven hundred charioteers and forty thousand horsemen of the Syrians, and struck Shobach the commander of their army, who died there. [19]And when all the kings *who were* servants to Hadadezer[a] saw that they were defeated by Israel, they made peace with Israel and served them. So the Syrians were afraid to help the people of Ammon anymore.

David, Bathsheba, and Uriah

11 It happened in the spring of the year, at the time when kings go out *to battle,* that David sent Joab and his servants with him, and all Israel; and they destroyed the people of Ammon and besieged Rabbah. But David remained at Jerusalem.

[2]Then it happened one evening that David arose from his bed and walked on the roof of the king's house. And from the roof he saw a woman bathing, and the woman *was* very beautiful to behold. [3]So David sent and inquired about the woman. And *someone* said, "*Is* this not Bathsheba, the daughter of Eliam, the wife of Uriah the Hittite?" [4]Then David sent messengers, and took her; and she came to him, and he lay with her, for she was cleansed from her impurity; and she returned to her house. [5]And the woman conceived; so she sent and told David, and said, "I *am* with child."

[6]Then David sent to Joab, *saying,* "Send me Uriah the Hittite." And Joab sent Uriah to David. [7]When Uriah had come to him, David asked how Joab was doing, and how the people were doing, and how the war prospered. [8]And David said to Uriah, "Go down to your house and wash your feet." So Uriah departed from the king's house, and a gift *of food* from the king followed him. [9]But Uriah slept at the door of the king's house with all the servants of his lord, and did not go down to his house. [10]So when they told David, saying, "Uriah did not go down to his house," David said to Uriah, "Did you not come from a journey? Why did you not go down to your house?"

[11]And Uriah said to David, "The ark and Israel and Judah are dwelling in tents, and my lord Joab and the servants of my lord are encamped in the open fields. Shall I then go to my house to eat and drink, and to lie with my wife? *As* you live, and *as* your soul lives, I will not do this thing."

[12]Then David said to Uriah, "Wait here today also, and tomorrow I will let you depart." So Uriah remained in Jerusalem that day and the next. [13]Now when David

---

10:16 [a]Hebrew *Hadarezer* [b]That is, the Euphrates
10:19 [a]Hebrew *Hadarezer*

called him, he ate and drank before him; and he made him drunk. And at evening he went out to lie on his bed with the servants of his lord, but he did not go down to his house.

14In the morning it happened that David wrote a letter to Joab and sent *it* by the hand of Uriah. 15And he wrote in the letter, saying, "Set Uriah in the forefront of the hottest battle, and retreat from him, that he may be struck down and die." 16So it was, while Joab besieged the city, that he assigned Uriah to a place where he knew there *were* valiant men. 17Then the men of the city came out and fought with Joab. And *some* of the people of the servants of David fell; and Uriah the Hittite died also.

18Then Joab sent and told David all the things concerning the war, 19and charged the messenger, saying, "When you have finished telling the matters of the war to the king, 20if it happens that the king's wrath rises, and he says to you: 'Why did you approach so near to the city when you fought? Did you not know that they would shoot from the wall? 21Who struck Abimelech the son of Jerubbesheth?a Was it not a woman who cast a piece of a millstone on him from the wall, so that he died in Thebez? Why did you go near the wall?'—then you shall say, 'Your servant Uriah the Hittite is dead also.'"

22So the messenger went, and came and told David all that Joab had sent by him. 23And the messenger said to David, "Surely the men prevailed against us and came out to us in the field; then we drove them back as far as the entrance of the gate. 24The archers shot from the wall at your servants; and *some* of the king's servants are dead, and your servant Uriah the Hittite is dead also."

25Then David said to the messenger, "Thus you shall say to Joab: 'Do not let this thing displease you, for the sword devours one as well as another. Strengthen your attack against the city, and overthrow it.' So encourage him."

26When the wife of Uriah heard that Uriah her husband was dead, she mourned for her husband. 27And when her mourning was over, David sent and brought her to his house, and she became his wife and bore him a son. But the thing that David had done displeased the LORD.

Nathan's Parable and David's Confession

12 Then the LORD sent Nathan to David. And he came to him, and said to him: "There were two men in one city, one rich and the other poor. 2The rich *man* had exceedingly many flocks and herds. 3But the poor *man* had nothing, except one little ewe lamb which he had bought and nourished; and it grew up together with him and with his children. It ate of his own food and drank from his own cup and lay in his bosom; and it was like a daughter to him. 4And a traveler came to the rich man, who refused to take from his own flock and from his own herd to prepare one for the wayfaring man who had come to him; but he took the poor man's lamb and prepared it for the man who had come to him."

5So David's anger was greatly aroused against the man, and he said to Nathan, "*As* the LORD lives, the man who has done this shall surely die! 6And he shall restore fourfold for the lamb, because he did this thing and because he had no pity."

7Then Nathan said to David, "You *are* the man! Thus says the LORD God of Israel: 'I anointed you king over Israel, and I delivered you from the hand of Saul. 8I gave you your master's house and your master's wives into your keeping, and gave you the house of Israel and Judah. And if *that had been* too little, I also would have given you much more! 9Why have you despised the commandment of the LORD, to do evil in His sight? You have killed Uriah the Hittite with the sword; you have taken his wife *to be* your wife, and have killed him with the sword of the people of Ammon. 10Now therefore, the sword shall never depart from your house, because you have despised Me, and have taken the wife of Uriah the Hittite to be your wife.' 11Thus says the LORD: 'Behold, I will raise up adversity against you from your own house; and I will take your wives before your eyes and give *them* to your neighbor, and he shall lie with your wives in the sight of this sun. 12For you did *it* secretly, but I will do this thing before all Israel, before the sun.'"

11:21 aSame as *Jerubbaal* (Gideon), Judges 6:32ff

[13]So David said to Nathan, "I have sinned against the LORD."

And Nathan said to David, "The LORD also has put away your sin; you shall not die. [14]However, because by this deed you have given great occasion to the enemies of the LORD to blaspheme, the child also *who is* born to you shall surely die." [15]Then Nathan departed to his house.

The Death of David's Son

And the LORD struck the child that Uriah's wife bore to David, and it became ill. [16]David therefore pleaded with God for the child, and David fasted and went in and lay all night on the ground. [17]So the elders of his house arose *and went* to him, to raise him up from the ground. But he would not, nor did he eat food with them. [18]Then on the seventh day it came to pass that the child died. And the servants of David were afraid to tell him that the child was dead. For they said, "Indeed, while the child was alive, we spoke to him, and he would not heed our voice. How can we tell him that the child is dead? He may do some harm!"

[19]When David saw that his servants were whispering, David perceived that the child was dead. Therefore David said to his servants, "Is the child dead?"

And they said, "He is dead."

[20]So David arose from the ground, washed and anointed himself, and changed his clothes; and he went into the house of the LORD and worshiped. Then he went to his own house; and when he requested, they set food before him, and he ate. [21]Then his servants said to him, "What *is* this that you have done? You fasted and wept for the child *while he was* alive, but when the child died, you arose and ate food."

[22]And he said, "While the child was alive, I fasted and wept; for I said, 'Who can tell *whether* the LORD[a] will be gracious to me, that the child may live?' [23]But now he is dead; why should I fast? Can I bring him back again? I shall go to him, but he shall not return to me."

Solomon Is Born

[24]Then David comforted Bathsheba his wife, and went in to her and lay with her. So she bore a son, and he[a] called his name Solomon. Now the LORD loved him, [25]and He sent *word* by the hand of Nathan the prophet: So he[a] called his name Jedidiah,[b] because of the LORD.

Rabbah Is Captured

[26]Now Joab fought against Rabbah of the people of Ammon, and took the royal city. [27]And Joab sent messengers to David, and said, "I have fought against Rabbah, and I have taken the city's water *supply.* [28]Now therefore, gather the rest of the people together and encamp against the city and take it, lest I take the city and it be called after my name." [29]So David gathered all the people together and went to Rabbah, fought against it, and took it. [30]Then he took their king's crown from his head. Its weight *was* a talent of gold, with precious stones. And it was *set* on David's head. Also he brought out the spoil of the city in great abundance. [31]And he brought out the people who *were* in it, and put *them to work* with saws and iron picks and iron axes, and made them cross over to the brick works. So he did to all the cities of the people of Ammon. Then David and all the people returned to Jerusalem.

Amnon and Tamar

13 After this Absalom the son of David had a lovely sister, whose name *was* Tamar; and Amnon the son of David loved her. [2]Amnon was so distressed over his sister Tamar that he became sick; for she *was* a virgin. And it was improper for Amnon to do anything to her. [3]But Amnon had a friend whose name *was* Jonadab the son of Shimeah, David's brother. Now Jonadab *was* a very crafty man. [4]And he said to him, "Why *are* you, the king's son, becoming thinner day after day? Will you not tell me?"

Amnon said to him, "I love Tamar, my brother Absalom's sister."

[5]So Jonadab said to him, "Lie down on your bed and pretend to be ill. And when your father comes to see you, say to him,

---

12:22 [a]A few Hebrew manuscripts and Syriac read *God.*   **12:24** [a]Following Kethib, Septuagint, and Vulgate; Qere, a few Hebrew manuscripts, Syriac, and Targum read *she.*   **12:25** [a]Qere, some Hebrew manuscripts, Syriac, and Targum read *she.* [b]Literally *Beloved of the LORD*

'Please let my sister Tamar come and give me food, and prepare the food in my sight, that I may see *it* and eat it from her hand.'" ⁶Then Amnon lay down and pretended to be ill; and when the king came to see him, Amnon said to the king, "Please let Tamar my sister come and make a couple of cakes for me in my sight, that I may eat from her hand."

⁷And David sent home to Tamar, saying, "Now go to your brother Amnon's house, and prepare food for him." ⁸So Tamar went to her brother Amnon's house; and he was lying down. Then she took flour and kneaded *it,* made cakes in his sight, and baked the cakes. ⁹And she took the pan and placed *them* out before him, but he refused to eat. Then Amnon said, "Have everyone go out from me." And they all went out from him. ¹⁰Then Amnon said to Tamar, "Bring the food into the bedroom, that I may eat from your hand." And Tamar took the cakes which she had made, and brought *them* to Amnon her brother in the bedroom. ¹¹Now when she had brought *them* to him to eat, he took hold of her and said to her, "Come, lie with me, my sister."

¹²But she answered him, "No, my brother, do not force me, for no such thing should be done in Israel. Do not do this disgraceful thing! ¹³And I, where could I take my shame? And as for you, you would be like one of the fools in Israel. Now therefore, please speak to the king; for he will not withhold me from you." ¹⁴However, he would not heed her voice; and being stronger than she, he forced her and lay with her.

¹⁵Then Amnon hated her exceedingly, so that the hatred with which he hated her *was* greater than the love with which he had loved her. And Amnon said to her, "Arise, be gone!"

¹⁶So she said to him, "No, indeed! This evil of sending me away *is* worse than the other that you did to me."

But he would not listen to her. ¹⁷Then he called his servant who attended him, and said, "Here! Put this *woman* out, away from me, and bolt the door behind her." ¹⁸Now she had on a robe of many colors, for the king's virgin daughters wore such apparel. And his servant put her out and bolted the door behind her.

¹⁹Then Tamar put ashes on her head, and tore her robe of many colors that *was* on her, and laid her hand on her head and went away crying bitterly. ²⁰And Absalom her brother said to her, "Has Amnon your brother been with you? But now hold your peace, my sister. He *is* your brother; do not take this thing to heart." So Tamar remained desolate in her brother Absalom's house.

²¹But when King David heard of all these things, he was very angry. ²²And Absalom spoke to his brother Amnon neither good nor bad. For Absalom hated Amnon, because he had forced his sister Tamar.

Absalom Murders Amnon

²³And it came to pass, after two full years, that Absalom had sheepshearers in Baal Hazor, which *is* near Ephraim; so Absalom invited all the king's sons. ²⁴Then Absalom came to the king and said, "Kindly note, your servant has sheepshearers; please, let the king and his servants go with your servant."

²⁵But the king said to Absalom, "No, my son, let us not all go now, lest we be a burden to you." Then he urged him, but he would not go; and he blessed him.

²⁶Then Absalom said, "If not, please let my brother Amnon go with us."

And the king said to him, "Why should he go with you?" ²⁷But Absalom urged him; so he let Amnon and all the king's sons go with him.

²⁸Now Absalom had commanded his servants, saying, "Watch now, when Amnon's heart is merry with wine, and when I say to you, 'Strike Amnon!' then kill him. Do not be afraid. Have I not commanded you? Be courageous and valiant." ²⁹So the servants of Absalom did to Amnon as Absalom had commanded. Then all the king's sons arose, and each one got on his mule and fled.

³⁰And it came to pass, while they were on the way, that news came to David, saying, "Absalom has killed all the king's sons, and not one of them is left!" ³¹So the king arose and tore his garments and lay on the ground, and all his servants stood by with their clothes torn. ³²Then Jonadab the son of Shimeah, David's brother, answered and

said, "Let not my lord suppose they have killed all the young men, the king's sons, for only Amnon is dead. For by the command of Absalom this has been determined from the day that he forced his sister Tamar. [33]Now therefore, let not my lord the king take the thing to his heart, to think that all the king's sons are dead. For only Amnon is dead."

Absalom Flees to Geshur

[34]Then Absalom fled. And the young man who was keeping watch lifted his eyes and looked, and there, many people were coming from the road on the hillside behind him.[a] [35]And Jonadab said to the king, "Look, the king's sons are coming; as your servant said, so it is." [36]So it was, as soon as he had finished speaking, that the king's sons indeed came, and they lifted up their voice and wept. Also the king and all his servants wept very bitterly.

[37]But Absalom fled and went to Talmai the son of Ammihud, king of Geshur. And David mourned for his son every day. [38]So Absalom fled and went to Geshur, and was there three years. [39]And King David[a] longed to go to[b] Absalom. For he had been comforted concerning Amnon, because he was dead.

Absalom Returns to Jerusalem

14 So Joab the son of Zeruiah perceived that the king's heart was concerned about Absalom. [2]And Joab sent to Tekoa and brought from there a wise woman, and said to her, "Please pretend to be a mourner, and put on mourning apparel; do not anoint yourself with oil, but act like a woman who has been mourning a long time for the dead. [3]Go to the king and speak to him in this manner." So Joab put the words in her mouth.

[4]And when the woman of Tekoa spoke[a] to the king, she fell on her face to the ground and prostrated herself, and said, "Help, O king!"

[5]Then the king said to her, "What troubles you?"

And she answered, "Indeed I am a widow, my husband is dead. [6]Now your maidservant had two sons; and the two fought with each other in the field, and there was no one

to part them, but the one struck the other and killed him. [7]And now the whole family has risen up against your maidservant, and they said, 'Deliver him who struck his brother, that we may execute him for the life of his brother whom he killed; and we will destroy the heir also.' So they would extinguish my ember that is left, and leave to my husband neither name nor remnant on the earth."

[8]Then the king said to the woman, "Go to your house, and I will give orders concerning you."

[9]And the woman of Tekoa said to the king, "My lord, O king, let the iniquity be on me and on my father's house, and the king and his throne be guiltless."

[10]So the king said, "Whoever says anything to you, bring him to me, and he shall not touch you anymore."

[11]Then she said, "Please let the king remember the LORD your God, and do not permit the avenger of blood to destroy anymore, lest they destroy my son."

And he said, "As the LORD lives, not one hair of your son shall fall to the ground."

[12]Therefore the woman said, "Please, let your maidservant speak another word to my lord the king."

And he said, "Say on."

[13]So the woman said: "Why then have you schemed such a thing against the people of God? For the king speaks this thing as one who is guilty, in that the king does not bring his banished one home again. [14]For we will surely die and become like water spilled on the ground, which cannot be gathered up again. Yet God does not take away a life; but He devises means, so that His banished ones are not expelled from Him. [15]Now therefore, I have come to speak of this thing to my lord the king because the people have made me afraid. And your maidservant said, 'I will now speak to the

---

13:34 [a]Septuagint adds And the watchman went and told the king, and said, "I see men from the way of Horonaim, from the regions of the mountains." **13:39** [a]Following Masoretic Text, Syriac, and Vulgate; Septuagint reads the spirit of the king; Targum reads the soul of King David. [b]Following Masoretic Text and Targum; Septuagint and Vulgate read ceased to pursue after. **14:4** [a]Many Hebrew manuscripts, Septuagint, Syriac, and Vulgate read came.

king; it may be that the king will perform the request of his maidservant. [16]For the king will hear and deliver his maidservant from the hand of the man *who would* destroy me and my son together from the inheritance of God.' [17]Your maidservant said, 'The word of my lord the king will now be comforting; for as the angel of God, so *is* my lord the king in discerning good and evil. And may the Lord your God be with you.'"

[18]Then the king answered and said to the woman, "Please do not hide from me anything that I ask you."

And the woman said, "Please, let my lord the king speak."

[19]So the king said, "*Is* the hand of Joab with you in all this?" And the woman answered and said, "*As* you live, my lord the king, no one can turn to the right hand or to the left from anything that my lord the king has spoken. For your servant Joab commanded me, and he put all these words in the mouth of your maidservant. [20]To bring about this change of affairs your servant Joab has done this thing; but my lord *is* wise, according to the wisdom of the angel of God, to know everything that *is* in the earth."

[21]And the king said to Joab, "All right, I have granted this thing. Go therefore, bring back the young man Absalom."

[22]Then Joab fell to the ground on his face and bowed himself, and thanked the king. And Joab said, "Today your servant knows that I have found favor in your sight, my lord, O king, in that the king has fulfilled the request of his servant." [23]So Joab arose and went to Geshur, and brought Absalom to Jerusalem. [24]And the king said, "Let him return to his own house, but do not let him see my face." So Absalom returned to his own house, but did not see the king's face.

David Forgives Absalom

[25]Now in all Israel there was no one who was praised as much as Absalom for his good looks. From the sole of his foot to the crown of his head there was no blemish in him. [26]And when he cut the hair of his head—at the end of every year he cut *it* because it was heavy on him—when he cut it, he weighed the hair of his head at two hundred shekels according to the king's standard.

[27]To Absalom were born three sons, and one daughter whose name *was* Tamar. She was a woman of beautiful appearance.

[28]And Absalom dwelt two full years in Jerusalem, but did not see the king's face. [29]Therefore Absalom sent for Joab, to send him to the king, but he would not come to him. And when he sent again the second time, he would not come. [30]So he said to his servants, "See, Joab's field is near mine, and he has barley there; go and set it on fire." And Absalom's servants set the field on fire.

[31]Then Joab arose and came to Absalom's house, and said to him, "Why have your servants set my field on fire?"

[32]And Absalom answered Joab, "Look, I sent to you, saying, 'Come here, so that I may send you to the king, to say, "Why have I come from Geshur? *It would be* better for me *to be* there still."' Now therefore, let me see the king's face; but if there is iniquity in me, let him execute me."

[33]So Joab went to the king and told him. And when he had called for Absalom, he came to the king and bowed himself on his face to the ground before the king. Then the king kissed Absalom.

Absalom's Treason

15 After this it happened that Absalom provided himself with chariots and horses, and fifty men to run before him. [2]Now Absalom would rise early and stand beside the way to the gate. *So* it was, whenever anyone who had a lawsuit came to the king for a decision, that Absalom would call to him and say, "What city *are* you from?" And he would say, "Your servant *is* from such and such a tribe of Israel." [3]Then Absalom would say to him, "Look, your case *is* good and right; but *there is* no deputy of the king to hear you." [4]Moreover Absalom would say, "Oh, that I were made judge in the land, and everyone who has any suit or cause would come to me; then I would give him justice." [5]And *so* it was, whenever anyone came near to bow down to him, that he would put out his hand and take him and kiss him. [6]In this manner Absalom acted toward all Israel who came to the king for judgment. So Absalom stole the hearts of the men of Israel.

⁷Now it came to pass after forty[a] years that Absalom said to the king, "Please, let me go to Hebron and pay the vow which I made to the LORD. ⁸For your servant took a vow while I dwelt at Geshur in Syria, saying, 'If the LORD indeed brings me back to Jerusalem, then I will serve the LORD.'"

⁹And the king said to him, "Go in peace." So he arose and went to Hebron.

¹⁰Then Absalom sent spies throughout all the tribes of Israel, saying, "As soon as you hear the sound of the trumpet, then you shall say, 'Absalom reigns in Hebron!'" ¹¹And with Absalom went two hundred men invited from Jerusalem, and they went along innocently and did not know anything. ¹²Then Absalom sent for Ahithophel the Gilonite, David's counselor, from his city—from Giloh—while he offered sacrifices. And the conspiracy grew strong, for the people with Absalom continually increased in number.

David Escapes from Jerusalem

¹³Now a messenger came to David, saying, "The hearts of the men of Israel are with Absalom."

¹⁴So David said to all his servants who were with him at Jerusalem, "Arise, and let us flee, or we shall not escape from Absalom. Make haste to depart, lest he overtake us suddenly and bring disaster upon us, and strike the city with the edge of the sword."

¹⁵And the king's servants said to the king, "We are your servants, ready to do whatever my lord the king commands." ¹⁶Then the king went out with all his household after him. But the king left ten women, concubines, to keep the house. ¹⁷And the king went out with all the people after him, and stopped at the outskirts. ¹⁸Then all his servants passed before him; and all the Cherethites, all the Pelethites, and all the Gittites, six hundred men who had followed him from Gath, passed before the king.

¹⁹Then the king said to Ittai the Gittite, "Why are you also going with us? Return and remain with the king. For you are a foreigner and also an exile from your own place. ²⁰In fact, you came only yesterday. Should I make you wander up and down with us today, since I go I know not where? Return, and take your brethren back. Mercy and truth be with you."

²¹But Ittai answered the king and said, "As the LORD lives, and as my lord the king lives, surely in whatever place my lord the king shall be, whether in death or life, even there also your servant will be."

²²So David said to Ittai, "Go, and cross over." Then Ittai the Gittite and all his men and all the little ones who were with him crossed over. ²³And all the country wept with a loud voice, and all the people crossed over. The king himself also crossed over the Brook Kidron, and all the people crossed over toward the way of the wilderness.

²⁴There was Zadok also, and all the Levites with him, bearing the ark of the covenant of God. And they set down the ark of God, and Abiathar went up until all the people had finished crossing over from the city. ²⁵Then the king said to Zadok, "Carry the ark of God back into the city. If I find favor in the eyes of the LORD, He will bring me back and show me both it and His dwelling place. ²⁶But if He says thus: 'I have no delight in you,' here I am, let Him do to me as seems good to Him." ²⁷The king also said to Zadok the priest, "Are you not a seer? Return to the city in peace, and your two sons with you, Ahimaaz your son, and Jonathan the son of Abiathar. ²⁸See, I will wait in the plains of the wilderness until word comes from you to inform me." ²⁹Therefore Zadok and Abiathar carried the ark of God back to Jerusalem. And they remained there.

³⁰So David went up by the Ascent of the Mount of Olives, and wept as he went up; and he had his head covered and went barefoot. And all the people who were with him covered their heads and went up, weeping as they went up. ³¹Then someone told David, saying, "Ahithophel is among the conspirators with Absalom." And David said, "O LORD, I pray, turn the counsel of Ahithophel into foolishness!"

³²Now it happened when David had come to the top of the mountain, where he worshiped God—there was Hushai the Archite coming to meet him with his robe torn and

---

15:7 [a]Septuagint manuscripts, Syriac, and Josephus read four.

dust on his head. 33David said to him, "If you go on with me, then you will become a burden to me. 34But if you return to the city, and say to Absalom, 'I will be your servant, O king; as I *was* your father's servant previously, so I *will* now also *be* your servant,' then you may defeat the counsel of Ahithophel for me. 35And *do* you not *have* Zadok and Abiathar the priests with you there? Therefore it will be *that* whatever you hear from the king's house, you shall tell to Zadok and Abiathar the priests. 36Indeed *they have* there with them their two sons, Ahimaaz, Zadok's *son,* and Jonathan, Abiathar's *son;* and by them you shall send me everything you hear."

37So Hushai, David's friend, went into the city. And Absalom came into Jerusalem.

Mephibosheth's Servant

16 When David was a little past the top *of the mountain,* there was Ziba the servant of Mephibosheth, who met him with a couple of saddled donkeys, and on them two hundred *loaves* of bread, one hundred clusters of raisins, one hundred summer fruits, and a skin of wine. 2And the king said to Ziba, "What do you mean to do with these?"

So Ziba said, "The donkeys *are* for the king's household to ride on, the bread and summer fruit for the young men to eat, and the wine for those who are faint in the wilderness to drink."

3Then the king said, "And where *is* your master's son?"

And Ziba said to the king, "Indeed he is staying in Jerusalem, for he said, 'Today the house of Israel will restore the kingdom of my father to me.'"

4So the king said to Ziba, "Here, all that *belongs* to Mephibosheth *is* yours."

And Ziba said, "I humbly bow before you, *that* I may find favor in your sight, my lord, O king!"

Shimei Curses David

5Now when King David came to Bahurim, there was a man from the family of the house of Saul, whose name *was* Shimei the son of Gera, coming from there. He came out, cursing continuously as he came. 6And he threw stones at David and at all the servants of King David. And all the people and all the mighty men *were* on his right hand and on his left. 7Also Shimei said thus when he cursed: "Come out! Come out! You bloodthirsty man, you rogue! 8The LORD has brought upon you all the blood of the house of Saul, in whose place you have reigned; and the LORD has delivered the kingdom into the hand of Absalom your son. So now you *are caught* in your own evil, because you are a bloodthirsty man!"

9Then Abishai the son of Zeruiah said to the king, "Why should this dead dog curse my lord the king? Please, let me go over and take off his head!"

10But the king said, "What have I to do with you, you sons of Zeruiah? So let him curse, because the LORD has said to him, 'Curse David.' Who then shall say, 'Why have you done so?'"

11And David said to Abishai and all his servants, "See how my son who came from my own body seeks my life. How much more now *may this* Benjamite? Let him alone, and let him curse; for so the LORD has ordered him. 12It may be that the LORD will look on my affliction,a and that the LORD will repay me with good for his cursing this day." 13And as David and his men went along the road, Shimei went along the hillside opposite him and cursed as he went, threw stones at him and kicked up dust. 14Now the king and all the people who *were* with him became weary; so they refreshed themselves there.

The Advice of Ahithophel

15Meanwhile Absalom and all the people, the men of Israel, came to Jerusalem; and Ahithophel *was* with him. 16And so it was, when Hushai the Archite, David's friend, came to Absalom, that Hushai said to Absalom, "*Long* live the king! *Long* live the king!"

17So Absalom said to Hushai, "*Is* this your loyalty to your friend? Why did you not go with your friend?"

18And Hushai said to Absalom, "No, but whom the LORD and this people and all the

---

16:12 aFollowing Kethib, Septuagint, Syriac, and Vulgate; Qere reads *my eyes;* Targum reads *tears of my eyes.*

men of Israel choose, his I will be, and with him I will remain. ¹⁹Furthermore, whom should I serve? *Should I* not *serve* in the presence of his son? As I have served in your father's presence, so will I be in your presence."

²⁰Then Absalom said to Ahithophel, "Give advice as to what we should do."

²¹And Ahithophel said to Absalom, "Go in to your father's concubines, whom he has left to keep the house; and all Israel will hear that you are abhorred by your father. Then the hands of all who are with you will be strong." ²²So they pitched a tent for Absalom on the top of the house, and Absalom went in to his father's concubines in the sight of all Israel.

²³Now the advice of Ahithophel, which he gave in those days, *was* as if one had inquired at the oracle of God. So *was* all the advice of Ahithophel both with David and with Absalom.

17 Moreover Ahithophel said to Absalom, "Now let me choose twelve thousand men, and I will arise and pursue David tonight. ²I will come upon him while he *is* weary and weak, and make him afraid. And all the people who *are* with him will flee, and I will strike only the king. ³Then I will bring back all the people to you. When all return except the man whom you seek, all the people will be at peace." ⁴And the saying pleased Absalom and all the elders of Israel.

The Advice of Hushai

⁵Then Absalom said, "Now call Hushai the Archite also, and let us hear what he says too." ⁶And when Hushai came to Absalom, Absalom spoke to him, saying, "Ahithophel has spoken in this manner. Shall we do as he says? If not, speak up."

⁷So Hushai said to Absalom: "The advice that Ahithophel has given *is* not good at this time. ⁸For," said Hushai, "you know your father and his men, that they *are* mighty men, and they *are* enraged in their minds, like a bear robbed of her cubs in the field; and your father *is* a man of war, and will not camp with the people. ⁹Surely by now he is hidden in some pit, or in some *other* place. And it will be, when some of them are overthrown at the first, that whoever

hears *it* will say, 'There is a slaughter among the people who follow Absalom.' ¹⁰And even he *who is* valiant, whose heart *is* like the heart of a lion, will melt completely. For all Israel knows that your father *is* a mighty man, and *those* who *are* with him *are* valiant men. ¹¹Therefore I advise that all Israel be fully gathered to you, from Dan to Beersheba, like the sand that *is* by the sea for multitude, and that you go to battle in person. ¹²So we will come upon him in some place where he may be found, and we will fall on him as the dew falls on the ground. And of him and all the men who *are* with him there shall not be left so much as one. ¹³Moreover, if he has withdrawn into a city, then all Israel shall bring ropes to that city; and we will pull it into the river, until there is not one small stone found there."

¹⁴So Absalom and all the men of Israel said, "The advice of Hushai the Archite *is* better than the advice of Ahithophel." For the LORD had purposed to defeat the good advice of Ahithophel, to the intent that the LORD might bring disaster on Absalom.

Hushai Warns David to Escape

¹⁵Then Hushai said to Zadok and Abiathar the priests, "Thus and so Ahithophel advised Absalom and the elders of Israel, and thus and so I have advised. ¹⁶Now therefore, send quickly and tell David, saying, 'Do not spend this night in the plains of the wilderness, but speedily cross over, lest the king and all the people who *are* with him be swallowed up.'" ¹⁷Now Jonathan and Ahimaaz stayed at En Rogel, for they dared not be seen coming into the city; so a female servant would come and tell them, and they would go and tell King David. ¹⁸Nevertheless a lad saw them, and told Absalom. But both of them went away quickly and came to a man's house in Bahurim, who had a well in his court; and they went down into it. ¹⁹Then the woman took and spread a covering over the well's mouth, and spread ground grain on it; and the thing was not known. ²⁰And when Absalom's servants came to the woman at the house, they said, "Where *are* Ahimaaz and Jonathan?"

So the woman said to them, "They have gone over the water brook."

And when they had searched and could not find *them,* they returned to Jerusalem. ²¹Now it came to pass, after they had departed, that they came up out of the well and went and told King David, and said to David, "Arise and cross over the water quickly. For thus has Ahithophel advised against you." ²²So David and all the people who *were* with him arose and crossed over the Jordan. By morning light not one of them was left who had not gone over the Jordan.

²³Now when Ahithophel saw that his advice was not followed, he saddled a donkey, and arose and went home to his house, to his city. Then he put his household in order, and hanged himself, and died; and he was buried in his father's tomb.

²⁴Then David went to Mahanaim. And Absalom crossed over the Jordan, he and all the men of Israel with him. ²⁵And Absalom made Amasa captain of the army instead of Joab. This Amasa *was* the son of a man whose name *was* Jithra,ᵃ an Israelite,ᵇ who had gone in to Abigail the daughter of Nahash, sister of Zeruiah, Joab's mother. ²⁶So Israel and Absalom encamped in the land of Gilead.

²⁷Now it happened, when David had come to Mahanaim, that Shobi the son of Nahash from Rabbah of the people of Ammon, Machir the son of Ammiel from Lo Debar, and Barzillai the Gileadite from Rogelim, ²⁸brought beds and basins, earthen vessels and wheat, barley and flour, parched *grain* and beans, lentils and parched *seeds,* ²⁹honey and curds, sheep and cheese of the herd, for David and the people who *were* with him to eat. For they said, "The people are hungry and weary and thirsty in the wilderness."

Absalom's Defeat and Death

18 And David numbered the people who *were* with him, and set captains of thousands and captains of hundreds over them. ²Then David sent out one third of the people under the hand of Joab, one third under the hand of Abishai the son of Zeruiah, Joab's brother, and one third under the hand of Ittai the Gittite. And the king said to the people, "I also will surely go out with you myself."

³But the people answered, "You shall not go out! For if we flee away, they will not care about us; nor if half of us die, will they care about us. But *you are* worth ten thousand of us now. For you are now more help to us in the city."

⁴Then the king said to them, "Whatever seems best to you I will do." So the king stood beside the gate, and all the people went out by hundreds and by thousands. ⁵Now the king had commanded Joab, Abishai, and Ittai, saying, "*Deal* gently for my sake with the young man Absalom." And all the people heard when the king gave all the captains orders concerning Absalom.

⁶So the people went out into the field of battle against Israel. And the battle was in the woods of Ephraim. ⁷The people of Israel were overthrown there before the servants of David, and a great slaughter of twenty thousand took place there that day. ⁸For the battle there was scattered over the face of the whole countryside, and the woods devoured more people that day than the sword devoured.

⁹Then Absalom met the servants of David. Absalom rode on a mule. The mule went under the thick boughs of a great terebinth tree, and his head caught in the terebinth; so he was left hanging between heaven and earth. And the mule which *was* under him went on. ¹⁰Now a certain man saw *it* and told Joab, and said, "I just saw Absalom hanging in a terebinth tree!"

¹¹So Joab said to the man who told him, "You just saw *him!* And why did you not strike him there to the ground? I would have given you ten *shekels* of silver and a belt."

¹²But the man said to Joab, "Though I were to receive a thousand *shekels* of silver in my hand, I would not raise my hand against the king's son. For in our hearing the king commanded you and Abishai and Ittai, saying, 'Beware lest anyone *touch* the young man Absalom!'ᵃ ¹³Otherwise I would

17:25 ᵃSpelled *Jether* in 1 Chronicles 2:17 and elsewhere ᵇFollowing Masoretic Text, some manuscripts of the Septuagint, and Targum; some manuscripts of the Septuagint read *Ishmaelite* (compare 1 Chronicles 2:17); Vulgate reads *of Jezrael.* **18:12** ᵃThe ancient versions read *'Protect the young man Absalom for me!'*

have dealt falsely against my own life. For there is nothing hidden from the king, and you yourself would have set yourself against *me*."

¹⁴Then Joab said, "I cannot linger with you." And he took three spears in his hand and thrust them through Absalom's heart, while he was *still* alive in the midst of the terebinth tree. ¹⁵And ten young men who bore Joab's armor surrounded Absalom, and struck and killed him.

¹⁶So Joab blew the trumpet, and the people returned from pursuing Israel. For Joab held back the people. ¹⁷And they took Absalom and cast him into a large pit in the woods, and laid a very large heap of stones over him. Then all Israel fled, everyone to his tent.

¹⁸Now Absalom in his lifetime had taken and set up a pillar for himself, which *is* in the King's Valley. For he said, "I have no son to keep my name in remembrance." He called the pillar after his own name. And to this day it is called Absalom's Monument.

David Hears of Absalom's Death

¹⁹Then Ahimaaz the son of Zadok said, "Let me run now and take the news to the king, how the LORD has avenged him of his enemies."

²⁰And Joab said to him, "You shall not take the news this day, for you shall take the news another day. But today you shall take no news, because the king's son is dead." ²¹Then Joab said to the Cushite, "Go, tell the king what you have seen." So the Cushite bowed himself to Joab and ran.

²²And Ahimaaz the son of Zadok said again to Joab, "But whatever happens, please let me also run after the Cushite."

So Joab said, "Why will you run, my son, since you have no news ready?"

²³"But whatever happens," *he said,* "let me run."

So he said to him, "Run." Then Ahimaaz ran by way of the plain, and outran the Cushite.

²⁴Now David was sitting between the two gates. And the watchman went up to the roof over the gate, to the wall, lifted his eyes and looked, and there was a man, running alone. ²⁵Then the watchman cried out and told the king. And the king said, "If he *is* alone, *there is* news in his mouth." And he came rapidly and drew near.

²⁶Then the watchman saw *another* man running, and the watchman called to the gatekeeper and said, "There is *another* man, running alone!"

And the king said, "He also brings news."

²⁷So the watchman said, "I think the running of the first is like the running of Ahimaaz the son of Zadok."

And the king said, "He *is* a good man, and comes with good news."

²⁸So Ahimaaz called out and said to the king, "All is well!" Then he bowed down with his face to the earth before the king, and said, "Blessed *be* the LORD your God, who has delivered up the men who raised their hand against my lord the king!"

²⁹The king said, "Is the young man Absalom safe?"

Ahimaaz answered, "When Joab sent the king's servant and *me* your servant, I saw a great tumult, but I did not know what *it was about.*"

³⁰And the king said, "Turn aside *and* stand here." So he turned aside and stood still.

³¹Just then the Cushite came, and the Cushite said, "There is good news, my lord the king! For the LORD has avenged you this day of all those who rose against you."

³²And the king said to the Cushite, "Is the young man Absalom safe?"

So the Cushite answered, "May the enemies of my lord the king, and all who rise against you to do harm, be like *that* young man!"

David's Mourning for Absalom

³³Then the king was deeply moved, and went up to the chamber over the gate, and wept. And as he went, he said thus: "O my son Absalom—my son, my son Absalom—if only I had died in your place! O Absalom my son, my son!"

19 And Joab was told, "Behold, the king is weeping and mourning for Absalom." ²So the victory that day was *turned* into mourning for all the people. For the people heard it said that day, "The king is grieved for his son." ³And the people stole

back into the city that day, as people who are ashamed steal away when they flee in battle. ⁴But the king covered his face, and the king cried out with a loud voice, "O my son Absalom! O Absalom, my son, my son!"

⁵Then Joab came into the house to the king, and said, "Today you have disgraced all your servants who today have saved your life, the lives of your sons and daughters, the lives of your wives and the lives of your concubines, ⁶in that you love your enemies and hate your friends. For you have declared today that you regard neither princes nor servants; for today I perceive that if Absalom had lived and all of us had died today, then it would have pleased you well. ⁷Now therefore, arise, go out and speak comfort to your servants. For I swear by the LORD, if you do not go out, not one will stay with you this night. And that will be worse for you than all the evil that has befallen you from your youth until now." ⁸Then the king arose and sat in the gate. And they told all the people, saying, "There is the king, sitting in the gate." So all the people came before the king.

For everyone of Israel had fled to his tent.

David Returns to Jerusalem

⁹Now all the people were in a dispute throughout all the tribes of Israel, saying, "The king saved us from the hand of our enemies, he delivered us from the hand of the Philistines, and now he has fled from the land because of Absalom. ¹⁰But Absalom, whom we anointed over us, has died in battle. Now therefore, why do you say nothing about bringing back the king?"

¹¹So King David sent to Zadok and Abiathar the priests, saying, "Speak to the elders of Judah, saying, 'Why are you the last to bring the king back to his house, since the words of all Israel have come to the king, to his *very* house? ¹²You *are* my brethren, you *are* my bone and my flesh. Why then are you the last to bring back the king?' ¹³And say to Amasa, '*Are* you not my bone and my flesh? God do so to me, and more also, if you are not commander of the army before me continually in place of Joab.'" ¹⁴So he swayed the hearts of all the men of Judah, just as *the heart of* one man,

so that they sent *this word* to the king: "Return, you and all your servants!"

¹⁵Then the king returned and came to the Jordan. And Judah came to Gilgal, to go to meet the king, to escort the king across the Jordan. ¹⁶And Shimei the son of Gera, a Benjamite, who *was* from Bahurim, hurried and came down with the men of Judah to meet King David. ¹⁷*There were* a thousand men of Benjamin with him, and Ziba the servant of the house of Saul, and his fifteen sons and his twenty servants with him; and they went over the Jordan before the king. ¹⁸Then a ferryboat went across to carry over the king's household, and to do what he thought good.

David's Mercy to Shimei

Now Shimei the son of Gera fell down before the king when he had crossed the Jordan. ¹⁹Then he said to the king, "Do not let my lord impute iniquity to me, or remember what wrong your servant did on the day that my lord the king left Jerusalem, that the king should take *it* to heart. ²⁰For I, your servant, know that I have sinned. Therefore here I am, the first to come today of all the house of Joseph to go down to meet my lord the king."

²¹But Abishai the son of Zeruiah answered and said, "Shall not Shimei be put to death for this, because he cursed the LORD's anointed?"

²²And David said, "What have I to do with you, you sons of Zeruiah, that you should be adversaries to me today? Shall any man be put to death today in Israel? For do I not know that today I *am* king over Israel?" ²³Therefore the king said to Shimei, "You shall not die." And the king swore to him.

David and Mephibosheth Meet

²⁴Now Mephibosheth the son of Saul came down to meet the king. And he had not cared for his feet, nor trimmed his mustache, nor washed his clothes, from the day the king departed until the day he returned in peace. ²⁵So it was, when he had come to Jerusalem to meet the king, that the king said to him, "Why did you not go with me, Mephibosheth?"

26And he answered, "My lord, O king, my servant deceived me. For your servant said, 'I will saddle a donkey for myself, that I may ride on it and go to the king,' because your servant *is* lame. 27And he has slandered your servant to my lord the king, but my lord the king *is* like the angel of God. Therefore do *what is* good in your eyes. 28For all my father's house were but dead men before my lord the king. Yet you set your servant among those who eat at your own table. Therefore what right have I still to cry out anymore to the king?"

29So the king said to him, "Why do you speak anymore of your matters? I have said, 'You and Ziba divide the land.'"

30Then Mephibosheth said to the king, "Rather, let him take it all, inasmuch as my lord the king has come back in peace to his own house."

David's Kindness to Barzillai

31And Barzillai the Gileadite came down from Rogelim and went across the Jordan with the king, to escort him across the Jordan. 32Now Barzillai was a very aged man, eighty years old. And he had provided the king with supplies while he stayed at Mahanaim, for he *was* a very rich man. 33And the king said to Barzillai, "Come across with me, and I will provide for you while you are with me in Jerusalem."

34But Barzillai said to the king, "How long have I to live, that I should go up with the king to Jerusalem? 35I *am* today eighty years old. Can I discern between the good and bad? Can your servant taste what I eat or what I drink? Can I hear any longer the voice of singing men and singing women? Why then should your servant be a further burden to my lord the king? 36Your servant will go a little way across the Jordan with the king. And why should the king repay me *with* such a reward? 37Please let your servant turn back again, that I may die in my own city, near the grave of my father and mother. But here is your servant Chimham; let him cross over with my lord the king, and do for him what seems good to you."

38And the king answered, "Chimham shall cross over with me, and I will do for him what seems good to you. Now whatever you request of me, I will do for you." 39Then all the people went over the Jordan. And when the king had crossed over, the king kissed Barzillai and blessed him, and he returned to his own place.

The Quarrel About the King

40Now the king went on to Gilgal, and Chimham[a] went on with him. And all the people of Judah escorted the king, and also half the people of Israel. 41Just then all the men of Israel came to the king, and said to the king, "Why have our brethren, the men of Judah, stolen you away and brought the king, his household, and all David's men with him across the Jordan?"

42So all the men of Judah answered the men of Israel, "Because the king *is* a close relative of ours. Why then are you angry over this matter? Have we ever eaten at the king's *expense?* Or has he given us any gift?"

43And the men of Israel answered the men of Judah, and said, "We have ten shares in the king; therefore we also have more *right* to David than you. Why then do you despise us—were we not the first to advise bringing back our king?"

Yet the words of the men of Judah were fiercer than the words of the men of Israel.

The Rebellion of Sheba

20 And there happened to be there a rebel,[a] whose name *was* Sheba the son of Bichri, a Benjamite. And he blew a trumpet, and said:

"We have no share in David,
  Nor do we have inheritance in
    the son of Jesse;
  Every man to his tents, O Israel!"

2So every man of Israel deserted David, *and* followed Sheba the son of Bichri. But the men of Judah, from the Jordan as far as Jerusalem, remained loyal to their king.

3Now David came to his house at Jerusalem. And the king took the ten women, his concubines whom he had left to keep

---

19:40 aMasoretic Text reads *Chimham.*
20:1 aLiterally *man of Belial*

the house, and put them in seclusion and supported them, but did not go in to them. So they were shut up to the day of their death, living in widowhood.

⁴And the king said to Amasa, "Assemble the men of Judah for me within three days, and be present here yourself." ⁵So Amasa went to assemble *the men of* Judah. But he delayed longer than the set time which David had appointed him. ⁶And David said to Abishai, "Now Sheba the son of Bichri will do us more harm than Absalom. Take your lord's servants and pursue him, lest he find for himself fortified cities, and escape us." ⁷So Joab's men, with the Cherethites, the Pelethites, and all the mighty men, went out after him. And they went out of Jerusalem to pursue Sheba the son of Bichri. ⁸When they *were* at the large stone which *is* in Gibeon, Amasa came before them. Now Joab was dressed in battle armor; on it was a belt *with* a sword fastened in its sheath at his hips; and as he was going forward, it fell out. ⁹Then Joab said to Amasa, "*Are* you in health, my brother?" And Joab took Amasa by the beard with his right hand to kiss him. ¹⁰But Amasa did not notice the sword that *was* in Joab's hand. And he struck him with it in the stomach, and his entrails poured out on the ground; and he did not *strike* him again. Thus he died.

Then Joab and Abishai his brother pursued Sheba the son of Bichri. ¹¹Meanwhile one of Joab's men stood near Amasa, and said, "Whoever favors Joab and whoever *is* for David—follow Joab!" ¹²But Amasa wallowed in *his* blood in the middle of the highway. And when the man saw that all the people stood still, he moved Amasa from the highway to the field and threw a garment over him, when he saw that everyone who came upon him halted. ¹³When he was removed from the highway, all the people went on after Joab to pursue Sheba the son of Bichri.

¹⁴And he went through all the tribes of Israel to Abel and Beth Maachah and all the Berites. So they were gathered together

SELFLESS

But the men of Judah . . . remained loyal to their king.

2 SAMUEL 20:2

PATRIOTISM

Noah Webster's *An American Dictionary of the English Language*, 1828

patriotism, n. Love of one's country; the passion which aims to serve one's country, either in defending it from invasion, or protecting its rights and maintaining its laws and institutions in vigor and purity. Patriotism is the characteristic of a good citizen, the noblest passion that animates a man in the character of a citizen.

Merriam-Webster's Collegiate® Dictionary, Eleventh Edition, copyright © 2004

patriotism, n. Love for or devotion to one's country.

Note how the definitions have changed. Noah Webster's patriot defends his country with objective actions, versus the vague, subjective patriotism of one who only feels and expresses love for his country. True patriotism is not just an emotional feeling; it is action.

Webster's original definition includes a love for country, service to country, defense of country, protection of the rights of country, maintenance of the laws and institutions of country, preservation of religion and morality in public and private life, and puts the needs of the country above personal or partisan desires as well as above the favor of foreign nations.

and also went after *Sheba.*ᵃ ¹⁵Then they came and besieged him in Abel of Beth Maachah; and they cast up a siege mound against the city, and it stood by the rampart. And all the people who *were* with Joab battered the wall to throw it down.

¹⁶Then a wise woman cried out from the city, "Hear, hear! Please say to Joab, 'Come nearby, that I may speak with you.'" ¹⁷When he had come near to her, the woman said, "*Are* you Joab?"

He answered, "I *am.*"

Then she said to him, "Hear the words of your maidservant."

And he answered, "I am listening."

¹⁸So she spoke, saying, "They used to talk in former times, saying, 'They shall surely seek *guidance* at Abel,' and so they would end *disputes.* ¹⁹I *am among the* peaceable *and* faithful in Israel. You seek to destroy a city and a mother in Israel. Why would you swallow up the inheritance of the LORD?"

²⁰And Joab answered and said, "Far be it, far be it from me, that I should swallow up or destroy! ²¹That *is* not so. But a man from the mountains of Ephraim, Sheba the son of Bichri by name, has raised his hand against the king, against David. Deliver him only, and I will depart from the city."

So the woman said to Joab, "Watch, his head will be thrown to you over the wall." ²²Then the woman in her wisdom went to all the people. And they cut off the head of Sheba the son of Bichri, and threw *it* out to Joab. Then he blew a trumpet, and they withdrew from the city, every man to his tent. So Joab returned to the king at Jerusalem.

David's Government Officers

²³And Joab *was* over all the army of Israel; Benaiah the son of Jehoiada *was* over the Cherethites and the Pelethites; ²⁴Adoram *was* in charge of revenue; Jehoshaphat the son of Ahilud *was* recorder; ²⁵Sheva *was* scribe; Zadok and Abiathar *were* the priests; ²⁶and Ira the Jairite was a chief minister under David.

David Avenges the Gibeonites

21 Now there was a famine in the days of David for three years, year after year; and David inquired of the LORD. And the LORD answered, "*It is* because of Saul and *his* bloodthirsty house, because he killed the Gibeonites." ²So the king called the Gibeonites and spoke to them. Now the Gibeonites *were* not of the children of Israel, but of the remnant of the Amorites; the children of Israel had sworn protection to them, but Saul had sought to kill them in his zeal for the children of Israel and Judah.

³Therefore David said to the Gibeonites, "What shall I do for you? And with what shall I make atonement, that you may bless the inheritance of the LORD?"

⁴And the Gibeonites said to him, "We will have no silver or gold from Saul or from his house, nor shall you kill any man in Israel for us."

So he said, "Whatever you say, I will do for you."

⁵Then they answered the king, "As for the man who consumed us and plotted against us, *that* we should be destroyed from remaining in any of the territories of Israel, ⁶let seven men of his descendants be delivered to us, and we will hang them before the LORD in Gibeah of Saul, *whom* the LORD chose."

And the king said, "I will give *them.*"

⁷But the king spared Mephibosheth the son of Jonathan, the son of Saul, because of the LORD's oath that *was* between them, between David and Jonathan the son of Saul. ⁸So the king took Armoni and Mephibosheth, the two sons of Rizpah the daughter of Aiah, whom she bore to Saul, and the five sons of Michalᵃ the daughter of Saul, whom she brought up for Adriel the son of Barzillai the Meholathite; ⁹and he delivered them into the hands of the Gibeonites, and they hanged them on the hill before the LORD. So they fell, *all* seven together, and were put to death in the days of harvest, in the first *days,* in the beginning of barley harvest.

¹⁰Now Rizpah the daughter of Aiah took sackcloth and spread it for herself on the rock, from the beginning of harvest until the late rains poured on them from heaven. And she did not allow the birds of the air

---

20:14 ᵃLiterally *him*   **21:8** ᵃOr *Merab* (compare 1 Samuel 18:19 and 25:44; 2 Samuel 3:14 and 6:23)

to rest on them by day nor the beasts of the field by night.

11And David was told what Rizpah the daughter of Aiah, the concubine of Saul, had done. 12Then David went and took the bones of Saul, and the bones of Jonathan his son, from the men of Jabesh Gilead who had stolen them from the street of Beth Shan,a where the Philistines had hung them up, after the Philistines had struck down Saul in Gilboa. 13So he brought up the bones of Saul and the bones of Jonathan his son from there; and they gathered the bones of those who had been hanged. 14They buried the bones of Saul and Jonathan his son in the country of Benjamin in Zelah, in the tomb of Kish his father. So they performed all that the king commanded. And after that God heeded the prayer for the land.

Philistine Giants Destroyed

15When the Philistines were at war again with Israel, David and his servants with him went down and fought against the Philistines; and David grew faint. 16Then Ishbi-Benob, who *was* one of the sons of the giant, the weight of whose bronze spear *was* three hundred *shekels,* who was bearing a new *sword,* thought he could kill David. 17But Abishai the son of Zeruiah came to his aid, and struck the Philistine and killed him. Then the men of David swore to him, saying, "You shall go out no more with us to battle, lest you quench the lamp of Israel."

18Now it happened afterward that there was again a battle with the Philistines at Gob. Then Sibbechai the Hushathite killed Saph,a who *was* one of the sons of the giant. 19Again there was war at Gob with the Philistines, where Elhanan the son of Jaare-Oregima the Bethlehemite killed *the brother of* Goliath the Gittite, the shaft of whose spear *was* like a weaver's beam.

20Yet again there was war at Gath, where there was a man of *great* stature, who had six fingers on each hand and six toes on each foot, twenty-four in number; and he also was born to the giant. 21So when he defied Israel, Jonathan the son of Shimea,a David's brother, killed him.

22These four were born to the giant in Gath, and fell by the hand of David and by the hand of his servants.

Praise for God's Deliverance

22 Then David spoke to the LORD the words of this song, on the day when the LORD had delivered him from the hand of all his enemies, and from the hand of Saul. 2And he said:a

"The LORD *is* my rock and my fortress
and my deliverer;
3 The God of my strength, in whom
I will trust;
My shield and the horn of my salvation,
My stronghold and my refuge;
My Savior, You save me from violence.
4 I will call upon the LORD, *who is worthy*
to be praised;
So shall I be saved from my enemies.

5 "When the waves of death surrounded me,
The floods of ungodliness made me afraid.
6 The sorrows of Sheol surrounded me;
The snares of death confronted me.
7 In my distress I called upon the LORD,
And cried out to my God;
He heard my voice from His temple,
And my cry *entered* His ears.

8 "Then the earth shook and trembled;
The foundations of heavena quaked
and were shaken,
Because He was angry.
9 Smoke went up from His nostrils,
And devouring fire from His mouth;
Coals were kindled by it.
10 He bowed the heavens also, and came down
With darkness under His feet.
11 He rode upon a cherub, and flew;
And He was seena upon the wings
of the wind.

21:12 aSpelled *Beth Shean* in Joshua 17:11 and elsewhere 21:18 aSpelled *Sippai* in 1 Chronicles 20:4 21:19 aSpelled *Jair* in 1 Chronicles 20:5 21:21 aSpelled *Shammah* in 1 Samuel 16:9 and elsewhere 22:2 aCompare Psalm 18 22:8 aFollowing Masoretic Text, Septuagint, and Targum; Syriac and Vulgate read *hills* (compare Psalm 18:7). 22:11 aFollowing Masoretic Text and Septuagint; many Hebrew manuscripts, Syriac, and Vulgate read *He flew* (compare Psalm 18:10); Targum reads *He spoke with power.*

12 He made darkness canopies around Him,
   Dark waters *and* thick clouds of the skies.
13 From the brightness before Him
   Coals of fire were kindled.

14 "The Lord thundered from heaven,
   And the Most High uttered His voice.
15 He sent out arrows and scattered them;
   Lightning bolts, and He vanquished them.
16 Then the channels of the sea were seen,
   The foundations of the world were uncovered,
   At the rebuke of the Lord,
   At the blast of the breath of His nostrils.

17 "He sent from above, He took me,
   He drew me out of many waters.
18 He delivered me from my strong enemy,
   From those who hated me;
   For they were too strong for me.
19 They confronted me in the day of my calamity,
   But the Lord was my support.
20 He also brought me out into a broad place;
   He delivered me because He delighted in me.

21 "The Lord rewarded me according to my righteousness;
   According to the cleanness of my hands He has recompensed me.
22 For I have kept the ways of the Lord,
   And have not wickedly departed from my God.
23 For all His judgments *were* before me;
   And *as for* His statutes, I did not depart from them.
24 I was also blameless before Him,
   And I kept myself from my iniquity.
25 Therefore the Lord has recompensed me according to my righteousness,
   According to my cleanness in His eyes.ᵃ

26 "With the merciful You will show Yourself merciful;
   With a blameless man You will show Yourself blameless;

27 With the pure You will show Yourself pure;
   And with the devious You will show Yourself shrewd.
28 You will save the humble people;
   But Your eyes *are* on the haughty,
   that You may bring *them* down.

29 "For You *are* my lamp, O Lord;
   The Lord shall enlighten my darkness.
30 For by You I can run against a troop;
   By my God I can leap over a wall.
31 *As for* God, His way *is* perfect;
   The word of the Lord *is* proven;
   He *is* a shield to all who trust in Him.

32 "For who *is* God, except the Lord?
   And who *is* a rock, except our God?
33 God *is* my strength *and* power,ᵃ
   And He makes myᵇ way perfect.
34 He makes myᵃ feet like the *feet* of deer,
   And sets me on my high places.
35 He teaches my hands to make war,
   So that my arms can bend a bow of bronze.

36 "You have also given me the shield of Your salvation;
   Your gentleness has made me great.
37 You enlarged my path under me;
   So my feet did not slip.

38 "I have pursued my enemies and destroyed them;
   Neither did I turn back again till they were destroyed.
39 And I have destroyed them and wounded them,
   So that they could not rise;
   They have fallen under my feet.
40 For You have armed me with strength for the battle;

22:25 ᵃSeptuagint, Syriac, and Vulgate read *the cleanness of my hands in His sight* (compare Psalm 18:24); Targum reads *my cleanness before His word.* **22:33** ᵃDead Sea Scrolls, Septuagint, Syriac, and Vulgate read *It is God who arms me with strength* (compare Psalm 18:32); Targum reads *It is God who sustains me with strength.* ᵇFollowing Qere, Septuagint, Syriac, Targum, and Vulgate (compare Psalm 18:32); Kethib reads *His.* **22:34** ᵃFollowing Qere, Septuagint, Syriac, Targum, and Vulgate (compare Psalm 18:33); Kethib reads *His.*

You have subdued under me those
   who rose against me.
41 You have also given me the necks
      of my enemies,
   So that I destroyed those who
      hated me.
42 They looked, but *there was* none
      to save;
   Even to the LORD, but He did not
      answer them.
43 Then I beat them as fine as the dust
      of the earth;
   I trod them like dirt in the streets,
   And I spread them out.

44 "You have also delivered me from the
      strivings of my people;
   You have kept me as the head of the
      nations.
   A people I have not known shall
      serve me.
45 The foreigners submit to me;
   As soon as they hear, they obey me.
46 The foreigners fade away,
   And come frightened[a] from their
      hideouts.

47 "The LORD lives!
   Blessed *be* my Rock!
   Let God be exalted,
   The Rock of my salvation!
48 *It is* God who avenges me,
   And subdues the peoples under me;
49 He delivers me from my enemies.
   You also lift me up above those who
      rise against me;
   You have delivered me from the
      violent man.
50 Therefore I will give thanks to You,
      O LORD, among the Gentiles,
   And sing praises to Your name.

51 *He is* the tower of salvation to His king,
   And shows mercy to His anointed,
   To David and his descendants
      forevermore."

David's Last Words

23 Now these *are* the last words of David.

   Thus says David the son of Jesse;
   Thus says the man raised up on high,

The anointed of the God of Jacob,
   And the sweet psalmist of Israel:

2 "The Spirit of the LORD spoke by me,
   And His word *was* on my tongue.
3 The God of Israel said,
   The Rock of Israel spoke to me:
   'He who rules over men *must be* just,
   Ruling in the fear of God.
4 And *he shall be* like the light of the
      morning *when* the sun rises,
   A morning without clouds,
   Like the tender grass *springing* out
      of the earth,
   By clear shining after rain.'

5 "Although my house *is* not so with God,
   Yet He has made with me an
      everlasting covenant,
   Ordered in all *things* and secure.
   For *this is* all my salvation and all *my*
      desire;
   Will He not make *it* increase?
6 But *the sons* of rebellion *shall* all *be*
      as thorns thrust away,
   Because they cannot be taken with
      hands.
7 But the man *who* touches them
   Must be armed with iron and the
      shaft of a spear,
   And they shall be utterly burned with
      fire in *their* place."

David's Mighty Men

8These *are* the names of the mighty men
whom David had: Josheb-Basshebeth[a] the
Tachmonite, chief among the captains.[b] He
was called Adino the Eznite, because he had
killed eight hundred men at one time. 9And
after him *was* Eleazar the son of Dodo,[a] the
Ahohite, *one* of the three mighty men with
David when they defied the Philistines *who*
were gathered there for battle, and the men
of Israel had retreated. 10He arose and
attacked the Philistines until his hand was
weary, and his hand stuck to the sword. The

22:46 [a]Following Septuagint, Targum, and Vulgate
(compare Psalm 18:45); Masoretic Text reads *gird
themselves.*   23:8 [a]Literally *One Who Sits in the Seat*
(compare 1 Chronicles 11:11) [b]Following Masoretic
Text and Targum; Septuagint and Vulgate read *the
three.*   23:9 [a]Spelled *Dodai* in 1 Chronicles 27:4

LORD brought about a great victory that day; and the people returned after him only to plunder. ¹¹And after him *was* Shammah the son of Agee the Hararite. The Philistines had gathered together into a troop where there was a piece of ground full of lentils. So the people fled from the Philistines. ¹²But he stationed himself in the middle of the field, defended it, and killed the Philistines. So the LORD brought about a great victory.

¹³Then three of the thirty chief men went down at harvest time and came to David at the cave of Adullam. And the troop of Philistines encamped in the Valley of Rephaim. ¹⁴David *was* then in the stronghold, and the garrison of the Philistines *was* then *in* Bethlehem. ¹⁵And David said with longing, "Oh, that someone would give me a drink of the water from the well of Bethlehem, which *is* by the gate!" ¹⁶So the three mighty men broke through the camp of the Philistines, drew water from the well of Bethlehem that *was* by the gate, and took it and brought *it* to David. Nevertheless he would not drink it, but poured it out to the LORD. ¹⁷And he said, "Far be it from me, O LORD, that I should do this! Is *this not* the blood of the men who went in *jeopardy of* their lives?" Therefore he would not drink it.

These things were done by the three mighty men.

¹⁸Now Abishai the brother of Joab, the son of Zeruiah, was chief of *another* three.ᵃ He lifted his spear against three hundred *men,* killed *them,* and won a name among *these* three. ¹⁹Was he not the most honored of three? Therefore he became their captain. However, he did not attain to the *first* three.

²⁰Benaiah *was* the son of Jehoiada, the son of a valiant man from Kabzeel, who had done many deeds. He had killed two lion-like heroes of Moab. He also had gone down and killed a lion in the midst of a pit on a snowy day. ²¹And he killed an Egyptian, a spectacular man. The Egyptian *had* a spear in his hand; so he went down to him with a staff, wrested the spear out of the Egyptian's hand, and killed him with his own spear. ²²These *things* Benaiah the son of Jehoiada did, and won a name among three mighty men. ²³He was more honored than the thirty, but he did not attain to the

first three. And David appointed him over his guard.

²⁴Asahel the brother of Joab *was* one of the thirty; Elhanan the son of Dodo of Bethlehem, ²⁵Shammah the Harodite, Elika the Harodite, ²⁶Helez the Paltite, Ira the son of Ikkesh the Tekoite, ²⁷Abiezer the Anathothite, Mebunnai the Hushathite, ²⁸Zalmon the Ahohite, Maharai the Netophathite, ²⁹Heleb the son of Baanah (the Netophathite), Ittai the son of Ribai from Gibeah of the children of Benjamin, ³⁰Benaiah a Pirathonite, Hiddai from the brooks of Gaash, ³¹Abi-Albon the Arbathite, Azmaveth the Barhumite, ³²Eliahba the Shaalbonite (of the sons of Jashen), Jonathan, ³³Shammah the Hararite, Ahiam the son of Sharar the Hararite, ³⁴Eliphelet the son of Ahasbai, the son of the Maachathite, Eliam the son of Ahithophel the Gilonite, ³⁵Hezraiᵃ the Carmelite, Paarai the Arbite, ³⁶Igal the son of Nathan of Zobah, Bani the Gadite, ³⁷Zelek the Ammonite, Naharai the Beerothite (armorbearer of Joab the son of Zeruiah), ³⁸Ira the Ithrite, Gareb the Ithrite, ³⁹*and* Uriah the Hittite: thirty-seven in all.

David's Census of Israel and Judah

24 Again the anger of the LORD was aroused against Israel, and He moved David against them to say, "Go, number Israel and Judah."

²So the king said to Joab the commander of the army who *was* with him, "Now go throughout all the tribes of Israel, from Dan to Beersheba, and count the people, that I may know the number of the people." ³And Joab said to the king, "Now may the LORD your God add to the people a hundred times more than there are, and may the eyes of my lord the king see *it.* But why does my lord the king desire this thing?" ⁴Nevertheless the king's word prevailed against Joab and against the captains of the army. Therefore Joab and the captains of the army went out from the presence of the king to count the people of Israel.

23:18 ᵃFollowing Masoretic Text, Septuagint, and Vulgate; some Hebrew manuscripts and Syriac read *thirty;* Targum reads *the mighty men.*
23:35 ᵃSpelled *Hezro* in 1 Chronicles 11:37

FREEDOM'S DEFENSE

FREDERICK DOUGLASS

DEFENDER

These are the names of the mighty men whom David had. . . .

2 SAMUEL 23:8

The soldier's heart, the soldier's spirit, the soldier's soul are everything. Unless the soldier's soul sustains him, he cannot be relied upon and will fail himself, his commander, and his country in the end.

GENERAL GEORGE C. MARSHALL

Wars may be fought with weapons, but they are won by men. It is the spirit of the men who follow and of the man who leads that gains that victory.

GENERAL GEORGE S. PATTON

God grants liberty only to those who love it and are always ready to guard and defend it.

DANIEL WEBSTER

Those who profess to favor freedom and yet depreciate agitation, are people who want crops without plowing the ground; they want rain without thunder and lightning; they want the ocean without the roar of its many waters. The struggle may be a moral one, or it may be a physical one, or it may be both. But it must be a struggle. Power concedes nothing without a demand; it never has and it never will.

FREDERICK DOUGLASS

This nation will remain the land of the free only so long as it is the home of the brave.

ELMER DAVIS

I only regret that I have but one life to lose for my country.

NATHAN HALE

A man who won't die for something is not fit to live.

MARTIN LUTHER KING JR.

The liberties of our country, the freedom of our civil Constitution, are worth defending at all hazards; and it is our duty to defend them against all attacks. We have received them as a fair inheritance from our worthy ancestors: they purchased them for us with toil and danger and expense of treasure and blood, and transmitted them to us with care and diligence. It will bring an everlasting mark of infamy on the present generation, enlightened as it is, if we should suffer them to be wrested from us by violence without a struggle or to be cheated out of them by the artifices of false and designing men.

SAMUEL ADAMS

⁵And they crossed over the Jordan and camped in Aroer, on the right side of the town which *is* in the midst of the ravine of Gad, and toward Jazer. ⁶Then they came to Gilead and to the land of Tahtim Hodshi; they came to Dan Jaan and around to Sidon; ⁷and they came to the stronghold of Tyre and to all the cities of the Hivites and the Canaanites. Then they went out to South Judah *as far as* Beersheba. ⁸So when they had gone through all the land, they came to Jerusalem at the end of nine months and twenty days. ⁹Then Joab gave the sum of the number of the people to the king. And there were in Israel eight hundred thousand valiant men who drew the sword, and the men of Judah were five hundred thousand men.

The Judgment on David's Sin

¹⁰And David's heart condemned him after he had numbered the people. So David said to the LORD, "I have sinned greatly in what I have done; but now, I pray, O LORD, take away the iniquity of Your servant, for I have done very foolishly."

¹¹Now when David arose in the morning, the word of the LORD came to the prophet Gad, David's seer, saying, ¹²"Go and tell David, 'Thus says the LORD: "I offer you three *things;* choose one of them for yourself, that I may do *it* to you."'" ¹³So Gad came to David and told him; and he said to him, "Shall sevenᵃ years of famine come to you in your land? Or shall you flee three months before your enemies, while they pursue you? Or shall there be three days' plague in your land? Now consider and see what answer I should take back to Him who sent me."

¹⁴And David said to Gad, "I am in great distress. Please let us fall into the hand of the LORD, for His mercies *are* great; but do not let me fall into the hand of man."

¹⁵So the LORD sent a plague upon Israel from the morning till the appointed time. From Dan to Beersheba seventy thousand men of the people died. ¹⁶And when the angelᵃ stretched out His hand over Jerusalem to destroy it, the LORD relented from the destruction, and said to the angel who was destroying the people, "It is enough; now restrain your hand." And the angel of the LORD was by the threshing floor of Araunahᵇ the Jebusite.

¹⁷Then David spoke to the LORD when he saw the angel who was striking the people, and said, "Surely I have sinned, and I have done wickedly; but these sheep, what have they done? Let Your hand, I pray, be against me and against my father's house."

The Altar on the Threshing Floor

¹⁸And Gad came that day to David and said to him, "Go up, erect an altar to the LORD on the threshing floor of Araunah the Jebusite." ¹⁹So David, according to the word of Gad, went up as the LORD commanded. ²⁰Now Araunah looked, and saw the king and his servants coming toward him. So Araunah went out and bowed before the king with his face to the ground.

²¹Then Araunah said, "Why has my lord the king come to his servant?"

And David said, "To buy the threshing floor from you, to build an altar to the LORD, that the plague may be withdrawn from the people."

²²Now Araunah said to David, "Let my lord the king take and offer up whatever *seems* good to him. Look, *here are* oxen for burnt sacrifice, and threshing implements and the yokes of the oxen for wood. ²³All these, O king, Araunah has given to the king."

And Araunah said to the king, "May the LORD your God accept you."

²⁴Then the king said to Araunah, "No, but I will surely buy *it* from you for a price; nor will I offer burnt offerings to the LORD my God with that which costs me nothing." So David bought the threshing floor and the oxen for fifty shekels of silver. ²⁵And David built there an altar to the LORD, and offered burnt offerings and peace offerings. So the LORD heeded the prayers for the land, and the plague was withdrawn from Israel.

24:13 ᵃFollowing Masoretic Text, Syriac, Targum, and Vulgate; Septuagint reads *three* (compare 1 Chronicles 21:12).   **24:16** ᵃOr *Angel* ᵇSpelled *Ornan* in 1 Chronicles 21:15

1 KINGS

Author: Unknown, attributed to Jeremiah

When Written: 560–538 B.C.

Theme: Division

Key Verses: 1 Kings 9:4, 5—"Now if you walk before Me as your father David walked, in integrity of heart and in uprightness, to do according to all that I have commanded you, and if you keep My statutes and My judgments, then I will establish the throne of your kingdom over Israel forever, as I promised David your father, saying, 'You shall not fail to have a man on the throne of Israel.' "

Key Chapter: 1 Kings 12—The crucial turning point in 1 Kings occurs in chapter 12 when, following the death of Solomon, the nation of Israel is torn asunder by internal conflict and becomes two separate warring kingdoms. Where there had once been unity of vision and spirit, there now exists ongoing discord and strife.

First Kings records the life and reign of Israel's King Solomon, considered the wisest man who ever lived. When Solomon heeded God's Word and followed the directives handed down through his father, King David, Israel enjoyed unprecedented peace, prosperity, and blessing. But when, toward the end of his life, Solomon took his eyes off the God-inspired vision for Israel, the nation began a slow decline.

Similarly, the far-reaching vision that led America's forefathers to found a nation governed by the rule of law could not prevent that nation from splintering less than 80 years later as self-centered ideologies and a militant spirit threatened to destroy this "one nation under God." Only God's mercy, righteous leadership, and the prayers of individuals and groups who love their God and their country have helped keep America as the "land of the free and the home of the brave."

1 KINGS

Adonijah Presumes to Be King

1 Now King David was old, advanced in years; and they put covers on him, but he could not get warm. [2]Therefore his servants said to him, "Let a young woman, a virgin, be sought for our lord the king, and let her stand before the king, and let her care for him; and let her lie in your bosom, that our lord the king may be warm." [3]So they sought for a lovely young woman throughout all the territory of Israel, and found Abishag the Shunammite, and brought her to the king. [4]The young woman *was* very lovely; and she cared for the king, and served him; but the king did not know her.

[5]Then Adonijah the son of Haggith exalted himself, saying, "I will be king"; and he prepared for himself chariots and horsemen, and fifty men to run before him. [6](And his father had not rebuked him at any time by saying, "Why have you done so?" He *was* also very good-looking. *His mother* had borne him after Absalom.) [7]Then he conferred with Joab the son of Zeruiah and with Abiathar the priest, and they followed and helped Adonijah. [8]But Zadok the priest, Benaiah the son of Jehoiada, Nathan the prophet, Shimei, Rei, and the mighty men who *belonged* to David were not with Adonijah.

[9]And Adonijah sacrificed sheep and oxen and fattened cattle by the stone of Zoheleth, which *is* by En Rogel; he also invited all his brothers, the king's sons, and all the men of Judah, the king's servants. [10]But he did not invite Nathan the prophet, Benaiah, the mighty men, or Solomon his brother.

[11]So Nathan spoke to Bathsheba the mother of Solomon, saying, "Have you not heard that Adonijah the son of Haggith has become king, and David our lord does not know *it?* [12]Come, please, let me now give you advice, that you may save your own life and the life of your son Solomon. [13]Go immediately to King David and say to him, 'Did you not, my lord, O king, swear to your maidservant, saying, "Assuredly your son Solomon shall reign after me, and he shall sit on my throne"? Why then has Adonijah become king?' [14]Then, while you are still talking there with the king, I also will come in after you and confirm your words."

[15]So Bathsheba went into the chamber to the king. (Now the king was very old, and Abishag the Shunammite was serving the king.) [16]And Bathsheba bowed and did homage to the king. Then the king said, "What is your wish?"

[17]Then she said to him, "My lord, you swore by the LORD your God to your maidservant, *saying,* 'Assuredly Solomon your son shall reign after me, and he shall sit on my throne.' [18]So now, look! Adonijah has become king; and now, my lord the king, you do not know about *it.* [19]He has sacrificed oxen and fattened cattle and sheep in abundance, and has invited all the sons of the king, Abiathar the priest, and Joab the commander of the army; but Solomon your servant he has not invited. [20]And as for you, my lord, O king, the eyes of all Israel *are* on you, that you should tell them who will sit on the throne of my lord the king after him. [21]Otherwise it will happen, when my lord the king rests with his fathers, that I and my son Solomon will be counted as offenders."

[22]And just then, while she was still talking with the king, Nathan the prophet also came in. [23]So they told the king, saying, "Here is Nathan the prophet." And when he came in before the king, he bowed down before the king with his face to the ground. [24]And Nathan said, "My lord, O king, have you said, 'Adonijah shall reign after me, and he shall sit on my throne'? [25]For he has gone down today, and has sacrificed oxen and fattened cattle and sheep in abundance, and has invited all the king's sons, and the commanders of the army, and Abiathar the priest; and look! They are eating and drinking before him; and they say,

'*Long* live King Adonijah!' [26]But he has not invited me—me your servant—nor Zadok the priest, nor Benaiah the son of Jehoiada, nor your servant Solomon. [27]Has this thing been done by my lord the king, and you have not told your servant who should sit on the throne of my lord the king after him?"

David Proclaims Solomon King

[28]Then King David answered and said, "Call Bathsheba to me." So she came into the king's presence and stood before the king. [29]And the king took an oath and said, "*As* the LORD lives, who has redeemed my life from every distress, [30]just as I swore to you by the LORD God of Israel, saying, 'Assuredly Solomon your son shall be king after me, and he shall sit on my throne in my place,' so I certainly will do this day." [31]Then Bathsheba bowed with *her* face to the earth, and paid homage to the king, and said, "Let my lord King David live forever!"

[32]And King David said, "Call to me Zadok the priest, Nathan the prophet, and Benaiah the son of Jehoiada." So they came before the king. [33]The king also said to them, "Take with you the servants of your lord, and have Solomon my son ride on my own mule, and take him down to Gihon. [34]There let Zadok the priest and Nathan the prophet anoint him king over Israel; and blow the horn, and say, '*Long* live King Solomon!' [35]Then you shall come up after him, and he shall come and sit on my throne, and he shall be king in my place. For I have appointed him to be ruler over Israel and Judah."

[36]Benaiah the son of Jehoiada answered the king and said, "Amen! May the LORD God of my lord the king say so *too.* [37]As the LORD has been with my lord the king, even so may He be with Solomon, and make his throne greater than the throne of my lord King David."

[38]So Zadok the priest, Nathan the prophet, Benaiah the son of Jehoiada, the Cherethites, and the Pelethites went down and had Solomon ride on King David's mule, and took him to Gihon. [39]Then Zadok the priest took a horn of oil from the tabernacle and anointed Solomon. And they blew the horn, and all the people said, "*Long* live

King Solomon!" [40]And all the people went up after him; and the people played the flutes and rejoiced with great joy, so that the earth *seemed to* split with their sound.

[41]Now Adonijah and all the guests who *were* with him heard *it* as they finished eating. And when Joab heard the sound of the horn, he said, "Why *is* the city in such a noisy uproar?" [42]While he was still speaking, there came Jonathan, the son of Abiathar the priest. And Adonijah said to him, "Come in, for you *are* a prominent man, and bring good news."

[43]Then Jonathan answered and said to Adonijah, "No! Our lord King David has made Solomon king. [44]The king has sent with him Zadok the priest, Nathan the prophet, Benaiah the son of Jehoiada, the Cherethites, and the Pelethites; and they have made him ride on the king's mule. [45]So Zadok the priest and Nathan the prophet have anointed him king at Gihon; and they have gone up from there rejoicing, so that the city is in an uproar. This *is* the noise that you have heard. [46]Also Solomon sits on the throne of the kingdom. [47]And moreover the king's servants have gone to bless our lord King David, saying, 'May God make the name of Solomon better than your name, and may He make his throne greater than your throne.' Then the king bowed himself on the bed. [48]Also the king said thus, 'Blessed *be* the LORD God of Israel, who has given *one* to sit on my throne this day, while my eyes see *it!*'"

[49]So all the guests who were with Adonijah were afraid, and arose, and each one went his way.

[50]Now Adonijah was afraid of Solomon; so he arose, and went and took hold of the horns of the altar. [51]And it was told Solomon, saying, "Indeed Adonijah is afraid of King Solomon; for look, he has taken hold of the horns of the altar, saying, 'Let King Solomon swear to me today that he will not put his servant to death with the sword.'"

[52]Then Solomon said, "If he proves himself a worthy man, not one hair of him shall fall to the earth; but if wickedness is found in him, he shall die." [53]So King Solomon sent them to bring him down from the altar. And he came and fell down before

King Solomon; and Solomon said to him, "Go to your house."

David's Instructions to Solomon

2 Now the days of David drew near that he should die, and he charged Solomon his son, saying: [2]"I go the way of all the earth; be strong, therefore, and prove yourself a man. [3]And keep the charge of the LORD your God: to walk in His ways, to keep His statutes, His commandments, His judgments, and His testimonies, as it is written in the Law of Moses, that you may prosper in all that you do and wherever you turn; [4]that the LORD may fulfill His word which He spoke concerning me, saying, 'If your sons take heed to their way, to walk before Me in truth with all their heart and with all their soul,' He said, 'you shall not lack a man on the throne of Israel.'

[5]"Moreover you know also what Joab the son of Zeruiah did to me, *and* what he did to the two commanders of the armies of Israel, to Abner the son of Ner and Amasa the son of Jether, whom he killed. And he shed the blood of war in peacetime, and put the blood of war on his belt that *was* around his waist, and on his sandals that *were* on his feet. [6]Therefore do according to your wisdom, and do not let his gray hair go down to the grave in peace.

[7]"But show kindness to the sons of Barzillai the Gileadite, and let them be among those who eat at your table, for so they came to me when I fled from Absalom your brother.

[8]"And see, *you have* with you Shimei the son of Gera, a Benjamite from Bahurim, who cursed me with a malicious curse in the day when I went to Mahanaim. But he came down to meet me at the Jordan, and I swore to him by the LORD, saying, 'I will not put you to death with the sword.' [9]Now therefore, do not hold him guiltless, for you *are* a wise man and know what you ought to do to him; but bring his gray hair down to the grave with blood."

Death of David

[10]So David rested with his fathers, and was buried in the City of David. [11]The period that David reigned over Israel *was* forty years; seven years he reigned in Hebron, and in Jerusalem he reigned thirty-three years. [12]Then Solomon sat on the throne of his father David; and his kingdom was firmly established.

Solomon Executes Adonijah

[13]Now Adonijah the son of Haggith came to Bathsheba the mother of Solomon. So she said, "Do you come peaceably?"

And he said, "Peaceably." [14]Moreover he said, "I have something *to say* to you."

And she said, "Say it."

[15]Then he said, "You know that the kingdom was mine, and all Israel had set their expectations on me, that I should reign. However, the kingdom has been turned over, and has become my brother's; for it was his from the LORD. [16]Now I ask one petition of you; do not deny me."

And she said to him, "Say it."

[17]Then he said, "Please speak to King Solomon, for he will not refuse you, that he may give me Abishag the Shunammite as wife."

[18]So Bathsheba said, "Very well, I will speak for you to the king."

[19]Bathsheba therefore went to King Solomon, to speak to him for Adonijah. And the king rose up to meet her and bowed down to her, and sat down on his throne and had a throne set for the king's mother; so she sat at his right hand. [20]Then she said, "I desire one small petition of you; do not refuse me."

And the king said to her, "Ask it, my mother, for I will not refuse you."

[21]So she said, "Let Abishag the Shunammite be given to Adonijah your brother as wife."

[22]And King Solomon answered and said to his mother, "Now why do you ask Abishag the Shunammite for Adonijah? Ask for him the kingdom also—for he *is* my older brother—for him, and for Abiathar the priest, and for Joab the son of Zeruiah." [23]Then King Solomon swore by the LORD, saying, "May God do so to me, and more also, if Adonijah has not spoken this word against his own life! [24]Now therefore, *as* the LORD lives, who has confirmed me and set me on the throne of David my

father, and who has established a house[a] for me, as He promised, Adonijah shall be put to death today!"

²⁵So King Solomon sent by the hand of Benaiah the son of Jehoiada; and he struck him down, and he died.

Abiathar Exiled, Joab Executed

²⁶And to Abiathar the priest the king said, "Go to Anathoth, to your own fields, for you *are* deserving of death; but I will not put you to death at this time, because you carried the ark of the Lord GOD before my father David, and because you were afflicted every time my father was afflicted." ²⁷So Solomon removed Abiathar from being priest to the LORD, that he might fulfill the word of the LORD which He spoke concerning the house of Eli at Shiloh.

²⁸Then news came to Joab, for Joab had defected to Adonijah, though he had not defected to Absalom. So Joab fled to the tabernacle of the LORD, and took hold of the horns of the altar. ²⁹And King Solomon was told, "Joab has fled to the tabernacle of the LORD; there *he is,* by the altar." Then Solomon sent Benaiah the son of Jehoiada, saying, "Go, strike him down." ³⁰So Benaiah went to the tabernacle of the LORD, and said to him, "Thus says the king, 'Come out!'"

And he said, "No, but I will die here." And Benaiah brought back word to the king, saying, "Thus said Joab, and thus he answered me."

³¹Then the king said to him, "Do as he has said, and strike him down and bury him, that you may take away from me and from the house of my father the innocent blood which Joab shed. ³²So the LORD will return his blood on his head, because he struck down two men more righteous and better than he, and killed them with the sword—Abner the son of Ner, the commander of the army of Israel, and Amasa the son of Jether, the commander of the army of Judah—though my father David did not know *it.* ³³Their blood shall therefore return upon the head of Joab and upon the head of his descendants forever. But upon David and his descendants, upon his house and his throne, there shall be peace forever from the LORD."

³⁴So Benaiah the son of Jehoiada went up and struck and killed him; and he was buried in his own house in the wilderness. ³⁵The king put Benaiah the son of Jehoiada in his place over the army, and the king put Zadok the priest in the place of Abiathar.

Shimei Executed

³⁶Then the king sent and called for Shimei, and said to him, "Build yourself a house in Jerusalem and dwell there, and do not go out from there anywhere. ³⁷For it shall be, on the day you go out and cross the Brook Kidron, know for certain you shall surely die; your blood shall be on your own head."

³⁸And Shimei said to the king, "The saying *is* good. As my lord the king has said, so your servant will do." So Shimei dwelt in Jerusalem many days.

³⁹Now it happened at the end of three years, that two slaves of Shimei ran away to Achish the son of Maachah, king of Gath. And they told Shimei, saying, "Look, your slaves *are* in Gath!" ⁴⁰So Shimei arose, saddled his donkey, and went to Achish at Gath to seek his slaves. And Shimei went and brought his slaves from Gath. ⁴¹And Solomon was told that Shimei had gone from Jerusalem to Gath and had come back. ⁴²Then the king sent and called for Shimei, and said to him, "Did I not make you swear by the LORD, and warn you, saying, 'Know for certain that on the day you go out and travel anywhere, you shall surely die'? And you said to me, 'The word I have heard *is* good.' ⁴³Why then have you not kept the oath of the LORD and the commandment that I gave you?" ⁴⁴The king said moreover to Shimei, "You know, as your heart acknowledges, all the wickedness that you did to my father David; therefore the LORD will return your wickedness on your own head. ⁴⁵But King Solomon *shall be* blessed, and the throne of David shall be established before the LORD forever."

⁴⁶So the king commanded Benaiah the son of Jehoiada; and he went out and struck him down, and he died. Thus the kingdom was established in the hand of Solomon.

2:24 [a]That is, a royal dynasty

Solomon Requests Wisdom

3 Now Solomon made a treaty with Pharaoh king of Egypt, and married Pharaoh's daughter; then he brought her to the City of David until he had finished building his own house, and the house of the LORD, and the wall all around Jerusalem. ²Meanwhile the people sacrificed at the high places, because there was no house built for the name of the LORD until those days. ³And Solomon loved the LORD, walking in the statutes of his father David, except that he sacrificed and burned incense at the high places.

⁴Now the king went to Gibeon to sacrifice there, for that *was* the great high place: Solomon offered a thousand burnt offerings on that altar. ⁵At Gibeon the LORD appeared to Solomon in a dream by night; and God said, "Ask! What shall I give you?"

⁶And Solomon said: "You have shown great mercy to Your servant David my father, because he walked before You in truth, in righteousness, and in uprightness of heart with You; You have continued this great kindness for him, and You have given him a son to sit on his throne, as *it is* this day. ⁷Now, O LORD my God, You have made Your servant king instead of my father David, but I *am* a little child; I do not know *how* to go out or come in. ⁸And Your servant *is* in the midst of Your people whom You have chosen, a great people, too numerous to be numbered or counted.

William Howard Taft placed his hand on 1 Kings 3:9–11 as he took the presidential oath of office in 1909.

---

⁹Therefore give to Your servant an understanding heart to judge Your people, that I may discern between good and evil. For who is able to judge this great people of Yours?"

¹⁰The speech pleased the Lord, that Solomon had asked this thing. ¹¹Then God said to him: "Because you have asked this thing, and have not asked long life for yourself, nor have asked riches for yourself, nor have asked the life of your enemies, but have asked for yourself understanding to discern justice, ¹²behold, I have done according to your words; see, I have given you a wise and understanding heart, so that there has not been anyone like you before you, nor shall any like you arise after you. ¹³And I have also given you what you have not asked: both riches and honor, so that there shall not be anyone like you among the kings all your days. ¹⁴So if you walk in My ways, to keep My statutes and My commandments, as your father David walked, then I will lengthen your days."

¹⁵Then Solomon awoke; and indeed it had been a dream. And he came to Jerusalem and stood before the ark of the covenant of the LORD, offered up burnt offerings, offered peace offerings, and made a feast for all his servants.

Solomon's Wise Judgment

¹⁶Now two women *who were* harlots came to the king, and stood before him. ¹⁷And one woman said, "O my lord, this woman and I dwell in the same house; and I gave birth while she *was* in the house. ¹⁸Then it happened, the third day after I had given birth, that this woman also gave birth. And we *were* together; no one *was* with us in the house, except the two of us in the house. ¹⁹And this woman's son died in the night, because she lay on him. ²⁰So she arose in the middle of the night and took my son from my side, while your maidservant slept, and laid him in her bosom, and laid her dead child in my bosom. ²¹And when I rose in the morning to nurse my son, there he was, dead. But when I had examined him in the morning, indeed, he was not my son whom I had borne."

²²Then the other woman said, "No! But the living one *is* my son, and the dead one *is* your son."

And the first woman said, "No! But the dead one *is* your son, and the living one *is* my son."

Thus they spoke before the king.

²³And the king said, "The one says, 'This *is* my son, who lives, and your son *is* the dead one'; and the other says, 'No! But your son *is* the dead one, and my son *is* the living one.'" ²⁴Then the king said, "Bring

me a sword." So they brought a sword before the king. ²⁵And the king said, "Divide the living child in two, and give half to one, and half to the other."

²⁶Then the woman whose son *was* living spoke to the king, for she yearned with compassion for her son; and she said, "O my lord, give her the living child, and by no means kill him!"

But the other said, "Let him be neither mine nor yours, *but* divide *him*."

²⁷So the king answered and said, "Give the first woman the living child, and by no means kill him; she *is* his mother."

²⁸And all Israel heard of the judgment which the king had rendered; and they feared the king, for they saw that the wisdom of God *was* in him to administer justice.

Solomon's Administration

4 So King Solomon was king over all Israel. ²And these *were* his officials: Azariah the son of Zadok, the priest; ³Elihoreph and Ahijah, the sons of Shisha, scribes; Jehoshaphat the son of Ahilud, the recorder; ⁴Benaiah the son of Jehoiada, over the army; Zadok and Abiathar, the priests; ⁵Azariah the son of Nathan, over the officers; Zabud the son of Nathan, a priest *and* the king's friend; ⁶Ahishar, over the household; and Adoniram the son of Abda, over the labor force.

⁷And Solomon had twelve governors over all Israel, who provided food for the king and his household; each one made provision for one month of the year. ⁸These *are* their names: Ben-Hur,ᵃ in the mountains of Ephraim; ⁹Ben-Deker,ᵃ in Makaz, Shaalbim, Beth Shemesh, and Elon Beth Hanan; ¹⁰Ben-Hesed,ᵃ in Arubboth; to him *belonged* Sochoh and all the land of Hepher; ¹¹Ben-Abinadab,ᵃ *in* all the regions of Dor; he had Taphath the daughter of Solomon as wife; ¹²Baana the son of Ahilud, *in* Taanach, Megiddo, and all Beth Shean, which *is* beside Zaretan below Jezreel, from Beth Shean to Abel Meholah, as far as the other side of Jokneam; ¹³Ben-Geber,ᵃ in Ramoth Gilead; to him *belonged* the towns of Jair the son of Manasseh, in Gilead; to him *also belonged* the region of Argob in Bashan—sixty large cities with walls and bronze gate-bars; ¹⁴Ahinadab the son of Iddo, *in* Mahanaim; ¹⁵Ahimaaz, in Naphtali; he also took Basemath the daughter of Solomon as wife; ¹⁶Baanah the son of Hushai, in Asher and Aloth; ¹⁷Jehoshaphat the son of Paruah, in Issachar; ¹⁸Shimei the son of Elah, in Benjamin; ¹⁹Geber the son of Uri, in the land of Gilead, *in* the country of Sihon king of the Amorites, and of Og king of Bashan. *He was* the only governor who *was* in the land.

Prosperity and Wisdom of Solomon's Reign

²⁰Judah and Israel *were* as numerous as the sand by the sea in multitude, eating and drinking and rejoicing. ²¹So Solomon reigned over all kingdoms from the Riverᵃ *to* the land of the Philistines, as far as the border of Egypt. *They* brought tribute and served Solomon all the days of his life.

²²Now Solomon's provision for one day was thirty kors of fine flour, sixty kors of meal, ²³ten fatted oxen, twenty oxen from the pastures, and one hundred sheep, besides deer, gazelles, roebucks, and fatted fowl.

²⁴For he had dominion over all *the region* on this side of the Riverᵃ from Tiphsah even to Gaza, namely over all the kings on this side of the River; and he had peace on every side all around him. ²⁵And Judah and Israel dwelt safely, each man under his vine and his fig tree, from Dan as far as Beersheba, all the days of Solomon.

²⁶Solomon had fortyᵃ thousand stalls of horses for his chariots, and twelve thousand horsemen. ²⁷And these governors, each man in his month, provided food for King Solomon and for all who came to King Solomon's table. There was no lack in their supply. ²⁸They also brought barley and straw to the proper place, for the horses and steeds, each man according to his charge.

²⁹And God gave Solomon wisdom and exceedingly great understanding, and largeness of heart like the sand on the seashore.

4:8 ᵃLiterally *Son of Hur*   **4:9** ᵃLiterally *Son of Deker*
4:10 ᵃLiterally *Son of Hesed*   **4:11** ᵃLiterally *Son of Abinadab*   **4:13** ᵃLiterally *Son of Geber*
4:21 ᵃThat is, the Euphrates   **4:24** ᵃThat is, the Euphrates   **4:26** ᵃFollowing Masoretic Text and most other authorities; some manuscripts of the Septuagint read *four* (compare 2 Chronicles 9:25).

[30]Thus Solomon's wisdom excelled the wisdom of all the men of the East and all the wisdom of Egypt. [31]For he was wiser than all men—than Ethan the Ezrahite, and Heman, Chalcol, and Darda, the sons of Mahol; and his fame was in all the surrounding nations. [32]He spoke three thousand proverbs, and his songs were one thousand and five. [33]Also he spoke of trees, from the cedar tree of Lebanon even to the hyssop that springs out of the wall; he spoke also of animals, of birds, of creeping things, and of fish. [34]And men of all nations, from all the kings of the earth who had heard of his wisdom, came to hear the wisdom of Solomon.

Solomon Prepares to Build the Temple

5 Now Hiram king of Tyre sent his servants to Solomon, because he heard that they had anointed him king in place of his father, for Hiram had always loved David. [2]Then Solomon sent to Hiram, saying:

[3]   You know how my father David could not build a house for the name of the LORD his God because of the wars which were fought against him on every side, until the LORD put *his foes*[a] under the soles of his feet.
[4]   But now the LORD my God has given me rest on every side; *there is* neither adversary nor evil occurrence.
[5]   And behold, I propose to build a house for the name of the LORD my God, as the LORD spoke to my father David, saying, "Your son, whom I will set on your throne in your place, he shall build the house for My name."
[6]   Now therefore, command that they cut down cedars for me from Lebanon; and my servants will be with your servants, and I will pay you wages for your servants according to whatever you say. For you know *there is* none among us who has skill to cut timber like the Sidonians.

[7]So it was, when Hiram heard the words of Solomon, that he rejoiced greatly and said,

   Blessed *be* the LORD this day, for He has given David a wise son over this great people!

[8]Then Hiram sent to Solomon, saying:

   I have considered *the message* which you sent me, *and* I will do all you desire concerning the cedar and cypress logs.
[9]   My servants shall bring *them* down from Lebanon to the sea; I will float them in rafts by sea to the place you indicate to me, and will have them broken apart there; then you can take *them* away. And you shall fulfill my desire by giving food for my household.

[10]Then Hiram gave Solomon cedar and cypress logs *according to* all his desire. [11]And Solomon gave Hiram twenty thousand kors of wheat *as* food for his household, and twenty[a] kors of pressed oil. Thus Solomon gave to Hiram year by year.

[12]So the LORD gave Solomon wisdom, as He had promised him; and there was peace between Hiram and Solomon, and the two of them made a treaty together.

[13]Then King Solomon raised up a labor force out of all Israel; and the labor force was thirty thousand men. [14]And he sent them to Lebanon, ten thousand a month in shifts: they were one month in Lebanon *and* two months at home; Adoniram *was* in charge of the labor force. [15]Solomon had seventy thousand who carried burdens, and eighty thousand who quarried *stone* in the mountains, [16]besides three thousand three hundred[a] from the chiefs of Solomon's deputies, who supervised the people who labored in the work. [17]And the king commanded them to quarry large stones, costly stones, *and* hewn stones, to lay the foundation of the temple.[a] [18]So Solomon's builders, Hiram's builders, and the Gebalites quarried *them;* and they prepared timber and stones to build the temple.

5:3 [a]Literally *them*   **5:11** [a]Following Masoretic Text, Targum, and Vulgate; Septuagint and Syriac read *twenty thousand.*   **5:16** [a]Following Masoretic Text, Targum, and Vulgate; Septuagint reads *three thousand six hundred.*   **5:17** [a]Literally *house,* and so frequently throughout this book

Solomon Builds the Temple

6 And it came to pass in the four hundred and eightieth[a] year after the children of Israel had come out of the land of Egypt, in the fourth year of Solomon's reign over Israel, in the month of Ziv, which *is* the second month, that he began to build the house of the LORD. [2]Now the house which King Solomon built for the LORD, its length *was* sixty cubits, its width twenty, and its height thirty cubits. [3]The vestibule in front of the sanctuary[a] of the house *was* twenty cubits long across the width of the house, *and* the width of *the vestibule*[b] extended ten cubits from the front of the house. [4]And he made for the house windows with beveled frames.

[5]Against the wall of the temple he built chambers all around, *against* the walls of the temple, all around the sanctuary and the inner sanctuary.[a] Thus he made side chambers all around it. [6]The lowest chamber *was* five cubits wide, the middle *was* six cubits wide, and the third *was* seven cubits wide; for he made narrow ledges around the outside of the temple, so that *the support beams* would not be fastened into the walls of the temple. [7]And the temple, when it was being built, was built with stone finished at the quarry, so that no hammer or chisel *or* any iron tool was heard in the temple while it was being built. [8]The doorway for the middle story[a] *was* on the right side of the temple. They went up by stairs to the middle *story,* and from the middle to the third.

[9]So he built the temple and finished it, and he paneled the temple with beams and boards of cedar. [10]And he built side chambers against the entire temple, each five cubits high; they were attached to the temple with cedar beams.

[11]Then the word of the LORD came to Solomon, saying: [12]"*Concerning* this temple which you are building, if you walk in My statutes, execute My judgments, keep all My commandments, and walk in them, then I will perform My word with you, which I spoke to your father David. [13]And I will dwell among the children of Israel, and will not forsake My people Israel."

[14]So Solomon built the temple and finished it. [15]And he built the inside walls of the temple with cedar boards; from the floor of the temple to the ceiling he paneled the inside with wood; and he covered the floor of the temple with planks of cypress. [16]Then he built the twenty-cubit room at the rear of the temple, from floor to ceiling, with cedar boards; he built *it* inside as the inner sanctuary, as the Most Holy *Place.* [17]And in front of it the temple sanctuary was forty cubits *long.* [18]The inside of the temple was cedar, carved with ornamental buds and open flowers. All *was* cedar; there was no stone *to be* seen.

[19]And he prepared the inner sanctuary inside the temple, to set the ark of the covenant of the LORD there. [20]The inner sanctuary *was* twenty cubits long, twenty cubits wide, and twenty cubits high. He overlaid it with pure gold, and overlaid the altar of cedar. [21]So Solomon overlaid the inside of the temple with pure gold. He stretched gold chains across the front of the inner sanctuary, and overlaid it with gold. [22]The whole temple he overlaid with gold, until he had finished all the temple; also he overlaid with gold the entire altar that *was* by the inner sanctuary.

[23]Inside the inner sanctuary he made two cherubim *of* olive wood, *each* ten cubits high. [24]One wing of the cherub *was* five cubits, and the other wing of the cherub five cubits: ten cubits from the tip of one wing to the tip of the other. [25]And the other cherub *was* ten cubits; both cherubim *were* of the same size and shape. [26]The height of one cherub *was* ten cubits, and so *was* the other cherub. [27]Then he set the cherubim inside the inner room;[a] and they stretched out the wings of the cherubim so that the wing of the one touched *one* wall, and the wing of the other cherub touched the other wall. And their wings touched each other in the middle of the room. [28]Also he overlaid the cherubim with gold.

6:1 [a]Following Masoretic Text, Targum, and Vulgate; Septuagint reads *fortieth.*   **6:3** [a]Hebrew *heykal;* here the main room of the temple, elsewhere called the holy place (compare Exodus 26:33 and Ezekiel 41:1) [b]Literally *it*   **6:5** [a]Hebrew *debir;* here the inner room of the temple, elsewhere called the Most Holy Place (compare verse 16)   **6:8** [a]Following Masoretic Text and Vulgate; Septuagint reads *upper story;* Targum reads *ground story.*   **6:27** [a]Literally *house*

²⁹Then he carved all the walls of the temple all around, both the inner and outer *sanctuaries,* with carved figures of cherubim, palm trees, and open flowers. ³⁰And the floor of the temple he overlaid with gold, both the inner and outer *sanctuaries.*

³¹For the entrance of the inner sanctuary he made doors *of* olive wood; the lintel *and* doorposts *were* one-fifth *of the wall.* ³²The two doors *were of* olive wood; and he carved on them figures of cherubim, palm trees, and open flowers, and overlaid *them* with gold; and he spread gold on the cherubim and on the palm trees. ³³So for the door of the sanctuary he also made doorposts *of* olive wood, one-fourth *of the wall.* ³⁴And the two doors *were of* cypress wood; two panels *comprised* one folding door, and two panels *comprised* the other folding door. ³⁵Then he carved cherubim, palm trees, and open flowers *on them,* and overlaid *them* with gold applied evenly on the carved work.

³⁶And he built the inner court with three rows of hewn stone and a row of cedar beams.

³⁷In the fourth year the foundation of the house of the LORD was laid, in the month of Ziv. ³⁸And in the eleventh year, in the month of Bul, which is the eighth month, the house was finished in all its details and according to all its plans. So he was seven years in building it.

Solomon's Other Buildings

7 But Solomon took thirteen years to build his own house; so he finished all his house.

²He also built the House of the Forest of Lebanon; its length *was* one hundred cubits, its width fifty cubits, and its height thirty cubits, with four rows of cedar pillars, and cedar beams on the pillars. ³And *it was* paneled with cedar above the beams that *were* on forty-five pillars, fifteen *to* a row. ⁴*There were* windows *with beveled frames in* three rows, and window *was* opposite window *in* three tiers. ⁵And all the doorways and doorposts had rectangular frames; and window *was* opposite window *in* three tiers.

⁶He also made the Hall of Pillars: its length *was* fifty cubits, and its width thirty cubits; and in front of them *was* a portico

with pillars, and a canopy *was* in front of them.

⁷Then he made a hall for the throne, the Hall of Judgment, where he might judge; and *it was* paneled with cedar from floor to ceiling.ᵃ

⁸And the house where he dwelt *had* another court inside the hall, of like workmanship. Solomon also made a house like this hall for Pharaoh's daughter, whom he had taken *as wife.*

⁹All these *were of* costly stones cut to size, trimmed with saws, inside and out, from the foundation to the eaves, and also on the outside to the great court. ¹⁰The foundation *was of* costly stones, large stones, some ten cubits and some eight cubits. ¹¹And above *were* costly stones, hewn to size, and cedar wood. ¹²The great court *was* enclosed with three rows of hewn stones and a row of cedar beams. So were the inner court of the house of the LORD and the vestibule of the temple.

Hiram the Craftsman

¹³Now King Solomon sent and brought Huramᵃ from Tyre. ¹⁴He *was* the son of a widow from the tribe of Naphtali, and his father *was* a man of Tyre, a bronze worker; he was filled with wisdom and understanding and skill in working with all kinds of bronze work. So he came to King Solomon and did all his work.

The Bronze Pillars for the Temple

¹⁵And he cast two pillars of bronze, each one eighteen cubits high, and a line of twelve cubits measured the circumference of each. ¹⁶Then he made two capitals *of* cast bronze, to set on the tops of the pillars. The height of one capital *was* five cubits, and the height of the other capital *was* five cubits. ¹⁷*He made* a lattice network, with wreaths of chainwork, for the capitals which *were* on top of the pillars: seven chains for one capital and seven for the other capital. ¹⁸So he made the pillars, and two rows of pomegranates above the network all around to cover the capitals that

---

7:7 ᵃLiterally *floor,* that is, of the upper level
7:13 ᵃHebrew *Hiram* (compare 2 Chronicles 2:13, 14)

were on top; and thus he did for the other capital. [19]The capitals which *were* on top of the pillars in the hall *were* in the shape of lilies, four cubits. [20]The capitals on the two pillars also *had pomegranates* above, by the convex surface which *was* next to the network; and there *were* two hundred such pomegranates in rows on each of the capitals all around.

[21]Then he set up the pillars by the vestibule of the temple; he set up the pillar on the right and called its name Jachin, and he set up the pillar on the left and called its name Boaz. [22]The tops of the pillars were in the shape of lilies. So the work of the pillars was finished.

The Sea and the Oxen

[23]And he made the Sea of cast bronze, ten cubits from one brim to the other; *it was* completely round. Its height *was* five cubits, and a line of thirty cubits measured its circumference. [24]Below its brim *were* ornamental buds encircling it all around, ten to a cubit, all the way around the Sea. The ornamental buds *were* cast in two rows when it was cast. [25]It stood on twelve oxen: three looking toward the north, three looking toward the west, three looking toward the south, and three looking toward the east; the Sea *was set* upon them, and all their back parts *pointed* inward. [26]It *was* a handbreadth thick; and its brim was shaped like the brim of a cup, *like* a lily blossom. It contained two thousand[a] baths.

The Carts and the Lavers

[27]He also made ten carts of bronze; four cubits *was* the length of each cart, four cubits its width, and three cubits its height. [28]And this *was* the design of the carts: They had panels, and the panels *were* between frames; [29]on the panels that *were* between the frames *were* lions, oxen, and cherubim. And on the frames *was* a pedestal on top. Below the lions and oxen *were* wreaths of plaited work. [30]Every cart had four bronze wheels and axles of bronze, and its four feet had supports. Under the laver *were* supports of cast *bronze* beside each wreath.

[31]Its opening inside the crown at the top *was* one cubit in diameter; and the opening *was* round, shaped *like* a pedestal, one and a half cubits in outside diameter; and also on the opening *were* engravings, but the panels were square, not round. [32]Under the panels *were* the four wheels, and the axles of the wheels *were joined* to the cart. The height of a wheel *was* one and a half cubits. [33]The workmanship of the wheels *was* like the workmanship of a chariot wheel; their axle pins, their rims, their spokes, and their hubs *were* all of cast *bronze*. [34]And *there were* four supports at the four corners of each cart; its supports *were* part of the cart itself. [35]On the top of the cart, at the height of half a cubit, *it was* perfectly round. And on the top of the cart, its flanges and its panels *were* of the same casting. [36]On the plates of its flanges and on its panels he engraved cherubim, lions, and palm trees, wherever there was a clear space on each, with wreaths all around. [37]Thus he made the ten carts. All of them were of the same mold, one measure, *and* one shape.

[38]Then he made ten lavers of bronze; each laver contained forty baths, *and* each laver *was* four cubits. On each of the ten carts *was* a laver. [39]And he put five carts on the right side of the house, and five on the left side of the house. He set the Sea on the right side of the house, toward the southeast.

Furnishings of the Temple

[40]Huram[a] made the lavers and the shovels and the bowls. So Huram finished doing all the work that he was to do for King Solomon *for* the house of the LORD: [41]the two pillars, the *two* bowl-shaped capitals that *were* on top of the two pillars; the two networks covering the two bowl-shaped capitals which *were* on top of the pillars; [42]four hundred pomegranates for the two networks (two rows of pomegranates for each network, to cover the two bowl-shaped capitals that *were* on top of the pillars); [43]the ten carts, and ten lavers on the carts; [44]one Sea, and twelve oxen under the Sea; [45]the pots, the shovels, and the bowls.

7:26 [a]Or *three thousand* (compare 2 Chronicles 4:5)
7:40 [a]Hebrew *Hiram* (compare 2 Chronicles 2:13, 14)

All these articles which Huram[a] made for King Solomon *for* the house of the LORD *were of* burnished bronze. 46In the plain of Jordan the king had them cast in clay molds, between Succoth and Zaretan. 47And Solomon did not weigh all the articles, because *there were* so many; the weight of the bronze was not determined.

48Thus Solomon had all the furnishings made for the house of the LORD: the altar of gold, and the table of gold on which *was* the showbread; 49the lampstands of pure gold, five on the right *side* and five on the left in front of the inner sanctuary, with the flowers and the lamps and the wick-trimmers of gold; 50the basins, the trimmers, the bowls, the ladles, and the censers of pure gold; and the hinges of gold, *both* for the doors of the inner room (the Most Holy *Place*) *and* for the doors of the main hall of the temple.

51So all the work that King Solomon had done for the house of the LORD was finished; and Solomon brought in the things which his father David had dedicated: the silver and the gold and the furnishings. He put them in the treasuries of the house of the LORD.

The Ark Brought into the Temple

8 Now Solomon assembled the elders of Israel and all the heads of the tribes, the chief fathers of the children of Israel, to King Solomon in Jerusalem, that they might bring up the ark of the covenant of the LORD from the City of David, which *is* Zion. 2Therefore all the men of Israel assembled with King Solomon at the feast in the month of Ethanim, which *is* the seventh month. 3So all the elders of Israel came, and the priests took up the ark. 4Then they brought up the ark of the LORD, the tabernacle of meeting, and all the holy furnishings that *were* in the tabernacle. The priests and the Levites brought them up. 5Also King Solomon, and all the congregation of Israel who were assembled with him, *were* with him before the ark, sacrificing sheep and oxen that could not be counted or numbered for multitude. 6Then the priests brought in the ark of the covenant of the LORD to its place, into the inner sanctuary of the temple, to the Most Holy *Place*, under the wings of the cherubim.

7For the cherubim spread *their* two wings over the place of the ark, and the cherubim overshadowed the ark and its poles. 8The poles extended so that the ends of the poles could be seen from the holy *place,* in front of the inner sanctuary; but they could not be seen from outside. And they are there to this day. 9Nothing *was* in the ark except the two tablets of stone which Moses put there at Horeb, when the LORD made *a covenant* with the children of Israel, when they came out of the land of Egypt.

10And it came to pass, when the priests came out of the holy *place,* that the cloud filled the house of the LORD, 11so that the priests could not continue ministering because of the cloud; for the glory of the LORD filled the house of the LORD.

12Then Solomon spoke:

"The LORD said He would dwell in the dark cloud.
13   I have surely built You an exalted house,
     And a place for You to dwell in forever."

Solomon's Speech at Completion of the Work

14Then the king turned around and blessed the whole assembly of Israel, while all the assembly of Israel was standing. 15And he said: "Blessed *be* the LORD God of Israel, who spoke with His mouth to my father David, and with His hand has fulfilled *it,* saying, 16'Since the day that I brought My people Israel out of Egypt, I have chosen no city from any tribe of Israel *in which* to build a house, that My name might be there; but I chose David to be over My people Israel.' 17Now it was in the heart of my father David to build a temple[a] for the name of the LORD God of Israel. 18But the LORD said to my father David, 'Whereas it was in your heart to build a temple for My name, you did well that it was in your heart. 19Nevertheless you shall not build the temple, but your son who will come from your body, he shall build the temple for My name.' 20So the LORD has fulfilled His word which He spoke;

7:45 [a]Hebrew *Hiram* (compare 2 Chronicles 2:13, 14)
8:17 [a]Literally *house,* and so in verses 18–20

and I have filled the position of my father David, and sit on the throne of Israel, as the Lord promised; and I have built a temple for the name of the Lord God of Israel. 21And there I have made a place for the ark, in which *is* the covenant of the Lord which He made with our fathers, when He brought them out of the land of Egypt."

Solomon's Prayer of Dedication

22Then Solomon stood before the altar of the Lord in the presence of all the assembly of Israel, and spread out his hands toward heaven; 23and he said: "Lord God of Israel, *there is* no God in heaven above or on earth below like You, who keep *Your* covenant and mercy with Your servants who walk before You with all their hearts. 24You have kept what You promised Your servant David my father; You have both spoken with Your mouth and fulfilled *it* with Your hand, as *it is* this day. 25Therefore, Lord God of Israel, now keep what You promised Your servant David my father, saying, 'You shall not fail to have a man sit before Me on the throne of Israel, only if your sons take heed to their way, that they walk before Me as you have walked before Me.' 26And now I pray, O God of Israel, let Your word come true, which You have spoken to Your servant David my father.

27"But will God indeed dwell on the earth? Behold, heaven and the heaven of heavens cannot contain You. How much less this temple which I have built! 28Yet regard the prayer of Your servant and his supplication, O Lord my God, and listen to the cry and the prayer which Your servant is praying before You today: 29that Your eyes may be open toward this temple night and day, toward the place of which You said, 'My name shall be there,' that You may hear the prayer which Your servant makes toward this place. 30And may You hear the supplication of Your servant and of Your people Israel, when they pray toward this place. Hear in heaven Your dwelling place; and when You hear, forgive.

31"When anyone sins against his neighbor, and is forced to take an oath, and comes *and* takes an oath before Your altar in this temple, 32then hear in heaven, and act, and judge Your servants, condemning the wicked, bringing his way on his head, and justifying the righteous by giving him according to his righteousness.

33"When Your people Israel are defeated before an enemy because they have sinned against You, and when they turn back to You and confess Your name, and pray and make supplication to You in this temple, 34then hear in heaven, and forgive the sin of Your people Israel, and bring them back to the land which You gave to their fathers.

35"When the heavens are shut up and there is no rain because they have sinned against You, when they pray toward this place and confess Your name, and turn from their sin because You afflict them, 36then hear in heaven, and forgive the sin of Your servants, Your people Israel, that You may teach them the good way in which they should walk; and send rain on Your land which You have given to Your people as an inheritance.

37"When there is famine in the land, pestilence *or* blight *or* mildew, locusts *or* grasshoppers; when their enemy besieges them in the land of their cities; whatever plague or whatever sickness *there is;* 38whatever prayer, whatever supplication is made by anyone, *or* by all Your people Israel, when each one knows the plague of his own heart, and spreads out his hands toward this temple: 39then hear in heaven Your dwelling place, and forgive, and act, and give to everyone according to all his ways, whose heart You know (for You alone know the hearts of all the sons of men), 40that they may fear You all the days that they live in the land which You gave to our fathers.

41"Moreover, concerning a foreigner, who *is* not of Your people Israel, but has come from a far country for Your name's sake 42(for they will hear of Your great name and Your strong hand and Your outstretched arm), when he comes and prays toward this temple, 43hear in heaven Your dwelling place, and do according to all for which the foreigner calls to You, that all peoples of the earth may know Your name and fear You, as *do* Your people Israel, and that they may know that this temple which I have built is called by Your name.

44"When Your people go out to battle against their enemy, wherever You send them, and when they pray to the Lord toward the city which You have chosen and the temple which I have built for Your name, 45then hear in heaven their prayer and their supplication, and maintain their cause.

46"When they sin against You (for *there is* no one who does not sin), and You become angry with them and deliver them to the enemy, and they take them captive to the land of the enemy, far or near; 47yet when they come to themselves in the land where they were carried captive, and repent, and make supplication to You in the land of those who took them captive, saying, 'We have sinned and done wrong, we have committed wickedness'; 48and *when* they return to You with all their heart and with all their soul in the land of their enemies who led them away captive, and pray to You toward their land which You gave to their fathers, the city which You have chosen and the temple which I have built for Your name: 49then hear in heaven Your dwelling place their prayer and their supplication, and maintain their cause, 50and forgive Your people who have sinned against You, and all their transgressions which they have transgressed against You; and grant them compassion before those who took them captive, that they may have compassion on them 51(for they *are* Your people and Your inheritance, whom You brought out of Egypt, out of the iron furnace), 52that Your eyes may be open to the supplication of Your servant and the supplication of Your people Israel, to listen to them whenever they call to You. 53For You separated them from among all the peoples of the earth *to be* Your inheritance, as You spoke by Your servant Moses, when You brought our fathers out of Egypt, O Lord God."

Solomon Blesses the Assembly

54And so it was, when Solomon had finished praying all this prayer and supplication to the Lord, that he arose from before the altar of the Lord, from kneeling on his knees with his hands spread up to heaven. 55Then he stood and blessed all the assembly of Israel with a loud voice, saying: 56"Blessed *be* the Lord, who has given rest to His people Israel, according to all that He promised. There has not failed one word of all His good promise, which He promised through His servant Moses. 57May the Lord our God be with us, as He was with our fathers. May He not leave us nor forsake us, 58that He may incline our hearts to Himself, to walk in all His ways, and to keep His commandments and His statutes and His judgments, which He commanded our fathers. 59And may these words of mine, with which I have made supplication before the Lord, be near the Lord our God day and night, that He may maintain the cause of His servant and the cause of His people Israel, as each day may require, 60that all the peoples of the earth may know that the Lord *is* God; *there is* no other. 61Let your heart therefore be loyal to the Lord our God, to walk in His statutes and keep His commandments, as at this day."

Solomon Dedicates the Temple

62Then the king and all Israel with him offered sacrifices before the Lord. 63And Solomon offered a sacrifice of peace offerings, which he offered to the Lord, twenty-two thousand bulls and one hundred and twenty thousand sheep. So the king and all the children of Israel dedicated the house of the Lord. 64On the same day the king consecrated the middle of the court that *was* in front of the house of the Lord; for there he offered burnt offerings, grain offerings, and the fat of the peace offerings, because the bronze altar that *was* before the Lord *was* too small to receive the burnt offerings, the grain offerings, and the fat of the peace offerings.

65At that time Solomon held a feast, and all Israel with him, a great assembly from the entrance of Hamath to the Brook of Egypt, before the Lord our God, seven days and seven *more* days—fourteen days. 66On the eighth day he sent the people away; and they blessed the king, and went to their tents joyful and glad of heart for all the good that the Lord had done for His servant David, and for Israel His people.

"MY COUNTRY, 'TIS OF THEE"

SAMUEL FRANCIS SMITH

Samuel Francis Smith wrote the words to "My Country, 'Tis of Thee," also known as "America," while studying at Andover Theological Seminary in 1831. The song's inspirational words are matched with a popular international melody used by many nations, including England, where it accompanies "God Save the King/Queen." The hymn soon became a national favorite, serving as a de facto national anthem of the United States for much of the nineteenth century.

My country, 'tis of thee, sweet land of liberty, of thee I sing:
Land where my fathers died, land of the pilgrims' pride,
From every mountainside let freedom ring!

My native country, thee, land of the noble free, thy name I love:
I love thy rocks and rills, thy woods and templed hills;
My heart with rapture thrills, like that above.

Let music swell the breeze, and ring from all the trees sweet
*   freedom's song:*
Let mortal tongues awake; let all that breathe partake;
Let rocks their silence break, the sound prolong.

Our fathers' God, to Thee, author of liberty, to Thee we sing:
Long may our land be bright with freedom's holy light.
Protect us by Thy might, great God, our King!

God's Second Appearance to Solomon

9 And it came to pass, when Solomon had finished building the house of the LORD and the king's house, and all Solomon's desire which he wanted to do, ²that the LORD appeared to Solomon the second time, as He had appeared to him at Gibeon. ³And the LORD said to him: "I have heard your prayer and your supplication that you have made before Me; I have consecrated this house which you have built to put My name there forever, and My eyes and My heart will be there perpetually. ⁴Now if you walk before Me as your father David walked, in integrity of heart and in uprightness, to do according to all that I have commanded you, *and* if you keep My statutes and My judgments, ⁵then I will establish the throne of your kingdom over Israel forever, as I promised David your father, saying, 'You shall not fail to have a man on the throne of Israel.' ⁶*But* if you or your sons at all turn from following Me, and do not keep My commandments *and* My statutes which I have set before you, but go and serve other gods and worship them, ⁷then I will cut off Israel from the land which I have given them; and this house which I have consecrated for My name I will cast out of My sight. Israel will be a proverb and a byword among all peoples. ⁸And *as for* this house, *which* is exalted, everyone who passes by it will be astonished and will hiss, and say, 'Why has the LORD done thus to this land and to this house?' ⁹Then they will answer, 'Because they forsook the LORD their God, who brought their fathers out of the land of Egypt, and have embraced other gods, and worshiped them and served them; therefore the LORD has brought all this calamity on them.'"

Solomon and Hiram Exchange Gifts

¹⁰Now it happened at the end of twenty years, when Solomon had built the two houses, the house of the LORD and the king's house ¹¹(Hiram the king of Tyre had supplied Solomon with cedar and cypress and gold, as much as he desired), *that* King Solomon then gave Hiram twenty cities in the land of Galilee. ¹²Then Hiram went from Tyre to see the cities which Solomon had given him, but they did not please him. ¹³So he said, "What *kind of* cities *are* these which you have given me, my brother?" And he called them the land of Cabul,ᵃ as they are to this day. ¹⁴Then Hiram sent the king one hundred and twenty talents of gold.

INTEGRITY

". . . walk before Me . . . in integrity of heart. . . ."

1 KINGS 9:4

The World's Best Currency

William McKinley, the 25th president of the United States (1897–1901), stated:

> There is no currency in this world that passes at such a premium anywhere as good Christian character. . . . The time has gone by when the young man or the young woman in the United States has to apologize for being a follower of Christ. . . . No cause but one could have brought together so many people, and that is the cause of our Master.

Solomon's Additional Achievements

¹⁵And this *is* the reason for the labor force which King Solomon raised: to build the house of the LORD, his own house, the Millo,ᵃ the wall of Jerusalem, Hazor, Megiddo, and Gezer. ¹⁶(Pharaoh king of Egypt had gone up and taken Gezer and burned it with fire, had killed the Canaanites who dwelt in the city, and had given it *as* a dowry to his daughter, Solomon's wife.) ¹⁷And Solomon built Gezer, Lower Beth Horon, ¹⁸Baalath, and Tadmor in the wilderness, in the land *of Judah,* ¹⁹all the storage cities that Solomon had, cities for his chariots and cities for his cavalry, and whatever Solomon desired to build in Jerusalem, in Lebanon, and in all the land of his dominion.

²⁰All the people *who were* left of the Amorites, Hittites, Perizzites, Hivites, and Jebusites, who *were* not of the children of Israel— ²¹that is, their descendants who were left in the land after them, whom the children of Israel had not been able to destroy completely—

9:13 ᵃLiterally *Good for Nothing*   **9:15** ᵃLiterally *The Landfill*

from these Solomon raised forced labor, as it is to this day. ²²But of the children of Israel Solomon made no forced laborers, because they *were* men of war and his servants: his officers, his captains, commanders of his chariots, and his cavalry.

²³Others *were* chiefs of the officials who *were* over Solomon's work: five hundred and fifty, who ruled over the people who did the work.

²⁴But Pharaoh's daughter came up from the City of David to her house which *Solomon*ᵃ had built for her. Then he built the Millo.

²⁵Now three times a year Solomon offered burnt offerings and peace offerings on the altar which he had built for the LORD, and he burned incense with them *on the altar* that *was* before the LORD. So he finished the temple.

²⁶King Solomon also built a fleet of ships at Ezion Geber, which *is* near Elathᵃ on the shore of the Red Sea, in the land of Edom. ²⁷Then Hiram sent his servants with the fleet, seamen who knew the sea, to work with the servants of Solomon. ²⁸And they went to Ophir, and acquired four hundred and twenty talents of gold from there, and brought *it* to King Solomon.

The Queen of Sheba's Praise of Solomon

10 Now when the queen of Sheba heard of the fame of Solomon concerning the name of the LORD, she came to test him with hard questions. ²She came to Jerusalem with a very great retinue, with camels that bore spices, very much gold, and precious stones; and when she came to Solomon, she spoke with him about all that was in her heart. ³So Solomon answered all her questions; there was nothing so difficult for the king that he could not explain *it* to her. ⁴And when the queen of Sheba had seen all the wisdom of Solomon, the house that he had built, ⁵the food on his table, the seating of his servants, the service of his waiters and their apparel, his cupbearers, and his entryway by which he went up to the house of the LORD, there was no more spirit in her. ⁶Then she said to the king: "It was a true report which I heard in my own land about your words and your wisdom.

⁷However I did not believe the words until I came and saw with my own eyes; and indeed the half was not told me. Your wisdom and prosperity exceed the fame of which I heard. ⁸Happy *are* your men and happy *are* these your servants, who stand continually before you *and* hear your wisdom! ⁹Blessed be the LORD your God, who delighted in you, setting you on the throne of Israel! Because the LORD has loved Israel forever, therefore He made you king, to do justice and righteousness."

¹⁰Then she gave the king one hundred and twenty talents of gold, spices in great quantity, and precious stones. There never again came such abundance of spices as the queen of Sheba gave to King Solomon. ¹¹Also, the ships of Hiram, which brought gold from Ophir, brought great quantities of almugᵃ wood and precious stones from Ophir. ¹²And the king made steps of the almug wood for the house of the LORD and for the king's house, also harps and stringed instruments for singers. There never again came such almug wood, nor has the like been seen to this day.

¹³Now King Solomon gave the queen of Sheba all she desired, whatever she asked, besides what Solomon had given her according to the royal generosity. So she turned and went to her own country, she and her servants.

Solomon's Great Wealth

¹⁴The weight of gold that came to Solomon yearly was six hundred and sixty-six talents of gold, ¹⁵besides *that* from the traveling merchants, from the income of traders, from all the kings of Arabia, and from the governors of the country.

¹⁶And King Solomon made two hundred large shields *of* hammered gold; six hundred *shekels* of gold went into each shield. ¹⁷He also *made* three hundred shields *of* hammered gold; three minas of gold went into each shield. The king put them in the House of the Forest of Lebanon.

¹⁸Moreover the king made a great throne of ivory, and overlaid it with pure gold.

9:24 ᵃLiterally *he* (compare 2 Chronicles 8:11)
9:26 ᵃHebrew *Eloth* (compare 2 Kings 14:22)
10:11 ᵃOr *algum* (compare 2 Chronicles 9:10, 11)

[19]The throne had six steps, and the top of the throne *was* round at the back; *there were* armrests on either side of the place of the seat, and two lions stood beside the armrests. [20]Twelve lions stood there, one on each side of the six steps; nothing like *this* had been made for any *other* kingdom.

[21]All King Solomon's drinking vessels *were* gold, and all the vessels of the House of the Forest of Lebanon *were* pure gold. Not *one was* silver, for this was accounted as nothing in the days of Solomon. [22]For the king had merchant ships[a] at sea with the fleet of Hiram. Once every three years the merchant ships came bringing gold, silver, ivory, apes, and monkeys.[b] [23]So King Solomon surpassed all the kings of the earth in riches and wisdom.

[24]Now all the earth sought the presence of Solomon to hear his wisdom, which God had put in his heart. [25]Each man brought his present: articles of silver and gold, garments, armor, spices, horses, and mules, at a set rate year by year.

[26]And Solomon gathered chariots and horsemen; he had one thousand four hundred chariots and twelve thousand horsemen, whom he stationed[a] in the chariot cities and with the king at Jerusalem. [27]The king made silver *as common* in Jerusalem as stones, and he made cedar trees as abundant as the sycamores which *are* in the lowland.

[28]Also Solomon had horses imported from Egypt and Keveh; the king's merchants bought them in Keveh at the *current* price. [29]Now a chariot that was imported from Egypt cost six hundred *shekels* of silver, and a horse one hundred and fifty; and thus, through their agents,[a] they exported *them* to all the kings of the Hittites and the kings of Syria.

Solomon's Heart Turns from the LORD

11 But King Solomon loved many foreign women, as well as the daughter of Pharaoh: women of the Moabites, Ammonites, Edomites, Sidonians, *and* Hittites— [2]from the nations of whom the LORD had said to the children of Israel, "You shall not intermarry with them, nor they with you. Surely they will turn away your hearts after their gods." Solomon clung to these in love. [3]And he had seven hundred wives, princesses, and three hundred concubines; and his wives turned away his heart. [4]For it was so, when Solomon was old, that his wives turned his heart after other gods; and his heart was not loyal to the LORD his God, as *was* the heart of his father David. [5]For Solomon went after Ashtoreth the goddess of the Sidonians, and after Milcom the abomination of the Ammonites. [6]Solomon did evil in the sight of the LORD, and did not fully follow the LORD, as *did* his father David. [7]Then Solomon built a high place for Chemosh the abomination of Moab, on the hill that *is* east of Jerusalem, and for Molech the abomination of the people of Ammon. [8]And he did likewise for all his foreign wives, who burned incense and sacrificed to their gods.

[9]So the LORD became angry with Solomon, because his heart had turned from the LORD God of Israel, who had appeared to him twice, [10]and had commanded him concerning this thing, that he should not go after other gods; but he did not keep what the LORD had commanded. [11]Therefore the LORD said to Solomon, "Because you have done this, and have not kept My covenant and My statutes, which I have commanded you, I will surely tear the kingdom away from you and give it to your servant. [12]Nevertheless I will not do it in your days, for the sake of your father David; I will tear it out of the hand of your son. [13]However I will not tear away the whole kingdom; I will give one tribe to your son for the sake of My servant David, and for the sake of Jerusalem which I have chosen."

Adversaries of Solomon

[14]Now the LORD raised up an adversary against Solomon, Hadad the Edomite; he *was* a descendant of the king in Edom. [15]For it happened, when David was in Edom, and Joab the commander of the army had gone up to bury the slain, after he had killed every

---

10:22 [a]Literally *ships of Tarshish,* deep-sea vessels [b]Or *peacocks*　　**10:26** [a]Following Septuagint, Syriac, Targum, and Vulgate (compare 2 Chronicles 9:25); Masoretic Text reads *led.*　　**10:29** [a]Literally *by their hands*

male in Edom ¹⁶(because for six months Joab remained there with all Israel, until he had cut down every male in Edom), ¹⁷that Hadad fled to go to Egypt, he and certain Edomites of his father's servants with him. Hadad *was* still a little child. ¹⁸Then they arose from Midian and came to Paran; and they took men with them from Paran and came to Egypt, to Pharaoh king of Egypt, who gave him a house, apportioned food for him, and gave him land. ¹⁹And Hadad found great favor in the sight of Pharaoh, so that he gave him as wife the sister of his own wife, that is, the sister of Queen Tahpenes. ²⁰Then the sister of Tahpenes bore him Genubath his son, whom Tahpenes weaned in Pharaoh's house. And Genubath was in Pharaoh's household among the sons of Pharaoh.

²¹So when Hadad heard in Egypt that David rested with his fathers, and that Joab the commander of the army was dead, Hadad said to Pharaoh, "Let me depart, that I may go to my own country."

²²Then Pharaoh said to him, "But what have you lacked with me, that suddenly you seek to go to your own country?"

So he answered, "Nothing, but do let me go anyway."

²³And God raised up *another* adversary against him, Rezon the son of Eliadah, who had fled from his lord, Hadadezer king of Zobah. ²⁴So he gathered men to him and became captain over a band *of raiders,* when David killed those *of Zobah.* And they went to Damascus and dwelt there, and reigned in Damascus. ²⁵He was an adversary of Israel all the days of Solomon (besides the trouble that Hadad *caused*); and he abhorred Israel, and reigned over Syria.

Jeroboam's Rebellion

²⁶Then Solomon's servant, Jeroboam the son of Nebat, an Ephraimite from Zereda, whose mother's name *was* Zeruah, a widow, also rebelled against the king. ²⁷And this *is* what caused him to rebel against the king: Solomon had built the Millo *and* repaired the damages to the City of David his father. ²⁸The man Jeroboam *was* a mighty man of valor; and Solomon, seeing that the young man was industrious,

made him the officer over all the labor force of the house of Joseph.

²⁹Now it happened at that time, when Jeroboam went out of Jerusalem, that the prophet Ahijah the Shilonite met him on the way; and he had clothed himself with a new garment, and the two *were* alone in the field. ³⁰Then Ahijah took hold of the new garment that *was* on him, and tore it *into* twelve pieces. ³¹And he said to Jeroboam, "Take for yourself ten pieces, for thus says the LORD, the God of Israel: 'Behold, I will tear the kingdom out of the hand of Solomon and will give ten tribes to you ³²(but he shall have one tribe for the sake of My servant David, and for the sake of Jerusalem, the city which I have chosen out of all the tribes of Israel), ³³because they haveᵃ forsaken Me, and worshiped Ashtoreth the goddess of the Sidonians, Chemosh the god of the Moabites, and Milcom the god of the people of Ammon, and have not walked in My ways to do *what is* right in My eyes and *keep* My statutes and My judgments, as *did* his father David. ³⁴However I will not take the whole kingdom out of his hand, because I have made him ruler all the days of his life for the sake of My servant David, whom I chose because he kept My commandments and My statutes. ³⁵But I will take the kingdom out of his son's hand and give it to you—ten tribes. ³⁶And to his son I will give one tribe, that My servant David may always have a lamp before Me in Jerusalem, the city which I have chosen for Myself, to put My name there. ³⁷So I will take you, and you shall reign over all your heart desires, and you shall be king over Israel. ³⁸Then it shall be, if you heed all that I command you, walk in My ways, and do *what is* right in My sight, to keep My statutes and My commandments, as My servant David did, then I will be with you and build for you an enduring house, as I built for David, and will give Israel to you. ³⁹And I will afflict the descendants of David because of this, but not forever.' "

⁴⁰Solomon therefore sought to kill Jeroboam. But Jeroboam arose and fled to

---

11:33 ᵃFollowing Masoretic Text and Targum; Septuagint, Syriac, and Vulgate read *he has.*

Egypt, to Shishak king of Egypt, and was in Egypt until the death of Solomon.

Death of Solomon

41Now the rest of the acts of Solomon, all that he did, and his wisdom, *are* they not written in the book of the acts of Solomon? 42And the period that Solomon reigned in Jerusalem over all Israel *was* forty years. 43Then Solomon rested with his fathers, and was buried in the City of David his father. And Rehoboam his son reigned in his place.

The Revolt Against Rehoboam

12 And Rehoboam went to Shechem, for all Israel had gone to Shechem to make him king. 2So it happened, when Jeroboam the son of Nebat heard *it* (he was still in Egypt, for he had fled from the presence of King Solomon and had been dwelling in Egypt), 3that they sent and called him. Then Jeroboam and the whole assembly of Israel came and spoke to Rehoboam, saying, 4"Your father made our yoke heavy; now therefore, lighten the burdensome service of your father, and his heavy yoke which he put on us, and we will serve you."

5So he said to them, "Depart *for* three days, then come back to me." And the people departed.

6Then King Rehoboam consulted the elders who stood before his father Solomon while he still lived, and he said, "How do you advise *me* to answer these people?"

7And they spoke to him, saying, "If you will be a servant to these people today, and serve them, and answer them, and speak good words to them, then they will be your servants forever."

8But he rejected the advice which the elders had given him, and consulted the young men who had grown up with him, who stood before him. 9And he said to them, "What advice do you give? How should we answer this people who have spoken to me, saying, 'Lighten the yoke which your father put on us'?"

10Then the young men who had grown up with him spoke to him, saying, "Thus you should speak to this people who have spoken to you, saying, 'Your father made our yoke heavy, but you make *it* lighter on us'—thus you shall say to them: 'My little *finger* shall be thicker than my father's waist! 11And now, whereas my father put a heavy yoke on you, I will add to your yoke; my father chastised you with whips, but I will chastise you with scourges!' "a

12So Jeroboam and all the people came to Rehoboam the third day, as the king had directed, saying, "Come back to me the third day." 13Then the king answered the people roughly, and rejected the advice which the elders had given him; 14and he spoke to them according to the advice of the young men, saying, "My father made your yoke heavy, but I will add to your yoke; my father chastised you with whips, but I will chastise you with scourges!"a 15So the king did not listen to the people; for the turn *of events* was from the LORD, that He might fulfill His word, which the LORD had spoken by Ahijah the Shilonite to Jeroboam the son of Nebat.

16Now when all Israel saw that the king did not listen to them, the people answered the king, saying:

"What share have we in David?
  We have no inheritance in the son
    of Jesse.
  To your tents, O Israel!
  Now, see to your own house, O David!"

So Israel departed to their tents. 17But Rehoboam reigned over the children of Israel who dwelt in the cities of Judah.

18Then King Rehoboam sent Adoram, who *was* in charge of the revenue; but all Israel stoned him with stones, and he died. Therefore King Rehoboam mounted his chariot in haste to flee to Jerusalem. 19So Israel has been in rebellion against the house of David to this day.

20Now it came to pass when all Israel heard that Jeroboam had come back, they sent for him and called him to the congregation, and made him king over all Israel. There was none who followed the house of David, but the tribe of Judah only.

21And when Rehoboam came to Jerusalem, he assembled all the house of Judah

---

12:11 aLiterally *scorpions*   **12:14** aLiterally *scorpions*

with the tribe of Benjamin, one hundred and eighty thousand chosen *men* who were warriors, to fight against the house of Israel, that he might restore the kingdom to Rehoboam the son of Solomon. [22]But the word of God came to Shemaiah the man of God, saying, [23]"Speak to Rehoboam the son of Solomon, king of Judah, to all the house of Judah and Benjamin, and to the rest of the people, saying, [24]'Thus says the LORD: "You shall not go up nor fight against your brethren the children of Israel. Let every man return to his house, for this thing is from Me." ' " Therefore they obeyed the word of the LORD, and turned back, according to the word of the LORD.

Jeroboam's Gold Calves

[25]Then Jeroboam built Shechem in the mountains of Ephraim, and dwelt there. Also he went out from there and built Penuel. [26]And Jeroboam said in his heart, "Now the kingdom may return to the house of David: [27]If these people go up to offer sacrifices in the house of the LORD at Jerusalem, then the heart of this people will turn back to their lord, Rehoboam king of Judah, and they will kill me and go back to Rehoboam king of Judah." [28]Therefore the king asked advice, made two calves of gold, and said to the people, "It is too much for you to go up to Jerusalem. Here are your gods, O Israel, which brought you up from the land of Egypt!" [29]And he set up one in Bethel, and the other he put in Dan. [30]Now this thing became a sin, for the people went *to worship* before the one as far as Dan. [31]He made shrines[a] on the high places, and made priests from every class of people, who were not of the sons of Levi. [32]Jeroboam ordained a feast on the fifteenth day of the eighth month, like the feast that *was* in Judah, and offered sacrifices on the altar. So he did at Bethel, sacrificing to the calves that he had made. And at Bethel he installed the priests of the high places which he had made. [33]So he made offerings on the altar which he had made at Bethel on the fifteenth day of the eighth month, in the month which he had devised in his own heart. And he ordained a feast for the children of Israel, and offered sacrifices on the altar and burned incense.

The Message of the Man of God

13 And behold, a man of God went from Judah to Bethel by the word of the LORD, and Jeroboam stood by the altar to burn incense. [2]Then he cried out against the altar by the word of the LORD, and said, "O altar, altar! Thus says the LORD: 'Behold, a child, Josiah by name, shall be born to the house of David; and on you he shall sacrifice the priests of the high places who burn incense on you, and men's bones shall be burned on you.' " [3]And he gave a sign the same day, saying, "This *is* the sign which the LORD has spoken: Surely the altar shall split apart, and the ashes on it shall be poured out."

[4]So it came to pass when King Jeroboam heard the saying of the man of God, who cried out against the altar in Bethel, that he stretched out his hand from the altar, saying, "Arrest him!" Then his hand, which he stretched out toward him, withered, so that he could not pull it back to himself. [5]The altar also was split apart, and the ashes poured out from the altar, according to the sign which the man of God had given by the word of the LORD. [6]Then the king answered and said to the man of God, "Please entreat the favor of the LORD your God, and pray for me, that my hand may be restored to me."

So the man of God entreated the LORD, and the king's hand was restored to him, and became as before. [7]Then the king said to the man of God, "Come home with me and refresh yourself, and I will give you a reward."

[8]But the man of God said to the king, "If you were to give me half your house, I would not go in with you; nor would I eat bread nor drink water in this place. [9]For so it was commanded me by the word of the LORD, saying, 'You shall not eat bread, nor drink water, nor return by the same way you came.' " [10]So he went another way and did not return by the way he came to Bethel.

12:31 [a]Literally *a house*

Death of the Man of God

[11]Now an old prophet dwelt in Bethel, and his sons came and told him all the works that the man of God had done that day in Bethel; they also told their father the words which he had spoken to the king. [12]And their father said to them, "Which way did he go?" For his sons had seen[a] which way the man of God went who came from Judah. [13]Then he said to his sons, "Saddle the donkey for me." So they saddled the donkey for him; and he rode on it, [14]and went after the man of God, and found him sitting under an oak. Then he said to him, "*Are* you the man of God who came from Judah?"

And he said, "I *am*."

[15]Then he said to him, "Come home with me and eat bread."

[16]And he said, "I cannot return with you nor go in with you; neither can I eat bread nor drink water with you in this place. [17]For I have been told by the word of the LORD, 'You shall not eat bread nor drink water there, nor return by going the way you came.'"

[18]He said to him, "I too *am* a prophet as you *are,* and an angel spoke to me by the word of the LORD, saying, 'Bring him back with you to your house, that he may eat bread and drink water.'" (He was lying to him.)

[19]So he went back with him, and ate bread in his house, and drank water.

[20]Now it happened, as they sat at the table, that the word of the LORD came to the prophet who had brought him back; [21]and he cried out to the man of God who came from Judah, saying, "Thus says the LORD: 'Because you have disobeyed the word of the LORD, and have not kept the commandment which the LORD your God commanded you, [22]but you came back, ate bread, and drank water in the place of which *the LORD* said to you, "Eat no bread and drink no water," your corpse shall not come to the tomb of your fathers.'"

[23]So it was, after he had eaten bread and after he had drunk, that he saddled the donkey for him, the prophet whom he had brought back. [24]When he was gone, a lion met him on the road and killed him. And his corpse was thrown on the road, and the donkey stood by it. The lion also stood by the corpse. [25]And there, men passed by and saw the corpse thrown on the road, and the lion standing by the corpse. Then they went and told *it* in the city where the old prophet dwelt.

[26]Now when the prophet who had brought him back from the way heard *it,* he said, "It *is* the man of God who was disobedient to the word of the LORD. Therefore the LORD has delivered him to the lion, which has torn him and killed him, according to the word of the LORD which He spoke to him." [27]And he spoke to his sons, saying, "Saddle the donkey for me." So they saddled *it.* [28]Then he went and found his corpse thrown on the road, and the donkey and the lion standing by the corpse. The lion had not eaten the corpse nor torn the donkey. [29]And the prophet took up the corpse of the man of God, laid it on the donkey, and brought it back. So the old prophet came to the city to mourn, and to bury him. [30]Then he laid the corpse in his own tomb; and they mourned over him, *saying,* "Alas, my brother!" [31]So it was, after he had buried him, that he spoke to his sons, saying, "When I am dead, then bury me in the tomb where the man of God *is* buried; lay my bones beside his bones. [32]For the saying which he cried out by the word of the LORD against the altar in Bethel, and against all the shrines[a] on the high places which *are* in the cities of Samaria, will surely come to pass."

[33]After this event Jeroboam did not turn from his evil way, but again he made priests from every class of people for the high places; whoever wished, he consecrated him, and he became *one* of the priests of the high places. [34]And this thing was the sin of the house of Jeroboam, so as to exterminate and destroy *it* from the face of the earth.

Judgment on the House of Jeroboam

14 At that time Abijah the son of Jeroboam became sick. [2]And Jeroboam said to his wife, "Please arise, and disguise yourself, that they may not recognize you

---

13:12 [a]Septuagint, Syriac, Targum, and Vulgate read *showed him.*   **13:32** [a]Literally *houses*

as the wife of Jeroboam, and go to Shiloh. Indeed, Ahijah the prophet *is* there, who told me that *I would be* king over this people. ³Also take with you ten loaves, *some* cakes, and a jar of honey, and go to him; he will tell you what will become of the child." ⁴And Jeroboam's wife did so; she arose and went to Shiloh, and came to the house of Ahijah. But Ahijah could not see, for his eyes were glazed by reason of his age.

⁵Now the Lord had said to Ahijah, "Here is the wife of Jeroboam, coming to ask you something about her son, for he *is* sick. Thus and thus you shall say to her; for it will be, when she comes in, that she will pretend *to be* another *woman.*"

⁶And so it was, when Ahijah heard the sound of her footsteps as she came through the door, he said, "Come in, wife of Jeroboam. Why do you pretend *to be* another *person?* For I *have been* sent to you *with* bad *news.* ⁷Go, tell Jeroboam, 'Thus says the Lord God of Israel: "Because I exalted you from among the people, and made you ruler over My people Israel, ⁸and tore the kingdom away from the house of David, and gave it to you; and *yet* you have not been as My servant David, who kept My commandments and who followed Me with all his heart, to do only *what was* right in My eyes; ⁹but you have done more evil than all who were before you, for you have gone and made for yourself other gods and molded images to provoke Me to anger, and have cast Me behind your back— ¹⁰therefore behold! I will bring disaster on the house of Jeroboam, and will cut off from Jeroboam every male in Israel, bond and free; I will take away the remnant of the house of Jeroboam, as one takes away refuse until it is all gone. ¹¹The dogs shall eat whoever belongs to Jeroboam and dies in the city, and the birds of the air shall eat whoever dies in the field; for the Lord has spoken!"' ¹²Arise therefore, go to your own house. When your feet enter the city, the child shall die. ¹³And all Israel shall mourn for him and bury him, for he is the only one of Jeroboam who shall come to the grave, because in him there is found something good toward the Lord God of Israel in the house of Jeroboam.

¹⁴"Moreover the Lord will raise up for Himself a king over Israel who shall cut off the house of Jeroboam; this is the day. What? Even now! ¹⁵For the Lord will strike Israel, as a reed is shaken in the water. He will uproot Israel from this good land which He gave to their fathers, and will scatter them beyond the River,ᵃ because they have made their wooden images,ᵇ provoking the Lord to anger. ¹⁶And He will give Israel up because of the sins of Jeroboam, who sinned and who made Israel sin."

¹⁷Then Jeroboam's wife arose and departed, and came to Tirzah. When she came to the threshold of the house, the child died. ¹⁸And they buried him; and all Israel mourned for him, according to the word of the Lord which He spoke through His servant Ahijah the prophet.

Death of Jeroboam

¹⁹Now the rest of the acts of Jeroboam, how he made war and how he reigned, indeed they *are* written in the book of the chronicles of the kings of Israel. ²⁰The period that Jeroboam reigned *was* twenty-two years. So he rested with his fathers. Then Nadab his son reigned in his place.

Rehoboam Reigns in Judah

²¹And Rehoboam the son of Solomon reigned in Judah. Rehoboam *was* forty-one years old when he became king. He reigned seventeen years in Jerusalem, the city which the Lord had chosen out of all the tribes of Israel, to put His name there. His mother's name *was* Naamah, an Ammonitess. ²²Now Judah did evil in the sight of the Lord, and they provoked Him to jealousy with their sins which they committed, more than all that their fathers had done. ²³For they also built for themselves high places, *sacred* pillars, and wooden images on every high hill and under every green tree. ²⁴And there were also perverted personsᵃ in the land. They did according to all the abominations of the nations which the Lord had cast out before the children of Israel.

14:15 ᵃThat is, the Euphrates ᵇHebrew *Asherim,* Canaanite deities   **14:24** ᵃHebrew *qadesh,* that is, one practicing sodomy and prostitution in religious rituals

25It happened in the fifth year of King Rehoboam *that* Shishak king of Egypt came up against Jerusalem. 26And he took away the treasures of the house of the LORD and the treasures of the king's house; he took away everything. He also took away all the gold shields which Solomon had made. 27Then King Rehoboam made bronze shields in their place, and committed *them* to the hands of the captains of the guard, who guarded the doorway of the king's house. 28And whenever the king entered the house of the LORD, the guards carried them, then brought them back into the guardroom.

29Now the rest of the acts of Rehoboam, and all that he did, *are* they not written in the book of the chronicles of the kings of Judah? 30And there was war between Rehoboam and Jeroboam all *their* days. 31So Rehoboam rested with his fathers, and was buried with his fathers in the City of David. His mother's name *was* Naamah, an Ammonitess. Then Abijam[a] his son reigned in his place.

Abijam Reigns in Judah

15 In the eighteenth year of King Jeroboam the son of Nebat, Abijam became king over Judah. 2He reigned three years in Jerusalem. His mother's name *was* Maachah the granddaughter of Abishalom. 3And he walked in all the sins of his father, which he had done before him; his heart was not loyal to the LORD his God, as was the heart of his father David. 4Nevertheless for David's sake the LORD his God gave him a lamp in Jerusalem, by setting up his son after him and by establishing Jerusalem; 5because David did *what was* right in the eyes of the LORD, and had not turned aside from anything that He commanded him all the days of his life, except in the matter of Uriah the Hittite. 6And there was war between Rehoboam[a] and Jeroboam all the days of his life. 7Now the rest of the acts of Abijam, and all that he did, *are* they not written in the book of the chronicles of the kings of Judah? And there was war between Abijam and Jeroboam.

8So Abijam rested with his fathers, and they buried him in the City of David. Then Asa his son reigned in his place.

Asa Reigns in Judah

9In the twentieth year of Jeroboam king of Israel, Asa became king over Judah. 10And he reigned forty-one years in Jerusalem. His grandmother's name *was* Maachah the granddaughter of Abishalom. 11Asa did *what was* right in the eyes of the LORD, as *did* his father David. 12And he banished the perverted persons[a] from the land, and removed all the idols that his fathers had made. 13Also he removed Maachah his grandmother from *being* queen mother, because she had made an obscene image of Asherah.[a] And Asa cut down her obscene image and burned *it* by the Brook Kidron. 14But the high places were not removed. Nevertheless Asa's heart was loyal to the LORD all his days. 15He also brought into the house of the LORD the things which his father had dedicated, and the things which he himself had dedicated: silver and gold and utensils.

16Now there was war between Asa and Baasha king of Israel all their days. 17And Baasha king of Israel came up against Judah, and built Ramah, that he might let none go out or come in to Asa king of Judah. 18Then Asa took all the silver and gold *that was* left in the treasuries of the house of the LORD and the treasuries of the king's house, and delivered them into the hand of his servants. And King Asa sent them to Ben-Hadad the son of Tabrimmon, the son of Hezion, king of Syria, who dwelt in Damascus, saying, 19"*Let there be* a treaty between you and me, as there was between my father and your father. See, I have sent you a present of silver and gold. Come and break your treaty with Baasha king of Israel, so that he will withdraw from me."

20So Ben-Hadad heeded King Asa, and sent the captains of his armies against the cities of Israel. He attacked Ijon, Dan, Abel Beth Maachah, and all Chinneroth, with all the land of Naphtali. 21Now it happened,

---

14:31 [a]Spelled *Abijah* in 2 Chronicles 12:16ff
15:6 [a]Following Masoretic Text, Septuagint, Targum, and Vulgate; some Hebrew manuscripts and Syriac read *Abijam*.   **15:12** [a]Hebrew *qedeshim,* that is, those practicing sodomy and prostitution in religious rituals   **15:13** [a]A Canaanite goddess

when Baasha heard *it,* that he stopped building Ramah, and remained in Tirzah.

²²Then King Asa made a proclamation throughout all Judah; none *was* exempted. And they took away the stones and timber of Ramah, which Baasha had used for building; and with them King Asa built Geba of Benjamin, and Mizpah.

²³The rest of all the acts of Asa, all his might, all that he did, and the cities which he built, *are* they not written in the book of the chronicles of the kings of Judah? But in the time of his old age he was diseased in his feet. ²⁴So Asa rested with his fathers, and was buried with his fathers in the City of David his father. Then Jehoshaphat his son reigned in his place.

Nadab Reigns in Israel

²⁵Now Nadab the son of Jeroboam became king over Israel in the second year of Asa king of Judah, and he reigned over Israel two years. ²⁶And he did evil in the sight of the LORD, and walked in the way of his father, and in his sin by which he had made Israel sin.

²⁷Then Baasha the son of Ahijah, of the house of Issachar, conspired against him. And Baasha killed him at Gibbethon, which *belonged* to the Philistines, while Nadab and all Israel laid siege to Gibbethon. ²⁸Baasha killed him in the third year of Asa king of Judah, and reigned in his place. ²⁹And it was so, when he became king, *that* he killed all the house of Jeroboam. He did not leave to Jeroboam anyone that breathed, until he had destroyed him, according to the word of the LORD which He had spoken by His servant Ahijah the Shilonite, ³⁰because of the sins of Jeroboam, which he had sinned and by which he had made Israel sin, because of his provocation with which he had provoked the LORD God of Israel to anger.

³¹Now the rest of the acts of Nadab, and all that he did, *are* they not written in the book of the chronicles of the kings of Israel? ³²And there was war between Asa and Baasha king of Israel all their days.

Baasha Reigns in Israel

³³In the third year of Asa king of Judah, Baasha the son of Ahijah became king over all Israel in Tirzah, and *reigned* twenty-four years. ³⁴He did evil in the sight of the LORD, and walked in the way of Jeroboam, and in his sin by which he had made Israel sin.

16 Then the word of the LORD came to Jehu the son of Hanani, against Baasha, saying: ²"Inasmuch as I lifted you out of the dust and made you ruler over My people Israel, and you have walked in the way of Jeroboam, and have made My people Israel sin, to provoke Me to anger with their sins, ³surely I will take away the posterity of Baasha and the posterity of his house, and I will make your house like the house of Jeroboam the son of Nebat. ⁴The dogs shall eat whoever belongs to Baasha and dies in the city, and the birds of the air shall eat whoever dies in the fields."

⁵Now the rest of the acts of Baasha, what he did, and his might, *are* they not written in the book of the chronicles of the kings of Israel? ⁶So Baasha rested with his fathers and was buried in Tirzah. Then Elah his son reigned in his place.

⁷And also the word of the LORD came by the prophet Jehu the son of Hanani against Baasha and his house, because of all the evil that he did in the sight of the LORD in provoking Him to anger with the work of his hands, in being like the house of Jeroboam, and because he killed them.

Elah Reigns in Israel

⁸In the twenty-sixth year of Asa king of Judah, Elah the son of Baasha became king over Israel, *and reigned* two years in Tirzah. ⁹Now his servant Zimri, commander of half *his* chariots, conspired against him as he was in Tirzah drinking himself drunk in the house of Arza, steward of *his* house in Tirzah. ¹⁰And Zimri went in and struck him and killed him in the twenty-seventh year of Asa king of Judah, and reigned in his place.

¹¹Then it came to pass, when he began to reign, as soon as he was seated on his throne, *that* he killed all the household of Baasha; he did not leave him one male, neither of his relatives nor of his friends. ¹²Thus Zimri destroyed all the household of Baasha, according to the word of the LORD, which He spoke against Baasha by Jehu the prophet, ¹³for all the sins of Baasha and

the sins of Elah his son, by which they had sinned and by which they had made Israel sin, in provoking the LORD God of Israel to anger with their idols. [14]Now the rest of the acts of Elah, and all that he did, *are* they not written in the book of the chronicles of the kings of Israel?

Zimri Reigns in Israel

[15]In the twenty-seventh year of Asa king of Judah, Zimri had reigned in Tirzah seven days. And the people *were* encamped against Gibbethon, which *belonged* to the Philistines. [16]Now the people *who were* encamped heard it said, "Zimri has conspired and also has killed the king." So all Israel made Omri, the commander of the army, king over Israel that day in the camp. [17]Then Omri and all Israel with him went up from Gibbethon, and they besieged Tirzah. [18]And it happened, when Zimri saw that the city was taken, that he went into the citadel of the king's house and burned the king's house down upon himself with fire, and died, [19]because of the sins which he had committed in doing evil in the sight of the LORD, in walking in the way of Jeroboam, and in his sin which he had committed to make Israel sin. [20]Now the rest of the acts of Zimri, and the treason he committed, *are* they not written in the book of the chronicles of the kings of Israel?

Omri Reigns in Israel

[21]Then the people of Israel were divided into two parts: half of the people followed Tibni the son of Ginath, to make him king, and half followed Omri. [22]But the people who followed Omri prevailed over the people who followed Tibni the son of Ginath. So Tibni died and Omri reigned. [23]In the thirty-first year of Asa king of Judah, Omri became king over Israel, *and reigned* twelve years. Six years he reigned in Tirzah. [24]And he bought the hill of Samaria from Shemer for two talents of silver; then he built on the hill, and called the name of the city which he built, Samaria, after the name of Shemer, owner of the hill. [25]Omri did evil in the eyes of the LORD, and did worse than all who *were* before him. [26]For he walked in all the ways of Jeroboam the son of Nebat, and in his sin by which he had made Israel sin, provoking the LORD God of Israel to anger with their idols. [27]Now the rest of the acts of Omri which he did, and the might that he showed, *are* they not written in the book of the chronicles of the kings of Israel? [28]So Omri rested with his fathers and was buried in Samaria. Then Ahab his son reigned in his place.

Ahab Reigns in Israel

[29]In the thirty-eighth year of Asa king of Judah, Ahab the son of Omri became king over Israel; and Ahab the son of Omri reigned over Israel in Samaria twenty-two years. [30]Now Ahab the son of Omri did evil in the sight of the LORD, more than all who *were* before him. [31]And it came to pass, as though it had been a trivial thing for him to walk in the sins of Jeroboam the son of Nebat, that he took as wife Jezebel the daughter of Ethbaal, king of the Sidonians; and he went and served Baal and worshiped him. [32]Then he set up an altar for Baal in the temple of Baal, which he had built in Samaria. [33]And Ahab made a wooden image.[a] Ahab did more to provoke the LORD God of Israel to anger than all the kings of Israel who were before him. [34]In his days Hiel of Bethel built Jericho. He laid its foundation with Abiram his firstborn, and with his youngest *son* Segub he set up its gates, according to the word of the LORD, which He had spoken through Joshua the son of Nun.[a]

Elijah Proclaims a Drought

17 And Elijah the Tishbite, of the inhabitants of Gilead, said to Ahab, "*As* the LORD God of Israel lives, before whom I stand, there shall not be dew nor rain these years, except at my word."

[2]Then the word of the LORD came to him, saying, [3]"Get away from here and turn eastward, and hide by the Brook Cherith, which flows into the Jordan. [4]And it will be *that* you shall drink from the brook, and I have commanded the ravens to feed you there."

16:33 [a]Hebrew *Asherah*, a Canaanite goddess
16:34 [a]Compare Joshua 6:26

⁵So he went and did according to the word of the LORD, for he went and stayed by the Brook Cherith, which flows into the Jordan. ⁶The ravens brought him bread and meat in the morning, and bread and meat in the evening; and he drank from the brook. ⁷And it happened after a while that the brook dried up, because there had been no rain in the land.

Elijah and the Widow

⁸Then the word of the LORD came to him, saying, ⁹"Arise, go to Zarephath, which *belongs* to Sidon, and dwell there. See, I have commanded a widow there to provide for you." ¹⁰So he arose and went to Zarephath. And when he came to the gate of the city, indeed a widow *was* there gathering sticks. And he called to her and said, "Please bring me a little water in a cup, that I may drink." ¹¹And as she was going to get *it,* he called to her and said, "Please bring me a morsel of bread in your hand."

¹²So she said, "As the LORD your God lives, I do not have bread, only a handful of flour in a bin, and a little oil in a jar; and see, I *am* gathering a couple of sticks that I may go in and prepare it for myself and my son, that we may eat it, and die."

¹³And Elijah said to her, "Do not fear; go *and* do as you have said, but make me a small cake from it first, and bring *it* to me; and afterward make *some* for yourself and your son. ¹⁴For thus says the LORD God of Israel: 'The bin of flour shall not be used up, nor shall the jar of oil run dry, until the day the LORD sends rain on the earth.'"

¹⁵So she went away and did according to the word of Elijah; and she and he and her household ate for *many* days. ¹⁶The bin of flour was not used up, nor did the jar of oil run dry, according to the word of the LORD which He spoke by Elijah.

Elijah Revives the Widow's Son

¹⁷Now it happened after these things *that* the son of the woman who owned the house became sick. And his sickness was so serious that there was no breath left in him. ¹⁸So she said to Elijah, "What have I to do with you, O man of God? Have you come to me to bring my sin to remembrance, and to kill my son?"

¹⁹And he said to her, "Give me your son." So he took him out of her arms and carried him to the upper room where he was staying, and laid him on his own bed. ²⁰Then he cried out to the LORD and said, "O LORD my God, have You also brought tragedy on the widow with whom I lodge, by killing her son?" ²¹And he stretched himself out on the child three times, and cried out to the LORD and said, "O LORD my God, I pray, let this child's soul come back to him." ²²Then the LORD heard the voice of Elijah; and the soul of the child came back to him, and he revived.

²³And Elijah took the child and brought him down from the upper room into the house, and gave him to his mother. And Elijah said, "See, your son lives!"

²⁴Then the woman said to Elijah, "Now by this I know that you *are* a man of God, *and* that the word of the LORD in your mouth *is* the truth."

Elijah's Message to Ahab

18 And it came to pass *after* many days that the word of the LORD came to Elijah, in the third year, saying, "Go, present yourself to Ahab, and I will send rain on the earth."

²So Elijah went to present himself to Ahab; and *there was* a severe famine in Samaria. ³And Ahab had called Obadiah, who *was* in charge of *his* house. (Now Obadiah feared the LORD greatly. ⁴For so it was, while Jezebel massacred the prophets of the LORD, that Obadiah had taken one hundred prophets and hidden them, fifty to a cave, and had fed them with bread and water.) ⁵And Ahab had said to Obadiah, "Go into the land to all the springs of water and to all the brooks; perhaps we may find grass to keep the horses and mules alive, so that we will not have to kill any livestock." ⁶So they divided the land between them to explore it; Ahab went one way by himself, and Obadiah went another way by himself.

⁷Now as Obadiah was on his way, suddenly Elijah met him; and he recognized him, and fell on his face, and said, "*Is that* you, my lord Elijah?"

⁸And he answered him, "*It is* I. Go, tell your master, 'Elijah *is here.*'"

⁹So he said, "How have I sinned, that you are delivering your servant into the hand of Ahab, to kill me? ¹⁰As the LORD your God lives, there is no nation or kingdom where my master has not sent someone to hunt for you; and when they said, '*He is* not *here,*' he took an oath from the kingdom or nation that they could not find you. ¹¹And now you say, 'Go, tell your master, "Elijah *is here*"'! ¹²And it shall come to pass, *as soon as* I am gone from you, that the Spirit of the LORD will carry you to a place I do not know; so when I go and tell Ahab, and he cannot find you, he will kill me. But I your servant have feared the LORD from my youth. ¹³Was it not reported to my lord what I did when Jezebel killed the prophets of the LORD, how I hid one hundred men of the LORD's prophets, fifty to a cave, and fed them with bread and water? ¹⁴And now you say, 'Go, tell your master, "Elijah *is here.*"' He will kill me!"

¹⁵Then Elijah said, "*As* the LORD of hosts lives, before whom I stand, I will surely present myself to him today."

¹⁶So Obadiah went to meet Ahab, and told him; and Ahab went to meet Elijah.

¹⁷Then it happened, when Ahab saw Elijah, that Ahab said to him, "*Is that* you, O troubler of Israel?"

¹⁸And he answered, "I have not troubled Israel, but you and your father's house *have,* in that you have forsaken the commandments of the LORD and have followed the Baals. ¹⁹Now therefore, send *and* gather all Israel to me on Mount Carmel, the four hundred and fifty prophets of Baal, and the four hundred prophets of Asherah,ª who eat at Jezebel's table."

Elijah's Mount Carmel Victory

²⁰So Ahab sent for all the children of Israel, and gathered the prophets together on Mount Carmel. ²¹And Elijah came to all the people, and said, "How long will you falter between two opinions? If the LORD *is* God, follow Him; but if Baal, follow him." But the people answered him not a word. ²²Then Elijah said to the people, "I alone am left a prophet of the LORD; but Baal's prophets *are* four hundred and fifty men. ²³Therefore let them give us two bulls; and

let them choose one bull for themselves, cut it in pieces, and lay *it* on the wood, but put no fire *under it;* and I will prepare the other bull, and lay *it* on the wood, but put no fire *under it.* ²⁴Then you call on the name of your gods, and I will call on the name of the LORD; and the God who answers by fire, He is God."

So all the people answered and said, "It is well spoken."

²⁵Now Elijah said to the prophets of Baal, "Choose one bull for yourselves and prepare *it* first, for you *are* many; and call on the name of your god, but put no fire *under it.*"

²⁶So they took the bull which was given them, and they prepared *it,* and called on the name of Baal from morning even till noon, saying, "O Baal, hear us!" But *there was* no voice; no one answered. Then they leaped about the altar which they had made.

²⁷And so it was, at noon, that Elijah mocked them and said, "Cry aloud, for he *is* a god; either he is meditating, or he is busy, or he is on a journey, *or* perhaps he is sleeping and must be awakened." ²⁸So they cried aloud, and cut themselves, as was their custom, with knives and lances, until the blood gushed out on them. ²⁹And when midday was past, they prophesied until the *time* of the offering of the *evening* sacrifice. But *there was* no voice; no one answered, no one paid attention.

³⁰Then Elijah said to all the people, "Come near to me." So all the people came near to him. And he repaired the altar of the LORD *that was* broken down. ³¹And Elijah took twelve stones, according to the number of the tribes of the sons of Jacob, to whom the word of the LORD had come, saying, "Israel shall be your name."ª ³²Then with the stones he built an altar in the name of the LORD; and he made a trench around the altar large enough to hold two seahs of seed. ³³And he put the wood in order, cut the bull in pieces, and laid *it* on the wood, and said, "Fill four waterpots with water, and pour *it* on the burnt sacrifice and on the wood." ³⁴Then he said, "Do *it* a second

---

18:19 ªA Canaanite goddess   **18:31** ªGenesis 32:28

time," and they did *it* a second time; and he said, "Do *it* a third time," and they did *it* a third time. ³⁵So the water ran all around the altar; and he also filled the trench with water.

³⁶And it came to pass, at *the time of* the offering of the *evening* sacrifice, that Elijah the prophet came near and said, "Lord God of Abraham, Isaac, and Israel, let it be known this day that You *are* God in Israel and I *am* Your servant, and *that* I have done all these things at Your word. ³⁷Hear me, O Lord, hear me, that this people may know that You *are* the Lord God, and *that* You have turned their hearts back *to You* again."

³⁸Then the fire of the Lord fell and consumed the burnt sacrifice, and the wood and the stones and the dust, and it licked up the water that *was* in the trench. ³⁹Now when all the people saw *it,* they fell on their faces; and they said, "The Lord, He *is* God! The Lord, He *is* God!"

⁴⁰And Elijah said to them, "Seize the prophets of Baal! Do not let one of them escape!" So they seized them; and Elijah brought them down to the Brook Kishon and executed them there.

The Drought Ends

⁴¹Then Elijah said to Ahab, "Go up, eat and drink; for *there is* the sound of abundance of rain." ⁴²So Ahab went up to eat and drink. And Elijah went up to the top of Carmel; then he bowed down on the ground, and put his face between his knees, ⁴³and said to his servant, "Go up now, look toward the sea."

So he went up and looked, and said, "*There is* nothing." And seven times he said, "Go again."

⁴⁴Then it came to pass the seventh *time,* that he said, "There is a cloud, as small as a man's hand, rising out of the sea!" So he said, "Go up, say to Ahab, 'Prepare *your* chariot, and go down before the rain stops you.'"

⁴⁵Now it happened in the meantime that the sky became black with clouds and wind, and there was a heavy rain. So Ahab rode away and went to Jezreel. ⁴⁶Then the hand of the Lord came upon Elijah; and he girded up his loins and ran ahead of Ahab to the entrance of Jezreel.

Elijah Escapes from Jezebel

19 And Ahab told Jezebel all that Elijah had done, also how he had executed all the prophets with the sword. ²Then Jezebel sent a messenger to Elijah, saying, "So let the gods do *to me,* and more also, if I do not make your life as the life of one of them by tomorrow about this time." ³And when he saw *that,* he arose and ran for his life, and went to Beersheba, which *belongs* to Judah, and left his servant there.

⁴But he himself went a day's journey into the wilderness, and came and sat down under a broom tree. And he prayed that he might die, and said, "It is enough! Now, Lord, take my life, for I *am* no better than my fathers!"

⁵Then as he lay and slept under a broom tree, suddenly an angelᵃ touched him, and said to him, "Arise *and* eat." ⁶Then he looked, and there by his head *was* a cake baked on coals, and a jar of water. So he ate and drank, and lay down again. ⁷And the angelᵃ of the Lord came back the second time, and touched him, and said, "Arise *and* eat, because the journey *is* too great for you." ⁸So he arose, and ate and drank; and he went in the strength of that food forty days and forty nights as far as Horeb, the mountain of God.

⁹And there he went into a cave, and spent the night in that place; and behold, the word of the Lord *came* to him, and He said to him, "What are you doing here, Elijah?"

¹⁰So he said, "I have been very zealous for the Lord God of hosts; for the children of Israel have forsaken Your covenant, torn down Your altars, and killed Your prophets with the sword. I alone am left; and they seek to take my life."

God's Revelation to Elijah

¹¹Then He said, "Go out, and stand on the mountain before the Lord." And behold, the Lord passed by, and a great and strong wind tore into the mountains and broke the rocks in pieces before the Lord, *but* the Lord *was* not in the wind; and after the wind an earthquake, *but* the Lord *was* not in the

19:5 ᵃOr *Angel*　　**19:7** ᵃOr *Angel*

earthquake; [12]and after the earthquake a fire, *but* the LORD *was* not in the fire; and after the fire a still small voice.

[13]So it was, when Elijah heard *it,* that he wrapped his face in his mantle and went out and stood in the entrance of the cave. Suddenly a voice *came* to him, and said, "What are you doing here, Elijah?"

[14]And he said, "I have been very zealous for the LORD God of hosts; because the children of Israel have forsaken Your covenant, torn down Your altars, and killed Your prophets with the sword. I alone am left; and they seek to take my life."

[15]Then the LORD said to him: "Go, return on your way to the Wilderness of Damascus; and when you arrive, anoint Hazael *as* king over Syria. [16]Also you shall anoint Jehu the son of Nimshi *as* king over Israel. And Elisha the son of Shaphat of Abel Meholah you shall anoint *as* prophet in your place. [17]It shall be *that* whoever escapes the sword of Hazael, Jehu will kill; and whoever escapes the sword of Jehu, Elisha will kill. [18]Yet I have reserved seven thousand in Israel, all whose knees have not bowed to Baal, and every mouth that has not kissed him."

Elisha Follows Elijah

[19]So he departed from there, and found Elisha the son of Shaphat, who *was* plowing *with* twelve yoke *of oxen* before him, and he was with the twelfth. Then Elijah passed by him and threw his mantle on him. [20]And he left the oxen and ran after Elijah, and said, "Please let me kiss my father and my mother, and *then* I will follow you."

And he said to him, "Go back again, for what have I done to you?"

[21]So *Elisha* turned back from him, and took a yoke of oxen and slaughtered them and boiled their flesh, using the oxen's equipment, and gave it to the people, and they ate. Then he arose and followed Elijah, and became his servant.

Ahab Defeats the Syrians

20 Now Ben-Hadad the king of Syria gathered all his forces together; thirty-two kings *were* with him, with horses and chariots. And he went up and besieged Samaria, and made war against it. [2]Then he sent messengers into the city to Ahab king of Israel, and said to him, "Thus says Ben-Hadad: [3]'Your silver and your gold *are* mine; your loveliest wives and children are mine.'"

[4]And the king of Israel answered and said, "My lord, O king, just as you say, I and all that I have *are* yours."

[5]Then the messengers came back and said, "Thus speaks Ben-Hadad, saying, 'Indeed I have sent to you, saying, "You shall deliver to me your silver and your gold, your wives and your children"; [6]but I will send my servants to you tomorrow about this time, and they shall search your house and the houses of your servants. And it shall be, *that* whatever is pleasant in your eyes, they will put *it* in their hands and take *it.*'"

[7]So the king of Israel called all the elders of the land, and said, "Notice, please, and see how this *man* seeks trouble, for he sent to me for my wives, my children, my silver, and my gold; and I did not deny him."

[8]And all the elders and all the people said to him, "Do not listen or consent."

[9]Therefore he said to the messengers of Ben-Hadad, "Tell my lord the king, 'All that you sent for to your servant the first time I will do, but this thing I cannot do.'"

And the messengers departed and brought back word to him.

[10]Then Ben-Hadad sent to him and said, "The gods do so to me, and more also, if enough dust is left of Samaria for a handful for each of the people who follow me."

[11]So the king of Israel answered and said, "Tell *him,* 'Let not the one who puts on *his* armor boast like the one who takes *it off.*'"

[12]And it happened when *Ben-Hadad* heard this message, as he and the kings *were* drinking at the command post, that he said to his servants, "Get ready." And they got ready to attack the city.

[13]Suddenly a prophet approached Ahab king of Israel, saying, "Thus says the LORD: 'Have you seen all this great multitude? Behold, I will deliver it into your hand today, and you shall know that I *am* the LORD.'"

[14]So Ahab said, "By whom?"

And he said, "Thus says the LORD: 'By the young leaders of the provinces.'"

Then he said, "Who will set the battle in order?"

And he answered, "You."

[15]Then he mustered the young leaders of the provinces, and there were two hundred and thirty-two; and after them he mustered all the people, all the children of Israel—seven thousand.

[16]So they went out at noon. Meanwhile Ben-Hadad and the thirty-two kings helping him were getting drunk at the command post. [17]The young leaders of the provinces went out first. And Ben-Hadad sent out *a patrol,* and they told him, saying, "Men are coming out of Samaria!" [18]So he said, "If they have come out for peace, take them alive; and if they have come out for war, take them alive."

[19]Then these young leaders of the provinces went out of the city with the army which followed them. [20]And each one killed his man; so the Syrians fled, and Israel pursued them; and Ben-Hadad the king of Syria escaped on a horse with the cavalry. [21]Then the king of Israel went out and attacked the horses and chariots, and killed the Syrians with a great slaughter.

[22]And the prophet came to the king of Israel and said to him, "Go, strengthen yourself; take note, and see what you should do, for in the spring of the year the king of Syria will come up against you."

The Syrians Again Defeated

[23]Then the servants of the king of Syria said to him, "Their gods *are* gods of the hills. Therefore they were stronger than we; but if we fight against them in the plain, surely we will be stronger than they. [24]So do this thing: Dismiss the kings, each from his position, and put captains in their places; [25]and you shall muster an army like the army that you have lost, horse for horse and chariot for chariot. Then we will fight against them in the plain; surely we will be stronger than they."

And he listened to their voice and did so.

[26]So it was, in the spring of the year, that Ben-Hadad mustered the Syrians and went up to Aphek to fight against Israel. [27]And the children of Israel were mustered and given provisions, and they went against them. Now the children of Israel encamped before them like two little flocks of goats, while the Syrians filled the countryside.

[28]Then a man of God came and spoke to the king of Israel, and said, "Thus says the LORD: 'Because the Syrians have said, "The LORD *is* God of the hills, but He *is* not God of the valleys," therefore I will deliver all this great multitude into your hand, and you shall know that I *am* the LORD.'" [29]And they encamped opposite each other for seven days. So it was that on the seventh day the battle was joined; and the children of Israel killed one hundred thousand foot soldiers *of* the Syrians in one day. [30]But the rest fled to Aphek, into the city; then a wall fell on twenty-seven thousand of the men *who were* left.

And Ben-Hadad fled and went into the city, into an inner chamber.

Ahab's Treaty with Ben-Hadad

[31]Then his servants said to him, "Look now, we have heard that the kings of the house of Israel *are* merciful kings. Please, let us put sackcloth around our waists and ropes around our heads, and go out to the king of Israel; perhaps he will spare your life." [32]So they wore sackcloth around their waists and *put* ropes around their heads, and came to the king of Israel and said, "Your servant Ben-Hadad says, 'Please let me live.'"

And he said, "*Is* he still alive? He *is* my brother."

[33]Now the men were watching closely to see whether *any sign of mercy would come* from him; and they quickly grasped *at this word* and said, "Your brother Ben-Hadad."

So he said, "Go, bring him." Then Ben-Hadad came out to him; and he had him come up into the chariot.

[34]So *Ben-Hadad* said to him, "The cities which my father took from your father I will restore; and you may set up marketplaces for yourself in Damascus, as my father did in Samaria."

Then *Ahab said,* "I will send you away with this treaty." So he made a treaty with him and sent him away.

Ahab Condemned

[35]Now a certain man of the sons of the prophets said to his neighbor by the word of the LORD, "Strike me, please." And the

man refused to strike him. ³⁶Then he said to him, "Because you have not obeyed the voice of the LORD, surely, as soon as you depart from me, a lion shall kill you." And as soon as he left him, a lion found him and killed him.

³⁷And he found another man, and said, "Strike me, please." So the man struck him, inflicting a wound. ³⁸Then the prophet departed and waited for the king by the road, and disguised himself with a bandage over his eyes. ³⁹Now as the king passed by, he cried out to the king and said, "Your servant went out into the midst of the battle; and there, a man came over and brought a man to me, and said, 'Guard this man; if by any means he is missing, your life shall be for his life, or else you shall pay a talent of silver.' ⁴⁰While your servant was busy here and there, he was gone."

Then the king of Israel said to him, "So *shall* your judgment *be*; you yourself have decided *it*."

⁴¹And he hastened to take the bandage away from his eyes; and the king of Israel recognized him as one of the prophets. ⁴²Then he said to him, "Thus says the LORD: 'Because you have let slip out of *your* hand a man whom I appointed to utter destruction, therefore your life shall go for his life, and your people for his people.' "

⁴³So the king of Israel went to his house sullen and displeased, and came to Samaria.

Naboth Is Murdered for His Vineyard

21 And it came to pass after these things *that* Naboth the Jezreelite had a vineyard which *was* in Jezreel, next to the palace of Ahab king of Samaria. ²So Ahab spoke to Naboth, saying, "Give me your vineyard, that I may have it for a vegetable garden, because it *is* near, next to my house; and for it I will give you a vineyard better than it. *Or,* if it seems good to you, I will give you its worth in money."

³But Naboth said to Ahab, "The LORD forbid that I should give the inheritance of my fathers to you!"

⁴So Ahab went into his house sullen and displeased because of the word which Naboth the Jezreelite had spoken to him; for he had said, "I will not give you the inheritance of my fathers." And he lay down on his bed, and turned away his face, and would eat no food. ⁵But Jezebel his wife came to him, and said to him, "Why is your spirit so sullen that you eat no food?"

⁶He said to her, "Because I spoke to Naboth the Jezreelite, and said to him, 'Give me your vineyard for money; or else, if it pleases you, I will give you *another* vineyard for it.' And he answered, 'I will not give you my vineyard.' "

⁷Then Jezebel his wife said to him, "You now exercise authority over Israel! Arise, eat food, and let your heart be cheerful; I will give you the vineyard of Naboth the Jezreelite."

⁸And she wrote letters in Ahab's name, sealed *them* with his seal, and sent the letters to the elders and the nobles who *were* dwelling in the city with Naboth. ⁹She wrote in the letters, saying,

> Proclaim a fast, and seat Naboth with high honor among the people; ¹⁰and seat two men, scoundrels, before him to bear witness against him, saying, "You have blasphemed God and the king." *Then* take him out, and stone him, that he may die.

¹¹So the men of his city, the elders and nobles who were inhabitants of his city, did as Jezebel had sent to them, as it *was* written in the letters which she had sent to them. ¹²They proclaimed a fast, and seated Naboth with high honor among the people. ¹³And two men, scoundrels, came in and sat before him; and the scoundrels witnessed against him, against Naboth, in the presence of the people, saying, "Naboth has blasphemed God and the king!" Then they took him outside the city and stoned him with stones, so that he died. ¹⁴Then they sent to Jezebel, saying, "Naboth has been stoned and is dead."

¹⁵And it came to pass, when Jezebel heard that Naboth had been stoned and was dead, that Jezebel said to Ahab, "Arise, take possession of the vineyard of Naboth the Jezreelite, which he refused to give you for money; for Naboth is not alive, but dead." ¹⁶So it was, when Ahab heard that Naboth

was dead, that Ahab got up and went down to take possession of the vineyard of Naboth the Jezreelite.

The LORD Condemns Ahab

¹⁷Then the word of the LORD came to Elijah the Tishbite, saying, ¹⁸"Arise, go down to meet Ahab king of Israel, who *lives* in Samaria. There *he is,* in the vineyard of Naboth, where he has gone down to take possession of it. ¹⁹You shall speak to him, saying, 'Thus says the LORD: "Have you murdered and also taken possession?"' And you shall speak to him, saying, 'Thus says the LORD: "In the place where dogs licked the blood of Naboth, dogs shall lick your blood, even yours."'"

²⁰So Ahab said to Elijah, "Have you found me, O my enemy?"

And he answered, "I have found *you,* because you have sold yourself to do evil in the sight of the LORD: ²¹'Behold, I will bring calamity on you. I will take away your posterity, and will cut off from Ahab every male in Israel, both bond and free. ²²I will make your house like the house of Jeroboam the son of Nebat, and like the house of Baasha the son of Ahijah, because of the provocation with which you have provoked *Me* to anger, and made Israel sin.' ²³And concerning Jezebel the LORD also spoke, saying, 'The dogs shall eat Jezebel by the wallª of Jezreel.' ²⁴The dogs shall eat whoever belongs to Ahab and dies in the city, and the birds of the air shall eat whoever dies in the field."

²⁵But there was no one like Ahab who sold himself to do wickedness in the sight of the LORD, because Jezebel his wife stirred him up. ²⁶And he behaved very abominably in following idols, according to all *that* the Amorites had done, whom the LORD had cast out before the children of Israel.

²⁷So it was, when Ahab heard those words, that he tore his clothes and put sackcloth on his body, and fasted and lay in sackcloth, and went about mourning.

²⁸And the word of the LORD came to Elijah the Tishbite, saying, ²⁹"See how Ahab has humbled himself before Me? Because he has humbled himself before Me, I will not bring the calamity in his days. In the days of his son I will bring the calamity on his house."

Micaiah Warns Ahab

22 Now three years passed without war between Syria and Israel. ²Then it came to pass, in the third year, that Jehoshaphat the king of Judah went down to *visit* the king of Israel.

³And the king of Israel said to his servants, "Do you know that Ramoth in Gilead *is* ours, but we hesitate to take it out of the hand of the king of Syria?" ⁴So he said to Jehoshaphat, "Will you go with me to fight at Ramoth Gilead?"

Jehoshaphat said to the king of Israel, "I *am* as you *are,* my people as your people, my horses as your horses." ⁵Also Jehoshaphat said to the king of Israel, "Please inquire for the word of the LORD today."

⁶Then the king of Israel gathered the prophets together, about four hundred men, and said to them, "Shall I go against Ramoth Gilead to fight, or shall I refrain?"

So they said, "Go up, for the Lord will deliver *it* into the hand of the king."

⁷And Jehoshaphat said, "*Is there* not still a prophet of the LORD here, that we may inquire of Him?"ª

⁸So the king of Israel said to Jehoshaphat, "*There is* still one man, Micaiah the son of Imlah, by whom we may inquire of the LORD; but I hate him, because he does not prophesy good concerning me, but evil."

And Jehoshaphat said, "Let not the king say such things!"

⁹Then the king of Israel called an officer and said, "Bring Micaiah the son of Imlah quickly!"

¹⁰The king of Israel and Jehoshaphat the king of Judah, having put on *their* robes, sat each on his throne, at a threshing floor at the entrance of the gate of Samaria; and all the prophets prophesied before them. ¹¹Now Zedekiah the son of Chenaanah had made horns of iron for himself; and he said, "Thus says the LORD: 'With these you shall

21:23 ªFollowing Masoretic Text and Septuagint; some Hebrew manuscripts, Syriac, Targum, and Vulgate read *plot of ground* (compare 2 Kings 9:36). **22:7** ªOr *him*

gore the Syrians until they are destroyed.' "
¹²And all the prophets prophesied so, saying, "Go up to Ramoth Gilead and prosper, for the Lord will deliver *it* into the king's hand."

¹³Then the messenger who had gone to call Micaiah spoke to him, saying, "Now listen, the words of the prophets with one accord encourage the king. Please, let your word be like the word of one of them, and speak encouragement."

¹⁴And Micaiah said, "*As* the Lord lives, whatever the Lord says to me, that I will speak."

¹⁵Then he came to the king; and the king said to him, "Micaiah, shall we go to war against Ramoth Gilead, or shall we refrain?"

And he answered him, "Go and prosper, for the Lord will deliver *it* into the hand of the king!"

¹⁶So the king said to him, "How many times shall I make you swear that you tell me nothing but the truth in the name of the Lord?"

¹⁷Then he said, "I saw all Israel scattered on the mountains, as sheep that have no shepherd. And the Lord said, 'These have no master. Let each return to his house in peace.' "

¹⁸And the king of Israel said to Jehoshaphat, "Did I not tell you he would not prophesy good concerning me, but evil?"

¹⁹Then *Micaiah* said, "Therefore hear the word of the Lord: I saw the Lord sitting on His throne, and all the host of heaven standing by, on His right hand and on His left. ²⁰And the Lord said, 'Who will persuade Ahab to go up, that he may fall at Ramoth Gilead?' So one spoke in this manner, and another spoke in that manner. ²¹Then a spirit came forward and stood before the Lord, and said, 'I will persuade him.' ²²The Lord said to him, 'In what way?' So he said, 'I will go out and be a lying spirit in the mouth of all his prophets.' And the Lord said, 'You shall persuade *him,* and also prevail. Go out and do so.' ²³Therefore look! The Lord has put a lying spirit in the mouth of all these prophets of yours, and the Lord has declared disaster against you."

²⁴Now Zedekiah the son of Chenaanah went near and struck Micaiah on the cheek, and said, "Which way did the spirit from the Lord go from me to speak to you?"

²⁵And Micaiah said, "Indeed, you shall see on that day when you go into an inner chamber to hide!"

²⁶So the king of Israel said, "Take Micaiah, and return him to Amon the governor of the city and to Joash the king's son; ²⁷and say, 'Thus says the king: "Put this *fellow* in prison, and feed him with bread of affliction and water of affliction, until I come in peace." ' "

²⁸But Micaiah said, "If you ever return in peace, the Lord has not spoken by me." And he said, "Take heed, all you people!"

Ahab Dies in Battle

²⁹So the king of Israel and Jehoshaphat the king of Judah went up to Ramoth Gilead. ³⁰And the king of Israel said to Jehoshaphat, "I will disguise myself and go into battle; but you put on your robes." So the king of Israel disguised himself and went into battle.

³¹Now the king of Syria had commanded the thirty-two captains of his chariots, saying, "Fight with no one small or great, but only with the king of Israel." ³²So it was, when the captains of the chariots saw Jehoshaphat, that they said, "Surely it *is* the king of Israel!" Therefore they turned aside to fight against him, and Jehoshaphat cried out. ³³And it happened, when the captains of the chariots saw that it *was* not the king of Israel, that they turned back from pursuing him. ³⁴Now a *certain* man drew a bow at random, and struck the king of Israel between the joints of his armor. So he said to the driver of his chariot, "Turn around and take me out of the battle, for I am wounded."

³⁵The battle increased that day; and the king was propped up in his chariot, facing the Syrians, and died at evening. The blood ran out from the wound onto the floor of the chariot. ³⁶Then, as the sun was going down, a shout went throughout the army, saying, "Every man to his city, and every man to his own country!"

³⁷So the king died, and was brought to Samaria. And they buried the king in

FREEDOM'S COST

NATHAN HALE

"As the LORD lives, whatever the LORD says to me, that I will speak."

1 KINGS 22:14

A wise person once said, "Freedom is never free," and that is certainly true in America.

Nathan Hale (1755–1776) was a schoolteacher when the Revolutionary War broke out in April 1775 at Concord and Lexington. Nathan's friend witnessed the siege of Boston and wrote a letter in which he said: "Was I in your condition . . . I think the more extensive service would be my choice. Our holy religion, the honor of our God, a glorious country, and a happy constitution is what we have to defend." Soon after receiving the letter, Hale joined his five brothers in the fight for independence against the British and quickly rose to the rank of captain.

Hale fought under General George Washington in New York, as British General William Howe began a military buildup on Long Island. Washington took his army onto Manhattan Island. At the battle of Harlem Heights, Washington asked for a volunteer to go on a spy mission behind enemy lines. Hale stepped forward and was sent out on his mission. For a week he gathered information on the position of British troops, but was captured while returning to the American side. Because of incriminating papers Hale possessed, the British knew he was a spy. Howe ordered the 20-year-old Hale to be hanged the following day without a trial.

Widely considered America's first spy, patriot Nathan Hale was hanged on September 22, 1776. Before he gave his life for his country, he made a short speech, ending with these famous words that have inspired Americans from every generation: "I only regret that I have but one life to lose for my country."

> *We have enjoyed so much freedom for so long that we are perhaps in danger of forgetting how much blood it cost to establish the Bill of Rights.*
>
> FELIX FRANKFURTER

> *We on this continent should never forget that men first crossed the Atlantic not to find soil for their ploughs but to secure liberty for their souls.*
>
> ROBERT J. MCCRACKEN

> *Posterity: you will never know how much it has cost my generation to preserve your freedom. I hope you will make good use of it.*
>
> JOHN QUINCY ADAMS

Samaria. ³⁸Then *someone* washed the chariot at a pool in Samaria, and the dogs licked up his blood while the harlots bathed,ᵃ according to the word of the LORD which He had spoken.

³⁹Now the rest of the acts of Ahab, and all that he did, the ivory house which he built and all the cities that he built, *are* they not written in the book of the chronicles of the kings of Israel? ⁴⁰So Ahab rested with his fathers. Then Ahaziah his son reigned in his place.

Jehoshaphat Reigns in Judah

⁴¹Jehoshaphat the son of Asa had become king over Judah in the fourth year of Ahab king of Israel. ⁴²Jehoshaphat *was* thirty-five years old when he became king, and he reigned twenty-five years in Jerusalem. His mother's name *was* Azubah the daughter of Shilhi. ⁴³And he walked in all the ways of his father Asa. He did not turn aside from them, doing *what was* right in the eyes of the LORD. Nevertheless the high places were not taken away, *for* the people offered sacrifices and burned incense on the high places. ⁴⁴Also Jehoshaphat made peace with the king of Israel.

⁴⁵Now the rest of the acts of Jehoshaphat, the might that he showed, and how he made war, *are* they not written in the book of the chronicles of the kings of Judah?

⁴⁶And the rest of the perverted persons,ᵃ who remained in the days of his father Asa, he banished from the land. ⁴⁷*There was* then no king in Edom, only a deputy of the king.

⁴⁸Jehoshaphat made merchant shipsᵃ to go to Ophir for gold; but they never sailed, for the ships were wrecked at Ezion Geber. ⁴⁹Then Ahaziah the son of Ahab said to Jehoshaphat, "Let my servants go with your servants in the ships." But Jehoshaphat would not.

⁵⁰And Jehoshaphat rested with his fathers, and was buried with his fathers in the City of David his father. Then Jehoram his son reigned in his place.

Ahaziah Reigns in Israel

⁵¹Ahaziah the son of Ahab became king over Israel in Samaria in the seventeenth year of Jehoshaphat king of Judah, and reigned two years over Israel. ⁵²He did evil in the sight of the LORD, and walked in the way of his father and in the way of his mother and in the way of Jeroboam the son of Nebat, who had made Israel sin; ⁵³for he served Baal and worshiped him, and provoked the LORD God of Israel to anger, according to all that his father had done.

22:38 ᵃSyriac and Targum read *they washed his armor.*
22:46 ᵃHebrew *qadesh,* that is, one practicing sodomy and prostitution in religious rituals   **22:48** ᵃOr *ships of Tarshish*

2 KINGS

Author: Unknown, attributed to Jeremiah

When Written: 560–538 B.C.

Theme: Destruction, Captivity

Key Verses: 2 Kings 23:27—And the Lord said, "I will also remove Judah from My sight, as I have removed Israel, and will cast off this city Jerusalem which I have chosen, and the house of which I said, 'My name shall be there.'"

Key Chapter: 2 Kings 25—The last chapter of this book records the utter destruction of Jerusalem and its glorious temple and the removal of all of its inhabitants (except the poorest) to bondage in Babylon. The final verses, however, offer hope for Judah and a subtle foreshadowing of the return of the Babylonian captives to their longed-for home.

Second Kings continues the account of the downward spiral of both Israel and Judah as the divided nations by and large walk a path of rebellion and disobedience to God. During this time, prophets such as Elijah and Elisha are sent to warn the people of sin, idolatry, and impending judgment. They explain the necessity of turning from evil and following the commandments given by God.

Just as God used spokesmen and prophets in Israel and Judah to encourage righteousness and warn against idolatry and evil, so throughout the generations of our own nation He has raised men and women to speak in defense of liberty, justice, morality, and righteousness. Individuals such as Jonathan Edwards, Charles Finney, Frederick Douglass, Harriet Beecher Stowe, D. L. Moody, Peter Marshall, Billy Graham, and many others have reminded this nation that from its foundations to the present time her significance will endure only as she seeks to be a "nation under God."

2 KINGS

God Judges Ahaziah

1 Moab rebelled against Israel after the death of Ahab.

²Now Ahaziah fell through the lattice of his upper room in Samaria, and was injured; so he sent messengers and said to them, "Go, inquire of Baal-Zebub, the god of Ekron, whether I shall recover from this injury." ³But the angelᵃ of the LORD said to Elijah the Tishbite, "Arise, go up to meet the messengers of the king of Samaria, and say to them, *'Is it* because *there is* no God in Israel *that* you are going to inquire of Baal-Zebub, the god of Ekron?' ⁴Now therefore, thus says the LORD: 'You shall not come down from the bed to which you have gone up, but you shall surely die.' " So Elijah departed.

⁵And when the messengers returned to him, he said to them, "Why have you come back?"

⁶So they said to him, "A man came up to meet us, and said to us, 'Go, return to the king who sent you, and say to him, "Thus says the LORD: *'Is it* because *there is* no God in Israel *that* you are sending to inquire of Baal-Zebub, the god of Ekron? Therefore you shall not come down from the bed to which you have gone up, but you shall surely die.' " ' "

⁷Then he said to them, "What kind of man *was it* who came up to meet you and told you these words?"

⁸So they answered him, "A hairy man wearing a leather belt around his waist."

And he said, "It *is* Elijah the Tishbite."

⁹Then the king sent to him a captain of fifty with his fifty men. So he went up to him; and there he was, sitting on the top of a hill. And he spoke to him: "Man of God, the king has said, 'Come down!'"

¹⁰So Elijah answered and said to the captain of fifty, "If I *am* a man of God, then let fire come down from heaven and consume you and your fifty men." And fire came down from heaven and consumed him and his fifty. ¹¹Then he sent to him another captain of fifty with his fifty men.

And he answered and said to him: "Man of God, thus has the king said, 'Come down quickly!'"

¹²So Elijah answered and said to them, "If I *am* a man of God, let fire come down from heaven and consume you and your fifty men." And the fire of God came down from heaven and consumed him and his fifty.

¹³Again, he sent a third captain of fifty with his fifty men. And the third captain of fifty went up, and came and fell on his knees before Elijah, and pleaded with him, and said to him: "Man of God, please let my life and the life of these fifty servants of yours be precious in your sight. ¹⁴Look, fire has come down from heaven and burned up the first two captains of fifties with their fifties. But let my life now be precious in your sight."

¹⁵And the angelᵃ of the LORD said to Elijah, "Go down with him; do not be afraid of him." So he arose and went down with him to the king. ¹⁶Then he said to him, "Thus says the LORD: 'Because you have sent messengers to inquire of Baal-Zebub, the god of Ekron, *is it* because *there is* no God in Israel to inquire of His word? Therefore you shall not come down from the bed to which you have gone up, but you shall surely die.' "

¹⁷So *Ahaziah* died according to the word of the LORD which Elijah had spoken. Because he had no son, Jehoramᵃ became king in his place, in the second year of Jehoram the son of Jehoshaphat, king of Judah.

¹⁸Now the rest of the acts of Ahaziah which he did, *are* they not written in the book of the chronicles of the kings of Israel?

Elijah Ascends to Heaven

2 And it came to pass, when the LORD was about to take up Elijah into heaven by a whirlwind, that Elijah went with Elisha

---

1:3 ᵃOr *Angel*   **1:15** ᵃOr *Angel*   **1:17** ᵃThe son of Ahab king of Israel (compare 3:1)

from Gilgal. [2]Then Elijah said to Elisha, "Stay here, please, for the LORD has sent me on to Bethel."

But Elisha said, "*As* the LORD lives, and *as* your soul lives, I will not leave you!" So they went down to Bethel.

[3]Now the sons of the prophets who *were* at Bethel came out to Elisha, and said to him, "Do you know that the LORD will take away your master from over you today?"

And he said, "Yes, I know; keep silent!"

[4]Then Elijah said to him, "Elisha, stay here, please, for the LORD has sent me on to Jericho."

But he said, "*As* the LORD lives, and *as* your soul lives, I will not leave you!" So they came to Jericho.

[5]Now the sons of the prophets who *were* at Jericho came to Elisha and said to him, "Do you know that the LORD will take away your master from over you today?"

So he answered, "Yes, I know; keep silent!"

[6]Then Elijah said to him, "Stay here, please, for the LORD has sent me on to the Jordan."

But he said, "*As* the LORD lives, and *as* your soul lives, I will not leave you!" So the two of them went on. [7]And fifty men of the sons of the prophets went and stood facing *them* at a distance, while the two of them stood by the Jordan. [8]Now Elijah took his mantle, rolled *it* up, and struck the water; and it was divided this way and that, so that the two of them crossed over on dry ground.

[9]And so it was, when they had crossed over, that Elijah said to Elisha, "Ask! What may I do for you, before I am taken away from you?"

Elisha said, "Please let a double portion of your spirit be upon me."

[10]So he said, "You have asked a hard thing. *Nevertheless,* if you see me *when I am* taken from you, it shall be so for you; but if not, it shall not be *so.*" [11]Then it happened, as they continued on and talked, that suddenly a chariot of fire *appeared* with horses of fire, and separated the two of them; and Elijah went up by a whirlwind into heaven.

[12]And Elisha saw *it,* and he cried out, "My father, my father, the chariot of Israel and its horsemen!" So he saw him no more. And he took hold of his own clothes and tore them into two pieces. [13]He also took up the mantle of Elijah that had fallen from him, and went back and stood by the bank of the Jordan. [14]Then he took the mantle of Elijah that had fallen from him, and struck the water, and said, "Where *is* the LORD God of Elijah?" And when he also had struck the water, it was divided this way and that; and Elisha crossed over.

[15]Now when the sons of the prophets who *were* from Jericho saw him, they said, "The spirit of Elijah rests on Elisha." And they came to meet him, and bowed to the ground before him. [16]Then they said to him, "Look now, there are fifty strong men with your servants. Please let them go and search for your master, lest perhaps the Spirit of the LORD has taken him up and cast him upon some mountain or into some valley."

And he said, "You shall not send anyone."

[17]But when they urged him till he was ashamed, he said, "Send *them!*" Therefore they sent fifty men, and they searched for three days but did not find him. [18]And when they came back to him, for he had stayed in Jericho, he said to them, "Did I not say to you, 'Do not go'?"

Elisha Performs Miracles

[19]Then the men of the city said to Elisha, "Please notice, the situation of this city *is* pleasant, as my lord sees; but the water *is* bad, and the ground barren."

[20]And he said, "Bring me a new bowl, and put salt in it." So they brought *it* to him. [21]Then he went out to the source of the water, and cast in the salt there, and said, "Thus says the LORD: 'I have healed this water; from it there shall be no more death or barrenness.'" [22]So the water remains healed to this day, according to the word of Elisha which he spoke.

[23]Then he went up from there to Bethel; and as he was going up the road, some youths came from the city and mocked him, and said to him, "Go up, you baldhead! Go up, you baldhead!"

[24]So he turned around and looked at them, and pronounced a curse on them in

the name of the Lord. And two female bears came out of the woods and mauled forty-two of the youths.

25Then he went from there to Mount Carmel, and from there he returned to Samaria.

Moab Rebels Against Israel

3 Now Jehoram the son of Ahab became king over Israel at Samaria in the eighteenth year of Jehoshaphat king of Judah, and reigned twelve years. 2And he did evil in the sight of the Lord, but not like his father and mother; for he put away the *sacred* pillar of Baal that his father had made. 3Nevertheless he persisted in the sins of Jeroboam the son of Nebat, who had made Israel sin; he did not depart from them.

4Now Mesha king of Moab was a sheep-breeder, and he regularly paid the king of Israel one hundred thousand lambs and the wool of one hundred thousand rams. 5But it happened, when Ahab died, that the king of Moab rebelled against the king of Israel.

6So King Jehoram went out of Samaria at that time and mustered all Israel. 7Then he went and sent to Jehoshaphat king of Judah, saying, "The king of Moab has rebelled against me. Will you go with me to fight against Moab?"

And he said, "I will go up; I *am* as you *are,* my people as your people, my horses as your horses." 8Then he said, "Which way shall we go up?"

And he answered, "By way of the Wilderness of Edom."

9So the king of Israel went with the king of Judah and the king of Edom, and they marched on that roundabout route seven days; and there was no water for the army, nor for the animals that followed them. 10And the king of Israel said, "Alas! For the Lord has called these three kings together to deliver them into the hand of Moab."

11But Jehoshaphat said, "*Is there* no prophet of the Lord here, that we may inquire of the Lord by him?"

So one of the servants of the king of Israel answered and said, "Elisha the son of Shaphat *is* here, who poured water on the hands of Elijah."

12And Jehoshaphat said, "The word of the Lord is with him." So the king of Israel and Jehoshaphat and the king of Edom went down to him.

13Then Elisha said to the king of Israel, "What have I to do with you? Go to the prophets of your father and the prophets of your mother."

But the king of Israel said to him, "No, for the Lord has called these three kings *together* to deliver them into the hand of Moab."

14And Elisha said, "*As* the Lord of hosts lives, before whom I stand, surely were it not that I regard the presence of Jehoshaphat king of Judah, I would not look at you, nor see you. 15But now bring me a musician."

Then it happened, when the musician played, that the hand of the Lord came upon him. 16And he said, "Thus says the Lord: 'Make this valley full of ditches.' 17For thus says the Lord: 'You shall not see wind, nor shall you see rain; yet that valley shall be filled with water, so that you, your cattle, and your animals may drink.' 18And this is a simple matter in the sight of the Lord; He will also deliver the Moabites into your hand. 19Also you shall attack every fortified city and every choice city, and shall cut down every good tree, and stop up every spring of water, and ruin every good piece of land with stones."

20Now it happened in the morning, when the grain offering was offered, that suddenly water came by way of Edom, and the land was filled with water.

21And when all the Moabites heard that the kings had come up to fight against them, all who were able to bear arms and older were gathered; and they stood at the border. 22Then they rose up early in the morning, and the sun was shining on the water; and the Moabites saw the water on the other side *as* red as blood. 23And they said, "This is blood; the kings have surely struck swords and have killed one another; now therefore, Moab, to the spoil!"

24So when they came to the camp of Israel, Israel rose up and attacked the Moabites, so that they fled before them; and they entered *their* land, killing the Moabites. 25Then they destroyed the cities, and each

man threw a stone on every good piece of land and filled it; and they stopped up all the springs of water and cut down all the good trees. But they left the stones of Kir Haraseth *intact*. However the slingers surrounded and attacked it.

26 And when the king of Moab saw that the battle was too fierce for him, he took with him seven hundred men who drew swords, to break through to the king of Edom, but they could not. 27 Then he took his eldest son who would have reigned in his place, and offered him *as* a burnt offering upon the wall; and there was great indignation against Israel. So they departed from him and returned to *their own* land.

Elisha and the Widow's Oil

4 A certain woman of the wives of the sons of the prophets cried out to Elisha, saying, "Your servant my husband is dead, and you know that your servant feared the LORD. And the creditor is coming to take my two sons to be his slaves."

2 So Elisha said to her, "What shall I do for you? Tell me, what do you have in the house?" And she said, "Your maidservant has nothing in the house but a jar of oil."

3 Then he said, "Go, borrow vessels from everywhere, from all your neighbors— empty vessels; do not gather just a few. 4 And when you have come in, you shall shut the door behind you and your sons; then pour it into all those vessels, and set aside the full ones."

5 So she went from him and shut the door behind her and her sons, who brought *the vessels* to her; and she poured *it* out. 6 Now it came to pass, when the vessels were full, that she said to her son, "Bring me another vessel."

And he said to her, "*There is* not another vessel." So the oil ceased. 7 Then she came and told the man of God. And he said, "Go, sell the oil and pay your debt; and you *and* your sons live on the rest."

Elisha Raises the Shunammite's Son

8 Now it happened one day that Elisha went to Shunem, where there *was* a notable woman, and she persuaded him to eat some food. So it was, as often as he passed

by, he would turn in there to eat some food. 9 And she said to her husband, "Look now, I know that this *is* a holy man of God, who passes by us regularly. 10 Please, let us make a small upper room on the wall; and let us put a bed for him there, and a table and a chair and a lampstand; so it will be, whenever he comes to us, he can turn in there."

11 And it happened one day that he came there, and he turned in to the upper room and lay down there. 12 Then he said to Gehazi his servant, "Call this Shunammite woman." When he had called her, she stood before him. 13 And he said to him, "Say now to her, 'Look, you have been concerned for us with all this care. What *can I* do for you? Do you want me to speak on your behalf to the king or to the commander of the army?'"

She answered, "I dwell among my own people."

14 So he said, "What then *is* to be done for her?"

And Gehazi answered, "Actually, she has no son, and her husband is old."

15 So he said, "Call her." When he had called her, she stood in the doorway. 16 Then he said, "About this time next year you shall embrace a son."

And she said, "No, my lord. Man of God, do not lie to your maidservant!"

17 But the woman conceived, and bore a son when the appointed time had come, of which Elisha had told her.

18 And the child grew. Now it happened one day that he went out to his father, to the reapers. 19 And he said to his father, "My head, my head!"

So he said to a servant, "Carry him to his mother." 20 When he had taken him and brought him to his mother, he sat on her knees till noon, and *then* died. 21 And she went up and laid him on the bed of the man of God, shut *the door* upon him, and went out. 22 Then she called to her husband, and said, "Please send me one of the young men and one of the donkeys, that I may run to the man of God and come back."

23 So he said, "Why are you going to him today? *It is* neither the New Moon nor the Sabbath."

And she said, "*It is* well." 24 Then she saddled a donkey, and said to her servant,

"Drive, and go forward; do not slacken the pace for me unless I tell you." [25]And so she departed, and went to the man of God at Mount Carmel.

So it was, when the man of God saw her afar off, that he said to his servant Gehazi, "Look, the Shunammite woman! [26]Please run now to meet her, and say to her, 'Is it well with you? Is it well with your husband? Is it well with the child?'"

And she answered, "It is well." [27]Now when she came to the man of God at the hill, she caught him by the feet, but Gehazi came near to push her away. But the man of God said, "Let her alone; for her soul is in deep distress, and the LORD has hidden it from me, and has not told me."

[28]So she said, "Did I ask a son of my lord? Did I not say, 'Do not deceive me'?"

[29]Then he said to Gehazi, "Get yourself ready, and take my staff in your hand, and be on your way. If you meet anyone, do not greet him; and if anyone greets you, do not answer him; but lay my staff on the face of the child."

[30]And the mother of the child said, "As the LORD lives, and as your soul lives, I will not leave you." So he arose and followed her. [31]Now Gehazi went on ahead of them, and laid the staff on the face of the child; but there was neither voice nor hearing. Therefore he went back to meet him, and told him, saying, "The child has not awakened."

[32]When Elisha came into the house, there was the child, lying dead on his bed. [33]He went in therefore, shut the door behind the two of them, and prayed to the LORD. [34]And he went up and lay on the child, and put his mouth on his mouth, his eyes on his eyes, and his hands on his hands; and he stretched himself out on the child, and the flesh of the child became warm. [35]He returned and walked back and forth in the house, and again went up and stretched himself out on him; then the child sneezed seven times, and the child opened his eyes. [36]And he called Gehazi and said, "Call this Shunammite woman." So he called her. And when she came in to him, he said, "Pick up your son." [37]So she went in, fell at his feet, and bowed to the ground; then she picked up her son and went out.

Elisha Purifies the Pot of Stew

[38]And Elisha returned to Gilgal, and there was a famine in the land. Now the sons of the prophets were sitting before him; and he said to his servant, "Put on the large pot, and boil stew for the sons of the prophets." [39]So one went out into the field to gather herbs, and found a wild vine, and gathered from it a lapful of wild gourds, and came and sliced them into the pot of stew, though they did not know what they were. [40]Then they served it to the men to eat. Now it happened, as they were eating the stew, that they cried out and said, "Man of God, there is death in the pot!" And they could not eat it.

[41]So he said, "Then bring some flour." And he put it into the pot, and said, "Serve it to the people, that they may eat." And there was nothing harmful in the pot.

Elisha Feeds One Hundred Men

[42]Then a man came from Baal Shalisha, and brought the man of God bread of the firstfruits, twenty loaves of barley bread, and newly ripened grain in his knapsack. And he said, "Give it to the people, that they may eat."

[43]But his servant said, "What? Shall I set this before one hundred men?"

He said again, "Give it to the people, that they may eat; for thus says the LORD: 'They shall eat and have some left over.'" [44]So he set it before them; and they ate and had some left over, according to the word of the LORD.

Naaman's Leprosy Healed

5 Now Naaman, commander of the army of the king of Syria, was a great and honorable man in the eyes of his master, because by him the LORD had given victory to Syria. He was also a mighty man of valor, but a leper. [2]And the Syrians had gone out on raids, and had brought back captive a young girl from the land of Israel. She waited on Naaman's wife. [3]Then she said to her mistress, "If only my master were with the prophet who is in Samaria! For he would heal him of his leprosy." [4]And Naaman went in and told his master, saying, "Thus and thus said the girl who is from the land of Israel."

⁵Then the king of Syria said, "Go now, and I will send a letter to the king of Israel."

So he departed and took with him ten talents of silver, six thousand *shekels* of gold, and ten changes of clothing. ⁶Then he brought the letter to the king of Israel, which said,

> Now be advised, when this letter comes to you, that I have sent Naaman my servant to you, that you may heal him of his leprosy.

⁷And it happened, when the king of Israel read the letter, that he tore his clothes and said, "*Am* I God, to kill and make alive, that this man sends a man to me to heal him of his leprosy? Therefore please consider, and see how he seeks a quarrel with me."

⁸So it was, when Elisha the man of God heard that the king of Israel had torn his clothes, that he sent to the king, saying, "Why have you torn your clothes? Please let him come to me, and he shall know that there is a prophet in Israel."

⁹Then Naaman went with his horses and chariot, and he stood at the door of Elisha's house. ¹⁰And Elisha sent a messenger to him, saying, "Go and wash in the Jordan seven times, and your flesh shall be restored to you, and *you shall* be clean." ¹¹But Naaman became furious, and went away and said, "Indeed, I said to myself, 'He will surely come out *to me,* and stand and call on the name of the LORD his God, and wave his hand over the place, and heal the leprosy.' ¹²*Are* not the Abanahᵃ and the Pharpar, the rivers of Damascus, better than all the waters of Israel? Could I not wash in them and be clean?" So he turned and went away in a rage. ¹³And his servants came near and spoke to him, and said, "My father, *if* the prophet had told you *to do* something great, would you not have done *it?* How much more then, when he *says* to you, 'Wash, and be clean'?" ¹⁴So he went down and dipped seven times in the Jordan, according to the saying of the man of God; and his flesh was restored like the flesh of a little child, and he was clean.

¹⁵And he returned to the man of God, he and all his aides, and came and stood before him; and he said, "Indeed, now I know that *there is* no God in all the earth, except in Israel; now therefore, please take a gift from your servant."

¹⁶But he said, "*As* the LORD lives, before whom I stand, I will receive nothing." And he urged him to take *it,* but he refused.

¹⁷So Naaman said, "Then, if not, please let your servant be given two mule-loads of earth; for your servant will no longer offer either burnt offering or sacrifice to other gods, but to the LORD. ¹⁸Yet in this thing may the LORD pardon your servant: when my master goes into the temple of Rimmon to worship there, and he leans on my hand, and I bow down in the temple of Rimmon— when I bow down in the temple of Rimmon, may the LORD please pardon your servant in this thing."

¹⁹Then he said to him, "Go in peace." So he departed from him a short distance.

Gehazi's Greed

²⁰But Gehazi, the servant of Elisha the man of God, said, "Look, my master has spared Naaman this Syrian, while not receiving from his hands what he brought; but *as* the LORD lives, I will run after him and take something from him." ²¹So Gehazi pursued Naaman. When Naaman saw *him* running after him, he got down from the chariot to meet him, and said, "*Is* all well?"

²²And he said, "All *is* well. My master has sent me, saying, 'Indeed, just now two young men of the sons of the prophets have come to me from the mountains of Ephraim. Please give them a talent of silver and two changes of garments.'"

²³So Naaman said, "Please, take two talents." And he urged him, and bound two talents of silver in two bags, with two changes of garments, and handed *them* to two of his servants; and they carried *them* on ahead of him. ²⁴When he came to the citadel, he took *them* from their hand, and stored *them* away in the house; then he let the men go, and they departed. ²⁵Now he went in and stood before his master. Elisha said to him, "Where *did you go,* Gehazi?"

5:12 ᵃFollowing Kethib, Septuagint, and Vulgate; Qere, Syriac, and Targum read *Amanah.*

And he said, "Your servant did not go anywhere."

²⁶Then he said to him, "Did not my heart go *with you* when the man turned back from his chariot to meet you? *Is it* time to receive money and to receive clothing, olive groves and vineyards, sheep and oxen, male and female servants? ²⁷Therefore the leprosy of Naaman shall cling to you and your descendants forever." And he went out from his presence leprous, *as white* as snow.

The Floating Ax Head

6 And the sons of the prophets said to Elisha, "See now, the place where we dwell with you is too small for us. ²Please, let us go to the Jordan, and let every man take a beam from there, and let us make there a place where we may dwell."

So he answered, "Go."

³Then one said, "Please consent to go with your servants."

And he answered, "I will go." ⁴So he went with them. And when they came to the Jordan, they cut down trees. ⁵But as one was cutting down a tree, the iron *ax head* fell into the water; and he cried out and said, "Alas, master! For it was borrowed."

⁶So the man of God said, "Where did it fall?" And he showed him the place. So he cut off a stick, and threw *it* in there; and he made the iron float. ⁷Therefore he said, "Pick *it* up for yourself." So he reached out his hand and took it.

The Blinded Syrians Captured

⁸Now the king of Syria was making war against Israel; and he consulted with his servants, saying, "My camp *will be* in such and such a place." ⁹And the man of God sent to the king of Israel, saying, "Beware that you do not pass this place, for the Syrians are coming down there." ¹⁰Then the king of Israel sent *someone* to the place of which the man of God had told him. Thus he warned him, and he was watchful there, not just once or twice.

¹¹Therefore the heart of the king of Syria was greatly troubled by this thing; and he called his servants and said to them, "Will you not show me which of us *is* for the king of Israel?"

¹²And one of his servants said, "None, my lord, O king; but Elisha, the prophet who *is* in Israel, tells the king of Israel the words that you speak in your bedroom."

¹³So he said, "Go and see where he *is*, that I may send and get him."

And it was told him, saying, "Surely *he is* in Dothan."

¹⁴Therefore he sent horses and chariots and a great army there, and they came by night and surrounded the city. ¹⁵And when the servant of the man of God arose early and went out, there was an army, surrounding the city with horses and chariots. And his servant said to him, "Alas, my master! What shall we do?"

¹⁶So he answered, "Do not fear, for those who *are* with us *are* more than those who *are* with them." ¹⁷And Elisha prayed, and said, "Lord, I pray, open his eyes that he may see." Then the Lord opened the eyes of the young man, and he saw. And behold, the mountain *was* full of horses and chariots of fire all around Elisha. ¹⁸So when *the Syrians* came down to him, Elisha prayed to the Lord, and said, "Strike this people, I pray, with blindness." And He struck them with blindness according to the word of Elisha.

¹⁹Now Elisha said to them, "This *is* not the way, nor *is* this the city. Follow me, and I will bring you to the man whom you seek." But he led them to Samaria.

²⁰So it was, when they had come to Samaria, that Elisha said, "Lord, open the eyes of these *men,* that they may see." And the Lord opened their eyes, and they saw; and there *they were,* inside Samaria!

²¹Now when the king of Israel saw them, he said to Elisha, "My father, shall I kill *them?* Shall I kill *them?*"

²²But he answered, "You shall not kill *them.* Would you kill those whom you have taken captive with your sword and your bow? Set food and water before them, that they may eat and drink and go to their master." ²³Then he prepared a great feast for them; and after they ate and drank, he sent them away and they went to their master. So the bands of Syrian *raiders* came no more into the land of Israel.

Syria Besieges Samaria in Famine

24And it happened after this that Ben-Hadad king of Syria gathered all his army, and went up and besieged Samaria. 25And there was a great famine in Samaria; and indeed they besieged it until a donkey's head was *sold* for eighty *shekels* of silver, and one-fourth of a kab of dove droppings for five *shekels* of silver.

26Then, as the king of Israel was passing by on the wall, a woman cried out to him, saying, "Help, my lord, O king!"

27And he said, "If the LORD does not help you, where can I find help for you? From the threshing floor or from the winepress?" 28Then the king said to her, "What is troubling you?"

And she answered, "This woman said to me, 'Give your son, that we may eat him today, and we will eat my son tomorrow.' 29So we boiled my son, and ate him. And I said to her on the next day, 'Give your son, that we may eat him'; but she has hidden her son."

30Now it happened, when the king heard the words of the woman, that he tore his clothes; and as he passed by on the wall, the people looked, and there underneath *he had* sackcloth on his body. 31Then he said, "God do so to me and more also, if the head of Elisha the son of Shaphat remains on him today!"

32But Elisha was sitting in his house, and the elders were sitting with him. And *the king* sent a man ahead of him, but before the messenger came to him, he said to the elders, "Do you see how this son of a murderer has sent someone to take away my head? Look, when the messenger comes, shut the door, and hold him fast at the door. *Is* not the sound of his master's feet behind him?" 33And while he was still talking with them, there was the messenger, coming down to him; and then *the king* said, "Surely this calamity *is* from the LORD; why should I wait for the LORD any longer?"

7 Then Elisha said, "Hear the word of the LORD. Thus says the LORD: 'Tomorrow about this time a seah of fine flour *shall be sold* for a shekel, and two seahs of barley for a shekel, at the gate of Samaria.'"

2So an officer on whose hand the king leaned answered the man of God and said, "Look, *if* the LORD would make windows in heaven, could this thing be?"

And he said, "In fact, you shall see *it* with your eyes, but you shall not eat of it."

The Syrians Flee

3Now there were four leprous men at the entrance of the gate; and they said to one another, "Why are we sitting here until we die? 4If we say, 'We will enter the city,' the famine *is* in the city, and we shall die there. And if we sit here, we die also. Now therefore, come, let us surrender to the army of the Syrians. If they keep us alive, we shall live; and if they kill us, we shall only die." 5And they rose at twilight to go to the camp of the Syrians; and when they had come to the outskirts of the Syrian camp, to their surprise no one *was* there. 6For the Lord had caused the army of the Syrians to hear the noise of chariots and the noise of horses—the noise of a great army; so they said to one another, "Look, the king of Israel has hired against us the kings of the Hittites and the kings of the Egyptians to attack us!" 7Therefore they arose and fled at twilight, and left the camp intact—their tents, their horses, and their donkeys—and they fled for their lives. 8And when these lepers came to the outskirts of the camp, they went into one tent and ate and drank, and carried from it silver and gold and clothing, and went and hid *them;* then they came back and entered another tent, and carried *some* from there *also,* and went and hid *it.*

9Then they said to one another, "We are not doing right. This day *is* a day of good news, and we remain silent. If we wait until morning light, some punishment will come upon us. Now therefore, come, let us go and tell the king's household." 10So they went and called to the gatekeepers of the city, and told them, saying, "We went to the Syrian camp, and surprisingly no one *was* there, not a human sound—only horses and donkeys tied, and the tents intact." 11And the gatekeepers called out, and they told *it* to the king's household inside.

12So the king arose in the night and said to his servants, "Let me now tell you what

"THE STAR-SPANGLED BANNER"

FREEDOM

"Look, if the LORD would make windows in heaven, could this thing be?"

2 KINGS 7:2

During the War of 1812, the British navy unleashed a fierce bombardment on Fort McHenry from the Baltimore harbor. On September 13, 1814, a young American lawyer named Francis Scott Key watched the relentless bombing throughout the night, then silence followed. Had the fort been forced to surrender? As the first rays of sunlight broke the darkness, Key could see the American flag waving proudly. In the inspiration of the moment, he began a poem titled "Defence of Fort McHenry," which was set to a popular tune and renamed "The Star-Spangled Banner." It became a well-known American patriotic song and was eventually made the national anthem by a congressional resolution on March 3, 1931. More than just a song, it expresses one man's deep gratitude for America's freedom and godly foundation.

O! say can you see by the dawn's early light
What so proudly we hailed at the twilight's last gleaming?
Whose broad stripes and bright stars through the perilous fight,
O'er the ramparts we watched were so gallantly streaming?
And the rockets' red glare, the bombs bursting in air,
Gave proof through the night that our flag was still there.
Oh, say does that star-spangled banner yet wave
O'er the land of the free and the home of the brave?

On the shore, dimly seen through the mists of the deep,
Where the foe's haughty host in dread silence reposes,
What is that which the breeze, o'er the towering steep,
As it fitfully blows, half conceals, half discloses?
Now it catches the gleam of the morning's first beam,
In full glory reflected now shines in the stream:
'Tis the star-spangled banner! Oh long may it wave
O'er the land of the free and the home of the brave!

O! thus be it ever, when freemen shall stand
Between their loved home and the war's desolation!
Blest with victory and peace, may the heav'n rescued land
Praise the Power that hath made and preserved us a nation.
Then conquer we must, when our cause it is just,
And this be our motto: "In God is our trust."
And the star-spangled banner in triumph shall wave
O'er the land of the free and the home of the brave!

(The third stanza is not included.)

the Syrians have done to us. They know that we *are* hungry; therefore they have gone out of the camp to hide themselves in the field, saying, 'When they come out of the city, we shall catch them alive, and get into the city.' "

¹³And one of his servants answered and said, "Please, let several *men* take five of the remaining horses which are left in the city. Look, they *may either become* like all the multitude of Israel that are left in it; or indeed, *I say,* they *may become* like all the multitude of Israel left from those who are consumed; so let us send them and see." ¹⁴Therefore they took two chariots with horses; and the king sent them in the direction of the Syrian army, saying, "Go and see." ¹⁵And they went after them to the Jordan; and indeed all the road *was* full of garments and weapons which the Syrians had thrown away in their haste. So the messengers returned and told the king. ¹⁶Then the people went out and plundered the tents of the Syrians. So a seah of fine flour was *sold* for a shekel, and two seahs of barley for a shekel, according to the word of the LORD.

¹⁷Now the king had appointed the officer on whose hand he leaned to have charge of the gate. But the people trampled him in the gate, and he died, just as the man of God had said, who spoke when the king came down to him. ¹⁸So it happened just as the man of God had spoken to the king, saying, "Two seahs of barley for a shekel, and a seah of fine flour for a shekel, shall be *sold* tomorrow about this time in the gate of Samaria."

¹⁹Then that officer had answered the man of God, and said, "Now look, *if* the LORD would make windows in heaven, could such a thing be?"

And he had said, "In fact, you shall see *it* with your eyes, but you shall not eat of it." ²⁰And so it happened to him, for the people trampled him in the gate, and he died.

The King Restores the Shunammite's Land

8 Then Elisha spoke to the woman whose son he had restored to life, saying, "Arise and go, you and your household, and stay wherever you can; for the LORD has called for a famine, and furthermore, it will come upon the land for seven years." ²So the woman arose and did according to the saying of the man of God, and she went with her household and dwelt in the land of the Philistines seven years.

³It came to pass, at the end of seven years, that the woman returned from the land of the Philistines; and she went to make an appeal to the king for her house and for her land. ⁴Then the king talked with Gehazi, the servant of the man of God, saying, "Tell me, please, all the great things Elisha has done." ⁵Now it happened, as he was telling the king how he had restored the dead to life, that there was the woman whose son he had restored to life, appealing to the king for her house and for her land. And Gehazi said, "My lord, O king, this *is* the woman, and this *is* her son whom Elisha restored to life." ⁶And when the king asked the woman, she told him.

So the king appointed a certain officer for her, saying, "Restore all that *was* hers, and all the proceeds of the field from the day that she left the land until now."

Death of Ben-Hadad

⁷Then Elisha went to Damascus, and Ben-Hadad king of Syria was sick; and it was told him, saying, "The man of God has come here." ⁸And the king said to Hazael, "Take a present in your hand, and go to meet the man of God, and inquire of the LORD by him, saying, 'Shall I recover from this disease?'" ⁹So Hazael went to meet him and took a present with him, of every good thing of Damascus, forty camel-loads; and he came and stood before him, and said, "Your son Ben-Hadad king of Syria has sent me to you, saying, 'Shall I recover from this disease?'"

¹⁰And Elisha said to him, "Go, say to him, 'You shall certainly recover.' However the LORD has shown me that he will really die." ¹¹Then he set his countenance in a stare until he was ashamed; and the man of God wept. ¹²And Hazael said, "Why is my lord weeping?"

He answered, "Because I know the evil that you will do to the children of Israel: Their strongholds you will set on fire, and their young men you will kill with the

sword; and you will dash their children, and rip open their women with child."

¹³So Hazael said, "But what *is* your servant—a dog, that he should do this gross thing?"

And Elisha answered, "The LORD has shown me that you *will become* king over Syria."

¹⁴Then he departed from Elisha, and came to his master, who said to him, "What did Elisha say to you?" And he answered, "He told me you would surely recover." ¹⁵But it happened on the next day that he took a thick cloth and dipped *it* in water, and spread *it* over his face so that he died; and Hazael reigned in his place.

Jehoram Reigns in Judah

¹⁶Now in the fifth year of Joram the son of Ahab, king of Israel, Jehoshaphat *having been* king of Judah, Jehoram the son of Jehoshaphat began to reign as king of Judah. ¹⁷He was thirty-two years old when he became king, and he reigned eight years in Jerusalem. ¹⁸And he walked in the way of the kings of Israel, just as the house of Ahab had done, for the daughter of Ahab was his wife; and he did evil in the sight of the LORD. ¹⁹Yet the LORD would not destroy Judah, for the sake of His servant David, as He promised him to give a lamp to him *and* his sons forever.

²⁰In his days Edom revolted against Judah's authority, and made a king over themselves. ²¹So Joramᵃ went to Zair, and all his chariots with him. Then he rose by night and attacked the Edomites who had surrounded him and the captains of the chariots; and the troops fled to their tents. ²²Thus Edom has been in revolt against Judah's authority to this day. And Libnah revolted at that time.

²³Now the rest of the acts of Joram, and all that he did, *are* they not written in the book of the chronicles of the kings of Judah? ²⁴So Joram rested with his fathers, and was buried with his fathers in the City of David. Then Ahaziah his son reigned in his place.

Ahaziah Reigns in Judah

²⁵In the twelfth year of Joram the son of Ahab, king of Israel, Ahaziah the son of Jehoram, king of Judah, began to reign. ²⁶Ahaziah *was* twenty-two years old when he became king, and he reigned one year in Jerusalem. His mother's name *was* Athaliah the granddaughter of Omri, king of Israel. ²⁷And he walked in the way of the house of Ahab, and did evil in the sight of the LORD, like the house of Ahab, for he *was* the son-in-law of the house of Ahab.

²⁸Now he went with Joram the son of Ahab to war against Hazael king of Syria at Ramoth Gilead; and the Syrians wounded Joram. ²⁹Then King Joram went back to Jezreel to recover from the wounds which the Syrians had inflicted on him at Ramah, when he fought against Hazael king of Syria. And Ahaziah the son of Jehoram, king of Judah, went down to see Joram the son of Ahab in Jezreel, because he was sick.

Jehu Anointed King of Israel

9 And Elisha the prophet called one of the sons of the prophets, and said to him, "Get yourself ready, take this flask of oil in your hand, and go to Ramoth Gilead. ²Now when you arrive at that place, look there for Jehu the son of Jehoshaphat, the son of Nimshi, and go in and make him rise up from among his associates, and take him to an inner room. ³Then take the flask of oil, and pour *it* on his head, and say, 'Thus says the LORD: "I have anointed you king over Israel."' Then open the door and flee, and do not delay."

⁴So the young man, the servant of the prophet, went to Ramoth Gilead. ⁵And when he arrived, there *were* the captains of the army sitting; and he said, "I have a message for you, Commander."

Jehu said, "For which *one* of us?"

And he said, "For you, Commander." ⁶Then he arose and went into the house. And he poured the oil on his head, and said to him, "Thus says the LORD God of Israel: 'I have anointed you king over the people of the LORD, over Israel. ⁷You shall strike down the house of Ahab your master, that I may avenge the blood of My servants the prophets, and the blood of all the servants of the LORD, at the hand of Jezebel. ⁸For the

---

8:21 ᵃSpelled *Jehoram* in verse 16

whole house of Ahab shall perish; and I will cut off from Ahab all the males in Israel, both bond and free. ⁹So I will make the house of Ahab like the house of Jeroboam the son of Nebat, and like the house of Baasha the son of Ahijah. ¹⁰The dogs shall eat Jezebel on the plot *of ground* at Jezreel, and *there shall be* none to bury *her.*'" And he opened the door and fled.

¹¹Then Jehu came out to the servants of his master, and *one* said to him, "*Is* all well? Why did this madman come to you?"

And he said to them, "You know the man and his babble."

¹²And they said, "A lie! Tell us now."

So he said, "Thus and thus he spoke to me, saying, 'Thus says the LORD: "I have anointed you king over Israel."'"

¹³Then each man hastened to take his garment and put *it* under him on the top of the steps; and they blew trumpets, saying, "Jehu is king!"

Joram of Israel Killed

¹⁴So Jehu the son of Jehoshaphat, the son of Nimshi, conspired against Joram. (Now Joram had been defending Ramoth Gilead, he and all Israel, against Hazael king of Syria. ¹⁵But King Joram had returned to Jezreel to recover from the wounds which the Syrians had inflicted on him when he fought with Hazael king of Syria.) And Jehu said, "If you are so minded, let no one leave *or* escape from the city to go and tell *it* in Jezreel." ¹⁶So Jehu rode in a chariot and went to Jezreel, for Joram was laid up there; and Ahaziah king of Judah had come down to see Joram.

¹⁷Now a watchman stood on the tower in Jezreel, and he saw the company of Jehu as he came, and said, "I see a company of men."

And Joram said, "Get a horseman and send him to meet them, and let him say, '*Is it* peace?'"

¹⁸So the horseman went to meet him, and said, "Thus says the king: '*Is it* peace?'"

And Jehu said, "What have you to do with peace? Turn around and follow me."

So the watchman reported, saying, "The messenger went to them, but is not coming back."

¹⁹Then he sent out a second horseman who came to them, and said, "Thus says the king: '*Is it* peace?'"

And Jehu answered, "What have you to do with peace? Turn around and follow me."

²⁰So the watchman reported, saying, "He went up to them and is not coming back; and the driving *is* like the driving of Jehu the son of Nimshi, for he drives furiously!"

²¹Then Joram said, "Make ready." And his chariot was made ready. Then Joram king of Israel and Ahaziah king of Judah went out, each in his chariot; and they went out to meet Jehu, and met him on the property of Naboth the Jezreelite. ²²Now it happened, when Joram saw Jehu, that he said, "*Is it* peace, Jehu?"

So he answered, "What peace, as long as the harlotries of your mother Jezebel and her witchcraft *are so* many?"

²³Then Joram turned around and fled, and said to Ahaziah, "Treachery, Ahaziah!" ²⁴Now Jehu drew his bow with full strength and shot Jehoram between his arms; and the arrow came out at his heart, and he sank down in his chariot. ²⁵Then *Jehu* said to Bidkar his captain, "Pick *him* up, *and* throw him into the tract of the field of Naboth the Jezreelite; for remember, when you and I were riding together behind Ahab his father, that the LORD laid this burden upon him: ²⁶'Surely I saw yesterday the blood of Naboth and the blood of his sons,' says the LORD, 'and I will repay you in this plot,' says the LORD. Now therefore, take *and* throw him on the plot *of ground,* according to the word of the LORD."

Ahaziah of Judah Killed

²⁷But when Ahaziah king of Judah saw *this,* he fled by the road to Beth Haggan.ᵃ So Jehu pursued him, and said, "Shoot him also in the chariot." *And they shot him* at the Ascent of Gur, which is by Ibleam. Then he fled to Megiddo, and died there. ²⁸And his servants carried him in the chariot to Jerusalem, and buried him in his tomb with his fathers in the City of David. ²⁹In the eleventh year of Joram the son of Ahab, Ahaziah had become king over Judah.

9:27 ᵃLiterally *The Garden House*

Jezebel's Violent Death

³⁰Now when Jehu had come to Jezreel, Jezebel heard *of it;* and she put paint on her eyes and adorned her head, and looked through a window. ³¹Then, as Jehu entered at the gate, she said, "*Is it* peace, Zimri, murderer of your master?"

³²And he looked up at the window, and said, "Who *is* on my side? Who?" So two *or* three eunuchs looked out at him. ³³Then he said, "Throw her down." So they threw her down, and *some* of her blood spattered on the wall and on the horses; and he trampled her underfoot. ³⁴And when he had gone in, he ate and drank. Then he said, "Go now, see to this accursed *woman,* and bury her, for she was a king's daughter." ³⁵So they went to bury her, but they found no more of her than the skull and the feet and the palms of *her* hands. ³⁶Therefore they came back and told him. And he said, "This *is* the word of the Lᴏʀᴅ, which He spoke by His servant Elijah the Tishbite, saying, 'On the plot *of ground* at Jezreel dogs shall eat the flesh of Jezebel;ᵃ ³⁷and the corpse of Jezebel shall be as refuse on the surface of the field, in the plot at Jezreel, so that they shall not say, "Here *lies* Jezebel." ' "

Ahab's Seventy Sons Killed

10 Now Ahab had seventy sons in Samaria. And Jehu wrote and sent letters to Samaria, to the rulers of Jezreel,ᵃ to the elders, and to those who reared Ahab's *sons,* saying:

² Now as soon as this letter comes to you, since your master's sons *are* with you, and you have chariots and horses, a fortified city also, and weapons, ³choose the best qualified of your master's sons, set *him* on his father's throne, and fight for your master's house.

⁴But they were exceedingly afraid, and said, "Look, two kings could not stand up to him; how then can we stand?" ⁵And he who *was* in charge of the house, and he who *was* in charge of the city, the elders also, and those who reared *the sons,* sent to Jehu, saying, "We *are* your servants, we will do all you tell us; but we will not make anyone king. Do *what is* good in your sight." ⁶Then he wrote a second letter to them, saying:

If you *are* for me and will obey my
voice, take the heads of the men,
your master's sons, and come to me
at Jezreel by this time tomorrow.

Now the king's sons, seventy persons, *were* with the great men of the city, *who* were rearing them. ⁷So it was, when the letter came to them, that they took the king's sons and slaughtered seventy persons, put their heads in baskets and sent *them* to him at Jezreel.

⁸Then a messenger came and told him, saying, "They have brought the heads of the king's sons."

And he said, "Lay them in two heaps at the entrance of the gate until morning."

⁹So it was, in the morning, that he went out and stood, and said to all the people, "You *are* righteous. Indeed I conspired against my master and killed him; but who killed all these? ¹⁰Know now that nothing shall fall to the earth of the word of the Lᴏʀᴅ which the Lᴏʀᴅ spoke concerning the house of Ahab; for the Lᴏʀᴅ has done what He spoke by His servant Elijah." ¹¹So Jehu killed all who remained of the house of Ahab in Jezreel, and all his great men and his close acquaintances and his priests, until he left him none remaining.

Ahaziah's Forty-two Brothers Killed

¹²And he arose and departed and went to Samaria. On the way, at Beth Ekedᵃ of the Shepherds, ¹³Jehu met with the brothers of Ahaziah king of Judah, and said, "Who *are* you?"

So they answered, "We *are* the brothers of Ahaziah; we have come down to greet the sons of the king and the sons of the queen mother."

¹⁴And he said, "Take them alive!" So they took them alive, and killed them at the well

9:36 ᵃ1 Kings 21:23   **10:1** ᵃFollowing Masoretic Text, Syriac, and Targum; Septuagint reads *Samaria;* Vulgate reads *city.*   **10:12** ᵃOr *The Shearing House*

of Beth Eked, forty-two men; and he left none of them.

The Rest of Ahab's Family Killed

15Now when he departed from there, he met Jehonadab the son of Rechab, *coming* to meet him; and he greeted him and said to him, "Is your heart right, as my heart *is* toward your heart?"

And Jehonadab answered, "It is."

Jehu said, "If it is, give *me* your hand." So he gave *him* his hand, and he took him up to him into the chariot. 16Then he said, "Come with me, and see my zeal for the Lord." So they had him ride in his chariot. 17And when he came to Samaria, he killed all who remained to Ahab in Samaria, till he had destroyed them, according to the word of the Lord which He spoke to Elijah.

Worshipers of Baal Killed

18Then Jehu gathered all the people together, and said to them, "Ahab served Baal a little, Jehu will serve him much. 19Now therefore, call to me all the prophets of Baal, all his servants, and all his priests. Let no one be missing, for I have a great sacrifice for Baal. Whoever is missing shall not live." But Jehu acted deceptively, with the intent of destroying the worshipers of Baal. 20And Jehu said, "Proclaim a solemn assembly for Baal." So they proclaimed *it.* 21Then Jehu sent throughout all Israel; and all the worshipers of Baal came, so that there was not a man left who did not come. So they came into the templeᵃ of Baal, and the temple of Baal was full from one end to the other. 22And he said to the one in charge of the wardrobe, "Bring out vestments for all the worshipers of Baal." So he brought out vestments for them. 23Then Jehu and Jehonadab the son of Rechab went into the temple of Baal, and said to the worshipers of Baal, "Search and see that no servants of the Lord are here with you, but only the worshipers of Baal." 24So they went in to offer sacrifices and burnt offerings. Now Jehu had appointed for himself eighty men on the outside, and had said, "*If* any of the men whom I have brought into your hands escapes, *whoever lets him escape, it shall be* his life for the life of the other."

25Now it happened, as soon as he had made an end of offering the burnt offering, that Jehu said to the guard and to the captains, "Go in *and* kill them; let no one come out!" And they killed them with the edge of the sword; then the guards and the officers threw *them* out, and went into the inner room of the temple of Baal. 26And they brought the *sacred* pillars out of the temple of Baal and burned them. 27Then they broke down the *sacred* pillar of Baal, and tore down the temple of Baal and made it a refuse dump to this day. 28Thus Jehu destroyed Baal from Israel.

29However Jehu did not turn away from the sins of Jeroboam the son of Nebat, who had made Israel sin, *that is,* from the golden calves that *were* at Bethel and Dan. 30And the Lord said to Jehu, "Because you have done well in doing *what is* right in My sight, *and* have done to the house of Ahab all that *was* in My heart, your sons shall sit on the throne of Israel to the fourth *generation.*" 31But Jehu took no heed to walk in the law of the Lord God of Israel with all his heart; for he did not depart from the sins of Jeroboam, who had made Israel sin.

Death of Jehu

32In those days the Lord began to cut off *parts* of Israel; and Hazael conquered them in all the territory of Israel 33from the Jordan eastward: all the land of Gilead—Gad, Reuben, and Manasseh—from Aroer, which *is* by the River Arnon, including Gilead and Bashan. 34Now the rest of the acts of Jehu, all that he did, and all his might, *are* they not written in the book of the chronicles of the kings of Israel? 35So Jehu rested with his fathers, and they buried him in Samaria. Then Jehoahaz his son reigned in his place. 36And the period that Jehu reigned over Israel in Samaria *was* twenty-eight years.

Athaliah Reigns in Judah

11 When Athaliah the mother of Ahaziah saw that her son was dead, she arose and destroyed all the royal heirs. 2But Jehosheba, the daughter of King Joram,

---

10:21 ᵃLiterally *house,* and so elsewhere in this chapter

sister of Ahaziah, took Joash the son of Ahaziah, and stole him away from among the king's sons *who were* being murdered; and they hid him and his nurse in the bedroom, from Athaliah, so that he was not killed. ³So he was hidden with her in the house of the LORD for six years, while Athaliah reigned over the land.

Joash Crowned King of Judah

⁴In the seventh year Jehoiada sent and brought the captains of hundreds—of the bodyguards and the escorts—and brought them into the house of the LORD to him. And he made a covenant with them and took an oath from them in the house of the LORD, and showed them the king's son. ⁵Then he commanded them, saying, "This *is* what you shall do: One-third of you who come on duty on the Sabbath shall be keeping watch over the king's house, ⁶one-third *shall be* at the gate of Sur, and one-third at the gate behind the escorts. You shall keep the watch of the house, lest it be broken down. ⁷The two contingents of you who go off duty on the Sabbath shall keep the watch of the house of the LORD for the king. ⁸But you shall surround the king on all sides, every man with his weapons in his hand; and whoever comes within range, let him be put to death. You are to be with the king as he goes out and as he comes in."

⁹So the captains of the hundreds did according to all that Jehoiada the priest commanded. Each of them took his men who were to be on duty on the Sabbath, with those who were going off duty on the Sabbath, and came to Jehoiada the priest. ¹⁰And the priest gave the captains of hundreds the spears and shields which *had belonged* to King David, that were in the temple of the LORD. ¹¹Then the escorts stood, every man with his weapons in his hand, all around the king, from the right side of the temple to the left side of the temple, by the altar and the house. ¹²And he brought out the king's son, put the crown on him, and *gave him* the Testimony;ᵃ they made him king and anointed him, and they clapped their hands and said, "Long live the king!"

Death of Athaliah

¹³Now when Athaliah heard the noise of the escorts *and* the people, she came to the people *in* the temple of the LORD. ¹⁴When she looked, there was the king standing by a pillar according to custom; and the leaders and the trumpeters were by the king. All the people of the land were rejoicing and blowing trumpets. So Athaliah tore her clothes and cried out, "Treason! Treason!"

¹⁵And Jehoiada the priest commanded the captains of the hundreds, the officers of the army, and said to them, "Take her outside under guard, and slay with the sword whoever follows her." For the priest had said, "Do not let her be killed in the house of the LORD." ¹⁶So they seized her; and she went by way of the horses' entrance *into* the king's house, and there she was killed.

¹⁷Then Jehoiada made a covenant between the LORD, the king, and the people, that they should be the LORD's people, and *also* between the king and the people. ¹⁸And all the people of the land went to the temple of Baal, and tore it down. They thoroughly broke in pieces its altars and images, and killed Mattan the priest of Baal before the altars. And the priest appointed officers over the house of the LORD. ¹⁹Then he took the captains of hundreds, the bodyguards, the escorts, and all the people of the land; and they brought the king down from the house of the LORD, and went by way of the gate of the escorts to the king's house. Then he sat on the throne of the kings. ²⁰So all the people of the land rejoiced; and the city was quiet, for they had slain Athaliah with the sword *in* the king's house. ²¹Jehoash *was* seven years old when he became king.

Jehoash Repairs the Temple

12 In the seventh year of Jehu, Jehoashᵃ became king, and he reigned forty years in Jerusalem. His mother's name *was* Zibiah of Beersheba. ²Jehoash did *what was* right in the sight of the LORD all the days in which Jehoiada the priest instructed him. ³But the high places were not taken away;

11:12 ᵃThat is, the Law (compare Exodus 25:16, 21 and Deuteronomy 31:9)   **12:1** ᵃSpelled *Joash* in 11:2ff

the people still sacrificed and burned incense on the high places.

⁴And Jehoash said to the priests, "All the money of the dedicated gifts that are brought into the house of the LORD—each man's census money, each man's assessment moneyᵃ—*and* all the money that a man purposes in his heart to bring into the house of the LORD, ⁵let the priests take *it* themselves, each from his constituency; and let them repair the damages of the temple, wherever any dilapidation is found."

⁶Now it was so, by the twenty-third year of King Jehoash, *that* the priests had not repaired the damages of the temple. ⁷So King Jehoash called Jehoiada the priest and the *other* priests, and said to them, "Why have you not repaired the damages of the temple? Now therefore, do not take *more* money from your constituency, but deliver it for repairing the damages of the temple." ⁸And the priests agreed that they would neither receive *more* money from the people, nor repair the damages of the temple.

⁹Then Jehoiada the priest took a chest, bored a hole in its lid, and set it beside the altar, on the right side as one comes into the house of the LORD; and the priests who kept the door put there all the money brought into the house of the LORD. ¹⁰So it was, whenever they saw that *there was* much money in the chest, that the king's scribe and the high priest came up and put it in bags, and counted the money that was found in the house of the LORD. ¹¹Then they gave the money, which had been apportioned, into the hands of those who did the work, who had the oversight of the house of the LORD; and they paid it out to the carpenters and builders who worked on the house of the LORD, ¹²and to masons and stonecutters, and for buying timber and hewn stone, to repair the damage of the house of the LORD, and for all that was paid out to repair the temple. ¹³However there were not made for the house of the LORD basins of silver, trimmers, sprinkling-bowls, trumpets, any articles of gold or articles of silver, from the money brought into the house of the LORD. ¹⁴But they gave that to the workmen, and they repaired the house of the LORD with it. ¹⁵Moreover they did not

require an account from the men into whose hand they delivered the money to be paid to workmen, for they dealt faithfully. ¹⁶The money from the trespass offerings and the money from the sin offerings was not brought into the house of the LORD. It belonged to the priests.

Hazael Threatens Jerusalem

¹⁷Hazael king of Syria went up and fought against Gath, and took it; then Hazael set his face to go up to Jerusalem. ¹⁸And Jehoash king of Judah took all the sacred things that his fathers, Jehoshaphat and Jehoram and Ahaziah, kings of Judah, had dedicated, and his own sacred things, and all the gold found in the treasuries of the house of the LORD and in the king's house, and sent *them* to Hazael king of Syria. Then he went away from Jerusalem.

Death of Joash

¹⁹Now the rest of the acts of Joash,ᵃ and all that he did, *are* they not written in the book of the chronicles of the kings of Judah? ²⁰And his servants arose and formed a conspiracy, and killed Joash in the house of the Millo,ᵃ which goes down to Silla. ²¹For Jozacharᵃ the son of Shimeath and Jehozabad the son of Shomer,ᵇ his servants, struck him. So he died, and they buried him with his fathers in the City of David. Then Amaziah his son reigned in his place.

Jehoahaz Reigns in Israel

13 In the twenty-third year of Joashᵃ the son of Ahaziah, king of Judah, Jehoahaz the son of Jehu became king over Israel in Samaria, *and reigned* seventeen years. ²And he did evil in the sight of the LORD, and followed the sins of Jeroboam the son of Nebat, who had made Israel sin. He did not depart from them.

³Then the anger of the LORD was aroused against Israel, and He delivered them into the hand of Hazael king of Syria, and into the hand of Ben-Hadad the son of Hazael,

---

12:4 ᵃCompare Leviticus 27:2ff   12:19 ᵃSpelled *Jehoash* in 12:1ff   12:20 ᵃLiterally *The Landfill* 12:21 ᵃCalled *Zabad* in 2 Chronicles 24:26 ᵇCalled *Shimrith* in 2 Chronicles 24:26   13:1 ᵃSpelled *Jehoash* in 12:1ff

all *their* days. ⁴So Jehoahaz pleaded with the LORD, and the LORD listened to him; for He saw the oppression of Israel, because the king of Syria oppressed them. ⁵Then the LORD gave Israel a deliverer, so that they escaped from under the hand of the Syrians; and the children of Israel dwelt in their tents as before. ⁶Nevertheless they did not depart from the sins of the house of Jeroboam, who had made Israel sin, *but* walked in them; and the wooden imageᵃ also remained in Samaria. ⁷For He left of the army of Jehoahaz only fifty horsemen, ten chariots, and ten thousand foot soldiers; for the king of Syria had destroyed them and made them like the dust at threshing.

⁸Now the rest of the acts of Jehoahaz, all that he did, and his might, *are* they not written in the book of the chronicles of the kings of Israel? ⁹So Jehoahaz rested with his fathers, and they buried him in Samaria. Then Joash his son reigned in his place.

Jehoash Reigns in Israel

¹⁰In the thirty-seventh year of Joash king of Judah, Jehoashᵃ the son of Jehoahaz became king over Israel in Samaria, *and* reigned sixteen years. ¹¹And he did evil in the sight of the LORD. He did not depart from all the sins of Jeroboam the son of Nebat, who made Israel sin, *but* walked in them.

¹²Now the rest of the acts of Joash, all that he did, and his might with which he fought against Amaziah king of Judah, *are* they not written in the book of the chronicles of the kings of Israel? ¹³So Joash rested with his fathers. Then Jeroboam sat on his throne. And Joash was buried in Samaria with the kings of Israel.

Death of Elisha

¹⁴Elisha had become sick with the illness of which he would die. Then Joash the king of Israel came down to him, and wept over his face, and said, "O my father, my father, the chariots of Israel and their horsemen!" ¹⁵And Elisha said to him, "Take a bow and some arrows." So he took himself a bow and some arrows. ¹⁶Then he said to the king of Israel, "Put your hand on the bow." So he put his hand *on it,* and Elisha put his hands on the king's hands. ¹⁷And he said, "Open

the east window"; and he opened *it.* Then Elisha said, "Shoot"; and he shot. And he said, "The arrow of the LORD's deliverance and the arrow of deliverance from Syria; for you must strike the Syrians at Aphek till you have destroyed *them.*" ¹⁸Then he said, "Take the arrows"; so he took *them.* And he said to the king of Israel, "Strike the ground"; so he struck three times, and stopped. ¹⁹And the man of God was angry with him, and said, "You should have struck five or six times; then you would have struck Syria till you had destroyed *it!* But now you will strike Syria *only* three times."

²⁰Then Elisha died, and they buried him. And the *raiding* bands from Moab invaded the land in the spring of the year. ²¹So it was, as they were burying a man, that suddenly they spied a band *of raiders;* and they put the man in the tomb of Elisha; and when the man was let down and touched the bones of Elisha, he revived and stood on his feet.

Israel Recaptures Cities from Syria

²²And Hazael king of Syria oppressed Israel all the days of Jehoahaz. ²³But the LORD was gracious to them, had compassion on them, and regarded them, because of His covenant with Abraham, Isaac, and Jacob, and would not yet destroy them or cast them from His presence.

²⁴Now Hazael king of Syria died. Then Ben-Hadad his son reigned in his place. ²⁵And Jehoashᵃ the son of Jehoahaz recaptured from the hand of Ben-Hadad, the son of Hazael, the cities which he had taken out of the hand of Jehoahaz his father by war. Three times Joash defeated him and recaptured the cities of Israel.

Amaziah Reigns in Judah

14 In the second year of Joash the son of Jehoahaz, king of Israel, Amaziah the son of Joash, king of Judah, became king. ²He was twenty-five years old when he became king, and he reigned twenty-nine years in Jerusalem. His mother's name

---

13:6 ᵃHebrew *Asherah,* a Canaanite goddess
13:10 ᵃSpelled *Joash* in verse 9   **13:25** ᵃSpelled *Joash* in verses 12–14, 25

was Jehoaddan of Jerusalem. ³And he did *what was* right in the sight of the LORD, yet not like his father David; he did everything as his father Joash had done. ⁴However the high places were not taken away, and the people still sacrificed and burned incense on the high places.

⁵Now it happened, as soon as the kingdom was established in his hand, that he executed his servants who had murdered his father the king. ⁶But the children of the murderers he did not execute, according to what is written in the Book of the Law of Moses, in which the LORD commanded, saying, "Fathers shall not be put to death for their children, nor shall children be put to death for their fathers; but a person shall be put to death for his own sin."ᵃ

⁷He killed ten thousand Edomites in the Valley of Salt, and took Sela by war, and called its name Joktheel to this day.

⁸Then Amaziah sent messengers to Jehoashᵃ the son of Jehoahaz, the son of Jehu, king of Israel, saying, "Come, let us face one another *in battle.*" ⁹And Jehoash king of Israel sent to Amaziah king of Judah, saying, "The thistle that *was* in Lebanon sent to the cedar that *was* in Lebanon, saying, 'Give your daughter to my son as wife'; and a wild beast that *was* in Lebanon passed by and trampled the thistle. ¹⁰You have indeed defeated Edom, and your heart has lifted you up. Glory *in that,* and stay at home; for why should you meddle with trouble so that you fall—you and Judah with you?"

¹¹But Amaziah would not heed. Therefore Jehoash king of Israel went out; so he and Amaziah king of Judah faced one another at Beth Shemesh, which *belongs* to Judah. ¹²And Judah was defeated by Israel, and every man fled to his tent. ¹³Then Jehoash king of Israel captured Amaziah king of Judah, the son of Jehoash, the son of Ahaziah, at Beth Shemesh; and he went to Jerusalem, and broke down the wall of Jerusalem from the Gate of Ephraim to the Corner Gate—four hundred cubits. ¹⁴And he took all the gold and silver, all the articles that were found in the house of the LORD and in the treasuries of the king's house, and hostages, and returned to Samaria.

¹⁵Now the rest of the acts of Jehoash which he did—his might, and how he fought with Amaziah king of Judah—*are* they not written in the book of the chronicles of the kings of Israel? ¹⁶So Jehoash rested with his fathers, and was buried in Samaria with the kings of Israel. Then Jeroboam his son reigned in his place.

¹⁷Amaziah the son of Joash, king of Judah, lived fifteen years after the death of Jehoash the son of Jehoahaz, king of Israel. ¹⁸Now the rest of the acts of Amaziah, *are* they not written in the book of the chronicles of the kings of Judah? ¹⁹And they formed a conspiracy against him in Jerusalem, and he fled to Lachish; but they sent after him to Lachish and killed him there. ²⁰Then they brought him on horses, and he was buried at Jerusalem with his fathers in the City of David.

²¹And all the people of Judah took Azariah,ᵃ who *was* sixteen years old, and made him king instead of his father Amaziah. ²²He built Elath and restored it to Judah, after the king rested with his fathers.

Jeroboam II Reigns in Israel

²³In the fifteenth year of Amaziah the son of Joash, king of Judah, Jeroboam the son of Joash, king of Israel, became king in Samaria, *and reigned* forty-one years. ²⁴And he did evil in the sight of the LORD; he did not depart from all the sins of Jeroboam the son of Nebat, who had made Israel sin. ²⁵He restored the territory of Israel from the entrance of Hamath to the Sea of the Arabah, according to the word of the LORD God of Israel, which He had spoken through His servant Jonah the son of Amittai, the prophet who *was* from Gath Hepher. ²⁶For the LORD saw *that* the affliction of Israel *was* very bitter; and whether bond or free, there was no helper for Israel. ²⁷And the LORD did not say that He would blot out the name of Israel from under heaven; but He saved them by the hand of Jeroboam the son of Joash.

²⁸Now the rest of the acts of Jeroboam, and all that he did—his might, how he made

---

14:6 ᵃDeuteronomy 24:16   **14:8** ᵃSpelled *Joash* in 13:12ff and 2 Chronicles 25:17ff   **14:21** ᵃCalled *Uzziah* in 2 Chronicles 26:1ff, Isaiah 6:1, and elsewhere

war, and how he recaptured for Israel, from Damascus and Hamath, *what had belonged to Judah*—*are* they not written in the book of the chronicles of the kings of Israel? ²⁹So Jeroboam rested with his fathers, the kings of Israel. Then Zechariah his son reigned in his place.

Azariah Reigns in Judah

15 In the twenty-seventh year of Jeroboam king of Israel, Azariah the son of Amaziah, king of Judah, became king. ²He was sixteen years old when he became king, and he reigned fifty-two years in Jerusalem. His mother's name *was* Jecholiah of Jerusalem. ³And he did *what was* right in the sight of the LORD, according to all that his father Amaziah had done, ⁴except that the high places were not removed; the people still sacrificed and burned incense on the high places. ⁵Then the LORD struck the

king, so that he was a leper until the day of his death; so he dwelt in an isolated house. And Jotham the king's son *was* over the *royal* house, judging the people of the land. ⁶Now the rest of the acts of Azariah, and all that he did, *are* they not written in the book of the chronicles of the kings of Judah? ⁷So Azariah rested with his fathers, and they buried him with his fathers in the City of David. Then Jotham his son reigned in his place.

Zechariah Reigns in Israel

⁸In the thirty-eighth year of Azariah king of Judah, Zechariah the son of Jeroboam reigned over Israel in Samaria six months. ⁹And he did evil in the sight of the LORD, as his fathers had done; he did not depart from the sins of Jeroboam the son of Nebat, who had made Israel sin. ¹⁰Then Shallum the son of Jabesh conspired against him,

---

FREEDOM

For the LORD saw that the affliction . . . there was no helper for Israel.

2 KINGS 14:26

Harriet Tubman

"I WAS FREE"

Harriet Tubman (1820–1913) was an escaped slave who repeatedly risked her life to free slaves using the network of antislavery activists and safe houses known as the Underground Railroad. Also known as "Moses," Tubman was an African-American abolitionist who inspired generations of African-Americans struggling for equality and civil rights. During the Civil War she served as a Union spy, and after the war she helped set up schools for freed slaves and struggled for women's suffrage.

To her biographer, Sarah H. Bradford, Harriet Tubman stated:

> I had crossed de line of which I had so long been dreaming. I was free; but dere was no one to welcome me to de land of freedom, I was a stranger in a strange land, and my home after all was down in de old cabin quarter, wid de ole folks, and my brudders and sisters. But to dis solemn resolution I came; I was free, and dey should be free also; I would make a home for dem in de North, and de Lord helping me, I would bring dem all dere. Oh, how I prayed den, lying all alone on de cold, damp ground; "Oh, dear Lord," I said, "I haint got no friend but you. Come to my help, Lord, for I'm in trouble!"
>
> 'Twant me, 'twas the Lord. I always told Him, "I trust to You. I don't know where to go or what to do, but I expect You to lead me," and He always did.

and struck and killed him in front of the people; and he reigned in his place.

¹¹Now the rest of the acts of Zechariah, indeed they *are* written in the book of the chronicles of the kings of Israel.

¹²This *was* the word of the LORD which He spoke to Jehu, saying, "Your sons shall sit on the throne of Israel to the fourth *generation*."ᵃ And so it was.

Shallum Reigns in Israel

¹³Shallum the son of Jabesh became king in the thirty-ninth year of Uzziahᵃ king of Judah; and he reigned a full month in Samaria. ¹⁴For Menahem the son of Gadi went up from Tirzah, came to Samaria, and struck Shallum the son of Jabesh in Samaria and killed him; and he reigned in his place.

¹⁵Now the rest of the acts of Shallum, and the conspiracy which he led, indeed they *are* written in the book of the chronicles of the kings of Israel. ¹⁶Then from Tirzah, Menahem attacked Tiphsah, all who *were* there, and its territory. Because they did not surrender, therefore he attacked *it*. All the women there who were with child he ripped open.

Menahem Reigns in Israel

¹⁷In the thirty-ninth year of Azariah king of Judah, Menahem the son of Gadi became king over Israel, *and reigned* ten years in Samaria. ¹⁸And he did evil in the sight of the LORD; he did not depart all his days from the sins of Jeroboam the son of Nebat, who had made Israel sin. ¹⁹Pulᵃ king of Assyria came against the land; and Menahem gave Pul a thousand talents of silver, that his hand might be with him to strengthen the kingdom under his control. ²⁰And Menahem exacted the money from Israel, from all the very wealthy, from each man fifty shekels of silver, to give to the king of Assyria. So the king of Assyria turned back, and did not stay there in the land.

²¹Now the rest of the acts of Menahem, and all that he did, *are* they not written in the book of the chronicles of the kings of Israel? ²²So Menahem rested with his fathers. Then Pekahiah his son reigned in his place.

Pekahiah Reigns in Israel

²³In the fiftieth year of Azariah king of Judah, Pekahiah the son of Menahem became king over Israel in Samaria, *and reigned* two years. ²⁴And he did evil in the sight of the LORD; he did not depart from the sins of Jeroboam the son of Nebat, who had made Israel sin. ²⁵Then Pekah the son of Remaliah, an officer of his, conspired against him and killed him in Samaria, in the citadel of the king's house, along with Argob and Arieh; and with him were fifty men of Gilead. He killed him and reigned in his place.

²⁶Now the rest of the acts of Pekahiah, and all that he did, indeed they *are* written in the book of the chronicles of the kings of Israel.

Pekah Reigns in Israel

²⁷In the fifty-second year of Azariah king of Judah, Pekah the son of Remaliah became king over Israel in Samaria, *and reigned* twenty years. ²⁸And he did evil in the sight of the LORD; he did not depart from the sins of Jeroboam the son of Nebat, who had made Israel sin. ²⁹In the days of Pekah king of Israel, Tiglath-Pileser king of Assyria came and took Ijon, Abel Beth Maachah, Janoah, Kedesh, Hazor, Gilead, and Galilee, all the land of Naphtali; and he carried them captive to Assyria. ³⁰Then Hoshea the son of Elah led a conspiracy against Pekah the son of Remaliah, and struck and killed him; so he reigned in his place in the twentieth year of Jotham the son of Uzziah.

³¹Now the rest of the acts of Pekah, and all that he did, indeed they *are* written in the book of the chronicles of the kings of Israel.

Jotham Reigns in Judah

³²In the second year of Pekah the son of Remaliah, king of Israel, Jotham the son of Uzziah, king of Judah, began to reign. ³³He was twenty-five years old when he became king, and he reigned sixteen years in Jerusalem. His mother's name *was* Jerushaᵃ

15:12 ᵃ2 Kings 10:30   **15:13** ᵃCalled *Azariah* in 14:21ff and 15:1ff   **15:19** ᵃThat is, Tiglath-Pileser III (compare verse 29)   **15:33** ᵃSpelled *Jerushah* in 2 Chronicles 27:1

the daughter of Zadok. [34]And he did *what was* right in the sight of the Lord; he did according to all that his father Uzziah had done. [35]However the high places were not removed; the people still sacrificed and burned incense on the high places. He built the Upper Gate of the house of the Lord.

[36]Now the rest of the acts of Jotham, and all that he did, *are* they not written in the book of the chronicles of the kings of Judah? [37]In those days the Lord began to send Rezin king of Syria and Pekah the son of Remaliah against Judah. [38]So Jotham rested with his fathers, and was buried with his fathers in the City of David his father. Then Ahaz his son reigned in his place.

Ahaz Reigns in Judah

16 In the seventeenth year of Pekah the son of Remaliah, Ahaz the son of Jotham, king of Judah, began to reign. [2]Ahaz *was* twenty years old when he became king, and he reigned sixteen years in Jerusalem; and he did not do *what was* right in the sight of the Lord his God, as his father David *had done*. [3]But he walked in the way of the kings of Israel; indeed he made his son pass through the fire, according to the abominations of the nations whom the Lord had cast out from before the children of Israel. [4]And he sacrificed and burned incense on the high places, on the hills, and under every green tree.

[5]Then Rezin king of Syria and Pekah the son of Remaliah, king of Israel, came up to Jerusalem to *make* war; and they besieged Ahaz but could not overcome *him*. [6]At that time Rezin king of Syria captured Elath for Syria, and drove the men of Judah from Elath. Then the Edomites[a] went to Elath, and dwell there to this day.

[7]So Ahaz sent messengers to Tiglath-Pileser king of Assyria, saying, "I *am* your servant and your son. Come up and save me from the hand of the king of Syria and from the hand of the king of Israel, who rise up against me." [8]And Ahaz took the silver and gold that was found in the house of the Lord, and in the treasuries of the king's house, and sent *it as* a present to the king of Assyria. [9]So the king of Assyria heeded him; for the king of Assyria went up against Damascus and took it, carried *its people* captive to Kir, and killed Rezin.

[10]Now King Ahaz went to Damascus to meet Tiglath-Pileser king of Assyria, and saw an altar that *was* at Damascus; and King Ahaz sent to Urijah the priest the design of the altar and its pattern, according to all its workmanship. [11]Then Urijah the priest built an altar according to all that King Ahaz had sent from Damascus. So Urijah the priest made *it* before King Ahaz came back from Damascus. [12]And when the king came back from Damascus, the king saw the altar; and the king approached the altar and made offerings on it. [13]So he burned his burnt offering and his grain offering; and he poured his drink offering and sprinkled the blood of his peace offerings on the altar. [14]He also brought the bronze altar which *was* before the Lord, from the front of the temple—from between the *new* altar and the house of the Lord—and put it on the north side of the *new* altar. [15]Then King Ahaz commanded Urijah the priest, saying, "On the great *new* altar burn the morning burnt offering, the evening grain offering, the king's burnt sacrifice, and his grain offering, with the burnt offering of all the people of the land, their grain offering, and their drink offerings; and sprinkle on it all the blood of the burnt offering and all the blood of the sacrifice. And the bronze altar shall be for me to inquire *by*." [16]Thus did Urijah the priest, according to all that King Ahaz commanded.

[17]And King Ahaz cut off the panels of the carts, and removed the lavers from them; and he took down the Sea from the bronze oxen that *were* under it, and put it on a pavement of stones. [18]Also he removed the Sabbath pavilion which they had built in the temple, and he removed the king's outer entrance from the house of the Lord, on account of the king of Assyria.

[19]Now the rest of the acts of Ahaz which he did, *are* they not written in the book of the chronicles of the kings of Judah? [20]So Ahaz rested with his fathers, and was buried with his fathers in the City of David. Then Hezekiah his son reigned in his place.

16:6 [a]Some ancient authorities read *Syrians*.

Hoshea Reigns in Israel

17 In the twelfth year of Ahaz king of Judah, Hoshea the son of Elah became king of Israel in Samaria, *and he reigned* nine years. ²And he did evil in the sight of the LORD, but not as the kings of Israel who were before him. ³Shalmaneser king of Assyria came up against him; and Hoshea became his vassal, and paid him tribute money. ⁴And the king of Assyria uncovered a conspiracy by Hoshea; for he had sent messengers to So, king of Egypt, and brought no tribute to the king of Assyria, as *he had done* year by year. Therefore the king of Assyria shut him up, and bound him in prison.

Israel Carried Captive to Assyria

⁵Now the king of Assyria went throughout all the land, and went up to Samaria and besieged it for three years. ⁶In the ninth year of Hoshea, the king of Assyria took Samaria and carried Israel away to Assyria, and placed them in Halah and by the Habor, the River of Gozan, and in the cities of the Medes.

⁷For so it was that the children of Israel had sinned against the LORD their God, who had brought them up out of the land of Egypt, from under the hand of Pharaoh king of Egypt; and they had feared other gods, ⁸and had walked in the statutes of the nations whom the LORD had cast out from before the children of Israel, and of the kings of Israel, which they had made. ⁹Also the children of Israel secretly did against the LORD their God things that *were* not right, and they built for themselves high places in all their cities, from watchtower to fortified city. ¹⁰They set up for themselves *sacred* pillars and wooden imagesᵃ on every high hill and under every green tree. ¹¹There they burned incense on all the high places, like the nations whom the LORD had carried away before them; and they did wicked things to provoke the LORD to anger, ¹²for they served idols, of which the LORD had said to them, "You shall not do this thing."

¹³Yet the LORD testified against Israel and against Judah, by all of His prophets, every seer, saying, "Turn from your evil ways, and keep My commandments *and* My statutes, according to all the law which I commanded your fathers, and which I sent to you by My servants the prophets." ¹⁴Nevertheless they would not hear, but stiffened their necks, like the necks of their fathers, who did not believe in the LORD their God. ¹⁵And they rejected His statutes and His covenant that He had made with their fathers, and His testimonies which He had testified against them; they followed idols, became idolaters, and *went* after the nations who *were* all around them, *concerning* whom the LORD had charged them that they should not do like them. ¹⁶So they left all the commandments of the LORD their God, made for themselves a molded image *and* two calves, made a wooden image and worshiped all the host of heaven, and served Baal. ¹⁷And they caused their sons and daughters to pass through the fire, practiced witchcraft and soothsaying, and sold themselves to do evil in the sight of the LORD, to provoke Him to anger. ¹⁸Therefore the LORD was very angry with Israel, and removed them from His sight; there was none left but the tribe of Judah alone.

¹⁹Also Judah did not keep the commandments of the LORD their God, but walked in the statutes of Israel which they made. ²⁰And the LORD rejected all the descendants of Israel, afflicted them, and delivered them into the hand of plunderers, until He had cast them from His sight. ²¹For He tore Israel from the house of David, and they made Jeroboam the son of Nebat king. Then Jeroboam drove Israel from following the LORD, and made them commit a great sin. ²²For the children of Israel walked in all the sins of Jeroboam which he did; they did not depart from them, ²³until the LORD removed Israel out of His sight, as He had said by all His servants the prophets. So Israel was carried away from their own land to Assyria, *as it is* to this day.

Assyria Resettles Samaria

²⁴Then the king of Assyria brought *people* from Babylon, Cuthah, Ava, Hamath, and from Sepharvaim, and placed *them* in the cities of Samaria instead of the children

---

17:10 ᵃHebrew *Asherim*, Canaanite deities

of Israel; and they took possession of Samaria and dwelt in its cities. 25And it was so, at the beginning of their dwelling there, *that* they did not fear the Lord; therefore the Lord sent lions among them, which killed *some* of them. 26So they spoke to the king of Assyria, saying, "The nations whom you have removed and placed in the cities of Samaria do not know the rituals of the God of the land; therefore He has sent lions among them, and indeed, they are killing them because they do not know the rituals of the God of the land." 27Then the king of Assyria commanded, saying, "Send there one of the priests whom you brought from there; let him go and dwell there, and let him teach them the rituals of the God of the land." 28Then one of the priests whom they had carried away from Samaria came and dwelt in Bethel, and taught them how they should fear the Lord.

29However every nation continued to make gods of its own, and put *them* in the shrines on the high places which the Samaritans had made, *every* nation in the cities where they dwelt. 30The men of Babylon made Succoth Benoth, the men of Cuth made Nergal, the men of Hamath made Ashima, 31and the Avites made Nibhaz and Tartak; and the Sepharvites burned their children in fire to Adrammelech and Anammelech, the gods of Sepharvaim. 32So they feared the Lord, and from every class they appointed for themselves priests of the high places, who sacrificed for them in the shrines of the high places. 33They feared the Lord, yet served their own gods—according to the rituals of the nations from among whom they were carried away.

34To this day they continue practicing the former rituals; they do not fear the Lord, nor do they follow their statutes or their ordinances, or the law and commandment which the Lord had commanded the children of Jacob, whom He named Israel, 35with whom the Lord had made a covenant and charged them, saying: "You shall not fear other gods, nor bow down to them nor serve them nor sacrifice to them; 36but the Lord, who brought you up from the land of Egypt with great power and an outstretched arm, Him you shall fear, Him you

shall worship, and to Him you shall offer sacrifice. 37And the statutes, the ordinances, the law, and the commandment which He wrote for you, you shall be careful to observe forever; you shall not fear other gods. 38And the covenant that I have made with you, you shall not forget, nor shall you fear other gods. 39But the Lord your God you shall fear; and He will deliver you from the hand of all your enemies." 40However they did not obey, but they followed their former rituals. 41So these nations feared the Lord, yet served their carved images; also their children and their children's children have continued doing as their fathers did, even to this day.

Hezekiah Reigns in Judah

18 Now it came to pass in the third year of Hoshea the son of Elah, king of Israel, *that* Hezekiah the son of Ahaz, king of Judah, began to reign. 2He was twenty-five years old when he became king, and he reigned twenty-nine years in Jerusalem. His mother's name *was* Abi[a] the daughter of Zechariah. 3And he did *what was* right in the sight of the Lord, according to all that his father David had done.

4He removed the high places and broke the *sacred* pillars, cut down the wooden image[a] and broke in pieces the bronze serpent that Moses had made; for until those days the children of Israel burned incense to it, and called it Nehushtan.[b] 5He trusted in the Lord God of Israel, so that after him was none like him among all the kings of Judah, nor who were before him. 6For he held fast to the Lord; he did not depart from following Him, but kept His commandments, which the Lord had commanded Moses. 7The Lord was with him; he prospered wherever he went. And he rebelled against the king of Assyria and did not serve him. 8He subdued the Philistines, as far as Gaza and its territory, from watchtower to fortified city.

9Now it came to pass in the fourth year of King Hezekiah, which *was* the seventh

---

18:2 [a]Called *Abijah* in 2 Chronicles 29:1ff
18:4 [a]Hebrew *Asherah,* a Canaanite goddess
[b]Literally *Bronze Thing*

year of Hoshea the son of Elah, king of Israel, *that* Shalmaneser king of Assyria came up against Samaria and besieged it. ¹⁰And at the end of three years they took it. In the sixth year of Hezekiah, that *is,* the ninth year of Hoshea king of Israel, Samaria was taken. ¹¹Then the king of Assyria carried Israel away captive to Assyria, and put them in Halah and by the Habor, the River of Gozan, and in the cities of the Medes, ¹²because they did not obey the voice of the LORD their God, but transgressed His covenant *and* all that Moses the servant of the LORD had commanded; and they would neither hear nor do *them.*

¹³And in the fourteenth year of King Hezekiah, Sennacherib king of Assyria came up against all the fortified cities of Judah and took them. ¹⁴Then Hezekiah king of Judah sent to the king of Assyria at Lachish, saying, "I have done wrong; turn away from me; whatever you impose on me I will pay." And the king of Assyria assessed Hezekiah king of Judah three hundred talents of silver and thirty talents of gold. ¹⁵So Hezekiah gave *him* all the silver that was found in the house of the LORD and in the treasuries of the king's house. ¹⁶At that time Hezekiah stripped *the gold from* the doors of the temple of the LORD, and *from* the pillars which Hezekiah king of Judah had overlaid, and gave it to the king of Assyria.

Sennacherib Boasts Against the LORD

¹⁷Then the king of Assyria sent *the* Tartan,ᵃ *the* Rabsaris,ᵇ *and the* Rabshakehᶜ from Lachish, with a great army against Jerusalem, to King Hezekiah. And they went

---

18:17 ᵃA title, probably *Commander in Chief* ᵇA title, probably *Chief Officer* ᶜA title, probably *Chief of Staff* or *Governor*

HONOR

He trusted in the LORD God of Israel....

2 KINGS 18:5

Scott O'Grady

"I AM AN AMERICAN"

On June 2, 1995, U.S. Air Force Captain Scott O'Grady was patrolling the United Nations designated no-fly zone over war torn Bosnia when his F-16 fighter was struck by a surface-to-air missile at 27,000 feet above the Earth. He desperately pulled his ejection lever and was catapulted into the sky at 350 miles per hour. Remarkably, he managed to land unscathed in enemy territory.

For six incredible days and nights, O'Grady eluded capture by the Bosnian Serbs who relentlessly hunted him. Utilizing his survival training to the maximum, O'Grady said it was also his faith in God that sustained him. On his third day on the ground, he experienced the love of God to such a level that it took away his fear of death. On the sixth day in a daring daylight rescue, an elite team of Marines moved in with a chopper, dodged enemy fire, and pulled the young American hero to safety.

At a national press conference following his triumphant return, O'Grady said, "If it wasn't for my love for God and God's love for me, I wouldn't be here right now." His inspirational and patriotic story is a brilliant testimony to Article Six of the United States Military Code of Conduct: "I will never forget that I am an American, fighting for freedom, responsible for my actions, and dedicated to the principles which made my country free. I will trust in my God and in the United States of America."

up and came to Jerusalem. When they had come up, they went and stood by the aqueduct from the upper pool, which *was* on the highway to the Fuller's Field. ¹⁸And when they had called to the king, Eliakim the son of Hilkiah, who *was* over the household, Shebna the scribe, and Joah the son of Asaph, the recorder, came out to them. ¹⁹Then *the* Rabshakeh said to them, "Say now to Hezekiah, 'Thus says the great king, the king of Assyria: "What confidence *is* this in which you trust? ²⁰You speak of *having* plans and power for war; but *they are* mere words. And in whom do you trust, that you rebel against me? ²¹Now look! You are trusting in the staff of this broken reed, Egypt, on which if a man leans, it will go into his hand and pierce it. So *is* Pharaoh king of Egypt to all who trust in him. ²²But if you say to me, 'We trust in the LORD our God,' *is* it not He whose high places and whose altars Hezekiah has taken away, and said to Judah and Jerusalem, 'You shall worship before this altar in Jerusalem'?" ²³Now therefore, I urge you, give a pledge to my master the king of Assyria, and I will give you two thousand horses—if you are able on your part to put riders on them! ²⁴How then will you repel one captain of the least of my master's servants, and put your trust in Egypt for chariots and horsemen? ²⁵Have I now come up without the LORD against this place to destroy it? The LORD said to me, 'Go up against this land, and destroy it.'"

²⁶Then Eliakim the son of Hilkiah, Shebna, and Joah said to *the* Rabshakeh, "Please speak to your servants in Aramaic, for we understand *it;* and do not speak to us in Hebrewᵃ in the hearing of the people who *are* on the wall."

²⁷But *the* Rabshakeh said to them, "Has my master sent me to your master and to you to speak these words, and not to the men who sit on the wall, who will eat and drink their own waste with you?"

²⁸Then *the* Rabshakeh stood and called out with a loud voice in Hebrew, and spoke, saying, "Hear the word of the great king, the king of Assyria! ²⁹Thus says the king: 'Do not let Hezekiah deceive you, for he shall not be able to deliver you from his hand; ³⁰nor let Hezekiah make you trust in the LORD, saying, "The LORD will surely deliver us; this city shall not be given into the hand of the king of Assyria."' ³¹Do not listen to Hezekiah; for thus says the king of Assyria: 'Make *peace* with me by a present and come out to me; and every one of you eat from his own vine and every one from his own fig tree, and every one of you drink the waters of his own cistern; ³²until I come and take you away to a land like your own land, a land of grain and new wine, a land of bread and vineyards, a land of olive groves and honey, that you may live and not die. But do not listen to Hezekiah, lest he persuade you, saying, "The LORD will deliver us." ³³Has any of the gods of the nations at all delivered its land from the hand of the king of Assyria? ³⁴Where *are* the gods of Hamath and Arpad? Where *are* the gods of Sepharvaim and Hena and Ivah? Indeed, have they delivered Samaria from my hand? ³⁵Who among all the gods of the lands have delivered their countries from my hand, that the LORD should deliver Jerusalem from my hand?'"

³⁶But the people held their peace and answered him not a word; for the king's commandment was, "Do not answer him." ³⁷Then Eliakim the son of Hilkiah, who *was* over the household, Shebna the scribe, and Joah the son of Asaph, the recorder, came to Hezekiah with *their* clothes torn, and told him the words of *the* Rabshakeh.

Isaiah Assures Deliverance

19 And so it was, when King Hezekiah heard *it,* that he tore his clothes, covered himself with sackcloth, and went into the house of the LORD. ²Then he sent Eliakim, who *was* over the household, Shebna the scribe, and the elders of the priests, covered with sackcloth, to Isaiah the prophet, the son of Amoz. ³And they said to him, "Thus says Hezekiah: 'This day *is* a day of trouble, and rebuke, and blasphemy; for the children have come to birth, but *there is* no strength to bring them forth. ⁴It may be that the LORD your God will hear all the words of *the* Rabshakeh, whom his master the king of Assyria has sent to reproach the

18:26 ᵃLiterally *Judean*

living God, and will rebuke the words which the LORD your God has heard. Therefore lift up *your* prayer for the remnant that is left.'"

⁵So the servants of King Hezekiah came to Isaiah. ⁶And Isaiah said to them, "Thus you shall say to your master, 'Thus says the LORD: "Do not be afraid of the words which you have heard, with which the servants of the king of Assyria have blasphemed Me. ⁷Surely I will send a spirit upon him, and he shall hear a rumor and return to his own land; and I will cause him to fall by the sword in his own land."'"

Sennacherib's Threat and Hezekiah's Prayer

⁸Then the Rabshakeh returned and found the king of Assyria warring against Libnah, for he heard that he had departed from Lachish. ⁹And the king heard concerning Tirhakah king of Ethiopia, "Look, he has come out to make war with you." So he again sent messengers to Hezekiah, saying, ¹⁰"Thus you shall speak to Hezekiah king of Judah, saying: 'Do not let your God in whom you trust deceive you, saying, "Jerusalem shall not be given into the hand of the king of Assyria." ¹¹Look! You have heard what the kings of Assyria have done to all lands by utterly destroying them; and shall you be delivered? ¹²Have the gods of the nations delivered those whom my fathers have destroyed, Gozan and Haran and Rezeph, and the people of Eden who *were* in Telassar? ¹³Where *is* the king of Hamath, the king of Arpad, and the king of the city of Sepharvaim, Hena, and Ivah?'"

¹⁴And Hezekiah received the letter from the hand of the messengers, and read it; and Hezekiah went up to the house of the LORD, and spread it before the LORD. ¹⁵Then Hezekiah prayed before the LORD, and said: "O LORD God of Israel, *the One* who dwells *between* the cherubim, You are God, You alone, of all the kingdoms of the earth. You have made heaven and earth. ¹⁶Incline Your ear, O LORD, and hear; open Your eyes, O LORD, and see; and hear the words of Sennacherib, which he has sent to reproach the living God. ¹⁷Truly, LORD, the kings of Assyria have laid waste the nations and their lands, ¹⁸and have cast their gods into the fire; for they *were* not gods, but the work

of men's hands—wood and stone. Therefore they destroyed them. ¹⁹Now therefore, O LORD our God, I pray, save us from his hand, that all the kingdoms of the earth may know that You *are* the LORD God, You alone."

FAITH

"You are God, You alone, of all the kingdoms of the earth."   2 KINGS 19:15

In God Alone

Tom Campbell Clark, an Associate Justice of the U.S. Supreme Court (1949–1967), stated:

> *The Founding Fathers believed devoutly that there was a God and that the unalienable rights of man were rooted—not in the state, nor the legislature, nor in any other human power—but in God alone.*

The Word of the LORD Concerning Sennacherib

²⁰Then Isaiah the son of Amoz sent to Hezekiah, saying, "Thus says the LORD God of Israel: 'Because you have prayed to Me against Sennacherib king of Assyria, I have heard.' ²¹This *is* the word which the LORD has spoken concerning him:

> 'The virgin, the daughter of Zion,
> Has despised you, laughed you to
>   scorn;
> The daughter of Jerusalem
> Has shaken *her* head behind your back!

²² 'Whom have you reproached and
>   blasphemed?
> Against whom have you raised *your*
>   voice,
> And lifted up your eyes on high?
> Against the Holy *One* of Israel.
²³ By your messengers you have
>   reproached the Lord,
> And said: "By the multitude of my
>   chariots
> I have come up to the height of the
>   mountains,
> To the limits of Lebanon;
> I will cut down its tall cedars
> *And* its choice cypress trees;

I will enter the extremity of its borders,
To its fruitful forest.
24 I have dug and drunk strange water,
And with the soles of my feet I have
    dried up
All the brooks of defense."

25 'Did you not hear long ago
How I made it,
From ancient times that I formed it?
Now I have brought it to pass,
That you should be
For crushing fortified cities *into* heaps
    of ruins.
26 Therefore their inhabitants had little
    power;
They were dismayed and confounded;
They were *as* the grass of the field
And the green herb,
As the grass on the housetops
And *grain* blighted before it is grown.

27 'But I know your dwelling place,
Your going out and your coming in,
And your rage against Me.
28 Because your rage against Me and
    your tumult
Have come up to My ears,
Therefore I will put My hook in
    your nose
And My bridle in your lips,
And I will turn you back
By the way which you came.

29'This *shall be* a sign to you:

You shall eat this year such as grows
    of itself,
And in the second year what springs
    from the same;
Also in the third year sow and reap,
Plant vineyards and eat the fruit of
    them.
30 And the remnant who have escaped
    of the house of Judah
Shall again take root downward,
And bear fruit upward.
31 For out of Jerusalem shall go a remnant,
And those who escape from Mount
    Zion.
The zeal of the LORD of hosts[a] will
    do this.'

32"Therefore thus says the LORD concerning the king of Assyria:

'He shall not come into this city,
Nor shoot an arrow there,
Nor come before it with shield,
Nor build a siege mound against it.
33 By the way that he came,
By the same shall he return;
And he shall not come into this city,'
Says the LORD.
34 'For I will defend this city, to save it
For My own sake and for My servant
    David's sake.' "

Sennacherib's Defeat and Death

35And it came to pass on a certain night that the angel[a] of the LORD went out, and killed in the camp of the Assyrians one hundred and eighty-five thousand; and when *people* arose early in the morning, there were the corpses—all dead. 36So Sennacherib king of Assyria departed and went away, returned *home,* and remained at Nineveh. 37Now it came to pass, as he was worshiping in the temple of Nisroch his god, that his sons Adrammelech and Sharezer struck him down with the sword; and they escaped into the land of Ararat. Then Esarhaddon his son reigned in his place.

Hezekiah's Life Extended

20 In those days Hezekiah was sick and near death. And Isaiah the prophet, the son of Amoz, went to him and said to him, "Thus says the LORD: 'Set your house in order, for you shall die, and not live.' "
2Then he turned his face toward the wall, and prayed to the LORD, saying, 3"Remember now, O LORD, I pray, how I have walked before You in truth and with a loyal heart, and have done *what was* good in Your sight." And Hezekiah wept bitterly.
4And it happened, before Isaiah had gone out into the middle court, that the word of the LORD came to him, saying, 5"Return and tell Hezekiah the leader of My people, 'Thus says the LORD, the God of David your father: "I have heard your prayer, I have seen your

---

19:31 [a]Following many Hebrew manuscripts and ancient versions (compare Isaiah 37:32); Masoretic Text omits *of hosts.*   19:35 [a]Or *Angel*

tears; surely I will heal you. On the third day you shall go up to the house of the LORD. [6]And I will add to your days fifteen years. I will deliver you and this city from the hand of the king of Assyria; and I will defend this city for My own sake, and for the sake of My servant David." ' "

[7]Then Isaiah said, "Take a lump of figs." So they took and laid it on the boil, and he recovered.

[8]And Hezekiah said to Isaiah, "What is the sign that the LORD will heal me, and that I shall go up to the house of the LORD the third day?"

[9]Then Isaiah said, "This is the sign to you from the LORD, that the LORD will do the thing which He has spoken: shall the shadow go forward ten degrees or go backward ten degrees?"

[10]And Hezekiah answered, "It is an easy thing for the shadow to go down ten degrees; no, but let the shadow go backward ten degrees."

[11]So Isaiah the prophet cried out to the LORD, and He brought the shadow ten degrees backward, by which it had gone down on the sundial of Ahaz.

The Babylonian Envoys

[12]At that time Berodach-Baladan[a] the son of Baladan, king of Babylon, sent letters and a present to Hezekiah, for he heard that Hezekiah had been sick. [13]And Hezekiah was attentive to them, and showed them all the house of his treasures—the silver and gold, the spices and precious ointment, and all[a] his armory—all that was found among his treasures. There was nothing in his house or in all his dominion that Hezekiah did not show them.

[14]Then Isaiah the prophet went to King Hezekiah, and said to him, "What did these men say, and from where did they come to you?"

So Hezekiah said, "They came from a far country, from Babylon."

[15]And he said, "What have they seen in your house?"

So Hezekiah answered, "They have seen all that is in my house; there is nothing among my treasures that I have not shown them."

[16]Then Isaiah said to Hezekiah, "Hear the word of the LORD: [17]'Behold, the days are coming when all that is in your house, and what your fathers have accumulated until this day, shall be carried to Babylon; nothing shall be left,' says the LORD. [18]'And they shall take away some of your sons who will descend from you, whom you will beget; and they shall be eunuchs in the palace of the king of Babylon.' "

[19]So Hezekiah said to Isaiah, "The word of the LORD which you have spoken is good!" For he said, "Will there not be peace and truth at least in my days?"

Death of Hezekiah

[20]Now the rest of the acts of Hezekiah—all his might, and how he made a pool and a tunnel and brought water into the city—are they not written in the book of the chronicles of the kings of Judah? [21]So Hezekiah rested with his fathers. Then Manasseh his son reigned in his place.

Manasseh Reigns in Judah

21 Manasseh was twelve years old when he became king, and he reigned fifty-five years in Jerusalem. His mother's name was Hephzibah. [2]And he did evil in the sight of the LORD, according to the abominations of the nations whom the LORD had cast out before the children of Israel. [3]For he rebuilt the high places which Hezekiah his father had destroyed; he raised up altars for Baal, and made a wooden image,[a] as Ahab king of Israel had done; and he worshiped all the host of heaven[b] and served them. [4]He also built altars in the house of the LORD, of which the LORD had said, "In Jerusalem I will put My name." [5]And he built altars for all the host of heaven in the two courts of the house of the LORD. [6]Also he made his son pass through the fire, practiced soothsaying, used witchcraft, and consulted spiritists and mediums. He did much evil in the sight of the LORD, to provoke Him to anger. [7]He even set a carved

---

20:12 [a]Spelled Merodach-Baladan in Isaiah 39:1
20:13 [a]Following many Hebrew manuscripts, Syriac, and Targum; Masoretic Text omits all.
21:3 [a]Hebrew Asherah, a Canaanite goddess
[b]The gods of the Assyrians

image of Asherah[a] that he had made, in the house of which the LORD had said to David and to Solomon his son, "In this house and in Jerusalem, which I have chosen out of all the tribes of Israel, I will put My name forever; [8]and I will not make the feet of Israel wander anymore from the land which I gave their fathers—only if they are careful to do according to all that I have commanded them, and according to all the law that My servant Moses commanded them." [9]But they paid no attention, and Manasseh seduced them to do more evil than the nations whom the LORD had destroyed before the children of Israel.

[10]And the LORD spoke by His servants the prophets, saying, [11]"Because Manasseh king of Judah has done these abominations (he has acted more wickedly than all the Amorites who *were* before him, and has also made Judah sin with his idols), [12]therefore thus says the LORD God of Israel: 'Behold, *I* am bringing *such* calamity upon Jerusalem and Judah, that whoever hears of it, both his ears will tingle. [13]And I will stretch over Jerusalem the measuring line of Samaria and the plummet of the house of Ahab; I will wipe Jerusalem as *one* wipes a dish, wiping *it* and turning *it* upside down. [14]So I will forsake the remnant of My inheritance and deliver them into the hand of their enemies; and they shall become victims of plunder to all their enemies, [15]because they have done evil in My sight, and have provoked Me to anger since the day their fathers came out of Egypt, even to this day.' "

[16]Moreover Manasseh shed very much innocent blood, till he had filled Jerusalem from one end to another, besides his sin by which he made Judah sin, in doing evil in the sight of the LORD.

[17]Now the rest of the acts of Manasseh—all that he did, and the sin that he committed—*are* they not written in the book of the chronicles of the kings of Judah? [18]So Manasseh rested with his fathers, and was buried in the garden of his own house, in the garden of Uzza. Then his son Amon reigned in his place.

Amon's Reign and Death

[19]Amon *was* twenty-two years old when he became king, and he reigned two years

in Jerusalem. His mother's name *was* Meshullemeth the daughter of Haruz of Jotbah. [20]And he did evil in the sight of the LORD, as his father Manasseh had done. [21]So he walked in all the ways that his father had walked; and he served the idols that his father had served, and worshiped them. [22]He forsook the LORD God of his fathers, and did not walk in the way of the LORD.

[23]Then the servants of Amon conspired against him, and killed the king in his own house. [24]But the people of the land executed all those who had conspired against King Amon. Then the people of the land made his son Josiah king in his place.

[25]Now the rest of the acts of Amon which he did, *are* they not written in the book of the chronicles of the kings of Judah? [26]And he was buried in his tomb in the garden of Uzza. Then Josiah his son reigned in his place.

Josiah Reigns in Judah

22 Josiah *was* eight years old when he became king, and he reigned thirty-one years in Jerusalem. His mother's name *was* Jedidah the daughter of Adaiah of Bozkath. [2]And he did *what was* right in the sight of the LORD, and walked in all the ways of his father David; he did not turn aside to the right hand or to the left.

Hilkiah Finds the Book of the Law

[3]Now it came to pass, in the eighteenth year of King Josiah, *that* the king sent Shaphan the scribe, the son of Azaliah, the son of Meshullam, to the house of the LORD, saying: [4]"Go up to Hilkiah the high priest, that he may count the money which has been brought into the house of the LORD, which the doorkeepers have gathered from the people. [5]And let them deliver it into the hand of those doing the work, who are the overseers in the house of the LORD; let them give it to those who *are* in the house of the LORD doing the work, to repair the damages of the house— [6]to carpenters and builders and masons—and to buy timber and hewn stone to repair the house. [7]However there need be no accounting made with them

---

21:7 [a]A Canaanite goddess

of the money delivered into their hand, because they deal faithfully."

8Then Hilkiah the high priest said to Shaphan the scribe, "I have found the Book of the Law in the house of the LORD." And Hilkiah gave the book to Shaphan, and he read it. 9So Shaphan the scribe went to the king, bringing the king word, saying, "Your servants have gathered the money that was found in the house, and have delivered it into the hand of those who do the work, who oversee the house of the LORD." 10Then Shaphan the scribe showed the king, saying, "Hilkiah the priest has given me a book." And Shaphan read it before the king.

11Now it happened, when the king heard the words of the Book of the Law, that he tore his clothes. 12Then the king commanded Hilkiah the priest, Ahikam the son of Shaphan, Achbora the son of Michaiah, Shaphan the scribe, and Asaiah a servant of the king, saying, 13"Go, inquire of the LORD for me, for the people and for all Judah, concerning the words of this book that has been found; for great *is* the wrath of the LORD that is aroused against us, because our fathers have not obeyed the words of this book, to do according to all that is written concerning us."

14So Hilkiah the priest, Ahikam, Achbor, Shaphan, and Asaiah went to Huldah the prophetess, the wife of Shallum the son of Tikvah, the son of Harhas, keeper of the wardrobe. (She dwelt in Jerusalem in the Second Quarter.) And they spoke with her. 15Then she said to them, "Thus says the LORD God of Israel, 'Tell the man who sent you to Me, 16"Thus says the LORD: 'Behold, I will bring calamity on this place and on its inhabitants—all the words of the book which the king of Judah has read— 17because they have forsaken Me and burned incense to other gods, that they might provoke Me to anger with all the works of their hands. Therefore My wrath shall be aroused against this place and shall not be quenched.'"' 18But as for the king of Judah, who sent you to inquire of the LORD, in this manner you shall speak to him, 'Thus says the LORD God of Israel: "*Concerning* the words which you have heard— 19because your heart was tender, and you humbled yourself before

the LORD when you heard what I spoke against this place and against its inhabitants, that they would become a desolation and a curse, and you tore your clothes and wept before Me, I also have heard *you*," says the LORD. 20"Surely, therefore, I will gather you to your fathers, and you shall be gathered to your grave in peace; and your eyes shall not see all the calamity which I will bring on this place."'" So they brought back word to the king.

Josiah Restores True Worship

23 Now the king sent them to gather all the elders of Judah and Jerusalem to him. 2The king went up to the house of the LORD with all the men of Judah, and with him all the inhabitants of Jerusalem—the priests and the prophets and all the people, both small and great. And he read in their hearing all the words of the Book of the Covenant which had been found in the house of the LORD.

3Then the king stood by a pillar and made a covenant before the LORD, to follow the LORD and to keep His commandments and His testimonies and His statutes, with all *his* heart and all *his* soul, to perform the words of this covenant that were written in this book. And all the people took a stand for the covenant. 4And the king commanded Hilkiah the high priest, the priests of the second order, and the doorkeepers, to bring out of the temple of the LORD all the articles that were made for Baal, for Asherah,a and for all the host of heaven;b and he burned them outside Jerusalem in the fields of Kidron, and carried their ashes to Bethel. 5Then he removed the idolatrous priests whom the kings of Judah had ordained to burn incense on the high places in the cities of Judah and in the places all around Jerusalem, and those who burned incense to Baal, to the sun, to the moon, to the constellations, and to all the host of heaven. 6And he brought out the wooden imagea from the house of the LORD, to the Brook Kidron outside Jerusalem, burned it at the

---

22:12 aAbdon the son of Micah in 2 Chronicles 34:20
23:4 aA Canaanite goddess bThe gods of the Assyrians
23:6 aHebrew *Asherah*, a Canaanite goddess

Brook Kidron and ground *it* to ashes, and threw its ashes on the graves of the common people. [7]Then he tore down the *ritual* booths of the perverted persons[a] that *were* in the house of the Lord, where the women wove hangings for the wooden image. [8]And he brought all the priests from the cities of Judah, and defiled the high places where the priests had burned incense, from Geba to Beersheba; also he broke down the high places at the gates which *were* at the entrance of the Gate of Joshua the governor of the city, which *were* to the left of the city gate. [9]Nevertheless the priests of the high places did not come up to the altar of the Lord in Jerusalem, but they ate unleavened bread among their brethren.

[10]And he defiled Topheth, which *is* in the Valley of the Son[a] of Hinnom, that no man might make his son or his daughter pass through the fire to Molech. [11]Then he removed the horses that the kings of Judah had dedicated to the sun, at the entrance to the house of the Lord, by the chamber of Nathan-Melech, the officer who *was* in the court; and he burned the chariots of the sun with fire. [12]The altars that *were* on the roof, the upper chamber of Ahaz, which the kings of Judah had made, and the altars which Manasseh had made in the two courts of the house of the Lord, the king broke down and pulverized there, and threw their dust into the Brook Kidron. [13]Then the king defiled the high places that *were* east of Jerusalem, which *were* on the south of the Mount of Corruption, which Solomon king of Israel had built for Ashtoreth the abomination of the Sidonians, for Chemosh the abomination of the Moabites, and for Milcom the abomination of the people of Ammon. [14]And he broke in pieces the *sacred* pillars and cut down the wooden images, and filled their places with the bones of men.

[15]Moreover the altar that *was* at Bethel, *and* the high place which Jeroboam the son of Nebat, who made Israel sin, had made, both that altar and the high place he broke down; and he burned the high place *and* crushed *it* to powder, and burned the wooden image. [16]As Josiah turned, he saw the tombs that *were* there on the mountain. And he sent and took the bones out of the tombs and burned *them* on the altar, and defiled it according to the word of the Lord which the man of God proclaimed, who proclaimed these words. [17]Then he said, "What gravestone *is* this that I see?"

So the men of the city told him, *"It is* the tomb of the man of God who came from Judah and proclaimed these things which you have done against the altar of Bethel."

[18]And he said, "Let him alone; let no one move his bones." So they let his bones alone, with the bones of the prophet who came from Samaria.

[19]Now Josiah also took away all the shrines of the high places that *were* in the cities of Samaria, which the kings of Israel had made to provoke the Lord[a] to anger; and he did to them according to all the deeds he had done in Bethel. [20]He executed all the priests of the high places who *were* there, on the altars, and burned men's bones on them; and he returned to Jerusalem.

[21]Then the king commanded all the people, saying, "Keep the Passover to the Lord your God, as *it is* written in this Book of the Covenant." [22]Such a Passover surely had never been held since the days of the judges who judged Israel, nor in all the days of the kings of Israel and the kings of Judah. [23]But in the eighteenth year of King Josiah this Passover was held before the Lord in Jerusalem. [24]Moreover Josiah put away those who consulted mediums and spiritists, the household gods and idols, all the abominations that were seen in the land of Judah and in Jerusalem, that he might perform the words of the law which were written in the book that Hilkiah the priest found in the house of the Lord. [25]Now before him there was no king like him, who turned to the Lord with all his heart, with all his soul, and with all his might, according to all the Law of Moses; nor after him did *any* arise like him.

Impending Judgment on Judah

[26]Nevertheless the Lord did not turn from the fierceness of His great wrath, with

---

23:7 [a]Hebrew *qedeshim,* that is, those practicing sodomy and prostitution in religious rituals
23:10 [a]Kethib reads *Sons.*   **23:19** [a]Following Septuagint, Syriac, and Vulgate; Masoretic Text and Targum omit *the Lord.*

which His anger was aroused against Judah, because of all the provocations with which Manasseh had provoked Him. ²⁷And the LORD said, "I will also remove Judah from My sight, as I have removed Israel, and will cast off this city Jerusalem which I have chosen, and the house of which I said, 'My name shall be there.' "ᵃ

Josiah Dies in Battle

²⁸Now the rest of the acts of Josiah, and all that he did, *are* they not written in the book of the chronicles of the kings of Judah? ²⁹In his days Pharaoh Necho king of Egypt went to the aid of the king of Assyria, to the River Euphrates; and King Josiah went against him. And *Pharaoh Necho* killed him at Megiddo when he confronted him. ³⁰Then his servants moved his body in a chariot from Megiddo, brought him to Jerusalem, and buried him in his own tomb. And the people of the land took Jehoahaz the son of Josiah, anointed him, and made him king in his father's place.

The Reign and Captivity of Jehoahaz

³¹Jehoahaz *was* twenty-three years old when he became king, and he reigned three months in Jerusalem. His mother's name *was* Hamutal the daughter of Jeremiah of Libnah. ³²And he did evil in the sight of the LORD, according to all that his fathers had done. ³³Now Pharaoh Necho put him in prison at Riblah in the land of Hamath, that he might not reign in Jerusalem; and he imposed on the land a tribute of one hundred talents of silver and a talent of gold. ³⁴Then Pharaoh Necho made Eliakim the son of Josiah king in place of his father Josiah, and changed his name to Jehoiakim. And *Pharaoh* took Jehoahaz and went to Egypt, and heᵃ died there.

Jehoiakim Reigns in Judah

³⁵So Jehoiakim gave the silver and gold to Pharaoh; but he taxed the land to give money according to the command of Pharaoh; he exacted the silver and gold from the people of the land, from every one according to his assessment, to give *it* to Pharaoh Necho. ³⁶Jehoiakim *was* twenty-five years old when he became king, and

he reigned eleven years in Jerusalem. His mother's name *was* Zebudah the daughter of Pedaiah of Rumah. ³⁷And he did evil in the sight of the LORD, according to all that his fathers had done.

Judah Overrun by Enemies

24 In his days Nebuchadnezzar king of Babylon came up, and Jehoiakim became his vassal *for* three years. Then he turned and rebelled against him. ²And the LORD sent against him *raiding* bands of Chaldeans, bands of Syrians, bands of Moabites, and bands of the people of Ammon; He sent them against Judah to destroy it, according to the word of the LORD which He had spoken by His servants the prophets. ³Surely at the commandment of the LORD *this* came upon Judah, to remove *them* from His sight because of the sins of Manasseh, according to all that he had done, ⁴and also because of the innocent blood that he had shed; for he had filled Jerusalem with innocent blood, which the LORD would not pardon.

⁵Now the rest of the acts of Jehoiakim, and all that he did, *are* they not written in the book of the chronicles of the kings of Judah? ⁶So Jehoiakim rested with his fathers. Then Jehoiachin his son reigned in his place.

⁷And the king of Egypt did not come out of his land anymore, for the king of Babylon had taken all that belonged to the king of Egypt from the Brook of Egypt to the River Euphrates.

The Reign and Captivity of Jehoiachin

⁸Jehoiachin *was* eighteen years old when he became king, and he reigned in Jerusalem three months. His mother's name *was* Nehushta the daughter of Elnathan of Jerusalem. ⁹And he did evil in the sight of the LORD, according to all that his father had done.

¹⁰At that time the servants of Nebuchadnezzar king of Babylon came up against Jerusalem, and the city was besieged. ¹¹And Nebuchadnezzar king of Babylon came against the city, as his servants were besieging it. ¹²Then Jehoiachin king of Judah, his

---

23:27 ᵃ1 Kings 8:29   23:34 ᵃThat is, Jehoahaz

mother, his servants, his princes, and his officers went out to the king of Babylon; and the king of Babylon, in the eighth year of his reign, took him prisoner.

The Captivity of Jerusalem

¹³And he carried out from there all the treasures of the house of the LORD and the treasures of the king's house, and he cut in pieces all the articles of gold which Solomon king of Israel had made in the temple of the LORD, as the LORD had said. ¹⁴Also he carried into captivity all Jerusalem: all the captains and all the mighty men of valor, ten thousand captives, and all the craftsmen and smiths. None remained except the poorest people of the land. ¹⁵And he carried Jehoiachin captive to Babylon. The king's mother, the king's wives, his officers, and the mighty of the land he carried into captivity from Jerusalem to Babylon. ¹⁶All the valiant men, seven thousand, and craftsmen and smiths, one thousand, all *who were* strong *and* fit for war, these the king of Babylon brought captive to Babylon.

Zedekiah Reigns in Judah

¹⁷Then the king of Babylon made Mattaniah, *Jehoiachin's*ᵃ uncle, king in his place, and changed his name to Zedekiah.

¹⁸Zedekiah *was* twenty-one years old when he became king, and he reigned eleven years in Jerusalem. His mother's name *was* Hamutal the daughter of Jeremiah of Libnah. ¹⁹He also did evil in the sight of the LORD, according to all that Jehoiakim had done. ²⁰For because of the anger of the LORD *this* happened in Jerusalem and Judah, that He finally cast them out from His presence. Then Zedekiah rebelled against the king of Babylon.

The Fall and Captivity of Judah

25 Now it came to pass in the ninth year of his reign, in the tenth month, on the tenth *day* of the month, *that* Nebuchadnezzar king of Babylon and all his army came against Jerusalem and encamped against it; and they built a siege wall against it all around. ²So the city was besieged until the eleventh year of King Zedekiah. ³By the ninth *day* of the *fourth* month the famine had become so severe in the city that there was no food for the people of the land.

⁴Then the city wall was broken through, and all the men of war *fled* at night by way of the gate between two walls, which was by the king's garden, even though the Chaldeans *were* still encamped all around against the city. And *the king*ᵃ went by way of the plain.ᵇ ⁵But the army of the Chaldeans pursued the king, and they overtook him in the plains of Jericho. All his army was scattered from him. ⁶So they took the king and brought him up to the king of Babylon at Riblah, and they pronounced judgment on him. ⁷Then they killed the sons of Zedekiah before his eyes, put out the eyes of Zedekiah, bound him with bronze fetters, and took him to Babylon.

⁸And in the fifth month, on the seventh *day* of the month (which *was* the nineteenth year of King Nebuchadnezzar king of Babylon), Nebuzaradan the captain of the guard, a servant of the king of Babylon, came to Jerusalem. ⁹He burned the house of the LORD and the king's house; all the houses of Jerusalem, that is, all the houses of the great, he burned with fire. ¹⁰And all the army of the Chaldeans who *were with* the captain of the guard broke down the walls of Jerusalem all around.

¹¹Then Nebuzaradan the captain of the guard carried away captive the rest of the people *who* remained in the city and the defectors who had deserted to the king of Babylon, with the rest of the multitude. ¹²But the captain of the guard left *some* of the poor of the land as vinedressers and farmers. ¹³The bronze pillars that *were* in the house of the LORD, and the carts and the bronze Sea that *were* in the house of the LORD, the Chaldeans broke in pieces, and carried their bronze to Babylon. ¹⁴They also took away the pots, the shovels, the trimmers, the spoons, and all the bronze utensils with which the priests ministered. ¹⁵The firepans and the basins, the things of solid gold and solid silver, the captain of the guard took away. ¹⁶The two pillars, one Sea, and the carts, which Solomon had made

---

24:17 ᵃLiterally *his*   25:4 ᵃLiterally *he* ᵇOr *Arabah,* that is, the Jordan Valley

for the house of the LORD, the bronze of all these articles was beyond measure. ¹⁷The height of one pillar *was* eighteen cubits, and the capital on it *was* of bronze. The height of the capital was three cubits, and the network and pomegranates all around the capital were all of bronze. The second pillar was the same, with a network.

¹⁸And the captain of the guard took Seraiah the chief priest, Zephaniah the second priest, and the three doorkeepers. ¹⁹He also took out of the city an officer who had charge of the men of war, five men of the king's close associates who were found in the city, the chief recruiting officer of the army, who mustered the people of the land, and sixty men of the people of the land *who were* found in the city. ²⁰So Nebuzaradan, captain of the guard, took these and brought them to the king of Babylon at Riblah. ²¹Then the king of Babylon struck them and put them to death at Riblah in the land of Hamath. Thus Judah was carried away captive from its own land.

Gedaliah Made Governor of Judah

²²Then he made Gedaliah the son of Ahikam, the son of Shaphan, governor over the people who remained in the land of Judah, whom Nebuchadnezzar king of Babylon had left. ²³Now when all the captains of the armies, they and *their* men, heard that the king of Babylon had made Gedaliah governor, they came to Gedaliah at Mizpah—Ishmael the son of Nethaniah, Johanan the son of Careah, Seraiah the son of Tanhumeth the Netophathite, and Jaazaniahᵃ the son of a Maachathite, they and their men. ²⁴And Gedaliah took an oath before them and their men, and said to them, "Do not be afraid of the servants of the Chaldeans. Dwell in the land and serve the king of Babylon, and it shall be well with you."

²⁵But it happened in the seventh month that Ishmael the son of Nethaniah, the son of Elishama, of the royal family, came with ten men and struck and killed Gedaliah, the Jews, as well as the Chaldeans who were with him at Mizpah. ²⁶And all the people, small and great, and the captains of the armies, arose and went to Egypt; for they were afraid of the Chaldeans.

Jehoiachin Released from Prison

²⁷Now it came to pass in the thirty-seventh year of the captivity of Jehoiachin king of Judah, in the twelfth month, on the twenty-seventh *day* of the month, *that* Evil-Merodachᵃ king of Babylon, in the year that he began to reign, released Jehoiachin king of Judah from prison. ²⁸He spoke kindly to him, and gave him a more prominent seat than those of the kings who *were* with him in Babylon. ²⁹So Jehoiachin changed from his prison garments, and he ate bread regularly before the king all the days of his life. ³⁰And as for his provisions, *there was* a regular ration given him by the king, a portion for each day, all the days of his life.

25:23 ᵃSpelled *Jezaniah* in Jeremiah 40:8
25:27 ᵃLiterally *Man of Marduk*

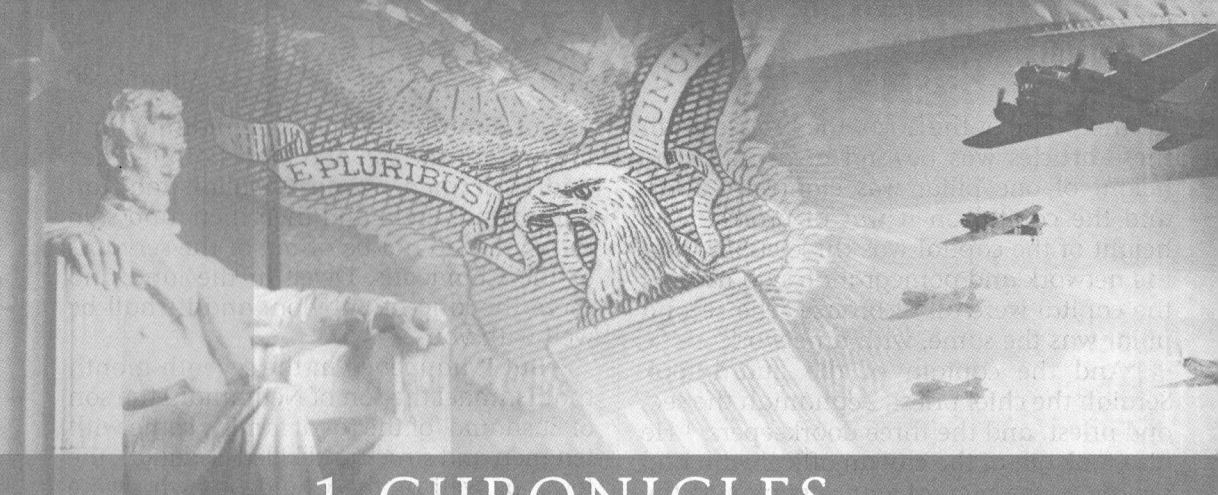

1 CHRONICLES

Author: Attributed to Ezra

When Written: 425–400 B.C.

Theme: Heritage, Covenant

Key Verse: 1 Chronicles 29:11—"Yours, O LORD, is the greatness, the power and the glory, the victory and the majesty; for all that is in heaven and in earth is Yours; Yours is the kingdom, O LORD, and You are exalted as head over all."

Key Chapter: 1 Chronicles 17—A pivotal passage for this book—and all of Scripture—is God's promise to David, recorded in chapter 17, that He would establish David's own Son (ultimately fulfilled through the Lord Jesus Christ) "in My house and in My kingdom forever; and his throne shall be established forever" (v. 14).

While the Books of Chronicles might appear to be a repeat of the narratives of 1 and 2 Samuel and 1 and 2 Kings, they were actually penned for the Israelites returning from their years of bondage in Babylon, to remind and encourage them concerning God's unchanging covenant with His people. Beginning with a list of all who form the chain of God's chosen family, 1 Chronicles goes on to recount the reign of one of the greatest heroes of Scripture, King David, and God's promise to establish his throne forever. Such a promise would have spoken great comfort to the returning exiles.

Heritage and history are important reference points for any nation, offering examples of both past successes and failures, of righteousness and shortcomings, that can serve as signposts and examples for future generations. How our forefathers fought for liberty in the American Revolution, battled and killed one another in our nation's great Civil War, or hammered out the essence of civil rights for all individuals during the middle part of the twentieth century—all are pieces of a large and rich tapestry of heritage from which every citizen can draw in the ongoing effort to maintain our liberties.

1 CHRONICLES

The Family of Adam—Seth to Abraham

1 Adam, Seth, Enosh, ²Cainan,ᵃ Mahalalel, Jared, ³Enoch, Methuselah, Lamech, ⁴Noah,ᵃ Shem, Ham, and Japheth.

⁵The sons of Japheth *were* Gomer, Magog, Madai, Javan, Tubal, Meshech, and Tiras. ⁶The sons of Gomer *were* Ashkenaz, Diphath,ᵃ and Togarmah. ⁷The sons of Javan *were* Elishah, Tarshishah,ᵃ Kittim, and Rodanim.ᵇ

⁸The sons of Ham *were* Cush, Mizraim, Put, and Canaan. ⁹The sons of Cush *were* Seba, Havilah, Sabta,ᵃ Raama,ᵇ and Sabtecha. The sons of Raama *were* Sheba and Dedan. ¹⁰Cush begot Nimrod; he began to be a mighty one on the earth. ¹¹Mizraim begot Ludim, Anamim, Lehabim, Naphtuhim, ¹²Pathrusim, Casluhim (from whom came the Philistines and the Caphtorim). ¹³Canaan begot Sidon, his firstborn, and Heth; ¹⁴the Jebusite, the Amorite, and the Girgashite; ¹⁵the Hivite, the Arkite, and the Sinite; ¹⁶the Arvadite, the Zemarite, and the Hamathite.

¹⁷The sons of Shem *were* Elam, Asshur, Arphaxad, Lud, Aram, Uz, Hul, Gether, and Meshech.ᵃ ¹⁸Arphaxad begot Shelah, and Shelah begot Eber. ¹⁹To Eber were born two sons: the name of one *was* Peleg,ᵃ for in his days the earth was divided; and his brother's name *was* Joktan. ²⁰Joktan begot Almodad, Sheleph, Hazarmaveth, Jerah, ²¹Hadoram, Uzal, Diklah, ²²Ebal,ᵃ Abimael, Sheba, ²³Ophir, Havilah, and Jobab. All these *were* the sons of Joktan.

²⁴Shem, Arphaxad, Shelah, ²⁵Eber, Peleg, Reu, ²⁶Serug, Nahor, Terah, ²⁷and Abram, who *is* Abraham. ²⁸The sons of Abraham *were* Isaac and Ishmael.

The Family of Ishmael

²⁹These *are* their genealogies: The firstborn of Ishmael *was* Nebajoth; then Kedar, Adbeel, Mibsam, ³⁰Mishma, Dumah, Massa, Hadad,ᵃ Tema, ³¹Jetur, Naphish, and Kedemah. These *were* the sons of Ishmael.

The Family of Keturah

³²Now the sons born to Keturah, Abraham's concubine, *were* Zimran, Jokshan, Medan, Midian, Ishbak, and Shuah. The sons of Jokshan *were* Sheba and Dedan. ³³The sons of Midian *were* Ephah, Epher, Hanoch, Abida, and Eldaah. All these were the children of Keturah.

The Family of Isaac

³⁴And Abraham begot Isaac. The sons of Isaac *were* Esau and Israel. ³⁵The sons of Esau *were* Eliphaz, Reuel, Jeush, Jaalam, and Korah. ³⁶And the sons of Eliphaz *were* Teman, Omar, Zephi,ᵃ Gatam, *and* Kenaz; and *by* Timna,ᵇ Amalek. ³⁷The sons of Reuel *were* Nahath, Zerah, Shammah, and Mizzah.

The Family of Seir

³⁸The sons of Seir *were* Lotan, Shobal, Zibeon, Anah, Dishon, Ezer, and Dishan. ³⁹And the sons of Lotan *were* Hori and Homam; Lotan's sister *was* Timna. ⁴⁰The sons of Shobal *were* Alian,ᵃ Manahath, Ebal, Shephi,ᵇ and Onam. The sons of Zibeon *were* Ajah and Anah. ⁴¹The son of Anah *was* Dishon. The sons of Dishon *were* Hamran,ᵃ Eshban, Ithran, and Cheran. ⁴²The sons of Ezer *were* Bilhan, Zaavan, *and* Jaakan.ᵃ The sons of Dishan *were* Uz and Aran.

The Kings of Edom

⁴³Now these *were* the kings who reigned in the land of Edom before a king reigned

---

1:2 ᵃHebrew *Qenan*   **1:4** ᵃFollowing Masoretic Text and Vulgate; Septuagint adds *the sons of Noah*. **1:6** ᵃSpelled *Riphath* in Genesis 10:3 **1:7** ᵃSpelled *Tarshish* in Genesis 10:4 ᵇSpelled *Dodanim* in Genesis 10:4   **1:9** ᵃSpelled *Sabtah* in Genesis 10:7 ᵇSpelled *Raamah* in Genesis 10:7   **1:17** ᵃSpelled *Mash* in Genesis 10:23   **1:19** ᵃLiterally *Division* **1:22** ᵃSpelled *Obal* in Genesis 10:28   **1:30** ᵃSpelled *Hadar* in Genesis 25:15   **1:36** ᵃSpelled *Zepho* in Genesis 36:11 ᵇCompare Genesis 36:12 **1:40** ᵃSpelled *Alvan* in Genesis 36:23 ᵇSpelled *Shepho* in Genesis 36:23   **1:41** ᵃSpelled *Hemdan* in Genesis 36:26   **1:42** ᵃSpelled *Akan* in Genesis 36:27

over the children of Israel: Bela the son of Beor, and the name of his city was Dinhabah. ⁴⁴And when Bela died, Jobab the son of Zerah of Bozrah reigned in his place. ⁴⁵When Jobab died, Husham of the land of the Temanites reigned in his place. ⁴⁶And when Husham died, Hadad the son of Bedad, who attacked Midian in the field of Moab, reigned in his place. The name of his city was Avith. ⁴⁷When Hadad died, Samlah of Masrekah reigned in his place. ⁴⁸And when Samlah died, Saul of Rehoboth-by-the-River reigned in his place. ⁴⁹When Saul died, Baal-Hanan the son of Achbor reigned in his place. ⁵⁰And when Baal-Hanan died, Hadadᵃ reigned in his place; and the name of his city was Pai.ᵇ His wife's name was Mehetabel the daughter of Matred, the daughter of Mezahab. ⁵¹Hadad died also. And the chiefs of Edom were Chief Timnah, Chief Aliah,ᵃ Chief Jetheth, ⁵²Chief Aholibamah, Chief Elah, Chief Pinon, ⁵³Chief Kenaz, Chief Teman, Chief Mibzar, ⁵⁴Chief Magdiel, and Chief Iram. These *were* the chiefs of Edom.

The Family of Israel

2 These *were* the sons of Israel: Reuben, Simeon, Levi, Judah, Issachar, Zebulun, ²Dan, Joseph, Benjamin, Naphtali, Gad, and Asher.

From Judah to David

³The sons of Judah *were* Er, Onan, and Shelah. *These* three were born to him by the daughter of Shua, the Canaanitess. Er, the firstborn of Judah, was wicked in the sight of the LORD; so He killed him. ⁴And Tamar, his daughter-in-law, bore him Perez and Zerah. All the sons of Judah *were* five. ⁵The sons of Perez *were* Hezron and Hamul. ⁶The sons of Zerah *were* Zimri, Ethan, Heman, Calcol, and Dara—five of them in all. ⁷The son of Carmi *was* Achar,ᵃ the troubler of Israel, who transgressed in the accursed thing.

⁸The son of Ethan *was* Azariah.

⁹Also the sons of Hezron who were born to him *were* Jerahmeel, Ram, and Chelubai.ᵃ ¹⁰Ram begot Amminadab, and Amminadab begot Nahshon, leader of the children of Judah; ¹¹Nahshon begot Salma,ᵃ

and Salma begot Boaz; ¹²Boaz begot Obed, and Obed begot Jesse; ¹³Jesse begot Eliab his firstborn, Abinadab the second, Shimeaᵃ the third, ¹⁴Nethanel the fourth, Raddai the fifth, ¹⁵Ozem the sixth, *and* David the seventh.

¹⁶Now their sisters *were* Zeruiah and Abigail. And the sons of Zeruiah *were* Abishai, Joab, and Asahel—three. ¹⁷Abigail bore Amasa; and the father of Amasa *was* Jether the Ishmaelite.ᵃ

The Family of Hezron

¹⁸Caleb the son of Hezron had children by Azubah, *his* wife, and by Jerioth. Now these were her sons: Jesher, Shobab, and Ardon. ¹⁹When Azubah died, Caleb took Ephrathᵃ as his wife, who bore him Hur. ²⁰And Hur begot Uri, and Uri begot Bezalel.

²¹Now afterward Hezron went in to the daughter of Machir the father of Gilead, whom he married when he *was* sixty years old; and she bore him Segub. ²²Segub begot Jair, who had twenty-three cities in the land of Gilead. ²³(Geshur and Syria took from them the towns of Jair, with Kenath and its towns—sixty towns.) All these *belonged to* the sons of Machir the father of Gilead. ²⁴After Hezron died in Caleb Ephrathah, Hezron's wife Abijah bore him Ashhur the father of Tekoa.

The Family of Jerahmeel

²⁵The sons of Jerahmeel, the firstborn of Hezron, *were* Ram, the firstborn, and Bunah, Oren, Ozem, *and* Ahijah. ²⁶Jerahmeel had another wife, whose name was Atarah; she was the mother of Onam. ²⁷The sons of Ram, the firstborn of Jerahmeel, were Maaz, Jamin, and Eker. ²⁸The sons of Onam were Shammai and Jada. The sons of Shammai *were* Nadab and Abishur.

²⁹And the name of the wife of Abishur *was* Abihail, and she bore him Ahban and Molid. ³⁰The sons of Nadab *were* Seled and

---

1:50 ᵃSpelled *Hadar* in Genesis 36:39   ᵇSpelled *Pau* in Genesis 36:39   **1:51** ᵃSpelled *Alvah* in Genesis 36:40   **2:7** ᵃSpelled *Achan* in Joshua 7:1 and elsewhere   **2:9** ᵃSpelled *Caleb* in 2:18, 42   **2:11** ᵃSpelled *Salmon* in Ruth 4:21 and Luke 3:32   **2:13** ᵃSpelled *Shammah* in 1 Samuel 16:9 and elsewhere   **2:17** ᵃCompare 2 Samuel 17:25   **2:19** ᵃSpelled *Ephrathah* elsewhere

Appaim; Seled died without children. ³¹The son of Appaim *was* Ishi, the son of Ishi *was* Sheshan, and Sheshan's son *was* Ahlai. ³²The sons of Jada, the brother of Shammai, *were* Jether and Jonathan; Jether died without children. ³³The sons of Jonathan *were* Peleth and Zaza. These were the sons of Jerahmeel.

³⁴Now Sheshan had no sons, only daughters. And Sheshan had an Egyptian servant whose name *was* Jarha. ³⁵Sheshan gave his daughter to Jarha his servant as wife, and she bore him Attai. ³⁶Attai begot Nathan, and Nathan begot Zabad; ³⁷Zabad begot Ephlal, and Ephlal begot Obed; ³⁸Obed begot Jehu, and Jehu begot Azariah; ³⁹Azariah begot Helez, and Helez begot Eleasah; ⁴⁰Eleasah begot Sismai, and Sismai begot Shallum; ⁴¹Shallum begot Jekamiah, and Jekamiah begot Elishama.

The Family of Caleb

⁴²The descendants of Caleb the brother of Jerahmeel *were* Mesha, his firstborn, who was the father of Ziph, and the sons of Mareshah the father of Hebron. ⁴³The sons of Hebron *were* Korah, Tappuah, Rekem, and Shema. ⁴⁴Shema begot Raham the father of Jorkoam, and Rekem begot Shammai. ⁴⁵And the son of Shammai *was* Maon, and Maon *was* the father of Beth Zur.

⁴⁶Ephah, Caleb's concubine, bore Haran, Moza, and Gazez; and Haran begot Gazez. ⁴⁷And the sons of Jahdai *were* Regem, Jotham, Geshan, Pelet, Ephah, and Shaaph.

⁴⁸Maachah, Caleb's concubine, bore Sheber and Tirhanah. ⁴⁹She also bore Shaaph the father of Madmannah, Sheva the father of Machbenah and the father of Gibea. And the daughter of Caleb *was* Achsah.

⁵⁰These were the descendants of Caleb: The sons of Hur, the firstborn of Ephrathah, *were* Shobal the father of Kirjath Jearim, ⁵¹Salma the father of Bethlehem, *and* Hareph the father of Beth Gader.

⁵²And Shobal the father of Kirjath Jearim had descendants: Haroeh, *and* half of the *families of* Manuhoth.ᵃ ⁵³The families of Kirjath Jearim *were* the Ithrites, the Puthites, the Shumathites, and the Mishraites. From these came the Zorathites and the Eshtaolites.

⁵⁴The sons of Salma *were* Bethlehem, the Netophathites, Atroth Beth Joab, half of the Manahethites, and the Zorites. ⁵⁵And the families of the scribes who dwelt at Jabez *were* the Tirathites, the Shimeathites, *and* the Suchathites. These *were* the Kenites who came from Hammath, the father of the house of Rechab.

The Family of David

3 Now these were the sons of David who were born to him in Hebron: The first-born *was* Amnon, by Ahinoam the Jezreelitess; the second, Daniel,ᵃ by Abigail the Carmelitess; ²the third, Absalom the son of Maacah, the daughter of Talmai, king of Geshur; the fourth, Adonijah the son of Haggith; ³the fifth, Shephatiah, by Abital; the sixth, Ithream, by his wife Eglah.

⁴*These* six were born to him in Hebron. There he reigned seven years and six months, and in Jerusalem he reigned thirty-three years. ⁵And these were born to him in Jerusalem: Shimea,ᵃ Shobab, Nathan, and Solomon—four by Bathshuaᵇ the daughter of Ammiel.ᶜ ⁶Also *there* were Ibhar, Elishama,ᵃ Eliphelet,ᵇ ⁷Nogah, Nepheg, Japhia, ⁸Elishama, Eliada,ᵃ and Eliphelet—nine *in all.* ⁹*These were* all the sons of David, besides the sons of the concubines, and Tamar their sister.

The Family of Solomon

¹⁰Solomon's son *was* Rehoboam; Abijahᵃ *was* his son, Asa his son, Jehoshaphat his son, ¹¹Joramᵃ his son, Ahaziah his son, Joashᵇ his son, ¹²Amaziah his son, Azariahᵃ his son, Jotham his son, ¹³Ahaz his son, Hezekiah his son, Manasseh his son, ¹⁴Amon his son, *and* Josiah his son. ¹⁵The sons of Josiah *were* Johanan the firstborn, the second Jehoiakim, the third Zedekiah,

---

2:52 ᵃSame as *the Manahethites,* verse 54
3:1 ᵃCalled *Chileab* in 2 Samuel 3:3   **3:5** ᵃSpelled *Shammua* in 14:4 and 2 Samuel 5:14 ᵇSpelled *Bathsheba* in 2 Samuel 11:3 ᶜCalled *Eliam* in 2 Samuel 11:3   **3:6** ᵃSpelled *Elishua* in 14:5 and 2 Samuel 5:15 ᵇSpelled *Elpelet* in 14:5
3:8 ᵃSpelled *Beeliada* in 14:7   **3:10** ᵃSpelled *Abijam* in 1 Kings 15:1   **3:11** ᵃSpelled *Jehoram* in 2 Kings 1:17 and 8:16 ᵇSpelled *Jehoash* in 2 Kings 12:1
3:12 ᵃCalled *Uzziah* in Isaiah 6:1

and the fourth Shallum.ᵃ ¹⁶The sons of Jehoiakim *were* Jeconiah his son *and* Zedekiahᵃ his son.

The Family of Jeconiah

¹⁷And the sons of Jeconiahᵃ *were* Assir,ᵇ Shealtiel his son, ¹⁸*and* Malchiram, Pedaiah, Shenazzar, Jecamiah, Hoshama, and Nedabiah. ¹⁹The sons of Pedaiah *were* Zerubbabel and Shimei. The sons of Zerubbabel *were* Meshullam, Hananiah, Shelomith their sister, ²⁰and Hashubah, Ohel, Berechiah, Hasadiah, and Jushab-Hesed—five *in all.*

²¹The sons of Hananiah *were* Pelatiah and Jeshaiah, the sons of Rephaiah, the sons of Arnan, the sons of Obadiah, and the sons of Shechaniah. ²²The son of Shechaniah was Shemaiah. The sons of Shemaiah *were* Hattush, Igal, Bariah, Neariah, and Shaphat—six *in all.* ²³The sons of Neariah *were* Elioenai, Hezekiah, and Azrikam—three *in all.* ²⁴The sons of Elioenai *were* Hodaviah, Eliashib, Pelaiah, Akkub, Johanan, Delaiah, and Anani—seven *in all.*

The Family of Judah

4 The sons of Judah *were* Perez, Hezron, Carmi, Hur, and Shobal. ²And Reaiah the son of Shobal begot Jahath, and Jahath begot Ahumai and Lahad. These *were* the families of the Zorathites. ³These *were the sons of* the father of Etam: Jezreel, Ishma, and Idbash; and the name of their sister *was* Hazelelponi; ⁴and Penuel *was* the father of Gedor, and Ezer *was the* father of Hushah.

These *were* the sons of Hur, the firstborn of Ephrathah the father of Bethlehem.

⁵And Ashhur the father of Tekoa had two wives, Helah and Naarah. ⁶Naarah bore him Ahuzzam, Hepher, Temeni, and Haahashtari. These *were* the sons of Naarah. ⁷The sons of Helah *were* Zereth, Zohar, and Ethnan; ⁸and Koz begot Anub, Zobebah, and the families of Aharhel the son of Harum.

⁹Now Jabez was more honorable than his brothers, and his mother called his name Jabez,ᵃ saying, "Because I bore *him* in pain." ¹⁰And Jabez called on the God of Israel saying, "Oh, that You would bless me indeed, and enlarge my territory, that Your hand would be with me, and that You would keep *me* from evil, that I may not cause pain!" So God granted him what he requested.

¹¹Chelub the brother of Shuhah begot Mehir, who *was* the father of Eshton. ¹²And Eshton begot Beth-Rapha, Paseah, and Tehinnah the father of Ir-Nahash. These *were* the men of Rechah.

¹³The sons of Kenaz *were* Othniel and Seraiah. The sons of Othniel *were* Hathath,ᵃ ¹⁴and Meonothai *who* begot Ophrah. Seraiah begot Joab the father of Ge Harashim,ᵃ for they were craftsmen. ¹⁵The sons of Caleb the son of Jephunneh *were* Iru, Elah, and Naam. The son of Elah *was* Kenaz. ¹⁶The sons of Jehallelel *were* Ziph, Ziphah, Tiria, and Asarel. ¹⁷The sons of Ezrah *were* Jether, Mered, Epher, and Jalon. And *Mered's wife*ᵃ bore Miriam, Shammai, and Ishbah the father of Eshtemoa. ¹⁸(His wife Jehudijahᵃ bore Jered the father of Gedor, Heber the father of Sochoh, and Jekuthiel the father of Zanoah.) And these were the sons of Bithiah the daughter of Pharaoh, whom Mered took.

¹⁹The sons of Hodiah's wife, the sister of Naham, *were* the fathers of Keilah the Garmite and of Eshtemoa the Maachathite. ²⁰And the sons of Shimon *were* Amnon, Rinnah, Ben-Hanan, and Tilon. And the sons of Ishi *were* Zoheth and Ben-Zoheth.

²¹The sons of Shelah the son of Judah *were* Er the father of Lecah, Laadah the father of Mareshah, and the families of the house of the linen workers of the house of Ashbea; ²²also Jokim, the men of Chozeba, and Joash; Saraph, who ruled in Moab, and Jashubi-Lehem. Now the records are ancient. ²³These *were* the potters and those who dwell at Netaimᵃ and Gederah;ᵇ there they dwelt with the king for his work.

3:15 ᵃCalled *Jehoahaz* in 2 Kings 23:31
3:16 ᵃCompare 2 Kings 24:17   **3:17** ᵃAlso called *Coniah* in Jeremiah 22:24 and *Jehoiachin* in 2 Kings 24:8   ᵇOr *Jeconiah the captive were*
4:9 ᵃLiterally *He Will Cause Pain*   **4:13** ᵃSeptuagint and Vulgate add *and Meonothai.*   **4:14** ᵃLiterally *Valley of Craftsmen*   **4:17** ᵃLiterally *she*
4:18 ᵃOr *His Judean wife*   **4:23** ᵃLiterally *Plants*
ᵇLiterally *Hedges*

The Family of Simeon

²⁴The sons of Simeon *were* Nemuel, Jamin, Jarib,ᵃ Zerah,ᵇ *and* Shaul, ²⁵Shallum his son, Mibsam his son, and Mishma his son. ²⁶And the sons of Mishma *were* Hamuel his son, Zacchur his son, and Shimei his son. ²⁷Shimei had sixteen sons and six daughters; but his brothers did not have many children, nor did any of their families multiply as much as the children of Judah.

²⁸They dwelt at Beersheba, Moladah, Hazar Shual, ²⁹Bilhah, Ezem, Tolad, ³⁰Bethuel, Hormah, Ziklag, ³¹Beth Marcaboth, Hazar Susim, Beth Biri, and at Shaaraim. These *were* their cities until the reign of David. ³²And their villages *were* Etam, Ain, Rimmon, Tochen, and Ashan— five cities— ³³and all the villages that *were* around these cities as far as Baal.ᵃ These *were* their dwelling places, and they maintained their genealogy: ³⁴Meshobab, Jamlech, and Joshah the son of Amaziah; ³⁵Joel, and Jehu the son of Joshibiah, the son of Seraiah, the son of Asiel; ³⁶Elioenai, Jaakobah, Jeshohaiah, Asaiah, Adiel, Jesimiel, and Benaiah; ³⁷Ziza the son of Shiphi, the son of Allon, the son of Jedaiah, the son of Shimri, the son of Shemaiah— ³⁸these mentioned by name *were* leaders in their families, and their father's house increased greatly.

³⁹So they went to the entrance of Gedor, as far as the east side of the valley, to seek pasture for their flocks. ⁴⁰And they found rich, good pasture, and the land *was* broad, quiet, and peaceful; for some Hamites formerly lived there. ⁴¹These recorded by name came in the days of Hezekiah king of Judah; and they attacked their tents and the Meunites who were found there, and utterly destroyed them, as it is to this day. So they dwelt in their place, because *there was* pasture for their flocks there. ⁴²Now *some* of them, five hundred men of the sons of Simeon, went to Mount Seir, having as their captains Pelatiah, Neariah, Rephaiah, and Uzziel, the sons of Ishi. ⁴³And they defeated the rest of the Amalekites who had escaped. They have dwelt there to this day.

The Family of Reuben

5 Now the sons of Reuben the firstborn of Israel—he *was* indeed the firstborn, but because he defiled his father's bed, his birthright was given to the sons of Joseph, the son of Israel, so that the genealogy is not listed according to the birthright; ²yet Judah prevailed over his brothers, and from him *came* a ruler, although the birthright was Joseph's— ³the sons of Reuben the firstborn of Israel were Hanoch, Pallu, Hezron, and Carmi.

⁴The sons of Joel *were* Shemaiah his son, Gog his son, Shimei his son, ⁵Micah his son, Reaiah his son, Baal his son, ⁶and Beerah his son, whom Tiglath-Pileserᵃ king of Assyria carried into captivity. He *was* leader of the Reubenites. ⁷And his brethren by their families, when the genealogy of their generations was registered: the chief, Jeiel, and Zechariah, ⁸and Bela the son of Azaz, the son of Shema, the son of Joel, who dwelt in Aroer, as far as Nebo and Baal Meon. ⁹Eastward they settled as far as the entrance of the wilderness this side of the River Euphrates, because their cattle had multiplied in the land of Gilead.

¹⁰Now in the days of Saul they made war with the Hagrites, who fell by their hand; and they dwelt in their tents throughout the entire *area* east of Gilead.

The Family of Gad

¹¹And the children of Gad dwelt next to them in the land of Bashan as far as Salcah: ¹²Joel *was* the chief, Shapham the next, then Jaanai and Shaphat in Bashan, ¹³and their brethren of their father's house: Michael, Meshullam, Sheba, Jorai, Jachan, Zia, and Eber—seven *in all*. ¹⁴These *were* the children of Abihail the son of Huri, the son of Jaroah, the son of Gilead, the son of Michael, the son of Jeshishai, the son of Jahdo, the son of Buz; ¹⁵Ahi the son of Abdiel, the son of Guni, *was* chief of their father's house. ¹⁶And *the Gadites* dwelt in Gilead, in Bashan and in its villages, and in all the common-lands of Sharon within their

---

4:24 ᵃCalled *Jachin* in Genesis 46:10 ᵇCalled *Zohar* in Genesis 46:10   **4:33** ᵃOr *Baalath Beer* (compare Joshua 19:8)   **5:6** ᵃHebrew *Tilgath-Pilneser*

"A CHRISTIAN NATION"

In 1892, the United States Supreme Court determined, in the case *The Church of the Holy Trinity vs. United States*, that an English minister was not a foreign laborer under the U.S. Code statute even though he was a foreigner. While this case was not specifically about religion and considered the legality of contracts for other foreign professionals, the court considered America's Christian identity to be a strong support for its conclusion that Congress could not have intended to prohibit foreign ministers.

Justice David Josiah Brewer penned the court's opinion, in which he stated that the United States was a "Christian nation." This statement is included as part of the dicta—that is, it is a gratuitous statement that is not essential to the Court's holding. The Court had already decided the issue before venturing its opinion as to the religious character of the country. Included was a remarkable list of 87 examples taken from pre-Constitutional documents, historical practice, colonial charters, and the like, which reveal our undisputed religious roots. They range from the commission of Christopher Columbus to the first charter of Virginia to the Declaration of Independence and include the following statements:

> *No purpose of action against religion can be imputed to any legislation, state or national, because this is a religious people. This is historically true. From the discovery of this continent to the present hour, there is a single voice making this affirmation. . . . There is no dissonance in these declarations. There is a universal language pervading them all, having one meaning; they affirm and reaffirm that this is a religious nation. These are not individual sayings, declarations of private persons: they are organic utterances; they speak the voice of the entire people. . . . These, and many other matters which might be noticed, add a volume of unofficial declarations to the mass of organic utterances that this is a Christian nation.*

Brewer later clarified his position on a "Christian nation," stating the U.S. is "Christian" in that many of its traditions are rooted in Christianity, not that Christianity should receive legal privileges or is established to the exclusion of other religions or to the exclusion of irreligion.

borders. ¹⁷All these were registered by genealogies in the days of Jotham king of Judah, and in the days of Jeroboam king of Israel.

¹⁸The sons of Reuben, the Gadites, and half the tribe of Manasseh *had* forty-four thousand seven hundred and sixty valiant men, men able to bear shield and sword, to shoot with the bow, and skillful in war, who went to war. ¹⁹They made war with the Hagrites, Jetur, Naphish, and Nodab. ²⁰And they were helped against them, and the Hagrites were delivered into their hand, and all who *were* with them, for they cried out to God in the battle. He heeded their prayer, because they put their trust in Him. ²¹Then they took away their livestock—fifty thousand of their camels, two hundred and fifty thousand of their sheep, and two thousand of their donkeys—also one hundred thousand of their men; ²²for many fell dead, because the war *was* God's. And they dwelt in their place until the captivity.

The Family of Manasseh (East)

²³So the children of the half-tribe of Manasseh dwelt in the land. Their *numbers* increased from Bashan to Baal Hermon, that is, to Senir, or Mount Hermon. ²⁴These *were* the heads of their fathers' houses: Epher, Ishi, Eliel, Azriel, Jeremiah, Hodaviah, and Jahdiel. They were mighty men of valor, famous men, *and* heads of their fathers' houses.

²⁵And they were unfaithful to the God of their fathers, and played the harlot after the gods of the peoples of the land, whom God had destroyed before them. ²⁶So the God of Israel stirred up the spirit of Pul king of Assyria, that is, Tiglath-Pileser^a king of Assyria. He carried the Reubenites, the Gadites, and the half-tribe of Manasseh into captivity. He took them to Halah, Habor, Hara, and the river of Gozan to this day.

The Family of Levi

6 The sons of Levi *were* Gershon, Kohath, and Merari. ²The sons of Kohath *were* Amram, Izhar, Hebron, and Uzziel. ³The children of Amram *were* Aaron, Moses, and Miriam. And the sons of Aaron *were* Nadab, Abihu, Eleazar, and Ithamar. ⁴Eleazar begot Phinehas, *and* Phinehas begot Abishua;

⁵Abishua begot Bukki, and Bukki begot Uzzi; ⁶Uzzi begot Zerahiah, and Zerahiah begot Meraioth; ⁷Meraioth begot Amariah, and Amariah begot Ahitub; ⁸Ahitub begot Zadok, and Zadok begot Ahimaaz; ⁹Ahimaaz begot Azariah, and Azariah begot Johanan; ¹⁰Johanan begot Azariah (it was he who ministered as priest in the temple that Solomon built in Jerusalem); ¹¹Azariah begot Amariah, and Amariah begot Ahitub; ¹²Ahitub begot Zadok, and Zadok begot Shallum; ¹³Shallum begot Hilkiah, and Hilkiah begot Azariah; ¹⁴Azariah begot Seraiah, and Seraiah begot Jehozadak. ¹⁵Jehozadak went *into captivity* when the LORD carried Judah and Jerusalem into captivity by the hand of Nebuchadnezzar.

¹⁶The sons of Levi *were* Gershon,^a Kohath, and Merari. ¹⁷These are the names of the sons of Gershon: Libni and Shimei. ¹⁸The sons of Kohath *were* Amram, Izhar, Hebron, and Uzziel. ¹⁹The sons of Merari *were* Mahli and Mushi. Now these *are* the families of the Levites according to their fathers: ²⁰Of Gershon *were* Libni his son, Jahath his son, Zimmah his son, ²¹Joah his son, Iddo his son, Zerah his son, *and* Jeatherai his son. ²²The sons of Kohath *were* Amminadab his son, Korah his son, Assir his son, ²³Elkanah his son, Ebiasaph his son, Assir his son, ²⁴Tahath his son, Uriel his son, Uzziah his son, and Shaul his son. ²⁵The sons of Elkanah *were* Amasai and Ahimoth. ²⁶*As for* Elkanah,^a the sons of Elkanah *were* Zophai^b his son, Nahath^c his son, ²⁷Eliab^a his son, Jeroham his son, *and* Elkanah his son. ²⁸The sons of Samuel *were* Joel^a the firstborn, and Abijah the second.^b ²⁹The sons of Merari *were* Mahli, Libni his son, Shimei his son, Uzzah his son, ³⁰Shimea his son, Haggiah his son, *and* Asaiah his son.

Musicians in the House of the LORD

³¹Now these are the men whom David appointed over the service of song in the

---

5:26 ^aHebrew *Tilgath-Pilneser*   **6:16** ^aHebrew *Gershom* (alternate spelling of *Gershon,* as in verses 1, 17, 20, 43, 62, and 71)   **6:26** ^aCompare verse 35 ^bSpelled *Zuph* in verse 35 and 1 Samuel 1:1 ^cCompare verse 34   **6:27** ^aCompare verse 34 **6:28** ^aFollowing Septuagint, Syriac, and Arabic (compare verse 33 and 1 Samuel 8:2) ^bHebrew *Vasheni*

house of the LORD, after the ark came to rest. ³²They were ministering with music before the dwelling place of the tabernacle of meeting, until Solomon had built the house of the LORD in Jerusalem, and they served in their office according to their order.

³³And these *are* the ones who ministered with their sons: Of the sons of the Kohathites *were* Heman the singer, the son of Joel, the son of Samuel, ³⁴the son of Elkanah, the son of Jeroham, the son of Eliel,ᵃ the son of Toah,ᵇ ³⁵the son of Zuph, the son of Elkanah, the son of Mahath, the son of Amasai, ³⁶the son of Elkanah, the son of Joel, the son of Azariah, the son of Zephaniah, ³⁷the son of Tahath, the son of Assir, the son of Ebiasaph, the son of Korah, ³⁸the son of Izhar, the son of Kohath, the son of Levi, the son of Israel. ³⁹And his brother Asaph, who stood at his right hand, *was* Asaph the son of Berachiah, the son of Shimea, ⁴⁰the son of Michael, the son of Baaseiah, the son of Malchijah, ⁴¹the son of Ethni, the son of Zerah, the son of Adaiah, ⁴²the son of Ethan, the son of Zimmah, the son of Shimei, ⁴³the son of Jahath, the son of Gershon, the son of Levi.

⁴⁴Their brethren, the sons of Merari, on the left hand, *were* Ethan the son of Kishi, the son of Abdi, the son of Malluch, ⁴⁵the son of Hashabiah, the son of Amaziah, the son of Hilkiah, ⁴⁶the son of Amzi, the son of Bani, the son of Shamer, ⁴⁷the son of Mahli, the son of Mushi, the son of Merari, the son of Levi.

⁴⁸And their brethren, the Levites, *were* appointed to every kind of service of the tabernacle of the house of God.

The Family of Aaron

⁴⁹But Aaron and his sons offered sacrifices on the altar of burnt offering and on the altar of incense, for all the work of the Most Holy *Place,* and to make atonement for Israel, according to all that Moses the servant of God had commanded. ⁵⁰Now these *are* the sons of Aaron: Eleazar his son, Phinehas his son, Abishua his son, ⁵¹Bukki his son, Uzzi his son, Zerahiah his son, ⁵²Meraioth his son, Amariah his son, Ahitub his son, ⁵³Zadok his son, *and* Ahimaaz his son.

Dwelling Places of the Levites

⁵⁴Now these *are* their dwelling places throughout their settlements in their territory, for they were *given* by lot to the sons of Aaron, of the family of the Kohathites: ⁵⁵They gave them Hebron in the land of Judah, with its surrounding common-lands. ⁵⁶But the fields of the city and its villages they gave to Caleb the son of Jephunneh. ⁵⁷And to the sons of Aaron they gave *one of* the cities of refuge, Hebron; also Libnah with its common-lands, Jattir, Eshtemoa with its common-lands, ⁵⁸Hilenᵃ with its common-lands, Debir with its common-lands, ⁵⁹Ashanᵃ with its common-lands, and Beth Shemesh with its common-lands. ⁶⁰And from the tribe of Benjamin: Geba with its common-lands, Alemethᵃ with its common-lands, and Anathoth with its common-lands. All their cities among their families *were* thirteen.

⁶¹To the rest of the family of the tribe of the Kohathites *they gave* by lot ten cities from half the tribe of Manasseh. ⁶²And to the sons of Gershon, throughout their families, *they gave* thirteen cities from the tribe of Issachar, from the tribe of Asher, from the tribe of Naphtali, and from the tribe of Manasseh in Bashan. ⁶³To the sons of Merari, throughout their families, *they gave* twelve cities from the tribe of Reuben, from the tribe of Gad, and from the tribe of Zebulun. ⁶⁴So the children of Israel gave *these* cities with their common-lands to the Levites. ⁶⁵And they gave by lot from the tribe of the children of Judah, from the tribe of the children of Simeon, and from the tribe of the children of Benjamin these cities which are called by *their* names.

⁶⁶Now some of the families of the sons of Kohath *were given* cities as their territory from the tribe of Ephraim. ⁶⁷And they gave them *one of* the cities of refuge, Shechem with its common-lands, in the mountains of Ephraim, also Gezer with its common-lands, ⁶⁸Jokmeam with its common-lands, Beth Horon with its common-lands, ⁶⁹Aijalon

---

6:34 ᵃSpelled *Elihu* in 1 Samuel 1:1 ᵇSpelled *Tohu* in 1 Samuel 1:1   **6:58** ᵃSpelled *Holon* in Joshua 21:15 **6:59** ᵃSpelled *Ain* in Joshua 21:16   **6:60** ᵃSpelled *Almon* in Joshua 21:18

with its common-lands, and Gath Rimmon with its common-lands. [70]And from the half-tribe of Manasseh: Aner with its common-lands and Bileam with its common-lands, for the rest of the family of the sons of Kohath.

[71]From the family of the half-tribe of Manasseh the sons of Gershon *were given* Golan in Bashan with its common-lands and Ashtaroth with its common-lands. [72]And from the tribe of Issachar: Kedesh with its common-lands, Daberath with its common-lands, [73]Ramoth with its common-lands, and Anem with its common-lands. [74]And from the tribe of Asher: Mashal with its common-lands, Abdon with its common-lands, [75]Hukok with its common-lands, and Rehob with its common-lands. [76]And from the tribe of Naphtali: Kedesh in Galilee with its common-lands, Hammon with its common-lands, and Kirjathaim with its common-lands.

[77]From the tribe of Zebulun the rest of the children of Merari *were given* Rimmon[a] with its common-lands and Tabor with its common-lands. [78]And on the other side of the Jordan, across from Jericho, on the east side of the Jordan, *they were given* from the tribe of Reuben: Bezer in the wilderness with its common-lands, Jahzah with its common-lands, [79]Kedemoth with its common-lands, and Mephaath with its common-lands. [80]And from the tribe of Gad: Ramoth in Gilead with its common-lands, Mahanaim with its common-lands, [81]Heshbon with its common-lands, and Jazer with its common-lands.

The Family of Issachar

7 The sons of Issachar *were* Tola, Puah,[a] Jashub, and Shimron—four *in all*. [2]The sons of Tola *were* Uzzi, Rephaiah, Jeriel, Jahmai, Jibsam, and Shemuel, heads of their father's house. *The sons* of Tola *were* mighty men of valor in their generations; their number in the days of David *was* twenty-two thousand six hundred. [3]The son of Uzzi *was* Izrahiah, and the sons of Izrahiah *were* Michael, Obadiah, Joel, and Ishiah. All five of them *were* chief men. [4]And with them, by their generations, according to their fathers' houses, *were* thirty-six thousand troops ready for war; for they had many wives and sons.

[5]Now their brethren among all the families of Issachar *were* mighty men of valor, listed by their genealogies, eighty-seven thousand in all.

The Family of Benjamin

[6]*The sons* of Benjamin *were* Bela, Becher, and Jediael—three *in all*. [7]The sons of Bela were Ezbon, Uzzi, Uzziel, Jerimoth, and Iri—five *in all*. They *were* heads of *their* fathers' houses, and they were listed by their genealogies, twenty-two thousand and thirty-four mighty men of valor.

[8]The sons of Becher *were* Zemirah, Joash, Eliezer, Elioenai, Omri, Jerimoth, Abijah, Anathoth, and Alemeth. All these *are* the sons of Becher. [9]And they were recorded by genealogy according to their generations, heads of their fathers' houses, twenty thousand two hundred mighty men of valor. [10]The son of Jediael *was* Bilhan, and the sons of Bilhan *were* Jeush, Benjamin, Ehud, Chenaanah, Zethan, Tharshish, and Ahishahar.

[11]All these sons of Jediael *were* heads of their fathers' houses; *there were* seventeen thousand two hundred mighty men of valor fit to go out for war *and* battle. [12]Shuppim and Huppim[a] *were* the sons of Ir, *and* Hushim *was* the son of Aher.

The Family of Naphtali

[13]The sons of Naphtali *were* Jahziel,[a] Guni, Jezer, and Shallum,[b] the sons of Bilhah.

The Family of Manasseh (West)

[14]The descendants of Manasseh: his Syrian concubine bore him Machir the father of Gilead, the father of Asriel.[a] [15]Machir took as his wife *the sister* of Huppim and Shuppim,[a] whose name *was* Maachah. The name of *Gilead's* grandson[b] *was* Zelophehad,[c] but Zelophehad begot only daughters.

6:77 [a]Hebrew *Rimmono*, alternate spelling of *Rimmon;* see 4:32   **7:1** [a]Spelled *Puvah* in Genesis 46:13
7:12 [a]Called *Hupham* in Numbers 26:39
7:13 [a]Spelled *Jahzeel* in Genesis 46:24 [b]Spelled *Shillem* in Genesis 46:24   **7:14** [a]The son of Gilead (compare Numbers 26:30, 31)   **7:15** [a]Compare verse 12
[b]Literally *the second* [c]Compare Numbers 26:30–33

¹⁶(Maachah the wife of Machir bore a son, and she called his name Peresh. The name of his brother *was* Sheresh, and his sons *were* Ulam and Rakem. ¹⁷The son of Ulam *was* Bedan.) These *were* the descendants of Gilead the son of Machir, the son of Manasseh.

¹⁸His sister Hammoleketh bore Ishhod, Abiezer, and Mahlah.

¹⁹And the sons of Shemida were Ahian, Shechem, Likhi, and Aniam.

The Family of Ephraim

²⁰The sons of Ephraim *were* Shuthelah, Bered his son, Tahath his son, Eladah his son, Tahath his son, ²¹Zabad his son, Shuthelah his son, and Ezer and Elead. The men of Gath who were born in *that* land killed *them* because they came down to take away their cattle. ²²Then Ephraim their father mourned many days, and his brethren came to comfort him.

²³And when he went in to his wife, she conceived and bore a son; and he called his name Beriah,ᵃ because tragedy had come upon his house. ²⁴Now his daughter *was* Sheerah, who built Lower and Upper Beth Horon and Uzzen Sheerah; ²⁵and Rephah *was* his son, *as well as* Resheph, and Telah his son, Tahan his son, ²⁶Laadan his son, Ammihud his son, Elishama his son, ²⁷Nunᵃ his son, and Joshua his son.

²⁸Now their possessions and dwelling places *were* Bethel and its towns: to the east Naaran, to the west Gezer and its towns, and Shechem and its towns, as far as Ayyahᵃ and its towns; ²⁹and by the borders of the children of Manasseh *were* Beth Shean and its towns, Taanach and its towns, Megiddo and its towns, Dor and its towns. In these dwelt the children of Joseph, the son of Israel.

The Family of Asher

³⁰The sons of Asher *were* Imnah, Ishvah, Ishvi, Beriah, and their sister Serah. ³¹The sons of Beriah *were* Heber and Malchiel, who was the father of Birzaith.ᵃ ³²And Heber begot Japhlet, Shomer,ᵃ Hotham,ᵇ and their sister Shua. ³³The sons of Japhlet *were* Pasach, Bimhal, and Ashvath. These *were* the children of Japhlet. ³⁴The sons of Shemer *were* Ahi, Rohgah, Jehubbah, and Aram. ³⁵And the sons of his brother Helem *were* Zophah, Imna, Shelesh, and Amal. ³⁶The sons of Zophah *were* Suah, Harnepher, Shual, Beri, Imrah, ³⁷Bezer, Hod, Shamma, Shilshah, Jithran,ᵃ and Beera. ³⁸The sons of Jether *were* Jephunneh, Pispah, and Ara. ³⁹The sons of Ulla *were* Arah, Haniel, and Rizia.

⁴⁰All these *were* the children of Asher, heads of *their* fathers' houses, choice men, mighty men of valor, chief leaders. And they were recorded by genealogies among the army fit for battle; their number *was* twenty-six thousand.

The Family Tree of King Saul of Benjamin

8 Now Benjamin begot Bela his firstborn, Ashbel the second, Aharahᵃ the third, ²Nohah the fourth, and Rapha the fifth. ³The sons of Bela *were* Addar,ᵃ Gera, Abihud, ⁴Abishua, Naaman, Ahoah, ⁵Gera, Shephuphan, and Huram.

⁶These *are* the sons of Ehud, who were the heads of the fathers' *houses* of the inhabitants of Geba, and who forced them to move to Manahath: ⁷Naaman, Ahijah, and Gera who forced them to move. He begot Uzza and Ahihud.

⁸Also Shaharaim had children in the country of Moab, after he had sent away Hushim and Baara his wives. ⁹By Hodesh his wife he begot Jobab, Zibia, Mesha, Malcam, ¹⁰Jeuz, Sachiah, and Mirmah. These *were* his sons, heads of their fathers' *houses*.

¹¹And by Hushim he begot Abitub and Elpaal. ¹²The sons of Elpaal *were* Eber, Misham, and Shemed, who built Ono and Lod with its towns; ¹³and Beriah and Shema, who *were* heads of their fathers' *houses* of the inhabitants of Aijalon, who drove out the inhabitants of Gath. ¹⁴Ahio, Shashak, Jeremoth, ¹⁵Zebadiah, Arad, Eder, ¹⁶Michael, Ispah, and Joha *were* the sons of Beriah.

7:23 ᵃLiterally *In Tragedy*   **7:27** ᵃHebrew *Non*
7:28 ᵃMany Hebrew manuscripts, Bomberg, Septuagint, Targum, and Vulgate read *Gazza*.
7:31 ᵃOr *Birzavith* or *Birzoth*   **7:32** ᵃSpelled *Shemer* in verse 34 ᵇSpelled *Helem* in verse 35
7:37 ᵃSpelled *Jether* in verse 38   **8:1** ᵃSpelled *Ahiram* in Numbers 26:38   **8:3** ᵃCalled *Ard* in Numbers 26:40

[17]Zebadiah, Meshullam, Hizki, Heber, [18]Ishmerai, Jizliah, and Jobab *were* the sons of Elpaal. [19]Jakim, Zichri, Zabdi, [20]Elienai, Zillethai, Eliel, [21]Adaiah, Beraiah, and Shimrath *were* the sons of Shimei. [22]Ishpan, Eber, Eliel, [23]Abdon, Zichri, Hanan, [24]Hananiah, Elam, Antothijah, [25]Iphdeiah, and Penuel *were* the sons of Shashak. [26]Shamsherai, Shehariah, Athaliah, [27]Jaareshiah, Elijah, and Zichri *were* the sons of Jeroham.

[28]These *were* heads of the fathers' *houses* by their generations, chief men. These dwelt in Jerusalem.

[29]Now the father of Gibeon, whose wife's name *was* Maacah, dwelt at Gibeon. [30]And his firstborn son *was* Abdon, then Zur, Kish, Baal, Nadab, [31]Gedor, Ahio, Zecher, [32]and Mikloth, *who* begot Shimeah.[a] They also dwelt alongside their relatives in Jerusalem, with their brethren. [33]Ner[a] begot Kish, Kish begot Saul, and Saul begot Jonathan, Malchishua, Abinadab,[b] and Esh-Baal.[c] [34]The son of Jonathan *was* Merib-Baal,[a] and Merib-Baal begot Micah. [35]The sons of Micah *were* Pithon, Melech, Tarea, and Ahaz. [36]And Ahaz begot Jehoaddah;[a] Jehoaddah begot Alemeth, Azmaveth, and Zimri; and Zimri begot Moza. [37]Moza begot Binea, Raphah[a] his son, Eleasah his son, *and* Azel his son.

[38]Azel had six sons whose names *were* these: Azrikam, Bocheru, Ishmael, Sheariah, Obadiah, and Hanan. All these *were* the sons of Azel. [39]And the sons of Eshek his brother *were* Ulam his firstborn, Jeush the second, and Eliphelet the third.

[40]The sons of Ulam were mighty men of valor—archers. *They* had many sons and grandsons, one hundred and fifty *in all*. These *were* all sons of Benjamin.

9 So all Israel was recorded by genealogies, and indeed, they *were* inscribed in the book of the kings of Israel. But Judah was carried away captive to Babylon because of their unfaithfulness. [2]And the first inhabitants who *dwelt* in their possessions in their cities *were* Israelites, priests, Levites, and the Nethinim.

Dwellers in Jerusalem

[3]Now in Jerusalem the children of Judah dwelt, and some of the children of Benjamin, and of the children of Ephraim and Manasseh: [4]Uthai the son of Ammihud, the son of Omri, the son of Imri, the son of Bani, of the descendants of Perez, the son of Judah. [5]Of the Shilonites: Asaiah the firstborn and his sons. [6]Of the sons of Zerah: Jeuel, and their brethren—six hundred and ninety. [7]Of the sons of Benjamin: Sallu the son of Meshullam, the son of Hodaviah, the son of Hassenuah; [8]Ibneiah the son of Jeroham; Elah the son of Uzzi, the son of Michri; Meshullam the son of Shephatiah, the son of Reuel, the son of Ibnijah; [9]and their brethren, according to their generations—nine hundred and fifty-six. All these men *were* heads of a father's *house* in their fathers' houses.

The Priests at Jerusalem

[10]Of the priests: Jedaiah, Jehoiarib, and Jachin; [11]Azariah the son of Hilkiah, the son of Meshullam, the son of Zadok, the son of Meraioth, the son of Ahitub, the officer over the house[a] of God; [12]Adaiah the son of Jeroham, the son of Pashur, the son of Malchijah; Maasai the son of Adiel, the son of Jahzerah, the son of Meshullam, the son of Meshillemith, the son of Immer; [13]and their brethren, heads of their fathers' houses—one thousand seven hundred and sixty. *They were* very able men for the work of the service of the house of God.

The Levites at Jerusalem

[14]Of the Levites: Shemaiah the son of Hasshub, the son of Azrikam, the son of Hashabiah, of the sons of Merari; [15]Bakbakkar, Heresh, Galal, and Mattaniah the son of Micah, the son of Zichri, the son of Asaph; [16]Obadiah the son of Shemaiah, the son of Galal, the son of Jeduthun; and Berechiah the son of Asa, the son of Elkanah, who lived in the villages of the Netophathites.

The Levite Gatekeepers

[17]And the gatekeepers *were* Shallum, Akkub, Talmon, Ahiman, and their brethren.

8:32 [a]Spelled *Shimeam* in 9:38 **8:33** [a]Also the son of Gibeon (compare 9:36, 39) [b]Called *Jishui* in 1 Samuel 14:49 [c]Called *Ishbosheth* in 2 Samuel 2:8 and elsewhere **8:34** [a]Called *Mephibosheth* in 2 Samuel 4:4 **8:36** [a]Spelled *Jarah* in 9:42 **8:37** [a]Spelled *Rephaiah* in 9:43

Shallum *was* the chief. [18]Until then *they had been* gatekeepers for the camps of the children of Levi at the King's Gate on the east.

[19]Shallum the son of Kore, the son of Ebiasaph, the son of Korah, and his brethren, from his father's house, the Korahites, *were* in charge of the work of the service, gatekeepers of the tabernacle. Their fathers had been keepers of the entrance to the camp of the LORD. [20]And Phinehas the son of Eleazar had been the officer over them in time past; the LORD *was* with him. [21]Zechariah the son of Meshelemiah *was* keeper of the door of the tabernacle of meeting.

[22]All those chosen as gatekeepers *were* two hundred and twelve. They were recorded by their genealogy, in their villages. David and Samuel the seer had appointed them to their trusted office. [23]So they and their children *were* in charge of the gates of the house of the LORD, the house of the tabernacle, by assignment. [24]The gatekeepers were assigned to the four directions: the east, west, north, and south. [25]And their brethren in their villages *had* to come with them from time to time for seven days. [26]For in this trusted office *were* four chief gatekeepers; they were Levites. And they had charge over the chambers and treasuries of the house of God. [27]And they lodged *all* around the house of God because they *had* the responsibility, and they *were* in charge of opening *it* every morning.

Other Levite Responsibilities

[28]Now *some* of them were in charge of the serving vessels, for they brought them in and took them out by count. [29]*Some* of them *were* appointed over the furnishings and over all the implements of the sanctuary, and over the fine flour and the wine and the oil and the incense and the spices. [30]And *some* of the sons of the priests made the ointment of the spices. [31]Mattithiah of the Levites, the firstborn of Shallum the Korahite, had the trusted office over the things that were baked in the pans. [32]And some of their brethren of the sons of the Kohathites *were* in charge of preparing the showbread for every Sabbath. [33]These are the singers, heads of the fathers' *houses* of the Levites, who *lodged* in the chambers, *and were* free *from other duties;* for they were employed in *that* work day and night. [34]These heads of the fathers' *houses* of the Levites *were* heads throughout their generations. They dwelt at Jerusalem.

The Family of King Saul

[35]Jeiel the father of Gibeon, whose wife's name *was* Maacah, dwelt at Gibeon. [36]His firstborn son *was* Abdon, then Zur, Kish, Baal, Ner, Nadab, [37]Gedor, Ahio, Zechariah,[a] and Mikloth. [38]And Mikloth begot Shimeam.[a] They also dwelt alongside their relatives in Jerusalem, with their brethren. [39]Ner begot Kish, Kish begot Saul, and Saul begot Jonathan, Malchishua, Abinadab, and Esh-Baal. [40]The son of Jonathan *was* Merib-Baal, and Merib-Baal begot Micah. [41]The sons of Micah *were* Pithon, Melech, Tahrea,[a] and Ahaz.[b] [42]And Ahaz begot Jarah;[a] Jarah begot Alemeth, Azmaveth, and Zimri; and Zimri begot Moza; [43]Moza begot Binea, Rephaiah[a] his son, Eleasah his son, and Azel his son.

[44]And Azel had six sons whose names *were* these: Azrikam, Bocheru, Ishmael, Sheariah, Obadiah, and Hanan; these *were* the sons of Azel.

Tragic End of Saul and His Sons

10Now the Philistines fought against Israel; and the men of Israel fled from before the Philistines, and fell slain on Mount Gilboa. [2]Then the Philistines followed hard after Saul and his sons. And the Philistines killed Jonathan, Abinadab, and Malchishua, Saul's sons. [3]The battle became fierce against Saul. The archers hit him, and he was wounded by the archers. [4]Then Saul said to his armorbearer, "Draw your sword, and thrust me through with it, lest these uncircumcised men come and abuse me." But his armorbearer would not, for he was greatly afraid. Therefore Saul took a sword and fell on it. [5]And when his armorbearer

9:37 [a]Called *Zecher* in 8:31　　**9:38** [a]Spelled *Shimeah* in 8:32　　**9:41** [a]Spelled *Tarea* in 8:35　[b]Following Arabic, Syriac, Targum, and Vulgate (compare 8:35); Masoretic Text and Septuagint omit *and Ahaz.*
9:42 [a]Spelled *Jehoaddah* in 8:36　　**9:43** [a]Spelled *Raphah* in 8:37

saw that Saul was dead, he also fell on his sword and died. ⁶So Saul and his three sons died, and all his house died together. ⁷And when all the men of Israel who *were* in the valley saw that they had fled and that Saul and his sons were dead, they forsook their cities and fled; then the Philistines came and dwelt in them.

⁸So it happened the next day, when the Philistines came to strip the slain, that they found Saul and his sons fallen on Mount Gilboa. ⁹And they stripped him and took his head and his armor, and sent word throughout the land of the Philistines to proclaim the news *in the temple* of their idols and among the people. ¹⁰Then they put his armor in the temple of their gods, and fastened his head in the temple of Dagon.

¹¹And when all Jabesh Gilead heard all that the Philistines had done to Saul, ¹²all the valiant men arose and took the body of Saul and the bodies of his sons; and they brought them to Jabesh, and buried their bones under the tamarisk tree at Jabesh, and fasted seven days.

¹³So Saul died for his unfaithfulness which he had committed against the LORD, because he did not keep the word of the LORD, and also because he consulted a medium for guidance. ¹⁴But *he* did not inquire of the LORD; therefore He killed him, and turned the kingdom over to David the son of Jesse.

David Made King over All Israel

11 Then all Israel came together to David at Hebron, saying, "Indeed we *are* your bone and your flesh. ²Also, in time past, even when Saul was king, you *were* the one who led Israel out and brought them in; and the LORD your God said to you, 'You shall shepherd My people Israel, and be ruler over My people Israel.'" ³Therefore all the elders of Israel came to the king at Hebron, and David made a covenant with them at Hebron before the LORD. And they anointed David king over Israel, according to the word of the LORD by Samuel.

The City of David

⁴And David and all Israel went to Jerusalem, which is Jebus, where the Jebusites *were*, the inhabitants of the land. ⁵But the inhabitants of Jebus said to David, "You shall not come in here!" Nevertheless David took the stronghold of Zion (that is, the City of David). ⁶Now David said, "Whoever attacks the Jebusites first shall be chief and captain." And Joab the son of Zeruiah went up first, and became chief. ⁷Then David dwelt in the stronghold; therefore they called it the City of David. ⁸And he built the city around it, from the Milloᵃ to the surrounding area. Joab repaired the rest of the city. ⁹So David went on and became great, and the LORD of hosts *was* with him.

The Mighty Men of David

¹⁰Now these *were* the heads of the mighty men whom David had, who strengthened themselves with him in his kingdom, with all Israel, to make him king, according to the word of the LORD concerning Israel.

¹¹And this *is* the number of the mighty men whom David had: Jashobeam the son of a Hachmonite, chief of the captains;ᵃ he had lifted up his spear against three hundred, killed *by him* at one time.

¹²After him *was* Eleazar the son of Dodo, the Ahohite, who *was one* of the three mighty men. ¹³He was with David at Pasdammim. Now there the Philistines were gathered for battle, and there was a piece of ground full of barley. So the people fled from the Philistines. ¹⁴But they stationed themselves in the middle of *that* field, defended it, and killed the Philistines. So the LORD brought about a great victory.

¹⁵Now three of the thirty chief men went down to the rock to David, into the cave of Adullam; and the army of the Philistines encamped in the Valley of Rephaim. ¹⁶David *was* then in the stronghold, and the garrison of the Philistines *was* then in Bethlehem. ¹⁷And David said with longing, "Oh, that someone would give me a drink of water from the well of Bethlehem, which is by the gate!" ¹⁸So the three broke through the camp of the Philistines, drew water from the well of Bethlehem that *was* by the gate, and took *it* and brought *it* to David. Nevertheless

---

11:8 ᵃLiterally *The Landfill*   **11:11** ᵃFollowing Qere; Kethib, Septuagint, and Vulgate read *the thirty* (compare 2 Samuel 23:8).

David would not drink it, but poured it out to the LORD. [19]And he said, "Far be it from me, O my God, that I should do this! Shall I drink the blood of these men *who have put their lives in jeopardy?* For at the risk of their lives they brought it." Therefore he would not drink it. These things were done by the three mighty men.

[20]Abishai the brother of Joab was chief of *another* three.[a] He had lifted up his spear against three hundred *men,* killed *them,* and won a name among *these* three. [21]Of the three he was more honored than the other two men. Therefore he became their captain. However he did not attain to the *first* three.

[22]Benaiah was the son of Jehoiada, the son of a valiant man from Kabzeel, who had done many deeds. He had killed two lion-like heroes of Moab. He also had gone down and killed a lion in the midst of a pit on a snowy day. [23]And he killed an Egyptian, a man of *great* height, five cubits tall. In the Egyptian's hand *there was* a spear like a weaver's beam; and he went down to him with a staff, wrested the spear out of the Egyptian's hand, and killed him with his own spear. [24]These *things* Benaiah the son of Jehoiada did, and won a name among three mighty men. [25]Indeed he was more honored than the thirty, but he did not attain to the *first* three. And David appointed him over his guard.

[26]Also the mighty warriors *were* Asahel the brother of Joab, Elhanan the son of Dodo of Bethlehem, [27]Shammoth the Harorite,[a] Helez the Pelonite,[b] [28]Ira the son of Ikkesh the Tekoite, Abiezer the Anathothite, [29]Sibbechai the Hushathite, Ilai the Ahohite, [30]Maharai the Netophathite, Heled[a] the son of Baanah the Netophathite, [31]Ithai[a] the son of Ribai of Gibeah, of the sons of Benjamin, Benaiah the Pirathonite, [32]Hurai[a] of the brooks of Gaash, Abiel[b] the Arbathite, [33]Azmaveth the Baharumite,[a] Eliahba the Shaalbonite, [34]the sons of Hashem the Gizonite, Jonathan the son of Shageh the Hararite, [35]Ahiam the son of Sacar the Hararite, Eliphal the son of Ur, [36]Hepher the Mecherathite, Ahijah the Pelonite, [37]Hezro the Carmelite, Naarai the son of Ezbai, [38]Joel the brother of Nathan, Mibhar the son of

Hagri, [39]Zelek the Ammonite, Naharai the Berothite[a] (the armorbearer of Joab the son of Zeruiah), [40]Ira the Ithrite, Gareb the Ithrite, [41]Uriah the Hittite, Zabad the son of Ahlai, [42]Adina the son of Shiza the Reubenite (a chief of the Reubenites) and thirty with him, [43]Hanan the son of Maachah, Joshaphat the Mithnite, [44]Uzzia the Ashterathite, Shama and Jeiel the sons of Hotham the Aroerite, [45]Jediael the son of Shimri, and Joha his brother, the Tizite, [46]Eliel the Mahavite, Jeribai and Joshaviah the sons of Elnaam, Ithmah the Moabite, [47]Eliel, Obed, and Jaasiel the Mezobaite.

The Growth of David's Army

12 Now these *were* the men who came to David at Ziklag while he was still a fugitive from Saul the son of Kish; and they *were* among the mighty men, helpers in the war, [2]armed with bows, using both the right hand and the left in *hurling* stones and *shooting* arrows with the bow. *They were* of Benjamin, Saul's brethren.

[3]The chief *was* Ahiezer, then Joash, the sons of Shemaah the Gibeathite; Jeziel and Pelet the sons of Azmaveth; Berachah, and Jehu the Anathothite; [4]Ishmaiah the Gibeonite, a mighty man among the thirty, and over the thirty; Jeremiah, Jahaziel, Johanan, and Jozabad the Gederathite; [5]Eluzai, Jerimoth, Bealiah, Shemariah, and Shephatiah the Haruphite; [6]Elkanah, Jisshiah, Azarel, Joezer, and Jashobeam, the Korahites; [7]and Joelah and Zebadiah the sons of Jeroham of Gedor.

[8]*Some* Gadites joined David at the stronghold in the wilderness, mighty men of valor, men trained for battle, who could handle shield and spear, whose faces *were like* the faces of lions, and *were* as swift as gazelles on the mountains: [9]Ezer the first, Obadiah the second, Eliab the third, [10]Mishmannah

---

11:20 [a]Following Masoretic Text, Septuagint, and Vulgate; Syriac reads *thirty.*   **11:27** [a]Spelled *Harodite* in 2 Samuel 23:25 [b]Called *Paltite* in 2 Samuel 23:26   **11:30** [a]Spelled *Heleb* in 2 Samuel 23:29 and *Heldai* in 1 Chronicles 27:15
11:31 [a]Spelled *Ittai* in 2 Samuel 23:29
11:32 [a]Spelled *Hiddai* in 2 Samuel 23:30 [b]Spelled *Abi-Albon* in 2 Samuel 23:31
11:33 [a]Spelled *Barhumite* in 2 Samuel 23:31
11:39 [a]Spelled *Beerothite* in 2 Samuel 23:37

the fourth, Jeremiah the fifth, [11]Attai the sixth, Eliel the seventh, [12]Johanan the eighth, Elzabad the ninth, [13]Jeremiah the tenth, and Machbanai the eleventh. [14]These *were* from the sons of Gad, captains of the army; the least was over a hundred, and the greatest was over a thousand. [15]These *are* the ones who crossed the Jordan in the first month, when it had overflowed all its banks; and they put to flight all *those* in the valleys, to the east and to the west.

[16]Then some of the sons of Benjamin and Judah came to David at the stronghold. [17]And David went out to meet them, and answered and said to them, "If you have come peaceably to me to help me, my heart will be united with you; but if to betray me to my enemies, since *there is* no wrong in my hands, may the God of our fathers look and bring judgment." [18]Then the Spirit came upon Amasai, chief of the captains, *and he said:*

"*We are* yours, O David;
We *are* on your side, O son of Jesse!
Peace, peace to you,
And peace to your helpers!
For your God helps you."

So David received them, and made them captains of the troop.

[19]And *some* from Manasseh defected to David when he was going with the Philistines to battle against Saul; but they did not help them, for the lords of the Philistines sent him away by agreement, saying, "He may defect to his master Saul *and endanger* our heads." [20]When he went to Ziklag, those of Manasseh who defected to him were Adnah, Jozabad, Jediael, Michael, Jozabad, Elihu, and Zillethai, captains of the thousands who *were* from Manasseh. [21]And they helped David against the bands *of raiders,* for they *were* all mighty men of valor, and they were captains in the army. [22]For at *that* time they came to David day by day to help him, until *it was* a great army, like the army of God.

David's Army at Hebron

[23]Now these *were* the numbers of the divisions *that were* equipped for war, *and* came to David at Hebron to turn *over* the kingdom of Saul to him, according to the word of the LORD: [24]of the sons of Judah bearing shield and spear, six thousand eight hundred armed for war; [25]of the sons

---

HONOR

. . . mighty men of valor, . . . whose faces were like the faces of lions. . . .

1 CHRONICLES 12:8

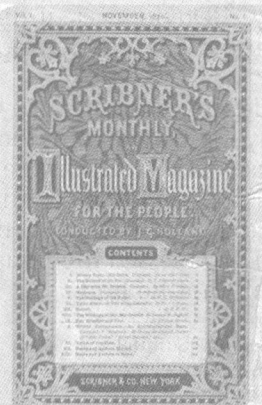

"GOD, GIVE US MEN"

Josiah Gilbert Holland (1819–1881), a poet and the founder and editor of the popular *Scribner's Monthly* (afterward the *Century Magazine*), penned these famous words:

*God, give us men! A time like this demands
    Strong minds, great hearts, true faith and ready hands;
    Men whom the lust of office does not kill;
Men whom the spoils of office can not buy;
    Men who possess opinions and a will;
Men who have honor; men who will not lie;
Men who can stand before a demagogue
    And damn his treacherous flatteries without winking!
Tall men, sun-crowned, who live above the fog
    In public duty, and in private thinking;
For while the rabble, with their thumb-worn creeds,
Their large professions and their little deeds,
Mingle in selfish strife, lo! Freedom weeps,
Wrong rules the land and waiting Justice sleeps.*

of Simeon, mighty men of valor fit for war, seven thousand one hundred; [26]of the sons of Levi four thousand six hundred; [27]Jehoiada, the leader of the Aaronites, and with him three thousand seven hundred; [28]Zadok, a young man, a valiant warrior, and from his father's house twenty-two captains; [29]of the sons of Benjamin, relatives of Saul, three thousand (until then the greatest part of them had remained loyal to the house of Saul); [30]of the sons of Ephraim twenty thousand eight hundred, mighty men of valor, famous men throughout their father's house; [31]of the half-tribe of Manasseh eighteen thousand, who were designated by name to come and make David king; [32]of the sons of Issachar who had understanding of the times, to know what Israel ought to do, their chiefs were two hundred; and all their brethren were at their command; [33]of Zebulun there were fifty thousand who went out to battle, expert in war with all weapons of war, stouthearted men who could keep ranks; [34]of Naphtali one thousand captains, and with them thirty-seven thousand with shield and spear; [35]of the Danites who could keep battle formation, twenty-eight thousand six hundred; [36]of Asher, those who could go out to war, able to keep battle formation, forty thousand; [37]of the Reubenites and the Gadites and the half-tribe of Manasseh, from the other side of the Jordan, one hundred and twenty thousand armed for battle with every *kind* of weapon of war.

[38]All these men of war, who could keep ranks, came to Hebron with a loyal heart, to make David king over all Israel; and all the rest of Israel *were* of one mind to make David king. [39]And they were there with David three days, eating and drinking, for their brethren had prepared for them. [40]Moreover those who were near to them, from as far away as Issachar and Zebulun and Naphtali, were bringing food on donkeys and camels, on mules and oxen—provisions of flour and cakes of figs and cakes of raisins, wine and oil and oxen and sheep abundantly, for *there was* joy in Israel.

The Ark Brought from Kirjath Jearim

13 Then David consulted with the captains of thousands and hundreds, *and* with every leader. [2]And David said to all the assembly of Israel, "If *it seems* good to you, and if it is of the LORD our God, let us send out to our brethren everywhere *who are* left in all the land of Israel, and with them to the priests and Levites *who are* in their cities *and* their common-lands, that they may gather together to us; [3]and let us bring the ark of our God back to us, for we have not inquired at it since the days of Saul." [4]Then all the assembly said that they would do so, for the thing was right in the eyes of all the people.

[5]So David gathered all Israel together, from Shihor in Egypt to as far as the entrance of Hamath, to bring the ark of God from Kirjath Jearim. [6]And David and all Israel went up to Baalah,[a] to Kirjath Jearim, which belonged to Judah, to bring up from there the ark of God the LORD, who dwells *between* the cherubim, where *His* name is proclaimed. [7]So they carried the ark of God on a new cart from the house of Abinadab, and Uzza and Ahio drove the cart. [8]Then David and all Israel played *music* before God with all *their* might, with singing, on harps, on stringed instruments, on tambourines, on cymbals, and with trumpets.

[9]And when they came to Chidon's[a] threshing floor, Uzza put out his hand to hold the ark, for the oxen stumbled. [10]Then the anger of the LORD was aroused against Uzza, and He struck him because he put his hand to the ark; and he died there before God. [11]And David became angry because of the LORD's outbreak against Uzza; therefore that place is called Perez Uzza[a] to this day. [12]David was afraid of God that day, saying, "How can I bring the ark of God to me?"

[13]So David would not move the ark with him into the City of David, but took it aside into the house of Obed-Edom the Gittite. [14]The ark of God remained with the family of Obed-Edom in his house three months. And the LORD blessed the house of Obed-Edom and all that he had.

13:6 [a]Called *Baale Judah* in 2 Samuel 6:2
13:9 [a]Called *Nachon* in 2 Samuel 6:6
13:11 [a]Literally *Outburst Against Uzza*

David Established at Jerusalem

14 Now Hiram king of Tyre sent messengers to David, and cedar trees, with masons and carpenters, to build him a house. ²So David knew that the LORD had established him as king over Israel, for his kingdom was highly exalted for the sake of His people Israel.

³Then David took more wives in Jerusalem, and David begot more sons and daughters. ⁴And these are the names of his children whom he had in Jerusalem: Shammua,ᵃ Shobab, Nathan, Solomon, ⁵Ibhar, Elishua,ᵃ Elpelet,ᵇ ⁶Nogah, Nepheg, Japhia, ⁷Elishama, Beeliada,ᵃ and Eliphelet.

The Philistines Defeated

⁸Now when the Philistines heard that David had been anointed king over all Israel, all the Philistines went up to search for David. And David heard *of it* and went out against them. ⁹Then the Philistines went and made a raid on the Valley of Rephaim. ¹⁰And David inquired of God, saying, "Shall I go up against the Philistines? Will You deliver them into my hand?"

The LORD said to him, "Go up, for I will deliver them into your hand."

¹¹So they went up to Baal Perazim, and David defeated them there. Then David said, "God has broken through my enemies by my hand like a breakthrough of water." Therefore they called the name of that place Baal Perazim.ᵃ ¹²And when they left their gods there, David gave a commandment, and they were burned with fire.

¹³Then the Philistines once again made a raid on the valley. ¹⁴Therefore David inquired again of God, and God said to him, "You shall not go up after them; circle around them, and come upon them in front of the mulberry trees. ¹⁵And it shall be, when you hear a sound of marching in the tops of the mulberry trees, then you shall go out to battle, for God has gone out before you to strike the camp of the Philistines." ¹⁶So David did as God commanded him, and they drove back the army of the Philistines from Gibeon as far as Gezer. ¹⁷Then the fame of David went out into all lands, and the LORD brought the fear of him upon all nations.

The Ark Brought to Jerusalem

15 *David* built houses for himself in the City of David; and he prepared a place for the ark of God, and pitched a tent for it. ²Then David said, "No one may carry the ark of God but the Levites, for the LORD has chosen them to carry the ark of God and to minister before Him forever." ³And David gathered all Israel together at Jerusalem, to bring up the ark of the LORD to its place, which he had prepared for it. ⁴Then David assembled the children of Aaron and the Levites: ⁵of the sons of Kohath, Uriel the chief, and one hundred and twenty of his brethren; ⁶of the sons of Merari, Asaiah the chief, and two hundred and twenty of his brethren; ⁷of the sons of Gershom, Joel the chief, and one hundred and thirty of his brethren; ⁸of the sons of Elizaphan, Shemaiah the chief, and two hundred of his brethren; ⁹of the sons of Hebron, Eliel the chief, and eighty of his brethren; ¹⁰of the sons of Uzziel, Amminadab the chief, and one hundred and twelve of his brethren.

¹¹And David called for Zadok and Abiathar the priests, and for the Levites: for Uriel, Asaiah, Joel, Shemaiah, Eliel, and Amminadab. ¹²He said to them, "You *are* the heads of the fathers' *houses* of the Levites; sanctify yourselves, you and your brethren, that you may bring up the ark of the LORD God of Israel to *the place* I have prepared for it. ¹³For because you *did* not *do it* the first *time,* the LORD our God broke out against us, because we did not consult Him about the proper order."

¹⁴So the priests and the Levites sanctified themselves to bring up the ark of the LORD God of Israel. ¹⁵And the children of the Levites bore the ark of God on their shoulders, by its poles, as Moses had commanded according to the word of the LORD.

¹⁶Then David spoke to the leaders of the Levites to appoint their brethren *to be* the singers accompanied by instruments of music, stringed instruments, harps, and cymbals, by raising the voice with resounding joy. ¹⁷So the Levites appointed Heman

---

14:4 ᵃSpelled *Shimea* in 3:5   **14:5** ᵃSpelled *Elishama* in 3:6   ᵇSpelled *Eliphelet* in 3:6   **14:7** ᵃSpelled *Eliada* in 3:8   **14:11** ᵃLiterally *Master of Breakthroughs*

the son of Joel; and of his brethren, Asaph the son of Berechiah; and of their brethren, the sons of Merari, Ethan the son of Kushaiah; [18]and with them their brethren of the second *rank:* Zechariah, Ben,[a] Jaaziel, Shemiramoth, Jehiel, Unni, Eliab, Benaiah, Maaseiah, Mattithiah, Elipheleh, Mikneiah, Obed-Edom, and Jeiel, the gatekeepers; [19]the singers, Heman, Asaph, and Ethan, *were* to sound the cymbals of bronze; [20]Zechariah, Aziel, Shemiramoth, Jehiel, Unni, Eliab, Maaseiah, and Benaiah, with strings according to Alamoth; [21]Mattithiah, Elipheleh, Mikneiah, Obed-Edom, Jeiel, and Azaziah, to direct with harps on the Sheminith; [22]Chenaniah, leader of the Levites, was instructor *in charge of* the music, because he *was* skillful; [23]Berechiah and Elkanah *were* doorkeepers for the ark; [24]Shebaniah, Joshaphat, Nethanel, Amasai, Zechariah, Benaiah, and Eliezer, the priests, were to blow the trumpets before the ark of God; and Obed-Edom and Jehiah, doorkeepers for the ark.

[25]So David, the elders of Israel, and the captains over thousands went to bring up the ark of the covenant of the LORD from the house of Obed-Edom with joy. [26]And so it was, when God helped the Levites who bore the ark of the covenant of the LORD, that they offered seven bulls and seven rams. [27]David was clothed with a robe of fine linen, as were all the Levites who bore the ark, the singers, and Chenaniah the music master *with* the singers. David also wore a linen ephod. [28]Thus all Israel brought up the ark of the covenant of the LORD with shouting and with the sound of the horn, with trumpets and with cymbals, making music with stringed instruments and harps.

[29]And it happened, *as* the ark of the covenant of the LORD came to the City of David, that Michal, Saul's daughter, looked through a window and saw King David whirling and playing music; and she despised him in her heart.

The Ark Placed in the Tabernacle

16 So they brought the ark of God, and set it in the midst of the tabernacle that David had erected for it. Then they offered burnt offerings and peace offerings before God. [2]And when David had finished offering the burnt offerings and the peace offerings, he blessed the people in the name of the LORD. [3]Then he distributed to everyone of Israel, both man and woman, to everyone a loaf of bread, a piece *of meat,* and a cake of raisins.

[4]And he appointed some of the Levites to minister before the ark of the LORD, to commemorate, to thank, and to praise the LORD God of Israel: [5]Asaph the chief, and next to him Zechariah, *then* Jeiel, Shemiramoth, Jehiel, Mattithiah, Eliab, Benaiah, and Obed-Edom: Jeiel with stringed instruments and harps, but Asaph made music with cymbals; [6]Benaiah and Jahaziel the priests regularly *blew* the trumpets before the ark of the covenant of God.

David's Song of Thanksgiving

[7]On that day David first delivered *this psalm* into the hand of Asaph and his brethren, to thank the LORD:

8 Oh, give thanks to the LORD!
   Call upon His name;
   Make known His deeds among the
      peoples!
9 Sing to Him, sing psalms to Him;
   Talk of all His wondrous works!
10 Glory in His holy name;
   Let the hearts of those rejoice who
      seek the LORD!
11 Seek the LORD and His strength;
   Seek His face evermore!
12 Remember His marvelous works
      which He has done,
   His wonders, and the judgments of
      His mouth,
13 O seed of Israel His servant,
   You children of Jacob, His chosen ones!

14 He *is* the LORD our God;
   His judgments *are* in all the earth.
15 Remember His covenant forever,
   The word which He commanded, for
      a thousand generations,
16 *The covenant which* He made with
      Abraham,

15:18 [a]Following Masoretic Text and Vulgate; Septuagint omits *Ben.*

And His oath to Isaac,
17 And confirmed it to Jacob for a statute,
To Israel *for* an everlasting covenant,
18 Saying, "To you I will give the land of
Canaan
As the allotment of your inheritance,"
19 When you were few in number,
Indeed very few, and strangers in it.

20 When they went from one nation
to another,
And from *one* kingdom to another
people,
21 He permitted no man to do them
wrong;
Yes, He rebuked kings for their sakes,
22 *Saying,* "Do not touch My anointed
ones,
And do My prophets no harm."[a]

23 Sing to the LORD, all the earth;
Proclaim the good news of His
salvation from day to day.
24 Declare His glory among the nations,
His wonders among all peoples.

HONOR

Remember His covenant forever. . . .

1 CHRONICLES 16:15

The First Expression of Americanism
In a National Day of Prayer Proclamation,
December 5, 1974, President Gerald Ford quoted
President Dwight Eisenhower's 1955 statement:

*Without God there could be no American form
of government, nor an American way of life.
Recognition of the Supreme Being is the first—
the most basic—expression of Americanism.
Thus, the Founding Fathers of America saw it,
and thus with God's help, it will continue to be.*

---

25 For the LORD *is* great and greatly to
be praised;
He *is* also to be feared above all gods.
26 For all the gods of the peoples *are*
idols,
But the LORD made the heavens.
27 Honor and majesty *are* before Him;
Strength and gladness are in His
place.

28 Give to the LORD, O families of the
peoples,
Give to the LORD glory and strength.
29 Give to the LORD the glory *due* His
name;
Bring an offering, and come before
Him.
Oh, worship the LORD in the beauty
of holiness!
30 Tremble before Him, all the earth.
The world also is firmly established,
It shall not be moved.

31 Let the heavens rejoice, and let the
earth be glad;
And let them say among the nations,
"The LORD reigns."
32 Let the sea roar, and all its fullness;
Let the field rejoice, and all that *is* in it.
33 Then the trees of the woods shall
rejoice before the LORD,
For He is coming to judge the earth.[a]

34 Oh, give thanks to the LORD, for *He
is* good!
For His mercy *endures* forever.[a]
35 And say, "Save us, O God of our
salvation;
Gather us together, and deliver us
from the Gentiles,
To give thanks to Your holy name,
To triumph in Your praise."

36 Blessed *be* the LORD God of Israel
From everlasting to everlasting![a]

And all the people said, "Amen!" and
praised the LORD.

Regular Worship Maintained

37So he left Asaph and his brothers there
before the ark of the covenant of the LORD
to minister before the ark regularly, as every
day's work required; 38and Obed-Edom with
his sixty-eight brethren, including Obed-
Edom the son of Jeduthun, and Hosah, *to
be* gatekeepers; 39and Zadok the priest and

16:22 [a]Compare verses 8–22 with Psalm 105:1–15
16:33 [a]Compare verses 23–33 with Psalm 96:1–13
16:34 [a]Compare verse 34 with Psalm 106:1
16:36 [a]Compare verses 35, 36 with Psalm 106:47, 48

his brethren the priests, before the tabernacle of the Lord at the high place that *was* at Gibeon, 40to offer burnt offerings to the Lord on the altar of burnt offering regularly morning and evening, and *to do* according to all that is written in the Law of the Lord which He commanded Israel; 41and with them Heman and Jeduthun and the rest who were chosen, who were designated by name, to give thanks to the Lord, because His mercy *endures* forever; 42and with them Heman and Jeduthun, to sound aloud with trumpets and cymbals and the musical instruments of God. Now the sons of Jeduthun *were* gatekeepers.

43Then all the people departed, every man to his house; and David returned to bless his house.

God's Covenant with David

17 Now it came to pass, when David was dwelling in his house, that David said to Nathan the prophet, "See now, I dwell in a house of cedar, but the ark of the covenant of the Lord *is* under tent curtains."

2Then Nathan said to David, "Do all that *is* in your heart, for God *is* with you."

3But it happened that night that the word of God came to Nathan, saying, 4"Go and tell My servant David, 'Thus says the Lord: "You shall not build Me a house to dwell in. 5For I have not dwelt in a house since the time that I brought up Israel, even to this day, but have gone from tent to tent, and from *one* tabernacle *to another*. 6Wherever I have moved about with all Israel, have I ever spoken a word to any of the judges of Israel, whom I commanded to shepherd My people, saying, 'Why have you not built Me a house of cedar?' " ' 7Now therefore, thus shall you say to My servant David, 'Thus says the Lord of hosts: "I took you from the sheepfold, from following the sheep, to be ruler over My people Israel. 8And I have been with you wherever you have gone, and have cut off all your enemies from before you, and have made you a name like the name of the great men who *are* on the earth. 9Moreover I will appoint a place for My people Israel, and will plant them, that they may dwell in a place of their own and move no more; nor shall the sons of wickedness

oppress them anymore, as previously, 10since the time that I commanded judges *to be* over My people Israel. Also I will subdue all your enemies. Furthermore I tell you that the Lord will build you a house.ᵃ 11And it shall be, when your days are fulfilled, when you must go *to be* with your fathers, that I will set up your seed after you, who will be of your sons; and I will establish his kingdom. 12He shall build Me a house, and I will establish his throne forever. 13I will be his Father, and he shall be My son; and I will not take My mercy away from him, as I took *it* from *him* who was before you. 14And I will establish him in My house and in My kingdom forever; and his throne shall be established forever." ' "

15According to all these words and according to all this vision, so Nathan spoke to David.

16Then King David went in and sat before the Lord; and he said: "Who *am* I, O Lord God? And what is my house, that You have brought me this far? 17And *yet* this was a small thing in Your sight, O God; and You have *also* spoken of Your servant's house for a great while to come, and have regarded me according to the rank of a man of high degree, O Lord God. 18What more can David *say* to You for the honor of Your servant? For You know Your servant. 19O Lord, for Your servant's sake, and according to Your own heart, You have done all this greatness, in making known all these great things. 20O Lord, *there is* none like You, nor *is there any* God besides You, according to all that we have heard with our ears. 21And who *is* like Your people Israel, the one nation on the earth whom God went to redeem for Himself *as* a people—to make for Yourself a name by great and awesome deeds, by driving out nations from before Your people whom You redeemed from Egypt? 22For You have made Your people Israel Your very own people forever; and You, Lord, have become their God.

23"And now, O Lord, the word which You have spoken concerning Your servant and concerning his house, *let it* be established forever, and do as You have said. 24So let it

---

17:10 ᵃThat is, a royal dynasty

be established, that Your name may be magnified forever, saying, 'The LORD of hosts, the God of Israel, *is* Israel's God.' And let the house of Your servant David be established before You. ²⁵For You, O my God, have revealed to Your servant that You will build him a house. Therefore Your servant has found it *in his heart* to pray before You. ²⁶And now, LORD, You are God, and have promised this goodness to Your servant. ²⁷Now You have been pleased to bless the house of Your servant, that it may continue before You forever; for You have blessed it, O LORD, and *it shall be* blessed forever."

David's Further Conquests

18 After this it came to pass that David attacked the Philistines, subdued them, and took Gath and its towns from the hand of the Philistines. ²Then he defeated Moab, and the Moabites became David's servants, *and* brought tribute.

³And David defeated Hadadezer[a] king of Zobah *as far as* Hamath, as he went to establish his power by the River Euphrates. ⁴David took from him one thousand chariots, seven thousand[a] horsemen, and twenty thousand foot soldiers. Also David hamstrung all the chariot *horses,* except that he spared enough of them for one hundred chariots.

⁵When the Syrians of Damascus came to help Hadadezer king of Zobah, David killed twenty-two thousand of the Syrians. ⁶Then David put *garrisons* in Syria of Damascus; and the Syrians became David's servants, *and* brought tribute. So the LORD preserved David wherever he went. ⁷And David took the shields of gold that were on the servants of Hadadezer, and brought them to Jerusalem. ⁸Also from Tibhath[a] and from Chun, cities of Hadadezer, David brought a large amount of bronze, with which Solomon made the bronze Sea, the pillars, and the articles of bronze.

⁹Now when Tou[a] king of Hamath heard that David had defeated all the army of Hadadezer king of Zobah, ¹⁰he sent Hadoram[a] his son to King David, to greet him and bless him, because he had fought against Hadadezer and defeated him (for Hadadezer had been at war with Tou); and

Hadoram brought with him all kinds of articles of gold, silver, and bronze. ¹¹King David also dedicated these to the LORD, along with the silver and gold that he had brought from all *these* nations—from Edom, from Moab, from the people of Ammon, from the Philistines, and from Amalek.

¹²Moreover Abishai the son of Zeruiah killed eighteen thousand Edomites[a] in the Valley of Salt. ¹³He also put garrisons in Edom, and all the Edomites became David's servants. And the LORD preserved David wherever he went.

David's Administration

¹⁴So David reigned over all Israel, and administered judgment and justice to all his people. ¹⁵Joab the son of Zeruiah *was* over the army; Jehoshaphat the son of Ahilud *was* recorder; ¹⁶Zadok the son of Ahitub and Abimelech the son of Abiathar *were* the priests; Shavsha[a] *was* the scribe; ¹⁷Benaiah the son of Jehoiada *was* over the Cherethites and the Pelethites; and David's sons *were* chief ministers at the king's side.

The Ammonites and Syrians Defeated

19 It happened after this that Nahash the king of the people of Ammon died, and his son reigned in his place. ²Then David said, "I will show kindness to Hanun the son of Nahash, because his father showed kindness to me." So David sent messengers to comfort him concerning his father. And David's servants came to Hanun in the land of the people of Ammon to comfort him.

³And the princes of the people of Ammon said to Hanun, "Do you think that David really honors your father because he has sent comforters to you? Did his servants not come to you to search and to overthrow and to spy out the land?"

⁴Therefore Hanun took David's servants, shaved them, and cut off their garments in

---

18:3 [a]Hebrew *Hadarezer,* and so throughout chapters 18 and 19   **18:4** [a]Or *seven hundred* (compare 2 Samuel 8:4)   **18:8** [a]Spelled *Betah* in 2 Samuel 8:8   **18:9** [a]Spelled *Toi* in 2 Samuel 8:9, 10   **18:10** [a]Spelled *Joram* in 2 Samuel 8:10   **18:12** [a]Or *Syrians* (compare 2 Samuel 8:13)   **18:16** [a]Spelled *Seraiah* in 2 Samuel 8:17

the middle, at their buttocks, and sent them away. [5]Then *some* went and told David about the men; and he sent to meet them, because the men were greatly ashamed. And the king said, "Wait at Jericho until your beards have grown, and *then* return."

[6]When the people of Ammon saw that they had made themselves repulsive to David, Hanun and the people of Ammon sent a thousand talents of silver to hire for themselves chariots and horsemen from Mesopotamia,[a] from Syrian Maacah, and from Zobah.[b] [7]So they hired for themselves thirty-two thousand chariots, with the king of Maacah and his people, who came and encamped before Medeba. Also the people of Ammon gathered together from their cities, and came to battle.

[8]Now when David heard *of it,* he sent Joab and all the army of the mighty men. [9]Then the people of Ammon came out and put themselves in battle array before the gate of the city, and the kings who had come *were* by themselves in the field.

[10]When Joab saw that the battle line was against him before and behind, he chose some of Israel's best, and put *them* in battle array against the Syrians. [11]And the rest of the people he put under the command of Abishai his brother, and they set *themselves* in battle array against the people of Ammon. [12]Then he said, "If the Syrians are too strong for me, then you shall help me; but if the people of Ammon are too strong for you, then I will help you. [13]Be of good courage, and let us be strong for our people and for the cities of our God. And may the LORD do *what is* good in His sight."

[14]So Joab and the people who *were* with him drew near for the battle against the Syrians, and they fled before him. [15]When the people of Ammon saw that the Syrians were fleeing, they also fled before Abishai his brother, and entered the city. So Joab went to Jerusalem.

[16]Now when the Syrians saw that they had been defeated by Israel, they sent messengers and brought the Syrians who were beyond the River,[a] and Shophach[b] the commander of Hadadezer's army *went* before them. [17]When it was told David, he gathered all Israel, crossed over the Jordan and came upon them, and set up in *battle* array against them. So when David had set up in battle array against the Syrians, they fought with him. [18]Then the Syrians fled before Israel; and David killed seven thousand[a] charioteers and forty thousand foot soldiers[b] of the Syrians, and killed Shophach the commander of the army. [19]And when the servants of Hadadezer saw that they were defeated by Israel, they made peace with David and became his servants. So the Syrians were not willing to help the people of Ammon anymore.

Rabbah Is Conquered

20 It happened in the spring of the year, at the time kings go out *to battle,* that Joab led out the armed forces and ravaged the country of the people of Ammon, and came and besieged Rabbah. But David stayed at Jerusalem. And Joab defeated Rabbah and overthrew it. [2]Then David took their king's crown from his head, and found it to weigh a talent of gold, and *there were* precious stones in it. And it was set on David's head. Also he brought out the spoil of the city in great abundance. [3]And he brought out the people who *were* in it, and put *them* to work[a] with saws, with iron picks, and with axes. So David did to all the cities of the people of Ammon. Then David and all the people returned *to* Jerusalem.

Philistine Giants Destroyed

[4]Now it happened afterward that war broke out at Gezer with the Philistines, at which time Sibbechai the Hushathite killed Sippai,[a] *who was one* of the sons of the giant. And they were subdued.

[5]Again there was war with the Philistines, and Elhanan the son of Jair[a] killed Lahmi the brother of Goliath the Gittite, the shaft of whose spear *was* like a weaver's beam.

[6]Yet again there was war at Gath, where there was a man of *great* stature, with

---

19:6 [a]Hebrew *Aram Naharaim* [b]Spelled *Zoba* in 2 Samuel 10:6   **19:16** [a]That is, the Euphrates [b]Spelled *Shobach* in 2 Samuel 10:16   **19:18** [a]Or *seven hundred* (compare 2 Samuel 10:18) [b]Or *horsemen* (compare 2 Samuel 10:18)   **20:3** [a]Septuagint reads *cut them.*   **20:4** [a]Spelled *Saph* in 2 Samuel 21:18 **20:5** [a]Spelled *Jaare-Oregim* in 2 Samuel 21:19

twenty-four fingers and toes, six *on each hand* and six *on each foot;* and he also was born to the giant. [7]So when he defied Israel, Jonathan the son of Shimea,[a] David's brother, killed him.

[8]These were born to the giant in Gath, and they fell by the hand of David and by the hand of his servants.

The Census of Israel and Judah

21 Now Satan stood up against Israel, and moved David to number Israel. [2]So David said to Joab and to the leaders of the people, "Go, number Israel from Beersheba to Dan, and bring the number of them to me that I may know *it.*"

[3]And Joab answered, "May the Lord make His people a hundred times more than they are. But, my lord the king, *are* they not all my lord's servants? Why then does my lord require this thing? Why should he be a cause of guilt in Israel?"

[4]Nevertheless the king's word prevailed against Joab. Therefore Joab departed and went throughout all Israel and came to Jerusalem. [5]Then Joab gave the sum of the number of the people to David. All Israel *had* one million one hundred thousand men who drew the sword, and Judah *had* four hundred and seventy thousand men who drew the sword. [6]But he did not count Levi and Benjamin among them, for the king's word was abominable to Joab.

[7]And God was displeased with this thing; therefore He struck Israel. [8]So David said to God, "I have sinned greatly, because I have done this thing; but now, I pray, take away the iniquity of Your servant, for I have done very foolishly."

[9]Then the Lord spoke to Gad, David's seer, saying, [10]"Go and tell David, saying, 'Thus says the Lord: "I offer you three *things;* choose one of them for yourself, that I may do *it* to you."'"

[11]So Gad came to David and said to him, "Thus says the Lord: 'Choose for yourself, [12]either three[a] years of famine, or three months to be defeated by your foes with the sword of your enemies overtaking *you,* or else for three days the sword of the Lord— the plague in the land, with the angel[b] of the Lord destroying throughout all the territory of Israel.' Now consider what answer I should take back to Him who sent me."

[13]And David said to Gad, "I am in great distress. Please let me fall into the hand of the Lord, for His mercies *are* very great; but do not let me fall into the hand of man."

[14]So the Lord sent a plague upon Israel, and seventy thousand men of Israel fell. [15]And God sent an angel to Jerusalem to destroy it. As he[a] was destroying, the Lord looked and relented of the disaster, and said to the angel who was destroying, "It is enough; now restrain your[b] hand." And the angel of the Lord stood by the threshing floor of Ornan[c] the Jebusite.

[16]Then David lifted his eyes and saw the angel of the Lord standing between earth and heaven, having in his hand a drawn sword stretched out over Jerusalem. So David and the elders, clothed in sackcloth, fell on their faces. [17]And David said to God, "Was it not I who commanded the people to be numbered? I am the one who has sinned and done evil indeed; but these sheep, what have they done? Let Your hand, I pray, O Lord my God, be against me and my father's house, but not against Your people that they should be plagued."

[18]Therefore, the angel of the Lord commanded Gad to say to David that David should go and erect an altar to the Lord on the threshing floor of Ornan the Jebusite. [19]So David went up at the word of Gad, which he had spoken in the name of the Lord. [20]Now Ornan turned and saw the angel; and his four sons *who were* with him hid themselves, but Ornan continued threshing wheat. [21]So David came to Ornan, and Ornan looked and saw David. And he went out from the threshing floor, and bowed before David with *his* face to the ground. [22]Then David said to Ornan, "Grant me the place of *this* threshing floor, that I may build an altar on it to the Lord. You shall grant it to me at the full price, that the plague may be withdrawn from the people."

20:7 [a]Spelled *Shimeah* in 2 Samuel 21:21 and *Shammah* in 1 Samuel 16:9   **21:12** [a]Or *seven* (compare 2 Samuel 24:13) [b]Or *Angel,* and so elsewhere in this chapter   **21:15** [a]Or *He* [b]Or *Your* [c]Spelled *Araunah* in 2 Samuel 24:16

[23]But Ornan said to David, "Take *it* to yourself, and let my lord the king do *what is* good in his eyes. Look, I *also* give *you* the oxen for burnt offerings, the threshing implements for wood, and the wheat for the grain offering; I give *it* all."

[24]Then King David said to Ornan, "No, but I will surely buy *it* for the full price, for I will not take what is yours for the LORD, nor offer burnt offerings with *that which* costs *me* nothing." [25]So David gave Ornan six hundred shekels of gold by weight for the place. [26]And David built there an altar to the LORD, and offered burnt offerings and peace offerings, and called on the LORD; and He answered him from heaven by fire on the altar of burnt offering.

[27]So the LORD commanded the angel, and he returned his sword to its sheath.

[28]At that time, when David saw that the LORD had answered him on the threshing floor of Ornan the Jebusite, he sacrificed there. [29]For the tabernacle of the LORD and the altar of the burnt offering, which Moses had made in the wilderness, *were* at that time at the high place in Gibeon. [30]But David could not go before it to inquire of God, for he was afraid of the sword of the angel of the LORD.

David Prepares to Build the Temple

22 Then David said, "This *is* the house of the LORD God, and this *is* the altar of burnt offering for Israel." [2]So David commanded to gather the aliens who *were* in the land of Israel; and he appointed masons to cut hewn stones to build the house of God. [3]And David prepared iron in abundance for the nails of the doors of the gates and for the joints, and bronze in abundance beyond measure, [4]and cedar trees in abundance; for the Sidonians and those from Tyre brought much cedar wood to David.

[5]Now David said, "Solomon my son *is* young and inexperienced, and the house to be built for the LORD *must be* exceedingly magnificent, famous and glorious throughout all countries. I will now make preparation for it." So David made abundant preparations before his death.

[6]Then he called for his son Solomon, and charged him to build a house for the LORD God of Israel. [7]And David said to Solomon: "My son, as for me, it was in my mind to build a house to the name of the LORD my God; [8]but the word of the LORD came to me, saying, 'You have shed much blood and have made great wars; you shall not build a house for My name, because you have shed much blood on the earth in My sight. [9]Behold, a son shall be born to you, who shall be a man of rest; and I will give him rest from all his enemies all around. His name shall be Solomon,[a] for I will give peace and quietness to Israel in his days. [10]He shall build a house for My name, and he shall be My son, and I *will be* his Father; and I will establish the throne of his kingdom over Israel forever.' [11]Now, my son, may the LORD be with you; and may you prosper, and build the house of the LORD your God, as He has said to you. [12]Only may the LORD give you wisdom and understanding, and give you charge concerning Israel, that you may keep the law of the LORD your God. [13]Then you will prosper, if you take care to fulfill the statutes and judgments with which the LORD charged Moses concerning Israel. Be strong and of good courage; do not fear nor be dismayed. [14]Indeed I have taken much trouble to prepare for the house of the LORD one hundred thousand talents of gold and one million talents of silver, and bronze and iron beyond measure, for it is so abundant. I have prepared timber and stone also, and you may add to them. [15]Moreover *there are* workmen with you in abundance: woodsmen and stonecutters, and all types of skillful men for every kind of work. [16]Of gold and silver and bronze and iron *there is* no limit. Arise and begin working, and the LORD be with you."

[17]David also commanded all the leaders of Israel to help Solomon his son, *saying,* [18]"*Is* not the LORD your God with you? And has He *not* given you rest on every side? For He has given the inhabitants of the land into my hand, and the land is subdued before the LORD and before His people. [19]Now set your heart and your soul to seek the LORD your God. Therefore arise and build the sanctuary of the LORD God, to bring the ark of the covenant of the LORD and the holy

---

22:9 [a]Literally *Peaceful*

articles of God into the house that is to be built for the name of the Lord."

The Divisions of the Levites

23 So when David was old and full of days, he made his son Solomon king over Israel.

2And he gathered together all the leaders of Israel, with the priests and the Levites. 3Now the Levites were numbered from the age of thirty years and above; and the number of individual males was thirty-eight thousand. 4Of these, twenty-four thousand *were* to look after the work of the house of the Lord, six thousand *were* officers and judges, 5four thousand *were* gatekeepers, and four thousand praised the Lord with *musical instruments,* "which I made," *said David,* "for giving praise."

6Also David separated them into divisions among the sons of Levi: Gershon, Kohath, and Merari.

7Of the Gershonites: Laadana and Shimei. 8The sons of Laadan: the first Jehiel, then Zetham and Joel—three *in all.* 9The sons of Shimei: Shelomith, Haziel, and Haran— three *in all.* These were the heads of the fathers' *houses* of Laadan. 10And the sons of Shimei: Jahath, Zina,a Jeush, and Beriah. These *were* the four sons of Shimei. 11Jahath was the first and Zizah the second. But Jeush and Beriah did not have many sons; therefore they were assigned as one father's house.

12The sons of Kohath: Amram, Izhar, Hebron, and Uzziel—four *in all.* 13The sons of Amram: Aaron and Moses; and Aaron was set apart, he and his sons forever, that he should sanctify the most holy things, to burn incense before the Lord, to minister to Him, and to give the blessing in His name forever. 14Now the sons of Moses the man of God were reckoned to the tribe of Levi. 15The sons of Moses *were* Gershona and Eliezer. 16Of the sons of Gershon, Shebuela *was* the first. 17Of the descendants of Eliezer, Rehabiah was the first. And Eliezer had no other sons, but the sons of Rehabiah were very many. 18Of the sons of Izhar, Shelomith *was* the first. 19Of the sons of Hebron, Jeriah *was* the first, Amariah the second, Jahaziel the third, and Jekameam the fourth. 20Of

the sons of Uzziel, Michah *was* the first and Jesshiah the second.

21The sons of Merari *were* Mahli and Mushi. The sons of Mahli *were* Eleazar and Kish. 22And Eleazar died, and had no sons, but only daughters; and their brethren, the sons of Kish, took them *as wives.* 23The sons of Mushi *were* Mahli, Eder, and Jeremoth— three *in all.*

24These *were* the sons of Levi by their fathers' houses—the heads of the fathers' *houses* as they were counted individually by the number of their names, who did the work for the service of the house of the Lord, from the age of twenty years and above.

25For David said, "The Lord God of Israel has given rest to His people, that they may dwell in Jerusalem forever"; 26and also to the Levites, "They shall no longer carry the tabernacle, or any of the articles for its service." 27For by the last words of David the Levites *were* numbered from twenty years old and above; 28because their duty *was* to help the sons of Aaron in the service of the house of the Lord, in the courts and in the chambers, in the purifying of all holy things and the work of the service of the house of God, 29both with the showbread and the fine flour for the grain offering, with the unleavened cakes and *what is baked in* the pan, with what is mixed and with all kinds of measures and sizes; 30to stand every morning to thank and praise the Lord, and likewise at evening; 31and at every presentation of a burnt offering to the Lord on the Sabbaths and on the New Moons and on the set feasts, by number according to the ordinance governing them, regularly before the Lord; 32and that they should attend to the needs of the tabernacle of meeting, the needs of the holy *place,* and the needs of the sons of Aaron their brethren in the work of the house of the Lord.

The Divisions of the Priests

24 Now *these are* the divisions of the sons of Aaron. The sons of Aaron *were*

23:7 aSpelled *Libni* in Exodus 6:17
23:10 aSeptuagint and Vulgate read *Zizah* (compare verse 11).   **23:15** aHebrew *Gershom* (compare 6:16)
23:16 aSpelled *Shubael* in 24:20

Nadab, Abihu, Eleazar, and Ithamar. ²And Nadab and Abihu died before their father, and had no children; therefore Eleazar and Ithamar ministered as priests. ³Then David with Zadok of the sons of Eleazar, and Ahimelech of the sons of Ithamar, divided them according to the schedule of their service.

⁴There were more leaders found of the sons of Eleazar than of the sons of Ithamar, and *thus* they were divided. Among the sons of Eleazar *were* sixteen heads of *their* fathers' houses, and eight heads of their fathers' houses among the sons of Ithamar. ⁵Thus they were divided by lot, one group as another, for there were officials of the sanctuary and officials *of the house* of God, from the sons of Eleazar and from the sons of Ithamar. ⁶And the scribe, Shemaiah the son of Nethanel, *one of* the Levites, wrote them down before the king, the leaders, Zadok the priest, Ahimelech the son of Abiathar, and the heads of the fathers' *houses* of the priests and Levites, one father's house taken for Eleazar and *one* for Ithamar.

⁷Now the first lot fell to Jehoiarib, the second to Jedaiah, ⁸the third to Harim, the fourth to Seorim, ⁹the fifth to Malchijah, the sixth to Mijamin, ¹⁰the seventh to Hakkoz, the eighth to Abijah, ¹¹the ninth to Jeshua, the tenth to Shecaniah, ¹²the eleventh to Eliashib, the twelfth to Jakim, ¹³the thirteenth to Huppah, the fourteenth to Jeshebeab, ¹⁴the fifteenth to Bilgah, the sixteenth to Immer, ¹⁵the seventeenth to Hezir, the eighteenth to Happizzez,ᵃ ¹⁶the nineteenth to Pethahiah, the twentieth to Jehezekel,ᵃ ¹⁷the twenty-first to Jachin, the twenty-second to Gamul, ¹⁸the twenty-third to Delaiah, the twenty-fourth to Maaziah.

¹⁹This *was* the schedule of their service for coming into the house of the Lord according to their ordinance by the hand of Aaron their father, as the Lord God of Israel had commanded him.

Other Levites

²⁰And the rest of the sons of Levi: of the sons of Amram, Shubael;ᵃ of the sons of Shubael, Jehdeiah. ²¹Concerning Rehabiah, of the sons of Rehabiah, the first *was* Isshiah. ²²Of the Izharites, Shelomoth;ᵃ of the sons of Shelomoth, Jahath. ²³Of the sons of

Hebron,ᵃ Jeriah *was the first,*ᵇ Amariah the second, Jahaziel the third, *and* Jekameam the fourth. ²⁴*Of* the sons of Uzziel, Michah; of the sons of Michah, Shamir. ²⁵The brother of Michah, Isshiah; of the sons of Isshiah, Zechariah. ²⁶The sons of Merari *were* Mahli and Mushi; the son of Jaaziah, Beno. ²⁷The sons of Merari by Jaaziah *were* Beno, Shoham, Zaccur, and Ibri. ²⁸Of Mahli: Eleazar, who had no sons. ²⁹Of Kish: the son of Kish, Jerahmeel.

³⁰Also the sons of Mushi *were* Mahli, Eder, and Jerimoth. These *were* the sons of the Levites according to their fathers' houses.

³¹These also cast lots just as their brothers the sons of Aaron did, in the presence of King David, Zadok, Ahimelech, and the heads of the fathers' *houses* of the priests and Levites. The chief fathers *did* just as their younger brethren.

The Musicians

25 Moreover David and the captains of the army separated for the service *some* of the sons of Asaph, of Heman, and of Jeduthun, who *should* prophesy with harps, stringed instruments, and cymbals. And the number of the skilled men performing their service was: ²Of the sons of Asaph: Zaccur, Joseph, Nethaniah, and Asharelah;ᵃ the sons of Asaph *were* under the direction of Asaph, who prophesied according to the order of the king. ³Of Jeduthun, the sons of Jeduthun: Gedaliah, Zeri,ᵃ Jeshaiah, *Shimei,* Hashabiah, and Mattithiah, six,ᵇ under the direction of their father Jeduthun, who prophesied with a harp to give thanks and to praise the Lord. ⁴Of Heman, the sons of Heman: Bukkiah, Mattaniah, Uzziel,ᵃ Shebuel,ᵇ Jerimoth,ᶜ

24:15 ᵃSeptuagint and Vulgate read *Aphses.*
24:16 ᵃMasoretic Text reads *Jehezkel.*
24:20 ᵃSpelled *Shebuel* in 23:16　　　**24:22** ᵃSpelled *Shelomith* in 23:18　　　**24:23** ᵃSupplied from 23:19 (following some Hebrew manuscripts and Septuagint manuscripts) ᵇSupplied from 23:19 (following some Hebrew manuscripts and Septuagint manuscripts)
25:2 ᵃSpelled *Jesharelah* in verse 14　　　**25:3** ᵃSpelled *Jizri* in verse 11 ᵇ*Shimei,* appearing in one Hebrew and several Septuagint manuscripts, completes the total of six sons (compare verse 17).　　　**25:4** ᵃSpelled *Azarel* in verse 18 ᵇSpelled *Shubael* in verse 20 ᶜSpelled *Jeremoth* in verse 22

Hananiah, Hanani, Eliathah, Giddalti, Romamti-Ezer, Joshbekashah, Mallothi, Hothir, *and* Mahazioth. ⁵All these *were* the sons of Heman the king's seer in the words of God, to exalt his horn.ᵃ For God gave Heman fourteen sons and three daughters.

⁶All these *were* under the direction of their father for the music *in* the house of the Lord, with cymbals, stringed instruments, and harps, for the service of the house of God. Asaph, Jeduthun, and Heman *were* under the authority of the king. ⁷So the number of them, with their brethren who were instructed in the songs of the Lord, all who were skillful, *was* two hundred and eighty-eight.

⁸And they cast lots for their duty, the small as well as the great, the teacher with the student.

⁹Now the first lot for Asaph came out for Joseph; the second for Gedaliah, him with his brethren and sons, twelve; ¹⁰the third for Zaccur, his sons and his brethren, twelve; ¹¹the fourth for Jizri,ᵃ his sons and his brethren, twelve; ¹²the fifth for Nethaniah, his sons and his brethren, twelve; ¹³the sixth for Bukkiah, his sons and his brethren, twelve; ¹⁴the seventh for Jesharelah,ᵃ his sons and his brethren, twelve; ¹⁵the eighth for Jeshaiah, his sons and his brethren, twelve; ¹⁶the ninth for Mattaniah, his sons and his brethren, twelve; ¹⁷the tenth for Shimei, his sons and his brethren, twelve; ¹⁸the eleventh for Azarel,ᵃ his sons and his brethren, twelve; ¹⁹the twelfth for Hashabiah, his sons and his brethren, twelve; ²⁰the thirteenth for Shubael,ᵃ his sons and his brethren, twelve; ²¹the fourteenth for Mattithiah, his sons and his brethren, twelve; ²²the fifteenth for Jeremoth,ᵃ his sons and his brethren, twelve; ²³the sixteenth for Hananiah, his sons and his brethren, twelve; ²⁴the seventeenth for Joshbekashah, his sons and his brethren, twelve; ²⁵the eighteenth for Hanani, his sons and his brethren, twelve; ²⁶the nineteenth for Mallothi, his sons and his brethren, twelve; ²⁷the twentieth for Eliathah, his sons and his brethren, twelve; ²⁸the twenty-first for Hothir, his sons and his brethren, twelve; ²⁹the twenty-second for Giddalti, his sons and his brethren, twelve; ³⁰the twenty-third for Mahazioth, his sons and his brethren, twelve; ³¹the twenty-fourth for Romamti-Ezer, his sons and his brethren, twelve.

The Gatekeepers

26 Concerning the divisions of the gatekeepers: of the Korahites, Meshelemiah the son of Kore, of the sons of Asaph. ²And the sons of Meshelemiah *were* Zechariah the firstborn, Jediael the second, Zebadiah the third, Jathniel the fourth, ³Elam the fifth, Jehohanan the sixth, Eliehoenai the seventh.

⁴Moreover the sons of Obed-Edom *were* Shemaiah the firstborn, Jehozabad the second, Joah the third, Sacar the fourth, Nethanel the fifth, ⁵Ammiel the sixth, Issachar the seventh, Peulthai the eighth; for God blessed him.

⁶Also to Shemaiah his son were sons born who governed their fathers' houses, because they *were* men of great ability. ⁷The sons of Shemaiah *were* Othni, Rephael, Obed, and Elzabad, whose brothers Elihu and Semachiah *were* able men.

⁸All these *were* of the sons of Obed-Edom, they and their sons and their brethren, able men with strength for the work: sixty-two of Obed-Edom.

⁹And Meshelemiah had sons and brethren, eighteen able men.

¹⁰Also Hosah, of the children of Merari, had sons: Shimri the first (for *though* he was not the firstborn, his father made him the first), ¹¹Hilkiah the second, Tebaliah the third, Zechariah the fourth; all the sons and brethren of Hosah *were* thirteen.

¹²Among these *were* the divisions of the gatekeepers, among the chief men, *having* duties just like their brethren, to serve in the house of the Lord. ¹³And they cast lots for each gate, the small as well as the great, according to their father's house. ¹⁴The lot for the East *Gate* fell to Shelemiah. Then they cast lots *for* his son Zechariah, a wise counselor, and his lot came out for the North Gate; ¹⁵to Obed-Edom the South Gate, and

---

25:5 ᵃThat is, to increase his power or influence
25:11 ᵃSpelled *Zeri* in verse 3   **25:14** ᵃSpelled *Asharelah* in verse 2   **25:18** ᵃSpelled *Uzziel* in verse 4   **25:20** ᵃSpelled *Shebuel* in verse 4
25:22 ᵃSpelled *Jerimoth* in verse 4

to his sons the storehouse.ᵃ ¹⁶To Shuppim and Hosah *the lot came out* for the West Gate, with the Shallecheth Gate on the ascending highway—watchman opposite watchman. ¹⁷On the east *were* six Levites, on the north four each day, on the south four each day, and for the storehouseᵃ two by two. ¹⁸As for the Parbarᵃ on the west, *there were* four on the highway *and* two at the Parbar. ¹⁹These were the divisions of the gatekeepers among the sons of Korah and among the sons of Merari.

The Treasuries and Other Duties

²⁰Of the Levites, Ahijah *was* over the treasuries of the house of God and over the treasuries of the dedicated things. ²¹The sons of Laadan, the descendants of the Gershonites of Laadan, heads of their fathers' *houses,* of Laadan the Gershonite: Jehieli. ²²The sons of Jehieli, Zetham and Joel his brother, *were* over the treasuries of the house of the LORD. ²³Of the Amramites, the Izharites, the Hebronites, and the Uzzielites: ²⁴Shebuel the son of Gershom, the son of Moses, *was* overseer of the treasuries. ²⁵And his brethren by Eliezer *were* Rehabiah his son, Jeshaiah his son, Joram his son, Zichri his son, and Shelomith his son.

²⁶This Shelomith and his brethren *were* over all the treasuries of the dedicated things which King David and the heads of fathers' *houses,* the captains over thousands and hundreds, and the captains of the army, had dedicated. ²⁷Some of the spoils won in battles they dedicated to maintain the house of the LORD. ²⁸And all that Samuel the seer, Saul the son of Kish, Abner the son of Ner, and Joab the son of Zeruiah had dedicated, every dedicated *thing,* was under the hand of Shelomith and his brethren.

²⁹Of the Izharites, Chenaniah and his sons *performed* duties as officials and judges over Israel outside Jerusalem.

³⁰Of the Hebronites, Hashabiah and his brethren, one thousand seven hundred able men, had the oversight of Israel on the west side of the Jordan for all the business of the LORD, and in the service of the king. ³¹Among the Hebronites, Jerijah *was* head of the Hebronites according to his genealogy of the fathers. In the fortieth year of the reign of David they were sought, and there were found among them capable men at Jazer of Gilead. ³²And his brethren *were* two thousand seven hundred able men, heads of fathers' *houses,* whom King David made officials over the Reubenites, the Gadites, and the half-tribe of Manasseh, for every matter pertaining to God and the affairs of the king.

The Military Divisions

27 And the children of Israel, according to their number, the heads of fathers' *houses,* the captains of thousands and hundreds and their officers, served the king in every matter of the *military* divisions. *These divisions* came in and went out month by month throughout all the months of the year, each division *having* twenty-four thousand.

²Over the first division for the first month *was* Jashobeam the son of Zabdiel, and in his division *were* twenty-four thousand; ³he was of the children of Perez, and the chief of all the captains of the army for the first month. ⁴Over the division of the second month *was* Dodaiᵃ an Ahohite, and of his division Mikloth also *was* the leader; in his division *were* twenty-four thousand. ⁵The third captain of the army for the third month *was* Benaiah, the son of Jehoiada the priest, who was chief; in his division *were* twenty-four thousand. ⁶This was the Benaiah *who was* mighty *among* the thirty, and was over the thirty; in his division *was* Ammizabad his son. ⁷The fourth *captain* for the fourth month *was* Asahel the brother of Joab, and Zebadiah his son after him; in his division *were* twenty-four thousand. ⁸The fifth captain for the fifth month *was* Shamhuthᵃ the Izrahite; in his division were twenty-four thousand. ⁹The sixth *captain* for the sixth month *was* Ira the son of Ikkesh the Tekoite; in his division *were* twenty-four thousand. ¹⁰The seventh *captain* for the seventh month *was* Helez the Pelonite, of the children of Ephraim; in his division *were* twenty-four

26:15 ᵃHebrew *asuppim*   **26:17** ᵃHebrew *asuppim*   **26:18** ᵃProbably a court or colonnade extending west of the temple   **27:4** ᵃHebrew *Dodai,* usually spelled *Dodo* (compare 2 Samuel 23:9)   **27:8** ᵃSpelled *Shammoth* in 11:27 and *Shammah* in 2 Samuel 23:11

thousand. [11]The eighth *captain* for the eighth month *was* Sibbechai the Hushathite, of the Zarhites; in his division *were* twenty-four thousand. [12]The ninth *captain* for the ninth month *was* Abiezer the Anathothite, of the Benjamites; in his division *were* twenty-four thousand. [13]The tenth *captain* for the tenth month *was* Maharai the Netophathite, of the Zarhites; in his division *were* twenty-four thousand. [14]The eleventh *captain* for the eleventh month *was* Benaiah the Pirathonite, of the children of Ephraim; in his division *were* twenty-four thousand. [15]The twelfth *captain* for the twelfth month *was* Heldai[a] the Netophathite, of Othniel; in his division *were* twenty-four thousand.

Leaders of Tribes

[16]Furthermore, over the tribes of Israel: the officer over the Reubenites *was* Eliezer the son of Zichri; over the Simeonites, Shephatiah the son of Maachah; [17]*over* the Levites, Hashabiah the son of Kemuel; over the Aaronites, Zadok; [18]*over* Judah, Elihu, *one* of David's brothers; *over* Issachar, Omri the son of Michael; [19]*over* Zebulun, Ishmaiah the son of Obadiah; *over* Naphtali, Jerimoth the son of Azriel; [20]*over* the children of Ephraim, Hoshea the son of Azaziah; *over* the half-tribe of Manasseh, Joel the son of Pedaiah; [21]*over* the half-*tribe* of Manasseh in Gilead, Iddo the son of Zechariah; *over* Benjamin, Jaasiel the son of Abner; [22]*over* Dan, Azarel the son of Jeroham. These *were* the leaders of the tribes of Israel.

[23]But David did not take the number of those twenty years old and under, because the LORD had said He would multiply Israel like the stars of the heavens. [24]Joab the son of Zeruiah began a census, but he did not finish, for wrath came upon Israel because of this census; nor was the number recorded in the account of the chronicles of King David.

Other State Officials

[25]And Azmaveth the son of Adiel *was* over the king's treasuries; and Jehonathan the son of Uzziah was over the storehouses in the field, in the cities, in the villages, and in the fortresses. [26]Ezri the son of Chelub was over those who did the work of the field for tilling the ground. [27]And Shimei the Ramathite *was* over the vineyards, and Zabdi the Shiphmite was over the produce of the vineyards for the supply of wine. [28]Baal-Hanan the Gederite was over the olive trees and the sycamore trees that *were* in the lowlands, and Joash *was* over the store of oil. [29]And Shitrai the Sharonite *was* over the herds that fed in Sharon, and Shaphat the son of Adlai was over the herds *that were* in the valleys. [30]Obil the Ishmaelite *was* over the camels, Jehdeiah the Meronothite *was* over the donkeys, [31]and Jaziz the Hagrite *was* over the flocks. All these *were* the officials over King David's property.

[32]Also Jehonathan, David's uncle, *was* a counselor, a wise man, and a scribe; and Jehiel the son of Hachmoni *was* with the king's sons. [33]Ahithophel *was* the king's counselor, and Hushai the Archite *was* the king's companion. [34]After Ahithophel *was* Jehoiada the son of Benaiah, then Abiathar. And the general of the king's army *was* Joab.

Solomon Instructed to Build the Temple

28 Now David assembled at Jerusalem all the leaders of Israel: the officers of the tribes and the captains of the divisions who served the king, the captains over thousands and captains over hundreds, and the stewards over all the substance and possessions of the king and of his sons, with the officials, the valiant men, and all the mighty men of valor.

[2]Then King David rose to his feet and said, "Hear me, my brethren and my people: I *had* it in my heart to build a house of rest for the ark of the covenant of the LORD, and for the footstool of our God, and had made preparations to build it. [3]But God said to me, 'You shall not build a house for My name, because you *have been* a man of war and have shed blood.' [4]However the LORD God of Israel chose me above all the house of my father to be king over Israel forever, for He has chosen Judah *to be* the ruler. And of the house of Judah, the house of my father, and among the sons of my father, He was pleased with me to make *me* king

---

27:15 [a]Spelled *Heled* in 11:30 and *Heleb* in 2 Samuel 23:29

over all Israel. ⁵And of all my sons (for the LORD has given me many sons) He has chosen my son Solomon to sit on the throne of the kingdom of the LORD over Israel. ⁶Now He said to me, 'It is your son Solomon *who* shall build My house and My courts; for I have chosen him *to be* My son, and I will be his Father. ⁷Moreover I will establish his kingdom forever, if he is steadfast to observe My commandments and My judgments, as it is this day.' ⁸Now therefore, in the sight of all Israel, the assembly of the LORD, and in the hearing of our God, be careful to seek out all the commandments of the LORD your God, that you may possess this good land, and leave *it* as an inheritance for your children after you forever.

⁹"As for you, my son Solomon, know the God of your father, and serve Him with a loyal heart and with a willing mind; for the LORD searches all hearts and understands all the intent of the thoughts. If you seek Him, He will be found by you; but if you forsake Him, He will cast you off forever. ¹⁰Consider now, for the LORD has chosen you to build a house for the sanctuary; be strong, and do it."

¹¹Then David gave his son Solomon the plans for the vestibule, its houses, its treasuries, its upper chambers, its inner chambers, and the place of the mercy seat; ¹²and the plans for all that he had by the Spirit, of the courts of the house of the LORD, of all the chambers all around, of the treasuries of the house of God, and of the treasuries for the dedicated things; ¹³also for the division of the priests and the Levites, for all the work of the service of the house of the LORD, and for all the articles of service in the house of the LORD. ¹⁴*He gave* gold by weight for *things* of gold, for all articles used in every kind of service; also *silver* for all articles of silver by weight, for all articles used in every kind of service; ¹⁵the weight for the lampstands of gold, and their lamps of gold, by weight for each lampstand and its lamps; for the lampstands of silver by weight, for the lampstand and its lamps, according to the use of each lampstand. ¹⁶And by weight *he gave* gold for the tables of the showbread, for each table, and silver for the tables of silver; ¹⁷also pure gold for the forks, the basins, the pitchers

of pure gold, and the golden bowls—*he gave gold* by weight for every bowl; and for the silver bowls, *silver* by weight for every bowl; ¹⁸and refined gold by weight for the altar of incense, and for the construction of the chariot, that is, the gold cherubim that spread *their wings* and overshadowed the ark of the covenant of the LORD. ¹⁹"All *this*," said David, "the LORD made me understand in writing, by *His* hand upon me, all the works of these plans."

FREEDOM
"If you seek Him, He will be found by you. . . ."
                                                    1 CHRONICLES 28:9

Freedom and the Soul of Man
Whittaker Chambers (1901–1961), an American writer and editor who had formerly been a Soviet communist spy before he recanted and defected to the West, stated:

> Freedom is a need of the soul, and nothing else. It is in striving toward God that the soul strives continually after a condition of freedom. God alone is the inciter and guarantor of freedom. He is the only guarantor.

> External freedom is only an aspect of interior freedom. Political freedom, as the Western world has known it, is only a political reading of the Bible. Religion and freedom are indivisible. Without freedom the soul dies. Without the soul there is no justification for freedom.

²⁰And David said to his son Solomon, "Be strong and of good courage, and do *it;* do not fear nor be dismayed, for the LORD God—my God—*will be* with you. He will not leave you nor forsake you, until you have finished all the work for the service of the house of the LORD. ²¹*Here are* the divisions of the priests and the Levites for all the service of the house of God; and every willing craftsman *will be* with you for all manner of workmanship, for every kind of service; also the leaders and all the people *will be* completely at your command."

Offerings for Building the Temple

29 Furthermore King David said to all the assembly: "My son Solomon, whom

alone God has chosen, *is* young and inexperienced; and the work *is* great, because the temple[a] *is* not for man but for the LORD God. [2]Now for the house of my God I have prepared with all my might: gold for *things to be made of* gold, silver for *things of* silver, bronze for *things of* bronze, iron for *things of* iron, wood for *things of* wood, onyx stones, *stones* to be set, glistening stones of various colors, all kinds of precious stones, and marble slabs in abundance. [3]Moreover, because I have set my affection on the house of my God, I have given to the house of my God, over and above all that I have prepared for the holy house, my own special treasure of gold and silver: [4]three thousand talents of gold, of the gold of Ophir, and seven thousand talents of refined silver, to overlay the walls of the houses; [5]the gold for *things of* gold and the silver for *things of* silver, and for all kinds of work *to be done* by the hands of craftsmen. Who *then* is willing to consecrate himself this day to the LORD?"

[6]Then the leaders of the fathers' *houses,* leaders of the tribes of Israel, the captains of thousands and of hundreds, with the officers over the king's work, offered willingly. [7]They gave for the work of the house of God five thousand talents and ten thousand darics of gold, ten thousand talents of silver, eighteen thousand talents of bronze, and one hundred thousand talents of iron. [8]And whoever had *precious* stones gave *them* to the treasury of the house of the LORD, into the hand of Jehiel[a] the Gershonite. [9]Then the people rejoiced, for they had offered willingly, because with a loyal heart they had offered willingly to the LORD; and King David also rejoiced greatly.

David's Praise to God

[10]Therefore David blessed the LORD before all the assembly; and David said:

"Blessed are You, LORD God of Israel,
    our Father, forever and ever.
[11]   Yours, O LORD, *is* the greatness,

29:1 [a]Literally *palace*   **29:8** [a]Possibly the same as *Jehieli* (compare 26:21, 22)

SERVICE

"Now for the house of my God I have prepared with all my might. . . ."

1 CHRONICLES 29:2

Elias Boudinot Jr.

AMERICAN BIBLE SOCIETY

Elias Boudinot Jr. (1740–1821) was an early American lawyer and statesman from Elizabeth, New Jersey. As an energetic patriot, he was elected as a delegate to the Continental Congress from 1777 to 1784, serving as its president from 1782 until 1783. He then served three terms in Congress, followed by the appointment to be the Director of the Mint for ten years. Boudinot supported many civic and educational causes during his life, including serving as one of Princeton's trustees for nearly half a century.

Boudinot was elected president of the American Bible Society at its founding in 1816 and served until his death in 1821. In his letter accepting the office of president, he stated that this was "the greatest honor" that could have been conferred upon him "on this side of the grave." He had an unwavering faith that God had called the men of the society to the work of making Bibles available in America. His ten thousand dollar gift, at a time when an annual salary of $400 was considered good, essentially enabled the formation and early organization of the American Bible Society, which still sponsors the work of Bible translation and distribution around the world.

The power and the glory,
The victory and the majesty;
For all *that is* in heaven and in earth
   is Yours;
Yours *is* the kingdom, O LORD,
And You are exalted as head over all.
12 Both riches and honor *come* from You,
And You reign over all.
In Your hand *is* power and might;
In Your hand *it is* to make great
And to give strength to all.

13 "Now therefore, our God,
We thank You
And praise Your glorious name.
14 But who *am* I, and who *are* my
   people,
That we should be able to offer so
   willingly as this?
For all things *come* from You,
And of Your own we have given You.
15 For we *are* aliens and pilgrims before
   You,
As *were* all our fathers;
Our days on earth *are* as a shadow,
And without hope.

16"O LORD our God, all this abundance that we have prepared to build You a house for Your holy name is from Your hand, and *is* all Your own. 17I know also, my God, that You test the heart and have pleasure in uprightness. As for me, in the uprightness of my heart I have willingly offered all these *things;* and now with joy I have seen Your people, who are present here to offer willingly to You. 18O LORD God of Abraham, Isaac, and Israel, our fathers, keep this forever in the intent of the thoughts of the heart of Your people, and fix their heart toward You. 19And give my son Solomon a loyal heart to keep Your commandments and Your testimonies and Your statutes, to do all *these things,* and to build the temple[a] for which I have made provision."

20Then David said to all the assembly, "Now bless the LORD your God." So all the assembly blessed the LORD God of their fathers, and bowed their heads and prostrated themselves before the LORD and the king.

Solomon Anointed King

21And they made sacrifices to the LORD and offered burnt offerings to the LORD on the next day: a thousand bulls, a thousand rams, a thousand lambs, with their drink offerings, and sacrifices in abundance for all Israel. 22So they ate and drank before the LORD with great gladness on that day. And they made Solomon the son of David king the second time, and anointed *him* before the LORD *to be* the leader, and Zadok *to be* priest. 23Then Solomon sat on the throne of the LORD as king instead of David his father, and prospered; and all Israel obeyed him. 24All the leaders and the mighty men, and also all the sons of King David, submitted themselves to King Solomon. 25So the LORD exalted Solomon exceedingly in the sight of all Israel, and bestowed on him *such* royal majesty as had not been on any king before him in Israel.

The Close of David's Reign

26Thus David the son of Jesse reigned over all Israel. 27And the period that he reigned over Israel *was* forty years; seven years he reigned in Hebron, and thirty-three *years* he reigned in Jerusalem. 28So he died in a good old age, full of days and riches and honor; and Solomon his son reigned in his place. 29Now the acts of King David, first and last, indeed they *are* written in the book of Samuel the seer, in the book of Nathan the prophet, and in the book of Gad the seer, 30with all his reign and his might, and the events that happened to him, to Israel, and to all the kingdoms of the lands.

29:19 [a]Literally *palace*

2 CHRONICLES

Author: Attributed to Ezra

When Written: 425–400 B.C.

Theme: Spiritual Heritage

Key Verse: 2 Chronicles 7:14—". . . if My people who are called by My name will humble themselves, and pray and seek My face, and turn from their wicked ways, then I will hear from heaven, and will forgive their sin and heal their land."

Key Chapter: 2 Chronicles 34—Second Chronicles records the righteous reforms that occurred under such kings as Asa, Jehoshaphat, Joash, Hezekiah, and Josiah. Chapter 34 traces the dramatic revival that took place under Josiah when the "Book of the Law" was discovered, read, and obeyed.

God's promise in 2 Chronicles 7 that He will hear the cry of a humble people has motivated America's leaders from our nation's earliest days. In 1775, the Continental Congress called for a day of prayer as it began the process of forming a new nation. At critical junctures during the Civil War, President Abraham Lincoln called for the nation to fast and pray. And in 1952, President Truman signed a bill establishing a National Day of Prayer to be called annually by the President of the United States.

Second Chronicles helps establish a model of national spiritual renewal, showing how a succession of righteous kings in Judah led reforms that brought the people back to true faith in God. Chapter 16, verse 9 of this challenging book assures us that God will "show Himself strong" toward those who place their trust in Him.

Solomon Requests Wisdom

1 Now Solomon the son of David was strengthened in his kingdom, and the LORD his God *was* with him and exalted him exceedingly.

²And Solomon spoke to all Israel, to the captains of thousands and of hundreds, to the judges, and to every leader in all Israel, the heads of the fathers' *houses.* ³Then Solomon, and all the assembly with him, went to the high place that *was* at Gibeon; for the tabernacle of meeting with God was there, which Moses the servant of the LORD had made in the wilderness. ⁴But David had brought up the ark of God from Kirjath Jearim to *the place* David had prepared for it, for he had pitched a tent for it at Jerusalem. ⁵Now the bronze altar that Bezalel the son of Uri, the son of Hur, had made, he put[a] before the tabernacle of the LORD; Solomon and the assembly sought Him *there.* ⁶And Solomon went up there to the bronze altar before the LORD, which *was* at the tabernacle of meeting, and offered a thousand burnt offerings on it.

⁷On that night God appeared to Solomon, and said to him, "Ask! What shall I give you?"

⁸And Solomon said to God: "You have shown great mercy to David my father, and have made me king in his place. ⁹Now, O LORD God, let Your promise to David my father be established, for You have made me king over a people like the dust of the

---

William McKinley placed his hand on 2 Chronicles 1:10 as he took the presidential oath of office in 1897.

---

earth in multitude. ¹⁰Now give me wisdom and knowledge, that I may go out and come in before this people; for who can judge this great people of Yours?"

¹¹Then God said to Solomon: "Because this was in your heart, and you have not asked riches or wealth or honor or the life of your enemies, nor have you asked long life—but have asked wisdom and knowledge for yourself, that you may judge My people over whom I have made you king—¹²wisdom and knowledge *are* granted to you; and I will give you riches and wealth and honor, such as none of the kings have had who *were* before you, nor shall any after you have the like."

Solomon's Military and Economic Power

¹³So Solomon came to Jerusalem from the high place that *was* at Gibeon, from before the tabernacle of meeting, and reigned over Israel. ¹⁴And Solomon gathered chariots and horsemen; he had one thousand four hundred chariots and twelve thousand horsemen, whom he stationed in the chariot cities and with the king in Jerusalem. ¹⁵Also the king made silver and gold as common in Jerusalem as stones, and he made cedars as abundant as the sycamores which *are* in the lowland. ¹⁶And Solomon had horses imported from Egypt and Keveh; the king's merchants bought them in Keveh at the *current* price. ¹⁷They also acquired and imported from Egypt a chariot for six hundred *shekels* of silver, and a horse for one hundred and fifty; thus, through their agents,[a] they exported them to all the kings of the Hittites and the kings of Syria.

Solomon Prepares to Build the Temple

2 Then Solomon determined to build a temple for the name of the LORD, and a royal house for himself. ²Solomon selected seventy thousand men to bear burdens, eighty thousand to quarry *stone* in the mountains, and three thousand six hundred to oversee them.

³Then Solomon sent to Hiram[a] king of Tyre, saying:

1:5 [a]Some authorities read *it was there.*
1:17 [a]Literally *by their hands* **2:3** [a]Hebrew *Huram* (compare 1 Kings 5:1)

As you have dealt with David my father, and sent him cedars to build himself a house to dwell in, *so deal with me.* [4]Behold, I am building a temple for the name of the Lord my God, to dedicate *it* to Him, to burn before Him sweet incense, for the continual showbread, for the burnt offerings morning and evening, on the Sabbaths, on the New Moons, and on the set feasts of the Lord our God. This *is an ordinance* forever to Israel.

[5] And the temple which I build *will be* great, for our God is greater than all gods. [6]But who is able to build Him a temple, since heaven and the heaven of heavens cannot contain Him? Who *am* I then, that I should build Him a temple, except to burn sacrifice before Him?

[7] Therefore send me at once a man skillful to work in gold and silver, in bronze and iron, in purple and crimson and blue, who has skill to engrave with the skillful men who are with me in Judah and Jerusalem, whom David my father provided. [8]Also send me cedar and cypress and algum logs from Lebanon, for I know that your servants have skill to cut timber in Lebanon; and indeed my servants *will be* with your servants, [9]to prepare timber for me in abundance, for the temple which I am about to build *shall be* great and wonderful.

[10] And indeed I will give to your servants, the woodsmen who cut timber, twenty thousand kors of ground wheat, twenty thousand kors of barley, twenty thousand baths of wine, and twenty thousand baths of oil.

[11]Then Hiram king of Tyre answered in writing, which he sent to Solomon:

Because the Lord loves His people, He has made you king over them.

[12]Hiram[a] also said:

Blessed *be* the Lord God of Israel, who made heaven and earth, for He has given King David a wise son, endowed with prudence and understanding, who will build a temple for the Lord and a royal house for himself!

[13] And now I have sent a skillful man, endowed with understanding, Huram[a] my master[b] *craftsman* [14](the son of a woman of the daughters of Dan, and his father was a man of Tyre), skilled to work in gold and silver, bronze and iron, stone and wood, purple and blue, fine linen and crimson, and to make any engraving and to accomplish any plan which may be given to him, with your skillful men and with the skillful men of my lord David your father.

[15] Now therefore, the wheat, the barley, the oil, and the wine which my lord has spoken of, let him send to his servants. [16]And we will cut wood from Lebanon, as much as you need; we will bring it to you in rafts by sea to Joppa, and you will carry it up to Jerusalem.

[17]Then Solomon numbered all the aliens who *were* in the land of Israel, after the census in which David his father had numbered them; and there were found to be one hundred and fifty-three thousand six hundred. [18]And he made seventy thousand of them bearers of burdens, eighty thousand stonecutters in the mountain, and three thousand six hundred overseers to make the people work.

Solomon Builds the Temple

3 Now Solomon began to build the house of the Lord at Jerusalem on Mount Moriah, where *the Lord*[a] had appeared to his father David, at the place that David had prepared on the threshing floor of Ornan[b] the Jebusite. [2]And he began to build on the

---

2:12 [a]Hebrew *Huram* (compare 1 Kings 5:1)
2:13 [a]Spelled *Hiram* in 1 Kings 7:13 [b]Literally *father* (compare 1 Kings 7:13, 14) **3:1** [a]Literally *He,* following Masoretic Text and Vulgate; Septuagint reads *the Lord;* Targum reads *the Angel of the Lord.* [b]Spelled *Araunah* in 2 Samuel 24:16ff

second *day* of the second month in the fourth year of his reign.

³This is the foundation which Solomon laid for building the house of God: The length *was* sixty cubits (by cubits according to the former measure) and the width twenty cubits. ⁴And the vestibule that *was* in front *of the sanctuary*^a was twenty cubits long across the width of the house, and the height *was* one hundred and^b twenty. He overlaid the inside with pure gold. ⁵The larger room^a he paneled with cypress which he overlaid with fine gold, and he carved palm trees and chainwork on it. ⁶And he decorated the house with precious stones for beauty, and the gold *was* gold from Parvaim. ⁷He also overlaid the house—the beams and doorposts, its walls and doors—with gold; and he carved cherubim on the walls.

⁸And he made the Most Holy Place. Its length was according to the width of the house, twenty cubits, and its width twenty cubits. He overlaid it with six hundred talents of fine gold. ⁹The weight of the nails *was* fifty shekels of gold; and he overlaid the upper area with gold. ¹⁰In the Most Holy Place he made two cherubim, fashioned by carving, and overlaid them with gold. ¹¹The wings of the cherubim *were* twenty cubits in *overall* length: one wing *of the one cherub was* five cubits, touching the wall of the room, and the other wing *was* five cubits, touching the wing of the other cherub; ¹²one wing of the other cherub *was* five cubits, touching the wall of the room, and the other wing *also was* five cubits, touching the wing of the other cherub. ¹³The wings of these cherubim spanned twenty cubits overall. They stood on their feet, and they faced inward. ¹⁴And he made the veil of blue, purple, crimson, and fine linen, and wove cherubim into it.

¹⁵Also he made in front of the temple^a two pillars thirty-five^b cubits high, and the capital that *was* on the top of each of *them* was five cubits. ¹⁶He made wreaths of chainwork, as in the inner sanctuary, and put *them* on top of the pillars; and he made one hundred pomegranates, and put *them* on the wreaths of chainwork. ¹⁷Then he set up the pillars before the temple, one on the right hand and the other on the left; he

called the name of the one on the right hand Jachin, and the name of the one on the left Boaz.

Furnishings of the Temple

4 Moreover he made a bronze altar: twenty cubits was its length, twenty cubits its width, and ten cubits its height.

²Then he made the Sea of cast *bronze,* ten cubits from one brim to the other; *it was* completely round. Its height *was* five cubits, and a line of thirty cubits measured its circumference. ³And under it *was* the likeness of oxen encircling it all around, ten to a cubit, all the way around the Sea. The oxen *were* cast in two rows, when it was cast. ⁴It stood on twelve oxen: three looking toward the north, three looking toward the west, three looking toward the south, and three looking toward the east; the Sea *was set* upon them, and all their back parts *pointed* inward. ⁵It *was* a handbreadth thick; and its brim was shaped like the brim of a cup, *like* a lily blossom. It contained three thousand^a baths.

⁶He also made ten lavers, and put five on the right side and five on the left, to wash in them; such things as they offered for the burnt offering they would wash in them, but the Sea *was* for the priests to wash in. ⁷And he made ten lampstands of gold according to their design, and set *them* in the temple, five on the right side and five on the left. ⁸He also made ten tables, and placed *them* in the temple, five on the right side and five on the left. And he made one hundred bowls of gold.

⁹Furthermore he made the court of the priests, and the great court and doors for the court; and he overlaid these doors with bronze. ¹⁰He set the Sea on the right side, toward the southeast.

¹¹Then Huram made the pots and the shovels and the bowls. So Huram finished

---

3:4 ^aThe main room of the temple; elsewhere called the holy place (compare 1 Kings 6:3) ^bFollowing Masoretic Text, Septuagint, and Vulgate; Arabic, some manuscripts of the Septuagint, and Syriac omit *one hundred and.*   **3:5** ^aLiterally *house*
3:15 ^aLiterally *house* ^bOr *eighteen* (compare 1 Kings 7:15; 2 Kings 25:17; and Jeremiah 52:21)
4:5 ^aOr *two thousand* (compare 1 Kings 7:26)

doing the work that he was to do for King Solomon for the house of God: ¹²the two pillars and the bowl-shaped capitals *that were* on top of the two pillars; the two networks covering the two bowl-shaped capitals which *were* on top of the pillars; ¹³four hundred pomegranates for the two networks (two rows of pomegranates for each network, to cover the two bowl-shaped capitals that *were* on the pillars); ¹⁴he also made carts and the lavers on the carts; ¹⁵one Sea and twelve oxen under it; ¹⁶also the pots, the shovels, the forks—and all their articles Huram his master[a] *craftsman* made of burnished bronze for King Solomon for the house of the Lord.

¹⁷In the plain of Jordan the king had them cast in clay molds, between Succoth and Zeredah.[a] ¹⁸And Solomon had all these articles made in such great abundance that the weight of the bronze was not determined.

¹⁹Thus Solomon had all the furnishings made for the house of God: the altar of gold and the tables on which *was* the showbread; ²⁰the lampstands with their lamps of pure gold, to burn in the prescribed manner in front of the inner sanctuary, ²¹with the flowers and the lamps and the wick-trimmers of gold, of purest gold; ²²the trimmers, the bowls, the ladles, and the censers of pure gold. As for the entry of the sanctuary, its inner doors to the Most Holy *Place,* and the doors of the main hall of the temple, *were* gold.

5 So all the work that Solomon had done for the house of the Lord was finished; and Solomon brought in the things which his father David had dedicated: the silver and the gold and all the furnishings. And he put *them* in the treasuries of the house of God.

The Ark Brought into the Temple

²Now Solomon assembled the elders of Israel and all the heads of the tribes, the chief fathers of the children of Israel, in Jerusalem, that they might bring the ark of the covenant of the Lord up from the City of David, which *is* Zion. ³Therefore all the men of Israel assembled with the king at the feast, which *was* in the seventh month. ⁴So all the elders of Israel came, and the

Levites took up the ark. ⁵Then they brought up the ark, the tabernacle of meeting, and all the holy furnishings that *were* in the tabernacle. The priests and the Levites brought them up. ⁶Also King Solomon, and all the congregation of Israel who were assembled with him before the ark, were sacrificing sheep and oxen that could not be counted or numbered for multitude. ⁷Then the priests brought in the ark of the covenant of the Lord to its place, into the inner sanctuary of the temple,[a] to the Most Holy *Place,* under the wings of the cherubim. ⁸For the cherubim spread *their* wings over the place of the ark, and the cherubim overshadowed the ark and its poles. ⁹The poles extended so that the ends of the poles of the ark could be seen from *the holy place,* in front of the inner sanctuary; but they could not be seen from outside. And they are there to this day. ¹⁰Nothing was in the ark except the two tablets which Moses put *there* at Horeb, when the Lord made *a covenant* with the children of Israel, when they had come out of Egypt.

¹¹And it came to pass when the priests came out of the *Most* Holy *Place* (for all the priests who *were* present had sanctified themselves, without keeping to their divisions), ¹²and the Levites *who were* the singers, all those of Asaph and Heman and Jeduthun, with their sons and their brethren, stood at the east end of the altar, clothed in white linen, having cymbals, stringed instruments and harps, and with them one hundred and twenty priests sounding with trumpets— ¹³indeed it came to pass, when the trumpeters and singers *were* as one, to make one sound to be heard in praising and thanking the Lord, and when they lifted up their voice with the trumpets and cymbals and instruments of music, and praised the Lord, *saying:*

"*For He is* good,
For His mercy *endures* forever,"[a]

that the house, the house of the Lord, was filled with a cloud, ¹⁴so that the priests could

---

4:16 [a]Literally *father*   **4:17** [a]Spelled *Zaretan* in 1 Kings 7:46   **5:7** [a]Literally *house*
5:13 [a]Compare Psalm 106:1

not continue ministering because of the cloud; for the glory of the LORD filled the house of God.

6 Then Solomon spoke:

"The LORD said He would dwell in the dark cloud.
2   I have surely built You an exalted house,
   And a place for You to dwell in forever."

Solomon's Speech upon Completion of the Work

³Then the king turned around and blessed the whole assembly of Israel, while all the assembly of Israel was standing. ⁴And he said: "Blessed *be* the LORD God of Israel, who has fulfilled with His hands *what* He spoke with His mouth to my father David, saying, ⁵'Since the day that I brought My people out of the land of Egypt, I have chosen no city from any tribe of Israel *in which* to build a house, that My name might be there, nor did I choose any man to be a ruler over My people Israel. ⁶Yet I have chosen Jerusalem, that My name may be there, and I have chosen David to be over My people Israel.' ⁷Now it was in the heart of my father David to build a temple*a* for the name of the LORD God of Israel. ⁸But the LORD said to my father David, 'Whereas it was in your heart to build a temple for My name, you did well in that it was in your heart. ⁹Nevertheless you shall not build the temple, but your son who will come from your body, he shall build the temple for My name.' ¹⁰So the LORD has fulfilled His word which He spoke, and I have filled the position of my father David, and sit on the throne of Israel, as the LORD promised; and I have built the temple for the name of the LORD God of Israel. ¹¹And there I have put the ark, in which *is* the covenant of the LORD which He made with the children of Israel."

Solomon's Prayer of Dedication

¹²Then *Solomon*ᵃ stood before the altar of the LORD in the presence of all the assembly of Israel, and spread out his hands ¹³(for Solomon had made a bronze platform five cubits long, five cubits wide, and three cubits high, and had set it in the midst of the court; and he stood on it, knelt down on his knees before all the assembly of Israel, and spread out his hands toward heaven); ¹⁴and he said: "LORD God of Israel, *there is* no God in heaven or on earth like You, who keep *Your* covenant and mercy with Your servants who walk before You with all their hearts. ¹⁵You have kept what You promised Your servant David my father; You have both spoken with Your mouth and fulfilled *it* with Your hand, as *it is* this day. ¹⁶Therefore, LORD God of Israel, now keep what You promised Your servant David my father, saying, 'You shall not fail to have a man sit before Me on the throne of Israel, only if your sons take heed to their way, that they walk in My law as you have walked before Me.' ¹⁷And now, O LORD God of Israel, let Your word come true, which You have spoken to Your servant David.

¹⁸"But will God indeed dwell with men on the earth? Behold, heaven and the heaven of heavens cannot contain You. How much less this temple*a* which I have built! ¹⁹Yet regard the prayer of Your servant and his supplication, O LORD my God, and listen to the cry and the prayer which Your servant is praying before You: ²⁰that Your eyes may be open toward this temple day and night, toward the place where *You* said *You would* put Your name, that You may hear the prayer which Your servant makes toward this place. ²¹And may You hear the supplications of Your servant and of Your people Israel, when they pray toward this place. Hear from heaven Your dwelling place, and when You hear, forgive.

²²"If anyone sins against his neighbor, and is forced to take an oath, and comes *and* takes an oath before Your altar in this temple, ²³then hear from heaven, and act, and judge Your servants, bringing retribution on the wicked by bringing his way on his own head, and justifying the righteous by giving him according to his righteousness.

²⁴"Or if Your people Israel are defeated before an enemy because they have sinned

---

6:7 ᵃLiterally *house,* and so in verses 8–10
6:12 ᵃLiterally *he* (compare 1 Kings 8:22)
6:18 ᵃLiterally *house*

against You, and return and confess Your name, and pray and make supplication before You in this temple, ²⁵then hear from heaven and forgive the sin of Your people Israel, and bring them back to the land which You gave to them and their fathers.

²⁶"When the heavens are shut up and there is no rain because they have sinned against You, when they pray toward this place and confess Your name, and turn from their sin because You afflict them, ²⁷then hear *in* heaven, and forgive the sin of Your servants, Your people Israel, that You may teach them the good way in which they should walk; and send rain on Your land which You have given to Your people as an inheritance.

²⁸"When there is famine in the land, pestilence or blight or mildew, locusts or grasshoppers; when their enemies besiege them in the land of their cities; whatever plague or whatever sickness *there is;* ²⁹whatever prayer, whatever supplication is *made* by anyone, or by all Your people Israel, when each one knows his own burden and his own grief, and spreads out his hands to this temple: ³⁰then hear from heaven Your dwelling place, and forgive, and give to everyone according to all his ways, whose heart You know (for You alone know the hearts of the sons of men), ³¹that they may fear You, to walk in Your ways as long as they live in the land which You gave to our fathers.

³²"Moreover, concerning a foreigner, who is not of Your people Israel, but has come from a far country for the sake of Your great name and Your mighty hand and Your outstretched arm, when they come and pray in this temple; ³³then hear from heaven Your dwelling place, and do according to all for which the foreigner calls to You, that all peoples of the earth may know Your name and fear You, as *do* Your people Israel, and that they may know that this temple which I have built is called by Your name.

³⁴"When Your people go out to battle against their enemies, wherever You send them, and when they pray to You toward this city which You have chosen and the temple which I have built for Your name, ³⁵then hear from heaven their prayer and their supplication, and maintain their cause.

³⁶"When they sin against You (for *there is* no one who does not sin), and You become angry with them and deliver them to the enemy, and they take them captive to a land far or near; ³⁷yet when they come to themselves in the land where they were carried captive, and repent, and make supplication to You in the land of their captivity, saying, 'We have sinned, we have done wrong, and have committed wickedness'; ³⁸and *when* they return to You with all their heart and with all their soul in the land of their captivity, where they have been carried captive, and pray toward their land which You gave to their fathers, the city which You have chosen, and toward the temple which I have built for Your name: ³⁹then hear from heaven Your dwelling place their prayer and their supplications, and maintain their cause, and forgive Your people who have sinned against You. ⁴⁰Now, my God, I pray, let Your eyes be open and *let* Your ears *be* attentive to the prayer *made* in this place.

⁴¹ "Now therefore,
Arise, O LORD God, to Your resting place,
You and the ark of Your strength.
Let Your priests, O LORD God, be clothed with salvation,
And let Your saints rejoice in goodness.

⁴² "O LORD God, do not turn away the face of Your Anointed;
Remember the mercies of Your servant David."^a

Solomon Dedicates the Temple

7 When Solomon had finished praying, fire came down from heaven and consumed the burnt offering and the sacrifices; and the glory of the LORD filled the temple.^a ²And the priests could not enter the house of the LORD, because the glory of the LORD had filled the LORD's house. ³When all the children of Israel saw how the fire came down, and the glory of the LORD on the temple,

---

6:42 ^aCompare Psalm 132:8–10   **7:1** ^aLiterally *house*

they bowed their faces to the ground on the pavement, and worshiped and praised the LORD, *saying:*

"For *He is* good,
    For His mercy *endures* forever."[a]

⁴Then the king and all the people offered sacrifices before the LORD. ⁵King Solomon offered a sacrifice of twenty-two thousand bulls and one hundred and twenty thousand sheep. So the king and all the people dedicated the house of God. ⁶And the priests attended to their services; the Levites also with instruments of the music of the LORD, which King David had made to praise the LORD, saying, "For His mercy *endures* forever,"[a] whenever David offered praise by their ministry. The priests sounded trumpets opposite them, while all Israel stood.

⁷Furthermore Solomon consecrated the middle of the court that *was* in front of the house of the LORD; for there he offered burnt offerings and the fat of the peace offerings, because the bronze altar which Solomon had made was not able to receive the burnt offerings, the grain offerings, and the fat.

⁸At that time Solomon kept the feast seven days, and all Israel with him, a very great assembly from the entrance of Hamath to the Brook of Egypt.[a] ⁹And on the eighth day they held a sacred assembly, for they observed the dedication of the altar seven days, and the feast seven days. ¹⁰On the twenty-third day of the seventh month he sent the people away to their tents, joyful and glad of heart for the good that the LORD had done for David, for Solomon, and for His people Israel. ¹¹Thus Solomon finished the house of the LORD and the king's house; and Solomon successfully accomplished all that came into his heart to make in the house of the LORD and in his own house.

God's Second Appearance to Solomon

¹²Then the LORD appeared to Solomon by night, and said to him: "I have heard your prayer, and have chosen this place for Myself as a house of sacrifice. ¹³When I shut up heaven and there is no rain, or command the locusts to devour the land, or send

---

Dwight D. Eisenhower placed his hand on Psalm 127:1 and 2 Chronicles 7:14 as he took the presidential oath of office in 1953.

Ronald Reagan placed his hand on 2 Chronicles 7:14 as he took the presidential oath of office in 1981 and 1985.

---

pestilence among My people, ¹⁴if My people who are called by My name will humble themselves, and pray and seek My face, and turn from their wicked ways, then I will hear from heaven, and will forgive their sin and heal their land. ¹⁵Now My eyes will be open and My ears attentive to prayer *made* in this place. ¹⁶For now I have chosen and sanctified this house, that My name may be there forever; and My eyes and My heart will be there perpetually. ¹⁷As for you, if you walk before Me as your father David walked, and do according to all that I have commanded you, and if you keep My statutes and My judgments, ¹⁸then I will establish the throne

---

PRAYER

". . . if My people . . . will humble themselves and pray. . . ."   2 CHRONICLES 7:14

National Day of Prayer
On January 25, 1988, the United States Congress, by a Joint Resolution of the 100th Congress, declared the first Thursday of each May to be recognized as a National Day of Prayer.

> *Be it enacted by the Senate and House of Representatives of the United States of America in Congress assembled, That the joint resolution entitled "Joint Resolution to provide for setting aside an appropriate day as a National Day of Prayer," approved April 17, 1952 (Public Law 82-324; 66 Stat. 64), is amended by striking "a suitable day each year, other than a Sunday," and inserting in lieu thereof "the first Thursday in May in each year."*

7:3 ᵃCompare Psalm 106:1   7:6 ᵃCompare Psalm 106:1   7:8 ᵃThat is, the Shihor (compare 1 Chronicles 13:5)

of your kingdom, as I covenanted with David your father, saying, 'You shall not fail *to have* a man as ruler in Israel.'

¹⁹"But if you turn away and forsake My statutes and My commandments which I have set before you, and go and serve other gods, and worship them, ²⁰then I will uproot them from My land which I have given them; and this house which I have sanctified for My name I will cast out of My sight, and will make it a proverb and a byword among all peoples.

²¹"And *as for* this house, which is exalted, everyone who passes by it will be astonished and say, 'Why has the Lord done thus to this land and this house?' ²²Then they will answer, 'Because they forsook the Lord God of their fathers, who brought them out of the land of Egypt, and embraced other gods, and worshiped them and served them; therefore He has brought all this calamity on them.'"

Solomon's Additional Achievements

8 It came to pass at the end of twenty years, when Solomon had built the house of the Lord and his own house, ²that the cities which Hiramª had given to Solomon, Solomon built them; and he settled the children of Israel there. ³And Solomon went to Hamath Zobah and seized it. ⁴He also built Tadmor in the wilderness, and all the storage cities which he built in Hamath. ⁵He built Upper Beth Horon and Lower Beth Horon, fortified cities *with* walls, gates, and bars, ⁶also Baalath and all the storage cities that Solomon had, and all the chariot cities and the cities of the cavalry, and all that Solomon desired to build in Jerusalem, in Lebanon, and in all the land of his dominion.

⁷All the people *who were* left of the Hittites, Amorites, Perizzites, Hivites, and Jebusites, who *were* not of Israel— ⁸that is, their descendants who were left in the land after them, whom the children of Israel did not destroy—from these Solomon raised forced labor, as it is to this day. ⁹But Solomon did not make the children of Israel servants for his work. Some *were* men of war, captains of his officers, captains of his chariots, and his cavalry. ¹⁰And others *were* chiefs of the officials of King Solomon: two hundred and fifty, who ruled over the people.

¹¹Now Solomon brought the daughter of Pharaoh up from the City of David to the house he had built for her, for he said, "My wife shall not dwell in the house of David king of Israel, because *the places* to which the ark of the Lord has come are holy."

¹²Then Solomon offered burnt offerings to the Lord on the altar of the Lord which he had built before the vestibule, ¹³according to the daily rate, offering according to the commandment of Moses, for the Sabbaths, the New Moons, and the three appointed yearly feasts—the Feast of Unleavened Bread, the Feast of Weeks, and the Feast of Tabernacles. ¹⁴And, according to the order of David his father, he appointed the divisions of the priests for their service, the Levites for their duties (to praise and serve before the priests) as the duty of each day required, and the gatekeepers by their divisions at each gate; for so David the man of God had commanded. ¹⁵They did not depart from the command of the king to the priests and Levites concerning any matter or concerning the treasuries.

¹⁶Now all the work of Solomon was well-ordered fromª the day of the foundation of the house of the Lord until it was finished. So the house of the Lord was completed.

¹⁷Then Solomon went to Ezion Geber and Elathª on the seacoast, in the land of Edom. ¹⁸And Hiram sent him ships by the hand of his servants, and servants who knew the sea. They went with the servants of Solomon to Ophir, and acquired four hundred and fifty talents of gold from there, and brought it to King Solomon.

The Queen of Sheba's Praise of Solomon

9 Now when the queen of Sheba heard of the fame of Solomon, she came to Jerusalem to test Solomon with hard questions, *having* a very great retinue, camels that bore spices, gold in abundance, and precious stones; and when she came to Solomon, she

---

8:2 ªHebrew *Huram* (compare 2 Chronicles 2:3)
8:16 ªFollowing Septuagint, Syriac, and Vulgate; Masoretic Text reads *as far as.*   **8:17** ªHebrew *Eloth* (compare 2 Kings 14:22)

spoke with him about all that was in her heart. [2]So Solomon answered all her questions; there was nothing so difficult for Solomon that he could not explain it to her. [3]And when the queen of Sheba had seen the wisdom of Solomon, the house that he had built, [4]the food on his table, the seating of his servants, the service of his waiters and their apparel, his cupbearers and their apparel, and his entryway by which he went up to the house of the LORD, there was no more spirit in her.

[5]Then she said to the king: "*It was* a true report which I heard in my own land about your words and your wisdom. [6]However I did not believe their words until I came and saw with my own eyes; and indeed the half of the greatness of your wisdom was not told me. You exceed the fame of which I heard. [7]Happy *are* your men and happy *are* these your servants, who stand continually before you and hear your wisdom! [8]Blessed be the LORD your God, who delighted in you, setting you on His throne *to be* king for the LORD your God! Because your God has loved Israel, to establish them forever, therefore He made you king over them, to do justice and righteousness."

[9]And she gave the king one hundred and twenty talents of gold, spices in great abundance, and precious stones; there never were any spices such as those the queen of Sheba gave to King Solomon.

[10]Also, the servants of Hiram and the servants of Solomon, who brought gold from Ophir, brought algum[a] wood and precious stones. [11]And the king made walkways *of* the algum[a] wood for the house of the LORD and for the king's house, also harps and stringed instruments for singers; and there were none such *as these* seen before in the land of Judah.

[12]Now King Solomon gave to the queen of Sheba all she desired, whatever she asked, *much more* than she had brought to the king. So she turned and went to her own country, she and her servants.

Solomon's Great Wealth

[13]The weight of gold that came to Solomon yearly was six hundred and sixty-six talents of gold, [14]besides *what* the traveling merchants and traders brought. And all the kings of Arabia and governors of the country brought gold and silver to Solomon. [15]And King Solomon made two hundred large shields of hammered gold; six hundred *shekels* of hammered gold went into each shield. [16]*He* also *made* three hundred shields of hammered gold; three hundred *shekels*[a] of gold went into each shield. The king put them in the House of the Forest of Lebanon.

[17]Moreover the king made a great throne of ivory, and overlaid it with pure gold. [18]The throne *had* six steps, with a footstool of gold, *which were* fastened to the throne; there were armrests on either side of the place of the seat, and two lions stood beside the armrests. [19]Twelve lions stood there, one on each side of the six steps; nothing like *this* had been made for any *other* kingdom.

[20]All King Solomon's drinking vessels *were* gold, and all the vessels of the House of the Forest of Lebanon *were* pure gold. Not *one was* silver, for this was accounted as nothing in the days of Solomon. [21]For the king's ships went to Tarshish with the servants of Hiram.[a] Once every three years the merchant ships[b] came, bringing gold, silver, ivory, apes, and monkeys.[c]

[22]So King Solomon surpassed all the kings of the earth in riches and wisdom. [23]And all the kings of the earth sought the presence of Solomon to hear his wisdom, which God had put in his heart. [24]Each man brought his present: articles of silver and gold, garments, armor, spices, horses, and mules, at a set rate year by year.

[25]Solomon had four thousand stalls for horses and chariots, and twelve thousand horsemen whom he stationed in the chariot cities and with the king at Jerusalem.

[26]So he reigned over all the kings from the River[a] to the land of the Philistines, as far as the border of Egypt. [27]The king made silver *as common* in Jerusalem as stones, and he made cedar trees as abundant as the

---

9:10 [a]Or *almug* (compare 1 Kings 10:11, 12)
9:11 [a]Or *almug* (compare 1 Kings 10:11, 12)
9:16 [a]Or *three minas* (compare 1 Kings 10:17)
9:21 [a]Hebrew *Huram* (compare 1 Kings 10:22)
[b]Literally *ships of Tarshish* (deep-sea vessels)
[c]Or *peacocks*   **9:26** [a]That is, the Euphrates

sycamores which *are* in the lowland. [28]And they brought horses to Solomon from Egypt and from all lands.

Death of Solomon

[29]Now the rest of the acts of Solomon, first and last, *are* they not written in the book of Nathan the prophet, in the prophecy of Ahijah the Shilonite, and in the visions of Iddo the seer concerning Jeroboam the son of Nebat? [30]Solomon reigned in Jerusalem over all Israel forty years. [31]Then Solomon rested with his fathers, and was buried in the City of David his father. And Rehoboam his son reigned in his place.

The Revolt Against Rehoboam

10And Rehoboam went to Shechem, for all Israel had gone to Shechem to make him king. [2]So it happened, when Jeroboam the son of Nebat heard *it* (he was in Egypt, where he had fled from the presence of King Solomon), that Jeroboam returned from Egypt. [3]Then they sent for him and called him. And Jeroboam and all Israel came and spoke to Rehoboam, saying, [4]"Your father made our yoke heavy; now therefore, lighten the burdensome service of your father and his heavy yoke which he put on us, and we will serve you."

[5]So he said to them, "Come back to me after three days." And the people departed.

[6]Then King Rehoboam consulted the elders who stood before his father Solomon while he still lived, saying, "How do you advise *me* to answer these people?"

[7]And they spoke to him, saying, "If you are kind to these people, and please them, and speak good words to them, they will be your servants forever."

[8]But he rejected the advice which the elders had given him, and consulted the young men who had grown up with him, who stood before him. [9]And he said to them, "What advice do you give? How should we answer this people who have spoken to me, saying, 'Lighten the yoke which your father put on us'?"

[10]Then the young men who had grown up with him spoke to him, saying, "Thus you should speak to the people who have spoken to you, saying, 'Your father made

our yoke heavy, but you make *it* lighter on us'—thus you shall say to them: 'My little *finger* shall be thicker than my father's waist! [11]And now, whereas my father put a heavy yoke on you, I will add to your yoke; my father chastised you with whips, but I *will chastise you* with scourges!' "[a]

[12]So Jeroboam and all the people came to Rehoboam on the third day, as the king had directed, saying, "Come back to me the third day." [13]Then the king answered them roughly. King Rehoboam rejected the advice of the elders, [14]and he spoke to them according to the advice of the young men, saying, "My father[a] made your yoke heavy, but I will add to it; my father chastised you with whips, but I *will chastise you* with scourges!"[b]

[15]So the king did not listen to the people; for the turn *of events* was from God, that the LORD might fulfill His word, which He had spoken by the hand of Ahijah the Shilonite to Jeroboam the son of Nebat.

[16]Now when all Israel *saw* that the king did not listen to them, the people answered the king, saying:

> "What share have we in David?
>   *We have* no inheritance in the son of
>   Jesse.
> Every man to your tents, O Israel!
> Now see to your own house, O David!"

So all Israel departed to their tents. [17]But Rehoboam reigned over the children of Israel who dwelt in the cities of Judah.

[18]Then King Rehoboam sent Hadoram, who *was* in charge of revenue; but the children of Israel stoned him with stones, and he died. Therefore King Rehoboam mounted *his* chariot in haste to flee to Jerusalem. [19]So Israel has been in rebellion against the house of David to this day.

11Now when Rehoboam came to Jerusalem, he assembled from the house of Judah and Benjamin one hundred and eighty thousand chosen *men* who were warriors, to fight against Israel, that he might restore the kingdom to Rehoboam.

10:11 [a]Literally *scorpions*   **10:14** [a]Following many Hebrew manuscripts, Septuagint, Syriac, and Vulgate (compare verse 10 and 1 Kings 12:14); Masoretic Text reads *I*. [b]Literally *scorpions*

²But the word of the LORD came to Shemaiah the man of God, saying, ³"Speak to Rehoboam the son of Solomon, king of Judah, and to all Israel in Judah and Benjamin, saying, ⁴'Thus says the LORD: "You shall not go up or fight against your brethren! Let every man return to his house, for this thing is from Me."'" Therefore they obeyed the words of the LORD, and turned back from attacking Jeroboam.

Rehoboam Fortifies the Cities

⁵So Rehoboam dwelt in Jerusalem, and built cities for defense in Judah. ⁶And he built Bethlehem, Etam, Tekoa, ⁷Beth Zur, Sochoh, Adullam, ⁸Gath, Mareshah, Ziph, ⁹Adoraim, Lachish, Azekah, ¹⁰Zorah, Aijalon, and Hebron, which are in Judah and Benjamin, fortified cities. ¹¹And he fortified the strongholds, and put captains in them, and stores of food, oil, and wine. ¹²Also in every city *he put* shields and spears, and made them very strong, having Judah and Benjamin on his side.

Priests and Levites Move to Judah

¹³And from all their territories the priests and the Levites who *were* in all Israel took their stand with him. ¹⁴For the Levites left their common-lands and their possessions and came to Judah and Jerusalem, for Jeroboam and his sons had rejected them from serving as priests to the LORD. ¹⁵Then he appointed for himself priests for the high places, for the demons, and the calf idols which he had made. ¹⁶And after *the Levites left,*ᵃ those from all the tribes of Israel, such as set their heart to seek the LORD God of Israel, came to Jerusalem to sacrifice to the LORD God of their fathers. ¹⁷So they strengthened the kingdom of Judah, and made Rehoboam the son of Solomon strong for three years, because they walked in the way of David and Solomon for three years.

The Family of Rehoboam

¹⁸Then Rehoboam took for himself as wife Mahalath the daughter of Jerimoth the son of David, *and of* Abihail the daughter of Eliah the son of Jesse. ¹⁹And she bore him children: Jeush, Shamariah, and Zaham. ²⁰After her he took Maachah the granddaughterᵃ of Absalom; and she bore him Abijah, Attai, Ziza, and Shelomith. ²¹Now Rehoboam loved Maachah the granddaughter of Absalom more than all his wives and his concubines; for he took eighteen wives and sixty concubines, and begot twenty-eight sons and sixty daughters. ²²And Rehoboam appointed Abijah the son of Maachah as chief, *to be* leader among his brothers; for he *intended* to make him king. ²³He dealt wisely, and dispersed some of his sons throughout all the territories of Judah and Benjamin, to every fortified city; and he gave them provisions in abundance. He also sought many wives *for them.*

Egypt Attacks Judah

12 Now it came to pass, when Rehoboam had established the kingdom and had strengthened himself, that he forsook the law of the LORD, and all Israel along with him. ²And it happened in the fifth year of King Rehoboam *that* Shishak king of Egypt came up against Jerusalem, because they had transgressed against the LORD, ³with twelve hundred chariots, sixty thousand horsemen, and people without number who came with him out of Egypt—the Lubim and the Sukkiim and the Ethiopians. ⁴And he took the fortified cities of Judah and came to Jerusalem.

⁵Then Shemaiah the prophet came to Rehoboam and the leaders of Judah, who were gathered together in Jerusalem because of Shishak, and said to them, "Thus says the LORD: 'You have forsaken Me, and therefore I also have left you in the hand of Shishak.'"

⁶So the leaders of Israel and the king humbled themselves; and they said, "The LORD *is* righteous."

⁷Now when the LORD saw that they humbled themselves, the word of the LORD came to Shemaiah, saying, "They have humbled themselves; *therefore* I will not destroy them, but I will grant them some deliverance. My wrath shall not be poured out on Jerusalem by the hand of Shishak.

11:16 ᵃLiterally *after them*   **11:20** ᵃLiterally *daughter,* but in the broader sense of granddaughter (compare 2 Chronicles 13:2)

[8]Nevertheless they will be his servants, that they may distinguish My service from the service of the kingdoms of the nations."

[9]So Shishak king of Egypt came up against Jerusalem, and took away the treasures of the house of the LORD and the treasures of the king's house; he took everything. He also carried away the gold shields which Solomon had made. [10]Then King Rehoboam made bronze shields in their place, and committed *them* to the hands of the captains of the guard, who guarded the doorway of the king's house. [11]And whenever the king entered the house of the LORD, the guard would go and bring them out; then they would take them back into the guardroom. [12]When he humbled himself, the wrath of the LORD turned from him, so as not to destroy *him* completely; and things also went well in Judah.

The End of Rehoboam's Reign

[13]Thus King Rehoboam strengthened himself in Jerusalem and reigned. Now Rehoboam *was* forty-one years old when he became king; and he reigned seventeen years in Jerusalem, the city which the LORD had chosen out of all the tribes of Israel, to put His name there. His mother's name *was* Naamah, an Ammonitess. [14]And he did evil, because he did not prepare his heart to seek the LORD.

[15]The acts of Rehoboam, first and last, *are* they not written in the book of Shemaiah the prophet, and of Iddo the seer concerning genealogies? And *there were* wars between Rehoboam and Jeroboam all their days. [16]So Rehoboam rested with his fathers, and was buried in the City of David. Then Abijah[a] his son reigned in his place.

Abijah Reigns in Judah

13 In the eighteenth year of King Jeroboam, Abijah became king over Judah. [2]He reigned three years in Jerusalem. His mother's name *was* Michaiah[a] the daughter of Uriel of Gibeah.

And there was war between Abijah and Jeroboam. [3]Abijah set the battle in order with an army of valiant warriors, four hundred thousand choice men. Jeroboam also drew up in battle formation against him with eight hundred thousand choice men, mighty men of valor.

[4]Then Abijah stood on Mount Zemaraim, which *is* in the mountains of Ephraim, and said, "Hear me, Jeroboam and all Israel: [5]Should you not know that the LORD God of Israel gave the dominion over Israel to David forever, to him and his sons, by a covenant of salt? [6]Yet Jeroboam the son of Nebat, the servant of Solomon the son of David, rose up and rebelled against his lord. [7]Then worthless rogues gathered to him, and strengthened themselves against Rehoboam the son of Solomon, when Rehoboam was young and inexperienced and could not withstand them. [8]And now you think to withstand the kingdom of the LORD, which is in the hand of the sons of David; and you *are* a great multitude, and with you are the gold calves which Jeroboam made for you as gods. [9]Have you not cast out the priests of the LORD, the sons of Aaron, and the Levites, and made for yourselves priests, like the peoples of *other* lands, so that whoever comes to consecrate himself with a young bull and seven rams may be a priest of *things that are* not gods? [10]But as for us, the LORD *is* our God, and we have not forsaken Him; and the priests who minister to the LORD *are* the sons of Aaron, and the Levites *attend* to *their* duties. [11]And they burn to the LORD every morning and every evening burnt sacrifices and sweet incense; *they* also *set* the showbread *in order on* the pure *gold* table, and the lampstand of gold with its lamps to burn every evening; for we keep the command of the LORD our God, but you have forsaken Him. [12]Now look, God Himself is with us as *our* head, and His priests with sounding trumpets to sound the alarm against you. O children of Israel, do not fight against the LORD God of your fathers, for you shall not prosper!"

[13]But Jeroboam caused an ambush to go around behind them; so they were in front of Judah, and the ambush *was* behind them. [14]And when Judah looked around, to their surprise the battle line *was* at both front and rear; and they cried out to the

---

12:16 [a]Spelled *Abijam* in 1 Kings 14:31
13:2 [a]Spelled *Maachah* in 11:20, 21 and 1 Kings 15:2

The GETTYSBURG ADDRESS

ABRAHAM LINCOLN

FREEDOM

And the children of Israel fled before Judah, . . . so five hundred thousand choice men of Israel fell slain.

2 CHRONICLES 13:16, 17

The Battle of Gettysburg (July 1–3, 1863) resulted in the largest number of casualties in the Civil War (over 51,000) and is frequently cited as the war's turning point. Abraham Lincoln's address at the dedication of the Soldiers' National Cemetery in Gettysburg, Pennsylvania, on November 19, 1863, has come to be regarded as one of the greatest speeches in American history. His opening words invoked the principles of human equality espoused by the Declaration of Independence and defined the Civil War as "a new birth of freedom" that would bring true equality to all of its citizens. His ending words symbolized the definition of democracy itself, and those words consecrated the living in the struggle to ensure that "government of the people, by the people, for the people, shall not perish from the earth."

Fourscore and seven years ago our fathers brought forth on this continent a new nation, conceived in liberty and dedicated to the proposition that all men are created equal. Now we are engaged in a great civil war, testing whether that nation or any nation so conceived and so dedicated can long endure. We are met on a great battlefield of that war. We have come to dedicate a portion of that field as a final resting-place for those who here gave their lives that that nation might live. It is altogether fitting and proper that we should do this. But in a larger sense, we cannot dedicate, we cannot consecrate, we cannot hallow this ground. The brave men, living and dead, who struggled here have consecrated it far above our poor power to add or detract. The world will little note nor long remember what we say here, but it can never forget what they did here. It is for us the living rather to be dedicated here to the unfinished work which they who fought here have thus far so nobly advanced. It is rather for us to be here dedicated to the great task remaining before us—that from these honored dead we take increased devotion to that cause for which they gave the last full measure of devotion—that we here highly resolve that these dead shall not have died in vain, that this nation under God shall have a new birth of freedom, and that government of the people, by the people, for the people shall not perish from the earth.

LORD, and the priests sounded the trumpets. [15]Then the men of Judah gave a shout; and as the men of Judah shouted, it happened that God struck Jeroboam and all Israel before Abijah and Judah. [16]And the children of Israel fled before Judah, and God delivered them into their hand. [17]Then Abijah and his people struck them with a great slaughter; so five hundred thousand choice men of Israel fell slain. [18]Thus the children of Israel were subdued at that time; and the children of Judah prevailed, because they relied on the LORD God of their fathers.

[19]And Abijah pursued Jeroboam and took cities from him: Bethel with its villages, Jeshanah with its villages, and Ephrain[a] with its villages. [20]So Jeroboam did not recover strength again in the days of Abijah; and the LORD struck him, and he died.

[21]But Abijah grew mighty, married fourteen wives, and begot twenty-two sons and sixteen daughters. [22]Now the rest of the acts of Abijah, his ways, and his sayings *are* written in the annals of the prophet Iddo.

14 So Abijah rested with his fathers, and they buried him in the City of David. Then Asa his son reigned in his place. In his days the land was quiet for ten years.

Asa Reigns in Judah

[2]Asa did *what was* good and right in the eyes of the LORD his God, [3]for he removed the altars of the foreign *gods* and the high places, and broke down the *sacred* pillars and cut down the wooden images. [4]He commanded Judah to seek the LORD God of their fathers, and to observe the law and the commandment. [5]He also removed the high places and the incense altars from all the cities of Judah, and the kingdom was quiet under him. [6]And he built fortified cities in Judah, for the land had rest; he had no war in those years, because the LORD had given him rest. [7]Therefore he said to Judah, "Let us build these cities and make walls around *them,* and towers, gates, and bars, *while* the land *is* yet before us, because we have sought the LORD our God; we have sought *Him,* and He has given us rest on every side." So they built and prospered. [8]And Asa had an army of three hundred thousand from Judah who carried shields and spears, and from Benjamin two hundred and eighty thousand men who carried shields and drew bows; all these *were* mighty men of valor.

[9]Then Zerah the Ethiopian came out against them with an army of a million men and three hundred chariots, and he came to Mareshah. [10]So Asa went out against him, and they set the troops in battle array in the Valley of Zephathah at Mareshah. [11]And Asa cried out to the LORD his God, and said, "LORD, *it is* nothing for You to help, whether with many or with those who have no power; help us, O LORD our God, for we rest on You, and in Your name we go against this multitude. O LORD, You *are* our God; do not let man prevail against You!"

[12]So the LORD struck the Ethiopians before Asa and Judah, and the Ethiopians fled. [13]And Asa and the people who *were* with him pursued them to Gerar. So the Ethiopians were overthrown, and they could not recover, for they were broken before the LORD and His army. And they carried away very much spoil. [14]Then they defeated all the cities around Gerar, for the fear of the LORD came upon them; and they plundered all the cities, for there was exceedingly much spoil in them. [15]They also attacked the livestock enclosures, and carried off sheep and camels in abundance, and returned to Jerusalem.

The Reforms of Asa

15 Now the Spirit of God came upon Azariah the son of Oded. [2]And he went out to meet Asa, and said to him: "Hear me, Asa, and all Judah and Benjamin. The LORD *is* with you while you are with Him. If you seek Him, He will be found by you; but if you forsake Him, He will forsake you. [3]For a long time Israel *has been* without the true God, without a teaching priest, and without law; [4]but when in their trouble they turned to the LORD God of Israel, and sought Him, He was found by them. [5]And in those times *there was* no peace to the one who went out, nor to the one who came in, but great turmoil *was* on all the inhabitants of the lands. [6]So nation was destroyed by nation, and city by city, for God troubled them with

---

13:19 [a]Or *Ephron*

every adversity. [7]But you, be strong and do not let your hands be weak, for your work shall be rewarded!"

[8]And when Asa heard these words and the prophecy of Oded[a] the prophet, he took courage, and removed the abominable idols from all the land of Judah and Benjamin and from the cities which he had taken in the mountains of Ephraim; and he restored the altar of the LORD that *was* before the vestibule of the LORD. [9]Then he gathered all Judah and Benjamin, and those who dwelt with them from Ephraim, Manasseh, and Simeon, for they came over to him in great numbers from Israel when they saw that the LORD his God was with him.

[10]So they gathered together at Jerusalem in the third month, in the fifteenth year of the reign of Asa. [11]And they offered to the LORD at that time seven hundred bulls and seven thousand sheep from the spoil they had brought. [12]Then they entered into a covenant to seek the LORD God of their fathers with all their heart and with all their soul; [13]and whoever would not seek the LORD God of Israel was to be put to death, whether small or great, whether man or woman. [14]Then they took an oath before the LORD with a loud voice, with shouting and trumpets and rams' horns. [15]And all Judah rejoiced at the oath, for they had sworn with all their heart and sought Him with all their soul; and He was found by them, and the LORD gave them rest all around.

[16]Also he removed Maachah, the mother of Asa the king, from *being* queen mother, because she had made an obscene image of Asherah;[a] and Asa cut down her obscene image, then crushed and burned *it* by the Brook Kidron. [17]But the high places were not removed from Israel. Nevertheless the heart of Asa was loyal all his days.

[18]He also brought into the house of God the things that his father had dedicated and that he himself had dedicated: silver and gold and utensils. [19]And there was no war until the thirty-fifth year of the reign of Asa.

Asa's Treaty with Syria

16 In the thirty-sixth year of the reign of Asa, Baasha king of Israel came up against Judah and built Ramah, that he might let none go out or come in to Asa king of Judah. [2]Then Asa brought silver and gold from the treasuries of the house of the LORD and of the king's house, and sent to Ben-Hadad king of Syria, who dwelt in Damascus, saying, [3]*"Let there be* a treaty between you and me, as there was between my father and your father. See, I have sent you silver and gold; come, break your treaty with Baasha king of Israel, so that he will withdraw from me."

[4]So Ben-Hadad heeded King Asa, and sent the captains of his armies against the cities of Israel. They attacked Ijon, Dan, Abel Maim, and all the storage cities of Naphtali. [5]Now it happened, when Baasha heard *it*, that he stopped building Ramah and ceased his work. [6]Then King Asa took all Judah, and they carried away the stones and timber of Ramah, which Baasha had used for building; and with them he built Geba and Mizpah.

Hanani's Message to Asa

[7]And at that time Hanani the seer came to Asa king of Judah, and said to him: "Because you have relied on the king of Syria, and have not relied on the LORD your God, therefore the army of the king of Syria has escaped from your hand. [8]Were the Ethiopians and the Lubim not a huge army with very many chariots and horsemen? Yet, because you relied on the LORD, He delivered them into your hand. [9]For the eyes of the LORD run to and fro throughout the whole earth, to show Himself strong on behalf of *those* whose heart *is* loyal to Him. In this you have done foolishly; therefore from now on you shall have wars." [10]Then Asa was angry with the seer, and put him in prison, for *he was* enraged at him because of this. And Asa oppressed *some* of the people at that time.

Illness and Death of Asa

[11]Note that the acts of Asa, first and last, are indeed written in the book of the kings of Judah and Israel. [12]And in the thirty-ninth year of his reign, Asa became diseased

---

15:8 [a]Following Masoretic Text and Septuagint; Syriac and Vulgate read *Azariah the son of Oded* (compare verse 1). **15:16** [a]A Canaanite deity

in his feet, and his malady was severe; yet in his disease he did not seek the LORD, but the physicians.

[13]So Asa rested with his fathers; he died in the forty-first year of his reign. [14]They buried him in his own tomb, which he had made for himself in the City of David; and they laid him in the bed which was filled with spices and various ingredients prepared in a mixture of ointments. They made a very great burning for him.

Jehoshaphat Reigns in Judah

17 Then Jehoshaphat his son reigned in his place, and strengthened himself against Israel. [2]And he placed troops in all the fortified cities of Judah, and set garrisons in the land of Judah and in the cities of Ephraim which Asa his father had taken. [3]Now the LORD was with Jehoshaphat, because he walked in the former ways of his father David; he did not seek the Baals, [4]but sought the God[a] of his father, and walked in His commandments and not according to the acts of Israel. [5]Therefore the LORD established the kingdom in his hand; and all Judah gave presents to Jehoshaphat, and he had riches and honor in abundance. [6]And his heart took delight in the ways of the LORD; moreover he removed the high places and wooden images from Judah.

[7]Also in the third year of his reign he sent his leaders, Ben-Hail, Obadiah, Zechariah, Nethanel, and Michaiah, to teach in the cities of Judah. [8]And with them *he sent* Levites: Shemaiah, Nethaniah, Zebadiah, Asahel, Shemiramoth, Jehonathan, Adonijah, Tobijah, and Tobadonijah—the Levites; and with them Elishama and Jehoram, the priests. [9]So they taught in Judah, and *had* the Book of the Law of the LORD with them; they went throughout all the cities of Judah and taught the people.

[10]And the fear of the LORD fell on all the kingdoms of the lands that *were* around Judah, so that they did not make war against Jehoshaphat. [11]Also *some* of the Philistines brought Jehoshaphat presents and silver as tribute; and the Arabians brought him flocks, seven thousand seven hundred rams and seven thousand seven hundred male goats.

[12]So Jehoshaphat became increasingly powerful, and he built fortresses and storage cities in Judah. [13]He had much property in the cities of Judah; and the men of war, mighty men of valor, *were* in Jerusalem.

[14]These *are* their numbers, according to their fathers' houses. Of Judah, the captains of thousands: Adnah the captain, and with him three hundred thousand mighty men of valor; [15]and next to him *was* Jehohanan the captain, and with him two hundred and eighty thousand; [16]and next to him *was* Amasiah the son of Zichri, who willingly offered himself to the LORD, and with him two hundred thousand mighty men of valor. [17]Of Benjamin: Eliada a mighty man of valor, and with him two hundred thousand men armed with bow and shield; [18]and next to him *was* Jehozabad, and with him one hundred and eighty thousand prepared for war. [19]These served the king, besides those the king put in the fortified cities throughout all Judah.

Micaiah Warns Ahab

18 Jehoshaphat had riches and honor in abundance; and by marriage he allied himself with Ahab. [2]After some years he went down to *visit* Ahab in Samaria; and Ahab killed sheep and oxen in abundance for him and the people who were with him, and persuaded him to go up *with him* to Ramoth Gilead. [3]So Ahab king of Israel said to Jehoshaphat king of Judah, "Will you go with me *against* Ramoth Gilead?"

And he answered him, "I *am* as you *are*, and my people as your people; *we will be* with you in the war."

[4]Also Jehoshaphat said to the king of Israel, "Please inquire for the word of the LORD today."

[5]Then the king of Israel gathered the prophets together, four hundred men, and said to them, "Shall we go to war against Ramoth Gilead, or shall I refrain?"

So they said, "Go up, for God will deliver it into the king's hand."

[6]But Jehoshaphat said, *"Is there* not still a prophet of the LORD here, that we may inquire of Him?"[a]

17:4 [a]Septuagint reads LORD God.   **18:6** [a]Or him

⁷So the king of Israel said to Jehoshaphat, "*There is* still one man by whom we may inquire of the Lᴏʀᴅ; but I hate him, because he never prophesies good concerning me, but always evil. He *is* Micaiah the son of Imla."

And Jehoshaphat said, "Let not the king say such things!"

⁸Then the king of Israel called one *of his* officers and said, "Bring Micaiah the son of Imla quickly!"

⁹The king of Israel and Jehoshaphat king of Judah, clothed in *their* robes, sat each on his throne; and they sat at a threshing floor at the entrance of the gate of Samaria; and all the prophets prophesied before them. ¹⁰Now Zedekiah the son of Chenaanah had made horns of iron for himself; and he said, "Thus says the Lᴏʀᴅ: 'With these you shall gore the Syrians until they are destroyed.'"

¹¹And all the prophets prophesied so, saying, "Go up to Ramoth Gilead and prosper, for the Lᴏʀᴅ will deliver *it* into the king's hand."

¹²Then the messenger who had gone to call Micaiah spoke to him, saying, "Now listen, the words of the prophets with one accord encourage the king. Therefore please let your word be like *the word of* one of them, and speak encouragement."

¹³And Micaiah said, "*As* the Lᴏʀᴅ lives, whatever my God says, that I will speak."

¹⁴Then he came to the king; and the king said to him, "Micaiah, shall we go to war against Ramoth Gilead, or shall I refrain?"

And he said, "Go and prosper, and they shall be delivered into your hand!"

¹⁵So the king said to him, "How many times shall I make you swear that you tell me nothing but the truth in the name of the Lᴏʀᴅ?"

¹⁶Then he said, "I saw all Israel scattered on the mountains, as sheep that have no shepherd. And the Lᴏʀᴅ said, 'These have no master. Let each return to his house in peace.'"

¹⁷And the king of Israel said to Jehoshaphat, "Did I not tell you he would not prophesy good concerning me, but evil?"

¹⁸Then *Micaiah* said, "Therefore hear the word of the Lᴏʀᴅ: I saw the Lᴏʀᴅ sitting on His throne, and all the host of heaven standing on His right hand and His left. ¹⁹And the Lᴏʀᴅ said, 'Who will persuade Ahab king of Israel to go up, that he may fall at Ramoth Gilead?' So one spoke in this manner, and another spoke in that manner. ²⁰Then a spirit came forward and stood before the Lᴏʀᴅ, and said, 'I will persuade him.' The Lᴏʀᴅ said to him, 'In what way?' ²¹So he said, 'I will go out and be a lying spirit in the mouth of all his prophets.' And *the* Lᴏʀᴅ said, 'You shall persuade *him* and also prevail; go out and do so.' ²²Therefore look! The Lᴏʀᴅ has put a lying spirit in the mouth of these prophets of yours, and the Lᴏʀᴅ has declared disaster against you."

²³Then Zedekiah the son of Chenaanah went near and struck Micaiah on the cheek, and said, "Which way did the spirit from the Lᴏʀᴅ go from me to speak to you?"

²⁴And Micaiah said, "Indeed you shall see on that day when you go into an inner chamber to hide!"

²⁵Then the king of Israel said, "Take Micaiah, and return him to Amon the governor of the city and to Joash the king's son; ²⁶and say, 'Thus says the king: "Put this *fellow* in prison, and feed him with bread of affliction and water of affliction, until I return in peace."'"

²⁷But Micaiah said, "If you ever return in peace, the Lᴏʀᴅ has not spoken by me." And he said, "Take heed, all you people!"

Ahab Dies in Battle

²⁸So the king of Israel and Jehoshaphat the king of Judah went up to Ramoth Gilead. ²⁹And the king of Israel said to Jehoshaphat, "I will disguise myself and go into battle; but you put on your robes." So the king of Israel disguised himself, and they went into battle.

³⁰Now the king of Syria had commanded the captains of the chariots who *were* with him, saying, "Fight with no one small or great, but only with the king of Israel."

³¹So it was, when the captains of the chariots saw Jehoshaphat, that they said, "It *is* the king of Israel!" Therefore they surrounded him to attack; but Jehoshaphat cried out, and the Lᴏʀᴅ helped him, and God diverted them from him. ³²For so it was, when the captains of the chariots saw

that it was not the king of Israel, that they turned back from pursuing him. 33Now a certain man drew a bow at random, and struck the king of Israel between the joints of his armor. So he said to the driver of his chariot, "Turn around and take me out of the battle, for I am wounded." 34The battle increased that day, and the king of Israel propped *himself* up in *his* chariot facing the Syrians until evening; and about the time of sunset he died.

19 Then Jehoshaphat the king of Judah returned safely to his house in Jerusalem. 2And Jehu the son of Hanani the seer went out to meet him, and said to King Jehoshaphat, "Should you help the wicked and love those who hate the LORD? Therefore the wrath of the LORD *is* upon you. 3Nevertheless good things are found in you, in that you have removed the wooden images from the land, and have prepared your heart to seek God."

The Reforms of Jehoshaphat

4So Jehoshaphat dwelt at Jerusalem; and he went out again among the people from Beersheba to the mountains of Ephraim, and brought them back to the LORD God of their fathers. 5Then he set judges in the land throughout all the fortified cities of Judah, city by city, 6and said to the judges, "Take heed to what you are doing, for you do not judge for man but for the LORD, who *is* with you in the judgment. 7Now therefore, let the fear of the LORD be upon you; take care and do *it,* for *there is* no iniquity with the LORD our God, no partiality, nor taking of bribes."

8Moreover in Jerusalem, for the judgment of the LORD and for controversies, Jehoshaphat appointed some of the Levites and priests, and some of the chief fathers of Israel, when they returned to Jerusalem.ª 9And he commanded them, saying, "Thus you shall act in the fear of the LORD, faithfully and with a loyal heart: 10Whatever case comes to you from your brethren who dwell in their cities, whether of bloodshed or offenses against law or commandment, against statutes or ordinances, you shall warn them, lest they trespass against the LORD and wrath come upon you and your brethren. Do this, and you will not be guilty. 11And take notice: Amariah the chief priest *is* over you in all matters of the LORD; and Zebadiah the son of Ishmael, the ruler of the house of Judah, for all the king's matters; also the Levites *will be* officials before you. Behave courageously, and the LORD will be with the good."

COURAGE

"Behave courageously, and the LORD will be with the good."   2 CHRONICLES 19:11

Dignity and Courage

Martin Luther King Jr. (1929–1968), a pivotal leader of the civil rights movement, stated:

> If you will protest courageously, and yet with dignity and Christian love, when the history books are written in future generations, the historians will have to pause and say, "There lived a great people—a black people—who injected new meaning and dignity into the veins of civilization."

Ammon, Moab, and Mount Seir Defeated

20 It happened after this *that* the people of Moab with the people of Ammon, and *others* with them besides the Ammonites,ª came to battle against Jehoshaphat. 2Then some came and told Jehoshaphat, saying, "A great multitude is coming against you from beyond the sea, from Syria;ª and they are in Hazazon Tamar" (which *is* En Gedi). 3And Jehoshaphat feared, and set himself to seek the LORD, and proclaimed a fast throughout all Judah. 4So Judah gathered together to ask *help* from the LORD; and from all the cities of Judah they came to seek the LORD.

5Then Jehoshaphat stood in the assembly of Judah and Jerusalem, in the house of the LORD, before the new court, 6and said: "O LORD God of our fathers, *are* You not God in heaven, and do You *not* rule over all the

---

19:8 ªSeptuagint and Vulgate read *for the inhabitants of Jerusalem.*   **20:1** ªFollowing Masoretic Text and Vulgate; Septuagint reads *Meunites* (compare 26:7). **20:2** ªFollowing Masoretic Text, Septuagint, and Vulgate; some Hebrew manuscripts and Old Latin read *Edom.*

kingdoms of the nations, and in Your hand *is there not* power and might, so that no one is able to withstand You? [7]*Are* You not our God, *who* drove out the inhabitants of this land before Your people Israel, and gave it to the descendants of Abraham Your friend forever? [8]And they dwell in it, and have built You a sanctuary in it for Your name, saying, [9]'If disaster comes upon us—sword, judgment, pestilence, or famine—we will stand before this temple and in Your presence (for Your name *is* in this temple), and cry out to You in our affliction, and You will hear and save.' [10]And now, here are the people of Ammon, Moab, and Mount Seir—whom You would not let Israel invade when they came out of the land of Egypt, but they turned from them and did not destroy them— [11]here they are, rewarding us by coming to throw us out of Your possession which You have given us to inherit. [12]O our God, will You not judge them? For we have no power against this great multitude that is coming against us; nor do we know what to do, but our eyes *are* upon You."

[13]Now all Judah, with their little ones, their wives, and their children, stood before the LORD.

[14]Then the Spirit of the LORD came upon Jahaziel the son of Zechariah, the son of Benaiah, the son of Jeiel, the son of Mattaniah, a Levite of the sons of Asaph, in the midst of the assembly. [15]And he said, "Listen, all you of Judah and you inhabitants of Jerusalem, and you, King Jehoshaphat! Thus says the LORD to you: 'Do not be afraid nor dismayed because of this great multitude, for the battle *is* not yours, but God's. [16]Tomorrow go down against them. They will surely come up by the Ascent of Ziz, and you will find them at *the* end of the brook before the Wilderness of Jeruel. [17]You will not *need* to fight in this *battle*. Position yourselves, stand still and see the salvation of the LORD, who is with you, O Judah and Jerusalem!' Do not fear or be dismayed; tomorrow go out against them, for the LORD *is* with you."

[18]And Jehoshaphat bowed his head with *his* face to the ground, and all Judah and the inhabitants of Jerusalem bowed before the LORD, worshiping the LORD. [19]Then the Levites of the children of the Kohathites and of the children of the Korahites stood up to praise the LORD God of Israel with voices loud and high.

[20]So they rose early in the morning and went out into the Wilderness of Tekoa; and as they went out, Jehoshaphat stood and said, "Hear me, O Judah and you inhabitants of Jerusalem: Believe in the LORD your God, and you shall be established; believe His prophets, and you shall prosper." [21]And when he had consulted with the people, he appointed those who should sing to the LORD, and who should praise the beauty of holiness, as they went out before the army and were saying:

> "Praise the LORD,
>   For His mercy *endures* forever."[a]

[22]Now when they began to sing and to praise, the LORD set ambushes against the people of Ammon, Moab, and Mount Seir, who had come against Judah; and they were defeated. [23]For the people of Ammon and Moab stood up against the inhabitants of Mount Seir to utterly kill and destroy *them.* And when they had made an end of the inhabitants of Seir, they helped to destroy one another.

[24]So when Judah came to a place overlooking the wilderness, they looked toward the multitude; and there *were* their dead bodies, fallen on the earth. No one had escaped. [25]When Jehoshaphat and his people came to take away their spoil, they found among them an abundance of valuables on the dead bodies,[a] and precious jewelry, which they stripped off for themselves, more than they could carry away; and they were three days gathering the spoil because there was so much. [26]And on the fourth day they assembled in the Valley of Berachah, for there they blessed the LORD; therefore the name of that place was called The Valley of Berachah[a] until this day. [27]Then they

---

20:21 [a]Compare Psalm 106:1   **20:25** [a]A few Hebrew manuscripts, Old Latin, and Vulgate read *garments;* Septuagint reads *armor.*   **20:26** [a]Literally *Blessing*

Now when they began to sing and to praise, the LORD set ambushes. . . .

2 CHRONICLES 20:22

"CHESTER"

When the Continental Army fought to defend the new nation's independence, it chose as its favorite marching song an adapted hymn, "Chester," by the Boston church composer William Billings around 1778. It became the song of the American Revolution, sung around the campfires of the Continental Army and played by fifers on the march to battle. The music and words express perfectly the burning desire for freedom that sustained the patriots as they risked their lives. One detects no "separation of church and state" in their convictions.

Let tyrants shake their iron rod,
And slavery clank her galling chains,
We fear them not, we trust in God,
New England's God forever reigns.

Howe and Burgoyne and Clinton too,
With Prescott and Cornwallis join'd,
Together plot our overthrow,
In one infernal league combin'd.

When God inspir'd us for the fight,
Their ranks were broke, their lines were forc'd,
Their ships were shatter'd in our sight
Or swiftly driven from our coast.

The foe comes on with haughty stride,
Our troops advance with martial noise,
Their vet'rans flee before our youth,
And gen'rals yield to beardless boys.

What grateful offerings shall we bring?
What shall we render to the Lord?
Loud Hallelujahs let us sing,
And praise His name on ev'ry chord.

returned, every man of Judah and Jerusalem, with Jehoshaphat in front of them, to go back to Jerusalem with joy, for the Lord had made them rejoice over their enemies. ²⁸So they came to Jerusalem, with stringed instruments and harps and trumpets, to the house of the Lord. ²⁹And the fear of God was on all the kingdoms of *those* countries when they heard that the Lord had fought against the enemies of Israel. ³⁰Then the realm of Jehoshaphat was quiet, for his God gave him rest all around.

The End of Jehoshaphat's Reign

³¹So Jehoshaphat was king over Judah. *He was* thirty-five years old when he became king, and he reigned twenty-five years in Jerusalem. His mother's name *was* Azubah the daughter of Shilhi. ³²And he walked in the way of his father Asa, and did not turn aside from it, doing *what was* right in the sight of the Lord. ³³Nevertheless the high places were not taken away, for as yet the people had not directed their hearts to the God of their fathers.

³⁴Now the rest of the acts of Jehoshaphat, first and last, indeed they *are* written in the book of Jehu the son of Hanani, which *is* mentioned in the book of the kings of Israel.

³⁵After this Jehoshaphat king of Judah allied himself with Ahaziah king of Israel, who acted very wickedly. ³⁶And he allied himself with him to make ships to go to Tarshish, and they made the ships in Ezion Geber. ³⁷But Eliezer the son of Dodavah of Mareshah prophesied against Jehoshaphat, saying, "Because you have allied yourself with Ahaziah, the Lord has destroyed your works." Then the ships were wrecked, so that they were not able to go to Tarshish.

Jehoram Reigns in Judah

21 And Jehoshaphat rested with his fathers, and was buried with his fathers in the City of David. Then Jehoram his son reigned in his place. ²He had brothers, the sons of Jehoshaphat: Azariah, Jehiel, Zechariah, Azaryahu, Michael, and Shephatiah; all these *were* the sons of Jehoshaphat king of Israel. ³Their father gave them great gifts of silver and gold and precious things, with fortified cities in Judah; but he gave the kingdom to Jehoram, because he *was* the firstborn.

⁴Now when Jehoram was established over the kingdom of his father, he strengthened himself and killed all his brothers with the sword, and also *others* of the princes of Israel.

⁵Jehoram *was* thirty-two years old when he became king, and he reigned eight years in Jerusalem. ⁶And he walked in the way of the kings of Israel, just as the house of Ahab had done, for he had the daughter of Ahab as a wife; and he did evil in the sight of the Lord. ⁷Yet the Lord would not destroy the house of David, because of the covenant that He had made with David, and since He had promised to give a lamp to him and to his sons forever.

⁸In his days Edom revolted against Judah's authority, and made a king over themselves. ⁹So Jehoram went out with his officers, and all his chariots with him. And he rose by night and attacked the Edomites who had surrounded him and the captains of the chariots. ¹⁰Thus Edom has been in revolt against Judah's authority to this day. At that time Libnah revolted against his rule, because he had forsaken the Lord God of his fathers. ¹¹Moreover he made high places in the mountains of Judah, and caused the inhabitants of Jerusalem to commit harlotry, and led Judah astray.

¹²And a letter came to him from Elijah the prophet, saying,

Thus says the Lord God of your father David:
Because you have not walked in the ways of Jehoshaphat your father, or in the ways of Asa king of Judah, ¹³but have walked in the way of the kings of Israel, and have made Judah and the inhabitants of Jerusalem to play the harlot like the harlotry of the house of Ahab, and also have killed your brothers, those of your father's household, *who were* better than yourself, ¹⁴behold, the Lord will strike your people with a serious affliction— your children, your wives, and all your possessions; ¹⁵and you *will become* very sick with a disease of your intestines,

until your intestines come out by reason of the sickness, day by day.

¹⁶Moreover the LORD stirred up against Jehoram the spirit of the Philistines and the Arabians who *were* near the Ethiopians. ¹⁷And they came up into Judah and invaded it, and carried away all the possessions that were found in the king's house, and also his sons and his wives, so that there was not a son left to him except Jehoahaz,ᵃ the youngest of his sons.

¹⁸After all this the LORD struck him in his intestines with an incurable disease. ¹⁹Then it happened in the course of time, after the end of two years, that his intestines came out because of his sickness; so he died in severe pain. And his people made no burning for him, like the burning for his fathers.

²⁰He was thirty-two years old when he became king. He reigned in Jerusalem eight years and, to no one's sorrow, departed. However they buried him in the City of David, but not in the tombs of the kings.

Ahaziah Reigns in Judah

22 Then the inhabitants of Jerusalem made Ahaziah his youngest son king in his place, for the raiders who came with the Arabians into the camp had killed all the older *sons*. So Ahaziah the son of Jehoram, king of Judah, reigned. ²Ahaziah *was* forty-twoᵃ years old when he became king, and he reigned one year in Jerusalem. His mother's name *was* Athaliah the granddaughter of Omri. ³He also walked in the ways of the house of Ahab, for his mother advised him to do wickedly. ⁴Therefore he did evil in the sight of the LORD, like the house of Ahab; for they were his counselors after the death of his father, to his destruction. ⁵He also followed their advice, and went with Jehoramᵃ the son of Ahab king of Israel to war against Hazael king of Syria at Ramoth Gilead; and the Syrians wounded Joram. ⁶Then he returned to Jezreel to recover from the wounds which he had received at Ramah, when he fought against Hazael king of Syria. And Azariahᵃ the son of Jehoram, king of Judah, went down to see Jehoram the son of Ahab in Jezreel, because he was sick.

⁷His going to Joram was God's occasion for Ahaziah's downfall; for when he arrived, he went out with Jehoram against Jehu the son of Nimshi, whom the LORD had anointed to cut off the house of Ahab. ⁸And it happened, when Jehu was executing judgment on the house of Ahab, and found the princes of Judah and the sons of Ahaziah's brothers who served Ahaziah, that he killed them. ⁹Then he searched for Ahaziah; and they caught him (he was hiding in Samaria), and brought him to Jehu. When they had killed him, they buried him, "because," they said, "he is the son of Jehoshaphat, who sought the LORD with all his heart."

So the house of Ahaziah had no one to assume power over the kingdom.

Athaliah Reigns in Judah

¹⁰Now when Athaliah the mother of Ahaziah saw that her son was dead, she arose and destroyed all the royal heirs of the house of Judah. ¹¹But Jehoshabeath,ᵃ the daughter of the king, took Joash the son of Ahaziah, and stole him away from among the king's sons who were being murdered, and put him and his nurse in a bedroom. So Jehoshabeath, the daughter of King Jehoram, the wife of Jehoiada the priest (for she was the sister of Ahaziah), hid him from Athaliah so that she did not kill him. ¹²And he was hidden with them in the house of God for six years, while Athaliah reigned over the land.

Joash Crowned King of Judah

23 In the seventh year Jehoiada strengthened himself, *and made a* covenant with the captains of hundreds: Azariah the son of Jeroham, Ishmael the son of Jehohanan, Azariah the son of Obed, Maaseiah the son of Adaiah, and Elishaphat the son of Zichri. ²And they went throughout Judah and gathered the Levites from all the cities

---

21:17 ᵃElsewhere called *Ahaziah* (compare 2 Chronicles 22:1)   **22:2** ᵃOr *twenty-two* (compare 2 Kings 8:26)   **22:5** ᵃAlso spelled *Joram* (compare verses 5 and 7; 2 Kings 8:28; and elsewhere)
22:6 ᵃSome Hebrew manuscripts, Septuagint, Syriac, Vulgate, and 2 Kings 8:29 read *Ahaziah.*
22:11 ᵃSpelled *Jehosheba* in 2 Kings 11:2

of Judah, and the chief fathers of Israel, and they came to Jerusalem.

3Then all the assembly made a covenant with the king in the house of God. And he said to them, "Behold, the king's son shall reign, as the LORD has said of the sons of David. 4This *is* what you shall do: One-third of you entering on the Sabbath, of the priests and the Levites, *shall be* keeping watch over the doors; 5one-third *shall be* at the king's house; and one-third at the Gate of the Foundation. All the people *shall be* in the courts of the house of the LORD. 6But let no one come into the house of the LORD except the priests and those of the Levites who serve. They may go in, for they *are* holy; but all the people shall keep the watch of the LORD. 7And the Levites shall surround the king on all sides, every man with his weapons in his hand; and whoever comes into the house, let him be put to death. You are to be with the king when he comes in and when he goes out."

8So the Levites and all Judah did according to all that Jehoiada the priest commanded. And each man took his men who were to be on duty on the Sabbath, with those who were going *off duty* on the Sabbath; for Jehoiada the priest had not dismissed the divisions. 9And Jehoiada the priest gave to the captains of hundreds the spears and the large and small shields which *had belonged* to King David, that *were* in the temple of God. 10Then he set all the people, every man with his weapon in his hand, from the right side of the temple to the left side of the temple, along by the altar and by the temple, all around the king. 11And they brought out the king's son, put the crown on him, *gave him* the Testimony,ᵃ and made him king. Then Jehoiada and his sons anointed him, and said, "*Long* live the king!"

Death of Athaliah

12Now when Athaliah heard the noise of the people running and praising the king, she came to the people *in* the temple of the LORD. 13*When* she looked, there was the king standing by his pillar at the entrance; and the leaders and the trumpeters *were* by the king. All the people of the land were

rejoicing and blowing trumpets, also the singers with musical instruments, and those who led in praise. So Athaliah tore her clothes and said, "Treason! Treason!"

14And Jehoiada the priest brought out the captains of hundreds who were set over the army, and said to them, "Take her outside under guard, and slay with the sword whoever follows her." For the priest had said, "Do not kill her in the house of the LORD."

15So they seized her; and she went by way of the entrance of the Horse Gate *into* the king's house, and they killed her there.

16Then Jehoiada made a covenant between himself, the people, and the king, that they should be the LORD's people. 17And all the people went to the templeᵃ of Baal, and tore it down. They broke in pieces its altars and images, and killed Mattan the priest of Baal before the altars. 18Also Jehoiada appointed the oversight of the house of the LORD to the hand of the priests, the Levites, whom David had assigned in the house of the LORD, to offer the burnt offerings of the LORD, as *it is* written in the Law of Moses, with rejoicing and with singing, *as it was established* by David. 19And he set the gatekeepers at the gates of the house of the LORD, so that no one *who was* in any way unclean should enter.

20Then he took the captains of hundreds, the nobles, the governors of the people, and all the people of the land, and brought the king down from the house of the LORD; and they went through the Upper Gate to the king's house, and set the king on the throne of the kingdom. 21So all the people of the land rejoiced; and the city was quiet, for they had slain Athaliah with the sword.

Joash Repairs the Temple

24 Joash *was* seven years old when he became king, and he reigned forty years in Jerusalem. His mother's name *was* Zibiah of Beersheba. 2Joash did *what was* right in the sight of the LORD all the days of Jehoiada the priest. 3And Jehoiada took two wives for him, and he had sons and daughters.

23:11 ᵃThat is, the Law (compare Exodus 25:16, 21; 31:18)   **23:17** ᵃLiterally *house*

⁴Now it happened after this *that* Joash set his heart on repairing the house of the Lord. ⁵Then he gathered the priests and the Levites, and said to them, "Go out to the cities of Judah, and gather from all Israel money to repair the house of your God from year to year, and see that you do it quickly."

However the Levites did not do it quickly. ⁶So the king called Jehoiada the chief *priest,* and said to him, "Why have you not required the Levites to bring in from Judah and from Jerusalem the collection, *according to the commandment* of Moses the servant of the Lord and of the assembly of Israel, for the tabernacle of witness?" ⁷For the sons of Athaliah, that wicked woman, had broken into the house of God, and had also presented all the dedicated things of the house of the Lord to the Baals.

⁸Then at the king's command they made a chest, and set it outside at the gate of the house of the Lord. ⁹And they made a proclamation throughout Judah and Jerusalem to bring to the Lord the collection *that* Moses the servant of God *had imposed* on Israel in the wilderness. ¹⁰Then all the leaders and all the people rejoiced, brought their contributions, and put *them* into the chest until all had given. ¹¹So it was, at that time, when the chest was brought to the king's official by the hand of the Levites, and when they saw that *there was* much money, that the king's scribe and the high priest's officer came and emptied the chest, and took it and returned it to its place. Thus they did day by day, and gathered money in abundance.

¹²The king and Jehoiada gave it to those who did the work of the service of the house of the Lord; and they hired masons and carpenters to repair the house of the Lord, and also those who worked in iron and bronze to restore the house of the Lord. ¹³So the workmen labored, and the work was completed by them; they restored the house of God to its original condition and reinforced it. ¹⁴When they had finished, they brought the rest of the money before the king and Jehoiada; they made from it articles for the house of the Lord, articles for serving and offering, spoons and vessels of gold and silver. And they offered burnt offerings in the house of the Lord continually all the days of Jehoiada.

Apostasy of Joash

¹⁵But Jehoiada grew old and was full of days, and he died; *he was* one hundred and thirty years old when he died. ¹⁶And they buried him in the City of David among the kings, because he had done good in Israel, both toward God and His house.

¹⁷Now after the death of Jehoiada the leaders of Judah came and bowed down to the king. And the king listened to them. ¹⁸Therefore they left the house of the Lord God of their fathers, and served wooden images and idols; and wrath came upon Judah and Jerusalem because of their trespass. ¹⁹Yet He sent prophets to them, to bring them back to the Lord; and they testified against them, but they would not listen.

²⁰Then the Spirit of God came upon Zechariah the son of Jehoiada the priest, who stood above the people, and said to them, "Thus says God: 'Why do you transgress the commandments of the Lord, so that you cannot prosper? Because you have forsaken the Lord, He also has forsaken you.'" ²¹So they conspired against him, and at the command of the king they stoned him with stones in the court of the house of the Lord. ²²Thus Joash the king did not remember the kindness which Jehoiada his father had done to him, but killed his son; and as he died, he said, "The Lord look on *it,* and repay!"

Death of Joash

²³So it happened in the spring of the year *that* the army of Syria came up against him; and they came to Judah and Jerusalem, and destroyed all the leaders of the people from among the people, and sent all their spoil to the king of Damascus. ²⁴For the army of the Syrians came with a small company of men; but the Lord delivered a very great army into their hand, because they had forsaken the Lord God of their fathers. So they executed judgment against Joash. ²⁵And when they had withdrawn from him (for they left him severely wounded), his own servants conspired against him because of the blood of the

sonsa of Jehoiada the priest, and killed him on his bed. So he died. And they buried him in the City of David, but they did not bury him in the tombs of the kings.

26These are the ones who conspired against him: Zabada the son of Shimeath the Ammonitess, and Jehozabad the son of Shimrithb the Moabitess. 27Now *concerning* his sons, and the many oracles about him, and the repairing of the house of God, indeed they *are* written in the annals of the book of the kings. Then Amaziah his son reigned in his place.

Amaziah Reigns in Judah

25 Amaziah *was* twenty-five years old *when* he became king, and he reigned twenty-nine years in Jerusalem. His mother's name *was* Jehoaddan of Jerusalem. 2And he did *what was* right in the sight of the LORD, but not with a loyal heart.

3Now it happened, as soon as the kingdom was established for him, that he executed his servants who had murdered his father the king. 4However he did not execute their children, but *did* as *it is* written in the Law in the Book of Moses, where the LORD commanded, saying, "The fathers shall not be put to death for their children, nor shall the children be put to death for their fathers; but a person shall die for his own sin."a

The War Against Edom

5Moreover Amaziah gathered Judah together and set over them captains of thousands and captains of hundreds, according to *their* fathers' houses, throughout all Judah and Benjamin; and he numbered them from twenty years old and above, and found them to be three hundred thousand choice *men, able* to go to war, who could handle spear and shield. 6He also hired one hundred thousand mighty men of valor from Israel for one hundred talents of silver. 7But a man of God came to him, saying, "O king, do not let the army of Israel go with you, for the LORD *is* not with Israel—*not with* any of the children of Ephraim. 8But if you go, be gone! Be strong in battle! *Even so,* God shall make you fall before the enemy; for God has power to help and to overthrow."

9Then Amaziah said to the man of God, "But what *shall we* do about the hundred talents which I have given to the troops of Israel?"

And the man of God answered, "The LORD is able to give you much more than this." 10So Amaziah discharged the troops that had come to him from Ephraim, to go back home. Therefore their anger was greatly aroused against Judah, and they returned home in great anger.

11Then Amaziah strengthened himself, and leading his people, he went to the Valley of Salt and killed ten thousand of the people of Seir. 12Also the children of Judah took captive ten thousand alive, brought them to the top of the rock, and cast them down from the top of the rock, so that they all were dashed in pieces.

13But as for the soldiers of the army which Amaziah had discharged, so that they would not go with him to battle, they raided the cities of Judah from Samaria to Beth Horon, killed three thousand in them, and took much spoil.

14Now it was so, after Amaziah came from the slaughter of the Edomites, that he brought the gods of the people of Seir, set them up *to be* his gods, and bowed down before them and burned incense to them. 15Therefore the anger of the LORD was aroused against Amaziah, and He sent him a prophet who said to him, "Why have you sought the gods of the people, which could not rescue their own people from your hand?"

16So it was, as he talked with him, that *the king* said to him, "Have we made you the king's counselor? Cease! Why should you be killed?"

Then the prophet ceased, and said, "I know that God has determined to destroy you, because you have done this and have not heeded my advice."

Israel Defeats Judah

17Now Amaziah king of Judah asked advice and sent to Joasha the son of Jehoahaz, the

---

24:25 aSeptuagint and Vulgate read *son* (compare verses 20–22).   24:26 aOr *Jozachar* (compare 2 Kings 12:21) bOr *Shomer* (compare 2 Kings 12:21) 25:4 aDeuteronomy 24:16   25:17 aSpelled *Jehoash* in 2 Kings 14:8ff

GIVE ME LIBERTY
or give me death!

THE AMERICAN REVOLUTION

ON MARCH 23, 1775, when Patrick Henry spoke the now famous phrase, "Give me liberty or give me death!" to arouse the Second Virginia Convention to arms against the tyranny of Great Britain, he noted that "we have done everything that could be done to avert the storm which is now coming upon us." During the critical years of 1765–1776, the American colonies had been forced to endure taxation without representation, searches and seizures without probable cause, the confiscation of firearms, and on and on. Though the colonial leaders had tried to remain loyal to the Crown and reconcile their differences, they were finally compelled to break away in revolt.

THE DECLARATION OF INDEPENDENCE was then written as a proclamation to the world of their reasons for separating from England. But while the Declaration gives a detailed list of legal offenses that England had left unresolved, the Founders saw these as more than isolated wrongs. Rather, they saw them as a part of a predetermined plan to take away their religious liberties and reestablish the Church of England to rule over their hearts and souls, thus enslaving the colonies. In that light, one understands the power of Patrick Henry's fiery words.

Faced with such prospects, the Declaration stated that the American colonists were set to defend "the laws of nature and of nature's God"— words that define the principle upon which the Founders stood. The *laws of nature* were understood to mean the will of God for man as revealed to man's reason. However, because man is fallen and his reason does not always comprehend this law, God gave His law in the Bible to make it absolutely clear.

WE OUGHT TO OBEY GOD RATHER THAN MEN

(Acts 5:29)

THUS, IT WAS THE CHURCHES THAT became the primary source that stirred the fires of liberty, telling the colonists that the English government was usurping their God-given rights, and the King and Parliament were violating the laws of God. The Founding Fathers were convinced that it was their sacred duty to start a revolution to uphold the law of God against the unjust and oppressive laws of men. And the fight for political liberty was seen as a sacred cause because civil liberty was an inalienable right, according to God's natural law.

The New England ministers, in particular, were decisive in rallying the popular moral support for war against England. They pressed their congregations to overthrow King George because they believed that rebellion to tyrants was obedience to God. From many pulpits, ministers recruited troops and strengthened them in battle with patriotic sermons.

While the church leaders were well schooled in the fact that the Bible placed great emphasis on due submission to civil authorities (Romans 13), they noted there are also many passages that approve resistance to ungodly authority. For instance, when the apostles were commanded by the Sanhedrin to cease preaching that Jesus Christ had risen from the dead, Peter boldly asserted: "We ought to obey God rather than men" (Acts 5:29).

Therefore, it is no coincidence that one of the watchwords of the American Revolution was "No King but King Jesus." For most of the patriots, their faith gave them the courage to stand on God's Word and risk their lives and properties to break the tyranny of an unjust human authority. In their Christian worldview, obedience to God took precedence over country or government, and their primary allegiance was to the Lord Jesus Christ.

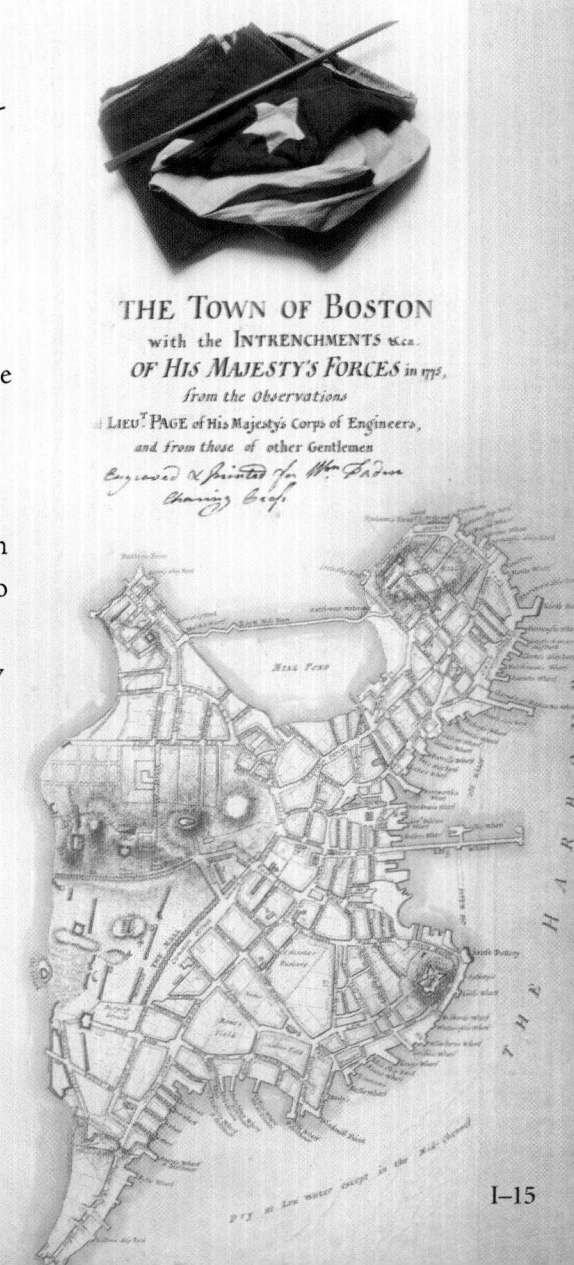

THE TOWN OF BOSTON
with the INTRENCHMENTS &c.a.
OF HIS MAJESTY'S FORCES in 1775,
from the Observations
of LIEUT. PAGE of His Majesty's Corps of Engineers,
and from those of other Gentlemen

INDICATIVE OF THIS SPIRIT, in 1775, the Lutheran pastor John Peter Gabriel Muhlenberg preached a sermon on Ecclesiastes 3:1, "To everything there is a season, a time for every purpose under heaven." Concluding the message, he declared, "In the language of the Holy Writ, there is a time for all things. There is a time to preach and a time to fight. And *now* is the time to fight." He then threw off his clerical robes to reveal the uniform of a Revolutionary Army officer. That afternoon, at the head of 300 men, he marched off to join General Washington's troops and became Colonel of the 8th Virginia Regiment.

Ministers turned the colonial resistance into a righteous cause and served at every level in the conflict, from military chaplains to members of state legislatures to taking up arms and leading troops into battle. And, ultimately, after two main British armies were captured by the Continental Army at Saratoga in 1777 and Yorktown in 1781, the other words of Patrick Henry to his fellow Virginians proved true: "Three millions of people, armed with the holy cause of liberty, and in such a country as that which we possess, are invincible by any force which our enemy can send against us."

son of Jehu, king of Israel, saying, "Come, let us face one another *in battle.*"

[18] And Joash king of Israel sent to Amaziah king of Judah, saying, "The thistle that *was* in Lebanon sent to the cedar that was in Lebanon, saying, 'Give your daughter to my son as wife'; and a wild beast that *was* in Lebanon passed by and trampled the thistle. [19] Indeed you say that you have defeated the Edomites, and your heart is lifted up to boast. Stay at home now; why should you meddle with trouble, that you should fall—you and Judah with you?"

[20] But Amaziah would not heed, for it *came* from God, that He might give them into the hand *of their enemies,* because they sought the gods of Edom. [21] So Joash king of Israel went out; and he and Amaziah king of Judah faced one another at Beth Shemesh, which *belongs* to Judah. [22] And Judah was defeated by Israel, and every man fled to his tent. [23] Then Joash the king of Israel captured Amaziah king of Judah, the son of Joash, the son of Jehoahaz, at Beth Shemesh; and he brought him to Jerusalem, and broke down the wall of Jerusalem from the Gate of Ephraim to the Corner Gate—four hundred cubits. [24] And *he took* all the gold and silver, all the articles that were found in the house of God with Obed-Edom, the treasures of the king's house, and hostages, and returned to Samaria.

Death of Amaziah

[25] Amaziah the son of Joash, king of Judah, lived fifteen years after the death of Joash the son of Jehoahaz, king of Israel. [26] Now the rest of the acts of Amaziah, from first to last, indeed *are* they not written in the book of the kings of Judah and Israel? [27] After the time that Amaziah turned away from following the LORD, they made a conspiracy against him in Jerusalem, and he fled to Lachish; but they sent after him to Lachish and killed him there. [28] Then they brought him on horses and buried him with his fathers in the City of Judah.

Uzziah Reigns in Judah

26 Now all the people of Judah took Uzziah,ᵃ who *was* sixteen years old, and made him king instead of his father

Amaziah. [2] He built Elathᵃ and restored it to Judah, after the king rested with his fathers.

[3] Uzziah *was* sixteen years old when he became king, and he reigned fifty-two years in Jerusalem. His mother's name was Jecholiah of Jerusalem. [4] And he did *what was* right in the sight of the LORD, according to all that his father Amaziah had done. [5] He sought God in the days of Zechariah, who had understanding in the visionsᵃ of God; and as long as he sought the LORD, God made him prosper.

[6] Now he went out and made war against the Philistines, and broke down the wall of Gath, the wall of Jabneh, and the wall of Ashdod; and he built cities *around* Ashdod and among the Philistines. [7] God helped him against the Philistines, against the Arabians who lived in Gur Baal, and against the Meunites. [8] Also the Ammonites brought tribute to Uzziah. His fame spread as far as the entrance of Egypt, for he became exceedingly strong.

[9] And Uzziah built towers in Jerusalem at the Corner Gate, at the Valley Gate, and at the corner buttress of the wall; then he fortified them. [10] Also he built towers in the desert. He dug many wells, for he had much livestock, both in the lowlands and in the plains; *he also had* farmers and vinedressers in the mountains and in Carmel, for he loved the soil.

[11] Moreover Uzziah had an army of fighting men who went out to war by companies, according to the number on their roll as prepared by Jeiel the scribe and Maaseiah the officer, under the hand of Hananiah, *one* of the king's captains. [12] The total number of chief officersᵃ of the mighty men of valor *was* two thousand six hundred. [13] And under their authority *was* an army of three hundred and seven thousand five hundred, that made war with mighty power, to help the king against the enemy. [14] Then Uzziah prepared for them, for the entire army, shields, spears, helmets, body armor, bows, and slings *to cast* stones. [15] And he

---

26:1 ᵃCalled *Azariah* in 2 Kings 14:21ff
26:2 ᵃHebrew *Eloth*   **26:5** ᵃSeveral Hebrew manuscripts, Septuagint, Syriac, Targum, and Arabic read *fear.*   **26:12** ᵃLiterally *chief fathers*

made devices in Jerusalem, invented by skillful men, to be on the towers and the corners, to shoot arrows and large stones. So his fame spread far and wide, for he was marvelously helped till he became strong.

The Penalty for Uzziah's Pride

16But when he was strong his heart was lifted up, to *his* destruction, for he transgressed against the Lord his God by entering the temple of the Lord to burn incense on the altar of incense. 17So Azariah the priest went in after him, and with him were eighty priests of the Lord—valiant men. 18And they withstood King Uzziah, and said to him, "*It is* not for you, Uzziah, to burn incense to the Lord, but for the priests, the sons of Aaron, who are consecrated to burn incense. Get out of the sanctuary, for you have trespassed! You *shall have* no honor from the Lord God."

19Then Uzziah became furious; and he *had* a censer in his hand to burn incense. And while he was angry with the priests, leprosy broke out on his forehead, before the priests in the house of the Lord, beside the incense altar. 20And Azariah the chief priest and all the priests looked at him, and there, on his forehead, he *was* leprous; so they thrust him out of that place. Indeed he also hurried to get out, because the Lord had struck him.

21King Uzziah was a leper until the day of his death. He dwelt in an isolated house, because he was a leper; for he was cut off from the house of the Lord. Then Jotham his son *was* over the king's house, judging the people of the land.

22Now the rest of the acts of Uzziah, from first to last, the prophet Isaiah the son of Amoz wrote. 23So Uzziah rested with his fathers, and they buried him with his fathers in the field of burial which *belonged* to the kings, for they said, "He is a leper." Then Jotham his son reigned in his place.

Jotham Reigns in Judah

27 Jotham *was* twenty-five years old when he became king, and he reigned sixteen years in Jerusalem. His mother's name *was* Jerushah[a] the daughter of Zadok. 2And he did *what was* right in the sight of the

Lord, according to all that his father Uzziah had done (although he did not enter the temple of the Lord). But still the people acted corruptly.

3He built the Upper Gate of the house of the Lord, and he built extensively on the wall of Ophel. 4Moreover he built cities in the mountains of Judah, and in the forests he built fortresses and towers. 5He also fought with the king of the Ammonites and defeated them. And the people of Ammon gave him in that year one hundred talents of silver, ten thousand kors of wheat, and ten thousand of barley. The people of Ammon paid this to him in the second and third years also. 6So Jotham became mighty, because he prepared his ways before the Lord his God.

7Now the rest of the acts of Jotham, and all his wars and his ways, indeed they *are* written in the book of the kings of Israel and Judah. 8He was twenty-five years old when he became king, and he reigned sixteen years in Jerusalem. 9So Jotham rested with his fathers, and they buried him in the City of David. Then Ahaz his son reigned in his place.

Ahaz Reigns in Judah

28 Ahaz *was* twenty years old when he became king, and he reigned sixteen years in Jerusalem; and he did not do *what was* right in the sight of the Lord, as his father David *had done*. 2For he walked in the ways of the kings of Israel, and made molded images for the Baals. 3He burned incense in the Valley of the Son of Hinnom, and burned his children in the fire, according to the abominations of the nations whom the Lord had cast out before the children of Israel. 4And he sacrificed and burned incense on the high places, on the hills, and under every green tree.

Syria and Israel Defeat Judah

5Therefore the Lord his God delivered him into the hand of the king of Syria. They defeated him, and carried away a great multitude of them as captives, and brought *them* to Damascus. Then he was also delivered into the hand of the king of Israel, who

---

27:1 [a]Spelled *Jerusha* in 2 Kings 15:33

defeated him with a great slaughter. [6]For Pekah the son of Remaliah killed one hundred and twenty thousand in Judah in one day, all valiant men, because they had forsaken the LORD God of their fathers. [7]Zichri, a mighty man of Ephraim, killed Maaseiah the king's son, Azrikam the officer over the house, and Elkanah *who was* second to the king. [8]And the children of Israel carried away captive of their brethren two hundred thousand women, sons, and daughters; and they also took away much spoil from them, and brought the spoil to Samaria.

Israel Returns the Captives

[9]But a prophet of the LORD was there, whose name *was* Oded; and he went out before the army that came to Samaria, and said to them: "Look, because the LORD God of your fathers was angry with Judah, He has delivered them into your hand; but you have killed them in a rage *that* reaches up to heaven. [10]And now you propose to force the children of Judah and Jerusalem to be your male and female slaves; *but are* you not also guilty before the LORD your God? [11]Now hear me, therefore, and return the captives, whom you have taken captive from your brethren, for the fierce wrath of the LORD *is* upon you."

[12]Then some of the heads of the children of Ephraim, Azariah the son of Johanan, Berechiah the son of Meshillemoth, Jehizkiah the son of Shallum, and Amasa the son of Hadlai, stood up against those who came from the war, [13]and said to them, "You shall not bring the captives here, for we *already* have offended the LORD. You intend to add to our sins and to our guilt; for our guilt is great, and *there is* fierce wrath against Israel." [14]So the armed men left the captives and the spoil before the leaders and all the assembly. [15]Then the men who were designated by name rose up and took the captives, and from the spoil they clothed all who were naked among them, dressed them and gave them sandals, gave them food and drink, and anointed them; and they let all the feeble ones ride on donkeys. So they brought them to their brethren at Jericho, the city of palm trees. Then they returned to Samaria.

Assyria Refuses to Help Judah

[16]At the same time King Ahaz sent to the kings[a] of Assyria to help him. [17]For again the Edomites had come, attacked Judah, and carried away captives. [18]The Philistines also had invaded the cities of the lowland and of the South of Judah, and had taken Beth Shemesh, Aijalon, Gederoth, Sochoh with its villages, Timnah with its villages, and Gimzo with its villages; and they dwelt there. [19]For the LORD brought Judah low because of Ahaz king of Israel, for he had encouraged moral decline in Judah and had been continually unfaithful to the LORD. [20]Also Tiglath-Pileser[a] king of Assyria came to him and distressed him, and did not assist him. [21]For Ahaz took part *of the treasures* from the house of the LORD, from the house of the king, and from the leaders, and he gave *it* to the king of Assyria; but he did not help him.

Apostasy and Death of Ahaz

[22]Now in the time of his distress King Ahaz became increasingly unfaithful to the LORD. This *is that* King Ahaz. [23]For he sacrificed to the gods of Damascus which had defeated him, saying, "Because the gods of the kings of Syria help them, I will sacrifice to them that they may help me." But they were the ruin of him and of all Israel. [24]So Ahaz gathered the articles of the house of God, cut in pieces the articles of the house of God, shut up the doors of the house of the LORD, and made for himself altars in every corner of Jerusalem. [25]And in every single city of Judah he made high places to burn incense to other gods, and provoked to anger the LORD God of his fathers.

[26]Now the rest of his acts and all his ways, from first to last, indeed they *are* written in the book of the kings of Judah and Israel. [27]So Ahaz rested with his fathers, and they buried him in the city, in Jerusalem; but they did not bring him into the tombs of the kings of Israel. Then Hezekiah his son reigned in his place.

28:16 [a]Septuagint, Syriac, and Vulgate read *king* (compare verse 20).   **28:20** [a]Hebrew *Tilgath-Pilneser*

Hezekiah Reigns in Judah

29 Hezekiah became king *when he was* twenty-five years old, and he reigned twenty-nine years in Jerusalem. His mother's name *was* Abijah[a] the daughter of Zechariah. [2]And he did *what was* right in the sight of the LORD, according to all that his father David had done.

Hezekiah Cleanses the Temple

[3]In the first year of his reign, in the first month, he opened the doors of the house of the LORD and repaired them. [4]Then he brought in the priests and the Levites, and gathered them in the East Square, [5]and said to them: "Hear me, Levites! Now sanctify yourselves, sanctify the house of the LORD God of your fathers, and carry out the rubbish from the holy *place*. [6]For our fathers have trespassed and done evil in the eyes of the LORD our God; they have forsaken Him, have turned their faces away from the dwelling place of the LORD, and turned *their* backs *on Him*. [7]They have also shut up the doors of the vestibule, put out the lamps, and have not burned incense or offered burnt offerings in the holy *place* to the God of Israel. [8]Therefore the wrath of the LORD fell upon Judah and Jerusalem, and He has given them up to trouble, to desolation, and to jeering, as you see with your eyes. [9]For indeed, because of this our fathers have fallen by the sword; and our sons, our daughters, and our wives *are* in captivity.

[10]"Now *it is* in my heart to make a covenant with the LORD God of Israel, that His fierce wrath may turn away from us. [11]My sons, do not be negligent now, for the LORD has chosen you to stand before Him, to serve Him, and that you should minister to Him and burn incense."

[12]Then these Levites arose: Mahath the son of Amasai and Joel the son of Azariah, of the sons of the Kohathites; of the sons of Merari, Kish the son of Abdi and Azariah the son of Jehallelel; of the Gershonites, Joah the son of Zimmah and Eden the son of Joah; [13]of the sons of Elizaphan, Shimri and Jeiel; of the sons of Asaph, Zechariah and Mattaniah; [14]of the sons of Heman, Jehiel and Shimei; and of the sons of Jeduthun, Shemaiah and Uzziel.

[15]And they gathered their brethren, sanctified themselves, and went according to the commandment of the king, at the words of the LORD, to cleanse the house of the LORD. [16]Then the priests went into the inner part of the house of the LORD to cleanse *it*, and brought out all the debris that they found in the temple of the LORD to the court of the house of the LORD. And the Levites took *it* out and carried *it* to the Brook Kidron. [17]Now they began to sanctify on the first *day* of the first month, and on the eighth day of the month they came to the vestibule of the LORD. So they sanctified the house of the LORD in eight days, and on the sixteenth day of the first month they finished. [18]Then they went in to King Hezekiah and said, "We have cleansed all the house of the LORD, the altar of burnt offerings with all its articles, and the table of the showbread with all its articles. [19]Moreover all the articles which King Ahaz in his reign had cast aside in his transgression we have prepared and sanctified; and there they *are*, before the altar of the LORD."

Hezekiah Restores Temple Worship

[20]Then King Hezekiah rose early, gathered the rulers of the city, and went up to the house of the LORD. [21]And they brought seven bulls, seven rams, seven lambs, and seven male goats for a sin offering for the kingdom, for the sanctuary, and for Judah. Then he commanded the priests, the sons of Aaron, to offer *them* on the altar of the LORD. [22]So they killed the bulls, and the priests received the blood and sprinkled *it* on the altar. Likewise they killed the rams and sprinkled the blood on the altar. They also killed the lambs and sprinkled the blood on the altar. [23]Then they brought out the male goats *for* the sin offering before the king and the assembly, and they laid their hands on them. [24]And the priests killed them; and they presented their blood on the altar as a sin offering to make an atonement for all Israel, for the king commanded *that* the burnt offering and the sin offering *be made* for all Israel. [25]And he stationed the Levites in the house of the LORD with cymbals, with stringed

29:1 [a]Spelled *Abi* in 2 Kings 18:2

instruments, and with harps, according to the commandment of David, of Gad the king's seer, and of Nathan the prophet; for thus *was* the commandment of the LORD by His prophets. 26The Levites stood with the instruments of David, and the priests with the trumpets. 27Then Hezekiah commanded *them* to offer the burnt offering on the altar. And when the burnt offering began, the song of the LORD *also* began, with the trumpets and with the instruments of David king of Israel. 28So all the assembly worshiped, the singers sang, and the trumpeters sounded; all *this continued* until the burnt offering was finished. 29And when they had finished offering, the king and all who were present with him bowed and worshiped. 30Moreover King Hezekiah and the leaders commanded the Levites to sing praise to the LORD with the words of David and of Asaph the seer. So they sang praises with gladness, and they bowed their heads and worshiped.

31Then Hezekiah answered and said, "Now *that* you have consecrated yourselves to the LORD, come near, and bring sacrifices and thank offerings into the house of the LORD." So the assembly brought in sacrifices and thank offerings, and as many as were of a willing heart *brought* burnt offerings. 32And the number of the burnt offerings which the assembly brought was seventy bulls, one hundred rams, *and* two hundred lambs; all these *were* for a burnt offering to the LORD. 33The consecrated things *were* six hundred bulls and three thousand sheep. 34But the priests were too few, so that they could not skin all the burnt offerings; therefore their brethren the Levites helped them until the work was ended and until the *other* priests had sanctified themselves, for the Levites were more diligent in sanctifying themselves than the priests. 35Also the burnt offerings *were* in abundance, with the fat of the peace offerings and *with* the drink offerings for *every* burnt offering.

So the service of the house of the LORD was set in order. 36Then Hezekiah and all the people rejoiced that God had prepared the people, since the events took place so suddenly.

Hezekiah Keeps the Passover

30 And Hezekiah sent to all Israel and Judah, and also wrote letters to Ephraim and Manasseh, that they should come to the house of the LORD at Jerusalem, to keep the Passover to the LORD God of Israel. 2For the king and his leaders and all the assembly in Jerusalem had agreed to keep the Passover in the second month. 3For they could not keep it at the regular time,a because a sufficient number of priests had not consecrated themselves, nor had the people gathered together at Jerusalem. 4And the matter pleased the king and all the assembly. 5So they resolved to make a proclamation throughout all Israel, from Beersheba to Dan, that they should come to keep the Passover to the LORD God of Israel at Jerusalem, since they had not done *it* for a long *time* in the *prescribed* manner.

6Then the runners went throughout all Israel and Judah with the letters from the king and his leaders, and spoke according to the command of the king: "Children of Israel, return to the LORD God of Abraham, Isaac, and Israel; then He will return to the remnant of you who have escaped from the hand of the kings of Assyria. 7And do not be like your fathers and your brethren, who trespassed against the LORD God of their fathers, so that He gave them up to desolation, as you see. 8Now do not be stiff-necked, as your fathers *were, but* yield yourselves to the LORD; and enter His sanctuary, which He has sanctified forever, and serve the LORD your God, that the fierceness of His wrath may turn away from you. 9For if you return to the LORD, your brethren and your children *will be treated* with compassion by those who lead them captive, so that they may come back to this land; for the LORD your God *is* gracious and merciful, and will not turn *His* face from you if you return to Him."

10So the runners passed from city to city through the country of Ephraim and Manasseh, as far as Zebulun; but they laughed at them and mocked them. 11Nevertheless

---

30:3 aThat is, the first month (compare Leviticus 23:5); literally *at that time*

some from Asher, Manasseh, and Zebulun humbled themselves and came to Jerusalem. [12]Also the hand of God was on Judah to give them singleness of heart to obey the command of the king and the leaders, at the word of the LORD.

[13]Now many people, a very great assembly, gathered at Jerusalem to keep the Feast of Unleavened Bread in the second month. [14]They arose and took away the altars that were in Jerusalem, and they took away all the incense altars and cast them into the Brook Kidron. [15]Then they slaughtered the Passover lambs on the fourteenth day of the second month. The priests and the Levites were ashamed, and sanctified themselves, and brought the burnt offerings to the house of the LORD. [16]They stood in their place according to their custom, according to the Law of Moses the man of God; the priests sprinkled the blood received from the hand of the Levites. [17]For there were many in the assembly who had not sanctified themselves; therefore the Levites had charge of the slaughter of the Passover lambs for everyone who was not clean, to sanctify them to the LORD. [18]For a multitude of the people, many from Ephraim, Manasseh, Issachar, and Zebulun, had not cleansed themselves, yet they ate the Passover contrary to what was written. But Hezekiah prayed for them, saying, "May the good LORD provide atonement for everyone [19]who prepares his heart to seek God, the LORD God of his fathers, though he is not cleansed according to the purification of the sanctuary." [20]And the LORD listened to Hezekiah and healed the people.

[21]So the children of Israel who were present at Jerusalem kept the Feast of Unleavened Bread seven days with great gladness; and the Levites and the priests praised the LORD day by day, singing to the LORD, accompanied by loud instruments. [22]And Hezekiah gave encouragement to all the Levites who taught the good knowledge of the LORD; and they ate throughout the feast seven days, offering peace offerings

PRAYER

. . . and their prayer came up to His holy dwelling place, to heaven.

2 CHRONICLES 30:27

Warren Earl Burger

GOVERNMENT PAID LEGISLATIVE CHAPLAINS

Warren Earl Burger was Chief Justice of the U.S. Supreme Court from 1969 to 1986. He delivered the court's opinion in the 1982 case of *Marsh v. Chambers*, regarding chaplains opening legislative sessions with prayer:

> The men who wrote the First Amendment religion clause did not view paid legislative chaplains and opening prayers as a violation of that amendment . . . the practice of opening sessions with prayer has continued without interruption ever since that early session of Congress.
>
> It can hardly be thought that in the same week the members of the first Congress voted to appoint and pay a chaplain for each House and also voted to approve the draft of the First Amendment . . . (that) they intended to forbid what they had just declared acceptable.
>
> [Prayer and chaplains] are deeply embedded in the history and tradition of this country.
>
> The legislature by majority vote invites a clergyman to give a prayer, neither the inviting nor the giving nor the hearing of the prayer is making a law. On this basis alone . . . the sayings of prayers, per se, in the legislative halls at the opening session in not prohibited by the First and Fourteenth Amendments.

and making confession to the Lord God of their fathers.

²³Then the whole assembly agreed to keep *the feast* another seven days, and they kept it *another* seven days with gladness. ²⁴For Hezekiah king of Judah gave to the assembly a thousand bulls and seven thousand sheep, and the leaders gave to the assembly a thousand bulls and ten thousand sheep; and a great number of priests sanctified themselves. ²⁵The whole assembly of Judah rejoiced, also the priests and Levites, all the assembly that came from Israel, the sojourners who came from the land of Israel, and those who dwelt in Judah. ²⁶So there was great joy in Jerusalem, for since the time of Solomon the son of David, king of Israel, *there had* been nothing like this in Jerusalem. ²⁷Then the priests, the Levites, arose and blessed the people, and their voice was heard; and their prayer came *up* to His holy dwelling place, to heaven.

The Reforms of Hezekiah

31 Now when all this was finished, all Israel who were present went out to the cities of Judah and broke the *sacred* pillars in pieces, cut down the wooden images, and threw down the high places and the altars—from all Judah, Benjamin, Ephraim, and Manasseh—until they had utterly destroyed them all. Then all the children of Israel returned to their own cities, every man to his possession.

²And Hezekiah appointed the divisions of the priests and the Levites according to their divisions, each man according to his service, the priests and Levites for burnt offerings and peace offerings, to serve, to give thanks, and to praise in the gates of the campᵃ of the Lord. ³The king also *appointed* a portion of his possessions for the burnt offerings: for the morning and evening burnt offerings, the burnt offerings for the Sabbaths and the New Moons and the set feasts, as *it is* written in the Law of the Lord. ⁴Moreover he commanded the people who dwelt in Jerusalem to contribute support for the priests and the Levites, that they might devote themselves to the Law of the Lord.

⁵As soon as the commandment was circulated, the children of Israel brought in abundance the firstfruits of grain and wine, oil and honey, and of all the produce of the field; and they brought in abundantly the tithe of everything. ⁶And the children of Israel and Judah, who dwelt in the cities of Judah, brought the tithe of oxen and sheep; also the tithe of holy things which were consecrated to the Lord their God they laid in heaps.

⁷In the third month they began laying them in heaps, and they finished in the seventh month. ⁸And when Hezekiah and the leaders came and saw the heaps, they blessed the Lord and His people Israel. ⁹Then Hezekiah questioned the priests and the Levites concerning the heaps. ¹⁰And Azariah the chief priest, from the house of Zadok, answered him and said, "Since *the people* began to bring the offerings into the house of the Lord, we have had enough to eat and have plenty left, for the Lord has blessed His people; and what is left *is* this great abundance."

¹¹Now Hezekiah commanded *them* to prepare rooms in the house of the Lord, and they prepared them. ¹²Then they faithfully brought in the offerings, the tithes, and the dedicated things; Cononiah the Levite had charge of them, and Shimei his brother *was* the next. ¹³Jehiel, Azaziah, Nahath, Asahel, Jerimoth, Jozabad, Eliel, Ismachiah, Mahath, and Benaiah *were* overseers under the hand of Cononiah and Shimei his brother, at the commandment of Hezekiah the king and Azariah the ruler of the house of God. ¹⁴Kore the son of Imnah the Levite, the keeper of the East Gate, *was* over the freewill offerings to God, to distribute the offerings of the Lord and the most holy things. ¹⁵And under him *were* Eden, Miniamin, Jeshua, Shemaiah, Amariah, and Shecaniah, *his* faithful assistants in the cities of the priests, to distribute allotments to their brethren by divisions, to the great as well as the small.

¹⁶Besides those males from three years old and up who were written in the genealogy, they distributed to everyone who entered

31:2 ᵃThat is, the temple

the house of the LORD his daily portion for the work of his service, by his division, [17]and to the priests who were written in the genealogy according to their father's house, and to the Levites from twenty years old and up according to their work, by their divisions, [18]and to all who were written in the genealogy—their little ones and their wives, their sons and daughters, the whole company of them—for in their faithfulness they sanctified themselves in holiness.

[19]Also for the sons of Aaron the priests, *who were* in the fields of the common-lands of their cities, in every single city, *there were* men who were designated by name to distribute portions to all the males among the priests and to all who were listed by genealogies among the Levites.

[20]Thus Hezekiah did throughout all Judah, and he did what *was* good and right and true before the LORD his God. [21]And in every work that he began in the service of the house of God, in the law and in the commandment, to seek his God, he did *it* with all his heart. So he prospered.

Sennacherib Boasts Against the LORD

32 After these deeds of faithfulness, Sennacherib king of Assyria came and entered Judah; he encamped against the fortified cities, thinking to win them over to himself. [2]And when Hezekiah saw that Sennacherib had come, and that his purpose was to make war against Jerusalem, [3]he consulted with his leaders and commanders[a] to stop the water from the springs which *were* outside the city; and they helped him. [4]Thus many people gathered together who stopped all the springs and the brook that ran through the land, saying, "Why should the kings[a] of Assyria come and find much water?" [5]And he strengthened himself, built up all the wall that was broken, raised *it* up to the towers, and *built* another wall outside; also he repaired the Millo[a] *in* the City of David, and made weapons and shields in abundance. [6]Then he set military captains over the people, gathered them together to him in the open square of the city gate, and gave them encouragement, saying, [7]"Be strong and courageous; do not be afraid nor dismayed before the king of Assyria, nor before all the multitude that *is* with him; for *there are* more with us than with him. [8]With him *is* an arm of flesh; but with us *is* the LORD our God, to help us and to fight our battles." And the people were strengthened by the words of Hezekiah king of Judah.

[9]After this Sennacherib king of Assyria sent his servants to Jerusalem (but he and all the forces with him *laid siege* against Lachish), to Hezekiah king of Judah, and to all Judah who *were* in Jerusalem, saying, [10]"Thus says Sennacherib king of Assyria: 'In what do you trust, that you remain under siege in Jerusalem? [11]Does not Hezekiah persuade you to give yourselves over to die by famine and by thirst, saying, "The LORD our God will deliver us from the hand of the king of Assyria"? [12]Has not the same Hezekiah taken away His high places and His altars, and commanded Judah and Jerusalem, saying, "You shall worship before one altar and burn incense on it"? [13]Do you not know what I and my fathers have done to all the peoples of *other* lands? Were the gods of the nations of those lands in any way able to deliver their lands out of my hand? [14]Who *was there* among all the gods of those nations that my fathers utterly destroyed that could deliver his people from my hand, that your God should be able to deliver you from my hand? [15]Now therefore, do not let Hezekiah deceive you or persuade you like this, and do not believe him; for no god of any nation or kingdom was able to deliver his people from my hand or the hand of my fathers. How much less will your God deliver you from my hand?'"

[16]Furthermore, his servants spoke against the LORD God and against His servant Hezekiah.

[17]He also wrote letters to revile the LORD God of Israel, and to speak against Him, saying, "As the gods of the nations of *other* lands have not delivered their people from my hand, so the God of Hezekiah will not deliver His people from my hand." [18]Then they called out with a loud voice in Hebrew[a]

32:3 [a]Literally *mighty men*   **32:4** [a]Following Masoretic Text and Vulgate; Arabic, Septuagint, and Syriac read *king*.   **32:5** [a]Literally *The Landfill*
32:18 [a]Literally *Judean*

to the people of Jerusalem who *were* on the wall, to frighten them and trouble them, that they might take the city. [19]And they spoke against the God of Jerusalem, as against the gods of the people of the earth—the work of men's hands.

Sennacherib's Defeat and Death

[20]Now because of this King Hezekiah and the prophet Isaiah, the son of Amoz, prayed and cried out to heaven. [21]Then the LORD sent an angel who cut down every mighty man of valor, leader, and captain in the camp of the king of Assyria. So he returned shamefaced to his own land. And when he had gone into the temple of his god, some of his own offspring struck him down with the sword there. [22]Thus the LORD saved Hezekiah and the inhabitants of Jerusalem from the hand of Sennacherib the king of Assyria, and from the hand of all *others,* and guided them[a] on every side. [23]And many brought gifts to the LORD at Jerusalem, and presents to Hezekiah king of Judah, so that he was exalted in the sight of all nations thereafter.

Hezekiah Humbles Himself

[24]In those days Hezekiah was sick and near death, and he prayed to the LORD; and He spoke to him and gave him a sign. [25]But Hezekiah did not repay according to the favor *shown* him, for his heart was lifted up; therefore wrath was looming over him and over Judah and Jerusalem. [26]Then Hezekiah humbled himself for the pride of his heart, he and the inhabitants of Jerusalem, so that the wrath of the LORD did not come upon them in the days of Hezekiah.

Hezekiah's Wealth and Honor

[27]Hezekiah had very great riches and honor. And he made himself treasuries for silver, for gold, for precious stones, for spices, for shields, and for all kinds of desirable items; [28]storehouses for the harvest of grain, wine, and oil; and stalls for all kinds of livestock, and folds for flocks.[a] [29]Moreover he provided cities for himself, and possessions of flocks and herds in abundance; for God had given him very much property. [30]This same Hezekiah also stopped the water outlet of Upper Gihon, and brought the water by tunnel[a] to the west side of the City of David. Hezekiah prospered in all his works.

[31]However, *regarding* the ambassadors of the princes of Babylon, whom they sent to him to inquire about the wonder that was *done* in the land, God withdrew from him, in order to test him, that He might know all *that was* in his heart.

Death of Hezekiah

[32]Now the rest of the acts of Hezekiah, and his goodness, indeed they *are* written in the vision of Isaiah the prophet, the son of Amoz, *and* in the book of the kings of Judah and Israel. [33]So Hezekiah rested with his fathers, and they buried him in the upper tombs of the sons of David; and all Judah and the inhabitants of Jerusalem honored him at his death. Then Manasseh his son reigned in his place.

Manasseh Reigns in Judah

33 Manasseh *was* twelve years old when he became king, and he reigned fifty-five years in Jerusalem. [2]But he did evil in the sight of the LORD, according to the abominations of the nations whom the LORD had cast out before the children of Israel. [3]For he rebuilt the high places which Hezekiah his father had broken down; he raised up altars for the Baals, and made wooden images; and he worshiped all the host of heaven[a] and served them. [4]He also built altars in the house of the LORD, of which the LORD had said, "In Jerusalem shall My name be forever." [5]And he built altars for all the host of heaven in the two courts of the house of the LORD. [6]Also he caused his sons to pass through the fire in the Valley of the Son of Hinnom; he practiced soothsaying, used witchcraft and sorcery, and consulted mediums and spiritists. He did much evil in the sight of the LORD, to provoke Him to anger. [7]He even set a carved image, the idol which

---

32:22 [a]Septuagint reads *gave them rest;* Vulgate reads *gave them treasures.*   **32:28** [a]Following Septuagint and Vulgate; Arabic and Syriac omit *folds for flocks;* Masoretic Text reads *flocks for sheepfolds.*
32:30 [a]Literally *brought it straight* (compare 2 Kings 20:20)   **33:3** [a]The gods of the Assyrians

he had made, in the house of God, of which God had said to David and to Solomon his son, "In this house and in Jerusalem, which I have chosen out of all the tribes of Israel, I will put My name forever; ⁸and I will not again remove the foot of Israel from the land which I have appointed for your fathers—only if they are careful to do all that I have commanded them, according to the whole law and the statutes and the ordinances by the hand of Moses." ⁹So Manasseh seduced Judah and the inhabitants of Jerusalem to do more evil than the nations whom the Lord had destroyed before the children of Israel.

Manasseh Restored After Repentance

¹⁰And the Lord spoke to Manasseh and his people, but they would not listen. ¹¹Therefore the Lord brought upon them the captains of the army of the king of Assyria, who took Manasseh with hooks,ᵃ bound him with bronze *fetters,* and carried him off to Babylon. ¹²Now when he was in affliction, he implored the Lord his God, and humbled himself greatly before the God of his fathers, ¹³and prayed to Him; and He received his entreaty, heard his supplication, and brought him back to Jerusalem into his kingdom. Then Manasseh knew that the Lord *was* God.

¹⁴After this he built a wall outside the City of David on the west side of Gihon, in the valley, as far as the entrance of the Fish Gate; and *it* enclosed Ophel, and he raised it to a very great height. Then he put military captains in all the fortified cities of Judah. ¹⁵He took away the foreign gods and the idol from the house of the Lord, and all the altars that he had built in the mount of the house of the Lord and in Jerusalem; and he cast *them* out of the city. ¹⁶He also repaired the altar of the Lord, sacrificed peace offerings and thank offerings on it, and commanded Judah to serve the Lord God of Israel. ¹⁷Nevertheless the people still sacrificed on the high places, *but* only to the Lord their God.

Death of Manasseh

¹⁸Now the rest of the acts of Manasseh, his prayer to his God, and the words of the seers who spoke to him in the name of the Lord God of Israel, indeed they *are written* in the bookᵃ of the kings of Israel. ¹⁹Also his prayer and *how God* received his entreaty, and all his sin and trespass, and the sites where he built high places and set up wooden images and carved images, before he was humbled, indeed they *are* written among the sayings of Hozai.ᵃ ²⁰So Manasseh rested with his fathers, and they buried him in his own house. Then his son Amon reigned in his place.

Amon's Reign and Death

²¹Amon *was* twenty-two years old when he became king, and he reigned two years in Jerusalem. ²²But he did evil in the sight of the Lord, as his father Manasseh had done; for Amon sacrificed to all the carved images which his father Manasseh had made, and served them. ²³And he did not humble himself before the Lord, as his father Manasseh had humbled himself; but Amon trespassed more and more.

²⁴Then his servants conspired against him, and killed him in his own house. ²⁵But the people of the land executed all those who had conspired against King Amon. Then the people of the land made his son Josiah king in his place.

Josiah Reigns in Judah

34 Josiah *was* eight years old when he became king, and he reigned thirty-one years in Jerusalem. ²And he did *what was* right in the sight of the Lord, and walked in the ways of his father David; *he* did *not* turn aside to the right hand or to the left.

³For in the eighth year of his reign, while he was still young, he began to seek the God of his father David; and in the twelfth year he began to purge Judah and Jerusalem of the high places, the wooden images, the carved images, and the molded images. ⁴They broke down the altars of the Baals in his presence, and the incense altars which *were* above them he cut down; and the

---

33:11 ᵃThat is, nose hooks (compare 2 Kings 19:28)
33:18 ᵃLiterally *words*   **33:19** ᵃSeptuagint reads *the seers.*

wooden images, the carved images, and the molded images he broke in pieces, and made dust of them and scattered *it* on the graves of those who had sacrificed to them. [5]He also burned the bones of the priests on their altars, and cleansed Judah and Jerusalem. [6]And *so he did* in the cities of Manasseh, Ephraim, and Simeon, as far as Naphtali and all around, with axes.[a] [7]When he had broken down the altars and the wooden images, had beaten the carved images into powder, and cut down all the incense altars throughout all the land of Israel, he returned to Jerusalem.

Hilkiah Finds the Book of the Law

[8]In the eighteenth year of his reign, when he had purged the land and the temple,[a] he sent Shaphan the son of Azaliah, Maaseiah the governor of the city, and Joah the son of Joahaz the recorder, to repair the house of the LORD his God. [9]When they came to Hilkiah the high priest, they delivered the money that was brought into the house of God, which the Levites who kept the doors had gathered from the hand of Manasseh and Ephraim, from all the remnant of Israel, from all Judah and Benjamin, and *which* they had brought back to Jerusalem. [10]Then they put *it* in the hand of the foremen who had the oversight of the house of the LORD; and they gave it to the workmen who worked in the house of the LORD, to repair and restore the house. [11]They gave *it* to the craftsmen and builders to buy hewn stone and timber for beams, and to floor the houses which the kings of Judah had destroyed. [12]And the men did the work faithfully. Their overseers *were* Jahath and Obadiah the Levites, of the sons of Merari, and Zechariah and Meshullam, of the sons of the Kohathites, to supervise. *Others of* the Levites, all of whom were skillful with instruments of music, [13]*were* over the burden bearers and *were* overseers of all who did work in any kind of service. And *some* of the Levites *were* scribes, officers, and gatekeepers.

[14]Now when they brought out the money that was brought into the house of the LORD, Hilkiah the priest found the Book of the Law of the LORD *given* by Moses. [15]Then Hilkiah answered and said to Shaphan the scribe, "I have found the Book of the Law in the house of the LORD." And Hilkiah gave the book to Shaphan. [16]So Shaphan carried the book to the king, bringing the king word, saying, "All that was committed to your servants they are doing. [17]And they have gathered the money that was found in the house of the LORD, and have delivered it into the hand of the overseers and the workmen." [18]Then Shaphan the scribe told the king, saying, "Hilkiah the priest has given me a book." And Shaphan read it before the king.

[19]Thus it happened, when the king heard the words of the Law, that he tore his clothes. [20]Then the king commanded Hilkiah, Ahikam the son of Shaphan, Abdon[a] the son of Micah, Shaphan the scribe, and Asaiah a servant of the king, saying, [21]"Go, inquire of the LORD for me, and for those who are left in Israel and Judah, concerning the words of the book that is found; for great *is* the wrath of the LORD that is poured out on us, because our fathers have not kept the word of the LORD, to do according to all that is written in this book."

[22]So Hilkiah and those the king *had appointed* went to Huldah the prophetess, the wife of Shallum the son of Tokhath,[a] the son of Hasrah,[b] keeper of the wardrobe. (She dwelt in Jerusalem in the Second Quarter.) And they spoke to her to that *effect*.

[23]Then she answered them, "Thus says the LORD God of Israel, 'Tell the man who sent you to Me, [24]"Thus says the LORD: 'Behold, I will bring calamity on this place and on its inhabitants, all the curses that are written in the book which they have read before the king of Judah, [25]because they have forsaken Me and burned incense to other gods, that they might provoke Me to anger with all the works of their hands. Therefore My wrath will be poured out on this place, and not be quenched.' " ' [26]But as for the king of Judah, who sent you to inquire of the LORD, in this manner you shall speak to him, 'Thus says the LORD God of Israel: "*Concerning* the words which you have heard—

34:6 [a]Literally *swords*   **34:8** [a]Literally *house*
34:20 [a]*Achbor the son of Michaiah* in 2 Kings 22:12
34:22 [a]Spelled *Tikvah* in 2 Kings 22:14   [b]Spelled *Harhas* in 2 Kings 22:14

²⁷because your heart was tender, and you humbled yourself before God when you heard His words against this place and against its inhabitants, and you humbled yourself before Me, and you tore your clothes and wept before Me, I also have heard *you*," says the LORD. ²⁸"Surely I will gather you to your fathers, and you shall be gathered to your grave in peace; and your eyes shall not see all the calamity which I will bring on this place and its inhabitants."'" So they brought back word to the king.

Josiah Restores True Worship

²⁹Then the king sent and gathered all the elders of Judah and Jerusalem. ³⁰The king went up to the house of the LORD, with all the men of Judah and the inhabitants of Jerusalem—the priests and the Levites, and all the people, great and small. And he read in their hearing all the words of the Book of the Covenant which had been found in the house of the LORD. ³¹Then the king stood in his place and made a covenant before the LORD, to follow the LORD, and to keep His commandments and His testimonies and His statutes with all his heart and all his soul, to perform the words of the covenant that were written in this book. ³²And he made all who were present in Jerusalem and Benjamin take a stand. So the inhabitants of Jerusalem did according to the covenant of God, the God of their fathers. ³³Thus Josiah removed all the abominations from all the country that *belonged* to the children of Israel, and made all who were present in Israel diligently serve the LORD their God. All his days they did not depart from following the LORD God of their fathers.

Josiah Keeps the Passover

35 Now Josiah kept a Passover to the LORD in Jerusalem, and they slaughtered the Passover *lambs* on the fourteenth *day* of the first month. ²And he set the priests in their duties and encouraged them for the service of the house of the LORD. ³Then he said to the Levites who taught all Israel, who were holy to the LORD: "Put the holy ark in the house which Solomon the son of David, king of Israel, built. *It shall* no longer *be* a burden on *your* shoulders. Now serve the LORD your God and His people Israel. ⁴Prepare *yourselves* according to your fathers' houses, according to your divisions, following the written instruction of David king of Israel and the written instruction of Solomon his son. ⁵And stand in the holy *place* according to the divisions of the fathers' houses of your brethren the *lay* people, and *according to* the division of the father's house of the Levites. ⁶So slaughter the Passover *offerings,* consecrate yourselves, and prepare *them* for your brethren, that *they* may do according to the word of the LORD by the hand of Moses."

⁷Then Josiah gave the *lay* people lambs and young goats from the flock, all for Passover *offerings* for all who were present, to the number of thirty thousand, as well as three thousand cattle; these *were* from the king's possessions. ⁸And his leaders gave willingly to the people, to the priests, and to the Levites. Hilkiah, Zechariah, and Jehiel, rulers of the house of God, gave to the priests for the Passover *offerings* two thousand six hundred *from the flock,* and three hundred cattle. ⁹Also Conaniah, his brothers Shemaiah and Nethanel, and Hashabiah and Jeiel and Jozabad, chief of the Levites, gave to the Levites for Passover *offerings* five thousand *from the flock* and five hundred cattle.

¹⁰So the service was prepared, and the priests stood in their places, and the Levites in their divisions, according to the king's command. ¹¹And they slaughtered the Passover *offerings;* and the priests sprinkled *the blood* with their hands, while the Levites skinned *the animals.* ¹²Then they removed the burnt offerings that *they* might give them to the divisions of the fathers' houses of the *lay* people, to offer to the LORD, as *it is* written in the Book of Moses. And so *they did* with the cattle. ¹³Also they roasted the Passover *offerings* with fire according to the ordinance; but the *other* holy *offerings* they boiled in pots, in caldrons, and in pans, and divided *them* quickly among all the *lay* people. ¹⁴Then afterward they prepared portions for themselves and for the priests, because the priests, the sons of Aaron, *were busy* in offering burnt offerings and fat until night; therefore the Levites prepared portions for themselves and for the priests,

the sons of Aaron. [15]And the singers, the sons of Asaph, *were* in their places, according to the command of David, Asaph, Heman, and Jeduthun the king's seer. Also the gatekeepers were at each gate; they did not have to leave their position, because their brethren the Levites prepared portions for them.

[16]So all the service of the LORD was prepared the same day, to keep the Passover and to offer burnt offerings on the altar of the LORD, according to the command of King Josiah. [17]And the children of Israel who were present kept the Passover at that time, and the Feast of Unleavened Bread for seven days. [18]There had been no Passover kept in Israel like that since the days of Samuel the prophet; and none of the kings of Israel had kept such a Passover as Josiah kept, with the priests and the Levites, all Judah and Israel who were present, and the inhabitants of Jerusalem. [19]In the eighteenth year of the reign of Josiah this Passover was kept.

Josiah Dies in Battle

[20]After all this, when Josiah had prepared the temple, Necho king of Egypt came up to fight against Carchemish by the Euphrates; and Josiah went out against him. [21]But he sent messengers to him, saying, "What have I to do with you, king of Judah? *I have* not *come* against you this day, but against the house with which I have war; for God commanded me to make haste. Refrain *from meddling with* God, who *is* with me, lest He destroy you." [22]Nevertheless Josiah would not turn his face from him, but disguised himself so that he might fight with him, and did not heed the words of Necho from the mouth of God. So he came to fight in the Valley of Megiddo.

[23]And the archers shot King Josiah; and the king said to his servants, "Take me away, for I am severely wounded." [24]His servants therefore took him out of that chariot and put him in the second chariot that he had, and they brought him to Jerusalem. So he died, and was buried in *one of* the tombs of his fathers. And all Judah and Jerusalem mourned for Josiah.

[25]Jeremiah also lamented for Josiah. And to this day all the singing men and the singing women speak of Josiah in their lamentations. They made it a custom in Israel; and indeed they *are* written in the Laments.

[26]Now the rest of the acts of Josiah and his goodness, according to *what was* written in the Law of the LORD, [27]and his deeds from first to last, indeed they *are* written in the book of the kings of Israel and Judah.

The Reign and Captivity of Jehoahaz

36 Then the people of the land took Jehoahaz the son of Josiah, and made him king in his father's place in Jerusalem. [2]Jehoahaz[a] *was* twenty-three years old when he became king, and he reigned three months in Jerusalem. [3]Now the king of Egypt deposed him at Jerusalem; and he imposed on the land a tribute of one hundred talents of silver and a talent of gold. [4]Then the king of Egypt made *Jehoahaz's*[a] brother Eliakim king over Judah and Jerusalem, and changed his name to Jehoiakim. And Necho took Jehoahaz[b] his brother and carried him off to Egypt.

The Reign and Captivity of Jehoiakim

[5]Jehoiakim *was* twenty-five years old when he became king, and he reigned eleven years in Jerusalem. And he did evil in the sight of the LORD his God. [6]Nebuchadnezzar king of Babylon came up against him, and bound him in bronze *fetters* to carry him off to Babylon. [7]Nebuchadnezzar also carried off *some* of the articles from the house of the LORD to Babylon, and put them in his temple at Babylon. [8]Now the rest of the acts of Jehoiakim, the abominations which he did, and what was found against him, indeed they *are* written in the book of the kings of Israel and Judah. Then Jehoiachin his son reigned in his place.

The Reign and Captivity of Jehoiachin

[9]Jehoiachin *was* eight[a] years old when he became king, and he reigned in Jerusalem three months and ten days. And he did evil in the sight of the LORD. [10]At the turn of the

---

36:2 [a]Masoretic Text reads *Joahaz*. **36:4** [a]Literally *his* [b]Masoretic Text reads *Joahaz*. **36:9** [a]Some Hebrew manuscripts, Septuagint, Syriac, and 2 Kings 24:8 read *eighteen*.

GOD'S PLACE IN AMERICA'S BIRTHRIGHT

ROBERT BYRD

Democratic Senator Robert Byrd, the longest-serving member in the history of the U.S. Senate, delivered a message on June 27, 1962, just two days after the Supreme Court declared prayer in schools unconstitutional, warning Congress about disastrous decisions such as this one:

> Inasmuch as our greatest leaders have shown no doubt about God's proper place in the American birthright, can we, in our day, dare do less? . . . In no other place in the United States are there so many, and such varied official evidences of deep and abiding faith in God on the part of government as there are in Washington. . . .

> Every session of the House and the Senate begins with prayer. Each house has its own chaplain.

> The Eighty-third Congress set aside a small room in the Capitol, just off the rotunda, for the private prayer and meditation of members of Congress. . . . The room's focal point is a stained glass window showing George Washington kneeling in prayer. Behind him is etched these words from Psalm 16:1: "Preserve me, O God, for in Thee do I put my trust."

> Inside the rotunda is a picture of the Pilgrims. . . . Very clear are the words, "The New Testament according to our Lord and Savior, Jesus Christ." On the sail is the motto of the Pilgrims, "In God We Trust, God With Us."

> The phrase, "In God We Trust," appears opposite the president of the Senate, who is the vice-president of the United States. The same phrase, in large words inscribed in the marble, backdrops the Speaker of the House of Representatives.

> Above the head of the Chief Justice of the Supreme Court are the Ten Commandments, with the great American eagle protecting them. Moses is included among the great lawgivers in Herman A. MacNeil's marble sculpture group on the east front. The crier who opens each session closes with the words, "God save the United States and this Honorable Court." . . .

> On the south banks of Washington's Tidal Basin, Thomas Jefferson still speaks:

> "God who gave us life gave us liberty. Can the liberties of a nation be secure when we have removed a conviction that these liberties are the gift of God? Indeed I tremble for my country when I reflect that God is just, that his justice cannot sleep forever."

> [Jefferson's words are] a forceful and explicit warning that to remove God from this country will destroy it.

year King Nebuchadnezzar summoned *him* and took him to Babylon, with the costly articles from the house of the Lord, and made Zedekiah, *Jehoiakim's*ᵃ brother, king over Judah and Jerusalem.

Zedekiah Reigns in Judah

¹¹Zedekiah *was* twenty-one years old when he became king, and he reigned eleven years in Jerusalem. ¹²He did evil in the sight of the Lord his God, *and* did not humble himself before Jeremiah the prophet, *who spoke* from the mouth of the Lord. ¹³And he also rebelled against King Nebuchadnezzar, who had made him swear *an oath* by God; but he stiffened his neck and hardened his heart against turning to the Lord God of Israel. ¹⁴Moreover all the leaders of the priests and the people transgressed more and more, *according* to all the abominations of the nations, and defiled the house of the Lord which He had consecrated in Jerusalem.

The Fall of Jerusalem

¹⁵And the Lord God of their fathers sent *warnings* to them by His messengers, rising up early and sending *them,* because He had compassion on His people and on His dwelling place. ¹⁶But they mocked the messengers of God, despised His words, and scoffed at His prophets, until the wrath of the Lord arose against His people, till *there was* no remedy. ¹⁷Therefore He brought against them the king of the Chaldeans, who killed their young men with the sword in the house of their sanctuary, and had no compassion on young man or virgin, on the aged or the weak; He gave *them* all into his hand. ¹⁸And all the articles from the house of God, great and small, the treasures of the house of the Lord, and the treasures of the king and of his leaders, all *these* he took to Babylon. ¹⁹Then they burned the house of God, broke down the wall of Jerusalem, burned all its palaces with fire, and destroyed all its precious possessions. ²⁰And those who escaped from the sword he carried away to Babylon, where they became servants to him and his sons until the rule of the kingdom of Persia, ²¹to fulfill the word of the Lord by the mouth of Jeremiah, until the land had enjoyed her Sabbaths. As long as she lay desolate she kept Sabbath, to fulfill seventy years.

The Proclamation of Cyrus

²²Now in the first year of Cyrus king of Persia, that the word of the Lord by the mouth of Jeremiah might be fulfilled, the Lord stirred up the spirit of Cyrus king of Persia, so that he made a proclamation throughout all his kingdom, and also *put it* in writing, saying,

23	Thus says Cyrus king of Persia:
	All the kingdoms of the earth the Lord
	God of heaven has given me. And He
	has commanded me to build Him a
	house at Jerusalem which is in Judah.
	Who *is* among you of all His people?
	May the Lord his God *be* with him,
	and let him go up!

36:10 ᵃLiterally *his* (compare 2 Kings 24:17)

EZRA

Author: Probably Ezra

When Written: 538–457 B.C.

Theme: Restoration

Key Verses: Ezra 7:10—For Ezra had prepared his heart to seek the Law of the LORD, and to do it, and to teach statutes and ordinances in Israel.

Key Chapter: Ezra 6—This passage records the completion and dedication of the temple, which prompts the children of Israel to keep the Passover and separate themselves "from the filth of the nations of the land in order to seek the LORD God of Israel" (v. 21).

As God's people returned to Jerusalem after years of exile, Ezra, a humble priest and unassuming leader, was instrumental in reestablishing worship and righteousness among the children of Israel. The Book of Ezra demonstrates how ordinary people submitted to God can accomplish extraordinary things.

The history of America is filled with similar accounts of unassuming individuals who rose to greatness through humble dedication to God and righteousness. One such example is Harriet Tubman, who, perhaps more than any other American, was responsible for helping slaves escape bondage and reach their promised land of freedom. An escaped slave herself, Tubman recalled that during the years she was an instrumental figure in the Underground Railroad—which took hundreds of slaves to freedom—she would tell God: "I trust You. I don't know where to go or what to do, but I expect You to lead me."

What a perfect reflection of the spirit of humility through which God is pleased to work His will in the earth!

EZRA

End of the Babylonian Captivity

1 Now in the first year of Cyrus king of Persia, that the word of the Lord by the mouth of Jeremiah might be fulfilled, the Lord stirred up the spirit of Cyrus king of Persia, so that he made a proclamation throughout all his kingdom, and also *put it* in writing, saying,

2 Thus says Cyrus king of Persia:
All the kingdoms of the earth the Lord God of heaven has given me. And He has commanded me to build Him a house at Jerusalem which *is* in Judah. ³Who *is* among you of all His people? May his God be with him, and let him go up to Jerusalem which *is* in Judah, and build the house of the Lord God of Israel (He *is* God), which *is* in Jerusalem. ⁴And whoever is left in any place where he dwells, let the men of his place help him with silver and gold, with goods and livestock, besides the freewill offerings for the house of God which *is* in Jerusalem.

⁵Then the heads of the fathers' *houses* of Judah and Benjamin, and the priests and the Levites, with all whose spirits God had moved, arose to go up and build the house of the Lord which *is* in Jerusalem. ⁶And all those who *were* around them encouraged them with articles of silver and gold, with goods and livestock, and with precious things, besides all *that* was willingly offered. ⁷King Cyrus also brought out the articles of the house of the Lord, which Nebuchadnezzar had taken from Jerusalem and put in the temple of his gods; ⁸and Cyrus king of Persia brought them out by the hand of Mithredath the treasurer, and counted them out to Sheshbazzar the prince of Judah. ⁹This *is* the number of them: thirty gold platters, one thousand silver platters, twenty-nine knives, ¹⁰thirty gold basins, four hundred and ten silver basins of a similar *kind,* and one thousand other articles. ¹¹All the articles of gold and silver *were* five thousand four hundred. All *these* Sheshbazzar took with the captives who were brought from Babylon to Jerusalem.

The Captives Who Returned to Jerusalem

2 Now[a] these *are* the people of the province who came back from the captivity, of those who had been carried away, whom Nebuchadnezzar the king of Babylon had carried away to Babylon, and who returned to Jerusalem and Judah, everyone to his *own* city.

²*Those* who came with Zerubbabel *were* Jeshua, Nehemiah, Seraiah, Reelaiah, Mordecai, Bilshan, Mispar,[a] Bigvai, Rehum,[b] *and* Baanah. The number of the men of the people of Israel: ³the people of Parosh, two thousand one hundred and seventy-two; ⁴the people of Shephatiah, three hundred and seventy-two; ⁵the people of Arah, seven hundred and seventy-five; ⁶the people of Pahath-Moab, of the people of Jeshua *and* Joab, two thousand eight hundred and twelve; ⁷the people of Elam, one thousand two hundred and fifty-four; ⁸the people of Zattu, nine hundred and forty-five; ⁹the people of Zaccai, seven hundred and sixty; ¹⁰the people of Bani,[a] six hundred and forty-two; ¹¹the people of Bebai, six hundred and twenty-three; ¹²the people of Azgad, one thousand two hundred and twenty-two; ¹³the people of Adonikam, six hundred and sixty-six; ¹⁴the people of Bigvai, two thousand and fifty-six; ¹⁵the people of Adin, four hundred and fifty-four; ¹⁶the people of Ater of Hezekiah, ninety-eight; ¹⁷the people of Bezai, three hundred and twenty-three; ¹⁸the people of Jorah,[a] one hundred and twelve; ¹⁹the people of Hashum, two hundred and

---

2:1 [a]Compare this chapter with Nehemiah 7:6–73. **2:2** [a]Spelled *Mispereth* in Nehemiah 7:7 [b]Spelled *Nehum* in Nehemiah 7:7 **2:10** [a]Spelled *Binnui* in Nehemiah 7:15 **2:18** [a]Called *Hariph* in Nehemiah 7:24

The EMANCIPATION PROCLAMATION

BOOKER T. WASHINGTON

The Emancipation Proclamation consists of two executive orders issued by President Abraham Lincoln during the American Civil War. The first one, issued September 22, 1862, declared the freedom of all slaves in any state of the Confederate States of America that did not return to Union control by January 1, 1863. The second order, issued January 1, 1863, named the specific states where it applied.

The Emancipation Proclamation was widely attacked at the time because it did not free any slaves of the border states (Kentucky, Missouri, Maryland, Delaware, and West Virginia) or any southern state (or part of a state) already under Union control. But in practice, it committed the Union to ending slavery, and as the Union armies conquered the Confederacy, thousands of slaves were freed each day.

President Lincoln stated the Bible moved him to issue this, the most controversial document in his presidency, which was met with both hostility and jubilation in the North. He noted especially the words of Exodus 6:5: "I [God] have also heard the groaning of the children of Israel whom the Egyptians keep in bondage." After the proclamation was made, Lincoln noted that "stocks have declined, and troops come forward more slowly than ever," but he later remarked, "I never, in my life, felt more certain that I was doing right, than I do in signing this paper."

Booker T. Washington, as a slave boy of nine, remembered the day of freedom for his family:

> As the great day drew nearer, there was more singing in the slave quarters than usual. It was bolder, had more ring, and lasted later into the night. Most of the verses of the plantation songs had some reference to freedom. . . . Some man who seemed to be a stranger (a United States officer, I presume) made a little speech and then read a rather long paper—the Emancipation Proclamation, I think. After the reading, we were told that we were all free and could go when and where we pleased. My mother, who was standing by my side, leaned over and kissed her children, while tears of joy ran down her cheeks. She explained to us what it all meant, that this was the day for which she had been so long praying, but fearing that she would never live to see.

twenty-three; ²⁰the people of Gibbar,^a ninety-five; ²¹the people of Bethlehem, one hundred and twenty-three; ²²the men of Netophah, fifty-six; ²³the men of Anathoth, one hundred and twenty-eight; ²⁴the people of Azmaveth,^a forty-two; ²⁵the people of Kirjath Arim,^a Chephirah, and Beeroth, seven hundred and forty-three; ²⁶the people of Ramah and Geba, six hundred and twenty-one; ²⁷the men of Michmas, one hundred and twenty-two; ²⁸the men of Bethel and Ai, two hundred and twenty-three; ²⁹the people of Nebo, fifty-two; ³⁰the people of Magbish, one hundred and fifty-six; ³¹the people of the other Elam, one thousand two hundred and fifty-four; ³²the people of Harim, three hundred and twenty; ³³the people of Lod, Hadid, and Ono, seven hundred and twenty-five; ³⁴the people of Jericho, three hundred and forty-five; ³⁵the people of Senaah, three thousand six hundred and thirty.

³⁶The priests: the sons of Jedaiah, of the house of Jeshua, nine hundred and seventy-three; ³⁷the sons of Immer, one thousand and fifty-two; ³⁸the sons of Pashhur, one thousand two hundred and forty-seven; ³⁹the sons of Harim, one thousand and seventeen.

⁴⁰The Levites: the sons of Jeshua and Kadmiel, of the sons of Hodaviah,^a seventy-four.

⁴¹The singers: the sons of Asaph, one hundred and twenty-eight.

⁴²The sons of the gatekeepers: the sons of Shallum, the sons of Ater, the sons of Talmon, the sons of Akkub, the sons of Hatita, and the sons of Shobai, one hundred and thirty-nine *in* all.

⁴³The Nethinim: the sons of Ziha, the sons of Hasupha, the sons of Tabbaoth, ⁴⁴the sons of Keros, the sons of Siaha,^a the sons of Padon, ⁴⁵the sons of Lebanah, the sons of Hagabah, the sons of Akkub, ⁴⁶the sons of Hagab, the sons of Shalmai, the sons of Hanan, ⁴⁷the sons of Giddel, the sons of Gahar, the sons of Reaiah, ⁴⁸the sons of Rezin, the sons of Nekoda, the sons of Gazzam, ⁴⁹the sons of Uzza, the sons of Paseah, the sons of Besai, ⁵⁰the sons of Asnah, the sons of Meunim, the sons of Nephusim,^a ⁵¹the sons of Bakbuk, the sons of Hakupha, the sons of Harhur, ⁵²the sons of Bazluth,^a the sons of Mehida, the sons of Harsha, ⁵³the sons of Barkos, the sons of Sisera, the sons

of Tamah, ⁵⁴the sons of Neziah, and the sons of Hatipha.

⁵⁵The sons of Solomon's servants: the sons of Sotai, the sons of Sophereth, the sons of Peruda,^a ⁵⁶the sons of Jaala, the sons of Darkon, the sons of Giddel, ⁵⁷the sons of Shephatiah, the sons of Hattil, the sons of Pochereth of Zebaim, and the sons of Ami.^a ⁵⁸All the Nethinim and the children of Solomon's servants were three hundred and ninety-two.

⁵⁹And these *were* the ones who came up from Tel Melah, Tel Harsha, Cherub, Addan,^a and Immer; but they could not identify their father's house or their genealogy,^b whether they *were* of Israel: ⁶⁰the sons of Delaiah, the sons of Tobiah, and the sons of Nekoda, six hundred and fifty-two; ⁶¹and of the sons of the priests: the sons of Habaiah, the sons of Koz,^a and the sons of Barzillai, who took a wife of the daughters of Barzillai the Gileadite, and was called by their name. ⁶²These sought their listing *among* those who were registered by genealogy, but they were not found; therefore they *were excluded* from the priesthood as defiled. ⁶³And the governor^a said to them that they should not eat of the most holy things till a priest could consult with the Urim and Thummim.

⁶⁴The whole assembly together *was* forty-two thousand three hundred *and* sixty, ⁶⁵besides their male and female servants, of whom *there were* seven thousand three hundred and thirty-seven; and they had two hundred men and women singers. ⁶⁶Their horses *were* seven hundred and thirty-six, their mules two hundred and forty-five, ⁶⁷their camels four hundred and thirty-five, and *their* donkeys six thousand seven hundred and twenty.

⁶⁸*Some* of the heads of the fathers' *houses,* when they came to the house of the LORD

2:20 ^aCalled *Gibeon* in Nehemiah 7:25
2:24 ^aCalled *Beth Azmaveth* in Nehemiah 7:28
2:25 ^aCalled *Kirjath Jearim* in Nehemiah 7:29
2:40 ^aSpelled *Hodevah* in Nehemiah 7:43
2:44 ^aSpelled *Sia* in Nehemiah 7:47   **2:50** ^aSpelled *Nephishesim* in Nehemiah 7:52   **2:52** ^aSpelled *Bazlith* in Nehemiah 7:54   **2:55** ^aSpelled *Perida* in Nehemiah 7:57   **2:57** ^aSpelled *Amon* in Nehemiah 7:59   **2:59** ^aSpelled *Addon* in Nehemiah 7:61 ^bLiterally *seed*   **2:61** ^aOr *Hakkoz*
2:63 ^aHebrew *Tirshatha*

520

which *is* in Jerusalem, offered freely for the house of God, to erect it in its place: [69]According to their ability, they gave to the treasury for the work sixty-one thousand gold drachmas, five thousand minas of silver, and one hundred priestly garments.

[70]So the priests and the Levites, *some* of the people, the singers, the gatekeepers, and the Nethinim, dwelt in their cities, and all Israel in their cities.

Worship Restored at Jerusalem

3 And when the seventh month had come, and the children of Israel *were* in the cities, the people gathered together as one man to Jerusalem. [2]Then Jeshua the son of Jozadak[a] and his brethren the priests, and Zerubbabel the son of Shealtiel and his brethren, arose and built the altar of the God of Israel, to offer burnt offerings on it, as *it is* written in the Law of Moses the man of God. [3]Though fear *had come* upon them because of the people of those countries, they set the altar on its bases; and they offered burnt offerings on it to the LORD, *both* the morning and evening burnt offerings. [4]They also kept the Feast of Tabernacles, as *it is* written, and *offered* the daily burnt offerings in the number required by ordinance for each day. [5]Afterwards *they offered* the regular burnt offering, and *those* for New Moons and for all the appointed feasts of the LORD that were consecrated, and *those* of everyone who willingly offered a freewill offering to the LORD. [6]From the first day of the seventh month they began to offer burnt offerings to the LORD, although the foundation of the temple of the LORD had not been laid. [7]They also gave money to the masons and the carpenters, and food, drink, and oil to the people of Sidon and Tyre to bring cedar logs from Lebanon to the sea, to Joppa, according to the permission which they had from Cyrus king of Persia.

Restoration of the Temple Begins

[8]Now in the second month of the second year of their coming to the house of God at Jerusalem, Zerubbabel the son of Shealtiel, Jeshua the son of Jozadak,[a] and the rest of their brethren the priests and the Levites, and all those who had come out of the captivity to Jerusalem, began *work* and appointed the Levites from twenty years old and above to oversee the work of the house of the LORD. [9]Then Jeshua *with* his sons and brothers, Kadmiel *with* his sons, and the sons of Judah,[a] arose as one to oversee those working on the house of God: the sons of Henadad *with* their sons and their brethren the Levites.

[10]When the builders laid the foundation of the temple of the LORD, the priests stood[a] in their apparel with trumpets, and the Levites, the sons of Asaph, with cymbals, to praise the LORD, according to the ordinance of David king of Israel. [11]And they sang responsively, praising and giving thanks to the LORD:

"For *He is* good,
For His mercy *endures* forever toward Israel."[a]

Then all the people shouted with a great shout, when they praised the LORD, because the foundation of the house of the LORD was laid.

[12]But many of the priests and Levites and heads of the fathers' *houses,* old men who had seen the first temple, wept with a loud voice when the foundation of this temple was laid before their eyes. Yet many shouted aloud for joy, [13]so that the people could not discern the noise of the shout of joy from the noise of the weeping of the people, for the people shouted with a loud shout, and the sound was heard afar off.

Resistance to Rebuilding the Temple

4 Now when the adversaries of Judah and Benjamin heard that the descendants of the captivity were building the temple of the LORD God of Israel, [2]they came to Zerubbabel and the heads of the fathers' *houses,* and said to them, "Let us build with you, for we seek your God as you *do;* and we have sacrificed to Him since the days of

---

3:2 [a]Spelled *Jehozadak* in 1 Chronicles 6:14
3:8 [a]Spelled *Jehozadak* in 1 Chronicles 6:14
3:9 [a]Or *Hodaviah* (compare 2:40)
3:10 [a]Following Septuagint, Syriac, and Vulgate; Masoretic Text reads *they stationed the priests.*
3:11 [a]Compare Psalm 136:1

Esarhaddon king of Assyria, who brought us here." ³But Zerubbabel and Jeshua and the rest of the heads of the fathers' *houses* of Israel said to them, "You may do nothing with us to build a house for our God; but we alone will build to the Lord God of Israel, as King Cyrus the king of Persia has commanded us." ⁴Then the people of the land tried to discourage the people of Judah. They troubled them in building, ⁵and hired counselors against them to frustrate their purpose all the days of Cyrus king of Persia, even until the reign of Darius king of Persia.

Rebuilding of Jerusalem Opposed

⁶In the reign of Ahasuerus, in the beginning of his reign, they wrote an accusation against the inhabitants of Judah and Jerusalem.

⁷In the days of Artaxerxes also, Bishlam, Mithredath, Tabel, and the rest of their companions wrote to Artaxerxes king of Persia; and the letter *was* written in Aramaic script, and translated into the Aramaic language. ⁸Rehumᵃ the commander and Shimshai the scribe wrote a letter against Jerusalem to King Artaxerxes in this fashion:

9   Fromᵃ Rehum the commander, Shimshai the scribe, and the rest of their companions—*representatives* of the Dinaites, the Apharsathchites, the Tarpelites, the people of Persia and Erech and Babylon and Shushan,ᵇ the Dehavites, the Elamites, ¹⁰and the rest of the nations whom the great and noble Osnapper took captive and settled in the cities of Samaria and the remainder beyond the Riverᵃ—and so forth.ᵇ

¹¹(This *is* a copy of the letter that they sent him)

To King Artaxerxes from your servants, the men *of the region* beyond the River, and so forth:ᵃ

12   Let it be known to the king that the Jews who came up from you have come to us at Jerusalem, and are building the rebellious and evil city,

and are finishing *its* walls and repairing the foundations. ¹³Let it now be known to the king that, if this city is built and the walls completed, they will not pay tax, tribute, or custom, and the king's treasury will be diminished. ¹⁴Now because we receive support from the palace, it was not proper for us to see the king's dishonor; therefore we have sent and informed the king, ¹⁵that search may be made in the book of the records of your fathers. And you will find in the book of the records and know that this city *is* a rebellious city, harmful to kings and provinces, and that they have incited sedition within the city in former times, for which cause this city was destroyed.

16   We inform the king that if this city is rebuilt and its walls are completed, the result will be that you will have no dominion beyond the River.

¹⁷The king sent an answer:

To Rehum the commander, *to* Shimshai the scribe, *to* the rest of their companions who dwell in Samaria, and *to* the remainder beyond the River:

Peace, and so forth.ᵃ

18   The letter which you sent to us has been clearly read before me. ¹⁹And I gave the command, and a search has been made, and it was found that this city in former times has revolted against kings, and rebellion and sedition have been fostered in it. ²⁰There have also been mighty kings over Jerusalem, who have ruled over all *the region* beyond the River; and tax, tribute, and custom were paid to them. ²¹Now give the command to make these men cease, that this city may not be built until the command is given by me.

4:8 ᵃThe original language of Ezra 4:8 through 6:18 is Aramaic.   **4:9** ᵃLiterally *Then* ᵇOr *Susa*   **4:10** ᵃThat is, the Euphrates ᵇLiterally *and now*   **4:11** ᵃLiterally *and now*   **4:17** ᵃLiterally *and now*

22 Take heed now that you do not fail to do this. Why should damage increase to the hurt of the kings?

23 Now when the copy of King Artaxerxes' letter *was* read before Rehum, Shimshai the scribe, and their companions, they went up in haste to Jerusalem against the Jews, and by force of arms made them cease. 24 Thus the work of the house of God which *is* at Jerusalem ceased, and it was discontinued until the second year of the reign of Darius king of Persia.

Restoration of the Temple Resumed

5 Then the prophet Haggai and Zechariah the son of Iddo, prophets, prophesied to the Jews who *were* in Judah and Jerusalem, in the name of the God of Israel, *who was* over them. 2 So Zerubbabel the son of Shealtiel and Jeshua the son of Jozadakᵃ rose up and began to build the house of God which *is* in Jerusalem; and the prophets of God *were* with them, helping them.

3 At the same time Tattenai the governor of *the region* beyond the Riverᵃ and Shethar-Boznai and their companions came to them and spoke thus to them: "Who has commanded you to build this temple and finish this wall?" 4 Then, accordingly, we told them the names of the men who were constructing this building. 5 But the eye of their God was upon the elders of the Jews, so that they could not make them cease till a report could go to Darius. Then a written answer was returned concerning this *matter.* 6 This is a copy of the letter that Tattenai sent:

The governor of *the region* beyond the River, and Shethar-Boznai, and his companions, the Persians who *were in the region* beyond the River, to Darius the king.

7 (They sent a letter to him, in which was written thus)

To Darius the king:

All peace.

8 Let it be known to the king that we went into the province of Judea, to the temple of the great God, which is being built with heavy stones, and timber is being laid in the walls; and this work goes on diligently and prospers in their hands.

9 Then we asked those elders, *and* spoke thus to them: "Who commanded you to build this temple and to finish these walls?" 10 We also asked them their names to inform you, that we might write the names of the men who *were* chief among them.

11 And thus they returned us an answer, saying: "We are the servants of the God of heaven and earth, and we are rebuilding the temple that was built many years ago, which a great king of Israel built and completed. 12 But because our fathers provoked the God of heaven to wrath, He gave them into the hand of Nebuchadnezzar king of Babylon, the Chaldean, *who* destroyed this temple and carried the people away to Babylon. 13 However, in the first year of Cyrus king of Babylon, King Cyrus issued a decree to build this house of God. 14 Also, the gold and silver articles of the house of God, which Nebuchadnezzar had taken from the temple that *was* in Jerusalem and carried into the temple of Babylon—those King Cyrus took from the temple of Babylon, and they were given to one named Sheshbazzar, whom he had made governor. 15 And he said to him, 'Take these articles; go, carry them to the temple *site* that *is* in Jerusalem, and let the house of God be rebuilt on its former site.' 16 Then the same Sheshbazzar came *and* laid the foundation of the house of God which *is* in Jerusalem; but from that time even until now it has been under construction, and it is not finished."

17 Now therefore, if *it seems* good to the king, let a search be made in the

---

5:2 ᵃSpelled *Jehozadak* in 1 Chronicles 6:14
5:3 ᵃThat is, the Euphrates

king's treasure house, which *is* there in Babylon, whether it is *so* that a decree was issued by King Cyrus to build this house of God at Jerusalem, and let the king send us his pleasure concerning this *matter.*

The Decree of Darius

6 Then King Darius issued a decree, and a search was made in the archives,[a] where the treasures were stored in Babylon. [2]And at Achmetha,[a] in the palace that *is* in the province of Media, a scroll was found, and in it a record *was* written thus:

[3] In the first year of King Cyrus, King Cyrus issued a decree *concerning* the house of God at Jerusalem: "Let the house be rebuilt, the place where they offered sacrifices; and let the foundations of it be firmly laid, its height sixty cubits *and* its width sixty cubits, [4]*with* three rows of heavy stones and one row of new timber. Let the expenses be paid from the king's treasury. [5]Also let the gold and silver articles of the house of God, which Nebuchadnezzar took from the temple which *is* in Jerusalem and brought to Babylon, be restored and taken back to the temple which *is* in Jerusalem, *each* to its place; and deposit *them* in the house of God"—

[6] Now *therefore,* Tattenai, governor of *the region* beyond the River, and Shethar-Boznai, and your companions the Persians who *are* beyond the River, keep yourselves far from there. [7]Let the work of this house of God alone; let the governor of the Jews and the elders of the Jews build this house of God on its site.

[8] Moreover I issue a decree *as to* what you shall do for the elders of these Jews, for the building of this house of God: Let the cost be paid at the king's expense from taxes *on the region* beyond the River; this is to be given immediately to these men, so that they are not hindered. [9]And whatever

they need—young bulls, rams, and lambs for the burnt offerings of the God of heaven, wheat, salt, wine, and oil, according to the request of the priests who *are* in Jerusalem—let it be given them day by day without fail, [10]that they may offer sacrifices of sweet aroma to the God of heaven, and pray for the life of the king and his sons.

[11] Also I issue a decree that whoever alters this edict, let a timber be pulled from his house and erected, and let him be hanged on it; and let his house be made a refuse heap because of this. [12]And may the God who causes His name to dwell there destroy any king or people who put their hand to alter it, or to destroy this house of God which is in Jerusalem. I Darius issue a decree; let it be done diligently.

SERVICE
Let the cost be paid at the king's expense. . . .
EZRA 6:8

State-Funded Ministers
The State of Massachusetts paid the salaries of the Congregational ministers in that state until 1833. Other states had cut official ties to a church previous to Massachusetts.

The Temple Completed and Dedicated

[13]Then Tattenai, governor of *the region* beyond the River, Shethar-Boznai, and their companions diligently did according to what King Darius had sent. [14]So the elders of the Jews built, and they prospered through the prophesying of Haggai the prophet and Zechariah the son of Iddo. And they built and finished *it,* according to the commandment of the God of Israel, and according to the command of Cyrus, Darius, and Artaxerxes king of Persia. [15]Now the temple was finished on the third day of the month of Adar, which was in the sixth year of the reign of King Darius. [16]Then the children of

6:1 [a]Literally *house of the scrolls* 6:2 [a]Probably *Ecbatana,* the ancient capital of Media

Israel, the priests and the Levites and the rest of the descendants of the captivity, celebrated the dedication of this house of God with joy. [17]And they offered sacrifices at the dedication of this house of God, one hundred bulls, two hundred rams, four hundred lambs, and as a sin offering for all Israel twelve male goats, according to the number of the tribes of Israel. [18]They assigned the priests to their divisions and the Levites to their divisions, over the service of God in Jerusalem, as it is written in the Book of Moses.

The Passover Celebrated

[19]And the descendants of the captivity kept the Passover on the fourteenth *day* of the first month. [20]For the priests and the Levites had purified themselves; all of them *were ritually* clean. And they slaughtered the Passover *lambs* for all the descendants of the captivity, for their brethren the priests, and for themselves. [21]Then the children of Israel who had returned from the captivity ate together with all who had separated themselves from the filth of the nations of the land in order to seek the LORD God of Israel. [22]And they kept the Feast of Unleavened Bread seven days with joy; for the LORD made them joyful, and turned the heart of the king of Assyria toward them, to strengthen their hands in the work of the house of God, the God of Israel.

The Arrival of Ezra

7 Now after these things, in the reign of Artaxerxes king of Persia, Ezra the son of Seraiah, the son of Azariah, the son of Hilkiah, [2]the son of Shallum, the son of Zadok, the son of Ahitub, [3]the son of Amariah, the son of Azariah, the son of Meraioth, [4]the son of Zerahiah, the son of Uzzi, the son of Bukki, [5]the son of Abishua, the son of Phinehas, the son of Eleazar, the son of Aaron the chief priest— [6]this Ezra came up from Babylon; and he *was* a skilled scribe in the Law of Moses, which the LORD God of Israel had given. The king granted him all his request, according to the hand of the LORD his God upon him. [7]*Some* of the children of Israel, the priests, the Levites, the singers, the gatekeepers, and the Nethinim

came up to Jerusalem in the seventh year of King Artaxerxes. [8]And Ezra came to Jerusalem in the fifth month, which *was* in the seventh year of the king. [9]On the first *day* of the first month he began *his* journey from Babylon, and on the first *day* of the fifth month he came to Jerusalem, according to the good hand of his God upon him. [10]For Ezra had prepared his heart to seek the Law of the LORD, and to do *it,* and to teach statutes and ordinances in Israel.

The Letter of Artaxerxes to Ezra

[11]This *is* a copy of the letter that King Artaxerxes gave Ezra the priest, the scribe, expert in the words of the commandments of the LORD, and of His statutes to Israel:

[12]   Artaxerxes,[a] king of kings,

To Ezra the priest, a scribe of the Law of the God of heaven:

Perfect *peace,* and so forth.[b]

[13]   I issue a decree that all those of the people of Israel and the priests and Levites in my realm, who volunteer to go up to Jerusalem, may go with you. [14]And whereas you are being sent by the king and his seven counselors to inquire concerning Judah and Jerusalem, with regard to the Law of your God which *is* in your hand; [15]and *whereas you are* to carry the silver and gold which the king and his counselors have freely offered to the God of Israel, whose dwelling *is* in Jerusalem; [16]and *whereas* all the silver and gold that you may find in all the province of Babylon, along with the freewill offering of the people and the priests, *are to be* freely offered for the house of their God in Jerusalem— [17]now therefore, be careful to buy with this money bulls, rams, and lambs, with their grain offerings and their drink offerings, and offer them on the altar of the house of your God in Jerusalem.

7:12 [a]The original language of Ezra 7:12–26 is Aramaic. [b]Literally *and now*

18 And whatever seems good to you and your brethren to do with the rest of the silver and the gold, do it according to the will of your God. 19Also the articles that are given to you for the service of the house of your God, deliver in full before the God of Jerusalem. 20And whatever more may be needed for the house of your God, which you may have occasion to provide, pay *for it* from the king's treasury.

21 And I, *even* I, Artaxerxes the king, issue a decree to all the treasurers who *are in the region* beyond the River, that whatever Ezra the priest, the scribe of the Law of the God of heaven, may require of you, let it be done diligently, 22up to one hundred talents of silver, one hundred kors of wheat, one hundred baths of wine, one hundred baths of oil, and salt without prescribed limit. 23Whatever is commanded by the God of heaven, let it diligently be done for the house of the God of heaven. For why should there be wrath against the realm of the king and his sons?

24 Also we inform you that it shall not be lawful to impose tax, tribute, or custom on any of the priests, Levites, singers, gatekeepers, Nethinim, or servants of this house of God. 25And you, Ezra, according to your God-given wisdom, set magistrates and judges who may judge all the people who *are in the region* beyond the River, all such as know the laws of your God; and teach those who do not know *them*. 26Whoever will not observe the law of your God and the law of the king, let judgment be executed speedily on him, whether *it be* death, or banishment, or confiscation of goods, or imprisonment.

27Blessed *be* the LORD God of our fathers, who has put *such a thing* as this in the king's heart, to beautify the house of the LORD which *is* in Jerusalem, 28and has extended mercy to me before the king and his counselors, and before all the king's mighty princes.

So I was encouraged, as the hand of the LORD my God *was* upon me; and I gathered leading men of Israel to go up with me.

Heads of Families Who Returned with Ezra

8These *are* the heads of their fathers' houses, and *this is* the genealogy of those who went up with me from Babylon, in the reign of King Artaxerxes: 2of the sons of Phinehas, Gershom; of the sons of Ithamar, Daniel; of the sons of David, Hattush; 3of the sons of Shecaniah, of the sons of Parosh, Zechariah; and registered with him *were* one hundred and fifty males; 4of the sons of Pahath-Moab, Eliehoenai the son of Zerahiah, and with him two hundred males; 5of the sons of Shechaniah,ᵃ Ben-Jahaziel, and with him three hundred males; 6of the sons of Adin, Ebed the son of Jonathan, and with him fifty males; 7of the sons of Elam, Jeshaiah the son of Athaliah, and with him seventy males; 8of the sons of Shephatiah, Zebadiah the son of Michael, and with him eighty males; 9of the sons of Joab, Obadiah the son of Jehiel, and with him two

FAITH
. . . set magistrates and judges . . . such as know the laws of your God. . . .   EZRA 7:25

State Constitutions After Declaring Independence
Following the declaration of independence from Great Britain, all the state governments, which had been controlled by the British, had to be established with new state constitutions. It is interesting to read what many of the Founders who signed the founding documents placed in their original new state constitutions. Delaware provides one example, but other states were similar:

Every person appointed to public office shall say "I do profess faith in God the Father, and in Jesus Christ His only Son, and in the Holy Ghost, one God, blessed for evermore; and I do acknowledge the Holy Scriptures of the Old and New Testament to be given by divine inspiration."

8:5 ᵃFollowing Masoretic Text and Vulgate; Septuagint reads *the sons of Zatho, Shechaniah.*

hundred and eighteen males; ¹⁰of the sons of Shelomith,ª Ben-Josiphiah, and with him one hundred and sixty males; ¹¹of the sons of Bebai, Zechariah the son of Bebai, and with him twenty-eight males; ¹²of the sons of Azgad, Johanan the son of Hakkatan, and with him one hundred and ten males; ¹³of the last sons of Adonikam, whose names *are* these—Eliphelet, Jeiel, and Shemaiah—and with them sixty males; ¹⁴also of the sons of Bigvai, Uthai and Zabbud, and with them seventy males.

Servants for the Temple

¹⁵Now I gathered them by the river that flows to Ahava, and we camped there three days. And I looked among the people and the priests, and found none of the sons of Levi there. ¹⁶Then I sent for Eliezer, Ariel, Shemaiah, Elnathan, Jarib, Elnathan, Nathan, Zechariah, and Meshullam, leaders; also for Joiarib and Elnathan, men of understanding. ¹⁷And I gave them a command for Iddo the chief man at the place Casiphia, and I told them what they should say to Iddo *and* his brethrenª the Nethinim at the place Casiphia—that they should bring us servants for the house of our God. ¹⁸Then, by the good hand of our God upon us, they brought us a man of understanding, of the sons of Mahli the son of Levi, the son of Israel, namely Sherebiah, with his sons and brothers, eighteen men; ¹⁹and Hashabiah, and with him Jeshaiah of the sons of Merari, his brothers and their sons, twenty men; ²⁰also of the Nethinim, whom David and the leaders had appointed for the service of the Levites, two hundred and twenty Nethinim. All of them were designated by name.

Fasting and Prayer for Protection

²¹Then I proclaimed a fast there at the river of Ahava, that we might humble ourselves before our God, to seek from Him the right way for us and our little ones and all our possessions. ²²For I was ashamed to request of the king an escort of soldiers and horsemen to help us against the enemy on the road, because we had spoken to the king, saying, "The hand of our God *is* upon all those for good who seek Him, but His power and His wrath *are* against all those who forsake Him." ²³So we fasted and entreated our God for this, and He answered our prayer.

Gifts for the Temple

²⁴And I separated twelve of the leaders of the priests—Sherebiah, Hashabiah, and ten of their brethren with them— ²⁵and weighed out to them the silver, the gold, and the articles, the offering for the house of our God which the king and his counselors and his princes, and all Israel *who were* present, had offered. ²⁶I weighed into their hand six hundred and fifty talents of silver, silver articles *weighing* one hundred talents, one hundred talents of gold, ²⁷twenty gold basins *worth* a thousand drachmas, and two vessels of fine polished bronze, precious as gold. ²⁸And I said to them, "You *are* holy to the Lᴏʀᴅ; the articles *are* holy also; and the silver and the gold *are* a freewill offering to the Lᴏʀᴅ God of your fathers. ²⁹Watch and keep *them* until you weigh *them* before the leaders of the priests and the Levites and heads of the fathers' *houses* of Israel in Jerusalem, *in* the chambers of the house of the Lᴏʀᴅ." ³⁰So the priests and the Levites received the silver and the gold and the articles by weight, to bring *them* to Jerusalem to the house of our God.

The Return to Jerusalem

³¹Then we departed from the river of Ahava on the twelfth *day* of the first month, to go to Jerusalem. And the hand of our God was upon us, and He delivered us from the hand of the enemy and from ambush along the road. ³²So we came to Jerusalem, and stayed there three days.

³³Now on the fourth day the silver and the gold and the articles were weighed in the house of our God by the hand of Meremoth the son of Uriah the priest, and with him *was* Eleazar the son of Phinehas; with them *were* the Levites, Jozabad the son of Jeshua and Noadiah the son of Binnui,

---

8:10 ªFollowing Masoretic Text and Vulgate; Septuagint reads *the sons of Banni, Shelomith.*
8:17 ªFollowing Vulgate; Masoretic Text reads *to Iddo his brother;* Septuagint reads *to their brethren.*

PRESIDENTS AND INAUGURAL ADDRESSES

RONALD REAGAN

Then I proclaimed a fast . . . that we might humble ourselves before our God. . . .

EZRA 8:21

Every president from George Washington forward has prayed, invoked prayer, or otherwise asked God for His continued blessing on the United States during their Inaugural Address. Here is a short sample that reflects this nation's dependence upon God:

No people can be bound to acknowledge and adore the Invisible Hand which conducts the affairs of men more than those of the United States.

GEORGE WASHINGTON, APRIL 30, 1789

I shall need, too, the favor of that Being in whose hands we are, who led our fathers, as Israel of old, from their native land and planted them in a country flowing with all the necessaries and comforts of life; who has covered our infancy with His providence and our riper years with His wisdom and power, and to whose goodness I ask you to join in supplications with me that He will so enlighten the minds of your servants, guide their councils, and prosper their measures. . . .

THOMAS JEFFERSON, MARCH 4, 1805

With malice toward none, with charity for all, with firmness in the right as God gives us to see the right, let us strive on to finish the work we are in, to bind up the nation's wounds, to care for him who shall have borne the battle and for his widow and his orphan, to do all which may achieve and cherish a just and lasting peace among ourselves and with all nations.

ABRAHAM LINCOLN, MARCH 4, 1865

The Almighty God has blessed our land in many ways. He has given our people stout hearts and strong arms with which to strike mighty blows for freedom and truth. He has given to our country a faith which has become the hope of all peoples in an anguished world. So we pray to Him now for the vision to see our way clearly—to see the way that leads to a better life for ourselves and for all our fellow men—to the achievement of His will to peace on earth.

FRANKLIN ROOSEVELT, JANUARY 20, 1945

And may He continue to hold us close as we fill the world with our sound—sound in unity, affection, and love—one people under God, dedicated to the dream of freedom that He has placed in the human heart, called upon now to pass that dream on to a waiting and hopeful world.

RONALD REAGAN, JANUARY 21, 1985

[34]with the number *and* weight of everything. All the weight was written down at that time.

[35]The children of those who had been carried away captive, who had come from the captivity, offered burnt offerings to the God of Israel: twelve bulls for all Israel, ninety-six rams, seventy-seven lambs, and twelve male goats *as* a sin offering. All *this was* a burnt offering to the LORD.

[36]And they delivered the king's orders to the king's satraps and the governors *in the region* beyond the River. So they gave support to the people and the house of God.

Intermarriage with Pagans

9 When these things were done, the leaders came to me, saying, "The people of Israel and the priests and the Levites have not separated themselves from the peoples of the lands, with respect to the abominations of the Canaanites, the Hittites, the Perizzites, the Jebusites, the Ammonites, the Moabites, the Egyptians, and the Amorites. [2]For they have taken some of their daughters *as wives* for themselves and their sons, so that the holy seed is mixed with the peoples of *those* lands. Indeed, the hand of the leaders and rulers has been foremost in this trespass." [3]So when I heard this thing, I tore my garment and my robe, and plucked out some of the hair of my head and beard, and sat down astonished. [4]Then everyone who trembled at the words of the God of Israel assembled to me, because of the transgression of those who had been carried away captive, and I sat astonished until the evening sacrifice.

[5]At the evening sacrifice I arose from my fasting; and having torn my garment and my robe, I fell on my knees and spread out my hands to the LORD my God. [6]And I said: "O my God, I am too ashamed and humiliated to lift up my face to You, my God; for our iniquities have risen higher than *our* heads, and our guilt has grown up to the heavens. [7]Since the days of our fathers to this day we *have been* very guilty, and for our iniquities we, our kings, *and* our priests have been delivered into the hand of the kings of the lands, to the sword, to captivity, to plunder, and to humiliation, as *it is* this day. [8]And now for a little while grace has been *shown* from the LORD our God, to leave us a remnant to escape, and to give us a peg in His holy place, that our God may enlighten our eyes and give us a measure of revival in our bondage. [9]For we *were* slaves. Yet our God did not forsake us in our bondage; but He extended mercy to us in the sight of the kings of Persia, to revive us, to repair the house of our God, to rebuild its ruins, and to give us a wall in Judah and Jerusalem. [10]And now, O our God, what shall we say after this? For we have forsaken Your commandments, [11]which You commanded by Your servants the prophets, saying, 'The land which you are entering to possess is an unclean land, with the uncleanness of the peoples of the lands, with their abominations which have filled it from one end to another with their impurity. [12]Now therefore, do not give your daughters as wives for their sons, nor take their daughters to your sons; and never seek their peace or prosperity, that you may be strong and eat the good of the land, and leave *it* as an inheritance to your children forever.' [13]And after all that has come upon us for our evil deeds and for our great guilt, since You our God have punished us less than our iniquities *deserve,* and have given us *such* deliverance as this, [14]should we again break Your commandments, and join in marriage with the people *committing* these abominations? Would You not be angry with us until You had consumed *us,* so that *there would be* no remnant or survivor? [15]O LORD God of Israel,

---

HUMILITY
. . . I fell on my knees. . . .

EZRA 9:5

When Wisdom Fails
After the Union Army's devastating loss at the Second Battle of Bull Run in August 1862, President Abraham Lincoln stated:

> *I have been driven many times upon my knees by the overwhelming conviction that I had nowhere else to go. My own wisdom, and that of all about me, seemed insufficient for that day.*

You *are* righteous, for we are left as a remnant, as *it is* this day. Here we *are* before You, in our guilt, though no one can stand before You because of this!"

Sins Forgiven

Peter Cartwright (1785–1872) was a Methodist circuit rider and evangelist in Tennessee, Kentucky, and surrounding states during the Second Great Awakening. He preached nearly 15,000 sermons, and personally baptized 12,000 people. In recalling his own conversion, he stated:

> I went with weeping multitudes and bowed before the preaching stand and earnestly prayed for mercy. In the midst of a solemn struggle of soul, an impression was made upon my mind, as though a voice said to me: "Thy sins are all forgiven thee."

Confession of Improper Marriages

10 Now while Ezra was praying, and while he was confessing, weeping, and bowing down before the house of God, a very large assembly of men, women, and children gathered to him from Israel; for the people wept very bitterly. ²And Shechaniah the son of Jehiel, *one* of the sons of Elam, spoke up and said to Ezra, "We have trespassed against our God, and have taken pagan wives from the peoples of the land; yet now there is hope in Israel in spite of this. ³Now therefore, let us make a covenant with our God to put away all these wives and those who have been born to them, according to the advice of my master and of those who tremble at the commandment of our God; and let it be done according to the law. ⁴Arise, for *this* matter *is* your *responsibility.* We also *are* with you. Be of good courage, and do *it.*"

⁵Then Ezra arose, and made the leaders of the priests, the Levites, and all Israel swear an oath that they would do according to this word. So they swore an oath. ⁶Then Ezra rose up from before the house of God, and went into the chamber of Jehohanan the son of Eliashib; and *when* he came there, he ate no bread and drank no water, for he mourned because of the guilt of those from the captivity.

⁷And they issued a proclamation throughout Judah and Jerusalem to all the descendants of the captivity, that they must gather at Jerusalem, ⁸and that whoever would not come within three days, according to the instructions of the leaders and elders, all his property would be confiscated, and he himself would be separated from the assembly of those from the captivity.

⁹So all the men of Judah and Benjamin gathered at Jerusalem within three days. It *was* the ninth month, on the twentieth of the month; and all the people sat in the open square of the house of God, trembling because of *this* matter and because of heavy rain. ¹⁰Then Ezra the priest stood up and said to them, "You have transgressed and have taken pagan wives, adding to the guilt of Israel. ¹¹Now therefore, make confession to the LORD God of your fathers, and do His will; separate yourselves from the peoples of the land, and from the pagan wives."

¹²Then all the assembly answered and said with a loud voice, "Yes! As you have said, so we must do. ¹³But *there are* many people; *it is* the season for heavy rain, and we are not able to stand outside. Nor *is this* the work of one or two days, for *there are* many of us who have transgressed in this matter. ¹⁴Please, let the leaders of our entire assembly stand; and let all those in our cities who have taken pagan wives come at appointed times, together with the elders and judges of their cities, until the fierce wrath of our God is turned away from us in this matter." ¹⁵Only Jonathan the son of Asahel and Jahaziah the son of Tikvah opposed this, and Meshullam and Shabbethai the Levite gave them support.

¹⁶Then the descendants of the captivity did so. And Ezra the priest, *with* certain heads of the fathers' *households,* were set apart by the fathers' households, each of them by name; and they sat down on the first day of the tenth month to examine the matter. ¹⁷By the first day of the first month they finished *questioning* all the men who had taken pagan wives.

Pagan Wives Put Away

18And among the sons of the priests who had taken pagan wives *the following* were found of the sons of Jeshua the son of Jozadak,ᵃ and his brothers: Maaseiah, Eliezer, Jarib, and Gedaliah. 19And they gave their promise that they would put away their wives; and *being* guilty, *they presented* a ram of the flock as their trespass offering.

20Also of the sons of Immer: Hanani and Zebadiah; 21of the sons of Harim: Maaseiah, Elijah, Shemaiah, Jehiel, and Uzziah; 22of the sons of Pashhur: Elioenai, Maaseiah, Ishmael, Nethanel, Jozabad, and Elasah.

23Also of the Levites: Jozabad, Shimei, Kelaiah (the same *is* Kelita), Pethahiah, Judah, and Eliezer.

24Also of the singers: Eliashib; and of the gatekeepers: Shallum, Telem, and Uri.

25And others of Israel: of the sons of Parosh: Ramiah, Jeziah, Malchiah, Mijamin, Eleazar, Malchijah, and Benaiah; 26of the sons of Elam: Mattaniah, Zechariah, Jehiel, Abdi, Jeremoth, and Eliah; 27of the sons of Zattu: Elioenai, Eliashib, Mattaniah, Jeremoth, Zabad, and Aziza; 28of the sons of

Bebai: Jehohanan, Hananiah, Zabbai, *and* Athlai; 29of the sons of Bani: Meshullam, Malluch, Adaiah, Jashub, Sheal, *and* Ramoth;ᵃ 30of the sons of Pahath-Moab: Adna, Chelal, Benaiah, Maaseiah, Mattaniah, Bezalel, Binnui, and Manasseh; 31*of* the sons of Harim: Eliezer, Ishijah, Malchijah, Shemaiah, Shimeon, 32Benjamin, Malluch, *and* Shemariah; 33of the sons of Hashum: Mattenai, Mattattah, Zabad, Eliphelet, Jeremai, Manasseh, *and* Shimei; 34of the sons of Bani: Maadai, Amram, Uel, 35Benaiah, Bedeiah, Cheluh,ᵃ 36Vaniah, Meremoth, Eliashib, 37Mattaniah, Mattenai, Jaasai,ᵃ 38Bani, Binnui, Shimei, 39Shelemiah, Nathan, Adaiah, 40Machnadebai, Shashai, Sharai, 41Azarel, Shelemiah, Shemariah, 42Shallum, Amariah, *and* Joseph; 43of the sons of Nebo: Jeiel, Mattithiah, Zabad, Zebina, Jaddai,ᵃ Joel, *and* Benaiah.

44All these had taken pagan wives, and *some* of them had wives *by whom* they had children.

10:18 ᵃSpelled *Jehozadak* in 1 Chronicles 6:14
10:29 ᵃOr *Jeremoth*   **10:35** ᵃOr *Cheluhi,* or *Cheluhu*
10:37 ᵃOr *Jaasu*   **10:43** ᵃOr *Jaddu*

NEHEMIAH

Author: Nehemiah

When Written: Around 423 B.C.

Theme: Godly Leadership

Key Verse: Nehemiah 6:15, 16—So the wall was finished on the twenty-fifth day of Elul, in fifty-two days. And it happened, when all our enemies heard of it, and all the nations around us saw these things, that they were very disheartened in their own eyes; for they perceived that this work was done by our God.

Key Chapter: Nehemiah 9—The theme and unifying factor of all of Scripture is God's unchanging covenant with His people. When Israel stayed true to God's Word and will, the nation prospered and was blessed. When the people disobeyed God and strayed, they faced some stiff consequences.

As America faced the beginnings of the Great Depression, President Franklin Roosevelt chose his first inaugural address to speak a bold word of encouragement to his fellow citizens. Assuring them that the only thing they had to fear was "fear itself," FDR challenged, "We face arduous days that lie before us in the warm courage of national unity; with the clear consciousness of seeking old and precious moral values." Beseeching God's blessing, the president added, "May He protect each and every one of us! May He guide me in the days to come!" FDR's courageous and selfless leadership would be a decisive factor in keeping America's resolve strong throughout the years of depression and world war that would follow.

The life of Nehemiah, who led the returning exiles in repairing the walls of Jerusalem, exemplifies true spirituality that is walked out in practical faith in action. Imagine the stress and demands of leading those who were doing the heavy lifting of rebuilding the broken down walls of Jerusalem. Nehemiah offers an incredible example of how one man's selfless leadership, dedication, and obedience to God helped restore not only Jerusalem's walls, but the hearts of the people as well.

Nehemiah Prays for His People

1The words of Nehemiah the son of Hachaliah.

It came to pass in the month of Chislev, *in* the twentieth year, as I was in Shushan[a] the citadel, [2]that Hanani one of my brethren came with men from Judah; and I asked them concerning the Jews who had escaped, who had survived the captivity, and concerning Jerusalem. [3]And they said to me, "The survivors who are left from the captivity in the province *are* there in great distress and reproach. The wall of Jerusalem *is* also broken down, and its gates are burned with fire."

[4]So it was, when I heard these words, that I sat down and wept, and mourned *for many* days; I was fasting and praying before the God of heaven.

[5]And I said: "I pray, LORD God of heaven, O great and awesome God, *You* who keep *Your* covenant and mercy with those who love You[a] and observe Your[b] commandments, [6]please let Your ear be attentive and Your eyes open, that You may hear the prayer of Your servant which I pray before You now, day and night, for the children of Israel Your servants, and confess the sins of the children of Israel which we have sinned against You. Both my father's house and I have sinned. [7]We have acted very corruptly against You, and have not kept the commandments, the statutes, nor the ordinances which You commanded Your servant Moses. [8]Remember, I pray, the word that You commanded Your servant Moses, saying, '*If* you are unfaithful, I will scatter you among the nations;[a] [9]but *if* you return to Me, and keep My commandments and do them, though some of you were cast out to the farthest part of the heavens, *yet* I will gather them from there, and bring them to the place which I have chosen as a dwelling for My name.'[a] [10]Now these *are* Your servants and Your people, whom You have redeemed by Your great power, and by Your strong hand.

[11]O Lord, I pray, please let Your ear be attentive to the prayer of Your servant, and to the prayer of Your servants who desire to fear Your name; and let Your servant prosper this day, I pray, and grant him mercy in the sight of this man."

For I was the king's cupbearer.

Nehemiah Sent to Judah

2And it came to pass in the month of Nisan, in the twentieth year of King Artaxerxes, *when* wine *was* before him, that I took the wine and gave it to the king. Now I had never been sad in his presence before. [2]Therefore the king said to me, "Why *is* your face sad, since you *are* not sick? This *is* nothing but sorrow of heart."

So I became dreadfully afraid, [3]and said to the king, "May the king live forever! Why should my face not be sad, when the city, the place of my fathers' tombs, *lies* waste, and its gates are burned with fire?"

[4]Then the king said to me, "What do you request?"

So I prayed to the God of heaven. [5]And I said to the king, "If it pleases the king, and if your servant has found favor in your sight, I ask that you send me to Judah, to the city of my fathers' tombs, that I may rebuild it."

[6]Then the king said to me (the queen also sitting beside him), "How long will your journey be? And when will you return?" So it pleased the king to send me; and I set him a time.

[7]Furthermore I said to the king, "If it pleases the king, let letters be given to me for the governors *of the region* beyond the River,[a] that they must permit me to pass through till I come to Judah, [8]and a letter to Asaph the keeper of the king's forest, that he must give me timber to make beams for the gates

---

1:1 [a]Or *Susa*   **1:5** [a]Literally *Him* [b]Literally *His*
1:8 [a]Leviticus 26:33   **1:9** [a]Deuteronomy 30:2–5
2:7 [a]That is, the Euphrates, and so elsewhere in this book

of the citadel which *pertains* to the temple,[a] for the city wall, and for the house that I will occupy." And the king granted *them* to me according to the good hand of my God upon me.

⁹Then I went to the governors *in the region* beyond the River, and gave them the king's letters. Now the king had sent captains of the army and horsemen with me. ¹⁰When Sanballat the Horonite and Tobiah the Ammonite official[a] heard *of it,* they were deeply disturbed that a man had come to seek the well-being of the children of Israel.

Nehemiah Views the Wall of Jerusalem

¹¹So I came to Jerusalem and was there three days. ¹²Then I arose in the night, I and a few men with me; I told no one what my God had put in my heart to do at Jerusalem; nor was there any animal with me, except the one on which I rode. ¹³And I went out by night through the Valley Gate to the Serpent Well and the Refuse Gate, and viewed the walls of Jerusalem which were broken down and its gates which were burned with fire. ¹⁴Then I went on to the Fountain Gate and to the King's Pool, but *there was* no room for the animal under me to pass. ¹⁵So I went up in the night by the valley, and viewed the wall; then I turned back and entered by the Valley Gate, and so returned. ¹⁶And the officials did not know where I had gone or what I had done; I had not yet told the Jews, the priests, the nobles, the officials, or the others who did the work.

¹⁷Then I said to them, "You see the distress that we *are* in, how Jerusalem *lies* waste, and its gates are burned with fire. Come and let us build the wall of Jerusalem, that we may no longer be a reproach." ¹⁸And I told them of the hand of my God which had been good upon me, and also of the king's words that he had spoken to me.

So they said, "Let us rise up and build." Then they set their hands to *this* good *work.*

¹⁹But when Sanballat the Horonite, Tobiah the Ammonite official, and Geshem the Arab heard *of it,* they laughed at us and despised us, and said, "What *is* this thing that you are doing? Will you rebel against the king?"

²⁰So I answered them, and said to them, "The God of heaven Himself will prosper us; therefore we His servants will arise and build, but you have no heritage or right or memorial in Jerusalem."

Rebuilding the Wall

3Then Eliashib the high priest rose up with his brethren the priests and built the Sheep Gate; they consecrated it and hung its doors. They built as far as the Tower of the Hundred,[a] *and* consecrated it, then as far as the Tower of Hananel. ²Next to *Eliashib*[a] the men of Jericho built. And next to them Zaccur the son of Imri built.

³Also the sons of Hassenaah built the Fish Gate; they laid its beams and hung its doors with its bolts and bars. ⁴And next to them Meremoth the son of Urijah, the son of Koz,[a] made repairs. Next to them Meshullam the son of Berechiah, the son of Meshezabel, made repairs. Next to them Zadok the son of Baana made repairs. ⁵Next to them the Tekoites made repairs; but their nobles did not put their shoulders[a] to the work of their Lord.

⁶Moreover Jehoiada the son of Paseah and Meshullam the son of Besodeiah repaired the Old Gate; they laid its beams and hung its doors, with its bolts and bars. ⁷And next to them Melatiah the Gibeonite, Jadon the Meronothite, the men of Gibeon and Mizpah, repaired the residence[a] of the governor *of the region* beyond the River. ⁸Next to him Uzziel the son of Harhaiah, one of the goldsmiths, made repairs. Also next to him Hananiah, one[a] of the perfumers, made repairs; and they fortified Jerusalem as far as the Broad Wall. ⁹And next to them Rephaiah the son of Hur, leader of half the district of Jerusalem, made repairs. ¹⁰Next to them Jedaiah the son of Harumaph made repairs in front of his house. And next to him Hattush the son of Hashabniah made repairs. ¹¹Malchijah the son of Harim and Hashub the son of Pahath-Moab repaired another section, as well as the Tower of the Ovens.

2:8 [a]Literally *house*   **2:10** [a]Literally *servant, and so elsewhere in this book*   **3:1** [a]Hebrew *Hammeah,* also at 12:39   **3:2** [a]Literally *On his hand*   **3:4** [a]Or *Hakkoz*   **3:5** [a]Literally *necks*   **3:7** [a]Literally *throne*   **3:8** [a]Literally *the son*

BOOKER T. WASHINGTON

A CLASS AT THE
TUSKEGEE INSTITUTE

*"Come and let
us build. . . ."*

NEHEMIAH 2:17

Booker T. Washington (1856–1915) was the most influential American black leader and educator of his time. He was the founder and head of the famous Tuskegee Institute, a vocational school for blacks in Tuskegee, Alabama, and his students became leaders and educators across the nation. He also advised two Presidents—Theodore Roosevelt and William Howard Taft—on racial issues and policies and was influential in the appointment of several blacks to federal office.

Born a slave in the hills of Virginia, from the age of nine Washington worked in coal mines and salt furnaces. Determined to get an education, at the age of sixteen he attended Hampton Institute, an industrial school for blacks in Hampton, Virginia. Upon graduating with honors in just three years (1875), Washington joined the faculty and was soon offered the position to lead a new school in Tuskegee, Alabama. He started this school in an old abandoned church and a shanty, and by 1915 he had built Tuskegee Institute into a school of 107 buildings on 2,000 acres with over 1,500 students and more than 200 teachers and professors—a phenomenal accomplishment, especially considering the times in which Washington lived.

As the presiding principal, Washington outlined several objectives for the new school. He not only offered the traditional academic courses, but industry and trade skills were also required. Students learned bricklaying, forestry and timber skills, sewing, cooking, and practical agriculture; in addition, every student was obligated to master at least two trades. Washington's goal was to produce independent small businessmen, farmers, and teachers.

He also insisted on high moral character for both students and faculty. His clear emphasis on the value of character and the training of the "head, hand, and heart" was filled with great insight. Christian faith was something Washington learned as a child in Sunday school, and it helped shape his ideals. Devotional exercises were held every morning at Tuskegee as well as evening prayers. He wrote that the support that "the Christ-like work which the Church of all denominations in America has done" would have convinced him of the value of the Christian life, if he wasn't already a believer.

¹²And next to him was Shallum the son of Hallohesh, leader of half the district of Jerusalem; he and his daughters made repairs.

¹³Hanun and the inhabitants of Zanoah repaired the Valley Gate. They built it, hung its doors with its bolts and bars, and *repaired* a thousand cubits of the wall as far as the Refuse Gate.

¹⁴Malchijah the son of Rechab, leader of the district of Beth Haccerem, repaired the Refuse Gate; he built it and hung its doors with its bolts and bars.

¹⁵Shallun the son of Col-Hozeh, leader of the district of Mizpah, repaired the Fountain Gate; he built it, covered it, hung its doors with its bolts and bars, and repaired the wall of the Pool of Shelah by the King's Garden, as far as the stairs that go down from the City of David. ¹⁶After him Nehemiah the son of Azbuk, leader of half the district of Beth Zur, made repairs as far as *the place* in front of the tombsᵃ of David, to the man-made pool, and as far as the House of the Mighty.

¹⁷After him the Levites, *under* Rehum the son of Bani, made repairs. Next to him Hashabiah, leader of half the district of Keilah, made repairs for his district. ¹⁸After him their brethren, *under* Bavaiᵃ the son of Henadad, leader of the *other* half of the district of Keilah, made repairs. ¹⁹And next to him Ezer the son of Jeshua, the leader of Mizpah, repaired another section in front of the Ascent to the Armory at the buttress. ²⁰After him Baruch the son of Zabbaiᵃ carefully repaired the other section, from the buttress to the door of the house of Eliashib the high priest. ²¹After him Meremoth the son of Urijah, the son of Koz,ᵃ repaired another section, from the door of the house of Eliashib to the end of the house of Eliashib.

²²And after him the priests, the men of the plain, made repairs. ²³After him Benjamin and Hasshub made repairs opposite their house. After them Azariah the son of Maaseiah, the son of Ananiah, made repairs by his house. ²⁴After him Binnui the son of Henadad repaired another section, from the house of Azariah to the buttress, even as far as the corner. ²⁵Palal the son of Uzai *made repairs* opposite the buttress, and on the tower which projects from the king's upper house that *was* by the court of the prison.

After him Pedaiah the son of Parosh *made repairs.*

²⁶Moreover the Nethinim who dwelt in Ophel *made repairs* as far as *the place* in front of the Water Gate toward the east, and on the projecting tower. ²⁷After them the Tekoites repaired another section, next to the great projecting tower, and as far as the wall of Ophel.

²⁸Beyond the Horse Gate the priests made repairs, each in front of his *own* house. ²⁹After them Zadok the son of Immer made repairs in front of his *own* house. After him Shemaiah the son of Shechaniah, the keeper of the East Gate, made repairs. ³⁰After him Hananiah the son of Shelemiah, and Hanun, the sixth son of Zalaph, repaired another section. After him Meshullam the son of Berechiah made repairs in front of his dwelling. ³¹After him Malchijah, one of the goldsmiths, made repairs as far as the house of the Nethinim and of the merchants, in front of the Miphkadᵃ Gate, and as far as the upper room at the corner. ³²And between the upper room at the corner, as far as the Sheep Gate, the goldsmiths and the merchants made repairs.

The Wall Defended Against Enemies

4 But it so happened, when Sanballat heard that we were rebuilding the wall, that he was furious and very indignant, and mocked the Jews. ²And he spoke before his brethren and the army of Samaria, and said, "What are these feeble Jews doing? Will they fortify themselves? Will they offer sacrifices? Will they complete it in a day? Will they revive the stones from the heaps of rubbish—*stones* that are burned?"

³Now Tobiah the Ammonite *was* beside him, and he said, "Whatever they build, if even a fox goes up *on it,* he will break down their stone wall."

⁴Hear, O our God, for we are despised; turn their reproach on their own heads, and give

---

3:16 ᵃSeptuagint, Syriac, and Vulgate read *tomb.*
3:18 ᵃFollowing Masoretic Text and Vulgate; some Hebrew manuscripts, Septuagint, and Syriac read *Binnui* (compare verse 24).   **3:20** ᵃA few Hebrew manuscripts, Syriac, and Vulgate read *Zaccai.*
3:21 ᵃOr *Hakkoz*   **3:31** ᵃLiterally *Inspection* or *Recruiting*

them as plunder to a land of captivity! ⁵Do not cover their iniquity, and do not let their sin be blotted out from before You; for they have provoked *You* to anger before the builders.

⁶So we built the wall, and the entire wall was joined together up to half its *height,* for the people had a mind to work.

⁷Now it happened, when Sanballat, Tobiah, the Arabs, the Ammonites, and the Ashdodites heard that the walls of Jerusalem were being restored and the gaps were beginning to be closed, that they became very angry, ⁸and all of them conspired together to come *and* attack Jerusalem and create confusion. ⁹Nevertheless we made our prayer to our God, and because of them we set a watch against them day and night.

¹⁰Then Judah said, "The strength of the laborers is failing, and *there is* so much rubbish that we are not able to build the wall."

¹¹And our adversaries said, "They will neither know nor see anything, till we come into their midst and kill them and cause the work to cease."

¹²So it was, when the Jews who dwelt near them came, that they told us ten times, "From whatever place you turn, *they will be* upon us."

¹³Therefore I positioned *men* behind the lower parts of the wall, at the openings; and I set the people according to their families, with their swords, their spears, and their bows. ¹⁴And I looked, and arose and said to the nobles, to the leaders, and to the rest of the people, "Do not be afraid of them. Remember the Lord, great and awesome, and fight for your brethren, your sons, your daughters, your wives, and your houses."

¹⁵And it happened, when our enemies heard that it was known to us, and *that* God had brought their plot to nothing, that all of us returned to the wall, everyone to his work. ¹⁶So it was, from that time on, *that* half of my servants worked at construction, while the other half held the spears, the shields, the bows, and *wore* armor; and the leaders *were* behind all the house of Judah. ¹⁷Those who built on the wall, and those who carried burdens, loaded themselves so that with one hand they worked at construction, and with the other held a weapon.

¹⁸Every one of the builders had his sword girded at his side as he built. And the one who sounded the trumpet *was* beside me.

¹⁹Then I said to the nobles, the rulers, and the rest of the people, "The work *is* great and extensive, and we are separated far from one another on the wall. ²⁰Wherever you hear the sound of the trumpet, rally to us there. Our God will fight for us."

²¹So we labored in the work, and half of *the men*ᵃ held the spears from daybreak until the stars appeared. ²²At the same time I also said to the people, "Let each man and his servant stay at night in Jerusalem, that they may be our guard by night and a working party by day." ²³So neither I, my brethren, my servants, nor the men of the guard who followed me took off our clothes, *except* that everyone took them off for washing.

Nehemiah Deals with Oppression

5 And there was a great outcry of the people and their wives against their Jewish brethren. ²For there were those who said, "We, our sons, and our daughters *are* many; therefore let us get grain, that we may eat and live."

³There were also *some* who said, "We have mortgaged our lands and vineyards and houses, that we might buy grain because of the famine."

⁴There were also those who said, "We have borrowed money for the king's tax *on* our lands and vineyards. ⁵Yet now our flesh *is* as the flesh of our brethren, our children as their children; and indeed we are forcing our sons and our daughters to be slaves, and *some* of our daughters have been brought into slavery. *It is* not in our power *to redeem them,* for other men have our lands and vineyards."

⁶And I became very angry when I heard their outcry and these words. ⁷After serious thought, I rebuked the nobles and rulers, and said to them, "Each of you is exacting usury from his brother." So I called a great assembly against them. ⁸And I said to them, "According to our ability we have redeemed our Jewish brethren who were sold to the

4:21 ᵃLiterally *them*

nations. Now indeed, will you even sell your brethren? Or should they be sold to us?"

Then they were silenced and found nothing *to say.* ⁹Then I said, "What you are doing *is* not good. Should you not walk in the fear of our God because of the reproach of the nations, our enemies? ¹⁰I also, *with* my brethren and my servants, am lending them money and grain. Please, let us stop this usury! ¹¹Restore now to them, even this day, their lands, their vineyards, their olive groves, and their houses, also a hundredth of the money and the grain, the new wine and the oil, that you have charged them."

¹²So they said, "We will restore *it,* and will require nothing from them; we will do as you say."

Then I called the priests, and required an oath from them that they would do according to this promise. ¹³Then I shook out the fold of my garmentª and said, "So may God shake out each man from his house, and from his property, who does not perform this promise. Even thus may he be shaken out and emptied."

And all the assembly said, "Amen!" and praised the Lord. Then the people did according to this promise.

The Generosity of Nehemiah

¹⁴Moreover, from the time that I was appointed to be their governor in the land of Judah, from the twentieth year until the thirty-second year of King Artaxerxes, twelve years, neither I nor my brothers ate the governor's provisions. ¹⁵But the former governors who *were* before me laid burdens on the people, and took from them bread and wine, besides forty shekels of silver. Yes, even their servants bore rule over the people, but I did not do so, because of the fear of God. ¹⁶Indeed, I also continued the work on this wall, and weª did not buy any land. All my servants *were* gathered there for the work.

¹⁷And at my table *were* one hundred and fifty Jews and rulers, besides those who came to us from the nations around us. ¹⁸Now *that* which was prepared daily *was* one ox *and* six choice sheep. Also fowl were prepared for me, and once every ten days an abundance of all kinds of wine. Yet in spite of this

I did not demand the governor's provisions, because the bondage was heavy on this people.

¹⁹Remember me, my God, for good, *according to* all that I have done for this people.

Conspiracy Against Nehemiah

6 Now it happened when Sanballat, Tobiah, Geshem the Arab, and the rest of our enemies heard that I had rebuilt the wall, and *that* there were no breaks left in it (though at that time I had not hung the doors in the gates), ²that Sanballat and Geshem sent to me, saying, "Come, let us meet together among the villages in the plain of Ono." But they thought to do me harm.

³So I sent messengers to them, saying, "I *am* doing a great work, so that I cannot come down. Why should the work cease while I leave it and go down to you?"

⁴But they sent me this message four times, and I answered them in the same manner.

⁵Then Sanballat sent his servant to me as before, the fifth time, with an open letter in his hand. ⁶In it *was* written:

It is reported among the nations, and Geshemª says, *that* you and the Jews plan to rebel; therefore, according to these rumors, you are rebuilding the wall, that you may be their king. ⁷And you have also appointed prophets to proclaim concerning you at Jerusalem, saying, "*There is* a king in Judah!" Now these matters will be reported to the king. So come, therefore, and let us consult together.

⁸Then I sent to him, saying, "No such things as you say are being done, but you invent them in your own heart."

⁹For they all *were trying to* make us afraid, saying, "Their hands will be weakened in the work, and it will not be done."

Now therefore, *O God,* strengthen my hands.

5:13 ªLiterally *my lap*   **5:16** ªFollowing Masoretic Text; Septuagint, Syriac, and Vulgate read *I.*
6:6 ªHebrew *Gashmu*

¹⁰Afterward I came to the house of Shemaiah the son of Delaiah, the son of Mehetabel, who *was* a secret informer; and he said, "Let us meet together in the house of God, within the temple, and let us close the doors of the temple, for they are coming to kill you; indeed, at night they will come to kill you." ¹¹And I said, "Should such a man as I flee? And who *is there* such as I who would go into the temple to save his life? I will not go in!" ¹²Then I perceived that God had not sent him at all, but that he pronounced *this* prophecy against me because Tobiah and Sanballat had hired him. ¹³For this reason he *was* hired, that I should be afraid and act that way and sin, so *that* they might have *cause* for an evil report, that they might reproach me.

¹⁴My God, remember Tobiah and Sanballat, according to these their works, and the prophetess Noadiah and the rest of the prophets who would have made me afraid.

The Wall Completed

¹⁵So the wall was finished on the twenty-fifth *day* of Elul, in fifty-two days. ¹⁶And it happened, when all our enemies heard *of it,* and all the nations around us saw *these things,* that they were very disheartened in their own eyes; for they perceived that this work was done by our God.

¹⁷Also in those days the nobles of Judah sent many letters to Tobiah, and *the letters of* Tobiah came to them. ¹⁸For many in Judah were pledged to him, because he was the son-in-law of Shechaniah the son of Arah, and his son Jehohanan had married the daughter of Meshullam the son of Berechiah. ¹⁹Also they reported his good deeds before me, and reported my words to him. Tobiah sent letters to frighten me.

7 Then it was, when the wall was built and I had hung the doors, when the gatekeepers, the singers, and the Levites had been appointed, ²that I gave the charge of Jerusalem to my brother Hanani, and Hananiah the leader of the citadel, for he *was* a faithful man and feared God more than many. ³And I said to them, "Do not let the gates of Jerusalem be opened until the sun is hot; and while they stand *guard,* let them shut and bar the doors; and appoint guards from among the inhabitants of Jerusalem, one at his watch station and another in front of his own house."

The Captives Who Returned to Jerusalem

⁴Now the city *was* large and spacious, but the people in it *were* few, and the houses *were* not rebuilt. ⁵Then my God put it into my heart to gather the nobles, the rulers, and the people, that they might be registered by genealogy. And I found a register of the genealogy of those who had come up in the first *return,* and found written in it:

6   Theseᵃ *are* the people of the province who came back from the captivity, of those who had been carried away, whom Nebuchadnezzar the king of Babylon had carried away, and who returned to Jerusalem and Judah, everyone to his city.

7   Those who came with Zerubbabel *were* Jeshua, Nehemiah, Azariah, Raamiah, Nahamani, Mordecai, Bilshan, Mispereth,ᵃ Bigvai, Nehum, and Baanah.

The number of the men of the people of Israel: ⁸the sons of Parosh, two thousand one hundred and seventy-two;

⁹the sons of Shephatiah, three hundred and seventy-two;

¹⁰the sons of Arah, six hundred and fifty-two;

¹¹the sons of Pahath-Moab, of the sons of Jeshua and Joab, two thousand eight hundred and eighteen;

¹²the sons of Elam, one thousand two hundred and fifty-four;

¹³the sons of Zattu, eight hundred and forty-five;

¹⁴the sons of Zaccai, seven hundred and sixty;

¹⁵the sons of Binnui,ᵃ six hundred and forty-eight;

7:6 ᵃCompare verses 6–72 with Ezra 2:1–70
7:7 ᵃSpelled *Mispar* in Ezra 2:2   **7:15** ᵃSpelled *Bani* in Ezra 2:10

¹⁶the sons of Bebai, six hundred and twenty-eight;
¹⁷the sons of Azgad, two thousand three hundred and twenty-two;
¹⁸the sons of Adonikam, six hundred and sixty-seven;
¹⁹the sons of Bigvai, two thousand and sixty-seven;
²⁰the sons of Adin, six hundred and fifty-five;
²¹the sons of Ater of Hezekiah, ninety-eight;
²²the sons of Hashum, three hundred and twenty-eight;
²³the sons of Bezai, three hundred and twenty-four;
²⁴the sons of Hariph,^a one hundred and twelve;
²⁵the sons of Gibeon,^a ninety-five;
²⁶the men of Bethlehem and Netophah, one hundred and eighty-eight;
²⁷the men of Anathoth, one hundred and twenty-eight;
²⁸the men of Beth Azmaveth,^a forty-two;
²⁹the men of Kirjath Jearim, Chephirah, and Beeroth, seven hundred and forty-three;
³⁰the men of Ramah and Geba, six hundred and twenty-one;
³¹the men of Michmas, one hundred and twenty-two;
³²the men of Bethel and Ai, one hundred and twenty-three;
³³the men of the other Nebo, fifty-two;
³⁴the sons of the other Elam, one thousand two hundred and fifty-four;
³⁵the sons of Harim, three hundred and twenty;
³⁶the sons of Jericho, three hundred and forty-five;
³⁷the sons of Lod, Hadid, and Ono, seven hundred and twenty-one;
³⁸the sons of Senaah, three thousand nine hundred and thirty.

³⁹ The priests: the sons of Jedaiah, of the house of Jeshua, nine hundred and seventy-three;
⁴⁰the sons of Immer, one thousand and fifty-two;

⁴¹the sons of Pashhur, one thousand two hundred and forty-seven;
⁴²the sons of Harim, one thousand and seventeen.

⁴³ The Levites: the sons of Jeshua, of Kadmiel, *and* of the sons of Hodevah,^a seventy-four.

⁴⁴ The singers: the sons of Asaph, one hundred and forty-eight.

⁴⁵ The gatekeepers: the sons of Shallum, the sons of Ater, the sons of Talmon, the sons of Akkub, the sons of Hatita, the sons of Shobai, one hundred and thirty-eight.

⁴⁶ The Nethinim: the sons of Ziha, the sons of Hasupha, the sons of Tabbaoth, ⁴⁷the sons of Keros, the sons of Sia,^a the sons of Padon, ⁴⁸the sons of Lebana,^a the sons of Hagaba,^b the sons of Salmai,^c ⁴⁹the sons of Hanan, the sons of Giddel, the sons of Gahar, ⁵⁰the sons of Reaiah, the sons of Rezin, the sons of Nekoda, ⁵¹the sons of Gazzam, the sons of Uzza, the sons of Paseah, ⁵²the sons of Besai, the sons of Meunim, the sons of Nephishesim,^a ⁵³the sons of Bakbuk, the sons of Hakupha, the sons of Harhur, ⁵⁴the sons of Bazlith,^a

---

7:24 ^aCalled *Jorah* in Ezra 2:18　　**7:25** ^aCalled *Gibbar* in Ezra 2:20　　**7:28** ^aCalled *Azmaveth* in Ezra 2:24　　**7:43** ^aSpelled *Hodaviah* in Ezra 2:40　　**7:47** ^aSpelled *Siaha* in Ezra 2:44　　**7:48** ^aMasoretic Text reads *Lebanah.* ^bMasoretic Text reads *Hogabah.* ^cOr *Shalmai,* or *Shamlai*　　**7:52** ^aSpelled *Nephusim* in Ezra 2:50　　**7:54** ^aSpelled *Bazluth* in Ezra 2:52

the sons of Mehida,
the sons of Harsha,
⁵⁵the sons of Barkos,
the sons of Sisera,
the sons of Tamah,
⁵⁶the sons of Neziah,
and the sons of Hatipha.

⁵⁷ The sons of Solomon's servants: the
sons of Sotai,
the sons of Sophereth,
the sons of Perida,ᵃ
⁵⁸the sons of Jaala,
the sons of Darkon,
the sons of Giddel,
⁵⁹the sons of Shephatiah,
the sons of Hattil,
the sons of Pochereth of Zebaim,
and the sons of Amon.ᵃ
⁶⁰All the Nethinim, and the sons
of Solomon's servants, *were* three
hundred and ninety-two.

⁶¹ And these *were* the ones who came up
from Tel Melah, Tel Harsha, Cherub,
Addon,ᵃ and Immer, but they could
not identify their father's house nor
their lineage, whether they *were* of
Israel: ⁶²the sons of Delaiah,
the sons of Tobiah,
the sons of Nekoda, six hundred and
forty-two;
⁶³and of the priests: the sons of
Habaiah,
the sons of Koz,ᵃ
the sons of Barzillai, who took a wife
of the daughters of Barzillai the
Gileadite, and was called by their
name.
⁶⁴These sought their listing *among*
those who were registered by
genealogy, but it was not found;
therefore they were excluded from the
priesthood as defiled. ⁶⁵And the
governorᵃ said to them that they
should not eat of the most holy things
till a priest could consult with the
Urim and Thummim.

⁶⁶ Altogether the whole assembly *was*
forty-two thousand three hundred and
sixty, ⁶⁷besides their male and female

servants, of whom *there were* seven
thousand three hundred and thirty-
seven; and they had two hundred and
forty-five men and women singers.
⁶⁸Their horses were seven hundred and
thirty-six, their mules two hundred
and forty-five, ⁶⁹*their* camels four
hundred and thirty-five, *and* donkeys
six thousand seven hundred and
twenty.

⁷⁰ And some of the heads of the fathers'
houses gave to the work. The governorᵃ
gave to the treasury one thousand
gold drachmas, fifty basins, and five
hundred and thirty priestly garments.
⁷¹Some of the heads of the fathers'
houses gave to the treasury of the work
twenty thousand gold drachmas, and
two thousand two hundred silver
minas. ⁷²And that which the rest of the
people gave *was* twenty thousand gold
drachmas, two thousand silver minas,
and sixty-seven priestly garments.

⁷³So the priests, the Levites, the gatekeepers, the singers, *some* of the people, the
Nethinim, and all Israel dwelt in their cities.

Ezra Reads the Law

When the seventh month came, the children of Israel *were* in their cities.

8 Now all the people gathered together as
one man in the open square that *was* in
front of the Water Gate; and they told Ezra
the scribe to bring the Book of the Law of
Moses, which the LORD had commanded
Israel. ²So Ezra the priest brought the Law
before the assembly of men and women and
all who *could* hear with understanding on
the first day of the seventh month. ³Then he
read from it in the open square that *was* in
front of the Water Gate from morning until
midday, before the men and women and
those who could understand; and the ears
of all the people *were attentive* to the Book of
the Law.

7:57 ᵃSpelled *Peruda* in Ezra 2:55   **7:59** ᵃSpelled
Ami in Ezra 2:57   **7:61** ᵃSpelled *Addan* in Ezra 2:59
7:63 ᵃOr *Hakkoz*   **7:65** ᵃHebrew *Tirshatha*
7:70 ᵃHebrew *Tirshatha*

[4]So Ezra the scribe stood on a platform of wood which they had made for the purpose; and beside him, at his right hand, stood Mattithiah, Shema, Anaiah, Urijah, Hilkiah, and Maaseiah; and at his left hand Pedaiah, Mishael, Malchijah, Hashum, Hashbadana, Zechariah, *and* Meshullam. [5]And Ezra opened the book in the sight of all the people, for he was *standing* above all the people; and when he opened it, all the people stood up. [6]And Ezra blessed the LORD, the great God.

Then all the people answered, "Amen, Amen!" while lifting up their hands. And they bowed their heads and worshiped the LORD with *their* faces to the ground.

[7]Also Jeshua, Bani, Sherebiah, Jamin, Akkub, Shabbethai, Hodijah, Maaseiah, Kelita, Azariah, Jozabad, Hanan, Pelaiah, and the Levites, helped the people to understand the Law; and the people *stood* in their place. [8]So they read distinctly from the book, in the Law of God; and they gave the sense, and helped *them* to understand the reading.

[9]And Nehemiah, who *was* the governor,[a] Ezra the priest *and* scribe, and the Levites who taught the people said to all the people, "This day *is* holy to the LORD your God; do not mourn nor weep." For all the people wept, when they heard the words of the Law.

[10]Then he said to them, "Go your way, eat the fat, drink the sweet, and send portions to those for whom nothing is prepared; for *this* day *is* holy to our Lord. Do not sorrow, for the joy of the LORD is your strength."

[11]So the Levites quieted all the people, saying, "Be still, for the day *is* holy; do not be grieved." [12]And all the people went their way to eat and drink, to send portions and rejoice greatly, because they understood the words that were declared to them.

The Feast of Tabernacles

[13]Now on the second day the heads of the fathers' *houses* of all the people, with the priests and Levites, were gathered to Ezra the scribe, in order to understand the words of the Law. [14]And they found written in the Law, which the LORD had commanded by Moses, that the children of Israel should dwell in booths during the feast of the seventh month, [15]and that they should

announce and proclaim in all their cities and in Jerusalem, saying, "Go out to the mountain, and bring olive branches, branches of oil trees, myrtle branches, palm branches, and branches of leafy trees, to make booths, as *it is* written."

[16]Then the people went out and brought *them* and made themselves booths, each one on the roof of his house, or in their courtyards or the courts of the house of God, and in the open square of the Water Gate and in the open square of the Gate of Ephraim. [17]So the whole assembly of those who had returned from the captivity made booths and sat under the booths; for since the days of Joshua the son of Nun until that day the children of Israel had not done so. And there was very great gladness. [18]Also day by day, from the first day until the last day, he read from the Book of the Law of God. And they kept the feast seven days; and on the eighth day *there was* a sacred assembly, according to the *prescribed* manner.

FAMILY VALUES

And there was very great gladness.

NEHEMIAH 8:17

Celebrating the Fourth of July

Erma Bombeck, one of America's most popular humorists in the second half of the twentieth century, wrote:

> *You have to love a nation that celebrates its independence every July 4, not with a parade of guns, tanks, and soldiers who file by the White House in a show of strength and muscle, but with family picnics where kids throw Frisbees, the potato salad gets "iffy," and the flies die from happiness. You may think you have overeaten, but it is patriotism.*

The People Confess Their Sins

9 Now on the twenty-fourth day of this month the children of Israel were assembled with fasting, in sackcloth, and with dust on their heads.[a] [2]Then those of Israelite lineage separated themselves from all

---

8:9 [a]Hebrew *Tirshatha*   **9:1** [a]Literally *earth on them*

foreigners; and they stood and confessed their sins and the iniquities of their fathers. ³And they stood up in their place and read from the Book of the Law of the LORD their God *for one*-fourth of the day; and *for another* fourth they confessed and worshiped the LORD their God.

⁴Then Jeshua, Bani, Kadmiel, Shebaniah, Bunni, Sherebiah, Bani, *and* Chenani stood on the stairs of the Levites and cried out with a loud voice to the LORD their God. ⁵And the Levites, Jeshua, Kadmiel, Bani, Hashabniah, Sherebiah, Hodijah, Shebaniah, *and* Pethahiah, said:

"Stand up *and* bless the LORD your God
Forever and ever!

"Blessed be Your glorious name,
  Which is exalted above all blessing
    and praise!
6 You alone *are* the LORD;
  You have made heaven,
  The heaven of heavens, with all their
    host,
  The earth and everything on it,
  The seas and all that is in them,
  And You preserve them all.
  The host of heaven worships You.

7 "You *are* the LORD God,
  Who chose Abram,
  And brought him out of Ur of the
    Chaldeans,
  And gave him the name Abraham;
8 You found his heart faithful before You,
  And made a covenant with him
  To give the land of the Canaanites,
  The Hittites, the Amorites,
  The Perizzites, the Jebusites,
  And the Girgashites—
  To give *it* to his descendants.
  You have performed Your words,
  For You *are* righteous.

9 "You saw the affliction of our fathers
    in Egypt,
  And heard their cry by the Red Sea.
10 You showed signs and wonders
    against Pharaoh,
  Against all his servants,
  And against all the people of his land.

For You knew that they acted proudly
  against them.
So You made a name for Yourself, as
  it is this day.
11 And You divided the sea before them,
  So that they went through the midst
    of the sea on the dry land;
  And their persecutors You threw into
    the deep,
  As a stone into the mighty waters.
12 Moreover You led them by day with
    a cloudy pillar,
  And by night with a pillar of fire,
  To give them light on the road
  Which they should travel.

13 "You came down also on Mount Sinai,
  And spoke with them from heaven,
  And gave them just ordinances and
    true laws,
  Good statutes and commandments.
14 You made known to them Your holy
    Sabbath,
  And commanded them precepts,
    statutes and laws,
  By the hand of Moses Your servant.
15 You gave them bread from heaven
    for their hunger,
  And brought them water out of the
    rock for their thirst,
  And told them to go in to possess the
    land
  Which You had sworn to give them.

16 "But they and our fathers acted
    proudly,
  Hardened their necks,
  And did not heed Your
    commandments.
17 They refused to obey,
  And they were not mindful of Your
    wonders
  That You did among them.
  But they hardened their necks,
  And in their rebellion[a]
  They appointed a leader
  To return to their bondage.
  But You *are* God,
  Ready to pardon,

9:17 [a]Following Masoretic Text and Vulgate; Septuagint reads *in Egypt*.

Gracious and merciful,
Slow to anger,
Abundant in kindness,
And did not forsake them.

18 "Even when they made a molded calf
   for themselves,
And said, 'This *is* your god
That brought you up out of Egypt,'
And worked great provocations,

19 Yet in Your manifold mercies
You did not forsake them in the
   wilderness.
The pillar of the cloud did not depart
   from them by day,
To lead them on the road;
Nor the pillar of fire by night,
To show them light,
And the way they should go.

20 You also gave Your good Spirit to
   instruct them,
And did not withhold Your manna
   from their mouth,
And gave them water for their thirst.

21 Forty years You sustained them in the
   wilderness;
They lacked nothing;
Their clothes did not wear out[a]
And their feet did not swell.

22 "Moreover You gave them kingdoms
   and nations,
And divided them into districts.[a]
So they took possession of the land of
   Sihon,
The land of[b] the king of Heshbon,
And the land of Og king of Bashan.

23 You also multiplied their children as
   the stars of heaven,
And brought them into the land
Which You had told their fathers
To go in and possess.

24 So the people went in
And possessed the land;
You subdued before them the
   inhabitants of the land,
The Canaanites,
And gave them into their hands,
With their kings
And the people of the land,
That they might do with them as they
   wished.

25 And they took strong cities and a rich
   land,
And possessed houses full of all goods,
Cisterns *already* dug, vineyards, olive
   groves,
And fruit trees in abundance.
So they ate and were filled and grew
   fat,
And delighted themselves in Your
   great goodness.

26 "Nevertheless they were disobedient
And rebelled against You,
Cast Your law behind their backs
And killed Your prophets, who testified
   against them
To turn them to Yourself;
And they worked great provocations.

27 Therefore You delivered them into the
   hand of their enemies,
Who oppressed them;
And in the time of their trouble,
When they cried to You,
You heard from heaven;
And according to Your abundant
   mercies
You gave them deliverers who saved
   them
From the hand of their enemies.

28 "But after they had rest,
They again did evil before You.
Therefore You left them in the hand of
   their enemies,
So that they had dominion over them;
Yet when they returned and cried out
   to You,
You heard from heaven;
And many times You delivered them
   according to Your mercies,

29 And testified against them,
That You might bring them back to
   Your law.
Yet they acted proudly,
And did not heed Your commandments,
But sinned against Your judgments,
' Which if a man does, he shall live by
   them.'[a]

9:21 [a]Compare Deuteronomy 29:5   **9:22** [a]Literally
corners [b]Following Masoretic Text and Vulgate;
Septuagint omits *The land of.*   **9:29** [a]Leviticus 18:5

And they shrugged their shoulders,
Stiffened their necks,
And would not hear.
30 Yet for many years You had patience
 with them,
And testified against them by Your
 Spirit in Your prophets.
Yet they would not listen;
Therefore You gave them into the
 hand of the peoples of the lands.
31 Nevertheless in Your great mercy
You did not utterly consume them
 nor forsake them;
For You *are* God, gracious and
 merciful.

32 "Now therefore, our God,
The great, the mighty, and awesome
 God,
Who keeps covenant and mercy:
Do not let all the trouble seem small
 before You
That has come upon us,
Our kings and our princes,
Our priests and our prophets,
Our fathers and on all Your people,
From the days of the kings of Assyria
 until this day.
33 However, You *are* just in all that has
 befallen us;
For You have dealt faithfully,
But we have done wickedly.
34 Neither our kings nor our princes,
Our priests nor our fathers,
Have kept Your law,
Nor heeded Your commandments and
 Your testimonies,
With which You testified against them.
35 For they have not served You in their
 kingdom,
Or in the many good *things* that You
 gave them,
Or in the large and rich land which
 You set before them;
Nor did they turn from their wicked
 works.

36 "Here we *are,* servants today!
And the land that You gave to our
 fathers,
To eat its fruit and its bounty,
Here we *are,* servants in it!

37 And it yields much increase to the
 kings
You have set over us,
Because of our sins;
Also they have dominion over our
 bodies and our cattle
At their pleasure;
And we *are* in great distress.

38 "And because of all this,
We make a sure *covenant* and write *it;*
Our leaders, our Levites, *and* our
 priests seal *it.*"

The People Who Sealed the Covenant

10 Now those who placed *their* seal on *the document were:*
Nehemiah the governor, the son of Hacaliah, and Zedekiah, [2]Seraiah, Azariah, Jeremiah, [3]Pashhur, Amariah, Malchijah, [4]Hattush, Shebaniah, Malluch, [5]Harim, Meremoth, Obadiah, [6]Daniel, Ginnethon, Baruch, [7]Meshullam, Abijah, Mijamin, [8]Maaziah, Bilgai, and Shemaiah. These were the priests.

[9]The Levites: Jeshua the son of Azaniah, Binnui of the sons of Henadad, *and* Kadmiel.

[10]Their brethren: Shebaniah, Hodijah, Kelita, Pelaiah, Hanan, [11]Micha, Rehob, Hashabiah, [12]Zaccur, Sherebiah, Shebaniah, [13]Hodijah, Bani, *and* Beninu.

[14]The leaders of the people: Parosh, Pahath-Moab, Elam, Zattu, Bani, [15]Bunni, Azgad, Bebai, [16]Adonijah, Bigvai, Adin, [17]Ater, Hezekiah, Azzur, [18]Hodijah, Hashum, Bezai, [19]Hariph, Anathoth, Nebai, [20]Magpiash, Meshullam, Hezir, [21]Meshezabel, Zadok, Jaddua, [22]Pelatiah, Hanan, Anaiah, [23]Hoshea, Hananiah, Hasshub, [24]Hallohesh, Pilha, Shobek, [25]Rehum, Hashabnah, Maaseiah, [26]Ahijah, Hanan, Anan, [27]Malluch, Harim, *and* Baanah.

The Covenant That Was Sealed

[28]Now the rest of the people—the priests, the Levites, the gatekeepers, the singers, the Nethinim, and all those who had separated themselves from the peoples of the lands to the Law of God, their wives, their sons, and their daughters, everyone who had knowledge and understanding— [29]these joined

with their brethren, their nobles, and entered into a curse and an oath to walk in God's Law, which was given by Moses the servant of God, and to observe and do all the commandments of the LORD our Lord, and His ordinances and His statutes: 30We would not give our daughters as wives to the peoples of the land, nor take their daughters for our sons; 31if the peoples of the land brought wares or any grain to sell on the Sabbath day, we would not buy it from them on the Sabbath, or on a holy day; and we would forego the seventh year's *produce* and the exacting of every debt.

32Also we made ordinances for ourselves, to exact from ourselves yearly one-third of a shekel for the service of the house of our God: 33for the showbread, for the regular grain offering, for the regular burnt offering of the Sabbaths, the New Moons, and the set feasts; for the holy things, for the sin offerings to make atonement for Israel, and all the work of the house of our God. 34We cast lots among the priests, the Levites, and the people, for bringing the wood offering into the house of our God, according to our fathers' houses, at the appointed times year by year, to burn on the altar of the LORD our God as *it is* written in the Law.

35And *we made ordinances* to bring the firstfruits of our ground and the firstfruits of all fruit of all trees, year by year, to the house of the LORD; 36to bring the firstborn of our sons and our cattle, as *it is* written in the Law, and the firstborn of our herds and our flocks, to the house of our God, to the priests who minister in the house of our God; 37to bring the firstfruits of our dough, our offerings, the fruit from all kinds of trees, *the* new wine and oil, to the priests, to the storerooms of the house of our God; and to bring the tithes of our land to the Levites, for the Levites should receive the tithes in all our farming communities. 38And the priest, the descendant of Aaron, shall be with the Levites when the Levites receive tithes; and the Levites shall bring up a tenth of the tithes to the house of our God, to the rooms of the storehouse.

39For the children of Israel and the children of Levi shall bring the offering of the grain, of the new wine and the oil, to the storerooms where the articles of the sanctuary *are, where* the priests who minister and the gatekeepers and the singers *are;* and we will not neglect the house of our God.

The People Dwelling in Jerusalem

11 Now the leaders of the people dwelt at Jerusalem; the rest of the people cast lots to bring one out of ten to dwell in Jerusalem, the holy city, and nine-tenths *were to dwell* in *other* cities. 2And the people blessed all the men who willingly offered themselves to dwell at Jerusalem.

3These *are* the heads of the province who dwelt in Jerusalem. (But in the cities of Judah everyone dwelt in his own possession in their cities—Israelites, priests, Levites, Nethinim, and descendants of Solomon's servants.) 4Also in Jerusalem dwelt *some* of the children of Judah and of the children of Benjamin.

The children of Judah: Athaiah the son of Uzziah, the son of Zechariah, the son of Amariah, the son of Shephatiah, the son of Mahalalel, of the children of Perez; 5and Maaseiah the son of Baruch, the son of Col-Hozeh, the son of Hazaiah, the son of Adaiah, the son of Joiarib, the son of Zechariah, the son of Shiloni. 6All the sons of Perez who dwelt at Jerusalem *were* four hundred and sixty-eight valiant men.

7And these are the sons of Benjamin: Sallu the son of Meshullam, the son of Joed, the son of Pedaiah, the son of Kolaiah, the son of Maaseiah, the son of Ithiel, the son of Jeshaiah; 8and after him Gabbai *and* Sallai, nine hundred and twenty-eight. 9Joel the son of Zichri *was* their overseer, and Judah the son of Senuah[a] *was* second over the city.

10Of the priests: Jedaiah the son of Joiarib, and Jachin; 11Seraiah the son of Hilkiah, the son of Meshullam, the son of Zadok, the son of Meraioth, the son of Ahitub, *was* the leader of the house of God. 12Their brethren who did the work of the house *were* eight hundred and twenty-two; and Adaiah the son of Jeroham, the son of Pelaliah, the son of Amzi, the son of Zechariah, the son of Pashhur, the son of Malchijah, 13and his

---

11:9 aOr *Hassenuah*

brethren, heads of the fathers' *houses, were* two hundred and forty-two; and Amashai the son of Azarel, the son of Ahzai, the son of Meshillemoth, the son of Immer, [14]and their brethren, mighty men of valor, *were* one hundred and twenty-eight. Their overseer *was* Zabdiel the son of *one of* the great men.[a]

[15]Also of the Levites: Shemaiah the son of Hasshub, the son of Azrikam, the son of Hashabiah, the son of Bunni; [16]Shabbethai and Jozabad, of the heads of the Levites, *had* the oversight of the business outside of the house of God; [17]Mattaniah the son of Micha,[a] the son of Zabdi, the son of Asaph, the leader *who* began the thanksgiving with prayer; Bakbukiah, the second among his brethren; and Abda the son of Shammua, the son of Galal, the son of Jeduthun. [18]All the Levites in the holy city *were* two hundred and eighty-four.

[19]Moreover the gatekeepers, Akkub, Talmon, and their brethren who kept the gates, *were* one hundred and seventy-two.

[20]And the rest of Israel, of the priests *and* Levites, *were* in all the cities of Judah, everyone in his inheritance. [21]But the Nethinim dwelt in Ophel. And Ziha and Gishpa *were* over the Nethinim.

[22]Also the overseer of the Levites at Jerusalem *was* Uzzi the son of Bani, the son of Hashabiah, the son of Mattaniah, the son of Micha, of the sons of Asaph, the singers in charge of the service of the house of God. [23]For *it was* the king's command concerning them that a certain portion should be for the singers, a quota day by day. [24]Pethahiah the son of Meshezabel, of the children of Zerah the son of Judah, *was* the king's deputy[a] in all matters concerning the people.

The People Dwelling Outside Jerusalem

[25]And as for the villages with their fields, *some* of the children of Judah dwelt in Kirjath Arba and its villages, Dibon and its villages, Jekabzeel and its villages; [26]in Jeshua, Moladah, Beth Pelet, [27]Hazar Shual, and Beersheba and its villages; [28]in Ziklag and Meconah and its villages; [29]in En Rimmon, Zorah, Jarmuth, [30]Zanoah, Adullam, and their villages; in Lachish and its fields;

in Azekah and its villages. They dwelt from Beersheba to the Valley of Hinnom.

[31]Also the children of Benjamin from Geba *dwelt in* Michmash, Aija, and Bethel, and their villages; [32]in Anathoth, Nob, Ananiah; [33]in Hazor, Ramah, Gittaim; [34]in Hadid, Zeboim, Neballat; [35]in Lod, Ono, *and* the Valley of Craftsmen. [36]Some of the Judean divisions of Levites *were* in Benjamin.

The Priests and Levites

12 Now these *are* the priests and the Levites who came up with Zerubbabel the son of Shealtiel, and Jeshua: Seraiah, Jeremiah, Ezra, [2]Amariah, Malluch, Hattush, [3]Shechaniah, Rehum, Meremoth, [4]Iddo, Ginnethoi,[a] Abijah, [5]Mijamin, Maadiah, Bilgah, [6]Shemaiah, Joiarib, Jedaiah, [7]Sallu, Amok, Hilkiah, *and* Jedaiah.

These *were* the heads of the priests and their brethren in the days of Jeshua.

[8]Moreover the Levites *were* Jeshua, Binnui, Kadmiel, Sherebiah, Judah, *and* Mattaniah *who led* the thanksgiving *psalms,* he and his brethren. [9]Also Bakbukiah and Unni, their brethren, *stood* across from them in *their* duties.

[10]Jeshua begot Joiakim, Joiakim begot Eliashib, Eliashib begot Joiada, [11]Joiada begot Jonathan, and Jonathan begot Jaddua.

[12]Now in the days of Joiakim, the priests, the heads of the fathers' *houses were:* of Seraiah, Meraiah; of Jeremiah, Hananiah; [13]of Ezra, Meshullam; of Amariah, Jehohanan; [14]of Melichu,[a] Jonathan; of Shebaniah,[b] Joseph; [15]of Harim,[a] Adna; of Meraioth,[b] Helkai; [16]of Iddo, Zechariah; of Ginnethon, Meshullam; [17]of Abijah, Zichri; *the son* of Minjamin;[a] of Moadiah,[b] Piltai; [18]of Bilgah, Shammua; of Shemaiah, Jehonathan; [19]of Joiarib, Mattenai; of Jedaiah, Uzzi; [20]of Sallai,[a] Kallai; of Amok, Eber; [21]of Hilkiah, Hashabiah; *and* of Jedaiah, Nethanel.

11:14 [a]Or *the son of Haggedolim*   **11:17** [a]Or *Michah*
11:24 [a]Literally *at the king's hand*   **12:4** [a]Or
Ginnethon (compare verse 16)   **12:14** [a]Or *Malluch*
(compare verse 2) [b]Or *Shechaniah* (compare verse 3)
12:15 [a]Or *Rehum* (compare verse 3) [b]Or *Meremoth*
(compare verse 3)   **12:17** [a]Or *Mijamin* (compare
verse 5) [b]Or *Maadiah* (compare verse 5)
12:20 [a]Or *Sallu* (compare verse 7)

²²During the reign of Darius the Persian, a record *was also kept* of the Levites and priests *who had been* heads of their fathers' *houses* in the days of Eliashib, Joiada, Johanan, and Jaddua. ²³The sons of Levi, the heads of the fathers' *houses* until the days of Johanan the son of Eliashib, *were* written in the book of the chronicles.

²⁴And the heads of the Levites *were* Hashabiah, Sherebiah, and Jeshua the son of Kadmiel, with their brothers across from them, to praise *and* give thanks, group alternating with group, according to the command of David the man of God. ²⁵Mattaniah, Bakbukiah, Obadiah, Meshullam, Talmon, and Akkub *were* gatekeepers keeping the watch at the storerooms of the gates. ²⁶These *lived* in the days of Joiakim the son of Jeshua, the son of Jozadak,ᵃ and in the days of Nehemiah the governor, and of Ezra the priest, the scribe.

HUMILITY

. . . to celebrate the dedication with gladness. . . .
NEHEMIAH 12:27

Early Settlements in America

In 1564, Rene de Laudonniere led a group of Huguenots (Protestants from France) to colonize and build Fort Caroline near present-day Jacksonville. He recorded on June 30, 1564:

We sang a psalm of thanksgiving unto God, beseeching Him that it would please Him to continue His accustomed goodness toward us.

Nehemiah Dedicates the Wall

²⁷Now at the dedication of the wall of Jerusalem they sought out the Levites in all their places, to bring them to Jerusalem to celebrate the dedication with gladness, both with thanksgivings and singing, *with* cymbals and stringed instruments and harps. ²⁸And the sons of the singers gathered together from the countryside around Jerusalem, from the villages of the Netophathites, ²⁹from the house of Gilgal, and from the fields of Geba and Azmaveth; for the singers had built themselves villages all around Jerusalem. ³⁰Then the priests and Levites purified themselves, and purified the people, the gates, and the wall.

³¹So I brought the leaders of Judah up on the wall, and appointed two large thanksgiving choirs. *One* went to the right hand on the wall toward the Refuse Gate. ³²After them went Hoshaiah and half of the leaders of Judah, ³³and Azariah, Ezra, Meshullam, ³⁴Judah, Benjamin, Shemaiah, Jeremiah, ³⁵and some of the priests' sons with trumpets—Zechariah the son of Jonathan, the son of Shemaiah, the son of Mattaniah, the son of Michaiah, the son of Zaccur, the son of Asaph, ³⁶and his brethren, Shemaiah, Azarel, Milalai, Gilalai, Maai, Nethanel, Judah, *and* Hanani, with the musical instruments of David the man of God. And Ezra the scribe *went* before them. ³⁷By the Fountain Gate, in front of them, they went up the stairs of the City of David, on the stairway of the wall, beyond the house of David, as far as the Water Gate eastward.

³⁸The other thanksgiving choir went the opposite *way,* and I *was* behind them with half of the people on the wall, going past the Tower of the Ovens as far as the Broad Wall, ³⁹and above the Gate of Ephraim, above the Old Gate, above the Fish Gate, the Tower of Hananel, the Tower of the Hundred, as far as the Sheep Gate; and they stopped by the Gate of the Prison.

⁴⁰So the two thanksgiving choirs stood in the house of God, likewise I and the half of the rulers with me; ⁴¹and the priests, Eliakim, Maaseiah, Minjamin,ᵃ Michaiah, Elioenai, Zechariah, *and* Hananiah, with trumpets; ⁴²also Maaseiah, Shemaiah, Eleazar, Uzzi, Jehohanan, Malchijah, Elam, and Ezer. The singers sang loudly with Jezrahiah the director.

⁴³Also that day they offered great sacrifices, and rejoiced, for God had made them rejoice with great joy; the women and the children also rejoiced, so that the joy of Jerusalem was heard afar off.

Temple Responsibilities

⁴⁴And at the same time some were appointed over the rooms of the storehouse

---

12:26 ᵃSpelled *Jehozadak* in 1 Chronicles 6:14
12:41 ᵃOr *Mijamin* (compare verse 5)

for the offerings, the firstfruits, and the tithes, to gather into them from the fields of the cities the portions specified by the Law for the priests and Levites; for Judah rejoiced over the priests and Levites who ministered. 45Both the singers and the gatekeepers kept the charge of their God and the charge of the purification, according to the command of David *and* Solomon his son. 46For in the days of David and Asaph of old *there were* chiefs of the singers, and songs of praise and thanksgiving to God. 47In the days of Zerubbabel and in the days of Nehemiah all Israel gave the portions for the singers and the gatekeepers, a portion for each day. They also consecrated *holy things* for the Levites, and the Levites consecrated *them* for the children of Aaron.

Principles of Separation

13 On that day they read from the Book of Moses in the hearing of the people, and in it was found written that no Ammonite or Moabite should ever come into the assembly of God, 2because they had not met the children of Israel with bread and water, but hired Balaam against them to curse them. However, our God turned the curse into a blessing. 3So it was, when they had heard the Law, that they separated all the mixed multitude from Israel.

The Reforms of Nehemiah

4Now before this, Eliashib the priest, having authority over the storerooms of the house of our God, *was* allied with Tobiah. 5And he had prepared for him a large room, where previously they had stored the grain offerings, the frankincense, the articles, the tithes of grain, the new wine and oil, which were commanded *to be given* to the Levites and singers and gatekeepers, and the offerings for the priests. 6But during all this I was not in Jerusalem, for in the thirty-second year of Artaxerxes king of Babylon I had returned to the king. Then after certain days I obtained leave from the king, 7and I came to Jerusalem and discovered the evil that Eliashib had done for Tobiah, in preparing a room for him in the courts of the house of God. 8And it grieved me bitterly; therefore I threw all the household goods of

Tobiah out of the room. 9Then I commanded them to cleanse the rooms; and I brought back into them the articles of the house of God, with the grain offering and the frankincense.

10I also realized that the portions for the Levites had not been given *them;* for each of the Levites and the singers who did the work had gone back to his field. 11So I contended with the rulers, and said, "Why is the house of God forsaken?" And I gathered them together and set them in their place. 12Then all Judah brought the tithe of the grain and the new wine and the oil to the storehouse. 13And I appointed as treasurers over the storehouse Shelemiah the priest and Zadok the scribe, and of the Levites, Pedaiah; and next to them *was* Hanan the son of Zaccur, the son of Mattaniah; for they were considered faithful, and their task *was* to distribute to their brethren.

14Remember me, O my God, concerning this, and do not wipe out my good deeds that I have done for the house of my God, and for its services!

15In those days I saw *people* in Judah treading wine presses on the Sabbath, and bringing in sheaves, and loading donkeys with wine, grapes, figs, and all *kinds of* burdens, which they brought into Jerusalem on the Sabbath day. And I warned *them* about the day on which they were selling provisions. 16Men of Tyre dwelt there also, who brought in fish and all kinds of goods, and sold *them* on the Sabbath to the children of Judah, and in Jerusalem.

17Then I contended with the nobles of Judah, and said to them, "What evil thing *is* this that you do, by which you profane the Sabbath day? 18Did not your fathers do thus, and did not our God bring all this disaster on us and on this city? Yet you bring added wrath on Israel by profaning the Sabbath."

19So it was, at the gates of Jerusalem, as it began to be dark before the Sabbath, that I commanded the gates to be shut, and charged that they must not be opened till after the Sabbath. Then I posted *some* of my servants at the gates, *so that* no burdens would be brought in on the Sabbath day. 20Now the merchants and sellers of all kinds

of wares lodged outside Jerusalem once or twice. ²¹Then I warned them, and said to them, "Why do you spend the night around the wall? If you do *so* again, I will lay hands on you!" From that time on they came no *more* on the Sabbath. ²²And I commanded the Levites that they should cleanse themselves, and that they should go and guard the gates, to sanctify the Sabbath day.

Remember me, O my God, *concerning* this also, and spare me according to the greatness of Your mercy!

²³In those days I also saw Jews *who* had married women of Ashdod, Ammon, *and* Moab. ²⁴And half of their children spoke the language of Ashdod, and could not speak the language of Judah, but spoke according to the language of one or the other people.

²⁵So I contended with them and cursed them, struck some of them and pulled out their hair, and made them swear by God, *saying,* "You shall not give your daughters as wives to their sons, nor take their daughters for your sons or yourselves. ²⁶Did not Solomon king of Israel sin by these things? Yet among many nations there was no king like him, who was beloved of his God; and God made him king over all Israel. Nevertheless pagan women caused even him to sin. ²⁷Should we then hear of your doing all this great evil, transgressing against our God by marrying pagan women?"

²⁸And *one* of the sons of Joiada, the son of Eliashib the high priest, *was* a son-in-law of Sanballat the Horonite; therefore I drove him from me.

²⁹Remember them, O my God, because they have defiled the priesthood and the covenant of the priesthood and the Levites.

³⁰Thus I cleansed them of everything pagan. I also assigned duties to the priests and the Levites, each to his service, ³¹and *to bringing* the wood offering and the firstfruits at appointed times.

Remember me, O my God, for good!

ESTHER

Author: Unknown

When Written: Shortly after 465 B.C.

Theme: Humility, Godly Fear

Key Verse: Esther 4:14—"For if you remain completely silent at this time, relief and deliverance will arise for the Jews from another place, but you and your father's house will perish. Yet who knows whether you have come to the kingdom for such a time as this?"

Key Chapter: Esther 8—The decree of Persian King Ahasuerus, which would have meant the destruction of the Jews living in exile there, is revised through the God-inspired intervention of Queen Esther, allowing the Jews to defend themselves against their enemies.

American journalist Robert Parry has noted, "From the Lexington Green to the Normandy beaches, from the Sons of Liberty to the Freedom Riders, it has been part of the American narrative that risks are taken to expand freedom, not freedoms sacrificed to avoid risk." Over the 200-plus years of the American republic, liberty has been protected only by the sacrifices of men and women who "more than self their country loved," as the patriotic hymn reminds us.

The heroic and righteous qualities that are required to protect liberty and life are graphically demonstrated to us in the Book of Esther. Although God's name is not mentioned in the book, His influence and character are demonstrated throughout the story. Esther, an orphaned Jewish girl, rises by divine intervention to become queen of Persia. In spite of great personal risk, Esther, along with her cousin Mordecai, position themselves to be God's agents for bringing deliverance to His people. Esther's fear of God over man is demonstrated throughout this tale of intrigue and adventure, and results in freedom for her people and honor and privilege being granted to her and her cousin Mordecai by the king.

ESTHER

The King Dethrones Queen Vashti

1 Now it came to pass in the days of Ahasuerus[a] (this *was* the Ahasuerus who reigned over one hundred and twenty-seven provinces, from India to Ethiopia), [2]in those days when King Ahasuerus sat on the throne of his kingdom, which *was* in Shushan[a] the citadel, [3]*that* in the third year of his reign he made a feast for all his officials and servants—the powers of Persia and Media, the nobles, and the princes of the provinces *being* before him— [4]when he showed the riches of his glorious kingdom and the splendor of his excellent majesty for many days, one hundred and eighty days *in all.*

[5]And when these days were completed, the king made a feast lasting seven days for all the people who were present in Shushan the citadel, from great to small, in the court of the garden of the king's palace. [6]*There were* white and blue linen *curtains* fastened with cords of fine linen and purple on silver rods and marble pillars; *and the* couches *were* of gold and silver on a *mosaic* pavement of alabaster, turquoise, and white and black marble. [7]And they served drinks in golden vessels, each vessel being different from the other, with royal wine in abundance, according to the generosity of the king. [8]In accordance with the law, the drinking was not compulsory; for so the king had ordered all the officers of his household, that they should do according to each man's pleasure.

[9]Queen Vashti also made a feast for the women *in* the royal palace which *belonged* to King Ahasuerus.

[10]On the seventh day, when the heart of the king was merry with wine, he commanded Mehuman, Biztha, Harbona, Bigtha, Abagtha, Zethar, and Carcas, seven eunuchs who served in the presence of King Ahasuerus, [11]to bring Queen Vashti before the king, *wearing* her royal crown, in order to show her beauty to the people and the officials, for she *was* beautiful to behold.

[12]But Queen Vashti refused to come at the king's command *brought* by *his* eunuchs; therefore the king was furious, and his anger burned within him.

[13]Then the king said to the wise men who understood the times (for this *was* the king's manner toward all who knew law and justice, [14]those closest to him *being* Carshena, Shethar, Admatha, Tarshish, Meres, Marsena, and Memucan, the seven princes of Persia and Media, who had access to the king's presence, *and* who ranked highest in the kingdom): [15]"What *shall we* do to Queen Vashti, according to law, because she did not obey the command of King Ahasuerus *brought to her* by the eunuchs?"

[16]And Memucan answered before the king and the princes: "Queen Vashti has not only wronged the king, but also all the princes, and all the people who *are* in all the provinces of King Ahasuerus. [17]For the queen's behavior will become known to all women, so that they will despise their husbands in their eyes, when they report, 'King Ahasuerus commanded Queen Vashti to be brought in before him, but she did not come.' [18]This very day the *noble* ladies of Persia and Media will say to all the king's officials that they have heard of the behavior of the queen. Thus *there will be* excessive contempt and wrath. [19]If it pleases the king, let a royal decree go out from him, and let it be recorded in the laws of the Persians and the Medes, so that it will not be altered, that Vashti shall come no more before King Ahasuerus; and let the king give her royal position to another who is better than she. [20]When the king's decree which he will make is proclaimed throughout all his empire (for it is great), all wives will honor their husbands, both great and small."

[21]And the reply pleased the king and the princes, and the king did according to the word of Memucan. [22]Then he sent letters to

1:1 [a]Generally identified with Xerxes I (485–464 B.C.)
1:2 [a]Or *Susa,* and so throughout this book

all the king's provinces, to each province in its own script, and to every people in their own language, that each man should be master in his own house, and speak in the language of his own people.

Esther Becomes Queen

2 After these things, when the wrath of King Ahasuerus subsided, he remembered Vashti, what she had done, and what had been decreed against her. ²Then the king's servants who attended him said: "Let beautiful young virgins be sought for the king; ³and let the king appoint officers in all the provinces of his kingdom, that they may gather all the beautiful young virgins to Shushan the citadel, into the women's quarters, under the custody of Hegai[a] the king's eunuch, custodian of the women. And let beauty preparations be given *them.* ⁴Then let the young woman who pleases the king be queen instead of Vashti."

This thing pleased the king, and he did so.

⁵In Shushan the citadel there was a certain Jew whose name *was* Mordecai the son of Jair, the son of Shimei, the son of Kish, a Benjamite. ⁶*Kish*[a] had been carried away from Jerusalem with the captives who had been captured with Jeconiah[b] king of Judah, whom Nebuchadnezzar the king of Babylon had carried away. ⁷And *Mordecai* had brought up Hadassah, that *is,* Esther, his uncle's daughter, for she had neither father nor mother. The young woman *was* lovely and beautiful. When her father and mother died, Mordecai took her as his own daughter.

⁸So it was, when the king's command and decree were heard, and when many young women were gathered at Shushan the citadel, *under* the custody of Hegai, that Esther also was taken to the king's palace, into the care of Hegai the custodian of the women. ⁹Now the young woman pleased him, and she obtained his favor; so he readily gave beauty preparations to her, besides her allowance. Then seven choice maidservants were provided for her from the king's palace, and he moved her and her maidservants to the best *place* in the house of the women.

¹⁰Esther had not revealed her people or family, for Mordecai had charged her not to reveal *it.* ¹¹And every day Mordecai paced in front of the court of the women's quarters, to learn of Esther's welfare and what was happening to her.

¹²Each young woman's turn came to go in to King Ahasuerus after she had completed twelve months' preparation, according to the regulations for the women, for thus were the days of their preparation apportioned: six months with oil of myrrh, and six months with perfumes and preparations for beautifying women. ¹³Thus *prepared, each* young woman went to the king, and she was given whatever she desired to take with her from the women's quarters to the king's palace. ¹⁴In the evening she went, and in the morning she returned to the second house of the women, to the custody of Shaashgaz, the king's eunuch who kept the concubines. She would not go in to the king again unless the king delighted in her and called for her by name.

¹⁵Now when the turn came for Esther the daughter of Abihail the uncle of Mordecai, who had taken her as his daughter, to go in to the king, she requested nothing but what Hegai the king's eunuch, the custodian of the women, advised. And Esther obtained favor in the sight of all who saw her. ¹⁶So Esther was taken to King Ahasuerus, into his royal palace, in the tenth month, which *is* the month of Tebeth, in the seventh year of his reign. ¹⁷The king loved Esther more than all the *other* women, and she obtained grace and favor in his sight more than all the virgins; so he set the royal crown upon her head and made her queen instead of Vashti. ¹⁸Then the king made a great feast, the Feast of Esther, for all his officials and servants; and he proclaimed a holiday in the provinces and gave gifts according to the generosity of a king.

Mordecai Discovers a Plot

¹⁹When virgins were gathered together a second time, Mordecai sat within the king's gate. ²⁰Now Esther had not revealed her family and her people, just as Mordecai had charged her, for Esther obeyed the command

---

2:3 ªHebrew *Hege*   **2:6** ªLiterally *Who* ᵇSame as *Jehoiachin,* 2 Kings 24:6 and elsewhere

of Mordecai as when she was brought up by him.

21In those days, while Mordecai sat within the king's gate, two of the king's eunuchs, Bigthan and Teresh, doorkeepers, became furious and sought to lay hands on King Ahasuerus. 22So the matter became known to Mordecai, who told Queen Esther, and Esther informed the king in Mordecai's name. 23And when an inquiry was made into the matter, it was confirmed, and both were hanged on a gallows; and it was written in the book of the chronicles in the presence of the king.

Haman's Conspiracy Against the Jews

3 After these things King Ahasuerus promoted Haman, the son of Hammedatha the Agagite, and advanced him and set his seat above all the princes who *were* with him. 2And all the king's servants who *were* within the king's gate bowed and paid homage to Haman, for so the king had commanded concerning him. But Mordecai would not bow or pay homage. 3Then the king's servants who *were* within the king's gate said to Mordecai, "Why do you transgress the king's command?" 4Now it happened, when they spoke to him daily and he would not listen to them, that they told *it* to Haman, to see whether Mordecai's words would stand; for *Mordecai* had told them that he *was* a Jew. 5When Haman saw that Mordecai did not bow or pay him homage, Haman was filled with wrath. 6But he disdained to lay hands on Mordecai alone, for they had told him of the people of Mordecai. Instead, Haman sought to destroy all the Jews who *were* throughout the whole kingdom of Ahasuerus—the people of Mordecai.

7In the first month, which is the month of Nisan, in the twelfth year of King Ahasuerus, they cast Pur (that *is,* the lot), before Haman to determine the day and the month,a until *it fell on the* twelfth *month,*b which *is* the month of Adar.

8Then Haman said to King Ahasuerus, "There is a certain people scattered and dispersed among the people in all the provinces of your kingdom; their laws *are* different from all *other* people's, and they do not keep the king's laws. Therefore it *is*

not fitting for the king to let them remain. 9If it pleases the king, let *a decree* be written that they be destroyed, and I will pay ten thousand talents of silver into the hands of those who do the work, to bring *it* into the king's treasuries."

10So the king took his signet ring from his hand and gave it to Haman, the son of Hammedatha the Agagite, the enemy of the Jews. 11And the king said to Haman, "The money and the people *are* given to you, to do with them as seems good to you."

12Then the king's scribes were called on the thirteenth day of the first month, and *a decree* was written according to all that Haman commanded—to the king's satraps, to the governors who *were* over each province, to the officials of all people, to every province according to its script, and to every people in their language. In the name of King Ahasuerus it was written, and sealed with the king's signet ring. 13And the letters were sent by couriers into all the king's provinces, to destroy, to kill, and to annihilate all the Jews, both young and old, little children and women, in one day, on the thirteenth *day* of the twelfth month, which *is* the month of Adar, and to plunder their possessions.a 14A copy of the document was to be issued as law in every province, being published for all people, that they should be ready for that day. 15The couriers went out, hastened by the king's command; and the decree was proclaimed in Shushan the citadel. So the king and Haman sat down to drink, but the city of Shushan was perplexed.

Esther Agrees to Help the Jews

4 When Mordecai learned all that had happened, he tore his clothes and put on sackcloth and ashes, and went out into the midst of the city. He cried out with a loud and bitter cry. 2He went as far as the front of the king's gate, for no one *might* enter the king's gate clothed with sackcloth. 3And in

---

3:7 aSeptuagint adds *to destroy the people of Mordecai in one day;* Vulgate adds *the nation of the Jews should be destroyed.* bFollowing Masoretic Text and Vulgate; Septuagint reads *and the lot fell on the fourteenth of the month.* **3:13** aSeptuagint adds the text of the letter here.

every province where the king's command and decree arrived, *there was* great mourning among the Jews, with fasting, weeping, and wailing; and many lay in sackcloth and ashes.

4So Esther's maids and eunuchs came and told her, and the queen was deeply distressed. Then she sent garments to clothe Mordecai and take his sackcloth away from him, but he would not accept *them*. 5Then Esther called Hathach, *one* of the king's eunuchs whom he had appointed to attend her, and she gave him a command concerning Mordecai, to learn what and why this *was*. 6So Hathach went out to Mordecai in the city square that *was* in front of the king's gate. 7And Mordecai told him all that had happened to him, and the sum of money that Haman had promised to pay into the king's treasuries to destroy the Jews. 8He also gave him a copy of the written decree for their destruction, which was given at Shushan, that he might show it to Esther and explain it to her, and that he might command her to go in to the king to make supplication to him and plead before him for her people. 9So Hathach returned and told Esther the words of Mordecai.

10Then Esther spoke to Hathach, and gave him a command for Mordecai: 11"All the king's servants and the people of the king's provinces know that any man or woman who goes into the inner court to the king, who has not been called, *he has* but one law: put *all* to death, except the one to whom the king holds out the golden scepter, that he may live. Yet I myself have not been called to go in to the king these thirty days." 12So they told Mordecai Esther's words.

13And Mordecai told *them* to answer Esther: "Do not think in your heart that you will escape in the king's palace any more than all the other Jews. 14For if you remain completely silent at this time, relief and deliverance will arise for the Jews from another place, but you and your father's house will perish. Yet who knows whether you have come to the kingdom for *such* a time as this?"

15Then Esther told *them* to reply to Mordecai: 16"Go, gather all the Jews who are present in Shushan, and fast for me; neither eat nor drink for three days, night or day. My maids and I will fast likewise. And so I will go to the king, which *is* against the law; and if I perish, I perish!"

17So Mordecai went his way and did according to all that Esther commanded him.ª

Esther's Banquet

5 Now it happened on the third day that Esther put on *her* royal *robes* and stood in the inner court of the king's palace, across from the king's house, while the king sat on his royal throne in the royal house, facing the entrance of the house.ª 2So it was, when the king saw Queen Esther standing in the court, *that* she found favor in his sight, and the king held out to Esther the golden scepter that *was* in his hand. Then Esther went near and touched the top of the scepter.

3And the king said to her, "What do you wish, Queen Esther? What *is* your request? It shall be given to you—up to half the kingdom!"

4So Esther answered, "If it pleases the king, let the king and Haman come today to the banquet that I have prepared for him."

5Then the king said, "Bring Haman quickly, that he may do as Esther has said." So the king and Haman went to the banquet that Esther had prepared.

6At the banquet of wine the king said to Esther, "What *is* your petition? It shall be granted you. What *is* your request, up to half the kingdom? It shall be done!"

7Then Esther answered and said, "My petition and request *is this:* 8If I have found favor in the sight of the king, and if it pleases the king to grant my petition and fulfill my request, then let the king and Haman come to the banquet which I will prepare for them, and tomorrow I will do as the king has said."

Haman's Plot Against Mordecai

9So Haman went out that day joyful and with a glad heart; but when Haman saw Mordecai in the king's gate, and that he did not stand or tremble before him, he was

---

4:17 ªSeptuagint adds a prayer of Mordecai here.
5:1 ªSeptuagint adds many extra details in verses 1 and 2.

SEPTEMBER 11, 2001

SELFLESS

*" . . . and if I perish,
I perish!"*

ESTHER 4:16

In his book *A Time for Heroes*, Lance Wubbels paid tribute to the patriotic heroes the world watched on September 11, 2001:

It was a day of unthinkable horror and destruction, but it became a day for American heroes. Heroes were everywhere you looked. Giants rose out of relative obscurity to cast long shadows across the smoke and dust and rubble. Ordinary American citizens, suddenly caught in the crossfire of terrorism, put their lives on the line to preserve the lives of others.

They emerged as the truly mighty and valiant ones of Flight 93. Among the smoldering wreckage of the Pentagon, they stood with undimmed spirits as fire fighters unfurled a gigantic flag from the roof of the burned-out structure. At Ground Zero, hundreds and thousands of people on dozens of fronts searched the mountain of unstable rubble in an epic battle to win back as many lives as could possibly be rescued.

Most of them remain nameless to us, but their undaunted faces are engraved forever upon our hearts. They are the fire fighters, the tireless fire fighters, who were forever captured by the photo of the three ashen-caked firemen raising the American flag on a pole that stuck up out of the debris of the World Trade Center. Framed against the monstrous heap of steel and concrete in the background, it was an easy reminder of the heroic Marines who raised the flag on Iwo Jima during another of this nation's great conflicts.

They are the police, paramedics, rescue workers, doctors, nurses, National Guard, Red Cross workers, and others we have so often taken for granted. And they are the janitors and security guards and office managers and the coworkers who said no to death and helped thousands escape who might have easily perished.

In that sudden moment of time, the real heroes of our world stood out as brilliant luminaries cast against the darkest night.

In a world where rock superstars, athletes, and celebrities have been elevated to hero status, we were given a lesson on true heroism and patriotism. Such acts of selfless devotion are nearly beyond our imaginations. It is little wonder that the world seems so empty when they are gone.

filled with indignation against Mordecai. [10]Nevertheless Haman restrained himself and went home, and he sent and called for his friends and his wife Zeresh. [11]Then Haman told them of his great riches, the multitude of his children, everything in which the king had promoted him, and how he had advanced him above the officials and servants of the king.

[12]Moreover Haman said, "Besides, Queen Esther invited no one but me to come in with the king to the banquet that she prepared; and tomorrow I am again invited by her, along with the king. [13]Yet all this avails me nothing, so long as I see Mordecai the Jew sitting at the king's gate."

[14]Then his wife Zeresh and all his friends said to him, "Let a gallows be made, fifty cubits high, and in the morning suggest to the king that Mordecai be hanged on it; then go merrily with the king to the banquet."

And the thing pleased Haman; so he had the gallows made.

The King Honors Mordecai

6 That night the king could not sleep. So one was commanded to bring the book of the records of the chronicles; and they were read before the king. [2]And it was found written that Mordecai had told of Bigthana and Teresh, two of the king's eunuchs, the doorkeepers who had sought to lay hands on King Ahasuerus. [3]Then the king said, "What honor or dignity has been bestowed on Mordecai for this?"

And the king's servants who attended him said, "Nothing has been done for him."

[4]So the king said, "Who *is* in the court?" Now Haman had *just* entered the outer court of the king's palace to suggest that the king hang Mordecai on the gallows that he had prepared for him.

[5]The king's servants said to him, "Haman is there, standing in the court."

And the king said, "Let him come in."

[6]So Haman came in, and the king asked him, "What shall be done for the man whom the king delights to honor?"

Now Haman thought in his heart, "Whom would the king delight to honor more than me?" [7]And Haman answered the king, "*For* the man whom the king delights to honor,

[8]let a royal robe be brought which the king has worn, and a horse on which the king has ridden, which has a royal crest placed on its head. [9]Then let this robe and horse be delivered to the hand of one of the king's most noble princes, that he may array the man whom the king delights to honor. Then parade him on horseback through the city square, and proclaim before him: 'Thus shall it be done to the man whom the king delights to honor!'"

[10]Then the king said to Haman, "Hurry, take the robe and the horse, as you have suggested, and do so for Mordecai the Jew who sits within the king's gate! Leave nothing undone of all that you have spoken."

[11]So Haman took the robe and the horse, arrayed Mordecai and led him on horseback through the city square, and proclaimed before him, "Thus shall it be done to the man whom the king delights to honor!"

[12]Afterward Mordecai went back to the king's gate. But Haman hurried to his house, mourning and with his head covered. [13]When Haman told his wife Zeresh and all his friends everything that had happened to him, his wise men and his wife Zeresh said to him, "If Mordecai, before whom you have begun to fall, is of Jewish descent, you will not prevail against him but will surely fall before him."

[14]While they *were* still talking with him, the king's eunuchs came, and hastened to bring Haman to the banquet which Esther had prepared.

Haman Hanged Instead of Mordecai

7 So the king and Haman went to dine with Queen Esther. [2]And on the second day, at the banquet of wine, the king again said to Esther, "What *is* your petition, Queen Esther? It shall be granted you. And what *is* your request, up to half the kingdom? It shall be done!"

[3]Then Queen Esther answered and said, "If I have found favor in your sight, O king, and if it pleases the king, let my life be given me at my petition, and my people at my request. [4]For we have been sold, my people and I, to be destroyed, to be killed, and to be annihilated. Had we been sold as male and female slaves, I would have held my

tongue, although the enemy could never compensate for the king's loss."

⁵So King Ahasuerus answered and said to Queen Esther, "Who is he, and where is he, who would dare presume in his heart to do such a thing?"

⁶And Esther said, "The adversary and enemy *is* this wicked Haman!"

So Haman was terrified before the king and queen.

⁷Then the king arose in his wrath from the banquet of wine *and went* into the palace garden; but Haman stood before Queen Esther, pleading for his life, for he saw that evil was determined against him by the king. ⁸When the king returned from the palace garden to the place of the banquet of wine, Haman had fallen across the couch where Esther *was.* Then the king said, "Will he also assault the queen while I *am* in the house?"

As the word left the king's mouth, they covered Haman's face. ⁹Now Harbonah, one of the eunuchs, said to the king, "Look! The gallows, fifty cubits high, which Haman made for Mordecai, who spoke good on the king's behalf, is standing at the house of Haman."

Then the king said, "Hang him on it!"

¹⁰So they hanged Haman on the gallows that he had prepared for Mordecai. Then the king's wrath subsided.

Esther Saves the Jews

8 On that day King Ahasuerus gave Queen Esther the house of Haman, the enemy of the Jews. And Mordecai came before the king, for Esther had told how he *was related* to her. ²So the king took off his signet ring, which he had taken from Haman, and gave it to Mordecai; and Esther appointed Mordecai over the house of Haman.

³Now Esther spoke again to the king, fell down at his feet, and implored him with tears to counteract the evil of Haman the Agagite, and the scheme which he had devised against the Jews. ⁴And the king held out the golden scepter toward Esther. So Esther arose and stood before the king, ⁵and said, "If it pleases the king, and if I have found favor in his sight and the thing *seems* right to the king and I am pleasing

in his eyes, let it be written to revoke the letters devised by Haman, the son of Hammedatha the Agagite, which he wrote to annihilate the Jews who *are* in all the king's provinces. ⁶For how can I endure to see the evil that will come to my people? Or how can I endure to see the destruction of my countrymen?"

⁷Then King Ahasuerus said to Queen Esther and Mordecai the Jew, "Indeed, I have given Esther the house of Haman, and they have hanged him on the gallows because he *tried to* lay his hand on the Jews. ⁸You yourselves write *a decree* concerning the Jews, as you please, in the king's name, and seal *it* with the king's signet ring; for whatever is written in the king's name and sealed with the king's signet ring no one can revoke."

⁹So the king's scribes were called at that time, in the third month, which *is* the month of Sivan, on the twenty-third *day;* and it was written, according to all that Mordecai commanded, to the Jews, the satraps, the governors, and the princes of the provinces from India to Ethiopia, one hundred and twenty-seven provinces *in all,* to every province in its own script, to every people in their own language, and to the Jews in their own script and language. ¹⁰And he wrote in the name of King Ahasuerus, sealed *it* with the king's signet ring, and sent letters by couriers on horseback, riding on royal horses bred from swift steeds.ᵃ

¹¹By these letters the king permitted the Jews who *were* in every city to gather together and protect their lives—to destroy, kill, and annihilate all the forces of any people or province that would assault them, *both* little children and women, and to plunder their possessions, ¹²on one day in all the provinces of King Ahasuerus, on the thirteenth *day* of the twelfth month, which *is* the month of Adar.ᵃ ¹³A copy of the document was to be issued as a decree in every province and published for all people, so that the Jews would be ready on that day to avenge themselves on their enemies. ¹⁴The couriers who rode on royal horses went out, hastened

---

8:10 ᵃLiterally *sons of the swift horses*
8:12 ᵃSeptuagint adds the text of the letter here.

and pressed on by the king's command. And the decree was issued in Shushan the citadel.

¹⁵So Mordecai went out from the presence of the king in royal apparel of blue and white, with a great crown of gold and a garment of fine linen and purple; and the city of Shushan rejoiced and was glad. ¹⁶The Jews had light and gladness, joy and honor. ¹⁷And in every province and city, wherever the king's command and decree came, the Jews had joy and gladness, a feast and a holiday. Then many of the people of the land became Jews, because fear of the Jews fell upon them.

The Jews Destroy Their Tormentors

9 Now in the twelfth month, that is, the month of Adar, on the thirteenth day, *the time* came for the king's command and his decree to be executed. On the day that the enemies of the Jews had hoped to overpower them, the opposite occurred, in that the Jews themselves overpowered those who hated them. ²The Jews gathered together in their cities throughout all the provinces of King Ahasuerus to lay hands on those who sought their harm. And no one could withstand them, because fear of them fell upon all people. ³And all the officials of the provinces, the satraps, the governors, and all those doing the king's work, helped the Jews, because the fear of Mordecai fell upon them. ⁴For Mordecai *was* great in the king's palace, and his fame spread throughout all the provinces; for this man Mordecai became increasingly prominent. ⁵Thus the Jews defeated all their enemies with the stroke of the sword, with slaughter and destruction, and did what they pleased with those who hated them.

⁶And in Shushan the citadel the Jews killed and destroyed five hundred men. ⁷Also Parshandatha, Dalphon, Aspatha, ⁸Poratha, Adalia, Aridatha, ⁹Parmashta, Arisai, Aridai, and Vajezatha— ¹⁰the ten sons of Haman the son of Hammedatha, the enemy of the Jews—they killed; but they did not lay a hand on the plunder.

¹¹On that day the number of those who were killed in Shushan the citadel was brought to the king. ¹²And the king said to Queen Esther, "The Jews have killed and destroyed five hundred men in Shushan the citadel, and the ten sons of Haman. What have they done in the rest of the king's provinces? Now what *is* your petition? It shall be granted to you. Or what *is* your further request? It shall be done."

¹³Then Esther said, "If it pleases the king, let it be granted to the Jews who *are* in Shushan to do again tomorrow according to today's decree, and let Haman's ten sons be hanged on the gallows."

¹⁴So the king commanded this to be done; the decree was issued in Shushan, and they hanged Haman's ten sons.

¹⁵And the Jews who *were* in Shushan gathered together again on the fourteenth day of the month of Adar and killed three hundred men at Shushan; but they did not lay a hand on the plunder.

¹⁶The remainder of the Jews in the king's provinces gathered together and protected their lives, had rest from their enemies, and killed seventy-five thousand of their enemies; but they did not lay a hand on the plunder. ¹⁷*This was* on the thirteenth day of the month of Adar. And on the fourteenth of *the month*ᵃ they rested and made it a day of feasting and gladness.

The Feast of Purim

¹⁸But the Jews who *were* at Shushan assembled together on the thirteenth *day*, as well as on the fourteenth; and on the fifteenth of *the month*ᵃ they rested, and made it a day of feasting and gladness. ¹⁹Therefore the Jews of the villages who dwelt in the unwalled towns celebrated the fourteenth day of the month of Adar *with* gladness and feasting, as a holiday, and for sending presents to one another.

²⁰And Mordecai wrote these things and sent letters to all the Jews, near and far, who *were* in all the provinces of King Ahasuerus, ²¹to establish among them that they should celebrate yearly the fourteenth and fifteenth days of the month of Adar, ²²as the days on which the Jews had rest from their enemies, as the month which was turned from sorrow to joy for them, and from mourning to a holiday; that they should

---

9:17 ᵃLiterally *it*   **9:18** ᵃLiterally *it*

make them days of feasting and joy, of sending presents to one another and gifts to the poor. ²³So the Jews accepted the custom which they had begun, as Mordecai had written to them, ²⁴because Haman, the son of Hammedatha the Agagite, the enemy of all the Jews, had plotted against the Jews to annihilate them, and had cast Pur (that *is*, the lot), to consume them and destroy them; ²⁵but when *Esther*[a] came before the king, he commanded by letter that this[b] wicked plot which *Haman* had devised against the Jews should return on his own head, and that he and his sons should be hanged on the gallows.

²⁶So they called these days Purim, after the name Pur. Therefore, because of all the words of this letter, what they had seen concerning this matter, and what had happened to them, ²⁷the Jews established and imposed it upon themselves and their descendants and all who would join them, that without fail they should celebrate these two days every year, according to the written *instructions* and according to the *prescribed* time, ²⁸that these days *should be* remembered and kept throughout every generation, every family, every province, and every city, that these days of Purim should not fail *to be observed* among the Jews, and *that* the memory of them should not perish among their descendants.

²⁹Then Queen Esther, the daughter of Abihail, with Mordecai the Jew, wrote with full authority to confirm this second letter about Purim. ³⁰And *Mordecai* sent letters to all the Jews, to the one hundred and twenty-seven provinces of the kingdom of Ahasuerus, *with* words of peace and truth, ³¹to confirm these days of Purim at their *appointed* time, as Mordecai the Jew and Queen Esther had prescribed for them, and as they had decreed for themselves and their descendants concerning matters of their fasting and lamenting. ³²So the decree of Esther confirmed these matters of Purim, and it was written in the book.

9:25 [a]Literally *she* or *it* [b]Literally *his*

INSPIRING

. . . that without fail they should celebrate these two days every year. . . .

ESTHER 9:27

THE FOURTH OF JULY CELEBRATION

On July 3, 1776, following the signing of the Declaration of Independence, John Adams wrote to his wife, reflecting on what he had shared in Congress concerning the importance of that day:

> *The second day of July 1776 will be the most memorable epoch in the history of America. I am apt to believe that it will be celebrated by succeeding generations as the great anniversary festival. It ought to be commemorated as the day of deliverance, by solemn acts of devotion to God Almighty. It ought to be solemnized with pomp and parade, with shows, games, sports, guns, bells, bonfires, and illuminations, from one end of this continent to the other, from this time forward forever.*
>
> *You will think me transported with enthusiasm, but I am not. I am well aware of the toil and blood and treasure that it will cost to maintain this Declaration and support and defend these States. Yet through all the gloom I can see the rays of ravishing light and glory. I can see that the end is worth more than all the means; that posterity will triumph in that day's transaction, even though we [may regret] it, which I trust in God we shall not.*

Mordecai's Advancement

10 And King Ahasuerus imposed tribute on the land and *on* the islands of the sea. ²Now all the acts of his power and his might, and the account of the greatness of Mordecai, to which the king advanced him, *are* they not written in the book of the chronicles of the kings of Media and Persia? ³For Mordecai the Jew *was* second to King Ahasuerus, and was great among the Jews and well received by the multitude of his brethren, seeking the good of his people and speaking peace to all his countrymen.ᵃ

10:3 ᵃLiterally *seed.* Septuagint and Vulgate add a dream of Mordecai here; Vulgate adds six more chapters.

JOB

Author: Unknown

When Written: 1500–200 B.C.

Theme: Suffering, God's Sovereignty

Key Verse: Job 13:15—"Though He slay me, yet will I trust Him. . . ."

Key Chapter: Job 42—The last chapter of this passionate and intense book records the climax of Job's long and difficult experience. Job's recognition of God's unquestionable majesty and sovereignty leads to a resolution within his own heart and mind and opens the door to a complete restoration of all that was taken from him.

In times of great stress and trial, God remains faithful. On September 16, 1775, Abigail Adams wrote to her husband, John Adams, expressing her decision to trust in God in the midst of intense uncertainty: "And unto Him who mounts the whirlwind and directs the storm, I will cheerfully leave the ordering of my lot and whether adverse or prosperous days should be my future portion, I will trust in His right hand to lead me safely through, and after a short rotation of events, fix me in a state immutable and happy. . . ."

The Book of Job chronicles the suffering and pain of a God-fearing man and prompts the reader to ask difficult questions about life. Why do bad things happen to good people? Does God really care when we suffer? Job walks through his personal wilderness posing many questions and concerns, but in the end he declares of His Lord, "I have heard of You by the hearing of the ears, but now my eye sees You" (42:5).

JOB

Job and His Family in Uz

1 There was a man in the land of Uz, whose name *was* Job; and that man was blameless and upright, and one who feared God and shunned evil. ²And seven sons and three daughters were born to him. ³Also, his possessions were seven thousand sheep, three thousand camels, five hundred yoke of oxen, five hundred female donkeys, and a very large household, so that this man was the greatest of all the people of the East.

⁴And his sons would go and feast *in their* houses, each on his *appointed* day, and would send and invite their three sisters to eat and drink with them. ⁵So it was, when the days of feasting had run their course, that Job would send and sanctify them, and he would rise early in the morning and offer burnt offerings *according to* the number of them all. For Job said, "It may be that my sons have sinned and cursedᵃ God in their hearts." Thus Job did regularly.

Satan Attacks Job's Character

⁶Now there was a day when the sons of God came to present themselves before the LORD, and Satanᵃ also came among them. ⁷And the LORD said to Satan, "From where do you come?"

So Satan answered the LORD and said, "From going to and fro on the earth, and from walking back and forth on it."

⁸Then the LORD said to Satan, "Have you considered My servant Job, that *there is* none like him on the earth, a blameless and upright man, one who fears God and shuns evil?"

⁹So Satan answered the LORD and said, "Does Job fear God for nothing? ¹⁰Have You not made a hedge around him, around his household, and around all that he has on every side? You have blessed the work of his hands, and his possessions have increased in the land. ¹¹But now, stretch out Your hand and touch all that he has, and he will surely curse You to Your face!"

¹²And the LORD said to Satan, "Behold, all that he has *is* in your power; only do not lay a hand on his *person.*"

So Satan went out from the presence of the LORD.

Job Loses His Property and Children

¹³Now there was a day when his sons and daughters *were* eating and drinking wine in their oldest brother's house; ¹⁴and a messenger came to Job and said, "The oxen were plowing and the donkeys feeding beside them, ¹⁵when the Sabeansᵃ raided *them* and took them away—indeed they have killed the servants with the edge of the sword; and I alone have escaped to tell you!"

¹⁶While he *was* still speaking, another also came and said, "The fire of God fell from heaven and burned up the sheep and the servants, and consumed them; and I alone have escaped to tell you!"

¹⁷While he *was* still speaking, another also came and said, "The Chaldeans formed three bands, raided the camels and took them away, yes, and killed the servants with the edge of the sword; and I alone have escaped to tell you!"

¹⁸While he *was* still speaking, another also came and said, "Your sons and daughters *were* eating and drinking wine in their oldest brother's house, ¹⁹and suddenly a great wind came from acrossᵃ the wilderness and struck the four corners of the house, and it fell on the young people, and they are dead; and I alone have escaped to tell you!"

²⁰Then Job arose, tore his robe, and shaved his head; and he fell to the ground and worshiped. ²¹And he said:

"Naked I came from my mother's womb,
    And naked shall I return there.

1:5 ᵃLiterally *blessed,* but used here in the evil sense, and so in verse 11 and 2:5, 9   **1:6** ᵃLiterally *the Adversary,* and so throughout this book   **1:15** ᵃLiterally *Sheba* (compare 6:19)   **1:19** ᵃSeptuagint omits *across.*

The LORD gave, and the LORD has
taken away;
Blessed be the name of the LORD."

22In all this Job did not sin nor charge
God with wrong.

Satan Attacks Job's Health

2 Again there was a day when the sons of
God came to present themselves before
the LORD, and Satan came also among them
to present himself before the LORD. 2And the
LORD said to Satan, "From where do you
come?"

Satan answered the LORD and said, "From
going to and fro on the earth, and from
walking back and forth on it."

3Then the LORD said to Satan, "Have you
considered My servant Job, that there is none
like him on the earth, a blameless and
upright man, one who fears God and shuns
evil? And still he holds fast to his integrity,
although you incited Me against him, to
destroy him without cause."

4So Satan answered the LORD and said,
"Skin for skin! Yes, all that a man has he
will give for his life. 5But stretch out Your
hand now, and touch his bone and his flesh,
and he will surely curse You to Your face!"

6And the LORD said to Satan, "Behold, he
is in your hand, but spare his life."

7So Satan went out from the presence of
the LORD, and struck Job with painful boils
from the sole of his foot to the crown of his
head. 8And he took for himself a potsherd
with which to scrape himself while he sat
in the midst of the ashes.

9Then his wife said to him, "Do you still
hold fast to your integrity? Curse God and
die!"

INTEGRITY

*"Do you still hold fast
to your integrity?"*

JOB 2:9

William Bross

HOW TO BE SUCCESSFUL

William Bross (1813–1890) was a highly successful American
journalist, the copublisher of the *Chicago Tribune*. In an inter-
view, he discussed his success:

Q. What maxims have had a strong influence on your life
and helped to your success?

A. *The Proverbs of Solomon and other Scriptures. They were quoted
a thousand times by my honored father and caused an effort to
do my duty each day, under a constant sense of obligation to my
Savior and fellow man.*

Q. What do you consider essential elements of success for a
young man entering upon such a profession as yours?

A. *Sterling, unflinching integrity in all matters, public and private.
Let everyone do his whole duty, both to God and man. Let
him follow earnestly the teachings of the Scriptures and
eschew infidelity in all its forms.*

Q. What, in your observation, have been the chief causes of
the numerous failures in the life of business and professional men?

A. *Want of integrity, careless of the truth, reckless in thought and
expression, lack of trust in God, and a disregard of the teachings of His Holy Word, bad company, and bad morals in any
of their many phases.*

¹⁰But he said to her, "You speak as one of the foolish women speaks. Shall we indeed accept good from God, and shall we not accept adversity?" In all this Job did not sin with his lips.

Job's Three Friends

¹¹Now when Job's three friends heard of all this adversity that had come upon him, each one came from his own place—Eliphaz the Temanite, Bildad the Shuhite, and Zophar the Naamathite. For they had made an appointment together to come and mourn with him, and to comfort him. ¹²And when they raised their eyes from afar, and did not recognize him, they lifted their voices and wept; and each one tore his robe and sprinkled dust on his head toward heaven. ¹³So they sat down with him on the ground seven days and seven nights, and no one spoke a word to him, for they saw that *his* grief was very great.

Job Deplores His Birth

3 After this Job opened his mouth and cursed the day of his *birth*. ²And Job spoke, and said:

3 "May the day perish on which I was
        born,
    And the night *in which* it was said,
    'A male child is conceived.'
4   May that day be darkness;
    May God above not seek it,
    Nor the light shine upon it.
5   May darkness and the shadow of
        death claim it;
    May a cloud settle on it;
    May the blackness of the day terrify it.
6   *As for* that night, may darkness seize it;
    May it not rejoiceª among the days of
        the year,
    May it not come into the number of
        the months.
7   Oh, may that night be barren!
    May no joyful shout come into it!
8   May those curse it who curse the day,
    Those who are ready to arouse
        Leviathan.
9   May the stars of its morning be dark;
    May it look for light, but *have* none,
    And not see the dawning of the day;

10 Because it did not shut up the doors
        of my *mother's* womb,
    Nor hide sorrow from my eyes.

11 "Why did I not die at birth?
    Why did I *not* perish when I came
        from the womb?
12 Why did the knees receive me?
    Or why the breasts, that I should nurse?
13 For now I would have lain still and
        been quiet,
    I would have been asleep;
    Then I would have been at rest
14 With kings and counselors of the earth,
    Who built ruins for themselves,
15 Or with princes who had gold,
    Who filled their houses *with* silver;
16 Or *why* was I not hidden like a
        stillborn child,
    Like infants who never saw light?
17 There the wicked cease *from* troubling,
    And there the weary are at rest.
18 *There* the prisoners rest together;
    They do not hear the voice of the
        oppressor.
19 The small and great are there,
    And the servant *is* free from his master.

20 "Why is light given to him who is in
        misery,
    And life to the bitter of soul,
21 Who long for death, but it does not
        come,
    And search for it more than hidden
        treasures;
22 Who rejoice exceedingly,
    And are glad when they can find the
        grave?
23 *Why is light given* to a man whose way
        is hidden,
    And whom God has hedged in?
24 For my sighing comes before I eat,ª
    And my groanings pour out like water.
25 For the thing I greatly feared has come
        upon me,
    And what I dreaded has happened
        to me.
26 I am not at ease, nor am I quiet;
    I have no rest, for trouble comes."

3:6 ªSeptuagint, Syriac, Targum, and Vulgate read *be joined*.   **3:24** ªLiterally *my bread*

THE GREAT AWAKENINGS

W HEN JONATHAN EDWARDS began preaching in Northampton, Massachusetts, in 1734, the moral conditions were at an extreme low, as was prevalent throughout most of the American colonies. Under his preaching that stressed the importance of an immediate, personal spiritual rebirth, a revival began in his church among the youth and then spread to the adults. Edwards wrote that "in the spring and summer following, anno 1735, the town seemed to be so full of the presence of God; it never was so full of love, nor of joy, and yet so full of distress, as it was then." In two years, 300 converts were added to the church, and news of the revival spread throughout New England.

Jonathan Edwards

THE BRITISH METHODIST PREACHER George Whitefield continued the movement, making seven separate trips to America and spending nine years preaching across the colonies. He preached to five thousand on the Boston Commons and eight thousand at once in the open fields. Between 1740 and 1742, an estimated 25,000 to 50,000 people were added to the New England church, changing the region's moral tone and gaining the name of a "Great Awakening."

The revival spread into the Middle Colonies, beginning in New Jersey largely among the Presbyterians trained under William Tennent, including his son Gilbert, who became the leading figure of the Great Awakening in the Middle Colonies. The revival reached the South with the preaching of Samuel Davies among the Presbyterians of Virginia (1748–1759), with the great success of the Baptists in North Carolina in the 1760s, and with the rapid spread of Methodism shortly before the American Revolution.

Because the First Great Awakening served to build up interests that were intercolonial in character and increased opposition to the Anglican Church and the royal officials who supported it, many historians say it helped set in motion a democratic spirit that eventually brought America its political freedoms. It also resulted in an outburst of missionary activity among Native Americans by such men as David Brainerd, and it was the impetus to the first movement of importance against slavery. In education, it led to the founding of a number of academies and colleges, notably Princeton, Brown, Rutgers, and Dartmouth.

BY THE YEAR 1800, nearly a million people had made their way west, settling in the area west of the Blue Ridge in Virginia, in Kentucky, Tennessee, the Northwest, and in the Indian Territory. Most did not have access to a church, and moral conditions once again went into decline. However, a second great spiritual revival began that continued into the 1830s. Many historians refer to Logan County in Kentucky as its starting point, where several Methodist and Presbyterian ministers joined efforts in 1799; and visitors to the revival would camp out for two or three nights. One such gathering was held at Cane Ridge, Kentucky, in 1801, and drew perhaps as many as 15,000 to 20,000 people. More than 10,000 people were swept into the Kentucky churches between 1800 and 1803.

The great revival quickly spread throughout Kentucky, Tennessee, and southern Ohio. The Methodists had created an efficient organization of "districts" of churches, each of which would be served by circuit riders—preachers who traveled from church to church to preach and minister, especially in rural areas. The circuit riders came from among the common people, which helped them establish a rapport with the frontier families they hoped to bring to faith. They promoted "Sunday schools," in which children were taught reading, writing, and arithmetic.

Camp Meeting of the Methodists in N. America

WHILE THE FOCUS OF THE Second Great Awakening was primarily on personal salvation experienced in revival meetings, it accomplished far more than that, for it had a greater impact on secular society than any other in American history through its vast social concern. Through a multitude of channels, this revival encouraged Christians to become involved in causes dealing with prison reform, temperance, women's suffrage, and the crusade to abolish slavery.

Charles Finney

For instance, Charles Finney, one of the greatest American preachers in the 1800s, became the president of Oberlin College in Ohio. He strongly supported giving freedom to the slaves, and the college was a busy station for the Underground Railroad, which secretly brought slaves to freedom. Oberlin was among the first American colleges to coeducate blacks and women with white men. Finney also helped form a great network of volunteer societies organized to aid in solving social problems. By 1834, the budget of these societies was nearly as large as the federal budget of that time.

During revivals that Finney held in Boston, fifty thousand people put their faith in Christ in just one week. Finney always demanded a verdict from his question: "What will you do with Jesus Christ?" Perhaps that is a fitting description of what happened across America through the Second Great Awakening. Hundreds of thousands put their faith in Christ and went on to exert a profound spiritual and social impact in their day.

Eliphaz: Job Has Sinned

4 Then Eliphaz the Temanite answered and said:

2 "If one attempts a word with you, will you become weary?
But who can withhold himself from speaking?
3 Surely you have instructed many,
And you have strengthened weak hands.
4 Your words have upheld him who was stumbling,
And you have strengthened the feeble knees;
5 But now it comes upon you, and you are weary;
It touches you, and you are troubled.
6 *Is* not your reverence your confidence?
And the integrity of your ways your hope?

7 "Remember now, who *ever* perished being innocent?
Or where were the upright *ever* cut off?
8 Even as I have seen,
Those who plow iniquity
And sow trouble reap the same.
9 By the blast of God they perish,
And by the breath of His anger they are consumed.
10 The roaring of the lion,
The voice of the fierce lion,
And the teeth of the young lions are broken.
11 The old lion perishes for lack of prey,
And the cubs of the lioness are scattered.

12 "Now a word was secretly brought to me,
And my ear received a whisper of it.
13 In disquieting thoughts from the visions of the night,
When deep sleep falls on men,
14 Fear came upon me, and trembling,
Which made all my bones shake.
15 Then a spirit passed before my face;
The hair on my body stood up.
16 It stood still,
But I could not discern its appearance.
A form *was* before my eyes;

There was silence;
Then I heard a voice *saying:*
17 'Can a mortal be more righteous than God?
Can a man be more pure than his Maker?
18 If He puts no trust in His servants,
If He charges His angels with error,
19 How much more those who dwell in houses of clay,
Whose foundation is in the dust,
Who are crushed before a moth?
20 They are broken in pieces from morning till evening;
They perish forever, with no one regarding.
21 Does not their own excellence go away?
They die, even without wisdom.'

Eliphaz: Job Is Chastened by God

5 "Call out now;
Is there anyone who will answer you?
And to which of the holy ones will you turn?
2 For wrath kills a foolish man,
And envy slays a simple one.
3 I have seen the foolish taking root,
But suddenly I cursed his dwelling place.
4 His sons are far from safety,
They are crushed in the gate,
And *there is* no deliverer.
5 Because the hungry eat up his harvest,
Taking it even from the thorns,[a]
And a snare snatches their substance.[b]
6 For affliction does not come from the dust,
Nor does trouble spring from the ground;
7 Yet man is born to trouble,
As the sparks fly upward.

8 "But as for me, I would seek God,
And to God I would commit my cause—
9 Who does great things, and unsearchable,
Marvelous things without number.

5:5 [a]Septuagint reads *They shall not be taken from evil men;* Vulgate reads *And the armed man shall take him by violence.* [b]Septuagint reads *The might shall draw them off;* Vulgate reads *And the thirsty shall drink up their riches.*

10 He gives rain on the earth,
And sends waters on the fields.
11 He sets on high those who are lowly,
And those who mourn are lifted to
safety.
12 He frustrates the devices of the crafty,
So that their hands cannot carry out
their plans.
13 He catches the wise in their own
craftiness,
And the counsel of the cunning comes
quickly upon them.
14 They meet with darkness in the daytime,
And grope at noontime as in the night.
15 But He saves the needy from the sword,
From the mouth of the mighty,
And from their hand.
16 So the poor have hope,
And injustice shuts her mouth.

17 "Behold, happy *is* the man whom God
corrects;
Therefore do not despise the
chastening of the Almighty.
18 For He bruises, but He binds up;
He wounds, but His hands make whole.
19 He shall deliver you in six troubles,
Yes, in seven no evil shall touch you.
20 In famine He shall redeem you from
death,
And in war from the power of the
sword.
21 You shall be hidden from the scourge
of the tongue,
And you shall not be afraid of
destruction when it comes.
22 You shall laugh at destruction and
famine,
And you shall not be afraid of the
beasts of the earth.
23 For you shall have a covenant with
the stones of the field,
And the beasts of the field shall be
at peace with you.
24 You shall know that your tent *is* in
peace;
You shall visit your dwelling and find
nothing amiss.
25 You shall also know that your
descendants *shall be* many,
And your offspring like the grass of
the earth.

26 You shall come to the grave at a full
age,
As a sheaf of grain ripens in its
season.
27 Behold, this we have searched out;
It *is* true.
Hear it, and know for yourself."

Job: My Complaint Is Just

6 Then Job answered and said:

2 "Oh, that my grief were fully weighed,
And my calamity laid with it on the
scales!
3 For then it would be heavier than the
sand of the sea—
Therefore my words have been rash.
4 For the arrows of the Almighty *are*
within me;
My spirit drinks in their poison;
The terrors of God are arrayed against
me.
5 Does the wild donkey bray when it
has grass,
Or does the ox low over its fodder?
6 Can flavorless food be eaten without
salt?
Or is there *any* taste in the white of
an egg?
7 My soul refuses to touch them;
They *are* as loathsome food to me.

8 "Oh, that I might have my request,
That God would grant *me* the thing
that I long for!
9 That it would please God to crush me,
That He would loose His hand and cut
me off!
10 Then I would still have comfort;
Though in anguish I would exult,
He will not spare;
For I have not concealed the words
of the Holy One.

11 "What strength do I have, that I should
hope?
And what *is* my end, that I should
prolong my life?
12 *Is* my strength the strength of stones?
Or is my flesh bronze?
13 *Is* my help not within me?
And is success driven from me?

14 "To him who is afflicted, kindness
    should be shown by his friend,
    Even though he forsakes the fear of
    the Almighty.
15 My brothers have dealt deceitfully
    like a brook,
    Like the streams of the brooks that
    pass away,
16 Which are dark because of the ice,
    And into which the snow vanishes.
17 When it is warm, they cease to flow;
    When it is hot, they vanish from their
    place.
18 The paths of their way turn aside,
    They go nowhere and perish.
19 The caravans of Tema look,
    The travelers of Sheba hope for them.
20 They are disappointed because they
    were confident;
    They come there and are confused.
21 For now you are nothing,
    You see terror and are afraid.
22 Did I ever say, 'Bring *something* to me'?
    Or, 'Offer a bribe for me from your
    wealth'?
23 Or, 'Deliver me from the enemy's hand'?
    Or, 'Redeem me from the hand of
    oppressors'?

24 "Teach me, and I will hold my tongue;
    Cause me to understand wherein I
    have erred.
25 How forceful are right words!
    But what does your arguing prove?
26 Do you intend to rebuke *my* words,
    And the speeches of a desperate one,
    which are as wind?
27 Yes, you overwhelm the fatherless,
    And you undermine your friend.
28 Now therefore, be pleased to look at me;
    For I would never lie to your face.
29 Yield now, let there be no injustice!
    Yes, concede, my righteousness still
    stands!
30 Is there injustice on my tongue?
    Cannot my taste discern the unsavory?

Job: My Suffering Is Comfortless

7 "Is there not a time of hard service for
    man on earth?
    Are not his days also like the days of a
    hired man?

2 Like a servant who earnestly desires
    the shade,
    And like a hired man who eagerly
    looks for his wages,
3 So I have been allotted months of
    futility,
    And wearisome nights have been
    appointed to me.
4 When I lie down, I say, 'When shall
    I arise,
    And the night be ended?'
    For I have had my fill of tossing till
    dawn.
5 My flesh is caked with worms and
    dust,
    My skin is cracked and breaks out
    afresh.

6 "My days are swifter than a weaver's
    shuttle,
    And are spent without hope.
7 Oh, remember that my life *is* a breath!
    My eye will never again see good.
8 The eye of him who sees me will see
    me no *more;*
    While your eyes *are* upon me, I shall
    no longer *be.*
9 *As* the cloud disappears and vanishes
    away,
    So he who goes down to the grave
    does not come up.
10 He shall never return to his house,
    Nor shall his place know him anymore.

11 "Therefore I will not restrain my mouth;
    I will speak in the anguish of my spirit;
    I will complain in the bitterness of my
    soul.
12 *Am* I a sea, or a sea serpent,
    That You set a guard over me?
13 When I say, 'My bed will comfort me,
    My couch will ease my complaint,'
14 Then You scare me with dreams
    And terrify me with visions,
15 So that my soul chooses strangling
    And death rather than my body.[a]
16 I loathe *my life;*
    I would not live forever.
    Let me alone,
    For my days *are but* a breath.

7:15 [a]Literally *my bones*

17 "What *is* man, that You should exalt
　　him,
　　That You should set Your heart on him,
18 That You should visit him every
　　morning,
　　And test him every moment?
19 How long?
　　Will You not look away from me,
　　And let me alone till I swallow my
　　saliva?
20 Have I sinned?
　　What have I done to You, O watcher
　　of men?
　　Why have You set me as Your target,
　　So that I am a burden to myself?ᵃ
21 Why then do You not pardon my
　　transgression,
　　And take away my iniquity?
　　For now I will lie down in the dust,
　　And You will seek me diligently,
　　But I *will* no longer *be*."

Bildad: Job Should Repent

8 Then Bildad the Shuhite answered and
said:

2 "How long will you speak these *things,*
　　And the words of your mouth *be like* a
　　strong wind?
3 Does God subvert judgment?
　　Or does the Almighty pervert justice?
4 If your sons have sinned against Him,
　　He has cast them away for their
　　transgression.
5 If you would earnestly seek God
　　And make your supplication to the
　　Almighty,
6 If you *were* pure and upright,
　　Surely now He would awake for you,
　　And prosper your rightful dwelling
　　place.
7 Though your beginning was small,
　　Yet your latter end would increase
　　abundantly.

8 "For inquire, please, of the former age,
　　And consider the things discovered by
　　their fathers;
9 For we *were born* yesterday, and know
　　nothing,
　　Because our days on earth *are* a
　　shadow.

10 Will they not teach you and tell you,
　　And utter words from their heart?
11 "Can the papyrus grow up without a
　　marsh?
　　Can the reeds flourish without water?
12 While it *is* yet green *and* not cut down,
　　It withers before any *other* plant.
13 So *are* the paths of all who forget God;
　　And the hope of the hypocrite shall
　　perish,
14 Whose confidence shall be cut off,
　　And whose trust *is* a spider's web.
15 He leans on his house, but it does not
　　stand.
　　He holds it fast, but it does not
　　endure.
16 He grows green in the sun,
　　And his branches spread out in his
　　garden.
17 His roots wrap around the rock heap,
　　And look for a place in the stones.
18 If he is destroyed from his place,
　　Then *it* will deny him, *saying,* 'I have
　　not seen you.'

19 "Behold, this is the joy of His way,
　　And out of the earth others will grow.
20 Behold, God will not cast away the
　　blameless,
　　Nor will He uphold the evildoers.
21 He will yet fill your mouth with
　　laughing,
　　And your lips with rejoicing.
22 Those who hate you will be clothed
　　with shame,
　　And the dwelling place of the wicked
　　will come to nothing."ᵃ

Job: There Is No Mediator

9 Then Job answered and said:

2 "Truly I know *it is* so,
　　But how can a man be righteous
　　before God?
3 If one wished to contend with Him,
　　He could not answer Him one time
　　out of a thousand.

7:20 ᵃFollowing Masoretic Text, Targum, and
Vulgate; Septuagint and Jewish tradition read *to You.*
8:22 ᵃLiterally *will not be*

4 *God is* wise in heart and mighty in strength.
Who has hardened *himself* against Him and prospered?

5 He removes the mountains, and they do not know
When He overturns them in His anger;

6 He shakes the earth out of its place,
And its pillars tremble;

7 He commands the sun, and it does not rise;
He seals off the stars;

8 He alone spreads out the heavens,
And treads on the waves of the sea;

9 He made the Bear, Orion, and the Pleiades,
And the chambers of the south;

10 He does great things past finding out,
Yes, wonders without number.

11 If He goes by me, I do not see *Him;*
If He moves past, I do not perceive Him;

12 If He takes away, who can hinder Him?
Who can say to Him, 'What are You doing?'

13 God will not withdraw His anger,
The allies of the proud[a] lie prostrate beneath Him.

14 "How then can I answer Him,
And choose my words *to reason* with Him?

15 For though I were righteous, I could not answer Him;
I would beg mercy of my Judge.

16 If I called and He answered me,
I would not believe that He was listening to my voice.

17 For He crushes me with a tempest,
And multiplies my wounds without cause.

18 He will not allow me to catch my breath,
But fills me with bitterness.

19 If *it is a matter* of strength, indeed *He is* strong;
And if of justice, who will appoint my day *in court?*

20 Though I were righteous, my own mouth would condemn me;
Though I *were* blameless, it would prove me perverse.

21 "I am blameless, yet I do not know myself;
I despise my life.

22 It *is* all one *thing;*
Therefore I say, 'He destroys the blameless and the wicked.'

23 If the scourge slays suddenly,
He laughs at the plight of the innocent.

24 The earth is given into the hand of the wicked.
He covers the faces of its judges.
If it is not *He,* who else could it be?

25 "Now my days are swifter than a runner;
They flee away, they see no good.

26 They pass by like swift ships,
Like an eagle swooping on its prey.

27 If I say, 'I will forget my complaint,
I will put off my sad face and wear a smile,'

28 I am afraid of all my sufferings;
I know that You will not hold me innocent.

29 *If* I am condemned,
Why then do I labor in vain?

30 If I wash myself with snow water,
And cleanse my hands with soap,

31 Yet You will plunge me into the pit,
And my own clothes will abhor me.

32 "For *He is* not a man, as I *am,*
That I may answer Him,
And that we should go to court together.

33 Nor is there any mediator between us,
Who may lay his hand on us both.

34 Let Him take His rod away from me,
And do not let dread of Him terrify me.

35 *Then* I would speak and not fear Him,
But it is not so with me.

Job: I Would Plead with God

10 "My soul loathes my life;
I will give free course to my complaint,
I will speak in the bitterness of my soul.

2 I will say to God, 'Do not condemn me;
Show me why You contend with me.

3 *Does it* seem good to You that You should oppress,

9:13 [a]Hebrew *rahab*

That You should despise the work of
　　Your hands,
And smile on the counsel of the wicked?
4　Do You have eyes of flesh?
　　Or do You see as man sees?
5　*Are* Your days like the days of a mortal
　　man?
　　Are Your years like the days of a
　　mighty man,
6　That You should seek for my iniquity
　　And search out my sin,
7　Although You know that I am not
　　wicked,
　　And *there is* no one who can deliver
　　from Your hand?

8　'Your hands have made me and
　　fashioned me,
　　An intricate unity;
　　Yet You would destroy me.
9　Remember, I pray, that You have
　　made me like clay.
　　And will You turn me into dust again?
10　Did You not pour me out like milk,
　　And curdle me like cheese,
11　Clothe me with skin and flesh,
　　And knit me together with bones and
　　sinews?
12　You have granted me life and favor,
　　And Your care has preserved my spirit.

13　'And these *things* You have hidden in
　　Your heart;
　　I know that this *was* with You:
14　If I sin, then You mark me,
　　And will not acquit me of my iniquity.
15　If I am wicked, woe to me;
　　Even *if* I am righteous, I cannot lift up
　　my head.
　　I am full of disgrace;
　　See my misery!
16　If *my head* is exalted,
　　You hunt me like a fierce lion,
　　And again You show Yourself
　　awesome against me.
17　You renew Your witnesses against me,
　　And increase Your indignation toward
　　me;
　　Changes and war are *ever* with me.

18　'Why then have You brought me out of
　　the womb?

Oh, that I had perished and no eye
　　had seen me!
19　I would have been as though I had
　　not been.
　　I would have been carried from the
　　womb to the grave.
20　Are not my days few?
　　Cease! Leave me alone, that I may
　　take a little comfort,
21　Before I go *to the place from which* I
　　shall not return,
　　To the land of darkness and the
　　shadow of death,
22　A land as dark as darkness *itself,*
　　As the shadow of death, without any
　　order,
　　Where even the light *is* like darkness.'"

Zophar Urges Job to Repent

11　Then Zophar the Naamathite an-
　　swered and said:

2　"Should not the multitude of words be
　　answered?
　　And should a man full of talk be
　　vindicated?
3　Should your empty talk make men
　　hold their peace?
　　And when you mock, should no one
　　rebuke you?
4　For you have said,
　　'My doctrine *is* pure,
　　And I am clean in your eyes.'
5　But oh, that God would speak,
　　And open His lips against you,
6　That He would show you the secrets
　　of wisdom!
　　For *they would* double *your* prudence.
　　Know therefore that God exacts from
　　you
　　Less than your iniquity *deserves.*

7　"Can you search out the deep things
　　of God?
　　Can you find out the limits of the
　　Almighty?
8　*They are* higher than heaven— what
　　can you do?
　　Deeper than Sheol— what can you
　　know?
9　Their measure *is* longer than the earth
　　And broader than the sea.

10 "If He passes by, imprisons, and gathers
     to judgment,
   Then who can hinder Him?
11 For He knows deceitful men;
   He sees wickedness also.
   Will He not then consider *it?*
12 For an empty-headed man will be wise,
   When a wild donkey's colt is born a
     man.

13 "If you would prepare your heart,
   And stretch out your hands toward Him;
14 If iniquity *were* in your hand, *and you*
     put it far away,
   And would not let wickedness dwell in
     your tents;
15 Then surely you could lift up your face
     without spot;
   Yes, you could be steadfast, and not fear;
16 Because you would forget *your* misery,
   And remember *it* as waters *that have*
     passed away,
17 And *your* life would be brighter than
     noonday.
   Though you were dark, you would be
     like the morning.
18 And you would be secure, because
     there is hope;
   Yes, you would dig *around you, and*
     take your rest in safety.
19 You would also lie down, and no one
     would make *you* afraid;
   Yes, many would court your favor.
20 But the eyes of the wicked will fail,
   And they shall not escape,
   And their hope—loss of life!"

Job Answers His Critics

12 Then Job answered and said:

2 "No doubt you *are* the people,
   And wisdom will die with you!
3 But I have understanding as well as
     you;
   I *am* not inferior to you.
   Indeed, who does not *know* such
     things as these?

4 "I am one mocked by his friends,
   Who called on God, and He answered
     him,
   The just and blameless *who is* ridiculed.

5 A lamp[a] is despised in the thought
     of one who is at ease;
   It is made ready for those whose feet
     slip.
6 The tents of robbers prosper,
   And those who provoke God are
     secure—
   In what God provides by His hand.

7 "But now ask the beasts, and they will
     teach you;
   And the birds of the air, and they will
     tell you;
8 Or speak to the earth, and it will
     teach you;
   And the fish of the sea will explain
     to you.
9 Who among all these does not know
   That the hand of the LORD has done
     this,
10 In whose hand *is* the life of every
     living thing,
   And the breath of all mankind?
11 Does not the ear test words
   And the mouth taste its food?
12 Wisdom *is* with aged men,
   And with length of days,
     understanding.

13 "With Him *are* wisdom and strength,
   He has counsel and understanding.
14 If He breaks *a thing* down, it cannot
     be rebuilt;
   If He imprisons a man, there can be
     no release.
15 If He withholds the waters, they dry
     up;
   If He sends them out, they overwhelm
     the earth.
16 With Him *are* strength and prudence.
   The deceived and the deceiver *are* His.
17 He leads counselors away plundered,
   And makes fools of the judges.
18 He loosens the bonds of kings,
   And binds their waist with a belt.
19 He leads princes[a] away plundered,
   And overthrows the mighty.
20 He deprives the trusted ones of speech,
   And takes away the discernment of
     the elders.

12:5 [a]Or *disaster*   **12:19** [a]Literally *priests,* but not
in a technical sense

21 He pours contempt on princes,
And disarms the mighty.
22 He uncovers deep things out of
darkness,
And brings the shadow of death to
light.
23 He makes nations great, and destroys
them;
He enlarges nations, and guides them.
24 He takes away the understanding[a] of
the chiefs of the people of the earth,
And makes them wander in a pathless
wilderness.
25 They grope in the dark without light,
And He makes them stagger like a
drunken *man.*

13 "Behold, my eye has seen all *this,*
My ear has heard and understood it.
2 What you know, I also know;
I *am* not inferior to you.
3 But I would speak to the Almighty,
And I desire to reason with God.
4 But you forgers of lies,
You *are* all worthless physicians.
5 Oh, that you would be silent,
And it would be your wisdom!
6 Now hear my reasoning,
And heed the pleadings of my lips.
7 Will you speak wickedly for God,
And talk deceitfully for Him?
8 Will you show partiality for Him?
Will you contend for God?
9 Will it be well when He searches you
out?
Or can you mock Him as one mocks
a man?
10 He will surely rebuke you
If you secretly show partiality.
11 Will not His excellence make you
afraid,
And the dread of Him fall upon you?
12 Your platitudes *are* proverbs of ashes,
Your defenses are defenses of clay.

13 "Hold your peace with me, and let me
speak,
Then let come on me what *may!*
14 Why do I take my flesh in my teeth,
And put my life in my hands?
15 Though He slay me, yet will I trust Him.
Even so, I will defend my own ways
before Him.

16 He also *shall* be my salvation,
For a hypocrite could not come before
Him.
17 Listen carefully to my speech,
And to my declaration with your ears.
18 See now, I have prepared *my* case,
I know that I shall be vindicated.
19 Who *is* he *who* will contend with me?
If now I hold my tongue, I perish.

Job's Despondent Prayer

20 "Only two *things* do not do to me,
Then I will not hide myself from You:
21 Withdraw Your hand far from me,
And let not the dread of You make
me afraid.
22 Then call, and I will answer;
Or let me speak, then You respond
to me.
23 How many *are* my iniquities and
sins?
Make me know my transgression
and my sin.
24 Why do You hide Your face,
And regard me as Your enemy?
25 Will You frighten a leaf driven to and
fro?
And will You pursue dry stubble?
26 For You write bitter things against me,
And make me inherit the iniquities
of my youth.
27 You put my feet in the stocks,
And watch closely all my paths.
You set a limit[a] for the soles of my
feet.

28 "Man[a] decays like a rotten thing,
Like a garment that is moth-eaten.

14 "Man *who is* born of woman
Is of few days and full of trouble.
2 He comes forth like a flower and fades
away;
He flees like a shadow and does not
continue.
3 And do You open Your eyes on such
a one,
And bring me[a] to judgment with
Yourself?

12:24 [a]Literally *heart*   **13:27** [a]Literally *inscribe a
print*   **13:28** [a]Literally *He*   **14:3** [a]Septuagint,
Syriac, and Vulgate read *him.*

4 Who can bring a clean *thing* out of an
   unclean?
   No one!
5 Since his days *are* determined,
   The number of his months *is* with You;
   You have appointed his limits, so that
   he cannot pass.
6 Look away from him that he may rest,
   Till like a hired man he finishes his day.

7 "For there is hope for a tree,
   If it is cut down, that it will sprout
   again,
   And that its tender shoots will not
   cease.
8 Though its root may grow old in the
   earth,
   And its stump may die in the ground,
9 *Yet* at the scent of water it will bud
   And bring forth branches like a plant.
10 But man dies and is laid away;
   Indeed he breathes his last
   And where *is* he?
11 *As* water disappears from the sea,
   And a river becomes parched and
   dries up,
12 So man lies down and does not rise.
   Till the heavens *are* no more,
   They will not awake
   Nor be roused from their sleep.

13 "Oh, that You would hide me in the
   grave,
   That You would conceal me until Your
   wrath is past,
   That You would appoint me a set
   time, and remember me!
14 If a man dies, shall he live *again?*
   All the days of my hard service I will
   wait,
   Till my change comes.
15 You shall call, and I will answer You;
   You shall desire the work of Your
   hands.
16 For now You number my steps,
   But do not watch over my sin.
17 My transgression *is* sealed up in a bag,
   And You cover[a] my iniquity.

18 "But *as* a mountain falls *and* crumbles
   away,
   And *as* a rock is moved from its place;

19 *As* water wears away stones,
   And as torrents wash away the soil
   of the earth;
   So You destroy the hope of man.
20 You prevail forever against him, and
   he passes on;
   You change his countenance and send
   him away.
21 His sons come to honor, and he does
   not know *it;*
   They are brought low, and he does not
   perceive *it.*
22 But his flesh will be in pain over it,
   And his soul will mourn over it."

Eliphaz Accuses Job of Folly

15 Then Eliphaz the Temanite answered
and said:

2 "Should a wise man answer with empty
   knowledge,
   And fill himself with the east wind?
3 Should he reason with unprofitable
   talk,
   Or by speeches with which he can do
   no good?
4 Yes, you cast off fear,
   And restrain prayer before God.
5 For your iniquity teaches your mouth,
   And you choose the tongue of the
   crafty.
6 Your own mouth condemns you, and
   not I;
   Yes, your own lips testify against you.

7 "*Are* you the first man *who* was born?
   Or were you made before the hills?
8 Have you heard the counsel of God?
   Do you limit wisdom to yourself?
9 What do you know that we do not
   know?
   What do you understand that *is* not
   in us?
10 Both the gray-haired and the aged
   are among us,
   Much older than your father.
11 *Are* the consolations of God too small
   for you,
   And the word *spoken* gently[a] with you?

14:17 [a]Literally *plaster over*   **15:11** [a]Septuagint
reads *a secret thing.*

12 Why does your heart carry you away,
And what do your eyes wink at,

13 That you turn your spirit against God,
And let *such* words go out of your
mouth?

14 "What *is* man, that he could be pure?
And *he who is* born of a woman, that
he could be righteous?

15 If *God* puts no trust in His saints,
And the heavens are not pure in His
sight,

16 How much less man, *who is*
abominable and filthy,
Who drinks iniquity like water!

17 "I will tell you, hear me;
What I have seen I will declare,

18 What wise men have told,
Not hiding *anything received* from their
fathers,

19 To whom alone the land was given,
And no alien passed among them:

20 The wicked man writhes with pain
all *his* days,
And the number of years is hidden
from the oppressor.

21 Dreadful sounds *are* in his ears;
In prosperity the destroyer comes
upon him.

22 He does not believe that he will return
from darkness,
For a sword is waiting for him.

23 He wanders about for bread, *saying,*
'Where *is it?*'
He knows that a day of darkness is
ready at his hand.

24 Trouble and anguish make him afraid;
They overpower him, like a king ready
for battle.

25 For he stretches out his hand against
God,
And acts defiantly against the Almighty,

26 Running stubbornly against Him
With his strong, embossed shield.

27 "Though he has covered his face with
his fatness,
And made *his* waist heavy with fat,

28 He dwells in desolate cities,
In houses which no one inhabits,
Which are destined to become ruins.

29 He will not be rich,
Nor will his wealth continue,
Nor will his possessions overspread
the earth.

30 He will not depart from darkness;
The flame will dry out his branches,
And by the breath of His mouth he
will go away.

31 Let him not trust in futile *things,*
deceiving himself,
For futility will be his reward.

32 It will be accomplished before his time,
And his branch will not be green.

33 He will shake off his unripe grape like
a vine,
And cast off his blossom like an olive
tree.

34 For the company of hypocrites *will be*
barren,
And fire will consume the tents of
bribery.

35 They conceive trouble and bring forth
futility;
Their womb prepares deceit."

Job Reproaches His Pitiless Friends

16 Then Job answered and said:

2 "I have heard many such things;
Miserable comforters *are* you all!

3 Shall words of wind have an end?
Or what provokes you that you
answer?

4 I also could speak as you *do,*
If your soul were in my soul's place.
I could heap up words against you,
And shake my head at you;

5 *But* I would strengthen you with my
mouth,
And the comfort of my lips would
relieve *your grief.*

6 "Though I speak, my grief is not
relieved;
And *if* I remain silent, how am I eased?

7 But now He has worn me out;
You have made desolate all my
company.

8 You have shriveled me up,
And it is a witness *against me;*
My leanness rises up against me
And bears witness to my face.

9 He tears *me* in His wrath, and hates
    me;
    He gnashes at me with His teeth;
    My adversary sharpens His gaze on me.
10 They gape at me with their mouth,
    They strike me reproachfully on the
    cheek,
    They gather together against me.
11 God has delivered me to the ungodly,
    And turned me over to the hands of
    the wicked.
12 I was at ease, but He has shattered me;
    He also has taken *me* by my neck, and
    shaken me to pieces;
    He has set me up for His target,
13 His archers surround me.
    He pierces my heart[a] and does not pity;
    He pours out my gall on the ground.
14 He breaks me with wound upon wound;
    He runs at me like a warrior.[a]

15 "I have sewn sackcloth over my skin,
    And laid my head[a] in the dust.
16 My face is flushed from weeping,
    And on my eyelids *is* the shadow of
    death;
17 Although no violence *is* in my hands,
    And my prayer *is* pure.

18 "O earth, do not cover my blood,
    And let my cry have no *resting* place!
19 Surely even now my witness *is* in
    heaven,
    And my evidence *is* on high.
20 My friends scorn me;
    My eyes pour out *tears* to God.
21 Oh, that one might plead for a man
    with God,
    As a man *pleads* for his neighbor!
22 For when a few years are finished,
    I shall go the way of no return.

Job Prays for Relief

17 "My spirit is broken,
    My days are extinguished,
    The grave *is ready* for me.
2 *Are* not mockers with me?
    And does not my eye dwell on their
    provocation?

3 "Now put down a pledge for me with
    Yourself.

    Who *is* he *who* will shake hands with
    me?
4 For You have hidden their heart from
    understanding;
    Therefore You will not exalt *them*.
5 He who speaks flattery to *his* friends,
    Even the eyes of his children will fail.

6 "But He has made me a byword of the
    people,
    And I have become one in whose face
    men spit.
7 My eye has also grown dim because
    of sorrow,
    And all my members *are* like shadows.
8 Upright *men* are astonished at this,
    And the innocent stirs himself up
    against the hypocrite.
9 Yet the righteous will hold to his way,
    And he who has clean hands will be
    stronger and stronger.

10 "But please, come back again, all
    of you,[a]
    For I shall not find *one* wise *man*
    among you.
11 My days are past,
    My purposes are broken off,
    Even the thoughts of my heart.
12 They change the night into day;
    'The light *is* near,' *they say,* in the face
    of darkness.
13 If I wait *for* the grave *as* my house,
    If I make my bed in the darkness,
14 If I say to corruption, 'You *are* my
    father,'
    And to the worm, 'You *are* my mother
    and my sister,'
15 Where then *is* my hope?
    As for my hope, who can see it?
16 *Will* they go down to the gates of Sheol?
    Shall *we have* rest together in the dust?"

Bildad: The Wicked Are Punished

18 Then Bildad the Shuhite answered
    and said:

16:13 [a]Literally *kidneys*   **16:14** [a]Vulgate reads
giant.   **16:15** [a]Literally *horn*   **17:10** [a]Following
some Hebrew manuscripts, Septuagint, Syriac, and
Vulgate; Masoretic Text and Targum read *all of them.*

2 "How long *till* you put an end to words?
Gain understanding, and afterward
we will speak.

3 Why are we counted as beasts,
And regarded as stupid in your sight?

4 You who tear yourself in anger,
Shall the earth be forsaken for you?
Or shall the rock be removed from its
place?

5 "The light of the wicked indeed goes out,
And the flame of his fire does not shine.

6 The light is dark in his tent,
And his lamp beside him is put out.

7 The steps of his strength are shortened,
And his own counsel casts him down.

8 For he is cast into a net by his own feet,
And he walks into a snare.

9 The net takes *him* by the heel,
And a snare lays hold of him.

10 A noose *is* hidden for him on the
ground,
And a trap for him in the road.

11 Terrors frighten him on every side,
And drive him to his feet.

12 His strength is starved,
And destruction *is* ready at his side.

13 It devours patches of his skin;
The firstborn of death devours his
limbs.

14 He is uprooted from the shelter of
his tent,
And they parade him before the king
of terrors.

15 They dwell in his tent *who are* none
of his;
Brimstone is scattered on his dwelling.

16 His roots are dried out below,
And his branch withers above.

17 The memory of him perishes from
the earth,
And he has no name among the
renowned.[a]

18:17 [a]Literally *before the outside,* meaning
distinguished, famous

HOPE

"Where then is my hope?"

JOB 17:15

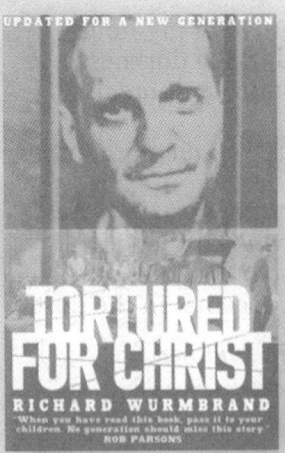

THE LAST BASTION OF FREEDOM

Richard Wurmbrand (1909–2001), a Romanian evangelical
Christian minister and author who spent a total of 14 years
imprisoned in Romania for his faith, was also the founder
of the Voice of the Martyrs, an interdenominational organization working with and for persecuted Christians around
the world. In 1967, he expressed this view of America:

> Every freedom-loving man has two fatherlands; his own
> and America. Today, America is the hope of every enslaved
> man, because it is the last bastion of freedom in the world.
> Only America has the power and spiritual resources to
> stand as a barrier between militant communism and the
> people of the world.
>
> It is the last "dike" holding back the rampaging flood-
> waters of militant communism. If it crumples, there is no
> other dike, no other dam; no other line of defense to fall
> back upon.
>
> America is the last hope of millions of enslaved peo-
> ples. They look to it as their second fatherland. In it lies
> their hopes and prayers.
>
> I have seen fellow-prisoners in communist prisons
> beaten, tortured, with 50 pounds of chains on their legs—
> praying for America . . . that the dike will not crumple;
> that it will remain free.

18 He is driven from light into darkness,
And chased out of the world.
19 He has neither son nor posterity
among his people,
Nor any remaining in his dwellings.
20 Those in the west are astonished at
his day,
As those in the east are frightened.
21 Surely such *are* the dwellings of the
wicked,
And this *is* the place *of him who* does
not know God."

Job Trusts in His Redeemer

19 Then Job answered and said:

2 "How long will you torment my soul,
And break me in pieces with words?
3 These ten times you have reproached
me;
You are not ashamed *that* you have
wronged me.ᵃ
4 And if indeed I have erred,
My error remains with me.
5 If indeed you exalt *yourselves* against
me,
And plead my disgrace against me,
6 Know then that God has wronged me,
And has surrounded me with His net.

7 "If I cry out concerning wrong, I am
not heard.
If I cry aloud, *there is* no justice.
8 He has fenced up my way, so that I
cannot pass;
And He has set darkness in my paths.
9 He has stripped me of my glory,
And taken the crown *from* my head.
10 He breaks me down on every side,
And I am gone;
My hope He has uprooted like a tree.
11 He has also kindled His wrath against
me,
And He counts me as *one of* His enemies.
12 His troops come together
And build up their road against me;
They encamp all around my tent.

13 "He has removed my brothers far from
me,
And my acquaintances are completely
estranged from me.

14 My relatives have failed,
And my close friends have forgotten me.
15 Those who dwell in my house, and
my maidservants,
Count me as a stranger;
I am an alien in their sight.
16 I call my servant, but he gives no
answer;
I beg him with my mouth.
17 My breath is offensive to my wife,
And I am repulsive to the children
of my own body.
18 Even young children despise me;
I arise, and they speak against me.
19 All my close friends abhor me,
And those whom I love have turned
against me.
20 My bone clings to my skin and to my
flesh,
And I have escaped by the skin of my
teeth.

21 "Have pity on me, have pity on me,
O you my friends,
For the hand of God has struck me!
22 Why do you persecute me as God *does,*
And are not satisfied with my flesh?

23 "Oh, that my words were written!
Oh, that they were inscribed in a book!
24 That they were engraved on a rock
With an iron pen and lead, forever!
25 For I know *that* my Redeemer lives,
And He shall stand at last on the earth;
26 And after my skin is destroyed, this *I
know,*
That in my flesh I shall see God,
27 Whom I shall see for myself,
And my eyes shall behold, and not
another.
How my heart yearns within me!
28 If you should say, 'How shall we
persecute him?'—
Since the root of the matter is found
in me,
29 Be afraid of the sword for yourselves;
For wrath *brings* the punishment of
the sword,
That you may know *there is* a
judgment."

19:3 ᵃA Jewish tradition reads *make yourselves
strange to me.*

FAITH
"... And after my skin is destroyed...."

JOB 19:26

A Resurrection Body
In his early twenties, Benjamin Franklin, one of America's renowned Founding Fathers, wrote this verse, reminiscent of words of Job, to serve as his epitaph:

The Body of
Benjamin Franklin, Printer,
(Like the cover of an old book,
Its contents torn out
And stripped of its lettering and gilding,)
Lies here, food for worms.
But the work shall not be lost;
For it will, as he believ'd, appear once more
In a new and more elegant edition,
Revised and Corrected
By the Author

Zophar's Sermon on the Wicked Man

20 Then Zophar the Naamathite answered and said:

2 "Therefore my anxious thoughts make me answer,
Because of the turmoil within me.
3 I have heard the rebuke that reproaches me,
And the spirit of my understanding causes me to answer.

4 "Do you *not* know this of old,
Since man was placed on earth,
5 That the triumphing of the wicked is short,
And the joy of the hypocrite is *but* for a moment?
6 Though his haughtiness mounts up to the heavens,
And his head reaches to the clouds,
7 *Yet* he will perish forever like his own refuse;
Those who have seen him will say, 'Where is he?'
8 He will fly away like a dream, and not be found;
Yes, he will be chased away like a vision of the night.

9 The eye *that* saw him will *see him* no more,
Nor will his place behold him anymore.
10 His children will seek the favor of the poor,
And his hands will restore his wealth.
11 His bones are full of his youthful vigor,
But it will lie down with him in the dust.

12 "Though evil is sweet in his mouth,
And he hides it under his tongue,
13 *Though* he spares it and does not forsake it,
But still keeps it in his mouth,
14 *Yet* his food in his stomach turns sour;
It becomes cobra venom within him.
15 He swallows down riches
And vomits them up again;
God casts them out of his belly.
16 He will suck the poison of cobras;
The viper's tongue will slay him.
17 He will not see the streams,
The rivers flowing with honey and cream.
18 He will restore that for which he labored,
And will not swallow *it* down;
From the proceeds of business
He will get no enjoyment.
19 For he has oppressed *and* forsaken the poor,
He has violently seized a house which he did not build.

20 "Because he knows no quietness in his heart,[a]
He will not save anything he desires.
21 Nothing is left for him to eat;
Therefore his well-being will not last.
22 In his self-sufficiency he will be in distress;
Every hand of misery will come against him.
23 *When* he is about to fill his stomach,
God will cast on him the fury of His wrath,
And will rain *it* on him while he is eating.
24 He will flee from the iron weapon;
A bronze bow will pierce him through.

20:20 [a]Literally *belly*

25 It is drawn, and comes out of the body;
  Yes, the glittering *point comes* out of
    his gall.
  Terrors *come* upon him;
26 Total darkness *is* reserved for his
    treasures.
  An unfanned fire will consume him;
  It shall go ill with him who is left in
    his tent.
27 The heavens will reveal his iniquity,
  And the earth will rise up against him.
28 The increase of his house will depart,
  And his goods will flow away in the
    day of His wrath.
29 This *is* the portion from God for a
    wicked man,
  The heritage appointed to him by God."

Job's Discourse on the Wicked

21 Then Job answered and said:

2 "Listen carefully to my speech,
  And let this be your consolation.
3 Bear with me that I may speak,
  And after I have spoken, keep mocking.

4 "As for me, *is* my complaint against
    man?
  And if *it were,* why should I not be
    impatient?
5 Look at me and be astonished;
  Put *your* hand over *your* mouth.
6 Even when I remember I am terrified,
  And trembling takes hold of my flesh.
7 Why do the wicked live *and* become
    old,
  Yes, become mighty in power?
8 Their descendants are established with
    them in their sight,
  And their offspring before their eyes.
9 Their houses *are* safe from fear,
  Neither *is* the rod of God upon them.
10 Their bull breeds without failure;
  Their cow calves without miscarriage.
11 They send forth their little ones like a
    flock,
  And their children dance.
12 They sing to the tambourine and harp,
  And rejoice to the sound of the flute.
13 They spend their days in wealth,
  And in a moment go down to the
    grave.ᵃ

14 Yet they say to God, 'Depart from us,
  For we do not desire the knowledge of
    Your ways.
15 Who *is* the Almighty, that we should
    serve Him?
  And what profit do we have if we pray
    to Him?'
16 Indeed their prosperity *is* not in their
    hand;
  The counsel of the wicked is far from
    me.

17 "How often is the lamp of the wicked
    put out?
  How often does their destruction come
    upon them,
  The sorrows *God* distributes in His
    anger?
18 They are like straw before the wind,
  And like chaff that a storm carries
    away.
19 *They say,* 'God lays up one'sᵃ iniquity
    for his children';
  Let Him recompense him, that he may
    know *it.*
20 Let his eyes see his destruction,
  And let him drink of the wrath of the
    Almighty.
21 For what does he care about his
    household after him,
  When the number of his months is cut
    in half?

22 "Can *anyone* teach God knowledge,
  Since He judges those on high?
23 One dies in his full strength,
  Being wholly at ease and secure;
24 His pailsᵃ are full of milk,
  And the marrow of his bones is moist.
25 Another man dies in the bitterness of
    his soul,
  Never having eaten with pleasure.
26 They lie down alike in the dust,
  And worms cover them.

27 "Look, I know your thoughts,
  And the schemes *with which* you would
    wrong me.

21:13 ᵃOr *Sheol*   **21:19** ᵃLiterally *his*
21:24 ᵃSeptuagint and Vulgate read *bowels;* Syriac
reads *sides;* Targum reads *breasts.*

28 For you say,
'Where *is* the house of the prince?
And where *is* the tent,[a]
The dwelling place of the wicked?'
29 Have you not asked those who travel
    the road?
And do you not know their signs?
30 For the wicked are reserved for the day
    of doom;
They shall be brought out on the day
    of wrath.
31 Who condemns his way to his face?
And who repays him *for what* he has
    done?
32 Yet he shall be brought to the grave,
And a vigil kept over the tomb.
33 The clods of the valley shall be sweet
    to him;
Everyone shall follow him,
As countless *have gone* before him.
34 How then can you comfort me with
    empty words,
Since falsehood remains in your
    answers?"

Eliphaz Accuses Job of Wickedness

22 Then Eliphaz the Temanite answered and said:

2 "Can a man be profitable to God,
Though he who is wise may be
    profitable to himself?
3 *Is it* any pleasure to the Almighty that
    you are righteous?
Or *is it* gain *to Him* that you make
    your ways blameless?

4 "Is it because of your fear of Him that
    He corrects you,
And enters into judgment with you?
5 *Is* not your wickedness great,
And your iniquity without end?
6 For you have taken pledges from your
    brother for no reason,
And stripped the naked of their
    clothing.
7 You have not given the weary water
    to drink,
And you have withheld bread from
    the hungry.
8 But the mighty man possessed the land,
And the honorable man dwelt in it.

9 You have sent widows away empty,
And the strength of the fatherless was
    crushed.
10 Therefore snares *are* all around you,
And sudden fear troubles you,
11 Or darkness *so that* you cannot see;
And an abundance of water covers you.

12 "Is not God in the height of heaven?
And see the highest stars, how lofty
    they are!
13 And you say, 'What does God know?
Can He judge through the deep
    darkness?
14 Thick clouds cover Him, so that He
    cannot see,
And He walks above the circle of
    heaven.'
15 Will you keep to the old way
Which wicked men have trod,
16 Who were cut down before their time,
Whose foundations were swept away
    by a flood?
17 They said to God, 'Depart from us!
What can the Almighty do to them?'[a]
18 Yet He filled their houses with good
    things;
But the counsel of the wicked is far
    from me.

19 "The righteous see *it* and are glad,
And the innocent laugh at them:
20 'Surely our adversaries[a] are cut down,
And the fire consumes their remnant.'

21 "Now acquaint yourself with Him, and
    be at peace;
Thereby good will come to you.
22 Receive, please, instruction from His
    mouth,
And lay up His words in your heart.
23 If you return to the Almighty, you will
    be built up;
You will remove iniquity far from your
    tents.
24 Then you will lay your gold in the dust,
And the *gold* of Ophir among the
    stones of the brooks.

21:28 [a]Vulgate omits *the tent.*
22:17 [a]Septuagint and Syriac read *us.*
22:20 [a]Septuagint reads *substance.*

25 Yes, the Almighty will be your gold[a]
    And your precious silver;
26 For then you will have your delight in
        the Almighty,
    And lift up your face to God.
27 You will make your prayer to Him,
    He will hear you,
    And you will pay your vows.
28 You will also declare a thing,
    And it will be established for you;
    So light will shine on your ways.
29 When they cast *you* down, and you
        say, 'Exaltation *will come!*'
    Then He will save the humble *person.*
30 He will *even* deliver one who is not
        innocent;
    Yes, he will be delivered by the purity
        of your hands."

Job Proclaims God's Righteous Judgments

23 Then Job answered and said:

2   "Even today my complaint is bitter;
    My[a] hand is listless because of my
        groaning.
3   Oh, that I knew where I might find
        Him,
    That I might come to His seat!
4   I would present *my* case before Him,
    And fill my mouth with arguments.
5   I would know the words *which* He
        would answer me,
    And understand what He would say
        to me.
6   Would He contend with me in His
        great power?
    No! But He would take *note* of me.
7   There the upright could reason with
        Him,
    And I would be delivered forever from
        my Judge.

8   "Look, I go forward, but He is not *there,*
    And backward, but I cannot perceive
        Him;
9   When He works on the left hand, I
        cannot behold *Him;*
    When He turns to the right hand, I
        cannot see *Him.*
10 But He knows the way that I take;
    When He has tested me, I shall come
        forth as gold.

11 My foot has held fast to His steps;
    I have kept His way and not turned
        aside.
12 I have not departed from the
        commandment of His lips;
    I have treasured the words of His
        mouth
    More than my necessary *food.*

13 "But He *is* unique, and who can make
        Him change?
    And *whatever* His soul desires, *that* He
        does.
14 For He performs *what is* appointed for
        me,
    And many such *things are* with Him.
15 Therefore I am terrified at His
        presence;
    When I consider *this,* I am afraid of
        Him.
16 For God made my heart weak,
    And the Almighty terrifies me;
17 Because I was not cut off from the
        presence of darkness,
    And He did *not* hide deep darkness
        from my face.

Job Complains of Violence on the Earth

24 "*Since* times are not hidden from
        the Almighty,
    Why do those who know Him see not
        His days?

2   "*Some* remove landmarks;
    They seize flocks violently and feed
        on them;
3   They drive away the donkey of the
        fatherless;
    They take the widow's ox as a pledge.
4   They push the needy off the road;
    All the poor of the land are forced to
        hide.
5   Indeed, *like* wild donkeys in the desert,
    They go out to their work, searching
        for food.
    The wilderness *yields* food for them
        and for *their* children.

22:25 [a]The ancient versions suggest *defense;* Hebrew
reads *gold* as in verse 24.   **23:2** [a]Following
Masoretic Text, Targum, and Vulgate; Septuagint
and Syriac read *His.*

6 They gather their fodder in the field
And glean in the vineyard of the
wicked.
7 They spend the night naked, without
clothing,
And have no covering in the cold.
8 They are wet with the showers of the
mountains,
And huddle around the rock for want
of shelter.

9 "*Some* snatch the fatherless from the
breast,
And take a pledge from the poor.
10 They cause *the poor* to go naked,
without clothing;
And they take away the sheaves from
the hungry.
11 They press out oil within their walls,
And tread winepresses, yet suffer
thirst.
12 The dying groan in the city,
And the souls of the wounded cry
out;
Yet God does not charge *them* with
wrong.

13 "There are those who rebel against
the light;
They do not know its ways
Nor abide in its paths.
14 The murderer rises with the light;
He kills the poor and needy;
And in the night he is like a thief.
15 The eye of the adulterer waits for the
twilight,
Saying, 'No eye will see me';
And he disguises *his* face.
16 In the dark they break into houses
Which they marked for themselves in
the daytime;
They do not know the light.
17 For the morning is the same to them
as the shadow of death;
If *someone* recognizes *them,*
They are in the terrors of the shadow
of death.

18 "They *should be* swift on the face of the
waters,
Their portion *should be* cursed in the
earth,

So that no *one would* turn into the way
of their vineyards.
19 As drought and heat consume the
snow waters,
So the grave[a] *consumes those who* have
sinned.
20 The womb *should* forget him,
The worm *should* feed sweetly on him;
He *should* be remembered no more,
And wickedness *should* be broken like
a tree.
21 For he preys on the barren *who* do not
bear,
And does no good for the widow.

22 "But *God* draws the mighty away with
His power;
He rises up, but no *man* is sure of life.
23 He gives them security, and they rely
on it;
Yet His eyes *are* on their ways.
24 They are exalted for a little while,
Then they are gone.
They are brought low;
They are taken out of the way like all
others;
They dry out like the heads of grain.

25 "Now if *it is* not *so,* who will prove me
a liar,
And make my speech worth nothing?"

Bildad: How Can Man Be Righteous?

25 Then Bildad the Shuhite answered
and said:

2 "Dominion and fear *belong* to Him;
He makes peace in His high places.
3 Is there any number to His armies?
Upon whom does His light not rise?
4 How then can man be righteous
before God?
Or how can he be pure *who is* born
of a woman?
5 If even the moon does not shine,
And the stars are not pure in His
sight,
6 How much less man, *who is* a maggot,
And a son of man, *who is* a worm?"

24:19 [a]Or *Sheol*

Job: Man's Frailty and God's Majesty

26 But Job answered and said:

2 "How have you helped *him who is*
without power?
How have you saved the arm *that has*
no strength?
3 How have you counseled *one who has*
no wisdom?
And *how* have you declared sound
advice to many?
4 To whom have you uttered words?
And whose spirit came from you?

5 "The dead tremble,
Those under the waters and those
inhabiting them.
6 Sheol *is* naked before Him,
And Destruction has no covering.
7 He stretches out the north over empty
space;
He hangs the earth on nothing.
8 He binds up the water in His thick
clouds,
Yet the clouds are not broken under it.
9 He covers the face of *His* throne,
And spreads His cloud over it.
10 He drew a circular horizon on the face
of the waters,
At the boundary of light and darkness.
11 The pillars of heaven tremble,
And are astonished at His rebuke.
12 He stirs up the sea with His power,
And by His understanding He breaks
up the storm.
13 By His Spirit He adorned the heavens;
His hand pierced the fleeing serpent.
14 Indeed these *are* the mere edges of His
ways,
And how small a whisper we hear of
Him!
But the thunder of His power who can
understand?"

Job Maintains His Integrity

27 Moreover Job continued his discourse,
and said:

2 "*As* God lives, *who* has taken away my
justice,
And the Almighty, *who* has made my
soul bitter,
3 As long as my breath *is* in me,
And the breath of God in my nostrils,
4 My lips will not speak wickedness,
Nor my tongue utter deceit.
5 Far be it from me
That I should say you are right;
Till I die I will not put away my
integrity from me.
6 My righteousness I hold fast, and will
not let it go;
My heart shall not reproach *me* as
long as I live.

7 "May my enemy be like the wicked,
And he who rises up against me like
the unrighteous.
8 For what is the hope of the hypocrite,
Though he may gain *much,*
If God takes away his life?
9 Will God hear his cry
When trouble comes upon him?
10 Will he delight himself in the Almighty?
Will he always call on God?

11 "I will teach you about the hand of God;
What *is* with the Almighty I will not
conceal.
12 Surely all of you have seen *it;*
Why then do you behave with
complete nonsense?

13 "This is the portion of a wicked man
with God,
And the heritage of oppressors,
received from the Almighty:
14 If his children are multiplied, *it is* for
the sword;
And his offspring shall not be satisfied
with bread.
15 Those who survive him shall be buried
in death,
And their[a] widows shall not weep,
16 Though he heaps up silver like dust,
And piles up clothing like clay—
17 He may pile *it* up, but the just will
wear *it,*
And the innocent will divide the silver.
18 He builds his house like a moth,[a]

27:15 [a]Literally *his*   27:18 [a]Following Masoretic
Text and Vulgate; Septuagint and Syriac read *spider*
(compare 8:14); Targum reads *decay.*

Like a booth *which* a watchman makes.
19 The rich man will lie down,
But not be gathered *up;*[a]
He opens his eyes,
And he *is* no more.
20 Terrors overtake him like a flood;
A tempest steals him away in the night.
21 The east wind carries him away, and
　　he is gone;
It sweeps him out of his place.
22 It hurls against him and does not spare;
He flees desperately from its power.
23 *Men* shall clap their hands at him,
And shall hiss him out of his place.

Job's Discourse on Wisdom

28 "Surely there is a mine for silver,
　　And a place *where* gold is refined.
2 Iron is taken from the earth,
And copper *is* smelted *from* ore.
3 *Man* puts an end to darkness,
And searches every recess
For ore in the darkness and the
　　shadow of death.
4 He breaks open a shaft away from
　　people;
In places forgotten by feet
They hang far away from men;
They swing to and fro.
5 *As for* the earth, from it comes bread,
But underneath it is turned up as by
　　fire;
6 Its stones *are* the source of sapphires,
And it contains gold dust.
7 *That* path no bird knows,
Nor has the falcon's eye seen it.
8 The proud lions[a] have not trodden it,
Nor has the fierce lion passed over it.
9 He puts his hand on the flint;
He overturns the mountains at the
　　roots.
10 He cuts out channels in the rocks,
And his eye sees every precious thing.
11 He dams up the streams from
　　trickling;
What is hidden he brings forth to light.

12 "But where can wisdom be found?
And where *is* the place of
　　understanding?
13 Man does not know its value,
Nor is it found in the land of the living.

14 The deep says, '*It is* not in me';
And the sea says, '*It is* not with me.'
15 It cannot be purchased for gold,
Nor can silver be weighed *for* its price.
16 It cannot be valued in the gold of Ophir,
In precious onyx or sapphire.
17 Neither gold nor crystal can equal it,
Nor can it be exchanged for jewelry
　　of fine gold.
18 No mention shall be made of coral
　　or quartz,
For the price of wisdom *is* above rubies.
19 The topaz of Ethiopia cannot equal it,
Nor can it be valued in pure gold.

20 "From where then does wisdom come?
And where *is* the place of
　　understanding?
21 It is hidden from the eyes of all living,
And concealed from the birds of the air.
22 Destruction and Death say,
'We have heard a report about it with
　　our ears.'
23 God understands its way,
And He knows its place.
24 For He looks to the ends of the earth,
And sees under the whole heavens,
25 To establish a weight for the wind,
And apportion the waters by measure.
26 When He made a law for the rain,
And a path for the thunderbolt,
27 Then He saw *wisdom*[a] and declared it;
He prepared it, indeed, He searched
　　it out.
28 And to man He said,
'Behold, the fear of the Lord, that *is*
　　wisdom,
And to depart from evil *is*
　　understanding.' "

Job's Summary Defense

29 Job further continued his discourse,
and said:

2 "Oh, that I were as *in* months past,
As *in* the days *when* God watched over
　　me;

27:19 [a]Following Masoretic Text and Targum;
Septuagint and Syriac read *But shall not add* (that is,
do it again); Vulgate reads *But take away nothing.*
28:8 [a]Literally *sons of pride,* figurative of the great
lions　　**28:27** [a]Literally *it*

3 When His lamp shone upon my head,
   And when by His light I walked *through*
       darkness;
4 Just as I was in the days of my prime,
   When the friendly counsel of God *was*
       over my tent;
5 When the Almighty *was* yet with me,
   When my children *were* around me;
6 When my steps were bathed with
       cream,[a]
   And the rock poured out rivers of oil
       for me!

7 "When I went out to the gate by the city,
   When I took my seat in the open
       square,
8 The young men saw me and hid,
   And the aged arose *and* stood;
9 The princes refrained from talking,
   And put *their* hand on their mouth;
10 The voice of nobles was hushed,
   And their tongue stuck to the roof of
       their mouth.
11 When the ear heard, then it blessed me,
   And when the eye saw, then it
       approved me;
12 Because I delivered the poor who cried
       out,
   The fatherless and *the one who* had no
       helper.
13 The blessing of a perishing *man* came
       upon me,
   And I caused the widow's heart to sing
       for joy.
14 I put on righteousness, and it clothed
       me;
   My justice *was* like a robe and a turban.
15 I *was* eyes to the blind,
   And I *was* feet to the lame.
16 I *was* a father to the poor,
   And I searched out the case *that* I did
       not know.
17 I broke the fangs of the wicked,
   And plucked the victim from his teeth.

18 "Then I said, 'I shall die in my nest,
   And multiply *my* days as the sand.
19 My root *is* spread out to the waters,
   And the dew lies all night on my
       branch.
20 My glory *is* fresh within me,
   And my bow is renewed in my hand.'

21 "*Men* listened to me and waited,
   And kept silence for my counsel.
22 After my words they did not speak
       again,
   And my speech settled on them *as*
       dew.
23 They waited for me *as* for the rain,
   And they opened their mouth wide
       as for the spring rain.
24 *If* I mocked at them, they did not
       believe *it,*
   And the light of my countenance they
       did not cast down.
25 I chose the way for them, and sat as
       chief;
   So I dwelt as a king in the army,
   As one *who* comforts mourners.

30 "But now they mock at me, *men*
       younger than I,
   Whose fathers I disdained to put with
       the dogs of my flock.
2 Indeed, what *profit* is the strength of
       their hands to me?
   Their vigor has perished.
3 *They are* gaunt from want and famine,
   Fleeing late to the wilderness, desolate
       and waste,
4 Who pluck mallow by the bushes,
   And broom tree roots *for* their food.
5 They were driven out from among *men,*
   They shouted at them as *at* a thief.
6 *They had* to live in the clefts of the
       valleys,
   In caves of the earth and the rocks.
7 Among the bushes they brayed,
   Under the nettles they nestled.
8 *They were* sons of fools,
   Yes, sons of vile men;
   They were scourged from the land.

9 "And now I am their taunting song;
   Yes, I am their byword.
10 They abhor me, they keep far from me;
   They do not hesitate to spit in my face.
11 Because He has loosed my[a] bowstring
       and afflicted me,
   They have cast off restraint before me.

29:6 [a]Masoretic Text reads *wrath;* ancient versions
and some Hebrew manuscripts read *cream* (compare
20:17).   **30:11** [a]Following Masoretic Text, Syriac,
and Targum; Septuagint and Vulgate read *His.*

THE RIGHTEOUSNESS OF NATIONS

When Germany started unrestricted submarine warfare in early 1917 and made an attempt to enlist Mexico as an ally, Woodrow Wilson, the 28th president of the United States, led America into World War I against the Central Powers. In his declaration of war speech, he stated that unless America threw its weight into the war, Western civilization itself could be destroyed. This excerpt from a speech given in 1911 is his view of the Word of God in society:

There are great problems before the American people. There are problems which will need purity of spirit and an integrity of purpose such as has never been called for before in the history of this country. I should be afraid to go forward if I did not believe that there lay at the foundation of all our schooling and of all our thought this incomparable and unimpeachable Word of God. If we cannot derive our strength thence, there is no source from which we can derive it, and so I would bid you go from this place, if I may, inspired once more with the feeling that the providence of God is the foundation of affairs, and that only those can guide, and only those can follow, who take this providence of God from the sources where it is authentically interpreted. . . .

The happiness of seeing a great company of people like this gathered together in the interest of the Sunday school is the happiness of knowing that there are they who seek light and who know that the lamp from which their spirits can be kindled is the lamp that glows in the Word of God.

Every Sunday school should be a place where this great book is not only opened, is not only studied, is not only revered, but is drunk of as if it were a fountain of life, is used as if it were the only source of inspiration and of guidance. No great nation can ever survive its own temptations and its own follies that does not indoctrinate its children in the Word of God; so that as schoolmaster and as Governor I know that my feet must rest with the feet of my fellowmen upon this foundation, and upon this foundation only; for the righteousness of nations, like the righteousness of men, must take its source from these foundations of inspiration.

12 At *my* right *hand* the rabble arises;
   They push away my feet,
   And they raise against me their ways
   of destruction.
13 They break up my path,
   They promote my calamity;
   They have no helper.
14 They come as broad breakers;
   Under the ruinous storm they roll along.
15 Terrors are turned upon me;
   They pursue my honor as the wind,
   And my prosperity has passed like
   a cloud.

16 "And now my soul is poured out
   because of my *plight;*
   The days of affliction take hold of me.
17 My bones are pierced in me at night,
   And my gnawing pains take no rest.
18 By great force my garment is
   disfigured;
   It binds me about as the collar of my
   coat.
19 He has cast me into the mire,
   And I have become like dust and ashes.

20 "I cry out to You, but You do not
   answer me;
   I stand up, and You regard me.
21 *But* You have become cruel to me;
   With the strength of Your hand You
   oppose me.
22 You lift me up to the wind and cause
   me to ride *on it;*
   You spoil my success.
23 For I know *that* You will bring me *to*
   death,
   And *to* the house appointed for all
   living.

24 "Surely He would not stretch out *His*
   hand against a heap of ruins,
   If they cry out when He destroys *it.*
25 Have I not wept for him who was in
   trouble?
   Has *not* my soul grieved for the poor?
26 But when I looked for good, evil came
   to me;
   And when I waited for light, then came
   darkness.
27 My heart is in turmoil and cannot rest;
   Days of affliction confront me.

28 I go about mourning, but not in the
   sun;
   I stand up in the assembly *and* cry
   out for help.
29 I am a brother of jackals,
   And a companion of ostriches.
30 My skin grows black and falls from me;
   My bones burn with fever.
31 My harp is *turned* to mourning,
   And my flute to the voice of those who
   weep.

31

"I have made a covenant with my
   eyes;
   Why then should I look upon a young
   woman?
2 For what *is* the allotment of God from
   above,
   And the inheritance of the Almighty
   from on high?
3 *Is* it not destruction for the wicked,
   And disaster for the workers of iniquity?
4 Does He not see my ways,
   And count all my steps?

5 "If I have walked with falsehood,
   Or if my foot has hastened to deceit,
6 Let me be weighed on honest scales,
   That God may know my integrity.
7 If my step has turned from the way,
   Or my heart walked after my eyes,
   Or if any spot adheres to my hands,
8 *Then* let me sow, and another eat;
   Yes, let my harvest be rooted out.

9 "If my heart has been enticed by a
   woman,
   Or *if* I have lurked at my neighbor's
   door,
10 *Then* let my wife grind for another,
   And let others bow down over her.
11 For that *would be* wickedness;
   Yes, it *would be* iniquity *deserving of*
   judgment.
12 For that *would be* a fire *that* consumes
   to destruction,
   And would root out all my increase.

13 "If I have despised the cause of my
   male or female servant
   When they complained against me,
14 What then shall I do when God
   rises up?

When He punishes, how shall I
answer Him?
15 Did not He who made me in the
womb make them?
Did not the same One fashion us
in the womb?

16 "If I have kept the poor from *their* desire,
Or caused the eyes of the widow to fail,
17 Or eaten my morsel by myself,
So that the fatherless could not eat of it
18 (But from my youth I reared him as a
father,
And from my mother's womb I guided
*the widow*ᵃ);
19 If I have seen anyone perish for lack
of clothing,
Or any poor *man* without covering;
20 If his heartᵃ has not blessed me,
And *if* he was *not* warmed with the
fleece of my sheep;
21 If I have raised my hand against the
fatherless,
When I saw I had help in the gate;
22 *Then* let my arm fall from my shoulder,
Let my arm be torn from the socket.
23 For destruction *from* God *is* a terror to
me,
And because of His magnificence I
cannot endure.

24 "If I have made gold my hope,
Or said to fine gold, '*You are* my
confidence';
25 If I have rejoiced because my wealth
was great,
And because my hand had gained
much;
26 If I have observed the sunᵃ when it
shines,
Or the moon moving *in* brightness,
27 So that my heart has been secretly
enticed,
And my mouth has kissed my hand;
28 This also *would be* an iniquity
deserving of judgment,
For I would have denied God *who is*
above.

29 "If I have rejoiced at the destruction of
him who hated me,
Or lifted myself up when evil found him

30 (Indeed I have not allowed my mouth
to sin
By asking for a curse on his soul);
31 If the men of my tent have not said,
'Who is there that has not been
satisfied with his meat?'
32 (*But* no sojourner had to lodge in the
street,
For I have opened my doors to the
travelerᵃ);
33 If I have covered my transgressions as
Adam,
By hiding my iniquity in my bosom,
34 Because I feared the great multitude,
And dreaded the contempt of families,
So that I kept silence
And did not go out of the door—
35 Oh, that I had one to hear me!
Here is my mark.
Oh, that the Almighty would answer
me,
That my Prosecutor had written a book!
36 Surely I would carry it on my
shoulder,
And bind it on me *like* a crown;
37 I would declare to Him the number of
my steps;
Like a prince I would approach Him.

38 "If my land cries out against me,
And its furrows weep together;
39 If I have eaten its fruitᵃ without money,
Or caused its owners to lose their lives;
40 *Then* let thistles grow instead of wheat,
And weeds instead of barley."

The words of Job are ended.

Elihu Contradicts Job's Friends

32 So these three men ceased answering
Job, because he *was* righteous in his
own eyes. ²Then the wrath of Elihu, the son
of Barachel the Buzite, of the family of Ram,
was aroused against Job; his wrath was
aroused because he justified himself rather
than God. ³Also against his three friends
his wrath was aroused, because they had

31:18 ᵃLiterally *her* (compare verse 16)
31:20 ᵃLiterally *loins*   **31:26** ᵃLiterally *light*
31:32 ᵃFollowing Septuagint, Syriac, Targum,
and Vulgate; Masoretic Text reads *road.*
31:39 ᵃLiterally *its strength*

found no answer, and *yet* had condemned Job.

⁴Now because they *were* years older than he, Elihu had waited to speak to Job.ᵃ ⁵When Elihu saw that *there was* no answer in the mouth of these three men, his wrath was aroused.

⁶So Elihu, the son of Barachel the Buzite, answered and said:

"I *am* young in years, and you *are* very old;
Therefore I was afraid,
And dared not declare my opinion to you.
7 I said, 'Ageᵃ should speak,
And multitude of years should teach wisdom.'
8 But *there is* a spirit in man,
And the breath of the Almighty gives him understanding.
9 Great menᵃ are not *always* wise,
Nor do the aged *always* understand justice.

10 "Therefore I say, 'Listen to me,
I also will declare my opinion.'
11 Indeed I waited for your words,
I listened to your reasonings, while you searched out what to say.
12 I paid close attention to you;
And surely not one of you convinced Job,
Or answered his words—
13 Lest you say,
'We have found wisdom';
God will vanquish him, not man.
14 Now he has not directed *his* words against me;
So I will not answer him with your words.

15 "They are dismayed and answer no more;
Words escape them.
16 And I have waited, because they did not speak,
Because they stood still *and* answered no more.
17 I also will answer my part,
I too will declare my opinion.
18 For I am full of words;

The spirit within me compels me.
19 Indeed my belly *is* like wine *that* has no vent;
It is ready to burst like new wineskins.
20 I will speak, that I may find relief;
I must open my lips and answer.
21 Let me not, I pray, show partiality to anyone;
Nor let me flatter any man.
22 For I do not know how to flatter,
Else my Maker would soon take me away.

Elihu Contradicts Job

33 "But please, Job, hear my speech,
And listen to all my words.
2 Now, I open my mouth;
My tongue speaks in my mouth.
3 My words *come* from my upright heart;
My lips utter pure knowledge.
4 The Spirit of God has made me,
And the breath of the Almighty gives me life.
5 If you can answer me,
Set *your words* in order before me;
Take your stand.
6 Truly I *am* as your spokesmanᵃ before God;
I also have been formed out of clay.
7 Surely no fear of me will terrify you,
Nor will my hand be heavy on you.

8 "Surely you have spoken in my hearing,
And I have heard the sound of *your* words, *saying,*
9 'I *am* pure, without transgression;
I *am* innocent, and *there is* no iniquity in me.
10 Yet He finds occasions against me,
He counts me as His enemy;
11 He puts my feet in the stocks,
He watches all my paths.'

12 "Look, *in* this you are not righteous.
I will answer you,
For God is greater than man.
13 Why do you contend with Him?

32:4 ᵃVulgate reads *till Job had spoken.*
32:7 ᵃLiterally *Days,* that is, years   **32:9** ᵃOr *Men of many years*   **33:6** ᵃLiterally *as your mouth*

For He does not give an accounting of any of His words.

14 For God may speak in one way, or in another,
Yet man does not perceive it.

15 In a dream, in a vision of the night,
When deep sleep falls upon men,
While slumbering on their beds,

16 Then He opens the ears of men,
And seals their instruction.

17 In order to turn man *from his* deed,
And conceal pride from man,

18 He keeps back his soul from the Pit,
And his life from perishing by the sword.

19 "*Man* is also chastened with pain on his bed,
And with strong *pain* in many of his bones,

20 So that his life abhors bread,
And his soul succulent food.

21 His flesh wastes away from sight,
And his bones stick out *which once* were not seen.

22 Yes, his soul draws near the Pit,
And his life to the executioners.

23 "If there is a messenger for him,
A mediator, one among a thousand,
To show man His uprightness,

24 Then He is gracious to him, and says,
'Deliver him from going down to the Pit;
I have found a ransom';

25 His flesh shall be young like a child's,
He shall return to the days of his youth.

26 He shall pray to God, and He will delight in him,
He shall see His face with joy,
For He restores to man His righteousness.

27 Then he looks at men and says,
'I have sinned, and perverted *what was* right,
And it did not profit me.'

28 He will redeem his[a] soul from going down to the Pit,
And his[b] life shall see the light.

29 "Behold, God works all these *things*,
Twice, *in fact*, three *times* with a man,

30 To bring back his soul from the Pit,
That he may be enlightened with the light of life.

31 "Give ear, Job, listen to me;
Hold your peace, and I will speak.

32 If you have anything to say, answer me;
Speak, for I desire to justify you.

33 If not, listen to me;
Hold your peace, and I will teach you wisdom."

Elihu Proclaims God's Justice

34 Elihu further answered and said:

2 "Hear my words, you wise *men*;
Give ear to me, you who have knowledge.

3 For the ear tests words
As the palate tastes food.

4 Let us choose justice for ourselves;
Let us know among ourselves what *is* good.

5 "For Job has said, 'I am righteous,
But God has taken away my justice;

6 Should I lie concerning my right?
My wound *is* incurable, *though I am* without transgression.'

7 What man *is* like Job,
Who drinks scorn like water,

8 Who goes in company with the workers of iniquity,
And walks with wicked men?

9 For he has said, 'It profits a man nothing
That he should delight in God.'

10 "Therefore listen to me, you men of understanding:
Far be it from God *to do* wickedness,
And *from* the Almighty to *commit* iniquity.

11 For He repays man *according to* his work,
And makes man to find a reward according to *his* way.

12 Surely God will never do wickedly,
Nor will the Almighty pervert justice.

33:28 [a]Or *my* (Kethib) [b]Or *my* (Kethib)

13 Who gave Him charge over the earth?
   Or who appointed *Him over* the whole
   world?
14 If He should set His heart on it,
   If He should gather to Himself His
   Spirit and His breath,
15 All flesh would perish together,
   And man would return to dust.

16 "If *you have* understanding, hear this;
   Listen to the sound of my words:
17 Should one who hates justice govern?
   Will you condemn *Him who is* most
   just?
18 *Is it fitting* to say to a king, 'You are
   worthless,'
   And to nobles, 'You are wicked'?
19 Yet He is not partial to princes,
   Nor does He regard the rich more than
   the poor;
   For they *are* all the work of His hands.
20 In a moment they die, in the middle
   of the night;
   The people are shaken and pass away;
   The mighty are taken away without a
   hand.

21 "For His eyes *are* on the ways of man,
   And He sees all his steps.
22 There is no darkness nor shadow of
   death
   Where the workers of iniquity may
   hide themselves.
23 For He need not further consider a man,
   That he should go before God in
   judgment.
24 He breaks in pieces mighty men
   without inquiry,
   And sets others in their place.
25 Therefore He knows their works;
   He overthrows *them* in the night,
   And they are crushed.
26 He strikes them as wicked *men*
   In the open sight of others,
27 Because they turned back from Him,
   And would not consider any of His
   ways,
28 So that they caused the cry of the poor
   to come to Him;
   For He hears the cry of the afflicted.
29 When He gives quietness, who then
   can make trouble?
   And when He hides *His* face, who then
   can see Him,
   Whether *it is* against a nation or a man
   alone?—
30 That the hypocrite should not reign,
   Lest the people be ensnared.

31 "For has *anyone* said to God,
   'I have borne *chastening;*
   I will offend no more;
32 Teach me *what* I do not see;
   If I have done iniquity, I will do no
   more'?
33 Should He repay *it* according to your
   terms,
   Just because you disavow it?
   You must choose, and not I;
   Therefore speak what you know.

34 "Men of understanding say to me,
   Wise men who listen to me:
35 'Job speaks without knowledge,
   His words *are* without wisdom.'
36 Oh, that Job were tried to the utmost,
   Because *his* answers *are* like those of
   wicked men!
37 For he adds rebellion to his sin;
   He claps *his hands* among us,
   And multiplies his words against God."

Elihu Condemns Self-Righteousness

35 Moreover Elihu answered and said:

2 "Do you think this is right?
   Do you say,
   'My righteousness is more than God's'?
3 For you say,
   'What advantage will it be to You?
   What profit shall I have, more than *if*
   I had sinned?'

4 "I will answer you,
   And your companions with you.
5 Look to the heavens and see;
   And behold the clouds—
   They are higher than you.
6 If you sin, what do you accomplish
   against Him?
   Or, *if* your transgressions are
   multiplied, what do you do to Him?
7 If you are righteous, what do you give
   Him?

Or what does He receive from your
hand?

8 Your wickedness affects a man such
as you,
And your righteousness a son of man.

9 "Because of the multitude of
oppressions they cry out;
They cry out for help because of the
arm of the mighty.

10 But no one says, 'Where *is* God my
Maker,
Who gives songs in the night,

11 Who teaches us more than the beasts
of the earth,
And makes us wiser than the birds
of heaven?'

12 There they cry out, but He does not
answer,
Because of the pride of evil men.

13 Surely God will not listen to empty *talk*,
Nor will the Almighty regard it.

14 Although you say you do not see Him,
Yet justice *is* before Him, and you must
wait for Him.

15 And now, because He has not
punished in His anger,
Nor taken much notice of folly,

16 Therefore Job opens his mouth in vain;
He multiplies words without
knowledge."

Elihu Proclaims God's Goodness

36 Elihu also proceeded and said:

2 "Bear with me a little, and I will show
you
That *there are* yet words to speak on
God's behalf.

3 I will fetch my knowledge from afar;
I will ascribe righteousness to my Maker.

4 For truly my words *are* not false;
One who is perfect in knowledge *is*
with you.

5 "Behold, God *is* mighty, but despises
no one;
He is mighty in strength of
understanding.

6 He does not preserve the life of the
wicked,
But gives justice to the oppressed.

7 He does not withdraw His eyes from
the righteous;
But *they are* on the throne with kings,
For He has seated them forever,
And they are exalted.

8 And if *they are* bound in fetters,
Held in the cords of affliction,

9 Then He tells them their work and
their transgressions—
That they have acted defiantly.

10 He also opens their ear to instruction,
And commands that they turn from
iniquity.

11 If they obey and serve *Him,*
They shall spend their days in
prosperity,
And their years in pleasures.

12 But if they do not obey,
They shall perish by the sword,
And they shall die without
knowledge.ᵃ

13 "But the hypocrites in heart store up
wrath;
They do not cry for help when He
binds them.

14 They die in youth,
And their life *ends* among the
perverted persons.ᵃ

15 He delivers the poor in their affliction,
And opens their ears in oppression.

16 "Indeed He would have brought you
out of dire distress,
Into a broad place where *there is* no
restraint;
And what is set on your table *would
be* full of richness.

17 But you are filled with the judgment
due the wicked;
Judgment and justice take hold *of you.*

18 Because *there is* wrath, *beware* lest He
take you away with *one* blow;
For a large ransom would not help
you avoid *it.*

19 Will your riches,
Or all the mighty forces,
Keep you from distress?

36:12 ᵃMasoretic Text reads *as one without knowledge.*
36:14 ᵃHebrew *qedeshim,* that is, those practicing
sodomy and prostitution in religious rituals

20 Do not desire the night,
When people are cut off in their
place.
21 Take heed, do not turn to iniquity,
For you have chosen this rather than
affliction.

22 "Behold, God is exalted by His power;
Who teaches like Him?
23 Who has assigned Him His way,
Or who has said, 'You have done
wrong'?

Elihu Proclaims God's Majesty

24 "Remember to magnify His work,
Of which men have sung.
25 Everyone has seen it;
Man looks on *it* from afar.

26 "Behold, God *is* great, and we do not
know *Him*;
Nor can the number of His years *be*
discovered.
27 For He draws up drops of water,
Which distill as rain from the mist,
28 Which the clouds drop down
And pour abundantly on man.
29 Indeed, can *anyone* understand the
spreading of clouds,
The thunder from His canopy?
30 Look, He scatters His light upon it,
And covers the depths of the sea.
31 For by these He judges the peoples;
He gives food in abundance.
32 He covers *His* hands with lightning,
And commands it to strike.
33 His thunder declares it,
The cattle also, concerning the rising
storm.

37 "At this also my heart trembles,
And leaps from its place.
2 Hear attentively the thunder of His
voice,
And the rumbling *that* comes from
His mouth.
3 He sends it forth under the whole
heaven,
His lightning to the ends of the earth.
4 After it a voice roars;
He thunders with His majestic voice,
And He does not restrain them when
His voice is heard.

5 God thunders marvelously with His
voice;
He does great things which we cannot
comprehend.
6 For He says to the snow, 'Fall *on* the
earth';
Likewise to the gentle rain and the
heavy rain of His strength.
7 He seals the hand of every man,
That all men may know His work.
8 The beasts go into dens,
And remain in their lairs.
9 From the chamber *of the south* comes
the whirlwind,
And cold from the scattering winds
of the north.
10 By the breath of God ice is given,
And the broad waters are frozen.
11 Also with moisture He saturates the
thick clouds;
He scatters His bright clouds.
12 And they swirl about, being turned
by His guidance,
That they may do whatever He
commands them
On the face of the whole earth.[a]
13 He causes it to come,
Whether for correction,
Or for His land,
Or for mercy.

14 "Listen to this, O Job;
Stand still and consider the wondrous
works of God.
15 Do you know when God dispatches
them,
And causes the light of His cloud to
shine?
16 Do you know how the clouds are
balanced,
Those wondrous works of Him who
is perfect in knowledge?
17 Why *are* your garments hot,
When He quiets the earth by the south
wind?
18 With Him, have you spread out the
skies,
Strong as a cast metal mirror?

19 "Teach us what we should say to Him,

37:12 [a]Literally *the world of the earth*

"GOD of OUR FATHERS"

"He comes from the north as golden splendor; with God is awesome majesty."

JOB 37:22

Daniel C. Roberts survived the Civil War and went on to become the rector of the small Episcopal parish in Brandon, Vermont. He wanted a new hymn for his congregation to celebrate the American Centennial in 1876, so he wrote "God of Our Fathers," which his congregation sang on July 4. In 1892, this hymn was chosen for the celebration of the centennial of the United States Constitution.

God of our fathers, whose almighty hand
Leads forth in beauty all the starry band
Of shining worlds in splendor through the skies
Our grateful songs before Thy throne arise.

Thy love divine hath led us in the past,
In this free land by Thee our lot is cast,
Be Thou our Ruler, Guardian, Guide and Stay,
Thy Word our law, Thy paths our chosen way.

From war's alarms, from deadly pestilence,
Be Thy strong arm our ever sure defense;
Thy true religion in our hearts increase,
Thy bounteous goodness nourish us in peace.

Refresh Thy people on their toilsome way,
Lead us from night to never ending day;
Fill all our lives with love and grace divine,
And glory, laud, and praise be ever Thine.

For we can prepare nothing because of
the darkness.
20 Should He be told that I *wish to* speak?
If a man were to speak, surely he
would be swallowed up.
21 Even now *men* cannot look at the light
when it is bright in the skies,
When the wind has passed and
cleared them.
22 He comes from the north *as* golden
splendor;
With God *is* awesome majesty.
23 *As for* the Almighty, we cannot find
Him;
He is excellent in power,
In judgment and abundant justice;
He does not oppress.
24 Therefore men fear Him;
He shows no partiality to any *who are*
wise of heart."

The Lord Reveals His Omnipotence to Job

38 Then the Lord answered Job out of
the whirlwind, and said:

2 "Who *is* this who darkens counsel
By words without knowledge?
3 Now prepare yourself like a man;
I will question you, and you shall
answer Me.

4 "Where were you when I laid the
foundations of the earth?
Tell *Me,* if you have understanding.
5 Who determined its measurements?
Surely you know!
Or who stretched the line upon it?
6 To what were its foundations fastened?
Or who laid its cornerstone,
7 When the morning stars sang
together,
And all the sons of God shouted for
joy?

8 "Or *who* shut in the sea with doors,
When it burst forth *and* issued from
the womb;
9 When I made the clouds its garment,
And thick darkness its swaddling band;
10 When I fixed My limit for it,
And set bars and doors;
11 When I said,

'This far you may come, but no farther,
And here your proud waves must stop!'

12 "Have you commanded the morning
since your days *began,*
And caused the dawn to know its place,
13 That it might take hold of the ends of
the earth,
And the wicked be shaken out of it?
14 It takes on form like clay *under* a seal,
And stands out like a garment.
15 From the wicked their light is withheld,
And the upraised arm is broken.

16 "Have you entered the springs of the
sea?
Or have you walked in search of the
depths?
17 Have the gates of death been revealed
to you?
Or have you seen the doors of the
shadow of death?
18 Have you comprehended the breadth
of the earth?
Tell *Me,* if you know all this.

19 "Where *is* the way *to* the dwelling
of light?
And darkness, where *is* its place,
20 That you may take it to its territory,
That you may know the paths *to* its
home?
21 Do you know *it,* because you were
born then,
Or *because* the number of your days
is great?

22 "Have you entered the treasury of snow,
Or have you seen the treasury of hail,
23 Which I have reserved for the time
of trouble,
For the day of battle and war?
24 By what way is light diffused,
Or the east wind scattered over the
earth?

25 "Who has divided a channel for the
overflowing *water,*
Or a path for the thunderbolt,
26 To cause it to rain on a land *where*
there is no one,
A wilderness in which *there is* no man;

27 To satisfy the desolate waste,
And cause to spring forth the growth
of tender grass?

28 Has the rain a father?
Or who has begotten the drops of dew?

29 From whose womb comes the ice?
And the frost of heaven, who gives it
birth?

30 The waters harden like stone,
And the surface of the deep is frozen.

31 "Can you bind the cluster of the
Pleiades,
Or loose the belt of Orion?

32 Can you bring out Mazzaroth[a] in its
season?
Or can you guide the Great Bear with
its cubs?

33 Do you know the ordinances of the
heavens?
Can you set their dominion over the
earth?

34 "Can you lift up your voice to the
clouds,
That an abundance of water may
cover you?

35 Can you send out lightnings, that
they may go,
And say to you, 'Here we *are!*'?

36 Who has put wisdom in the mind?[a]
Or who has given understanding to
the heart?

37 Who can number the clouds by
wisdom?
Or who can pour out the bottles of
heaven,

38 When the dust hardens in clumps,
And the clods cling together?

39 "Can you hunt the prey for the lion,
Or satisfy the appetite of the young
lions,

40 When they crouch in *their* dens,
Or lurk in their lairs to lie in wait?

41 Who provides food for the raven,
When its young ones cry to God,
And wander about for lack of food?

39 "Do you know the time when the
wild mountain goats bear young?
Or can you mark when the deer gives
birth?

2 Can you number the months *that*
they fulfill?
Or do you know the time when they
bear young?

3 They bow down,
They bring forth their young,
They deliver their offspring.[a]

4 Their young ones are healthy,
They grow strong with grain;
They depart and do not return to them.

5 "Who set the wild donkey free?
Who loosed the bonds of the onager,

6 Whose home I have made the
wilderness,
And the barren land his dwelling?

7 He scorns the tumult of the city;
He does not heed the shouts of the
driver.

8 The range of the mountains *is* his
pasture,
And he searches after every green thing.

9 "Will the wild ox be willing to serve you?
Will he bed by your manger?

10 Can you bind the wild ox in the
furrow with ropes?
Or will he plow the valleys behind you?

11 Will you trust him because his strength
is great?
Or will you leave your labor to him?

12 Will you trust him to bring home your
grain,
And gather it to your threshing floor?

13 "The wings of the ostrich wave proudly,
But are her wings and pinions *like the*
kindly stork's?

14 For she leaves her eggs on the ground,
And warms them in the dust;

15 She forgets that a foot may crush them,
Or that a wild beast may break them.

16 She treats her young harshly, as
though *they were* not hers;
Her labor is in vain, without concern,

17 Because God deprived her of wisdom,
And did not endow her with
understanding.

38:32 [a]Literally *Constellations* **38:36** [a]Literally
inward parts **39:3** [a]Literally *pangs,* figurative of
offspring

18 When she lifts herself on high,
She scorns the horse and its rider.

19 "Have you given the horse strength?
Have you clothed his neck with
thunder?[a]
20 Can you frighten him like a locust?
His majestic snorting strikes terror.
21 He paws in the valley, and rejoices
in *his* strength;
He gallops into the clash of arms.
22 He mocks at fear, and is not
frightened;
Nor does he turn back from the sword.
23 The quiver rattles against him,
The glittering spear and javelin.
24 He devours the distance with
fierceness and rage;
Nor does he come to a halt because
the trumpet *has* sounded.
25 At *the blast of* the trumpet he says,
'Aha!'
He smells the battle from afar,
The thunder of captains and shouting.

26 "Does the hawk fly by your wisdom,
And spread its wings toward the
south?
27 Does the eagle mount up at your
command,
And make its nest on high?
28 On the rock it dwells and resides,
On the crag of the rock and the
stronghold.
29 From there it spies out the prey;
Its eyes observe from afar.
30 Its young ones suck up blood;
And where the slain *are,* there it *is."*

40 Moreover the LORD answered Job, and
said:

2 "Shall the one who contends with the
Almighty correct *Him?*
He who rebukes God, let him answer
it."

Job's Response to God

3 Then Job answered the LORD and said:

4 "Behold, I am vile;
What shall I answer You?
I lay my hand over my mouth.

5 Once I have spoken, but I will not
answer;
Yes, twice, but I will proceed no further."

God's Challenge to Job

6 Then the LORD answered Job out of the
whirlwind, and said:

7 "Now prepare yourself like a man;
I will question you, and you shall
answer Me:

8 "Would you indeed annul My judgment?
Would you condemn Me that you may
be justified?
9 Have you an arm like God?
Or can you thunder with a voice like
His?
10 Then adorn yourself *with* majesty and
splendor,
And array yourself with glory and
beauty.
11 Disperse the rage of your wrath;
Look on everyone *who is* proud, and
humble him.
12 Look on everyone *who is* proud, *and*
bring him low;
Tread down the wicked in their place.
13 Hide them in the dust together,
Bind their faces in hidden *darkness.*
14 Then I will also confess to you
That your own right hand can save you.

15 "Look now at the behemoth,[a] which
I made *along* with you;
He eats grass like an ox.
16 See now, his strength *is* in his hips,
And his power *is* in his stomach
muscles.
17 He moves his tail like a cedar;
The sinews of his thighs are tightly knit.
18 His bones *are like* beams of bronze,
His ribs like bars of iron.
19 He *is* the first of the ways of God;
Only He who made him can bring
near His sword.
20 Surely the mountains yield food for him,
And all the beasts of the field play
there.

39:19 [a]Or *a mane*   **40:15** [a]A large animal, exact
identity unknown

21 He lies under the lotus trees,
In a covert of reeds and marsh.
22 The lotus trees cover him *with* their
shade;
The willows by the brook surround him.
23 Indeed the river may rage,
Yet he is not disturbed;
He is confident, though the Jordan
gushes into his mouth,
24 *Though* he takes it in his eyes,
Or one pierces *his* nose with a snare.

41 "Can you draw out Leviathanª with
a hook,
Or *snare* his tongue with a line *which*
you lower?
2 Can you put a reed through his nose,
Or pierce his jaw with a hook?
3 Will he make many supplications to
you?
Will he speak softly to you?
4 Will he make a covenant with you?
Will you take him as a servant
forever?
5 Will you play with him as *with* a bird,
Or will you leash him for your
maidens?
6 Will *your* companions make a
banquetª of him?
Will they apportion him among the
merchants?
7 Can you fill his skin with harpoons,
Or his head with fishing spears?
8 Lay your hand on him;
Remember the battle—
Never do it again!
9 Indeed, *any* hope of *overcoming* him
is false;
Shall *one not* be overwhelmed at the
sight of him?
10 No one *is* so fierce that he would dare
stir him up.
Who then is able to stand against Me?
11 Who has preceded Me, that I should
pay *him?*
Everything under heaven is Mine.

12 "I will not concealª his limbs,
His mighty power, or his graceful
proportions.
13 Who can remove his outer coat?
Who can approach *him* with a double
bridle?

14 Who can open the doors of his face,
With his terrible teeth all around?
15 *His* rows of scales are *his* pride,
Shut up tightly *as with* a seal;
16 One is so near another
That no air can come between them;
17 They are joined one to another,
They stick together and cannot be
parted.
18 His sneezings flash forth light,
And his eyes *are* like the eyelids of the
morning.
19 Out of his mouth go burning lights;
Sparks of fire shoot out.
20 Smoke goes out of his nostrils,
As *from* a boiling pot and burning
rushes.
21 His breath kindles coals,
And a flame goes out of his mouth.
22 Strength dwells in his neck,
And sorrow dances before him.
23 The folds of his flesh are joined
together;
They are firm on him and cannot
be moved.
24 His heart is as hard as stone,
Even as hard as the lower *millstone.*
25 When he raises himself up, the
mighty are afraid;
Because of his crashings they are
besideª themselves.
26 *Though* the sword reaches him, it
cannot avail;
Nor does spear, dart, or javelin.
27 He regards iron as straw,
And bronze as rotten wood.
28 The arrow cannot make him flee;
Slingstones become like stubble to him.
29 Darts are regarded as straw;
He laughs at the threat of javelins.
30 His undersides *are* like sharp potsherds;
He spreads pointed *marks* in the mire.
31 He makes the deep boil like a pot;
He makes the sea like a pot of
ointment.
32 He leaves a shining wake behind him;
One would think the deep had white
hair.

41:1 ªA large sea creature, exact identity unknown
41:6 ªOr *bargain over him*   **41:12** ªLiterally *keep
silent about*   **41:25** ªOr *purify themselves*

33 On earth there is nothing like him,
     Which is made without fear.
34 He beholds every high *thing;*
     He *is* king over all the children of
        pride.”

Job's Repentance and Restoration

42 Then Job answered the LORD and said:

2 “I know that You can do everything,
    And that no purpose *of Yours* can be
       withheld from You.
3 *You asked,* ‘Who *is* this who hides
       counsel without knowledge?’
    Therefore I have uttered what I did not
       understand,
    Things too wonderful for me, which
       I did not know.
4 Listen, please, and let me speak;
    You said, ‘I will question you, and you
       shall answer Me.’

5 “I have heard of You by the hearing
       of the ear,
    But now my eye sees You.
6 Therefore I abhor *myself,*
    And repent in dust and ashes.”

7 And so it was, after the LORD had spoken these words to Job, that the LORD said to Eliphaz the Temanite, “My wrath is aroused against you and your two friends, for you have not spoken of Me *what is* right, as My servant Job *has.* 8 Now therefore, take for yourselves seven bulls and seven rams, go to My servant Job, and offer up for yourselves a burnt offering; and My servant Job shall pray for you. For I will accept him, lest I deal with you *according to your* folly; because you have not spoken of Me *what is* right, as My servant Job *has.*”

9 So Eliphaz the Temanite and Bildad the Shuhite *and* Zophar the Naamathite went and did as the LORD commanded them; for the LORD had accepted Job. 10 And the LORD restored Job's losses[a] when he prayed for his friends. Indeed the LORD gave Job twice as much as he had before. 11 Then all his brothers, all his sisters, and all those who had been his acquaintances before, came to him and ate food with him in his house; and they consoled him and comforted him for all the adversity that the LORD had brought upon him. Each one gave him a piece of silver and each a ring of gold.

12 Now the LORD blessed the latter *days* of Job more than his beginning; for he had fourteen thousand sheep, six thousand camels, one thousand yoke of oxen, and one thousand female donkeys. 13 He also had seven sons and three daughters. 14 And he called the name of the first Jemimah, the name of the second Keziah, and the name of the third Keren-Happuch. 15 In all the land were found no women *so* beautiful as the daughters of Job; and their father gave them an inheritance among their brothers.

16 After this Job lived one hundred and forty years, and saw his children and grandchildren *for* four generations. 17 So Job died, old and full of days.

42:10 [a]Literally *Job's captivity,* that is, what was captured from Job

PSALMS

Author: David, Solomon, Asaph, Sons of Korah, Others

When Written: 1000–300 B.C.

Theme: Worship

Key Verse: Psalm 19:14—Let the words of my mouth and the meditation of my heart be acceptable in Your sight, O LORD, my strength and my Redeemer.

Key Chapter: Psalm 100—While the Psalms are filled with divinely inspired counsel that believers throughout history have claimed as favorites, no chapter more beautifully depicts the central themes of worship and praise than Psalm 100.

The Book of Psalms is a profoundly deep and personal guide to intimate worship and praise to God. Containing some of the most beautiful poetry ever penned, the Psalms can help us express our deepest needs, thoughts, and desires to our heavenly Father—both in times of great joy and great sorrow. A wonderful resource of spiritual encouragement, the Psalms are the richest scriptural resource for worship, prayer, meditation, and instruction about God.

One of America's most beloved sacred lyricists, Fanny Crosby, no doubt received much of her mentoring from time spent in the Book of Psalms. Despite the fact that she was blind from infancy, she went on to pen more than 8,000 songs of praise to God, including such classic hymns as "Near The Cross," "Praise Him, Praise Him," and "To God Be the Glory." The chorus of one of her most well-known hymns, "Blessed Assurance," sums up the theme of Psalms:

> This is my story, this is my song,
> praising my Savior all the day long;
> this is my story, this is my song,
> praising my Savior all the day long.

PSALMS

Book One: Psalms 1—41

PSALM 1

The Way of the Righteous and the End of the Ungodly

1 Blessed *is* the man
  Who walks not in the counsel of the
    ungodly,
    Nor stands in the path of sinners,
    Nor sits in the seat of the scornful;
2 But his delight *is* in the law of the LORD,
    And in His law he meditates day and
    night.
3 He shall be like a tree
    Planted by the rivers of water,
    That brings forth its fruit in its season,
    Whose leaf also shall not wither;
  And whatever he does shall prosper.

4 The ungodly *are* not so,
  But *are* like the chaff which the wind
    drives away.
5 Therefore the ungodly shall not stand
    in the judgment,
  Nor sinners in the congregation of the
    righteous.

6 For the LORD knows the way of the
    righteous,
  But the way of the ungodly shall perish.

PSALM 2

The Messiah's Triumph and Kingdom

1 Why do the nations rage,
  And the people plot a vain thing?
2 The kings of the earth set themselves,
  And the rulers take counsel together,
  Against the LORD and against His
    Anointed, *saying,*
3 "Let us break Their bonds in pieces
  And cast away Their cords from us."

4 He who sits in the heavens shall laugh;
  The Lord shall hold them in derision.

5 Then He shall speak to them in
    His wrath,
  And distress them in His deep
    displeasure:
6 "Yet I have set My King
  On My holy hill of Zion."

7 "I will declare the decree:
  The LORD has said to Me,
  'You *are* My Son,
  Today I have begotten You.
8 Ask of Me, and I will give *You*
  The nations *for* Your inheritance,
  And the ends of the earth *for* Your
    possession.
9 You shall break[a] them with a rod of
    iron;
  You shall dash them to pieces like a
    potter's vessel.' "

10 Now therefore, be wise, O kings;
  Be instructed, you judges of the earth.
11 Serve the LORD with fear,
  And rejoice with trembling.
12 Kiss the Son,[a] lest He[b] be angry,
  And you perish *in* the way,
  When His wrath is kindled but a little.
  Blessed *are* all those who put their
    trust in Him.

PSALM 3

The LORD Helps His Troubled People

A Psalm of David when he fled
from Absalom his son.

1 LORD, how they have increased who
    trouble me!
  Many *are* they who rise up against me.
2 Many *are* they who say of me,
  "*There is* no help for him in God."
                                        Selah

2:9 [a]Following Masoretic Text and Targum;
Septuagint, Syriac, and Vulgate read *rule* (compare
Revelation 2:27).   **2:12** [a]Septuagint and Vulgate
read *Embrace discipline;* Targum reads *Receive
instruction.* [b]Septuagint reads *the LORD.*

3 But You, O LORD, *are* a shield for me,
  My glory and the One who lifts up
      my head.
4 I cried to the LORD with my voice,
  And He heard me from His holy hill.
                                    Selah

5 I lay down and slept;
  I awoke, for the LORD sustained me.
6 I will not be afraid of ten thousands
      of people
  Who have set *themselves* against me
      all around.

7 Arise, O LORD;
  Save me, O my God!
  For You have struck all my enemies
      on the cheekbone;
  You have broken the teeth of the
      ungodly.
8 Salvation *belongs* to the LORD.
  Your blessing *is* upon Your people.
                                    Selah

PSALM 4

The Safety of the Faithful

To the Chief Musician. With stringed instruments.
A Psalm of David.

1 Hear me when I call, O God of my
      righteousness!
  You have relieved me in *my* distress;
  Have mercy on me, and hear my
      prayer.

2 How long, O you sons of men,
  Will you turn my glory to shame?
  How long will you love worthlessness
  And seek falsehood?   Selah
3 But know that the LORD has set apart[a]
      for Himself him who is godly;
  The LORD will hear when I call to
      Him.

4 Be angry, and do not sin.
  Meditate within your heart on your
      bed, and be still.   Selah
5 Offer the sacrifices of righteousness,
  And put your trust in the LORD.

6 *There are* many who say,
  "Who will show us *any* good?"

LORD, lift up the light of Your
      countenance upon us.
7 You have put gladness in my heart,
  More than in the season that their
      grain and wine increased.
8 I will both lie down in peace, and sleep;
  For You alone, O LORD, make me dwell
      in safety.

PSALM 5

A Prayer for Guidance

To the Chief Musician. With flutes.[a]
A Psalm of David.

1 Give ear to my words, O LORD,
  Consider my meditation.
2 Give heed to the voice of my cry,
  My King and my God,
  For to You I will pray.
3 My voice You shall hear in the
      morning, O LORD;
  In the morning I will direct *it* to You,
  And I will look up.

4 For You *are* not a God who takes
      pleasure in wickedness,
  Nor shall evil dwell with You.
5 The boastful shall not stand in Your
      sight;
  You hate all workers of iniquity.
6 You shall destroy those who speak
      falsehood;
  The LORD abhors the bloodthirsty
      and deceitful man.

7 But as for me, I will come into Your
      house in the multitude of Your mercy;
  In fear of You I will worship toward
      Your holy temple.
8 Lead me, O LORD, in Your
      righteousness because of my enemies;
  Make Your way straight before my face.

9 For *there is* no faithfulness in their
      mouth;
  Their inward part *is* destruction;
  Their throat *is* an open tomb;
  They flatter with their tongue.

4:3 [a]Many Hebrew manuscripts, Septuagint,
Targum, and Vulgate read *made wonderful*.
5:title [a]Hebrew *nehiloth*

10 Pronounce them guilty, O God!
   Let them fall by their own counsels;
   Cast them out in the multitude of
      their transgressions,
   For they have rebelled against You.

11 But let all those rejoice who put their
      trust in You;
   Let them ever shout for joy, because
      You defend them;
   Let those also who love Your name
   Be joyful in You.
12 For You, O Lord, will bless the righteous;
   With favor You will surround him as
      with a shield.

PSALM 6

A Prayer of Faith in Time of Distress

To the Chief Musician. With stringed instruments.
On an eight-stringed harp.[a] A Psalm of David.

1 O Lord, do not rebuke me in Your anger,
   Nor chasten me in Your hot displeasure.
2 Have mercy on me, O Lord, for I *am*
      weak;
   O Lord, heal me, for my bones are
      troubled.
3 My soul also is greatly troubled;
   But You, O Lord—how long?

4 Return, O Lord, deliver me!
   Oh, save me for Your mercies' sake!
5 For in death *there is* no remembrance
      of You;
   In the grave who will give You thanks?

6 I am weary with my groaning;
   All night I make my bed swim;
   I drench my couch with my tears.
7 My eye wastes away because of grief;
   It grows old because of all my enemies.

8 Depart from me, all you workers of
      iniquity;
   For the Lord has heard the voice of
      my weeping.
9 The Lord has heard my supplication;
   The Lord will receive my prayer.
10 Let all my enemies be ashamed and
      greatly troubled;
   Let them turn back *and* be ashamed
      suddenly.

PSALM 7

Prayer and Praise for Deliverance from Enemies

A Meditation[a] of David, which he sang to the Lord
concerning the words of Cush, a Benjamite.

1 O Lord my God, in You I put my trust;
   Save me from all those who persecute
      me;
   And deliver me,
2 Lest they tear me like a lion,
   Rending *me* in pieces, while *there is*
      none to deliver.

3 O Lord my God, if I have done this:
   If there is iniquity in my hands,
4 If I have repaid evil to him who was
      at peace with me,
   Or have plundered my enemy without
      cause,
5 Let the enemy pursue me and overtake
      me;
   Yes, let him trample my life to the earth,
   And lay my honor in the dust.   Selah

6 Arise, O Lord, in Your anger;
   Lift Yourself up because of the rage
      of my enemies;
   Rise up for me[a] *to* the judgment You
      have commanded!
7 So the congregation of the peoples
      shall surround You;
   For their sakes, therefore, return on
      high.
8 The Lord shall judge the peoples;
   Judge me, O Lord, according to
      my righteousness,
   And according to my integrity
      within me.

9 Oh, let the wickedness of the wicked
      come to an end,
   But establish the just;
   For the righteous God tests the hearts
      and minds.
10 My defense *is* of God,
   Who saves the upright in heart.

6:title [a]Hebrew *sheminith*   **7:title** [a]Hebrew
Shiggaion   **7:6** [a]Following Masoretic Text, Targum,
and Vulgate; Septuagint reads *O Lord my God.*

11 God *is* a just judge,
   And God is angry *with the wicked* every
      day.
12 If he does not turn back,
   He will sharpen His sword;
   He bends His bow and makes it ready.
13 He also prepares for Himself
      instruments of death;
   He makes His arrows into fiery shafts.

14 Behold, *the wicked* brings forth iniquity;
   Yes, he conceives trouble and brings
      forth falsehood.
15 He made a pit and dug it out,
   And has fallen into the ditch *which* he
      made.
16 His trouble shall return upon his own
      head,
   And his violent dealing shall come
      down on his own crown.

17 I will praise the Lord according to His
      righteousness,
   And will sing praise to the name of the
      Lord Most High.

PSALM 8

The Glory of the Lord in Creation

To the Chief Musician. On the instrument of Gath.ᵃ
A Psalm of David.

1 O Lord, our Lord,
   How excellent *is* Your name in all
      the earth,
   Who have set Your glory above the
      heavens!

2 Out of the mouth of babes and
      nursing infants
   You have ordained strength,
   Because of Your enemies,
   That You may silence the enemy
      and the avenger.

3 When I consider Your heavens, the
      work of Your fingers,
   The moon and the stars, which You
      have ordained,
4 What is man that You are mindful
      of him,
   And the son of man that You visit
      him?

5 For You have made him a little lower
      than the angels,ᵃ
   And You have crowned him with glory
      and honor.

6 You have made him to have dominion
      over the works of Your hands;
   You have put all *things* under his feet,
7 All sheep and oxen—
   Even the beasts of the field,
8 The birds of the air,
   And the fish of the sea
   That pass through the paths of the
      seas.

9 O Lord, our Lord,
   How excellent *is* Your name in all
      the earth!

PSALM 9

Prayer and Thanksgiving for the Lord's Righteous Judgments

To the Chief Musician. To *the tune of*
"Death of the Son."ᵃ A Psalm of David.

1 I will praise *You,* O Lord, with my
      whole heart;
   I will tell of all Your marvelous works.
2 I will be glad and rejoice in You;
   I will sing praise to Your name,
   O Most High.

3 When my enemies turn back,
   They shall fall and perish at Your
      presence.
4 For You have maintained my right
      and my cause;
   You sat on the throne judging in
      righteousness.
5 You have rebuked the nations,
   You have destroyed the wicked;
   You have blotted out their name
      forever and ever.

6 O enemy, destructions are finished
      forever!
   And you have destroyed cities;
   Even their memory has perished.

8:title ᵃHebrew *Al Gittith*　　**8:5** ᵃHebrew *Elohim, God;*
Septuagint, Syriac, Targum, and Jewish tradition
translate as *angels.*　　**9:title** ᵃHebrew *Muth Labben*

7 But the LORD shall endure forever;
He has prepared His throne for judgment.
8 He shall judge the world in righteousness,
And He shall administer judgment for the peoples in uprightness.

9 The LORD also will be a refuge for the oppressed,
A refuge in times of trouble.
10 And those who know Your name will put their trust in You;
For You, LORD, have not forsaken those who seek You.

11 Sing praises to the LORD, who dwells in Zion!
Declare His deeds among the people.
12 When He avenges blood, He remembers them;
He does not forget the cry of the humble.

13 Have mercy on me, O LORD!
Consider my trouble from those who hate me,
You who lift me up from the gates of death,
14 That I may tell of all Your praise
In the gates of the daughter of Zion.
I will rejoice in Your salvation.

15 The nations have sunk down in the pit *which* they made;
In the net which they hid, their own foot is caught.
16 The LORD is known *by* the judgment He executes;
The wicked is snared in the work of his own hands.
Meditation.[a]   Selah

17 The wicked shall be turned into hell,
And all the nations that forget God.
18 For the needy shall not always be forgotten;
The expectation of the poor shall *not* perish forever.

19 Arise, O LORD,
Do not let man prevail;
Let the nations be judged in Your sight.
20 Put them in fear, O LORD,
That the nations may know themselves *to be but* men.   Selah

PSALM 10

A Song of Confidence in God's Triumph over Evil

1 Why do You stand afar off, O LORD?
Why do You hide in times of trouble?
2 The wicked in *his* pride persecutes the poor;
Let them be caught in the plots which they have devised.

3 For the wicked boasts of his heart's desire;
He blesses the greedy *and* renounces the LORD.
4 The wicked in his proud countenance does not seek *God;*
God *is* in none of his thoughts.

5 His ways are always prospering;
Your judgments *are* far above, out of his sight;
As for all his enemies, he sneers at them.
6 He has said in his heart, "I shall not be moved;
I shall never be in adversity."
7 His mouth is full of cursing and deceit and oppression;
Under his tongue *is* trouble and iniquity.

8 He sits in the lurking places of the villages;
In the secret places he murders the innocent;
His eyes are secretly fixed on the helpless.
9 He lies in wait secretly, as a lion in his den;
He lies in wait to catch the poor;
He catches the poor when he draws him into his net.
10 So he crouches, he lies low,
That the helpless may fall by his strength.
11 He has said in his heart,

9:16 [a]Hebrew *Higgaion*

"God has forgotten;
He hides His face;
He will never see."

12 Arise, O LORD!
O God, lift up Your hand!
Do not forget the humble.
13 Why do the wicked renounce God?
He has said in his heart,
"You will not require *an account*."

14 But You have seen, for You observe
trouble and grief,
To repay *it* by Your hand.
The helpless commits himself to You;
You are the helper of the fatherless.
15 Break the arm of the wicked and the
evil *man*;
Seek out his wickedness *until* You find
none.

16 The LORD *is* King forever and ever;
The nations have perished out of His
land.
17 LORD, You have heard the desire of
the humble;
You will prepare their heart;
You will cause Your ear to hear,
18 To do justice to the fatherless and the
oppressed,
That the man of the earth may oppress
no more.

PSALM 11

Faith in the LORD's Righteousness

To the Chief Musician. *A Psalm* of David.

1 In the LORD I put my trust;
How can you say to my soul,
"Flee *as* a bird to your mountain"?
2 For look! The wicked bend *their* bow,
They make ready their arrow on the
string,
That they may shoot secretly at the
upright in heart.
3 If the foundations are destroyed,
What can the righteous do?

4 The LORD *is* in His holy temple,
The LORD's throne *is* in heaven;
His eyes behold,
His eyelids test the sons of men.

5 The LORD tests the righteous,
But the wicked and the one who loves
violence His soul hates.
6 Upon the wicked He will rain coals;
Fire and brimstone and a burning
wind
Shall be the portion of their cup.

7 For the LORD *is* righteous,
He loves righteousness;
His countenance beholds the upright.[a]

PSALM 12

Man's Treachery and God's Constancy

To the Chief Musician. On an eight-stringed harp.[a]
A Psalm of David.

1 Help, LORD, for the godly man ceases!
For the faithful disappear from among
the sons of men.
2 They speak idly everyone with his
neighbor;
With flattering lips *and* a double heart
they speak.

3 May the LORD cut off all flattering lips,
And the tongue that speaks proud
things,
4 Who have said,
"With our tongue we will prevail;
Our lips *are* our own;
Who *is* lord over us?"

5 "For the oppression of the poor, for the
sighing of the needy,
Now I will arise," says the LORD;
"I will set *him* in the safety for which
he yearns."

6 The words of the LORD *are* pure words,
Like silver tried in a furnace of earth,
Purified seven times.
7 You shall keep them, O LORD,
You shall preserve them from this
generation forever.

8 The wicked prowl on every side,
When vileness is exalted among the
sons of men.

11:7 [a]Or *The upright beholds His countenance*
12:title [a]Hebrew *sheminith*

"IF THE FOUNDATIONS BE DESTROYED. . . ."

Jedidiah Morse (1761–1826) was a pioneer American educator, clergyman, geographer, and the father of Samuel Morse, inventor of the telegraph and "Morse Code." After the American Revolution, he taught school to earn money while a graduate student at Yale. The students needed a good geography text, so he wrote *Geography Made Easy* and published it in 1784. It was the first geography book published in the United States and went through over 25 editions. Morse later published other American and world geographies, earning the informal title of "Father of American Geography."

While at Yale, Jedidiah studied for the ministry. In 1789, he accepted a call to the First Church of Charlestown, Massachusetts, one of the oldest churches in America. He was highly alarmed by how far the Boston clergy had moved away from doctrinal orthodoxy as well as by the growing influence of European rationalism in the United States. In 1799, he preached an insightful Election Sermon: "If the foundations be destroyed, what can the righteous do?" In it, he said:

> *Our dangers are of two kinds, those which affect our religion, and those which affect our government. They are, however, so closely allied that they cannot, with propriety, be separated. The foundations which support the interest of Christianity, are also necessary to support a free and equal government like our own. . . .*

> *To the kindly influence of Christianity we owe that degree of civil freedom, and political and social happiness which mankind now enjoys. In proportion as the genuine effects of Christianity are diminished in any nation, either through unbelief or the corruption of its doctrine, or the neglect of its institutions; in the same proportion will the people of that nation recede from the blessings of genuine freedom, and approximate the miseries of complete despotism. I hold this to be a truth confirmed by experience. If so, it follows, that all efforts made to destroy the foundations of our holy religion, ultimately tend to the subversion also of our political freedom and happiness. Whenever the pillars of Christianity shall be overthrown, our present republican forms of government, and all the blessings which flow from them, must fall with them.*

PSALM 13

Trust in the Salvation of the LORD

To the Chief Musician. A Psalm of David.

1 How long, O LORD? Will You forget
      me forever?
   How long will You hide Your face
      from me?
2 How long shall I take counsel in my
      soul,
   Having sorrow in my heart daily?
   How long will my enemy be exalted
      over me?

3 Consider *and* hear me, O LORD my God;
   Enlighten my eyes,
   Lest I sleep the *sleep of* death;
4 Lest my enemy say,
   "I have prevailed against him";
   Lest those who trouble me rejoice
      when I am moved.

5 But I have trusted in Your mercy;
   My heart shall rejoice in Your salvation.
6 I will sing to the LORD,
   Because He has dealt bountifully
      with me.

PSALM 14

Folly of the Godless, and God's Final Triumph

To the Chief Musician. *A Psalm* of David.

1 The fool has said in his heart,
   "*There is* no God."
   They are corrupt,
   They have done abominable works,
   There is none who does good.

2 The LORD looks down from heaven
      upon the children of men,
   To see if there are any who understand,
      who seek God.
3 They have all turned aside,
   They have together become corrupt;
   There is none who does good,
   No, not one.

4 Have all the workers of iniquity no
      knowledge,
   Who eat up my people *as* they eat
      bread,
   And do not call on the LORD?

5 There they are in great fear,
   For God *is* with the generation of the
      righteous.
6 You shame the counsel of the poor,
   But the LORD *is* his refuge.

7 Oh, that the salvation of Israel *would*
      come out of Zion!
   When the LORD brings back the
      captivity of His people,
   Let Jacob rejoice *and* Israel be glad.

PSALM 15

*The Character of Those Who May Dwell
with the LORD*

A Psalm of David.

1 LORD, who may abide in Your
      tabernacle?
   Who may dwell in Your holy hill?

2 He who walks uprightly,
      And works righteousness,
      And speaks the truth in his heart;
3 He *who* does not backbite with his
      tongue,
      Nor does evil to his neighbor,
      Nor does he take up a reproach
         against his friend;
4 In whose eyes a vile person is despised,
      But he honors those who fear the LORD;
   He *who* swears to his own hurt and
      does not change;
5 He *who* does not put out his money at
      usury,
      Nor does he take a bribe against the
         innocent.

   He who does these *things* shall never
      be moved.

PSALM 16

*The Hope of the Faithful, and the Messiah's
Victory*

A Michtam of David.

1 Preserve me, O God, for in You I put
      my trust.

2 *O my soul,* you have said to the LORD,
   "You *are* my Lord,

My goodness is nothing apart from
   You."
3 As for the saints who *are* on the earth,
   "They are the excellent ones, in whom
      is all my delight."

4 Their sorrows shall be multiplied who
      hasten *after* another *god;*
   Their drink offerings of blood I will
      not offer,
   Nor take up their names on my lips.

5 O LORD, *You are* the portion of my
      inheritance and my cup;
   You maintain my lot.
6 The lines have fallen to me in
      pleasant *places;*
   Yes, I have a good inheritance.

7 I will bless the LORD who has given
      me counsel;
   My heart also instructs me in the
      night seasons.
8 I have set the LORD always before me;
   Because *He is* at my right hand I shall
      not be moved.

9 Therefore my heart is glad, and my
      glory rejoices;
   My flesh also will rest in hope.
10 For You will not leave my soul in
      Sheol,
   Nor will You allow Your Holy One to
      see corruption.
11 You will show me the path of life;
   In Your presence *is* fullness of joy;
   At Your right hand *are* pleasures
      forevermore.

PSALM 17

Prayer with Confidence in Final Salvation

A Prayer of David.

1 Hear a just cause, O LORD,
   Attend to my cry;
   Give ear to my prayer *which is* not
      from deceitful lips.
2 Let my vindication come from Your
      presence;
   Let Your eyes look on the things that
      are upright.

3 You have tested my heart;
   You have visited *me* in the night;
   You have tried me and have found
      nothing;
   I have purposed that my mouth shall
      not transgress.
4 Concerning the works of men,
   By the word of Your lips,
   I have kept away from the paths
      of the destroyer.
5 Uphold my steps in Your paths,
   That my footsteps may not slip.

6 I have called upon You, for You will
      hear me, O God;
   Incline Your ear to me, *and* hear my
      speech.
7 Show Your marvelous lovingkindness
      by Your right hand,
   O You who save those who trust *in
      You*
   From those who rise up *against them.*
8 Keep me as the apple of Your eye;
   Hide me under the shadow of Your
      wings,
9 From the wicked who oppress me,
   From my deadly enemies who
      surround me.

10 They have closed up their fat *hearts;*
   With their mouths they speak
      proudly.
11 They have now surrounded us in our
      steps;
   They have set their eyes, crouching
      down to the earth,
12 As a lion is eager to tear his prey,
   And like a young lion lurking in secret
      places.

13 Arise, O LORD,
   Confront him, cast him down;
   Deliver my life from the wicked with
      Your sword,
14 With Your hand from men, O LORD,
   From men of the world *who have* their
      portion in *this* life,
   And whose belly You fill with Your
      hidden treasure.
   They are satisfied with children,
   And leave the rest of their *possession*
      for their babes.

15 As for me, I will see Your face in
    righteousness;
  I shall be satisfied when I awake
    in Your likeness.

PSALM 18

God the Sovereign Savior

To the Chief Musician. *A Psalm* of David
the servant of the Lord, who spoke to the Lord
the words of this song on the day that the Lord
delivered him from the hand of all his enemies
and from the hand of Saul. And he said:

1 I will love You, O Lord, my strength.
2 The Lord is my rock and my fortress
    and my deliverer;
  My God, my strength, in whom I will
    trust;
  My shield and the horn of my
    salvation, my stronghold.
3 I will call upon the Lord, *who is worthy*
    to be praised;
  So shall I be saved from my enemies.

4 The pangs of death surrounded me,
  And the floods of ungodliness made
    me afraid.
5 The sorrows of Sheol surrounded me;
  The snares of death confronted me.
6 In my distress I called upon the Lord,
  And cried out to my God;
  He heard my voice from His temple,
  And my cry came before Him, *even* to
    His ears.

7 Then the earth shook and trembled;
  The foundations of the hills also
    quaked and were shaken,
  Because He was angry.
8 Smoke went up from His nostrils,
  And devouring fire from His mouth;
  Coals were kindled by it.
9 He bowed the heavens also, and came
    down
  With darkness under His feet.
10 And He rode upon a cherub, and flew;
  He flew upon the wings of the wind.
11 He made darkness His secret place;
  His canopy around Him *was* dark waters
  And thick clouds of the skies.
12 From the brightness before Him,
  His thick clouds passed with hailstones
    and coals of fire.

13 The Lord thundered from heaven,
  And the Most High uttered His voice,
  Hailstones and coals of fire.[a]
14 He sent out His arrows and scattered
    the foe,
  Lightnings in abundance, and He
    vanquished them.
15 Then the channels of the sea were seen,
  The foundations of the world were
    uncovered
  At Your rebuke, O Lord,
  At the blast of the breath of Your nostrils.

16 He sent from above, He took me;
  He drew me out of many waters.
17 He delivered me from my strong enemy,
  From those who hated me,
  For they were too strong for me.
18 They confronted me in the day of my
    calamity,
  But the Lord was my support.
19 He also brought me out into a broad
    place;
  He delivered me because He delighted
    in me.

20 The Lord rewarded me according to my
    righteousness;
  According to the cleanness of my hands
  He has recompensed me.
21 For I have kept the ways of the Lord,
  And have not wickedly departed from
    my God.
22 For all His judgments *were* before me,
  And I did not put away His statutes
    from me.
23 I was also blameless before Him,
  And I kept myself from my iniquity.
24 Therefore the Lord has recompensed
    me according to my righteousness,
  According to the cleanness of my
    hands in His sight.

25 With the merciful You will show
    Yourself merciful;
  With a blameless man You will show
    Yourself blameless;
26 With the pure You will show Yourself
    pure;

18:13 ᵃFollowing Masoretic Text, Targum, and
Vulgate; a few Hebrew manuscripts and Septuagint
omit *Hailstones and coals of fire.*

And with the devious You will show
    Yourself shrewd.
27 For You will save the humble people,
    But will bring down haughty looks.

28 For You will light my lamp;
    The LORD my God will enlighten my
        darkness.
29 For by You I can run against a troop,
    By my God I can leap over a wall.
30 *As for* God, His way *is* perfect;
    The word of the LORD is proven;
    He *is* a shield to all who trust in Him.

31 For who *is* God, except the LORD?
    And who *is* a rock, except our God?
32 *It is* God who arms me with strength,
    And makes my way perfect.
33 He makes my feet like the *feet of* deer,
    And sets me on my high places.
34 He teaches my hands to make war,
    So that my arms can bend a bow of
        bronze.

35 You have also given me the shield
    of Your salvation;
    Your right hand has held me up,
    Your gentleness has made me great.
36 You enlarged my path under me,
    So my feet did not slip.

37 I have pursued my enemies and
    overtaken them;
    Neither did I turn back again till they
        were destroyed.
38 I have wounded them,
    So that they could not rise;
    They have fallen under my feet.
39 For You have armed me with strength
    for the battle;
    You have subdued under me those
        who rose up against me.
40 You have also given me the necks
    of my enemies,
    So that I destroyed those who
        hated me.
41 They cried out, but *there was* none
    to save;
    Even to the LORD, but He did not
        answer them.
42 Then I beat them as fine as the dust
    before the wind;

I cast them out like dirt in the streets.

43 You have delivered me from the
    strivings of the people;
    You have made me the head of the
        nations;
    A people I have not known shall
        serve me.
44 As soon as they hear of me they
    obey me;
    The foreigners submit to me.
45 The foreigners fade away,
    And come frightened from their
        hideouts.

46 The LORD lives!
    Blessed *be* my Rock!
    Let the God of my salvation be exalted.
47 *It is* God who avenges me,
    And subdues the peoples under me;
48 He delivers me from my enemies.
    You also lift me up above those who
        rise against me;
    You have delivered me from the
        violent man.
49 Therefore I will give thanks to You,
    O LORD, among the Gentiles,
    And sing praises to Your name.

50 Great deliverance He gives to His king,
    And shows mercy to His anointed,
    To David and his descendants
        forevermore.

PSALM 19

The Perfect Revelation of the LORD

To the Chief Musician. A Psalm of David.

1 The heavens declare the glory of God;
    And the firmament shows His
        handiwork.
2 Day unto day utters speech,
    And night unto night reveals knowledge.
3 *There is* no speech nor language
    Where their voice is not heard.
4 Their line[a] has gone out through all
    the earth,
    And their words to the end of the
        world.

19:4 [a]Septuagint, Syriac, and Vulgate read *sound;*
Targum reads *business.*

In them He has set a tabernacle for
the sun,

5 Which *is* like a bridegroom coming
out of his chamber,
And rejoices like a strong man to run
its race.

6 Its rising *is* from one end of heaven,
And its circuit to the other end;
And there is nothing hidden from its
heat.

7 The law of the LORD *is* perfect,
converting the soul;
The testimony of the LORD *is* sure,
making wise the simple;

8 The statutes of the LORD *are* right,
rejoicing the heart;
The commandment of the LORD *is*
pure, enlightening the eyes;

9 The fear of the LORD *is* clean, enduring
forever;
The judgments of the LORD *are* true
and righteous altogether.

10 More to be desired *are they* than gold,
Yea, than much fine gold;
Sweeter also than honey and the
honeycomb.

11 Moreover by them Your servant is
warned,
And in keeping them *there is* great
reward.

12 Who can understand *his* errors?
Cleanse me from secret *faults.*

13 Keep back Your servant also from
presumptuous *sins;*
Let them not have dominion over me.
Then I shall be blameless,
And I shall be innocent of great
transgression.

14 Let the words of my mouth and
the meditation of my heart
Be acceptable in Your sight,
O LORD, my strength and my
Redeemer.

FAITH

*The heavens declare the
glory of God. . . .*

PSALM 19:1

John Glenn

JOHN GLENN

Between 1957 and 1975, the competition of space exploration between the Soviet Union and the United States became a heated part of the Cold War, both because of its potential military and technological applications and its morale-boosting social benefits. The Soviets were the first to achieve a manned orbit of the earth in 1961, putting America behind in the "Space Race."

On February 20, 1962, atop an Atlas rocket, Colonel John Glenn piloted the first American manned orbital mission aboard Friendship 7, circling the globe three times. Fulfilling America's political and scientific hopes and dreams as declared by President John F. Kennedy, Glenn returned to Earth as virtually every American's hero.

From 1974 to 1999, John Glenn served as a United States senator. In 1998, NASA invited him to rejoin the space program as a member of the Space Shuttle Discovery Crew. On October 29, 1998, Glenn became the oldest human, at the age of 77, ever to venture into space. It was a vivid reminder of the heroic spirit that makes space exploration possible.

As Glenn observed the heavens and earth from the windows of Discovery, he said, "To look out at this kind of creation out here and not believe in God is to me impossible. It just strengthens my faith. I wish there were words to describe what it's like."

PSALM 20

The Assurance of God's Saving Work

To the Chief Musician. A Psalm of David.

1 May the LORD answer you in the day
      of trouble;
   May the name of the God of Jacob
      defend you;
2 May He send you help from the
      sanctuary,
   And strengthen you out of Zion;
3 May He remember all your offerings,
   And accept your burnt sacrifice.   Selah

4 May He grant you according to your
      heart's *desire,*
   And fulfill all your purpose.
5 We will rejoice in your salvation,
   And in the name of our God we will
      set up *our* banners!
   May the LORD fulfill all your petitions.

6 Now I know that the LORD saves His
      anointed;
   He will answer him from His holy
      heaven
   With the saving strength of His right
      hand.

7 Some *trust* in chariots, and some in
      horses;
   But we will remember the name of the
      LORD our God.
8 They have bowed down and fallen;
   But we have risen and stand upright.

9 Save, LORD!
   May the King answer us when we call.

PSALM 21

Joy in the Salvation of the LORD

To the Chief Musician. A Psalm of David.

1 The king shall have joy in Your
      strength, O LORD;
   And in Your salvation how greatly
      shall he rejoice!
2 You have given him his heart's
      desire,
   And have not withheld the request
      of his lips.   Selah

3 For You meet him with the blessings of
      goodness;
   You set a crown of pure gold upon his
      head.
4 He asked life from You, *and* You gave
      it to him—
   Length of days forever and ever.
5 His glory *is* great in Your salvation;
   Honor and majesty You have placed
      upon him.
6 For You have made him most blessed
      forever;
   You have made him exceedingly glad
      with Your presence.
7 For the king trusts in the LORD,
   And through the mercy of the Most
      High he shall not be moved.

8 Your hand will find all Your enemies;
   Your right hand will find those who
      hate You.
9 You shall make them as a fiery oven
      in the time of Your anger;
   The LORD shall swallow them up in
      His wrath,
   And the fire shall devour them.
10 Their offspring You shall destroy from
      the earth,
   And their descendants from among
      the sons of men.
11 For they intended evil against You;
   They devised a plot *which* they are not
      able *to perform.*
12 Therefore You will make them turn
      their back;
   You will make ready *Your arrows* on
      Your string toward their faces.

13 Be exalted, O LORD, in Your own
      strength!
   We will sing and praise Your power.

PSALM 22

The Suffering, Praise, and Posterity
of the Messiah

*To the Chief Musician. Set to
"The Deer of the Dawn."ª A Psalm of David.*

1 My God, My God, why have You
      forsaken Me?

22:title ªHebrew *Aijeleth Hashahar*

Why are You so far from helping Me,
And from the words of My groaning?

2 O My God, I cry in the daytime, but
You do not hear;
And in the night season, and am not
silent.

3 But You *are* holy,
Enthroned in the praises of Israel.
4 Our fathers trusted in You;
They trusted, and You delivered them.
5 They cried to You, and were delivered;
They trusted in You, and were not
ashamed.

6 But I *am* a worm, and no man;
A reproach of men, and despised by
the people.
7 All those who see Me ridicule Me;
They shoot out the lip, they shake the
head, *saying,*
8 "He trusted[a] in the LORD, let Him rescue
Him;
Let Him deliver Him, since He delights
in Him!"

9 But You *are* He who took Me out
of the womb;
You made Me trust *while* on My
mother's breasts.
10 I was cast upon You from birth.
From My mother's womb
You *have been* My God.
11 Be not far from Me,
For trouble *is* near;
For *there is* none to help.

12 Many bulls have surrounded Me;
Strong *bulls* of Bashan have
encircled Me.
13 They gape at Me *with* their mouths,
Like a raging and roaring lion.

14 I am poured out like water,
And all My bones are out of joint;
My heart is like wax;
It has melted within Me.
15 My strength is dried up like a
potsherd,
And My tongue clings to My jaws;
You have brought Me to the dust
of death.

16 For dogs have surrounded Me;
The congregation of the wicked has
enclosed Me.
They pierced[a] My hands and My feet;
17 I can count all My bones.
They look *and* stare at Me.
18 They divide My garments among them,
And for My clothing they cast lots.

19 But You, O LORD, do not be far from Me;
O My Strength, hasten to help Me!
20 Deliver Me from the sword,
My precious *life* from the power of the
dog.
21 Save Me from the lion's mouth
And from the horns of the wild oxen!

You have answered Me.

22 I will declare Your name to My brethren;
In the midst of the assembly I will
praise You.
23 You who fear the LORD, praise Him!
All you descendants of Jacob, glorify
Him,
And fear Him, all you offspring of Israel!
24 For He has not despised nor abhorred
the affliction of the afflicted;
Nor has He hidden His face from Him;
But when He cried to Him, He heard.

25 My praise *shall be* of You in the great
assembly;
I will pay My vows before those who
fear Him.
26 The poor shall eat and be satisfied;
Those who seek Him will praise the
LORD.
Let your heart live forever!

27 All the ends of the world
Shall remember and turn to the LORD,
And all the families of the nations
Shall worship before You.[a]
28 For the kingdom *is* the LORD's,
And He rules over the nations.

22:8 [a]Septuagint, Syriac, and Vulgate read *hoped;*
Targum reads *praised.*   **22:16** [a]Following some
Hebrew manuscripts, Septuagint, Syriac, Vulgate;
Masoretic Text reads *Like a lion.*   **22:27** [a]Following
Masoretic Text, Septuagint, and Targum; Arabic,
Syriac, and Vulgate read *Him.*

29 All the prosperous of the earth
    Shall eat and worship;
    All those who go down to the dust
    Shall bow before Him,
    Even he who cannot keep himself alive.

30 A posterity shall serve Him.
    It will be recounted of the Lord to the
        next generation,
31 They will come and declare His
        righteousness to a people who will
        be born,
    That He has done *this.*

PSALM 23

The Lord the Shepherd of His People

A Psalm of David.

1 The Lord *is* my shepherd;
    I shall not want.
2 He makes me to lie down in green
        pastures;
    He leads me beside the still waters.
3 He restores my soul;
    He leads me in the paths of
        righteousness
    For His name's sake.

4 Yea, though I walk through the
        valley of the shadow of death,
    I will fear no evil;
    For You *are* with me;
    Your rod and Your staff, they
        comfort me.

5 You prepare a table before me in
        the presence of my enemies;
    You anoint my head with oil;
    My cup runs over.
6 Surely goodness and mercy shall
        follow me
    All the days of my life;
    And I will dwell[a] in the house of
        the Lord
    Forever.

PSALM 24

The King of Glory and His Kingdom

A Psalm of David.

1 The earth *is* the Lord's, and all its
        fullness,

The world and those who dwell therein.
2 For He has founded it upon the seas,
    And established it upon the waters.

3 Who may ascend into the hill of the
        Lord?
    Or who may stand in His holy place?
4 He who has clean hands and a pure
        heart,
    Who has not lifted up his soul to an
        idol,
    Nor sworn deceitfully.
5 He shall receive blessing from the Lord,
    And righteousness from the God of his
        salvation.
6 This *is* Jacob, the generation of those
        who seek Him,
    Who seek Your face.   Selah

7 Lift up your heads, O you gates!
    And be lifted up, you everlasting doors!
    And the King of glory shall come in.
8 Who *is* this King of glory?
    The Lord strong and mighty,
    The Lord mighty in battle.
9 Lift up your heads, O you gates!
    Lift up, you everlasting doors!
    And the King of glory shall come in.
10 Who is this King of glory?
    The Lord of hosts,
    He *is* the King of glory.   Selah

PSALM 25

A Plea for Deliverance and Forgiveness

A *Psalm* of David.

1 To You, O Lord, I lift up my soul.
2 O my God, I trust in You;
    Let me not be ashamed;
    Let not my enemies triumph over me.
3 Indeed, let no one who waits on You
        be ashamed;
    Let those be ashamed who deal
        treacherously without cause.

4 Show me Your ways, O Lord;
    Teach me Your paths.
5 Lead me in Your truth and teach me,
    For You *are* the God of my salvation;

23:6 [a]Following Septuagint, Syriac, Targum, and
Vulgate; Masoretic Text reads *return.*

On You I wait all the day.

6 Remember, O LORD, Your tender
    mercies and Your lovingkindnesses,
For they *are* from of old.
7 Do not remember the sins of my
    youth, nor my transgressions;
According to Your mercy remember me,
For Your goodness' sake, O LORD.

8 Good and upright *is* the LORD;
Therefore He teaches sinners in the way.
9 The humble He guides in justice,
And the humble He teaches His way.
10 All the paths of the LORD *are* mercy
    and truth,
To such as keep His covenant and His
    testimonies.
11 For Your name's sake, O LORD,
Pardon my iniquity, for it *is* great.

12 Who *is* the man that fears the LORD?
Him shall He[a] teach in the way He[b]
    chooses.
13 He himself shall dwell in prosperity,
And his descendants shall inherit the
    earth.
14 The secret of the LORD *is* with those who
    fear Him,
And He will show them His covenant.
15 My eyes *are* ever toward the LORD,
For He shall pluck my feet out of the net.

16 Turn Yourself to me, and have mercy
    on me,
For I *am* desolate and afflicted.
17 The troubles of my heart have enlarged;
Bring me out of my distresses!
18 Look on my affliction and my pain,
And forgive all my sins.
19 Consider my enemies, for they are
    many;
And they hate me with cruel hatred.
20 Keep my soul, and deliver me;
Let me not be ashamed, for I put
    my trust in You.
21 Let integrity and uprightness
    preserve me,
For I wait for You.

22 Redeem Israel, O God,
Out of all their troubles!

PSALM 26

A Prayer for Divine Scrutiny and Redemption

A Psalm of David.

1 Vindicate me, O LORD,
For I have walked in my integrity.
I have also trusted in the LORD;
I shall not slip.
2 Examine me, O LORD, and prove me;
Try my mind and my heart.
3 For Your lovingkindness *is* before my
    eyes,
And I have walked in Your truth.
4 I have not sat with idolatrous mortals,
Nor will I go in with hypocrites.
5 I have hated the assembly of evildoers,
And will not sit with the wicked.

6 I will wash my hands in innocence;
So I will go about Your altar, O LORD,
7 That I may proclaim with the voice
    of thanksgiving,
And tell of all Your wondrous works.
8 LORD, I have loved the habitation of
    Your house,
And the place where Your glory dwells.

9 Do not gather my soul with sinners,
Nor my life with bloodthirsty men,
10 In whose hands *is* a sinister scheme,
And whose right hand is full of bribes.

11 But as for me, I will walk in my
    integrity;
Redeem me and be merciful to me.
12 My foot stands in an even place;
In the congregations I will bless the
    LORD.

PSALM 27

An Exuberant Declaration of Faith

A Psalm of David.

1 The LORD *is* my light and my salvation;
Whom shall I fear?
The LORD *is* the strength of my life;
Of whom shall I be afraid?
2 When the wicked came against me
To eat up my flesh,
My enemies and foes,

25:12 [a]Or *he* [b]Or *he*

They stumbled and fell.

3 Though an army may encamp
   against me,
My heart shall not fear;
Though war may rise against me,
In this I *will be* confident.

4 One *thing* I have desired of the LORD,
That will I seek:
That I may dwell in the house of the
   LORD
All the days of my life,
To behold the beauty of the LORD,
And to inquire in His temple.

5 For in the time of trouble
He shall hide me in His pavilion;
In the secret place of His tabernacle
He shall hide me;
He shall set me high upon a rock.

6 And now my head shall be lifted up
   above my enemies all around me;
Therefore I will offer sacrifices of joy
   in His tabernacle;
I will sing, yes, I will sing praises to
   the LORD.

7 Hear, O LORD, *when* I cry with my voice!
Have mercy also upon me, and
   answer me.

8 *When You said,* "Seek My face,"
My heart said to You, "Your face, LORD,
   I will seek."

9 Do not hide Your face from me;
Do not turn Your servant away in anger;
You have been my help;
Do not leave me nor forsake me,
O God of my salvation.

10 When my father and my mother
    forsake me,
Then the LORD will take care of me.

11 Teach me Your way, O LORD,
And lead me in a smooth path,
   because of my enemies.

12 Do not deliver me to the will of my
    adversaries;
For false witnesses have risen
   against me,
And such as breathe out violence.

13 *I would have lost heart,* unless I had
    believed

That I would see the goodness
   of the LORD
In the land of the living.

14 Wait on the LORD;
Be of good courage,
And He shall strengthen your heart;
Wait, I say, on the LORD!

PSALM 28

Rejoicing in Answered Prayer

A Psalm of David.

1 To You I will cry, O LORD my Rock:
Do not be silent to me,
Lest, if You *are* silent to me,
I become like those who go down to
   the pit.

2 Hear the voice of my supplications
When I cry to You,
When I lift up my hands toward Your
   holy sanctuary.

3 Do not take me away with the wicked
And with the workers of iniquity,
Who speak peace to their neighbors,
But evil *is* in their hearts.

4 Give them according to their deeds,
And according to the wickedness of
   their endeavors;
Give them according to the work of
   their hands;
Render to them what they deserve.

5 Because they do not regard the works
   of the LORD,
Nor the operation of His hands,
He shall destroy them
And not build them up.

6 Blessed *be* the LORD,
Because He has heard the voice of my
   supplications!

7 The LORD *is* my strength and my shield;
My heart trusted in Him, and I am
   helped;
Therefore my heart greatly rejoices,
And with my song I will praise Him.

8 The LORD *is* their strength,[a]

28:8 [a]Following Masoretic Text and Targum; Septuagint,
Syriac, and Vulgate read *the strength of His people.*

And He *is* the saving refuge of His anointed.
9 Save Your people,
And bless Your inheritance;
Shepherd them also,
And bear them up forever.

PSALM 29

Praise to God in His Holiness and Majesty

A Psalm of David.

1 Give unto the LORD, O you mighty ones,
Give unto the LORD glory and strength.
2 Give unto the LORD the glory due to His name;
Worship the LORD in the beauty of holiness.

3 The voice of the LORD *is* over the waters;
The God of glory thunders;
The LORD *is* over many waters.
4 The voice of the LORD *is* powerful;
The voice of the LORD *is* full of majesty.

5 The voice of the LORD breaks the cedars,
Yes, the LORD splinters the cedars of Lebanon.
6 He makes them also skip like a calf,
Lebanon and Sirion like a young wild ox.
7 The voice of the LORD divides the flames of fire.

8 The voice of the LORD shakes the wilderness;
The LORD shakes the Wilderness of Kadesh.
9 The voice of the LORD makes the deer give birth,
And strips the forests bare;
And in His temple everyone says, "Glory!"

10 The LORD sat *enthroned* at the Flood,
And the LORD sits as King forever.
11 The LORD will give strength to His people;
The LORD will bless His people with peace.

PSALM 30

The Blessedness of Answered Prayer

A Psalm. A Song at the dedication of the house of David.

1 I will extol You, O LORD, for You have lifted me up,
And have not let my foes rejoice over me.
2 O LORD my God, I cried out to You,
And You healed me.
3 O LORD, You brought my soul up from the grave;
You have kept me alive, that I should not go down to the pit.ᵃ

4 Sing praise to the LORD, you saints of His,
And give thanks at the remembrance of His holy name.ᵃ
5 For His anger *is but for* a moment,
His favor *is for* life;
Weeping may endure for a night,
But joy *comes* in the morning.

6 Now in my prosperity I said,
"I shall never be moved."
7 LORD, by Your favor You have made my mountain stand strong;
You hid Your face, *and* I was troubled.

8 I cried out to You, O LORD;
And to the LORD I made supplication:
9 "What profit *is there* in my blood,
When I go down to the pit?
Will the dust praise You?
Will it declare Your truth?
10 Hear, O LORD, and have mercy on me;
LORD, be my helper!"

11 You have turned for me my mourning into dancing;
You have put off my sackcloth and clothed me with gladness,
12 To the end that *my* glory may sing praise to You and not be silent.
O LORD my God, I will give thanks to You forever.

30:3 ᵃFollowing Qere and Targum; Kethib, Septuagint, Syriac, and Vulgate read *from those who descend to the pit.*   **30:4** ᵃOr *His holiness*

Chester A. Arthur placed his hand on Psalm 31:1–3 as he took the presidential oath of office in 1881.

PSALM 31

The Lord a Fortress in Adversity

To the Chief Musician. A Psalm of David.

1 In You, O Lord, I put my trust;
Let me never be ashamed;
Deliver me in Your righteousness.

2 Bow down Your ear to me,
Deliver me speedily;
Be my rock of refuge,
A fortress of defense to save me.

3 For You *are* my rock and my fortress;
Therefore, for Your name's sake,
Lead me and guide me.

4 Pull me out of the net which they
have secretly laid for me,
For You *are* my strength.

5 Into Your hand I commit my spirit;
You have redeemed me, O Lord God
of truth.

6 I have hated those who regard useless
idols;
But I trust in the Lord.

7 I will be glad and rejoice in Your mercy,
For You have considered my trouble;
You have known my soul in adversities,

8 And have not shut me up into the
hand of the enemy;
You have set my feet in a wide place.

9 Have mercy on me, O Lord, for I am
in trouble;
My eye wastes away with grief,
Yes, my soul and my body!

10 For my life is spent with grief,
And my years with sighing;
My strength fails because of my
iniquity,
And my bones waste away.

11 I am a reproach among all my
enemies,
But especially among my neighbors,
And *am* repulsive to my acquaintances;
Those who see me outside flee
from me.

12 I am forgotten like a dead man,
out of mind;
I am like a broken vessel.

13 For I hear the slander of many;
Fear *is* on every side;
While they take counsel together
against me,
They scheme to take away my life.

14 But as for me, I trust in You, O Lord;
I say, "You *are* my God."

15 My times *are* in Your hand;
Deliver me from the hand of my
enemies,
And from those who persecute me.

16 Make Your face shine upon Your
servant;
Save me for Your mercies' sake.

17 Do not let me be ashamed, O Lord,
for I have called upon You;
Let the wicked be ashamed;
Let them be silent in the grave.

18 Let the lying lips be put to silence,
Which speak insolent things proudly
and contemptuously against the
righteous.

19 Oh, how great *is* Your goodness,
Which You have laid up for those
who fear You,
Which You have prepared for those
who trust in You
In the presence of the sons of men!

20 You shall hide them in the secret
place of Your presence
From the plots of man;
You shall keep them secretly in a
pavilion
From the strife of tongues.

21 Blessed *be* the Lord,
For He has shown me His marvelous
kindness in a strong city!

22 For I said in my haste,
"I am cut off from before Your eyes";
Nevertheless You heard the voice of
my supplications
When I cried out to You.

23 Oh, love the Lord, all you His saints!
For the Lord preserves the faithful,
And fully repays the proud person.

24 Be of good courage,
And He shall strengthen your heart,
All you who hope in the LORD.

PSALM 32

The Joy of Forgiveness

A Psalm of David. A Contemplation.^a

1 Blessed *is he whose* transgression *is*
forgiven,
Whose sin *is* covered.
2 Blessed *is* the man to whom the LORD
does not impute iniquity,
And in whose spirit *there is* no deceit.

3 When I kept silent, my bones grew old
Through my groaning all the day long.
4 For day and night Your hand was
heavy upon me;
My vitality was turned into the
drought of summer.　　Selah
5 I acknowledged my sin to You,
And my iniquity I have not hidden.
I said, "I will confess my
transgressions to the LORD,"
And You forgave the iniquity of
my sin.　　　　　　Selah

6 For this cause everyone who is godly
shall pray to You
In a time when You may be found;
Surely in a flood of great waters
They shall not come near him.
7 You *are* my hiding place;
You shall preserve me from trouble;
You shall surround me with songs
of deliverance.　　　Selah

8 I will instruct you and teach you in
the way you should go;
I will guide you with My eye.
9 Do not be like the horse *or* like the mule,
Which have no understanding,
Which must be harnessed with bit
and bridle,
Else they will not come near you.

10 Many sorrows *shall be* to the wicked;
But he who trusts in the LORD, mercy
shall surround him.
11 Be glad in the LORD and rejoice, you
righteous;

And shout for joy, all *you* upright in
heart!

PSALM 33

The Sovereignty of the LORD in Creation and History

1 Rejoice in the LORD, O you righteous!
For praise from the upright is beautiful.
2 Praise the LORD with the harp;
Make melody to Him with an
instrument of ten strings.
3 Sing to Him a new song;
Play skillfully with a shout of joy.

4 For the word of the LORD *is* right,
And all His work *is done* in truth.
5 He loves righteousness and justice;
The earth is full of the goodness of
the LORD.

6 By the word of the LORD the heavens
were made,
And all the host of them by the breath
of His mouth.
7 He gathers the waters of the sea
together as a heap;^a
He lays up the deep in storehouses.

8 Let all the earth fear the LORD;
Let all the inhabitants of the world
stand in awe of Him.
9 For He spoke, and it was *done;*
He commanded, and it stood fast.

10 The LORD brings the counsel of the
nations to nothing;
He makes the plans of the peoples of
no effect.
11 The counsel of the LORD stands forever,
The plans of His heart to all generations.

Dwight D. Eisenhower placed his hand
on Psalm 33:12 as he took the presidential
oath of office in 1957.

12 Blessed *is* the nation whose God *is* the
LORD,
The people He has chosen as His own
inheritance.

32:title ^aHebrew *Maschil*　　**33:7** ^aSeptuagint,
Targum, and Vulgate read *in a vessel.*

13 The LORD looks from heaven;
He sees all the sons of men.
14 From the place of His dwelling He looks
On all the inhabitants of the earth;
15 He fashions their hearts individually;
He considers all their works.

FAITH

Blessed is the nation whose God is the LORD. . . .
PSALM 33:12

The Soul of America

Charles Malik (1906–1967), the ambassador to the United Nations from Lebanon and president of the 13th Session of the United Nations General Assembly in 1959, stated:

The good [in the United States] would never have come into being without the blessing and power of Jesus Christ. . . .Whoever tries to conceive the American word without taking full account of the suffering and love and salvation of Christ is only dreaming. I know how embarrassing this matter is to politicians, bureaucrats, businessmen, and cynics; but, whatever these honored men think, the irrefutable truth is that the soul of America is, at its best and highest, Christian.

16 No king is saved by the multitude of an army;
A mighty man is not delivered by great strength.
17 A horse is a vain hope for safety;
Neither shall it deliver any by its great strength.
18 Behold, the eye of the LORD is on those who fear Him,
On those who hope in His mercy,
19 To deliver their soul from death,
And to keep them alive in famine.

20 Our soul waits for the LORD;
He is our help and our shield.
21 For our heart shall rejoice in Him,
Because we have trusted in His holy name.
22 Let Your mercy, O LORD, be upon us,
Just as we hope in You.

PSALM 34

The Happiness of Those Who Trust in God

A Psalm of David when he pretended madness before Abimelech, who drove him away, and he departed.

1 I will bless the LORD at all times;
His praise *shall* continually *be* in my mouth.
2 My soul shall make its boast in the LORD;
The humble shall hear *of it* and be glad.
3 Oh, magnify the LORD with me,
And let us exalt His name together.

4 I sought the LORD, and He heard me,
And delivered me from all my fears.
5 They looked to Him and were radiant,
And their faces were not ashamed.
6 This poor man cried out, and the LORD heard *him,*
And saved him out of all his troubles.
7 The angel[a] of the LORD encamps all around those who fear Him,
And delivers them.

8 Oh, taste and see that the LORD *is* good;
Blessed *is* the man *who* trusts in Him!
9 Oh, fear the LORD, you His saints!
There is no want to those who fear Him.
10 The young lions lack and suffer hunger;
But those who seek the LORD shall not lack any good *thing.*

11 Come, you children, listen to me;
I will teach you the fear of the LORD.
12 Who *is* the man *who* desires life,
And loves *many* days, that he may see good?
13 Keep your tongue from evil,
And your lips from speaking deceit.
14 Depart from evil and do good;
Seek peace and pursue it.

15 The eyes of the LORD *are* on the righteous,
And His ears *are open* to their cry.

34:7 ªOr Angel

16 The face of the Lord *is* against those
who do evil,
To cut off the remembrance of them
from the earth.

17 *The righteous* cry out, and the Lord
hears,
And delivers them out of all their
troubles.

18 The Lord *is* near to those who have
a broken heart,
And saves such as have a contrite
spirit.

19 Many *are* the afflictions of the righteous,
But the Lord delivers him out of
them all.

20 He guards all his bones;
Not one of them is broken.

21 Evil shall slay the wicked,
And those who hate the righteous
shall be condemned.

22 The Lord redeems the soul of His
servants,
And none of those who trust in Him
shall be condemned.

PSALM 35

The Lord the Avenger of His People

A Psalm of David.

1 Plead *my cause,* O Lord, with those
who strive with me;
Fight against those who fight
against me.

2 Take hold of shield and buckler,
And stand up for my help.

3 Also draw out the spear,
And stop those who pursue me.
Say to my soul,
"I *am* your salvation."

4 Let those be put to shame and brought
to dishonor
Who seek after my life;
Let those be turned back and brought
to confusion
Who plot my hurt.

5 Let them be like chaff before the wind,
And let the angel[a] of the Lord chase
them.

6 Let their way be dark and slippery,
And let the angel of the Lord pursue
them.

7 For without cause they have hidden
their net for me *in* a pit,
Which they have dug without cause
for my life.

8 Let destruction come upon him
unexpectedly,
And let his net that he has hidden
catch himself;
Into that very destruction let him fall.

9 And my soul shall be joyful in the Lord;
It shall rejoice in His salvation.

10 All my bones shall say,
"Lord, who *is* like You,
Delivering the poor from him who is
too strong for him,
Yes, the poor and the needy from him
who plunders him?"

11 Fierce witnesses rise up;
They ask me *things* that I do not know.

12 They reward me evil for good,
To the sorrow of my soul.

13 But as for me, when they were sick,
My clothing *was* sackcloth;
I humbled myself with fasting;
And my prayer would return to my
own heart.

14 I paced about as though *he were* my
friend *or* brother;
I bowed down heavily, as one who
mourns *for his* mother.

15 But in my adversity they rejoiced
And gathered together;
Attackers gathered against me,
And I did not know *it;*
They tore *at me* and did not cease;

16 With ungodly mockers at feasts
They gnashed at me with their teeth.

17 Lord, how long will You look on?
Rescue me from their destructions,
My precious *life* from the lions.

18 I will give You thanks in the great
assembly;
I will praise You among many people.

35:5 [a]Or Angel

THE FIRST PRAYER OF CONGRESS

JACOB DUCHÉ

*Fight against those
who fight against me.*

PSALM 35:1

When the first Congress of the United States met on September 7, 1774, it began with prayer. On that morning, Congress was very concerned about Great Britain's recent attack on Boston. Reverend Jacob Duché, Rector of Christ Church of Philadelphia, was summoned to lead the opening prayers. He first read Psalm 35, after which John Adams stated in a letter to his wife: "I never saw a greater effect upon an audience. It seemed as if Heaven had ordained that Psalm to be read on the morning."

Then rather than read a general prayer as was commonly done, Reverence Duché broke into extemporaneous prayer:

O Lord our Heavenly Father, high and mighty King of kings and Lord of lords, who dost from Thy throne behold all the dwellers on earth and reignest with power supreme and uncontrolled over all the kingdoms, empires and governments; look down in mercy, we beseech Thee, on these our American States, who have fled to Thee from the rod of the oppressor and thrown themselves on Thy gracious protection, desiring to be henceforth dependent only on Thee. To Thee have they appealed for the righteousness of their cause; to Thee do they now look up for that countenance and support, which Thou alone canst give. Take them, therefore, Heavenly Father, under Thy nurturing care; give them wisdom in council and valor in the field; defeat the malicious designs of our cruel adversaries; convince them of the unrighteousness of their cause and if they persist in their sanguinary purposes, of own unerring justice, sounding in their hearts, constrain them to drop the weapons of war from their unnerved hands in the day of battle!

Be Thou present, O God of wisdom, and direct the councils of this honorable assembly; enable them to settle things on the best and surest foundation. That the scene of blood may be speedily closed; that order, harmony, and peace may be effectually restored, and truth and justice, religion and piety, prevail and flourish amongst the people. Preserve the health of their bodies and vigor of their minds; shower down on them and the millions they here represent, such temporal blessings as Thou seest expedient for them in this world and crown them with everlasting glory in the world to come. All this we ask in the name and through the merits of Jesus Christ, Thy Son and our Savior.

Amen.

What an amazing way to start Congress!

19 Let them not rejoice over me who are
        wrongfully my enemies;
    Nor let them wink with the eye who
        hate me without a cause.
20 For they do not speak peace,
    But they devise deceitful matters
    Against *the* quiet ones in the land.
21 They also opened their mouth wide
        against me,
    And said, "Aha, aha!
    Our eyes have seen *it.*"

22 *This* You have seen, O LORD;
    Do not keep silence.
    O Lord, do not be far from me.
23 Stir up Yourself, and awake to my
        vindication,
    To my cause, my God and my Lord.
24 Vindicate me, O LORD my God,
        according to Your righteousness;
    And let them not rejoice over me.
25 Let them not say in their hearts,
        "Ah, so we would have it!"
    Let them not say, "We have swallowed
        him up."

26 Let them be ashamed and brought to
        mutual confusion
    Who rejoice at my hurt;
    Let them be clothed with shame and
        dishonor
    Who exalt themselves against me.

27 Let them shout for joy and be glad,
    Who favor my righteous cause;
    And let them say continually,
    "Let the LORD be magnified,
    Who has pleasure in the prosperity
        of His servant."
28 And my tongue shall speak of Your
        righteousness
    And of Your praise all the day long.

PSALM 36

Man's Wickedness and God's Perfections

To the Chief Musician.
A Psalm of David the servant of the LORD.

1   An oracle within my heart concerning
        the transgression of the wicked:
    There is no fear of God before his eyes.
2   For he flatters himself in his own eyes,

When he finds out his iniquity *and*
        when he hates.
3   The words of his mouth *are* wickedness
        and deceit;
    He has ceased to be wise *and* to do good.
4   He devises wickedness on his bed;
    He sets himself in a way *that is* not
        good;
    He does not abhor evil.

5   Your mercy, O LORD, *is* in the heavens;
    Your faithfulness *reaches* to the clouds.
6   Your righteousness *is* like the great
        mountains;
    Your judgments *are* a great deep;
    O LORD, You preserve man and beast.

7   How precious *is* Your lovingkindness,
        O God!
    Therefore the children of men put their
        trust under the shadow of Your wings.
8   They are abundantly satisfied with the
        fullness of Your house,
    And You give them drink from the
        river of Your pleasures.
9   For with You *is* the fountain of life;
    In Your light we see light.

10 Oh, continue Your lovingkindness
        to those who know You,
    And Your righteousness to the
        upright in heart.
11 Let not the foot of pride come
        against me,
    And let not the hand of the wicked
        drive me away.
12 There the workers of iniquity have
        fallen;
    They have been cast down and are
        not able to rise.

PSALM 37

*The Heritage of the Righteous and the
Calamity of the Wicked*

A Psalm of David.

1   Do not fret because of evildoers,
    Nor be envious of the workers of
        iniquity.
2   For they shall soon be cut down like
        the grass,
    And wither as the green herb.

3 Trust in the LORD, and do good;
Dwell in the land, and feed on His
    faithfulness.
4 Delight yourself also in the LORD,
And He shall give you the desires
    of your heart.

5 Commit your way to the LORD,
Trust also in Him,
And He shall bring *it* to pass.
6 He shall bring forth your
    righteousness as the light,
And your justice as the noonday.

7 Rest in the LORD, and wait patiently
    for Him;
Do not fret because of him who
    prospers in his way,
Because of the man who brings
    wicked schemes to pass.
8 Cease from anger, and forsake wrath;
Do not fret—*it* only *causes* harm.

9 For evildoers shall be cut off;
But those who wait on the LORD,
They shall inherit the earth.
10 For yet a little while and the wicked
    shall be no *more;*
Indeed, you will look carefully for his
    place,
But it *shall be* no *more.*
11 But the meek shall inherit the earth,
And shall delight themselves in the
    abundance of peace.

12 The wicked plots against the just,
And gnashes at him with his teeth.
13 The Lord laughs at him,
For He sees that his day is coming.
14 The wicked have drawn the sword
And have bent their bow,
To cast down the poor and needy,
To slay those who are of upright
    conduct.
15 Their sword shall enter their own heart,
And their bows shall be broken.

16 A little that a righteous man has
Is better than the riches of many wicked.
17 For the arms of the wicked shall be
    broken,
But the LORD upholds the righteous.

18 The LORD knows the days of the upright,
And their inheritance shall be forever.
19 They shall not be ashamed in the evil
    time,
And in the days of famine they shall
    be satisfied.
20 But the wicked shall perish;
And the enemies of the LORD,
Like the splendor of the meadows,
    shall vanish.
Into smoke they shall vanish away.

21 The wicked borrows and does not repay,
But the righteous shows mercy and
    gives.
22 For *those* blessed by Him shall inherit
    the earth,
But *those* cursed by Him shall be cut
    off.

23 The steps of a *good* man are ordered
    by the LORD,
And He delights in his way.
24 Though he fall, he shall not be utterly
    cast down;
For the LORD upholds *him with* His hand.

25 I have been young, and *now* am old;
Yet I have not seen the righteous
    forsaken,
Nor his descendants begging bread.
26 *He is* ever merciful, and lends;
And his descendants *are* blessed.

27 Depart from evil, and do good;
And dwell forevermore.
28 For the LORD loves justice,
And does not forsake His saints;
They are preserved forever,
But the descendants of the wicked
    shall be cut off.
29 The righteous shall inherit the land,
And dwell in it forever.

30 The mouth of the righteous speaks
    wisdom,
And his tongue talks of justice.
31 The law of his God *is* in his heart;
None of his steps shall slide.

32 The wicked watches the righteous,
And seeks to slay him.

33 The LORD will not leave him in his hand,
   Nor condemn him when he is judged.

34 Wait on the LORD,
   And keep His way,
   And He shall exalt you to inherit the
      land;
   When the wicked are cut off, you shall
      see *it.*
35 I have seen the wicked in great power,
   And spreading himself like a native
      green tree.
36 Yet he passed away,[a] and behold, he
   was no *more;*
   Indeed I sought him, but he could not
      be found.

37 Mark the blameless *man,* and observe
      the upright;
   For the future of *that* man *is* peace.
38 But the transgressors shall be
      destroyed together;
   The future of the wicked shall be cut off.

39 But the salvation of the righteous *is*
      from the LORD;
   He is their strength in the time of
      trouble.
40 And the LORD shall help them and
      deliver them;
   He shall deliver them from the wicked,
   And save them,
   Because they trust in Him.

PSALM 38

Prayer in Time of Chastening

A Psalm of David. To bring to remembrance.

1 O LORD, do not rebuke me in Your wrath,
   Nor chasten me in Your hot displeasure!
2 For Your arrows pierce me deeply,
   And Your hand presses me down.

3 *There is* no soundness in my flesh
   Because of Your anger,
   Nor *any* health in my bones
   Because of my sin.
4 For my iniquities have gone over my
      head;
   Like a heavy burden they are too
      heavy for me.

5 My wounds are foul *and* festering
   Because of my foolishness.

6 I am troubled, I am bowed down
      greatly;
   I go mourning all the day long.
7 For my loins are full of inflammation,
   And *there is* no soundness in my flesh.
8 I am feeble and severely broken;
   I groan because of the turmoil of my
      heart.

9 Lord, all my desire *is* before You;
   And my sighing is not hidden from You.
10 My heart pants, my strength fails me;
   As for the light of my eyes, it also has
      gone from me.

11 My loved ones and my friends stand
      aloof from my plague,
   And my relatives stand afar off.
12 Those also who seek my life lay snares
      for me;
   Those who seek my hurt speak of
      destruction,
   And plan deception all the day long.

13 But I, like a deaf *man,* do not hear;
   And *I am* like a mute *who* does not
      open his mouth.
14 Thus I am like a man who does not
      hear,
   And in whose mouth *is* no response.

15 For in You, O LORD, I hope;
   You will hear, O Lord my God.
16 For I said, "*Hear me,* lest they rejoice
      over me,
   Lest, when my foot slips, they exalt
      themselves against me."

17 For I *am* ready to fall,
   And my sorrow *is* continually before me.
18 For I will declare my iniquity;
   I will be in anguish over my sin.
19 But my enemies *are* vigorous, *and* they
      are strong;
   And those who hate me wrongfully
      have multiplied.

37:36 [a]Following Masoretic Text, Septuagint, and
Targum; Syriac and Vulgate read *I passed by.*

20 Those also who render evil for good,
They are my adversaries, because I
follow *what is* good.

21 Do not forsake me, O LORD;
O my God, be not far from me!
22 Make haste to help me,
O Lord, my salvation!

PSALM 39

Prayer for Wisdom and Forgiveness

*To the Chief Musician. To Jeduthun.
A Psalm of David.*

1 I said, "I will guard my ways,
Lest I sin with my tongue;
I will restrain my mouth with a
muzzle,
While the wicked are before me."
2 I was mute with silence,
I held my peace *even* from good;
And my sorrow was stirred up.
3 My heart was hot within me;
While I was musing, the fire burned.
Then I spoke with my tongue:

4 "LORD, make me to know my end,
And what *is* the measure of my days,
That I may know how frail I *am.*
5 Indeed, You have made my days *as*
handbreadths,
And my age *is* as nothing before You;
Certainly every man at his best state
is but vapor.   Selah
6 Surely every man walks about like a
shadow;
Surely they busy themselves in vain;
He heaps up *riches,*
And does not know who will gather
them.

7 "And now, Lord, what do I wait for?
My hope *is* in You.
8 Deliver me from all my
transgressions;
Do not make me the reproach of
the foolish.
9 I was mute, I did not open my mouth,
Because it was You who did *it.*
10 Remove Your plague from me;
I am consumed by the blow of Your
hand.

11 When with rebukes You correct man
for iniquity,
You make his beauty melt away like
a moth;
Surely every man *is* vapor.   Selah

12 "Hear my prayer, O LORD,
And give ear to my cry;
Do not be silent at my tears;
For I *am* a stranger with You,
A sojourner, as all my fathers *were.*
13 Remove Your gaze from me, that I
may regain strength,
Before I go away and am no more."

PSALM 40

Faith Persevering in Trial

To the Chief Musician. A Psalm of David.

1 I waited patiently for the LORD;
And He inclined to me,
And heard my cry.
2 He also brought me up out of a
horrible pit,
Out of the miry clay,
And set my feet upon a rock,
And established my steps.
3 He has put a new song in my
mouth—
Praise to our God;
Many will see *it* and fear,
And will trust in the LORD.

4 Blessed *is* that man who makes the
LORD his trust,
And does not respect the proud, nor
such as turn aside to lies.
5 Many, O LORD my God, *are* Your
wonderful works
Which You have done;
And Your thoughts toward us
Cannot be recounted to You in order;
If I would declare and speak *of them,*
They are more than can be
numbered.

6 Sacrifice and offering You did not
desire;
My ears You have opened.
Burnt offering and sin offering
You did not require.

7 Then I said, "Behold, I come;
   In the scroll of the book *it is* written
      of me.
8 I delight to do Your will, O my God,
   And Your law *is* within my heart."

9 I have proclaimed the good news of
      righteousness
   In the great assembly;
   Indeed, I do not restrain my lips,
   O LORD, You Yourself know.
10 I have not hidden Your righteousness
      within my heart;
   I have declared Your faithfulness and
      Your salvation;
   I have not concealed Your
      lovingkindness and Your truth
   From the great assembly.

11 Do not withhold Your tender mercies
      from me, O LORD;
   Let Your lovingkindness and Your
      truth continually preserve me.
12 For innumerable evils have
      surrounded me;
   My iniquities have overtaken me,
      so that I am not able to look up;
   They are more than the hairs of my
      head;
   Therefore my heart fails me.

13 Be pleased, O LORD, to deliver me;
   O LORD, make haste to help me!
14 Let them be ashamed and brought to
      mutual confusion
   Who seek to destroy my life;
   Let them be driven backward and
      brought to dishonor
   Who wish me evil.
15 Let them be confounded because of
      their shame,
   Who say to me, "Aha, aha!"

16 Let all those who seek You rejoice and
      be glad in You;
   Let such as love Your salvation say
      continually,
    "The LORD be magnified!"
17 But I *am* poor and needy;
   Yet the LORD thinks upon me.
   You *are* my help and my deliverer;
   Do not delay, O my God.

PSALM 41

The Blessing and Suffering of the Godly

To the Chief Musician. A Psalm of David.

1 Blessed *is* he who considers the poor;
   The LORD will deliver him in time of
      trouble.
2 The LORD will preserve him and keep
      him alive,
   And he will be blessed on the earth;
   You will not deliver him to the will of
      his enemies.
3 The LORD will strengthen him on his
      bed of illness;
   You will sustain him on his sickbed.

4 I said, "LORD, be merciful to me;
   Heal my soul, for I have sinned
      against You."
5 My enemies speak evil of me:
   "When will he die, and his name
      perish?"
6 And if he comes to see *me,* he speaks
      lies;
   His heart gathers iniquity to itself;
   When he goes out, he tells *it.*

7 All who hate me whisper together
      against me;
   Against me they devise my hurt.
8 "An evil disease," *they say,* "clings to him.
   And *now* that he lies down, he will rise
      up no more."
9 Even my own familiar friend in whom
      I trusted,
   Who ate my bread,
   Has lifted up *his* heel against me.

10 But You, O LORD, be merciful to me,
      and raise me up,
   That I may repay them.
11 By this I know that You are well
      pleased with me,
   Because my enemy does not triumph
      over me.
12 As for me, You uphold me in my
      integrity,
   And set me before Your face forever.

13 Blessed *be* the LORD God of Israel
   From everlasting to everlasting!
   Amen and Amen.

THE BIBLE
AND
AMERICAN EDUCATION

$\mathcal{T}$HE BOOK OF PROVERBS tells us that "the fear of the LORD is the beginning of knowledge" (1:7). The American Founders certainly understood this truth, and from the beginning stressed the relationship between a sound education based upon biblical absolutes and the future of the nation.

In 1776, the future President John Adams said, "Statesmen . . . may plan and speculate for liberty, but it is *religion* and *morality* alone, which can establish the principles upon which freedom can securely stand." That mind-set was widely held among the Founders who helped shape the political, educational, and legal foundations of the new nation. Men such as Daniel Webster, Benjamin Franklin, Benjamin Rush, Samuel Adams, and George Washington echoed these same sentiments, believing that the strength of the republic was dependent upon the morality of her people, and that religion must undergird it. They saw the education of young minds being at the heart of it.

NOT SURPRISINGLY, most of America's oldest universities were started by preachers and churches. Harvard, William and Mary, Yale, Princeton, King's College, Brown, Rutgers, and Dartmouth were all founded by Christian preachers and church affiliations.

Harvard University, for example, which was founded in 1636 by the Puritans, adopted the "Rules and Precepts" of the university that stated: "Let every student be plainly instructed, and earnestly pressed to consider well, the main end of his life and studies is, to know God and Jesus Christ which is eternal life (John 17:3) and therefore lay Christ at the bottom, as the only foundation of all sound knowledge and learning." Even Harvard's original seal, which can be seen etched in the walls of the campus today, states upon it these words: "Truth for Christ and the Church."

Yale College was established in 1701 with a stated goal that "every student shall consider the main end of his study to wit to know God in Jesus Christ and answerably to lead a godly, sober life." The College of William and Mary was founded in 1693 to supply the church of Virginia "with a seminary of ministers" that the "Christian faith may be propagated." And King's College, known today as Columbia University, purposed to "inculcate upon [students'] tender minds the great principles of Christianity and morality." Princeton had as one of its founding statements: "Cursed is all learning that is contrary to the Cross of Christ."

IN COLONIAL AMERICA, in addition to the Bible and the *Bay Psalm Book*, the first textbook for schoolchildren, *The New England Primer*, taught the ABC's by children memorizing basic biblical truths and lessons about life: *A—In Adam's fall, we sinned all. B—Heaven to find, the Bible Mind. C—Christ crucify'd for sinners died*, and so on. Included in the *Primer* were the names of the Old and New Testament books, the Lord's Prayer, the Apostles' Creed, the Ten Commandments, the Westminster Assembly Shorter Catechism, and John Cotton's "Spiritual Milk for American Babes." The *Primer* was the second best-selling book in the American colonies (the Bible was number one).

IN 1836, NOAH WEBSTER, often called "The Father of American Education," expressed the purpose of schools was meant for the advancement of the Christian faith: "In my view, the Christian religion is the most important and one of the first things in which all children, under a free government ought to be instructed.... No truth is more evident to my mind than that the Christian religion must be the basis of any government intended to secure the rights and privileges of a free people."

Unfortunately, in time, a philosophical shift took place in America, and the biblical principles for education were slowly eroded and abandoned, with sad and tragic consequences that continue to unfold. John Dewey, known as "The Architect of Modern Education," said, "There is no God, and there is no soul. Hence, there are no needs for the props of traditional religion." Those props have been knocked away, and the loss of moral standards has opened the door to untold numbers of unwanted teen pregnancies, abortions, drug abuse, alcoholism, violence, and suicide.

If we believe that the Founders were correct in asserting that America would fail if it lost its religious foundation, it is primarily incumbent upon Christian believers to reaffirm and reclaim our Christian educational heritage with the same passion and commitment of the Founders. There are many ways and many levels at which to instigate change, but it begins with a willingness to become engaged in the battle.

Book Two: Psalms 42—72

PSALM 42

Yearning for God in the Midst of Distresses

To the Chief Musician.
A Contemplation[a] of the sons of Korah.

1   As the deer pants for the water brooks,
    So pants my soul for You, O God.
2   My soul thirsts for God, for the living
    God.
    When shall I come and appear before
    God?[a]
3   My tears have been my food day and
    night,
    While they continually say to me,
    "Where *is* your God?"

4   When I remember these *things,*
    I pour out my soul within me.
    For I used to go with the multitude;
    I went with them to the house of God,
    With the voice of joy and praise,
    With a multitude that kept a pilgrim
    feast.

5   Why are you cast down, O my soul?
    And *why* are you disquieted within me?
    Hope in God, for I shall yet praise
    Him
    For the help of His countenance.[a]

6   O my God,[a] my soul is cast down
    within me;
    Therefore I will remember You from
    the land of the Jordan,
    And from the heights of Hermon,
    From the Hill Mizar.
7   Deep calls unto deep at the noise of
    Your waterfalls;
    All Your waves and billows have gone
    over me.
8   The LORD will command His
    lovingkindness in the daytime,
    And in the night His song *shall be*
    with me—
    A prayer to the God of my life.

9   I will say to God my Rock,
    "Why have You forgotten me?
    Why do I go mourning because of the
    oppression of the enemy?"

10 *As* with a breaking of my bones,
    My enemies reproach me,
    While they say to me all day long,
    "Where *is* your God?"

11 Why are you cast down, O my soul?
    And why are you disquieted
    within me?
    Hope in God;
    For I shall yet praise Him,
    The help of my countenance and
    my God.

PSALM 43

Prayer to God in Time of Trouble

1   Vindicate me, O God,
    And plead my cause against an
    ungodly nation;
    Oh, deliver me from the deceitful
    and unjust man!
2   For You *are* the God of my strength;
    Why do You cast me off?
    Why do I go mourning because of
    the oppression of the enemy?

3   Oh, send out Your light and Your
    truth!
    Let them lead me;
    Let them bring me to Your holy hill
    And to Your tabernacle.
4   Then I will go to the altar of God,
    To God my exceeding joy;
    And on the harp I will praise You,
    O God, my God.

5   Why are you cast down, O my soul?
    And why are you disquieted
    within me?
    Hope in God;
    For I shall yet praise Him,
    The help of my countenance and
    my God.

42:title [a]Hebrew *Maschil*   42:2 [a]Following
Masoretic Text and Vulgate; some Hebrew
manuscripts, Septuagint, Syriac, and Targum read *I
see the face of God.*   42:5 [a]Following Masoretic Text
and Targum; a few Hebrew manuscripts, Septuagint,
Syriac, and Vulgate read *The help of my countenance,
my God.*   42:6 [a]Following Masoretic Text and
Targum; a few Hebrew manuscripts, Septuagint,
Syriac, and Vulgate put *my God* at the end of verse 5.

PSALM 44

Redemption Remembered in Present Dishonor

To the Chief Musician.
A Contemplation[a] of the sons of Korah.

1 We have heard with our ears, O God,
   Our fathers have told us,
   The deeds You did in their days,
   In days of old:
2 You drove out the nations with Your
   hand,
   But them You planted;
   You afflicted the peoples, and cast
   them out.
3 For they did not gain possession of the
   land by their own sword,
   Nor did their own arm save them;
   But it was Your right hand, Your arm,
   and the light of Your countenance,
   Because You favored them.

4 You are my King, O God;[a]
   Command[b] victories for Jacob.
5 Through You we will push down our
   enemies;
   Through Your name we will trample
   those who rise up against us.
6 For I will not trust in my bow,
   Nor shall my sword save me.
7 But You have saved us from our
   enemies,
   And have put to shame those who
   hated us.
8 In God we boast all day long,
   And praise Your name forever.   Selah

9 But You have cast *us* off and put us to
   shame,
   And You do not go out with our armies.
10 You make us turn back from the enemy,
   And those who hate us have taken
   spoil for themselves.
11 You have given us up like sheep
   intended for food,
   And have scattered us among the
   nations.
12 You sell Your people for *next to* nothing,
   And are not enriched by selling them.

13 You make us a reproach to our
   neighbors,

A scorn and a derision to those all
   around us.
14 You make us a byword among the
   nations,
   A shaking of the head among the
   peoples.
15 My dishonor *is* continually before me,
   And the shame of my face has
   covered me,
16 Because of the voice of him who
   reproaches and reviles,
   Because of the enemy and the avenger.

17 All this has come upon us;
   But we have not forgotten You,
   Nor have we dealt falsely with Your
   covenant.
18 Our heart has not turned back,
   Nor have our steps departed from
   Your way;
19 But You have severely broken us in
   the place of jackals,
   And covered us with the shadow of
   death.

20 If we had forgotten the name of our
   God,
   Or stretched out our hands to a foreign
   god,
21 Would not God search this out?
   For He knows the secrets of the heart.
22 Yet for Your sake we are killed all day
   long;
   We are accounted as sheep for the
   slaughter.

23 Awake! Why do You sleep, O Lord?
   Arise! Do not cast *us* off forever.
24 Why do You hide Your face,
   And forget our affliction and our
   oppression?
25 For our soul is bowed down to the
   dust;
   Our body clings to the ground.
26 Arise for our help,
   And redeem us for Your mercies' sake.

44:title [a]Hebrew *Maschil*   **44:4** [a]Following
Masoretic Text and Targum; Septuagint and Vulgate
read *and my God.* [b]Following Masoretic Text and
Targum; Septuagint, Syriac, and Vulgate read *Who
commands.*

PSALM 45

The Glories of the Messiah and His Bride

To the Chief Musician. Set to "The Lilies."ᵃ
A Contemplationᵇ of the sons of Korah.
A Song of Love.

1 My heart is overflowing with a good
       theme;
   I recite my composition concerning
       the King;
   My tongue *is* the pen of a ready writer.

2 You are fairer than the sons of men;
   Grace is poured upon Your lips;
   Therefore God has blessed You forever.
3 Gird Your sword upon *Your* thigh,
       O Mighty One,
   With Your glory and Your majesty.
4 And in Your majesty ride prosperously
       because of truth, humility, *and*
       righteousness;
   And Your right hand shall teach You
       awesome things.
5 Your arrows *are* sharp in the heart of
       the King's enemies;
   The peoples fall under You.

6 Your throne, O God, *is* forever and ever;
   A scepter of righteousness *is* the
       scepter of Your kingdom.
7 You love righteousness and hate
       wickedness;
   Therefore God, Your God, has anointed
       You
   With the oil of gladness more than
       Your companions.
8 All Your garments *are scented* with
       myrrh and aloes *and* cassia,
   Out of the ivory palaces, by which they
       have made You glad.
9 Kings' daughters *are* among Your
       honorable women;
   At Your right hand stands the queen
       in gold from Ophir.

10 Listen, O daughter,
    Consider and incline your ear;
    Forget your own people also, and your
        father's house;
11 So the King will greatly desire your
        beauty;
    Because He *is* your Lord, worship Him.

12 And the daughter of Tyre *will come*
        with a gift;
    The rich among the people will seek
        your favor.

13 The royal daughter *is* all glorious
        within *the palace;*
    Her clothing *is* woven with gold.
14 She shall be brought to the King in
        robes of many colors;
    The virgins, her companions who
        follow her, shall be brought to You.
15 With gladness and rejoicing they shall
        be brought;
    They shall enter the King's palace.

16 Instead of Your fathers shall be Your
        sons,
    Whom You shall make princes in all
        the earth.
17 I will make Your name to be
        remembered in all generations;
    Therefore the people shall praise You
        forever and ever.

Woodrow Wilson placed his hand on
Psalm 46 as he took the presidential oath
of office in 1917.

PSALM 46

*God the Refuge of His People and Conqueror
of the Nations*

To the Chief Musician. *A Psalm* of the sons of Korah.
A Song for Alamoth.

1 God *is* our refuge and strength,
   A very present help in trouble.
2 Therefore we will not fear,
   Even though the earth be removed,
   And though the mountains be carried
       into the midst of the sea;
3 *Though* its waters roar *and* be troubled,
   Though the mountains shake with its
       swelling.   Selah

4 *There is* a river whose streams shall
       make glad the city of God,
   The holy *place* of the tabernacle of
       the Most High.

45:title ᵃHebrew *Shoshannim* ᵇHebrew *Maschil*

5 God *is* in the midst of her, she shall not
  be moved;
  God shall help her, just at the break of
  dawn.
6 The nations raged, the kingdoms were
  moved;
  He uttered His voice, the earth melted.

7 The LORD of hosts *is* with us;
  The God of Jacob *is* our refuge.   Selah

8 Come, behold the works of the LORD,
  Who has made desolations in the earth.
9 He makes wars cease to the end of the
  earth;
  He breaks the bow and cuts the spear
  in two;
  He burns the chariot in the fire.

10 Be still, and know that I *am* God;
   I will be exalted among the nations,
   I will be exalted in the earth!

11 The LORD of hosts *is* with us;
   The God of Jacob *is* our refuge.   Selah

PSALM 47

Praise to God, the Ruler of the Earth

To the Chief Musician. A Psalm of the sons of Korah.

1 Oh, clap your hands, all you peoples!
  Shout to God with the voice of triumph!
2 For the LORD Most High *is* awesome;
  He is a great King over all the earth.
3 He will subdue the peoples under us,
  And the nations under our feet.
4 He will choose our inheritance for us,
  The excellence of Jacob whom He
    loves.   Selah

5 God has gone up with a shout,
  The LORD with the sound of a trumpet.
6 Sing praises to God, sing praises!
  Sing praises to our King, sing praises!
7 For God *is* the King of all the earth;
  Sing praises with understanding.

8 God reigns over the nations;
  God sits on His holy throne.
9 The princes of the people have
    gathered together,

The people of the God of Abraham.
For the shields of the earth *belong* to
  God;
He is greatly exalted.

PSALM 48

The Glory of God in Zion

A Song. A Psalm of the sons of Korah.

1 Great *is* the LORD, and greatly to
    be praised
  In the city of our God,
  In His holy mountain.
2 Beautiful in elevation,
  The joy of the whole earth,
  Is Mount Zion *on* the sides of the north,
  The city of the great King.
3 God *is* in her palaces;
  He is known as her refuge.

4 For behold, the kings assembled,
  They passed by together.
5 They saw *it, and* so they marveled;
  They were troubled, they hastened
    away.
6 Fear took hold of them there,
  And pain, as of a woman in birth pangs,
7 *As when* You break the ships of Tarshish
  With an east wind.

8 As we have heard,
  So we have seen
  In the city of the LORD of hosts,
  In the city of our God:
  God will establish it forever.   Selah

9 We have thought, O God, on Your
    lovingkindness,
  In the midst of Your temple.
10 According to Your name, O God,
   So *is* Your praise to the ends of the
     earth;
   Your right hand is full of
     righteousness.
11 Let Mount Zion rejoice,
   Let the daughters of Judah be glad,
   Because of Your judgments.

12 Walk about Zion,
   And go all around her.
   Count her towers;

13 Mark well her bulwarks;
Consider her palaces;
That you may tell *it* to the generation
following.

14 For this *is* God,
Our God forever and ever;
He will be our guide
Even to death.[a]

PSALM 49

The Confidence of the Foolish

To the Chief Musician. A Psalm of the sons of Korah.

1 Hear this, all peoples;
Give ear, all inhabitants of the world,

2 Both low and high,
Rich and poor together.

3 My mouth shall speak wisdom,
And the meditation of my heart *shall
give* understanding.

4 I will incline my ear to a proverb;
I will disclose my dark saying on the
harp.

5 Why should I fear in the days of evil,
When the iniquity at my heels
surrounds me?

6 Those who trust in their wealth
And boast in the multitude of their
riches,

7 None *of them* can by any means
redeem *his* brother,
Nor give to God a ransom for him—

8 For the redemption of their souls *is* costly,
And it shall cease forever—

9 That he should continue to live
eternally,
And not see the Pit.

10 For he sees wise men die;
Likewise the fool and the senseless
person perish,
And leave their wealth to others.

11 Their inner thought *is that* their
houses *will last* forever,[a]
Their dwelling places to all generations;
They call *their* lands after their own
names.

12 Nevertheless man, *though* in honor,
does not remain;[a]
He is like the beasts *that* perish.

13 This is the way of those who *are* foolish,
And of their posterity who approve
their sayings.   Selah

14 Like sheep they are laid in the grave;
Death shall feed on them;
The upright shall have dominion over
them in the morning;
And their beauty shall be consumed in
the grave, far from their dwelling.

15 But God will redeem my soul from the
power of the grave,
For He shall receive me.   Selah

16 Do not be afraid when one becomes
rich,
When the glory of his house is
increased;

17 For when he dies he shall carry
nothing away;
His glory shall not descend after him.

18 Though while he lives he blesses himself
(For *men* will praise you when you do
well for yourself),

19 He shall go to the generation of his
fathers;
They shall never see light.

20 A man *who is* in honor, yet does not
understand,
Is like the beasts *that* perish.

PSALM 50

God the Righteous Judge

A Psalm of Asaph.

1 The Mighty One, God the LORD,
Has spoken and called the earth
From the rising of the sun to its going
down.

2 Out of Zion, the perfection of beauty,
God will shine forth.

3 Our God shall come, and shall not
keep silent;
A fire shall devour before Him,
And it shall be very tempestuous all
around Him.

48:14 [a]Following Masoretic Text and Syriac;
Septuagint and Vulgate read *Forever.*
49:11 [a]Septuagint, Syriac, Targum, and Vulgate read
Their graves shall be their houses forever.
49:12 [a]Following Masoretic Text and Targum;
Septuagint, Syriac, and Vulgate read *understand*
(compare verse 20).

4 He shall call to the heavens from above,
  And to the earth, that He may judge
    His people:
5 "Gather My saints together to Me,
  Those who have made a covenant
    with Me by sacrifice."
6 Let the heavens declare His
    righteousness,
  For God Himself *is* Judge.   Selah

7 "Hear, O My people, and I will speak,
  O Israel, and I will testify against you;
  I *am* God, your God!
8 I will not rebuke you for your sacrifices
  Or your burnt offerings,
  Which are continually before Me.
9 I will not take a bull from your house,
  Nor goats out of your folds.
10 For every beast of the forest *is* Mine,
   And the cattle on a thousand hills.
11 I know all the birds of the mountains,
   And the wild beasts of the field *are*
     Mine.

12 "If I were hungry, I would not tell you;
   For the world *is* Mine, and all its
     fullness.
13 Will I eat the flesh of bulls,
   Or drink the blood of goats?
14 Offer to God thanksgiving,
   And pay your vows to the Most High.
15 Call upon Me in the day of trouble;
   I will deliver you, and you shall
     glorify Me."

16 But to the wicked God says:
   "What *right* have you to declare My
     statutes,
   Or take My covenant in your mouth,
17 Seeing you hate instruction
   And cast My words behind you?
18 When you saw a thief, you consented[a]
     with him,
   And have been a partaker with
     adulterers.
19 You give your mouth to evil,
   And your tongue frames deceit.
20 You sit *and* speak against your
     brother;
   You slander your own mother's son.
21 These *things* you have done, and I
     kept silent;

You thought that I was altogether like
  you;
But I will rebuke you,
And set *them* in order before your eyes.

22 "Now consider this, you who forget God,
   Lest I tear *you* in pieces,
   And *there be* none to deliver:
23 Whoever offers praise glorifies Me;
   And to him who orders *his* conduct
     aright
   I will show the salvation of God."

PSALM 51

A Prayer of Repentance

To the Chief Musician. A Psalm of David when
Nathan the prophet went to him, after he had gone
in to Bathsheba.

1 Have mercy upon me, O God,
  According to Your lovingkindness;
  According to the multitude of Your
    tender mercies,
  Blot out my transgressions.
2 Wash me thoroughly from my iniquity,
  And cleanse me from my sin.

3 For I acknowledge my transgressions,
  And my sin *is* always before me.
4 Against You, You only, have I sinned,
  And done *this* evil in Your sight—
  That You may be found just when You
    speak,[a]
  And blameless when You judge.

5 Behold, I was brought forth in iniquity,
  And in sin my mother conceived me.
6 Behold, You desire truth in the inward
    parts,
  And in the hidden *part* You will make
    me to know wisdom.

7 Purge me with hyssop, and I shall be
    clean;
  Wash me, and I shall be whiter than
    snow.
8 Make me hear joy and gladness,
  That the bones You have broken may
    rejoice.

50:18 [a]Septuagint, Syriac, Targum, and Vulgate read
ran.   **51:4** [a]Septuagint, Targum, and Vulgate read
in Your words.

9 Hide Your face from my sins,
And blot out all my iniquities.

10 Create in me a clean heart, O God,
And renew a steadfast spirit
within me.
11 Do not cast me away from Your
presence,
And do not take Your Holy Spirit
from me.

12 Restore to me the joy of Your salvation,
And uphold me *by Your* generous
Spirit.
13 *Then* I will teach transgressors Your
ways,
And sinners shall be converted to You.

14 Deliver me from the guilt of bloodshed,
O God,
The God of my salvation,
And my tongue shall sing aloud of
Your righteousness.
15 O Lord, open my lips,
And my mouth shall show forth Your
praise.
16 For You do not desire sacrifice, or else
I would give *it;*
You do not delight in burnt offering.
17 The sacrifices of God *are* a broken spirit,
A broken and a contrite heart—
These, O God, You will not despise.

18 Do good in Your good pleasure to Zion;
Build the walls of Jerusalem.
19 Then You shall be pleased with the
sacrifices of righteousness,
With burnt offering and whole burnt
offering;
Then they shall offer bulls on Your altar.

PSALM 52

*The End of the Wicked and the Peace
of the Godly*

To the Chief Musician. A Contemplation[a] of David
when Doeg the Edomite went and told Saul, and said
to him, "David has gone to the house of Ahimelech."

1 Why do you boast in evil, O mighty
man?
The goodness of God *endures*
continually.

2 Your tongue devises destruction,
Like a sharp razor, working deceitfully.
3 You love evil more than good,
Lying rather than speaking
righteousness.   Selah
4 You love all devouring words,
You deceitful tongue.

5 God shall likewise destroy you forever;
He shall take you away, and pluck
you out of *your* dwelling place,
And uproot you from the land
of the living.   Selah
6 The righteous also shall see and fear,
And shall laugh at him, *saying,*
7 "Here is the man *who* did not make
God his strength,
But trusted in the abundance of his
riches,
And strengthened himself in his
wickedness."

8 But I *am* like a green olive tree in
the house of God;
I trust in the mercy of God forever
and ever.
9 I will praise You forever,
Because You have done *it;*
And in the presence of Your saints
I will wait on Your name, for *it is*
good.

PSALM 53

*Folly of the Godless, and the Restoration
of Israel*

To the Chief Musician. Set to "Mahalath."
A Contemplation[a] of David.

1 The fool has said in his heart,
"*There is* no God."
They are corrupt, and have done
abominable iniquity;
There is none who does good.

2 God looks down from heaven upon
the children of men,
To see if there are *any* who understand,
who seek God.
3 Every one of them has turned aside;
They have together become corrupt;

52:title [a]Hebrew *Maschil*   **53:title** [a]Hebrew *Maschil*

There is none who does good,
No, not one.

4 Have the workers of iniquity no
      knowledge,
Who eat up my people *as* they eat
      bread,
And do not call upon God?
5 There they are in great fear
Where no fear was,
For God has scattered the bones of
      him who encamps against you;
You have put *them* to shame,
Because God has despised them.

6 Oh, that the salvation of Israel would
      come out of Zion!
When God brings back the captivity of
      His people,
Let Jacob rejoice *and* Israel be glad.

PSALM 54

Answered Prayer for Deliverance from Adversaries

To the Chief Musician. With stringed instruments.[a]
A Contemplation[b] of David when the Ziphites went
and said to Saul, "Is David not hiding with us?"

1 Save me, O God, by Your name,
And vindicate me by Your strength.
2 Hear my prayer, O God;
Give ear to the words of my mouth.
3 For strangers have risen up against me,
And oppressors have sought after my
      life;
They have not set God before them.
                      Selah

4 Behold, God *is* my helper;
The Lord *is* with those who uphold my
      life.
5 He will repay my enemies for their
      evil.
Cut them off in Your truth.

6 I will freely sacrifice to You;
I will praise Your name, O LORD, for
      it is good.
7 For He has delivered me out of all
      trouble;
And my eye has seen *its desire* upon
      my enemies.

PSALM 55

Trust in God Concerning the Treachery of Friends

To the Chief Musician. With stringed instruments.[a]
A Contemplation[b] of David.

1 Give ear to my prayer, O God,
And do not hide Yourself from my
      supplication.
2 Attend to me, and hear me;
I am restless in my complaint, and
      moan noisily,
3 Because of the voice of the enemy,
Because of the oppression of the wicked;
For they bring down trouble upon me,
And in wrath they hate me.

4 My heart is severely pained within me,
And the terrors of death have fallen
      upon me.
5 Fearfulness and trembling have come
      upon me,
And horror has overwhelmed me.
6 So I said, "Oh, that I had wings like
      a dove!
I would fly away and be at rest.
7 Indeed, I would wander far off,
And remain in the wilderness.   Selah
8 I would hasten my escape
From the windy storm *and* tempest."

9 Destroy, O Lord, *and* divide their
      tongues,
For I have seen violence and strife
      in the city.
10 Day and night they go around it on
      its walls;
Iniquity and trouble *are* also in the
      midst of it.
11 Destruction *is* in its midst;
Oppression and deceit do not depart
      from its streets.

12 For *it is* not an enemy *who* reproaches
      me;
Then I could bear *it*.
Nor *is it* one *who* hates me who has
      exalted *himself* against me;
Then I could hide from him.

54:title [a]Hebrew *neginoth* [b]Hebrew *Maschil*
55:title [a]Hebrew *neginoth* [b]Hebrew *Maschil*

13 But *it was* you, a man my equal,
My companion and my acquaintance.
14 We took sweet counsel together,
And walked to the house of God in the
throng.

15 Let death seize them;
Let them *go* down alive into hell,
For wickedness *is* in their dwellings
and among them.

16 As for me, I will call upon God,
And the Lord shall save me.
17 Evening and morning and at noon
I will pray, and cry aloud,
And He shall hear my voice.
18 He has redeemed my soul in peace
from the battle *that was* against me,
For there were many against me.
19 God will hear, and afflict them,
Even He who abides from of old. Selah
Because they do not change,
Therefore they do not fear God.

20 He has put forth his hands against
those who were at peace with him;
He has broken his covenant.
21 *The words* of his mouth were smoother
than butter,
But war *was* in his heart;
His words were softer than oil,
Yet they *were* drawn swords.

22 Cast your burden on the Lord,
And He shall sustain you;
He shall never permit the righteous
to be moved.

23 But You, O God, shall bring them
down to the pit of destruction;
Bloodthirsty and deceitful men shall
not live out half their days;
But I will trust in You.

PSALM 56

Prayer for Relief from Tormentors

To the Chief Musician. Set to "The Silent Dove
in Distant Lands."ᵃ A Michtam of David when
the Philistines captured him in Gath.

1 Be merciful to me, O God, for man
would swallow me up;
Fighting all day he oppresses me.

2 My enemies would hound *me* all day,
For *there are* many who fight against
me, O Most High.

3 Whenever I am afraid,
I will trust in You.
4 In God (I will praise His word),
In God I have put my trust;
I will not fear.
What can flesh do to me?

5 All day they twist my words;
All their thoughts *are* against me for
evil.
6 They gather together,
They hide, they mark my steps,
When they lie in wait for my life.
7 Shall they escape by iniquity?
In anger cast down the peoples, O God!

8 You number my wanderings;
Put my tears into Your bottle;
Are they not in Your book?
9 When I cry out *to You,*
Then my enemies will turn back;
This I know, because God *is* for me.
10 In God (I will praise *His* word),
In the Lord (I will praise *His* word),
11 In God I have put my trust;
I will not be afraid.
What can man do to me?

12 Vows *made* to You *are binding* upon me,
O God;
I will render praises to You,
13 For You have delivered my soul from
death.
Have You not *kept* my feet from falling,
That I may walk before God
In the light of the living?

PSALM 57

Prayer for Safety from Enemies

To the Chief Musician. Set to "Do Not Destroy."ᵃ
A Michtam of David when he fled from Saul
into the cave.

1 Be merciful to me, O God, be merciful
to me!

56:title ᵃHebrew *Jonath Elem Rechokim*
57:title ᵃHebrew *Al Tashcheth*

For my soul trusts in You;
And in the shadow of Your wings I will
    make my refuge,
Until *these* calamities have passed by.

2   I will cry out to God Most High,
To God who performs *all things* for me.
3   He shall send from heaven and save
    me;
He reproaches the one who would
    swallow me up.   Selah
God shall send forth His mercy and
    His truth.

4   My soul *is* among lions;
I lie *among* the sons of men
Who are set on fire,
Whose teeth *are* spears and arrows,
And their tongue a sharp sword.
5   Be exalted, O God, above the heavens;
Let Your glory *be* above all the earth.

6   They have prepared a net for my steps;
My soul is bowed down;
They have dug a pit before me;
Into the midst of it they *themselves*
    have fallen.   Selah

7   My heart is steadfast, O God, my
    heart is steadfast;
I will sing and give praise.
8   Awake, my glory!
Awake, lute and harp!
I will awaken the dawn.

9   I will praise You, O Lord, among the
    peoples;
I will sing to You among the nations.
10 For Your mercy reaches unto the
    heavens,
And Your truth unto the clouds.

11 Be exalted, O God, above the heavens;
Let Your glory *be* above all the earth.

PSALM 58

The Just Judgment of the Wicked

To the Chief Musician. Set to "Do Not Destroy."ᵃ
A Michtam of David.

1   Do you indeed speak righteousness,
    you silent ones?

Do you judge uprightly, you
    sons of men?
2   No, in heart you work
    wickedness;
You weigh out the violence of
    your hands in the earth.

3   The wicked are estranged from
    the womb;
They go astray as soon as they
    are born, speaking lies.
4   Their poison *is* like the poison of
    a serpent;
They are like the deaf cobra *that*
    stops its ear,
5   Which will not heed the voice of
    charmers,
Charming ever so skillfully.

6   Break their teeth in their mouth,
    O God!
Break out the fangs of the young
    lions, O LORD!
7   Let them flow away as waters
    which run continually;
When he bends *his bow*,
Let his arrows be as if cut in
    pieces.
8   *Let them be* like a snail which
    melts away as it goes,
Like a stillborn child of a woman,
    that they may not see the sun.

9   Before your pots can feel *the
    burning* thorns,
He shall take them away as with
    a whirlwind,
As in His living and burning
    wrath.
10 The righteous shall rejoice when
    he sees the vengeance;
He shall wash his feet in the blood
    of the wicked,
11 So that men will say,
"Surely *there is* a reward for the
    righteous;
Surely He is God who judges in
    the earth."

58:title ᵃHebrew *Al Tashcheth*

PSALM 59

The Assured Judgment of the Wicked

To the Chief Musician. Set to "Do Not Destroy."[a]
A Michtam of David when Saul sent men,
and they watched the house in order to kill him.

1   Deliver me from my enemies, O my
        God;
    Defend me from those who rise up
        against me.
2   Deliver me from the workers of iniquity,
    And save me from bloodthirsty men.

3   For look, they lie in wait for my life;
    The mighty gather against me,
    Not *for* my transgression nor *for* my sin,
        O Lord.
4   They run and prepare themselves
        through no fault *of mine.*

    Awake to help me, and behold!
5   You therefore, O Lord God of hosts,
        the God of Israel,
    Awake to punish all the nations;
    Do not be merciful to any wicked
        transgressors.   Selah

6   At evening they return,
    They growl like a dog,
    And go all around the city.
7   Indeed, they belch with their mouth;
    Swords *are* in their lips;
    For *they say,* "Who hears?"

8   But You, O Lord, shall laugh at them;
    You shall have all the nations in
        derision.
9   I will wait for You, O You his Strength;[a]
    For God *is* my defense.
10 My God of mercy[a] shall come to
        meet me;
    God shall let me see *my desire* on my
        enemies.

11 Do not slay them, lest my people
        forget;
    Scatter them by Your power,
    And bring them down,
    O Lord our shield.
12 *For* the sin of their mouth *and* the
        words of their lips,
    Let them even be taken in their pride,

    And for the cursing and lying *which*
        they speak.
13 Consume *them* in wrath, consume *them,*
    That they *may* not *be;*
    And let them know that God rules in
        Jacob
    To the ends of the earth.   Selah

14 And at evening they return,
    They growl like a dog,
    And go all around the city.
15 They wander up and down for food,
    And howl[a] if they are not satisfied.

16 But I will sing of Your power;
    Yes, I will sing aloud of Your mercy in
        the morning;
    For You have been my defense
    And refuge in the day of my trouble.
17 To You, O my Strength, I will sing
        praises;
    For God *is* my defense,
    My God of mercy.

PSALM 60

Urgent Prayer for the Restored Favor of God

To the Chief Musician. Set to "Lily of the Testimony."[a]
A Michtam of David. For teaching. When he fought
against Mesopotamia and Syria of Zobah, and Joab
returned and killed twelve thousand Edomites in the
Valley of Salt.

1   O God, You have cast us off;
    You have broken us down;
    You have been displeased;
    Oh, restore us again!
2   You have made the earth tremble;
    You have broken it;
    Heal its breaches, for it is shaking.
3   You have shown Your people hard
        things;
    You have made us drink the wine
        of confusion.

59:title [a]Hebrew *Al Tashcheth*   59:9 [a]Following
Masoretic Text and Syriac; some Hebrew manuscripts,
Septuagint, Targum, and Vulgate read *my Strength.*
59:10 [a]Following Qere; some Hebrew manuscripts,
Septuagint, and Vulgate read *My God, His mercy;*
Kethib, some Hebrew manuscripts and Targum read
O God, my mercy; Syriac reads *O God, Your mercy.*
59:15 [a]Following Septuagint and Vulgate; Masoretic
Text, Syriac, and Targum read *spend the night.*
60:title [a]Hebrew *Shushan Eduth*

4 You have given a banner to those who
    fear You,
  That it may be displayed because
    of the truth.   Selah
5 That Your beloved may be delivered,
  Save *with* Your right hand, and hear me.

6 God has spoken in His holiness:
  "I will rejoice;
  I will divide Shechem
  And measure out the Valley of Succoth.
7 Gilead *is* Mine, and Manasseh *is* Mine;
  Ephraim also *is* the helmet for My head;
  Judah *is* My lawgiver.
8 Moab *is* My washpot;
  Over Edom I will cast My shoe;
  Philistia, shout in triumph because
    of Me."

9 Who will bring me *to* the strong city?
  Who will lead me to Edom?
10 *Is it* not You, O God, *who* cast us off?
  And You, O God, *who* did not go out
    with our armies?
11 Give us help from trouble,
  For the help of man *is* useless.
12 Through God we will do valiantly,
  For *it is* He *who* shall tread down our
    enemies.ᵃ

PSALM 61

Assurance of God's Eternal Protection

To the Chief Musician. On a stringed instrument.ᵃ
A Psalm of David.

1 Hear my cry, O God;
  Attend to my prayer.
2 From the end of the earth I will cry to
    You,
  When my heart is overwhelmed;
  Lead me to the rock that is higher
    than I.

3 For You have been a shelter for me,
  A strong tower from the enemy.
4 I will abide in Your tabernacle forever;
  I will trust in the shelter of Your wings.
                                    Selah

5 For You, O God, have heard my vows;
  You have given *me* the heritage of
    those who fear Your name.

6 You will prolong the king's life,
  His years as many generations.
7 He shall abide before God forever.
  Oh, prepare mercy and truth, *which*
    may preserve him!

8 So I will sing praise to Your name
    forever,
  That I may daily perform my vows.

PSALM 62

A Calm Resolve to Wait for the Salvation of God

To the Chief Musician. To Jeduthun.
A Psalm of David.

1 Truly my soul silently *waits* for God;
  From Him *comes* my salvation.
2 He only *is* my rock and my salvation;
  He is my defense;
  I shall not be greatly moved.

3 How long will you attack a man?
  You shall be slain, all of you,
  Like a leaning wall and a tottering
    fence.
4 They only consult to cast *him* down
    from his high position;
  They delight in lies;
  They bless with their mouth,
  But they curse inwardly.   Selah

5 My soul, wait silently for God alone,
  For my expectation *is* from Him.
6 He only *is* my rock and my salvation;
  He is my defense;
  I shall not be moved.
7 In God *is* my salvation and my glory;
  The rock of my strength,
  And my refuge, *is* in God.

8 Trust in Him at all times, you people;
  Pour out your heart before Him;
  God *is* a refuge for us.   Selah

9 Surely men of low degree *are* a vapor,
  Men of high degree *are* a lie;
  If they are weighed on the scales,
  They *are* altogether *lighter* than vapor.

60:12 ᵃCompare verses 5–12 with 108:6–13
61:title ᵃHebrew *neginah*

10 Do not trust in oppression,
    Nor vainly hope in robbery;
    If riches increase,
    Do not set *your* heart *on them.*

11 God has spoken once,
    Twice I have heard this:
    That power *belongs* to God.
12 Also to You, O Lord, *belongs* mercy;
    For You render to each one according
        to his work.

PSALM 63

Joy in the Fellowship of God

A Psalm of David when he was
in the wilderness of Judah.

1   O God, You *are* my God;
    Early will I seek You;
    My soul thirsts for You;
    My flesh longs for You
    In a dry and thirsty land
    Where there is no water.
2   So I have looked for You in the
        sanctuary,
    To see Your power and Your glory.

3   Because Your lovingkindness *is* better
        than life,
    My lips shall praise You.
4   Thus I will bless You while I live;
    I will lift up my hands in Your name.
5   My soul shall be satisfied as with
        marrow and fatness,
    And my mouth shall praise *You* with
        joyful lips.

6   When I remember You on my bed,
    I meditate on You in the *night*
        watches.
7   Because You have been my help,
    Therefore in the shadow of Your wings
        I will rejoice.
8   My soul follows close behind You;
    Your right hand upholds me.

9   But those *who* seek my life, to
        destroy *it,*
    Shall go into the lower parts of the
        earth.
10 They shall fall by the sword;
    They shall be a portion for jackals.

11 But the king shall rejoice in God;
    Everyone who swears by Him shall
        glory;
    But the mouth of those who speak lies
        shall be stopped.

PSALM 64

*Oppressed by the Wicked but Rejoicing
in the LORD*

To the Chief Musician. A Psalm of David.

1   Hear my voice, O God, in my
        meditation;
    Preserve my life from fear of the
        enemy.
2   Hide me from the secret plots of
        the wicked,
    From the rebellion of the workers
        of iniquity,
3   Who sharpen their tongue like a
        sword,
    And bend *their bows to shoot* their
        arrows—bitter words,
4   That they may shoot in secret at the
        blameless;
    Suddenly they shoot at him and do
        not fear.

5   They encourage themselves *in* an evil
        matter;
    They talk of laying snares secretly;
    They say, "Who will see them?"
6   They devise iniquities:
    "We have perfected a shrewd scheme."
    Both the inward thought and the
        heart of man are deep.

7   But God shall shoot at them *with* an
        arrow;
    Suddenly they shall be wounded.
8   So He will make them stumble over
        their own tongue;
    All who see them shall flee away.
9   All men shall fear,
    And shall declare the work of God;
    For they shall wisely consider His doing.

10 The righteous shall be glad in the
        LORD, and trust in Him.
    And all the upright in heart shall
        glory.

PSALM 65

Praise to God for His Salvation and Providence

To the Chief Musician. A Psalm of David. A Song.

1 Praise is awaiting You, O God, in Zion;
   And to You the vow shall be performed.
2 O You who hear prayer,
   To You all flesh will come.
3 Iniquities prevail against me;
   As for our transgressions,
   You will provide atonement for them.

4 Blessed *is the man* You choose,
   And cause to approach *You,*
   That he may dwell in Your courts.
   We shall be satisfied with the
      goodness of Your house,
   Of Your holy temple.

5 *By* awesome deeds in righteousness
      You will answer us,
   O God of our salvation,
   You who are the confidence of all the
      ends of the earth,
   And of the far-off seas;
6 Who established the mountains by
      His strength,
   Being clothed with power;
7 You who still the noise of the seas,
   The noise of their waves,
   And the tumult of the peoples.
8 They also who dwell in the farthest
      parts are afraid of Your signs;
   You make the outgoings of the
      morning and evening rejoice.

9 You visit the earth and water it,
   You greatly enrich it;
   The river of God is full of water;
   You provide their grain,
   For so You have prepared it.
10 You water its ridges abundantly,
   You settle its furrows;
   You make it soft with showers,
   You bless its growth.

11 You crown the year with Your goodness,
   And Your paths drip *with* abundance.
12 They drop *on* the pastures of the
      wilderness,
   And the little hills rejoice on every side.

13 The pastures are clothed with flocks;
   The valleys also are covered with grain;
   They shout for joy, they also sing.

PSALM 66

Praise to God for His Awesome Works

To the Chief Musician. A Song. A Psalm.

1 Make a joyful shout to God, all the
      earth!
2 Sing out the honor of His name;
   Make His praise glorious.
3 Say to God,
   "How awesome are Your works!
   Through the greatness of Your power
   Your enemies shall submit themselves
      to You.
4 All the earth shall worship You
   And sing praises to You;
   They shall sing praises *to* Your name."
                                    Selah

5 Come and see the works of God;
   He is awesome *in His* doing toward
      the sons of men.
6 He turned the sea into dry *land;*
   They went through the river on foot.
   There we will rejoice in Him.
7 He rules by His power forever;
   His eyes observe the nations;
   Do not let the rebellious exalt
      themselves.   Selah

8 Oh, bless our God, you peoples!
   And make the voice of His praise to
      be heard,
9 Who keeps our soul among the living,
   And does not allow our feet to be moved.
10 For You, O God, have tested us;
   You have refined us as silver is refined.
11 You brought us into the net;
   You laid affliction on our backs.
12 You have caused men to ride over our
      heads;
   We went through fire and through
      water;
   But You brought us out to rich
   fulfillment.

13 I will go into Your house with burnt
   offerings;

I will pay You my vows,
14 Which my lips have uttered
And my mouth has spoken when I
   was in trouble.
15 I will offer You burnt sacrifices of fat
   animals,
With the sweet aroma of rams;
I will offer bulls with goats.   Selah

16 Come *and* hear, all you who fear God,
And I will declare what He has done
   for my soul.
17 I cried to Him with my mouth,
And He was extolled with my tongue.
18 If I regard iniquity in my heart,
The Lord will not hear.
19 *But* certainly God has heard *me;*
He has attended to the voice of my
   prayer.

20 Blessed *be* God,
Who has not turned away my prayer,
Nor His mercy from me!

PSALM 67

An Invocation and a Doxology

To the Chief Musician. On stringed instruments.ᵃ
A Psalm. A Song.

1 God be merciful to us and bless us,
And cause His face to shine upon us,
                                      Selah
2 That Your way may be known on
   earth,
Your salvation among all nations.

3 Let the peoples praise You, O God;
Let all the peoples praise You.
4 Oh, let the nations be glad and sing
   for joy!
For You shall judge the people
   righteously,
And govern the nations on earth.
                                      Selah

5 Let the peoples praise You, O God;
Let all the peoples praise You.
6 *Then* the earth shall yield her increase;
God, our own God, shall bless us.
7 God shall bless us,
And all the ends of the earth shall
   fear Him.

PSALM 68

The Glory of God in His Goodness to Israel

To the Chief Musician. A Psalm of David. A Song.

1 Let God arise,
Let His enemies be scattered;
Let those also who hate Him flee
   before Him.
2 As smoke is driven away,
So drive *them* away;
As wax melts before the fire,
So let the wicked perish at the
   presence of God.
3 But let the righteous be glad;
Let them rejoice before God;
Yes, let them rejoice exceedingly.

4 Sing to God, sing praises to His name;
Extol Him who rides on the clouds,ᵃ
By His name YAH,
And rejoice before Him.

5 A father of the fatherless, a defender
   of widows,
Is God in His holy habitation.
6 God sets the solitary in families;
He brings out those who are bound
   into prosperity;
But the rebellious dwell in a dry *land.*

7 O God, when You went out before
   Your people,
When You marched through the
   wilderness,   Selah
8 The earth shook;
The heavens also dropped *rain* at the
   presence of God;
Sinai itself *was moved* at the presence
   of God, the God of Israel.
9 You, O God, sent a plentiful rain,
Whereby You confirmed Your
   inheritance,
When it was weary.
10 Your congregation dwelt in it;
You, O God, provided from Your
   goodness for the poor.

11 The Lord gave the word;

67:title ᵃHebrew *neginoth*   **68:4** ᵃMasoretic Text
reads *deserts;* Targum reads *heavens* (compare verse 34
and Isaiah 19:1).

Great *was* the company of those who
proclaimed *it:*

12 "Kings of armies flee, they flee,
And she who remains at home divides
the spoil.

13 Though you lie down among the
sheepfolds,
You will be like the wings of a dove
covered with silver,
And her feathers with yellow gold."

14 When the Almighty scattered kings
in it,
It was *white* as snow in Zalmon.

15 A mountain of God *is* the mountain
of Bashan;
A mountain *of many* peaks *is* the
mountain of Bashan.

16 Why do you fume with envy, you
mountains of *many* peaks?
This is the mountain *which* God desires
to dwell in;
Yes, the LORD will dwell *in it* forever.

17 The chariots of God *are* twenty
thousand,
Even thousands of thousands;
The Lord is among them *as in* Sinai, in
the Holy *Place.*

18 You have ascended on high,
You have led captivity captive;
You have received gifts among men,
Even *from* the rebellious,
That the LORD God might dwell *there.*

19 Blessed *be* the Lord,
Who daily loads us *with benefits,*
The God of our salvation!　　　　Selah

20 Our God *is* the God of salvation;
And to GOD the Lord *belong* escapes
from death.

21 But God will wound the head of His
enemies,
The hairy scalp of the one who still
goes on in his trespasses.

22 The Lord said, "I will bring back from
Bashan,
I will bring *them* back from the depths
of the sea,

23 That your foot may crush *them*ᵃ in
blood,

And the tongues of your dogs *may have*
their portion from *your* enemies."

24 They have seen Your procession, O God,
The procession of my God, my King,
into the sanctuary.

25 The singers went before, the players
on instruments *followed* after;
Among *them were* the maidens
playing timbrels.

26 Bless God in the congregations,
The Lord, from the fountain of Israel.

27 There *is* little Benjamin, their leader,
The princes of Judah *and* their company,
The princes of Zebulun *and* the princes
of Naphtali.

28 Your God has commandedᵃ your
strength;
Strengthen, O God, what You have
done for us.

29 Because of Your temple at Jerusalem,
Kings will bring presents to You.

30 Rebuke the beasts of the reeds,
The herd of bulls with the calves of
the peoples,
Till everyone submits himself with
pieces of silver.
Scatter the peoples *who* delight in war.

31 Envoys will come out of Egypt;
Ethiopia will quickly stretch out her
hands to God.

32 Sing to God, you kingdoms of the earth;
Oh, sing praises to the Lord,　　　Selah

33 To Him who rides on the heaven of
heavens, *which were* of old!
Indeed, He sends out His voice, a
mighty voice.

34 Ascribe strength to God;
His excellence *is* over Israel,
And His strength *is* in the clouds.

35 O God, *You are* more awesome than
Your holy places.
The God of Israel *is* He who gives
strength and power to *His* people.

Blessed *be* God!

68:23 ᵃSeptuagint, Syriac, Targum, and Vulgate read
you may dip your foot.　　**68:28** ᵃSeptuagint, Syriac,
Targum, and Vulgate read *Command, O God.*

PSALM 69

An Urgent Plea for Help in Trouble

To the Chief Musician. Set to "The Lilies."ᵃ
A Psalm of David.

1 Save me, O God!
For the waters have come up to *my* neck.
2 I sink in deep mire,
Where *there is* no standing;
I have come into deep waters,
Where the floods overflow me.
3 I am weary with my crying;
My throat is dry;
My eyes fail while I wait for my God.

4 Those who hate me without a cause
Are more than the hairs of my head;
They are mighty who would destroy me,
Being my enemies wrongfully;
Though I have stolen nothing,
I *still* must restore *it*.

5 O God, You know my foolishness;
And my sins are not hidden from You.
6 Let not those who wait for You, O Lord
God of hosts, be ashamed because
of me;
Let not those who seek You be
confounded because of me, O God
of Israel.
7 Because for Your sake I have borne
reproach;
Shame has covered my face.
8 I have become a stranger to my
brothers,
And an alien to my mother's children;
9 Because zeal for Your house has eaten
me up,
And the reproaches of those who
reproach You have fallen on me.
10 When I wept *and chastened* my soul
with fasting,
That became my reproach.
11 I also made sackcloth my garment;
I became a byword to them.
12 Those who sit in the gate speak
against me,
And I *am* the song of the drunkards.

13 But as for me, my prayer *is* to You,
O Lord, *in* the acceptable time;
O God, in the multitude of Your mercy,
Hear me in the truth of Your salvation.
14 Deliver me out of the mire,
And let me not sink;
Let me be delivered from those who
hate me,
And out of the deep waters.
15 Let not the floodwater overflow me,
Nor let the deep swallow me up;
And let not the pit shut its mouth
on me.

16 Hear me, O LORD, for Your
lovingkindness *is* good;
Turn to me according to the multitude
of Your tender mercies.
17 And do not hide Your face from Your
servant,
For I am in trouble;
Hear me speedily.
18 Draw near to my soul, *and* redeem it;
Deliver me because of my enemies.

19 You know my reproach, my shame,
and my dishonor;
My adversaries *are* all before You.
20 Reproach has broken my heart,
And I am full of heaviness;
I looked *for someone* to take pity, but
there was none;
And for comforters, but I found none.
21 They also gave me gall for my food,
And for my thirst they gave me
vinegar to drink.

22 Let their table become a snare before
them,
And their well-being a trap.
23 Let their eyes be darkened, so that they
do not see;
And make their loins shake continually.
24 Pour out Your indignation upon them,
And let Your wrathful anger take hold
of them.
25 Let their dwelling place be desolate;
Let no one live in their tents.
26 For they persecute the *ones* You have
struck,
And talk of the grief of those You have
wounded.

69:title ᵃHebrew *Shoshannim*

27 Add iniquity to their iniquity,
   And let them not come into Your
      righteousness.
28 Let them be blotted out of the book
      of the living,
   And not be written with the
      righteous.

29 But I *am* poor and sorrowful;
   Let Your salvation, O God, set me up
      on high.
30 I will praise the name of God with a
      song,
   And will magnify Him with
      thanksgiving.
31 *This* also shall please the Lord better
      than an ox *or* bull,
   Which has horns and hooves.
32 The humble shall see *this and* be
      glad;
   And you who seek God, your hearts
      shall live.
33 For the Lord hears the poor,
   And does not despise His prisoners.

34 Let heaven and earth praise Him,
   The seas and everything that moves
      in them.
35 For God will save Zion
   And build the cities of Judah,
   That they may dwell there and
      possess it.
36 Also, the descendants of His servants
      shall inherit it,
   And those who love His name shall
      dwell in it.

PSALM 70

Prayer for Relief from Adversaries

To the Chief Musician. *A Psalm* of David.
To bring to remembrance.

1 *Make haste,* O God, to deliver me!
   Make haste to help me, O Lord!

2 Let them be ashamed and confounded
   Who seek my life;
   Let them be turned back[a] and confused
   Who desire my hurt.
3 Let them be turned back because of
      their shame,
   Who say, "Aha, aha!"

4 Let all those who seek You rejoice and
      be glad in You;
   And let those who love Your salvation
      say continually,
   "Let God be magnified!"

5 But I *am* poor and needy;
   Make haste to me, O God!
   You *are* my help and my deliverer;
   O Lord, do not delay.

PSALM 71

God the Rock of Salvation

1 In You, O Lord, I put my trust;
   Let me never be put to shame.
2 Deliver me in Your righteousness, and
      cause me to escape;
   Incline Your ear to me, and save me.
3 Be my strong refuge,
   To which I may resort continually;
   You have given the commandment to
      save me,
   For You *are* my rock and my fortress.

4 Deliver me, O my God, out of the hand
      of the wicked,
   Out of the hand of the unrighteous and
      cruel man.
5 For You are my hope, O Lord God;
   You are my trust from my youth.
6 By You I have been upheld from birth;
   You are He who took me out of my
      mother's womb.
   My praise *shall be* continually of You.

7 I have become as a wonder to many,
   But You *are* my strong refuge.
8 Let my mouth be filled *with* Your praise
   And with Your glory all the day.

9 Do not cast me off in the time of old
      age;
   Do not forsake me when my strength
      fails.
10 For my enemies speak against me;
   And those who lie in wait for my life
      take counsel together,

70:2 [a]Following Masoretic Text, Septuagint, Targum, and Vulgate; some Hebrew manuscripts and Syriac read *be appalled* (compare 40:15).

11 Saying, "God has forsaken him;
Pursue and take him, for *there is* none
to deliver *him.*"

12 O God, do not be far from me;
O my God, make haste to help me!
13 Let them be confounded *and* consumed
Who are adversaries of my life;
Let them be covered *with* reproach and
dishonor
Who seek my hurt.

14 But I will hope continually,
And will praise You yet more and more.
15 My mouth shall tell of Your
righteousness
And Your salvation all the day,
For I do not know *their* limits.
16 I will go in the strength of the Lord GOD;
I will make mention of Your
righteousness, of Yours only.

17 O God, You have taught me from
my youth;
And to this *day* I declare Your
wondrous works.
18 Now also when *I am* old and
grayheaded,
O God, do not forsake me,
Until I declare Your strength to *this*
generation,
Your power to everyone *who* is to come.

19 Also Your righteousness, O God, *is*
very high,
You who have done great things;
O God, who *is* like You?
20 *You,* who have shown me great and
severe troubles,
Shall revive me again,
And bring me up again from the
depths of the earth.
21 You shall increase my greatness,
And comfort me on every side.

22 Also with the lute I will praise You—
And Your faithfulness, O my God!
To You I will sing with the harp,
O Holy One of Israel.
23 My lips shall greatly rejoice when I
sing to You,
And my soul, which You have redeemed.

24 My tongue also shall talk of Your
righteousness all the day long;
For they are confounded,
For they are brought to shame
Who seek my hurt.

PSALM 72

Glory and Universality of the Messiah's Reign

A *Psalm* of Solomon.

1 Give the king Your judgments, O God,
And Your righteousness to the king's
Son.
2 He will judge Your people with
righteousness,
And Your poor with justice.
3 The mountains will bring peace to the
people,
And the little hills, by righteousness.
4 He will bring justice to the poor of the
people;
He will save the children of the needy,
And will break in pieces the oppressor.

5 They shall fear You[a]
As long as the sun and moon endure,
Throughout all generations.
6 He shall come down like rain upon
the grass before mowing,
Like showers *that* water the earth.
7 In His days the righteous shall flourish,
And abundance of peace,
Until the moon is no more.

8 He shall have dominion also from sea
to sea,
And from the River to the ends of the
earth.
9 Those who dwell in the wilderness will
bow before Him,
And His enemies will lick the dust.
10 The kings of Tarshish and of the isles
Will bring presents;
The kings of Sheba and Seba
Will offer gifts.
11 Yes, all kings shall fall down before
Him;
All nations shall serve Him.

72:5 [a]Following Masoretic Text and Targum;
Septuagint and Vulgate read *They shall continue.*

12 For He will deliver the needy when
    he cries,
The poor also, and *him* who has no
    helper.
13 He will spare the poor and needy,
And will save the souls of the needy.
14 He will redeem their life from
    oppression and violence;
And precious shall be their blood
    in His sight.

15 And He shall live;
And the gold of Sheba will be given
    to Him;
Prayer also will be made for Him
    continually,
And daily He shall be praised.

16 There will be an abundance of grain
    in the earth,
On the top of the mountains;

Its fruit shall wave like Lebanon;
And *those* of the city shall flourish like
    grass of the earth.

17 His name shall endure forever;
His name shall continue as long as
    the sun.
And *men* shall be blessed in Him;
All nations shall call Him blessed.

18 Blessed *be* the L ORD God, the God of
    Israel,
Who only does wondrous things!
19 And blessed *be* His glorious name
    forever!
And let the whole earth be filled *with*
    His glory.
Amen and Amen.

20 The prayers of David the son of Jesse
    are ended.

WORSHIP

*And let the whole earth
be filled with His glory.*

PSALM 72:19

John Hancock

FILL THE WORLD WITH HIS GLORY

To celebrate the victorious conclusion of the Revolutionary War, Governor John Hancock of Massachusetts issued a Proclamation for a Day of Thanksgiving on December 11, 1783:

Whereas . . . these United States are not only happily rescued from the danger and calamities to which they have been so long exposed, but their freedom, sovereignty, and independence ultimately acknowledged.

And whereas . . . the interposition of Divine Providence in our favor hath been most abundantly and most graciously manifested, and the citizens of these United States have every reason for praise and gratitude to the God of their salvation.

Impressed therefore with an exalted sense of the blessings by which we are surrounded, and of our entire dependence on that Almighty Being from whose goodness and bounty they are derived; I do by and with the Advice of the Council appoint Thursday the eleventh day of December next (the day recommended by the Congress to all the States) to be religiously observed as a day of Thanksgiving and Prayer, that all the people may then assemble to celebrate . . . that He hath been pleased to continue to us the Light of the blessed Gospel; . . . That we also offer up fervent supplications . . . to cause pure religion and virtue to flourish . . . and to fill the world with His glory.

Book Three: Psalms 73—89

PSALM 73

The Tragedy of the Wicked, and the Blessedness of Trust in God

A Psalm of Asaph.

1 Truly God *is* good to Israel,
   To such as are pure in heart.
2 But as for me, my feet had almost stumbled;
   My steps had nearly slipped.
3 For I *was* envious of the boastful,
   When I saw the prosperity of the wicked.

4 For *there are* no pangs in their death,
   But their strength *is* firm.
5 They *are* not in trouble *as other* men,
   Nor are they plagued like *other* men.
6 Therefore pride serves as their necklace;
   Violence covers them *like* a garment.
7 Their eyes bulgeᵃ with abundance;
   They have more than heart could wish.
8 They scoff and speak wickedly *concerning* oppression;
   They speak loftily.
9 They set their mouth against the heavens,
   And their tongue walks through the earth.

10 Therefore his people return here,
    And waters of a full *cup* are drained by them.
11 And they say, "How does God know?
    And is there knowledge in the Most High?"
12 Behold, these *are* the ungodly,
    Who are always at ease;
    They increase *in* riches.
13 Surely I have cleansed my heart *in* vain,
    And washed my hands in innocence.
14 For all day long I have been plagued,
    And chastened every morning.

15 If I had said, "I will speak thus,"
    Behold, I would have been untrue to the generation of Your children.
16 When I thought *how* to understand this,
    It *was* too painful for me—

17 Until I went into the sanctuary of God;
   Then I understood their end.

18 Surely You set them in slippery places;
   You cast them down to destruction.
19 Oh, how they are *brought* to desolation, as in a moment!
   They are utterly consumed with terrors.
20 As a dream when *one* awakes,
   So, Lord, when You awake,
   You shall despise their image.

21 Thus my heart was grieved,
   And I was vexed in my mind.
22 I *was* so foolish and ignorant;
   I was *like* a beast before You.
23 Nevertheless I *am* continually with You;
   You hold *me* by my right hand.
24 You will guide me with Your counsel,
   And afterward receive me *to* glory.

25 Whom have I in heaven *but You?*
   And *there is* none upon earth *that* I desire besides You.
26 My flesh and my heart fail;
   But God *is* the strength of my heart and my portion forever.

27 For indeed, those who are far from You shall perish;
   You have destroyed all those who desert You for harlotry.
28 But *it is* good for me to draw near to God;
   I have put my trust in the Lord GOD,
   That I may declare all Your works.

PSALM 74

A Plea for Relief from Oppressors

A Contemplationᵃ of Asaph.

1 O God, why have You cast *us* off forever?
   Why does Your anger smoke against the sheep of Your pasture?
2 Remember Your congregation, *which* You have purchased of old,

---

73:7 ᵃTargum reads *face bulges;* Septuagint, Syriac, and Vulgate read *iniquity bulges.*
74:title ᵃHebrew *Maschil*

The tribe of Your inheritance, *which*
  You have redeemed—
This Mount Zion where You have dwelt.
3 Lift up Your feet to the perpetual
    desolations.
The enemy has damaged everything
  in the sanctuary.
4 Your enemies roar in the midst of Your
    meeting place;
They set up their banners *for* signs.
5 They seem like men who lift up
Axes among the thick trees.
6 And now they break down its carved
    work, all at once,
With axes and hammers.
7 They have set fire to Your sanctuary;
They have defiled the dwelling place
  of Your name to the ground.
8 They said in their hearts,
"Let us destroy them altogether."
They have burned up all the meeting
  places of God in the land.

9 We do not see our signs;
There is no longer any prophet;
Nor *is there* any among us who knows
  how long.
10 O God, how long will the adversary
    reproach?
Will the enemy blaspheme Your name
  forever?
11 Why do You withdraw Your hand,
    even Your right hand?
Take it out of Your bosom and destroy
  them.
12 For God *is* my King from of old,
Working salvation in the midst of the
  earth.
13 You divided the sea by Your strength;
You broke the heads of the sea
  serpents in the waters.
14 You broke the heads of Leviathan in
    pieces,
And gave him *as* food to the people
  inhabiting the wilderness.
15 You broke open the fountain and the
    flood;
You dried up mighty rivers.
16 The day *is* Yours, the night also *is* Yours;
You have prepared the light and the sun.
17 You have set all the borders of the earth;
You have made summer and winter.

18 Remember this, *that* the enemy has
    reproached, O Lord,
And *that* a foolish people has
  blasphemed Your name.
19 Oh, do not deliver the life of Your
    turtledove to the wild beast!
Do not forget the life of Your poor
  forever.
20 Have respect to the covenant;
For the dark places of the earth are
  full of the haunts of cruelty.
21 Oh, do not let the oppressed return
    ashamed!
Let the poor and needy praise Your
  name.

22 Arise, O God, plead Your own cause;
Remember how the foolish man
  reproaches You daily.
23 Do not forget the voice of Your enemies;
The tumult of those who rise up
  against You increases continually.

PSALM 75

Thanksgiving for God's Righteous Judgment

To the Chief Musician. Set to "Do Not Destroy."[a]
A Psalm of Asaph. A Song.

1 We give thanks to You, O God, we give
    thanks!
For Your wondrous works declare *that*
  Your name is near.

2 "When I choose the proper time,
I will judge uprightly.
3 The earth and all its inhabitants are
    dissolved;
I set up its pillars firmly.   Selah

4 "I said to the boastful, 'Do not deal
    boastfully,'
And to the wicked, 'Do not lift up the
  horn.
5 Do not lift up your horn on high;
Do *not* speak with a stiff neck.' "

6 For exaltation *comes* neither from the
    east
Nor from the west nor from the south.
7 But God *is* the Judge:

75:title [a]Hebrew *Al Tashcheth*

He puts down one,
And exalts another.
8 For in the hand of the LORD *there is a* cup,
And the wine is red;
It is fully mixed, and He pours it out;
Surely its dregs shall all the wicked of the earth
Drain *and* drink down.

9 But I will declare forever,
I will sing praises to the God of Jacob.

10 "All the horns of the wicked I will also cut off,
But the horns of the righteous shall be exalted."

PSALM 76

The Majesty of God in Judgment

To the Chief Musician. On stringed instruments.ᵃ
A Psalm of Asaph. A Song.

1 In Judah God *is* known;
His name *is* great in Israel.
2 In Salemᵃ also is His tabernacle,
And His dwelling place in Zion.
3 There He broke the arrows of the bow,
The shield and sword of battle.   Selah

4 You *are* more glorious and excellent
Than the mountains of prey.
5 The stouthearted were plundered;
They have sunk into their sleep;
And none of the mighty men have found the use of their hands.
6 At Your rebuke, O God of Jacob,
Both the chariot and horse were cast into a dead sleep.

7 You, Yourself, *are* to be feared;
And who may stand in Your presence
When once You are angry?
8 You caused judgment to be heard from heaven;
The earth feared and was still,
9 When God arose to judgment,
To deliver all the oppressed of the earth.   Selah

10 Surely the wrath of man shall praise You;

With the remainder of wrath You shall gird Yourself.

11 Make vows to the LORD your God, and pay *them;*
Let all who are around Him bring presents to Him who ought to be feared.
12 He shall cut off the spirit of princes;
He is awesome to the kings of the earth.

PSALM 77

The Consoling Memory of God's Redemptive Works

To the Chief Musician. To Jeduthun.
A Psalm of Asaph.

1 I cried out to God with my voice—
To God with my voice;
And He gave ear to me.
2 In the day of my trouble I sought the Lord;
My hand was stretched out in the night without ceasing;
My soul refused to be comforted.
3 I remembered God, and was troubled;
I complained, and my spirit was overwhelmed.   Selah

4 You hold my eyelids *open;*
I am so troubled that I cannot speak.
5 I have considered the days of old,
The years of ancient times.
6 I call to remembrance my song in the night;
I meditate within my heart,
And my spirit makes diligent search.

7 Will the Lord cast off forever?
And will He be favorable no more?
8 Has His mercy ceased forever?
Has *His* promise failed forevermore?
9 Has God forgotten to be gracious?
Has He in anger shut up His tender mercies?   Selah

10 And I said, "This *is* my anguish;
But I will remember the years of the right hand of the Most High."

76:title ᵃHebrew *neginoth*   **76:2** ᵃThat is, Jerusalem

11 I will remember the works of the LORD;
   Surely I will remember Your wonders
      of old.
12 I will also meditate on all Your work,
   And talk of Your deeds.
13 Your way, O God, *is* in the sanctuary;
   Who *is* so great a God as *our* God?
14 You *are* the God who does wonders;
   You have declared Your strength
      among the peoples.
15 You have with *Your* arm redeemed
      Your people,
   The sons of Jacob and Joseph.   Selah

16 The waters saw You, O God;
   The waters saw You, they were afraid;
   The depths also trembled.
17 The clouds poured out water;
   The skies sent out a sound;
   Your arrows also flashed about.
18 The voice of Your thunder *was* in the
      whirlwind;
   The lightnings lit up the world;
   The earth trembled and shook.
19 Your way *was* in the sea,
   Your path in the great waters,
   And Your footsteps were not known.
20 You led Your people like a flock
   By the hand of Moses and Aaron.

PSALM 78

God's Kindness to Rebellious Israel

A Contemplation[a] of Asaph.

1 Give ear, O my people, *to* my law;
   Incline your ears to the words of my
      mouth.
2 I will open my mouth in a parable;
   I will utter dark sayings of old,
3 Which we have heard and known,
   And our fathers have told us.
4 We will not hide *them* from their
      children,
   Telling to the generation to come the
      praises of the LORD,
   And His strength and His wonderful
      works that He has done.

5 For He established a testimony in Jacob,
   And appointed a law in Israel,
   Which He commanded our fathers,

That they should make them known
   to their children;
6 That the generation to come might
   know *them,*
The children *who* would be born,
That they may arise and declare *them*
   to their children,
7 That they may set their hope in God,
   And not forget the works of God,
   But keep His commandments;
8 And may not be like their fathers,
   A stubborn and rebellious generation,
   A generation *that* did not set its heart
      aright,
   And whose spirit was not faithful to God.

9 The children of Ephraim, *being* armed
      and carrying bows,
   Turned back in the day of battle.
10 They did not keep the covenant of God;
   They refused to walk in His law,
11 And forgot His works
   And His wonders that He had shown
      them.

12 Marvelous things He did in the sight
      of their fathers,
   In the land of Egypt, *in* the field of Zoan.
13 He divided the sea and caused them
      to pass through;
   And He made the waters stand up like
      a heap.
14 In the daytime also He led them with
      the cloud,
   And all the night with a light of fire.
15 He split the rocks in the wilderness,
   And gave *them* drink in abundance
      like the depths.
16 He also brought streams out of the rock,
   And caused waters to run down like
      rivers.

17 But they sinned even more against Him
   By rebelling against the Most High in
      the wilderness.
18 And they tested God in their heart
   By asking for the food of their fancy.
19 Yes, they spoke against God:
   They said, "Can God prepare a table
      in the wilderness?

78:title [a]Hebrew *Maschil*

20 Behold, He struck the rock,
So that the waters gushed out,
And the streams overflowed.
Can He give bread also?
Can He provide meat for His people?"

21 Therefore the LORD heard *this* and was
furious;
So a fire was kindled against Jacob,
And anger also came up against Israel,
22 Because they did not believe in God,
And did not trust in His salvation.
23 Yet He had commanded the clouds
above,
And opened the doors of heaven,
24 Had rained down manna on them to
eat,
And given them of the bread of heaven.
25 Men ate angels' food;
He sent them food to the full.

26 He caused an east wind to blow in the
heavens;
And by His power He brought in the
south wind.
27 He also rained meat on them like the
dust,
Feathered fowl like the sand of the seas;
28 And He let *them* fall in the midst of
their camp,
All around their dwellings.
29 So they ate and were well filled,
For He gave them their own desire.
30 They were not deprived of their craving;
But while their food *was* still in their
mouths,
31 The wrath of God came against them,
And slew the stoutest of them,
And struck down the choice *men* of
Israel.

32 In spite of this they still sinned,
And did not believe in His wondrous
works.
33 Therefore their days He consumed in
futility,
And their years in fear.

34 When He slew them, then they sought
Him;
And they returned and sought
earnestly for God.

35 Then they remembered that God *was*
their rock,
And the Most High God their Redeemer.
36 Nevertheless they flattered Him with
their mouth,
And they lied to Him with their tongue;
37 For their heart was not steadfast with
Him,
Nor were they faithful in His covenant.
38 But He, *being* full of compassion,
forgave *their* iniquity,
And did not destroy *them*.
Yes, many a time He turned His anger
away,
And did not stir up all His wrath;
39 For He remembered that they *were but*
flesh,
A breath that passes away and does
not come again.

40 How often they provoked Him in the
wilderness,
And grieved Him in the desert!
41 Yes, again and again they tempted God,
And limited the Holy One of Israel.
42 They did not remember His power:
The day when He redeemed them
from the enemy,
43 When He worked His signs in Egypt,
And His wonders in the field of Zoan;
44 Turned their rivers into blood,
And their streams, that they could not
drink.
45 He sent swarms of flies among them,
which devoured them,
And frogs, which destroyed them.
46 He also gave their crops to the
caterpillar,
And their labor to the locust.
47 He destroyed their vines with hail,
And their sycamore trees with frost.
48 He also gave up their cattle to the hail,
And their flocks to fiery lightning.
49 He cast on them the fierceness of His
anger,
Wrath, indignation, and trouble,
By sending angels of destruction
among them.
50 He made a path for His anger;
He did not spare their soul from
death,
But gave their life over to the plague,

51 And destroyed all the firstborn in Egypt,
The first of *their* strength in the tents of Ham.

52 But He made His own people go forth like sheep,
And guided them in the wilderness like a flock;

53 And He led them on safely, so that they did not fear;
But the sea overwhelmed their enemies.

54 And He brought them to His holy border,
This mountain *which* His right hand had acquired.

55 He also drove out the nations before them,
Allotted them an inheritance by survey,
And made the tribes of Israel dwell in their tents.

56 Yet they tested and provoked the Most High God,
And did not keep His testimonies,

57 But turned back and acted unfaithfully like their fathers;
They were turned aside like a deceitful bow.

58 For they provoked Him to anger with their high places,
And moved Him to jealousy with their carved images.

59 When God heard *this,* He was furious,
And greatly abhorred Israel,

60 So that He forsook the tabernacle of Shiloh,
The tent He had placed among men,

61 And delivered His strength into captivity,
And His glory into the enemy's hand.

62 He also gave His people over to the sword,
And was furious with His inheritance.

63 The fire consumed their young men,
And their maidens were not given in marriage.

64 Their priests fell by the sword,
And their widows made no lamentation.

65 Then the Lord awoke as *from* sleep,
Like a mighty man who shouts because of wine.

66 And He beat back His enemies;
He put them to a perpetual reproach.

67 Moreover He rejected the tent of Joseph,
And did not choose the tribe of Ephraim,

68 But chose the tribe of Judah,
Mount Zion which He loved.

69 And He built His sanctuary like the heights,
Like the earth which He has established forever.

70 He also chose David His servant,
And took him from the sheepfolds;

71 From following the ewes that had young He brought him,
To shepherd Jacob His people,
And Israel His inheritance.

72 So he shepherded them according to the integrity of his heart,
And guided them by the skillfulness of his hands.

PSALM 79

A Dirge and a Prayer for Israel, Destroyed by Enemies

A Psalm of Asaph.

1 O God, the nations have come into Your inheritance;
Your holy temple they have defiled;
They have laid Jerusalem in heaps.

2 The dead bodies of Your servants
They have given *as* food for the birds of the heavens,
The flesh of Your saints to the beasts of the earth.

3 Their blood they have shed like water all around Jerusalem,
And *there was* no one to bury *them.*

4 We have become a reproach to our neighbors,
A scorn and derision to those who are around us.

5 How long, LORD?
Will You be angry forever?
Will Your jealousy burn like fire?

6 Pour out Your wrath on the nations that do not know You,
And on the kingdoms that do not call on Your name.

7 For they have devoured Jacob,
And laid waste his dwelling place.

8 Oh, do not remember former iniquities
    against us!
  Let Your tender mercies come speedily
    to meet us,
  For we have been brought very low.
9 Help us, O God of our salvation,
  For the glory of Your name;
  And deliver us, and provide atonement
    for our sins,
  For Your name's sake!
10 Why should the nations say,
  "Where *is* their God?"
  Let there be known among the nations
    in our sight
  The avenging of the blood of Your
    servants *which has been* shed.

11 Let the groaning of the prisoner come
    before You;
  According to the greatness of Your power
  Preserve those who are appointed to die;
12 And return to our neighbors sevenfold
    into their bosom
  Their reproach with which they have
    reproached You, O Lord.

13 So we, Your people and sheep of Your
    pasture,
  Will give You thanks forever;
  We will show forth Your praise to all
    generations.

PSALM 80

Prayer for Israel's Restoration

To the Chief Musician. Set to "The Lilies."[a]
A Testimony[b] of Asaph. A Psalm.

1 Give ear, O Shepherd of Israel,
  You who lead Joseph like a flock;
  You who dwell *between* the cherubim,
    shine forth!
2 Before Ephraim, Benjamin, and
    Manasseh,
  Stir up Your strength,
  And come *and* save us!

3 Restore us, O God;
  Cause Your face to shine,
  And we shall be saved!

4 O LORD God of hosts,
  How long will You be angry

Against the prayer of Your people?
5 You have fed them with the bread
    of tears,
  And given them tears to drink in
    great measure.
6 You have made us a strife to our
    neighbors,
  And our enemies laugh among
    themselves.

7 Restore us, O God of hosts;
  Cause Your face to shine,
  And we shall be saved!

8 You have brought a vine out of Egypt;
  You have cast out the nations, and
    planted it.
9 You prepared *room* for it,
  And caused it to take deep root,
  And it filled the land.
10 The hills were covered with its shadow,
  And the mighty cedars with its boughs.
11 She sent out her boughs to the Sea,[a]
  And her branches to the River.[b]

12 Why have You broken down her hedges,
  So that all who pass by the way pluck
    her *fruit?*
13 The boar out of the woods uproots it,
  And the wild beast of the field
    devours it.

14 Return, we beseech You, O God of hosts;
  Look down from heaven and see,
  And visit this vine
15 And the vineyard which Your right
    hand has planted,
  And the branch *that* You made strong
    for Yourself.
16 *It is* burned with fire, *it is* cut down;
  They perish at the rebuke of Your
    countenance.
17 Let Your hand be upon the man of
    Your right hand,
  Upon the son of man *whom* You made
    strong for Yourself.
18 Then we will not turn back from You;
  Revive us, and we will call upon Your
    name.

80:title [a]Hebrew *Shoshannim* [b]Hebrew *Eduth*
80:11 [a]That is, the Mediterranean [b]That is, the
Euphrates

19   Restore us, O LORD God of hosts;
      Cause Your face to shine,
      And we shall be saved!

PSALM 81

An Appeal for Israel's Repentance

To the Chief Musician. On an instrument of Gath.[a]
A Psalm of Asaph.

1   Sing aloud to God our strength;
      Make a joyful shout to the God of
        Jacob.
2   Raise a song and strike the timbrel,
      The pleasant harp with the lute.

3   Blow the trumpet at the time of the
        New Moon,
      At the full moon, on our solemn feast
        day.
4   For this *is* a statute for Israel,
      A law of the God of Jacob.
5   This He established in Joseph *as* a
        testimony,
      When He went throughout the land
        of Egypt,
      Where I heard a language I did not
        understand.

6   "I removed his shoulder from the burden;
      His hands were freed from the baskets.
7   You called in trouble, and I delivered
        you;
      I answered you in the secret place of
        thunder;
      I tested you at the waters of Meribah.
                      Selah

8   "Hear, O My people, and I will
        admonish you!
      O Israel, if you will listen to Me!
9   There shall be no foreign god among
        you;
      Nor shall you worship any foreign god.
10   I *am* the LORD your God,
      Who brought you out of the land of
        Egypt;
      Open your mouth wide, and I will
        fill it.

11   "But My people would not heed My
        voice,
      And Israel would *have* none of Me.

12   So I gave them over to their own
        stubborn heart,
      To walk in their own counsels.

13   "Oh, that My people would listen to Me,
      That Israel would walk in My ways!
14   I would soon subdue their enemies,
      And turn My hand against their
        adversaries.
15   The haters of the LORD would pretend
        submission to Him,
      But their fate would endure forever.
16   He would have fed them also with the
        finest of wheat;
      And with honey from the rock I would
        have satisfied you."

PSALM 82

A Plea for Justice

A Psalm of Asaph.

1   God stands in the congregation of
        the mighty;
      He judges among the gods.[a]
2   How long will you judge unjustly,
      And show partiality to the wicked?
                      Selah
3   Defend the poor and fatherless;
      Do justice to the afflicted and needy.
4   Deliver the poor and needy;
      Free *them* from the hand of the
        wicked.

5   They do not know, nor do they
        understand;
      They walk about in darkness;
      All the foundations of the earth are
        unstable.

6   I said, "You *are* gods,[a]
      And all of you *are* children of the
        Most High.
7   But you shall die like men,
      And fall like one of the princes."

8   Arise, O God, judge the earth;
      For You shall inherit all nations.

81:title [a]Hebrew *Al Gittith*   **82:1** [a]Hebrew *elohim,*
mighty ones; that is, the judges   **82:6** [a]Hebrew
elohim, mighty ones; that is, the judges

PSALM 83

Prayer to Frustrate Conspiracy Against Israel

A Song. A Psalm of Asaph.

1 Do not keep silent, O God!
  Do not hold Your peace,
  And do not be still, O God!
2 For behold, Your enemies make a
    tumult;
  And those who hate You have lifted
    up their head.
3 They have taken crafty counsel
    against Your people,
  And consulted together against Your
    sheltered ones.
4 They have said, "Come, and let us cut
    them off from *being* a nation,
  That the name of Israel may be
    remembered no more."

5 For they have consulted together with
    one consent;
  They form a confederacy against You:
6 The tents of Edom and the Ishmaelites;
  Moab and the Hagrites;
7 Gebal, Ammon, and Amalek;
  Philistia with the inhabitants of Tyre;
8 Assyria also has joined with them;
  They have helped the children of Lot.
                                    Selah

9 Deal with them as *with* Midian,
  As *with* Sisera,
  As *with* Jabin at the Brook Kishon,
10 Who perished at En Dor,
   Who became as refuse on the earth.
11 Make their nobles like Oreb and like
     Zeeb,
   Yes, all their princes like Zebah and
     Zalmunna,
12 Who said, "Let us take for ourselves
   The pastures of God for a possession."

13 O my God, make them like the
     whirling dust,
   Like the chaff before the wind!
14 As the fire burns the woods,
   And as the flame sets the mountains
     on fire,
15 So pursue them with Your tempest,
   And frighten them with Your storm.

16 Fill their faces with shame,
   That they may seek Your name, O LORD.
17 Let them be confounded and dismayed
     forever;
   Yes, let them be put to shame and
     perish,
18 That they may know that You, whose
     name alone *is* the LORD,
   Are the Most High over all the earth.

PSALM 84

*The Blessedness of Dwelling in the House
of God*

To the Chief Musician. On an instrument of Gath.[a]
A Psalm of the sons of Korah.

1 How lovely *is* Your tabernacle,
  O LORD of hosts!
2 My soul longs, yes, even faints
  For the courts of the LORD;
  My heart and my flesh cry out for
    the living God.

3 Even the sparrow has found a home,
  And the swallow a nest for herself,
  Where she may lay her young—
  Even Your altars, O LORD of hosts,
  My King and my God.
4 Blessed *are* those who dwell in Your
    house;
  They will still be praising You.   Selah

5 Blessed *is* the man whose strength *is*
    in You,
  Whose heart *is* set on pilgrimage.
6 *As they* pass through the Valley of Baca,
  They make it a spring;
  The rain also covers it with pools.
7 They go from strength to strength;
  Each one appears before God in Zion.[a]

8 O LORD God of hosts, hear my prayer;
  Give ear, O God of Jacob!   Selah
9 O God, behold our shield,
  And look upon the face of Your
    anointed.

10 For a day in Your courts *is* better than
     a thousand.

84:title [a]Hebrew *Al Gittith*   **84:7** [a]Septuagint,
Syriac, and Vulgate read *The God of gods shall be seen.*

I would rather be a doorkeeper in the
   house of my God
Than dwell in the tents of wickedness.
11 For the LORD God *is* a sun and shield;
The LORD will give grace and glory;
No good *thing* will He withhold
From those who walk uprightly.

12 O LORD of hosts,
Blessed *is* the man who trusts in You!

PSALM 85

*Prayer that the LORD Will Restore Favor
to the Land*

To the Chief Musician. A Psalm of the sons of Korah.

1 LORD, You have been favorable to Your
   land;
You have brought back the captivity
   of Jacob.
2 You have forgiven the iniquity of Your
   people;
You have covered all their sin.   Selah
3 You have taken away all Your wrath;
You have turned from the fierceness
   of Your anger.

4 Restore us, O God of our salvation,
And cause Your anger toward us to
   cease.
5 Will You be angry with us forever?
Will You prolong Your anger to all
   generations?
6 Will You not revive us again,
That Your people may rejoice in You?
7 Show us Your mercy, LORD,
And grant us Your salvation.

8 I will hear what God the LORD will
   speak,
For He will speak peace
To His people and to His saints;
But let them not turn back to folly.
9 Surely His salvation *is* near to those
   who fear Him,
That glory may dwell in our land.

10 Mercy and truth have met together;
Righteousness and peace have kissed.
11 Truth shall spring out of the earth,
And righteousness shall look down
   from heaven.

12 Yes, the LORD will give *what is* good;
And our land will yield its increase.
13 Righteousness will go before Him,
And shall make His footsteps *our*
   pathway.

PSALM 86

*Prayer for Mercy, with Meditation on the
Excellencies of the LORD*

A Prayer of David.

1 Bow down Your ear, O LORD,
   hear me;
For I *am* poor and needy.
2 Preserve my life, for I *am* holy;
You are my God;
Save Your servant who trusts in You!
3 Be merciful to me, O Lord,
For I cry to You all day long.
4 Rejoice the soul of Your servant,
For to You, O Lord, I lift up my soul.
5 For You, Lord, *are* good, and ready
   to forgive,
And abundant in mercy to all those
   who call upon You.

6 Give ear, O LORD, to my prayer;
And attend to the voice of my
   supplications.
7 In the day of my trouble I will call
   upon You,
For You will answer me.

8 Among the gods *there is* none like You,
   O Lord;
Nor *are there any works* like Your works.
9 All nations whom You have made
Shall come and worship before You,
   O Lord,
And shall glorify Your name.
10 For You *are* great, and do wondrous
   things;
You alone *are* God.

11 Teach me Your way, O LORD;
I will walk in Your truth;
Unite my heart to fear Your name.
12 I will praise You, O Lord my God,
   with all my heart,
And I will glorify Your name
   forevermore.

13 For great *is* Your mercy toward me,
And You have delivered my soul from
   the depths of Sheol.

14 O God, the proud have risen
   against me,
And a mob of violent *men* have
   sought my life,
And have not set You before them.

15 But You, O Lord, *are* a God full of
   compassion, and gracious,
Longsuffering and abundant in mercy
   and truth.

16 Oh, turn to me, and have mercy on me!
Give Your strength to Your servant,
And save the son of Your maidservant.

17 Show me a sign for good,
That those who hate me may see *it*
   and be ashamed,
Because You, Lord, have helped me
   and comforted me.

PSALM 87

The Glories of the City of God

A Psalm of the sons of Korah. A Song.

1 His foundation *is* in the holy
   mountains.

2 The Lord loves the gates of Zion
More than all the dwellings of Jacob.

3 Glorious things are spoken of you,
O city of God!   Selah

4 "I will make mention of Rahab and
   Babylon to those who know Me;
Behold, O Philistia and Tyre, with
   Ethiopia:
'This *one* was born there.'"

5 And of Zion it will be said,
"This *one* and that *one* were born in her;
And the Most High Himself shall
   establish her."

6 The Lord will record,
When He registers the peoples:
"This *one* was born there."   Selah

7 Both the singers and the players on
   instruments *say,*
"All my springs *are* in you."

PSALM 88

A Prayer for Help in Despondency

A Song. A Psalm of the sons of Korah.
To the Chief Musician. Set to "Mahalath Leannoth."
A Contemplation[a] of Heman the Ezrahite.

1 O Lord, God of my salvation,
I have cried out day and night before
   You.

2 Let my prayer come before You;
Incline Your ear to my cry.

3 For my soul is full of troubles,
And my life draws near to the grave.

4 I am counted with those who go down
   to the pit;
I am like a man *who has* no strength,

5 Adrift among the dead,
Like the slain who lie in the grave,
Whom You remember no more,
And who are cut off from Your hand.

6 You have laid me in the lowest pit,
In darkness, in the depths.

7 Your wrath lies heavy upon me,
And You have afflicted *me* with all
   Your waves.   Selah

8 You have put away my acquaintances
   far from me;
You have made me an abomination
   to them;
I am shut up, and I cannot get out;

9 My eye wastes away because of
   affliction.

Lord, I have called daily upon You;
I have stretched out my hands to
   You.

10 Will You work wonders for the dead?
Shall the dead arise *and* praise You?
            Selah

11 Shall Your lovingkindness be declared
   in the grave?
Or Your faithfulness in the place of
   destruction?

12 Shall Your wonders be known in the
   dark?
And Your righteousness in the land
   of forgetfulness?

88:title [a]Hebrew *Maschil*

13 But to You I have cried out, O Lord,
And in the morning my prayer comes
before You.
14 Lord, why do You cast off my soul?
Why do You hide Your face from me?
15 I *have been* afflicted and ready to die
from *my* youth;
I suffer Your terrors;
I am distraught.
16 Your fierce wrath has gone over me;
Your terrors have cut me off.
17 They came around me all day long
like water;
They engulfed me altogether.
18 Loved one and friend You have put
far from me,
And my acquaintances into darkness.

PSALM 89

*Remembering the Covenant with David,
and Sorrow for Lost Blessings*

A Contemplation[a] of Ethan the Ezrahite.

1 I will sing of the mercies of the Lord
forever;
With my mouth will I make known
Your faithfulness to all generations.
2 For I have said, "Mercy shall be built
up forever;
Your faithfulness You shall establish in
the very heavens."

3 "I have made a covenant with My
chosen,
I have sworn to My servant David:
4 'Your seed I will establish forever,
And build up your throne to all
generations.'"   Selah

5 And the heavens will praise Your
wonders, O Lord;
Your faithfulness also in the assembly
of the saints.
6 For who in the heavens can be
compared to the Lord?
Who among the sons of the mighty
can be likened to the Lord?
7 God is greatly to be feared in the
assembly of the saints,
And to be held in reverence by all
those around Him.

8 O Lord God of hosts,
Who *is* mighty like You, O Lord?
Your faithfulness also surrounds You.
9 You rule the raging of the sea;
When its waves rise, You still them.
10 You have broken Rahab in pieces, as
one who is slain;
You have scattered Your enemies with
Your mighty arm.

11 The heavens *are* Yours, the earth also
is Yours;
The world and all its fullness, You have
founded them.
12 The north and the south, You have
created them;
Tabor and Hermon rejoice in Your name.
13 You have a mighty arm;
Strong is Your hand, *and* high is Your
right hand.
14 Righteousness and justice *are* the
foundation of Your throne;
Mercy and truth go before Your face.
15 Blessed *are* the people who know the
joyful sound!
They walk, O Lord, in the light of
Your countenance.
16 In Your name they rejoice all day long,
And in Your righteousness they are
exalted.
17 For You *are* the glory of their strength,
And in Your favor our horn is exalted.
18 For our shield *belongs* to the Lord,
And our king to the Holy One of Israel.

19 Then You spoke in a vision to Your
holy one,[a]
And said: "I have given help to *one
who is* mighty;
I have exalted one chosen from the
people.
20 I have found My servant David;
With My holy oil I have anointed him,
21 With whom My hand shall be
established;
Also My arm shall strengthen him.
22 The enemy shall not outwit him,
Nor the son of wickedness afflict him.

89:title [a]Hebrew *Maschil*   **89:19** [a]Following many
Hebrew manuscripts; Masoretic Text, Septuagint,
Targum, and Vulgate read *holy ones*.

23 I will beat down his foes before his face,
And plague those who hate him.

24 "But My faithfulness and My mercy
shall be with him,
And in My name his horn shall be
exalted.
25 Also I will set his hand over the sea,
And his right hand over the rivers.
26 He shall cry to Me, 'You *are* my Father,
My God, and the rock of my salvation.'
27 Also I will make him *My* firstborn,
The highest of the kings of the earth.
28 My mercy I will keep for him forever,
And My covenant shall stand firm
with him.
29 His seed also I will make *to endure*
forever,
And his throne as the days of heaven.

30 "If his sons forsake My law
And do not walk in My judgments,
31 If they break My statutes
And do not keep My commandments,
32 Then I will punish their transgression
with the rod,
And their iniquity with stripes.
33 Nevertheless My lovingkindness I will
not utterly take from him,
Nor allow My faithfulness to fail.
34 My covenant I will not break,
Nor alter the word that has gone out
of My lips.
35 Once I have sworn by My holiness;
I will not lie to David:
36 His seed shall endure forever,
And his throne as the sun before Me;
37 It shall be established forever like the
moon,
Even *like* the faithful witness in the
sky." Selah

38 But You have cast off and abhorred,
You have been furious with Your
anointed.
39 You have renounced the covenant of
Your servant;
You have profaned his crown *by
casting it* to the ground.
40 You have broken down all his hedges;
You have brought his strongholds to
ruin.

41 All who pass by the way plunder him;
He is a reproach to his neighbors.
42 You have exalted the right hand of his
adversaries;
You have made all his enemies rejoice.
43 You have also turned back the edge of
his sword,
And have not sustained him in the
battle.
44 You have made his glory cease,
And cast his throne down to the
ground.
45 The days of his youth You have
shortened;
You have covered him with shame.
Selah

46 How long, LORD?
Will You hide Yourself forever?
Will Your wrath burn like fire?
47 Remember how short my time is;
For what futility have You created all
the children of men?
48 What man can live and not see death?
Can he deliver his life from the power
of the grave? Selah

49 Lord, where *are* Your former
lovingkindnesses,
Which You swore to David in Your truth?
50 Remember, Lord, the reproach of Your
servants—
How I bear in my bosom *the reproach
of* all the many peoples,
51 With which Your enemies have
reproached, O LORD,
With which they have reproached the
footsteps of Your anointed.

52 Blessed *be* the LORD forevermore!
Amen and Amen.

Book Four: Psalms 90—106

PSALM 90

The Eternity of God, and Man's Frailty

A Prayer of Moses the man of God.

1 Lord, You have been our dwelling
placeª in all generations.

90:1 ªSeptuagint, Targum, and Vulgate read *refuge.*

2 Before the mountains were brought
forth,
Or ever You had formed the earth and
the world,
Even from everlasting to everlasting,
You *are* God.

3 You turn man to destruction,
And say, "Return, O children of men."
4 For a thousand years in Your sight
Are like yesterday when it is past,
And *like* a watch in the night.
5 You carry them away *like* a flood;
They are like a sleep.
In the morning they are like grass
which grows up:
6 In the morning it flourishes and
grows up;
In the evening it is cut down and
withers.

7 For we have been consumed by Your
anger,
And by Your wrath we are terrified.
8 You have set our iniquities before You,
Our secret *sins* in the light of Your
countenance.
9 For all our days have passed away in
Your wrath;
We finish our years like a sigh.
10 The days of our lives *are* seventy years;
And if by reason of strength *they are*
eighty years,
Yet their boast *is* only labor and sorrow;
For it is soon cut off, and we fly away.
11 Who knows the power of Your anger?
For as the fear of You, *so is* Your wrath.
12 So teach *us* to number our days,
That we may gain a heart of wisdom.

13 Return, O LORD!
How long?
And have compassion on Your
servants.
14 Oh, satisfy us early with Your mercy,
That we may rejoice and be glad all
our days!
15 Make us glad according to the days
in which You have afflicted us,
The years *in which* we have seen evil.
16 Let Your work appear to Your servants,
And Your glory to their children.

17 And let the beauty of the LORD our God
be upon us,
And establish the work of our hands
for us;
Yes, establish the work of our hands.

PSALM 91

Safety of Abiding in the Presence of God

1 He who dwells in the secret place of
the Most High
Shall abide under the shadow of the
Almighty.
2 I will say of the LORD, "*He is* my refuge
and my fortress;
My God, in Him I will trust."

3 Surely He shall deliver you from the
snare of the fowler[a]
And from the perilous pestilence.
4 He shall cover you with His feathers,
And under His wings you shall take
refuge;
His truth *shall be your* shield and
buckler.
5 You shall not be afraid of the terror
by night,
Nor of the arrow *that* flies by day,
6 *Nor* of the pestilence *that* walks in
darkness,
Nor of the destruction *that* lays waste
at noonday.

7 A thousand may fall at your side,
And ten thousand at your right
hand;
But it shall not come near you.
8 Only with your eyes shall you look,
And see the reward of the wicked.

9 Because you have made the LORD,
who is my refuge,
Even the Most High, your dwelling
place,
10 No evil shall befall you,
Nor shall any plague come near your
dwelling;
11 For He shall give His angels charge
over you,
To keep you in all your ways.

91:3 [a]That is, one who catches birds in a trap or snare

Grover Cleveland placed his hand on Psalm 91:12–16 as he took the presidential oath of office in 1893.

12 In *their* hands they shall bear you up,
   Lest you dash your foot against a stone.
13 You shall tread upon the lion and the cobra,
   The young lion and the serpent you shall trample underfoot.

14 "Because he has set his love upon Me,
   therefore I will deliver him;
   I will set him on high, because he has known My name.
15 He shall call upon Me, and I will answer him;
   I *will be* with him in trouble;
   I will deliver him and honor him.
16 With long life I will satisfy him,
   And show him My salvation."

PSALM 92

Praise to the Lord for His Love and Faithfulness

A Psalm. A Song for the Sabbath day.

1 *It is* good to give thanks to the Lord,
   And to sing praises to Your name,
   O Most High;
2 To declare Your lovingkindness in the morning,
   And Your faithfulness every night,
3 On an instrument of ten strings,
   On the lute,
   And on the harp,
   With harmonious sound.
4 For You, Lord, have made me glad through Your work;
   I will triumph in the works of Your hands.

5 O Lord, how great are Your works!
   Your thoughts are very deep.
6 A senseless man does not know,
   Nor does a fool understand this.
7 When the wicked spring up like grass,
   And when all the workers of iniquity flourish,
   It is that they may be destroyed forever.

8 But You, Lord, *are* on high forevermore.
9 For behold, Your enemies, O Lord,
   For behold, Your enemies shall perish;
   All the workers of iniquity shall be scattered.

10 But my horn You have exalted like a wild ox;
   I have been anointed with fresh oil.
11 My eye also has seen *my desire* on my enemies;
   My ears hear *my desire* on the wicked Who rise up against me.

12 The righteous shall flourish like a palm tree,
   He shall grow like a cedar in Lebanon.
13 Those who are planted in the house of the Lord
   Shall flourish in the courts of our God.
14 They shall still bear fruit in old age;
   They shall be fresh and flourishing,
15 To declare that the Lord is upright;
   He is my rock, and *there is* no unrighteousness in Him.

PSALM 93

The Eternal Reign of the Lord

1 The Lord reigns, He is clothed with majesty;
   The Lord is clothed,
   He has girded Himself with strength.
   Surely the world is established,
   so that it cannot be moved.
2 Your throne *is* established from of old;
   You *are* from everlasting.

3 The floods have lifted up, O Lord,
   The floods have lifted up their voice;
   The floods lift up their waves.
4 The Lord on high *is* mightier
   Than the noise of many waters,
   Than the mighty waves of the sea.

5 Your testimonies are very sure;
   Holiness adorns Your house,
   O Lord, forever.

PSALM 94

God the Refuge of the Righteous

1 O LORD God, to whom vengeance
     belongs—
   O God, to whom vengeance belongs,
     shine forth!
2 Rise up, O Judge of the earth;
   Render punishment to the proud.
3 LORD, how long will the wicked,
   How long will the wicked triumph?

4 They utter speech, *and* speak insolent
     things;
   All the workers of iniquity boast in
     themselves.
5 They break in pieces Your people,
     O LORD,
   And afflict Your heritage.
6 They slay the widow and the stranger,
   And murder the fatherless.
7 Yet they say, "The LORD does not see,
   Nor does the God of Jacob understand."

8 Understand, you senseless among the
     people;
   And *you* fools, when will you be wise?
9 He who planted the ear, shall He not
     hear?
   He who formed the eye, shall He not
     see?
10 He who instructs the nations, shall
      He not correct,
    He who teaches man knowledge?
11 The LORD knows the thoughts of man,
    That they *are* futile.

12 Blessed *is* the man whom You instruct,
      O LORD,
    And teach out of Your law,
13 That You may give him rest from the
      days of adversity,
    Until the pit is dug for the wicked.
14 For the LORD will not cast off His people,
    Nor will He forsake His inheritance.
15 But judgment will return to
      righteousness,
    And all the upright in heart will
      follow it.

16 Who will rise up for me against the
      evildoers?

Who will stand up for me against the
  workers of iniquity?
17 Unless the LORD *had been* my help,
    My soul would soon have settled in
      silence.
18 If I say, "My foot slips,"
    Your mercy, O LORD, will hold me up.
19 In the multitude of my anxieties
      within me,
    Your comforts delight my soul.

20 Shall the throne of iniquity, which
      devises evil by law,
    Have fellowship with You?
21 They gather together against the life
      of the righteous,
    And condemn innocent blood.
22 But the LORD has been my defense,
    And my God the rock of my refuge.
23 He has brought on them their own
      iniquity,
    And shall cut them off in their own
      wickedness;
    The LORD our God shall cut them off.

PSALM 95

A Call to Worship and Obedience

1 Oh come, let us sing to the LORD!
   Let us shout joyfully to the Rock of
     our salvation.
2 Let us come before His presence with
     thanksgiving;
   Let us shout joyfully to Him with
     psalms.
3 For the LORD *is* the great God,
   And the great King above all gods.
4 In His hand *are* the deep places of
     the earth;
   The heights of the hills *are* His also.
5 The sea *is* His, for He made it;
   And His hands formed the dry *land.*

6 Oh come, let us worship and bow
     down;
   Let us kneel before the LORD our
     Maker.
7 For He *is* our God,
   And we *are* the people of His pasture,
   And the sheep of His hand.

Today, if you will hear His voice:

8 "Do not harden your hearts, as in the
   rebellion,ᵃ
   As *in* the day of trialᵇ in the wilderness,
9 When your fathers tested Me;
   They tried Me, though they saw My
   work.
10 For forty years I was grieved with *that*
   generation,
   And said, 'It *is* a people who go astray
   in their hearts,
   And they do not know My ways.'
11 So I swore in My wrath,
   'They shall not enter My rest.' "

PSALM 96

A Song of Praise to God Coming in Judgment

1 Oh, sing to the LORD a new song!
   Sing to the LORD, all the earth.
2 Sing to the LORD, bless His name;
   Proclaim the good news of His
   salvation from day to day.
3 Declare His glory among the nations,
   His wonders among all peoples.

4 For the LORD *is* great and greatly to be
   praised;
   He *is* to be feared above all gods.
5 For all the gods of the peoples *are* idols,
   But the LORD made the heavens.
6 Honor and majesty *are* before Him;
   Strength and beauty *are* in His
   sanctuary.

7 Give to the LORD, O families of the
   peoples,
   Give to the LORD glory and strength.
8 Give to the LORD the glory *due* His name;
   Bring an offering, and come into His
   courts.
9 Oh, worship the LORD in the beauty
   of holiness!
   Tremble before Him, all the earth.

10 Say among the nations, "The LORD
   reigns;
   The world also is firmly established,
   It shall not be moved;
   He shall judge the peoples righteously."

11 Let the heavens rejoice, and let the
   earth be glad;

Let the sea roar, and all its fullness;
12 Let the field be joyful, and all that *is*
   in it.
   Then all the trees of the woods will
   rejoice before the LORD.
13 For He is coming, for He is coming to
   judge the earth.
   He shall judge the world with
   righteousness,
   And the peoples with His truth.

PSALM 97

A Song of Praise to the Sovereign LORD

1 The LORD reigns;
   Let the earth rejoice;
   Let the multitude of isles be glad!

2 Clouds and darkness surround Him;
   Righteousness and justice *are* the
   foundation of His throne.
3 A fire goes before Him,
   And burns up His enemies round about.
4 His lightnings light the world;
   The earth sees and trembles.
5 The mountains melt like wax at the
   presence of the LORD,
   At the presence of the Lord of the
   whole earth.
6 The heavens declare His righteousness,
   And all the peoples see His glory.

7 Let all be put to shame who serve
   carved images,
   Who boast of idols.
   Worship Him, all *you* gods.
8 Zion hears and is glad,
   And the daughters of Judah rejoice
   Because of Your judgments, O LORD.
9 For You, LORD, *are* most high above
   all the earth;
   You are exalted far above all gods.

10 You who love the LORD, hate evil!
   He preserves the souls of His saints;
   He delivers them out of the hand of
   the wicked.
11 Light is sown for the righteous,
   And gladness for the upright in heart.
12 Rejoice in the LORD, you righteous,

95:8 ᵃOr *Meribah* ᵇOr *Massah*

And give thanks at the remembrance of His holy name.ᵃ

PSALM 98

A Song of Praise to the LORD for His Salvation and Judgment

A Psalm.

1 Oh, sing to the LORD a new song!
For He has done marvelous things;
His right hand and His holy arm
have gained Him the victory.

2 The LORD has made known His salvation;
His righteousness He has revealed in the sight of the nations.

3 He has remembered His mercy and His faithfulness to the house of Israel;
All the ends of the earth have seen the salvation of our God.

4 Shout joyfully to the LORD, all the earth;
Break forth in song, rejoice, and sing praises.

5 Sing to the LORD with the harp,
With the harp and the sound of a psalm,

6 With trumpets and the sound of a horn;
Shout joyfully before the LORD, the King.

7 Let the sea roar, and all its fullness,
The world and those who dwell in it;

8 Let the rivers clap *their* hands;
Let the hills be joyful together before the LORD,

9 For He is coming to judge the earth.
With righteousness He shall judge the world,
And the peoples with equity.

PSALM 99

Praise to the LORD for His Holiness

1 The LORD reigns;
Let the peoples tremble!
He dwells *between* the cherubim;
Let the earth be moved!

2 The LORD *is* great in Zion,

97:12 ᵃOr *His holiness*

DEFENDER

*The LORD reigns;
let the peoples tremble!*

PSALM 99:1

Thomas Paine

COMMON SENSE BY THOMAS PAINE

In early 1776, Americans still hoped for reconciliation with Britain, and the British were preparing to take advantage of that sentiment with a generous offer for peace that many Americans would have welcomed. But then Thomas Paine anonymously published the political pamphlet *Common Sense* in January 1776, which presented the American colonists with a convincing argument for independence from British rule that resonated with the colonists. In the first year alone, over 500,000 copies were sold, and the revolution caught fire.

Paine structured *Common Sense* like a sermon and relied on biblical references and allusions, such as, "But where says some is the king of America? I'll tell you, friend, He reigns above," to make his case to the people. His vision stirred the colonists to strengthen their resolve. By spring 1776, there was significant support for American independence, and Virginia's convention voted to instruct their delegates to Congress to propose that the colonies formally declare their independence. On June 7, Richard Henry Lee moved that Congress declare the United Colonies to be free and independent, resulting in the first successful anti-colonial action in modern history.

And He *is* high above all the peoples.
3 Let them praise Your great and
     awesome name—
He *is* holy.

4 The King's strength also loves justice;
You have established equity;
You have executed justice and
     righteousness in Jacob.
5 Exalt the LORD our God,
And worship at His footstool—
He *is* holy.

6 Moses and Aaron were among His
     priests,
And Samuel was among those who
     called upon His name;
They called upon the LORD, and He
     answered them.
7 He spoke to them in the cloudy pillar;
They kept His testimonies and the
     ordinance He gave them.

8 You answered them, O LORD our God;
You were to them God-Who-Forgives,
Though You took vengeance on their
     deeds.
9 Exalt the LORD our God,
And worship at His holy hill;
For the LORD our God *is* holy.

PSALM 100

*A Song of Praise for the Faithfulness
to His People*

A Psalm of Thanksgiving.

1 Make a joyful shout to the LORD, all
     you lands!
2 Serve the LORD with gladness;
Come before His presence with singing.
3 Know that the LORD, He *is* God;
It is He *who* has made us, and not we
     ourselves;ᵃ
We are His people and the sheep of His
     pasture.

4 Enter into His gates with thanksgiving,
And into His courts with praise.
Be thankful to Him, *and* bless His name.
5 For the LORD *is* good;
His mercy *is* everlasting,
And His truth *endures* to all generations.

PSALM 101

Promised Faithfulness to the LORD

A Psalm of David.

1 I will sing of mercy and justice;
To You, O LORD, I will sing praises.

2 I will behave wisely in a perfect way.
Oh, when will You come to me?
I will walk within my house with a
     perfect heart.

3 I will set nothing wicked before my eyes;
I hate the work of those who fall away;
It shall not cling to me.
4 A perverse heart shall depart from me;
I will not know wickedness.

5 Whoever secretly slanders his neighbor,
Him I will destroy;
The one who has a haughty look and
     a proud heart,
Him I will not endure.

6 My eyes *shall be* on the faithful
     of the land,
That they may dwell with me;
He who walks in a perfect way,
He shall serve me.
7 He who works deceit shall not dwell
     within my house;
He who tells lies shall not continue
     in my presence.
8 Early I will destroy all the wicked of
     the land,
That I may cut off all the evildoers
     from the city of the LORD.

PSALM 102

The LORD's Eternal Love

A Prayer of the afflicted, when he is overwhelmed
and pours out his complaint before the LORD.

1 Hear my prayer, O LORD,
And let my cry come to You.
2 Do not hide Your face from me in the
     day of my trouble;
Incline Your ear to me;

100:3 ᵃFollowing Kethib, Septuagint, and Vulgate;
Qere, many Hebrew manuscripts, and Targum read
we are His.

In the day that I call, answer me
   speedily.

3 For my days are consumed like smoke,
   And my bones are burned like a hearth.
4 My heart is stricken and withered like
      grass,
   So that I forget to eat my bread.
5 Because of the sound of my groaning
   My bones cling to my skin.
6 I am like a pelican of the wilderness;
   I am like an owl of the desert.
7 I lie awake,
   And am like a sparrow alone on the
      housetop.

8 My enemies reproach me all day long;
   Those who deride me swear an oath
      against me.
9 For I have eaten ashes like bread,
   And mingled my drink with weeping,
10 Because of Your indignation and Your
      wrath;
   For You have lifted me up and cast
      me away.
11 My days *are* like a shadow that
      lengthens,
   And I wither away like grass.

12 But You, O LORD, shall endure forever,
   And the remembrance of Your name
      to all generations.
13 You will arise *and* have mercy on Zion;
   For the time to favor her,
   Yes, the set time, has come.
14 For Your servants take pleasure in
      her stones,
   And show favor to her dust.
15 So the nations shall fear the name
      of the LORD,
   And all the kings of the earth Your
      glory.
16 For the LORD shall build up Zion;
   He shall appear in His glory.
17 He shall regard the prayer of the
      destitute,
   And shall not despise their prayer.

18 This will be written for the generation
      to come,
   That a people yet to be created may
      praise the LORD.

19 For He looked down from the height of
      His sanctuary;
   From heaven the LORD viewed the earth,
20 To hear the groaning of the prisoner,
   To release those appointed to death,
21 To declare the name of the LORD in Zion,
   And His praise in Jerusalem,
22 When the peoples are gathered together,
   And the kingdoms, to serve the LORD.

23 He weakened my strength in the way;
   He shortened my days.
24 I said, "O my God,
   Do not take me away in the midst
      of my days;
   Your years *are* throughout all
      generations.
25 Of old You laid the foundation of the
      earth,
   And the heavens *are* the work of Your
      hands.
26 They will perish, but You will endure;
   Yes, they will all grow old like a
      garment;
   Like a cloak You will change them,
   And they will be changed.
27 But You *are* the same,
   And Your years will have no end.
28 The children of Your servants will
      continue,
   And their descendants will be
      established before You."

PSALM 103

Praise for the LORD's Mercies

A Psalm of David.

1 Bless the LORD, O my soul;
   And all that is within me, *bless* His
      holy name!
2 Bless the LORD, O my soul,
   And forget not all His benefits:
3 Who forgives all your iniquities,
   Who heals all your diseases,
4 Who redeems your life from destruction,
   Who crowns you with lovingkindness
      and tender mercies,
5 Who satisfies your mouth with good
      things,
   So that your youth is renewed like
      the eagle's.

6 The Lord executes righteousness
And justice for all who are oppressed.
7 He made known His ways to Moses,
His acts to the children of Israel.
8 The Lord *is* merciful and gracious,
Slow to anger, and abounding in mercy.
9 He will not always strive *with us,*
Nor will He keep *His anger* forever.
10 He has not dealt with us according
to our sins,
Nor punished us according to our
iniquities.

11 For as the heavens are high above
the earth,
So great is His mercy toward those
who fear Him;
12 As far as the east is from the west,
So far has He removed our
transgressions from us.
13 As a father pities *his* children,
So the Lord pities those who fear Him.
14 For He knows our frame;
He remembers that we *are* dust.

15 *As for* man, his days *are* like grass;
As a flower of the field, so he flourishes.
16 For the wind passes over it, and it is
gone,
And its place remembers it no more.[a]
17 But the mercy of the Lord *is* from
everlasting to everlasting
On those who fear Him,
And His righteousness to children's
children,
18 To such as keep His covenant,
And to those who remember His
commandments to do them.

19 The Lord has established His throne
in heaven,
And His kingdom rules over all.

20 Bless the Lord, you His angels,
Who excel in strength, who do His word,
Heeding the voice of His word.
21 Bless the Lord, all *you* His hosts,
You ministers of His, who do His
pleasure.
22 Bless the Lord, all His works,
In all places of His dominion.

Bless the Lord, O my soul!

PSALM 104

Praise to the Sovereign Lord for His Creation and Providence

1 Bless the Lord, O my soul!

O Lord my God, You are very great:
You are clothed with honor and majesty,
2 Who cover *Yourself* with light as *with a*
garment,
Who stretch out the heavens like a
curtain.

3 He lays the beams of His upper
chambers in the waters,
Who makes the clouds His chariot,
Who walks on the wings of the wind,
4 Who makes His angels spirits,
His ministers a flame of fire.

5 *You who* laid the foundations of the
earth,
So *that* it should not be moved forever,
6 You covered it with the deep as *with a*
garment;
The waters stood above the mountains.
7 At Your rebuke they fled;
At the voice of Your thunder they
hastened away.
8 They went up over the mountains;
They went down into the valleys,
To the place which You founded for
them.
9 You have set a boundary that they
may not pass over,
That they may not return to cover
the earth.

10 He sends the springs into the valleys;
They flow among the hills.
11 They give drink to every beast of the
field;
The wild donkeys quench their thirst.
12 By them the birds of the heavens have
their home;
They sing among the branches.
13 He waters the hills from His upper
chambers;
The earth is satisfied with the fruit
of Your works.

103:16 [a]Compare Job 7:10

14 He causes the grass to grow for the
     cattle,
   And vegetation for the service of man,
   That he may bring forth food from
     the earth,
15 And wine *that* makes glad the heart
     of man,
   Oil to make *his* face shine,
   And bread *which* strengthens man's
     heart.
16 The trees of the Lord are full *of sap,*
   The cedars of Lebanon which He
     planted,
17 Where the birds make their nests;
   The stork has her home in the fir trees.
18 The high hills *are* for the wild goats;
   The cliffs are a refuge for the rock
     badgers.ᵃ

19 He appointed the moon for seasons;
   The sun knows its going down.
20 You make darkness, and it is night,
   In which all the beasts of the forest
     creep about.
21 The young lions roar after their prey,
   And seek their food from God.
22 *When* the sun rises, they gather
     together
   And lie down in their dens.
23 Man goes out to his work
   And to his labor until the evening.

24 O Lord, how manifold are Your works!
   In wisdom You have made them all.
   The earth is full of Your possessions—
25 This great and wide sea,
   In which *are* innumerable teeming
     things,
   Living things both small and great.
26 There the ships sail about;
   There is that Leviathan
   Which You have made to play there.

27 These all wait for You,
   That You may give *them* their food in
     due season.
28 *What* You give them they gather in;
   You open Your hand, they are filled
     with good.
29 You hide Your face, they are troubled;
   You take away their breath, they die
     and return to their dust.

30 You send forth Your Spirit, they are
     created;
   And You renew the face of the earth.

31 May the glory of the Lord endure
     forever;
   May the Lord rejoice in His works.
32 He looks on the earth, and it trembles;
   He touches the hills, and they smoke.

33 I will sing to the Lord as long as I live;
   I will sing praise to my God while I
     have my being.
34 May my meditation be sweet to Him;
   I will be glad in the Lord.
35 May sinners be consumed from the
     earth,
   And the wicked be no more.

Bless the Lord, O my soul!
Praise the Lord!

PSALM 105

The Eternal Faithfulness of the Lord

1 Oh, give thanks to the Lord!
   Call upon His name;
   Make known His deeds among the
     peoples!
2 Sing to Him, sing psalms to Him;
   Talk of all His wondrous works!
3 Glory in His holy name;
   Let the hearts of those rejoice who seek
     the Lord!
4 Seek the Lord and His strength;
   Seek His face evermore!
5 Remember His marvelous works which
     He has done,
   His wonders, and the judgments of His
     mouth,
6 O seed of Abraham His servant,
   You children of Jacob, His chosen ones!

7 He *is* the Lord our God;
   His judgments *are* in all the earth.
8 He remembers His covenant forever,
   The word *which* He commanded, for a
     thousand generations,
9 *The covenant* which He made with
     Abraham,

104:18 ᵃOr *rock hyrax* (compare Leviticus 11:5)

And His oath to Isaac,
10 And confirmed it to Jacob for a statute,
To Israel *as* an everlasting covenant,
11 Saying, "To you I will give the land of Canaan
As the allotment of your inheritance,"
12 When they were few in number,
Indeed very few, and strangers in it.

13 When they went from one nation to another,
From *one* kingdom to another people,
14 He permitted no one to do them wrong;
Yes, He rebuked kings for their sakes,
15 *Saying,* "Do not touch My anointed ones,
And do My prophets no harm."

16 Moreover He called for a famine in the land;
He destroyed all the provision of bread.
17 He sent a man before them—
Joseph—*who* was sold as a slave.
18 They hurt his feet with fetters,
He was laid in irons.
19 Until the time that his word came to pass,
The word of the Lord tested him.
20 The king sent and released him,
The ruler of the people let him go free.
21 He made him lord of his house,
And ruler of all his possessions,
22 To bind his princes at his pleasure,
And teach his elders wisdom.

23 Israel also came into Egypt,
And Jacob dwelt in the land of Ham.
24 He increased His people greatly,
And made them stronger than their enemies.
25 He turned their heart to hate His people,
To deal craftily with His servants.

26 He sent Moses His servant,
And Aaron whom He had chosen.
27 They performed His signs among them,
And wonders in the land of Ham.
28 He sent darkness, and made *it* dark;
And they did not rebel against His word.
29 He turned their waters into blood,
And killed their fish.
30 Their land abounded with frogs,
Even in the chambers of their kings.

31 He spoke, and there came swarms of flies,
And lice in all their territory.
32 He gave them hail for rain,
And flaming fire in their land.
33 He struck their vines also, and their fig trees,
And splintered the trees of their territory.
34 He spoke, and locusts came,
Young locusts without number,
35 And ate up all the vegetation in their land,
And devoured the fruit of their ground.
36 He also destroyed all the firstborn in their land,
The first of all their strength.

37 He also brought them out with silver and gold,
And *there was* none feeble among His tribes.
38 Egypt was glad when they departed,
For the fear of them had fallen upon them.
39 He spread a cloud for a covering,
And fire to give light in the night.
40 *The people* asked, and He brought quail,
And satisfied them with the bread of heaven.
41 He opened the rock, and water gushed out;
It ran in the dry places *like* a river.

42 For He remembered His holy promise,
And Abraham His servant.
43 He brought out His people with joy,
His chosen ones with gladness.
44 He gave them the lands of the Gentiles,
And they inherited the labor of the nations,
45 That they might observe His statutes
And keep His laws.

Praise the Lord!

PSALM 106

Joy in Forgiveness of Israel's Sins

1 Praise the Lord!

Oh, give thanks to the Lord, for *He is* good!

For His mercy *endures* forever.

2 Who can utter the mighty acts of the
     LORD?
Who can declare all His praise?
3 Blessed *are* those who keep justice,
And he who does^a righteousness at all
     times!

4 Remember me, O LORD, with the favor
     You have toward Your people.
Oh, visit me with Your salvation,
5 That I may see the benefit of Your
     chosen ones,
That I may rejoice in the gladness of
     Your nation,
That I may glory with Your
     inheritance.

6 We have sinned with our fathers,
We have committed iniquity,
We have done wickedly.
7 Our fathers in Egypt did not
     understand Your wonders;
They did not remember the multitude
     of Your mercies,
But rebelled by the sea—the Red Sea.

8 Nevertheless He saved them for His
     name's sake,
That He might make His mighty
     power known.
9 He rebuked the Red Sea also, and it
     dried up;
So He led them through the depths,
As through the wilderness.
10 He saved them from the hand of him
     who hated *them,*
And redeemed them from the hand of
     the enemy.
11 The waters covered their enemies;
There was not one of them left.
12 Then they believed His words;
They sang His praise.

13 They soon forgot His works;
They did not wait for His counsel,
14 But lusted exceedingly in the
     wilderness,
And tested God in the desert.
15 And He gave them their request,
But sent leanness into their soul.

16 When they envied Moses in the camp,
And Aaron the saint of the LORD,
17 The earth opened up and swallowed
     Dathan,
And covered the faction of Abiram.
18 A fire was kindled in their company;
The flame burned up the wicked.

19 They made a calf in Horeb,
And worshiped the molded image.
20 Thus they changed their glory
Into the image of an ox that eats grass.
21 They forgot God their Savior,
Who had done great things in Egypt,
22 Wondrous works in the land of Ham,
Awesome things by the Red Sea.
23 Therefore He said that He would
     destroy them,
Had not Moses His chosen one stood
     before Him in the breach,
To turn away His wrath, lest He
     destroy *them.*

24 Then they despised the pleasant land;
They did not believe His word,
25 But complained in their tents,
And did not heed the voice of the LORD.
26 Therefore He raised His hand *in an
     oath* against them,
To overthrow them in the wilderness,
27 To overthrow their descendants
     among the nations,
And to scatter them in the lands.

28 They joined themselves also to Baal
     of Peor,
And ate sacrifices made to the dead.
29 Thus they provoked *Him* to anger with
     their deeds,
And the plague broke out among them.
30 Then Phinehas stood up and
     intervened,
And the plague was stopped.
31 And that was accounted to him for
     righteousness
To all generations forevermore.

32 They angered *Him* also at the waters
     of strife,^a

106:3 ^aSeptuagint, Syriac, Targum, and Vulgate read
those who do.   **106:32** ^aOr *Meribah*

So that it went ill with Moses on
    account of them;
33 Because they rebelled against His Spirit,
So that he spoke rashly with his lips.

34 They did not destroy the peoples,
Concerning whom the LORD had
    commanded them,
35 But they mingled with the Gentiles
And learned their works;
36 They served their idols,
Which became a snare to them.
37 They even sacrificed their sons
And their daughters to demons,
38 And shed innocent blood,
The blood of their sons and daughters,
Whom they sacrificed to the idols of
    Canaan;
And the land was polluted with blood.
39 Thus they were defiled by their own
    works,
And played the harlot by their own
    deeds.

40 Therefore the wrath of the LORD was
    kindled against His people,
So that He abhorred His own
    inheritance.
41 And He gave them into the hand of
    the Gentiles,
And those who hated them ruled over
    them.
42 Their enemies also oppressed them,
And they were brought into subjection
    under their hand.
43 Many times He delivered them;
But they rebelled in their counsel,
And were brought low for their iniquity.

44 Nevertheless He regarded their
    affliction,
When He heard their cry;
45 And for their sake He remembered His
    covenant,
And relented according to the
    multitude of His mercies.
46 He also made them to be pitied
By all those who carried them away
    captive.

47 Save us, O LORD our God,
And gather us from among the Gentiles,

To give thanks to Your holy name,
To triumph in Your praise.

48 Blessed *be* the LORD God of Israel
From everlasting to everlasting!
And let all the people say, "Amen!"

Praise the LORD!

Book Five: Psalms 107—150

PSALM 107

Thanksgiving to the LORD for His Great Works of Deliverance

1 Oh, give thanks to the LORD, for *He is*
    good!
For His mercy *endures* forever.
2 Let the redeemed of the LORD say *so,*
Whom He has redeemed from the
    hand of the enemy,
3 And gathered out of the lands,
From the east and from the west,
From the north and from the south.

4 They wandered in the wilderness in
    a desolate way;
They found no city to dwell in.
5 Hungry and thirsty,
Their soul fainted in them.
6 Then they cried out to the LORD in
    their trouble,
And He delivered them out of their
    distresses.
7 And He led them forth by the right
    way,
That they might go to a city for a
    dwelling place.
8 Oh, that *men* would give thanks to the
    LORD *for* His goodness,
And *for* His wonderful works to the
    children of men!
9 For He satisfies the longing soul,
And fills the hungry soul with
    goodness.

10 Those who sat in darkness and in the
    shadow of death,
Bound in affliction and irons—
11 Because they rebelled against the
    words of God,

And despised the counsel of the Most
   High,
12 Therefore He brought down their heart
   with labor;
   They fell down, and *there was* none
   to help.
13 Then they cried out to the LORD in
   their trouble,
   And He saved them out of their
   distresses.
14 He brought them out of darkness
   and the shadow of death,
   And broke their chains in pieces.
15 Oh, that *men* would give thanks to the
   LORD *for* His goodness,
   And *for* His wonderful works to the
   children of men!
16 For He has broken the gates of bronze,
   And cut the bars of iron in two.

17 Fools, because of their transgression,
   And because of their iniquities, were
   afflicted.
18 Their soul abhorred all manner of
   food,
   And they drew near to the gates of
   death.
19 Then they cried out to the LORD in
   their trouble,
   And He saved them out of their
   distresses.
20 He sent His word and healed them,
   And delivered *them* from their
   destructions.
21 Oh, that *men* would give thanks to
   the LORD *for* His goodness,
   And *for* His wonderful works to the
   children of men!
22 Let them sacrifice the sacrifices of
   thanksgiving,
   And declare His works with rejoicing.

23 Those who go down to the sea in ships,
   Who do business on great waters,
24 They see the works of the LORD,
   And His wonders in the deep.
25 For He commands and raises the
   stormy wind,
   Which lifts up the waves of the sea.
26 They mount up to the heavens,
   They go down again to the depths;
   Their soul melts because of trouble.

27 They reel to and fro, and stagger like
   a drunken man,
   And are at their wits' end.
28 Then they cry out to the LORD in their
   trouble,
   And He brings them out of their
   distresses.
29 He calms the storm,
   So that its waves are still.
30 Then they are glad because they are
   quiet;
   So He guides them to their desired
   haven.
31 Oh, that *men* would give thanks to
   the LORD *for* His goodness,
   And *for* His wonderful works to the
   children of men!
32 Let them exalt Him also in the
   assembly of the people,
   And praise Him in the company of
   the elders.

33 He turns rivers into a wilderness,
   And the watersprings into dry ground;
34 A fruitful land into barrenness,
   For the wickedness of those who dwell
   in it.
35 He turns a wilderness into pools of
   water,
   And dry land into watersprings.
36 There He makes the hungry dwell,
   That they may establish a city for a
   dwelling place,
37 And sow fields and plant vineyards,
   That they may yield a fruitful harvest.
38 He also blesses them, and they
   multiply greatly;
   And He does not let their cattle
   decrease.

39 When they are diminished and
   brought low
   Through oppression, affliction,
   and sorrow,
40 He pours contempt on princes,
   And causes them to wander in the
   wilderness *where there is* no way;
41 Yet He sets the poor on high, far from
   affliction,
   And makes *their* families like a flock.
42 The righteous see *it* and rejoice,
   And all iniquity stops its mouth.

43 Whoever *is* wise will observe these
   things,
   And they will understand the
   lovingkindness of the LORD.

PSALM 108

Assurance of God's Victory over Enemies

A Song. A Psalm of David.

1 O God, my heart is steadfast;
  I will sing and give praise, even with
  my glory.
2 Awake, lute and harp!
  I will awaken the dawn.
3 I will praise You, O LORD, among the
  peoples,
  And I will sing praises to You among
  the nations.
4 For Your mercy *is* great above the
  heavens,
  And Your truth *reaches* to the clouds.

5 Be exalted, O God, above the heavens,
  And Your glory above all the earth;
6 That Your beloved may be delivered,
  Save *with* Your right hand, and
  hear me.

7 God has spoken in His holiness:
  "I will rejoice;
  I will divide Shechem
  And measure out the Valley of
  Succoth.
8 Gilead *is* Mine; Manasseh *is* Mine;
  Ephraim also *is* the helmet for My
  head;
  Judah *is* My lawgiver.
9 Moab *is* My washpot;
  Over Edom I will cast My shoe;
  Over Philistia I will triumph."

10 Who will bring me *into* the strong city?
   Who will lead me to Edom?
11 *Is it* not You, O God, *who* cast us off?
   And You, O God, *who* did not go out
   with our armies?
12 Give us help from trouble,
   For the help of man is useless.
13 Through God we will do valiantly,
   For *it is* He *who* shall tread down our
   enemies.ᵃ

PSALM 109

Plea for Judgment of False Accusers

To the Chief Musician. A Psalm of David.

1 Do not keep silent,
  O God of my praise!
2 For the mouth of the wicked and the
  mouth of the deceitful
  Have opened against me;
  They have spoken against me with a
  lying tongue.
3 They have also surrounded me with
  words of hatred,
  And fought against me without a cause.
4 In return for my love they are my
  accusers,
  But I *give myself to* prayer.
5 Thus they have rewarded me evil for
  good,
  And hatred for my love.

6 Set a wicked man over him,
  And let an accuserᵃ stand at his right
  hand.
7 When he is judged, let him be found
  guilty,
  And let his prayer become sin.
8 Let his days be few,
  And let another take his office.
9 Let his children be fatherless,
  And his wife a widow.
10 Let his children continually be
   vagabonds, and beg;
   Let them seek *their bread*ᵃ also from
   their desolate places.
11 Let the creditor seize all that he has,
   And let strangers plunder his labor.
12 Let there be none to extend mercy to
   him,
   Nor let there be any to favor his
   fatherless children.
13 Let his posterity be cut off,
   And in the generation following let
   their name be blotted out.

14 Let the iniquity of his fathers be
   remembered before the LORD,

108:13 ᵃCompare verses 6–13 with 60:5–12
109:6 ᵃHebrew *satan*   **109:10** ᵃFollowing
Masoretic Text and Targum; Septuagint and Vulgate
read *be cast out.*

And let not the sin of his mother be blotted out.

15 Let them be continually before the Lord,
That He may cut off the memory of them from the earth;

16 Because he did not remember to show mercy,
But persecuted the poor and needy man,
That he might even slay the broken in heart.

17 As he loved cursing, so let it come to him;
As he did not delight in blessing, so let it be far from him.

18 As he clothed himself with cursing as with his garment,
So let it enter his body like water,
And like oil into his bones.

19 Let it be to him like the garment which covers him,
And for a belt with which he girds himself continually.

20 *Let* this *be* the Lord's reward to my accusers,
And to those who speak evil against my person.

21 But You, O God the Lord,
Deal with me for Your name's sake;
Because Your mercy *is* good, deliver me.

22 For I *am* poor and needy,
And my heart is wounded within me.

23 I am gone like a shadow when it lengthens;
I am shaken off like a locust.

24 My knees are weak through fasting,
And my flesh is feeble from lack of fatness.

25 I also have become a reproach to them;
When they look at me, they shake their heads.

26 Help me, O Lord my God!
Oh, save me according to Your mercy,

27 That they may know that this *is* Your hand—
That You, Lord, have done it!

28 Let them curse, but You bless;
When they arise, let them be ashamed,
But let Your servant rejoice.

29 Let my accusers be clothed with shame,

And let them cover themselves with their own disgrace as with a mantle.

30 I will greatly praise the Lord with my mouth;
Yes, I will praise Him among the multitude.

31 For He shall stand at the right hand of the poor,
To save *him* from those who condemn him.

PSALM 110

Announcement of the Messiah's Reign

A Psalm of David.

1 The Lord said to my Lord,
"Sit at My right hand,
Till I make Your enemies Your footstool."

2 The Lord shall send the rod of Your strength out of Zion.
Rule in the midst of Your enemies!

3 Your people *shall be* volunteers
In the day of Your power;
In the beauties of holiness, from the womb of the morning,
You have the dew of Your youth.

4 The Lord has sworn
And will not relent,
"You *are* a priest forever
According to the order of Melchizedek."

5 The Lord *is* at Your right hand;
He shall execute kings in the day of His wrath.

6 He shall judge among the nations,
He shall fill *the places* with dead bodies,
He shall execute the heads of many countries.

7 He shall drink of the brook by the wayside;
Therefore He shall lift up the head.

PSALM 111

Praise to God for His Faithfulness and Justice

1 Praise the Lord!

I will praise the Lord with *my* whole heart,

In the assembly of the upright and *in* the congregation.

2 The works of the LORD *are* great,
Studied by all who have pleasure in them.
3 His work *is* honorable and glorious,
And His righteousness endures forever.
4 He has made His wonderful works to be remembered;
The LORD *is* gracious and full of compassion.
5 He has given food to those who fear Him;
He will ever be mindful of His covenant.
6 He has declared to His people the power of His works,
In giving them the heritage of the nations.

7 The works of His hands *are* verity and justice;
All His precepts *are* sure.
8 They stand fast forever and ever,
And are done in truth and uprightness.
9 He has sent redemption to His people;
He has commanded His covenant forever:
Holy and awesome *is* His name.

10 The fear of the LORD *is* the beginning of wisdom;
A good understanding have all those who do *His commandments.*
His praise endures forever.

PSALM 112

The Blessed State of the Righteous

1 Praise the LORD!

Blessed *is* the man *who* fears the LORD,
Who delights greatly in His commandments.

2 His descendants will be mighty on earth;
The generation of the upright will be blessed.
3 Wealth and riches *will be* in his house,
And his righteousness endures forever.

> **Grover Cleveland** placed his hand on Psalm 112:4–10 as he took the presidential oath of office in 1885.

4 Unto the upright there arises light in the darkness;
He is gracious, and full of compassion, and righteous.
5 A good man deals graciously and lends;
He will guide his affairs with discretion.
6 Surely he will never be shaken;
The righteous will be in everlasting remembrance.
7 He will not be afraid of evil tidings;
His heart is steadfast, trusting in the LORD.
8 His heart *is* established;
He will not be afraid,
Until he sees *his desire* upon his enemies.

9 He has dispersed abroad,
He has given to the poor;
His righteousness endures forever;
His horn will be exalted with honor.
10 The wicked will see *it* and be grieved;
He will gnash his teeth and melt away;
The desire of the wicked shall perish.

PSALM 113

The Majesty and Condescension of God

1 Praise the LORD!

Praise, O servants of the LORD,
Praise the name of the LORD!
2 Blessed be the name of the LORD
From this time forth and forevermore!
3 From the rising of the sun to its going down
The LORD's name *is* to be praised.

4 The LORD *is* high above all nations,
His glory above the heavens.
5 Who *is* like the LORD our God,
Who dwells on high,
6 Who humbles Himself to behold
The things that are in the heavens and in the earth?

7 He raises the poor out of the dust,
And lifts the needy out of the ash heap,

8 That He may seat *him* with princes—
With the princes of His people.
9 He grants the barren woman a home,
Like a joyful mother of children.

Praise the LORD!

PSALM 114

The Power of God in His Deliverance of Israel

1 When Israel went out of Egypt,
The house of Jacob from a people
   of strange language,
2 Judah became His sanctuary,
And Israel His dominion.

3 The sea saw *it* and fled;
Jordan turned back.
4 The mountains skipped like rams,
The little hills like lambs.
5 What ails you, O sea, that you fled?
O Jordan, *that* you turned back?
6 O mountains, *that* you skipped like
   rams?
O little hills, like lambs?

7 Tremble, O earth, at the presence of
   the Lord,
At the presence of the God of Jacob,
8 Who turned the rock *into* a pool of
   water,
The flint into a fountain of waters.

PSALM 115

*The Futility of Idols and the Trustworthiness
of God*

1 Not unto us, O LORD, not unto us,
But to Your name give glory,
Because of Your mercy,
Because of Your truth.
2 Why should the Gentiles say,
"So where *is* their God?"

3 But our God *is* in heaven;
He does whatever He pleases.
4 Their idols *are* silver and gold,
The work of men's hands.
5 They have mouths, but they do not
   speak;
Eyes they have, but they do not see;
6 They have ears, but they do not hear;

Noses they have, but they do not smell;
7 They have hands, but they do not
   handle;
Feet they have, but they do not walk;
Nor do they mutter through their throat.
8 Those who make them are like them;
So is everyone who trusts in them.

9 O Israel, trust in the LORD;
He *is* their help and their shield.
10 O house of Aaron, trust in the LORD;
He *is* their help and their shield.
11 You who fear the LORD, trust in the LORD;
He *is* their help and their shield.

12 The LORD has been mindful of *us;*
He will bless us;
He will bless the house of Israel;
He will bless the house of Aaron.
13 He will bless those who fear the LORD,
Both small and great.

14 May the LORD give you increase more
   and more,
You and your children.
15 *May* you *be* blessed by the LORD,
Who made heaven and earth.

16 The heaven, *even* the heavens, *are*
   the LORD's;
But the earth He has given to the
   children of men.
17 The dead do not praise the LORD,
Nor any who go down into silence.
18 But we will bless the LORD
From this time forth and forevermore.

Praise the LORD!

PSALM 116

Thanksgiving for Deliverance from Death

1 I love the LORD, because He has heard
My voice *and* my supplications.
2 Because He has inclined His ear to me,
Therefore I will call *upon Him* as long
   as I live.

3 The pains of death surrounded me,
And the pangs of Sheol laid hold
   of me;
I found trouble and sorrow.

4   Then I called upon the name of the
      LORD:
      "O LORD, I implore You, deliver my soul!"

5   Gracious *is* the LORD, and righteous;
      Yes, our God *is* merciful.
6   The LORD preserves the simple;
      I was brought low, and He saved me.
7   Return to your rest, O my soul,
      For the LORD has dealt bountifully
        with you.

8   For You have delivered my soul
        from death,
      My eyes from tears,
      And my feet from falling.
9   I will walk before the LORD
      In the land of the living.
10   I believed, therefore I spoke,
      "I am greatly afflicted."
11   I said in my haste,
      "All men *are* liars."

12   What shall I render to the LORD
      For all His benefits toward me?
13   I will take up the cup of salvation,
      And call upon the name of the LORD.
14   I will pay my vows to the LORD
      Now in the presence of all His people.

15   Precious in the sight of the LORD
      Is the death of His saints.

16   O LORD, truly I *am* Your servant;
      I *am* Your servant, the son of Your
        maidservant;
      You have loosed my bonds.
17   I will offer to You the sacrifice of
        thanksgiving,
      And will call upon the name of the LORD.

18   I will pay my vows to the LORD
      Now in the presence of all His people,
19   In the courts of the LORD's house,
      In the midst of you, O Jerusalem.

      Praise the LORD!

PSALM 117

Let All Peoples Praise the LORD

1   Praise the LORD, all you Gentiles!
      Laud Him, all you peoples!

2   For His merciful kindness is great
        toward us,
      And the truth of the LORD *endures*
        forever.

      Praise the LORD!

PSALM 118

Praise to God for His Everlasting Mercy

1   Oh, give thanks to the LORD, for
      He is good!
      For His mercy *endures* forever.

2   Let Israel now say,
      "His mercy *endures* forever."
3   Let the house of Aaron now say,
      "His mercy *endures* forever."
4   Let those who fear the LORD now say,
      "His mercy *endures* forever."

5   I called on the LORD in distress;
      The LORD answered me *and set me* in
        a broad place.
6   The LORD *is* on my side;
      I will not fear.
      What can man do to me?
7   The LORD is for me among those who
        help me;
      Therefore I shall see *my desire* on those
        who hate me.
8   *It is* better to trust in the LORD
      Than to put confidence in man.
9   *It is* better to trust in the LORD
      Than to put confidence in princes.

10   All nations surrounded me,
      But in the name of the LORD I will
        destroy them.

> **Rutherford B. Hayes** placed his hand on Psalm 118:11–13 as he took the presidential oath of office in 1877.

11   They surrounded me,
      Yes, they surrounded me;
      But in the name of the LORD I will
        destroy them.
12   They surrounded me like bees;
      They were quenched like a fire of
        thorns;

For in the name of the LORD I will
destroy them.
13 You pushed me violently, that I might
fall,
But the LORD helped me.
14 The LORD *is* my strength and song,
And He has become my salvation.ᵃ

15 The voice of rejoicing and salvation
Is in the tents of the righteous;
The right hand of the LORD does
valiantly.
16 The right hand of the LORD is exalted;
The right hand of the LORD does
valiantly.
17 I shall not die, but live,
And declare the works of the LORD.
18 The LORD has chastened me severely,
But He has not given me over to death.

19 Open to me the gates of righteousness;
I will go through them,
And I will praise the LORD.
20 This is the gate of the LORD,
Through which the righteous shall enter.

21 I will praise You,
For You have answered me,
And have become my salvation.

22 The stone *which* the builders rejected
Has become the chief cornerstone.
23 This was the LORD's doing;
It *is* marvelous in our eyes.
24 This *is* the day the LORD has made;
We will rejoice and be glad in it.

25 Save now, I pray, O LORD;
O LORD, I pray, send now prosperity.
26 Blessed *is* he who comes in the name
of the LORD!
We have blessed you from the house
of the LORD.
27 God *is* the LORD,
And He has given us light;
Bind the sacrifice with cords to the
horns of the altar.
28 You *are* my God, and I will praise You;
You are my God, I will exalt You.

29 Oh, give thanks to the LORD, for *He is*
good!
For His mercy *endures* forever.

Woodrow Wilson placed his hand on
Psalm 119 as he took the presidential oath
of office in 1913.

PSALM 119

*Meditations on the Excellencies of the Word
of God*

א   ALEPH
1 Blessed *are* the undefiled in the way,
Who walk in the law of the LORD!
2 Blessed *are* those who keep His
testimonies,
Who seek Him with the whole heart!
3 They also do no iniquity;
They walk in His ways.
4 You have commanded *us*
To keep Your precepts diligently.
5 Oh, that my ways were directed
To keep Your statutes!
6 Then I would not be ashamed,
When I look into all Your
commandments.
7 I will praise You with uprightness of
heart,
When I learn Your righteous
judgments.
8 I will keep Your statutes;
Oh, do not forsake me utterly!

ב   BETH
9 How can a young man cleanse his way?
By taking heed according to Your word.
10 With my whole heart I have sought
You;
Oh, let me not wander from Your
commandments!
11 Your word I have hidden in my heart,
That I might not sin against You.
12 Blessed *are* You, O LORD!
Teach me Your statutes.
13 With my lips I have declared
All the judgments of Your mouth.
14 I have rejoiced in the way of Your
testimonies,
As *much as* in all riches.
15 I will meditate on Your precepts,
And contemplate Your ways.

118:14 ᵃCompare Exodus 15:2

16 I will delight myself in Your statutes;
I will not forget Your word.

ב GIMEL
17 Deal bountifully with Your servant,
That I may live and keep Your word.
18 Open my eyes, that I may see
Wondrous things from Your law.
19 I *am* a stranger in the earth;
Do not hide Your commandments
from me.
20 My soul breaks with longing
For Your judgments at all times.
21 You rebuke the proud—the cursed,
Who stray from Your commandments.
22 Remove from me reproach and
contempt,
For I have kept Your testimonies.
23 Princes also sit *and* speak against me,
But Your servant meditates on Your
statutes.
24 Your testimonies also *are* my delight
And my counselors.

ד DALETH
25 My soul clings to the dust;
Revive me according to Your word.
26 I have declared my ways, and You
answered me;
Teach me Your statutes.

MORAL STRENGTH
How can a young man cleanse his way?
PSALM 119:9

The Bible as a School Textbook
Fisher Ames (1758–1808), a Founder and politician
who helped formulate the Bill of Rights, stated:

*We have a dangerous trend beginning to take
place in our education. We're starting to put
more and more textbooks into our schools. . . .
We've become accustomed of late of putting little books into the hands of children containing
fables and moral lessons. . . .*

*We are spending less time in the classroom on
the Bible, which should be the principal text of
our schools. . . . The Bible states these great
moral lessons better than any other manmade
book.*

27 Make me understand the way of Your
precepts;
So shall I meditate on Your wonderful
works.
28 My soul melts from heaviness;
Strengthen me according to Your word.
29 Remove from me the way of lying,
And grant me Your law graciously.
30 I have chosen the way of truth;
Your judgments I have laid *before me.*
31 I cling to Your testimonies;
O LORD, do not put me to shame!
32 I will run the course of Your
commandments,
For You shall enlarge my heart.

ה HE
33 Teach me, O LORD, the way of Your
statutes,
And I shall keep it *to* the end.
34 Give me understanding, and I shall
keep Your law;
Indeed, I shall observe it with *my*
whole heart.
35 Make me walk in the path of Your
commandments,
For I delight in it.
36 Incline my heart to Your testimonies,
And not to covetousness.
37 Turn away my eyes from looking at
worthless things,
And revive me in Your way.[a]
38 Establish Your word to Your servant,
Who *is devoted* to fearing You.
39 Turn away my reproach which I dread,
For Your judgments *are* good.
40 Behold, I long for Your precepts;
Revive me in Your righteousness.

ו WAW
41 Let Your mercies come also to me,
O LORD—
Your salvation according to Your word.
42 So shall I have an answer for him
who reproaches me,
For I trust in Your word.
43 And take not the word of truth utterly
out of my mouth,
For I have hoped in Your ordinances.

119:37 [a]Following Masoretic Text, Septuagint, and
Vulgate; Targum reads *Your words.*

44 So shall I keep Your law continually,
   Forever and ever.
45 And I will walk at liberty,
   For I seek Your precepts.
46 I will speak of Your testimonies also
      before kings,
   And will not be ashamed.
47 And I will delight myself in Your
      commandments,
   Which I love.
48 My hands also I will lift up to Your
      commandments,
   Which I love,
   And I will meditate on Your statutes.

ז ZAYIN
49 Remember the word to Your servant,
   Upon which You have caused me to
      hope.
50 This *is* my comfort in my affliction,
   For Your word has given me life.
51 The proud have me in great derision,
   Yet I do not turn aside from Your law.
52 I remembered Your judgments of old,
      O LORD,
   And have comforted myself.
53 Indignation has taken hold of me
   Because of the wicked, who forsake
      Your law.
54 Your statutes have been my songs
   In the house of my pilgrimage.
55 I remember Your name in the night,
      O LORD,
   And I keep Your law.
56 This has become mine,
   Because I kept Your precepts.

ח HETH
57 *You are* my portion, O LORD;
   I have said that I would keep Your
      words.
58 I entreated Your favor with *my* whole
      heart;
   Be merciful to me according to Your
      word.
59 I thought about my ways,
   And turned my feet to Your testimonies.
60 I made haste, and did not delay
   To keep Your commandments.
61 The cords of the wicked have
      bound me,
   But I have not forgotten Your law.

62 At midnight I will rise to give thanks
      to You,
   Because of Your righteous judgments.
63 I *am* a companion of all who fear You,
   And of those who keep Your precepts.
64 The earth, O LORD, is full of Your mercy;
   Teach me Your statutes.

ט TETH
65 You have dealt well with Your servant,
   O LORD, according to Your word.
66 Teach me good judgment and
      knowledge,
   For I believe Your commandments.
67 Before I was afflicted I went astray,
   But now I keep Your word.
68 You *are* good, and do good;
   Teach me Your statutes.
69 The proud have forged a lie against me,
   But I will keep Your precepts with *my*
      whole heart.
70 Their heart is as fat as grease,
   But I delight in Your law.
71 *It is* good for me that I have been
      afflicted,
   That I may learn Your statutes.
72 The law of Your mouth *is* better to me
   Than thousands of *coins of* gold and
      silver.

י YOD
73 Your hands have made me and
      fashioned me;
   Give me understanding, that I may
      learn Your commandments.
74 Those who fear You will be glad when
      they see me,
   Because I have hoped in Your word.
75 I know, O LORD, that Your judgments
      are right,
   And *that* in faithfulness You have
      afflicted me.
76 Let, I pray, Your merciful kindness be
      for my comfort,
   According to Your word to Your servant.
77 Let Your tender mercies come to me,
      that I may live;
   For Your law *is* my delight.
78 Let the proud be ashamed,
   For they treated me wrongfully with
      falsehood;
   But I will meditate on Your precepts.

⁷⁹ Let those who fear You turn to me,
Those who know Your testimonies.
⁸⁰ Let my heart be blameless regarding
Your statutes,
That I may not be ashamed.

כ KAPH
⁸¹ My soul faints for Your salvation,
But I hope in Your word.
⁸² My eyes fail *from searching* Your word,
Saying, "When will You comfort me?"
⁸³ For I have become like a wineskin in
smoke,
Yet I do not forget Your statutes.
⁸⁴ How many *are* the days of Your servant?
When will You execute judgment on
those who persecute me?
⁸⁵ The proud have dug pits for me,
Which *is* not according to Your law.
⁸⁶ All Your commandments *are* faithful;
They persecute me wrongfully;
Help me!
⁸⁷ They almost made an end of me on
earth,
But I did not forsake Your precepts.
⁸⁸ Revive me according to Your
lovingkindness,
So that I may keep the testimony of
Your mouth.

ל LAMED
⁸⁹ Forever, O Lord,
Your word is settled in heaven.
⁹⁰ Your faithfulness *endures* to all
generations;
You established the earth, and it abides.
⁹¹ They continue this day according to
Your ordinances,
For all *are* Your servants.
⁹² Unless Your law *had been* my delight,
I would then have perished in my
affliction.
⁹³ I will never forget Your precepts,
For by them You have given me life.
⁹⁴ I *am* Yours, save me;
For I have sought Your precepts.
⁹⁵ The wicked wait for me to destroy me,
But I will consider Your testimonies.
⁹⁶ I have seen the consummation of all
perfection,
But Your commandment *is* exceedingly
broad.

מ MEM
⁹⁷ Oh, how I love Your law!
It *is* my meditation all the day.
⁹⁸ You, through Your commandments,
make me wiser than my enemies;
For they *are* ever with me.
⁹⁹ I have more understanding than all
my teachers,
For Your testimonies *are* my meditation.
¹⁰⁰ I understand more than the ancients,
Because I keep Your precepts.
¹⁰¹ I have restrained my feet from every
evil way,
That I may keep Your word.
¹⁰² I have not departed from Your
judgments,
For You Yourself have taught me.
¹⁰³ How sweet are Your words to my taste,
Sweeter than honey to my mouth!
¹⁰⁴ Through Your precepts I get
understanding;
Therefore I hate every false way.

נ NUN
¹⁰⁵ Your word *is* a lamp to my feet
And a light to my path.
¹⁰⁶ I have sworn and confirmed
That I will keep Your righteous
judgments.
¹⁰⁷ I am afflicted very much;
Revive me, O Lord, according to Your
word.
¹⁰⁸ Accept, I pray, the freewill offerings
of my mouth, O Lord,
And teach me Your judgments.
¹⁰⁹ My life *is* continually in my hand,
Yet I do not forget Your law.
¹¹⁰ The wicked have laid a snare for me,
Yet I have not strayed from Your
precepts.
¹¹¹ Your testimonies I have taken as a
heritage forever,
For they *are* the rejoicing of my heart.
¹¹² I have inclined my heart to perform
Your statutes
Forever, to the very end.

ס SAMEK
¹¹³ I hate the double-minded,
But I love Your law.
¹¹⁴ You *are* my hiding place and my shield;
I hope in Your word.

115 Depart from me, you evildoers,
For I will keep the commandments
of my God!
116 Uphold me according to Your word,
that I may live;
And do not let me be ashamed of
my hope.
117 Hold me up, and I shall be safe,
And I shall observe Your statutes
continually.
118 You reject all those who stray from
Your statutes,
For their deceit *is* falsehood.
119 You put away all the wicked of the
earth *like* dross;
Therefore I love Your testimonies.
120 My flesh trembles for fear of You,
And I am afraid of Your judgments.

ע   AYIN
121 I have done justice and righteousness;
Do not leave me to my oppressors.
122 Be surety for Your servant for good;
Do not let the proud oppress me.
123 My eyes fail *from seeking* Your
salvation
And Your righteous word.

124 Deal with Your servant according
to Your mercy,
And teach me Your statutes.
125 I *am* Your servant;
Give me understanding,
That I may know Your testimonies.
126 *It is* time for *You* to act, O LORD,
For they have regarded Your law as
void.
127 Therefore I love Your commandments
More than gold, yes, than fine gold!
128 Therefore all *Your* precepts *concerning*
all *things*
I consider *to be* right;
I hate every false way.

פ   PE
129 Your testimonies are wonderful;
Therefore my soul keeps them.
130 The entrance of Your words gives
light;
It gives understanding to the simple.
131 I opened my mouth and panted,
For I longed for Your commandments.
132 Look upon me and be merciful to me,
As Your custom *is* toward those who
love Your name.

TRUTH

*Your word is a lamp to my
feet and a light to my path.*

PSALM 119:105

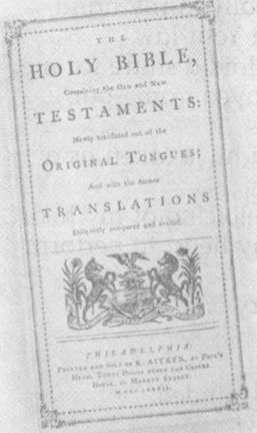

Aitken Bible 1782

THE BIBLE OF THE REVOLUTION

Until the American Revolution, America's Bibles had been shipped in from England. When that supply was cut off and supplies dwindled in 1777, Congress resolved to import 20,000 copies of the Bible from other countries, based on a Congressional committee's determination that "the use of the Bible is so universal and its importance so great."

That resolution was not acted upon, though, and the need remained. Robert Aitken of Philadelphia published a New Testament in 1777 and followed it with three additional editions. In early 1781, he petitioned Congress and received the approval to print the entire Bible. Thus originated the first American printing of the English Bible in 1782, what has come to be called the "Bible of the Revolution."

W. P. Strickland, an early American historian, said of this Bible publication: "Who, in view of this fact, will call in question the assertion that this is a Bible nation? Who will charge the government with indifference to religion when the first Congress of the States assumed all the rights and performed all the duties of a Bible society long before such an institution had an existence in the world?"

133 Direct my steps by Your word,
And let no iniquity have dominion
over me.
134 Redeem me from the oppression of man,
That I may keep Your precepts.
135 Make Your face shine upon Your
servant,
And teach me Your statutes.
136 Rivers of water run down from my eyes,
Because *men* do not keep Your law.

צ   TSADDE
137 Righteous *are* You, O LORD,
And upright *are* Your judgments.
138 Your testimonies, *which* You have
commanded,
Are righteous and very faithful.
139 My zeal has consumed me,
Because my enemies have forgotten
Your words.
140 Your word *is* very pure;
Therefore Your servant loves it.
141 I *am* small and despised,
Yet I do not forget Your precepts.
142 Your righteousness *is* an everlasting
righteousness,
And Your law *is* truth.
143 Trouble and anguish have
overtaken me,
Yet Your commandments *are* my
delights.
144 The righteousness of Your testimonies
is everlasting;
Give me understanding, and I shall
live.

ק   QOPH
145 I cry out with *my* whole heart;
Hear me, O LORD!
I will keep Your statutes.
146 I cry out to You;
Save me, and I will keep Your
testimonies.
147 I rise before the dawning of the
morning,
And cry for help;
I hope in Your word.
148 My eyes are awake through the *night*
watches,
That I may meditate on Your word.
149 Hear my voice according to Your
lovingkindness;

O LORD, revive me according to Your
justice.
150 They draw near who follow after
wickedness;
They are far from Your law.
151 You *are* near, O LORD,
And all Your commandments *are* truth.
152 Concerning Your testimonies,
I have known of old that You have
founded them forever.

ר   RESH
153 Consider my affliction and deliver me,
For I do not forget Your law.
154 Plead my cause and redeem me;
Revive me according to Your word.
155 Salvation *is* far from the wicked,
For they do not seek Your statutes.
156 Great *are* Your tender mercies, O LORD;
Revive me according to Your judgments.
157 Many *are* my persecutors and my
enemies,
Yet I do not turn from Your testimonies.
158 I see the treacherous, and am disgusted,
Because they do not keep Your word.
159 Consider how I love Your precepts;
Revive me, O LORD, according to Your
lovingkindness.
160 The entirety of Your word *is* truth,
And every one of Your righteous
judgments *endures* forever.

ש   SHIN
161 Princes persecute me without a cause,
But my heart stands in awe of Your
word.
162 I rejoice at Your word
As one who finds great treasure.
163 I hate and abhor lying,
But I love Your law.
164 Seven times a day I praise You,
Because of Your righteous judgments.
165 Great peace have those who love Your
law,
And nothing causes them to stumble.
166 LORD, I hope for Your salvation,
And I do Your commandments.
167 My soul keeps Your testimonies,
And I love them exceedingly.
168 I keep Your precepts and Your
testimonies,
For all my ways *are* before You.

ת   TAU

169 Let my cry come before You, O Lord;
     Give me understanding according to
        Your word.
170 Let my supplication come before You;
     Deliver me according to Your word.
171 My lips shall utter praise,
     For You teach me Your statutes.
172 My tongue shall speak of Your word,
     For all Your commandments *are*
        righteousness.
173 Let Your hand become my help,
     For I have chosen Your precepts.
174 I long for Your salvation, O Lord,
     And Your law *is* my delight.
175 Let my soul live, and it shall praise You;
     And let Your judgments help me.
176 I have gone astray like a lost sheep;
     Seek Your servant,
     For I do not forget Your commandments.

PSALM 120

Plea for Relief from Bitter Foes

A Song of Ascents.

1 In my distress I cried to the Lord,
   And He heard me.
2 Deliver my soul, O Lord, from lying lips
   And from a deceitful tongue.

3 What shall be given to you,
   Or what shall be done to you,
   You false tongue?
4 Sharp arrows of the warrior,
   With coals of the broom tree!

5 Woe is me, that I dwell in Meshech,
   That I dwell among the tents of Kedar!
6 My soul has dwelt too long
   With one who hates peace.
7 I *am for* peace;
   But when I speak, they *are* for war.

PSALM 121

God the Help of Those Who Seek Him

A Song of Ascents.

1 I will lift up my eyes to the hills—
   From whence comes my help?
2 My help *comes* from the Lord,
   Who made heaven and earth.

Benjamin Harrison placed his hand on
Psalm 121:1–6 as he took the presidential
oath of office in 1889.

3 He will not allow your foot to be moved;
   He who keeps you will not slumber.
4 Behold, He who keeps Israel
   Shall neither slumber nor sleep.

5 The Lord *is* your keeper;
   The Lord *is* your shade at your right
      hand.
6 The sun shall not strike you by day,
   Nor the moon by night.

7 The Lord shall preserve you from all evil;
   He shall preserve your soul.
8 The Lord shall preserve your going
      out and your coming in
   From this time forth, and even
      forevermore.

PSALM 122

The Joy of Going to the House of the Lord

A Song of Ascents. Of David.

1 I was glad when they said to me,
   "Let us go into the house of the Lord."
2 Our feet have been standing
   Within your gates, O Jerusalem!

3 Jerusalem is built
   As a city that is compact together,
4 Where the tribes go up,
   The tribes of the Lord,
   To the Testimony of Israel,
   To give thanks to the name of the Lord.
5 For thrones are set there for judgment,
   The thrones of the house of David.

6 Pray for the peace of Jerusalem:
   "May they prosper who love you.
7 Peace be within your walls,
   Prosperity within your palaces."
8 For the sake of my brethren and
      companions,
   I will now say, "Peace *be* within you."
9 Because of the house of the Lord our
      God
   I will seek your good.

GOD'S CROWNING HELP

Confederate General Robert E. Lee is among the most celebrated generals in American history, admired equally for his character and his military prowess. One historian has written, "Robert Lee was one of the small company of great men in whom there is no inconsistency to be explained, no enigma to be solved. What he seemed, he was—a wholly human gentleman, the essential elements of whose positive character were two and only two, simplicity and spirituality."

We get a glimpse of Lee's character in this Christmas greeting to his wife written from Fredericksburg on Christmas Day 1862. His words underscore President Lincoln's ironic summary of the Civil War: "Both invokes [God's] aid against the other."

FAITH

My help comes from the LORD, who made heaven and earth.

PSALM 121:2

I will commence this holy day, dearest Mary, by writing to you. My heart is filled with gratitude to Almighty God for His unspeakable mercies with which He has blessed us in this day, for those He has granted us from the beginning of life, and particularly for those He has vouchsafed us during the past year. What should have become of us without His crowning help and protection? Oh, if our people would only recognize it and cease from vain self-boasting and adulation, how strong would be my belief in final success and happiness to our country! For in Him alone I know is our trust and safety.

Cut off from you and my children, my greatest pleasure is to write to you and them. Yet I have no time to indulge in it. You must tell them so, and say I constantly think of them and love them fervently with all my heart. But what a cruel thing is war; to separate and destroy families and friends, and mar the purest joys and happiness God has granted us in this world; to fill our hearts with hatred instead of love for our neighbors, and to devastate the fair face of this beautiful world!

I pray that, on this day when only peace and goodwill are preached to mankind, better thoughts may fill the hearts of our enemies and turn them to peace. . . . My heart bleeds at the death of every one of our gallant men.

PSALM 123

Prayer for Relief from Contempt

A Song of Ascents.

1 Unto You I lift up my eyes,
O You who dwell in the heavens.
2 Behold, as the eyes of servants *look*
to the hand of their masters,
As the eyes of a maid to the hand of
her mistress,
So our eyes *look* to the LORD our God,
Until He has mercy on us.

3 Have mercy on us, O LORD, have mercy
on us!
For we are exceedingly filled with
contempt.
4 Our soul is exceedingly filled
With the scorn of those who are at ease,
With the contempt of the proud.

PSALM 124

The LORD the Defense of His People

A Song of Ascents. Of David.

1 "If it had not been the LORD who was
on our side,"
Let Israel now say—
2 "If it had not been the LORD who was
on our side,
When men rose up against us,
3 Then they would have swallowed us
alive,
When their wrath was kindled against
us;
4 Then the waters would have
overwhelmed us,
The stream would have gone over our
soul;
5 Then the swollen waters
Would have gone over our soul."

6 Blessed *be* the LORD,
Who has not given us *as* prey to their
teeth.
7 Our soul has escaped as a bird from
the snare of the fowlers;[a]
The snare is broken, and we have
escaped.
8 Our help *is* in the name of the LORD,
Who made heaven and earth.

PSALM 125

The LORD the Strength of His People

A Song of Ascents.

1 Those who trust in the LORD
Are like Mount Zion,
Which cannot be moved, *but* abides
forever.
2 As the mountains surround Jerusalem,
So the LORD surrounds His people
From this time forth and forever.

3 For the scepter of wickedness shall not
rest
On the land allotted to the righteous,
Lest the righteous reach out their
hands to iniquity.

4 Do good, O LORD, to *those who are* good,
And to *those who are* upright in their
hearts.

5 As for such as turn aside to their
crooked ways,
The LORD shall lead them away
With the workers of iniquity.

Peace *be* upon Israel!

PSALM 126

A Joyful Return to Zion

A Song of Ascents.

1 When the LORD brought back the
captivity of Zion,
We were like those who dream.
2 Then our mouth was filled with laughter,
And our tongue with singing.
Then they said among the nations,
"The LORD has done great things for
them."
3 The LORD has done great things for us,
And we are glad.

4 Bring back our captivity, O LORD,
As the streams in the South.

5 Those who sow in tears
Shall reap in joy.

124:7 [a]That is, persons who catch birds in a trap
or snare

6 He who continually goes forth weeping,
Bearing seed for sowing,
Shall doubtless come again with
   rejoicing,
Bringing his sheaves *with him.*

PSALM 127

Laboring and Prospering with the LORD

A Song of Ascents. Of Solomon.

> **Dwight D. Eisenhower** placed his hand on
> Psalm 127:1 and 2 Chronicles 7:14 as he
> took the presidential oath of office in 1953.

1 Unless the LORD builds the house,
They labor in vain who build it;
Unless the LORD guards the city,
The watchman stays awake in vain.
2 *It is* vain for you to rise up early,
To sit up late,
To eat the bread of sorrows;
For so He gives His beloved sleep.

3 Behold, children *are* a heritage from
   the LORD,
The fruit of the womb *is* a reward.
4 Like arrows in the hand of a warrior,
So *are* the children of one's youth.
5 Happy *is* the man who has his quiver
   full of them;
They shall not be ashamed,
But shall speak with their enemies in
   the gate.

PSALM 128

Blessings of Those Who Fear the LORD

A Song of Ascents.

1 Blessed *is* every one who fears the LORD,
Who walks in His ways.

2 When you eat the labor of your hands,
You *shall be* happy, and *it shall be* well
   with you.
3 Your wife *shall be* like a fruitful vine
In the very heart of your house,
Your children like olive plants
All around your table.
4 Behold, thus shall the man be blessed
Who fears the LORD.

5 The LORD bless you out of Zion,
And may you see the good of
   Jerusalem
All the days of your life.
6 Yes, may you see your children's
   children.

Peace *be* upon Israel!

PSALM 129

Song of Victory over Zion's Enemies

A Song of Ascents.

1 "Many a time they have afflicted me
   from my youth,"
Let Israel now say—
2 "Many a time they have afflicted me
   from my youth;
Yet they have not prevailed against me.
3 The plowers plowed on my back;
They made their furrows long."
4 The LORD *is* righteous;
He has cut in pieces the cords of the
   wicked.

5 Let all those who hate Zion
Be put to shame and turned back.
6 Let them be as the grass *on* the
   housetops,
Which withers before it grows up,
7 With which the reaper does not fill
   his hand,
Nor he who binds sheaves, his arms.
8 Neither let those who pass by them say,
"The blessing of the LORD *be* upon you;
We bless you in the name of the LORD!"

PSALM 130

Waiting for the Redemption of the LORD

A Song of Ascents.

1 Out of the depths I have cried to You,
   O LORD;
2 Lord, hear my voice!
Let Your ears be attentive
To the voice of my supplications.

3 If You, LORD, should mark iniquities,
O Lord, who could stand?
4 But *there is* forgiveness with You,
That You may be feared.

FRANKLIN SUGGESTS PRAYER
FOR THE CONSTITUTION

BENJAMIN FRANKLIN

In the summer of 1787, as America's Founders met at Independence Hall in Philadelphia to hammer out the specifics of our nation's governing constitution, tempers flared among the delegates of the 13 colonies to such an extent that the entire convention was in danger of breaking down. Into this atmosphere thick with division and conflict, an 81-year-old statesman slowly rose to speak words of profound wisdom.

Although one of the least religious of our nation's Founders, Dr. Benjamin Franklin nonetheless understood how crucial moral and biblical virtues would be to this newborn republic. Appealing to the words of Psalm 127:1, Franklin addressed George Washington, president of the convention, and counseled his fellow delegates to beseech the aid of Almighty God before they proceeded further:

> *I have lived, sir, a long time, and the longer I live, the more convincing proofs I see of this truth, that God governs in the affairs of men. And if a sparrow cannot fall to the ground without His notice, is it probable that an empire can rise without His aid? We have been assured, sir, in the Sacred Writings, that "except the Lord builds the house, they labor in vain that build it." I firmly believe this; and I also believe that without His concurring aid we shall succeed in this political building no better than the builders of Babel: We shall be divided by our partial local interests; our projects will be confounded, and we ourselves shall become a reproach and bye word down to future ages. And what is worse, mankind may hereafter from this unfortunate instance, despair of establishing governments by human wisdom and leave it to chance, war, and conquest.*
>
> *I therefore beg leave to move that henceforth prayers imploring the assistance of Heaven, and its blessings on our deliberations, be held in this assembly every morning before we proceed to business, and that one or more of the clergy of this city be requested to officiate in that service.*

God, indeed, answered the prayers of the Founding Fathers, as on September 17, 1787, the drafting of the U.S. Constitution was completed, the greatest political document ever written. Franklin's words remain forever true: as our nation faces today's political, moral, and spiritual issues, we shall fail in this "grand experiment" of liberty unless we seek the "assistance of Heaven."

5   I wait for the LORD, my soul waits,
    And in His word I do hope.
6   My soul *waits* for the Lord
    More than those who watch for the
      morning—
    Yes, more than those who watch for
      the morning.

7   O Israel, hope in the LORD;
    For with the LORD *there is* mercy,
    And with Him *is* abundant
      redemption.
8   And He shall redeem Israel
    From all his iniquities.

PSALM 131

Simple Trust in the LORD

A Song of Ascents. Of David.

1   LORD, my heart is not haughty,
    Nor my eyes lofty.
    Neither do I concern myself with great
      matters,
    Nor with things too profound for me.

2   Surely I have calmed and quieted my
      soul,
    Like a weaned child with his mother;
    Like a weaned child *is* my soul
      within me.

3   O Israel, hope in the LORD
    From this time forth and forever.

PSALM 132

The Eternal Dwelling of God in Zion

A Song of Ascents.

1   LORD, remember David
    And all his afflictions;
2   How he swore to the LORD,
    And vowed to the Mighty One of
      Jacob:
3   "Surely I will not go into the chamber
      of my house,
    Or go up to the comfort of my bed;
4   I will not give sleep to my eyes
    Or slumber to my eyelids,
5   Until I find a place for the LORD,
    A dwelling place for the Mighty One
      of Jacob."

6   Behold, we heard of it in Ephrathah;
    We found it in the fields of the woods.ᵃ
7   Let us go into His tabernacle;
    Let us worship at His footstool.
8   Arise, O LORD, to Your resting place,
    You and the ark of Your strength.
9   Let Your priests be clothed with
      righteousness,
    And let Your saints shout for joy.

10 For Your servant David's sake,
    Do not turn away the face of Your
      Anointed.

11 The LORD has sworn *in* truth to David;
    He will not turn from it:
    "I will set upon your throne the fruit of
      your body.
12 If your sons will keep My covenant
    And My testimony which I shall teach
      them,
    Their sons also shall sit upon your
      throne forevermore."

13 For the LORD has chosen Zion;
    He has desired *it* for His dwelling
      place:
14 "This *is* My resting place forever;
    Here I will dwell, for I have desired it.
15 I will abundantly bless her provision;
    I will satisfy her poor with bread.
16 I will also clothe her priests with
      salvation,
    And her saints shall shout aloud for
      joy.
17 There I will make the horn of David
      grow;
    I will prepare a lamp for My Anointed.
18 His enemies I will clothe with shame,
    But upon Himself His crown shall
      flourish."

PSALM 133

Blessed Unity of the People of God

A Song of Ascents. Of David.

1   Behold, how good and how pleasant
      it is
    For brethren to dwell together in unity!

132:6 ᵃHebrew *Jaar*

2   *It is* like the precious oil upon the head,
    Running down on the beard,
    The beard of Aaron,
    Running down on the edge of his
       garments.
3   *It is* like the dew of Hermon,
    Descending upon the mountains of
       Zion;
    For there the Lord commanded the
       blessing—
    Life forevermore.

PSALM 134

Praising the Lord in His House at Night

A Song of Ascents.

1   Behold, bless the Lord,
    All *you* servants of the Lord,
    Who by night stand in the house of
       the Lord!
2   Lift up your hands *in* the sanctuary,
    And bless the Lord.

3   The Lord who made heaven and earth
    Bless you from Zion!

PSALM 135

Praise to God in Creation and Redemption

1   Praise the Lord!

    Praise the name of the Lord;
    Praise *Him,* O you servants of the Lord!
2   You who stand in the house of the Lord,
    In the courts of the house of our God,
3   Praise the Lord, for the Lord *is* good;
    Sing praises to His name, for *it is*
       pleasant.
4   For the Lord has chosen Jacob for
       Himself,
    Israel for His special treasure.

5   For I know that the Lord *is* great,
    And our Lord *is* above all gods.
6   Whatever the Lord pleases He does,
    In heaven and in earth,
    In the seas and in all deep places.
7   He causes the vapors to ascend from
       the ends of the earth;
    He makes lightning for the rain;
    He brings the wind out of His
       treasuries.

8   He destroyed the firstborn of Egypt,
    Both of man and beast.
9   He sent signs and wonders into the
       midst of you, O Egypt,
    Upon Pharaoh and all his servants.
10 He defeated many nations
    And slew mighty kings—
11 Sihon king of the Amorites,
    Og king of Bashan,
    And all the kingdoms of Canaan—
12 And gave their land *as* a heritage,
    A heritage to Israel His people.

13 Your name, O Lord, *endures* forever,
    Your fame, O Lord, throughout all
       generations.
14 For the Lord will judge His people,
    And He will have compassion on His
       servants.

15 The idols of the nations *are* silver and
       gold,
    The work of men's hands.
16 They have mouths, but they do not
       speak;
    Eyes they have, but they do not see;
17 They have ears, but they do not hear;
    Nor is there *any* breath in their
       mouths.
18 Those who make them are like them;
    So is everyone who trusts in them.

19 Bless the Lord, O house of Israel!
    Bless the Lord, O house of Aaron!
20 Bless the Lord, O house of Levi!
    You who fear the Lord, bless the
       Lord!
21 Blessed be the Lord out of Zion,
    Who dwells in Jerusalem!

    Praise the Lord!

PSALM 136

Thanksgiving to God for His Enduring Mercy

1   Oh, give thanks to the Lord, for *He
       is* good!
    For His mercy *endures* forever.
2   Oh, give thanks to the God of gods!
    For His mercy *endures* forever.
3   Oh, give thanks to the Lord of lords!
    For His mercy *endures* forever:

4 To Him who alone does great wonders,
For His mercy *endures* forever;
5 To Him who by wisdom made the
heavens,
For His mercy *endures* forever;
6 To Him who laid out the earth above
the waters,
For His mercy *endures* forever;
7 To Him who made great lights,
For His mercy *endures* forever—
8 The sun to rule by day,
For His mercy *endures* forever;
9 The moon and stars to rule by night,
For His mercy *endures* forever.

10 To Him who struck Egypt in their
firstborn,
For His mercy *endures* forever;
11 And brought out Israel from among
them,
For His mercy *endures* forever;
12 With a strong hand, and with an
outstretched arm,
For His mercy *endures* forever;
13 To Him who divided the Red Sea in two,
For His mercy *endures* forever;
14 And made Israel pass through the
midst of it,
For His mercy *endures* forever;
15 But overthrew Pharaoh and his army
in the Red Sea,
For His mercy *endures* forever;
16 To Him who led His people through
the wilderness,
For His mercy *endures* forever;
17 To Him who struck down great kings,
For His mercy *endures* forever;
18 And slew famous kings,
For His mercy *endures* forever—
19 Sihon king of the Amorites,
For His mercy *endures* forever;
20 And Og king of Bashan,
For His mercy *endures* forever—
21 And gave their land as a heritage,
For His mercy *endures* forever;
22 A heritage to Israel His servant,
For His mercy *endures* forever.

23 Who remembered us in our lowly state,
For His mercy *endures* forever;
24 And rescued us from our enemies,
For His mercy *endures* forever;

25 Who gives food to all flesh,
For His mercy *endures* forever.

26 Oh, give thanks to the God of heaven!
For His mercy *endures* forever.

PSALM 137

Longing for Zion in a Foreign Land

1 By the rivers of Babylon,
There we sat down, yea, we wept
When we remembered Zion.
2 We hung our harps
Upon the willows in the midst of it.
3 For there those who carried us away
captive asked of us a song,
And those who plundered us *requested*
mirth,
Saying, "Sing us *one* of the songs of
Zion!"

4 How shall we sing the Lord's song
In a foreign land?
5 If I forget you, O Jerusalem,
Let my right hand forget *its skill!*
6 If I do not remember you,
Let my tongue cling to the roof of
my mouth—
If I do not exalt Jerusalem
Above my chief joy.

7 Remember, O Lord, against the sons
of Edom
The day of Jerusalem,
Who said, "Raze *it*, raze *it*,
To its very foundation!"

8 O daughter of Babylon, who are to be
destroyed,
Happy the one who repays you as you
have served us!
9 Happy the one who takes and dashes
Your little ones against the rock!

PSALM 138

The Lord's Goodness to the Faithful

A Psalm of David.

1 I will praise You with my whole heart;
Before the gods I will sing praises to
You.

AMERICAN SUPPORT
FOR THE JEWISH STATE, 1948

PROTECTOR

*If I forget you,
O Jerusalem. . . .*

PSALM 137:5

Margaret Truman said the most difficult decision Harry Truman ever faced as president was whether he should support the creation of a Jewish homeland in Palestine after World War II. "What I am trying to do is make the whole world safe for Jews," he wrote as he wrestled over the decision. Deeply affected by the full revelation of the Holocaust as well as his moral and religious upbringing and familiarity with the Bible, Truman sympathized with Jewish aspirations for a homeland. In November 1947, he lobbied for the United Nations' resolution that divided Palestine into Jewish and Arab states.

Great Britain announced it would transfer authority over Palestine to the U.N. by May 14, 1948. On the eve of British withdrawal, which would be followed immediately by the Jewish declaration of independence, Secretary of State George Marshall and most of the American foreign service experts strongly opposed the creation of a Jewish state in Palestine, warning Truman that Arab countries would cut off oil and unite to destroy the Jews. But Truman weighed the multifaceted concerns and held firm despite the heated opposition.

On May 14, David Ben-Gurion read a declaration of Jewish independence in front of a small audience at the Tel Aviv Art Museum. Striking the speaker's table for emphasis, he announced, "The name of our state shall be Israel." At midnight, British rule over Palestine lapsed; eleven minutes later, White House spokesman Charlie Ross announced U.S. recognition. The American statement recognizing the new State of Israel bears President Truman's last-minute handwritten changes.

"God put you in your mother's womb," the Chief Rabbi of Israel, Isaac Halevi Herzog, later told Truman, "so you would be the instrument to bring about Israel's rebirth after 2000 years." With Truman's decision, the hopes of the Jewish people were realized, but so too were Marshall's fears. Arab opponents of the new nation immediately declared war, prompting a bloody struggle over Israel's existence that continues today.

Truman's favorite Psalm was 137, which begins: "By the rivers of Babylon, there we sat down, yea, we wept when we remembered Zion."

2 I will worship toward Your holy temple,
  And praise Your name
  For Your lovingkindness and Your truth;
  For You have magnified Your word
    above all Your name.
3 In the day when I cried out, You
    answered me,
  And made me bold *with* strength in
    my soul.

4 All the kings of the earth shall praise
    You, O LORD,
  When they hear the words of Your
    mouth.
5 Yes, they shall sing of the ways of
    the LORD,
  For great *is* the glory of the LORD.
6 Though the LORD *is* on high,
  Yet He regards the lowly;
  But the proud He knows from afar.

7 Though I walk in the midst of trouble,
    You will revive me;
  You will stretch out Your hand
  Against the wrath of my enemies,
  And Your right hand will save me.
8 The LORD will perfect *that which*
    concerns me;
  Your mercy, O LORD, *endures* forever;
  Do not forsake the works of Your hands.

PSALM 139

God's Perfect Knowledge of Man

For the Chief Musician. A Psalm of David.

1 O LORD, You have searched me and
    known *me.*
2 You know my sitting down and my
    rising up;
  You understand my thought afar off.
3 You comprehend my path and my
    lying down,
  And are acquainted with all my ways.
4 For *there is* not a word on my tongue,
  But behold, O LORD, You know it
    altogether.
5 You have hedged me behind and
    before,
  And laid Your hand upon me.
6 *Such* knowledge *is* too wonderful for me;
  It is high, I cannot *attain* it.

7 Where can I go from Your Spirit?
  Or where can I flee from Your presence?
8 If I ascend into heaven, You *are* there;
  If I make my bed in hell, behold, You
    are there.
9 *If* I take the wings of the morning,
  And dwell in the uttermost parts of
    the sea,
10 Even there Your hand shall lead me,
  And Your right hand shall hold me.
11 If I say, "Surely the darkness shall fall[a]
    on me,"
  Even the night shall be light
    about me;
12 Indeed, the darkness shall not hide
    from You,
  But the night shines as the day;
  The darkness and the light *are* both
    alike *to* You.

13 For You formed my inward parts;
  You covered me in my mother's womb.
14 I will praise You, for I am fearfully *and*
    wonderfully made;[a]
  Marvelous are Your works,
  And *that* my soul knows very well.
15 My frame was not hidden from You,
  When I was made in secret,
  And skillfully wrought in the lowest
    parts of the earth.
16 Your eyes saw my substance, being
    yet unformed.
  And in Your book they all were written,
  The days fashioned for me,
  When *as yet there were* none of them.

17 How precious also are Your thoughts
    to me, O God!
  How great is the sum of them!
18 *If* I should count them, they would be
    more in number than the sand;
  When I awake, I am still with You.

19 Oh, that You would slay the wicked,
    O God!
  Depart from me, therefore, you
    bloodthirsty men.

139:11 [a]Vulgate and Symmachus read *cover.*
139:14 [a]Following Masoretic Text and Targum;
Septuagint, Syriac, and Vulgate read *You are fearfully
wonderful.*

20 For they speak against You wickedly;
   Your enemies take *Your name* in
   vain.ª

21 Do I not hate them, O LORD, who
   hate You?
   And do I not loathe those who rise
   up against You?

22 I hate them with perfect hatred;
   I count them my enemies.

23 Search me, O God, and know my heart;
   Try me, and know my anxieties;

24 And see if *there is any* wicked way
   in me,
   And lead me in the way everlasting.

PSALM 140

Prayer for Deliverance from Evil Men

To the Chief Musician. A Psalm of David.

1 Deliver me, O LORD, from evil men;
  Preserve me from violent men,

2 Who plan evil things in *their* hearts;
  They continually gather together *for* war.

3 They sharpen their tongues like a
  serpent;
  The poison of asps *is* under their lips.
  Selah

139:20 ªSeptuagint and Vulgate read *They take your
cities in vain.*

DEFENDER

*For You formed my
inward parts; You covered me
in my mother's womb.*

PSALM 139:13

Pope John Paul II

IN DEFENSE OF LIFE

Pope John Paul II addressed a crowd of over 375,000 people
from 70 different countries in a Mass celebrated at Cherry
Creek State Park, Colorado, as a part of "World Youth Day"
on August 15, 1993. He stated:

*A "culture of death" seeks to impose itself on our
desire to live, and live to the full. . . . In our own century,
as at no other time in history, the "culture of death" has
assumed a social and institutional form of legality to justify the most horrible crimes against humanity: genocide,
"final solutions," "ethnic cleansings," and massive taking of lives of human beings even before they are born,
or before they reach the natural point of death. . . .*

*In much of contemporary thinking, any reference to a
"law" guaranteed by the Creator is absent. There remains
only each individual's choice of this or that objective as
convenient or useful in a given set of circumstances. No
longer is anything considered intrinsically "good" and
"universally binding."*

*The family especially is under attack. And the sacred
character of Human Life is denied. Naturally, the weakest members of society are the most at risk. The unborn,
children, the sick, the handicapped, the old, the poor and
unemployed, the immigrant and refugee. . . .*

*You must feel the full urgency of the task. Woe to you
if you do not succeed in defending life. The church needs
your energies, your enthusiasm, your youthful ideas, in
order to make the Gospel of Life penetrate the fabric of
society, transforming people's hearts and the structures
of society in order to create a civilization of true justice
and love.*

4 Keep me, O Lord, from the hands of
     the wicked;
   Preserve me from violent men,
   Who have purposed to make my steps
     stumble.
5 The proud have hidden a snare for
     me, and cords;
   They have spread a net by the wayside;
   They have set traps for me.   Selah

6 I said to the Lord: "You *are* my God;
   Hear the voice of my supplications,
     O Lord.
7 O God the Lord, the strength of my
     salvation,
   You have covered my head in the day
     of battle.
8 Do not grant, O Lord, the desires of
     the wicked;
   Do not further his *wicked* scheme,
   Lest they be exalted.   Selah

9 "*As for* the head of those who surround
     me,
   Let the evil of their lips cover them;
10 Let burning coals fall upon them;
   Let them be cast into the fire,
   Into deep pits, that they rise not up
     again.
11 Let not a slanderer be established in
     the earth;
   Let evil hunt the violent man to
     overthrow *him*."

12 I know that the Lord will maintain
   The cause of the afflicted,
   And justice for the poor.
13 Surely the righteous shall give thanks
     to Your name;
   The upright shall dwell in Your presence.

PSALM 141

Prayer for Safekeeping from Wickedness

A Psalm of David.

1 Lord, I cry out to You;
   Make haste to me!
   Give ear to my voice when I cry out
     to You.
2 Let my prayer be set before You *as*
   incense,

The lifting up of my hands *as* the
     evening sacrifice.

3 Set a guard, O Lord, over my mouth;
   Keep watch over the door of my lips.
4 Do not incline my heart to any evil
     thing,
   To practice wicked works
   With men who work iniquity;
   And do not let me eat of their delicacies.

5 Let the righteous strike me;
   It shall be a kindness.
   And let him rebuke me;
   It shall be as excellent oil;
   Let my head not refuse it.

   For still my prayer *is* against the deeds
     of the wicked.
6 Their judges are overthrown by the
     sides of the cliff,
   And they hear my words, for they are
     sweet.
7 Our bones are scattered at the mouth
     of the grave,
   As when one plows and breaks up the
     earth.

8 But my eyes *are* upon You, O God the
     Lord;
   In You I take refuge;
   Do not leave my soul destitute.
9 Keep me from the snares they have
     laid for me,
   And from the traps of the workers of
     iniquity.
10 Let the wicked fall into their own nets,
   While I escape safely.

PSALM 142

A Plea for Relief from Persecutors

A Contemplation[a] of David.
A Prayer when he was in the cave.

1 I cry out to the Lord with my voice;
   With my voice to the Lord I make my
     supplication.
2 I pour out my complaint before Him;
   I declare before Him my trouble.

142:title [a]Hebrew *Maschil*

3 When my spirit was overwhelmed
    within me,
  Then You knew my path.
  In the way in which I walk
  They have secretly set a snare for me.
4 Look on *my* right hand and see,
  For *there is* no one who
    acknowledges me;
  Refuge has failed me;
  No one cares for my soul.

5 I cried out to You, O LORD:
  I said, "You *are* my refuge,
  My portion in the land of the living.
6 Attend to my cry,
  For I am brought very low;
  Deliver me from my persecutors,
  For they are stronger than I.
7 Bring my soul out of prison,
  That I may praise Your name;
  The righteous shall surround me,
  For You shall deal bountifully with me."

PSALM 143

An Earnest Appeal for Guidance and Deliverance

A Psalm of David.

1 Hear my prayer, O LORD,
  Give ear to my supplications!
  In Your faithfulness answer me,
  And in Your righteousness.
2 Do not enter into judgment with Your
    servant,
  For in Your sight no one living is
    righteous.

3 For the enemy has persecuted my soul;
  He has crushed my life to the ground;
  He has made me dwell in darkness,
  Like those who have long been dead.
4 Therefore my spirit is overwhelmed
    within me;
  My heart within me is distressed.

5 I remember the days of old;
  I meditate on all Your works;
  I muse on the work of Your hands.
6 I spread out my hands to You;
  My soul *longs* for You like a thirsty
    land.   Selah

7 Answer me speedily, O LORD;
  My spirit fails!
  Do not hide Your face from me,
  Lest I be like those who go down into
    the pit.
8 Cause me to hear Your lovingkindness
    in the morning,
  For in You do I trust;
  Cause me to know the way in which
    I should walk,
  For I lift up my soul to You.

9 Deliver me, O LORD, from my enemies;
  In You I take shelter.[a]
10 Teach me to do Your will,
  For You *are* my God;
  Your Spirit *is* good.
  Lead me in the land of uprightness.

11 Revive me, O LORD, for Your name's
    sake!
  For Your righteousness' sake bring my
    soul out of trouble.
12 In Your mercy cut off my enemies,
  And destroy all those who afflict my
    soul;
  For I *am* Your servant.

PSALM 144

A Song to the LORD Who Preserves and Prospers His People

A *Psalm* of David.

1 Blessed *be* the LORD my Rock,
  Who trains my hands for war,
  And my fingers for battle—
2 My lovingkindness and my fortress,
  My high tower and my deliverer,
  My shield and *the One* in whom I take
    refuge,
  Who subdues my people[a] under me.

3 LORD, what *is* man, that You take
    knowledge of him?
  Or the son of man, that You are
    mindful of him?
4 Man is like a breath;
  His days *are* like a passing shadow.

143:9 [a]Septuagint and Vulgate read *To You I flee.*
144:2 [a]Following Masoretic Text, Septuagint, and Vulgate; Syriac and Targum read *the peoples* (compare 18:47).

5 Bow down Your heavens, O LORD, and
   come down;
   Touch the mountains, and they shall
   smoke.
6 Flash forth lightning and scatter them;
   Shoot out Your arrows and destroy
   them.
7 Stretch out Your hand from above;
   Rescue me and deliver me out of great
   waters,
   From the hand of foreigners,
8 Whose mouth speaks lying words,
   And whose right hand *is* a right hand
   of falsehood.

9 I will sing a new song to You, O God;
   On a harp of ten strings I will sing
   praises to You,
10 *The One* who gives salvation to kings,
   Who delivers David His servant
   From the deadly sword.

11 Rescue me and deliver me from the
   hand of foreigners,
   Whose mouth speaks lying words,
   And whose right hand *is* a right hand
   of falsehood—
12 That our sons *may be* as plants grown
   up in their youth;
   That our daughters *may be* as pillars,
   Sculptured in palace style;
13 *That* our barns *may be* full,
   Supplying all kinds of produce;
   That our sheep may bring forth
   thousands
   And ten thousands in our fields;
14 *That* our oxen *may be* well laden;
   That there be no breaking in or going
   out;
   That there be no outcry in our streets.
15 Happy *are* the people who are in such
   a state;
   Happy *are* the people whose God *is*
   the LORD!

PSALM 145

A Song of God's Majesty and Love

A Praise of David.

1 I will extol You, my God, O King;
   And I will bless Your name forever
   and ever.

2 Every day I will bless You,
   And I will praise Your name forever
   and ever.
3 Great *is* the LORD, and greatly to be
   praised;
   And His greatness *is* unsearchable.

4 One generation shall praise Your
   works to another,
   And shall declare Your mighty acts.
5 I[a] will meditate on the glorious
   splendor of Your majesty,
   And on Your wondrous works.[b]
6 *Men* shall speak of the might of Your
   awesome acts,
   And I will declare Your greatness.
7 They shall utter the memory of Your
   great goodness,
   And shall sing of Your righteousness.

8 The LORD *is* gracious and full of
   compassion,
   Slow to anger and great in mercy.
9 The LORD *is* good to all,
   And His tender mercies *are* over all
   His works.

10 All Your works shall praise You, O LORD,
   And Your saints shall bless You.
11 They shall speak of the glory of Your
   kingdom,
   And talk of Your power,
12 To make known to the sons of men
   His mighty acts,
   And the glorious majesty of His
   kingdom.
13 Your kingdom *is* an everlasting
   kingdom,
   And Your dominion *endures*
   throughout all generations.[a]

14 The LORD upholds all who fall,
   And raises up all *who are* bowed down.
15 The eyes of all look expectantly to You,
   And You give them their food in due
   season.

145:5 [a]Following Masoretic Text and Targum; Dead
Sea Scrolls, Septuagint, Syriac, and Vulgate read *They.*
[b]Literally *on the words of Your wondrous works*
145:13 [a]Following Masoretic Text and Targum; Dead
Sea Scrolls, Septuagint, Syriac, and Vulgate add *The
LORD is faithful in all His words, And holy in all His works.*

KATHARINE LEE BATES

"AMERICA THE BEAUTIFUL"

"America the Beautiful" was written by the professor, poet, and writer Katharine Lee Bates (1859–1929), after an inspiring trip to Pikes Peak, Colorado, in 1893. When she got to the top of Pike's Peak, she said, "All the wonder of America seemed displayed there, with the sea-like expanse." It inspired her to write the song that is considered the American national hymn, as opposed to "The Star-Spangled Banner," which is the national anthem.

*O beautiful for spacious skies,
For amber waves of grain,
For purple mountain majesties
Above the fruited plain!
America! America!
God shed His grace on thee,
And crown thy good with brotherhood
From sea to shining sea!*

*O beautiful for pilgrim feet
Whose stern impassion'd stress
A thoroughfare for freedom beat
Across the wilderness.
America! America!
God mend thine ev'ry flaw,
Confirm thy soul in self-control,
Thy liberty in law.*

*O beautiful for heroes prov'd
In liberating strife,
Who more than self their country loved,
And mercy more than life.
America! America!
May God thy gold refine
Till all success be nobleness,
And ev'ry gain divine.*

*O beautiful for patriot dream
That sees beyond the years
Thine alabaster cities gleam
Undimmed by human tears.
America! America!
God shed His grace on thee,
And crown thy good with brotherhood
From sea to shining sea.*

16 You open Your hand
    And satisfy the desire of every living
        thing.

17 The LORD *is* righteous in all His ways,
    Gracious in all His works.
18 The LORD *is* near to all who call upon
        Him,
    To all who call upon Him in truth.
19 He will fulfill the desire of those who
        fear Him;
    He also will hear their cry and save
        them.
20 The LORD preserves all who love Him,
    But all the wicked He will destroy.
21 My mouth shall speak the praise of
        the LORD,
    And all flesh shall bless His holy name
    Forever and ever.

PSALM 146

*The Happiness of Those Whose Help Is
the LORD*

1   Praise the LORD!

    Praise the LORD, O my soul!
2   While I live I will praise the LORD;
    I will sing praises to my God while I
        have my being.

3   Do not put your trust in princes,
    Nor in a son of man, in whom *there
        is* no help.
4   His spirit departs, he returns to his
        earth;
    In that very day his plans perish.

5   Happy *is he* who *has* the God of Jacob
        for his help,
    Whose hope *is* in the LORD his God,
6   Who made heaven and earth,
    The sea, and all that *is* in them;
    Who keeps truth forever,
7   Who executes justice for the oppressed,
    Who gives food to the hungry.
    The LORD gives freedom to the prisoners.

8   The LORD opens *the eyes of* the blind;
    The LORD raises those who are bowed
        down;
    The LORD loves the righteous.

9   The LORD watches over the strangers;
    He relieves the fatherless and widow;
    But the way of the wicked He turns
        upside down.

10 The LORD shall reign forever—
    Your God, O Zion, to all generations.

    Praise the LORD!

PSALM 147

Praise to God for His Word and Providence

1   Praise the LORD!
    For *it is* good to sing praises to our God;
    For *it is* pleasant, *and* praise is beautiful.

2   The LORD builds up Jerusalem;
    He gathers together the outcasts of
        Israel.
3   He heals the brokenhearted
    And binds up their wounds.
4   He counts the number of the stars;
    He calls them all by name.
5   Great *is* our Lord, and mighty in power;
    His understanding *is* infinite.
6   The LORD lifts up the humble;
    He casts the wicked down to the ground.

7   Sing to the LORD with thanksgiving;
    Sing praises on the harp to our God,
8   Who covers the heavens with clouds,
    Who prepares rain for the earth,
    Who makes grass to grow on the
        mountains.
9   He gives to the beast its food,
    And to the young ravens that cry.

10 He does not delight in the strength of
        the horse;
    He takes no pleasure in the legs of a
        man.
11 The LORD takes pleasure in those who
        fear Him,
    In those who hope in His mercy.

12 Praise the LORD, O Jerusalem!
    Praise your God, O Zion!
13 For He has strengthened the bars of
        your gates;
    He has blessed your children within
        you.

14 He makes peace *in* your borders,
 And fills you with the finest wheat.

15 He sends out His command *to the*
 earth;
 His word runs very swiftly.

16 He gives snow like wool;
 He scatters the frost like ashes;

17 He casts out His hail like morsels;
 Who can stand before His cold?

18 He sends out His word and melts
 them;
 He causes His wind to blow, *and* the
 waters flow.

19 He declares His word to Jacob,
 His statutes and His judgments to
 Israel.

20 He has not dealt thus with any
 nation;
 And *as for His* judgments, they have
 not known them.

Praise the LORD!

PSALM 148

Praise to the LORD from Creation

1 Praise the LORD!

 Praise the LORD from the heavens;
 Praise Him in the heights!

2 Praise Him, all His angels;
 Praise Him, all His hosts!

3 Praise Him, sun and moon;
 Praise Him, all you stars of light!

4 Praise Him, you heavens of heavens,
 And you waters above the heavens!

5 Let them praise the name of the
 LORD,
 For He commanded and they were
 created.

6 He also established them forever and
 ever;
 He made a decree which shall not
 pass away.

7 Praise the LORD from the earth,
 You great sea creatures and all the
 depths;

8 Fire and hail, snow and clouds;

 Stormy wind, fulfilling His word;

9 Mountains and all hills;
 Fruitful trees and all cedars;

10 Beasts and all cattle;
 Creeping things and flying fowl;

11 Kings of the earth and all peoples;
 Princes and all judges of the earth;

12 Both young men and maidens;
 Old men and children.

13 Let them praise the name of the
 LORD,
 For His name alone is exalted;
 His glory *is* above the earth and
 heaven.

14 And He has exalted the horn of
 His people,
 The praise of all His saints—
 Of the children of Israel,
 A people near to Him.

 Praise the LORD!

PSALM 149

Praise to God for His Salvation and Judgment

1 Praise the LORD!

 Sing to the LORD a new song,
 And His praise in the assembly of
 saints.

2 Let Israel rejoice in their Maker;
 Let the children of Zion be joyful in
 their King.

3 Let them praise His name with the
 dance;
 Let them sing praises to Him with
 the timbrel and harp.

4 For the LORD takes pleasure in His
 people;
 He will beautify the humble with
 salvation.

5 Let the saints be joyful in glory;
 Let them sing aloud on their beds.

6 *Let* the high praises of God *be* in their
 mouth,
 And a two-edged sword in their hand,

7 To execute vengeance on the nations,
 And punishments on the peoples;

8 To bind their kings with chains,

And their nobles with fetters of iron;
9 To execute on them the written
    judgment—
This honor have all His saints.

Praise the LORD!

PSALM 150

Let All Things Praise the LORD

1 Praise the LORD!

Praise God in His sanctuary;
Praise Him in His mighty firmament!

2 Praise Him for His mighty acts;

Praise Him according to His excellent
    greatness!

3 Praise Him with the sound of the
    trumpet;
Praise Him with the lute and harp!
4 Praise Him with the timbrel and dance;
Praise Him with stringed instruments
    and flutes!
5 Praise Him with loud cymbals;
Praise Him with clashing cymbals!

6 Let everything that has breath praise
    the LORD.

Praise the LORD!

PROVERBS

Author: Solomon, with parts by Agur and King Lemuel

When Written: About 950 B.C., with some sections penned about 720 B.C.

Theme: Wisdom and Instruction for Life

Key Verses: Proverbs 3:5, 6—Trust in the LORD with all your heart, and lean not on your own understanding; in all your ways acknowledge Him, and He shall direct your paths.

Key Chapter: While each chapter of Proverbs is packed with crucial wisdom for godly and upright living, chapter 31 is highly unique, revealing the supreme value and treasure a man has in a virtuous woman.

The Book of Proverbs offers practical wisdom and instruction for how one can live an upright and righteous life. Its counsel is not just relevant to individuals, however, but to nations as well. Proverbs 14:34 provides a maxim that godly leaders have pointed to for generations: "Righteousness exalts a nation, but sin is a reproach to any people."

Patrick Henry, one of early America's most outspoken Revolutionary leaders, predicted that whether or not the newly formed United States would prove "a blessing or a curse will depend upon the use our people make of the blessings which a gracious God hath bestowed on us. If they are wise, they will be great and happy. If they are of a contrary character, they will be miserable. Righteousness alone can exalt them as a nation."

PROVERBS

The Beginning of Knowledge

1 The proverbs of Solomon the son of David, king of Israel:

2 To know wisdom and instruction,
To perceive the words of understanding,
3 To receive the instruction of wisdom,
Justice, judgment, and equity;
4 To give prudence to the simple,
To the young man knowledge and
discretion—
5 A wise *man* will hear and increase
learning,
And a man of understanding will
attain wise counsel,
6 To understand a proverb and an
enigma,
The words of the wise and their riddles.

7 The fear of the LORD *is* the beginning
of knowledge,
But fools despise wisdom and instruction.

Shun Evil Counsel

8 My son, hear the instruction of your
father,
And do not forsake the law of your
mother;
9 For they *will be* a graceful ornament
on your head,
And chains about your neck.

10 My son, if sinners entice you,
Do not consent.
11 If they say, "Come with us,
Let us lie in wait to *shed* blood;
Let us lurk secretly for the innocent
without cause;
12 Let us swallow them alive like Sheol,ᵃ
And whole, like those who go down
to the Pit;
13 We shall find all *kinds* of precious
possessions,
We shall fill our houses with spoil;
14 Cast in your lot among us,
Let us all have one purse"—

15 My son, do not walk in the way with
them,
Keep your foot from their path;
16 For their feet run to evil,
And they make haste to shed blood.
17 Surely, in vain the net is spread
In the sight of any bird;
18 But they lie in wait for their *own* blood,
They lurk secretly for their *own* lives.
19 So *are* the ways of everyone who is
greedy for gain;
It takes away the life of its owners.

The Call of Wisdom

20 Wisdom calls aloud outside;
She raises her voice in the open squares.
21 She cries out in the chief concourses,ᵃ
At the openings of the gates in the city
She speaks her words:
22 "How long, you simple ones, will you
love simplicity?
For scorners delight in their scorning,
And fools hate knowledge.
23 Turn at my rebuke;
Surely I will pour out my spirit on you;
I will make my words known to you.
24 Because I have called and you refused,
I have stretched out my hand and no
one regarded,
25 Because you disdained all my counsel,
And would have none of my rebuke,
26 I also will laugh at your calamity;
I will mock when your terror comes,
27 When your terror comes like a storm,
And your destruction comes like a
whirlwind,
When distress and anguish come
upon you.

28 "Then they will call on me, but I will
not answer;
They will seek me diligently, but they
will not find me.

1:12 ᵃOr *the grave*   **1:21** ᵃSeptuagint, Syriac, and
Targum read *top of the walls;* Vulgate reads *the head of
multitudes.*

29 Because they hated knowledge
   And did not choose the fear of the LORD,
30 They would have none of my counsel
   And despised my every rebuke.
31 Therefore they shall eat the fruit of
   their own way,
   And be filled to the full with their
   own fancies.
32 For the turning away of the simple
   will slay them,
   And the complacency of fools will
   destroy them;
33 But whoever listens to me will dwell
   safely,
   And will be secure, without fear of evil."

The Value of Wisdom

2 My son, if you receive my words,
   And treasure my commands within
   you,
2 So that you incline your ear to wisdom,
   And apply your heart to understanding;
3 Yes, if you cry out for discernment,
   And lift up your voice for understanding,
4 If you seek her as silver,
   And search for her *as for* hidden
   treasures;
5 Then you will understand the fear
   of the LORD,
   And find the knowledge of God.
6 For the LORD gives wisdom;
   From His mouth *come* knowledge and
   understanding;
7 He stores up sound wisdom for the
   upright;
   He is a shield to those who walk
   uprightly;
8 He guards the paths of justice,
   And preserves the way of His saints.
9 Then you will understand
   righteousness and justice,
   Equity *and* every good path.

10 When wisdom enters your heart,
   And knowledge is pleasant to your soul,
11 Discretion will preserve you;
   Understanding will keep you,
12 To deliver you from the way of evil,
   From the man who speaks perverse
   things,
13 From those who leave the paths of
   uprightness

To walk in the ways of darkness;
14 Who rejoice in doing evil,
   And delight in the perversity of the
   wicked;
15 Whose ways *are* crooked,
   And *who are* devious in their paths;
16 To deliver you from the immoral
   woman,
   From the seductress *who* flatters with
   her words,
17 Who forsakes the companion of her
   youth,
   And forgets the covenant of her God.
18 For her house leads down to death,
   And her paths to the dead;
19 None who go to her return,
   Nor do they regain the paths of life—
20 So you may walk in the way of
   goodness,
   And keep *to* the paths of
   righteousness.
21 For the upright will dwell in the land,
   And the blameless will remain in it;
22 But the wicked will be cut off from
   the earth,
   And the unfaithful will be uprooted
   from it.

Guidance for the Young

3 My son, do not forget my law,
   But let your heart keep my commands;
2 For length of days and long life
   And peace they will add to you.

3 Let not mercy and truth forsake you;
   Bind them around your neck,
   Write them on the tablet of your heart,
4 *And* so find favor and high esteem
   In the sight of God and man.

> **Gerald R. Ford** placed his hand on Proverbs
> 3:5, 6 as he took the presidential oath of
> office in 1974.

5 Trust in the LORD with all your heart,
   And lean not on your own
   understanding;
6 In all your ways acknowledge Him,
   And He shall direct[a] your paths.

3:6 [a]Or *make smooth* or *straight*

OUR NATION'S COINS AND CURRENCY

Trust in the LORD with all your heart. . . .

PROVERBS 3:5

Our nation's coins have not always had "In God We Trust" stamped on them. The motto was placed on United States coins largely because of the increased religious sentiment existing during the Civil War. From Treasury Department records it appears that the first suggestion that God be recognized on U.S. coinage can be traced to a letter addressed to the Secretary of Treasury Salmon P. Chase from a small-town Pennsylvania minister in 1861.

As a result, in a letter dated November 20, 1861, Secretary Chase instructed James Pollock, Director of the Mint at Philadelphia, to prepare a motto: "Dear Sir: No nation can be strong except in the strength of God, or safe except in His defense. The trust of our people in God should be declared on our national coins."

"In God We Trust" first appeared on the 1864 two-cent coin. An Act of Congress passed on March 3, 1865, allowed the Mint Director, with the Secretary's approval, to place the motto on all gold and silver coins that "shall admit the inscription thereon." Under the Act, the motto was placed on the gold double-eagle coin, the gold eagle coin, and the gold half-eagle coin. It was also placed on the silver dollar coin, the half-dollar coin, the quarter-dollar coin, the nickel, and the three-cent coin beginning in 1866.

The motto was omitted from the new gold coins issued in 1907, causing a storm of public criticism. As a result, legislation passed in May 1908 made "In God We Trust" mandatory on all coins on which it had previously appeared. Legislation approved July 11, 1955, made the appearance of "In God We Trust" mandatory on all coins and paper currency of the United States. By an act of Congress, July 30, 1956, "In God We Trust" became the national motto of the United States.

Since 1955, all the United States coins and currency have carried the motto "In God We Trust." Not until 1970 and 1978 were the laws authorizing its use legally challenged. Responding to atheist Madalyn Murray O'Hair's charge, the federal courts rejected her argument that the motto violated the First Amendment.

7 Do not be wise in your own eyes;
   Fear the LORD and depart from evil.
8 It will be health to your flesh,[a]
   And strength[b] to your bones.

9 Honor the LORD with your possessions,
   And with the firstfruits of all your
     increase;
10 So your barns will be filled with plenty,
   And your vats will overflow with new
     wine.

11 My son, do not despise the chastening
     of the LORD,
   Nor detest His correction;
12 For whom the LORD loves He corrects,
   Just as a father the son *in whom* he
     delights.

13 Happy *is* the man *who* finds wisdom,
   And the man *who* gains understanding;
14 For her proceeds *are* better than the
     profits of silver,
   And her gain than fine gold.
15 She *is* more precious than rubies,
   And all the things you may desire
     cannot compare with her.
16 Length of days *is* in her right hand,
   In her left hand riches and honor.

> Martin Van Buren placed his hand on
> Proverbs 3:17 as he took the presidential
> oath of office in 1837.

17 Her ways *are* ways of pleasantness,
   And all her paths *are* peace.
18 She *is* a tree of life to those who take
     hold of her,
   And happy *are all* who retain her.

19 The LORD by wisdom founded the
     earth;
   By understanding He established the
     heavens;
20 By His knowledge the depths were
     broken up,
   And clouds drop down the dew.

21 My son, let them not depart from
     your eyes—
   Keep sound wisdom and discretion;

22 So they will be life to your soul
   And grace to your neck.
23 Then you will walk safely in your way,
   And your foot will not stumble.
24 When you lie down, you will not be
     afraid;
   Yes, you will lie down and your sleep
     will be sweet.
25 Do not be afraid of sudden terror,
   Nor of trouble from the wicked when
     it comes;
26 For the LORD will be your confidence,
   And will keep your foot from being
     caught.

27 Do not withhold good from those to
     whom it is due,
   When it is in the power of your hand
     to do *so.*
28 Do not say to your neighbor,
  "Go, and come back,
   And tomorrow I will give *it,*"
   When you have it with you.
29 Do not devise evil against your
     neighbor,
   For he dwells by you for safety's sake.
30 Do not strive with a man without
     cause,
   If he has done you no harm.

31 Do not envy the oppressor,
   And choose none of his ways;
32 For the perverse *person is* an
     abomination to the LORD,
   But His secret counsel *is* with the
     upright.
33 The curse of the LORD *is* on the house
     of the wicked,
   But He blesses the home of the just.
34 Surely He scorns the scornful,
   But gives grace to the humble.
35 The wise shall inherit glory,
   But shame shall be the legacy of fools.

Security in Wisdom

4 Hear, *my* children, the instruction
     of a father,
   And give attention to know
     understanding;

3:8 [a]Literally *navel,* figurative of the body [b]Literally *drink* or *refreshment*

2 For I give you good doctrine:
Do not forsake my law.
3 When I was my father's son,
Tender and the only one in the sight
of my mother,
4 He also taught me, and said to me:
"Let your heart retain my words;
Keep my commands, and live.
5 Get wisdom! Get understanding!
Do not forget, nor turn away from
the words of my mouth.
6 Do not forsake her, and she will
preserve you;
Love her, and she will keep you.
7 Wisdom *is* the principal thing;
Therefore get wisdom.
And in all your getting, get
understanding.
8 Exalt her, and she will promote you;
She will bring you honor, when you
embrace her.
9 She will place on your head an
ornament of grace;
A crown of glory she will deliver to you."

10 Hear, my son, and receive my sayings,
And the years of your life will be many.
11 I have taught you in the way of wisdom;
I have led you in right paths.
12 When you walk, your steps will not
be hindered,
And when you run, you will not
stumble.
13 Take firm hold of instruction, do not
let go;
Keep her, for she *is* your life.

14 Do not enter the path of the wicked,
And do not walk in the way of evil.
15 Avoid it, do not travel on it;
Turn away from it and pass on.
16 For they do not sleep unless they have
done evil;
And their sleep is taken away unless
they make *someone* fall.
17 For they eat the bread of wickedness,
And drink the wine of violence.

18 But the path of the just *is* like the
shining sun,[a]
That shines ever brighter unto the
perfect day.

19 The way of the wicked *is* like darkness;
They do not know what makes them
stumble.

20 My son, give attention to my words;
Incline your ear to my sayings.
21 Do not let them depart from your eyes;
Keep them in the midst of your heart;
22 For they *are* life to those who find
them,
And health to all their flesh.
23 Keep your heart with all diligence,
For out of it *spring* the issues of life.
24 Put away from you a deceitful mouth,
And put perverse lips far from you.
25 Let your eyes look straight ahead,
And your eyelids look right before you.
26 Ponder the path of your feet,
And let all your ways be established.
27 Do not turn to the right or the left;
Remove your foot from evil.

HOPE

But the path of the just is like the shining sun. . . .

PROVERBS 4:18

The Whole Hope of Human Progress

William Henry Seward (1801–1872), the Secretary of State under Presidents Abraham Lincoln and Andrew Johnson who negotiated the purchase of Alaska from Russia, stated:

> *I do not believe human society, including not merely a few persons in any state, but whole masses of men, ever have attained, or ever can attain, a high state of intelligence, virtue, security, liberty, or happiness without the Holy Scriptures; even the whole hope of human progress is suspended on the ever-growing influence of the Bible.*

The Peril of Adultery

5 My son, pay attention to my wisdom;
Lend your ear to my understanding,
2 That you may preserve discretion,
And your lips may keep knowledge.
3 For the lips of an immoral woman
drip honey,
And her mouth *is* smoother than oil;

4:18 [a]Literally *light*

4 But in the end she is bitter as
     wormwood,
     Sharp as a two-edged sword.
5 Her feet go down to death,
     Her steps lay hold of hell.ᵃ
6 Lest you ponder *her* path of life—
     Her ways are unstable;
     You do not know *them.*

7 Therefore hear me now, *my* children,
     And do not depart from the words of
     my mouth.
8 Remove your way far from her,
     And do not go near the door of her
     house,
9 Lest you give your honor to others,
     And your years to the cruel *one;*
10 Lest aliens be filled with your wealth,
     And your labors *go* to the house of a
     foreigner;
11 And you mourn at last,
     When your flesh and your body are
     consumed,
12 And say:
     "How I have hated instruction,
     And my heart despised correction!
13 I have not obeyed the voice of my
     teachers,
     Nor inclined my ear to those who
     instructed me!
14 I was on the verge of total ruin,
     In the midst of the assembly and
     congregation."

15 Drink water from your own cistern,
     And running water from your own
     well.
16 Should your fountains be dispersed
     abroad,
     Streams of water in the streets?
17 Let them be only your own,
     And not for strangers with you.
18 Let your fountain be blessed,
     And rejoice with the wife of your youth.
19 *As a* loving deer and a graceful doe,
     Let her breasts satisfy you at all times;
     And always be enraptured with her
     love.
20 For why should you, my son, be
     enraptured by an immoral woman,
     And be embraced in the arms of a
     seductress?

21 For the ways of man *are* before the
     eyes of the LORD,
     And He ponders all his paths.
22 His own iniquities entrap the wicked
     man,
     And he is caught in the cords of his sin.
23 He shall die for lack of instruction,
     And in the greatness of his folly he
     shall go astray.

Dangerous Promises

6 My son, if you become surety for your
     friend,
     If you have shaken hands in pledge
     for a stranger,
2 You are snared by the words of your
     mouth;
     You are taken by the words of your
     mouth.
3 So do this, my son, and deliver yourself;
     For you have come into the hand of
     your friend:
     Go and humble yourself;
     Plead with your friend.
4 Give no sleep to your eyes,
     Nor slumber to your eyelids.
5 Deliver yourself like a gazelle from the
     hand *of the hunter,*
     And like a bird from the hand of the
     fowler.ᵃ

The Folly of Indolence

6 Go to the ant, you sluggard!
     Consider her ways and be wise,
7 Which, having no captain,
     Overseer or ruler,
8 Provides her supplies in the summer,
     And gathers her food in the harvest.
9 How long will you slumber, O sluggard?
     When will you rise from your sleep?
10 A little sleep, a little slumber,
     A little folding of the hands to sleep—
11 So shall your poverty come on you
     like a prowler,
     And your need like an armed man.

The Wicked Man

12 A worthless person, a wicked man,
     Walks with a perverse mouth;

5:5 ᵃOr *Sheol*   **6:5** ᵃThat is, one who catches birds
in a trap or snare

13 He winks with his eyes,
   He shuffles his feet,
   He points with his fingers;
14 Perversity *is* in his heart,
   He devises evil continually,
   He sows discord.
15 Therefore his calamity shall come
       suddenly;
   Suddenly he shall be broken without
       remedy.

16 These six *things* the LORD hates,
   Yes, seven *are* an abomination to Him:
17 A proud look,
   A lying tongue,
   Hands that shed innocent blood,
18 A heart that devises wicked plans,
   Feet that are swift in running to evil,
19 A false witness *who* speaks lies,
   And one who sows discord among
       brethren.

Beware of Adultery

20 My son, keep your father's command,
   And do not forsake the law of your
       mother.
21 Bind them continually upon your heart;
   Tie them around your neck.
22 When you roam, they[a] will lead you;
   When you sleep, they will keep you;
   And *when* you awake, they will speak
       with you.
23 For the commandment *is* a lamp,
   And the law a light;
   Reproofs of instruction *are* the way
       of life,
24 To keep you from the evil woman,
   From the flattering tongue of a
       seductress.
25 Do not lust after her beauty in your
       heart,
   Nor let her allure you with her eyelids.
26 For by means of a harlot
   A man is reduced to a crust of bread;
   And an adulteress[a] will prey upon his
       precious life.
27 Can a man take fire to his bosom,
   And his clothes not be burned?
28 Can one walk on hot coals,
   And his feet not be seared?
29 So *is* he who goes in to his neighbor's
       wife;

   Whoever touches her shall not be
       innocent.

30 *People* do not despise a thief
   If he steals to satisfy himself when he
       is starving.
31 Yet *when* he is found, he must restore
       sevenfold;
   He may have to give up all the
       substance of his house.
32 Whoever commits adultery with a
       woman lacks understanding;
   He *who* does so destroys his own soul.
33 Wounds and dishonor he will get,
   And his reproach will not be wiped
       away.
34 For jealousy *is* a husband's fury;
   Therefore he will not spare in the day
       of vengeance.
35 He will accept no recompense,
   Nor will he be appeased though you
       give many gifts.

7 My son, keep my words,
   And treasure my commands within you.
2 Keep my commands and live,
   And my law as the apple of your eye.
3 Bind them on your fingers;
   Write them on the tablet of your heart.
4 Say to wisdom, "You *are* my sister,"
   And call understanding *your* nearest
       kin,
5 That they may keep you from the
       immoral woman,
   From the seductress *who* flatters with
       her words.

The Crafty Harlot

6 For at the window of my house
   I looked through my lattice,
7 And saw among the simple,
   I perceived among the youths,
   A young man devoid of
       understanding,
8 Passing along the street near her
       corner;
   And he took the path to her house
9 In the twilight, in the evening,
   In the black and dark night.

6:22 [a]Literally *it*   **6:26** [a]Literally *a man's wife,* that
is, of another

10 And there a woman met him,
With the attire of a harlot, and a
crafty heart.
11 She *was* loud and rebellious,
Her feet would not stay at home.
12 At times *she was* outside, at times in
the open square,
Lurking at every corner.
13 So she caught him and kissed him;
With an impudent face she said to him:
14 "*I have* peace offerings with me;
Today I have paid my vows.
15 So I came out to meet you,
Diligently to seek your face,
And I have found you.
16 I have spread my bed with tapestry,
Colored coverings of Egyptian linen.
17 I have perfumed my bed
With myrrh, aloes, and cinnamon.
18 Come, let us take our fill of love until
morning;
Let us delight ourselves with love.
19 For my husband *is* not at home;
He has gone on a long journey;
20 He has taken a bag of money with him,
And will come home on the appointed
day."

21 With her enticing speech she caused
him to yield,
With her flattering lips she seduced
him.
22 Immediately he went after her, as
an ox goes to the slaughter,
Or as a fool to the correction of the
stocks,a
23 Till an arrow struck his liver.
As a bird hastens to the snare,
He did not know it *would cost* his life.

24 Now therefore, listen to me, *my*
children;
Pay attention to the words of my
mouth:
25 Do not let your heart turn aside to
her ways,
Do not stray into her paths;
26 For she has cast down many wounded,
And all who were slain by her were
strong *men.*
27 Her house *is* the way to hell,a
Descending to the chambers of death.

The Excellence of Wisdom

8 Does not wisdom cry out,
And understanding lift up her voice?
2 She takes her stand on the top of the
high hill,
Beside the way, where the paths meet.
3 She cries out by the gates, at the entry
of the city,
At the entrance of the doors:
4 "To you, O men, I call,
And my voice *is* to the sons of men.
5 O you simple ones, understand
prudence,
And you fools, be of an understanding
heart.
6 Listen, for I will speak of excellent
things,
And from the opening of my lips *will
come* right things;
7 For my mouth will speak truth;
Wickedness *is* an abomination to my
lips.
8 All the words of my mouth *are* with
righteousness;
Nothing crooked or perverse *is* in them.
9 They *are* all plain to him who
understands,
And right to those who find knowledge.
10 Receive my instruction, and not silver,
And knowledge rather than choice
gold;
11 For wisdom *is* better than rubies,
And all the things one may desire
cannot be compared with her.

12 "I, wisdom, dwell with prudence,
And find out knowledge *and* discretion.
13 The fear of the LORD *is* to hate evil;
Pride and arrogance and the evil way
And the perverse mouth I hate.
14 Counsel *is* mine, and sound wisdom;
I *am* understanding, I have strength.
15 By me kings reign,
And rulers decree justice.
16 By me princes rule, and nobles,
All the judges of the earth.a

7:22 aSeptuagint, Syriac, and Targum read *as a dog
to bonds;* Vulgate reads *as a lamb . . . to bonds.*
7:27 aOr *Sheol*   **8:16** aMasoretic Text, Syriac,
Targum, and Vulgate read *righteousness;* Septuagint,
Bomberg, and some manuscripts and editions read
earth.

17 I love those who love me,
And those who seek me diligently
will find me.
18 Riches and honor *are* with me,
Enduring riches and righteousness.
19 My fruit *is* better than gold, yes, than
fine gold,
And my revenue than choice silver.
20 I traverse the way of righteousness,
In the midst of the paths of justice,
21 That I may cause those who love me
to inherit wealth,
That I may fill their treasuries.

22 "The LORD possessed me at the
beginning of His way,
Before His works of old.
23 I have been established from
everlasting,
From the beginning, before there
was ever an earth.
24 When *there were* no depths I was
brought forth,
When *there were* no fountains
abounding with water.
25 Before the mountains were settled,
Before the hills, I was brought forth;
26 While as yet He had not made the
earth or the fields,
Or the primal dust of the world.
27 When He prepared the heavens, I *was*
there,
When He drew a circle on the face of
the deep,
28 When He established the clouds above,
When He strengthened the fountains
of the deep,
29 When He assigned to the sea its limit,
So that the waters would not
transgress His command,
When He marked out the foundations
of the earth,
30 Then I was beside Him *as* a master
craftsman;ᵃ
And I was daily *His* delight,
Rejoicing always before Him,
31 Rejoicing in His inhabited world,
And my delight *was* with the sons of
men.

32 "Now therefore, listen to me, *my* children,
For blessed *are those who* keep my ways.

33 Hear instruction and be wise,
And do not disdain *it*.
34 Blessed is the man who listens to me,
Watching daily at my gates,
Waiting at the posts of my doors.
35 For whoever finds me finds life,
And obtains favor from the LORD;
36 But he who sins against me wrongs
his own soul;
All those who hate me love death."

The Way of Wisdom

9 Wisdom has built her house,
She has hewn out her seven pillars;
2 She has slaughtered her meat,
She has mixed her wine,
She has also furnished her table.
3 She has sent out her maidens,
She cries out from the highest places
of the city,
4 "Whoever *is* simple, let him turn in
here!"
As for him who lacks understanding,
she says to him,
5 "Come, eat of my bread
And drink of the wine I have mixed.
6 Forsake foolishness and live,
And go in the way of understanding.

7 "He who corrects a scoffer gets shame
for himself,
And he who rebukes a wicked *man*
only harms himself.
8 Do not correct a scoffer, lest he hate you;
Rebuke a wise *man*, and he will love
you.
9 Give *instruction* to a wise *man*, and he
will be still wiser;
Teach a just *man*, and he will increase
in learning.

10 "The fear of the LORD *is* the beginning
of wisdom,
And the knowledge of the Holy One *is*
understanding.
11 For by me your days will be multiplied,
And years of life will be added to you.
12 If you are wise, you are wise for
yourself,
And *if* you scoff, you will bear *it* alone."

8:30 ᵃA Jewish tradition reads *one brought up*.

The Way of Folly

13 A foolish woman is clamorous;
    She is simple, and knows nothing.
14 For she sits at the door of her house,
    On a seat *by* the highest places of the
      city,
15 To call to those who pass by,
    Who go straight on their way:
16 "Whoever *is* simple, let him turn in
      here";
    And *as for* him who lacks
      understanding, she says to him,
17 "Stolen water is sweet,
    And bread *eaten* in secret is pleasant."
18 But he does not know that the dead
      are there,
    That her guests *are* in the depths of hell.ª

Wise Sayings of Solomon

10 The proverbs of Solomon:

    A wise son makes a glad father,
    But a foolish son *is* the grief of his
      mother.

2 Treasures of wickedness profit nothing,
    But righteousness delivers from death.
3 The Lord will not allow the righteous
      soul to famish,
    But He casts away the desire of the
      wicked.

4 He who has a slack hand becomes
      poor,
    But the hand of the diligent makes
      rich.
5 He who gathers in summer *is* a wise
      son;
    He who sleeps in harvest *is* a son
      who causes shame.

6 Blessings *are* on the head of the
      righteous,
    But violence covers the mouth of the
      wicked.
7 The memory of the righteous *is* blessed,
    But the name of the wicked will rot.

8 The wise in heart will receive
      commands,
    But a prating fool will fall.

9 He who walks with integrity walks
      securely,
    But he who perverts his ways will
      become known.

10 He who winks with the eye causes
      trouble,
    But a prating fool will fall.

11 The mouth of the righteous *is* a well
      of life,
    But violence covers the mouth of the
      wicked.

12 Hatred stirs up strife,
    But love covers all sins.

13 Wisdom is found on the lips of him
      who has understanding,
    But a rod *is* for the back of him who
      is devoid of understanding.

14 Wise *people* store up knowledge,
    But the mouth of the foolish *is* near
      destruction.

15 The rich man's wealth *is* his strong
      city;
    The destruction of the poor *is* their
      poverty.

16 The labor of the righteous *leads* to life,
    The wages of the wicked to sin.

17 He who keeps instruction *is in* the way
      of life,
    But he who refuses correction goes
      astray.

18 Whoever hides hatred *has* lying lips,
    And whoever spreads slander *is* a fool.

19 In the multitude of words sin is not
      lacking,
    But he who restrains his lips *is* wise.
20 The tongue of the righteous *is* choice
      silver;
    The heart of the wicked *is worth* little.
21 The lips of the righteous feed many,
    But fools die for lack of wisdom.ª

9:18 ªOr *Sheol*   **10:21** ªLiterally *heart*

22 The blessing of the LORD makes *one* rich,
And He adds no sorrow with it.

23 To do evil *is* like sport to a fool,
But a man of understanding has
wisdom.
24 The fear of the wicked will come upon
him,
And the desire of the righteous will
be granted.
25 When the whirlwind passes by, the
wicked *is* no *more,*
But the righteous *has* an everlasting
foundation.

26 As vinegar to the teeth and smoke to
the eyes,
So *is* the lazy *man* to those who send
him.

27 The fear of the LORD prolongs days,
But the years of the wicked will be
shortened.
28 The hope of the righteous *will be*
gladness,
But the expectation of the wicked will
perish.
29 The way of the LORD *is* strength for the
upright,
But destruction *will come* to the
workers of iniquity.

30 The righteous will never be removed,
But the wicked will not inhabit the
earth.
31 The mouth of the righteous brings
forth wisdom,
But the perverse tongue will be cut out.
32 The lips of the righteous know what is
acceptable,
But the mouth of the wicked *what is*
perverse.

11

Dishonest scales *are* an abomination
to the LORD,
But a just weight *is* His delight.

2 When pride comes, then comes shame;
But with the humble *is* wisdom.

3 The integrity of the upright will guide
them,
But the perversity of the unfaithful
will destroy them.
4 Riches do not profit in the day of wrath,
But righteousness delivers from death.
5 The righteousness of the blameless
will direct[a] his way aright,
But the wicked will fall by his own
wickedness.
6 The righteousness of the upright will
deliver them,
But the unfaithful will be caught by
their lust.

7 When a wicked man dies, *his*
expectation will perish,
And the hope of the unjust perishes.
8 The righteous is delivered from
trouble,
And it comes to the wicked instead.
9 The hypocrite with *his* mouth destroys
his neighbor,
But through knowledge the righteous
will be delivered.
10 When it goes well with the righteous,
the city rejoices;
And when the wicked perish, *there is*
jubilation.
11 By the blessing of the upright the city
is exalted,
But it is overthrown by the mouth of
the wicked.

12 He who is devoid of wisdom despises
his neighbor,
But a man of understanding holds his
peace.

13 A talebearer reveals secrets,
But he who is of a faithful spirit
conceals a matter.

14 Where *there is* no counsel, the people
fall;
But in the multitude of counselors
there is safety.

15 He who is surety for a stranger will
suffer,
But one who hates being surety is
secure.

11:5 [a]Or *make smooth* or *straight*

16 A gracious woman retains honor,
But ruthless *men* retain riches.
17 The merciful man does good for his
own soul,
But *he who is* cruel troubles his own
flesh.
18 The wicked *man* does deceptive work,
But he who sows righteousness *will
have* a sure reward.
19 As righteousness *leads* to life,
So he who pursues evil *pursues it* to his
own death.
20 Those who are of a perverse heart *are*
an abomination to the LORD,
But *the* blameless in their ways *are* His
delight.
21 *Though they join* forces,[a] the wicked
will not go unpunished;
But the posterity of the righteous will
be delivered.

22 *As* a ring of gold in a swine's snout,
So is a lovely woman who lacks
discretion.

23 The desire of the righteous *is* only good,
But the expectation of the wicked *is*
wrath.

24 There is *one* who scatters, yet increases
more;
And there is *one* who withholds more
than is right,
But it *leads* to poverty.
25 The generous soul will be made rich,
And he who waters will also be
watered himself.
26 The people will curse him who
withholds grain,
But blessing *will be* on the head of him
who sells *it.*

27 He who earnestly seeks good finds favor,
But trouble will come to him who
seeks *evil.*

28 He who trusts in his riches will fall,
But the righteous will flourish like
foliage.

29 He who troubles his own house will
inherit the wind,

And the fool *will be* servant to the wise
of heart.

30 The fruit of the righteous *is a* tree of life,
And he who wins souls *is* wise.

31 If the righteous will be recompensed
on the earth,
How much more the ungodly and the
sinner.

12 Whoever loves instruction loves
knowledge,
But he who hates correction *is* stupid.

2 A good *man* obtains favor from the
LORD,
But a man of wicked intentions He
will condemn.

3 A man is not established by wickedness,
But the root of the righteous cannot be
moved.

4 An excellent[a] wife *is* the crown of her
husband,
But she who causes shame *is* like
rottenness in his bones.

5 The thoughts of the righteous *are* right,
But the counsels of the wicked *are*
deceitful.
6 The words of the wicked *are,* "Lie in
wait for blood,"
But the mouth of the upright will
deliver them.

7 The wicked are overthrown and *are*
no more,
But the house of the righteous will
stand.

8 A man will be commended according
to his wisdom,
But he who is of a perverse heart will
be despised.

9 Better *is the one* who is slighted but
has a servant,

11:21 [a]Literally *hand to hand*
12:4 [a]Literally *A wife of valor*

Than he who honors himself but lacks bread.

10 A righteous *man* regards the life of his animal,
But the tender mercies of the wicked *are* cruel.

11 He who tills his land will be satisfied with bread,
But he who follows frivolity *is* devoid of understanding.ᵃ

12 The wicked covet the catch of evil *men,*
But the root of the righteous yields *fruit.*

13 The wicked is ensnared by the transgression of *his* lips,
But the righteous will come through trouble.

14 A man will be satisfied with good by the fruit of *his* mouth,
And the recompense of a man's hands will be rendered to him.

15 The way of a fool *is* right in his own eyes,
But he who heeds counsel *is* wise.

16 A fool's wrath is known at once,
But a prudent *man* covers shame.

17 He *who* speaks truth declares righteousness,
But a false witness, deceit.

18 There is one who speaks like the piercings of a sword,
But the tongue of the wise *promotes* health.

19 The truthful lip shall be established forever,
But a lying tongue *is* but for a moment.

20 Deceit is in the heart of those who devise evil,
But counselors of peace have joy.

21 No grave trouble will overtake the righteous,
But the wicked shall be filled with evil.

22 Lying lips *are* an abomination to the LORD,
But those who deal truthfully *are* His delight.

23 A prudent man conceals knowledge,
But the heart of fools proclaims foolishness.

24 The hand of the diligent will rule,
But the lazy *man* will be put to forced labor.

25 Anxiety in the heart of man causes depression,
But a good word makes it glad.

26 The righteous should choose his friends carefully,
For the way of the wicked leads them astray.

27 The lazy *man* does not roast what he took in hunting,
But diligence *is* man's precious possession.

28 In the way of righteousness *is* life,
And in *its* pathway *there is* no death.

13 A wise son *heeds* his father's instruction,
But a scoffer does not listen to rebuke.

2 A man shall eat well by the fruit of *his* mouth,
But the soul of the unfaithful feeds on violence.

3 He who guards his mouth preserves his life,
But he who opens wide his lips shall have destruction.

4 The soul of a lazy *man* desires, and *has* nothing;
But the soul of the diligent shall be made rich.

5 A righteous *man* hates lying,
But a wicked *man* is loathsome and comes to shame.

6 Righteousness guards *him whose* way is blameless,
But wickedness overthrows the sinner.

12:11 ᵃLiterally *heart*

7 There is one who makes himself rich,
    yet *has* nothing;
And one who makes himself poor, yet
    has great riches.

8 The ransom of a man's life *is* his riches,
But the poor does not hear rebuke.

9 The light of the righteous rejoices,
But the lamp of the wicked will be
    put out.

10 By pride comes nothing but strife,
But with the well-advised *is* wisdom.

11 Wealth *gained by* dishonesty will be
    diminished,
But he who gathers by labor will
    increase.

12 Hope deferred makes the heart sick,
But *when* the desire comes, *it is* a tree
    of life.

HOPE

Hope deferred makes the heart sick. . . .
                          PROVERBS 13:12

The Last Best Hope of Earth

In December 1862, President Lincoln concluded
his Second Annual Message to Congress:

> *In giving freedom to the slave, we assure free-
> dom to the free—honorable alike in what we
> give and what we preserve. We shall nobly
> save—or meanly lose—the last best hope of
> earth. Other means may succeed; this could
> not fail. The way is plain, peaceful, generous,
> just—a way which if followed the world will
> forever applaud and God must forever bless.*

13 He who despises the word will be
    destroyed,
But he who fears the commandment
    will be rewarded.
14 The law of the wise *is* a fountain of life,
To turn *one* away from the snares of
    death.

15 Good understanding gains favor,
But the way of the unfaithful *is* hard.

16 Every prudent *man* acts with knowledge,
But a fool lays open *his* folly.

17 A wicked messenger falls into trouble,
But a faithful ambassador *brings*
    health.

18 Poverty and shame *will come* to him
    who disdains correction,
But he who regards a rebuke will be
    honored.

19 A desire accomplished is sweet to the
    soul,
But *it is* an abomination to fools to
    depart from evil.

20 He who walks with wise *men* will be
    wise,
But the companion of fools will be
    destroyed.

21 Evil pursues sinners,
But to the righteous, good shall be
    repaid.

22 A good *man* leaves an inheritance to
    his children's children,
But the wealth of the sinner is stored
    up for the righteous.

23 Much food *is in* the fallow *ground* of
    the poor,
And for lack of justice there is waste.[a]

24 He who spares his rod hates his son,
But he who loves him disciplines him
    promptly.

25 The righteous eats to the satisfying of
    his soul,
But the stomach of the wicked shall be
    in want.

14 The wise woman builds her house,
But the foolish pulls it down with
    her hands.

2 He who walks in his uprightness fears
    the LORD,

13:23 [a]Literally *what is swept away*

But *he who is* perverse in his ways
  despises Him.

3   In the mouth of a fool *is* a rod of pride,
  But the lips of the wise will preserve
  them.

4   Where no oxen *are,* the trough *is* clean;
  But much increase *comes* by the strength
  of an ox.

5   A faithful witness does not lie,
  But a false witness will utter lies.

6   A scoffer seeks wisdom and does not
  find it,
  But knowledge *is* easy to him who
  understands.

7   Go from the presence of a foolish man,
  When you do not perceive *in him* the
  lips of knowledge.

8   The wisdom of the prudent *is* to
  understand his way,
  But the folly of fools *is* deceit.

9   Fools mock at sin,
  But among the upright *there is* favor.

10   The heart knows its own bitterness,
  And a stranger does not share its joy.

11   The house of the wicked will be
  overthrown,
  But the tent of the upright will flourish.

12   There is a way *that seems* right to a
  man,
  But its end *is* the way of death.

13   Even in laughter the heart may sorrow,
  And the end of mirth *may be* grief.

14   The backslider in heart will be filled
  with his own ways,
  But a good man *will be satisfied* from
  above.ᵃ

15   The simple believes every word,
  But the prudent considers well his steps.

16   A wise *man* fears and departs from
  evil,
  But a fool rages and is self-confident.

17   A quick-tempered *man* acts foolishly,
  And a man of wicked intentions is
  hated.

18   The simple inherit folly,
  But the prudent are crowned with
  knowledge.

19   The evil will bow before the good,
  And the wicked at the gates of the
  righteous.

20   The poor *man* is hated even by his
  own neighbor,
  But the rich *has* many friends.

21   He who despises his neighbor sins;
  But he who has mercy on the poor,
  happy *is* he.

22   Do they not go astray who devise evil?
  But mercy and truth *belong* to those
  who devise good.

23   In all labor there is profit,
  But idle chatterᵃ *leads* only to
  poverty.

24   The crown of the wise is their riches,
  But the foolishness of fools *is* folly.

25   A true witness delivers souls,
  But a deceitful *witness* speaks lies.

26   In the fear of the LORD *there is* strong
  confidence,
  And His children will have a place
  of refuge.

27   The fear of the LORD *is* a fountain of
  life,
  To turn *one* away from the snares of
  death.

28   In a multitude of people *is* a king's
  honor,
  But in the lack of people *is* the
  downfall of a prince.

29   *He who is* slow to wrath has great
  understanding,
  But *he who is* impulsiveᵃ exalts folly.

14:14 ᵃLiterally *from above himself*
14:23 ᵃLiterally *talk of the lips*
14:29 ᵃLiterally *short of spirit*

30 A sound heart *is* life to the body,
But envy *is* rottenness to the bones.

31 He who oppresses the poor reproaches
his Maker,
But he who honors Him has mercy on
the needy.

32 The wicked is banished in his
wickedness,
But the righteous has a refuge in his
death.

33 Wisdom rests in the heart of him who
has understanding,
But *what is* in the heart of fools is
made known.

34 Righteousness exalts a nation,
But sin *is* a reproach to *any* people.

35 The king's favor *is* toward a wise
servant,
But his wrath *is against* him who
causes shame.

MORAL STRENGTH
Righteousness exalts a nation. . . .
PROVERBS 14:34

Righteousness Exalts a Nation
Patrick Henry, an American Revolutionary leader
who pushed through the Stamp Act Resolves in
May 1765, the most anti-British political action to
that point, wrote:

*Whether this will prove a blessing or a curse will
depend upon the use our people make of the
blessings, which a gracious God hath bestowed
on us. If they are wise, they will be great and
happy. If they are of a contrary character, they
will be miserable.*

*Righteousness alone can exalt them as a
nation. Reader! Whoever thou art, remember
this, and in thy sphere practice virtue thyself,
and encourage it in others.*

15 A soft answer turns away wrath,
But a harsh word stirs up anger.
2 The tongue of the wise uses knowledge
rightly,

But the mouth of fools pours forth
foolishness.

3 The eyes of the LORD *are* in every place,
Keeping watch on the evil and the good.

4 A wholesome tongue *is* a tree of life,
But perverseness in it breaks the spirit.

5 A fool despises his father's instruction,
But he who receives correction is
prudent.

6 *In* the house of the righteous *there
is* much treasure,
But in the revenue of the wicked is
trouble.

7 The lips of the wise disperse knowledge,
But the heart of the fool *does* not *do* so.

8 The sacrifice of the wicked *is* an
abomination to the LORD,
But the prayer of the upright *is* His
delight.

9 The way of the wicked *is* an
abomination to the LORD,
But He loves him who follows
righteousness.

10 Harsh discipline *is* for him who
forsakes the way,
And he who hates correction will die.

11 Hell[a] and Destruction[b] *are* before the
LORD;
So how much more the hearts of the
sons of men.

12 A scoffer does not love one who
corrects him,
Nor will he go to the wise.

13 A merry heart makes a cheerful
countenance,
But by sorrow of the heart the spirit
is broken.

14 The heart of him who has
understanding seeks knowledge,

15:11 [a]Or *Sheol* [b]Hebrew *Abaddon*

But the mouth of fools feeds on
  foolishness.

15 All the days of the afflicted *are* evil,
  But he who is of a merry heart *has a*
  continual feast.

16 Better *is* a little with the fear of the
  LORD,
  Than great treasure with trouble.
17 Better *is* a dinner of herbs[a] where
  love is,
  Than a fatted calf with hatred.

18 A wrathful man stirs up strife,
  But *he who is* slow to anger allays
  contention.

19 The way of the lazy *man is* like a hedge
  of thorns,
  But the way of the upright *is* a highway.

20 A wise son makes a father glad,
  But a foolish man despises his mother.

21 Folly *is* joy *to him who is* destitute of
  discernment,
  But a man of understanding walks
  uprightly.

22 Without counsel, plans go awry,
  But in the multitude of counselors
  they are established.

23 A man has joy by the answer of his
  mouth,
  And a word *spoken* in due season, how
  good *it is!*

24 The way of life *winds* upward for the
  wise,
  That he may turn away from hell[a]
  below.

25 The LORD will destroy the house of the
  proud,
  But He will establish the boundary of
  the widow.

26 The thoughts of the wicked *are* an
  abomination to the LORD,
  But the words of the pure *are* pleasant.

27 He who is greedy for gain troubles his
  own house,
  But he who hates bribes will live.

28 The heart of the righteous studies how
  to answer,
  But the mouth of the wicked pours
  forth evil.

29 The LORD *is* far from the wicked,
  But He hears the prayer of the righteous.

30 The light of the eyes rejoices the heart,
  And a good report makes the bones
  healthy.[a]

31 The ear that hears the rebukes of life
  Will abide among the wise.
32 He who disdains instruction despises
  his own soul,
  But he who heeds rebuke gets
  understanding.
33 The fear of the LORD *is* the instruction
  of wisdom,
  And before honor *is* humility.

William **McKinley** placed his hand on
Proverbs 16 as he took the presidential
oath of office in 1901.

16 The preparations of the heart *belong*
  to man,
  But the answer of the tongue *is* from
  the LORD.

2 All the ways of a man *are* pure in
  his own eyes,
  But the LORD weighs the spirits.

3 Commit your works to the LORD,
  And your thoughts will be established.

4 The LORD has made all for Himself,
  Yes, even the wicked for the day of
  doom.

5 Everyone proud in heart *is* an
  abomination to the LORD;

15:17 [a]Or *vegetables*   15:24 [a]Or *Sheol*
15:30 [a]Literally *fat*

Though they join forces,[a] none will go unpunished.

6   In mercy and truth
Atonement is provided for iniquity;
And by the fear of the LORD *one* departs from evil.

7   When a man's ways please the LORD,
He makes even his enemies to be at peace with him.

8   Better *is* a little with righteousness,
Than vast revenues without justice.

9   A man's heart plans his way,
But the LORD directs his steps.

10   Divination *is* on the lips of the king;
His mouth must not transgress in judgment.

11   Honest weights and scales *are* the LORD's;
All the weights in the bag *are* His work.

12   *It is* an abomination for kings to commit wickedness,
For a throne is established by righteousness.

13   Righteous lips *are* the delight of kings,
And they love him who speaks *what is* right.

14   As messengers of death *is* the king's wrath,
But a wise man will appease it.

15   In the light of the king's face *is* life,
And his favor *is* like a cloud of the latter rain.

16   How much better to get wisdom than gold!
And to get understanding is to be chosen rather than silver.

17   The highway of the upright *is* to depart from evil;
He who keeps his way preserves his soul.

18   Pride *goes* before destruction,
And a haughty spirit before a fall.

19   Better *to be* of a humble spirit with the lowly,
Than to divide the spoil with the proud.

20   He who heeds the word wisely will find good,
And whoever trusts in the LORD, happy *is* he.

21   The wise in heart will be called prudent,
And sweetness of the lips increases learning.

22   Understanding *is* a wellspring of life to him who has it.
But the correction of fools *is* folly.

23   The heart of the wise teaches his mouth,
And adds learning to his lips.

24   Pleasant words *are like* a honeycomb,
Sweetness to the soul and health to the bones.

25   There is a way *that seems* right to a man,
But its end *is* the way of death.

26   The person who labors, labors for himself,
For his *hungry* mouth drives him *on.*

27   An ungodly man digs up evil,
And *it is* on his lips like a burning fire.

28   A perverse man sows strife,
And a whisperer separates the best of friends.

29   A violent man entices his neighbor,
And leads him in a way *that is* not good.

30   He winks his eye to devise perverse things;
He purses his lips *and* brings about evil.

31   The silver-haired head *is* a crown of glory,
If it is found in the way of righteousness.

32   *He who is* slow to anger *is* better than the mighty,
And he who rules his spirit than he who takes a city.

33   The lot is cast into the lap,
But its every decision *is* from the LORD.

16:5 [a]Literally *hand to hand*

17 Better *is* a dry morsel with quietness,
Than a house full of feasting[a] *with* strife.

2 A wise servant will rule over a son who causes shame,
And will share an inheritance among the brothers.

3 The refining pot *is* for silver and the furnace for gold,
But the LORD tests the hearts.

4 An evildoer gives heed to false lips;
A liar listens eagerly to a spiteful tongue.

5 He who mocks the poor reproaches his Maker;
He who is glad at calamity will not go unpunished.

6 Children's children *are* the crown of old men,
And the glory of children *is* their father.

7 Excellent speech is not becoming to a fool,
Much less lying lips to a prince.

8 A present *is* a precious stone in the eyes of its possessor;
Wherever he turns, he prospers.

9 He who covers a transgression seeks love,
But he who repeats a matter separates friends.

10 Rebuke is more effective for a wise *man*
Than a hundred blows on a fool.

11 An evil *man* seeks only rebellion;
Therefore a cruel messenger will be sent against him.

12 Let a man meet a bear robbed of her cubs,
Rather than a fool in his folly.

13 Whoever rewards evil for good,
Evil will not depart from his house.

14 The beginning of strife *is like* releasing water;
Therefore stop contention before a quarrel starts.

15 He who justifies the wicked, and he who condemns the just,
Both of them alike *are* an abomination to the LORD.

16 Why *is there* in the hand of a fool the purchase price of wisdom,
Since *he has* no heart *for it?*

17 A friend loves at all times,
And a brother is born for adversity.

18 A man devoid of understanding shakes hands in a pledge,
And becomes surety for his friend.

19 He who loves transgression loves strife,
And he who exalts his gate seeks destruction.

20 He who has a deceitful heart finds no good,
And he who has a perverse tongue falls into evil.

21 He who begets a scoffer *does so* to his sorrow,
And the father of a fool has no joy.

22 A merry heart does good, *like* medicine,[a]
But a broken spirit dries the bones.

23 A wicked *man* accepts a bribe behind the back[a]
To pervert the ways of justice.

24 Wisdom *is* in the sight of him who has understanding,
But the eyes of a fool *are* on the ends of the earth.

25 A foolish son *is* a grief to his father,
And bitterness to her who bore him.

17:1 [a]Or *sacrificial meals*   **17:22** [a]Or *makes medicine even better*   **17:23** [a]Literally *from the bosom*

26 Also, to punish the righteous *is* not good,
Nor to strike princes for *their* uprightness.

27 He who has knowledge spares his words,
And a man of understanding is of a calm spirit.

28 Even a fool is counted wise when he holds his peace;
When he shuts his lips, *he is considered* perceptive.

18 A man who isolates himself seeks his own desire;
He rages against all wise judgment.

2 A fool has no delight in understanding,
But in expressing his own heart.

3 When the wicked comes, contempt comes also;
And with dishonor *comes* reproach.

4 The words of a man's mouth *are* deep waters;
The wellspring of wisdom *is* a flowing brook.

5 *It is* not good to show partiality to the wicked,
Or to overthrow the righteous in judgment.

6 A fool's lips enter into contention,
And his mouth calls for blows.

7 A fool's mouth *is* his destruction,
And his lips *are* the snare of his soul.

8 The words of a talebearer *are* like tasty trifles,[a]
And they go down into the inmost body.

9 He who is slothful in his work
Is a brother to him who is a great destroyer.

10 The name of the LORD *is* a strong tower;
The righteous run to it and are safe.

11 The rich man's wealth *is* his strong city,
And like a high wall in his own esteem.

12 Before destruction the heart of a man is haughty,
And before honor *is* humility.

13 He who answers a matter before he hears *it,*
It *is* folly and shame to him.

14 The spirit of a man will sustain him in sickness,
But who can bear a broken spirit?

15 The heart of the prudent acquires knowledge,
And the ear of the wise seeks knowledge.

HONOR

. . . with dishonor comes reproach.

PROVERBS 18:3

The Minutemen

In 1774, the Massachusetts Provincial Congress reorganized the Massachusetts militia, providing that one-fourth of the entire militia was made up of "Minutemen"—patriots who vowed to be ready to fight at a minute's notice. The Massachusetts Provincial Congress charged the Minutemen:

You . . . are placed by Providence in the post of honor, because it is the post of danger. . . . The eyes not only of North America and the whole British Empire, but of all Europe, are upon you. Let us be, therefore, altogether solicitous that no disorderly behavior, nothing unbecoming our characters as Americans, as citizens and Christians, be justly chargeable to us.

16 A man's gift makes room for him,
And brings him before great men.

17 The first *one* to plead his cause *seems* right,
Until his neighbor comes and examines him.

18 Casting lots causes contentions to cease,
And keeps the mighty apart.

18:8 [a]A Jewish tradition reads *wounds.*

19 A brother offended *is harder to win*
than a strong city,
And contentions *are* like the bars of
a castle.

20 A man's stomach shall be satisfied
from the fruit of his mouth;
From the produce of his lips he shall
be filled.

21 Death and life *are* in the power of the
tongue,
And those who love it will eat its fruit.

22 *He who* finds a wife finds a good *thing*,
And obtains favor from the LORD.

23 The poor *man* uses entreaties,
But the rich answers roughly.

24 A man *who has* friends must himself
be friendly,[a]
But there is a friend *who* sticks closer
than a brother.

19 Better *is* the poor who walks in his
integrity
Than *one who is* perverse in his lips,
and is a fool.

2 Also it is not good *for* a soul *to be*
without knowledge,
And he sins who hastens with *his* feet.

3 The foolishness of a man twists his
way,
And his heart frets against the LORD.

4 Wealth makes many friends,
But the poor is separated from his
friend.

5 A false witness will not go
unpunished,
And *he who* speaks lies will not escape.

6 Many entreat the favor of the nobility,
And every man *is* a friend to one who
gives gifts.

7 All the brothers of the poor hate him;
How much more do his friends go far
from him!

He may pursue *them with* words, *yet*
they abandon *him*.

8 He who gets wisdom loves his own
soul;
He who keeps understanding will
find good.

9 A false witness will not go
unpunished,
And *he who* speaks lies shall perish.

10 Luxury is not fitting for a fool,
Much less for a servant to rule over
princes.

11 The discretion of a man makes him
slow to anger,
And his glory *is* to overlook a
transgression.

12 The king's wrath *is* like the roaring
of a lion,
But his favor *is* like dew on the grass.

13 A foolish son *is* the ruin of his
father,
And the contentions of a wife *are*
a continual dripping.

14 Houses and riches *are* an inheritance
from fathers,
But a prudent wife *is* from the LORD.

15 Laziness casts *one* into a deep sleep,
And an idle person will suffer
hunger.

16 He who keeps the commandment
keeps his soul,
But he who is careless[a] of his ways
will die.

17 He who has pity on the poor lends
to the LORD,
And He will pay back what he has
given.

18:24 [a]Following Greek manuscripts, Syriac, Targum,
and Vulgate; Masoretic Text reads *may come to ruin*.
19:16 [a]Literally *despises*, figurative of recklessness or
carelessness

18 Chasten your son while there is hope,
   And do not set your heart on his
      destruction.ª

19 A *man of* great wrath will suffer
      punishment;
   For if you rescue *him,* you will have
      to do it again.

20 Listen to counsel and receive
      instruction,
   That you may be wise in your latter
      days.

21 There are many plans in a man's
      heart,
   Nevertheless the LORD's counsel—that
      will stand.

22 What is desired in a man is kindness,
   And a poor man is better than a liar.

23 The fear of the LORD *leads* to life,
   And *he who has it* will abide in
      satisfaction;
   He will not be visited with evil.

24 A lazy *man* buries his hand in the
      bowl,ª
   And will not so much as bring it to his
      mouth again.

25 Strike a scoffer, and the simple will
      become wary;
   Rebuke one who has understanding,
      and he will discern knowledge.

26 He who mistreats *his* father *and* chases
      away *his* mother
   Is a son who causes shame and brings
      reproach.

27 Cease listening to instruction, my son,
   And you will stray from the words of
      knowledge.

28 A disreputable witness scorns justice,
   And the mouth of the wicked devours
      iniquity.

29 Judgments are prepared for scoffers,
   And beatings for the backs of fools.

20 Wine *is* a mocker,
   Strong drink *is* a brawler,
   And whoever is led astray by it is not
      wise.

2 The wrathª of a king *is* like the roaring
      of a lion;
   Whoever provokes him to anger sins
      against his own life.

3 *It is* honorable for a man to stop
      striving,
   Since any fool can start a quarrel.

4 The lazy *man* will not plow because
      of winter;
   He will beg during harvest and *have*
      nothing.

5 Counsel in the heart of man *is* like
      deep water,
   But a man of understanding will
      draw it out.

6 Most men will proclaim each his own
      goodness,
   But who can find a faithful man?

7 The righteous *man* walks in his
      integrity;
   His children *are* blessed after him.

8 A king who sits on the throne of
      judgment
   Scatters all evil with his eyes.

9 Who can say, "I have made my heart
      clean,
   I am pure from my sin"?

10 Diverse weights *and* diverse measures,
   They *are* both alike, an abomination
      to the LORD.

11 Even a child is known by his deeds,
   Whether what he does *is* pure and
      right.

19:18 ªLiterally *to put him to death;* a Jewish tradition
reads *on his crying.*   **19:24** ªSeptuagint and Syriac
read *bosom;* Targum and Vulgate read *armpit.*
20:2 ªLiterally *fear* or *terror* which is produced by the
king's wrath

12 The hearing ear and the seeing eye,
The LORD has made them both.

13 Do not love sleep, lest you come to
   poverty;
Open your eyes, *and* you will be
   satisfied with bread.

14 "*It is* good for nothing,"ᵃ cries the buyer;
But when he has gone his way, then
   he boasts.

15 There is gold and a multitude of rubies,
But the lips of knowledge *are* a
   precious jewel.

16 Take the garment of one who is surety
   for a stranger,
And hold it as a pledge *when it* is for a
   seductress.

17 Bread gained by deceit *is* sweet to a
   man,
But afterward his mouth will be filled
   with gravel.

18 Plans are established by counsel;
By wise counsel wage war.

19 He who goes about *as* a talebearer
   reveals secrets;
Therefore do not associate with one
   who flatters with his lips.

20 Whoever curses his father or his mother,
His lamp will be put out in deep
   darkness.

21 An inheritance gained hastily at the
   beginning
Will not be blessed at the end.

22 Do not say, "I will recompense evil";
Wait for the LORD, and He will save you.

23 Diverse weights *are* an abomination to
   the LORD,
And dishonest scales *are* not good.

24 A man's steps *are* of the LORD;
How then can a man understand his
   own way?

25 *It is* a snare for a man to devote
   rashly *something as* holy,
And afterward to reconsider *his* vows.

26 A wise king sifts out the wicked,
And brings the threshing wheel over
   them.

27 The spirit of a man *is* the lamp of the
   LORD,
Searching all the inner depths of his
   heart.ᵃ

28 Mercy and truth preserve the king,
And by lovingkindness he upholds his
   throne.

29 The glory of young men *is* their
   strength,
And the splendor of old men *is* their
   gray head.

30 Blows that hurt cleanse away evil,
As *do* stripes the inner depths of the
   heart.ᵃ

Andrew Johnson placed his hand on
Proverbs 21 as he took the presidential oath
of office in 1865.

James A. Garfield placed his hand on
Proverbs 21:1 as he took the presidential
oath of office in 1881.

---

21 The king's heart *is* in the hand
   of the LORD,
Like the rivers of water;
He turns it wherever He wishes.

2 Every way of a man *is* right in his
   own eyes,
But the LORD weighs the hearts.

3 To do righteousness and justice
Is more acceptable to the LORD than
   sacrifice.

20:14 ᵃLiterally *evil, evil*   **20:27** ᵃLiterally *the rooms*
of the belly   **20:30** ᵃLiterally *the rooms of the belly*

4 A haughty look, a proud heart,
   And the plowing^a of the wicked *are* sin.

5 The plans of the diligent *lead* surely
      to plenty,
   But *those of* everyone *who is* hasty,
      surely to poverty.

6 Getting treasures by a lying tongue
   Is the fleeting fantasy of those who
      seek death.^a

7 The violence of the wicked will destroy
      them,^a
   Because they refuse to do justice.

8 The way of a guilty man *is* perverse;^a
   But *as for* the pure, his work *is* right.

9 Better to dwell in a corner of a
      housetop,
   Than in a house shared with a
      contentious woman.

10 The soul of the wicked desires evil;
   His neighbor finds no favor in his eyes.

11 When the scoffer is punished, the
      simple is made wise;
   But when the wise is instructed, he
      receives knowledge.

12 The righteous *God* wisely considers the
      house of the wicked,
   Overthrowing the wicked for *their*
      wickedness.

13 Whoever shuts his ears to the cry of the
      poor
   Will also cry himself and not be heard.

14 A gift in secret pacifies anger,
   And a bribe behind the back,^a strong
      wrath.

15 *It is* a joy for the just to do justice,
   But destruction *will come* to the
      workers of iniquity.

16 A man who wanders from the way of
      understanding
   Will rest in the assembly of the dead.

17 He who loves pleasure *will be* a poor
      man;
   He who loves wine and oil will not be
      rich.

18 The wicked *shall be* a ransom for the
      righteous,
   And the unfaithful for the upright.

19 Better to dwell in the wilderness,
   Than with a contentious and angry
      woman.

20 *There is* desirable treasure,
   And oil in the dwelling of the wise,
   But a foolish man squanders it.

21 He who follows righteousness and mercy
   Finds life, righteousness, and honor.

22 A wise *man* scales the city of the mighty,
   And brings down the trusted stronghold.

23 Whoever guards his mouth and tongue
   Keeps his soul from troubles.

24 A proud *and* haughty *man*—"Scoffer"
      is his name;
   He acts with arrogant pride.

25 The desire of the lazy *man* kills him,
   For his hands refuse to labor.
26 He covets greedily all day long,
   But the righteous gives and does not
      spare.

27 The sacrifice of the wicked *is* an
      abomination;
   How much more *when* he brings
      it with wicked intent!

28 A false witness shall perish,
   But the man who hears *him* will
      speak endlessly.

21:4 ^aOr *lamp*   **21:6** ^aSeptuagint reads *Pursue
vanity on the snares of death;* Vulgate reads *Is vain
and foolish, and shall stumble on the snares of death;*
Targum reads *They shall be destroyed, and they shall
fall who seek death.*   **21:7** ^aLiterally *drag them away*
21:8 ^aOr *The way of a man is perverse and strange*
21:14 ^aLiterally *in the bosom*

29 A wicked man hardens his face,
But *as for* the upright, he establishes[a]
his way.

30 *There is* no wisdom or understanding
Or counsel *against* the LORD.

31 The horse *is* prepared for the day of
battle,
But deliverance *is* of the LORD.

22 A *good* name is to be chosen rather
than great riches,
Loving favor rather than silver and
gold.

2 The rich and the poor have this in
common,
The LORD *is* the maker of them all.

3 A prudent *man* foresees evil and hides
himself,
But the simple pass on and are
punished.

4 By humility *and* the fear of the LORD
Are riches and honor and life.

5 Thorns *and* snares *are* in the way of
the perverse;
He who guards his soul will be far
from them.

6 Train up a child in the way he
should go,
And when he is old he will not
depart from it.

7 The rich rules over the poor,
And the borrower *is* servant to the
lender.

8 He who sows iniquity will reap sorrow,
And the rod of his anger will fail.

9 He who has a generous eye will be
blessed,
For he gives of his bread to the poor.

10 Cast out the scoffer, and contention
will leave;
Yes, strife and reproach will cease.

11 He who loves purity of heart
And has grace on his lips,
The king *will be* his friend.

12 The eyes of the LORD preserve
knowledge,
But He overthrows the words of
the faithless.

13 The lazy *man* says, "*There is* a lion
outside!
I shall be slain in the streets!"

14 The mouth of an immoral woman *is*
a deep pit;
He who is abhorred by the LORD will
fall there.

15 Foolishness *is* bound up in the heart
of a child;
The rod of correction will drive it far
from him.

16 He who oppresses the poor to increase
his *riches,*
And he who gives to the rich, *will*
surely *come* to poverty.

Sayings of the Wise

17 Incline your ear and hear the words of
the wise,
And apply your heart to my knowledge;
18 For *it is* a pleasant thing if you keep
them within you;
Let them all be fixed upon your lips,
19 So that your trust may be in the LORD;
I have instructed you today, even you.
20 Have I not written to you excellent
things
Of counsels and knowledge,
21 That I may make you know the
certainty of the words of truth,
That you may answer words of truth
To those who send to you?

22 Do not rob the poor because he *is* poor,
Nor oppress the afflicted at the gate;
23 For the LORD will plead their cause,
And plunder the soul of those who
plunder them.

21:29 [a]Qere and Septuagint read *understands.*

24 Make no friendship with an angry man,
    And with a furious man do not go,
25 Lest you learn his ways
    And set a snare for your soul.

26 Do not be one of those who shakes
        hands in a pledge,
    One of those who is surety for debts;
27 If you have nothing *with which* to pay,
    Why should he take away your bed
        from under you?

28 Do not remove the ancient landmark
    Which your fathers have set.

29 Do you see a man *who* excels in his
        work?
    He will stand before kings;
    He will not stand before unknown *men.*

23 When you sit down to eat with a ruler,
    Consider carefully what *is* before you;
2 And put a knife to your throat
    If you *are* a man given to appetite.
3 Do not desire his delicacies,
    For they *are* deceptive food.

4 Do not overwork to be rich;
    Because of your own understanding,
        cease!
5 Will you set your eyes on that which
        is not?
    For *riches* certainly make themselves
        wings;
    They fly away like an eagle *toward*
        heaven.

6 Do not eat the bread of a miser,[a]
    Nor desire his delicacies;
7 For as he thinks in his heart, so *is* he.
    "Eat and drink!" he says to you,
    But his heart is not with you.
8 The morsel you have eaten, you will
        vomit up,
    And waste your pleasant words.

9 Do not speak in the hearing of a fool,
    For he will despise the wisdom of your
        words.

10 Do not remove the ancient landmark,
    Nor enter the fields of the fatherless;

11 For their Redeemer *is* mighty;
    He will plead their cause against you.

12 Apply your heart to instruction,
    And your ears to words of knowledge.

13 Do not withhold correction from
        a child,
    For *if* you beat him with a rod,
        he will not die.
14 You shall beat him with a rod,
    And deliver his soul from hell.[a]

15 My son, if your heart is wise,
    My heart will rejoice—indeed, I myself;
16 Yes, my inmost being will rejoice
    When your lips speak right things.

17 Do not let your heart envy sinners,
    But *be zealous* for the fear of the LORD
        all the day;
18 For surely there is a hereafter,
    And your hope will not be cut off.

19 Hear, my son, and be wise;
    And guide your heart in the way.
20 Do not mix with winebibbers,
    Or with gluttonous eaters of meat;
21 For the drunkard and the glutton will
        come to poverty,
    And drowsiness will clothe *a man* with
        rags.

22 Listen to your father who begot you,
    And do not despise your mother when
        she is old.

23 Buy the truth, and do not sell *it,*
    Also wisdom and instruction and
        understanding.

24 The father of the righteous will greatly
        rejoice,
    And he who begets a wise *child* will
        delight in him.
25 Let your father and your mother be
        glad,
    And let her who bore you rejoice.

23:6 [a]Literally *one who has an evil eye*
23:14 [a]Or *Sheol*

THE CENSORING OF RELIGIOUS ACTIVITIES IN PUBLIC SCHOOLS

SUPREME COURT
OF THE UNITED STATES

In Supreme Court decisions rendered in 1962 and 1963, the inclusion of religious activities, such as school prayer and Bible reading, in major activities of daily student life in public schools was struck down. It was the first time in the history of the United States that any branch of the federal government took such a stand, censoring religious activities long considered an integral part of education.

This sudden restructuring of educational policies was precipitated by the Court's controversial reinterpretation of the phrase "separation of church and state" as it relates to the First Amendment, which simply states: "Congress shall make no law respecting an establishment of religion or prohibit the free exercise thereof." The Court decided that the First Amendment includes a prohibition against including religious activities in public affairs, inviting skyrocketing numbers of lawsuits that challenge any presence of religion in public life. The Court has already delivered far-reaching decisions to:

- Remove student prayer: "Prayer in its public school system breaches the constitution's wall of separation between Church and State." *Engle v. Vitale*, 1962

- Remove school Bible readings: "No state law or school board may require that passages from the Bible be read or that the Lord's Prayer be recited in the public schools of a state at the beginning of each school day." *Abington v. Schempp*, 1963

- Remove the Ten Commandments from view: "If the posted copies of the Ten Commandments are to have any effect at all, it will be to induce the schoolchildren to read, meditate upon, perhaps to venerate and obey the Commandments ... this ... is not a permissible state objective under the establishment clause." *Stone v. Graham*, 1980

- Remove benedictions and invocations from school activities: "Religious invocation ... in high school commencement exercises conveyed the message that district had given its endorsement to prayer and religion, so that school district was properly [prohibited] from including invocation in commencement exercise." *Graham v. Central*, 1985; *Kay v. Douglas*, 1986; *Jager v. Douglas*, 1989; *Lee v. Weisman*, 1992

26 My son, give me your heart,
   And let your eyes observe my ways.
27 For a harlot *is* a deep pit,
   And a seductress *is* a narrow well.
28 She also lies in wait as *for* a victim,
   And increases the unfaithful among
      men.

29 Who has woe?
   Who has sorrow?
   Who has contentions?
   Who has complaints?
   Who has wounds without cause?
   Who has redness of eyes?
30 Those who linger long at the wine,
   Those who go in search of mixed wine.
31 Do not look on the wine when it is red,
   When it sparkles in the cup,
   When it swirls around smoothly;
32 At the last it bites like a serpent,
   And stings like a viper.
33 Your eyes will see strange things,
   And your heart will utter perverse
      things.
34 Yes, you will be like one who lies down
      in the midst of the sea,
   Or like one who lies at the top of the
      mast, *saying:*
35 "They have struck me, *but* I was not
      hurt;
   They have beaten me, but I did not
      feel *it.*
   When shall I awake, that I may seek
      another *drink?*"

24 Do not be envious of evil men,
   Nor desire to be with them;
2 For their heart devises violence,
   And their lips talk of troublemaking.

3 Through wisdom a house is built,
   And by understanding it is established;
4 By knowledge the rooms are filled
   With all precious and pleasant riches.

5 A wise man *is* strong,
   Yes, a man of knowledge increases
      strength;
6 For by wise counsel you will wage
      your own war,
   And in a multitude of counselors
      there is safety.

7 Wisdom *is* too lofty for a fool;
   He does not open his mouth in the gate.

8 He who plots to do evil
   Will be called a schemer.
9 The devising of foolishness *is* sin,
   And the scoffer *is* an abomination
      to men.

10 *If* you faint in the day of adversity,
   Your strength *is* small.

11 Deliver *those who* are drawn toward
      death,
   And hold back *those* stumbling to the
      slaughter.
12 If you say, "Surely we did not know
      this,"
   Does not He who weighs the hearts
      consider *it?*
   He who keeps your soul, does He *not*
      know *it?*
   And will He *not* render to *each* man
      according to his deeds?

13 My son, eat honey because *it is* good,
   And the honeycomb *which is* sweet to
      your taste;
14 So *shall* the knowledge of wisdom *be*
      to your soul;
   If you have found *it,* there is a prospect,
   And your hope will not be cut off.

15 Do not lie in wait, O wicked *man,*
      against the dwelling of the righteous;
   Do not plunder his resting place;
16 For a righteous *man* may fall seven
      times
   And rise again,
   But the wicked shall fall by calamity.

17 Do not rejoice when your enemy falls,
   And do not let your heart be glad
      when he stumbles;
18 Lest the LORD see *it,* and it displease
      Him,
   And He turn away His wrath from him.

19 Do not fret because of evildoers,
   Nor be envious of the wicked;
20 For there will be no prospect for the
      evil *man;*

The lamp of the wicked will be put out.

21 My son, fear the LORD and the king;
　　Do not associate with those given to
　　change;
22 For their calamity will rise suddenly,
　　And who knows the ruin those two
　　can bring?

Further Sayings of the Wise

23These *things* also *belong* to the wise:

It is not good to show partiality in
　judgment.
24 He who says to the wicked, "You *are*
　righteous,"
　Him the people will curse;
　Nations will abhor him.
25 But those who rebuke *the wicked* will
　have delight,
　And a good blessing will come upon
　them.

26 He who gives a right answer kisses
　the lips.

27 Prepare your outside work,
　Make it fit for yourself in the field;
　And afterward build your house.

28 Do not be a witness against your
　neighbor without cause,
　For would you deceive[a] with your lips?
29 Do not say, "I will do to him just as he
　has done to me;
　I will render to the man according to
　his work."

30 I went by the field of the lazy *man,*
　And by the vineyard of the man
　devoid of understanding;
31 And there it was, all overgrown with
　thorns;
　Its surface was covered with nettles;
　Its stone wall was broken down.
32 When I saw *it,* I considered *it* well;
　I looked on *it and* received instruction:
33 A little sleep, a little slumber,
　A little folding of the hands to rest;
34 So shall your poverty come *like* a
　prowler,
　And your need like an armed man.

Further Wise Sayings of Solomon

25 These also *are* proverbs of Solomon
　which the men of Hezekiah king of
Judah copied:

2 *It is* the glory of God to conceal a
　matter,
　But the glory of kings *is* to search
　out a matter.

3 *As* the heavens for height and the
　earth for depth,
　So the heart of kings *is* unsearchable.

4 Take away the dross from silver,
　And it will go to the silversmith *for*
　jewelry.
5 Take away the wicked from before
　the king,
　And his throne will be established in
　righteousness.

6 Do not exalt yourself in the presence
　of the king,
　And do not stand in the place of the
　great;
7 For *it is* better that he say to you,
　"Come up here,"
　Than that you should be put lower in
　the presence of the prince,
　Whom your eyes have seen.

8 Do not go hastily to court;
　For what will you do in the end,
　When your neighbor has put you to
　shame?
9 Debate your case with your neighbor,
　And do not disclose the secret to
　another;
10 Lest he who hears *it* expose your shame,
　And your reputation be ruined.

11 A word fitly spoken *is like* apples
　of gold
　In settings of silver.
12 *Like* an earring of gold and an
　ornament of fine gold
　Is a wise rebuker to an obedient ear.

24:28 [a]Septuagint and Vulgate read *Do not deceive.*

13 Like the cold of snow in time of harvest
Is a faithful messenger to those who
   send him,
For he refreshes the soul of his masters.

14 Whoever falsely boasts of giving
Is like clouds and wind without rain.

15 By long forbearance a ruler is
   persuaded,
And a gentle tongue breaks a bone.

16 Have you found honey?
Eat only as much as you need,
Lest you be filled with it and vomit.

17 Seldom set foot in your neighbor's
   house,
Lest he become weary of you and
   hate you.

18 A man who bears false witness
   against his neighbor
Is like a club, a sword, and a sharp
   arrow.

19 Confidence in an unfaithful *man* in
   time of trouble
Is like a bad tooth and a foot out of
   joint.

20 *Like* one who takes away a garment in
   cold weather,
And like vinegar on soda,
Is one who sings songs to a heavy heart.

21 If your enemy is hungry, give him
   bread to eat;
And if he is thirsty, give him water to
   drink;

22 For *so* you will heap coals of fire on
   his head,
And the LORD will reward you.

23 The north wind brings forth rain,
And a backbiting tongue an angry
   countenance.

24 *It is* better to dwell in a corner of
   a housetop,
Than in a house shared with a
   contentious woman.

25 *As* cold water to a weary soul,
So *is* good news from a far country.

26 A righteous *man* who falters before
   the wicked
Is like a murky spring and a polluted
   well.

27 *It is* not good to eat much honey;
So to seek one's own glory *is not* glory.

28 Whoever *has* no rule over his own spirit
Is like a city broken down, without walls.

26 As snow in summer and rain in
   harvest,
So honor is not fitting for a fool.

2 Like a flitting sparrow, like a flying
   swallow,
So a curse without cause shall not
   alight.

3 A whip for the horse,
A bridle for the donkey,
And a rod for the fool's back.

4 Do not answer a fool according to
   his folly,
Lest you also be like him.

5 Answer a fool according to his folly,
Lest he be wise in his own eyes.

6 He who sends a message by the hand
   of a fool
Cuts off *his own* feet *and* drinks violence.

7 *Like* the legs of the lame that hang limp
Is a proverb in the mouth of fools.

8 Like one who binds a stone in a sling
Is he who gives honor to a fool.

9 *Like* a thorn *that* goes into the hand of
   a drunkard
Is a proverb in the mouth of fools.

10 The great *God* who formed everything
Gives the fool *his* hire and the
   transgressor *his* wages.[a]

11 As a dog returns to his own vomit,
So a fool repeats his folly.

12 Do you see a man wise in his own eyes?
There is more hope for a fool than for
   him.

26:10 [a]The Hebrew is difficult; ancient and modern translators differ greatly.

13 The lazy *man* says, "*There is* a lion
   in the road!
   A fierce lion *is* in the streets!"

14 *As* a door turns on its hinges,
   So *does* the lazy *man* on his bed.

15 The lazy *man* buries his hand in the
   bowl;ᵃ
   It wearies him to bring it back to his
   mouth.

16 The lazy *man is* wiser in his own eyes
   Than seven men who can answer
   sensibly.

17 He who passes by *and* meddles in a
   quarrel not his own
   Is like one who takes a dog by the ears.

18 Like a madman who throws
   firebrands, arrows, and death,

19 *Is* the man *who* deceives his neighbor,
   And says, "I was only joking!"

20 Where *there is* no wood, the fire goes
   out;
   And where *there is* no talebearer, strife
   ceases.

21 *As* charcoal *is* to burning coals, and
   wood to fire,
   So *is* a contentious man to kindle strife.

22 The words of a talebearer *are* like tasty
   trifles,
   And they go down into the inmost
   body.

23 Fervent lips with a wicked heart
   Are like earthenware covered with
   silver dross.

24 He who hates, disguises *it* with his
   lips,
   And lays up deceit within himself;

25 When he speaks kindly, do not believe
   him,
   For *there are* seven abominations in
   his heart;

26 *Though his* hatred is covered by deceit,
   His wickedness will be revealed before
   the assembly.

27 Whoever digs a pit will fall into it,
   And he who rolls a stone will have it
   roll back on him.

28 A lying tongue hates *those who are*
   crushed by it,
   And a flattering mouth works ruin.

27 Do not boast about tomorrow,
     For you do not know what a day
     may bring forth.

2 Let another man praise you, and not
   your own mouth;
   A stranger, and not your own lips.

3 A stone *is* heavy and sand *is* weighty,
   But a fool's wrath *is* heavier than both
   of them.

4 Wrath *is* cruel and anger a torrent,
   But who *is* able to stand before jealousy?

5 Open rebuke *is* better
   Than love carefully concealed.

6 Faithful *are* the wounds of a friend,
   But the kisses of an enemy *are* deceitful.

7 A satisfied soul loathes the
   honeycomb,
   But to a hungry soul every bitter
   thing *is* sweet.

8 Like a bird that wanders from its nest
   Is a man who wanders from his place.

9 Ointment and perfume delight the
   heart,
   And the sweetness of a man's friend
   gives delight by hearty counsel.

10 Do not forsake your own friend or
   your father's friend,
   Nor go to your brother's house in the
   day of your calamity;
   Better *is* a neighbor nearby than a
   brother far away.

11 My son, be wise, and make my heart
   glad,
   That I may answer him who
   reproaches me.

26:15 ᵃCompare 19:24

12 A prudent *man* foresees evil *and* hides
    himself;
    The simple pass on *and* are punished.

13 Take the garment of him who is surety
    for a stranger,
    And hold it in pledge *when* he is surety
    for a seductress.

14 He who blesses his friend with a loud
    voice, rising early in the morning,
    It will be counted a curse to him.

15 A continual dripping on a very rainy
    day
    And a contentious woman are alike;
16 Whoever restrains her restrains the
    wind,
    And grasps oil with his right hand.

17 *As* iron sharpens iron,
    So a man sharpens the countenance
    of his friend.

18 Whoever keeps the fig tree will eat its
    fruit;
    So he who waits on his master will be
    honored.

19 As in water face *reflects* face,
    So a man's heart *reveals* the man.

20 Hell[a] and Destruction[b] are never full;
    So the eyes of man are never satisfied.

21 The refining pot *is* for silver and the
    furnace for gold,
    And a man *is valued* by what others
    say of him.

22 Though you grind a fool in a mortar
    with a pestle along with crushed
    grain,
    Yet his foolishness will not depart from
    him.

23 Be diligent to know the state of your
    flocks,
    And attend to your herds;
24 For riches *are* not forever,
    Nor does a crown *endure* to all
    generations.

25 *When* the hay is removed, and the
    tender grass shows itself,
    And the herbs of the mountains are
    gathered in,
26 The lambs *will provide* your clothing,
    And the goats the price of a field;
27 *You shall have* enough goats' milk for
    your food,
    For the food of your household,
    And the nourishment of your
    maidservants.

28

The wicked flee when no one
    pursues,
But the righteous are bold as a
    lion.

2 Because of the transgression of a
    land, many *are* its princes;
    But by a man of understanding *and*
    knowledge
    Right will be prolonged.

3 A poor man who oppresses the poor
    Is like a driving rain which leaves no
    food.

4 Those who forsake the law praise the
    wicked,
    But such as keep the law contend with
    them.

5 Evil men do not understand justice,
    But those who seek the Lord
    understand all.

6 Better *is* the poor who walks in his
    integrity
    Than one perverse *in his* ways, though
    he *be* rich.

7 Whoever keeps the law *is* a discerning
    son,
    But a companion of gluttons shames
    his father.

8 One who increases his possessions by
    usury and extortion
    Gathers it for him who will pity the
    poor.

27:20 [a]Or *Sheol* [b]Hebrew *Abaddon*

9 One who turns away his ear from
      hearing the law,
   Even his prayer *is* an abomination.

10 Whoever causes the upright to go
      astray in an evil way,
   He himself will fall into his own pit;
   But the blameless will inherit good.

11 The rich man *is* wise in his own eyes,
   But the poor who has understanding
      searches him out.

12 When the righteous rejoice, *there is*
      great glory;
   But when the wicked arise, men hide
      themselves.

13 He who covers his sins will not prosper,
   But whoever confesses and forsakes
      them will have mercy.

14 Happy *is* the man who is always
      reverent,
   But he who hardens his heart will
      fall into calamity.

15 *Like* a roaring lion and a charging
      bear
   Is a wicked ruler over poor people.

16 A ruler who lacks understanding *is*
      a great oppressor,
   But he who hates covetousness will
      prolong *his* days.

17 A man burdened with bloodshed will
      flee into a pit;
   Let no one help him.

18 Whoever walks blamelessly will be
      saved,
   But *he who is* perverse *in his* ways will
      suddenly fall.

19 He who tills his land will have plenty
      of bread,
   But he who follows frivolity will have
      poverty enough!

20 A faithful man will abound with
      blessings,

But he who hastens to be rich will not
   go unpunished.

21 To show partiality *is* not good,
   Because for a piece of bread a man
      will transgress.

22 A man with an evil eye hastens after
      riches,
   And does not consider that poverty
      will come upon him.

23 He who rebukes a man will find more
      favor afterward
   Than he who flatters with the tongue.

24 Whoever robs his father or his mother,
   And says, "*It is* no transgression,"
   The same *is* companion to a destroyer.

25 He who is of a proud heart stirs up
      strife,
   But he who trusts in the LORD will be
      prospered.

26 He who trusts in his own heart is a fool,
   But whoever walks wisely will be
      delivered.

27 He who gives to the poor will not lack,
   But he who hides his eyes will have
      many curses.

28 When the wicked arise, men hide
      themselves;
   But when they perish, the righteous
      increase.

29 He who is often rebuked, *and*
      hardens *his* neck,
   Will suddenly be destroyed, and that
      without remedy.

2 When the righteous are in authority,
      the people rejoice;
   But when a wicked *man* rules, the
      people groan.

3 Whoever loves wisdom makes his
      father rejoice,
   But a companion of harlots wastes *his*
      wealth.

4 The king establishes the land by
     justice,
   But he who receives bribes
     overthrows it.

5 A man who flatters his neighbor
   Spreads a net for his feet.

6 By transgression an evil man is snared,
   But the righteous sings and rejoices.

7 The righteous considers the cause of
     the poor,
   But the wicked does not understand
     such knowledge.

8 Scoffers set a city aflame,
   But wise *men* turn away wrath.

9 *If* a wise man contends with a foolish
     man,
   Whether *the fool* rages or laughs, *there
     is* no peace.

10 The bloodthirsty hate the blameless,
    But the upright seek his well-being.[a]

11 A fool vents all his feelings,[a]
    But a wise *man* holds them back.

12 If a ruler pays attention to lies,
    All his servants *become* wicked.

13 The poor *man* and the oppressor have
      this in common:
    The LORD gives light to the eyes of both.

14 The king who judges the poor with
      truth,
    His throne will be established forever.

15 The rod and rebuke give wisdom,
    But a child left *to himself* brings shame
      to his mother.

16 When the wicked are multiplied,
      transgression increases;
    But the righteous will see their fall.

17 Correct your son, and he will give you
      rest;
    Yes, he will give delight to your soul.

Herbert Hoover placed his hand on Proverbs 29:18 as he took the presidential oath of office in 1929.

---

18 Where *there is* no revelation,[a] the
      people cast off restraint;
    But happy *is* he who keeps the law.

19 A servant will not be corrected by
      mere words;
    For though he understands, he will
      not respond.

20 Do you see a man hasty in his
      words?
    There is more hope for a fool than
      for him.

21 He who pampers his servant from
      childhood
    Will have him as a son in the end.

22 An angry man stirs up strife,
    And a furious man abounds in
      transgression.

23 A man's pride will bring him low,
    But the humble in spirit will retain
      honor.

24 Whoever is a partner with a thief
      hates his own life;
    He swears to tell the truth,[a] but reveals
      nothing.

25 The fear of man brings a snare,
    But whoever trusts in the LORD shall
      be safe.

26 Many seek the ruler's favor,
    But justice for man *comes* from the
      LORD.

27 An unjust man *is* an abomination
      to the righteous,
    And *he who is* upright in the way *is*
      an abomination to the wicked.

29:10 [a]Literally *soul*   **29:11** [a]Literally *spirit*
29:18 [a]Or *prophetic vision*   **29:24** [a]Literally *hears
the adjuration*

The Wisdom of Agur

30 The words of Agur the son of Jakeh, *his* utterance. This man declared to Ithiel—to Ithiel and Ucal:

2 Surely I *am* more stupid than *any* man,
  And do not have the understanding of
    a man.
3 I neither learned wisdom
  Nor have knowledge of the Holy One.

4 Who has ascended into heaven, or
    descended?
  Who has gathered the wind in His
    fists?
  Who has bound the waters in a
    garment?
  Who has established all the ends of
    the earth?
  What *is* His name, and what *is* His
    Son's name,
  If you know?

5 Every word of God *is* pure;
  He *is* a shield to those who put their
    trust in Him.
6 Do not add to His words,
  Lest He rebuke you, and you be found
    a liar.

7 Two *things* I request of You
  (Deprive me not before I die):
8 Remove falsehood and lies far
    from me;
  Give me neither poverty nor riches—
  Feed me with the food allotted to me;
9 Lest I be full and deny *You,*
  And say, "Who *is* the LORD?"
  Or lest I be poor and steal,
  And profane the name of my God.

10 Do not malign a servant to his master,
   Lest he curse you, and you be found
     guilty.

11 *There is* a generation *that* curses its
     father,
   And does not bless its mother.
12 *There is* a generation *that is* pure in
     its own eyes,
   Yet is not washed from its filthiness.

13 *There is* a generation—oh, how lofty
     are their eyes!
   And their eyelids are lifted up.
14 *There is* a generation whose teeth *are
     like* swords,
   And whose fangs *are like* knives,
   To devour the poor from off the earth,
   And the needy from *among* men.

15 The leech has two daughters—
   Give *and* Give!

   There are three *things that* are never
     satisfied,
   Four never say, "Enough!":
16 The grave,ª
   The barren womb,
   The earth *that* is not satisfied with
     water—
   And the fire never says, "Enough!"

17 The eye *that* mocks *his* father,
   And scorns obedience to *his* mother,
   The ravens of the valley will pick it out,
   And the young eagles will eat it.

18 There are three *things which* are too
     wonderful for me,
   Yes, four *which* I do not understand:
19 The way of an eagle in the air,
   The way of a serpent on a rock,
   The way of a ship in the midst of
     the sea,
   And the way of a man with a virgin.

20 This *is* the way of an adulterous woman:
   She eats and wipes her mouth,
   And says, "I have done no wickedness."

21 For three *things* the earth is perturbed,
   Yes, for four it cannot bear up:
22 For a servant when he reigns,
   A fool when he is filled with food,
23 A hateful *woman* when she is married,
   And a maidservant who succeeds her
     mistress.

24 There are four *things which* are little
     on the earth,
   But they *are* exceedingly wise:

30:16 ªOr *Sheol*

The UNIVERSAL EDUCATION of YOUTH

Dr. Benjamin Rush, a signer of the Declaration of Independence and one of America's most influential Founding Fathers, was one of the first Founders to call for free, national, public schools. A distinguished physician and scientist, he understood the role of an educated citizenry as regards the stability of a republic, stating:

> *I believe no man was ever early instructed in the truths of the Bible without having been made wiser or better by the early operation of these impressions upon his mind. . . .*
>
> *If moral precepts alone could have reformed mankind, the mission of the Son of God into our world would have been unnecessary. He came to promulgate a system of doctrines, as well as a system of morals. The perfect morality of the Gospel rests upon a doctrine which, though often controverted, has never been refuted; I mean the vicarious life and death of the Son of God. This sublime and ineffable doctrine delivers us from the absurd hypothesis of modern philosophers concerning the foundation of moral obligation, and fixes it upon the eternal and self-moving principle of LOVE. It concentrates a whole system of ethics in a single text of Scripture: "A new commandment I give unto you, that ye love one another, even as I have loved you." By withholding the knowledge of this doctrine from children, we deprive ourselves of the best means of awakening moral sensibility in their minds. We do more; we furnish an argument for withholding from them a knowledge of the morality of the Gospel likewise; for this, in many instances, is as supernatural, and therefore as liable to be controverted, as any of the doctrines or miracles which are mentioned in the New Testament. The miraculous conception of the Savior of the world by a virgin is not more opposed to the ordinary course of natural events, nor is the doctrine of the atonement more above human reason, than those moral precepts which command us to love our enemies or to die for our friends. . . .*
>
> *Contemplating merely the political institutions of the United States, I lament that we waste so much time and money in punishing crimes and take so little pains to prevent them. We profess to be republicans, and yet we neglect the only means of establishing and perpetuating our republican forms of government; that is, the universal education of our youth in the principles of Christianity by means of the Bible; for this divine book, above all others, favors that equality among mankind, that respect for just laws, and all those sober and frugal virtues which constitute the soul of republicanism.*

25 The ants *are* a people not strong,
Yet they prepare their food in the summer;
26 The rock badgers^a are a feeble folk,
Yet they make their homes in the crags;
27 The locusts have no king,
Yet they all advance in ranks;
28 The spider^a skillfully grasps with its hands,
And it is in kings' palaces.

29 There are three *things which* are majestic in pace,
Yes, four *which* are stately in walk:
30 A lion, *which is* mighty among beasts
And does not turn away from any;
31 A greyhound,^a
A male goat also,
And a king *whose* troops *are* with him.^b

32 If you have been foolish in exalting yourself,
Or if you have devised evil, *put your* hand on *your* mouth.
33 For *as* the churning of milk produces butter,
And wringing the nose produces blood,
So the forcing of wrath produces strife.

The Words of King Lemuel's Mother

31 The words of King Lemuel, the utterance which his mother taught him:

2 What, my son?
And what, son of my womb?
And what, son of my vows?
3 Do not give your strength to women,
Nor your ways to that which destroys kings.

4 *It is* not for kings, O Lemuel,
It is not for kings to drink wine,
Nor for princes intoxicating drink;
5 Lest they drink and forget the law,
And pervert the justice of all the afflicted.
6 Give strong drink to him who is perishing,
And wine to those who are bitter of heart.
7 Let him drink and forget his poverty,
And remember his misery no more.

8 Open your mouth for the speechless,
In the cause of all *who are* appointed to die.^a
9 Open your mouth, judge righteously,
And plead the cause of the poor and needy.

The Virtuous Wife

10 Who^a can find a virtuous^b wife?
For her worth *is* far above rubies.
11 The heart of her husband safely trusts her;
So he will have no lack of gain.
12 She does him good and not evil
All the days of her life.
13 She seeks wool and flax,
And willingly works with her hands.
14 She is like the merchant ships,
She brings her food from afar.
15 She also rises while it is yet night,
And provides food for her household,
And a portion for her maidservants.
16 She considers a field and buys it;
From her profits she plants a vineyard.
17 She girds herself with strength,
And strengthens her arms.
18 She perceives that her merchandise *is* good,
And her lamp does not go out by night.
19 She stretches out her hands to the distaff,
And her hand holds the spindle.
20 She extends her hand to the poor,
Yes, she reaches out her hands to the needy.
21 She is not afraid of snow for her household,
For all her household *is* clothed with scarlet.
22 She makes tapestry for herself;
Her clothing *is* fine linen and purple.
23 Her husband is known in the gates,
When he sits among the elders of the land.

30:26 ^aOr *hyraxes*   **30:28** ^aOr *lizard*
30:31 ^aExact identity unknown ^bA Jewish tradition reads *a king against whom there is no uprising.*
31:8 ^aLiterally *sons of passing away*   **31:10** ^aVerses 10 through 31 are an alphabetic acrostic in Hebrew (compare Psalm 119). ^bLiterally *a wife of valor,* in the sense of all forms of excellence

24 She makes linen garments and sells
   them,
   And supplies sashes for the merchants.
25 Strength and honor *are* her clothing;
   She shall rejoice in time to come.
26 She opens her mouth with wisdom,
   And on her tongue *is* the law of
   kindness.
27 She watches over the ways of her
   household,
   And does not eat the bread of
   idleness.

28 Her children rise up and call her
   blessed;
   Her husband *also,* and he praises her:
29 "Many daughters have done well,
   But you excel them all."
30 Charm *is* deceitful and beauty *is*
   passing,
   But a woman *who* fears the LORD, she
   shall be praised.
31 Give her of the fruit of her hands,
   And let her own works praise her in
   the gates.

ECCLESIASTES

Author: Solomon

When Written: Around 931 B.C.

Theme: Life's Meaning Begins and Ends With God

Key Verse: Ecclesiastes 12:13—Let us hear the conclusion of the whole matter: Fear God and keep His commandments, for this is man's all.

Key Chapter: Ecclesiastes 12—At the end of a life given to embracing every experience and pleasure available to him, the author concludes that the only value is living life from the perspective of God's eternal economy.

All of humankind searches for meaning and purpose in life. In his own pursuit, the "preacher" of Ecclesiastes finds that earthly goals that do not lead to God only bring dissatisfaction, frustration, and uncertainty.

American businessman James Cash (J. C.) Penney came to a similar conclusion. Through hard work and a thrifty lifestyle, J. C. Penney succeeded in building one of America's most prosperous retail franchises. But during the Great Depression, heavy financial losses caused him enormous stress, which led to a life-threatening illness. While in the hospital, believing he was going to die, Penney wrote farewell letters to his wife and son. When he awoke the next morning, he went for a walk down the hallway of the hospital and heard singing coming from the chapel. He went in and listened with a heavy heart. The song "God Will Take Care of You" spoke to him deeply.

In a life-transforming instant, Penney discovered that God was there to help. "From that day to this, my life has been free from worry," he later declared. Even in the midst of potentially life-altering circumstances, J. C. Penney, along with the preacher of Ecclesiastes, found the answer to all of life—love of God.

ECCLESIASTES

The Vanity of Life

1 The words of the Preacher, the son of David, king in Jerusalem.

2 "Vanity[a] of vanities," says the Preacher;
"Vanity of vanities, all *is* vanity."

3 What profit has a man from all his
  labor
  In which he toils under the sun?
4 *One* generation passes away, and
  another generation comes;
  But the earth abides forever.
5 The sun also rises, and the sun goes
  down,
  And hastens to the place where it
  arose.
6 The wind goes toward the south,
  And turns around to the north;
  The wind whirls about continually,
  And comes again on its circuit.
7 All the rivers run into the sea,
  Yet the sea *is* not full;
  To the place from which the rivers
  come,
  There they return again.
8 All things *are* full of labor;
  Man cannot express *it.*
  The eye is not satisfied with seeing,
  Nor the ear filled with hearing.

9 That which has been *is* what will be,
  That which *is* done is what will be
  done,
  And *there is* nothing new under the sun.
10 Is there anything of which it may be
  said,
  "See, this *is* new"?
  It has already been in ancient times
  before us.
11 *There is* no remembrance of former
  things,
  Nor will there be any remembrance of
  things that are to come
  By *those* who will come after.

The Grief of Wisdom

12 I, the Preacher, was king over Israel in Jerusalem. 13 And I set my heart to seek and search out by wisdom concerning all that is done under heaven; this burdensome task God has given to the sons of man, by which they may be exercised. 14 I have seen all the works that are done under the sun; and indeed, all *is* vanity and grasping for the wind.

15 *What is* crooked cannot be made
  straight,
  And what is lacking cannot be
  numbered.

16 I communed with my heart, saying, "Look, I have attained greatness, and have gained more wisdom than all who were before me in Jerusalem. My heart has understood great wisdom and knowledge." 17 And I set my heart to know wisdom and to know madness and folly. I perceived that this also is grasping for the wind.

18 For in much wisdom *is* much grief,
  And he who increases knowledge
  increases sorrow.

The Vanity of Pleasure

2 I said in my heart, "Come now, I will test you with mirth; therefore enjoy pleasure"; but surely, this also *was* vanity. 2 I said of laughter—"Madness!"; and of mirth, "What does it accomplish?" 3 I searched in my heart *how* to gratify my flesh with wine, while guiding my heart with wisdom, and how to lay hold on folly, till I might see what *was* good for the sons of men to do under heaven all the days of their lives.

4 I made my works great, I built myself houses, and planted myself vineyards. 5 I made myself gardens and orchards, and I

1:2 [a] Or *Absurdity, Frustration, Futility, Nonsense;* and so throughout this book

planted all *kinds* of fruit trees in them. [6]I made myself water pools from which to water the growing trees of the grove. [7]I acquired male and female servants, and had servants born in my house. Yes, I had greater possessions of herds and flocks than all who were in Jerusalem before me. [8]I also gathered for myself silver and gold and the special treasures of kings and of the provinces. I acquired male and female singers, the delights of the sons of men, *and* musical instruments[a] of all kinds.

[9]So I became great and excelled more than all who were before me in Jerusalem. Also my wisdom remained with me.

10 Whatever my eyes desired I did not
        keep from them.
    I did not withhold my heart from any
        pleasure,
    For my heart rejoiced in all my labor;
    And this was my reward from all my
        labor.
11 Then I looked on all the works that
        my hands had done

And on the labor in which I had toiled;
    And indeed all *was* vanity and
        grasping for the wind.
    There was no profit under the sun.

The End of the Wise and the Fool

12 Then I turned myself to consider
        wisdom and madness and folly;
    For what *can* the man *do* who
        succeeds the king?—
    Only what he has already done.
13 Then I saw that wisdom excels folly
    As light excels darkness.
14 The wise man's eyes *are* in his head,
    But the fool walks in darkness.
    Yet I myself perceived
    That the same event happens to them
        all.

15 So I said in my heart,
    "As it happens to the fool,
      It also happens to me,
      And why was I then more wise?"

2:8 [a]Exact meaning unknown

TRUTH

... the wind whirls about continually, and comes again on its circuit.

ECCLESIASTES 1:6

Matthew Maury

CHRISTIAN MEN OF SCIENCE

Matthew Maury (1806–1873), nicknamed the "Pathfinder of the Seas" for having charted the ocean and wind currents while serving in the U.S. Navy, was considered the "Father of Modern Oceanography and Naval Meteorology" and later the "Scientist of the Seas." He wrote:

I have always found in my scientific studies, that, when I could get the Bible to say anything on the subject, it afforded me a firm platform to stand upon and a round in the ladder by which I could safely ascend.

As our knowledge of nature and her laws has increased, so has our knowledge of many passages of the Bible improved.

The Bible called the earth "the round world," yet for ages it was . . . heresy for Christian men to say that the world is round; and, finally, sailors circumnavigated the globe and proved the Bible to be right, and saved Christian men of science from the stake.

And as for the general system of circulation which I have been so long endeavoring to describe, the Bible tells it all in a single sentence: "The wind goeth toward the South . . . and returneth again to his circuits."

Then I said in my heart,
"This also *is* vanity."

16 For *there is* no more remembrance of
    the wise than of the fool forever,
Since all that now *is* will be forgotten
    in the days to come.
And how does a wise *man* die?
As the fool!

17Therefore I hated life because the work that was done under the sun *was* distressing to me, for all *is* vanity and grasping for the wind.

18Then I hated all my labor in which I had toiled under the sun, because I must leave it to the man who will come after me. 19And who knows whether he will be wise or a fool? Yet he will rule over all my labor in which I toiled and in which I have shown myself wise under the sun. This also *is* vanity. 20Therefore I turned my heart and despaired of all the labor in which I had toiled under the sun. 21For there is a man whose labor *is* with wisdom, knowledge, and skill; yet he must leave his heritage to a man who has not labored for it. This also *is* vanity and a great evil. 22For what has man for all his labor, and for the striving of his heart with which he has toiled under the sun? 23For all his days *are* sorrowful, and his work burdensome; even in the night his heart takes no rest. This also is vanity.

24Nothing *is* better for a man *than* that he should eat and drink, and *that* his soul should enjoy good in his labor. This also, I saw, was from the hand of God. 25For who can eat, or who can have enjoyment, more than I?ᵃ 26For *God* gives wisdom and knowledge and joy to a man who *is* good in His sight; but to the sinner He gives the work of gathering and collecting, that he may give to *him who is* good before God. This also *is* vanity and grasping for the wind.

Everything Has Its Time

3 To everything *there is* a season,
A time for every purpose under heaven:

2   A time to be born,
    And a time to die;
  A time to plant,
    And a time to pluck *what is* planted;

3   A time to kill,
    And a time to heal;
  A time to break down,
    And a time to build up;
4   A time to weep,
    And a time to laugh;
  A time to mourn,
    And a time to dance;
5   A time to cast away stones,
    And a time to gather stones;
  A time to embrace,
    And a time to refrain from
     embracing;
6   A time to gain,
    And a time to lose;
  A time to keep,
    And a time to throw away;
7   A time to tear,
    And a time to sew;
  A time to keep silence,
    And a time to speak;
8   A time to love,
    And a time to hate;
  A time of war,
    And a time of peace.

The God-Given Task

9What profit has the worker from that in which he labors? 10I have seen the God-given task with which the sons of men are to be occupied. 11He has made everything beautiful in its time. Also He has put eternity in their hearts, except that no one can find out the work that God does from beginning to end.

12I know that nothing *is* better for them than to rejoice, and to do good in their lives, 13and also that every man should eat and drink and enjoy the good of all his labor—it *is* the gift of God.

14   I know that whatever God does,
    It shall be forever.
  Nothing can be added to it,
    And nothing taken from it.
  God does *it*, that men should fear
    before Him.
15 That which is has already been,

2:25 ᵃFollowing Masoretic Text, Targum, and Vulgate; some Hebrew manuscripts, Septuagint, and Syriac read *without Him.*

And what is to be has already been;
And God requires an account of what
   is past.

Injustice Seems to Prevail

[16]Moreover I saw under the sun:

In the place of judgment,
Wickedness was there;
And in the place of righteousness,
Iniquity was there.

[17]I said in my heart,

"God shall judge the righteous and the
   wicked,
For there is a time there for every
   purpose and for every work."

[18]I said in my heart, "Concerning the condition of the sons of men, God tests them, that they may see that they themselves are like animals." [19]For what happens to the sons of men also happens to animals; one thing befalls them: as one dies, so dies the other. Surely, they all have one breath; man has no advantage over animals, for all is vanity. [20]All go to one place: all are from the dust, and all return to dust. [21]Who knows the spirit of the sons of men, which goes upward, and the spirit of the animal, which goes down to the earth?[a] [22]So I perceived that nothing is better than that a man should rejoice in his own works, for

---

3:21 [a]Septuagint, Syriac, Targum, and Vulgate read Who knows whether the spirit . . . goes upward, and whether . . . goes downward to the earth?

PROTECTOR

Moreover I saw . . . in the
place of righteousness,
iniquity was there.

ECCLESIASTES 3:16

Andrew Jackson

CORRECTING ABUSES

In July 1832, President Andrew Jackson vetoed the Bank Renewal Bill, preventing the rechartering of the Bank of the United States. Believing the bank was unauthorized by the Constitution and concentrated too much economic power in the hands of a small moneyed elite, he stated:

In the full enjoyment of the gifts of Heaven and the fruits of superior industry, economy, and virtue, every man is equally entitled to protection by law; but when the laws undertake to add to these natural and just advantages artificial distinctions, to grant titles, gratuities, and exclusive privileges, to make the rich richer and the potent more powerful, the humble members of society—the farmers, mechanics, and laborers— . . . have a right to complain of the injustice of their Government.

There are no necessary evils in government. Its evils exist only in its abuses. If it would confine itself to equal protection, and, as Heaven does its rains, shower its favors alike on the high and the low, the rich and the poor, it would be an unqualified blessing. In the act before me there seems to be a wide and unnecessary departure from these just principles. . . .

For relief and deliverance let us firmly rely on that kind Providence which I am sure watches with peculiar care over the destinies of our Republic, and on the intelligence and wisdom of our countrymen. Through His abundant goodness and their patriotic devotion our liberty and Union will be preserved.

that *is* his heritage. For who can bring him to see what will happen after him?

4 Then I returned and considered all the oppression that is done under the sun:

> And look! The tears of the oppressed,
> But they have no comforter—
> On the side of their oppressors *there is* power,
> But they have no comforter.

2 Therefore I praised the dead who were already dead,
> More than the living who are still alive.

3 Yet, better than both *is he* who has never existed,
> Who has not seen the evil work that is done under the sun.

The Vanity of Selfish Toil

4Again, I saw that for all toil and every skillful work a man is envied by his neighbor. This also *is* vanity and grasping for the wind.

5 The fool folds his hands
> And consumes his own flesh.

6 Better a handful *with* quietness
> Than both hands full, *together with* toil and grasping for the wind.

7Then I returned, and I saw vanity under the sun:

8 There is one alone, without companion:
> He has neither son nor brother.
> Yet *there is* no end to all his labors,
> Nor is his eye satisfied with riches.
> *But he never asks,*
> "For whom do I toil and deprive myself of good?"
> This also *is* vanity and a grave misfortune.

The Value of a Friend

9 Two *are* better than one,
> Because they have a good reward for their labor.

10 For if they fall, one will lift up his companion.
> But woe to him *who is* alone when he falls,

> For *he has* no one to help him up.

11 Again, if two lie down together, they will keep warm;
> But how can one be warm *alone?*

12 Though one may be overpowered by another, two can withstand him.
> And a threefold cord is not quickly broken.

Popularity Passes Away

13 Better a poor and wise youth
> Than an old and foolish king who will be admonished no more.

14 For he comes out of prison to be king,
> Although he was born poor in his kingdom.

15 I saw all the living who walk under the sun;
> They were with the second youth who stands in his place.

16 *There was* no end of all the people over whom he was made king;
> Yet those who come afterward will not rejoice in him.
> Surely this also *is* vanity and grasping for the wind.

Fear God, Keep Your Vows

5 Walk prudently when you go to the house of God; and draw near to hear rather than to give the sacrifice of fools, for they do not know that they do evil.

2 Do not be rash with your mouth,
> And let not your heart utter anything hastily before God.
> For God *is* in heaven, and you on earth;
> Therefore let your words be few.

3 For a dream comes through much activity,
> And a fool's voice *is known* by *his* many words.

4 When you make a vow to God, do not delay to pay it;
> For *He has* no pleasure in fools.
> Pay what you have vowed—

5 Better not to vow than to vow and not pay.

6Do not let your mouth cause your flesh to sin, nor say before the messenger *of God*

that it *was* an error. Why should God be angry at your excuse[a] and destroy the work of your hands? [7]For in the multitude of dreams and many words *there is* also vanity. But fear God.

The Vanity of Gain and Honor

[8]If you see the oppression of the poor, and the violent perversion of justice and righteousness in a province, do not marvel at the matter; for high official watches over high official, and higher officials are over them. [9]Moreover the profit of the land is for all; *even* the king is served from the field.

[10] He who loves silver will not be
    satisfied with silver;
Nor he who loves abundance, with
    increase.
This also *is* vanity.

[11] When goods increase,
They increase who eat them;
So what profit have the owners
Except to see *them* with their eyes?

[12] The sleep of a laboring man *is* sweet,
Whether he eats little or much;
But the abundance of the rich will not
    permit him to sleep.

[13] There is a severe evil *which* I have seen
    under the sun:
Riches kept for their owner to his hurt.
[14] But those riches perish through
    misfortune;
When he begets a son, *there is* nothing
    in his hand.
[15] As he came from his mother's womb,
    naked shall he return,
To go as he came;
And he shall take nothing from his
    labor
Which he may carry away in his
    hand.

[16] And this also *is* a severe evil—
Just exactly as he came, so shall he go.
And what profit has he who has
    labored for the wind?
[17] All his days he also eats in darkness,

And *he has* much sorrow and sickness
    and anger.

[18]Here is what I have seen: *It is* good and fitting *for one* to eat and drink, and to enjoy the good of all his labor in which he toils under the sun all the days of his life which God gives him; for it *is* his heritage. [19]As for every man to whom God has given riches and wealth, and given him power to eat of it, to receive his heritage and rejoice in his labor—this *is* the gift of God. [20]For he will not dwell unduly on the days of his life, because God keeps *him* busy with the joy of his heart.

6 There is an evil which I have seen under the sun, and it *is* common among men: [2]A man to whom God has given riches and wealth and honor, so that he lacks nothing for himself of all he desires; yet God does not give him power to eat of it, but a foreigner consumes it. This *is* vanity, and it *is* an evil affliction.

[3]If a man begets a hundred *children* and lives many years, so that the days of his years are many, but his soul is not satisfied with goodness, or indeed he has no burial, I say *that* a stillborn child *is* better than he— [4]for it comes in vanity and departs in darkness, and its name is covered with darkness. [5]Though it has not seen the sun or known *anything,* this has more rest than that man, [6]even if he lives a thousand years twice—but has not seen goodness. Do not all go to one place?

[7] All the labor of man *is* for his mouth,
    And yet the soul is not satisfied.
[8] For what more has the wise *man* than
    the fool?
What does the poor man have,
Who knows *how* to walk before the
    living?
[9] Better *is* the sight of the eyes than the
    wandering of desire.
This also *is* vanity and grasping for
    the wind.

[10] Whatever one is, he has been named
    already,

5:6 [a]Literally *voice*

For it is known that he *is* man;
And he cannot contend with Him who
is mightier than he.
11 Since there are many things that
increase vanity,
How *is* man the better?

12For who knows what *is* good for man in
life, all the days of his vain life which he
passes like a shadow? Who can tell a man
what will happen after him under the sun?

The Value of Practical Wisdom

7 A good name *is* better than precious
ointment,
And the day of death than the day of
one's birth;
2 Better to go to the house of
mourning
Than to go to the house of feasting,
For that *is* the end of all men;
And the living will take *it* to heart.
3 Sorrow *is* better than laughter,
For by a sad countenance the heart is
made better.
4 The heart of the wise *is* in the house of
mourning,
But the heart of fools *is* in the house of
mirth.

5 *It is* better to hear the rebuke of the
wise
Than for a man to hear the song of
fools.
6 For like the crackling of thorns under
a pot,
So *is* the laughter of the fool.
This also is vanity.
7 Surely oppression destroys a wise
man's reason,
And a bribe debases the heart.

8 The end of a thing *is* better than its
beginning;
The patient in spirit *is* better than the
proud in spirit.
9 Do not hasten in your spirit to be
angry,
For anger rests in the bosom of fools.
10 Do not say,
"Why were the former days better than
these?"

For you do not inquire wisely
concerning this.

11 Wisdom *is* good with an inheritance,
And profitable to those who see the
sun.
12 For wisdom *is* a defense *as* money *is*
a defense,
But the excellence of knowledge *is*
that wisdom gives life to those
who have it.

13 Consider the work of God;
For who can make straight what He
has made crooked?
14 In the day of prosperity be joyful,
But in the day of adversity consider:
Surely God has appointed the one as
well as the other,
So that man can find out nothing *that*
will come after him.

15I have seen everything in my days of
vanity:

There is a just *man* who perishes in his
righteousness,
And there is a wicked *man* who
prolongs *life* in his wickedness.

16 Do not be overly righteous,
Nor be overly wise:
Why should you destroy yourself?
17 Do not be overly wicked,
Nor be foolish:
Why should you die before your time?
18 *It is* good that you grasp this,
And also not remove your hand from
the other;
For he who fears God will escape
them all.

19 Wisdom strengthens the wise
More than ten rulers of the city.

20 For *there is* not a just man on earth
who does good
And does not sin.

21 Also do not take to heart everything
people say,
Lest you hear your servant cursing you.

22 For many times, also, your own heart has known
That even you have cursed others.

23 All this I have proved by wisdom.
I said, "I will be wise";
But it *was* far from me.
24 As for that which is far off and exceedingly deep,
Who can find it out?
25 I applied my heart to know,
To search and seek out wisdom and the reason *of things,*
To know the wickedness of folly,
Even of foolishness *and* madness.
26 And I find more bitter than death
The woman whose heart *is* snares and nets,
Whose hands *are* fetters.
He who pleases God shall escape from her,
But the sinner shall be trapped by her.

27 "Here is what I have found," says the Preacher,
"*Adding* one thing to the other to find out the reason,
28 Which my soul still seeks but I cannot find:
One man among a thousand I have found,
But a woman among all these I have not found.
29 Truly, this only I have found:
That God made man upright,
But they have sought out many schemes."

8 Who *is* like a wise *man?*
And who knows the interpretation of a thing?
A man's wisdom makes his face shine,
And the sternness of his face is changed.

Obey Authorities for God's Sake

2 I *say,* "Keep the king's commandment for the sake of your oath to God. 3 Do not be hasty to go from his presence. Do not take your stand for an evil thing, for he does whatever pleases him."

4 Where the word of a king *is, there is* power;
And who may say to him, "What are you doing?"
5 He who keeps his command will experience nothing harmful;
And a wise man's heart discerns both time and judgment,
6 Because for every matter there is a time and judgment,
Though the misery of man increases greatly.
7 For he does not know what will happen;
So who can tell him when it will occur?
8 No one has power over the spirit to retain the spirit,
And no one has power in the day of death.
There is no release from that war,
And wickedness will not deliver those who are given to it.

9 All this I have seen, and applied my heart to every work that is done under the sun: *There is* a time in which one man rules over another to his own hurt.

Death Comes to All

10 Then I saw the wicked buried, who had come and gone from the place of holiness, and they were forgotten[a] in the city where they had so done. This also *is* vanity. 11 Because the sentence against an evil work is not executed speedily, therefore the heart of the sons of men is fully set in them to do evil. 12 Though a sinner does evil a hundred *times,* and his *days* are prolonged, yet I surely know that it will be well with those who fear God, who fear before Him. 13 But it will not be well with the wicked; nor will he prolong *his* days, *which are* as a shadow, because he does not fear before God.

14 There is a vanity which occurs on earth, that there are just *men* to whom it happens according to the work of the wicked; again, there are wicked *men* to whom it happens according to the work of the righteous. I said that this also *is* vanity.

8:10 [a]Some Hebrew manuscripts, Septuagint, and Vulgate read *praised.*

¹⁵So I commended enjoyment, because a man has nothing better under the sun than to eat, drink, and be merry; for this will remain with him in his labor *all* the days of his life which God gives him under the sun.

¹⁶When I applied my heart to know wisdom and to see the business that is done on earth, even though one sees no sleep day or night, ¹⁷then I saw all the work of God, that a man cannot find out the work that is done under the sun. For though a man labors to discover *it,* yet he will not find *it;* moreover, though a wise *man* attempts to know *it,* he will not be able to find *it.*

9 For I considered all this in my heart, so that I could declare it all: that the righteous and the wise and their works *are* in the hand of God. People know neither love nor hatred *by* anything *they see* before them. ²All things *come* alike to all:

One event *happens* to the righteous
  and the wicked;
To the good,ᵃ the clean, and the
  unclean;
To him who sacrifices and him who
  does not sacrifice.
As is the good, so *is* the sinner;
He who takes an oath as *he* who fears
  an oath.

³This *is* an evil in all that is done under the sun: that one thing *happens* to all. Truly the hearts of the sons of men are full of evil; madness *is* in their hearts while they live, and after that *they go* to the dead. ⁴But for him who is joined to all the living there is hope, for a living dog is better than a dead lion.

⁵ For the living know that they will die;
  But the dead know nothing,
  And they have no more reward,
  For the memory of them is forgotten.
⁶ Also their love, their hatred, and their
    envy have now perished;
  Nevermore will they have a share
  In anything done under the sun.

⁷ Go, eat your bread with joy,

And drink your wine with a merry
    heart;
  For God has already accepted your
    works.
⁸ Let your garments always be white,
  And let your head lack no oil.

⁹Live joyfully with the wife whom you love all the days of your vain life which He has given you under the sun, all your days of vanity; for that *is* your portion in life, and in the labor which you perform under the sun.

¹⁰Whatever your hand finds to do, do *it* with your might; for *there is* no work or device or knowledge or wisdom in the grave where you are going.

¹¹I returned and saw under the sun that—

The race *is* not to the swift,
  Nor the battle to the strong,
  Nor bread to the wise,
  Nor riches to men of understanding,
  Nor favor to men of skill;
  But time and chance happen to them
    all.
¹² For man also does not know his time:
  Like fish taken in a cruel net,
  Like birds caught in a snare,
  So the sons of men *are* snared in an
    evil time,
  When it falls suddenly upon them.

Wisdom Superior to Folly

¹³This wisdom I have also seen under the sun, and it *seemed* great to me: ¹⁴*There was* a little city with few men in it; and a great king came against it, besieged it, and built great snaresᵃ around it. ¹⁵Now there was found in it a poor wise man, and he by his wisdom delivered the city. Yet no one remembered that same poor man.

¹⁶Then I said:

"Wisdom *is* better than strength.
  Nevertheless the poor man's wisdom *is*
    despised,
  And his words are not heard.

9:2 ᵃSeptuagint, Syriac, and Vulgate read *good and bad.*
9:14 ᵃSeptuagint, Syriac, and Vulgate read *bulwarks.*

17 Words of the wise, *spoken* quietly,
  should be heard
  Rather than the shout of a ruler of
  fools.
18 Wisdom *is* better than weapons of
  war;
  But one sinner destroys much good."

10 Dead flies putrefy[a] the perfumer's
  ointment,
  And cause it to give off a foul odor;
  So does a little folly to one respected
  for wisdom *and* honor.
2 A wise man's heart *is* at his right
  hand,
  But a fool's heart at his left.
3 Even when a fool walks along the
  way,
  He lacks wisdom,
  And he shows everyone *that* he *is* a
  fool.
4 If the spirit of the ruler rises against
  you,
  Do not leave your post;
  For conciliation pacifies great offenses.

5 There is an evil I have seen under the
  sun,
  As an error proceeding from the ruler:
6 Folly is set in great dignity,
  While the rich sit in a lowly place.
7 I have seen servants on horses,
  While princes walk on the ground like
  servants.

8 He who digs a pit will fall into it,
  And whoever breaks through a wall
  will be bitten by a serpent.
9 He who quarries stones may be hurt
  by them,
  And he who splits wood may be
  endangered by it.
10 If the ax is dull,
  And one does not sharpen the edge,
  Then he must use more strength;
  But wisdom brings success.

11 A serpent may bite when *it is* not
  charmed;
  The babbler is no different.
12 The words of a wise man's mouth *are*
  gracious,

But the lips of a fool shall swallow
  him up;
13 The words of his mouth begin with
  foolishness,
  And the end of his talk *is* raving
  madness.
14 A fool also multiplies words.
  No man knows what is to be;
  Who can tell him what will be after
  him?
15 The labor of fools wearies them,
  For they do not even know how to go
  to the city!

16 Woe to you, O land, when your king *is*
  a child,
  And your princes feast in the
  morning!
17 Blessed *are* you, O land, when your
  king *is* the son of nobles,
  And your princes feast at the proper
  time—
  For strength and not for drunkenness!
18 Because of laziness the building
  decays,
  And through idleness of hands the
  house leaks.
19 A feast is made for laughter,
  And wine makes merry;
  But money answers everything.

20 Do not curse the king, even in your
  thought;
  Do not curse the rich, even in your
  bedroom;
  For a bird of the air may carry your
  voice,
  And a bird in flight may tell the
  matter.

The Value of Diligence

11 Cast your bread upon the waters,
  For you will find it after many days.
2 Give a serving to seven, and also to
  eight,
  For you do not know what evil will be
  on the earth.

3 If the clouds are full of rain,
  They empty *themselves* upon the earth;

10:1 [a]Targum and Vulgate omit *putrefy.*

And if a tree falls to the south or the
   north,
In the place where the tree falls, there
   it shall lie.
4 He who observes the wind will not sow,
   And he who regards the clouds will
     not reap.

5 As you do not know what *is* the way
   of the wind,[a]
Or how the bones *grow* in the womb of
   her who is with child,
So you do not know the works of God
   who makes everything.
6 In the morning sow your seed,
   And in the evening do not withhold
     your hand;
For you do not know which will
     prosper,
Either this or that,
Or whether both alike *will be* good.

7 Truly the light is sweet,
   And *it is* pleasant for the eyes to
     behold the sun;
8 But if a man lives many years
   And rejoices in them all,
Yet let him remember the days of
     darkness,
For they will be many.
All that is coming *is* vanity.

Seek God in Early Life

9 Rejoice, O young man, in your youth,
   And let your heart cheer you in the
     days of your youth;
Walk in the ways of your heart,
   And in the sight of your eyes;
But know that for all these
   God will bring you into judgment.
10 Therefore remove sorrow from your
     heart,
And put away evil from your flesh,
For childhood and youth *are* vanity.

12 Remember now your Creator in the
     days of your youth,
Before the difficult days come,
And the years draw near when you
     say,
"I have no pleasure in them":
2 While the sun and the light,
The moon and the stars,
Are not darkened,
And the clouds do not return after the
     rain;

11:5 [a]*Or spirit*

HONOR

Remember now your Creator in the days of your youth. . . .

ECCLESIASTES 12:1

James Madison

RENDER HONOR TO THE CREATOR

James Madison, the fourth president of the United States and "Chief Architect of the Constitution," wrote:

The religion then of every man must be left to the conviction and conscience of every man; and it is the right of every man to exercise it as these may dictate. This right is in its nature an unalienable right. It is unalienable, because the opinions of men, depending only on the evidence contemplated by their own minds cannot follow the dictates of other men. It is unalienable also, because what is here a right toward men, is a duty toward the Creator. It is the duty of every man to render to the Creator such homage and such only as he believes to be acceptable to him. This duty is precedent, both in order of time and in degree of obligation, to the claims of civil society. Before any man can be considered as a member of civil society, he must be considered as a sub-ject of the Governor of the Universe. . . .

3 In the day when the keepers of the
house tremble,
And the strong men bow down;
When the grinders cease because they
are few,
And those that look through the
windows grow dim;
4 When the doors are shut in the streets,
And the sound of grinding is low;
When one rises up at the sound of a
bird,
And all the daughters of music are
brought low.
5 Also they are afraid of height,
And of terrors in the way;
When the almond tree blossoms,
The grasshopper is a burden,
And desire fails.
For man goes to his eternal home,
And the mourners go about the
streets.

6 *Remember your Creator* before the silver
cord is loosed,ᵃ
Or the golden bowl is broken,
Or the pitcher shattered at the
fountain,
Or the wheel broken at the well.
7 Then the dust will return to the earth
as it was,
And the spirit will return to God who
gave it.

8 "Vanity of vanities," says the Preacher,
"All *is* vanity."

The Whole Duty of Man

9And moreover, because the Preacher
was wise, he still taught the people knowledge; yes, he pondered and sought out *and*
set in order many proverbs. 10The Preacher
sought to find acceptable words; and *what
was* written *was* upright—words of truth.
11The words of the wise are like goads, and
the words of scholarsᵃ are like well-driven
nails, given by one Shepherd. 12And further, my son, be admonished by these. Of
making many books *there is* no end, and
much study *is* wearisome to the flesh.
13Let us hear the conclusion of the whole
matter:

Fear God and keep His
commandments,
For this is man's all.
14 For God will bring every work into
judgment,
Including every secret thing,
Whether good or evil.

12:6 ᵃFollowing Qere and Targum; Kethib reads
removed; Septuagint and Vulgate read *broken.*
12:11 ᵃLiterally *masters of the assemblies*

SONG OF SOLOMON

Author: Solomon

When Written: 970–930 B.C.

Theme: Covenant Love

Key Verse: Song of Solomon 7:10—I am my beloved's, and his desire is toward me.

Key Chapter: All eight chapters of this unified book form a key that beautifully depicts the love of a man for a woman, and the love of Christ for His bride.

The Song of Solomon is a beautiful love story full of metaphors and imagery. While it may be read as a poetic account of intimate love between a man and a woman, its highest value is found allegorically as the description of deep spiritual passion and intimacy that exists between Christ and His bride, the Church.

The great early American preacher Jonathan Edwards was convinced that this unique book "was designed for a divine song and of divine authority, for we read in 1 Kings 4:32 that Solomon's songs were 'a thousand and five.' This he called the 'Song of Songs.' " Edwards noted that such a designation proves that God considers it "a song of the most excellent subject, treating of the love, union, and communion between Christ and His spouse, of which marriage and conjugal love was but a shadow. These are the most excellent lovers and their love the most excellent love."

1 The song of songs, which *is* Solomon's.

The Banquet

THE SHULAMITE[a]

2 Let him kiss me with the kisses of his
  mouth—
  For your[b] love *is* better than wine.
3 Because of the fragrance of your good
  ointments,
  Your name *is* ointment poured forth;
  Therefore the virgins love you.
4 Draw me away!

THE DAUGHTERS OF JERUSALEM

We will run after you.[a]

THE SHULAMITE

The king has brought me into his
chambers.

THE DAUGHTERS OF JERUSALEM

We will be glad and rejoice in you.[b]

We will remember your[c] love more
than wine.

THE SHULAMITE

Rightly do they love you.[d]

5 I *am* dark, but lovely,
  O daughters of Jerusalem,
  Like the tents of Kedar,
  Like the curtains of Solomon.
6 Do not look upon me, because I *am*
  dark,
  Because the sun has tanned me.
  My mother's sons were angry with me;
  They made me the keeper of the
  vineyards,
  But my own vineyard I have not kept.

(TO HER BELOVED)

7 Tell me, O you whom I love,
  Where you feed *your flock*,
  Where you make *it* rest at noon.
  For why should I be as one who veils
  herself[a]
  By the flocks of your companions?

THE BELOVED

8 If you do not know, O fairest among
  women,
  Follow in the footsteps of the flock,
  And feed your little goats
  Beside the shepherds' tents.
9 I have compared you, my love,
  To my filly among Pharaoh's chariots.
10 Your cheeks are lovely with
  ornaments,
  Your neck with chains *of gold*.

THE DAUGHTERS OF JERUSALEM

11 We will make you[a] ornaments of gold
  With studs of silver.

THE SHULAMITE

12 While the king *is* at his table,
  My spikenard sends forth its
  fragrance.
13 A bundle of myrrh *is* my beloved
  to me,
  That lies all night between my breasts.
14 My beloved *is* to me a cluster of henna
  blooms
  In the vineyards of En Gedi.

THE BELOVED

15 Behold, you *are* fair, my love!
  Behold, you *are* fair!
  You *have* dove's eyes.

1:2 [a]A young woman from the town of Shulam or
Shunem (compare 6:13). The speaker and audience
are identified according to the number, gender, and
person of the Hebrew words. Occasionally the identity
is not certain. [b]Masculine singular, that is, the
Beloved   **1:4** [a]Masculine singular, that is, the
Beloved [b]Feminine singular, that is, the Shulamite
[c]Masculine singular, that is, the Beloved [d]Masculine
singular, that is, the Beloved   **1:7** [a]Septuagint,
Syriac, and Vulgate read *wanders*.   **1:11** [a]Feminine
singular, that is, the Shulamite

The Shulamite

16 Behold, you *are* handsome, my beloved!
Yes, pleasant!
Also our bed *is* green.
17 The beams of our houses *are* cedar,
And our rafters of fir.

2 I *am* the rose of Sharon,
And the lily of the valleys.

The Beloved

2 Like a lily among thorns,
So *is* my love among the daughters.

The Shulamite

3 Like an apple tree among the trees
of the woods,
So *is* my beloved among the sons.
I sat down in his shade with great
delight,
And his fruit *was* sweet to my taste.

The Shulamite to the Daughters of Jerusalem

4 He brought me to the banqueting
house,
And his banner over me *was* love.
5 Sustain me with cakes of raisins,
Refresh me with apples,
For I *am* lovesick.

6 His left hand *is* under my head,
And his right hand embraces me.
7 I charge you, O daughters of Jerusalem,
By the gazelles or by the does of the
field,
Do not stir up nor awaken love
Until it pleases.

The Beloved's Request

The Shulamite

8 The voice of my beloved!
Behold, he comes
Leaping upon the mountains,
Skipping upon the hills.
9 My beloved is like a gazelle or a
young stag.
Behold, he stands behind our wall;
He is looking through the windows,
Gazing through the lattice.

10 My beloved spoke, and said to me:
"Rise up, my love, my fair one,
And come away.
11 For lo, the winter is past,
The rain is over *and* gone.
12 The flowers appear on the earth;
The time of singing has come,
And the voice of the turtledove
Is heard in our land.
13 The fig tree puts forth her green figs,
And the vines *with* the tender grapes
Give a *good* smell.
Rise up, my love, my fair one,
And come away!

14 "O my dove, in the clefts of the rock,
In the secret *places* of the cliff,
Let me see your face,
Let me hear your voice;
For your voice *is* sweet,
And your face *is* lovely."

Her Brothers

15 Catch us the foxes,
The little foxes that spoil the vines,
For our vines *have* tender grapes.

The Shulamite

16 My beloved *is* mine, and I *am* his.
He feeds *his* flock among the lilies.

(To Her Beloved)

17 Until the day breaks
And the shadows flee away,
Turn, my beloved,
And be like a gazelle
Or a young stag
Upon the mountains of Bether.[a]

A Troubled Night

The Shulamite

3 By night on my bed I sought the one
I love;
I sought him, but I did not find him.
2 "I will rise now," *I said,*
"And go about the city;
In the streets and in the squares
I will seek the one I love."
I sought him, but I did not find him.

2:17 [a]Literally *Separation*

3 The watchmen who go about the city
    found me;
  I said,
  "Have you seen the one I love?"

4 Scarcely had I passed by them,
  When I found the one I love.
  I held him and would not let him go,
  Until I had brought him to the house
    of my mother,
  And into the chamber of her who
    conceived me.

5 I charge you, O daughters of
    Jerusalem,
  By the gazelles or by the does of
    the field,
  Do not stir up nor awaken love
  Until it pleases.

The Coming of Solomon

THE SHULAMITE

6 Who *is* this coming out of the
    wilderness
  Like pillars of smoke,
  Perfumed with myrrh and
    frankincense,
  With all the merchant's fragrant
    powders?
7 Behold, it *is* Solomon's couch,
  With sixty valiant men around it,
  Of the valiant of Israel.
8 They all hold swords,
  Being expert in war.
  Every man *has* his sword on his thigh
  Because of fear in the night.

9 Of the wood of Lebanon
  Solomon the King
  Made himself a palanquin:ª
10 He made its pillars *of* silver,
   Its support *of* gold,
   Its seat *of* purple,
   Its interior paved *with* love
   By the daughters of Jerusalem.
11 Go forth, O daughters of Zion,
   And see King Solomon with the crown
   With which his mother crowned him
   On the day of his wedding,
   The day of the gladness of his heart.

The Bridegroom Praises the Bride

THE BELOVED

4 Behold, you *are* fair, my love!
  Behold, you *are* fair!
  You *have* dove's eyes behind your veil.
  Your hair *is* like a flock of goats,
  Going down from Mount Gilead.
2 Your teeth *are* like a flock of shorn *sheep*
  Which have come up from the
    washing,
  Every one of which bears twins,
  And none *is* barren among them.
3 Your lips *are* like a strand of scarlet,
  And your mouth is lovely.
  Your temples behind your veil
  Are like a piece of pomegranate.
4 Your neck *is* like the tower of David,
  Built for an armory,
  On which hang a thousand bucklers,
  All shields of mighty men.
5 Your two breasts *are* like two fawns,
  Twins of a gazelle,
  Which feed among the lilies.

6 Until the day breaks
  And the shadows flee away,
  I will go my way to the mountain
    of myrrh
  And to the hill of frankincense.

7 You *are* all fair, my love,
  And *there is* no spot in you.
8 Come with me from Lebanon, *my*
    spouse,
  With me from Lebanon.
  Look from the top of Amana,
  From the top of Senir and Hermon,
  From the lions' dens,
  From the mountains of the leopards.

9 You have ravished my heart,
  My sister, *my* spouse;
  You have ravished my heart
  With one *look* of your eyes,
  With one link of your necklace.
10 How fair is your love,
   My sister, *my* spouse!
   How much better than wine is your
     love,

3:9 ªA portable enclosed chair

And the scent of your perfumes
Than all spices!
11 Your lips, O *my* spouse,
Drip as the honeycomb;
Honey and milk *are* under your tongue;
And the fragrance of your garments
Is like the fragrance of Lebanon.

12 A garden enclosed
Is my sister, *my* spouse,
A spring shut up,
A fountain sealed.
13 Your plants *are* an orchard of
pomegranates
With pleasant fruits,
Fragrant henna with spikenard,
14 Spikenard and saffron,
Calamus and cinnamon,
With all trees of frankincense,
Myrrh and aloes,
With all the chief spices—
15 A fountain of gardens,
A well of living waters,
And streams from Lebanon.

THE SHULAMITE

16 Awake, O north *wind,*
And come, O south!
Blow upon my garden,
That its spices may flow out.
Let my beloved come to his garden
And eat its pleasant fruits.

THE BELOVED

5 I have come to my garden, my sister,
my spouse;
I have gathered my myrrh with my
spice;
I have eaten my honeycomb with my
honey;
I have drunk my wine with my milk.

(TO HIS FRIENDS)

Eat, O friends!
Drink, yes, drink deeply,
O beloved ones!

The Shulamite's Troubled Evening

THE SHULAMITE

2 I sleep, but my heart is awake;
It is the voice of my beloved!

He knocks, *saying,*
"Open for me, my sister, my love,
My dove, my perfect one;
For my head is covered with dew,
My locks with the drops of the night."

3 I have taken off my robe;
How can I put it on *again?*
I have washed my feet;
How can I defile them?
4 My beloved put his hand
By the latch *of the door,*
And my heart yearned for him.
5 I arose to open for my beloved,
And my hands dripped *with* myrrh,
My fingers with liquid myrrh,
On the handles of the lock.

6 I opened for my beloved,
But my beloved had turned away *and*
was gone.
My heart leaped up when he spoke.
I sought him, but I could not find him;
I called him, but he gave me no answer.
7 The watchmen who went about the
city found me.
They struck me, they wounded me;
The keepers of the walls
Took my veil away from me.
8 I charge you, O daughters of
Jerusalem,
If you find my beloved,
That you tell him I *am* lovesick!

THE DAUGHTERS OF JERUSALEM

9 What *is* your beloved
More than *another* beloved,
O fairest among women?
What *is* your beloved
More than *another* beloved,
That you so charge us?

THE SHULAMITE

10 My beloved *is* white and ruddy,
Chief among ten thousand.
11 His head *is like* the finest gold;
His locks *are* wavy,
And black as a raven.
12 His eyes *are like* doves
By the rivers of waters,
Washed with milk,
And fitly set.

13 His cheeks *are* like a bed of spices,
Banks of scented herbs.
His lips *are* lilies,
Dripping liquid myrrh.

14 His hands *are* rods of gold
Set with beryl.
His body *is* carved ivory
Inlaid *with* sapphires.
15 His legs *are* pillars of marble
Set on bases of fine gold.
His countenance *is* like Lebanon,
Excellent as the cedars.
16 His mouth *is* most sweet,
Yes, he *is* altogether lovely.
This *is* my beloved,
And this *is* my friend,
O daughters of Jerusalem!

HOPE
. . . chief among ten thousand.
SONG OF SOLOMON 5:10

The Infallible Word of God
William Strong, an Associate Justice of the U.S. Supreme Court (1870–1880), stated:

You ask me what I think of Christ? He is the chiefest among ten thousand, and altogether lovely—my Lord, my Savior, and my God.

What do I think of the Bible? It is the infallible Word of God, a light erected all along the shores of time to warn against the rocks and breakers, and to show the only way to the harbor of eternal rest.

THE DAUGHTERS OF JERUSALEM

6 Where has your beloved gone,
O fairest among women?
Where has your beloved turned aside,
That we may seek him with you?

THE SHULAMITE

2 My beloved has gone to his garden,
To the beds of spices,
To feed *his flock* in the gardens,
And to gather lilies.
3 I *am* my beloved's,
And my beloved *is* mine.
He feeds *his flock* among the lilies.

Praise of the Shulamite's Beauty

THE BELOVED

4 O my love, you *are as* beautiful as Tirzah,
Lovely as Jerusalem,
Awesome as *an army* with banners!
5 Turn your eyes away from me,
For they have overcome me.
Your hair *is* like a flock of goats
Going down from Gilead.
6 Your teeth *are* like a flock of sheep
Which have come up from the washing;
Every one bears twins,
And none *is* barren among them.
7 Like a piece of pomegranate
Are your temples behind your veil.

8 There are sixty queens
And eighty concubines,
And virgins without number.
9 My dove, my perfect one,
Is the only one,
The only one of her mother,
The favorite of the one who bore her.
The daughters saw her
And called her blessed,
The queens and the concubines,
And they praised her.

10 Who is she who looks forth as the morning,
Fair as the moon,
Clear as the sun,
Awesome as *an army* with banners?

THE SHULAMITE

11 I went down to the garden of nuts
To see the verdure of the valley,
To see whether the vine had budded
And the pomegranates had bloomed.
12 Before I was even aware,
My soul had made me
As the chariots of my noble people.[a]

THE BELOVED AND HIS FRIENDS

13 Return, return, O Shulamite;
Return, return, that we may look upon you!

6:12 [a]Hebrew *Ammi Nadib*

The Shulamite

What would you see in the Shulamite—
As it were, the dance of the two camps?[a]

Expressions of Praise

The Beloved

7 How beautiful are your feet in sandals,
O prince's daughter!
The curves of your thighs *are* like jewels,
The work of the hands of a skillful
workman.

2 Your navel *is* a rounded goblet;
It lacks no blended beverage.
Your waist *is* a heap of wheat
Set about with lilies.

3 Your two breasts *are* like two fawns,
Twins of a gazelle.

4 Your neck *is* like an ivory tower,
Your eyes *like* the pools in Heshbon
By the gate of Bath Rabbim.
Your nose *is* like the tower of Lebanon
Which looks toward Damascus.

5 Your head *crowns* you like *Mount* Carmel,
And the hair of your head *is* like purple;
A king *is* held captive by *your* tresses.

6 How fair and how pleasant you are,
O love, with your delights!

7 This stature of yours is like a palm tree,
And your breasts *like* its clusters.

8 I said, "I will go up to the palm tree,
I will take hold of its branches."
Let now your breasts be like clusters of
the vine,
The fragrance of your breath like apples,

9 And the roof of your mouth like the
best wine.

The Shulamite

The wine goes *down* smoothly for my
beloved,
Moving gently the lips of sleepers.[a]

10 I *am* my beloved's,
And his desire *is* toward me.

11 Come, my beloved,
Let us go forth to the field;
Let us lodge in the villages.

12 Let us get up early to the vineyards;
Let us see if the vine has budded,
Whether the grape blossoms are open,
And the pomegranates are in bloom.
There I will give you my love.

13 The mandrakes give off a fragrance,
And at our gates *are* pleasant *fruits,*
All manner, new and old,
Which I have laid up for you, my
beloved.

8 Oh, that you were like my brother,
Who nursed at my mother's breasts!
If I should find you outside,
I would kiss you;
I would not be despised.

2 I would lead you *and* bring you
Into the house of my mother,
She *who* used to instruct me.
I would cause you to drink of spiced
wine,
Of the juice of my pomegranate.

(To the Daughters of Jerusalem)

3 His left hand *is* under my head,
And his right hand embraces me.

4 I charge you, O daughters of
Jerusalem,
Do not stir up nor awaken love
Until it pleases.

Love Renewed in Lebanon

A Relative

5 Who *is* this coming up from the
wilderness,
Leaning upon her beloved?

I awakened you under the apple tree.
There your mother brought you forth;
There she *who* bore you brought *you*
forth.

The Shulamite to Her Beloved

6 Set me as a seal upon your heart,
As a seal upon your arm;
For love *is as* strong as death,
Jealousy *as* cruel as the grave;[a]
Its flames *are* flames of fire,
A most vehement flame.[b]

6:13 [a]Hebrew *Mahanaim*   7:9 [a]Septuagint, Syriac,
and Vulgate read *lips and teeth.*   8:6 [a]Or *Sheol*
[b]Literally *A flame of* Yah (a poetic form of *YHWH,*
the Lord)

7 Many waters cannot quench love,
Nor can the floods drown it.
If a man would give for love
All the wealth of his house,
It would be utterly despised.

THE SHULAMITE'S BROTHERS

8 We have a little sister,
And she has no breasts.
What shall we do for our sister
In the day when she is spoken for?
9 If she *is* a wall,
We will build upon her
A battlement of silver;
And if she *is* a door,
We will enclose her
With boards of cedar.

THE SHULAMITE

10 I *am* a wall,
And my breasts like towers;
Then I became in his eyes
As one who found peace.

11 Solomon had a vineyard at Baal
Hamon;
He leased the vineyard to keepers;
Everyone was to bring for its fruit
A thousand silver *coins*.

(TO SOLOMON)

12 My own vineyard *is* before me.
You, O Solomon, *may have* a thousand,
And those who tend its fruit two
hundred.

THE BELOVED

13 You who dwell in the gardens,
The companions listen for your
voice—
Let me hear it!

THE SHULAMITE

14 Make haste, my beloved,
And be like a gazelle
Or a young stag
On the mountains of spices.

ISAIAH

Author: Isaiah

When Written: 700–690 B.C.

Theme: Salvation Is of the Lord

Key Verse: Isaiah 53:6—All we like sheep have gone astray; we have turned, every one, to his own way; and the LORD has laid on Him the iniquity of us all.

Key Chapter: Isaiah 53—Along with Psalm 22, Isaiah 53 details the most remarkable and specific prophecies concerning the Messiah and the atonement He made.

The theme for Isaiah is found in the meaning of the prophet's own name: "Yahweh is Salvation." This book contains some of the most meaningful and eloquent writings of the Old Testament, with the prophet Isaiah warning the people of Judah of impending judgment because of their sin, depravity, and spiritual idolatry. In spite of this, God remains faithful to His covenant, promising deliverance and salvation to His people through the coming Messiah.

Jonathan Edwards (1703–1757), whose preaching began America's First Great Awakening, is famous for his "Sinners in the Hands of an Angry God" sermon, which emphasized the just wrath of God against sin. But as Isaiah did, he was passionate about declaring the glory of the Suffering Messiah:

> All the virtues that appeared in Christ shone brightest in the close of His life, under the trials He then met. Eminent virtue always shows brightest in the fire. Pure gold shows its purity chiefly in the furnace. It was chiefly under those trials that Christ endured in the close of His life that His love to God, His honor of God's majesty, His regard to the honor of His law, His spirit of obedience, His humility, contempt of the world, His patience, meekness, and spirit of forgiveness toward men, appeared. Indeed, everything that Christ did to work out redemption for us appears mainly in the close of His life.

ISAIAH

1 The vision of Isaiah the son of Amoz, which he saw concerning Judah and Jerusalem in the days of Uzziah, Jotham, Ahaz, *and* Hezekiah, kings of Judah.

The Wickedness of Judah

2   Hear, O heavens, and give ear,
        O earth!
     For the LORD has spoken:
     "I have nourished and brought up
        children,
     And they have rebelled against Me;
3   The ox knows its owner
     And the donkey its master's crib;
     But Israel does not know,
     My people do not consider."

4   Alas, sinful nation,
     A people laden with iniquity,
     A brood of evildoers,
     Children who are corrupters!
     They have forsaken the LORD,
     They have provoked to anger
     The Holy One of Israel,
     They have turned away backward.

5   Why should you be stricken again?
     You will revolt more and more.
     The whole head is sick,
     And the whole heart faints.
6   From the sole of the foot even to the
        head,
     There is no soundness in it,
     But wounds and bruises and putrefying
        sores;
     They have not been closed or bound up,
     Or soothed with ointment.

7   Your country *is* desolate,
     Your cities *are* burned with fire;
     Strangers devour your land in your
        presence;
     And *it is* desolate, as overthrown by
        strangers.
8   So the daughter of Zion is left as a
        booth in a vineyard,

     As a hut in a garden of cucumbers,
     As a besieged city.
9   Unless the LORD of hosts
     Had left to us a very small remnant,
     We would have become like Sodom,
     We would have been made like
        Gomorrah.

10   Hear the word of the LORD,
     You rulers of Sodom;
     Give ear to the law of our God,
     You people of Gomorrah:
11   "To what purpose *is* the multitude of
        your sacrifices to Me?"
     Says the LORD.
     "I have had enough of burnt offerings
        of rams
     And the fat of fed cattle.
     I do not delight in the blood of bulls,
     Or of lambs or goats.

12   "When you come to appear before Me,
     Who has required this from your hand,
     To trample My courts?
13   Bring no more futile sacrifices;
     Incense is an abomination to Me.
     The New Moons, the Sabbaths, and
        the calling of assemblies—
     I cannot endure iniquity and the
        sacred meeting.
14   Your New Moons and your appointed
        feasts
     My soul hates;
     They are a trouble to Me,
     I am weary of bearing *them.*
15   When you spread out your hands,
     I will hide My eyes from you;
     Even though you make many prayers,
     I will not hear.
     Your hands are full of blood.

16   "Wash yourselves, make yourselves
        clean;
     Put away the evil of your doings
        from before My eyes.
     Cease to do evil,

17 Learn to do good;
    Seek justice,
    Rebuke the oppressor;ᵃ
    Defend the fatherless,
    Plead for the widow.

18 "Come now, and let us reason together,"
    Says the LORD,
    "Though your sins are like scarlet,
    They shall be as white as snow;
    Though they are red like crimson,
    They shall be as wool.
19 If you are willing and obedient,
    You shall eat the good of the land;
20 But if you refuse and rebel,
    You shall be devoured by the sword";
    For the mouth of the LORD has spoken.

The Degenerate City

21 How the faithful city has become
       a harlot!
    It was full of justice;
    Righteousness lodged in it,
    But now murderers.
22 Your silver has become dross,
    Your wine mixed with water.

23 Your princes *are* rebellious,
    And companions of thieves;
    Everyone loves bribes,
    And follows after rewards.
    They do not defend the fatherless,
    Nor does the cause of the widow
       come before them.

24 Therefore the Lord says,
    The LORD of hosts, the Mighty One
       of Israel,
    "Ah, I will rid Myself of My adversaries,
    And take vengeance on My enemies.
25 I will turn My hand against you,
    And thoroughly purge away your dross,
    And take away all your alloy.
26 I will restore your judges as at the first,
    And your counselors as at the
       beginning.
    Afterward you shall be called the city
       of righteousness, the faithful city."

27 Zion shall be redeemed with justice,
    And her penitents with righteousness.
28 The destruction of transgressors and
       of sinners *shall be* together,
    And those who forsake the LORD shall
       be consumed.
29 For theyᵃ shall be ashamed of the
       terebinth trees
    Which you have desired;
    And you shall be embarrassed
       because of the gardens
    Which you have chosen.
30 For you shall be as a terebinth whose
       leaf fades,
    And as a garden that has no water.
31 The strong shall be as tinder,
    And the work of it as a spark;
    Both will burn together,
    And no one shall quench *them.*

The Future House of God

2 The word that Isaiah the son of Amoz
   saw concerning Judah and Jerusalem.

2 Now it shall come to pass in the latter
       days

1:17 ᵃSome ancient versions read *the oppressed.*
1:29 ᵃFollowing Masoretic Text, Septuagint, and
Vulgate; some Hebrew manuscripts and Targum
read *you.*

That the mountain of the LORD's house
Shall be established on the top of the
mountains,
And shall be exalted above the hills;
And all nations shall flow to it.
3   Many people shall come and say,
"Come, and let us go up to the
mountain of the LORD,
To the house of the God of Jacob;
He will teach us His ways,
And we shall walk in His paths."
For out of Zion shall go forth the law,
And the word of the LORD from
Jerusalem.

Richard M. Nixon placed his hand on Isaiah 2:4 as he took the presidential oath of office in 1969 and 1973.

---

4   He shall judge between the nations,
And rebuke many people;
They shall beat their swords into
plowshares,
And their spears into pruning hooks;
Nation shall not lift up sword against
nation,
Neither shall they learn war anymore.

The Day of the LORD

5   O house of Jacob, come and let us walk
In the light of the LORD.

6   For You have forsaken Your people, the
house of Jacob,
Because they are filled with eastern
ways;
They *are* soothsayers like the Philistines,
And they are pleased with the children
of foreigners.
7   Their land is also full of silver and gold,
And there is no end to their treasures;
Their land is also full of horses,
And there is no end to their chariots.
8   Their land is also full of idols;
They worship the work of their own
hands,
That which their own fingers have
made.
9   People bow down,
And each man humbles himself;
Therefore do not forgive them.

10   Enter into the rock, and hide in
the dust,
From the terror of the LORD
And the glory of His majesty.
11   The lofty looks of man shall be
humbled,
The haughtiness of men shall be
bowed down,
And the LORD alone shall be exalted
in that day.

12   For the day of the LORD of hosts
Shall come upon everything proud and
lofty,
Upon everything lifted up—
And it shall be brought low—
13   Upon all the cedars of Lebanon *that
are* high and lifted up,
And upon all the oaks of Bashan;
14   Upon all the high mountains,
And upon all the hills *that are* lifted up;
15   Upon every high tower,
And upon every fortified wall;
16   Upon all the ships of Tarshish,
And upon all the beautiful sloops.
17   The loftiness of man shall be bowed
down,
And the haughtiness of men shall be
brought low;
The LORD alone will be exalted in that
day,
18   But the idols He shall utterly abolish.

19   They shall go into the holes of the rocks,
And into the caves of the earth,
From the terror of the LORD
And the glory of His majesty,
When He arises to shake the earth
mightily.

20   In that day a man will cast away his
idols of silver
And his idols of gold,
Which they made, *each* for himself to
worship,
To the moles and bats,
21   To go into the clefts of the rocks,
And into the crags of the rugged rocks,
From the terror of the LORD
And the glory of His majesty,
When He arises to shake the earth
mightily.

22 Sever yourselves from such a man,
  Whose breath *is* in his nostrils;
  For of what account is he?

Judgment on Judah and Jerusalem

3 For behold, the Lord, the LORD of hosts,
  Takes away from Jerusalem and from
    Judah
  The stock and the store,
  The whole supply of bread and the
    whole supply of water;
2 The mighty man and the man of war,
  The judge and the prophet,
  And the diviner and the elder;
3 The captain of fifty and the honorable
    man,
  The counselor and the skillful artisan,
  And the expert enchanter.

4 "I will give children *to be* their princes,
  And babes shall rule over them.
5 The people will be oppressed,
  Every one by another and every one
    by his neighbor;
  The child will be insolent toward the
    elder,
  And the base toward the honorable."

6 When a man takes hold of his brother
  In the house of his father, *saying,*
  "You have clothing;
  You be our ruler,
  And *let* these ruins *be* under your
    power,"ᵃ
7 In that day he will protest, saying,
  "I cannot cure *your* ills,
  For in my house *is* neither food nor
    clothing;
  Do not make me a ruler of the people."

8 For Jerusalem stumbled,
  And Judah is fallen,
  Because their tongue and their doings
  Are against the LORD,
  To provoke the eyes of His glory.
9 The look on their countenance
    witnesses against them,
  And they declare their sin as Sodom;
  They do not hide *it.*
  Woe to their soul!
  For they have brought evil upon
    themselves.

10 "Say to the righteous that *it shall be*
    well *with them,*
  For they shall eat the fruit of their
    doings.
11 Woe to the wicked! *It shall be* ill *with*
    him,
  For the reward of his hands shall be
    given him.
12 *As for* My people, children *are* their
    oppressors,
  And women rule over them.
  O My people! Those who lead you
    cause *you* to err,
  And destroy the way of your paths."

Oppression and Luxury Condemned

13 The LORD stands up to plead,
  And stands to judge the people.
14 The LORD will enter into judgment
  With the elders of His people
  And His princes:
  "For you have eaten up the vineyard;
  The plunder of the poor *is* in your
    houses.
15 What do you mean by crushing My
    people
  And grinding the faces of the poor?"
  Says the Lord GOD of hosts.

16Moreover the LORD says:

  "Because the daughters of Zion are
    haughty,
  And walk with outstretched necks
  And wanton eyes,
  Walking and mincing *as* they go,
  Making a jingling with their feet,
17 Therefore the Lord will strike with a
    scab
  The crown of the head of the
    daughters of Zion,
  And the LORD will uncover their secret
    parts."

18 In that day the Lord will take away
    the finery:
  The jingling anklets, the scarves, and
    the crescents;
19 The pendants, the bracelets, and the
    veils;

3:6 ᵃLiterally *hand*

20 The headdresses, the leg ornaments,
     and the headbands;
   The perfume boxes, the charms,
21   and the rings;
   The nose jewels,
22   the festal apparel, and the mantles;
   The outer garments, the purses,
23   and the mirrors;
   The fine linen, the turbans, and the
     robes.

24And so it shall be:

   Instead of a sweet smell there will
     be a stench;
   Instead of a sash, a rope;
   Instead of well-set hair, baldness;
   Instead of a rich robe, a girding of
     sackcloth;
   And branding instead of beauty.
25 Your men shall fall by the sword,
   And your mighty in the war.

26 Her gates shall lament and mourn,
   And she *being* desolate shall sit on
     the ground.

4 And in that day seven women shall take
   hold of one man, saying,
   "We will eat our own food and wear
     our own apparel;
   Only let us be called by your name,
   To take away our reproach."

The Renewal of Zion

2   In that day the Branch of the LORD
     shall be beautiful and glorious;
   And the fruit of the earth *shall be*
     excellent and appealing
   For those of Israel who have escaped.

3And it shall come to pass that *he who is*
left in Zion and remains in Jerusalem will
be called holy—everyone who is recorded
among the living in Jerusalem. 4When the
Lord has washed away the filth of the
daughters of Zion, and purged the blood of
Jerusalem from her midst, by the spirit of
judgment and by the spirit of burning, 5then
the LORD will create above every dwelling
place of Mount Zion, and above her assemblies, a cloud and smoke by day and the
shining of a flaming fire by night. For over
all the glory there *will be* a covering. 6And
there will be a tabernacle for shade in the
daytime from the heat, for a place of refuge,
and for a shelter from storm and rain.

God's Disappointing Vineyard

5 Now let me sing to my Well-beloved
   A song of my Beloved regarding His
     vineyard:

   My Well-beloved has a vineyard
   On a very fruitful hill.
2   He dug it up and cleared out its stones,
   And planted it with the choicest vine.
   He built a tower in its midst,
   And also made a winepress in it;
   So He expected *it* to bring forth *good*
     grapes,
   But it brought forth wild grapes.

3   "And now, O inhabitants of Jerusalem
     and men of Judah,
   Judge, please, between Me and My
     vineyard.
4   What more could have been done to
     My vineyard
   That I have not done in it?
   Why then, when I expected *it* to bring
     forth *good* grapes,
   Did it bring forth wild grapes?
5   And now, please let Me tell you what
     I will do to My vineyard:
   I will take away its hedge, and it shall
     be burned;
   And break down its wall, and it shall
     be trampled down.
6   I will lay it waste;
   It shall not be pruned or dug,
   But there shall come up briers and
     thorns.
   I will also command the clouds
   That they rain no rain on it."

7   For the vineyard of the LORD of hosts
     is the house of Israel,
   And the men of Judah are His
     pleasant plant.
   He looked for justice, but behold,
     oppression;
   For righteousness, but behold, a cry
     for help.

Impending Judgment on Excesses

8 Woe to those who join house to house;
   They add field to field,
   Till *there is* no place
   Where they may dwell alone in the
      midst of the land!

9 In my hearing the Lord of hosts *said,*
   "Truly, many houses shall be desolate,
   Great and beautiful ones, without
      inhabitant.

10 For ten acres of vineyard shall yield
      one bath,
   And a homer of seed shall yield one
      ephah."

11 Woe to those who rise early in the
      morning,
   That they may follow intoxicating drink;
   Who continue until night, *till* wine
      inflames them!

12 The harp and the strings,
   The tambourine and flute,
   And wine are in their feasts;
   But they do not regard the work of the
      Lord,
   Nor consider the operation of His hands.

13 Therefore my people have gone into
      captivity,
   Because *they have* no knowledge;
   Their honorable men *are* famished,
   And their multitude dried up with
      thirst.

14 Therefore Sheol has enlarged itself
   And opened its mouth beyond measure;
   Their glory and their multitude and
      their pomp,
   And he who is jubilant, shall descend
      into it.

15 People shall be brought down,
   Each man shall be humbled,
   And the eyes of the lofty shall be
      humbled.

16 But the Lord of hosts shall be exalted
      in judgment,
   And God who is holy shall be
      hallowed in righteousness.

17 Then the lambs shall feed in their
      pasture,
   And in the waste places of the fat
      ones strangers shall eat.

18 Woe to those who draw iniquity with
      cords of vanity,
   And sin as if with a cart rope;

19 That say, "Let Him make speed *and*
      hasten His work,
   That we may see *it;*
   And let the counsel of the Holy One
      of Israel draw near and come,
   That we may know *it.*"

20 Woe to those who call evil good, and
      good evil;
   Who put darkness for light, and light
      for darkness;
   Who put bitter for sweet, and sweet
      for bitter!

21 Woe to *those who are* wise in their
      own eyes,
   And prudent in their own sight!

22 Woe to men mighty at drinking wine,
   Woe to men valiant for mixing
      intoxicating drink,

23 Who justify the wicked for a bribe,
   And take away justice from the
      righteous man!

24 Therefore, as the fire devours the
      stubble,
   And the flame consumes the chaff,
   So their root will be as rottenness,
   And their blossom will ascend like dust;
   Because they have rejected the law of
      the Lord of hosts,
   And despised the word of the Holy One
      of Israel.

25 Therefore the anger of the Lord is
      aroused against His people;
   He has stretched out His hand against
      them
   And stricken them,
   And the hills trembled.
   Their carcasses *were* as refuse in the
      midst of the streets.

   For all this His anger is not turned
      away,
   But His hand *is* stretched out still.

26 He will lift up a banner to the nations
      from afar,

And will whistle to them from the end
   of the earth;
Surely they shall come with speed,
   swiftly.
27 No one will be weary or stumble
   among them,
No one will slumber or sleep;
Nor will the belt on their loins be
   loosed,
Nor the strap of their sandals be broken;
28 Whose arrows *are* sharp,
And all their bows bent;
Their horses' hooves will seem like flint,
And their wheels like a whirlwind.
29 Their roaring *will be* like a lion,
They will roar like young lions;
Yes, they will roar
And lay hold of the prey;
They will carry *it* away safely,
And no one will deliver.
30 In that day they will roar against them
Like the roaring of the sea.
And if *one* looks to the land,
Behold, darkness *and* sorrow;
And the light is darkened by the clouds.

Isaiah Called to Be a Prophet

6 In the year that King Uzziah died, I saw the Lord sitting on a throne, high and lifted up, and the train of His *robe* filled the temple. 2Above it stood seraphim; each one had six wings: with two he covered his face, with two he covered his feet, and with two he flew. 3And one cried to another and said:

"Holy, holy, holy *is* the Lord of hosts;
The whole earth *is* full of His glory!"

4And the posts of the door were shaken by the voice of him who cried out, and the house was filled with smoke.
  5So I said:

"Woe *is* me, for I am undone!
Because I *am* a man of unclean lips,
And I dwell in the midst of a people
   of unclean lips;
For my eyes have seen the King,
The Lord of hosts."

6Then one of the seraphim flew to me, having in his hand a live coal *which* he had taken with the tongs from the altar. 7And he touched my mouth *with it,* and said:

"Behold, this has touched your lips;
Your iniquity is taken away,
And your sin purged."

8Also I heard the voice of the Lord, saying:

"Whom shall I send,
And who will go for Us?"

Then I said, "Here *am* I! Send me."
9And He said, "Go, and tell this people:

'Keep on hearing, but do not
   understand;
Keep on seeing, but do not perceive.'

10 "Make the heart of this people dull,
And their ears heavy,
And shut their eyes;
Lest they see with their eyes,
And hear with their ears,
And understand with their heart,
And return and be healed."

11Then I said, "Lord, how long?"
And He answered:

"Until the cities are laid waste and
   without inhabitant,
The houses are without a man,
The land is utterly desolate,
12 The Lord has removed men far away,
And the forsaken places *are* many in
   the midst of the land.
13 But yet a tenth *will be* in it,
And will return and be for consuming,
As a terebinth tree or as an oak,
Whose stump *remains* when it is cut
   down.
So the holy seed *shall be* its stump."

Isaiah Sent to King Ahaz

7 Now it came to pass in the days of Ahaz the son of Jotham, the son of Uzziah, king of Judah, *that* Rezin king of Syria and Pekah the son of Remaliah, king of Israel, went up to Jerusalem to *make* war against it, but could not prevail against it. 2And it was told to the house of David, saying, "Syria's forces

are deployed in Ephraim." So his heart and the heart of his people were moved as the trees of the woods are moved with the wind.

³Then the LORD said to Isaiah, "Go out now to meet Ahaz, you and Shear-Jashub[a] your son, at the end of the aqueduct from the upper pool, on the highway to the Fuller's Field, ⁴and say to him: 'Take heed, and be quiet; do not fear or be fainthearted for these two stubs of smoking firebrands, for the fierce anger of Rezin and Syria, and the son of Remaliah. ⁵Because Syria, Ephraim, and the son of Remaliah have plotted evil against you, saying, ⁶"Let us go up against Judah and trouble it, and let us make a gap in its wall for ourselves, and set a king over them, the son of Tabel"— ⁷thus says the Lord GOD:

"It shall not stand,
   Nor shall it come to pass.
8   For the head of Syria is Damascus,
   And the head of Damascus is Rezin.
   Within sixty-five years Ephraim will be broken,
   So that it will not be a people.
9   The head of Ephraim is Samaria,
   And the head of Samaria is Remaliah's son.
   If you will not believe,
   Surely you shall not be established."'"

The Immanuel Prophecy

¹⁰Moreover the LORD spoke again to Ahaz, saying, ¹¹"Ask a sign for yourself from the LORD your God; ask it either in the depth or in the height above." ¹²But Ahaz said, "I will not ask, nor will I test the LORD!" ¹³Then he said, "Hear now, O house of David! Is it a small thing for you to weary men, but will you weary my God also? ¹⁴Therefore the Lord Himself will give you a sign: Behold, the virgin shall conceive and bear a Son, and shall call His name Immanuel.[a] ¹⁵Curds and honey He shall eat, that He may know to refuse the evil and choose the good. ¹⁶For before the Child shall know to refuse the evil and choose the good, the land that you dread will be forsaken by both her kings. ¹⁷The LORD will bring the king of Assyria upon you and your people and your father's house—days that have not come since the day that Ephraim departed from Judah."

18   And it shall come to pass in that day
   That the LORD will whistle for the fly
   That is in the farthest part of the rivers of Egypt,
   And for the bee that is in the land of Assyria.
19   They will come, and all of them will rest
   In the desolate valleys and in the clefts of the rocks,
   And on all thorns and in all pastures.

20   In the same day the Lord will shave with a hired razor,
   With those from beyond the River,[a] with the king of Assyria,
   The head and the hair of the legs,
   And will also remove the beard.

21   It shall be in that day
   That a man will keep alive a young cow and two sheep;
22   So it shall be, from the abundance of milk they give,
   That he will eat curds;
   For curds and honey everyone will eat who is left in the land.

23   It shall happen in that day,
   That wherever there could be a thousand vines
   Worth a thousand shekels of silver,
   It will be for briers and thorns.
24   With arrows and bows men will come there,
   Because all the land will become briers and thorns.

25   And to any hill which could be dug with the hoe,
   You will not go there for fear of briers and thorns;
   But it will become a range for oxen
   And a place for sheep to roam.

7:3 ᵃLiterally A Remnant Shall Return
7:14 ᵃLiterally God-With-Us   7:20 ᵃThat is, the Euphrates

Assyria Will Invade the Land

8 Moreover the Lord said to me, "Take a large scroll, and write on it with a man's pen concerning Maher-Shalal-Hash-Baz.ᵃ ²And I will take for Myself faithful witnesses to record, Uriah the priest and Zechariah the son of Jeberechiah."

³Then I went to the prophetess, and she conceived and bore a son. Then the Lord said to me, "Call his name Maher-Shalal-Hash-Baz; ⁴for before the child shall have knowledge to cry 'My father' and 'My mother,' the riches of Damascus and the spoil of Samaria will be taken away before the king of Assyria."

⁵The Lord also spoke to me again, saying:

6   "Inasmuch as these people refused
    The waters of Shiloah that flow softly,
    And rejoice in Rezin and in Remaliah's
      son;
7   Now therefore, behold, the Lord brings
      up over them
    The waters of the River,ᵃ strong and
      mighty—
    The king of Assyria and all his glory;
    He will go up over all his channels
    And go over all his banks.
8   He will pass through Judah,
    He will overflow and pass over,
    He will reach up to the neck;
    And the stretching out of his wings
    Will fill the breadth of Your land,
      O Immanuel.ᵃ

9   "Be shattered, O you peoples, and be
      broken in pieces!
    Give ear, all you from far countries.
    Gird yourselves, but be broken in
      pieces;
    Gird yourselves, but be broken in
      pieces.
10 Take counsel together, but it will come
      to nothing;
    Speak the word, but it will not stand,
    For God is with us."ᵃ

Fear God, Heed His Word

¹¹For the Lord spoke thus to me with a strong hand, and instructed me that I should not walk in the way of this people, saying:

12 "Do not say, 'A conspiracy,'
    Concerning all that this people call
      a conspiracy,
    Nor be afraid of their threats, nor be
      troubled.
13 The Lord of hosts, Him you shall
      hallow;
    Let Him be your fear,
    And let Him be your dread.
14 He will be as a sanctuary,
    But a stone of stumbling and a rock
      of offense
    To both the houses of Israel,
    As a trap and a snare to the
      inhabitants of Jerusalem.
15 And many among them shall
      stumble;
    They shall fall and be broken,
    Be snared and taken."

16 Bind up the testimony,
    Seal the law among my disciples.
17 And I will wait on the Lord,
    Who hides His face from the house of
      Jacob;
    And I will hope in Him.
18 Here am I and the children whom the
      Lord has given me!
    We are for signs and wonders in Israel
    From the Lord of hosts,
    Who dwells in Mount Zion.

¹⁹And when they say to you, "Seek those who are mediums and wizards, who whisper and mutter," should not a people seek their God? Should they seek the dead on behalf of the living? ²⁰To the law and to the testimony! If they do not speak according to this word, it is because there is no light in them.

²¹They will pass through it hard-pressed and hungry; and it shall happen, when they are hungry, that they will be enraged and curse their king and their God, and look upward. ²²Then they will look to the earth, and see trouble and darkness, gloom of anguish; and they will be driven into darkness.

8:1 ᵃLiterally *Speed the Spoil, Hasten the Booty*
8:7 ᵃThat is, the Euphrates   **8:8** ᵃLiterally *God-With-Us*   **8:10** ᵃHebrew *Immanuel*

The Government of the Promised Son

9 Nevertheless the gloom *will* not *be* upon
    her who *is* distressed,
As when at first He lightly esteemed
The land of Zebulun and the land of
    Naphtali,
And afterward more heavily oppressed
    her,
By the way of the sea, beyond the
    Jordan,
In Galilee of the Gentiles.
2   The people who walked in darkness
Have seen a great light;
Those who dwelt in the land of the
    shadow of death,
Upon them a light has shined.

3   You have multiplied the nation
And increased its joy;[a]
They rejoice before You
According to the joy of harvest,
As *men* rejoice when they divide the
    spoil.
4   For You have broken the yoke of his
    burden
And the staff of his shoulder,
The rod of his oppressor,
As in the day of Midian.
5   For every warrior's sandal from the
    noisy battle,
And garments rolled in blood,
Will be used for burning *and* fuel of
    fire.

6   For unto us a Child is born,
Unto us a Son is given;
And the government will be upon
    His shoulder.
And His name will be called
Wonderful, Counselor, Mighty God,
Everlasting Father, Prince of Peace.
7   Of the increase of *His* government
    and peace
There will be no end,
Upon the throne of David and over
    His kingdom,
To order it and establish it with
    judgment and justice
From that time forward, even forever.
The zeal of the LORD of hosts will
    perform this.

PROTECTOR

. . . and the government will be upon His
shoulder. . . .   ISAIAH 9:6

The Government of God

Lyman Beecher (1775–1863), a renowned Presbyterian clergyman in New England who later became president of Lane Theological Seminary, wrote:

> The government of God is the only government which will hold society, against depravity within and temptation without; and this it must do by the force of its own law written upon the heart.

> This is that unity of the Spirit and that bond of peace which can alone perpetuate national purity and tranquility—that law of universal and impartial love by which alone nations can be kept back from ruin. There is no safety for republics but in self-government, under the influence of a holy heart, swayed by the government of God.

The Punishment of Samaria

8   The Lord sent a word against Jacob,
And it has fallen on Israel.
9   All the people will know—
Ephraim and the inhabitant of
    Samaria—
Who say in pride and arrogance of
    heart:
10   "The bricks have fallen down,
But we will rebuild with hewn stones;
The sycamores are cut down,
But we will replace *them* with cedars."
11   Therefore the LORD shall set up
The adversaries of Rezin against him,
And spur his enemies on,
12   The Syrians before and the Philistines
    behind;
And they shall devour Israel with an
    open mouth.

For all this His anger is not turned
    away,
But His hand *is* stretched out still.

9:3 [a]Following Qere and Targum; Kethib and Vulgate read *not increased joy;* Septuagint reads *Most of the people You brought down in Your joy.*

13 For the people do not turn to Him who
       strikes them,
    Nor do they seek the LORD of hosts.
14 Therefore the LORD will cut off head
       and tail from Israel,
    Palm branch and bulrush in one day.
15 The elder and honorable, he *is* the head;
    The prophet who teaches lies, he *is* the
       tail.
16 For the leaders of this people cause
       them to err,
    And *those who are* led by them are
       destroyed.
17 Therefore the Lord will have no joy
       in their young men,
    Nor have mercy on their fatherless
       and widows;
    For everyone *is* a hypocrite and an
       evildoer,
    And every mouth speaks folly.

    For all this His anger is not turned
       away,
    But His hand *is* stretched out still.

18 For wickedness burns as the fire;
    It shall devour the briers and thorns,
    And kindle in the thickets of the forest;
    They shall mount up *like* rising smoke.
19 Through the wrath of the LORD of hosts
    The land is burned up,
    And the people shall be as fuel for the
       fire;
    No man shall spare his brother.
20 And he shall snatch on the right hand
    And be hungry;
    He shall devour on the left hand
    And not be satisfied;
    Every man shall eat the flesh of his
       own arm.
21 Manasseh *shall devour* Ephraim, and
       Ephraim Manasseh;
    Together they *shall be* against Judah.

    For all this His anger is not turned
       away,
    But His hand *is* stretched out still.

10 "Woe to those who decree unrighteous
       decrees,
    Who write misfortune,
    Which they have prescribed

2 To rob the needy of justice,
    And to take what is right from the
       poor of My people,
    That widows may be their prey,
    And *that* they may rob the fatherless.
3 What will you do in the day of
       punishment,
    And in the desolation *which* will come
       from afar?
    To whom will you flee for help?
    And where will you leave your glory?
4 Without Me they shall bow down
       among the prisoners,
    And they shall fall among the slain."

    For all this His anger is not turned
       away,
    But His hand *is* stretched out still.

Arrogant Assyria Also Judged

5 "Woe to Assyria, the rod of My anger
    And the staff in whose hand is My
       indignation.
6 I will send him against an ungodly
       nation,
    And against the people of My wrath
    I will give him charge,
    To seize the spoil, to take the prey,
    And to tread them down like the mire
       of the streets.
7 Yet he does not mean so,
    Nor does his heart think so;
    But *it is* in his heart to destroy,
    And cut off not a few nations.
8 For he says,
    '*Are* not my princes altogether kings?
9 *Is* not Calno like Carchemish?
    Is not Hamath like Arpad?
    Is not Samaria like Damascus?
10 As my hand has found the kingdoms
       of the idols,
    Whose carved images excelled those
       of Jerusalem and Samaria,
11 As I have done to Samaria and her
       idols,
    Shall I not do also to Jerusalem and
       her idols?' "

12 Therefore it shall come to pass, when the
Lord has performed all His work on Mount
Zion and on Jerusalem, *that* He will say, "I
will punish the fruit of the arrogant heart

of the king of Assyria, and the glory of his haughty looks."

¹³For he says:

"By the strength of my hand I have done *it,*
And by my wisdom, for I am prudent;
Also I have removed the boundaries of the people,
And have robbed their treasuries;
So I have put down the inhabitants like a valiant *man.*

14   My hand has found like a nest the riches of the people,
And as one gathers eggs *that are* left,
I have gathered all the earth;
And there was no one who moved *his* wing,
Nor opened *his* mouth with even a peep."

15   Shall the ax boast itself against him who chops with it?
Or shall the saw exalt itself against him who saws with it?
As if a rod could wield *itself* against those who lift it up,
Or as if a staff could lift up, *as if it were* not wood!

16   Therefore the Lord, the Lordª of hosts,
Will send leanness among his fat ones;
And under his glory
He will kindle a burning
Like the burning of a fire.

17   So the Light of Israel will be for a fire,
And his Holy One for a flame;
It will burn and devour
His thorns and his briers in one day.

18   And it will consume the glory of his forest and of his fruitful field,
Both soul and body;
And they will be as when a sick man wastes away.

19   Then the rest of the trees of his forest
Will be so few in number
That a child may write them.

The Returning Remnant of Israel

20   And it shall come to pass in that day
That the remnant of Israel,
And such as have escaped of the house of Jacob,
Will never again depend on him who defeated them,
But will depend on the LORD, the Holy One of Israel, in truth.

21   The remnant will return, the remnant of Jacob,
To the Mighty God.

22   For though your people, O Israel, be as the sand of the sea,
A remnant of them will return;
The destruction decreed shall overflow with righteousness.

23   For the Lord GOD of hosts
Will make a determined end
In the midst of all the land.

²⁴Therefore thus says the Lord GOD of hosts: "O My people, who dwell in Zion, do not be afraid of the Assyrian. He shall strike you with a rod and lift up his staff against you, in the manner of Egypt. ²⁵For yet a very little while and the indignation will cease, as will My anger in their destruction." ²⁶And the LORD of hosts will stir up a scourge for him like the slaughter of Midian at the rock of Oreb; *as* His rod was on the sea, so will He lift it up in the manner of Egypt.

27   It shall come to pass in that day
That his burden will be taken away from your shoulder,
And his yoke from your neck,
And the yoke will be destroyed because of the anointing oil.

28   He has come to Aiath,
He has passed Migron;
At Michmash he has attended to his equipment.

29   They have gone along the ridge,
They have taken up lodging at Geba.
Ramah is afraid,
Gibeah of Saul has fled.

30   Lift up your voice,
O daughter of Gallim!
Cause it to be heard as far as Laish—
O poor Anathoth!ª

10:16 ªFollowing Bomberg; Masoretic Text and Dead Sea Scrolls read *YHWH* (the LORD).
10:30 ªFollowing Masoretic Text, Targum, and Vulgate; Septuagint and Syriac read *Listen to her, O Anathoth.*

31 Madmenah has fled,
The inhabitants of Gebim seek refuge.
32 As yet he will remain at Nob that day;
He will shake his fist at the mount of
the daughter of Zion,
The hill of Jerusalem.

33 Behold, the Lord,
The LORD of hosts,
Will lop off the bough with terror;
Those of high stature *will be* hewn
down,
And the haughty will be humbled.
34 He will cut down the thickets of the
forest with iron,
And Lebanon will fall by the Mighty
One.

The Reign of Jesse's Offspring

Ulysses S. Grant placed his hand on Isaiah
11:1–3 as he took the presidential oath of
office in 1873.

11 There shall come forth a Rod from
the stem of Jesse,
And a Branch shall grow out of his
roots.
2 The Spirit of the LORD shall rest upon
Him,
The Spirit of wisdom and
understanding,
The Spirit of counsel and might,
The Spirit of knowledge and of the
fear of the LORD.

3 His delight *is* in the fear of the LORD,
And He shall not judge by the sight
of His eyes,
Nor decide by the hearing of His ears;
4 But with righteousness He shall judge
the poor,
And decide with equity for the meek
of the earth;
He shall strike the earth with the rod
of His mouth,
And with the breath of His lips He
shall slay the wicked.
5 Righteousness shall be the belt of His
loins,
And faithfulness the belt of His waist.

6 "The wolf also shall dwell with the lamb,
The leopard shall lie down with the
young goat,
The calf and the young lion and the
fatling together;
And a little child shall lead them.
7 The cow and the bear shall graze;
Their young ones shall lie down
together;
And the lion shall eat straw like
the ox.
8 The nursing child shall play by the
cobra's hole,
And the weaned child shall put his
hand in the viper's den.
9 They shall not hurt nor destroy in all
My holy mountain,
For the earth shall be full of the
knowledge of the LORD
As the waters cover the sea.

10 "And in that day there shall be a Root
of Jesse,
Who shall stand as a banner to the
people;
For the Gentiles shall seek Him,
And His resting place shall be glorious."

11 It shall come to pass in that day
That the Lord shall set His hand again
the second time
To recover the remnant of His people
who are left,
From Assyria and Egypt,
From Pathros and Cush,
From Elam and Shinar,
From Hamath and the islands of
the sea.

12 He will set up a banner for the nations,
And will assemble the outcasts of Israel,
And gather together the dispersed of
Judah
From the four corners of the earth.
13 Also the envy of Ephraim shall depart,
And the adversaries of Judah shall be
cut off;
Ephraim shall not envy Judah,
And Judah shall not harass Ephraim.
14 But they shall fly down upon the
shoulder of the Philistines toward
the west;

Together they shall plunder the people
of the East;
They shall lay their hand on Edom
and Moab;
And the people of Ammon shall obey
them.

15 The LORD will utterly destroy[a] the
tongue of the Sea of Egypt;
With His mighty wind He will shake
His fist over the River,[b]
And strike it in the seven streams,
And make *men* cross over dry-shod.

16 There will be a highway for the
remnant of His people
Who will be left from Assyria,
As it was for Israel
In the day that he came up from the
land of Egypt.

A Hymn of Praise

12 And in that day you will say:

"O LORD, I will praise You;
Though You were angry with me,
Your anger is turned away, and You
comfort me.

2 Behold, God *is* my salvation,
I will trust and not be afraid;
'For YAH, the LORD, *is* my strength and
song;
He also has become my salvation.' "[a]

3 Therefore with joy you will draw water
From the wells of salvation.

4 And in that day you will say:

"Praise the LORD, call upon His name;
Declare His deeds among the peoples,
Make mention that His name is
exalted.

5 Sing to the LORD,
For He has done excellent things;
This *is* known in all the earth.

6 Cry out and shout, O inhabitant of
Zion,
For great *is* the Holy One of Israel in
your midst!"

Proclamation Against Babylon

13 The burden against Babylon which
Isaiah the son of Amoz saw.

2 "Lift up a banner on the high mountain,
Raise your voice to them;
Wave your hand, that they may enter
the gates of the nobles.

3 I have commanded My sanctified ones;
I have also called My mighty ones for
My anger—
Those who rejoice in My exaltation."

4 The noise of a multitude in the
mountains,
Like that of many people!
A tumultuous noise of the kingdoms
of nations gathered together!
The LORD of hosts musters
The army for battle.

5 They come from a far country,
From the end of heaven—
The LORD and His weapons of
indignation,
To destroy the whole land.

6 Wail, for the day of the LORD *is* at
hand!
It will come as destruction from
the Almighty.

7 Therefore all hands will be limp,
Every man's heart will melt,

8 And they will be afraid.
Pangs and sorrows will take hold
of *them*;
They will be in pain as a woman in
childbirth;
They will be amazed at one another;
Their faces *will be like* flames.

9 Behold, the day of the LORD comes,
Cruel, with both wrath and fierce anger,
To lay the land desolate;
And He will destroy its sinners from it.

10 For the stars of heaven and their
constellations
Will not give their light;
The sun will be darkened in its going
forth,
And the moon will not cause its light
to shine.

11:15 [a]Following Masoretic Text and Vulgate;
Septuagint, Syriac, and Targum read *dry up.* [b]That is,
the Euphrates   **12:2** [a]Exodus 15:2

11 "I will punish the world for *its* evil,
    And the wicked for their iniquity;
    I will halt the arrogance of the proud,
    And will lay low the haughtiness of
        the terrible.
12 I will make a mortal more rare than
        fine gold,
    A man more than the golden wedge
        of Ophir.
13 Therefore I will shake the heavens,
    And the earth will move out of her
        place,
    In the wrath of the LORD of hosts
    And in the day of His fierce anger.
14 It shall be as the hunted gazelle,
    And as a sheep that no man takes up;
    Every man will turn to his own people,
    And everyone will flee to his own land.
15 Everyone who is found will be thrust
        through,
    And everyone who is captured will fall
        by the sword.
16 Their children also will be dashed to
        pieces before their eyes;
    Their houses will be plundered
    And their wives ravished.

17 "Behold, I will stir up the Medes against
        them,
    Who will not regard silver;
    And *as for* gold, they will not delight
        in it.
18 Also *their* bows will dash the young
        men to pieces,
    And they will have no pity on the fruit
        of the womb;
    Their eye will not spare children.
19 And Babylon, the glory of kingdoms,
    The beauty of the Chaldeans' pride,
    Will be as when God overthrew Sodom
        and Gomorrah.
20 It will never be inhabited,
    Nor will it be settled from generation
        to generation;
    Nor will the Arabian pitch tents there,
    Nor will the shepherds make their
        sheepfolds there.
21 But wild beasts of the desert will lie
        there,
    And their houses will be full of owls;
    Ostriches will dwell there,
    And wild goats will caper there.

22 The hyenas will howl in their citadels,
    And jackals in their pleasant palaces.
    Her time *is* near to come,
    And her days will not be prolonged."

Mercy on Jacob

14 For the LORD will have mercy on Jacob, and will still choose Israel, and settle them in their own land. The strangers will be joined with them, and they will cling to the house of Jacob. 2Then people will take them and bring them to their place, and the house of Israel will possess them for servants and maids in the land of the LORD; they will take them captive whose captives they were, and rule over their oppressors.

Fall of the King of Babylon

3It shall come to pass in the day the LORD gives you rest from your sorrow, and from your fear and the hard bondage in which you were made to serve, 4that you will take up this proverb against the king of Babylon, and say:

    "How the oppressor has ceased,
    The golden[a] city ceased!
5 The LORD has broken the staff of the
        wicked,
    The scepter of the rulers;
6 He who struck the people in wrath
        with a continual stroke,
    He who ruled the nations in anger,
    Is persecuted *and* no one hinders.
7 The whole earth is at rest *and* quiet;
    They break forth into singing.
8 Indeed the cypress trees rejoice over you,
    And the cedars of Lebanon,
    Saying, 'Since you were cut down,
    No woodsman has come up against us.'

9 "Hell from beneath is excited about you,
    To meet *you* at your coming;
    It stirs up the dead for you,
    All the chief ones of the earth;
    It has raised up from their thrones
    All the kings of the nations.
10 They all shall speak and say to you:
    'Have you also become as weak as we?
    Have you become like us?

14:4 [a]Or *insolent*

11 Your pomp is brought down to Sheol,
  And the sound of your stringed
    instruments;
  The maggot is spread under you,
  And worms cover you.'

The Fall of Lucifer

12 "How you are fallen from heaven,
  O Lucifer,ᵃ son of the morning!
  How you are cut down to the ground,
  You who weakened the nations!
13 For you have said in your heart:
  'I will ascend into heaven,
  I will exalt my throne above the stars
    of God;
  I will also sit on the mount of the
    congregation
  On the farthest sides of the north;
14 I will ascend above the heights of the
    clouds,
  I will be like the Most High.'
15 Yet you shall be brought down to Sheol,
  To the lowest depths of the Pit.

16 "Those who see you will gaze at you,
  And consider you, *saying:*
  '*Is* this the man who made the earth
    tremble,
  Who shook kingdoms,
17 Who made the world as a wilderness
  And destroyed its cities,
  Who did not open the house of his
    prisoners?'

18 "All the kings of the nations,
  All of them, sleep in glory,
  Everyone in his own house;
19 But you are cast out of your grave
  Like an abominable branch,
  Like the garment of those who are slain,
  Thrust through with a sword,
  Who go down to the stones of the pit,
  Like a corpse trodden underfoot.
20 You will not be joined with them in
    burial,
  Because you have destroyed your land
  And slain your people.
  The brood of evildoers shall never be
    named.
21 Prepare slaughter for his children
  Because of the iniquity of their fathers,
  Lest they rise up and possess the land,
  And fill the face of the world with
    cities."

Babylon Destroyed

22 "For I will rise up against them," says
    the Lᴏʀᴅ of hosts,
  "And cut off from Babylon the name
    and remnant,
  And offspring and posterity," says the
    Lᴏʀᴅ.
23 "I will also make it a possession for the
    porcupine,
  And marshes of muddy water;
  I will sweep it with the broom of
    destruction," says the Lᴏʀᴅ of hosts.

Assyria Destroyed

24 The Lᴏʀᴅ of hosts has sworn, saying,
  "Surely, as I have thought, so it shall
    come to pass,
  And as I have purposed, *so* it shall
    stand:
25 That I will break the Assyrian in My
    land,
  And on My mountains tread him
    underfoot.
  Then his yoke shall be removed from
    them,
  And his burden removed from their
    shoulders.
26 This *is* the purpose that is purposed
    against the whole earth,
  And this *is* the hand that is stretched
    out over all the nations.
27 For the Lᴏʀᴅ of hosts has purposed,
  And who will annul *it?*
  His hand *is* stretched out,
  And who will turn it back?"

Philistia Destroyed

28This is the burden which came in the
year that King Ahaz died.

29 "Do not rejoice, all you of Philistia,
  Because the rod that struck you is
    broken;
  For out of the serpent's roots will come
    forth a viper,
  And its offspring *will be* a fiery flying
    serpent.

14:12 ᵃLiterally *Day Star*

30 The firstborn of the poor will feed,
And the needy will lie down in safety;
I will kill your roots with famine,
And it will slay your remnant.
31 Wail, O gate! Cry, O city!
All you of Philistia *are* dissolved;
For smoke will come from the north,
And no one *will be* alone in his
appointed times."

32 What will they answer the messengers
of the nation?
That the Lord has founded Zion,
And the poor of His people shall take
refuge in it.

Proclamation Against Moab

15 The burden against Moab.

Because in the night Ar of Moab is
laid waste
And destroyed,
Because in the night Kir of Moab is
laid waste
And destroyed,
2 He has gone up to the temple[a] and
Dibon,
To the high places to weep.
Moab will wail over Nebo and over
Medeba;
On all their heads *will be* baldness,
And every beard cut off.
3 In their streets they will clothe
themselves with sackcloth;
On the tops of their houses
And in their streets
Everyone will wail, weeping bitterly.
4 Heshbon and Elealeh will cry out,
Their voice shall be heard as far as
Jahaz;
Therefore the armed soldiers[a] of Moab
will cry out;
His life will be burdensome to him.

5 "My heart will cry out for Moab;
His fugitives *shall flee* to Zoar,
Like a three-year-old heifer.[a]
For by the Ascent of Luhith
They will go up with weeping;
For in the way of Horonaim
They will raise up a cry of
destruction,

6 For the waters of Nimrim will be
desolate,
For the green grass has withered away;
The grass fails, there is nothing green.
7 Therefore the abundance they have
gained,
And what they have laid up,
They will carry away to the Brook of
the Willows.
8 For the cry has gone all around the
borders of Moab,
Its wailing to Eglaim
And its wailing to Beer Elim.
9 For the waters of Dimon[a] will be full
of blood;
Because I will bring more upon Dimon,[b]
Lions upon him who escapes from
Moab,
And on the remnant of the land."

Moab Destroyed

16 Send the lamb to the ruler of the
land,
From Sela to the wilderness,
To the mount of the daughter of Zion.
2 For it shall be as a wandering bird
thrown out of the nest;
So shall be the daughters of Moab at
the fords of the Arnon.

3 "Take counsel, execute judgment;
Make your shadow like the night in
the middle of the day;
Hide the outcasts,
Do not betray him who escapes.
4 Let My outcasts dwell with you,
O Moab;
Be a shelter to them from the face
of the spoiler.
For the extortioner is at an end,
Devastation ceases,
The oppressors are consumed out of
the land.

15:2 [a]Hebrew *bayith,* literally *house*
15:4 [a]Following Masoretic Text, Targum, and Vulgate;
Septuagint and Syriac read *loins.* **15:5** [a]Or *The
Third Eglath,* an unknown city (compare Jeremiah
48:34) **15:9** [a]Following Masoretic Text and
Targum; Dead Sea Scrolls and Vulgate read *Dibon;*
Septuagint reads *Rimon.* [b]Following Masoretic Text
and Targum; Dead Sea Scrolls and Vulgate read *Dibon;*
Septuagint reads *Rimon.*

5 In mercy the throne will be established;
　And One will sit on it in truth, in the
　　tabernacle of David,
　Judging and seeking justice and
　　hastening righteousness."

6 We have heard of the pride of Moab—
　He is very proud—
　Of his haughtiness and his pride and
　　his wrath;
　But his lies *shall* not *be* so.
7 Therefore Moab shall wail for Moab;
　Everyone shall wail.
　For the foundations of Kir Hareseth
　　you shall mourn;
　Surely *they are* stricken.

8 For the fields of Heshbon languish,
　And the vine of Sibmah;
　The lords of the nations have broken
　　down its choice plants,
　Which have reached to Jazer
　And wandered through the wilderness.
　Her branches are stretched out,
　They are gone over the sea.
9 Therefore I will bewail the vine of
　　Sibmah,
　With the weeping of Jazer;
　I will drench you with my tears,
　O Heshbon and Elealeh;
　For battle cries have fallen
　Over your summer fruits and your
　　harvest.

10 Gladness is taken away,
　And joy from the plentiful field;
　In the vineyards there will be no
　　singing,
　Nor will there be shouting;
　No treaders will tread out wine in the
　　presses;
　I have made their shouting cease.
11 Therefore my heart shall resound like
　　a harp for Moab,
　And my inner being for Kir Heres.

12 And it shall come to pass,
　When it is seen that Moab is weary
　　on the high place,
　That he will come to his sanctuary
　　to pray;
　But he will not prevail.

13 This *is* the word which the Lord has spoken concerning Moab since that time. 14 But now the Lord has spoken, saying, "Within three years, as the years of a hired man, the glory of Moab will be despised with all that great multitude, and the remnant *will be* very small *and* feeble."

Proclamation Against Syria and Israel

17 The burden against Damascus.

　"Behold, Damascus will cease from
　　being a city,
　And it will be a ruinous heap.
2 The cities of Aroer *are* forsaken;ᵃ
　They will be for flocks
　Which lie down, and no one will
　　make *them* afraid.
3 The fortress also will cease from
　　Ephraim,
　The kingdom from Damascus,
　And the remnant of Syria;
　They will be as the glory of the
　　children of Israel,"
　Says the Lord of hosts.

4 "In that day it shall come to pass
　That the glory of Jacob will wane,
　And the fatness of his flesh grow
　　lean.
5 It shall be as when the harvester
　　gathers the grain,
　And reaps the heads with his arm;
　It shall be as he who gathers heads
　　of grain
　In the Valley of Rephaim.
6 Yet gleaning grapes will be left in it,
　Like the shaking of an olive tree,
　Two *or* three olives at the top of the
　　uppermost bough,
　Four *or* five in its most fruitful
　　branches,"
　Says the Lord God of Israel.

7 In that day a man will look to his
　　Maker,
　And his eyes will have respect for
　　the Holy One of Israel.

17:2 ᵃFollowing Masoretic Text and Vulgate; Septuagint reads *It shall be forsaken forever;* Targum reads *Its cities shall be forsaken and desolate.*

⁸ He will not look to the altars,
The work of his hands;
He will not respect what his fingers
have made,
Nor the wooden images^a nor the
incense altars.

⁹ In that day his strong cities will be as
a forsaken bough^a
And an uppermost branch,^b
Which they left because of the children
of Israel;
And there will be desolation.

¹⁰ Because you have forgotten the God
of your salvation,
And have not been mindful of the
Rock of your stronghold,
Therefore you will plant pleasant plants
And set out foreign seedlings;
¹¹ In the day you will make your plant
to grow,
And in the morning you will make
your seed to flourish;
But the harvest *will be* a heap of ruins
In the day of grief and desperate sorrow.

¹² Woe to the multitude of many people
Who make a noise like the roar of the
seas,
And to the rushing of nations
That make a rushing like the rushing
of mighty waters!
¹³ The nations will rush like the rushing
of many waters;
But *God* will rebuke them and they
will flee far away,
And be chased like the chaff of the
mountains before the wind,
Like a rolling thing before the
whirlwind.
¹⁴ Then behold, at eventide, trouble!
And before the morning, he *is* no more.
This *is* the portion of those who
plunder us,
And the lot of those who rob us.

Proclamation Against Ethiopia

18 Woe to the land shadowed with
buzzing wings,
Which *is* beyond the rivers of Ethiopia,
² Which sends ambassadors by sea,

Even in vessels of reed on the waters,
saying,
"Go, swift messengers, to a nation
tall and smooth *of skin,*
To a people terrible from their
beginning onward,
A nation powerful and treading down,
Whose land the rivers divide."

³ All inhabitants of the world and
dwellers on the earth:
When he lifts up a banner on the
mountains, you see *it;*
And when he blows a trumpet, you
hear *it.*
⁴ For so the LORD said to me,
"I will take My rest,
And I will look from My dwelling place
Like clear heat in sunshine,
Like a cloud of dew in the heat of
harvest."
⁵ For before the harvest, when the bud
is perfect
And the sour grape is ripening in the
flower,
He will both cut off the sprigs with
pruning hooks
And take away *and* cut down the
branches.
⁶ They will be left together for the
mountain birds of prey
And for the beasts of the earth;
The birds of prey will summer on them,
And all the beasts of the earth will
winter on them.

⁷ In that time a present will be brought
to the LORD of hosts
From^a a people tall and smooth *of skin,*
And from a people terrible from their
beginning onward,
A nation powerful and treading down,
Whose land the rivers divide—
To the place of the name of the LORD
of hosts,
To Mount Zion.

17:8 ^aHebrew *Asherim,* Canaanite deities
17:9 ^aSeptuagint reads *Hivites;* Targum reads *laid waste;* Vulgate reads *as the plows.* ^bSeptuagint reads *Amorites;* Targum reads *in ruins;* Vulgate reads *corn.*
18:7 ^aFollowing Dead Sea Scrolls, Septuagint, and Vulgate; Masoretic Text omits *From;* Targum reads *To.*

Proclamation Against Egypt

19
The burden against Egypt.

Behold, the LORD rides on a swift cloud,
And will come into Egypt;
The idols of Egypt will totter at His presence,
And the heart of Egypt will melt in its midst.

2 "I will set Egyptians against Egyptians;
Everyone will fight against his brother,
And everyone against his neighbor,
City against city, kingdom against kingdom.
3 The spirit of Egypt will fail in its midst;
I will destroy their counsel,
And they will consult the idols and the charmers,
The mediums and the sorcerers.
4 And the Egyptians I will give
Into the hand of a cruel master,
And a fierce king will rule over them,"
Says the Lord, the LORD of hosts.

5 The waters will fail from the sea,
And the river will be wasted and dried up.
6 The rivers will turn foul;
The brooks of defense will be emptied and dried up;
The reeds and rushes will wither.
7 The papyrus reeds by the River,ᵃ by the mouth of the River,
And everything sown by the River,
Will wither, be driven away, and be no more.
8 The fishermen also will mourn;
All those will lament who cast hooks into the River,
And they will languish who spread nets on the waters.
9 Moreover those who work in fine flax
And those who weave fine fabric will be ashamed;
10 And its foundations will be broken.
All who make wages *will be* troubled of soul.

11 Surely the princes of Zoan *are* fools;
Pharaoh's wise counselors give foolish counsel.

How do you say to Pharaoh, "I *am* the son of the wise,
The son of ancient kings?"
12 Where *are* they?
Where are your wise men?
Let them tell you now,
And let them know what the LORD of hosts has purposed against Egypt.
13 The princes of Zoan have become fools;
The princes of Nophᵃ are deceived;
They have also deluded Egypt,
Those who are the mainstay of its tribes.
14 The LORD has mingled a perverse spirit in her midst;
And they have caused Egypt to err in all her work,
As a drunken man staggers in his vomit.
15 Neither will there be *any* work for Egypt,
Which the head or tail,
Palm branch or bulrush, may do.ᵃ

16 In that day Egypt will be like women, and will be afraid and fear because of the waving of the hand of the LORD of hosts, which He waves over it. 17 And the land of Judah will be a terror to Egypt; everyone who makes mention of it will be afraid in himself, because of the counsel of the LORD of hosts which He has determined against it.

Egypt, Assyria, and Israel Blessed

18 In that day five cities in the land of Egypt will speak the language of Canaan and swear by the LORD of hosts; one will be called the City of Destruction.ᵃ
19 In that day there will be an altar to the LORD in the midst of the land of Egypt, and a pillar to the LORD at its border. 20 And it will be for a sign and for a witness to the LORD of hosts in the land of Egypt; for they will cry to the LORD because of the oppressors, and He will send them a Savior and a Mighty One, and He will deliver them. 21 Then the LORD will be known to Egypt, and the Egyptians will know the LORD in that day, and will make sacrifice and offering;

19:7 ᵃThat is, the Nile   **19:13** ᵃThat is, ancient Memphis   **19:15** ᵃCompare Isaiah 9:14–16
19:18 ᵃSome Hebrew manuscripts, Arabic, Dead Sea Scrolls, Targum, and Vulgate read *Sun;* Septuagint reads *Asedek* (literally *Righteousness*).

yes, they will make a vow to the Lord and perform *it*. ²²And the Lord will strike Egypt, He will strike and heal *it;* they will return to the Lord, and He will be entreated by them and heal them.

²³In that day there will be a highway from Egypt to Assyria, and the Assyrian will come into Egypt and the Egyptian into Assyria, and the Egyptians will serve with the Assyrians.

²⁴In that day Israel will be one of three with Egypt and Assyria—a blessing in the midst of the land, ²⁵whom the Lord of hosts shall bless, saying, "Blessed *is* Egypt My people, and Assyria the work of My hands, and Israel My inheritance."

The Sign Against Egypt and Ethiopia

20 In the year that Tartan[a] came to Ashdod, when Sargon the king of Assyria sent him, and he fought against Ashdod and took it, ²at the same time the Lord spoke by Isaiah the son of Amoz, saying, "Go, and remove the sackcloth from your body, and take your sandals off your feet." And he did so, walking naked and barefoot.

³Then the Lord said, "Just as My servant Isaiah has walked naked and barefoot three years *for* a sign and a wonder against Egypt and Ethiopia, ⁴so shall the king of Assyria lead away the Egyptians as prisoners and the Ethiopians as captives, young and old, naked and barefoot, with their buttocks uncovered, to the shame of Egypt. ⁵Then they shall be afraid and ashamed of Ethiopia their expectation and Egypt their glory. ⁶And the inhabitant of this territory will say in that day, 'Surely such *is* our expectation, wherever we flee for help to be delivered from the king of Assyria; and how shall we escape?'"

The Fall of Babylon Proclaimed

21 The burden against the Wilderness of the Sea.

As whirlwinds in the South pass
     through,
So it comes from the desert, from a
     terrible land.
2   A distressing vision is declared to me;
     The treacherous dealer deals
        treacherously,

And the plunderer plunders.
     Go up, O Elam!
     Besiege, O Media!
     All its sighing I have made to cease.

3   Therefore my loins are filled with
        pain;
     Pangs have taken hold of me, like
        the pangs of a woman in labor.
     I was distressed when *I* heard *it;*
     I was dismayed when *I* saw *it.*
4   My heart wavered, fearfulness
        frightened me;
     The night for which I longed He
        turned into fear for me.
5   Prepare the table,
     Set a watchman in the tower,
     Eat and drink.
     Arise, you princes,
     Anoint the shield!

6   For thus has the Lord said to me:
     "Go, set a watchman,
     Let him declare what he sees."
7   And he saw a chariot *with* a pair of
        horsemen,
     A chariot of donkeys, *and* a chariot
        of camels,
     And he listened earnestly with great
        care.
8   Then he cried, "A lion,[a] my Lord!
     I stand continually on the watchtower
        in the daytime;
     I have sat at my post every night.
9   And look, here comes a chariot of
        men *with* a pair of horsemen!"
     Then he answered and said,
     "Babylon is fallen, is fallen!
     And all the carved images of her
        gods
     He has broken to the ground."

10   Oh, my threshing and the grain
        of my floor!
     That which I have heard from the
        Lord of hosts,
     The God of Israel,
     I have declared to you.

20:1 [a]Or *the Commander in Chief*   **21:8** [a]Dead Sea Scrolls read *Then the observer cried.*

Proclamation Against Edom

¹¹The burden against Dumah.

He calls to me out of Seir,
"Watchman, what of the night?
Watchman, what of the night?"
¹² The watchman said,
"The morning comes, and also the night.
If you will inquire, inquire;
Return! Come back!"

Proclamation Against Arabia

¹³The burden against Arabia.

In the forest in Arabia you will lodge,
O you traveling companies of
Dedanites.
¹⁴ O inhabitants of the land of Tema,
Bring water to him who is thirsty;
With their bread they met him who fled.
¹⁵ For they fled from the swords, from the
drawn sword,
From the bent bow, and from the
distress of war.

¹⁶For thus the LORD has said to me: "Within a year, according to the year of a hired man, all the glory of Kedar will fail; ¹⁷and the remainder of the number of archers, the mighty men of the people of Kedar, will be diminished; for the LORD God of Israel has spoken it."

Proclamation Against Jerusalem

22 The burden against the Valley of Vision.

What ails you now, that you have all
gone up to the housetops,
² You who are full of noise,
A tumultuous city, a joyous city?
Your slain *men are* not slain with the
sword,
Nor dead in battle.
³ All your rulers have fled together;
They are captured by the archers.
All who are found in you are bound
together;
They have fled from afar.
⁴ Therefore I said, "Look away from me,
I will weep bitterly;

Do not labor to comfort me
Because of the plundering of the
daughter of my people."

⁵ For *it is* a day of trouble and treading
down and perplexity
By the Lord GOD of hosts
In the Valley of Vision—
Breaking down the walls
And of crying to the mountain.
⁶ Elam bore the quiver
With chariots of men *and* horsemen,
And Kir uncovered the shield.
⁷ It shall come to pass *that* your choicest
valleys
Shall be full of chariots,
And the horsemen shall set
themselves in array at the gate.

⁸ He removed the protection of Judah.
You looked in that day to the armor
of the House of the Forest;
⁹ You also saw the damage to the city
of David,
That it was great;
And you gathered together the waters
of the lower pool.
¹⁰ You numbered the houses of
Jerusalem,
And the houses you broke down
To fortify the wall.
¹¹ You also made a reservoir between the
two walls
For the water of the old pool.
But you did not look to its Maker,
Nor did you have respect for Him who
fashioned it long ago.

¹² And in that day the Lord GOD of hosts
Called for weeping and for mourning,
For baldness and for girding with
sackcloth.
¹³ But instead, joy and gladness,
Slaying oxen and killing sheep,
Eating meat and drinking wine:
"Let us eat and drink, for tomorrow we
die!"

¹⁴ Then it was revealed in my hearing by
the LORD of hosts,
"Surely for this iniquity there will be no
atonement for you,

Even to your death," says the Lord
  GOD of hosts.

The Judgment on Shebna

¹⁵Thus says the Lord GOD of hosts:

"Go, proceed to this steward,
  To Shebna, who *is* over the house,
  and say:
¹⁶ 'What have you here, and whom
    have you here,
  That you have hewn a sepulcher
    here,
  As he who hews himself a sepulcher
    on high,
  Who carves a tomb for himself in a
    rock?
¹⁷ Indeed, the LORD will throw you away
    violently,
  O mighty man,
  And will surely seize you.
¹⁸ He will surely turn violently and toss
    you like a ball
  Into a large country;
  There you shall die, and there your
    glorious chariots
  Shall be the shame of your master's
    house.
¹⁹ So I will drive you out of your office,
  And from your position he will pull
    you down.^a

²⁰ 'Then it shall be in that day,
  That I will call My servant Eliakim
    the son of Hilkiah;
²¹ I will clothe him with your robe
  And strengthen him with your belt;
  I will commit your responsibility into
    his hand.
  He shall be a father to the inhabitants
    of Jerusalem
  And to the house of Judah.
²² The key of the house of David
  I will lay on his shoulder;
  So he shall open, and no one shall
    shut;
  And he shall shut, and no one shall
    open.
²³ I will fasten him *as* a peg in a secure
    place,
  And he will become a glorious throne
    to his father's house.

²⁴'They will hang on him all the glory of
his father's house, the offspring and the posterity, all vessels of small quantity, from the
cups to all the pitchers. ²⁵In that day,' says
the LORD of hosts, 'the peg that is fastened in
the secure place will be removed and be cut
down and fall, and the burden that *was* on
it will be cut off; for the LORD has spoken.'"

Proclamation Against Tyre

23 The burden against Tyre.

  Wail, you ships of Tarshish!
  For it is laid waste,
  So that there is no house, no harbor;
  From the land of Cyprus^a it is revealed
    to them.

² Be still, you inhabitants of the
    coastland,
  You merchants of Sidon,
  Whom those who cross the sea have
    filled.^a
³ And on great waters the grain of Shihor,
  The harvest of the River,^a *is* her revenue;
  And she is a marketplace for the
    nations.

⁴ Be ashamed, O Sidon;
  For the sea has spoken,
  The strength of the sea, saying,
  "I do not labor, nor bring forth children;
  Neither do I rear young men,
  Nor bring up virgins."
⁵ When the report *reaches* Egypt,
  They also will be in agony at the
    report of Tyre.

⁶ Cross over to Tarshish;
  Wail, you inhabitants of the coastland!
⁷ *Is* this your joyous *city,*
  Whose antiquity *is* from ancient days,
  Whose feet carried her far off to dwell?
⁸ Who has taken this counsel against
    Tyre, the crowning *city,*

22:19 ^aSeptuagint omits *he will pull you down;* Syriac,
Targum, and Vulgate read *I will pull you down.*
23:1 ^aHebrew *Kittim,* western lands, especially Cyprus
23:2 ^aFollowing Masoretic Text and Vulgate;
Septuagint and Targum read *Passing over the water;*
Dead Sea Scrolls read *Your messengers passing over
the sea.*   **23:3** ^aThat is, the Nile

Whose merchants *are* princes,
Whose traders *are* the honorable of
the earth?
9 The Lord of hosts has purposed it,
To bring to dishonor the pride of all
glory,
To bring into contempt all the
honorable of the earth.

10 Overflow through your land like the
River,[a]
O daughter of Tarshish;
There is no more strength.
11 He stretched out His hand over the sea,
He shook the kingdoms;
The Lord has given a commandment
against Canaan
To destroy its strongholds.
12 And He said, "You will rejoice no more,
O you oppressed virgin daughter of
Sidon.
Arise, cross over to Cyprus;
There also you will have no rest."

13 Behold, the land of the Chaldeans,
This people *which* was not;
Assyria founded it for wild beasts of
the desert.
They set up its towers,
They raised up its palaces,
And brought it to ruin.

14 Wail, you ships of Tarshish!
For your strength is laid waste.

15Now it shall come to pass in that day
that Tyre will be forgotten seventy years,
according to the days of one king. At the
end of seventy years it will happen to Tyre
as *in* the song of the harlot:

16 "Take a harp, go about the city,
You forgotten harlot;
Make sweet melody, sing many songs,
That you may be remembered."

17And it shall be, at the end of seventy
years, that the Lord will deal with Tyre. She
will return to her hire, and commit fornication with all the kingdoms of the world
on the face of the earth. 18Her gain and her
pay will be set apart for the Lord; it will
not be treasured nor laid up, for her gain
will be for those who dwell before the Lord,
to eat sufficiently, and for fine clothing.

Impending Judgment on the Earth

24 Behold, the Lord makes the earth
empty and makes it waste,
Distorts its surface
And scatters abroad its inhabitants.
2 And it shall be:
As with the people, so with the priest;
As with the servant, so with his master;
As with the maid, so with her mistress;
As with the buyer, so with the seller;
As with the lender, so with the borrower;
As with the creditor, so with the debtor.
3 The land shall be entirely emptied and
utterly plundered,
For the Lord has spoken this word.

4 The earth mourns *and* fades away,
The world languishes *and* fades away;
The haughty people of the earth
languish.
5 The earth is also defiled under its
inhabitants,
Because they have transgressed the laws,
Changed the ordinance,
Broken the everlasting covenant.
6 Therefore the curse has devoured the
earth,
And those who dwell in it are desolate.
Therefore the inhabitants of the earth
are burned,
And few men *are* left.

7 The new wine fails, the vine languishes,
All the merry-hearted sigh.
8 The mirth of the tambourine ceases,
The noise of the jubilant ends,
The joy of the harp ceases.
9 They shall not drink wine with a song;
Strong drink is bitter to those who
drink it.
10 The city of confusion is broken down;
Every house is shut up, so that none
may go in.
11 *There is* a cry for wine in the streets,
All joy is darkened,
The mirth of the land is gone.

23:10 [a]That is, the Nile

12 In the city desolation is left,
And the gate is stricken with destruction.
13 When it shall be thus in the midst of
the land among the people,
It shall be like the shaking of an olive
tree,
Like the gleaning of grapes when the
vintage is done.

14 They shall lift up their voice, they
shall sing;
For the majesty of the LORD
They shall cry aloud from the sea.
15 Therefore glorify the LORD in the
dawning light,
The name of the LORD God of Israel
in the coastlands of the sea.
16 From the ends of the earth we have
heard songs:
"Glory to the righteous!"
But I said, "I am ruined, ruined!
Woe to me!
The treacherous dealers have dealt
treacherously,
Indeed, the treacherous dealers have
dealt very treacherously."

17 Fear and the pit and the snare
Are upon you, O inhabitant of the earth.
18 And it shall be
That he who flees from the noise of
the fear
Shall fall into the pit,
And he who comes up from the midst
of the pit
Shall be caught in the snare;
For the windows from on high are open,
And the foundations of the earth are
shaken.

19 The earth is violently broken,
The earth is split open,
The earth is shaken exceedingly.
20 The earth shall reel to and fro like a
drunkard,
And shall totter like a hut;
Its transgression shall be heavy upon it,
And it will fall, and not rise again.

21 It shall come to pass in that day
That the LORD will punish on high the
host of exalted ones,

And on the earth the kings of the earth.
22 They will be gathered together,
As prisoners are gathered in the pit,
And will be shut up in the prison;
After many days they will be punished.
23 Then the moon will be disgraced
And the sun ashamed;
For the LORD of hosts will reign
On Mount Zion and in Jerusalem
And before His elders, gloriously.

Praise to God

25 O LORD, You *are* my God.
I will exalt You,
I will praise Your name,
For You have done wonderful *things;*
Your counsels of old *are* faithfulness
and truth.
2 For You have made a city a ruin,
A fortified city a ruin,
A palace of foreigners to be a city no
more;
It will never be rebuilt.
3 Therefore the strong people will glorify
You;
The city of the terrible nations will
fear You.
4 For You have been a strength to the
poor,
A strength to the needy in his distress,
A refuge from the storm,
A shade from the heat;
For the blast of the terrible ones *is* as a
storm *against* the wall.
5 You will reduce the noise of aliens,
As heat in a dry place;
As heat in the shadow of a cloud,
The song of the terrible ones will be
diminished.

6 And in this mountain
The LORD of hosts will make for all
people
A feast of choice pieces,
A feast of wines on the lees,
Of fat things full of marrow,
Of well-refined wines on the lees.
7 And He will destroy on this mountain
The surface of the covering cast over
all people,
And the veil that is spread over all
nations.

8 He will swallow up death forever,
   And the Lord GOD will wipe away
      tears from all faces;
   The rebuke of His people
   He will take away from all the earth;
   For the LORD has spoken.

9 And it will be said in that day:
   "Behold, this *is* our God;
   We have waited for Him, and He
      will save us.
   This *is* the LORD;
   We have waited for Him;
   We will be glad and rejoice in His
      salvation."

10 For on this mountain the hand of the
      LORD will rest,
   And Moab shall be trampled down
      under Him,
   As straw is trampled down for the
      refuse heap.
11 And He will spread out His hands in
      their midst
   As a swimmer reaches out to swim,
   And He will bring down their pride
   Together with the trickery of their hands.
12 The fortress of the high fort of your walls
   He will bring down, lay low,
   And bring to the ground, down to the
      dust.

DEFENDER
"You will keep him in perfect peace. . . ."

ISAIAH 26:3

Christianity in American Society
Samuel Chase, a signer of the Declaration of
Independence and Justice of the United States
Supreme Court, gave the court's opinion in the
1799 case of *Runkel v. Winemiller*:

> *Religion is of general and public concern, and
> on its support depend, in great measure, the
> peace and good order of government, the
> safety and happiness of the people. By our
> form of government, the Christian religion is
> the established religion; and all sects and
> denominations of Christians are placed upon
> the same equal footing, and are equally enti-
> tled to protection in their religious liberty.*

A Song of Salvation

26 In that day this song will be sung in
the land of Judah:

   "We have a strong city;
   God will appoint salvation *for* walls
      and bulwarks.
2 Open the gates,
   That the righteous nation which keeps
      the truth may enter in.
3 You will keep *him* in perfect peace,
   Whose mind *is* stayed *on You,*
   Because he trusts in You.
4 Trust in the LORD forever,
   For in YAH, the LORD, *is* everlasting
      strength.ᵃ
5 For He brings down those who dwell
      on high,
   The lofty city;
   He lays it low,
   He lays it low to the ground,
   He brings it down to the dust.
6 The foot shall tread it down—
   The feet of the poor
   And the steps of the needy."

7 The way of the just *is* uprightness;
   O Most Upright,
   You weigh the path of the just.
8 Yes, in the way of Your judgments,
   O LORD, we have waited for You;
   The desire of *our* soul *is* for Your
      name
   And for the remembrance of You.
9 With my soul I have desired You in
      the night,
   Yes, by my spirit within me I will seek
      You early;
   For when Your judgments *are* in the
      earth,
   The inhabitants of the world will
      learn righteousness.

10 Let grace be shown to the wicked,
   Yet he will not learn righteousness;
   In the land of uprightness he will
      deal unjustly,
   And will not behold the majesty of
      the LORD.

26:4 ᵃOr *Rock of Ages*

¹¹ LORD, *when* Your hand is lifted up, they
    will not see.
But they will see and be ashamed
For *their* envy of people;
Yes, the fire of Your enemies shall
    devour them.

¹² LORD, You will establish peace for us,
For You have also done all our works
    in us.
¹³ O LORD our God, masters besides You
Have had dominion over us;
But by You only we make mention of
    Your name.
¹⁴ *They are* dead, they will not live;
They are deceased, they will not rise.
Therefore You have punished and
    destroyed them,
And made all their memory to perish.
¹⁵ You have increased the nation, O LORD,
You have increased the nation;
You are glorified;
You have expanded all the borders of
    the land.

¹⁶ LORD, in trouble they have visited You,
They poured out a prayer *when* Your
    chastening *was* upon them.
¹⁷ As a woman with child
Is in pain and cries out in her pangs,
When she draws near the time of her
    delivery,
So have we been in Your sight, O LORD.
¹⁸ We have been with child, we have
    been in pain;
We have, as it were, brought forth wind;
We have not accomplished any
    deliverance in the earth,
Nor have the inhabitants of the world
    fallen.

¹⁹ Your dead shall live;
Together with my dead body^a they shall
    arise.
Awake and sing, you who dwell in dust;
For your dew *is like* the dew of herbs,
And the earth shall cast out the dead.

Take Refuge from the Coming Judgment

²⁰ Come, my people, enter your
    chambers,
And shut your doors behind you;

Hide yourself, as it were, for a little
    moment,
Until the indignation is past.
²¹ For behold, the LORD comes out of His
    place
To punish the inhabitants of the earth
    for their iniquity;
The earth will also disclose her blood,
And will no more cover her slain.

27 In that day the LORD with His severe
    sword, great and strong,
Will punish Leviathan the fleeing
    serpent,
Leviathan that twisted serpent;
And He will slay the reptile that *is*
    in the sea.

The Restoration of Israel

² In that day sing to her,
"A vineyard of red wine!^a
³ I, the LORD, keep it,
I water it every moment;
Lest any hurt it,
I keep it night and day.
⁴ Fury *is* not in Me.
Who would set briers *and* thorns
Against Me in battle?
I would go through them,
I would burn them together.
⁵ Or let him take hold of My strength,
That he may make peace with Me;
And he shall make peace with Me."

⁶ Those who come He shall cause to
    take root in Jacob;
Israel shall blossom and bud,
And fill the face of the world with
    fruit.

⁷ Has He struck Israel as He struck those
    who struck him?
Or has He been slain according to the
    slaughter of those who were slain
    by Him?

26:19 ^aFollowing Masoretic Text and Vulgate; Syriac
and Targum read *their dead bodies;* Septuagint reads
those in the tombs.   **27:2** ^aFollowing Masoretic Text
(Kittel's *Biblia Hebraica*), Bomberg, and Vulgate;
Masoretic Text (*Biblia Hebraica Stuttgartensia*), some
Hebrew manuscripts, and Septuagint read *delight;*
Targum reads *choice vineyard.*

8 In measure, by sending it away,
  You contended with it.
  He removes *it* by His rough wind
  In the day of the east wind.
9 Therefore by this the iniquity of Jacob
    will be covered;
  And this *is* all the fruit of taking away
    his sin:
  When he makes all the stones of the
    altar
  Like chalkstones that are beaten to dust,
  Wooden images[a] and incense altars
    shall not stand.

10 Yet the fortified city *will be* desolate,
   The habitation forsaken and left like
     a wilderness;
   There the calf will feed, and there it
     will lie down
   And consume its branches.
11 When its boughs are withered, they
     will be broken off;
   The women come *and* set them on fire.
   For it *is* a people of no understanding;
   Therefore He who made them will not
     have mercy on them,
   And He who formed them will show
     them no favor.

12 And it shall come to pass in that day
   That the LORD will thresh,
   From the channel of the River[a] to the
     Brook of Egypt;
   And you will be gathered one by one,
   O you children of Israel.

13 So it shall be in that day:
   The great trumpet will be blown;
   They will come, who are about to
     perish in the land of Assyria,
   And they who are outcasts in the
     land of Egypt,
   And shall worship the LORD in the
     holy mount at Jerusalem.

Woe to Ephraim and Jerusalem

28 Woe to the crown of pride, to the
       drunkards of Ephraim,
   Whose glorious beauty *is* a fading flower
   Which *is* at the head of the verdant
     valleys,
   To those who are overcome with wine!

2 Behold, the Lord has a mighty and
    strong one,
  Like a tempest of hail and a destroying
    storm,
  Like a flood of mighty waters
    overflowing,
  Who will bring *them* down to the
    earth with *His* hand.
3 The crown of pride, the drunkards
    of Ephraim,
  Will be trampled underfoot;
4 And the glorious beauty is a fading
    flower
  Which *is* at the head of the verdant
    valley,
  Like the first fruit before the summer,
  Which an observer sees;
  He eats it up while it is still in his hand.

5 In that day the LORD of hosts will be
  For a crown of glory and a diadem
    of beauty
  To the remnant of His people,
6 For a spirit of justice to him who sits
    in judgment,
  And for strength to those who turn
    back the battle at the gate.

7 But they also have erred through wine,
  And through intoxicating drink are
    out of the way;
  The priest and the prophet have erred
    through intoxicating drink,
  They are swallowed up by wine,
  They are out of the way through
    intoxicating drink;
  They err in vision, they stumble *in*
    judgment.
8 For all tables are full of vomit *and* filth;
  No place *is clean.*

9 "Whom will he teach knowledge?
  And whom will he make to
    understand the message?
  Those *just* weaned from milk?
  Those *just* drawn from the breasts?
10 For precept *must be* upon precept,
     precept upon precept,
   Line upon line, line upon line,
   Here a little, there a little."

27:9 [a]Hebrew *Asherim,* Canaanite deities
27:12 [a]That is, the Euphrates

11 For with stammering lips and another
     tongue
   He will speak to this people,
12 To whom He said, "This *is* the rest *with
     which*
   You may cause the weary to rest,"
   And, "This *is* the refreshing";
   Yet they would not hear.
13 But the word of the Lord was to them,
   "Precept upon precept, precept upon
     precept,
   Line upon line, line upon line,
   Here a little, there a little,"
   That they might go and fall
     backward, and be broken
   And snared and caught.

14 Therefore hear the word of the Lord,
     you scornful men,
   Who rule this people who *are* in
     Jerusalem,
15 Because you have said, "We have
     made a covenant with death,
   And with Sheol we are in agreement.
   When the overflowing scourge passes
     through,
   It will not come to us,
   For we have made lies our refuge,
   And under falsehood we have hidden
     ourselves."

A Cornerstone in Zion

   16Therefore thus says the Lord God:

   "Behold, I lay in Zion a stone for a
     foundation,
   A tried stone, a precious cornerstone,
     a sure foundation;
   Whoever believes will not act hastily.
17 Also I will make justice the measuring
     line,
   And righteousness the plummet;
   The hail will sweep away the refuge
     of lies,
   And the waters will overflow the
     hiding place.
18 Your covenant with death will be
     annulled,
   And your agreement with Sheol will
     not stand;
   When the overflowing scourge passes
     through,

Then you will be trampled down by it.
19 As often as it goes out it will take you;
   For morning by morning it will pass
     over,
   And by day and by night;
   It will be a terror just to understand
     the report."

20 For the bed is too short to stretch
     out *on,*
   And the covering so narrow that one
     cannot wrap himself *in it.*
21 For the Lord will rise up as *at* Mount
     Perazim,
   He will be angry as in the Valley of
     Gibeon—
   That He may do His work, His awesome
     work,
   And bring to pass His act, His unusual
     act.
22 Now therefore, do not be mockers,
   Lest your bonds be made strong;
   For I have heard from the Lord God
     of hosts,
   A destruction determined even upon
     the whole earth.

Listen to the Teaching of God

23 Give ear and hear my voice,
   Listen and hear my speech.
24 Does the plowman keep plowing all
     day to sow?
   Does he keep turning his soil and
     breaking the clods?
25 When he has leveled its surface,
   Does he not sow the black cummin
   And scatter the cummin,
   Plant the wheat in rows,
   The barley in the appointed place,
   And the spelt in its place?
26 For He instructs him in right judgment,
   His God teaches him.

27 For the black cummin is not threshed
     with a threshing sledge,
   Nor is a cartwheel rolled over the
     cummin;
   But the black cummin is beaten out
     with a stick,
   And the cummin with a rod.
28 Bread *flour* must be ground;
   Therefore he does not thresh it forever,

Break *it with* his cartwheel,
Or crush *it with* his horsemen.
29 This also comes from the LORD of hosts,
Who is wonderful in counsel *and*
excellent in guidance.

Woe to Jerusalem

29 "Woe to Ariel,ᵃ to Ariel, the city
where David dwelt!
Add year to year;
Let feasts come around.
2 Yet I will distress Ariel;
There shall be heaviness and sorrow,
And it shall be to Me as Ariel.
3 I will encamp against you all around,
I will lay siege against you with a
mound,
And I will raise siegeworks against you.
4 You shall be brought down,
You shall speak out of the ground;
Your speech shall be low, out of the dust;
Your voice shall be like a medium's,
out of the ground;
And your speech shall whisper out of
the dust.

5 "Moreover the multitude of your foes
Shall be like fine dust,
And the multitude of the terrible ones
Like chaff that passes away;
Yes, it shall be in an instant, suddenly.
6 You will be punished by the LORD of
hosts
With thunder and earthquake and
great noise,
With storm and tempest
And the flame of devouring fire.
7 The multitude of all the nations who
fight against Ariel,
Even all who fight against her and
her fortress,
And distress her,
Shall be as a dream of a night vision.
8 It shall even be as when a hungry
man dreams,
And look—he eats;
But he awakes, and his soul is still
empty;
Or as when a thirsty man dreams,
And look—he drinks;
But he awakes, and indeed *he is* faint,
And his soul still craves:

So the multitude of all the nations
shall be,
Who fight against Mount Zion."

The Blindness of Disobedience

9 Pause and wonder!
Blind yourselves and be blind!
They are drunk, but not with wine;
They stagger, but not with
intoxicating drink.
10 For the LORD has poured out on you
The spirit of deep sleep,
And has closed your eyes, namely,
the prophets;
And He has covered your heads,
namely, the seers.

11The whole vision has become to you like
the words of a book that is sealed, which
men deliver to one who is literate, saying,
"Read this, please."
And he says, "I cannot, for it *is* sealed."
12Then the book is delivered to one who
is illiterate, saying, "Read this, please."
And he says, "I am not literate."
13Therefore the Lord said:

"Inasmuch as these people draw near
with their mouths
And honor Me with their lips,
But have removed their hearts far
from Me,
And their fear toward Me is taught
by the commandment of men,
14 Therefore, behold, I will again do a
marvelous work
Among this people,
A marvelous work and a wonder;
For the wisdom of their wise *men* shall
perish,
And the understanding of their
prudent *men* shall be hidden."

15 Woe to those who seek deep to hide
their counsel far from the LORD,
And their works are in the dark;
They say, "Who sees us?" and, "Who
knows us?"
16 Surely you have things turned around!
Shall the potter be esteemed as the clay;

29:1 ᵃThat is, Jerusalem

For shall the thing made say of him
    who made it,
"He did not make me"?
Or shall the thing formed say of him
    who formed it,
"He has no understanding"?

Future Recovery of Wisdom

17 *Is* it not yet a very little while
    Till Lebanon shall be turned into a
        fruitful field,
    And the fruitful field be esteemed as
        a forest?
18 In that day the deaf shall hear the
        words of the book,
    And the eyes of the blind shall see out
        of obscurity and out of darkness.
19 The humble also shall increase *their*
        joy in the Lord,
    And the poor among men shall rejoice
    In the Holy One of Israel.
20 For the terrible one is brought to
        nothing,
    The scornful one is consumed,
    And all who watch for iniquity are
        cut off—
21 Who make a man an offender by a
        word,
    And lay a snare for him who reproves
        in the gate,
    And turn aside the just by empty words.

22Therefore thus says the Lord, who
redeemed Abraham, concerning the house
of Jacob:

"Jacob shall not now be ashamed,
    Nor shall his face now grow pale;
23 But when he sees his children,
    The work of My hands, in his midst,
    They will hallow My name,
    And hallow the Holy One of Jacob,
    And fear the God of Israel.
24 These also who erred in spirit will
        come to understanding,
    And those who complained will learn
        doctrine."

Futile Confidence in Egypt

30 "Woe to the rebellious children,"
        says the Lord,
"Who take counsel, but not of Me,

And who devise plans, but not of
    My Spirit,
That they may add sin to sin;
2 Who walk to go down to Egypt,
    And have not asked My advice,
    To strengthen themselves in the
        strength of Pharaoh,
    And to trust in the shadow of Egypt!
3 Therefore the strength of Pharaoh
    Shall be your shame,
    And trust in the shadow of Egypt
    Shall be *your* humiliation.
4 For his princes were at Zoan,
    And his ambassadors came to Hanes.
5 They were all ashamed of a people
    who could not benefit them,
    Or be help or benefit,
    But a shame and also a reproach."

6The burden against the beasts of the
South.

Through a land of trouble and anguish,
From which *came* the lioness and lion,
The viper and fiery flying serpent,
They will carry their riches on the
    backs of young donkeys,
And their treasures on the humps
    of camels,
To a people *who* shall not profit;
7 For the Egyptians shall help in vain
        and to no purpose.
    Therefore I have called her
    Rahab-Hem-Shebeth.ª

A Rebellious People

8 Now go, write it before them on a
        tablet,
    And note it on a scroll,
    That it may be for time to come,
    Forever and ever:
9 That this *is* a rebellious people,
    Lying children,
    Children *who* will not hear the law
        of the Lord;
10 Who say to the seers, "Do not see,"
    And to the prophets, "Do not
        prophesy to us right things;
    Speak to us smooth things, prophesy
        deceits.

30:7 ªLiterally *Rahab Sits Idle*

11   Get out of the way,
      Turn aside from the path,
      Cause the Holy One of Israel
      To cease from before us."

¹²Therefore thus says the Holy One of Israel:

      "Because you despise this word,
      And trust in oppression and perversity,
      And rely on them,
13   Therefore this iniquity shall be to you
      Like a breach ready to fall,
      A bulge in a high wall,
      Whose breaking comes suddenly,
          in an instant.
14   And He shall break it like the
          breaking of the potter's vessel,
      Which is broken in pieces;
      He shall not spare.
      So there shall not be found among
          its fragments
      A shard to take fire from the hearth,
      Or to take water from the cistern."

¹⁵For thus says the Lord GOD, the Holy One of Israel:

      "In returning and rest you shall be
          saved;
      In quietness and confidence shall be
          your strength."
      But you would not,
16   And you said, "No, for we will flee on
          horses"—
      Therefore you shall flee!
      And, "We will ride on swift *horses*"—
      Therefore those who pursue you shall
          be swift!

17   One thousand *shall flee* at the threat
          of one,
      At the threat of five you shall flee,
      Till you are left as a pole on top of
          a mountain
      And as a banner on a hill.

God Will Be Gracious

18   Therefore the LORD will wait, that He
          may be gracious to you;
      And therefore He will be exalted, that
          He may have mercy on you.

      For the LORD *is* a God of justice;
      Blessed *are* all those who wait for Him.

19   For the people shall dwell in Zion at
          Jerusalem;
      You shall weep no more.
      He will be very gracious to you at the
          sound of your cry;
      When He hears it, He will answer you.
20   And *though* the Lord gives you
      The bread of adversity and the water
          of affliction,
      Yet your teachers will not be moved
          into a corner anymore,
      But your eyes shall see your teachers.
21   Your ears shall hear a word behind
          you, saying,
      "This *is* the way, walk in it,"
      Whenever you turn to the right hand
      Or whenever you turn to the left.
22   You will also defile the covering of
          your images of silver,
      And the ornament of your molded
          images of gold.
      You will throw them away as an
          unclean thing;
      You will say to them, "Get away!"

23   Then He will give the rain for your seed
      With which you sow the ground,
      And bread of the increase of the earth;
      It will be fat and plentiful.
      In that day your cattle will feed
      In large pastures.
24   Likewise the oxen and the young
          donkeys that work the ground
      Will eat cured fodder,
      Which has been winnowed with the
          shovel and fan.
25   There will be on every high mountain
      And on every high hill
      Rivers *and* streams of waters,
      In the day of the great slaughter,
      When the towers fall.
26   Moreover the light of the moon will
          be as the light of the sun,
      And the light of the sun will be
          sevenfold,
      As the light of seven days,
      In the day that the LORD binds up the
          bruise of His people
      And heals the stroke of their wound.

Judgment on Assyria

27 Behold, the name of the Lord comes
      from afar,
    Burning *with* His anger,
    And *His* burden *is* heavy;
    His lips are full of indignation,
    And His tongue like a devouring fire.
28 His breath is like an overflowing
      stream,
    Which reaches up to the neck,
    To sift the nations with the sieve of
      futility;
    And *there shall be* a bridle in the jaws
      of the people,
    Causing *them* to err.

29 You shall have a song
    As in the night *when* a holy festival is
      kept,
    And gladness of heart as when one
      goes with a flute,
    To come into the mountain of the Lord,
    To the Mighty One of Israel.
30 The Lord will cause His glorious voice
      to be heard,
    And show the descent of His arm,
    With the indignation of *His* anger
    And the flame of a devouring fire,
    With scattering, tempest, and
      hailstones.
31 For through the voice of the Lord
    Assyria will be beaten down,
    As He strikes with the rod.
32 And *in* every place where the staff of
      punishment passes,
    Which the Lord lays on him,
    It will be with tambourines and harps;
    And in battles of brandishing He will
      fight with it.
33 For Tophet *was* established of old,
    Yes, for the king it is prepared.
    He has made *it* deep and large;
    Its pyre *is* fire with much wood;
    The breath of the Lord, like a stream
      of brimstone,
    Kindles it.

The Folly of Not Trusting God

31 Woe to those who go down to Egypt
      for help,
    And rely on horses,

    Who trust in chariots because *they
      are* many,
    And in horsemen because they are
      very strong,
    But who do not look to the Holy One
      of Israel,
    Nor seek the Lord!
2 Yet He also *is* wise and will bring
      disaster,
    And will not call back His words,
    But will arise against the house of
      evildoers,
    And against the help of those who
      work iniquity.
3 Now the Egyptians *are* men, and not
      God;
    And their horses are flesh, and not
      spirit.
    When the Lord stretches out His hand,
    Both he who helps will fall,
    And he who is helped will fall down;
    They all will perish together.

God Will Deliver Jerusalem

4 For thus the Lord has spoken to me:

    "As a lion roars,
    And a young lion over his prey
    (When a multitude of shepherds is
      summoned against him,
    He will not be afraid of their voice
    Nor be disturbed by their noise),
    So the Lord of hosts will come down
    To fight for Mount Zion and for its hill.
5 Like birds flying about,
    So will the Lord of hosts defend
      Jerusalem.
    Defending, He will also deliver *it;*
    Passing over, He will preserve *it.*"

6 Return *to Him* against whom the children of Israel have deeply revolted. 7 For in
that day every man shall throw away his
idols of silver and his idols of gold—sin,
which your own hands have made for
yourselves.

8 "Then Assyria shall fall by a sword
      not of man,
    And a sword not of mankind shall
      devour him.
    But he shall flee from the sword,

And his young men shall become
  forced labor.
9 He shall cross over to his stronghold
  for fear,
And his princes shall be afraid of the
  banner,"
Says the LORD,
Whose fire *is* in Zion
And whose furnace *is* in Jerusalem.

A Reign of Righteousness

32 Behold, a king will reign in
     righteousness,
And princes will rule with justice.
2 A man will be as a hiding place from
  the wind,
And a cover from the tempest,
As rivers of water in a dry place,
As the shadow of a great rock in a
  weary land.
3 The eyes of those who see will not be
  dim,
And the ears of those who hear will
  listen.
4 Also the heart of the rash will
  understand knowledge,
And the tongue of the stammerers will
  be ready to speak plainly.

5 The foolish person will no longer
  be called generous,
Nor the miser said *to be* bountiful;
6 For the foolish person will speak
  foolishness,
And his heart will work iniquity:
To practice ungodliness,
To utter error against the LORD,
To keep the hungry unsatisfied,
And he will cause the drink of the
  thirsty to fail.
7 Also the schemes of the schemer *are*
  evil;
He devises wicked plans
To destroy the poor with lying words,
Even when the needy speaks justice.
8 But a generous man devises generous
  things,
And by generosity he shall stand.

Consequences of Complacency

9 Rise up, you women who are at ease,
Hear my voice;

You complacent daughters,
Give ear to my speech.
10 In a year and *some* days
You will be troubled, you complacent
  women;
For the vintage will fail,
The gathering will not come.
11 Tremble, you *women* who are at ease;
Be troubled, you complacent ones;
Strip yourselves, make yourselves bare,
And gird *sackcloth* on *your* waists.

12 People shall mourn upon their breasts
For the pleasant fields, for the fruitful
  vine.
13 On the land of my people will come
  up thorns *and* briers,
Yes, on all the happy homes *in the*
  joyous city;
14 Because the palaces will be forsaken,
The bustling city will be deserted.
The forts and towers will become lairs
  forever,
A joy of wild donkeys, a pasture of
  flocks—
15 Until the Spirit is poured upon us from
  on high,
And the wilderness becomes a fruitful
  field,
And the fruitful field is counted as a
  forest.

The Peace of God's Reign

16 Then justice will dwell in the wilderness,
And righteousness remain in the
  fruitful field.
17 The work of righteousness will be peace,
And the effect of righteousness,
  quietness and assurance forever.
18 My people will dwell in a peaceful
  habitation,
In secure dwellings, and in quiet
  resting places,
19 Though hail comes down on the
  forest,
And the city is brought low in
  humiliation.

20 Blessed *are* you who sow beside all
  waters,
Who send out freely the feet of the ox
  and the donkey.

A Prayer in Deep Distress

33 Woe to you who plunder, though
you *have* not *been* plundered;
And you who deal treacherously,
though they have not dealt
treacherously with you!
When you cease plundering,
You will be plundered;
When you make an end of dealing
treacherously,
They will deal treacherously with you.

2 O LORD, be gracious to us;
We have waited for You.
Be their[a] arm every morning,
Our salvation also in the time of trouble.
3 At the noise of the tumult the people
shall flee;
When You lift Yourself up, the nations
shall be scattered;
4 And Your plunder shall be gathered
Like the gathering of the caterpillar;
As the running to and fro of locusts,
He shall run upon them.

5 The LORD is exalted, for He dwells on
high;
He has filled Zion with justice and
righteousness.
6 Wisdom and knowledge will be the
stability of your times,
And the strength of salvation;
The fear of the LORD *is* His treasure.

7 Surely their valiant ones shall cry
outside,
The ambassadors of peace shall weep
bitterly.
8 The highways lie waste,
The traveling man ceases.
He has broken the covenant,
He has despised the cities,[a]
He regards no man.
9 The earth mourns *and* languishes,
Lebanon is shamed *and* shriveled;
Sharon is like a wilderness,
And Bashan and Carmel shake off
their fruits.

Impending Judgment on Zion

10 "Now I will rise," says the LORD;
"Now I will be exalted,
Now I will lift Myself up.
11 You shall conceive chaff,
You shall bring forth stubble;
Your breath, *as* fire, shall devour you.
12 And the people shall be *like* the
burnings of lime;
Like thorns cut up they shall be
burned in the fire.
13 Hear, you *who are* afar off, what I
have done;
And you *who are* near, acknowledge
My might."

14 The sinners in Zion are afraid;
Fearfulness has seized the hypocrites:
"Who among us shall dwell with the
devouring fire?
Who among us shall dwell with
everlasting burnings?"
15 He who walks righteously and speaks
uprightly,
He who despises the gain of oppressions,
Who gestures with his hands, refusing
bribes,
Who stops his ears from hearing of
bloodshed,
And shuts his eyes from seeing evil:
16 He will dwell on high;
His place of defense *will be* the fortress
of rocks;
Bread will be given him,
His water *will be* sure.

The Land of the Majestic King

17 Your eyes will see the King in His
beauty;
They will see the land that is very
far off.
18 Your heart will meditate on terror:
"Where *is* the scribe?
Where *is* he who weighs?
Where *is* he who counts the towers?"
19 You will not see a fierce people,
A people of obscure speech, beyond
perception,
Of a stammering tongue *that you*
cannot understand.

33:2 [a]Septuagint omits *their*; Syriac, Targum, and
Vulgate read *our*.   **33:8** [a]Following Masoretic Text
and Vulgate; Dead Sea Scrolls read *witnesses*;
Septuagint omits *cities*; Targum reads *They have been
removed from their cities.*

20 Look upon Zion, the city of our
appointed feasts;
Your eyes will see Jerusalem, a quiet
home,
A tabernacle *that* will not be taken
down;
Not one of its stakes will ever be
removed,
Nor will any of its cords be broken.
21 But there the majestic LORD *will be*
for us
A place of broad rivers *and* streams,
In which no galley with oars will sail,
Nor majestic ships pass by
22 (For the LORD *is* our Judge,
The LORD *is* our Lawgiver,
The LORD *is* our King;
He will save us);
23 Your tackle is loosed,
They could not strengthen their mast,
They could not spread the sail.

Then the prey of great plunder is
divided;
The lame take the prey.
24 And the inhabitant will not say,
"I am sick";
The people who dwell in it *will be*
forgiven *their* iniquity.

Judgment on the Nations

34 Come near, you nations, to hear;
And heed, you people!
Let the earth hear, and all that is
in it,
The world and all things that come
forth from it.
2 For the indignation of the LORD is
against all nations,
And *His* fury against all their armies;
He has utterly destroyed them,
He has given them over to the
slaughter.

HONOR

*"And you who are near,
acknowledge My might."*

ISAIAH 33:13

The New York State Capitol

GOD AND STATE CONSTITUTIONS

While there have been revisions to state constitutions over the years, forty-three state constitutions acknowledge God or a higher power in their preambles (introductory clause of explanation), and the other seven states acknowledge God in their religious freedom provisions. You may want to read your state constitution and discover how your state government acknowledges God.

The following is a short sample from various state constitutions:

Connecticut 1818, Preamble. "The People of Connecticut, acknowledging with gratitude the good Providence of God in permitting them to enjoy a free government. . . ."

Maine 1820, Preamble. "We the People of Maine . . . acknowledging with grateful hearts the goodness of the Sovereign Ruler of the Universe in affording us an opportunity . . . and imploring His aid and direction in its accomplishment. . . ."

Massachusetts 1780, Preamble. "We, therefore, the people of Massachusetts, acknowledging with grateful hearts, the goodness of the Great Legislator of the Universe, in affording us, in the course of His Providence, an opportunity . . . and devoutly imploring His direction. . . ."

New York 1846, Preamble. "We, the people of the State of New York, grateful to Almighty God for our freedom, in order to secure its blessings. . . ."

3 Also their slain shall be thrown out;
Their stench shall rise from their
corpses,
And the mountains shall be melted
with their blood.
4 All the host of heaven shall be
dissolved,
And the heavens shall be rolled up
like a scroll;
All their host shall fall down
As the leaf falls from the vine,
And as *fruit* falling from a fig tree.

5 "For My sword shall be bathed in
heaven;
Indeed it shall come down on Edom,
And on the people of My curse, for
judgment.
6 The sword of the LORD is filled with
blood,
It is made overflowing with fatness,
With the blood of lambs and goats,
With the fat of the kidneys of rams.
For the LORD has a sacrifice in Bozrah,
And a great slaughter in the land of
Edom.
7 The wild oxen shall come down with
them,
And the young bulls with the mighty
bulls;
Their land shall be soaked with blood,
And their dust saturated with fatness."

8 For *it is* the day of the LORD's vengeance,
The year of recompense for the cause
of Zion.
9 Its streams shall be turned into pitch,
And its dust into brimstone;
Its land shall become burning pitch.
10 It shall not be quenched night or day;
Its smoke shall ascend forever.
From generation to generation it shall
lie waste;
No one shall pass through it forever
and ever.
11 But the pelican and the porcupine
shall possess it,
Also the owl and the raven shall dwell
in it.
And He shall stretch out over it
The line of confusion and the stones
of emptiness.

12 They shall call its nobles to the
kingdom,
But none *shall be* there, and all its
princes shall be nothing.

13 And thorns shall come up in its
palaces,
Nettles and brambles in its fortresses;
It shall be a habitation of jackals,
A courtyard for ostriches.
14 The wild beasts of the desert shall also
meet with the jackals,
And the wild goat shall bleat to its
companion;
Also the night creature shall rest there,
And find for herself a place of rest.
15 There the arrow snake shall make her
nest and lay *eggs*
And hatch, and gather *them* under her
shadow;
There also shall the hawks be gathered,
Every one with her mate.

16 "Search from the book of the LORD,
and read:
Not one of these shall fail;
Not one shall lack her mate.
For My mouth has commanded it,
and His Spirit has gathered them.
17 He has cast the lot for them,
And His hand has divided it among
them with a measuring line.
They shall possess it forever;
From generation to generation they
shall dwell in it."

The Future Glory of Zion

35 The wilderness and the wasteland
shall be glad for them,
And the desert shall rejoice and
blossom as the rose;
2 It shall blossom abundantly and
rejoice,
Even with joy and singing.
The glory of Lebanon shall be given
to it,
The excellence of Carmel and Sharon.
They shall see the glory of the LORD,
The excellency of our God.

3 Strengthen the weak hands,
And make firm the feeble knees.

4 Say to those *who are* fearful-hearted,
"Be strong, do not fear!
Behold, your God will come *with*
    vengeance,
With the recompense of God;
He will come and save you."

5 Then the eyes of the blind shall be
    opened,
And the ears of the deaf shall be
    unstopped.
6 Then the lame shall leap like a deer,
And the tongue of the dumb sing.
For waters shall burst forth in the
    wilderness,
And streams in the desert.
7 The parched ground shall become
    a pool,
And the thirsty land springs of water;
In the habitation of jackals, where
    each lay,
There shall be grass with reeds and
    rushes.

8 A highway shall be there, and a road,
And it shall be called the Highway of
    Holiness.
The unclean shall not pass over it,
But it *shall be* for others.
Whoever walks the road, although
    a fool,
Shall not go astray.
9 No lion shall be there,
Nor shall *any* ravenous beast go up
    on it;
It shall not be found there.
But the redeemed shall walk *there,*
10 And the ransomed of the LORD shall
    return,
And come to Zion with singing,
With everlasting joy on their heads.
They shall obtain joy and gladness,
And sorrow and sighing shall flee
    away.

Sennacherib Boasts Against the LORD

36 Now it came to pass in the fourteenth year of King Hezekiah *that* Sennacherib king of Assyria came up against all the fortified cities of Judah and took them. [2]Then the king of Assyria sent *the* Rabshakeh[a] with a great army from Lachish to King Hezekiah at Jerusalem. And he stood by the aqueduct from the upper pool, on the highway to the Fuller's Field. [3]And Eliakim the son of Hilkiah, who was over the household, Shebna the scribe, and Joah the son of Asaph, the recorder, came out to him.

[4]Then *the* Rabshakeh said to them, "Say now to Hezekiah, 'Thus says the great king, the king of Assyria: "What confidence is this in which you trust? [5]I say you speak of having plans and power for war; but *they are* mere words. Now in whom do you trust, that you rebel against me? [6]Look! You are trusting in the staff of this broken reed, Egypt, on which if a man leans, it will go into his hand and pierce it. So *is* Pharaoh king of Egypt to all who trust in him. [7]"But if you say to me, 'We trust in the LORD our God,' *is it* not He whose high places and whose altars Hezekiah has taken away, and said to Judah and Jerusalem, 'You shall worship before this altar'?"' [8]Now therefore, I urge you, give a pledge to my master the king of Assyria, and I will give you two thousand horses—if you are able on your part to put riders on them! [9]How then will you repel one captain of the least of my master's servants, and put your trust in Egypt for chariots and horsemen? [10]Have I now come up without the LORD against this land to destroy it? The LORD said to me, 'Go up against this land, and destroy it.'"

[11]Then Eliakim, Shebna, and Joah said to *the* Rabshakeh, "Please speak to your servants in Aramaic, for we understand *it;* and do not speak to us in Hebrew[a] in the hearing of the people who *are* on the wall."

[12]But *the* Rabshakeh said, "Has my master sent me to your master and to you to speak these words, and not to the men who sit on the wall, who will eat and drink their own waste with you?"

[13]Then *the* Rabshakeh stood and called out with a loud voice in Hebrew, and said, "Hear the words of the great king, the king of Assyria! [14]Thus says the king: 'Do not let Hezekiah deceive you, for he will not be able to deliver you; [15]nor let Hezekiah make you trust in the LORD, saying, "The LORD will

---

36:2 [a]A title, probably *Chief of Staff* or *Governor*
36:11 [a]Literally *Judean*

surely deliver us; this city will not be given into the hand of the king of Assyria.' " [16]Do not listen to Hezekiah; for thus says the king of Assyria: 'Make *peace* with me *by a present* and come out to me; and every one of you eat from his own vine and every one from his own fig tree, and every one of you drink the waters of his own cistern; [17]until I come and take you away to a land like your own land, a land of grain and new wine, a land of bread and vineyards. [18]*Beware* lest Hezekiah persuade you, saying, "The LORD will deliver us." Has any one of the gods of the nations delivered its land from the hand of the king of Assyria? [19]Where *are* the gods of Hamath and Arpad? Where *are* the gods of Sepharvaim? Indeed, have they delivered Samaria from my hand? [20]Who among all the gods of these lands have delivered their countries from my hand, that the LORD should deliver Jerusalem from my hand?' "

[21]But they held their peace and answered him not a word; for the king's commandment was, "Do not answer him." [22]Then Eliakim the son of Hilkiah, who *was* over the household, Shebna the scribe, and Joah the son of Asaph, the recorder, came to Hezekiah with *their* clothes torn, and told him the words of *the* Rabshakeh.

Isaiah Assures Deliverance

37 And so it was, when King Hezekiah heard *it,* that he tore his clothes, covered himself with sackcloth, and went into the house of the LORD. [2]Then he sent Eliakim, who *was* over the household, Shebna the scribe, and the elders of the priests, covered with sackcloth, to Isaiah the prophet, the son of Amoz. [3]And they said to him, "Thus says Hezekiah: 'This day *is* a day of trouble and rebuke and blasphemy; for the children have come to birth, but *there is* no strength to bring them forth. [4]It may be that the LORD your God will hear the words of *the* Rabshakeh, whom his master the king of Assyria has sent to reproach the living God, and will rebuke the words which the LORD your God has heard. Therefore lift up *your* prayer for the remnant that is left.' "

[5]So the servants of King Hezekiah came to Isaiah. [6]And Isaiah said to them, "Thus you shall say to your master, 'Thus says the LORD: "Do not be afraid of the words which you have heard, with which the servants of the king of Assyria have blasphemed Me. [7]Surely I will send a spirit upon him, and he shall hear a rumor and return to his own land; and I will cause him to fall by the sword in his own land." ' "

Sennacherib's Threat and Hezekiah's Prayer

[8]Then *the* Rabshakeh returned, and found the king of Assyria warring against Libnah, for he heard that he had departed from Lachish. [9]And the king heard concerning Tirhakah king of Ethiopia, "He has come out to make war with you." So when he heard *it,* he sent messengers to Hezekiah, saying, [10]"Thus you shall speak to Hezekiah king of Judah, saying: 'Do not let your God in whom you trust deceive you, saying, "Jerusalem shall not be given into the hand of the king of Assyria." [11]Look! You have heard what the kings of Assyria have done to all lands by utterly destroying them; and shall you be delivered? [12]Have the gods of the nations delivered those whom my fathers have destroyed, Gozan and Haran and Rezeph, and the people of Eden who *were* in Telassar? [13]Where *is* the king of Hamath, the king of Arpad, and the king of the city of Sepharvaim, Hena, and Ivah?' "

[14]And Hezekiah received the letter from the hand of the messengers, and read it; and Hezekiah went up to the house of the LORD, and spread it before the LORD. [15]Then Hezekiah prayed to the LORD, saying: [16]"O LORD of hosts, God of Israel, *the One* who dwells *between* the cherubim, You *are* God, You alone, of all the kingdoms of the earth. You have made heaven and earth. [17]Incline Your ear, O LORD, and hear; open Your eyes, O LORD, and see; and hear all the words of Sennacherib, which he has sent to reproach the living God. [18]Truly, LORD, the kings of Assyria have laid waste all the nations and their lands, [19]and have cast their gods into the fire; for they *were* not gods, but the work of men's hands—wood and stone. Therefore they destroyed them. [20]Now therefore, O LORD our God, save us from his hand, that all the kingdoms of the earth may know that You *are* the LORD, You alone."

AMERICA on ITS KNEES

Conrad Hilton (1887–1979), founder of the Hilton Hotel chain, being a man of conviction during the fight against communism in the Cold War, published this prayer on full-page ads in major magazines on July 4, 1952:

Our Father in heaven.

We pray that You save us from ourselves.

The world that You have made for us, to live in peace, we have made into an armed camp. We live in fear of war to come. We are afraid of "the terror that flies by night, and the arrow that flies by day, the pestilence that walks in darkness and the destruction that wastes at noon-day."

We have turned from You to go our selfish way. We have broken Your commandments and denied Your truth. We have left Your altars to serve the false gods of money and pleasure and power.

Forgive us and help us.

Now, darkness gathers around us, and we are confused in all our counsels. Losing faith in You, we lose faith in ourselves.

Inspire us with wisdom, all of us of every color, race, and creed, to use our wealth, our strength to help our brother, instead of destroying him. Help us to do Your will as it is done in heaven and to be worthy of Your promise of peace on earth. Fill us with new faith, new strength and new courage, that we may win the Battle for Peace.

Be swift to save us, dear God, before the darkness falls.

The Word of the LORD Concerning Sennacherib

²¹Then Isaiah the son of Amoz sent to Hezekiah, saying, "Thus says the LORD God of Israel, 'Because you have prayed to Me against Sennacherib king of Assyria, ²²this *is* the word which the LORD has spoken concerning him:

"The virgin, the daughter of Zion,
  Has despised you, laughed you to
    scorn;
  The daughter of Jerusalem
  Has shaken *her* head behind your back!

²³ "Whom have you reproached and
    blasphemed?
  Against whom have you raised *your*
    voice,
  And lifted up your eyes on high?
  Against the Holy One of Israel.
²⁴ By your servants you have reproached
    the Lord,
  And said, 'By the multitude of my
    chariots
  I have come up to the height of the
    mountains,
  To the limits of Lebanon;
  I will cut down its tall cedars
  And its choice cypress trees;
  I will enter its farthest height,
  To its fruitful forest.
²⁵ I have dug and drunk water,
  And with the soles of my feet I have
    dried up
  All the brooks of defense.'

²⁶ "Did you not hear long ago
  How I made it,
  From ancient times that I formed it?
  Now I have brought it to pass,
  That you should be
  For crushing fortified cities *into* heaps
    of ruins.
²⁷ Therefore their inhabitants *had* little
    power;
  They were dismayed and confounded;
  They were *as* the grass of the field
  And the green herb,
  As the grass on the housetops
  And *grain* blighted before it is grown.

²⁸ "But I know your dwelling place,
  Your going out and your coming in,
  And your rage against Me.
²⁹ Because your rage against Me and
    your tumult
  Have come up to My ears,
  Therefore I will put My hook in
    your nose
  And My bridle in your lips,
  And I will turn you back
  By the way which you came." '

³⁰"This *shall be* a sign to you:

You shall eat this year such as grows
  of itself,
And the second year what springs
  from the same;
Also in the third year sow and reap,
Plant vineyards and eat the fruit of
  them.
³¹ And the remnant who have escaped
  of the house of Judah
Shall again take root downward,
And bear fruit upward.
³² For out of Jerusalem shall go a remnant,
And those who escape from Mount
  Zion.
The zeal of the LORD of hosts will do
  this.

³³"Therefore thus says the LORD concerning the king of Assyria:

'He shall not come into this city,
  Nor shoot an arrow there,
  Nor come before it with shield,
  Nor build a siege mound against it.
³⁴ By the way that he came,
  By the same shall he return;
  And he shall not come into this city,'
  Says the LORD.
³⁵ 'For I will defend this city, to save it
  For My own sake and for My servant
    David's sake.' "

Sennacherib's Defeat and Death

³⁶Then the angelᵃ of the LORD went out, and killed in the camp of the Assyrians one hundred and eighty-five thousand; and

---

37:36 ᵃOr *Angel*

when *people* arose early in the morning, there were the corpses—all dead. ³⁷So Sennacherib king of Assyria departed and went away, returned *home,* and remained at Nineveh. ³⁸Now it came to pass, as he was worshiping in the house of Nisroch his god, that his sons Adrammelech and Sharezer struck him down with the sword; and they escaped into the land of Ararat. Then Esarhaddon his son reigned in his place.

Hezekiah's Life Extended

38 In those days Hezekiah was sick and near death. And Isaiah the prophet, the son of Amoz, went to him and said to him, "Thus says the LORD: 'Set your house in order, for you shall die and not live.'"

²Then Hezekiah turned his face toward the wall, and prayed to the LORD, ³and said, "Remember now, O LORD, I pray, how I have walked before You in truth and with a loyal heart, and have done *what is* good in Your sight." And Hezekiah wept bitterly.

⁴And the word of the LORD came to Isaiah, saying, ⁵"Go and tell Hezekiah, 'Thus says the LORD, the God of David your father: "I have heard your prayer, I have seen your tears; surely I will add to your days fifteen years. ⁶I will deliver you and this city from the hand of the king of Assyria, and I will defend this city."' ⁷And this *is* the sign to you from the LORD, that the LORD will do this thing which He has spoken: ⁸Behold, I will bring the shadow on the sundial, which has gone down with the sun on the sundial of Ahaz, ten degrees backward." So the sun returned ten degrees on the dial by which it had gone down.

⁹This is the writing of Hezekiah king of Judah, when he had been sick and had recovered from his sickness:

¹⁰ I said,
"In the prime of my life
  I shall go to the gates of Sheol;
  I am deprived of the remainder of
    my years."
¹¹ I said,
"I shall not see YAH,
  The LORDᵃ in the land of the living;
  I shall observe man no more among
    the inhabitants of the world.ᵇ

¹² My life span is gone,
  Taken from me like a shepherd's tent;
  I have cut off my life like a weaver.
  He cuts me off from the loom;
  From day until night You make an
    end of me.
¹³ I have considered until morning—
  Like a lion,
  So He breaks all my bones;
  From day until night You make
    an end of me.
¹⁴ Like a crane *or* a swallow, so I
    chattered;
  I mourned like a dove;
  My eyes fail *from looking* upward.
  O LORD,ᵃ I am oppressed;
  Undertake for me!

¹⁵ "What shall I say?
  He has both spoken to me,ᵃ
  And He Himself has done *it.*
  I shall walk carefully all my years
  In the bitterness of my soul.
¹⁶ O Lord, by these *things men* live;
  And in all these *things is* the life of
    my spirit;
  So You will restore me and make me
    live.
¹⁷ Indeed *it was* for *my own* peace
  That I had great bitterness;
  But You have lovingly *delivered* my
    soul from the pit of corruption,
  For You have cast all my sins behind
    Your back.
¹⁸ For Sheol cannot thank You,
  Death cannot praise You;
  Those who go down to the pit cannot
    hope for Your truth.
¹⁹ The living, the living man, he shall
    praise You,
  As I *do* this day;
  The father shall make known Your
    truth to the children.

38:11 ᵃHebrew *YAH, YAH* ᵇFollowing some Hebrew manuscripts; Masoretic Text and Vulgate read *rest;* Septuagint omits *among the inhabitants of the world;* Targum reads *land.* **38:14** ᵃFollowing Bomberg; Masoretic Text and Dead Sea Scrolls read *Lord.* **38:15** ᵃFollowing Masoretic Text and Vulgate; Dead Sea Scrolls and Targum read *And shall I say to Him;* Septuagint omits first half of this verse.

20 "The LORD *was ready* to save me;
  Therefore we will sing my songs with
    stringed instruments
  All the days of our life, in the house
    of the LORD."

21Now Isaiah had said, "Let them take a lump of figs, and apply *it* as a poultice on the boil, and he shall recover."

22And Hezekiah had said, "What *is* the sign that I shall go up to the house of the LORD?"

The Babylonian Envoys

39 At that time Merodach-Baladan[a] the son of Baladan, king of Babylon, sent letters and a present to Hezekiah, for he heard that he had been sick and had recovered. 2And Hezekiah was pleased with them, and showed them the house of his treasures—the silver and gold, the spices and precious ointment, and all his armory—all that was found among his treasures. There was nothing in his house or in all his dominion that Hezekiah did not show them.

3Then Isaiah the prophet went to King Hezekiah, and said to him, "What did these men say, and from where did they come to you?"

So Hezekiah said, "They came to me from a far country, from Babylon."

4And he said, "What have they seen in your house?"

So Hezekiah answered, "They have seen all that *is* in my house; there is nothing among my treasures that I have not shown them."

5Then Isaiah said to Hezekiah, "Hear the word of the LORD of hosts: 6'Behold, the days are coming when all that *is* in your house, and what your fathers have accumulated until this day, shall be carried to Babylon; nothing shall be left,' says the LORD. 7'And they shall take away *some* of your sons who will descend from you, whom you will beget; and they shall be eunuchs in the palace of the king of Babylon.'"

8So Hezekiah said to Isaiah, "The word of the LORD which you have spoken *is* good!" For he said, "At least there will be peace and truth in my days."

God's People Are Comforted

40 "Comfort, yes, comfort My people!"
  Says your God.
2 "Speak comfort to Jerusalem, and cry
    out to her,
  That her warfare is ended,
  That her iniquity is pardoned;
  For she has received from the LORD's
    hand
  Double for all her sins."

3 The voice of one crying in the
    wilderness:
  "Prepare the way of the LORD;
  Make straight in the desert[a]
  A highway for our God.
4 Every valley shall be exalted
  And every mountain and hill brought
    low;
  The crooked places shall be made
    straight
  And the rough places smooth;
5 The glory of the LORD shall be revealed,
  And all flesh shall see *it* together;
  For the mouth of the LORD has spoken."

6 The voice said, "Cry out!"
  And he[a] said, "What shall I cry?"

  "All flesh *is* grass,
  And all its loveliness *is* like the flower
    of the field.
7 The grass withers, the flower fades,
  Because the breath of the LORD blows
    upon it;
  Surely the people *are* grass.
8 The grass withers, the flower fades,
  But the word of our God stands forever."

9 O Zion,
  You who bring good tidings,
  Get up into the high mountain;
  O Jerusalem,
  You who bring good tidings,
  Lift up your voice with strength,
  Lift *it* up, be not afraid;

39:1 [a]Spelled *Berodach-Baladan* in 2 Kings 20:12
40:3 [a]Following Masoretic Text, Targum, and Vulgate; Septuagint omits *in the desert*.   **40:6** [a]Following Masoretic Text and Targum; Dead Sea Scrolls, Septuagint, and Vulgate read *I*.

"I HAVE A DREAM"

MARTIN LUTHER KING JR.

Every valley shall be exalted and every mountain and hill brought low. . . .

ISAIAH 40:4

Martin Luther King Jr. was a driving force in the push to end segregation and racial discrimination through civil disobedience and other non-violent means in the turbulent 1950s and the 1960s. His efforts led to the 1963 March on Washington, where King delivered his "I Have a Dream" speech, which is credited with mobilizing supporters of desegregation and prompting the 1964 Civil Rights Act. On the steps of the Lincoln Memorial, he delivered these unforgettable words:

Now is the time to rise from the dark and desolate valley of segregation to the sunlit path of racial justice. . . . Now is the time to make justice a reality for all of God's children. . . .

I have a dream that one day this nation will rise up and live out the true meaning of its creed: "We hold these truths to be self-evident: that all men are created equal."

I have a dream that one day on the red hills of Georgia the sons of former slaves and the sons of former slave owners will be able to sit down together at the table of brotherhood. . . .

I have a dream that my four little children will one day live in a nation where they will not be judged by the color of their skin but by the content of their character. . . .

This is our hope. This is the faith that I go back to the South with. With this faith we will be able to hew out of the mountain of despair a stone of hope. With this faith we will be able to transform the jangling discords of our nation into a beautiful symphony of brotherhood. With this faith we will be able to work together, to pray together, to struggle together, to go to jail together, to stand up for freedom together, knowing that we will be free one day. . . .

From every mountainside, let freedom ring. And when this happens, when we allow freedom to ring, when we let it ring from every village and every hamlet, from every state and every city, we will be able to speed up that day when all of God's children, black men and white men, Jews and Gentiles, Protestants and Catholics, will be able to join hands and sing in the words of the old Negro spiritual, "Free at last! Free at last! Thank God Almighty, we are free at last!"

Say to the cities of Judah, "Behold
your God!"

10 Behold, the Lord God shall come with
a strong *hand,*
And His arm shall rule for Him;
Behold, His reward *is* with Him,
And His work before Him.
11 He will feed His flock like a shepherd;
He will gather the lambs with His arm,
And carry *them* in His bosom,
And gently lead those who are with
young.

12 Who has measured the waters[a] in the
hollow of His hand,
Measured heaven with a span
And calculated the dust of the earth
in a measure?
Weighed the mountains in scales
And the hills in a balance?
13 Who has directed the Spirit of the Lord,
Or *as* His counselor has taught Him?
14 With whom did He take counsel, and
who instructed Him,
And taught Him in the path of justice?
Who taught Him knowledge,
And showed Him the way of
understanding?

15 Behold, the nations *are* as a drop in
a bucket,
And are counted as the small dust on
the scales;
Look, He lifts up the isles as a very
little thing.
16 And Lebanon *is* not sufficient to burn,
Nor its beasts sufficient for a burnt
offering.
17 All nations before Him *are* as nothing,
And they are counted by Him less
than nothing and worthless.

18 To whom then will you liken God?
Or what likeness will you compare to
Him?
19 The workman molds an image,
The goldsmith overspreads it with gold,
And the silversmith casts silver chains.
20 Whoever *is* too impoverished for *such*
a contribution
Chooses a tree *that* will not rot;

He seeks for himself a skillful
workman
To prepare a carved image *that* will
not totter.

21 Have you not known?
Have you not heard?
Has it not been told you from the
beginning?
Have you not understood from the
foundations of the earth?
22 *It is* He who sits above the circle of
the earth,
And its inhabitants *are* like
grasshoppers,
Who stretches out the heavens like
a curtain,
And spreads them out like a tent to
dwell in.
23 He brings the princes to nothing;
He makes the judges of the earth
useless.

24 Scarcely shall they be planted,
Scarcely shall they be sown,
Scarcely shall their stock take root in
the earth,
When He will also blow on them,
And they will wither,
And the whirlwind will take them
away like stubble.

25 "To whom then will you liken Me,
Or *to whom* shall I be equal?" says
the Holy One.
26 Lift up your eyes on high,
And see who has created these *things,*
Who brings out their host by number;
He calls them all by name,
By the greatness of His might
And the strength of *His* power;
Not one is missing.

27 Why do you say, O Jacob,
And speak, O Israel:
"My way is hidden from the Lord,
And my just claim is passed over by
my God"?

40:12 [a]Following Masoretic Text, Septuagint, and
Vulgate; Dead Sea Scrolls read *waters of the sea;*
Targum reads *waters of the world.*

28 Have you not known?
   Have you not heard?
   The everlasting God, the Lord,
   The Creator of the ends of the earth,
   Neither faints nor is weary.
   His understanding is unsearchable.
29 He gives power to the weak,
   And to *those who have* no might He
      increases strength.
30 Even the youths shall faint and be
      weary,
   And the young men shall utterly fall,
31 But those who wait on the Lord
   Shall renew *their* strength;
   They shall mount up with wings like
      eagles,
   They shall run and not be weary,
   They shall walk and not faint.

Israel Assured of God's Help

41 "Keep silence before Me, O coastlands,
   And let the people renew *their*
      strength!
   Let them come near, then let them
      speak;
   Let us come near together for judgment.

2 "Who raised up one from the east?
   Who in righteousness called him to
      His feet?
   Who gave the nations before him,
   And made *him* rule over kings?
   Who gave *them* as the dust *to* his
      sword,
   As driven stubble to his bow?
3 Who pursued them, *and* passed safely
   By the way *that* he had not gone with
      his feet?
4 Who has performed and done *it,*
   Calling the generations from the
      beginning?
   'I, the Lord, am the first;
   And with the last I *am* He.'"

5 The coastlands saw *it* and feared,
   The ends of the earth were afraid;
   They drew near and came.
6 Everyone helped his neighbor,
   And said to his brother,
   "Be of good courage!"
7 So the craftsman encouraged the
      goldsmith;

He who smooths *with* the hammer
   inspired him who strikes the anvil,
Saying, "It *is* ready for the soldering";
Then he fastened it with pegs,
That it might not totter.

8 "But you, Israel, *are* My servant,
   Jacob whom I have chosen,
   The descendants of Abraham My friend.
9 *You* whom I have taken from the ends
      of the earth,
   And called from its farthest regions,
   And said to you,
   'You *are* My servant,
   I have chosen you and have not cast
      you away:
10 Fear not, for I *am* with you;
   Be not dismayed, for I *am* your God.
   I will strengthen you,
   Yes, I will help you,
   I will uphold you with My righteous
      right hand.'

11 "Behold, all those who were incensed
      against you
   Shall be ashamed and disgraced;
   They shall be as nothing,
   And those who strive with you shall
      perish.
12 You shall seek them and not find
      them—
   Those who contended with you.
   Those who war against you
   Shall be as nothing,
   As a nonexistent thing.
13 For I, the Lord your God, will hold your
      right hand,
   Saying to you, 'Fear not, I will help you.'

14 "Fear not, you worm Jacob,
   You men of Israel!
   I will help you," says the Lord
   And your Redeemer, the Holy One
      of Israel.
15 "Behold, I will make you into a new
      threshing sledge with sharp teeth;
   You shall thresh the mountains and
      beat *them* small,
   And make the hills like chaff.
16 You shall winnow them, the wind
      shall carry them away,
   And the whirlwind shall scatter them;

You shall rejoice in the LORD,
And glory in the Holy One of Israel.

17 "The poor and needy seek water, but
    there is none,
Their tongues fail for thirst.
I, the LORD, will hear them;
I, the God of Israel, will not forsake
    them.
18 I will open rivers in desolate heights,
And fountains in the midst of the
    valleys;
I will make the wilderness a pool of
    water,
And the dry land springs of water.
19 I will plant in the wilderness the cedar
    and the acacia tree,
The myrtle and the oil tree;
I will set in the desert the cypress tree
    and the pine
And the box tree together,
20 That they may see and know,
And consider and understand together,
That the hand of the LORD has done
    this,
And the Holy One of Israel has
    created it.

The Futility of Idols

21 "Present your case," says the LORD.
"Bring forth your strong *reasons,*" says
    the King of Jacob.
22 "Let them bring forth and show us
    what will happen;
Let them show the former things,
    what they *were,*
That we may consider them,
And know the latter end of them;
Or declare to us things to come.
23 Show the things that are to come
    hereafter,
That we may know that you *are* gods;
Yes, do good or do evil,
That we may be dismayed and see *it*
    together.
24 Indeed you *are* nothing,
And your work *is* nothing;
He who chooses you *is* an
    abomination.

25 "I have raised up one from the north,
And he shall come;

From the rising of the sun he shall call
    on My name;
And he shall come against princes as
    though mortar,
As the potter treads clay.
26 Who has declared from the beginning,
    that we may know?
And former times, that we may say,
    '*He is* righteous'?
Surely *there is* no one who shows,
Surely *there is* no one who declares,
Surely *there is* no one who hears your
    words.
27 The first time *I said* to Zion,
    'Look, there they are!'
And I will give to Jerusalem one who
    brings good tidings.
28 For I looked, and *there was* no man;
I looked among them, but *there was*
    no counselor,
Who, when I asked of them, could
    answer a word.
29 Indeed they *are* all worthless;ᵃ
Their works *are* nothing;
Their molded images *are* wind and
    confusion.

The Servant of the LORD

42 "Behold! My Servant whom I uphold,
My Elect One *in whom* My soul
    delights!
I have put My Spirit upon Him;
He will bring forth justice to the
    Gentiles.
2 He will not cry out, nor raise *His voice,*
Nor cause His voice to be heard in the
    street.
3 A bruised reed He will not break,
And smoking flax He will not quench;
He will bring forth justice for truth.
4 He will not fail nor be discouraged,
Till He has established justice in the
    earth;
And the coastlands shall wait for His
    law."

5 Thus says God the LORD,
Who created the heavens and
    stretched them out,

41:29 ᵃFollowing Masoretic Text and Vulgate; Dead
Sea Scrolls, Syriac, and Targum read *nothing;*
Septuagint omits the first line.

Who spread forth the earth and that
 which comes from it,
Who gives breath to the people on it,
And spirit to those who walk on it:
6 "I, the LORD, have called You in
 righteousness,
And will hold Your hand;
I will keep You and give You as
 a covenant to the people,
As a light to the Gentiles,
7 To open blind eyes,
To bring out prisoners from the prison,
Those who sit in darkness from the
 prison house.
8 I *am* the LORD, that *is* My name;
And My glory I will not give to another,
Nor My praise to carved images.
9 Behold, the former things have come
 to pass,
And new things I declare;
Before they spring forth I tell you of
 them."

Praise to the LORD

10 Sing to the LORD a new song,
 And His praise from the ends of the
 earth,
You who go down to the sea, and all
 that is in it,
You coastlands and you inhabitants
 of them!
11 Let the wilderness and its cities lift up
 their voice,
The villages *that* Kedar inhabits.
Let the inhabitants of Sela sing,
Let them shout from the top of the
 mountains.
12 Let them give glory to the LORD,
And declare His praise in the
 coastlands.
13 The LORD shall go forth like a mighty
 man;
He shall stir up *His* zeal like a man of
 war.
He shall cry out, yes, shout aloud;
He shall prevail against His enemies.

Promise of the LORD's Help

14 "I have held My peace a long time,
I have been still and restrained Myself.
Now I will cry like a woman in labor,
I will pant and gasp at once.

15 I will lay waste the mountains and
 hills,
And dry up all their vegetation;
I will make the rivers coastlands,
And I will dry up the pools.
16 I will bring the blind by a way they
 did not know;
I will lead them in paths they have
 not known.
I will make darkness light before them,
And crooked places straight.
These things I will do for them,
And not forsake them.
17 They shall be turned back,
They shall be greatly ashamed,
Who trust in carved images,
Who say to the molded images,
'You *are* our gods.'

18 "Hear, you deaf;
And look, you blind, that you may see.
19 Who *is* blind but My servant,
Or deaf as My messenger *whom* I send?
Who *is* blind as *he who is* perfect,
And blind as the LORD's servant?
20 Seeing many things, but you do not
 observe;
Opening the ears, but he does not
 hear."

Israel's Obstinate Disobedience

21 The LORD is well pleased for His
 righteousness' sake;
He will exalt the law and make *it*
 honorable.
22 But this *is* a people robbed and
 plundered;
All of them are snared in holes,
And they are hidden in prison houses;
They are for prey, and no one delivers;
For plunder, and no one says,
 "Restore!"

23 Who among you will give ear to this?
Who will listen and hear for the time
 to come?
24 Who gave Jacob for plunder, and
 Israel to the robbers?
Was it not the LORD,
He against whom we have sinned?
For they would not walk in His ways,
Nor were they obedient to His law.

25 Therefore He has poured on him the
  fury of His anger
And the strength of battle;
It has set him on fire all around,
Yet he did not know;
And it burned him,
Yet he did not take *it* to heart.

The Redeemer of Israel

43 But now, thus says the LORD, who
  created you, O Jacob,
And He who formed you, O Israel:
"Fear not, for I have redeemed you;
I have called *you* by your name;
You *are* Mine.
2 When you pass through the waters,
  I *will be* with you;
And through the rivers, they shall not
  overflow you.
When you walk through the fire, you
  shall not be burned,
Nor shall the flame scorch you.
3 For I *am* the LORD your God,
The Holy One of Israel, your Savior;
I gave Egypt for your ransom,
Ethiopia and Seba in your place.
4 Since you were precious in My sight,
You have been honored,
And I have loved you;
Therefore I will give men for you,
And people for your life.
5 Fear not, for I *am* with you;
I will bring your descendants from the
  east,
And gather you from the west;
6 I will say to the north, 'Give them up!'
And to the south, 'Do not keep them
  back!'
Bring My sons from afar,
And My daughters from the ends of
  the earth—
7 Everyone who is called by My name,
Whom I have created for My glory;
I have formed him, yes, I have made
  him."

8 Bring out the blind people who have
  eyes,
And the deaf who have ears.
9 Let all the nations be gathered
  together,
And let the people be assembled.

Who among them can declare this,
And show us former things?
Let them bring out their witnesses,
  that they may be justified;
Or let them hear and say, "*It is* truth."
10 "You *are* My witnesses," says the LORD,
"And My servant whom I have chosen,
That you may know and believe Me,
And understand that I *am* He.
Before Me there was no God formed,
Nor shall there be after Me.
11 I, *even* I, *am* the LORD,
And besides Me *there is* no savior.
12 I have declared and saved,
I have proclaimed,
And *there was* no foreign *god* among
  you;
Therefore you *are* My witnesses,"
Says the LORD, "that I *am* God.
13 Indeed before the day *was,* I *am* He;
And *there is* no one who can deliver
  out of My hand;
I work, and who will reverse it?"

14 Thus says the LORD, your Redeemer,
The Holy One of Israel:
"For your sake I will send to Babylon,
And bring them all down as fugitives—
The Chaldeans, who rejoice in their
  ships.
15 I *am* the LORD, your Holy One,
The Creator of Israel, your King."

16 Thus says the LORD, who makes a way
  in the sea
And a path through the mighty waters,
17 Who brings forth the chariot and horse,
The army and the power
(They shall lie down together, they
  shall not rise;
They are extinguished, they are
  quenched like a wick):
18 "Do not remember the former things,
Nor consider the things of old.
19 Behold, I will do a new thing,
Now it shall spring forth;
Shall you not know it?
I will even make a road in the
  wilderness
And rivers in the desert.
20 The beast of the field will honor Me,
The jackals and the ostriches,

Because I give waters in the wilderness
And rivers in the desert,
To give drink to My people, My chosen.
21 This people I have formed for Myself;
They shall declare My praise.

Pleading with Unfaithful Israel

22 "But you have not called upon Me,
O Jacob;
And you have been weary of Me,
O Israel.
23 You have not brought Me the sheep
for your burnt offerings,
Nor have you honored Me with your
sacrifices.
I have not caused you to serve with
grain offerings,
Nor wearied you with incense.
24 You have bought Me no sweet cane
with money,
Nor have you satisfied Me with the
fat of your sacrifices;
But you have burdened Me with your
sins,
You have wearied Me with your
iniquities.

25 "I, *even* I, *am* He who blots out your
transgressions for My own sake;
And I will not remember your sins.
26 Put Me in remembrance;
Let us contend together;
State your *case,* that you may be
acquitted.
27 Your first father sinned,
And your mediators have transgressed
against Me.
28 Therefore I will profane the princes of
the sanctuary;
I will give Jacob to the curse,
And Israel to reproaches.

God's Blessing on Israel

44 "Yet hear now, O Jacob My
servant,
And Israel whom I have chosen.
2 Thus says the LORD who made you
And formed you from the womb,
who will help you:
'Fear not, O Jacob My servant;
And you, Jeshurun, whom I have
chosen.

3 For I will pour water on him who
is thirsty,
And floods on the dry ground;
I will pour My Spirit on your
descendants,
And My blessing on your offspring;
4 They will spring up among the grass
Like willows by the watercourses.'
5 One will say, 'I *am* the LORD's';
Another will call *himself* by the name
of Jacob;
Another will write *with* his hand,
'The LORD's,'
And name *himself* by the name of
Israel.

There Is No Other God

6 "Thus says the LORD, the King of Israel,
And his Redeemer, the LORD of hosts:
'I *am* the First and I *am* the Last;
Besides Me *there is* no God.
7 And who can proclaim as I do?
Then let him declare it and set it in
order for Me,
Since I appointed the ancient people.
And the things that are coming and
shall come,
Let them show these to them.
8 Do not fear, nor be afraid;
Have I not told you from that time,
and declared *it?*
You *are* My witnesses.
Is there a God besides Me?
Indeed *there is* no other Rock;
I know not *one.*' "

Idolatry Is Foolishness

9 Those who make an image, all of
them *are* useless,
And their precious things shall not
profit;
They *are* their own witnesses;
They neither see nor know, that they
may be ashamed.
10 Who would form a god or mold an
image
That profits him nothing?
11 Surely all his companions would be
ashamed;
And the workmen, they *are* mere men.
Let them all be gathered together,
Let them stand up;

Yet they shall fear,
They shall be ashamed together.

12   The blacksmith with the tongs works
      one in the coals,
      Fashions it with hammers,
      And works it with the strength of his
      arms.
      Even so, he is hungry, and his strength
      fails;
      He drinks no water and is faint.

13   The craftsman stretches out *his* rule,
      He marks one out with chalk;
      He fashions it with a plane,
      He marks it out with the compass,
      And makes it like the figure of a man,
      According to the beauty of a man,
      that it may remain in the house.
14   He cuts down cedars for himself,
      And takes the cypress and the oak;
      He secures *it* for himself among the
      trees of the forest.
      He plants a pine, and the rain
      nourishes *it*.

15   Then it shall be for a man to burn,
      For he will take some of it and warm
      himself;
      Yes, he kindles *it* and bakes bread;
      Indeed he makes a god and
      worships *it*;
      He makes it a carved image, and falls
      down to it.
16   He burns half of it in the fire;
      With this half he eats meat;
      He roasts a roast, and is satisfied.
      He even warms *himself* and says,
      "Ah! I am warm,
      I have seen the fire."
17   And the rest of it he makes into a god,
      His carved image.
      He falls down before it and
      worships *it*,
      Prays to it and says,
      "Deliver me, for you *are* my god!"

18   They do not know nor understand;
      For He has shut their eyes, so that
      they cannot see,
      And their hearts, so that they cannot
      understand.

19   And no one considers in his heart,
      Nor *is there* knowledge nor
      understanding to say,
      "I have burned half of it in the fire,
      Yes, I have also baked bread on its coals;
      I have roasted meat and eaten *it*;
      And shall I make the rest of it an
      abomination?
      Shall I fall down before a block of
      wood?"
20   He feeds on ashes;
      A deceived heart has turned him aside;
      And he cannot deliver his soul,
      Nor say, "*Is there* not a lie in my right
      hand?"

Israel Is Not Forgotten

21   "Remember these, O Jacob,
      And Israel, for you *are* My servant;
      I have formed you, you *are* My servant;
      O Israel, you will not be forgotten
      by Me!
22   I have blotted out, like a thick cloud,
      your transgressions,
      And like a cloud, your sins.
      Return to Me, for I have redeemed you."

23   Sing, O heavens, for the LORD has
      done *it*!
      Shout, you lower parts of the earth;
      Break forth into singing, you
      mountains,
      O forest, and every tree in it!
      For the LORD has redeemed Jacob,
      And glorified Himself in Israel.

Judah Will Be Restored

24   Thus says the LORD, your Redeemer,
      And He who formed you from the
      womb:
      "I *am* the LORD, who makes all *things*,
      Who stretches out the heavens all alone,
      Who spreads abroad the earth by
      Myself;
25   Who frustrates the signs of the babblers,
      And drives diviners mad;
      Who turns wise men backward,
      And makes their knowledge
      foolishness;
26   Who confirms the word of His servant,
      And performs the counsel of His
      messengers;

Who says to Jerusalem, 'You shall be
  inhabited,'
To the cities of Judah, 'You shall be
  built,'
And I will raise up her waste places;
27 Who says to the deep, 'Be dry!
And I will dry up your rivers';
28 Who says of Cyrus, '*He is* My
  shepherd,
And he shall perform all My pleasure,
Saying to Jerusalem, "You shall be
  built,"
And to the temple, "Your foundation
  shall be laid."'

Cyrus, God's Instrument

45 "Thus says the Lord to His anointed,
  To Cyrus, whose right hand I have
  held—
To subdue nations before him
And loose the armor of kings,
To open before him the double doors,
So that the gates will not be shut:
2 'I will go before you
And make the crooked places[a] straight;
I will break in pieces the gates of bronze
And cut the bars of iron.
3 I will give you the treasures of darkness
And hidden riches of secret places,
That you may know that I, the Lord,
Who call *you* by your name,
Am the God of Israel.
4 For Jacob My servant's sake,
And Israel My elect,
I have even called you by your name;
I have named you, though you have
  not known Me.
5 I *am* the Lord, and *there is* no other;
There is no God besides Me.
I will gird you, though you have not
  known Me,
6 That they may know from the rising
  of the sun to its setting
That *there is* none besides Me.
I *am* the Lord, and *there is* no other;
7 I form the light and create darkness,
I make peace and create calamity;
I, the Lord, do all these *things.*'

8 "Rain down, you heavens, from above,
And let the skies pour down
  righteousness;

Let the earth open, let them bring
  forth salvation,
And let righteousness spring up
  together.
I, the Lord, have created it.

9 "Woe to him who strives with his
  Maker!
Let the potsherd *strive* with the
  potsherds of the earth!
Shall the clay say to him who forms it,
  'What are you making?'
Or shall your handiwork *say,* 'He has
  no hands'?
10 Woe to him who says to *his* father,
  'What are you begetting?'
Or to the woman, 'What have you
  brought forth?' "

11 Thus says the Lord,
The Holy One of Israel, and his Maker:
"Ask Me of things to come concerning
  My sons;
And concerning the work of My
  hands, you command Me.
12 I have made the earth,
And created man on it.
I—My hands—stretched out the
  heavens,
And all their host I have commanded.
13 I have raised him up in righteousness,
And I will direct all his ways;
He shall build My city
And let My exiles go free,
Not for price nor reward,"
Says the Lord of hosts.

The Lord, the Only Savior

14Thus says the Lord:

"The labor of Egypt and merchandise
  of Cush
And of the Sabeans, men of stature,
Shall come over to you, and they shall
  be yours;
They shall walk behind you,
They shall come over in chains;
And they shall bow down to you.

45:2 [a]Dead Sea Scrolls and Septuagint read
mountains; Targum reads *I will trample down the walls;*
Vulgate reads *I will humble the great ones of the earth.*

They will make supplication to you,
  saying, 'Surely God *is* in you,
And *there is* no other;
There is no other God.' "

15 Truly You *are* God, who hide Yourself,
   O God of Israel, the Savior!
16 They shall be ashamed
   And also disgraced, all of them;
   They shall go in confusion together,
   Who are makers of idols.
17 *But* Israel shall be saved by the LORD
   With an everlasting salvation;
   You shall not be ashamed or disgraced
   Forever and ever.

18 For thus says the LORD,
   Who created the heavens,
   Who is God,
   Who formed the earth and made it,
   Who has established it,
   Who did not create it in vain,
   Who formed it to be inhabited:
   "I *am* the LORD, and *there is* no other.
19 I have not spoken in secret,

In a dark place of the earth;
   I did not say to the seed of Jacob,
   'Seek Me in vain';
   I, the LORD, speak righteousness,
   I declare things that are right.

20 "Assemble yourselves and come;
   Draw near together,
   You *who have* escaped from the nations.
   They have no knowledge,
   Who carry the wood of their carved
     image,
   And pray to a god *that* cannot save.
21 Tell and bring forth *your case*;
   Yes, let them take counsel together.
   Who has declared this from ancient
     time?
   Who has told it from that time?
   Have not I, the LORD?
   And *there is* no other God besides Me,
   A just God and a Savior;
   There is none besides Me.

22 "Look to Me, and be saved,
   All you ends of the earth!

FAITH

*"Woe to him who strives
with his Maker!"*

ISAIAH 45:9

Wernher von Braun

THE DESIGNER OF THE UNIVERSE

Wernher von Braun (1912–1977), the director of NASA and known as "The Father of the American Space Program," stated in a published article in May 1974:

One cannot be exposed to the law and order of the universe without concluding that there must be design and purpose behind it all. . . . The better we understand the intricacies of the universe and all it harbors, the more reason we have found to marvel at the inherent design upon which it is based. . . .

To be forced to believe only one conclusion—that everything in the universe happened by chance—would violate the very objectivity of science itself. . . . What random process could produce the brains of a man or the system of the human eye? . . .

They [evolutionists] challenge science to prove the existence of God. But must we really light a candle to see the sun? . . . They say they cannot visualize a Designer. Well, can a physicist visualize an electron? . . . What strange rationale makes some physicists accept the inconceivable electron as real while refusing to accept the reality of a Designer on the ground that they cannot conceive Him?

For I *am* God, and *there is* no other.

23 I have sworn by Myself;
The word has gone out of My mouth
　in righteousness,
And shall not return,
That to Me every knee shall bow,
Every tongue shall take an oath.

24 He shall say,
'Surely in the LORD I have righteousness
　and strength.
To Him *men* shall come,
And all shall be ashamed
Who are incensed against Him.

25 In the LORD all the descendants of Israel
Shall be justified, and shall glory.'"

Dead Idols and the Living God

46 Bel bows down, Nebo stoops;
Their idols were on the beasts and
　on the cattle.
Your carriages *were* heavily loaded,
A burden to the weary *beast.*

2 They stoop, they bow down together;
They could not deliver the burden,
But have themselves gone into captivity.

3 "Listen to Me, O house of Jacob,
And all the remnant of the house of
　Israel,
Who have been upheld *by Me* from
　birth,
Who have been carried from the
　womb:

4 Even to *your* old age, I *am* He,
And *even* to gray hairs I will carry *you!*
I have made, and I will bear;
Even I will carry, and will deliver *you.*

5 "To whom will you liken Me, and make
　Me equal
And compare Me, that we should be
　alike?

6 They lavish gold out of the bag,
And weigh silver on the scales;
They hire a goldsmith, and he makes
　it a god;
They prostrate themselves, yes, they
　worship.

7 They bear it on the shoulder, they
　carry it
And set it in its place, and it stands;
From its place it shall not move.

Though *one* cries out to it, yet it
　cannot answer
Nor save him out of his trouble.

8 "Remember this, and show yourselves
　men;
Recall to mind, O you transgressors.

9 Remember the former things of old,
For I *am* God, and *there is* no other;
I am God, and *there is* none like Me,

10 Declaring the end from the
　beginning,
And from ancient times *things* that
　are not *yet* done,
Saying, 'My counsel shall stand,
And I will do all My pleasure,'

11 Calling a bird of prey from the east,
The man who executes My counsel,
　from a far country.
Indeed I have spoken *it;*
I will also bring it to pass.
I have purposed *it;*
I will also do it.

12 "Listen to Me, you stubborn-hearted,
Who *are* far from righteousness:

13 I bring My righteousness near, it shall
　not be far off;
My salvation shall not linger.
And I will place salvation in Zion,
For Israel My glory.

The Humiliation of Babylon

47 "Come down and sit in the dust,
O virgin daughter of Babylon;
Sit on the ground without a throne,
O daughter of the Chaldeans!
For you shall no more be called
Tender and delicate.

2 Take the millstones and grind meal.
Remove your veil,
Take off the skirt,
Uncover the thigh,
Pass through the rivers.

3 Your nakedness shall be uncovered,
Yes, your shame will be seen;
I will take vengeance,
And I will not arbitrate with a man."

4 *As for* our Redeemer, the LORD of hosts
　is His name,
The Holy One of Israel.

5 "Sit in silence, and go into darkness,
   O daughter of the Chaldeans;
   For you shall no longer be called
   The Lady of Kingdoms.
6 I was angry with My people;
   I have profaned My inheritance,
   And given them into your hand.
   You showed them no mercy;
   On the elderly you laid your yoke very
      heavily.
7 And you said, 'I shall be a lady forever,'
   So that you did not take these *things* to
      heart,
   Nor remember the latter end of them.

8 "Therefore hear this now, *you who are*
      given to pleasures,
   Who dwell securely,
   Who say in your heart, 'I *am,* and
      there is no one else besides me;
   I shall not sit *as* a widow,
   Nor shall I know the loss of children';
9 But these two *things* shall come to you
   In a moment, in one day:
   The loss of children, and widowhood.
   They shall come upon you in their
      fullness
   Because of the multitude of your
      sorceries,
   For the great abundance of your
      enchantments.

10 "For you have trusted in your wickedness;
    You have said, 'No one sees me';
    Your wisdom and your knowledge
       have warped you;
    And you have said in your heart,
    'I *am,* and *there is* no one else
       besides me.'
11 Therefore evil shall come upon you;
    You shall not know from where it
       arises.
    And trouble shall fall upon you;
    You will not be able to put it off.
    And desolation shall come upon you
       suddenly,
    Which you shall not know.

12 "Stand now with your enchantments
    And the multitude of your sorceries,
    In which you have labored from your
       youth—

Perhaps you will be able to profit,
Perhaps you will prevail.
13 You are wearied in the multitude of
       your counsels;
    Let now the astrologers, the stargazers,
    And the monthly prognosticators
    Stand up and save you
    From what shall come upon you.
14 Behold, they shall be as stubble,
    The fire shall burn them;
    They shall not deliver themselves
    From the power of the flame;
    It shall not *be* a coal to be warmed by,
    Nor a fire to sit before!
15 Thus shall they be to you
    With whom you have labored,
    Your merchants from your youth;
    They shall wander each one to his
       quarter.
    No one shall save you.

Israel Refined for God's Glory

48 "Hear this, O house of Jacob,
   Who are called by the name of
      Israel,
   And have come forth from the
      wellsprings of Judah;
   Who swear by the name of the LORD,
   And make mention of the God of
      Israel,
   But not in truth or in righteousness;
2 For they call themselves after the holy
      city,
   And lean on the God of Israel;
   The LORD of hosts *is* His name:

3 "I have declared the former things
      from the beginning;
   They went forth from My mouth, and
      I caused them to hear it.
   Suddenly I did *them,* and they came
      to pass.
4 Because I knew that you *were*
      obstinate,
   And your neck *was* an iron sinew,
   And your brow bronze,
5 Even from the beginning I have
      declared *it* to you;
   Before it came to pass I proclaimed *it*
      to you,
   Lest you should say, 'My idol has done
      them,

And my carved image and my molded
    image
Have commanded them.'

6 "You have heard;
See all this.
And will you not declare *it?*
I have made you hear new things
    from this time,
Even hidden things, and you did not
    know them.
7 They are created now and not from
    the beginning;
And before this day you have not
    heard them,
Lest you should say, 'Of course I knew
    them.'
8 Surely you did not hear,
Surely you did not know;
Surely from long ago your ear was not
    opened.
For I knew that you would deal very
    treacherously,
And were called a transgressor from
    the womb.

9 "For My name's sake I will defer My
    anger,
And *for* My praise I will restrain it
    from you,
So that I do not cut you off.
10 Behold, I have refined you, but not as
    silver;
I have tested you in the furnace of
    affliction.
11 For My own sake, for My own sake,
    I will do *it;*
For how should *My name* be profaned?
And I will not give My glory to
    another.

God's Ancient Plan to Redeem Israel

12 "Listen to Me, O Jacob,
And Israel, My called:
I *am* He, I *am* the First,
I *am* also the Last.
13 Indeed My hand has laid the
    foundation of the earth,
And My right hand has stretched
    out the heavens;
When I call to them,
They stand up together.

14 "All of you, assemble yourselves, and
    hear!
Who among them has declared these
    things?
The LORD loves him;
He shall do His pleasure on Babylon,
And His arm *shall be against* the
    Chaldeans.
15 I, *even* I, have spoken;
Yes, I have called him,
I have brought him, and his way will
    prosper.

16 "Come near to Me, hear this:
I have not spoken in secret from the
    beginning;
From the time that it was, I *was* there.
And now the Lord GOD and His Spirit
Have[a] sent Me."

17 Thus says the LORD, your Redeemer,
The Holy One of Israel:
"I *am* the LORD your God,
Who teaches you to profit,
Who leads you by the way you
    should go.
18 Oh, that you had heeded My
    commandments!
Then your peace would have been like
    a river,
And your righteousness like the waves
    of the sea.
19 Your descendants also would have
    been like the sand,
And the offspring of your body like
    the grains of sand;
His name would not have been cut off
Nor destroyed from before Me."

20 Go forth from Babylon!
Flee from the Chaldeans!
With a voice of singing,
Declare, proclaim this,
Utter it to the end of the earth;
Say, "The LORD has redeemed
His servant Jacob!"
21 And they did not thirst
When He led them through the deserts;
He caused the waters to flow from the
    rock for them;

48:16 [a]The Hebrew verb is singular.

CHRISTIANITY
AND THE
AMERICAN FRONTIER

AS THE AMERICAN FRONTIER opened up between 1776 and 1850, American colonists first expanded out as far west as Appalachia, then pushed the frontier to the Mississippi River. By 1850, American pioneers pushed the edge of settlement to Texas, the Southwest, and the Pacific Northwest, seeking cheap land and inspired by the belief that they had a "manifest destiny" to stretch across the continent.

In 1835, Alexis de Tocqueville, a French historian, traveled America as it was coming into its own as a nation. He wrote down his observations in *Democracy in America*. This classic book provides unique insights into what made America such a rapid success, which clearly he believed to be Christianity. One of his observations describes what he saw happen as the American settlers spread across the continent: "I have

Alexis de Tocqueville

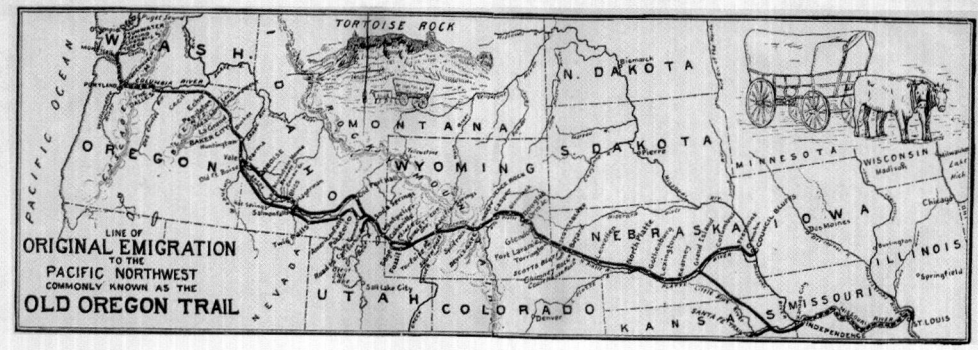

known of societies formed by the Americans to send out ministers of the Gospel into the new Western States to found schools and churches there, lest religion should be suffered to die away in those remote settlements, and the rising States be less fitted to enjoy free institutions than the people from which they emanated. I met with wealthy New Englanders who abandoned the country in which they were born in order to lay the foundations of Christianity and of freedom on the banks of the Missouri or in the prairies of Illinois."

FOLLOWING THE MIGRATION west from the Appalachian cabins to settlements along the Oregon Trail, the American Sunday School Union (ASSU) undertook a great campaign to establish a Sunday school in every new community on the western frontier and sent out a large number of Sunday school missionaries. Thousands of churches eventually sprang up from these Sunday schools.

One example of the tremendous influence the Sunday school movement had in American frontier life was the Mississippi Valley Enterprise (MVE), which was a missionary enterprise of the ASSU to "establish a Sunday school in every destitute place where it is practicable throughout the Valley of the Mississippi." The MVE established over 61,000 Sunday schools and enrolled 2,650,000 pupils in fifty years. Remarkably, one missionary, Stephen Paxson, who was born with a speech impediment and later nicknamed "Stuttering Stephen," started 1,314 Sunday schools with 83,000 students during his twenty years of service with the mission.

PORTLAND, OREGON, THE METROPOLIS OF THE PACIFIC NORTHWEST.

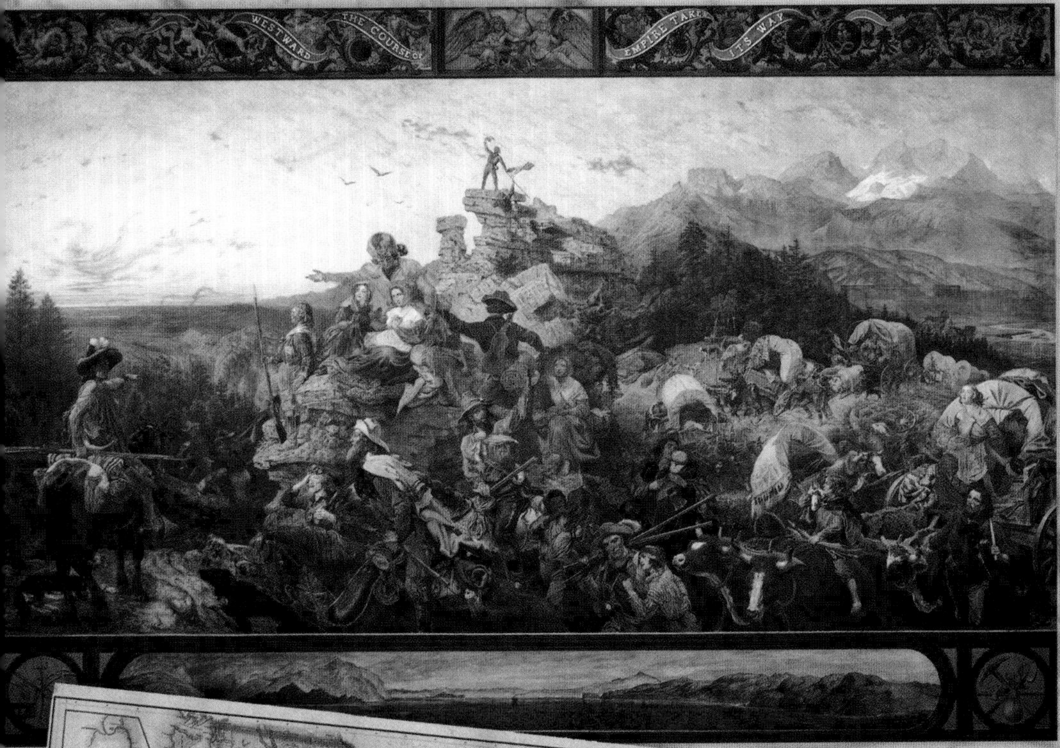
WESTWARD THE COURSE OF EMPIRE TAKES ITS WAY

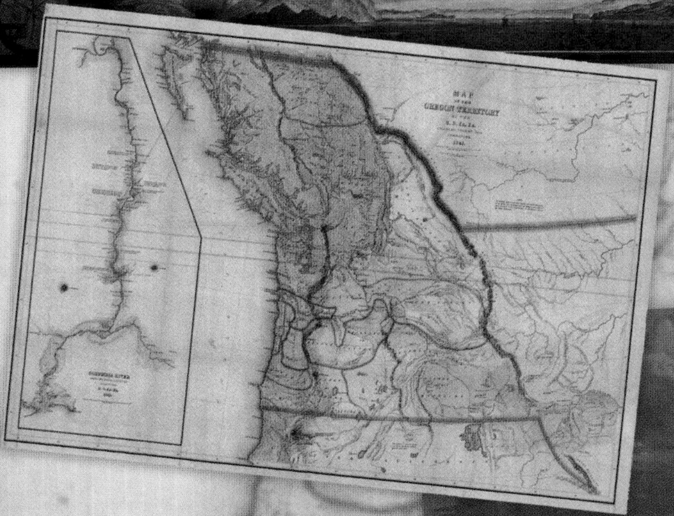

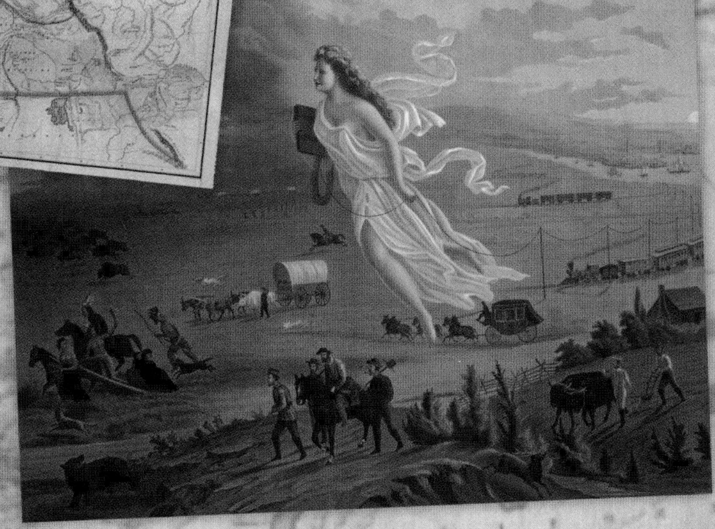

THE REV. FRANCIS ASBURY.
Bishop of the Methodist Episcopal Church in the United States.

ALSO FOLLOWING THE EXPANSION WEST

were the Methodist circuit riders, preachers on horseback who braved the cold weather and lack of roads and danger of Indian attacks to bring the Gospel to the pioneers. Led by the colossal efforts of Francis Asbury, who traveled nearly 300,000 miles on horseback and preached more than 16,000 sermons from 1771 to 1816, an army of circuit riders were inspired to go where the pioneers went. In that span of time, the Methodists grew in number from only 300 members with four ministers to over 200,000 with 2,000 ministers, many with little formal education but who spoke the language of the frontier folk. The Methodists also gave unprecedented freedom to both women and African-Americans to participate and make a significant contribution.

Simultaneously, the Baptists sent out their "farmer-preachers." As was true of the Methodists, the Baptists developed systems that made it easy for committed laypeople to enter the ministry and to be deployed quickly where the greatest opportunities were. Most of their preachers had little education and were poorly paid, but they were in touch with the pioneers' lives. With an emphasis on the need for a personal conversion and salvation from sin through faith in Jesus Christ, these ministers spread the Gospel far and wide.

As was true in the founding of the American colonies, Christians planted many of America's colleges as the nation moved west, including such notable institutions as Northwestern University in Chicago, which was founded by the Methodists, and the University of California at Berkeley, which was founded by the Presbyterians before becoming a state university.

He also split the rock, and the waters gushed out.

22 "*There is* no peace," says the LORD, "for the wicked."

The Servant, the Light to the Gentiles

49 "Listen, O coastlands, to Me,
And take heed, you peoples from afar!
The LORD has called Me from the womb;
From the matrix of My mother He has made mention of My name.
2 And He has made My mouth like a sharp sword;
In the shadow of His hand He has hidden Me,
And made Me a polished shaft;
In His quiver He has hidden Me."

3 "And He said to me,
'You *are* My servant, O Israel,
In whom I will be glorified.'
4 Then I said, 'I have labored in vain,
I have spent my strength for nothing and in vain;
Yet surely my just reward *is* with the LORD,
And my work with my God.'"

5 "And now the LORD says,
Who formed Me from the womb *to be* His Servant,
To bring Jacob back to Him,
So that Israel is gathered to Him^a
(For I shall be glorious in the eyes of the LORD,
And My God shall be My strength),
6 Indeed He says,
'It is too small a thing that You should be My Servant
To raise up the tribes of Jacob,
And to restore the preserved ones of Israel;
I will also give You as a light to the Gentiles,
That You should be My salvation to the ends of the earth.'"

7 Thus says the LORD,
The Redeemer of Israel, their Holy One,
To Him whom man despises,
To Him whom the nation abhors,
To the Servant of rulers:
"Kings shall see and arise,
Princes also shall worship,
Because of the LORD who is faithful,
The Holy One of Israel;
And He has chosen You."

8 Thus says the LORD:

"In an acceptable time I have heard You,
And in the day of salvation I have helped You;
I will preserve You and give You
As a covenant to the people,
To restore the earth,
To cause them to inherit the desolate heritages;
9 That You may say to the prisoners, 'Go forth,'
To those who *are* in darkness, 'Show yourselves.'

"They shall feed along the roads,
And their pastures *shall be* on all desolate heights.
10 They shall neither hunger nor thirst,
Neither heat nor sun shall strike them;
For He who has mercy on them will lead them,
Even by the springs of water He will guide them.
11 I will make each of My mountains a road,
And My highways shall be elevated.
12 Surely these shall come from afar;
Look! Those from the north and the west,
And these from the land of Sinim."

13 Sing, O heavens!
Be joyful, O earth!
And break out in singing, O mountains!
For the LORD has comforted His people,
And will have mercy on His afflicted.

God Will Remember Zion

14 But Zion said, "The LORD has forsaken me,
And my Lord has forgotten me."

49:5 ^aQere, Dead Sea Scrolls, and Septuagint read *is gathered to Him;* Kethib reads *is not gathered.*

15 "Can a woman forget her nursing child,
    And not have compassion on the son
       of her womb?
    Surely they may forget,
    Yet I will not forget you.
16 See, I have inscribed you on the palms
       of My hands;
    Your walls *are* continually before Me.
17 Your sons[a] shall make haste;
    Your destroyers and those who laid
       you waste
    Shall go away from you.
18 Lift up your eyes, look around and see;
    All these gather together *and* come to
       you.
    As I live," says the LORD,
    "You shall surely clothe yourselves with
       them all as an ornament,
    And bind them *on you* as a bride *does.*

19 "For your waste and desolate places,
    And the land of your destruction,
    Will even now be too small for the
       inhabitants;
    And those who swallowed you up
       will be far away.
20 The children you will have,
    After you have lost the others,
    Will say again in your ears,
    'The place *is* too small for me;
    Give me a place where I may dwell.'
21 Then you will say in your heart,
    'Who has begotten these for me,
    Since I have lost my children and am
       desolate,
    A captive, and wandering to and fro?
    And who has brought these up?
    There I was, left alone;
    But these, where *were* they?' "

22 Thus says the Lord GOD:

    "Behold, I will lift My hand in an oath
       to the nations,
    And set up My standard for the peoples;
    They shall bring your sons in *their* arms,
    And your daughters shall be carried
       on *their* shoulders;
23 Kings shall be your foster fathers,
    And their queens your nursing mothers;
    They shall bow down to you with *their*
    faces to the earth,

    And lick up the dust of your feet.
    Then you will know that I *am* the LORD,
    For they shall not be ashamed who
       wait for Me."

24 Shall the prey be taken from the mighty,
    Or the captives of the righteous[a] be
       delivered?
25 But thus says the LORD:

    "Even the captives of the mighty shall
       be taken away,
    And the prey of the terrible be delivered;
    For I will contend with him who
       contends with you,
    And I will save your children.
26 I will feed those who oppress you with
       their own flesh,
    And they shall be drunk with their
       own blood as with sweet wine.
    All flesh shall know
    That I, the LORD, *am* your Savior,
    And your Redeemer, the Mighty One
       of Jacob."

The Servant, Israel's Hope

50 Thus says the LORD:

    "Where *is* the certificate of your
       mother's divorce,
    Whom I have put away?
    Or which of My creditors *is it* to
       whom I have sold you?
    For your iniquities you have sold
       yourselves,
    And for your transgressions your
       mother has been put away.
2   Why, when I came, *was there* no man?
    Why, when I called, *was there* none to
       answer?
    Is My hand shortened at all that it
       cannot redeem?
    Or have I no power to deliver?
    Indeed with My rebuke I dry up the
       sea,
    I make the rivers a wilderness;

49:17 [a]Dead Sea Scrolls, Septuagint, Targum, and
Vulgate read *builders.*   49:24 [a]Following Masoretic
Text and Targum; Dead Sea Scrolls, Syriac, and
Vulgate read *the mighty;* Septuagint reads *unjustly.*

Their fish stink because *there is* no
water,
And die of thirst.
3 I clothe the heavens with blackness,
And I make sackcloth their covering."

4 "The Lord GOD has given Me
The tongue of the learned,
That I should know how to speak
A word in season to *him who is* weary.
He awakens Me morning by morning,
He awakens My ear
To hear as the learned.
5 The Lord GOD has opened My ear;
And I was not rebellious,
Nor did I turn away.
6 I gave My back to those who struck *Me,*
And My cheeks to those who plucked
out the beard;
I did not hide My face from shame
and spitting.

MORAL STRENGTH

"... therefore I have set My face like a flint...."
ISAIAH 50:7

Determination

Abraham Lincoln, the 16th president of the United States (1861–1865), in a Special Session Message to Congress at the beginning of the Civil War, concluded:

Having thus chosen our course, without guile and with pure purpose, let us renew our trust in God and go forward without fear and with manly hearts.

---

7 "For the Lord GOD will help Me;
Therefore I will not be disgraced;
Therefore I have set My face like a flint,
And I know that I will not be ashamed.
8 *He is* near who justifies Me;
Who will contend with Me?
Let us stand together.
Who *is* My adversary?
Let him come near Me.
9 Surely the Lord GOD will help Me;
Who *is* he *who* will condemn Me?
Indeed they will all grow old like a
garment;
The moth will eat them up.

10 "Who among you fears the LORD?
Who obeys the voice of His Servant?
Who walks in darkness
And has no light?
Let him trust in the name of the LORD
And rely upon his God.
11 Look, all you who kindle a fire,
Who encircle *yourselves* with sparks:
Walk in the light of your fire and in
the sparks you have kindled—
This you shall have from My hand:
You shall lie down in torment.

The LORD Comforts Zion

51 "Listen to Me, you who follow after
righteousness,
You who seek the LORD:
Look to the rock *from which* you were
hewn,
And to the hole of the pit *from which*
you were dug.
2 Look to Abraham your father,
And to Sarah *who* bore you;
For I called him alone,
And blessed him and increased him."

3 For the LORD will comfort Zion,
He will comfort all her waste places;
He will make her wilderness like Eden,
And her desert like the garden of the
LORD;
Joy and gladness will be found in it,
Thanksgiving and the voice of melody.

4 "Listen to Me, My people;
And give ear to Me, O My nation:
For law will proceed from Me,
And I will make My justice rest
As a light of the peoples.
5 My righteousness *is* near,
My salvation has gone forth,
And My arms will judge the peoples;
The coastlands will wait upon Me,
And on My arm they will trust.
6 Lift up your eyes to the heavens,
And look on the earth beneath.
For the heavens will vanish away
like smoke,
The earth will grow old like a
garment,
And those who dwell in it will die
in like manner;

But My salvation will be forever,
And My righteousness will not be
  abolished.

7 "Listen to Me, you who know
  righteousness,
You people in whose heart *is* My law:
Do not fear the reproach of men,
Nor be afraid of their insults.
8 For the moth will eat them up like a
  garment,
And the worm will eat them like wool;
But My righteousness will be forever,
And My salvation from generation to
  generation."

9 Awake, awake, put on strength,
O arm of the LORD!
Awake as in the ancient days,
In the generations of old.
Are You not *the arm* that cut Rahab
  apart,
And wounded the serpent?

10 *Are* You not *the One* who dried up the
  sea,
The waters of the great deep;
That made the depths of the sea a road
For the redeemed to cross over?
11 So the ransomed of the LORD shall
  return,
And come to Zion with singing,
With everlasting joy on their heads.
They shall obtain joy and gladness;
Sorrow and sighing shall flee away.

12 "I, *even* I, *am* He who comforts you.
Who *are* you that you should be afraid
Of a man *who* will die,
And of the son of a man *who* will be
  made like grass?
13 And you forget the LORD your Maker,
Who stretched out the heavens
And laid the foundations of the earth;
You have feared continually every day
Because of the fury of the oppressor,
When *he has* prepared to destroy.
And where *is* the fury of the oppressor?
14 The captive exile hastens, that he may
  be loosed,
That he should not die in the pit,
And that his bread should not fail.

15 But I *am* the LORD your God,
Who divided the sea whose waves
  roared—
The LORD of hosts *is* His name.
16 And I have put My words in your
  mouth;
I have covered you with the shadow
  of My hand,
That I may plant the heavens,
Lay the foundations of the earth,
And say to Zion, 'You *are* My people.'"

God's Fury Removed

17 Awake, awake!
Stand up, O Jerusalem,
You who have drunk at the hand of
  the LORD
The cup of His fury;
You have drunk the dregs of the cup
  of trembling,
And drained *it* out.
18 *There is* no one to guide her
Among all the sons she has brought
  forth;
Nor *is there any* who takes her by the
  hand
Among all the sons she has brought up.
19 These two *things* have come to you;
Who will be sorry for you?—
Desolation and destruction, famine
  and sword—
By whom will I comfort you?
20 Your sons have fainted,
They lie at the head of all the streets,
Like an antelope in a net;
They are full of the fury of the LORD,
The rebuke of your God.

21 Therefore please hear this, you afflicted,
And drunk but not with wine.
22 Thus says your Lord,
The LORD and your God,
Who pleads the cause of His people:
"See, I have taken out of your hand
The cup of trembling,
The dregs of the cup of My fury;
You shall no longer drink it.
23 But I will put it into the hand of those
  who afflict you,
Who have said to you,ᵃ

51:23 ᵃLiterally *your soul*

'Lie down, that we may walk over you.'
And you have laid your body like the
     ground,
And as the street, for those who walk
     over."

God Redeems Jerusalem

52 Awake, awake!
Put on your strength, O Zion;
Put on your beautiful garments,
O Jerusalem, the holy city!
For the uncircumcised and the unclean
Shall no longer come to you.
2 Shake yourself from the dust, arise;
Sit down, O Jerusalem!
Loose yourself from the bonds of your
     neck,
O captive daughter of Zion!

³For thus says the LORD:

"You have sold yourselves for nothing,
And you shall be redeemed without
     money."

⁴For thus says the Lord GOD:

"My people went down at first
Into Egypt to dwell there;
Then the Assyrian oppressed them
     without cause.
5 Now therefore, what have I here,"
     says the LORD,
"That My people are taken away for
     nothing?
Those who rule over them
Make them wail,"ᵃ says the LORD,
"And My name *is* blasphemed
     continually every day.
6 Therefore My people shall know My
     name;
Therefore *they shall know* in that day
That I *am* He who speaks:
'Behold, *it is* I.'"

7 How beautiful upon the mountains
Are the feet of him who brings good
     news,
Who proclaims peace,
Who brings glad tidings of good *things,*
Who proclaims salvation,
Who says to Zion,

"Your God reigns!"
8 Your watchmen shall lift up *their*
     voices,
With their voices they shall sing
     together;
For they shall see eye to eye
When the LORD brings back Zion.
9 Break forth into joy, sing together,
You waste places of Jerusalem!
For the LORD has comforted His
     people,
He has redeemed Jerusalem.
10 The LORD has made bare His holy arm
In the eyes of all the nations;
And all the ends of the earth shall see
The salvation of our God.

11 Depart! Depart! Go out from there,
Touch no unclean *thing;*
Go out from the midst of her,
Be clean,
You who bear the vessels of the LORD.
12 For you shall not go out with haste,
Nor go by flight;
For the LORD will go before you,
And the God of Israel *will be* your rear
     guard.

The Sin-Bearing Servant

13 Behold, My Servant shall deal
     prudently;
He shall be exalted and extolled and
     be very high.
14 Just as many were astonished at you,
So His visage was marred more than
     any man,
And His form more than the sons of
     men;
15 So shall He sprinkleᵃ many nations.
Kings shall shut their mouths at Him;
For what had not been told them they
     shall see,
And what they had not heard they
     shall consider.

53 Who has believed our report?
And to whom has the arm of the
     LORD been revealed?

52:5 ᵃDead Sea Scrolls read *Mock;* Septuagint reads
Marvel and wail; Targum reads *Boast themselves;*
Vulgate reads *Treat them unjustly.*   **52:15** ᵃOr *startle*

2 For He shall grow up before Him as a
  tender plant,
And as a root out of dry ground.
He has no form or comeliness;
And when we see Him,
There is no beauty that we should
  desire Him.
3 He is despised and rejected by men,
A Man of sorrows and acquainted
  with grief.
And we hid, as it were, *our* faces from
  Him;
He was despised, and we did not
  esteem Him.

4 Surely He has borne our griefs
And carried our sorrows;
Yet we esteemed Him stricken,
Smitten by God, and afflicted.

5 But He *was* wounded for our
  transgressions,
He was bruised for our iniquities;
The chastisement for our peace *was*
  upon Him,
And by His stripes we are healed.
6 All we like sheep have gone astray;
We have turned, every one, to his
  own way;
And the LORD has laid on Him the
  iniquity of us all.

7 He was oppressed and He was
  afflicted,
Yet He opened not His mouth;
He was led as a lamb to the slaughter,
And as a sheep before its shearers is
  silent,
So He opened not His mouth.

FREEDOM

*The LORD has made bare
His holy arm. . . .*

ISAIAH 52:10

The Boston Tea Party

BOSTON TEA PARTY

The Stamp Act of 1765 and the Townshend Acts of 1767 had angered American colonists regarding British decisions on imposing intolerable taxes on the colonies without representation in the Westminster Parliament. In March 1770, the crisis culminated in the deaths of five American colonists killed by British soldiers who were commandeering homes. Early in 1773, the men of Marlborough, Massachusetts, declared unanimously:

> *Death is more eligible than slavery. A free-born people are not required by the religion of Jesus Christ to submit to tyranny, but may make use of such power as God has given them to recover and support their laws and liberties. . . . [We] implore the Ruler above the skies, that He would make bare His arm in defense of His Church and people, and let Israel go.*

On December 16, 1773, the Sons of Liberty, a band of Boston patriots, threw the cargo of 342 chests of tea from a British East India Company ship into the Boston Harbor. The British government responded by closing the port of Boston, enacting other laws that were known as the "Intolerable Acts," and charging John Hancock, Samuel Adams, Joseph Warren, and Benjamin Church with the "Crime of High Treason." At the very least, the Boston Tea Party rallied the support for revolutionaries in the 13 colonies and sparked the Revolution.

8 He was taken from prison and from
    judgment,
  And who will declare His generation?
  For He was cut off from the land of
    the living;
  For the transgressions of My people He
    was stricken.
9 And they[a] made His grave with the
    wicked—
  But with the rich at His death,
  Because He had done no violence,
  Nor *was any* deceit in His mouth.

10 Yet it pleased the LORD to bruise Him;
  He has put *Him* to grief.
  When You make His soul an offering
    for sin,
  He shall see *His* seed, He shall prolong
    His days,
  And the pleasure of the LORD shall
    prosper in His hand.
11 He shall see the labor of His soul,[a] *and*
    be satisfied.
  By His knowledge My righteous
    Servant shall justify many,
  For He shall bear their iniquities.
12 Therefore I will divide Him a portion
    with the great,
  And He shall divide the spoil with the
    strong,
  Because He poured out His soul unto
    death,
  And He was numbered with the
    transgressors,
  And He bore the sin of many,
  And made intercession for the
    transgressors.

A Perpetual Covenant of Peace

54 "Sing, O barren,
    You *who* have not borne!
  Break forth into singing, and cry aloud,
  You *who* have not labored with child!
  For more *are* the children of the desolate
  Than the children of the married
    woman," says the LORD.
2 "Enlarge the place of your tent,
  And let them stretch out the curtains
    of your dwellings;
  Do not spare;
  Lengthen your cords,
  And strengthen your stakes.

3 For you shall expand to the right and
    to the left,
  And your descendants will inherit the
    nations,
  And make the desolate cities inhabited.

4 "Do not fear, for you will not be
    ashamed;
  Neither be disgraced, for you will not
    be put to shame;
  For you will forget the shame of your
    youth,
  And will not remember the reproach
    of your widowhood anymore.
5 For your Maker *is* your husband,
  The LORD of hosts *is* His name;
  And your Redeemer *is* the Holy One
    of Israel;
  He is called the God of the whole earth.
6 For the LORD has called you
  Like a woman forsaken and grieved in
    spirit,
  Like a youthful wife when you were
    refused,"
  Says your God.
7 "For a mere moment I have forsaken you,
  But with great mercies I will gather you.
8 With a little wrath I hid My face from
    you for a moment;
  But with everlasting kindness I will
    have mercy on you,"
  Says the LORD, your Redeemer.

9 "For this *is* like the waters of Noah to Me;
  For as I have sworn
  That the waters of Noah would no
    longer cover the earth,
  So have I sworn
  That I would not be angry with you,
    nor rebuke you.
10 For the mountains shall depart
  And the hills be removed,
  But My kindness shall not depart from
    you,
  Nor shall My covenant of peace be
    removed,"
  Says the LORD, who has mercy on you.

53:9 [a]Literally *he* or *He*   53:11 [a]Following
Masoretic Text, Targum, and Vulgate; Dead Sea Scrolls
and Septuagint read *From the labor of His soul He shall
see light.*

11 "O you afflicted one,
　Tossed with tempest, *and* not comforted,
　Behold, I will lay your stones with
　　colorful gems,
　And lay your foundations with
　　sapphires.
12 I will make your pinnacles of rubies,
　Your gates of crystal,
　And all your walls of precious stones.
13 All your children *shall be* taught by
　　the LORD,
　And great *shall be* the peace of your
　　children.
14 In righteousness you shall be
　　established;
　You shall be far from oppression, for
　　you shall not fear;
　And from terror, for it shall not come
　　near you.
15 Indeed they shall surely assemble, *but*
　　not because of Me.
　Whoever assembles against you shall
　　fall for your sake.

16 "Behold, I have created the blacksmith
　Who blows the coals in the fire,
　Who brings forth an instrument for
　　his work;
　And I have created the spoiler to destroy.
17 No weapon formed against you shall
　　prosper,
　And every tongue *which* rises against
　　you in judgment
　You shall condemn.
　This *is* the heritage of the servants of
　　the LORD,
　And their righteousness *is* from Me,"
　Says the LORD.

An Invitation to Abundant Life

55 "Ho! Everyone who thirsts,
　Come to the waters;
　And you who have no money,
　Come, buy and eat.
　Yes, come, buy wine and milk
　Without money and without price.
2 Why do you spend money for *what is*
　　not bread,
　And your wages for *what* does not
　　satisfy?
　Listen carefully to Me, and eat *what*
　　is good,

　And let your soul delight itself in
　　abundance.
3 Incline your ear, and come to Me.
　Hear, and your soul shall live;
　And I will make an everlasting
　　covenant with you—
　The sure mercies of David.
4 Indeed I have given him *as* a witness
　　to the people,
　A leader and commander for the people.
5 Surely you shall call a nation you do
　　not know,
　And nations *who* do not know you
　　shall run to you,
　Because of the LORD your God,
　And the Holy One of Israel;
　For He has glorified you."

6 Seek the LORD while He may be found,
　Call upon Him while He is near.
7 Let the wicked forsake his way,
　And the unrighteous man his thoughts;
　Let him return to the LORD,
　And He will have mercy on him;
　And to our God,
　For He will abundantly pardon.

8 "For My thoughts *are* not your thoughts,
　Nor *are* your ways My ways," says the
　　LORD.
9 "For *as* the heavens are higher than
　　the earth,
　So are My ways higher than your ways,
　And My thoughts than your thoughts.

10 "For as the rain comes down, and the
　　snow from heaven,
　And do not return there,
　But water the earth,
　And make it bring forth and bud,
　That it may give seed to the sower
　And bread to the eater,
11 So shall My word be that goes forth
　　from My mouth;
　It shall not return to Me void,
　But it shall accomplish what I please,
　And it shall prosper *in the thing* for
　　which I sent it.

12 "For you shall go out with joy,
　And be led out with peace;
　The mountains and the hills

Shall break forth into singing before
you,
And all the trees of the field shall clap
their hands.
13 Instead of the thorn shall come up the
cypress tree,
And instead of the brier shall come up
the myrtle tree;
And it shall be to the Lord for a
name,
For an everlasting sign *that* shall not
be cut off."

Salvation for the Gentiles

56 Thus says the Lord:

"Keep justice, and do righteousness,
For My salvation *is* about to come,
And My righteousness to be revealed.

2 Blessed *is* the man *who* does this,
And the son of man *who* lays hold
on it;
Who keeps from defiling the Sabbath,
And keeps his hand from doing any
evil."

3 Do not let the son of the foreigner
Who has joined himself to the Lord
Speak, saying,
"The Lord has utterly separated
me from His people";
Nor let the eunuch say,
"Here I am, a dry tree."
4 For thus says the Lord:
"To the eunuchs who keep My
Sabbaths,
And choose what pleases Me,
And hold fast My covenant,

INSPIRING

*"So shall My word be
that goes forth from My
mouth. . . ."*

Isaiah 55:11

THE BIBLE'S INFLUENCE ON THE FOUNDING FATHERS

In 1984, political scientists Donald Lutz and Charles Hyneman at the University of Houston wrote a paper regarding the research they had done to determine the sources that most influenced the development of American political thought during our nation's founding period. Over the course of ten years, they analyzed some 15,000 items of American political commentary published between 1760 and 1805, the Founding Era. This research paper, "The Relative Influence of European Writers on Late Eighteenth-Century American Political Thought," was published in *The American Political Science Review*, 78 (1984).

The researchers isolated 3,154 direct quotes made by the Founders over this period of time and identified the source of those quotes. The researchers discovered that 34 percent of the Founders' quotes came directly out of the Bible. Baron Charles de Montesquieu, a French legal philosopher, was quoted 8.3 percent of the time. Sir William Blackstone, a renowned English jurist whose *Commentaries on the Laws of England* were highly accepted in America, was next at 7.9 percent of the Founders' quotes, and John Locke, an English philosopher, was fourth with 2.9 percent.

While it is true that three-fourths of the biblical citations in the 1760 to 1805 sample came from reprinted sermons (one of the most popular types of political writing during these years), and only 9 percent of all citations came from secular literature, it is a reflection of the powerful role of the Bible upon the thinking of the Founding Fathers.

5 Even to them I will give in My house
And within My walls a place and a
name
Better than that of sons and daughters;
I will give them[a] an everlasting name
That shall not be cut off.

6 "Also the sons of the foreigner
Who join themselves to the LORD, to
serve Him,
And to love the name of the LORD, to
be His servants—
Everyone who keeps from defiling the
Sabbath,
And holds fast My covenant—

7 Even them I will bring to My holy
mountain,
And make them joyful in My house
of prayer.
Their burnt offerings and their
sacrifices
Will be accepted on My altar;
For My house shall be called a house
of prayer for all nations."

8 The Lord GOD, who gathers the
outcasts of Israel, says,
"Yet I will gather to him
Others besides those who are gathered
to him."

Israel's Irresponsible Leaders

9 All you beasts of the field, come
to devour,
All you beasts in the forest.

10 His watchmen are blind,
They are all ignorant;
They are all dumb dogs,
They cannot bark;
Sleeping, lying down, loving to
slumber.

11 Yes, they are greedy dogs
Which never have enough.
And they are shepherds
Who cannot understand;
They all look to their own way,
Every one for his own gain,
From his own territory.

12 "Come," one says, "I will bring wine,
And we will fill ourselves with
intoxicating drink;
Tomorrow will be as today,
And much more abundant."

Israel's Futile Idolatry

57 The righteous perishes,
And no man takes it to heart;
Merciful men are taken away,
While no one considers
That the righteous is taken away from
evil.

2 He shall enter into peace;
They shall rest in their beds,
Each one walking in his uprightness.

3 "But come here,
You sons of the sorceress,
You offspring of the adulterer and the
harlot!

4 Whom do you ridicule?
Against whom do you make a wide
mouth
And stick out the tongue?
Are you not children of transgression,
Offspring of falsehood,

5 Inflaming yourselves with gods under
every green tree,
Slaying the children in the valleys,
Under the clefts of the rocks?

6 Among the smooth stones of the
stream
Is your portion;
They, they, are your lot!
Even to them you have poured a
drink offering,
You have offered a grain offering.
Should I receive comfort in these?

7 "On a lofty and high mountain
You have set your bed;
Even there you went up
To offer sacrifice.

8 Also behind the doors and their posts
You have set up your remembrance;
For you have uncovered yourself to
those other than Me,
And have gone up to them;
You have enlarged your bed
And made a covenant with them;
You have loved their bed,
Where you saw their nudity.[a]

9 You went to the king with ointment,
And increased your perfumes;

56:5 [a]Literally him   57:8 [a]Literally hand,
a euphemism

You sent your messengers far off,
And *even* descended to Sheol.
10 You are wearied in the length of your
way;
Yet you did not say, 'There is no hope.'
You have found the life of your hand;
Therefore you were not grieved.

11 "And of whom have you been afraid,
or feared,
That you have lied
And not remembered Me,
Nor taken *it* to your heart?
Is it not because I have held My peace
from of old
That you do not fear Me?
12 I will declare your righteousness
And your works,
For they will not profit you.
13 When you cry out,
Let your collection *of idols* deliver you.
But the wind will carry them all away,
A breath will take *them.*
But he who puts his trust in Me shall
possess the land,
And shall inherit My holy mountain."

Healing for the Backslider

14 And one shall say,
"Heap it up! Heap it up!
Prepare the way,
Take the stumbling block out of the
way of My people."

15 For thus says the High and Lofty One
Who inhabits eternity, whose name *is*
Holy:
"I dwell in the high and holy *place,*
With him *who* has a contrite and
humble spirit,
To revive the spirit of the humble,
And to revive the heart of the contrite
ones.
16 For I will not contend forever,
Nor will I always be angry;
For the spirit would fail before Me,
And the souls *which* I have made.
17 For the iniquity of his covetousness
I was angry and struck him;
I hid and was angry,
And he went on backsliding in the
way of his heart.

18 I have seen his ways, and will heal him;
I will also lead him,
And restore comforts to him
And to his mourners.

19 "I create the fruit of the lips:
Peace, peace to *him who is* far off and
to *him who is* near,"
Says the Lord,
"And I will heal him."
20 But the wicked *are* like the troubled sea,
When it cannot rest,
Whose waters cast up mire and dirt.

21 "*There is* no peace,"
Says my God, "for the wicked."

Fasting that Pleases God

58 "Cry aloud, spare not;
Lift up your voice like a trumpet;
Tell My people their transgression,
And the house of Jacob their sins.
2 Yet they seek Me daily,
And delight to know My ways,
As a nation that did righteousness,
And did not forsake the ordinance of
their God.
They ask of Me the ordinances of
justice;
They take delight in approaching God.
3 'Why have we fasted,' *they say,* 'and
You have not seen?
Why have we afflicted our souls, and
You take no notice?'

"In fact, in the day of your fast you
find pleasure,
And exploit all your laborers.
4 Indeed you fast for strife and debate,
And to strike with the fist of wickedness.
You will not fast as *you do* this day,
To make your voice heard on high.
5 Is it a fast that I have chosen,
A day for a man to afflict his soul?
Is it to bow down his head like a
bulrush,
And to spread out sackcloth and ashes?
Would you call this a fast,
And an acceptable day to the Lord?

6 "*Is* this not the fast that I have chosen:
To loose the bonds of wickedness,

To undo the heavy burdens,
To let the oppressed go free,
And that you break every yoke?
7 *Is it* not to share your bread with the
   hungry,
And that you bring to your house the
   poor who are cast out;
When you see the naked, that you
   cover him,
And not hide yourself from your own
   flesh?
8 Then your light shall break forth like
   the morning,
Your healing shall spring forth speedily,
And your righteousness shall go
   before you;
The glory of the LORD shall be your
   rear guard.

9 Then you shall call, and the LORD will
   answer;
You shall cry, and He will say, 'Here
   I *am.*'

"If you take away the yoke from your
   midst,
The pointing of the finger, and
   speaking wickedness,
10 *If* you extend your soul to the hungry
And satisfy the afflicted soul,
Then your light shall dawn in the
   darkness,
And your darkness shall *be* as the
   noonday.
11 The LORD will guide you continually,
And satisfy your soul in drought,
And strengthen your bones;

HUMILITY

"Is this not the fast that I have chosen: to loose the bonds of wickedness. . . ."

ISAIAH 58:6

Abraham Lincoln

NATIONAL BLESSING

Abraham Lincoln, anguished by the ravages of civil war, declared a "Proclamation of a National Fast Day" on March 30, 1863:

Whereas it is the duty of nations as well as of men to own their dependence upon the overruling power of God, to confess their sins and transgressions in humble sorrow, yet with assured hope that genuine repentance will lead to mercy and pardon, and to recognize the sublime truth, announced in the Holy Scriptures and proven by all history, that those nations only are blessed whose God is the Lord.

. . . We have been the recipients of the choicest bounties of Heaven; we have been preserved these many years in peace and prosperity; we have grown in numbers, wealth, and power as no other nation has ever grown. But we have forgotten God. We have forgotten the gracious hand which preserved us in peace and multiplied and enriched and strengthened us, and we have vainly imagined, in the deceitfulness of our hearts, that all these blessings were produced by some superior wisdom and virtue of our own. Intoxicated with unbroken success, we have become too self-sufficient to feel the necessity of redeeming and preserving grace, too proud to pray to the God that made us.

It behooves us, then, to humble ourselves before the offended Power, to confess our national sins, and to pray for clemency and forgiveness.

You shall be like a watered
  garden,
And like a spring of water,
  whose waters do not fail.

Bill Clinton placed his hand on Isaiah 58:12
as he took the presidential oath of office in
1997.

---

12 Those from among you
   Shall build the old waste places;
   You shall raise up the foundations of
     many generations;
   And you shall be called the Repairer
     of the Breach,
   The Restorer of Streets to Dwell In.

13 "If you turn away your foot from the
     Sabbath,
   From doing your pleasure on My holy
     day,
   And call the Sabbath a delight,
   The holy *day* of the LORD honorable,
   And shall honor Him, not doing your
     own ways,
   Nor finding your own pleasure,
   Nor speaking *your own* words,
14 Then you shall delight yourself in the
     LORD;
   And I will cause you to ride on the
     high hills of the earth,
   And feed you with the heritage of
     Jacob your father.
   The mouth of the LORD has spoken."

Separated from God

59 Behold, the LORD's hand is not
     shortened,
   That it cannot save;
   Nor His ear heavy,
   That it cannot hear.
2 But your iniquities have separated
     you from your God;
   And your sins have hidden *His* face
     from you,
   So that He will not hear.
3 For your hands are defiled with
     blood,
   And your fingers with iniquity;
   Your lips have spoken lies,
   Your tongue has muttered perversity.

4 No one calls for justice,
   Nor does *any* plead for truth.
   They trust in empty words and speak
     lies;
   They conceive evil and bring forth
     iniquity.
5 They hatch vipers' eggs and weave
     the spider's web;
   He who eats of their eggs dies,
   And *from* that which is crushed a
     viper breaks out.

6 Their webs will not become garments,
   Nor will they cover themselves with
     their works;
   Their works *are* works of iniquity,
   And the act of violence *is* in their hands.
7 Their feet run to evil,
   And they make haste to shed innocent
     blood;
   Their thoughts *are* thoughts of iniquity;
   Wasting and destruction *are* in their
     paths.
8 The way of peace they have not known,
   And *there is* no justice in their ways;
   They have made themselves crooked
     paths;
   Whoever takes that way shall not
     know peace.

Sin Confessed

9 Therefore justice is far from us,
   Nor does righteousness overtake us;
   We look for light, but there is darkness!
   For brightness, *but* we walk in blackness!
10 We grope for the wall like the blind,
   And we grope as if *we had* no eyes;
   We stumble at noonday as at twilight;
   We are as dead *men* in desolate places.
11 We all growl like bears,
   And moan sadly like doves;
   We look for justice, but *there is* none;
   For salvation, *but* it is far from us.
12 For our transgressions are multiplied
     before You,
   And our sins testify against us;
   For our transgressions *are* with us,
   And *as for* our iniquities, we know them:
13 In transgressing and lying against the
     LORD,
   And departing from our God,
   Speaking oppression and revolt,

Conceiving and uttering from the
heart words of falsehood.
14 Justice is turned back,
And righteousness stands afar off;
For truth is fallen in the street,
And equity cannot enter.
15 So truth fails,
And he *who* departs from evil makes
himself a prey.

The Redeemer of Zion

Then the LORD saw *it,* and it displeased
Him
That *there was* no justice.
16 He saw that *there was* no man,
And wondered that *there was* no
intercessor;
Therefore His own arm brought
salvation for Him;
And His own righteousness, it
sustained Him.
17 For He put on righteousness as a
breastplate,
And a helmet of salvation on His head;
He put on the garments of vengeance
for clothing,
And was clad with zeal as a cloak.
18 According to *their* deeds, accordingly
He will repay,
Fury to His adversaries,
Recompense to His enemies;
The coastlands He will fully repay.
19 So shall they fear
The name of the LORD from the west,
And His glory from the rising of the sun;
When the enemy comes in like a flood,
The Spirit of the LORD will lift up a
standard against him.

20 "The Redeemer will come to Zion,
And to those who turn from
transgression in Jacob,"
Says the LORD.

21 "As for Me," says the LORD, "this *is* My
covenant with them: My Spirit who *is* upon
you, and My words which I have put in your
mouth, shall not depart from your mouth,
nor from the mouth of your descendants,
nor from the mouth of your descendants'
descendants," says the LORD, "from this time
and forevermore."

The Gentiles Bless Zion

60 Arise, shine;
For your light has come!
And the glory of the LORD is risen
upon you.
2 For behold, the darkness shall cover
the earth,
And deep darkness the people;
But the LORD will arise over you,
And His glory will be seen upon you.
3 The Gentiles shall come to your light,
And kings to the brightness of your
rising.

4 "Lift up your eyes all around, and see:
They all gather together, they come
to you;
Your sons shall come from afar,
And your daughters shall be nursed
at *your* side.
5 Then you shall see and become radiant,
And your heart shall swell with joy;
Because the abundance of the sea
shall be turned to you,
The wealth of the Gentiles shall come
to you.
6 The multitude of camels shall cover
your *land,*
The dromedaries of Midian and Ephah;
All those from Sheba shall come;
They shall bring gold and incense,
And they shall proclaim the praises
of the LORD.
7 All the flocks of Kedar shall be
gathered together to you,
The rams of Nebaioth shall minister
to you;
They shall ascend with acceptance on
My altar,
And I will glorify the house of My glory.

8 "Who *are* these *who* fly like a cloud,
And like doves to their roosts?
9 Surely the coastlands shall wait for Me;
And the ships of Tarshish *will come*
first,
To bring your sons from afar,
Their silver and their gold with them,
To the name of the LORD your God,
And to the Holy One of Israel,
Because He has glorified you.

10 "The sons of foreigners shall build up
    your walls,
And their kings shall minister to you;
For in My wrath I struck you,
But in My favor I have had mercy on
    you.

11 Therefore your gates shall be open
    continually;
They shall not be shut day or night,
That *men* may bring to you the wealth
    of the Gentiles,
And their kings in procession.

12 For the nation and kingdom which
    will not serve you shall perish,
And *those* nations shall be utterly
    ruined.

13 "The glory of Lebanon shall come to
    you,
The cypress, the pine, and the box
    tree together,
To beautify the place of My sanctuary;
And I will make the place of My feet
    glorious.

14 Also the sons of those who afflicted
    you
Shall come bowing to you,
And all those who despised you shall
    fall prostrate at the soles of your feet;
And they shall call you The City of the
    LORD,
Zion of the Holy One of Israel.

15 "Whereas you have been forsaken and
    hated,
So that no one went through *you,*
I will make you an eternal excellence,
A joy of many generations.

16 You shall drink the milk of the
    Gentiles,
And milk the breast of kings;
You shall know that I, the LORD, *am*
    your Savior
And your Redeemer, the Mighty One
    of Jacob.

17 "Instead of bronze I will bring gold,
Instead of iron I will bring silver,
Instead of wood, bronze,
And instead of stones, iron.
I will also make your officers peace,
And your magistrates righteousness.

18 Violence shall no longer be heard in
    your land,
Neither wasting nor destruction within
    your borders;
But you shall call your walls Salvation,
And your gates Praise.

God the Glory of His People

19 "The sun shall no longer be your light
    by day,
Nor for brightness shall the moon give
    light to you;
But the LORD will be to you an
    everlasting light,
And your God your glory.

20 Your sun shall no longer go down,
Nor shall your moon withdraw itself;
For the LORD will be your everlasting
    light,
And the days of your mourning shall
    be ended.

21 Also your people *shall* all *be* righteous;
They shall inherit the land forever,
The branch of My planting,
The work of My hands,
That I may be glorified.

22 A little one shall become a thousand,
And a small one a strong nation.
I, the LORD, will hasten it in its time."

The Good News of Salvation

61 "The Spirit of the Lord GOD *is* upon Me,
    Because the LORD has anointed Me
To preach good tidings to the poor;
He has sent Me to heal the
    brokenhearted,
To proclaim liberty to the captives,
And the opening of the prison to *those
    who are* bound;

2 To proclaim the acceptable year of the
    LORD,
And the day of vengeance of our God;
To comfort all who mourn,

3 To console those who mourn in Zion,
To give them beauty for ashes,
The oil of joy for mourning,
The garment of praise for the spirit of
    heaviness;
That they may be called trees of
    righteousness,
The planting of the LORD, that He may
    be glorified."

4 And they shall rebuild the old ruins,
They shall raise up the former
desolations,
And they shall repair the ruined cities,
The desolations of many generations.
5 Strangers shall stand and feed your
flocks,
And the sons of the foreigner
Shall be your plowmen and your
vinedressers.
6 But you shall be named the priests
of the LORD,
They shall call you the servants of
our God.
You shall eat the riches of the
Gentiles,
And in their glory you shall boast.
7 Instead of your shame *you shall have*
double *honor,*
And *instead of* confusion they shall
rejoice in their portion.
Therefore in their land they shall
possess double;
Everlasting joy shall be theirs.

8 "For I, the LORD, love justice;
I hate robbery for burnt offering;
I will direct their work in truth,
And will make with them an
everlasting covenant.
9 Their descendants shall be known
among the Gentiles,
And their offspring among the
people.
All who see them shall acknowledge
them,
That they *are* the posterity *whom* the
LORD has blessed."

10 I will greatly rejoice in the LORD,
My soul shall be joyful in my God;
For He has clothed me with the
garments of salvation,
He has covered me with the robe of
righteousness,
As a bridegroom decks *himself* with
ornaments,
And as a bride adorns *herself* with her
jewels.
11 For as the earth brings forth its bud,
As the garden causes the things that
are sown in it to spring forth,

So the Lord GOD will cause
righteousness and praise to spring
forth before all the nations.

Assurance of Zion's Salvation

62 For Zion's sake I will not hold My
peace,
And for Jerusalem's sake I will not rest,
Until her righteousness goes forth as
brightness,
And her salvation as a lamp *that* burns.
2 The Gentiles shall see your
righteousness,
And all kings your glory.
You shall be called by a new name,
Which the mouth of the LORD will name.
3 You shall also be a crown of glory
In the hand of the LORD,
And a royal diadem
In the hand of your God.
4 You shall no longer be termed Forsaken,
Nor shall your land any more be
termed Desolate;
But you shall be called Hephzibah,[a]
and your land Beulah;[b]
For the LORD delights in you,
And your land shall be married.
5 For *as* a young man marries a virgin,
So shall your sons marry you;
And *as* the bridegroom rejoices over
the bride,
So shall your God rejoice over you.

6 I have set watchmen on your walls,
O Jerusalem;
They shall never hold their peace day
or night.
You who make mention of the LORD,
do not keep silent,
7 And give Him no rest till He establishes
And till He makes Jerusalem a praise
in the earth.

8 The LORD has sworn by His right hand
And by the arm of His strength:
"Surely I will no longer give your grain
As food for your enemies;
And the sons of the foreigner shall not
drink your new wine,
For which you have labored.

62:4 [a]Literally *My Delight Is in Her* [b]Literally *Married*

9 But those who have gathered it shall
   eat it,
   And praise the LORD;
   Those who have brought it together
   shall drink it in My holy courts."

10 Go through,
   Go through the gates!
   Prepare the way for the people;
   Build up,
   Build up the highway!
   Take out the stones,
   Lift up a banner for the peoples!

11 Indeed the LORD has proclaimed
   To the end of the world:
   "Say to the daughter of Zion,
   'Surely your salvation is coming;
   Behold, His reward is with Him,
   And His work before Him.'"
12 And they shall call them The Holy
   People,
   The Redeemed of the LORD;
   And you shall be called Sought Out,
   A City Not Forsaken.

The LORD in Judgment and Salvation

63 Who is this who comes from Edom,
   With dyed garments from Bozrah,
   This One who is glorious in His apparel,
   Traveling in the greatness of His
   strength?—

   "I who speak in righteousness, mighty
   to save."

2 Why is Your apparel red,
   And Your garments like one who
   treads in the winepress?

3 "I have trodden the winepress alone,
   And from the peoples no one was
   with Me.
   For I have trodden them in My anger,
   And trampled them in My fury;
   Their blood is sprinkled upon My
   garments,
   And I have stained all My robes.
4 For the day of vengeance is in My heart,
   And the year of My redeemed has come.
5 I looked, but there was no one to help,
   And I wondered

   That there was no one to uphold;
   Therefore My own arm brought
   salvation for Me;
   And My own fury, it sustained Me.
6 I have trodden down the peoples in
   My anger,
   Made them drunk in My fury,
   And brought down their strength to
   the earth."

God's Mercy Remembered

7 I will mention the lovingkindnesses
   of the LORD
   And the praises of the LORD,
   According to all that the LORD has
   bestowed on us,
   And the great goodness toward the
   house of Israel,
   Which He has bestowed on them
   according to His mercies,
   According to the multitude of His
   lovingkindnesses.
8 For He said, "Surely they are My
   people,
   Children who will not lie."
   So He became their Savior.
9 In all their affliction He was afflicted,
   And the Angel of His Presence saved
   them;
   In His love and in His pity He
   redeemed them;
   And He bore them and carried them
   All the days of old.
10 But they rebelled and grieved His Holy
   Spirit;
   So He turned Himself against them
   as an enemy,
   And He fought against them.

11 Then he remembered the days of old,
   Moses and his people, saying:
   "Where is He who brought them up
   out of the sea
   With the shepherd of His flock?
   Where is He who put His Holy Spirit
   within them,
12 Who led them by the right hand of
   Moses,
   With His glorious arm,
   Dividing the water before them
   To make for Himself an everlasting
   name,

13 Who led them through the deep,
As a horse in the wilderness,
That they might not stumble?"

14 As a beast goes down into the valley,
And the Spirit of the LORD causes him
to rest,
So You lead Your people,
To make Yourself a glorious name.

A Prayer of Penitence

15 Look down from heaven,
And see from Your habitation, holy
and glorious.
Where *are* Your zeal and Your strength,
The yearning of Your heart and Your
mercies toward me?
Are they restrained?

16 Doubtless You *are* our Father,
Though Abraham was ignorant of us,
And Israel does not acknowledge us.
You, O LORD, *are* our Father;
Our Redeemer from Everlasting *is* Your
name.

17 O LORD, why have You made us stray
from Your ways,
And hardened our heart from Your fear?
Return for Your servants' sake,
The tribes of Your inheritance.

18 Your holy people have possessed *it* but
a little while;
Our adversaries have trodden down
Your sanctuary.

19 We have become *like* those of old, over
whom You never ruled,
Those who were never called by Your
name.

64 Oh, that You would rend the heavens!
That You would come down!
That the mountains might shake at
Your presence—

2 As fire burns brushwood,
As fire causes water to boil—
To make Your name known to Your
adversaries,
That the nations may tremble at Your
presence!

3 When You did awesome things *for
which* we did not look,
You came down,
The mountains shook at Your presence.

4 For since the beginning of the world
Men have not heard nor perceived by
the ear,
Nor has the eye seen any God besides
You,
Who acts for the one who waits for Him.

5 You meet him who rejoices and does
righteousness,
Who remembers You in Your ways.
You are indeed angry, for we have
sinned—
In these ways we continue;
And we need to be saved.

6 But we are all like an unclean *thing,*
And all our righteousnesses *are* like
filthy rags;
We all fade as a leaf,
And our iniquities, like the wind,
Have taken us away.

7 And *there is* no one who calls on Your
name,
Who stirs himself up to take hold of
You;
For You have hidden Your face from us,
And have consumed us because of our
iniquities.

8 But now, O LORD,
You *are* our Father;
We *are* the clay, and You our potter;
And all we *are* the work of Your hand.

9 Do not be furious, O LORD,
Nor remember iniquity forever;
Indeed, please look—we all *are* Your
people!

10 Your holy cities are a wilderness,
Zion is a wilderness,
Jerusalem a desolation.

11 Our holy and beautiful temple,
Where our fathers praised You,
Is burned up with fire;
And all our pleasant things are laid
waste.

12 Will You restrain Yourself because of
these *things,* O LORD?
Will You hold Your peace, and afflict
us very severely?

The Righteousness of God's Judgment

65 "I was sought by *those who* did not
ask *for Me;*

I was found by *those who* did not
    seek Me.
I said, 'Here I am, here I am,'
To a nation *that* was not called by
    My name.
2 I have stretched out My hands all
    day long to a rebellious people,
Who walk in a way *that is* not good,
According to their own thoughts;
3 A people who provoke Me to anger
    continually to My face;
Who sacrifice in gardens,
And burn incense on altars of brick;
4 Who sit among the graves,
And spend the night in the tombs;
Who eat swine's flesh,
And the broth of abominable things
    is *in* their vessels;
5 Who say, 'Keep to yourself,
Do not come near me,
For I am holier than you!'
These *are* smoke in My nostrils,
A fire that burns all the day.

6 "Behold, *it is* written before Me:
I will not keep silence, but will repay—
Even repay into their bosom—
7 Your iniquities and the iniquities of
    your fathers together,"
Says the LORD,
"Who have burned incense on the
    mountains
And blasphemed Me on the hills;
Therefore I will measure their former
    work into their bosom."

8 Thus says the LORD:

"As the new wine is found in the cluster,
And *one* says, 'Do not destroy it,
For a blessing *is* in it,'
So will I do for My servants' sake,
That I may not destroy them all.
9 I will bring forth descendants from
    Jacob,
And from Judah an heir of My
    mountains;
My elect shall inherit it,
And My servants shall dwell there.
10 Sharon shall be a fold of flocks,
And the Valley of Achor a place for
    herds to lie down,

For My people who have sought Me.

11 "But you *are* those who forsake the LORD,
Who forget My holy mountain,
Who prepare a table for Gad,[a]
And who furnish a drink offering for
    Meni.[b]
12 Therefore I will number you for the
    sword,
And you shall all bow down to the
    slaughter;
Because, when I called, you did not
    answer;
When I spoke, you did not hear,
But did evil before My eyes,
And chose *that* in which I do not
    delight."

13 Therefore thus says the Lord GOD:

"Behold, My servants shall eat,
But you shall be hungry;
Behold, My servants shall drink,
But you shall be thirsty;
Behold, My servants shall rejoice,
But you shall be ashamed;
14 Behold, My servants shall sing for joy
    of heart,
But you shall cry for sorrow of heart,
And wail for grief of spirit.
15 You shall leave your name as a curse
    to My chosen;
For the Lord GOD will slay you,
And call His servants by another name;
16 So that he who blesses himself in the
    earth
Shall bless himself in the God of truth;
And he who swears in the earth
Shall swear by the God of truth;
Because the former troubles are
    forgotten,
And because they are hidden from
    My eyes.

The Glorious New Creation

17 "For behold, I create new heavens
    and a new earth;
And the former shall not be
    remembered or come to mind.

65:11 [a]Literally *Troop* or *Fortune,* a pagan deity
[b]Literally *Number* or *Destiny,* a pagan deity

18 But be glad and rejoice forever in
       what I create;
   For behold, I create Jerusalem *as a*
       rejoicing,
   And her people a joy.
19 I will rejoice in Jerusalem,
   And joy in My people;
   The voice of weeping shall no longer
       be heard in her,
   Nor the voice of crying.

20 "No more shall an infant from there
       live but a few days,
   Nor an old man who has not fulfilled
       his days;
   For the child shall die one hundred
       years old,
   But the sinner *being* one hundred
       years old shall be accursed.
21 They shall build houses and inhabit
       them;
   They shall plant vineyards and eat
       their fruit.
22 They shall not build and another
       inhabit;
   They shall not plant and another eat;
   For as the days of a tree, *so shall be* the
       days of My people,
   And My elect shall long enjoy the
       work of their hands.
23 They shall not labor in vain,
   Nor bring forth children for trouble;
   For they *shall be* the descendants of
       the blessed of the LORD,
   And their offspring with them.

24 "It shall come to pass
   That before they call, I will answer;
   And while they are still speaking, I
       will hear.
25 The wolf and the lamb shall feed
       together,
   The lion shall eat straw like the ox,
   And dust *shall be* the serpent's food.
   They shall not hurt nor destroy in all
       My holy mountain,"
   Says the LORD.

True Worship and False

66 Thus says the LORD:

   "Heaven *is* My throne,
   And earth *is* My footstool.
   Where *is* the house that you will
       build Me?
   And where *is* the place of My rest?
2 For all those *things* My hand has made,
   And all those *things* exist,"
   Says the LORD.
   "But on this *one* will I look:
   On *him who is* poor and of a contrite
       spirit,
   And who trembles at My word.

3 "He who kills a bull *is as if* he slays
       a man;
   He who sacrifices a lamb, *as if* he
       breaks a dog's neck;
   He who offers a grain offering, *as if*
       he offers swine's blood;
   He who burns incense, *as if* he blesses
       an idol.
   Just as they have chosen their own
       ways,
   And their soul delights in their
       abominations,
4 So will I choose their delusions,
   And bring their fears on them;
   Because, when I called, no one
       answered,
   When I spoke they did not hear;
   But they did evil before My eyes,
   And chose *that* in which I do not
       delight."

The LORD Vindicates Zion

5 Hear the word of the LORD,
   You who tremble at His word:
   "Your brethren who hated you,
   Who cast you out for My name's sake,
       said,
   'Let the LORD be glorified,
   That we may see your joy.'
   But they shall be ashamed."

6 The sound of noise from the city!
   A voice from the temple!
   The voice of the LORD,
   Who fully repays His enemies!

7 "Before she was in labor, she gave birth;
   Before her pain came,
   She delivered a male child.
8 Who has heard such a thing?
   Who has seen such things?

Shall the earth be made to give birth
   in one day?
Or shall a nation be born at once?
For as soon as Zion was in labor,
She gave birth to her children.
9 Shall I bring to the time of birth, and
   not cause delivery?" says the LORD.
  "Shall I who cause delivery shut up *the*
   womb?" says your God.
10 "Rejoice with Jerusalem,
   And be glad with her, all you who
    love her;
   Rejoice for joy with her, all you who
    mourn for her;
11 That you may feed and be satisfied
   With the consolation of her bosom,
   That you may drink deeply and be
    delighted
   With the abundance of her glory."

12For thus says the LORD:

"Behold, I will extend peace to her like
   a river,
   And the glory of the Gentiles like a
    flowing stream.
   Then you shall feed;
   On *her* sides shall you be carried,
   And be dandled on *her* knees.
13 As one whom his mother comforts,
   So I will comfort you;
   And you shall be comforted in
    Jerusalem."

The Reign and Indignation of God

14 When you see *this,* your heart shall
   rejoice,
   And your bones shall flourish like
    grass;
   The hand of the LORD shall be known
    to His servants,
   And *His* indignation to His enemies.
15 For behold, the LORD will come with
   fire
   And with His chariots, like a
    whirlwind,
   To render His anger with fury,
   And His rebuke with flames of fire.
16 For by fire and by His sword
   The LORD will judge all flesh;
   And the slain of the LORD shall be
    many.

17 "Those who sanctify themselves and
   purify themselves,
   To go to the gardens
   After an *idol* in the midst,
   Eating swine's flesh and the
    abomination and the mouse,
   Shall be consumed together," says
    the LORD.

18"For I *know* their works and their thoughts. It shall be that I will gather all nations and tongues; and they shall come and see My glory. 19I will set a sign among them; and those among them who escape I will send to the nations: *to* Tarshish and Pul[a] and Lud, who draw the bow, and Tubal and Javan, *to* the coastlands afar off who have not heard My fame nor seen My glory. And they shall declare My glory among the Gentiles. 20Then they shall bring all your brethren for an offering to the LORD out of all nations, on horses and in chariots and in litters, on mules and on camels, to My holy mountain Jerusalem," says the LORD, "as the children of Israel bring an offering in a clean vessel into the house of the LORD. 21And I will also take some of them for priests *and* Levites," says the LORD.

22 "For as the new heavens and the new
   earth
   Which I will make shall remain before
    Me," says the LORD,
  "So shall your descendants and your
   name remain.
23 And it shall come to pass
   That from one New Moon to
    another,
   And from one Sabbath to another,
   All flesh shall come to worship
    before Me," says the LORD.

24 "And they shall go forth and look
   Upon the corpses of the men
   Who have transgressed against Me.
   For their worm does not die,
   And their fire is not quenched.
   They shall be an abhorrence to all
    flesh."

66:19 [a]Following Masoretic Text and Targum;
Septuagint reads *Put* (compare Jeremiah 46:9).

JEREMIAH

Author: Jeremiah

When Written: 626–586 B.C.

Theme: Repentance and Restoration

Key Verses: Jeremiah 7:23, 24—"But this is what I commanded them, saying, 'Obey My voice, and I will be your God, and you shall be My people. And walk in all the ways that I have commanded you, that it may be well with you.' Yet they did not obey or incline their ear, but followed the counsels and the dictates of their evil hearts, and went backward and not forward."

Key Chapter: Jeremiah 31—Even though the Book of Jeremiah contains stern judgment and condemnation of Judah for its disobedience and rebellion against God, chapter 31 offers hope of a new covenant, as God promises to write His law on the hearts of His people and to be their God (v. 33).

The prophet Jeremiah was just a youth when God called him to take a message of repentance to the rebellious nation of Judah. From a compassionate heart, Jeremiah agonized over Judah's sin and condemned the people for their idolatry. But even in the midst of the severe judgment that he was called to declare over God's children, Jeremiah promised that God would respond to their repentance and bring restoration.

The great American statesman Daniel Webster understood how crucial it is for a nation "under God" to steadfastly guard its foundations of righteousness. In 1852, he warned of his own beloved America, "If we and our posterity reject religious instruction and authority, violate the rules of eternal justice, trifle with the injunctions of morality, and recklessly destroy the political constitution which holds us together, no man can tell how sudden a catastrophe may overwhelm us, that shall bury all our glory in profound obscurity."

1 The words of Jeremiah the son of Hilkiah, of the priests who *were* in Anathoth in the land of Benjamin, ²to whom the word of the LORD came in the days of Josiah the son of Amon, king of Judah, in the thirteenth year of his reign. ³It came also in the days of Jehoiakim the son of Josiah, king of Judah, until the end of the eleventh year of Zedekiah the son of Josiah, king of Judah, until the carrying away of Jerusalem captive in the fifth month.

The Prophet Is Called

⁴Then the word of the LORD came to me, saying:

5 "Before I formed you in the womb I
        knew you;
    Before you were born I sanctified
        you;
    I ordained you a prophet to the
        nations."

⁶Then said I:

"Ah, Lord GOD!
    Behold, I cannot speak, for I *am* a
        youth."

⁷But the LORD said to me:

"Do not say, 'I *am* a youth,'
    For you shall go to all to whom I send
        you,
    And whatever I command you, you
        shall speak.
8   Do not be afraid of their faces,
    For I *am* with you to deliver you," says
        the LORD.

⁹Then the LORD put forth His hand and touched my mouth, and the LORD said to me:

"Behold, I have put My words in your
        mouth.

10 See, I have this day set you over the
        nations and over the kingdoms,
    To root out and to pull down,
    To destroy and to throw down,
    To build and to plant."

¹¹Moreover the word of the LORD came to me, saying, "Jeremiah, what do you see?"

And I said, "I see a branch of an almond tree."

¹²Then the LORD said to me, "You have seen well, for I am ready to perform My word."

¹³And the word of the LORD came to me the second time, saying, "What do you see?"

And I said, "I see a boiling pot, and it is facing away from the north."

¹⁴Then the LORD said to me:

"Out of the north calamity shall break
        forth
    On all the inhabitants of the land.
15 For behold, I am calling
    All the families of the kingdoms of the
        north," says the LORD;
    "They shall come and each one set his
        throne
    At the entrance of the gates of
        Jerusalem,
    Against all its walls all around,
    And against all the cities of Judah.
16 I will utter My judgments
    Against them concerning all their
        wickedness,
    Because they have forsaken Me,
    Burned incense to other gods,
    And worshiped the works of their own
        hands.

17 "Therefore prepare yourself and arise,
    And speak to them all that I
        command you.
    Do not be dismayed before their faces,
    Lest I dismay you before them.
18 For behold, I have made you this day

THE DIGNITY OF HUMAN LIFE

PROTECTOR

*"Before I formed
you in the womb
I knew you. . . ."*

JEREMIAH 1:5

Our Founding Fathers held to the biblical principle that human life is precious and created equal. In the Declaration of Independence, it is God the "Creator" who endowed every man, woman, and child with the right to "life, liberty, and the pursuit of happiness." The signers called them self-evident truths. Each life has inherent dignity and matchless value, apparently from conception until death.

The Founders knew that if God the "Creator" is taken out of the national value system, our rights as citizens are no longer absolute and become subject to the relative values of those who are in a position to make or change the laws. In truth, we are no longer equal in value as people, and typically it is the weakest and most vulnerable members of society who are the first to pay the price as others take the role of determining what rights we do and do not have. Universal moral laws that promote the good of all people and protect the innocent and vulnerable give way to the selfish pursuits of those who demand the moral license to do what they want.

The dignity of human life is not just a biblical principle, it is a principle of a decent life. Every human being, born or unborn, deserves the equal protection of the law, and the value of life is not conditional upon its usefulness to others or to the state. Neither scientific progress nor the desire to help others can justify the sacrifice of any human being's life or inherent dignity, whether it takes the form of abortion, euthanasia, or any of the many new forms of biotechnology. We must reaffirm our steadfast determination to defend the sanctity of human life.

A fortified city and an iron pillar,
And bronze walls against the whole
    land—
Against the kings of Judah,
Against its princes,
Against its priests,
And against the people of the land.
19 They will fight against you,
But they shall not prevail against you.
For I *am* with you," says the Lord, "to
    deliver you."

God's Case Against Israel

2 Moreover the word of the Lord came to
me, saying, 2"Go and cry in the hearing
of Jerusalem, saying, 'Thus says the Lord:

"I remember you,
The kindness of your youth,
The love of your betrothal,
When you went after Me in the
    wilderness,
In a land not sown.
3 Israel *was* holiness to the Lord,
The firstfruits of His increase.
All that devour him will offend;
Disaster will come upon them," says
    the Lord.'"

4Hear the word of the Lord, O house of
Jacob and all the families of the house of
Israel. 5Thus says the Lord:

"What injustice have your fathers
    found in Me,
That they have gone far from Me,
Have followed idols,
And have become idolaters?
6 Neither did they say, 'Where *is* the Lord,
Who brought us up out of the land of
    Egypt,
Who led us through the wilderness,
Through a land of deserts and pits,
Through a land of drought and the
    shadow of death,
Through a land that no one crossed
And where no one dwelt?'
7 I brought you into a bountiful
    country,
To eat its fruit and its goodness.
But when you entered, you defiled My
    land

And made My heritage an
    abomination.
8 The priests did not say, 'Where *is* the
    Lord?'
And those who handle the law did not
    know Me;
The rulers also transgressed against
    Me;
The prophets prophesied by Baal,
And walked after *things that* do not
    profit.

9 "Therefore I will yet bring charges
    against you," says the Lord,
"And against your children's children I
    will bring charges.
10 For pass beyond the coasts of Cyprusᵃ
    and see,
Send to Kedarᵇ and consider diligently,
And see if there has been such *a thing.*
11 Has a nation changed *its* gods,
Which *are* not gods?
But My people have changed their
    Glory
For *what* does not profit.
12 Be astonished, O heavens, at this,
And be horribly afraid;
Be very desolate," says the Lord.
13 "For My people have committed two
    evils:
They have forsaken Me, the fountain
    of living waters,
And hewn themselves cisterns—broken
    cisterns that can hold no water.

14 "*Is* Israel a servant?
Is he a homeborn *slave?*
Why is he plundered?
15 The young lions roared at him, *and*
    growled;
They made his land waste;
His cities are burned, without
    inhabitant.
16 Also the people of Nophᵃ and
    Tahpanhes
Have broken the crown of your head.
17 Have you not brought this on yourself,

2:10 ᵃHebrew *Kittim,* western lands, especially Cyprus
ᵇIn the northern Arabian desert, representative of the
eastern cultures   **2:16** ᵃThat is, Memphis in
ancient Egypt

In that you have forsaken the Lord
    your God
When He led you in the way?
18 And now why take the road to Egypt,
To drink the waters of Sihor?
Or why take the road to Assyria,
To drink the waters of the River?ᵃ
19 Your own wickedness will correct you,
And your backslidings will rebuke
    you.
Know therefore and see that *it is* an
    evil and bitter *thing*
That you have forsaken the Lord your
    God,
And the fear of Me *is* not in you,"
Says the Lord God of hosts.

20 "For of old I have broken your yoke
    and burst your bonds;
And you said, 'I will not transgress,'
When on every high hill and under
    every green tree
You lay down, playing the harlot.
21 Yet I had planted you a noble vine, a
    seed of highest quality.
How then have you turned before Me
Into the degenerate plant of an alien
    vine?
22 For though you wash yourself with
    lye, and use much soap,
Yet your iniquity is marked before
    Me," says the Lord God.

23 "How can you say, 'I am not polluted,
I have not gone after the Baals'?
See your way in the valley;
Know what you have done:
You are a swift dromedary breaking
    loose in her ways,
24 A wild donkey used to the
    wilderness,
That sniffs at the wind in her desire;
In her time of mating, who can turn
    her away?
All those who seek her will not weary
    themselves;
In her month they will find her.
25 Withhold your foot from being
    unshod, and your throat from thirst.
But you said, 'There is no hope.
No! For I have loved aliens, and after
    them I will go.'

26 "As the thief is ashamed when he is
    found out,
So is the house of Israel ashamed;
They and their kings and their
    princes, and their priests and their
    prophets,
27 Saying to a tree, 'You *are* my father,'
And to a stone, 'You gave birth to me.'
For they have turned *their* back to Me,
    and not *their* face.
But in the time of their trouble
They will say, 'Arise and save us.'
28 But where *are* your gods that you have
    made for yourselves?
Let them arise,
If they can save you in the time of
    your trouble;
For *according to* the number of your
    cities
Are your gods, O Judah.

29 "Why will you plead with Me?
You all have transgressed against Me,"
    says the Lord.
30 "In vain I have chastened your
    children;
They received no correction.
Your sword has devoured your
    prophets
Like a destroying lion.

31 "O generation, see the word of the
    Lord!
Have I been a wilderness to Israel,
Or a land of darkness?
Why do My people say, 'We are lords;
We will come no more to You'?
32 Can a virgin forget her ornaments,
Or a bride her attire?
Yet My people have forgotten Me days
    without number.

33 "Why do you beautify your way to seek
    love?
Therefore you have also taught
The wicked women your ways.
34 Also on your skirts is found
The blood of the lives of the poor
    innocents.
I have not found it by secret search,

2:18 ᵃThat is, the Euphrates

But plainly on all these things.
35 Yet you say, 'Because I am innocent,
    Surely His anger shall turn from me.'
    Behold, I will plead My case against
        you,
    Because you say, 'I have not sinned.'
36 Why do you gad about so much to
        change your way?
    Also you shall be ashamed of Egypt as
        you were ashamed of Assyria.
37 Indeed you will go forth from him
    With your hands on your head;
    For the LORD has rejected your trusted
        allies,
    And you will not prosper by them.

Israel Is Shameless

3 "They say, 'If a man divorces his wife,
    And she goes from him
    And becomes another man's,
    May he return to her again?'
    Would not that land be greatly
        polluted?
    But you have played the harlot with
        many lovers;
    Yet return to Me," says the LORD.

2 "Lift up your eyes to the desolate
        heights and see:
    Where have you not lain *with men?*
    By the road you have sat for them
    Like an Arabian in the wilderness;
    And you have polluted the land
    With your harlotries and your
        wickedness.
3 Therefore the showers have been
        withheld,
    And there has been no latter rain.
    You have had a harlot's forehead;
    You refuse to be ashamed.
4 Will you not from this time cry to Me,
    'My Father, You *are* the guide of my
        youth?
5 Will He remain angry forever?
    Will He keep it to the end?'
    Behold, you have spoken and done
        evil things,
    As you were able."

A Call to Repentance

6 The LORD said also to me in the days of
Josiah the king: "Have you seen what
backsliding Israel has done? She has gone
up on every high mountain and under
every green tree, and there played the harlot. 7 And I said, after she had done all
these *things,* 'Return to Me.' But she did not
return. And her treacherous sister Judah saw
it. 8 Then I saw that for all the causes for
which backsliding Israel had committed
adultery, I had put her away and given her
a certificate of divorce; yet her treacherous
sister Judah did not fear, but went and
played the harlot also. 9 So it came to pass,
through her casual harlotry, that she defiled
the land and committed adultery with
stones and trees. 10 And yet for all this her
treacherous sister Judah has not turned to
Me with her whole heart, but in pretense,"
says the LORD.

11 Then the LORD said to me, "Backsliding
Israel has shown herself more righteous
than treacherous Judah. 12 Go and proclaim
these words toward the north, and say:

    'Return, backsliding Israel,' says the
        LORD;
    'I will not cause My anger to fall on you.
    For I *am* merciful,' says the LORD;
    'I will not remain angry forever.
13 Only acknowledge your iniquity,
    That you have transgressed against
        the LORD your God,
    And have scattered your charms
    To alien deities under every green tree,
    And you have not obeyed My voice,'
        says the LORD.

14 "Return, O backsliding children," says
the LORD; "for I am married to you. I will
take you, one from a city and two from a
family, and I will bring you to Zion. 15 And
I will give you shepherds according to My
heart, who will feed you with knowledge
and understanding.

16 "Then it shall come to pass, when you
are multiplied and increased in the land in
those days," says the LORD, "that they will
say no more, 'The ark of the covenant of
the LORD.' It shall not come to mind, nor
shall they remember it, nor shall they visit
it, nor shall it be made anymore.

17 "At that time Jerusalem shall be called
The Throne of the LORD, and all the

nations shall be gathered to it, to the name of the LORD, to Jerusalem. No more shall they follow the dictates of their evil hearts.

18"In those days the house of Judah shall walk with the house of Israel, and they shall come together out of the land of the north to the land that I have given as an inheritance to your fathers.

19"But I said:

'How can I put you among the
    children
And give you a pleasant land,
A beautiful heritage of the hosts of
    nations?'

"And I said:

'You shall call Me, "My Father,"
And not turn away from Me.'
20 Surely, *as* a wife treacherously departs
    from her husband,
So have you dealt treacherously
    with Me,
O house of Israel," says the LORD.

21 A voice was heard on the desolate
    heights,
Weeping *and* supplications of the
    children of Israel.
For they have perverted their way;
They have forgotten the LORD their God.

22 "Return, you backsliding children,
And I will heal your backslidings."

"Indeed we do come to You,
For You are the LORD our God.
23 Truly, in vain *is salvation hoped for*
    from the hills,
And from the multitude of mountains;
Truly, in the LORD our God
Is the salvation of Israel.
24 For shame has devoured
The labor of our fathers from our
    youth—
Their flocks and their herds,
Their sons and their daughters.
25 We lie down in our shame,
And our reproach covers us.
For we have sinned against the LORD
    our God,

We and our fathers,
From our youth even to this day,
And have not obeyed the voice of the
    LORD our God."

4 "If you will return, O Israel," says
    the LORD,
"Return to Me;
And if you will put away your
    abominations out of My sight,
Then you shall not be moved.
2   And you shall swear, 'The LORD lives,'
In truth, in judgment, and in
    righteousness;
The nations shall bless themselves in
    Him,
And in Him they shall glory."

3For thus says the LORD to the men of Judah and Jerusalem:

"Break up your fallow ground,
And do not sow among thorns.
4   Circumcise yourselves to the LORD,
And take away the foreskins of your
    hearts,
You men of Judah and inhabitants of
    Jerusalem,
Lest My fury come forth like fire,
And burn so that no one can quench *it,*
Because of the evil of your doings."

An Imminent Invasion

5Declare in Judah and proclaim in Jerusalem, and say:

"Blow the trumpet in the land;
Cry, 'Gather together,'
And say, 'Assemble yourselves,
And let us go into the fortified cities.'
6   Set up the standard toward Zion.
Take refuge! Do not delay!
For I will bring disaster from the
    north,
And great destruction."

7   The lion has come up from his
    thicket,
And the destroyer of nations is on
    his way.
He has gone forth from his place
To make your land desolate.

Your cities will be laid waste,
Without inhabitant.
8 For this, clothe yourself with
    sackcloth,
Lament and wail.
For the fierce anger of the LORD
Has not turned back from us.

9 "And it shall come to pass in that day,"
    says the LORD,
"*That* the heart of the king shall perish,
And the heart of the princes;
The priests shall be astonished,
And the prophets shall wonder."

10 Then I said, "Ah, Lord GOD!
Surely You have greatly deceived this
    people and Jerusalem,
Saying, 'You shall have peace,'
Whereas the sword reaches to the
    heart."

11 At that time it will be said
To this people and to Jerusalem,
"A dry wind of the desolate heights
    blows in the wilderness
Toward the daughter of My people—
Not to fan or to cleanse—
12 A wind too strong for these will come
    for Me;
Now I will also speak judgment
    against them."

13 "Behold, he shall come up like clouds,
And his chariots like a whirlwind.
His horses are swifter than eagles.
Woe to us, for we are plundered!"

14 O Jerusalem, wash your heart from
    wickedness,
That you may be saved.
How long shall your evil thoughts
    lodge within you?
15 For a voice declares from Dan
And proclaims affliction from Mount
    Ephraim:
16 "Make mention to the nations,
Yes, proclaim against Jerusalem,
That watchers come from a far
    country
And raise their voice against the cities
    of Judah.

17 Like keepers of a field they are against
    her all around,
Because she has been rebellious
    against Me," says the LORD.
18 "Your ways and your doings
Have procured these *things* for you.
This *is* your wickedness,
Because it is bitter,
Because it reaches to your heart."

Sorrow for the Doomed Nation

19 O my soul, my soul!
I am pained in my very heart!
My heart makes a noise in me;
I cannot hold my peace,
Because you have heard, O my soul,
The sound of the trumpet,
The alarm of war.
20 Destruction upon destruction is
    cried,
For the whole land is plundered.
Suddenly my tents are plundered,
And my curtains in a moment.
21 How long will I see the standard,
And hear the sound of the trumpet?

22 "For My people *are* foolish,
They have not known Me.
They *are* silly children,
And they have no understanding.
They *are* wise to do evil,
But to do good they have no
    knowledge."

23 I beheld the earth, and indeed *it was*
    without form, and void;
And the heavens, they *had* no light.
24 I beheld the mountains, and indeed
    they trembled,
And all the hills moved back and
    forth.
25 I beheld, and indeed *there was* no
    man,
And all the birds of the heavens had
    fled.
26 I beheld, and indeed the fruitful land
    was a wilderness,
And all its cities were broken down
At the presence of the LORD,
By His fierce anger.

27 For thus says the LORD:

"The whole land shall be desolate;
Yet I will not make a full end.
28 For this shall the earth mourn,
And the heavens above be black,
Because I have spoken.
I have purposed and will not relent,
Nor will I turn back from it.
29 The whole city shall flee from the
noise of the horsemen and bowmen.
They shall go into thickets and climb
up on the rocks.
Every city *shall be* forsaken,
And not a man shall dwell in it.

30 "And *when* you *are* plundered,
What will you do?
Though you clothe yourself with
crimson,
Though you adorn *yourself* with
ornaments of gold,
Though you enlarge your eyes with
paint,
In vain you will make yourself fair;
Your lovers will despise you;
They will seek your life.

31 "For I have heard a voice as of a
woman in labor,
The anguish as of her who brings
forth her first child,
The voice of the daughter of Zion
bewailing herself;
She spreads her hands, *saying,*
'Woe *is* me now, for my soul is weary
Because of murderers!'

The Justice of God's Judgment

5 "Run to and fro through the streets
of Jerusalem;
See now and know;
And seek in her open places
If you can find a man,
If there is *anyone* who executes
judgment,
Who seeks the truth,
And I will pardon her.
2 Though they say, 'As the LORD lives,'
Surely they swear falsely."

3 O LORD, *are* not Your eyes on the
truth?
You have stricken them,
But they have not grieved;
You have consumed them,
But they have refused to receive
correction.
They have made their faces harder
than rock;
They have refused to return.

4 Therefore I said, "Surely these *are*
poor.
They are foolish;
For they do not know the way of the
LORD,
The judgment of their God.
5 I will go to the great men and speak
to them,
For they have known the way of the
LORD,
The judgment of their God."
But these have altogether broken the
yoke
And burst the bonds.
6 Therefore a lion from the forest shall
slay them,
A wolf of the deserts shall destroy
them;
A leopard will watch over their cities.
Everyone who goes out from there
shall be torn in pieces,
Because their transgressions are many;
Their backslidings have increased.

7 "How shall I pardon you for this?
Your children have forsaken Me
And sworn by *those that are* not gods.
When I had fed them to the full,
Then they committed adultery
And assembled themselves by troops
in the harlots' houses.
8 They were *like* well-fed lusty stallions;
Every one neighed after his neighbor's
wife.
9 Shall I not punish *them* for these
things?" says the LORD.
"And shall I not avenge Myself on such
a nation as this?

10 "Go up on her walls and destroy,
But do not make a complete end.
Take away her branches,
For they *are* not the LORD's.

11 For the house of Israel and the house
    of Judah
Have dealt very treacherously with
    Me," says the LORD.

12 They have lied about the LORD,
    And said, "*It is* not He.
    Neither will evil come upon us,
    Nor shall we see sword or famine.
13 And the prophets become wind,
    For the word *is* not in them.
    Thus shall it be done to them."

14Therefore thus says the LORD God of
hosts:

"Because you speak this word,
    Behold, I will make My words in your
        mouth fire,
    And this people wood,
    And it shall devour them.
15 Behold, I will bring a nation against
        you from afar,
    O house of Israel," says the LORD.
"It *is* a mighty nation,
    It *is* an ancient nation,
    A nation whose language you do not
        know,
    Nor can you understand what they
        say.
16 Their quiver *is* like an open tomb;
    They *are* all mighty men.
17 And they shall eat up your harvest
        and your bread,
    Which your sons and daughters should
        eat.
    They shall eat up your flocks and your
        herds;
    They shall eat up your vines and your
        fig trees;
    They shall destroy your fortified
        cities,
    In which you trust, with the sword.

18"Nevertheless in those days," says the
LORD, "I will not make a complete end of
you. 19And it will be when you say, 'Why
does the LORD our God do all these *things* to
us?' then you shall answer them, 'Just as
you have forsaken Me and served foreign
gods in your land, so you shall serve aliens
in a land *that is* not yours.'

20 "Declare this in the house of Jacob
    And proclaim it in Judah, saying,
21 'Hear this now, O foolish people,
    Without understanding,
    Who have eyes and see not,
    And who have ears and hear not:
22 Do you not fear Me?' says the LORD.
    'Will you not tremble at My presence,
    Who have placed the sand as the
        bound of the sea,
    By a perpetual decree, that it cannot
        pass beyond it?
    And though its waves toss to and fro,
    Yet they cannot prevail;
    Though they roar, yet they cannot
        pass over it.
23 But this people has a defiant and
        rebellious heart;
    They have revolted and departed.
24 They do not say in their heart,
    "Let us now fear the LORD our God,
    Who gives rain, both the former and
        the latter, in its season.
    He reserves for us the appointed weeks
        of the harvest."
25 Your iniquities have turned these
        things away,
    And your sins have withheld good
        from you.

26 'For among My people are found
        wicked *men;*
    They lie in wait as one who sets
        snares;
    They set a trap;
    They catch men.
27 As a cage is full of birds,
    So their houses *are* full of deceit.
    Therefore they have become great and
        grown rich.
28 They have grown fat, they are sleek;
    Yes, they surpass the deeds of the
        wicked;
    They do not plead the cause,
    The cause of the fatherless;
    Yet they prosper,
    And the right of the needy they do not
        defend.
29 Shall I not punish *them* for these
        things?' says the LORD.
    'Shall I not avenge Myself on such a
        nation as this?'

30 "An astonishing and horrible thing
   Has been committed in the land:
31 The prophets prophesy falsely,
   And the priests rule by their *own*
      power;
   And My people love *to have it* so.
   But what will you do in the end?

Impending Destruction from the North

6 "O you children of Benjamin,
   Gather yourselves to flee from the
      midst of Jerusalem!
   Blow the trumpet in Tekoa,
   And set up a signal-fire in Beth
      Haccerem;
   For disaster appears out of the north,
   And great destruction.
2 I have likened the daughter of Zion
   To a lovely and delicate woman.
3 The shepherds with their flocks shall
      come to her.
   They shall pitch *their* tents against her
      all around.
   Each one shall pasture in his own
      place."

4 "Prepare war against her;
   Arise, and let us go up at noon.
   Woe to us, for the day goes away,
   For the shadows of the evening are
      lengthening.
5 Arise, and let us go by night,
   And let us destroy her palaces."

6 For thus has the Lord of hosts said:

   "Cut down trees,
   And build a mound against
      Jerusalem.
   This *is* the city to be punished.
   She *is* full of oppression in her
      midst.
7 As a fountain wells up with water,
   So she wells up with her wickedness.
   Violence and plundering are heard
      in her.
   Before Me continually *are* grief
      and wounds.
8 Be instructed, O Jerusalem,
   Lest My soul depart from you;
   Lest I make you desolate,
   A land not inhabited."

9 Thus says the Lord of hosts:

   "They shall thoroughly glean as a vine
      the remnant of Israel;
   As a grape-gatherer, put your hand
      back into the branches."

10 To whom shall I speak and give
      warning,
   That they may hear?
   Indeed their ear *is* uncircumcised,
   And they cannot give heed.
   Behold, the word of the Lord is a
      reproach to them;
   They have no delight in it.
11 Therefore I am full of the fury of the
      Lord.
   I am weary of holding *it* in.
   "I will pour it out on the children
      outside,
   And on the assembly of young men
      together;
   For even the husband shall be taken
      with the wife,
   The aged with *him who is* full of days.
12 And their houses shall be turned over
      to others,
   Fields and wives together;
   For I will stretch out My hand
   Against the inhabitants of the land,"
      says the Lord.
13 "Because from the least of them even
      to the greatest of them,
   Everyone *is* given to covetousness;
   And from the prophet even to the
      priest,
   Everyone deals falsely.
14 They have also healed the hurt of My
      people slightly,
   Saying, 'Peace, peace!'
   When *there is* no peace.
15 Were they ashamed when they had
      committed abomination?
   No! They were not at all ashamed;
   Nor did they know how to blush.
   Therefore they shall fall among those
      who fall;
   At the time I punish them,
   They shall be cast down," says the
      Lord.

16 Thus says the Lord:

"Stand in the ways and see,
    And ask for the old paths, where the
        good way *is,*
    And walk in it;
Then you will find rest for your souls.
    But they said, 'We will not walk *in it.*'
17 Also, I set watchmen over you, *saying,*
    'Listen to the sound of the trumpet!'
    But they said, 'We will not listen.'
18 Therefore hear, you nations,
    And know, O congregation, what *is*
        among them.
19 Hear, O earth!
    Behold, I will certainly bring calamity
        on this people—
    The fruit of their thoughts,
    Because they have not heeded My
        words
    Nor My law, but rejected it.
20 For what purpose to Me
    Comes frankincense from Sheba,
    And sweet cane from a far country?
    Your burnt offerings *are* not
        acceptable,
    Nor your sacrifices sweet to Me."

21Therefore thus says the LORD:

"Behold, I will lay stumbling blocks
        before this people,
    And the fathers and the sons together
        shall fall on them.
    The neighbor and his friend shall
        perish."

22Thus says the LORD:

"Behold, a people comes from the
        north country,
    And a great nation will be raised from
        the farthest parts of the earth.
23 They will lay hold on bow and spear;
    They *are* cruel and have no mercy;
    Their voice roars like the sea;
    And they ride on horses,
    As men of war set in array against
        you, O daughter of Zion."

24 We have heard the report of it;
    Our hands grow feeble.
    Anguish has taken hold of us,
    Pain as of a woman in labor.

25 Do not go out into the field,
    Nor walk by the way.
    Because of the sword of the enemy,
    Fear *is* on every side.
26 O daughter of my people,
    Dress in sackcloth
    And roll about in ashes!
    Make mourning *as for* an only son,
        most bitter lamentation;
    For the plunderer will suddenly come
        upon us.

27 "I have set you *as* an assayer *and* a
        fortress among My people,
    That you may know and test their way.
28 They *are* all stubborn rebels, walking
        as slanderers.
    They are bronze and iron,
    They *are* all corrupters;
29 The bellows blow fiercely,
    The lead is consumed by the fire;
    The smelter refines in vain,
    For the wicked are not drawn off.
30 *People* will call them rejected silver,
    Because the LORD has rejected them."

Trusting in Lying Words

7 The word that came to Jeremiah from the LORD, saying, 2"Stand in the gate of the LORD's house, and proclaim there this word, and say, 'Hear the word of the LORD, all *you of* Judah who enter in at these gates to worship the LORD!'" 3Thus says the LORD of hosts, the God of Israel: "Amend your ways and your doings, and I will cause you to dwell in this place. 4Do not trust in these lying words, saying, 'The temple of the LORD, the temple of the LORD, the temple of the LORD *are* these.'

5"For if you thoroughly amend your ways and your doings, if you thoroughly execute judgment between a man and his neighbor, 6if you do not oppress the stranger, the fatherless, and the widow, and do not shed innocent blood in this place, or walk after other gods to your hurt, 7then I will cause you to dwell in this place, in the land that I gave to your fathers forever and ever.

8"Behold, you trust in lying words that cannot profit. 9Will you steal, murder, commit adultery, swear falsely, burn incense to

Baal, and walk after other gods whom you do not know, [10]and *then* come and stand before Me in this house which is called by My name, and say, 'We are delivered to do all these abominations'? [11]Has this house, which is called by My name, become a den of thieves in your eyes? Behold, I, even I, have seen *it*," says the LORD.

[12]"But go now to My place which *was* in Shiloh, where I set My name at the first, and see what I did to it because of the wickedness of My people Israel. [13]And now, because you have done all these works," says the LORD, "and I spoke to you, rising up early and speaking, but you did not hear, and I called you, but you did not answer, [14]therefore I will do to the house which is called by My name, in which you trust, and to this place which I gave to you and your fathers, as I have done to Shiloh. [15]And I will cast you out of My sight, as I have cast out all your brethren—the whole posterity of Ephraim.

[16]"Therefore do not pray for this people, nor lift up a cry or prayer for them, nor make intercession to Me; for I will not hear you. [17]Do you not see what they do in the cities of Judah and in the streets of Jerusalem? [18]The children gather wood, the fathers kindle the fire, and the women knead dough, to make cakes for the queen of heaven; and *they* pour out drink offerings to other gods, that they may provoke Me to anger. [19]Do they provoke Me to anger?" says the LORD. "*Do they* not *provoke* themselves, to the shame of their own faces?"

[20]Therefore thus says the Lord GOD: "Behold, My anger and My fury will be poured out on this place—on man and on beast, on the trees of the field and on the fruit of the ground. And it will burn and not be quenched."

[21]Thus says the LORD of hosts, the God of Israel: "Add your burnt offerings to your sacrifices and eat meat. [22]For I did not speak to your fathers, or command them in the day that I brought them out of the land of Egypt, concerning burnt offerings or sacrifices. [23]But this is what I commanded them, saying, 'Obey My voice, and I will be your God, and you shall be My people. And walk in all the ways that I have commanded you, that it may be well with you.' [24]Yet they did not obey or incline their ear, but followed the counsels *and* the dictates of their evil hearts, and went backward and not forward. [25]Since the day that your fathers came out of the land of Egypt until this day, I have even sent to you all My servants the prophets, daily rising up early and sending *them*. [26]Yet they did not obey Me or incline their ear, but stiffened their neck. They did worse than their fathers.

[27]"Therefore you shall speak all these words to them, but they will not obey you. You shall also call to them, but they will not answer you.

Judgment on Obscene Religion

[28]"So you shall say to them, 'This *is* a nation that does not obey the voice of the LORD their God nor receive correction. Truth has perished and has been cut off from their mouth. [29]Cut off your hair and cast *it* away, and take up a lamentation on the desolate heights; for the LORD has rejected and forsaken the generation of His wrath.' [30]For the children of Judah have done evil in My sight," says the LORD. "They have set their abominations in the house which is called by My name, to pollute it. [31]And they have built the high places of Tophet, which *is* in the Valley of the Son of Hinnom, to burn their sons and their daughters in the fire, which I did not command, nor did it come into My heart.

[32]"Therefore behold, the days are coming," says the LORD, "when it will no more be called Tophet, or the Valley of the Son of Hinnom, but the Valley of Slaughter; for they will bury in Tophet until there is no room. [33]The corpses of this people will be food for the birds of the heaven and for the beasts of the earth. And no one will frighten *them away*. [34]Then I will cause to cease from the cities of Judah and from the streets of Jerusalem the voice of mirth and the voice of gladness, the voice of the bridegroom and the voice of the bride. For the land shall be desolate.

8 "At that time," says the LORD, "they shall bring out the bones of the kings of Judah, and the bones of its princes, and the bones of the priests, and the bones of

the prophets, and the bones of the inhabitants of Jerusalem, out of their graves. ²They shall spread them before the sun and the moon and all the host of heaven, which they have loved and which they have served and after which they have walked, which they have sought and which they have worshiped. They shall not be gathered nor buried; they shall be like refuse on the face of the earth. ³Then death shall be chosen rather than life by all the residue of those who remain of this evil family, who remain in all the places where I have driven them," says the LORD of hosts.

The Peril of False Teaching

⁴"Moreover you shall say to them, 'Thus says the LORD:

"Will they fall and not rise?
Will one turn away and not return?
5   Why has this people slidden back,
     Jerusalem, in a perpetual backsliding?
     They hold fast to deceit,
     They refuse to return.
6   I listened and heard,
     But they do not speak aright.
     No man repented of his wickedness,
     Saying, 'What have I done?'
     Everyone turned to his own course,
     As the horse rushes into the battle.

7   "Even the stork in the heavens
     Knows her appointed times;
     And the turtledove, the swift, and the
        swallow
     Observe the time of their coming.
     But My people do not know the
        judgment of the LORD.

8   "How can you say, 'We *are* wise,
     And the law of the LORD *is* with us'?
     Look, the false pen of the scribe
        certainly works falsehood.
9   The wise men are ashamed,
     They are dismayed and taken.
     Behold, they have rejected the word of
        the LORD;
     So what wisdom do they have?
10   Therefore I will give their wives to
        others,

And their fields to those who will
   inherit *them;*
Because from the least even to the
   greatest
Everyone is given to covetousness;
From the prophet even to the priest
Everyone deals falsely.
11   For they have healed the hurt of the
        daughter of My people slightly,
     Saying, 'Peace, peace!'
     When *there is* no peace.
12   Were they ashamed when they had
        committed abomination?
     No! They were not at all ashamed,
     Nor did they know how to blush.
     Therefore they shall fall among those
        who fall;
     In the time of their punishment
     They shall be cast down," says the
        LORD.

13   "I will surely consume them," says the
        LORD.
     "No grapes *shall be* on the vine,
     Nor figs on the fig tree,
     And the leaf shall fade;
     And *the things* I have given them shall
        pass away from them."'"

14   "Why do we sit still?
     Assemble yourselves,
     And let us enter the fortified cities,
     And let us be silent there.
     For the LORD our God has put us to
        silence
     And given us water of gall to drink,
     Because we have sinned against the
        LORD.

15   "*We* looked for peace, but no good *came;*
     And for a time of health, and there
        was trouble!
16   The snorting of His horses was heard
        from Dan.
     The whole land trembled at the sound
        of the neighing of His strong ones;
     For they have come and devoured the
        land and all that is in it,
     The city and those who dwell in it."

17   "For behold, I will send serpents among
        you,

Vipers which cannot be charmed,
And they shall bite you," says the
LORD.

The Prophet Mourns for the People

18 I would comfort myself in sorrow;
My heart *is* faint in me.
19 Listen! The voice,
The cry of the daughter of my people
From a far country:
"*Is* not the LORD in Zion?
Is not her King in her?"

"Why have they provoked Me to anger
With their carved images—
With foreign idols?"

20 "The harvest is past,
The summer is ended,
And we are not saved!"

21 For the hurt of the daughter of my
people I am hurt.
I am mourning;
Astonishment has taken hold of me.
22 *Is there* no balm in Gilead,
Is there no physician there?
Why then is there no recovery
For the health of the daughter of my
people?

9 Oh, that my head were waters,
And my eyes a fountain of tears,
That I might weep day and night
For the slain of the daughter of my
people!
2 Oh, that I had in the wilderness
A lodging place for travelers;
That I might leave my people,
And go from them!
For they *are* all adulterers,
An assembly of treacherous men.

3 "And *like* their bow they have bent
their tongues *for* lies.
They are not valiant for the truth on
the earth.
For they proceed from evil to evil,
And they do not know Me," says the
LORD.
4 "Everyone take heed to his neighbor,
And do not trust any brother;

For every brother will utterly
supplant,
And every neighbor will walk with
slanderers.
5 Everyone will deceive his neighbor,
And will not speak the truth;
They have taught their tongue to
speak lies;
They weary themselves to commit
iniquity.
6 Your dwelling place *is* in the midst of
deceit;
Through deceit they refuse to know
Me," says the LORD.

7Therefore thus says the LORD of hosts:

"Behold, I will refine them and try
them;
For how shall I deal with the daughter
of My people?
8 Their tongue *is* an arrow shot out;
It speaks deceit;
One speaks peaceably to his neighbor
with his mouth,
But in his heart he lies in wait.
9 Shall I not punish them for these
things?" says the LORD.
"Shall I not avenge Myself on such a
nation as this?"

10 I will take up a weeping and wailing
for the mountains,
And for the dwelling places of the
wilderness a lamentation,
Because they are burned up,
So that no one can pass through;
Nor can *men* hear the voice of the
cattle.
Both the birds of the heavens and the
beasts have fled;
They are gone.

11 "I will make Jerusalem a heap of ruins,
a den of jackals.
I will make the cities of Judah
desolate, without an inhabitant."

12Who *is* the wise man who may understand this? And *who is he* to whom the
mouth of the LORD has spoken, that he
may declare it? Why does the land perish

and burn up like a wilderness, so that no one can pass through?

¹³And the LORD said, "Because they have forsaken My law which I set before them, and have not obeyed My voice, nor walked according to it, ¹⁴but they have walked according to the dictates of their own hearts and after the Baals, which their fathers taught them," ¹⁵therefore thus says the LORD of hosts, the God of Israel: "Behold, I will feed them, this people, with wormwood, and give them water of gall to drink. ¹⁶I will scatter them also among the Gentiles, whom neither they nor their fathers have known. And I will send a sword after them until I have consumed them."

The People Mourn in Judgment

¹⁷Thus says the LORD of hosts:

"Consider and call for the mourning women,
   That they may come;
And send for skillful *wailing* women,
   That they may come.
¹⁸ Let them make haste
   And take up a wailing for us,
   That our eyes may run with tears,
   And our eyelids gush with water.
¹⁹ For a voice of wailing is heard from Zion:
   'How we are plundered!
   We are greatly ashamed,
   Because we have forsaken the land,
   Because we have been cast out of our dwellings.' "

²⁰ Yet hear the word of the LORD,
      O women,
   And let your ear receive the word of His mouth;
   Teach your daughters wailing,
   And everyone her neighbor a lamentation.
²¹ For death has come through our windows,
   Has entered our palaces,
   To kill off the children—*no longer to be* outside!
   And the young men—*no longer* on the streets!

²² Speak, "Thus says the LORD:

'Even the carcasses of men shall fall as refuse on the open field,
   Like cuttings after the harvester,
   And no one shall gather *them.*' "

²³Thus says the LORD:

"Let not the wise *man* glory in his wisdom,
   Let not the mighty *man* glory in his might,
   Nor let the rich *man* glory in his riches;
²⁴ But let him who glories glory in this,
   That he understands and knows Me,
   That I *am* the LORD, exercising lovingkindness, judgment, and righteousness in the earth.
   For in these I delight," says the LORD.

²⁵"Behold, the days are coming," says the LORD, "that I will punish all *who are* circumcised with the uncircumcised— ²⁶Egypt, Judah, Edom, the people of Ammon, Moab, and all *who are* in the farthest corners, who dwell in the wilderness. For all *these* nations *are* uncircumcised, and all the house of Israel *are* uncircumcised in the heart."

Idols and the True God

10 Hear the word which the LORD speaks to you, O house of Israel. ²Thus says the LORD:

"Do not learn the way of the Gentiles;
Do not be dismayed at the signs of heaven,
For the Gentiles are dismayed at them.
³ For the customs of the peoples *are* futile;
For *one* cuts a tree from the forest,
The work of the hands of the workman, with the ax.
⁴ They decorate it with silver and gold;
They fasten it with nails and hammers
So that it will not topple.
⁵ They *are* upright, like a palm tree,
And they cannot speak;
They must be carried,

Because they cannot go *by themselves.*
Do not be afraid of them,
For they cannot do evil,
Nor can they do any good."

6 Inasmuch as *there is* none like You,
O LORD
(You *are* great, and Your name *is* great
in might),
7 Who would not fear You, O King of
the nations?
For this is Your rightful due.
For among all the wise *men* of the
nations,
And in all their kingdoms,
There is none like You.
8 But they are altogether dull-hearted
and foolish;
A wooden idol *is* a worthless doctrine.
9 Silver is beaten into plates;
It is brought from Tarshish,
And gold from Uphaz,
The work of the craftsman
And of the hands of the metalsmith;
Blue and purple *are* their clothing;
They *are* all the work of skillful *men.*
10 But the LORD *is* the true God;
He *is* the living God and the
everlasting King.
At His wrath the earth will tremble,
And the nations will not be able to
endure His indignation.

11 Thus you shall say to them: "The gods
that have not made the heavens and the
earth shall perish from the earth and from
under these heavens."

12 He has made the earth by His
power,
He has established the world by His
wisdom,
And has stretched out the heavens at
His discretion.
13 When He utters His voice,
There is a multitude of waters in the
heavens:
"And He causes the vapors to ascend
from the ends of the earth.
He makes lightning for the rain,
He brings the wind out of His
treasuries."[a]

14 Everyone is dull-hearted, without
knowledge;
Every metalsmith is put to shame by
an image;
For his molded image *is* falsehood,
And *there is* no breath in them.
15 They *are* futile, a work of errors;
In the time of their punishment they
shall perish.
16 The Portion of Jacob *is* not like them,
For He *is* the Maker of all *things,*
And Israel *is* the tribe of His
inheritance;
The LORD of hosts *is* His name.

The Coming Captivity of Judah

17 Gather up your wares from the land,
O inhabitant of the fortress!

18 For thus says the LORD:

"Behold, I will throw out at this time
The inhabitants of the land,
And will distress them,
That they may find *it* so."

19 Woe is me for my hurt!
My wound is severe.
But I say, "Truly this *is* an infirmity,
And I must bear it."
20 My tent is plundered,
And all my cords are broken;
My children have gone from me,
And they *are* no more.
There is no one to pitch my tent
anymore,
Or set up my curtains.

21 For the shepherds have become
dull-hearted,
And have not sought the LORD;
Therefore they shall not prosper,
And all their flocks shall be scattered.
22 Behold, the noise of the report has
come,
And a great commotion out of the
north country,
To make the cities of Judah desolate, a
den of jackals.

10:13 [a] Psalm 135:7

23 O LORD, I know the way of man *is* not
   in himself;
   It is not in man who walks to direct
   his own steps.
24 O LORD, correct me, but with justice;
   Not in Your anger, lest You bring me
   to nothing.
25 Pour out Your fury on the Gentiles,
   who do not know You,
   And on the families who do not call
   on Your name;
   For they have eaten up Jacob,
   Devoured him and consumed him,
   And made his dwelling place desolate.

The Broken Covenant

11 The word that came to Jeremiah from
the LORD, saying, 2"Hear the words of
this covenant, and speak to the men of
Judah and to the inhabitants of Jerusalem;
3and say to them, 'Thus says the LORD God
of Israel: "Cursed *is* the man who does not
obey the words of this covenant 4which I
commanded your fathers in the day I
brought them out of the land of Egypt,
from the iron furnace, saying, 'Obey My
voice, and do according to all that I command you; so shall you be My people, and
I will be your God,' 5that I may establish
the oath which I have sworn to your
fathers, to give them 'a land flowing with
milk and honey,'ᵃ as *it is* this day." ' "

And I answered and said, "So be it,
LORD."

6Then the LORD said to me, "Proclaim all
these words in the cities of Judah and in
the streets of Jerusalem, saying: 'Hear the
words of this covenant and do them. 7For I
earnestly exhorted your fathers in the day
I brought them up out of the land of Egypt,
until this day, rising early and exhorting,
saying, "Obey My voice." 8Yet they did not
obey or incline their ear, but everyone followed the dictates of his evil heart; therefore I will bring upon them all the words of
this covenant, which I commanded *them* to
do, but *which* they have not done.' "

9And the LORD said to me, "A conspiracy
has been found among the men of Judah
and among the inhabitants of Jerusalem.
10They have turned back to the iniquities of
their forefathers who refused to hear My

words, and they have gone after other gods
to serve them; the house of Israel and the
house of Judah have broken My covenant
which I made with their fathers."

11Therefore thus says the LORD: "Behold,
I will surely bring calamity on them which
they will not be able to escape; and though
they cry out to Me, I will not listen to them.
12Then the cities of Judah and the inhabitants of Jerusalem will go and cry out to
the gods to whom they offer incense, but
they will not save them at all in the time of
their trouble. 13For *according to* the number
of your cities were your gods, O Judah; and
according to the number of the streets of
Jerusalem you have set up altars to *that*
shameful thing, altars to burn incense to
Baal.

14"So do not pray for this people, or lift
up a cry or prayer for them; for I will not
hear *them* in the time that they cry out to
Me because of their trouble.

15 "What has My beloved to do in My
      house,
    Having done lewd deeds with many?
    And the holy flesh has passed from
      you.
    When you do evil, then you rejoice.
16   The LORD called your name,
    Green Olive Tree, Lovely *and* of Good
      Fruit.
    With the noise of a great tumult
    He has kindled fire on it,
    And its branches are broken.

17"For the LORD of hosts, who planted
you, has pronounced doom against you
for the evil of the house of Israel and of the
house of Judah, which they have done
against themselves to provoke Me to anger
in offering incense to Baal."

Jeremiah's Life Threatened

18Now the LORD gave me knowledge *of it,*
and I know *it;* for You showed me their
doings. 19But I *was* like a docile lamb
brought to the slaughter; and I did not
know that they had devised schemes
against me, *saying,* "Let us destroy the tree

11:5 ᵃExodus 3:8

with its fruit, and let us cut him off from the land of the living, that his name may be remembered no more."

20   But, O LORD of hosts,
      You who judge righteously,
      Testing the mind and the heart,
      Let me see Your vengeance on them,
      For to You I have revealed my cause.

21 "Therefore thus says the LORD concerning the men of Anathoth who seek your life, saying, 'Do not prophesy in the name of the LORD, lest you die by our hand'— 22therefore thus says the LORD of hosts: 'Behold, I will punish them. The young men shall die by the sword, their sons and their daughters shall die by famine; 23and there shall be no remnant of them, for I will bring catastrophe on the men of Anathoth, *even* the year of their punishment.'"

Jeremiah's Question

12 Righteous *are* You, O LORD, when I plead with You;
      Yet let me talk with You about *Your* judgments.
      Why does the way of the wicked prosper?
      Why are those happy who deal so treacherously?
2   You have planted them, yes, they have taken root;
      They grow, yes, they bear fruit.
      You *are* near in their mouth
      But far from their mind.

3   But You, O LORD, know me;
      You have seen me,
      And You have tested my heart toward You.
      Pull them out like sheep for the slaughter,
      And prepare them for the day of slaughter.
4   How long will the land mourn,
      And the herbs of every field wither?
      The beasts and birds are consumed,
      For the wickedness of those who dwell there,
      Because they said, "He will not see our final end."

The LORD Answers Jeremiah

5   "If you have run with the footmen, and they have wearied you,
      Then how can you contend with horses?
      And *if* in the land of peace,
      In which you trusted, *they wearied you*,
      Then how will you do in the floodplaina of the Jordan?
6   For even your brothers, the house of your father,
      Even they have dealt treacherously with you;
      Yes, they have called a multitude after you.
      Do not believe them,
      Even though they speak smooth words to you.

7   "I have forsaken My house, I have left My heritage;
      I have given the dearly beloved of My soul into the hand of her enemies.
8   My heritage is to Me like a lion in the forest;
      It cries out against Me;
      Therefore I have hated it.
9   My heritage *is* to Me *like* a speckled vulture;
      The vultures all around *are* against her.
      Come, assemble all the beasts of the field,
      Bring them to devour!

10   "Many rulersa have destroyed My vineyard,
      They have trodden My portion underfoot;
      They have made My pleasant portion a desolate wilderness.
11   They have made it desolate;
      Desolate, it mourns to Me;
      The whole land is made desolate,
      Because no one takes *it* to heart.
12   The plunderers have come
      On all the desolate heights in the wilderness,

12:5 aOr *thicket*   **12:10** aLiterally *shepherds* or *pastors*

For the sword of the Lord shall devour
From *one* end of the land to the *other*
   end of the land;
No flesh shall have peace.
13 They have sown wheat but reaped
       thorns;
They have put themselves to pain *but*
   do not profit.
But be ashamed of your harvest
Because of the fierce anger of the
   Lord."

14Thus says the Lord: "Against all My evil neighbors who touch the inheritance which I have caused My people Israel to inherit—behold, I will pluck them out of their land and pluck out the house of Judah from among them. 15Then it shall be, after I have plucked them out, that I will return and have compassion on them and bring them back, everyone to his heritage and everyone to his land. 16And it shall be, if they will learn carefully the ways of My people, to swear by My name, 'As the Lord lives,' as they taught My people to swear by Baal, then they shall be established in the midst of My people. 17But if they do not obey, I will utterly pluck up and destroy that nation," says the Lord.

Symbol of the Linen Sash

13 Thus the Lord said to me: "Go and get yourself a linen sash, and put it around your waist, but do not put it in water." 2So I got a sash according to the word of the Lord, and put *it* around my waist.

3And the word of the Lord came to me the second time, saying, 4"Take the sash that you acquired, which *is* around your waist, and arise, go to the Euphrates,a and hide it there in a hole in the rock." 5So I went and hid it by the Euphrates, as the Lord commanded me.

6Now it came to pass after many days that the Lord said to me, "Arise, go to the Euphrates, and take from there the sash which I commanded you to hide there." 7Then I went to the Euphrates and dug, and I took the sash from the place where I had hidden it; and there was the sash, ruined. It was profitable for nothing.

8Then the word of the Lord came to me, saying, 9"Thus says the Lord: 'In this manner I will ruin the pride of Judah and the great pride of Jerusalem. 10This evil people, who refuse to hear My words, who follow the dictates of their hearts, and walk after other gods to serve them and worship them, shall be just like this sash which is profitable for nothing. 11For as the sash clings to the waist of a man, so I have caused the whole house of Israel and the whole house of Judah to cling to Me,' says the Lord, 'that they may become My people, for renown, for praise, and for glory; but they would not hear.'

Symbol of the Wine Bottles

12"Therefore you shall speak to them this word: 'Thus says the Lord God of Israel: "Every bottle shall be filled with wine."'

"And they will say to you, 'Do we not certainly know that every bottle will be filled with wine?'

13"Then you shall say to them, 'Thus says the Lord: "Behold, I will fill all the inhabitants of this land—even the kings who sit on David's throne, the priests, the prophets, and all the inhabitants of Jerusalem—with drunkenness! 14And I will dash them one against another, even the fathers and the sons together," says the Lord. "I will not pity nor spare nor have mercy, but will destroy them."'"

Pride Precedes Captivity

15   Hear and give ear:
       Do not be proud,
       For the Lord has spoken.
16   Give glory to the Lord your God
       Before He causes darkness,
       And before your feet stumble
       On the dark mountains,
       And while you are looking for light,
       He turns it into the shadow of death
       And makes *it* dense darkness.
17   But if you will not hear it,
       My soul will weep in secret for *your*
          pride;
       My eyes will weep bitterly
       And run down with tears,

13:4 aHebrew *Perath*

WHY THE WALL OF SEPARATION?

THOMAS JEFFERSON

When the Founding Fathers fashioned the First Amendment to the Constitution, they began with these forceful words: "Congress shall make no law respecting an establishment of religion, or prohibiting the free exercise thereof." For over one hundred and fifty years, this mandate was understood to prohibit the establishment of a national religion by Congress or the preference of one religion over another, or religion over non-religion. Clearly, while limiting the federal government from exercising any authority in matters of religion, there was no hint that it was meant to exclude people of faith or their values from impacting, participating in, or shaping government.

But in 1947, the *Everson v. Board of Education* decision took up Thomas Jefferson's "wall of church and state" metaphor, which is not in the Constitution and was not even in discussions leading up to the Constitution. It was written in a letter 13 years after the constitution, and announced: "The First Amendment has erected a wall between church and state. That wall must be kept high and impregnable. We could not approve the slightest breach."

What has followed from decisions rendered by the Supreme Court on down through many lower courts is the highly successful silencing of religion. Those decisions have declared verbal prayer offered in a school as unconstitutional, restricted religious speech in schools, removed the Ten Commandments from schools and public buildings, proclaimed that the display of a nativity scene on public property is unconstitutional unless surrounded by sufficient secular displays to prevent it from appearing religious—the list goes on and on.

Soon after the *Emerson* decision, another wall was erected against religious freedom. Prior to 1954 and the revision of the IRS tax code, religious groups and other nonprofits could oppose or support political candidates without risking their nonprofit status. The revision changed that, stating that all 501 (c)(3)s (nonprofits) are tax exempt and are therefore prohibited from endorsing or opposing candidates running for public office. The IRS says clergy speaking in an official capacity also should not indirectly imply who they endorse or oppose.

Since 1947, the religious freedom established by the Founders has undergone and continues to undergo serious erosion in America. The riches and wisdom of faith are no longer welcome in the public square. It is time for a new generation to pray and take action in reestablishing the primacy of faith in every level of American life and maintaining America as "one nation, under God."

Because the LORD's flock has been
     taken captive.

18 Say to the king and to the queen
     mother,
"Humble yourselves;
Sit down,
For your rule shall collapse, the crown
     of your glory."
19 The cities of the South shall be shut
     up,
And no one shall open *them;*
Judah shall be carried away captive,
     all of it;
It shall be wholly carried away captive.

20 Lift up your eyes and see
Those who come from the north.
Where *is* the flock *that* was given to
     you,
Your beautiful sheep?
21 What will you say when He punishes
     you?
For you have taught them
To be chieftains, to be head over you.
Will not pangs seize you,
Like a woman in labor?
22 And if you say in your heart,
"Why have these things come upon
     me?"
For the greatness of your iniquity
Your skirts have been uncovered,
Your heels made bare.
23 Can the Ethiopian change his skin or
     the leopard its spots?
Then may you also do good who are
     accustomed to do evil.

24 "Therefore I will scatter them like
     stubble
That passes away by the wind of the
     wilderness.
25 This is your lot,
The portion of your measures from
     Me," says the LORD,
"Because you have forgotten Me
And trusted in falsehood.
26 Therefore I will uncover your skirts
     over your face,
That your shame may appear.
27 I have seen your adulteries
And your *lustful* neighings,

The lewdness of your harlotry,
Your abominations on the hills in the
     fields.
Woe to you, O Jerusalem!
Will you still not be made clean?"

Sword, Famine, and Pestilence

14 The word of the LORD that came to
     Jeremiah concerning the droughts.

2 "Judah mourns,
And her gates languish;
They mourn for the land,
And the cry of Jerusalem has gone up.
3 Their nobles have sent their lads for
     water;
They went to the cisterns *and* found
     no water.
They returned with their vessels
     empty;
They were ashamed and confounded
And covered their heads.
4 Because the ground is parched,
For there was no rain in the land,
The plowmen were ashamed;
They covered their heads.
5 Yes, the deer also gave birth in the
     field,
But left because there was no grass.
6 And the wild donkeys stood in the
     desolate heights;
They sniffed at the wind like jackals;
Their eyes failed because *there was* no
     grass."

7 O LORD, though our iniquities testify
     against us,
Do it for Your name's sake;
For our backslidings are many,
We have sinned against You.
8 O the Hope of Israel, his Savior in
     time of trouble,
Why should You be like a stranger in
     the land,
And like a traveler *who* turns aside to
     tarry for a night?
9 Why should You be like a man
     astonished,
Like a mighty one *who* cannot save?
Yet You, O LORD, *are* in our midst,
And we are called by Your name;
Do not leave us!

¹⁰Thus says the Lord to this people:

"Thus they have loved to wander;
  They have not restrained their feet.
Therefore the Lord does not accept
  them;
He will remember their iniquity now,
  And punish their sins."

¹¹Then the Lord said to me, "Do not pray for this people, for *their* good. ¹²When they fast, I will not hear their cry; and when they offer burnt offering and grain offering, I will not accept them. But I will consume them by the sword, by the famine, and by the pestilence."

¹³Then I said, "Ah, Lord God! Behold, the prophets say to them, 'You shall not see the sword, nor shall you have famine, but I will give you assured peace in this place.'"

¹⁴And the Lord said to me, "The prophets prophesy lies in My name. I have not sent them, commanded them, nor spoken to them; they prophesy to you a false vision, divination, a worthless thing, and the deceit of their heart. ¹⁵Therefore thus says the Lord concerning the prophets who prophesy in My name, whom I did not send, and who say, 'Sword and famine shall not be in this land'—'By sword and famine those prophets shall be consumed! ¹⁶And the people to whom they prophesy shall be cast out in the streets of Jerusalem because of the famine and the sword; they will have no one to bury them—them nor their wives, their sons nor their daughters—for I will pour their wickedness on them.'

¹⁷"Therefore you shall say this word to them:

'Let my eyes flow with tears night and
  day,
And let them not cease;
For the virgin daughter of my people
Has been broken with a mighty stroke,
  with a very severe blow.
18 If I go out to the field,
Then behold, those slain with the
  sword!
And if I enter the city,
Then behold, those sick from
  famine!

Yes, both prophet and priest go about
  in a land they do not know.'"

The People Plead for Mercy

19 Have You utterly rejected Judah?
    Has Your soul loathed Zion?
    Why have You stricken us so that *there
      is* no healing for us?
    We looked for peace, but *there was* no
      good;
    And for the time of healing, and there
      was trouble.
20 We acknowledge, O Lord, our
      wickedness
    And the iniquity of our fathers,
    For we have sinned against You.
21 Do not abhor *us,* for Your name's sake;
    Do not disgrace the throne of Your
      glory.
    Remember, do not break Your
      covenant with us.
22 Are there any among the idols of the
      nations that can cause rain?
    Or can the heavens give showers?
    Are You not He, O Lord our God?
    Therefore we will wait for You,
    Since You have made all these.

The Lord Will Not Relent

15 Then the Lord said to me, "*Even* if Moses and Samuel stood before Me, My mind *would* not *be* favorable toward this people. Cast *them* out of My sight, and let them go forth. ²And it shall be, if they say to you, 'Where should we go?' then you shall tell them, 'Thus says the Lord:

"Such as *are* for death, to death;
  And such as *are* for the sword, to the
    sword;
  And such as *are* for the famine, to the
    famine;
  And such as *are* for the captivity, to
    the captivity."'

³"And I will appoint over them four forms *of destruction,*" says the Lord: "the sword to slay, the dogs to drag, the birds of the heavens and the beasts of the earth to devour and destroy. ⁴I will hand them over to trouble, to all kingdoms of the earth, because of Manasseh the son of Hezekiah,

king of Judah, for what he did in Jerusalem.

5 "For who will have pity on you,
  O Jerusalem?
  Or who will bemoan you?
  Or who will turn aside to ask how you
  are doing?
6 You have forsaken Me," says the LORD,
  "You have gone backward.
  Therefore I will stretch out My hand
  against you and destroy you;
  I am weary of relenting!
7 And I will winnow them with a
  winnowing fan in the gates of the
  land;
  I will bereave *them* of children;
  I will destroy My people,
  Since they do not return from their
  ways.
8 Their widows will be increased to Me
  more than the sand of the seas;
  I will bring against them,
  Against the mother of the young men,
  A plunderer at noonday;
  I will cause anguish and terror to fall
  on them suddenly.

9 "She languishes who has borne seven;
  She has breathed her last;
  Her sun has gone down
  While *it was* yet day;
  She has been ashamed and
  confounded.
  And the remnant of them I will
  deliver to the sword
  Before their enemies," says the LORD.

Jeremiah's Dejection

10 Woe is me, my mother,
   That you have borne me,
   A man of strife and a man of
   contention to the whole earth!
   I have neither lent for interest,
   Nor have men lent to me for
   interest.
   Every one of them curses me.

11The LORD said:

"Surely it will be well with your
  remnant;

Surely I will cause the enemy to
  intercede with you
In the time of adversity and in the
  time of affliction.
12 Can anyone break iron,
   The northern iron and the bronze?
13 Your wealth and your treasures
   I will give as plunder without price,
   Because of all your sins,
   Throughout your territories.
14 And I will make *you* cross over with[a]
   your enemies
   Into a land *which* you do not know;
   For a fire is kindled in My anger,
   Which shall burn upon you."

15 O LORD, You know;
   Remember me and visit me,
   And take vengeance for me on my
   persecutors.
   In Your enduring patience, do not take
   me away.
   Know that for Your sake I have
   suffered rebuke.
16 Your words were found, and I ate
   them,
   And Your word was to me the joy and
   rejoicing of my heart;
   For I am called by Your name,
   O LORD God of hosts.
17 I did not sit in the assembly of the
   mockers,
   Nor did I rejoice;
   I sat alone because of Your hand,
   For You have filled me with
   indignation.
18 Why is my pain perpetual
   And my wound incurable,
   Which refuses to be healed?
   Will You surely be to me like an
   unreliable stream,
   As waters *that* fail?

The LORD Reassures Jeremiah

19Therefore thus says the LORD:

"If you return,
  Then I will bring you back;

15:14 [a]Following Masoretic Text and Vulgate;
Septuagint, Syriac, and Targum read *cause you to serve*
(compare 17:4).

You shall stand before Me;
If you take out the precious from the
    vile,
You shall be as My mouth.
Let them return to you,
But you must not return to them.
20 And I will make you to this people a
    fortified bronze wall;
And they will fight against you,
But they shall not prevail against you;
For I *am* with you to save you
And deliver you," says the LORD.
21 "I will deliver you from the hand of the
    wicked,
And I will redeem you from the grip of
    the terrible."

Jeremiah's Life-Style and Message

16 The word of the LORD also came to me, saying, 2"You shall not take a wife, nor shall you have sons or daughters in this place." 3For thus says the LORD concerning the sons and daughters who are born in this place, and concerning their mothers who bore them and their fathers who begot them in this land: 4"They shall die gruesome deaths; they shall not be lamented nor shall they be buried, *but* they shall be like refuse on the face of the earth. They shall be consumed by the sword and by famine, and their corpses shall be meat for the birds of heaven and for the beasts of the earth."

5For thus says the LORD: "Do not enter the house of mourning, nor go to lament or bemoan them; for I have taken away My peace from this people," says the LORD, "lovingkindness and mercies. 6Both the great and the small shall die in this land. They shall not be buried; neither shall men lament for them, cut themselves, nor make themselves bald for them. 7Nor shall *men* break *bread* in mourning for them, to comfort them for the dead; nor shall *men* give them the cup of consolation to drink for their father or their mother. 8Also you shall not go into the house of feasting to sit with them, to eat and drink."

9For thus says the LORD of hosts, the God of Israel: "Behold, I will cause to cease from this place, before your eyes and in your days, the voice of mirth and the voice of gladness, the voice of the bridegroom and the voice of the bride.

10"And it shall be, when you show this people all these words, and they say to you, 'Why has the LORD pronounced all this great disaster against us? Or what *is* our iniquity? Or what *is* our sin that we have committed against the LORD our God?' 11then you shall say to them, 'Because your fathers have forsaken Me,' says the LORD; 'they have walked after other gods and have served them and worshiped them, and have forsaken Me and not kept My law. 12And you have done worse than your fathers, for behold, each one follows the dictates of his own evil heart, so that no one listens to Me. 13Therefore I will cast you out of this land into a land that you do not know, neither you nor your fathers; and there you shall serve other gods day and night, where I will not show you favor.'

God Will Restore Israel

14"Therefore behold, the days are coming," says the LORD, "that it shall no more be said, 'The LORD lives who brought up the children of Israel from the land of Egypt,' 15but, 'The LORD lives who brought up the children of Israel from the land of the north and from all the lands where He had driven them.' For I will bring them back into their land which I gave to their fathers.

16"Behold, I will send for many fishermen," says the LORD, "and they shall fish them; and afterward I will send for many hunters, and they shall hunt them from every mountain and every hill, and out of the holes of the rocks. 17For My eyes *are* on all their ways; they are not hidden from My face, nor is their iniquity hidden from My eyes. 18And first I will repay double for their iniquity and their sin, because they have defiled My land; they have filled My inheritance with the carcasses of their detestable and abominable idols."

19 O LORD, my strength and my fortress,
My refuge in the day of affliction,
The Gentiles shall come to You
From the ends of the earth and say,

"Surely our fathers have inherited lies,
Worthlessness and unprofitable
things."

20 Will a man make gods for himself,
Which *are* not gods?

21 "Therefore behold, I will this once
cause them to know,
I will cause them to know
My hand and My might;
And they shall know that My name *is*
the LORD.

Judah's Sin and Punishment

17 "The sin of Judah *is* written with
a pen of iron;
With the point of a diamond *it is*
engraved
On the tablet of their heart,
And on the horns of your altars,

2 While their children remember
Their altars and their wooden images[a]
By the green trees on the high hills.

3 O My mountain in the field,
I will give as plunder your wealth, all
your treasures,
And your high places of sin within all
your borders.

4 And you, even yourself,
Shall let go of your heritage which I
gave you;
And I will cause you to serve your
enemies
In the land which you do not know;
For you have kindled a fire in My
anger *which* shall burn forever."

5 Thus says the LORD:

"Cursed *is* the man who trusts in man
And makes flesh his strength,
Whose heart departs from the LORD.

6 For he shall be like a shrub in the
desert,
And shall not see when good comes,
But shall inhabit the parched places
in the wilderness,
In a salt land *which is* not inhabited.

7 "Blessed *is* the man who trusts in the
LORD,
And whose hope is the LORD.

8 For he shall be like a tree planted by
the waters,
Which spreads out its roots by the
river,
And will not fear[a] when heat comes;
But its leaf will be green,
And will not be anxious in the year of
drought,
Nor will cease from yielding fruit.

9 "The heart *is* deceitful above all *things,*
And desperately wicked;
Who can know it?

10 I, the LORD, search the heart,
I test the mind,
Even to give every man according to
his ways,
According to the fruit of his doings.

11 "*As* a partridge that broods but does
not hatch,
So is he who gets riches, but not by
right;
It will leave him in the midst of his
days,
And at his end he will be a fool."

HOPE
"O LORD, the hope of Israel. . . ."
JEREMIAH 17:13

In God We Hope
On the Seal of the State of Rhode Island, over the picture of an anchor, is inscribed the motto:

IN GOD WE HOPE

12 A glorious high throne from the
beginning
Is the place of our sanctuary.

13 O LORD, the hope of Israel,
All who forsake You shall be ashamed.

"Those who depart from Me
Shall be written in the earth,
Because they have forsaken the LORD,
The fountain of living waters."

17:2 [a]Hebrew *Asherim,* Canaanite deities
17:8 [a]Qere and Targum read *see.*

Jeremiah Prays for Deliverance

14 Heal me, O LORD, and I shall be
       healed;
   Save me, and I shall be saved,
   For You *are* my praise.
15 Indeed they say to me,
   "Where *is* the word of the LORD?
   Let it come now!"
16 As for me, I have not hurried away
       from *being* a shepherd *who* follows
       You,
   Nor have I desired the woeful day;
   You know what came out of my lips;
   It was right there before You.
17 Do not be a terror to me;
   You *are* my hope in the day of doom.
18 Let them be ashamed who persecute
       me,
   But do not let me be put to shame;
   Let them be dismayed,
   But do not let me be dismayed.
   Bring on them the day of doom,
   And destroy them with double
       destruction!

Hallow the Sabbath Day

19Thus the LORD said to me: "Go and stand in the gate of the children of the people, by which the kings of Judah come in and by which they go out, and in all the gates of Jerusalem; 20and say to them, 'Hear the word of the LORD, you kings of Judah, and all Judah, and all the inhabitants of Jerusalem, who enter by these gates. 21Thus says the LORD: "Take heed to yourselves, and bear no burden on the Sabbath day, nor bring *it* in by the gates of Jerusalem; 22nor carry a burden out of your houses on the Sabbath day, nor do any work, but hallow the Sabbath day, as I commanded your fathers. 23But they did not obey nor incline their ear, but made their neck stiff, that they might not hear nor receive instruction.

24"And it shall be, if you heed Me carefully," says the LORD, "to bring no burden through the gates of this city on the Sabbath day, but hallow the Sabbath day, to do no work in it, 25then shall enter the gates of this city kings and princes sitting on the throne of David, riding in chariots and on horses, they and their princes, accompanied by the men of Judah and the inhabitants of Jerusalem; and this city shall remain forever. 26And they shall come from the cities of Judah and from the places around Jerusalem, from the land of Benjamin and from the lowland, from the mountains and from the South, bringing burnt offerings and sacrifices, grain offerings and incense, bringing sacrifices of praise to the house of the LORD. 27"But if you will not heed Me to hallow the Sabbath day, such as not carrying a burden when entering the gates of Jerusalem on the Sabbath day, then I will kindle a fire in its gates, and it shall devour the palaces of Jerusalem, and it shall not be quenched." ' "

The Potter and the Clay

18 The word which came to Jeremiah from the LORD, saying: 2"Arise and go down to the potter's house, and there I will cause you to hear My words." 3Then I went down to the potter's house, and there he was, making something at the wheel. 4And the vessel that he made of clay was marred in the hand of the potter; so he made it again into another vessel, as it seemed good to the potter to make.

5Then the word of the LORD came to me, saying: 6"O house of Israel, can I not do with you as this potter?" says the LORD. "Look, as the clay *is* in the potter's hand, so *are* you in My hand, O house of Israel! 7The instant I speak concerning a nation and concerning a kingdom, to pluck up, to pull down, and to destroy *it,* 8if that nation against whom I have spoken turns from its evil, I will relent of the disaster that I thought to bring upon it. 9And the instant I speak concerning a nation and concerning a kingdom, to build and to plant *it,* 10if it does evil in My sight so that it does not obey My voice, then I will relent concerning the good with which I said I would benefit it.

11"Now therefore, speak to the men of Judah and to the inhabitants of Jerusalem, saying, 'Thus says the LORD: "Behold, I am fashioning a disaster and devising a plan against you. Return now every one from

his evil way, and make your ways and your doings good." ' "

God's Warning Rejected

¹²And they said, "That is hopeless! So we will walk according to our own plans, and we will every one obey the dictates of his evil heart."

¹³Therefore thus says the Lord:

"Ask now among the Gentiles,
Who has heard such things?
The virgin of Israel has done a very
horrible thing.
¹⁴ Will *a man* leave the snow water of
Lebanon,
Which comes from the rock of the
field?
Will the cold flowing waters be
forsaken for strange waters?

¹⁵ "Because My people have forgotten Me,
They have burned incense to worthless
idols.
And they have caused themselves to
stumble in their ways,
From the ancient paths,
To walk in pathways and not on a
highway,
¹⁶ To make their land desolate *and* a
perpetual hissing;
Everyone who passes by it will be
astonished
And shake his head.
¹⁷ I will scatter them as with an east
wind before the enemy;
I will show themᵃ the back and not
the face
In the day of their calamity."

Jeremiah Persecuted

¹⁸Then they said, "Come and let us devise plans against Jeremiah; for the law shall not perish from the priest, nor counsel from the wise, nor the word from the prophet. Come and let us attack him with the tongue, and let us not give heed to any of his words."

¹⁹ Give heed to me, O Lord,
And listen to the voice of those who
contend with me!

²⁰ Shall evil be repaid for good?
For they have dug a pit for my life.
Remember that I stood before You
To speak good for them,
To turn away Your wrath from
them.
²¹ Therefore deliver up their children to
the famine,
And pour out their *blood*
By the force of the sword;
Let their wives *become* widows
And bereaved of their children.
Let their men be put to death,
Their young men *be* slain
By the sword in battle.
²² Let a cry be heard from their houses,
When You bring a troop suddenly
upon them;
For they have dug a pit to take me,
And hidden snares for my feet.
²³ Yet, Lord, You know all their counsel
Which is against me, to slay *me*.
Provide no atonement for their
iniquity,
Nor blot out their sin from Your
sight;
But let them be overthrown before
You.
Deal *thus* with them
In the time of Your anger.

The Sign of the Broken Flask

19Thus says the Lord: "Go and get a potter's earthen flask, and *take* some of the elders of the people and some of the elders of the priests. ²And go out to the Valley of the Son of Hinnom, which *is* by the entry of the Potsherd Gate; and proclaim there the words that I will tell you, ³and say, 'Hear the word of the Lord, O kings of Judah and inhabitants of Jerusalem. Thus says the Lord of hosts, the God of Israel: "Behold, I will bring such a catastrophe on this place, that whoever hears of it, his ears will tingle.

⁴"Because they have forsaken Me and made this an alien place, because they have burned incense in it to other gods whom neither they, their fathers, nor the

---

18:17 ᵃFollowing Septuagint, Syriac, Targum, and Vulgate; Masoretic Text reads *look them in.*

kings of Judah have known, and have filled this place with the blood of the innocents ⁵(they have also built the high places of Baal, to burn their sons with fire *for* burnt offerings to Baal, which I did not command or speak, nor did it come into My mind), ⁶therefore behold, the days are coming," says the LORD, "that this place shall no more be called Tophet or the Valley of the Son of Hinnom, but the Valley of Slaughter. ⁷And I will make void the counsel of Judah and Jerusalem in this place, and I will cause them to fall by the sword before their enemies and by the hands of those who seek their lives; their corpses I will give as meat for the birds of the heaven and for the beasts of the earth. ⁸I will make this city desolate and a hissing; everyone who passes by it will be astonished and hiss because of all its plagues. ⁹And I will cause them to eat the flesh of their sons and the flesh of their daughters, and everyone shall eat the flesh of his friend in the siege and in the desperation with which their enemies and those who seek their lives shall drive them to despair.' '

¹⁰"Then you shall break the flask in the sight of the men who go with you, ¹¹and say to them, 'Thus says the LORD of hosts: "Even so I will break this people and this city, as *one* breaks a potter's vessel, which cannot be made whole again; and they shall bury *them* in Tophet till *there is* no place to bury. ¹²Thus I will do to this place," says the LORD, "and to its inhabitants, and make this city like Tophet. ¹³And the houses of Jerusalem and the houses of the kings of Judah shall be defiled like the place of Tophet, because of all the houses on whose roofs they have burned incense to all the host of heaven, and poured out drink offerings to other gods." ' "

¹⁴Then Jeremiah came from Tophet, where the LORD had sent him to prophesy; and he stood in the court of the Lord's house and said to all the people, ¹⁵"Thus says the LORD of hosts, the God of Israel: 'Behold, I will bring on this city and on all her towns all the doom that I have pronounced against it, because they have stiffened their necks that they might not hear My words.' "

The Word of God to Pashhur

20 Now Pashhur the son of Immer, the priest who *was* also chief governor in the house of the LORD, heard that Jeremiah prophesied these things. ²Then Pashhur struck Jeremiah the prophet, and put him in the stocks that *were* in the high gate of Benjamin, which *was* by the house of the LORD.

³And it happened on the next day that Pashhur brought Jeremiah out of the stocks. Then Jeremiah said to him, "The LORD has not called your name Pashhur, but Magor-Missabib.ᵃ ⁴For thus says the LORD: 'Behold, I will make you a terror to yourself and to all your friends; and they shall fall by the sword of their enemies, and your eyes shall see *it*. I will give all Judah into the hand of the king of Babylon, and he shall carry them captive to Babylon and slay them with the sword. ⁵Moreover I will deliver all the wealth of this city, all its produce, and all its precious things; all the treasures of the kings of Judah I will give into the hand of their enemies, who will plunder them, seize them, and carry them to Babylon. ⁶And you, Pashhur, and all who dwell in your house, shall go into captivity. You shall go to Babylon, and there you shall die, and be buried there, you and all your friends, to whom you have prophesied lies.' "

Jeremiah's Unpopular Ministry

7   O LORD, You induced me, and I was
        persuaded;
    You are stronger than I, and have
        prevailed.
    I am in derision daily;
    Everyone mocks me.
8   For when I spoke, I cried out;
    I shouted, "Violence and plunder!"
    Because the word of the LORD was
        made to me
    A reproach and a derision daily.
9   Then I said, "I will not make mention
        of Him,
    Nor speak anymore in His name."
    But *His word* was in my heart like a
        burning fire
    Shut up in my bones;

20:3 ᵃLiterally *Fear on Every Side*

I was weary of holding *it* back,
And I could not.

10 For I heard many mocking:
"Fear on every side!"
"Report," *they say,* "and we will report
it!"
All my acquaintances watched for my
stumbling, *saying,*
"Perhaps he can be induced;
Then we will prevail against him,
And we will take our revenge on
him."

11 But the Lord *is* with me as a mighty,
awesome One.
Therefore my persecutors will stumble,
and will not prevail.
They will be greatly ashamed, for they
will not prosper.
Their everlasting confusion will never
be forgotten.

12 But, O Lord of hosts,
You who test the righteous,
And see the mind and heart,
Let me see Your vengeance on them;
For I have pleaded my cause before
You.

13 Sing to the Lord! Praise the Lord!
For He has delivered the life of the
poor
From the hand of evildoers.

14 Cursed *be* the day in which I was born!
Let the day not be blessed in which
my mother bore me!

15 Let the man *be* cursed
Who brought news to my father,
saying,
"A male child has been born to you!"
Making him very glad.

16 And let that man be like the cities
Which the Lord overthrew, and did
not relent;
Let him hear the cry in the morning
And the shouting at noon,

17 Because he did not kill me from the
womb,
That my mother might have been
my grave,
And her womb always enlarged
with me.

18 Why did I come forth from the womb
to see labor and sorrow,
That my days should be consumed
with shame?

Jerusalem's Doom Is Sealed

21 The word which came to Jeremiah from the Lord when King Zedekiah sent to him Pashhur the son of Melchiah, and Zephaniah the son of Maaseiah, the priest, saying, 2"Please inquire of the Lord for us, for Nebuchadnezzar[a] king of Babylon makes war against us. Perhaps the Lord will deal with us according to all His wonderful works, that *the king* may go away from us."

3Then Jeremiah said to them, "Thus you shall say to Zedekiah, 4'Thus says the Lord God of Israel: "Behold, I will turn back the weapons of war that *are* in your hands, with which you fight against the king of Babylon and the Chaldeans[a] who besiege you outside the walls; and I will assemble them in the midst of this city. 5I Myself will fight against you with an outstretched hand and with a strong arm, even in anger and fury and great wrath. 6I will strike the inhabitants of this city, both man and beast; they shall die of a great pestilence. 7And afterward," says the Lord, "I will deliver Zedekiah king of Judah, his servants and the people, and such as are left in this city from the pestilence and the sword and the famine, into the hand of Nebuchadnezzar king of Babylon, into the hand of their enemies, and into the hand of those who seek their life; and he shall strike them with the edge of the sword. He shall not spare them, or have pity or mercy." '

8"Now you shall say to this people, 'Thus says the Lord: "Behold, I set before you the way of life and the way of death. 9He who remains in this city shall die by the sword, by famine, and by pestilence; but he who goes out and defects to the Chaldeans who besiege you, he shall live, and his life shall be as a prize to him. 10For I have set My face against this city for adversity and not for good," says the Lord. "It shall be given

---
21:2 [a]Hebrew *Nebuchadrezzar,* and so elsewhere
21:4 [a]Or *Babylonians*

into the hand of the king of Babylon, and he shall burn it with fire."'

Message to the House of David

¹¹"And concerning the house of the king of Judah, *say,* 'Hear the word of the LORD, ¹²O house of David! Thus says the LORD:

"Execute judgment in the morning;
  And deliver *him who is* plundered
Out of the hand of the oppressor,
Lest My fury go forth like fire
And burn so that no one can quench *it,*
Because of the evil of your doings.

¹³ "Behold, I *am* against you,
  O inhabitant of the valley,
  And rock of the plain," says the LORD,
"Who say, 'Who shall come down
  against us?
Or who shall enter our dwellings?'
¹⁴ But I will punish you according to the
  fruit of your doings," says the LORD;
"I will kindle a fire in its forest,
  And it shall devour all things around
  it."'"

22 Thus says the LORD: "Go down to the house of the king of Judah, and there speak this word, ²and say, 'Hear the word of the LORD, O king of Judah, you who sit on the throne of David, you and your servants and your people who enter these gates! ³Thus says the LORD: "Execute judgment and righteousness, and deliver the plundered out of the hand of the oppressor. Do no wrong and do no violence to the stranger, the fatherless, or the widow, nor shed innocent blood in this place. ⁴For if you indeed do this thing, then shall enter the gates of this house, riding on horses and in chariots, accompanied by servants and people, kings who sit on the throne of David. ⁵But if you will not hear these words, I swear by Myself," says the LORD, "that this house shall become a desolation."'"

⁶For thus says the LORD to the house of the king of Judah:

"You *are* Gilead to Me,
  The head of Lebanon;

Yet I surely will make you a
  wilderness,
Cities *which* are not inhabited.
⁷ I will prepare destroyers against you,
  Everyone with his weapons;
They shall cut down your choice
  cedars
And cast *them* into the fire.

⁸And many nations will pass by this city; and everyone will say to his neighbor, 'Why has the LORD done so to this great city?' ⁹Then they will answer, 'Because they have forsaken the covenant of the LORD their God, and worshiped other gods and served them.'"

¹⁰ Weep not for the dead, nor bemoan
  him;
Weep bitterly for him who goes
  away,
For he shall return no more,
Nor see his native country.

Message to the Sons of Josiah

¹¹For thus says the LORD concerning Shallum[a] the son of Josiah, king of Judah, who reigned instead of Josiah his father, who went from this place: "He shall not return here anymore, ¹²but he shall die in the place where they have led him captive, and shall see this land no more.

¹³ "Woe to him who builds his house by
  unrighteousness
And his chambers by injustice,
Who uses his neighbor's service
  without wages
And gives him nothing for his work,
¹⁴ Who says, 'I will build myself a wide
  house with spacious chambers,
And cut out windows for it,
Paneling *it* with cedar
And painting *it* with vermilion.'

¹⁵ "Shall you reign because you enclose
  yourself in cedar?
Did not your father eat and drink,
And do justice and righteousness?
Then *it was* well with him.

22:11 ᵃAlso called *Jehoahaz*

¹⁶ He judged the cause of the poor and
   needy;
   Then *it was* well.
   Was not this knowing Me?" says the
   LORD.
¹⁷ "Yet your eyes and your heart *are* for
   nothing but your covetousness,
   For shedding innocent blood,
   And practicing oppression and
   violence."

¹⁸Therefore thus says the LORD concerning Jehoiakim the son of Josiah, king of Judah:

"They shall not lament for him,
   Saying, 'Alas, my brother!' or 'Alas, my
   sister!'
They shall not lament for him,
   Saying, 'Alas, master!' or 'Alas, his
   glory!'
¹⁹ He shall be buried with the burial of a
   donkey,
   Dragged and cast out beyond the
   gates of Jerusalem.

²⁰ "Go up to Lebanon, and cry out,
   And lift up your voice in Bashan;
   Cry from Abarim,
   For all your lovers are destroyed.
²¹ I spoke to you in your prosperity,
   But you said, 'I will not hear.'
   This *has been* your manner from your
   youth,
   That you did not obey My voice.
²² The wind shall eat up all your rulers,
   And your lovers shall go into
   captivity;
   Surely then you will be ashamed and
   humiliated
   For all your wickedness.
²³ O inhabitant of Lebanon,
   Making your nest in the cedars,
   How gracious will you be when pangs
   come upon you,
   Like the pain of a woman in labor?

Message to Coniah

²⁴"As I live," says the LORD, "though Coniah[a] the son of Jehoiakim, king of Judah, were the signet on My right hand, yet I would pluck you off; ²⁵and I will give

you into the hand of those who seek your life, and into the hand *of those* whose face you fear—the hand of Nebuchadnezzar king of Babylon and the hand of the Chaldeans. ²⁶So I will cast you out, and your mother who bore you, into another country where you were not born; and there you shall die. ²⁷But to the land to which they desire to return, there they shall not return.

²⁸ "Is this man Coniah a despised, broken
   idol—
   A vessel in which *is* no pleasure?
   Why are they cast out, he and his
   descendants,
   And cast into a land which they do
   not know?
²⁹ O earth, earth, earth,
   Hear the word of the LORD!
³⁰ Thus says the LORD:
   'Write this man down as childless,
   A man *who* shall not prosper in his
   days;
   For none of his descendants shall
   prosper,
   Sitting on the throne of David,
   And ruling anymore in Judah.' "

The Branch of Righteousness

23 "Woe to the shepherds who destroy and scatter the sheep of My pasture!" says the LORD. ²Therefore thus says the LORD God of Israel against the shepherds who feed My people: "You have scattered My flock, driven them away, and not attended to them. Behold, I will attend to you for the evil of your doings," says the LORD. ³"But I will gather the remnant of My flock out of all countries where I have driven them, and bring them back to their folds; and they shall be fruitful and increase. ⁴I will set up shepherds over them who will feed them; and they shall fear no more, nor be dismayed, nor shall they be lacking," says the LORD.

⁵ "Behold, *the* days are coming," says the
   LORD,
   "That I will raise to David a Branch of
   righteousness;

22:24 [a]Also called *Jeconiah* and *Jehoiachin*

A King shall reign and prosper,
And execute judgment and
   righteousness in the earth.
6 In His days Judah will be saved,
And Israel will dwell safely;
Now this *is* His name by which He will
   be called:

THE LORD OUR RIGHTEOUSNESS.[a]

7"Therefore, behold, *the* days are coming," says the LORD, "that they shall no longer say, 'As the LORD lives who brought up the children of Israel from the land of Egypt,' 8but, 'As the LORD lives who brought up and led the descendants of the house of Israel from the north country and from all the countries where I had driven them.' And they shall dwell in their own land."

False Prophets and Empty Oracles

9 My heart within me is broken
   Because of the prophets;
All my bones shake.
I am like a drunken man,
And like a man whom wine has
   overcome,
Because of the LORD,
And because of His holy words.
10 For the land is full of adulterers;
For because of a curse the land
   mourns.
The pleasant places of the wilderness
   are dried up.
Their course of life is evil,
And their might *is* not right.

11 "For both prophet and priest are
   profane;
Yes, in My house I have found their
   wickedness," says the LORD.
12 "Therefore their way shall be to them
Like slippery *ways;*
In the darkness they shall be
   driven on
And fall in them;
For I will bring disaster on them,
The year of their punishment," says
   the LORD.
13 "And I have seen folly in the prophets
   of Samaria:
They prophesied by Baal
And caused My people Israel to err.

14 Also I have seen a horrible thing in
   the prophets of Jerusalem:
They commit adultery and walk in
   lies;
They also strengthen the hands of
   evildoers,
So that no one turns back from his
   wickedness.
All of them are like Sodom to Me,
And her inhabitants like Gomorrah.

15"Therefore thus says the LORD of hosts concerning the prophets:

'Behold, I will feed them with
   wormwood,
And make them drink the water of
   gall;
For from the prophets of Jerusalem
Profaneness has gone out into all the
   land.'"

16Thus says the LORD of hosts:

"Do not listen to the words of the
   prophets who prophesy to you.
They make you worthless;
They speak a vision of their own
   heart,
Not from the mouth of the LORD.
17 They continually say to those who
   despise Me,
'The LORD has said, "You shall have
   peace"';
And *to* everyone who walks according
   to the dictates of his own heart, they
   say,
'No evil shall come upon you.'"

18 For who has stood in the counsel of
   the LORD,
And has perceived and heard His
   word?
Who has marked His word and
   heard *it?*
19 Behold, a whirlwind of the LORD has
   gone forth in fury—
A violent whirlwind!
It will fall violently on the head of
   the wicked.

23:6 [a]Hebrew *YHWH Tsidkenu*

²⁰ The anger of the LORD will not turn
back
Until He has executed and performed
the thoughts of His heart.
In the latter days you will understand
it perfectly.

²¹ "I have not sent these prophets, yet
they ran.
I have not spoken to them, yet they
prophesied.
²² But if they had stood in My counsel,
And had caused My people to hear
My words,
Then they would have turned them
from their evil way
And from the evil of their doings.

DEFENDER

"... so I shall not see him?"

JEREMIAH 23:24

Known Only to God

The Tomb of the Unknowns was originated after the end of World War I (November 1921) in Arlington National Cemetery, Virginia. It contains the remains of unknown American soldiers from World Wars I and II, the Korean Conflict, and the Vietnam War (until 1998) and represents the missing and unknown service members who died so our country could remain free. The Tomb gives their families a place to grieve and pray and has been guarded continuously, 24 hours a day, 7 days a week, since July 1937, by specially trained Tomb Guards, who ensure they rest in peace.

The Tomb's inscription reads:

Here Rests in Honored Glory an American Soldier Known Only to God.

---

²³ "*Am* I a God near at hand," says the
LORD,
"And not a God afar off?
²⁴ Can anyone hide himself in secret
places,
So I shall not see him?" says the LORD;
"Do I not fill heaven and earth?" says
the LORD.

²⁵"I have heard what the prophets have said who prophesy lies in My name, saying,

'I have dreamed, I have dreamed!' ²⁶How long will *this* be in the heart of the prophets who prophesy lies? Indeed *they are* prophets of the deceit of their own heart, ²⁷who try to make My people forget My name by their dreams which everyone tells his neighbor, as their fathers forgot My name for Baal.

²⁸ "The prophet who has a dream, let
him tell a dream;
And he who has My word, let him
speak My word faithfully.
What *is* the chaff to the wheat?" says
the LORD.
²⁹ "*Is* not My word like a fire?" says the
LORD,
"And like a hammer *that* breaks the
rock in pieces?

³⁰"Therefore behold, I *am* against the prophets," says the LORD, "who steal My words every one from his neighbor. ³¹Behold, I *am* against the prophets," says the LORD, "who use their tongues and say, 'He says.' ³²Behold, I *am* against those who prophesy false dreams," says the LORD, "and tell them, and cause My people to err by their lies and by their recklessness. Yet I did not send them or command them; therefore they shall not profit this people at all," says the LORD.

³³"So when these people or the prophet or the priest ask you, saying, 'What is the oracle of the LORD?' you shall then say to them, 'What oracle?'^a I will even forsake you," says the LORD. ³⁴"And *as for* the prophet and the priest and the people who say, 'The oracle of the LORD!' I will even punish that man and his house. ³⁵Thus every one of you shall say to his neighbor, and every one to his brother, 'What has the LORD answered?' and, 'What has the LORD spoken?' ³⁶And the oracle of the LORD you shall mention no more. For every man's word will be his oracle, for you have perverted the words of the living God, the LORD of hosts, our God. ³⁷Thus you shall say to the prophet, 'What has the LORD answered you?' and, 'What has the LORD spoken?'

23:33 ^aSeptuagint, Targum, and Vulgate read *'You are the burden.'*

³⁸But since you say, 'The oracle of the LORD!' therefore thus says the LORD: 'Because you say this word, "The oracle of the LORD!" and I have sent to you, saying, "Do not say, 'The oracle of the LORD!'"' ³⁹therefore behold, I, even I, will utterly forget you and forsake you, and the city that I gave you and your fathers, and *will cast you* out of My presence. ⁴⁰And I will bring an everlasting reproach upon you, and a perpetual shame, which shall not be forgotten.'"

The Sign of Two Baskets of Figs

24 The LORD showed me, and there were two baskets of figs set before the temple of the LORD, after Nebuchadnezzar king of Babylon had carried away captive Jeconiah the son of Jehoiakim, king of Judah, and the princes of Judah with the craftsmen and smiths, from Jerusalem, and had brought them to Babylon. ²One basket *had* very good figs, like the figs *that are* first ripe; and the other basket *had* very bad figs which could not be eaten, they were so bad. ³Then the LORD said to me, "What do you see, Jeremiah?"

And I said, "Figs, the good figs, very good; and the bad, very bad, which cannot be eaten, they are so bad."

⁴Again the word of the LORD came to me, saying, ⁵"Thus says the LORD, the God of Israel: 'Like these good figs, so will I acknowledge those who are carried away captive from Judah, whom I have sent out of this place for *their own* good, into the land of the Chaldeans. ⁶For I will set My eyes on them for good, and I will bring them back to this land; I will build them and not pull *them* down, and I will plant them and not pluck *them* up. ⁷Then I will give them a heart to know Me, that I *am* the LORD; and they shall be My people, and I will be their God, for they shall return to Me with their whole heart.

⁸'And as the bad figs which cannot be eaten, they are so bad'—surely thus says the LORD—'so will I give up Zedekiah the king of Judah, his princes, the residue of Jerusalem who remain in this land, and those who dwell in the land of Egypt. ⁹I will deliver them to trouble into all the kingdoms of the earth, for *their* harm, *to be a* reproach and a byword, a taunt and a curse, in all places where I shall drive them. ¹⁰And I will send the sword, the famine, and the pestilence among them, till they are consumed from the land that I gave to them and their fathers.'"

Seventy Years of Desolation

25 The word that came to Jeremiah concerning all the people of Judah, in the fourth year of Jehoiakim the son of Josiah, king of Judah (which *was* the first year of Nebuchadnezzar king of Babylon), ²which Jeremiah the prophet spoke to all the people of Judah and to all the inhabitants of Jerusalem, saying: ³"From the thirteenth year of Josiah the son of Amon, king of Judah, even to this day, this *is* the twenty-third year in which the word of the LORD has come to me; and I have spoken to you, rising early and speaking, but you have not listened. ⁴And the LORD has sent to you all His servants the prophets, rising early and sending *them,* but you have not listened nor inclined your ear to hear. ⁵They said, 'Repent now everyone of his evil way and his evil doings, and dwell in the land that the LORD has given to you and your fathers forever and ever. ⁶Do not go after other gods to serve them and worship them, and do not provoke Me to anger with the works of your hands; and I will not harm you.' ⁷Yet you have not listened to Me," says the LORD, "that you might provoke Me to anger with the works of your hands to your own hurt.

⁸"Therefore thus says the LORD of hosts: 'Because you have not heard My words, ⁹behold, I will send and take all the families of the north,' says the LORD, 'and Nebuchadnezzar the king of Babylon, My servant, and will bring them against this land, against its inhabitants, and against these nations all around, and will utterly destroy them, and make them an astonishment, a hissing, and perpetual desolations. ¹⁰Moreover I will take from them the voice of mirth and the voice of gladness, the voice of the bridegroom and the voice of the bride, the sound of the millstones and the light of the lamp. ¹¹And this whole land shall be a desolation *and* an astonishment,

and these nations shall serve the king of Babylon seventy years.

¹²'Then it will come to pass, when seventy years are completed, *that* I will punish the king of Babylon and that nation, the land of the Chaldeans, for their iniquity,' says the LORD; 'and I will make it a perpetual desolation. ¹³So I will bring on that land all My words which I have pronounced against it, all that is written in this book, which Jeremiah has prophesied concerning all the nations. ¹⁴(For many nations and great kings shall be served by them also; and I will repay them according to their deeds and according to the works of their own hands.)'"

Judgment on the Nations

¹⁵For thus says the LORD God of Israel to me: "Take this wine cup of fury from My hand, and cause all the nations, to whom I send you, to drink it. ¹⁶And they will drink and stagger and go mad because of the sword that I will send among them."

¹⁷Then I took the cup from the LORD's hand, and made all the nations drink, to whom the LORD had sent me: ¹⁸Jerusalem and the cities of Judah, its kings and its princes, to make them a desolation, an astonishment, a hissing, and a curse, as *it is* this day; ¹⁹Pharaoh king of Egypt, his servants, his princes, and all his people; ²⁰all the mixed multitude, all the kings of the land of Uz, all the kings of the land of the Philistines (namely, Ashkelon, Gaza, Ekron, and the remnant of Ashdod); ²¹Edom, Moab, and the people of Ammon; ²²all the kings of Tyre, all the kings of Sidon, and the kings of the coastlands which *are* across the sea; ²³Dedan, Tema, Buz, and all *who are* in the farthest corners; ²⁴all the kings of Arabia and all the kings of the mixed multitude who dwell in the desert; ²⁵all the kings of Zimri, all the kings of Elam, and all the kings of the Medes; ²⁶all the kings of the north, far and near, one with another; and all the kingdoms of the world which *are* on the face of the earth. Also the king of Sheshach^a shall drink after them.

²⁷"Therefore you shall say to them, 'Thus says the LORD of hosts, the God of Israel: "Drink, be drunk, and vomit! Fall and rise no more, because of the sword which I will send among you."' ²⁸And it shall be, if they refuse to take the cup from your hand to drink, then you shall say to them, 'Thus says the LORD of hosts: "You shall certainly drink! ²⁹For behold, I begin to bring calamity on the city which is called by My name, and should you be utterly unpunished? You shall not be unpunished, for I will call for a sword on all the inhabitants of the earth," says the LORD of hosts.'

³⁰"Therefore prophesy against them all these words, and say to them:

'The LORD will roar from on high,
    And utter His voice from His holy
        habitation;
    He will roar mightily against His fold.
    He will give a shout, as those who
        tread *the grapes,*
    Against all the inhabitants of the
        earth.
31 A noise will come to the ends of the
        earth—
    For the LORD has a controversy with
        the nations;
    He will plead His case with all flesh.
    He will give those *who are* wicked to
        the sword,' says the LORD."

³²Thus says the LORD of hosts:

"Behold, disaster shall go forth
    From nation to nation,
    And a great whirlwind shall be
        raised up
    From the farthest parts of the earth.

³³"And at that day the slain of the LORD shall be from *one* end of the earth even to the *other* end of the earth. They shall not be lamented, or gathered, or buried; they shall become refuse on the ground.

34 "Wail, shepherds, and cry!
    Roll about *in the ashes,*
    You leaders of the flock!
    For the days of your slaughter and
        your dispersions are fulfilled;
    You shall fall like a precious vessel.

25:26 ^aA code word for Babylon (compare 51:41)

35 And the shepherds will have no way
     to flee,
   Nor the leaders of the flock to escape.
36 A voice of the cry of the shepherds,
   And a wailing of the leaders to the
     flock *will be heard.*
   For the LORD has plundered their
     pasture,
37 And the peaceful dwellings are cut
     down
   Because of the fierce anger of the
     LORD.
38 He has left His lair like the lion;
   For their land is desolate
   Because of the fierceness of the
     Oppressor,
   And because of His fierce anger."

Jeremiah Saved from Death

26 In the beginning of the reign of Jehoiakim the son of Josiah, king of Judah, this word came from the LORD, saying, 2"Thus says the LORD: 'Stand in the court of the LORD's house, and speak to all the cities of Judah, which come to worship *in* the LORD's house, all the words that I command you to speak to them. Do not diminish a word. 3Perhaps everyone will listen and turn from his evil way, that I may relent concerning the calamity which I purpose to bring on them because of the evil of their doings.' 4And you shall say to them, 'Thus says the LORD: "If you will not listen to Me, to walk in My law which I have set before you, 5to heed the words of My servants the prophets whom I sent to you, both rising up early and sending *them* (but you have not heeded), 6then I will make this house like Shiloh, and will make this city a curse to all the nations of the earth."'"

7So the priests and the prophets and all the people heard Jeremiah speaking these words in the house of the LORD. 8Now it happened, when Jeremiah had made an end of speaking all that the LORD had commanded *him* to speak to all the people, that the priests and the prophets and all the people seized him, saying, "You will surely die! 9Why have you prophesied in the name of the LORD, saying, 'This house shall be like Shiloh, and this city shall be

desolate, without an inhabitant'?" And all the people were gathered against Jeremiah in the house of the LORD.

10When the princes of Judah heard these things, they came up from the king's house to the house of the LORD and sat down in the entry of the New Gate of the LORD's *house.* 11And the priests and the prophets spoke to the princes and all the people, saying, "This man deserves to die! For he has prophesied against this city, as you have heard with your ears."

12Then Jeremiah spoke to all the princes and all the people, saying: "The LORD sent me to prophesy against this house and against this city with all the words that you have heard. 13Now therefore, amend your ways and your doings, and obey the voice of the LORD your God; then the LORD will relent concerning the doom that He has pronounced against you. 14As for me, here I am, in your hand; do with me as seems good and proper to you. 15But know for certain that if you put me to death, you will surely bring innocent blood on yourselves, on this city, and on its inhabitants; for truly the LORD has sent me to you to speak all these words in your hearing."

16So the princes and all the people said to the priests and the prophets, "This man does not deserve to die. For he has spoken to us in the name of the LORD our God."

17Then certain of the elders of the land rose up and spoke to all the assembly of the people, saying: 18"Micah of Moresheth prophesied in the days of Hezekiah king of Judah, and spoke to all the people of Judah, saying, 'Thus says the LORD of hosts:

   "Zion shall be plowed *like* a field,
     Jerusalem shall become heaps of
       ruins,
   And the mountain of the temple[a]
     Like the bare hills of the forest." '[b]

19Did Hezekiah king of Judah and all Judah ever put him to death? Did he not fear the LORD and seek the LORD's favor? And the LORD relented concerning the doom which He had pronounced against

---

26:18 [a]Literally *house* [b]Compare Micah 3:12

them. But we are doing great evil against ourselves."

20Now there was also a man who prophesied in the name of the LORD, Urijah the son of Shemaiah of Kirjath Jearim, who prophesied against this city and against this land according to all the words of Jeremiah. 21And when Jehoiakim the king, with all his mighty men and all the princes, heard his words, the king sought to put him to death; but when Urijah heard *it,* he was afraid and fled, and went to Egypt. 22Then Jehoiakim the king sent men to Egypt: Elnathan the son of Achbor, and *other* men *who went* with him to Egypt. 23And they brought Urijah from Egypt and brought him to Jehoiakim the king, who killed him with the sword and cast his dead body into the graves of the common people.

24Nevertheless the hand of Ahikam the son of Shaphan was with Jeremiah, so that they should not give him into the hand of the people to put him to death.

Symbol of the Bonds and Yokes

27 In the beginning of the reign of Jehoiakim[a] the son of Josiah, king of Judah, this word came to Jeremiah from the LORD, saying,[b] 2"Thus says the LORD to me: 'Make for yourselves bonds and yokes, and put them on your neck, 3and send them to the king of Edom, the king of Moab, the king of the Ammonites, the king of Tyre, and the king of Sidon, by the hand of the messengers who come to Jerusalem to Zedekiah king of Judah. 4And command them to say to their masters, "Thus says the LORD of hosts, the God of Israel—thus you shall say to your masters: 5'I have made the earth, the man and the beast that *are* on the ground, by My great power and by My outstretched arm, and have given it to whom it seemed proper to Me. 6And now I have given all these lands into the hand of Nebuchadnezzar the king of Babylon, My servant; and the beasts of the field I have also given him to serve him. 7So all nations shall serve him and his son and his son's son, until the time of his land comes; and then many nations and great kings shall make him serve them. 8And it shall be, *that* the nation and kingdom

which will not serve Nebuchadnezzar the king of Babylon, and which will not put its neck under the yoke of the king of Babylon, that nation I will punish,' says the LORD, 'with the sword, the famine, and the pestilence, until I have consumed them by his hand. 9Therefore do not listen to your prophets, your diviners, your dreamers, your soothsayers, or your sorcerers, who speak to you, saying, "You shall not serve the king of Babylon." 10For they prophesy a lie to you, to remove you far from your land; and I will drive you out, and you will perish. 11But the nations that bring their necks under the yoke of the king of Babylon and serve him, I will let them remain in their own land,' says the LORD, 'and they shall till it and dwell in it.'" '"

12I also spoke to Zedekiah king of Judah according to all these words, saying, "Bring your necks under the yoke of the king of Babylon, and serve him and his people, and live! 13Why will you die, you and your people, by the sword, by the famine, and by the pestilence, as the LORD has spoken against the nation that will not serve the king of Babylon? 14Therefore do not listen to the words of the prophets who speak to you, saying, 'You shall not serve the king of Babylon,' for they prophesy a lie to you; 15for I have not sent them," says the LORD, "yet they prophesy a lie in My name, that I may drive you out, and that you may perish, you and the prophets who prophesy to you."

16Also I spoke to the priests and to all this people, saying, "Thus says the LORD: 'Do not listen to the words of your prophets who prophesy to you, saying, "Behold, the vessels of the LORD's house will now shortly be brought back from Babylon"; for they prophesy a lie to you. 17Do not listen to them; serve the king of Babylon, and live! Why should this city be laid waste? 18But if they *are* prophets, and if the word of the LORD is with them, let them now make intercession to the LORD of hosts, that the

---

27:1 [a]Following Masoretic Text, Targum, and Vulgate; some Hebrew manuscripts, Arabic, and Syriac read *Zedekiah* (compare 27:3, 12; 28:1). [b]Septuagint omits verse 1.

vessels which are left in the house of the LORD, *in* the house of the king of Judah, and at Jerusalem, do not go to Babylon.'

¹⁹"For thus says the LORD of hosts concerning the pillars, concerning the Sea, concerning the carts, and concerning the remainder of the vessels that remain in this city, ²⁰which Nebuchadnezzar king of Babylon did not take, when he carried away captive Jeconiah the son of Jehoiakim, king of Judah, from Jerusalem to Babylon, and all the nobles of Judah and Jerusalem— ²¹yes, thus says the LORD of hosts, the God of Israel, concerning the vessels that remain in the house of the LORD, and in the house of the king of Judah and of Jerusalem: ²²'They shall be carried to Babylon, and there they shall be until the day that I visit them,' says the LORD. 'Then I will bring them up and restore them to this place.'"

Hananiah's Falsehood and Doom

28 And it happened in the same year, at the beginning of the reign of Zedekiah king of Judah, in the fourth year *and* in the fifth month, *that* Hananiah the son of Azur the prophet, who *was* from Gibeon, spoke to me in the house of the LORD in the presence of the priests and of all the people, saying, ²"Thus speaks the LORD of hosts, the God of Israel, saying: 'I have broken the yoke of the king of Babylon. ³Within two full years I will bring back to this place all the vessels of the LORD's house, that Nebuchadnezzar king of Babylon took away from this place and carried to Babylon. ⁴And I will bring back to this place Jeconiah the son of Jehoiakim, king of Judah, with all the captives of Judah who went to Babylon,' says the LORD, 'for I will break the yoke of the king of Babylon.'"

⁵Then the prophet Jeremiah spoke to the prophet Hananiah in the presence of the priests and in the presence of all the people who stood in the house of the LORD, ⁶and the prophet Jeremiah said, "Amen! The LORD do so; the LORD perform your words which you have prophesied, to bring back the vessels of the LORD's house and all who were carried away captive, from Babylon to this place. ⁷Nevertheless hear now this word that I speak in your hearing and in the hearing of all the people: ⁸The prophets who have been before me and before you of old prophesied against many countries and great kingdoms—of war and disaster and pestilence. ⁹As for the prophet who prophesies of peace, when the word of the prophet comes to pass, the prophet will be known *as* one whom the LORD has truly sent."

¹⁰Then Hananiah the prophet took the yoke off the prophet Jeremiah's neck and broke it. ¹¹And Hananiah spoke in the presence of all the people, saying, "Thus says the LORD: 'Even so I will break the yoke of Nebuchadnezzar king of Babylon from the neck of all nations within the space of two full years.'" And the prophet Jeremiah went his way.

¹²Now the word of the LORD came to Jeremiah, after Hananiah the prophet had broken the yoke from the neck of the prophet Jeremiah, saying, ¹³"Go and tell Hananiah, saying, 'Thus says the LORD: "You have broken the yokes of wood, but you have made in their place yokes of iron." ¹⁴For thus says the LORD of hosts, the God of Israel: "I have put a yoke of iron on the neck of all these nations, that they may serve Nebuchadnezzar king of Babylon; and they shall serve him. I have given him the beasts of the field also."'"

¹⁵Then the prophet Jeremiah said to Hananiah the prophet, "Hear now, Hananiah, the LORD has not sent you, but you make this people trust in a lie. ¹⁶Therefore thus says the LORD: 'Behold, I will cast you from the face of the earth. This year you shall die, because you have taught rebellion against the LORD.'"

¹⁷So Hananiah the prophet died the same year in the seventh month.

Jeremiah's Letter to the Captives

29 Now these *are* the words of the letter that Jeremiah the prophet sent from Jerusalem to the remainder of the elders who were carried away captive—to the priests, the prophets, and all the people whom Nebuchadnezzar had carried away captive from Jerusalem to Babylon. ²(This happened after Jeconiah the king, the queen mother, the eunuchs, the princes of

Judah and Jerusalem, the craftsmen, and the smiths had departed from Jerusalem.) ³*The letter was sent* by the hand of Elasah the son of Shaphan, and Gemariah the son of Hilkiah, whom Zedekiah king of Judah sent to Babylon, to Nebuchadnezzar king of Babylon, saying,

4   Thus says the LORD of hosts, the God of Israel, to all who were carried away captive, whom I have caused to be carried away from Jerusalem to Babylon:

5   Build houses and dwell *in them;* plant gardens and eat their fruit. ⁶Take wives and beget sons and daughters; and take wives for your sons and give your daughters to husbands, so that they may bear sons and daughters— that you may be increased there, and not diminished. ⁷And seek the peace of the city where I have caused you to be carried away captive, and pray to the LORD for it; for in its peace you will have peace. ⁸For thus says the LORD of hosts, the God of Israel: Do not let your prophets and your diviners who are in your midst deceive you, nor listen to your dreams which you cause to be dreamed. ⁹For they prophesy falsely to you in My name; I have not sent them, says the LORD.

10 For thus says the LORD: After seventy years are completed at Babylon, I will visit you and perform My good word toward you, and cause you to return to this place. ¹¹For I know the thoughts that I think toward you, says the LORD, thoughts of peace and not of evil, to give you a future and a hope. ¹²Then you will call upon Me and go and pray to Me, and I will listen to you. ¹³And you will seek Me and find *Me,* when you search for Me with all your heart. ¹⁴I will be found by you, says the LORD, and I will bring you back

INSPIRING

. . . to give you a future and a hope.

JEREMIAH 29:11

Ronald Reagan

"THE AMERICAN SOUND"

Few presidents had the ability to ignite hope in the hearts of those who love liberty more than President Ronald Reagan. In his Second Inaugural Address in 1985, he stated:

History is a ribbon, always unfurling; history is a journey. And as we continue our journey, we think of those who traveled before us. . . . Now we hear again the echoes of our past: a general falls to his knees in the hard snow of Valley Forge; a lonely president paces the darkened halls and ponders his struggle to preserve the Union; the men of the Alamo call out encouragement to each other; a settler pushes west and sings a song, and the song echoes out forever and fills the unknowing air.

It is the American sound. It is hopeful, big-hearted, idealistic, daring, decent, and fair. That's our heritage; that is our song. We sing it still. For all our problems, our differences, we are together as of old, as we raise our voices to the God who is the Author of this most tender music. And may He continue to hold us close as we fill the world with our sound—sound in unity, affection, and love—one people under God, dedicated to the dream of freedom that He has placed in the human heart, called upon now to pass that dream on to a waiting and hopeful world.

from your captivity; I will gather you from all the nations and from all the places where I have driven you, says the LORD, and I will bring you to the place from which I cause you to be carried away captive.

15 Because you have said, "The LORD has raised up prophets for us in Babylon"— 16therefore thus says the LORD concerning the king who sits on the throne of David, concerning all the people who dwell in this city, and concerning your brethren who have not gone out with you into captivity— 17thus says the LORD of hosts: Behold, I will send on them the sword, the famine, and the pestilence, and will make them like rotten figs that cannot be eaten, they are so bad. 18And I will pursue them with the sword, with famine, and with pestilence; and I will deliver them to trouble among all the kingdoms of the earth—to be a curse, an astonishment, a hissing, and a reproach among all the nations where I have driven them, 19because they have not heeded My words, says the LORD, which I sent to them by My servants the prophets, rising up early and sending *them;* neither would you heed, says the LORD. 20Therefore hear the word of the LORD, all you of the captivity, whom I have sent from Jerusalem to Babylon.

21 Thus says the LORD of hosts, the God of Israel, concerning Ahab the son of Kolaiah, and Zedekiah the son of Maaseiah, who prophesy a lie to you in My name: Behold, I will deliver them into the hand of Nebuchadnezzar king of Babylon, and he shall slay them before your eyes. 22And because of them a curse shall be taken up by all the captivity of Judah who *are* in Babylon, saying, "The LORD make you like Zedekiah and Ahab, whom the king of Babylon roasted in the fire"; 23because they have done disgraceful things in Israel, have committed adultery with their neighbors' wives, and have spoken lying words in My name, which I have not commanded them. Indeed I know, and *am* a witness, says the LORD.

24 You shall also speak to Shemaiah the Nehelamite, saying, 25Thus speaks the LORD of hosts, the God of Israel, saying: You have sent letters in your name to all the people who *are* at Jerusalem, to Zephaniah the son of Maaseiah the priest, and to all the priests, saying, 26"The LORD has made you priest instead of Jehoiada the priest, so that there should be officers *in* the house of the LORD over every man *who* is demented and considers himself a prophet, that you should put him in prison and in the stocks. 27Now therefore, why have you not rebuked Jeremiah of Anathoth who makes himself a prophet to you? 28For he has sent to us *in* Babylon, saying, 'This *captivity is* long; build houses and dwell *in them,* and plant gardens and eat their fruit.'"

29 Now Zephaniah the priest read this letter in the hearing of Jeremiah the prophet. 30Then the word of the LORD came to Jeremiah, saying: 31Send to all those in captivity, saying, Thus says the LORD concerning Shemaiah the Nehelamite: Because Shemaiah has prophesied to you, and I have not sent him, and he has caused you to trust in a lie— 32therefore thus says the LORD: Behold, I will punish Shemaiah the Nehelamite and his family: he shall not have anyone to dwell among this people, nor shall he see the good that I will do for My people, says the LORD, because he has taught rebellion against the LORD.

Restoration of Israel and Judah

30 The word that came to Jeremiah from the LORD, saying, 2"Thus speaks the LORD God of Israel, saying: 'Write in a book for yourself all the words that I have spoken to you. 3For behold, the days are coming,' says the LORD, 'that I will bring back from

captivity My people Israel and Judah,' says the LORD. 'And I will cause them to return to the land that I gave to their fathers, and they shall possess it.'"

⁴Now these *are* the words that the LORD spoke concerning Israel and Judah.

⁵"For thus says the LORD:

'We have heard a voice of trembling,
Of fear, and not of peace.
6 Ask now, and see,
   Whether a man is ever in labor with
      child?
   So why do I see every man *with* his
      hands on his loins
   Like a woman in labor,
   And all faces turned pale?
7 Alas! For that day *is* great,
   So that none *is* like it;
   And it *is* the time of Jacob's trouble,
   But he shall be saved out of it.

8 'For it shall come to pass in that day,'
   Says the LORD of hosts,
   '*That* I will break his yoke from your
      neck,
   And will burst your bonds;
   Foreigners shall no more enslave
      them.
9 But they shall serve the LORD their
      God,
   And David their king,
   Whom I will raise up for them.

10 'Therefore do not fear, O My servant
      Jacob,' says the LORD,
   'Nor be dismayed, O Israel;
   For behold, I will save you from afar,
   And your seed from the land of their
      captivity.
   Jacob shall return, have rest and be
      quiet,
   And no one shall make *him* afraid.
11 For I *am* with you,' says the LORD, 'to
      save you;
   Though I make a full end of all
      nations where I have scattered you,
   Yet I will not make a complete end of
      you.
   But I will correct you in justice,
   And will not let you go altogether
      unpunished.'

12"For thus says the LORD:

'Your affliction *is* incurable,
Your wound *is* severe.
13   *There is* no one to plead your cause,
     That you may be bound up;
     You have no healing medicines.
14   All your lovers have forgotten you;
     They do not seek you;
     For I have wounded you with the
        wound of an enemy,
     With the chastisement of a cruel one,
     For the multitude of your iniquities,
     Because your sins have increased.
15   Why do you cry about your
        affliction?
     Your sorrow *is* incurable.
     Because of the multitude of your
        iniquities,
     Because your sins have increased,
     I have done these things to you.

16   'Therefore all those who devour you
        shall be devoured;
     And all your adversaries, every one of
        them, shall go into captivity;
     Those who plunder you shall become
        plunder,
     And all who prey upon you I will
        make a prey.
17   For I will restore health to you
     And heal you of your wounds,' says
        the LORD,
     'Because they called you an outcast
        saying:
     "This *is* Zion;
     No one seeks her."'

18"Thus says the LORD:

'Behold, I will bring back the captivity
   of Jacob's tents,
And have mercy on his dwelling
   places;
The city shall be built upon its own
   mound,
And the palace shall remain
   according to its own plan.
19   Then out of them shall proceed
        thanksgiving
     And the voice of those who make
        merry;

I will multiply them, and they shall
    not diminish;
I will also glorify them, and they shall
    not be small.
20 Their children also shall be as before,
And their congregation shall be
    established before Me;
And I will punish all who oppress them.
21 Their nobles shall be from among
    them,
And their governor shall come from
    their midst;
Then I will cause him to draw near,
And he shall approach Me;
For who *is* this who pledged his heart
    to approach Me?' says the LORD.
22 'You shall be My people,
And I will be your God.'"

23 Behold, the whirlwind of the LORD
Goes forth with fury,
A continuing whirlwind;
It will fall violently on the head of the
    wicked.
24 The fierce anger of the LORD will not
    return until He has done it,
And until He has performed the
    intents of His heart.

In the latter days you will consider it.

The Remnant of Israel Saved

31 "At the same time," says the LORD, "I
    will be the God of all the families of
Israel, and they shall be My people."
    2 Thus says the LORD:

"The people who survived the sword
Found grace in the wilderness—
Israel, when I went to give him rest."

3 The LORD has appeared of old to me,
    saying:
"Yes, I have loved you with an
    everlasting love;
Therefore with lovingkindness I have
    drawn you.
4 Again I will build you, and you shall
    be rebuilt,
O virgin of Israel!
You shall again be adorned with your
    tambourines,

And shall go forth in the dances of
    those who rejoice.
5 You shall yet plant vines on the
    mountains of Samaria;
The planters shall plant and eat *them*
    as ordinary food.
6 For there shall be a day
When the watchmen will cry on
    Mount Ephraim,
'Arise, and let us go up *to* Zion,
To the LORD our God.'"

7 For thus says the LORD:

"Sing with gladness for Jacob,
And shout among the chief of the
    nations;
Proclaim, give praise, and say,
'O LORD, save Your people,
The remnant of Israel!'
8 Behold, I will bring them from the
    north country,
And gather them from the ends of the
    earth,
Among them the blind and the lame,
The woman with child
And the one who labors with child,
    together;
A great throng shall return there.
9 They shall come with weeping,
And with supplications I will lead
    them.
I will cause them to walk by the rivers
    of waters,
In a straight way in which they shall
    not stumble;
For I am a Father to Israel,
And Ephraim *is* My firstborn.

10 "Hear the word of the LORD, O nations,
And declare *it* in the isles afar off, and
    say,
'He who scattered Israel will gather him,
And keep him as a shepherd *does* his
    flock.'
11 For the LORD has redeemed Jacob,
And ransomed him from the hand of
    one stronger than he.
12 Therefore they shall come and sing in
    the height of Zion,
Streaming to the goodness of the
    LORD—

THE CIVIL WAR

$\mathcal{I}$T WAS A WAR PEOPLE THOUGHT would be over in three months but lasted four horrible years (1861–1865), and the cost was more American lives than in all other American wars combined. By the end of the Civil War, over 360,000 Union and approximately 260,000 Confederate soldiers would be dead. It remains the greatest, and the most tragic, event in American history, where an incalculable sacrifice of "brothers' blood" was spilled to restore to one a nation bitterly torn in two.

While the reasons for the Revolutionary War were abundantly clear, the reasons for the Civil War are still being debated. Political disagreements between the North and South began soon after the American Revolution ended in 1782, and those arguments mounted between

1800 and 1860. Quarrels over unfair taxes paid on goods brought into the South from foreign countries as well as perceived shifts of political power in the federal government to favor the Northern and Midwestern states fueled the Southern call away from the central federal authority in Washington and to a restoration of states' rights.

HOWEVER, SLAVERY WAS THE DEFINING ISSUE that drove the Southern resolve to make war on the Union rather than accept Abraham Lincoln's election as president in 1860. Slavery had been a part of life for well over 200 years of America's history and was protected by state and federal laws regarding unlawful seizure of property. In the early 1800s, slavery was first seen as an economic issue and second as a moral issue, but it became the pivotal issue that divided the nation's political leaders. Extensive theological debate was waged over a biblical understanding of slavery, which Scripture never expressly denounces, though abolitionists gave convincing argument that the spirit of the Bible condemned slavery. But the bottom line was that if the South lost her slaves, her socioeconomic system would collapse.

The presidential election of Abraham Lincoln in 1860 was the last straw for the South. As a member of the Republican Party, Lincoln was considered friendly to abolitionists and northern businessmen. South Carolina became the first state to officially secede from the United States, and they were followed by six other Southern states. Together, they formed the "Confederate States of America" and

General Stonewall Jackson

General Robert E. Lee

Stone Mountain Memorial

elected Jefferson Davis, a Democratic senator and champion of states' rights from Mississippi, as their first president.

The South believed that the North was threatening their way of life, that it was their sovereign right to secede from the Union, and that the "peculiar institution" of slavery was ordained by God and upheld in the Bible. The North believed the South was in rebellion and, if allowed to secede, would destroy the republic. In a famous letter to Horace Greeley, whose strong anti-slavery newspaper editorials helped to stir the North to oppose slavery, Lincoln said that his first priority was saving the Union, not destroying slavery. But to save the Union meant to solve the problem of slavery: a constitutional government founded on the principle of equality for all had come to the breaking point.

Paradoxically, each side believed unequivocally that God was on its side in the conflict. From early colonial days, New England political and religious leaders had considered themselves as God's "chosen people." With the start of the Civil War, Southerners

invoked "the favor and guidance of Almighty God" in their constitution, proclaiming themselves a Christian nation. People of all walks of life—ministers, generals, political leaders, and newspaper editors—went so far as to claim that God had ordained the war and was sovereign to determine all its outcomes.

Nowhere was the religious paradox stated clearer than in Lincoln's Second Inaugural Address of March 1865, at one of the darkest moments of the war: "Both [North and South] read the same Bible, and pray to the same God; and each invokes His aid against the other. It may seem strange that any men should dare to ask a just God's assistance in wringing their bread from the sweat of other men's faces; but let us judge not that we be not judged. The prayers of both could not be answered; that of neither has been answered fully. The Almighty has His own purposes."

IN THE END, OVER THREE MILLION AMERICANS fought in the Civil War, and two percent of the population perished. It saw the end of slavery and ushered in a new political and economic order. As the era of Southern plantation aristocracy ended, the powers of the federal government expanded, and the days of big industry and business began. The clash over federal and states' rights finally came down to a struggle over the meaning of freedom in America. At Lincoln's Gettysburg Address in 1863, perhaps he was prophetic when he said the war was about a "new birth of freedom."

President Abraham Lincoln reading the Bible to his son

THE GETTYSBURG ADDRESS

DELIVERED BY ABRAHAM LINCOLN NOV. 19 1863

AT THE DEDICATION SERVICES ON THE BATTLE FIELD

Fourscore and seven years ago our fathers brought forth on this continent a new nation, conceived in liberty, and dedicated to the proposition that all men are created equal. * * * Now we are engaged in a great civil war, testing whether that nation, or any nation so conceived and so dedicated, can long endure. * * We are met on a great battle-field of that war. * We have come to dedicate a portion of that field as a final resting place for those who here gave their lives that that nation might live. * * It is altogether fitting and proper that we should do this. * * But in a larger sense we cannot dedicate, we cannot consecrate, we cannot hallow this ground. * The brave men, living and dead, who struggled here, have consecrated it far above our poor power to add or detract. The world will little note, nor long remember what we say here, but it can never forget what they did here. * * It is for us, the living, rather to be dedicated here to the unfinished work which they who fought here have thus far so nobly advanced. It is rather for us to be here dedicated to the great task remaining before us, that from these honored dead we take increased devotion to that cause for which they gave the last full measure of devotion; * that we here highly resolve that these dead shall not have died in vain; that this nation, under God, shall have a new birth of freedom, and that the government of the people, by the people, and for the people, shall not perish from the earth

For wheat and new wine and oil,
For the young of the flock and the
    herd;
Their souls shall be like a well-watered
    garden,
And they shall sorrow no more at all.

13 "Then shall the virgin rejoice in the
    dance,
And the young men and the old,
    together;
For I will turn their mourning to joy,
Will comfort them,
And make them rejoice rather than
    sorrow.
14 I will satiate the soul of the priests
    with abundance,
And My people shall be satisfied with
    My goodness, says the LORD."

Mercy on Ephraim

15Thus says the LORD:

"A voice was heard in Ramah,
Lamentation *and* bitter weeping,
Rachel weeping for her children,
Refusing to be comforted for her
    children,
Because they *are* no more."

16Thus says the LORD:

"Refrain your voice from weeping,
And your eyes from tears;
For your work shall be rewarded, says
    the LORD,
And they shall come back from the
    land of the enemy.
17 There is hope in your future, says the
    LORD,
That *your* children shall come back to
    their own border.

18 "I have surely heard Ephraim
    bemoaning himself:
' You have chastised me, and I was
    chastised,
Like an untrained bull;
Restore me, and I will return,
For You *are* the LORD my God.
19 Surely, after my turning, I repented;

And after I was instructed, I struck
    myself on the thigh;
I was ashamed, yes, even humiliated,
Because I bore the reproach of my
    youth.'
20 *Is* Ephraim My dear son?
    Is he a pleasant child?
For though I spoke against him,
I earnestly remember him still;
Therefore My heart yearns for him;
I will surely have mercy on him, says
    the LORD.

21 "Set up signposts,
Make landmarks;
Set your heart toward the highway,
The way in *which* you went.
Turn back, O virgin of Israel,
Turn back to these your cities.
22 How long will you gad about,
O you backsliding daughter?
For the LORD has created a new thing
    in the earth—
A woman shall encompass a man."

Future Prosperity of Judah

23Thus says the LORD of hosts, the God of Israel: "They shall again use this speech in the land of Judah and in its cities, when I bring back their captivity: 'The LORD bless you, O home of justice, *and* mountain of holiness!' 24And there shall dwell in Judah itself, and in all its cities together, farmers and those going out with flocks. 25For I have satiated the weary soul, and I have replenished every sorrowful soul."

26After this I awoke and looked around, and my sleep was sweet to me.

27"Behold, the days are coming, says the LORD, that I will sow the house of Israel and the house of Judah with the seed of man and the seed of beast. 28And it shall come to pass, *that* as I have watched over them to pluck up, to break down, to throw down, to destroy, and to afflict, so I will watch over them to build and to plant, says the LORD. 29In those days they shall say no more:

'The fathers have eaten sour grapes,
And the children's teeth are set on
    edge.'

30But every one shall die for his own iniquity; every man who eats the sour grapes, his teeth shall be set on edge.

A New Covenant

31"Behold, the days are coming, says the LORD, when I will make a new covenant with the house of Israel and with the house of Judah— 32not according to the covenant that I made with their fathers in the day *that* I took them by the hand to lead them out of the land of Egypt, My covenant which they broke, though I was a husband to them,ᵃ says the LORD. 33But this *is* the covenant that I will make with the house of Israel after those days, says the LORD: I will put My law in their minds, and write it on their hearts; and I will be their God, and they shall be My people. 34No more shall every man teach his neighbor, and every man his brother, saying, 'Know the LORD,' for they all shall know Me, from the least of them to the greatest of them, says the LORD. For I will forgive their iniquity, and their sin I will remember no more."

35   Thus says the LORD,
       Who gives the sun for a light by day,
       The ordinances of the moon and the
            stars for a light by night,
       Who disturbs the sea,
       And its waves roar
       (The LORD of hosts *is* His name):

36   "If those ordinances depart
       From before Me, says the LORD,
       Then the seed of Israel shall also cease
       From being a nation before Me forever."

37Thus says the LORD:

       "If heaven above can be measured,
       And the foundations of the earth
            searched out beneath,
       I will also cast off all the seed of Israel
       For all that they have done, says the
            LORD.

38"Behold, the days are coming, says the LORD, that the city shall be built for the LORD from the Tower of Hananel to the Corner Gate. 39The surveyor's line shall again extend straight forward over the hill Gareb; then it shall turn toward Goath. 40And the whole valley of the dead bodies and of the ashes, and all the fields as far as the Brook Kidron, to the corner of the Horse Gate toward the east, *shall be* holy to the LORD. It shall not be plucked up or thrown down anymore forever."

Jeremiah Buys a Field

32 The word that came to Jeremiah from the LORD in the tenth year of Zedekiah king of Judah, which was the eighteenth year of Nebuchadnezzar. 2For then the king of Babylon's army besieged Jerusalem, and Jeremiah the prophet was shut up in the court of the prison, which *was in* the king of Judah's house. 3For Zedekiah king of Judah had shut him up, saying, "Why do you prophesy and say, 'Thus says the LORD: "Behold, I will give this city into the hand of the king of Babylon, and he shall take it; 4and Zedekiah king of Judah shall not escape from the hand of the Chaldeans, but shall surely be delivered into the hand of the king of Babylon, and shall speak with him face to face,ᵃ and see him eye to eye; 5then he shall lead Zedekiah to Babylon, and there he shall be until I visit him," says the LORD; "though you fight with the Chaldeans, you shall not succeed" '?"

6And Jeremiah said, "The word of the LORD came to me, saying, 7'Behold, Hanamel the son of Shallum your uncle will come to you, saying, "Buy my field which *is* in Anathoth, for the right of redemption *is* yours to buy *it*." ' 8Then Hanamel my uncle's son came to me in the court of the prison according to the word of the LORD, and said to me, 'Please buy my field that *is* in Anathoth, which *is* in the country of Benjamin; for the right of inheritance *is* yours, and the redemption yours; buy *it* for yourself.' Then I knew that this was the word of the LORD. 9So I bought the field from Hanamel, the son of my uncle who *was* in Anathoth, and weighed *out to* him the money— seventeen shekels of silver. 10And I signed

---

31:32 ᵃFollowing Masoretic Text, Targum, and Vulgate; Septuagint and Syriac read *and I turned away from them.*   **32:4** ᵃLiterally *mouth to mouth*

the deed and sealed *it,* took witnesses, and weighed the money on the scales. ¹¹So I took the purchase deed, *both* that which was sealed *according* to the law and custom, and that which was open; ¹²and I gave the purchase deed to Baruch the son of Neriah, son of Mahseiah, in the presence of Hanamel my uncle's *son,* and in the presence of the witnesses who signed the purchase deed, before all the Jews who sat in the court of the prison. ¹³"Then I charged Baruch before them, saying, ¹⁴'Thus says the LORD of hosts, the God of Israel: "Take these deeds, both this purchase deed which is sealed and this deed which is open, and put them in an earthen vessel, that they may last many days." ¹⁵For thus says the LORD of hosts, the God of Israel: "Houses and fields and vineyards shall be possessed again in this land." '

Jeremiah Prays for Understanding

¹⁶"Now when I had delivered the purchase deed to Baruch the son of Neriah, I prayed to the LORD, saying: ¹⁷'Ah, Lord GOD! Behold, You have made the heavens and the earth by Your great power and outstretched arm. There is nothing too hard for You. ¹⁸*You* show lovingkindness to thousands, and repay the iniquity of the fathers into the bosom of their children after them—the Great, the Mighty God, whose name *is* the LORD of hosts. ¹⁹*You are* great in counsel and mighty in work, for Your eyes *are* open to all the ways of the sons of men, to give everyone according to his ways and according to the fruit of his doings. ²⁰You have set signs and wonders in the land of Egypt, to this day, and in Israel and among *other* men; and You have made Yourself a name, as it is this day. ²¹You have brought Your people Israel out of the land of Egypt with signs and wonders, with a strong hand and an outstretched arm, and with great terror; ²²You have given them this land, of which You swore to their fathers to give them—"a land flowing with milk and honey."ᵃ ²³And they came in and took possession of it, but they have not obeyed Your voice or walked in Your law. They have done nothing of all that You commanded them to do; therefore You have caused all this calamity to come upon them.

²⁴'Look, the siege mounds! They have come to the city to take it; and the city has been given into the hand of the Chaldeans who fight against it, because of the sword and famine and pestilence. What You have spoken has happened; there You see *it!* ²⁵And You have said to me, O Lord GOD, "Buy the field for money, and take witnesses"!—yet the city has been given into the hand of the Chaldeans.' "

God's Assurance of the People's Return

²⁶Then the word of the LORD came to Jeremiah, saying, ²⁷"Behold, I *am* the LORD, the God of all flesh. Is there anything too hard for Me? ²⁸Therefore thus says the LORD: 'Behold, I will give this city into the hand of the Chaldeans, into the hand of Nebuchadnezzar king of Babylon, and he shall take it. ²⁹And the Chaldeans who fight against this city shall come and set fire to this city and burn it, with the houses on whose roofs they have offered incense to Baal and poured out drink offerings to other gods, to provoke Me to anger; ³⁰because the children of Israel and the children of Judah have done only evil before Me from their youth. For the children of Israel have provoked Me only to anger with the work of their hands,' says the LORD. ³¹'For this city has been to Me *a provocation of* My anger and My fury from the day that they built it, even to this day; so I will remove it from before My face ³²because of all the evil of the children of Israel and the children of Judah, which they have done to provoke Me to anger— they, their kings, their princes, their priests, their prophets, the men of Judah, and the inhabitants of Jerusalem. ³³And they have turned to Me the back, and not the face; though I taught them, rising up early and teaching *them,* yet they have not listened to receive instruction. ³⁴But they set their abominations in the house which is called by My name, to defile it. ³⁵And they built the high places of Baal which *are* in the Valley of the Son of Hinnom, to cause their sons and their daughters to pass through *the fire* to Molech, which I did not command them, nor did it come into My mind

---

32:22 ᵃExodus 3:8

that they should do this abomination, to cause Judah to sin.'

36"Now therefore, thus says the LORD, the God of Israel, concerning this city of which you say, 'It shall be delivered into the hand of the king of Babylon by the sword, by the famine, and by the pestilence: 37Behold, I will gather them out of all countries where I have driven them in My anger, in My fury, and in great wrath; I will bring them back to this place, and I will cause them to dwell safely. 38They shall be My people, and I will be their God; 39then I will give them one heart and one way, that they may fear Me forever, for the good of them and their children after them. 40And I will make an everlasting covenant with them, that I will not turn away from doing them good; but I will put My fear in their hearts so that they will not depart from Me. 41Yes, I will rejoice over them to do them good, and I will assuredly plant them in this land, with all My heart and with all My soul.'

42"For thus says the LORD: 'Just as I have brought all this great calamity on this people, so I will bring on them all the good that I have promised them. 43And fields will be bought in this land of which you say, "It is desolate, without man or beast; it has been given into the hand of the Chaldeans." 44Men will buy fields for money, sign deeds

---

FAITH

"... the LORD who formed it to establish it. ..."
                                        JEREMIAH 33:2

The Signature of the Creator

Charles Stine (1882–1954), the Director of Research for the E.I. Dupont Company and leader in the development of significant new products and patents, most of which were connected with propellant powder, high explosives, dyes, artificial leather, and paints, stated:

> The world about us, far more intricate than any watch, filled with checks and balances of a hundred varieties, marvelous beyond even the imagination of the most skilled scientific investigator, this beautiful and intricate creation, bears the signature of its Creator, graven in its works.

---

and seal *them,* and take witnesses, in the land of Benjamin, in the places around Jerusalem, in the cities of Judah, in the cities of the mountains, in the cities of the lowland, and in the cities of the South; for I will cause their captives to return,' says the LORD."

Excellence of the Restored Nation

33 Moreover the word of the LORD came to Jeremiah a second time, while he was still shut up in the court of the prison, saying, 2"Thus says the LORD who made it, the LORD who formed it to establish it (the LORD *is* His name): 3'Call to Me, and I will answer you, and show you great and mighty things, which you do not know.'

4"For thus says the LORD, the God of Israel, concerning the houses of this city and the houses of the kings of Judah, which have been pulled down *to fortify*ᵃ against the siege mounds and the sword: 5'They come to fight with the Chaldeans, but *only* to fill their placesᵃ with the dead bodies of men whom I will slay in My anger and My fury, all for whose wickedness I have hidden My face from this city. 6Behold, I will bring it health and healing; I will heal them and reveal to them the abundance of peace and truth. 7And I will cause the captives of Judah and the captives of Israel to return, and will rebuild those places as at the first. 8I will cleanse them from all their iniquity by which they have sinned against Me, and I will pardon all their iniquities by which they have sinned and by which they have transgressed against Me. 9Then it shall be to Me a name of joy, a praise, and an honor before all nations of the earth, who shall hear all the good that I do to them; they shall fear and tremble for all the goodness and all the prosperity that I provide for it.'

10"Thus says the LORD: 'Again there shall be heard in this place—of which you say, "It *is* desolate, without man and without beast"—in the cities of Judah, in the streets of Jerusalem that are desolate, without man and without inhabitant and without beast, 11the voice of joy and the voice of gladness,

---

33:4 ᵃCompare Isaiah 22:10   **33:5** ᵃCompare 2 Kings 23:14

the voice of the bridegroom and the voice of the bride, the voice of those who will say:

> "Praise the Lord of hosts,
> For the Lord *is* good,
> For His mercy *endures* forever"—

and of those *who will* bring the sacrifice of praise into the house of the Lord. For I will cause the captives of the land to return as at the first,' says the Lord.

¹²"Thus says the Lord of hosts: 'In this place which is desolate, without man and without beast, and in all its cities, there shall again be a dwelling place of shepherds causing *their* flocks to lie down. ¹³In the cities of the mountains, in the cities of the lowland, in the cities of the South, in the land of Benjamin, in the places around Jerusalem, and in the cities of Judah, the flocks shall again pass under the hands of him who counts *them*,' says the Lord.

¹⁴'Behold, the days are coming,' says the Lord, 'that I will perform that good thing which I have promised to the house of Israel and to the house of Judah:

> ¹⁵ 'In those days and at that time
> I will cause to grow up to David
> A Branch of righteousness;
> He shall execute judgment and
> righteousness in the earth.
> ¹⁶ In those days Judah will be saved,
> And Jerusalem will dwell safely.
> And this *is the name* by which she
> will be called:

THE LORD OUR RIGHTEOUSNESS.'ᵃ

¹⁷"For thus says the Lord: 'David shall never lack a man to sit on the throne of the house of Israel; ¹⁸nor shall the priests, the Levites, lack a man to offer burnt offerings before Me, to kindle grain offerings, and to sacrifice continually.' "

The Permanence of God's Covenant

¹⁹And the word of the Lord came to Jeremiah, saying, ²⁰"Thus says the Lord: 'If you can break My covenant with the day and My covenant with the night, so that there will not be day and night in their season, ²¹then My covenant may also be broken with David My servant, so that he shall not have a son to reign on his throne, and with the Levites, the priests, My ministers. ²²As the host of heaven cannot be numbered, nor the sand of the sea measured, so will I multiply the descendants of David My servant and the Levites who minister to Me.' "

²³Moreover the word of the Lord came to Jeremiah, saying, ²⁴"Have you not considered what these people have spoken, saying, 'The two families which the Lord has chosen, He has also cast them off'? Thus they have despised My people, as if they should no more be a nation before them.

²⁵"Thus says the Lord: 'If My covenant *is* not with day and night, *and if* I have not appointed the ordinances of heaven and earth, ²⁶then I will cast away the descendants of Jacob and David My servant, *so* that I will not take *any* of his descendants *to be* rulers over the descendants of Abraham, Isaac, and Jacob. For I will cause their captives to return, and will have mercy on them.' "

Zedekiah Warned by God

34 The word which came to Jeremiah from the Lord, when Nebuchadnezzar king of Babylon and all his army, all the kingdoms of the earth under his dominion, and all the people, fought against Jerusalem and all its cities, saying, ²"Thus says the Lord, the God of Israel: 'Go and speak to Zedekiah king of Judah and tell him, "Thus says the Lord: 'Behold, I will give this city into the hand of the king of Babylon, and he shall burn it with fire. ³And you shall not escape from his hand, but shall surely be taken and delivered into his hand; your eyes shall see the eyes of the king of Babylon, he shall speak with you face to face,ᵃ and you shall go to Babylon.' " ' ⁴Yet hear the word of the Lord, O Zedekiah king of Judah! Thus says the Lord concerning you: 'You shall not die by the sword. ⁵You shall die in peace; as in the ceremonies of your fathers, the former kings who were before you, so they shall burn *incense* for you and lament for you, *saying,* "Alas, lord!"

33:16 ᵃCompare 23:5, 6   **34:3** ᵃLiterally *mouth to mouth*

For I have pronounced the word, says the Lord.'"

⁶Then Jeremiah the prophet spoke all these words to Zedekiah king of Judah in Jerusalem, ⁷when the king of Babylon's army fought against Jerusalem and all the cities of Judah that were left, against Lachish and Azekah; for *only* these fortified cities remained of the cities of Judah.

Treacherous Treatment of Slaves

⁸*This is* the word that came to Jeremiah from the Lord, after King Zedekiah had made a covenant with all the people who *were* at Jerusalem to proclaim liberty to them: ⁹that every man should set free his male and female slave—a Hebrew man or woman—that no one should keep a Jewish brother in bondage. ¹⁰Now when all the princes and all the people, who had entered into the covenant, heard that everyone should set free his male and female slaves, that no one should keep them in bondage anymore, they obeyed and let *them* go. ¹¹But afterward they changed their minds and made the male and female slaves return, whom they had set free, and brought them into subjection as male and female slaves.

¹²Therefore the word of the Lord came to Jeremiah from the Lord, saying, ¹³"Thus says the Lord, the God of Israel: 'I made a covenant with your fathers in the day that I brought them out of the land of Egypt, out of the house of bondage, saying, ¹⁴"At the end of seven years let every man set free his Hebrew brother, who has been sold to him; and when he has served you six years, you shall let him go free from you." But your fathers did not obey Me nor incline their ear. ¹⁵Then you recently turned and did what was right in My sight—every man proclaiming liberty to his neighbor; and you made a covenant before Me in the house which is called by My name. ¹⁶Then you turned around and profaned My name, and every one of you brought back his male and female slaves, whom you had set at liberty, at their pleasure, and brought them back into subjection, to be your male and female slaves.'

¹⁷"Therefore thus says the Lord: 'You have not obeyed Me in proclaiming liberty, every one to his brother and every one to his neighbor. Behold, I proclaim liberty to you,' says the Lord—'to the sword, to pestilence, and to famine! And I will deliver you to trouble among all the kingdoms of the earth. ¹⁸And I will give the men who have transgressed My covenant, who have not performed the words of the covenant which they made before Me, when they cut the calf in two and passed between the parts of it— ¹⁹the princes of Judah, the princes of Jerusalem, the eunuchs, the priests, and all the people of the land who passed between the parts of the calf— ²⁰I will give them into the hand of their enemies and into the hand of those who seek their life. Their dead bodies shall be for meat for the birds of the heaven and the beasts of the earth. ²¹And I will give Zedekiah king of Judah and his princes into the hand of their enemies, into the hand of those who seek their life, and into the hand of the king of Babylon's army which has gone back from you. ²²Behold, I will command,' says the Lord, 'and cause them to return to this city. They will fight against it and take it and burn it with fire; and I will make the cities of Judah a desolation without inhabitant.'"

The Obedient Rechabites

35 The word which came to Jeremiah from the Lord in the days of Jehoiakim the son of Josiah, king of Judah, saying, ²"Go to the house of the Rechabites, speak to them, and bring them into the house of the Lord, into one of the chambers, and give them wine to drink."

³Then I took Jaazaniah the son of Jeremiah, the son of Habazziniah, his brothers and all his sons, and the whole house of the Rechabites, ⁴and I brought them into the house of the Lord, into the chamber of the sons of Hanan the son of Igdaliah, a man of God, which *was* by the chamber of the princes, above the chamber of Maaseiah the son of Shallum, the keeper of the door. ⁵Then I set before the sons of the house of the Rechabites bowls full of wine, and cups; and I said to them, "Drink wine."

⁶But they said, "We will drink no wine, for Jonadab the son of Rechab, our father, commanded us, saying, 'You shall drink no wine,

you nor your sons, forever. ⁷You shall not build a house, sow seed, plant a vineyard, nor have *any of these;* but all your days you shall dwell in tents, that you may live many days in the land where you are sojourners.' ⁸Thus we have obeyed the voice of Jonadab the son of Rechab, our father, in all that he charged us, to drink no wine all our days, we, our wives, our sons, or our daughters, ⁹nor to build ourselves houses to dwell in; nor do we have vineyard, field, or seed. ¹⁰But we have dwelt in tents, and have obeyed and done according to all that Jonadab our father commanded us. ¹¹But it came to pass, when Nebuchadnezzar king of Babylon came up into the land, that we said, 'Come, let us go to Jerusalem for fear of the army of the Chaldeans and for fear of the army of the Syrians.' So we dwell at Jerusalem."

¹²Then came the word of the LORD to Jeremiah, saying, ¹³"Thus says the LORD of hosts, the God of Israel: 'Go and tell the men of Judah and the inhabitants of Jerusalem, "Will you not receive instruction to obey My words?" says the LORD. ¹⁴"The words of Jonadab the son of Rechab, which he commanded his sons, not to drink wine, are performed; for to this day they drink none, and obey their father's commandment. But although I have spoken to you, rising early and speaking, you did not obey Me. ¹⁵I have also sent to you all My servants the prophets, rising up early and sending *them,* saying, 'Turn now everyone from his evil way, amend your doings, and do not go after other gods to serve them; then you will dwell in the land which I have given you and your fathers.' But you have not inclined your ear, nor obeyed Me. ¹⁶Surely the sons of Jonadab the son of Rechab have performed the commandment of their father, which he commanded them, but this people has not obeyed Me."'

¹⁷"Therefore thus says the LORD God of hosts, the God of Israel: 'Behold, I will bring on Judah and on all the inhabitants of Jerusalem all the doom that I have pronounced against them; because I have spoken to them but they have not heard, and I have called to them but they have not answered.'"

¹⁸And Jeremiah said to the house of the Rechabites, "Thus says the LORD of hosts, the God of Israel: 'Because you have obeyed the commandment of Jonadab your father, and kept all his precepts and done according to all that he commanded you, ¹⁹therefore thus says the LORD of hosts, the God of Israel: "Jonadab the son of Rechab shall not lack a man to stand before Me forever."'"

The Scroll Read in the Temple

36 Now it came to pass in the fourth year of Jehoiakim the son of Josiah, king of Judah, *that* this word came to Jeremiah from the LORD, saying: ²"Take a scroll of a book and write on it all the words that I have spoken to you against Israel, against Judah, and against all the nations, from the day I spoke to you, from the days of Josiah even to this day. ³It may be that the house of Judah will hear all the adversities which I purpose to bring upon them, that everyone may turn from his evil way, that I may forgive their iniquity and their sin."

⁴Then Jeremiah called Baruch the son of Neriah; and Baruch wrote on a scroll of a book, at the instruction of Jeremiah,ᵃ all the words of the LORD which He had spoken to him. ⁵And Jeremiah commanded Baruch, saying, "I *am* confined, I cannot go into the house of the LORD. ⁶You go, therefore, and read from the scroll which you have written at my instruction,ᵃ the words of the LORD, in the hearing of the people in the LORD's house on the day of fasting. And you shall also read them in the hearing of all Judah who come from their cities. ⁷It may be that they will present their supplication before the LORD, and everyone will turn from his evil way. For great *is* the anger and the fury that the LORD has pronounced against this people." ⁸And Baruch the son of Neriah did according to all that Jeremiah the prophet commanded him, reading from the book the words of the LORD in the LORD's house.

⁹Now it came to pass in the fifth year of Jehoiakim the son of Josiah, king of Judah, in the ninth month, *that* they proclaimed a fast before the LORD to all the people in

---

36:4 ᵃLiterally *from Jeremiah's mouth*
36:6 ᵃLiterally *from my mouth*

Jerusalem, and to all the people who came from the cities of Judah to Jerusalem. ¹⁰Then Baruch read from the book the words of Jeremiah in the house of the Lord, in the chamber of Gemariah the son of Shaphan the scribe, in the upper court at the entry of the New Gate of the Lord's house, in the hearing of all the people.

The Scroll Read in the Palace

¹¹When Michaiah the son of Gemariah, the son of Shaphan, heard all the words of the Lord from the book, ¹²he then went down to the king's house, into the scribe's chamber; and there all the princes were sitting—Elishama the scribe, Delaiah the son of Shemaiah, Elnathan the son of Achbor, Gemariah the son of Shaphan, Zedekiah the son of Hananiah, and all the princes. ¹³Then Michaiah declared to them all the words that he had heard when Baruch read the book in the hearing of the people. ¹⁴Therefore all the princes sent Jehudi the son of Nethaniah, the son of Shelemiah, the son of Cushi, to Baruch, saying, "Take in your hand the scroll from which you have read in the hearing of the people, and come." So Baruch the son of Neriah took the scroll in his hand and came to them. ¹⁵And they said to him, "Sit down now, and read it in our hearing." So Baruch read it in their hearing.

¹⁶Now it happened, when they had heard all the words, that they looked in fear from one to another, and said to Baruch, "We will surely tell the king of all these words." ¹⁷And they asked Baruch, saying, "Tell us now, how did you write all these words—at his instruction?"ᵃ

¹⁸So Baruch answered them, "He proclaimed with his mouth all these words to me, and I wrote them with ink in the book."

¹⁹Then the princes said to Baruch, "Go and hide, you and Jeremiah; and let no one know where you are."

The King Destroys Jeremiah's Scroll

²⁰And they went to the king, into the court; but they stored the scroll in the chamber of Elishama the scribe, and told all the words in the hearing of the king. ²¹So the king sent Jehudi to bring the scroll, and he took it from Elishama the scribe's chamber. And Jehudi read it in the hearing of the king and in the hearing of all the princes who stood beside the king. ²²Now the king was sitting in the winter house in the ninth month, with a fire burning on the hearth before him. ²³And it happened, when Jehudi had read three or four columns, that the king cut it with the scribe's knife and cast it into the fire that was on the hearth, until all the scroll was consumed in the fire that was on the hearth. ²⁴Yet they were not afraid, nor did they tear their garments, the king nor any of his servants who heard all these words. ²⁵Nevertheless Elnathan, Delaiah, and Gemariah implored the king not to burn the scroll; but he would not listen to them. ²⁶And the king commanded Jerahmeel the king'sᵃ son, Seraiah the son of Azriel, and Shelemiah the son of Abdeel, to seize Baruch the scribe and Jeremiah the prophet, but the Lord hid them.

Jeremiah Rewrites the Scroll

²⁷Now after the king had burned the scroll with the words which Baruch had written at the instruction of Jeremiah,ᵃ the word of the Lord came to Jeremiah, saying: ²⁸"Take yet another scroll, and write on it all the former words that were in the first scroll which Jehoiakim the king of Judah has burned. ²⁹And you shall say to Jehoiakim king of Judah, 'Thus says the Lord: "You have burned this scroll, saying, 'Why have you written in it that the king of Babylon will certainly come and destroy this land, and cause man and beast to cease from here?'" ³⁰Therefore thus says the Lord concerning Jehoiakim king of Judah: "He shall have no one to sit on the throne of David, and his dead body shall be cast out to the heat of the day and the frost of the night. ³¹I will punish him, his family, and his servants for their iniquity; and I will bring on them, on the inhabitants of Jerusalem, and on the men of Judah all the doom that I have pronounced against them; but they did not heed."'"

³²Then Jeremiah took another scroll and gave it to Baruch the scribe, the son of

---

36:17 ᵃLiterally with his mouth **36:26** ᵃHebrew Hammelech **36:27** ᵃLiterally from Jeremiah's mouth

Neriah, who wrote on it at the instruction of Jeremiah[a] all the words of the book which Jehoiakim king of Judah had burned in the fire. And besides, there were added to them many similar words.

Zedekiah's Vain Hope

37 Now King Zedekiah the son of Josiah reigned instead of Coniah the son of Jehoiakim, whom Nebuchadnezzar king of Babylon made king in the land of Judah. [2]But neither he nor his servants nor the people of the land gave heed to the words of the LORD which He spoke by the prophet Jeremiah.

[3]And Zedekiah the king sent Jehucal the son of Shelemiah, and Zephaniah the son of Maaseiah, the priest, to the prophet Jeremiah, saying, "Pray now to the LORD our God for us." [4]Now Jeremiah was coming and going among the people, for they had not *yet* put him in prison. [5]Then Pharaoh's army came up from Egypt; and when the Chaldeans who were besieging Jerusalem heard news of them, they departed from Jerusalem.

[6]Then the word of the LORD came to the prophet Jeremiah, saying, [7]"Thus says the LORD, the God of Israel, 'Thus you shall say to the king of Judah, who sent you to Me to inquire of Me: "Behold, Pharaoh's army which has come up to help you will return to Egypt, to their own land. [8]And the Chaldeans shall come back and fight against this city, and take it and burn it with fire."' [9]Thus says the LORD: 'Do not deceive yourselves, saying, "The Chaldeans will surely depart from us," for they will not depart. [10]For though you had defeated the whole army of the Chaldeans who fight against you, and there remained *only* wounded men among them, they would rise up, every man in his tent, and burn the city with fire.' "

Jeremiah Imprisoned

[11]And it happened, when the army of the Chaldeans left *the siege* of Jerusalem for fear of Pharaoh's army, [12]that Jeremiah went out of Jerusalem to go into the land of Benjamin to claim his property there among the people. [13]And when he was in the Gate of Benjamin, a captain of the guard

was there whose name *was* Irijah the son of Shelemiah, the son of Hananiah; and he seized Jeremiah the prophet, saying, "You are defecting to the Chaldeans!"

[14]Then Jeremiah said, "False! I am not defecting to the Chaldeans." But he did not listen to him.

So Irijah seized Jeremiah and brought him to the princes. [15]Therefore the princes were angry with Jeremiah, and they struck him and put him in prison in the house of Jonathan the scribe. For they had made that the prison.

[16]When Jeremiah entered the dungeon and the cells, and Jeremiah had remained there many days, [17]then Zedekiah the king sent and took him *out*. The king asked him secretly in his house, and said, "Is there *any* word from the LORD?"

And Jeremiah said, "There is." Then he said, "You shall be delivered into the hand of the king of Babylon!"

[18]Moreover Jeremiah said to King Zedekiah, "What offense have I committed against you, against your servants, or against this people, that you have put me in prison? [19]Where now *are* your prophets who prophesied to you, saying, 'The king of Babylon will not come against you or against this land'? [20]Therefore please hear now, O my lord the king. Please, let my petition be accepted before you, and do not make me return to the house of Jonathan the scribe, lest I die there."

[21]Then Zedekiah the king commanded that they should commit Jeremiah to the court of the prison, and that they should give him daily a piece of bread from the bakers' street, until all the bread in the city was gone. Thus Jeremiah remained in the court of the prison.

Jeremiah in the Dungeon

38 Now Shephatiah the son of Mattan, Gedaliah the son of Pashhur, Jucal[a] the son of Shelemiah, and Pashhur the son of Malchiah heard the words that Jeremiah had spoken to all the people, saying, [2]"Thus says the LORD: 'He who remains in this city

---

36:32 [a]Literally *from Jeremiah's mouth*   **38:1** [a]Same as *Jehucal* (compare 37:3)

shall die by the sword, by famine, and by pestilence; but he who goes over to the Chaldeans shall live; his life shall be as a prize to him, and he shall live.'[a] 3Thus says the Lord: 'This city shall surely be given into the hand of the king of Babylon's army, which shall take it.'"

4Therefore the princes said to the king, "Please, let this man be put to death, for thus he weakens the hands of the men of war who remain in this city, and the hands of all the people, by speaking such words to them. For this man does not seek the welfare of this people, but their harm."

5Then Zedekiah the king said, "Look, he *is* in your hand. For the king can *do* nothing against you." 6So they took Jeremiah and cast him into the dungeon of Malchiah the king's[a] son, which *was* in the court of the prison, and they let Jeremiah down with ropes. And in the dungeon *there was* no water, but mire. So Jeremiah sank in the mire.

7Now Ebed-Melech the Ethiopian, one of the eunuchs, who was in the king's house, heard that they had put Jeremiah in the dungeon. When the king was sitting at the Gate of Benjamin, 8Ebed-Melech went out of the king's house and spoke to the king, saying: 9"My lord the king, these men have done evil in all that they have done to Jeremiah the prophet, whom they have cast into the dungeon, and he is likely to die from hunger in the place where he is. For *there is* no more bread in the city." 10Then the king commanded Ebed-Melech the Ethiopian, saying, "Take from here thirty men with you, and lift Jeremiah the prophet out of the dungeon before he dies." 11So Ebed-Melech took the men with him and went into the house of the king under the treasury, and took from there old clothes and old rags, and let them down by ropes into the dungeon to Jeremiah. 12Then Ebed-Melech the Ethiopian said to Jeremiah, "Please put these old clothes and rags under your armpits, under the ropes." And Jeremiah did so. 13So they pulled Jeremiah up with ropes and lifted him out of the dungeon. And Jeremiah remained in the court of the prison.

Zedekiah's Fears and Jeremiah's Advice

14Then Zedekiah the king sent and had Jeremiah the prophet brought to him at the third entrance of the house of the Lord. And the king said to Jeremiah, "I will ask you something. Hide nothing from me."

15Jeremiah said to Zedekiah, "If I declare *it* to you, will you not surely put me to death? And if I give you advice, you will not listen to me."

16So Zedekiah the king swore secretly to Jeremiah, saying, "*As* the Lord lives, who made our very souls, I will not put you to death, nor will I give you into the hand of these men who seek your life."

17Then Jeremiah said to Zedekiah, "Thus says the Lord, the God of hosts, the God of Israel: 'If you surely surrender to the king of Babylon's princes, then your soul shall live; this city shall not be burned with fire, and you and your house shall live. 18But if you do not surrender to the king of Babylon's princes, then this city shall be given into the hand of the Chaldeans; they shall burn it with fire, and you shall not escape from their hand.'"

19And Zedekiah the king said to Jeremiah, "I am afraid of the Jews who have defected to the Chaldeans, lest they deliver me into their hand, and they abuse me."

20But Jeremiah said, "They shall not deliver *you.* Please, obey the voice of the Lord which I speak to you. So it shall be well with you, and your soul shall live. 21But if you refuse to surrender, this *is* the word that the Lord has shown me: 22'Now behold, all the women who are left in the king of Judah's house *shall be* surrendered to the king of Babylon's princes, and those *women* shall say:

"Your close friends have set upon you
    And prevailed against you;
Your feet have sunk in the mire,
    And they have turned away again."

23'So they shall surrender all your wives and children to the Chaldeans. You shall not escape from their hand, but shall be taken

---

38:2 [a]Compare 21:9   **38:6** [a]Hebrew *Hammelech*

by the hand of the king of Babylon. And you shall cause this city to be burned with fire.'"

24Then Zedekiah said to Jeremiah, "Let no one know of these words, and you shall not die. 25But if the princes hear that I have talked with you, and they come to you and say to you, 'Declare to us now what you have said to the king, and also what the king said to you; do not hide *it* from us, and we will not put you to death,' 26then you shall say to them, 'I presented my request before the king, that he would not make me return to Jonathan's house to die there.'"

27Then all the princes came to Jeremiah and asked him. And he told them according to all these words that the king had commanded. So they stopped speaking with him, for the conversation had not been heard. 28Now Jeremiah remained in the court of the prison until the day that Jerusalem was taken. And he was *there* when Jerusalem was taken.

The Fall of Jerusalem

39 In the ninth year of Zedekiah king of Judah, in the tenth month, Nebuchadnezzar king of Babylon and all his army came against Jerusalem, and besieged it. 2In the eleventh year of Zedekiah, in the fourth month, on the ninth *day* of the month, the city was penetrated.

3Then all the princes of the king of Babylon came in and sat in the Middle Gate: Nergal-Sharezer, Samgar-Nebo, Sarsechim, Rabsaris,a Nergal-Sarezer, Rabmag,b with the rest of the princes of the king of Babylon.

4So it was, when Zedekiah the king of Judah and all the men of war saw them, that they fled and went out of the city by night, by way of the king's garden, by the gate between the two walls. And he went out by way of the plain.a 5But the Chaldean army pursued them and overtook Zedekiah in the plains of Jericho. And when they had captured him, they brought him up to Nebuchadnezzar king of Babylon, to Riblah in the land of Hamath, where he pronounced judgment on him. 6Then the king of Babylon killed the sons of Zedekiah

before his eyes in Riblah; the king of Babylon also killed all the nobles of Judah. 7Moreover he put out Zedekiah's eyes, and bound him with bronze fetters to carry him off to Babylon. 8And the Chaldeans burned the king's house and the houses of the people with fire, and broke down the walls of Jerusalem. 9Then Nebuzaradan the captain of the guard carried away captive to Babylon the remnant of the people who remained in the city and those who defected to him, with the rest of the people who remained. 10But Nebuzaradan the captain of the guard left in the land of Judah the poor people, who had nothing, and gave them vineyards and fields at the same time.

Jeremiah Goes Free

11Now Nebuchadnezzar king of Babylon gave charge concerning Jeremiah to Nebuzaradan the captain of the guard, saying, 12"Take him and look after him, and do him no harm; but do to him just as he says to you." 13So Nebuzaradan the captain of the guard sent Nebushasban, Rabsaris, Nergal-Sharezer, Rabmag, and all the king of Babylon's chief officers; 14then they sent *someone* to take Jeremiah from the court of the prison, and committed him to Gedaliah the son of Ahikam, the son of Shaphan, that he should take him home. So he dwelt among the people.

15Meanwhile the word of the LORD had come to Jeremiah while he was shut up in the court of the prison, saying, 16"Go and speak to Ebed-Melech the Ethiopian, saying, 'Thus says the LORD of hosts, the God of Israel: "Behold, I will bring My words upon this city for adversity and not for good, and they shall be *performed* in that day before you. 17But I will deliver you in that day," says the LORD, "and you shall not be given into the hand of the men of whom you *are* afraid. 18For I will surely deliver you, and you shall not fall by the sword; but your life shall be as a prize to you, because you have put your trust in Me," says the LORD.'"

39:3 aA title, probably *Chief Officer;* also verse 13
bA title, probably *Troop Commander;* also verse 13
39:4 aOr *the Arabah,* that is, the Jordan Valley

Jeremiah with Gedaliah the Governor

40 The word that came to Jeremiah from the LORD after Nebuzaradan the captain of the guard had let him go from Ramah, when he had taken him bound in chains among all who were carried away captive from Jerusalem and Judah, who were carried away captive to Babylon. [2]And the captain of the guard took Jeremiah and said to him: "The LORD your God has pronounced this doom on this place. [3]Now the LORD has brought *it,* and has done just as He said. Because you *people* have sinned against the LORD, and not obeyed His voice, therefore this thing has come upon you. [4]And now look, I free you this day from the chains that *were* on your hand. If it seems good to you to come with me to Babylon, come, and I will look after you. But if it seems wrong for you to come with me to Babylon, remain here. See, all the land *is* before you; wherever it seems good and convenient for you to go, go there."

[5]Now while Jeremiah had not yet gone back, *Nebuzaradan said,* "Go back to Gedaliah the son of Ahikam, the son of Shaphan, whom the king of Babylon has made governor over the cities of Judah, and dwell with him among the people. Or go wherever it seems convenient for you to go." So the captain of the guard gave him rations and a gift and let him go. [6]Then Jeremiah went to Gedaliah the son of Ahikam, to Mizpah, and dwelt with him among the people who were left in the land.

[7]And when all the captains of the armies who *were* in the fields, they and their men, heard that the king of Babylon had made Gedaliah the son of Ahikam governor in the land, and had committed to him men, women, children, and the poorest of the land who had not been carried away captive to Babylon, [8]then they came to Gedaliah at Mizpah—Ishmael the son of Nethaniah, Johanan and Jonathan the sons of Kareah, Seraiah the son of Tanhumeth, the sons of Ephai the Netophathite, and Jezaniah[a] the son of a Maachathite, they and their men. [9]And Gedaliah the son of Ahikam, the son of Shaphan, took an oath before them and their men, saying, "Do not be afraid to serve the Chaldeans. Dwell in the land and serve the king of Babylon, and it shall be well with you. [10]As for me, I will indeed dwell at Mizpah and serve the Chaldeans who come to us. But you, gather wine and summer fruit and oil, put *them* in your vessels, and dwell in your cities that you have taken."

[11]Likewise, when all the Jews who *were* in Moab, among the Ammonites, in Edom, and who *were* in all the countries, heard that the king of Babylon had left a remnant of Judah, and that he had set over them Gedaliah the son of Ahikam, the son of Shaphan, [12]then all the Jews returned out of all places where they had been driven, and came to the land of Judah, to Gedaliah at Mizpah, and gathered wine and summer fruit in abundance.

[13]Moreover Johanan the son of Kareah and all the captains of the forces that *were* in the fields came to Gedaliah at Mizpah, [14]and said to him, "Do you certainly know that Baalis the king of the Ammonites has sent Ishmael the son of Nethaniah to murder you?" But Gedaliah the son of Ahikam did not believe them.

[15]Then Johanan the son of Kareah spoke secretly to Gedaliah in Mizpah, saying, "Let me go, please, and I will kill Ishmael the son of Nethaniah, and no one will know *it.* Why should he murder you, so that all the Jews who are gathered to you would be scattered, and the remnant in Judah perish?"

[16]But Gedaliah the son of Ahikam said to Johanan the son of Kareah, "You shall not do this thing, for you speak falsely concerning Ishmael."

Insurrection Against Gedaliah

41 Now it came to pass in the seventh month *that* Ishmael the son of Nethaniah, the son of Elishama, of the royal family and of the officers of the king, came with ten men to Gedaliah the son of Ahikam, at Mizpah. And there they ate bread together in Mizpah. [2]Then Ishmael the son of Nethaniah, and the ten men who were with him, arose and struck Gedaliah the son of Ahikam, the son of Shaphan, with the sword, and killed him whom the king of Babylon

---

40:8 [a]Spelled *Jaazaniah* in 2 Kings 25:23

had made governor over the land. ³Ishmael also struck down all the Jews who were with him, *that is,* with Gedaliah at Mizpah, and the Chaldeans who were found there, the men of war.

⁴And it happened, on the second day after he had killed Gedaliah, when as yet no one knew *it,* ⁵that certain men came from Shechem, from Shiloh, and from Samaria, eighty men with their beards shaved and their clothes torn, having cut themselves, with offerings and incense in their hand, to bring *them* to the house of the LORD. ⁶Now Ishmael the son of Nethaniah went out from Mizpah to meet them, weeping as he went along; and it happened as he met them that he said to them, "Come to Gedaliah the son of Ahikam!" ⁷So it was, when they came into the midst of the city, that Ishmael the son of Nethaniah killed them *and cast them* into the midst of a pit, he and the men who were with him. ⁸But ten men were found among them who said to Ishmael, "Do not kill us, for we have treasures of wheat, barley, oil, and honey in the field." So he desisted and did not kill them among their brethren. ⁹Now the pit into which Ishmael had cast all the dead bodies of the men whom he had slain, because of Gedaliah, *was* the same one Asa the king had made for fear of Baasha king of Israel. Ishmael the son of Nethaniah filled it with *the* slain. ¹⁰Then Ishmael carried away captive all the rest of the people who *were* in Mizpah, the king's daughters and all the people who remained in Mizpah, whom Nebuzaradan the captain of the guard had committed to Gedaliah the son of Ahikam. And Ishmael the son of Nethaniah carried them away captive and departed to go over to the Ammonites.

¹¹But when Johanan the son of Kareah and all the captains of the forces that *were* with him heard of all the evil that Ishmael the son of Nethaniah had done, ¹²they took all the men and went to fight with Ishmael the son of Nethaniah; and they found him by the great pool that *is* in Gibeon. ¹³So it was, when all the people who *were* with Ishmael saw Johanan the son of Kareah, and all the captains of the forces who *were* with him, that they were glad. ¹⁴Then all

the people whom Ishmael had carried away captive from Mizpah turned around and came back, and went to Johanan the son of Kareah. ¹⁵But Ishmael the son of Nethaniah escaped from Johanan with eight men and went to the Ammonites.

¹⁶Then Johanan the son of Kareah, and all the captains of the forces that were with him, took from Mizpah all the rest of the people whom he had recovered from Ishmael the son of Nethaniah after he had murdered Gedaliah the son of Ahikam—the mighty men of war and the women and the children and the eunuchs, whom he had brought back from Gibeon. ¹⁷And they departed and dwelt in the habitation of Chimham, which is near Bethlehem, as they went on their way to Egypt, ¹⁸because of the Chaldeans; for they were afraid of them, because Ishmael the son of Nethaniah had murdered Gedaliah the son of Ahikam, whom the king of Babylon had made governor in the land.

The Flight to Egypt Forbidden

42 Now all the captains of the forces, Johanan the son of Kareah, Jezaniah the son of Hoshaiah, and all the people, from the least to the greatest, came near ²and said to Jeremiah the prophet, "Please, let our petition be acceptable to you, and pray for us to the LORD your God, for all this remnant (since we are left *but* a few of many, as you can see), ³that the LORD your God may show us the way in which we should walk and the thing we should do."

⁴Then Jeremiah the prophet said to them, "I have heard. Indeed, I will pray to the LORD your God according to your words, and it shall be, *that* whatever the LORD answers you, I will declare *it* to you. I will keep nothing back from you."

⁵So they said to Jeremiah, "Let the LORD be a true and faithful witness between us, if we do not do according to everything which the LORD your God sends us by you. ⁶Whether *it is* pleasing or displeasing, we will obey the voice of the LORD our God to whom we send you, that it may be well with us when we obey the voice of the LORD our God."

⁷And it happened after ten days that the word of the LORD came to Jeremiah. ⁸Then

he called Johanan the son of Kareah, all the captains of the forces which *were* with him, and all the people from the least even to the greatest, [9]and said to them, "Thus says the Lord, the God of Israel, to whom you sent me to present your petition before Him: [10]'If you will still remain in this land, then I will build you and not pull *you* down, and I will plant you and not pluck *you* up. For I relent concerning the disaster that I have brought upon you. [11]Do not be afraid of the king of Babylon, of whom you are afraid; do not be afraid of him,' says the Lord, 'for I *am* with you, to save you and deliver you from his hand. [12]And I will show you mercy, that he may have mercy on you and cause you to return to your own land.'

[13]"But if you say, 'We will not dwell in this land,' disobeying the voice of the Lord your God, [14]saying, 'No, but we will go to the land of Egypt where we shall see no war, nor hear the sound of the trumpet, nor be hungry for bread, and there we will dwell'— [15]Then hear now the word of the Lord, O remnant of Judah! Thus says the Lord of hosts, the God of Israel: 'If you wholly set your faces to enter Egypt, and go to dwell there, [16]then it shall be *that* the sword which you feared shall overtake you there in the land of Egypt; the famine of which you were afraid shall follow close after you there *in* Egypt; and there you shall die. [17]So shall it be with all the men who set their faces to go to Egypt to dwell there. They shall die by the sword, by famine, and by pestilence. And none of them shall remain or escape from the disaster that I will bring upon them.'

[18]"For thus says the Lord of hosts, the God of Israel: 'As My anger and My fury have been poured out on the inhabitants of Jerusalem, so will My fury be poured out on you when you enter Egypt. And you shall be an oath, an astonishment, a curse, and a reproach; and you shall see this place no more.'

[19]"The Lord has said concerning you, O remnant of Judah, 'Do not go to Egypt!' Know certainly that I have admonished you this day. [20]For you were hypocrites in your hearts when you sent me to the Lord your God, saying, 'Pray for us to the Lord our God, and according to all that the Lord your God says, so declare to us and we will do *it*.' [21]And I have this day declared *it* to you, but you have not obeyed the voice of the Lord your God, or anything which He has sent you by me. [22]Now therefore, know certainly that you shall die by the sword, by famine, and by pestilence in the place where you desire to go to dwell."

Jeremiah Taken to Egypt

43 Now it happened, when Jeremiah had stopped speaking to all the people all the words of the Lord their God, for which the Lord their God had sent him to them, all these words, [2]that Azariah the son of Hoshaiah, Johanan the son of Kareah, and all the proud men spoke, saying to Jeremiah, "You speak falsely! The Lord our God has not sent you to say, 'Do not go to Egypt to dwell there.' [3]But Baruch the son of Neriah has set you against us, to deliver us into the hand of the Chaldeans, that they may put us to death or carry us away captive to Babylon." [4]So Johanan the son of Kareah, all the captains of the forces, and all the people would not obey the voice of the Lord, to remain in the land of Judah. [5]But Johanan the son of Kareah and all the captains of the forces took all the remnant of Judah who had returned to dwell in the land of Judah, from all nations where they had been driven— [6]men, women, children, the king's daughters, and every person whom Nebuzaradan the captain of the guard had left with Gedaliah the son of Ahikam, the son of Shaphan, and Jeremiah the prophet and Baruch the son of Neriah. [7]So they went to the land of Egypt, for they did not obey the voice of the Lord. And they went as far as Tahpanhes.

[8]Then the word of the Lord came to Jeremiah in Tahpanhes, saying, [9]"Take large stones in your hand, and hide them in the sight of the men of Judah, in the clay in the brick courtyard which *is* at the entrance to Pharaoh's house in Tahpanhes; [10]and say to them, 'Thus says the Lord of hosts, the God of Israel: "Behold, I will send and bring Nebuchadnezzar the king of Babylon, My servant, and will set his throne above these stones that I have hidden. And he will spread his royal pavilion over them. [11]When he

comes, he shall strike the land of Egypt *and deliver* to death *those appointed* for death, and to captivity *those appointed* for captivity, and to the sword *those appointed* for the sword. [12]I[a] will kindle a fire in the houses of the gods of Egypt, and he shall burn them and carry them away captive. And he shall array himself with the land of Egypt, as a shepherd puts on his garment, and he shall go out from there in peace. [13]He shall also break the *sacred* pillars of Beth Shemesh[a] that *are* in the land of Egypt; and the houses of the gods of the Egyptians he shall burn with fire." ' "

Israelites Will Be Punished in Egypt

44 The word that came to Jeremiah concerning all the Jews who dwell in the land of Egypt, who dwell at Migdol, at Tahpanhes, at Noph,[a] and in the country of Pathros, saying, [2]"Thus says the LORD of hosts, the God of Israel: 'You have seen all the calamity that I have brought on Jerusalem and on all the cities of Judah; and behold, this day they *are* a desolation, and no one dwells in them, [3]because of their wickedness which they have committed to provoke Me to anger, in that they went to burn incense *and* to serve other gods whom they did not know, they nor you nor your fathers. [4]However I have sent to you all My servants the prophets, rising early and sending *them,* saying, "Oh, do not do this abominable thing that I hate!" [5]But they did not listen or incline their ear to turn from their wickedness, to burn no incense to other gods. [6]So My fury and My anger were poured out and kindled in the cities of Judah and in the streets of Jerusalem; and they are wasted *and* desolate, as it is this day.'

[7]"Now therefore, thus says the LORD, the God of hosts, the God of Israel: 'Why do you commit *this* great evil against yourselves, to cut off from you man and woman, child and infant, out of Judah, leaving none to remain, [8]in that you provoke Me to wrath with the works of your hands, burning incense to other gods in the land of Egypt where you have gone to dwell, that you may cut yourselves off and be a curse and a reproach among all the nations of the earth? [9]Have you forgotten the wickedness

of your fathers, the wickedness of the kings of Judah, the wickedness of their wives, your own wickedness, and the wickedness of your wives, which they committed in the land of Judah and in the streets of Jerusalem? [10]They have not been humbled, to this day, nor have they feared; they have not walked in My law or in My statutes that I set before you and your fathers.'

[11]"Therefore thus says the LORD of hosts, the God of Israel: 'Behold, I will set My face against you for catastrophe and for cutting off all Judah. [12]And I will take the remnant of Judah who have set their faces to go into the land of Egypt to dwell there, and they shall all be consumed *and* fall in the land of Egypt. They shall be consumed by the sword *and* by famine. They shall die, from the least to the greatest, by the sword and by famine; and they shall be an oath, an astonishment, a curse and a reproach! [13]For I will punish those who dwell in the land of Egypt, as I have punished Jerusalem, by the sword, by famine, and by pestilence, [14]so that none of the remnant of Judah who have gone into the land of Egypt to dwell there shall escape or survive, lest they return to the land of Judah, to which they desire to return and dwell. For none shall return except those who escape.' "

[15]Then all the men who knew that their wives had burned incense to other gods, with all the women who stood by, a great multitude, and all the people who dwelt in the land of Egypt, in Pathros, answered Jeremiah, saying: [16]"*As for* the word that you have spoken to us in the name of the LORD, we will not listen to you! [17]But we will certainly do whatever has gone out of our own mouth, to burn incense to the queen of heaven and pour out drink offerings to her, as we have done, we and our fathers, our kings and our princes, in the cities of Judah and in the streets of Jerusalem. For *then* we had plenty of food, were well-off, and saw no trouble. [18]But since we stopped burning incense to the queen of heaven and pouring

---

43:12 [a]Following Masoretic Text and Targum; Septuagint, Syriac, and Vulgate read *He.*
43:13 [a]Literally *House of the Sun,* ancient On; later called Heliopolis   **44:1** [a]That is, ancient Memphis

out drink offerings to her, we have lacked everything and have been consumed by the sword and by famine."

[19]*The women also said,* "And when we burned incense to the queen of heaven and poured out drink offerings to her, did we make cakes for her, to worship her, and pour out drink offerings to her without our husbands' *permission?*"

[20]Then Jeremiah spoke to all the people—the men, the women, and all the people who had given him *that* answer—saying: [21]"The incense that you burned in the cities of Judah and in the streets of Jerusalem, you and your fathers, your kings and your princes, and the people of the land, did not the LORD remember them, and did it *not* come into His mind? [22]So the LORD could no longer bear *it,* because of the evil of your doings *and* because of the abominations which you committed. Therefore your land is a desolation, an astonishment, a curse, and without an inhabitant, as *it is* this day. [23]Because you have burned incense and because you have sinned against the LORD, and have not obeyed the voice of the LORD or walked in His law, in His statutes or in His testimonies, therefore this calamity has happened to you, as *at* this day."

[24]Moreover Jeremiah said to all the people and to all the women, "Hear the word of the LORD, all Judah who *are* in the land of Egypt! [25]Thus says the LORD of hosts, the God of Israel, saying: 'You and your wives have spoken with your mouths and fulfilled with your hands, saying, "We will surely keep our vows that we have made, to burn incense to the queen of heaven and pour out drink offerings to her." You will surely keep your vows and perform your vows!' [26]Therefore hear the word of the LORD, all Judah who dwell in the land of Egypt: 'Behold, I have sworn by My great name,' says the LORD, 'that My name shall no more be named in the mouth of any man of Judah in all the land of Egypt, saying, "The Lord GOD lives." [27]Behold, I will watch over them for adversity and not for good. And all the men of Judah who *are* in the land of Egypt shall be consumed by the sword and by famine, until there is an end to them. [28]Yet a small number who escape the sword shall return

from the land of Egypt to the land of Judah; and all the remnant of Judah, who have gone to the land of Egypt to dwell there, shall know whose words will stand, Mine or theirs. [29]And this *shall be* a sign to you,' says the LORD, 'that I will punish you in this place, that you may know that My words will surely stand against you for adversity.'

[30]"Thus says the LORD: 'Behold, I will give Pharaoh Hophra king of Egypt into the hand of his enemies and into the hand of those who seek his life, as I gave Zedekiah king of Judah into the hand of Nebuchadnezzar king of Babylon, his enemy who sought his life.'"

Assurance to Baruch

45 The word that Jeremiah the prophet spoke to Baruch the son of Neriah, when he had written these words in a book at the instruction of Jeremiah,[a] in the fourth year of Jehoiakim the son of Josiah, king of Judah, saying, [2]"Thus says the LORD, the God of Israel, to you, O Baruch: [3]'You said, "Woe is me now! For the LORD has added grief to my sorrow. I fainted in my sighing, and I find no rest."'

[4]"Thus you shall say to him, 'Thus says the LORD: "Behold, what I have built I will break down, and what I have planted I will pluck up, that is, this whole land. [5]And do you seek great things for yourself? Do not seek *them;* for behold, I will bring adversity on all flesh," says the LORD. "But I will give your life to you as a prize in all places, wherever you go."'"

Judgment on Egypt

46 The word of the LORD which came to Jeremiah the prophet against the nations. [2]Against Egypt.

Concerning the army of Pharaoh Necho, king of Egypt, which was by the River Euphrates in Carchemish, and which Nebuchadnezzar king of Babylon defeated in the fourth year of Jehoiakim the son of Josiah, king of Judah:

[3] "Order the buckler and shield,
     And draw near to battle!

45:1 [a]Literally *from Jeremiah's mouth*

4 Harness the horses,
    And mount up, you horsemen!
    Stand forth with *your* helmets,
    Polish the spears,
    Put on the armor!
5 Why have I seen them dismayed *and*
        turned back?
    Their mighty ones are beaten down;
    They have speedily fled,
    And did not look back,
    For fear *was* all around," says the LORD.
6 "Do not let the swift flee away,
    Nor the mighty man escape;
    They will stumble and fall
    Toward the north, by the River
        Euphrates.

7 "Who *is* this coming up like a flood,
    Whose waters move like the rivers?
8 Egypt rises up like a flood,
    And *its* waters move like the rivers;
    And he says, 'I will go up *and* cover
        the earth,
    I will destroy the city and its
        inhabitants.'
9 Come up, O horses, and rage,
        O chariots!
    And let the mighty men come forth:
    The Ethiopians and the Libyans who
        handle the shield,
    And the Lydians who handle *and*
        bend the bow.
10 For this *is* the day of the Lord GOD
        of hosts,
    A day of vengeance,
    That He may avenge Himself on His
        adversaries.
    The sword shall devour;
    It shall be satiated and made drunk
        with their blood;
    For the Lord GOD of hosts has a sacrifice
    In the north country by the River
        Euphrates.

11 "Go up to Gilead and take balm,
        O virgin, the daughter of Egypt;
    In vain you will use many medicines;
    You shall not be cured.
12 The nations have heard of your shame,
    And your cry has filled the land;
    For the mighty man has stumbled
        against the mighty;
    They both have fallen together."

Babylonia Will Strike Egypt

13 The word that the LORD spoke to Jeremiah the prophet, how Nebuchadnezzar king of Babylon would come *and* strike the land of Egypt.

14 "Declare in Egypt, and proclaim in
        Migdol;
    Proclaim in Noph[a] and in Tahpanhes;
    Say, 'Stand fast and prepare
        yourselves,
    For the sword devours all around you.'
15 Why are your valiant *men* swept
        away?
    They did not stand
    Because the LORD drove them away.
16 He made many fall;
    Yes, one fell upon another.
    And they said, 'Arise!
    Let us go back to our own people
    And to the land of our nativity
    From the oppressing sword.'
17 They cried there,
    'Pharaoh, king of Egypt, *is but* a noise.
    He has passed by the appointed time!'

18 "*As* I live," says the King,
    Whose name *is* the LORD of hosts,
    "Surely as Tabor *is* among the
        mountains
    And as Carmel by the sea, *so* he
        shall come.
19 O you daughter dwelling in Egypt,
    Prepare yourself to go into captivity!
    For Noph[a] shall be waste and
        desolate, without inhabitant.

20 "Egypt *is* a very pretty heifer,
    But destruction comes, it comes from
        the north.
21 Also her mercenaries are in her midst
        like fat bulls,
    For they also are turned back,
    They have fled away together.
    They did not stand,
    For the day of their calamity had
        come upon them,
    The time of their punishment.

46:14 [a]That is, ancient Memphis   **46:19** [a]That is, ancient Memphis

22 Her noise shall go like a serpent,
For they shall march with an army
And come against her with axes,
Like those who chop wood.

23 "They shall cut down her forest,"
    says the LORD,
"Though it cannot be searched,
Because they *are* innumerable,
And more numerous than
    grasshoppers.
24 The daughter of Egypt shall be
    ashamed;
She shall be delivered into the hand
Of the people of the north."

25The LORD of hosts, the God of Israel, says: "Behold, I will bring punishment on Amon[a] of No,[b] and Pharaoh and Egypt, with their gods and their kings—Pharaoh and those who trust in him. 26And I will deliver them into the hand of those who seek their lives, into the hand of Nebuchadnezzar king of Babylon and the hand of his servants. Afterward it shall be inhabited as in the days of old," says the LORD.

God Will Preserve Israel

27 "But do not fear, O My servant Jacob,
And do not be dismayed, O Israel!
For behold, I will save you from afar,
And your offspring from the land of
    their captivity;
Jacob shall return, have rest and be
    at ease;
No one shall make *him* afraid.
28 Do not fear, O Jacob My servant,"
    says the LORD,
"For I *am* with you;
For I will make a complete end of all
    the nations
To which I have driven you,
But I will not make a complete end
    of you.
I will rightly correct you,
For I will not leave you wholly
    unpunished."

Judgment on Philistia

47 The word of the LORD that came to Jeremiah the prophet against the Philistines, before Pharaoh attacked Gaza.

2Thus says the LORD:

"Behold, waters rise out of the north,
And shall be an overflowing flood;
They shall overflow the land and all
    that is in it,
The city and those who dwell within;
Then the men shall cry,
And all the inhabitants of the land
    shall wail.
3   At the noise of the stamping hooves
        of his strong horses,
    At the rushing of his chariots,
    At the rumbling of his wheels,
    The fathers will not look back for *their*
        children,
    Lacking courage,
4   Because of the day that comes to
        plunder all the Philistines,
    To cut off from Tyre and Sidon every
        helper who remains;
    For the LORD shall plunder the
        Philistines,
    The remnant of the country of Caphtor.
5   Baldness has come upon Gaza,
    Ashkelon is cut off
    With the remnant of their valley.
    How long will you cut yourself?

6   "O you sword of the LORD,
    How long until you are quiet?
    Put yourself up into your scabbard,
    Rest and be still!
7   How can it be quiet,
    Seeing the LORD has given it a charge
    Against Ashkelon and against the
        seashore?
    There He has appointed it."

Judgment on Moab

48 Against Moab.
Thus says the LORD of hosts, the God of Israel:

"Woe to Nebo!
For it is plundered,
Kirjathaim is shamed *and* taken;
The high stronghold[a] is shamed and
    dismayed—

46:25 [a]A sun god [b]That is, ancient Thebes
48:1 [a]Hebrew *Misgab*

2 No more praise of Moab.
   In Heshbon they have devised evil
      against her:
   'Come, and let us cut her off as
      a nation.'
   You also shall be cut down,
      O Madmen!ᵃ
   The sword shall pursue you;
3 A voice of crying *shall be* from
      Horonaim:
   'Plundering and great destruction!'

4 "Moab is destroyed;
   Her little ones have caused a cry to
      be heard;ᵃ
5 For in the Ascent of Luhith they
      ascend with continual weeping;
   For in the descent of Horonaim the
      enemies have heard a cry of
      destruction.

6 "Flee, save your lives!
   And be like the juniperᵃ in the
      wilderness.
7 For because you have trusted in your
      works and your treasures,
   You also shall be taken.
   And Chemosh shall go forth into
      captivity,
   His priests and his princes together.
8 And the plunderer shall come against
      every city;
   No one shall escape.
   The valley also shall perish,
   And the plain shall be destroyed,
   As the LORD has spoken.

9 "Give wings to Moab,
   That she may flee and get away;
   For her cities shall be desolate,
   Without any to dwell in them.
10 Cursed *is* he who does the work of
      the LORD deceitfully,
   And cursed *is* he who keeps back
      his sword from blood.

11 "Moab has been at ease from hisᵃ
      youth;
   He has settled on his dregs,
   And has not been emptied from
      vessel to vessel,
   Nor has he gone into captivity.

Therefore his taste remained in him,
   And his scent has not changed.

12 "Therefore behold, the days are
      coming," says the LORD,
   "That I shall send him wine-workers
   Who will tip him over
   And empty his vessels
   And break the bottles.
13 Moab shall be ashamed of Chemosh,
   As the house of Israel was ashamed of
      Bethel, their confidence.

14 "How can you say, 'We *are* mighty
   And strong men for the war'?
15 Moab is plundered and gone up *from*
      her cities;
   Her chosen young men have gone down
      to the slaughter," says the King,
   Whose name *is* the LORD of hosts.

16 "The calamity of Moab *is* near at hand,
   And his affliction comes quickly.
17 Bemoan him, all you who are around
      him;
   And all you who know his name,
   Say, 'How the strong staff is broken,
   The beautiful rod!'

18 "O daughter inhabiting Dibon,
   Come down from *your* glory,
   And sit in thirst;
   For the plunderer of Moab has come
      against you,
   He has destroyed your strongholds.
19 O inhabitant of Aroer,
   Stand by the way and watch;
   Ask him who flees
   And her who escapes;
   Say, 'What has happened?'
20 Moab is shamed, for he is broken down.
   Wail and cry!
   Tell it in Arnon, that Moab is plundered.

21 "And judgment has come on the plain
      country:
   On Holon and Jahzah and Mephaath,

48:2 ᵃA city of Moab   **48:4** ᵃFollowing Masoretic
Text, Targum, and Vulgate; Septuagint reads *Proclaim
it in Zoar.*   **48:6** ᵃOr *Aroer,* a city of Moab
48:11 ᵃThe Hebrew uses masculine and feminine
pronouns interchangeably in this chapter.

22 On Dibon and Nebo and Beth
        Diblathaim,
23 On Kirjathaim and Beth Gamul
        and Beth Meon,
24 On Kerioth and Bozrah,
     On all the cities of the land of Moab,
        Far or near.
25 The horn of Moab is cut off,
     And his arm is broken," says the LORD.

26 "Make him drunk,
     Because he exalted *himself* against
        the LORD.
     Moab shall wallow in his vomit,
     And he shall also be in derision.
27 For was not Israel a derision to you?
     Was he found among thieves?
     For whenever you speak of him,
     You shake *your head in scorn.*
28 You who dwell in Moab,
     Leave the cities and dwell in the rock,
     And be like the dove *which* makes her
        nest
     In the sides of the cave's mouth.

29 "We have heard the pride of Moab
     (He *is* exceedingly proud),
     Of his loftiness and arrogance and
        pride,
     And of the haughtiness of his heart."

30 "I know his wrath," says the LORD,
     "But it *is* not right;
     His lies have made nothing right.
31 Therefore I will wail for Moab,
     And I will cry out for all Moab;
     I[a] will mourn for the men of Kir
        Heres.
32 O vine of Sibmah! I will weep for
        you with the weeping of Jazer.
     Your plants have gone over the sea,
     They reach to the sea of Jazer.
     The plunderer has fallen on your
        summer fruit and your vintage.
33 Joy and gladness are taken
     From the plentiful field
     And from the land of Moab;
     I have caused wine to fail from the
        winepresses;
     No one will tread with joyous
        shouting—
     Not joyous shouting!

34 "From the cry of Heshbon to Elealeh
        and to Jahaz
     They have uttered their voice,
     From Zoar to Horonaim,
     Like a three-year-old heifer;[a]
     For the waters of Nimrim also shall
        be desolate.

35 "Moreover," says the LORD,
     "I will cause to cease in Moab
     The one who offers *sacrifices* in the
        high places
     And burns incense to his gods.
36 Therefore My heart shall wail like
        flutes for Moab,
     And like flutes My heart shall wail
     For the men of Kir Heres.
     Therefore the riches they have
        acquired have perished.

37 "For every head *shall be* bald, and
        every beard clipped;
     On all the hands *shall be* cuts, and
        on the loins sackcloth—
38 A general lamentation
     On all the housetops of Moab,
     And in its streets;
     For I have broken Moab like a vessel in
        which *is* no pleasure," says the LORD.
39 "They shall wail:
     'How she is broken down!
     How Moab has turned her back with
        shame!'
     So Moab shall be a derision
     And a dismay to all those about her."

40 For thus says the LORD:

     "Behold, one shall fly like an eagle,
     And spread his wings over Moab.
41 Kerioth is taken,
     And the strongholds are surprised;
     The mighty men's hearts in Moab on
        that day shall be
     Like the heart of a woman in birth
        pangs.
42 And Moab shall be destroyed as a
        people,

48:31 [a]Following Dead Sea Scrolls, Septuagint, and
Vulgate; Masoretic Text reads *He.*   **48:34** [a]Or *The
Third Eglath,* an unknown city (compare Isaiah 15:5)

Because he exalted *himself* against the
LORD.
43 Fear and the pit and the snare *shall be*
upon you,
O inhabitant of Moab," says the LORD.
44 "He who flees from the fear shall fall
into the pit,
And he who gets out of the pit shall
be caught in the snare.
For upon Moab, upon it I will bring
The year of their punishment," says
the LORD.

45 "Those who fled stood under the
shadow of Heshbon
Because of exhaustion.
But a fire shall come out of Heshbon,
A flame from the midst of Sihon,
And shall devour the brow of Moab,
The crown of the head of the sons of
tumult.
46 Woe to you, O Moab!
The people of Chemosh perish;
For your sons have been taken captive,
And your daughters captive.

47 "Yet I will bring back the captives of
Moab
In the latter days," says the LORD.

Thus far *is* the judgment of Moab.

Judgment on Ammon

49 Against the Ammonites.
Thus says the LORD:

"Has Israel no sons?
Has he no heir?
Why *then* does Milcom[a] inherit Gad,
And his people dwell in its cities?
2 Therefore behold, the days are
coming," says the LORD,
"That I will cause to be heard an alarm
of war
In Rabbah of the Ammonites;
It shall be a desolate mound,
And her villages shall be burned with
fire.
Then Israel shall take possession of his
inheritance," says the LORD.

3 "Wail, O Heshbon, for Ai is plundered!

Cry, you daughters of Rabbah,
Gird yourselves with sackcloth!
Lament and run to and fro by the
walls;
For Milcom shall go into captivity
With his priests and his princes
together.
4 Why do you boast in the valleys,
Your flowing valley, O backsliding
daughter?
Who trusted in her treasures, *saying,*
'Who will come against me?'
5 Behold, I will bring fear upon you,"
Says the Lord GOD of hosts,
"From all those who are around you;
You shall be driven out, everyone
headlong,
And no one will gather those who
wander off.
6 But afterward I will bring back
The captives of the people of Ammon,"
says the LORD.

Judgment on Edom

7 Against Edom.
Thus says the LORD of hosts:

"*Is* wisdom no more in Teman?
Has counsel perished from the prudent?
Has their wisdom vanished?
8 Flee, turn back, dwell in the depths,
O inhabitants of Dedan!
For I will bring the calamity of Esau
upon him,
The time *that* I will punish him.
9 If grape-gatherers came to you,
Would they not leave *some* gleaning
grapes?
If thieves by night,
Would they not destroy until they
have enough?
10 But I have made Esau bare;
I have uncovered his secret places,[a]
And he shall not be able to hide
himself.
His descendants are plundered,
His brethren and his neighbors,
And he *is* no more.

49:1 [a]Hebrew *Malcam,* literally *their king,* a god of the
Ammonites; also called *Molech* (compare verse 3)
49:10 [a]Compare Obadiah 5, 6

11 Leave your fatherless children,
    I will preserve *them* alive;
    And let your widows trust in Me.”

12For thus says the Lord: “Behold, those whose judgment *was* not to drink of the cup have assuredly drunk. And *are* you the one who will altogether go unpunished? You shall not go unpunished, but you shall surely drink *of it*. 13For I have sworn by Myself,” says the Lord, “that Bozrah shall become a desolation, a reproach, a waste, and a curse. And all its cities shall be perpetual wastes.”

14 I have heard a message from the Lord,
    And an ambassador has been sent to
        the nations:
    “Gather together, come against her,
    And rise up to battle!

15 “For indeed, I will make you small
        among nations,
    Despised among men.
16 Your fierceness has deceived you,
    The pride of your heart,
    O you who dwell in the clefts of the
        rock,
    Who hold the height of the hill!
    Though you make your nest as high
        as the eagle,
    I will bring you down from there,”
    says the Lord.ᵃ

17 “Edom also shall be an astonishment;
    Everyone who goes by it will be
        astonished
    And will hiss at all its plagues.
18 As in the overthrow of Sodom and
        Gomorrah
    And their neighbors,” says the Lord,
    “No one shall remain there,
    Nor shall a son of man dwell in it.

19 “Behold, he shall come up like a lion
        from the floodplainᵃ of the Jordan
    Against the dwelling place of the
        strong;
    But I will suddenly make him run
        away from her.
    And who *is* a chosen *man that* I may
        appoint over her?

For who *is* like Me?
    Who will arraign Me?
    And who *is* that shepherd
    Who will withstand Me?”

20 Therefore hear the counsel of the Lord
        that He has taken against Edom,
    And His purposes that He has
        proposed against the inhabitants of
        Teman:
    Surely the least of the flock shall draw
        them out;
    Surely He shall make their dwelling
        places desolate with them.
21 The earth shakes at the noise of their
        fall;
    At the cry its noise is heard at the
        Red Sea.
22 Behold, He shall come up and fly like
        the eagle,
    And spread His wings over Bozrah;
    The heart of the mighty men of Edom
        in that day shall be
    Like the heart of a woman in birth
        pangs.

Judgment on Damascus

23Against Damascus.

    “Hamath and Arpad are shamed,
    For they have heard bad news.
    They are fainthearted;
    There is trouble on the sea;
    It cannot be quiet.
24 Damascus has grown feeble;
    She turns to flee,
    And fear has seized *her*.
    Anguish and sorrows have taken her
        like a woman in labor.
25 Why is the city of praise not deserted,
        the city of My joy?
26 Therefore her young men shall fall in
        her streets,
    And all the men of war shall be cut off
        in that day,” says the Lord of hosts.
27 “I will kindle a fire in the wall of
        Damascus,
    And it shall consume the palaces of
        Ben-Hadad.”ᵃ

49:16 ᵃCompare Obadiah 3, 4   **49:19** ᵃOr *thicket*
49:27 ᵃCompare Amos 1:4

Judgment on Kedar and Hazor

²⁸Against Kedar and against the kingdoms of Hazor, which Nebuchadnezzar king of Babylon shall strike.
Thus says the LORD:

"Arise, go up to Kedar,
And devastate the men of the East!
²⁹ Their tents and their flocks they shall take away.
They shall take for themselves their curtains,
All their vessels and their camels;
And they shall cry out to them,
'Fear *is* on every side!'

³⁰ "Flee, get far away! Dwell in the depths,
O inhabitants of Hazor!" says the LORD.
"For Nebuchadnezzar king of Babylon
has taken counsel against you,
And has conceived a plan against you.

³¹ "Arise, go up to the wealthy nation
that dwells securely," says the LORD,
"Which has neither gates nor bars,
Dwelling alone.
³² Their camels shall be for booty,
And the multitude of their cattle for plunder.
I will scatter to all winds those in the farthest corners,
And I will bring their calamity from all its sides," says the LORD.
³³ "Hazor shall be a dwelling for jackals,
a desolation forever;
No one shall reside there,
Nor son of man dwell in it."

Judgment on Elam

³⁴The word of the LORD that came to Jeremiah the prophet against Elam, in the beginning of the reign of Zedekiah king of Judah, saying, ³⁵"Thus says the LORD of hosts:

'Behold, I will break the bow of Elam,
The foremost of their might.
³⁶ Against Elam I will bring the four winds
From the four quarters of heaven,
And scatter them toward all those winds;
There shall be no nations where the outcasts of Elam will not go.

³⁷ For I will cause Elam to be dismayed
before their enemies
And before those who seek their life.
I will bring disaster upon them,
My fierce anger,' says the LORD;
'And I will send the sword after them
Until I have consumed them.
³⁸ I will set My throne in Elam,
And will destroy from there the king
and the princes,' says the LORD.

³⁹ 'But it shall come to pass in the latter days:
I will bring back the captives of Elam,'
says the LORD."

Judgment on Babylon and Babylonia

50 The word that the LORD spoke against Babylon *and* against the land of the Chaldeans by Jeremiah the prophet.

² "Declare among the nations,
Proclaim, and set up a standard;
Proclaim—do not conceal *it*—
Say, 'Babylon is taken, Bel is shamed.
Merodachᵃ is broken in pieces;
Her idols are humiliated,
Her images are broken in pieces.'
³ For out of the north a nation comes up against her,
Which shall make her land desolate,
And no one shall dwell therein.
They shall move, they shall depart,
Both man and beast.

⁴ "In those days and in that time,"
says the LORD,
"The children of Israel shall come,
They and the children of Judah together;
With continual weeping they shall come,
And seek the LORD their God.
⁵ They shall ask the way to Zion,
With their faces toward it, *saying,*
'Come and let us join ourselves to the LORD
In a perpetual covenant
That will not be forgotten.'

50:2 ᵃA Babylonian god; sometimes spelled *Marduk*

6 "My people have been lost sheep.
  Their shepherds have led them astray;
  They have turned them away *on* the
    mountains.
  They have gone from mountain to
    hill;
  They have forgotten their resting place.
7 All who found them have devoured
    them;
  And their adversaries said, 'We have
    not offended,
  Because they have sinned against the
    LORD, the habitation of justice,
  The LORD, the hope of their fathers.'

8 "Move from the midst of Babylon,
  Go out of the land of the Chaldeans;
  And be like the rams before the flocks.
9 For behold, I will raise and cause to
    come up against Babylon
  An assembly of great nations from
    the north country,

And they shall array themselves
    against her;
  From there she shall be captured.
  Their arrows *shall be* like *those* of an
    expert warrior;ᵃ
  None shall return in vain.
10 And Chaldea shall become plunder;
  All who plunder her shall be
    satisfied," says the LORD.

11 "Because you were glad, because you
    rejoiced,
  You destroyers of My heritage,
  Because you have grown fat like a
    heifer threshing grain,
  And you bellow like bulls,
12 Your mother shall be deeply ashamed;
  She who bore you shall be ashamed.

50:9 ᵃFollowing some Hebrew manuscripts, Septuagint, and Syriac; Masoretic Text, Targum, and Vulgate read *a warrior who makes childless.*

DEFENDER

"My people have been lost sheep. Their shepherds have led them astray...."

JEREMIAH 50:6

United States Capitol,
House of Representatives
Chamber

HOW FAR HAVE WE GONE?

Many states have adopted laws approving the posting of our national motto, "In God We Trust," in public buildings and school classrooms. For instance, in 1992 the State of Kentucky passed Kentucky Revised Statute, Title XIII, Education, 158.195, regarding conduct of schools:

> *Reading and posting in public schools of texts and documents on American history and heritage.—Local school boards may allow any teacher or administrator in a public school district of the Commonwealth to read or post in a public school building, classroom, or event any excerpts or portions of the National Motto, the National Anthem, the Pledge of Allegiance, the Preamble to the Kentucky Constitution, the Declaration of Independence, the Mayflower Pact, the writings, speeches, documents, and proclamations of the founding fathers and presidents of the United States, U.S. Supreme Court decisions, and acts of the U.S. Congress, including the published text of the Congressional Record.*
>
> *There shall be no content-based censorship of American history of heritage in the Commonwealth based on religious references in these writings, documents, and records.*

How far astray have we gone that we have to pass such laws?

Behold, the least of the nations *shall
be* a wilderness,
A dry land and a desert.
13 Because of the wrath of the LORD
She shall not be inhabited,
But she shall be wholly desolate.
Everyone who goes by Babylon shall
be horrified
And hiss at all her plagues.

14 "Put yourselves in array against
Babylon all around,
All you who bend the bow;
Shoot at her, spare no arrows,
For she has sinned against the LORD.
15 Shout against her all around;
She has given her hand,
Her foundations have fallen,
Her walls are thrown down;
For it *is* the vengeance of the LORD.
Take vengeance on her.
As she has done, so do to her.
16 Cut off the sower from Babylon,
And him who handles the sickle at
harvest time.
For fear of the oppressing sword
Everyone shall turn to his own people,
And everyone shall flee to his own land.

17 "Israel *is* like scattered sheep;
The lions have driven *him* away.
First the king of Assyria devoured him;
Now at last this Nebuchadnezzar king
of Babylon has broken his bones."

18 Therefore thus says the LORD of hosts,
the God of Israel:

"Behold, I will punish the king of
Babylon and his land,
As I have punished the king of Assyria.
19 But I will bring back Israel to his home,
And he shall feed on Carmel and
Bashan;
His soul shall be satisfied on Mount
Ephraim and Gilead.
20 In those days and in that time," says
the LORD,
"The iniquity of Israel shall be sought,
but *there shall be* none;
And the sins of Judah, but they shall
not be found;
For I will pardon those whom I preserve.

21 "Go up against the land of Merathaim,
against it,
And against the inhabitants of Pekod.
Waste and utterly destroy them," says
the LORD,
"And do according to all that I have
commanded you.
22 A sound of battle *is* in the land,
And of great destruction.
23 How the hammer of the whole earth
has been cut apart and broken!
How Babylon has become a desolation
among the nations!
24 I have laid a snare for you;
You have indeed been trapped,
O Babylon,
And you were not aware;
You have been found and also caught,
Because you have contended against
the LORD.
25 The LORD has opened His armory,
And has brought out the weapons
of His indignation;
For this *is* the work of the Lord GOD
of hosts
In the land of the Chaldeans.
26 Come against her from the farthest
border;
Open her storehouses;
Cast her up as heaps of ruins,
And destroy her utterly;
Let nothing of her be left.
27 Slay all her bulls,
Let them go down to the slaughter.
Woe to them!
For their day has come, the time of
their punishment.
28 The voice of those who flee and escape
from the land of Babylon
Declares in Zion the vengeance of the
LORD our God,
The vengeance of His temple.

29 "Call together the archers against
Babylon.
All you who bend the bow, encamp
against it all around;
Let none of them escape.ᵃ
Repay her according to her work;

50:29 ᵃQere, some Hebrew manuscripts, Septuagint,
and Targum add *to her.*

According to all she has done, do to
   her;
For she has been proud against the
   LORD,
Against the Holy One of Israel.
30 Therefore her young men shall fall in
   the streets,
And all her men of war shall be cut
   off in that day," says the LORD.
31 "Behold, I *am* against you,
   O most haughty one!" says the Lord
   GOD of hosts;
"For your day has come,
The time *that* I will punish you.ᵃ
32 The most proud shall stumble and fall,
And no one will raise him up;
I will kindle a fire in his cities,
And it will devour all around him."

33 Thus says the LORD of hosts:

"The children of Israel *were* oppressed,
Along with the children of Judah;
All who took them captive have held
   them fast;
They have refused to let them go.
34 Their Redeemer *is* strong;
The LORD of hosts *is* His name.
He will thoroughly plead their case,
That He may give rest to the land,
And disquiet the inhabitants of Babylon.

35 "A sword *is* against the Chaldeans,"
   says the LORD,
"Against the inhabitants of Babylon,
And against her princes and her wise
   men.
36 A sword *is* against the soothsayers,
   and they will be fools.
A sword *is* against her mighty men,
   and they will be dismayed.
37 A sword *is* against their horses,
Against their chariots,
And against all the mixed peoples
   who *are* in her midst;
And they will become like women.
A sword *is* against her treasures, and
   they will be robbed.
38 A droughtᵃ *is* against her waters, and
   they will be dried up.
For it *is* the land of carved images,
And they are insane with *their* idols.

39 "Therefore the wild desert beasts shall
   dwell *there* with the jackals,
And the ostriches shall dwell in it.
It shall be inhabited no more forever,
Nor shall it be dwelt in from
   generation to generation.
40 As God overthrew Sodom and
   Gomorrah
And their neighbors," says the LORD,
"*So* no one shall reside there,
Nor son of man dwell in it.

41 "Behold, a people shall come from the
   north,
And a great nation and many kings
Shall be raised up from the ends of
   the earth.
42 They shall hold the bow and the
   lance;
They *are* cruel and shall not show
   mercy.
Their voice shall roar like the sea;
They shall ride on horses,
Set in array, like a man for the battle,
Against you, O daughter of Babylon.

43 "The king of Babylon has heard the
   report about them,
And his hands grow feeble;
Anguish has taken hold of him,
Pangs as of a woman in childbirth.

44 "Behold, he shall come up like a lion
   from the floodplainᵃ of the Jordan
Against the dwelling place of the strong;
But I will make them suddenly run
   away from her.
And who *is* a chosen *man that* I may
   appoint over her?
For who *is* like Me?
Who will arraign Me?
And who *is* that shepherd
Who will withstand Me?"

45 Therefore hear the counsel of the LORD
   that He has taken against Babylon,

50:31 ᵃFollowing Masoretic Text and Targum;
Septuagint and Vulgate read *The time of your
punishment.*   **50:38** ᵃFollowing Masoretic Text,
Targum, and Vulgate; Syriac reads *sword;* Septuagint
omits *A drought is.*   **50:44** ᵃOr *thicket*

And His purposes that He has
　　proposed against the land of the
　　Chaldeans:
Surely the least of the flock shall draw
　　them out;
Surely He will make their dwelling
　　place desolate with them.
46 At the noise of the taking of Babylon
　　The earth trembles,
　　And the cry is heard among the nations.

The Utter Destruction of Babylon

51 Thus says the LORD:

"Behold, I will raise up against Babylon,
Against those who dwell in Leb Kamai,[a]
A destroying wind.
2 And I will send winnowers to Babylon,
Who shall winnow her and empty her
　　land.
For in the day of doom
They shall be against her all around.
3 Against *her* let the archer bend his bow,
And lift himself up against *her* in his
　　armor.
Do not spare her young men;
Utterly destroy all her army.
4 Thus the slain shall fall in the land
　　of the Chaldeans,
And *those* thrust through in her
　　streets.
5 For Israel is not forsaken, nor Judah,
By his God, the LORD of hosts,
Though their land was filled with sin
　　against the Holy One of Israel."

6 Flee from the midst of Babylon,
And every one save his life!
Do not be cut off in her iniquity,
For this *is* the time of the LORD's
　　vengeance;
He shall recompense her.
7 Babylon *was* a golden cup in the
　　LORD's hand,
That made all the earth drunk.
The nations drank her wine;
Therefore the nations are deranged.
8 Babylon has suddenly fallen and
　　been destroyed.
Wail for her!
Take balm for her pain;
Perhaps she may be healed.

9 We would have healed Babylon,
But she is not healed.
Forsake her, and let us go everyone to
　　his own country;
For her judgment reaches to heaven
　　and is lifted up to the skies.
10 The LORD has revealed our
　　righteousness.
Come and let us declare in Zion the
　　work of the LORD our God.

11 Make the arrows bright!
Gather the shields!
The LORD has raised up the spirit of
　　the kings of the Medes.
For His plan *is* against Babylon to
　　destroy it,
Because it *is* the vengeance of the LORD,
The vengeance for His temple.
12 Set up the standard on the walls of
　　Babylon;
Make the guard strong,
Set up the watchmen,
Prepare the ambushes.
For the LORD has both devised and
　　done
What He spoke against the
　　inhabitants of Babylon.
13 O you who dwell by many waters,
Abundant in treasures,
Your end has come,
The measure of your covetousness.
14 The LORD of hosts has sworn by Himself:
"Surely I will fill you with men, as with
　　locusts,
And they shall lift up a shout against
　　you."

15 He has made the earth by His power;
He has established the world by His
　　wisdom,
And stretched out the heaven by His
　　understanding.
16 When He utters *His* voice—
There is a multitude of waters in the
　　heavens:
"He causes the vapors to ascend from
　　the ends of the earth;
He makes lightnings for the rain;

51:1 [a]A code word for Chaldea (Babylonia); may be
translated *The Midst of Those Who Rise Up Against Me*

He brings the wind out of His
treasuries."ᵃ

17 Everyone is dull-hearted, without
knowledge;
Every metalsmith is put to shame by
the carved image;
For his molded image *is* falsehood,
And *there is* no breath in them.
18 They *are* futile, a work of errors;
In the time of their punishment they
shall perish.
19 The Portion of Jacob *is* not like them,
For He *is* the Maker of all things;
And *Israel is* the tribe of His
inheritance.
The LORD of hosts *is* His name.

20 "You *are* My battle-ax *and* weapons
of war:
For with you I will break the nation
in pieces;
With you I will destroy kingdoms;
21 With you I will break in pieces the
horse and its rider;
With you I will break in pieces the
chariot and its rider;
22 With you also I will break in pieces
man and woman;
With you I will break in pieces old
and young;
With you I will break in pieces the
young man and the maiden;
23 With you also I will break in pieces
the shepherd and his flock;
With you I will break in pieces the
farmer and his yoke of oxen;
And with you I will break in pieces
governors and rulers.

24 "And I will repay Babylon
And all the inhabitants of Chaldea
For all the evil they have done
In Zion in your sight," says the LORD.

25 "Behold, I *am* against you, O destroying
mountain,
Who destroys all the earth," says the
LORD.
"And I will stretch out My hand against
you,
Roll you down from the rocks,

And make you a burnt mountain.
26 They shall not take from you a stone
for a corner
Nor a stone for a foundation,
But you shall be desolate forever,"
says the LORD.

27 Set up a banner in the land,
Blow the trumpet among the nations!
Prepare the nations against her,
Call the kingdoms together against her:
Ararat, Minni, and Ashkenaz.
Appoint a general against her;
Cause the horses to come up like the
bristling locusts.
28 Prepare against her the nations,
With the kings of the Medes,
Its governors and all its rulers,
All the land of his dominion.
29 And the land will tremble and
sorrow;
For every purpose of the LORD shall
be performed against Babylon,
To make the land of Babylon a
desolation without inhabitant.
30 The mighty men of Babylon have
ceased fighting,
They have remained in their
strongholds;
Their might has failed,
They became *like* women;
They have burned her dwelling places,
The bars of her *gate* are broken.
31 One runner will run to meet another,
And one messenger to meet another,
To show the king of Babylon that his
city is taken on *all* sides;
32 The passages are blocked,
The reeds they have burned with fire,
And the men of war are terrified.

33 For thus says the LORD of hosts, the God
of Israel:

"The daughter of Babylon *is* like a
threshing floor
When it is time to thresh her;
Yet a little while
And the time of her harvest will come."

51:16 ᵃPsalm 135:7

³⁴ "Nebuchadnezzar the king of Babylon
    Has devoured me, he has crushed me;
    He has made me an empty vessel,
    He has swallowed me up like a
        monster;
    He has filled his stomach with my
        delicacies,
    He has spit me out.
³⁵ Let the violence *done* to me and my
        flesh *be* upon Babylon,"
    The inhabitant of Zion will say;
    "And my blood be upon the
        inhabitants of Chaldea!"
    Jerusalem will say.

³⁶Therefore thus says the LORD:

    "Behold, I will plead your case and
        take vengeance for you.
    I will dry up her sea and make her
        springs dry.
³⁷ Babylon shall become a heap,
    A dwelling place for jackals,
    An astonishment and a hissing,
    Without an inhabitant.
³⁸ They shall roar together like lions,
    They shall growl like lions' whelps.
³⁹ In their excitement I will prepare
        their feasts;
    I will make them drunk,
    That they may rejoice,
    And sleep a perpetual sleep
    And not awake," says the LORD.
⁴⁰ "I will bring them down
    Like lambs to the slaughter,
    Like rams with male goats.

⁴¹ "Oh, how Sheshachᵃ is taken!
    Oh, how the praise of the whole earth
        is seized!
    How Babylon has become desolate
        among the nations!
⁴² The sea has come up over Babylon;
    She is covered with the multitude of
        its waves.
⁴³ Her cities are a desolation,
    A dry land and a wilderness,
    A land where no one dwells,
    Through which no son of man passes.
⁴⁴ I will punish Bel in Babylon,
    And I will bring out of his mouth
        what he has swallowed;

And the nations shall not stream to
        him anymore.
    Yes, the wall of Babylon shall fall.

⁴⁵ "My people, go out of the midst of her!
    And let everyone deliver himself from
        the fierce anger of the LORD.
⁴⁶ And lest your heart faint,
    And you fear for the rumor that *will
        be* heard in the land
    (A rumor will come *one* year,
    And after that, in *another* year
    A rumor *will come,*
    And violence in the land,
    Ruler against ruler),
⁴⁷ Therefore behold, the days are coming
    That I will bring judgment on the
        carved images of Babylon;
    Her whole land shall be ashamed,
    And all her slain shall fall in her midst.
⁴⁸ Then the heavens and the earth and
        all that *is* in them
    Shall sing joyously over Babylon;
    For the plunderers shall come to her
        from the north," says the LORD.

⁴⁹ As Babylon *has caused* the slain of
        Israel to fall,
    So at Babylon the slain of all the
        earth shall fall.
⁵⁰ You who have escaped the sword,
    Get away! Do not stand still!
    Remember the LORD afar off,
    And let Jerusalem come to your mind.

⁵¹ We are ashamed because we have
        heard reproach.
    Shame has covered our faces,
    For strangers have come into the
        sanctuaries of the LORD's house.

⁵² "Therefore behold, the days are
        coming," says the LORD,
    "That I will bring judgment on her
        carved images,
    And throughout all her land the
        wounded shall groan.
⁵³ Though Babylon were to mount up
        to heaven,

51:41 ᵃA code word for Babylon (compare
Jeremiah 25:26)

And though she were to fortify the
    height of her strength,
Yet from Me plunderers would come
    to her," says the Lord.

54 The sound of a cry *comes* from Babylon,
    And great destruction from the land of
    the Chaldeans,
55 Because the Lord is plundering Babylon
    And silencing her loud voice,
    Though her waves roar like great
    waters,
    And the noise of their voice is uttered,
56 Because the plunderer comes against
    her, against Babylon,
    And her mighty men are taken.
    Every one of their bows is broken;
    For the Lord *is* the God of recompense,
    He will surely repay.

57 "And I will make drunk
    Her princes and wise men,
    Her governors, her deputies, and her
    mighty men.
    And they shall sleep a perpetual sleep
    And not awake," says the King,
    Whose name *is* the Lord of hosts.

58 Thus says the Lord of hosts:

"The broad walls of Babylon shall be
    utterly broken,
    And her high gates shall be burned
    with fire;
    The people will labor in vain,
    And the nations, because of the fire;
    And they shall be weary."

Jeremiah's Command to Seraiah

59 The word which Jeremiah the prophet commanded Seraiah the son of Neriah, the son of Mahseiah, when he went with Zedekiah the king of Judah to Babylon in the fourth year of his reign. And Seraiah *was* the quartermaster. 60 So Jeremiah wrote in a book all the evil that would come upon Babylon, all these words that are written against Babylon. 61 And Jeremiah said to Seraiah, "When you arrive in Babylon and see it, and read all these words, 62 then you shall say, 'O Lord, You have spoken against this place to cut it off, so that none shall remain in it, neither man nor beast, but it shall be desolate forever.' 63 Now it shall be, when you have finished reading this book, *that* you shall tie a stone to it and throw it out into the Euphrates. 64 Then you shall say, 'Thus Babylon shall sink and not rise from the catastrophe that I will bring upon her. And they shall be weary.' "

Thus far *are* the words of Jeremiah.

The Fall of Jerusalem Reviewed

52 Zedekiah *was* twenty-one years old when he became king, and he reigned eleven years in Jerusalem. His mother's name *was* Hamutal the daughter of Jeremiah of Libnah. 2 He also did evil in the sight of the Lord, according to all that Jehoiakim had done. 3 For because of the anger of the Lord *this* happened in Jerusalem and Judah, till He finally cast them out from His presence. Then Zedekiah rebelled against the king of Babylon.

4 Now it came to pass in the ninth year of his reign, in the tenth month, on the tenth *day* of the month, *that* Nebuchadnezzar king of Babylon and all his army came against Jerusalem and encamped against it; and *they* built a siege wall against it all around. 5 So the city was besieged until the eleventh year of King Zedekiah. 6 By the fourth month, on the ninth day of the month, the famine had become so severe in the city that there was no food for the people of the land. 7 Then the city *wall* was broken through, and all the men of war fled and went out of the city at night by way of the gate between the two walls, which *was* by the king's garden, even though the Chaldeans *were* near the city all around. And they went by way of the plain.ᵃ

8 But the army of the Chaldeans pursued the king, and they overtook Zedekiah in the plains of Jericho. All his army was scattered from him. 9 So they took the king and brought him up to the king of Babylon at Riblah in the land of Hamath, and he pronounced judgment on him. 10 Then the king of Babylon killed the sons of Zedekiah before his eyes. And he killed all the princes of Judah in Riblah. 11 He also put out the eyes of Zedekiah; and the king of Babylon bound

---

52:7 ᵃOr *the Arabah,* that is, the Jordan Valley

him in bronze fetters, took him to Babylon, and put him in prison till the day of his death.

The Temple and City Plundered and Burned

¹²Now in the fifth month, on the tenth *day* of the month (which *was* the nineteenth year of King Nebuchadnezzar king of Babylon), Nebuzaradan, the captain of the guard, *who* served the king of Babylon, came to Jerusalem. ¹³He burned the house of the Lord and the king's house; all the houses of Jerusalem, that is, all the houses of the great, he burned with fire. ¹⁴And all the army of the Chaldeans who *were* with the captain of the guard broke down all the walls of Jerusalem all around. ¹⁵Then Nebuzaradan the captain of the guard carried away captive *some* of the poor people, the rest of the people who remained in the city, the defectors who had deserted to the king of Babylon, and the rest of the craftsmen. ¹⁶But Nebuzaradan the captain of the guard left *some* of the poor of the land as vinedressers and farmers.

¹⁷The bronze pillars that *were* in the house of the Lord, and the carts and the bronze Sea that *were* in the house of the Lord, the Chaldeans broke in pieces, and carried all their bronze to Babylon. ¹⁸They also took away the pots, the shovels, the trimmers, the bowls, the spoons, and all the bronze utensils with which the *priests* ministered. ¹⁹The basins, the firepans, the bowls, the pots, the lampstands, the spoons, and the cups, whatever *was* solid gold and whatever *was* solid silver, the captain of the guard took away. ²⁰The two pillars, one Sea, the twelve bronze bulls which *were* under *it, and* the carts, which King Solomon had made for the house of the Lord—the bronze of all these articles was beyond measure. ²¹Now *concerning* the pillars: the height of one pillar *was* eighteen cubits, a measuring line of twelve cubits could measure its circumference, and its thickness *was* four fingers; *it was* hollow. ²²A capital of bronze *was* on it; and the height of one capital *was* five cubits, with a network and pomegranates all around the capital, all of bronze. The second pillar, with pomegranates was the same. ²³There were ninety-six pomegranates on the sides; all the pomegranates, all around on the network, *were* one hundred.

The People Taken Captive to Babylonia

²⁴The captain of the guard took Seraiah the chief priest, Zephaniah the second priest, and the three doorkeepers. ²⁵He also took out of the city an officer who had charge of the men of war, seven men of the king's close associates who were found in the city, the principal scribe of the army who mustered the people of the land, and sixty men of the people of the land who were found in the midst of the city. ²⁶And Nebuzaradan the captain of the guard took these and brought them to the king of Babylon at Riblah. ²⁷Then the king of Babylon struck them and put them to death at Riblah in the land of Hamath. Thus Judah was carried away captive from its own land.

²⁸These *are* the people whom Nebuchadnezzar carried away captive: in the seventh year, three thousand and twenty-three Jews; ²⁹in the eighteenth year of Nebuchadnezzar he carried away captive from Jerusalem eight hundred and thirty-two persons; ³⁰in the twenty-third year of Nebuchadnezzar, Nebuzaradan the captain of the guard carried away captive of the Jews seven hundred and forty-five persons. All the persons *were* four thousand six hundred.

Jehoiachin Released from Prison

³¹Now it came to pass in the thirty-seventh year of the captivity of Jehoiachin king of Judah, in the twelfth month, on the twenty-fifth *day* of the month, *that* Evil-Merodach^a king of Babylon, in the *first* year of his reign, lifted up the head of Jehoiachin king of Judah and brought him out of prison. ³²And he spoke kindly to him and gave him a more prominent seat than those of the kings who *were* with him in Babylon. ³³So Jehoiachin changed from his prison garments, and he ate bread regularly before the *king* all the days of his life. ³⁴And as for his provisions, there was a regular ration given him by the king of Babylon, a portion for each day until the day of his death, all the days of his life.

52:31 ^aOr *Awil-Marduk*

LAMENTATIONS

Author: Probably Jeremiah

When Written: 587 B.C.

Theme: Punishment for Sin

Key Verses: Lamentations 3:22, 23—Through the Lord's mercies we are not consumed, because His compassions fail not. They are new every morning; great is Your faithfulness.

Key Chapter: Lamentations 3—In the midst of a narration devoted to ruin, destruction, and hopelessness, Jeremiah rises to declare God's faithfulness and mercy.

Written soon after the destruction of Jerusalem, Lamentations describes the suffering of a nation as a result of the sin and rebellion of its people. But this heartrending account doesn't merely focus on the tragic events that have left the children of God in despair, but emphasizes God's unrelenting grace, mercy, and faithfulness.

While the United States of America has faced a number of potentially catastrophic periods in its own history, perhaps nothing threatened its utter destruction more than the issue of slavery. In her classic novel, *Uncle Tom's Cabin*, published in 1852, Harriet Beecher Stowe attacked the cruelty of slavery, making the slavery issue tangible to millions and energizing anti-slavery forces in the American North. Her book ends by saying: "A day of grace is yet held out to us. Both North and South have been guilty before God; and the Christian church has a heavy account to answer. Not by combining together, to protect injustice and cruelty, and making a common capital of sin, is this Union to be saved, but by repentance, justice, and mercy."

LAMENTATIONS

Jerusalem in Affliction

1 How lonely sits the city
That was full of people!
How like a widow is she,
Who *was* great among the nations!
The princess among the provinces
Has become a slave!

2 She weeps bitterly in the night,
Her tears *are* on her cheeks;
Among all her lovers
She has none to comfort *her.*
All her friends have dealt
   treacherously with her;
They have become her enemies.

3 Judah has gone into captivity,
Under affliction and hard servitude;
She dwells among the nations,
She finds no rest;
All her persecutors overtake her in dire
   straits.

4 The roads to Zion mourn
Because no one comes to the set
   feasts.
All her gates are desolate;
Her priests sigh,
Her virgins are afflicted,
And she *is* in bitterness.

5 Her adversaries have become the
   master,
Her enemies prosper;
For the LORD has afflicted her
Because of the multitude of her
   transgressions.
Her children have gone into captivity
   before the enemy.

6 And from the daughter of Zion
All her splendor has departed.
Her princes have become like deer
That find no pasture,
That flee without strength
Before the pursuer.

7 In the days of her affliction and
   roaming,
Jerusalem remembers all her pleasant
   things
That she had in the days of old.
When her people fell into the hand
   of the enemy,
With no one to help her,
The adversaries saw her
And mocked at her downfall.[a]

8 Jerusalem has sinned gravely,
Therefore she has become vile.[a]
All who honored her despise her
Because they have seen her nakedness;
Yes, she sighs and turns away.

9 Her uncleanness *is* in her skirts;
She did not consider her destiny;
Therefore her collapse was awesome;
She had no comforter.
"O LORD, behold my affliction,
For *the* enemy is exalted!"

10 The adversary has spread his hand
Over all her pleasant things;
For she has seen the nations enter her
   sanctuary,
Those whom You commanded
Not to enter Your assembly.

11 All her people sigh,
They seek bread;
They have given their valuables for
   food to restore life.
"See, O LORD, and consider,
For I am scorned."

12 "*Is it* nothing to you, all you who
   pass by?
Behold and see
If there is any sorrow like my sorrow,
Which has been brought on me,

1:7 [a]Vulgate reads *her Sabbaths.*   **1:8** [a]Septuagint
and Vulgate read *moved* or *removed.*

Which the LORD has inflicted
In the day of His fierce anger.

13 "From above He has sent fire into
my bones,
And it overpowered them;
He has spread a net for my feet
And turned me back;
He has made me desolate
And faint all the day.

14 "The yoke of my transgressions was
bound;ᵃ
They were woven together by His
hands,
And thrust upon my neck.
He made my strength fail;
The Lord delivered me into the hands
of *those whom* I am not able to
withstand.

15 "The Lord has trampled underfoot all
my mighty *men* in my midst;
He has called an assembly against me
To crush my young men;
The Lord trampled *as* in a winepress
The virgin daughter of Judah.

16 "For these *things* I weep;
My eye, my eye overflows with water;
Because the comforter, who should
restore my life,
Is far from me.
My children are desolate
Because the enemy prevailed."

17 Zion spreads out her hands,
But no one comforts her;

1:14 ᵃFollowing Masoretic Text and Targum;
Septuagint, Syriac, and Vulgate read *watched over.*

INSPIRING

*She did not consider
her destiny; therefore her
collapse was awesome....*

LAMENTATIONS 1:9

Calvin Coolidge

"THE DESTINY OF AMERICA"

Calvin Coolidge, the 30th President of the United States
(1923–1929), spoke on the motives of the Puritan forefathers
in a message entitled "The Destiny of America":

> If there be a destiny, it is of no avail to us unless we
> work with it. The ways of Providence will be of no advan-
> tage to us unless we proceed in the same direction. If we
> perceive a destiny in America, if we believe that Providence
> has been our guide, our own success, our own salvation
> requires that we should act and serve in harmony and
> obedience. . . .
>
> Settlers came here from mixed motives, some for pil-
> lage and adventure, some for trade and refuge, but those
> who have set their imperishable mark upon our institu-
> tions came from far higher motives. Generally defined,
> they were seeking a broader freedom. They were intent
> upon establishing a Christian commonwealth in accor-
> dance to the principle of self-government.
>
> They were an inspired body of men. It has been said
> that God sifted the nations that He might send choice
> grain into the wilderness. They had a genius for orga-
> nized society on the foundations of piety, righteousness,
> liberty, and obedience of the law. They brought with them
> the accumulated wisdom and experience of the ages. . . .
> Who can fail to see in it the hand of destiny? Who can
> doubt that it has been guided by a Divine Providence?

The LORD has commanded concerning
  Jacob
That those around him *become* his
  adversaries;
Jerusalem has become an unclean
  thing among them.

18 "The LORD is righteous,
For I rebelled against His
  commandment.
Hear now, all peoples,
And behold my sorrow;
My virgins and my young men
Have gone into captivity.

19 "I called for my lovers,
But they deceived me;
My priests and my elders
Breathed their last in the city,
While they sought food
To restore their life.

20 "See, O LORD, that I *am* in distress;
My soul is troubled;
My heart is overturned within me,
For I have been very rebellious.
Outside the sword bereaves,
At home *it is* like death.

21 "They have heard that I sigh,
But no one comforts me.
All my enemies have heard of my
  trouble;
They are glad that You have done *it*.
Bring on the day You have announced,
That they may become like me.

22 "Let all their wickedness come before
  You,
And do to them as You have done to me
For all my transgressions;
For my sighs *are* many,
And my heart *is* faint."

God's Anger with Jerusalem

2 How the Lord has covered the daughter
    of Zion
With a cloud in His anger!
He cast down from heaven to the earth
The beauty of Israel,
And did not remember His footstool
In the day of His anger.

2 The Lord has swallowed up and has
    not pitied
All the dwelling places of Jacob.
He has thrown down in His wrath
The strongholds of the daughter of
  Judah;
He has brought *them* down to the
  ground;
He has profaned the kingdom and
  its princes.

3 He has cut off in fierce anger
Every horn of Israel;
He has drawn back His right hand
From before the enemy.
He has blazed against Jacob like a
  flaming fire
Devouring all around.

4 Standing like an enemy, He has bent
    His bow;
With His right hand, like an adversary,
He has slain all *who were* pleasing to
  His eye;
On the tent of the daughter of Zion,
He has poured out His fury like fire.

5 The Lord was like an enemy.
He has swallowed up Israel,
He has swallowed up all her palaces;
He has destroyed her strongholds,
And has increased mourning and
  lamentation
In the daughter of Judah.

6 He has done violence to His tabernacle,
As if it were a garden;
He has destroyed His place of assembly;
The LORD has caused
The appointed feasts and Sabbaths to
  be forgotten in Zion.
In His burning indignation He has
  spurned the king and the priest.

7 The Lord has spurned His altar,
He has abandoned His sanctuary;
He has given up the walls of her
  palaces
Into the hand of the enemy.
They have made a noise in the house
  of the LORD
As on the day of a set feast.

8 The LORD has purposed to destroy
   The wall of the daughter of Zion.
   He has stretched out a line;
   He has not withdrawn His hand from
      destroying;
   Therefore He has caused the rampart
      and wall to lament;
   They languished together.

9 Her gates have sunk into the ground;
   He has destroyed and broken her bars.
   Her king and her princes *are* among
      the nations;
   The Law *is* no *more*,
   And her prophets find no vision from
      the LORD.

10 The elders of the daughter of Zion
   Sit on the ground *and* keep silence;
   They throw dust on their heads
   And gird themselves with sackcloth.
   The virgins of Jerusalem
   Bow their heads to the ground.

11 My eyes fail with tears,
   My heart is troubled;
   My bile is poured on the ground
   Because of the destruction of the
      daughter of my people,
   Because the children and the infants
   Faint in the streets of the city.

12 They say to their mothers,
   "Where *is* grain and wine?"
   As they swoon like the wounded
   In the streets of the city,
   As their life is poured out
   In their mothers' bosom.

13 How shall I console you?
   To what shall I liken you,
   O daughter of Jerusalem?
   What shall I compare with you, that
      I may comfort you,
   O virgin daughter of Zion?
   For your ruin *is* spread wide as the sea;
   Who can heal you?

14 Your prophets have seen for you
   False and deceptive visions;
   They have not uncovered your iniquity,
   To bring back your captives,
   But have envisioned for you false
      prophecies and delusions.

15 All who pass by clap *their* hands at you;
   They hiss and shake their heads
   At the daughter of Jerusalem:
   "*Is* this the city that is called
   'The perfection of beauty,
   The joy of the whole earth'?"

16 All your enemies have opened their
      mouth against you;
   They hiss and gnash *their* teeth.
   They say, "We have swallowed *her* up!
   Surely this *is* the day we have waited
      for;
   We have found *it,* we have seen *it!*"

17 The LORD has done what He purposed;
   He has fulfilled His word
   Which He commanded in days of old.
   He has thrown down and has not
      pitied,
   And He has caused an enemy to
      rejoice over you;
   He has exalted the horn of your
      adversaries.

18 Their heart cried out to the Lord,
   "O wall of the daughter of Zion,
   Let tears run down like a river day
      and night;
   Give yourself no relief;
   Give your eyes no rest.

19 "Arise, cry out in the night,
   At the beginning of the watches;
   Pour out your heart like water before
      the face of the Lord.
   Lift your hands toward Him
   For the life of your young children,
   Who faint from hunger at the head
      of every street."

20 "See, O LORD, and consider!
   To whom have You done this?
   Should the women eat their offspring,
   The children they have cuddled?[a]
   Should the priest and prophet be slain
   In the sanctuary of the Lord?

2:20 [a]Vulgate reads *a span long.*

21 "Young and old lie
On the ground in the streets;
My virgins and my young men
Have fallen by the sword;
You have slain *them* in the day of Your
anger,
You have slaughtered *and* not pitied.

22 "You have invited as to a feast day
The terrors that surround me.
In the day of the LORD's anger
There was no refugee or survivor.
Those whom I have borne and
brought up
My enemies have destroyed."

The Prophet's Anguish and Hope

3 I *am* the man *who* has seen affliction by
the rod of His wrath.
2 He has led me and made *me* walk
In darkness and not *in* light.
3 Surely He has turned His hand
against me
Time and time again throughout
the day.

4 He has aged my flesh and my skin,
And broken my bones.
5 He has besieged me
And surrounded *me* with bitterness
and woe.
6 He has set me in dark places
Like the dead of long ago.

7 He has hedged me in so that I cannot
get out;
He has made my chain heavy.
8 Even when I cry and shout,
He shuts out my prayer.
9 He has blocked my ways with hewn
stone;
He has made my paths crooked.

10 He *has been* to me a bear lying in
wait,
Like a lion in ambush.
11 He has turned aside my ways and
torn me in pieces;
He has made me desolate.
12 He has bent His bow
And set me up as a target for the
arrow.

13 He has caused the arrows of His quiver
To pierce my loins.ª
14 I have become the ridicule of all my
people—
Their taunting song all the day.
15 He has filled me with bitterness,
He has made me drink wormwood.
16 He has also broken my teeth with
gravel,
And covered me with ashes.
17 You have moved my soul far from
peace;
I have forgotten prosperity.
18 And I said, "My strength and my hope
Have perished from the LORD."

19 Remember my affliction and roaming,
The wormwood and the gall.
20 My soul still remembers
And sinks within me.
21 This I recall to my mind,
Therefore I have hope.

22 *Through* the LORD's mercies we are not
consumed,
Because His compassions fail not.
23 *They are* new every morning;
Great *is* Your faithfulness.
24 "The LORD *is* my portion," says my soul,
"Therefore I hope in Him!"

25 The LORD *is* good to those who wait
for Him,
To the soul *who* seeks Him.
26 *It is* good that *one* should hope and
wait quietly
For the salvation of the LORD.
27 *It is* good for a man to bear
The yoke in his youth.

28 Let him sit alone and keep silent,
Because *God* has laid *it* on him;
29 Let him put his mouth in the dust—
There may yet be hope.
30 Let him give *his* cheek to the one
who strikes him,
And be full of reproach.

31 For the Lord will not cast off forever.

3:13 ªLiterally *kidneys*

HOPE

It is good that one should hope. . . .

LAMENTATIONS 3:26

The Last Best Hope of Man

In 1974, Ronald Reagan gave his famous "Shining City Upon a Hill" speech and concluded by saying:

We cannot escape our destiny, nor should we try to do so. The leadership of the free world was thrust upon us two centuries ago in that little hall of Philadelphia. In the days following World War II, when the economic strength and power of America was all that stood between the world and the return to the dark ages, Pope Pius XII said, "The American people have a great genius for splendid and unselfish actions. Into the hands of America God has placed the destinies of an afflicted mankind."

We are indeed, and we are today, the last best hope of man on earth.

32 Though He causes grief,
Yet He will show compassion
According to the multitude of His
mercies.
33 For He does not afflict willingly,
Nor grieve the children of men.

34 To crush under one's feet
All the prisoners of the earth,
35 To turn aside the justice *due* a man
Before the face of the Most High,
36 Or subvert a man in his cause—
The Lord does not approve.

37 Who *is* he *who* speaks and it comes to
pass,
When the Lord has not commanded *it?*
38 *Is it* not from the mouth of the Most
High
That woe and well-being proceed?
39 Why should a living man complain,
A man for the punishment of his
sins?

40 Let us search out and examine our
ways,
And turn back to the LORD;
41 Let us lift our hearts and hands
To God in heaven.

42 We have transgressed and rebelled;
You have not pardoned.

43 You have covered *Yourself* with anger
And pursued us;
You have slain *and* not pitied.
44 You have covered Yourself with a cloud,
That prayer should not pass through.
45 You have made us an offscouring and
refuse
In the midst of the peoples.

46 All our enemies
Have opened their mouths against us.
47 Fear and a snare have come upon us,
Desolation and destruction.
48 My eyes overflow with rivers of water
For the destruction of the daughter of
my people.

49 My eyes flow and do not cease,
Without interruption,
50 Till the LORD from heaven
Looks down and sees.
51 My eyes bring suffering to my soul
Because of all the daughters of my city.

52 My enemies without cause
Hunted me down like a bird.
53 They silenced[a] my life in the pit
And threw stones at me.
54 The waters flowed over my head;
I said, "I am cut off!"

55 I called on Your name, O LORD,
From the lowest pit.
56 You have heard my voice:
"Do not hide Your ear
From my sighing, from my cry for help."
57 You drew near on the day I called
on You,
And said, "Do not fear!"

58 O Lord, You have pleaded the case
for my soul;
You have redeemed my life.
59 O LORD, You have seen *how* I am
wronged;
Judge my case.
60 You have seen all their vengeance,
All their schemes against me.

3:53 [a]Septuagint reads *put to death.*

61 You have heard their reproach, O LORD,
All their schemes against me,
62 The lips of my enemies
And their whispering against me all
the day.
63 Look at their sitting down and their
rising up;
I *am* their taunting song.

64 Repay them, O LORD,
According to the work of their hands.
65 Give them a veiled[a] heart;
Your curse *be* upon them!
66 In Your anger,
Pursue and destroy them
From under the heavens of the LORD.

The Degradation of Zion

4 How the gold has become dim!
How changed the fine gold!
The stones of the sanctuary are scattered
At the head of every street.

2 The precious sons of Zion,
Valuable as fine gold,
How they are regarded as clay pots,
The work of the hands of the potter!

3 Even the jackals present their breasts
To nurse their young;
But the daughter of my people *is* cruel,
Like ostriches in the wilderness.

4 The tongue of the infant clings
To the roof of its mouth for thirst;
The young children ask for bread,
But no one breaks *it* for them.

5 Those who ate delicacies
Are desolate in the streets;
Those who were brought up in scarlet
Embrace ash heaps.

6 The punishment of the iniquity of the
daughter of my people
Is greater than the punishment of the
sin of Sodom,
Which was overthrown in a moment,
With no hand to help her!

7 Her Nazirites[a] were brighter than snow
And whiter than milk;

They were more ruddy in body than
rubies,
Like sapphire in their appearance.

8 *Now* their appearance is blacker than
soot;
They go unrecognized in the streets;
Their skin clings to their bones,
It has become as dry as wood.

9 *Those* slain by the sword are better off
Than *those* who die of hunger;
For these pine away,
Stricken *for lack* of the fruits of the field.

10 The hands of the compassionate women
Have cooked their own children;
They became food for them
In the destruction of the daughter of
my people.

11 The LORD has fulfilled His fury,
He has poured out His fierce anger.
He kindled a fire in Zion,
And it has devoured its foundations.

12 The kings of the earth,
And all inhabitants of the world,
Would not have believed
That the adversary and the enemy
Could enter the gates of Jerusalem—

13 Because of the sins of her prophets
And the iniquities of her priests,
Who shed in her midst
The blood of the just.

14 They wandered blind in the streets;
They have defiled themselves with
blood,
So that no one would touch their
garments.

15 They cried out to them,
"Go away, unclean!
Go away, go away,
Do not touch us!"
When they fled and wandered,
Those among the nations said,
"They shall no longer dwell *here.*"

3:65 [a]A Jewish tradition reads *sorrow of.*
4:7 [a]Or *nobles*

16 The face[a] of the LORD scattered them;
   He no longer regards them.
   The people do not respect the priests
   Nor show favor to the elders.

17 Still our eyes failed us,
   Watching vainly for our help;
   In our watching we watched
   For a nation *that* could not save *us*.

18 They tracked our steps
   So that we could not walk in our streets.
   Our end was near;
   Our days were over,
   For our end had come.

19 Our pursuers were swifter
   Than the eagles of the heavens.
   They pursued us on the mountains
   And lay in wait for us in the wilderness.

20 The breath of our nostrils, the anointed
      of the LORD,
   Was caught in their pits,
   Of whom we said, "Under his shadow
   We shall live among the nations."

21 Rejoice and be glad, O daughter of
      Edom,
   You who dwell in the land of Uz!
   The cup shall also pass over to you
   And you shall become drunk and
      make yourself naked.

22 *The punishment of* your iniquity is
      accomplished,
   O daughter of Zion;
   He will no longer send you into
      captivity.
   He will punish your iniquity,
   O daughter of Edom;
   He will uncover your sins!

A Prayer for Restoration

5 Remember, O LORD, what has come
      upon us;
   Look, and behold our reproach!

2 Our inheritance has been turned over
      to aliens,
   And our houses to foreigners.

3 We have become orphans and waifs,
   Our mothers *are* like widows.

4 We pay for the water we drink,
   And our wood comes at a price.

5 *They* pursue at our heels;[a]
   We labor *and* have no rest.

6 We have given our hand *to* the
      Egyptians
   And the Assyrians, to be satisfied with
      bread.

7 Our fathers sinned *and are* no more,
   But we bear their iniquities.

8 Servants rule over us;
   There is none to deliver *us* from their
      hand.

9 We get our bread *at the risk* of our lives,
   Because of the sword in the wilderness.

10 Our skin is hot as an oven,
   Because of the fever of famine.

11 They ravished the women in Zion,
   The maidens in the cities of Judah.

12 Princes were hung up by their hands,
   And elders were not respected.

13 Young men ground at the millstones;
   Boys staggered under *loads of* wood.

14 The elders have ceased *gathering at* the
      gate,
   And the young men from their music.

15 The joy of our heart has ceased;
   Our dance has turned into mourning.

16 The crown has fallen *from* our head.
   Woe to us, for we have sinned!

17 Because of this our heart is faint;
   Because of these *things* our eyes grow
      dim;

18 Because of Mount Zion which is
      desolate,
   With foxes walking about on it.

19 You, O LORD, remain forever;
   Your throne from generation to
      generation.

20 Why do You forget us forever,
   And forsake us for so long a time?

21 Turn us back to You, O LORD, and we
      will be restored;
   Renew our days as of old,

22 Unless You have utterly rejected us,
   And are very angry with us!

4:16 [a]Targum reads *anger*.　　**5:5** [a]Literally *necks*

EZEKIEL

Author: Ezekiel

When Written: 593–587 B.C.

Theme: Destruction and Restoration of Jerusalem

Key Verses: Ezekiel 36:24–26—"For I will take you from among the nations, gather you out of all countries, and bring you into your own land. Then I will sprinkle clean water on you, and you shall be clean; I will cleanse you from all your filthiness and from all your idols. I will give you a new heart and put a new spirit within you; I will take the heart of stone out of your flesh and give you a heart of flesh."

Key Chapter: Ezekiel 37—Central to Israel's hope of restoration is Ezekiel's vision of the valley of dry bones. With passion and clear vision, this chapter outlines the future hope of God's people.

George Bancroft, who served as Secretary of the Navy in 1845 under President James Polk, wrote that for eternal salvation to come to all people "it was requisite that the Divine Being should enter the abodes and hearts of men and dwell there," and that He should be known, "not as a distant Providence of boundless power and uncertain and inactive will, but as God present in the flesh."

From his position of exile with the nation of Judah in Babylon, the prophet Ezekiel offered a similar message of hope for God's children. While sin and rebellion had caused the glory of the Lord to depart from the people of God, He promised to return with a fresh wind of His Spirit and life. Like the dry bones that come to life in Ezekiel's vision, the despair and hopelessness of God's exiled children would be replaced by a double portion of His glory, and they would be given a new heart to know and love Him.

EZEKIEL

Ezekiel's Vision of God

1 Now it came to pass in the thirtieth year, in the fourth *month,* on the fifth *day* of the month, as I *was* among the captives by the River Chebar, *that* the heavens were opened and I saw visions[a] of God. ²On the fifth *day* of the month, which *was* in the fifth year of King Jehoiachin's captivity, ³the word of the LORD came expressly to Ezekiel the priest, the son of Buzi, in the land of the Chaldeans[a] by the River Chebar; and the hand of the LORD was upon him there.

⁴Then I looked, and behold, a whirlwind was coming out of the north, a great cloud with raging fire engulfing itself; and brightness *was* all around it and radiating out of its midst like the color of amber, out of the midst of the fire. ⁵Also from within it *came* the likeness of four living creatures. And this *was* their appearance: they had the likeness of a man. ⁶Each one had four faces, and each one had four wings. ⁷Their legs *were* straight, and the soles of their feet *were* like the soles of calves' feet. They sparkled like the color of burnished bronze. ⁸The hands of a man *were* under their wings on their four sides; and each of the four had faces and wings. ⁹Their wings touched one another. *The creatures* did not turn when they went, but each one went straight forward.

¹⁰As for the likeness of their faces, *each* had the face of a man; each of the four had the face of a lion on the right side, each of the four had the face of an ox on the left side, and each of the four had the face of an eagle. ¹¹Thus *were* their faces. Their wings stretched upward; two *wings* of each one touched one another, and two covered their bodies. ¹²And each one went straight forward; they went wherever the spirit wanted to go, and they did not turn when they went.

¹³As for the likeness of the living creatures, their appearance *was* like burning coals of fire, like the appearance of torches going back and forth among the living creatures. The fire was bright, and out of the fire went

lightning. ¹⁴And the living creatures ran back and forth, in appearance like a flash of lightning.

¹⁵Now as I looked at the living creatures, behold, a wheel *was* on the earth beside each living creature with its four faces. ¹⁶The appearance of the wheels and their workings *was* like the color of beryl, and all four had the same likeness. The appearance of their workings *was,* as it were, a wheel in the middle of a wheel. ¹⁷When they moved, they went toward any one of four directions; they did not turn aside when they went. ¹⁸As for their rims, they were so high they were awesome; and their rims *were* full of eyes, all around the four of them. ¹⁹When the living creatures went, the wheels went beside them; and when the living creatures were lifted up from the earth, the wheels were lifted up. ²⁰Wherever the spirit wanted to go, they went, *because* there the spirit went; and the wheels were lifted together with them, for the spirit of the living creatures[a] *was* in the wheels. ²¹When those went, *these* went; when those stood, *these* stood; and when those were lifted up from the earth, the wheels were lifted up together with them, for the spirit of the living creatures[a] *was* in the wheels.

²²The likeness of the firmament above the heads of the living creatures[a] *was* like the color of an awesome crystal, stretched out over their heads. ²³And under the firmament their wings *spread out* straight, one toward another. Each one had two which covered one side, and each one had two which covered the other side of the body. ²⁴When they went, I heard the noise of their

---

1:1 [a]Following Masoretic Text, Septuagint, and Vulgate; Syriac and Targum read *a vision.*
1:3 [a]Or *Babylonians,* and so elsewhere in this book
1:20 [a]Literally *living creature;* Septuagint and Vulgate read *spirit of life;* Targum reads *creatures.*
1:21 [a]Literally *living creature;* Septuagint and Vulgate read *spirit of life;* Targum reads *creatures.*
1:22 [a]Following Septuagint, Targum, and Vulgate; Masoretic Text reads *living creature.*

wings, like the noise of many waters, like the voice of the Almighty, a tumult like the noise of an army; and when they stood still, they let down their wings. 25A voice came from above the firmament that *was* over their heads; whenever they stood, they let down their wings.

26And above the firmament over their heads *was* the likeness of a throne, in appearance like a sapphire stone; on the likeness of the throne *was* a likeness with the appearance of a man high above it. 27Also from the appearance of His waist and upward I saw, as it were, the color of amber with the appearance of fire all around within it; and from the appearance of His waist and downward I saw, as it were, the appearance of fire with brightness all around. 28Like the appearance of a rainbow in a cloud on a rainy day, so *was* the appearance of the brightness all around it. This *was* the appearance of the likeness of the glory of the LORD.

Ezekiel Sent to Rebellious Israel

So when I saw *it,* I fell on my face, and I heard a voice of One speaking.

2 And He said to me, "Son of man, stand on your feet, and I will speak to you." 2Then the Spirit entered me when He spoke to me, and set me on my feet; and I heard Him who spoke to me. 3And He said to me: "Son of man, I am sending you to the children of Israel, to a rebellious nation that has rebelled against Me; they and their fathers have transgressed against Me to this very day. 4For *they are* impudent and stubborn children. I am sending you to them, and you shall say to them, 'Thus says the Lord GOD.' 5As for them, whether they hear or whether they refuse—for they *are* a rebellious house— yet they will know that a prophet has been among them.

6"And you, son of man, do not be afraid of them nor be afraid of their words, though briers and thorns *are* with you and you dwell among scorpions; do not be afraid of their words or dismayed by their looks, though they *are* a rebellious house. 7You shall speak My words to them, whether they hear or whether they refuse, for they *are* rebellious. 8But you, son of man, hear what I say to you. Do not be rebellious like that rebellious house; open your mouth and eat what I give you."

9Now when I looked, there was a hand stretched out to me; and behold, a scroll of a book *was* in it. 10Then He spread it before me; and *there was* writing on the inside and on the outside, and written on it *were* lamentations and mourning and woe.

3 Moreover He said to me, "Son of man, eat what you find; eat this scroll, and go, speak to the house of Israel." 2So I opened my mouth, and He caused me to eat that scroll.

3And He said to me, "Son of man, feed your belly, and fill your stomach with this scroll that I give you." So I ate, and it was in my mouth like honey in sweetness.

4Then He said to me: "Son of man, go to the house of Israel and speak with My words to them. 5For you *are* not sent to a people of unfamiliar speech and of hard language, *but* to the house of Israel, 6not to many people of unfamiliar speech and of hard language, whose words you cannot understand. Surely, had I sent you to them, they would have listened to you. 7But the house of Israel will not listen to you, because they will not listen to Me; for all the house of Israel *are* impudent and hard-hearted. 8Behold, I have made your face strong against their faces, and your forehead strong against their foreheads. 9Like adamant stone, harder than flint, I have made your forehead; do not be afraid of them, nor be dismayed at their looks, though they *are* a rebellious house."

10Moreover He said to me: "Son of man, receive into your heart all My words that I speak to you, and hear with your ears. 11And go, get to the captives, to the children of your people, and speak to them and tell them, 'Thus says the Lord GOD,' whether they hear, or whether they refuse."

12Then the Spirit lifted me up, and I heard behind me a great thunderous voice: "Blessed *is* the glory of the LORD from His place!" 13I also *heard* the noise of the wings of the living creatures that touched one another, and the noise of the wheels beside them, and a great thunderous noise. 14So the Spirit lifted me up and took me away, and I went in bitterness, in the heat of my

spirit; but the hand of the LORD was strong upon me. ¹⁵Then I came to the captives at Tel Abib, who dwelt by the River Chebar; and I sat where they sat, and remained there astonished among them seven days.

Ezekiel Is a Watchman

¹⁶Now it came to pass at the end of seven days that the word of the LORD came to me, saying, ¹⁷"Son of man, I have made you a watchman for the house of Israel; therefore hear a word from My mouth, and give them warning from Me: ¹⁸When I say to the wicked, 'You shall surely die,' and you give him no warning, nor speak to warn the wicked from his wicked way, to save his life, that same wicked *man* shall die in his iniquity; but his blood I will require at your hand. ¹⁹Yet, if you warn the wicked, and he does not turn from his wickedness, nor from his wicked way, he shall die in his iniquity; but you have delivered your soul. ²⁰"Again, when a righteous *man* turns from his righteousness and commits iniquity, and I lay a stumbling block before him, he shall die; because you did not give him warning, he shall die in his sin, and his righteousness which he has done shall not be remembered; but his blood I will require at your hand. ²¹Nevertheless if you warn the righteous *man* that the righteous should not sin, and he does not sin, he shall surely live because he took warning; also you will have delivered your soul."

²²Then the hand of the LORD was upon me there, and He said to me, "Arise, go out into the plain, and there I shall talk with you." ²³So I arose and went out into the plain, and behold, the glory of the LORD stood there, like the glory which I saw by the River Chebar; and I fell on my face. ²⁴Then the Spirit entered me and set me on my feet, and spoke with me and said to me: "Go, shut yourself inside your house. ²⁵And you, O son of man, surely they will put ropes on you and bind you with them, so that you cannot go out among them. ²⁶I will make your tongue cling to the roof of your mouth, so that you shall be mute and not be one to rebuke them, for they *are* a rebellious house. ²⁷But when I speak with you, I will open your mouth, and you shall say to them,

'Thus says the Lord GOD.' He who hears, let him hear; and he who refuses, let him refuse; for they *are* a rebellious house.

The Siege of Jerusalem Portrayed

4 "You also, son of man, take a clay tablet and lay it before you, and portray on it a city, Jerusalem. ²Lay siege against it, build a siege wall against it, and heap up a mound against it; set camps against it also, and place battering rams against it all around. ³Moreover take for yourself an iron plate, and set it *as* an iron wall between you and the city. Set your face against it, and it shall be besieged, and you shall lay siege against it. This *will be* a sign to the house of Israel.

⁴"Lie also on your left side, and lay the iniquity of the house of Israel upon it. *According* to the number of the days that you lie on it, you shall bear their iniquity. ⁵For I have laid on you the years of their iniquity, according to the number of the days, three hundred and ninety days; so you shall bear the iniquity of the house of Israel. ⁶And when you have completed them, lie again on your right side; then you shall bear the iniquity of the house of Judah forty days. I have laid on you a day for each year.

⁷"Therefore you shall set your face toward the siege of Jerusalem; your arm *shall be* uncovered, and you shall prophesy against it. ⁸And surely I will restrain you so that you cannot turn from one side to another till you have ended the days of your siege.

⁹"Also take for yourself wheat, barley, beans, lentils, millet, and spelt; put them into one vessel, and make bread of them for yourself. *During* the number of days that you lie on your side, three hundred and ninety days, you shall eat it. ¹⁰And your food which you eat *shall be* by weight, twenty shekels a day; from time to time you shall eat it. ¹¹You shall also drink water by measure, one-sixth of a hin; from time to time you shall drink. ¹²And you shall eat it *as* barley cakes; and bake it using fuel of human waste in their sight."

¹³Then the LORD said, "So shall the children of Israel eat their defiled bread among the Gentiles, where I will drive them."

[14]So I said, "Ah, Lord GOD! Indeed I have never defiled myself from my youth till now; I have never eaten what died of itself or was torn by beasts, nor has abominable flesh ever come into my mouth."

[15]Then He said to me, "See, I am giving you cow dung instead of human waste, and you shall prepare your bread over it."

[16]Moreover He said to me, "Son of man, surely I will cut off the supply of bread in Jerusalem; they shall eat bread by weight and with anxiety, and shall drink water by measure and with dread, [17]that they may lack bread and water, and be dismayed with one another, and waste away because of their iniquity.

A Sword Against Jerusalem

5 "And you, son of man, take a sharp sword, take it as a barber's razor, and pass *it* over your head and your beard; then take scales to weigh and divide the *hair*. [2]You shall burn with fire one-third in the midst of the city, when the days of the siege are finished; then you shall take one-third and strike around *it* with the sword, and one-third you shall scatter in the wind: I will draw out a sword after them. [3]You shall also take a small number of them and bind them in the edge of your *garment*. [4]Then take some of them again and throw them into the midst of the fire, and burn them in the fire. From there a fire will go out into all the house of Israel.

[5]"Thus says the Lord GOD: 'This *is* Jerusalem; I have set her in the midst of the nations and the countries all around her. [6]She has rebelled against My judgments by doing wickedness more than the nations, and against My statutes more than the countries that *are* all around her; for they have refused My judgments, and they have not walked in My statutes.' [7]Therefore thus says the Lord GOD: 'Because you have multiplied *disobedience* more than the nations that *are* all around you, have not walked in My statutes nor kept My judgments, nor even done[a] according to the judgments of the nations that *are* all around you'— [8]therefore thus says the Lord GOD: 'Indeed I, even I, *am* against you and will execute judgments in your midst in the sight of the nations. [9]And I will do among you what I have never done, and the like of which I will never do again, because of all your abominations. [10]Therefore fathers shall eat *their* sons in your midst, and sons shall eat their fathers; and I will execute judgments among you, and all of you who remain I will scatter to all the winds.

[11]'Therefore, *as* I live,' says the Lord GOD, 'surely, because you have defiled My sanctuary with all your detestable things and with all your abominations, therefore I will also diminish *you;* My eye will not spare, nor will I have any pity. [12]One-third of you shall die of the pestilence, and be consumed with famine in your midst; and one-third shall fall by the sword all around you; and I will scatter another third to all the winds, and I will draw out a sword after them.

[13]'Thus shall My anger be spent, and I will cause My fury to rest upon them, and I will be avenged; and they shall know that I, the LORD, have spoken *it* in My zeal, when I have spent My fury upon them. [14]Moreover I will make you a waste and a reproach among the nations that *are* all around you, in the sight of all who pass by.

[15]'So it[a] shall be a reproach, a taunt, a lesson, and an astonishment to the nations that *are* all around you, when I execute judgments among you in anger and in fury and in furious rebukes. I, the LORD, have spoken. [16]When I send against them the terrible arrows of famine which shall be for destruction, which I will send to destroy you, I will increase the famine upon you and cut off your supply of bread. [17]So I will send against you famine and wild beasts, and they will bereave you. Pestilence and blood shall pass through you, and I will bring the sword against you. I, the LORD, have spoken.'"

Judgment on Idolatrous Israel

6 Now the word of the LORD came to me, saying: [2]"Son of man, set your face toward the mountains of Israel, and

---

5:7 [a]Following Masoretic Text, Septuagint, Targum, and Vulgate; many Hebrew manuscripts and Syriac read *but have done* (compare 11:12).
5:15 [a]Septuagint, Syriac, Targum, and Vulgate read *you.*

prophesy against them, ³and say, 'O mountains of Israel, hear the word of the Lord GOD! Thus says the Lord GOD to the mountains, to the hills, to the ravines, and to the valleys: "Indeed I, *even* I, will bring a sword against you, and I will destroy your high places. ⁴Then your altars shall be desolate, your incense altars shall be broken, and I will cast down your slain *men* before your idols. ⁵And I will lay the corpses of the children of Israel before their idols, and I will scatter your bones all around your altars. ⁶In all your dwelling places the cities shall be laid waste, and the high places shall be desolate, so that your altars may be laid waste and made desolate, your idols may be broken and made to cease, your incense altars may be cut down, and your works may be abolished. ⁷The slain shall fall in your midst, and you shall know that I *am* the LORD.

⁸"Yet I will leave a remnant, so that you may have *some* who escape the sword among the nations, when you are scattered through the countries. ⁹Then those of you who escape will remember Me among the nations where they are carried captive, because I was crushed by their adulterous heart which has departed from Me, and by their eyes which play the harlot after their idols; they will loathe themselves for the evils which they committed in all their abominations. ¹⁰And they shall know that I *am* the LORD; I have not said in vain that I would bring this calamity upon them."

¹¹'Thus says the Lord GOD: "Pound your fists and stamp your feet, and say, 'Alas, for all the evil abominations of the house of Israel! For they shall fall by the sword, by famine, and by pestilence. ¹²He who is far off shall die by the pestilence, he who is near shall fall by the sword, and he who remains and is besieged shall die by the famine. Thus will I spend My fury upon them. ¹³Then you shall know that I *am* the LORD, when their slain are among their idols all around their altars, on every high hill, on all the mountaintops, under every green tree, and under every thick oak, wherever they offered sweet incense to all their idols. ¹⁴So I will stretch out My hand against them and make the land desolate, yes, more desolate than the wilderness toward Diblah, in all their dwelling places. Then they shall know that I *am* the LORD.'"'"

Judgment on Israel Is Near

7 Moreover the word of the LORD came to me, saying, ²"And you, son of man, thus says the Lord GOD to the land of Israel:

'An end! The end has come upon the four corners of the land.
3 Now the end *has come* upon you,
  And I will send My anger against you;
  I will judge you according to your ways,
  And I will repay you for all your abominations.
4 My eye will not spare you,
  Nor will I have pity;
  But I will repay your ways,
  And your abominations will be in your midst;
  Then you shall know that I *am* the LORD!'

⁵"Thus says the Lord GOD:

'A disaster, a singular disaster;
  Behold, it has come!
6 An end has come,
  The end has come;
  It has dawned for you;
  Behold, it has come!
7 Doom has come to you, you who dwell in the land;
  The time has come,
  A day of trouble *is* near,
  And not of rejoicing in the mountains.
8 Now upon you I will soon pour out My fury,
  And spend My anger upon you;
  I will judge you according to your ways,
  And I will repay you for all your abominations.

9 'My eye will not spare,
  Nor will I have pity;
  I will repay you according to your ways,
  And your abominations will be in your midst.
  Then you shall know that I *am* the LORD who strikes.

10 'Behold, the day!
Behold, it has come!
Doom has gone out;
The rod has blossomed,
Pride has budded.
11 Violence has risen up into a rod of
wickedness;
None of them *shall remain,*
None of their multitude,
None of them;
Nor *shall there be* wailing for them.
12 The time has come,
The day draws near.

'Let not the buyer rejoice,
Nor the seller mourn,
For wrath *is* on their whole multitude.
13 For the seller shall not return to what
has been sold,
Though he may still be alive;
For the vision concerns the whole
multitude,
And it shall not turn back;
No one will strengthen himself
Who lives in iniquity.

14 'They have blown the trumpet and
made everyone ready,
But no one goes to battle;
For My wrath *is* on all their multitude.
15 The sword *is* outside,
And the pestilence and famine within.
Whoever *is* in the field
Will die by the sword;
And whoever *is* in the city,
Famine and pestilence will devour him.

16 'Those who survive will escape and be
on the mountains
Like doves of the valleys,
All of them mourning,
Each for his iniquity.
17 Every hand will be feeble,
And every knee will be *as* weak *as* water.
18 They will also be girded with sackcloth;
Horror will cover them;
Shame *will be* on every face,
Baldness on all their heads.

19 'They will throw their silver into the
streets,
And their gold will be like refuse;

Their silver and their gold will not be
able to deliver them
In the day of the wrath of the LORD;
They will not satisfy their souls,
Nor fill their stomachs,
Because it became their stumbling
block of iniquity.

20 'As for the beauty of his ornaments,
He set it in majesty;
But they made from it
The images of their abominations—
Their detestable things;
Therefore I have made it
Like refuse to them.
21 I will give it as plunder
Into the hands of strangers,
And to the wicked of the earth as spoil;
And they shall defile it.
22 I will turn My face from them,
And they will defile My secret place;
For robbers shall enter it and defile it.

23 'Make a chain,
For the land is filled with crimes of
blood,
And the city is full of violence.
24 Therefore I will bring the worst of the
Gentiles,
And they will possess their houses;
I will cause the pomp of the strong
to cease,
And their holy places shall be defiled.
25 Destruction comes;
They will seek peace, but *there shall be*
none.
26 Disaster will come upon disaster,
And rumor will be upon rumor.
Then they will seek a vision from a
prophet;
But the law will perish from the priest,
And counsel from the elders.
27 'The king will mourn,
The prince will be clothed with
desolation,
And the hands of the common people
will tremble.
I will do to them according to their
way,
And according to what they deserve I
will judge them;

Then they shall know that I *am* the LORD!' "

Abominations in the Temple

8 And it came to pass in the sixth year, in the sixth *month,* on the fifth *day* of the month, as I sat in my house with the elders of Judah sitting before me, that the hand of the Lord GOD fell upon me there. ²Then I looked, and there was a likeness, like the appearance of fire—from the appearance of His waist and downward, fire; and from His waist and upward, like the appearance of brightness, like the color of amber. ³He stretched out the form of a hand, and took me by a lock of my hair; and the Spirit lifted me up between earth and heaven, and brought me in visions of God to Jerusalem, to the door of the north gate of the inner *court,* where the seat of the image of jealousy *was,* which provokes to jealousy. ⁴And behold, the glory of the God of Israel *was* there, like the vision that I saw in the plain.

⁵Then He said to me, "Son of man, lift your eyes now toward the north." So I lifted my eyes toward the north, and there, north of the altar gate, was this image of jealousy in the entrance.

⁶Furthermore He said to me, "Son of man, do you see what they are doing, the great abominations that the house of Israel commits here, to make Me go far away from My sanctuary? Now turn again, you will see greater abominations." ⁷So He brought me to the door of the court; and when I looked, there was a hole in the wall. ⁸Then He said to me, "Son of man, dig into the wall"; and when I dug into the wall, there was a door.

⁹And He said to me, "Go in, and see the wicked abominations which they are doing there." ¹⁰So I went in and saw, and there—every sort of creeping thing, abominable beasts, and all the idols of the house of Israel, portrayed all around on the walls. ¹¹And there stood before them seventy men of the elders of the house of Israel, and in their midst stood Jaazaniah the son of Shaphan. Each man had a censer in his hand, and a thick cloud of incense went up. ¹²Then He said to me, "Son of man, have you seen what the elders of the house of Israel do in the dark, every man in the room

of his idols? For they say, 'The LORD does not see us, the LORD has forsaken the land.' "

¹³And He said to me, "Turn again, *and* you will see greater abominations that they are doing." ¹⁴So He brought me to the door of the north gate of the LORD's house; and to my dismay, women were sitting there weeping for Tammuz.

¹⁵Then He said to me, "Have you seen *this,* O son of man? Turn again, you will see greater abominations than these." ¹⁶So He brought me into the inner court of the LORD's house; and there, at the door of the temple of the LORD, between the porch and the altar, *were* about twenty-five men with their backs toward the temple of the LORD and their faces toward the east, and they were worshiping the sun toward the east.

¹⁷And He said to me, "Have you seen *this,* O son of man? Is it a trivial thing to the house of Judah to commit the abominations which they commit here? For they have filled the land with violence; then they have returned to provoke Me to anger. Indeed they put the branch to their nose. ¹⁸Therefore I also will act in fury. My eye will not spare nor will I have pity; and though they cry in My ears with a loud voice, I will not hear them."

The Wicked Are Slain

9 Then He called out in my hearing with a loud voice, saying, "Let those who have charge over the city draw near, each *with* a deadly weapon in his hand." ²And suddenly six men came from the direction of the upper gate, which faces north, each with his battle-ax in his hand. One man among them *was* clothed with linen and had a writer's inkhorn at his side. They went in and stood beside the bronze altar.

³Now the glory of the God of Israel had gone up from the cherub, where it had been, to the threshold of the temple.ᵃ And He called to the man clothed with linen, who *had* the writer's inkhorn at his side; ⁴and the LORD said to him, "Go through the midst of the city, through the midst of Jerusalem, and put a mark on the foreheads of the men who sigh and cry over all the abominations that are done within it."

9:3 ᵃLiterally *house*

⁵To the others He said in my hearing, "Go after him through the city and kill; do not let your eye spare, nor have any pity. ⁶Utterly slay old *and* young men, maidens and little children and women; but do not come near anyone on whom *is* the mark; and begin at My sanctuary." So they began with the elders who *were* before the temple. ⁷Then He said to them, "Defile the temple, and fill the courts with the slain. Go out!" And they went out and killed in the city.

⁸So it was, that while they were killing them, I was left *alone;* and I fell on my face and cried out, and said, "Ah, Lord GOD! Will You destroy all the remnant of Israel in pouring out Your fury on Jerusalem?"

⁹Then He said to me, "The iniquity of the house of Israel and Judah *is* exceedingly great, and the land is full of bloodshed, and the city full of perversity; for they say, 'The LORD has forsaken the land, and the LORD does not see!' ¹⁰And as for Me also, My eye will neither spare, nor will I have pity, *but* I will recompense their deeds on their own head."

¹¹Just then, the man clothed with linen, who *had* the inkhorn at his side, reported back and said, "I have done as You commanded me."

The Glory Departs from the Temple

10And I looked, and there in the firmament that was above the head of the cherubim, there appeared something like a sapphire stone, having the appearance of the likeness of a throne. ²Then He spoke to the man clothed with linen, and said, "Go in among the wheels, under the cherub, fill your hands with coals of fire from among the cherubim, and scatter *them* over the city." And he went in as I watched.

³Now the cherubim were standing on the south side of the templeᵃ when the man went in, and the cloud filled the inner court. ⁴Then the glory of the LORD went up from the cherub, *and paused* over the threshold of the temple; and the house was filled with the cloud, and the court was full of the brightness of the LORD's glory. ⁵And the sound of the wings of the cherubim was heard *even* in the outer court, like the voice of Almighty God when He speaks.

⁶Then it happened, when He commanded the man clothed in linen, saying, "Take fire from among the wheels, from among the cherubim," that he went in and stood beside the wheels. ⁷And the cherub stretched out his hand from among the cherubim to the fire that *was* among the cherubim, and took *some of it* and put *it* into the hands of the *man* clothed with linen, who took *it* and went out. ⁸The cherubim appeared to have the form of a man's hand under their wings.

⁹And when I looked, there were four wheels by the cherubim, one wheel by one cherub and another wheel by each other cherub; the wheels appeared *to have* the color of a beryl stone. ¹⁰*As for* their appearance, all four looked alike—as it were, a wheel in the middle of a wheel. ¹¹When they went, they went toward *any of* their four directions; they did not turn aside when they went, but followed in the direction the head was facing. They did not turn aside when they went. ¹²And their whole body, with their back, their hands, their wings, and the wheels that the four had, *were* full of eyes all around. ¹³As for the wheels, they were called in my hearing, "Wheel."

¹⁴Each one had four faces: the first face *was* the face of a cherub, the second face the face of a man, the third the face of a lion, and the fourth the face of an eagle. ¹⁵And the cherubim were lifted up. This *was* the living creature I saw by the River Chebar. ¹⁶When the cherubim went, the wheels went beside them; and when the cherubim lifted their wings to mount up from the earth, the same wheels also did not turn from beside them. ¹⁷When *the cherubim*ᵃ stood still, *the wheels* stood still, and when *one*ᵇ was lifted up, *the other*ᶜ lifted itself up, for the spirit of the living creature *was* in them.

¹⁸Then the glory of the LORD departed from the threshold of the temple and stood over the cherubim. ¹⁹And the cherubim lifted their wings and mounted up from the earth in my sight. When they went out, the wheels *were* beside them; and they stood at the door of the east gate of the LORD's house, and the glory of the God of Israel *was* above them.

10:3 ᵃLiterally *house,* also in verses 4 and 18
10:17 ᵃLiterally *they* ᵇLiterally *they* ᶜLiterally *they*

²⁰This *is* the living creature I saw under the God of Israel by the River Chebar, and I knew they *were* cherubim. ²¹Each one had four faces and each one four wings, and the likeness of the hands of a man *was* under their wings. ²²And the likeness of their faces *was* the same *as* the faces which I had seen by the River Chebar, their appearance and their persons. They each went straight forward.

Judgment on Wicked Counselors

11 Then the Spirit lifted me up and brought me to the East Gate of the LORD's house, which faces eastward; and there at the door of the gate were twenty-five men, among whom I saw Jaazaniah the son of Azzur, and Pelatiah the son of Benaiah, princes of the people. ²And He said to me: "Son of man, these *are* the men who devise iniquity and give wicked counsel in this city, ³who say, '*The time is* not near to build houses; this *city is* the caldron, and we *are* the meat.' ⁴Therefore prophesy against them, prophesy, O son of man!"

⁵Then the Spirit of the LORD fell upon me, and said to me, "Speak! 'Thus says the LORD: "Thus you have said, O house of Israel; for I know the things that come into your mind. ⁶You have multiplied your slain in this city, and you have filled its streets with the slain." ⁷Therefore thus says the Lord GOD: "Your slain whom you have laid in its midst, they *are* the meat, and this *city is* the caldron; but I shall bring you out of the midst of it. ⁸You have feared the sword; and I will bring a sword upon you," says the Lord GOD. ⁹"And I will bring you out of its midst, and deliver you into the hands of strangers, and execute judgments on you. ¹⁰You shall fall by the sword. I will judge you at the border of Israel. Then you shall know that I *am* the LORD. ¹¹This *city* shall not be your caldron, nor shall you be the meat in its midst. I will judge you at the border of Israel. ¹²And you shall know that I *am* the LORD; for you have not walked in My statutes nor executed My judgments, but have done according to the customs of the Gentiles which *are* all around you."'"

¹³Now it happened, while I was prophesying, that Pelatiah the son of Benaiah died. Then I fell on my face and cried with a loud voice, and said, "Ah, Lord GOD! Will You make a complete end of the remnant of Israel?"

God Will Restore Israel

¹⁴Again the word of the LORD came to me, saying, ¹⁵"Son of man, your brethren, your relatives, your countrymen, and all the house of Israel in its entirety, *are* those about whom the inhabitants of Jerusalem have said, 'Get far away from the LORD; this land has been given to us as a possession.' ¹⁶Therefore say, 'Thus says the Lord GOD: "Although I have cast them far off among the Gentiles, and although I have scattered them among the countries, yet I shall be a little sanctuary for them in the countries where they have gone."' ¹⁷Therefore say, 'Thus says the Lord GOD: "I will gather you from the peoples, assemble you from the countries where you have been scattered, and I will give you the land of Israel."' ¹⁸And they will go there, and they will take away all its detestable things and all its abominations from there. ¹⁹Then I will give them one heart, and I will put a new spirit within them,ᵃ and take the stony heart out of their flesh, and give them a heart of flesh, ²⁰that they may walk in My statutes and keep My judgments and do them; and they shall be My people, and I will be their God. ²¹But *as for those* whose hearts follow the desire for their detestable things and their abominations, I will recompense their deeds on their own heads," says the Lord GOD.

²²So the cherubim lifted up their wings, with the wheels beside them, and the glory of the God of Israel *was* high above them. ²³And the glory of the LORD went up from the midst of the city and stood on the mountain, which *is* on the east side of the city.

²⁴Then the Spirit took me up and brought me in a vision by the Spirit of God into Chaldea,ᵃ to those in captivity. And the vision that I had seen went up from me. ²⁵So I spoke to those in captivity of all the things the LORD had shown me.

11:19 ᵃLiterally *you*   **11:24** ᵃOr *Babylon*, and so elsewhere in this book

Judah's Captivity Portrayed

12 Now the word of the LORD came to me, saying: 2"Son of man, you dwell in the midst of a rebellious house, which has eyes to see but does not see, and ears to hear but does not hear; for they *are* a rebellious house.

3"Therefore, son of man, prepare your belongings for captivity, and go into captivity by day in their sight. You shall go from your place into captivity to another place in their sight. It may be that they will consider, though they *are* a rebellious house. 4By day you shall bring out your belongings in their sight, as though going into captivity; and at evening you shall go in their sight, like those who go into captivity. 5Dig through the wall in their sight, and carry *your belongings* out through it. 6In their sight you shall bear *them* on *your* shoulders *and* carry *them* out at twilight; you shall cover your face, so that you cannot see the ground, for I have made you a sign to the house of Israel."

7So I did as I was commanded. I brought out my belongings by day, as though going into captivity, and at evening I dug through the wall with my hand. I brought *them* out at twilight, *and* I bore *them* on *my* shoulder in their sight.

8And in the morning the word of the LORD came to me, saying, 9"Son of man, has not the house of Israel, the rebellious house, said to you, 'What are you doing?' 10Say to them, 'Thus says the Lord GOD: "This burden *concerns* the prince in Jerusalem and all the house of Israel who are among them."' 11Say, 'I *am* a sign to you. As I have done, so shall it be done to them; they shall be carried away into captivity.' 12And the prince who *is* among them shall bear *his* belongings on *his* shoulder at twilight and go out. They shall dig through the wall to carry *them* out through it. He shall cover his face, so that he cannot see the ground with *his* eyes. 13I will also spread My net over him, and he shall be caught in My snare. I will bring him to Babylon, *to* the land of the Chaldeans; yet he shall not see it, though he shall die there. 14I will scatter to every wind all who *are* around him to help him, and all his troops; and I will draw out the sword after them.

15"Then they shall know that I *am* the LORD, when I scatter them among the nations and disperse them throughout the countries. 16But I will spare a few of their men from the sword, from famine, and from pestilence, that they may declare all their abominations among the Gentiles wherever they go. Then they shall know that I *am* the LORD."

Judgment Not Postponed

17Moreover the word of the LORD came to me, saying, 18"Son of man, eat your bread with quaking, and drink your water with trembling and anxiety. 19And say to the people of the land, 'Thus says the Lord GOD to the inhabitants of Jerusalem *and* to the land of Israel: "They shall eat their bread with anxiety, and drink their water with dread, so that her land may be emptied of all who are in it, because of the violence of all those who dwell in it. 20Then the cities that are inhabited shall be laid waste, and the land shall become desolate; and you shall know that I *am* the LORD."'"

21And the word of the LORD came to me, saying, 22"Son of man, what *is* this proverb

that you *people* have about the land of Israel, which says, 'The days are prolonged, and every vision fails'? [23]Tell them therefore, 'Thus says the Lord God: "I will lay this proverb to rest, and they shall no more use it as a proverb in Israel." ' But say to them, ' "The days are at hand, and the fulfillment of every vision. [24]For no more shall there be any false vision or flattering divination within the house of Israel. [25]For I *am* the Lord. I speak, and the word which I speak will come to pass; it will no more be postponed; for in your days, O rebellious house, I will say the word and perform it," says the Lord God.' "

[26]Again the word of the Lord came to me, saying, [27]"Son of man, look, the house of Israel is saying, 'The vision that he sees *is* for many days *from now,* and he prophesies of times far off.' [28]Therefore say to them, 'Thus says the Lord God: "None of My words will be postponed any more, but the word which I speak will be done," says the Lord God.' "

Woe to Foolish Prophets

13 And the word of the Lord came to me, saying, [2]"Son of man, prophesy against the prophets of Israel who prophesy, and say to those who prophesy out of their own heart, 'Hear the word of the Lord!' "

[3]Thus says the Lord God: "Woe to the foolish prophets, who follow their own spirit and have seen nothing! [4]O Israel, your prophets are like foxes in the deserts. [5]You have not gone up into the gaps to build a wall for the house of Israel to stand in battle on the day of the Lord. [6]They have envisioned futility and false divination, saying, 'Thus says the Lord!' But the Lord has not sent them; yet they hope that the word may be confirmed. [7]Have you not seen a futile vision, and have you not spoken false divination? You say, 'The Lord says,' but I have not spoken."

[8]Therefore thus says the Lord God: "Because you have spoken nonsense and envisioned lies, therefore I *am* indeed against you," says the Lord God. [9]"My hand will be against the prophets who envision futility and who divine lies; they shall not be in the assembly of My people, nor be written in the record of the house of Israel, nor shall they enter into the land of Israel. Then you shall know that I *am* the Lord God.

[10]"Because, indeed, because they have seduced My people, saying, 'Peace!' when *there is* no peace—and one builds a wall, and they plaster it with untempered *mortar*— [11]say to those who plaster *it* with untempered *mortar,* that it will fall. There will be flooding rain, and you, O great hailstones, shall fall; and a stormy wind shall tear *it* down. [12]Surely, when the wall has fallen, will it not be said to you, 'Where *is* the mortar with which you plastered *it?*' "

[13]Therefore thus says the Lord God: "I will cause a stormy wind to break forth in My fury; and there shall be a flooding rain in My anger, and great hailstones in fury to consume *it.* [14]So I will break down the wall you have plastered with untempered *mortar,* and bring it down to the ground, so that its foundation will be uncovered; it will fall, and you shall be consumed in the midst of it. Then you shall know that I *am* the Lord.

[15]"Thus will I accomplish My wrath on the wall and on those who have plastered it with untempered *mortar;* and I will say to you, 'The wall *is* no *more,* nor those who plastered it, [16]that is, the prophets of Israel who prophesy concerning Jerusalem, and who see visions of peace for her when *there is* no peace,' " says the Lord God.

[17]"Likewise, son of man, set your face against the daughters of your people, who prophesy out of their own heart; prophesy against them, [18]and say, 'Thus says the Lord God: "Woe to the *women* who sew *magic* charms on their sleeves[a] and make veils for the heads of people of every height to hunt souls! Will you hunt the souls of My people, and keep yourselves alive? [19]And will you profane Me among My people for handfuls of barley and for pieces of bread, killing people who should not die, and keeping people alive who should not live, by your lying to My people who listen to lies?"

13:18 [a]Literally *over all the joints of My hands;* Vulgate reads *under every elbow;* Septuagint and Targum read *on all elbows of the hands.*

The FOUR FREEDOMS

FRANKLIN D. ROOSEVELT

With Germany, Italy, and Japan already waging warfare on four continents in January 1941, President Franklin D. Roosevelt urged Americans that if democracy was to survive, mobilization was necessary to rid the world of dictatorships and military rule. He then described "four essential human freedoms" that the United States hoped to secure for the world community:

No realistic American can expect from a dictator's peace international generosity, or return of true independence, or world disarmament, or freedom of expression, or freedom of religion—or even good business. Such a peace would bring no security for us or for our neighbors. Those who would give up essential liberty to purchase a little temporary safety deserve neither liberty nor safety. ...

In the future days, which we seek to make secure, we look forward to a world founded upon four essential human freedoms.

The first is freedom of speech and expression—everywhere in the world.

The second is freedom of every person to worship God in his own way—everywhere in the world.

The third is freedom from want—which, translated into world terms, means economic understandings which will secure to every nation a healthy peacetime life for its inhabitants—everywhere in the world.

The fourth is freedom from fear—which, translated into world terms, means a worldwide reduction of armaments to such a point and in such a thorough fashion that no nation will be in a position to commit an act of physical aggression against any neighbor—anywhere in the world.

That is no vision of a distant millennium. It is a definite basis for a kind of world attainable in our own time and generation. That kind of world is the very antithesis of the so-called new order of tyranny which the dictators seek to create with the crash of a bomb. ...

This nation has placed its destiny in the hands and heads and hearts of its millions of free men and women; and its faith in freedom under the guidance of God. Freedom means the supremacy of human rights everywhere. Our support goes to those who struggle to gain those rights or keep them. Our strength is our unity of purpose.

To that high concept there can be no end save victory.

²⁰'Therefore thus says the Lord GOD: "Behold, I *am* against your *magic* charms by which you hunt souls there like birds. I will tear them from your arms, and let the souls go, the souls you hunt like birds. ²¹I will also tear off your veils and deliver My people out of your hand, and they shall no longer be as prey in your hand. Then you shall know that I *am* the LORD.

²²"Because with lies you have made the heart of the righteous sad, whom I have not made sad; and you have strengthened the hands of the wicked, so that he does not turn from his wicked way to save his life. ²³Therefore you shall no longer envision futility nor practice divination; for I will deliver My people out of your hand, and you shall know that I *am* the LORD."'"

Idolatry Will Be Punished

14 Now some of the elders of Israel came to me and sat before me. ²And the word of the LORD came to me, saying, ³"Son of man, these men have set up their idols in their hearts, and put before them that which causes them to stumble into iniquity. Should I let Myself be inquired of at all by them?

⁴"Therefore speak to them, and say to them, 'Thus says the Lord GOD: "Everyone of the house of Israel who sets up his idols in his heart, and puts before him what causes him to stumble into iniquity, and then comes to the prophet, I the LORD will answer him who comes, according to the multitude of his idols, ⁵that I may seize the house of Israel by their heart, because they are all estranged from Me by their idols."'

⁶"Therefore say to the house of Israel, 'Thus says the Lord GOD: "Repent, turn away from your idols, and turn your faces away from all your abominations. ⁷For anyone of the house of Israel, or of the strangers who dwell in Israel, who separates himself from Me and sets up his idols in his heart and puts before him what causes him to stumble into iniquity, then comes to a prophet to inquire of him concerning Me, I the LORD will answer him by Myself. ⁸I will set My face against that man and make him a sign and a proverb, and I will cut him off from the midst of My people. Then you shall know that I *am* the LORD.

⁹"And if the prophet is induced to speak anything, I the LORD have induced that prophet, and I will stretch out My hand against him and destroy him from among My people Israel. ¹⁰And they shall bear their iniquity; the punishment of the prophet shall be the same as the punishment of the one who inquired, ¹¹that the house of Israel may no longer stray from Me, nor be profaned anymore with all their transgressions, but that they may be My people and I may be their God," says the Lord GOD.'"

Judgment on Persistent Unfaithfulness

¹²The word of the LORD came again to me, saying: ¹³"Son of man, when a land sins against Me by persistent unfaithfulness, I will stretch out My hand against it; I will cut off its supply of bread, send famine on it, and cut off man and beast from it. ¹⁴Even *if* these three men, Noah, Daniel, and Job, were in it, they would deliver *only* themselves by their righteousness," says the Lord GOD.

¹⁵"If I cause wild beasts to pass through the land, and they empty it, and make it so desolate that no man may pass through because of the beasts, ¹⁶*even though* these three men *were* in it, *as* I live," says the Lord GOD, "they would deliver neither sons nor daughters; only they would be delivered, and the land would be desolate.

¹⁷"Or *if* I bring a sword on that land, and say, 'Sword, go through the land,' and I cut off man and beast from it, ¹⁸even *though* these three men *were* in it, *as* I live," says the Lord GOD, "they would deliver neither sons nor daughters, but only they themselves would be delivered.

¹⁹"Or *if* I send a pestilence into that land and pour out My fury on it in blood, and cut off from it man and beast, ²⁰even *though* Noah, Daniel, and Job *were* in it, *as* I live," says the Lord GOD, "they would deliver neither son nor daughter; they would deliver *only* themselves by their righteousness."

²¹For thus says the Lord GOD: "How much more it shall be when I send My four severe judgments on Jerusalem—the sword and famine and wild beasts and pestilence—to

cut off man and beast from it? ²²Yet behold, there shall be left in it a remnant who will be brought out, *both* sons and daughters; surely they will come out to you, and you will see their ways and their doings. Then you will be comforted concerning the disaster that I have brought upon Jerusalem, all that I have brought upon it. ²³And they will comfort you, when you see their ways and their doings; and you shall know that I have done nothing without cause that I have done in it," says the Lord GOD.

The Outcast Vine

15 Then the word of the LORD came to me, saying: ²"Son of man, how is the wood of the vine *better* than any other wood, the vine branch which is among the trees of the forest? ³Is wood taken from it to make any object? Or can *men* make a peg from it to hang any vessel on? ⁴Instead, it is thrown into the fire for fuel; the fire devours both ends of it, and its middle is burned. Is it useful for *any* work? ⁵Indeed, when it was whole, no object could be made from it. How much less will it be useful for *any* work when the fire has devoured it, and it is burned?

⁶"Therefore thus says the Lord GOD: 'Like the wood of the vine among the trees of the forest, which I have given to the fire for fuel, so I will give up the inhabitants of Jerusalem; ⁷and I will set My face against them. They will go out from *one* fire, but *another* fire shall devour them. Then you shall know that I *am* the LORD, when I set My face against them. ⁸Thus I will make the land desolate, because they have persisted in unfaithfulness,' says the Lord GOD."

God's Love for Jerusalem

16 Again the word of the LORD came to me, saying, ²"Son of man, cause Jerusalem to know her abominations, ³and say, 'Thus says the Lord GOD to Jerusalem: "Your birth and your nativity *are* from the land of Canaan; your father *was* an Amorite and your mother a Hittite. ⁴*As for* your nativity, on the day you were born your navel cord was not cut, nor were you washed in water to cleanse *you;* you were not rubbed with salt nor wrapped in swaddling cloths. ⁵No

eye pitied you, to do any of these things for you, to have compassion on you; but you were thrown out into the open field, when you yourself were loathed on the day you were born.

⁶"And when I passed by you and saw you struggling in your own blood, I said to you in your blood, 'Live!' Yes, I said to you in your blood, 'Live!' ⁷I made you thrive like a plant in the field; and you grew, matured, and became very beautiful. *Your* breasts were formed, your hair grew, but you *were* naked and bare.

⁸"When I passed by you again and looked upon you, indeed your time *was* the time of love; so I spread My wing over you and covered your nakedness. Yes, I swore an oath to you and entered into a covenant with you, and you became Mine," says the Lord GOD.

⁹"Then I washed you in water; yes, I thoroughly washed off your blood, and I anointed you with oil. ¹⁰I clothed you in embroidered cloth and gave you sandals of badger skin; I clothed you with fine linen and covered you with silk. ¹¹I adorned you with ornaments, put bracelets on your wrists, and a chain on your neck. ¹²And I put a jewel in your nose, earrings in your ears, and a beautiful crown on your head. ¹³Thus you were adorned with gold and silver, and your clothing *was of* fine linen, silk, and embroidered cloth. You ate *pastry of* fine flour, honey, and oil. You were exceedingly beautiful, and succeeded to royalty. ¹⁴Your fame went out among the nations because of your beauty, for it *was* perfect through My splendor which I had bestowed on you," says the Lord GOD.

Jerusalem's Harlotry

¹⁵"But you trusted in your own beauty, played the harlot because of your fame, and poured out your harlotry on everyone passing by who *would have* it. ¹⁶You took some of your garments and adorned multicolored high places for yourself, and played the harlot on them. *Such* things should not happen, nor be. ¹⁷You have also taken your beautiful jewelry from My gold and My silver, which I had given you, and made for yourself male images and played the harlot with them. ¹⁸You took your embroidered

garments and covered them, and you set My oil and My incense before them. ¹⁹Also My food which I gave you—the pastry of fine flour, oil, and honey *which* I fed you—you set it before them as sweet incense; and *so* it was," says the Lord GOD.

²⁰"Moreover you took your sons and your daughters, whom you bore to Me, and these you sacrificed to them to be devoured. *Were* your *acts* of harlotry a small matter, ²¹that you have slain My children and offered them up to them by causing them to pass through *the fire?* ²²And in all your abominations and acts of harlotry you did not remember the days of your youth, when you were naked and bare, struggling in your blood.

²³"Then it was so, after all your wickedness—'Woe, woe to you!' says the Lord GOD— ²⁴*that* you also built for yourself a shrine, and made a high place for yourself in every street. ²⁵You built your high places at the head of every road, and made your beauty to be abhorred. You offered yourself to everyone who passed by, and multiplied your acts of harlotry. ²⁶You also committed harlotry with the Egyptians, your very fleshly neighbors, and increased your acts of harlotry to provoke Me to anger.

²⁷"Behold, therefore, I stretched out My hand against you, diminished your allotment, and gave you up to the will of those who hate you, the daughters of the Philistines, who were ashamed of your lewd behavior. ²⁸You also played the harlot with the Assyrians, because you were insatiable; indeed you played the harlot with them and still were not satisfied. ²⁹Moreover you multiplied your acts of harlotry as far as the land of the trader, Chaldea; and even then you were not satisfied.

³⁰"How degenerate is your heart!" says the Lord GOD, "seeing you do all these *things,* the deeds of a brazen harlot.

Jerusalem's Adultery

³¹"You erected your shrine at the head of every road, and built your high place in every street. Yet you were not like a harlot, because you scorned payment. ³²*You are* an adulterous wife, *who* takes strangers instead

of her husband. ³³Men make payment to all harlots, but you made your payments to all your lovers, and hired them to come to you from all around for your harlotry. ³⁴You are the opposite of *other* women in your harlotry, because no one solicited you to be a harlot. In that you gave payment but no payment was given you, therefore you are the opposite."

Jerusalem's Lovers Will Abuse Her

³⁵'Now then, O harlot, hear the word of the LORD! ³⁶Thus says the Lord GOD: "Because your filthiness was poured out and your nakedness uncovered in your harlotry with your lovers, and with all your abominable idols, and because of the blood of your children which you gave to them, ³⁷surely, therefore, I will gather all your lovers with whom you took pleasure, all those you loved, *and* all those you hated; I will gather them from all around against you and will uncover your nakedness to them, that they may see all your nakedness. ³⁸And I will judge you as women who break wedlock or shed blood are judged; I will bring blood upon you in fury and jealousy. ³⁹I will also give you into their hand, and they shall throw down your shrines and break down your high places. They shall also strip you of your clothes, take your beautiful jewelry, and leave you naked and bare.

⁴⁰"They shall also bring up an assembly against you, and they shall stone you with stones and thrust you through with their swords. ⁴¹They shall burn your houses with fire, and execute judgments on you in the sight of many women; and I will make you cease playing the harlot, and you shall no longer hire lovers. ⁴²So I will lay to rest My fury toward you, and My jealousy shall depart from you. I will be quiet, and be angry no more. ⁴³Because you did not remember the days of your youth, but agitated Meª with all these *things,* surely I will also recompense your deeds on *your own* head," says the Lord GOD. "And you shall not commit lewdness in addition to all your abominations.

16:43 ªFollowing Septuagint, Syriac, Targum, and Vulgate; Masoretic Text reads *were agitated with Me.*

More Wicked than Samaria and Sodom

44"Indeed everyone who quotes proverbs will use *this* proverb against you: 'Like mother, like daughter!' 45You *are* your mother's daughter, loathing husband and children; and you *are* the sister of your sisters, who loathed their husbands and children; your mother *was* a Hittite and your father an Amorite.

46"Your elder sister *is* Samaria, who dwells with her daughters to the north of you; and your younger sister, who dwells to the south of you, *is* Sodom and her daughters. 47You did not walk in their ways nor act according to their abominations; but, as *if that were* too little, you became more corrupt than they in all your ways.

48"*As* I live," says the Lord GOD, "neither your sister Sodom nor her daughters have done as you and your daughters have done. 49Look, this was the iniquity of your sister Sodom: She and her daughter had pride, fullness of food, and abundance of idleness; neither did she strengthen the hand of the poor and needy. 50And they were haughty and committed abomination before Me; therefore I took them away as I saw *fit*.ª

51"Samaria did not commit half of your sins; but you have multiplied your abominations more than they, and have justified your sisters by all the abominations which you have done. 52You who judged your sisters, bear your own shame also, because the sins which you committed were more abominable than theirs; they are more righteous than you. Yes, be disgraced also, and bear your own shame, because you justified your sisters.

53"When I bring back their captives, the captives of Sodom and her daughters, and the captives of Samaria and her daughters, then *I will also bring back* the captives of your captivity among them, 54that you may bear your own shame and be disgraced by all that you did when you comforted them. 55When your sisters, Sodom and her daughters, return to their former state, and Samaria and her daughters return to their former state, then you and your daughters will return to your former state. 56For your sister Sodom was not a byword in your mouth in the days of your pride, 57before your wickedness was uncovered. It was like the time of the reproach of the daughters of Syriaª and all *those* around her, and of the daughters of the Philistines, who despise you everywhere. 58You have paid for your lewdness and your abominations," says the LORD. 59For thus says the Lord GOD: "I will deal with you as you have done, who despised the oath by breaking the covenant.

An Everlasting Covenant

60"Nevertheless I will remember My covenant with you in the days of your youth, and I will establish an everlasting covenant with you. 61Then you will remember your ways and be ashamed, when you receive your older and your younger sisters; for I will give them to you for daughters, but not because of My covenant with you. 62And I will establish My covenant with you. Then you shall know that I *am* the LORD, 63that you may remember and be ashamed, and never open your mouth anymore because of your shame, when I provide you an atonement for all you have done," says the Lord GOD.'"

The Eagles and the Vine

17 And the word of the LORD came to me, saying, 2"Son of man, pose a riddle, and speak a parable to the house of Israel, 3and say, 'Thus says the Lord GOD:

"A great eagle with large wings and
    long pinions,
Full of feathers of various colors,
Came to Lebanon
And took from the cedar the highest
    branch.
4   He cropped off its topmost young
    twig
And carried it to a land of trade;
He set it in a city of merchants.
5   Then he took some of the seed of
    the land
And planted it in a fertile field;

16:50 ªVulgate reads *you saw*; Septuagint reads *he saw*; Targum reads *as was revealed to Me.*
16:57 ªFollowing Masoretic Text, Septuagint, Targum, and Vulgate; many Hebrew manuscripts and Syriac read *Edom*.

He placed *it* by abundant waters
And set it like a willow tree.
6 And it grew and became a spreading
    vine of low stature;
Its branches turned toward him,
But its roots were under it.
So it became a vine,
Brought forth branches,
And put forth shoots.

7 "But there was another[a] great eagle with
    large wings and many feathers;
And behold, this vine bent its roots
    toward him,
And stretched its branches toward him,
From the garden terrace where it had
    been planted,
That he might water it.
8 It was planted in good soil by many
    waters,
To bring forth branches, bear fruit,
And become a majestic vine." '

9 "Say, 'Thus says the Lord GOD:

"Will it thrive?
Will he not pull up its roots,
Cut off its fruit,
And leave it to wither?
All of its spring leaves will wither,
And no great power or many people
Will be needed to pluck it up by its
    roots.
10 Behold, *it is* planted,
Will it thrive?
Will it not utterly wither when the east
    wind touches it?
It will wither in the garden terrace
    where it grew." ' "

11 Moreover the word of the LORD came to me, saying, 12 "Say now to the rebellious house: 'Do you not know what these *things* mean?' Tell *them*, 'Indeed the king of Babylon went to Jerusalem and took its king and princes, and led them with him to Babylon. 13 And he took the king's offspring, made a covenant with him, and put him under oath. He also took away the mighty of the land, 14 that the kingdom might be brought low and not lift itself up, *but* that by keeping his covenant it might stand. 15 But he

rebelled against him by sending his ambassadors to Egypt, that they might give him horses and many people. Will he prosper? Will he who does such *things* escape? Can he break a covenant and still be delivered? 16 'As I live,' says the Lord GOD, 'surely in the place *where* the king *dwells* who made him king, whose oath he despised and whose covenant he broke—with him in the midst of Babylon he shall die. 17 Nor will Pharaoh with *his* mighty army and great company do anything in the war, when they heap up a siege mound and build a wall to cut off many persons. 18 Since he despised the oath by breaking the covenant, and in fact gave his hand and still did all these *things*, he shall not escape.' "

19 Therefore thus says the Lord GOD: "As I live, surely My oath which he despised, and My covenant which he broke, I will recompense on his own head. 20 I will spread My net over him, and he shall be taken in My snare. I will bring him to Babylon and try him there for the treason which he committed against Me. 21 All his fugitives[a] with all his troops shall fall by the sword, and those who remain shall be scattered to every wind; and you shall know that I, the LORD, have spoken."

Israel Exalted at Last

22 Thus says the Lord GOD: "I will take also *one* of the highest branches of the high cedar and set *it* out. I will crop off from the topmost of its young twigs a tender one, and will plant *it* on a high and prominent mountain. 23 On the mountain height of Israel I will plant it; and it will bring forth boughs, and bear fruit, and be a majestic cedar. Under it will dwell birds of every sort; in the shadow of its branches they will dwell. 24 And all the trees of the field shall know that I, the LORD, have brought down the high tree and exalted the low tree, dried up the green tree and made the dry tree flourish; I, the LORD, have spoken and have done *it*."

17:7 [a]Following Septuagint, Syriac, and Vulgate; Masoretic Text and Targum read *one*.
17:21 [a]Following Masoretic Text and Vulgate; many Hebrew manuscripts and Syriac read *choice men*; Targum reads *mighty men*; Septuagint omits *All his fugitives*.

A False Proverb Refuted

18 The word of the LORD came to me again, saying, 2"What do you mean when you use this proverb concerning the land of Israel, saying:

'The fathers have eaten sour grapes,
    And the children's teeth are set on
        edge'?

3"As I live," says the Lord GOD, "you shall no longer use this proverb in Israel.

4   "Behold, all souls are Mine;
    The soul of the father
    As well as the soul of the son is Mine;
    The soul who sins shall die.
5   But if a man is just
    And does what is lawful and right;
6   If he has not eaten on the mountains,
    Nor lifted up his eyes to the idols of
        the house of Israel,
    Nor defiled his neighbor's wife,
    Nor approached a woman during her
        impurity;
7   If he has not oppressed anyone,
    But has restored to the debtor his
        pledge;
    Has robbed no one by violence,
    But has given his bread to the hungry
    And covered the naked with clothing;
8   If he has not exacted usury
    Nor taken any increase,
    But has withdrawn his hand from
        iniquity
    And executed true judgment between
        man and man;
9   If he has walked in My statutes
    And kept My judgments faithfully—
    He is just;
    He shall surely live!"
    Says the Lord GOD.

10 "If he begets a son who is a robber
    Or a shedder of blood,
    Who does any of these things
11 And does none of those duties,
    But has eaten on the mountains
    Or defiled his neighbor's wife;
12 If he has oppressed the poor and needy,
    Robbed by violence,

    Not restored the pledge,
    Lifted his eyes to the idols,
    Or committed abomination;
13 If he has exacted usury
    Or taken increase—
    Shall he then live?
    He shall not live!
    If he has done any of these
        abominations,
    He shall surely die;
    His blood shall be upon him.

14 "If, however, he begets a son
    Who sees all the sins which his father
        has done,
    And considers but does not do likewise;
15 Who has not eaten on the mountains,
    Nor lifted his eyes to the idols of the
        house of Israel,
    Nor defiled his neighbor's wife;
16 Has not oppressed anyone,
    Nor withheld a pledge,
    Nor robbed by violence,
    But has given his bread to the hungry
    And covered the naked with clothing;
17 Who has withdrawn his hand from
        the poor[a]
    And not received usury or increase,
    But has executed My judgments
    And walked in My statutes—
    He shall not die for the iniquity of
        his father;
    He shall surely live!

18 "As for his father,
    Because he cruelly oppressed,
    Robbed his brother by violence,
    And did what is not good among his
        people,
    Behold, he shall die for his iniquity.

Turn and Live

19"Yet you say, 'Why should the son not bear the guilt of the father?' Because the son has done what is lawful and right, and has kept all My statutes and observed them, he shall surely live. 20The soul who sins shall die. The son shall not bear the guilt of the father, nor the father bear the guilt of

---

18:17 [a]Following Masoretic Text, Targum, and Vulgate; Septuagint reads iniquity (compare verse 8).

the son. The righteousness of the righteous shall be upon himself, and the wickedness of the wicked shall be upon himself.

²¹"But if a wicked man turns from all his sins which he has committed, keeps all My statutes, and does what is lawful and right, he shall surely live; he shall not die. ²²None of the transgressions which he has committed shall be remembered against him; because of the righteousness which he has done, he shall live. ²³Do I have any pleasure at all that the wicked should die?" says the Lord GOD, "and not that he should turn from his ways and live?

²⁴"But when a righteous man turns away from his righteousness and commits iniquity, and does according to all the abominations that the wicked *man* does, shall he live? All the righteousness which he has done shall not be remembered; because of the unfaithfulness of which he is guilty and the sin which he has committed, because of them he shall die.

²⁵"Yet you say, 'The way of the Lord is not fair.' Hear now, O house of Israel, is it not My way which is fair, and your ways which are not fair? ²⁶When a righteous *man* turns away from his righteousness, commits iniquity, and dies in it, it is because of the iniquity which he has done that he dies. ²⁷Again, when a wicked *man* turns away from the wickedness which he committed, and does what is lawful and right, he preserves himself alive. ²⁸Because he considers and turns away from all the transgressions which he committed, he shall surely live; he shall not die. ²⁹Yet the house of Israel says, 'The way of the Lord is not fair.' O house of Israel, is it not My ways which are fair, and your ways which are not fair?

³⁰"Therefore I will judge you, O house of Israel, every one according to his ways," says the Lord GOD. "Repent, and turn from all your transgressions, so that iniquity will not be your ruin. ³¹Cast away from you all the transgressions which you have committed, and get yourselves a new heart and a new spirit. For why should you die, O house of Israel? ³²For I have no pleasure in the death of one who dies," says the Lord GOD. "Therefore turn and live!"

Israel Degraded

19 "Moreover take up a lamentation for the princes of Israel, ²and say:

'What *is* your mother? A lioness:
She lay down among the lions;
Among the young lions she nourished
   her cubs.
³ She brought up one of her cubs,
And he became a young lion;
He learned to catch prey,
And he devoured men.
⁴ The nations also heard of him;
He was trapped in their pit,
And they brought him with chains to
   the land of Egypt.

⁵ 'When she saw that she waited, *that*
   her hope was lost,
She took another of her cubs *and*
   made him a young lion.
⁶ He roved among the lions,
And became a young lion;
He learned to catch prey;
He devoured men.
⁷ He knew their desolate places,ᵃ
And laid waste their cities;
The land with its fullness was desolated
By the noise of his roaring.
⁸ Then the nations set against him from
   the provinces on every side,
And spread their net over him;
He was trapped in their pit.
⁹ They put him in a cage with chains,
And brought him to the king of
   Babylon;
They brought him in nets,
That his voice should no longer be
   heard on the mountains of Israel.

¹⁰ 'Your mother *was* like a vine in your
   bloodline,ᵃ
Planted by the waters,
Fruitful and full of branches
Because of many waters.

19:7 ᵃSeptuagint reads *He stood in insolence;* Targum reads *He destroyed its palaces;* Vulgate reads *He learned to make widows.*   **19:10** ᵃLiterally *blood,* following Masoretic Text, Syriac, and Vulgate; Septuagint reads *like a flower on a pomegranate tree;* Targum reads *in your likeness.*

11 She had strong branches for scepters
    of rulers.
    She towered in stature above the thick
    branches,
    And was seen in her height amid the
    dense foliage.
12 But she was plucked up in fury,
    She was cast down to the ground,
    And the east wind dried her fruit.
    Her strong branches were broken and
    withered;
    The fire consumed them.
13 And now she *is* planted in the
    wilderness,
    In a dry and thirsty land.
14 Fire has come out from a rod of her
    branches
    And devoured her fruit,
    So that she has no strong branch— a
    scepter for ruling.' "

This *is* a lamentation, and has become a
lamentation.

The Rebellions of Israel

20 It came to pass in the seventh year,
in the fifth *month,* on the tenth *day*
of the month, *that* certain of the elders of
Israel came to inquire of the Lord, and sat
before me. ²Then the word of the Lord came
to me, saying, ³"Son of man, speak to the
elders of Israel, and say to them, 'Thus says
the Lord God: "Have you come to inquire
of Me? *As* I live," says the Lord God, "I will
not be inquired of by you." ' ⁴Will you judge
them, son of man, will you judge *them?*
Then make known to them the abominations of their fathers.

⁵"Say to them, 'Thus says the Lord God:
"On the day when I chose Israel and raised
My hand in an oath to the descendants of
the house of Jacob, and made Myself known
to them in the land of Egypt, I raised My
hand in an oath to them, saying, 'I *am* the
Lord your God.' ⁶On that day I raised My
hand in an oath to them, to bring them
out of the land of Egypt into a land that I
had searched out for them, 'flowing with
milk and honey,'ᵃ the glory of all lands.
⁷Then I said to them, 'Each of you, throw
away the abominations which are before
his eyes, and do not defile yourselves with

the idols of Egypt. I *am* the Lord your God.'
⁸But they rebelled against Me and would
not obey Me. They did not all cast away the
abominations which were before their eyes,
nor did they forsake the idols of Egypt. Then
I said, 'I will pour out My fury on them and
fulfill My anger against them in the midst
of the land of Egypt.' ⁹But I acted for My
name's sake, that it should not be profaned
before the Gentiles among whom they *were,*
in whose sight I had made Myself known
to them, to bring them out of the land of
Egypt.

¹⁰"Therefore I made them go out of the
land of Egypt and brought them into the
wilderness. ¹¹And I gave them My statutes
and showed them My judgments, 'which, *if*
a man does, he shall live by them.'ᵃ ¹²Moreover I also gave them My Sabbaths, to be a
sign between them and Me, that they might
know that I *am* the Lord who sanctifies
them. ¹³Yet the house of Israel rebelled
against Me in the wilderness; they did not
walk in My statutes; they despised My judgments, 'which, *if* a man does, he shall live
by them';ᵃ and they greatly defiled My Sabbaths. Then I said I would pour out My
fury on them in the wilderness, to consume
them. ¹⁴But I acted for My name's sake, that
it should not be profaned before the Gentiles, in whose sight I had brought them
out. ¹⁵So I also raised My hand in an oath
to them in the wilderness, that I would not
bring them into the land which I had given
them, 'flowing with milk and honey,'ᵃ the
glory of all lands, ¹⁶because they despised
My judgments and did not walk in My
statutes, but profaned My Sabbaths; for
their heart went after their idols. ¹⁷Nevertheless My eye spared them from destruction. I did not make an end of them in the
wilderness.

¹⁸"But I said to their children in the
wilderness, 'Do not walk in the statutes of
your fathers, nor observe their judgments,
nor defile yourselves with their idols. ¹⁹I *am*
the Lord your God: Walk in My statutes,
keep My judgments, and do them; ²⁰hal-
low My Sabbaths, and they will be a sign

20:6 ᵃExodus 3:8   **20:11** ᵃLeviticus 18:5
20:13 ᵃLeviticus 18:5   **20:15** ᵃExodus 3:8

between Me and you, that you may know that I *am* the Lord your God.'

²¹"Notwithstanding, the children rebelled against Me; they did not walk in My statutes, and were not careful to observe My judgments, 'which, *if* a man does, he shall live by them';ᵃ but they profaned My Sabbaths. Then I said I would pour out My fury on them and fulfill My anger against them in the wilderness. ²²Nevertheless I withdrew My hand and acted for My name's sake, that it should not be profaned in the sight of the Gentiles, in whose sight I had brought them out. ²³Also I raised My hand in an oath to those in the wilderness, that I would scatter them among the Gentiles and disperse them throughout the countries, ²⁴because they had not executed My judgments, but had despised My statutes, profaned My Sabbaths, and their eyes were fixed on their fathers' idols.

²⁵"Therefore I also gave them up to statutes *that were* not good, and judgments by which they could not live; ²⁶and I pronounced them unclean because of their ritual gifts, in that they caused all their firstborn to pass through *the fire,* that I might make them desolate and that they might know that I am the Lord."'

²⁷"Therefore, son of man, speak to the house of Israel, and say to them, 'Thus says the Lord God: "In this too your fathers have blasphemed Me, by being unfaithful to Me. ²⁸When I brought them into the land *concerning* which I had raised My hand in an oath to give them, and they saw all the high hills and all the thick trees, there they offered their sacrifices and provoked Me with their offerings. There they also sent up their sweet aroma and poured out their drink offerings. ²⁹Then I said to them, 'What *is* this high place to which you go?' So its name is called Bamahᵃ to this day."'

³⁰Therefore say to the house of Israel, 'Thus says the Lord God: "Are you defiling yourselves in the manner of your fathers, and committing harlotry according to their abominations? ³¹For when you offer your gifts and make your sons pass through the fire, you defile yourselves with all your idols, even to this day. So shall I be inquired of by you, O house of Israel? *As* I live," says

the Lord God, "I will not be inquired of by you. ³²What you have in your mind shall never be, when you say, 'We will be like the Gentiles, like the families in other countries, serving wood and stone.'

God Will Restore Israel

³³"*As* I live," says the Lord God, "surely with a mighty hand, with an outstretched arm, and with fury poured out, I will rule over you. ³⁴I will bring you out from the peoples and gather you out of the countries where you are scattered, with a mighty hand, with an outstretched arm, and with fury poured out. ³⁵And I will bring you into the wilderness of the peoples, and there I will plead My case with you face to face. ³⁶Just as I pleaded My case with your fathers in the wilderness of the land of Egypt, so I will plead My case with you," says the Lord God.

³⁷"I will make you pass under the rod, and I will bring you into the bond of the covenant; ³⁸I will purge the rebels from among you, and those who transgress against Me; I will bring them out of the country where they dwell, but they shall not enter the land of Israel. Then you will know that I *am* the Lord.

³⁹"As for you, O house of Israel," thus says the Lord God: "Go, serve every one of you his idols—and hereafter—if you will not obey Me; but profane My holy name no more with your gifts and your idols. ⁴⁰For on My holy mountain, on the mountain height of Israel," says the Lord God, "there all the house of Israel, all of them in the land, shall serve Me; there I will accept them, and there I will require your offerings and the firstfruits of your sacrifices, together with all your holy things. ⁴¹I will accept you as a sweet aroma when I bring you out from the peoples and gather you out of the countries where you have been scattered; and I will be hallowed in you before the Gentiles. ⁴²Then you shall know that I *am* the Lord, when I bring you into the land of Israel, into the country *for* which I raised My hand in an oath to give to your fathers. ⁴³And there you shall remember your ways and

---

20:21 ᵃLeviticus 18:5   **20:29** ᵃLiterally *High Place*

all your doings with which you were defiled; and you shall loathe yourselves in your own sight because of all the evils that you have committed. ⁴⁴Then you shall know that I *am* the LORD, when I have dealt with you for My name's sake, not according to your wicked ways nor according to your corrupt doings, O house of Israel," says the Lord GOD.'"

Fire in the Forest

⁴⁵Furthermore the word of the LORD came to me, saying, ⁴⁶"Son of man, set your face toward the south; preach against the south and prophesy against the forest land, the South,^a ⁴⁷and say to the forest of the South, 'Hear the word of the LORD! Thus says the Lord GOD: "Behold, I will kindle a fire in you, and it shall devour every green tree and every dry tree in you; the blazing flame shall not be quenched, and all faces from the south to the north shall be scorched by it. ⁴⁸All flesh shall see that I, the LORD, have kindled it; it shall not be quenched."'" ⁴⁹Then I said, "Ah, Lord GOD! They say of me, 'Does he not speak parables?'"

Babylon, the Sword of God

21 And the word of the LORD came to me, saying, ²"Son of man, set your face toward Jerusalem, preach against the holy places, and prophesy against the land of Israel; ³and say to the land of Israel, 'Thus says the LORD: "Behold, I *am* against you, and I will draw My sword out of its sheath and cut off both righteous and wicked from you. ⁴Because I will cut off both righteous and wicked from you, therefore My sword shall go out of its sheath against all flesh from south *to* north, ⁵that all flesh may know that I, the LORD, have drawn My sword out of its sheath; it shall not return anymore."' ⁶Sigh therefore, son of man, with a breaking heart, and sigh with bitterness before their eyes. ⁷And it shall be when they say to you, 'Why are you sighing?' that you shall answer, 'Because of the news; when it comes, every heart will melt, all hands will be feeble, every spirit will faint, and all knees will be weak *as* water. Behold, it is coming and shall be brought to pass,' says the Lord GOD."

⁸Again the word of the LORD came to me, saying, ⁹"Son of man, prophesy and say, 'Thus says the LORD!' Say:

'A sword, a sword is sharpened
And also polished!
¹⁰ Sharpened to make a dreadful slaughter,
Polished to flash like lightning!
Should we then make mirth?
It despises the scepter of My son,
As it does all wood.
¹¹ And He has given it to be polished,
That it may be handled;
This sword is sharpened, and it is polished
To be given into the hand of the slayer.'

¹² "Cry and wail, son of man;
For it will be against My people,
Against all the princes of Israel.
Terrors including the sword will be against My people;
Therefore strike *your* thigh.

¹³ "Because *it is* a testing,
And what if *the sword* despises even the scepter?
The scepter shall be no *more*,"

says the Lord GOD.

¹⁴ "You therefore, son of man, prophesy,
And strike *your* hands together.
The third time let the sword do double *damage*.
It *is* the sword *that* slays,
The sword that slays the great *men*,
That enters their private chambers.
¹⁵ I have set the point of the sword against all their gates,
That the heart may melt and many may stumble.
Ah! *It is* made bright;
It is grasped for slaughter:

¹⁶ "Swords at the ready!
Thrust right!
Set your blade!
Thrust left—
Wherever your edge is ordered!

20:46 ^aHebrew *Negev*

17 "I also will beat My fists together,
And I will cause My fury to rest;
I, the Lord, have spoken."

18The word of the Lord came to me again, saying: 19"And son of man, appoint for yourself two ways for the sword of the king of Babylon to go; both of them shall go from the same land. Make a sign; put *it* at the head of the road to the city. 20Appoint a road for the sword to go to Rabbah of the Ammonites, and to Judah, into fortified Jerusalem. 21For the king of Babylon stands at the parting of the road, at the fork of the two roads, to use divination: he shakes the arrows, he consults the images, he looks at the liver. 22In his right hand is the divination for Jerusalem: to set up battering rams, to call for a slaughter, to lift the voice with shouting, to set battering rams against the gates, to heap up a *siege* mound, and to build a wall. 23And it will be to them like a false divination in the eyes of those who have sworn oaths with them; but he will bring their iniquity to remembrance, that they may be taken.

24"Therefore thus says the Lord God: 'Because you have made your iniquity to be remembered, in that your transgressions are uncovered, so that in all your doings your sins appear—because you have come to remembrance, you shall be taken in hand. 25'Now to you, O profane, wicked prince of Israel, whose day has come, whose iniquity *shall* end, 26thus says the Lord God:

"Remove the turban, and take off
the crown;
Nothing *shall remain* the same.
Exalt the humble, and humble the
exalted.
27 Overthrown, overthrown,
I will make it overthrown!
It shall be no *longer,*
Until He comes whose right it is,
And I will give it *to Him.*"'

A Sword Against the Ammonites

28"And you, son of man, prophesy and say, 'Thus says the Lord God concerning the Ammonites and concerning their reproach,' and say:

'A sword, a sword *is* drawn,
Polished for slaughter,
For consuming, for flashing—
29 While they see false visions for you,
While they divine a lie to you,
To bring you on the necks of the
wicked, the slain
Whose day has come,
Whose iniquity *shall* end.

30 'Return *it* to its sheath.
I will judge you
In the place where you were created,
In the land of your nativity.
31 I will pour out My indignation on you;
I will blow against you with the fire of
My wrath,
And deliver you into the hands of
brutal men *who are* skillful to destroy.
32 You shall be fuel for the fire;
Your blood shall be in the midst of
the land.
You shall not be remembered,
For I the Lord have spoken.'"

Sins of Jerusalem

22 Moreover the word of the Lord came to me, saying, 2"Now, son of man, will you judge, will you judge the bloody city? Yes, show her all her abominations! 3Then say, 'Thus says the Lord God: "The city sheds blood in her own midst, that her time may come; and she makes idols within herself to defile herself. 4You have become guilty by the blood which you have shed, and have defiled yourself with the idols which you have made. You have caused your days to draw near, and have come to *the end of* your years; therefore I have made you a reproach to the nations, and a mockery to all countries. 5*Those* near and *those* far from you will mock you as infamous *and* full of tumult.

6"Look, the princes of Israel: each one has used his power to shed blood in you. 7In you they have made light of father and mother; in your midst they have oppressed the stranger; in you they have mistreated the fatherless and the widow. 8You have despised My holy things and profaned My Sabbaths. 9In you are men who slander to cause bloodshed; in you are those who eat on the

IN GOD WE TRUST
Annuit Coeptis
THIS NATION UNDER GOD

MONUMENTS TO AMERICAN PATRIOTISM

IT IS AMAZING THAT, at a time when such a concerted effort is underway to erase the role of God and faith in America's public life, our nation's capital, Washington, D.C., is filled with Christian religious symbols that adorn its buildings and monuments as an abiding evidence of God's role in America's heritage. From the halls of Congress, to the monuments, to nearly every landmark building, biblical and religious quotations and images are inscribed and preserved as an official testimony to the true place God has in our nation's birthright and history.

THE WASHINGTON MONUMENT

Engraved on the aluminum capstone is the Latin phrase *Laus Deo*, which means "Praise be to God." Lining the walls of the stairwell are carved tribute blocks that declare such biblical phrases as "Holiness to the Lord"; "Search the Scriptures"; "The memory of the just is blessed"; and "Train up a child in the way he should go, and when he is old, he will not depart from it."

NO PEOPLE CAN BE BOUND TO ACKNOWLEDGE AND ADORE THE INVISIBLE HAND WHICH CONDUCTS THE AFFAIRS OF MEN MORE THEN THOSE OF THE UNITED STATES.

GEORGE WASHINGTON

THE U.S. CAPITOL

In the House chamber is the inscription, "In God We Trust." Also in the House chamber, above the Gallery door, stands a marble relief of Moses, surrounded by twenty-two other lawgivers. At the east entrance to the Senate chamber are the words *Annuit Coeptis*, which is Latin for "he has favored our undertakings." The words "In God We Trust" are also written over the southern entrance.

In the Rotunda is the painting of "The Baptism of Pocahontas," and also "The Embarkation of the Pilgrims" that shows the Pilgrims praying on shipboard led by William Brewster. Clearly seen in an open Bible are the words, "the New Testament according to our Lord and Savior, Jesus Christ." The words "God With Us" are inscribed on the sail of the ship.

In the Capitol's chapel is a stained glass window depicting George Washington in prayer under the inscription "This Nation Under God." Also, the prayer from Psalm 16:1 is etched in the window, which states, "Preserve me, God, for in Thee do I put my trust."

THE SUPREME COURT

The Supreme Court building has a number of places where there are images of Moses with the Ten Commandments. Moses is included among the great lawgivers in Herman MacNeil's marble sculpture group on the east front. As you enter the Supreme Court courtroom, the two huge doors have the Ten Commandments engraved on each lower portion of each door and a display of the Ten Commandments is also engraved over the chair of the Chief Justice.

THE JEFFERSON MEMORIAL

When you enter the Jefferson Memorial, you will find many references to God. A quote that runs around the interior dome says, "I have sworn upon the altar of God, eternal hostility against every form of tyranny over the minds of man." One of the panels reads: "God who gave us life gave us liberty. Can the liberties of a nation be secure when we have removed a conviction that these liberties are the gift of God? Indeed I tremble for my country when I reflect that God is just, that His justice cannot sleep forever."

THE LINCOLN MEMORIAL

Millions have entered the Lincoln Memorial and gazed up at the magnificent statue of Abraham Lincoln. His famous speeches are inscribed into the walls. On the left side is the Gettysburg Address. He said, "We here highly resolved that these dead shall not have died in vain, that this nation, under God, shall have a new birth of freedom." On the right side is Lincoln's Second Inaugural Address, which mentions God fourteen times and quotes the Bible twice. He concludes with a lament over the destruction caused by the Civil War, and appeals to charity in healing the wounds of the war. "With malice toward none, with charity for all, with firmness in the right as God gives us to see the right, let us strive on to finish the work we are in, to bind up the nation's wounds, to care for him who shall have borne the battle and for his widow and his orphan, to do all which may achieve and cherish a just and lasting peace among ourselves and with all nations."

mountains; in your midst they commit lewdness. [10]In you men uncover their fathers' nakedness; in you they violate women who are set apart during their impurity. [11]One commits abomination with his neighbor's wife; another lewdly defiles his daughter-in-law; and another in you violates his sister, his father's daughter. [12]In you they take bribes to shed blood; you take usury and increase; you have made profit from your neighbors by extortion, and have forgotten Me," says the Lord GOD.

[13]"Behold, therefore, I beat My fists at the dishonest profit which you have made, and at the bloodshed which has been in your midst. [14]Can your heart endure, or can your hands remain strong, in the days when I shall deal with you? I, the LORD, have spoken, and will do *it*. [15]I will scatter you among the nations, disperse you throughout the countries, and remove your filthiness completely from you. [16]You shall defile yourself in the sight of the nations; then you shall know that I *am* the LORD." ' "

Israel in the Furnace

[17]The word of the LORD came to me, saying, [18]"Son of man, the house of Israel has become dross to Me; they *are* all bronze, tin, iron, and lead, in the midst of a furnace; they have become dross from silver. [19]Therefore thus says the Lord GOD: 'Because you have all become dross, therefore behold, I will gather you into the midst of Jerusalem. [20]*As men* gather silver, bronze, iron, lead, and tin into the midst of a furnace, to blow fire on it, to melt *it;* so I will gather *you* in My anger and in My fury, and I will leave *you there* and melt you. [21]Yes, I will gather you and blow on you with the fire of My wrath, and you shall be melted in its midst. [22]As silver is melted in the midst of a furnace, so shall you be melted in its midst; then you shall know that I, the LORD, have poured out My fury on you.' "

Israel's Wicked Leaders

[23]And the word of the LORD came to me, saying, [24]"Son of man, say to her: 'You *are* a land that is not cleansed[a] or rained on in the day of indignation.' [25]The conspiracy of her prophets[a] in her midst is like a roaring lion tearing the prey; they have devoured people; they have taken treasure and precious things; they have made many widows in her midst. [26]Her priests have violated My law and profaned My holy things; they have not distinguished between the holy and unholy, nor have they made known *the difference* between the unclean and the clean; and they have hidden their eyes from My Sabbaths, so that I am profaned among them. [27]Her princes in her midst *are* like wolves tearing the prey, to shed blood, to destroy people, and to get dishonest gain. [28]Her prophets plastered them with untempered *mortar,* seeing false visions, and divining lies for them, saying, 'Thus says the Lord GOD,' when the LORD had not spoken. [29]The people of the land have used oppressions, committed robbery, and mistreated the poor and needy; and they wrongfully oppress the stranger. [30]So I sought for a man among them who would make a wall, and stand in the gap before Me on behalf of the land, that I should not destroy it; but I found no one. [31]Therefore I have poured out My indignation on them; I have consumed them with the fire of My wrath; and I have recompensed their deeds on their own heads," says the Lord GOD.

Two Harlot Sisters

23 The word of the LORD came again to me, saying:

2   "Son of man, there were two women,
     The daughters of one mother.
3   They committed harlotry in Egypt,
     They committed harlotry in their youth;
     Their breasts were there embraced,
     Their virgin bosom was there pressed.
4   Their names: Oholah[a] the elder and
        Oholibah[b] her sister;
     They were Mine,
     And they bore sons and daughters.
     As for their names,
     Samaria *is* Oholah, and Jerusalem *is*
        Oholibah.

22:24 [a]Following Masoretic Text, Syriac, and Vulgate; Septuagint reads *showered upon.*   **22:25** [a]Following Masoretic Text and Vulgate; Septuagint reads *princes;* Targum reads *scribes.*   **23:4** [a]Literally *Her Own Tabernacle* [b]Literally *My Tabernacle Is in Her*

PATRICK HENRY

Patrick Henry (1736–1799) was one of the most passionate and fiery advocates of the American Revolution and republicanism. Many have compared him to an Old Testament prophet in his powerful denunciations of corruption in government officials and his defense of the colonists' rights. Elected to the Virginia legislature in 1775, it was his influence that rallied the state of Virginia, the largest of the thirteen colonies, into military preparedness.

Rebellion against unjust taxes had begun in the colonies, and the British had posted troops throughout the colonies and warships in America's harbors. During the Second Virginia Convention's debates on whether to declare independence or negotiate with the British, Patrick Henry rose up on March 23, 1775, and declared, "Should I keep back my opinions at such a time, . . . I should consider myself as guilty of treason toward my country, and of an act of disloyalty toward the Majesty of Heaven, which I revere above all earthly kings." Then he called upon his countrymen to trust God and use all the means that He had placed in their power: "Three million of people, armed in the holy cause of liberty, and in such a country as that we possess, are invincible by any force which our enemy can send us. Besides, sirs, we shall not fight our battles alone. There is a just God who presides over the destinies of nations, and who will raise up friends to fight our battles for us. The battle, sir, is not to the strong alone; it is to the vigilant, the active, the brave."

Patrick concluded his argument with a passionate call, "Gentlemen may cry, Peace, Peace—but there is no peace. The war is actually begun! . . . Our brethren are already in the field! Why stand we here idle? . . . Is life so dear, or peace so sweet, as to be purchased at the price of chains and slavery? Forbid it, Almighty God! I know not what course others may take; but as for me, give me liberty or give me death!"

During the war, he served as the first post-colonial governor of Virginia. After the Revolution, Henry was an outspoken critic of the United States Constitution and urged against its adoption, arguing it gave the federal government too much power. He was instrumental in forcing the adoption of the Bill of Rights to amend the new Constitution. He served five terms as governor of Virginia.

The Older Sister, Samaria

5 "Oholah played the harlot even
      though she was Mine;
   And she lusted for her lovers, the
      neighboring Assyrians,
6 *Who were* clothed in purple,
   Captains and rulers,
   All of them desirable young men,
   Horsemen riding on horses.
7 Thus she committed her harlotry
      with them,
   All of them choice men of Assyria;
   And with all for whom she lusted,
   With all their idols, she defiled herself.
8 She has never given up her harlotry
      brought from Egypt,
   For in her youth they had lain with her,
   Pressed her virgin bosom,
   And poured out their immorality upon
      her.

9 "Therefore I have delivered her
   Into the hand of her lovers,
   Into the hand of the Assyrians,
   For whom she lusted.
10 They uncovered her nakedness,
    Took away her sons and daughters,
    And slew her with the sword;
    She became a byword among women,
    For they had executed judgment on
       her.

The Younger Sister, Jerusalem

11 "Now although her sister Oholibah saw
this, she became more corrupt in her lust
than she, and in her harlotry more corrupt
than her sister's harlotry.

12 "She lusted for the neighboring
       Assyrians,
    Captains and rulers,
    Clothed most gorgeously,
    Horsemen riding on horses,
    All of them desirable young men.
13 Then I saw that she was defiled;
    Both *took* the same way.
14 But she increased her harlotry;
    She looked at men portrayed on
       the wall,
    Images of Chaldeans portrayed
       in vermilion,

15 Girded with belts around their waists,
    Flowing turbans on their heads,
    All of them looking like captains,
    In the manner of the Babylonians
       of Chaldea,
    The land of their nativity.
16 As soon as her eyes saw them,
    She lusted for them
    And sent messengers to them in
       Chaldea.

17 "Then the Babylonians came to her,
       into the bed of love,
    And they defiled her with their
       immorality;
    So she was defiled by them, and
       alienated herself from them.
18 She revealed her harlotry and
       uncovered her nakedness.
    Then I alienated Myself from her,
    As I had alienated Myself from her
       sister.

19 "Yet she multiplied her harlotry
    In calling to remembrance the days
       of her youth,
    When she had played the harlot in
       the land of Egypt.
20 For she lusted for her paramours,
    Whose flesh *is like* the flesh of donkeys,
    And whose issue *is like* the issue of
       horses.
21 Thus you called to remembrance the
       lewdness of your youth,
    When the Egyptians pressed your
       bosom
    Because of your youthful breasts.

Judgment on Jerusalem

22 "Therefore, Oholibah, thus says the Lord
GOD:

    'Behold, I will stir up your lovers
       against you,
    From whom you have alienated
       yourself,
    And I will bring them against you
       from every side:
23 The Babylonians,
    All the Chaldeans,
    Pekod, Shoa, Koa,
    All the Assyrians with them,

All of them desirable young men,
Governors and rulers,
Captains and men of renown,
All of them riding on horses.
24 And they shall come against you
With chariots, wagons, and war-horses,
With a horde of people.
They shall array against you
Buckler, shield, and helmet all around.

'I will delegate judgment to them,
And they shall judge you according to
    their judgments.
25 I will set My jealousy against you,
And they shall deal furiously with you;
They shall remove your nose and your
    ears,
And your remnant shall fall by the
    sword;
They shall take your sons and your
    daughters,
And your remnant shall be devoured
    by fire.
26 They shall also strip you of your clothes
And take away your beautiful jewelry.

27 'Thus I will make you cease your
    lewdness and your harlotry
Brought from the land of Egypt,
So that you will not lift your eyes to
    them,
Nor remember Egypt anymore.'

28 "For thus says the Lord GOD: 'Surely I will deliver you into the hand of those you hate, into the hand *of those* from whom you alienated yourself. 29They will deal hatefully with you, take away all you have worked for, and leave you naked and bare. The nakedness of your harlotry shall be uncovered, both your lewdness and your harlotry. 30I will do these *things* to you because you have gone as a harlot after the Gentiles, because you have become defiled by their idols. 31You have walked in the way of your sister; therefore I will put her cup in your hand.'

32"Thus says the Lord GOD:

'You shall drink of your sister's cup,
The deep and wide one;
You shall be laughed to scorn

And held in derision;
It contains much.
33 You will be filled with drunkenness
    and sorrow,
The cup of horror and desolation,
The cup of your sister Samaria.
34 You shall drink and drain it,
You shall break its shards,
And tear at your own breasts;
For I have spoken,'
Says the Lord GOD.

35"Therefore thus says the Lord GOD:

'Because you have forgotten Me and
    cast Me behind your back,
Therefore you shall bear the *penalty*
Of your lewdness and your harlotry.'"

Both Sisters Judged

36The LORD also said to me: "Son of man, will you judge Oholah and Oholibah? Then declare to them their abominations. 37For they have committed adultery, and blood *is* on their hands. They have committed adultery with their idols, and even *sacrificed* their sons whom they bore to Me, passing them through *the fire,* to devour *them.* 38Moreover they have done this to Me: They have defiled My sanctuary on the same day and profaned My Sabbaths. 39For after they had slain their children for their idols, on the same day they came into My sanctuary to profane it; and indeed thus they have done in the midst of My house.

40"Furthermore you sent for men to come from afar, to whom a messenger *was* sent; and there they came. And you washed yourself for them, painted your eyes, and adorned yourself with ornaments. 41You sat on a stately couch, with a table prepared before it, on which you had set My incense and My oil. 42The sound of a carefree multitude *was* with her, and Sabeans *were* brought from the wilderness with men of the common sort, who put bracelets on their wrists and beautiful crowns on their heads. 43Then I said concerning *her who had grown* old in adulteries, 'Will they commit harlotry with her now, and she *with them?'* 44Yet they went in to her, as men go in to a woman who plays the harlot; thus

they went in to Oholah and Oholibah, the lewd women. 45But righteous men will judge them after the manner of adulteresses, and after the manner of women who shed blood, because they *are* adulteresses, and blood *is* on their hands.

46"For thus says the Lord GOD: 'Bring up an assembly against them, give them up to trouble and plunder. 47The assembly shall stone them with stones and execute them with their swords; they shall slay their sons and their daughters, and burn their houses with fire. 48Thus I will cause lewdness to cease from the land, that all women may be taught not to practice your lewdness. 49They shall repay you for your lewdness, and you shall pay for your idolatrous sins. Then you shall know that I *am* the Lord GOD.'"

Symbol of the Cooking Pot

24 Again, in the ninth year, in the tenth month, on the tenth *day* of the month, the word of the LORD came to me, saying, 2"Son of man, write down the name of the day, this very day—the king of Babylon started his siege against Jerusalem this very day. 3And utter a parable to the rebellious house, and say to them, 'Thus says the Lord GOD:

"Put on a pot, set *it* on,
And also pour water into it.
4 Gather pieces *of meat* in it,
Every good piece,
The thigh and the shoulder.
Fill *it* with choice cuts;
5 Take the choice of the flock.
Also pile *fuel* bones under it,
Make it boil well,
And let the cuts simmer in it."

6'Therefore thus says the Lord GOD:

"Woe to the bloody city,
To the pot whose scum *is* in it,
And whose scum is not gone from it!
Bring it out piece by piece,
On which no lot has fallen.
7 For her blood is in her midst;
She set it on top of a rock;
She did not pour it on the ground,
To cover it with dust.

8 That it may raise up fury and take
vengeance,
I have set her blood on top of a rock,
That it may not be covered."

9'Therefore thus says the Lord GOD:

"Woe to the bloody city!
I too will make the pyre great.
10 Heap on the wood,
Kindle the fire;
Cook the meat well,
Mix in the spices,
And let the cuts be burned up.

11 "Then set the pot empty on the coals,
That it may become hot and its
bronze may burn,
That its filthiness may be melted in it,
That its scum may be consumed.
12 She has grown weary with lies,
And her great scum has not gone
from her.
Let her scum *be* in the fire!
13 In your filthiness *is* lewdness.
Because I have cleansed you, and you
were not cleansed,
You will not be cleansed of your
filthiness anymore,
Till I have caused My fury to rest
upon you.
14 I, the LORD, have spoken *it;*
It shall come to pass, and I will do *it;*
I will not hold back,
Nor will I spare,
Nor will I relent;
According to your ways
And according to your deeds
They[a] will judge you,"
Says the Lord GOD.'"

The Prophet's Wife Dies

15Also the word of the LORD came to me, saying, 16"Son of man, behold, I take away from you the desire of your eyes with one stroke; yet you shall neither mourn nor weep, nor shall your tears run down. 17Sigh in silence, make no mourning for the dead; bind your turban on your head, and put your sandals on your feet; do not cover

---

24:14 [a]Septuagint, Syriac, Targum, and Vulgate read *I.*

your lips, and do not eat man's bread *of sorrow.*"

[18]So I spoke to the people in the morning, and at evening my wife died; and the next morning I did as I was commanded.

[19]And the people said to me, "Will you not tell us what these *things signify* to us, that you behave so?"

[20]Then I answered them, "The word of the LORD came to me, saying, [21]'Speak to the house of Israel, "Thus says the Lord GOD: 'Behold, I will profane My sanctuary, your arrogant boast, the desire of your eyes, the delight of your soul; and your sons and daughters whom you left behind shall fall by the sword. [22]And you shall do as I have done; you shall not cover *your* lips nor eat man's bread *of sorrow.* [23]Your turbans shall be on your heads and your sandals on your feet; you shall neither mourn nor weep, but you shall pine away in your iniquities and mourn with one another. [24]Thus Ezekiel is a sign to you; according to all that he has done you shall do; and when this comes, you shall know that I *am* the Lord GOD.' "

[25]'And you, son of man—*will it* not *be* in the day when I take from them their stronghold, their joy and their glory, the desire of their eyes, and that on which they set their minds, their sons and their daughters: [26]*that* on that day one who escapes will come to you to let *you* hear *it* with *your* ears? [27]On that day your mouth will be opened to him who has escaped; you shall speak and no longer be mute. Thus you will be a sign to them, and they shall know that I *am* the LORD.' "

Proclamation Against Ammon

25 The word of the LORD came to me, saying, [2]"Son of man, set your face against the Ammonites, and prophesy against them. [3]Say to the Ammonites, 'Hear the word of the Lord GOD! Thus says the Lord GOD: "Because you said, 'Aha!' against My sanctuary when it was profaned, and against the land of Israel when it was desolate, and against the house of Judah when they went into captivity, [4]indeed, therefore, I will deliver you as a possession to the men of the East, and they shall set their encampments among you and make their dwellings among you; they shall eat your fruit, and they shall drink your milk. [5]And I will make Rabbah a stable for camels and Ammon a resting place for flocks. Then you shall know that I *am* the LORD."

[6]'For thus says the Lord GOD: "Because you clapped *your* hands, stamped your feet, and rejoiced in heart with all your disdain for the land of Israel, [7]indeed, therefore, I will stretch out My hand against you, and give you as plunder to the nations; I will cut you off from the peoples, and I will cause you to perish from the countries; I will destroy you, and you shall know that I *am* the LORD."

Proclamation Against Moab

[8]'Thus says the Lord GOD: "Because Moab and Seir say, 'Look! The house of Judah *is* like all the nations,' [9]therefore, behold, I will clear the territory of Moab of cities, of the cities on its frontier, the glory of the country, Beth Jeshimoth, Baal Meon, and Kirjathaim. [10]To the men of the East I will give it as a possession, together with the Ammonites, that the Ammonites may not be remembered among the nations. [11]And I will execute judgments upon Moab, and they shall know that I *am* the LORD."

Proclamation Against Edom

[12]'Thus says the Lord GOD: "Because of what Edom did against the house of Judah by taking vengeance, and has greatly offended by avenging itself on them," [13]therefore thus says the Lord GOD: "I will also stretch out My hand against Edom, cut off man and beast from it, and make it desolate from Teman; Dedan shall fall by the sword. [14]I will lay My vengeance on Edom by the hand of My people Israel, that they may do in Edom according to My anger and according to My fury; and they shall know My vengeance," says the Lord GOD.

Proclamation Against Philistia

[15]'Thus says the Lord GOD: "Because the Philistines dealt vengefully and took vengeance with a spiteful heart, to destroy because of the old hatred," [16]therefore thus says the Lord GOD: "I will stretch out My hand against the Philistines, and I will cut off the Cherethites and destroy the remnant

of the seacoast. [17]I will execute great vengeance on them with furious rebukes; and they shall know that I *am* the Lord, when I lay My vengeance upon them.” ’ ”

Proclamation Against Tyre

26 And it came to pass in the eleventh year, on the first *day* of the month, *that* the word of the Lord came to me, saying, [2]“Son of man, because Tyre has said against Jerusalem, ‘Aha! She is broken who *was* the gateway of the peoples; now she is turned over to me; I shall be filled; she is laid waste.’

[3]“Therefore thus says the Lord God: ‘Behold, I *am* against you, O Tyre, and will cause many nations to come up against you, as the sea causes its waves to come up. [4]And they shall destroy the walls of Tyre and break down her towers; I will also scrape her dust from her, and make her like the top of a rock. [5]It shall be *a place for* spreading nets in the midst of the sea, for I have spoken,’ says the Lord God; ‘it shall become plunder for the nations. [6]Also her daughter *villages* which *are* in the fields shall be slain by the sword. Then they shall know that I am the Lord.’

[7]“For thus says the Lord God: ‘Behold, I will bring against Tyre from the north Nebuchadnezzar[a] king of Babylon, king of kings, with horses, with chariots, and with horsemen, and an army with many people. [8]He will slay with the sword your daughter *villages* in the fields; he will heap up a siege mound against you, build a wall against you, and raise a defense against you. [9]He will direct his battering rams against your walls, and with his axes he will break down your towers. [10]Because of the abundance of his horses, their dust will cover you; your walls will shake at the noise of the horsemen, the wagons, and the chariots, when he enters your gates, as men enter a city that has been breached. [11]With the hooves of his horses he will trample all your streets; he will slay your people by the sword, and your strong pillars will fall to the ground. [12]They will plunder your riches and pillage your merchandise; they will break down your walls and destroy your pleasant houses; they will lay your stones, your timber, and your soil in the midst of the water. [13]I will put an end to the sound of your songs, and the sound of your harps shall be heard no more. [14]I will make you like the top of a rock; you shall be *a place for* spreading nets, and you shall never be rebuilt, for I the Lord have spoken,’ says the Lord God.

[15]“Thus says the Lord God to Tyre: ‘Will the coastlands not shake at the sound of your fall, when the wounded cry, when slaughter is made in the midst of you? [16]Then all the princes of the sea will come down from their thrones, lay aside their robes, and take off their embroidered garments; they will clothe themselves with trembling; they will sit on the ground, tremble *every* moment, and be astonished at you. [17]And they will take up a lamentation for you, and say to you:

“How you have perished,
  O one inhabited by seafaring men,
  O renowned city,
Who was strong at sea,
  She and her inhabitants,
Who caused their terror *to be* on all
  her inhabitants!
[18] Now the coastlands tremble on the
    day of your fall;
  Yes, the coastlands by the sea are
    troubled at your departure.” ’

[19]“For thus says the Lord God: ‘When I make you a desolate city, like cities that are not inhabited, when I bring the deep upon you, and great waters cover you, [20]then I will bring you down with those who descend into the Pit, to the people of old, and I will make you dwell in the lowest part of the earth, in places desolate from antiquity, with those who go down to the Pit, so that you may never be inhabited; and I shall establish glory in the land of the living. [21]I will make you a terror, and you *shall be* no *more;* though you are sought for, you will never be found again,’ says the Lord God.”

26:7 [a]Hebrew *Nebuchadrezzar,* and so elsewhere in this book

Lamentation for Tyre

27 The word of the LORD came again to me, saying, [2]"Now, son of man, take up a lamentation for Tyre, [3]and say to Tyre, 'You who are situated at the entrance of the sea, merchant of the peoples on many coastlands, thus says the Lord GOD:

"O Tyre, you have said,
'I *am* perfect in beauty.'
4   Your borders *are* in the midst of the seas.
     Your builders have perfected your
        beauty.
5   They made all *your* planks of fir trees
        from Senir;
     They took a cedar from Lebanon to
        make you a mast.
6   *Of* oaks from Bashan they made your
        oars;
     The company of Ashurites have inlaid
        your planks
     With ivory from the coasts of Cyprus.[a]
7   Fine embroidered linen from Egypt
        was what you spread for your sail;
     Blue and purple from the coasts of
        Elishah was what covered you.

8   "Inhabitants of Sidon and Arvad were
        your oarsmen;
     Your wise men, O Tyre, were in you;
     They became your pilots.
9   Elders of Gebal and its wise men
     Were in you to caulk your seams;
     All the ships of the sea
     And their oarsmen were in you
     To market your merchandise.

10   "Those from Persia, Lydia,[a] and Libya[b]
     Were in your army as men of war;
     They hung shield and helmet in you;
     They gave splendor to you.
11   Men of Arvad with your army *were* on
        your walls *all* around,
     And the men of Gammad were in
        your towers;
     They hung their shields on your walls
        all around;
     They made your beauty perfect.

[12]"Tarshish *was* your merchant because of your many luxury goods. They gave you silver, iron, tin, and lead for your goods.

[13]Javan, Tubal, and Meshech *were* your traders. They bartered human lives and vessels of bronze for your merchandise. [14]Those from the house of Togarmah traded for your wares with horses, steeds, and mules. [15]The men of Dedan *were* your traders; many isles *were* the market of your hand. They brought you ivory tusks and ebony as payment. [16]Syria *was* your merchant because of the abundance of goods you made. They gave you for your wares emeralds, purple, embroidery, fine linen, corals, and rubies. [17]Judah and the land of Israel *were* your traders. They traded for your merchandise wheat of Minnith, millet, honey, oil, and balm. [18]Damascus *was* your merchant because of the abundance of goods you made, because of your many luxury items, with the wine of Helbon and with white wool. [19]Dan and Javan paid for your wares, traversing back and forth. Wrought iron, cassia, and cane were among your merchandise. [20]Dedan *was* your merchant in saddlecloths for riding. [21]Arabia and all the princes of Kedar *were* your regular merchants. They traded with you in lambs, rams, and goats. [22]The merchants of Sheba and Raamah *were* your merchants. They traded for your wares the choicest spices, all kinds of precious stones, and gold. [23]Haran, Canneh, Eden, the merchants of Sheba, Assyria, *and* Chilmad *were* your merchants. [24]These *were* your merchants in choice items—in purple clothes, in embroidered garments, in chests of multicolored apparel, in sturdy woven cords, which were in your marketplace.

25   "The ships of Tarshish were carriers
        of your merchandise.
     You were filled and very glorious in
        the midst of the seas.
26   Your oarsmen brought you into many
        waters,
     But the east wind broke you in the
        midst of the seas.

27   "Your riches, wares, and merchandise,
     Your mariners and pilots,
     Your caulkers and merchandisers,

27:6 [a]Hebrew *Kittim*, western lands, especially Cyprus
27:10 [a]Hebrew *Lud* [b]Hebrew *Put*

All your men of war who *are* in you,
And the entire company which *is* in
your midst,
Will fall into the midst of the seas on
the day of your ruin.
28 The common-land will shake at the
sound of the cry of your pilots.

29 "All who handle the oar,
The mariners,
All the pilots of the sea
Will come down from their ships *and*
stand on the shore.
30 They will make their voice heard
because of you;
They will cry bitterly and cast dust on
their heads;
They will roll about in ashes;
31 They will shave themselves completely
bald because of you,
Gird themselves with sackcloth,
And weep for you
With bitterness of heart *and* bitter
wailing.
32 In their wailing for you
They will take up a lamentation,
And lament for you:
'What *city is* like Tyre,
Destroyed in the midst of the sea?

33 'When your wares went out by sea,
You satisfied many people;
You enriched the kings of the earth
With your many luxury goods and
your merchandise.
34 But you are broken by the seas in the
depths of the waters;
Your merchandise and the entire
company will fall in your midst.
35 All the inhabitants of the isles will be
astonished at you;
Their kings will be greatly afraid,
And *their* countenance will be troubled.
36 The merchants among the peoples
will hiss at you;
You will become a horror, and *be* no
more forever.' " ' "

Proclamation Against the King of Tyre

28 The word of the Lord came to me
again, saying, 2"Son of man, say to
the prince of Tyre, 'Thus says the Lord God:

"Because your heart *is* lifted up,
And you say, 'I *am* a god,
I sit *in* the seat of gods,
In the midst of the seas,'
Yet you *are* a man, and not a god,
Though you set your heart as the
heart of a god
3 (Behold, you *are* wiser than Daniel!
There is no secret that can be hidden
from you!
4 With your wisdom and your
understanding
You have gained riches for yourself,
And gathered gold and silver into
your treasuries;
5 By your great wisdom in trade you
have increased your riches,
And your heart is lifted up because of
your riches),"

6'Therefore thus says the Lord God:

"Because you have set your heart as
the heart of a god,
7 Behold, therefore, I will bring
strangers against you,
The most terrible of the nations;
And they shall draw their swords
against the beauty of your wisdom,
And defile your splendor.
8 They shall throw you down into the
Pit,
And you shall die the death of the
slain
In the midst of the seas.

9 "Will you still say before him who slays
you,
'I *am* a god'?
But you *shall be* a man, and not a god,
In the hand of him who slays you.
10 You shall die the death of the
uncircumcised
By the hand of aliens;
For I have spoken," says the Lord
God.' "

Lamentation for the King of Tyre

11Moreover the word of the Lord came to
me, saying, 12"Son of man, take up a
lamentation for the king of Tyre, and say
to him, 'Thus says the Lord God:

"You *were* the seal of perfection,
Full of wisdom and perfect in beauty.
13 You were in Eden, the garden of God;
Every precious stone *was* your covering:
The sardius, topaz, and diamond,
Beryl, onyx, and jasper,
Sapphire, turquoise, and emerald with
    gold.
The workmanship of your timbrels
    and pipes
Was prepared for you on the day you
    were created.

14 "You *were* the anointed cherub who
    covers;
I established you;
You were on the holy mountain of God;
You walked back and forth in the
    midst of fiery stones.
15 You *were* perfect in your ways from the
    day you were created,
Till iniquity was found in you.

16 "By the abundance of your trading
You became filled with violence within,
And you sinned;
Therefore I cast you as a profane thing
Out of the mountain of God;
And I destroyed you, O covering cherub,
From the midst of the fiery stones.

17 "Your heart was lifted up because of
    your beauty;
You corrupted your wisdom for the
    sake of your splendor;
I cast you to the ground,
I laid you before kings,
That they might gaze at you.

18 "You defiled your sanctuaries
By the multitude of your iniquities,
By the iniquity of your trading;
Therefore I brought fire from your
    midst;
It devoured you,
And I turned you to ashes upon the
    earth
In the sight of all who saw you.
19 All who knew you among the peoples
    are astonished at you;
You have become a horror,
And *shall be* no more forever." ' "

Proclamation Against Sidon

20 Then the word of the LORD came to me, saying, 21 "Son of man, set your face toward Sidon, and prophesy against her, 22 and say, 'Thus says the Lord GOD:

"Behold, I *am* against you, O Sidon;
I will be glorified in your midst;
And they shall know that I *am* the
    LORD,
When I execute judgments in her and
    am hallowed in her.
23 For I will send pestilence upon her,
And blood in her streets;
The wounded shall be judged in her
    midst
By the sword against her on every side;
Then they shall know that I *am* the
    LORD.

24 "And there shall no longer be a pricking brier or a painful thorn for the house of Israel from among all *who are* around them, who despise them. Then they shall know that I *am* the Lord GOD."

Israel's Future Blessing

25 'Thus says the Lord GOD: "When I have gathered the house of Israel from the peoples among whom they are scattered, and am hallowed in them in the sight of the Gentiles, then they will dwell in their own land which I gave to My servant Jacob. 26 And they will dwell safely there, build houses, and plant vineyards; yes, they will dwell securely, when I execute judgments on all those around them who despise them. Then they shall know that I *am* the LORD their God." ' "

Proclamation Against Egypt

29 In the tenth year, in the tenth *month*, on the twelfth *day* of the month, the word of the LORD came to me, saying, 2 "Son of man, set your face against Pharaoh king of Egypt, and prophesy against him, and against all Egypt. 3 Speak, and say, 'Thus says the Lord GOD:

"Behold, I *am* against you,
O Pharaoh king of Egypt,

O great monster who lies in the midst
    of his rivers,
Who has said, 'My River[a] *is* my own;
I have made *it* for myself.'
4 But I will put hooks in your jaws,
    And cause the fish of your rivers to
      stick to your scales;
    I will bring you up out of the midst
      of your rivers,
    And all the fish in your rivers will
      stick to your scales.
5 I will leave you in the wilderness,
    You and all the fish of your rivers;
    You shall fall on the open field;
    You shall not be picked up or
      gathered.[a]
    I have given you as food
    To the beasts of the field
    And to the birds of the heavens.

6 "Then all the inhabitants of Egypt
    Shall know that I *am* the LORD,
    Because they have been a staff of reed
      to the house of Israel.
7 When they took hold of you with the
      hand,
    You broke and tore all their shoulders;[a]
    When they leaned on you,
    You broke and made all their backs
      quiver."

8'Therefore thus says the Lord GOD: "Surely I will bring a sword upon you and cut off from you man and beast. 9And the land of Egypt shall become desolate and waste; then they will know that I *am* the LORD, because he said, 'The River *is* mine, and I have made *it.*' 10Indeed, therefore, I *am* against you and against your rivers, and I will make the land of Egypt utterly waste and desolate, from Migdol[a] *to* Syene, as far as the border of Ethiopia. 11Neither foot of man shall pass through it nor foot of beast pass through it, and it shall be uninhabited forty years. 12I will make the land of Egypt desolate in the midst of the countries *that are* desolate; and among the cities *that are* laid waste, her cities shall be desolate forty years; and I will scatter the Egyptians among the nations and disperse them throughout the countries."

13'Yet, thus says the Lord GOD: "At the end of forty years I will gather the Egyptians from the peoples among whom they were scattered. 14I will bring back the captives of Egypt and cause them to return to the land of Pathros, to the land of their origin, and there they shall be a lowly kingdom. 15It shall be the lowliest of kingdoms; it shall never again exalt itself above the nations, for I will diminish them so that they will not rule over the nations anymore. 16No longer shall it be the confidence of the house of Israel, but will remind them of *their* iniquity when they turned to follow them. Then they shall know that I *am* the Lord GOD." ' "

Babylonia Will Plunder Egypt

17And it came to pass in the twenty-seventh year, in the first *month,* on the first *day* of the month, *that* the word of the LORD came to me, saying, 18"Son of man, Nebuchadnezzar king of Babylon caused his army to labor strenuously against Tyre; every head *was* made bald, and every shoulder rubbed raw; yet neither he nor his army received wages from Tyre, for the labor which they expended on it. 19Therefore thus says the Lord GOD: 'Surely I will give the land of Egypt to Nebuchadnezzar king of Babylon; he shall take away her wealth, carry off her spoil, and remove her pillage; and that will be the wages for his army. 20I have given him the land of Egypt *for* his labor, because they worked for Me,' says the Lord GOD. 21'In that day I will cause the horn of the house of Israel to spring forth, and I will open your mouth to speak in their midst. Then they shall know that I *am* the LORD.' "

Egypt and Her Allies Will Fall

30 The word of the LORD came to me again, saying, 2"Son of man, prophesy and say, 'Thus says the Lord GOD:

    "Wail, 'Woe to the day!'
3   For the day *is* near,
      Even the day of the LORD *is* near;
      It will be a day of clouds, the time
        of the Gentiles.

29:3 [a]That is, the Nile   **29:5** [a]Following Masoretic Text, Septuagint, and Vulgate; some Hebrew manuscripts and Targum read *buried.*
29:7 [a]Following Masoretic Text and Vulgate; Septuagint and Syriac read *hand.*   **29:10** [a]Or *tower*

4 The sword shall come upon Egypt,
 And great anguish shall be in Ethiopia,
 When the slain fall in Egypt,
 And they take away her wealth,
 And her foundations are broken down.

5 "Ethiopia, Libya,ᵃ Lydia,ᵇ all the mingled people, Chub, and the men of the lands who are allied, shall fall with them by the sword."
6 'Thus says the LORD:

 "Those who uphold Egypt shall fall,
 And the pride of her power shall
    come down.
 From Migdol *to* Syene
 Those within her shall fall by the
    sword,"
 Says the Lord GOD.

7 "They shall be desolate in the midst of
    the desolate countries,
 And her cities shall be in the midst of
    the cities *that are* laid waste.
8 Then they will know that I *am* the LORD,
 When I have set a fire in Egypt
 And all her helpers are destroyed.
9 On that day messengers shall go forth
    from Me in ships
 To make the careless Ethiopians afraid,
 And great anguish shall come upon
    them,
 As on the day of Egypt;
 For indeed it is coming!"

10 'Thus says the Lord GOD:

 "I will also make a multitude of Egypt
    to cease
 By the hand of Nebuchadnezzar king
    of Babylon.
11 He and his people with him, the most
    terrible of the nations,
 Shall be brought to destroy the land;
 They shall draw their swords against
    Egypt,
 And fill the land with the slain.
12 I will make the rivers dry,
 And sell the land into the hand of the
    wicked;
 I will make the land waste, and all
    that is in it,

 By the hand of aliens.
 I, the LORD, have spoken."

13 'Thus says the Lord GOD:

 "I will also destroy the idols,
 And cause the images to cease from
    Noph;ᵃ
 There shall no longer be princes from
    the land of Egypt;
 I will put fear in the land of Egypt.
14 I will make Pathros desolate,
 Set fire to Zoan,
 And execute judgments in No.ᵃ
15 I will pour My fury on Sin,ᵃ the
    strength of Egypt;
 I will cut off the multitude of No,
16 And set a fire in Egypt;
 Sin shall have great pain,
 No shall be split open,
 And Noph *shall be in* distress daily.
17 The young men of Avenᵃ and Pi
    Beseth shall fall by the sword,
 And these *cities* shall go into captivity.
18 At Tehaphnehesᵃ the day shall also
    be darkened,ᵇ
 When I break the yokes of Egypt there.
 And her arrogant strength shall cease
    in her;
 As for her, a cloud shall cover her,
 And her daughters shall go into
    captivity.
19 Thus I will execute judgments on Egypt,
 Then they shall know that I *am* the
    LORD." ' "

Proclamation Against Pharaoh

20 And it came to pass in the eleventh year, in the first *month,* on the seventh *day* of the month, *that* the word of the LORD came to me, saying, 21 "Son of man, I have broken the arm of Pharaoh king of Egypt; and see, it has not been bandaged for healing, nor a splint put on to bind it, to make it strong enough to hold a sword. 22 Therefore thus

---

30:5 ᵃHebrew *Put* ᵇHebrew *Lud*   **30:13** ᵃThat is, ancient Memphis   **30:14** ᵃThat is, ancient Thebes **30:15** ᵃThat is, ancient Pelusium   **30:17** ᵃThat is, ancient On (Heliopolis)   **30:18** ᵃSpelled *Tahpanhes* in Jeremiah 43:7 and elsewhere ᵇFollowing many Hebrew manuscripts, Bomberg, Septuagint, Syriac, Targum, and Vulgate; Masoretic Text reads *refrained.*

says the Lord GOD: 'Surely I *am* against Pharaoh king of Egypt, and will break his arms, both the strong one and the one that was broken; and I will make the sword fall out of his hand. ²³I will scatter the Egyptians among the nations, and disperse them throughout the countries. ²⁴I will strengthen the arms of the king of Babylon and put My sword in his hand; but I will break Pharaoh's arms, and he will groan before him with the groanings of a mortally wounded *man.* ²⁵Thus I will strengthen the arms of the king of Babylon, but the arms of Pharaoh shall fall down; they shall know that I *am* the LORD, when I put My sword into the hand of the king of Babylon and he stretches it out against the land of Egypt. ²⁶I will scatter the Egyptians among the nations and disperse them throughout the countries. Then they shall know that I *am* the LORD.' "

Egypt Cut Down Like a Great Tree

31 Now it came to pass in the eleventh year, in the third *month,* on the first *day* of the month, *that* the word of the LORD came to me, saying, ²"Son of man, say to Pharaoh king of Egypt and to his multitude:

'Whom are you like in your greatness?
3   Indeed Assyria *was* a cedar in
        Lebanon,
     With fine branches that shaded the
        forest,
     And of high stature;
     And its top was among the thick
        boughs.
4   The waters made it grow;
     Underground waters gave it height,
     With their rivers running around the
        place where it was planted,
     And sent out rivulets to all the trees
        of the field.

5   'Therefore its height was exalted above
        all the trees of the field;
     Its boughs were multiplied,
     And its branches became long because
        of the abundance of water,
     As it sent them out.
6   All the birds of the heavens made
        their nests in its boughs;

Under its branches all the beasts of
        the field brought forth their young;
     And in its shadow all great nations
        made their home.

7   'Thus it was beautiful in greatness and
        in the length of its branches,
     Because its roots reached to abundant
        waters.
8   The cedars in the garden of God could
        not hide it;
     The fir trees were not like its boughs,
     And the chestnutᵃ trees were not like
        its branches;
     No tree in the garden of God was like
        it in beauty.
9   I made it beautiful with a multitude
        of branches,
     So that all the trees of Eden envied it,
     That *were* in the garden of God.'

¹⁰"Therefore thus says the Lord GOD: 'Because you have increased in height, and it set its top among the thick boughs, and its heart was lifted up in its height, ¹¹therefore I will deliver it into the hand of the mighty one of the nations, and he shall surely deal with it; I have driven it out for its wickedness. ¹²And aliens, the most terrible of the nations, have cut it down and left it; its branches have fallen on the mountains and in all the valleys; its boughs lie broken by all the rivers of the land; and all the peoples of the earth have gone from under its shadow and left it.

13   'On its ruin will remain all the birds of
        the heavens,
     And all the beasts of the field will come
        to its branches—

¹⁴'So that no trees by the waters may ever again exalt themselves for their height, nor set their tops among the thick boughs, that no tree which drinks water may ever be high enough to reach up to them.

'For they have all been delivered to
        death,
     To the depths of the earth,

31:8 ᵃHebrew *armon*

Among the children of men who go down to the Pit.'

15"Thus says the Lord GOD: 'In the day when it went down to hell, I caused mourning. I covered the deep because of it. I restrained its rivers, and the great waters were held back. I caused Lebanon to mourn for it, and all the trees of the field wilted because of it. 16I made the nations shake at the sound of its fall, when I cast it down to hell together with those who descend into the Pit; and all the trees of Eden, the choice and best of Lebanon, all that drink water, were comforted in the depths of the earth. 17They also went down to hell with it, with those slain by the sword; and *those who were* its *strong* arm dwelt in its shadows among the nations.

18'To which of the trees in Eden will you then be likened in glory and greatness? Yet you shall be brought down with the trees of Eden to the depths of the earth; you shall lie in the midst of the uncircumcised, with *those* slain by the sword. This *is* Pharaoh and all his multitude,' says the Lord GOD."

Lamentation for Pharaoh and Egypt

32 And it came to pass in the twelfth year, in the twelfth *month,* on the first *day* of the month, *that* the word of the LORD came to me, saying, 2"Son of man, take up a lamentation for Pharaoh king of Egypt, and say to him:

'You are like a young lion among
    the nations,
And you *are* like a monster in the
    seas,
Bursting forth in your rivers,
Troubling the waters with your feet,
And fouling their rivers.

3'Thus says the Lord GOD:

"I will therefore spread My net over you
    with a company of many people,
And they will draw you up in My net.
4   Then I will leave you on the land;
I will cast you out on the open fields,
And cause to settle on you all the
    birds of the heavens.

And with you I will fill the beasts of
    the whole earth.
5   I will lay your flesh on the mountains,
And fill the valleys with your carcass.

6   "I will also water the land with the
    flow of your blood,
Even to the mountains;
And the riverbeds will be full of you.
7   When *I* put out your light,
I will cover the heavens, and make its
    stars dark;
I will cover the sun with a cloud,
And the moon shall not give her light.
8   All the bright lights of the heavens I
    will make dark over you,
And bring darkness upon your land,"
Says the Lord GOD.

9'I will also trouble the hearts of many peoples, when I bring your destruction among the nations, into the countries which you have not known. 10Yes, I will make many peoples astonished at you, and their kings shall be horribly afraid of you when I brandish My sword before them; and they shall tremble *every* moment, every man for his own life, in the day of your fall.

11'For thus says the Lord GOD: "The sword of the king of Babylon shall come upon you. 12By the swords of the mighty warriors, all of them the most terrible of the nations, I will cause your multitude to fall.

"They shall plunder the pomp of Egypt,
And all its multitude shall be destroyed.
13   Also I will destroy all its animals
From beside its great waters;
The foot of man shall muddy them
    no more,
Nor shall the hooves of animals
    muddy them.
14   Then I will make their waters clear,
And make their rivers run like oil,"
Says the Lord GOD.

15   "When I make the land of Egypt
    desolate,
And the country is destitute of all that
    once filled it,
When I strike all who dwell in it,
Then they shall know that I *am* the
    LORD.

16 "This *is* the lamentation
  With which they shall lament her;
  The daughters of the nations shall
    lament her;
  They shall lament for her, for Egypt,
  And for all her multitude,"
  Says the Lord GOD.' "

Egypt and Others Consigned to the Pit

17 It came to pass also in the twelfth year, on the fifteenth *day* of the month, *that* the word of the LORD came to me, saying:

18 "Son of man, wail over the multitude
    of Egypt,
  And cast them down to the depths of
    the earth,
  Her and the daughters of the famous
    nations,
  With those who go down to the Pit:
19 'Whom do you surpass in beauty?
  Go down, be placed with the
    uncircumcised.'

20 "They shall fall in the midst of *those*
    slain by the sword;
  She is delivered to the sword,
  Drawing her and all her multitudes.
21 The strong among the mighty
  Shall speak to him out of the midst
    of hell
  With those who help him:
  'They have gone down,
  They lie with the uncircumcised, slain
    by the sword.'

22 "Assyria *is* there, and all her company,
  With their graves all around her,
  All of them slain, fallen by the sword.
23 Her graves are set in the recesses of
    the Pit,
  And her company is all around her
    grave,
  All of them slain, fallen by the sword,
  Who caused terror in the land of the
    living.

24 "There *is* Elam and all her multitude,
  All around her grave,
  All of them slain, fallen by the sword,
  Who have gone down uncircumcised
    to the lower parts of the earth,
  Who caused their terror in the land of
    the living;
  Now they bear their shame with those
    who go down to the Pit.
25 They have set her bed in the midst of
    the slain,
  With all her multitude,
  With her graves all around it,
  All of them uncircumcised, slain by
    the sword;
  Though their terror was caused
  In the land of the living,
  Yet they bear their shame
  With those who go down to the Pit;
  It was put in the midst of the slain.

26 "There *are* Meshech and Tubal and all
    their multitudes,
  With all their graves around it,
  All of them uncircumcised, slain by
    the sword,
  Though they caused their terror in the
    land of the living.
27 They do not lie with the mighty
  Who are fallen of the uncircumcised,
  Who have gone down to hell with
    their weapons of war;
  They have laid their swords under
    their heads,
  But their iniquities will be on their
    bones,
  Because of the terror of the mighty in
    the land of the living.
28 Yes, you shall be broken in the midst
    of the uncircumcised,
  And lie with *those* slain by the sword.

29 "There *is* Edom,
  Her kings and all her princes,
  Who despite their might
  Are laid beside *those* slain by the sword;
  They shall lie with the uncircumcised,
  And with those who go down to the Pit.
30 There *are* the princes of the north,
  All of them, and all the Sidonians,
  Who have gone down with the slain
  In shame at the terror which they
    caused by their might;
  They lie uncircumcised with *those*
    slain by the sword,
  And bear their shame with those who
    go down to the Pit.

31 "Pharaoh will see them
And be comforted over all his
multitude,
Pharaoh and all his army,
Slain by the sword,"
Says the Lord GOD.

32 "For I have caused My terror in the
land of the living;
And he shall be placed in the midst
of the uncircumcised
With *those* slain by the sword,
Pharaoh and all his multitude,"
Says the Lord GOD.

The Watchman and His Message

33 Again the word of the LORD came to me, saying, 2"Son of man, speak to the children of your people, and say to them: 'When I bring the sword upon a land, and the people of the land take a man from their territory and make him their watchman, 3when he sees the sword coming upon the land, if he blows the trumpet and warns the people, 4then whoever hears the sound of the trumpet and does not take warning, if the sword comes and takes him away, his blood shall be on his *own* head. 5He heard the sound of the trumpet, but did not take warning; his blood shall be upon himself. But he who takes warning will save his life. 6But if the watchman sees the sword coming and does not blow the trumpet, and the people are not warned, and the sword comes and takes *any* person from among them, he is taken away in his iniquity; but his blood I will require at the watchman's hand.'

7"So you, son of man: I have made you a watchman for the house of Israel; therefore you shall hear a word from My mouth and warn them for Me. 8When I say to the wicked, 'O wicked *man,* you shall surely die!' and you do not speak to warn the wicked from his way, that wicked *man* shall die in his iniquity; but his blood I will require at your hand. 9Nevertheless if you warn the wicked to turn from his way, and he does not turn from his way, he shall die in his iniquity; but you have delivered your soul.

10"Therefore you, O son of man, say to the house of Israel: 'Thus you say, "If our transgressions and our sins *lie* upon us, and we pine away in them, how can we then live?"' 11Say to them: '*As* I live,' says the Lord GOD, 'I have no pleasure in the death of the wicked, but that the wicked turn from his way and live. Turn, turn from your evil ways! For why should you die, O house of Israel?'

The Fairness of God's Judgment

12"Therefore you, O son of man, say to the children of your people: 'The righteousness of the righteous man shall not deliver him in the day of his transgression; as for the wickedness of the wicked, he shall not fall because of it in the day that he turns from his wickedness; nor shall the righteous be able to live because of *his righteousness* in the day that he sins.' 13When I say to the righteous *that* he shall surely live, but he trusts in his own righteousness and commits iniquity, none of his righteous works shall be remembered; but because of the iniquity that he has committed, he shall die. 14Again, when I say to the wicked, 'You shall surely die,' if he turns from his sin and does what is lawful and right, 15if the wicked restores the pledge, gives back what he has stolen, and walks in the statutes of life without committing iniquity, he shall surely live; he shall not die. 16None of his sins which he has committed shall be remembered against him; he has done what is lawful and right; he shall surely live.

17"Yet the children of your people say, 'The way of the Lord is not fair.' But it is their way which is not fair! 18When the righteous turns from his righteousness and commits iniquity, he shall die because of it. 19But when the wicked turns from his wickedness and does what is lawful and right, he shall live because of it. 20Yet you say, 'The way of the Lord is not fair.' O house of Israel, I will judge every one of you according to his own ways."

The Fall of Jerusalem

21And it came to pass in the twelfth year of our captivity, in the tenth *month,* on the fifth *day* of the month, *that* one who had escaped from Jerusalem came to me and said, "The city has been captured!" 22Now the hand of the LORD had been upon me the evening before the man came

who had escaped. And He had opened my mouth; so when he came to me in the morning, my mouth was opened, and I was no longer mute.

The Cause of Judah's Ruin

²³Then the word of the LORD came to me, saying: ²⁴"Son of man, they who inhabit those ruins in the land of Israel are saying, 'Abraham was only one, and he inherited the land. But we *are* many; the land has been given to us as a possession.'

²⁵"Therefore say to them, 'Thus says the Lord GOD: "You eat *meat* with blood, you lift up your eyes toward your idols, and shed blood. Should you then possess the land? ²⁶You rely on your sword, you commit abominations, and you defile one another's wives. Should you then possess the land?"'

²⁷"Say thus to them, 'Thus says the Lord GOD: "*As* I live, surely those who *are* in the ruins shall fall by the sword, and the one who *is* in the open field I will give to the beasts to be devoured, and those who *are* in the strongholds and caves shall die of the pestilence. ²⁸For I will make the land most desolate, her arrogant strength shall cease, and the mountains of Israel shall be so desolate that no one will pass through. ²⁹Then they shall know that I *am* the LORD, when I have made the land most desolate because of all their abominations which they have committed."'

Hearing and Not Doing

³⁰"As for you, son of man, the children of your people are talking about you beside the walls and in the doors of the houses; and they speak to one another, everyone saying to his brother, 'Please come and hear what the word is that comes from the LORD.' ³¹So they come to you as people do, they sit before you *as* My people, and they hear your words, but they do not do them; for with their mouth they show much love, *but* their hearts pursue their *own* gain. ³²Indeed you *are* to them as a very lovely song of one who has a pleasant voice and can play well on an instrument; for they hear your words, but they do not do them. ³³And when this comes to pass—surely it will come—then they will know that a prophet has been among them."

Irresponsible Shepherds

34 And the word of the LORD came to me, saying, ²"Son of man, prophesy against the shepherds of Israel, prophesy and say to them, 'Thus says the Lord GOD to the shepherds: "Woe to the shepherds of Israel who feed themselves! Should not the shepherds feed the flocks? ³You eat the fat and clothe yourselves with the wool; you slaughter the fatlings, *but* you do not feed the flock. ⁴The weak you have not strengthened, nor have you healed those who were sick, nor bound up the broken, nor brought back what was driven away, nor sought what was lost; but with force and cruelty you have ruled them. ⁵So they were scattered because *there was* no shepherd; and they became food for all the beasts of the field when they were scattered. ⁶My sheep wandered through all the mountains, and on every high hill; yes, My flock was scattered over the whole face of the earth, and no one was seeking or searching *for them*."

⁷'Therefore, you shepherds, hear the word of the LORD: ⁸"*As* I live," says the Lord GOD, "surely because My flock became a prey, and My flock became food for every beast of the field, because *there was* no shepherd, nor did My shepherds search for My flock, but the shepherds fed themselves and did not feed My flock"— ⁹therefore, O shepherds, hear the word of the LORD! ¹⁰Thus says the Lord GOD: "Behold, I *am* against the shepherds, and I will require My flock at their hand; I will cause them to cease feeding the sheep, and the shepherds shall feed themselves no more; for I will deliver My flock from their mouths, that they may no longer be food for them."

God, the True Shepherd

¹¹'For thus says the Lord GOD: "Indeed I Myself will search for My sheep and seek them out. ¹²As a shepherd seeks out his flock on the day he is among his scattered sheep, so will I seek out My sheep and deliver them from all the places where they were scattered on a cloudy and dark day. ¹³And I will bring them out from the peoples and gather them from the countries, and will bring them to their own land; I will feed them on

the mountains of Israel, in the valleys and in all the inhabited places of the country. ¹⁴I will feed them in good pasture, and their fold shall be on the high mountains of Israel. There they shall lie down in a good fold and feed in rich pasture on the mountains of Israel. ¹⁵I will feed My flock, and I will make them lie down," says the Lord God. ¹⁶"I will seek what was lost and bring back what was driven away, bind up the broken and strengthen what was sick; but I will destroy the fat and the strong, and feed them in judgment."

¹⁷'And *as for* you, O My flock, thus says the Lord God: "Behold, I shall judge between sheep and sheep, between rams and goats. ¹⁸*Is it* too little for you to have eaten up the good pasture, that you must tread down with your feet the residue of your pasture—and to have drunk of the clear waters, that you must foul the residue with your feet? ¹⁹And *as for* My flock, they eat what you have trampled with your feet, and they drink what you have fouled with your feet."

²⁰'Therefore thus says the Lord God to them: "Behold, I Myself will judge between the fat and the lean sheep. ²¹Because you have pushed with side and shoulder, butted all the weak ones with your horns, and scattered them abroad, ²²therefore I will save My flock, and they shall no longer be a prey; and I will judge between sheep and sheep. ²³I will establish one shepherd over them, and he shall feed them—My servant David. He shall feed them and be their shepherd. ²⁴And I, the Lord, will be their God, and My servant David a prince among them; I, the Lord, have spoken.

²⁵"I will make a covenant of peace with them, and cause wild beasts to cease from the land; and they will dwell safely in the wilderness and sleep in the woods. ²⁶I will make them and the places all around My hill a blessing; and I will cause showers to come down in their season; there shall be showers of blessing. ²⁷Then the trees of the field shall yield their fruit, and the earth shall yield her increase. They shall be safe in their land; and they shall know that I *am* the Lord, when I have broken the bands of their yoke and delivered them from the hand of those who enslaved them. ²⁸And

they shall no longer be a prey for the nations, nor shall beasts of the land devour them; but they shall dwell safely, and no one shall make *them* afraid. ²⁹I will raise up for them a garden of renown, and they shall no longer be consumed with hunger in the land, nor bear the shame of the Gentiles anymore. ³⁰Thus they shall know that I, the Lord their God, *am* with them, and they, the house of Israel, *are* My people," says the Lord God.'

³¹"You are My flock, the flock of My pasture; you *are* men, *and* I *am* your God," says the Lord God.

Judgment on Mount Seir

35 Moreover the word of the Lord came to me, saying, ²"Son of man, set your face against Mount Seir and prophesy against it, ³and say to it, 'Thus says the Lord God:

"Behold, O Mount Seir, I *am* against you;
   I will stretch out My hand against you,
   And make you most desolate;
⁴ I shall lay your cities waste,
   And you shall be desolate.
   Then you shall know that I *am* the Lord.

⁵"Because you have had an ancient hatred, and have shed *the blood of* the children of Israel by the power of the sword at the time of their calamity, when their iniquity *came to an* end, ⁶therefore, *as* I live," says the Lord God, "I will prepare you for blood, and blood shall pursue you; since you have not hated blood, therefore blood shall pursue you. ⁷Thus I will make Mount Seir most desolate, and cut off from it the one who leaves and the one who returns. ⁸And I will fill its mountains with the slain; on your hills and in your valleys and in all your ravines those who are slain by the sword shall fall. ⁹I will make you perpetually desolate, and your cities shall be uninhabited; then you shall know that I *am* the Lord.

¹⁰"Because you have said, 'These two nations and these two countries shall be mine, and we will possess them,' although the Lord was there, ¹¹therefore, *as* I live," says the Lord God, "I will do according to

your anger and according to the envy which you showed in your hatred against them; and I will make Myself known among them when I judge you. ¹²Then you shall know that I *am* the LORD. I have heard all your blasphemies which you have spoken against the mountains of Israel, saying, 'They are desolate; they are given to us to consume.' ¹³Thus with your mouth you have boasted against Me and multiplied your words against Me; I have heard *them.*"

¹⁴'Thus says the Lord GOD: "The whole earth will rejoice when I make you desolate. ¹⁵As you rejoiced because the inheritance of the house of Israel was desolate, so I will do to you; you shall be desolate, O Mount Seir, as well as all of Edom—all of it! Then they shall know that I *am* the LORD."'

Blessing on Israel

36 "And you, son of man, prophesy to the mountains of Israel, and say, 'O mountains of Israel, hear the word of the LORD! ²Thus says the Lord GOD: "Because the enemy has said of you, 'Aha! The ancient heights have become our possession,'"' ³therefore prophesy, and say, 'Thus says the Lord GOD: "Because they made *you* desolate and swallowed you up on every side, so that you became the possession of the rest of the nations, and you are taken up by the lips of talkers and slandered by the people"— ⁴therefore, O mountains of Israel, hear the word of the Lord GOD! Thus says the Lord GOD to the mountains, the hills, the rivers, the valleys, the desolate wastes, and the cities that have been forsaken, which became plunder and mockery to the rest of the nations all around— ⁵therefore thus says the Lord GOD: "Surely I have spoken in My burning jealousy against the rest of the nations and against all Edom, who gave My land to themselves as a possession, with wholehearted joy *and* spiteful minds, in order to plunder its open country."'

⁶"Therefore prophesy concerning the land of Israel, and say to the mountains, the hills, the rivers, and the valleys, 'Thus says the Lord GOD: "Behold, I have spoken in My jealousy and My fury, because you have borne the shame of the nations." ⁷Therefore thus says the Lord GOD: "I have raised My hand in an oath that surely the nations that *are* around you shall bear their own shame. ⁸But you, O mountains of Israel, you shall shoot forth your branches and yield your fruit to My people Israel, for they are about to come. ⁹For indeed I *am* for you, and I will turn to you, and you shall be tilled and sown. ¹⁰I will multiply men upon you, all the house of Israel, all of it; and the cities shall be inhabited and the ruins rebuilt. ¹¹I will multiply upon you man and beast; and they shall increase and bear young; I will make you inhabited as in former times, and do better *for you* than at your beginnings. Then you shall know that I *am* the LORD. ¹²Yes, I will cause men to walk on you, My people Israel; they shall take possession of you, and you shall be their inheritance; no more shall you bereave them *of children.*"

¹³'Thus says the Lord GOD: "Because they say to you, 'You devour men and bereave your nation *of children,*' ¹⁴therefore you shall devour men no more, nor bereave your nation anymore," says the Lord GOD. ¹⁵"Nor will I let you hear the taunts of the nations anymore, nor bear the reproach of the peoples anymore, nor shall you cause your nation to stumble anymore," says the Lord GOD.'"

The Renewal of Israel

¹⁶Moreover the word of the LORD came to me, saying: ¹⁷"Son of man, when the house of Israel dwelt in their own land, they defiled it by their own ways and deeds; to Me their way was like the uncleanness of a woman in her customary impurity. ¹⁸Therefore I poured out My fury on them for the blood they had shed on the land, and for their idols *with which* they had defiled it. ¹⁹So I scattered them among the nations, and they were dispersed throughout the countries; I judged them according to their ways and their deeds. ²⁰When they came to the nations, wherever they went, they profaned My holy name—when they said of them, 'These *are* the people of the LORD, *and* yet they have gone out of His land.' ²¹But I had concern for My holy name, which the house of Israel had profaned among the nations wherever they went.

22"Therefore say to the house of Israel, 'Thus says the Lord God: "I do not do *this* for your sake, O house of Israel, but for My holy name's sake, which you have profaned among the nations wherever you went. 23And I will sanctify My great name, which has been profaned among the nations, which you have profaned in their midst; and the nations shall know that I *am* the Lord," says the Lord God, "when I am hallowed in you before their eyes. 24For I will take you from among the nations, gather you out of all countries, and bring you into your own land. 25Then I will sprinkle clean water on you, and you shall be clean; I will cleanse you from all your filthiness and from all your idols. 26I will give you a new heart and put a new spirit within you; I will take the heart of stone out of your flesh and give you a heart of flesh. 27I will put My Spirit within you and cause you to walk in My statutes, and you will keep My judgments and do *them.* 28Then you shall dwell in the land that I gave to your fathers; you shall be My people, and I will be your God. 29I will deliver you from all your uncleannesses. I will call for the grain and multiply it, and bring no famine upon you. 30And I will multiply the fruit of your trees and the increase of your fields, so that you need never again bear the reproach of famine among the nations. 31Then you will remember your evil ways and your deeds that *were* not good; and you will loathe yourselves in your own sight, for your iniquities and your abominations. 32Not for your sake do I do *this,*" says the Lord God, "let it be known to you. Be ashamed and confounded for your own ways, O house of Israel!"

33'Thus says the Lord God: "On the day that I cleanse you from all your iniquities, I will also enable *you* to dwell in the cities, and the ruins shall be rebuilt. 34The desolate land shall be tilled instead of lying desolate in the sight of all who pass by. 35So they will say, 'This land that was desolate has become like the garden of Eden; and the wasted, desolate, and ruined cities *are now* fortified *and* inhabited.' 36Then the nations which are left all around you shall know that I, the Lord, have rebuilt the ruined places *and* planted what was desolate. I, the Lord, have spoken *it,* and I will do *it.*"

37'Thus says the Lord God: "I will also let the house of Israel inquire of Me to do this for them: I will increase their men like a flock. 38Like a flock *offered as* holy *sacrifices,* like the flock at Jerusalem on its feast days, so shall the ruined cities be filled with flocks of men. Then they shall know that I *am* the Lord."'"

The Dry Bones Live

37 The hand of the Lord came upon me and brought me out in the Spirit of the Lord, and set me down in the midst of the valley; and it *was* full of bones. 2Then He caused me to pass by them all around, and behold, *there were* very many in the open valley; and indeed *they were* very dry. 3And He said to me, "Son of man, can these bones live?"

So I answered, "O Lord God, You know."

4Again He said to me, "Prophesy to these bones, and say to them, 'O dry bones, hear the word of the Lord! 5Thus says the Lord God to these bones: "Surely I will cause breath to enter into you, and you shall live. 6I will put sinews on you and bring flesh upon you, cover you with skin and put breath in you; and you shall live. Then you shall know that I *am* the Lord."'"

7So I prophesied as I was commanded; and as I prophesied, there was a noise, and suddenly a rattling; and the bones came together, bone to bone. 8Indeed, as I looked, the sinews and the flesh came upon them, and the skin covered them over; but *there was* no breath in them.

9Also He said to me, "Prophesy to the breath, prophesy, son of man, and say to the breath, 'Thus says the Lord God: "Come from the four winds, O breath, and breathe on these slain, that they may live."'" 10So I prophesied as He commanded me, and breath came into them, and they lived, and stood upon their feet, an exceedingly great army.

11Then He said to me, "Son of man, these bones are the whole house of Israel. They indeed say, 'Our bones are dry, our hope is lost, and we ourselves are cut off!' 12Therefore prophesy and say to them, 'Thus says

the Lord GOD: "Behold, O My people, I will open your graves and cause you to come up from your graves, and bring you into the land of Israel. ¹³Then you shall know that I *am* the LORD, when I have opened your graves, O My people, and brought you up from your graves. ¹⁴I will put My Spirit in you, and you shall live, and I will place you in your own land. Then you shall know that I, the LORD, have spoken *it* and performed *it,*" says the LORD.'"

One Kingdom, One King

¹⁵Again the word of the LORD came to me, saying, ¹⁶"As for you, son of man, take a stick for yourself and write on it: 'For Judah and for the children of Israel, his companions.' Then take another stick and write on it, 'For Joseph, the stick of Ephraim, and *for* all the house of Israel, his companions.' ¹⁷Then join them one to another for yourself into one stick, and they will become one in your hand.

¹⁸"And when the children of your people speak to you, saying, 'Will you not show us what you *mean* by these?'— ¹⁹say to them, 'Thus says the Lord GOD: "Surely I will take the stick of Joseph, which *is* in the hand of Ephraim, and the tribes of Israel, his companions; and I will join them with it, with the stick of Judah, and make them one stick, and they will be one in My hand."' ²⁰And the sticks on which you write will be in your hand before their eyes.

²¹"Then say to them, 'Thus says the Lord GOD: "Surely I will take the children of Israel from among the nations, wherever they have gone, and will gather them from every side and bring them into their own land; ²²and I will make them one nation in the land, on the mountains of Israel; and one king shall be king over them all; they shall no longer be two nations, nor shall they ever be divided into two kingdoms again. ²³They shall not defile themselves anymore with their idols, nor with their detestable things, nor with any of their transgressions; but I will deliver them from all their dwelling places in which they have sinned, and will cleanse them. Then they shall be My people, and I will be their God. ²⁴"David My servant *shall be* king over them, and they shall all have one shepherd;

they shall also walk in My judgments and observe My statutes, and do them. ²⁵Then they shall dwell in the land that I have given to Jacob My servant, where your fathers dwelt; and they shall dwell there, they, their children, and their children's children, forever; and My servant David *shall be* their prince forever. ²⁶Moreover I will make a covenant of peace with them, and it shall be an everlasting covenant with them; I will establish them and multiply them, and I will set My sanctuary in their midst forevermore. ²⁷My tabernacle also shall be with them; indeed I will be their God, and they shall be My people. ²⁸The nations also will know that I, the LORD, sanctify Israel, when My sanctuary is in their midst forevermore."'"

Gog and Allies Attack Israel

38 Now the word of the LORD came to me, saying, ²"Son of man, set your face against Gog, of the land of Magog, the prince of Rosh,ᵃ Meshech, and Tubal, and prophesy against him, ³and say, 'Thus says the Lord GOD: "Behold, I *am* against you, O Gog, the prince of Rosh, Meshech, and Tubal. ⁴I will turn you around, put hooks into your jaws, and lead you out, with all your army, horses, and horsemen, all splendidly clothed, a great company *with* bucklers and shields, all of them handling swords. ⁵Persia, Ethiopia,ᵃ and Libyaᵇ are with them, all of them *with* shield and helmet; ⁶Gomer and all its troops; the house of Togarmah *from* the far north and all its troops—many people *are* with you.

⁷"Prepare yourself and be ready, you and all your companies that are gathered about you; and be a guard for them. ⁸After many days you will be visited. In the latter years you will come into the land of those brought back from the sword *and* gathered from many people on the mountains of Israel, which had long been desolate; they were brought out of the nations, and now all of them dwell safely. ⁹You will ascend, coming like a storm, covering the land like a cloud, you and all your troops and many peoples with you."

38:2 ᵃTargum, Vulgate, and Aquila read *chief prince of* (also verse 3).   **38:5** ᵃHebrew *Cush* ᵇHebrew *Put*

10Thus says the Lord GOD: "On that day it shall come to pass *that* thoughts will arise in your mind, and you will make an evil plan: 11You will say, 'I will go up against a land of unwalled villages; I will go to a peaceful people, who dwell safely, all of them dwelling without walls, and having neither bars nor gates'— 12to take plunder and to take booty, to stretch out your hand against the waste places *that are again* inhabited, and against a people gathered from the nations, who have acquired livestock and goods, who dwell in the midst of the land. 13Sheba, Dedan, the merchants of Tarshish, and all their young lions will say to you, 'Have you come to take plunder? Have you gathered your army to take booty, to carry away silver and gold, to take away livestock and goods, to take great plunder?' " '

14"Therefore, son of man, prophesy and say to Gog, 'Thus says the Lord GOD: "On that day when My people Israel dwell safely, will you not know *it?* 15Then you will come from your place out of the far north, you and many peoples with you, all of them riding on horses, a great company and a mighty army. 16You will come up against My people Israel like a cloud, to cover the land. It will be in the latter days that I will bring you against My land, so that the nations may know Me, when I am hallowed in you, O Gog, before their eyes." 17Thus says the Lord GOD: "Are *you* he of whom I have spoken in former days by My servants the prophets of Israel, who prophesied for years in those days that I would bring you against them?

Judgment on Gog

18"And it will come to pass at the same time, when Gog comes against the land of Israel," says the Lord GOD, "*that* My fury will show in My face. 19For in My jealousy *and* in the fire of My wrath I have spoken: 'Surely in that day there shall be a great earthquake in the land of Israel, 20so that the fish of the sea, the birds of the heavens, the beasts of the field, all creeping things that creep on the earth, and all men who *are* on the face of the earth shall shake at My presence. The mountains shall be thrown down, the steep places shall fall, and every wall shall fall to the ground.' 21I will call for a sword against Gog throughout all My mountains," says the Lord GOD. "Every man's sword will be against his brother. 22And I will bring him to judgment with pestilence and bloodshed; I will rain down on him, on his troops, and on the many peoples who *are* with him, flooding rain, great hailstones, fire, and brimstone. 23Thus I will magnify Myself and sanctify Myself, and I will be known in the eyes of many nations. Then they shall know that I *am* the LORD." '

Gog's Armies Destroyed

39 "And you, son of man, prophesy against Gog, and say, 'Thus says the Lord GOD: "Behold, I *am* against you, O Gog, the prince of Rosh,a Meshech, and Tubal; 2and I will turn you around and lead you on, bringing you up from the far north, and bring you against the mountains of Israel. 3Then I will knock the bow out of your left hand, and cause the arrows to fall out of your right hand. 4You shall fall upon the mountains of Israel, you and all your troops and the peoples who *are* with you; I will give you to birds of prey of every sort and *to* the beasts of the field to be devoured. 5You shall fall on the open field; for I have spoken," says the Lord GOD. 6"And I will send fire on Magog and on those who live in security in the coastlands. Then they shall know that I *am* the LORD. 7So I will make My holy name known in the midst of My people Israel, and I will not *let them* profane My holy name anymore. Then the nations shall know that *I am* the LORD, the Holy One in Israel. 8Surely it is coming, and it shall be done," says the Lord GOD. "This *is* the day of which I have spoken.

9"Then those who dwell in the cities of Israel will go out and set on fire and burn the weapons, both the shields and bucklers, the bows and arrows, the javelins and spears; and they will make fires with them for seven years. 10They will not take wood from the field nor cut down *any* from the forests, because they will make fires with the weapons; and they will plunder those

---

39:1 aTargum, Vulgate and Aquila read *chief prince of.*

who plundered them, and pillage those who pillaged them," says the Lord GOD.

The Burial of Gog

¹¹"It will come to pass in that day *that* I will give Gog a burial place there in Israel, the valley of those who pass by east of the sea; and it will obstruct travelers, because there they will bury Gog and all his multitude. Therefore they will call *it* the Valley of Hamon Gog.ᵃ ¹²For seven months the house of Israel will be burying them, in order to cleanse the land. ¹³Indeed all the people of the land will be burying, and they will gain renown for it on the day that I am glorified," says the Lord GOD. ¹⁴"They will set apart men regularly employed, with the help of a search party,ᵃ to pass through the land and bury those bodies remaining on the ground, in order to cleanse it. At the end of seven months they will make a search. ¹⁵The search party will pass through the land; and *when anyone* sees a man's bone, he shall set up a marker by it, till the buriers have buried it in the Valley of Hamon Gog. ¹⁶*The* name of *the* city *will* also *be* Hamonah. Thus they shall cleanse the land."'

A Triumphant Festival

¹⁷"And as for you, son of man, thus says the Lord GOD, 'Speak to every sort of bird and to every beast of the field:

"Assemble yourselves and come;
   Gather together from all sides to
      My sacrificial meal
   Which I am sacrificing for you,
   A great sacrificial meal on the
      mountains of Israel,
   That you may eat flesh and drink
      blood.
¹⁸   You shall eat the flesh of the mighty,
   Drink the blood of the princes of the
      earth,
   Of rams and lambs,
   Of goats and bulls,
   All of them fatlings of Bashan.
¹⁹   You shall eat fat till you are full,
   And drink blood till you are drunk,
   At My sacrificial meal
   Which I am sacrificing for you.

²⁰   You shall be filled at My table
   With horses and riders,
   With mighty men
   And with all the men of war,"
      says the Lord GOD.

Israel Restored to the Land

²¹"I will set My glory among the nations; all the nations shall see My judgment which I have executed, and My hand which I have laid on them. ²²So the house of Israel shall know that I *am* the LORD their God from that day forward. ²³The Gentiles shall know that the house of Israel went into captivity for their iniquity; because they were unfaithful to Me, therefore I hid My face from them. I gave them into the hand of their enemies, and they all fell by the sword. ²⁴According to their uncleanness and according to their transgressions I have dealt with them, and hidden My face from them."'

²⁵"Therefore thus says the Lord GOD: 'Now I will bring back the captives of Jacob, and have mercy on the whole house of Israel; and I will be jealous for My holy name— ²⁶after they have borne their shame, and all their unfaithfulness in which they were unfaithful to Me, when they dwelt safely in their *own* land and no one made *them* afraid. ²⁷When I have brought them back from the peoples and gathered them out of their enemies' lands, and I am hallowed in them in the sight of many nations, ²⁸then they shall know that I *am* the LORD their God, who sent them into captivity among the nations, but also brought them back to their land, and left none of them captive any longer. ²⁹And I will not hide My face from them anymore; for I shall have poured out My Spirit on the house of Israel,' says the Lord GOD."

A New City, a New Temple

40 In the twenty-fifth year of our captivity, at the beginning of the year, on the tenth *day* of the month, in the fourteenth year after the city was captured, on the very same day the hand of the LORD was upon me; and He took me there. ²In the

39:11 ᵃLiterally *The Multitude of Gog*
39:14 ᵃLiterally *those who pass through*

visions of God He took me into the land of Israel and set me on a very high mountain; on it toward the south *was* something like the structure of a city. ³He took me there, and behold, *there was* a man whose appearance *was* like the appearance of bronze. He had a line of flax and a measuring rod in his hand, and he stood in the gateway.

⁴And the man said to me, "Son of man, look with your eyes and hear with your ears, and fix your mind on everything I show you; for you *were* brought here so that I might show *them* to you. Declare to the house of Israel everything you see." ⁵Now there was a wall all around the outside of the temple.ᵃ In the man's hand was a measuring rod six cubits *long, each being a* cubit and a handbreadth; and he measured the width of the wall structure, one rod; and the height, one rod.

The Eastern Gateway of the Temple

⁶Then he went to the gateway which faced east; and he went up its stairs and measured the threshold of the gateway, *which was* one rod wide, and the other threshold *was* one rod wide. ⁷Each gate chamber *was* one rod long and one rod wide; between the gate chambers *was a space of* five cubits; and the threshold of the gateway by the vestibule of the inside gate *was* one rod. ⁸He also measured the vestibule of the inside gate, one rod. ⁹Then he measured the vestibule of the gateway, eight cubits; and the gateposts, two cubits. The vestibule of the gate *was* on the inside. ¹⁰In the eastern gateway *were* three gate chambers on one side and three on the other; the three *were* all the same size; also the gateposts were of the same size on this side and that side.

¹¹He measured the width of the entrance to the gateway, ten cubits; *and* the length of the gate, thirteen cubits. ¹²*There was a* space in front of the gate chambers, one cubit *on this side* and one cubit on that side; the gate chambers *were* six cubits on this side and six cubits on that side. ¹³Then he measured the gateway from the roof of *one* gate chamber to the roof of the other; the width *was* twenty-five cubits, as door faces door. ¹⁴He measured the gateposts, sixty cubits high, and the court all around the gateway

extended to the gatepost. ¹⁵*From* the front of the entrance gate to the front of the vestibule of the inner gate *was* fifty cubits. ¹⁶*There were* beveled window *frames* in the gate chambers and in their intervening archways on the inside of the gateway all around, and likewise in the vestibules. *There were* windows all around on the inside. And on each gatepost *were* palm trees.

The Outer Court

¹⁷Then he brought me into the outer court; and *there were* chambers and a pavement made all around the court; thirty chambers faced the pavement. ¹⁸The pavement was by the side of the gateways, corresponding to the length of the gateways; *this was* the lower pavement. ¹⁹Then he measured the width from the front of the lower gateway to the front of the inner court exterior, one hundred cubits toward the east and the north.

The Northern Gateway

²⁰On the outer court was also a gateway facing north, and he measured its length and its width. ²¹Its gate chambers, three on this side and three on that side, its gateposts and its archways, had the same measurements as the first gate; its length *was* fifty cubits and its width twenty-five cubits. ²²Its windows and those of its archways, and also its palm trees, *had* the same measurements as the gateway facing east; it was ascended by seven steps, and its archway *was* in front of it. ²³A gate of the inner court was opposite the northern gateway, just as the eastern *gateway;* and he measured from gateway to gateway, one hundred cubits.

The Southern Gateway

²⁴After that he brought me toward the south, and there a gateway was facing south; and he measured its gateposts and archways according to these same measurements. ²⁵*There were* windows in it and in its archways all around like those windows; its length *was* fifty cubits and its width twenty-five cubits. ²⁶Seven steps led up to it, and its archway *was* in front of them; and

---

40:5 ᵃLiterally *house,* and so elsewhere in this book

it had palm trees on its gateposts, one on this side and one on that side. ²⁷*There was* also a gateway on the inner court, facing south; and he measured from gateway to gateway toward the south, one hundred cubits.

Gateways of the Inner Court

²⁸Then he brought me to the inner court through the southern gateway; he measured the southern gateway according to these same measurements. ²⁹Also its gate chambers, its gateposts, and its archways *were* according to these same measurements; *there were* windows in it and in its archways all around; *it was* fifty cubits long and twenty-five cubits wide. ³⁰*There were* archways all around, twenty-five cubits long and five cubits wide. ³¹Its archways faced the outer court, palm trees *were* on its gateposts, and going up to it *were* eight steps.

³²And he brought me into the inner court facing east; he measured the gateway according to these same measurements. ³³Also its gate chambers, its gateposts, and its archways *were* according to these same measurements; and *there were* windows in it and in its archways all around; *it was* fifty cubits long and twenty-five cubits wide. ³⁴Its archways faced the outer court, and palm trees *were* on its gateposts on this side and on that side; and going up to it *were* eight steps.

³⁵Then he brought me to the north gateway and measured *it* according to these same measurements— ³⁶also its gate chambers, its gateposts, and its archways. It had windows all around; its length *was* fifty cubits and its width twenty-five cubits. ³⁷Its gateposts faced the outer court, palm trees *were* on its gateposts on this side and on that side, and going up to it *were* eight steps.

Where Sacrifices Were Prepared

³⁸*There was* a chamber and its entrance by the gateposts of the gateway, where they washed the burnt offering. ³⁹In the vestibule of the gateway *were* two tables on this side and two tables on that side, on which to slay the burnt offering, the sin offering, and the trespass offering. ⁴⁰At the outer side of the *vestibule,* as one goes up to the entrance of

the northern gateway, *were* two tables; and on the other side of the *vestibule* of the gateway *were* two tables. ⁴¹Four tables *were* on this side and four tables on that side, by the side of the gateway, eight tables on which they slaughtered *the sacrifices.* ⁴²*There were* also four tables of hewn stone for the burnt offering, one cubit and a half long, one cubit and a half wide, and one cubit high; on these they laid the instruments with which they slaughtered the burnt offering and the sacrifice. ⁴³Inside *were* hooks, a handbreadth wide, fastened all around; and the flesh of the sacrifices *was* on the tables.

Chambers for Singers and Priests

⁴⁴Outside the inner gate *were* the chambers for the singers in the inner court, one facing south at the side of the northern gateway, and the other facing north at the side of the southernᵃ gateway. ⁴⁵Then he said to me, "This chamber which faces south *is* for the priests who have charge of the temple. ⁴⁶The chamber which faces north *is* for the priests who have charge of the altar; these *are* the sons of Zadok, from the sons of Levi, who come near the LORD to minister to Him."

Dimensions of the Inner Court and Vestibule

⁴⁷And he measured the court, one hundred cubits long and one hundred cubits wide, foursquare. The altar *was* in front of the temple. ⁴⁸Then he brought me to the vestibule of the temple and measured the doorposts of the vestibule, five cubits on this side and five cubits on that side; and the width of the gateway was three cubits on this side and three cubits on that side. ⁴⁹The length of the vestibule *was* twenty cubits, and the width eleven cubits; and by the steps which led up to it *there were* pillars by the doorposts, one on this side and another on that side.

Dimensions of the Sanctuary

41 Then he brought me into the sanctuaryᵃ and measured the doorposts, six

---

40:44 ᵃFollowing Septuagint; Masoretic Text and Vulgate read *eastern.*   **41:1** ᵃHebrew *heykal,* here the main room of the temple, sometimes called the *holy place* (compare Exodus 26:33)

cubits wide on one side and six cubits wide on the other side—the width of the tabernacle. [2]The width of the entryway *was* ten cubits, and the side walls of the entrance *were* five cubits on this side and five cubits on the other side; and he measured its length, forty cubits, and its width, twenty cubits.

[3]Also he went inside and measured the doorposts, two cubits; and the entrance, six cubits *high;* and the width of the entrance, seven cubits. [4]He measured the length, twenty cubits; and the width, twenty cubits, beyond the sanctuary; and he said to me, "This *is* the Most Holy *Place.*"

The Side Chambers on the Wall

[5]Next, he measured the wall of the temple, six cubits. The width of each side chamber all around the temple *was* four cubits on every side. [6]The side chambers *were* in three stories, one above the other, thirty chambers in each story; they rested on ledges which *were* for the side chambers all around, that they might be supported, but not fastened to the wall of the temple. [7]As one went up from story to story, the side chambers became wider all around, because their supporting ledges in the wall of the temple ascended like steps; therefore the width of the structure increased as one went up *from* the lowest *story* to the highest by way of the middle one. [8]I also saw an elevation all around the temple; it was the foundation of the side chambers, a full rod, *that is,* six cubits *high.* [9]The thickness of the outer wall of the side chambers *was* five cubits, and so also the remaining terrace by the place of the side chambers of the temple. [10]And between *it and* the *wall* chambers was a width of twenty cubits all around the temple on every side. [11]The doors of the side chambers opened on the terrace, one door toward the north and another toward the south; and the width of the terrace *was* five cubits all around.

The Building at the Western End

[12]The building that faced the separating courtyard at its western end *was* seventy cubits wide; the wall of the building *was* five cubits thick all around, and its length ninety cubits.

Dimensions and Design of the Temple Area

[13]So he measured the temple, one hundred cubits long; and the separating courtyard with the building and its walls *was* one hundred cubits long; [14]also the width of the eastern face of the temple, including the separating courtyard, *was* one hundred cubits. [15]He measured the length of the building behind it, facing the separating courtyard, with its galleries on the one side and on the other side, one hundred cubits, as well as the inner temple and the porches of the court, [16]their doorposts and the beveled window frames. And the galleries all around their three stories opposite the threshold were paneled with wood from the ground to the windows—the windows were covered— [17]from the space above the door, even to the inner room,[a] as well as outside, and on every wall all around, inside and outside, by measure.

[18]And *it was* made with cherubim and palm trees, a palm tree between cherub and cherub. *Each* cherub had two faces, [19]so that the face of a man *was* toward a palm tree on one side, and the face of a young lion toward a palm tree on the other side; thus *it was* made throughout the temple all around. [20]From the floor to the space above the door, and on the wall of the sanctuary, cherubim and palm trees *were* carved.

[21]The doorposts of the temple *were* square, *as was* the front of the sanctuary; their appearance was similar. [22]The altar *was* of wood, three cubits high, and its length two cubits. Its corners, its length, and its sides *were* of wood; and he said to me, "This *is* the table that *is* before the LORD."

[23]The temple and the sanctuary had two doors. [24]The doors had two panels *apiece,* two folding panels: two *panels* for one door and two panels for the other *door.* [25]Cherubim and palm trees *were* carved on the doors of the temple just as they *were* carved on the walls. A wooden canopy *was* on the front of the vestibule outside. [26]*There were* beveled window *frames* and palm trees on one side and on the other, on the sides of the vestibule—also on the side chambers of the temple and on the canopies.

41:17 [a]Literally *house,* here the Most Holy Place

The Chambers for the Priests

42 Then he brought me out into the outer court, by the way toward the north; and he brought me into the chamber which *was* opposite the separating courtyard, and which *was* opposite the building toward the north. ²Facing the length, *which was* one hundred cubits (the width was fifty cubits), was the north door. ³Opposite the inner court of twenty *cubits,* and opposite the pavement of the outer court, *was* gallery against gallery in three *stories.* ⁴In front of the chambers, toward the inside, *was* a walk ten cubits wide, at a distance of one cubit; and their doors faced north. ⁵Now the upper chambers *were* shorter, because the galleries took away *space* from them more than from the lower and middle stories of the building. ⁶For they *were* in three *stories* and did not have pillars like the pillars of the courts; therefore *the upper level* was shortened more than the lower and middle levels from the ground up. ⁷And a wall which *was* outside ran parallel to the chambers, at the front of the chambers, toward the outer court; its length *was* fifty cubits. ⁸The length of the chambers toward the outer court *was* fifty cubits, whereas that facing the temple *was* one hundred cubits. ⁹At the lower chambers *was* the entrance on the east side, as one goes into them from the outer court.

¹⁰Also *there were* chambers in the thickness of the wall of the court toward the east, opposite the separating courtyard and opposite the building. ¹¹*There was* a walk in front of them also, and their appearance *was* like the chambers which *were* toward the north; they *were* as long and as wide as the others, and all their exits and entrances *were* according to plan. ¹²And corresponding to the doors of the chambers that *were* facing south, as one enters them, *there was* a door in front of the walk, the way directly in front of the wall toward the east.

¹³Then he said to me, "The north chambers *and* the south chambers, which *are* opposite the separating courtyard, *are* the holy chambers where the priests who approach the Lord shall eat the most holy offerings. There they shall lay the most holy offerings—the grain offering, the sin offering, and the trespass offering—for the place *is* holy. ¹⁴When the priests enter them, they shall not go out of the holy *chamber* into the outer court; but there they shall leave their garments in which they minister, for they *are* holy. They shall put on other garments; then they may approach *that* which *is* for the people."

Outer Dimensions of the Temple

¹⁵Now when he had finished measuring the inner temple, he brought me out through the gateway that faces toward the east, and measured it all around. ¹⁶He measured the east side with the measuring rod,ᵃ five hundred rods by the measuring rod all around. ¹⁷He measured the north side, five hundred rods by the measuring rod all around. ¹⁸He measured the south side, five hundred rods by the measuring rod. ¹⁹He came around to the west side *and* measured five hundred rods by the measuring rod. ²⁰He measured it on the four sides; it had a wall all around, five hundred *cubits* long and five hundred wide, to separate the holy areas from the common.

The Temple, the Lord's Dwelling Place

43 Afterward he brought me to the gate, the gate that faces toward the east. ²And behold, the glory of the God of Israel came from the way of the east. His voice *was* like the sound of many waters; and the earth shone with His glory. ³*It was* like the appearance of the vision which I saw—like the vision which I saw when Iᵃ came to destroy the city. The visions *were* like the vision which I saw by the River Chebar; and I fell on my face. ⁴And the glory of the Lord came into the temple by way of the gate which faces toward the east. ⁵The Spirit lifted me up and brought me into the inner court; and behold, the glory of the Lord filled the temple.

⁶Then I heard *Him* speaking to me from the temple, while a man stood beside me. ⁷And He said to me, "Son of man, *this is* the place of My throne and the place of the soles of My feet, where I will dwell in the midst of

---

42:16 ᵃCompare 40:5   **43:3** ᵃSome Hebrew manuscripts and Vulgate read *He.*

the children of Israel forever. No more shall the house of Israel defile My holy name, they nor their kings, by their harlotry or with the carcasses of their kings on their high places. [8]When they set their threshold by My threshold, and their doorpost by My doorpost, with a wall between them and Me, they defiled My holy name by the abominations which they committed; therefore I have consumed them in My anger. [9]Now let them put their harlotry and the carcasses of their kings far away from Me, and I will dwell in their midst forever.

[10]"Son of man, describe the temple to the house of Israel, that they may be ashamed of their iniquities; and let them measure the pattern. [11]And if they are ashamed of all that they have done, make known to them the design of the temple and its arrangement, its exits and its entrances, its entire design and all its ordinances, all its forms and all its laws. Write *it* down in their sight, so that they may keep its whole design and all its ordinances, and perform them. [12]This *is* the law of the temple: The whole area surrounding the mountaintop *is* most holy. Behold, this *is* the law of the temple.

Dimensions of the Altar

[13]"These are the measurements of the altar in cubits (the cubit *is* one cubit and a handbreadth): the base one cubit high and one cubit wide, with a rim all around its edge of one span. This *is* the height of the altar: [14]from the base on the ground to the lower ledge, two cubits; the width of the ledge, one cubit; from the smaller ledge to the larger ledge, four cubits; and the width of the ledge, *one* cubit. [15]The altar hearth *is* four cubits high, with four horns extending upward from the hearth. [16]The altar hearth *is* twelve *cubits* long, twelve wide, square at its four corners; [17]the ledge, fourteen *cubits* long and fourteen wide on its four sides, with a rim of half a cubit around it; its base, one cubit all around; and its steps face toward the east."

Consecrating the Altar

[18]And He said to me, "Son of man, thus says the Lord GOD: 'These *are* the ordinances for the altar on the day when it is made, for sacrificing burnt offerings on it, and for sprinkling blood on it. [19]You shall give a young bull for a sin offering to the priests, the Levites, who are of the seed of Zadok, who approach Me to minister to Me,' says the Lord GOD. [20]'You shall take some of its blood and put *it* on the four horns of the altar, on the four corners of the ledge, and on the rim around it; thus you shall cleanse it and make atonement for it. [21]Then you shall also take the bull of the sin offering, and burn it in the appointed place of the temple, outside the sanctuary. [22]On the second day you shall offer a kid of the goats without blemish for a sin offering; and they shall cleanse the altar, as they cleansed *it* with the bull. [23]When you have finished cleansing *it,* you shall offer a young bull without blemish, and a ram from the flock without blemish. [24]When you offer them before the LORD, the priests shall throw salt on them, and they will offer them up *as* a burnt offering to the LORD. [25]Every day for seven days you shall prepare a goat *for* a sin offering; they shall also prepare a young bull and a ram from the flock, both without blemish. [26]Seven days they shall make atonement for the altar and purify it, and so consecrate *it.* [27]When these days are over it shall be, on the eighth day and thereafter, that the priests shall offer your burnt offerings and your peace offerings on the altar; and I will accept you,' says the Lord GOD."

The East Gate and the Prince

44 Then He brought me back to the outer gate of the sanctuary which faces toward the east, but it *was* shut. [2]And the LORD said to me, "This gate shall be shut; it shall not be opened, and no man shall enter by it, because the LORD God of Israel has entered by it; therefore it shall be shut. [3]*As for* the prince, *because* he *is* the prince, he may sit in it to eat bread before the LORD; he shall enter by way of the vestibule of the gateway, and go out the same way."

Those Admitted to the Temple

[4]Also He brought me by way of the north gate to the front of the temple; so I looked, and behold, the glory of the LORD filled the house of the LORD; and I fell on my face. [5]And the LORD said to me, "Son of man,

mark well, see with your eyes and hear with your ears, all that I say to you concerning all the ordinances of the house of the LORD and all its laws. Mark well who may enter the house and all who go out from the sanctuary.

⁶"Now say to the rebellious, to the house of Israel, 'Thus says the Lord GOD: "O house of Israel, let Us have no more of all your abominations. ⁷When you brought in foreigners, uncircumcised in heart and uncircumcised in flesh, to be in My sanctuary to defile it—My house—and when you offered My food, the fat and the blood, then they broke My covenant because of all your abominations. ⁸And you have not kept charge of My holy things, but you have set *others* to keep charge of My sanctuary for you." ⁹Thus says the Lord GOD: "No foreigner, uncircumcised in heart or uncircumcised in flesh, shall enter My sanctuary, including any foreigner who *is* among the children of Israel.

Laws Governing Priests

¹⁰"And the Levites who went far from Me, when Israel went astray, who strayed away from Me after their idols, they shall bear their iniquity. ¹¹Yet they shall be ministers in My sanctuary, *as* gatekeepers of the house and ministers of the house; they shall slay the burnt offering and the sacrifice for the people, and they shall stand before them to minister to them. ¹²Because they ministered to them before their idols and caused the house of Israel to fall into iniquity, therefore I have raised My hand in an oath against them," says the Lord GOD, "that they shall bear their iniquity. ¹³And they shall not come near Me to minister to Me as priest, nor come near any of My holy things, nor into the Most Holy *Place;* but they shall bear their shame and their abominations which they have committed. ¹⁴Nevertheless I will make them keep charge of the temple, for all its work, and for all that has to be done in it.

¹⁵"But the priests, the Levites, the sons of Zadok, who kept charge of My sanctuary when the children of Israel went astray from Me, they shall come near Me to minister to Me; and they shall stand before Me to offer to Me the fat and the blood," says the Lord GOD. ¹⁶"They shall enter My sanctuary, and they shall come near My table to minister to Me, and they shall keep My charge. ¹⁷And it shall be, whenever they enter the gates of the inner court, that they shall put on linen garments; no wool shall come upon them while they minister within the gates of the inner court or within the house. ¹⁸They shall have linen turbans on their heads and linen trousers on their bodies; they shall not clothe themselves with *anything that causes* sweat. ¹⁹When they go out to the outer court, to the outer court to the people, they shall take off their garments in which they have ministered, leave them in the holy chambers, and put on other garments; and in their holy garments they shall not sanctify the people.

²⁰"They shall neither shave their heads nor let their hair grow long, but they shall keep their hair well trimmed. ²¹No priest shall drink wine when he enters the inner court. ²²They shall not take as wife a widow or a divorced woman, but take virgins of the descendants of the house of Israel, or widows of priests.

²³"And they shall teach My people *the difference* between the holy and the unholy, and cause them to discern between the unclean and the clean. ²⁴In controversy they shall stand as judges, *and* judge it according to My judgments. They shall keep My laws and My statutes in all My appointed meetings, and they shall hallow My Sabbaths.

²⁵"They shall not defile *themselves* by coming near a dead person. Only for father or mother, for son or daughter, for brother or unmarried sister may they defile themselves. ²⁶After he is cleansed, they shall count seven days for him. ²⁷And on the day that he goes to the sanctuary to minister in the sanctuary, he must offer his sin offering in the inner court," says the Lord GOD.

²⁸"It shall be, in regard to their inheritance, *that* I *am* their inheritance. You shall give them no possession in Israel, for I *am* their possession. ²⁹They shall eat the grain offering, the sin offering, and the trespass offering; every dedicated thing in Israel shall be theirs. ³⁰The best of all firstfruits of any kind, and every sacrifice of any kind from all your sacrifices, shall be the priest's;

also you shall give to the priest the first of your ground meal, to cause a blessing to rest on your house. [31]The priests shall not eat anything, bird or beast, that died naturally or was torn *by wild beasts.*

The Holy District

45 "Moreover, when you divide the land by lot into inheritance, you shall set apart a district for the LORD, a holy section of the land; its length *shall be* twenty-five thousand *cubits,* and the width ten thousand. It *shall be* holy throughout its territory all around. [2]Of this there shall be a square plot for the sanctuary, five hundred by five hundred *rods,* with fifty cubits around it for an open space. [3]So this is the district you shall measure: twenty-five thousand *cubits* long and ten thousand wide; in it shall be the sanctuary, the Most Holy *Place.* [4]It shall be a holy *section* of the land, belonging to the priests, the ministers of the sanctuary, who come near to minister to the LORD; it shall be a place for their houses and a holy place for the sanctuary. [5]*An area* twenty-five thousand *cubits* long and ten thousand wide shall belong to the Levites, the ministers of the temple; they shall have twenty chambers as a possession.[a]

Properties of the City and the Prince

[6]"You shall appoint as the property of the city *an area* five thousand *cubits* wide and twenty-five thousand long, adjacent to the district of the holy *section;* it shall belong to the whole house of Israel. [7]"The prince shall have *a section* on one side and the other of the holy district and the city's property; and bordering on the holy district and the city's property, extending westward on the west side and eastward on the east side, the length *shall be* side by side with one of the *tribal* portions, from the west border to the east border. [8]The land shall be his possession in Israel; and My princes shall no more oppress My people, but they shall give *the rest of* the land to the house of Israel, according to their tribes."

Laws Governing the Prince

[9]'Thus says the Lord GOD: "Enough, O princes of Israel! Remove violence and plundering, execute justice and righteousness, and stop dispossessing My people," says the Lord GOD. [10]"You shall have honest scales, an honest ephah, and an honest bath. [11]The ephah and the bath shall be of the same measure, so that the bath contains one-tenth of a homer, and the ephah one-tenth of a homer; their measure shall be according to the homer. [12]The shekel *shall be* twenty gerahs; twenty shekels, twenty-five shekels, *and* fifteen shekels shall be your mina.

[13]"This *is* the offering which you shall offer: you shall give one-sixth of an ephah from a homer of wheat, and one-sixth of an ephah from a homer of barley. [14]The ordinance concerning oil, the bath of oil, *is* one-tenth of a bath from a kor. *A kor is* a homer or ten baths, for ten baths *are* a homer. [15]And one lamb shall be given from a flock of two hundred, from the rich pastures of Israel. These shall be for grain offerings, burnt offerings, and peace offerings, to make atonement for them," says the Lord GOD. [16]"All the people of the land shall give this offering for the prince in Israel. [17]Then it shall be the prince's part *to give* burnt offerings, grain offerings, and drink offerings, at the feasts, the New Moons, the Sabbaths, and at all the appointed seasons of the house of Israel. He shall prepare the sin offering, the grain offering, the burnt offering, and the peace offerings to make atonement for the house of Israel."

Keeping the Feasts

[18]'Thus says the Lord GOD: "In the first *month,* on the first *day* of the month, you shall take a young bull without blemish and cleanse the sanctuary. [19]The priest shall take some of the blood of the sin offering and put *it* on the doorposts of the temple, on the four corners of the ledge of the altar, and on the gateposts of the gate of the inner court. [20]And so you shall do on the seventh *day* of the month for everyone who has sinned unintentionally or in ignorance. Thus you shall make atonement for the temple.

45:5 [a]Following Masoretic Text, Targum, and Vulgate; Septuagint reads *a possession, cities of dwelling.*

21"In the first *month,* on the fourteenth day of the month, you shall observe the Passover, a feast of seven days; unleavened bread shall be eaten. 22And on that day the prince shall prepare for himself and for all the people of the land a bull *for* a sin offering. 23On the seven days of the feast he shall prepare a burnt offering to the LORD, seven bulls and seven rams without blemish, daily for seven days, and a kid of the goats daily *for* a sin offering. 24And he shall prepare a grain offering of one ephah for each bull and one ephah for each ram, together with a hin of oil for each ephah.

25"In the seventh *month,* on the fifteenth day of the month, at the feast, he shall do likewise for seven days, according to the sin offering, the burnt offering, the grain offering, and the oil."

The Manner of Worship

46 'Thus says the Lord GOD: "The gateway of the inner court that faces toward the east shall be shut the six working days; but on the Sabbath it shall be opened, and on the day of the New Moon it shall be opened. 2The prince shall enter by way of the vestibule of the gateway from the outside, and stand by the gatepost. The priests shall prepare his burnt offering and his peace offerings. He shall worship at the threshold of the gate. Then he shall go out, but the gate shall not be shut until evening. 3Likewise the people of the land shall worship at the entrance to this gateway before the LORD on the Sabbaths and the New Moons. 4The burnt offering that the prince offers to the LORD on the Sabbath day *shall be* six lambs without blemish, and a ram without blemish; 5and the grain offering *shall be one* ephah for a ram, and the grain offering for the lambs, as much as he wants to give, as well as a hin of oil with every ephah. 6On the day of the New Moon *it shall be* a young bull without blemish, six lambs, and a ram; they shall be without blemish. 7He shall prepare a grain offering of an ephah for a bull, an ephah for a ram, as much as he wants to give for the lambs, and a hin of oil with every ephah. 8When the prince enters, he shall go in by way of the vestibule of the gateway, and go out the same way.

9"But when the people of the land come before the LORD on the appointed feast days, whoever enters by way of the north gate to worship shall go out by way of the south gate; and whoever enters by way of the south gate shall go out by way of the north gate. He shall not return by way of the gate through which he came, but shall go out through the opposite gate. 10The prince shall then be in their midst. When they go in, he shall go in; and when they go out, he shall go out. 11At the festivals and the appointed feast days the grain offering shall be an ephah for a bull, an ephah for a ram, as much as he wants to give for the lambs, and a hin of oil with every ephah.

12"Now when the prince makes a voluntary burnt offering or voluntary peace offering to the LORD, the gate that faces toward the east shall then be opened for him; and he shall prepare his burnt offering and his peace offerings as he did on the Sabbath day. Then he shall go out, and after he goes out the gate shall be shut.

13"You shall daily make a burnt offering to the LORD *of a* lamb of the first year without blemish; you shall prepare it every morning. 14And you shall prepare a grain offering with it every morning, a sixth of an ephah, and a third of a hin of oil to moisten the fine flour. This grain offering is a perpetual ordinance, to be made regularly to the LORD. 15Thus they shall prepare the lamb, the grain offering, and the oil, *as a* regular burnt offering every morning."

The Prince and Inheritance Laws

16'Thus says the Lord GOD: "If the prince gives a gift *of some* of his inheritance to any of his sons, it shall belong to his sons; it is their possession by inheritance. 17But if he gives a gift of some of his inheritance to one of his servants, it shall be his until the year of liberty, after which it shall return to the prince. But his inheritance shall belong to his sons; it shall become theirs. 18Moreover the prince shall not take any of the people's inheritance by evicting them from their property; he shall provide an inheritance for his sons from his own property, so that none of My people may be scattered from his property." ' "

How the Offerings Were Prepared

¹⁹Now he brought me through the entrance, which *was* at the side of the gate, into the holy chambers of the priests which face toward the north; and there a place *was* situated at their extreme western end. ²⁰And he said to me, "This *is* the place where the priests shall boil the trespass offering and the sin offering, *and* where they shall bake the grain offering, so that they do not bring *them* out into the outer court to sanctify the people."

²¹Then he brought me out into the outer court and caused me to pass by the four corners of the court; and in fact, in every corner of the court *there was another* court. ²²In the four corners of the court *were* enclosed courts, forty *cubits* long and thirty wide; all four corners *were* the same size. ²³*There was* a row *of building stones* all around in them, all around the four of them; and cooking hearths were made under the rows of stones all around. ²⁴And he said to me, "These *are* the kitchens where the ministers of the temple shall boil the sacrifices of the people."

The Healing Waters and Trees

47 Then he brought me back to the door of the temple; and there was water, flowing from under the threshold of the temple toward the east, for the front of the temple faced east; the water was flowing from under the right side of the temple, south of the altar. ²He brought me out by way of the north gate, and led me around on the outside to the outer gateway that faces east; and there was water, running out on the right side.

³And when the man went out to the east with the line in his hand, he measured one thousand cubits, and he brought me through the waters; the water *came up to my* ankles. ⁴Again he measured one thousand and brought me through the waters; the water *came up to my* knees. Again he measured one thousand and brought me through; the water *came up to my* waist. ⁵Again he measured one thousand, *and it was* a river that I could not cross; for the water was too deep, water in which one must swim, a river that could not be crossed. ⁶He said to me, "Son of

man, have you seen *this?*" Then he brought me and returned me to the bank of the river.

⁷When I returned, there, along the bank of the river, *were* very many trees on one side and the other. ⁸Then he said to me: "This water flows toward the eastern region, goes down into the valley, and enters the sea. *When it* reaches the sea, *its* waters are healed. ⁹And it shall be *that* every living thing that moves, wherever the rivers go, will live. There will be a very great multitude of fish, because these waters go there; for they will be healed, and everything will live wherever the river goes. ¹⁰It shall be *that* fishermen will stand by it from En Gedi to En Eglaim; they will be *places* for spreading their nets. Their fish will be of the same kinds as the fish of the Great Sea, exceedingly many. ¹¹But its swamps and marshes will not be healed; they will be given over to salt. ¹²Along the bank of the river, on this side and that, will grow all *kinds of* trees used for food; their leaves will not wither, and their fruit will not fail. They will bear fruit every month, because their water flows from the sanctuary. Their fruit will be for food, and their leaves for medicine."

Borders of the Land

¹³Thus says the Lord GOD: "These *are* the borders by which you shall divide the land as an inheritance among the twelve tribes of Israel. Joseph *shall have two* portions. ¹⁴You shall inherit it equally with one another; for I raised My hand in an oath to give it to your fathers, and this land shall fall to you as your inheritance.

¹⁵"This *shall be* the border of the land on the north: from the Great Sea, *by* the road to Hethlon, as one goes to Zedad, ¹⁶Hamath, Berothah, Sibraim (which *is* between the border of Damascus and the border of Hamath), to Hazar Hatticon (which *is* on the border of Hauran). ¹⁷Thus the boundary shall be from the Sea to Hazar Enan, the border of Damascus; and as for the north, northward, it is the border of Hamath. *This is* the north side.

¹⁸"On the east side you shall mark out the border from between Hauran and Damascus, and between Gilead and the land of Israel, along the Jordan, and along the eastern side of the sea. *This is* the east side.

¹⁹"The south side, toward the South,ᵃ *shall be* from Tamar to the waters of Meribah by Kadesh, along the brook to the Great Sea. *This is* the south side, toward the South.

²⁰"The west side *shall be* the Great Sea, from the *southern* boundary until one comes to a point opposite Hamath. This *is* the west side.

²¹"Thus you shall divide this land among yourselves according to the tribes of Israel. ²²It shall be that you will divide it by lot as an inheritance for yourselves, and for the strangers who dwell among you and who bear children among you. They shall be to you as native-born among the children of Israel; they shall have an inheritance with you among the tribes of Israel. ²³And it shall be *that* in whatever tribe the stranger dwells, there you shall give *him* his inheritance," says the Lord GOD.

Division of the Land

48 "Now these *are* the names of the tribes: From the northern border along the road to Hethlon at the entrance of Hamath, to Hazar Enan, the border of Damascus northward, in the direction of Hamath, *there shall be* one *section for* Dan from its east to its west side; ²by the border of Dan, from the east side to the west, one *section for* Asher; ³by the border of Asher, from the east side to the west, one *section for* Naphtali; ⁴by the border of Naphtali, from the east side to the west, one *section for* Manasseh; ⁵by the border of Manasseh, from the east side to the west, one *section for* Ephraim; ⁶by the border of Ephraim, from the east side to the west, one *section for* Reuben; ⁷by the border of Reuben, from the east side to the west, one *section for* Judah; ⁸by the border of Judah, from the east side to the west, shall be the district which you shall set apart, twenty-five thousand *cubits* in width, and *in* length the same as one of the *other* portions, from the east side to the west, with the sanctuary in the center.

⁹"The district that you shall set apart for the LORD *shall be* twenty-five thousand *cubits* in length and ten thousand in width. ¹⁰To these—to the priests—the holy district shall belong: on the north twenty-five thousand *cubits in length,* on the west ten thousand in width, on the east ten thousand in width, and on the south twenty-five thousand in length. The sanctuary of the LORD shall be in the center. ¹¹*It shall be* for the priests of the sons of Zadok, who are sanctified, who have kept My charge, who did not go astray when the children of Israel went astray, as the Levites went astray. ¹²And *this* district of land that is set apart shall be to them a thing most holy by the border of the Levites.

¹³"Opposite the border of the priests, the Levites *shall have an area* twenty-five thousand *cubits* in length and ten thousand in width; its entire length *shall be* twenty-five thousand and its width ten thousand. ¹⁴And they shall not sell or exchange any of it; they may not alienate this best *part* of the land, for *it is* holy to the LORD.

¹⁵"The five thousand *cubits* in width that remain, along the edge of the twenty-five thousand, shall be for general use by the city, for dwellings and common-land; and the city shall be in the center. ¹⁶These *shall be* its measurements: the north side four thousand five hundred *cubits,* the south side four thousand five hundred, the east side four thousand five hundred, and the west side four thousand five hundred. ¹⁷The common-land of the city shall be: to the north two hundred and fifty *cubits,* to the south two hundred and fifty, to the east two hundred and fifty, and to the west two hundred and fifty. ¹⁸The rest of the length, alongside the district of the holy *section, shall be* ten thousand *cubits* to the east and ten thousand to the west. It shall be adjacent to the district of the holy *section,* and its produce shall be food for the workers of the city. ¹⁹The workers of the city, from all the tribes of Israel, shall cultivate it. ²⁰The entire district *shall be* twenty-five thousand *cubits* by twenty-five thousand *cubits,* foursquare. You shall set apart the holy district with the property of the city.

²¹"The rest *shall belong* to the prince, on one side and on the other of the holy district and of the city's property, next to the twenty-five thousand *cubits* of the *holy* district as far as the eastern border, and westward next to the twenty-five thousand as

---

47:19 ᵃHebrew *Negev*

far as the western border, adjacent to the *tribal* portions; *it shall belong* to the prince. It shall be the holy district, and the sanctuary of the temple *shall be* in the center. [22]Moreover, apart from the possession of the Levites and the possession of the city *which are* in the midst of what *belongs* to the prince, *the area* between the border of Judah and the border of Benjamin shall belong to the prince.

[23]"As for the rest of the tribes, from the east side to the west, Benjamin *shall have* one *section;* [24]by the border of Benjamin, from the east side to the west, Simeon *shall have* one *section;* [25]by the border of Simeon, from the east side to the west, Issachar *shall have* one *section;* [26]by the border of Issachar, from the east side to the west, Zebulun *shall have* one *section;* [27]by the border of Zebulun, from the east side to the west, Gad *shall have* one *section;* [28]by the border of Gad, on the south side, toward the South,[a] the border shall be from Tamar *to* the waters of Meribah *by* Kadesh, along the brook to the Great Sea. [29]This *is* the land which you shall divide by lot as an inheritance among the tribes of Israel, and these *are* their portions," says the Lord GOD.

The Gates of the City and Its Name

[30]"These *are* the exits of the city. On the north side, measuring four thousand five hundred *cubits* [31](the gates of the city *shall be* named after the tribes of Israel), the three gates northward: one gate for Reuben, one gate for Judah, and one gate for Levi; [32]on the east side, four thousand five hundred *cubits,* three gates: one gate for Joseph, one gate for Benjamin, and one gate for Dan; [33]on the south side, measuring four thousand five hundred *cubits,* three gates: one gate for Simeon, one gate for Issachar, and one gate for Zebulun; [34]on the west side, four thousand five hundred *cubits* with their three gates: one gate for Gad, one gate for Asher, and one gate for Naphtali. [35]All the way around *shall be* eighteen thousand *cubits;* and the name of the city from *that* day *shall be:* THE LORD *IS* THERE."[a]

48:28 [a]Hebrew *Negev*   **48:35** [a]Hebrew *YHWH Shammah*

DANIEL

Author: Daniel

When Written: Late Sixth Century B.C.

Theme: God Is in Control

Key Verses: Daniel 2:44—"And in the days of these kings the God of heaven will set up a kingdom which shall never be destroyed; and the kingdom shall not be left to other people; it shall break in pieces and consume all these kingdoms, and it shall stand forever."

Key Chapter: Daniel 9—Daniel's prophecy of the 70 weeks (9:24–27) provides a framework which many see as fulfilling both Christ's first and second comings.

Taken into captivity as a teenager and chosen for service in the Babylonian government, Daniel stood before the exiled children of Israel as a clear example of godly and upright behavior among their godless captors. As a prophet, he encouraged the exiled Jews that their captivity would not last forever, but that their restoration would come at God's appointed time and would open the door to an everlasting Kingdom of God's chosen Messiah.

Like the prophet Daniel, General Robert E. Lee stood as a bright example of integrity, honor, character, and courage during one of America's darkest historical chapters. "My trust is in the mercy and wisdom of a kind Providence, who ordereth all things for our good," he wrote as he led the vastly outnumbered Army of Northern Virginia in America's Civil War. While his soldiers placed great confidence in his ability as a military leader, he remained deeply humble, writing, "I tremble for my country when I hear of confidence expressed in me. I know too well my weakness, that our only hope is in God."

Daniel and His Friends Obey God

1 In the third year of the reign of Jehoiakim king of Judah, Nebuchadnezzar king of Babylon came to Jerusalem and besieged it. ²And the Lord gave Jehoiakim king of Judah into his hand, with some of the articles of the house of God, which he carried into the land of Shinar to the house of his god; and he brought the articles into the treasure house of his god.

³Then the king instructed Ashpenaz, the master of his eunuchs, to bring some of the children of Israel and some of the king's descendants and some of the nobles, ⁴young men in whom *there was* no blemish, but good-looking, gifted in all wisdom, possessing knowledge and quick to understand, who *had* ability to serve in the king's palace, and whom they might teach the language and literature of the Chaldeans. ⁵And the king appointed for them a daily provision of the king's delicacies and of the wine which he drank, and three years of training for them, so that at the end of *that time* they might serve before the king. ⁶Now from among those of the sons of Judah were Daniel, Hananiah, Mishael, and Azariah. ⁷To them the chief of the eunuchs gave names: he gave Daniel *the name* Belteshazzar; to Hananiah, Shadrach; to Mishael, Meshach; and to Azariah, Abed-Nego.

⁸But Daniel purposed in his heart that he would not defile himself with the portion of the king's delicacies, nor with the wine which he drank; therefore he requested of the chief of the eunuchs that he might not defile himself. ⁹Now God had brought Daniel into the favor and goodwill of the chief of the eunuchs. ¹⁰And the chief of the eunuchs said to Daniel, "I fear my lord the king, who has appointed your food and drink. For why should he see your faces looking worse than the young men who *are* your age? Then you would endanger my head before the king."

¹¹So Daniel said to the steward[a] whom the chief of the eunuchs had set over Daniel, Hananiah, Mishael, and Azariah, ¹²"Please test your servants for ten days, and let them give us vegetables to eat and water to drink. ¹³Then let our appearance be examined before you, and the appearance of the young men who eat the portion of the king's delicacies; and as you see fit, *so* deal with your servants." ¹⁴So he consented with them in this matter, and tested them ten days.

¹⁵And at the end of ten days their features appeared better and fatter in flesh than all the young men who ate the portion of the king's delicacies. ¹⁶Thus the steward took away their portion of delicacies and the wine that they were to drink, and gave them vegetables.

¹⁷As for these four young men, God gave them knowledge and skill in all literature and wisdom; and Daniel had understanding in all visions and dreams.

¹⁸Now at the end of the days, when the king had said that they should be brought in, the chief of the eunuchs brought them in before Nebuchadnezzar. ¹⁹Then the king interviewed[a] them, and among them all none was found like Daniel, Hananiah, Mishael, and Azariah; therefore they served before the king. ²⁰And in all matters of wisdom *and* understanding about which the king examined them, he found them ten times better than all the magicians *and* astrologers who *were* in all his realm. ²¹Thus Daniel continued until the first year of King Cyrus.

Nebuchadnezzar's Dream

2 Now in the second year of Nebuchadnezzar's reign, Nebuchadnezzar had dreams; and his spirit was *so* troubled that his sleep left him. ²Then the king gave the command to call the magicians, the astrologers,

---

1:11 ªHebrew *Melzar*, also in verse 16
1:19 ªLiterally *talked with them*

the sorcerers, and the Chaldeans to tell the king his dreams. So they came and stood before the king. ³And the king said to them, "I have had a dream, and my spirit is anxious to know the dream."

⁴Then the Chaldeans spoke to the king in Aramaic,ª "O king, live forever! Tell your servants the dream, and we will give the interpretation."

⁵The king answered and said to the Chaldeans, "My decision is firm: if you do not make known the dream to me, and its interpretation, you shall be cut in pieces, and your houses shall be made an ash heap. ⁶However, if you tell the dream and its interpretation, you shall receive from me gifts, rewards, and great honor. Therefore tell me the dream and its interpretation."

⁷They answered again and said, "Let the king tell his servants the dream, and we will give its interpretation."

⁸The king answered and said, "I know for certain that you would gain time, because you see that my decision is firm: ⁹if you do not make known the dream to me, *there is only* one decree for you! For you have agreed to speak lying and corrupt words before me till the time has changed. Therefore tell me the dream, and I shall know that you can give me its interpretation."

¹⁰The Chaldeans answered the king, and said, "There is not a man on earth who can tell the king's matter; therefore no king, lord, or ruler has *ever* asked such things of any magician, astrologer, or Chaldean. ¹¹*It is a* difficult thing that the king requests, and there is no other who can tell it to the king except the gods, whose dwelling is not with flesh."

¹²For this reason the king was angry and very furious, and gave the command to destroy all the wise *men* of Babylon. ¹³So the decree went out, and they began killing the wise *men;* and they sought Daniel and his companions, to kill *them.*

God Reveals Nebuchadnezzar's Dream

¹⁴Then with counsel and wisdom Daniel answered Arioch, the captain of the king's guard, who had gone out to kill the wise *men* of Babylon; ¹⁵he answered and said to Arioch the king's captain, "Why is the decree from the king so urgent?" Then Arioch made the decision known to Daniel.

¹⁶So Daniel went in and asked the king to give him time, that he might tell the king the interpretation. ¹⁷Then Daniel went to his house, and made the decision known to Hananiah, Mishael, and Azariah, his companions, ¹⁸that they might seek mercies from the God of heaven concerning this secret, so that Daniel and his companions might not perish with the rest of the wise *men* of Babylon. ¹⁹Then the secret was revealed to Daniel in a night vision. So Daniel blessed the God of heaven.

²⁰Daniel answered and said:

"Blessed be the name of God forever
    and ever,
    For wisdom and might are His.
21 And He changes the times and the
    seasons;
    He removes kings and raises up kings;
    He gives wisdom to the wise
    And knowledge to those who have
    understanding.
22 He reveals deep and secret things;
    He knows what *is* in the darkness,
    And light dwells with Him.

23 "I thank You and praise You,
    O God of my fathers;
    You have given me wisdom and might,
    And have now made known to me
    what we asked of You,
    For You have made known to us the
    king's demand."

Daniel Explains the Dream

²⁴Therefore Daniel went to Arioch, whom the king had appointed to destroy the wise *men* of Babylon. He went and said thus to him: "Do not destroy the wise *men* of Babylon; take me before the king, and I will tell the king the interpretation."

²⁵Then Arioch quickly brought Daniel before the king, and said thus to him, "I have found a man of the captivesª of Judah, who will make known to the king the interpretation."

2:4 ªThe original language of Daniel 2:4b through 7:28 is Aramaic.   **2:25** ªLiterally *of the sons of the captivity*

26The king answered and said to Daniel, whose name *was* Belteshazzar, "Are you able to make known to me the dream which I have seen, and its interpretation?" 27Daniel answered in the presence of the king, and said, "The secret which the king has demanded, the wise *men,* the astrologers, the magicians, and the soothsayers cannot declare to the king. 28But there is a God in heaven who reveals secrets, and He has made known to King Nebuchadnezzar what will be in the latter days. Your dream, and the visions of your head upon your bed, were these: 29As for you, O king, thoughts came *to* your *mind while* on your bed, *about* what would come to pass after this; and He who reveals secrets has made known to you what will be. 30But as for me, this secret has not been revealed to me because I have more wisdom than anyone living, but for *our* sakes who make known the interpretation to the king, and that you may know the thoughts of your heart.

31"You, O king, were watching; and behold, a great image! This great image, whose splendor *was* excellent, stood before you; and its form *was* awesome. 32This image's head *was* of fine gold, its chest and arms of silver, its belly and thighsª of bronze, 33its legs of iron, its feet partly of iron and partly of clay.ª 34You watched while a stone was cut out without hands, which struck the image on its feet of iron and clay, and broke them in pieces. 35Then the iron, the clay, the bronze, the silver, and the gold were crushed together, and became like chaff from the summer threshing floors; the wind carried them away so that no trace of them was found. And the stone that struck the image became a great mountain and filled the whole earth.

36"This *is* the dream. Now we will tell the interpretation of it before the king. 37You,

---

2:32 ªOr *sides*   **2:33** ªOr *baked clay,* and so in verses 34, 35, and 42

INSPIRING

"But there is a God in heaven who reveals secrets. . . ."

Daniel 2:28

George Washington Carver

"THE GOD WHO MADE THE PEANUT"

George Washington Carver (1864–1943) was a fabulous chemist of international fame in the field of agriculture. Much of his fame was based on his research and promotion of alternative crops to soil-depleting cotton, such as the peanut, soybean, pecan, and sweet potato. He wanted poor farmers to grow alternative crops as both a source of their own food as well as a source of other products to improve their quality of life.

In 1921, Carver spoke in favor of a peanut tariff before the Ways and Means Committee of the United States House of Representatives. At the time, it was unusual for a black person to be called as an expert. He also detailed the potential uses of the peanut and other new crops to improve the economy of the South. At the end of his address, the Chairman of the Committee asked:

"Dr. Carver, how did you learn all of these things?"
Carver answered: *"From an old book."*
"What book?"
Carver replied, *"The Bible."*
The Senator inquired, *"Does the Bible tell about peanuts?"*
"No, sir," Dr. Carver replied, *"but it tells about the God who made the peanut. I asked Him to show me what to do with the peanut, and He did."*

O king, *are* a king of kings. For the God of heaven has given you a kingdom, power, strength, and glory; [38]and wherever the children of men dwell, or the beasts of the field and the birds of the heaven, He has given *them* into your hand, and has made you ruler over them all—you *are* this head of gold. [39]But after you shall arise another kingdom inferior to yours; then another, a third kingdom of bronze, which shall rule over all the earth. [40]And the fourth kingdom shall be as strong as iron, inasmuch as iron breaks in pieces and shatters everything; and like iron that crushes, *that kingdom* will break in pieces and crush all the others. [41]Whereas you saw the feet and toes, partly of potter's clay and partly of iron, the kingdom shall be divided; yet the strength of the iron shall be in it, just as you saw the iron mixed with ceramic clay. [42]And *as* the toes of the feet *were* partly of iron and partly of clay, *so* the kingdom shall be partly strong and partly fragile. [43]As you saw iron mixed with ceramic clay, they will mingle with the seed of men; but they will not adhere to one another, just as iron does not mix with clay. [44]And in the days of these kings the God of heaven will set up a kingdom which shall never be destroyed; and the kingdom shall not be left to other people; it shall break in pieces and consume all these kingdoms, and it shall stand forever. [45]Inasmuch as you saw that the stone was cut out of the mountain without hands, and that it broke in pieces the iron, the bronze, the clay, the silver, and the gold—the great God has made known to the king what will come to pass after this. The dream is certain, and its interpretation is sure."

Daniel and His Friends Promoted

[46]Then King Nebuchadnezzar fell on his face, prostrate before Daniel, and commanded that they should present an offering and incense to him. [47]The king answered Daniel, and said, "Truly your God *is* the God of gods, the Lord of kings, and a revealer of secrets, since you could reveal this secret." [48]Then the king promoted Daniel and gave him many great gifts; and he made him ruler over the whole province of Babylon, and chief administrator over all the wise

men of Babylon. [49]Also Daniel petitioned the king, and he set Shadrach, Meshach, and Abed-Nego over the affairs of the province of Babylon; but Daniel *sat* in the gate[a] of the king.

The Image of Gold

3 Nebuchadnezzar the king made an image of gold, whose height *was* sixty cubits *and* its width six cubits. He set it up in the plain of Dura, in the province of Babylon. [2]And King Nebuchadnezzar sent *word* to gather together the satraps, the administrators, the governors, the counselors, the treasurers, the judges, the magistrates, and all the officials of the provinces, to come to the dedication of the image which King Nebuchadnezzar had set up. [3]So the satraps, the administrators, the governors, the counselors, the treasurers, the judges, the magistrates, and all the officials of the provinces gathered together for the dedication of the image that King Nebuchadnezzar had set up; and they stood before the image that Nebuchadnezzar had set up. [4]Then a herald cried aloud: "To you it is commanded, O peoples, nations, and languages, [5]*that* at the time you hear the sound of the horn, flute, harp, lyre, *and* psaltery, in symphony with all kinds of music, you shall fall down and worship the gold image that King Nebuchadnezzar has set up; [6]and whoever does not fall down and worship shall be cast immediately into the midst of a burning fiery furnace."

[7]So at that time, when all the people heard the sound of the horn, flute, harp, *and* lyre, in symphony with all kinds of music, all the people, nations, and languages fell down *and* worshiped the gold image which King Nebuchadnezzar had set up.

Daniel's Friends Disobey the King

[8]Therefore at that time certain Chaldeans came forward and accused the Jews. [9]They spoke and said to King Nebuchadnezzar, "O king, live forever! [10]You, O king, have made a decree that everyone who hears the sound of the horn, flute, harp, lyre, *and* psaltery, in symphony with all kinds of music, shall

---

2:49 [a]That is, the king's court

fall down and worship the gold image; [11]and whoever does not fall down and worship shall be cast into the midst of a burning fiery furnace. [12]There are certain Jews whom you have set over the affairs of the province of Babylon: Shadrach, Meshach, and Abed-Nego; these men, O king, have not paid due regard to you. They do not serve your gods or worship the gold image which you have set up."

[13]Then Nebuchadnezzar, in rage and fury, gave the command to bring Shadrach, Meshach, and Abed-Nego. So they brought these men before the king. [14]Nebuchadnezzar spoke, saying to them, "*Is it* true, Shadrach, Meshach, and Abed-Nego, *that* you do not serve my gods or worship the gold image which I have set up? [15]Now if you are ready at the time you hear the sound of the horn, flute, harp, lyre, *and* psaltery, in symphony with all kinds of music, and you fall down and worship the image which I have made, *good!* But if you do not worship, you shall be cast immediately into the midst of a burning fiery furnace. And who *is* the god who will deliver you from my hands?"

[16]Shadrach, Meshach, and Abed-Nego answered and said to the king, "O Nebuchadnezzar, we have no need to answer you in this matter. [17]If that *is the case,* our God whom we serve is able to deliver us from the burning fiery furnace, and He will deliver *us* from your hand, O king. [18]But if not, let it be known to you, O king, that we do not serve your gods, nor will we worship the gold image which you have set up."

Saved in Fiery Trial

[19]Then Nebuchadnezzar was full of fury, and the expression on his face changed toward Shadrach, Meshach, and Abed-Nego. He spoke and commanded that they heat the furnace seven times more than it was usually heated. [20]And he commanded certain mighty men of valor who *were* in his army to bind Shadrach, Meshach, and Abed-Nego, *and* cast *them* into the burning fiery furnace. [21]Then these men were bound in their coats, their trousers, their turbans, and their *other* garments, and were cast into the midst of the burning fiery furnace. [22]Therefore, because the king's command was urgent, and the furnace exceedingly hot, the flame of the fire killed those men who took up Shadrach, Meshach, and Abed-Nego. [23]And these three men, Shadrach, Meshach, and Abed-Nego, fell down bound into the midst of the burning fiery furnace.

[24]Then King Nebuchadnezzar was astonished; and he rose in haste *and* spoke, saying to his counselors, "Did we not cast three men bound into the midst of the fire?"

They answered and said to the king, "True, O king."

[25]"Look!" he answered, "I see four men loose, walking in the midst of the fire; and they are not hurt, and the form of the fourth is like the Son of God."[a]

Nebuchadnezzar Praises God

[26]Then Nebuchadnezzar went near the mouth of the burning fiery furnace *and* spoke, saying, "Shadrach, Meshach, and Abed-Nego, servants of the Most High God, come out, and come *here.*" Then Shadrach, Meshach, and Abed-Nego came from the midst of the fire. [27]And the satraps, administrators, governors, and the king's counselors gathered together, and they saw these men on whose bodies the fire had no power; the hair of their head was not singed nor were their garments affected, and the smell of fire was not on them.

[28]Nebuchadnezzar spoke, saying, "Blessed be the God of Shadrach, Meshach, and Abed-Nego, who sent His Angel[a] and delivered His servants who trusted in Him, and they have frustrated the king's word, and yielded their bodies, that they should not serve nor worship any god except their own God! [29]Therefore I make a decree that any people, nation, or language which speaks anything amiss against the God of Shadrach, Meshach, and Abed-Nego shall be cut in pieces, and their houses shall be made an ash heap; because there is no other God who can deliver like this."

[30]Then the king promoted Shadrach, Meshach, and Abed-Nego in the province of Babylon.

3:25 [a]Or *a son of the gods*   **3:28** [a]Or *angel*

Nebuchadnezzar's Second Dream

4 Nebuchadnezzar the king,

To all peoples, nations, and languages that dwell in all the earth:

Peace be multiplied to you.

2 I thought it good to declare the signs and wonders that the Most High God has worked for me.

3 How great *are* His signs,
And how mighty His wonders!
His kingdom *is* an everlasting kingdom,
And His dominion *is* from generation
    to generation.

4 I, Nebuchadnezzar, was at rest in my house, and flourishing in my palace. ⁵I saw a dream which made me afraid, and the thoughts on my bed and the visions of my head troubled me. ⁶Therefore I issued a decree to bring in all the wise *men* of Babylon before me, that they might make known to me the interpretation of the dream. ⁷Then the magicians, the astrologers, the Chaldeans, and the soothsayers came in, and I told them the dream; but they did not make known to me its interpretation. ⁸But at last Daniel came before me (his name *is* Belteshazzar, according to the name of my god; in him *is* the Spirit of the Holy God), and I told the dream before him, *saying:* ⁹"Belteshazzar, chief of the magicians, because I know that the Spirit of the Holy God *is* in you, and no secret troubles you, explain to me the visions of my dream that I have seen, and its interpretation.

SELFLESS

A FIREMAN'S PRAYER

"*. . . from the burning
fiery furnace. . . .*"
DANIEL 3:17

American Fireman,
Rushing to the Conflict
by Currier & Ives

*When I am called to duty, God,
Wherever flame may rage,
Give me the strength to save some life,
Whatever be its age.*

*Help me embrace a little child
Before it is too late,
Or save an older person from
The horror of that fate.*

*Enable me to be alert
And hear the weakest shout,
And quickly and efficiently
To put the fire out.*

*I want to fill my calling and
To give the best in me,
To guard my every neighbor
And protect his property.*

*And if according to my fate,
I am to lose my life,
Please bless with Your protecting hand
My children and my wife.*

Author Unknown

10 "These *were* the visions of my head
while on my bed:

I was looking, and behold,
A tree in the midst of the earth,
And its height was great.
11 The tree grew and became strong;
Its height reached to the heavens,
And it could be seen to the ends
    of all the earth.
12 Its leaves *were* lovely,
Its fruit abundant,
And in it *was* food for all.
The beasts of the field found shade
    under it,
The birds of the heavens dwelt in its
    branches,
And all flesh was fed from it.

13 "I saw in the visions of my head
while on my bed, and there was a
watcher, a holy one, coming down
from heaven. 14He cried aloud and
said thus:

'Chop down the tree and cut off its
    branches,
Strip off its leaves and scatter its fruit.
Let the beasts get out from under it,
And the birds from its branches.
15 Nevertheless leave the stump and
    roots in the earth,
Bound with a band of iron and
    bronze,
In the tender grass of the field.
Let it be wet with the dew of heaven,
And *let* him graze with the beasts
On the grass of the earth.
16 Let his heart be changed from *that of*
    a man,
Let him be given the heart of a beast,
And let seven times^a pass over him.

17 'This decision *is* by the decree of the
    watchers,
And the sentence by the word of the
    holy ones,
In order that the living may know
That the Most High rules in the
    kingdom of men,
Gives it to whomever He will,
And sets over it the lowest of men.'

18 "This dream I, King Nebuchadnezzar,
have seen. Now you, Belteshazzar,
declare its interpretation, since all
the wise *men* of my kingdom are
not able to make known to me the
interpretation; but you *are* able, for
the Spirit of the Holy God *is* in you."

Daniel Explains the Second Dream

19 Then Daniel, whose name *was*
Belteshazzar, was astonished for
a time, and his thoughts troubled
him. *So* the king spoke, and said,
"Belteshazzar, do not let the dream
or its interpretation trouble you."
    Belteshazzar answered and said,
"My lord, *may* the dream concern those
who hate you, and its interpretation
concern your enemies!

20 "The tree that you saw, which grew and
became strong, whose height reached
to the heavens and which *could be*
seen by all the earth, 21whose leaves
were lovely and its fruit abundant, in
which *was* food for all, under which
the beasts of the field dwelt, and in
whose branches the birds of the heaven
had their home— 22it *is* you, O king,
who have grown and become strong;
for your greatness has grown and
reaches to the heavens, and your
dominion to the end of the earth.

23 "And inasmuch as the king saw a
watcher, a holy one, coming down
from heaven and saying, 'Chop down
the tree and destroy it, but leave its
stump and roots in the earth, *bound*
with a band of iron and bronze in the
tender grass of the field; let it be wet
with the dew of heaven, and let him
graze with the beasts of the field, till
seven times pass over him'; 24this is the
interpretation, O king, and this is the
decree of the Most High, which has
come upon my lord the king: 25They
shall drive you from men, your dwelling
shall be with the beasts of the field,

4:16 ^aPossibly *seven years,* and so in verses 23, 25,
and 32

and they shall make you eat grass like oxen. They shall wet you with the dew of heaven, and seven times shall pass over you, till you know that the Most High rules in the kingdom of men, and gives it to whomever He chooses.

26 "And inasmuch as they gave the command to leave the stump *and* roots of the tree, your kingdom shall be assured to you, after you come to know that Heaven rules. 27Therefore, O king, let my advice be acceptable to you; break off your sins by *being* righteous, and your iniquities by showing mercy to *the* poor. Perhaps there may be a lengthening of your prosperity."

Nebuchadnezzar's Humiliation

28 All *this* came upon King Nebuchadnezzar. 29At the end of the twelve months he was walking about the royal palace of Babylon. 30The king spoke, saying, "Is not this great Babylon, that I have built for a royal dwelling by my mighty power and for the honor of my majesty?"

31 While the word *was still* in the king's mouth, a voice fell from heaven: "King Nebuchadnezzar, to you it is spoken: the kingdom has departed from you! 32And they shall drive you from men, and your dwelling *shall be* with the beasts of the field. They shall make you eat grass like oxen; and seven times shall pass over you, until you know that the Most High rules in the kingdom of men, and gives it to whomever He chooses."

33 That very hour the word was fulfilled concerning Nebuchadnezzar; he was driven from men and ate grass like oxen; his body was wet with the dew of heaven till his hair had grown like eagles' *feathers* and his nails like birds' *claws.*

Nebuchadnezzar Praises God

34 And at the end of the time[a] I, Nebuchadnezzar, lifted my eyes to heaven, and my understanding returned to me; and I blessed the Most High and praised and honored Him who lives forever:

For His dominion *is* an everlasting dominion,
And His kingdom *is* from generation to generation.
35 All the inhabitants of the earth *are* reputed as nothing;
He does according to His will in the army of heaven
And *among* the inhabitants of the earth.
No one can restrain His hand
Or say to Him, "What have You done?"

36 At the same time my reason returned to me, and for the glory of my kingdom, my honor and splendor returned to me. My counselors and nobles resorted to me, I was restored to my kingdom, and excellent majesty was added to me. 37Now I, Nebuchadnezzar, praise and extol and honor the King of heaven, all of whose works *are* truth, and His ways justice. And those who walk in pride He is able to put down.

Belshazzar's Feast

5 Belshazzar the king made a great feast for a thousand of his lords, and drank wine in the presence of the thousand. 2While he tasted the wine, Belshazzar gave the command to bring the gold and silver vessels which his father Nebuchadnezzar had taken from the temple which *had been* in Jerusalem, that the king and his lords, his wives, and his concubines might drink from them. 3Then they brought the gold vessels that had been taken from the temple of the house of God which *had been* in Jerusalem; and the king and his lords, his wives, and his concubines drank from them. 4They drank wine, and praised the gods of gold and silver, bronze and iron, wood and stone.

5In the same hour the fingers of a man's hand appeared and wrote opposite the lampstand on the plaster of the wall of the king's palace; and the king saw the part of the

---

4:34 [a]Literally *days*

hand that wrote. [6]Then the king's countenance changed, and his thoughts troubled him, so that the joints of his hips were loosened and his knees knocked against each other. [7]The king cried aloud to bring in the astrologers, the Chaldeans, and the soothsayers. The king spoke, saying to the wise *men* of Babylon, "Whoever reads this writing, and tells me its interpretation, shall be clothed with purple and *have* a chain of gold around his neck; and he shall be the third ruler in the kingdom." [8]Now all the king's wise *men* came, but they could not read the writing, or make known to the king its interpretation. [9]Then King Belshazzar was greatly troubled, his countenance was changed, and his lords were astonished.

[10]The queen, because of the words of the king and his lords, came to the banquet hall. The queen spoke, saying, "O king, live forever! Do not let your thoughts trouble you, nor let your countenance change. [11]There is a man in your kingdom in whom *is* the Spirit of the Holy God. And in the days of your father, light and understanding and wisdom, like the wisdom of the gods, were found in him; and King Nebuchadnezzar your father—your father the king—made him chief of the magicians, astrologers, Chaldeans, *and* soothsayers. [12]Inasmuch as an excellent spirit, knowledge, understanding, interpreting dreams, solving riddles, and explaining enigmas[a] were found in this Daniel, whom the king named Belteshazzar, now let Daniel be called, and he will give the interpretation."

The Writing on the Wall Explained

[13]Then Daniel was brought in before the king. The king spoke, and said to Daniel, "*Are* you that Daniel who is one of the captives[a] from Judah, whom my father the king brought from Judah? [14]I have heard of you, that the Spirit of God *is* in you, and *that* light and understanding and excellent wisdom are found in you. [15]Now the wise *men*, the astrologers, have been brought in before me, that they should read this writing and make known to me its interpretation, but they could not give the interpretation of the thing. [16]And I have heard of you, that

you can give interpretations and explain enigmas. Now if you can read the writing and make known to me its interpretation, you shall be clothed with purple and *have* a chain of gold around your neck, and shall be the third ruler in the kingdom."

[17]Then Daniel answered, and said before the king, "Let your gifts be for yourself, and give your rewards to another; yet I will read the writing to the king, and make known to him the interpretation. [18]O king, the Most High God gave Nebuchadnezzar your father a kingdom and majesty, glory and honor. [19]And because of the majesty that He gave him, all peoples, nations, and languages trembled and feared before him. Whomever he wished, he executed; whomever he wished, he kept alive; whomever he wished, he set up; and whomever he wished, he put down. [20]But when his heart was lifted up, and his spirit was hardened in pride, he was deposed from his kingly throne, and they took his glory from him. [21]Then he was driven from the sons of men, his heart was made like the beasts, and his dwelling *was* with the wild donkeys. They fed him with grass like oxen, and his body was wet with the dew of heaven, till he knew that the Most High God rules in the kingdom of men, and appoints over it whomever He chooses.

[22]"But you his son, Belshazzar, have not humbled your heart, although you knew all this. [23]And you have lifted yourself up against the Lord of heaven. They have brought the vessels of His house before you, and you and your lords, your wives and your concubines, have drunk wine from them. And you have praised the gods of silver and gold, bronze and iron, wood and stone, which do not see or hear or know; and the God who *holds* your breath in His hand and owns all your ways, you have not glorified. [24]Then the fingers[a] of the hand were sent from Him, and this writing was written.

[25]"And this is the inscription that was written:

5:12 [a]Literally *untying knots,* and so in verse 16
5:13 [a]Literally *of the sons of the captivity*
5:24 [a]Literally *palm*

MENE,[a] MENE, TEKEL,[b] UPHARSIN.[c]

[26]This *is* the interpretation of *each* word. MENE: God has numbered your kingdom, and finished it; [27]TEKEK: You have been weighed in the balances, and found wanting; [28]PERES: Your kingdom has been divided, and given to the Medes and Persians."[a] [29]Then Belshazzar gave the command, and they clothed Daniel with purple and *put* a chain of gold around his neck, and made a proclamation concerning him that he should be the third ruler in the kingdom.

Belshazzar's Fall

[30]That very night Belshazzar, king of the Chaldeans, was slain. [31]And Darius the Mede received the kingdom, *being* about sixty-two years old.

The Plot Against Daniel

6 It pleased Darius to set over the kingdom one hundred and twenty satraps, to be over the whole kingdom; [2]and over these, three governors, of whom Daniel *was* one, that the satraps might give account to them, so that the king would suffer no loss. [3]Then this Daniel distinguished himself above the governors and satraps, because an excellent spirit *was* in him; and the king gave thought to setting him over the whole realm. [4]So the governors and satraps sought to find *some* charge against Daniel concerning the kingdom; but they could find no charge or fault, because he *was* faithful; nor was there any error or fault found in him. [5]Then these men said, "We shall not find any charge against this Daniel unless we find *it* against him concerning the law of his God."

[6]So these governors and satraps thronged before the king, and said thus to him: "King Darius, live forever! [7]All the governors of the kingdom, the administrators and satraps, the counselors and advisors, have consulted together to establish a royal statute and to make a firm decree, that whoever petitions any god or man for thirty days, except you, O king, shall be cast into the den of lions. [8]Now, O king, establish the decree and sign the writing, so that it cannot be changed, according to the law of the Medes and Persians, which does not alter." [9]Therefore King Darius signed the written decree.

Daniel in the Lions' Den

[10]Now when Daniel knew that the writing was signed, he went home. And in his upper room, with his windows open toward Jerusalem, he knelt down on his knees three times that day, and prayed and gave thanks before his God, as was his custom since early days.

[11]Then these men assembled and found Daniel praying and making supplication before his God. [12]And they went before the king, and spoke concerning the king's decree: "Have you not signed a decree that every man who petitions any god or man within thirty days, except you, O king, shall be cast into the den of lions?"

The king answered and said, "The thing *is* true, according to the law of the Medes and Persians, which does not alter."

[13]So they answered and said before the king, "That Daniel, who is one of the captives[a] from Judah, does not show due regard for you, O king, or for the decree that you have signed, but makes his petition three times a day."

[14]And the king, when he heard *these* words, was greatly displeased with himself, and set *his* heart on Daniel to deliver him; and he labored till the going down of the sun to deliver him. [15]Then these men approached the king, and said to the king, "Know, O king, that *it is* the law of the Medes and Persians that no decree or statute which the king establishes may be changed."

[16]So the king gave the command, and they brought Daniel and cast *him* into the den of lions. *But* the king spoke, saying to Daniel, "Your God, whom you serve continually, He will deliver you." [17]Then a stone was brought and laid on the mouth of the den, and the king sealed it with his own signet ring and with the signets of his lords, that the purpose concerning Daniel might not be changed.

5:25 [a]Literally *a mina* (50 shekels) from the verb "to number" [b]Literally *a shekel* from the verb "to weigh" [c]Literally *and half-shekels* from the verb "to divide" **5:28** [a]Aramaic *Paras,* consonant with *Peres* **6:13** [a]Literally *of the sons of the captivity*

Daniel Saved from the Lions

[18]Now the king went to his palace and spent the night fasting; and no musicians[a] were brought before him. Also his sleep went from him. [19]Then the king arose very early in the morning and went in haste to the den of lions. [20]And when he came to the den, he cried out with a lamenting voice to Daniel. The king spoke, saying to Daniel, "Daniel, servant of the living God, has your God, whom you serve continually, been able to deliver you from the lions?"

[21]Then Daniel said to the king, "O king, live forever! [22]My God sent His angel and shut the lions' mouths, so that they have not hurt me, because I was found innocent before Him; and also, O king, I have done no wrong before you."

[23]Now the king was exceedingly glad for him, and commanded that they should take Daniel up out of the den. So Daniel was taken up out of the den, and no injury whatever was found on him, because he believed in his God.

Darius Honors God

[24]And the king gave the command, and they brought those men who had accused Daniel, and they cast *them* into the den of lions—them, their children, and their wives; and the lions overpowered them, and broke all their bones in pieces before they ever came to the bottom of the den. [25]Then King Darius wrote:

To all peoples, nations, and languages that dwell in all the earth:

Peace be multiplied to you.

[26]   I make a decree that in every dominion of my kingdom *men must* tremble and fear before the God of Daniel.

For He *is* the living God,
And steadfast forever;
His kingdom *is the one* which shall not be destroyed,
And His dominion *shall endure* to the end.

[27]   He delivers and rescues,
And He works signs and wonders
In heaven and on earth,
Who has delivered Daniel from the power of the lions.

[28]So this Daniel prospered in the reign of Darius and in the reign of Cyrus the Persian.

Vision of the Four Beasts

7 In the first year of Belshazzar king of Babylon, Daniel had a dream and visions of his head *while* on his bed. Then he wrote down the dream, telling the main facts.[a]

[2]Daniel spoke, saying, "I saw in my vision by night, and behold, the four winds of heaven were stirring up the Great Sea. [3]And four great beasts came up from the sea, each different from the other. [4]The first *was* like a lion, and had eagle's wings. I watched till its wings were plucked off; and it was lifted up from the earth and made to stand on two feet like a man, and a man's heart was given to it.

[5]"And suddenly another beast, a second, like a bear. It was raised up on one side, and *had* three ribs in its mouth between its teeth. And they said thus to it: 'Arise, devour much flesh!'

[6]"After this I looked, and there was another, like a leopard, which had on its back four wings of a bird. The beast also had four heads, and dominion was given to it.

[7]"After this I saw in the night visions, and behold, a fourth beast, dreadful and terrible, exceedingly strong. It had huge iron teeth; it was devouring, breaking in pieces, and trampling the residue with its feet. It *was* different from all the beasts that *were* before it, and it had ten horns. [8]I was considering the horns, and there was another horn, a little one, coming up among them, before whom three of the first horns were plucked out by the roots. And there, in this horn, *were* eyes like the eyes of a man, and a mouth speaking pompous words.

6:18 [a]Exact meaning unknown   **7:1** [a]Literally *the head* (or *chief*) *of the words*

Vision of the Ancient of Days

9 "I watched till thrones were put in place,
And the Ancient of Days was seated;
His garment *was* white as snow,
And the hair of His head *was* like pure wool.
His throne *was* a fiery flame,
Its wheels a burning fire;

10 A fiery stream issued
And came forth from before Him.
A thousand thousands ministered to Him;
Ten thousand times ten thousand stood before Him.
The court[a] was seated,
And the books were opened.

11 "I watched then because of the sound of the pompous words which the horn was speaking; I watched till the beast was slain, and its body destroyed and given to the burning flame. 12As for the rest of the beasts, they had their dominion taken away, yet their lives were prolonged for a season and a time.

13 "I was watching in the night visions,
And behold, *One* like the Son of Man,
Coming with the clouds of heaven!
He came to the Ancient of Days,
And they brought Him near before Him.

14 Then to Him was given dominion and glory and a kingdom,
That all peoples, nations, and languages should serve Him.
His dominion *is* an everlasting dominion,
Which shall not pass away,
And His kingdom *the one*
Which shall not be destroyed.

Daniel's Visions Interpreted

15"I, Daniel, was grieved in my spirit within *my* body, and the visions of my head troubled me. 16I came near to one of those who stood by, and asked him the truth of all this. So he told me and made known to me the interpretation of these things: 17'Those great beasts, which are four, *are* four kings[a] which arise out of the earth. 18But the saints of the Most High shall receive the kingdom, and possess the kingdom forever, even forever and ever.'

19"Then I wished to know the truth about the fourth beast, which was different from all the others, exceedingly dreadful, *with* its teeth of iron and its nails of bronze, *which* devoured, broke in pieces, and trampled the residue with its feet; 20and the ten horns that *were* on its head, and the other *horn* which came up, before which three fell, namely, that horn which had eyes and a mouth which spoke pompous words, whose appearance *was* greater than his fellows.

21"I was watching; and the same horn was making war against the saints, and prevailing against them, 22until the Ancient of Days came, and a judgment was made *in favor* of the saints of the Most High, and the time came for the saints to possess the kingdom.

23"Thus he said:

'The fourth beast shall be
A fourth kingdom on earth,
Which shall be different from all *other* kingdoms,
And shall devour the whole earth,
Trample it and break it in pieces.

24 The ten horns *are* ten kings
Who shall arise from this kingdom.
And another shall rise after them;
He shall be different from the first *ones,*
And shall subdue three kings.

25 He shall speak *pompous* words against the Most High,
Shall persecute[a] the saints of the Most High,
And shall intend to change times and law.
Then *the saints* shall be given into his hand
For a time and times and half a time.

26 'But the court shall be seated,
And they shall take away his dominion,
To consume and destroy *it* forever.

7:10 [a]Or *judgment*   **7:17** [a]Representing their kingdoms (compare verse 23)   **7:25** [a]Literally *wear out*

27 Then the kingdom and dominion,
  And the greatness of the kingdoms
    under the whole heaven,
  Shall be given to the people, the saints
    of the Most High.
  His kingdom *is* an everlasting kingdom,
  And all dominions shall serve and
    obey Him.'

28"This *is* the end of the account.ᵃ As for me, Daniel, my thoughts greatly troubled me, and my countenance changed; but I kept the matter in my heart."

Vision of a Ram and a Goat

8 In the third year of the reign of King Belshazzar a vision appeared *to* me—to me, Daniel—after the one that appeared to me the first time. 2I saw in the vision, and it so happened while I was looking, that I *was* in Shushan, the citadel, which *is* in the province of Elam; and I saw in the vision that I was by the River Ulai. 3Then I lifted my eyes and saw, and there, standing beside the river, was a ram which had two horns, and the two horns *were* high; but one *was* higher than the other, and the higher *one* came up last. 4I saw the ram pushing westward, northward, and southward, so that no animal could withstand him; nor *was there any* that could deliver from his hand, but he did according to his will and became great.

5And as I was considering, suddenly a male goat came from the west, across the surface of the whole earth, without touching the ground; and the goat *had* a notable horn between his eyes. 6Then he came to the ram that had two horns, which I had seen standing beside the river, and ran at him with furious power. 7And I saw him confronting the ram; he was moved with rage against him, attacked the ram, and broke his two horns. There was no power in the ram to withstand him, but he cast him down to the ground and trampled him; and there was no one that could deliver the ram from his hand.

8Therefore the male goat grew very great; but when he became strong, the large horn was broken, and in place of it four notable ones came up toward the four winds of heaven. 9And out of one of them came a little horn which grew exceedingly great toward the south, toward the east, and toward the Glorious *Land.* 10And it grew up to the host of heaven; and it cast down *some* of the host and *some* of the stars to the ground, and trampled them. 11He even exalted *himself* as high as the Prince of the host; and by him the daily *sacrifices* were taken away, and the place of His sanctuary was cast down. 12Because of transgression, an army was given over *to the horn* to oppose the daily *sacrifices;* and he cast truth down to the ground. He did *all this* and prospered.

13Then I heard a holy one speaking; and *another* holy one said to that certain *one* who was speaking, "How long *will* the vision *be, concerning* the daily *sacrifices* and the transgression of desolation, the giving of both the sanctuary and the host to be trampled underfoot?"

14And he said to me, "For two thousand three hundred days;ᵃ then the sanctuary shall be cleansed."

Gabriel Interprets the Vision

15Then it happened, when I, Daniel, had seen the vision and was seeking the meaning, that suddenly there stood before me one having the appearance of a man. 16And I heard a man's voice between *the banks of* the Ulai, who called, and said, "Gabriel, make this *man* understand the vision." 17So he came near where I stood, and when he came I was afraid and fell on my face; but he said to me, "Understand, son of man, that the vision *refers* to the time of the end."

18Now, as he was speaking with me, I was in a deep sleep with my face to the ground; but he touched me, and stood me upright. 19And he said, "Look, I am making known to you what shall happen in the latter time of the indignation; for at the appointed time the end *shall be.* 20The ram which you saw, having the two horns—*they are* the kings of Media and Persia. 21And the male goat *is* the kingdomᵃ of Greece. The large horn that *is* between its eyes *is* the first king. 22As for the broken *horn* and the four

---

7:28 ᵃLiterally *the word*   **8:14** ᵃLiterally *evening-mornings*   **8:21** ᵃLiterally *king,* representing his kingdom (compare 7:17, 23)

PRAYER FOR THE PEOPLE

U.S. ARMY'S FIRST DIVISION,
OMAHA BEACH

PRAYER

*Then I set my
face toward the
Lord God. . . .*

DANIEL 9:3

The circumstances were different, but centuries later another leader went before God for his people's sake, praying for His mercy and help. This is the prayer originally entitled "Let Our Hearts Be Stout," read to the nation on radio by President Franklin D. Roosevelt as Allied troops were invading Nazi-occupied Europe on D-Day, June 6, 1944:

Almighty God, our sons, pride of our nation, this day have set upon a mighty endeavor, a struggle to preserve our Republic, our religion, and our civilization, and to set free a suffering humanity. Lead them straight and true; give strength to their arms, stoutness to their hearts, steadfastness in their faith.

They will need Thy blessings. Their road will be long and hard. For the enemy is strong. He may hurl back our forces. Success may not come with rushing speed, but we shall return again and again; and we know that by Thy grace, and by the righteousness of our cause, our sons will triumph.

. . . For these men are lately drawn from the ways of peace. They fight not for the lust of conquest. They fight to end conquest. They fight to liberate. They fight to let justice arise and tolerance and goodwill among all Thy people. They yearn but for the end of battle, for their return to the haven of home. Some will never return. Embrace these, Father, and receive them, Thy heroic servants, into Thy kingdom.

And for us at home—fathers, mothers, children, wives, sisters, and brothers of brave men overseas, whose thoughts and prayers are ever with them—help us, Almighty God, to rededicate ourselves in renewed faith in Thee in this hour of great sacrifice. . . . And let our hearts be stout, to wait out the long travail, to bear sorrows that may come, to impart our courage unto our sons wheresoever they may be.

. . . With Thy blessing, we shall prevail over the unholy forces of our enemy. Help us to conquer the apostles of greed and racial arrogances. Lead us to the saving of our country, and with our sister nations into a world unity that will spell a sure peace—a peace invulnerable to the schemings of unworthy men. And a peace that will let all of men live in freedom, reaping the just rewards of their honest toil.

Thy will be done, Almighty God. Amen.

that stood up in its place, four kingdoms shall arise out of that nation, but not with its power.

23 "And in the latter time of their kingdom,
When the transgressors have reached their fullness,
A king shall arise,
Having fierce features,
Who understands sinister schemes.
24 His power shall be mighty, but not by his own power;
He shall destroy fearfully,
And shall prosper and thrive;
He shall destroy the mighty, and *also* the holy people.

25 "Through his cunning
He shall cause deceit to prosper under his rule;ᵃ
And he shall exalt *himself* in his heart.
He shall destroy many in *their* prosperity.
He shall even rise against the Prince of princes;
But he shall be broken without *human* means.ᵇ

26 "And the vision of the evenings and mornings
Which was told is true;
Therefore seal up the vision,
For *it refers* to many days *in the future.*"

27 And I, Daniel, fainted and was sick for days; afterward I arose and went about the king's business. I was astonished by the vision, but no one understood it.

Daniel's Prayer for the People

9 In the first year of Darius the son of Ahasuerus, of the lineage of the Medes, who was made king over the realm of the Chaldeans— 2in the first year of his reign I, Daniel, understood by the books the number of the years *specified* by the word of the LORD through Jeremiah the prophet, that He would accomplish seventy years in the desolations of Jerusalem.

3Then I set my face toward the Lord God to make request by prayer and supplications, with fasting, sackcloth, and ashes. 4And I

prayed to the LORD my God, and made confession, and said, "O Lord, great and awesome God, who keeps His covenant and mercy with those who love Him, and with those who keep His commandments, 5we have sinned and committed iniquity, we have done wickedly and rebelled, even by departing from Your precepts and Your judgments. 6Neither have we heeded Your servants the prophets, who spoke in Your name to our kings and our princes, to our fathers and all the people of the land. 7O Lord, righteousness *belongs* to You, but to us shame of face, as *it is* this day—to the men of Judah, to the inhabitants of Jerusalem and all Israel, those near and those far off in all the countries to which You have driven them, because of the unfaithfulness which they have committed against You.

8"O Lord, to us *belongs* shame of face, to our kings, our princes, and our fathers, because we have sinned against You. 9To the Lord our God *belong* mercy and forgiveness, though we have rebelled against Him. 10We have not obeyed the voice of the LORD our God, to walk in His laws, which He set before us by His servants the prophets. 11Yes, all Israel has transgressed Your law, and has departed so as not to obey Your voice; therefore the curse and the oath written in the Law of Moses the servant of God have been poured out on us, because we have sinned against Him. 12And He has confirmed His words, which He spoke against us and against our judges who judged us, by bringing upon us a great disaster; for under the whole heaven such has never been done as what has been done to Jerusalem.

13"As *it is* written in the Law of Moses, all this disaster has come upon us; yet we have not made our prayer before the LORD our God, that we might turn from our iniquities and understand Your truth. 14Therefore the LORD has kept the disaster in mind, and brought it upon us; for the LORD our God *is* righteous in all the works which He does, though we have not obeyed His voice. 15And now, O Lord our God, who brought Your people out of the land of Egypt with a mighty hand, and made Yourself a name,

---

8:25 ᵃLiterally *hand* ᵇLiterally *hand*

as *it is* this day—we have sinned, we have done wickedly!

¹⁶"O Lord, according to all Your righteousness, I pray, let Your anger and Your fury be turned away from Your city Jerusalem, Your holy mountain; because for our sins, and for the iniquities of our fathers, Jerusalem and Your people *are* a reproach to all *those* around us. ¹⁷Now therefore, our God, hear the prayer of Your servant, and his supplications, and for the Lord's sake cause Your face to shine on Your sanctuary, which is desolate. ¹⁸O my God, incline Your ear and hear; open Your eyes and see our desolations, and the city which is called by Your name; for we do not present our supplications before You because of our righteous deeds, but because of Your great mercies. ¹⁹O Lord, hear! O Lord, forgive! O Lord, listen and act! Do not delay for Your own sake, my God, for Your city and Your people are called by Your name."

The Seventy-Weeks Prophecy

²⁰Now while I *was* speaking, praying, and confessing my sin and the sin of my people Israel, and presenting my supplication before the Lord my God for the holy mountain of my God, ²¹yes, while I *was* speaking in prayer, the man Gabriel, whom I had seen in the vision at the beginning, being caused to fly swiftly, reached me about the time of the evening offering. ²²And he informed *me,* and talked with me, and said, "O Daniel, I have now come forth to give you skill to understand. ²³At the beginning of your supplications the command went out, and I have come to tell *you,* for you *are* greatly beloved; therefore consider the matter, and understand the vision:

²⁴ "Seventy weeks^a are determined
    For your people and for your holy city,
    To finish the transgression,
    To make an end of^b sins,
    To make reconciliation for iniquity,
    To bring in everlasting righteousness,
    To seal up vision and prophecy,
    And to anoint the Most Holy.

²⁵ "Know therefore and understand,
    That from the going forth of the
      command

    To restore and build Jerusalem
    Until Messiah the Prince,
    There shall be seven weeks and sixty-
      two weeks;
    The street^a shall be built again, and
      the wall,^b
    Even in troublesome times.

²⁶ "And after the sixty-two weeks
    Messiah shall be cut off, but not for
      Himself;
    And the people of the prince who is
      to come
    Shall destroy the city and the sanctuary.
    The end of it *shall be* with a flood,
    And till the end of the war desolations
      are determined.

²⁷   Then he shall confirm a covenant
      with many for one week;
    But in the middle of the week
    He shall bring an end to sacrifice and
      offering.
    And on the wing of abominations
      shall be one who makes desolate,
    Even until the consummation, which
      is determined,
    Is poured out on the desolate."

Vision of the Glorious Man

10 In the third year of Cyrus king of Persia a message was revealed to Daniel, whose name was called Belteshazzar. The message *was* true, but the appointed time *was* long;^a and he understood the message, and had understanding of the vision. ²In those days I, Daniel, was mourning three full weeks. ³I ate no pleasant food, no meat or wine came into my mouth, nor did I anoint myself at all, till three whole weeks were fulfilled.

⁴Now on the twenty-fourth day of the first month, as I was by the side of the great river, that *is,* the Tigris,^a ⁵I lifted my eyes and looked, and behold, a certain man clothed in linen, whose waist *was* girded with gold of Uphaz! ⁶His body *was* like beryl, his face like the appearance of lightning, his eyes

---

9:24 ^aLiterally *sevens,* and so throughout the chapter ^bFollowing Qere, Septuagint, Syriac, and Vulgate; Kethib and Theodotion read *To seal up.*
9:25 ^aOr *open square* ^bOr *moat*   **10:1** ^aOr *and of great conflict*   **10:4** ^aHebrew *Hiddekel*

like torches of fire, his arms and feet like burnished bronze in color, and the sound of his words like the voice of a multitude.

[7]And I, Daniel, alone saw the vision, for the men who were with me did not see the vision; but a great terror fell upon them, so that they fled to hide themselves. [8]Therefore I was left alone when I saw this great vision, and no strength remained in me; for my vigor was turned to frailty in me, and I retained no strength. [9]Yet I heard the sound of his words; and while I heard the sound of his words I was in a deep sleep on my face, with my face to the ground.

Prophecies Concerning Persia and Greece

[10]Suddenly, a hand touched me, which made me tremble on my knees and *on* the palms of my hands. [11]And he said to me, "O Daniel, man greatly beloved, understand the words that I speak to you, and stand upright, for I have now been sent to you." While he was speaking this word to me, I stood trembling.

[12]Then he said to me, "Do not fear, Daniel, for from the first day that you set your heart to understand, and to humble yourself before your God, your words were heard; and I have come because of your words. [13]But the prince of the kingdom of Persia withstood me twenty-one days; and behold, Michael, one of the chief princes, came to help me, for I had been left alone there with the kings of Persia. [14]Now I have come to make you understand what will happen to your people in the latter days, for the vision *refers* to *many* days yet *to come.*"

[15]When he had spoken such words to me, I turned my face toward the ground and became speechless. [16]And suddenly, *one* having the likeness of the sons[a] of men touched my lips; then I opened my mouth and spoke, saying to him who stood before me, "My lord, because of the vision my sorrows have overwhelmed me, and I have retained no strength. [17]For how can this servant of my lord talk with you, my lord? As for me, no strength remains in me now, nor is any breath left in me."

[18]Then again, *the one* having the likeness of a man touched me and strengthened me. [19]And he said, "O man greatly beloved, fear not! Peace *be* to you; be strong, yes, be strong!"

So when he spoke to me I was strengthened, and said, "Let my lord speak, for you have strengthened me."

[20]Then he said, "Do you know why I have come to you? And now I must return to fight with the prince of Persia; and when I have gone forth, indeed the prince of Greece will come. [21]But I will tell you what is noted in the Scripture of Truth. (No one upholds me against these, except Michael your prince.

11 "Also in the first year of Darius the Mede, I, *even* I, stood up to confirm and strengthen him.) [2]And now I will tell you the truth: Behold, three more kings will arise in Persia, and the fourth shall be far richer than *them* all; by his strength, through his riches, he shall stir up all against the realm of Greece. [3]Then a mighty king shall arise, who shall rule with great dominion, and do according to his will. [4]And when he has arisen, his kingdom shall be broken up and divided toward the four winds of heaven, but not among his posterity nor according to his dominion with which he ruled; for his kingdom shall be uprooted, even for others besides these.

Warring Kings of North and South

[5]"Also the king of the South shall become strong, as well as *one* of his princes; and he shall gain power over him and have dominion. His dominion *shall be* a great dominion. [6]And at the end of *some* years they shall join forces, for the daughter of the king of the South shall go to the king of the North to make an agreement; but she shall not retain the power of her authority,[a] and neither he nor his authority[b] shall stand; but she shall be given up, with those who brought her, and with him who begot her, and with him who strengthened her in *those* times. [7]But from a branch of her roots *one* shall arise in his place, who shall come with an army, enter the fortress of the king of the North, and deal with them and prevail.

10:16 [a]Theodotion and Vulgate read *the son;* Septuagint reads *a hand.*   **11:6** [a]Literally *arm* [b]Literally *arm*

⁸And he shall also carry their gods captive to Egypt, with their princesᵃ *and* their precious articles of silver and gold; and he shall continue *more* years than the king of the North.

⁹"Also *the king of the North* shall come to the kingdom of the king of the South, but shall return to his own land. ¹⁰However his sons shall stir up strife, and assemble a multitude of great forces; and *one* shall certainly come and overwhelm and pass through; then he shall return to his fortress and stir up strife.

¹¹"And the king of the South shall be moved with rage, and go out and fight with him, with the king of the North, who shall muster a great multitude; but the multitude shall be given into the hand of his *enemy.* ¹²When he has taken away the multitude, his heart will be lifted up; and he will cast down tens of thousands, but he will not prevail. ¹³For the king of the North will return and muster a multitude greater than the former, and shall certainly come at the end of some years with a great army and much equipment.

¹⁴"Now in those times many shall rise up against the king of the South. Also, violent menᵃ of your people shall exalt themselves in fulfillment of the vision, but they shall fall. ¹⁵So the king of the North shall come and build a siege mound, and take a fortified city; and the forcesᵃ of the South shall not withstand *him.* Even his choice troops *shall have* no strength to resist. ¹⁶But he who comes against him shall do according to his own will, and no one shall stand against him. He shall stand in the Glorious Land with destruction in his power.ᵃ

¹⁷"He shall also set his face to enter with the strength of his whole kingdom, and upright onesᵃ with him; thus shall he do. And he shall give him the daughter of women to destroy it; but she shall not stand *with him,* or be for him. ¹⁸After this he shall turn his face to the coastlands, and shall take many. But a ruler shall bring the reproach against them to an end; and with the reproach removed, he shall turn back on him. ¹⁹Then he shall turn his face toward the fortress of his own land; but he shall stumble and fall, and not be found.

²⁰"There shall arise in his place one who imposes taxes *on* the glorious kingdom; but within a few days he shall be destroyed, but not in anger or in battle. ²¹And in his place shall arise a vile person, to whom they will not give the honor of royalty; but he shall come in peaceably, and seize the kingdom by intrigue. ²²With the forceᵃ of a flood they shall be swept away from before him and be broken, and also the prince of the covenant. ²³And after the league *is made* with him he shall act deceitfully, for he shall come up and become strong with a small *number of* people. ²⁴He shall enter peaceably, even into the richest places of the province; and he shall do *what* his fathers have not done, nor his forefathers: he shall disperse among them the plunder, spoil, and riches; and he shall devise his plans against the strongholds, but *only* for a time.

²⁵"He shall stir up his power and his courage against the king of the South with a great army. And the king of the South shall be stirred up to battle with a very great and mighty army; but he shall not stand, for they shall devise plans against him. ²⁶Yes, those who eat of the portion of his delicacies shall destroy him; his army shall be swept away, and many shall fall down slain. ²⁷Both these kings' hearts *shall be* bent on evil, and they shall speak lies at the same table; but it shall not prosper, for the end *will* still *be* at the appointed time. ²⁸While returning to his land with great riches, his heart shall be *moved* against the holy covenant; so he shall do *damage* and return to his own land.

The Northern King's Blasphemies

²⁹"At the appointed time he shall return and go toward the south; but it shall not be like the former or the latter. ³⁰For ships from Cyprusᵃ shall come against him; therefore he shall be grieved, and return in rage against the holy covenant, and do *damage.*

"So he shall return and show regard for those who forsake the holy covenant. ³¹And

---

11:8 ᵃOr *molded images*   **11:14** ᵃOr *robbers,* literally *sons of breakage*   **11:15** ᵃLiterally *arms*   **11:16** ᵃLiterally *hand*   **11:17** ᵃOr *bring equitable terms*   **11:22** ᵃLiterally *arms*   **11:30** ᵃHebrew *Kittim,* western lands, especially Cyprus

forces[a] shall be mustered by him, and they shall defile the sanctuary fortress; then they shall take away the daily *sacrifices,* and place *there* the abomination of desolation. [32]Those who do wickedly against the covenant he shall corrupt with flattery; but the people who know their God shall be strong, and carry out *great exploits.* [33]And those of the people who understand shall instruct many; yet *for many* days they shall fall by sword and flame, by captivity and plundering. [34]Now when they fall, they shall be aided with a little help; but many shall join with them by intrigue. [35]And *some* of those of understanding shall fall, to refine them, purify *them,* and make *them* white, *until* the time of the end; because *it is* still for the appointed time.

[36]"Then the king shall do according to his own will: he shall exalt and magnify himself above every god, shall speak blasphemies against the God of gods, and shall prosper till the wrath has been accomplished; for what has been determined shall be done. [37]He shall regard neither the God[a] of his fathers nor the desire of women, nor regard any god; for he shall exalt himself above *them* all. [38]But in their place he shall honor a god of fortresses; and a god which his fathers did not know he shall honor with gold and silver, with precious stones and pleasant things. [39]Thus he shall act against the strongest fortresses with a foreign god, which he shall acknowledge, *and* advance *its* glory; and he shall cause them to rule over many, and divide the land for gain.

The Northern King's Conquests

[40]"At the time of the end the king of the South shall attack him; and the king of the North shall come against him like a whirlwind, with chariots, horsemen, and with many ships; and he shall enter the countries, overwhelm *them,* and pass through. [41]He shall also enter the Glorious Land, and many *countries* shall be overthrown; but these shall escape from his hand: Edom, Moab, and the prominent people of Ammon. [42]He shall stretch out his hand against the countries, and the land of Egypt shall not escape. [43]He shall have

power over the treasures of gold and silver, and over all the precious things of Egypt; also the Libyans and Ethiopians *shall follow* at his heels. [44]But news from the east and the north shall trouble him; therefore he shall go out with great fury to destroy and annihilate many. [45]And he shall plant the tents of his palace between the seas and the glorious holy mountain; yet he shall come to his end, and no one will help him.

Prophecy of the End Time

12 "At that time Michael shall stand up,
The great prince who stands *watch*
    over the sons of your people;
And there shall be a time of trouble,
Such as never was since there was a
    nation,
Even to that time.
And at that time your people shall
    be delivered,
Every one who is found written in
    the book.
2   And many of those who sleep in the
        dust of the earth shall awake,
Some to everlasting life,
Some to shame *and* everlasting
    contempt.
3   Those who are wise shall shine
Like the brightness of the firmament,
And those who turn many to
    righteousness
Like the stars forever and ever.

[4]"But you, Daniel, shut up the words, and seal the book until the time of the end; many shall run to and fro, and knowledge shall increase."

[5]Then I, Daniel, looked; and there stood two others, one on this riverbank and the other on that riverbank. [6]And *one* said to the man clothed in linen, who *was* above the waters of the river, "How long shall the fulfillment of these wonders *be?*"

[7]Then I heard the man clothed in linen, who *was* above the waters of the river, when he held up his right hand and his left hand to heaven, and swore by Him who lives forever, that *it shall be* for a time,

---

11:31 [a]Literally *arms*   **11:37** [a]Or *gods*

times, and half *a time;* and when the power of the holy people has been completely shattered, all these *things* shall be finished.

⁸Although I heard, I did not understand. Then I said, "My lord, what *shall be* the end of these *things?"*

⁹And he said, "Go *your way,* Daniel, for the words *are* closed up and sealed till the time of the end. ¹⁰Many shall be purified, made white, and refined, but the wicked shall do wickedly; and none of the wicked shall understand, but the wise shall understand.

¹¹"And from the time *that* the daily *sacrifice* is taken away, and the abomination of desolation is set up, *there shall be* one thousand two hundred and ninety days. ¹²Blessed *is* he who waits, and comes to the one thousand three hundred and thirty-five days.

¹³"But you, go *your way* till the end; for you shall rest, and will arise to your inheritance at the end of the days."

HOSEA

Author: Hosea

When Written: Around 750 B.C.

Theme: Return to God

Key Verses: Hosea 4:1—Hear the word of the LORD, you children of Israel, for the LORD brings a charge against the inhabitants of the land: "There is no truth or mercy or knowledge of God in the land."

Key Chapter: Hosea 4—This key chapter illustrates how the nation of Israel left the knowledge of the truth in favor of the idolatry of their pagan neighbors.

The theme of Hosea—a man's love for his unfaithful spouse—illustrates the faithful love that God has for his people even when they turn from Him. Just as Hosea pursued his adulterous wife, so too God pursues His people in order to show them His love and forgiveness.

Charles Colson, founder of Prison Fellowship, experienced a first-hand encounter with this pursuing love of God. As a high-powered attorney and member of President Richard Nixon's White House inner circle, Colson was considered one of the most powerful men in Washington, D.C. His ruthless tactics as Mr. Nixon's political "hatchet man" also made him one of the most hated. But when the consequences of the infamous Watergate scandal sent him to federal prison, the cynical and self-sufficient Colson was confronted with something he could not earn and did not deserve—the love and mercy of God.

HOSEA

1 The word of the LORD that came to Hosea the son of Beeri, in the days of Uzziah, Jotham, Ahaz, *and* Hezekiah, kings of Judah, and in the days of Jeroboam the son of Joash, king of Israel.

The Family of Hosea

²When the LORD began to speak by Hosea, the LORD said to Hosea:

> "Go, take yourself a wife of harlotry
> And children of harlotry,
> For the land has committed great
>   harlotry
> *By departing* from the LORD."

³So he went and took Gomer the daughter of Diblaim, and she conceived and bore him a son. ⁴Then the LORD said to him:

> "Call his name Jezreel,
> For in a little *while*
> I will avenge the bloodshed of Jezreel
>   on the house of Jehu,
> And bring an end to the kingdom of
>   the house of Israel.
> ⁵ It shall come to pass in that day
> That I will break the bow of Israel in
>   the Valley of Jezreel."

⁶And she conceived again and bore a daughter. Then *God* said to him:

> "Call her name Lo-Ruhamah,ᵃ
> For I will no longer have mercy on the
>   house of Israel,
> But I will utterly take them away.ᵇ
> ⁷ Yet I will have mercy on the house of
>   Judah,
> Will save them by the LORD their God,
> And will not save them by bow,
> Nor by sword or battle,
> By horses or horsemen."

⁸Now when she had weaned Lo-Ruhamah, she conceived and bore a son. ⁹Then *God* said:

> "Call his name Lo-Ammi,ᵃ
> For you *are* not My people,
> And I will not be your *God*.

The Restoration of Israel

> ¹⁰ "Yet the number of the children of Israel
>   Shall be as the sand of the sea,
>   Which cannot be measured or
>   numbered.
>   And it shall come to pass
>   In the place where it was said to them,
>   'You *are* not My people,'ᵃ
>   *There* it shall be said to them,
>   '*You are* sons of the living God.'
> ¹¹ Then the children of Judah and the
>   children of Israel
>   Shall be gathered together,
>   And appoint for themselves one head;
>   And they shall come up out of the
>   land,
>   For great *will be* the day of Jezreel!

2 Say to your brethren, 'My people,'ᵃ
And to your sisters, 'Mercyᵇ *is shown*.'

God's Unfaithful People

> ² "Bring charges against your mother,
>   bring charges;
>   For she *is* not My wife, nor *am* I her
>   Husband!
>   Let her put away her harlotries from
>   her sight,
>   And her adulteries from between her
>   breasts;
> ³ Lest I strip her naked
>   And expose her, as in the day she was
>   born,
>   And make her like a wilderness,
>   And set her like a dry land,
>   And slay her with thirst.

1:6 ᵃLiterally *No-Mercy* ᵇOr *That I may forgive them at all*   **1:9** ᵃLiterally *Not-My-People*
1:10 ᵃHebrew *lo-ammi* (compare verse 9)
2:1 ᵃHebrew *Ammi* (compare 1:9, 10) ᵇHebrew *Ruhamah* (compare 1:6)

4 "I will not have mercy on her children,
  For they *are* the children of harlotry.
5 For their mother has played the harlot;
  She who conceived them has behaved
    shamefully.
  For she said, 'I will go after my lovers,
  Who give *me* my bread and my water,
  My wool and my linen,
  My oil and my drink.'

6 "Therefore, behold,
  I will hedge up your way with thorns,
  And wall her in,
  So that she cannot find her paths.
7 She will chase her lovers,
  But not overtake them;
  Yes, she will seek them, but not find
    them.
  Then she will say,
  'I will go and return to my first husband,
  For then *it was* better for me than now.'
8 For she did not know
  That I gave her grain, new wine, and
    oil,
  And multiplied her silver and gold—
  Which they prepared for Baal.

9 "Therefore I will return and take away
  My grain in its time
  And My new wine in its season,
  And will take back My wool and My
    linen,
  Given to cover her nakedness.
10 Now I will uncover her lewdness in
    the sight of her lovers,
  And no one shall deliver her from
    My hand.
11 I will also cause all her mirth to
    cease,
  Her feast days,
  Her New Moons,
  Her Sabbaths—
  All her appointed feasts.

12 "And I will destroy her vines and her
    fig trees,
  Of which she has said,
  'These *are* my wages that my lovers
    have given me.'
  So I will make them a forest,
  And the beasts of the field shall eat
    them.

13 I will punish her
  For the days of the Baals to which she
    burned incense.
  She decked herself with her earrings
    and jewelry,
  And went after her lovers;
  But Me she forgot," says the LORD.

God's Mercy on His People

14 "Therefore, behold, I will allure her,
  Will bring her into the wilderness,
  And speak comfort to her.
15 I will give her her vineyards from
    there,
  And the Valley of Achor as a door
    of hope;
  She shall sing there,
  As in the days of her youth,
  As in the day when she came up
    from the land of Egypt.

16 "And it shall be, in that day,"
  Says the LORD,
  "*That* you will call Me 'My Husband,'[a]
  And no longer call Me 'My Master,'[b]
17 For I will take from her mouth the
    names of the Baals,
  And they shall be remembered by
    their name no more.
18 In that day I will make a covenant
    for them
  With the beasts of the field,
  With the birds of the air,
  And *with* the creeping things of the
    ground.
  Bow and sword of battle I will shatter
    from the earth,
  To make them lie down safely.

19 "I will betroth you to Me forever;
  Yes, I will betroth you to Me
  In righteousness and justice,
  In lovingkindness and mercy;
20 I will betroth you to Me in faithfulness,
  And you shall know the LORD.

21 "It shall come to pass in that day
  That I will answer," says the LORD;
  "I will answer the heavens,
  And they shall answer the earth.

2:16 [a]Hebrew *Ishi* [b]Hebrew *Baali*

22 The earth shall answer
With grain,
With new wine,
And with oil;
They shall answer Jezreel.ᵃ
23 Then I will sow her for Myself in the earth,
And I will have mercy on *her who had* not obtained mercy;ᵃ
Then I will say to *those who were* not My people,ᵇ
'You *are* My people!'
And they shall say, '*You are* my God!'"

Israel Will Return to God

3 Then the LORD said to me, "Go again, love a woman *who is* loved by a loverᵃ and is committing adultery, just like the love of the LORD for the children of Israel, who look to other gods and love *the* raisin cakes *of the pagans.*"

²So I bought her for myself for fifteen *shekels* of silver, and one and one-half *homers* of barley. ³And I said to her, "You shall stay with me many days; you shall not play the harlot, nor shall you have a man—so, too, *will* I *be* toward you."

⁴For the children of Israel shall abide many days without king or prince, without sacrifice or *sacred* pillar, without ephod or teraphim. ⁵Afterward the children of Israel shall return and seek the LORD their God and David their king. They shall fear the LORD and His goodness in the latter days.

God's Charge Against Israel

4 Hear the word of the LORD,
You children of Israel,
For the LORD *brings* a charge against the inhabitants of the land:

"There is no truth or mercy
Or knowledge of God in the land.
2 *By* swearing and lying,
Killing and stealing and committing adultery,
They break all restraint,
With bloodshed upon bloodshed.
3 Therefore the land will mourn;
And everyone who dwells there will waste away
With the beasts of the field

And the birds of the air;
Even the fish of the sea will be taken away.

4 "Now let no man contend, or rebuke another;
For your people *are* like those who contend with the priest.
5 Therefore you shall stumble in the day;
The prophet also shall stumble with you in the night;
And I will destroy your mother.
6 My people are destroyed for lack of knowledge.
Because you have rejected knowledge,
I also will reject you from being priest for Me;
Because you have forgotten the law of your God,
I also will forget your children.

7 "The more they increased,
The more they sinned against Me;
I will changeᵃ their gloryᵇ into shame.
8 They eat up the sin of My people;
They set their heart on their iniquity.
9 And it shall be: like people, like priest.
So I will punish them for their ways,
And reward them for their deeds.
10 For they shall eat, but not have enough;
They shall commit harlotry, but not increase;
Because they have ceased obeying the LORD.

The Idolatry of Israel

11 "Harlotry, wine, and new wine enslave the heart.
12 My people ask counsel from their wooden *idols,*
And their staff informs them.
For the spirit of harlotry has caused *them* to stray,
And they have played the harlot against their God.

2:22 ᵃLiterally *God Will Sow* **2:23** ᵃHebrew *lo-ruhamah* ᵇHebrew *lo-ammi* **3:1** ᵃLiterally *friend* or *husband* **4:7** ᵃFollowing Masoretic Text, Septuagint, and Vulgate; scribal tradition, Syriac, and Targum read *They will change.* ᵇFollowing Masoretic Text, Septuagint, Syriac, Targum, and Vulgate; scribal tradition reads *My glory.*

13 They offer sacrifices on the
    mountaintops,
  And burn incense on the hills,
  Under oaks, poplars, and terebinths,
  Because their shade *is* good.
  Therefore your daughters commit
    harlotry,
  And your brides commit adultery.

14 "I will not punish your daughters when
    they commit harlotry,
  Nor your brides when they commit
    adultery;
  For *the men* themselves go apart with
    harlots,
  And offer sacrifices with a ritual harlot.ᵃ
  Therefore people *who* do not
    understand will be trampled.

15 "Though you, Israel, play the harlot,
  Let not Judah offend.
  Do not come up to Gilgal,

  Nor go up to Beth Aven,
  Nor swear an oath, *saying,* 'As the
    LORD lives'—

16 "For Israel is stubborn
  Like a stubborn calf;
  Now the LORD will let them forage
  Like a lamb in open country.

17 "Ephraim *is* joined to idols,
  Let him alone.
18 Their drink is rebellion,
  They commit harlotry continually.
  Her rulers dearlyᵃ love dishonor.
19 The wind has wrapped her up in its
    wings,
  And they shall be ashamed because of
    their sacrifices.

4:14 ᵃCompare Deuteronomy 23:18
4:18 ᵃHebrew is difficult; a Jewish tradition reads
Her rulers shamefully love, 'Give!'

TRUTH

*"Because you have forgotten
the law of your God. . . ."*

HOSEA 4:6

Justice James Wilson

RELIGION AND LAW

Justice James Wilson was one of the Supreme Court's original members and a signer of both the Declaration of Independence and the Constitution. A major force in the drafting
of the Constitution, he wrote several legal works, including
a 1792 *Commentary on the Constitution of the United States of
America* and a three-volume set of legal lectures, delivered to
law students. Wilson played a significant role in laying the
early foundation of an American system of jurisprudence.
Notice what he taught his students:

> *It should always be remembered that this law, . . .
> made for men or for nations, flows from the same Divine
> source: it is the law of God. . . . What we do, indeed, must
> be founded on what He has done; and the deficiencies of
> our laws must be supplied by the perfections of His.
> Human law must rest its authority, ultimately, upon the
> authority of that law which is Divine. . . . We now see the
> deep and the solid foundations of human law. . . . From
> this short, but plain and, I hope, just statement of
> things, we perceive a principle of connection between all
> the learned professions; but especially between the two
> last mentioned [the profession of Divinity and the pro-
> fession of law]. Far from being rivals or enemies, religion
> and law are twin sisters, friends, and mutual assistants.
> Indeed, these two sciences run into each other.*

Impending Judgment on Israel and Judah

5 "Hear this, O priests!
  Take heed, O house of Israel!
  Give ear, O house of the king!
  For yours *is* the judgment,
  Because you have been a snare to
      Mizpah
  And a net spread on Tabor.
2 The revolters are deeply involved
      in slaughter,
  Though I rebuke them all.
3 I know Ephraim,
  And Israel is not hidden from Me;
  For now, O Ephraim, you commit
      harlotry;
  Israel is defiled.

4 "They do not direct their deeds
  Toward turning to their God,
  For the spirit of harlotry is in their midst,
  And they do not know the LORD.
5 The pride of Israel testifies to his face;
  Therefore Israel and Ephraim stumble
      in their iniquity;
  Judah also stumbles with them.

6 "With their flocks and herds
  They shall go to seek the LORD,
  But they will not find *Him;*
  He has withdrawn Himself from them.
7 They have dealt treacherously with
      the LORD,
  For they have begotten pagan children.
  Now a New Moon shall devour them
      and their heritage.

8 "Blow the ram's horn in Gibeah,
  The trumpet in Ramah!
  Cry aloud *at* Beth Aven,
  'Look behind you, O Benjamin!'
9 Ephraim shall be desolate in the day
      of rebuke;
  Among the tribes of Israel I make
      known what is sure.

10 "The princes of Judah are like those
      who remove a landmark;
  I will pour out My wrath on them like
      water.
11 Ephraim is oppressed *and* broken in
      judgment,

Because he willingly walked by *human*
      precept.
12 Therefore I *will be* to Ephraim like a
      moth,
  And to the house of Judah like
      rottenness.

13 "When Ephraim saw his sickness,
  And Judah *saw* his wound,
  Then Ephraim went to Assyria
  And sent to King Jareb;
  Yet he cannot cure you,
  Nor heal you of your wound.
14 For I *will be* like a lion to Ephraim,
  And like a young lion to the house
      of Judah.
  I, *even* I, will tear *them* and go away;
  I will take *them* away, and no one
      shall rescue.
15 I will return again to My place
  Till they acknowledge their offense.
  Then they will seek My face;
  In their affliction they will earnestly
      seek Me."

A Call to Repentance

6 Come, and let us return to the LORD;
  For He has torn, but He will heal us;
  He has stricken, but He will bind us up.
2 After two days He will revive us;
  On the third day He will raise us up,
  That we may live in His sight.
3 Let us know,
  Let us pursue the knowledge of the LORD.
  His going forth is established as the
      morning;
  He will come to us like the rain,
  Like the latter *and* former rain to the
      earth.

Impenitence of Israel and Judah

4 "O Ephraim, what shall I do to you?
  O Judah, what shall I do to you?
  For your faithfulness is like a morning
      cloud,
  And like the early dew it goes away.
5 Therefore I have hewn *them* by the
      prophets,
  I have slain them by the words of My
      mouth;
  And your judgments *are like* light *that*
      goes forth.

6 For I desire mercy and not sacrifice,
And the knowledge of God more than
burnt offerings.

7 "But like men[a] they transgressed the
covenant;
There they dealt treacherously with Me.
8 Gilead *is* a city of evildoers
And defiled with blood.
9 As bands of robbers lie in wait for a
man,
So the company of priests murder on
the way to Shechem;
Surely they commit lewdness.
10 I have seen a horrible thing in the
house of Israel:
There *is* the harlotry of Ephraim;
Israel is defiled.
11 Also, O Judah, a harvest is appointed
for you,
When I return the captives of My
people.

7 "When I would have healed Israel,
Then the iniquity of Ephraim was
uncovered,
And the wickedness of Samaria.
For they have committed fraud;
A thief comes in;
A band of robbers takes spoil outside.
2 They do not consider in their hearts
That I remember all their wickedness;
Now their own deeds have surrounded
them;
They are before My face.
3 They make a king glad with their
wickedness,
And princes with their lies.

4 "They *are* all adulterers.
Like an oven heated by a baker—
He ceases stirring *the fire* after
kneading the dough,
Until it is leavened.
5 In the day of our king
Princes have made *him* sick, inflamed
with wine;
He stretched out his hand with scoffers.
6 They prepare their heart like an oven,
While they lie in wait;
Their baker[a] sleeps all night;
In the morning it burns like a flaming
fire.

7 They are all hot, like an oven,
And have devoured their judges;
All their kings have fallen.
None among them calls upon Me.

8 "Ephraim has mixed himself among
the peoples;
Ephraim is a cake unturned.
9 Aliens have devoured his strength,
But he does not know *it;*
Yes, gray hairs are here and there on
him,
Yet he does not know *it.*
10 And the pride of Israel testifies to his
face,
But they do not return to the LORD
their God,
Nor seek Him for all this.

Futile Reliance on the Nations

11 "Ephraim also is like a silly dove,
without sense—
They call to Egypt,
They go to Assyria.
12 Wherever they go, I will spread My
net on them;
I will bring them down like birds of
the air;
I will chastise them
According to what their congregation
has heard.

13 "Woe to them, for they have fled from
Me!
Destruction to them,
Because they have transgressed
against Me!
Though I redeemed them,
Yet they have spoken lies against Me.
14 They did not cry out to Me with their
heart
When they wailed upon their beds.

"They assemble together for[a] grain and
new wine,

6:7 [a]Or *like Adam*   **7:6** [a]Following Masoretic Text
and Vulgate; Syriac and Targum read *Their anger;*
Septuagint reads *Ephraim.*   **7:14** [a]Following
Masoretic Text and Targum; Vulgate reads *thought
upon;* Septuagint reads *slashed themselves for* (compare
1 Kings 18:28).

They rebel against Me;[b]

15 Though I disciplined *and* strengthened
their arms,
Yet they devise evil against Me;
16 They return, *but* not to the Most High;[a]
They are like a treacherous bow.
Their princes shall fall by the sword
For the cursings of their tongue.
This *shall be* their derision in the land
of Egypt.

The Apostasy of Israel

8 "*Set* the trumpet[a] to your mouth!
He shall come like an eagle against
the house of the LORD,
Because they have transgressed My
covenant
And rebelled against My law.
2 Israel will cry to Me,
'My God, we know You!'
3 Israel has rejected the good;
The enemy will pursue him.

4 "They set up kings, but not by Me;
They made princes, but I did not
acknowledge *them*.
From their silver and gold
They made idols for themselves—
That they might be cut off.
5 Your calf is rejected, O Samaria!
My anger is aroused against them—
How long until they attain to innocence?
6 For from Israel *is* even this:
A workman made it, and it *is* not God;
But the calf of Samaria shall be
broken to pieces.

7 "They sow the wind,
And reap the whirlwind.
The stalk has no bud;
It shall never produce meal.
If it should produce,
Aliens would swallow it up.
8 Israel is swallowed up;
Now they are among the Gentiles
Like a vessel in which *is* no pleasure.
9 For they have gone up to Assyria,
Like a wild donkey alone by itself;
Ephraim has hired lovers.
10 Yes, though they have hired among
the nations,
Now I will gather them;

And they shall sorrow a little,[a]
Because of the burden[b] of the king
of princes.

11 "Because Ephraim has made many
altars for sin,
They have become for him altars for
sinning.
12 I have written for him the great things
of My law,
But they were considered a strange
thing.
13 *For* the sacrifices of My offerings they
sacrifice flesh and eat *it*,
But the LORD does not accept them.
Now He will remember their iniquity
and punish their sins.
They shall return to Egypt.

HONOR
"For Israel has forgotten his Maker. . . ."
HOSEA 8:14

America, Never Forget
Carlos Romulo (1899–1985), a Philippine general
renowned for his heroic activities during World
War II, stated:

*Never forget, Americans, that yours is a spiri-
tual country. Yes, I know you're a practical
people. Like others, I've marveled at your fac-
tories, your skyscrapers, and your arsenals.
But underlying everything else is the fact that
America began as a God-loving, God-fearing,
God-worshipping people.*

14 "For Israel has forgotten his Maker,
And has built temples;[a]
Judah also has multiplied fortified cities;
But I will send fire upon his cities,
And it shall devour his palaces."

Judgment of Israel's Sin

9 Do not rejoice, O Israel, with joy like
other peoples,
For you have played the harlot
against your God.

7:14 [b]Following Masoretic Text, Syriac, and Targum;
Septuagint omits *They rebel against Me*; Vulgate reads
They departed from Me.   **7:16** [a]Or *upward*
8:1 [a]Hebrew *shophar*, ram's horn   **8:10** [a]Or *begin
to diminish* [b]Or *oracle*   **8:14** [a]Or *palaces*

You have made love *for* hire on every
   threshing floor.
2 The threshing floor and the winepress
Shall not feed them,
And the new wine shall fail in her.

3 They shall not dwell in the Lord's land,
But Ephraim shall return to Egypt,
And shall eat unclean *things* in Assyria.
4 They shall not offer wine *offerings* to
   the Lord,
Nor shall their sacrifices be pleasing
   to Him.
It shall be like bread of mourners to
   them;
All who eat it shall be defiled.
For their bread *shall be* for their *own* life;
It shall not come into the house of the
   Lord.

5 What will you do in the appointed day,
And in the day of the feast of the Lord?
6 For indeed they are gone because of
   destruction.
Egypt shall gather them up;
Memphis shall bury them.
Nettles shall possess their valuables
   of silver;
Thorns *shall be* in their tents.

7 The days of punishment have come;
The days of recompense have come.
Israel knows!
The prophet *is* a fool,
The spiritual man *is* insane,
Because of the greatness of your
   iniquity and great enmity.
8 The watchman of Ephraim *is* with my
   God;
But the prophet *is* a fowler's[a] snare in
   all his ways—
Enmity in the house of his God.
9 They are deeply corrupted,
As in the days of Gibeah.
He will remember their iniquity;
He will punish their sins.

10 "I found Israel
Like grapes in the wilderness;
I saw your fathers
As the firstfruits on the fig tree in its
   first season.

But they went to Baal Peor,
And separated themselves *to that*
   shame;
They became an abomination like
   the thing they loved.
11 *As for* Ephraim, their glory shall fly
   away like a bird—
No birth, no pregnancy, and no
   conception!
12 Though they bring up their children,
Yet I will bereave them to the last man.
Yes, woe to them when I depart from
   them!
13 Just as I saw Ephraim like Tyre,
   planted in a pleasant place,
So Ephraim will bring out his children
   to the murderer."

14 Give them, O Lord—
What will You give?
Give them a miscarrying womb
And dry breasts!

15 "All their wickedness *is* in Gilgal,
For there I hated them.
Because of the evil of their deeds
I will drive them from My house;
I will love them no more.
All their princes *are* rebellious.
16 Ephraim is stricken,
Their root is dried up;
They shall bear no fruit.
Yes, were they to bear children,
I would kill the darlings of their womb."

17 My God will cast them away,
Because they did not obey Him;
And they shall be wanderers among
   the nations.

Israel's Sin and Captivity

10 Israel empties *his* vine;
   He brings forth fruit for himself.
According to the multitude of his fruit
He has increased the altars;
According to the bounty of his land
They have embellished *his sacred*
   pillars.
2 Their heart is divided;
Now they are held guilty.

9:8 [a]That is, one who catches birds in a trap or snare

He will break down their altars;
He will ruin their *sacred* pillars.

3   For now they say,
"We have no king,
Because we did not fear the LORD.
And as for a king, what would he do
    for us?"
4   They have spoken words,
Swearing falsely in making a covenant.
Thus judgment springs up like
    hemlock in the furrows of the field.

5   The inhabitants of Samaria fear
Because of the calf[a] of Beth Aven.
For its people mourn for it,
And its priests shriek for it—
Because its glory has departed from it.
6   *The idol* also shall be carried to Assyria
As a present for King Jareb.
Ephraim shall receive shame,
And Israel shall be ashamed of his
    own counsel.

7   *As for* Samaria, her king is cut off
Like a twig on the water.
8   Also the high places of Aven, the sin
    of Israel,
Shall be destroyed.
The thorn and thistle shall grow on
    their altars;
They shall say to the mountains,
"Cover us!"
And to the hills, "Fall on us!"

9   "O Israel, you have sinned from the
    days of Gibeah;
There they stood.
The battle in Gibeah against the
    children of iniquity[a]
Did not overtake them.
10   When *it is* My desire, I will chasten
    them.
Peoples shall be gathered against them
When I bind them for their two
    transgressions.[a]
11   Ephraim *is* a trained heifer
That loves to thresh *grain;*
But I harnessed her fair neck,
I will make Ephraim pull *a plow.*
Judah shall plow;
Jacob shall break his clods."

12   Sow for yourselves righteousness;
Reap in mercy;
Break up your fallow ground,
For *it is* time to seek the LORD,
Till He comes and rains righteousness
    on you.

13   You have plowed wickedness;
You have reaped iniquity.
You have eaten the fruit of lies,
Because you trusted in your own way,
In the multitude of your mighty men.
14   Therefore tumult shall arise among
    your people,
And all your fortresses shall be
    plundered
As Shalman plundered Beth Arbel in
    the day of battle—
A mother dashed in pieces upon *her*
    children.
15   Thus it shall be done to you, O Bethel,
Because of your great wickedness.
At dawn the king of Israel
Shall be cut off utterly.

God's Continuing Love for Israel

11 "When Israel *was* a child, I loved him,
And out of Egypt I called My son.
2   *As* they called them,[a]
So they went from them;[b]
They sacrificed to the Baals,
And burned incense to carved images.

3   "I taught Ephraim to walk,
Taking them by their arms;[a]
But they did not know that I healed
    them.
4   I drew them with gentle cords,[a]
With bands of love,
And I was to them as those who take
    the yoke from their neck.[b]
I stooped *and* fed them.

10:5 [a]Literally *calves*   **10:9** [a]So read many Hebrew
manuscripts, Septuagint, and Vulgate; Masoretic Text
reads *unruliness.*   **10:10** [a]Or *in their two habitations*
11:2 [a]Following Masoretic Text and Vulgate;
Septuagint reads *Just as I called them;* Targum
interprets as *I sent prophets to a thousand of them.*
[b]Following Masoretic Text, Targum, and Vulgate;
Septuagint reads *from My face.*   **11:3** [a]Some
Hebrew manuscripts, Septuagint, Syriac, and Vulgate
read *My arms.*   **11:4** [a]Literally *cords of a man*
[b]Literally *jaws*

5 "He shall not return to the land of Egypt;
But the Assyrian shall be his king,
Because they refused to repent.
6 And the sword shall slash in his cities,
Devour his districts,
And consume *them,*
Because of their own counsels.
7 My people are bent on backsliding
    from Me.
Though they call to the Most High,ᵃ
None at all exalt *Him.*

8 "How can I give you up, Ephraim?
How can I hand you over, Israel?
How can I make you like Admah?
How can I set you like Zeboiim?
My heart churns within Me;
My sympathy is stirred.
9 I will not execute the fierceness of
    My anger;
I will not again destroy Ephraim.
For I *am* God, and not man,
The Holy One in your midst;
And I will not come with terror.ᵃ

10 "They shall walk after the LORD.
He will roar like a lion.
When He roars,
Then *His* sons shall come trembling
    from the west;
11 They shall come trembling like a bird
    from Egypt,
Like a dove from the land of Assyria.
And I will let them dwell in their
    houses,"
Says the LORD.

God's Charge Against Ephraim

12 "Ephraim has encircled Me with lies,
And the house of Israel with deceit;
But Judah still walks with God,
Even with the Holy Oneᵃ *who is* faithful.

12 "Ephraim feeds on the wind,
And pursues the east wind;
He daily increases lies and desolation.
Also they make a covenant with the
    Assyrians,
And oil is carried to Egypt.

2 "The LORD also *brings* a charge against
    Judah,

And will punish Jacob according to
    his ways;
According to his deeds He will
    recompense him.
3 He took his brother by the heel in the
    womb,
And in his strength he struggled with
    God.ᵃ
4 Yes, he struggled with the Angel and
    prevailed;
He wept, and sought favor from Him.
He found Him *in* Bethel,
And there He spoke to us—
5 That is, the LORD God of hosts.
The LORD *is* His memorable name.
6 So you, by *the help of* your God, return;
Observe mercy and justice,
And wait on your God continually.

7 "A cunning Canaanite!
Deceitful scales *are* in his hand;
He loves to oppress.
8 And Ephraim said,
'Surely I have become rich,
I have found wealth for myself;
In all my labors
They shall find in me no iniquity
    that *is* sin.'

9 "But I *am* the LORD your God,
Ever since the land of Egypt;
I will again make you dwell in tents,
As in the days of the appointed feast.
10 I have also spoken by the prophets,
And have multiplied visions;
I have given symbols through the
    witness of the prophets."

11 Though Gilead *has* idols—
Surely they are vanity—
Though they sacrifice bulls in Gilgal,
Indeed their altars *shall be* heaps in
    the furrows of the field.

12 Jacob fled to the country of Syria;
Israel served for a spouse,
And for a wife he tended *sheep.*
13 By a prophet the LORD brought Israel
    out of Egypt,

11:7 ᵃOr *upward*   **11:9** ᵃOr *I will not enter a city*
11:12 ᵃOr *holy ones*   **12:3** ᵃCompare Genesis 32:28

And by a prophet he was preserved.
14 Ephraim provoked *Him* to anger most
    bitterly;
Therefore his Lord will leave the guilt
    of his bloodshed upon him,
And return his reproach upon him.

Relentless Judgment on Israel

13 When Ephraim spoke, trembling,
He exalted *himself* in Israel;
But when he offended through Baal
    worship, he died.
2 Now they sin more and more,
And have made for themselves molded
    images,
Idols of their silver, according to their
    skill;
All of it *is* the work of craftsmen.
They say of them,
"Let the men who sacrifice[a] kiss the
    calves!"
3 Therefore they shall be like the morning
    cloud
And like the early dew that passes away,
Like chaff blown off from a threshing
    floor
And like smoke from a chimney.

4 "Yet I *am* the Lord your God
Ever since the land of Egypt,
And you shall know no God but Me;
For *there is* no savior besides Me.
5 I knew you in the wilderness,
In the land of great drought.
6 When they had pasture, they were
    filled;
They were filled and their heart was
    exalted;
Therefore they forgot Me.

7 "So I will be to them like a lion;
Like a leopard by the road I will lurk;
8 I will meet them like a bear deprived
    of her cubs;
I will tear open their rib cage,
And there I will devour them like a lion.
The wild beast shall tear them.

9 "O Israel, you are destroyed,[a]
But your help[b] *is* from Me.
10 I will be your King;[a]
Where *is any other,*

That he may save you in all your cities?
And your judges to whom you said,
'Give me a king and princes'?
11 I gave you a king in My anger,
And took *him* away in My wrath.

12 "The iniquity of Ephraim *is* bound up;
His sin *is* stored up.
13 The sorrows of a woman in childbirth
    shall come upon him.
He *is* an unwise son,
For he should not stay long where
    children are born.

14 "I will ransom them from the power
    of the grave;[a]
I will redeem them from death.
O Death, I will be your plagues![b]
O Grave,[c] I will be your destruction![d]
Pity is hidden from My eyes."

15 Though he is fruitful among *his*
    brethren,
An east wind shall come;
The wind of the Lord shall come up
    from the wilderness.
Then his spring shall become dry,
And his fountain shall be dried up.
He shall plunder the treasury of every
    desirable prize.
16 Samaria is held guilty,[a]
For she has rebelled against her God.
They shall fall by the sword,
Their infants shall be dashed in pieces,
And their women with child ripped
    open.

Israel Restored at Last

14 O Israel, return to the Lord your God,
For you have stumbled because of
    your iniquity;
2 Take words with you,
And return to the Lord.
Say to Him,
"Take away all iniquity;

13:2 [a]Or *those who offer human sacrifice*
13:9 [a]Literally *it* or *he destroyed you* [b]Literally *in your help*   13:10 [a]Septuagint, Syriac, Targum, and Vulgate read *Where is your king?*   13:14 [a]Or *Sheol* [b]Septuagint reads *where is your punishment?* [c]Or *Sheol* [d]Septuagint reads *where is your sting?* 13:16 [a]Septuagint reads *shall be disfigured*

Receive *us* graciously,
For we will offer the sacrifices[a] of our
    lips.
3 Assyria shall not save us,
We will not ride on horses,
Nor will we say anymore to the work
    of our hands, '*You are* our gods.'
For in You the fatherless finds mercy."

4 "I will heal their backsliding,
I will love them freely,
For My anger has turned away from
    him.
5 I will be like the dew to Israel;
He shall grow like the lily,
And lengthen his roots like Lebanon.
6 His branches shall spread;
His beauty shall be like an olive tree,
And his fragrance like Lebanon.
7 Those who dwell under his shadow
    shall return;

They shall be revived *like* grain,
And grow like a vine.
Their scent[a] *shall be* like the wine of
    Lebanon.

8 "Ephraim *shall say,* 'What have I to do
    anymore with idols?'
I have heard and observed him.
I *am* like a green cypress tree;
Your fruit is found in Me."

9 Who *is* wise?
Let him understand these things.
Who is prudent?
Let him know them.
For the ways of the LORD *are* right;
The righteous walk in them,
But transgressors stumble in them.

14:2 [a]Literally *bull calves;* Septuagint reads *fruit.*
14:7 [a]Literally *remembrance*

JOEL

Author: Joel

When Written: Probably 835–805 B.C.

Theme: The Day of the Lord

Key Verses: Joel 2:28, 29—"And it shall come to pass afterward that I will pour out My Spirit on all flesh; your sons and your daughters shall prophesy, your old men shall dream dreams, your young men shall see visions. And also on My menservants and on My maidservants I will pour out My Spirit in those days."

Key Chapter: Joel 2—As the prophet calls the nation of Judah to repentance for its rebellion against God, he looks forward to the day when God will extend His mercy and pour out His Spirit "on all flesh."

The Book of Joel is not only a warning to the people of Judah of coming destruction for their sin and rebellion against God. It also includes a promise of God's restoration and deliverance to all who will call upon Him.

One of America's most favorite patriotic hymns, Julia Ward Howe's *The Battle Hymn of the Republic,* speaks of the same delivering power that will be unleashed to destroy oppression and bring freedom to all humanity: "Mine eyes have seen the glory of the coming of the Lord: He is trampling out the vintage where the grapes of wrath are stored; He has loosed the fateful lightning of His terrible swift sword: His truth is marching on."

JOEL

1 The word of the LORD that came to Joel the son of Pethuel.

The Land Laid Waste

2 Hear this, you elders,
And give ear, all you inhabitants of
the land!
Has *anything like* this happened in
your days,
Or even in the days of your fathers?
3 Tell your children about it,
Let your children *tell* their children,
And their children another generation.

4 What the chewing locust[a] left, the
swarming locust has eaten;
What the swarming locust left, the
crawling locust has eaten;
And what the crawling locust left, the
consuming locust has eaten.

5 Awake, you drunkards, and weep;
And wail, all you drinkers of wine,
Because of the new wine,
For it has been cut off from your
mouth.
6 For a nation has come up against
My land,
Strong, and without number;
His teeth *are* the teeth of a lion,
And he has the fangs of a fierce lion.
7 He has laid waste My vine,
And ruined My fig tree;
He has stripped it bare and thrown
it away;
Its branches are made white.

8 Lament like a virgin girded with
sackcloth
For the husband of her youth.
9 The grain offering and the drink
offering
Have been cut off from the house of
the LORD;
The priests mourn, who minister to
the LORD.

10 The field is wasted,
The land mourns;
For the grain is ruined,
The new wine is dried up,
The oil fails.

11 Be ashamed, you farmers,
Wail, you vinedressers,
For the wheat and the barley;
Because the harvest of the field has
perished.
12 The vine has dried up,
And the fig tree has withered;
The pomegranate tree,
The palm tree also,
And the apple tree—
All the trees of the field are withered;
Surely joy has withered away from
the sons of men.

Mourning for the Land

13 Gird yourselves and lament, you priests;
Wail, you who minister before the
altar;
Come, lie all night in sackcloth,
You who minister to my God;
For the grain offering and the drink
offering
Are withheld from the house of your
God.
14 Consecrate a fast,
Call a sacred assembly;
Gather the elders
And all the inhabitants of the land
Into the house of the LORD your God,
And cry out to the LORD.

15 Alas for the day!
For the day of the LORD *is* at hand;
It shall come as destruction from the
Almighty.
16 Is not the food cut off before our eyes,
Joy and gladness from the house of
our God?

1:4 [a]Exact identity of these locusts is unknown.

17 The seed shrivels under the clods,
Storehouses are in shambles;
Barns are broken down,
For the grain has withered.
18 How the animals groan!
The herds of cattle are restless,
Because they have no pasture;
Even the flocks of sheep suffer
punishment.ᵃ

19 O LORD, to You I cry out;
For fire has devoured the open pastures,
And a flame has burned all the trees
of the field.
20 The beasts of the field also cry out to
You,
For the water brooks are dried up,
And fire has devoured the open
pastures.

The Day of the LORD

2 Blow the trumpet in Zion,
And sound an alarm in My holy
mountain!
Let all the inhabitants of the land
tremble;
For the day of the LORD is coming,
For it is at hand:
2 A day of darkness and gloominess,
A day of clouds and thick darkness,
Like the morning *clouds* spread over
the mountains.
A people *come,* great and strong,
The like of whom has never been;
Nor will there ever be any *such* after
them,
Even for many successive generations.

3 A fire devours before them,
And behind them a flame burns;
The land *is* like the Garden of Eden
before them,
And behind them a desolate wilderness;
Surely nothing shall escape them.
4 Their appearance is like the
appearance of horses;
And like swift steeds, so they run.
5 With a noise like chariots
Over mountaintops they leap,
Like the noise of a flaming fire that
devours the stubble,
Like a strong people set in battle array.

6 Before them the people writhe in pain;
All faces are drained of color.ᵃ
7 They run like mighty men,
They climb the wall like men of war;
Every one marches in formation,
And they do not break ranks.
8 They do not push one another;
Every one marches in his own column.ᵃ
Though they lunge between the
weapons,
They are not cut down.ᵇ
9 They run to and fro in the city,
They run on the wall;
They climb into the houses,
They enter at the windows like a thief.

10 The earth quakes before them,
The heavens tremble;
The sun and moon grow dark,
And the stars diminish their brightness.
11 The LORD gives voice before His army,
For His camp is very great;
For strong *is the One* who executes His
word.
For the day of the LORD *is* great and
very terrible;
Who can endure it?

A Call to Repentance

12 "Now, therefore," says the LORD,
"Turn to Me with all your heart,
With fasting, with weeping, and with
mourning."
13 So rend your heart, and not your
garments;
Return to the LORD your God,
For He *is* gracious and merciful,
Slow to anger, and of great kindness;
And He relents from doing harm.
14 Who knows *if* He will turn and relent,
And leave a blessing behind Him—
A grain offering and a drink offering
For the LORD your God?

15 Blow the trumpet in Zion,
Consecrate a fast,
Call a sacred assembly;

1:18 ᵃSeptuagint and Vulgate read *are made desolate.*
2:6 ᵃSeptuagint, Targum, and Vulgate read *gather
blackness.*   **2:8** ᵃLiterally *his own highway* ᵇThat is,
they are not halted by losses

16 Gather the people,
   Sanctify the congregation,
   Assemble the elders,
   Gather the children and nursing babes;
   Let the bridegroom go out from his
     chamber,
   And the bride from her dressing room.
17 Let the priests, who minister to the LORD,
   Weep between the porch and the altar;
   Let them say, "Spare Your people,
     O LORD,
   And do not give Your heritage to
     reproach,
   That the nations should rule over them.
   Why should they say among the
     peoples,
   'Where is their God?'"

The Land Refreshed

18 Then the LORD will be zealous for His
     land,
   And pity His people.
19 The LORD will answer and say to His
     people,

"Behold, I will send you grain and new
   wine and oil,
And you will be satisfied by them;
I will no longer make you a reproach
   among the nations.

20 "But I will remove far from you the
     northern *army*,
   And will drive him away into a barren
     and desolate land,
   With his face toward the eastern sea
   And his back toward the western sea;
   His stench will come up,
   And his foul odor will rise,
   Because he has done monstrous things."

21 Fear not, O land;
   Be glad and rejoice,
   For the LORD has done marvelous things!
22 Do not be afraid, you beasts of the field;
   For the open pastures are springing up,
   And the tree bears its fruit;
   The fig tree and the vine yield their
     strength.

HUMILITY

*"Turn to Me with all
your heart, with fasting,
with weeping, and with
mourning."*

JOEL 2:12

The Boston Tea Party

DAYS OF FASTING

After the Boston Tea Party, the British navy retaliated by blockading the port of Boston. The colonies surrounding Massachusetts responded with sympathy and action. On May 24, 1773, the House of Burgesses in Virginia proposed and approved a Day of Fasting, Humiliation, and Prayer:

> *This House, being deeply impressed with apprehension of the great dangers to be derived to British America from the hostile invasion of the city of Boston in our Sister Colony of Massachusetts Bay, whose commerce and harbor are, on the first day of June next, to be stopped by an armed force, deem it highly necessary that the said first day of June be set apart, by the members of this House, as a Day of Fasting, Humiliation, and Prayer, devoutly to implore the Divine interposition, for averting the heavy calamity which threatens destruction to our civil rights and the evils of civil war; to give us one heart and mind firmly opposed, by all just and proper means, every injury to American rights; and that the minds of his Majesty and his Parliament, may be inspired from above with wisdom, moderation, and justice, to remove from the loyal people of America all cause of danger from a continued pursuit of measures pregnant with their ruin.*

23 Be glad then, you children of Zion,
And rejoice in the LORD your God;
For He has given you the former rain
faithfully,ᵃ
And He will cause the rain to come
down for you—
The former rain,
And the latter rain in the first *month*.
24 The threshing floors shall be full of
wheat,
And the vats shall overflow with new
wine and oil.

25 "So I will restore to you the years that
the swarming locust has eaten,
The crawling locust,
The consuming locust,
And the chewing locust,ᵃ
My great army which I sent among
you.
26 You shall eat in plenty and be
satisfied,
And praise the name of the LORD
your God,
Who has dealt wondrously with you;
And My people shall never be put to
shame.
27 Then you shall know that I *am* in the
midst of Israel:
I *am* the LORD your God
And there is no other.
My people shall never be put to shame.

God's Spirit Poured Out

28 "And it shall come to pass afterward
That I will pour out My Spirit on all
flesh;
Your sons and your daughters shall
prophesy,
Your old men shall dream dreams,
Your young men shall see visions.
29 And also on *My* menservants and on
My maidservants
I will pour out My Spirit in those days.

30 "And I will show wonders in the
heavens and in the earth:
Blood and fire and pillars of smoke.
31 The sun shall be turned into darkness,
And the moon into blood,
Before the coming of the great and
awesome day of the LORD.

32 And it shall come to pass
That whoever calls on the name of
the LORD
Shall be saved.
For in Mount Zion and in Jerusalem
there shall be deliverance,
As the LORD has said,
Among the remnant whom the LORD
calls.

God Judges the Nations

3 "For behold, in those days and at
that time,
When I bring back the captives of
Judah and Jerusalem,
2 I will also gather all nations,
And bring them down to the Valley
of Jehoshaphat;
And I will enter into judgment with
them there
On account of My people, My heritage
Israel,
Whom they have scattered among
the nations;
They have also divided up My land.
3 They have cast lots for My people,
Have given a boy *as payment* for a
harlot,
And sold a girl for wine, that they
may drink.

4 "Indeed, what have you to do
with Me,
O Tyre and Sidon, and all the coasts
of Philistia?
Will you retaliate against Me?
But if you retaliate against Me,
Swiftly and speedily I will return your
retaliation upon your own head;
5 Because you have taken My silver
and My gold,
And have carried into your temples
My prized possessions.
6 Also the people of Judah and the
people of Jerusalem
You have sold to the Greeks,
That you may remove them far from
their borders.

2:23 ᵃOr *the teacher of righteousness*
2:25 ᵃCompare 1:4

7 "Behold, I will raise them
    Out of the place to which you have
        sold them,
    And will return your retaliation upon
        your own head.
8 I will sell your sons and your
        daughters
    Into the hand of the people of Judah,
    And they will sell them to the Sabeans,ᵃ
    To a people far off;
    For the LORD has spoken."

9 Proclaim this among the nations:
    "Prepare for war!
    Wake up the mighty men,
    Let all the men of war draw near,
    Let them come up.
10 Beat your plowshares into swords
    And your pruning hooks into spears;
    Let the weak say, 'I *am* strong.'"
11 Assemble and come, all you nations,
    And gather together all around.
    Cause Your mighty ones to go down
        there, O LORD.

12 "Let the nations be wakened, and come
        up to the Valley of Jehoshaphat;
    For there I will sit to judge all the
        surrounding nations.
13 Put in the sickle, for the harvest is ripe.
    Come, go down;
    For the winepress is full,
    The vats overflow—
    For their wickedness *is* great."

14 Multitudes, multitudes in the valley
        of decision!
    For the day of the LORD *is* near in the
        valley of decision.
15 The sun and moon will grow dark,
    And the stars will diminish their
        brightness.

16 The LORD also will roar from Zion,
    And utter His voice from Jerusalem;
    The heavens and earth will shake;
    But the LORD will be a shelter for His
        people,
    And the strength of the children of
        Israel.

17 "So you shall know that I *am* the LORD
        your God,
    Dwelling in Zion My holy mountain.
    Then Jerusalem shall be holy,
    And no aliens shall ever pass through
        her again."

God Blesses His People

18   And it will come to pass in that day
    That the mountains shall drip with
        new wine,
    The hills shall flow with milk,
    And all the brooks of Judah shall be
        flooded with water;
    A fountain shall flow from the house
        of the LORD
    And water the Valley of Acacias.

19 "Egypt shall be a desolation,
    And Edom a desolate wilderness,
    Because of violence *against* the people
        of Judah,
    For they have shed innocent blood in
        their land.
20   But Judah shall abide forever,
    And Jerusalem from generation to
        generation.
21   For I will acquit them of the guilt of
        bloodshed, whom I had not
        acquitted;
    For the LORD dwells in Zion."

3:8 ᵃLiterally *Shebaites* (compare Isaiah 60:6 and
Ezekiel 27:22)

AMOS

Author: Amos

When Written: 760–750 B.C.

Theme: Judgment

Key Verses: Amos 8:11—"Behold, the days are coming," says the Lord GOD, "that I will send a famine on the land, not a famine of bread, nor a thirst for water, but of hearing the words of the LORD."

Key Chapter: Amos 9—Even as the prophet pronounces the terrible judgment that God will visit upon the nation of Israel, he concludes with the promise that God will redeem His people.

The Book of Amos covers a period of economic prosperity for the nation of Israel. But underneath the surface, the hearts of the people are given over to greed and avarice, as they deal heartlessly with the poor and disadvantaged among them. Amos, a farmer by trade, is called by God to raise a prophetic challenge to the people of Israel to repent of their sin and return to their covenant relationship with God before it is too late.

A similar challenge exists today for the people of America to return to the roots of God's justice and mercy as it did during America's Great Awakening, which was sparked largely by George Whitefield's preaching tour of 1739–1740. Though only 25 years old, the evangelist took America by storm. His farewell sermon on Boston Common drew 23,000 people—more than Boston's entire population. He was known to preach:

> *I offer you salvation this day; the door of mercy is not yet shut, there does yet remain a sacrifice for sin, for all that will accept of the Lord Jesus Christ. He will embrace you in the arms of His love. O turn to Him, turn in a sense of your own unworthiness; tell Him how polluted you are, how vile, and be not faithless, but believing. Why fear ye that the Lord Jesus Christ will not accept of you? Your sins will be no hindrance, your unworthiness no hindrance; if your own corrupt hearts do not keep you back, nothing will hinder Christ from receiving of you.*

AMOS

1 The words of Amos, who was among the sheepbreeders[a] of Tekoa, which he saw concerning Israel in the days of Uzziah king of Judah, and in the days of Jeroboam the son of Joash, king of Israel, two years before the earthquake.

2 And he said:

> "The LORD roars from Zion,
> And utters His voice from Jerusalem;
> The pastures of the shepherds mourn,
> And the top of Carmel withers."

Judgment on the Nations

3 Thus says the LORD:

> "For three transgressions of Damascus,
>   and for four,
> I will not turn away its *punishment,*
> Because they have threshed Gilead
>   with implements of iron.
> 4 But I will send a fire into the house
>   of Hazael,
> Which shall devour the palaces of
>   Ben-Hadad.
> 5 I will also break the *gate* bar of
>   Damascus,
> And cut off the inhabitant from the
>   Valley of Aven,
> And the one who holds the scepter
>   from Beth Eden.
> The people of Syria shall go captive
>   to Kir,"
> Says the LORD.

6 Thus says the LORD:

> "For three transgressions of Gaza, and
>   for four,
> I will not turn away its *punishment,*
> Because they took captive the whole
>   captivity
> To deliver *them* up to Edom.
> 7 But I will send a fire upon the wall
>   of Gaza,
> Which shall devour its palaces.

> 8 I will cut off the inhabitant from
>   Ashdod,
> And the one who holds the scepter
>   from Ashkelon;
> I will turn My hand against Ekron,
> And the remnant of the Philistines
>   shall perish,"
> Says the Lord GOD.

9 Thus says the LORD:

> "For three transgressions of Tyre, and
>   for four,
> I will not turn away its *punishment,*
> Because they delivered up the whole
>   captivity to Edom,
> And did not remember the covenant
>   of brotherhood.
> 10 But I will send a fire upon the wall
>   of Tyre,
> Which shall devour its palaces."

11 Thus says the LORD:

> "For three transgressions of Edom, and
>   for four,
> I will not turn away its *punishment,*
> Because he pursued his brother with
>   the sword,
> And cast off all pity;
> His anger tore perpetually,
> And he kept his wrath forever.
> 12 But I will send a fire upon Teman,
> Which shall devour the palaces of
>   Bozrah."

13 Thus says the LORD:

> "For three transgressions of the people
>   of Ammon, and for four,
> I will not turn away its *punishment,*
> Because they ripped open the women
>   with child in Gilead,
> That they might enlarge their
>   territory.

1:1 [a]Compare 2 Kings 3:4

14 But I will kindle a fire in the wall
    of Rabbah,
And it shall devour its palaces,
Amid shouting in the day of battle,
And a tempest in the day of the
    whirlwind.
15 Their king shall go into captivity,
He and his princes together,"
Says the LORD.

2 Thus says the LORD:

"For three transgressions of Moab,
    and for four,
I will not turn away its *punishment,*
Because he burned the bones of the
    king of Edom to lime.
2 But I will send a fire upon Moab,
And it shall devour the palaces of
    Kerioth;
Moab shall die with tumult,
With shouting *and* trumpet sound.
3 And I will cut off the judge from its
    midst,
And slay all its princes with him,"
Says the LORD.

Judgment on Judah

4 Thus says the LORD:

"For three transgressions of Judah,
    and for four,
I will not turn away its *punishment,*
Because they have despised the law
    of the LORD,
And have not kept His
    commandments.
Their lies lead them astray,
Lies which their fathers followed.
5 But I will send a fire upon Judah,
And it shall devour the palaces of
    Jerusalem."

Judgment on Israel

6 Thus says the LORD:

"For three transgressions of Israel,
    and for four,
I will not turn away its *punishment,*
Because they sell the righteous for
    silver,
And the poor for a pair of sandals.

7 They pant after[a] the dust of the earth
    which is on the head of the poor,
And pervert the way of the humble.
A man and his father go in to the
    same girl,
To defile My holy name.
8 They lie down by every altar on
    clothes taken in pledge,
And drink the wine of the condemned
    in the house of their god.

HONOR

". . . they have despised the law of the LORD. . . ."

AMOS 2:4

A Christian Republic

Judge Nathaniel Freeman in 1802 charged the Massachusetts Grand Juries as follows:

The laws of the Christian system, as embraced by the Bible, must be respected as of high authority in all our courts, and it cannot be thought improper for the officers of such government to acknowledge their obligation to be governed by its rule. . . . [Our government] originating in the voluntary compact of a people who in that very instrument profess the Christian religion, it may be considered, not as republic Rome was, a pagan, but a Christian republic.

9 "Yet *it was* I *who* destroyed the Amorite
    before them,
Whose height *was* like the height of
    the cedars,
And he *was as* strong as the oaks;
Yet I destroyed his fruit above
And his roots beneath.
10 Also *it was* I *who* brought you up from
    the land of Egypt,
And led you forty years through the
    wilderness,
To possess the land of the Amorite.
11 I raised up some of your sons as
    prophets,
And some of your young men as
    Nazirites.
Is it not so, O you children of Israel?"
Says the LORD.

2:7 [a]Or *trample on*

12 "But you gave the Nazirites wine to
   drink,
   And commanded the prophets saying,
   'Do not prophesy!'

13 "Behold, I am weighed down by you,
   As a cart full of sheaves is weighed
      down.
14 Therefore flight shall perish from the
      swift,
   The strong shall not strengthen his
      power,
   Nor shall the mighty deliver himself;
15 He shall not stand who handles the
      bow,
   The swift of foot shall not escape,
   Nor shall he who rides a horse deliver
      himself.
16 The most courageous men of might
   Shall flee naked in that day,"
   Says the LORD.

Authority of the Prophet's Message

3 Hear this word that the LORD has spoken against you, O children of Israel,
against the whole family which I brought
up from the land of Egypt, saying:

2 "You only have I known of all the
      families of the earth;
   Therefore I will punish you for all
      your iniquities."

3 Can two walk together, unless they
      are agreed?
4 Will a lion roar in the forest, when he
      has no prey?
   Will a young lion cry out of his den,
      if he has caught nothing?
5 Will a bird fall into a snare on the
      earth, where there is no trap for it?
   Will a snare spring up from the earth,
      if it has caught nothing at all?
6 If a trumpet is blown in a city, will not
      the people be afraid?
   If there is calamity in a city, will not
      the LORD have done it?

7 Surely the Lord GOD does nothing,
   Unless He reveals His secret to His
      servants the prophets.
8 A lion has roared!
   Who will not fear?

The Lord GOD has spoken!
   Who can but prophesy?

Punishment of Israel's Sins

9 "Proclaim in the palaces at Ashdod,ᵃ
   And in the palaces in the land of
      Egypt, and say:
   'Assemble on the mountains of Samaria;
   See great tumults in her midst,
   And the oppressed within her.
10   For they do not know to do right,'
   Says the LORD,
   'Who store up violence and robbery in
      their palaces.'"

11Therefore thus says the Lord GOD:

"An adversary *shall be* all around the
      land;
   He shall sap your strength from you,
   And your palaces shall be plundered."

12Thus says the LORD:

"As a shepherd takes from the mouth
      of a lion
   Two legs or a piece of an ear,
   So shall the children of Israel be taken
      out
   Who dwell in Samaria—
   In the corner of a bed and on the
      edgeᵃ of a couch!
13   Hear and testify against the house of
      Jacob,"
   Says the Lord GOD, the God of hosts,
14 "That in the day I punish Israel for
      their transgressions,
   I will also visit *destruction* on the altars
      of Bethel;
   And the horns of the altar shall be cut
      off
   And fall to the ground.
15   I will destroy the winter house along
      with the summer house;
   The houses of ivory shall perish,
   And the great houses shall have an
      end,"
   Says the LORD.

3:9 ᵃFollowing Masoretic Text; Septuagint reads
Assyria.   **3:12** ᵃThe Hebrew is uncertain.

4 Hear this word, you cows of Bashan,
　　who *are* on the mountain of Samaria,
Who oppress the poor,
Who crush the needy,
Who say to your husbands,ᵃ "Bring
　　wine, let us drink!"

2　The Lord God has sworn by His holiness:
"Behold, the days shall come upon you
　　When He will take you away with
　　　　fishhooks,
And your posterity with fishhooks.

3　You will go out *through* broken *walls,*
　　Each one straight ahead of her,
And you will be cast into Harmon,"
　　Says the Lord.

4　"Come to Bethel and transgress,
　　At Gilgal multiply transgression;
Bring your sacrifices every morning,
Your tithes every three days.ᵃ

5　Offer a sacrifice of thanksgiving with
　　leaven,
Proclaim *and* announce the freewill
　　offerings;
For this you love,
You children of Israel!"
　　Says the Lord God.

Israel Did Not Accept Correction

6　"Also I gave you cleanness of teeth in
　　all your cities,
And lack of bread in all your places;
Yet you have not returned to Me,"
　　Says the Lord.

7　"I also withheld rain from you,
　　When *there were* still three months
　　　　to the harvest.
I made it rain on one city,
I withheld rain from another city.
One part was rained upon,
And where it did not rain the part
　　withered.

8　So two *or* three cities wandered to
　　another city to drink water,
But they were not satisfied;
Yet you have not returned to Me,"
　　Says the Lord.

9　"I blasted you with blight and mildew.
　　When your gardens increased,
Your vineyards,
Your fig trees,
And your olive trees,
The locust devoured *them;*
Yet you have not returned to Me,"
Says the Lord.

10　"I sent among you a plague after the
　　manner of Egypt;
Your young men I killed with a sword,
Along with your captive horses;
I made the stench of your camps come
　　up into your nostrils;
Yet you have not returned to Me,"
Says the Lord.

11　"I overthrew *some* of you,
　　As God overthrew Sodom and
　　　　Gomorrah,
And you were like a firebrand plucked
　　from the burning;
Yet you have not returned to Me,"
Says the Lord.

12　"Therefore thus will I do to you,
　　O Israel;
Because I will do this to you,
Prepare to meet your God, O Israel!"

13　For behold,
He who forms mountains,
And creates the wind,
Who declares to man what hisᵃ
　　thought *is,*
And makes the morning darkness,
Who treads the high places of the
　　earth—
The Lord God of hosts *is* His name.

A Lament for Israel

5 Hear this word which I take up against
　　you, a lamentation, O house of Israel:

2　The virgin of Israel has fallen;
She will rise no more.
She lies forsaken on her land;
There is no one to raise her up.

³For thus says the Lord God:

4:1 ᵃLiterally *their lords* or *their masters*　　**4:4** ᵃOr
years (compare Deuteronomy 14:28)　　**4:13** ᵃOr *His*

"The city that goes out by a thousand
Shall have a hundred left,
And that which goes out by a hundred
Shall have ten left to the house of
    Israel."

A Call to Repentance

⁴For thus says the LORD to the house of Israel:

"Seek Me and live;
5 But do not seek Bethel,
Nor enter Gilgal,
Nor pass over to Beersheba;
For Gilgal shall surely go into captivity,
And Bethel shall come to nothing.
6 Seek the LORD and live,
Lest He break out like fire *in* the house
    of Joseph,
And devour *it*,
With no one to quench *it* in Bethel—
7 You who turn justice to wormwood,
And lay righteousness to rest in the
    earth!"

DEFENDER

". . . you who turn justice to wormwood. . . ."

AMOS 5:7

Where Justice Is Denied

Frederick Douglass (1818–1895), an abolitionist, orator, author, statesman, and one of the most prominent figures in African-American and American history, stated:

Where justice is denied, where poverty is enforced, where ignorance prevails, and where any one class is made to feel that society is an organized conspiracy to oppress, rob and degrade them, neither persons nor property will be safe.

---

8 He made the Pleiades and Orion;
He turns the shadow of death into
    morning
And makes the day dark as night;
He calls for the waters of the sea
And pours them out on the face of
    the earth;
The LORD *is* His name.
9 He rains ruin upon the strong,
So that fury comes upon the fortress.

10 They hate the one who rebukes in
    the gate,
And they abhor the one who speaks
    uprightly.
11 Therefore, because you tread down
    the poor
And take grain taxes from him,
Though you have built houses of
    hewn stone,
Yet you shall not dwell in them;
You have planted pleasant vineyards,
But you shall not drink wine from them.
12 For I know your manifold transgressions
And your mighty sins:
Afflicting the just *and* taking bribes;
Diverting the poor *from justice* at the
    gate.
13 Therefore the prudent keep silent at
    that time,
For it *is* an evil time.

14 Seek good and not evil,
That you may live;
So the LORD God of hosts will be with
    you,
As you have spoken.
15 Hate evil, love good;
Establish justice in the gate.
It may be that the LORD God of hosts
Will be gracious to the remnant of
    Joseph.

The Day of the LORD

¹⁶Therefore the LORD God of hosts, the Lord, says this:

"*There shall be* wailing in all streets,
And they shall say in all the highways,
'Alas! Alas!'
They shall call the farmer to mourning,
And skillful lamenters to wailing.
17 In all vineyards *there shall be* wailing,
For I will pass through you,"
Says the LORD.

18 Woe to you who desire the day of the
    LORD!
For what good *is* the day of the LORD
    to you?
It *will be* darkness, and not light.
19 It *will be* as though a man fled from
    a lion,
And a bear met him!

Or *as though* he went into the house,
Leaned his hand on the wall,
And a serpent bit him!

20 *Is* not the day of the LORD darkness,
and not light?
Is it not very dark, with no brightness
in it?

21 "I hate, I despise your feast days,
And I do not savor your sacred
assemblies.
22 Though you offer Me burnt offerings
and your grain offerings,
I will not accept *them,*
Nor will I regard your fattened peace
offerings.
23 Take away from Me the noise of your
songs,
For I will not hear the melody of your
stringed instruments.
24 But let justice run down like water,
And righteousness like a mighty stream.

25 "Did you offer Me sacrifices and offerings
In the wilderness forty years, O house
of Israel?
26 You also carried Sikkuth^a your king^b
And Chiun,^c your idols,
The star of your gods,
Which you made for yourselves.
27 Therefore I will send you into captivity
beyond Damascus,"
Says the LORD, whose name *is* the God
of hosts.

Warnings to Zion and Samaria

6 Woe to you *who are* at ease in Zion,
And trust in Mount Samaria,
Notable persons in the chief nation,
To whom the house of Israel comes!
2 Go over to Calneh and see;
And from there go to Hamath the great;
Then go down to Gath of the Philistines.
Are you better than these kingdoms?
Or is their territory greater than your
territory?

3 *Woe to* you who put far off the day
of doom,
Who cause the seat of violence to
come near;
4 Who lie on beds of ivory,
Stretch out on your couches,

Eat lambs from the flock
And calves from the midst of the stall;
5 Who sing idly to the sound of stringed
instruments,
And invent for yourselves musical
instruments like David;
6 Who drink wine from bowls,
And anoint yourselves with the best
ointments,
But are not grieved for the affliction
of Joseph.
7 Therefore they shall now go captive
as the first of the captives,
And those who recline at banquets
shall be removed.

8 The Lord GOD has sworn by Himself,
The LORD God of hosts says:
"I abhor the pride of Jacob,
And hate his palaces;
Therefore I will deliver up *the* city
And all that is in it."

9Then it shall come to pass, that if ten men remain in one house, they shall die. 10And when a relative *of the dead,* with one who will burn *the bodies,* picks up the bodies^a to take them out of the house, he will say to one inside the house, "*Are there* any more with you?"
Then someone will say, "None."
And he will say, "Hold your tongue! For we dare not mention the name of the LORD."

11 For behold, the LORD gives a command:
He will break the great house into bits,
And the little house into pieces.

12 Do horses run on rocks?
Does *one* plow *there* with oxen?
Yet you have turned justice into gall,
And the fruit of righteousness into
wormwood,
13 You who rejoice over Lo Debar,^a
Who say, "Have we not taken
Karnaim^b for ourselves
By our own strength?"

5:26 ^aA pagan deity ^bSeptuagint and Vulgate read *tabernacle of Moloch.* ^cA pagan deity
6:10 ^aLiterally *bones* 6:13 ^aLiterally *Nothing*
^bLiterally *Horns,* symbol of strength

14 "But, behold, I will raise up a nation
      against you,
    O house of Israel,"
    Says the LORD God of hosts;
    "And they will afflict you from the
      entrance of Hamath
    To the Valley of the Arabah."

Vision of the Locusts

7 Thus the Lord GOD showed me: Behold,
  He formed locust swarms at the beginning of the late crop; indeed *it was* the late
crop after the king's mowings. 2And so it
was, when they had finished eating the
grass of the land, that I said:

    "O Lord GOD, forgive, I pray!
     Oh, that Jacob may stand,
     For he *is* small!"
3   *So* the LORD relented concerning this.
    "It shall not be," said the LORD.

Vision of the Fire

4Thus the Lord GOD showed me: Behold,
the Lord GOD called for conflict by fire, and
it consumed the great deep and devoured
the territory. 5Then I said:

    "O Lord GOD, cease, I pray!
     Oh, that Jacob may stand,
     For he *is* small!"
6   *So* the LORD relented concerning this.
    "This also shall not be," said the Lord
      GOD.

Vision of the Plumb Line

7Thus He showed me: Behold, the Lord
stood on a wall *made* with a plumb line,
with a plumb line in His hand. 8And the
LORD said to me, "Amos, what do you see?"
    And I said, "A plumb line."
    Then the Lord said:

    "Behold, I am setting a plumb line
     In the midst of My people Israel;
     I will not pass by them anymore.
9   The high places of Isaac shall be
      desolate,
     And the sanctuaries of Israel shall
      be laid waste.
     I will rise with the sword against
      the house of Jeroboam."

Amaziah's Complaint

10Then Amaziah the priest of Bethel sent
to Jeroboam king of Israel, saying, "Amos
has conspired against you in the midst of
the house of Israel. The land is not able to
bear all his words. 11For thus Amos has said:

    'Jeroboam shall die by the sword,
     And Israel shall surely be led away
      captive
     From their own land.'"

12Then Amaziah said to Amos:

    "Go, you seer!
     Flee to the land of Judah.
     There eat bread,
     And there prophesy.
13   But never again prophesy at Bethel,
     For it *is* the king's sanctuary,
     And it *is* the royal residence."

14Then Amos answered, and said to
Amaziah:

    "I *was* no prophet,
     Nor *was* I a son of a prophet,
     But I *was* a sheepbreeder[a]
     And a tender of sycamore fruit.
15   Then the LORD took me as I followed
      the flock,
     And the LORD said to me,
     'Go, prophesy to My people Israel.'
16   Now therefore, hear the word of the
      LORD:
     You say, 'Do not prophesy against Israel,
     And do not spout against the house of
      Isaac.'

17"Therefore thus says the LORD:

    'Your wife shall be a harlot in the city;
     Your sons and daughters shall fall by
      the sword;
     Your land shall be divided by *survey* line;
     You shall die in a defiled land;
     And Israel shall surely be led away
      captive
     From his own land.'"

7:14 [a]Compare 2 Kings 3:4

Vision of the Summer Fruit

8 Thus the Lord GOD showed me: Behold, a basket of summer fruit. [2]And He said, "Amos, what do you see?"

So I said, "A basket of summer fruit."

Then the LORD said to me:

"The end has come upon My people
   Israel;
I will not pass by them anymore.
[3] And the songs of the temple
Shall be wailing in that day,"
Says the Lord GOD—
"Many dead bodies everywhere,
They shall be thrown out in silence."

[4] Hear this, you who swallow up[a] the
   needy,
And make the poor of the land fail,

[5]Saying:

"When will the New Moon be past,
That we may sell grain?
And the Sabbath,
That we may trade wheat?
Making the ephah small and the
   shekel large,
Falsifying the scales by deceit,
[6] That we may buy the poor for silver,
And the needy for a pair of sandals—
Even sell the bad wheat?"

[7] The LORD has sworn by the pride of
   Jacob:
"Surely I will never forget any of their
   works.
[8] Shall the land not tremble for this,
And everyone mourn who dwells in it?
All of it shall swell like the River,[a]
Heave and subside
Like the River of Egypt.

[9] "And it shall come to pass in that day,"
   says the Lord GOD,
"That I will make the sun go down at
   noon,
And I will darken the earth in broad
   daylight;
[10] I will turn your feasts into mourning,
And all your songs into lamentation;

I will bring sackcloth on every waist,
And baldness on every head;
I will make it like mourning for an
   only son,
And its end like a bitter day.

[11] "Behold, the days are coming," says
   the Lord GOD,
"That I will send a famine on the land,
Not a famine of bread,
Nor a thirst for water,
But of hearing the words of the LORD.
[12] They shall wander from sea to sea,
And from north to east;
They shall run to and fro, seeking the
   word of the LORD,
But shall not find it.

[13] "In that day the fair virgins
And strong young men
Shall faint from thirst.
[14] Those who swear by the sin[a] of Samaria,
Who say,
'As your god lives, O Dan!'
And, 'As the way of Beersheba lives!'
They shall fall and never rise again."

The Destruction of Israel

9 I saw the Lord standing by the altar, and He said:

"Strike the doorposts, that the
   thresholds may shake,
And break them on the heads of them
   all.
I will slay the last of them with the
   sword.
He who flees from them shall not get
   away,
And he who escapes from them shall
   not be delivered.

[2] "Though they dig into hell,[a]
From there My hand shall take them;
Though they climb up to heaven,
From there I will bring them down;

8:4 [a]Or *trample on* (compare 2:7)   **8:8** [a]That is, the Nile; some Hebrew manuscripts, Septuagint, Syriac, Targum, and Vulgate read *River;* Masoretic Text reads *the light.*   **8:14** [a]Or *Ashima,* a Syrian goddess   **9:2** [a]Or *Sheol*

3 And though they hide themselves on
    top of Carmel,
  From there I will search and take them;
  Though they hide from My sight at
    the bottom of the sea,
  From there I will command the
    serpent, and it shall bite them;
4 Though they go into captivity before
    their enemies,
  From there I will command the sword,
  And it shall slay them.
  I will set My eyes on them for harm
    and not for good."

5 The Lord GOD of hosts,
  He who touches the earth and it melts,
  And all who dwell there mourn;
  All of it shall swell like the River,ª
  And subside like the River of Egypt.
6 He who builds His layers in the sky,
  And has founded His strata in the earth;
  Who calls for the waters of the sea,
  And pours them out on the face of the
    earth—
  The LORD is His name.

7 "Are you not like the people of Ethiopia
    to Me,
  O children of Israel?" says the LORD.
  "Did I not bring up Israel from the land
    of Egypt,
  The Philistines from Caphtor,
  And the Syrians from Kir?

8 "Behold, the eyes of the Lord GOD are
    on the sinful kingdom,
  And I will destroy it from the face of
    the earth;
  Yet I will not utterly destroy the house
    of Jacob,"
  Says the LORD.

9 "For surely I will command,
  And will sift the house of Israel
    among all nations,
  As grain is sifted in a sieve;
  Yet not the smallest grain shall fall to
    the ground.
10 All the sinners of My people shall die
    by the sword,
  Who say, 'The calamity shall not
    overtake nor confront us.'

Israel Will Be Restored

11 "On that day I will raise up
  The tabernacleª of David, which has
    fallen down,
  And repair its damages;
  I will raise up its ruins,
  And rebuild it as in the days of old;
12 That they may possess the remnant of
    Edom,ª
  And all the Gentiles who are called by
    My name,"
  Says the LORD who does this thing.

13 "Behold, the days are coming," says
    the LORD,
  "When the plowman shall overtake the
    reaper,
  And the treader of grapes him who
    sows seed;
  The mountains shall drip with sweet
    wine,
  And all the hills shall flow with it.
14 I will bring back the captives of My
    people Israel;
  They shall build the waste cities and
    inhabit them;
  They shall plant vineyards and drink
    wine from them;
  They shall also make gardens and eat
    fruit from them.
15 I will plant them in their land,
  And no longer shall they be pulled up
  From the land I have given them,"
  Says the LORD your God.

9:5 ªThat is, the Nile   **9:11** ªLiterally *booth*, figure of
a deposed dynasty   **9:12** ªSeptuagint reads *mankind*.

OBADIAH

Author: Obadiah

When Written: Shortly After 586 B.C.

Theme: God's Judgment on Edom

Key Verse: Obadiah 21—Then saviors shall come to Mount Zion to judge the mountains of Esau, and the kingdom shall be the LORD's.

"Though force can protect in emergency," declared America's 34th President, Dwight David Eisenhower, "only justice, fairness, consideration, and cooperation can finally lead men to the dawn of eternal peace."

The Book of Obadiah speaks directly to the issues of justice and fairness. God's people had a long-standing feud with the neighboring nation of Edom, even though the two peoples were distant blood relatives. When Judah was conquered by Babylon, Edom not only rejoiced but looted Judah and captured those trying to escape, turning them over to their enemies. Obadiah condemns Edom's treachery and arrogance, declaring that God will destroy them for coming against His people. Moreover, Obadiah prophesies the future restoration of Israel through His own faithfulness.

OBADIAH

The Coming Judgment on Edom

The vision of Obadiah.

Thus says the Lord GOD concerning
Edom
(We have heard a report from the LORD,
And a messenger has been sent
among the nations, *saying,*
"Arise, and let us rise up against her
for battle"):

2 "Behold, I will make you small among
the nations;
You shall be greatly despised.
3 The pride of your heart has deceived
you,
You who dwell in the clefts of the rock,
Whose habitation *is* high;
You who say in your heart, 'Who will
bring me down to the ground?'
4 Though you ascend *as* high as the
eagle,
And though you set your nest among
the stars,
From there I will bring you down,"
says the LORD.

5 "If thieves had come to you,
If robbers by night—
Oh, how you will be cut off!—
Would they not have stolen till they
had enough?
If grape-gatherers had come to you,
Would they not have left *some*
gleanings?

6 "Oh, how Esau shall be searched out!
How his hidden treasures shall be
sought after!
7 All the men in your confederacy
Shall force you to the border;
The men at peace with you
Shall deceive you *and* prevail against
you.
Those who eat your bread shall lay a
trap[a] for you.
No one is aware of it.

8 "Will I not in that day," says the LORD,
"Even destroy the wise *men* from Edom,
And understanding from the
mountains of Esau?
9 Then your mighty men, O Teman,
shall be dismayed,
To the end that everyone from the
mountains of Esau
May be cut off by slaughter.

Edom Mistreated His Brother

10 "For violence against your brother
Jacob,
Shame shall cover you,
And you shall be cut off forever.
11 In the day that you stood on the
other side—
In the day that strangers carried
captive his forces,
When foreigners entered his gates
And cast lots for Jerusalem—
Even you *were* as one of them.

12 "But you should not have gazed on
the day of your brother
In the day of his captivity;[a]
Nor should you have rejoiced over the
children of Judah
In the day of their destruction;
Nor should you have spoken proudly
In the day of distress.
13 You should not have entered the gate
of My people
In the day of their calamity.
Indeed, you should not have gazed
on their affliction
In the day of their calamity,
Nor laid *hands* on their substance
In the day of their calamity.
14 You should not have stood at the
crossroads
To cut off those among them who
escaped;

---

7 [a]Or *wound,* or *plot*   **12** [a]Literally *on the day he
became a foreigner*

Nor should you have delivered up
   those among them who remained
In the day of distress.

15 "For the day of the LORD upon all the
   nations *is* near;
As you have done, it shall be done to
   you;
Your reprisal shall return upon your
   own head.

16 For as you drank on My holy mountain,
So shall all the nations drink
   continually;
Yes, they shall drink, and swallow,
And they shall be as though they had
   never been.

Israel's Final Triumph

17 "But on Mount Zion there shall be
   deliverance,

And there shall be holiness;
The house of Jacob shall possess their
   possessions.

18 The house of Jacob shall be a fire,
And the house of Joseph a flame;
But the house of Esau *shall be* stubble;
They shall kindle them and devour
   them,
And no survivor shall *remain* of the
   house of Esau,"
For the LORD has spoken.

19 The South[a] shall possess the mountains
   of Esau,
And the Lowland shall possess Philistia.
They shall possess the fields of Ephraim
And the fields of Samaria.
Benjamin *shall possess* Gilead.

---

19 [a]Hebrew *Negev*

HOPE

"But on Mount Zion there shall be deliverance. . . ."

OBADIAH 17

Henry Wadsworth Longfellow

"SAIL ON, O SHIP OF STATE!"

Henry Wadsworth Longfellow (1807–1882) was by far the most widely known and best-loved American poet of his time. He achieved a level of national and international prominence possibly unequaled in the literary history of the United States. A fervent abolitionist, his poem "The Building of a Ship" was a pro-Union allegory that speaks of his fear that the slavery issue would destroy the Union. Upon hearing the poem recited, President Lincoln was said to have wept:

Thou, too, sail on, O Ship of State!
Sail on, O Union, strong and great!
Humanity with all its fears,
With all the hopes of future years,
Is hanging breathless on thy fate! . . .

Our hearts, our hopes, are all with thee,
Our hearts, our hopes, our prayers, our tears,
Our faith triumphant o'er our fears,
Are all with thee—are all with thee!

In early 1941, President Franklin Roosevelt sent a handwritten letter to English Prime Minister Churchill and included the first five lines of Longfellow's poem, stating the verse "applies to you people as it does to us." Churchill wrote back that he was "deeply moved" and cited the letter as a symbol of the growing partnership between England and the United States. "Give us the tools," he told the president, "and we will finish the job!"

20 And the captives of this host of the
     children of Israel
Shall possess the land of the Canaanites
As far as Zarephath.
The captives of Jerusalem who are in
     Sepharad

Shall possess the cities of the South.[a]

21 Then saviors[a] shall come to Mount Zion
To judge the mountains of Esau,
And the kingdom shall be the LORD's.

---

20 [a]Hebrew *Negev*   **21** [a]Or *deliverers*

JONAH

Author: Probably Jonah

When Written: About 760 B.C. or After 612 B.C.

Theme: God's Compassion for All Humanity

Key Verse: Jonah 2:9—"I will sacrifice to You with the voice of thanksgiving; I will pay what I have vowed. Salvation is of the LORD."

Key Chapter: Jonah 3—The third chapter of this unique Old Testament prophetic book records one of the greatest spiritual revivals in history, revealing the extent to which God is willing to go to show His mercy to sinful humanity.

When God called the prophet Jonah to preach repentance to the wicked people of Nineveh, Jonah instead ran the other way. After Jonah spent three harrowing days in the belly of a big fish, he agreed to go to Nineveh, where the people openly received and responded to God's message of repentance. The Book of Jonah illustrates God's eagerness to extend His forgiveness and mercy to even the most undeserving of sinners.

In the depths of the Civil War, President Abraham Lincoln appealed to God's mercy when he proclaimed a National Fast Day for March 30, 1863, admonishing the American people to "rest humbly in the hope authorized by the Divine teachings, that the united cry of the nation will be heard on high and answered with blessing no less than the pardon of our national sins and the restoration of our now divided and suffering country to its former happy condition of unity and peace."

JONAH

Jonah's Disobedience

1 Now the word of the LORD came to Jonah the son of Amittai, saying, ²"Arise, go to Nineveh, that great city, and cry out against it; for their wickedness has come up before Me." ³But Jonah arose to flee to Tarshish from the presence of the LORD. He went down to Joppa, and found a ship going to Tarshish; so he paid the fare, and went down into it, to go with them to Tarshish from the presence of the LORD.

The Storm at Sea

⁴But the LORD sent out a great wind on the sea, and there was a mighty tempest on the sea, so that the ship was about to be broken up.

⁵Then the mariners were afraid; and every man cried out to his god, and threw the cargo that *was* in the ship into the sea, to lighten the load.ᵃ But Jonah had gone down into the lowest parts of the ship, had lain down, and was fast asleep.

⁶So the captain came to him, and said to him, "What do you mean, sleeper? Arise, call on your God; perhaps your God will consider us, so that we may not perish."

⁷And they said to one another, "Come, let us cast lots, that we may know for whose cause this trouble *has come* upon us." So they cast lots, and the lot fell on Jonah. ⁸Then they said to him, "Please tell us! For whose cause *is* this trouble upon us? What is your occupation? And where do you come from? What is your country? And of what people are you?"

⁹So he said to them, "I *am* a Hebrew; and I fear the LORD, the God of heaven, who made the sea and the dry *land.*"

Jonah Thrown into the Sea

¹⁰Then the men were exceedingly afraid, and said to him, "Why have you done this?" For the men knew that he fled from the presence of the LORD, because he had told them. ¹¹Then they said to him, "What shall we do to you that the sea may be calm for us?"—for the sea was growing more tempestuous.

¹²And he said to them, "Pick me up and throw me into the sea; then the sea will become calm for you. For I know that this great tempest *is* because of me."

¹³Nevertheless the men rowed hard to return to land, but they could not, for the sea continued to grow more tempestuous against them. ¹⁴Therefore they cried out to the LORD and said, "We pray, O LORD, please do not let us perish for this man's life, and do not charge us with innocent blood; for You, O LORD, have done as it pleased You." ¹⁵So they picked up Jonah and threw him into the sea, and the sea ceased from its raging. ¹⁶Then the men feared the LORD exceedingly, and offered a sacrifice to the LORD and took vows.

Jonah's Prayer and Deliverance

¹⁷Now the LORD had prepared a great fish to swallow Jonah. And Jonah was in the belly of the fish three days and three nights.

2 Then Jonah prayed to the LORD his God from the fish's belly. ²And he said:

"I cried out to the LORD because of my
    affliction,
And He answered me.

"Out of the belly of Sheol I cried,
    And You heard my voice.
3   For You cast me into the deep,
    Into the heart of the seas,
    And the floods surrounded me;
    All Your billows and Your waves
        passed over me.
4   Then I said, 'I have been cast out
        of Your sight;
    Yet I will look again toward Your
        holy temple.'
5   The waters surrounded me, *even* to
        my soul;

1:5 ᵃLiterally *from upon them*

The deep closed around me;
Weeds were wrapped around my head.
6 I went down to the moorings of the
      mountains;
   The earth with its bars *closed* behind
      me forever;
   Yet You have brought up my life from
      the pit,
   O LORD, my God.

7 "When my soul fainted within me,
   I remembered the LORD;
   And my prayer went *up* to You,
   Into Your holy temple.

8 "Those who regard worthless idols
   Forsake their own Mercy.
9 But I will sacrifice to You
   With the voice of thanksgiving;
   I will pay what I have vowed.
   Salvation *is* of the LORD."

¹⁰So the LORD spoke to the fish, and it vomited Jonah onto dry *land.*

INSPIRING

So the people of Nineveh believed God. . . .

JONAH 3:5

Revival Fires

William W. Bennett was a Confederate chaplain who published a first-hand account of the spiritual renewal that swept through every corps, division, brigade, and regiment in General Robert E. Lee's Army of Northern Virginia.

Up to January 1865, it was estimated that nearly 150,000 soldiers had been converted during the progress of the war, and it was believed that fully one-third of all the soldiers in the field were praying men and members of some branch of the Christian church.

Jonah Preaches at Nineveh

3 Now the word of the LORD came to Jonah the second time, saying, ²"Arise, go to Nineveh, that great city, and preach to it the message that I tell you." ³So Jonah arose and went to Nineveh, according to the word of the LORD. Now Nineveh was an exceedingly great city, a three-day journey[a]

MORAL STRENGTH

Then God saw . . . that they turned from their evil way. . . .

JONAH 3:10

On Moral Decay

General Douglas MacArthur, Supreme Commander of the Allied Forces in the Pacific during World War II, said in December 1951:

In this day of gathering storms, as moral deterioration of political power spreads its growing infection, it is essential that every spiritual force be mobilized to defend and preserve the religious base upon which this nation is founded; for it has been that base which has been the motivating impulse to our moral and national growth. History fails to record a single precedent in which nations subject to moral decay have not passed into political and economic decline. There has been either a spiritual reawakening to overcome the moral lapse or a progressive deterioration leading to ultimate national disaster.

---

in extent. ⁴And Jonah began to enter the city on the first day's walk. Then he cried out and said, "Yet forty days, and Nineveh shall be overthrown!"

The People of Nineveh Believe

⁵So the people of Nineveh believed God, proclaimed a fast, and put on sackcloth, from the greatest to the least of them. ⁶Then word came to the king of Nineveh; and he arose from his throne and laid aside his robe, covered *himself* with sackcloth and sat in ashes. ⁷And he caused *it* to be proclaimed and published throughout Nineveh by the decree of the king and his nobles, saying,

Let neither man nor beast, herd nor flock, taste anything; do not let them eat, or drink water. ⁸But let man and beast be covered with sackcloth, and cry mightily to God; yes, let every one turn from his evil way and from the violence that is in his hands. ⁹Who can tell *if* God will turn and relent, and turn away from His fierce anger, so that we may not perish?

3:3 ᵃExact meaning unknown

¹⁰Then God saw their works, that they turned from their evil way; and God relented from the disaster that He had said He would bring upon them, and He did not do it.

Jonah's Anger and God's Kindness

4 But it displeased Jonah exceedingly, and he became angry. ²So he prayed to the LORD, and said, "Ah, LORD, was not this what I said when I was still in my country? Therefore I fled previously to Tarshish; for I know that You *are* a gracious and merciful God, slow to anger and abundant in lovingkindness, One who relents from doing harm. ³Therefore now, O LORD, please take my life from me, for *it is* better for me to die than to live!"

⁴Then the LORD said, "*Is it* right for you to be angry?"

⁵So Jonah went out of the city and sat on the east side of the city. There he made himself a shelter and sat under it in the shade, till he might see what would become of the city. ⁶And the LORD God prepared a plant[a] and made it come up over Jonah, that it might be shade for his head to deliver him from his misery. So Jonah was very grateful for the plant. ⁷But as morning dawned the next day God prepared a worm, and it *so* damaged the plant that it withered. ⁸And it happened, when the sun arose, that God prepared a vehement east wind; and the sun beat on Jonah's head, so that he grew faint. Then he wished death for himself, and said, "*It is* better for me to die than to live."

⁹Then God said to Jonah, "*Is it* right for you to be angry about the plant?"

And he said, "*It is* right for me to be angry, even to death!"

¹⁰But the LORD said, "You have had pity on the plant for which you have not labored, nor made it grow, which came up in a night and perished in a night. ¹¹And should I not pity Nineveh, that great city, in which are more than one hundred and twenty thousand persons who cannot discern between their right hand and their left—and much livestock?"

4:6 ᵃHebrew *kikayon*, exact identity unknown

MICAH

Author: Micah

When Written: 704–696 B.C.

Theme: God's Incomparable Compassion

Key Verse: Micah 7:18—Who is a God like You, pardoning iniquity and passing over the transgression of the remnant of His heritage? He does not retain His anger forever, because He delights in mercy.

Key Chapter: Micah 7—The prophet offers the promise that the same God who executes judgment against Judah will turn His heart back to His people, extending mercy and restoration.

The powerful Assyrian empire was expanding and demanded surrender from Israel. When the people rebelled, the Assyrians destroyed the capital city of Samaria and took many into exile. The prophet Micah wrote to the people to warn them of God's approaching judgment because they had rejected Him and His law. Nonetheless, Micah offers hope to the faithful few who have kept the word of the Lord, assuring them that God will one day restore their nation.

John Winthrop, founder and governor of the Massachusetts Bay Colony, in his classic work *A Model of Christian Charity*, referenced the Book of Micah in 1630, noting that "to provide for our posterity, is to follow the counsel of Micah, to do justly, to love mercy, to walk humbly with our God. For this end, we must be knit together in this work as one man. We must hold a familiar commerce together in each other in all meekness, gentleness, patience, and liberality. We must delight in each other; make others' conditions our own; rejoice together, mourn together, labor and suffer together, always having before our eyes our commission and community in the work, as members of the same body. So shall we keep the unity of the spirit in the bond of peace."

MICAH

1 The word of the LORD that came to Micah of Moresheth in the days of Jotham, Ahaz, *and* Hezekiah, kings of Judah, which he saw concerning Samaria and Jerusalem.

The Coming Judgment on Israel

2 Hear, all you peoples!
   Listen, O earth, and all that is in it!
   Let the Lord GOD be a witness against you,
   The Lord from His holy temple.

3 For behold, the LORD is coming out of His place;
   He will come down
   And tread on the high places of the earth.
4 The mountains will melt under Him,
   And the valleys will split
   Like wax before the fire,
   Like waters poured down a steep place.
5 All this is for the transgression of Jacob
   And for the sins of the house of Israel.
   What *is* the transgression of Jacob?
   Is it not Samaria?
   And what *are* the high places of Judah?
   Are they not Jerusalem?

6 "Therefore I will make Samaria a heap of ruins in the field,
   Places for planting a vineyard;
   I will pour down her stones into the valley,
   And I will uncover her foundations.
7 All her carved images shall be beaten to pieces,
   And all her pay as a harlot shall be burned with the fire;
   All her idols I will lay desolate,
   For she gathered *it* from the pay of a harlot,
   And they shall return to the pay of a harlot."

Mourning for Israel and Judah

8 Therefore I will wail and howl,
   I will go stripped and naked;
   I will make a wailing like the jackals
   And a mourning like the ostriches,
9 For her wounds *are* incurable.
   For it has come to Judah;
   It has come to the gate of My people—
   To Jerusalem.

10 Tell *it* not in Gath,
   Weep not at all;
   In Beth Aphrah[a]
   Roll yourself in the dust.
11 Pass by in naked shame, you inhabitant of Shaphir;
   The inhabitant of Zaanan[a] does not go out.
   Beth Ezel mourns;
   Its place to stand is taken away from you.

12 For the inhabitant of Maroth pined[a] for good,
   But disaster came down from the LORD
   To the gate of Jerusalem.
13 O inhabitant of Lachish,
   Harness the chariot to the swift steeds
   (She *was* the beginning of sin to the daughter of Zion),
   For the transgressions of Israel were found in you.

14 Therefore you shall give presents to Moresheth Gath;[a]
   The houses of Achzib[b] *shall be* a lie to the kings of Israel.
15 I will yet bring an heir to you,
   O inhabitant of Mareshah;[a]
   The glory of Israel shall come to Adullam.

1:10 [a]Literally *House of Dust*   1:11 [a]Literally *Going Out*   1:12 [a]Literally *was sick*   1:14 [a]Literally *Possession of Gath* [b]Literally *Lie*   1:15 [a]Literally *Inheritance*

16 Make yourself bald and cut off your
      hair,
Because of your precious children;
Enlarge your baldness like an eagle,
For they shall go from you into
      captivity.

Woe to Evildoers

2 Woe to those who devise iniquity,
   And work out evil on their beds!
   At morning light they practice it,
   Because it is in the power of their hand.
2 They covet fields and take *them* by
      violence,
   Also houses, and seize *them.*
   So they oppress a man and his house,
   A man and his inheritance.

³Therefore thus says the LORD:

"Behold, against this family I am
      devising disaster,
From which you cannot remove your
      necks;
Nor shall you walk haughtily,
For this *is* an evil time.
4 In that day *one* shall take up a
      proverb against you,
   And lament with a bitter lamentation,
      saying:
   'We are utterly destroyed!
   He has changed the heritage of my
      people;
   How He has removed *it* from me!
   To a turncoat He has divided our
      fields.' "

5 Therefore you will have no one to
      determine boundariesᵃ by lot
   In the assembly of the LORD.

Lying Prophets

6 "Do not prattle," *you say to those* who
      prophesy.
   So they shall not prophesy to you;ᵃ
   They shall not return insult for insult.ᵇ
7 *You who are* named the house of
      Jacob:
   "Is the Spirit of the LORD restricted?
   Are these His doings?
   Do not My words do good
   To him who walks uprightly?

8 "Lately My people have risen up as an
      enemy—
   You pull off the robe with the garment
   From those who trust *you,* as they
      pass by,
   Like men returned from war.
9 The women of My people you cast out
   From their pleasant houses;
   From their children
   You have taken away My glory forever.

10 "Arise and depart,
   For this *is* not *your* rest;
   Because it is defiled, it shall destroy,
   Yes, with utter destruction.
11 If a man should walk in a false spirit
   And speak a lie, *saying,*
   'I will prophesy to you of wine and
      drink,'
   Even he would be the prattler of this
      people.

Israel Restored

12 "I will surely assemble all of you,
      O Jacob,
   I will surely gather the remnant of
      Israel;
   I will put them together like sheep
      of the fold,ᵃ
   Like a flock in the midst of their
      pasture;
   They shall make a loud noise because
      of *so many* people.
13 The one who breaks open will come
      up before them;
   They will break out,
   Pass through the gate,
   And go out by it;
   Their king will pass before them,
   With the LORD at their head."

Wicked Rulers and Prophets

3 And I said:

"Hear now, O heads of Jacob,
   And you rulers of the house of Israel:
   Is it not for you to know justice?
2 You who hate good and love evil;

2:5 ᵃLiterally *one casting a surveyor's line*
2:6 ᵃLiterally *to these* ᵇVulgate reads *He shall not
take shame.* **2:12** ᵃHebrew *Bozrah*

Who strip the skin from My people,[a]
And the flesh from their bones;
3 Who also eat the flesh of My people,
Flay their skin from them,
Break their bones,
And chop *them* in pieces
Like *meat* for the pot,
Like flesh in the caldron."

4 Then they will cry to the LORD,
But He will not hear them;
He will even hide His face from them
    at that time,
Because they have been evil in their
    deeds.

5 Thus says the LORD concerning the
    prophets
Who make my people stray;
Who chant "Peace"
While they chew with their teeth,
But who prepare war against him
Who puts nothing into their mouths:
6 "Therefore you shall have night
    without vision,
And you shall have darkness without
    divination;
The sun shall go down on the prophets,
And the day shall be dark for them.
7 So the seers shall be ashamed,
And the diviners abashed;
Indeed they shall all cover their lips;
For *there is* no answer from God."

8 But truly I am full of power by the
    Spirit of the LORD,
And of justice and might,
To declare to Jacob his transgression
And to Israel his sin.
9 Now hear this,
You heads of the house of Jacob
And rulers of the house of Israel,
Who abhor justice
And pervert all equity,
10 Who build up Zion with bloodshed
And Jerusalem with iniquity:
11 Her heads judge for a bribe,
Her priests teach for pay,
And her prophets divine for money.
Yet they lean on the LORD, and say,
"Is not the LORD among us?
No harm can come upon us."

12 Therefore because of you
Zion shall be plowed *like* a field,
Jerusalem shall become heaps of ruins,
And the mountain of the temple[a]
Like the bare hills of the forest.

The LORD's Reign in Zion

4 Now it shall come to pass in the latter
    days
That the mountain of the LORD's house
Shall be established on the top of the
    mountains,
And shall be exalted above the hills;
And peoples shall flow to it.
2 Many nations shall come and say,
"Come, and let us go up to the
    mountain of the LORD,
To the house of the God of Jacob;
He will teach us His ways,
And we shall walk in His paths."
For out of Zion the law shall go forth,
And the word of the LORD from
    Jerusalem.
3 He shall judge between many peoples,
And rebuke strong nations afar off;
They shall beat their swords into
    plowshares,
And their spears into pruning hooks;
Nation shall not lift up sword against
    nation,
Neither shall they learn war
    anymore.[a]

4 But everyone shall sit under his vine
    and under his fig tree,
And no one shall make *them* afraid;
For the mouth of the LORD of hosts has
    spoken.
5 For all people walk each in the name
    of his god,
But we will walk in the name of the
    LORD our God
Forever and ever.

Zion's Future Triumph

6 "In that day," says the LORD,
"I will assemble the lame,
I will gather the outcast
And those whom I have afflicted;

3:2 [a]Literally *them*   **3:12** [a]Literally *house*
4:3 [a]Compare Isaiah 2:2–4

7 I will make the lame a remnant,
And the outcast a strong nation;
So the LORD will reign over them in
   Mount Zion
From now on, even forever.

8 And you, O tower of the flock,
The stronghold of the daughter of
   Zion,
To you shall it come,
Even the former dominion shall come,
The kingdom of the daughter of
   Jerusalem."

9 Now why do you cry aloud?
Is there no king in your midst?
Has your counselor perished?
For pangs have seized you like a
   woman in labor.

10 Be in pain, and labor to bring forth,
O daughter of Zion,
Like a woman in birth pangs.
For now you shall go forth from the
   city,
You shall dwell in the field,
And to Babylon you shall go.
There you shall be delivered;
There the LORD will redeem you
From the hand of your enemies.

11 Now also many nations have
   gathered against you,
Who say, "Let her be defiled,
And let our eye look upon Zion."

12 But they do not know the thoughts of
   the LORD,
Nor do they understand His counsel;
For He will gather them like sheaves
   to the threshing floor.

13 "Arise and thresh, O daughter of Zion;
For I will make your horn iron,
And I will make your hooves bronze;
You shall beat in pieces many peoples;
I will consecrate their gain to the LORD,
And their substance to the Lord of the
   whole earth."

5 Now gather yourself in troops,
O daughter of troops;
He has laid siege against us;
They will strike the judge of Israel
   with a rod on the cheek.

TRUTH

"... out of you shall come forth to Me the One
to be Ruler in Israel. ..."   MICAH 5:2

Inexplicable Evidences

Robert Morris Page (1903–1970), the physicist known as the "Father of U.S. Radar," wrote:

The authenticity of the writings of the prophets . . . is established by such things as the prediction of highly significant events far in the future that could be accomplished only through a knowledge obtained from a realm that is not subject to the laws of time as we know them.

One of the great evidences is the long series of prophecies concerning Jesus the Messiah. These prophecies extend hundreds of years prior to the birth of Christ. They include a vast amount of detail concerning Christ himself, His nature and the things He would do when He came— things which to the natural world, or the scientific world, remain to this day completely inexplicable.

The Coming Messiah

2 "But you, Bethlehem Ephrathah,
Though you are little among the
   thousands of Judah,
Yet out of you shall come forth to Me
The One to be Ruler in Israel,
Whose goings forth *are* from of old,
From everlasting."

3 Therefore He shall give them up,
Until the time *that* she who is in labor
   has given birth;
Then the remnant of His brethren
Shall return to the children of Israel.

4 And He shall stand and feed *His flock*
In the strength of the LORD,
In the majesty of the name of the
   LORD His God;
And they shall abide,
For now He shall be great
To the ends of the earth;

5 And this *One* shall be peace.

Judgment on Israel's Enemies

When the Assyrian comes into our land,
And when he treads in our palaces,

Then we will raise against him
Seven shepherds and eight princely
men.
6 They shall waste with the sword the
land of Assyria,
And the land of Nimrod at its
entrances;
Thus He shall deliver *us* from the
Assyrian,
When he comes into our land
And when he treads within our borders.

7 Then the remnant of Jacob
Shall be in the midst of many peoples,
Like dew from the LORD,
Like showers on the grass,
That tarry for no man
Nor wait for the sons of men.
8 And the remnant of Jacob
Shall be among the Gentiles,
In the midst of many peoples,
Like a lion among the beasts of the
forest,
Like a young lion among flocks of
sheep,
Who, if he passes through,
Both treads down and tears in pieces,
And none can deliver.
9 Your hand shall be lifted against your
adversaries,
And all your enemies shall be cut off.

10 "And it shall be in that day," says the
LORD,
"That I will cut off your horses from
your midst
And destroy your chariots.
11 I will cut off the cities of your land
And throw down all your strongholds.
12 I will cut off sorceries from your hand,
And you shall have no soothsayers.
13 Your carved images I will also cut off,
And your *sacred* pillars from your
midst;
You shall no more worship the work of
your hands;
14 I will pluck your wooden images[a] from
your midst;
Thus I will destroy your cities.
15 And I will execute vengeance in anger
and fury
On the nations that have not heard."[a]

God Pleads with Israel

6 Hear now what the LORD says:

"Arise, plead your case before the
mountains,
And let the hills hear your voice.
2 Hear, O you mountains, the LORD's
complaint,
And you strong foundations of the
earth;
For the LORD has a complaint against
His people,
And He will contend with Israel.

3 "O My people, what have I done to you?
And how have I wearied you?
Testify against Me.
4 For I brought you up from the land
of Egypt,
I redeemed you from the house of
bondage;
And I sent before you Moses, Aaron,
and Miriam.
5 O My people, remember now
What Balak king of Moab counseled,
And what Balaam the son of Beor
answered him,
From Acacia Grove[a] to Gilgal,
That you may know the righteousness
of the LORD."

6 With what shall I come before the LORD,
And bow myself before the High God?
Shall I come before Him with burnt
offerings,
With calves a year old?
7 Will the LORD be pleased with
thousands of rams,
Ten thousand rivers of oil?
Shall I give my firstborn *for* my
transgression,
The fruit of my body *for* the sin of
my soul?

Warren G. Harding placed his hand on
Micah 6:8 as he took the presidential oath
of office in 1921.

5:14 [a]Hebrew *Asherim,* Canaanite deities
5:15 [a]Or *obeyed*   **6:5** [a]Hebrew *Shittim* (compare
Numbers 25:1; Joshua 2:1; 3:1)

Jimmy Carter placed his hand on Micah 6:8 as he took the presidential oath of office in 1977.

8 He has shown you, O man, what *is* good;
And what does the LORD require of you
But to do justly,
To love mercy,
And to walk humbly with your God?

Punishment of Israel's Injustice

9 The LORD's voice cries to the city—
Wisdom shall see Your name:

"Hear the rod!
Who has appointed it?

10 Are there yet the treasures of wickedness
In the house of the wicked,
And the short measure *that is* an abomination?
11 Shall I count pure *those* with the wicked scales,
And with the bag of deceitful weights?
12 For her rich men are full of violence,
Her inhabitants have spoken lies,
And their tongue is deceitful in their mouth.

13 "Therefore I will also make *you* sick by striking you,
By making *you* desolate because of your sins.

PROTECTOR

He has shown you, O man, what is good. . . .

MICAH 6:8

Thomas Jefferson

A WISE AND FRUGAL GOVERNMENT

In his 1801 Inaugural Address, President Thomas Jefferson stated:

Sometimes it is said that man cannot be trusted with the government of himself. Can he, then, be trusted with the government of others? Or have we found angels in the forms of kings to govern him? Let history answer this question. Let us, then, with courage and confidence pursue our own federal and republican principles. . . .

Enlightened by a benign religion, professed, indeed, and practiced in various forms, yet all of them inculcating honesty, truth, temperance, gratitude, and the love of man; acknowledging and adoring an overruling Providence, which by all its dispensations proves that it delights in the happiness of man here and his greater happiness hereafter. With all these blessings, what more is necessary to make us a happy and prosperous people? Still one thing more, fellow citizens—a wise and frugal government, which shall restrain men from injuring one another, shall leave them otherwise free to regulate their own pursuits of industry and improvement, and shall not take from the mouth of labor the bread it has earned. . . .

You should understand what I deem the essential principles of our government. . . . Equal and exact justice to all men, of whatever state or persuasion, religious or political . . . the arraignment of all abuses at the bar of the public reason; freedom of religion; freedom of the press, and freedom of person under the protection of the habeas corpus and trial by jury impartially selected. . . .

14 You shall eat, but not be satisfied;
   Hunger^a *shall be* in your midst.
   You may carry *some* away,^b but shall
      not save *them;*
   And what you do rescue I will give
      over to the sword.

15 "You shall sow, but not reap;
   You shall tread the olives, but not
      anoint yourselves with oil;
   And *make* sweet wine, but not drink
      wine.

16 For the statutes of Omri are kept;
   All the works of Ahab's house *are done;*
   And you walk in their counsels,
   That I may make you a desolation,
   And your inhabitants a hissing.
   Therefore you shall bear the reproach
      of My people."^a

Sorrow for Israel's Sins

7 Woe is me!
   For I am like those who gather summer
      fruits,
   Like those who glean vintage grapes;
   There is no cluster to eat
   Of the first-ripe fruit *which* my soul
      desires.
2 The faithful *man* has perished from
      the earth,
   And *there is* no one upright among men.
   They all lie in wait for blood;
   Every man hunts his brother with a net.

3 That they may successfully do evil
      with both hands—
   The prince asks *for gifts,*
   The judge *seeks* a bribe,
   And the great *man* utters his evil desire;
   So they scheme together.
4 The best of them *is* like a brier;
   The most upright *is sharper* than a
      thorn hedge;
   The day of your watchman and your
      punishment comes;
   Now shall be their perplexity.

5 Do not trust in a friend;
   Do not put your confidence in a
      companion;
   Guard the doors of your mouth
   From her who lies in your bosom.

6 For son dishonors father,
   Daughter rises against her mother,
   Daughter-in-law against her mother-
      in-law;
   A man's enemies *are* the men of his
      own household.
7 Therefore I will look to the LORD;
   I will wait for the God of my salvation;
   My God will hear me.

Israel's Confession and Comfort

8 Do not rejoice over me, my enemy;
   When I fall, I will arise;
   When I sit in darkness,
   The LORD *will be* a light to me.
9 I will bear the indignation of the LORD,
   Because I have sinned against Him,
   Until He pleads my case
   And executes justice for me.
   He will bring me forth to the light;
   I will see His righteousness.
10 Then *she who is* my enemy will see,
   And shame will cover her who said
      to me,
   "Where is the LORD your God?"
   My eyes will see her;
   Now she will be trampled down
   Like mud in the streets.

11 *In* the day when your walls are to be
      built,
   In that day the decree shall go far and
      wide.^a
12 *In* that day they^a shall come to you
   From Assyria and the fortified cities,^b
   From the fortress^c to the River,^d
   From sea to sea,
   And mountain *to* mountain.
13 Yet the land shall be desolate
   Because of those who dwell in it,
   And for the fruit of their deeds.

God Will Forgive Israel

14 Shepherd Your people with Your staff,
   The flock of Your heritage,

6:14 ^aOr *Emptiness* or *Humiliation* ^bTargum and
Vulgate read *You shall take hold.* **6:16** ^aFollowing
Masoretic Text, Targum, and Vulgate; Septuagint
reads *of nations.* **7:11** ^aOr *the boundary shall be
extended* **7:12** ^aLiterally *he,* collective of the
captives ^bHebrew *arey mazor,* possibly *cities of Egypt*
^cHebrew *mazor,* possibly *Egypt* ^dThat is, the Euphrates

Who dwell solitarily *in* a woodland,
In the midst of Carmel;
Let them feed *in* Bashan and Gilead,
As in days of old.

15 "As in the days when you came out of
   the land of Egypt,
   I will show them[a] wonders."

16 The nations shall see and be ashamed
   of all their might;
   They shall put *their* hand over *their*
   mouth;
   Their ears shall be deaf.
17 They shall lick the dust like a serpent;
   They shall crawl from their holes like
   snakes of the earth.
   They shall be afraid of the LORD our God,
   And shall fear because of You.

18 Who *is* a God like You,
   Pardoning iniquity
   And passing over the transgression of
   the remnant of His heritage?

   He does not retain His anger forever,
   Because He delights *in* mercy.
19 He will again have compassion on us,
   And will subdue our iniquities.

   You will cast all our[a] sins
   Into the depths of the sea.
20 You will give truth to Jacob
   And mercy to Abraham,
   Which You have sworn to our fathers
   From days of old.

7:15 [a]Literally *him,* collective for the captives
7:19 [a]Literally *their*

NAHUM

Author: Nahum

When Written: Shortly Before 612 B.C.

Theme: Judgment Against Nineveh

Key Verse: Nahum 1:7—The LORD is good, a stronghold in the day of trouble; and He knows those who trust in Him.

Key Chapter: The opening chapter of Nahum records the principles guiding God's judgment against wicked Nineveh, as well as His mercy and deliverance on Judah.

Nahum was written approximately one hundred years after God had extended mercy to a repentant Nineveh through the preaching of the prophet Jonah. As the years passed, the Assyrian leaders once again hardened their hearts against God and His people, bringing God's swift and terrible judgment against the city of Nineveh. Through this, the nation of Judah sees a God who is all-powerful, holy, just, merciful, and always true to His Word. He assures them that evil will not last forever and that God will fulfill His plan and bring permanent restoration to Israel.

In the long struggle for civil rights, Martin Luther King Jr. held on to the hope that equality and justice would finally come for all Americans: "I refuse to accept the view that mankind is so tragically bound to the starless midnight of racism and war that the bright daybreak of peace and brotherhood can never become reality. I believe that unarmed truth and unconditional love will have the final word."

NAHUM

1 The burden[a] against Nineveh. The book of the vision of Nahum the Elkoshite.

God's Wrath on His Enemies

2 God *is* jealous, and the LORD avenges;
The LORD avenges and *is* furious.
The LORD will take vengeance on His
adversaries,
And He reserves *wrath* for His enemies;
3 The LORD *is* slow to anger and great in
power,
And will not at all acquit *the wicked.*

The LORD has His way
In the whirlwind and in the storm,
And the clouds *are* the dust of His feet.
4 He rebukes the sea and makes it dry,
And dries up all the rivers.
Bashan and Carmel wither,
And the flower of Lebanon wilts.
5 The mountains quake before Him,
The hills melt,
And the earth heaves[a] at His presence,
Yes, the world and all who dwell in it.

6 Who can stand before His indignation?
And who can endure the fierceness of
His anger?
His fury is poured out like fire,
And the rocks are thrown down by
Him.

7 The LORD *is* good,
A stronghold in the day of trouble;
And He knows those who trust in Him.
8 But with an overflowing flood
He will make an utter end of its place,
And darkness will pursue His enemies.

9 What do you conspire against the LORD?
He will make an utter end *of it.*
Affliction will not rise up a second time.
10 For while tangled *like* thorns,
And while drunken *like* drunkards,
They shall be devoured like stubble
fully dried.

11 From you comes forth *one*
Who plots evil against the LORD,
A wicked counselor.

12 Thus says the LORD:

"Though *they are* safe, and likewise
many,
Yet in this manner they will be cut
down
When he passes through.
Though I have afflicted you,
I will afflict you no more;
13 For now I will break off his yoke from
you,
And burst your bonds apart."

14 The LORD has given a command
concerning you:
"Your name shall be perpetuated no
longer.
Out of the house of your gods
I will cut off the carved image and
the molded image.
I will dig your grave,
For you are vile."

15 Behold, on the mountains
The feet of him who brings good tidings,
Who proclaims peace!
O Judah, keep your appointed feasts,
Perform your vows.
For the wicked one shall no more pass
through you;
He is utterly cut off.

The Destruction of Nineveh

2 He who scatters[a] has come up before
your face.
Man the fort!
Watch the road!
Strengthen *your* flanks!
Fortify *your* power mightily.

1:1 [a]Or *oracle*   1:5 [a]Targum reads *burns.*
2:1 [a]Vulgate reads *He who destroys.*

2 For the LORD will restore the excellence
       of Jacob
    Like the excellence of Israel,
    For the emptiers have emptied them
       out
    And ruined their vine branches.

3 The shields of his mighty men *are*
       made red,
    The valiant men *are* in scarlet.
    The chariots *come* with flaming
       torches
    In the day of his preparation,
    And the spears are brandished.ᵃ
4 The chariots rage in the streets,
    They jostle one another in the broad
       roads;
    They seem like torches,
    They run like lightning.

5 He remembers his nobles;
    They stumble in their walk;
    They make haste to her walls,
    And the defense is prepared.
6 The gates of the rivers are opened,
    And the palace is dissolved.
7 It is decreed:ᵃ
    She shall be led away captive,
    She shall be brought up;

    And her maidservants shall lead *her*
       as with the voice of doves,
    Beating their breasts.

8 Though Nineveh of old *was* like a pool
       of water,
    Now they flee away.
    "Halt! Halt!" *they cry;*
    But no one turns back.
9 Take spoil of silver!
    Take spoil of gold!
    There is no end of treasure,
    Or wealth of every desirable prize.
10 She is empty, desolate, and waste!
    The heart melts, and the knees shake;
    Much pain *is* in every side,
    And all their faces are drained of color.ᵃ

11 Where *is* the dwelling of the lions,
    And the feeding place of the young
       lions,
    Where the lion walked, the lioness *and*
       lion's cub,
    And no one made *them* afraid?
12 The lion tore in pieces enough for his
       cubs,
    Killed for his lionesses,
    Filled his caves with prey,
    And his dens with flesh.

13"Behold, I *am* against you," says the
LORD of hosts, "I will burn yourᵃ chariots in
smoke, and the sword shall devour your
young lions; I will cut off your prey from
the earth, and the voice of your messengers shall be heard no more."

The Woe of Nineveh

3 Woe to the bloody city!
    It *is* all full of lies *and* robbery.
    Its victim never departs.
2 The noise of a whip
    And the noise of rattling wheels,
    Of galloping horses,
    Of clattering chariots!
3 Horsemen charge with bright sword
       and glittering spear.

2:3 ᵃLiterally *the cypresses are shaken;* Septuagint and
Syriac read *the horses rush about;* Vulgate reads *the
drivers are stupefied.*   **2:7** ᵃHebrew *Huzzab*
2:10 ᵃCompare Joel 2:6   **2:13** ᵃLiterally *her*

There is a multitude of slain,
A great number of bodies,
Countless corpses—
They stumble over the corpses—

4 Because of the multitude of harlotries
   of the seductive harlot,
The mistress of sorceries,
Who sells nations through her
   harlotries,
And families through her sorceries.

5 "Behold, I *am* against you," says the
   LORD of hosts;
"I will lift your skirts over your face,
I will show the nations your nakedness,
And the kingdoms your shame.

6 I will cast abominable filth upon you,
Make you vile,
And make you a spectacle.

7 It shall come to pass *that* all who
   look upon you
Will flee from you, and say,
'Nineveh is laid waste!
Who will bemoan her?'
Where shall I seek comforters for you?"

8 Are you better than No Amon[a]
That was situated by the River,[b]
That had the waters around her,
Whose rampart *was* the sea,
Whose wall *was* the sea?

9 Ethiopia and Egypt *were* her strength,
And *it was* boundless;
Put and Lubim were your[a] helpers.

10 Yet she *was* carried away,
She went into captivity;
Her young children also were dashed
   to pieces
At the head of every street;
They cast lots for her honorable men,
And all her great men were bound in
   chains.

11 You also will be drunk;
You will be hidden;
You also will seek refuge from the
   enemy.

12 All your strongholds *are* fig trees with
   ripened figs:

If they are shaken,
They fall into the mouth of the eater.

13 Surely, your people in your midst *are*
   women!
The gates of your land are wide open
   for your enemies;
Fire shall devour the bars of your *gates.*

14 Draw your water for the siege!
Fortify your strongholds!
Go into the clay and tread the mortar!
Make strong the brick kiln!

15 There the fire will devour you,
The sword will cut you off;
It will eat you up like a locust.

Make yourself many—like the locust!
Make yourself many— like the
   swarming locusts!

16 You have multiplied your merchants
   more than the stars of heaven.
The locust plunders and flies away.

17 Your commanders *are* like *swarming*
   locusts,
And your generals like great
   grasshoppers,
Which camp in the hedges on a cold
   day;
When the sun rises they flee away,
And the place where they *are* is not
   known.

18 Your shepherds slumber, O king of
   Assyria;
Your nobles rest *in the dust.*
Your people are scattered on the
   mountains,
And no one gathers them.

19 Your injury *has* no healing,
Your wound is severe.
All who hear news of you
Will clap *their* hands over you,
For upon whom has not your
   wickedness passed continually?

3:8 [a]That is, ancient Thebes; Targum and Vulgate
read *populous Alexandria.* [b]Literally *rivers,* that is, the
Nile and the surrounding canals   **3:9** [a]Septuagint
reads *her.*

HABAKKUK

Author: Habakkuk

When Written: Around 600 B.C.

Theme: The Just Shall Live by Faith

Key Verse: Habakkuk 2:4—"Behold the proud, his soul is not upright in him; but the just shall live by his faith."

Key Chapter: Habakkuk 3—Building to a triumphant climax in its last three verses, chapter three of this prophetic book records the glory of God that reaches from the distant past to the hopeful future.

As America suffered defeat after defeat in the War of 1812 with the British, Canadians, and First Nations allies, President James Madison proclaimed a national day of prayer in July 1813, emphasizing the importance of a nation humbling itself before Almighty God and pleading for His help against injustice: "Whereas in times of public calamity, such as that of the war brought on the United States by the injustice of a foreign government, it is especially becoming that the hearts of all should be touched with the same and the eyes of all be turned to that Almighty Power in whose hands are the welfare and the destiny of nations."

The Book of Habakkuk records the prophet's personal struggle with God on the issues of injustice and evil. Habakkuk anguished over the sins of his people and wondered why this evil and the evil of the conquering Babylonians went unpunished. God assured Habakkuk that His justice will always prevail, prompting Habakkuk to turn from despondency to powerful praise and a declaration that no matter the circumstances, "Yet I will rejoice in the LORD, I will joy in the God of my salvation" (3:18).

HABAKKUK

1 The burden[a] which the prophet Habakkuk saw.

The Prophet's Question

2 O LORD, how long shall I cry,
And You will not hear?
Even cry out to You, "Violence!"
And You will not save.
3 Why do You show me iniquity,
And cause *me* to see trouble?
For plundering and violence *are*
before me;
There is strife, and contention arises.
4 Therefore the law is powerless,
And justice never goes forth.
For the wicked surround the righteous;
Therefore perverse judgment proceeds.

The LORD's Reply

5 "Look among the nations and watch—
Be utterly astounded!
For *I will* work a work in your days
Which you would not believe, though
it were told *you*.
6 For indeed I am raising up the
Chaldeans,
A bitter and hasty nation
Which marches through the breadth
of the earth,
To possess dwelling places *that are* not
theirs.
7 They are terrible and dreadful;
Their judgment and their dignity
proceed from themselves.
8 Their horses also are swifter than
leopards,
And more fierce than evening wolves.
Their chargers charge ahead;
Their cavalry comes from afar;
They fly as the eagle *that* hastens to eat.

9 "They all come for violence;
Their faces are set *like* the east wind.
They gather captives like sand.
10 They scoff at kings,
And princes are scorned by them.
They deride every stronghold,

For they heap up earthen *mounds*
and seize it.
11 Then *his* mind[a] changes, and he
transgresses;
He commits offense,
Ascribing this power to his god."

The Prophet's Second Question

12 Are You not from everlasting,
O LORD my God, my Holy One?
We shall not die.
O LORD, You have appointed them for
judgment;
O Rock, You have marked them for
correction.
13 *You are* of purer eyes than to behold
evil,
And cannot look on wickedness.
Why do You look on those who deal
treacherously,
And hold Your tongue when the
wicked devours
A *person* more righteous than he?
14 *Why* do You make men like fish of the
sea,
Like creeping things *that have* no ruler
over them?

15 They take up all of them with a hook,
They catch them in their net,
And gather them in their dragnet.
Therefore they rejoice and are glad.
16 Therefore they sacrifice to their net,
And burn incense to their dragnet;
Because by them their share *is*
sumptuous
And their food plentiful.
17 Shall they therefore empty their net,
And continue to slay nations without
pity?

2 I will stand my watch
And set myself on the rampart,
And watch to see what He will say
to me,

1:1 [a]Or *oracle*   **1:11** [a]Literally *spirit* or *wind*

And what I will answer when I am
corrected.

The Just Live by Faith

²Then the LORD answered me and said:

"Write the vision
And make *it* plain on tablets,
That he may run who reads it.
3   For the vision *is* yet for an appointed
time;
But at the end it will speak, and it
will not lie.
Though it tarries, wait for it;
Because it will surely come,
It will not tarry.

4   "Behold the proud,
His soul is not upright in him;
But the just shall live by his faith.

FAITH

". . . the just shall live by his faith."

HABAKKUK 2:4

Faith of the Founding Fathers

George H.W. Bush, the 41st president of the United
States, stated:

*The great faith that led our nation's Founding
Fathers to pursue this bold experience in self-
government has sustained us in uncertain and
perilous times; it has given us strength and
inspiration to this very day.*

*Like them, we do very well to recall our "firm
reliance on the protection of Divine Providence,"
to give thanks for the freedom and prosperity
this nation enjoys, and to pray for continued
help and guidance from our wise and loving
Creator.*

Woe to the Wicked

5   "Indeed, because he transgresses by
wine,
He is a proud man,
And he does not stay at home.
Because he enlarges his desire as hell,ᵃ
And he *is* like death, and cannot be
satisfied,
He gathers to himself all nations
And heaps up for himself all peoples.

6   "Will not all these take up a proverb
against him,
And a taunting riddle against him,
and say,
'Woe to him who increases
What is not his—how long?
And to him who loads himself with
many pledges'?ᵃ
7   Will not your creditorsᵃ rise up
suddenly?
Will they not awaken who oppress
you?
And you will become their booty.
8   Because you have plundered many
nations,
All the remnant of the people shall
plunder you,
Because of men's blood
And the violence of the land *and*
the city,
And of all who dwell in it.

9   "Woe to him who covets evil gain
for his house,
That he may set his nest on high,
That he may be delivered from the
power of disaster!
10   You give shameful counsel to your
house,
Cutting off many peoples,
And sin *against* your soul.
11   For the stone will cry out from the
wall,
And the beam from the timbers will
answer it.

12   "Woe to him who builds a town with
bloodshed,
Who establishes a city by iniquity!
13   Behold, *is it* not of the LORD of hosts
That the peoples labor to feed the
fire,ᵃ
And nations weary themselves in vain?
14   For the earth will be filled
With the knowledge of the glory
of the LORD,
As the waters cover the sea.

2:5 ᵃOr *Sheol*   **2:6** ᵃSyriac and Vulgate read *thick
clay.*   **2:7** ᵃLiterally *those who bite you*
2:13 ᵃLiterally *for what satisfies fire,* that is, for what is
of no lasting value

¹⁵ "Woe to him who gives drink to his
　　neighbor,
Pressing^a *him to* your bottle,
Even to make *him* drunk,
That you may look on his nakedness!
¹⁶ You are filled with shame instead of
　　glory.
You also—drink!
And be exposed as uncircumcised!^a
The cup of the LORD's right hand *will
　　be* turned against you,
And utter shame will be on your glory.
¹⁷ For the violence *done to* Lebanon will
　　cover you,
And the plunder of beasts *which* made
　　them afraid,
Because of men's blood
And the violence of the land *and* the city,
And of all who dwell in it.

¹⁸ "What profit is the image, that its
　　maker should carve it,
The molded image, a teacher of lies,
That the maker of its mold should
　　trust in it,
To make mute idols?
¹⁹ Woe to him who says to wood, 'Awake!'
To silent stone, 'Arise! It shall teach!'
Behold, it is overlaid with gold and
　　silver,
Yet in it there is no breath at all.

²⁰ "But the LORD is in His holy temple.
Let all the earth keep silence before
　　Him."

The Prophet's Prayer

3 A prayer of Habakkuk the prophet, on
Shigionoth.^a

²　O LORD, I have heard Your speech *and*
　　was afraid;
O LORD, revive Your work in the midst
　　of the years!
In the midst of the years make *it* known;
In wrath remember mercy.

³　God came from Teman,
The Holy One from Mount Paran. *Selah*

His glory covered the heavens,
And the earth was full of His praise.

⁴　*His* brightness was like the light;
He had rays *flashing* from His hand,
And there His power *was* hidden.
⁵　Before Him went pestilence,
And fever followed at His feet.

⁶　He stood and measured the earth;
He looked and startled the nations.
And the everlasting mountains were
　　scattered,
The perpetual hills bowed.
His ways *are* everlasting.
⁷　I saw the tents of Cushan in affliction;
The curtains of the land of Midian
　　trembled.

⁸　O LORD, were *You* displeased with the
　　rivers,
Was Your anger against the rivers,
Was Your wrath against the sea,
That You rode on Your horses,
Your chariots of salvation?
⁹　Your bow was made quite ready;
Oaths were sworn over *Your* arrows.^a
　　　　　　　　　　　　　　　Selah

You divided the earth with rivers.
¹⁰ The mountains saw You *and* trembled;
The overflowing of the water passed by.
The deep uttered its voice,
And lifted its hands on high.
¹¹ The sun and moon stood still in their
　　habitation;
At the light of Your arrows they went,
At the shining of Your glittering spear.

¹² You marched through the land in
　　indignation;
You trampled the nations in anger.
¹³ You went forth for the salvation of
　　Your people,
For salvation with Your Anointed.
You struck the head from the house
　　of the wicked,
By laying bare from foundation to
　　neck.　　　　　　　　　　　*Selah*

2:15 ^aLiterally *Attaching* or *Joining*　　**2:16** ^aDead Sea
Scrolls and Septuagint read *And reel!;* Syriac and
Vulgate read *And fall fast asleep!*　　**3:1** ^aExact
meaning unknown　　**3:9** ^aLiterally *rods* or *tribes*
(compare verse 14)

14 You thrust through with his own
    arrows
  The head of his villages.
  They came out like a whirlwind to
    scatter me;
  Their rejoicing was like feasting on
    the poor in secret.
15 You walked through the sea with
    Your horses,
  Through the heap of great waters.

16 When I heard, my body trembled;
  My lips quivered at *the* voice;
  Rottenness entered my bones;
  And I trembled in myself,
  That I might rest in the day of
    trouble.
  When he comes up to the people,
  He will invade them with his
    troops.

A Hymn of Faith

17 Though the fig tree may not blossom,
  Nor fruit be on the vines;
  Though the labor of the olive may fail,
  And the fields yield no food;
  Though the flock may be cut off from
    the fold,
  And there be no herd in the stalls—
18 Yet I will rejoice in the LORD,
  I will joy in the God of my salvation.

19 The LORD God[a] is my strength;
  He will make my feet like deer's *feet*,
  And He will make me walk on my
    high hills.

  To the Chief Musician. With my stringed
  instruments.

_____

3:19 [a]Hebrew *YHWH Adonai*

HUMILITY

... *in wrath*
remember mercy.

HABAKKUK 3:2

Abraham Lincoln

THE FIRST NATIONAL DAY OF THANKSGIVING

In the midst of the Civil War, President Abraham Lincoln initiated the first annual National Day of Thanksgiving and Praise on October 3, 1863, issuing a formal Proclamation, passed by an Act of Congress:

  ... No human counsel hath devised nor hath any mortal hand worked out these great things. They are the gracious gifts of the Most High God, who, while dealing with us in anger for our sins, hath nevertheless remembered mercy. It has seemed to me fit and proper that they should be solemnly, reverently, and gratefully acknowledged as with one heart and one voice by the whole American People. I do therefore invite my fellow citizens in every part of the United States, and also those who are at sea and those who are sojourning in foreign lands, to set apart and observe the last Thursday of November next, as a day of Thanksgiving and Praise to our beneficent Father who dwelleth in the Heavens.
  And I recommend to them that while offering up the ascriptions justly due to Him for such singular deliverances and blessings, they do also, with humble penitence for our national perverseness and disobedience, commend to His tender care all those who have become widows, orphans, mourners, or sufferers in the lamentable civil strife in which we are unavoidably engaged, and fervently implore the interposition of the Almighty Hand to heal the wounds of the nation and to restore it as soon as may be consistent with the Divine purposes to the full enjoyment of peace, harmony, tranquility, and Union.

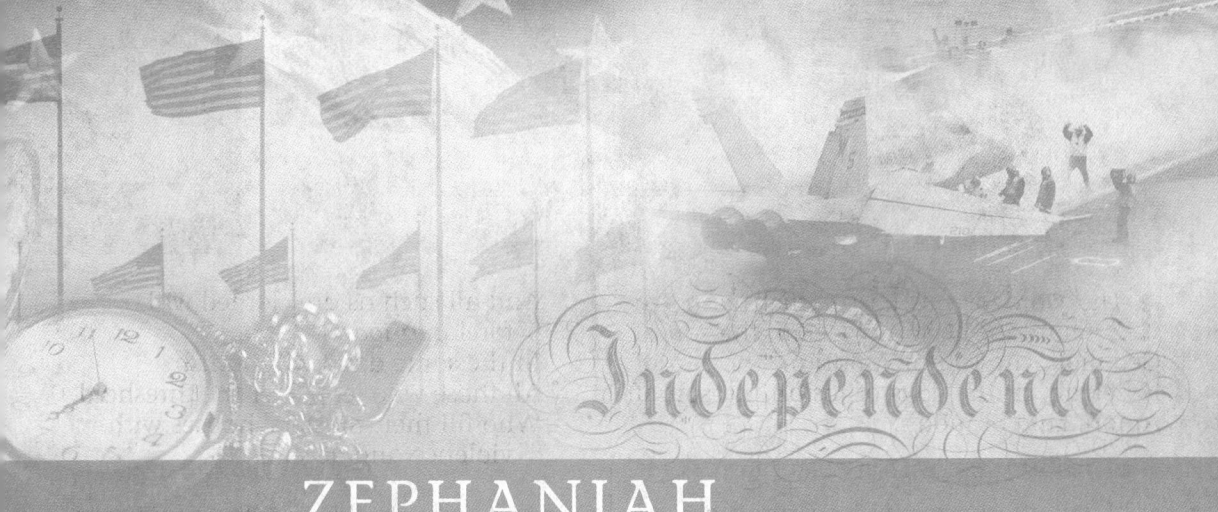

ZEPHANIAH

Author: Zephaniah

When Written: Around 630 B.C.

Theme: Judgment of a Loving God

Key Verse: Zephaniah 2:3—Seek the LORD, all you meek of the earth, who have upheld His justice. Seek righteousness, seek humility. It may be that you will be hidden in the day of the LORD's anger.

Key Chapter: Zephaniah 3—The last chapter of Zephaniah records the two distinct parts of the day of the Lord: judgment and restoration.

In 1843, Emma Willard, a historian and pioneer who founded the first women's school of higher education, wrote: "The government of the United States is acknowledged by the wise and good of other nations, to be the most free, impartial, and righteous government of the world; but all agree, that for such a government to be sustained for many years, the principles of truth and righteousness, taught in the Holy Scriptures, must be practiced. The rulers must govern in the fear of God, and the people obey the laws."

In Zephaniah's day, the civil and religious leaders of Judah had grown corrupt and idolatry was widespread. The prophet wrote to the people of Judah to warn them of impending judgment and the coming of the "day of the LORD" (1:14, 15). But he tempers the message of judgment with one of mercy, declaring that God is also gracious and compassionate. What begins as a prophecy of doom concludes triumphantly as Zephaniah reveals God's unending love and righteousness.

ZEPHANIAH

1 The word of the LORD which came to Zephaniah the son of Cushi, the son of Gedaliah, the son of Amariah, the son of Hezekiah, in the days of Josiah the son of Amon, king of Judah.

The Great Day of the LORD

2 "I will utterly consume everything
    From the face of the land,"
    Says the LORD;
3 "I will consume man and beast;
    I will consume the birds of the heavens,
    The fish of the sea,
    And the stumbling blocks[a] along with
      the wicked.
    I will cut off man from the face of the
      land,"
    Says the LORD.

4 "I will stretch out My hand against
      Judah,
    And against all the inhabitants of
      Jerusalem.
    I will cut off every trace of Baal from
      this place,
    The names of the idolatrous priests[a]
      with the *pagan* priests—
5 Those who worship the host of heaven
      on the housetops;
    Those who worship and swear *oaths*
      by the LORD,
    But who *also* swear by Milcom;[a]
6 Those who have turned back from
      following the LORD,
    And have not sought the LORD, nor
      inquired of Him."

7 Be silent in the presence of the Lord GOD;
    For the day of the LORD *is* at hand,
    For the LORD has prepared a sacrifice;
    He has invited[a] His guests.

8 "And it shall be,
    In the day of the LORD's sacrifice,
    That I will punish the princes and the
      king's children,
    And all such as are clothed with
      foreign apparel.
9 In the same day I will punish
    All those who leap over the threshold,[a]
    Who fill their masters' houses with
      violence and deceit.

10 "And there shall be on that day," says
      the LORD,
    "The sound of a mournful cry from the
      Fish Gate,
    A wailing from the Second Quarter,
    And a loud crashing from the hills.
11 Wail, you inhabitants of Maktesh![a]
    For all the merchant people are cut
      down;
    All those who handle money are cut
      off.

12 "And it shall come to pass at that time
    That I will search Jerusalem with lamps,
    And punish the men
    Who are settled in complacency,[a]
    Who say in their heart,
    'The LORD will not do good,
    Nor will He do evil.'
13 Therefore their goods shall become
      booty,
    And their houses a desolation;
    They shall build houses, but not
      inhabit *them;*
    They shall plant vineyards, but not
      drink their wine."

14 The great day of the LORD *is* near;
    It is near and hastens quickly.
    The noise of the day of the LORD is
      bitter;
    There the mighty men shall cry out.

1:3 [a]Figurative of idols   1:4 [a]Hebrew *chemarim*
1:5 [a]Or *Malcam,* an Ammonite god, also called *Molech* (compare Leviticus 18:21)   1:7 [a]Literally *set apart, consecrated*   1:9 [a]Compare 1 Samuel 5:5
1:11 [a]Literally *Mortar,* a market district of Jerusalem
1:12 [a]Literally *on their lees,* that is, settled like the dregs of wine

15 That day *is* a day of wrath,
A day of trouble and distress,
A day of devastation and desolation,
A day of darkness and gloominess,
A day of clouds and thick darkness,
16 A day of trumpet and alarm
Against the fortified cities
And against the high towers.

17 "I will bring distress upon men,
And they shall walk like blind men,
Because they have sinned against the
Lord;
Their blood shall be poured out like
dust,
And their flesh like refuse."

18 Neither their silver nor their gold
Shall be able to deliver them
In the day of the Lord's wrath;
But the whole land shall be devoured
By the fire of His jealousy,
For He will make speedy riddance
Of all those who dwell in the land.

A Call to Repentance

2 Gather yourselves together, yes, gather together,
O undesirable[a] nation,
2 Before the decree is issued,
Or the day passes like chaff,
Before the Lord's fierce anger comes
upon you,
Before the day of the Lord's anger
comes upon you!
3 Seek the Lord, all you meek of the earth,
Who have upheld His justice.
Seek righteousness, seek humility.
It may be that you will be hidden
In the day of the Lord's anger.

Judgment on Nations

4 For Gaza shall be forsaken,
And Ashkelon desolate;
They shall drive out Ashdod at noonday,
And Ekron shall be uprooted.
5 Woe to the inhabitants of the seacoast,
The nation of the Cherethites!
The word of the Lord *is* against you,
O Canaan, land of the Philistines:
"I will destroy you;
So there shall be no inhabitant."

6 The seacoast shall be pastures,
With shelters[a] for shepherds and folds
for flocks.
7 The coast shall be for the remnant of
the house of Judah;
They shall feed *their* flocks there;
In the houses of Ashkelon they shall
lie down at evening.
For the Lord their God will intervene
for them,
And return their captives.

MORAL STRENGTH
Seek righteousness, seek humility.
ZEPHANIAH 2:3

One Great Political Idea
Frederick Douglass, the greatest civil rights leader
of the nineteenth century, declared:

*I have one great political idea. . . . That idea is
an old one. It is widely and generally assented
to; nevertheless, it is very generally trampled
upon and disregarded. The best expression of
it, I have found in the Bible. It is in substance:
"Righteousness exalteth a nation; sin is a
reproach to any people." This constitutes my
politics—the negative and positive of my politics, and the whole of my politics. . . . I feel it my
duty to do all in my power to infuse this idea
into the public mind, that it may speedily be
recognized and practiced upon by our people.*

8 "I have heard the reproach of Moab,
And the insults of the people of
Ammon,
With which they have reproached
My people,
And made arrogant threats against
their borders.
9 Therefore, as I live,"
Says the Lord of hosts, the God of
Israel,
"Surely Moab shall be like Sodom,
And the people of Ammon like
Gomorrah—
Overrun with weeds and saltpits,
And a perpetual desolation.

2:1 [a]Or *shameless*   **2:6** [a]Literally *excavations*, either
underground huts or cisterns

The residue of My people shall
    plunder them,
And the remnant of My people shall
    possess them."

10 This they shall have for their pride,
    Because they have reproached and
        made arrogant threats
    Against the people of the LORD of hosts.
11 The LORD *will be* awesome to them,
    For He will reduce to nothing all the
        gods of the earth;
    People shall worship Him,
    Each one from his place,
    Indeed all the shores of the nations.

12 "You Ethiopians also,
    You shall be slain by My sword."

13 And He will stretch out His hand
        against the north,
    Destroy Assyria,
    And make Nineveh a desolation,
    As dry as the wilderness.
14 The herds shall lie down in her midst,
    Every beast of the nation.
    Both the pelican and the bittern
    Shall lodge on the capitals *of* her *pillars;*
    Their voice shall sing in the windows;
    Desolation *shall be* at the threshold;
    For He will lay bare the cedar work.
15 This is the rejoicing city
    That dwelt securely,
    That said in her heart,
    "I *am it,* and *there is* none besides me."
    How has she become a desolation,
    A place for beasts to lie down!
    Everyone who passes by her
    Shall hiss and shake his fist.

The Wickedness of Jerusalem

3 Woe to her who is rebellious and
    polluted,
    To the oppressing city!
2 She has not obeyed *His* voice,
    She has not received correction;
    She has not trusted in the LORD,
    She has not drawn near to her God.

3 Her princes in her midst *are* roaring
    lions;
    Her judges *are* evening wolves

That leave not a bone till morning.
4 Her prophets are insolent, treacherous
    people;
    Her priests have polluted the sanctuary,
    They have done violence to the law.
5 The LORD *is* righteous in her midst,
    He will do no unrighteousness.
    Every morning He brings His justice
        to light;
    He never fails,
    But the unjust knows no shame.

6 "I have cut off nations,
    Their fortresses are devastated;
    I have made their streets desolate,
    With none passing by.
    Their cities are destroyed;
    There is no one, no inhabitant.
7 I said, 'Surely you will fear Me,
    You will receive instruction'—
    So that her dwelling would not be
        cut off,
    Despite everything for which I
        punished her.
    But they rose early and corrupted
        all their deeds.

A Faithful Remnant

8 "Therefore wait for Me," says the
    LORD,
    "Until the day I rise up for plunder;a
    My determination *is* to gather the
        nations
    To My assembly of kingdoms,
    To pour on them My indignation,
    All My fierce anger;
    All the earth shall be devoured
    With the fire of My jealousy.

9 "For then I will restore to the peoples
        a pure language,
    That they all may call on the name
        of the LORD,
    To serve Him with one accord.
10 From beyond the rivers of Ethiopia
    My worshipers,
    The daughter of My dispersed ones,
    Shall bring My offering.

3:8 aSeptuagint and Syriac read *for witness;* Targum
reads *for the day of My revelation for judgment;* Vulgate
reads *for the day of My resurrection that is to come.*

11 In that day you shall not be shamed
     for any of your deeds
   In which you transgress against Me;
   For then I will take away from your
     midst
   Those who rejoice in your pride,
   And you shall no longer be haughty
   In My holy mountain.
12 I will leave in your midst
   A meek and humble people,
   And they shall trust in the name of
     the LORD.
13 The remnant of Israel shall do no
     unrighteousness
   And speak no lies,
   Nor shall a deceitful tongue be found
     in their mouth;
   For they shall feed *their* flocks and lie
     down,
   And no one shall make *them* afraid."

Joy in God's Faithfulness

14 Sing, O daughter of Zion!
   Shout, O Israel!

Be glad and rejoice with all *your* heart,
     O daughter of Jerusalem!
15 The LORD has taken away your
     judgments,
   He has cast out your enemy.
   The King of Israel, the LORD, *is* in your
     midst;
   You shall see[a] disaster no more.

16 In that day it shall be said to Jerusalem:
   "Do not fear;
   Zion, let not your hands be weak.
17 The LORD your God in your midst,
   The Mighty One, will save;
   He will rejoice over you with gladness,
   He will quiet *you* with His love,
   He will rejoice over you with singing."

18 "I will gather those who sorrow over
     the appointed assembly,

3:15 [a]Some Hebrew manuscripts, Septuagint, and
Bomberg read *see;* Masoretic Text and Vulgate read
fear.

INSPIRING

*"Do not fear; Zion,
let not your
hands be weak."*

ZEPHANIAH 3:16

Franklin Delano Roosevelt

FACING FEAR IN DARK HOURS

In his First Inaugural Address, Franklin Delano Roosevelt,
the 32nd President of the United States (1933–1945), proclaimed to the nation, as it just entered the Depression:

> First of all, let me assert my firm belief that the only
> thing we have to fear is fear itself—nameless, unreason-
> ing, unjustified terror which paralyzes needed efforts to
> convert retreat into advance. . . . In such a spirit on my
> part and on yours we face our common difficulties. They
> concern, thank God, only material things. . . .
>
> Practices of the unscrupulous moneychangers stand
> indicted in the court of public opinion, rejected by the
> hearts and minds of men. . . . They know only the rules
> of a generation of self-seekers. They have no vision, and
> where there is no vision the people perish [Proverbs 29:18].
> The moneychangers have fled from their high seats in
> the temple of our civilization. We may now restore that
> temple to the ancient truths. . . .
>
> We face arduous days that lie before us in the warm
> courage of national unity; with the clear consciousness
> of seeking old and precious moral values. . . .
>
> In this dedication of a nation we humbly ask the bless-
> ing of God. May He protect each and every one of us!
> May He guide me in the days to come.

Who are among you,
To whom its reproach *is* a burden.
19 Behold, at that time
I will deal with all who afflict you;
I will save the lame,
And gather those who were driven
   out;
I will appoint them for praise and
   fame

In every land where they were put
   to shame.
20 At that time I will bring you back,
Even at the time I gather you;
For I will give you fame and praise
Among all the peoples of the earth,
When I return your captives before
   your eyes,"
Says the Lord.

HAGGAI

Author: Haggai

When Written: 520 B.C.

Theme: Rebuilding the Temple

Key Verse: Haggai 2:9—" 'The glory of this latter temple shall be greater than the former,' says the LORD of hosts. 'And in this place I will give peace,' says the LORD of hosts."

Key Chapter: Haggai 2—In chapter 2, the prophet Haggai declares the glorious restoration of God's house, which is ultimately fulfilled in the coming of the Messiah.

With the Babylonian exile behind them, the children of Israel returned to their land and enthusiastically began to rebuild the temple. But their initial joy was dampened by hard work, fear, and other hardships, causing them to become despondent and to put the project aside. When the project was still uncompleted after 16 years, the prophet Haggai stepped in to show the people that they had been putting their own priorities above God's. When they repented, put God first, and completed the temple, God responded by blessing them with joy and prosperity.

In 1966, Senator Robert F. Kennedy described what happens when citizens join together in a righteous cause: "Few will have the greatness to bend history itself, but each of us can work to change a small portion of events, and in the total of all those acts will be written the history of this generation. . . . It is from numberless diverse acts of courage and belief that human history is shaped. Each time a man stands up for an ideal, or acts to improve the lot of others, or strikes out against injustice, he sends forth a tiny ripple of hope, and crossing each other from a million different centers of energy and daring, those ripples build a current that can sweep down the mightiest walls of oppression and resistance."

HAGGAI

The Command to Build God's House

1 In the second year of King Darius, in the sixth month, on the first day of the month, the word of the LORD came by Haggai the prophet to Zerubbabel the son of Shealtiel, governor of Judah, and to Joshua the son of Jehozadak, the high priest, saying, ²"Thus speaks the LORD of hosts, saying: 'This people says, "The time has not come, the time that the LORD's house should be built."'"

³Then the word of the LORD came by Haggai the prophet, saying, ⁴"*Is it* time for you yourselves to dwell in your paneled houses, and this templeª *to lie* in ruins?" ⁵Now therefore, thus says the LORD of hosts: "Consider your ways!

6 "You have sown much, and bring in little;
    You eat, but do not have enough;
    You drink, but you are not filled with drink;
    You clothe yourselves, but no one is warm;
    And he who earns wages,
    Earns wages *to put* into a bag with holes."

⁷Thus says the LORD of hosts: "Consider your ways! ⁸Go up to the mountains and bring wood and build the temple, that I may take pleasure in it and be glorified," says the LORD. ⁹"*You* looked for much, but indeed *it came to* little; and when you brought it home, I blew it away. Why?" says the LORD of hosts. "Because of My house that *is in* ruins, while every one of you runs to his own house. ¹⁰Therefore the heavens above you withhold the dew, and the earth withholds its fruit. ¹¹For I called for a drought on the land and the mountains, on the grain and the new wine and the oil, on whatever the ground brings forth, on men and livestock, and on all the labor of *your* hands."

The People's Obedience

¹²Then Zerubbabel the son of Shealtiel, and Joshua the son of Jehozadak, the high priest, with all the remnant of the people, obeyed the voice of the LORD their God, and the words of Haggai the prophet, as the LORD their God had sent him; and the people feared the presence of the LORD. ¹³Then Haggai, the LORD's messenger, spoke the LORD's message to the people, saying, "I *am* with you, says the LORD." ¹⁴So the LORD stirred up the spirit of Zerubbabel the son of Shealtiel, governor of Judah, and the spirit of Joshua the son of Jehozadak, the high priest, and the spirit of all the remnant of the people; and they came and worked on the house of the LORD of hosts, their God, ¹⁵on the twenty-fourth day of the sixth month, in the second year of King Darius.

The Coming Glory of God's House

2 In the seventh *month*, on the twenty-first of the month, the word of the LORD came by Haggai the prophet, saying: ²"Speak now to Zerubbabel the son of Shealtiel, governor of Judah, and to Joshua the son of Jehozadak, the high priest, and to the remnant of the people, saying: ³'Who is left among you who saw this templeª in its former glory? And how do you see it now? In comparison with it, *is this* not in your eyes as nothing? ⁴Yet now be strong, Zerubbabel,' says the LORD; 'and be strong, Joshua, son of Jehozadak, the high priest; and be strong, all you people of the land,' says the LORD, 'and work; for I *am* with you,' says the LORD of hosts. ⁵'*According to* the word that I covenanted with you when you came out of Egypt, so My Spirit remains among you; do not fear!'

⁶"For thus says the LORD of hosts: 'Once more (it *is* a little while) I will shake heaven and earth, the sea and dry land; ⁷and I will

---

1:4 ªLiterally *house,* and so in verse 8
2:3 ªLiterally *house,* and so in verses 7 and 9

shake all nations, and they shall come to the Desire of All Nations,ᵃ and I will fill this temple with glory,' says the LORD of hosts. ⁸'The silver *is* Mine, and the gold *is* Mine,' says the LORD of hosts. ⁹'The glory of this latter temple shall be greater than the former,' says the LORD of hosts. 'And in this place I will give peace,' says the LORD of hosts."

HOPE

"... and I will fill this temple with glory. ..."

HAGGAI 2:7

Eternal Hope

James Garfield, the 20th president of the United States (1881), who was assassinated after serving only four months, wrote:

> The world's history is a Divine poem, of which the history of every nation is a canto and every man a word. Its strains have been pealing along down the centuries, and though there have been mingled the discords of warring cannons and dying men, yet to the Christian philosopher and historian—the humble listener—there has been a Divine melody running through the song which speaks of hope and halcyon days to come.

The People Are Defiled

¹⁰On the twenty-fourth *day* of the ninth *month,* in the second year of Darius, the word of the LORD came by Haggai the prophet, saying, ¹¹"Thus says the LORD of hosts: 'Now, ask the priests *concerning the* law, saying, ¹²"If one carries holy meat in the fold of his garment, and with the edge he touches bread or stew, wine or oil, or any food, will it become holy?" ' "

Then the priests answered and said, "No."

¹³And Haggai said, "If *one who is* unclean *because* of a dead body touches any of these, will it be unclean?"

So the priests answered and said, "It shall be unclean."

¹⁴Then Haggai answered and said, " 'So is this people, and so is this nation before Me,' says the LORD, 'and so is every work of their hands; and what they offer there is unclean.

Promised Blessing

¹⁵'And now, carefully consider from this day forward: from before stone was laid upon stone in the temple of the LORD—¹⁶since those *days,* when *one* came to a heap of twenty ephahs, there were *but* ten; when *one* came to the wine vat to draw out fifty baths from the press, there were *but* twenty. ¹⁷I struck you with blight and mildew and hail in all the labors of your hands; yet you did not *turn* to Me,' says the LORD. ¹⁸'Consider now from this day forward, from the twenty-fourth day of the ninth month, from the day that the foundation of the LORD's temple was laid—consider it: ¹⁹Is the seed still in the barn? As yet the vine, the fig tree, the pomegranate, and the olive tree have not yielded *fruit. But* from this day I will bless *you.* ' "

Zerubbabel Chosen as a Signet

²⁰And again the word of the LORD came to Haggai on the twenty-fourth day of the month, saying, ²¹"Speak to Zerubbabel, governor of Judah, saying:

'I will shake heaven and earth.
²² I will overthrow the throne of
　　kingdoms;
I will destroy the strength of the
　　Gentile kingdoms.
I will overthrow the chariots
And those who ride in them;
The horses and their riders shall
　　come down,
Every one by the sword of his brother.

²³'In that day,' says the LORD of hosts, 'I will take you, Zerubbabel My servant, the son of Shealtiel,' says the LORD, 'and will make you like a signet *ring;* for I have chosen you,' says the LORD of hosts."

2:7 ᵃOr *the desire of all nations*

ZECHARIAH

Author: Zechariah

When Written: 520–475 B.C.

Theme: The Lord Remembers Zion

Key Verse: Zechariah 8:3—"Thus says the LORD: 'I will return to Zion, and dwell in the midst of Jerusalem. Jerusalem shall be called the City of Truth, the Mountain of the LORD of hosts, the Holy Mountain.'"

Key Chapter: Zechariah 14—The last chapter of Zechariah builds to a dramatic climax as the prophet discloses the initial victory of the enemies of Israel, the Lord's defense of Jerusalem, and His restoration of a Holy City and a holy people.

God's richest blessings are bestowed with certain responsibilities. As he took his place as America's 23rd President in 1889, Benjamin Harrison admonished his fellow citizens, "No other people have a government more worthy of their respect and love, or a land so magnificent in extent, so pleasant to look upon, and so full of generous suggestion to enterprise and labor. God has placed upon our head a diadem and has laid at our feet power and wealth beyond definition or calculation. But we must not forget that we take these gifts upon the condition that justice and mercy shall hold the reins of power and the upward avenues of hope shall be free to all people."

Like the prophet Haggai, the prophet Zechariah was called by God to exhort the remnant of God to finish the task of rebuilding the temple. Zechariah spurs them to action by reminding them that one day the Messiah's glory will fill the temple they are building. But their future blessing hinges upon their present obedience. As they recognize that they are building for the future, they enter into the project with renewed zeal. Zechariah declares that the children of Israel will be blessed because Yahweh remembered His covenant with their forefathers.

A Call to Repentance

1 In the eighth month of the second year of Darius, the word of the Lord came to Zechariah the son of Berechiah, the son of Iddo the prophet, saying, [2]"The Lord has been very angry with your fathers. [3]Therefore say to them, 'Thus says the Lord of hosts: "Return to Me," says the Lord of hosts, "and I will return to you," says the Lord of hosts. [4]"Do not be like your fathers, to whom the former prophets preached, saying, 'Thus says the Lord of hosts: "Turn now from your evil ways and your evil deeds." ' But they did not hear nor heed Me," says the Lord.

[5]   "Your fathers, where *are* they?
        And the prophets, do they live forever?
[6]   Yet surely My words and My statutes,
        Which I commanded My servants the
            prophets,
        Did they not overtake your fathers?

    "So they returned and said:

    'Just as the Lord of hosts determined to
        do to us,
    According to our ways and according
        to our deeds,
    So He has dealt with us.' " ' "

Vision of the Horses

[7]On the twenty-fourth day of the eleventh month, which is the month Shebat, in the second year of Darius, the word of the Lord came to Zechariah the son of Berechiah, the son of Iddo the prophet: [8]I saw by night, and behold, a man riding on a red horse, and it stood among the myrtle trees in the hollow; and behind him *were* horses: red, sorrel, and white. [9]Then I said, "My lord, what *are* these?" So the angel who talked with me said to me, "I will show you what they *are*." [10]And the man who stood among the myrtle trees answered and said, "These *are the ones* whom the Lord has sent to walk to and fro throughout the earth."

[11]So they answered the Angel of the Lord, who stood among the myrtle trees, and said, "We have walked to and fro throughout the earth, and behold, all the earth is resting quietly."

The Lord Will Comfort Zion

[12]Then the Angel of the Lord answered and said, "O Lord of hosts, how long will You not have mercy on Jerusalem and on the cities of Judah, against which You were angry these seventy years?" [13]And the Lord answered the angel who talked to me, *with* good *and* comforting words. [14]So the angel who spoke with me said to me, "Proclaim, saying, 'Thus says the Lord of hosts:

    "I am zealous for Jerusalem
        And for Zion with great zeal.
[15]   I am exceedingly angry with the
            nations at ease;
        For I was a little angry,
        And they helped—*but* with evil *intent*."

[16]'Therefore thus says the Lord:

    "I am returning to Jerusalem with mercy;
        My house shall be built in it," says the
            Lord of hosts,
    "And a *surveyor's* line shall be stretched
        out over Jerusalem."'

[17]"Again proclaim, saying, 'Thus says the Lord of hosts:

    "My cities shall again spread out
        through prosperity;
        The Lord will again comfort Zion,
        And will again choose Jerusalem." ' "

Vision of the Horns

[18]Then I raised my eyes and looked, and there *were* four horns. [19]And I said to the angel who talked with me, "What *are* these?"

So he answered me, "These *are* the horns that have scattered Judah, Israel, and Jerusalem."

²⁰Then the LORD showed me four craftsmen. ²¹And I said, "What are these coming to do?"

So he said, "These *are* the horns that scattered Judah, so that no one could lift up his head; but the craftsmenᵃ are coming to terrify them, to cast out the horns of the nations that lifted up *their* horn against the land of Judah to scatter it."

Vision of the Measuring Line

2 Then I raised my eyes and looked, and behold, a man with a measuring line in his hand. ²So I said, "Where are you going?"

And he said to me, "To measure Jerusalem, to see what *is* its width and what *is* its length."

³And there *was* the angel who talked with me, going out; and another angel was coming out to meet him, ⁴who said to him, "Run, speak to this young man, saying: 'Jerusalem shall be inhabited *as* towns without walls, because of the multitude of men and livestock in it. ⁵For I,' says the LORD, 'will be a wall of fire all around her, and I will be the glory in her midst.' "

Future Joy of Zion and Many Nations

⁶"Up, up! Flee from the land of the north," says the LORD; "for I have spread you abroad like the four winds of heaven," says the LORD. ⁷"Up, Zion! Escape, you who dwell with the daughter of Babylon."

⁸For thus says the LORD of hosts: "He sent Me after glory, to the nations which plunder you; for he who touches you touches the apple of His eye. ⁹For surely I will shake My hand against them, and they shall become spoil for their servants. Then you will know that the LORD of hosts has sent Me.

¹⁰"Sing and rejoice, O daughter of Zion! For behold, I am coming and I will dwell in your midst," says the LORD. ¹¹"Many nations shall be joined to the LORD in that day, and they shall become My people. And I will dwell in your midst. Then you will know that the LORD of hosts has sent Me to you. ¹²And the LORD will take possession of Judah as His inheritance in the Holy Land, and

will again choose Jerusalem. ¹³Be silent, all flesh, before the LORD, for He is aroused from His holy habitation!"

Vision of the High Priest

3 Then he showed me Joshua the high priest standing before the Angel of the LORD, and Satan standing at his right hand to oppose him. ²And the LORD said to Satan, "The LORD rebuke you, Satan! The LORD who has chosen Jerusalem rebuke you! *Is this* not a brand plucked from the fire?"

³Now Joshua was clothed with filthy garments, and was standing before the Angel. ⁴Then He answered and spoke to those who stood before Him, saying, "Take away the filthy garments from him." And to him He said, "See, I have removed your iniquity from you, and I will clothe you with rich robes."

⁵And I said, "Let them put a clean turban on his head."

So they put a clean turban on his head, and they put the clothes on him. And the Angel of the LORD stood by.

The Coming Branch

⁶Then the Angel of the LORD admonished Joshua, saying, ⁷"Thus says the LORD of hosts:

'If you will walk in My ways,
And if you will keep My command,
Then you shall also judge My house,
And likewise have charge of My courts;
I will give you places to walk
Among these who stand here.

8 'Hear, O Joshua, the high priest,
  You and your companions who sit
    before you,
  For they are a wondrous sign;
  For behold, I am bringing forth My
    Servant the BRANCH.
9 For behold, the stone
  That I have laid before Joshua:
  Upon the stone *are* seven eyes.
  Behold, I will engrave its inscription,'
  Says the LORD of hosts,
  'And I will remove the iniquity of that
    land in one day.

10   In that day,' says the LORD of hosts,
'Everyone will invite his neighbor
Under his vine and under his fig tree.' "

Vision of the Lampstand and Olive Trees

4 Now the angel who talked with me came back and wakened me, as a man who is wakened out of his sleep. ²And he said to me, "What do you see?"

So I said, "I am looking, and there is a lampstand of solid gold with a bowl on top of it, and on the *stand* seven lamps with seven pipes to the seven lamps. ³Two olive trees *are* by it, one at the right of the bowl and the other at its left." ⁴So I answered and spoke to the angel who talked with me, saying, "What *are* these, my lord?"

⁵Then the angel who talked with me answered and said to me, "Do you not know what these are?"

And I said, "No, my lord."

⁶So he answered and said to me:

"This *is* the word of the LORD to
Zerubbabel:
'Not by might nor by power, but by
My Spirit,'
Says the LORD of hosts.

⁷ 'Who *are* you, O great mountain?
Before Zerubbabel *you shall become*
a plain!
And he shall bring forth the
capstone
With shouts of "Grace, grace to it!" ' "

⁸Moreover the word of the LORD came to me, saying:

⁹ "The hands of Zerubbabel
Have laid the foundation of this
temple;ᵃ
His hands shall also finish *it*.
Then you will know
That the LORD of hosts has sent Me
to you.
10   For who has despised the day of
small things?
For these seven rejoice to see
The plumb line in the hand of
Zerubbabel.
They are the eyes of the LORD,
Which scan to and fro throughout
the whole earth."

4:9 ᵃLiterally *house*

MORAL STRENGTH

"For who has despised the day of small things?"

ZECHARIAH 4:10

Theodore Roosevelt

TRUE CHRISTIAN, TRUE CITIZEN

Theodore Roosevelt, the 26th President of the United States (1901–1909), the youngest man to hold the office, stated:

The true Christian is the true citizen, lofty of purpose, resolute in endeavor, ready for a hero's deeds, but never looking down on his task because it is cast in the day of small things; scornful of baseness, awake to his own duties as well as to his rights, following the higher law with reverence, and in this world doing all that in his power lies, so that when death comes he may feel that mankind is in some degree better because he lived.

Every thinking man, when he thinks, realizes that the teachings of the Bible are so interwoven and entwined with our whole civic and social life that it would be literally impossible for us to figure ourselves what that life would be if these standards were removed. We would lose almost all the standards by which we now judge both public and private morals; all the standards toward which we, with more or less resolution, strive to raise ourselves.

¹¹Then I answered and said to him, "What *are* these two olive trees—at the right of the lampstand and at its left?" ¹²And I further answered and said to him, "What *are* these two olive branches that *drip* into the receptacles[a] of the two gold pipes from which the golden *oil* drains?"

¹³Then he answered me and said, "Do you not know what these *are?*"

And I said, "No, my lord."

¹⁴So he said, "These *are* the two anointed ones, who stand beside the Lord of the whole earth."

Vision of the Flying Scroll

5 Then I turned and raised my eyes, and saw there a flying scroll.

²And he said to me, "What do you see?"

So I answered, "I see a flying scroll. Its length *is* twenty cubits and its width ten cubits."

³Then he said to me, "This *is* the curse that goes out over the face of the whole earth: 'Every thief shall be expelled,' according *to* this side of *the scroll;* and, 'Every perjurer shall be expelled,' according *to* that side of it."

⁴ "I will send out *the curse,*" says the LORD of hosts;
"It shall enter the house of the thief
And the house of the one who swears falsely by My name.
It shall remain in the midst of his house
And consume it, with its timber and stones."

Vision of the Woman in a Basket

⁵Then the angel who talked with me came out and said to me, "Lift your eyes now, and see what this *is* that goes forth."

⁶So I asked, "What *is* it?" And he said, "It *is* a basket[a] that is going forth."

He also said, "This *is* their resemblance throughout the earth: ⁷Here *is* a lead disc lifted up, and this *is* a woman sitting inside the basket"; ⁸then he said, "This *is* Wickedness!" And he thrust her down into the basket, and threw the lead cover[a] over its mouth. ⁹Then I raised my eyes and looked, and there *were* two women, coming with the wind in their wings; for they had wings like the wings of a stork, and they lifted up the basket between earth and heaven.

¹⁰So I said to the angel who talked with me, "Where are they carrying the basket?"

¹¹And he said to me, "To build a house for it in the land of Shinar;[a] when it is ready, *the basket* will be set there on its base."

Vision of the Four Chariots

6 Then I turned and raised my eyes and looked, and behold, four chariots *were* coming from between two mountains, and the mountains *were* mountains of bronze. ²With the first chariot *were* red horses, with the second chariot black horses, ³with the third chariot white horses, and with the fourth chariot dappled horses—strong *steeds.* ⁴Then I answered and said to the angel who talked with me, "What *are* these, my lord?"

⁵And the angel answered and said to me, "These *are* four spirits of heaven, who go out from *their* station before the Lord of all the earth. ⁶The one with the black horses is going to the north country, the white are going after them, and the dappled are going toward the south country." ⁷Then the strong *steeds* went out, eager to go, that they might walk to and fro throughout the earth. And He said, "Go, walk to and fro throughout the earth." So they walked to and fro throughout the earth. ⁸And He called to me, and spoke to me, saying, "See, those who go toward the north country have given rest to My Spirit in the north country."

The Command to Crown Joshua

⁹Then the word of the LORD came to me, saying: ¹⁰"Receive *the gift* from the captives—from Heldai, Tobijah, and Jedaiah, who have come from Babylon—and go the same day and enter the house of Josiah the son of Zephaniah. ¹¹Take the silver and gold, make an elaborate crown, and set *it* on the head of Joshua the son of Jehozadak, the high priest. ¹²Then speak to him, saying, 'Thus says the LORD of hosts, saying:

4:12 [a]Literally *into the hands of* **5:6** [a]Hebrew *ephah,* a measuring container, and so elsewhere **5:8** [a]Literally *stone* **5:11** [a]That is, Babylon

"Behold, the Man whose name *is* the
    BRANCH!
From His place He shall branch out,
And He shall build the temple of the
    LORD;
13 Yes, He shall build the temple of the
    LORD.
He shall bear the glory,
And shall sit and rule on His throne;
So He shall be a priest on His throne,
And the counsel of peace shall be
    between them both."'

14"Now the elaborate crown shall be for a memorial in the temple of the LORD for Helem,[a] Tobijah, Jedaiah, and Hen the son of Zephaniah. 15Even those from afar shall come and build the temple of the LORD. Then you shall know that the LORD of hosts has sent Me to you. And *this* shall come to pass if you diligently obey the voice of the LORD your God."

Obedience Better than Fasting

7 Now in the fourth year of King Darius it came to pass *that* the word of the LORD came to Zechariah, on the fourth *day* of the ninth month, Chislev, 2when *the people*[a] sent Sherezer,[b] with Regem-Melech and his men, *to* the house of God,[c] to pray before the LORD, 3*and* to ask the priests who *were* in the house of the LORD of hosts, and the prophets, saying, "Should I weep in the fifth month and fast as I have done for so many years?"

4Then the word of the LORD of hosts came to me, saying, 5"Say to all the people of the land, and to the priests: 'When you fasted and mourned in the fifth and seventh *months* during those seventy years, did you really fast for Me—for Me? 6When you eat and when you drink, do you not eat and drink *for yourselves?* 7*Should you* not *have obeyed* the words which the LORD proclaimed through the former prophets when Jerusalem and the cities around it were inhabited and prosperous, and the South[a] and the Lowland were inhabited?'"

Disobedience Resulted in Captivity

8Then the word of the LORD came to Zechariah, saying, 9"Thus says the LORD of hosts:

'Execute true justice,
Show mercy and compassion
    Everyone to his brother.
10 Do not oppress the widow or the
    fatherless,
The alien or the poor.
Let none of you plan evil in his heart
    Against his brother.'

DEFENDER

"Thus says the LORD of hosts: 'Execute true justice. . . .'" ZECHARIAH 7:9

Saving Principles

Frederick Douglass (1818–1895), an abolitionist, orator, author, statesman, and one of the most prominent figures in African-American and American history, stated:

> *The Declaration of Independence is the ring-bolt to the chain of your nation's destiny; so, indeed, I regard it. The principles contained in that instrument are saving principles. Stand by those principles, be true to them on all occasions, in all places, against all foes, and at whatever cost.*

11"But they refused to heed, shrugged their shoulders, and stopped their ears so that they could not hear. 12Yes, they made their hearts like flint, refusing to hear the law and the words which the LORD of hosts had sent by His Spirit through the former prophets. Thus great wrath came from the LORD of hosts. 13Therefore it happened, *that* just as He proclaimed and they would not hear, so they called out and I would not listen," says the LORD of hosts. 14"But I scattered them with a whirlwind among all the nations which they had not known. Thus the land became desolate after them, so that no one passed through or returned; for they made the pleasant land desolate."

Jerusalem, Holy City of the Future

8 Again the word of the LORD of hosts came, saying, 2"Thus says the LORD of hosts:

6:14 [a]Following Masoretic Text, Targum, and Vulgate; Syriac reads *for Heldai* (compare verse 10); Septuagint reads *for the patient ones.* **7:2** [a]Literally *they* (compare verse 5) [b]Or *Sar-Ezer* [c]Hebrew *Bethel* **7:7** [a]Hebrew *Negev*

'I am zealous for Zion with great zeal;
With great fervor I am zealous for her.'

3"Thus says the LORD:

'I will return to Zion,
And dwell in the midst of Jerusalem.
Jerusalem shall be called the City of
    Truth,
The Mountain of the LORD of hosts,
The Holy Mountain.'

4"Thus says the LORD of hosts:

'Old men and old women shall again sit
In the streets of Jerusalem,
Each one with his staff in his hand
Because of great age.
5   The streets of the city
Shall be full of boys and girls
Playing in its streets.'

6"Thus says the LORD of hosts:

'If it is marvelous in the eyes of the
    remnant of this people in these days,
Will it also be marvelous in My eyes?'
Says the LORD of hosts.

7"Thus says the LORD of hosts:

'Behold, I will save My people from
    the land of the east
And from the land of the west;
8   I will bring them *back*,
And they shall dwell in the midst of
    Jerusalem.
They shall be My people
And I will be their God,
In truth and righteousness.'

9"Thus says the LORD of hosts:

'Let your hands be strong,
You who have been hearing in these
    days
These words by the mouth of the
    prophets,
Who *spoke* in the day the foundation
    was laid
For the house of the LORD of hosts,
That the temple might be built.

10   For before these days
There were no wages for man nor any
    hire for beast;
There was no peace from the enemy
    for whoever went out or came in;
For I set all men, everyone, against his
    neighbor.

11But now I *will* not *treat* the remnant of
this people as in the former days,' says the
LORD of hosts.

12   'For the seed *shall be* prosperous,
The vine shall give its fruit,
The ground shall give her increase,
And the heavens shall give their dew—
I will cause the remnant of this people
To possess all these.
13   And it shall come to pass
That just as you were a curse among
    the nations,
O house of Judah and house of Israel,
So I will save you, and you shall be a
    blessing.
Do not fear,
Let your hands be strong.'

14"For thus says the LORD of hosts:

'Just as I determined to punish you
When your fathers provoked Me to
    wrath,'
Says the LORD of hosts,
'And I would not relent,
15   So again in these days
I am determined to do good
To Jerusalem and to the house of
    Judah.
Do not fear.
16   These *are* the things you shall do:
Speak each man the truth to his
    neighbor;
Give judgment in your gates for truth,
    justice, and peace;
17   Let none of you think evil in your[a]
    heart against your neighbor;
And do not love a false oath.
For all these *are things* that I hate,'
Says the LORD."

8:17 [a]Literally *his*

18Then the word of the LORD of hosts came to me, saying, 19"Thus says the LORD of hosts:

'The fast of the fourth *month,*
The fast of the fifth,
The fast of the seventh,
And the fast of the tenth,
Shall be joy and gladness and cheerful
    feasts
For the house of Judah.
Therefore love truth and peace.'

20"Thus says the LORD of hosts:

'Peoples shall yet come,
Inhabitants of many cities;
21   The inhabitants of one *city* shall go to
        another, saying,
"Let us continue to go and pray before
    the LORD,
And seek the LORD of hosts.
I myself will go also."
22   Yes, many peoples and strong nations
Shall come to seek the LORD of hosts in
    Jerusalem,
And to pray before the LORD.'

23"Thus says the LORD of hosts: 'In those days ten men from every language of the nations shall grasp the sleeve of a Jewish man, saying, "Let us go with you, for we have heard *that* God *is* with you." ' "

Israel Defended Against Enemies

9 The burdenᵃ of the word of the LORD
Against the land of Hadrach,
And Damascus its resting place
(For the eyes of men
And all the tribes of Israel
Are on the LORD);
2   Also *against* Hamath, *which* borders
        on it,
And *against* Tyre and Sidon, though
    they are very wise.

3   For Tyre built herself a tower,
Heaped up silver like the dust,
And gold like the mire of the streets.
4   Behold, the Lord will cast her out;
He will destroy her power in the sea,
And she will be devoured by fire.

5   Ashkelon shall see *it* and fear;
Gaza also shall be very sorrowful;
And Ekron, for He dried up her
    expectation.
The king shall perish from Gaza,
And Ashkelon shall not be inhabited.

6   "A mixed race shall settle in Ashdod,
And I will cut off the pride of the
    Philistines.
7   I will take away the blood from his
    mouth,
And the abominations from between
    his teeth.
But he who remains, even he *shall be*
    for our God,
And shall be like a leader in Judah,
And Ekron like a Jebusite.
8   I will camp around My house
Because of the army,
Because of him who passes by and
    him who returns.
No more shall an oppressor pass
    through them,
For now I have seen with My eyes.

The Coming King

9   "Rejoice greatly, O daughter of Zion!
Shout, O daughter of Jerusalem!
Behold, your King is coming to you;
He *is* just and having salvation,
Lowly and riding on a donkey,
A colt, the foal of a donkey.
10   I will cut off the chariot from Ephraim
And the horse from Jerusalem;
The battle bow shall be cut off.
He shall speak peace to the nations;
His dominion *shall be* 'from sea to sea,
And from the River to the ends of the
    earth.'ᵃ

God Will Save His People

11   "As for you also,
Because of the blood of your covenant,
I will set your prisoners free from the
    waterless pit.
12   Return to the stronghold,
You prisoners of hope.
Even today I declare
That I will restore double to you.

9:1 ᵃOr *oracle*   9:10 ᵃPsalm 72:8

CHRISTOPHER COLUMBUS

CHRISTOPHER COLUMBUS

Christopher Columbus (1451–1506) was an Italian navigator and explorer whose voyages across the Atlantic Ocean ushered in the first period of sustained contact between Europe and the Americas. Though he was preceded by hundreds of years by other explorers, such as Leif Ericson, Columbus initiated widespread contact between Europeans and indigenous Americans in the Western Hemisphere.

When Columbus sailed from Spain in 1492, his motives may have been many. To open a trade route to the untapped wealth of the Orient would win glory and vast riches. He may have also felt it would secure a way to diminish the power of the Ottoman Turks who were threatening Europe at the time. But there certainly was a Christian motive as well that underlay his mission.

Columbus was a devout Catholic who felt predestined, chosen for a mission. He felt his name, Christopher, which means "Christ-bearer," was evidence of his destiny. He searched the Scriptures and thought he found assurance for a call to sail to the far reaches of the globe with the Christian message. Zechariah 9:10 said that "He shall speak peace to the nations; His dominion shall be 'from sea to sea, and from the River to the ends of the earth.'" And Psalm 107:23, 24 promised that "those who go down to the sea in ships, who do business on great waters, they see the works of the LORD, and His wonders in the deep."

Describing his motive, Columbus stated: "Who can doubt that this fire was not merely mine, but also the Holy Spirit who encouraged me with a radiance of marvelous illumination from his sacred Scriptures, . . . urging me to press forward?" He felt that Almighty God had directly brought about his journey: "With a hand that could be felt, the Lord opened my mind to the fact that it would be possible . . . and He opened my will to desire to accomplish that project. . . . The Lord purposed that there should be something miraculous in this matter of the voyage to the Indies."

Although Columbus has come under criticism in recent years, his sense of having a mission from God eventually opened the way for millions of unreached people to hear the good news of salvation through Jesus Christ. As Pulitzer-Prize-winning biographer Samuel Eliot Morison wrote, "This conviction that God destined him to be an instrument for spreading the faith was far more potent than the desire to win glory, wealth, and worldly honors, to which he was certainly far from indifferent."

13 For I have bent Judah, My *bow,*
Fitted the bow with Ephraim,
And raised up your sons, O Zion,
Against your sons, O Greece,
And made you like the sword of a
  mighty man."

14 Then the LORD will be seen over them,
And His arrow will go forth like
  lightning.
The Lord GOD will blow the trumpet,
And go with whirlwinds from the south.
15 The LORD of hosts will defend them;
They shall devour and subdue with
  slingstones.
They shall drink *and* roar as if with
  wine;
They shall be filled *with blood* like
  basins,
Like the corners of the altar.
16 The LORD their God will save them
  in that day,
As the flock of His people.
For they *shall be like* the jewels of a
  crown,
Lifted like a banner over His land—
17 For how great is its[a] goodness
And how great its[b] beauty!
Grain shall make the young men thrive,
And new wine the young women.

Restoration of Judah and Israel

10 Ask the LORD for rain
In the time of the latter rain.[a]
The LORD will make flashing clouds;
He will give them showers of rain,
Grass in the field for everyone.

2 For the idols[a] speak delusion;
The diviners envision lies,
And tell false dreams;
They comfort in vain.
Therefore *the people* wend their way
  like sheep;
They are in trouble because *there is*
  no shepherd.

3 "My anger is kindled against the
  shepherds,
And I will punish the goatherds.
For the LORD of hosts will visit His flock,
The house of Judah,

And will make them as His royal
  horse in the battle.
4 From him comes the cornerstone,
From him the tent peg,
From him the battle bow,
From him every ruler[a] together.
5 They shall be like mighty men,
Who tread down *their enemies*
In the mire of the streets in the battle.
They shall fight because the LORD is
  with them,
And the riders on horses shall be put
  to shame.

6 "I will strengthen the house of Judah,
And I will save the house of Joseph.
I will bring them back,
Because I have mercy on them.
They shall be as though I had not cast
  them aside;
For I *am* the LORD their God,
And I will hear them.
7 *Those of* Ephraim shall be like a
  mighty man,
And their heart shall rejoice as if with
  wine.
Yes, their children shall see *it* and be
  glad;
Their heart shall rejoice in the LORD.
8 I will whistle for them and gather them,
For I will redeem them;
And they shall increase as they once
  increased.

9 "I will sow them among the peoples,
And they shall remember Me in far
  countries;
They shall live, together with their
  children,
And they shall return.
10 I will also bring them back from the
  land of Egypt,
And gather them from Assyria.
I will bring them into the land of
  Gilead and Lebanon,
Until no *more room* is found for them.
11 He shall pass through the sea with
  affliction,
And strike the waves of the sea:

9:17 [a]Or *His* [b]Or *His*   10:1 [a]That is, spring rain
10:2 [a]Hebrew *teraphim*   10:4 [a]Or *despot*

All the depths of the River[a] shall dry up.
Then the pride of Assyria shall be
    brought down,
And the scepter of Egypt shall depart.

12 "So I will strengthen them in the LORD,
    And they shall walk up and down in
      His name,"
    Says the LORD.

Desolation of Israel

11 Open your doors, O Lebanon,
    That fire may devour your cedars.
2 Wail, O cypress, for the cedar has fallen,
    Because the mighty *trees* are ruined.
    Wail, O oaks of Bashan,
    For the thick forest has come down.
3 *There is* the sound of wailing
      shepherds!
    For their glory is in ruins.
    There is the sound of roaring lions!
    For the pride[a] of the Jordan is in ruins.

Prophecy of the Shepherds

4Thus says the LORD my God, "Feed the flock for slaughter, 5whose owners slaughter them and feel no guilt; those who sell them say, 'Blessed be the LORD, for I am rich'; and their shepherds do not pity them. 6For I will no longer pity the inhabitants of the land," says the LORD. "But indeed I will give everyone into his neighbor's hand and into the hand of his king. They shall attack the land, and I will not deliver *them* from their hand."

7So I fed the flock for slaughter, in particular the poor of the flock.[a] I took for myself two staffs: the one I called Beauty,[b] and the other I called Bonds;[c] and I fed the flock. 8I dismissed the three shepherds in one month. My soul loathed them, and their soul also abhorred me. 9Then I said, "I will not feed you. Let what is dying die, and what is perishing perish. Let those that are left eat each other's flesh." 10And I took my staff, Beauty, and cut it in two, that I might break the covenant which I had made with all the peoples. 11So it was broken on that day. Thus the poor[a] of the flock, who were watching me, knew that it *was* the word of the LORD. 12Then I said to them, "If it is agreeable to you, give *me* my wages; and if

not, refrain." So they weighed out for my wages thirty *pieces* of silver.

13And the LORD said to me, "Throw it to the potter"—that princely price they set on me. So I took the thirty *pieces* of silver and threw them into the house of the LORD for the potter. 14Then I cut in two my other staff, Bonds, that I might break the brotherhood between Judah and Israel.

15And the LORD said to me, "Next, take for yourself the implements of a foolish shepherd. 16For indeed I will raise up a shepherd in the land *who* will not care for those who are cut off, nor seek the young, nor heal those that are broken, nor feed those that still stand. But he will eat the flesh of the fat and tear their hooves in pieces.

17 "Woe to the worthless shepherd,
    Who leaves the flock!
    A sword *shall be* against his arm
    And against his right eye;
    His arm shall completely wither,
    And his right eye shall be totally
      blinded."

The Coming Deliverance of Judah

12 The burden[a] of the word of the LORD against Israel. Thus says the LORD, who stretches out the heavens, lays the foundation of the earth, and forms the spirit of man within him: 2"Behold, I will make Jerusalem a cup of drunkenness to all the surrounding peoples, when they lay siege against Judah and Jerusalem. 3And it shall happen in that day that I will make Jerusalem a very heavy stone for all peoples; all who would heave it away will surely be cut in pieces, though all nations of the earth are gathered against it. 4In that day," says the LORD, "I will strike every horse with confusion, and its rider with madness; I will open My eyes on the house of Judah, and will strike every horse of the peoples with blindness. 5And the governors of Judah shall say

---

10:11 [a]That is, the Nile   **11:3** [a]Or *floodplain, thicket*
11:7 [a]Following Masoretic Text, Targum, and Vulgate; Septuagint reads *for the Canaanites.*   [b]Or *Grace,* and so in verse 10   [c]Or *Unity,* and so in verse 14
11:11 [a]Following Masoretic Text, Targum, and Vulgate; Septuagint reads *the Canaanites.*
12:1 [a]Or *oracle*

in their heart, 'The inhabitants of Jerusalem *are* my strength in the LORD of hosts, their God.' 6In that day I will make the governors of Judah like a firepan in the woodpile, and like a fiery torch in the sheaves; they shall devour all the surrounding peoples on the right hand and on the left, but Jerusalem shall be inhabited again in her own place—Jerusalem.

7"The LORD will save the tents of Judah first, so that the glory of the house of David and the glory of the inhabitants of Jerusalem shall not become greater than that of Judah. 8In that day the LORD will defend the inhabitants of Jerusalem; the one who is feeble among them in that day shall be like David, and the house of David *shall be* like God, like the Angel of the LORD before them. 9It shall be in that day *that* I will seek to destroy all the nations that come against Jerusalem.

Mourning for the Pierced One

10"And I will pour on the house of David and on the inhabitants of Jerusalem the Spirit of grace and supplication; then they will look on Me whom they pierced. Yes, they will mourn for Him as one mourns for *his* only *son,* and grieve for Him as one grieves for a firstborn. 11In that day there shall be a great mourning in Jerusalem, like the mourning at Hadad Rimmon in the plain of Megiddo.ᵃ 12And the land shall mourn, every family by itself: the family of the house of David by itself, and their wives by themselves; the family of the house of Nathan by itself, and their wives by themselves; 13the family of the house of Levi by itself, and their wives by themselves; the family of Shimei by itself, and their wives by themselves; 14all the families that remain, every family by itself, and their wives by themselves.

Idolatry Cut Off

13 "In that day a fountain shall be opened for the house of David and for the inhabitants of Jerusalem, for sin and for uncleanness.

2"It shall be in that day," says the LORD of hosts, "that I will cut off the names of the idols from the land, and they shall no longer be remembered. I will also cause the prophets and the unclean spirit to depart from the land. 3It shall come to pass *that* if anyone still prophesies, then his father and mother who begot him will say to him, 'You shall not live, because you have spoken lies in the name of the LORD.' And his father and mother who begot him shall thrust him through when he prophesies.

4"And it shall be in that day *that* every prophet will be ashamed of his vision when he prophesies; they will not wear a robe of coarse hair to deceive. 5But he will say, 'I *am* no prophet, I *am* a farmer; for a man taught me to keep cattle from my youth.' 6And *one* will say to him, 'What are these wounds between your arms?'ᵃ Then he will answer, 'Those with which I was wounded in the house of my friends.'

The Shepherd Savior

7 "Awake, O sword, against My Shepherd,
   Against the Man who is My
      Companion,"
   Says the LORD of hosts.
   "Strike the Shepherd,
   And the sheep will be scattered;
   Then I will turn My hand against the
      little ones.
8 And it shall come to pass in all the
      land,"
   Says the LORD,
   "That two-thirds in it shall be cut off
      and die,
   But *one*-third shall be left in it:
9 I will bring the *one*-third through the
      fire,
   Will refine them as silver is refined,
   And test them as gold is tested.
   They will call on My name,
   And I will answer them.
   I will say, 'This *is* My people';
   And each one will say, 'The LORD *is*
      my God.'"

The Day of the LORD

14 Behold, the day of the LORD is
      coming,
   And your spoil will be divided in your
      midst.

12:11 ᵃHebrew *Megiddon*   **13:6** ᵃOr *hands*

2 For I will gather all the nations to
　　battle against Jerusalem;
　The city shall be taken,
　The houses rifled,
　And the women ravished.
　Half of the city shall go into
　　captivity,
　But the remnant of the people shall
　　not be cut off from the city.

3 Then the LORD will go forth
　And fight against those nations,
　As He fights in the day of battle.
4 And in that day His feet will stand
　　on the Mount of Olives,
　Which faces Jerusalem on the east.
　And the Mount of Olives shall be
　　split in two,
　From east to west,
　Making a very large valley;
　Half of the mountain shall move
　　toward the north
　And half of it toward the south.

5 Then you shall flee *through* My
　　mountain valley,
　For the mountain valley shall reach
　　to Azal.
　Yes, you shall flee
　As you fled from the earthquake
　In the days of Uzziah king of Judah.

　Thus the LORD my God will come,
　And all the saints with You.[a]

6 It shall come to pass in that day
　That there will be no light;
　The lights will diminish.
7 It shall be one day
　Which is known to the LORD—
　Neither day nor night.
　But at evening time it shall happen
　That it will be light.

8 And in that day it shall be
　That living waters shall flow from
　　Jerusalem,
　Half of them toward the eastern sea
　And half of them toward the western
　　sea;
　In both summer and winter it shall
　　occur.

9 And the LORD shall be King over all
　　the earth.
　In that day it shall be—
　"The LORD *is* one,"[a]
　And His name one.

10 All the land shall be turned into a plain from Geba to Rimmon south of Jerusalem. *Jerusalem*[a] shall be raised up and inhabited in her place from Benjamin's Gate to the place of the First Gate and the Corner Gate, and *from* the Tower of Hananel to the king's winepresses.

11 *The people* shall dwell in it;
　And no longer shall there be utter
　　destruction,
　But Jerusalem shall be safely inhabited.

12 And this shall be the plague with which the LORD will strike all the people who fought against Jerusalem:

　Their flesh shall dissolve while they
　　stand on their feet,
　Their eyes shall dissolve in their sockets,
　And their tongues shall dissolve in
　　their mouths.

13 It shall come to pass in that day
　That a great panic from the LORD will
　　be among them.
　Everyone will seize the hand of his
　　neighbor,
　And raise his hand against his
　　neighbor's hand;
14 Judah also will fight at Jerusalem.
　And the wealth of all the surrounding
　　nations
　Shall be gathered together:
　Gold, silver, and apparel in great
　　abundance.

15 Such also shall be the plague
　On the horse *and* the mule,
　On the camel and the donkey,
　And on all the cattle that will be in
　　those camps.
　So *shall* this plague *be.*

14:5 [a]Or *you*; Septuagint, Targum, and Vulgate read *Him.*　　**14:9** [a]Compare Deuteronomy 6:4　　**14:10** [a]Literally *She*

The Nations Worship the King

¹⁶And it shall come to pass *that* everyone who is left of all the nations which came against Jerusalem shall go up from year to year to worship the King, the Lord of hosts, and to keep the Feast of Tabernacles. ¹⁷And it shall be *that* whichever of the families of the earth do not come up to Jerusalem to worship the King, the Lord of hosts, on them there will be no rain. ¹⁸If the family of Egypt will not come up and enter in, they *shall have* no *rain;* they shall receive the plague with which the Lord strikes the nations who do not come up to keep the Feast of Tabernacles. ¹⁹This shall be the punishment of Egypt and the punishment of all the nations that do not come up to keep the Feast of Tabernacles.

²⁰In that day "HOLINESS TO THE LORD" shall be *engraved* on the bells of the horses. The pots in the Lord's house shall be like the bowls before the altar. ²¹Yes, every pot in Jerusalem and Judah shall be holiness to the Lord of hosts.^a Everyone who sacrifices shall come and take them and cook in them. In that day there shall no longer be a Canaanite in the house of the Lord of hosts.

14:21 ^aOr *on every pot . . . shall be (engraved)* *"HOLINESS TO THE LORD OF HOSTS"*

MALACHI

Author: Malachi

When Written: Around 450 B.C.

Theme: God's Love and Justice

Key Verse: Malachi 4:5, 6—"Behold, I will send you Elijah the prophet before the coming of the great and dreadful day of the LORD. And he will turn the hearts of the fathers to the children, and the hearts of the children to their fathers, lest I come and strike the earth with a curse."

Key Chapter: Malachi 3—The last book of the Old Testament concludes with a compelling prophecy of the coming of John the Baptist, who will prepare the way for the promised Messiah, and of the Messiah Himself, who will come "with healing in His wings" (4:2).

The message of Malachi was directed to a people plagued by corrupt priests and wickedness. The prophet confronted the people of Israel for their hypocrisy, infidelity, divorce, pride, greed, and arrogance. The nation was so complacent in their sin that God's word no longer had any impact on them. Malachi challenged them to turn from merely "going through the motions" to a relationship with God filled with faith, obedience, and worship. God loves us passionately and wants us to return that love to Him by being people of integrity, purity, and justice.

In May 1775, Harvard College president Samuel Langdon delivered a message to the Provincial Congress of Massachusetts that is reminiscent of Malachi's prophecy—and which echoes eloquently through history to today's America: "We have rebelled against God. We have lost the true spirit of Christianity, though we retain the outward profession and form of it. . . . My brethren, let us repent and implore the divine mercy. . . . May the Lord hear us in this day of trouble. . . . We will rejoice in His salvation, and in the name of our God, we will set up our banners!"

MALACHI

1 The burden[a] of the word of the LORD to
Israel by Malachi.

Israel Beloved of God

2 "I have loved you," says the LORD.
"Yet you say, 'In what way have You
loved us?'
Was not Esau Jacob's brother?"
Says the LORD.
"Yet Jacob I have loved;
3 But Esau I have hated,
And laid waste his mountains and
his heritage
For the jackals of the wilderness."

4 Even though Edom has said,
"We have been impoverished,
But we will return and build the
desolate places,"

Thus says the LORD of hosts:

"They may build, but I will throw
down;
They shall be called the Territory
of Wickedness,
And the people against whom
the LORD will have indignation
forever.
5 Your eyes shall see,
And you shall say,
'The LORD is magnified beyond the
border of Israel.'

Polluted Offerings

6 "A son honors *his* father,
And a servant *his* master.
If then I am the Father,
Where *is* My honor?
And if I *am* a Master,
Where *is* My reverence?
Says the LORD of hosts
To you priests who despise My name.
Yet you say, 'In what way have we
despised Your name?'

7 "You offer defiled food on My altar,
But say,
'In what way have we defiled You?'
By saying,
'The table of the LORD is contemptible.'
8 And when you offer the blind as a
sacrifice,
Is it not evil?
And when you offer the lame and sick,
Is it not evil?
Offer it then to your governor!
Would he be pleased with you?
Would he accept you favorably?"
Says the LORD of hosts.

9 "But now entreat God's favor,
That He may be gracious to us.
While this is being *done* by your hands,
Will He accept you favorably?"
Says the LORD of hosts.
10 "Who *is there* even among you who
would shut the doors,
So that you would not kindle fire *on*
My altar in vain?
I have no pleasure in you,"
Says the LORD of hosts,
"Nor will I accept an offering from
your hands.
11 For from the rising of the sun, even
to its going down,
My name *shall be* great among the
Gentiles;
In every place incense *shall be* offered
to My name,
And a pure offering;
For My name shall be great among
the nations,"
Says the LORD of hosts.

12 "But you profane it,
In that you say,
'The table of the LORD[a] is defiled;
And its fruit, its food, *is* contemptible.'

1:1 [a]Or *oracle*   **1:12** [a]Following Bomberg;
Masoretic Text reads *Lord.*

13 You also say,
'Oh, what a weariness!'
And you sneer at it,"
Says the LORD of hosts.
"And you bring the stolen, the lame,
and the sick;
Thus you bring an offering!
Should I accept this from your hand?"
Says the LORD.
14 "But cursed *be* the deceiver
Who has in his flock a male,
And takes a vow,
But sacrifices to the Lord what is
blemished—
For I *am* a great King,"
Says the LORD of hosts,
"And My name *is to be* feared among
the nations.

Corrupt Priests

2 "And now, O priests, this commandment
is for you.
2 If you will not hear,
And if you will not take *it* to heart,
To give glory to My name,"
Says the LORD of hosts,
"I will send a curse upon you,
And I will curse your blessings.
Yes, I have cursed them already,
Because you do not take *it* to heart.

3 "Behold, I will rebuke your descendants
And spread refuse on your faces,
The refuse of your solemn feasts;
And *one* will take you away with it.
4 Then you shall know that I have sent
this commandment to you,
That My covenant with Levi may
continue,"
Says the LORD of hosts.
5 "My covenant was with him, *one* of life
and peace,
And I gave them to him *that he might*
fear *Me*;
So he feared Me
And was reverent before My name.
6 The law of truth[a] was in his mouth,
And injustice was not found on his
lips.
He walked with Me in peace and
equity,
And turned many away from iniquity.

7 "For the lips of a priest should keep
knowledge,
And *people* should seek the law from
his mouth;
For he is the messenger of the LORD of
hosts.
8 But you have departed from the way;
You have caused many to stumble at
the law.
You have corrupted the covenant of
Levi,"
Says the LORD of hosts.
9 "Therefore I also have made you
contemptible and base
Before all the people,
Because you have not kept My ways
But have shown partiality in the law."

FREEDOM
Have we not all one Father?

MALACHI 2:10

Liberty, a Gift of the Creator
Alexander Hamilton (1755–1804), a Founding
Father who cowrote the *Federalist Papers*, stated
concerning the nature of liberty:

*The fundamental source of all your errors,
sophisms, and false reasonings, is a total ignorance of the natural rights of mankind. Were
you once to become acquainted with these, you
could never entertain a thought that all men
are not, by nature, entitled to a parity of privileges. You would be convinced that natural
liberty is a gift of the beneficent Creator to the
whole human race; and that civil liberty is
founded in that and cannot be wrested from
any people, without the most manifest violation of justice.*

Treachery of Infidelity

10 Have we not all one Father?
Has not one God created us?
Why do we deal treacherously with
one another
By profaning the covenant of the
fathers?
11 Judah has dealt treacherously,
And an abomination has been
committed in Israel and in Jerusalem,

2:6 [a]Or *true instruction*

For Judah has profaned
The LORD's holy *institution* which He
loves:
He has married the daughter of a
foreign god.
12 May the LORD cut off from the tents
of Jacob
The man who does this, being awake
and aware,ᵃ
Yet who brings an offering to the LORD
of hosts!

13 And this is the second thing you do:
You cover the altar of the LORD with
tears,
With weeping and crying;
So He does not regard the offering
anymore,
Nor receive *it* with goodwill from your
hands.
14 Yet you say, "For what reason?"
Because the LORD has been witness
Between you and the wife of your youth,
With whom you have dealt
treacherously;
Yet she is your companion
And your wife by covenant.
15 But did He not make *them* one,
Having a remnant of the Spirit?
And why one?
He seeks godly offspring.
Therefore take heed to your spirit,
And let none deal treacherously with
the wife of his youth.

16 "For the LORD God of Israel says
That He hates divorce,
For it covers one's garment with
violence,"
Says the LORD of hosts.
"Therefore take heed to your spirit,
That you do not deal treacherously."

17 You have wearied the LORD with your
words;
Yet you say,
"In what way have we wearied *Him?*"
In that you say,
"Everyone who does evil
Is good in the sight of the LORD,
And He delights in them,"
Or, "Where *is* the God of justice?"

The Coming Messenger

3 "Behold, I send My messenger,
And he will prepare the way before Me.
And the Lord, whom you seek,
Will suddenly come to His temple,
Even the Messenger of the covenant,
In whom you delight.
Behold, He is coming,"
Says the LORD of hosts.

2 "But who can endure the day of His
coming?
And who can stand when He appears?
For He *is* like a refiner's fire
And like launderers' soap.
3 He will sit as a refiner and a purifier
of silver;
He will purify the sons of Levi,
And purge them as gold and silver,
That they may offer to the LORD
An offering in righteousness.

4 "Then the offering of Judah and
Jerusalem
Will be pleasant to the LORD,
As in the days of old,
As in former years.
5 And I will come near you for judgment;
I will be a swift witness
Against sorcerers,
Against adulterers,
Against perjurers,
Against those who exploit wage
earners and widows and orphans,
And against those who turn away an
alien—
Because they do not fear Me,"
Says the LORD of hosts.

6 "For I *am* the LORD, I do not change;
Therefore you are not consumed,
O sons of Jacob.
7 Yet from the days of your fathers
You have gone away from My
ordinances
And have not kept *them.*
Return to Me, and I will return to you,"
Says the LORD of hosts.
"But you said,
'In what way shall we return?'

2:12 ᵃTalmud and Vulgate read *teacher and student.*

Do Not Rob God

8 "Will a man rob God?
   Yet you have robbed Me!
   But you say,
   'In what way have we robbed You?'
   In tithes and offerings.
9 You are cursed with a curse,
   For you have robbed Me,
   Even this whole nation.
10 Bring all the tithes into the storehouse,
   That there may be food in My house,
   And try Me now in this,"
   Says the LORD of hosts,
   "If I will not open for you the windows
      of heaven
   And pour out for you *such* blessing
   That *there will* not *be room* enough *to
      receive it.*

11 "And I will rebuke the devourer for
      your sakes,
   So that he will not destroy the fruit of
      your ground,
   Nor shall the vine fail to bear fruit for
      you in the field,"
   Says the LORD of hosts;

DEVOTION
". . . open for you the windows of heaven. . . ."
                                MALACHI 3:10

Loving Devotion of a Free People
In his Inaugural Address, Rutherford Hayes, the
19th president of the United States (1877–1881),
stated:

> *Looking for the guidance of that Divine Hand
> by which the destinies of nations and individ-
> uals are shaped, I call upon you, Senators, Rep-
> resentatives, judges, fellow citizens, here and
> everywhere, to unite with me in an earnest
> effort to secure to our country the blessings, not
> only of material property, but of justice, peace,
> and union—a union depending not upon the
> constraint of force but upon the loving devo-
> tion of a free people; and that all things may
> be so ordered and settled upon the best and
> surest foundations that peace and happiness,
> truth and justice, religion and piety, may be
> established among us for all generations.*

12 "And all nations will call you blessed,
   For you will be a delightful land,"
   Says the LORD of hosts.

The People Complain Harshly

13 "Your words have been harsh against
      Me,"
   Says the LORD,
   "Yet you say,
   'What have we spoken against You?'
14 You have said,
   'It is useless to serve God;
   What profit *is it* that we have kept His
      ordinance,
   And that we have walked as mourners
   Before the LORD of hosts?
15 So now we call the proud blessed,
   For those who do wickedness are
      raised up;
   They even tempt God and go free.'"

A Book of Remembrance

16 Then those who feared the LORD spoke
      to one another,
   And the LORD listened and heard *them;*
   So a book of remembrance was
      written before Him
   For those who fear the LORD
   And who meditate on His name.

17 "They shall be Mine," says the LORD
      of hosts,
   "On the day that I make them My
      jewels.ᵃ
   And I will spare them
   As a man spares his own son who
      serves him."
18 Then you shall again discern
   Between the righteous and the wicked,
   Between one who serves God
   And one who does not serve Him.

The Great Day of God

4 "For behold, the day is coming,
   Burning like an oven,
   And all the proud, yes, all who do
      wickedly will be stubble.
   And the day which is coming shall
      burn them up,"
   Says the LORD of hosts,

3:17 ᵃLiterally *special treasure*

"That will leave them neither root nor
   branch.
2 But to you who fear My name
   The Sun of Righteousness shall arise
   With healing in His wings;
   And you shall go out
   And grow fat like stall-fed calves.

INSPIRING

"The Sun of Righteousness shall arise. . . ."

MALACHI 4:2

The Sun of Righteousness

Rutgers University (originally chartered as Queen's College) was founded in New Jersey in 1766. Inspired by the motto of the University of Utrecht, Netherlands, which was "Sun of Righteousness, Shine Upon Us," Rutgers University chose for its official motto:

Sun of Righteousness, Shine Upon the West Also

---

3 You shall trample the wicked,
   For they shall be ashes under the
    soles of your feet
   On the day that I do *this*,"
   Says the LORD of hosts.

4 "Remember the Law of Moses, My
    servant,
   Which I commanded him in Horeb
    for all Israel,
   With the statutes and judgments.
5 Behold, I will send you Elijah the
    prophet
   Before the coming of the great and
    dreadful day of the LORD.
6 And he will turn
   The hearts of the fathers to the
    children,
   And the hearts of the children to
    their fathers,
   Lest I come and strike the earth with
    a curse."

THE NEW TESTAMENT

...in the most humble terms...

...against their Country to become the executioners...

...but endeavoured to bring on the inhabitants of our frontiers, the merciless Indian savages... In every stage of these Oppressions We have Petitioned for Redress... A Prince whose character is thus marked by every act which may define a Tyrant, is unfit to be the ruler of a free people. Nor have We been wanting in attentions to our British brethren. We have warned them from time to time of attempts by their legislature to extend an unwarrantable jurisdiction over us. We have reminded them of the circumstances of our emigration and settlement here. We have appealed to their native justice and magnanimity, and we have conjured them by the ties of our common kindred to disavow these usurpations, which would inevitably interrupt our connections and correspondence. They too have been deaf to the voice of justice and of consanguinity. We must, therefore, acquiesce in the necessity, which denounces our Separation, and hold them, as we hold the rest of mankind, Enemies in War, in Peace Friends.

We, therefore, the Representatives of the united States of America, in General Congress, Assembled, appealing to the Supreme Judge of the world for the rectitude of our intentions, do, in the Name, and by Authority of the good People of these Colonies, solemnly publish and declare, That these United Colonies are, and of Right ought to be Free and Independent States; that they are Absolved from all Allegiance to the British Crown, and that all political connexion between them and the State of Great Britain, is and ought to be totally dissolved; and that as Free and Independent States, they have full Power to levy War, conclude Peace, contract Alliances, establish Commerce, and to do all other Acts and Things which Independent States may of right do. And for the support of this Declaration, **With a firm reliance on the Protection of Divine Providence**, we mutually pledge to each other our Lives, our Fortunes and our sacred Honor.

John Hancock

Button Gwinnett

Lyman Hall

Geo Walton

Edward Rutledge

Thos Heyward Junr.

Thomas Lynch Junr.

Arthur Middleton

Saml Chase

Wm Paca

Thos Stone

Charles Carroll of Carrollton

George Wythe

Richard Henry Lee

Th Jefferson

Benja Harrison

Robt Morris

Benjamin Rush

Benja Franklin

John Morton

Geo Clymer

Jas Smith

Geo Taylor

James Wilson

Geo Ross

Caesar Rodney

MATTHEW

Author: Matthew

When Written: A.D. 50–60

Theme: Jesus the King

Key Verse: Matthew 16:16—"Simon Peter answered and said, 'You are the Christ, the Son of the living God.'"

Key Chapter: Matthew 12—This chapter is the turning point when the Pharisees, acting as the leadership of the nation of Israel, formally reject Jesus Christ as their Messiah, stating that He comes not from God but from Satan.

The Old Testament prophets predicted and longed for the coming of the Messiah, who would enter history to bring redemption and deliverance. Through a carefully selected series of Old Testament quotations, Matthew documents Jesus Christ's claim to be the King of the Jews. Matthew also outlines the characteristics of the kingdom of God, both for Israel and the church. Jesus' genealogy, baptism, messages, and miracles all point to the same inescapable conclusion: Jesus is King, the long-awaited Messiah.

President Thomas Jefferson believed the teachings of Jesus embodied the "most sublime system of morals" in the whole world. He stated, "We all agree in the obligation of the moral precepts of Jesus, and nowhere will they be found delivered in greater purity than in His discourses." The Book of Matthew details Jesus' discourses, especially through the Sermon on the Mount (chs. 5–7), as no other of the Gospels.

The Genealogy of Jesus Christ

1 The book of the genealogy of Jesus Christ, the Son of David, the Son of Abraham: ²Abraham begot Isaac, Isaac begot Jacob, and Jacob begot Judah and his brothers. ³Judah begot Perez and Zerah by Tamar, Perez begot Hezron, and Hezron begot Ram. ⁴Ram begot Amminadab, Amminadab begot Nahshon, and Nahshon begot Salmon. ⁵Salmon begot Boaz by Rahab, Boaz begot Obed by Ruth, Obed begot Jesse, ⁶and Jesse begot David the king.

David the king begot Solomon by her *who had been the wife*[a] of Uriah. ⁷Solomon begot Rehoboam, Rehoboam begot Abijah, and Abijah begot Asa.[a] ⁸Asa begot Jehoshaphat, Jehoshaphat begot Joram, and Joram begot Uzziah. ⁹Uzziah begot Jotham, Jotham begot Ahaz, and Ahaz begot Hezekiah. ¹⁰Hezekiah begot Manasseh, Manasseh begot Amon,[a] and Amon begot Josiah. ¹¹Josiah begot Jeconiah and his brothers about the time they were carried away to Babylon.

¹²And after they were brought to Babylon, Jeconiah begot Shealtiel, and Shealtiel begot Zerubbabel. ¹³Zerubbabel begot Abiud, Abiud begot Eliakim, and Eliakim begot Azor. ¹⁴Azor begot Zadok, Zadok begot Achim, and Achim begot Eliud. ¹⁵Eliud begot Eleazar, Eleazar begot Matthan, and Matthan begot Jacob. ¹⁶And Jacob begot Joseph the husband of Mary, of whom was born Jesus who is called Christ.

¹⁷So all the generations from Abraham to David *are* fourteen generations, from David until the captivity in Babylon *are* fourteen generations, and from the captivity in Babylon until the Christ *are* fourteen generations.

Christ Born of Mary

¹⁸Now the birth of Jesus Christ was as follows: After His mother Mary was betrothed to Joseph, before they came together, she was found with child of the Holy Spirit. ¹⁹Then Joseph her husband, being a just *man,* and not wanting to make her a public example, was minded to put her away secretly. ²⁰But while he thought about these things, behold, an angel of the Lord appeared to him in a dream, saying, "Joseph, son of David, do not be afraid to take to you Mary your wife, for that which is conceived in her is of the Holy Spirit. ²¹And she will bring forth a Son, and you shall call His name JESUS, for He will save His people from their sins."

²²So all this was done that it might be fulfilled which was spoken by the Lord through the prophet, saying: ²³*"Behold, the virgin shall be with child, and bear a Son, and they shall call His name Immanuel,"*[a] which is translated, "God with us."

²⁴Then Joseph, being aroused from sleep, did as the angel of the Lord commanded him and took to him his wife, ²⁵and did not know her till she had brought forth her firstborn Son.[a] And he called His name JESUS.

Wise Men from the East

2 Now after Jesus was born in Bethlehem of Judea in the days of Herod the king, behold, wise men from the East came to Jerusalem, ²saying, "Where is He who has been born King of the Jews? For we have seen His star in the East and have come to worship Him."

³When Herod the king heard *this,* he was troubled, and all Jerusalem with him. ⁴And when he had gathered all the chief priests and scribes of the people together, he inquired of them where the Christ was to be born.

⁵So they said to him, "In Bethlehem of Judea, for thus it is written by the prophet:

1:6 [a]Words in italic type have been added for clarity. They are not found in the original Greek. **1:7** [a]NU-Text reads *Asaph.* **1:10** [a]NU-Text reads *Amos.* **1:23** [a]Isaiah 7:14. Words in oblique type in the New Testament are quoted from the Old Testament. **1:25** [a]NU-Text reads *a Son.*

6 'But you, Bethlehem, in the land of
  Judah,
  Are not the least among the rulers
  of Judah;
  For out of you shall come a Ruler
  Who will shepherd My people Israel.'"ᵃ

7Then Herod, when he had secretly called the wise men, determined from them what time the star appeared. 8And he sent them to Bethlehem and said, "Go and search carefully for the young Child, and when you have found *Him*, bring back word to me, that I may come and worship Him also."

9When they heard the king, they departed; and behold, the star which they had seen in the East went before them, till it came and stood over where the young Child was. 10When they saw the star, they rejoiced with exceedingly great joy. 11And when they had come into the house, they saw the young Child with Mary His mother, and fell down and worshiped Him. And when they had opened their treasures, they presented gifts to Him: gold, frankincense, and myrrh.

12Then, being divinely warned in a dream that they should not return to Herod, they departed for their own country another way.

The Flight into Egypt

13Now when they had departed, behold, an angel of the Lord appeared to Joseph in a dream, saying, "Arise, take the young Child and His mother, flee to Egypt, and stay there until I bring you word; for Herod will seek the young Child to destroy Him." 14When he arose, he took the young Child and His mother by night and departed for Egypt, 15and was there until the death of Herod, that it might be fulfilled which was spoken by the Lord through the prophet, saying, *"Out of Egypt I called My Son."*ᵃ

Massacre of the Innocents

16Then Herod, when he saw that he was deceived by the wise men, was exceedingly angry; and he sent forth and put to death all the male children who were in Bethlehem and in all its districts, from two years

---

2:6 ᵃMicah 5:2   **2:15** ᵃHosea 11:1

FREEDOM

. . . they saw the young Child with Mary His mother, and fell down and worshiped Him.

MATTHEW 2:11

Warren Earl Burger

THE GOVERNMENT AND NATIVITY SCENES

Warren Earl Burger, Chief Justice of the United States from 1969 to 1986, delivered the Supreme Court's opinion in the 1985 case of Lynch v. Donnelly, which upheld that the city of Pawtucket, Rhode Island, did not violate the Constitution by displaying a Nativity scene. Noting that presidential orders and proclamations from Congress have designated Christmas as a national holiday in religious terms for two centuries and in the Western world for twenty centuries, he wrote:

> There is an unbroken history of official acknowledgment by all three branches of government of the role of religion in American life. . . . The Constitution does not require a complete separation of church and state. It affirmatively mandates accommodation, not merely tolerance, of all religions and forbids hostility towards any. . . . Anything less would require the "callous indifference" we have said was never intended by the Establishment Clause. Indeed, we have observed, such hostility would bring us into a "war with our national tradition as embodied in the First Amendment's guaranty of the free exercise of religion."

old and under, according to the time which he had determined from the wise men. [17]Then was fulfilled what was spoken by Jeremiah the prophet, saying:

[18] *"A voice was heard in Ramah,*
　　Lamentation, weeping, and great
　　　mourning,
　　Rachel weeping for her children,
　　Refusing to be comforted,
　　Because they are no more."[a]

The Home in Nazareth

[19]Now when Herod was dead, behold, an angel of the Lord appeared in a dream to Joseph in Egypt, [20]saying, "Arise, take the young Child and His mother, and go to the land of Israel, for those who sought the young Child's life are dead." [21]Then he arose, took the young Child and His mother, and came into the land of Israel. [22]But when he heard that Archelaus was reigning over Judea instead of his father Herod, he was afraid to go there. And being warned by God in a dream, he turned aside into the region of Galilee. [23]And he came and dwelt in a city called Nazareth, that it might be fulfilled which was spoken by the prophets, "He shall be called a Nazarene."

John the Baptist Prepares the Way

3 In those days John the Baptist came preaching in the wilderness of Judea, [2]and saying, "Repent, for the kingdom of heaven is at hand!" [3]For this is he who was spoken of by the prophet Isaiah, saying:

　"The voice of one crying in the
　　wilderness:
　'Prepare the way of the LORD;
　Make His paths straight.' "[a]

[4]Now John himself was clothed in camel's hair, with a leather belt around his waist; and his food was locusts and wild honey. [5]Then Jerusalem, all Judea, and all the region around the Jordan went out to him [6]and were baptized by him in the Jordan, confessing their sins.

[7]But when he saw many of the Pharisees and Sadducees coming to his baptism, he said to them, "Brood of vipers! Who warned you to flee from the wrath to come? [8]Therefore bear fruits worthy of repentance, [9]and do not think to say to yourselves, 'We have Abraham as *our* father.' For I say to you that God is able to raise up children to Abraham from these stones. [10]And even now the ax is laid to the root of the trees. Therefore every tree which does not bear good fruit is cut down and thrown into the fire. [11]I indeed baptize you with water unto repentance, but He who is coming after me is mightier than I, whose sandals I am not worthy to carry. He will baptize you with the Holy Spirit and fire.[a] [12]His winnowing fan *is* in His hand, and He will thoroughly clean out His threshing floor, and gather His wheat into the barn; but He will burn up the chaff with unquenchable fire."

John Baptizes Jesus

[13]Then Jesus came from Galilee to John at the Jordan to be baptized by him. [14]And John *tried to* prevent Him, saying, "I need to be baptized by You, and are You coming to me?" [15]But Jesus answered and said to him, "Permit *it to be so* now, for thus it is fitting for us to fulfill all righteousness." Then he allowed Him.

[16]When He had been baptized, Jesus came up immediately from the water; and behold, the heavens were opened to Him, and He[a] saw the Spirit of God descending like a dove and alighting upon Him. [17]And suddenly a voice *came* from heaven, saying, "This is My beloved Son, in whom I am well pleased."

Satan Tempts Jesus

4 Then Jesus was led up by the Spirit into the wilderness to be tempted by the devil. [2]And when He had fasted forty days and forty nights, afterward He was hungry. [3]Now when the tempter came to Him, he said, "If You are the Son of God, command that these stones become bread."

[4]But He answered and said, "It is written, *'Man shall not live by bread alone, but by every word that proceeds from the mouth of God.' "*[a]

2:18 [a]Jeremiah 31:15　　**3:3** [a]Isaiah 40:3
3:11 [a]M-Text omits *and fire.*　　**3:16** [a]Or *he*
4:4 [a]Deuteronomy 8:3

5Then the devil took Him up into the holy city, set Him on the pinnacle of the temple, 6and said to Him, "If You are the Son of God, throw Yourself down. For it is written:

'He shall give His angels charge over you,'

and,

'In their hands they shall bear you up, Lest you dash your foot against a stone.'"a

7Jesus said to him, "It is written again, 'You shall not tempt the LORD your God.'"a
8Again, the devil took Him up on an exceedingly high mountain, and showed Him all the kingdoms of the world and their glory. 9And he said to Him, "All these things I will give You if You will fall down and worship me."
10Then Jesus said to him, "Away with you,a Satan! For it is written, 'You shall worship the LORD your God, and Him only you shall serve.'"b
11Then the devil left Him, and behold, angels came and ministered to Him.

Jesus Begins His Galilean Ministry

12Now when Jesus heard that John had been put in prison, He departed to Galilee. 13And leaving Nazareth, He came and dwelt in Capernaum, which is by the sea, in the regions of Zebulun and Naphtali, 14that it might be fulfilled which was spoken by Isaiah the prophet, saying:

15 "The land of Zebulun and the land of Naphtali,
     By the way of the sea, beyond the Jordan,
     Galilee of the Gentiles:
16 The people who sat in darkness have seen a great light,
     And upon those who sat in the region and shadow of death
     Light has dawned."a

17From that time Jesus began to preach and to say, "Repent, for the kingdom of heaven is at hand."

Four Fishermen Called as Disciples

18And Jesus, walking by the Sea of Galilee, saw two brothers, Simon called Peter, and Andrew his brother, casting a net into the sea; for they were fishermen. 19Then He said to them, "Follow Me, and I will make you fishers of men." 20They immediately left their nets and followed Him.
21Going on from there, He saw two other brothers, James the son of Zebedee, and John his brother, in the boat with Zebedee their father, mending their nets. He called them, 22and immediately they left the boat and their father, and followed Him.

Jesus Heals a Great Multitude

23And Jesus went about all Galilee, teaching in their synagogues, preaching the gospel of the kingdom, and healing all kinds of sickness and all kinds of disease among the people. 24Then His fame went throughout all Syria; and they brought to Him all sick people who were afflicted with various diseases and torments, and those who were demon-possessed, epileptics, and paralytics; and He healed them. 25Great multitudes followed Him—from Galilee, and from Decapolis, Jerusalem, Judea, and beyond the Jordan.

> **George H.W. Bush** placed his hand on Matthew 5 as he took the presidential oath of office in 1989.

The Beatitudes

5 And seeing the multitudes, He went up on a mountain, and when He was seated His disciples came to Him. 2Then He opened His mouth and taught them, saying:

> **Harry S. Truman** placed his hand on Matthew 5:3–11 and Exodus 20:3–17 as he took the presidential oath of office in 1949.

4:6 aPsalm 91:11, 12   **4:7** aDeuteronomy 6:16
4:10 aM-Text reads Get behind Me. bDeuteronomy 6:13
4:16 aIsaiah 9:1, 2

3 "Blessed *are* the poor in spirit,
    For theirs is the kingdom of heaven.
4 Blessed *are* those who mourn,
    For they shall be comforted.
5 Blessed *are* the meek,
    For they shall inherit the earth.
6 Blessed *are* those who hunger and
      thirst for righteousness,
    For they shall be filled.
7 Blessed *are* the merciful,
    For they shall obtain mercy.
8 Blessed *are* the pure in heart,
    For they shall see God.
9 Blessed *are* the peacemakers,
    For they shall be called sons of God.
10 Blessed *are* those who are persecuted
      for righteousness' sake,
    For theirs is the kingdom of heaven.

11 "Blessed are you when they revile and persecute you, and say all kinds of evil against you falsely for My sake. 12Rejoice and be exceedingly glad, for great *is* your reward in heaven, for so they persecuted the prophets who were before you.

MORAL STRENGTH
Then He opened His mouth and taught them. . . .
MATTHEW 5:2

The Moral Precepts of Jesus
In a letter to Dr. Benjamin Rush in 1803, President Thomas Jefferson stated:

The practice of morality being necessary for the well-being of society, He [God] has taken care to impress its precepts so indelibly on our hearts that they shall not be effaced by the subtleties of our brain. We all agree in the obligation of the moral precepts of Jesus, and nowhere will they be found delivered in greater purity than in His discourses.

Believers Are Salt and Light

13 "You are the salt of the earth; but if the salt loses its flavor, how shall it be seasoned? It is then good for nothing but to be thrown out and trampled underfoot by men. 14"You are the light of the world. A city that is set on a hill cannot be hidden. 15Nor do they light a lamp and put it under a

HONOR
"A city that is set on a hill cannot be hidden."
MATTHEW 5:14

God's Covenant People
Peter Bulkley (1583–1659) was the Puritan leader who founded the city of Concord, Massachusetts. In his book of sermons, *The Gospel Covenant*, he stated:

We are as a city set upon a hill, in the open view of all the earth. . . . We profess ourselves to be a people in covenant with God, and therefore . . . the Lord our God . . . will cry shame upon us if we walk contrary to the covenant which we have promised to walk in. If we open the mouths of men against our profession, by reason of the scandalousness of our lives, we (of all men) shall have the greater sin.

basket, but on a lampstand, and it gives light to all *who are* in the house. 16Let your light so shine before men, that they may see your good works and glorify your Father in heaven.

Christ Fulfills the Law

17 "Do not think that I came to destroy the Law or the Prophets. I did not come to destroy but to fulfill. 18For assuredly, I say to you, till heaven and earth pass away, one jot or one tittle will by no means pass from the law till all is fulfilled. 19Whoever therefore breaks one of the least of these commandments, and teaches men so, shall be called least in the kingdom of heaven; but whoever does and teaches *them,* he shall be called great in the kingdom of heaven. 20For I say to you, that unless your righteousness exceeds *the righteousness* of the scribes and Pharisees, you will by no means enter the kingdom of heaven.

Murder Begins in the Heart

21 "You have heard that it was said to those of old, *'You shall not murder,*ᵃ and whoever murders will be in danger of the judgment.' 22But I say to you that whoever is angry with his brother without a causeᵃ shall be in danger of the judgment. And

5:21 ᵃExodus 20:13; Deuteronomy 5:17
5:22 ᵃNU-Text omits *without a cause.*

whoever says to his brother, 'Raca!' shall be in danger of the council. But whoever says, 'You fool!' shall be in danger of hell fire. [23]Therefore if you bring your gift to the altar, and there remember that your brother has something against you, [24]leave your gift there before the altar, and go your way. First be reconciled to your brother, and then come and offer your gift. [25]Agree with your adversary quickly, while you are on the way with him, lest your adversary deliver you to the judge, the judge hand you over to the officer, and you be thrown into prison. [26]Assuredly, I say to you, you will by no means get out of there till you have paid the last penny.

Adultery in the Heart

[27]"You have heard that it was said to those of old,[a] 'You shall not commit adultery.'[b] [28]But I say to you that whoever looks at a woman to lust for her has already committed adultery with her in his heart. [29]If your right eye causes you to sin, pluck it out and cast it from you; for it is more profitable for you that one of your members perish, than for your whole body to be cast into hell. [30]And if your right hand causes you to sin, cut it off and cast it from you; for it is more profitable for you that one of your members perish, than for your whole body to be cast into hell.

Marriage Is Sacred and Binding

[31]"Furthermore it has been said, 'Whoever divorces his wife, let him give her a certificate of divorce.' [32]But I say to you that whoever divorces his wife for any reason except sexual immorality[a] causes her to commit adultery; and whoever marries a woman who is divorced commits adultery.

Jesus Forbids Oaths

[33]"Again you have heard that it was said to those of old, 'You shall not swear falsely, but shall perform your oaths to the Lord.' [34]But I say to you, do not swear at all: neither by heaven, for it is God's throne; [35]nor by the earth, for it is His footstool; nor by Jerusalem, for it is the city of the great King. [36]Nor shall you swear by your head, because you cannot make one hair white or black. [37]But let your 'Yes' be 'Yes,' and your 'No,' 'No.' For whatever is more than these is from the evil one.

Go the Second Mile

[38]"You have heard that it was said, 'An eye for an eye and a tooth for a tooth.'[a] [39]But I tell you not to resist an evil person. But whoever slaps you on your right cheek, turn the other to him also. [40]If anyone wants to sue you and take away your tunic, let him have your cloak also. [41]And whoever compels you to go one mile, go with him two. [42]Give to him who asks you, and from him who wants to borrow from you do not turn away.

Love Your Enemies

[43]"You have heard that it was said, 'You shall love your neighbor[a] and hate your enemy.' [44]But I say to you, love your enemies, bless those who curse you, do good to those who hate you, and pray for those who spitefully use you and persecute you,[a] [45]that you may be sons of your Father in heaven; for He makes His sun rise on the evil and on the good, and sends rain on the just and on the unjust. [46]For if you love those who love you, what reward have you? Do not even the tax collectors do the same? [47]And if you greet your brethren[a] only, what do you do more than others? Do not even the tax collectors[b] do so? [48]Therefore you shall be perfect, just as your Father in heaven is perfect.

Do Good to Please God

6 "Take heed that you do not do your charitable deeds before men, to be seen by them. Otherwise you have no reward from your Father in heaven. [2]Therefore, when you do a charitable deed, do not sound a trumpet before you as the hypocrites do in the synagogues and in the streets, that they

---

5:27 [a]NU-Text and M-Text omit *to those of old.* [b]Exodus 20:14; Deuteronomy 5:18   **5:32** [a]Or *fornication*   **5:38** [a]Exodus 21:24; Leviticus 24:20; Deuteronomy 19:21   **5:43** [a]Compare Leviticus 19:18   **5:44** [a]NU-Text omits three clauses from this verse, leaving, "*But I say to you, love your enemies and pray for those who persecute you.*"   **5:47** [a]M-Text reads *friends.* [b]NU-Text reads *Gentiles.*

may have glory from men. Assuredly, I say to you, they have their reward. [3]But when you do a charitable deed, do not let your left hand know what your right hand is doing, [4]that your charitable deed may be in secret; and your Father who sees in secret will Himself reward you openly.[a]

The Model Prayer

[5]"And when you pray, you shall not be like the hypocrites. For they love to pray standing in the synagogues and on the corners of the streets, that they may be seen by men. Assuredly, I say to you, they have their reward. [6]But you, when you pray, go into your room, and when you have shut your door, pray to your Father who *is* in the secret *place;* and your Father who sees in secret will reward you openly.[a] [7]And when you pray, do not use vain repetitions as the heathen *do.* For they think that they will be heard for their many words. [8]"Therefore do not be like them. For your Father knows the things you have need of before you ask Him. [9]In this manner, therefore, pray:

Our Father in heaven,
Hallowed be Your name.
[10] Your kingdom come.
Your will be done
On earth as *it is* in heaven.
[11] Give us this day our daily bread.
[12] And forgive us our debts,
As we forgive our debtors.
[13] And do not lead us into temptation,
But deliver us from the evil one.
For Yours is the kingdom and the
    power and the glory forever. Amen.[a]

[14]"For if you forgive men their trespasses, your heavenly Father will also forgive you. [15]But if you do not forgive men their trespasses, neither will your Father forgive your trespasses.

Fasting to Be Seen Only by God

[16]"Moreover, when you fast, do not be like the hypocrites, with a sad countenance. For they disfigure their faces that they may appear to men to be fasting. Assuredly, I say to you, they have their reward. [17]But you, when you fast, anoint your head and wash your face, [18]so that you do not appear to men to be fasting, but to your Father who *is* in the secret *place;* and your Father who sees in secret will reward you openly.[a]

Lay Up Treasures in Heaven

[19]"Do not lay up for yourselves treasures on earth, where moth and rust destroy and where thieves break in and steal; [20]but lay up for yourselves treasures in heaven, where neither moth nor rust destroys and where thieves do not break in and steal. [21]For where your treasure is, there your heart will be also.

The Lamp of the Body

[22]"The lamp of the body is the eye. If therefore your eye is good, your whole body will be full of light. [23]But if your eye is bad, your whole body will be full of darkness. If therefore the light that is in you is darkness, how great *is* that darkness!

You Cannot Serve God and Riches

[24]"No one can serve two masters; for either he will hate the one and love the other, or else he will be loyal to the one and despise the other. You cannot serve God and mammon.

Do Not Worry

[25]"Therefore I say to you, do not worry about your life, what you will eat or what you will drink; nor about your body, what you will put on. Is not life more than food and the body more than clothing? [26]Look at the birds of the air, for they neither sow nor reap nor gather into barns; yet your heavenly Father feeds them. Are you not of more value than they? [27]Which of you by worrying can add one cubit to his stature? [28]"So why do you worry about clothing? Consider the lilies of the field, how they grow: they neither toil nor spin; [29]and yet I say to you that even Solomon in all his glory was not arrayed like one of these. [30]Now if God so clothes the grass of the field,

---

6:4 [a]NU-Text omits *openly.*   **6:6** [a]NU-Text omits *openly.*   **6:13** [a]NU-Text omits *For Yours* through *Amen.*   **6:18** [a]NU-Text and M-Text omit *openly.*

which today is, and tomorrow is thrown into the oven, *will He* not much more *clothe* you, O you of little faith?

[31]"Therefore do not worry, saying, 'What shall we eat?' or 'What shall we drink?' or 'What shall we wear?' [32]For after all these things the Gentiles seek. For your heavenly Father knows that you need all these things. [33]But seek first the kingdom of God and His righteousness, and all these things shall be added to you. [34]Therefore do not worry about tomorrow, for tomorrow will worry about its own things. Sufficient for the day *is* its own trouble.

> **Abraham Lincoln** placed his hand on Matthew 7:1, 18:7, and Revelation 16:7 as he took the presidential oath of office in 1865.

Do Not Judge

7 "Judge not, that you be not judged. [2]For with what judgment you judge, you will be judged; and with the measure you use, it will be measured back to you. [3]And why do you look at the speck in your brother's eye, but do not consider the plank in your own eye? [4]Or how can you say to your brother, 'Let me remove the speck from your eye'; and look, a plank *is* in your own eye? [5]Hypocrite! First remove the plank from your own eye, and then you will see clearly to remove the speck from your brother's eye.

[6]"Do not give what is holy to the dogs; nor cast your pearls before swine, lest they trample them under their feet, and turn and tear you in pieces.

Keep Asking, Seeking, Knocking

[7]"Ask, and it will be given to you; seek, and you will find; knock, and it will be opened to you. [8]For everyone who asks receives, and he who seeks finds, and to him who knocks it will be opened. [9]Or what man is there among you who, if his son asks for bread, will give him a stone? [10]Or if he asks for a fish, will he give him a serpent? [11]If you then, being evil, know how to give good gifts to your children, how much more will your Father who is in heaven give good things to those who ask

Him! [12]Therefore, whatever you want men to do to you, do also to them, for this is the Law and the Prophets.

The Narrow Way

[13]"Enter by the narrow gate; for wide *is* the gate and broad *is* the way that leads to destruction, and there are many who go in by it. [14]Because[a] narrow *is* the gate and difficult *is* the way which leads to life, and there are few who find it.

You Will Know Them by Their Fruits

[15]"Beware of false prophets, who come to you in sheep's clothing, but inwardly they are ravenous wolves. [16]You will know them by their fruits. Do men gather grapes from thornbushes or figs from thistles? [17]Even so, every good tree bears good fruit, but a bad tree bears bad fruit. [18]A good tree cannot bear bad fruit, nor *can* a bad tree bear good fruit. [19]Every tree that does not bear good fruit is cut down and thrown into the fire. [20]Therefore by their fruits you will know them.

I Never Knew You

[21]"Not everyone who says to Me, 'Lord, Lord,' shall enter the kingdom of heaven, but he who does the will of My Father in heaven. [22]Many will say to Me in that day, 'Lord, Lord, have we not prophesied in Your name, cast out demons in Your name, and done many wonders in Your name?' [23]And then I will declare to them, 'I never knew you; depart from Me, you who practice lawlessness!'

Build on the Rock

[24]"Therefore whoever hears these sayings of Mine, and does them, I will liken him to a wise man who built his house on the rock: [25]and the rain descended, the floods came, and the winds blew and beat on that house; and it did not fall, for it was founded on the rock.

[26]"But everyone who hears these sayings of Mine, and does not do them, will be like a foolish man who built his house on the sand: [27]and the rain descended, the floods

7:14 [a]NU-Text and M-Text read *How . . . !*

came, and the winds blew and beat on that house; and it fell. And great was its fall."

28And so it was, when Jesus had ended these sayings, that the people were astonished at His teaching, 29for He taught them as one having authority, and not as the scribes.

Jesus Cleanses a Leper

8 When He had come down from the mountain, great multitudes followed Him. 2And behold, a leper came and worshiped Him, saying, "Lord, if You are willing, You can make me clean."

3Then Jesus put out *His* hand and touched him, saying, "I am willing; be cleansed." Immediately his leprosy was cleansed.

4And Jesus said to him, "See that you tell no one; but go your way, show yourself to the priest, and offer the gift that Moses commanded, as a testimony to them."

Jesus Heals a Centurion's Servant

5Now when Jesus had entered Capernaum, a centurion came to Him, pleading with Him, 6saying, "Lord, my servant is lying at home paralyzed, dreadfully tormented."

7And Jesus said to him, "I will come and heal him."

8The centurion answered and said, "Lord, I am not worthy that You should come under my roof. But only speak a word, and my servant will be healed. 9For I also am a man under authority, having soldiers under me. And I say to this *one,* 'Go,' and he goes; and to another, 'Come,' and he comes; and to my servant, 'Do this,' and he does *it.*"

10When Jesus heard *it,* He marveled, and said to those who followed, "Assuredly, I say to you, I have not found such great faith, not even in Israel! 11And I say to you that many will come from east and west,

---

MORAL STRENGTH

"Therefore whoever hears these sayings of Mine, and does them. . . ."

MATTHEW 7:24

Robert Winthrop

RELIGION SUPPORTS THE STATE

Robert Winthrop, a lawyer and philanthropist who served as the Speaker of the United States House of Representatives (1847–1849), stated:

> The voice of experience and the voice of our own reason speak but one language. . . . Both united in teaching us that men may as well build their houses upon the sand and expect to see them stand, when the rains fall, and the winds blow, and the floods come, as to found free institutions upon any other basis than that of morality and virtue, of which the Word of God is the only authoritative rule, and the only adequate sanction.
>
> All societies of men must be governed in some way or other. The less they have of stringent state government, the more they must have of individual self-government. The less they rely on public law or physical force, the more they must rely on private moral restraint.
>
> Men, in a word, must necessarily be controlled either by a power within them or a power without them; either by the Word of God or by the strong arm of man; either by the Bible or by the bayonet.
>
> It may do for other countries and other governments to talk about the state supporting religion. Here, under our own free institutions, it is religion which must support the state.

and sit down with Abraham, Isaac, and Jacob in the kingdom of heaven. ¹²But the sons of the kingdom will be cast out into outer darkness. There will be weeping and gnashing of teeth." ¹³Then Jesus said to the centurion, "Go your way; and as you have believed, *so* let it be done for you." And his servant was healed that same hour.

Peter's Mother-in-Law Healed

¹⁴Now when Jesus had come into Peter's house, He saw his wife's mother lying sick with a fever. ¹⁵So He touched her hand, and the fever left her. And she arose and served them.ª

Many Healed in the Evening

¹⁶When evening had come, they brought to Him many who were demon-possessed. And He cast out the spirits with a word, and healed all who were sick, ¹⁷that it might be fulfilled which was spoken by Isaiah the prophet, saying:

> *"He Himself took our infirmities*
> *And bore our sicknesses."*ª

The Cost of Discipleship

¹⁸And when Jesus saw great multitudes about Him, He gave a command to depart to the other side. ¹⁹Then a certain scribe came and said to Him, "Teacher, I will follow You wherever You go."
²⁰And Jesus said to him, "Foxes have holes and birds of the air *have* nests, but the Son of Man has nowhere to lay *His* head."
²¹Then another of His disciples said to Him, "Lord, let me first go and bury my father."
²²But Jesus said to him, "Follow Me, and let the dead bury their own dead."

Wind and Wave Obey Jesus

²³Now when He got into a boat, His disciples followed Him. ²⁴And suddenly a great tempest arose on the sea, so that the boat was covered with the waves. But He was asleep. ²⁵Then His disciples came to *Him* and awoke Him, saying, "Lord, save us! We are perishing!"
²⁶But He said to them, "Why are you fearful, O you of little faith?" Then He arose and rebuked the winds and the sea, and there was a great calm. ²⁷So the men marveled, saying, "Who can this be, that even the winds and the sea obey Him?"

Two Demon-Possessed Men Healed

²⁸When He had come to the other side, to the country of the Gergesenes,ª there met Him two demon-possessed *men,* coming out of the tombs, exceedingly fierce, so that no one could pass that way. ²⁹And suddenly they cried out, saying, "What have we to do with You, Jesus, You Son of God? Have You come here to torment us before the time?"
³⁰Now a good way off from them there was a herd of many swine feeding. ³¹So the demons begged Him, saying, "If You cast us out, permit us to go awayª into the herd of swine."
³²And He said to them, "Go." So when they had come out, they went into the herd of swine. And suddenly the whole herd of swine ran violently down the steep place into the sea, and perished in the water.
³³Then those who kept *them* fled; and they went away into the city and told everything, including what *had happened* to the demon-possessed *men.* ³⁴And behold, the whole city came out to meet Jesus. And when they saw Him, they begged *Him* to depart from their region.

Jesus Forgives and Heals a Paralytic

9 So He got into a boat, crossed over, and came to His own city. ²Then behold, they brought to Him a paralytic lying on a bed. When Jesus saw their faith, He said to the paralytic, "Son, be of good cheer; your sins are forgiven you."
³And at once some of the scribes said within themselves, "This Man blasphemes!"
⁴But Jesus, knowing their thoughts, said, "Why do you think evil in your hearts? ⁵For which is easier, to say, '*Your* sins are forgiven you,' or to say, 'Arise and walk'? ⁶But that you may know that the Son of Man has power on earth to forgive sins"—then He

---

8:15 ªNU-Text and M-Text read *Him.*
8:17 ªIsaiah 53:4   **8:28** ªNU-Text reads *Gadarenes.*
8:31 ªNU-Text reads *send us.*

said to the paralytic, "Arise, take up your bed, and go to your house." [7]And he arose and departed to his house.

[8]Now when the multitudes saw *it,* they marveled[a] and glorified God, who had given such power to men.

Matthew the Tax Collector

[9]As Jesus passed on from there, He saw a man named Matthew sitting at the tax office. And He said to him, "Follow Me." So he arose and followed Him.

[10]Now it happened, as Jesus sat at the table in the house, *that* behold, many tax collectors and sinners came and sat down with Him and His disciples. [11]And when the Pharisees saw *it,* they said to His disciples, "Why does your Teacher eat with tax collectors and sinners?"

[12]When Jesus heard *that,* He said to them, "Those who are well have no need of a physician, but those who are sick. [13]But go and learn what *this* means: *'I desire mercy and not sacrifice.'*[a] For I did not come to call the righteous, but sinners, to repentance."[b]

Jesus Is Questioned About Fasting

[14]Then the disciples of John came to Him, saying, "Why do we and the Pharisees fast often,[a] but Your disciples do not fast?"

[15]And Jesus said to them, "Can the friends of the bridegroom mourn as long as the bridegroom is with them? But the days will come when the bridegroom will be taken away from them, and then they will fast. [16]No one puts a piece of unshrunk cloth on an old garment; for the patch pulls away from the garment, and the tear is made worse. [17]Nor do they put new wine into old wineskins, or else the wineskins break, the wine is spilled, and the wineskins are ruined. But they put new wine into new wineskins, and both are preserved."

A Girl Restored to Life and a Woman Healed

[18]While He spoke these things to them, behold, a ruler came and worshiped Him, saying, "My daughter has just died, but come and lay Your hand on her and she will live." [19]So Jesus arose and followed him, and so *did* His disciples.

[20]And suddenly, a woman who had a flow of blood for twelve years came from behind and touched the hem of His garment. [21]For she said to herself, "If only I may touch His garment, I shall be made well." [22]But Jesus turned around, and when He saw her He said, "Be of good cheer, daughter; your faith has made you well." And the woman was made well from that hour.

[23]When Jesus came into the ruler's house, and saw the flute players and the noisy crowd wailing, [24]He said to them, "Make room, for the girl is not dead, but sleeping." And they ridiculed Him. [25]But when the crowd was put outside, He went in and took her by the hand, and the girl arose. [26]And the report of this went out into all that land.

Two Blind Men Healed

[27]When Jesus departed from there, two blind men followed Him, crying out and saying, "Son of David, have mercy on us!"

[28]And when He had come into the house, the blind men came to Him. And Jesus said to them, "Do you believe that I am able to do this?"

They said to Him, "Yes, Lord."

[29]Then He touched their eyes, saying, "According to your faith let it be to you." [30]And their eyes were opened. And Jesus sternly warned them, saying, "See *that* no one knows *it.*" [31]But when they had departed, they spread the news about Him in all that country.

A Mute Man Speaks

[32]As they went out, behold, they brought to Him a man, mute and demon-possessed. [33]And when the demon was cast out, the mute spoke. And the multitudes marveled, saying, "It was never seen like this in Israel!"

[34]But the Pharisees said, "He casts out demons by the ruler of the demons."

The Compassion of Jesus

[35]Then Jesus went about all the cities and villages, teaching in their synagogues, preaching the gospel of the kingdom, and

---

9:8 [a]NU-Text reads *were afraid.* 9:13 [a]Hosea 6:6
[b]NU-Text omits *to repentance.* 9:14 [a]NU-Text brackets *often* as disputed.

healing every sickness and every disease among the people.[a] 36But when He saw the multitudes, He was moved with compassion for them, because they were weary[a] and scattered, like sheep having no shepherd. 37Then He said to His disciples, "The harvest truly *is* plentiful, but the laborers *are* few. 38Therefore pray the Lord of the harvest to send out laborers into His harvest."

The Twelve Apostles

10 And when He had called His twelve disciples to *Him,* He gave them power *over* unclean spirits, to cast them out, and to heal all kinds of sickness and all kinds of disease. 2Now the names of the twelve apostles are these: first, Simon, who is called Peter, and Andrew his brother; James the *son* of Zebedee, and John his brother; 3Philip and Bartholomew; Thomas and Matthew the tax collector; James the *son* of Alphaeus, and Lebbaeus, whose surname was[a] Thaddaeus; 4Simon the Cananite,[a] and Judas Iscariot, who also betrayed Him.

Sending Out the Twelve

5These twelve Jesus sent out and commanded them, saying: "Do not go into the way of the Gentiles, and do not enter a city of the Samaritans. 6But go rather to the lost sheep of the house of Israel. 7And as you go, preach, saying, 'The kingdom of heaven is at hand.' 8Heal the sick, cleanse the lepers, raise the dead,[a] cast out demons. Freely you have received, freely give. 9Provide neither gold nor silver nor copper in your money belts, 10nor bag for *your* journey, nor two tunics, nor sandals, nor staffs; for a worker is worthy of his food.

11"Now whatever city or town you enter, inquire who in it is worthy, and stay there till you go out. 12And when you go into a household, greet it. 13If the household is worthy, let your peace come upon it. But if it is not worthy, let your peace return to you. 14And whoever will not receive you nor hear your words, when you depart from that house or city, shake off the dust from your feet. 15Assuredly, I say to you, it will be more tolerable for the land of Sodom and Gomorrah in the day of judgment than for that city!

Persecutions Are Coming

16"Behold, I send you out as sheep in the midst of wolves. Therefore be wise as serpents and harmless as doves. 17But beware of men, for they will deliver you up to councils and scourge you in their synagogues. 18You will be brought before governors and kings for My sake, as a testimony to them and to the Gentiles. 19But when they deliver you up, do not worry about how or what you should speak. For it will be given to you in that hour what you should speak; 20for it is not you who speak, but the Spirit of your Father who speaks in you.

21"Now brother will deliver up brother to death, and a father *his* child; and children will rise up against parents and cause them to be put to death. 22And you will be hated by all for My name's sake. But he who endures to the end will be saved. 23When they persecute you in this city, flee to another. For assuredly, I say to you, you will not have gone through the cities of Israel before the Son of Man comes.

24"A disciple is not above *his* teacher, nor a servant above his master. 25It is enough for a disciple that he be like his teacher, and a servant like his master. If they have called the master of the house Beelzebub,[a] how much more *will they call* those of his household! 26Therefore do not fear them. For there is nothing covered that will not be revealed, and hidden that will not be known.

Jesus Teaches the Fear of God

27"Whatever I tell you in the dark, speak in the light; and what you hear in the ear, preach on the housetops. 28And do not fear those who kill the body but cannot kill the soul. But rather fear Him who is able to destroy both soul and body in hell. 29Are not two sparrows sold for a copper coin? And not one of them falls to the ground apart

---

9:35 [a]NU-Text omits *among the people.*
9:36 [a]NU-Text and M-Text read *harassed.*
10:3 [a]NU-Text omits *Lebbaeus, whose surname was.*
10:4 [a]NU-Text reads *Cananaean.*   **10:8** [a]NU-Text reads *raise the dead, cleanse the lepers;* M-Text omits *raise the dead.*   **10:25** [a]NU-Text and M-Text read *Beelzebul.*

from your Father's will. ³⁰But the very hairs of your head are all numbered. ³¹Do not fear therefore; you are of more value than many sparrows.

Confess Christ Before Men

³²"Therefore whoever confesses Me before men, him I will also confess before My Father who is in heaven. ³³But whoever denies Me before men, him I will also deny before My Father who is in heaven.

Christ Brings Division

³⁴"Do not think that I came to bring peace on earth. I did not come to bring peace but a sword. ³⁵For I have come to 'set a man against his father, a daughter against her mother, and a daughter-in-law against her mother-in-law'; ³⁶and 'a man's enemies will be those of his own household.'ᵃ ³⁷He who loves father or mother more than Me is not worthy of Me. And he who loves son or daughter more than Me is not worthy of Me. ³⁸And he who does not take his cross and follow after Me is not worthy of Me. ³⁹He who finds his life will lose it, and he who loses his life for My sake will find it.

A Cup of Cold Water

⁴⁰"He who receives you receives Me, and he who receives Me receives Him who sent Me. ⁴¹He who receives a prophet in the name of a prophet shall receive a prophet's reward. And he who receives a righteous man in the name of a righteous man shall receive a righteous man's reward. ⁴²And whoever gives one of these little ones only a cup of cold water in the name of a disciple, assuredly, I say to you, he shall by no means lose his reward."

John the Baptist Sends Messengers to Jesus

11 Now it came to pass, when Jesus finished commanding His twelve disciples, that He departed from there to teach and to preach in their cities.

²And when John had heard in prison about the works of Christ, he sent two ofᵃ his disciples ³and said to Him, "Are You the Coming One, or do we look for another?"

⁴Jesus answered and said to them, "Go and tell John the things which you hear

and see: ⁵The blind see and the lame walk; the lepers are cleansed and the deaf hear; the dead are raised up and the poor have the gospel preached to them. ⁶And blessed is he who is not offended because of Me."

⁷As they departed, Jesus began to say to the multitudes concerning John: "What did you go out into the wilderness to see? A reed shaken by the wind? ⁸But what did you go out to see? A man clothed in soft garments? Indeed, those who wear soft clothing are in kings' houses. ⁹But what did you go out to see? A prophet? Yes, I say to you, and more than a prophet. ¹⁰For this is he of whom it is written:

> 'Behold, I send My messenger before Your face,
> Who will prepare Your way before You.'ᵃ

¹¹"Assuredly, I say to you, among those born of women there has not risen one greater than John the Baptist; but he who is least in the kingdom of heaven is greater than he. ¹²And from the days of John the Baptist until now the kingdom of heaven suffers violence, and the violent take it by force. ¹³For all the prophets and the law prophesied until John. ¹⁴And if you are willing to receive it, he is Elijah who is to come. ¹⁵He who has ears to hear, let him hear!

¹⁶"But to what shall I liken this generation? It is like children sitting in the marketplaces and calling to their companions, ¹⁷and saying:

> 'We played the flute for you,
> And you did not dance;
> We mourned to you,
> And you did not lament.'

¹⁸For John came neither eating nor drinking, and they say, 'He has a demon.' ¹⁹The Son of Man came eating and drinking, and they say, 'Look, a glutton and a winebibber, a friend of tax collectors and sinners!' But wisdom is justified by her children."ᵃ

10:36 ᵃMicah 7:6   **11:2** ᵃNU-Text reads by for two of.
11:10 ᵃMalachi 3:1   **11:19** ᵃNU-Text reads works.

Woe to the Impenitent Cities

20Then He began to rebuke the cities in which most of His mighty works had been done, because they did not repent: 21"Woe to you, Chorazin! Woe to you, Bethsaida! For if the mighty works which were done in you had been done in Tyre and Sidon, they would have repented long ago in sackcloth and ashes. 22But I say to you, it will be more tolerable for Tyre and Sidon in the day of judgment than for you. 23And you, Capernaum, who are exalted to heaven, will be[a] brought down to Hades; for if the mighty works which were done in you had been done in Sodom, it would have remained until this day. 24But I say to you that it shall be more tolerable for the land of Sodom in the day of judgment than for you."

Jesus Gives True Rest

25At that time Jesus answered and said, "I thank You, Father, Lord of heaven and earth, that You have hidden these things from the wise and prudent and have revealed them to babes. 26Even so, Father, for so it seemed good in Your sight. 27All things have been delivered to Me by My Father, and no one knows the Son except the Father. Nor does anyone know the Father except the Son, and the one to whom the Son wills to reveal Him. 28Come to Me, all you who labor and are heavy laden, and I will give you rest. 29Take My yoke upon you and learn from Me, for I am gentle and lowly in heart, and you will find rest for your souls. 30For My yoke is easy and My burden is light."

Jesus Is Lord of the Sabbath

12 At that time Jesus went through the grainfields on the Sabbath. And His disciples were hungry, and began to pluck heads of grain and to eat. 2And when the Pharisees saw it, they said to Him, "Look, Your disciples are doing what is not lawful to do on the Sabbath!"

3But He said to them, "Have you not read what David did when he was hungry, he and those who were with him: 4how he entered the house of God and ate the showbread which was not lawful for him to eat,

nor for those who were with him, but only for the priests? 5Or have you not read in the law that on the Sabbath the priests in the temple profane the Sabbath, and are blameless? 6Yet I say to you that in this place there is One greater than the temple. 7But if you had known what this means, 'I desire mercy and not sacrifice,'[a] you would not have condemned the guiltless. 8For the Son of Man is Lord even[a] of the Sabbath."

Healing on the Sabbath

9Now when He had departed from there, He went into their synagogue. 10And behold, there was a man who had a withered hand. And they asked Him, saying, "Is it lawful to heal on the Sabbath?"—that they might accuse Him.

11Then He said to them, "What man is there among you who has one sheep, and if it falls into a pit on the Sabbath, will not lay hold of it and lift it out? 12Of how much more value then is a man than a sheep? Therefore it is lawful to do good on the Sabbath." 13Then He said to the man, "Stretch out your hand." And he stretched it out, and it was restored as whole as the other. 14Then the Pharisees went out and plotted against Him, how they might destroy Him.

Behold, My Servant

15But when Jesus knew it, He withdrew from there. And great multitudes[a] followed Him, and He healed them all. 16Yet He warned them not to make Him known, 17that it might be fulfilled which was spoken by Isaiah the prophet, saying:

18 "Behold! My Servant whom I have
       chosen,
     My Beloved in whom My soul is
       well pleased!
     I will put My Spirit upon Him,
     And He will declare justice to the
       Gentiles.
19 He will not quarrel nor cry out,
     Nor will anyone hear His voice in
       the streets.

11:23 [a]NU-Text reads will you be exalted to heaven? No, you will be. **12:7** [a]Hosea 6:6 **12:8** [a]NU-Text and M-Text omit even. **12:15** [a]NU-Text brackets multitudes as disputed.

20 *A bruised reed He will not break,*
    And smoking flax He will not quench,
    Till He sends forth justice to victory;
21 *And in His name Gentiles will trust."*ᵃ

A House Divided Cannot Stand

22Then one was brought to Him who was demon-possessed, blind and mute; and He healed him, so that the blind andᵃ mute man both spoke and saw. 23And all the multitudes were amazed and said, "Could this be the Son of David?"

24Now when the Pharisees heard *it* they said, "This *fellow* does not cast out demons except by Beelzebub,ᵃ the ruler of the demons."

25But Jesus knew their thoughts, and said to them: "Every kingdom divided against itself is brought to desolation, and every city or house divided against itself will not stand. 26If Satan casts out Satan, he is divided against himself. How then will his kingdom stand? 27And if I cast out demons by Beelzebub, by whom do your sons cast *them* out? Therefore they shall be your judges. 28But if I cast out demons by the Spirit of God, surely the kingdom of God has come upon you. 29Or how can one enter a strong man's house and plunder his goods, unless he first binds the strong man? And then he will plunder his house. 30He who is not with Me is against Me, and he who does not gather with Me scatters abroad.

The Unpardonable Sin

31"Therefore I say to you, every sin and blasphemy will be forgiven men, but the blasphemy *against* the Spirit will not be forgiven men. 32Anyone who speaks a word against the Son of Man, it will be forgiven him; but whoever speaks against the Holy Spirit, it will not be forgiven him, either in this age or in the *age* to come.

A Tree Known by Its Fruit

33"Either make the tree good and its fruit good, or else make the tree bad and its fruit bad; for a tree is known by *its* fruit. 34Brood of vipers! How can you, being evil, speak good things? For out of the abundance of the heart the mouth speaks. 35A good man out of the good treasure of his heartᵃ brings forth good things, and an evil man out of the evil treasure brings forth evil things. 36But I say to you that for every idle word men may speak, they will give account of it in the day of judgment. 37For by your words you will be justified, and by your words you will be condemned."

The Scribes and Pharisees Ask for a Sign

38Then some of the scribes and Pharisees answered, saying, "Teacher, we want to see a sign from You."

39But He answered and said to them, "An evil and adulterous generation seeks after a sign, and no sign will be given to it except the sign of the prophet Jonah. 40For as Jonah was three days and three nights in the belly of the great fish, so will the Son of Man be three days and three nights in the heart of the earth. 41The men of Nineveh will rise up in the judgment with this generation and condemn it, because they repented at the preaching of Jonah; and indeed a greater than Jonah *is* here. 42The queen of the South will rise up in the judgment with this generation and condemn it, for she came from the ends of the earth to hear the wisdom of Solomon; and indeed a greater than Solomon *is* here.

An Unclean Spirit Returns

43"When an unclean spirit goes out of a man, he goes through dry places, seeking rest, and finds none. 44Then he says, 'I will return to my house from which I came.' And when he comes, he finds *it* empty, swept, and put in order. 45Then he goes and takes with him seven other spirits more wicked than himself, and they enter and dwell there; and the last *state* of that man is worse than the first. So shall it also be with this wicked generation."

Jesus' Mother and Brothers Send for Him

46While He was still talking to the multitudes, behold, His mother and brothers stood outside, seeking to speak with Him. 47Then one said to Him, "Look, Your mother and

12:21 ᵃIsaiah 42:1–4   **12:22** ᵃNU-Text omits *blind and.*   **12:24** ᵃNU-Text and M-Text read *Beelzebul.*   **12:35** ᵃNU-Text and M-Text omit *of his heart.*

Your brothers are standing outside, seeking to speak with You."

⁴⁸But He answered and said to the one who told Him, "Who is My mother and who are My brothers?" ⁴⁹And He stretched out His hand toward His disciples and said, "Here are My mother and My brothers! ⁵⁰For whoever does the will of My Father in heaven is My brother and sister and mother."

The Parable of the Sower

13 On the same day Jesus went out of the house and sat by the sea. ²And great multitudes were gathered together to Him, so that He got into a boat and sat; and the whole multitude stood on the shore. ³Then He spoke many things to them in parables, saying: "Behold, a sower went out to sow. ⁴And as he sowed, some *seed* fell by the wayside; and the birds came and devoured them. ⁵Some fell on stony places, where they did not have much earth; and they immediately sprang up because they had no depth of earth. ⁶But when the sun was up they were scorched, and because they had no root they withered away. ⁷And some fell among thorns, and the thorns sprang up and choked them. ⁸But others fell on good ground and yielded a crop: some a hundredfold, some sixty, some thirty. ⁹He who has ears to hear, let him hear!"

The Purpose of Parables

¹⁰And the disciples came and said to Him, "Why do You speak to them in parables?"

¹¹He answered and said to them, "Because it has been given to you to know the mysteries of the kingdom of heaven, but to them it has not been given. ¹²For whoever has, to him more will be given, and he will have

WORSHIP

". . . a tree is known by its fruit."

MATTHEW 12:33

Benjamin Franklin

GOOD WORKS

Benjamin Franklin, one of America's renowned Founding Fathers, wrote:

I can only show my gratitude for these mercies from God, by a readiness to help His other children and my brethren. For I do not think that thanks and compliments, though repeated weekly, can discharge our real obligations to each other, and much less those to our Creator.

You will see in this my notion of good works, that I am far from expecting to merit heaven by them. By heaven we understand a state of happiness, infinite in degree, and eternal in duration. I can do nothing to deserve such rewards. . . .

The faith you mention has certainly its use in the world. I do not desire to see it diminished, nor would I endeavor to lessen it in any man. But I wish it were more productive of good works than I have generally seen it; I mean real good works; works of kindness, charity, mercy, and public spirit; not holiday keeping, sermon reading or hearing; performing church ceremonies, or making long prayers, filled with flatteries and compliments. . . .

The worship of God is a duty; the hearing and reading of sermons may be useful; but, if men rest in hearing and praying, as too many do, it is as if a tree should value itself on being watered and putting forth leaves, though it never produce any fruit.

abundance; but whoever does not have, even what he has will be taken away from him. [13]Therefore I speak to them in parables, because seeing they do not see, and hearing they do not hear, nor do they understand. [14]And in them the prophecy of Isaiah is fulfilled, which says:

> 'Hearing you will hear and shall
>   not understand,
> And seeing you will see and not
>   perceive;
> [15] For the hearts of this people have
>   grown dull.
> Their ears are hard of hearing,
> And their eyes they have closed,
> Lest they should see with their eyes
>   and hear with their ears,
> Lest they should understand with
>   their hearts and turn,
> So that I should[a] heal them.'[b]

[16]But blessed *are* your eyes for they see, and your ears for they hear; [17]for assuredly, I say to you that many prophets and righteous *men* desired to see what you see, and did not see *it,* and to hear what you hear, and did not hear *it.*

The Parable of the Sower Explained

[18]"Therefore hear the parable of the sower: [19]When anyone hears the word of the kingdom, and does not understand *it,* then the wicked *one* comes and snatches away what was sown in his heart. This is he who received seed by the wayside. [20]But he who received the seed on stony places, this is he who hears the word and immediately receives it with joy; [21]yet he has no root in himself, but endures only for a while. For when tribulation or persecution arises because of the word, immediately he stumbles. [22]Now he who received seed among the thorns is he who hears the word, and the cares of this world and the deceitfulness of riches choke the word, and he becomes unfruitful. [23]But he who received seed on the good ground is he who hears the word and understands *it,* who indeed bears fruit and produces: some a hundredfold, some sixty, some thirty."

The Parable of the Wheat and the Tares

[24]Another parable He put forth to them, saying: "The kingdom of heaven is like a man who sowed good seed in his field; [25]but while men slept, his enemy came and sowed tares among the wheat and went his way. [26]But when the grain had sprouted and produced a crop, then the tares also appeared. [27]So the servants of the owner came and said to him, 'Sir, did you not sow good seed in your field? How then does it have tares?' [28]He said to them, 'An enemy has done this.' The servants said to him, 'Do you want us then to go and gather them up?' [29]But he said, 'No, lest while you gather up the tares you also uproot the wheat with them. [30]Let both grow together until the harvest, and at the time of harvest I will say to the reapers, "First gather together the tares and bind them in bundles to burn them, but gather the wheat into my barn." ' "

The Parable of the Mustard Seed

[31]Another parable He put forth to them, saying: "The kingdom of heaven is like a mustard seed, which a man took and sowed in his field, [32]which indeed is the least of all the seeds; but when it is grown it is greater than the herbs and becomes a tree, so that the birds of the air come and nest in its branches."

The Parable of the Leaven

[33]Another parable He spoke to them: "The kingdom of heaven is like leaven, which a woman took and hid in three measures[a] of meal till it was all leavened."

Prophecy and the Parables

[34]All these things Jesus spoke to the multitude in parables; and without a parable He did not speak to them, [35]that it might be fulfilled which was spoken by the prophet, saying:

> "I will open My mouth in parables;
> I will utter things kept secret from
>   the foundation of the world."[a]

13:15 [a]NU-Text and M-Text read *would.* [b]Isaiah 6:9, 10   **13:33** [a]Greek *sata,* approximately two pecks in all   **13:35** [a]Psalm 78:2

The Parable of the Tares Explained

³⁶Then Jesus sent the multitude away and went into the house. And His disciples came to Him, saying, "Explain to us the parable of the tares of the field."

³⁷He answered and said to them: "He who sows the good seed is the Son of Man. ³⁸The field is the world, the good seeds are the sons of the kingdom, but the tares are the sons of the wicked *one.* ³⁹The enemy who sowed them is the devil, the harvest is the end of the age, and the reapers are the angels. ⁴⁰Therefore as the tares are gathered and burned in the fire, so it will be at the end of this age. ⁴¹The Son of Man will send out His angels, and they will gather out of His kingdom all things that offend, and those who practice lawlessness, ⁴²and will cast them into the furnace of fire. There will be wailing and gnashing of teeth. ⁴³Then the righteous will shine forth as the sun in the kingdom of their Father. He who has ears to hear, let him hear!

The Parable of the Hidden Treasure

⁴⁴"Again, the kingdom of heaven is like treasure hidden in a field, which a man found and hid; and for joy over it he goes and sells all that he has and buys that field.

The Parable of the Pearl of Great Price

⁴⁵"Again, the kingdom of heaven is like a merchant seeking beautiful pearls, ⁴⁶who, when he had found one pearl of great price, went and sold all that he had and bought it.

The Parable of the Dragnet

⁴⁷"Again, the kingdom of heaven is like a dragnet that was cast into the sea and gathered some of every kind, ⁴⁸which, when it was full, they drew to shore; and they sat down and gathered the good into vessels, but threw the bad away. ⁴⁹So it will be at the end of the age. The angels will come forth, separate the wicked from among the just, ⁵⁰and cast them into the furnace of fire. There will be wailing and gnashing of teeth."

⁵¹Jesus said to them,^a "Have you understood all these things?"

They said to Him, "Yes, Lord."^b

⁵²Then He said to them, "Therefore every scribe instructed concerning^a the kingdom of heaven is like a householder who brings out of his treasure *things* new and old."

Jesus Rejected at Nazareth

⁵³Now it came to pass, when Jesus had finished these parables, that He departed from there. ⁵⁴When He had come to His own country, He taught them in their synagogue, so that they were astonished and said, "Where did this *Man* get this wisdom and *these* mighty works? ⁵⁵Is this not the carpenter's son? Is not His mother called Mary? And His brothers James, Joses,^a Simon, and Judas? ⁵⁶And His sisters, are they not all with us? Where then did this *Man* get all these things?" ⁵⁷So they were offended at Him.

But Jesus said to them, "A prophet is not without honor except in his own country and in his own house." ⁵⁸Now He did not do many mighty works there because of their unbelief.

John the Baptist Beheaded

14 At that time Herod the tetrarch heard the report about Jesus ²and said to his servants, "This is John the Baptist; he is risen from the dead, and therefore these powers are at work in him." ³For Herod had laid hold of John and bound him, and put *him* in prison for the sake of Herodias, his brother Philip's wife. ⁴Because John had said to him, "It is not lawful for you to have her." ⁵And although he wanted to put him to death, he feared the multitude, because they counted him as a prophet.

⁶But when Herod's birthday was celebrated, the daughter of Herodias danced before them and pleased Herod. ⁷Therefore he promised with an oath to give her whatever she might ask.

⁸So she, having been prompted by her mother, said, "Give me John the Baptist's head here on a platter."

⁹And the king was sorry; nevertheless, because of the oaths and because of those

---

13:51 ^aNU-Text omits *Jesus said to them.* ^bNU-Text omits *Lord.*   **13:52** ^aOr *for*   **13:55** ^aNU-Text reads *Joseph.*

who sat with him, he commanded *it* to be given to *her.* [10]So he sent and had John beheaded in prison. [11]And his head was brought on a platter and given to the girl, and she brought *it* to her mother. [12]Then his disciples came and took away the body and buried it, and went and told Jesus.

Feeding the Five Thousand

[13]When Jesus heard *it,* He departed from there by boat to a deserted place by Himself. But when the multitudes heard it, they followed Him on foot from the cities. [14]And when Jesus went out He saw a great multitude; and He was moved with compassion for them, and healed their sick. [15]When it was evening, His disciples came to Him, saying, "This is a deserted place, and the hour is already late. Send the multitudes away, that they may go into the villages and buy themselves food."

[16]But Jesus said to them, "They do not need to go away. You give them something to eat."

[17]And they said to Him, "We have here only five loaves and two fish."

[18]He said, "Bring them here to Me." [19]Then He commanded the multitudes to sit down on the grass. And He took the five loaves and the two fish, and looking up to heaven, He blessed and broke and gave the loaves to the disciples; and the disciples gave to the multitudes. [20]So they all ate and were filled, and they took up twelve baskets full of the fragments that remained. [21]Now those who had eaten were about five thousand men, besides women and children.

Jesus Walks on the Sea

[22]Immediately Jesus made His disciples get into the boat and go before Him to the other side, while He sent the multitudes away. [23]And when He had sent the multitudes away, He went up on the mountain by Himself to pray. Now when evening came, He was alone there. [24]But the boat was now in the middle of the sea,[a] tossed by the waves, for the wind was contrary. [25]Now in the fourth watch of the night Jesus went to them, walking on the sea. [26]And when the disciples saw Him walking

on the sea, they were troubled, saying, "It is a ghost!" And they cried out for fear. [27]But immediately Jesus spoke to them, saying, "Be of good cheer! It is I; do not be afraid."

[28]And Peter answered Him and said, "Lord, if it is You, command me to come to You on the water."

[29]So He said, "Come." And when Peter had come down out of the boat, he walked on the water to go to Jesus. [30]But when he saw that the wind *was* boisterous,[a] he was afraid; and beginning to sink he cried out, saying, "Lord, save me!"

[31]And immediately Jesus stretched out *His* hand and caught him, and said to him, "O you of little faith, why did you doubt?" [32]And when they got into the boat, the wind ceased.

[33]Then those who were in the boat came and[a] worshiped Him, saying, "Truly You are the Son of God."

Many Touch Him and Are Made Well

[34]When they had crossed over, they came to the land of[a] Gennesaret. [35]And when the men of that place recognized Him, they sent out into all that surrounding region, brought to Him all who were sick, [36]and begged Him that they might only touch the hem of His garment. And as many as touched *it* were made perfectly well.

Defilement Comes from Within

15 Then the scribes and Pharisees who were from Jerusalem came to Jesus, saying, [2]"Why do Your disciples transgress the tradition of the elders? For they do not wash their hands when they eat bread."

[3]He answered and said to them, "Why do you also transgress the commandment of God because of your tradition? [4]For God commanded, saying, *'Honor your father and your mother'*;[a] and, *'He who curses father or mother, let him be put to death.'*[b] [5]But you say, 'Whoever says to his father or mother, "Whatever profit you might have

---

14:24 [a]NU-Text reads *many furlongs away from the land.*   **14:30** [a]NU-Text brackets *that* and *boisterous* as disputed.   **14:33** [a]NU-Text omits *came and.*
14:34 [a]NU-Text reads *came to land at.*
15:4 [a]Exodus 20:12; Deuteronomy 5:16 [b]Exodus 21:17

received from me *is a gift to God*"— [6]then he need not honor his father or mother.'[a] Thus you have made the commandment[b] of God of no effect by your tradition. [7]Hypocrites! Well did Isaiah prophesy about you, saying:

[8] 'These people draw near to Me with
        their mouth,
     And[a] honor Me with their lips,
     But their heart is far from Me.
[9]   And in vain they worship Me,
     Teaching as doctrines the
        commandments of men.' "[a]

[10]When He had called the multitude to *Himself*, He said to them, "Hear and understand: [11]Not what goes into the mouth defiles a man; but what comes out of the mouth, this defiles a man."

[12]Then His disciples came and said to Him, "Do You know that the Pharisees were offended when they heard this saying?"

[13]But He answered and said, "Every plant which My heavenly Father has not planted will be uprooted. [14]Let them alone. They are blind leaders of the blind. And if the blind leads the blind, both will fall into a ditch."

[15]Then Peter answered and said to Him, "Explain this parable to us."

[16]So Jesus said, "Are you also still without understanding? [17]Do you not yet understand that whatever enters the mouth goes into the stomach and is eliminated? [18]But those things which proceed out of the mouth come from the heart, and they defile a man. [19]For out of the heart proceed evil thoughts, murders, adulteries, fornications, thefts, false witness, blasphemies. [20]These are *the things* which defile a man, but to eat with unwashed hands does not defile a man."

A Gentile Shows Her Faith

[21]Then Jesus went out from there and departed to the region of Tyre and Sidon. [22]And behold, a woman of Canaan came from that region and cried out to Him, saying, "Have mercy on me, O Lord, Son of David! My daughter is severely demon-possessed."

[23]But He answered her not a word.

And His disciples came and urged Him, saying, "Send her away, for she cries out after us."

[24]But He answered and said, "I was not sent except to the lost sheep of the house of Israel."

[25]Then she came and worshiped Him, saying, "Lord, help me!"

[26]But He answered and said, "It is not good to take the children's bread and throw *it* to the little dogs."

[27]And she said, "Yes, Lord, yet even the little dogs eat the crumbs which fall from their masters' table."

[28]Then Jesus answered and said to her, "O woman, great *is* your faith! Let it be to you as you desire." And her daughter was healed from that very hour.

Jesus Heals Great Multitudes

[29]Jesus departed from there, skirted the Sea of Galilee, and went up on the mountain and sat down there. [30]Then great multitudes came to Him, having with them *the* lame, blind, mute, maimed, and many others; and they laid them down at Jesus' feet, and He healed them. [31]So the multitude marveled when they saw *the* mute speaking, *the* maimed made whole, *the* lame walking, and *the* blind seeing; and they glorified the God of Israel.

Feeding the Four Thousand

[32]Now Jesus called His disciples to *Himself* and said, "I have compassion on the multitude, because they have now continued with Me three days and have nothing to eat. And I do not want to send them away hungry, lest they faint on the way."

[33]Then His disciples said to Him, "Where could we get enough bread in the wilderness to fill such a great multitude?"

[34]Jesus said to them, "How many loaves do you have?"

And they said, "Seven, and a few little fish."

[35]So He commanded the multitude to sit down on the ground. [36]And He took the

---

15:6 [a]NU-Text omits *or mother.* [b]NU-Text reads *word.*
15:8 [a]NU-Text omits *draw near to Me with their mouth, And.*   **15:9** [a]Isaiah 29:13

seven loaves and the fish and gave thanks, broke *them* and gave *them* to His disciples; and the disciples *gave* to the multitude. 37So they all ate and were filled, and they took up seven large baskets full of the fragments that were left. 38Now those who ate were four thousand men, besides women and children. 39And He sent away the multitude, got into the boat, and came to the region of Magdala.ᵃ

The Pharisees and Sadducees Seek a Sign

16 Then the Pharisees and Sadducees came, and testing Him asked that He would show them a sign from heaven. 2He answered and said to them, "When it is evening you say, '*It will be* fair weather, for the sky is red'; 3and in the morning, '*It will be* foul weather today, for the sky is red and threatening.' Hypocrites!ᵃ You know how to discern the face of the sky, but you cannot *discern* the signs of the times. 4A wicked and adulterous generation seeks after a sign, and no sign shall be given to it except the sign of the prophetᵃ Jonah." And He left them and departed.

The Leaven of the Pharisees and Sadducees

5Now when His disciples had come to the other side, they had forgotten to take bread. 6Then Jesus said to them, "Take heed and beware of the leaven of the Pharisees and the Sadducees."

7And they reasoned among themselves, saying, "*It is* because we have taken no bread."

8But Jesus, being aware of *it,* said to them, "O you of little faith, why do you reason among yourselves because you have brought no bread?ᵃ 9Do you not yet understand, or remember the five loaves of the five thousand and how many baskets you took up? 10Nor the seven loaves of the four thousand and how many large baskets you took up? 11How is it you do not understand that I did not speak to you concerning bread?—*but* to beware of the leaven of the Pharisees and Sadducees."

12Then they understood that He did not tell *them* to beware of the leaven of bread, but of the doctrine of the Pharisees and Sadducees.

Peter Confesses Jesus as the Christ

13When Jesus came into the region of Caesarea Philippi, He asked His disciples, saying, "Who do men say that I, the Son of Man, am?"

14So they said, "Some *say* John the Baptist, some Elijah, and others Jeremiah or one of the prophets."

15He said to them, "But who do you say that I am?"

16Simon Peter answered and said, "You are the Christ, the Son of the living God."

17Jesus answered and said to him, "Blessed are you, Simon Bar-Jonah, for flesh and blood has not revealed *this* to you, but My Father who is in heaven. 18And I also say to you that you are Peter, and on this rock I will build My church, and the gates of Hades shall not prevail against it. 19And I will give you the keys of the kingdom of heaven, and whatever you bind on earth will be bound in heaven, and whatever you loose on earth will be loosedᵃ in heaven."

20Then He commanded His disciples that they should tell no one that He was Jesus the Christ.

Jesus Predicts His Death and Resurrection

21From that time Jesus began to show to His disciples that He must go to Jerusalem, and suffer many things from the elders and chief priests and scribes, and be killed, and be raised the third day.

22Then Peter took Him aside and began to rebuke Him, saying, "Far be it from You, Lord; this shall not happen to You!"

23But He turned and said to Peter, "Get behind Me, Satan! You are an offense to Me, for you are not mindful of the things of God, but the things of men."

Take Up the Cross and Follow Him

24Then Jesus said to His disciples, "If anyone desires to come after Me, let him deny himself, and take up his cross, and follow Me. 25For whoever desires to save his life will lose it, but whoever loses his life for My

---

15:39 ᵃNU-Text reads *Magadan.* **16:3** ᵃNU-Text omits *Hypocrites.* **16:4** ᵃNU-Text omits *the prophet.* **16:8** ᵃNU-Text reads *you have no bread.* **16:19** ᵃOr *will have been bound . . . will have been loosed*

sake will find it. ²⁶For what profit is it to a man if he gains the whole world, and loses his own soul? Or what will a man give in exchange for his soul? ²⁷For the Son of Man will come in the glory of His Father with His angels, and then He will reward each according to his works. ²⁸Assuredly, I say to you, there are some standing here who shall not taste death till they see the Son of Man coming in His kingdom."

Jesus Transfigured on the Mount

17 Now after six days Jesus took Peter, James, and John his brother, led them up on a high mountain by themselves; ²and He was transfigured before them. His face shone like the sun, and His clothes became as white as the light. ³And behold, Moses and Elijah appeared to them, talking with Him. ⁴Then Peter answered and said to Jesus, "Lord, it is good for us to be here; if You wish, let us[a] make here three tabernacles: one for You, one for Moses, and one for Elijah."

⁵While he was still speaking, behold, a bright cloud overshadowed them; and suddenly a voice came out of the cloud, saying, "This is My beloved Son, in whom I am well pleased. Hear Him!" ⁶And when the disciples heard *it,* they fell on their faces and were greatly afraid. ⁷But Jesus came and touched them and said, "Arise, and do not be afraid." ⁸When they had lifted up their eyes, they saw no one but Jesus only.

⁹Now as they came down from the mountain, Jesus commanded them, saying, "Tell the vision to no one until the Son of Man is risen from the dead."

¹⁰And His disciples asked Him, saying, "Why then do the scribes say that Elijah must come first?"

¹¹Jesus answered and said to them, "Indeed, Elijah is coming first[a] and will restore all things. ¹²But I say to you that Elijah has come already, and they did not know him but did to him whatever they wished. Likewise the Son of Man is also about to suffer at their hands." ¹³Then the disciples understood that He spoke to them of John the Baptist.

A Boy Is Healed

¹⁴And when they had come to the multitude, a man came to Him, kneeling down to Him and saying, ¹⁵"Lord, have mercy on my son, for he is an epileptic[a] and suffers severely; for he often falls into the fire and often into the water. ¹⁶So I brought him to Your disciples, but they could not cure him."

¹⁷Then Jesus answered and said, "O faithless and perverse generation, how long shall I be with you? How long shall I bear with you? Bring him here to Me." ¹⁸And Jesus rebuked the demon, and it came out of him; and the child was cured from that very hour.

¹⁹Then the disciples came to Jesus privately and said, "Why could we not cast it out?"

²⁰So Jesus said to them, "Because of your unbelief;[a] for assuredly, I say to you, if you have faith as a mustard seed, you will say to this mountain, 'Move from here to there,' and it will move; and nothing will be impossible for you. ²¹However, this kind does not go out except by prayer and fasting."[a]

Jesus Again Predicts His Death and Resurrection

²²Now while they were staying[a] in Galilee, Jesus said to them, "The Son of Man is about to be betrayed into the hands of men, ²³and they will kill Him, and the third day He will be raised up." And they were exceedingly sorrowful.

Peter and His Master Pay Their Taxes

²⁴When they had come to Capernaum,[a] those who received the *temple* tax came to Peter and said, "Does your Teacher not pay the *temple* tax?"

²⁵He said, "Yes."

And when he had come into the house, Jesus anticipated him, saying, "What do you think, Simon? From whom do the kings

---

17:4 [a]NU-Text reads *I will.*   **17:11** [a]NU-Text omits *first.*   **17:15** [a]Literally *moonstruck*   **17:20** [a]NU-Text reads *little faith.*   **17:21** [a]NU-Text omits this verse.   **17:22** [a]NU-Text reads *gathering together.*   **17:24** [a]NU-Text reads *Capharnaum* (here and elsewhere).

of the earth take customs or taxes, from their sons or from strangers?"

26Peter said to Him, "From strangers."

Jesus said to him, "Then the sons are free. 27Nevertheless, lest we offend them, go to the sea, cast in a hook, and take the fish that comes up first. And when you have opened its mouth, you will find a piece of money;a take that and give it to them for Me and you."

Who Is the Greatest?

18 At that time the disciples came to Jesus, saying, "Who then is greatest in the kingdom of heaven?"

2Then Jesus called a little child to Him, set him in the midst of them, 3and said, "Assuredly, I say to you, unless you are converted and become as little children, you will by no means enter the kingdom of heaven. 4Therefore whoever humbles himself as this little child is the greatest in the kingdom of heaven. 5Whoever receives one little child like this in My name receives Me.

Jesus Warns of Offenses

6"Whoever causes one of these little ones who believe in Me to sin, it would be better for him if a millstone were hung around his neck, and he were drowned in the depth

---

Abraham Lincoln placed his hand on Matthew 7:1, 18:7, and Revelation 16:7 as he took the presidential oath of office in 1865.

---

of the sea. 7Woe to the world because of offenses! For offenses must come, but woe to that man by whom the offense comes!

8"If your hand or foot causes you to sin, cut it off and cast it from you. It is better for you to enter into life lame or maimed, rather than having two hands or two feet, to be cast into the everlasting fire. 9And if your eye causes you to sin, pluck it out and cast it from you. It is better for you to enter into life with one eye, rather than having two eyes, to be cast into hell fire.

The Parable of the Lost Sheep

10"Take heed that you do not despise one of these little ones, for I say to you that in heaven their angels always see the face of My Father who is in heaven. 11For the Son of Man has come to save that which was lost.a

12"What do you think? If a man has a hundred sheep, and one of them goes astray, does he not leave the ninety-nine and go to the mountains to seek the one that is straying? 13And if he should find it, assuredly, I say to you, he rejoices more over that *sheep* than over the ninety-nine that did not go astray. 14Even so it is not the will of your Father who is in heaven that one of these little ones should perish.

Dealing with a Sinning Brother

15"Moreover if your brother sins against you, go and tell him his fault between you and him alone. If he hears you, you have gained your brother. 16But if he will not hear, take with you one or two more, that '*by the mouth of two or three witnesses every word may be established.*'a 17And if he refuses to hear them, tell *it* to the church. But if he refuses even to hear the church, let him be to you like a heathen and a tax collector.

18"Assuredly, I say to you, whatever you bind on earth will be bound in heaven, and whatever you loose on earth will be loosed in heaven.

19"Again I saya to you that if two of you agree on earth concerning anything that they ask, it will be done for them by My Father in heaven. 20For where two or three are gathered together in My name, I am there in the midst of them."

The Parable of the Unforgiving Servant

21Then Peter came to Him and said, "Lord, how often shall my brother sin against me, and I forgive him? Up to seven times?"

22Jesus said to him, "I do not say to you, up to seven times, but up to seventy times seven. 23Therefore the kingdom of heaven is like a certain king who wanted to settle accounts with his servants. 24And when he had begun to settle accounts, one was

---

17:27 aGreek *stater,* the exact amount to pay the temple tax (didrachma) for two   18:11 aNU-Text omits this verse.   18:16 aDeuteronomy 19:15
18:19 aNU-Text and M-Text read *Again, assuredly, I say.*

brought to him who owed him ten thousand talents. ²⁵But as he was not able to pay, his master commanded that he be sold, with his wife and children and all that he had, and that payment be made. ²⁶The servant therefore fell down before him, saying, 'Master, have patience with me, and I will pay you all.' ²⁷Then the master of that servant was moved with compassion, released him, and forgave him the debt.

²⁸"But that servant went out and found one of his fellow servants who owed him a hundred denarii; and he laid hands on him and took *him* by the throat, saying, 'Pay me what you owe!' ²⁹So his fellow servant fell down at his feet^a and begged him, saying, 'Have patience with me, and I will pay you all.'^a ³⁰And he would not, but went and threw him into prison till he should pay the debt. ³¹So when his fellow servants saw what had been done, they were very grieved, and came and told their master all that had been done. ³²Then his master, after he had called him, said to him, 'You wicked servant! I forgave you all that debt because you begged me. ³³Should you not also have had compassion on your fellow servant, just as I had pity on you?' ³⁴And his master was angry, and delivered him to the torturers until he should pay all that was due to him.

³⁵"So My heavenly Father also will do to you if each of you, from his heart, does not forgive his brother his trespasses."^a

Marriage and Divorce

19 Now it came to pass, when Jesus had finished these sayings, *that* He departed from Galilee and came to the region of Judea beyond the Jordan. ²And great multitudes followed Him, and He healed them there.

³The Pharisees also came to Him, testing Him, and saying to Him, "Is it lawful for a man to divorce his wife for *just* any reason?"

⁴And He answered and said to them, "Have you not read that He who made^a *them* at the beginning 'made them male and female,'^b ⁵and said, 'For this reason a man shall leave his father and mother and be joined to his wife, and the two shall

become *one flesh'*?^a ⁶So then, they are no longer two but one flesh. Therefore what God has joined together, let not man separate."

⁷They said to Him, "Why then did Moses command to give a certificate of divorce, and to put her away?"

⁸He said to them, "Moses, because of the hardness of your hearts, permitted you to divorce your wives, but from the beginning it was not so. ⁹And I say to you, whoever divorces his wife, except for sexual immorality,^a and marries another, commits adultery; and whoever marries her who is divorced commits adultery."

¹⁰His disciples said to Him, "If such is the case of the man with *his* wife, it is better not to marry."

Jesus Teaches on Celibacy

¹¹But He said to them, "All cannot accept this saying, but only *those* to whom it has been given: ¹²For there are eunuchs who were born thus from *their* mother's womb, and there are eunuchs who were made eunuchs by men, and there are eunuchs who have made themselves eunuchs for the kingdom of heaven's sake. He who is able to accept *it*, let him accept *it*."

Jesus Blesses Little Children

¹³Then little children were brought to Him that He might put *His* hands on them and pray, but the disciples rebuked them. ¹⁴But Jesus said, "Let the little children come to Me, and do not forbid them; for of such is the kingdom of heaven." ¹⁵And He laid *His* hands on them and departed from there.

Jesus Counsels the Rich Young Ruler

¹⁶Now behold, one came and said to Him, "Good^a Teacher, what good thing shall I do that I may have eternal life?"

¹⁷So He said to him, "Why do you call Me good?^a No one *is* good but One, *that is,*

18:29 ^aNU-Text omits *at his feet.* ^bNU-Text and M-Text omit *all.* **18:35** ^aNU-Text omits *his trespasses.*
19:4 ^aNU-Text reads *created.* ^bGenesis 1:27; 5:2
19:5 ^aGenesis 2:24   **19:9** ^aOr *fornication*
19:16 ^aNU-Text omits *Good.*   **19:17** ^aNU-Text reads *Why do you ask Me about what is good?*

THE BIBLE AND MARRIAGE

FAMILY VALUES

"For this reason a man shall leave his father and mother and be joined to his wife, and the two shall become one flesh."

MATTHEW 19:5

Our American society has been based upon the belief that the biblical view of a traditional marriage and family is the backbone of a civilized people. The biblical basis for understanding God's intention for marriage is found in Genesis 2:24: "Therefore a man shall leave his father and mother and be joined to his wife, and they shall become one flesh." The creation of Adam and Eve (male and female) was the foundation of human civilization, and their union was the first marriage. Jesus also reminded us in the New Testament that marriage is an institution of God designed as a lifelong covenant relationship between a man and woman (Matthew 19:1–6).

God's command to Adam and Eve was to "be fruitful and multiply; fill the earth and subdue it" (Genesis 1:28). God's design for procreation demanded the union of a man and woman. From this sanctified union come children, who are born into a secure home with a father and a mother to love, nurture, and teach them how to become healthy, productive, and responsible citizens. God's plan, nature's plan, and common sense's plan all support a man and woman producing children within the institution of marriage.

Preserving the traditional family is vital to the future of America. We must join together to maintain the heritage given to us—marriage is one man and one woman lovingly committed to each other for life. The family is a sacred institution; it is the basic unit of our society and essential to the well being of the greater community.

God.[b] But if you want to enter into life, keep the commandments."

[18]He said to Him, "Which ones?"

Jesus said, "'*You shall not murder,*' '*You shall not commit adultery,*' '*You shall not steal,*' '*You shall not bear false witness,*' [19]'*Honor your father and your mother,*'[a] and, '*You shall love your neighbor as yourself.*'"[b]

[20]The young man said to Him, "All these things I have kept from my youth.[a] What do I still lack?"

[21]Jesus said to him, "If you want to be perfect, go, sell what you have and give to the poor, and you will have treasure in heaven; and come, follow Me."

[22]But when the young man heard that saying, he went away sorrowful, for he had great possessions.

With God All Things Are Possible

[23]Then Jesus said to His disciples, "Assuredly, I say to you that it is hard for a rich man to enter the kingdom of heaven. [24]And again I say to you, it is easier for a camel to go through the eye of a needle than for a rich man to enter the kingdom of God."

[25]When His disciples heard *it,* they were greatly astonished, saying, "Who then can be saved?"

[26]But Jesus looked at *them* and said to them, "With men this is impossible, but with God all things are possible."

[27]Then Peter answered and said to Him, "See, we have left all and followed You. Therefore what shall we have?"

[28]So Jesus said to them, "Assuredly I say to you, that in the regeneration, when the Son of Man sits on the throne of His glory, you who have followed Me will also sit on twelve thrones, judging the twelve tribes of Israel. [29]And everyone who has left houses or brothers or sisters or father or mother or wife[a] or children or lands, for My name's sake, shall receive a hundredfold, and inherit eternal life. [30]But many *who are* first will be last, and the last first.

The Parable of the Workers in the Vineyard

20 "For the kingdom of heaven is like a landowner who went out early in the morning to hire laborers for his vineyard.

[2]Now when he had agreed with the laborers for a denarius a day, he sent them into his vineyard. [3]And he went out about the third hour and saw others standing idle in the marketplace, [4]and said to them, 'You also go into the vineyard, and whatever is right I will give you.' So they went. [5]Again he went out about the sixth and the ninth hour, and did likewise. [6]And about the eleventh hour he went out and found others standing idle,[a] and said to them, 'Why have you been standing here idle all day?' [7]They said to him, 'Because no one hired us.' He said to them, 'You also go into the vineyard, and whatever is right you will receive.'[a]

[8]"So when evening had come, the owner of the vineyard said to his steward, 'Call the laborers and give them *their* wages, beginning with the last to the first.' [9]And when those came who *were hired* about the eleventh hour, they each received a denarius. [10]But when the first came, they supposed that they would receive more; and they likewise received each a denarius. [11]And when they had received *it,* they complained against the landowner, [12]saying, 'These last *men* have worked *only* one hour, and you made them equal to us who have borne the burden and the heat of the day.' [13]But he answered one of them and said, 'Friend, I am doing you no wrong. Did you not agree with me for a denarius? [14]Take *what is* yours and go your way. I wish to give to this last man *the same* as to you. [15]Is it not lawful for me to do what I wish with my own things? Or is your eye evil because I am good?' [16]So the last will be first, and the first last. For many are called, but few chosen."[a]

Jesus a Third Time Predicts His Death and Resurrection

[17]Now Jesus, going up to Jerusalem, took the twelve disciples aside on the road and said to them, [18]"Behold, we are going up to

---

19:17 [b]NU-Text reads *There is One who is good.*
19:19 [a]Exodus 20:12–16; Deuteronomy 5:16–20
[b]Leviticus 19:18   **19:20** [a]NU-Text omits *from my youth.*   **19:29** [a]NU-Text omits *or wife.*
20:6 [a]NU-Text omits *idle.*   **20:7** [a]NU-Text omits the last clause of this verse.   **20:16** [a]NU-Text omits the last sentence of this verse.

Jerusalem, and the Son of Man will be betrayed to the chief priests and to the scribes; and they will condemn Him to death, ¹⁹and deliver Him to the Gentiles to mock and to scourge and to crucify. And the third day He will rise again."

Greatness Is Serving

²⁰Then the mother of Zebedee's sons came to Him with her sons, kneeling down and asking something from Him.

²¹And He said to her, "What do you wish?"

She said to Him, "Grant that these two sons of mine may sit, one on Your right hand and the other on the left, in Your kingdom."

²²But Jesus answered and said, "You do not know what you ask. Are you able to drink the cup that I am about to drink, and be baptized with the baptism that I am baptized with?"ᵃ

They said to Him, "We are able."

²³So He said to them, "You will indeed drink My cup, and be baptized with the baptism that I am baptized with;ᵃ but to sit on My right hand and on My left is not Mine to give, but *it is for those* for whom it is prepared by My Father."

²⁴And when the ten heard *it,* they were greatly displeased with the two brothers. ²⁵But Jesus called them to *Himself* and said, "You know that the rulers of the Gentiles lord it over them, and those who are great exercise authority over them. ²⁶Yet it shall not be so among you; but whoever desires to become great among you, let him be your servant. ²⁷And whoever desires to be first among you, let him be your slave— ²⁸just as the Son of Man did not come to be served, but to serve, and to give His life a ransom for many."

Two Blind Men Receive Their Sight

²⁹Now as they went out of Jericho, a great multitude followed Him. ³⁰And behold, two blind men sitting by the road, when they heard that Jesus was passing by, cried out, saying, "Have mercy on us, O Lord, Son of David!"

³¹Then the multitude warned them that they should be quiet; but they cried out all the more, saying, "Have mercy on us, O Lord, Son of David!"

³²So Jesus stood still and called them, and said, "What do you want Me to do for you?"

³³They said to Him, "Lord, that our eyes may be opened." ³⁴So Jesus had compassion and touched their eyes. And immediately their eyes received sight, and they followed Him.

The Triumphal Entry

21 Now when they drew near Jerusalem, and came to Bethphage,ᵃ at the Mount of Olives, then Jesus sent two disciples, ²saying to them, "Go into the village opposite you, and immediately you will find a donkey tied, and a colt with her. Loose *them* and bring *them* to Me. ³And if anyone says anything to you, you shall say, 'The Lord has need of them,' and immediately he will send them."

⁴Allᵃ this was done that it might be fulfilled which was spoken by the prophet, saying:

⁵ *"Tell the daughter of Zion,*
   'Behold, your King is coming to you,
   Lowly, and sitting on a donkey,
   *A colt, the foal of a donkey.' "*ᵃ

⁶So the disciples went and did as Jesus commanded them. ⁷They brought the donkey and the colt, laid their clothes on them, and set *Him*ᵃ on them. ⁸And a very great multitude spread their clothes on the road; others cut down branches from the trees and spread *them* on the road. ⁹Then the multitudes who went before and those who followed cried out, saying:

"Hosanna to the Son of David!
'*Blessed is He who comes in the name*
   of the LORD!'ᵃ
Hosanna in the highest!"

20:22 ᵃNU-Text omits *and be baptized with the baptism that I am baptized with.*   **20:23** ᵃNU-Text omits *and be baptized with the baptism that I am baptized with.* **21:1** ᵃM-Text reads *Bethphage.*   **21:4** ᵃNU-Text omits *All.*   **21:5** ᵃZechariah 9:9   **21:7** ᵃNU-Text reads *and He sat.*   **21:9** ᵃPsalm 118:26

¹⁰And when He had come into Jerusalem, all the city was moved, saying, "Who is this?"

¹¹So the multitudes said, "This is Jesus, the prophet from Nazareth of Galilee."

Jesus Cleanses the Temple

¹²Then Jesus went into the temple of Godᵃ and drove out all those who bought and sold in the temple, and overturned the tables of the money changers and the seats of those who sold doves. ¹³And He said to them, "It is written, *'My house shall be called a house of prayer,'*ᵃ but you have made it a *'den of thieves.'*"ᵇ

¹⁴Then *the* blind and *the* lame came to Him in the temple, and He healed them. ¹⁵But when the chief priests and scribes saw the wonderful things that He did, and the children crying out in the temple and saying, "Hosanna to the Son of David!" they were indignant ¹⁶and said to Him, "Do You hear what these are saying?"

And Jesus said to them, "Yes. Have you never read,

> *'Out of the mouth of babes and*
>   *nursing infants*
> *You have perfected praise'?"*ᵃ

¹⁷Then He left them and went out of the city to Bethany, and He lodged there.

The Fig Tree Withered

¹⁸Now in the morning, as He returned to the city, He was hungry. ¹⁹And seeing a fig tree by the road, He came to it and found nothing on it but leaves, and said to it, "Let no fruit grow on you ever again." Immediately the fig tree withered away.

The Lesson of the Withered Fig Tree

²⁰And when the disciples saw *it,* they marveled, saying, "How did the fig tree wither away so soon?"

²¹So Jesus answered and said to them, "Assuredly, I say to you, if you have faith and do not doubt, you will not only do what was done to the fig tree, but also if you say to this mountain, 'Be removed and be cast into the sea,' it will be done. ²²And whatever things you ask in prayer, believing, you will receive."

Jesus' Authority Questioned

²³Now when He came into the temple, the chief priests and the elders of the people confronted Him as He was teaching, and said, "By what authority are You doing these things? And who gave You this authority?"

²⁴But Jesus answered and said to them, "I also will ask you one thing, which if you tell Me, I likewise will tell you by what authority I do these things: ²⁵The baptism of John—where was it from? From heaven or from men?"

And they reasoned among themselves, saying, "If we say, 'From heaven,' He will say to us, 'Why then did you not believe him?' ²⁶But if we say, 'From men,' we fear the multitude, for all count John as a prophet." ²⁷So they answered Jesus and said, "We do not know."

And He said to them, "Neither will I tell you by what authority I do these things.

The Parable of the Two Sons

²⁸"But what do you think? A man had two sons, and he came to the first and said, 'Son, go, work today in my vineyard.' ²⁹He answered and said, 'I will not,' but afterward he regretted it and went. ³⁰Then he came to the second and said likewise. And he answered and said, 'I *go,* sir,' but he did not go. ³¹Which of the two did the will of *his* father?"

They said to Him, "The first."

Jesus said to them, "Assuredly, I say to you that tax collectors and harlots enter the kingdom of God before you. ³²For John came to you in the way of righteousness, and you did not believe him; but tax collectors and harlots believed him; and when you saw *it,* you did not afterward relent and believe him.

The Parable of the Wicked Vinedressers

³³"Hear another parable: There was a certain landowner who planted a vineyard and set a hedge around it, dug a winepress in it and built a tower. And he leased it to vinedressers and went into a far country.

21:12 ᵃNU-Text omits *of God.*   **21:13** ᵃIsaiah 56:7
ᵇJeremiah 7:11   **21:16** ᵃPsalm 8:2

³⁴Now when vintage-time drew near, he sent his servants to the vinedressers, that they might receive its fruit. ³⁵And the vinedressers took his servants, beat one, killed one, and stoned another. ³⁶Again he sent other servants, more than the first, and they did likewise to them. ³⁷Then last of all he sent his son to them, saying, 'They will respect my son.' ³⁸But when the vinedressers saw the son, they said among themselves, 'This is the heir. Come, let us kill him and seize his inheritance.' ³⁹So they took him and cast *him* out of the vineyard and killed *him.*

⁴⁰"Therefore, when the owner of the vineyard comes, what will he do to those vinedressers?"

⁴¹They said to Him, "He will destroy those wicked men miserably, and lease *his* vineyard to other vinedressers who will render to him the fruits in their seasons."

⁴²Jesus said to them, "Have you never read in the Scriptures:

'The stone which the builders rejected
Has become the chief cornerstone.
This was the Lᴏʀᴅ's doing,
And it is marvelous in our eyes'?ᵃ

⁴³"Therefore I say to you, the kingdom of God will be taken from you and given to a nation bearing the fruits of it. ⁴⁴And whoever falls on this stone will be broken; but on whomever it falls, it will grind him to powder."

⁴⁵Now when the chief priests and Pharisees heard His parables, they perceived that He was speaking of them. ⁴⁶But when they sought to lay hands on Him, they feared the multitudes, because they took Him for a prophet.

The Parable of the Wedding Feast

22 And Jesus answered and spoke to them again by parables and said: ²"The kingdom of heaven is like a certain king who arranged a marriage for his son, ³and sent out his servants to call those who were invited to the wedding; and they were not willing to come. ⁴Again, he sent out other servants, saying, 'Tell those who are invited, "See, I have prepared my dinner; my oxen and fatted cattle *are* killed, and all

things *are* ready. Come to the wedding."' ⁵But they made light of it and went their ways, one to his own farm, another to his business. ⁶And the rest seized his servants, treated *them* spitefully, and killed *them.* ⁷But when the king heard *about it,* he was furious. And he sent out his armies, destroyed those murderers, and burned up their city. ⁸Then he said to his servants, 'The wedding is ready, but those who were invited were not worthy. ⁹Therefore go into the highways, and as many as you find, invite to the wedding.' ¹⁰So those servants went out into the highways and gathered together all whom they found, both bad and good. And the wedding *hall* was filled with guests.

¹¹"But when the king came in to see the guests, he saw a man there who did not have on a wedding garment. ¹²So he said to him, 'Friend, how did you come in here without a wedding garment?' And he was speechless. ¹³Then the king said to the servants, 'Bind him hand and foot, take him away, andᵃ cast *him* into outer darkness; there will be weeping and gnashing of teeth.'

¹⁴"For many are called, but few *are* chosen."

The Pharisees: Is It Lawful to Pay Taxes to Caesar?

¹⁵Then the Pharisees went and plotted how they might entangle Him in *His* talk. ¹⁶And they sent to Him their disciples with the Herodians, saying, "Teacher, we know that You are true, and teach the way of God in truth; nor do You care about anyone, for You do not regard the person of men. ¹⁷Tell us, therefore, what do You think? Is it lawful to pay taxes to Caesar, or not?"

¹⁸But Jesus perceived their wickedness, and said, "Why do you test Me, *you* hypocrites? ¹⁹Show Me the tax money."

So they brought Him a denarius.

²⁰And He said to them, "Whose image and inscription *is* this?"

²¹They said to Him, "Caesar's."

And He said to them, "Render therefore to Caesar the things that are Caesar's, and to God the things that are God's." ²²When

---

21:42 ᵃPsalm 118:22, 23   **22:13** ᵃNU-Text omits *take him away, and.*

they had heard *these words,* they marveled, and left Him and went their way.

The Sadducees: What About the Resurrection?

23The same day the Sadducees, who say there is no resurrection, came to Him and asked Him, 24saying: "Teacher, Moses said that if a man dies, having no children, his brother shall marry his wife and raise up offspring for his brother. 25Now there were with us seven brothers. The first died after he had married, and having no offspring, left his wife to his brother. 26Likewise the second also, and the third, even to the seventh. 27Last of all the woman died also. 28Therefore, in the resurrection, whose wife of the seven will she be? For they all had her."

29Jesus answered and said to them, "You are mistaken, not knowing the Scriptures nor the power of God. 30For in the resurrection they neither marry nor are given in marriage, but are like angels of God\a in heaven. 31But concerning the resurrection of the dead, have you not read what was spoken to you by God, saying, 32*'I am the God of Abraham, the God of Isaac, and the God of Jacob'*?\a God is not the God of the dead, but of the living." 33And when the multitudes heard *this,* they were astonished at His teaching.

The Scribes: Which Is the First Commandment of All?

34But when the Pharisees heard that He had silenced the Sadducees, they gathered together. 35Then one of them, a lawyer, asked *Him a question,* testing Him, and saying, 36"Teacher, which *is* the great commandment in the law?"

37Jesus said to him, " '*You shall love the LORD your God with all your heart, with all your soul, and with all your mind.'*\a 38This is *the* first and great commandment. 39And *the* second *is* like it: '*You shall love your neighbor as yourself.'*\a 40On these two commandments hang all the Law and the Prophets."

Jesus: How Can David Call His Descendant Lord?

41While the Pharisees were gathered together, Jesus asked them, 42saying, "What do you think about the Christ? Whose Son is He?"

They said to Him, "*The Son* of David."

43He said to them, "How then does David in the Spirit call Him '*Lord,*' saying:

44 '*The LORD said to my Lord,
"Sit at My right hand,
Till I make Your enemies Your
footstool"* '?\a

45If David then calls Him '*Lord,*' how is He his Son?" 46And no one was able to answer Him a word, nor from that day on did anyone dare question Him anymore.

Woe to the Scribes and Pharisees

23Then Jesus spoke to the multitudes and to His disciples, 2saying: "The scribes and the Pharisees sit in Moses' seat. 3Therefore whatever they tell you to observe,\a *that* observe and do, but do not do according to their works; for they say, and do not do. 4For they bind heavy burdens, hard to bear, and lay *them* on men's shoulders; but they *themselves* will not move them with one of their fingers. 5But all their works they do to be seen by men. They make their phylacteries broad and enlarge the borders of their garments. 6They love the best places at feasts, the best seats in the synagogues, 7greetings in the marketplaces, and to be called by men, 'Rabbi, Rabbi.' 8But you, do not be called 'Rabbi'; for One is your Teacher, the Christ,\a and you are all brethren. 9Do not call anyone on earth your father; for One is your Father, He who is in heaven. 10And do not be called teachers; for One is your Teacher, the Christ. 11But he who is greatest among you shall be your servant. 12And whoever exalts himself will be humbled, and he who humbles himself will be exalted.

13"But woe to you, scribes and Pharisees, hypocrites! For you shut up the kingdom of heaven against men; for you neither go in *yourselves,* nor do you allow those who are

---

22:30 \aNU-Text omits *of God.*　　**22:32** \aExodus 3:6, 15
22:37 \aDeuteronomy 6:5　　**22:39** \aLeviticus 19:18
22:44 \aPsalm 110:1　　**23:3** \aNU-Text omits *to observe.*　　**23:8** \aNU-Text omits *the Christ.*

entering to go in. [14]Woe to you, scribes and Pharisees, hypocrites! For you devour widows' houses, and for a pretense make long prayers. Therefore you will receive greater condemnation.[a]

[15]"Woe to you, scribes and Pharisees, hypocrites! For you travel land and sea to win one proselyte, and when he is won, you make him twice as much a son of hell as yourselves.

[16]"Woe to you, blind guides, who say, 'Whoever swears by the temple, it is nothing; but whoever swears by the gold of the temple, he is obliged *to perform it.*' [17]Fools and blind! For which is greater, the gold or the temple that sanctifies[a] the gold? [18]And, 'Whoever swears by the altar, it is nothing; but whoever swears by the gift that is on it, he is obliged *to perform it.*' [19]Fools and blind! For which is greater, the gift or the altar that sanctifies the gift? [20]Therefore he who swears by the altar, swears by it and by all things on it. [21]He who swears by the temple, swears by it and by Him who dwells[a] in it. [22]And he who swears by heaven, swears by the throne of God and by Him who sits on it.

[23]"Woe to you, scribes and Pharisees, hypocrites! For you pay tithe of mint and anise and cummin, and have neglected the weightier *matters* of the law: justice and mercy and faith. These you ought to have done, without leaving the others undone. [24]Blind guides, who strain out a gnat and swallow a camel!

[25]"Woe to you, scribes and Pharisees, hypocrites! For you cleanse the outside of the cup and dish, but inside they are full of extortion and self-indulgence.[a] [26]Blind Pharisee, first cleanse the inside of the cup and dish, that the outside of them may be clean also.

[27]"Woe to you, scribes and Pharisees, hypocrites! For you are like whitewashed tombs which indeed appear beautiful outwardly, but inside are full of dead *men's* bones and all uncleanness. [28]Even so you also outwardly appear righteous to men, but inside you are full of hypocrisy and lawlessness.

[29]"Woe to you, scribes and Pharisees, hypocrites! Because you build the tombs of the prophets and adorn the monuments of the righteous, [30]and say, 'If we had lived in the days of our fathers, we would not have been partakers with them in the blood of the prophets.'

[31]"Therefore you are witnesses against yourselves that you are sons of those who murdered the prophets. [32]Fill up, then, the measure of your fathers' *guilt.* [33]Serpents, brood of vipers! How can you escape the condemnation of hell? [34]Therefore, indeed, I send you prophets, wise men, and scribes: *some* of them you will kill and crucify, and *some* of them you will scourge in your synagogues and persecute from city to city, [35]that on you may come all the righteous blood shed on the earth, from the blood of righteous Abel to the blood of Zechariah, son of Berechiah, whom you murdered between the temple and the altar. [36]Assuredly, I say to you, all these things will come upon this generation.

Jesus Laments over Jerusalem

[37]"O Jerusalem, Jerusalem, the one who kills the prophets and stones those who are sent to her! How often I wanted to gather your children together, as a hen gathers her chicks under *her* wings, but you were not willing! [38]See! Your house is left to you desolate; [39]for I say to you, you shall see Me no more till you say, '*Blessed is He who comes in the name of the LORD!*'"[a]

Jesus Predicts the Destruction of the Temple

24 Then Jesus went out and departed from the temple, and His disciples came up to show Him the buildings of the temple. [2]And Jesus said to them, "Do you not see all these things? Assuredly, I say to you, not *one* stone shall be left here upon another, that shall not be thrown down."

The Signs of the Times and the End of the Age

[3]Now as He sat on the Mount of Olives, the disciples came to Him privately, saying,

---

23:14 [a]NU-Text omits this verse.   **23:17** [a]NU-Text reads *sanctified.*   **23:21** [a]M-Text reads *dwelt.*
23:25 [a]M-Text reads *unrighteousness.*
23:39 [a]Psalm 118:26

"Tell us, when will these things be? And what *will be* the sign of Your coming, and of the end of the age?"

[4]And Jesus answered and said to them: "Take heed that no one deceives you. [5]For many will come in My name, saying, 'I am the Christ,' and will deceive many. [6]And you will hear of wars and rumors of wars. See that you are not troubled; for all[a] *these things* must come to pass, but the end is not yet. [7]For nation will rise against nation, and kingdom against kingdom. And there will be famines, pestilences,[a] and earthquakes in various places. [8]All these *are* the beginning of sorrows.

[9]"Then they will deliver you up to tribulation and kill you, and you will be hated by all nations for My name's sake. [10]And then many will be offended, will betray one another, and will hate one another. [11]Then many false prophets will rise up and deceive many. [12]And because lawlessness will abound, the love of many will grow cold. [13]But he who endures to the end shall be saved. [14]And this gospel of the kingdom will be preached in all the world as a witness to all the nations, and then the end will come.

The Great Tribulation

[15]"Therefore when you see the '*abomination of desolation,*'[a] spoken of by Daniel the prophet, standing in the holy place" (whoever reads, let him understand), [16]"then let those who are in Judea flee to the mountains. [17]Let him who is on the housetop not go down to take anything out of his house. [18]And let him who is in the field not go back to get his clothes. [19]But woe to those who are pregnant and to those who are nursing babies in those days! [20]And pray that your flight may not be in winter or on the Sabbath. [21]For then there will be great tribulation, such as has not been since the beginning of the world until this time, no, nor ever shall be. [22]And unless those days were shortened, no flesh would be saved; but for the elect's sake those days will be shortened.

[23]"Then if anyone says to you, 'Look, here *is* the Christ!' or 'There!' do not believe *it.* [24]For false christs and false prophets will rise and show great signs and wonders to deceive, if possible, even the elect. [25]See, I have told you beforehand.

[26]"Therefore if they say to you, 'Look, He is in the desert!' do not go out; *or* 'Look, *He is* in the inner rooms!' do not believe *it.* [27]For as the lightning comes from the east and flashes to the west, so also will the coming of the Son of Man be. [28]For wherever the carcass is, there the eagles will be gathered together.

The Coming of the Son of Man

[29]"Immediately after the tribulation of those days the sun will be darkened, and the moon will not give its light; the stars will fall from heaven, and the powers of the heavens will be shaken. [30]Then the sign of the Son of Man will appear in heaven, and then all the tribes of the earth will mourn, and they will see the Son of Man coming on the clouds of heaven with power and great glory. [31]And He will send His angels with a great sound of a trumpet, and they will gather together His elect from the four winds, from one end of heaven to the other.

The Parable of the Fig Tree

[32]"Now learn this parable from the fig tree: When its branch has already become tender and puts forth leaves, you know that summer *is* near. [33]So you also, when you see all these things, know that it[a] is near—at the doors! [34]Assuredly, I say to you, this generation will by no means pass away till all these things take place. [35]Heaven and earth will pass away, but My words will by no means pass away.

No One Knows the Day or Hour

[36]"But of that day and hour no one knows, not even the angels of heaven,[a] but My Father only. [37]But as the days of Noah *were,* so also will the coming of the Son of Man be. [38]For as in the days before the flood, they were eating and drinking, marrying and giving in marriage, until the day that

---

24:6 [a]NU-Text omits *all.*　　**24:7** [a]NU-Text omits *pestilences.*　　**24:15** [a]Daniel 11:31; 12:11　　**24:33** [a]Or *He*　　**24:36** [a]NU-Text adds *nor the Son.*

Noah entered the ark, [39]and did not know until the flood came and took them all away, so also will the coming of the Son of Man be. [40]Then two *men* will be in the field: one will be taken and the other left. [41]Two *women will be* grinding at the mill: one will be taken and the other left. [42]Watch therefore, for you do not know what hour[a] your Lord is coming. [43]But know this, that if the master of the house had known what hour the thief would come, he would have watched and not allowed his house to be broken into. [44]Therefore you also be ready, for the Son of Man is coming at an hour you do not expect.

The Faithful Servant and the Evil Servant

[45]"Who then is a faithful and wise servant, whom his master made ruler over his household, to give them food in due season? [46]Blessed *is* that servant whom his master, when he comes, will find so doing. [47]Assuredly, I say to you that he will make him ruler over all his goods. [48]But if that evil servant says in his heart, 'My master is delaying his coming,'[a] [49]and begins to beat *his* fellow servants, and to eat and drink with the drunkards, [50]the master of that servant will come on a day when he is not looking for *him* and at an hour that he is not aware of, [51]and will cut him in two and appoint *him* his portion with the hypocrites. There shall be weeping and gnashing of teeth.

The Parable of the Wise and Foolish Virgins

25 "Then the kingdom of heaven shall be likened to ten virgins who took their lamps and went out to meet the bridegroom. [2]Now five of them were wise, and five *were* foolish. [3]Those who *were* foolish took their lamps and took no oil with them, [4]but the wise took oil in their vessels with their lamps. [5]But while the bridegroom was delayed, they all slumbered and slept. [6]"And at midnight a cry was *heard:* 'Behold, the bridegroom is coming;[a] go out to meet him!' [7]Then all those virgins arose and trimmed their lamps. [8]And the foolish said to the wise, 'Give us *some* of your oil, for our lamps are going out.' [9]But the wise answered, saying, '*No,* lest there should not

be enough for us and you; but go rather to those who sell, and buy for yourselves.' [10]And while they went to buy, the bridegroom came, and those who were ready went in with him to the wedding; and the door was shut.

[11]"Afterward the other virgins came also, saying, 'Lord, Lord, open to us!' [12]But he answered and said, 'Assuredly, I say to you, I do not know you.'

[13]"Watch therefore, for you know neither the day nor the hour[a] in which the Son of Man is coming.

The Parable of the Talents

[14]"For *the kingdom of heaven is* like a man traveling to a far country, *who* called his own servants and delivered his goods to them. [15]And to one he gave five talents, to another two, and to another one, to each according to his own ability; and immediately he went on a journey. [16]Then he who had received the five talents went and traded with them, and made another five talents. [17]And likewise he who *had received* two gained two more also. [18]But he who had received one went and dug in the ground, and hid his lord's money. [19]After a long time the lord of those servants came and settled accounts with them.

[20]"So he who had received five talents came and brought five other talents, saying, 'Lord, you delivered to me five talents; look, I have gained five more talents besides them.' [21]His lord said to him, 'Well *done,* good and faithful servant; you were faithful over a few things, I will make you ruler over many things. Enter into the joy of your lord.' [22]He also who had received two talents came and said, 'Lord, you delivered to me two talents; look, I have gained two more talents besides them.' [23]His lord said to him, 'Well *done,* good and faithful servant; you have been faithful over a few things, I will make you ruler over many things. Enter into the joy of your lord.'

[24]"Then he who had received the one talent came and said, 'Lord, I knew you to be

---

24:42 [a]NU-Text reads *day.*   **24:48** [a]NU-Text omits *his coming.*   **25:6** [a]NU-Text omits *is coming.* **25:13** [a]NU-Text omits the rest of this verse.

a hard man, reaping where you have not sown, and gathering where you have not scattered seed. ²⁵And I was afraid, and went and hid your talent in the ground. Look, *there* you have *what is* yours.'

²⁶"But his lord answered and said to him, 'You wicked and lazy servant, you knew that I reap where I have not sown, and gather where I have not scattered seed. ²⁷So you ought to have deposited my money with the bankers, and at my coming I would have received back my own with interest. ²⁸So take the talent from him, and give *it* to him who has ten talents.

²⁹'For to everyone who has, more will be given, and he will have abundance; but from him who does not have, even what he has will be taken away. ³⁰And cast the unprofitable servant into the outer darkness. There will be weeping and gnashing of teeth.'

The Son of Man Will Judge the Nations

³¹"When the Son of Man comes in His glory, and all the holyᵃ angels with Him, then He will sit on the throne of His glory.

³²All the nations will be gathered before Him, and He will separate them one from another, as a shepherd divides *his* sheep from the goats. ³³And He will set the sheep on His right hand, but the goats on the left. ³⁴Then the King will say to those on His right hand, 'Come, you blessed of My Father, inherit the kingdom prepared for you from the foundation of the world: ³⁵for I was hungry and you gave Me food; I was thirsty and you gave Me drink; I was a stranger and you took Me in; ³⁶I *was* naked and you clothed Me; I was sick and you visited Me; I was in prison and you came to Me.'

³⁷"Then the righteous will answer Him, saying, 'Lord, when did we see You hungry and feed *You,* or thirsty and give *You* drink? ³⁸When did we see You a stranger and take *You* in, or naked and clothe *You?* ³⁹Or when did we see You sick, or in prison, and come to You?' ⁴⁰And the King will answer and say to them, 'Assuredly, I say to you, inasmuch as you did *it* to one of the least of these My brethren, you did *it* to Me.'

25:31 ᵃNU-Text omits *holy.*

DEFENDER

". . . inasmuch as you did it to one of the least of these My brethren, you did it to Me."

MATTHEW 25:40

Henry Hyde

DEFENDING THE UNBORN

Henry Hyde served thirty-two years in the House of Representatives and was described as a passionate, eloquent champion and powerful defender of the unborn and of American freedom. On July 16, 1993, he stated:

"That all men are created equal and are endowed by their Creator"—human beings upon creation, not upon birth. That is where our human dignity comes from. It comes from the Creator. It is an endowment, not an achievement.

By membership in the human family, we are endowed by our Creator with "inalienable rights." They can't be voted away by a jury or a court.

"Among which are life"—the first inalienable right, the first endowment from the Creator. That is mainstream America, the predicate for our Constitution, our country's birth certificate. To respect the right to life as an endowment from the Creator. . . .

It is the unborn who are the least of God's creatures. We have been told that whatsoever we do for the least of these we do unto Jesus.

41"Then He will also say to those on the left hand, 'Depart from Me, you cursed, into the everlasting fire prepared for the devil and his angels: 42for I was hungry and you gave Me no food; I was thirsty and you gave Me no drink; 43I was a stranger and you did not take Me in, naked and you did not clothe Me, sick and in prison and you did not visit Me.'

44"Then they also will answer Him,a saying, 'Lord, when did we see You hungry or thirsty or a stranger or naked or sick or in prison, and did not minister to You?' 45Then He will answer them, saying, 'Assuredly, I say to you, inasmuch as you did not do it to one of the least of these, you did not do it to Me.' 46And these will go away into everlasting punishment, but the righteous into eternal life."

The Plot to Kill Jesus

26 Now it came to pass, when Jesus had finished all these sayings, that He said to His disciples, 2"You know that after two days is the Passover, and the Son of Man will be delivered up to be crucified."

3Then the chief priests, the scribes,a and the elders of the people assembled at the palace of the high priest, who was called Caiaphas, 4and plotted to take Jesus by trickery and kill Him. 5But they said, "Not during the feast, lest there be an uproar among the people."

The Anointing at Bethany

6And when Jesus was in Bethany at the house of Simon the leper, 7a woman came to Him having an alabaster flask of very costly fragrant oil, and she poured it on His head as He sat at the table. 8But when His disciples saw it, they were indignant, saying, "Why this waste? 9For this fragrant oil might have been sold for much and given to the poor." 10But when Jesus was aware of it, He said to them, "Why do you trouble the woman? For she has done a good work for Me. 11For you have the poor with you always, but Me you do not have always. 12For in pouring this fragrant oil on My body, she did it for My burial. 13Assuredly, I say to you, wherever this gospel is preached in the whole world, what this woman has done will also be told as a memorial to her."

Judas Agrees to Betray Jesus

14Then one of the twelve, called Judas Iscariot, went to the chief priests 15and said, "What are you willing to give me if I deliver Him to you?" And they counted out to him thirty pieces of silver. 16So from that time he sought opportunity to betray Him.

Jesus Celebrates Passover with His Disciples

17Now on the first day of the Feast of the Unleavened Bread the disciples came to Jesus, saying to Him, "Where do You want us to prepare for You to eat the Passover?"

18And He said, "Go into the city to a certain man, and say to him, 'The Teacher says, "My time is at hand; I will keep the Passover at your house with My disciples."'"

19So the disciples did as Jesus had directed them; and they prepared the Passover.

20When evening had come, He sat down with the twelve. 21Now as they were eating, He said, "Assuredly, I say to you, one of you will betray Me."

22And they were exceedingly sorrowful, and each of them began to say to Him, "Lord, is it I?"

23He answered and said, "He who dipped his hand with Me in the dish will betray Me. 24The Son of Man indeed goes just as it is written of Him, but woe to that man by whom the Son of Man is betrayed! It would have been good for that man if he had not been born."

25Then Judas, who was betraying Him, answered and said, "Rabbi, is it I?"

He said to him, "You have said it."

Jesus Institutes the Lord's Supper

26And as they were eating, Jesus took bread, blesseda and broke it, and gave it to the disciples and said, "Take, eat; this is My body."

27Then He took the cup, and gave thanks, and gave it to them, saying, "Drink from it, all of you. 28For this is My blood of the newa

---

25:44 aNU-Text and M-Text omit Him.
26:3 aNU-Text omits the scribes.   **26:26** aM-Text reads gave thanks for.   **26:28** aNU-Text omits new.

covenant, which is shed for many for the remission of sins. 29But I say to you, I will not drink of this fruit of the vine from now on until that day when I drink it new with you in My Father's kingdom."

30And when they had sung a hymn, they went out to the Mount of Olives.

Jesus Predicts Peter's Denial

31Then Jesus said to them, "All of you will be made to stumble because of Me this night, for it is written:

'I will strike the Shepherd,
And the sheep of the flock will be scattered.'a

32But after I have been raised, I will go before you to Galilee."

33Peter answered and said to Him, "Even if all are made to stumble because of You, I will never be made to stumble."

34Jesus said to him, "Assuredly, I say to you that this night, before the rooster crows, you will deny Me three times."

35Peter said to Him, "Even if I have to die with You, I will not deny You!"

And so said all the disciples.

The Prayer in the Garden

36Then Jesus came with them to a place called Gethsemane, and said to the disciples, "Sit here while I go and pray over there." 37And He took with Him Peter and the two sons of Zebedee, and He began to be sorrowful and deeply distressed. 38Then He said to them, "My soul is exceedingly sorrowful, even to death. Stay here and watch with Me."

39He went a little farther and fell on His face, and prayed, saying, "O My Father, if it is possible, let this cup pass from Me; nevertheless, not as I will, but as You will."

40Then He came to the disciples and found them sleeping, and said to Peter, "What! Could you not watch with Me one hour? 41Watch and pray, lest you enter into temptation. The spirit indeed is willing, but the flesh is weak."

42Again, a second time, He went away and prayed, saying, "O My Father, if this cup cannot pass away from Me unlessa I

drink it, Your will be done." 43And He came and found them asleep again, for their eyes were heavy.

44So He left them, went away again, and prayed the third time, saying the same words. 45Then He came to His disciples and said to them, "Are you still sleeping and resting? Behold, the hour is at hand, and the Son of Man is being betrayed into the hands of sinners. 46Rise, let us be going. See, My betrayer is at hand."

Betrayal and Arrest in Gethsemane

47And while He was still speaking, behold, Judas, one of the twelve, with a great multitude with swords and clubs, came from the chief priests and elders of the people. 48Now His betrayer had given them a sign, saying, "Whomever I kiss, He is the One; seize Him." 49Immediately he went up to Jesus and said, "Greetings, Rabbi!" and kissed Him.

50But Jesus said to him, "Friend, why have you come?"

Then they came and laid hands on Jesus and took Him. 51And suddenly, one of those who were with Jesus stretched out his hand and drew his sword, struck the servant of the high priest, and cut off his ear.

52But Jesus said to him, "Put your sword in its place, for all who take the sword will perisha by the sword. 53Or do you think that I cannot now pray to My Father, and He will provide Me with more than twelve legions of angels? 54How then could the Scriptures be fulfilled, that it must happen thus?"

55In that hour Jesus said to the multitudes, "Have you come out, as against a robber, with swords and clubs to take Me? I sat daily with you, teaching in the temple, and you did not seize Me. 56But all this was done that the Scriptures of the prophets might be fulfilled."

Then all the disciples forsook Him and fled.

Jesus Faces the Sanhedrin

57And those who had laid hold of Jesus led Him away to Caiaphas the high priest,

---

26:31 aZechariah 13:7　　**26:42** aNU-Text reads if this may not pass away unless.　　**26:52** aM-Text reads die.

where the scribes and the elders were assembled. [58]But Peter followed Him at a distance to the high priest's courtyard. And he went in and sat with the servants to see the end.

[59]Now the chief priests, the elders,[a] and all the council sought false testimony against Jesus to put Him to death, [60]but found none. Even though many false witnesses came forward, they found none.[a] But at last two false witnesses[b] came forward [61]and said, "This *fellow* said, 'I am able to destroy the temple of God and to build it in three days.'"

[62]And the high priest arose and said to Him, "Do You answer nothing? What *is it* these men testify against You?" [63]But Jesus kept silent. And the high priest answered and said to Him, "I put You under oath by the living God: Tell us if You are the Christ, the Son of God!"

[64]Jesus said to him, "*It is as* you said. Nevertheless, I say to you, hereafter you will see the Son of Man sitting at the right hand of the Power, and coming on the clouds of heaven."

[65]Then the high priest tore his clothes, saying, "He has spoken blasphemy! What further need do we have of witnesses? Look, now you have heard His blasphemy! [66]What do you think?"

They answered and said, "He is deserving of death."

[67]Then they spat in His face and beat Him; and others struck *Him* with the palms of their hands, [68]saying, "Prophesy to us, Christ! Who is the one who struck You?"

Peter Denies Jesus, and Weeps Bitterly

[69]Now Peter sat outside in the courtyard. And a servant girl came to him, saying, "You also were with Jesus of Galilee."

[70]But he denied it before *them* all, saying, "I do not know what you are saying."

[71]And when he had gone out to the gateway, another *girl* saw him and said to those *who were* there, "This *fellow* also was with Jesus of Nazareth."

[72]But again he denied with an oath, "I do not know the Man!"

[73]And a little later those who stood by came up and said to Peter, "Surely you also are *one* of them, for your speech betrays you."

[74]Then he began to curse and swear, *saying,* "I do not know the Man!"

Immediately a rooster crowed. [75]And Peter remembered the word of Jesus who had said to him, "Before the rooster crows, you will deny Me three times." So he went out and wept bitterly.

Jesus Handed Over to Pontius Pilate

27 When morning came, all the chief priests and elders of the people plotted against Jesus to put Him to death. [2]And when they had bound Him, they led Him away and delivered Him to Pontius[a] Pilate the governor.

Judas Hangs Himself

[3]Then Judas, His betrayer, seeing that He had been condemned, was remorseful and brought back the thirty pieces of silver to the chief priests and elders, [4]saying, "I have sinned by betraying innocent blood."

And they said, "What *is that* to us? You see *to it!*"

[5]Then he threw down the pieces of silver in the temple and departed, and went and hanged himself.

[6]But the chief priests took the silver pieces and said, "It is not lawful to put them into the treasury, because they are the price of blood." [7]And they consulted together and bought with them the potter's field, to bury strangers in. [8]Therefore that field has been called the Field of Blood to this day.

[9]Then was fulfilled what was spoken by Jeremiah the prophet, saying, *"And they took the thirty pieces of silver, the value of Him who was priced,* whom they of the children of Israel priced, [10]*and gave them for the potter's field, as the LORD directed me."*[a]

Jesus Faces Pilate

[11]Now Jesus stood before the governor. And the governor asked Him, saying, "Are You the King of the Jews?"

26:59 [a]NU-Text omits *the elders.*   **26:60** [a]NU-Text puts a comma after *but found none,* does not capitalize *Even,* and omits *they found none.* [b]NU-Text omits *false witnesses.*   **27:2** [a]NU-Text omits *Pontius.* **27:10** [a]Jeremiah 32:6–9

Jesus said to him, "*It is as* you say." ¹²And while He was being accused by the chief priests and elders, He answered nothing.

¹³Then Pilate said to Him, "Do You not hear how many things they testify against You?" ¹⁴But He answered him not one word, so that the governor marveled greatly.

Taking the Place of Barabbas

¹⁵Now at the feast the governor was accustomed to releasing to the multitude one prisoner whom they wished. ¹⁶And at that time they had a notorious prisoner called Barabbas.ª ¹⁷Therefore, when they had gathered together, Pilate said to them, "Whom do you want me to release to you? Barabbas, or Jesus who is called Christ?" ¹⁸For he knew that they had handed Him over because of envy.

¹⁹While he was sitting on the judgment seat, his wife sent to him, saying, "Have nothing to do with that just Man, for I have suffered many things today in a dream because of Him."

²⁰But the chief priests and elders persuaded the multitudes that they should ask for Barabbas and destroy Jesus. ²¹The governor answered and said to them, "Which of the two do you want me to release to you?"

They said, "Barabbas!"

²²Pilate said to them, "What then shall I do with Jesus who is called Christ?"

They all said to him, "Let Him be crucified!"

²³Then the governor said, "Why, what evil has He done?"

But they cried out all the more, saying, "Let Him be crucified!"

²⁴When Pilate saw that he could not prevail at all, but rather *that* a tumult was rising, he took water and washed *his* hands before the multitude, saying, "I am innocent of the blood of this just Person.ª You see *to it*."

²⁵And all the people answered and said, "His blood *be* on us and on our children."

²⁶Then he released Barabbas to them; and when he had scourged Jesus, he delivered *Him* to be crucified.

The Soldiers Mock Jesus

²⁷Then the soldiers of the governor took Jesus into the Praetorium and gathered the whole garrison around Him. ²⁸And they stripped Him and put a scarlet robe on Him. ²⁹When they had twisted a crown of thorns, they put *it* on His head, and a reed in His right hand. And they bowed the knee before Him and mocked Him, saying, "Hail, King of the Jews!" ³⁰Then they spat on Him, and took the reed and struck Him on the head. ³¹And when they had mocked Him, they took the robe off Him, put His *own* clothes on Him, and led Him away to be crucified.

The King on a Cross

³²Now as they came out, they found a man of Cyrene, Simon by name. Him they compelled to bear His cross. ³³And when they had come to a place called Golgotha, that is to say, Place of a Skull, ³⁴they gave Him sourª wine mingled with gall to drink. But when He had tasted *it,* He would not drink.

³⁵Then they crucified Him, and divided His garments, casting lots,ª that it might be fulfilled which was spoken by the prophet:

> "They divided My garments among
>   them,
>   And for My clothing they cast lots."ᵇ

³⁶Sitting down, they kept watch over Him there. ³⁷And they put up over His head the accusation written against Him:

THIS IS JESUS THE KING OF THE JEWS.

³⁸Then two robbers were crucified with Him, one on the right and another on the left.

³⁹And those who passed by blasphemed Him, wagging their heads ⁴⁰and saying, "You who destroy the temple and build *it* in three days, save Yourself! If You are the Son of God, come down from the cross."

⁴¹Likewise the chief priests also, mocking with the scribes and elders,ª said, ⁴²"He

---

27:16 ªNU-Text reads *Jesus Barabbas.*
27:24 ªNU-Text omits *just.*   **27:34** ªNU-Text omits *sour.*   **27:35** ªNU-Text and M-Text omit the rest of this verse. ᵇPsalm 22:18   **27:41** ªM-Text reads *with the scribes, the Pharisees, and the elders.*

saved others; Himself He cannot save. If He is the King of Israel,ᵃ let Him now come down from the cross, and we will believe Him.ᵇ ⁴³He trusted in God; let Him deliver Him now if He will have Him; for He said, 'I am the Son of God.' "

⁴⁴Even the robbers who were crucified with Him reviled Him with the same thing.

Jesus Dies on the Cross

⁴⁵Now from the sixth hour until the ninth hour there was darkness over all the land. ⁴⁶And about the ninth hour Jesus cried out with a loud voice, saying, "Eli, Eli, lama sabachthani?" that is, *"My God, My God, why have You forsaken Me?"*ᵃ ⁴⁷Some of those who stood there, when they heard *that,* said, "This Man is calling for Elijah!" ⁴⁸Immediately one of them ran and took a sponge, filled *it* with sour wine and put *it* on a reed, and offered it to Him to drink.

⁴⁹The rest said, "Let Him alone; let us see if Elijah will come to save Him."

⁵⁰And Jesus cried out again with a loud voice, and yielded up His spirit.

⁵¹Then, behold, the veil of the temple was torn in two from top to bottom; and the earth quaked, and the rocks were split, ⁵²and the graves were opened; and many bodies of the saints who had fallen asleep were raised; ⁵³and coming out of the graves after His resurrection, they went into the holy city and appeared to many.

⁵⁴So when the centurion and those with him, who were guarding Jesus, saw the earthquake and the things that had happened, they feared greatly, saying, "Truly this was the Son of God!"

⁵⁵And many women who followed Jesus from Galilee, ministering to Him, were there looking on from afar, ⁵⁶among whom were Mary Magdalene, Mary the mother of James and Joses,ᵃ and the mother of Zebedee's sons.

Jesus Buried in Joseph's Tomb

⁵⁷Now when evening had come, there came a rich man from Arimathea, named Joseph, who himself had also become a disciple of Jesus. ⁵⁸This man went to Pilate and asked for the body of Jesus. Then Pilate commanded the body to be given to him. ⁵⁹When Joseph had taken the body, he wrapped it in a clean linen cloth, ⁶⁰and laid it in his new tomb which he had hewn out of the rock; and he rolled a large stone against the door of the tomb, and departed. ⁶¹And Mary Magdalene was there, and the other Mary, sitting opposite the tomb.

Pilate Sets a Guard

⁶²On the next day, which followed the Day of Preparation, the chief priests and Pharisees gathered together to Pilate, ⁶³saying, "Sir, we remember, while He was still alive, how that deceiver said, 'After three days I will rise.' ⁶⁴Therefore command that the tomb be made secure until the third day, lest His disciples come by nightᵃ and steal Him *away,* and say to the people, 'He has risen from the dead.' So the last deception will be worse than the first."

⁶⁵Pilate said to them, "You have a guard; go your way, make *it* as secure as you know how." ⁶⁶So they went and made the tomb secure, sealing the stone and setting the guard.

He Is Risen

28 Now after the Sabbath, as the first *day* of the week began to dawn, Mary Magdalene and the other Mary came to see the tomb. ²And behold, there was a great earthquake; for an angel of the Lord descended from heaven, and came and rolled back the stone from the door,ᵃ and sat on it. ³His countenance was like lightning, and his clothing as white as snow. ⁴And the guards shook for fear of him, and became like dead *men.*

⁵But the angel answered and said to the women, "Do not be afraid, for I know that you seek Jesus who was crucified. ⁶He is not here; for He is risen, as He said. Come, see the place where the Lord lay. ⁷And go quickly and tell His disciples that He is risen from the dead, and indeed He is going

---

27:42 ᵃNU-Text reads *He is the King of Israel!* ᵇNU-Text and M-Text read *we will believe in Him.*
27:46 ᵃPsalm 22:1   **27:56** ᵃNU-Text reads *Joseph.*
27:64 ᵃNU-Text omits *by night.*   **28:2** ᵃNU-Text omits *from the door.*

JOHN ELIOT, "APOSTLE TO THE INDIANS"

The 1628 charter of the Massachusetts Bay Company stated that one of the chief purposes of establishing a colony in New England was "to win the natives of the country to the knowledge and obedience of the only true God and Savior of mankind." The seal of the colony had the picture of an Indian and the words of the Macedonian to Paul from Acts 16:9, "Come Over and Help Us." During the earliest years of the colony, however, the Puritans did all they could do just to survive and establish homes in the American wilderness.

In 1637, the Puritans became involved in an inter-tribal war between the Narragansett and Pequot Indians. Though one might have expected otherwise, the Puritans often treated the Indians brutally. Many Pequot people were killed, and more were captured and sold into slavery. Later, in 1675 and 1676, a bitter armed conflict broke out in which over 600 colonists and 3,000 Native Americans died. Several hundred native captives were tried and executed or sold as slaves.

Surprisingly, the Pequot war triggered the earliest Puritan missions to the Indians. John Eliot, later known as the "Apostle to the Indians," began learning the Algonquian language, spoken by most New England Indians, from captured Indians. Teaching Christian truths to the Indians in their own language, Eliot saw many of the Indians put their faith in Christ and leave their nomadic lives to form villages that separated them from their pagan backgrounds. These became "praying Indian towns," over a dozen self-governing communities where the Indians often made strict biblical laws punishing their former practices, including wife beating, polygamy, lying, and stealing.

John Eliot translated the entire Bible into Algonquian. In 1663, this translation became the first Bible printed in America. Eliot also composed an Indian primer, an Indian grammar, and an Indian psalter. Other successful missionary endeavors followed. Harvard University (1636) began a training program for young Indian men to minister to their people. At least six Boston area communities, thriving today, were started by Christian Indians. The famous island, Martha's Vineyard, once was the site of Indian Christian congregations through the missionary endeavors of the Mayhew family. Dartmouth University had its beginning through the efforts of a Connecticut Puritan to train Indian young men to preach the Gospel.

before you into Galilee; there you will see Him. Behold, I have told you."

[8]So they went out quickly from the tomb with fear and great joy, and ran to bring His disciples word.

The Women Worship the Risen Lord

[9]And as they went to tell His disciples,[a] behold, Jesus met them, saying, "Rejoice!" So they came and held Him by the feet and worshiped Him. [10]Then Jesus said to them, "Do not be afraid. Go *and* tell My brethren to go to Galilee, and there they will see Me."

The Soldiers Are Bribed

[11]Now while they were going, behold, some of the guard came into the city and reported to the chief priests all the things that had happened. [12]When they had assembled with the elders and consulted together, they gave a large sum of money to the soldiers, [13]saying, "Tell them, 'His disciples came at night and stole Him *away* while we slept.' [14]And if this comes to the governor's ears, we will appease him and make you secure." [15]So they took the money and did as they were instructed; and this saying is commonly reported among the Jews until this day.

The Great Commission

[16]Then the eleven disciples went away into Galilee, to the mountain which Jesus had appointed for them. [17]When they saw Him, they worshiped Him; but some doubted.

[18]And Jesus came and spoke to them, saying, "All authority has been given to Me in heaven and on earth. [19]Go therefore[a] and make disciples of all the nations, baptizing them in the name of the Father and of the Son and of the Holy Spirit, [20]teaching them to observe all things that I have commanded you; and lo, I am with you always, *even* to the end of the age." Amen.[a]

28:9 [a]NU-Text omits the first clause of this verse.
28:19 [a]M-Text omits *therefore*.   **28:20** [a]NU-Text omits *Amen*.

MARK

Author: Mark

When Written: Around A.D. 65

Theme: Jesus the Servant

Key Verses: Mark 10:44, 45—"And whoever of you desires to be first shall be slave of all. For even the Son of Man did not come to be served, but to serve, and to give His life a ransom for many."

Key Chapter: Mark 8—The pivotal event of the book lies in Peter's confession, "You are the Christ." That faith-inspired response triggers a new phase in Jesus' ministry, where He begins to forti-fy His disciples for His coming suffering and death at the hands of the Jewish religious leaders.

Mark, the shortest of the four gospels, gives a crisp and fast-moving look at the dual focus of the life of Christ—His service and sacrifice. Through His teaching, preaching, and healing, Jesus constantly ministers to the needs of others, even to the point of death. Mark traces the steady building of hostility and opposi-tion to Jesus as He resolutely moves toward the fulfillment of His earthy ministry—to give His life as a ransom for many.

When Benjamin Franklin, the most famous Founding Father at our country's birth, was confronted by a disgruntled American that his country had failed to provide him with the happiness it had promised, Franklin is said to have smiled and calmly replied, "The Constitution only gives people the right to pursue happiness. You have to catch it yourself." Similarly, Jesus gave His life to ran-som our lives, but we must join Peter and confess that Jesus is the Christ, our personal Savior, to receive the eternal life He has for us.

MARK

John the Baptist Prepares the Way

1 The beginning of the gospel of Jesus Christ, the Son of God. ²As it is written in the Prophets:ᵃ

"Behold, I send My messenger before Your face,
Who will prepare Your way before You." ᵇ
³ "The voice of one crying in the wilderness:
'Prepare the way of the LORD;
Make His paths straight.' "ᵃ

⁴John came baptizing in the wilderness and preaching a baptism of repentance for the remission of sins. ⁵Then all the land of Judea, and those from Jerusalem, went out to him and were all baptized by him in the Jordan River, confessing their sins. ⁶Now John was clothed with camel's hair and with a leather belt around his waist, and he ate locusts and wild honey. ⁷And he preached, saying, "There comes One after me who is mightier than I, whose sandal strap I am not worthy to stoop down and loose. ⁸I indeed baptized you with water, but He will baptize you with the Holy Spirit."

John Baptizes Jesus

⁹It came to pass in those days that Jesus came from Nazareth of Galilee, and was baptized by John in the Jordan. ¹⁰And immediately, coming up fromᵃ the water, He saw the heavens parting and the Spirit descending upon Him like a dove. ¹¹Then a voice came from heaven, "You are My beloved Son, in whom I am well pleased."

Satan Tempts Jesus

¹²Immediately the Spirit drove Him into the wilderness. ¹³And He was there in the wilderness forty days, tempted by Satan, and was with the wild beasts; and the angels ministered to Him.

Jesus Begins His Galilean Ministry

¹⁴Now after John was put in prison, Jesus came to Galilee, preaching the gospel of the kingdomᵃ of God, ¹⁵and saying, "The time is fulfilled, and the kingdom of God is at hand. Repent, and believe in the gospel."

Four Fishermen Called as Disciples

¹⁶And as He walked by the Sea of Galilee, He saw Simon and Andrew his brother casting a net into the sea; for they were fishermen. ¹⁷Then Jesus said to them, "Follow Me, and I will make you become fishers of men." ¹⁸They immediately left their nets and followed Him.

¹⁹When He had gone a little farther from there, He saw James the son of Zebedee, and John his brother, who also were in the boat mending their nets. ²⁰And immediately He called them, and they left their father Zebedee in the boat with the hired servants, and went after Him.

Jesus Casts Out an Unclean Spirit

²¹Then they went into Capernaum, and immediately on the Sabbath He entered the synagogue and taught. ²²And they were astonished at His teaching, for He taught them as one having authority, and not as the scribes.

²³Now there was a man in their synagogue with an unclean spirit. And he cried out, ²⁴saying, "Let us alone! What have we to do with You, Jesus of Nazareth? Did You come to destroy us? I know who You are—the Holy One of God!"

²⁵But Jesus rebuked him, saying, "Be quiet, and come out of him!" ²⁶And when the unclean spirit had convulsed him and cried out with a loud voice, he came out of him. ²⁷Then they were all amazed, so that they questioned among themselves, saying,

---

1:2 ᵃNU-Text reads Isaiah the prophet. ᵇMalachi 3:1
1:3 ᵃIsaiah 40:3   **1:10** ᵃNU-Text reads out of.
1:14 ᵃNU-Text omits of the kingdom.

"What is this? What new doctrine *is* this? For with authority[a] He commands even the unclean spirits, and they obey Him." [28]And immediately His fame spread throughout all the region around Galilee.

Peter's Mother-in-Law Healed

[29]Now as soon as they had come out of the synagogue, they entered the house of Simon and Andrew, with James and John. [30]But Simon's wife's mother lay sick with a fever, and they told Him about her at once. [31]So He came and took her by the hand and lifted her up, and immediately the fever left her. And she served them.

Many Healed After Sabbath Sunset

[32]At evening, when the sun had set, they brought to Him all who were sick and those who were demon-possessed. [33]And the whole city was gathered together at the door. [34]Then He healed many who were sick with various diseases, and cast out many demons; and He did not allow the demons to speak, because they knew Him.

Preaching in Galilee

[35]Now in the morning, having risen a long while before daylight, He went out and departed to a solitary place; and there He prayed. [36]And Simon and those *who were* with Him searched for Him. [37]When they found Him, they said to Him, "Everyone is looking for You."

[38]But He said to them, "Let us go into the next towns, that I may preach there also, because for this purpose I have come forth." [39]And He was preaching in their synagogues throughout all Galilee, and casting out demons.

Jesus Cleanses a Leper

[40]Now a leper came to Him, imploring Him, kneeling down to Him and saying to Him, "If You are willing, You can make me clean." [41]Then Jesus, moved with compassion, stretched out *His* hand and touched him, and said to him, "I am willing; be cleansed." [42]As soon as He had spoken, immediately the leprosy left him, and he was cleansed.

[43]And He strictly warned him and sent him away at once, [44]and said to him, "See that you say nothing to anyone; but go your way, show yourself to the priest, and offer for your cleansing those things which Moses commanded, as a testimony to them."

[45]However, he went out and began to proclaim *it* freely, and to spread the matter, so that Jesus could no longer openly enter the city, but was outside in deserted places; and they came to Him from every direction.

Jesus Forgives and Heals a Paralytic

2 And again He entered Capernaum after *some* days, and it was heard that He was in the house. [2]Immediately[a] many gathered together, so that there was no longer room to receive *them,* not even near the door. And He preached the word to them. [3]Then they came to Him, bringing a paralytic who was carried by four *men.* [4]And when they could not come near Him because of the crowd, they uncovered the roof where He was. So when they had broken through, they let down the bed on which the paralytic was lying. [5]When Jesus saw their faith, He said to the paralytic, "Son, your sins are forgiven you."

[6]And some of the scribes were sitting there and reasoning in their hearts, [7]"Why does this *Man* speak blasphemies like this? Who can forgive sins but God alone?"

[8]But immediately, when Jesus perceived in His spirit that they reasoned thus within themselves, He said to them, "Why do you reason about these things in your hearts? [9]Which is easier, to say to the paralytic, '*Your* sins are forgiven you,' or to say, 'Arise, take up your bed and walk'? [10]But that you may know that the Son of Man has power on earth to forgive sins"—He said to the paralytic, [11]"I say to you, arise, take up your bed, and go to your house." [12]Immediately he arose, took up the bed, and went out in the presence of them all, so that all were amazed and glorified God, saying, "We never saw *anything* like this!"

1:27 [a]NU-Text reads *What is this? A new doctrine with authority.*   **2:2** [a]NU-Text omits *Immediately.*

Matthew the Tax Collector

¹³Then He went out again by the sea; and all the multitude came to Him, and He taught them. ¹⁴As He passed by, He saw Levi the *son* of Alphaeus sitting at the tax office. And He said to him, "Follow Me." So he arose and followed Him.

¹⁵Now it happened, as He was dining in *Levi's* house, that many tax collectors and sinners also sat together with Jesus and His disciples; for there were many, and they followed Him. ¹⁶And when the scribes andª Pharisees saw Him eating with the tax collectors and sinners, they said to His disciples, "How *is it* that He eats and drinks with tax collectors and sinners?"

¹⁷When Jesus heard *it,* He said to them, "Those who are well have no need of a physician, but those who are sick. I did not come to call *the* righteous, but sinners, to repentance."ª

Jesus Is Questioned About Fasting

¹⁸The disciples of John and of the Pharisees were fasting. Then they came and said to Him, "Why do the disciples of John and of the Pharisees fast, but Your disciples do not fast?"

¹⁹And Jesus said to them, "Can the friends of the bridegroom fast while the bridegroom is with them? As long as they have the bridegroom with them they cannot fast. ²⁰But the days will come when the bridegroom will be taken away from them, and then they will fast in those days. ²¹No one sews a piece of unshrunk cloth on an old garment; or else the new piece pulls away from the old, and the tear is made worse. ²²And no one puts new wine into old wineskins; or else the new wine bursts the wineskins, the wine is spilled, and the wineskins are ruined. But new wine must be put into new wineskins."

Jesus Is Lord of the Sabbath

²³Now it happened that He went through the grainfields on the Sabbath; and as they went His disciples began to pluck the heads of grain. ²⁴And the Pharisees said to Him, "Look, why do they do what is not lawful on the Sabbath?"

²⁵But He said to them, "Have you never read what David did when he was in need and hungry, he and those with him: ²⁶how he went into the house of God *in the days* of Abiathar the high priest, and ate the showbread, which is not lawful to eat except for the priests, and also gave some to those who were with him?"

2:16 ªNU-Text reads *of the.* **2:17** ªNU-Text omits *to repentance.*

INSPIRING

"We never saw anything like this!"

MARK 2:12

William Cullen Bryant

THE BLESSED INFLUENCE OF JESUS

William Cullen Bryant (1794–1878), known as the "Father of American Poets" and long-time editor of the *New York Evening Post*, wrote:

> The very men who, in the pride of their investigations into the secrets of the internal world, turn a look of scorn upon the Christian system of belief, are not aware how much of the peace and order of society, how much the happiness of households, and the purest of those who are the dearest to them, are owing to the influence of that religion extending beyond their sphere. . . .
>
> In my view, the life, the teachings, the labors, and the sufferings of the blessed Jesus, there can be no admiration too profound, no love of which the human heart is capable too warm, no gratitude too earnest and deep of which He is justly the object.

[27]And He said to them, "The Sabbath was made for man, and not man for the Sabbath. [28]Therefore the Son of Man is also Lord of the Sabbath."

Healing on the Sabbath

3 And He entered the synagogue again, and a man was there who had a withered hand. [2]So they watched Him closely, whether He would heal him on the Sabbath, so that they might accuse Him. [3]And He said to the man who had the withered hand, "Step forward." [4]Then He said to them, "Is it lawful on the Sabbath to do good or to do evil, to save life or to kill?" But they kept silent. [5]And when He had looked around at them with anger, being grieved by the hardness of their hearts, He said to the man, "Stretch out your hand." And he stretched *it* out, and his hand was restored as whole as the other.[a] [6]Then the Pharisees went out and immediately plotted with the Herodians against Him, how they might destroy Him.

A Great Multitude Follows Jesus

[7]But Jesus withdrew with His disciples to the sea. And a great multitude from Galilee followed Him, and from Judea [8]and Jerusalem and Idumea and beyond the Jordan; and those from Tyre and Sidon, a great multitude, when they heard how many things He was doing, came to Him. [9]So He told His disciples that a small boat should be kept ready for Him because of the multitude, lest they should crush Him. [10]For He healed many, so that as many as had afflictions pressed about Him to touch Him. [11]And the unclean spirits, whenever they saw Him, fell down before Him and cried out, saying, "You are the Son of God." [12]But He sternly warned them that they should not make Him known.

The Twelve Apostles

[13]And He went up on the mountain and called to *Him* those He Himself wanted. And they came to Him. [14]Then He appointed twelve,[a] that they might be with Him and that He might send them out to preach, [15]and to have power to heal sicknesses and[a] to cast out demons: [16]Simon,[a] to whom He gave the name Peter; [17]James the *son* of Zebedee and John the brother of James, to whom He gave the name Boanerges, that is, "Sons of Thunder"; [18]Andrew, Philip, Bartholomew, Matthew, Thomas, James the *son* of Alphaeus, Thaddaeus, Simon the Cananite; [19]and Judas Iscariot, who also betrayed Him. And they went into a house.

A House Divided Cannot Stand

[20]Then the multitude came together again, so that they could not so much as eat bread. [21]But when His own people heard *about this,* they went out to lay hold of Him, for they said, "He is out of His mind." [22]And the scribes who came down from Jerusalem said, "He has Beelzebub," and, "By the ruler of the demons He casts out demons." [23]So He called them to *Himself* and said to them in parables: "How can Satan cast out Satan? [24]If a kingdom is divided against itself, that kingdom cannot stand. [25]And if a house is divided against itself, that house cannot stand. [26]And if Satan has risen up against himself, and is divided, he cannot stand, but has an end. [27]No one can enter a strong man's house and plunder his goods, unless he first binds the strong man. And then he will plunder his house.

The Unpardonable Sin

[28]"Assuredly, I say to you, all sins will be forgiven the sons of men, and whatever blasphemies they may utter; [29]but he who blasphemes against the Holy Spirit never has forgiveness, but is subject to eternal condemnation"— [30]because they said, "He has an unclean spirit."

Jesus' Mother and Brothers Send for Him

[31]Then His brothers and His mother came, and standing outside they sent to Him, calling Him. [32]And a multitude was sitting around Him; and they said to Him, "Look, Your mother and Your brothers[a] are outside seeking You."

3:5 [a]NU-Text omits *as whole as the other.*
3:14 [a]NU-Text adds *whom He also named apostles.*
3:15 [a]NU-Text omits *to heal sicknesses and.*
3:16 [a]NU-Text reads *and He appointed the twelve: Simon. . . .* **3:32** [a]NU-Text and M-Text add *and Your sisters.*

33But He answered them, saying, "Who is My mother, or My brothers?" 34And He looked around in a circle at those who sat about Him, and said, "Here are My mother and My brothers! 35For whoever does the will of God is My brother and My sister and mother."

The Parable of the Sower

4 And again He began to teach by the sea. And a great multitude was gathered to Him, so that He got into a boat and sat *in it* on the sea; and the whole multitude was on the land facing the sea. 2Then He taught them many things by parables, and said to them in His teaching:

3"Listen! Behold, a sower went out to sow. 4And it happened, as he sowed, *that* some *seed* fell by the wayside; and the birds of the air[a] came and devoured it. 5Some fell on stony ground, where it did not have much earth; and immediately it sprang up because it had no depth of earth. 6But when the sun was up it was scorched, and because it had no root it withered away. 7And some *seed* fell among thorns; and the thorns grew up and choked it, and it yielded no crop. 8But other *seed* fell on good ground and yielded a crop that sprang up, increased and produced: some thirtyfold, some sixty, and some a hundred."

9And He said to them,[a] "He who has ears to hear, let him hear!"

The Purpose of Parables

10But when He was alone, those around Him with the twelve asked Him about the parable. 11And He said to them, "To you it has been given to know the mystery of the kingdom of God; but to those who are outside, all things come in parables, 12so that

'Seeing they may see and not perceive,
  And hearing they may hear and not
    understand;
  Lest they should turn,
  And their sins be forgiven them.' "[a]

The Parable of the Sower Explained

13And He said to them, "Do you not understand this parable? How then will you understand all the parables? 14The sower sows the word. 15And these are the ones by the wayside where the word is sown. When they hear, Satan comes immediately and takes away the word that was sown in their hearts. 16These likewise are the ones sown on stony ground who, when they hear the word, immediately receive it with gladness; 17and they have no root in themselves, and so endure only for a time. Afterward, when tribulation or persecution arises for the word's sake, immediately they stumble. 18Now these are the ones sown among thorns; *they are* the ones who hear the word, 19and the cares of this world, the deceitfulness of riches, and the desires for other things entering in choke the word, and it becomes unfruitful. 20But these are the ones sown on good ground, those who hear the word, accept *it,* and bear fruit: some thirtyfold, some sixty, and some a hundred."

Light Under a Basket

21Also He said to them, "Is a lamp brought to be put under a basket or under a bed? Is it not to be set on a lampstand? 22For there is nothing hidden which will not be revealed, nor has anything been kept secret but that it should come to light. 23If anyone has ears to hear, let him hear."

24Then He said to them, "Take heed what you hear. With the same measure you use, it will be measured to you; and to you who hear, more will be given. 25For whoever has, to him more will be given; but whoever does not have, even what he has will be taken away from him."

The Parable of the Growing Seed

26And He said, "The kingdom of God is as if a man should scatter seed on the ground, 27and should sleep by night and rise by day, and the seed should sprout and grow, he himself does not know how. 28For the earth yields crops by itself: first the blade, then the head, after that the full grain in the head. 29But when the grain ripens, immediately he puts in the sickle, because the harvest has come."

4:4 [a]NU-Text and M-Text omit *of the air.*   **4:9** [a]NU-Text and M-Text omit *to them.*   **4:12** [a]Isaiah 6:9, 10

The Parable of the Mustard Seed

30Then He said, "To what shall we liken the kingdom of God? Or with what parable shall we picture it? 31*It is* like a mustard seed which, when it is sown on the ground, is smaller than all the seeds on earth; 32but when it is sown, it grows up and becomes greater than all herbs, and shoots out large branches, so that the birds of the air may nest under its shade."

Jesus' Use of Parables

33And with many such parables He spoke the word to them as they were able to hear *it.* 34But without a parable He did not speak to them. And when they were alone, He explained all things to His disciples.

Wind and Wave Obey Jesus

35On the same day, when evening had come, He said to them, "Let us cross over to the other side." 36Now when they had left the multitude, they took Him along in the boat as He was. And other little boats were also with Him. 37And a great windstorm arose, and the waves beat into the boat, so that it was already filling. 38But He was in the stern, asleep on a pillow. And they awoke Him and said to Him, "Teacher, do You not care that we are perishing?"

39Then He arose and rebuked the wind, and said to the sea, "Peace, be still!" And the wind ceased and there was a great calm. 40But He said to them, "Why are you so fearful? How *is it* that you have no faith?"a 41And they feared exceedingly, and said to one another, "Who can this be, that even the wind and the sea obey Him!"

A Demon-Possessed Man Healed

5 Then they came to the other side of the sea, to the country of the Gadarenes.a 2And when He had come out of the boat, immediately there met Him out of the tombs a man with an unclean spirit, 3who had *his* dwelling among the tombs; and no one could bind him,a not even with chains, 4because he had often been bound with shackles and chains. And the chains had been pulled apart by him, and the shackles broken in pieces; neither could anyone

tame him. 5And always, night and day, he was in the mountains and in the tombs, crying out and cutting himself with stones.

6When he saw Jesus from afar, he ran and worshiped Him. 7And he cried out with a loud voice and said, "What have I to do with You, Jesus, Son of the Most High God? I implore You by God that You do not torment me."

8For He said to him, "Come out of the man, unclean spirit!" 9Then He asked him, "What *is* your name?"

And he answered, saying, "My name *is* Legion; for we are many." 10Also he begged Him earnestly that He would not send them out of the country.

11Now a large herd of swine was feeding there near the mountains. 12So all the demons begged Him, saying, "Send us to the swine, that we may enter them." 13And at once Jesusa gave them permission. Then the unclean spirits went out and entered the swine (there were about two thousand); and the herd ran violently down the steep place into the sea, and drowned in the sea.

14So those who fed the swine fled, and they told *it* in the city and in the country. And they went out to see what it was that had happened. 15Then they came to Jesus, and saw the one *who had been* demon-possessed and had the legion, sitting and clothed and in his right mind. And they were afraid. 16And those who saw it told them how it happened to him *who had been* demon-possessed, and about the swine. 17Then they began to plead with Him to depart from their region.

18And when He got into the boat, he who had been demon-possessed begged Him that he might be with Him. 19However, Jesus did not permit him, but said to him, "Go home to your friends, and tell them what great things the Lord has done for you, and how He has had compassion on you." 20And he departed and began to proclaim in Decapolis all that Jesus had done for him; and all marveled.

4:40 aNU-Text reads *Have you still no faith?*
5:1 aNU-Text reads *Gerasenes.*   **5:3** aNU-Text adds *anymore.*   **5:13** aNU-Text reads *And He gave.*

A Girl Restored to Life and a Woman Healed

21Now when Jesus had crossed over again by boat to the other side, a great multitude gathered to Him; and He was by the sea. 22And behold, one of the rulers of the synagogue came, Jairus by name. And when he saw Him, he fell at His feet 23and begged Him earnestly, saying, "My little daughter lies at the point of death. Come and lay Your hands on her, that she may be healed, and she will live." 24So *Jesus* went with him, and a great multitude followed Him and thronged Him.

25Now a certain woman had a flow of blood for twelve years, 26and had suffered many things from many physicians. She had spent all that she had and was no better, but rather grew worse. 27When she heard about Jesus, she came behind *Him* in the crowd and touched His garment. 28For she said, "If only I may touch His clothes, I shall be made well."

29Immediately the fountain of her blood was dried up, and she felt in *her* body that she was healed of the affliction. 30And Jesus, immediately knowing in Himself that power had gone out of Him, turned around in the crowd and said, "Who touched My clothes?"

31But His disciples said to Him, "You see the multitude thronging You, and You say, 'Who touched Me?'"

32And He looked around to see her who had done this thing. 33But the woman, fearing and trembling, knowing what had

---

WORSHIP

"Who can this be, that even the wind and the sea obey Him!"

MARK 4:41

Ezra Stiles

"WHO BUT THE RULER OF THE WINDS? . . ."

As the president of Yale College (1778–1795), Ezra Stiles gave a major Election Address entitled "The United States Elevated to Glory and Honor," before the governor and the General Assembly of Connecticut in May 1783, stating:

> In our lowest and most dangerous state, in 1776 and 1777, we sustained ourselves against the British Army of sixty thousand troops, commanded by . . . the ablest generals Britain could procure throughout Europe, with a naval force of twenty-two thousand seamen in above eighty men-of-war.
>
> Who but a Washington, inspired by heaven, could have conceived the surprise move upon the enemy at Princeton—that Christmas eve when Washington and his army crossed the Delaware?
>
> Who but the Ruler of the winds could have delayed the British reinforcements by three months of contrary ocean winds at a critical point of the war?
>
> Or what but "a providential miracle" at the last minute detected the treacherous scheme of traitor Benedict Arnold, which would have delivered the American army, including George Washington himself, into the hands of the enemy?
>
> On the French role in the Revolution, it is God who so ordered the balancing interests of nations as to produce an irresistible motive in the European maritime powers to take our part. . . .
>
> The United States are under peculiar obligations to become a holy people unto the Lord our God.

"Once I prophesied that this generation of Americans had a rendezvous with destiny. That prophecy comes true."

Franklin D. Roosevelt

WORLD WAR II

IN THE CLOSE OF HIS ANNUAL State of the Union message to Congress in January 1939, and with war about to break out in Europe, President Franklin Delano Roosevelt quoted Abraham Lincoln and said, "Once I prophesied that this generation of Americans had a rendezvous with destiny. That prophecy comes true. To us much is given; more is expected. This generation will nobly save or meanly lose the last best hope of earth. . . . The way is plain, peaceful, generous, just—a way which if followed the world will forever applaud and God must forever bless.'"

One wonders if Roosevelt realized just how true his words would become for the great generation of young Americans he addressed. By 1940, most of mainland Europe had fallen to Nazi aggression. With German troops controlling Paris, Stalin and the communists in the east were rapidly building up one of history's largest ground armies to defend Russia. Japan had signed a ten-year military pact with Germany and Italy, forming an Axis power they were confident would eventually rule the world.

WITH THE JAPANESE ATTACK ON PEARL HARBOR on December 7, 1941, Americans whose lives had been shaped by the trying times of the Great Depression volunteered by the hundreds of thousands to fight the enemies abroad and to save the world from tyranny. The majority of the world's nations split into two opposing military alliances: the Allies and the Axis powers. Over 100 million military personnel would engage in the battle, and over 60 million people, including about 20 million soldiers and 40 million civilians, were killed, making it the deadliest and most widespread war in history.

By the D-Day invasion of Europe on June 6, 1944, 12 million Americans were in uniform, and over 16 million Americans would eventually fight in the Second World War. War production had taken over the nation's industry, representing over 40 percent of the gross national product. When the Battle of the Bulge was fought in December 1944, over 6.5 million women had been added to the nation's work force since 1939.

Valiant Marines planted the flag on Iwo Jima in February 1945, and on September 2, the Japanese signed the surrender agreement. Over 400,000 of America's heroic young people gave their final measure of devotion in this war.

FROM OVERCOMING THE MISERY OF LONG years of economic depression in the 1930s, to defeating Nazism and Japanese imperialism, to the Herculean task of remaking the postwar American society, this generation of Americans born for "a rendezvous with destiny" was undoubtedly the most influential of the twentieth century. But what was it that made them a generation of patriots, heroes, and builders?

Perhaps the answer was expressed through one of their own, Mitchell Paige, a recipient of the Congressional Medal of Honor, the nation's most prestigious military honor, for his actions at the Battle of Guadalcanal in the Solomon Islands. On October 26, 1942, after all of the other Marines in his platoon were killed or wounded, for hours Paige operated four machine guns, single-handedly stopping an entire Japanese regiment. Had that position fallen and the Japanese regained the airfield the Marines had taken, it is possible that the outcome of World War II may have significantly changed.

In the years to come, Paige was repeatedly asked why he would be willing to put his life on the line for his country. He said that the answers took him back to a Pennsylvania three-room country school where the children were so steeped in the traditions of America that they literally felt themselves a part of a glorious heritage—where the teacher opened the school day with a Bible verse and the Pledge of Allegiance, and where they memorized all the great documents that established the bedrock of America, such as the Gettysburg Address.

Mitchell Paige

"TRUST IN THE LORD WITH ALL YOUR HEART, AND LEAN NOT ON YOUR OWN UNDERSTANDING; IN ALL YOUR WAYS ACKNOWLEDGE HIM, AND HE WILL DIRECT YOUR PATHS."

His response went this way: "My undying love of country, and my strong loyalty to the Marines fighting by my side, gave me no choice but to fight on unswervingly throughout my battles, utilizing my God-given ability to make use of what I had been taught and learned."

WHEN PAIGE LEFT HOME TO WALK the two-hundred miles to the nearest Marine recruiting station in 1936, his mother packed him a lunch in which she included the note: "Trust in the Lord, son, and He will guide you always." He said those words remained forever in his mind, and whenever fear would overtake him, he was comforted by them.

Paige said, "I will never forget sitting in a foxhole, bloody, burned, and injured the morning after our all-night, fierce, hand-to-hand battle against an overwhelming Japanese force on Guadalcanal. I was alone except for hundreds of dead bodies of the enemy surrounding me. I emptied my pack looking for something to stop the bleeding from a bayonet wound and out fell my small Bible. Picking it up in my dirty, bloody hands, I could scarcely believe it when providentially it opened at Proverbs 3 and there were my mother's words, "Trust in the LORD with all your heart, and lean not on your own understanding; in all your ways acknowledge Him, and He will direct your paths."

Mitchell Paige was a true servant and patriot of America . . . and America is proud to have had hundreds of thousands of valiant soldiers cut from the same cloth.

happened to her, came and fell down before Him and told Him the whole truth. ³⁴And He said to her, "Daughter, your faith has made you well. Go in peace, and be healed of your affliction."

³⁵While He was still speaking, *some* came from the ruler of the synagogue's *house* who said, "Your daughter is dead. Why trouble the Teacher any further?"

³⁶As soon as Jesus heard the word that was spoken, He said to the ruler of the synagogue, "Do not be afraid; only believe." ³⁷And He permitted no one to follow Him except Peter, James, and John the brother of James. ³⁸Then He came to the house of the ruler of the synagogue, and saw a tumult and those who wept and wailed loudly. ³⁹When He came in, He said to them, "Why make this commotion and weep? The child is not dead, but sleeping."

⁴⁰And they ridiculed Him. But when He had put them all outside, He took the father and the mother of the child, and those *who were* with Him, and entered where the child was lying. ⁴¹Then He took the child by the hand, and said to her, "Talitha, cumi," which is translated, "Little girl, I say to you, arise." ⁴²Immediately the girl arose and walked, for she was twelve years *of age*. And they were overcome with great amazement. ⁴³But He commanded them strictly that no one should know it, and said that *something* should be given her to eat.

Jesus Rejected at Nazareth

6 Then He went out from there and came to His own country, and His disciples followed Him. ²And when the Sabbath had come, He began to teach in the synagogue. And many hearing *Him* were astonished, saying, "Where *did* this Man *get* these things? And what wisdom *is* this which is given to Him, that such mighty works are performed by His hands! ³Is this not the carpenter, the Son of Mary, and brother of James, Joses, Judas, and Simon? And are not His sisters here with us?" So they were offended at Him.

⁴But Jesus said to them, "A prophet is not without honor except in his own country, among his own relatives, and in his own house." ⁵Now He could do no mighty work there, except that He laid His hands on a few sick people and healed *them*. ⁶And He marveled because of their unbelief. Then He went about the villages in a circuit, teaching.

Sending Out the Twelve

⁷And He called the twelve to *Himself,* and began to send them out two *by* two, and gave them power over unclean spirits. ⁸He commanded them to take nothing for the journey except a staff—no bag, no bread, no copper in *their* money belts— ⁹but to wear sandals, and not to put on two tunics.

¹⁰Also He said to them, "In whatever place you enter a house, stay there till you depart from that place. ¹¹And whoeverᵃ will not receive you nor hear you, when you depart from there, shake off the dust under your feet as a testimony against them.ᵇ Assuredly, I say to you, it will be more tolerable for Sodom and Gomorrah in the day of judgment than for that city!"

¹²So they went out and preached that *people* should repent. ¹³And they cast out many demons, and anointed with oil many who were sick, and healed *them*.

John the Baptist Beheaded

¹⁴Now King Herod heard *of Him,* for His name had become well known. And he said, "John the Baptist is risen from the dead, and therefore these powers are at work in him."

¹⁵Others said, "It is Elijah."

And others said, "It is the Prophet, orᵃ like one of the prophets."

¹⁶But when Herod heard, he said, "This is John, whom I beheaded; he has been raised from the dead!" ¹⁷For Herod himself had sent and laid hold of John, and bound him in prison for the sake of Herodias, his brother Philip's wife; for he had married her. ¹⁸Because John had said to Herod, "It is not lawful for you to have your brother's wife." ¹⁹Therefore Herodias held it against him and wanted to kill him, but she could not; ²⁰for Herod feared John, knowing that he

---

6:11 ᵃNU-Text reads *whatever place.* ᵇNU-Text omits the rest of this verse.   **6:15** ᵃNU-Text and M-Text omit *or.*

was a just and holy man, and he protected him. And when he heard him, he did many things, and heard him gladly.

[21]Then an opportune day came when Herod on his birthday gave a feast for his nobles, the high officers, and the chief *men* of Galilee. [22]And when Herodias' daughter herself came in and danced, and pleased Herod and those who sat with him, the king said to the girl, "Ask me whatever you want, and I will give *it* to you." [23]He also swore to her, "Whatever you ask me, I will give you, up to half my kingdom."

[24]So she went out and said to her mother, "What shall I ask?"

And she said, "The head of John the Baptist!"

[25]Immediately she came in with haste to the king and asked, saying, "I want you to give me at once the head of John the Baptist on a platter."

[26]And the king was exceedingly sorry; *yet,* because of the oaths and because of those who sat with him, he did not want to refuse her. [27]Immediately the king sent an executioner and commanded his head to be brought. And he went and beheaded him in prison, [28]brought his head on a platter, and gave it to the girl; and the girl gave it to her mother. [29]When his disciples heard *of it,* they came and took away his corpse and laid it in a tomb.

Feeding the Five Thousand

[30]Then the apostles gathered to Jesus and told Him all things, both what they had done and what they had taught. [31]And He said to them, "Come aside by yourselves to a deserted place and rest a while." For there were many coming and going, and they did not even have time to eat. [32]So they departed to a deserted place in the boat by themselves.

[33]But the multitudes[a] saw them departing, and many knew Him and ran there on foot from all the cities. They arrived before them and came together to Him. [34]And Jesus, when He came out, saw a great multitude and was moved with compassion for them, because they were like sheep not having a shepherd. So He began to teach them many things. [35]When the day was now far

spent, His disciples came to Him and said, "This is a deserted place, and already the hour *is* late. [36]Send them away, that they may go into the surrounding country and villages and buy themselves bread;[a] for they have nothing to eat."

[37]But He answered and said to them, "You give them something to eat."

And they said to Him, "Shall we go and buy two hundred denarii worth of bread and give them *something* to eat?"

[38]But He said to them, "How many loaves do you have? Go and see."

And when they found out they said, "Five, and two fish."

[39]Then He commanded them to make them all sit down in groups on the green grass. [40]So they sat down in ranks, in hundreds and in fifties. [41]And when He had taken the five loaves and the two fish, He looked up to heaven, blessed and broke the loaves, and gave *them* to His disciples to set before them; and the two fish He divided among *them* all. [42]So they all ate and were filled. [43]And they took up twelve baskets full of fragments and of the fish. [44]Now those who had eaten the loaves were about[a] five thousand men.

Jesus Walks on the Sea

[45]Immediately He made His disciples get into the boat and go before Him to the other side, to Bethsaida, while He sent the multitude away. [46]And when He had sent them away, He departed to the mountain to pray. [47]Now when evening came, the boat was in the middle of the sea; and He *was* alone on the land. [48]Then He saw them straining at rowing, for the wind was against them. Now about the fourth watch of the night He came to them, walking on the sea, and would have passed them by. [49]And when they saw Him walking on the sea, they supposed it was a ghost, and cried out; [50]for they all saw Him and were troubled. But immediately He talked with them and said to them, "Be of good cheer!

6:33 [a]NU-Text and M-Text read *they.*
6:36 [a]NU-Text reads *something to eat* and omits the rest of this verse.   **6:44** [a]NU-Text and M-Text omit *about.*

It is I; do not be afraid." [51]Then He went up into the boat to them, and the wind ceased. And they were greatly amazed in themselves beyond measure, and marveled. [52]For they had not understood about the loaves, because their heart was hardened.

Many Touch Him and Are Made Well

[53]When they had crossed over, they came to the land of Gennesaret and anchored there. [54]And when they came out of the boat, immediately the people recognized Him, [55]ran through that whole surrounding region, and began to carry about on beds those who were sick to wherever they heard He was. [56]Wherever He entered, into villages, cities, or the country, they laid the sick in the marketplaces, and begged Him that they might just touch the hem of His garment. And as many as touched Him were made well.

Defilement Comes from Within

7 Then the Pharisees and some of the scribes came together to Him, having come from Jerusalem. [2]Now when[a] they saw some of His disciples eat bread with defiled, that is, with unwashed hands, they found fault. [3]For the Pharisees and all the Jews do not eat unless they wash *their* hands in a special way, holding the tradition of the elders. [4]*When they come* from the marketplace, they do not eat unless they wash. And there are many other things which they have received and hold, *like* the washing of cups, pitchers, copper vessels, and couches.

[5]Then the Pharisees and scribes asked Him, "Why do Your disciples not walk according to the tradition of the elders, but eat bread with unwashed hands?"

[6]He answered and said to them, "Well did Isaiah prophesy of you hypocrites, as it is written:

'This people honors Me with their lips,
　But their heart is far from Me.
[7]　And in vain they worship Me,
　Teaching as doctrines the
　　commandments of men.'[a]

[8]For laying aside the commandment of God, you hold the tradition of men[a]—the washing of pitchers and cups, and many other such things you do."

[9]He said to them, "*All too* well you reject the commandment of God, that you may keep your tradition. [10]For Moses said, '*Honor your father and your mother*';[a] and, '*He who curses father or mother, let him be put to death.*'[b] [11]But you say, 'If a man says to his father or mother, "Whatever profit you might have received from me *is* Corban"—' (that is, a gift *to* God), [12]then you no longer let him do anything for his father or his mother, [13]making the word of God of no effect through your tradition which you have handed down. And many such things you do."

[14]When He had called all the multitude to *Himself,* He said to them, "Hear Me, everyone, and understand: [15]There is nothing that enters a man from outside which can defile him; but the things which come out of him, those are the things that defile a man. [16]If anyone has ears to hear, let him hear!"[a]

[17]When He had entered a house away from the crowd, His disciples asked Him concerning the parable. [18]So He said to them, "Are you thus without understanding also? Do you not perceive that whatever enters a man from outside cannot defile him, [19]because it does not enter his heart but his stomach, and is eliminated, *thus* purifying all foods?"[a] [20]And He said, "What comes out of a man, that defiles a man. [21]For from within, out of the heart of men, proceed evil thoughts, adulteries, fornications, murders, [22]thefts, covetousness, wickedness, deceit, lewdness, an evil eye, blasphemy, pride, foolishness. [23]All these evil things come from within and defile a man."

A Gentile Shows Her Faith

[24]From there He arose and went to the region of Tyre and Sidon.[a] And He entered

---

7:2 [a]NU-Text omits *when* and *they found fault.*
7:7 [a]Isaiah 29:13　　**7:8** [a]NU-Text omits the rest of this verse.　　**7:10** [a]Exodus 20:12; Deuteronomy 5:16 [a]Exodus 21:17　　**7:16** [a]NU-Text omits this verse.
7:19 [a]NU-Text ends quotation with *eliminated,* setting off the final clause as Mark's comment that Jesus has declared all foods clean.　　**7:24** [a]NU-Text omits *and Sidon.*

a house and wanted no one to know *it,* but He could not be hidden. ²⁵For a woman whose young daughter had an unclean spirit heard about Him, and she came and fell at His feet. ²⁶The woman was a Greek, a Syro-Phoenician by birth, and she kept asking Him to cast the demon out of her daughter. ²⁷But Jesus said to her, "Let the children be filled first, for it is not good to take the children's bread and throw *it* to the little dogs."

²⁸And she answered and said to Him, "Yes, Lord, yet even the little dogs under the table eat from the children's crumbs."

²⁹Then He said to her, "For this saying go your way; the demon has gone out of your daughter."

³⁰And when she had come to her house, she found the demon gone out, and her daughter lying on the bed.

Jesus Heals a Deaf-Mute

³¹Again, departing from the region of Tyre and Sidon, He came through the midst of the region of Decapolis to the Sea of Galilee. ³²Then they brought to Him one who was deaf and had an impediment in his speech, and they begged Him to put His hand on him. ³³And He took him aside from the multitude, and put His fingers in his ears, and He spat and touched his tongue. ³⁴Then, looking up to heaven, He sighed, and said to him, "Ephphatha," that is, "Be opened."

³⁵Immediately his ears were opened, and the impediment of his tongue was loosed, and he spoke plainly. ³⁶Then He commanded them that they should tell no one; but the more He commanded them, the more widely they proclaimed *it.* ³⁷And they were astonished beyond measure, saying, "He has done all things well. He makes both the deaf to hear and the mute to speak."

Feeding the Four Thousand

8 In those days, the multitude being very great and having nothing to eat, Jesus called His disciples *to Him* and said to them, ²"I have compassion on the multitude, because they have now continued with Me three days and have nothing to eat. ³And if I send them away hungry to their own

houses, they will faint on the way; for some of them have come from afar."

⁴Then His disciples answered Him, "How can one satisfy these people with bread here in the wilderness?"

⁵He asked them, "How many loaves do you have?"

And they said, "Seven."

⁶So He commanded the multitude to sit down on the ground. And He took the seven loaves and gave thanks, broke *them* and gave *them* to His disciples to set before *them;* and they set *them* before the multitude. ⁷They also had a few small fish; and having blessed them, He said to set them also before *them.* ⁸So they ate and were filled, and they took up seven large baskets of leftover fragments. ⁹Now those who had eaten were about four thousand. And He sent them away, ¹⁰immediately got into the boat with His disciples, and came to the region of Dalmanutha.

The Pharisees Seek a Sign

¹¹Then the Pharisees came out and began to dispute with Him, seeking from Him a sign from heaven, testing Him. ¹²But He sighed deeply in His spirit, and said, "Why does this generation seek a sign? Assuredly, I say to you, no sign shall be given to this generation."

Beware of the Leaven of the Pharisees and Herod

¹³And He left them, and getting into the boat again, departed to the other side. ¹⁴Now the disciples[a] had forgotten to take bread, and they did not have more than one loaf with them in the boat. ¹⁵Then He charged them, saying, "Take heed, beware of the leaven of the Pharisees and the leaven of Herod."

¹⁶And they reasoned among themselves, saying, "*It is* because we have no bread."

¹⁷But Jesus, being aware of *it,* said to them, "Why do you reason because you have no bread? Do you not yet perceive nor understand? Is your heart still[a] hardened? ¹⁸Having eyes, do you not see? And

8:14 ᵃNU-Text and M-Text read *they.*
8:17 ᵃNU-Text omits *still.*

having ears, do you not hear? And do you not remember? ¹⁹When I broke the five loaves for the five thousand, how many baskets full of fragments did you take up?"

They said to Him, "Twelve."

²⁰"Also, when I broke the seven for the four thousand, how many large baskets full of fragments did you take up?"

And they said, "Seven."

²¹So He said to them, "How *is it* you do not understand?"

A Blind Man Healed at Bethsaida

²²Then He came to Bethsaida; and they brought a blind man to Him, and begged Him to touch him. ²³So He took the blind man by the hand and led him out of the town. And when He had spit on his eyes and put His hands on him, He asked him if he saw anything.

²⁴And he looked up and said, "I see men like trees, walking."

²⁵Then He put *His* hands on his eyes again and made him look up. And he was restored and saw everyone clearly. ²⁶Then He sent him away to his house, saying, "Neither go into the town, nor tell anyone in the town."ᵃ

Peter Confesses Jesus as the Christ

²⁷Now Jesus and His disciples went out to the towns of Caesarea Philippi; and on the road He asked His disciples, saying to them, "Who do men say that I am?"

²⁸So they answered, "John the Baptist; but some *say,* Elijah; and others, one of the prophets."

²⁹He said to them, "But who do you say that I am?"

Peter answered and said to Him, "You are the Christ."

³⁰Then He strictly warned them that they should tell no one about Him.

Jesus Predicts His Death and Resurrection

³¹And He began to teach them that the Son of Man must suffer many things, and be rejected by the elders and chief priests and scribes, and be killed, and after three days rise again. ³²He spoke this word openly. Then Peter took Him aside and began to rebuke Him. ³³But when He had turned around and looked at His disciples, He rebuked Peter, saying, "Get behind Me, Satan! For you are not mindful of the things of God, but the things of men."

Take Up the Cross and Follow Him

³⁴When He had called the people to *Himself,* with His disciples also, He said to them, "Whoever desires to come after Me, let him deny himself, and take up his cross, and follow Me. ³⁵For whoever desires to save his life will lose it, but whoever loses his life for My sake and the gospel's will save it. ³⁶For what will it profit a man if he gains the whole world, and loses his own soul? ³⁷Or what will a man give in exchange for his soul? ³⁸For whoever is ashamed of Me and My words in this adulterous and sinful generation, of him the Son of Man also will be ashamed when He comes in the glory of His Father with the holy angels."

9 And He said to them, "Assuredly, I say to you that there are some standing here who will not taste death till they see the kingdom of God present with power."

Jesus Transfigured on the Mount

²Now after six days Jesus took Peter, James, and John, and led them up on a high mountain apart by themselves; and He was transfigured before them. ³His clothes became shining, exceedingly white, like snow, such as no launderer on earth can whiten them. ⁴And Elijah appeared to them with Moses, and they were talking with Jesus. ⁵Then Peter answered and said to Jesus, "Rabbi, it is good for us to be here; and let us make three tabernacles: one for You, one for Moses, and one for Elijah"— ⁶because he did not know what to say, for they were greatly afraid.

⁷And a cloud came and overshadowed them; and a voice came out of the cloud, saying, "This is My beloved Son. Hear Him!" ⁸Suddenly, when they had looked around, they saw no one anymore, but only Jesus with themselves.

⁹Now as they came down from the mountain, He commanded them that they should tell no one the things they had

---

8:26 ᵃNU-Text reads *"Do not even go into the town."*

seen, till the Son of Man had risen from the dead. ¹⁰So they kept this word to themselves, questioning what the rising from the dead meant.

¹¹And they asked Him, saying, "Why do the scribes say that Elijah must come first?"

¹²Then He answered and told them, "Indeed, Elijah is coming first and restores all things. And how is it written concerning the Son of Man, that He must suffer many things and be treated with contempt? ¹³But I say to you that Elijah has also come, and they did to him whatever they wished, as it is written of him."

A Boy Is Healed

¹⁴And when He came to the disciples, He saw a great multitude around them, and scribes disputing with them. ¹⁵Immediately, when they saw Him, all the people were greatly amazed, and running to *Him,* greeted Him. ¹⁶And He asked the scribes, "What are you discussing with them?"

¹⁷Then one of the crowd answered and said, "Teacher, I brought You my son, who has a mute spirit. ¹⁸And wherever it seizes him, it throws him down; he foams at the mouth, gnashes his teeth, and becomes rigid. So I spoke to Your disciples, that they should cast it out, but they could not."

¹⁹He answered him and said, "O faithless generation, how long shall I be with you? How long shall I bear with you? Bring him to Me." ²⁰Then they brought him to Him. And when he saw Him, immediately the spirit convulsed him, and he fell on the ground and wallowed, foaming at the mouth.

²¹So He asked his father, "How long has this been happening to him?"

And he said, "From childhood. ²²And often he has thrown him both into the fire and into the water to destroy him. But if You can do anything, have compassion on us and help us."

²³Jesus said to him, "If you can believe,ᵃ all things *are* possible to him who believes."

²⁴Immediately the father of the child cried out and said with tears, "Lord, I believe; help my unbelief!"

²⁵When Jesus saw that the people came running together, He rebuked the unclean spirit, saying to it, "Deaf and dumb spirit, I command you, come out of him and enter him no more!" ²⁶Then *the spirit* cried out, convulsed him greatly, and came out of him. And he became as one dead, so that many said, "He is dead." ²⁷But Jesus took him by the hand and lifted him up, and he arose.

²⁸And when He had come into the house, His disciples asked Him privately, "Why could we not cast it out?"

²⁹So He said to them, "This kind can come out by nothing but prayer and fasting."ᵃ

FAITH

". . . all things are possible to him who believes."

MARK 9:23

The Motto of the State of Ohio
With God All Things Are Possible

Jesus Again Predicts His Death and Resurrection

³⁰Then they departed from there and passed through Galilee, and He did not want anyone to know *it.* ³¹For He taught His disciples and said to them, "The Son of Man is being betrayed into the hands of men, and they will kill Him. And after He is killed, He will rise the third day." ³²But they did not understand this saying, and were afraid to ask Him.

Who Is the Greatest?

³³Then He came to Capernaum. And when He was in the house He asked them, "What was it you disputed among yourselves on the road?" ³⁴But they kept silent, for on the road they had disputed among themselves who *would be the* greatest. ³⁵And He sat down, called the twelve, and said to them, "If anyone desires to be first, he shall be last of all and servant of all." ³⁶Then He took a little child and set him in the midst of them. And when He had taken him in His arms, He said to them, ³⁷"Whoever receives one of these little children in

---

9:23 ᵃNU-Text reads "*'If You can!' All things. . . .*"
9:29 ᵃNU-Text omits *and fasting.*

My name receives Me; and whoever receives Me, receives not Me but Him who sent Me."

Jesus Forbids Sectarianism

38Now John answered Him, saying, "Teacher, we saw someone who does not follow us casting out demons in Your name, and we forbade him because he does not follow us."

39But Jesus said, "Do not forbid him, for no one who works a miracle in My name can soon afterward speak evil of Me. 40For he who is not against us is on our a side. 41For whoever gives you a cup of water to drink in My name, because you belong to Christ, assuredly, I say to you, he will by no means lose his reward.

Jesus Warns of Offenses

42"But whoever causes one of these little ones who believe in Me to stumble, it would be better for him if a millstone were hung around his neck, and he were thrown into the sea. 43If your hand causes you to sin, cut it off. It is better for you to enter into life maimed, rather than having two hands, to go to hell, into the fire that shall never be quenched— 44where

'Their worm does not die
And the fire is not quenched.'a

45And if your foot causes you to sin, cut it off. It is better for you to enter life lame, rather than having two feet, to be cast into hell, into the fire that shall never be quenched— 46where

'Their worm does not die
And the fire is not quenched.'a

47And if your eye causes you to sin, pluck it out. It is better for you to enter the kingdom of God with one eye, rather than having two eyes, to be cast into hell fire— 48where

'Their worm does not die
And the fire is not quenched.'a

Tasteless Salt Is Worthless

49"For everyone will be seasoned with fire,a and every sacrifice will be seasoned with salt. 50Salt is good, but if the salt loses its flavor, how will you season it? Have salt in yourselves, and have peace with one another."

Marriage and Divorce

10 Then He arose from there and came to the region of Judea by the other side of the Jordan. And multitudes gathered to Him again, and as He was accustomed, He taught them again.

2The Pharisees came and asked Him, "Is it lawful for a man to divorce his wife?" testing Him.

3And He answered and said to them, "What did Moses command you?"

4They said, "Moses permitted a man to write a certificate of divorce, and to dismiss her."

5And Jesus answered and said to them, "Because of the hardness of your heart he wrote you this precept. 6But from the beginning of the creation, God 'made them male and female.'a 7'For this reason a man shall leave his father and mother and be joined to his wife, 8and the two shall become one flesh';a so then they are no longer two, but one flesh. 9Therefore what God has joined together, let not man separate."

10In the house His disciples also asked Him again about the same matter. 11So He said to them, "Whoever divorces his wife and marries another commits adultery against her. 12And if a woman divorces her husband and marries another, she commits adultery."

Jesus Blesses Little Children

13Then they brought little children to Him, that He might touch them; but the disciples rebuked those who brought them. 14But when Jesus saw it, He was greatly displeased and said to them, "Let the little children come to Me, and do not forbid them; for of such is the kingdom of God. 15Assuredly, I say to you, whoever does not

---

9:40 aM-Text reads against you is on your side. 9:44 aNU-Text omits this verse.   9:46 aNU-Text omits the last clause of verse 45 and all of verse 46. 9:48 aIsaiah 66:24   9:49 aNU-Text omits the rest of this verse.   10:6 aGenesis 1:27; 5:2 10:8 aGenesis 2:24

receive the kingdom of God as a little child will by no means enter it." ¹⁶And He took them up in His arms, laid *His* hands on them, and blessed them.

Jesus Counsels the Rich Young Ruler

¹⁷Now as He was going out on the road, one came running, knelt before Him, and asked Him, "Good Teacher, what shall I do that I may inherit eternal life?"

¹⁸So Jesus said to him, "Why do you call Me good? No one *is* good but One, *that is,* God. ¹⁹You know the commandments: *'Do not commit adultery,' 'Do not murder,' 'Do not steal,' 'Do not bear false witness,' 'Do not defraud,' 'Honor your father and your mother.' "*[a]

²⁰And he answered and said to Him, "Teacher, all these things I have kept from my youth."

²¹Then Jesus, looking at him, loved him, and said to him, "One thing you lack: Go your way, sell whatever you have and give to the poor, and you will have treasure in heaven; and come, take up the cross, and follow Me."

²²But he was sad at this word, and went away sorrowful, for he had great possessions.

With God All Things Are Possible

²³Then Jesus looked around and said to His disciples, "How hard it is for those who have riches to enter the kingdom of God!" ²⁴And the disciples were astonished at His words. But Jesus answered again and said to them, "Children, how hard it is for those who trust in riches[a] to enter the kingdom of God! ²⁵It is easier for a camel to go through the eye of a needle than for a rich man to enter the kingdom of God."

²⁶And they were greatly astonished, saying among themselves, "Who then can be saved?"

²⁷But Jesus looked at them and said, "With men *it is* impossible, but not with God; for with God all things are possible."

²⁸Then Peter began to say to Him, "See, we have left all and followed You."

²⁹So Jesus answered and said, "Assuredly, I say to you, there is no one who has left house or brothers or sisters or father or mother or wife[a] or children or lands, for My sake and the gospel's, ³⁰who shall not receive a hundredfold now in this time—houses and brothers and sisters and mothers and children and lands, with persecutions—and in the age to come, eternal life. ³¹But many *who are* first will be last, and the last first."

Jesus a Third Time Predicts His Death and Resurrection

³²Now they were on the road, going up to Jerusalem, and Jesus was going before them; and they were amazed. And as they followed they were afraid. Then He took the twelve aside again and began to tell them the things that would happen to Him: ³³"Behold, we are going up to Jerusalem, and the Son of Man will be betrayed to the chief priests and to the scribes; and they will condemn Him to death and deliver Him to the Gentiles; ³⁴and they will mock Him, and scourge Him, and spit on Him, and kill Him. And the third day He will rise again."

Greatness Is Serving

³⁵Then James and John, the sons of Zebedee, came to Him, saying, "Teacher, we want You to do for us whatever we ask."

³⁶And He said to them, "What do you want Me to do for you?"

³⁷They said to Him, "Grant us that we may sit, one on Your right hand and the other on Your left, in Your glory."

³⁸But Jesus said to them, "You do not know what you ask. Are you able to drink the cup that I drink, and be baptized with the baptism that I am baptized with?"

³⁹They said to Him, "We are able."

So Jesus said to them, "You will indeed drink the cup that I drink, and with the baptism I am baptized with you will be baptized; ⁴⁰but to sit on My right hand and on My left is not Mine to give, but *it is for those* for whom it is prepared."

⁴¹And when the ten heard *it,* they began to be greatly displeased with James and John. ⁴²But Jesus called them to *Himself* and

---

10:19 [a]Exodus 20:12–16; Deuteronomy 5:16–20
10:24 [a]NU-Text omits *for those who trust in riches.*
10:29 [a]NU-Text omits *or wife.*

said to them, "You know that those who are considered rulers over the Gentiles lord it over them, and their great ones exercise authority over them. ⁴³Yet it shall not be so among you; but whoever desires to become great among you shall be your servant. ⁴⁴And whoever of you desires to be first shall be slave of all. ⁴⁵For even the Son of Man did not come to be served, but to serve, and to give His life a ransom for many."

Jesus Heals Blind Bartimaeus

⁴⁶Now they came to Jericho. As He went out of Jericho with His disciples and a great multitude, blind Bartimaeus, the son of Timaeus, sat by the road begging. ⁴⁷And when he heard that it was Jesus of Nazareth, he began to cry out and say, "Jesus, Son of David, have mercy on me!"

⁴⁸Then many warned him to be quiet; but he cried out all the more, "Son of David, have mercy on me!"

⁴⁹So Jesus stood still and commanded him to be called.

Then they called the blind man, saying to him, "Be of good cheer. Rise, He is calling you."

⁵⁰And throwing aside his garment, he rose and came to Jesus.

⁵¹So Jesus answered and said to him, "What do you want Me to do for you?"

The blind man said to Him, "Rabboni, that I may receive my sight."

⁵²Then Jesus said to him, "Go your way; your faith has made you well." And immediately he received his sight and followed Jesus on the road.

The Triumphal Entry

11 Now when they drew near Jerusalem, to Bethphageᵃ and Bethany, at the Mount of Olives, He sent two of His disciples; ²and He said to them, "Go into the village opposite you; and as soon as you have entered it you will find a colt tied, on which no one has sat. Loose it and bring *it.* ³And if anyone says to you, 'Why are you doing this?' say, 'The Lord has need of it,' and immediately he will send it here."

⁴So they went their way, and found theᵃ colt tied by the door outside on the street, and they loosed it. ⁵But some of those who stood there said to them, "What are you doing, loosing the colt?"

11:1 ᵃM-Text reads *Bethsphage.*   **11:4** ᵃNU-Text and M-Text read *a.*

SERVICE

". . . whoever desires to become great among you shall be your servant."

MARK 10:43

President George H.W. Bush

THE USE OF POWER

In his 1989 Inaugural Address, George H.W. Bush stated:

We meet on democracy's front porch, a good place to talk as neighbors and as friends. For this is a day when our nation is made whole, when our differences, for a moment, are suspended.

And my first act as President is a prayer. I ask you to bow your heads:

Heavenly Father, we bow our heads and thank You for Your love. Accept our thanks for the peace that yields this day and the shared faith that makes its continuance likely. Make us strong to do Your work, willing to heed and hear Your will, and write on our hearts these words: "Use power to help people." For we are given power not to advance our own purposes, nor to make a great show in the world, nor a name. There is but one just use of power, and it is to serve people. Help us to remember it, Lord. Amen.

6And they spoke to them just as Jesus had commanded. So they let them go. 7Then they brought the colt to Jesus and threw their clothes on it, and He sat on it. 8And many spread their clothes on the road, and others cut down leafy branches from the trees and spread *them* on the road. 9Then those who went before and those who followed cried out, saying:

"Hosanna!
*'Blessed is He who comes in the name of the LORD!'*a
10   Blessed *is* the kingdom of our father David
    That comes in the name of the Lord!a
    Hosanna in the highest!"

11And Jesus went into Jerusalem and into the temple. So when He had looked around at all things, as the hour was already late, He went out to Bethany with the twelve.

The Fig Tree Withered

12Now the next day, when they had come out from Bethany, He was hungry. 13And seeing from afar a fig tree having leaves, He went to see if perhaps He would find something on it. When He came to it, He found nothing but leaves, for it was not the season for figs. 14In response Jesus said to it, "Let no one eat fruit from you ever again."

And His disciples heard *it.*

Jesus Cleanses the Temple

15So they came to Jerusalem. Then Jesus went into the temple and began to drive out those who bought and sold in the temple, and overturned the tables of the money changers and the seats of those who sold doves. 16And He would not allow anyone to carry wares through the temple. 17Then He taught, saying to them, "Is it not written, *'My house shall be called a house of prayer for all nations'*?a But you have made it a *'den of thieves.'"*b

18And the scribes and chief priests heard it and sought how they might destroy Him; for they feared Him, because all the people were astonished at His teaching. 19When evening had come, He went out of the city.

The Lesson of the Withered Fig Tree

20Now in the morning, as they passed by, they saw the fig tree dried up from the roots. 21And Peter, remembering, said to Him, "Rabbi, look! The fig tree which You cursed has withered away."

22So Jesus answered and said to them, "Have faith in God. 23For assuredly, I say to you, whoever says to this mountain, 'Be removed and be cast into the sea,' and does not doubt in his heart, but believes that those things he says will be done, he will have whatever he says. 24Therefore I say to you, whatever things you ask when you pray, believe that you receive *them,* and you will have *them.*

Forgiveness and Prayer

25"And whenever you stand praying, if you have anything against anyone, forgive him, that your Father in heaven may also forgive you your trespasses. 26But if you do not forgive, neither will your Father in heaven forgive your trespasses."a

Jesus' Authority Questioned

27Then they came again to Jerusalem. And as He was walking in the temple, the chief priests, the scribes, and the elders came to Him. 28And they said to Him, "By what authority are You doing these things? And who gave You this authority to do these things?"

29But Jesus answered and said to them, "I also will ask you one question; then answer Me, and I will tell you by what authority I do these things: 30The baptism of John—was it from heaven or from men? Answer Me."

31And they reasoned among themselves, saying, "If we say, 'From heaven,' He will say, 'Why then did you not believe him?' 32But if we say, 'From men'"—they feared the people, for all counted John to have been a prophet indeed. 33So they answered and said to Jesus, "We do not know."

And Jesus answered and said to them, "Neither will I tell you by what authority I do these things."

11:9 aPsalm 118:26   **11:10** aNU-Text omits *in the name of the Lord.*   **11:17** aIsaiah 56:7   bJeremiah 7:11   **11:26** aNU-Text omits this verse.

The Parable of the Wicked Vinedressers

12 Then He began to speak to them in parables: "A man planted a vineyard and set a hedge around *it,* dug *a place for* the wine vat and built a tower. And he leased it to vinedressers and went into a far country. ²Now at vintage-time he sent a servant to the vinedressers, that he might receive some of the fruit of the vineyard from the vinedressers. ³And they took *him* and beat him and sent *him* away empty-handed. ⁴Again he sent them another servant, and at him they threw stones,ᵃ wounded *him* in the head, and sent *him* away shamefully treated. ⁵And again he sent another, and him they killed; and many others, beating some and killing some. ⁶Therefore still having one son, his beloved, he also sent him to them last, saying, 'They will respect my son.' ⁷But those vinedressers said among themselves, 'This is the heir. Come, let us kill him, and the inheritance will be ours.' ⁸So they took him and killed *him* and cast *him* out of the vineyard.

⁹"Therefore what will the owner of the vineyard do? He will come and destroy the vinedressers, and give the vineyard to others. ¹⁰Have you not even read this Scripture:

'The stone which the builders rejected
Has become the chief cornerstone.
¹¹   This was the LORD's doing,
And it is marvelous in our eyes'?"ᵃ

¹²And they sought to lay hands on Him, but feared the multitude, for they knew He had spoken the parable against them. So they left Him and went away.

The Pharisees: Is It Lawful to Pay Taxes to Caesar?

¹³Then they sent to Him some of the Pharisees and the Herodians, to catch Him in *His* words. ¹⁴When they had come, they said to Him, "Teacher, we know that You are true, and care about no one; for You do not regard the person of men, but teach the way of God in truth. Is it lawful to pay taxes to Caesar, or not? ¹⁵Shall we pay, or shall we not pay?"

But He, knowing their hypocrisy, said to them, "Why do you test Me? Bring Me a denarius that I may see *it.*" ¹⁶So they brought *it.*

And He said to them, "Whose image and inscription *is* this?" They said to Him, "Caesar's."

¹⁷And Jesus answered and said to them, "Render to Caesar the things that are Caesar's, and to God the things that are God's."

And they marveled at Him.

HONOR

"Render to Caesar the things that are Caesar's. . . ."   MARK 12:17

Christ or Chaos

Peter Marshall, the chaplain of the U.S. Senate (1947–1949), issued a call for Americans to honor God:

> The choice before us is plain: Christ or chaos, conviction or compromise, discipline or disintegration. I am rather tired of hearing about our rights and privileges as American citizens. The time is come—it is now—when we ought to hear about the duties and responsibilities of our citizenship. America's future depends upon her accepting and demonstrating God's government.

The Sadducees: What About the Resurrection?

¹⁸Then *some* Sadducees, who say there is no resurrection, came to Him; and they asked Him, saying: ¹⁹"Teacher, Moses wrote to us that if a man's brother dies, and leaves *his* wife behind, and leaves no children, his brother should take his wife and raise up offspring for his brother. ²⁰Now there were seven brothers. The first took a wife; and dying, he left no offspring. ²¹And the second took her, and he died; nor did he leave any offspring. And the third likewise. ²²So the seven had her and left no offspring. Last of all the woman died also. ²³Therefore, in the resurrection, when they rise, whose wife will she be? For all seven had her as wife."

12:4 ᵃNU-Text omits *and at him they threw stones.*
12:11 ᵃPsalm 118:22, 23

24Jesus answered and said to them, "Are you not therefore mistaken, because you do not know the Scriptures nor the power of God? 25For when they rise from the dead, they neither marry nor are given in marriage, but are like angels in heaven. 26But concerning the dead, that they rise, have you not read in the book of Moses, in the *burning* bush *passage*, how God spoke to him, saying, *'I am the God of Abraham, the God of Isaac, and the God of Jacob'*?ᵃ 27He is not the God of the dead, but the God of the living. You are therefore greatly mistaken."

The Scribes: Which Is the First Commandment of All?

28Then one of the scribes came, and having heard them reasoning together, perceivingᵃ that He had answered them well, asked Him, "Which is the first commandment of all?"

29Jesus answered him, "The first of all the commandments *is: 'Hear, O Israel, the* LORD *our God, the* LORD *is one.* 30And you shall love the LORD your God with all your heart, with all your soul, with all your mind, and with all your strength.'ᵃ This *is* the first commandment.ᵇ 31And the second, like *it, is* this: *'You shall love your neighbor as yourself.'ᵃ* There is no other commandment greater than these."

32So the scribe said to Him, "Well *said,* Teacher. You have spoken the truth, for there is one God, and there is no other but He. 33And to love Him with all the heart, with all the understanding, with all the soul,ᵃ and with all the strength, and to love one's neighbor as oneself, is more than all the whole burnt offerings and sacrifices."

34Now when Jesus saw that he answered wisely, He said to him, "You are not far from the kingdom of God."

But after that no one dared question Him.

Jesus: How Can David Call His Descendant Lord?

35Then Jesus answered and said, while He taught in the temple, "How *is it* that the scribes say that the Christ is the Son of David? 36For David himself said by the Holy Spirit:

'The LORD said to my Lord,
  "Sit at My right hand,
    Till I make Your enemies Your
      footstool." 'ᵃ

37Therefore David himself calls Him *'Lord';* how is He *then* his Son?"

And the common people heard Him gladly.

Beware of the Scribes

38Then He said to them in His teaching, "Beware of the scribes, who desire to go around in long robes, *love* greetings in the marketplaces, 39the best seats in the synagogues, and the best places at feasts, 40who devour widows' houses, and for a pretense make long prayers. These will receive greater condemnation."

The Widow's Two Mites

41Now Jesus sat opposite the treasury and saw how the people put money into the treasury. And many *who were* rich put in much. 42Then one poor widow came and threw in two mites,ᵃ which make a quadrans. 43So He called His disciples to *Himself* and said to them, "Assuredly, I say to you that this poor widow has put in more than all those who have given to the treasury; 44for they all put in out of their abundance, but she out of her poverty put in all that she had, her whole livelihood."

Jesus Predicts the Destruction of the Temple

13 Then as He went out of the temple, one of His disciples said to Him, "Teacher, see what manner of stones and what buildings *are here!*"

2And Jesus answered and said to him, "Do you see these great buildings? Not *one* stone shall be left upon another, that shall not be thrown down."

The Signs of the Times and the End of the Age

3Now as He sat on the Mount of Olives opposite the temple, Peter, James, John, and

---

12:26 ᵃExodus 3:6, 15   **12:28** ᵃNU-Text reads *seeing.*   **12:30** ᵃDeuteronomy 6:4, 5 ᵇNU-Text omits this sentence.   **12:31** ᵃLeviticus 19:18   **12:33** ᵃNU-Text omits *with all the soul.*   **12:36** ᵃPsalm 110:1   **12:42** ᵃGreek *lepta,* very small copper coins worth a fraction of a penny

Andrew asked Him privately, [4]"Tell us, when will these things be? And what *will be* the sign when all these things will be fulfilled?"

[5]And Jesus, answering them, began to say: "Take heed that no one deceives you. [6]For many will come in My name, saying, 'I am *He*,' and will deceive many. [7]But when you hear of wars and rumors of wars, do not be troubled; for *such things* must happen, but the end *is* not yet. [8]For nation will rise against nation, and kingdom against kingdom. And there will be earthquakes in various places, and there will be famines and troubles.[a] These *are* the beginnings of sorrows.

[9]"But watch out for yourselves, for they will deliver you up to councils, and you will be beaten in the synagogues. You will be brought[a] before rulers and kings for My sake, for a testimony to them. [10]And the gospel must first be preached to all the nations. [11]But when they arrest *you* and deliver you up, do not worry beforehand, or premeditate[a] what you will speak. But whatever is given you in that hour, speak that; for it is not you who speak, but the Holy Spirit. [12]Now brother will betray brother to death, and a father *his* child; and children will rise up against parents and cause them to be put to death. [13]And you will be hated by all for My name's sake. But he who endures to the end shall be saved.

The Great Tribulation

[14]"So when you see the '*abomination of desolation,*'[a] spoken of by Daniel the prophet,[b] standing where it ought not" (let the reader understand), "then let those who are in Judea flee to the mountains. [15]Let him who is on the housetop not go down into the house, nor enter to take anything out of his house. [16]And let him who is in the field not go back to get his clothes. [17]But woe to those who are pregnant and to those who are nursing babies in those days! [18]And pray that your flight may not be in winter. [19]For *in* those days there will be tribulation, such as has not been since the beginning of the creation which God created until this time, nor ever shall be. [20]And unless the Lord had shortened those days, no flesh would be saved; but for the elect's sake, whom He chose, He shortened the days.

[21]"Then if anyone says to you, 'Look, here *is* the Christ!' or, 'Look, *He is* there!' do not believe it. [22]For false christs and false prophets will rise and show signs and wonders to deceive, if possible, even the elect. [23]But take heed; see, I have told you all things beforehand.

The Coming of the Son of Man

[24]"But in those days, after that tribulation, the sun will be darkened, and the moon will not give its light; [25]the stars of heaven will fall, and the powers in the heavens will be shaken. [26]Then they will see the Son of Man coming in the clouds with great power and glory. [27]And then He will send His angels, and gather together His elect from the four winds, from the farthest part of earth to the farthest part of heaven.

The Parable of the Fig Tree

[28]"Now learn this parable from the fig tree: When its branch has already become tender, and puts forth leaves, you know that summer is near. [29]So you also, when you see these things happening, know that it[a] is near—at the doors! [30]Assuredly, I say to you, this generation will by no means pass away till all these things take place. [31]Heaven and earth will pass away, but My words will by no means pass away.

No One Knows the Day or Hour

[32]"But of that day and hour no one knows, not even the angels in heaven, nor the Son, but only the Father. [33]Take heed, watch and pray; for you do not know when the time is. [34]*It is* like a man going to a far country, who left his house and gave authority to his servants, and to each his work, and commanded the doorkeeper to watch. [35]Watch therefore, for you do not know when the master of the house is coming—in the evening, at midnight, at the crowing

---

13:8 [a]NU-Text omits *and troubles.*   **13:9** [a]NU-Text and M-Text read *will stand.*   **13:11** [a]NU-Text omits *or premeditate.*   **13:14** [a]Daniel 11:31; 12:11 [b]NU-Text omits *spoken of by Daniel the prophet.*   **13:29** [a]Or *He*

of the rooster, or in the morning— ³⁶lest, coming suddenly, he find you sleeping. ³⁷And what I say to you, I say to all: Watch!"

The Plot to Kill Jesus

14 After two days it was the Passover and *the Feast* of Unleavened Bread. And the chief priests and the scribes sought how they might take Him by trickery and put *Him* to death. ²But they said, "Not during the feast, lest there be an uproar of the people."

The Anointing at Bethany

³And being in Bethany at the house of Simon the leper, as He sat at the table, a woman came having an alabaster flask of very costly oil of spikenard. Then she broke the flask and poured *it* on His head. ⁴But there were some who were indignant among themselves, and said, "Why was this fragrant oil wasted? ⁵For it might have been sold for more than three hundred denarii and given to the poor." And they criticized her sharply.

⁶But Jesus said, "Let her alone. Why do you trouble her? She has done a good work for Me. ⁷For you have the poor with you always, and whenever you wish you may do them good; but Me you do not have always. ⁸She has done what she could. She has come beforehand to anoint My body for burial. ⁹Assuredly, I say to you, wherever this gospel is preached in the whole world, what this woman has done will also be told as a memorial to her."

Judas Agrees to Betray Jesus

¹⁰Then Judas Iscariot, one of the twelve, went to the chief priests to betray Him to them. ¹¹And when they heard *it,* they were glad, and promised to give him money. So he sought how he might conveniently betray Him.

Jesus Celebrates the Passover with His Disciples

¹²Now on the first day of Unleavened Bread, when they killed the Passover *lamb,* His disciples said to Him, "Where do You want us to go and prepare, that You may eat the Passover?"

¹³And He sent out two of His disciples and said to them, "Go into the city, and a man will meet you carrying a pitcher of water; follow him. ¹⁴Wherever he goes in, say to the master of the house, 'The Teacher says, "Where is the guest room in which I may eat the Passover with My disciples?"' ¹⁵Then he will show you a large upper room, furnished *and* prepared; there make ready for us."

¹⁶So His disciples went out, and came into the city, and found it just as He had said to them; and they prepared the Passover.

¹⁷In the evening He came with the twelve. ¹⁸Now as they sat and ate, Jesus said, "Assuredly, I say to you, one of you who eats with Me will betray Me."

¹⁹And they began to be sorrowful, and to say to Him one by one, "*Is it I?*" And another *said,* "*Is it I?*"ᵃ

²⁰He answered and said to them, "*It is* one of the twelve, who dips with Me in the dish. ²¹The Son of Man indeed goes just as it is written of Him, but woe to that man by whom the Son of Man is betrayed! It would have been good for that man if he had never been born."

Jesus Institutes the Lord's Supper

²²And as they were eating, Jesus took bread, blessed and broke *it,* and gave *it* to them and said, "Take, eat;ᵃ this is My body."

²³Then He took the cup, and when He had given thanks He gave *it* to them, and they all drank from it. ²⁴And He said to them, "This is My blood of the newᵃ covenant, which is shed for many. ²⁵Assuredly, I say to you, I will no longer drink of the fruit of the vine until that day when I drink it new in the kingdom of God."

²⁶And when they had sung a hymn, they went out to the Mount of Olives.

Jesus Predicts Peter's Denial

²⁷Then Jesus said to them, "All of you will be made to stumble because of Me this night,ᵃ for it is written:

14:19 ᵃNU-Text omits this sentence.
14:22 ᵃNU-Text omits *eat.*   **14:24** ᵃNU-Text omits *new.*   **14:27** ᵃNU-Text omits *because of Me this night.*

*'I will strike the Shepherd,
And the sheep will be scattered.'*[b]

[28]"But after I have been raised, I will go before you to Galilee."

[29]Peter said to Him, "Even if all are made to stumble, yet I *will* not *be*."

[30]Jesus said to him, "Assuredly, I say to you that today, *even* this night, before the rooster crows twice, you will deny Me three times."

[31]But he spoke more vehemently, "If I have to die with You, I will not deny You!" And they all said likewise.

The Prayer in the Garden

[32]Then they came to a place which was named Gethsemane; and He said to His disciples, "Sit here while I pray." [33]And He took Peter, James, and John with Him, and He began to be troubled and deeply distressed. [34]Then He said to them, "My soul is exceedingly sorrowful, *even* to death. Stay here and watch."

[35]He went a little farther, and fell on the ground, and prayed that if it were possible, the hour might pass from Him. [36]And He said, "Abba, Father, all things *are* possible for You. Take this cup away from Me; nevertheless, not what I will, but what You *will*."

[37]Then He came and found them sleeping, and said to Peter, "Simon, are you sleeping? Could you not watch one hour? [38]Watch and pray, lest you enter into temptation. The spirit indeed *is* willing, but the flesh *is* weak."

[39]Again He went away and prayed, and spoke the same words. [40]And when He returned, He found them asleep again, for their eyes were heavy; and they did not know what to answer Him.

[41]Then He came the third time and said to them, "Are you still sleeping and resting? It is enough! The hour has come; behold, the Son of Man is being betrayed into the hands of sinners. [42]Rise, let us be going. See, My betrayer is at hand."

Betrayal and Arrest in Gethsemane

[43]And immediately, while He was still speaking, Judas, one of the twelve, with a great multitude with swords and clubs, came from the chief priests and the scribes and the elders. [44]Now His betrayer had given them a signal, saying, "Whomever I kiss, He is the One; seize Him and lead *Him* away safely."

[45]As soon as he had come, immediately he went up to Him and said to Him, "Rabbi, Rabbi!" and kissed Him. [46]Then they laid their hands on Him and took Him. [47]And one of those who stood by drew his sword and struck the servant of the high priest, and cut off his ear.

[48]Then Jesus answered and said to them, "Have you come out, as against a robber, with swords and clubs to take Me? [49]I was daily with you in the temple teaching, and you did not seize Me. But the Scriptures must be fulfilled."

[50]Then they all forsook Him and fled.

A Young Man Flees Naked

[51]Now a certain young man followed Him, having a linen cloth thrown around *his* naked *body*. And the young men laid hold of him, [52]and he left the linen cloth and fled from them naked.

Jesus Faces the Sanhedrin

[53]And they led Jesus away to the high priest; and with him were assembled all the chief priests, the elders, and the scribes. [54]But Peter followed Him at a distance, right into the courtyard of the high priest. And he sat with the servants and warmed himself at the fire.

[55]Now the chief priests and all the council sought testimony against Jesus to put Him to death, but found none. [56]For many bore false witness against Him, but their testimonies did not agree.

[57]Then some rose up and bore false witness against Him, saying, [58]"We heard Him say, 'I will destroy this temple made with hands, and within three days I will build another made without hands.'" [59]But not even then did their testimony agree.

[60]And the high priest stood up in the midst and asked Jesus, saying, "Do You answer nothing? What *is it* these men testify

14:27 [b]Zechariah 13:7

against You?" [61]But He kept silent and answered nothing.

Again the high priest asked Him, saying to Him, "Are You the Christ, the Son of the Blessed?"

[62]Jesus said, "I am. And you will see the Son of Man sitting at the right hand of the Power, and coming with the clouds of heaven."

[63]Then the high priest tore his clothes and said, "What further need do we have of witnesses? [64]You have heard the blasphemy! What do you think?"

And they all condemned Him to be deserving of death.

[65]Then some began to spit on Him, and to blindfold Him, and to beat Him, and to say to Him, "Prophesy!" And the officers struck Him with the palms of their hands.[a]

Peter Denies Jesus, and Weeps

[66]Now as Peter was below in the courtyard, one of the servant girls of the high priest came. [67]And when she saw Peter warming himself, she looked at him and said, "You also were with Jesus of Nazareth."

[68]But he denied it, saying, "I neither know nor understand what you are saying." And he went out on the porch, and a rooster crowed.

[69]And the servant girl saw him again, and began to say to those who stood by, "This is one of them." [70]But he denied it again.

And a little later those who stood by said to Peter again, "Surely you are one of them; for you are a Galilean, and your speech shows it."[a]

[71]Then he began to curse and swear, "I do not know this Man of whom you speak!"

[72]A second time the rooster crowed. Then Peter called to mind the word that Jesus had said to him, "Before the rooster crows twice, you will deny Me three times." And when he thought about it, he wept.

Jesus Faces Pilate

15 Immediately, in the morning, the chief priests held a consultation with the elders and scribes and the whole council; and they bound Jesus, led Him away, and delivered Him to Pilate. [2]Then Pilate asked Him, "Are You the King of the Jews?"

He answered and said to him, "It is as you say."

[3]And the chief priests accused Him of many things, but He answered nothing. [4]Then Pilate asked Him again, saying, "Do You answer nothing? See how many things they testify against You!"[a] [5]But Jesus still answered nothing, so that Pilate marveled.

Taking the Place of Barabbas

[6]Now at the feast he was accustomed to releasing one prisoner to them, whomever they requested. [7]And there was one named Barabbas, who was chained with his fellow rebels; they had committed murder in the rebellion. [8]Then the multitude, crying aloud,[a] began to ask him to do just as he had always done for them. [9]But Pilate answered them, saying, "Do you want me to release to you the King of the Jews?" [10]For he knew that the chief priests had handed Him over because of envy.

[11]But the chief priests stirred up the crowd, so that he should rather release Barabbas to them. [12]Pilate answered and said to them again, "What then do you want me to do with Him whom you call the King of the Jews?"

[13]So they cried out again, "Crucify Him!"

[14]Then Pilate said to them, "Why, what evil has He done?"

But they cried out all the more, "Crucify Him!"

[15]So Pilate, wanting to gratify the crowd, released Barabbas to them; and he delivered Jesus, after he had scourged Him, to be crucified.

The Soldiers Mock Jesus

[16]Then the soldiers led Him away into the hall called Praetorium, and they called together the whole garrison. [17]And they clothed Him with purple; and they twisted a crown of thorns, put it on His head, [18]and began to salute Him, "Hail, King of the Jews!" [19]Then they struck Him on the head

---

14:65 [a]NU-Text reads received Him with slaps.
14:70 [a]NU-Text omits and your speech shows it.
15:4 [a]NU-Text reads of which they accuse You.
15:8 [a]NU-Text reads going up.

with a reed and spat on Him; and bowing the knee, they worshiped Him. [20]And when they had mocked Him, they took the purple off Him, put His own clothes on Him, and led Him out to crucify Him.

The King on a Cross

[21]Then they compelled a certain man, Simon a Cyrenian, the father of Alexander and Rufus, as he was coming out of the country and passing by, to bear His cross. [22]And they brought Him to the place Golgotha, which is translated, Place of a Skull. [23]Then they gave Him wine mingled with myrrh to drink, but He did not take *it*. [24]And when they crucified Him, they divided His garments, casting lots for them *to determine* what every man should take.

[25]Now it was the third hour, and they crucified Him. [26]And the inscription of His accusation was written above:

THE KING OF THE JEWS.

[27]With Him they also crucified two robbers, one on His right and the other on His left. [28]So the Scripture was fulfilled[a] which says, *"And He was numbered with the transgressors."*[b]

[29]And those who passed by blasphemed Him, wagging their heads and saying, "Aha! *You* who destroy the temple and build *it* in three days, [30]save Yourself, and come down from the cross!"

[31]Likewise the chief priests also, mocking among themselves with the scribes, said, "He saved others; Himself He cannot save. [32]Let the Christ, the King of Israel, descend now from the cross, that we may see and believe."[a]

Even those who were crucified with Him reviled Him.

Jesus Dies on the Cross

[33]Now when the sixth hour had come, there was darkness over the whole land until the ninth hour. [34]And at the ninth hour Jesus cried out with a loud voice, saying, "Eloi, Eloi, lama sabachthani?" which is translated, *"My God, My God, why have You forsaken Me?"*[a]

[35]Some of those who stood by, when they heard *that*, said, "Look, He is calling for Elijah!" [36]Then someone ran and filled a sponge full of sour wine, put *it* on a reed, and offered *it* to Him to drink, saying, "Let Him alone; let us see if Elijah will come to take Him down."

[37]And Jesus cried out with a loud voice, and breathed His last.

[38]Then the veil of the temple was torn in two from top to bottom. [39]So when the centurion, who stood opposite Him, saw that He cried out like this and breathed His last,[a] he said, "Truly this Man was the Son of God!"

[40]There were also women looking on from afar, among whom were Mary Magdalene, Mary the mother of James the Less and of Joses, and Salome, [41]who also followed Him and ministered to Him when He was in Galilee, and many other women who came up with Him to Jerusalem.

Jesus Buried in Joseph's Tomb

[42]Now when evening had come, because it was the Preparation Day, that is, the day before the Sabbath, [43]Joseph of Arimathea, a prominent council member, who was himself waiting for the kingdom of God, coming and taking courage, went in to Pilate and asked for the body of Jesus. [44]Pilate marveled that He was already dead; and summoning the centurion, he asked him if He had been dead for some time. [45]So when he found out from the centurion, he granted the body to Joseph. [46]Then he bought fine linen, took Him down, and wrapped Him in the linen. And he laid Him in a tomb which had been hewn out of the rock, and rolled a stone against the door of the tomb. [47]And Mary Magdalene and Mary *the mother* of Joses observed where He was laid.

He Is Risen

16 Now when the Sabbath was past, Mary Magdalene, Mary *the mother* of James, and Salome bought spices, that they might come and anoint Him. [2]Very

---

15:28 [a]Isaiah 53:12 [b]NU-Text omits this verse.
15:32 [a]M-Text reads *believe Him.*
15:34 [a]Psalm 22:1   **15:39** [a]NU-Text reads *that He thus breathed His last.*

early in the morning, on the first *day* of the week, they came to the tomb when the sun had risen. [3]And they said among themselves, "Who will roll away the stone from the door of the tomb for us?" [4]But when they looked up, they saw that the stone had been rolled away—for it was very large. [5]And entering the tomb, they saw a young man clothed in a long white robe sitting on the right side; and they were alarmed.

[6]But he said to them, "Do not be alarmed. You seek Jesus of Nazareth, who was crucified. He is risen! He is not here. See the place where they laid Him. [7]But go, tell His disciples—and Peter—that He is going before you into Galilee; there you will see Him, as He said to you."

[8]So they went out quickly[a] and fled from the tomb, for they trembled and were amazed. And they said nothing to anyone, for they were afraid.

Mary Magdalene Sees the Risen Lord

[9]Now when *He* rose early on the first *day* of the week, He appeared first to Mary Magdalene, out of whom He had cast seven demons. [10]She went and told those who had been with Him, as they mourned and wept. [11]And when they heard that He was alive and had been seen by her, they did not believe.

Jesus Appears to Two Disciples

[12]After that, He appeared in another form to two of them as they walked and went into the country. [13]And they went and told *it* to the rest, *but* they did not believe them either.

16:8 [a]NU-Text and M-Text omit *quickly.*

INSPIRING

"Go into all the world and preach the gospel to every creature."

Mark 16:15

Haystack Monument
Williams College

THE HAYSTACK PRAYER MEETING

In August 1806, five Williams College students met in a field for one of their twice-weekly prayer meetings, when a thunderstorm drove them to take refuge in a nearby haystack. Continuing in prayer, Samuel John Mills shared his burden that Christianity be sent abroad, and the group prayed that American missions would spread Christianity through the East. The Haystack Prayer Meeting held in Williamstown, Massachusetts, is viewed by many scholars as the spark that ignited American support for world missions for subsequent decades.

In 1808, the Haystack Prayer group and other Williams students formed "The Brethren," a society organized to "effect, in the persons of its members, a mission to the heathen." Within a few years, they inspired the founding of the American Board of Commissioners for Foreign Missions (ABCFM). Several of the students, including Adoniram Judson, went to Asia as missionaries (the first foreign missionaries sent from America in 1812), and Samuel Mills stayed stateside to recruit others and later helped organize the American Bible Society and the United Foreign Missionary Society.

In its first fifty years, the ABCFM sent out over 1,250 missionaries. In 1961, the American Board merged to form the United Church Board for World Missions (UCBWM). After 150 years, the American Board had sent out nearly 5,000 missionaries to 34 different fields, and it all began with five young men praying in a haystack.

The Great Commission

¹⁴Later He appeared to the eleven as they sat at the table; and He rebuked their unbelief and hardness of heart, because they did not believe those who had seen Him after He had risen. ¹⁵And He said to them, "Go into all the world and preach the gospel to every creature. ¹⁶He who believes and is baptized will be saved; but he who does not believe will be condemned. ¹⁷And these signs will follow those who believe: In My name they will cast out demons; they will speak with new tongues; ¹⁸they[a] will take up serpents; and if they drink anything deadly, it will by no means hurt them; they will lay hands on the sick, and they will recover."

Christ Ascends to God's Right Hand

¹⁹So then, after the Lord had spoken to them, He was received up into heaven, and sat down at the right hand of God. ²⁰And they went out and preached everywhere, the Lord working with *them* and confirming the word through the accompanying signs. Amen.[a]

16:18 [a]NU-Text reads *and in their hands they will.*
16:20 [a]Verses 9–20 are bracketed in NU-Text as not original. They are lacking in Codex Sinaiticus and Codex Vaticanus, although nearly all other manuscripts of Mark contain them.

LUKE

Author: Luke

When Written: Around A.D. 62

Theme: Jesus the Son of Man

Key Verse: Luke 19:10—". . . for the Son of Man has come to seek and to save that which was lost."

Key Chapter: Luke 15—The three parables of the Lost Sheep, the Lost Coin, and the Lost Son capture the crux of this gospel: that God through Christ has come to seek and to save lost people.

Luke, a physician, writes with the compassion of a family doctor as he carefully documents the perfect humanity of the Son of Man, Jesus Christ. He builds the gospel narrative on the foundation of historical reliability, emphasizing Jesus' ancestry, birth, and early life before moving chronologically through His earthly ministry. Growing belief and growing opposition develop side by side, with the opposition finally leading to the death of the Son of Man on the cross. But Jesus' resurrection insures that His purpose of saving the lost is fulfilled.

Christianity welcomes examination into its authenticity, that the inquirer might "know the certainty" of its truths (Luke 1:4). Alexander Hamilton, a signer of the Constitution and one of America's first constitutional lawyers, made such an investigation and concluded, "I have carefully examined the evidences of the Christian religion, and if I was sitting as a juror upon its authenticity, I would unhesitatingly give my verdict in its favor. I can prove its truth as clearly as any proposition ever submitted to the mind of man."

LUKE

Dedication to Theophilus

1 Inasmuch as many have taken in hand to set in order a narrative of those things which have been fulfilled[a] among us, ²just as those who from the beginning were eyewitnesses and ministers of the word delivered them to us, ³it seemed good to me also, having had perfect understanding of all things from the very first, to write to you an orderly account, most excellent Theophilus, ⁴that you may know the certainty of those things in which you were instructed.

John's Birth Announced to Zacharias

⁵There was in the days of Herod, the king of Judea, a certain priest named Zacharias, of the division of Abijah. His wife *was* of the daughters of Aaron, and her name *was* Elizabeth. ⁶And they were both righteous before God, walking in all the commandments and ordinances of the Lord blameless. ⁷But they had no child, because Elizabeth was barren, and they were both well advanced in years.

⁸So it was, that while he was serving as priest before God in the order of his division, ⁹according to the custom of the priesthood, his lot fell to burn incense when he went into the temple of the Lord. ¹⁰And the whole multitude of the people was praying outside at the hour of incense. ¹¹Then an angel of the Lord appeared to him, standing on the right side of the altar of incense. ¹²And when Zacharias saw *him,* he was troubled, and fear fell upon him.

¹³But the angel said to him, "Do not be afraid, Zacharias, for your prayer is heard; and your wife Elizabeth will bear you a son, and you shall call his name John. ¹⁴And you will have joy and gladness, and many will rejoice at his birth. ¹⁵For he will be great in the sight of the Lord, and shall drink neither wine nor strong drink. He will also be filled with the Holy Spirit, even from his mother's womb. ¹⁶And he will turn many of the children of Israel to the Lord their God. ¹⁷He will also go before Him in the spirit and power of Elijah, *'to turn the hearts of the fathers to the children,'*[a] and the disobedient to the wisdom of the just, to make ready a people prepared for the Lord."

¹⁸And Zacharias said to the angel, "How shall I know this? For I am an old man, and my wife is well advanced in years."

¹⁹And the angel answered and said to him, "I am Gabriel, who stands in the presence of God, and was sent to speak to you and bring you these glad tidings. ²⁰But behold, you will be mute and not able to speak until the day these things take place, because you did not believe my words which will be fulfilled in their own time."

²¹And the people waited for Zacharias, and marveled that he lingered so long in the temple. ²²But when he came out, he could not speak to them; and they perceived that he had seen a vision in the temple, for he beckoned to them and remained speechless.

²³So it was, as soon as the days of his service were completed, that he departed to his own house. ²⁴Now after those days his wife Elizabeth conceived; and she hid herself five months, saying, ²⁵"Thus the Lord has dealt with me, in the days when He looked on *me,* to take away my reproach among people."

Christ's Birth Announced to Mary

²⁶Now in the sixth month the angel Gabriel was sent by God to a city of Galilee named Nazareth, ²⁷to a virgin betrothed to a man whose name was Joseph, of the house of David. The virgin's name *was* Mary. ²⁸And having come in, the angel said to her, "Rejoice, highly favored *one,* the Lord *is* with you; blessed *are* you among women!"[a]

1:1 [a]Or *are most surely believed*
1:17 [a]Malachi 4:5, 6   **1:28** [a]NU-Text omits *blessed are you among women.*

29But when she saw *him*,ᵃ she was troubled at his saying, and considered what manner of greeting this was. 30Then the angel said to her, "Do not be afraid, Mary, for you have found favor with God. 31And behold, you will conceive in your womb and bring forth a Son, and shall call His name JESUS. 32He will be great, and will be called the Son of the Highest; and the Lord God will give Him the throne of His father David. 33And He will reign over the house of Jacob forever, and of His kingdom there will be no end."

34Then Mary said to the angel, "How can this be, since I do not know a man?"

35And the angel answered and said to her, "*The* Holy Spirit will come upon you, and the power of the Highest will overshadow you; therefore, also, that Holy One who is to be born will be called the Son of God. 36Now indeed, Elizabeth your relative has also conceived a son in her old age; and this is now the sixth month for her who was called barren. 37For with God nothing will be impossible."

38Then Mary said, "Behold the maidservant of the Lord! Let it be to me according to your word." And the angel departed from her.

Mary Visits Elizabeth

39Now Mary arose in those days and went into the hill country with haste, to a city of Judah, 40and entered the house of Zacharias and greeted Elizabeth. 41And it happened, when Elizabeth heard the greeting of Mary, that the babe leaped in her womb; and Elizabeth was filled with the Holy Spirit. 42Then she spoke out with a loud voice and said, "Blessed *are* you among women, and blessed *is* the fruit of your womb! 43But why *is* this *granted* to me, that the mother of my Lord should come to me? 44For indeed, as soon as the voice of your greeting sounded in my ears, the babe leaped in my womb for joy. 45Blessed *is* she who believed, for there will be a fulfillment of those things which were told her from the Lord."

The Song of Mary

46And Mary said:

"My soul magnifies the Lord,

47   And my spirit has rejoiced in God my
          Savior.
48   For He has regarded the lowly state
          of His maidservant;
      For behold, henceforth all generations
          will call me blessed.
49   For He who is mighty has done great
          things for me,
      And holy *is* His name.
50   And His mercy *is* on those who fear
          Him
      From generation to generation.
51   He has shown strength with His arm;
      He has scattered *the* proud in the
          imagination of their hearts.
52   He has put down the mighty from
          their thrones,
      And exalted *the* lowly.
53   He has filled *the* hungry with good
          things,
      And *the* rich He has sent away empty.
54   He has helped His servant Israel,
      In remembrance of *His* mercy,
55   As He spoke to our fathers,
      To Abraham and to his seed forever."

56And Mary remained with her about three months, and returned to her house.

Birth of John the Baptist

57Now Elizabeth's full time came for her to be delivered, and she brought forth a son. 58When her neighbors and relatives heard how the Lord had shown great mercy to her, they rejoiced with her.

Circumcision of John the Baptist

59So it was, on the eighth day, that they came to circumcise the child; and they would have called him by the name of his father, Zacharias. 60His mother answered and said, "No; he shall be called John."

61But they said to her, "There is no one among your relatives who is called by this name." 62So they made signs to his father—what he would have him called.

63And he asked for a writing tablet, and wrote, saying, "His name is John." So they all marveled. 64Immediately his mouth was opened and his tongue *loosed*, and he

---

1:29 ᵃNU-Text omits *when she saw him.*

spoke, praising God. ⁶⁵Then fear came on all who dwelt around them; and all these sayings were discussed throughout all the hill country of Judea. ⁶⁶And all those who heard *them* kept *them* in their hearts, saying, "What kind of child will this be?" And the hand of the Lord was with him.

Zacharias' Prophecy

⁶⁷Now his father Zacharias was filled with the Holy Spirit, and prophesied, saying:

68 "Blessed *is* the Lord God of Israel,
　　For He has visited and redeemed His
　　　people,
69 And has raised up a horn of salvation
　　　for us
　　In the house of His servant David,
70 As He spoke by the mouth of His holy
　　　prophets,
　　Who *have been* since the world began,
71 That we should be saved from our
　　　enemies
　　And from the hand of all who hate us,
72 To perform the mercy *promised* to our
　　　fathers
　　And to remember His holy covenant,
73 The oath which He swore to our father
　　　Abraham:
74 To grant us that we,
　　Being delivered from the hand of our
　　　enemies,
　　Might serve Him without fear,
75 In holiness and righteousness before
　　　Him all the days of our life.

76 "And you, child, will be called the
　　　prophet of the Highest;
　　For you will go before the face of the
　　　Lord to prepare His ways,
77 To give knowledge of salvation to His
　　　people
　　By the remission of their sins,
78 Through the tender mercy of our God,
　　With which the Dayspring from on
　　　high has visitedᵃ us;
79 To give light to those who sit in
　　　darkness and the shadow of death,
　　To guide our feet into the way of
　　　peace."

⁸⁰So the child grew and became strong in spirit, and was in the deserts till the day of his manifestation to Israel.

Christ Born of Mary

2 And it came to pass in those days *that* a decree went out from Caesar Augustus that all the world should be registered. ²This census first took place while Quirinius was governing Syria. ³So all went to be registered, everyone to his own city.

⁴Joseph also went up from Galilee, out of the city of Nazareth, into Judea, to the city of David, which is called Bethlehem, because he was of the house and lineage of David, ⁵to be registered with Mary, his betrothed wife,ᵃ who was with child. ⁶So it was, that while they were there, the days were completed for her to be delivered. ⁷And she brought forth her firstborn Son, and wrapped Him in swaddling cloths, and laid Him in a manger, because there was no room for them in the inn.

Glory in the Highest

⁸Now there were in the same country shepherds living out in the fields, keeping watch over their flock by night. ⁹And behold,ᵃ an angel of the Lord stood before them, and the glory of the Lord shone around them, and they were greatly afraid. ¹⁰Then the angel said to them, "Do not be afraid, for behold, I bring you good tidings of great joy which will be to all people. ¹¹For there is born to you this day in the city of David a Savior, who is Christ the Lord. ¹²And this *will be* the sign to you: You will find a Babe wrapped in swaddling cloths, lying in a manger."

¹³And suddenly there was with the angel a multitude of the heavenly host praising God and saying:

14 "Glory to God in the highest,
　　And on earth peace, goodwill
　　　toward men!"ᵃ

1:78 ᵃNU-Text reads *shall visit.*　　2:5 ᵃNU-Text omits *wife.*　　2:9 ᵃNU-Text omits *behold.*　　2:14 ᵃNU-Text reads *toward men of goodwill.*

15So it was, when the angels had gone away from them into heaven, that the shepherds said to one another, "Let us now go to Bethlehem and see this thing that has come to pass, which the Lord has made known to us." 16And they came with haste and found Mary and Joseph, and the Babe lying in a manger. 17Now when they had seen *Him,* they made widelyª known the saying which was told them concerning this Child. 18And all those who heard *it* marveled at those things which were told them by the shepherds. 19But Mary kept all these things and pondered *them* in her heart. 20Then the shepherds returned, glorifying and praising God for all the things that they had heard and seen, as it was told them.

DEFENDER

"... and on earth peace, goodwill toward men!"

LUKE 2:14

Watchmen on the Walls

These are the unforgettable words President John F. Kennedy was to deliver in a luncheon speech on the day he was assassinated in Dallas, Texas, November 22, 1963:

We in this country, in this generation are, by destiny rather than choice, the watchmen on the walls of world freedom. We ask, therefore, that we may be worthy of our power and responsibility, that we may exercise our strength with wisdom and restraint, and that we may achieve in our time and for all time the ancient vision of "peace on earth, goodwill toward men." That must always be our goal. For as was written long ago, "Except the Lord keep the city, the watchman waketh but in vain."

Circumcision of Jesus

21And when eight days were completed for the circumcision of the Child,ª His name was called JESUS, the name given by the angel before He was conceived in the womb.

Jesus Presented in the Temple

22Now when the days of her purification according to the law of Moses were completed, they brought Him to Jerusalem to present *Him* to the Lord 23(as it is written in the law of the Lord, *"Every male who opens the womb shall be called holy to the* LORD"),ª 24and to offer a sacrifice according to what is said in the law of the Lord, *"A pair of turtledoves or two young pigeons."*ª

Simeon Sees God's Salvation

25And behold, there was a man in Jerusalem whose name *was* Simeon, and this man *was* just and devout, waiting for the Consolation of Israel, and the Holy Spirit was upon him. 26And it had been revealed to him by the Holy Spirit that he would not see death before he had seen the Lord's Christ. 27So he came by the Spirit into the temple. And when the parents brought in the Child Jesus, to do for Him according to the custom of the law, 28he took Him up in his arms and blessed God and said:

29 "Lord, now You are letting Your servant
    depart in peace,
    According to Your word;
30 For my eyes have seen Your salvation
31 Which You have prepared before the
    face of all peoples,
32 A light to *bring* revelation to the
    Gentiles,
    And the glory of Your people Israel."

33And Joseph and His motherª marveled at those things which were spoken of Him. 34Then Simeon blessed them, and said to Mary His mother, "Behold, this *Child* is destined for the fall and rising of many in Israel, and for a sign which will be spoken against 35(yes, a sword will pierce through your own soul also), that the thoughts of many hearts may be revealed."

Anna Bears Witness to the Redeemer

36Now there was one, Anna, a prophetess, the daughter of Phanuel, of the tribe of Asher. She was of a great age, and had lived with a husband seven years from her virginity; 37and this woman *was* a widow of about eighty-four years,ª who did not

---

2:17 ªNU-Text omits *widely.*   **2:21** ªNU-Text reads *for His circumcision.*   **2:23** ªExodus 13:2, 12, 15   **2:24** ªLeviticus 12:8   **2:33** ªNU-Text reads *And His father and mother.*   **2:37** ªNU-Text reads *a widow until she was eighty-four.*

depart from the temple, but served *God* with fastings and prayers night and day. ³⁸And coming in that instant she gave thanks to the Lord,^a and spoke of Him to all those who looked for redemption in Jerusalem.

The Family Returns to Nazareth

³⁹So when they had performed all things according to the law of the Lord, they returned to Galilee, to their *own* city, Nazareth. ⁴⁰And the Child grew and became strong in spirit,^a filled with wisdom; and the grace of God was upon Him.

The Boy Jesus Amazes the Scholars

⁴¹His parents went to Jerusalem every year at the Feast of the Passover. ⁴²And when He was twelve years old, they went up to Jerusalem according to the custom of the feast. ⁴³When they had finished the days, as they returned, the Boy Jesus lingered behind in Jerusalem. And Joseph and His mother^a did not know *it;* ⁴⁴but supposing Him to have been in the company, they went a day's journey, and sought Him among *their* relatives and acquaintances. ⁴⁵So when they did not find Him, they returned to Jerusalem, seeking Him. ⁴⁶Now so it was *that* after three days they found Him in the temple, sitting in the midst of the teachers, both listening to them and asking them questions. ⁴⁷And all who heard Him were astonished at His understanding and answers. ⁴⁸So when they saw Him, they were amazed; and His mother said to Him, "Son, why have You done this to us? Look, Your father and I have sought You anxiously."

⁴⁹And He said to them, "Why did you seek Me? Did you not know that I must be about My Father's business?" ⁵⁰But they did not understand the statement which He spoke to them.

Jesus Advances in Wisdom and Favor

⁵¹Then He went down with them and came to Nazareth, and was subject to them, but His mother kept all these things in her heart. ⁵²And Jesus increased in wisdom and stature, and in favor with God and men.

John the Baptist Prepares the Way

3 Now in the fifteenth year of the reign of Tiberius Caesar, Pontius Pilate being governor of Judea, Herod being tetrarch of Galilee, his brother Philip tetrarch of Iturea and the region of Trachonitis, and Lysanias tetrarch of Abilene, ²while Annas and Caiaphas were high priests,^a the word of God came to John the son of Zacharias in the wilderness. ³And he went into all the region around the Jordan, preaching a baptism of repentance for the remission of sins, ⁴as it is written in the book of the words of Isaiah the prophet, saying:

> "The voice of one crying in the
> 　wilderness:
> 'Prepare the way of the LORD;
> 　Make His paths straight.
> 5　Every valley shall be filled
> 　And every mountain and hill brought
> 　　low;
> 　The crooked places shall be made
> 　　straight
> 　And the rough ways smooth;
> 6　And all flesh shall see the salvation
> 　　of God.' "^a

John Preaches to the People

⁷Then he said to the multitudes that came out to be baptized by him, "Brood of vipers! Who warned you to flee from the wrath to come? ⁸Therefore bear fruits worthy of repentance, and do not begin to say to yourselves, 'We have Abraham as *our* father.' For I say to you that God is able to raise up children to Abraham from these stones. ⁹And even now the ax is laid to the root of the trees. Therefore every tree which does not bear good fruit is cut down and thrown into the fire."

¹⁰So the people asked him, saying, "What shall we do then?"

¹¹He answered and said to them, "He who has two tunics, let him give to him who has none; and he who has food, let him do likewise."

2:38 ^aNU-Text reads *to God.*　**2:40** ^aNU-Text omits *in spirit.*　**2:43** ^aNU-Text reads *And His parents.* **3:2** ^aNU-Text and M-Text read *in the high priesthood of Annas and Caiaphas.*　**3:6** ^aIsaiah 40:3–5

¹²Then tax collectors also came to be baptized, and said to him, "Teacher, what shall we do?"

¹³And he said to them, "Collect no more than what is appointed for you."

¹⁴Likewise the soldiers asked him, saying, "And what shall we do?"

So he said to them, "Do not intimidate anyone or accuse falsely, and be content with your wages."

¹⁵Now as the people were in expectation, and all reasoned in their hearts about John, whether he was the Christ *or* not, ¹⁶John answered, saying to all, "I indeed baptize you with water; but One mightier than I is coming, whose sandal strap I am not worthy to loose. He will baptize you with the Holy Spirit and fire. ¹⁷His winnowing fan *is* in His hand, and He will thoroughly clean out His threshing floor, and gather the wheat into His barn; but the chaff He will burn with unquenchable fire."

¹⁸And with many other exhortations he preached to the people. ¹⁹But Herod the tetrarch, being rebuked by him concerning Herodias, his brother Philip's wife,ᵃ and for all the evils which Herod had done, ²⁰also added this, above all, that he shut John up in prison.

John Baptizes Jesus

²¹When all the people were baptized, it came to pass that Jesus also was baptized; and while He prayed, the heaven was opened. ²²And the Holy Spirit descended in bodily form like a dove upon Him, and a voice came from heaven which said, "You are My beloved Son; in You I am well pleased."

The Genealogy of Jesus Christ

²³Now Jesus Himself began *His ministry at* about thirty years of age, being (as was supposed) *the* son of Joseph, *the son* of Heli, ²⁴*the son* of Matthat,ᵃ *the son* of Levi, *the son* of Melchi, *the son* of Janna, *the son* of Joseph, ²⁵*the son* of Mattathiah, *the son* of Amos, *the son* of Nahum, *the son* of Esli, *the son* of Naggai, ²⁶*the son* of Maath, *the son* of Mattathiah, *the son* of Semei, *the son* of Joseph, *the son* of Judah, ²⁷*the son* of Joannas, *the son* of Rhesa, *the son* of Zerubbabel,

the son of Shealtiel, *the son* of Neri, ²⁸*the son* of Melchi, *the son* of Addi, *the son* of Cosam, *the son* of Elmodam, *the son* of Er, ²⁹*the son* of Jose, *the son* of Eliezer, *the son* of Jorim, *the son* of Matthat, *the son* of Levi, ³⁰*the son* of Simeon, *the son* of Judah, *the son* of Joseph, *the son* of Jonan, *the son* of Eliakim, ³¹*the son* of Melea, *the son* of Menan, *the son* of Mattathah, *the son* of Nathan, *the son* of David, ³²*the son* of Jesse, *the son* of Obed, *the son* of Boaz, *the son* of Salmon, *the son* of Nahshon, ³³*the son* of Amminadab, *the son* of Ram, *the son* of Hezron, *the son* of Perez, *the son* of Judah, ³⁴*the son* of Jacob, *the son* of Isaac, *the son* of Abraham, *the son* of Terah, *the son* of Nahor, ³⁵*the son* of Serug, *the son* of Reu, *the son* of Peleg, *the son* of Eber, *the son* of Shelah, ³⁶*the son* of Cainan, *the son* of Arphaxad, *the son* of Shem, *the son* of Noah, *the son* of Lamech, ³⁷*the son* of Methuselah, *the son* of Enoch, *the son* of Jared, *the son* of Mahalalel, *the son* of Cainan, ³⁸*the son* of Enosh, *the son* of Seth, *the son* of Adam, *the son* of God.

Satan Tempts Jesus

4 Then Jesus, being filled with the Holy Spirit, returned from the Jordan and was led by the Spirit intoᵃ the wilderness, ²being tempted for forty days by the devil. And in those days He ate nothing, and afterward, when they had ended, He was hungry.

³And the devil said to Him, "If You are the Son of God, command this stone to become bread."

⁴But Jesus answered him, saying,ᵃ "It is written, *'Man shall not live by bread alone, but by every word of God.'*"ᵇ

⁵Then the devil, taking Him up on a high mountain, showed Himᵃ all the kingdoms of the world in a moment of time. ⁶And the devil said to Him, "All this authority I will

---

3:19 ᵃNU-Text reads *his brother's wife.*   **3:24** ᵃThis and several other names in the genealogy are spelled somewhat differently in the NU-Text. Since the New King James Version uses the Old Testament spelling for persons mentioned in the New Testament, these variations, which come from the Greek, have not been footnoted.   **4:1** ᵃNU-Text reads *in.*   **4:4** ᵃDeuteronomy 8:3 ᵇNU-Text omits *but by every word of God.*   **4:5** ᵃNU-Text reads *And taking Him up, he showed Him.*

give You, and their glory; for *this* has been delivered to me, and I give it to whomever I wish. [7]Therefore, if You will worship before me, all will be Yours."

[8]And Jesus answered and said to him, "Get behind Me, Satan![a] For[b] it is written, '*You shall worship the L*ORD *your God, and Him only you shall serve.*'"[c]

[9]Then he brought Him to Jerusalem, set Him on the pinnacle of the temple, and said to Him, "If You are the Son of God, throw Yourself down from here. [10]For it is written:

'*He shall give His angels charge over you,*
To keep you,'

[11]and,

'*In their hands they shall bear you up,*
Lest you dash your foot against a stone.'"[a]

[12]And Jesus answered and said to him, "It has been said, '*You shall not tempt the L*ORD *your God.*'"[a]

[13]Now when the devil had ended every temptation, he departed from Him until an opportune time.

Jesus Begins His Galilean Ministry

[14]Then Jesus returned in the power of the Spirit to Galilee, and news of Him went out through all the surrounding region. [15]And He taught in their synagogues, being glorified by all.

Jesus Rejected at Nazareth

[16]So He came to Nazareth, where He had been brought up. And as His custom was, He went into the synagogue on the Sabbath day, and stood up to read. [17]And He was handed the book of the prophet Isaiah. And when He had opened the book, He found the place where it was written:

[18] "*The Spirit of the L*ORD *is upon Me,*
Because He has anointed Me
To preach the gospel to the poor;
He has sent Me to heal the brokenhearted,[a]

To proclaim liberty to the captives
And recovery of sight to the blind,
To set at liberty those who are oppressed;
[19] *To proclaim the acceptable year of the L*ORD."[a]

[20]Then He closed the book, and gave *it* back to the attendant and sat down. And the eyes of all who were in the synagogue were fixed on Him. [21]And He began to say to them, "Today this Scripture is fulfilled in your hearing." [22]So all bore witness to Him, and marveled at the gracious words which proceeded out of His mouth. And they said, "Is this not Joseph's son?"

[23]He said to them, "You will surely say this proverb to Me, 'Physician, heal yourself! Whatever we have heard done in Capernaum,[a] do also here in Your country.'" [24]Then He said, "Assuredly, I say to you, no prophet is accepted in his own country. [25]But I tell you truly, many widows were in Israel in the days of Elijah, when the heaven was shut up three years and six months, and there was a great famine throughout all the land; [26]but to none of them was Elijah sent except to Zarephath,[a] *in the region* of Sidon, to a woman *who was* a widow. [27]And many lepers were in Israel in the time of Elisha the prophet, and none of them was cleansed except Naaman the Syrian."

[28]So all those in the synagogue, when they heard these things, were filled with wrath, [29]and rose up and thrust Him out of the city; and they led Him to the brow of the hill on which their city was built, that they might throw Him down over the cliff. [30]Then passing through the midst of them, He went His way.

Jesus Casts Out an Unclean Spirit

[31]Then He went down to Capernaum, a city of Galilee, and was teaching them on the Sabbaths. [32]And they were astonished

---

4:8 [a]NU-Text omits *Get behind Me, Satan.* [b]NU-Text and M-Text omit *For.* [c]Deuteronomy 6:13
4:11 [a]Psalm 91:11, 12　　**4:12** [a]Deuteronomy 6:16
4:18 [a]NU-Text omits *to heal the brokenhearted.*
4:19 [a]Isaiah 61:1, 2　　**4:23** [a]Here and elsewhere the NU-Text spelling is *Capharnaum.*　　**4:26** [a]Greek *Sarepta*

at His teaching, for His word was with authority. ³³Now in the synagogue there was a man who had a spirit of an unclean demon. And he cried out with a loud voice, ³⁴saying, "Let *us* alone! What have we to do with You, Jesus of Nazareth? Did You come to destroy us? I know who You are— the Holy One of God!"

³⁵But Jesus rebuked him, saying, "Be quiet, and come out of him!" And when the demon had thrown him in *their* midst, it came out of him and did not hurt him. ³⁶Then they were all amazed and spoke among themselves, saying, "What a word this *is!* For with authority and power He commands the unclean spirits, and they come out." ³⁷And the report about Him went out into every place in the surrounding region.

Peter's Mother-in-Law Healed

³⁸Now He arose from the synagogue and entered Simon's house. But Simon's wife's mother was sick with a high fever, and they made request of Him concerning her. ³⁹So He stood over her and rebuked the fever, and it left her. And immediately she arose and served them.

Many Healed After Sabbath Sunset

⁴⁰When the sun was setting, all those who had any that were sick with various diseases brought them to Him; and He laid His hands on every one of them and healed them. ⁴¹And demons also came out of many, crying out and saying, "You are the Christ,^a the Son of God!"

And He, rebuking *them,* did not allow them to speak, for they knew that He was the Christ.

Jesus Preaches in Galilee

⁴²Now when it was day, He departed and went into a deserted place. And the crowd sought Him and came to Him, and tried to keep Him from leaving them; ⁴³but He said

4:41 ^aNU-Text omits *the Christ.*

FREEDOM

". . . to set at liberty those who are oppressed. . . ."

LUKE 4:18

THE STATUE OF LIBERTY

The Statue of Liberty was presented to the United States by the people of France in 1886. Located in New York Harbor, it stands on Liberty Island as a symbol of freedom and a welcome to all visitors, immigrants, and returning Americans. Engraved on a bronze plaque and mounted inside the Statue of Liberty is the renowned sonnet by Emma Lazarus:

The New Colossus

Not like the brazen giant of Greek fame,
With conquering limbs astride from land to land;
Here at our sea-washed, sunset gates shall stand
A mighty woman with a torch, whose flame
Is the imprisoned lightning, and her name
Mother of Exiles. From her beacon-hand
Glows worldwide welcome; her mild eyes command
The air-bridged harbor that twin cities frame.
"Keep, ancient lands, your storied pomp!" cries she
With silent lips. "Give me your tired, your poor,
Your huddled masses yearning to breathe free,
The wretched refuse of your teeming shore.
Send these, the homeless, tempest-tost to me,
I lift my lamp beside the golden door!"

to them, "I must preach the kingdom of God to the other cities also, because for this purpose I have been sent." [44]And He was preaching in the synagogues of Galilee.[a]

Four Fishermen Called as Disciples

5 So it was, as the multitude pressed about Him to hear the word of God, that He stood by the Lake of Gennesaret, [2]and saw two boats standing by the lake; but the fishermen had gone from them and were washing *their* nets. [3]Then He got into one of the boats, which was Simon's, and asked him to put out a little from the land. And He sat down and taught the multitudes from the boat.

[4]When He had stopped speaking, He said to Simon, "Launch out into the deep and let down your nets for a catch."

[5]But Simon answered and said to Him, "Master, we have toiled all night and caught nothing; nevertheless at Your word I will let down the net." [6]And when they had done this, they caught a great number of fish, and their net was breaking. [7]So they signaled to *their* partners in the other boat to come and help them. And they came and filled both the boats, so that they began to sink. [8]When Simon Peter saw *it,* he fell down at Jesus' knees, saying, "Depart from me, for I am a sinful man, O Lord!"

[9]For he and all who were with him were astonished at the catch of fish which they had taken; [10]and so also *were* James and John, the sons of Zebedee, who were partners with Simon. And Jesus said to Simon, "Do not be afraid. From now on you will catch men." [11]So when they had brought their boats to land, they forsook all and followed Him.

Jesus Cleanses a Leper

[12]And it happened when He was in a certain city, that behold, a man who was full of leprosy saw Jesus; and he fell on *his* face and implored Him, saying, "Lord, if You are willing, You can make me clean."

[13]Then He put out *His* hand and touched him, saying, "I am willing; be cleansed." Immediately the leprosy left him. [14]And He charged him to tell no one, "But go and show yourself to the priest, and make an offering for your cleansing, as a testimony to them, just as Moses commanded."

[15]However, the report went around concerning Him all the more; and great multitudes came together to hear, and to be healed by Him of their infirmities. [16]So He Himself *often* withdrew into the wilderness and prayed.

Jesus Forgives and Heals a Paralytic

[17]Now it happened on a certain day, as He was teaching, that there were Pharisees and teachers of the law sitting by, who had come out of every town of Galilee, Judea, and Jerusalem. And the power of the Lord was *present* to heal them.[a] [18]Then behold, men brought on a bed a man who was paralyzed, whom they sought to bring in and lay before Him. [19]And when they could not find how they might bring him in, because of the crowd, they went up on the housetop and let him down with *his* bed through the tiling into the midst before Jesus.

[20]When He saw their faith, He said to him, "Man, your sins are forgiven you."

[21]And the scribes and the Pharisees began to reason, saying, "Who is this who speaks blasphemies? Who can forgive sins but God alone?"

[22]But when Jesus perceived their thoughts, He answered and said to them, "Why are you reasoning in your hearts? [23]Which is easier, to say, 'Your sins are forgiven you,' or to say, 'Rise up and walk'? [24]But that you may know that the Son of Man has power on earth to forgive sins"— He said to the man who was paralyzed, "I say to you, arise, take up your bed, and go to your house."

[25]Immediately he rose up before them, took up what he had been lying on, and departed to his own house, glorifying God. [26]And they were all amazed, and they glorified God and were filled with fear, saying, "We have seen strange things today!"

Matthew the Tax Collector

[27]After these things He went out and saw a tax collector named Levi, sitting at the

---

4:44 [a]NU-Text reads *Judea.* **5:17** [a]NU-Text reads *present with Him to heal.*

tax office. And He said to him, "Follow Me." ²⁸So he left all, rose up, and followed Him.

²⁹Then Levi gave Him a great feast in his own house. And there were a great number of tax collectors and others who sat down with them. ³⁰And their scribes and the Pharisees^a complained against His disciples, saying, "Why do You eat and drink with tax collectors and sinners?"

³¹Jesus answered and said to them, "Those who are well have no need of a physician, but those who are sick. ³²I have not come to call the righteous, but sinners, to repentance."

Jesus Is Questioned About Fasting

³³Then they said to Him, "Why do^a the disciples of John fast often and make prayers, and likewise those of the Pharisees, but Yours eat and drink?"

³⁴And He said to them, "Can you make the friends of the bridegroom fast while the bridegroom is with them? ³⁵But the days will come when the bridegroom will be taken away from them; then they will fast in those days."

³⁶Then He spoke a parable to them: "No one puts a piece from a new garment on an old one;^a otherwise the new makes a tear, and also the piece that was *taken* out of the new does not match the old. ³⁷And no one puts new wine into old wineskins; or else the new wine will burst the wineskins and be spilled, and the wineskins will be ruined. ³⁸But new wine must be put into new wineskins, and both are preserved.^a ³⁹And no one, having drunk old *wine,* immediately^a desires new; for he says, 'The old is better.' "^b

Jesus Is Lord of the Sabbath

6 Now it happened on the second Sabbath after the first^a that He went through the grainfields. And His disciples plucked the heads of grain and ate *them,* rubbing *them* in *their* hands. ²And some of the Pharisees said to them, "Why are you doing what is not lawful to do on the Sabbath?"

³But Jesus answering them said, "Have you not even read this, what David did when he was hungry, he and those who were with him: ⁴how he went into the

house of God, took and ate the showbread, and also gave some to those with him, which is not lawful for any but the priests to eat?" ⁵And He said to them, "The Son of Man is also Lord of the Sabbath."

Healing on the Sabbath

⁶Now it happened on another Sabbath, also, that He entered the synagogue and taught. And a man was there whose right hand was withered. ⁷So the scribes and Pharisees watched Him closely, whether He would heal on the Sabbath, that they might find an accusation against Him. ⁸But He knew their thoughts, and said to the man who had the withered hand, "Arise and stand here." And he arose and stood. ⁹Then Jesus said to them, "I will ask you one thing: Is it lawful on the Sabbath to do good or to do evil, to save life or to destroy?"^a ¹⁰And when He had looked around at them all, He said to the man,^a "Stretch out your hand." And he did so, and his hand was restored as whole as the other.^b ¹¹But they were filled with rage, and discussed with one another what they might do to Jesus.

The Twelve Apostles

¹²Now it came to pass in those days that He went out to the mountain to pray, and continued all night in prayer to God. ¹³And when it was day, He called His disciples to *Himself;* and from them He chose twelve whom He also named apostles: ¹⁴Simon, whom He also named Peter, and Andrew his brother; James and John; Philip and Bartholomew; ¹⁵Matthew and Thomas; James the *son* of Alphaeus, and Simon called the Zealot; ¹⁶Judas *the son* of James, and Judas Iscariot who also became a traitor.

Jesus Heals a Great Multitude

¹⁷And He came down with them and stood on a level place with a crowd of His

---

5:30 ^aNU-Text reads *But the Pharisees and their scribes.* **5:33** ^aNU-Text omits *Why do,* making the verse a statement. **5:36** ^aNU-Text reads *No one tears a piece from a new garment and puts it on an old one.* **5:38** ^aNU-Text omits *and both are preserved.* **5:39** ^aNU-Text omits *immediately.* ^bNU-Text reads *good.* **6:1** ^aNU-Text reads *on a Sabbath.* **6:9** ^aM-Text reads *to kill.* **6:10** ^aNU-Text and M-Text read *to him.* ^bNU-Text omits *as whole as the other.*

BENEDICT ARNOLD,
AN AMERICAN TRAITOR

BENEDICT ARNOLD

*. . . Judas Iscariot who
also became a traitor.*

LUKE 6:16

Benedict Arnold (1741–1801) was considered by many to be the best general and most accomplished leader in the Continental Army during the Revolutionary War. Without his early contributions to the American cause, some historians feel the American Revolution might have been lost. He secured the vital Lake Champlain route to Canada and led a daring march through the wilderness of Maine to attack Quebec. His heroic actions during the pivotal fighting leading up to defeat of Burgoyne at Saratoga was key to the American victory, which sealed the French alliance that helped guarantee independence for the country. Thanks in part to his friend George Washington, his rank was adjusted to Major General, as of February 1777.

But despite being imaginative, daring, and courageous, his name has become a byword for treason in the United States. After marrying a beautiful young British Loyalist, Peggy Shippen, getting into deep debt, becoming frustrated over the lack of recognition he received, and being disgusted with congressional politics, Arnold negotiated his treason with Sir Henry Clinton, the British commander, promising to deliver the well fortified American stronghold at West Point and its 3,000 defenders for 20,300 sterling (about one million dollars today), an act that would devastate the American cause.

Persuading Washington to place the fort under his command, Arnold moved in September 1780 to execute his treacherous plan. Fortunately, the plot was discovered just before the British attack, but Arnold was able to escape. He was rewarded with a commission as a Brigadier General in the British Army, and he served the British with the same dynamic energy and daring, leading devastating attacks and causing much destruction against the Americans. After the war, he returned to England and later died there, virtually unknown.

The traitor Benedict Arnold abused his position of authority and trust, being willing to betray the entire war for American independence in order to win his own selfish success. He could have been one of the great heroes of the American Revolution, but selfishness and self-pity are formidable foes.

disciples and a great multitude of people from all Judea and Jerusalem, and from the seacoast of Tyre and Sidon, who came to hear Him and be healed of their diseases, [18]as well as those who were tormented with unclean spirits. And they were healed. [19]And the whole multitude sought to touch Him, for power went out from Him and healed *them* all.

The Beatitudes

[20]Then He lifted up His eyes toward His disciples, and said:

"Blessed *are you* poor,
    For yours is the kingdom of God.
[21] Blessed *are you* who hunger now,
    For you shall be filled.
Blessed *are you* who weep now,
    For you shall laugh.
[22] Blessed are you when men hate you,
    And when they exclude you,
    And revile *you,* and cast out your
        name as evil,
    For the Son of Man's sake.
[23] Rejoice in that day and leap for joy!
    For indeed your reward *is* great in
        heaven,
    For in like manner their fathers did
        to the prophets.

Jesus Pronounces Woes

[24] "But woe to you who are rich,
    For you have received your
        consolation.
[25] Woe to you who are full,
    For you shall hunger.
Woe to you who laugh now,
    For you shall mourn and weep.
[26] Woe to you[a] when all[b] men speak well
        of you,
    For so did their fathers to the false
        prophets.

Love Your Enemies

[27]"But I say to you who hear: Love your enemies, do good to those who hate you, [28]bless those who curse you, and pray for those who spitefully use you. [29]To him who strikes you on the *one* cheek, offer the other also. And from him who takes away your cloak, do not withhold *your* tunic either.

[30]Give to everyone who asks of you. And from him who takes away your goods do not ask *them* back. [31]And just as you want men to do to you, you also do to them likewise.

[32]"But if you love those who love you, what credit is that to you? For even sinners love those who love them. [33]And if you do good to those who do good to you, what credit is that to you? For even sinners do the same. [34]And if you lend *to those* from whom you hope to receive back, what credit is that to you? For even sinners lend to sinners to receive as much back. [35]But love your enemies, do good, and lend, hoping for nothing in return; and your reward will be great, and you will be sons of the Most High. For He is kind to the unthankful and evil. [36]Therefore be merciful, just as your Father also is merciful.

Do Not Judge

[37]"Judge not, and you shall not be judged. Condemn not, and you shall not be condemned. Forgive, and you will be forgiven. [38]Give, and it will be given to you: good measure, pressed down, shaken together, and running over will be put into your bosom. For with the same measure that you use, it will be measured back to you."

[39]And He spoke a parable to them: "Can the blind lead the blind? Will they not both fall into the ditch? [40]A disciple is not above his teacher, but everyone who is perfectly trained will be like his teacher. [41]And why do you look at the speck in your brother's eye, but do not perceive the plank in your own eye? [42]Or how can you say to your brother, 'Brother, let me remove the speck that *is* in your eye,' when you yourself do not see the plank that *is* in your own eye? Hypocrite! First remove the plank from your own eye, and then you will see clearly to remove the speck that is in your brother's eye.

A Tree Is Known by Its Fruit

[43]"For a good tree does not bear bad fruit, nor does a bad tree bear good fruit. [44]For

---

6:26 [a]NU-Text and M-Text omit *to you.* [b]M-Text omits *all.*

every tree is known by its own fruit. For *men* do not gather figs from thorns, nor do they gather grapes from a bramble bush. ⁴⁵A good man out of the good treasure of his heart brings forth good; and an evil man out of the evil treasure of his heartᵃ brings forth evil. For out of the abundance of the heart his mouth speaks.

Build on the Rock

⁴⁶"But why do you call Me 'Lord, Lord,' and not do the things which I say? ⁴⁷Whoever comes to Me, and hears My sayings and does them, I will show you whom he is like: ⁴⁸He is like a man building a house, who dug deep and laid the foundation on the rock. And when the flood arose, the stream beat vehemently against that house, and could not shake it, for it was founded on the rock.ᵃ ⁴⁹But he who heard and did nothing is like a man who built a house on the earth without a foundation, against which the stream beat vehemently; and immediately it fell.ᵃ And the ruin of that house was great."

HOPE

". . . laid the foundation on the rock."

LUKE 6:48

The Last Hope of Liberty

Theodore Frelinghuysen (1787–1862), a U.S. senator and president of Rutgers College wrote:

Let [the Bible] find its way into every cottage until the whole mass of our population shall yield to its elevating power; and under the benignant smiles of Him who delights to bless the Word, our government, the last hope of liberty, will rest on foundations against which the winds and waves shall beat in vain.

Jesus Heals a Centurion's Servant

7 Now when He concluded all His sayings in the hearing of the people, He entered Capernaum. ²And a certain centurion's servant, who was dear to him, was sick and ready to die. ³So when he heard about Jesus, he sent elders of the Jews to Him, pleading with Him to come and heal his servant. ⁴And when they came to Jesus,

they begged Him earnestly, saying that the one for whom He should do this was deserving, ⁵"for he loves our nation, and has built us a synagogue."

⁶Then Jesus went with them. And when He was already not far from the house, the centurion sent friends to Him, saying to Him, "Lord, do not trouble Yourself, for I am not worthy that You should enter under my roof. ⁷Therefore I did not even think myself worthy to come to You. But say the word, and my servant will be healed. ⁸For I also am a man placed under authority, having soldiers under me. And I say to one, 'Go,' and he goes; and to another, 'Come,' and he comes; and to my servant, 'Do this,' and he does *it*."

⁹When Jesus heard these things, He marveled at him, and turned around and said to the crowd that followed Him, "I say to you, I have not found such great faith, not even in Israel!" ¹⁰And those who were sent, returning to the house, found the servant well who had been sick.ᵃ

Jesus Raises the Son of the Widow of Nain

¹¹Now it happened, the day after, *that* He went into a city called Nain; and many of His disciples went with Him, and a large crowd. ¹²And when He came near the gate of the city, behold, a dead man was being carried out, the only son of his mother; and she was a widow. And a large crowd from the city was with her. ¹³When the Lord saw her, He had compassion on her and said to her, "Do not weep." ¹⁴Then He came and touched the open coffin, and those who carried *him* stood still. And He said, "Young man, I say to you, arise." ¹⁵So he who was dead sat up and began to speak. And He presented him to his mother.

¹⁶Then fear came upon all, and they glorified God, saying, "A great prophet has risen up among us"; and, "God has visited His people." ¹⁷And this report about Him went throughout all Judea and all the surrounding region.

6:45 ᵃNU-Text omits *treasure of his heart.*
6:48 ᵃNU-Text reads *for it was well built.*
6:49 ᵃNU-Text reads *collapsed.*   **7:10** ᵃNU-Text omits *who had been sick.*

John the Baptist Sends Messengers to Jesus

18Then the disciples of John reported to him concerning all these things. 19And John, calling two of his disciples to *him,* sent *them* to Jesus,ª saying, "Are You the Coming One, or do we look for another?"

20When the men had come to Him, they said, "John the Baptist has sent us to You, saying, 'Are You the Coming One, or do we look for another?'" 21And that very hour He cured many of infirmities, afflictions, and evil spirits; and to many blind He gave sight.

22Jesus answered and said to them, "Go and tell John the things you have seen and heard: that *the* blind see, *the* lame walk, *the* lepers are cleansed, *the* deaf hear, *the* dead are raised, *the* poor have the gospel preached to them. 23And blessed is *he* who is not offended because of Me."

24When the messengers of John had departed, He began to speak to the multitudes concerning John: "What did you go out into the wilderness to see? A reed shaken by the wind? 25But what did you go out to see? A man clothed in soft garments? Indeed those who are gorgeously appareled and live in luxury are in kings' courts. 26But what did you go out to see? A prophet? Yes, I say to you, and more than a prophet. 27This is *he* of whom it is written:

'Behold, I send My messenger before
    Your face,
Who will prepare Your way before
    You.'ª

28For I say to you, among those born of women there is not a greater prophet than John the Baptist;ª but he who is least in the kingdom of God is greater than he."

29And when all the people heard *Him,* even the tax collectors justified God, having been baptized with the baptism of John. 30But the Pharisees and lawyers rejected the will of God for themselves, not having been baptized by him.

31And the Lord said,ª "To what then shall I liken the men of this generation, and what are they like? 32They are like children sitting in the marketplace and calling to one another, saying:

'We played the flute for you,
    And you did not dance;
We mourned to you,
    And you did not weep.'

33For John the Baptist came neither eating bread nor drinking wine, and you say, 'He has a demon.' 34The Son of Man has come eating and drinking, and you say, 'Look, a glutton and a winebibber, a friend of tax collectors and sinners!' 35But wisdom is justified by all her children."

A Sinful Woman Forgiven

36Then one of the Pharisees asked Him to eat with him. And He went to the Pharisee's house, and sat down to eat. 37And behold, a woman in the city who was a sinner, when she knew that *Jesus* sat at the table in the Pharisee's house, brought an alabaster flask of fragrant oil, 38and stood at His feet behind *Him* weeping; and she began to wash His feet with her tears, and wiped *them* with the hair of her head; and she kissed His feet and anointed *them* with the fragrant oil. 39Now when the Pharisee who had invited Him saw *this,* he spoke to himself, saying, "This Man, if He were a prophet, would know who and what manner of woman *this is* who is touching Him, for she is a sinner."

40And Jesus answered and said to him, "Simon, I have something to say to you."

So he said, "Teacher, say it."

41"There was a certain creditor who had two debtors. One owed five hundred denarii, and the other fifty. 42And when they had nothing with which to repay, he freely forgave them both. Tell Me, therefore, which of them will love him more?"

43Simon answered and said, "I suppose the *one* whom he forgave more."

And He said to him, "You have rightly judged." 44Then He turned to the woman and said to Simon, "Do you see this woman? I entered your house; you gave Me no water for My feet, but she has washed My feet with her tears and wiped *them* with the hair

---

7:19 ªNU-Text reads *the Lord.*   **7:27** ªMalachi 3:1
7:28 ªNU-Text reads *there is none greater than John.*
7:31 ªNU-Text and M-Text omit *And the Lord said.*

of her head. ⁴⁵You gave Me no kiss, but this woman has not ceased to kiss My feet since the time I came in. ⁴⁶You did not anoint My head with oil, but this woman has anointed My feet with fragrant oil. ⁴⁷Therefore I say to you, her sins, which *are* many, are forgiven, for she loved much. But to whom little is forgiven, *the same* loves little."

⁴⁸Then He said to her, "Your sins are forgiven."

⁴⁹And those who sat at the table with Him began to say to themselves, "Who is this who even forgives sins?"

⁵⁰Then He said to the woman, "Your faith has saved you. Go in peace."

Many Women Minister to Jesus

8 Now it came to pass, afterward, that He went through every city and village, preaching and bringing the glad tidings of the kingdom of God. And the twelve *were* with Him, ²and certain women who had been healed of evil spirits and infirmities— Mary called Magdalene, out of whom had come seven demons, ³and Joanna the wife of Chuza, Herod's steward, and Susanna, and many others who provided for Himᵃ from their substance.

The Parable of the Sower

⁴And when a great multitude had gathered, and they had come to Him from every city, He spoke by a parable: ⁵"A sower went out to sow his seed. And as he sowed, some fell by the wayside; and it was trampled down, and the birds of the air devoured it. ⁶Some fell on rock; and as soon as it sprang up, it withered away because it lacked moisture. ⁷And some fell among thorns, and the thorns sprang up with it and choked it. ⁸But others fell on good ground, sprang up, and yielded a crop a hundredfold." When He had said these things He cried, "He who has ears to hear, let him hear!"

The Purpose of Parables

⁹Then His disciples asked Him, saying, "What does this parable mean?"

¹⁰And He said, "To you it has been given to know the mysteries of the kingdom of God, but to the rest *it is* given in parables, that

'Seeing they may not see,
And hearing they may not understand.'ᵃ

The Parable of the Sower Explained

¹¹"Now the parable is this: The seed is the word of God. ¹²Those by the wayside are the ones who hear; then the devil comes and takes away the word out of their hearts, lest they should believe and be saved. ¹³But the ones on the rock *are those* who, when they hear, receive the word with joy; and these have no root, who believe for a while and in time of temptation fall away. ¹⁴Now the ones *that* fell among thorns are those who, when they have heard, go out and are choked with cares, riches, and pleasures of life, and bring no fruit to maturity. ¹⁵But the ones *that* fell on the good ground are those who, having heard the word with a noble and good heart, keep *it* and bear fruit with patience.

The Parable of the Revealed Light

¹⁶"No one, when he has lit a lamp, covers it with a vessel or puts *it* under a bed, but sets *it* on a lampstand, that those who enter may see the light. ¹⁷For nothing is secret that will not be revealed, nor *anything* hidden that will not be known and come to light. ¹⁸Therefore take heed how you hear. For whoever has, to him *more* will be given; and whoever does not have, even what he seems to have will be taken from him."

Jesus' Mother and Brothers Come to Him

¹⁹Then His mother and brothers came to Him, and could not approach Him because of the crowd. ²⁰And it was told Him *by some*, who said, "Your mother and Your brothers are standing outside, desiring to see You."

²¹But He answered and said to them, "My mother and My brothers are these who hear the word of God and do it."

Wind and Wave Obey Jesus

²²Now it happened, on a certain day, that He got into a boat with His disciples. And He said to them, "Let us cross over to

---

8:3 ᵃNU-Text and M-Text read *them*.
8:10 ᵃIsaiah 6:9

the other side of the lake." And they launched out. ²³But as they sailed He fell asleep. And a windstorm came down on the lake, and they were filling *with water,* and were in jeopardy. ²⁴And they came to Him and awoke Him, saying, "Master, Master, we are perishing!"

Then He arose and rebuked the wind and the raging of the water. And they ceased, and there was a calm. ²⁵But He said to them, "Where is your faith?"

And they were afraid, and marveled, saying to one another, "Who can this be? For He commands even the winds and water, and they obey Him!"

A Demon-Possessed Man Healed

²⁶Then they sailed to the country of the Gadarenes,ª which is opposite Galilee. ²⁷And when He stepped out on the land, there met Him a certain man from the city who had demons for a long time. And he wore no clothes,ª nor did he live in a house but in the tombs. ²⁸When he saw Jesus, he cried out, fell down before Him, and with a loud voice said, "What have I to do with You, Jesus, Son of the Most High God? I beg You, do not torment me!" ²⁹For He had commanded the unclean spirit to come out of the man. For it had often seized him, and he was kept under guard, bound with chains and shackles; and he broke the bonds and was driven by the demon into the wilderness.

³⁰Jesus asked him, saying, "What is your name?"

And he said, "Legion," because many demons had entered him. ³¹And they begged Him that He would not command them to go out into the abyss.

³²Now a herd of many swine was feeding there on the mountain. So they begged Him that He would permit them to enter them. And He permitted them. ³³Then the demons went out of the man and entered the swine, and the herd ran violently down the steep place into the lake and drowned.

³⁴When those who fed *them* saw what had happened, they fled and told *it* in the city and in the country. ³⁵Then they went out to see what had happened, and came to Jesus, and found the man from whom the demons had departed, sitting at the feet of Jesus, clothed and in his right mind. And they were afraid. ³⁶They also who had seen *it* told them by what means he who had been demon-possessed was healed. ³⁷Then the whole multitude of the surrounding region of the Gadarenesª asked Him to depart from them, for they were seized with great fear. And He got into the boat and returned.

³⁸Now the man from whom the demons had departed begged Him that he might be with Him. But Jesus sent him away, saying, ³⁹"Return to your own house, and tell what great things God has done for you." And he went his way and proclaimed throughout the whole city what great things Jesus had done for him.

A Girl Restored to Life and a Woman Healed

⁴⁰So it was, when Jesus returned, that the multitude welcomed Him, for they were all waiting for Him. ⁴¹And behold, there came a man named Jairus, and he was a ruler of the synagogue. And he fell down at Jesus' feet and begged Him to come to his house, ⁴²for he had an only daughter about twelve years of age, and she was dying.

But as He went, the multitudes thronged Him. ⁴³Now a woman, having a flow of blood for twelve years, who had spent all her livelihood on physicians and could not be healed by any, ⁴⁴came from behind and touched the border of His garment. And immediately her flow of blood stopped.

⁴⁵And Jesus said, "Who touched Me?"

When all denied it, Peter and those with himª said, "Master, the multitudes throng and press You, and You say, 'Who touched Me?'"ᵇ

⁴⁶But Jesus said, "Somebody touched Me, for I perceived power going out from Me." ⁴⁷Now when the woman saw that she was not hidden, she came trembling; and falling down before Him, she declared to Him in the presence of all the people the reason she had touched Him and how she was healed immediately.

8:26 ªNU-Text reads *Gerasenes.* **8:27** ªNU-Text reads *who had demons and for a long time wore no clothes.* **8:37** ªNU-Text reads *Gerasenes.* **8:45** ªNU-Text omits *and those with him.* ᵇNU-Text omits *and You say, 'Who touched Me?'*

⁴⁸And He said to her, "Daughter, be of good cheer;ᵃ your faith has made you well. Go in peace."

⁴⁹While He was still speaking, someone came from the ruler of the synagogue's *house,* saying to him, "Your daughter is dead. Do not trouble the Teacher."ᵃ

⁵⁰But when Jesus heard *it,* He answered him, saying, "Do not be afraid; only believe, and she will be made well." ⁵¹When He came into the house, He permitted no one to go inᵃ except Peter, James, and John,ᵇ and the father and mother of the girl. ⁵²Now all wept and mourned for her; but He said, "Do not weep; she is not dead, but sleeping." ⁵³And they ridiculed Him, knowing that she was dead.

⁵⁴But He put them all outside,ᵃ took her by the hand and called, saying, "Little girl, arise." ⁵⁵Then her spirit returned, and she arose immediately. And He commanded that she be given *something* to eat. ⁵⁶And her parents were astonished, but He charged them to tell no one what had happened.

Sending Out the Twelve

9 Then He called His twelve disciples together and gave them power and authority over all demons, and to cure diseases. ²He sent them to preach the kingdom of God and to heal the sick. ³And He said to them, "Take nothing for the journey, neither staffs nor bag nor bread nor money; and do not have two tunics apiece. ⁴"Whatever house you enter, stay there, and from there depart. ⁵And whoever will not receive you, when you go out of that city, shake off the very dust from your feet as a testimony against them."

⁶So they departed and went through the towns, preaching the gospel and healing everywhere.

Herod Seeks to See Jesus

⁷Now Herod the tetrarch heard of all that was done by Him; and he was perplexed, because it was said by some that John had risen from the dead, ⁸and by some that Elijah had appeared, and by others that one of the old prophets had risen again. ⁹Herod said, "John I have beheaded, but who is this of whom I hear such things?" So he sought to see Him.

Feeding the Five Thousand

¹⁰And the apostles, when they had returned, told Him all that they had done. Then He took them and went aside privately into a deserted place belonging to the city called Bethsaida. ¹¹But when the multitudes knew *it,* they followed Him; and He received them and spoke to them about the kingdom of God, and healed those who had need of healing. ¹²When the day began to wear away, the twelve came and said to Him, "Send the multitude away, that they may go into the surrounding towns and country, and lodge and get provisions; for we are in a deserted place here."

¹³But He said to them, "You give them something to eat."

And they said, "We have no more than five loaves and two fish, unless we go and buy food for all these people." ¹⁴For there were about five thousand men.

Then He said to His disciples, "Make them sit down in groups of fifty." ¹⁵And they did so, and made them all sit down.

¹⁶Then He took the five loaves and the two fish, and looking up to heaven, He blessed and broke them, and gave *them* to the disciples to set before the multitude. ¹⁷So they all ate and were filled, and twelve baskets of the leftover fragments were taken up by them.

Peter Confesses Jesus as the Christ

¹⁸And it happened, as He was alone praying, *that* His disciples joined Him, and He asked them, saying, "Who do the crowds say that I am?"

¹⁹So they answered and said, "John the Baptist, but some *say* Elijah; and others *say* that one of the old prophets has risen again."

²⁰He said to them, "But who do you say that I am?"

Peter answered and said, "The Christ of God."

8:48 ᵃNU-Text omits *be of good cheer.*
8:49 ᵃNU-Text adds *anymore.*   **8:51** ᵃNU-Text adds *with Him.* ᵇNU-Text and M-Text read *Peter, John, and James.*   **8:54** ᵃNU-Text omits *put them all outside.*

Jesus Predicts His Death and Resurrection

²¹And He strictly warned and commanded them to tell this to no one, ²²saying, "The Son of Man must suffer many things, and be rejected by the elders and chief priests and scribes, and be killed, and be raised the third day."

Take Up the Cross and Follow Him

²³Then He said to *them* all, "If anyone desires to come after Me, let him deny himself, and take up his cross daily,^a and follow Me. ²⁴For whoever desires to save his life will lose it, but whoever loses his life for My sake will save it. ²⁵For what profit is it to a man if he gains the whole world, and is himself destroyed or lost? ²⁶For whoever is ashamed of Me and My words, of him the Son of Man will be ashamed when He comes in His *own* glory, and *in His* Father's, and of the holy angels. ²⁷But I tell you truly, there are some standing here who shall not taste death till they see the kingdom of God."

Jesus Transfigured on the Mount

²⁸Now it came to pass, about eight days after these sayings, that He took Peter, John, and James and went up on the mountain to pray. ²⁹As He prayed, the appearance of His face was altered, and His robe *became* white *and* glistening. ³⁰And behold, two men talked with Him, who were Moses and Elijah, ³¹who appeared in glory and spoke of His decease which He was about to accomplish at Jerusalem. ³²But Peter and those with him were heavy with sleep; and when they were fully awake, they saw His glory and the two men who stood with Him. ³³Then it happened, as they were parting from Him, *that* Peter said to Jesus, "Master, it is good for us to be here; and let us make three tabernacles: one for You, one for Moses, and one for Elijah"—not knowing what he said.

³⁴While he was saying this, a cloud came and overshadowed them; and they were fearful as they entered the cloud. ³⁵And a voice came out of the cloud, saying, "This is My beloved Son.^a Hear Him!" ³⁶When the voice had ceased, Jesus was found alone.

But they kept quiet, and told no one in those days any of the things they had seen.

A Boy Is Healed

³⁷Now it happened on the next day, when they had come down from the mountain, that a great multitude met Him. ³⁸Suddenly a man from the multitude cried out, saying, "Teacher, I implore You, look on my son, for he is my only child. ³⁹And behold, a spirit seizes him, and he suddenly cries out; it convulses him so that he foams *at the mouth;* and it departs from him with great difficulty, bruising him. ⁴⁰So I implored Your disciples to cast it out, but they could not."

⁴¹Then Jesus answered and said, "O faithless and perverse generation, how long shall I be with you and bear with you? Bring your son here." ⁴²And as he was still coming, the demon threw him down and convulsed *him.* Then Jesus rebuked the unclean spirit, healed the child, and gave him back to his father.

Jesus Again Predicts His Death

⁴³And they were all amazed at the majesty of God.

But while everyone marveled at all the things which Jesus did, He said to His disciples, ⁴⁴"Let these words sink down into your ears, for the Son of Man is about to be betrayed into the hands of men." ⁴⁵But they did not understand this saying, and it was hidden from them so that they did not perceive it; and they were afraid to ask Him about this saying.

Who Is the Greatest?

⁴⁶Then a dispute arose among them as to which of them would be greatest. ⁴⁷And Jesus, perceiving the thought of their heart, took a little child and set him by Him, ⁴⁸and said to them, "Whoever receives this little child in My name receives Me; and whoever receives Me receives Him who sent Me. For he who is least among you all will be great."

9:23 ^aM-Text omits *daily.* **9:35** ^aNU-Text reads *This is My Son, the Chosen One.*

Jesus Forbids Sectarianism

⁴⁹Now John answered and said, "Master, we saw someone casting out demons in Your name, and we forbade him because he does not follow with us."

⁵⁰But Jesus said to him, "Do not forbid *him,* for he who is not against us[a] is on our[b] side."

A Samaritan Village Rejects the Savior

⁵¹Now it came to pass, when the time had come for Him to be received up, that He steadfastly set His face to go to Jerusalem, ⁵²and sent messengers before His face. And as they went, they entered a village of the Samaritans, to prepare for Him. ⁵³But they did not receive Him, because His face was *set* for the journey to Jerusalem. ⁵⁴And when His disciples James and John saw *this,* they said, "Lord, do You want us to command fire to come down from heaven and consume them, just as Elijah did?"[a]

⁵⁵But He turned and rebuked them,[a] and said, "You do not know what manner of spirit you are of. ⁵⁶For the Son of Man did not come to destroy men's lives but to save *them.*"[a] And they went to another village.

The Cost of Discipleship

⁵⁷Now it happened as they journeyed on the road, *that* someone said to Him, "Lord, I will follow You wherever You go."

⁵⁸And Jesus said to him, "Foxes have holes and birds of the air *have* nests, but the Son of Man has nowhere to lay *His* head."

⁵⁹Then He said to another, "Follow Me."

But he said, "Lord, let me first go and bury my father."

⁶⁰Jesus said to him, "Let the dead bury their own dead, but you go and preach the kingdom of God."

⁶¹And another also said, "Lord, I will follow You, but let me first go *and* bid them farewell who are at my house."

⁶²But Jesus said to him, "No one, having put his hand to the plow, and looking back, is fit for the kingdom of God."

The Seventy Sent Out

10After these things the Lord appointed seventy others also,[a] and sent them two by two before His face into every city and place where He Himself was about to go. ²Then He said to them, "The harvest truly *is* great, but the laborers *are* few; therefore pray the Lord of the harvest to send out laborers into His harvest. ³Go your way; behold, I send you out as lambs among wolves. ⁴Carry neither money bag, knapsack, nor sandals; and greet no one along the road. ⁵But whatever house you enter, first say, 'Peace to this house.' ⁶And if a son of peace is there, your peace will rest on it; if not, it will return to you. ⁷And remain in the same house, eating and drinking such things as they give, for the laborer is worthy of his wages. Do not go from house to house. ⁸Whatever city you enter, and they receive you, eat such things as are set before you. ⁹And heal the sick there, and say to them, 'The kingdom of God has come near to you.' ¹⁰But whatever city you enter, and they do not receive you, go out into its streets and say, ¹¹'The very dust of your city which clings to us[a] we wipe off against you. Nevertheless know this, that the kingdom of God has come near you.' ¹²But[a] I say to you that it will be more tolerable in that Day for Sodom than for that city.

Woe to the Impenitent Cities

¹³"Woe to you, Chorazin! Woe to you, Bethsaida! For if the mighty works which were done in you had been done in Tyre and Sidon, they would have repented long ago, sitting in sackcloth and ashes. ¹⁴But it will be more tolerable for Tyre and Sidon at the judgment than for you. ¹⁵And you, Capernaum, who are exalted to heaven, will be brought down to Hades.[a] ¹⁶He who hears you hears Me, he who rejects you rejects Me, and he who rejects Me rejects Him who sent Me."

9:50 [a]NU-Text reads *you.* [b]NU-Text reads *your.*
9:54 [a]NU-Text omits *just as Elijah did.*
9:55 [a]NU-Text omits the rest of this verse.
9:56 [a]NU-Text omits the first sentence of this verse.
10:1 [a]NU-Text reads *seventy-two others.*
10:11 [a]NU-Text reads *our feet.*   **10:12** [a]NU-Text and M-Text omit *But.*   **10:15** [a]NU-Text reads *will you be exalted to heaven? You will be thrust down to Hades!*

The Seventy Return with Joy

17Then the seventy[a] returned with joy, saying, "Lord, even the demons are subject to us in Your name."

18And He said to them, "I saw Satan fall like lightning from heaven. 19Behold, I give you the authority to trample on serpents and scorpions, and over all the power of the enemy, and nothing shall by any means hurt you. 20Nevertheless do not rejoice in this, that the spirits are subject to you, but rather[a] rejoice because your names are written in heaven."

Jesus Rejoices in the Spirit

21In that hour Jesus rejoiced in the Spirit and said, "I thank You, Father, Lord of heaven and earth, that You have hidden these things from *the* wise and prudent and revealed them to babes. Even so, Father, for so it seemed good in Your sight. 22All[a] things have been delivered to Me by My Father, and no one knows who the Son is except the Father, and who the Father is except the Son, and *the one* to whom the Son wills to reveal *Him*."

23Then He turned to *His* disciples and said privately, "Blessed *are* the eyes which see the things you see; 24for I tell you that many prophets and kings have desired to see what you see, and have not seen *it,* and to hear what you hear, and have not heard *it.*"

The Parable of the Good Samaritan

25And behold, a certain lawyer stood up and tested Him, saying, "Teacher, what shall I do to inherit eternal life?"

26He said to him, "What is written in the law? What is your reading *of it?*"

10:17 [a]NU-Text reads *seventy-two.* **10:20** [a]NU-Text and M-Text omit *rather.* **10:22** [a]M-Text reads *And turning to the disciples He said, "All. . . .*

EQUIPPER

"'You shall love . . . your neighbor as yourself.'"

LUKE 10:27

Noah Webster

ON CIVIL LIBERTY

Noah Webster (1758–1843) was an American lexicographer, textbook author, spelling reformer, political writer, word enthusiast, and editor. He has been called the "Father of American Scholarship and Education." In his public school textbook *History of the United States,* published in 1832, he stated:

Almost all the civil liberty now enjoyed in the world owes its origin to the principles of the Christian religion.

It is the sincere desire of the writer that our citizens should early understand that the genuine source of correct republican principles is the Bible, particularly the New Testament or the Christian religion.

The religion which has introduced civil liberty is the religion of Christ and His apostles, which enjoins humility, piety, and benevolence; which acknowledges in every person a brother, or a sister, and a citizen with equal rights. This is genuine Christianity, and to this we owe our free constitutions of government.

The moral principles and precepts contained in the Scriptures ought to form the basis of all of our civil constitutions and laws. . . . All the miseries and evils which men suffer from vice, crime, ambition, injustice, oppression, slavery, and war, proceed from their despising or neglecting the precepts contained in the Bible.

²⁷So he answered and said, "'*You shall love the* L<small>ORD</small> *your God with all your heart, with all your soul, with all your strength, and with all your mind,*'ᵃ and '*your neighbor as yourself.*'"ᵇ

²⁸And He said to him, "You have answered rightly; do this and you will live."

²⁹But he, wanting to justify himself, said to Jesus, "And who is my neighbor?"

³⁰Then Jesus answered and said: "A certain *man* went down from Jerusalem to Jericho, and fell among thieves, who stripped him of his clothing, wounded *him,* and departed, leaving *him* half dead. ³¹Now by chance a certain priest came down that road. And when he saw him, he passed by on the other side. ³²Likewise a Levite, when he arrived at the place, came and looked, and passed by on the other side. ³³But a certain Samaritan, as he journeyed, came where he was. And when he saw him, he had compassion. ³⁴So he went to *him* and bandaged his wounds, pouring on oil and wine; and he set him on his own animal, brought him to an inn, and took care of him. ³⁵On the next day, when he departed,ᵃ he took out two denarii, gave *them* to the innkeeper, and said to him, 'Take care of him; and whatever more you spend, when I come again, I will repay you.' ³⁶So which of these three do you think was neighbor to him who fell among the thieves?"

³⁷And he said, "He who showed mercy on him."

Then Jesus said to him, "Go and do likewise."

Mary and Martha Worship and Serve

³⁸Now it happened as they went that He entered a certain village; and a certain woman named Martha welcomed Him into her house. ³⁹And she had a sister called Mary, who also sat at Jesus'ᵃ feet and heard His word. ⁴⁰But Martha was distracted with much serving, and she approached Him and said, "Lord, do You not care that my sister has left me to serve alone? Therefore tell her to help me."

⁴¹And Jesusᵃ answered and said to her, "Martha, Martha, you are worried and troubled about many things. ⁴²But one thing is needed, and Mary has chosen that good part, which will not be taken away from her."

The Model Prayer

11 Now it came to pass, as He was praying in a certain place, when He ceased, *that* one of His disciples said to Him, "Lord, teach us to pray, as John also taught his disciples."

²So He said to them, "When you pray, say:

> Our Father in heaven,ᵃ
> Hallowed be Your name.
> Your kingdom come.ᵇ
> Your will be done
> On earth as *it is* in heaven.
> ³ Give us day by day our daily bread.
> ⁴ And forgive us our sins,
> For we also forgive everyone who is indebted to us.
> And do not lead us into temptation,
> But deliver us from the evil one."ᵃ

A Friend Comes at Midnight

⁵And He said to them, "Which of you shall have a friend, and go to him at midnight and say to him, 'Friend, lend me three loaves; ⁶for a friend of mine has come to me on his journey, and I have nothing to set before him'; ⁷and he will answer from within and say, 'Do not trouble me; the door is now shut, and my children are with me in bed; I cannot rise and give to you'? ⁸I say to you, though he will not rise and give to him because he is his friend, yet because of his persistence he will rise and give him as many as he needs.

Keep Asking, Seeking, Knocking

⁹"So I say to you, ask, and it will be given to you; seek, and you will find; knock, and it will be opened to you. ¹⁰For everyone who asks receives, and he who seeks finds,

---

10:27 ᵃDeuteronomy 6:5 ᵇLeviticus 19:18
10:35 ᵃNU-Text omits *when he departed.*
10:39 ᵃNU-Text reads *the Lord's.*   **10:41** ᵃNU-Text reads *the Lord.*   **11:2** ᵃNU-Text omits *Our* and *in heaven.* ᵇNU-Text omits the rest of this verse.
11:4 ᵃNU-Text omits *But deliver us from the evil one.*

and to him who knocks it will be opened. [11]If a son asks for bread[a] from any father among you, will he give him a stone? Or if *he asks* for a fish, will he give him a serpent instead of a fish? [12]Or if he asks for an egg, will he offer him a scorpion? [13]If you then, being evil, know how to give good gifts to your children, how much more will *your* heavenly Father give the Holy Spirit to those who ask Him!"

A House Divided Cannot Stand

[14]And He was casting out a demon, and it was mute. So it was, when the demon had gone out, that the mute spoke; and the multitudes marveled. [15]But some of them said, "He casts out demons by Beelzebub,[a] the ruler of the demons."

[16]Others, testing *Him,* sought from Him a sign from heaven. [17]But He, knowing their thoughts, said to them: "Every kingdom divided against itself is brought to desolation, and a house *divided* against a house falls. [18]If Satan also is divided against himself, how will his kingdom stand? Because you say I cast out demons by Beelzebub. [19]And if I cast out demons by Beelzebub, by whom do your sons cast *them* out? Therefore they will be your judges. [20]But if I cast out demons with the finger of God, surely the kingdom of God has come upon you. [21]When a strong man, fully armed, guards his own palace, his goods are in peace. [22]But when a stronger than he comes upon him and overcomes him, he takes from him all his armor in which he trusted, and divides his spoils. [23]He who is not with Me is against Me, and he who does not gather with Me scatters.

An Unclean Spirit Returns

[24]"When an unclean spirit goes out of a man, he goes through dry places, seeking rest; and finding none, he says, 'I will return to my house from which I came.' [25]And when he comes, he finds *it* swept and put in order. [26]Then he goes and takes with *him* seven other spirits more wicked than himself, and they enter and dwell there; and the last *state* of that man is worse than the first."

Keeping the Word

[27]And it happened, as He spoke these things, that a certain woman from the crowd raised her voice and said to Him, "Blessed *is* the womb that bore You, and *the* breasts which nursed You!"

[28]But He said, "More than that, blessed *are* those who hear the word of God and keep it!"

Seeking a Sign

[29]And while the crowds were thickly gathered together, He began to say, "This is an evil generation. It seeks a sign, and no sign will be given to it except the sign of Jonah the prophet.[a] [30]For as Jonah became a sign to the Ninevites, so also the Son of Man will be to this generation. [31]The queen of the South will rise up in the judgment with the men of this generation and condemn them, for she came from the ends of the earth to hear the wisdom of Solomon; and indeed a greater than Solomon *is* here. [32]The men of Nineveh will rise up in the judgment with this generation and condemn it, for they repented at the preaching of Jonah; and indeed a greater than Jonah *is* here.

The Lamp of the Body

[33]"No one, when he has lit a lamp, puts *it* in a secret place or under a basket, but on a lampstand, that those who come in may see the light. [34]The lamp of the body is the eye. Therefore, when your eye is good, your whole body also is full of light. But when *your eye* is bad, your body also *is* full of darkness. [35]Therefore take heed that the light which is in you is not darkness. [36]If then your whole body *is* full of light, having no part dark, *the* whole *body* will be full of light, as when the bright shining of a lamp gives you light."

Woe to the Pharisees and Lawyers

[37]And as He spoke, a certain Pharisee asked Him to dine with him. So He went in

---

11:11 [a]NU-Text omits the words from *bread* through *for* in the next sentence. **11:15** [a]NU-Text and M-Text read *Beelzebul.* **11:29** [a]NU-Text omits *the prophet.*

and sat down to eat. [38]When the Pharisee saw *it,* he marveled that He had not first washed before dinner.

[39]Then the Lord said to him, "Now you Pharisees make the outside of the cup and dish clean, but your inward part is full of greed and wickedness. [40]Foolish ones! Did not He who made the outside make the inside also? [41]But rather give alms of such things as you have; then indeed all things are clean to you.

[42]"But woe to you Pharisees! For you tithe mint and rue and all manner of herbs, and pass by justice and the love of God. These you ought to have done, without leaving the others undone. [43]Woe to you Pharisees! For you love the best seats in the synagogues and greetings in the marketplaces. [44]Woe to you, scribes and Pharisees, hypocrites![a] For you are like graves which are not seen, and the men who walk over *them* are not aware *of them.*"

[45]Then one of the lawyers answered and said to Him, "Teacher, by saying these things You reproach us also."

[46]And He said, "Woe to you also, lawyers! For you load men with burdens hard to bear, and you yourselves do not touch the burdens with one of your fingers. [47]Woe to you! For you build the tombs of the prophets, and your fathers killed them. [48]In fact, you bear witness that you approve the deeds of your fathers; for they indeed killed them, and you build their tombs. [49]Therefore the wisdom of God also said, 'I will send them prophets and apostles, and *some* of them they will kill and persecute,' [50]that the blood of all the prophets which was shed from the foundation of the world may be required of this generation, [51]from the blood of Abel to the blood of Zechariah who perished between the altar and the temple. Yes, I say to you, it shall be required of this generation.

[52]"Woe to you lawyers! For you have taken away the key of knowledge. You did not enter in yourselves, and those who were entering in you hindered."

[53]And as He said these things to them,[a] the scribes and the Pharisees began to assail *Him* vehemently, and to cross-examine Him about many things, [54]lying in wait for Him, and seeking to catch Him in something He might say, that they might accuse Him.[a]

Beware of Hypocrisy

12 In the meantime, when an innumerable multitude of people had gathered together, so that they trampled one another, He began to say to His disciples first *of all,* "Beware of the leaven of the Pharisees, which is hypocrisy. [2]For there is nothing covered that will not be revealed, nor hidden that will not be known. [3]Therefore whatever you have spoken in the dark will be heard in the light, and what you have spoken in the ear in inner rooms will be proclaimed on the housetops.

Jesus Teaches the Fear of God

[4]"And I say to you, My friends, do not be afraid of those who kill the body, and after that have no more that they can do. [5]But I will show you whom you should fear: Fear Him who, after He has killed, has power to cast into hell; yes, I say to you, fear Him! [6]"Are not five sparrows sold for two copper coins?[a] And not one of them is forgotten before God. [7]But the very hairs of your head are all numbered. Do not fear therefore; you are of more value than many sparrows.

Confess Christ Before Men

[8]"Also I say to you, whoever confesses Me before men, him the Son of Man also will confess before the angels of God. [9]But he who denies Me before men will be denied before the angels of God.

[10]"And anyone who speaks a word against the Son of Man, it will be forgiven him; but to him who blasphemes against the Holy Spirit, it will not be forgiven. [11]"Now when they bring you to the synagogues and magistrates and authorities, do not worry about how or what you should answer, or what you should say. [12]For the Holy Spirit will teach you in that very hour what you ought to say."

11:44 [a]NU-Text omits *scribes and Pharisees, hypocrites.*
11:53 [a]NU-Text reads *And when He left there.*
11:54 [a]NU-Text omits *and seeking* and *that they might accuse Him.*   **12:6** [a]Greek *assarion,* a coin of very small value

The Parable of the Rich Fool

13Then one from the crowd said to Him, "Teacher, tell my brother to divide the inheritance with me."

14But He said to him, "Man, who made Me a judge or an arbitrator over you?" 15And He said to them, "Take heed and beware of covetousness,ᵃ for one's life does not consist in the abundance of the things he possesses."

16Then He spoke a parable to them, saying: "The ground of a certain rich man yielded plentifully. 17And he thought within himself, saying, 'What shall I do, since I have no room to store my crops?' 18So he said, 'I will do this: I will pull down my barns and build greater, and there I will store all my crops and my goods. 19And I will say to my soul, "Soul, you have many goods laid up for many years; take your ease; eat, drink, and be merry." ' 20But God said to him, 'Fool! This night your soul will be required of you; then whose will those things be which you have provided?'

21"So is he who lays up treasure for himself, and is not rich toward God."

Do Not Worry

22Then He said to His disciples, "Therefore I say to you, do not worry about your life, what you will eat; nor about the body, what you will put on. 23Life is more than food, and the body is more than clothing. 24Consider the ravens, for they neither sow nor reap, which have neither storehouse nor barn; and God feeds them. Of how much more value are you than the birds? 25And which of you by worrying can add one cubit to his stature? 26If you then are not able to do the least, why are you anxious for the rest? 27Consider the lilies, how they grow: they neither toil nor spin; and yet I say to you, even Solomon in all his glory was not arrayed like one of these. 28If then God so clothes the grass, which today is in the field and tomorrow is thrown into the oven, how much more will He clothe you, O you of little faith?

29"And do not seek what you should eat or what you should drink, nor have an anxious mind. 30For all these things the nations of the world seek after, and your Father knows that you need these things. 31But seek the kingdom of God, and all these thingsᵃ shall be added to you.

32"Do not fear, little flock, for it is your Father's good pleasure to give you the kingdom. 33Sell what you have and give alms; provide yourselves money bags which do not grow old, a treasure in the heavens that does not fail, where no thief approaches nor moth destroys. 34For where your treasure is, there your heart will be also.

The Faithful Servant and the Evil Servant

35"Let your waist be girded and your lamps burning; 36and you yourselves be like men who wait for their master, when he will return from the wedding, that when he comes and knocks they may open to him immediately. 37Blessed are those servants whom the master, when he comes, will find watching. Assuredly, I say to you that he will gird himself and have them sit down to eat, and will come and serve them. 38And if he should come in the second watch, or come in the third watch, and find them so, blessed are those servants. 39But know this, that if the master of the house had known what hour the thief would come, he would have watched andᵃ not allowed his house to be broken into. 40Therefore you also be ready, for the Son of Man is coming at an hour you do not expect."

41Then Peter said to Him, "Lord, do You speak this parable only to us, or to all people?"

42And the Lord said, "Who then is that faithful and wise steward, whom his master will make ruler over his household, to give them their portion of food in due season? 43Blessed is that servant whom his master will find so doing when he comes. 44Truly, I say to you that he will make him ruler over all that he has. 45But if that servant says in his heart, 'My master is delaying his coming,' and begins to beat the male and female servants, and to eat and

12:15 ᵃNU-Text reads all covetousness.
12:31 ᵃNU-Text reads His kingdom, and these things.
12:39 ᵃNU-Text reads he would not have allowed.

drink and be drunk, ⁴⁶the master of that servant will come on a day when he is not looking for *him,* and at an hour when he is not aware, and will cut him in two and appoint *him* his portion with the unbelievers. ⁴⁷And that servant who knew his master's will, and did not prepare *himself* or do according to his will, shall be beaten with many *stripes.* ⁴⁸But he who did not know, yet committed things deserving of stripes, shall be beaten with few. For everyone to whom much is given, from him much will be required; and to whom much has been committed, of him they will ask the more.

Christ Brings Division

⁴⁹"I came to send fire on the earth, and how I wish it were already kindled! ⁵⁰But I have a baptism to be baptized with, and how distressed I am till it is accomplished! ⁵¹Do *you* suppose that I came to give peace on earth? I tell you, not at all, but rather division. ⁵²For from now on five in one house will be divided: three against two, and two against three. ⁵³Father will be divided against son and son against father, mother against daughter and daughter against mother, mother-in-law against her daughter-in-law and daughter-in-law against her mother-in-law."

Discern the Time

⁵⁴Then He also said to the multitudes, "Whenever you see a cloud rising out of the west, immediately you say, 'A shower is coming'; and so it is. ⁵⁵And when *you see* the south wind blow, you say, 'There will be hot weather'; and there is. ⁵⁶Hypocrites! You can discern the face of the sky and of the earth, but how *is it* you do not discern this time?

Make Peace with Your Adversary

⁵⁷"Yes, and why, even of yourselves, do you not judge what is right? ⁵⁸When you go with your adversary to the magistrate, make every effort along the way to settle with him, lest he drag you to the judge, the judge deliver you to the officer, and the officer throw you into prison. ⁵⁹I tell you, you shall not depart from there till you have paid the very last mite."

Repent or Perish

13 There were present at that season some who told Him about the Galileans whose blood Pilate had mingled with their sacrifices. ²And Jesus answered and said to them, "Do you suppose that these Galileans were worse sinners than all *other* Galileans, because they suffered such things? ³I tell you, no; but unless you repent you will all likewise perish. ⁴Or those eighteen on whom the tower in Siloam fell and killed them, do you think that they were worse sinners than all *other* men who dwelt in Jerusalem? ⁵I tell you, no; but unless you repent you will all likewise perish."

The Parable of the Barren Fig Tree

⁶He also spoke this parable: "A certain *man* had a fig tree planted in his vineyard, and he came seeking fruit on it and found none. ⁷Then he said to the keeper of his vineyard, 'Look, for three years I have come seeking fruit on this fig tree and find none. Cut it down; why does it use up the ground?' ⁸But he answered and said to him, 'Sir, let it alone this year also, until I dig around it and fertilize *it.* ⁹And if it bears fruit, *well.* But if not, after that ᵃ you can cut it down.'"

A Spirit of Infirmity

¹⁰Now He was teaching in one of the synagogues on the Sabbath. ¹¹And behold, there was a woman who had a spirit of infirmity eighteen years, and was bent over and could in no way raise *herself* up. ¹²But when Jesus saw her, He called *her* to Him and said to her, "Woman, you are loosed from your infirmity." ¹³And He laid His hands on her, and immediately she was made straight, and glorified God.

¹⁴But the ruler of the synagogue answered with indignation, because Jesus had healed on the Sabbath; and he said to the crowd, "There are six days on which men ought to work; therefore come and be healed on them, and not on the Sabbath day."

¹⁵The Lord then answered him and said, "Hypocrite!ᵃ Does not each one of you on

---

13:9 ᵃNU-Text reads *And if it bears fruit after that, well. But if not, you can cut it down.*   **13:15** ᵃNU-Text and M-Text read *Hypocrites.*

the Sabbath loose his ox or donkey from the stall, and lead *it* away to water it? ¹⁶So ought not this woman, being a daughter of Abraham, whom Satan has bound—think of it—for eighteen years, be loosed from this bond on the Sabbath?" ¹⁷And when He said these things, all His adversaries were put to shame; and all the multitude rejoiced for all the glorious things that were done by Him.

The Parable of the Mustard Seed

¹⁸Then He said, "What is the kingdom of God like? And to what shall I compare it? ¹⁹It is like a mustard seed, which a man took and put in his garden; and it grew and became a large*ᵃ* tree, and the birds of the air nested in its branches."

The Parable of the Leaven

²⁰And again He said, "To what shall I liken the kingdom of God? ²¹It is like leaven, which a woman took and hid in three measures*ᵃ* of meal till it was all leavened."

The Narrow Way

²²And He went through the cities and villages, teaching, and journeying toward Jerusalem. ²³Then one said to Him, "Lord, are there few who are saved?"

And He said to them, ²⁴"Strive to enter through the narrow gate, for many, I say to you, will seek to enter and will not be able. ²⁵When once the Master of the house has risen up and shut the door, and you begin to stand outside and knock at the door, saying, 'Lord, Lord, open for us,' and He will answer and say to you, 'I do not know you, where you are from,' ²⁶then you will begin to say, 'We ate and drank in Your presence, and You taught in our streets.' ²⁷But He will say, 'I tell you I do not know you, where you are from. Depart from Me, all you workers of iniquity.' ²⁸There will be weeping and gnashing of teeth, when you see Abraham and Isaac and Jacob and all the prophets in the kingdom of God, and yourselves thrust out. ²⁹They will come from the east and the west, from the north and the south, and sit down in the kingdom of God. ³⁰And indeed there are last who will be first, and there are first who will be last."

³¹On that very day*ᵃ* some Pharisees came, saying to Him, "Get out and depart from here, for Herod wants to kill You."

³²And He said to them, "Go, tell that fox, 'Behold, I cast out demons and perform cures today and tomorrow, and the third *day* I shall be perfected.' ³³Nevertheless I must journey today, tomorrow, and the *day* following; for it cannot be that a prophet should perish outside of Jerusalem.

Jesus Laments over Jerusalem

³⁴"O Jerusalem, Jerusalem, the one who kills the prophets and stones those who are sent to her! How often I wanted to gather your children together, as a hen *gathers* her brood under *her* wings, but you were not willing! ³⁵See! Your house is left to you desolate; and assuredly,*ᵃ* I say to you, you shall not see Me until *the time* comes when you say, '*Blessed is He who comes in the name of the LORD!* '*ᵇ*

A Man with Dropsy Healed on the Sabbath

14 Now it happened, as He went into the house of one of the rulers of the Pharisees to eat bread on the Sabbath, that they watched Him closely. ²And behold, there was a certain man before Him who had dropsy. ³And Jesus, answering, spoke to the lawyers and Pharisees, saying, "Is it lawful to heal on the Sabbath?"*ᵃ*

⁴But they kept silent. And He took *him* and healed him, and let him go. ⁵Then He answered them, saying, "Which of you, having a donkey*ᵃ* or an ox that has fallen into a pit, will not immediately pull him out on the Sabbath day?" ⁶And they could not answer Him regarding these things.

Take the Lowly Place

⁷So He told a parable to those who were invited, when He noted how they chose the best places, saying to them: ⁸"When you are invited by anyone to a wedding feast, do not sit down in the best place, lest one more honorable than you be invited by

---

13:19 *ᵃ*NU-Text omits *large*. **13:21** *ᵃ*Greek *sata*, approximately two pecks in all **13:31** *ᵃ*NU-Text reads *In that very hour*. **13:35** *ᵃ*NU-Text and M-Text omit *assuredly*. *ᵇ*Psalm 118:26 **14:3** *ᵃ*NU-Text adds *or not*. **14:5** *ᵃ*NU-Text and M-Text read *son*.

him; ⁹and he who invited you and him come and say to you, 'Give place to this man,' and then you begin with shame to take the lowest place. ¹⁰But when you are invited, go and sit down in the lowest place, so that when he who invited you comes he may say to you, 'Friend, go up higher.' Then you will have glory in the presence of those who sit at the table with you. ¹¹For whoever exalts himself will be humbled, and he who humbles himself will be exalted."

¹²Then He also said to him who invited Him, "When you give a dinner or a supper, do not ask your friends, your brothers, your relatives, nor rich neighbors, lest they also invite you back, and you be repaid. ¹³But when you give a feast, invite *the* poor, *the* maimed, *the* lame, *the* blind. ¹⁴And you will be blessed, because they cannot repay you; for you shall be repaid at the resurrection of the just."

The Parable of the Great Supper

¹⁵Now when one of those who sat at the table with Him heard these things, he said to Him, "Blessed *is* he who shall eat bread^a in the kingdom of God!"

¹⁶Then He said to him, "A certain man gave a great supper and invited many, ¹⁷and sent his servant at supper time to say to those who were invited, 'Come, for all things are now ready.' ¹⁸But they all with one *accord* began to make excuses. The first said to him, 'I have bought a piece of ground, and I must go and see it. I ask you to have me excused.' ¹⁹And another said, 'I have bought five yoke of oxen, and I am going to test them. I ask you to have me excused.' ²⁰Still another said, 'I have married a wife, and therefore I cannot come.' ²¹So that servant came and reported these things to his master. Then the master of the house, being angry, said to his servant, 'Go out quickly into the streets and lanes of the city, and bring in here *the* poor and *the* maimed and *the* lame and *the* blind.' ²²And the servant said, 'Master, it is done as you commanded, and still there is room.' ²³Then the master said to the servant, 'Go out into the highways and hedges, and compel *them* to come in, that my house may be filled. ²⁴For I say to you that none

of those men who were invited shall taste my supper.'"

Leaving All to Follow Christ

²⁵Now great multitudes went with Him. And He turned and said to them, ²⁶"If anyone comes to Me and does not hate his father and mother, wife and children, brothers and sisters, yes, and his own life also, he cannot be My disciple. ²⁷And whoever does not bear his cross and come after Me cannot be My disciple. ²⁸For which of you, intending to build a tower, does not sit down first and count the cost, whether he has *enough* to finish *it*— ²⁹lest, after he has laid the foundation, and is not able to finish, all who see *it* begin to mock him, ³⁰saying, 'This man began to build and was not able to finish'? ³¹Or what king, going to make war against another king, does not sit down first and consider whether he is able with ten thousand to meet him who comes against him with twenty thousand? ³²Or else, while the other is still a great way off, he sends a delegation and asks conditions of peace. ³³So likewise, whoever of you does not forsake all that he has cannot be My disciple.

Tasteless Salt Is Worthless

³⁴"Salt *is* good; but if the salt has lost its flavor, how shall it be seasoned? ³⁵It is neither fit for the land nor for the dunghill, *but* men throw it out. He who has ears to hear, let him hear!"

The Parable of the Lost Sheep

15 Then all the tax collectors and the sinners drew near to Him to hear Him. ²And the Pharisees and scribes complained, saying, "This Man receives sinners and eats with them." ³So He spoke this parable to them, saying:

⁴"What man of you, having a hundred sheep, if he loses one of them, does not leave the ninety-nine in the wilderness, and go after the one which is lost until he finds it? ⁵And when he has found *it,* he lays *it* on his shoulders, rejoicing. ⁶And when he comes home, he calls together *his* friends

---

14:15 ^a M-Text reads *dinner.*

and neighbors, saying to them, 'Rejoice with me, for I have found my sheep which was lost!' ⁷I say to you that likewise there will be more joy in heaven over one sinner who repents than over ninety-nine just persons who need no repentance.

The Parable of the Lost Coin

⁸"Or what woman, having ten silver coins,ᵃ if she loses one coin, does not light a lamp, sweep the house, and search carefully until she finds *it?* ⁹And when she has found *it,* she calls *her* friends and neighbors together, saying, 'Rejoice with me, for I have found the piece which I lost!' ¹⁰Likewise, I say to you, there is joy in the presence of the angels of God over one sinner who repents."

The Parable of the Lost Son

¹¹Then He said: "A certain man had two sons. ¹²And the younger of them said to *his* father, 'Father, give me the portion of goods that falls *to me.*' So he divided to them *his* livelihood. ¹³And not many days after, the younger son gathered all together, journeyed to a far country, and there wasted his possessions with prodigal living. ¹⁴But when he had spent all, there arose a severe famine in that land, and he began to be in want. ¹⁵Then he went and joined himself to a citizen of that country, and he sent him into his fields to feed swine. ¹⁶And he would gladly have filled his stomach with the pods that the swine ate, and no one gave him *anything.*

¹⁷"But when he came to himself, he said, 'How many of my father's hired servants have bread enough and to spare, and I perish with hunger! ¹⁸I will arise and go to my father, and will say to him, "Father, I have sinned against heaven and before you, ¹⁹and I am no longer worthy to be called your son. Make me like one of your hired servants."' ²⁰And he arose and came to his father. But when he was still a great way off, his father saw him and had compassion, and ran and fell on his neck and kissed him. ²¹And the son said to him, 'Father, I have sinned against heaven and in your sight, and am no longer worthy to be called your son.'

²²"But the father said to his servants, 'Bringᵃ out the best robe and put *it* on him, and put a ring on his hand and sandals on *his* feet. ²³And bring the fatted calf here and kill *it,* and let us eat and be merry; ²⁴for this my son was dead and is alive again; he was lost and is found.' And they began to be merry.

²⁵"Now his older son was in the field. And as he came and drew near to the house, he heard music and dancing. ²⁶So he called one of the servants and asked what these things meant. ²⁷And he said to him, 'Your brother has come, and because he has received him safe and sound, your father has killed the fatted calf.'

²⁸"But he was angry and would not go in. Therefore his father came out and pleaded with him. ²⁹So he answered and said to *his* father, 'Lo, these many years I have been serving you; I never transgressed your commandment at any time; and yet you never gave me a young goat, that I might make merry with my friends. ³⁰But as soon as this son of yours came, who has devoured your livelihood with harlots, you killed the fatted calf for him.'

³¹"And he said to him, 'Son, you are always with me, and all that I have is yours. ³²It was right that we should make merry and be glad, for your brother was dead and is alive again, and was lost and is found.'"

The Parable of the Unjust Steward

16 He also said to His disciples: "There was a certain rich man who had a steward, and an accusation was brought to him that this man was wasting his goods. ²So he called him and said to him, 'What is this I hear about you? Give an account of your stewardship, for you can no longer be steward.'

³"Then the steward said within himself, 'What shall I do? For my master is taking the stewardship away from me. I cannot dig; I am ashamed to beg. ⁴I have resolved what to do, that when I am put out of the

---

15:8 ᵃGreek *drachma,* a valuable coin often worn in a ten-piece garland by married women
15:22 ᵃNU-Text reads *Quickly bring.*

stewardship, they may receive me into their houses.'

⁵"So he called every one of his master's debtors to *him,* and said to the first, 'How much do you owe my master?' ⁶And he said, 'A hundred measures[a] of oil.' So he said to him, 'Take your bill, and sit down quickly and write fifty.' ⁷Then he said to another, 'And how much do you owe?' So he said, 'A hundred measures[a] of wheat.' And he said to him, 'Take your bill, and write eighty.' ⁸So the master commended the unjust steward because he had dealt shrewdly. For the sons of this world are more shrewd in their generation than the sons of light.

⁹"And I say to you, make friends for yourselves by unrighteous mammon, that when you fail,[a] they may receive you into an everlasting home. ¹⁰He who *is* faithful in *what is* least is faithful also in much; and he who is unjust in *what is* least is unjust also in much. ¹¹Therefore if you have not been faithful in the unrighteous mammon, who will commit to your trust the true *riches?* ¹²And if you have not been faithful in what is another man's, who will give you what is your own?

¹³"No servant can serve two masters; for either he will hate the one and love the other, or else he will be loyal to the one and despise the other. You cannot serve God and mammon."

The Law, the Prophets, and the Kingdom

¹⁴Now the Pharisees, who were lovers of money, also heard all these things, and they derided Him. ¹⁵And He said to them, "You are those who justify yourselves before men, but God knows your hearts. For what is highly esteemed among men is an abomination in the sight of God.

¹⁶"The law and the prophets *were* until John. Since that time the kingdom of God has been preached, and everyone is pressing into it. ¹⁷And it is easier for heaven and earth to pass away than for one tittle of the law to fail.

¹⁸"Whoever divorces his wife and marries another commits adultery; and whoever marries her who is divorced from *her* husband commits adultery.

The Rich Man and Lazarus

¹⁹"There was a certain rich man who was clothed in purple and fine linen and fared sumptuously every day. ²⁰But there was a certain beggar named Lazarus, full of sores, who was laid at his gate, ²¹desiring to be fed with the crumbs which fell[a] from the rich man's table. Moreover the dogs came and licked his sores. ²²So it was that the beggar died, and was carried by the angels to Abraham's bosom. The rich man also died and was buried. ²³And being in torments in Hades, he lifted up his eyes and saw Abraham afar off, and Lazarus in his bosom.

²⁴"Then he cried and said, 'Father Abraham, have mercy on me, and send Lazarus that he may dip the tip of his finger in water and cool my tongue; for I am tormented in this flame.' ²⁵But Abraham said, 'Son, remember that in your lifetime you received your good things, and likewise Lazarus evil things; but now he is comforted and you are tormented. ²⁶And besides all this, between us and you there is a great gulf fixed, so that those who want to pass from here to you cannot, nor can those from there pass to us.'

²⁷"Then he said, 'I beg you therefore, father, that you would send him to my father's house, ²⁸for I have five brothers, that he may testify to them, lest they also come to this place of torment.' ²⁹Abraham said to him, 'They have Moses and the prophets; let them hear them.' ³⁰And he said, 'No, father Abraham; but if one goes to them from the dead, they will repent.' ³¹But he said to him, 'If they do not hear Moses and the prophets, neither will they be persuaded though one rise from the dead.'"

Jesus Warns of Offenses

17 Then He said to the disciples, "It is impossible that no offenses should come, but woe *to him* through whom they do come! ²It would be better for him if a millstone were hung around his neck, and he were thrown into the sea, than that he

---

16:6 [a]Greek *batos,* eight or nine gallons each (Old Testament *bath*)   **16:7** [a]Greek *koros,* ten or twelve bushels each (Old Testament *kor*)   **16:9** [a]NU-Text reads *it fails.*   **16:21** [a]NU-Text reads *with what fell.*

should offend one of these little ones. ³Take heed to yourselves. If your brother sins against you,ª rebuke him; and if he repents, forgive him. ⁴And if he sins against you seven times in a day, and seven times in a day returns to you,ª saying, 'I repent,' you shall forgive him."

Faith and Duty

⁵And the apostles said to the Lord, "Increase our faith."

⁶So the Lord said, "If you have faith as a mustard seed, you can say to this mulberry tree, 'Be pulled up by the roots and be planted in the sea,' and it would obey you. ⁷And which of you, having a servant plowing or tending sheep, will say to him when he has come in from the field, 'Come at once and sit down to eat'? ⁸But will he not rather say to him, 'Prepare something for my supper, and gird yourself and serve me till I have eaten and drunk, and afterward you will eat and drink'? ⁹Does he thank that servant because he did the things that were commanded him? I think not.ª ¹⁰So likewise you, when you have done all those things which you are commanded, say, 'We are unprofitable servants. We have done what was our duty to do.' "

Ten Lepers Cleansed

¹¹Now it happened as He went to Jerusalem that He passed through the midst of Samaria and Galilee. ¹²Then as He entered a certain village, there met Him ten men who were lepers, who stood afar off. ¹³And they lifted up *their* voices and said, "Jesus, Master, have mercy on us!"

17:3 ªNU-Text omits *against you*.   **17:4** ªM-Text omits *to you*.   **17:9** ªNU-Text ends verse with *commanded;* M-Text omits *him*.

FREEDOM

"We have done what was our duty to do."

LUKE 17:10

Boy Scouts of America
1941

"DUTY TO GOD"

The Boy Scouts of America believes that no member can grow into the best kind of citizen without recognizing an obligation to God. Accordingly, youth members and adult volunteer leaders obligate themselves to do their duty to God and be reverent as embodied in the Scout Oath and the Scout Law. But it hasn't been without its share of legal battles.

In the 1993 case of *Welsh v. Boy Scouts of America*, the United States Court of Appeals—Seventh Circuit ruled that the Boy Scouts could keep the phrase "duty to God" in their oath, and as a private organization they had the right to exclude anyone who refused to take the oath. It stated:

> The leadership of many in our government is a testimonial to the success of Boy Scout activities. . . . In recent years, single-parent families, gang activity, the availability of drugs, and other factors have increased the dire need for support structures like the Scouts.
>
> When the government, in this instance, through the courts, seeks to regulate the membership of an organization like the Boy Scouts in a way that scuttles its founding principles, we run the risk of undermining one of the seedbeds of virtue that cultivate the sorts of citizens our nation so desperately needs.

Cases in 1995 and 1998 upheld the "duty to God" requirements for Scouts as well as leaders.

¹⁴So when He saw *them,* He said to them, "Go, show yourselves to the priests." And so it was that as they went, they were cleansed.

¹⁵And one of them, when he saw that he was healed, returned, and with a loud voice glorified God, ¹⁶and fell down on *his* face at His feet, giving Him thanks. And he was a Samaritan.

¹⁷So Jesus answered and said, "Were there not ten cleansed? But where *are* the nine? ¹⁸Were there not any found who returned to give glory to God except this foreigner?" ¹⁹And He said to him, "Arise, go your way. Your faith has made you well."

The Coming of the Kingdom

²⁰Now when He was asked by the Pharisees when the kingdom of God would come, He answered them and said, "The kingdom of God does not come with observation; ²¹nor will they say, 'See here!' or 'See there!'ᵃ For indeed, the kingdom of God is within you."

²²Then He said to the disciples, "The days will come when you will desire to see one of the days of the Son of Man, and you will not see *it.* ²³And they will say to you, 'Look here!' or 'Look there!'ᵃ Do not go after *them* or follow *them.* ²⁴For as the lightning that flashes out of one *part* under heaven shines to the other *part* under heaven, so also the Son of Man will be in His day. ²⁵But first He must suffer many things and be rejected by this generation. ²⁶And as it was in the days of Noah, so it will be also in the days of the Son of Man: ²⁷They ate, they drank, they married wives, they were given in marriage, until the day that Noah entered the ark, and the flood came and destroyed them all. ²⁸Likewise as it was also in the days of Lot: They ate, they drank, they bought, they sold, they planted, they built; ²⁹but on the day that Lot went out of Sodom it rained fire and brimstone from heaven and destroyed *them* all. ³⁰Even so will it be in the day when the Son of Man is revealed.

³¹"In that day, he who is on the housetop, and his goods *are* in the house, let him not come down to take them away. And likewise the one who is in the field, let him not turn back. ³²Remember Lot's wife.

³³Whoever seeks to save his life will lose it, and whoever loses his life will preserve it. ³⁴I tell you, in that night there will be two *men* in one bed: the one will be taken and the other will be left. ³⁵Two *women* will be grinding together: the one will be taken and the other left. ³⁶Two *men* will be in the field: the one will be taken and the other left."ᵃ

³⁷And they answered and said to Him, "Where, Lord?"

So He said to them, "Wherever the body is, there the eagles will be gathered together."

The Parable of the Persistent Widow

18 Then He spoke a parable to them, that men always ought to pray and not lose heart, ²saying: "There was in a certain city a judge who did not fear God nor regard man. ³Now there was a widow in that city; and she came to him, saying, 'Get justice for me from my adversary.' ⁴And he would not for a while; but afterward he said within himself, 'Though I do not fear God nor regard man, ⁵yet because this widow troubles me I will avenge her, lest by her continual coming she weary me.'"

⁶Then the Lord said, "Hear what the unjust judge said. ⁷And shall God not avenge His own elect who cry out day and night to Him, though He bears long with them? ⁸I tell you that He will avenge them speedily. Nevertheless, when the Son of Man comes, will He really find faith on the earth?"

The Parable of the Pharisee and the Tax Collector

⁹Also He spoke this parable to some who trusted in themselves that they were righteous, and despised others: ¹⁰"Two men went up to the temple to pray, one a Pharisee and the other a tax collector. ¹¹The Pharisee stood and prayed thus with himself, 'God, I thank You that I am not like other men—extortioners, unjust, adulterers, or even as this tax collector. ¹²I fast twice a week; I give tithes of all that I possess.' ¹³And the tax collector, standing afar

---

17:21 ᵃNU-Text reverses *here* and *there.*
17:23 ᵃNU-Text reverses *here* and *there.*
17:36 ᵃNU-Text and M-Text omit verse 36.

off, would not so much as raise *his* eyes to heaven, but beat his breast, saying, 'God, be merciful to me a sinner!' ¹⁴I tell you, this man went down to his house justified *rather* than the other; for everyone who exalts himself will be humbled, and he who humbles himself will be exalted."

Jesus Blesses Little Children

¹⁵Then they also brought infants to Him that He might touch them; but when the disciples saw *it,* they rebuked them. ¹⁶But Jesus called them to *Him* and said, "Let the little children come to Me, and do not forbid them; for of such is the kingdom of God. ¹⁷Assuredly, I say to you, whoever does not receive the kingdom of God as a little child will by no means enter it."

Jesus Counsels the Rich Young Ruler

¹⁸Now a certain ruler asked Him, saying, "Good Teacher, what shall I do to inherit eternal life?"

¹⁹So Jesus said to him, "Why do you call Me good? No one *is* good but One, *that is,* God. ²⁰You know the commandments: *'Do not commit adultery,' 'Do not murder,' 'Do not steal,' 'Do not bear false witness,' 'Honor your father and your mother.' "*ᵃ

²¹And he said, "All these things I have kept from my youth."

²²So when Jesus heard these things, He said to him, "You still lack one thing. Sell all that you have and distribute to the poor, and you will have treasure in heaven; and come, follow Me."

²³But when he heard this, he became very sorrowful, for he was very rich.

With God All Things Are Possible

²⁴And when Jesus saw that he became very sorrowful, He said, "How hard it is for those who have riches to enter the kingdom of God! ²⁵For it is easier for a camel to go through the eye of a needle than for a rich man to enter the kingdom of God."

²⁶And those who heard it said, "Who then can be saved?"

²⁷But He said, "The things which are impossible with men are possible with God."

²⁸Then Peter said, "See, we have left allᵃ and followed You."

²⁹So He said to them, "Assuredly, I say to you, there is no one who has left house or parents or brothers or wife or children, for the sake of the kingdom of God, ³⁰who shall not receive many times more in this present time, and in the age to come eternal life."

Jesus a Third Time Predicts His Death and Resurrection

³¹Then He took the twelve aside and said to them, "Behold, we are going up to Jerusalem, and all things that are written by the prophets concerning the Son of Man will be accomplished. ³²For He will be delivered to the Gentiles and will be mocked and insulted and spit upon. ³³They will scourge *Him* and kill Him. And the third day He will rise again."

³⁴But they understood none of these things; this saying was hidden from them, and they did not know the things which were spoken.

A Blind Man Receives His Sight

³⁵Then it happened, as He was coming near Jericho, that a certain blind man sat by the road begging. ³⁶And hearing a multitude passing by, he asked what it meant. ³⁷So they told him that Jesus of Nazareth was passing by. ³⁸And he cried out, saying, "Jesus, Son of David, have mercy on me!"

³⁹Then those who went before warned him that he should be quiet; but he cried out all the more, "Son of David, have mercy on me!"

⁴⁰So Jesus stood still and commanded him to be brought to Him. And when he had come near, He asked him, ⁴¹saying, "What do you want Me to do for you?"

He said, "Lord, that I may receive my sight."

⁴²Then Jesus said to him, "Receive your sight; your faith has made you well." ⁴³And immediately he received his sight, and followed Him, glorifying God. And all the people, when they saw *it,* gave praise to God.

18:20 ᵃExodus 20:12–16; Deuteronomy 5:16–20
18:28 ᵃNU-Text reads *our own.*

Jesus Comes to Zacchaeus' House

19 Then *Jesus* entered and passed through Jericho. ²Now behold, *there was* a man named Zacchaeus who was a chief tax collector, and he was rich. ³And he sought to see who Jesus was, but could not because of the crowd, for he was of short stature. ⁴So he ran ahead and climbed up into a sycamore tree to see Him, for He was going to pass that *way.* ⁵And when Jesus came to the place, He looked up and saw him,ᵃ and said to him, "Zacchaeus, make haste and come down, for today I must stay at your house." ⁶So he made haste and came down, and received Him joyfully. ⁷But when they saw *it,* they all complained, saying, "He has gone to be a guest with a man who is a sinner."

⁸Then Zacchaeus stood and said to the Lord, "Look, Lord, I give half of my goods to the poor; and if I have taken anything from anyone by false accusation, I restore fourfold."

⁹And Jesus said to him, "Today salvation has come to this house, because he also is a son of Abraham; ¹⁰for the Son of Man has come to seek and to save that which was lost."

The Parable of the Minas

¹¹Now as they heard these things, He spoke another parable, because He was near Jerusalem and because they thought the kingdom of God would appear immediately. ¹²Therefore He said: "A certain nobleman went into a far country to receive for himself a kingdom and to return. ¹³So he called ten of his servants, delivered to them ten minas,ᵃ and said to them, 'Do business till I come.' ¹⁴But his citizens hated him, and sent a delegation after him, saying, 'We will not have this *man* to reign over us.'

¹⁵"And so it was that when he returned, having received the kingdom, he then commanded these servants, to whom he had given the money, to be called to him, that he might know how much every man had gained by trading. ¹⁶Then came the first, saying, 'Master, your mina has earned ten minas.' ¹⁷And he said to him,

'Well *done,* good servant; because you were faithful in a very little, have authority over ten cities.' ¹⁸And the second came, saying, 'Master, your mina has earned five minas.' ¹⁹Likewise he said to him, 'You also be over five cities.'

²⁰"Then another came, saying, 'Master, here is your mina, which I have kept put away in a handkerchief. ²¹For I feared you, because you are an austere man. You collect what you did not deposit, and reap what you did not sow.' ²²And he said to him, 'Out of your own mouth I will judge you, *you* wicked servant. You knew that I was an austere man, collecting what I did not deposit and reaping what I did not sow. ²³Why then did you not put my money in the bank, that at my coming I might have collected it with interest?'

²⁴"And he said to those who stood by, 'Take the mina from him, and give *it* to him who has ten minas.' ²⁵(But they said to him, 'Master, he has ten minas.') ²⁶'For I say to you, that to everyone who has will be given; and from him who does not have,

---

19:5 ᵃNU-Text omits *and saw him.*   **19:13** ᵃThe *mina* (Greek *mna,* Hebrew *minah*) was worth about three months' salary.

even what he has will be taken away from him. ²⁷But bring here those enemies of mine, who did not want me to reign over them, and slay *them* before me.' "

The Triumphal Entry

²⁸When He had said this, He went on ahead, going up to Jerusalem. ²⁹And it came to pass, when He drew near to Bethphage^a and Bethany, at the mountain called Olivet, *that* He sent two of His disciples, ³⁰saying, "Go into the village opposite *you,* where as you enter you will find a colt tied, on which no one has ever sat. Loose it and bring *it here.* ³¹And if anyone asks you, 'Why are you loosing *it?*' thus you shall say to him, 'Because the Lord has need of it.' "

³²So those who were sent went their way and found *it* just as He had said to them. ³³But as they were loosing the colt, the owners of it said to them, "Why are you loosing the colt?"

³⁴And they said, "The Lord has need of him." ³⁵Then they brought him to Jesus. And they threw their own clothes on the colt, and they set Jesus on him. ³⁶And as He went, *many* spread their clothes on the road.

³⁷Then, as He was now drawing near the descent of the Mount of Olives, the whole multitude of the disciples began to rejoice and praise God with a loud voice for all the mighty works they had seen, ³⁸saying:

" '*Blessed is the King who comes in
the name of the LORD!*'^a
Peace in heaven and glory in the
highest!"

³⁹And some of the Pharisees called to Him from the crowd, "Teacher, rebuke Your disciples."

⁴⁰But He answered and said to them, "I tell you that if these should keep silent, the stones would immediately cry out."

Jesus Weeps over Jerusalem

⁴¹Now as He drew near, He saw the city and wept over it, ⁴²saying, "If you had known, even you, especially in this your day, the things *that make* for your peace! But now they are hidden from your eyes. ⁴³For days will come upon you when your enemies will build an embankment around you, surround you and close you in on every side, ⁴⁴and level you, and your children within you, to the ground; and they will not leave in you one stone upon another, because you did not know the time of your visitation."

Jesus Cleanses the Temple

⁴⁵Then He went into the temple and began to drive out those who bought and sold in it,^a ⁴⁶saying to them, "It is written, '*My house is*^a *a house of prayer,*'^b but you have made it a '*den of thieves.*' "^c

⁴⁷And He was teaching daily in the temple. But the chief priests, the scribes, and the leaders of the people sought to destroy Him, ⁴⁸and were unable to do anything; for all the people were very attentive to hear Him.

Jesus' Authority Questioned

20 Now it happened on one of those days, as He taught the people in the temple and preached the gospel, *that* the chief priests and the scribes, together with the elders, confronted *Him* ²and spoke to Him, saying, "Tell us, by what authority are You doing these things? Or who is he who gave You this authority?"

³But He answered and said to them, "I also will ask you one thing, and answer Me: ⁴The baptism of John—was it from heaven or from men?"

⁵And they reasoned among themselves, saying, "If we say, 'From heaven,' He will say, 'Why then^a did you not believe him?' ⁶But if we say, 'From men,' all the people will stone us, for they are persuaded that John was a prophet." ⁷So they answered that they did not know where *it was* from.

⁸And Jesus said to them, "Neither will I tell you by what authority I do these things."

The Parable of the Wicked Vinedressers

⁹Then He began to tell the people this parable: "A certain man planted a vineyard,

---

19:29 ^aM-Text reads *Bethsphage.*
19:38 ^aPsalm 118:26   **19:45** ^aNU-Text reads *those who were selling.*   **19:46** ^aNU-Text reads *shall be.* ^bIsaiah 56:7 ^cJeremiah 7:11   **20:5** ^aNU-Text and M-Text omit *then.*

leased it to vinedressers, and went into a far country for a long time. ¹⁰Now at vintage-time he sent a servant to the vinedressers, that they might give him some of the fruit of the vineyard. But the vinedressers beat him and sent *him* away empty-handed. ¹¹Again he sent another servant; and they beat him also, treated *him* shamefully, and sent *him* away empty-handed. ¹²And again he sent a third; and they wounded him also and cast *him* out.

¹³"Then the owner of the vineyard said, 'What shall I do? I will send my beloved son. Probably they will respect *him* when they see him.' ¹⁴But when the vinedressers saw him, they reasoned among themselves, saying, 'This is the heir. Come, let us kill him, that the inheritance may be ours.' ¹⁵So they cast him out of the vineyard and killed *him*. Therefore what will the owner of the vineyard do to them? ¹⁶He will come and destroy those vinedressers and give the vineyard to others."

And when they heard *it* they said, "Certainly not!"

¹⁷Then He looked at them and said, "What then is this that is written:

'The stone which the builders rejected
Has become the chief cornerstone'?ᵃ

¹⁸Whoever falls on that stone will be broken; but on whomever it falls, it will grind him to powder."

¹⁹And the chief priests and the scribes that very hour sought to lay hands on Him, but they feared the peopleᵃ—for they knew He had spoken this parable against them.

The Pharisees: Is It Lawful to Pay Taxes to Caesar?

²⁰So they watched *Him,* and sent spies who pretended to be righteous, that they might seize on His words, in order to deliver Him to the power and the authority of the governor. ²¹Then they asked Him, saying, "Teacher, we know that You say and teach rightly, and You do not show personal favoritism, but teach the way of God in truth: ²²Is it lawful for us to pay taxes to Caesar or not?"

²³But He perceived their craftiness, and said to them, "Why do you test Me?ᵃ ²⁴Show Me a denarius. Whose image and inscription does it have?"

They answered and said, "Caesar's."

²⁵And He said to them, "Render therefore to Caesar the things that are Caesar's, and to God the things that are God's."

²⁶But they could not catch Him in His words in the presence of the people. And they marveled at His answer and kept silent.

The Sadducees: What About the Resurrection?

²⁷Then some of the Sadducees, who deny that there is a resurrection, came to *Him* and asked Him, ²⁸saying: "Teacher, Moses wrote to us *that* if a man's brother dies, having a wife, and he dies without children, his brother should take his wife and raise up offspring for his brother. ²⁹Now there were seven brothers. And the first took a wife, and died without children. ³⁰And the secondᵃ took her as wife, and he died childless. ³¹Then the third took her, and in like manner the seven also; and they left no children,ᵃ and died. ³²Last of all the woman died also. ³³Therefore, in the resurrection, whose wife does she become? For all seven had her as wife."

³⁴Jesus answered and said to them, "The sons of this age marry and are given in marriage. ³⁵But those who are counted worthy to attain that age, and the resurrection from the dead, neither marry nor are given in marriage; ³⁶nor can they die anymore, for they are equal to the angels and are sons of God, being sons of the resurrection. ³⁷But even Moses showed in the *burning* bush *passage* that the dead are raised, when he called the Lord '*the God of Abraham, the God of Isaac, and the God of Jacob.*'ᵃ ³⁸For He is not the God of the dead but of the living, for all live to Him."

³⁹Then some of the scribes answered and said, "Teacher, You have spoken well." ⁴⁰But

---

20:17 ᵃPsalm 118:22   **20:19** ᵃM-Text reads *but they were afraid.*   **20:23** ᵃNU-Text omits *Why do you test Me?*   **20:30** ᵃNU-Text ends verse 30 here. **20:31** ᵃNU-Text and M-Text read *the seven also left no children.*   **20:37** ᵃExodus 3:6, 15

after that they dared not question Him anymore.

Jesus: How Can David Call His Descendant Lord?

41And He said to them, "How can they say that the Christ is the Son of David? 42Now David himself said in the Book of Psalms:

'The Lord said to my Lord,
"Sit at My right hand,
43 Till I make Your enemies Your
     footstool." 'a

44Therefore David calls Him 'Lord'; how is He then his Son?"

Beware of the Scribes

45Then, in the hearing of all the people, He said to His disciples, 46"Beware of the scribes, who desire to go around in long robes, love greetings in the marketplaces, the best seats in the synagogues, and the best places at feasts, 47who devour widows' houses, and for a pretense make long prayers. These will receive greater condemnation."

The Widow's Two Mites

21 And He looked up and saw the rich putting their gifts into the treasury, 2and He saw also a certain poor widow putting in two mites. 3So He said, "Truly I say to you that this poor widow has put in more than all; 4for all these out of their abundance have put in offerings for God,a but she out of her poverty put in all the livelihood that she had."

Jesus Predicts the Destruction of the Temple

5Then, as some spoke of the temple, how it was adorned with beautiful stones and donations, He said, 6"These things which you see—the days will come in which not one stone shall be left upon another that shall not be thrown down."

The Signs of the Times and the End of the Age

7So they asked Him, saying, "Teacher, but when will these things be? And what sign will there be when these things are about to take place?"

8And He said: "Take heed that you not be deceived. For many will come in My name, saying, 'I am He,' and, 'The time has drawn near.' Thereforea do not go after them. 9But when you hear of wars and commotions, do not be terrified; for these things must come to pass first, but the end will not come immediately."

10Then He said to them, "Nation will rise against nation, and kingdom against kingdom. 11And there will be great earthquakes in various places, and famines and pestilences; and there will be fearful sights and great signs from heaven. 12But before all these things, they will lay their hands on you and persecute you, delivering you up to the synagogues and prisons. You will be brought before kings and rulers for My name's sake. 13But it will turn out for you as an occasion for testimony. 14Therefore settle it in your hearts not to meditate beforehand on what you will answer; 15for I will give you a mouth and wisdom which all your adversaries will not be able to contradict or resist. 16You will be betrayed even by parents and brothers, relatives and friends; and they will put some of you to death. 17And you will be hated by all for My name's sake. 18But not a hair of your head shall be lost. 19By your patience possess your souls.

The Destruction of Jerusalem

20"But when you see Jerusalem surrounded by armies, then know that its desolation is near. 21Then let those who are in Judea flee to the mountains, let those who are in the midst of her depart, and let not those who are in the country enter her. 22For these are the days of vengeance, that all things which are written may be fulfilled. 23But woe to those who are pregnant and to those who are nursing babies in those days! For there will be great distress in the land and wrath upon this people. 24And they will fall by the edge of the sword, and be led away captive into all nations.

20:43 aPsalm 110:1   **21:4** aNU-Text omits for God. **21:8** aNU-Text omits Therefore.

And Jerusalem will be trampled by Gentiles until the times of the Gentiles are fulfilled.

The Coming of the Son of Man

25"And there will be signs in the sun, in the moon, and in the stars; and on the earth distress of nations, with perplexity, the sea and the waves roaring; 26men's hearts failing them from fear and the expectation of those things which are coming on the earth, for the powers of the heavens will be shaken. 27Then they will see the Son of Man coming in a cloud with power and great glory. 28Now when these things begin to happen, look up and lift up your heads, because your redemption draws near."

The Parable of the Fig Tree

29Then He spoke to them a parable: "Look at the fig tree, and all the trees. 30When they are already budding, you see and know for yourselves that summer is now near. 31So you also, when you see these things happening, know that the kingdom of God is near. 32Assuredly, I say to you, this generation will by no means pass away till all things take place. 33Heaven and earth will pass away, but My words will by no means pass away.

The Importance of Watching

34"But take heed to yourselves, lest your hearts be weighed down with carousing, drunkenness, and cares of this life, and that Day come on you unexpectedly. 35For it will come as a snare on all those who dwell on the face of the whole earth. 36Watch therefore, and pray always that you may be counted worthy[a] to escape all these things that will come to pass, and to stand before the Son of Man."

37And in the daytime He was teaching in the temple, but at night He went out and stayed on the mountain called Olivet. 38Then early in the morning all the people came to Him in the temple to hear Him.

The Plot to Kill Jesus

22 Now the Feast of Unleavened Bread drew near, which is called Passover. 2And the chief priests and the scribes sought how they might kill Him, for they feared the people.

3Then Satan entered Judas, surnamed Iscariot, who was numbered among the twelve. 4So he went his way and conferred with the chief priests and captains, how he

---

21:36 aNU-Text reads *may have strength.*

THE GENERAL PRINCIPLES OF LIBERTY

In a letter to Thomas Jefferson on June 28, 1813, John Adams wrote:

The general principles, on which the Fathers achieved independence, were the only principles in which that beautiful assembly of young gentlemen could unite. . . . And what were these general principles? I answer, the general principles of Christianity, in which all these sects were united: And the general principles of English and American liberty, in which all those young men united, and which had united all parties in America, in majorities sufficient to assert and maintain her independence.

Now I will avow, that I then believe, and now believe, that those general principles of Christianity, are as eternal and immutable, as the existence and attributes of God; and that those principles of liberty, are as unalterable as human nature and our terrestrial, mundane system.

might betray Him to them. ⁵And they were glad, and agreed to give him money. ⁶So he promised and sought opportunity to betray Him to them in the absence of the multitude.

Jesus and His Disciples Prepare the Passover

⁷Then came the Day of Unleavened Bread, when the Passover must be killed. ⁸And He sent Peter and John, saying, "Go and prepare the Passover for us, that we may eat."

⁹So they said to Him, "Where do You want us to prepare?"

¹⁰And He said to them, "Behold, when you have entered the city, a man will meet you carrying a pitcher of water; follow him into the house which he enters. ¹¹Then you shall say to the master of the house, 'The Teacher says to you, "Where is the guest room where I may eat the Passover with My disciples?"' ¹²Then he will show you a large, furnished upper room; there make ready."

¹³So they went and found it just as He had said to them, and they prepared the Passover.

Jesus Institutes the Lord's Supper

¹⁴When the hour had come, He sat down, and the twelveᵃ apostles with Him. ¹⁵Then He said to them, "With *fervent* desire I have desired to eat this Passover with you before I suffer; ¹⁶for I say to you, I will no longer eat of it until it is fulfilled in the kingdom of God."

¹⁷Then He took the cup, and gave thanks, and said, "Take this and divide *it* among yourselves; ¹⁸for I say to you,ᵃ I will not drink of the fruit of the vine until the kingdom of God comes."

¹⁹And He took bread, gave thanks and broke *it,* and gave *it* to them, saying, "This is My body which is given for you; do this in remembrance of Me."

²⁰Likewise He also *took* the cup after supper, saying, "This cup *is* the new covenant in My blood, which is shed for you. ²¹But behold, the hand of My betrayer *is* with Me on the table. ²²And truly the Son of Man goes as it has been determined, but woe to that man by whom He is betrayed!"

²³Then they began to question among themselves, which of them it was who would do this thing.

The Disciples Argue About Greatness

²⁴Now there was also a dispute among them, as to which of them should be considered the greatest. ²⁵And He said to them, "The kings of the Gentiles exercise lordship over them, and those who exercise authority over them are called 'benefactors.' ²⁶But not so *among* you; on the contrary, he who is greatest among you, let him be as the younger, and he who governs as he who serves. ²⁷For who *is* greater, he who sits at the table, or he who serves? *Is* it not he who sits at the table? Yet I am among you as the One who serves.

²⁸"But you are those who have continued with Me in My trials. ²⁹And I bestow upon you a kingdom, just as My Father bestowed *one* upon Me, ³⁰that you may eat and drink at My table in My kingdom, and sit on thrones judging the twelve tribes of Israel."

Jesus Predicts Peter's Denial

³¹And the Lord said,ᵃ "Simon, Simon! Indeed, Satan has asked for you, that he may sift *you* as wheat. ³²But I have prayed for you, that your faith should not fail; and when you have returned to *Me,* strengthen your brethren."

³³But he said to Him, "Lord, I am ready to go with You, both to prison and to death."

³⁴Then He said, "I tell you, Peter, the rooster shall not crow this day before you will deny three times that you know Me."

Supplies for the Road

³⁵And He said to them, "When I sent you without money bag, knapsack, and sandals, did you lack anything?"

So they said, "Nothing."

³⁶Then He said to them, "But now, he who has a money bag, let him take *it,* and likewise a knapsack; and he who has no sword, let him sell his garment and buy one. ³⁷For I say to you that this which is

---

22:14 ᵃNU-Text omits *twelve.*   **22:18** ᵃNU-Text adds *from now on.*   **22:31** ᵃNU-Text omits *And the Lord said.*

written must still be accomplished in Me: 'And He was numbered with the transgressors.'ᵃ For the things concerning Me have an end."

³⁸So they said, "Lord, look, here *are* two swords."

And He said to them, "It is enough."

The Prayer in the Garden

³⁹Coming out, He went to the Mount of Olives, as He was accustomed, and His disciples also followed Him. ⁴⁰When He came to the place, He said to them, "Pray that you may not enter into temptation." ⁴¹And He was withdrawn from them about a stone's throw, and He knelt down and prayed, ⁴²saying, "Father, if it is Your will, take this cup away from Me; nevertheless not My will, but Yours, be done." ⁴³Then an angel appeared to Him from heaven, strengthening Him. ⁴⁴And being in agony, He prayed more earnestly. Then His sweat became like great drops of blood falling down to the ground.ᵃ

⁴⁵When He rose up from prayer, and had come to His disciples, He found them sleeping from sorrow. ⁴⁶Then He said to them, "Why do you sleep? Rise and pray, lest you enter into temptation."

Betrayal and Arrest in Gethsemane

⁴⁷And while He was still speaking, behold, a multitude; and he who was called Judas, one of the twelve, went before them and drew near to Jesus to kiss Him. ⁴⁸But Jesus said to him, "Judas, are you betraying the Son of Man with a kiss?"

⁴⁹When those around Him saw what was going to happen, they said to Him, "Lord, shall we strike with the sword?" ⁵⁰And one of them struck the servant of the high priest and cut off his right ear.

⁵¹But Jesus answered and said, "Permit even this." And He touched his ear and healed him.

⁵²Then Jesus said to the chief priests, captains of the temple, and the elders who had come to Him, "Have you come out, as against a robber, with swords and clubs? ⁵³When I was with you daily in the temple, you did not try to seize Me. But this is your hour, and the power of darkness."

Peter Denies Jesus, and Weeps Bitterly

⁵⁴Having arrested Him, they led *Him* and brought Him into the high priest's house. But Peter followed at a distance. ⁵⁵Now when they had kindled a fire in the midst of the courtyard and sat down together, Peter sat among them. ⁵⁶And a certain servant girl, seeing him as he sat by the fire, looked intently at him and said, "This man was also with Him."

⁵⁷But he denied Him,ᵃ saying, "Woman, I do not know Him."

⁵⁸And after a little while another saw him and said, "You also are of them."

But Peter said, "Man, I am not!"

⁵⁹Then after about an hour had passed, another confidently affirmed, saying, "Surely this *fellow* also was with Him, for he is a Galilean."

⁶⁰But Peter said, "Man, I do not know what you are saying!"

Immediately, while he was still speaking, the roosterᵃ crowed. ⁶¹And the Lord turned and looked at Peter. Then Peter remembered the word of the Lord, how He had said to him, "Before the rooster crows,ᵃ you will deny Me three times." ⁶²So Peter went out and wept bitterly.

Jesus Mocked and Beaten

⁶³Now the men who held Jesus mocked Him and beat Him. ⁶⁴And having blindfolded Him, they struck Him on the face and asked Him,ᵃ saying, "Prophesy! Who is the one who struck You?" ⁶⁵And many other things they blasphemously spoke against Him.

Jesus Faces the Sanhedrin

⁶⁶As soon as it was day, the elders of the people, both chief priests and scribes, came together and led Him into their council, saying, ⁶⁷"If You are the Christ, tell us."

But He said to them, "If I tell you, you will by no means believe. ⁶⁸And if I also

---

22:37 ᵃIsaiah 53:12   **22:44** ᵃNU-Text brackets verses 43 and 44 as not in the original text.
22:57 ᵃNU-Text reads *denied it.*   **22:60** ᵃNU-Text and M-Text read *a rooster.*   **22:61** ᵃNU-Text adds *today.*   **22:64** ᵃNU-Text reads *And having blindfolded Him, they asked Him.*

ask *you,* you will by no means answer Me or let *Me* go.ª ⁶⁹Hereafter the Son of Man will sit on the right hand of the power of God."

⁷⁰Then they all said, "Are You then the Son of God?"

So He said to them, "You *rightly* say that I am."

⁷¹And they said, "What further testimony do we need? For we have heard it ourselves from His own mouth."

Jesus Handed Over to Pontius Pilate

23 Then the whole multitude of them arose and led Him to Pilate. ²And they began to accuse Him, saying, "We found this *fellow* perverting theª nation, and forbidding to pay taxes to Caesar, saying that He Himself is Christ, a King."

³Then Pilate asked Him, saying, "Are You the King of the Jews?"

He answered him and said, *"It is as* you say."

⁴So Pilate said to the chief priests and the crowd, "I find no fault in this Man."

⁵But they were the more fierce, saying, "He stirs up the people, teaching throughout all Judea, beginning from Galilee to this place."

Jesus Faces Herod

⁶When Pilate heard of Galilee,ª he asked if the Man were a Galilean. ⁷And as soon as he knew that He belonged to Herod's jurisdiction, he sent Him to Herod, who was also in Jerusalem at that time. ⁸Now when Herod saw Jesus, he was exceedingly glad; for he had desired for a long *time* to see Him, because he had heard many things about Him, and he hoped to see some miracle done by Him. ⁹Then he questioned Him with many words, but He answered him nothing. ¹⁰And the chief priests and scribes stood and vehemently accused Him. ¹¹Then Herod, with his men of war, treated Him with contempt and mocked *Him,* arrayed Him in a gorgeous robe, and sent Him back to Pilate. ¹²That very day Pilate and Herod became friends with each other, for previously they had been at enmity with each other.

Taking the Place of Barabbas

¹³Then Pilate, when he had called together the chief priests, the rulers, and the people, ¹⁴said to them, "You have brought this Man to me, as one who misleads the people. And indeed, having examined *Him* in your presence, I have found no fault in this Man concerning those things of which you accuse Him; ¹⁵no, neither did Herod, for I sent you back to him;ª and indeed nothing deserving of death has been done by Him. ¹⁶I will therefore chastise Him and release *Him"* ¹⁷(for it was necessary for him to release one to them at the feast).ª

¹⁸And they all cried out at once, saying, "Away with this *Man,* and release to us Barabbas"— ¹⁹who had been thrown into prison for a certain rebellion made in the city, and for murder.

²⁰Pilate, therefore, wishing to release Jesus, again called out to them. ²¹But they shouted, saying, "Crucify *Him,* crucify Him!"

²²Then he said to them the third time, "Why, what evil has He done? I have found no reason for death in Him. I will therefore chastise Him and let *Him* go."

²³But they were insistent, demanding with loud voices that He be crucified. And the voices of these men and of the chief priests prevailed.ª ²⁴So Pilate gave sentence that it should be as they requested. ²⁵And he released to themª the one they requested, who for rebellion and murder had been thrown into prison; but he delivered Jesus to their will.

The King on a Cross

²⁶Now as they led Him away, they laid hold of a certain man, Simon a Cyrenian, who was coming from the country, and on him they laid the cross that he might bear *it* after Jesus.

²⁷And a great multitude of the people followed Him, and women who also mourned and lamented Him. ²⁸But Jesus, turning to

---

22:68 ªNU-Text omits *also* and *Me or let Me go.*
23:2 ªNU-Text reads *our.*   **23:6** ªNU-Text omits *of Galilee.*   **23:15** ªNU-Text reads *for he sent Him back to us.*   **23:17** ªNU-Text omits verse 17.
23:23 ªNU-Text omits *and of the chief priests.*
23:25 ªNU-Text and M-Text omit *to them.*

them, said, "Daughters of Jerusalem, do not weep for Me, but weep for yourselves and for your children. ²⁹For indeed the days are coming in which they will say, 'Blessed *are* the barren, wombs that never bore, and breasts which never nursed!' ³⁰Then they will begin *'to say to the mountains, "Fall on us!" and to the hills, "Cover us!"'* ᵃ ³¹For if they do these things in the green wood, what will be done in the dry?"

³²There were also two others, criminals, led with Him to be put to death. ³³And when they had come to the place called Calvary, there they crucified Him, and the criminals, one on the right hand and the other on the left. ³⁴Then Jesus said, "Father, forgive them, for they do not know what they do."ᵃ

And they divided His garments and cast lots. ³⁵And the people stood looking on. But even the rulers with them sneered, saying, "He saved others; let Him save Himself if He is the Christ, the chosen of God."

³⁶The soldiers also mocked Him, coming and offering Him sour wine, ³⁷and saying, "If You are the King of the Jews, save Yourself."

³⁸And an inscription also was written over Him in letters of Greek, Latin, and Hebrew:ᵃ

THIS IS THE KING OF THE JEWS.

³⁹Then one of the criminals who were hanged blasphemed Him, saying, "If You are the Christ,ᵃ save Yourself and us."

⁴⁰But the other, answering, rebuked him, saying, "Do you not even fear God, seeing you are under the same condemnation? ⁴¹And we indeed justly, for we receive the due reward of our deeds; but this Man has done nothing wrong." ⁴²Then he said to Jesus, "Lord,ᵃ remember me when You come into Your kingdom."

⁴³And Jesus said to him, "Assuredly, I say to you, today you will be with Me in Paradise."

Jesus Dies on the Cross

⁴⁴Now it wasᵃ about the sixth hour, and there was darkness over all the earth until the ninth hour. ⁴⁵Then the sun was darkened,ᵃ and the veil of the temple was torn in two. ⁴⁶And when Jesus had cried out with a loud voice, He said, "Father, *'into Your hands I commit My spirit.'*"ᵃ Having said this, He breathed His last.

⁴⁷So when the centurion saw what had happened, he glorified God, saying, "Certainly this was a righteous Man!"

⁴⁸And the whole crowd who came together to that sight, seeing what had been done, beat their breasts and returned. ⁴⁹But all His acquaintances, and the women who followed Him from Galilee, stood at a distance, watching these things.

Jesus Buried in Joseph's Tomb

⁵⁰Now behold, *there was* a man named Joseph, a council member, a good and just man. ⁵¹He had not consented to their decision and deed. *He was* from Arimathea, a city of the Jews, who himself was also waitingᵃ for the kingdom of God. ⁵²This man went to Pilate and asked for the body of Jesus. ⁵³Then he took it down, wrapped it in linen, and laid it in a tomb *that was* hewn out of the rock, where no one had ever lain before. ⁵⁴That day was the Preparation, and the Sabbath drew near.

⁵⁵And the women who had come with Him from Galilee followed after, and they observed the tomb and how His body was laid. ⁵⁶Then they returned and prepared spices and fragrant oils. And they rested on the Sabbath according to the commandment.

He Is Risen

24 Now on the first *day* of the week, very early in the morning, they, and certain *other women* with them,ᵃ came to the tomb bringing the spices which they had prepared. ²But they found the stone rolled away from the tomb. ³Then they went in and did not find the body of the Lord Jesus. ⁴And it happened, as they were

---

23:30 ᵃHosea 10:8 **23:34** ᵃNU-Text brackets the first sentence as a later addition. **23:38** ᵃNU-Text omits *written* and *in letters of Greek, Latin, and Hebrew.* **23:39** ᵃNU-Text reads *Are You not the Christ?* **23:42** ᵃNU-Text reads *And he said, "Jesus, remember me.* **23:44** ᵃNU-Text adds *already.* **23:45** ᵃNU-Text reads *obscured.* **23:46** ᵃPsalm 31:5 **23:51** ᵃNU-Text reads *who was waiting.* **24:1** ᵃNU-Text omits *and certain other women with them.*

greatly[a] perplexed about this, that behold, two men stood by them in shining garments. [5]Then, as they were afraid and bowed *their* faces to the earth, they said to them, "Why do you seek the living among the dead? [6]He is not here, but is risen! Remember how He spoke to you when He was still in Galilee, [7]saying, 'The Son of Man must be delivered into the hands of sinful men, and be crucified, and the third day rise again.'"

[8]And they remembered His words. [9]Then they returned from the tomb and told all these things to the eleven and to all the rest. [10]It was Mary Magdalene, Joanna, Mary *the mother* of James, and the other *women* with them, who told these things to the apostles. [11]And their words seemed to them like idle tales, and they did not believe them. [12]But Peter arose and ran to the tomb; and stooping down, he saw the linen cloths lying[a] by themselves; and he departed, marveling to himself at what had happened.

The Road to Emmaus

[13]Now behold, two of them were traveling that same day to a village called Emmaus, which was seven miles[a] from Jerusalem. [14]And they talked together of all these things which had happened. [15]So it was, while they conversed and reasoned, that Jesus Himself drew near and went with them. [16]But their eyes were restrained, so that they did not know Him.

[17]And He said to them, "What kind of conversation *is* this that you have with one another as you walk and are sad?"[a]

[18]Then the one whose name was Cleopas answered and said to Him, "Are You the only stranger in Jerusalem, and have You not known the things which happened there in these days?"

[19]And He said to them, "What things?"

So they said to Him, "The things concerning Jesus of Nazareth, who was a Prophet mighty in deed and word before God and all the people, [20]and how the chief priests and our rulers delivered Him to be condemned to death, and crucified Him. [21]But we were hoping that it was He who was going to redeem Israel. Indeed, besides all

this, today is the third day since these things happened. [22]Yes, and certain women of our company, who arrived at the tomb early, astonished us. [23]When they did not find His body, they came saying that they had also seen a vision of angels who said He was alive. [24]And certain of those *who were* with us went to the tomb and found *it* just as the women had said; but Him they did not see."

[25]Then He said to them, "O foolish ones, and slow of heart to believe in all that the prophets have spoken! [26]Ought not the Christ to have suffered these things and to enter into His glory?" [27]And beginning at Moses and all the Prophets, He expounded to them in all the Scriptures the things concerning Himself.

The Disciples' Eyes Opened

[28]Then they drew near to the village where they were going, and He indicated that He would have gone farther. [29]But they constrained Him, saying, "Abide with us, for it is toward evening, and the day is far spent." And He went in to stay with them.

[30]Now it came to pass, as He sat at the table with them, that He took bread, blessed and broke *it,* and gave it to them. [31]Then their eyes were opened and they knew Him; and He vanished from their sight. [32]And they said to one another, "Did not our heart burn within us while He talked with us on the road, and while He opened the Scriptures to us?" [33]So they rose up that very hour and returned to Jerusalem, and found the eleven and those *who were* with them gathered together, [34]saying, "The Lord is risen indeed, and has appeared to Simon!" [35]And they told about the things *that had happened* on the road, and how He was known to them in the breaking of bread.

Jesus Appears to His Disciples

[36]Now as they said these things, Jesus Himself stood in the midst of them, and said to them, "Peace to you." [37]But they

---

24:4 [a]NU-Text omits *greatly.* **24:12** [a]NU-Text omits *lying.* **24:13** [a]Literally *sixty stadia* **24:17** [a]NU-Text reads *as you walk? And they stood still, looking sad.*

were terrified and frightened, and supposed they had seen a spirit. [38]And He said to them, "Why are you troubled? And why do doubts arise in your hearts? [39]Behold My hands and My feet, that it is I Myself. Handle Me and see, for a spirit does not have flesh and bones as you see I have."

[40]When He had said this, He showed them His hands and His feet.[a] [41]But while they still did not believe for joy, and marveled, He said to them, "Have you any food here?" [42]So they gave Him a piece of a broiled fish and some honeycomb.[a] [43]And He took *it* and ate in their presence.

The Scriptures Opened

[44]Then He said to them, "These *are* the words which I spoke to you while I was still with you, that all things must be fulfilled which were written in the Law of Moses and *the* Prophets and *the* Psalms concerning Me." [45]And He opened their understanding, that they might comprehend the Scriptures.

[46]Then He said to them, "Thus it is written, and thus it was necessary for the Christ to suffer and to rise[a] from the dead the third day, [47]and that repentance and remission of sins should be preached in His name to all nations, beginning at Jerusalem. [48]And you are witnesses of these things. [49]Behold, I send the Promise of My Father upon you; but tarry in the city of Jerusalem[a] until you are endued with power from on high."

The Ascension

[50]And He led them out as far as Bethany, and He lifted up His hands and blessed them. [51]Now it came to pass, while He blessed them, that He was parted from them and carried up into heaven. [52]And they worshiped Him, and returned to Jerusalem with great joy, [53]and were continually in the temple praising and[a] blessing God. Amen.[b]

24:40 [a]Some printed New Testaments omit this verse. It is found in nearly all Greek manuscripts.
24:42 [a]NU-Text omits *and some honeycomb.*
24:46 [a]NU-Text reads *written, that the Christ should suffer and rise.*   **24:49** [a]NU-Text omits *of Jerusalem.*
24:53 [a]NU-Text omits *praising and.* [b]NU-Text omits *Amen.*

JOHN

Author: John

When Written: Around A.D. 90

Theme: Believe That Jesus Is the Son of God

Key Verses: John 20:30, 31—And truly Jesus did many other signs in the presence of His disciples, which are not written in this book; but these are written that you may believe that Jesus is the Christ, the Son of God, and that believing you may have life in His name.

Key Chapter: John 3—Captured in the one verse (v. 16), is the gospel in its clearest and simplest form: salvation and eternal life are gifts of God and are obtainable only through belief in Him.

The Gospel of John is easily the simplest and yet most profound of the Gospels, and for many people it is the greatest and most powerful. John sets forth Jesus in His deity and His work for the specific purpose of bringing his readers to spiritual life through belief in Jesus Christ. John's Gospel is topical, not primarily chronological, and it revolves around seven miracles and seven "I am" statements of Christ.

When a student entered Harvard University in 1646, under the "Rules and Precepts" of the university, he agreed the "the main end of his life and studies" was found specifically in John 17:3: "And this is eternal life, that they may know You, the only true God, and Jesus Christ whom You have sent." In those days, a Harvard education placed the knowing of Christ as the "only foundation of all sound knowledge and learning."

SUSAN B. ANTHONY

CHRISTIANITY AND EQUAL RIGHTS

WHEN WE LOOK AT THE HISTORY of the American Revolution, the abolitionist movement, the women's suffrage movement, and the civil rights movement, we discover that when a monumental fight for freedom and justice was at hand, faith in God was there to strengthen the activists. We also see, unfortunately, that too often the staunchest opposition to any of these movements came from sectors of the religious establishment of the day.

The women's rights movement in America was largely birthed out of the ranks of the abolitionist movement to end slavery. In 1848, at the Seneca Falls Convention in New York, activists including Elizabeth Cady Stanton and Susan B. Anthony began a seventy-year struggle to secure the right to vote for women. Nearly all of the major leaders of the suffrage movement came from Christian backgrounds—women who believed that God created women as equals to men, and thus they demanded that the same rights guaranteed to men in the Constitution be extended to women.

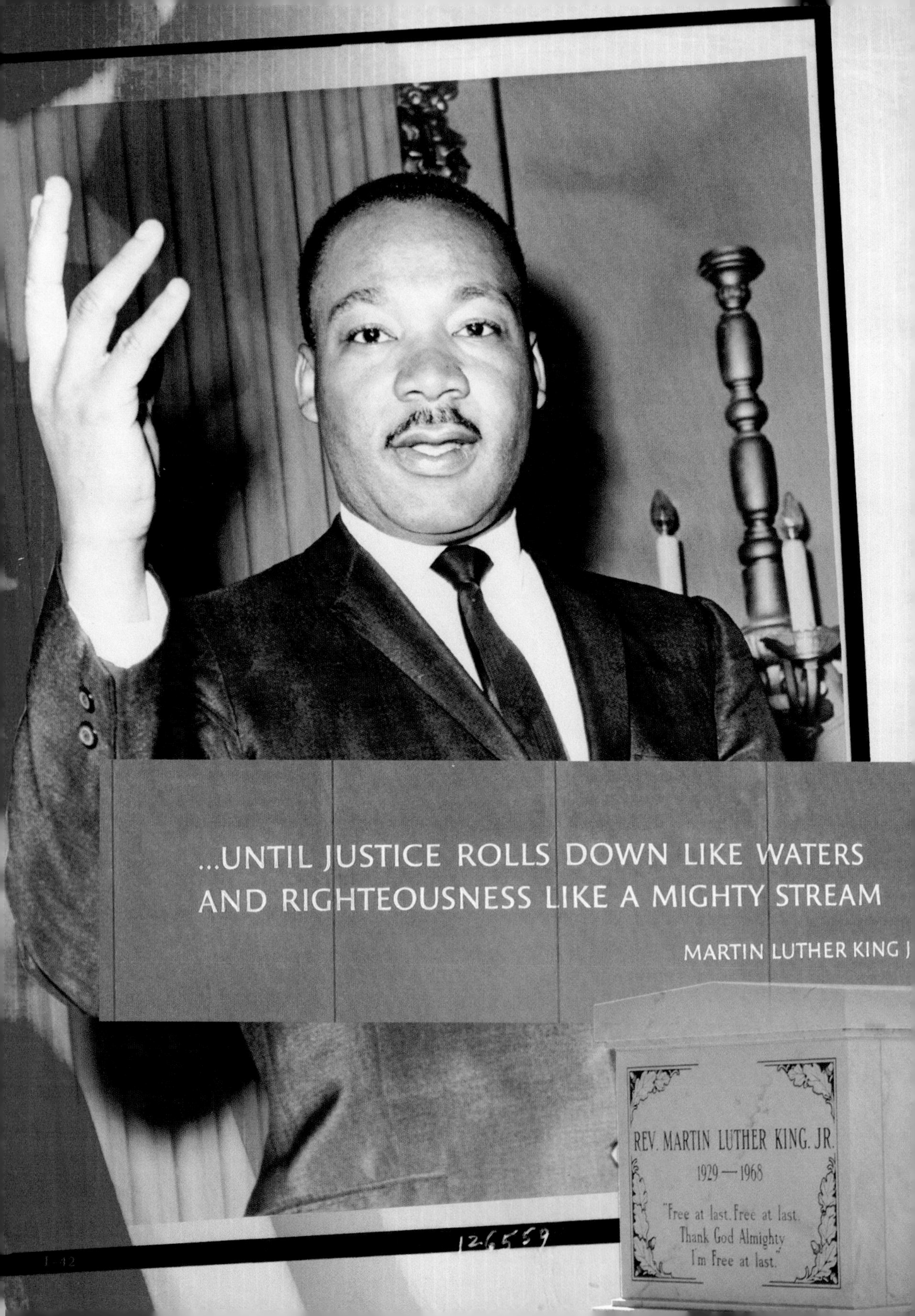

...UNTIL JUSTICE ROLLS DOWN LIKE WATERS
AND RIGHTEOUSNESS LIKE A MIGHTY STREAM

MARTIN LUTHER KING J

REV. MARTIN LUTHER KING. JR.

1929 — 1968

"Free at last. Free at last.
Thank God Almighty
I'm Free at last.

Some of these women included Lucretia Mott, an evangelical Quaker who helped to found the Anti-Slavery Society in 1833; Angelina Grimké, who presented female anti-slavery petitions to the Massachusetts state legislature; as well as Lucy Stone.

NOT ONLY DID MANY CHURCH ministers oppose suffrage, but they were also opposed to women owning property, getting university educations, and competing with men for wages. Most of the activists suffered mistreatment, were subject to arrests, and many were jailed. However, during the beginning of the twentieth century, women's suffrage gained in popularity as more and more people began to realize that there was no biblical support for inequality between the sexes. Finally, President Woodrow Wilson urged Congress to pass what became, when it was ratified in 1920, the Nineteenth Amendment, which stated, "The right of citizens of the United States to vote shall not be denied or abridged by the United States or by any State on account of sex."

"I LOOK TO A DAY WHEN
PEOPLE WILL NOT BE JUDGED
by the color of their skin, but by the content
OF THEIR CHARACTER."

DR. MARTIN LUTHER KING JR.

The civil rights movement of the 1950s and 1960s was led primarily by Dr. Martin Luther King Jr., who became the pastor of Dexter Avenue Baptist Church in Montgomery, Alabama, in 1954. At that time, the world around him was filled with inequality, oppression, and segregation of black citizens. Refusing to stoop to hate and bitterness, Dr. King connected his deep love of God with a powerful determination to achieve civil rights for African-Americans. He rose to national prominence as the leader of the movement through nonviolent, mass demonstrations, beginning with the Montgomery bus boycott (1956), which started after Rosa Parks was arrested for refusing to give her seat on a bus to a white man. The movement produced scores of men and women who risked . . . and some who gave . . . their lives to secure a more just and inclusive society.

KING AND ANOTHER MONTGOMERY minister, Ralph David Abernathy, organized the Southern Christian Leadership Conference in 1957, which attracted such civil rights activists as Ella Baker, T. J. Jemison, Stanley Levison, Joseph Lowery, Bayard Rustin, Fred Shuttlesworth, C. K. Steele, and others. The organization drew its strength from leaders of the black church in the South. As president of the conference, King focused on the goal of black voting rights.

Dr. King pursued his dream of a color-blind society through lectures, nonviolent marches, and protests. He suffered harassment, threats, beatings, incarceration—even his house being bombed—but he kept marching for justice, equality, and peace. In 1963, during the March on Washington, D.C., at the Lincoln Memorial, King delivered his famous "I Have a Dream" speech before 200,000 to 300,000 marchers, saying, "I look to a day when people will not be judged by the color of their skin, but by the content of their character." The speech beautifully and forcefully articulated the hopes and aspirations of the civil rights movement as rooted in two cherished national treasures—the Bible and the promise of true equality in the American Constitution.

PRESIDENT BARACK OBAMA

Strongly criticized by segregationists and militant blacks, Dr. King was assassinated before he could see victory over inequality. His message, however, lives on: "Our actions must be guided by the deepest principles of our Christian faith. Love must be our regulating ideal. Once again we must hear the words of Jesus echoing across the centuries: 'Love your enemies, bless them that curse you, and pray for them that despitefully use you.'... If you will protest courageously, and yet with dignity and Christian love, when the history books are written in future generations, the historians will pause and say, 'There lived a great people—a black people—who injected new meaning and dignity into the veins of civilization.'"

Barack Obama was two years old when Dr. King shared his dream for America in 1963. Obama's historic inauguration on January 20, 2009, as the first African-American to be elected President of the United States, reflects a fulfillment at least in part of Dr. King's vision for equal opportunity in America. As Obama proclaimed in his victory speech on November 4, 2008, "Change has come to America."

JOHN

The Eternal Word

1 In the beginning was the Word, and the Word was with God, and the Word was God. [2]He was in the beginning with God. [3]All things were made through Him, and without Him nothing was made that was made. [4]In Him was life, and the life was the light of men. [5]And the light shines in the darkness, and the darkness did not comprehend[a] it.

John's Witness: The True Light

[6]There was a man sent from God, whose name *was* John. [7]This man came for a witness, to bear witness of the Light, that all through him might believe. [8]He was not that Light, but *was sent* to bear witness of that Light. [9]That was the true Light which gives light to every man coming into the world.[a]

[10]He was in the world, and the world was made through Him, and the world did not know Him. [11]He came to His own,[a] and His own[b] did not receive Him. [12]But as many as received Him, to them He gave the right to become children of God, to those who believe in His name: [13]who were born, not of blood, nor of the will of the flesh, nor of the will of man, but of God.

The Word Becomes Flesh

[14]And the Word became flesh and dwelt among us, and we beheld His glory, the glory as of the only begotten of the Father, full of grace and truth.

[15]John bore witness of Him and cried out, saying, "This was He of whom I said, 'He who comes after me is preferred before me, for He was before me.'"

[16]And[a] of His fullness we have all received, and grace for grace. [17]For the law was given through Moses, *but* grace and truth came through Jesus Christ. [18]No one has seen God at any time. The only begotten Son,[a] who is in the bosom of the Father, He has declared *Him*.

A Voice in the Wilderness

[19]Now this is the testimony of John, when the Jews sent priests and Levites from Jerusalem to ask him, "Who are you?"

[20]He confessed, and did not deny, but confessed, "I am not the Christ."

[21]And they asked him, "What then? Are you Elijah?"

He said, "I am not."

"Are you the Prophet?"

And he answered, "No."

INSPIRING

And the light shines in the darkness. . . .

JOHN 1:5

Lighting the World

Samuel Colgate (1822–1897), an American manufacturer and philanthropist of what has become the Colgate-Palmolive Company, stated:

The only spiritual light in the world comes through Jesus Christ and the inspired Book; redemption and forgiveness of sin alone through Christ. Without His presence and the teachings of the Bible, we would be enshrouded in moral darkness and despair.

The condition of those nations without a Christ, contrasted with those where Christ is accepted, reveals so marked a difference that no arguments are needed. It is an object lesson so plain that it can be seen and understood by all. May "the earth be full of the knowledge of the Lord, as the waters cover the sea."

1:5 [a]Or *overcome*   **1:9** [a]Or *That was the true Light which, coming into the world, gives light to every man.* **1:11** [a]That is, His own things or domain [b]That is, His own people   **1:16** [a]NU-Text reads *For.* **1:18** [a]NU-Text reads *only begotten God.*

²²Then they said to him, "Who are you, that we may give an answer to those who sent us? What do you say about yourself?" ²³He said: "I *am*

'*The voice of one crying in the wilderness:*
"*Make straight the way of the LORD,*" 'ᵃ

as the prophet Isaiah said."

²⁴Now those who were sent were from the Pharisees. ²⁵And they asked him, saying, "Why then do you baptize if you are not the Christ, nor Elijah, nor the Prophet?" ²⁶John answered them, saying, "I baptize with water, but there stands One among you whom you do not know. ²⁷It is He who, coming after me, is preferred before me, whose sandal strap I am not worthy to loose." ²⁸These things were done in Bethabaraᵃ beyond the Jordan, where John was baptizing.

The Lamb of God

²⁹The next day John saw Jesus coming toward him, and said, "Behold! The Lamb of God who takes away the sin of the world! ³⁰This is He of whom I said, 'After me comes a Man who is preferred before me, for He was before me.' ³¹I did not know Him; but that He should be revealed to Israel, therefore I came baptizing with water." ³²And John bore witness, saying, "I saw the Spirit descending from heaven like a dove, and He remained upon Him. ³³I did not know Him, but He who sent me to baptize with water said to me, 'Upon whom you see the Spirit descending, and remaining on Him, this is He who baptizes with the Holy Spirit.' ³⁴And I have seen and testified that this is the Son of God."

The First Disciples

³⁵Again, the next day, John stood with two of his disciples. ³⁶And looking at Jesus as He walked, he said, "Behold the Lamb of God!" ³⁷The two disciples heard him speak, and they followed Jesus. ³⁸Then Jesus turned, and seeing them following, said to them, "What do you seek?"

They said to Him, "Rabbi" (which is to say, when translated, Teacher), "where are You staying?"

³⁹He said to them, "Come and see." They came and saw where He was staying, and remained with Him that day (now it was about the tenth hour). ⁴⁰One of the two who heard John *speak,* and followed Him, was Andrew, Simon Peter's brother. ⁴¹He first found his own brother Simon, and said to him, "We have found the Messiah" (which is translated, the Christ). ⁴²And he brought him to Jesus.

Now when Jesus looked at him, He said, "You are Simon the son of Jonah.ᵃ You shall be called Cephas" (which is translated, A Stone).

Philip and Nathanael

⁴³The following day Jesus wanted to go to Galilee, and He found Philip and said to him, "Follow Me." ⁴⁴Now Philip was from Bethsaida, the city of Andrew and Peter. ⁴⁵Philip found Nathanael and said to him, "We have found Him of whom Moses in the law, and also the prophets, wrote—Jesus of Nazareth, the son of Joseph."

⁴⁶And Nathanael said to him, "Can anything good come out of Nazareth?"

Philip said to him, "Come and see."

⁴⁷Jesus saw Nathanael coming toward Him, and said of him, "Behold, an Israelite indeed, in whom is no deceit!"

⁴⁸Nathanael said to Him, "How do You know me?"

Jesus answered and said to him, "Before Philip called you, when you were under the fig tree, I saw you."

⁴⁹Nathanael answered and said to Him, "Rabbi, You are the Son of God! You are the King of Israel!"

⁵⁰Jesus answered and said to him, "Because I said to you, 'I saw you under the fig tree,' do you believe? You will see greater things than these." ⁵¹And He said to him, "Most assuredly, I say to you, hereafterᵃ you shall see heaven open, and the angels of God ascending and descending upon the Son of Man."

1:23 ᵃIsaiah 40:3   **1:28** ᵃNU-Text and M-Text read *Bethany.*   **1:42** ᵃNU-Text reads *John.*   **1:51** ᵃNU-Text omits *hereafter.*

Water Turned to Wine

2 On the third day there was a wedding in Cana of Galilee, and the mother of Jesus was there. ²Now both Jesus and His disciples were invited to the wedding. ³And when they ran out of wine, the mother of Jesus said to Him, "They have no wine."

⁴Jesus said to her, "Woman, what does your concern have to do with Me? My hour has not yet come."

⁵His mother said to the servants, "Whatever He says to you, do *it.*"

⁶Now there were set there six waterpots of stone, according to the manner of purification of the Jews, containing twenty or thirty gallons apiece. ⁷Jesus said to them, "Fill the waterpots with water." And they filled them up to the brim. ⁸And He said to them, "Draw *some* out now, and take *it* to the master of the feast." And they took *it.* ⁹When the master of the feast had tasted the water that was made wine, and did not know where it came from (but the servants who had drawn the water knew), the master of the feast called the bridegroom. ¹⁰And he said to him, "Every man at the beginning sets out the good wine, and when the *guests* have well drunk, then the inferior. You have kept the good wine until now!"

¹¹This beginning of signs Jesus did in Cana of Galilee, and manifested His glory; and His disciples believed in Him.

¹²After this He went down to Capernaum, He, His mother, His brothers, and His disciples; and they did not stay there many days.

Jesus Cleanses the Temple

¹³Now the Passover of the Jews was at hand, and Jesus went up to Jerusalem. ¹⁴And He found in the temple those who sold oxen and sheep and doves, and the money changers doing business. ¹⁵When He had made a whip of cords, He drove them all out of the temple, with the sheep and the oxen, and poured out the changers' money and overturned the tables. ¹⁶And He said to those who sold doves, "Take these things away! Do not make My Father's house a house of merchandise!" ¹⁷Then His disciples remembered that it was written, *"Zeal for Your house has eaten*ᵃ *Me up."*ᵇ

¹⁸So the Jews answered and said to Him, "What sign do You show to us, since You do these things?"

¹⁹Jesus answered and said to them, "Destroy this temple, and in three days I will raise it up."

²⁰Then the Jews said, "It has taken forty-six years to build this temple, and will You raise it up in three days?"

²¹But He was speaking of the temple of His body. ²²Therefore, when He had risen from the dead, His disciples remembered that He had said this to them;ᵃ and they believed the Scripture and the word which Jesus had said.

The Discerner of Hearts

²³Now when He was in Jerusalem at the Passover, during the feast, many believed in His name when they saw the signs which He did. ²⁴But Jesus did not commit Himself to them, because He knew all *men,* ²⁵and had no need that anyone should testify of man, for He knew what was in man.

The New Birth

3 There was a man of the Pharisees named Nicodemus, a ruler of the Jews. ²This man came to Jesus by night and said to Him, "Rabbi, we know that You are a teacher come from God; for no one can do these signs that You do unless God is with him."

³Jesus answered and said to him, "Most assuredly, I say to you, unless one is born again, he cannot see the kingdom of God."

⁴Nicodemus said to Him, "How can a man be born when he is old? Can he enter a second time into his mother's womb and be born?"

⁵Jesus answered, "Most assuredly, I say to you, unless one is born of water and the Spirit, he cannot enter the kingdom of God. ⁶That which is born of the flesh is flesh, and that which is born of the Spirit is spirit. ⁷Do not marvel that I said to you, 'You must be born again.' ⁸The wind blows where it wishes, and you hear the sound of it, but cannot tell where it comes from and where it goes. So is everyone who is born of the Spirit."

2:17 ᵃNU-Text and M-Text read *will eat.* ᵇPsalm 69:9
2:22 ᵃNU-Text and M-Text omit *to them.*

⁹Nicodemus answered and said to Him, "How can these things be?"

¹⁰Jesus answered and said to him, "Are you the teacher of Israel, and do not know these things? ¹¹Most assuredly, I say to you, We speak what We know and testify what We have seen, and you do not receive Our witness. ¹²If I have told you earthly things and you do not believe, how will you believe if I tell you heavenly things? ¹³No one has ascended to heaven but He who came down from heaven, *that is,* the Son of Man who is in heaven.ᵃ ¹⁴And as Moses lifted up the serpent in the wilderness, even so must the Son of Man be lifted up, ¹⁵that whoever believes in Him should not perish butᵃ have eternal life. ¹⁶For God so loved the world that He gave His only begotten Son, that whoever believes in Him should not perish but have everlasting life. ¹⁷For God did not send His Son into the world to condemn the world, but that the world through Him might be saved.

¹⁸"He who believes in Him is not condemned; but he who does not believe is condemned already, because he has not believed in the name of the only begotten Son of God. ¹⁹And this is the condemnation, that the light has come into the world, and men loved darkness rather than light, because their deeds were evil. ²⁰For everyone practicing evil hates the light and does not come to the light, lest his deeds should be exposed. ²¹But he who does the truth comes to the light, that his deeds may be clearly seen, that they have been done in God."

John the Baptist Exalts Christ

²²After these things Jesus and His disciples came into the land of Judea, and there He remained with them and baptized. ²³Now John also was baptizing in Aenon near Salim, because there was much water there. And they came and were baptized. ²⁴For John had not yet been thrown into prison. ²⁵Then there arose a dispute between *some* of John's disciples and the Jews about purification. ²⁶And they came to John and said to him, "Rabbi, He who was with you beyond the Jordan, to whom you have testified—behold, He is baptizing, and all are coming to Him!"

²⁷John answered and said, "A man can receive nothing unless it has been given to him from heaven. ²⁸You yourselves bear me witness, that I said, 'I am not the Christ,' but, 'I have been sent before Him.' ²⁹He who has the bride is the bridegroom; but the friend of the bridegroom, who stands and hears him, rejoices greatly because of the bridegroom's voice. Therefore this joy of mine is fulfilled. ³⁰He must increase, but I *must* decrease. ³¹He who comes from above is above all; he who is of the earth is earthly and speaks of the earth. He who comes from heaven is above all. ³²And what He has seen and heard, that He testifies; and no one receives His testimony. ³³He who has received His testimony has certified that God is true. ³⁴For He whom God has sent speaks the words of God, for God does not give the Spirit by measure. ³⁵The Father loves the Son, and has given all things into His hand. ³⁶He who believes in the Son has everlasting life; and he who does not believe the Son shall not see life, but the wrath of God abides on him."

SELFLESS

"For God so loved the world that He gave. . . ."

JOHN 3:16

Freedom Abroad

Colin Powell, the U.S. Secretary of State (2001–2005), serving under President George W. Bush, stated:

Over the years, the United States has sent many of its fine young men and women into great peril to fight for freedom beyond our borders. The only amount of land we have ever asked for in return is enough to bury those who did not return.

A Samaritan Woman Meets Her Messiah

4 Therefore, when the Lord knew that the Pharisees had heard that Jesus made and baptized more disciples than John ²(though Jesus Himself did not baptize, but His disciples), ³He left Judea and departed

---

3:13 ᵃNU-Text omits *who is in heaven.*
3:15 ᵃNU-Text omits *not perish but.*

again to Galilee. ⁴But He needed to go through Samaria.

⁵So He came to a city of Samaria which is called Sychar, near the plot of ground that Jacob gave to his son Joseph. ⁶Now Jacob's well was there. Jesus therefore, being wearied from *His* journey, sat thus by the well. It was about the sixth hour.

⁷A woman of Samaria came to draw water. Jesus said to her, "Give Me a drink." ⁸For His disciples had gone away into the city to buy food.

⁹Then the woman of Samaria said to Him, "How is it that You, being a Jew, ask a drink from me, a Samaritan woman?" For Jews have no dealings with Samaritans.

¹⁰Jesus answered and said to her, "If you knew the gift of God, and who it is who says to you, 'Give Me a drink,' you would have asked Him, and He would have given you living water."

¹¹The woman said to Him, "Sir, You have nothing to draw with, and the well is deep. Where then do You get that living water? ¹²Are You greater than our father Jacob, who gave us the well, and drank from it himself, as well as his sons and his livestock?"

¹³Jesus answered and said to her, "Whoever drinks of this water will thirst again, ¹⁴but whoever drinks of the water that I shall give him will never thirst. But the water that I shall give him will become in him a fountain of water springing up into everlasting life."

¹⁵The woman said to Him, "Sir, give me this water, that I may not thirst, nor come here to draw."

¹⁶Jesus said to her, "Go, call your husband, and come here."

¹⁷The woman answered and said, "I have no husband."

Jesus said to her, "You have well said, 'I have no husband,' ¹⁸for you have had five husbands, and the one whom you now have is not your husband; in that you spoke truly."

¹⁹The woman said to Him, "Sir, I perceive that You are a prophet. ²⁰Our fathers worshiped on this mountain, and you *Jews* say that in Jerusalem is the place where one ought to worship."

²¹Jesus said to her, "Woman, believe Me, the hour is coming when you will neither on this mountain, nor in Jerusalem, worship the Father. ²²You worship what you do not know; we know what we worship, for salvation is of the Jews. ²³But the hour is coming, and now is, when the true worshipers will worship the Father in spirit and truth; for the Father is seeking such to worship Him. ²⁴God *is* Spirit, and those who worship Him must worship in spirit and truth."

²⁵The woman said to Him, "I know that Messiah is coming" (who is called Christ). "When He comes, He will tell us all things."

²⁶Jesus said to her, "I who speak to you am *He.*"

The Whitened Harvest

²⁷And at this *point* His disciples came, and they marveled that He talked with a woman; yet no one said, "What do You seek?" or, "Why are You talking with her?"

²⁸The woman then left her waterpot, went her way into the city, and said to the men, ²⁹"Come, see a Man who told me all things that I ever did. Could this be the Christ?" ³⁰Then they went out of the city and came to Him.

³¹In the meantime His disciples urged Him, saying, "Rabbi, eat."

³²But He said to them, "I have food to eat of which you do not know."

³³Therefore the disciples said to one another, "Has anyone brought Him *anything* to eat?"

³⁴Jesus said to them, "My food is to do the will of Him who sent Me, and to finish His work. ³⁵Do you not say, 'There are still four months and *then* comes the harvest'? Behold, I say to you, lift up your eyes and look at the fields, for they are already white for harvest! ³⁶And he who reaps receives wages, and gathers fruit for eternal life, that both he who sows and he who reaps may rejoice together. ³⁷For in this the saying is true: 'One sows and another reaps.' ³⁸I sent you to reap that for which you have not labored; others have labored, and you have entered into their labors."

The Savior of the World

39And many of the Samaritans of that city believed in Him because of the word of the woman who testified, "He told me all that I *ever* did." 40So when the Samaritans had come to Him, they urged Him to stay with them; and He stayed there two days. 41And many more believed because of His own word.

42Then they said to the woman, "Now we believe, not because of what you said, for we ourselves have heard *Him* and we know that this is indeed the Christ,ª the Savior of the world."

Welcome at Galilee

43Now after the two days He departed from there and went to Galilee. 44For Jesus Himself testified that a prophet has no honor in his own country. 45So when He came to Galilee, the Galileans received Him, having seen all the things He did in Jerusalem at the feast; for they also had gone to the feast.

A Nobleman's Son Healed

46So Jesus came again to Cana of Galilee where He had made the water wine. And there was a certain nobleman whose son was sick at Capernaum. 47When he heard that Jesus had come out of Judea into Galilee, he went to Him and implored Him to come down and heal his son, for he was at the point of death. 48Then Jesus said to him, "Unless you *people* see signs and wonders, you will by no means believe."

49The nobleman said to Him, "Sir, come down before my child dies!"

50Jesus said to him, "Go your way; your son lives." So the man believed the word that Jesus spoke to him, and he went his way. 51And as he was now going down, his servants met him and told *him,* saying, "Your son lives!"

52Then he inquired of them the hour when he got better. And they said to him, "Yesterday at the seventh hour the fever left him." 53So the father knew that *it was* at the same hour in which Jesus said to him, "Your son lives." And he himself believed, and his whole household.

54This again *is* the second sign Jesus did when He had come out of Judea into Galilee.

A Man Healed at the Pool of Bethesda

5 After this there was a feast of the Jews, and Jesus went up to Jerusalem. 2Now there is in Jerusalem by the Sheep *Gate* a pool, which is called in Hebrew, Bethesda,ª having five porches. 3In these lay a great multitude of sick people, blind, lame, paralyzed, waiting for the moving of the water. 4For an angel went down at a certain time into the pool and stirred up the water; then whoever stepped in first, after the stirring of the water, was made well of whatever disease he had.ª 5Now a certain man was there who had an infirmity thirty-eight years. 6When Jesus saw him lying there, and knew that he already had been *in that condition* a long time, He said to him, "Do you want to be made well?"

7The sick man answered Him, "Sir, I have no man to put me into the pool when the water is stirred up; but while I am coming, another steps down before me."

8Jesus said to him, "Rise, take up your bed and walk." 9And immediately the man was made well, took up his bed, and walked.

And that day was the Sabbath. 10The Jews therefore said to him who was cured, "It is the Sabbath; it is not lawful for you to carry your bed."

11He answered them, "He who made me well said to me, 'Take up your bed and walk.'"

12Then they asked him, "Who is the Man who said to you, 'Take up your bed and walk'?" 13But the one who was healed did not know who it was, for Jesus had withdrawn, a multitude being in *that* place. 14Afterward Jesus found him in the temple, and said to him, "See, you have been made well. Sin no more, lest a worse thing come upon you."

15The man departed and told the Jews that it was Jesus who had made him well.

4:42 ªNU-Text omits *the Christ.*   5:2 ªNU-Text reads *Bethzatha.*   5:4 ªNU-Text omits *waiting for the moving of the water* at the end of verse 3, and all of verse 4.

Honor the Father and the Son

16For this reason the Jews persecuted Jesus, and sought to kill Him,a because He had done these things on the Sabbath. 17But Jesus answered them, "My Father has been working until now, and I have been working."

18Therefore the Jews sought all the more to kill Him, because He not only broke the Sabbath, but also said that God was His Father, making Himself equal with God. 19Then Jesus answered and said to them, "Most assuredly, I say to you, the Son can do nothing of Himself, but what He sees the Father do; for whatever He does, the Son also does in like manner. 20For the Father loves the Son, and shows Him all things that He Himself does; and He will show Him greater works than these, that you may marvel. 21For as the Father raises the dead and gives life to *them,* even so the Son gives life to whom He will. 22For the Father judges no one, but has committed all judgment to the Son, 23that all should honor the Son just as they honor the Father. He who does not honor the Son does not honor the Father who sent Him.

Life and Judgment Are Through the Son

24"Most assuredly, I say to you, he who hears My word and believes in Him who sent Me has everlasting life, and shall not come into judgment, but has passed from death into life. 25Most assuredly, I say to you, the hour is coming, and now is, when the dead will hear the voice of the Son of God; and those who hear will live. 26For as the Father has life in Himself, so He has granted the Son to have life in Himself, 27and has given Him authority to execute judgment also, because He is the Son of Man. 28Do not marvel at this; for the hour is coming in which all who are in the graves will hear His voice 29and come forth—those who have done good, to the resurrection of life, and those who have done evil, to the resurrection of condemnation. 30I can of Myself do nothing. As I hear, I judge; and My judgment is righteous, because I do not seek My own will but the will of the Father who sent Me.

The Fourfold Witness

31"If I bear witness of Myself, My witness is not true. 32There is another who bears witness of Me, and I know that the witness which He witnesses of Me is true. 33You have sent to John, and he has borne witness to the truth. 34Yet I do not receive testimony from man, but I say these things that you may be saved. 35He was the burning and shining lamp, and you were willing for a time to rejoice in his light. 36But I have a greater witness than John's; for the works which the Father has given Me to finish—the very works that I do—bear witness of Me, that the Father has sent Me. 37And the Father Himself, who sent Me, has testified of Me. You have neither heard His voice at any time, nor seen His form. 38But you do not have His word abiding in you, because whom He sent, Him you do not believe. 39You search the Scriptures, for in them you think you have eternal life; and these are they which testify of Me. 40But you are not willing to come to Me that you may have life.

41"I do not receive honor from men. 42But I know you, that you do not have the love of God in you. 43I have come in My Father's name, and you do not receive Me; if another comes in his own name, him you will receive. 44How can you believe, who receive honor from one another, and do not seek the honor that *comes* from the only God? 45Do not think that I shall accuse you to the Father; there is *one* who accuses you—Moses, in whom you trust. 46For if you believed Moses, you would believe Me; for he wrote about Me. 47But if you do not believe his writings, how will you believe My words?"

Feeding the Five Thousand

6 After these things Jesus went over the Sea of Galilee, which is *the Sea* of Tiberias. 2Then a great multitude followed Him, because they saw His signs which He performed on those who were diseased. 3And Jesus went up on the mountain, and there He sat with His disciples.

5:16 aNU-Text omits *and sought to kill Him.*

⁴Now the Passover, a feast of the Jews, was near. ⁵Then Jesus lifted up *His* eyes, and seeing a great multitude coming toward Him, He said to Philip, "Where shall we buy bread, that these may eat?" ⁶But this He said to test him, for He Himself knew what He would do.

⁷Philip answered Him, "Two hundred denarii worth of bread is not sufficient for them, that every one of them may have a little."

⁸One of His disciples, Andrew, Simon Peter's brother, said to Him, ⁹"There is a lad here who has five barley loaves and two small fish, but what are they among so many?"

¹⁰Then Jesus said, "Make the people sit down." Now there was much grass in the place. So the men sat down, in number about five thousand. ¹¹And Jesus took the loaves, and when He had given thanks He distributed *them* to the disciples, and the disciplesᵃ to those sitting down; and likewise of the fish, as much as they wanted. ¹²So when they were filled, He said to His disciples, "Gather up the fragments that remain, so that nothing is lost." ¹³Therefore they gathered *them* up, and filled twelve baskets with the fragments of the five barley loaves which were left over by those who had eaten. ¹⁴Then those men, when they had seen the sign that Jesus did, said, "This is truly the Prophet who is to come into the world."

Jesus Walks on the Sea

¹⁵Therefore when Jesus perceived that they were about to come and take Him by force to make Him king, He departed again to the mountain by Himself alone.

¹⁶Now when evening came, His disciples went down to the sea, ¹⁷got into the boat, and went over the sea toward Capernaum. And it was already dark, and Jesus had not come to them. ¹⁸Then the sea arose because a great wind was blowing. ¹⁹So when they had rowed about three or four miles,ᵃ they saw Jesus walking on the sea and drawing near the boat; and they were afraid. ²⁰But He said to them, "It is I; do not be afraid." ²¹Then they willingly received Him into the boat, and immediately the boat was at the land where they were going.

The Bread from Heaven

²²On the following day, when the people who were standing on the other side of the sea saw that there was no other boat there, except that one which His disciples had entered,ᵃ and that Jesus had not entered the boat with His disciples, but His disciples had gone away alone— ²³however, other boats came from Tiberias, near the place where they ate bread after the Lord had given thanks— ²⁴when the people therefore saw that Jesus was not there, nor His disciples, they also got into boats and came to Capernaum, seeking Jesus. ²⁵And when they found Him on the other side of the sea, they said to Him, "Rabbi, when did You come here?"

²⁶Jesus answered them and said, "Most assuredly, I say to you, you seek Me, not because you saw the signs, but because you ate of the loaves and were filled. ²⁷Do not labor for the food which perishes, but for the food which endures to everlasting life, which the Son of Man will give you, because God the Father has set His seal on Him."

²⁸Then they said to Him, "What shall we do, that we may work the works of God?"

²⁹Jesus answered and said to them, "This is the work of God, that you believe in Him whom He sent."

³⁰Therefore they said to Him, "What sign will You perform then, that we may see it and believe You? What work will You do? ³¹Our fathers ate the manna in the desert; as it is written, *'He gave them bread from heaven to eat.'* "ᵃ

³²Then Jesus said to them, "Most assuredly, I say to you, Moses did not give you the bread from heaven, but My Father gives you the true bread from heaven. ³³For the bread of God is He who comes down from heaven and gives life to the world."

³⁴Then they said to Him, "Lord, give us this bread always."

³⁵And Jesus said to them, "I am the bread of life. He who comes to Me shall never

---

6:11 ᵃNU-Text omits *to the disciples, and the disciples.*
6:19 ᵃLiterally *twenty-five or thirty stadia*
6:22 ᵃNU-Text omits *that* and *which His disciples had entered.*   **6:31** ᵃExodus 16:4; Nehemiah 9:15; Psalm 78:24

hunger, and he who believes in Me shall never thirst. [36]But I said to you that you have seen Me and yet do not believe. [37]All that the Father gives Me will come to Me, and the one who comes to Me I will by no means cast out. [38]For I have come down from heaven, not to do My own will, but the will of Him who sent Me. [39]This is the will of the Father who sent Me, that of all He has given Me I should lose nothing, but should raise it up at the last day. [40]And this is the will of Him who sent Me, that everyone who sees the Son and believes in Him may have everlasting life; and I will raise him up at the last day."

Rejected by His Own

[41]The Jews then complained about Him, because He said, "I am the bread which came down from heaven." [42]And they said, "Is not this Jesus, the son of Joseph, whose father and mother we know? How is it then that He says, 'I have come down from heaven'?"

[43]Jesus therefore answered and said to them, "Do not murmur among yourselves. [44]No one can come to Me unless the Father who sent Me draws him; and I will raise him up at the last day. [45]It is written in the prophets, *And they shall all be taught by God.*[a] Therefore everyone who has heard and learned[b] from the Father comes to Me. [46]Not that anyone has seen the Father, except He who is from God; He has seen the Father. [47]Most assuredly, I say to you, he who believes in Me[a] has everlasting life. [48]I am the bread of life. [49]Your fathers ate the manna in the wilderness, and are dead. [50]This is the bread which comes down from heaven, that one may eat of it and not die. [51]I am the living bread which came down from heaven. If anyone eats of this bread, he will live forever; and the bread that I shall give is My flesh, which I shall give for the life of the world."

[52]The Jews therefore quarreled among themselves, saying, "How can this Man give us *His* flesh to eat?"

[53]Then Jesus said to them, "Most assuredly, I say to you, unless you eat the flesh of the Son of Man and drink His blood, you have no life in you. [54]Whoever eats My flesh

and drinks My blood has eternal life, and I will raise him up at the last day. [55]For My flesh is food indeed,[a] and My blood is drink indeed. [56]He who eats My flesh and drinks My blood abides in Me, and I in him. [57]As the living Father sent Me, and I live because of the Father, so he who feeds on Me will live because of Me. [58]This is the bread which came down from heaven—not as your fathers ate the manna, and are dead. He who eats this bread will live forever."

[59]These things He said in the synagogue as He taught in Capernaum.

Many Disciples Turn Away

[60]Therefore many of His disciples, when they heard *this,* said, "This is a hard saying; who can understand it?"

[61]When Jesus knew in Himself that His disciples complained about this, He said to them, "Does this offend you? [62]*What* then if you should see the Son of Man ascend where He was before? [63]It is the Spirit who gives life; the flesh profits nothing. The words that I speak to you are spirit, and *they* are life. [64]But there are some of you who do not believe." For Jesus knew from the beginning who they were who did not believe, and who would betray Him. [65]And He said, "Therefore I have said to you that no one can come to Me unless it has been granted to him by My Father."

[66]From that *time* many of His disciples went back and walked with Him no more. [67]Then Jesus said to the twelve, "Do you also want to go away?"

[68]But Simon Peter answered Him, "Lord, to whom shall we go? You have the words of eternal life. [69]Also we have come to believe and know that You are the Christ, the Son of the living God."[a]

[70]Jesus answered them, "Did I not choose you, the twelve, and one of you is a devil?" [71]He spoke of Judas Iscariot, *the son* of Simon, for it was he who would betray Him, being one of the twelve.

6:45 [a]Isaiah 54:13 [b]M-Text reads *hears and has learned.*   **6:47** [a]NU-Text omits *in Me.*
6:55 [a]NU-Text reads *true food* and *true drink.*
6:69 [a]NU-Text reads *You are the Holy One of God.*

Jesus' Brothers Disbelieve

7 After these things Jesus walked in Galilee; for He did not want to walk in Judea, because the Jews[a] sought to kill Him. ²Now the Jews' Feast of Tabernacles was at hand. ³His brothers therefore said to Him, "Depart from here and go into Judea, that Your disciples also may see the works that You are doing. ⁴For no one does anything in secret while he himself seeks to be known openly. If You do these things, show Yourself to the world." ⁵For even His brothers did not believe in Him.

⁶Then Jesus said to them, "My time has not yet come, but your time is always ready. ⁷The world cannot hate you, but it hates Me because I testify of it that its works are evil. ⁸You go up to this feast. I am not yet[a] going up to this feast, for My time has not yet fully come." ⁹When He had said these things to them, He remained in Galilee.

The Heavenly Scholar

¹⁰But when His brothers had gone up, then He also went up to the feast, not openly, but as it were in secret. ¹¹Then the Jews sought Him at the feast, and said, "Where is He?" ¹²And there was much complaining among the people concerning Him. Some said, "He is good"; others said, "No, on the contrary, He deceives the people." ¹³However, no one spoke openly of Him for fear of the Jews.

¹⁴Now about the middle of the feast Jesus went up into the temple and taught. ¹⁵And the Jews marveled, saying, "How does this Man know letters, having never studied?"

¹⁶Jesus[a] answered them and said, "My doctrine is not Mine, but His who sent Me. ¹⁷If anyone wills to do His will, he shall know concerning the doctrine, whether it is from God or *whether* I speak on My own *authority*. ¹⁸He who speaks from himself seeks his own glory; but He who seeks the glory of the One who sent Him is true, and no unrighteousness is in Him. ¹⁹Did not Moses give you the law, yet none of you keeps the law? Why do you seek to kill Me?"

²⁰The people answered and said, "You have a demon. Who is seeking to kill You?"

²¹Jesus answered and said to them, "I did one work, and you all marvel. ²²Moses therefore gave you circumcision (not that it is from Moses, but from the fathers), and you circumcise a man on the Sabbath. ²³If a man receives circumcision on the Sabbath, so that the law of Moses should not be broken, are you angry with Me because I made a man completely well on the Sabbath? ²⁴Do not judge according to appearance, but judge with righteous judgment."

FAITH
". . . whether it is from God. . . ."

JOHN 7:17

The Bible's Divine Character
Simon Greenleaf (1783–1853) was the Royall Professor of Law at Harvard and contributed extensively to the school's development. In correspondence with the American Bible Society, he wrote:

> Of the Divine character of the Bible, I think no man who deals honestly with his own mind and heart can entertain a reasonable doubt. For myself, I must say, that having for many years made the evidences of Christianity the subject of close study, the result has been a firm and increasing conviction of the authenticity and plenary inspiration of the Bible. It is indeed the Word of God.

Could This Be the Christ?

²⁵Now some of them from Jerusalem said, "Is this not He whom they seek to kill? ²⁶But look! He speaks boldly, and they say nothing to Him. Do the rulers know indeed that this is truly[a] the Christ? ²⁷However, we know where this Man is from; but when the Christ comes, no one knows where He is from."

²⁸Then Jesus cried out, as He taught in the temple, saying, "You both know Me, and you know where I am from; and I have not come of Myself, but He who sent Me is true, whom you do not know. ²⁹But[a] I know Him, for I am from Him, and He sent Me."

³⁰Therefore they sought to take Him; but no one laid a hand on Him, because His hour had not yet come. ³¹And many of the

---

7:1 ªThat is, the ruling authorities **7:8** ªNU-Text omits *yet.* **7:16** ªNU-Text and M-Text read *So Jesus.* **7:26** ªNU-Text omits *truly.* **7:29** ªNU-Text and M-Text omit *But.*

people believed in Him, and said, "When the Christ comes, will He do more signs than these which this *Man* has done?"

Jesus and the Religious Leaders

[32]The Pharisees heard the crowd murmuring these things concerning Him, and the Pharisees and the chief priests sent officers to take Him. [33]Then Jesus said to them,[a] "I shall be with you a little while longer, and *then* I go to Him who sent Me. [34]You will seek Me and not find *Me,* and where I am you cannot come."

[35]Then the Jews said among themselves, "Where does He intend to go that we shall not find Him? Does He intend to go to the Dispersion among the Greeks and teach the Greeks? [36]What is this thing that He said, 'You will seek Me and not find Me, and where I am you cannot come'?"

The Promise of the Holy Spirit

[37]On the last day, that great *day* of the feast, Jesus stood and cried out, saying, "If anyone thirsts, let him come to Me and drink. [38]He who believes in Me, as the Scripture has said, out of his heart will flow rivers of living water." [39]But this He spoke concerning the Spirit, whom those believing[a] in Him would receive; for the Holy[b] Spirit was not yet *given,* because Jesus was not yet glorified.

Who Is He?

[40]Therefore many[a] from the crowd, when they heard this saying, said, "Truly this is the Prophet." [41]Others said, "This is the Christ."

But some said, "Will the Christ come out of Galilee? [42]Has not the Scripture said that the Christ comes from the seed of David and from the town of Bethlehem, where David was?" [43]So there was a division among the people because of Him. [44]Now some of them wanted to take Him, but no one laid hands on Him.

Rejected by the Authorities

[45]Then the officers came to the chief priests and Pharisees, who said to them, "Why have you not brought Him?"

[46]The officers answered, "No man ever spoke like this Man!"

[47]Then the Pharisees answered them, "Are you also deceived? [48]Have any of the rulers or the Pharisees believed in Him? [49]But this crowd that does not know the law is accursed."

[50]Nicodemus (he who came to Jesus by night,[a] being one of them) said to them, [51]"Does our law judge a man before it hears him and knows what he is doing?"

[52]They answered and said to him, "Are you also from Galilee? Search and look, for no prophet has arisen[a] out of Galilee."

An Adulteress Faces the Light of the World

[53]And everyone went to his *own* house.[a]

8 But Jesus went to the Mount of Olives. [2]Now early[a] in the morning He came again into the temple, and all the people came to Him; and He sat down and taught them. [3]Then the scribes and Pharisees brought to Him a woman caught in adultery. And when they had set her in the midst, [4]they said to Him, "Teacher, this woman was caught[a] in adultery, in the very act. [5]Now Moses, in the law, commanded[a] us that such should be stoned.[b] But what do You say?"[c] [6]This they said, testing Him, that they might have *something* of which to accuse Him. But Jesus stooped down and wrote on the ground with *His* finger, as though He did not hear.[a]

[7]So when they continued asking Him, He raised Himself up[a] and said to them, "He who is without sin among you, let him throw a stone at her first." [8]And again He stooped down and wrote on the ground. [9]Then those who heard *it,* being convicted by *their* conscience,[a] went out one by one, beginning with the oldest *even* to the last.

7:33 [a]NU-Text and M-Text omit *to them.*
7:39 [a]NU-Text reads *who believed.* [b]NU-Text omits Holy.   **7:40** [a]NU-Text reads *some.*
7:50 [a]NU-Text reads *before.*   **7:52** [a]NU-Text reads *is to rise.*   **7:53** [a]The words *And everyone* through *sin no more* (8:11) are bracketed by NU-Text as not original. They are present in over 900 manuscripts.
8:2 [a]M-Text reads *very early.*   **8:4** [a]M-Text reads *we found this woman.*   **8:5** [a]M-Text reads *in our law Moses commanded.* [b]NU-Text and M-Text read *to stone such.* [c]M-Text adds *about her.*   **8:6** [a]NU-Text and M-Text omit *as though He did not hear.*   **8:7** [a]M-Text reads *He looked up.*   **8:9** [a]NU-Text and M-Text omit *being convicted by their conscience.*

And Jesus was left alone, and the woman standing in the midst. [10]When Jesus had raised Himself up and saw no one but the woman, He said to her,[a] "Woman, where are those accusers of yours?[b] Has no one condemned you?"

[11]She said, "No one, Lord."

And Jesus said to her, "Neither do I condemn you; go and[a] sin no more."

[12]Then Jesus spoke to them again, saying, "I am the light of the world. He who follows Me shall not walk in darkness, but have the light of life."

Jesus Defends His Self-Witness

[13]The Pharisees therefore said to Him, "You bear witness of Yourself; Your witness is not true."

[14]Jesus answered and said to them, "Even if I bear witness of Myself, My witness is true, for I know where I came from and where I am going; but you do not know where I come from and where I am going. [15]You judge according to the flesh; I judge no one. [16]And yet if I do judge, My judgment is true; for I am not alone, but I *am* with the Father who sent Me. [17]It is also written in your law that the testimony of two men is true. [18]I am One who bears witness of Myself, and the Father who sent Me bears witness of Me."

[19]Then they said to Him, "Where is Your Father?"

Jesus answered, "You know neither Me nor My Father. If you had known Me, you would have known My Father also."

[20]These words Jesus spoke in the treasury, as He taught in the temple; and no one laid hands on Him, for His hour had not yet come.

Jesus Predicts His Departure

[21]Then Jesus said to them again, "I am going away, and you will seek Me, and will die in your sin. Where I go you cannot come."

[22]So the Jews said, "Will He kill Himself, because He says, 'Where I go you cannot come'?"

[23]And He said to them, "You are from beneath; I am from above. You are of this world; I am not of this world. [24]Therefore I said to you that you will die in your sins; for if you do not believe that I am *He,* you will die in your sins."

[25]Then they said to Him, "Who are You?"

And Jesus said to them, "Just what I have been saying to you from the beginning. [26]I have many things to say and to judge concerning you, but He who sent Me is true; and I speak to the world those things which I heard from Him."

[27]They did not understand that He spoke to them of the Father.

[28]Then Jesus said to them, "When you lift up the Son of Man, then you will know that I am *He,* and *that* I do nothing of Myself; but as My Father taught Me, I speak these things. [29]And He who sent Me is with Me. The Father has not left Me alone, for I always do those things that please Him." [30]As He spoke these words, many believed in Him.

The Truth Shall Make You Free

[31]Then Jesus said to those Jews who believed Him, "If you abide in My word, you are My disciples indeed. [32]And you shall know the truth, and the truth shall make you free."

[33]They answered Him, "We are Abraham's descendants, and have never been in bondage to anyone. How *can* You say, 'You will be made free'?"

[34]Jesus answered them, "Most assuredly, I say to you, whoever commits sin is a slave of sin. [35]And a slave does not abide in the house forever, *but* a son abides forever. [36]Therefore if the Son makes you free, you shall be free indeed.

Abraham's Seed and Satan's

[37]"I know that you are Abraham's descendants, but you seek to kill Me, because My word has no place in you. [38]I speak what I have seen with My Father, and you do what you have seen with[a] your father."

[39]They answered and said to Him, "Abraham is our father."

8:10 [a]NU-Text omits *and saw no one but the woman;* M-Text reads *He saw her and said.* [b]NU-Text and M-Text omit *of yours.*   **8:11** [a]NU-Text and M-Text add *from now on.*   **8:38** [a]NU-Text reads *heard from.*

THE BILL OF RIGHTS

During the debates on the adoption of the U.S. Constitution, some of its opponents, including prominent Founding Fathers, argued that it failed to protect the basic principles of human liberty. While the Constitution spelled out the new government's delegated powers, it did not define the citizens' rights or insure that the federal government would not infringe on the most basic of civil rights at a later point in time, as the British had done before and during the Revolution. In their formal ratification of the Constitution, several state conventions either asked for or understood that such amendments would be offered.

The Bill of Rights is the first ten amendments to the Constitution. They were introduced by James Madison to the First U.S. Congress in 1791 as a series of constitutional amendments and came into effect on December 15, 1791, after being ratified by three-fourths of the states. In drafting the Bill of Rights, the Framers further defined the role of the federal government by defining certain actions it would not do.

Without the Bill of Rights, basic human rights such as the freedom of religion and of speech, the freedom to assemble and to petition, the right to a free press, and the right to keep and bear arms could have potentially been denied or repressed. The Bill of Rights prohibits unreasonable search and seizure, cruel and unusual punishment, and compelled self-incrimination. In federal criminal cases, it requires indictment by grand jury for any capital or "infamous crime," guarantees a speedy public trial with an impartial jury composed of members of the state or judicial district in which the crime occurred, and prohibits double jeopardy. In addition, the Bill of Rights reserves all powers not granted to the federal government to the citizenry or states.

After over two hundred years, the United States Supreme Court still frequently hears cases related to the Bill of Rights. For instance, the First Amendment, which states that "Congress shall make no law respecting an establishment of religion, or prohibiting the free exercise thereof," remains a hotly debated issue. In today's courts and culture, interpretation of this amendment as an impassable "wall of separation" between church and state seeks to prohibit religion from entering the halls of government, public schools, and numerous other community sectors. Freedom "of religion" lies within the balance.

Jesus said to them, "If you were Abraham's children, you would do the works of Abraham. ⁴⁰But now you seek to kill Me, a Man who has told you the truth which I heard from God. Abraham did not do this. ⁴¹You do the deeds of your father."

Then they said to Him, "We were not born of fornication; we have one Father—God."

⁴²Jesus said to them, "If God were your Father, you would love Me, for I proceeded forth and came from God; nor have I come of Myself, but He sent Me. ⁴³Why do you not understand My speech? Because you are not able to listen to My word. ⁴⁴You are of *your* father the devil, and the desires of your father you want to do. He was a murderer from the beginning, and does not stand in the truth, because there is no truth in him. When he speaks a lie, he speaks from his own *resources*, for he is a liar and the father of it. ⁴⁵But because I tell the truth, you do not believe Me. ⁴⁶Which of you convicts Me of sin? And if I tell the truth, why do you not believe Me? ⁴⁷He who is of God hears God's words; therefore you do not hear, because you are not of God."

Before Abraham Was, I AM

⁴⁸Then the Jews answered and said to Him, "Do we not say rightly that You are a Samaritan and have a demon?"

⁴⁹Jesus answered, "I do not have a demon; but I honor My Father, and you dishonor Me. ⁵⁰And I do not seek My *own* glory; there is One who seeks and judges. ⁵¹Most assuredly, I say to you, if anyone keeps My word he shall never see death."

⁵²Then the Jews said to Him, "Now we know that You have a demon! Abraham is dead, and the prophets; and You say, 'If anyone keeps My word he shall never taste death.' ⁵³Are You greater than our father Abraham, who is dead? And the prophets are dead. Who do You make Yourself out to be?"

⁵⁴Jesus answered, "If I honor Myself, My honor is nothing. It is My Father who honors Me, of whom you say that He is your^a God. ⁵⁵Yet you have not known Him, but I know Him. And if I say, 'I do not know Him,' I shall be a liar like you; but I do know Him and keep His word. ⁵⁶Your father Abraham rejoiced to see My day, and he saw *it* and was glad."

⁵⁷Then the Jews said to Him, "You are not yet fifty years old, and have You seen Abraham?"

⁵⁸Jesus said to them, "Most assuredly, I say to you, before Abraham was, I AM."

⁵⁹Then they took up stones to throw at Him; but Jesus hid Himself and went out of the temple,^a going through the midst of them, and so passed by.

A Man Born Blind Receives Sight

9 Now as *Jesus* passed by, He saw a man who was blind from birth. ²And His disciples asked Him, saying, "Rabbi, who sinned, this man or his parents, that he was born blind?"

³Jesus answered, "Neither this man nor his parents sinned, but that the works of God should be revealed in him. ⁴I^a must work the works of Him who sent Me while it is day; *the* night is coming when no one can work. ⁵As long as I am in the world, I am the light of the world."

⁶When He had said these things, He spat on the ground and made clay with the saliva; and He anointed the eyes of the blind man with the clay. ⁷And He said to him, "Go, wash in the pool of Siloam" (which is translated, Sent). So he went and washed, and came back seeing.

⁸Therefore the neighbors and those who previously had seen that he was blind^a said, "Is not this he who sat and begged?"

⁹Some said, "This is he." Others *said,* "He is like him."^a

He said, "I am *he.*"

¹⁰Therefore they said to him, "How were your eyes opened?"

¹¹He answered and said, "A Man called Jesus made clay and anointed my eyes and said to me, 'Go to the pool of^a Siloam and wash.' So I went and washed, and I received sight."

¹²Then they said to him, "Where is He?" He said, "I do not know."

8:54 ^aNU-Text and M-Text read *our.*
8:59 ^aNU-Text omits the rest of this verse.
9:4 ^aNU-Text reads *We.*   **9:8** ^aNU-Text reads *a beggar.*   **9:9** ^aNU-Text reads *"No, but he is like him."*
9:11 ^aNU-Text omits *the pool of.*

The Pharisees Excommunicate the Healed Man

[13]They brought him who formerly was blind to the Pharisees. [14]Now it was a Sabbath when Jesus made the clay and opened his eyes. [15]Then the Pharisees also asked him again how he had received his sight. He said to them, "He put clay on my eyes, and I washed, and I see."

[16]Therefore some of the Pharisees said, "This Man is not from God, because He does not keep the Sabbath."

Others said, "How can a man who is a sinner do such signs?" And there was a division among them.

[17]They said to the blind man again, "What do you say about Him because He opened your eyes?"

He said, "He is a prophet."

[18]But the Jews did not believe concerning him, that he had been blind and received his sight, until they called the parents of him who had received his sight. [19]And they asked them, saying, "Is this your son, who you say was born blind? How then does he now see?"

[20]His parents answered them and said, "We know that this is our son, and that he was born blind; [21]but by what means he now sees we do not know, or who opened his eyes we do not know. He is of age; ask him. He will speak for himself." [22]His parents said these things because they feared the Jews, for the Jews had agreed already that if anyone confessed that He was Christ, he would be put out of the synagogue. [23]Therefore his parents said, "He is of age; ask him."

[24]So they again called the man who was blind, and said to him, "Give God the glory! We know that this Man is a sinner."

[25]He answered and said, "Whether He is a sinner or not I do not know. One thing I know: that though I was blind, now I see."

[26]Then they said to him again, "What did He do to you? How did He open your eyes?"

[27]He answered them, "I told you already, and you did not listen. Why do you want to hear it again? Do you also want to become His disciples?"

[28]Then they reviled him and said, "You are His disciple, but we are Moses' disciples.

[29]We know that God spoke to Moses; as for this fellow, we do not know where He is from."

[30]The man answered and said to them, "Why, this is a marvelous thing, that you do not know where He is from; yet He has opened my eyes! [31]Now we know that God does not hear sinners; but if anyone is a worshiper of God and does His will, He hears him. [32]Since the world began it has been unheard of that anyone opened the eyes of one who was born blind. [33]If this Man were not from God, He could do nothing."

[34]They answered and said to him, "You were completely born in sins, and are you teaching us?" And they cast him out.

True Vision and True Blindness

[35]Jesus heard that they had cast him out; and when He had found him, He said to him, "Do you believe in the Son of God?"[a]

[36]He answered and said, "Who is He, Lord, that I may believe in Him?"

[37]And Jesus said to him, "You have both seen Him and it is He who is talking with you."

[38]Then he said, "Lord, I believe!" And he worshiped Him.

[39]And Jesus said, "For judgment I have come into this world, that those who do not see may see, and that those who see may be made blind."

[40]Then some of the Pharisees who were with Him heard these words, and said to Him, "Are we blind also?"

[41]Jesus said to them, "If you were blind, you would have no sin; but now you say, 'We see.' Therefore your sin remains.

Jesus the True Shepherd

10 "Most assuredly, I say to you, he who does not enter the sheepfold by the door, but climbs up some other way, the same is a thief and a robber. [2]But he who enters by the door is the shepherd of the sheep. [3]To him the doorkeeper opens, and the sheep hear his voice; and he calls his own sheep by name and leads them out. [4]And when he brings out his own sheep, he goes before them; and the sheep follow him,

9:35 [a]NU-Text reads Son of Man.

for they know his voice. ⁵Yet they will by no means follow a stranger, but will flee from him, for they do not know the voice of strangers." ⁶Jesus used this illustration, but they did not understand the things which He spoke to them.

Jesus the Good Shepherd

⁷Then Jesus said to them again, "Most assuredly, I say to you, I am the door of the sheep. ⁸All who *ever* came before Meᵃ are thieves and robbers, but the sheep did not hear them. ⁹I am the door. If anyone enters by Me, he will be saved, and will go in and out and find pasture. ¹⁰The thief does not come except to steal, and to kill, and to destroy. I have come that they may have life, and that they may have *it* more abundantly.

¹¹"I am the good shepherd. The good shepherd gives His life for the sheep. ¹²But a hireling, *he who is* not the shepherd, one who does not own the sheep, sees the wolf coming and leaves the sheep and flees; and the wolf catches the sheep and scatters them. ¹³The hireling flees because he is a hireling and does not care about the sheep. ¹⁴I am the good shepherd; and I know My *sheep,* and am known by My own. ¹⁵As the Father knows Me, even so I know the Father; and I lay down My life for the sheep. ¹⁶And other sheep I have which are not of this fold; them also I must bring, and they will hear My voice; and there will be one flock *and* one shepherd.

¹⁷"Therefore My Father loves Me, because I lay down My life that I may take it again. ¹⁸No one takes it from Me, but I lay it down of Myself. I have power to lay it down, and I have power to take it again. This command I have received from My Father."

¹⁹Therefore there was a division again among the Jews because of these sayings. ²⁰And many of them said, "He has a demon and is mad. Why do you listen to Him?" ²¹Others said, "These are not the words of one who has a demon. Can a demon open the eyes of the blind?"

The Shepherd Knows His Sheep

²²Now it was the Feast of Dedication in Jerusalem, and it was winter. ²³And Jesus walked in the temple, in Solomon's porch. ²⁴Then the Jews surrounded Him and said to Him, "How long do You keep us in doubt? If You are the Christ, tell us plainly."

²⁵Jesus answered them, "I told you, and you do not believe. The works that I do in My Father's name, they bear witness of Me. ²⁶But you do not believe, because you are not of My sheep, as I said to you.ᵃ ²⁷My sheep hear My voice, and I know them, and they follow Me. ²⁸And I give them eternal life, and they shall never perish; neither shall anyone snatch them out of My hand. ²⁹My Father, who has given *them* to Me, is greater than all; and no one is able to snatch *them* out of My Father's hand. ³⁰I and *My* Father are one."

Renewed Efforts to Stone Jesus

³¹Then the Jews took up stones again to stone Him. ³²Jesus answered them, "Many good works I have shown you from My Father. For which of those works do you stone Me?"

³³The Jews answered Him, saying, "For a good work we do not stone You, but for blasphemy, and because You, being a Man, make Yourself God."

³⁴Jesus answered them, "Is it not written in your law, *'I said, "You are gods" '*?ᵃ ³⁵If He called them gods, to whom the word of God came (and the Scripture cannot be broken), ³⁶do you say of Him whom the Father sanctified and sent into the world, 'You are blaspheming,' because I said, 'I am the Son of God'? ³⁷If I do not do the works of My Father, do not believe Me; ³⁸but if I do, though you do not believe Me, believe the works, that you may know and believeᵃ that the Father *is* in Me, and I in Him." ³⁹Therefore they sought again to seize Him, but He escaped out of their hand.

The Believers Beyond Jordan

⁴⁰And He went away again beyond the Jordan to the place where John was baptizing at first, and there He stayed. ⁴¹Then

---

10:8 ᵃM-Text omits *before Me.* **10:26** ᵃNU-Text omits *as I said to you.* **10:34** ᵃPsalm 82:6 **10:38** ᵃNU-Text reads *understand.*

many came to Him and said, "John performed no sign, but all the things that John spoke about this Man were true." ⁴²And many believed in Him there.

The Death of Lazarus

11 Now a certain *man* was sick, Lazarus of Bethany, the town of Mary and her sister Martha. ²It was *that* Mary who anointed the Lord with fragrant oil and wiped His feet with her hair, whose brother Lazarus was sick. ³Therefore the sisters sent to Him, saying, "Lord, behold, he whom You love is sick."

⁴When Jesus heard *that,* He said, "This sickness is not unto death, but for the glory of God, that the Son of God may be glorified through it."

⁵Now Jesus loved Martha and her sister and Lazarus. ⁶So, when He heard that he was sick, He stayed two more days in the place where He was. ⁷Then after this He said to *the* disciples, "Let us go to Judea again."

⁸*The* disciples said to Him, "Rabbi, lately the Jews sought to stone You, and are You going there again?"

⁹Jesus answered, "Are there not twelve hours in the day? If anyone walks in the day, he does not stumble, because he sees the light of this world. ¹⁰But if one walks in the night, he stumbles, because the light is not in him." ¹¹These things He said, and after that He said to them, "Our friend Lazarus sleeps, but I go that I may wake him up."

¹²Then His disciples said, "Lord, if he sleeps he will get well." ¹³However, Jesus spoke of his death, but they thought that He was speaking about taking rest in sleep.

¹⁴Then Jesus said to them plainly, "Lazarus is dead. ¹⁵And I am glad for your sakes that I was not there, that you may believe. Nevertheless let us go to him."

¹⁶Then Thomas, who is called the Twin, said to his fellow disciples, "Let us also go, that we may die with Him."

I Am the Resurrection and the Life

¹⁷So when Jesus came, He found that he had already been in the tomb four days. ¹⁸Now Bethany was near Jerusalem, about two miles^a away. ¹⁹And many of the Jews

had joined the women around Martha and Mary, to comfort them concerning their brother.

²⁰Now Martha, as soon as she heard that Jesus was coming, went and met Him, but Mary was sitting in the house. ²¹Now Martha said to Jesus, "Lord, if You had been here, my brother would not have died. ²²But even now I know that whatever You ask of God, God will give You."

²³Jesus said to her, "Your brother will rise again."

²⁴Martha said to Him, "I know that he will rise again in the resurrection at the last day."

²⁵Jesus said to her, "I am the resurrection and the life. He who believes in Me, though he may die, he shall live. ²⁶And whoever lives and believes in Me shall never die. Do you believe this?"

²⁷She said to Him, "Yes, Lord, I believe that You are the Christ, the Son of God, who is to come into the world."

Jesus and Death, the Last Enemy

²⁸And when she had said these things, she went her way and secretly called Mary her sister, saying, "The Teacher has come and is calling for you." ²⁹As soon as she heard *that,* she arose quickly and came to Him. ³⁰Now Jesus had not yet come into the town, but was^a in the place where Martha met Him. ³¹Then the Jews who were with her in the house, and comforting her, when they saw that Mary rose up quickly and went out, followed her, saying, "She is going to the tomb to weep there."^a

³²Then, when Mary came where Jesus was, and saw Him, she fell down at His feet, saying to Him, "Lord, if You had been here, my brother would not have died."

³³Therefore, when Jesus saw her weeping, and the Jews who came with her weeping, He groaned in the spirit and was troubled. ³⁴And He said, "Where have you laid him?"

They said to Him, "Lord, come and see."

³⁵Jesus wept. ³⁶Then the Jews said, "See how He loved him!"

11:18 ^aLiterally *fifteen stadia*   **11:30** ^aNU-Text adds *still.*   **11:31** ^aNU-Text reads *supposing that she was going to the tomb to weep there.*

37And some of them said, "Could not this Man, who opened the eyes of the blind, also have kept this man from dying?"

Lazarus Raised from the Dead

38Then Jesus, again groaning in Himself, came to the tomb. It was a cave, and a stone lay against it. 39Jesus said, "Take away the stone."

Martha, the sister of him who was dead, said to Him, "Lord, by this time there is a stench, for he has been *dead* four days."

40Jesus said to her, "Did I not say to you that if you would believe you would see the glory of God?" 41Then they took away the stone *from the place* where the dead man was lying.ᵃ And Jesus lifted up *His* eyes and said, "Father, I thank You that You have heard Me. 42And I know that You always hear Me, but because of the people who are standing by I said *this,* that they may believe that You sent Me." 43Now when He had said these things, He cried with a loud voice, "Lazarus, come forth!" 44And he who had died came out bound hand and foot with graveclothes, and his face was wrapped with a cloth. Jesus said to them, "Loose him, and let him go."

The Plot to Kill Jesus

45Then many of the Jews who had come to Mary, and had seen the things Jesus did, believed in Him. 46But some of them went away to the Pharisees and told them the things Jesus did. 47Then the chief priests and the Pharisees gathered a council and said, "What shall we do? For this Man works many signs. 48If we let Him alone like this, everyone will believe in Him, and the Romans will come and take away both our place and nation."

49And one of them, Caiaphas, being high priest that year, said to them, "You know nothing at all, 50nor do you consider that it is expedient for usᵃ that one man should die for the people, and not that the whole nation should perish." 51Now this he did not say on his own *authority;* but being high priest that year he prophesied that Jesus would die for the nation, 52and not for that nation only, but also that He would gather together in one the children of God who were scattered abroad.

53Then, from that day on, they plotted to put Him to death. 54Therefore Jesus no longer walked openly among the Jews, but went from there into the country near the wilderness, to a city called Ephraim, and there remained with His disciples.

55And the Passover of the Jews was near, and many went from the country up to Jerusalem before the Passover, to purify themselves. 56Then they sought Jesus, and spoke among themselves as they stood in the temple, "What do you think—that He will not come to the feast?" 57Now both the chief priests and the Pharisees had given a command, that if anyone knew where He was, he should report *it,* that they might seize Him.

The Anointing at Bethany

12 Then, six days before the Passover, Jesus came to Bethany, where Lazarus was who had been dead,ᵃ whom He had raised from the dead. 2There they made Him a supper; and Martha served, but Lazarus was one of those who sat at the table with Him. 3Then Mary took a pound of very costly oil of spikenard, anointed the feet of Jesus, and wiped His feet with her hair. And the house was filled with the fragrance of the oil.

4But one of His disciples, Judas Iscariot, Simon's *son,* who would betray Him, said, 5"Why was this fragrant oil not sold for three hundred denariiᵃ and given to the poor?" 6This he said, not that he cared for the poor, but because he was a thief, and had the money box; and he used to take what was put in it.

7But Jesus said, "Let her alone; she has keptᵃ this for the day of My burial. 8For the poor you have with you always, but Me you do not have always."

The Plot to Kill Lazarus

9Now a great many of the Jews knew that He was there; and they came, not for

---

11:41 ᵃNU-Text omits *from the place where the dead man was lying.*   **11:50** ᵃNU-Text reads *you.*
12:1 ᵃNU-Text omits *who had been dead.*
12:5 ᵃAbout one year's wages for a worker
12:7 ᵃNU-Text reads *that she may keep.*

Jesus' sake only, but that they might also see Lazarus, whom He had raised from the dead. [10]But the chief priests plotted to put Lazarus to death also, [11]because on account of him many of the Jews went away and believed in Jesus.

The Triumphal Entry

[12]The next day a great multitude that had come to the feast, when they heard that Jesus was coming to Jerusalem, [13]took branches of palm trees and went out to meet Him, and cried out:

"Hosanna!
'Blessed is He who comes in the name
  of the LORD!'[a]
The King of Israel!"

[14]Then Jesus, when He had found a young donkey, sat on it; as it is written:

[15] *"Fear not, daughter of Zion;*
Behold, your King is coming,
Sitting on a donkey's colt."[a]

[16]His disciples did not understand these things at first; but when Jesus was glorified, then they remembered that these things were written about Him and *that* they had done these things to Him. [17]Therefore the people, who were with Him when He called Lazarus out of his tomb and raised him from the dead, bore witness. [18]For this reason the people also met Him, because they heard that He had done this sign. [19]The Pharisees therefore said among themselves, "You see that you are accomplishing nothing. Look, the world has gone after Him!"

The Fruitful Grain of Wheat

[20]Now there were certain Greeks among those who came up to worship at the feast. [21]Then they came to Philip, who was from Bethsaida of Galilee, and asked him, saying, "Sir, we wish to see Jesus." [22]Philip came and told Andrew, and in turn Andrew and Philip told Jesus. [23]But Jesus answered them, saying, "The hour has come that the Son of Man should be glorified. [24]Most assuredly, I say to you, unless a grain of wheat falls into the ground and dies, it remains alone; but if it dies, it produces much grain. [25]He who loves his life will lose it, and he who hates his life in this world will keep it for eternal life. [26]If anyone serves Me, let him follow Me; and where I am, there My servant will be also. If anyone serves Me, him *My* Father will honor.

Jesus Predicts His Death on the Cross

[27]"Now My soul is troubled, and what shall I say? 'Father, save Me from this hour'? But for this purpose I came to this hour. [28]Father, glorify Your name."

Then a voice came from heaven, *saying,* "I have both glorified *it* and will glorify *it* again."

[29]Therefore the people who stood by and heard *it* said that it had thundered. Others said, "An angel has spoken to Him."

[30]Jesus answered and said, "This voice did not come because of Me, but for your sake. [31]Now is the judgment of this world; now the ruler of this world will be cast out. [32]And I, if I am lifted up from the earth, will draw all *peoples* to Myself." [33]This He said, signifying by what death He would die.

[34]The people answered Him, "We have heard from the law that the Christ remains forever; and how *can* You say, 'The Son of Man must be lifted up'? Who is this Son of Man?"

[35]Then Jesus said to them, "A little while longer the light is with you. Walk while you have the light, lest darkness overtake you; he who walks in darkness does not know where he is going. [36]While you have the light, believe in the light, that you may become sons of light." These things Jesus spoke, and departed, and was hidden from them.

Who Has Believed Our Report?

[37]But although He had done so many signs before them, they did not believe in Him, [38]that the word of Isaiah the prophet might be fulfilled, which he spoke:

12:13 [a]Psalm 118:26   **12:15** [a]Zechariah 9:9

"Lord, who has believed our report?
    And to whom has the arm of the LORD
    been revealed?"[a]

[39]Therefore they could not believe, because Isaiah said again:

[40] "He has blinded their eyes and
    hardened their hearts,
    Lest they should see with their eyes,
    Lest they should understand with their
        hearts and turn,
    So that I should heal them."[a]

[41]These things Isaiah said when[a] he saw His glory and spoke of Him.

Walk in the Light

[42]Nevertheless even among the rulers many believed in Him, but because of the Pharisees they did not confess *Him,* lest they should be put out of the synagogue; [43]for they loved the praise of men more than the praise of God.

[44]Then Jesus cried out and said, "He who believes in Me, believes not in Me but in Him who sent Me. [45]And he who sees Me sees Him who sent Me. [46]I have come *as a* light into the world, that whoever believes in Me should not abide in darkness. [47]And if anyone hears My words and does not believe,[a] I do not judge him; for I did not come to judge the world but to save the world. [48]He who rejects Me, and does not receive My words, has that which judges him—the word that I have spoken will judge him in the last day. [49]For I have not spoken on My own *authority;* but the Father who sent Me gave Me a command, what I should say and what I should speak. [50]And I know that His command is everlasting life. Therefore, whatever I speak, just as the Father has told Me, so I speak."

Jesus Washes the Disciples' Feet

13 Now before the Feast of the Passover, when Jesus knew that His hour had come that He should depart from this world to the Father, having loved His own who were in the world, He loved them to the end.

[2]And supper being ended,[a] the devil having already put it into the heart of Judas Iscariot, Simon's *son,* to betray Him, [3]Jesus, knowing that the Father had given all things into His hands, and that He had come from God and was going to God, [4]rose from supper and laid aside His garments, took a towel and girded Himself. [5]After that, He poured water into a basin and began to wash the disciples' feet, and to wipe *them* with the towel with which He was girded. [6]Then He came to Simon Peter. And *Peter* said to Him, "Lord, are You washing my feet?"

[7]Jesus answered and said to him, "What I am doing you do not understand now, but you will know after this."

[8]Peter said to Him, "You shall never wash my feet!"

Jesus answered him, "If I do not wash you, you have no part with Me."

[9]Simon Peter said to Him, "Lord, not my feet only, but also *my* hands and *my* head!"

[10]Jesus said to him, "He who is bathed needs only to wash *his* feet, but is completely clean; and you are clean, but not all of you." [11]For He knew who would betray Him; therefore He said, "You are not all clean."

[12]So when He had washed their feet, taken His garments, and sat down again, He said to them, "Do you know what I have done to you? [13]You call Me Teacher and Lord, and you say well, for *so* I am. [14]If I then, *your* Lord and Teacher, have washed your feet, you also ought to wash one another's feet. [15]For I have given you an example, that you should do as I have done to you. [16]Most assuredly, I say to you, a servant is not greater than his master; nor is he who is sent greater than he who sent him. [17]If you know these things, blessed are you if you do them.

Jesus Identifies His Betrayer

[18]"I do not speak concerning all of you. I know whom I have chosen; but that the

---

12:38 [a]Isaiah 53:1   **12:40** [a]Isaiah 6:10
12:41 [a]NU-Text reads *because.*   **12:47** [a]NU-Text reads *keep them.*   **13:2** [a]NU-Text reads *And during supper.*

Scripture may be fulfilled, '*He who eats bread with Me*[a] *has lifted up his heel against Me.*'[b] [19]Now I tell you before it comes, that when it does come to pass, you may believe that I am *He.* [20]Most assuredly, I say to you, he who receives whomever I send receives Me; and he who receives Me receives Him who sent Me."

[21]When Jesus had said these things, He was troubled in spirit, and testified and said, "Most assuredly, I say to you, one of you will betray Me." [22]Then the disciples looked at one another, perplexed about whom He spoke.

[23]Now there was leaning on Jesus' bosom one of His disciples, whom Jesus loved. [24]Simon Peter therefore motioned to him to ask who it was of whom He spoke.

[25]Then, leaning back[a] on Jesus' breast, he said to Him, "Lord, who is it?"

[26]Jesus answered, "It is he to whom I shall give a piece of bread when I have dipped *it.*" And having dipped the bread, He gave *it* to Judas Iscariot, *the son* of Simon. [27]Now after the piece of bread, Satan entered him. Then Jesus said to him, "What you do, do quickly." [28]But no one at the table knew for what reason He said this to him. [29]For some thought, because Judas had the money box, that Jesus had said to him, "Buy *those things* we need for the feast," or that he should give something to the poor.

[30]Having received the piece of bread, he then went out immediately. And it was night.

The New Commandment

[31]So, when he had gone out, Jesus said, "Now the Son of Man is glorified, and God is glorified in Him. [32]If God is glorified in Him, God will also glorify Him in Himself, and glorify Him immediately. [33]Little children, I shall be with you a little while longer. You will seek Me; and as I said to the Jews, 'Where I am going, you cannot come,' so now I say to you. [34]A new commandment I give to you, that you love one another; as I have loved you, that you also love one another. [35]By this all will know that you are My disciples, if you have love for one another."

Jesus Predicts Peter's Denial

[36]Simon Peter said to Him, "Lord, where are You going?"

Jesus answered him, "Where I am going you cannot follow Me now, but you shall follow Me afterward."

[37]Peter said to Him, "Lord, why can I not follow You now? I will lay down my life for Your sake."

[38]Jesus answered him, "Will you lay down your life for My sake? Most assuredly, I say to you, the rooster shall not crow till you have denied Me three times.

The Way, the Truth, and the Life

14 "Let not your heart be troubled; you believe in God, believe also in Me. [2]In My Father's house are many mansions;[a] if *it were* not *so,* I would have told you. I go to prepare a place for you.[b] [3]And if I go and prepare a place for you, I will come again and receive you to Myself; that where I am, *there* you may be also. [4]And where I go you know, and the way you know."

[5]Thomas said to Him, "Lord, we do not know where You are going, and how can we know the way?"

[6]Jesus said to him, "I am the way, the truth, and the life. No one comes to the Father except through Me.

The Father Revealed

[7]"If you had known Me, you would have known My Father also; and from now on you know Him and have seen Him."

[8]Philip said to Him, "Lord, show us the Father, and it is sufficient for us."

[9]Jesus said to him, "Have I been with you so long, and yet you have not known Me, Philip? He who has seen Me has seen the Father; so how can you say, 'Show us the Father'? [10]Do you not believe that I am in the Father, and the Father in Me? The words that I speak to you I do not speak on

---

13:18 [a]NU-Text reads *My bread.* [b]Psalm 41:9
13:25 [a]NU-Text and M-Text add *thus.*
14:2 [a]Literally *dwellings* [b]NU-Text adds a word which would cause the text to read either *if it were not so, would I have told you that I go to prepare a place for you?* or *if it were not so I would have told you; for I go to prepare a place for you.*

My own *authority;* but the Father who dwells in Me does the works. ¹¹Believe Me that I *am* in the Father and the Father in Me, or else believe Me for the sake of the works themselves.

The Answered Prayer

¹²"Most assuredly, I say to you, he who believes in Me, the works that I do he will do also; and greater *works* than these he will do, because I go to My Father. ¹³And whatever you ask in My name, that I will do, that the Father may be glorified in the Son. ¹⁴If you ask[a] anything in My name, I will do *it.*

Jesus Promises Another Helper

¹⁵"If you love Me, keep[a] My commandments. ¹⁶And I will pray the Father, and He will give you another Helper, that He may abide with you forever— ¹⁷the Spirit of truth, whom the world cannot receive, because it neither sees Him nor knows Him; but you know Him, for He dwells with you and will be in you. ¹⁸I will not leave you orphans; I will come to you.

Indwelling of the Father and the Son

¹⁹"A little while longer and the world will see Me no more, but you will see Me. Because I live, you will live also. ²⁰At that day you will know that I *am* in My Father, and you in Me, and I in you. ²¹He who has My commandments and keeps them, it is he who loves Me. And he who loves Me will

---

14:14 [a]NU-Text adds *Me.*   **14:15** [a]NU-Text reads *you will keep.*

TRUTH

"No one comes to the Father except through Me."

JOHN 14:6

Simon Greenleaf

NO ORDINARY CLAIMS

Simon Greenleaf (1783–1853) was the Royall Professor of Law at Harvard and considered one of the greatest legal minds in Western history. In his *Testimony of the Evangelists*, Greenleaf stated:

> The religion of Jesus Christ aims at nothing less than the utter overthrow of all other systems of religion in the world; denouncing them as inadequate to the wants of man, false in their foundations, and dangerous in their tendency. It not only solicits the grave attention of all, to whom its doctrines are presented, but it demands their cordial belief, as a matter of vital concernment.
>
> These are no ordinary claims; and it seems hardly possible for a rational being to regard them with even a subdued interest; much less to treat them with mere indifference and contempt. If not true, they are little else than the pretensions of a bold imposture, which, not satisfied with having already enslaved millions of the human race, seeks to continue its encroachments upon human liberty, until all nations shall be subjugated under its iron rule.
>
> But if they are well-founded and just, they can be no less than the high requirements of heaven, addressed by the voice of God to the reason and understanding of man, concerning things deeply affecting his relations to his sovereign, and essential to the formation of his character and of course to his destiny, both for this life and for the life to come.

be loved by My Father, and I will love him and manifest Myself to him.”

²²Judas (not Iscariot) said to Him, “Lord, how is it that You will manifest Yourself to us, and not to the world?”

²³Jesus answered and said to him, “If anyone loves Me, he will keep My word; and My Father will love him, and We will come to him and make Our home with him. ²⁴He who does not love Me does not keep My words; and the word which you hear is not Mine but the Father's who sent Me.

The Gift of His Peace

²⁵“These things I have spoken to you while being present with you. ²⁶But the Helper, the Holy Spirit, whom the Father will send in My name, He will teach you all things, and bring to your remembrance all things that I said to you. ²⁷Peace I leave with you, My peace I give to you; not as the world gives do I give to you. Let not your heart be troubled, neither let it be afraid. ²⁸You have heard Me say to you, ‘I am going away and coming *back* to you.’ If you loved Me, you would rejoice because I said,ᵃ ‘I am going to the Father,’ for My Father is greater than I.

²⁹“And now I have told you before it comes, that when it does come to pass, you may believe. ³⁰I will no longer talk much with you, for the ruler of this world is coming, and he has nothing in Me. ³¹But that the world may know that I love the Father, and as the Father gave Me commandment, so I do. Arise, let us go from here.

The True Vine

15 “I am the true vine, and My Father is the vinedresser. ²Every branch in Me that does not bear fruit He takes away;ᵃ and every *branch* that bears fruit He prunes, that it may bear more fruit. ³You are already clean because of the word which I have spoken to you. ⁴Abide in Me, and I in you. As the branch cannot bear fruit of itself, unless it abides in the vine, neither can you, unless you abide in Me.

⁵“I am the vine, you *are* the branches. He who abides in Me, and I in him, bears much fruit; for without Me you can do nothing. ⁶If anyone does not abide in Me, he is cast out as a branch and is withered; and they gather them and throw *them* into

14:28 ᵃNU-Text omits *I said.*   **15:2** ᵃOr *lifts up*

WORSHIP

“I am the vine. . . .”

JOHN 15:5

Buzz Aldrin

COMMUNION ON THE MOON

As the Lunar Module pilot on the Apollo 11 space mission, with the first lunar landing on July 20, 1969, Buzz Aldrin was the second person to walk on the moon, after Mission Commander Neil Armstrong. Aldrin had brought with him a tiny communion kit, given him by his church. During the morning, he radioed, “Houston, this is Eagle. . . . I would like to request a few moments of silence. I would like to invite each person listening in . . . to contemplate for a moment the events of the last few hours, and to give thanks in his own individual way.”

During the radio blackout, Aldrin took the communion elements and read John 15:5: “I am the vine, you are the branches. He who abides in Me, and I in him, bears much fruit.” Aldrin had been asked not to read the verse publicly because of a legal challenge NASA faced from famed atheist Madalyn Murray O'Hair regarding the reading of the biblical creation story from Genesis during the Apollo 8 mission.

How incredible is it that the first thing this American patriot did when he arrived on the moon was to worship God?

the fire, and they are burned. ⁷If you abide in Me, and My words abide in you, you willᵃ ask what you desire, and it shall be done for you. ⁸By this My Father is glorified, that you bear much fruit; so you will be My disciples.

Love and Joy Perfected

⁹"As the Father loved Me, I also have loved you; abide in My love. ¹⁰If you keep My commandments, you will abide in My love, just as I have kept My Father's commandments and abide in His love.

¹¹"These things I have spoken to you, that My joy may remain in you, and *that* your joy may be full. ¹²This is My commandment, that you love one another as I have loved you. ¹³Greater love has no one than this, than to lay down one's life for his friends. ¹⁴You are My friends if you do whatever I command you. ¹⁵No longer do I call you servants, for a servant does not know what his master is doing; but I have called you friends, for all things that I heard from My Father I have made known to you. ¹⁶You did not choose Me, but I chose you and appointed you that you should go and bear fruit, and *that* your fruit should remain, that whatever you ask the Father in My name He may give you. ¹⁷These things I command you, that you love one another.

The World's Hatred

¹⁸"If the world hates you, you know that it hated Me before *it hated* you. ¹⁹If you were of the world, the world would love its own. Yet because you are not of the world, but I chose you out of the world, therefore the world hates you. ²⁰Remember the word that I said to you, 'A servant is not greater than his master.' If they persecuted Me, they will also persecute you. If they kept My word, they will keep yours also. ²¹But all these things they will do to you for My name's sake, because they do not know Him who sent Me. ²²If I had not come and spoken to them, they would have no sin, but now they have no excuse for their sin. ²³He who hates Me hates My Father also. ²⁴If I had not done among them the works which no one else did, they would have no sin; but now they have seen and also hated both Me and My Father. ²⁵But *this happened* that the word might be fulfilled which is written in their law, 'They hated Me without a cause.'ᵃ

The Coming Rejection

²⁶"But when the Helper comes, whom I shall send to you from the Father, the Spirit of truth who proceeds from the Father, He will testify of Me. ²⁷And you also will bear witness, because you have been with Me from the beginning.

16 "These things I have spoken to you, that you should not be made to stumble. ²They will put you out of the synagogues; yes, the time is coming that whoever kills you will think that he offers God service. ³And these things they will do to youᵃ because they have not known the Father nor Me. ⁴But these things I have told you, that when theᵃ time comes, you may remember that I told you of them.

"And these things I did not say to you at the beginning, because I was with you.

The Work of the Holy Spirit

⁵"But now I go away to Him who sent Me, and none of you asks Me, 'Where are You going?' ⁶But because I have said these things to you, sorrow has filled your heart. ⁷Nevertheless I tell you the truth. It is to your advantage that I go away; for if I do not go away, the Helper will not come to you; but if I depart, I will send Him to you. ⁸And when He has come, He will convict the world of sin, and of righteousness, and of judgment: ⁹of sin, because they do not believe in Me; ¹⁰of righteousness, because I go to My Father and you see Me no more; ¹¹of judgment, because the ruler of this world is judged.

¹²"I still have many things to say to you, but you cannot bear *them* now. ¹³However, when He, the Spirit of truth, has come, He will guide you into all truth; for He will not speak on His own *authority*, but whatever He hears He will speak; and He will tell you

---

15:7 ᵃNU-Text omits *you will.*   15:25 ᵃPsalm 69:4
16:3 ᵃNU-Text and M-Text omit *to you.*
16:4 ᵃNU-Text reads *their.*

FOUR IMMORTAL CHAPLAINS

SELFLESS

*"Greater love has
no one than this. . . ."*

JOHN 15:13

Shortly before 1 A.M. on February 2, 1943, the American transport ship *Dorchester* was steaming through the icy North Atlantic from Newfoundland toward an American base in Greenland, carrying 902 service men, merchant seamen, and civilian workers, when a German torpedo struck the starboard side, amid ship, far below the water line. The blast killed scores of men, and many more were seriously wounded. Others, stunned by the explosion, groped in the darkness.

Through the pandemonium, according to eyewitnesses, four Army chaplains brought hope in despair and light in darkness to the men who struggled to find their way out. Those army chaplains were Lt. George L. Fox, Methodist; Lt. Alexander D. Goode, Jewish; Lt. John P. Washington, Roman Catholic; and Lt. Clark V. Poling, Dutch Reformed. Above the din, the four chaplains could be heard urging the frightened to be brave, praying for the dying, and guiding the disoriented toward the lifeboats.

Men jumped from the ship into lifeboats, overcrowding them to the point of capsizing. Other rafts, tossed into the Atlantic, drifted away before soldiers could get in them. As most of the men reached topside, the chaplains opened a storage locker and began distributing life jackets. When there were no more lifejackets available, the chaplains astonished onlookers, taking off theirs and giving them to four frightened young men.

"It was the finest thing I have seen or hope to see this side of heaven," said John Ladd, one of the survivors.

Then in the darkness, the four chaplains linked arms, grasped the railing of the ship together as it began to slip into the ocean, and began singing and shouting biblical encouragement in English, Hebrew, and Latin to the men in the sea. William Bednar, floating among his dead comrades, later said, "Their voices were the only thing that kept me going."

Of the men aboard the *Dorchester*, 672 died, including the chaplains. Their sacrificial action constitutes one of the purest spiritual and ethical acts a person can make. In their devotion to their troops, these men of God captured the best of what a military chaplain strives to be. Their heroic conduct set a vision of greatness that stunned America as did the magnitude of the tragedy.

things to come. ¹⁴He will glorify Me, for He will take of what is Mine and declare *it* to you. ¹⁵All things that the Father has are Mine. Therefore I said that He will take of Mine and declare *it* to you.ᵃ

Sorrow Will Turn to Joy

¹⁶"A little while, and you will not see Me; and again a little while, and you will see Me, because I go to the Father."

¹⁷Then *some* of His disciples said among themselves, "What is this that He says to us, 'A little while, and you will not see Me; and again a little while, and you will see Me'; and, 'because I go to the Father'?" ¹⁸They said therefore, "What is this that He says, 'A little while'? We do not know what He is saying."

¹⁹Now Jesus knew that they desired to ask Him, and He said to them, "Are you inquiring among yourselves about what I said, 'A little while, and you will not see Me; and again a little while, and you will see Me'? ²⁰Most assuredly, I say to you that you will weep and lament, but the world will rejoice; and you will be sorrowful, but your sorrow will be turned into joy. ²¹A woman, when she is in labor, has sorrow because her hour has come; but as soon as she has given birth to the child, she no longer remembers the anguish, for joy that a human being has been born into the world. ²²Therefore you now have sorrow; but I will see you again and your heart will rejoice, and your joy no one will take from you.

²³"And in that day you will ask Me nothing. Most assuredly, I say to you, whatever you ask the Father in My name He will give you. ²⁴Until now you have asked nothing in My name. Ask, and you will receive, that your joy may be full.

Jesus Christ Has Overcome the World

²⁵"These things I have spoken to you in figurative language; but the time is coming when I will no longer speak to you in figurative language, but I will tell you plainly about the Father. ²⁶In that day you will ask in My name, and I do not say to you that I shall pray the Father for you; ²⁷for the Father Himself loves you, because you have loved Me, and have believed that

I came forth from God. ²⁸I came forth from the Father and have come into the world. Again, I leave the world and go to the Father."

²⁹His disciples said to Him, "See, now You are speaking plainly, and using no figure of speech! ³⁰Now we are sure that You know all things, and have no need that anyone should question You. By this we believe that You came forth from God."

³¹Jesus answered them, "Do you now believe? ³²Indeed the hour is coming, yes, has now come, that you will be scattered, each to his own, and will leave Me alone. And yet I am not alone, because the Father is with Me. ³³These things I have spoken to you, that in Me you may have peace. In the world you willᵃ have tribulation; but be of good cheer, I have overcome the world."

Jesus Prays for Himself

17 Jesus spoke these words, lifted up His eyes to heaven, and said: "Father, the hour has come. Glorify Your Son, that Your Son also may glorify You, ²as You have given Him authority over all flesh, that He shouldᵃ give eternal life to as many as You have given Him. ³And this is eternal life, that they may know You, the only true God, and Jesus Christ whom You have sent. ⁴I have glorified You on the earth. I have finished the work which You have given Me to do. ⁵And now, O Father, glorify Me together with Yourself, with the glory which I had with You before the world was.

Jesus Prays for His Disciples

⁶"I have manifested Your name to the men whom You have given Me out of the world. They were Yours, You gave them to Me, and they have kept Your word. ⁷Now they have known that all things which You have given Me are from You. ⁸For I have given to them the words which You have given Me; and they have received *them,* and have known surely that I came forth from You; and they have believed that You sent Me.

16:15 ᵃNU-Text and M-Text read *He takes of Mine and will declare it to you.*   **16:33** ᵃNU-Text and M-Text omit *will.*   **17:2** ᵃM-Text reads *shall.*

9"I pray for them. I do not pray for the world but for those whom You have given Me, for they are Yours. 10And all Mine are Yours, and Yours are Mine, and I am glorified in them. 11Now I am no longer in the world, but these are in the world, and I come to You. Holy Father, keep through Your name those whom You have given Me,ᵃ that they may be one as We *are*. 12While I was with them in the world,ᵃ I kept them in Your name. Those whom You gave Me I have kept;ᵇ and none of them is lost except the son of perdition, that the Scripture might be fulfilled. 13But now I come to You, and these things I speak in the world, that they may have My joy fulfilled in themselves. 14I have given them Your word; and the world has hated them because they are not of the world, just as I am not of the world. 15I do not pray that You should take them out of the world, but that You should keep them from the evil one. 16They are not of the world, just as I am not of the world. 17Sanctify them by Your truth. Your word is truth. 18As You sent Me into the world, I also have sent them into the world. 19And for their sakes I sanctify Myself, that they also may be sanctified by the truth.

Jesus Prays for All Believers

20"I do not pray for these alone, but also for those who willᵃ believe in Me through their word; 21that they all may be one, as You, Father, *are* in Me, and I in You; that they also may be one in Us, that the world may believe that You sent Me. 22And the glory which You gave Me I have given them, that they may be one just as We are one: 23I in them, and You in Me; that they may be made perfect in one, and that the world may know that You have sent Me, and have loved them as You have loved Me.

24"Father, I desire that they also whom You gave Me may be with Me where I am, that they may behold My glory which You have given Me; for You loved Me before the foundation of the world. 25O righteous Father! The world has not known You, but I have known You; and these have known that You sent Me. 26And I have declared to them Your name, and will declare *it*, that

the love with which You loved Me may be in them, and I in them."

Betrayal and Arrest in Gethsemane

18 When Jesus had spoken these words, He went out with His disciples over the Brook Kidron, where there was a garden, which He and His disciples entered. 2And Judas, who betrayed Him, also knew the place; for Jesus often met there with His disciples. 3Then Judas, having received a detachment *of troops,* and officers from the chief priests and Pharisees, came there with lanterns, torches, and weapons. 4Jesus therefore, knowing all things that would come upon Him, went forward and said to them, "Whom are you seeking?"

5They answered Him, "Jesus of Nazareth."

Jesus said to them, "I am *He.*" And Judas, who betrayed Him, also stood with them. 6Now when He said to them, "I am *He,*" they drew back and fell to the ground.

7Then He asked them again, "Whom are you seeking?"

And they said, "Jesus of Nazareth."

8Jesus answered, "I have told you that I am *He.* Therefore, if you seek Me, let these go their way," 9that the saying might be fulfilled which He spoke, "Of those whom You gave Me I have lost none."

10Then Simon Peter, having a sword, drew it and struck the high priest's servant, and cut off his right ear. The servant's name was Malchus.

11So Jesus said to Peter, "Put your sword into the sheath. Shall I not drink the cup which My Father has given Me?"

Before the High Priest

12Then the detachment *of troops* and the captain and the officers of the Jews arrested Jesus and bound Him. 13And they led Him away to Annas first, for he was the father-in-law of Caiaphas who was high priest that year. 14Now it was Caiaphas who advised the Jews that it was expedient that one man should die for the people.

17:11 ᵃNU-Text and M-Text read *keep them through Your name which You have given Me.* **17:12** ᵃNU-Text omits *in the world.* ᵇNU-Text reads *in Your name which You gave Me. And I guarded them;* (or *it;*). **17:20** ᵃNU-Text and M-Text omit *will.*

Peter Denies Jesus

15And Simon Peter followed Jesus, and so *did* another[a] disciple. Now that disciple was known to the high priest, and went with Jesus into the courtyard of the high priest. 16But Peter stood at the door outside. Then the other disciple, who was known to the high priest, went out and spoke to her who kept the door, and brought Peter in. 17Then the servant girl who kept the door said to Peter, "You are not also *one* of this Man's disciples, are you?"

He said, "I am not."

18Now the servants and officers who had made a fire of coals stood there, for it was cold, and they warmed themselves. And Peter stood with them and warmed himself.

Jesus Questioned by the High Priest

19The high priest then asked Jesus about His disciples and His doctrine.

20Jesus answered him, "I spoke openly to the world. I always taught in synagogues and in the temple, where the Jews always meet,[a] and in secret I have said nothing. 21Why do you ask Me? Ask those who have heard Me what I said to them. Indeed they know what I said."

22And when He had said these things, one of the officers who stood by struck Jesus with the palm of his hand, saying, "Do You answer the high priest like that?"

23Jesus answered him, "If I have spoken evil, bear witness of the evil; but if well, why do you strike Me?"

24Then Annas sent Him bound to Caiaphas the high priest.

Peter Denies Twice More

25Now Simon Peter stood and warmed himself. Therefore they said to him, "You are not also *one* of His disciples, are you?"

He denied *it* and said, "I am not!"

26One of the servants of the high priest, a relative *of him* whose ear Peter cut off, said, "Did I not see you in the garden with Him?" 27Peter then denied again; and immediately a rooster crowed.

In Pilate's Court

28Then they led Jesus from Caiaphas to the Praetorium, and it was early morning. But they themselves did not go into the Praetorium, lest they should be defiled, but that they might eat the Passover. 29Pilate then went out to them and said, "What accusation do you bring against this Man?"

30They answered and said to him, "If He were not an evildoer, we would not have delivered Him up to you."

31Then Pilate said to them, "You take Him and judge Him according to your law."

Therefore the Jews said to him, "It is not lawful for us to put anyone to death," 32that the saying of Jesus might be fulfilled which He spoke, signifying by what death He would die.

33Then Pilate entered the Praetorium again, called Jesus, and said to Him, "Are You the King of the Jews?"

34Jesus answered him, "Are you speaking for yourself about this, or did others tell you this concerning Me?"

35Pilate answered, "Am I a Jew? Your own nation and the chief priests have delivered You to me. What have You done?"

36Jesus answered, "My kingdom is not of this world. If My kingdom were of this world, My servants would fight, so that I should not be delivered to the Jews; but now My kingdom is not from here."

37Pilate therefore said to Him, "Are You a king then?"

Jesus answered, "You say *rightly* that I am a king. For this cause I was born, and for this cause I have come into the world, that I should bear witness to the truth. Everyone who is of the truth hears My voice."

38Pilate said to Him, "What is truth?" And when he had said this, he went out again to the Jews, and said to them, "I find no fault in Him at all.

Taking the Place of Barabbas

39"But you have a custom that I should release someone to you at the Passover. Do you therefore want me to release to you the King of the Jews?"

40Then they all cried again, saying, "Not this Man, but Barabbas!" Now Barabbas was a robber.

18:15 [a]M-Text reads *the other.*   **18:20** [a]NU-Text reads *where all the Jews meet.*

The Soldiers Mock Jesus

19 So then Pilate took Jesus and scourged *Him.* [2]And the soldiers twisted a crown of thorns and put *it* on His head, and they put on Him a purple robe. [3]Then they said,[a] "Hail, King of the Jews!" And they struck Him with their hands.

[4]Pilate then went out again, and said to them, "Behold, I am bringing Him out to you, that you may know that I find no fault in Him."

Pilate's Decision

[5]Then Jesus came out, wearing the crown of thorns and the purple robe. And *Pilate* said to them, "Behold the Man!"

[6]Therefore, when the chief priests and officers saw Him, they cried out, saying, "Crucify *Him,* crucify *Him!*"

Pilate said to them, "You take Him and crucify *Him,* for I find no fault in Him."

[7]The Jews answered him, "We have a law, and according to our[a] law He ought to die, because He made Himself the Son of God."

[8]Therefore, when Pilate heard that saying, he was the more afraid, [9]and went again into the Praetorium, and said to Jesus, "Where are You from?" But Jesus gave him no answer.

[10]Then Pilate said to Him, "Are You not speaking to me? Do You not know that I have power to crucify You, and power to release You?"

[11]Jesus answered, "You could have no power at all against Me unless it had been given you from above. Therefore the one who delivered Me to you has the greater sin."

[12]From then on Pilate sought to release Him, but the Jews cried out, saying, "If you let this Man go, you are not Caesar's friend. Whoever makes himself a king speaks against Caesar."

[13]When Pilate therefore heard that saying, he brought Jesus out and sat down in the judgment seat in a place that is called *The* Pavement, but in Hebrew, Gabbatha. [14]Now it was the Preparation Day of the Passover, and about the sixth hour. And he said to the Jews, "Behold your King!"

[15]But they cried out, "Away with *Him,* away with *Him!* Crucify Him!"

Pilate said to them, "Shall I crucify your King?"

The chief priests answered, "We have no king but Caesar!"

[16]Then he delivered Him to them to be crucified. Then they took Jesus and led *Him* away.[a]

The King on a Cross

[17]And He, bearing His cross, went out to a place called *the Place* of a Skull, which is called in Hebrew, Golgotha, [18]where they crucified Him, and two others with Him, one on either side, and Jesus in the center. [19]Now Pilate wrote a title and put *it* on the cross. And the writing was:

JESUS OF NAZARETH,
THE KING OF THE JEWS.

[20]Then many of the Jews read this title, for the place where Jesus was crucified was near the city; and it was written in Hebrew, Greek, *and* Latin.

[21]Therefore the chief priests of the Jews said to Pilate, "Do not write, 'The King of the Jews,' but, 'He said, "I am the King of the Jews."'"

[22]Pilate answered, "What I have written, I have written."

[23]Then the soldiers, when they had crucified Jesus, took His garments and made four parts, to each soldier a part, and also the tunic. Now the tunic was without seam, woven from the top in one piece. [24]They said therefore among themselves, "Let us not tear it, but cast lots for it, whose it shall be," that the Scripture might be fulfilled which says:

"They divided My garments among them,
     And for My clothing they cast lots."[a]

Therefore the soldiers did these things.

Behold Your Mother

[25]Now there stood by the cross of Jesus His mother, and His mother's sister, Mary

---

19:3 [a]NU-Text reads *And they came up to Him and said.*
19:7 [a]NU-Text reads *the law.*   19:16 [a]NU-Text omits *and led Him away.*   19:24 [a]Psalm 22:18

the *wife* of Clopas, and Mary Magdalene. ²⁶When Jesus therefore saw His mother, and the disciple whom He loved standing by, He said to His mother, "Woman, behold your son!" ²⁷Then He said to the disciple, "Behold your mother!" And from that hour that disciple took her to his own *home.*

It Is Finished

²⁸After this, Jesus, knowing[a] that all things were now accomplished, that the Scripture might be fulfilled, said, "I thirst!" ²⁹Now a vessel full of sour wine was sitting there; and they filled a sponge with sour wine, put *it* on hyssop, and put *it* to His mouth. ³⁰So when Jesus had received the sour wine, He said, "It is finished!" And bowing His head, He gave up His spirit.

Jesus' Side Is Pierced

³¹Therefore, because it was the Preparation *Day,* that the bodies should not remain on the cross on the Sabbath (for that Sabbath was a high day), the Jews asked Pilate that their legs might be broken, and *that* they might be taken away. ³²Then the soldiers came and broke the legs of the first and of the other who was crucified with Him. ³³But when they came to Jesus and saw that He was already dead, they did not break His legs. ³⁴But one of the soldiers pierced His side with a spear, and immediately blood and water came out. ³⁵And he who has seen has testified, and his testimony is true; and he knows that he is telling the truth, so that you may believe. ³⁶For these things were done that the Scripture should be fulfilled, *"Not one of His bones shall be broken."*[a] ³⁷And again another Scripture says, *"They shall look on Him whom they pierced."*[a]

Jesus Buried in Joseph's Tomb

³⁸After this, Joseph of Arimathea, being a disciple of Jesus, but secretly, for fear of the Jews, asked Pilate that he might take away the body of Jesus; and Pilate gave *him* permission. So he came and took the body of Jesus. ³⁹And Nicodemus, who at first came to Jesus by night, also came, bringing a mixture of myrrh and aloes, about a hundred pounds. ⁴⁰Then they took the body of Jesus, and bound it in strips of linen with the spices, as the custom of the Jews is to bury. ⁴¹Now in the place where He was crucified there was a garden, and in the garden a new tomb in which no one had yet been laid. ⁴²So there they laid Jesus, because of the Jews' Preparation *Day,* for the tomb was nearby.

The Empty Tomb

20 Now the first *day* of the week Mary Magdalene went to the tomb early, while it was still dark, and saw *that* the stone had been taken away from the tomb. ²Then she ran and came to Simon Peter, and to the other disciple, whom Jesus loved, and said to them, "They have taken away the Lord out of the tomb, and we do not know where they have laid Him."

³Peter therefore went out, and the other disciple, and were going to the tomb. ⁴So they both ran together, and the other disciple outran Peter and came to the tomb first. ⁵And he, stooping down and looking in, saw the linen cloths lying *there;* yet he did not go in. ⁶Then Simon Peter came, following him, and went into the tomb; and he saw the linen cloths lying *there,* ⁷and the handkerchief that had been around His head, not lying with the linen cloths, but folded together in a place by itself. ⁸Then the other disciple, who came to the tomb first, went in also; and he saw and believed. ⁹For as yet they did not know the Scripture, that He must rise again from the dead. ¹⁰Then the disciples went away again to their own homes.

Mary Magdalene Sees the Risen Lord

¹¹But Mary stood outside by the tomb weeping, and as she wept she stooped down *and looked* into the tomb. ¹²And she saw two angels in white sitting, one at the head and the other at the feet, where the body of Jesus had lain. ¹³Then they said to her, "Woman, why are you weeping?"

She said to them, "Because they have taken away my Lord, and I do not know where they have laid Him."

19:28 [a]M-Text reads *seeing.*   **19:36** [a]Exodus 12:46; Numbers 9:12; Psalm 34:20   **19:37** [a]Zechariah 12:10

[14]Now when she had said this, she turned around and saw Jesus standing *there,* and did not know that it was Jesus. [15]Jesus said to her, "Woman, why are you weeping? Whom are you seeking?"

She, supposing Him to be the gardener, said to Him, "Sir, if You have carried Him away, tell me where You have laid Him, and I will take Him away."

[16]Jesus said to her, "Mary!"

She turned and said to Him,[a] "Rabboni!" (which is to say, Teacher).

[17]Jesus said to her, "Do not cling to Me, for I have not yet ascended to My Father; but go to My brethren and say to them, 'I am ascending to My Father and your Father, and *to* My God and your God.'"

[18]Mary Magdalene came and told the disciples that she had seen the Lord,[a] and *that* He had spoken these things to her.

The Apostles Commissioned

[19]Then, the same day at evening, being the first *day* of the week, when the doors were shut where the disciples were assembled,[a] for fear of the Jews, Jesus came and stood in the midst, and said to them, "Peace *be* with you." [20]When He had said this, He showed them *His* hands and His side. Then the disciples were glad when they saw the Lord.

[21]So Jesus said to them again, "Peace to you! As the Father has sent Me, I also send you." [22]And when He had said this, He breathed on *them,* and said to them, "Receive the Holy Spirit. [23]If you forgive the sins of any, they are forgiven them; if you retain the *sins* of any, they are retained."

Seeing and Believing

[24]Now Thomas, called the Twin, one of the twelve, was not with them when Jesus came. [25]The other disciples therefore said to him, "We have seen the Lord."

So he said to them, "Unless I see in His hands the print of the nails, and put my finger into the print of the nails, and put my hand into His side, I will not believe."

[26]And after eight days His disciples were again inside, and Thomas with them. Jesus came, the doors being shut, and stood in the midst, and said, "Peace to you!" [27]Then He said to Thomas, "Reach your finger here, and look at My hands; and reach your hand *here,* and put *it* into My side. Do not be unbelieving, but believing."

[28]And Thomas answered and said to Him, "My Lord and my God!"

[29]Jesus said to him, "Thomas,[a] because you have seen Me, you have believed. Blessed *are* those who have not seen and *yet* have believed."

That You May Believe

[30]And truly Jesus did many other signs in the presence of His disciples, which are not written in this book; [31]but these are written that you may believe that Jesus is the Christ, the Son of God, and that believing you may have life in His name.

Breakfast by the Sea

21 After these things Jesus showed Himself again to the disciples at the Sea of Tiberias, and in this way He showed *Himself:* [2]Simon Peter, Thomas called the Twin, Nathanael of Cana in Galilee, the *sons* of Zebedee, and two others of His disciples were together. [3]Simon Peter said to them, "I am going fishing."

They said to him, "We are going with you also." They went out and immediately[a] got into the boat, and that night they caught nothing. [4]But when the morning had now come, Jesus stood on the shore; yet the disciples did not know that it was Jesus. [5]Then Jesus said to them, "Children, have you any food?"

They answered Him, "No."

[6]And He said to them, "Cast the net on the right side of the boat, and you will find *some.*" So they cast, and now they were not able to draw it in because of the multitude of fish.

[7]Therefore that disciple whom Jesus loved said to Peter, "It is the Lord!" Now when Simon Peter heard that it was the

---

20:16 [a]NU-Text adds *in Hebrew.*   **20:18** [a]NU-Text reads *disciples, "I have seen the Lord,"* . . .
20:19 [a]NU-Text omits *assembled.*   **20:29** [a]NU-Text and M-Text omit *Thomas.*   **21:3** [a]NU-Text omits *immediately.*

Lord, he put on *his* outer garment (for he had removed it), and plunged into the sea. [8]But the other disciples came in the little boat (for they were not far from land, but about two hundred cubits), dragging the net with fish. [9]Then, as soon as they had come to land, they saw a fire of coals there, and fish laid on it, and bread. [10]Jesus said to them, "Bring some of the fish which you have just caught."

[11]Simon Peter went up and dragged the net to land, full of large fish, one hundred and fifty-three; and although there were so many, the net was not broken. [12]Jesus said to them, "Come *and* eat breakfast." Yet none of the disciples dared ask Him, "Who are You?"—knowing that it was the Lord. [13]Jesus then came and took the bread and gave it to them, and likewise the fish.

[14]This *is* now the third time Jesus showed Himself to His disciples after He was raised from the dead.

Jesus Restores Peter

[15]So when they had eaten breakfast, Jesus said to Simon Peter, "Simon, *son* of Jonah,ᵃ do you love Me more than these?"

He said to Him, "Yes, Lord; You know that I love You."

He said to him, "Feed My lambs."

[16]He said to him again a second time, "Simon, *son* of Jonah,ᵃ do you love Me?"

He said to Him, "Yes, Lord; You know that I love You."

He said to him, "Tend My sheep."

[17]He said to him the third time, "Simon, *son* of Jonah,ᵃ do you love Me?" Peter was grieved because He said to him the third time, "Do you love Me?"

And he said to Him, "Lord, You know all things; You know that I love You."

Jesus said to him, "Feed My sheep. [18]Most assuredly, I say to you, when you were younger, you girded yourself and walked where you wished; but when you are old, you will stretch out your hands, and another will gird you and carry *you* where you do not wish." [19]This He spoke, signifying by what death he would glorify God. And when He had spoken this, He said to him, "Follow Me."

The Beloved Disciple and His Book

[20]Then Peter, turning around, saw the disciple whom Jesus loved following, who also had leaned on His breast at the supper, and said, "Lord, who is the one who betrays You?" [21]Peter, seeing him, said to Jesus, "But Lord, what *about* this man?"

[22]Jesus said to him, "If I will that he remain till I come, what *is that* to you? You follow Me."

[23]Then this saying went out among the brethren that this disciple would not die. Yet Jesus did not say to him that he would not die, but, "If I will that he remain till I come, what *is that* to you?"

[24]This is the disciple who testifies of these things, and wrote these things; and we know that his testimony is true.

[25]And there are also many other things that Jesus did, which if they were written one by one, I suppose that even the world itself could not contain the books that would be written. Amen.

21:15 ᵃNU-Text reads *John.*   **21:16** ᵃNU-Text reads *John.*   **21:17** ᵃNU-Text reads *John.*

ACTS

Author: Luke

When Written: Around A.D. 60

Theme: The Growth of the Church

Key Verse: Acts 1:8—"But you shall receive power when the Holy Spirit has come upon you; and you shall be witnesses to Me in Jerusalem, and in all Judea and Samaria, and to the end of the earth."

Key Chapter: Acts 2—This chapter contains the world-changing events of the Day of Pentecost when the Holy Spirit comes, transforming a small group of fearful disciples into a thriving, worldwide church that is ever moving forward and fulfilling the Great Commission.

The histories behind the founding of both our beloved nation and Christ's glorious church share some inspiring parallels. Just as America's Founders gathered at Independence Hall on July 4, 1776, to establish a nation destined to serve as a beacon of hope and freedom to countless millions throughout the generations, so Christ's disciples gathered in Jerusalem in "one accord" (Acts 1:14) to establish a church destined to take the hope of the Gospel to the ends of the earth.

Acts recounts the bold steps of faith the apostles took, after they were filled with the power of the Holy Spirit, to establish an ever-growing community of believers prepared to model lives of Christian virtue and faith in a world of darkness and sin.

As was true of America's own early citizens, those early Christians faced many imposing challenges, dangers, and oppositions that struck at the very heart of their determination to succeed. But through their shared values, prayer, hard work, and a steadfast reliance on God and His unchanging Word, the truth of the Gospel went forth with power and continues today as the only hope for peace upon which individuals—or nations—can rely.

ACTS

Prologue

1 The former account I made, O Theophilus, of all that Jesus began both to do and teach, [2]until the day in which He was taken up, after He through the Holy Spirit had given commandments to the apostles whom He had chosen, [3]to whom He also presented Himself alive after His suffering by many infallible proofs, being seen by them during forty days and speaking of the things pertaining to the kingdom of God.

The Holy Spirit Promised

[4]And being assembled together with *them,* He commanded them not to depart from Jerusalem, but to wait for the Promise of the Father, "which," *He said,* "you have heard from Me; [5]for John truly baptized with water, but you shall be baptized with the Holy Spirit not many days from now." [6]Therefore, when they had come together, they asked Him, saying, "Lord, will You at this time restore the kingdom to Israel?" [7]And He said to them, "It is not for you to know times or seasons which the Father has put in His own authority. [8]But you shall receive power when the Holy Spirit has come upon you; and you shall be witnesses to Me[a] in Jerusalem, and in all Judea and Samaria, and to the end of the earth."

Jesus Ascends to Heaven

[9]Now when He had spoken these things, while they watched, He was taken up, and a cloud received Him out of their sight. [10]And while they looked steadfastly toward heaven as He went up, behold, two men stood by them in white apparel, [11]who also said, "Men of Galilee, why do you stand gazing up into heaven? This *same* Jesus, who was taken up from you into heaven, will so come in like manner as you saw Him go into heaven."

The Upper Room Prayer Meeting

[12]Then they returned to Jerusalem from the mount called Olivet, which is near Jerusalem, a Sabbath day's journey. [13]And when they had entered, they went up into the upper room where they were staying: Peter, James, John, and Andrew; Philip and Thomas; Bartholomew and Matthew; James *the son* of Alphaeus and Simon the Zealot; and Judas *the son* of James. [14]These all continued with one accord in prayer and supplication,[a] with the women and Mary the mother of Jesus, and with His brothers.

Matthias Chosen

[15]And in those days Peter stood up in the midst of the disciples[a] (altogether the number of names was about a hundred and twenty), and said, [16]"Men *and* brethren, this Scripture had to be fulfilled, which the Holy Spirit spoke before by the mouth of David concerning Judas, who became a guide to those who arrested Jesus; [17]for he was numbered with us and obtained a part in this ministry."

[18](Now this man purchased a field with the wages of iniquity; and falling headlong, he burst open in the middle and all his entrails gushed out. [19]And it became known to all those dwelling in Jerusalem; so that field is called in their own language, Akel Dama, that is, Field of Blood.)

[20]"For it is written in the Book of Psalms:

'Let his dwelling place be desolate,
   And let no one live in it';[a]

and,

'Let[b] another take his office.'[c]

[21]"Therefore, of these men who have accompanied us all the time that the Lord Jesus went in and out among us, [22]beginning from the baptism of John to that day

---

1:8 [a]NU-Text reads *My witnesses.* **1:14** [a]NU-Text omits *and supplication.* **1:15** [a]NU-Text reads *brethren.* **1:20** [a]Psalm 69:25 [b]Psalm 109:8 [c]Greek *episkopen,* position of overseer

when He was taken up from us, one of these must become a witness with us of His resurrection."

23And they proposed two: Joseph called Barsabas, who was surnamed Justus, and Matthias. 24And they prayed and said, "You, O Lord, who know the hearts of all, show which of these two You have chosen 25to take part in this ministry and apostleship from which Judas by transgression fell, that he might go to his own place." 26And they cast their lots, and the lot fell on Matthias. And he was numbered with the eleven apostles.

Coming of the Holy Spirit

2 When the Day of Pentecost had fully come, they were all with one accord[a] in one place. 2And suddenly there came a sound from heaven, as of a rushing mighty wind, and it filled the whole house where they were sitting. 3Then there appeared to them divided tongues, as of fire, and one sat upon each of them. 4And they were all filled with the Holy Spirit and began to speak with other tongues, as the Spirit gave them utterance.

The Crowd's Response

5And there were dwelling in Jerusalem Jews, devout men, from every nation under heaven. 6And when this sound occurred, the multitude came together, and were confused, because everyone heard them speak in his own language. 7Then they were all amazed and marveled, saying to one another, "Look, are not all these who speak Galileans? 8And how is it that we hear, each in our own language in which we were born? 9Parthians and Medes and Elamites, those dwelling in Mesopotamia, Judea and Cappadocia, Pontus and Asia, 10Phrygia and Pamphylia, Egypt and the parts of Libya adjoining Cyrene, visitors from Rome, both Jews and proselytes, 11Cretans and Arabs—we hear them speaking in our own tongues the wonderful works of God." 12So they were all amazed and perplexed, saying to one another, "Whatever could this mean?"

13Others mocking said, "They are full of new wine."

Peter's Sermon

14But Peter, standing up with the eleven, raised his voice and said to them, "Men of Judea and all who dwell in Jerusalem, let this be known to you, and heed my words. 15For these are not drunk, as you suppose, since it is only the third hour of the day. 16But this is what was spoken by the prophet Joel:

17 'And it shall come to pass in the last days, says God,
That I will pour out of My Spirit on all flesh;
Your sons and your daughters shall prophesy,
Your young men shall see visions,
Your old men shall dream dreams.
18 And on My menservants and on My maidservants
I will pour out My Spirit in those days;
And they shall prophesy.
19 I will show wonders in heaven above
And signs in the earth beneath:
Blood and fire and vapor of smoke.
20 The sun shall be turned into darkness,
And the moon into blood,
Before the coming of the great and awesome day of the LORD.
21 And it shall come to pass
That whoever calls on the name of the LORD
Shall be saved.'[a]

22"Men of Israel, hear these words: Jesus of Nazareth, a Man attested by God to you by miracles, wonders, and signs which God did through Him in your midst, as you yourselves also know— 23Him, being delivered by the determined purpose and foreknowledge of God, you have taken[a] by lawless hands, have crucified, and put to death; 24whom God raised up, having loosed the pains of death, because it was not possible that He should be held by it. 25For David says concerning Him:

'I foresaw the LORD always before my face,

2:1 aNU-Text reads together. 2:21 aJoel 2:28–32
2:23 aNU-Text omits have taken.

> For He is at my right hand, that I may
>   not be shaken.
> 26 Therefore my heart rejoiced, and my
>   tongue was glad;
>   Moreover my flesh also will rest in
>   hope.
> 27 For You will not leave my soul in
>   Hades,
>   Nor will You allow Your Holy One to
>   see corruption.
> 28 You have made known to me the ways
>   of life;
>   You will make me full of joy in Your
>   presence.'ᵃ

29"Men and brethren, let me speak freely to you of the patriarch David, that he is both dead and buried, and his tomb is with us to this day. 30Therefore, being a prophet, and knowing that God had sworn with an oath to him that of the fruit of his body, according to the flesh, He would raise up the Christ to sit on his throne,ᵃ 31he, fore-seeing this, spoke concerning the resurrection of the Christ, that His soul was not left in Hades, nor did His flesh see corruption. 32This Jesus God has raised up, of which we are all witnesses. 33Therefore being exalted to the right hand of God, and having received from the Father the promise of the Holy Spirit, He poured out this which you now see and hear.

34"For David did not ascend into the heavens, but he says himself:

> 'The LORD said to my Lord,
>   "Sit at My right hand,
> 35   Till I make Your enemies Your
>   footstool." 'ᵃ

36"Therefore let all the house of Israel know assuredly that God has made this Jesus, whom you crucified, both Lord and Christ."

37Now when they heard this, they were cut to the heart, and said to Peter and the rest of the apostles, "Men and brethren, what shall we do?"

38Then Peter said to them, "Repent, and let every one of you be baptized in the name of Jesus Christ for the remission of sins; and you shall receive the gift of the Holy Spirit. 39For the promise is to you and to your children, and to all who are afar off, as many as the Lord our God will call."

A Vital Church Grows

40And with many other words he testified and exhorted them, saying, "Be saved from this perverse generation." 41Then those who gladlyᵃ received his word were baptized; and that day about three thousand souls were added to them. 42And they continued steadfastly in the apostles' doctrine and fellowship, in the breaking of bread, and in prayers. 43Then fear came upon every soul, and many wonders and signs were done through the apostles. 44Now all who believed were together, and had all things in common, 45and sold their possessions and goods, and divided them among all, as anyone had need.

46So continuing daily with one accord in the temple, and breaking bread from house to house, they ate their food with gladness and simplicity of heart, 47praising God and having favor with all the people. And the Lord added to the churchᵃ daily those who were being saved.

A Lame Man Healed

3 Now Peter and John went up together to the temple at the hour of prayer, the ninth hour. 2And a certain man lame from his mother's womb was carried, whom they laid daily at the gate of the temple which is called Beautiful, to ask alms from those who entered the temple; 3who, seeing Peter and John about to go into the temple, asked for alms. 4And fixing his eyes on him, with John, Peter said, "Look at us." 5So he gave them his attention, expecting to receive something from them. 6Then Peter said, "Silver and gold I do not have, but what I do have I give you: In the name of Jesus Christ of Nazareth, rise up and walk." 7And he took him by the right hand and lifted him up, and immediately his feet and

---

2:28 ᵃPsalm 16:8–11   2:30 ᵃNU-Text omits *according to the flesh,* He would raise up the Christ and completes the verse with He would seat one on his throne.   2:35 ᵃPsalm 110:1   2:41 ᵃNU-Text omits gladly.   2:47 ᵃNU-Text omits to the church.

ankle bones received strength. ⁸So he, leaping up, stood and walked and entered the temple with them—walking, leaping, and praising God. ⁹And all the people saw him walking and praising God. ¹⁰Then they knew that it was he who sat begging alms at the Beautiful Gate of the temple; and they were filled with wonder and amazement at what had happened to him.

Preaching in Solomon's Portico

¹¹Now as the lame man who was healed held on to Peter and John, all the people ran together to them in the porch which is called Solomon's, greatly amazed. ¹²So when Peter saw *it,* he responded to the people: "Men of Israel, why do you marvel at this? Or why look so intently at us, as though by our own power or godliness we had made this man walk? ¹³The God of Abraham, Isaac, and Jacob, the God of our fathers, glorified His Servant Jesus, whom you delivered up and denied in the presence of Pilate, when he was determined to let *Him* go. ¹⁴But you denied the Holy One and the Just, and asked for a murderer to be granted to you, ¹⁵and killed the Prince of life, whom God raised from the dead, of which we are witnesses. ¹⁶And His name, through faith in His name, has made this man strong, whom you see and know. Yes, the faith which *comes* through Him has given him this perfect soundness in the presence of you all.

¹⁷"Yet now, brethren, I know that you did *it* in ignorance, as *did* also your rulers. ¹⁸But those things which God foretold by the mouth of all His prophets, that the Christ would suffer, He has thus fulfilled. ¹⁹Repent therefore and be converted, that your sins may be blotted out, so that times of refreshing may come from the presence of the Lord, ²⁰and that He may send Jesus Christ, who was preached to you before,ᵃ ²¹whom heaven must receive until the times of restoration of all things, which God has spoken by the mouth of all His holy prophets since the world began. ²²For Moses truly said to the fathers, *'The LORD your God will raise up for you a Prophet like me from your brethren. Him you shall hear in all things, whatever He says to you.* ²³*And it shall be that every soul who will*

*not hear that Prophet shall be utterly destroyed from among the people.'*ᵃ ²⁴Yes, and all the prophets, from Samuel and those who follow, as many as have spoken, have also foretoldᵃ these days. ²⁵You are sons of the prophets, and of the covenant which God made with our fathers, saying to Abraham, *'And in your seed all the families of the earth shall be blessed.'*ᵃ ²⁶To you first, God, having raised up His Servant Jesus, sent Him to bless you, in turning away every one *of you* from your iniquities."

Peter and John Arrested

4 Now as they spoke to the people, the priests, the captain of the temple, and the Sadducees came upon them, ²being greatly disturbed that they taught the people and preached in Jesus the resurrection from the dead. ³And they laid hands on them, and put *them* in custody until the next day, for it was already evening. ⁴However, many of those who heard the word believed; and the number of the men came to be about five thousand.

Addressing the Sanhedrin

⁵And it came to pass, on the next day, that their rulers, elders, and scribes, ⁶as well as Annas the high priest, Caiaphas, John, and Alexander, and as many as were of the family of the high priest, were gathered together at Jerusalem. ⁷And when they had set them in the midst, they asked, "By what power or by what name have you done this?"

⁸Then Peter, filled with the Holy Spirit, said to them, "Rulers of the people and elders of Israel: ⁹If we this day are judged for a good deed *done* to a helpless man, by what means he has been made well, ¹⁰let it be known to you all, and to all the people of Israel, that by the name of Jesus Christ of Nazareth, whom you crucified, whom God raised from the dead, by Him this man stands here before you whole. ¹¹This is the *'stone which was rejected by you builders, which has become the chief cornerstone.'*ᵃ

3:20 ᵃNU-Text and M-Text read *Christ Jesus, who was ordained for you before.* **3:23** ᵃDeuteronomy 18:15, 18, 19 **3:24** ᵃNU-Text and M-Text read *proclaimed.* **3:25** ᵃGenesis 22:18; 26:4; 28:14 **4:11** ᵃPsalm 118:22

¹²Nor is there salvation in any other, for there is no other name under heaven given among men by which we must be saved."

The Name of Jesus Forbidden

¹³Now when they saw the boldness of Peter and John, and perceived that they were uneducated and untrained men, they marveled. And they realized that they had been with Jesus. ¹⁴And seeing the man who had been healed standing with them, they could say nothing against it. ¹⁵But when they had commanded them to go aside out of the council, they conferred among themselves, ¹⁶saying, "What shall we do to these men? For, indeed, that a notable miracle has been done through them *is* evident to all who dwell in Jerusalem, and we cannot deny *it*. ¹⁷But so that it spreads no further among the people, let us severely threaten them, that from now on they speak to no man in this name."

¹⁸So they called them and commanded them not to speak at all nor teach in the name of Jesus. ¹⁹But Peter and John answered and said to them, "Whether it is right in the sight of God to listen to you more than to God, you judge. ²⁰For we cannot but speak

the things which we have seen and heard." ²¹So when they had further threatened them, they let them go, finding no way of punishing them, because of the people, since they all glorified God for what had been done. ²²For the man was over forty years old on whom this miracle of healing had been performed.

Prayer for Boldness

²³And being let go, they went to their own *companions* and reported all that the chief priests and elders had said to them. ²⁴So when they heard that, they raised their voice to God with one accord and said: "Lord, You *are* God, who made heaven and earth and the sea, and all that is in them, ²⁵who by the mouth of Your servant David[a] have said:

'Why did the nations rage,
And the people plot vain things?
²⁶ The kings of the earth took their
stand,
And the rulers were gathered together
Against the LORD and against His
Christ.'[a]

²⁷"For truly against Your holy Servant Jesus, whom You anointed, both Herod and Pontius Pilate, with the Gentiles and the people of Israel, were gathered together ²⁸to do whatever Your hand and Your purpose determined before to be done. ²⁹Now, Lord, look on their threats, and grant to Your servants that with all boldness they may speak Your word, ³⁰by stretching out Your hand to heal, and that signs and wonders may be done through the name of Your holy Servant Jesus."

³¹And when they had prayed, the place where they were assembled together was shaken; and they were all filled with the Holy Spirit, and they spoke the word of God with boldness.

Sharing in All Things

³²Now the multitude of those who believed were of one heart and one soul;

FAITH
. . . they all glorified God for what had been done. ACTS 4:21

The Divine Origin of Jesus
David Dixon Porter (1813–1891), an admiral in the U.S. Navy and later the superintendent of U.S. Naval Academy at Annapolis, stated:

> When one sees how much has been done for the world by the disciples of Christ and those professing the Christian religion, he must be astonished to find anyone who hesitates to believe in the Divine origin of Jesus and the wonderful works He performed, all of which are so beautifully portrayed by the Author of the work under consideration; and no man or woman of real intelligence would hesitate to believe that it is only through Christ that sinners can be saved, unless their vanity is so great that they are capable of saving themselves without an intermediary.

4:25 [a]NU-Text reads *who through the Holy Spirit, by the mouth of our father, Your servant David.* **4:26** [a]Psalm 2:1, 2

neither did anyone say that any of the things he possessed was his own, but they had all things in common. ³³And with great power the apostles gave witness to the resurrection of the Lord Jesus. And great grace was upon them all. ³⁴Nor was there anyone among them who lacked; for all who were possessors of lands or houses sold them, and brought the proceeds of the things that were sold, ³⁵and laid *them* at the apostles' feet; and they distributed to each as anyone had need.

³⁶And Joses,^a who was also named Barnabas by the apostles (which is translated Son of Encouragement), a Levite of the country of Cyprus, ³⁷having land, sold *it,* and brought the money and laid *it* at the apostles' feet.

Lying to the Holy Spirit

5 But a certain man named Ananias, with Sapphira his wife, sold a possession. ²And he kept back *part* of the proceeds, his wife also being aware *of it,* and brought a certain part and laid *it* at the apostles' feet. ³But Peter said, "Ananias, why has Satan filled your heart to lie to the Holy Spirit and keep back *part* of the price of the land for yourself? ⁴While it remained, was it not your own? And after it was sold, was it not in your own control? Why have you conceived this thing in your heart? You have not lied to men but to God."

⁵Then Ananias, hearing these words, fell down and breathed his last. So great fear came upon all those who heard these things. ⁶And the young men arose and wrapped him up, carried *him* out, and buried *him.*

⁷Now it was about three hours later when his wife came in, not knowing what had happened. ⁸And Peter answered her, "Tell me whether you sold the land for so much?"

She said, "Yes, for so much."

⁹Then Peter said to her, "How is it that you have agreed together to test the Spirit of the Lord? Look, the feet of those who have buried your husband *are* at the door, and they will carry you out." ¹⁰Then immediately she fell down at his feet and breathed her last. And the young men came

in and found her dead, and carrying *her* out, buried *her* by her husband. ¹¹So great fear came upon all the church and upon all who heard these things.

Continuing Power in the Church

¹²And through the hands of the apostles many signs and wonders were done among the people. And they were all with one accord in Solomon's Porch. ¹³Yet none of the rest dared join them, but the people esteemed them highly. ¹⁴And believers were increasingly added to the Lord, multitudes of both men and women, ¹⁵so that they brought the sick out into the streets and laid *them* on beds and couches, that at least the shadow of Peter passing by might fall on some of them. ¹⁶Also a multitude gathered from the surrounding cities to Jerusalem, bringing sick people and those who were tormented by unclean spirits, and they were all healed.

Imprisoned Apostles Freed

¹⁷Then the high priest rose up, and all those who *were* with him (which is the sect of the Sadducees), and they were filled with indignation, ¹⁸and laid their hands on the apostles and put them in the common prison. ¹⁹But at night an angel of the Lord opened the prison doors and brought them out, and said, ²⁰"Go, stand in the temple and speak to the people all the words of this life."

²¹And when they heard *that,* they entered the temple early in the morning and taught. But the high priest and those with him came and called the council together, with all the elders of the children of Israel, and sent to the prison to have them brought.

Apostles on Trial Again

²²But when the officers came and did not find them in the prison, they returned and reported, ²³saying, "Indeed we found the prison shut securely, and the guards standing outside^a before the doors; but when we

---

4:36 ^aNU-Text reads *Joseph.*   **5:23** ^aNU-Text and M-Text omit *outside.*

opened them, we found no one inside!" [24]Now when the high priest,[a] the captain of the temple, and the chief priests heard these things, they wondered what the outcome would be. [25]So one came and told them, saying,[a] "Look, the men whom you put in prison are standing in the temple and teaching the people!"

[26]Then the captain went with the officers and brought them without violence, for they feared the people, lest they should be stoned. [27]And when they had brought them, they set *them* before the council. And the high priest asked them, [28]saying, "Did we not strictly command you not to teach in this name? And look, you have filled Jerusalem with your doctrine, and intend to bring this Man's blood on us!"

FREEDOM

"We ought to obey God rather than men."

ACTS 5:29

The Right to Dissent

Considered by historians as among journalism's greatest figures, Edward R. Murrow (1908–1965) stated:

If we confuse dissent with disloyalty—if we deny the right of the individual to be wrong, unpopular, eccentric, or unorthodox—if we deny the essence of racial equality, then hundreds of millions in Asia and Africa who are shopping about for a new allegiance will conclude that we are concerned to defend a myth and our present privileged status. Every act that denies or limits the freedom of the individual in this country costs us the . . . confidence of men and women who aspire to that freedom and independence of which we speak and for which our ancestors fought.

---

[29]But Peter and the *other* apostles answered and said: "We ought to obey God rather than men. [30]The God of our fathers raised up Jesus whom you murdered by hanging on a tree. [31]Him God has exalted to His right hand *to be* Prince and Savior, to give repentance to Israel and forgiveness of sins. [32]And we are His witnesses to these things, and *so* also *is* the Holy Spirit whom God has given to those who obey Him."

Gamaliel's Advice

[33]When they heard *this,* they were furious and plotted to kill them. [34]Then one in the council stood up, a Pharisee named Gamaliel, a teacher of the law held in respect by all the people, and commanded them to put the apostles outside for a little while. [35]And he said to them: "Men of Israel, take heed to yourselves what you intend to do regarding these men. [36]For some time ago Theudas rose up, claiming to be somebody. A number of men, about four hundred, joined him. He was slain, and all who obeyed him were scattered and came to nothing. [37]After this man, Judas of Galilee rose up in the days of the census, and drew away many people after him. He also perished, and all who obeyed him were dispersed. [38]And now I say to you, keep away from these men and let them alone; for if this plan or this work is of men, it will come to nothing; [39]but if it is of God, you cannot overthrow it—lest you even be found to fight against God."

[40]And they agreed with him, and when they had called for the apostles and beaten *them,* they commanded that they should not speak in the name of Jesus, and let them go. [41]So they departed from the presence of the council, rejoicing that they were counted worthy to suffer shame for His[a] name. [42]And daily in the temple, and in every house, they did not cease teaching and preaching Jesus *as* the Christ.

Seven Chosen to Serve

6 Now in those days, when *the number of* the disciples was multiplying, there arose a complaint against the Hebrews by the Hellenists,[a] because their widows were neglected in the daily distribution. [2]Then the twelve summoned the multitude of the disciples and said, "It is not desirable that we should leave the word of God and serve tables. [3]Therefore, brethren, seek out from among you seven men of *good* reputation, full of the Holy Spirit and wisdom, whom

---

5:24 [a]NU-Text omits *the high priest.*   **5:25** [a]NU-Text and M-Text omit *saying.*   **5:41** [a]NU-Text reads *the name;* M-Text reads *the name of Jesus.*   **6:1** [a]That is, Greek-speaking Jews

we may appoint over this business; [4]but we will give ourselves continually to prayer and to the ministry of the word."

[5]And the saying pleased the whole multitude. And they chose Stephen, a man full of faith and the Holy Spirit, and Philip, Prochorus, Nicanor, Timon, Parmenas, and Nicolas, a proselyte from Antioch, [6]whom they set before the apostles; and when they had prayed, they laid hands on them.

[7]Then the word of God spread, and the number of the disciples multiplied greatly in Jerusalem, and a great many of the priests were obedient to the faith.

Stephen Accused of Blasphemy

[8]And Stephen, full of faith[a] and power, did great wonders and signs among the people. [9]Then there arose some from what is called the Synagogue of the Freedmen (Cyrenians, Alexandrians, and those from Cilicia and Asia), disputing with Stephen. [10]And they were not able to resist the wisdom and the Spirit by which he spoke. [11]Then they secretly induced men to say, "We have heard him speak blasphemous words against Moses and God." [12]And they stirred up the people, the elders, and the scribes; and they came upon *him,* seized him, and brought *him* to the council. [13]They also set up false witnesses who said, "This man does not cease to speak blasphemous[a] words against this holy place and the law; [14]for we have heard him say that this Jesus of Nazareth will destroy this place and change the customs which Moses delivered to us." [15]And all who sat in the council, looking steadfastly at him, saw his face as the face of an angel.

Stephen's Address: The Call of Abraham

7 Then the high priest said, "Are these things so?"

[2]And he said, "Brethren and fathers, listen: The God of glory appeared to our father Abraham when he was in Mesopotamia, before he dwelt in Haran, [3]and said to him, 'Get out of your country and from your relatives, and come to a land that I will show you.'[a] [4]Then he came out of the land of the Chaldeans and dwelt in Haran. And from there, when his father

was dead, He moved him to this land in which you now dwell. [5]And *God* gave him no inheritance in it, not even *enough* to set his foot on. But even when *Abraham* had no child, He promised to give it to him for a possession, and to his descendants after him. [6]But God spoke in this way: that his descendants would dwell in a foreign land, and that they would bring them into bondage and oppress *them* four hundred years. [7]*And the nation to whom they will be in bondage I will judge,'*[a] said God, '*and after that they shall come out and serve Me in this place.'*[b] [8]Then He gave him the covenant of circumcision; and so *Abraham* begot Isaac and circumcised him on the eighth day; and Isaac *begot* Jacob, and Jacob *begot* the twelve patriarchs.

The Patriarchs in Egypt

[9]"And the patriarchs, becoming envious, sold Joseph into Egypt. But God was with him [10]and delivered him out of all his troubles, and gave him favor and wisdom in the presence of Pharaoh, king of Egypt; and he made him governor over Egypt and all his house. [11]Now a famine and great trouble came over all the land of Egypt and Canaan, and our fathers found no sustenance. [12]But when Jacob heard that there was grain in Egypt, he sent out our fathers first. [13]And the second *time* Joseph was made known to his brothers, and Joseph's family became known to the Pharaoh. [14]Then Joseph sent and called his father Jacob and all his relatives to *him,* seventy-five[a] people. [15]So Jacob went down to Egypt; and he died, he and our fathers. [16]And they were carried back to Shechem and laid in the tomb that Abraham bought for a sum of money from the sons of Hamor, *the father* of Shechem.

God Delivers Israel by Moses

[17]"But when the time of the promise drew near which God had sworn to Abraham, the people grew and multiplied in Egypt

6:8 [a]NU-Text reads *grace.* **6:13** [a]NU-Text omits *blasphemous.* **7:3** [a]Genesis 12:1 **7:7** [a]Genesis 15:14 [b]Exodus 3:12 **7:14** [a]Or *seventy* (compare Exodus 1:5)

[18]till another king arose who did not know Joseph. [19]This man dealt treacherously with our people, and oppressed our forefathers, making them expose their babies, so that they might not live. [20]At this time Moses was born, and was well pleasing to God; and he was brought up in his father's house for three months. [21]But when he was set out, Pharaoh's daughter took him away and brought him up as her own son. [22]And Moses was learned in all the wisdom of the Egyptians, and was mighty in words and deeds.

[23]"Now when he was forty years old, it came into his heart to visit his brethren, the children of Israel. [24]And seeing one of *them* suffer wrong, he defended and avenged him who was oppressed, and struck down the Egyptian. [25]For he supposed that his brethren would have understood that God would deliver them by his hand, but they did not understand. [26]And the next day he appeared to *two of* them as they were fighting, and *tried to* reconcile them, saying, 'Men, you are brethren; why do you wrong one another?' [27]But he who did his neighbor wrong pushed him away, saying, *'Who made you a ruler and a judge over us?* [28]*Do you want to kill me as you did the Egyptian yesterday?'*[a] [29]Then, at this saying, Moses fled and became a dweller in the land of Midian, where he had two sons.

[30]"And when forty years had passed, an Angel of the Lord[a] appeared to him in a flame of fire in a bush, in the wilderness of Mount Sinai. [31]When Moses saw *it,* he marveled at the sight; and as he drew near to observe, the voice of the Lord came to him, [32]saying, *'I am the God of your fathers—the God of Abraham, the God of Isaac, and the God of Jacob.'*[a] And Moses trembled and dared not look. [33]'Then the LORD said to him, *"Take your sandals off your feet, for the place where you stand is holy ground.* [34]*I have surely seen the oppression of My people who are in Egypt; I have heard their groaning and have come down to deliver them. And now come, I will send you to Egypt."'*[a]

[35]"This Moses whom they rejected, saying, *'Who made you a ruler and a judge?'*[a] is the one God sent *to be* a ruler and a deliverer by the hand of the Angel who appeared to him in the bush. [36]He brought them out, after he had shown wonders and signs in the land of Egypt, and in the Red Sea, and in the wilderness forty years.

Israel Rebels Against God

[37]"This is that Moses who said to the children of Israel,[a] *'The LORD your God will raise up for you a Prophet like me from your brethren. Him you shall hear.'*[b] [38]"This is he who was in the congregation in the wilderness with the Angel who spoke to him on Mount Sinai, and *with* our fathers, the one who received the living oracles to give to us, [39]whom our fathers would not obey, but rejected. And in their hearts they turned back to Egypt, [40]saying to Aaron, *'Make us gods to go before us; as for this Moses who brought us out of the land of Egypt, we do not know what has become of him.'*[a] [41]And they made a calf in those days, offered sacrifices to the idol, and rejoiced in the works of their own hands. [42]Then God turned and gave them up to worship the host of heaven, as it is written in the book of the Prophets:

> *'Did you offer Me slaughtered animals*
>   *and sacrifices during forty years in*
>   *the wilderness,*
>   *O house of Israel?*
> [43] *You also took up the tabernacle of*
>   *Moloch,*
>   *And the star of your god Remphan,*
>   *Images which you made to worship;*
>   *And I will carry you away beyond*
>   *Babylon.'*[a]

God's True Tabernacle

[44]"Our fathers had the tabernacle of witness in the wilderness, as He appointed, instructing Moses to make it according to the pattern that he had seen, [45]which our fathers, having received it in turn, also brought with Joshua into the land possessed by the Gentiles, whom God drove out before the face of our fathers until the days of

---

7:28 [a]Exodus 2:14   **7:30** [a]NU-Text omits *of the Lord.*   **7:32** [a]Exodus 3:6, 15   **7:34** [a]Exodus 3:5, 7, 8, 10   **7:35** [a]Exodus 2:14   **7:37** [a]Deuteronomy 18:15 [b]NU-Text and M-Text omit *Him you shall hear.*   **7:40** [a]Exodus 32:1, 23   **7:43** [a]Amos 5:25–27

David, [46]who found favor before God and asked to find a dwelling for the God of Jacob. [47]But Solomon built Him a house.

[48]"However, the Most High does not dwell in temples made with hands, as the prophet says:

[49] 'Heaven is My throne,
    And earth is My footstool.
    What house will you build for Me?
      says the LORD,
    Or what is the place of My rest?
[50] Has My hand not made all these
      things?'[a]

Israel Resists the Holy Spirit

[51]"*You* stiff-necked and uncircumcised in heart and ears! You always resist the Holy Spirit; as your fathers *did,* so *do* you. [52]Which of the prophets did your fathers not persecute? And they killed those who foretold the coming of the Just One, of whom you now have become the betrayers and murderers, [53]who have received the law by the direction of angels and have not kept *it.*"

Stephen the Martyr

[54]When they heard these things they were cut to the heart, and they gnashed at him with *their* teeth. [55]But he, being full of the Holy Spirit, gazed into heaven and saw the glory of God, and Jesus standing at the right hand of God, [56]and said, "Look! I see the heavens opened and the Son of Man standing at the right hand of God!" [57]Then they cried out with a loud voice, stopped their ears, and ran at him with one accord; [58]and they cast *him* out of the city and stoned *him.* And the witnesses laid down their clothes at the feet of a young man named Saul. [59]And they stoned Stephen as he was calling on *God* and saying, "Lord Jesus, receive my spirit." [60]Then he knelt down and cried out with a loud voice, "Lord, do not charge them with this sin." And when he had said this, he fell asleep.

Saul Persecutes the Church

8 Now Saul was consenting to his death. At that time a great persecution arose against the church which was at Jerusalem; and they were all scattered throughout the regions of Judea and Samaria, except the apostles. [2]And devout men carried Stephen *to his burial,* and made great lamentation over him.

[3]As for Saul, he made havoc of the church, entering every house, and dragging off men and women, committing *them* to prison.

Christ Is Preached in Samaria

[4]Therefore those who were scattered went everywhere preaching the word. [5]Then Philip went down to the[a] city of Samaria and preached Christ to them. [6]And the multitudes with one accord heeded the things spoken by Philip, hearing and seeing the miracles which he did. [7]For unclean spirits, crying with a loud voice, came out of many who were possessed; and many who were paralyzed and lame were healed. [8]And there was great joy in that city.

The Sorcerer's Profession of Faith

[9]But there was a certain man called Simon, who previously practiced sorcery in the city and astonished the people of Samaria, claiming that he was someone great, [10]to whom they all gave heed, from the least to the greatest, saying, "This man is the great power of God." [11]And they heeded him because he had astonished them with his sorceries for a long time. [12]But when they believed Philip as he preached the things concerning the kingdom of God and the name of Jesus Christ, both men and women were baptized. [13]Then Simon himself also believed; and when he was baptized he continued with Philip, and was amazed, seeing the miracles and signs which were done.

The Sorcerer's Sin

[14]Now when the apostles who were at Jerusalem heard that Samaria had received the word of God, they sent Peter and John to them, [15]who, when they had come down, prayed for them that they might receive the Holy Spirit. [16]For as yet He had fallen upon none of them. They had only been baptized in the name of the Lord Jesus. [17]Then they laid hands on them, and they received the Holy Spirit.

7:50 [a]Isaiah 66:1, 2   **8:5** [a]Or *a*

[18]And when Simon saw that through the laying on of the apostles' hands the Holy Spirit was given, he offered them money, [19]saying, "Give me this power also, that anyone on whom I lay hands may receive the Holy Spirit."

[20]But Peter said to him, "Your money perish with you, because you thought that the gift of God could be purchased with money! [21]You have neither part nor portion in this matter, for your heart is not right in the sight of God. [22]Repent therefore of this your wickedness, and pray God if perhaps the thought of your heart may be forgiven you. [23]For I see that you are poisoned by bitterness and bound by iniquity."

[24]Then Simon answered and said, "Pray to the Lord for me, that none of the things which you have spoken may come upon me."

[25]So when they had testified and preached the word of the Lord, they returned to Jerusalem, preaching the gospel in many villages of the Samaritans.

Christ Is Preached to an Ethiopian

[26]Now an angel of the Lord spoke to Philip, saying, "Arise and go toward the south along the road which goes down from Jerusalem to Gaza." This is desert. [27]So he arose and went. And behold, a man of Ethiopia, a eunuch of great authority under Candace the queen of the Ethiopians, who had charge of all her treasury, and had come to Jerusalem to worship, [28]was returning. And sitting in his chariot, he was reading Isaiah the prophet. [29]Then the Spirit said to Philip, "Go near and overtake this chariot."

[30]So Philip ran to him, and heard him reading the prophet Isaiah, and said, "Do you understand what you are reading?"

[31]And he said, "How can I, unless someone guides me?" And he asked Philip to come up and sit with him. [32]The place in the Scripture which he read was this:

"He was led as a sheep to the
    slaughter;
And as a lamb before its shearer is
    silent,
So He opened not His mouth.

[33]   In His humiliation His justice was
        taken away,
    And who will declare His generation?
    For His life is taken from the earth."[a]

[34]So the eunuch answered Philip and said, "I ask you, of whom does the prophet say this, of himself or of some other man?" [35]Then Philip opened his mouth, and beginning at this Scripture, preached Jesus to him. [36]Now as they went down the road, they came to some water. And the eunuch said, "See, here is water. What hinders me from being baptized?"

[37]Then Philip said, "If you believe with all your heart, you may."

And he answered and said, "I believe that Jesus Christ is the Son of God."[a]

[38]So he commanded the chariot to stand still. And both Philip and the eunuch went down into the water, and he baptized him. [39]Now when they came up out of the water, the Spirit of the Lord caught Philip away, so that the eunuch saw him no more; and he went on his way rejoicing. [40]But Philip was found at Azotus. And passing through, he preached in all the cities till he came to Caesarea.

The Damascus Road: Saul Converted

9 Then Saul, still breathing threats and murder against the disciples of the Lord, went to the high priest [2]and asked letters from him to the synagogues of Damascus, so that if he found any who were of the Way, whether men or women, he might bring them bound to Jerusalem.

[3]As he journeyed he came near Damascus, and suddenly a light shone around him from heaven. [4]Then he fell to the ground, and heard a voice saying to him, "Saul, Saul, why are you persecuting Me?"

[5]And he said, "Who are You, Lord?"

Then the Lord said, "I am Jesus, whom you are persecuting.[a] It is hard for you to kick against the goads."

8:33 [a]Isaiah 53:7, 8   **8:37** [a]NU-Text and M-Text omit this verse. It is found in Western texts, including the Latin tradition.   **9:5** [a]NU-Text and M-Text omit the last sentence of verse 5 and begin verse 6 with *But arise and go.*

⁶So he, trembling and astonished, said, "Lord, what do You want me to do?"

Then the Lord *said* to him, "Arise and go into the city, and you will be told what you must do."

⁷And the men who journeyed with him stood speechless, hearing a voice but seeing no one. ⁸Then Saul arose from the ground, and when his eyes were opened he saw no one. But they led him by the hand and brought *him* into Damascus. ⁹And he was three days without sight, and neither ate nor drank.

Ananias Baptizes Saul

¹⁰Now there was a certain disciple at Damascus named Ananias; and to him the Lord said in a vision, "Ananias."

And he said, "Here I am, Lord."

¹¹So the Lord *said* to him, "Arise and go to the street called Straight, and inquire at the house of Judas for *one* called Saul of Tarsus, for behold, he is praying. ¹²And in a vision he has seen a man named Ananias coming in and putting *his* hand on him, so that he might receive his sight."

¹³Then Ananias answered, "Lord, I have heard from many about this man, how much harm he has done to Your saints in Jerusalem. ¹⁴And here he has authority from the chief priests to bind all who call on Your name."

¹⁵But the Lord said to him, "Go, for he is a chosen vessel of Mine to bear My name before Gentiles, kings, and the children of Israel. ¹⁶For I will show him how many things he must suffer for My name's sake."

¹⁷And Ananias went his way and entered the house; and laying his hands on him he said, "Brother Saul, the Lord Jesus,ᵃ who appeared to you on the road as you came, has sent me that you may receive your sight and be filled with the Holy Spirit." ¹⁸Immediately there fell from his eyes *something* like scales, and he received his sight at once; and he arose and was baptized. ¹⁹So when he had received food, he was strengthened. Then Saul spent some days with the disciples at Damascus.

Saul Preaches Christ

²⁰Immediately he preached the Christᵃ in the synagogues, that He is the Son of God.

²¹Then all who heard were amazed, and said, "Is this not he who destroyed those who called on this name in Jerusalem, and has come here for that purpose, so that he might bring them bound to the chief priests?"

²²But Saul increased all the more in strength, and confounded the Jews who dwelt in Damascus, proving that this *Jesus* is the Christ.

Saul Escapes Death

²³Now after many days were past, the Jews plotted to kill him. ²⁴But their plot became known to Saul. And they watched the gates day and night, to kill him. ²⁵Then the disciples took him by night and let *him* down through the wall in a large basket.

Saul at Jerusalem

²⁶And when Saul had come to Jerusalem, he tried to join the disciples; but they were all afraid of him, and did not believe that he was a disciple. ²⁷But Barnabas took him and brought *him* to the apostles. And he declared to them how he had seen the Lord on the road, and that He had spoken to him, and how he had preached boldly at Damascus in the name of Jesus. ²⁸So he was with them at Jerusalem, coming in and going out. ²⁹And he spoke boldly in the name of the Lord Jesus and disputed against the Hellenists, but they attempted to kill him. ³⁰When the brethren found out, they brought him down to Caesarea and sent him out to Tarsus.

The Church Prospers

³¹Then the churchesᵃ throughout all Judea, Galilee, and Samaria had peace and were edified. And walking in the fear of the Lord and in the comfort of the Holy Spirit, they were multiplied.

Aeneas Healed

³²Now it came to pass, as Peter went through all *parts of the country,* that he also came down to the saints who dwelt in Lydda. ³³There he found a certain man named Aeneas, who had been bedridden

---

9:17 ᵃM-Text omits *Jesus.*   **9:20** ᵃNU-Text reads *Jesus.*   **9:31** ᵃNU-Text reads *church . . . was edified.*

eight years and was paralyzed. ³⁴And Peter said to him, "Aeneas, Jesus the Christ heals you. Arise and make your bed." Then he arose immediately. ³⁵So all who dwelt at Lydda and Sharon saw him and turned to the Lord.

Dorcas Restored to Life

³⁶At Joppa there was a certain disciple named Tabitha, which is translated Dorcas. This woman was full of good works and charitable deeds which she did. ³⁷But it happened in those days that she became sick and died. When they had washed her, they laid *her* in an upper room. ³⁸And since Lydda was near Joppa, and the disciples had heard that Peter was there, they sent two men to him, imploring *him* not to delay in coming to them. ³⁹Then Peter arose and went with them. When he had come, they brought *him* to the upper room. And all the widows stood by him weeping, showing the tunics and garments which Dorcas had made while she was with them. ⁴⁰But Peter put them all out, and knelt down and prayed. And turning to the body he said, "Tabitha, arise." And she opened her eyes, and when she saw Peter she sat up. ⁴¹Then he gave her *his* hand and lifted her up; and when he had called the saints and widows, he presented her alive. ⁴²And it became known throughout all Joppa, and many believed on the Lord. ⁴³So it was that he stayed many days in Joppa with Simon, a tanner.

Cornelius Sends a Delegation

10 There was a certain man in Caesarea called Cornelius, a centurion of what was called the Italian Regiment, ²a devout *man* and one who feared God with all his household, who gave alms generously to the people, and prayed to God always. ³About the ninth hour of the day he saw clearly in a vision an angel of God coming in and saying to him, "Cornelius!"

⁴And when he observed him, he was afraid, and said, "What is it, lord?"

So he said to him, "Your prayers and your alms have come up for a memorial before God. ⁵Now send men to Joppa, and send for Simon whose surname is Peter. ⁶He is lodging with Simon, a tanner, whose house is by the sea.ᵃ He will tell you what you must do." ⁷And when the angel who spoke to him had departed, Cornelius called two of his household servants and a devout soldier from among those who waited on him continually. ⁸So when he had explained all *these* things to them, he sent them to Joppa.

Peter's Vision

⁹The next day, as they went on their journey and drew near the city, Peter went up on the housetop to pray, about the sixth hour. ¹⁰Then he became very hungry and wanted to eat; but while they made ready, he fell into a trance ¹¹and saw heaven opened and an object like a great sheet bound at the four corners, descending to him and let down to the earth. ¹²In it were all kinds of four-footed animals of the earth, wild beasts, creeping things, and birds of the air. ¹³And a voice came to him, "Rise, Peter; kill and eat."

¹⁴But Peter said, "Not so, Lord! For I have never eaten anything common or unclean."

¹⁵And a voice *spoke* to him again the second time, "What God has cleansed you must not call common." ¹⁶This was done three times. And the object was taken up into heaven again.

Summoned to Caesarea

¹⁷Now while Peter wondered within himself what this vision which he had seen meant, behold, the men who had been sent from Cornelius had made inquiry for Simon's house, and stood before the gate. ¹⁸And they called and asked whether Simon, whose surname was Peter, was lodging there.

¹⁹While Peter thought about the vision, the Spirit said to him, "Behold, three men are seeking you. ²⁰Arise therefore, go down and go with them, doubting nothing; for I have sent them."

²¹Then Peter went down to the men who had been sent to him from Cornelius,ᵃ and said, "Yes, I am he whom you seek. For what reason have you come?"

10:6 ᵃNU-Text and M-Text omit the last sentence of this verse. **10:21** ᵃNU-Text and M-Text omit *who had been sent to him from Cornelius.*

²²And they said, "Cornelius *the* centurion, a just man, one who fears God and has a good reputation among all the nation of the Jews, was divinely instructed by a holy angel to summon you to his house, and to hear words from you." ²³Then he invited them in and lodged *them.*

On the next day Peter went away with them, and some brethren from Joppa accompanied him.

Peter Meets Cornelius

²⁴And the following day they entered Caesarea. Now Cornelius was waiting for them, and had called together his relatives and close friends. ²⁵As Peter was coming in, Cornelius met him and fell down at his feet and worshiped *him.* ²⁶But Peter lifted him up, saying, "Stand up; I myself am also a man." ²⁷And as he talked with him, he went in and found many who had come together. ²⁸Then he said to them, "You know how unlawful it is for a Jewish man to keep company with or go to one of another nation. But God has shown me that I should not call any man common or unclean. ²⁹Therefore I came without objection as soon as I was sent for. I ask, then, for what reason have you sent for me?"

³⁰So Cornelius said, "Four days ago I was fasting until this hour; and at the ninth hour[a] I prayed in my house, and behold, a man stood before me in bright clothing, ³¹and said, 'Cornelius, your prayer has been heard, and your alms are remembered in the sight of God. ³²Send therefore to Joppa and call Simon here, whose surname is Peter. He is lodging in the house of Simon, a tanner, by the sea.[a] When he comes, he will speak to you.' ³³So I sent to you immediately, and you have done well to come. Now therefore, we are all present before God, to hear all the things commanded you by God."

Preaching to Cornelius' Household

³⁴Then Peter opened *his* mouth and said: "In truth I perceive that God shows no partiality. ³⁵But in every nation whoever fears Him and works righteousness is accepted by Him. ³⁶The word which *God* sent to the children of Israel, preaching peace through Jesus Christ—He is Lord of all— ³⁷that word you know, which was proclaimed throughout all Judea, and began from Galilee after the baptism which John preached: ³⁸how God anointed Jesus of Nazareth with the Holy Spirit and with power, who went about doing good and healing all who were oppressed by the devil, for God was with Him. ³⁹And we are witnesses of all things which He did both in the land of the Jews and in Jerusalem, whom they[a] killed by hanging on a tree. ⁴⁰Him God raised up on the third day, and showed Him openly, ⁴¹not to all the people, but to witnesses chosen before by God, *even* to us who ate and drank with Him after He arose from the dead. ⁴²And He commanded us to preach to the people, and to testify that it is He who was ordained by God *to be* Judge of the living and the dead. ⁴³To Him all the prophets witness that, through His name, whoever believes in Him will receive remission of sins."

The Holy Spirit Falls on the Gentiles

⁴⁴While Peter was still speaking these words, the Holy Spirit fell upon all those who heard the word. ⁴⁵And those of the circumcision who believed were astonished, as many as came with Peter, because the gift of the Holy Spirit had been poured out on the Gentiles also. ⁴⁶For they heard them speak with tongues and magnify God.

Then Peter answered, ⁴⁷"Can anyone forbid water, that these should not be baptized who have received the Holy Spirit just as we *have?*" ⁴⁸And he commanded them to be baptized in the name of the Lord. Then they asked him to stay a few days.

Peter Defends God's Grace

11 Now the apostles and brethren who were in Judea heard that the Gentiles had also received the word of God. ²And when Peter came up to Jerusalem, those of the circumcision contended with him, ³saying, "You went in to uncircumcised men and ate with them!"

10:30 [a]NU-Text reads *Four days ago to this hour, at the ninth hour.*   **10:32** [a]NU-Text omits the last sentence of this verse.   **10:39** [a]NU-Text and M-Text add *also.*

⁴But Peter explained *it* to them in order from the beginning, saying: ⁵"I was in the city of Joppa praying; and in a trance I saw a vision, an object descending like a great sheet, let down from heaven by four corners; and it came to me. ⁶When I observed it intently and considered, I saw four-footed animals of the earth, wild beasts, creeping things, and birds of the air. ⁷And I heard a voice saying to me, 'Rise, Peter; kill and eat.' ⁸But I said, 'Not so, Lord! For nothing common or unclean has at any time entered my mouth.' ⁹But the voice answered me again from heaven, 'What God has cleansed you must not call common.' ¹⁰Now this was done three times, and all were drawn up again into heaven. ¹¹At that very moment, three men stood before the house where I was, having been sent to me from Caesarea. ¹²Then the Spirit told me to go with them, doubting nothing. Moreover these six brethren accompanied me, and we entered the man's house. ¹³And he told us how he had seen an angel standing in his house, who said to him, 'Send men to Joppa, and call for Simon whose surname is Peter, ¹⁴who will tell you words by which you and all your household will be saved.' ¹⁵And as I began to speak, the Holy Spirit fell upon them, as upon us at the beginning. ¹⁶Then I remembered the word of the Lord, how He said, 'John indeed baptized with water, but you shall be baptized with the Holy Spirit.' ¹⁷If therefore God gave them the same gift as *He gave* us when we believed on the Lord Jesus Christ, who was I that I could withstand God?"

¹⁸When they heard these things they became silent; and they glorified God, saying, "Then God has also granted to the Gentiles repentance to life."

Barnabas and Saul at Antioch

¹⁹Now those who were scattered after the persecution that arose over Stephen traveled as far as Phoenicia, Cyprus, and Antioch, preaching the word to no one but the Jews only. ²⁰But some of them were men from Cyprus and Cyrene, who, when they had come to Antioch, spoke to the Hellenists, preaching the Lord Jesus. ²¹And the hand of the Lord was with them, and a great number believed and turned to the Lord.

²²Then news of these things came to the ears of the church in Jerusalem, and they sent out Barnabas to go as far as Antioch. ²³When he came and had seen the grace of God, he was glad, and encouraged them all that with purpose of heart they should continue with the Lord. ²⁴For he was a good man, full of the Holy Spirit and of faith. And a great many people were added to the Lord.

²⁵Then Barnabas departed for Tarsus to seek Saul. ²⁶And when he had found him, he brought him to Antioch. So it was that for a whole year they assembled with the church and taught a great many people. And the disciples were first called Christians in Antioch.

Relief to Judea

²⁷And in these days prophets came from Jerusalem to Antioch. ²⁸Then one of them, named Agabus, stood up and showed by the Spirit that there was going to be a great famine throughout all the world, which also happened in the days of Claudius Caesar. ²⁹Then the disciples, each according to his ability, determined to send relief to the brethren dwelling in Judea. ³⁰This they also did, and sent it to the elders by the hands of Barnabas and Saul.

Herod's Violence to the Church

12 Now about that time Herod the king stretched out *his* hand to harass some from the church. ²Then he killed James the brother of John with the sword. ³And because he saw that it pleased the Jews, he proceeded further to seize Peter also. Now it was *during* the Days of Unleavened Bread. ⁴So when he had arrested him, he put *him* in prison, and delivered *him* to four squads of soldiers to keep him, intending to bring him before the people after Passover.

Peter Freed from Prison

⁵Peter was therefore kept in prison, but constantᵃ prayer was offered to God for him by the church. ⁶And when Herod was

---

12:5 ᵃNU-Text reads *constantly* (or *earnestly*).

about to bring him out, that night Peter was sleeping, bound with two chains between two soldiers; and the guards before the door were keeping the prison. [7]Now behold, an angel of the Lord stood by *him,* and a light shone in the prison; and he struck Peter on the side and raised him up, saying, "Arise quickly!" And his chains fell off *his* hands. [8]Then the angel said to him, "Gird yourself and tie on your sandals"; and so he did. And he said to him, "Put on your garment and follow me." [9]So he went out and followed him, and did not know that what was done by the angel was real, but thought he was seeing a vision. [10]When they were past the first and the second guard posts, they came to the iron gate that leads to the city, which opened to them of its own accord; and they went out and went down one street, and immediately the angel departed from him.

[11]And when Peter had come to himself, he said, "Now I know for certain that the Lord has sent His angel, and has delivered me from the hand of Herod and *from* all the expectation of the Jewish people."

[12]So, when he had considered *this,* he came to the house of Mary, the mother of John whose surname was Mark, where many were gathered together praying. [13]And as Peter knocked at the door of the gate, a girl named Rhoda came to answer. [14]When she recognized Peter's voice, because of *her* gladness she did not open the gate, but ran in and announced that Peter stood before the gate. [15]But they said to her, "You are beside yourself!" Yet she kept insisting that it was so. So they said, "It is his angel."

[16]Now Peter continued knocking; and when they opened *the door* and saw him, they were astonished. [17]But motioning to them with his hand to keep silent, he declared to them how the Lord had brought him out of the prison. And he said, "Go, tell these things to James and to the brethren." And he departed and went to another place.

[18]Then, as soon as it was day, there was no small stir among the soldiers about what had become of Peter. [19]But when Herod had searched for him and not found him, he examined the guards and commanded that *they* should be put to death.

And he went down from Judea to Caesarea, and stayed *there.*

Herod's Violent Death

[20]Now Herod had been very angry with the people of Tyre and Sidon; but they came to him with one accord, and having made Blastus the king's personal aide their friend, they asked for peace, because their country was supplied with food by the king's *country.*

[21]So on a set day Herod, arrayed in royal apparel, sat on his throne and gave an oration to them. [22]And the people kept shouting, "The voice of a god and not of a man!" [23]Then immediately an angel of the Lord struck him, because he did not give glory to God. And he was eaten by worms and died.

[24]But the word of God grew and multiplied.

Barnabas and Saul Appointed

[25]And Barnabas and Saul returned from[a] Jerusalem when they had fulfilled *their* ministry, and they also took with them John whose surname was Mark.

13 Now in the church that was at Antioch there were certain prophets and teachers: Barnabas, Simeon who was called Niger, Lucius of Cyrene, Manaen who had been brought up with Herod the tetrarch, and Saul. [2]As they ministered to the Lord and fasted, the Holy Spirit said, "Now separate to Me Barnabas and Saul for the work to which I have called them." [3]Then, having fasted and prayed, and laid hands on them, they sent *them* away.

Preaching in Cyprus

[4]So, being sent out by the Holy Spirit, they went down to Seleucia, and from there they sailed to Cyprus. [5]And when they arrived in Salamis, they preached the word of God in the synagogues of the Jews. They also had John as *their* assistant. [6]Now when they had gone through the island[a] to Paphos, they found a certain

---

12:25 [a]NU-Text and M-Text read *to.*   **13:6** [a]NU-Text reads *the whole island.*

sorcerer, a false prophet, a Jew whose name *was* Bar-Jesus, [7]who was with the proconsul, Sergius Paulus, an intelligent man. This man called for Barnabas and Saul and sought to hear the word of God. [8]But Elymas the sorcerer (for so his name is translated) withstood them, seeking to turn the proconsul away from the faith. [9]Then Saul, who also *is called* Paul, filled with the Holy Spirit, looked intently at him [10]and said, "O full of all deceit and all fraud, *you* son of the devil, *you* enemy of all righteousness, will you not cease perverting the straight ways of the Lord? [11]And now, indeed, the hand of the Lord *is* upon you, and you shall be blind, not seeing the sun for a time."

And immediately a dark mist fell on him, and he went around seeking someone to lead him by the hand. [12]Then the proconsul believed, when he saw what had been done, being astonished at the teaching of the Lord.

At Antioch in Pisidia

[13]Now when Paul and his party set sail from Paphos, they came to Perga in Pamphylia; and John, departing from them, returned to Jerusalem. [14]But when they departed from Perga, they came to Antioch in Pisidia, and went into the synagogue on the Sabbath day and sat down. [15]And after the reading of the Law and the Prophets, the rulers of the synagogue sent to them, saying, "Men *and* brethren, if you have any word of exhortation for the people, say on."

[16]Then Paul stood up, and motioning with *his* hand said, "Men of Israel, and you who fear God, listen: [17]The God of this people Israel[a] chose our fathers, and exalted the people when they dwelt as strangers in the land of Egypt, and with an uplifted arm He brought them out of it. [18]Now for a time of about forty years He put up with their ways in the wilderness. [19]And when He had destroyed seven nations in the land of Canaan, He distributed their land to them by allotment.

[20]"After that He gave *them* judges for about four hundred and fifty years, until Samuel the prophet. [21]And afterward they asked for a king; so God gave them Saul the son of Kish, a man of the tribe of Benjamin, for forty years. [22]And when He had removed him, He raised up for them David as king, to whom also He gave testimony and said, 'I have found David[a] the *son* of Jesse, *a man after My own heart, who will do all My will.'*[b] [23]From this man's seed, according to *the* promise, God raised up for Israel a Savior—Jesus—[a] [24]after John had first preached, before His coming, the baptism of repentance to all the people of Israel. [25]And as John was finishing his course, he said, 'Who do you think I am? I am not *He.* But behold, there comes One after me, the sandals of whose feet I am not worthy to loose.'

[26]"Men *and* brethren, sons of the family of Abraham, and those among you who fear God, to you the word of this salvation has been sent. [27]For those who dwell in Jerusalem, and their rulers, because they did not know Him, nor even the voices of the Prophets which are read every Sabbath, have fulfilled *them* in condemning *Him.* [28]And though they found no cause for death *in Him,* they asked Pilate that He should be put to death. [29]Now when they had fulfilled all that was written concerning Him, they took *Him* down from the tree and laid *Him* in a tomb. [30]But God raised Him from the dead. [31]He was seen for many days by those who came up with Him from Galilee to Jerusalem, who are His witnesses to the people. [32]And we declare to you glad tidings—

13:17 [a]M-Text omits *Israel.* **13:22** [a]Psalm 89:20 [b]1 Samuel 13:14 **13:23** [a]M-Text reads *for Israel salvation.*

that promise which was made to the fathers. [33]God has fulfilled this for us their children, in that He has raised up Jesus. As it is also written in the second Psalm:

'You are My Son,
  Today I have begotten You.'[a]

[34]And that He raised Him from the dead, no more to return to corruption, He has spoken thus:

'I will give you the sure mercies of
  David.'[a]

[35]Therefore He also says in another Psalm:

'You will not allow Your Holy One to
  see corruption.'[a]

[36]"For David, after he had served his own generation by the will of God, fell asleep, was buried with his fathers, and saw corruption; [37]but He whom God raised up saw no corruption. [38]Therefore let it be known to you, brethren, that through this Man is preached to you the forgiveness of sins; [39]and by Him everyone who believes is justified from all things from which you could not be justified by the law of Moses. [40]Beware therefore, lest what has been spoken in the prophets come upon you:

[41] 'Behold, you despisers,
  Marvel and perish!
  For I work a work in your days,
  A work which you will by no means
    believe,
  Though one were to declare it to
    you.' "[a]

Blessing and Conflict at Antioch

[42]So when the Jews went out of the synagogue,[a] the Gentiles begged that these words might be preached to them the next Sabbath. [43]Now when the congregation had broken up, many of the Jews and devout proselytes followed Paul and Barnabas, who, speaking to them, persuaded them to continue in the grace of God.

[44]On the next Sabbath almost the whole city came together to hear the word of God.

[45]But when the Jews saw the multitudes, they were filled with envy; and contradicting and blaspheming, they opposed the things spoken by Paul. [46]Then Paul and Barnabas grew bold and said, "It was necessary that the word of God should be spoken to you first; but since you reject it, and judge yourselves unworthy of everlasting life, behold, we turn to the Gentiles. [47]For so the Lord has commanded us:

'I have set you as a light to the
  Gentiles,
  That you should be for salvation to
    the ends of the earth.' "[a]

[48]Now when the Gentiles heard this, they were glad and glorified the word of the Lord. And as many as had been appointed to eternal life believed.

[49]And the word of the Lord was being spread throughout all the region. [50]But the Jews stirred up the devout and prominent women and the chief men of the city, raised up persecution against Paul and Barnabas, and expelled them from their region. [51]But they shook off the dust from their feet against them, and came to Iconium. [52]And the disciples were filled with joy and with the Holy Spirit.

At Iconium

14 Now it happened in Iconium that they went together to the synagogue of the Jews, and so spoke that a great multitude both of the Jews and of the Greeks believed. [2]But the unbelieving Jews stirred up the Gentiles and poisoned their minds against the brethren. [3]Therefore they stayed there a long time, speaking boldly in the Lord, who was bearing witness to the word of His grace, granting signs and wonders to be done by their hands.

[4]But the multitude of the city was divided: part sided with the Jews, and part with the apostles. [5]And when a violent attempt was made by both the Gentiles and Jews,

---

13:33 [a]Psalm 2:7   **13:34** [a]Isaiah 55:3
13:35 [a]Psalm 16:10   **13:41** [a]Habakkuk 1:5
13:42 [a]Or And when they went out of the synagogue of the Jews; NU-Text reads And when they went out, they begged.   **13:47** [a]Isaiah 49:6

with their rulers, to abuse and stone them, [6]they became aware of it and fled to Lystra and Derbe, cities of Lycaonia, and to the surrounding region. [7]And they were preaching the gospel there.

Idolatry at Lystra

[8]And in Lystra a certain man without strength in his feet was sitting, a cripple from his mother's womb, who had never walked. [9]*This* man heard Paul speaking. Paul, observing him intently and seeing that he had faith to be healed, [10]said with a loud voice, "Stand up straight on your feet!" And he leaped and walked. [11]Now when the people saw what Paul had done, they raised their voices, saying in the Lycaonian *language*, "The gods have come down to us in the likeness of men!" [12]And Barnabas they called Zeus, and Paul, Hermes, because he was the chief speaker. [13]Then the priest of Zeus, whose temple was in front of their city, brought oxen and garlands to the gates, intending to sacrifice with the multitudes.

[14]But when the apostles Barnabas and Paul heard this, they tore their clothes and ran in among the multitude, crying out [15]and saying, "Men, why are you doing these things? We also are men with the same nature as you, and preach to you that you should turn from these useless things to the living God, who made the heaven, the earth, the sea, and all things that are in them, [16]who in bygone generations allowed all nations to walk in their own ways. [17]Nevertheless He did not leave Himself without witness, in that He did good, gave us rain from heaven and fruitful seasons, filling our hearts with food and gladness." [18]And with these sayings they could scarcely restrain the multitudes from sacrificing to them.

Stoning, Escape to Derbe

[19]Then Jews from Antioch and Iconium came there; and having persuaded the multitudes, they stoned Paul *and* dragged *him* out of the city, supposing him to be dead. [20]However, when the disciples gathered around him, he rose up and went into the city. And the next day he departed with Barnabas to Derbe.

Strengthening the Converts

[21]And when they had preached the gospel to that city and made many disciples, they returned to Lystra, Iconium, and Antioch, [22]strengthening the souls of the disciples, exhorting *them* to continue in the faith, and *saying,* "We must through many tribulations enter the kingdom of God." [23]So when they had appointed elders in every church, and prayed with fasting, they commended them to the Lord in whom they had believed. [24]And after they had passed through Pisidia, they came to Pamphylia. [25]Now when they had preached the word in Perga, they went down to Attalia. [26]From there they sailed to Antioch, where they had been commended to the grace of God for the work which they had completed.

[27]Now when they had come and gathered the church together, they reported all that God had done with them, and that He had opened the door of faith to the Gentiles. [28]So they stayed there a long time with the disciples.

Conflict over Circumcision

15 And certain *men* came down from Judea and taught the brethren, "Unless you are circumcised according to the custom of Moses, you cannot be saved." [2]Therefore, when Paul and Barnabas had no small dissension and dispute with them, they determined that Paul and Barnabas and certain others of them should go up to Jerusalem, to the apostles and elders, about this question.

[3]So, being sent on their way by the church, they passed through Phoenicia and Samaria, describing the conversion of the Gentiles; and they caused great joy to all the brethren. [4]And when they had come to Jerusalem, they were received by the church and the apostles and the elders; and they reported all things that God had done with them. [5]But some of the sect of the Pharisees who believed rose up, saying, "It is necessary to circumcise them, and to command *them* to keep the law of Moses."

The Jerusalem Council

[6]Now the apostles and elders came together to consider this matter. [7]And when

Now the apostles and elders came together to consider this matter.

ACTS 15:6

"A LITTLE SHORT OF A MIRACLE"

The U.S. Constitution was the first written constitution in the world, and one that defined a government of, by, and for the people. It has served Americans well, enhancing freedom and prosperity while withstanding over two centuries of trial by fire, tears, and bloodshed. Frequently copied over the past two hundred years, nearly every nation in the world has since adopted written constitutions, and the U.S. Constitution served as the model.

On September 17, 1787, George Washington witnessed the signing of the U.S. Constitution and later declared it as "little short of a miracle," and for good reason. The leaders from the thirteen states were deeply divided on many fundamental issues, particularly on the extent to which the states would cede any power to a national government. To create a strong central government meant confronting seemingly irresolvable differences on how to allocate the components of national power between large and small states. The delegates spent over three months in secret sessions, because they were fearful that if their debates were reported to the people before the entire document was ready for submission, the opposition would unite to kill their efforts.

It was so remarkable that the delegates were able to agree on a strong central government that Benjamin Franklin said, "To conclude, I beg I may not be understood to infer, that our General Convention was divinely inspired when it formed the new Federal Constitution, . . . yet I must own I have so much faith in the general government of the world by Providence, that I can hardly conceive a transaction of such momentous importance to the welfare of millions now existing, and to exist in the posterity of a great nation, should be suffered to pass without being in some degree influenced, guided, and governed by that omnipotent, omnipresent, and beneficent Ruler, in whom all inferior spirits live and move and have their being."

Charles Pinckney, another of the Framers, said, "Nothing less than that superintending hand of Providence, that so miraculously carried us through the war (in my humble opinion), could have brought it [the Constitution] about so complete, upon the whole."

Alexander Hamilton, who represented New York at the Constitutional Convention, expressed a similar view: "For my own part, I sincerely esteem it a system, which, without the finger of *God*, never could have been suggested and agreed upon by such a diversity of interests."

there had been much dispute, Peter rose up *and* said to them: "Men *and* brethren, you know that a good while ago God chose among us, that by my mouth the Gentiles should hear the word of the gospel and believe. 8So God, who knows the heart, acknowledged them by giving them the Holy Spirit, just as *He did* to us, 9and made no distinction between us and them, purifying their hearts by faith. 10Now therefore, why do you test God by putting a yoke on the neck of the disciples which neither our fathers nor we were able to bear? 11But we believe that through the grace of the Lord Jesus Christᵃ we shall be saved in the same manner as they."

12Then all the multitude kept silent and listened to Barnabas and Paul declaring how many miracles and wonders God had worked through them among the Gentiles. 13And after they had become silent, James answered, saying, "Men *and* brethren, listen to me: 14Simon has declared how God at the first visited the Gentiles to take out of them a people for His name. 15And with this the words of the prophets agree, just as it is written:

16 'After this I will return
And will rebuild the tabernacle of
    David, which has fallen down;
I will rebuild its ruins,
And I will set it up;
17 So that the rest of mankind may seek
    the Lord,
Even all the Gentiles who are called
    by My name,
Says the Lord who does all these
    things.'ᵃ

18"Known to God from eternity are all His works.ᵃ 19Therefore I judge that we should not trouble those from among the Gentiles who are turning to God, 20but that we write to them to abstain from things polluted by idols, *from* sexual immorality,ᵃ *from* things strangled, and *from* blood. 21For Moses has had throughout many generations those who preach him in every city, being read in the synagogues every Sabbath."

The Jerusalem Decree

22Then it pleased the apostles and elders, with the whole church, to send chosen men of their own company to Antioch with Paul and Barnabas, *namely,* Judas who was also named Barsabas,ᵃ and Silas, leading men among the brethren. 23They wrote this *letter* by them:

The apostles, the elders, and the brethren,

To the brethren who are of the Gentiles in Antioch, Syria, and Cilicia:

Greetings.

24 Since we have heard that some who went out from us have troubled you with words, unsettling your souls, saying, "*You must* be circumcised and keep the law"ᵃ—to whom we gave no such commandment—25it seemed good to us, being assembled with one accord, to send chosen men to you with our beloved Barnabas and Paul, 26men who have risked their lives for the name of our Lord Jesus Christ. 27We have therefore sent Judas and Silas, who will also report the same things by word of mouth. 28For it seemed good to the Holy Spirit, and to us, to lay upon you no greater burden than these necessary things: 29that you abstain from things offered to idols, from blood, from things strangled, and from sexual immorality.ᵃ If you keep yourselves from these, you will do well.

Farewell.

Continuing Ministry in Syria

30So when they were sent off, they came to Antioch; and when they had gathered

---

15:11 ᵃNU-Text and M-Text omit *Christ.*
15:17 ᵃAmos 9:11, 12   15:18 ᵃNU-Text (combining with verse 17) reads *Says the Lord, who makes these things known from eternity (of old).*   15:20 ᵃOr *fornication*   15:22 ᵃNU-Text and M-Text read *Barsabbas.*   15:24 ᵃNU-Text omits *saying, "You must be circumcised and keep the law."*   15:29 ᵃOr *fornication*

the multitude together, they delivered the letter. [31]When they had read it, they rejoiced over its encouragement. [32]Now Judas and Silas, themselves being prophets also, exhorted and strengthened the brethren with many words. [33]And after they had stayed *there* for a time, they were sent back with greetings from the brethren to the apostles.[a]

[34]However, it seemed good to Silas to remain there.[a] [35]Paul and Barnabas also remained in Antioch, teaching and preaching the word of the Lord, with many others also.

Division over John Mark

[36]Then after some days Paul said to Barnabas, "Let us now go back and visit our brethren in every city where we have preached the word of the Lord, *and see* how they are doing." [37]Now Barnabas was determined to take with them John called Mark. [38]But Paul insisted that they should not take with them the one who had departed from them in Pamphylia, and had not gone with them to the work. [39]Then the contention became so sharp that they parted from one another. And so Barnabas took Mark and sailed to Cyprus; [40]but Paul chose Silas and departed, being commended by the brethren to the grace of God. [41]And he went through Syria and Cilicia, strengthening the churches.

Timothy Joins Paul and Silas

16 Then he came to Derbe and Lystra. And behold, a certain disciple was there, named Timothy, *the* son of a certain Jewish woman who believed, but his father *was* Greek. [2]He was well spoken of by the brethren who were at Lystra and Iconium. [3]Paul wanted to have him go on with him. And he took *him* and circumcised him because of the Jews who were in that region, for they all knew that his father was Greek. [4]And as they went through the cities, they delivered to them the decrees to keep, which were determined by the apostles and elders at Jerusalem. [5]So the churches were strengthened in the faith, and increased in number daily.

The Macedonian Call

[6]Now when they had gone through Phrygia and the region of Galatia, they were forbidden by the Holy Spirit to preach the word in Asia. [7]After they had come to Mysia, they tried to go into Bithynia, but the Spirit[a] did not permit them. [8]So passing by Mysia, they came down to Troas. [9]And a vision appeared to Paul in the night. A man of Macedonia stood and pleaded with him, saying, "Come over to Macedonia and help us." [10]Now after he had seen the vision, immediately we sought to go to Macedonia, concluding that the Lord had called us to preach the gospel to them.

Lydia Baptized at Philippi

[11]Therefore, sailing from Troas, we ran a straight course to Samothrace, and the next *day* came to Neapolis, [12]and from there to Philippi, which is the foremost city of that part of Macedonia, a colony. And we were staying in that city for some days. [13]And on the Sabbath day we went out of the city to the riverside, where prayer was customarily made; and we sat down and spoke to the women who met *there*. [14]Now a certain woman named Lydia heard *us*. She was a seller of purple from the city of Thyatira, who worshiped God. The Lord opened her heart to heed the things spoken by Paul. [15]And when she and her household were baptized, she begged *us*, saying, "If you have judged me to be faithful to the Lord, come to my house and stay." So she persuaded us.

Paul and Silas Imprisoned

[16]Now it happened, as we went to prayer, that a certain slave girl possessed with a spirit of divination met us, who brought her masters much profit by fortune-telling. [17]This girl followed Paul and us, and cried out, saying, "These men are the servants of the Most High God, who proclaim to us the way of salvation." [18]And this she did for many days.

But Paul, greatly annoyed, turned and said to the spirit, "I command you in the

15:33 [a]NU-Text reads *to those who had sent them.*
15:34 [a]NU-Text and M-Text omit this verse.
16:7 [a]NU-Text adds *of Jesus.*

name of Jesus Christ to come out of her." And he came out that very hour. ¹⁹But when her masters saw that their hope of profit was gone, they seized Paul and Silas and dragged *them* into the marketplace to the authorities.

²⁰And they brought them to the magistrates, and said, "These men, being Jews, exceedingly trouble our city; ²¹and they teach customs which are not lawful for us, being Romans, to receive or observe." ²²Then the multitude rose up together against them; and the magistrates tore off their clothes and commanded *them* to be beaten with rods. ²³And when they had laid many stripes on them, they threw *them* into prison, commanding the jailer to keep them securely. ²⁴Having received such a charge, he put them into the inner prison and fastened their feet in the stocks.

The Philippian Jailer Saved

²⁵But at midnight Paul and Silas were praying and singing hymns to God, and the prisoners were listening to them. ²⁶Suddenly there was a great earthquake, so that the foundations of the prison were shaken; and immediately all the doors were opened and everyone's chains were loosed. ²⁷And the keeper of the prison, awaking from sleep and seeing the prison doors open, supposing the prisoners had fled, drew his sword and was about to kill himself. ²⁸But Paul called with a loud voice, saying, "Do yourself no harm, for we are all here."

²⁹Then he called for a light, ran in, and fell down trembling before Paul and Silas. ³⁰And he brought them out and said, "Sirs, what must I do to be saved?"

³¹So they said, "Believe on the Lord Jesus Christ, and you will be saved, you and your household." ³²Then they spoke the word of the Lord to him and to all who were in his house. ³³And he took them the same hour of the night and washed *their* stripes. And immediately he and all his *family* were baptized. ³⁴Now when he had brought them into his house, he set food before them; and he rejoiced, having believed in God with all his household.

Paul Refuses to Depart Secretly

³⁵And when it was day, the magistrates sent the officers, saying, "Let those men go." ³⁶So the keeper of the prison reported these words to Paul, saying, "The magistrates have sent to let you go. Now therefore depart, and go in peace."

³⁷But Paul said to them, "They have beaten us openly, uncondemned Romans, *and* have thrown *us* into prison. And now do they put us out secretly? No indeed! Let them come themselves and get us out."

³⁸And the officers told these words to the magistrates, and they were afraid when they heard that they were Romans. ³⁹Then they came and pleaded with them and brought *them* out, and asked *them* to depart from the city. ⁴⁰So they went out of the prison and entered *the house of* Lydia; and when they had seen the brethren, they encouraged them and departed.

Preaching Christ at Thessalonica

17 Now when they had passed through Amphipolis and Apollonia, they came to Thessalonica, where there was a synagogue of the Jews. ²Then Paul, as his custom was, went in to them, and for three Sabbaths reasoned with them from the Scriptures, ³explaining and demonstrating that the Christ had to suffer and rise again from the dead, and *saying,* "This Jesus whom I preach to you is the Christ." ⁴And some of them were persuaded; and a great multitude of the devout Greeks, and not a few of the leading women, joined Paul and Silas.

Assault on Jason's House

⁵But the Jews who were not persuaded, becoming envious,ᵃ took some of the evil men from the marketplace, and gathering a mob, set all the city in an uproar and attacked the house of Jason, and sought to bring them out to the people. ⁶But when they did not find them, they dragged Jason and some brethren to the rulers of the city, crying out, "These who have turned the world upside down have come here too.

17:5 ᵃNU-Text omits *who were not persuaded;* M-Text omits *becoming envious.*

⁷Jason has harbored them, and these are all acting contrary to the decrees of Caesar, saying there is another king—Jesus." ⁸And they troubled the crowd and the rulers of the city when they heard these things. ⁹So when they had taken security from Jason and the rest, they let them go.

INSPIRING

. . . searched the Scriptures daily. . . .
                                                                    ACTS 17:11

Search the Scriptures

John Quincy Adams, the sixth President of the United States, proclaimed:

I speak as a man of the world to men of the world; and I say to you, Search the Scriptures! The Bible is the book of all others, to be read at all ages, and in all conditions of human life; not to be read once or twice or thrice through, and then laid aside, but to be read in small portions of one or two chapters every day, and never to be intermitted, unless by some overruling necessity.

Ministering at Berea

¹⁰Then the brethren immediately sent Paul and Silas away by night to Berea. When they arrived, they went into the synagogue of the Jews. ¹¹These were more fair-minded than those in Thessalonica, in that they received the word with all readiness, and searched the Scriptures daily *to find out* whether these things were so. ¹²Therefore many of them believed, and also not a few of the Greeks, prominent women as well as men. ¹³But when the Jews from Thessalonica learned that the word of God was preached by Paul at Berea, they came there also and stirred up the crowds. ¹⁴Then immediately the brethren sent Paul away, to go to the sea; but both Silas and Timothy remained there. ¹⁵So those who conducted Paul brought him to Athens; and receiving a command for Silas and Timothy to come to him with all speed, they departed.

The Philosophers at Athens

¹⁶Now while Paul waited for them at Athens, his spirit was provoked within him when he saw that the city was given over to idols. ¹⁷Therefore he reasoned in the synagogue with the Jews and with the *Gentile* worshipers, and in the marketplace daily with those who happened to be there. ¹⁸Thenª certain Epicurean and Stoic philosophers encountered him. And some said, "What does this babbler want to say?"

Others said, "He seems to be a proclaimer of foreign gods," because he preached to them Jesus and the resurrection.

¹⁹And they took him and brought him to the Areopagus, saying, "May we know what this new doctrine *is* of which you speak? ²⁰For you are bringing some strange things to our ears. Therefore we want to know what these things mean." ²¹For all the Athenians and the foreigners who were there spent their time in nothing else but either to tell or to hear some new thing.

Addressing the Areopagus

²²Then Paul stood in the midst of the Areopagus and said, "Men of Athens, I perceive that in all things you are very religious; ²³for as I was passing through and considering the objects of your worship, I even found an altar with this inscription:

TO THE UNKNOWN GOD.

Therefore, the One whom you worship without knowing, Him I proclaim to you: ²⁴God, who made the world and everything in it, since He is Lord of heaven and earth, does not dwell in temples made with hands. ²⁵Nor is He worshiped with men's hands, as though He needed anything, since He gives to all life, breath, and all things. ²⁶And He has made from one bloodª every nation of men to dwell on all the face of the earth, and has determined their preappointed times and the boundaries of their dwellings, ²⁷so that they should seek the Lord, in the hope that they might grope for Him and find Him, though He is not far from each one of us; ²⁸for in Him we live and move and have our being, as also some of your own poets have said, 'For we are also His offspring.' ²⁹Therefore, since we are the offspring of

---

17:18 ªNU-Text and M-Text add *also.*   **17:26** ªNU-Text omits *blood.*

God, we ought not to think that the Divine Nature is like gold or silver or stone, something shaped by art and man's devising. [30]Truly, these times of ignorance God overlooked, but now commands all men everywhere to repent, [31]because He has appointed a day on which He will judge the world in righteousness by the Man whom He has ordained. He has given assurance of this to all by raising Him from the dead."

[32]And when they heard of the resurrection of the dead, some mocked, while others said, "We will hear you again on this *matter.*" [33]So Paul departed from among them. [34]However, some men joined him and believed, among them Dionysius the Areopagite, a woman named Damaris, and others with them.

Ministering at Corinth

18 After these things Paul departed from Athens and went to Corinth. [2]And he found a certain Jew named Aquila, born in Pontus, who had recently come from Italy with his wife Priscilla (because Claudius had commanded all the Jews to depart from Rome); and he came to them. [3]So, because he was of the same trade, he stayed with them and worked; for by occupation they were tentmakers. [4]And he reasoned in the synagogue every Sabbath, and persuaded both Jews and Greeks.

[5]When Silas and Timothy had come from Macedonia, Paul was compelled by the Spirit, and testified to the Jews *that* Jesus *is* the Christ. [6]But when they opposed him and blasphemed, he shook *his* garments and said to them, "Your blood *be* upon your *own* heads; I *am* clean. From now on I will go to the Gentiles." [7]And he departed from there and entered the house of a certain *man* named Justus,[a] *one* who worshiped

---

18:7 [a]NU-Text reads *Titius Justus.*

SERVICE

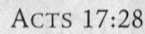

". . . in Him we live and move and have our being. . . ."

ACTS 17:28

George Washington Carver
in his laboratory

MAN AS GOD'S COWORKER

George Washington Carver (1864–1943), an agricultural chemist who discovered three hundred uses for peanuts and hundreds more uses for soybeans, pecans, and sweet potatoes, shared some of his observations about God:

As a very small boy exploring the almost virgin woods of the old Carver place, I had the impression someone had just been there ahead of me. Things were so orderly, so clean, so harmoniously beautiful. A few years later in this same woods, I was to understand the meaning of this boyish impression . . . because I was practically overwhelmed with the sense of some Great Presence. Not only had someone been there. Someone was there. . . .

Years later when I read in the Scriptures, "In Him we live and move and have our being," I knew what the writer meant. Never since have I been without this consciousness of the Creator speaking to me. . . . The out-of-doors has been to me more and more a great cathedral in which God could be continuously spoken to and heard from. . . .

Man, who needed a purpose, a mission, to keep him alive, had one. He could be . . . God's coworker. . . . My purpose alone must be God's purpose—to increase the welfare and happiness of His people. . . . Why, then, should we who believe in Christ be so surprised at what God can do with a willing man in a laboratory?

God, whose house was next door to the synagogue. ⁸Then Crispus, the ruler of the synagogue, believed on the Lord with all his household. And many of the Corinthians, hearing, believed and were baptized.

⁹Now the Lord spoke to Paul in the night by a vision, "Do not be afraid, but speak, and do not keep silent; ¹⁰for I am with you, and no one will attack you to hurt you; for I have many people in this city." ¹¹And he continued *there* a year and six months, teaching the word of God among them.

¹²When Gallio was proconsul of Achaia, the Jews with one accord rose up against Paul and brought him to the judgment seat, ¹³saying, "This *fellow* persuades men to worship God contrary to the law."

¹⁴And when Paul was about to open *his* mouth, Gallio said to the Jews, "If it were a matter of wrongdoing or wicked crimes, O Jews, there would be reason why I should bear with you. ¹⁵But if it is a question of words and names and your own law, look *to it* yourselves; for I do not want to be a judge of such *matters*." ¹⁶And he drove them from the judgment seat. ¹⁷Then all the Greeks[a] took Sosthenes, the ruler of the synagogue, and beat *him* before the judgment seat. But Gallio took no notice of these things.

Paul Returns to Antioch

¹⁸So Paul still remained a good while. Then he took leave of the brethren and sailed for Syria, and Priscilla and Aquila *were* with him. He had *his* hair cut off at Cenchrea, for he had taken a vow. ¹⁹And he came to Ephesus, and left them there; but he himself entered the synagogue and reasoned with the Jews. ²⁰When they asked *him* to stay a longer time with them, he did not consent, ²¹but took leave of them, saying, "I must by all means keep this coming feast in Jerusalem;[a] but I will return again to you, God willing." And he sailed from Ephesus.

²²And when he had landed at Caesarea, and gone up and greeted the church, he went down to Antioch. ²³After he had spent some time *there,* he departed and went over the region of Galatia and Phrygia in order, strengthening all the disciples.

Ministry of Apollos

²⁴Now a certain Jew named Apollos, born at Alexandria, an eloquent man *and* mighty in the Scriptures, came to Ephesus. ²⁵This man had been instructed in the way of the Lord; and being fervent in spirit, he spoke and taught accurately the things of the Lord, though he knew only the baptism of John. ²⁶So he began to speak boldly in the synagogue. When Aquila and Priscilla heard him, they took him aside and explained to him the way of God more accurately. ²⁷And when he desired to cross to Achaia, the brethren wrote, exhorting the disciples to receive him; and when he arrived, he greatly helped those who had believed through grace; ²⁸for he vigorously refuted the Jews publicly, showing from the Scriptures that Jesus is the Christ.

Paul at Ephesus

19 And it happened, while Apollos was at Corinth, that Paul, having passed through the upper regions, came to Ephesus. And finding some disciples ²he said to them, "Did you receive the Holy Spirit when you believed?"

So they said to him, "We have not so much as heard whether there is a Holy Spirit."

³And he said to them, "Into what then were you baptized?"

So they said, "Into John's baptism."

⁴Then Paul said, "John indeed baptized with a baptism of repentance, saying to the people that they should believe on Him who would come after him, that is, on Christ Jesus."

⁵When they heard *this,* they were baptized in the name of the Lord Jesus. ⁶And when Paul had laid hands on them, the Holy Spirit came upon them, and they spoke with tongues and prophesied. ⁷Now the men were about twelve in all.

⁸And he went into the synagogue and spoke boldly for three months, reasoning and persuading concerning the things of the kingdom of God. ⁹But when some were

---

18:17 [a]NU-Text reads *they all.*　**18:21** [a]NU-Text omits *I must* through *Jerusalem.*

hardened and did not believe, but spoke evil of the Way before the multitude, he departed from them and withdrew the disciples, reasoning daily in the school of Tyrannus. [10]And this continued for two years, so that all who dwelt in Asia heard the word of the Lord Jesus, both Jews and Greeks.

Miracles Glorify Christ

[11]Now God worked unusual miracles by the hands of Paul, [12]so that even handkerchiefs or aprons were brought from his body to the sick, and the diseases left them and the evil spirits went out of them. [13]Then some of the itinerant Jewish exorcists took it upon themselves to call the name of the Lord Jesus over those who had evil spirits, saying, "We[a] exorcise you by the Jesus whom Paul preaches." [14]Also there were seven sons of Sceva, a Jewish chief priest, who did so.

[15]And the evil spirit answered and said, "Jesus I know, and Paul I know; but who are you?"

[16]Then the man in whom the evil spirit was leaped on them, overpowered[a] them, and prevailed against them,[b] so that they fled out of that house naked and wounded. [17]This became known both to all Jews and Greeks dwelling in Ephesus; and fear fell on them all, and the name of the Lord Jesus was magnified. [18]And many who had believed came confessing and telling their deeds. [19]Also, many of those who had practiced magic brought their books together and burned *them* in the sight of all. And they counted up the value of them, and *it* totaled fifty thousand *pieces* of silver. [20]So the word of the Lord grew mightily and prevailed.

The Riot at Ephesus

[21]When these things were accomplished, Paul purposed in the Spirit, when he had passed through Macedonia and Achaia, to go to Jerusalem, saying, "After I have been there, I must also see Rome." [22]So he sent into Macedonia two of those who ministered to him, Timothy and Erastus, but he himself stayed in Asia for a time.

[23]And about that time there arose a great commotion about the Way. [24]For a certain man named Demetrius, a silversmith, who made silver shrines of Diana,[a] brought no small profit to the craftsmen. [25]He called them together with the workers of similar occupation, and said: "Men, you know that we have our prosperity by this trade. [26]Moreover you see and hear that not only at Ephesus, but throughout almost all Asia, this Paul has persuaded and turned away many people, saying that they are not gods which are made with hands. [27]So not only is this trade of ours in danger of falling into disrepute, but also the temple of the great goddess Diana may be despised and her magnificence destroyed,[a] whom all Asia and the world worship."

[28]Now when they heard *this,* they were full of wrath and cried out, saying, "Great *is* Diana of the Ephesians!" [29]So the whole city was filled with confusion, and rushed into the theater with one accord, having seized Gaius and Aristarchus, Macedonians, Paul's travel companions. [30]And when Paul wanted to go in to the people, the disciples would not allow him. [31]Then some of the officials of Asia, who were his friends, sent to him pleading that he would not venture into the theater. [32]Some therefore cried one thing and some another, for the assembly was confused, and most of them did not know why they had come together. [33]And they drew Alexander out of the multitude, the Jews putting him forward. And Alexander motioned with his hand, and wanted to make his defense to the people. [34]But when they found out that he was a Jew, all with one voice cried out for about two hours, "Great *is* Diana of the Ephesians!"

[35]And when the city clerk had quieted the crowd, he said: "Men of Ephesus, what man is there who does not know that the city of the Ephesians is temple guardian of the great goddess Diana, and of the *image* which fell down from Zeus? [36]Therefore, since these things cannot be denied, you

---

19:13 [a]NU-Text reads *I.*   **19:16** [a]M-Text reads *and they overpowered.* [b]NU-Text reads *both of them.*
19:24 [a]Greek *Artemis*   **19:27** [a]NU-Text reads *she be deposed from her magnificence.*

ought to be quiet and do nothing rashly.
³⁷For you have brought these men here who are neither robbers of temples nor blasphemers of your^a goddess. ³⁸Therefore, if Demetrius and his fellow craftsmen have a case against anyone, the courts are open and there are proconsuls. Let them bring charges against one another. ³⁹But if you have any other inquiry to make, it shall be determined in the lawful assembly. ⁴⁰For we are in danger of being called in question for today's uproar, there being no reason which we may give to account for this disorderly gathering." ⁴¹And when he had said these things, he dismissed the assembly.

Journeys in Greece

20 After the uproar had ceased, Paul called the disciples to *himself,* embraced *them,* and departed to go to Macedonia. ²Now when he had gone over that region and encouraged them with many words, he came to Greece ³and stayed three months. And when the Jews plotted against him as he was about to sail to Syria, he decided to return through Macedonia. ⁴And Sopater of Berea accompanied him to Asia—also Aristarchus and Secundus of the Thessalonians, and Gaius of Derbe, and Timothy, and Tychicus and Trophimus of Asia. ⁵These men, going ahead, waited for us at Troas. ⁶But we sailed away from Philippi after the Days of Unleavened Bread, and in five days joined them at Troas, where we stayed seven days.

Ministering at Troas

⁷Now on the first *day* of the week, when the disciples came together to break bread, Paul, ready to depart the next day, spoke to them and continued his message until midnight. ⁸There were many lamps in the upper room where they^a were gathered together. ⁹And in a window sat a certain young man named Eutychus, who was sinking into a deep sleep. He was overcome by sleep; and as Paul continued speaking, he fell down from the third story and was taken up dead. ¹⁰But Paul went down, fell on him, and embracing *him* said, "Do not trouble yourselves, for his life is in him." ¹¹Now when he had come up, had broken bread and eaten, and talked a long while, even till daybreak, he departed. ¹²And they brought the young man in alive, and they were not a little comforted.

From Troas to Miletus

¹³Then we went ahead to the ship and sailed to Assos, there intending to take Paul on board; for so he had given orders, intending himself to go on foot. ¹⁴And when he met us at Assos, we took him on board and came to Mitylene. ¹⁵We sailed from there, and the next *day* came opposite Chios. The following *day* we arrived at Samos and stayed at Trogyllium. The next *day* we came to Miletus. ¹⁶For Paul had decided to sail past Ephesus, so that he would not have to spend time in Asia; for he was hurrying to be at Jerusalem, if possible, on the Day of Pentecost.

The Ephesian Elders Exhorted

¹⁷From Miletus he sent to Ephesus and called for the elders of the church. ¹⁸And when they had come to him, he said to them: "You know, from the first day that I came to Asia, in what manner I always lived among you, ¹⁹serving the Lord with all humility, with many tears and trials which happened to me by the plotting of the Jews; ²⁰how I kept back nothing that was helpful, but proclaimed it to you, and taught you publicly and from house to house, ²¹testifying to Jews, and also to Greeks, repentance toward God and faith toward our Lord Jesus Christ. ²²And see, now I go bound in the spirit to Jerusalem, not knowing the things that will happen to me there, ²³except that the Holy Spirit testifies in every city, saying that chains and tribulations await me. ²⁴But none of these things move me; nor do I count my life dear to myself,^a so that I may finish my race with joy, and the ministry which I received from the Lord Jesus, to testify to the gospel of the grace of God. ²⁵"And indeed, now I know that you all, among whom I have gone preaching the kingdom of God, will see my face no more.

19:37 ^aNU-Text reads *our.* **20:8** ^aNU-Text and M-Text read *we.* **20:24** ^aNU-Text reads *But I do not count my life of any value or dear to myself.*

THE BIBLE AND BENEVOLENT SOCIETIES

CHARLES G. FINNEY

"The evidence of God's grace," said the Presbyterian revivalist Charles G. Finney, "was a person's benevolence toward others," and this principle was borne out of the Second Great Awakening (1800–1830s) in the United States. During the powerful evangelical revivalism of these years, church growth was stimulated, particularly in America's mainline denominations, and from the extraordinary energies generated by the evangelical movement, numerous benevolent societies emerged. Originally devoted to the salvation of souls, the mission of some of these societies eventually expanded to the eradication of every kind of social ill, such as drinking and gambling.

The earliest and most important of these organizations included the American Education Society (1815), the American Bible Society (1816), the American Sunday School Union (1824), the American Tract Society (1825), and the American Home Missionary Society (1826). This powerful network of benevolent organizations had local branches existing in almost every town and city, though their greatest influence was in the Northeast. All of them were voluntary, passionately Christian, and many had no ties to any single religious group. Most were interdenominational, and cooperative enterprises often took place among the societies.

The "Mississippi Valley Plan," devised by John Beck to evangelize the upper Mississippi Valley in 1826, illustrated how these agencies worked together. He went to the Baptist General Convention and the American Home Missionary Society and convinced them that every missionary could sell Bibles for the American Bible Society, distribute tracts for the American Tract Society, and start Sunday schools for the American Sunday School Union. The agencies adopted the plan, and as a result, 23,000 Bibles and $18,000 worth of tracts were shipped to Ohio and Kentucky in 1830 alone.

Members of the evangelical movement of the nineteenth century considered themselves as American patriots who subscribed to the views of the Founders that religion was a "necessary spring" for republican government. In that light, the benevolent societies assumed the role of helping to form the virtuous citizenry of which the Founders spoke. The conversion of souls was also seen as helping to save the republic. For instance, the American Home Missionary Society assured its supporters in 1826 that "we are doing the work of patriotism no less than Christianity."

26Therefore I testify to you this day that I *am* innocent of the blood of all *men.* 27For I have not shunned to declare to you the whole counsel of God. 28Therefore take heed to yourselves and to all the flock, among which the Holy Spirit has made you overseers, to shepherd the church of Godª which He purchased with His own blood. 29For I know this, that after my departure savage wolves will come in among you, not sparing the flock. 30Also from among yourselves men will rise up, speaking perverse things, to draw away the disciples after themselves. 31Therefore watch, and remember that for three years I did not cease to warn everyone night and day with tears.

32"So now, brethren, I commend you to God and to the word of His grace, which is able to build you up and give you an inheritance among all those who are sanctified. 33I have coveted no one's silver or gold or apparel. 34Yes,ª you yourselves know that these hands have provided for my necessities, and for those who were with me. 35I have shown you in every way, by laboring like this, that you must support the weak. And remember the words of the Lord Jesus, that He said, 'It is more blessed to give than to receive.'"

36And when he had said these things, he knelt down and prayed with them all. 37Then they all wept freely, and fell on Paul's neck and kissed him, 38sorrowing most of all for the words which he spoke, that they would see his face no more. And they accompanied him to the ship.

Warnings on the Journey to Jerusalem

21 Now it came to pass, that when we had departed from them and set sail, running a straight course we came to Cos, the following *day* to Rhodes, and from there to Patara. 2And finding a ship sailing over to Phoenicia, we went aboard and set sail. 3When we had sighted Cyprus, we passed it on the left, sailed to Syria, and landed at Tyre; for there the ship was to unload her cargo. 4And finding disciples,ª we stayed there seven days. They told Paul through the Spirit not to go up to Jerusalem. 5When we had come to the end of those days, we departed and went on our way; and they all accompanied us, with wives and children, till *we were* out of the city. And we knelt down on the shore and prayed. 6When we had taken our leave of one another, we boarded the ship, and they returned home.

7And when we had finished *our* voyage from Tyre, we came to Ptolemais, greeted the brethren, and stayed with them one day. 8On the next *day* we who were Paul's companionsª departed and came to Caesarea, and entered the house of Philip the evangelist, who was *one* of the seven, and stayed with him. 9Now this man had four virgin daughters who prophesied. 10And as we stayed many days, a certain prophet named Agabus came down from Judea. 11When he had come to us, he took Paul's belt, bound his *own* hands and feet, and said, "Thus says the Holy Spirit, 'So shall the Jews at Jerusalem bind the man who owns this belt, and deliver *him* into the hands of the Gentiles.'"

12Now when we heard these things, both we and those from that place pleaded with him not to go up to Jerusalem. 13Then Paul answered, "What do you mean by weeping and breaking my heart? For I am ready not only to be bound, but also to die at Jerusalem for the name of the Lord Jesus." 14So when he would not be persuaded, we ceased, saying, "The will of the Lord be done."

Paul Urged to Make Peace

15And after those days we packed and went up to Jerusalem. 16Also some of the disciples from Caesarea went with us and brought with them a certain Mnason of Cyprus, an early disciple, with whom we were to lodge.

17And when we had come to Jerusalem, the brethren received us gladly. 18On the following *day* Paul went in with us to James, and all the elders were present. 19When he had greeted them, he told in

---

20:28 ªM-Text reads *of the Lord and God.*
20:34 ªNU-Text and M-Text omit *Yes.*   **21:4** ªNU-Text reads *the disciples.*   **21:8** ªNU-Text omits *who were Paul's companions.*

detail those things which God had done among the Gentiles through his ministry. [20]And when they heard *it,* they glorified the Lord. And they said to him, "You see, brother, how many myriads of Jews there are who have believed, and they are all zealous for the law; [21]but they have been informed about you that you teach all the Jews who are among the Gentiles to forsake Moses, saying that they ought not to circumcise *their* children nor to walk according to the customs. [22]What then? The assembly must certainly meet, for they will[a] hear that you have come. [23]Therefore do what we tell you: We have four men who have taken a vow. [24]Take them and be purified with them, and pay their expenses so that they may shave *their* heads, and that all may know that those things of which they were informed concerning you are nothing, but *that* you yourself also walk orderly and keep the law. [25]But concerning the Gentiles who believe, we have written *and* decided that they should observe no such thing, except[a] that they should keep themselves from *things* offered to idols, from blood, from things strangled, and from sexual immorality."

Arrested in the Temple

[26]Then Paul took the men, and the next day, having been purified with them, entered the temple to announce the expiration of the days of purification, at which time an offering should be made for each one of them.

[27]Now when the seven days were almost ended, the Jews from Asia, seeing him in the temple, stirred up the whole crowd and laid hands on him, [28]crying out, "Men of Israel, help! This is the man who teaches all *men* everywhere against the people, the law, and this place; and furthermore he also brought Greeks into the temple and has defiled this holy place." [29](For they had previously[a] seen Trophimus the Ephesian with him in the city, whom they supposed that Paul had brought into the temple.)

[30]And all the city was disturbed; and the people ran together, seized Paul, and dragged him out of the temple; and immediately the doors were shut. [31]Now as they were seeking to kill him, news came to the commander of the garrison that all Jerusalem was in an uproar. [32]He immediately took soldiers and centurions, and ran down to them. And when they saw the commander and the soldiers, they stopped beating Paul. [33]Then the commander came near and took him, and commanded *him* to be bound with two chains; and he asked who he was and what he had done. [34]And some among the multitude cried one thing and some another.

So when he could not ascertain the truth because of the tumult, he commanded him to be taken into the barracks. [35]When he reached the stairs, he had to be carried by the soldiers because of the violence of the mob. [36]For the multitude of the people followed after, crying out, "Away with him!"

Addressing the Jerusalem Mob

[37]Then as Paul was about to be led into the barracks, he said to the commander, "May I speak to you?"

He replied, "Can you speak Greek? [38]Are you not the Egyptian who some time ago stirred up a rebellion and led the four thousand assassins out into the wilderness?"

[39]But Paul said, "I am a Jew from Tarsus, in Cilicia, a citizen of no mean city; and I implore you, permit me to speak to the people."

[40]So when he had given him permission, Paul stood on the stairs and motioned with his hand to the people. And when there was a great silence, he spoke to *them* in the Hebrew language, saying,

22 "Brethren and fathers, hear my defense before you now." [2]And when they heard that he spoke to them in the Hebrew language, they kept all the more silent.

Then he said: [3]"I am indeed a Jew, born in Tarsus of Cilicia, but brought up in this city at the feet of Gamaliel, taught according to the strictness of our fathers' law, and was zealous toward God as you all are today. [4]I persecuted this Way to the death,

---

21:22 [a]NU-Text reads *What then is to be done? They will certainly.*   **21:25** [a]NU-Text omits *that they should observe no such thing, except.*   **21:29** [a]M-Text omits *previously.*

THE BIBLE
AND
FAMOUS AMERICANS

OFTEN CALLED THE "BOOK OF BOOKS," the Bible holds a unique place in American history, politics, religion, and popular culture. Unfortunately, though, biblical illiteracy is so prevalent today that when President Ronald Reagan spoke so eloquently of a "shining city on a hill," few people realized he was referring to a sermon given by John Winthrop, the first governor of the Massachusetts Bay Colony, in 1630, which was based on the words of Jesus Christ in Matthew 5. When people hear Martin Luther King Jr.'s magnificent "I Have a Dream" speech, most do not recognize its numerous biblical allusions and quotes. Nevertheless, the transforming power of the Word of God remains to impact lives everywhere.

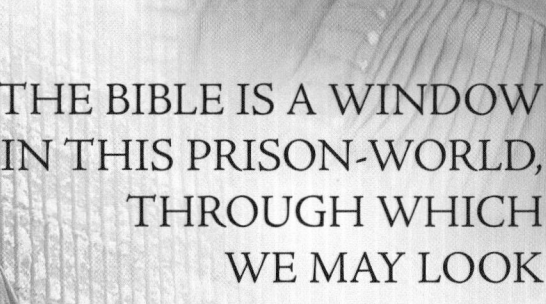

Unless we form the habit of going to the Bible in bright moments as well as in trouble, we cannot fully respond to its consolations because we lack equilibrium between light and darkness.

HELEN KELLER,
Writer and Social Reformer

John
Winthrop

THE BIBLE IS A WINDOW IN THIS PRISON-WORLD, THROUGH WHICH WE MAY LOOK INTO ETERNITY.

TIMOTHY DWIGHT,
President of Yale University

The most remarkable thing, though, is the difference Scripture makes in the lives of those who sincerely follow it. I've never heard anyone who said, "I've studied the Bible; I've lived it for years—and it doesn't work for me." The people I've talked to say that the more they truly absorb Scripture and seek to live by its precepts, they find God is able to accomplish amazing things for His purposes through their lives.

CHARLES COLSON,
Founder of Prison Fellowship

> *In all my perplexities and distresses, the Bible has never failed to give me light and strength.*
>
> ROBERT E. LEE,
> General of the Confederate Army

GENˡ ROBᵀ E. LEE

> *A Bible and a newspaper in every house, a good school in every district—all studied and appreciated as they merit—are the principal support of virtue, morality, and civil liberty.*
>
> BENJAMIN FRANKLIN,
> Statesman, Inventor, and Scientist

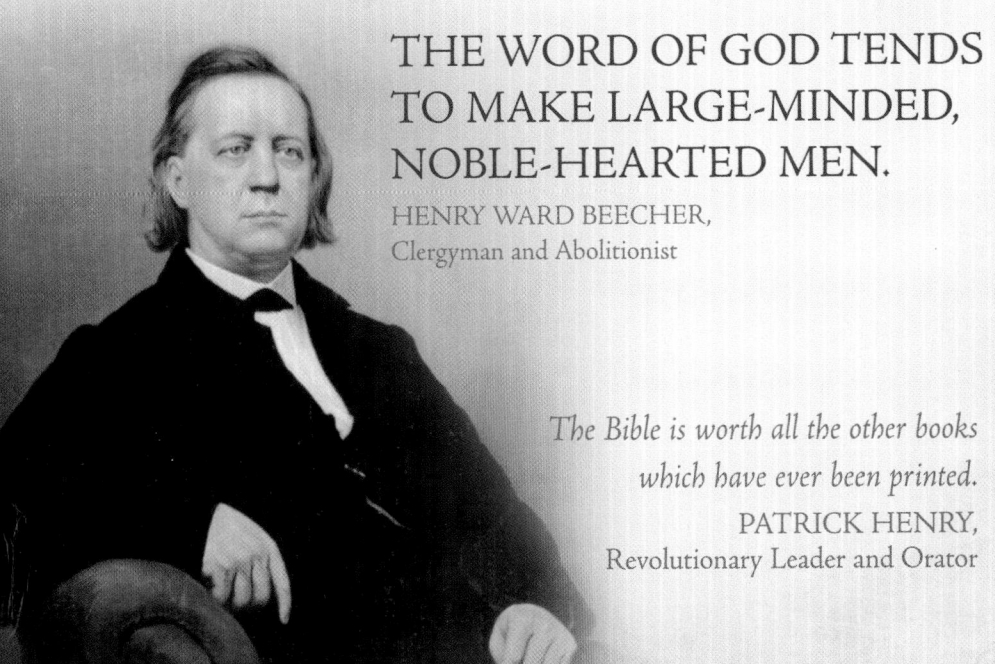

THE WORD OF GOD TENDS TO MAKE LARGE-MINDED, NOBLE-HEARTED MEN.

HENRY WARD BEECHER,
Clergyman and Abolitionist

> *The Bible is worth all the other books which have ever been printed.*
>
> PATRICK HENRY,
> Revolutionary Leader and Orator

George Washington Carver

The secret of my success?
It is simple. It is found in the Bible,
"In all thy ways acknowledge Him and
He shall direct thy paths."

George Washington Carver | INVENTOR
AND HORTICULTURALIST

If we abide by the principles taught
in the Bible, our country will go on prospering
and to prosper; but if we and our posterity
neglect its instructions and authority,
no man can tell how sudden a catastrophe
may overwhelm us and bury all our glory
in profound obscurity.

Daniel Webster | STATESMAN, LAWYER,
AND ORATOR

The Bible towers in content
above all earlier religious literature;
and it towers just as impressively
over all subsequent literature
in the direct simplicity of its message
and the catholicity of its appeal
to men of all lands and times.

William Foxwell Albright | ARCHAEOLOGIST

Should not the Bible regain the place
it once held as a schoolbook? Its morals are pure,
its examples captivating and noble. . . .
In no book is there so good English, so pure
and so elegant, and by teaching all the same book
they will speak alike, and the Bible
will justly remain the standard of language
as well as of faith.

Fischer Ames | AUTHOR OF THE
FIRST AMENDMENT

To call the Bible a great book
is an understatement. It is, quite simply,
the cornerstone of Western civilization.

Charlton Heston | ACTOR

Daniel
Webster

binding and delivering into prisons both men and women, [5]as also the high priest bears me witness, and all the council of the elders, from whom I also received letters to the brethren, and went to Damascus to bring in chains even those who were there to Jerusalem to be punished.

[6]"Now it happened, as I journeyed and came near Damascus at about noon, suddenly a great light from heaven shone around me. [7]And I fell to the ground and heard a voice saying to me, 'Saul, Saul, why are you persecuting Me?' [8]So I answered, 'Who are You, Lord?' And He said to me, 'I am Jesus of Nazareth, whom you are persecuting.'

[9]"And those who were with me indeed saw the light and were afraid,[a] but they did not hear the voice of Him who spoke to me. [10]So I said, 'What shall I do, Lord?' And the Lord said to me, 'Arise and go into Damascus, and there you will be told all things which are appointed for you to do.' [11]And since I could not see for the glory of that light, being led by the hand of those who were with me, I came into Damascus.

[12]"Then a certain Ananias, a devout man according to the law, having a good testimony with all the Jews who dwelt *there,* [13]came to me; and he stood and said to me, 'Brother Saul, receive your sight.' And at that same hour I looked up at him. [14]Then he said, 'The God of our fathers has chosen you that you should know His will, and see the Just One, and hear the voice of His mouth. [15]For you will be His witness to all men of what you have seen and heard. [16]And now why are you waiting? Arise and be baptized, and wash away your sins, calling on the name of the Lord.'

[17]"Now it happened, when I returned to Jerusalem and was praying in the temple, that I was in a trance [18]and saw Him saying to me, 'Make haste and get out of Jerusalem quickly, for they will not receive your testimony concerning Me.' [19]So I said, 'Lord, they know that in every synagogue I imprisoned and beat those who believe on You. [20]And when the blood of Your martyr Stephen was shed, I also was standing by consenting to his death,[a] and guarding the clothes of those who were killing him.'

[21]Then He said to me, 'Depart, for I will send you far from here to the Gentiles.'"

Paul's Roman Citizenship

[22]And they listened to him until this word, and *then* they raised their voices and said, "Away with such a *fellow* from the earth, for he is not fit to live!" [23]Then, as they cried out and tore off *their* clothes and threw dust into the air, [24]the commander ordered him to be brought into the barracks, and said that he should be examined under scourging, so that he might know why they shouted so against him. [25]And as they bound him with thongs, Paul said to the centurion who stood by, "Is it lawful for you to scourge a man who is a Roman, and uncondemned?"

[26]When the centurion heard *that,* he went and told the commander, saying, "Take care what you do, for this man is a Roman."

[27]Then the commander came and said to him, "Tell me, are you a Roman?"

He said, "Yes."

[28]The commander answered, "With a large sum I obtained this citizenship."

And Paul said, "But I was born *a citizen.*"

[29]Then immediately those who were about to examine him withdrew from him; and the commander was also afraid after he found out that he was a Roman, and because he had bound him.

The Sanhedrin Divided

[30]The next day, because he wanted to know for certain why he was accused by the Jews, he released him from *his* bonds, and commanded the chief priests and all their council to appear, and brought Paul down and set him before them.

23 Then Paul, looking earnestly at the council, said, "Men *and* brethren, I have lived in all good conscience before God until this day." [2]And the high priest Ananias commanded those who stood by him to strike him on the mouth. [3]Then Paul said to him, "God will strike you, *you* whitewashed wall! For you sit to judge me

22:9 [a]NU-Text omits *and were afraid.*   **22:20** [a]NU-Text omits *to his death.*

according to the law, and do you command me to be struck contrary to the law?"

⁴And those who stood by said, "Do you revile God's high priest?"

⁵Then Paul said, "I did not know, brethren, that he was the high priest; for it is written, 'You shall not speak evil of a ruler of your people.' "ᵃ

⁶But when Paul perceived that one part were Sadducees and the other Pharisees, he cried out in the council, "Men and brethren, I am a Pharisee, the son of a Pharisee; concerning the hope and resurrection of the dead I am being judged!"

⁷And when he had said this, a dissension arose between the Pharisees and the Sadducees; and the assembly was divided. ⁸For Sadducees say that there is no resurrection—and no angel or spirit; but the Pharisees confess both. ⁹Then there arose a loud outcry. And the scribes of the Pharisees' party arose and protested, saying, "We find no evil in this man; but if a spirit or an angel has spoken to him, let us not fight against God."ᵃ

¹⁰Now when there arose a great dissension, the commander, fearing lest Paul might be pulled to pieces by them, commanded the soldiers to go down and take him by force from among them, and bring him into the barracks.

The Plot Against Paul

¹¹But the following night the Lord stood by him and said, "Be of good cheer, Paul; for as you have testified for Me in Jerusalem, so you must also bear witness at Rome."

¹²And when it was day, some of the Jews banded together and bound themselves under an oath, saying that they would neither eat nor drink till they had killed Paul. ¹³Now there were more than forty who had formed this conspiracy. ¹⁴They came to the chief priests and elders, and said, "We have bound ourselves under a great oath that we will eat nothing until we have killed Paul. ¹⁵Now you, therefore, together with the council, suggest to the commander that he be brought down to you tomorrow,ᵃ as though you were going to make further inquiries concerning him; but we are ready to kill him before he comes near."

¹⁶So when Paul's sister's son heard of their ambush, he went and entered the barracks and told Paul. ¹⁷Then Paul called one of the centurions to him and said, "Take this young man to the commander, for he has something to tell him." ¹⁸So he took him and brought him to the commander and said, "Paul the prisoner called me to him and asked me to bring this young man to you. He has something to say to you."

¹⁹Then the commander took him by the hand, went aside, and asked privately, "What is it that you have to tell me?"

²⁰And he said, "The Jews have agreed to ask that you bring Paul down to the council tomorrow, as though they were going to inquire more fully about him. ²¹But do not yield to them, for more than forty of them lie in wait for him, men who have bound themselves by an oath that they will neither eat nor drink till they have killed him; and now they are ready, waiting for the promise from you."

²²So the commander let the young man depart, and commanded him, "Tell no one that you have revealed these things to me."

Sent to Felix

²³And he called for two centurions, saying, "Prepare two hundred soldiers, seventy horsemen, and two hundred spearmen to go to Caesarea at the third hour of the night; ²⁴and provide mounts to set Paul on, and bring him safely to Felix the governor." ²⁵He wrote a letter in the following manner:

²⁶ Claudius Lysias,

To the most excellent governor Felix:

Greetings.

²⁷ This man was seized by the Jews and was about to be killed by them. Coming with the troops I rescued him, having learned that he was a Roman. ²⁸And when I wanted to know the reason they accused him, I brought

---

23:5 ᵃExodus 22:28   **23:9** ᵃNU-Text omits last clause and reads what if a spirit or an angel has spoken to him?   **23:15** ᵃNU-Text omits tomorrow.

him before their council. ²⁹I found out that he was accused concerning questions of their law, but had nothing charged against him deserving of death or chains. ³⁰And when it was told me that the Jews lay in wait for the man,ᵃ I sent him immediately to you, and also commanded his accusers to state before you the charges against him.

Farewell.

³¹Then the soldiers, as they were commanded, took Paul and brought *him* by night to Antipatris. ³²The next day they left the horsemen to go on with him, and returned to the barracks. ³³When they came to Caesarea and had delivered the letter to the governor, they also presented Paul to him. ³⁴And when the governor had read *it*, he asked what province he was from. And when he understood that *he was* from Cilicia, ³⁵he said, "I will hear you when your accusers also have come." And he commanded him to be kept in Herod's Praetorium.

Accused of Sedition

24 Now after five days Ananias the high priest came down with the elders and a certain orator *named* Tertullus. These gave evidence to the governor against Paul. ²And when he was called upon, Tertullus began his accusation, saying: "Seeing that through you we enjoy great peace, and prosperity is being brought to this nation by your foresight, ³we accept *it* always and in all places, most noble Felix, with all thankfulness. ⁴Nevertheless, not to be tedious to you any further, I beg you to hear, by your courtesy, a few words from us. ⁵For we have found this man a plague, a creator of dissension among all the Jews throughout the world, and a ringleader of the sect of the Nazarenes. ⁶He even tried to profane the temple, and we seized him,ᵃ and wanted to judge him according to our law. ⁷But the commander Lysias came by and with great violence took *him* out of our hands, ⁸commanding his accusers to come to you. By

examining him yourself you may ascertain all these things of which we accuse him." ⁹And the Jews also assented,ᵃ maintaining that these things were so.

The Defense Before Felix

¹⁰Then Paul, after the governor had nodded to him to speak, answered: "Inasmuch as I know that you have been for many years a judge of this nation, I do the more cheerfully answer for myself, ¹¹because you may ascertain that it is no more than twelve days since I went up to Jerusalem to worship. ¹²And they neither found me in the temple disputing with anyone nor inciting the crowd, either in the synagogues or in the city. ¹³Nor can they prove the things of which they now accuse me. ¹⁴But this I confess to you, that according to the Way which they call a sect, so I worship the God of my fathers, believing all things which are written in the Law and in the Prophets. ¹⁵I have hope in God, which they themselves also accept, that there will be a resurrection of *the* dead,ᵃ both of *the* just and *the* unjust. ¹⁶This *being* so, I myself always strive to have a conscience without offense toward God and men.

¹⁷"Now after many years I came to bring alms and offerings to my nation, ¹⁸in the midst of which some Jews from Asia found me purified in the temple, neither with a mob nor with tumult. ¹⁹They ought to have been here before you to object if they had anything against me. ²⁰Or else let those who are *here* themselves say if they found any wrongdoingᵃ in me while I stood before the council, ²¹unless *it is* for this one statement which I cried out, standing among them, 'Concerning the resurrection of the dead I am being judged by you this day.'"

Felix Procrastinates

²²But when Felix heard these things, having more accurate knowledge of *the* Way,

---

23:30 ᵃNU-Text reads *there would be a plot against the man.* **24:6** ᵃNU-Text ends the sentence here and omits the rest of verse 6, all of verse 7, and the first clause of verse 8. **24:9** ᵃNU-Text and M-Text read *joined the attack.* **24:15** ᵃNU-Text omits *of the dead.* **24:20** ᵃNU-Text and M-Text read *say what wrongdoing they found.*

he adjourned the proceedings and said, "When Lysias the commander comes down, I will make a decision on your case." 23So he commanded the centurion to keep Paul and to let *him* have liberty, and told him not to forbid any of his friends to provide for or visit him.

24And after some days, when Felix came with his wife Drusilla, who was Jewish, he sent for Paul and heard him concerning the faith in Christ. 25Now as he reasoned about righteousness, self-control, and the judgment to come, Felix was afraid and answered, "Go away for now; when I have a convenient time I will call for you." 26Meanwhile he also hoped that money would be given him by Paul, that he might release him.a Therefore he sent for him more often and conversed with him.

27But after two years Porcius Festus succeeded Felix; and Felix, wanting to do the Jews a favor, left Paul bound.

Paul Appeals to Caesar

25 Now when Festus had come to the province, after three days he went up from Caesarea to Jerusalem. 2Then the high priesta and the chief men of the Jews informed him against Paul; and they petitioned him, 3asking a favor against him, that he would summon him to Jerusalem—while *they* lay in ambush along the road to kill him. 4But Festus answered that Paul should be kept at Caesarea, and that he himself was going *there* shortly. 5"Therefore," he said, "let those who have authority among you go down with *me* and accuse this man, to see if there is any fault in him."

6And when he had remained among them more than ten days, he went down to Caesarea. And the next day, sitting on the judgment seat, he commanded Paul to be brought. 7When he had come, the Jews who had come down from Jerusalem stood about and laid many serious complaints against Paul, which they could not prove, 8while he answered for himself, "Neither against the law of the Jews, nor against the temple, nor against Caesar have I offended in anything at all."

9But Festus, wanting to do the Jews a favor, answered Paul and said, "Are you willing to go up to Jerusalem and there be judged before me concerning these things?"

10So Paul said, "I stand at Caesar's judgment seat, where I ought to be judged. To the Jews I have done no wrong, as you very well know. 11For if I am an offender, or have committed anything deserving of death, I do not object to dying; but if there is nothing in these things of which these men accuse me, no one can deliver me to them. I appeal to Caesar."

12Then Festus, when he had conferred with the council, answered, "You have appealed to Caesar? To Caesar you shall go!"

DEFENDER
"I appeal to Caesar."

ACTS 25:11

Resistance to Tyranny
In 1774, the Massachusetts Provincial Congress resolved:

> *Resistance to tyranny becomes the Christian and social duty of each individual. . . . Continue steadfast, and with a proper sense of your dependence on God, nobly defend those rights which heaven gave, and no man ought to take from us.*

Paul Before Agrippa

13And after some days King Agrippa and Bernice came to Caesarea to greet Festus. 14When they had been there many days, Festus laid Paul's case before the king, saying: "There is a certain man left a prisoner by Felix, 15about whom the chief priests and the elders of the Jews informed *me*, when I was in Jerusalem, asking for a judgment against him. 16To them I answered, 'It is not the custom of the Romans to deliver any man to destructiona before the accused meets the accusers face to face, and has opportunity to answer for himself concerning the charge against him.' 17Therefore when they had come together, without any

---

24:26 aNU-Text omits *that he might release him.*
25:2 aNU-Text reads *chief priests.*   25:16 aNU-Text omits *to destruction,* although it is implied.

delay, the next day I sat on the judgment seat and commanded the man to be brought in. ¹⁸When the accusers stood up, they brought no accusation against him of such things as I supposed, ¹⁹but had some questions against him about their own religion and about a certain Jesus, who had died, whom Paul affirmed to be alive. ²⁰And because I was uncertain of such questions, I asked whether he was willing to go to Jerusalem and there be judged concerning these matters. ²¹But when Paul appealed to be reserved for the decision of Augustus, I commanded him to be kept till I could send him to Caesar."

²²Then Agrippa said to Festus, "I also would like to hear the man myself."

"Tomorrow," he said, "you shall hear him."

²³So the next day, when Agrippa and Bernice had come with great pomp, and had entered the auditorium with the commanders and the prominent men of the city, at Festus' command Paul was brought in. ²⁴And Festus said: "King Agrippa and all the men who are here present with us, you see this man about whom the whole assembly of the Jews petitioned me, both at Jerusalem and here, crying out that he was not fit to live any longer. ²⁵But when I found that he had committed nothing deserving of death, and that he himself had appealed to Augustus, I decided to send him. ²⁶I have nothing certain to write to my lord concerning him. Therefore I have brought him out before you, and especially before you, King Agrippa, so that after the examination has taken place I may have something to write. ²⁷For it seems to me unreasonable to send a prisoner and not to specify the charges against him."

Paul's Early Life

26 Then Agrippa said to Paul, "You are permitted to speak for yourself."

So Paul stretched out his hand and answered for himself: ²"I think myself happy, King Agrippa, because today I shall answer for myself before you concerning all the things of which I am accused by the Jews, ³especially because you are expert in all customs and questions which have to do with the Jews. Therefore I beg you to hear me patiently.

⁴"My manner of life from my youth, which was spent from the beginning among my own nation at Jerusalem, all the Jews know. ⁵They knew me from the first, if they were willing to testify, that according to the strictest sect of our religion I lived a Pharisee. ⁶And now I stand and am judged for the hope of the promise made by God to our fathers. ⁷To this *promise* our twelve tribes, earnestly serving *God* night and day, hope to attain. For this hope's sake, King Agrippa, I am accused by the Jews. ⁸Why should it be thought incredible by you that God raises the dead?

⁹"Indeed, I myself thought I must do many things contrary to the name of Jesus of Nazareth. ¹⁰This I also did in Jerusalem, and many of the saints I shut up in prison, having received authority from the chief priests; and when they were put to death, I cast my vote against *them*. ¹¹And I punished them often in every synagogue and compelled *them* to blaspheme; and being exceedingly enraged against them, I persecuted *them* even to foreign cities.

Paul Recounts His Conversion

¹²"While thus occupied, as I journeyed to Damascus with authority and commission from the chief priests, ¹³at midday, O king, along the road I saw a light from heaven, brighter than the sun, shining around me and those who journeyed with me. ¹⁴And when we all had fallen to the ground, I heard a voice speaking to me and saying in the Hebrew language, 'Saul, Saul, why are you persecuting Me? *It is* hard for you to kick against the goads.' ¹⁵So I said, 'Who are You, Lord?' And He said, 'I am Jesus, whom you are persecuting. ¹⁶But rise and stand on your feet; for I have appeared to you for this purpose, to make you a minister and a witness both of the things which you have seen and of the things which I will yet reveal to you. ¹⁷I will deliver you from the *Jewish* people, as well as *from* the Gentiles, to whom I nowᵃ send you, ¹⁸to open their eyes, *in order* to turn *them* from

26:17 ᵃNU-Text and M-Text omit *now*.

darkness to light, and *from* the power of Satan to God, that they may receive forgiveness of sins and an inheritance among those who are sanctified by faith in Me.'

Paul's Post-Conversion Life

19"Therefore, King Agrippa, I was not disobedient to the heavenly vision, 20but declared first to those in Damascus and in Jerusalem, and throughout all the region of Judea, and *then* to the Gentiles, that they should repent, turn to God, and do works befitting repentance. 21For these reasons the Jews seized me in the temple and tried to kill *me.* 22Therefore, having obtained help from God, to this day I stand, witnessing both to small and great, saying no other things than those which the prophets and Moses said would come— 23that the Christ would suffer, that He would be the first to rise from the dead, and would proclaim light to the *Jewish* people and to the Gentiles."

Agrippa Parries Paul's Challenge

24Now as he thus made his defense, Festus said with a loud voice, "Paul, you are beside yourself! Much learning is driving you mad!"

25But he said, "I am not mad, most noble Festus, but speak the words of truth and reason. 26For the king, before whom I also speak freely, knows these things; for I am convinced that none of these things escapes his attention, since this thing was not done in a corner. 27King Agrippa, do you believe the prophets? I know that you do believe."

28Then Agrippa said to Paul, "You almost persuade me to become a Christian."

29And Paul said, "I would to God that not only you, but also all who hear me today, might become both almost and altogether such as I am, except for these chains."

30When he had said these things, the king stood up, as well as the governor and Bernice and those who sat with them; 31and when they had gone aside, they talked among themselves, saying, "This man is doing nothing deserving of death or chains."

32Then Agrippa said to Festus, "This man might have been set free if he had not appealed to Caesar."

The Voyage to Rome Begins

27 And when it was decided that we should sail to Italy, they delivered Paul and some other prisoners to *one* named Julius, a centurion of the Augustan Regiment. 2So, entering a ship of Adramyttium, we put to sea, meaning to sail along the coasts of Asia. Aristarchus, a Macedonian of Thessalonica, was with us. 3And the next *day* we landed at Sidon. And Julius treated Paul kindly and gave *him* liberty to go to his friends and receive care. 4When we had put to sea from there, we sailed under *the shelter of* Cyprus, because the winds were contrary. 5And when we had sailed over the sea which is off Cilicia and Pamphylia, we came to Myra, *a city* of Lycia. 6There the centurion found an Alexandrian ship sailing to Italy, and he put us on board.

7When we had sailed slowly many days, and arrived with difficulty off Cnidus, the wind not permitting us to proceed, we sailed under *the shelter of* Crete off Salmone. 8Passing it with difficulty, we came to a place called Fair Havens, near the city *of* Lasea.

Paul's Warning Ignored

9Now when much time had been spent, and sailing was now dangerous because the Fast was already over, Paul advised them, 10saying, "Men, I perceive that this voyage will end with disaster and much loss, not only of the cargo and ship, but also our lives." 11Nevertheless the centurion was more persuaded by the helmsman and the owner of the ship than by the things spoken by Paul. 12And because the harbor was not suitable to winter in, the majority advised to set sail from there also, if by any means they could reach Phoenix, a harbor of Crete opening toward the southwest and northwest, *and* winter *there.*

In the Tempest

13When the south wind blew softly, supposing that they had obtained *their* desire, putting out to sea, they sailed close by Crete. 14But not long after, a tempestuous head wind arose, called Euroclydon.ᵃ 15So

---

27:14 ᵃNU-Text reads *Euraquilon.*

when the ship was caught, and could not head into the wind, we let *her* drive. [16]And running under *the shelter of* an island called Clauda,[a] we secured the skiff with difficulty. [17]When they had taken it on board, they used cables to undergird the ship; and fearing lest they should run aground on the Syrtis[a] *Sands*, they struck sail and so were driven. [18]And because we were exceedingly tempest-tossed, the next *day* they lightened the ship. [19]On the third *day* we threw the ship's tackle overboard with our own hands. [20]Now when neither sun nor stars appeared for many days, and no small tempest beat on *us*, all hope that we would be saved was finally given up.

[21]But after long abstinence from food, then Paul stood in the midst of them and said, "Men, you should have listened to me, and not have sailed from Crete and incurred this disaster and loss. [22]And now I urge you to take heart, for there will be no loss of life among you, but only of the ship. [23]For there stood by me this night an angel of the God to whom I belong and whom I serve, [24]saying, 'Do not be afraid, Paul; you must be brought before Caesar; and

indeed God has granted you all those who sail with you.' [25]Therefore take heart, men, for I believe God that it will be just as it was told me. [26]However, we must run aground on a certain island."

[27]Now when the fourteenth night had come, as we were driven up and down in the Adriatic *Sea*, about midnight the sailors sensed that they were drawing near some land. [28]And they took soundings and found *it* to be twenty fathoms; and when they had gone a little farther, they took soundings again and found *it* to be fifteen fathoms. [29]Then, fearing lest we should run aground on the rocks, they dropped four anchors from the stern, and prayed for day to come. [30]And as the sailors were seeking to escape from the ship, when they had let down the skiff into the sea, under pretense of putting out anchors from the prow, [31]Paul said to the centurion and the soldiers, "Unless these men stay in the ship, you cannot be saved." [32]Then the soldiers cut away the ropes of the skiff and let it fall off.

27:16 [a]NU-Text reads *Cauda.*   **27:17** [a]M-Text reads *Syrtes.*

SELFLESS

But the centurion . . . kept them from their purpose. . . .

ACTS 27:43

A POLICEMAN'S PRAYER

When I start my tour of duty, God,
Wherever crime may be,
As I walk the darkened streets alone,
Let me be close to thee.

Please give me understanding
With both the young and old.
Let me listen with attention
Until their story's told.

Let me never make a judgment
In a rash or callous way,
But let me hold my patience . . .
Let each man have his say.

Lord, if some dark and dreary night,
I must give my life,
Lord, with your everlasting love
protect my children and my wife.

Author Unknown

[33]And as day was about to dawn, Paul implored *them* all to take food, saying, "Today is the fourteenth day you have waited and continued without food, and eaten nothing. [34]Therefore I urge you to take nourishment, for this is for your survival, since not a hair will fall from the head of any of you." [35]And when he had said these things, he took bread and gave thanks to God in the presence of them all; and when he had broken *it* he began to eat. [36]Then they were all encouraged, and also took food themselves. [37]And in all we were two hundred and seventy-six persons on the ship. [38]So when they had eaten enough, they lightened the ship and threw out the wheat into the sea.

Shipwrecked on Malta

[39]When it was day, they did not recognize the land; but they observed a bay with a beach, onto which they planned to run the ship if possible. [40]And they let go the anchors and left *them* in the sea, meanwhile loosing the rudder ropes; and they hoisted the mainsail to the wind and made for shore. [41]But striking a place where two seas met, they ran the ship aground; and the prow stuck fast and remained immovable, but the stern was being broken up by the violence of the waves.

[42]And the soldiers' plan was to kill the prisoners, lest any of them should swim away and escape. [43]But the centurion, wanting to save Paul, kept them from *their* purpose, and commanded that those who could swim should jump *overboard* first and get to land, [44]and the rest, some on boards and some on *parts* of the ship. And so it was that they all escaped safely to land.

Paul's Ministry on Malta

28 Now when they had escaped, they then found out that the island was called Malta. [2]And the natives showed us unusual kindness; for they kindled a fire and made us all welcome, because of the rain that was falling and because of the cold. [3]But when Paul had gathered a bundle of sticks and laid *them* on the fire, a viper came out because of the heat, and fastened on his hand. [4]So when the natives saw the creature hanging from his hand,

they said to one another, "No doubt this man is a murderer, whom, though he has escaped the sea, yet justice does not allow to live." [5]But he shook off the creature into the fire and suffered no harm. [6]However, they were expecting that he would swell up or suddenly fall down dead. But after they had looked for a long time and saw no harm come to him, they changed their minds and said that he was a god.

[7]In that region there was an estate of the leading citizen of the island, whose name was Publius, who received us and entertained us courteously for three days. [8]And it happened that the father of Publius lay sick of a fever and dysentery. Paul went in to him and prayed, and he laid his hands on him and healed him. [9]So when this was done, the rest of those on the island who had diseases also came and were healed. [10]They also honored us in many ways; and when we departed, they provided such things as were necessary.

Arrival at Rome

[11]After three months we sailed in an Alexandrian ship whose figurehead was the Twin Brothers, which had wintered at the island. [12]And landing at Syracuse, we stayed three days. [13]From there we circled round and reached Rhegium. And after one day the south wind blew; and the next day we came to Puteoli, [14]where we found brethren, and were invited to stay with them seven days. And so we went toward Rome. [15]And from there, when the brethren heard about us, they came to meet us as far as Appii Forum and Three Inns. When Paul saw them, he thanked God and took courage.

[16]Now when we came to Rome, the centurion delivered the prisoners to the captain of the guard; but Paul was permitted to dwell by himself with the soldier who guarded him.

Paul's Ministry at Rome

[17]And it came to pass after three days that Paul called the leaders of the Jews together. So when they had come together, he said to them: "Men *and* brethren, though I have done nothing against our people or the customs of our fathers, yet I

was delivered as a prisoner from Jerusalem into the hands of the Romans, [18]who, when they had examined me, wanted to let *me* go, because there was no cause for putting me to death. [19]But when the Jews[a] spoke against *it*, I was compelled to appeal to Caesar, not that I had anything of which to accuse my nation. [20]For this reason therefore I have called for you, to see *you* and speak with *you*, because for the hope of Israel I am bound with this chain."

[21]Then they said to him, "We neither received letters from Judea concerning you, nor have any of the brethren who came reported or spoken any evil of you. [22]But we desire to hear from you what you think; for concerning this sect, we know that it is spoken against everywhere."

[23]So when they had appointed him a day, many came to him at *his* lodging, to whom he explained and solemnly testified of the kingdom of God, persuading them concerning Jesus from both the Law of Moses and the Prophets, from morning till evening. [24]And some were persuaded by the things which were spoken, and some disbelieved. [25]So when they did not agree among themselves, they departed after Paul had said one word: "The Holy Spirit spoke rightly through Isaiah the prophet to our[a] fathers, [26]saying,

'Go to this people and say:
"Hearing you will hear, and shall not
  understand;
And seeing you will see, and not
  perceive;
[27] For the hearts of this people have
  grown dull.
Their ears are hard of hearing,
And their eyes they have closed,
Lest they should see with their eyes
  and hear with their ears,
Lest they should understand with their
  hearts and turn,
So that I should heal them." '[a]

[28]"Therefore let it be known to you that the salvation of God has been sent to the Gentiles, and they will hear it!" [29]And when he had said these words, the Jews departed and had a great dispute among themselves.[a]

[30]Then Paul dwelt two whole years in his own rented house, and received all who came to him, [31]preaching the kingdom of God and teaching the things which concern the Lord Jesus Christ with all confidence, no one forbidding him.

28:19 [a]That is, the ruling authorities   **28:25** [a]NU-Text reads *your*.   **28:27** [a]Isaiah 6:9, 10   **28:29** [a]NU-Text omits this verse.

ROMANS

Author: Paul

When Written: Around A.D. 57

Theme: The Righteousness of God

Key Verses: Romans 1:16, 17—For I am not ashamed of the gospel of Christ, for it is the power of God to salvation for everyone who believes, for the Jew first and also for the Greek. For in it the righteousness of God is revealed from faith to faith; as it is written, "The just shall live by faith."

Key Chapters: Romans 6 through 8—These chapters contain the foundational teachings on the spiritual life. They answer questions on how to be delivered from sin, how to live a balanced life under grace, and how to live in the power of the Holy Spirit.

While the four Gospels present the words and works of Jesus Christ, Romans explores the significance of His sacrificial death. Using a question-and-answer format, Paul records the most systematic presentation of doctrine in the Bible and balances it with practical exhortation. The Good News at work in the life of a believer results in a life to be lived in righteousness reflective of the free grace of God.

In his famous address, "The Bible and Progress," delivered in Denver, Colorado, in 1911, President Woodrow Wilson told his audience, "America was born a Christian nation. America was born to exemplify that devotion to the elements of righteousness which are derived from the revelations of Holy Scripture." Out of the foundation laid by the Declaration of Independence and Constitution, America has a life to be lived in righteousness, or as presidential candidate Jimmy Carter stated in 1976, "We have a responsibility to try to shape government so that it does exemplify the will of God."

ROMANS

Greeting

1 Paul, a bondservant of Jesus Christ, called *to be* an apostle, separated to the gospel of God ²which He promised before through His prophets in the Holy Scriptures, ³concerning His Son Jesus Christ our Lord, who was born of the seed of David according to the flesh, ⁴*and* declared *to be* the Son of God with power according to the Spirit of holiness, by the resurrection from the dead. ⁵Through Him we have received grace and apostleship for obedience to the faith among all nations for His name, ⁶among whom you also are the called of Jesus Christ;

⁷To all who are in Rome, beloved of God, called *to be* saints:

Grace to you and peace from God our Father and the Lord Jesus Christ.

Desire to Visit Rome

⁸First, I thank my God through Jesus Christ for you all, that your faith is spoken of throughout the whole world. ⁹For God is my witness, whom I serve with my spirit in the gospel of His Son, that without ceasing I make mention of you always in my prayers, ¹⁰making request if, by some means, now at last I may find a way in the will of God to come to you. ¹¹For I long to see you, that I may impart to you some spiritual gift, so that you may be established— ¹²that is, that I may be encouraged together with you by the mutual faith both of you and me. ¹³Now I do not want you to be unaware, brethren, that I often planned to come to you (but was hindered until now), that I might have some fruit among you also, just as among the other Gentiles. ¹⁴I am a debtor both to Greeks and to barbarians, both to wise and to unwise. ¹⁵So, as much as is in me, *I am* ready to preach the gospel to you who are in Rome also.

The Just Live by Faith

¹⁶For I am not ashamed of the gospel of Christ,ᵃ for it is the power of God to salvation for everyone who believes, for the Jew first and also for the Greek. ¹⁷For in it the righteousness of God is revealed from faith to faith; as it is written, *"The just shall live by faith."*ᵃ

God's Wrath on Unrighteousness

¹⁸For the wrath of God is revealed from heaven against all ungodliness and unrighteousness of men, who suppress the truth in unrighteousness, ¹⁹because what may be known of God is manifest in them, for God has shown *it* to them. ²⁰For since the creation of the world His invisible *attributes* are clearly seen, being understood by the things that are made, *even* His eternal power and Godhead, so that they are without excuse, ²¹because, although they knew God, they did not glorify *Him* as God, nor were thankful, but became futile in their thoughts, and their foolish hearts were darkened. ²²Professing to be wise, they became fools, ²³and changed the glory of the incorruptible God into an image made like corruptible man—and birds and four-footed animals and creeping things.

²⁴Therefore God also gave them up to uncleanness, in the lusts of their hearts, to dishonor their bodies among themselves, ²⁵who exchanged the truth of God for the lie, and worshiped and served the creature rather than the Creator, who is blessed forever. Amen.

²⁶For this reason God gave them up to vile passions. For even their women exchanged the natural use for what is against nature. ²⁷Likewise also the men, leaving the natural use of the woman, burned in their lust for one another, men with men committing what is shameful,

---

1:16 ᵃNU-Text omits *of Christ.*
1:17 ᵃHabakkuk 2:4

The LAWS of NATURE AND of NATURE'S GOD

The first paragraph of the Declaration of Independence sets the stage for the American Revolution and its absolute reliance on the laws of God:

> When in the Course of human events, it becomes necessary for one people to dissolve the political bands which have connected them with one another, and to assume among the powers of the earth, the separate and equal station to which the Laws of Nature and of Nature's God entitles them, a decent respect to the opinions of mankind requires that they should declare the causes which impel them to the separation.

The "Laws of Nature and of Nature's God" had been defined by historic legal writers, such as Sir William Blackstone and others, as the laws that God, the Creator of the universe, had established for the governance of people, nations, and nature. *Blackstone's Commentaries on the Law,* which had become the primary law book of the Founding Fathers, explained "the laws of nature" as the will of God for man, which can be ascertained by people through an examination of God's creation, the text of the Bible, and to a certain degree, instinct or reason. Blackstone stated:

> Man, considered as a creature, must necessarily be subject to the laws of his Creator, for he is entirely a dependent being. . . . And consequently, as man depends absolutely upon his Maker for everything, it is necessary that he should in all points conform to his Maker's will. This will of his Maker is called the law of nature. . . . This law of nature, being coeval [coexistent] with mankind and dictated by God Himself, is of course superior in obligation to any other. It is binding over all the globe, in all countries, and at all times; no human laws are of any validity, if contrary to this. . . .
>
> And if our reason were always . . . clear and perfect . . . the task would be pleasant and easy; we should need no other guide but this [the law of nature]. But every man now finds the contrary in his own experience; that his reason is corrupt, and his understanding full of ignorance and error. This has given manifold occasion for the benign interposition of Divine Providence; which . . . hath been pleased, at sundry times and in diverse manners, to discover and enforce its laws by an immediate and direct revelation. The doctrines thus delivered we call the revealed or divine law, and they are to be found only in the Holy Scriptures. . . .
>
> Upon these two foundations, the law of nature and the law of revelation, depend all human laws; that is to say, no human laws should be suffered to contradict these.

and receiving in themselves the penalty of their error which was due.

[28]And even as they did not like to retain God in *their* knowledge, God gave them over to a debased mind, to do those things which are not fitting; [29]being filled with all unrighteousness, sexual immorality,[a] wickedness, covetousness, maliciousness; full of envy, murder, strife, deceit, evil-mindedness; *they are* whisperers, [30]backbiters, haters of God, violent, proud, boasters, inventors of evil things, disobedient to parents, [31]undiscerning, untrustworthy, unloving, unforgiving,[a] unmerciful; [32]who, knowing the righteous judgment of God, that those who practice such things are deserving of death, not only do the same but also approve of those who practice them.

God's Righteous Judgment

2 Therefore you are inexcusable, O man, whoever you are who judge, for in whatever you judge another you condemn yourself; for you who judge practice the same things. [2]But we know that the judgment of God is according to truth against those who practice such things. [3]And do you think this, O man, you who judge those practicing such things, and doing the same, that you will escape the judgment of God? [4]Or do you despise the riches of His goodness, forbearance, and longsuffering, not knowing that the goodness of God leads you to repentance? [5]But in accordance with your hardness and your impenitent heart you are treasuring up for yourself wrath in the day of wrath and revelation of the righteous judgment of God, [6]who *"will render to each one according to his deeds"*:[a] [7]eternal life to those who by patient continuance in doing good seek for glory, honor, and immortality; [8]but to those who are self-seeking and do not obey the truth, but obey unrighteousness—indignation and wrath, [9]tribulation and anguish, on every soul of man who does evil, of the Jew first and also of the Greek; [10]but glory, honor, and peace to everyone who works what is good, to the Jew first and also to the Greek. [11]For there is no partiality with God.

[12]For as many as have sinned without law will also perish without law, and as many as have sinned in the law will be judged by the law [13](for not the hearers of the law *are* just in the sight of God, but the doers of the law will be justified; [14]for when Gentiles, who do not have the law, by nature do the things in the law, these, although not having the law, are a law to themselves, [15]who show the work of the law written in their hearts, their conscience also bearing witness, and between themselves *their* thoughts accusing or else excusing *them*) [16]in the day when God will judge the secrets of men by Jesus Christ, according to my gospel.

The Jews Guilty as the Gentiles

[17]Indeed[a] you are called a Jew, and rest on the law, and make your boast in God, [18]and know *His* will, and approve the things that are excellent, being instructed out of the law, [19]and are confident that you yourself are a guide to the blind, a light to those who are in darkness, [20]an instructor of the foolish, a teacher of babes, having the form of knowledge and truth in the law. [21]You, therefore, who teach another, do you not teach yourself? You who preach that a man should not steal, do you steal? [22]You who say, "Do not commit adultery," do you commit adultery? You who abhor idols, do you rob temples? [23]You who make your boast in the law, do you dishonor God through breaking the law? [24]For *"the name of God is blasphemed among the Gentiles because of you,"*[a] as it is written.

Circumcision of No Avail

[25]For circumcision is indeed profitable if you keep the law; but if you are a breaker of the law, your circumcision has become uncircumcision. [26]Therefore, if an uncircumcised man keeps the righteous requirements of the law, will not his uncircumcision be counted as circumcision? [27]And will not the physically uncircumcised, if he fulfills the law, judge you who, *even* with *your* written code and circumcision, *are* a transgressor of

---

1:29 [a]NU-Text omits *sexual immorality*. **1:31** [a]NU-Text omits *unforgiving*. **2:6** [a]Psalm 62:12; Proverbs 24:12 **2:17** [a]NU-Text reads *But if*. **2:24** [a]Isaiah 52:5; Ezekiel 36:22

the law? [28]For he is not a Jew who *is one* outwardly, nor *is* circumcision that which *is* outward in the flesh; [29]but *he is* a Jew who *is one* inwardly; and circumcision *is that* of the heart, in the Spirit, not in the letter; whose praise *is* not from men but from God.

God's Judgment Defended

3 What advantage then has the Jew, or what *is* the profit of circumcision? [2]Much in every way! Chiefly because to them were committed the oracles of God. [3]For what if some did not believe? Will their unbelief make the faithfulness of God without effect? [4]Certainly not! Indeed, let God be true but every man a liar. As it is written:

"*That You may be justified in Your words, And may overcome when You are judged.*"[a]

[5]But if our unrighteousness demonstrates the righteousness of God, what shall we say? *Is* God unjust who inflicts wrath? (I speak as a man.) [6]Certainly not! For then how will God judge the world? [7]For if the truth of God has increased through my lie to His glory, why am I also still judged as a sinner? [8]And *why* not *say,* "Let us do evil that good may come"?—as we are slanderously reported and as some affirm that we say. Their condemnation is just.

All Have Sinned

[9]What then? Are we better *than they?* Not at all. For we have previously charged both Jews and Greeks that they are all under sin. [10]As it is written:

"*There is none righteous, no, not one;*
[11] *There is none who understands; There is none who seeks after God.*
[12] *They have all turned aside; They have together become unprofitable; There is none who does good, no, not one.*"[a]
[13] "*Their throat is an open tomb; With their tongues they have practiced deceit*";[a]

"*The poison of asps is under their lips*";[b]
[14] "*Whose mouth is full of cursing and bitterness.*"[a]
[15] "*Their feet are swift to shed blood;*
[16] *Destruction and misery are in their ways;*
[17] *And the way of peace they have not known.*"[a]
[18] "*There is no fear of God before their eyes.*"[a]

[19]Now we know that whatever the law says, it says to those who are under the law, that every mouth may be stopped, and all the world may become guilty before God. [20]Therefore by the deeds of the law no flesh will be justified in His sight, for by the law *is* the knowledge of sin.

God's Righteousness Through Faith

[21]But now the righteousness of God apart from the law is revealed, being witnessed by the Law and the Prophets, [22]even the righteousness of God, through faith in Jesus Christ, to all and on all[a] who believe. For there is no difference; [23]for all have sinned and fall short of the glory of God, [24]being justified freely by His grace through the redemption that is in Christ Jesus, [25]whom God set forth *as* a propitiation by His blood, through faith, to demonstrate His righteousness, because in His forbearance God had passed over the sins that were previously committed, [26]to demonstrate at the present time His righteousness, that He might be just and the justifier of the one who has faith in Jesus.

Boasting Excluded

[27]Where *is* boasting then? It is excluded. By what law? Of works? No, but by the law of faith. [28]Therefore we conclude that a man is justified by faith apart from the deeds of the law. [29]Or *is* He the God of the Jews only? *Is He* not also the God of the Gentiles? Yes, of the Gentiles also, [30]since *there is* one

---

3:4 [a]Psalm 51:4   **3:12** [a]Psalms 14:1–3; 53:1–3;
Ecclesiastes 7:20   **3:13** [a]Psalm 5:9 [b]Psalm 140:3
3:14 [a]Psalm 10:7   **3:17** [a]Isaiah 59:7, 8
3:18 [a]Psalm 36:1   **3:22** [a]NU-Text omits *and on all.*

God who will justify the circumcised by faith and the uncircumcised through faith. [31]Do we then make void the law through faith? Certainly not! On the contrary, we establish the law.

Abraham Justified by Faith

4 What then shall we say that Abraham our father has found according to the flesh?[a] [2]For if Abraham was justified by works, he has *something* to boast about, but not before God. [3]For what does the Scripture say? *"Abraham believed God, and it was accounted to him for righteousness."*[a] [4]Now to him who works, the wages are not counted as grace but as debt.

David Celebrates the Same Truth

[5]But to him who does not work but believes on Him who justifies the ungodly, his faith is accounted for righteousness, [6]just as David also describes the blessedness of the man to whom God imputes righteousness apart from works:

[7]   *"Blessed are those whose lawless deeds*
       are forgiven,
       And whose sins are covered;
[8]   *Blessed is the man to whom the Lord*
       shall not impute sin."[a]

Abraham Justified Before Circumcision

[9]*Does* this blessedness then *come* upon the circumcised *only,* or upon the uncircumcised also? For we say that faith was accounted to Abraham for righteousness. [10]How then was it accounted? While he was circumcised, or uncircumcised? Not while

---

4:1 [a]Or *Abraham our (fore)father according to the flesh has found?*   **4:3** [a]Genesis 15:6   **4:8** [a]Psalm 32:1, 2

LEADERSHIP

    ... was strengthened in faith,
    giving glory to God. ...
       Romans 4:20

Henry John Heinz

A LEGACY OF SUCCESS

At age six, Henry John Heinz (1844–1919) started helping his mother tend a small garden behind the family home. At twelve, he was working three and one-half acres of garden, using a horse and cart for his three-times-a-week deliveries to grocery stores in Pittsburgh. He went on to found his own company and named it 57 Varieties. H. J. Heinz Company was incorporated in 1905, which today sells more than 1,300 products worldwide ranging from ketchup to baby food.

Henry Heinz was deeply involved in the promotion of the Sunday school in Pittsburgh and around the world. His company was noted for pioneering safe and sanitary food preparation and for being ahead of its time in employee relations, providing free medical benefits and swimming and gymnasium facilities. Women held positions of larger responsibilities in his business, including making them supervisors. Heinz earned his reputation for enhancing the working and living conditions of his workers.

In his will, Heinz said, "I desire to set forth at the very beginning of this will, as the most important item in it, a confession of my faith in Jesus Christ as my Savior. I also desire to bear witness to the fact that throughout my life, in which there were unusual joys and sorrows, I have been wonderfully sustained by my faith in God through Jesus Christ. This legacy was left me by my consecrated mother, a woman of strong faith, and to it I attribute any success I have attained."

circumcised, but while uncircumcised. [11]And he received the sign of circumcision, a seal of the righteousness of the faith which *he had while still* uncircumcised, that he might be the father of all those who believe, though they are uncircumcised, that righteousness might be imputed to them also, [12]and the father of circumcision to those who not only *are* of the circumcision, but who also walk in the steps of the faith which our father Abraham *had while still* uncircumcised.

The Promise Granted Through Faith

[13]For the promise that he would be the heir of the world *was* not to Abraham or to his seed through the law, but through the righteousness of faith. [14]For if those who are of the law *are* heirs, faith is made void and the promise made of no effect, [15]because the law brings about wrath; for where there is no law *there is* no transgression.

[16]Therefore *it is* of faith that *it might be* according to grace, so that the promise might be sure to all the seed, not only to those who are of the law, but also to those who are of the faith of Abraham, who is the father of us all [17](as it is written, *"I have made you a father of many nations"*[a]) in the presence of Him whom he believed—God, who gives life to the dead and calls those things which do not exist as though they did; [18]who, contrary to hope, in hope believed, so that he became the father of many nations, according to what was spoken, *"So shall your descendants be."*[a] [19]And not being weak in faith, he did not consider his own body, already dead (since he was about a hundred years old), and the deadness of Sarah's womb. [20]He did not waver at the promise of God through unbelief, but was strengthened in faith, giving glory to God, [21]and being fully convinced that what He had promised He was also able to perform. [22]And therefore *"it was accounted to him for righteousness."*[a]

[23]Now it was not written for his sake alone that it was imputed to him, [24]but also for us. It shall be imputed to us who believe in Him who raised up Jesus our Lord from the dead, [25]who was delivered up because of our offenses, and was raised because of our justification.

Faith Triumphs in Trouble

5 Therefore, having been justified by faith, we have[a] peace with God through our Lord Jesus Christ, [2]through whom also we have access by faith into this grace in which we stand, and rejoice in hope of the glory of God. [3]And not only *that,* but we also glory in tribulations, knowing that tribulation produces perseverance; [4]and perseverance, character; and character, hope. [5]Now hope does not disappoint, because the love of God has been poured out in our hearts by the Holy Spirit who was given to us.

Christ in Our Place

[6]For when we were still without strength, in due time Christ died for the ungodly. [7]For scarcely for a righteous man will one die; yet perhaps for a good man someone would even dare to die. [8]But God demonstrates His own love toward us, in that while we were still sinners, Christ died for us. [9]Much more then, having now been justified by His blood, we shall be saved from wrath through Him. [10]For if when we were enemies we were reconciled to God through the death of His Son, much more, having been reconciled, we shall be saved by His life. [11]And not only *that,* but we also rejoice in God through our Lord Jesus Christ, through whom we have now received the reconciliation.

Death in Adam, Life in Christ

[12]Therefore, just as through one man sin entered the world, and death through sin, and thus death spread to all men, because all sinned— [13](For until the law sin was in the world, but sin is not imputed when there is no law. [14]Nevertheless death reigned from Adam to Moses, even over those who had not sinned according to the likeness of the transgression of Adam, who is a type of Him who was to come. [15]But the free gift *is* not like the offense. For if by the one man's offense many died, much more the grace of God and the gift by the grace of the one Man, Jesus Christ, abounded to

---

4:17 [a]Genesis 17:5   **4:18** [a]Genesis 15:5
4:22 [a]Genesis 15:6   **5:1** [a]Another ancient reading is, *let us have peace.*

many. [16]And the gift *is* not like *that which came* through the one who sinned. For the judgment *which came* from one *offense resulted* in condemnation, but the free gift *which came* from many offenses *resulted* in justification. [17]For if by the one man's offense death reigned through the one, much more those who receive abundance of grace and of the gift of righteousness will reign in life through the One, Jesus Christ.)

[18]Therefore, as through one man's offense *judgment came* to all men, resulting in condemnation, even so through one Man's righteous act *the free gift came* to all men, resulting in justification of life. [19]For as by one man's disobedience many were made sinners, so also by one Man's obedience many will be made righteous.

[20]Moreover the law entered that the offense might abound. But where sin abounded, grace abounded much more, [21]so that as sin reigned in death, even so grace might reign through righteousness to eternal life through Jesus Christ our Lord.

Dead to Sin, Alive to God

6 What shall we say then? Shall we continue in sin that grace may abound? [2]Certainly not! How shall we who died to sin live any longer in it? [3]Or do you not know that as many of us as were baptized into Christ Jesus were baptized into His death? [4]Therefore we were buried with Him through baptism into death, that just as Christ was raised from the dead by the glory of the Father, even so we also should walk in newness of life.

[5]For if we have been united together in the likeness of His death, certainly we also shall be *in the likeness* of *His* resurrection, [6]knowing this, that our old man was crucified with *Him,* that the body of sin might be done away with, that we should no longer be slaves of sin. [7]For he who died has been freed from sin. [8]Now if we died with Christ, we believe that we shall also live with Him, [9]knowing that Christ, having been raised from the dead, dies no more. Death no longer has dominion over Him. [10]For *the death* that He died, He died to sin once for all; but *the life* that He lives, He lives to God. [11]Likewise you also, reckon yourselves to be dead indeed to sin, but alive to God in Christ Jesus our Lord.

[12]Therefore do not let sin reign in your mortal body, that you should obey it in its lusts. [13]And do not present your members *as* instruments of unrighteousness to sin, but present yourselves to God as being alive from the dead, and your members *as* instruments of righteousness to God. [14]For sin shall not have dominion over you, for you are not under law but under grace.

From Slaves of Sin to Slaves of God

[15]What then? Shall we sin because we are not under law but under grace? Certainly not! [16]Do you not know that to whom you present yourselves slaves to obey, you are that one's slaves whom you obey, whether of sin *leading* to death, or of obedience *leading* to righteousness? [17]But God be thanked that *though* you were slaves of sin, yet you obeyed from the heart that form of doctrine to which you were delivered. [18]And having been set free from sin, you became slaves of righteousness. [19]I speak in human *terms* because of the weakness of your flesh. For just as you presented your members *as* slaves of uncleanness, and of lawlessness *leading* to *more* lawlessness, so now present your members *as* slaves *of* righteousness for holiness.

[20]For when you were slaves of sin, you were free in regard to righteousness. [21]What fruit did you have then in the things of which you are now ashamed? For the end of those things *is* death. [22]But now having been set free from sin, and having become slaves of God, you have your fruit to holiness, and the end, everlasting life. [23]For the wages of sin *is* death, but the gift of God *is* eternal life in Christ Jesus our Lord.

Freed from the Law

7 Or do you not know, brethren (for I speak to those who know the law), that the law has dominion over a man as long as he lives? [2]For the woman who has a husband is bound by the law to *her* husband as long as he lives. But if the husband dies, she is released from the law of *her* husband. [3]So then if, while *her* husband lives, she marries another man, she

FREEDOM

For the law of the Spirit of life in Christ Jesus has made me free....

ROMANS 8:2

THE DECLARATION OF INDEPENDENCE

The Declaration of Independence, considered the founding document of the United States, is an act of the Second Continental Congress, adopted on July 4, 1776, which declared that the 13 American colonies were "Free and Independent States" and that "all political connection between them and the State of Great Britain, is and ought to be totally dissolved." In it, our Founding Fathers were quick to acknowledge God as the source of our rights, and they were wise to not separate God from state. The placement of Judeo-Christian values and biblical morality into our founding documents and laws was clearly intentional. As Benjamin Rush, one of the Founders, said, "Without [religion] there can be no virtue, and without virtue there can be no liberty, and liberty is the object and life of all republican governments."

When in the Course of human events, it becomes necessary for one people to dissolve the political bands which have connected them with another, and to assume among the powers of the earth, the separate and equal station to which the Laws of Nature and of Nature's God entitle them. . . .

We hold these truths to be self-evident, that all men are created equal, that they are endowed by their Creator with certain unalienable Rights, that among these are Life, Liberty and the pursuit of Happiness. That to secure these rights, Governments are instituted among Men, deriving their just Powers from the consent of the governed, — That whenever any Form of Government becomes destructive of these ends, it is the Right of the People to alter or to abolish it, and to institute new Government, laying its foundation on such principles and organizing its powers in such form, as to them shall seem most likely to effect their Safety and Happiness. . . .

We, therefore, the Representatives of the united States of America, in General Congress, Assembled, appealing to the Supreme Judge of the world for the rectitude of our intentions . . . And for the support of this Declaration, with a firm reliance on the protection of Divine Providence, we mutually pledge to each other our Lives, our Fortunes and our sacred Honor.

will be called an adulteress; but if her husband dies, she is free from that law, so that she is no adulteress, though she has married another man. ⁴Therefore, my brethren, you also have become dead to the law through the body of Christ, that you may be married to another—to Him who was raised from the dead, that we should bear fruit to God. ⁵For when we were in the flesh, the sinful passions which were aroused by the law were at work in our members to bear fruit to death. ⁶But now we have been delivered from the law, having died to what we were held by, so that we should serve in the newness of the Spirit and not *in* the oldness of the letter.

Sin's Advantage in the Law

⁷What shall we say then? *Is* the law sin? Certainly not! On the contrary, I would not have known sin except through the law. For I would not have known covetousness unless the law had said, *"You shall not covet."*ᵃ ⁸But sin, taking opportunity by the commandment, produced in me all *manner of* evil desire. For apart from the law sin *was* dead. ⁹I was alive once without the law, but when the commandment came, sin revived and I died. ¹⁰And the commandment, which *was* to *bring* life, I found to *bring* death. ¹¹For sin, taking occasion by the commandment, deceived me, and by it killed *me.* ¹²Therefore the law *is* holy, and the commandment holy and just and good.

Law Cannot Save from Sin

¹³Has then what is good become death to me? Certainly not! But sin, that it might appear sin, was producing death in me through what is good, so that sin through the commandment might become exceedingly sinful. ¹⁴For we know that the law is spiritual, but I am carnal, sold under sin. ¹⁵For what I am doing, I do not understand. For what I will to do, that I do not practice; but what I hate, that I do. ¹⁶If, then, I do what I will not to do, I agree with the law that *it is* good. ¹⁷But now, *it is* no longer I who do it, but sin that dwells in me. ¹⁸For I know that in me (that is, in my flesh) nothing good dwells; for to will is present with me, but *how* to perform what

is good I do not find. ¹⁹For the good that I will *to do,* I do not do; but the evil I will not *to do,* that I practice. ²⁰Now if I do what I will not *to do,* it is no longer I who do it, but sin that dwells in me.

²¹I find then a law, that evil is present with me, the one who wills to do good. ²²For I delight in the law of God according to the inward man. ²³But I see another law in my members, warring against the law of my mind, and bringing me into captivity to the law of sin which is in my members. ²⁴O wretched man that I am! Who will deliver me from this body of death? ²⁵I thank God—through Jesus Christ our Lord!

So then, with the mind I myself serve the law of God, but with the flesh the law of sin.

Free from Indwelling Sin

8 *There is* therefore now no condemnation to those who are in Christ Jesus,ᵃ who do not walk according to the flesh, but according to the Spirit. ²For the law of the Spirit of life in Christ Jesus has made me free from the law of sin and death. ³For what the law could not do in that it was weak through the flesh, God *did* by sending His own Son in the likeness of sinful flesh, on account of sin: He condemned sin in the flesh, ⁴that the righteous requirement of the law might be fulfilled in us who do not walk according to the flesh but according to the Spirit. ⁵For those who live according to the flesh set their minds on the things of the flesh, but those *who live* according to the Spirit, the things of the Spirit. ⁶For to be carnally minded *is* death, but to be spiritually minded *is* life and peace. ⁷Because the carnal mind *is* enmity against God; for it is not subject to the law of God, nor indeed can be. ⁸So then, those who are in the flesh cannot please God.

⁹But you are not in the flesh but in the Spirit, if indeed the Spirit of God dwells in you. Now if anyone does not have the Spirit of Christ, he is not His. ¹⁰And if Christ *is* in you, the body *is* dead because of sin, but the Spirit *is* life because of righteousness. ¹¹But if the Spirit of Him who raised

---

7:7 ᵃExodus 20:17; Deuteronomy 5:21   **8:1** ᵃNU-Text omits the rest of this verse.

Jesus from the dead dwells in you, He who raised Christ from the dead will also give life to your mortal bodies through His Spirit who dwells in you.

Sonship Through the Spirit

12Therefore, brethren, we are debtors—not to the flesh, to live according to the flesh. 13For if you live according to the flesh you will die; but if by the Spirit you put to death the deeds of the body, you will live. 14For as many as are led by the Spirit of God, these are sons of God. 15For you did not receive the spirit of bondage again to fear, but you received the Spirit of adoption by whom we cry out, "Abba, Father." 16The Spirit Himself bears witness with our spirit that we are children of God, 17and if children, then heirs—heirs of God and joint heirs with Christ, if indeed we suffer with *Him,* that we may also be glorified together.

From Suffering to Glory

18For I consider that the sufferings of this present time are not worthy *to be compared* with the glory which shall be revealed in us. 19For the earnest expectation of the creation eagerly waits for the revealing of the sons of God. 20For the creation was subjected to futility, not willingly, but because of Him who subjected *it* in hope; 21because the creation itself also will be delivered from the bondage of corruption into the glorious liberty of the children of God. 22For we know that the whole creation groans and labors with birth pangs together until now. 23Not only *that,* but we also who have the firstfruits of the Spirit, even we ourselves groan within ourselves, eagerly waiting for the adoption, the redemption of our body. 24For we were saved in this hope, but hope that is seen is not hope; for why does one still hope for what he sees? 25But if we hope for what we do not see, we eagerly wait for *it* with perseverance.

26Likewise the Spirit also helps in our weaknesses. For we do not know what we should pray for as we ought, but the Spirit Himself makes intercession for us[a] with groanings which cannot be uttered. 27Now He who searches the hearts knows what the mind of the Spirit *is,* because He makes intercession for the saints according to *the will of* God.

28And we know that all things work together for good to those who love God, to those who are the called according to *His* purpose. 29For whom He foreknew, He also predestined *to be* conformed to the image of His Son, that He might be the firstborn among many brethren. 30Moreover whom He predestined, these He also called; whom He called, these He also justified; and whom He justified, these He also glorified.

God's Everlasting Love

31What then shall we say to these things? If God *is* for us, who *can be* against us? 32He who did not spare His own Son, but delivered Him up for us all, how shall He not with Him also freely give us all things? 33Who shall bring a charge against God's elect? *It is* God who justifies. 34Who *is* he who condemns? *It is* Christ who died, and furthermore is also risen, who is even at the right hand of God, who also makes intercession for us. 35Who shall separate us from the love of Christ? *Shall* tribulation, or distress, or persecution, or famine, or nakedness, or peril, or sword? 36As it is written:

> "For Your sake we are killed all day
>   long;
> We are accounted as sheep for the
>   slaughter."[a]

37Yet in all these things we are more than conquerors through Him who loved us. 38For I am persuaded that neither death nor life, nor angels nor principalities nor powers, nor things present nor things to come, 39nor height nor depth, nor any other created thing, shall be able to separate us from the love of God which is in Christ Jesus our Lord.

Israel's Rejection of Christ

9 I tell the truth in Christ, I am not lying, my conscience also bearing me witness in the Holy Spirit, 2that I have great sorrow and continual grief in my heart. 3For I could wish that I myself were accursed from

---

8:26 [a]NU-Text omits *for us.* **8:36** [a]Psalm 44:22

Christ for my brethren, my countrymen[a] according to the flesh, [4]who are Israelites, to whom *pertain* the adoption, the glory, the covenants, the giving of the law, the service *of God,* and the promises; [5]of whom *are* the fathers and from whom, according to the flesh, Christ *came,* who is over all, *the* eternally blessed God. Amen.

Israel's Rejection and God's Purpose

[6]But it is not that the word of God has taken no effect. For they *are* not all Israel who *are* of Israel, [7]nor *are they* all children because they are the seed of Abraham; but, *"In Isaac your seed shall be called."*[a] [8]That is, those who *are* the children of the flesh, these *are* not the children of God; but the children of the promise are counted as the seed. [9]For this *is* the word of promise: *"At this time I will come and Sarah shall have a son."*[a]

[10]And not only *this,* but when Rebecca also had conceived by one man, *even* by our father Isaac [11](for *the children* not yet being born, nor having done any good or evil, that the purpose of God according to election might stand, not of works but of Him who calls), [12]it was said to her, *"The older shall serve the younger."*[a] [13]As it is written, *"Jacob I have loved, but Esau I have hated."*[a]

Israel's Rejection and God's Justice

[14]What shall we say then? *Is there* unrighteousness with God? Certainly not! [15]For He says to Moses, *"I will have mercy on whomever I will have mercy, and I will have compassion on whomever I will have compassion."*[a] [16]So then *it is* not of him who wills, nor of him who runs, but of God who shows mercy. [17]For the Scripture says to the Pharaoh, *"For this very purpose I have raised you up, that I may show My power in you, and that My name may be declared in all the earth."*[a] [18]Therefore He has mercy on whom He wills, and whom He wills He hardens.

[19]You will say to me then, "Why does He still find fault? For who has resisted His will?" [20]But indeed, O man, who are you to reply against God? Will the thing formed say to him who formed *it,* "Why have you made me like this?" [21]Does not the potter have power over the clay, from the same lump to make one vessel for honor and another for dishonor?

[22]*What* if God, wanting to show *His* wrath and to make His power known, endured with much longsuffering the vessels of wrath prepared for destruction, [23]and that He might make known the riches of His glory on the vessels of mercy, which He had prepared beforehand for glory, [24]even us whom He called, not of the Jews only, but also of the Gentiles?

[25]As He says also in Hosea:

"I will call them My people, who were
    not My people,
And her beloved, who was not
    beloved."[a]
[26] *"And it shall come to pass in the place*
    where it was said to them,
'You are not My people,'
There they shall be called sons of the
    living God."[a]

[27]Isaiah also cries out concerning Israel:[a]

"Though the number of the children of
    Israel be as the sand of the sea,
The remnant will be saved.
[28] *For He will finish the work and cut it*
    short in righteousness,
Because the LORD will make a short
    work upon the earth."[a]

[29]And as Isaiah said before:

"Unless the LORD of Sabaoth[a] *had left*
    us a seed,
We would have become like Sodom,
And we would have been made like
    Gomorrah."[b]

Present Condition of Israel

[30]What shall we say then? That Gentiles, who did not pursue righteousness, have

---

9:3 [a]Or *relatives*   **9:7** [a]Genesis 21:12
9:9 [a]Genesis 18:10, 14   **9:12** [a]Genesis 25:23
9:13 [a]Malachi 1:2, 3   **9:15** [a]Exodus 33:19
9:17 [a]Exodus 9:16   **9:25** [a]Hosea 2:23
9:26 [a]Hosea 1:10   **9:27** [a]Isaiah 10:22, 23
9:28 [a]NU-Text reads *For the LORD will finish the work and cut it short upon the earth.*   **9:29** [a]Literally, in Hebrew, *Hosts* [b]Isaiah 1:9

attained to righteousness, even the righteousness of faith; ³¹but Israel, pursuing the law of righteousness, has not attained to the law of righteousness.ᵃ ³²Why? Because *they did* not *seek it* by faith, but as it were, by the works of the law.ᵃ For they stumbled at that stumbling stone. ³³As it is written:

> "Behold, I lay in Zion a stumbling
>   stone and rock of offense,
> And whoever believes on Him will not
>   be put to shame."ᵃ

Israel Needs the Gospel

10 Brethren, my heart's desire and prayer to God for Israelᵃ is that they may be saved. ²For I bear them witness that they have a zeal for God, but not according to knowledge. ³For they being ignorant of God's righteousness, and seeking to establish their own righteousness, have not submitted to the righteousness of God. ⁴For Christ *is* the end of the law for righteousness to everyone who believes.

⁵For Moses writes about the righteousness which is of the law, *"The man who does those things shall live by them."*ᵃ ⁶But the righteousness of faith speaks in this way, *"Do not say in your heart, 'Who will* ascend into heaven?' "ᵃ (that is, to bring Christ down *from above*) ⁷or, *"'Who will descend into the abyss?' "*ᵃ (that is, to bring Christ up from the dead). ⁸But what does it say? *"The word is near you, in your mouth and in your heart"*ᵃ (that is, the word of faith which we preach): ⁹that if you confess with your mouth the Lord Jesus and believe in your heart that God has raised Him from the dead, you will be saved. ¹⁰For with the heart one believes unto righteousness, and with the mouth confession is made unto salvation. ¹¹For the Scripture says, *"Whoever believes on Him will not be put to shame."*ᵃ ¹²For there is no distinction between Jew and Greek, for the same Lord over all is rich to all who call upon Him. ¹³For *"whoever calls on the name of the* LORD *shall be saved."*ᵃ

Israel Rejects the Gospel

¹⁴How then shall they call on Him in whom they have not believed? And how

---

9:31 ᵃNU-Text omits *of righteousness.* **9:32** ᵃNU-Text reads *by works.* **9:33** ᵃIsaiah 8:14; 28:16 **10:1** ᵃNU-Text reads *them.* **10:5** ᵃLeviticus 18:5 **10:6** ᵃDeuteronomy 30:12 **10:7** ᵃDeuteronomy 30:13 **10:8** ᵃDeuteronomy 30:14 **10:11** ᵃIsaiah 28:16 **10:13** ᵃJoel 2:32

FREEDOM

So then faith comes by hearing, and hearing by the word of God.

ROMANS 10:17

RELIGIOUS BROADCASTING RIGHTS

In July 1993, the Oklahoma State Court, Tulsa County, in the case of *Crowley, Gaines, and Ries v. Tilton,* granted the defendants summary judgment, stating:

> Initially Christianity was taught by Christ. He then taught disciples who went out over the world to teach others. This process has spread to a major world body of believers.
> Religion should be permitted to use contemporary means to communicate religious messages in the form of TV appeal to mass audiences, follow-up communication by computerized mailing designed to convert and symbolic tokens to cause response to the messages.
> The context of the message is belief, and the freedom for belief is absolute. When a minister or a church urges one to take certain actions based upon a representation that God will act toward that person in positive and rewarding ways, they are entitled to absolute protection as a belief.

shall they believe in Him of whom they have not heard? And how shall they hear without a preacher? ¹⁵And how shall they preach unless they are sent? As it is written:

> "How beautiful are the feet of those
>   who preach the gospel of peace,ᵃ
> Who bring glad tidings of good
>   things!"ᵇ

¹⁶But they have not all obeyed the gospel. For Isaiah says, "LORD, who has believed our report?"ᵃ ¹⁷So then faith *comes* by hearing, and hearing by the word of God.

¹⁸But I say, have they not heard? Yes indeed:

> "Their sound has gone out to all the
>   earth,
> And their words to the ends of the
>   world."ᵃ

¹⁹But I say, did Israel not know? First Moses says:

> "I will provoke you to jealousy by those
>   who are not a nation,
> I will move you to anger by a foolish
>   nation."ᵃ

²⁰But Isaiah is very bold and says:

> "I was found by those who did not seek
>   Me;
> I was made manifest to those who did
>   not ask for Me."ᵃ

²¹But to Israel he says:

> "All day long I have stretched out My
>   hands
> To a disobedient and contrary people."ᵃ

Israel's Rejection Not Total

11 I say then, has God cast away His people? Certainly not! For I also am an Israelite, of the seed of Abraham, of the tribe of Benjamin. ²God has not cast away His people whom He foreknew. Or do you not know what the Scripture says of Elijah, how he pleads with God against Israel, saying, ³"LORD, they have killed Your

prophets and torn down Your altars, and I alone am left, and they seek my life"?ᵃ ⁴But what does the divine response say to him? "I have reserved for Myself seven thousand men who have not bowed the knee to Baal."ᵃ ⁵Even so then, at this present time there is a remnant according to the election of grace. ⁶And if by grace, then *it is* no longer of works; otherwise grace is no longer grace.ᵃ But if *it is* of works, it is no longer grace; otherwise work is no longer work.

⁷What then? Israel has not obtained what it seeks; but the elect have obtained it, and the rest were blinded. ⁸Just as it is written:

> "God has given them a spirit of stupor,
> Eyes that they should not see
> And ears that they should not hear,
> To this very day."ᵃ

⁹And David says:

> "Let their table become a snare and a
>   trap,
> A stumbling block and a recompense
>   to them.
> 10 Let their eyes be darkened, so that
>   they do not see,
> And bow down their back always."ᵃ

Israel's Rejection Not Final

¹¹I say then, have they stumbled that they should fall? Certainly not! But through their fall, to provoke them to jealousy, salvation *has come* to the Gentiles. ¹²Now if their fall *is* riches for the world, and their failure riches for the Gentiles, how much more their fullness!

¹³For I speak to you Gentiles; inasmuch as I am an apostle to the Gentiles, I magnify my ministry, ¹⁴if by any means I may provoke to jealousy *those who are* my flesh and save some of them. ¹⁵For if their being

---

10:15 ᵃNU-Text omits *preach the gospel of peace, Who.* ᵇIsaiah 52:7; Nahum 1:15   **10:16** ᵃIsaiah 53:1
10:18 ᵃPsalm 19:4   **10:19** ᵃDeuteronomy 32:21
10:20 ᵃIsaiah 65:1   **10:21** ᵃIsaiah 65:2
11:3 ᵃ1 Kings 19:10, 14   **11:4** ᵃ1 Kings 19:18
11:6 ᵃNU-Text omits the rest of this verse.
11:8 ᵃDeuteronomy 29:4; Isaiah 29:10
11:10 ᵃPsalm 69:22, 23

cast away *is* the reconciling of the world, what *will* their acceptance *be* but life from the dead?

¹⁶For if the firstfruit *is* holy, the lump *is* also *holy;* and if the root *is* holy, so *are* the branches. ¹⁷And if some of the branches were broken off, and you, being a wild olive tree, were grafted in among them, and with them became a partaker of the root and fatness of the olive tree, ¹⁸do not boast against the branches. But if you do boast, *remember that* you do not support the root, but the root *supports* you.

¹⁹You will say then, "Branches were broken off that I might be grafted in." ²⁰Well *said.* Because of unbelief they were broken off, and you stand by faith. Do not be haughty, but fear. ²¹For if God did not spare the natural branches, He may not spare you either. ²²Therefore consider the goodness and severity of God: on those who fell, severity; but toward you, goodness,ᵃ if you continue in *His* goodness. Otherwise you also will be cut off. ²³And they also, if they do not continue in unbelief, will be grafted in, for God is able to graft them in again. ²⁴For if you were cut out of the olive tree which is wild by nature, and were grafted contrary to nature into a cultivated olive tree, how much more will these, who *are* natural *branches,* be grafted into their own olive tree?

²⁵For I do not desire, brethren, that you should be ignorant of this mystery, lest you should be wise in your own opinion, that blindness in part has happened to Israel until the fullness of the Gentiles has come in. ²⁶And so all Israel will be saved,ᵃ as it is written:

"The Deliverer will come out of Zion,
　And He will turn away ungodliness
　　from Jacob;
²⁷　For this is My covenant with them,
　When I take away their sins."ᵃ

²⁸Concerning the gospel *they are* enemies for your sake, but concerning the election *they are* beloved for the sake of the fathers. ²⁹For the gifts and the calling of God *are* irrevocable. ³⁰For as you were once disobedient to God, yet have now obtained mercy through their disobedience, ³¹even so these also have now been disobedient, that through the mercy shown you they also may obtain mercy. ³²For God has committed them all to disobedience, that He might have mercy on all.

³³Oh, the depth of the riches both of the wisdom and knowledge of God! How unsearchable *are* His judgments and His ways past finding out!

³⁴ *"For who has known the mind of the*
　　LORD?
　　*Or who has become His counselor?"*ᵃ
³⁵ *"Or who has first given to Him*
　　*And it shall be repaid to him?"*ᵃ

³⁶For of Him and through Him and to Him *are* all things, to whom *be* glory forever. Amen.

Living Sacrifices to God

12 I beseech you therefore, brethren, by the mercies of God, that you present your bodies a living sacrifice, holy, acceptable to God, *which is* your reasonable service. ²And do not be conformed to this world, but be transformed by the renewing of your mind, that you may prove what *is* that good and acceptable and perfect will of God.

Serve God with Spiritual Gifts

³For I say, through the grace given to me, to everyone who is among you, not to think *of himself* more highly than he ought to think, but to think soberly, as God has dealt to each one a measure of faith. ⁴For as we have many members in one body, but all the members do not have the same function, ⁵so we, *being* many, are one body in Christ, and individually members of one another. ⁶Having then gifts differing according to the grace that is given to us, *let us use them:* if prophecy, *let us prophesy* in proportion to our faith; ⁷or ministry, *let us use it* in *our* ministering; he who teaches, in teaching; ⁸he who exhorts, in exhortation;

11:22 ᵃNU-Text adds *of God.*　　**11:26** ᵃOr *delivered*
11:27 ᵃIsaiah 59:20, 21　　**11:34** ᵃIsaiah 40:13;
Jeremiah 23:18　　**11:35** ᵃJob 41:11

he who gives, with liberality; he who leads, with diligence; he who shows mercy, with cheerfulness.

Behave Like a Christian

⁹*Let* love *be* without hypocrisy. Abhor what is evil. Cling to what is good. ¹⁰*Be* kindly affectionate to one another with brotherly love, in honor giving preference to one another; ¹¹not lagging in diligence, fervent in spirit, serving the Lord; ¹²rejoicing in hope, patient in tribulation, continuing steadfastly in prayer; ¹³distributing to the needs of the saints, given to hospitality. ¹⁴Bless those who persecute you; bless and do not curse. ¹⁵Rejoice with those who rejoice, and weep with those who weep. ¹⁶Be of the same mind toward one another. Do not set your mind on high things, but associate with the humble. Do not be wise in your own opinion.

¹⁷Repay no one evil for evil. Have regard for good things in the sight of all men. ¹⁸If it is possible, as much as depends on you, live peaceably with all men. ¹⁹Beloved, do not avenge yourselves, but *rather* give place to wrath; for it is written, *"Vengeance is Mine, I will repay,"*ᵃ says the Lord. ²⁰Therefore

"If your enemy is hungry, feed him;
If he is thirsty, give him a drink;
For in so doing you will heap coals of
    fire on his head."ᵃ

²¹Do not be overcome by evil, but overcome evil with good.

Submit to Government

13 Let every soul be subject to the governing authorities. For there is no authority except from God, and the authorities that exist are appointed by God. ²Therefore whoever resists the authority resists the ordinance of God, and those who resist will bring judgment on themselves. ³For rulers are not a terror to good works, but to evil. Do you want to be unafraid of the authority? Do what is good, and you will have praise from the same. ⁴For he is God's minister to you for good. But if you do evil, be afraid; for he does not bear the sword in vain; for he is God's minister, an avenger to *execute* wrath on him who practices evil. ⁵Therefore *you* must be subject, not only because of wrath but also for conscience' sake. ⁶For because of this you also pay taxes, for they are God's ministers attending continually to this very thing. ⁷Render therefore to all their due: taxes to whom taxes *are due,* customs to whom customs, fear to whom fear, honor to whom honor.

SERVICE
"If your enemy is hungry, feed him. . . ."
                                    ROMANS 12:20

Feed the Hungry
Henry Ward Beecher (1813–1887) was a leading American clergyman, editor, and abolitionist. He observed:

> *Christianity works while infidelity talks. She feeds the hungry, clothes the naked, visits and cheers the sick, and seeks the lost, while infidelity abuses her and babbles nonsense and profanity. "By their fruits ye shall know them."*

He also said:

> *The Bible is God's chart for you to steer by, to keep you from the bottom of the sea, and to show you where the harbor is, and how to reach it without running on the rocks or bars.*

Love Your Neighbor

⁸Owe no one anything except to love one another, for he who loves another has fulfilled the law. ⁹For the commandments, *"You shall not commit adultery," "You shall not murder," "You shall not steal," "You shall not bear false witness,"*ᵃ *"You shall not covet,"*ᵇ and if *there is* any other commandment, are *all* summed up in this saying, namely, *"You shall love your neighbor as yourself."*ᶜ ¹⁰Love does no harm to a neighbor; therefore love *is* the fulfillment of the law.

12:19 ᵃDeuteronomy 32:35   **12:20** ᵃProverbs 25:21, 22   **13:9** ᵃNU-Text omits *"You shall not bear false witness."* ᵇExodus 20:13–15, 17; Deuteronomy 5:17–19, 21 ᶜLeviticus 19:18

Put on Christ

¹¹And *do* this, knowing the time, that now *it is* high time to awake out of sleep; for now our salvation *is* nearer than when we *first* believed. ¹²The night is far spent, the day is at hand. Therefore let us cast off the works of darkness, and let us put on the armor of light. ¹³Let us walk properly, as in the day, not in revelry and drunkenness, not in lewdness and lust, not in strife and envy. ¹⁴But put on the Lord Jesus Christ, and make no provision for the flesh, to *fulfill its* lusts.

The Law of Liberty

14 Receive one who is weak in the faith, *but* not to disputes over doubtful things. ²For one believes he may eat all things, but he who is weak eats *only* vegetables. ³Let not him who eats despise him who does not eat, and let not him who does not eat judge him who eats; for God has received him. ⁴Who are you to judge another's servant? To his own master he stands or falls. Indeed, he will be made to stand, for God is able to make him stand.

⁵One person esteems *one* day above another; another esteems every day *alike.* Let each be fully convinced in his own mind. ⁶He who observes the day, observes *it* to the Lord;ᵃ and he who does not observe the day, to the Lord he does not observe *it.* He who eats, eats to the Lord, for he gives God thanks; and he who does not eat, to the Lord he does not eat, and gives God thanks. ⁷For none of us lives to himself, and no one dies to himself. ⁸For if we live, we live to the Lord; and if we die, we die to the Lord. Therefore, whether we live or die, we are the Lord's. ⁹For to this end Christ died and roseᵃ and lived again, that He might be Lord of both the dead and the living. ¹⁰But why do you judge your brother? Or why do you show contempt for your brother? For we shall all stand before the judgment seat of Christ.ᵃ ¹¹For it is written:

"As I live, says the LORD,

14:6 ᵃNU-Text omits the rest of this sentence. **14:9** ᵃNU-Text omits *and rose.* **14:10** ᵃNU-Text reads *of God.*

DEFENDER

Let every soul be subject to the governing authorities.

ROMANS 13:1

THE LAND OF THE BIBLE

Benjamin Franklin Morris (1810–1867), the Congregational minister and historian who wrote *The Christian Life and Character of the Civil Institutions of the United States* in 1864, stated:

These fundamental objects of the Constitution are in perfect harmony with the revealed objects of the Christian religion. Union, justice, peace, the general welfare, and the blessings of civil and religious liberty, are the objects of Christianity, and always secured under its practical and beneficent reign.

The state must rest upon the basis of religion, and it must preserve this basis, or itself must fall. But the support which religion gives to the state will obviously cease the moment religion loses its hold upon the popular mind.

This is a Christian nation, first in name, and secondly because of the many and mighty elements of a pure Christianity which have given it character and shaped its destiny from the beginning. It is preeminently the land of the Bible, of the Christian Church, and of the Christian Sabbath. . . . The chief security and glory of the United States of America has been, is now, and will be forever, the prevalence and domination of the Christian faith.

Every knee shall bow to Me,
And every tongue shall confess to
God."ᵃ

¹²So then each of us shall give account of himself to God. ¹³Therefore let us not judge one another anymore, but rather resolve this, not to put a stumbling block or a cause to fall in *our* brother's way.

The Law of Love

¹⁴I know and am convinced by the Lord Jesus that *there is* nothing unclean of itself; but to him who considers anything to be unclean, to him *it is* unclean. ¹⁵Yet if your brother is grieved because of *your* food, you are no longer walking in love. Do not destroy with your food the one for whom Christ died. ¹⁶Therefore do not let your good be spoken of as evil; ¹⁷for the kingdom of God is not eating and drinking, but righteousness and peace and joy in the Holy Spirit. ¹⁸For he who serves Christ in these thingsᵃ *is* acceptable to God and approved by men.

¹⁹Therefore let us pursue the things *which* make for peace and the things by which one may edify another. ²⁰Do not destroy the work of God for the sake of food. All things indeed *are* pure, but *it is* evil for the man who eats with offense. ²¹*It is* good neither to eat meat nor drink wine nor *do anything* by which your brother stumbles or is offended or is made weak.ᵃ ²²Do you have faith?ᵃ Have *it* to yourself before God. Happy *is* he who does not condemn himself in what he approves. ²³But he who doubts is condemned if he eats, because *he does* not *eat* from faith; for whatever *is* not from faith is sin.ᵃ

Bearing Others' Burdens

15 We then who are strong ought to bear with the scruples of the weak, and not to please ourselves. ²Let each of us please *his* neighbor for *his* good, leading to edification.

14:11 ᵃIsaiah 45:23   **14:18** ᵃNU-Text reads *this.*
14:21 ᵃNU-Text omits *or is offended or is made weak.*
14:22 ᵃNU-Text reads *The faith which you have—have.*
14:23 ᵃM-Text puts Romans 16:25–27 here.

EQUIPPER

For whatever things were written before were written for our learning....

ROMANS 15:4

William Holmes McGuffy

MCGUFFEY READERS

William Holmes McGuffey (1800–1873), considered the "Schoolmaster of the Nation," published the first edition of his *McGuffey Reader* in 1836, one of the nation's first and most widely used series of textbooks in public education. It is estimated that at least 120 million copies of *McGuffey Readers* were sold between 1836 and 1960, placing its sales in a category with the Bible and *Webster's Dictionary*. In the preface of his *Eclectic Third Reader*, McGuffey wrote:

Selections [have been] drawn from the purest fountains of English literature. . . . Copious extracts made from the Sacred Scripture.

Upon a review of the work . . . an apology may be due for not having still more liberally transferred to pages the chaste simplicity, the thrilling pathos, the living descriptions, and the matchless sublimity of the Sacred Writings.

From no source has the author drawn more copiously than from the Sacred Scriptures. . . . This certainly apprehends no censure. In a Christian country, that man is to be pitied, who, at this day, can honestly object to imbuing the minds of youth with the language and spirit of the Word of God.

[3]For even Christ did not please Himself; but as it is written, *"The reproaches of those who reproached You fell on Me."*[a] [4]For whatever things were written before were written for our learning, that we through the patience and comfort of the Scriptures might have hope. [5]Now may the God of patience and comfort grant you to be like-minded toward one another, according to Christ Jesus, [6]that you may with one mind *and* one mouth glorify the God and Father of our Lord Jesus Christ.

Glorify God Together

[7]Therefore receive one another, just as Christ also received us,[a] to the glory of God. [8]Now I say that Jesus Christ has become a servant to the circumcision for the truth of God, to confirm the promises *made* to the fathers, [9]and that the Gentiles might glorify God for *His* mercy, as it is written:

> *"For this reason I will confess to You*
> *   among the Gentiles,*
> *And sing to Your name."*[a]

[10]And again he says:

> *"Rejoice, O Gentiles, with His people!"*[a]

[11]And again:

> *"Praise the* Lord, *all you Gentiles!*
> *Laud Him, all you peoples!"*[a]

[12]And again, Isaiah says:

> *"There shall be a root of Jesse;*
> *And He who shall rise to reign over*
> *   the Gentiles,*
> *In Him the Gentiles shall hope."*[a]

[13]Now may the God of hope fill you with all joy and peace in believing, that you may abound in hope by the power of the Holy Spirit.

From Jerusalem to Illyricum

[14]Now I myself am confident concerning you, my brethren, that you also are full of goodness, filled with all knowledge, able also to admonish one another.[a] [15]Nevertheless, brethren, I have written more boldly to you on *some* points, as reminding you, because of the grace given to me by God, [16]that I might be a minister of Jesus Christ to the Gentiles, ministering the gospel of God, that the offering of the Gentiles might be acceptable, sanctified by the Holy Spirit. [17]Therefore I have reason to glory in Christ Jesus in the things *which pertain* to God. [18]For I will not dare to speak of any of those things which Christ has not accomplished through me, in word and deed, to make the Gentiles obedient— [19]in mighty signs and wonders, by the power of the Spirit of God, so that from Jerusalem and round about to Illyricum I have fully preached the gospel of Christ. [20]And so I have made it my aim to preach the gospel, not where Christ was named, lest I should build on another man's foundation, [21]but as it is written:

> *"To whom He was not announced, they*
> *   shall see;*
> *And those who have not heard shall*
> *   understand."*[a]

Plan to Visit Rome

[22]For this reason I also have been much hindered from coming to you. [23]But now no longer having a place in these parts, and having a great desire these many years to come to you, [24]whenever I journey to Spain, I shall come to you.[a] For I hope to see you on my journey, and to be helped on my way there by you, if first I may enjoy your *company* for a while. [25]But now I am going to Jerusalem to minister to the saints. [26]For it pleased those from Macedonia and Achaia to make a certain contribution for the poor among the saints who are in Jerusalem. [27]It pleased them indeed, and they are their debtors. For if the Gentiles have been partakers of their spiritual things, their duty is also to minister to them in material things. [28]Therefore, when I have performed this and have sealed to

---

15:3 [a]Psalm 69:9   **15:7** [a]NU-Text and M-Text read *you.*   **15:9** [a]2 Samuel 22:50; Psalm 18:49
15:10 [a]Deuteronomy 32:43   **15:11** [a]Psalm 117:1
15:12 [a]Isaiah 11:10   **15:14** [a]M-Text reads *others.*
15:21 [a]Isaiah 52:15   **15:24** [a]NU-Text omits *I shall come to you* (and joins *Spain* with the next sentence).

them this fruit, I shall go by way of you to Spain. [29]But I know that when I come to you, I shall come in the fullness of the blessing of the gospel[a] of Christ.

[30]Now I beg you, brethren, through the Lord Jesus Christ, and through the love of the Spirit, that you strive together with me in prayers to God for me, [31]that I may be delivered from those in Judea who do not believe, and that my service for Jerusalem may be acceptable to the saints, [32]that I may come to you with joy by the will of God, and may be refreshed together with you. [33]Now the God of peace *be* with you all. Amen.

Sister Phoebe Commended

16 I commend to you Phoebe our sister, who is a servant of the church in Cenchrea, [2]that you may receive her in the Lord in a manner worthy of the saints, and assist her in whatever business she has need of you; for indeed she has been a helper of many and of myself also.

Greeting Roman Saints

[3]Greet Priscilla and Aquila, my fellow workers in Christ Jesus, [4]who risked their own necks for my life, to whom not only I give thanks, but also all the churches of the Gentiles. [5]Likewise *greet* the church that is in their house.

Greet my beloved Epaenetus, who is the firstfruits of Achaia[a] to Christ. [6]Greet Mary, who labored much for us. [7]Greet Andronicus and Junia, my countrymen and my fellow prisoners, who are of note among the apostles, who also were in Christ before me.

[8]Greet Amplias, my beloved in the Lord. [9]Greet Urbanus, our fellow worker in Christ, and Stachys, my beloved. [10]Greet Apelles, approved in Christ. Greet those who are of the *household* of Aristobulus. [11]Greet Herodion, my countryman.[a] Greet those who are of the *household* of Narcissus who are in the Lord.

[12]Greet Tryphena and Tryphosa, who have labored in the Lord. Greet the beloved Persis, who labored much in the Lord. [13]Greet Rufus, chosen in the Lord, and his mother and mine. [14]Greet Asyncritus, Phlegon, Hermas, Patrobas, Hermes, and the brethren who are with them. [15]Greet Philologus and Julia, Nereus and his sister, and Olympas, and all the saints who are with them.

[16]Greet one another with a holy kiss. The[a] churches of Christ greet you.

Avoid Divisive Persons

[17]Now I urge you, brethren, note those who cause divisions and offenses, contrary to the doctrine which you learned, and avoid them. [18]For those who are such do not serve our Lord Jesus[a] Christ, but their own belly, and by smooth words and flattering speech deceive the hearts of the simple. [19]For your obedience has become known to all. Therefore I am glad on your behalf; but I want you to be wise in what is good, and simple concerning evil. [20]And the God of peace will crush Satan under your feet shortly.

The grace of our Lord Jesus Christ *be* with you. Amen.

Greetings from Paul's Friends

[21]Timothy, my fellow worker, and Lucius, Jason, and Sosipater, my countrymen, greet you.

[22]I, Tertius, who wrote *this* epistle, greet you in the Lord.

[23]Gaius, my host and *the host* of the whole church, greets you. Erastus, the treasurer of the city, greets you, and Quartus, a brother. [24]The grace of our Lord Jesus Christ *be* with you all. Amen.[a]

Benediction

[25]Now to Him who is able to establish you according to my gospel and the preaching of Jesus Christ, according to the revelation of the mystery kept secret since the world began [26]but now made manifest, and by the prophetic Scriptures made known to all nations, according to the commandment of the everlasting God, for obedience to the faith— [27]to God, alone wise, *be* glory through Jesus Christ forever. Amen.[a]

15:29 [a]NU-Text omits *of the gospel.*   **16:5** [a]NU-Text reads *Asia.*   **16:11** [a]Or *relative*   **16:16** [a]NU-Text reads *All the churches.*   **16:18** [a]NU-Text and M-Text omit *Jesus.*   **16:24** [a]NU-Text omits this verse. **16:27** [a]M-Text puts Romans 16:25–27 after Romans 14:23.

1 CORINTHIANS

Author: Paul

When Written: Around A.D. 56

Theme: Correction for a Troubled Church

Key Verses: 1 Corinthians 6:19, 20—Or do you not know that your body is the temple of the Holy Spirit who is in you, whom you have from God, and you are not your own? For you were bought at a price; therefore glorify God in your body and in your spirit, which are God's.

Key Chapter: 1 Corinthians 13—The apostle Paul's definition of "love" is the best ever penned. Standing in stark contrast to the idea that love is an emotion, that one can fall into or out of love, this chapter reveals that true love is primarily an action.

Paul founded the church in this important Greek city, but the pagan life-style of the degraded culture exerts a profound influence upon the Christians. Paul must take the risk of addressing by letter a variety of problems in the church: factions, lawsuits, immorality, questionable practices, abuse of the Lord's Supper, and spiritual gifts. Paul also gives a series of perspectives on various questions and controversial issues raised by the Corinthians in a letter to Paul.

Presidents face momentous decisions and risks in confronting problems of the day. In October 1962, President John F. Kennedy faced the problem of Soviet's building an intermediate-range ballistic missile site in Cuba. If the U.S. attacked the sites, it might lead to nuclear war with the Soviets, but if the U.S. did nothing, it would endure the threat of nuclear weapons being launched from close range. Through negotiations with the Russians, Kennedy averted the crisis, which had brought the world closer to nuclear war than at any point before or since. President Kennedy said, "There are risks and costs to a program of action. But they are far less than the long-range risks and costs of comfortable inaction."

Greeting

1 Paul, called *to be* an apostle of Jesus Christ through the will of God, and Sosthenes *our* brother,

²To the church of God which is at Corinth, to those who are sanctified in Christ Jesus, called *to be* saints, with all who in every place call on the name of Jesus Christ our Lord, both theirs and ours:

³Grace to you and peace from God our Father and the Lord Jesus Christ.

Spiritual Gifts at Corinth

⁴I thank my God always concerning you for the grace of God which was given to you by Christ Jesus, ⁵that you were enriched in everything by Him in all utterance and all knowledge, ⁶even as the testimony of Christ was confirmed in you, ⁷so that you come short in no gift, eagerly waiting for the revelation of our Lord Jesus Christ, ⁸who will also confirm you to the end, *that you may be* blameless in the day of our Lord Jesus Christ. ⁹God *is* faithful, by whom you were called into the fellowship of His Son, Jesus Christ our Lord.

Sectarianism Is Sin

¹⁰Now I plead with you, brethren, by the name of our Lord Jesus Christ, that you all speak the same thing, and *that* there be no divisions among you, but *that* you be perfectly joined together in the same mind and in the same judgment. ¹¹For it has been declared to me concerning you, my brethren, by those of Chloe's *household,* that there are contentions among you. ¹²Now I say this, that each of you says, "I am of Paul," or "I am of Apollos," or "I am of Cephas," or "I am of Christ." ¹³Is Christ divided? Was Paul crucified for you? Or were you baptized in the name of Paul? ¹⁴I thank God that I baptized none of you except Crispus and Gaius, ¹⁵lest anyone should say that I had baptized in my own name. ¹⁶Yes, I also baptized the household of Stephanas. Besides, I do not know whether I baptized any other. ¹⁷For Christ did not send me to baptize, but to preach the gospel, not with wisdom of words, lest the cross of Christ should be made of no effect.

Christ the Power and Wisdom of God

¹⁸For the message of the cross is foolishness to those who are perishing, but to us who are being saved it is the power of God. ¹⁹For it is written:

> "I will destroy the wisdom of the wise,
> And bring to nothing the
>   understanding of the prudent."ᵃ

²⁰Where *is* the wise? Where *is* the scribe? Where *is* the disputer of this age? Has not God made foolish the wisdom of this world? ²¹For since, in the wisdom of God, the world through wisdom did not know God, it pleased God through the foolishness of the message preached to save those who believe. ²²For Jews request a sign, and Greeks seek after wisdom; ²³but we preach Christ crucified, to the Jews a stumbling block and to the Greeksᵃ foolishness, ²⁴but to those who are called, both Jews and Greeks, Christ the power of God and the wisdom of God. ²⁵Because the foolishness of God is wiser than men, and the weakness of God is stronger than men.

Glory Only in the Lord

²⁶For you see your calling, brethren, that not many wise according to the flesh, not many mighty, not many noble, *are called.* ²⁷But God has chosen the foolish things of the world to put to shame the wise, and God has chosen the weak things of the world to put to shame the things which are mighty;

1:19 ᵃIsaiah 29:14   **1:23** ᵃNU-Text reads *Gentiles.*

28and the base things of the world and the things which are despised God has chosen, and the things which are not, to bring to nothing the things that are, 29that no flesh should glory in His presence. 30But of Him you are in Christ Jesus, who became for us wisdom from God—and righteousness and sanctification and redemption— 31that, as it is written, *"He who glories, let him glory in the Lord."*a

Christ Crucified

2 And I, brethren, when I came to you, did not come with excellence of speech or of wisdom declaring to you the testimonya of God. 2For I determined not to know anything among you except Jesus Christ and Him crucified. 3I was with you in weakness, in fear, and in much trembling. 4And my speech and my preaching *were* not with persuasive words of humana wisdom, but in demonstration of the Spirit and of power, 5that your faith should not be in the wisdom of men but in the power of God.

Spiritual Wisdom

6However, we speak wisdom among those who are mature, yet not the wisdom of this age, nor of the rulers of this age, who are

1:31 aJeremiah 9:24   **2:1** aNU-Text reads *mystery.*
2:4 aNU-Text omits *human.*

EQUIPPER

". . . the things which God has prepared for those who love Him."

1 Corinthians 2:9

James McHenry

THE BIBLE'S IMPACT ON SOCIETY

James McHenry (1753–1816) was a physician, one of the signers of the Constitution, a member of the Continental Congress, and the U.S. Secretary of War. In 1813, he became the president of the first Bible society in Baltimore, Maryland, and stated the importance of distributing the Bible into society:

Neither, in considering this subject, let it be overlooked, that public utility pleads most forcibly for the general distribution of the Holy Scriptures. The doctrine they preach, the obligations they impose, the punishment they threaten, the rewards they promise, the stamp and image of divinity they bear, which produces a conviction of their truths, can alone secure to society, order and peace, and to our courts of justice and constitutions of government, purity, stability and usefulness.

In vain, without the Bible, we increase penal laws and draw entrenchments around our institutions. Bibles are strong entrenchments. Where they abound, men cannot pursue wicked courses and at the same time enjoy quiet conscience.

Consider also, the rich do not possess aught more precious than their Bible, and that the poor cannot be presented by the rich with anything of greater value. Withhold it not from the poor. It is a book of councils and directions, fitted to every situation in which man can be placed. It is an oracle which reveals to mortals the secrets of heavens and the hidden will of the Almighty. . . . It is an estate, whose title is guaranteed by Christ, whose delicious fruits ripen every season, survive the worm, and keep through eternity.

coming to nothing. [7]But we speak the wisdom of God in a mystery, the hidden *wisdom* which God ordained before the ages for our glory, [8]which none of the rulers of this age knew; for had they known, they would not have crucified the Lord of glory.

[9]But as it is written:

> "Eye has not seen, nor ear heard,
> Nor have entered into the heart of man
> The things which God has prepared
> for those who love Him."[a]

[10]But God has revealed *them* to us through His Spirit. For the Spirit searches all things, yes, the deep things of God. [11]For what man knows the things of a man except the spirit of the man which is in him? Even so no one knows the things of God except the Spirit of God. [12]Now we have received, not the spirit of the world, but the Spirit who is from God, that we might know the things that have been freely given to us by God.

[13]These things we also speak, not in words which man's wisdom teaches but which the Holy[a] Spirit teaches, comparing spiritual things with spiritual. [14]But the natural man does not receive the things of the Spirit of God, for they are foolishness to him; nor can he know *them,* because they are spiritually discerned. [15]But he who is spiritual judges all things, yet he himself is *rightly* judged by no one. [16]For *"who has known the mind of the LORD that he may instruct Him?"*[a] But we have the mind of Christ.

Sectarianism Is Carnal

3 And I, brethren, could not speak to you as to spiritual *people* but as to carnal, as to babes in Christ. [2]I fed you with milk and not with solid food; for until now you were not able *to receive it,* and even now you are still not able; [3]for you are still carnal. For where *there are* envy, strife, and divisions among you, are you not carnal and behaving like *mere* men? [4]For when one says, "I am of Paul," and another, "I *am* of Apollos," are you not carnal?

Watering, Working, Warning

[5]Who then is Paul, and who *is* Apollos, but ministers through whom you believed, as the Lord gave to each one? [6]I planted, Apollos watered, but God gave the increase. [7]So then neither he who plants is anything, nor he who waters, but God who gives the increase. [8]Now he who plants and he who waters are one, and each one will receive his own reward according to his own labor.

[9]For we are God's fellow workers; you are God's field, *you are* God's building. [10]According to the grace of God which was given to me, as a wise master builder I have laid the foundation, and another builds on it. But let each one take heed how he builds on it. [11]For no other foundation can anyone lay than that which is laid, which is Jesus Christ. [12]Now if anyone builds on this foundation *with* gold, silver, precious stones, wood, hay, straw, [13]each one's work will become clear; for the Day will declare it, because it will be revealed by fire; and the fire will test each one's work, of what sort it is. [14]If anyone's work which he has built on *it* endures, he will receive a reward. [15]If anyone's work is burned, he will suffer loss; but he himself will be saved, yet so as through fire.

[16]Do you not know that you are the temple of God and *that* the Spirit of God dwells in you? [17]If anyone defiles the temple of God, God will destroy him. For the temple of God is holy, which *temple* you are.

Avoid Worldly Wisdom

[18]Let no one deceive himself. If anyone among you seems to be wise in this age, let him become a fool that he may become wise. [19]For the wisdom of this world is foolishness with God. For it is written, *"He catches the wise in their own craftiness"*;[a] [20]and again, *"The LORD knows the thoughts of the wise, that they are futile."*[a] [21]Therefore let no one boast in men. For all things are yours: [22]whether Paul or Apollos or Cephas, or the world or life or death, or things present or things to come—all are yours. [23]And you *are* Christ's, and Christ *is* God's.

Stewards of the Mysteries of God

4 Let a man so consider us, as servants of Christ and stewards of the mysteries of

---

2:9 [a]Isaiah 64:4   **2:13** [a]NU-Text omits *Holy.*
2:16 [a]Isaiah 40:13   **3:19** [a]Job 5:13   **3:20** [a]Psalm 94:11

God. ²Moreover it is required in stewards that one be found faithful. ³But with me it is a very small thing that I should be judged by you or by a human court.ᵃ In fact, I do not even judge myself. ⁴For I know of nothing against myself, yet I am not justified by this; but He who judges me is the Lord. ⁵Therefore judge nothing before the time, until the Lord comes, who will both bring to light the hidden things of darkness and reveal the counsels of the hearts. Then each one's praise will come from God.

Fools for Christ's Sake

⁶Now these things, brethren, I have figuratively transferred to myself and Apollos for your sakes, that you may learn in us not to think beyond what is written, that none of you may be puffed up on behalf of one against the other. ⁷For who makes you differ *from another?* And what do you have that you did not receive? Now if you did indeed receive *it,* why do you boast as if you had not received *it?*

⁸You are already full! You are already rich! You have reigned as kings without us—and indeed I could wish you did reign, that we also might reign with you! ⁹For I think that God has displayed us, the apostles, last, as men condemned to death; for we have been made a spectacle to the world, both to angels and to men. ¹⁰We *are* fools for Christ's sake, but you *are* wise in Christ! We *are* weak, but you *are* strong! You *are* distinguished, but we *are* dishonored! ¹¹To the present hour we both hunger and thirst, and we are poorly clothed, and beaten, and homeless. ¹²And we labor, working with our own hands. Being reviled, we bless; being persecuted, we endure; ¹³being defamed, we entreat. We have been made as the filth of the world, the offscouring of all things until now.

Paul's Paternal Care

¹⁴I do not write these things to shame you, but as my beloved children I warn *you.* ¹⁵For though you might have ten thousand instructors in Christ, yet *you do* not *have* many fathers; for in Christ Jesus I have begotten you through the gospel. ¹⁶Therefore I urge you, imitate me. ¹⁷For this reason I have sent Timothy to you, who is my beloved and faithful son in the Lord, who will remind you of my ways in Christ, as I teach everywhere in every church.

¹⁸Now some are puffed up, as though I were not coming to you. ¹⁹But I will come to you shortly, if the Lord wills, and I will know, not the word of those who are puffed up, but the power. ²⁰For the kingdom of God *is* not in word but in power. ²¹What do you want? Shall I come to you with a rod, or in love and a spirit of gentleness?

Immorality Defiles the Church

5 It is actually reported *that there is* sexual immorality among you, and such sexual immorality as is not even namedᵃ among the Gentiles—that a man has his father's wife! ²And you are puffed up, and have not rather mourned, that he who has done this deed might be taken away from among you. ³For I indeed, as absent in body but present in spirit, have already judged (as though I were present) him who has so done this deed. ⁴In the name of our Lord Jesus Christ, when you are gathered together, along with my spirit, with the power of our Lord Jesus Christ, ⁵deliver such a one to Satan for the destruction of the flesh, that his spirit may be saved in the day of the Lord Jesus.ᵃ

⁶Your glorying *is* not good. Do you not know that a little leaven leavens the whole lump? ⁷Therefore purge out the old leaven, that you may be a new lump, since you truly are unleavened. For indeed Christ, our Passover, was sacrificed for us.ᵃ ⁸Therefore let us keep the feast, not with old leaven, nor with the leaven of malice and wickedness, but with the unleavened *bread* of sincerity and truth.

Immorality Must Be Judged

⁹I wrote to you in my epistle not to keep company with sexually immoral people. ¹⁰Yet *I* certainly *did* not *mean* with the sexually immoral people of this world, or with the covetous, or extortioners, or idolaters, since then you would need to go out of the world. ¹¹But now I have written to you not

---

4:3 ᵃLiterally *day*   **5:1** ᵃNU-Text omits *named.*
5:5 ᵃNU-Text omits *Jesus.*   **5:7** ᵃNU-Text omits *for us.*

to keep company with anyone named a brother, who is sexually immoral, or covetous, or an idolater, or a reviler, or a drunkard, or an extortioner—not even to eat with such a person.

¹²For what *have* I *to do* with judging those also who are outside? Do you not judge those who are inside? ¹³But those who are outside God judges. Therefore *"put away from yourselves the evil person."*ᵃ

Do Not Sue the Brethren

6 Dare any of you, having a matter against another, go to law before the unrighteous, and not before the saints? ²Do you not know that the saints will judge the world? And if the world will be judged by you, are you unworthy to judge the smallest matters? ³Do you not know that we shall judge angels? How much more, things that

pertain to this life? ⁴If then you have judgments concerning things pertaining to this life, do you appoint those who are least esteemed by the church to judge? ⁵I say this to your shame. Is it so, that there is not a wise man among you, not even one, who will be able to judge between his brethren? ⁶But brother goes to law against brother, and that before unbelievers!

⁷Now therefore, it is already an utter failure for you that you go to law against one another. Why do you not rather accept wrong? Why do you not rather *let yourselves* be cheated? ⁸No, you yourselves do wrong and cheat, and *you do* these things *to your* brethren! ⁹Do you not know that the unrighteous will not inherit the kingdom of God? Do not be deceived. Neither

---

5:13 ᵃDeuteronomy 17:7; 19:19; 22:21, 24; 24:7

Joseph Story

TRUTH

. . . nor thieves, nor covetous, nor drunkards, nor revilers, nor extortioners. . . .

1 CORINTHIANS 6:10

CHRISTIANITY AND COMMON LAW

At the age of 32, Joseph Story became the youngest Associate Justice of the Supreme Court and served from 1811 to 1845, writing 286 opinions. He was also the Dane Professor of Law at Harvard and wrote many legal texts now considered classics. His three-volume set of *Commentaries on the Constitution of the United States* is still the standard treatise on the subject.

At a point in his life where Story doubted the truth of Christianity, he "labored and read with assiduous attention all of the arguments of its proof" and became committed to the principles of Christianity, which he repeatedly expressed throughout his lengthy legal career. It was his conviction that American law and legal practices must never be separated from Christian principles. As he explained:

One of the beautiful boasts of our municipal jurisprudence is that Christianity is a part of the Common Law. . . . There never has been a period in which the Common Law did not recognize Christianity as lying at its foundations. . . . [The law] pronounces illegal every contract offensive to [Christianity's] morals. It recognizes with profound humility [Christianity's] holidays and festivals, and obeys them [even to the point of suspending all government functions on those days]. It still attaches to persons believing in [Christianity's] divine authority the highest degree of competency as witnesses.

fornicators, nor idolaters, nor adulterers, nor homosexuals,[a] nor sodomites, [10]nor thieves, nor covetous, nor drunkards, nor revilers, nor extortioners will inherit the kingdom of God. [11]And such were some of you. But you were washed, but you were sanctified, but you were justified in the name of the Lord Jesus and by the Spirit of our God.

FAMILY VALUES
. . . let each man have his own wife. . . .

1 CORINTHIANS 7:2

One Man, One Woman
In the 1885 Utah Territory case of *Murphy v. Ramsey*, the U.S. Supreme Court recognized the fundamental importance of the traditional institution of marriage:

> *Every person who has a husband or wife living . . . and marries another . . . is guilty of polygamy, and shall be punished. . . . For certainly no legislation can be supposed more wholesome and necessary in the founding of a free, self-governing commonwealth, fit to take rank as one of the coordinate States of the Union, than that which seeks to establish it on the basis of the idea of the family, as consisting in and springing from the union for life of one man and one woman in the holy estate of matrimony; the sure foundation of all that is stable and noble in our civilization; the best guaranty of that reverent morality which is the source of all beneficent progress in social and political improvement.*

Glorify God in Body and Spirit

[12]All things are lawful for me, but all things are not helpful. All things are lawful for me, but I will not be brought under the power of any. [13]Foods for the stomach and the stomach for foods, but God will destroy both it and them. Now the body *is* not for sexual immorality but for the Lord, and the Lord for the body. [14]And God both raised up the Lord and will also raise us up by His power.

[15]Do you not know that your bodies are members of Christ? Shall I then take the members of Christ and make *them* members of a harlot? Certainly not! [16]Or do you not know that he who is joined to a harlot is one body *with her*? For *"the two,"* He says, *"shall become one flesh."*[a] [17]But he who is joined to the Lord is one spirit *with Him*.

[18]Flee sexual immorality. Every sin that a man does is outside the body, but he who commits sexual immorality sins against his own body. [19]Or do you not know that your body is the temple of the Holy Spirit *who is* in you, whom you have from God, and you are not your own? [20]For you were bought at a price; therefore glorify God in your body[a] and in your spirit, which are God's.

Principles of Marriage

7 Now concerning the things of which you wrote to me:

It is good for a man not to touch a woman. [2]Nevertheless, because of sexual immorality, let each man have his own wife, and let each woman have her own husband. [3]Let the husband render to his wife the affection due her, and likewise also the wife to her husband. [4]The wife does not have authority over her own body, but the husband *does*. And likewise the husband does not have authority over his own body, but the wife *does*. [5]Do not deprive one another except with consent for a time, that you may give yourselves to fasting and prayer; and come together again so that Satan does not tempt you because of your lack of self-control. [6]But I say this as a concession, not as a commandment. [7]For I wish that all men were even as I myself. But each one has his own gift from God, one in this manner and another in that.

[8]But I say to the unmarried and to the widows: It is good for them if they remain even as I am; [9]but if they cannot exercise self-control, let them marry. For it is better to marry than to burn *with passion*.

Keep Your Marriage Vows

[10]Now to the married I command, *yet* not I but the Lord: A wife is not to depart from *her* husband. [11]But even if she does depart, let her remain unmarried or be reconciled to *her* husband. And a husband is not to divorce *his* wife.

6:9 [a]That is, catamites   **6:16** [a]Genesis 2:24
6:20 [a]NU-Text ends the verse at *body*.

¹²But to the rest I, not the Lord, say: If any brother has a wife who does not believe, and she is willing to live with him, let him not divorce her. ¹³And a woman who has a husband who does not believe, if he is willing to live with her, let her not divorce him. ¹⁴For the unbelieving husband is sanctified by the wife, and the unbelieving wife is sanctified by the husband; otherwise your children would be unclean, but now they are holy. ¹⁵But if the unbeliever departs, let him depart; a brother or a sister is not under bondage in such *cases.* But God has called us to peace. ¹⁶For how do you know, O wife, whether you will save *your* husband? Or how do you know, O husband, whether you will save *your* wife?

Live as You Are Called

¹⁷But as God has distributed to each one, as the Lord has called each one, so let him walk. And so I ordain in all the churches. ¹⁸Was anyone called while circumcised? Let him not become uncircumcised. Was anyone called while uncircumcised? Let him not be circumcised. ¹⁹Circumcision is nothing and uncircumcision is nothing, but keeping the commandments of God *is what matters.* ²⁰Let each one remain in the same calling in which he was called. ²¹Were you called *while* a slave? Do not be concerned about it; but if you can be made free, rather use *it.* ²²For he who is called in the Lord *while* a slave is the Lord's freedman. Likewise he who is called *while* free is Christ's slave. ²³You were bought at a price; do not become slaves of men. ²⁴Brethren, let each one remain with God in that *state* in which he was called.

To the Unmarried and Widows

²⁵Now concerning virgins: I have no commandment from the Lord; yet I give judgment as one whom the Lord in His mercy has made trustworthy. ²⁶I suppose therefore that this is good because of the present distress—that *it is* good for a man to remain as he is: ²⁷Are you bound to a wife? Do not seek to be loosed. Are you loosed from a wife? Do not seek a wife. ²⁸But even if you do marry, you have not sinned; and if a virgin marries, she has not sinned. Nevertheless such will have trouble in the flesh, but I would spare you.

²⁹But this I say, brethren, the time *is* short, so that from now on even those who have wives should be as though they had none, ³⁰those who weep as though they did not weep, those who rejoice as though they did not rejoice, those who buy as though they did not possess, ³¹and those who use this world as not misusing *it.* For the form of this world is passing away.

³²But I want you to be without care. He who is unmarried cares for the things of the Lord—how he may please the Lord. ³³But he who is married cares about the things of the world—how he may please *his* wife. ³⁴There isª a difference between a wife and a virgin. The unmarried woman cares about the things of the Lord, that she may be holy both in body and in spirit. But she who is married cares about the things of the world—how she may please *her* husband. ³⁵And this I say for your own profit, not that I may put a leash on you, but for what is proper, and that you may serve the Lord without distraction.

³⁶But if any man thinks he is behaving improperly toward his virgin, if she is past the flower of youth, and thus it must be, let him do what he wishes. He does not sin; let them marry. ³⁷Nevertheless he who stands steadfast in his heart, having no necessity, but has power over his own will, and has so determined in his heart that he will keep his virgin,ª does well. ³⁸So then he who gives herª in marriage does well, but he who does not give *her* in marriage does better.

³⁹A wife is bound by law as long as her husband lives; but if her husband dies, she is at liberty to be married to whom she wishes, only in the Lord. ⁴⁰But she is happier if she remains as she is, according to my judgment—and I think I also have the Spirit of God.

Be Sensitive to Conscience

8 Now concerning things offered to idols: We know that we all have knowledge. Knowledge puffs up, but love edifies. ²And

---

7:34 ªM-Text adds *also.*   **7:37** ªOr *virgin daughter*
7:38 ªNU-Text reads *his own virgin.*

if anyone thinks that he knows anything, he knows nothing yet as he ought to know. ³But if anyone loves God, this one is known by Him.

⁴Therefore concerning the eating of things offered to idols, we know that an idol *is* nothing in the world, and that *there is* no other God but one. ⁵For even if there are so-called gods, whether in heaven or on earth (as there are many gods and many lords), ⁶yet for us *there is* one God, the Father, of whom *are* all things, and we for Him; and one Lord Jesus Christ, through whom *are* all things, and through whom we *live.*

⁷However, *there is* not in everyone that knowledge; for some, with consciousness of the idol, until now eat *it* as a thing offered to an idol; and their conscience, being weak, is defiled. ⁸But food does not commend us to God; for neither if we eat are we the better, nor if we do not eat are we the worse.

⁹But beware lest somehow this liberty of yours become a stumbling block to those who are weak. ¹⁰For if anyone sees you who have knowledge eating in an idol's temple, will not the conscience of him who is weak be emboldened to eat those things offered to idols? ¹¹And because of your knowledge shall the weak brother perish, for whom Christ died? ¹²But when you thus sin against the brethren, and wound their weak conscience, you sin against Christ. ¹³Therefore, if food makes my brother stumble, I will never again eat meat, lest I make my brother stumble.

A Pattern of Self-Denial

9 Am I not an apostle? Am I not free? Have I not seen Jesus Christ our Lord? Are you not my work in the Lord? ²If I am not an apostle to others, yet doubtless I am to you. For you are the seal of my apostleship in the Lord.

³My defense to those who examine me is this: ⁴Do we have no right to eat and drink? ⁵Do we have no right to take along a believing wife, as *do* also the other apostles, the brothers of the Lord, and Cephas? ⁶Or *is it* only Barnabas and I *who* have no right to refrain from working? ⁷Who ever goes to war at his own expense? Who plants a vineyard and does not eat of its fruit? Or

who tends a flock and does not drink of the milk of the flock?

⁸Do I say these things as a *mere* man? Or does not the law say the same also? ⁹For it is written in the law of Moses, *"You shall not muzzle an ox while it treads out the grain."*ᵃ Is it oxen God is concerned about? ¹⁰Or does He say *it* altogether for our sakes? For our sakes, no doubt, *this* is written, that he who plows should plow in hope, and he who threshes in hope should be partaker of his hope. ¹¹If we have sown spiritual things for you, *is it* a great thing if we reap your material things? ¹²If others are partakers of *this* right over you, *are* we not even more?

Nevertheless we have not used this right, but endure all things lest we hinder the gospel of Christ. ¹³Do you not know that those who minister the holy things eat *of the things* of the temple, and those who serve at the altar partake of *the offerings of* the altar? ¹⁴Even so the Lord has commanded that those who preach the gospel should live from the gospel.

¹⁵But I have used none of these things, nor have I written these things that it should be done so to me; for it *would be* better for me to die than that anyone should make my boasting void. ¹⁶For if I preach the gospel, I have nothing to boast of, for necessity is laid upon me; yes, woe is me if I do not preach the gospel! ¹⁷For if I do this willingly, I have a reward; but if against my will, I have been entrusted with a stewardship. ¹⁸What is my reward then? That when I preach the gospel, I may present the gospel of Christᵃ without charge, that I may not abuse my authority in the gospel.

Serving All Men

¹⁹For though I am free from all *men,* I have made myself a servant to all, that I might win the more; ²⁰and to the Jews I became as a Jew, that I might win Jews; to those *who are* under the law, as under the law,ᵃ that I might win those *who are* under the law; ²¹to those *who are* without law, as without law (not being without law toward

---

9:9 ᵃDeuteronomy 25:4   **9:18** ᵃNU-Text omits *of Christ.*   **9:20** ᵃNU-Text adds *though not being myself under the law.*

God,[a] but under law toward Christ[b]), that I might win those *who are* without law; [22]to the weak I became as[a] weak, that I might win the weak. I have become all things to all *men,* that I might by all means save some. [23]Now this I do for the gospel's sake, that I may be partaker of it with *you.*

Striving for a Crown

[24]Do you not know that those who run in a race all run, but one receives the prize? Run in such a way that you may obtain *it.* [25]And everyone who competes *for the prize* is temperate in all things. Now they *do it* to obtain a perishable crown, but we *for* an imperishable *crown.* [26]Therefore I run thus: not with uncertainty. Thus I fight: not as *one who* beats the air. [27]But I discipline my body and bring *it* into subjection, lest, when I have preached to others, I myself should become disqualified.

Old Testament Examples

10 Moreover, brethren, I do not want you to be unaware that all our fathers were under the cloud, all passed through the sea, [2]all were baptized into Moses in the cloud and in the sea, [3]all ate the same spiritual food, [4]and all drank the same spiritual drink. For they drank of that spiritual Rock that followed them, and that Rock was Christ. [5]But with most of them God was not well pleased, for *their bodies* were scattered in the wilderness.

[6]Now these things became our examples, to the intent that we should not lust after evil things as they also lusted. [7]And do not become idolaters as *were* some of them. As it is written, *"The people sat down to eat and drink, and rose up to play."*[a] [8]Nor let us commit sexual immorality, as some of them did, and in one day twenty-three thousand fell; [9]nor let us tempt Christ, as some of them also tempted, and were destroyed by serpents; [10]nor complain, as some of them also complained, and were destroyed by the destroyer. [11]Now all[a] these things happened to them as examples, and they were written for our admonition, upon whom the ends of the ages have come.

[12]Therefore let him who thinks he stands take heed lest he fall. [13]No temptation has overtaken you except such as is common to man; but God *is* faithful, who will not allow you to be tempted beyond what you are able, but with the temptation will also make the way of escape, that you may be able to bear *it.*

Flee from Idolatry

[14]Therefore, my beloved, flee from idolatry. [15]I speak as to wise men; judge for yourselves what I say. [16]The cup of blessing which we bless, is it not the communion of the blood of Christ? The bread which we break, is it not the communion of the body of Christ? [17]For we, *though* many, are one bread *and* one body; for we all partake of that one bread.

[18]Observe Israel after the flesh: Are not those who eat of the sacrifices partakers of the altar? [19]What am I saying then? That an idol is anything, or what is offered to idols is anything? [20]Rather, that the things which the Gentiles sacrifice they sacrifice to demons and not to God, and I do not want you to have fellowship with demons. [21]You cannot drink the cup of the Lord and the cup of demons; you cannot partake of the Lord's table and of the table of demons. [22]Or do we provoke the Lord to jealousy? Are we stronger than He?

All to the Glory of God

[23]All things are lawful for me,[a] but not all things are helpful; all things are lawful for me,[b] but not all things edify. [24]Let no one seek his own, but each one the other's *well-being.*

[25]Eat whatever is sold in the meat market, asking no questions for conscience' sake; [26]for *"the earth is the LORD's, and all its fullness."*[a]

[27]If any of those who do not believe invites you *to dinner,* and you desire to go, eat whatever is set before you, asking no question for conscience' sake. [28]But if anyone says to you, "This was offered to idols," do not eat it for the sake of the one who

---

9:21 [a]NU-Text reads *God's law.* [b]NU-Text reads *Christ's law.* **9:22** [a]NU-Text omits *as.* **10:7** [a]Exodus 32:6 **10:11** [a]NU-Text omits *all.* **10:23** [a]NU-Text omits *for me.* [b]NU-Text omits *for me.* **10:26** [a]Psalm 24:1

told you, and for conscience' sake;[a] for *"the earth is the LORD's, and all its fullness."*[b] [29]"Conscience," I say, not your own, but that of the other. For why is my liberty judged by another *man's* conscience? [30]But if I partake with thanks, why am I evil spoken of for *the food* over which I give thanks?

[31]Therefore, whether you eat or drink, or whatever you do, do all to the glory of God. [32]Give no offense, either to the Jews or to the Greeks or to the church of God, [33]just as I also please all *men* in all *things,* not seeking my own profit, but the *profit* of many, that they may be saved.

11 Imitate me, just as I also *imitate* Christ.

Head Coverings

[2]Now I praise you, brethren, that you remember me in all things and keep the traditions just as I delivered *them* to you. [3]But I want you to know that the head of every man is Christ, the head of woman *is* man, and the head of Christ *is* God. [4]Every man praying or prophesying, having *his* head covered, dishonors his head. [5]But every woman who prays or prophesies with *her* head uncovered dishonors her head, for that is one and the same as if her head were shaved. [6]For if a woman is not covered, let her also be shorn. But if it is shameful for a woman to be shorn or shaved, let her be covered. [7]For a man indeed ought not to cover *his* head, since he is the image and glory of God; but woman is the glory of man. [8]For man is not from woman, but woman from man. [9]Nor was man created for the woman, but woman for the man. [10]For this reason the woman ought to have *a symbol of* authority on *her* head, because of the angels. [11]Nevertheless, neither *is* man independent of woman, nor woman independent of man, in the Lord. [12]For as woman *came* from man, even so man also *comes* through woman; but all things are from God.

[13]Judge among yourselves. Is it proper for a woman to pray to God with her head uncovered? [14]Does not even nature itself teach you that if a man has long hair, it is a dishonor to him? [15]But if a woman has

long hair, it is a glory to her; for *her* hair is given to her[a] for a covering. [16]But if anyone seems to be contentious, we have no such custom, nor *do* the churches of God.

Conduct at the Lord's Supper

[17]Now in giving these instructions I do not praise *you,* since you come together not for the better but for the worse. [18]For first of all, when you come together as a church, I hear that there are divisions among you, and in part I believe it. [19]For there must also be factions among you, that those who are approved may be recognized among you. [20]Therefore when you come together in one place, it is not to eat the Lord's Supper. [21]For in eating, each one takes his own supper ahead of *others;* and one is hungry and another is drunk. [22]What! Do you not have houses to eat and drink in? Or do you despise the church of God and shame those who have nothing? What shall I say to you? Shall I praise you in this? I do not praise *you.*

Institution of the Lord's Supper

[23]For I received from the Lord that which I also delivered to you: that the Lord Jesus on the *same* night in which He was betrayed took bread; [24]and when He had given thanks, He broke *it* and said, "Take, eat;[a] this is My body which is broken[b] for you; do this in remembrance of Me." [25]In the same manner *He* also *took* the cup after supper, saying, "This cup is the new covenant in My blood. This do, as often as you drink *it,* in remembrance of Me."

[26]For as often as you eat this bread and drink this cup, you proclaim the Lord's death till He comes.

Examine Yourself

[27]Therefore whoever eats this bread or drinks *this* cup of the Lord in an unworthy manner will be guilty of the body and blood[a] of the Lord. [28]But let a man examine

---

10:28 [a]NU-Text omits the rest of this verse. [b]Psalm 24:1 **11:15** [a]M-Text omits *to her.* **11:24** [a]NU-Text omits *Take, eat.* [b]NU-Text omits *broken.* **11:27** [a]NU-Text and M-Text read *the blood.*

himself, and so let him eat of the bread and drink of the cup. ²⁹For he who eats and drinks in an unworthy manner[a] eats and drinks judgment to himself, not discerning the Lord's[b] body. ³⁰For this reason many *are* weak and sick among you, and many sleep. ³¹For if we would judge ourselves, we would not be judged. ³²But when we are judged, we are chastened by the Lord, that we may not be condemned with the world.

³³Therefore, my brethren, when you come together to eat, wait for one another. ³⁴But if anyone is hungry, let him eat at home, lest you come together for judgment. And the rest I will set in order when I come.

Spiritual Gifts: Unity in Diversity

12 Now concerning spiritual *gifts,* brethren, I do not want you to be ignorant: ²You know that[a] you were Gentiles, carried away to these dumb idols, however you were led. ³Therefore I make known to you that no one speaking by the Spirit of God calls Jesus accursed, and no one can say that Jesus is Lord except by the Holy Spirit.

⁴There are diversities of gifts, but the same Spirit. ⁵There are differences of ministries, but the same Lord. ⁶And there are diversities of activities, but it is the same God who works all in all. ⁷But the manifestation of the Spirit is given to each one for the profit *of all:* ⁸for to one is given the word of wisdom through the Spirit, to another the word of knowledge through the same Spirit, ⁹to another faith by the same Spirit, to another gifts of healings by the same[a] Spirit, ¹⁰to another the working of miracles, to another prophecy, to another discerning of spirits, to another *different* kinds of tongues, to another the interpretation of tongues. ¹¹But one and the same Spirit works all these things, distributing to each one individually as He wills.

Unity and Diversity in One Body

¹²For as the body is one and has many members, but all the members of that one body, being many, are one body, so also *is* Christ. ¹³For by one Spirit we were all baptized into one body—whether Jews or Greeks, whether slaves or free—and have all been made to drink into[a] one Spirit. ¹⁴For in fact the body is not one member but many.

¹⁵If the foot should say, "Because I am not a hand, I am not of the body," is it therefore not of the body? ¹⁶And if the ear should say, "Because I am not an eye, I am not of the body," is it therefore not of the body? ¹⁷If the whole body *were* an eye, where *would be* the hearing? If the whole *were* hearing, where *would be* the smelling? ¹⁸But now God has set the members, each one of them, in the body just as He pleased. ¹⁹And if they were all one member, where *would* the body *be?*

²⁰But now indeed *there are* many members, yet one body. ²¹And the eye cannot say to the hand, "I have no need of you"; nor again the head to the feet, "I have no need of you." ²²No, much rather, those members of the body which seem to be weaker are necessary. ²³And those *members* of the body which we think to be less honorable, on these we bestow greater honor; and our unpresentable *parts* have greater modesty, ²⁴but our presentable *parts* have no need. But God composed the body, having given greater honor to that *part* which lacks it, ²⁵that there should be no schism in the body, but *that* the members should have the same care for one another. ²⁶And if one member suffers, all the members suffer with *it;* or if one member is honored, all the members rejoice with *it.*

²⁷Now you are the body of Christ, and members individually. ²⁸And God has appointed these in the church: first apostles, second prophets, third teachers, after that miracles, then gifts of healings, helps, administrations, varieties of tongues. ²⁹*Are* all apostles? *Are* all prophets? *Are* all teachers? *Are* all workers of miracles? ³⁰Do all have gifts of healings? Do all speak with tongues? Do all interpret? ³¹But earnestly desire the best[a] gifts. And yet I show you a more excellent way.

11:29 [a]NU-Text omits *in an unworthy manner.* [b]NU-Text omits *Lord's.*   **12:2** [a]NU-Text and M-Text add *when.*   **12:9** [a]NU-Text reads *one.*   **12:13** [a]NU-Text omits *into.*   **12:31** [a]NU-Text reads *greater.*

Franklin D. Roosevelt placed his hand on 1 Corinthians 13 as he took the presidential oath of office in 1933, 1937, 1941, and 1945.

The Greatest Gift

13 Though I speak with the tongues of men and of angels, but have not love, I have become sounding brass or a clanging cymbal. ²And though I have *the gift of* prophecy, and understand all mysteries and all knowledge, and though I have all faith, so that I could remove mountains, but have not love, I am nothing. ³And though I bestow all my goods to feed *the poor,* and though I give my body to be burned,ᵃ but have not love, it profits me nothing.

⁴Love suffers long *and* is kind; love does not envy; love does not parade itself, is not puffed up; ⁵does not behave rudely, does not seek its own, is not provoked, thinks no evil; ⁶does not rejoice in iniquity, but rejoices in the truth; ⁷bears all things, believes all things, hopes all things, endures all things.

⁸Love never fails. But whether *there are* prophecies, they will fail; whether *there are* tongues, they will cease; whether *there is* knowledge, it will vanish away. ⁹For we know in part and we prophesy in part. ¹⁰But when that which is perfect has come, then that which is in part will be done away.

¹¹When I was a child, I spoke as a child, I understood as a child, I thought as a child; but when I became a man, I put away childish things. ¹²For now we see in a mirror, dimly, but then face to face. Now I know in part, but then I shall know just as I also am known.

¹³And now abide faith, hope, love, these three; but the greatest of these *is* love.

Prophecy and Tongues

14 Pursue love, and desire spiritual *gifts,* but especially that you may prophesy. ²For he who speaks in a tongue does not speak to men but to God, for no one understands *him;* however, in the spirit he speaks mysteries. ³But he who prophesies speaks edification and exhortation and comfort to men. ⁴He who speaks in a tongue edifies himself, but he who prophesies edifies the church. ⁵I wish you all spoke with tongues, but even more that you prophesied; forᵃ he who prophesies *is* greater than he who speaks with tongues, unless indeed he interprets, that the church may receive edification.

Tongues Must Be Interpreted

⁶But now, brethren, if I come to you speaking with tongues, what shall I profit you unless I speak to you either by revelation, by knowledge, by prophesying, or by teaching? ⁷Even things without life, whether flute or harp, when they make a sound, unless they make a distinction in the sounds, how will it be known what is piped or played? ⁸For if the trumpet makes an uncertain sound, who will prepare for battle? ⁹So likewise you, unless you utter by the tongue words easy to understand, how will it be known what is spoken? For you will be speaking into the air. ¹⁰There are, it may be, so many kinds of languages in the world, and none of them *is* without significance. ¹¹Therefore, if I do not know the meaning of the language, I shall be a foreigner to him who speaks, and he who speaks *will be* a foreigner to me. ¹²Even so you, since you are zealous for spiritual *gifts, let it be* for the edification of the church *that* you seek to excel.

¹³Therefore let him who speaks in a tongue pray that he may interpret. ¹⁴For if I pray in a tongue, my spirit prays, but my understanding is unfruitful. ¹⁵What is *the conclusion* then? I will pray with the spirit, and I will also pray with the understanding. I will sing with the spirit, and I will also sing with the understanding. ¹⁶Otherwise, if you bless with the spirit, how will he who occupies the place of the uninformed say "Amen" at your giving of thanks, since he does not understand what you say? ¹⁷For you indeed give thanks well, but the other is not edified.

¹⁸I thank my God I speak with tongues more than you all; ¹⁹yet in the church I

13:3 ᵃNU-Text reads *so I may boast.*   **14:5** ᵃNU-Text reads *and.*

WAR HERO WITHOUT A GUN

DESMOND DOSS

When Desmond Doss was inducted into the U.S. Army in April 1942, he entered service as a conscientious objector for his religious beliefs and served as a medic for the 77th Infantry Division. From the beginning, the other men in his company harassed and threatened Doss for his beliefs and his quiet reading of the pocket-sized Bible his wife had given him, even trying to get him transferred out of their unit.

On Okinawa, in the late spring of 1945, his battalion assaulted a jagged escarpment 400 feet high. As the troops gained the summit, a heavy concentration of artillery, mortar, and machine-gun fire crashed into them, inflicting approximately 75 casualties and driving the others back. Doss refused to seek cover and remained in the fire-swept area with the many stricken, carrying them one by one to the edge of the escarpment and there lowering them on a rope-supported litter down the face of a cliff to friendly hands. Each time he got one of them to safety, he prayed, "Dear God, let me get just one more man."

In three more battles in May, he unhesitatingly braved enemy artillery and mortar shells, small arms fire, and showers of grenades to dress his comrades' wounds and evacuate them to safety. On May 21, while giving aid to the injured, he was seriously wounded in the legs by the explosion of a grenade. Caring for his own injuries, he waited five hours before litter bearers reached him and started carrying him to cover. Along the way, Doss insisted on giving his stretcher to a badly injured GI. Awaiting the litter bearers' return, he was struck by a bullet, suffering a compound fracture of one arm. With magnificent fortitude, he bound a rifle stock to his shattered arm as a splint and then crawled 300 yards over rough terrain to the aid station.

Discovering he had lost his Bible, Doss sent word asking if the men could keep an eye out for it. An entire battalion combed the battlefield until that Bible was found. A sergeant carefully dried it out and mailed it to Doss.

Through his outstanding bravery and unflinching determination in the face of desperately dangerous conditions, Private First Class Doss saved the lives of many soldiers and became the first conscientious objector to receive the Congressional Medal of Honor for outstanding gallantry far above and beyond the call of duty.

would rather speak five words with my understanding, that I may teach others also, than ten thousand words in a tongue.

Tongues a Sign to Unbelievers

20Brethren, do not be children in understanding; however, in malice be babes, but in understanding be mature.

21In the law it is written:

> "With men of other tongues and other
> lips
> I will speak to this people;
> And yet, for all that, they will not
> hear Me,"a

says the Lord.

22Therefore tongues are for a sign, not to those who believe but to unbelievers; but prophesying is not for unbelievers but for those who believe. 23Therefore if the whole church comes together in one place, and all speak with tongues, and there come in those who are uninformed or unbelievers, will they not say that you are out of your mind? 24But if all prophesy, and an unbeliever or an uninformed person comes in, he is convinced by all, he is convicted by all. 25And thusa the secrets of his heart are revealed; and so, falling down on his face, he will worship God and report that God is truly among you.

Order in Church Meetings

26How is it then, brethren? Whenever you come together, each of you has a psalm, has a teaching, has a tongue, has a revelation, has an interpretation. Let all things be done for edification. 27If anyone speaks in a tongue, let there be two or at the most three, each in turn, and let one interpret. 28But if there is no interpreter, let him keep silent in church, and let him speak to himself and to God. 29Let two or three prophets speak, and let the others judge. 30But if anything is revealed to another who sits by, let the first keep silent. 31For you can all prophesy one by one, that all may learn and all may be encouraged. 32And the spirits of the prophets are subject to the prophets. 33For God is not the author of confusion but of peace, as in all the churches of the saints.

34Let youra women keep silent in the churches, for they are not permitted to speak; but they are to be submissive, as the law also says. 35And if they want to learn something, let them ask their own husbands at home; for it is shameful for women to speak in church.

36Or did the word of God come originally from you? Or was it you only that it reached? 37If anyone thinks himself to be a prophet or spiritual, let him acknowledge that the things which I write to you are the commandments of the Lord. 38But if anyone is ignorant, let him be ignorant.a

39Therefore, brethren, desire earnestly to prophesy, and do not forbid to speak with tongues. 40Let all things be done decently and in order.

The Risen Christ, Faith's Reality

15 Moreover, brethren, I declare to you the gospel which I preached to you, which also you received and in which you stand, 2by which also you are saved, if you hold fast that word which I preached to you— unless you believed in vain.

3For I delivered to you first of all that which I also received: that Christ died for our sins according to the Scriptures, 4and that He was buried, and that He rose again the third day according to the Scriptures, 5and that He was seen by Cephas, then by the twelve. 6After that He was seen by over five hundred brethren at once, of whom the greater part remain to the present, but some have fallen asleep. 7After that He was seen by James, then by all the apostles. 8Then last of all He was seen by me also, as by one born out of due time.

9For I am the least of the apostles, who am not worthy to be called an apostle, because I persecuted the church of God. 10But by the grace of God I am what I am, and His grace toward me was not in vain; but I labored more abundantly than they all, yet not I, but the grace of God which was with me. 11Therefore, whether it was I or they, so we preach and so you believed.

14:21 aIsaiah 28:11, 12   14:25 aNU-Text omits And thus.   14:34 aNU-Text omits your.   14:38 aNU-Text reads if anyone does not recognize this, he is not recognized.

The Risen Christ, Our Hope

¹²Now if Christ is preached that He has been raised from the dead, how do some among you say that there is no resurrection of the dead? ¹³But if there is no resurrection of the dead, then Christ is not risen. ¹⁴And if Christ is not risen, then our preaching *is* empty and your faith *is* also empty. ¹⁵Yes, and we are found false witnesses of God, because we have testified of God that He raised up Christ, whom He did not raise up— if in fact the dead do not rise. ¹⁶For if *the* dead do not rise, then Christ is not risen. ¹⁷And if Christ is not risen, your faith *is* futile; you are still in your sins! ¹⁸Then also those who have fallen asleep in Christ have perished. ¹⁹If in this life only we have hope in Christ, we are of all men the most pitiable.

The Last Enemy Destroyed

²⁰But now Christ is risen from the dead, *and* has become the firstfruits of those who have fallen asleep. ²¹For since by man *came* death, by Man also *came* the resurrection of the dead. ²²For as in Adam all die, even so in Christ all shall be made alive. ²³But each one in his own order: Christ the firstfruits, afterward those *who are* Christ's at His coming. ²⁴Then *comes* the end, when He delivers the kingdom to God the Father, when He puts an end to all rule and all authority and power. ²⁵For He must reign till He has put all enemies under His feet. ²⁶The last enemy *that* will be destroyed *is* death. ²⁷For *"He has put all things under His feet."*ᵃ But when He says "all things are put under *Him,*" *it is* evident that He who put all things under Him is excepted. ²⁸Now when all things are made subject to Him, then the Son Himself will also be subject to Him who put all things under Him, that God may be all in all.

15:27 ᵃPsalm 8:6

TRUTH

And if Christ is not risen, your faith is futile. . . .

1 CORINTHIANS 15:17

Daniel Webster

TRUE HISTORY OR CONSUMMATE FRAUD?

Daniel Webster (1782–1852), a leading American statesman during the nation's Antebellum Period, declared:

> *The Gospel is either true history, or it is a consummate fraud; it is either a reality or an imposition. Christ was what He professed to be, or He was an imposter. There is no other alternative.*
>
> *His spotless life in His earnest enforcement of the truth—His suffering in its defense, forbid us to suppose that He was suffering an illusion of a heated brain. Every act of His pure and holy life shows that He was the author of truth, the advocate of truth, the earnest defender of truth, and the uncompromising sufferer for truth.*
>
> *Now, considering the purity of His doctrines, the simplicity of His life, and the sublimity of His death, is it possible that He would have died for an illusion? In all His preaching the Savior made no popular appeals; His discourses were always directed to the individual. Christ and His apostles sought to impress upon every man the conviction that he must stand or fall alone—he must live for himself, and die for himself, and give up his account to the omniscient God as though he were the only dependent creature in the universe. The Gospel leaves the individual sinner alone with himself and his God.*

Effects of Denying the Resurrection

29Otherwise, what will they do who are baptized for the dead, if the dead do not rise at all? Why then are they baptized for the dead? 30And why do we stand in jeopardy every hour? 31I affirm, by the boasting in you which I have in Christ Jesus our Lord, I die daily. 32If, in the manner of men, I have fought with beasts at Ephesus, what advantage *is it* to me? If *the* dead do not rise, *"Let us eat and drink, for tomorrow we die!"*a

33Do not be deceived: "Evil company corrupts good habits." 34Awake to righteousness, and do not sin; for some do not have the knowledge of God. I speak *this* to your shame.

A Glorious Body

35But someone will say, "How are the dead raised up? And with what body do they come?" 36Foolish one, what you sow is not made alive unless it dies. 37And what you sow, you do not sow that body that shall be, but mere grain—perhaps wheat or some other *grain.* 38But God gives it a body as He pleases, and to each seed its own body.

39All flesh *is* not the same flesh, but *there is* one *kind of* flesha of men, another flesh of animals, another of fish, *and* another of birds.

40*There are* also celestial bodies and terrestrial bodies; but the glory of the celestial *is* one, and the *glory* of the terrestrial *is* another. 41*There is* one glory of the sun, another glory of the moon, and another glory of the stars; for *one* star differs from *another* star in glory.

42So also *is* the resurrection of the dead. *The body* is sown in corruption, it is raised in incorruption. 43It is sown in dishonor, it is raised in glory. It is sown in weakness, it is raised in power. 44It is sown a natural body, it is raised a spiritual body. There is a natural body, and there is a spiritual body. 45And so it is written, *"The first man Adam became a living being."*a The last Adam *became* a life-giving spirit.

46However, the spiritual is not first, but the natural, and afterward the spiritual.

47The first man *was* of the earth, *made* of dust; the second Man *is* the Lorda from heaven. 48As *was* the *man* of dust, so also *are* those *who are made* of dust; and as *is* the heavenly *Man,* so also *are* those *who are* heavenly. 49And as we have borne the image of the *man* of dust, we shall also beara the image of the heavenly *Man.*

Our Final Victory

50Now this I say, brethren, that flesh and blood cannot inherit the kingdom of God; nor does corruption inherit incorruption. 51Behold, I tell you a mystery: We shall not all sleep, but we shall all be changed— 52in a moment, in the twinkling of an eye, at the last trumpet. For the trumpet will sound, and the dead will be raised incorruptible, and we shall be changed. 53For this corruptible must put on incorruption, and this mortal *must* put on immortality. 54So when this corruptible has put on incorruption, and this mortal has put on immortality, then shall be brought to pass the saying that is written: *"Death is swallowed up in victory."*a

55 *"O Death, where is your sting?*a
     *O Hades, where is your victory?"*b

56The sting of death *is* sin, and the strength of sin *is* the law. 57But thanks *be* to God, who gives us the victory through our Lord Jesus Christ.

58Therefore, my beloved brethren, be steadfast, immovable, always abounding in the work of the Lord, knowing that your labor is not in vain in the Lord.

Collection for the Saints

16 Now concerning the collection for the saints, as I have given orders to the churches of Galatia, so you must do also: 2On the first *day* of the week let each one of you lay something aside, storing up as he

---

15:32 aIsaiah 22:13   **15:39** aNU-Text and M-Text omit *of flesh.*   **15:45** aGenesis 2:7
15:47 aNU-Text omits *the Lord.*   **15:49** aM-Text reads *let us also bear.*   **15:54** aIsaiah 25:8
15:55 aHosea 13:14 bNU-Text reads *O Death, where is your victory? O Death, where is your sting?*

may prosper, that there be no collections when I come. ³And when I come, whomever you approve by *your* letters I will send to bear your gift to Jerusalem. ⁴But if it is fitting that I go also, they will go with me.

Personal Plans

⁵Now I will come to you when I pass through Macedonia (for I am passing through Macedonia). ⁶And it may be that I will remain, or even spend the winter with you, that you may send me on my journey, wherever I go. ⁷For I do not wish to see you now on the way; but I hope to stay a while with you, if the Lord permits.

⁸But I will tarry in Ephesus until Pentecost. ⁹For a great and effective door has opened to me, and *there are* many adversaries.

¹⁰And if Timothy comes, see that he may be with you without fear; for he does the work of the Lord, as I also *do.* ¹¹Therefore let no one despise him. But send him on his journey in peace, that he may come to me; for I am waiting for him with the brethren.

¹²Now concerning *our* brother Apollos, I strongly urged him to come to you with the brethren, but he was quite unwilling to come at this time; however, he will come when he has a convenient time.

Final Exhortations

¹³Watch, stand fast in the faith, be brave, be strong. ¹⁴Let all *that* you *do* be done with love.

¹⁵I urge you, brethren—you know the household of Stephanas, that it is the firstfruits of Achaia, and *that* they have devoted themselves to the ministry of the saints— ¹⁶that you also submit to such, and to everyone who works and labors with *us.*

¹⁷I am glad about the coming of Stephanas, Fortunatus, and Achaicus, for what was lacking on your part they supplied. ¹⁸For they refreshed my spirit and yours. Therefore acknowledge such men.

Greetings and a Solemn Farewell

¹⁹The churches of Asia greet you. Aquila and Priscilla greet you heartily in the Lord, with the church that is in their house. ²⁰All the brethren greet you.

Greet one another with a holy kiss.

²¹The salutation with my own hand—Paul's.

²²If anyone does not love the Lord Jesus Christ, let him be accursed.ᵃ O Lord, come!ᵇ

²³The grace of our Lord Jesus Christ *be* with you. ²⁴My love *be* with you all in Christ Jesus. Amen.

16:22 ᵃGreek *anathema* ᵇAramaic *Maranatha*

2 CORINTHIANS

Author: Paul

When Written: Around A.D. 56

Theme: Paul's Defense of His Ministry

Key Verse: 2 Corinthians 5:17—Therefore, if anyone is in Christ, he is a new creation; old things have passed away; behold, all things have become new.

Key Chapters: 2 Corinthians 8 and 9—These are really one unit and comprise the most complete revelation of God's plan for giving found anywhere in the Scriptures—the principles and purposes for giving, the policies to be followed in giving, and the promises to those who give.

Since Paul's first letter, the Corinthian church has been swayed by false teachers who turned the people against Paul. They claimed he was proud, unimpressive, and unqualified as an apostle of Jesus Christ. Paul sent Titus to Corinth to deal with these matters and, upon his return, rejoiced to hear of the Corinthians' change of heart. Paul wrote this letter to express his thanksgiving and to appeal to any who were still rejecting his authority.

Whether it is a problem of immorality or of false teachers, church leaders must take the appropriate action to remedy the problem. The same is true of government. President Thomas Jefferson stated, "When once a republic is corrupted, there is no possibility of remedying any of the growing evils but by removing the corruption and restoring its lost principles; every other correction is either useless or a new evil."

Greeting

1 Paul, an apostle of Jesus Christ by the will of God, and Timothy *our* brother,

To the church of God which is at Corinth, with all the saints who are in all Achaia:

²Grace to you and peace from God our Father and the Lord Jesus Christ.

Comfort in Suffering

³Blessed *be* the God and Father of our Lord Jesus Christ, the Father of mercies and God of all comfort, ⁴who comforts us in all our tribulation, that we may be able to comfort those who are in any trouble, with the comfort with which we ourselves are comforted by God. ⁵For as the sufferings of Christ abound in us, so our consolation also abounds through Christ. ⁶Now if we are afflicted, *it is* for your consolation and salvation, which is effective for enduring the same sufferings which we also suffer. Or if we are comforted, *it is* for your consolation and salvation. ⁷And our hope for you *is* steadfast, because we know that as you are partakers of the sufferings, so also *you will partake* of the consolation.

Delivered from Suffering

⁸For we do not want you to be ignorant, brethren, of our trouble which came to us in Asia: that we were burdened beyond measure, above strength, so that we despaired even of life. ⁹Yes, we had the sentence of death in ourselves, that we should not trust in ourselves but in God who raises the dead, ¹⁰who delivered us from so great a death, and does[a] deliver us; in whom we trust that He will still deliver *us*, ¹¹you also helping together in prayer for us, that thanks may be given by many persons on our[a] behalf for the gift *granted* to us through many.

Paul's Sincerity

¹²For our boasting is this: the testimony of our conscience that we conducted ourselves in the world in simplicity and godly sincerity, not with fleshly wisdom but by the grace of God, and more abundantly toward you. ¹³For we are not writing any other things to you than what you read or understand. Now I trust you will understand, even to the end ¹⁴(as also you have understood us in part), that we are your boast as you also *are* ours, in the day of the Lord Jesus.

Sparing the Church

¹⁵And in this confidence I intended to come to you before, that you might have a second benefit— ¹⁶to pass by way of you to Macedonia, to come again from Macedonia to you, and be helped by you on my way to Judea. ¹⁷Therefore, when I was planning this, did I do it lightly? Or the things I plan, do I plan according to the flesh, that with me there should be Yes, Yes, and No, No? ¹⁸But *as* God *is* faithful, our word to you was not Yes and No. ¹⁹For the Son of God, Jesus Christ, who was preached among you by us—by me, Silvanus, and Timothy—was not Yes and No, but in Him was Yes. ²⁰For all the promises of God in Him *are* Yes, and in Him Amen, to the glory of God through us. ²¹Now He who establishes us with you in Christ and has anointed us *is* God, ²²who also has sealed us and given us the Spirit in our hearts as a guarantee.

²³Moreover I call God as witness against my soul, that to spare you I came no more to Corinth. ²⁴Not that we have dominion over your faith, but are fellow workers for your joy; for by faith you stand.

2 But I determined this within myself, that I would not come again to you in sorrow. ²For if I make you sorrowful, then who is he who makes me glad but the one who is made sorrowful by me?

1:10 [a]NU-Text reads *shall.* **1:11** [a]M-Text reads *your behalf.*

Forgive the Offender

³And I wrote this very thing to you, lest, when I came, I should have sorrow over those from whom I ought to have joy, having confidence in you all that my joy is *the joy* of you all. ⁴For out of much affliction and anguish of heart I wrote to you, with many tears, not that you should be grieved, but that you might know the love which I have so abundantly for you.

⁵But if anyone has caused grief, he has not grieved me, but all of you to some extent—not to be too severe. ⁶This punishment which *was inflicted* by the majority *is* sufficient for such a man, ⁷so that, on the contrary, you *ought* rather to forgive and comfort *him,* lest perhaps such a one be swallowed up with too much sorrow. ⁸Therefore I urge you to reaffirm *your* love to him. ⁹For to this end I also wrote, that I might put you to the test, whether you are obedient in all things. ¹⁰Now whom you forgive anything, I also *forgive.* For if indeed I have forgiven anything, I have forgiven that one[a] for your sakes in the presence of Christ, ¹¹lest Satan should take advantage of us; for we are not ignorant of his devices.

Triumph in Christ

¹²Furthermore, when I came to Troas to *preach* Christ's gospel, and a door was opened to me by the Lord, ¹³I had no rest in my spirit, because I did not find Titus my brother; but taking my leave of them, I departed for Macedonia.

¹⁴Now thanks *be* to God who always leads us in triumph in Christ, and through us diffuses the fragrance of His knowledge in every place. ¹⁵For we are to God the fragrance of Christ among those who are being saved and among those who are perishing. ¹⁶To the one *we are* the aroma of death *leading* to death, and to the other the aroma of life *leading* to life. And who *is* sufficient for these things? ¹⁷For we are not, as so many,[a] peddling the word of God; but as of sincerity, but as from God, we speak in the sight of God in Christ.

Christ's Epistle

3 Do we begin again to commend ourselves? Or do we need, as some *others,*

epistles of commendation to you or *letters* of commendation from you? ²You are our epistle written in our hearts, known and read by all men; ³clearly you are an epistle of Christ, ministered by us, written not with ink but by the Spirit of the living God, not on tablets of stone but on tablets of flesh, *that is,* of the heart.

INSPIRING

. . . where the Spirit of the Lord is, there is liberty.
2 CORINTHIANS 3:17

Christianity, Liberty, and Science

Elaborating on the excesses inherent within the hierarchal state-controlled church, Thomas Jefferson, third president of the United States and author of the Declaration of Independence, wrote:

> The Christian religion, when divested of the rags in which they [the clergy] have enveloped it, and brought to the original purity and simplicity of its benevolent Institutor, is a religion of all others most friendly to liberty, science, and the freest expansion of the human mind.

The Spirit, Not the Letter

⁴And we have such trust through Christ toward God. ⁵Not that we are sufficient of ourselves to think of anything as *being* from ourselves, but our sufficiency *is* from God, ⁶who also made us sufficient as ministers of the new covenant, not of the letter but of the Spirit;[a] for the letter kills, but the Spirit gives life.

Glory of the New Covenant

⁷But if the ministry of death, written *and* engraved on stones, was glorious, so that the children of Israel could not look steadily at the face of Moses because of the glory of his countenance, which *glory* was passing away, ⁸how will the ministry of the Spirit not be more glorious? ⁹For if the ministry of condemnation *had* glory, the ministry of righteousness exceeds much more in glory. ¹⁰For even what was made glorious had no glory in this respect, because of the glory that

---

2:10 [a]NU-Text reads *For indeed, what I have forgiven, if I have forgiven anything, I did it.*   **2:17** [a]M-Text reads *the rest.*   **3:6** [a]Or *spirit*

excels. [11]For if what is passing away *was* glorious, what remains *is* much more glorious.

[12]Therefore, since we have such hope, we use great boldness of speech— [13]unlike Moses, *who* put a veil over his face so that the children of Israel could not look steadily at the end of what was passing away. [14]But their minds were blinded. For until this day the same veil remains unlifted in the reading of the Old Testament, because the *veil* is taken away in Christ. [15]But even to this day, when Moses is read, a veil lies on their heart. [16]Nevertheless when one turns to the Lord, the veil is taken away. [17]Now the Lord is the Spirit; and where the Spirit of the Lord *is,* there *is* liberty. [18]But we all, with unveiled face, beholding as in a mirror the glory of the Lord, are being transformed into the same image from glory to glory, just as by the Spirit of the Lord.

The Light of Christ's Gospel

4 Therefore, since we have this ministry, as we have received mercy, we do not lose heart. [2]But we have renounced the hidden things of shame, not walking in craftiness nor handling the word of God deceitfully, but by manifestation of the truth commending ourselves to every man's conscience in the sight of God. [3]But even if our gospel is veiled, it is veiled to those who are perishing, [4]whose minds the god of this age has blinded, who do not believe, lest the light of the gospel of the glory of Christ, who is the image of God, should shine on them. [5]For we do not preach ourselves, but Christ Jesus the Lord, and ourselves your bondservants for Jesus' sake. [6]For it is the God who commanded light to shine out of darkness, who has shone in our hearts to *give* the light of the knowledge of the glory of God in the face of Jesus Christ.

Cast Down but Unconquered

[7]But we have this treasure in earthen vessels, that the excellence of the power may be of God and not of us. [8]*We are* hard-pressed on every side, yet not crushed; *we are* perplexed, but not in despair; [9]persecuted, but not forsaken; struck down, but not destroyed— [10]always carrying about in the body the

---

HOPE

*... shone in our hearts
to give the light....*

2 CORINTHIANS 4:6

John McLean

LIFE AND IMMORTALITY

John McLean (1785–1861), a U.S. Postmaster General and Justice of the U.S. Supreme Court, wrote:

> No one can estimate or describe the salutary influence of the Bible. What would the world be without it? Compare the dark places of the earth, where the light of the Gospel has not penetrated, with those where it has been proclaimed and embraced in all its purity. Life and immortality are brought to light by the Scriptures.
>
> Aside from Revelation, darkness rests upon the world and upon the future. There is no ray of light to shine upon our pathway; there is no star of hope. We begin our speculations as to our destiny in conjecture, and they end in uncertainty. We know not that there is a God, a heaven, or a hell, or any day of general account, when the wicked and the righteous shall be judged.
>
> The Bible has shed a glorious light upon the world. It shows us that in the coming day we must answer for the deeds done in the body. It has opened us to a new and living way, so plainly marked out that no one can mistake it. The price paid for our redemption shows the value of our immortal souls.

dying of the Lord Jesus, that the life of Jesus also may be manifested in our body. [11]For we who live are always delivered to death for Jesus' sake, that the life of Jesus also may be manifested in our mortal flesh. [12]So then death is working in us, but life in you.

[13]And since we have the same spirit of faith, according to what is written, *"I believed and therefore I spoke,"*[a] we also believe and therefore speak, [14]knowing that He who raised up the Lord Jesus will also raise us up with Jesus, and will present *us* with you. [15]For all things *are* for your sakes, that grace, having spread through the many, may cause thanksgiving to abound to the glory of God.

Seeing the Invisible

[16]Therefore we do not lose heart. Even though our outward man is perishing, yet the inward *man* is being renewed day by day. [17]For our light affliction, which is but for a moment, is working for us a far more exceeding *and* eternal weight of glory, [18]while we do not look at the things which are seen, but at the things which are not seen. For the things which are seen *are* temporary, but the things which are not seen *are* eternal.

HOPE

. . . and eternal weight of glory. . . .

2 CORINTHIANS 4:17

An Exceeding Weight of Glory

Thomas "Stonewall" Jackson (1824–1863), the revered Civil War general whose death was a severe setback for the Confederacy, had written in a letter to his wife:

> *Don't trouble yourself . . . these things are earthly and transitory. There are real and glorious blessings, I trust, in reserve for us, beyond this life. It is best for us to keep our eyes fixed upon the throne of God. . . . It is gratifying to be beloved, and to have our conduct approved by our fellowmen; but this is not worthy to be compared with the glory that is in reservation for us, in the presence of the glorified Redeemer . . . knowing that there awaits us "a far more exceeding and eternal weight of glory."*

Assurance of the Resurrection

5 For we know that if our earthly house, *this* tent, is destroyed, we have a building from God, a house not made with hands, eternal in the heavens. [2]For in this we groan, earnestly desiring to be clothed with our habitation which is from heaven, [3]if indeed, having been clothed, we shall not be found naked. [4]For we who are in *this* tent groan, being burdened, not because we want to be unclothed, but further clothed, that mortality may be swallowed up by life. [5]Now He who has prepared us for this very thing *is* God, who also has given us the Spirit as a guarantee.

[6]So *we are* always confident, knowing that while we are at home in the body we are absent from the Lord. [7]For we walk by faith, not by sight. [8]We are confident, yes, well pleased rather to be absent from the body and to be present with the Lord.

The Judgment Seat of Christ

[9]Therefore we make it our aim, whether present or absent, to be well pleasing to Him. [10]For we must all appear before the judgment seat of Christ, that each one may receive the things *done* in the body, according to what he has done, whether good or bad. [11]Knowing, therefore, the terror of the Lord, we persuade men; but we are well known to God, and I also trust are well known in your consciences.

Be Reconciled to God

[12]For we do not commend ourselves again to you, but give you opportunity to boast on our behalf, that you may have *an answer* for those who boast in appearance and not in heart. [13]For if we are beside ourselves, *it is* for God; or if we are of sound mind, *it is* for you. [14]For the love of Christ compels us, because we judge thus: that if One died for all, then all died; [15]and He died for all, that those who live should live no longer for themselves, but for Him who died for them and rose again.

[16]Therefore, from now on, we regard no one according to the flesh. Even though we have known Christ according to the flesh, yet now we know *Him thus* no longer.

4:13 [a]Psalm 116:10

17Therefore, if anyone *is* in Christ, *he is a* new creation; old things have passed away; behold, all things have become new. 18Now all things *are* of God, who has reconciled us to Himself through Jesus Christ, and has given us the ministry of reconciliation, 19that is, that God was in Christ reconciling the world to Himself, not imputing their trespasses to them, and has committed to us the word of reconciliation.

20Now then, we are ambassadors for Christ, as though God were pleading through us: we implore *you* on Christ's behalf, be reconciled to God. 21For He made Him who knew no sin *to be* sin for us, that we might become the righteousness of God in Him.

Marks of the Ministry

6 We then, *as* workers together *with Him* also plead with *you* not to receive the grace of God in vain. 2For He says:

> "In an acceptable time I have heard
> you,
> And in the day of salvation I have
> helped you."a

Behold, now *is* the accepted time; behold, now *is* the day of salvation. 3We give no offense in anything, that our ministry may not be blamed. 4But in all *things* we commend ourselves as ministers of God: in much patience, in tribulations, in needs, in distresses, 5in stripes, in imprisonments, in tumults, in labors, in sleeplessness, in fastings; 6by purity, by knowledge, by longsuffering, by kindness, by the Holy Spirit, by sincere love, 7by the word of truth, by the power of God, by the armor of righteousness on the right hand and on the left, 8by honor and dishonor, by evil report and good report; as deceivers, and *yet* true; 9as unknown, and *yet* well known; as dying, and behold we live; as chastened, and *yet* not killed; 10as sorrowful, yet always rejoicing; as poor, yet making many rich; as having nothing, and *yet* possessing all things.

Be Holy

11O Corinthians! We have spoken openly to you, our heart is wide open. 12You are not restricted by us, but you are restricted by your *own* affections. 13Now in return for the same (I speak as to children), you also be open.

14Do not be unequally yoked together with unbelievers. For what fellowship has righteousness with lawlessness? And what communion has light with darkness? 15And what accord has Christ with Belial? Or what part has a believer with an unbeliever? 16And what agreement has the temple of God with idols? For youa are the temple of the living God. As God has said:

> "I will dwell in them
> And walk among them.
> I will be their God,
> And they shall be My people."b

17Therefore

> "Come out from among them
> And be separate, says the Lord.
> Do not touch what is unclean,
> And I will receive you."a
> 18 "I will be a Father to you,
> And you shall be My sons and
> daughters,
> Says the LORD Almighty."a

7 Therefore, having these promises, beloved, let us cleanse ourselves from all filthiness of the flesh and spirit, perfecting holiness in the fear of God.

The Corinthians' Repentance

2Open *your hearts* to us. We have wronged no one, we have corrupted no one, we have cheated no one. 3I do not say *this* to condemn; for I have said before that you are in our hearts, to die together and to live together. 4Great *is* my boldness of speech toward you, great *is* my boasting on your behalf. I am filled with comfort. I am exceedingly joyful in all our tribulation.

5For indeed, when we came to Macedonia, our bodies had no rest, but we were troubled on every side. Outside *were* conflicts, inside *were* fears. 6Nevertheless God, who comforts the downcast, comforted us by the coming of Titus, 7and not only by his coming, but also

---

6:2 aIsaiah 49:8   **6:16** aNU-Text reads *we.* bLeviticus 26:12; Jeremiah 32:38; Ezekiel 37:27   **6:17** aIsaiah 52:11; Ezekiel 20:34, 41   **6:18** a2 Samuel 7:14

by the consolation with which he was comforted in you, when he told us of your earnest desire, your mourning, your zeal for me, so that I rejoiced even more.

⁸For even if I made you sorry with my letter, I do not regret it; though I did regret it. For I perceive that the same epistle made you sorry, though only for a while. ⁹Now I rejoice, not that you were made sorry, but that your sorrow led to repentance. For you were made sorry in a godly manner, that you might suffer loss from us in nothing. ¹⁰For godly sorrow produces repentance *leading* to salvation, not to be regretted; but the sorrow of the world produces death. ¹¹For observe this very thing, that you sorrowed in a godly manner: What diligence it produced in you, *what* clearing *of yourselves, what* indignation, *what* fear, *what* vehement desire, *what* zeal, *what* vindication! In all *things* you proved yourselves to be clear in this matter. ¹²Therefore, although I wrote to you, *I did* not *do it* for the sake of him who had done the wrong, nor for the sake of him who suffered wrong, but that our care for you in the sight of God might appear to you.

The Joy of Titus

¹³Therefore we have been comforted in your comfort. And we rejoiced exceedingly more for the joy of Titus, because his spirit has been refreshed by you all. ¹⁴For if in anything I have boasted to him about you, I am not ashamed. But as we spoke all things to you in truth, even so our boasting to Titus was found true. ¹⁵And his affections are greater for you as he remembers the obedience of you all, how with fear and trembling you received him. ¹⁶Therefore I rejoice that I have confidence in you in everything.

Excel in Giving

8 Moreover, brethren, we make known to you the grace of God bestowed on the churches of Macedonia: ²that in a great trial of affliction the abundance of their joy and their deep poverty abounded in the riches of their liberality. ³For I bear witness that according to *their* ability, yes, and beyond *their* ability, *they were* freely willing, ⁴imploring us with much urgency that we

would receiveᵃ the gift and the fellowship of the ministering to the saints. ⁵And not *only* as we had hoped, but they first gave themselves to the Lord, and *then* to us by the will of God. ⁶So we urged Titus, that as he had begun, so he would also complete this grace in you as well. ⁷But as you abound in everything—in faith, in speech, in knowledge, in all diligence, and in your love for us—*see* that you abound in this grace also.

Christ Our Pattern

⁸I speak not by commandment, but I am testing the sincerity of your love by the diligence of others. ⁹For you know the grace of our Lord Jesus Christ, that though He was rich, yet for your sakes He became poor, that you through His poverty might become rich.

¹⁰And in this I give advice: It is to your advantage not only to be doing what you began and were desiring to do a year ago; ¹¹but now you also must complete the doing *of it;* that as *there was* a readiness to desire *it,* so *there* also *may be* a completion out of what *you* have. ¹²For if there is first a willing mind, *it is* accepted according to what one has, *and* not according to what he does not have.

¹³For *I do* not *mean* that others should be eased and you burdened; ¹⁴but by an equality, *that* now at this time your abundance *may supply* their lack, that their abundance also may *supply* your lack—that there may be equality. ¹⁵As it is written, *"He who gathered much had nothing left over, and he who gathered little had no lack."*ᵃ

Collection for the Judean Saints

¹⁶But thanks *be* to God who putsᵃ the same earnest care for you into the heart of Titus. ¹⁷For he not only accepted the exhortation, but being more diligent, he went to you of his own accord. ¹⁸And we have sent with him the brother whose praise *is* in the gospel throughout all the churches, ¹⁹and not only *that,* but who was also chosen by

---

8:4 ᵃNU-Text and M-Text omit *that we would receive,* thus changing text to *urgency for the favor and fellowship. . . .*   **8:15** ᵃExodus 16:18
8:16 ᵃNU-Text reads *has put.*

"GOD HAS A BIGGER SHOVEL"

R. G. LeTourneau

. . . and he who sows bountifully will also reap bountifully.

2 CORINTHIANS 9:6

R. G. LeTourneau (1888–1969) was a prolific inventor in the earth-moving industry and one of the most amazing "rags to riches" stories in America. He began his career in obscurity in Stockton, California, where frustrations with his first job of moving dirt drove him to find a better, more efficient way. As the father of the modern earthmoving industry, he was responsible for nearly 300 inventions, including the bulldozer, scrapers of all sorts, dredgers, portable cranes, rollers, dump wagons, bridge spans, logging equipment, mobile sea platforms for oil exploration, the electric wheel, and many others. During World War II, he produced 70 percent of all the army's earthmoving machinery.

LeTourneau felt that he was clearly called to be a "businessman for God," and he spoke of God as the Chairman of his board. He said that the money came in faster than he could give it away. He established the LeTourneau Foundation to channel 90 percent of his personal multimillion-dollar salary to Christian endeavors, especially the training of Christian workers in practical skills that are needed on mission fields. LeTourneau was convinced that he could not out-give God. "I shovel it out," he would say, "and God shovels it back, but God has a bigger shovel."

He also said, "You will never know what you can accomplish until you say a great big yes to the Lord," and he proved those words true. His business efforts—although incredibly successful—never deterred him from what he felt was his reason for existence: to glorify God and spread the Gospel message. He shared his faith with millions during his life and founded missionary efforts in Liberia and Peru. He and his wife also founded a college in Longview, Texas, which is a lasting spiritual legacy. LeTourneau University continues to hold to its spiritual foundations and has produced more than 10,000 alumni who are faithfully serving the Lord in all 50 states and 55 nations.

Many people see LeTourneau as one of the most influential people of the past hundred years. His attitude was always positive toward ultimate accomplishment, and he was known to say, "The only difference between can and can't is a little extra effort." His life's verse was Matthew 6:33: "But seek first the kingdom of God and His righteousness, and all these things shall be added to you."

the churches to travel with us with this gift, which is administered by us to the glory of the Lord Himself and *to show* your ready mind, 20avoiding this: that anyone should blame us in this lavish gift which is administered by us— 21providing honorable things, not only in the sight of the Lord, but also in the sight of men.

22And we have sent with them our brother whom we have often proved diligent in many things, but now much more diligent, because of the great confidence which *we have* in you. 23If *anyone inquires* about Titus, *he is* my partner and fellow worker concerning you. Or if our brethren *are inquired about, they are* messengers of the churches, the glory of Christ. 24Therefore show to them, anda before the churches, the proof of your love and of our boasting on your behalf.

Administering the Gift

9 Now concerning the ministering to the saints, it is superfluous for me to write to you; 2for I know your willingness, about which I boast of you to the Macedonians, that Achaia was ready a year ago; and your zeal has stirred up the majority. 3Yet I have sent the brethren, lest our boasting of you should be in vain in this respect, that, as I said, you may be ready; 4lest if *some* Macedonians come with me and find you unprepared, we (not to mention you!) should be ashamed of this confident boasting.a 5Therefore I thought it necessary to

exhort the brethren to go to you ahead of time, and prepare your generous gift beforehand, which *you had* previously promised, that it may be ready as *a matter of* generosity and not as a grudging obligation.

The Cheerful Giver

6But this *I say:* He who sows sparingly will also reap sparingly, and he who sows bountifully will also reap bountifully. 7So *let* each one *give* as he purposes in his heart, not grudgingly or of necessity; for God loves a cheerful giver. 8And God *is* able to make all grace abound toward you, that you, always having all sufficiency in all *things,* may have an abundance for every good work. 9As it is written:

> "He has dispersed abroad,
>   He has given to the poor;
>   His righteousness endures forever."a

10Now maya He who supplies seed to the sower, and bread for food, supply and multiply the seed you have *sown* and increase the fruits of your righteousness, 11while *you are* enriched in everything for all liberality, which causes thanksgiving through us to God. 12For the administration of this service not only supplies the needs of the saints, but also is abounding through many thanksgivings to God, 13while, through the proof of this ministry, they glorify God for the obedience of your confession to the gospel of Christ, and for *your* liberal sharing with them and all *men,* 14and by their prayer for you, who long for you because of the exceeding grace of God in you. 15Thanks *be* to God for His indescribable gift!

The Spiritual War

10 Now I, Paul, myself am pleading with you by the meekness and gentleness of Christ—who in presence *am* lowly among you, but being absent am bold toward you. 2But I beg *you* that when I am present I may not be bold with that confidence by which I intend to be bold against some, who think of us as if we walked according to the flesh.

INSPIRING
Thanks be to God for His indescribable gift!
                                2 CORINTHIANS 9:15

The Unspeakable Gift
John Sherman (1823–1900), a longtime American political leader noted for having introduced the Sherman Anti-Trust Act (1879) in an effort to curb the monopolies of big businesses, stated:

> I appreciate the Holy Bible as the highest gift of God to man, unless it be the "unspeakable Gift" of Jesus Christ as the Savior of the world. It is the Divine assurance that our life does not end with death, and it is the strongest incentive to honorable, charitable Christian deeds.

8:24 aNU-Text and M-Text omit *and.*   **9:4** aNU-Text reads *this confidence.*   **9:9** aPsalm 112:9   **9:10** aNU-Text reads *Now He who supplies . . . will supply. . . .*

3For though we walk in the flesh, we do not war according to the flesh. 4For the weapons of our warfare *are* not carnal but mighty in God for pulling down strongholds, 5casting down arguments and every high thing that exalts itself against the knowledge of God, bringing every thought into captivity to the obedience of Christ, 6and being ready to punish all disobedience when your obedience is fulfilled.

FAITH

For the weapons of our warfare are . . . mighty in God. . . .   2 CORINTHIANS 10:4

A Nation's Most Powerful Resource

Dwight David Eisenhower, the 34th president of the United States (1953–1961), signed into law the Congressional Act, Joint Resolution 243, which added the phrase "one Nation under God" to the Pledge of Allegiance. Concerning it, he stated:

> In this way we are reaffirming the transcendence of religious faith in America's heritage and future; in this way we shall constantly strengthen those spiritual weapons which forever will be our country's most powerful resource in peace and war.

Reality of Paul's Authority

7Do you look at things according to the outward appearance? If anyone is convinced in himself that he is Christ's, let him again consider this in himself, that just as he *is* Christ's, even so we *are* Christ's.ᵃ 8For even if I should boast somewhat more about our authority, which the Lord gave usᵃ for edification and not for your destruction, I shall not be ashamed— 9lest I seem to terrify you by letters. 10"For *his* letters," they say, "*are* weighty and powerful, but *his* bodily presence *is* weak, and *his* speech contemptible." 11Let such a person consider this, that what we are in word by letters when we are absent, such *we will* also *be* in deed when we are present.

Limits of Paul's Authority

12For we dare not class ourselves or compare ourselves with those who commend themselves. But they, measuring themselves by themselves, and comparing themselves among themselves, are not wise. 13We, however, will not boast beyond measure, but within the limits of the sphere which God appointed us—a sphere which especially includes you. 14For we are not overextending ourselves (as though *our authority* did not extend to you), for it was to you that we came with the gospel of Christ; 15not boasting of things beyond measure, *that is,* in other men's labors, but having hope, *that* as your faith is increased, we shall be greatly enlarged by you in our sphere, 16to preach the gospel in the *regions* beyond you, *and* not to boast in another man's sphere of accomplishment.

17But *"he who glories, let him glory in the* LORD."ᵃ 18For not he who commends himself is approved, but whom the Lord commends.

Concern for Their Faithfulness

11 Oh, that you would bear with me in a little folly—and indeed you do bear with me. 2For I am jealous for you with godly jealousy. For I have betrothed you to one husband, that I may present *you as* a chaste virgin to Christ. 3But I fear, lest somehow, as the serpent deceived Eve by his craftiness, so your minds may be corrupted from the simplicityᵃ that is in Christ. 4For if he who comes preaches another Jesus whom we have not preached, or *if* you receive a different spirit which you have not received, or a different gospel which you have not accepted—you may well put up with it!

Paul and False Apostles

5For I consider that I am not at all inferior to the most eminent apostles. 6Even though *I am* untrained in speech, yet *I am* not in knowledge. But we have been thoroughly manifestedᵃ among you in all things.

7Did I commit sin in humbling myself that you might be exalted, because I preached the gospel of God to you free of charge? 8I robbed other churches, taking wages *from them* to minister to you. 9And when I was present with you, and in need,

---

10:7 ᵃNU-Text reads *even as we are.*   10:8 ᵃNU-Text omits *us.*   10:17 ᵃJeremiah 9:24   11:3 ᵃNU-Text adds *and purity.*   11:6 ᵃNU-Text omits *been.*

I was a burden to no one, for what I lacked the brethren who came from Macedonia supplied. And in everything I kept myself from being burdensome to you, and so I will keep *myself.* ¹⁰As the truth of Christ is in me, no one shall stop me from this boasting in the regions of Achaia. ¹¹Why? Because I do not love you? God knows!

¹²But what I do, I will also continue to do, that I may cut off the opportunity from those who desire an opportunity to be regarded just as we are in the things of which they boast. ¹³For such *are* false apostles, deceitful workers, transforming themselves into apostles of Christ. ¹⁴And no wonder! For Satan himself transforms himself into an angel of light. ¹⁵Therefore *it is* no great thing if his ministers also transform themselves into ministers of righteousness, whose end will be according to their works.

Reluctant Boasting

¹⁶I say again, let no one think me a fool. If otherwise, at least receive me as a fool, that I also may boast a little. ¹⁷What I speak, I speak not according to the Lord, but as it were, foolishly, in this confidence of boasting. ¹⁸Seeing that many boast according to the flesh, I also will boast. ¹⁹For you put up with fools gladly, since you *yourselves* are wise! ²⁰For you put up with it if one brings you into bondage, if one devours *you,* if one takes *from you,* if one exalts himself, if one strikes you on the face. ²¹To *our* shame I say that we were too weak for that! But in whatever anyone is bold—I speak foolishly—I am bold also.

Suffering for Christ

²²Are they Hebrews? So *am* I. Are they Israelites? So *am* I. Are they the seed of Abraham? So *am* I. ²³Are they ministers of Christ?—I speak as a fool—I *am* more: in labors more abundant, in stripes above measure, in prisons more frequently, in deaths often. ²⁴From the Jews five times I received forty *stripes* minus one. ²⁵Three times I was beaten with rods; once I was stoned; three times I was shipwrecked; a night and a day I have been in the deep; ²⁶*in* journeys often, *in* perils of waters, *in* perils of robbers, *in* perils of *my own* countrymen, *in* perils of the Gentiles, *in* perils in the city,

in perils in the wilderness, *in* perils in the sea, *in* perils among false brethren; ²⁷in weariness and toil, in sleeplessness often, in hunger and thirst, in fastings often, in cold and nakedness— ²⁸besides the other things, what comes upon me daily: my deep concern for all the churches. ²⁹Who is weak, and I am not weak? Who is made to stumble, and I do not burn *with indignation?*

³⁰If I must boast, I will boast in the things which concern my infirmity. ³¹The God and Father of our Lord Jesus Christ, who is blessed forever, knows that I am not lying. ³²In Damascus the governor, under Aretas the king, was guarding the city of the Damascenes with a garrison, desiring to arrest me; ³³but I was let down in a basket through a window in the wall, and escaped from his hands.

The Vision of Paradise

12 It is doubtless[a] not profitable for me to boast. I will come to visions and revelations of the Lord: ²I know a man in Christ who fourteen years ago—whether in the body I do not know, or whether out of the body I do not know, God knows—such a one was caught up to the third heaven. ³And I know such a man—whether in the body or out of the body I do not know, God knows— ⁴how he was caught up into Paradise and heard inexpressible words, which it is not lawful for a man to utter. ⁵Of such a one I will boast; yet of myself I will not boast, except in my infirmities. ⁶For though I might desire to boast, I will not be a fool; for I will speak the truth. But I refrain, lest anyone should think of me above what he sees me *to be* or hears from me.

The Thorn in the Flesh

⁷And lest I should be exalted above measure by the abundance of the revelations, a thorn in the flesh was given to me, a messenger of Satan to buffet me, lest I be exalted above measure. ⁸Concerning this thing I pleaded with the Lord three times that it might depart from me. ⁹And He said to me, "My grace is sufficient for you, for My strength is made perfect in weakness."

12:1 [a]NU-Text reads *necessary, though not profitable, to boast.*

Therefore most gladly I will rather boast in my infirmities, that the power of Christ may rest upon me. [10]Therefore I take pleasure in infirmities, in reproaches, in needs, in persecutions, in distresses, for Christ's sake. For when I am weak, then I am strong.

Signs of an Apostle

[11]I have become a fool in boasting;[a] you have compelled me. For I ought to have been commended by you; for in nothing was I behind the most eminent apostles, though I am nothing. [12]Truly the signs of an apostle were accomplished among you with all perseverance, in signs and wonders and mighty deeds. [13]For what is it in which you were inferior to other churches, except that I myself was not burdensome to you? Forgive me this wrong!

Love for the Church

[14]Now *for* the third time I am ready to come to you. And I will not be burdensome to you; for I do not seek yours, but you. For the children ought not to lay up for the parents, but the parents for the children. [15]And I will very gladly spend and be spent for your souls; though the more abundantly I love you, the less I am loved.

[16]But be that *as it may,* I did not burden you. Nevertheless, being crafty, I caught you by cunning! [17]Did I take advantage of you by any of those whom I sent to you? [18]I urged Titus, and sent our brother with *him.* Did Titus take advantage of you? Did we not walk in the same spirit? Did *we* not *walk* in the same steps?

[19]Again, do you think[a] that we excuse ourselves to you? We speak before God in Christ. But *we do* all things, beloved, for your edification. [20]For I fear lest, when I come, I shall not find you such as I wish, and *that* I shall be found by you such as you do not wish; lest *there be* contentions, jealousies, outbursts of wrath, selfish ambitions, backbitings, whisperings, conceits, tumults; [21]lest, when I come again, my God will humble me among you, and I shall mourn for many who have sinned before and have not repented of the uncleanness, fornication, and lewdness which they have practiced.

Coming with Authority

13 This *will be* the third *time* I am coming to you. *"By the mouth of two or three witnesses every word shall be established."*[a] [2]I have told you before, and foretell as if I were present the second time, and now being absent I write[a] to those who have sinned before, and to all the rest, that if I come again I will not spare— [3]since you seek a proof of Christ speaking in me, who is not weak toward you, but mighty in you. [4]For though He was crucified in weakness, yet He lives by the power of God. For we also are weak in Him, but we shall live with Him by the power of God toward you.

[5]Examine yourselves *as to* whether you are in the faith. Test yourselves. Do you not know yourselves, that Jesus Christ is in you?—unless indeed you are disqualified. [6]But I trust that you will know that we are not disqualified.

Paul Prefers Gentleness

[7]Now I[a] pray to God that you do no evil, not that we should appear approved, but that you should do what is honorable, though we may seem disqualified. [8]For we can do nothing against the truth, but for the truth. [9]For we are glad when we are weak and you are strong. And this also we pray, that you may be made complete. [10]Therefore I write these things being absent, lest being present I should use sharpness, according to the authority which the Lord has given me for edification and not for destruction.

Greetings and Benediction

[11]Finally, brethren, farewell. Become complete. Be of good comfort, be of one mind, live in peace; and the God of love and peace will be with you. [12]Greet one another with a holy kiss. [13]All the saints greet you. [14]The grace of the Lord Jesus Christ, and the love of God, and the communion of the Holy Spirit *be* with you all. Amen.

12:11 [a]NU-Text omits *in boasting.*   **12:19** [a]NU-Text reads *You have been thinking for a long time. . . .*
13:1 [a]Deuteronomy 19:15   **13:2** [a]NU-Text omits *I write.*   **13:7** [a]NU-Text reads *we.*

GALATIANS

Author: Paul

When Written: Around A.D. 52

Theme: Freedom from the Law

Key Verse: Galatians 5:1—Stand fast therefore in the liberty by which Christ has made us free, and do not be entangled again with a yoke of bondage.

Key Chapter: Galatians 5—The impact of the truth concerning freedom is amazing: freedom must be used not as an opportunity for the flesh, but by love to serve one another. It records the power of walking in the Spirit as well as the resulting fruit of the Spirit.

The Galatians, who had believed in Christ by faith through the preaching of Paul, are beginning to surrender their priceless liberty through a gospel of works. Paul writes this forceful epistle to do away with the false gospel of works and demonstrates the superiority of justification by faith. This is Paul's manifesto of justification by faith, and the resulting liberty that no believer should ever trade away.

It was the oppressive theology of certain Jewish legalizers that had caused the Galatian believers to yield their freedoms in Christ. Paul's stern warning to the Galatians is similar to that given to America by President Abraham Lincoln: "America will never be destroyed from the outside. If we falter and lose our freedoms, it will be because we destroyed ourselves."

GALATIANS

Greeting

1 Paul, an apostle (not from men nor through man, but through Jesus Christ and God the Father who raised Him from the dead), ²and all the brethren who are with me,

To the churches of Galatia:

³Grace to you and peace from God the Father and our Lord Jesus Christ, ⁴who gave Himself for our sins, that He might deliver us from this present evil age, according to the will of our God and Father, ⁵to whom *be* glory forever and ever. Amen.

Only One Gospel

⁶I marvel that you are turning away so soon from Him who called you in the grace of Christ, to a different gospel, ⁷which is not another; but there are some who trouble you and want to pervert the gospel of Christ. ⁸But even if we, or an angel from heaven, preach any other gospel to you than what we have preached to you, let him be accursed. ⁹As we have said before, so now I say again, if anyone preaches any other gospel to you than what you have received, let him be accursed.

¹⁰For do I now persuade men, or God? Or do I seek to please men? For if I still pleased men, I would not be a bondservant of Christ.

Call to Apostleship

¹¹But I make known to you, brethren, that the gospel which was preached by me is not according to man. ¹²For I neither received it from man, nor was I taught *it,* but *it came* through the revelation of Jesus Christ.

¹³For you have heard of my former conduct in Judaism, how I persecuted the church of God beyond measure and *tried to* destroy it. ¹⁴And I advanced in Judaism beyond many of my contemporaries in my own nation, being more exceedingly zealous for the traditions of my fathers.

¹⁵But when it pleased God, who separated me from my mother's womb and called *me* through His grace, ¹⁶to reveal His Son in me, that I might preach Him among the Gentiles, I did not immediately confer with flesh and blood, ¹⁷nor did I go up to Jerusalem to those *who were* apostles before me; but I went to Arabia, and returned again to Damascus.

Contacts at Jerusalem

¹⁸Then after three years I went up to Jerusalem to see Peter,ᵃ and remained with him fifteen days. ¹⁹But I saw none of the other apostles except James, the Lord's brother. ²⁰(Now *concerning* the things which I write to you, indeed, before God, I do not lie.)

²¹Afterward I went into the regions of Syria and Cilicia. ²²And I was unknown by face to the churches of Judea which *were* in Christ. ²³But they were hearing only, "He who formerly persecuted us now preaches the faith which he once *tried to* destroy." ²⁴And they glorified God in me.

Defending the Gospel

2 Then after fourteen years I went up again to Jerusalem with Barnabas, and also took Titus with *me.* ²And I went up by revelation, and communicated to them that gospel which I preach among the Gentiles, but privately to those who were of reputation, lest by any means I might run, or had run, in vain. ³Yet not even Titus who *was* with me, being a Greek, was compelled to be circumcised. ⁴And *this occurred* because of false brethren secretly brought in (who came in by stealth to spy out our liberty which we have in Christ Jesus, that they might bring us into bondage), ⁵to whom we did not yield submission even for

---

1:18 ᵃNU-Text reads *Cephas.*

RICHARD ALLEN

But when I saw that they were not straightforward about the truth of the gospel. . . .

GALATIANS 2:14

Richard Allen (1760–1831) was born into slavery in Philadelphia. He came to faith in Christ at age 17, joined the Methodist Society, began attending classes, and started preaching on his plantation and at local Methodist churches. His owner allowed Allen to purchase his freedom for $2,000 by working for the Revolutionary forces, and he became one of the first blacks to be emancipated during the Revolutionary Era. For the next six years, Allen traveled the Methodist circuit in the mid Atlantic states, preaching to black and white congregants alike.

In 1786, he returned to Philadelphia and joined St. George's Methodist Church, where he preached at 5:00 A.M. so his services would not interfere with the whites. His leadership attracted dozens of blacks into the church, and with them came increased racial tension. Although whites and blacks often worshiped together, segregated seating was typical, and blacks enjoyed no real freedom or equality. Allen recognized that blacks needed a place they could worship without restriction and harassment, and where they could control their religious lives. He, along with Rev. Absalom Jones and a few others, formed the Free African Society in 1787. In 1794, he purchased an old frame building and started the Bethel African Methodist Episcopal Church.

Also in 1794, Allen and representatives from four other black Methodist congregations in Baltimore, Wilmington, Attleboro, and Salem met at the Bethel Church to organize a new denomination, the African Methodist Episcopal Church (AME). Allen was chosen as the first bishop of the church, the first fully independent black denomination in America, whose motto has always been, "God our father, man our brother, and Christ our redeemer."

Richard Allen remained a Methodist, continued preaching throughout his life, and oversaw the amazing growth of the AME's mother church in Philadelphia, which grew to 7,500 members in the 1820s. By 1846, the AME church had grown to 176 clergy, 296 churches, and over 17,000 members. Its expansion was not only as a spiritual force but also in civil and social activism, and the AME is considered one of the most enduring and influential black institutions ever organized. In the 1990s, the AME included over 2,000,000 members, 8,000 ministers, and 7,000 congregations in more than 30 nations in North and South America, Africa, and Europe.

A strong patriot, Allen supported the War of 1812 and denounced the notion of sending blacks to colonize in Africa, making the compelling argument: "This land which we have watered with our tears and our blood is now our mother country."

an hour, that the truth of the gospel might continue with you.

⁶But from those who seemed to be something—whatever they were, it makes no difference to me; God shows personal favoritism to no man—for those who seemed *to be something* added nothing to me. ⁷But on the contrary, when they saw that the gospel for the uncircumcised had been committed to me, as *the gospel* for the circumcised *was* to Peter ⁸(for He who worked effectively in Peter for the apostleship to the circumcised also worked effectively in me toward the Gentiles), ⁹and when James, Cephas, and John, who seemed to be pillars, perceived the grace that had been given to me, they gave me and Barnabas the right hand of fellowship, that we *should go* to the Gentiles and they to the circumcised. ¹⁰*They desired* only that we should remember the poor, the very thing which I also was eager to do.

No Return to the Law

¹¹Now when Peterᵃ had come to Antioch, I withstood him to his face, because he was to be blamed; ¹²for before certain men came from James, he would eat with the Gentiles; but when they came, he withdrew and separated himself, fearing those who were of the circumcision. ¹³And the rest of the Jews also played the hypocrite with him, so that even Barnabas was carried away with their hypocrisy.

¹⁴But when I saw that they were not straightforward about the truth of the gospel, I said to Peter before *them* all, "If you, being a Jew, live in the manner of Gentiles and not as the Jews, why do youᵃ compel Gentiles to live as Jews?ᵇ ¹⁵We *who are* Jews by nature, and not sinners of the Gentiles, ¹⁶knowing that a man is not justified by the works of the law but by faith in Jesus Christ, even we have believed in Christ Jesus, that we might be justified by faith in Christ and not by the works of the law; for by the works of the law no flesh shall be justified.

¹⁷"But if, while we seek to be justified by Christ, we ourselves also are found sinners, *is* Christ therefore a minister of sin? Certainly

not! ¹⁸For if I build again those things which I destroyed, I make myself a transgressor. ¹⁹For I through the law died to the law that I might live to God. ²⁰I have been crucified with Christ; it is no longer I who live, but Christ lives in me; and the *life* which I now live in the flesh I live by faith in the Son of God, who loved me and gave Himself for me. ²¹I do not set aside the grace of God; for if righteousness *comes* through the law, then Christ died in vain."

Justification by Faith

3 O foolish Galatians! Who has bewitched you that you should not obey the truth,ᵃ before whose eyes Jesus Christ was clearly portrayed among youᵇ as crucified? ²This only I want to learn from you: Did you receive the Spirit by the works of the law, or by the hearing of faith? ³Are you so foolish? Having begun in the Spirit, are you now being made perfect by the flesh? ⁴Have you suffered so many things in vain—if indeed *it was* in vain?

⁵Therefore He who supplies the Spirit to you and works miracles among you, *does He do it* by the works of the law, or by the hearing of faith?— ⁶just as Abraham *"believed God, and it was accounted to him for righteousness."*ᵃ ⁷Therefore know that *only* those who are of faith are sons of Abraham. ⁸And the Scripture, foreseeing that God would justify the Gentiles by faith, preached the gospel to Abraham beforehand, *saying, "In you all the nations shall be blessed."*ᵃ ⁹So then those who *are* of faith are blessed with believing Abraham.

The Law Brings a Curse

¹⁰For as many as are of the works of the law are under the curse; for it is written, *"Cursed is everyone who does not continue in all things which are written in the book of the law, to do them."*ᵃ ¹¹But that no one is justified by the law in the sight of God *is* evident, for *"the just shall live by faith."*ᵃ

2:11 ᵃNU-Text reads *Cephas.* **2:14** ᵃNU-Text reads *how can you.* ᵇSome interpreters stop the quotation here. **3:1** ᵃNU-Text omits *that you should not obey the truth.* ᵇNU-Text omits *among you.* **3:6** ᵃGenesis 15:6 **3:8** ᵃGenesis 12:3; 18:18; 22:18; 26:4; 28:14 **3:10** ᵃDeuteronomy 27:26 **3:11** ᵃHabakkuk 2:4

¹²Yet the law is not of faith, but *"the man who does them shall live by them."*ᵃ

¹³Christ has redeemed us from the curse of the law, having become a curse for us (for it is written, *"Cursed is everyone who hangs on a tree"*ᵃ), ¹⁴that the blessing of Abraham might come upon the Gentiles in Christ Jesus, that we might receive the promise of the Spirit through faith.

The Changeless Promise

¹⁵Brethren, I speak in the manner of men: Though *it is* only a man's covenant, yet *if it is* confirmed, no one annuls or adds to it. ¹⁶Now to Abraham and his Seed were the promises made. He does not say, "And to seeds," as of many, but as of one, *"And to your Seed,"*ᵃ who is Christ. ¹⁷And this I say, *that* the law, which was four hundred and thirty years later, cannot annul the covenant that was confirmed before by God in Christ,ᵃ that it should make the promise of no effect. ¹⁸For if the inheritance *is* of the law, *it is* no longer of promise; but God gave *it* to Abraham by promise.

Purpose of the Law

¹⁹What purpose then *does* the law *serve?* It was added because of transgressions, till the Seed should come to whom the promise was made; *and it was* appointed through angels by the hand of a mediator. ²⁰Now a mediator does not *mediate* for one *only,* but God is one.

²¹*Is* the law then against the promises of God? Certainly not! For if there had been a law given which could have given life, truly righteousness would have been by the law. ²²But the Scripture has confined all under sin, that the promise by faith in Jesus Christ might be given to those who believe. ²³But before faith came, we were kept under guard by the law, kept for the faith which would afterward be revealed. ²⁴Therefore the law was our tutor *to bring us* to Christ, that we might be justified by faith. ²⁵But after faith has come, we are no longer under a tutor.

Sons and Heirs

²⁶For you are all sons of God through faith in Christ Jesus. ²⁷For as many of you as were baptized into Christ have put on Christ. ²⁸There is neither Jew nor Greek, there is neither slave nor free, there is neither male nor female; for you are all one in Christ Jesus. ²⁹And if you *are* Christ's, then you are Abraham's seed, and heirs according to the promise.

4 Now I say *that* the heir, as long as he is a child, does not differ at all from a slave, though he is master of all, ²but is under guardians and stewards until the time appointed by the father. ³Even so we, when we were children, were in bondage under the elements of the world. ⁴But when the fullness of the time had come, God sent forth His Son, bornᵃ of a woman, born under the law, ⁵to redeem those who were under the law, that we might receive the adoption as sons.

⁶And because you are sons, God has sent forth the Spirit of His Son into your hearts, crying out, "Abba, Father!" ⁷Therefore you are no longer a slave but a son, and if a son, then an heir ofᵃ God through Christ.

Fears for the Church

⁸But then, indeed, when you did not know God, you served those which by nature are not gods. ⁹But now after you have known God, or rather are known by God, how *is it that* you turn again to the weak and beggarly elements, to which you desire *again* to be in bondage? ¹⁰You observe days and months and seasons and years. ¹¹I am afraid for you, lest I have labored for you in vain.

¹²Brethren, I urge you to become like me, for I *became* like you. You have not injured me at all. ¹³You know that because of physical infirmity I preached the gospel to you at the first. ¹⁴And my trial which was in my flesh you did not despise or reject, but you received me as an angel of God, *even* as Christ Jesus. ¹⁵Whatᵃ then was the blessing you *enjoyed?* For I bear you witness that, if possible, you would have plucked out your own eyes and given them to me. ¹⁶Have I

3:12 ᵃLeviticus 18:5   **3:13** ᵃDeuteronomy 21:23
3:16 ᵃGenesis 12:7; 13:15; 24:7   **3:17** ᵃNU-Text omits *in Christ.*   **4:4** ᵃOr *made*   **4:7** ᵃNU-Text reads *through God* and omits *through Christ.*
4:15 ᵃNU-Text reads *Where.*

The CHURCH'S ROLE in the WORLD

HARRY TRUMAN

PROTECTOR

*Stand fast therefore in the
liberty by which Christ
has made us free. . . .*

GALATIANS 5:1

President Harry Truman held office during the end of World War II, one of the most difficult periods of the twentieth century. In this 1946 excerpt, he reminds Americans of what we fought for and how to preserve it.

We have just come through a decade in which forces of evil in various parts of the world have been lined up in a bitter fight to banish from the face of the earth . . . religion and democracy. For these forces of evil have long realized that both religion and democracy are founded on one basic principle, the worth and dignity of the individual man and woman. Dictatorship, on the other hand, has always rejected that principle. Dictatorship, by whatever name, is founded on the doctrine that the individual amounts to nothing; that the State is the only thing that counts; and that men and women and children were put on earth solely for the purpose of serving the State.

In that long struggle between these two doctrines, the cause of decency and righteousness has been victorious. The right of every human being to live in dignity and freedom, the right to worship his God in his own way, the right to fix his own relationship to his fellow men and to his Creator—these again have been saved for mankind.

The fight to preserve these rights was hard-won. The victory took a toll of human life and treasure so large that it should bring home to us forever how precious, how invaluable, is our liberty which we had just begun to take for granted. Now that we have preserved our freedom of conscience and religion, . . . let us make use of it to save a world which is beset by so many threats of new conflicts, new terror, and new destruction. . . .

If men and nations would but live by the precepts of the ancient prophets and the teachings of the Sermon on the Mount, problems which now seem so difficult would soon disappear. . . .

This is a supreme opportunity for the Church to continue to fulfill its mission on earth . . . [and to] provide the shock forces to accomplish this moral and spiritual awakening. No other agency can do it. Unless it is done, we are headed for the disaster we would deserve. Oh for an Isaiah or a Saint Paul to reawaken this sick world to its moral responsibilities.

therefore become your enemy because I tell you the truth?

¹⁷They zealously court you, *but* for no good; yes, they want to exclude you, that you may be zealous for them. ¹⁸But it is good to be zealous in a good thing always, and not only when I am present with you. ¹⁹My little children, for whom I labor in birth again until Christ is formed in you, ²⁰I would like to be present with you now and to change my tone; for I have doubts about you.

Two Covenants

²¹Tell me, you who desire to be under the law, do you not hear the law? ²²For it is written that Abraham had two sons: the one by a bondwoman, the other by a freewoman. ²³But he *who was* of the bondwoman was born according to the flesh, and he of the freewoman through promise, ²⁴which things are symbolic. For these are theᵃ two covenants: the one from Mount Sinai which gives birth to bondage, which is Hagar— ²⁵for this Hagar is Mount Sinai in Arabia, and corresponds to Jerusalem which now is, and is in bondage with her children— ²⁶but the Jerusalem above is free, which is the mother of us all. ²⁷For it is written:

"Rejoice, O barren,
 You who do not bear!
 Break forth and shout,
 You who are not in labor!
 For the desolate has many more
    children
 Than she who has a husband."ᵃ

²⁸Now we, brethren, as Isaac *was,* are children of promise. ²⁹But, as he who was born according to the flesh then persecuted him *who was born* according to the Spirit, even so *it is* now. ³⁰Nevertheless what does the Scripture say? *"Cast out the bondwoman and her son, for the son of the bondwoman shall not be heir with the son of the freewoman."*ᵃ ³¹So then, brethren, we are not children of the bondwoman but of the free.

Christian Liberty

5 Stand fast therefore in the liberty by which Christ has made us free,ᵃ and do not be entangled again with a yoke of bondage. ²Indeed I, Paul, say to you that if you become circumcised, Christ will profit you nothing. ³And I testify again to every man who becomes circumcised that he is a debtor to keep the whole law. ⁴You have become estranged from Christ, you who *attempt to* be justified by law; you have fallen from grace. ⁵For we through the Spirit eagerly wait for the hope of righteousness by faith. ⁶For in Christ Jesus neither circumcision nor uncircumcision avails anything, but faith working through love.

MORAL STRENGTH

. . . beware lest you be consumed by one another!
GALATIANS 5:15

A Constitution for Moral People

John Adams (1735–1826) is one of America's Founding Fathers and served as the second president of the United States. In an October 1798 letter to the Militia of Massachusetts, he stated:

> We have no government armed with power capable of contending with human passions unbridled by morality and religion. Avarice, ambition, revenge, or gallantry would break the strongest cords of our Constitution as a whale goes through a net. Our Constitution was made only for a moral and religious people. It is wholly inadequate to the government of any other.

Love Fulfills the Law

⁷You ran well. Who hindered you from obeying the truth? ⁸This persuasion does not *come* from Him who calls you. ⁹A little leaven leavens the whole lump. ¹⁰I have confidence in you, in the Lord, that you will have no other mind; but he who troubles you shall bear his judgment, whoever he is.

¹¹And I, brethren, if I still preach circumcision, why do I still suffer persecution? Then the offense of the cross has ceased. ¹²I could wish that those who trouble you would even cut themselves off!

4:24 ᵃNU-Text and M-Text omit *the.*   **4:27** ᵃIsaiah 54:1   **4:30** ᵃGenesis 21:10   **5:1** ᵃNU-Text reads *For freedom Christ has made us free; stand fast therefore.*

[13]For you, brethren, have been called to liberty; only do not *use* liberty as an opportunity for the flesh, but through love serve one another. [14]For all the law is fulfilled in one word, *even* in this: "*You shall love your neighbor as yourself.*"[a] [15]But if you bite and devour one another, beware lest you be consumed by one another!

Walking in the Spirit

[16]I say then: Walk in the Spirit, and you shall not fulfill the lust of the flesh. [17]For the flesh lusts against the Spirit, and the Spirit against the flesh; and these are contrary to one another, so that you do not do the things that you wish. [18]But if you are led by the Spirit, you are not under the law.

[19]Now the works of the flesh are evident, which are: adultery,[a] fornication, uncleanness, lewdness, [20]idolatry, sorcery, hatred, contentions, jealousies, outbursts of wrath, selfish ambitions, dissensions, heresies, [21]envy, murders,[a] drunkenness, revelries, and the like; of which I tell you beforehand, just as I also told *you* in time past, that those who practice such things will not inherit the kingdom of God.

[22]But the fruit of the Spirit is love, joy, peace, longsuffering, kindness, goodness, faithfulness, [23]gentleness, self-control. Against such there is no law. [24]And those *who are* Christ's have crucified the flesh with its passions and desires. [25]If we live in the Spirit, let us also walk in the Spirit. [26]Let us not become conceited, provoking one another, envying one another.

Bear and Share the Burdens

6 Brethren, if a man is overtaken in any trespass, you who *are* spiritual restore such a one in a spirit of gentleness, considering yourself lest you also be tempted. [2]Bear one another's burdens, and so fulfill the law of Christ. [3]For if anyone thinks himself to be something, when he is nothing, he deceives himself. [4]But let each one examine his own work, and then he will have rejoicing in himself alone, and not in another. [5]For each one shall bear his own load.

Be Generous and Do Good

[6]Let him who is taught the word share in all good things with him who teaches.

[7]Do not be deceived, God is not mocked; for whatever a man sows, that he will also

> **Bill Clinton** placed his hand on Galatians 6:8 as he took the presidential oath of office in 1993.

reap. [8]For he who sows to his flesh will of the flesh reap corruption, but he who sows to the Spirit will of the Spirit reap everlasting life. [9]And let us not grow weary while doing good, for in due season we shall reap if we do not lose heart. [10]Therefore, as we have opportunity, let us do good to all, especially to those who are of the household of faith.

Glory Only in the Cross

[11]See with what large letters I have written to you with my own hand! [12]As many as desire to make a good showing in the flesh, these *would* compel you to be circumcised, only that they may not suffer persecution for the cross of Christ. [13]For not even those who are circumcised keep the law, but they desire to have you circumcised that they may boast in your flesh. [14]But God forbid that I should boast except in the cross of our Lord Jesus Christ, by whom[a] the world has been crucified to me, and I to the world. [15]For in Christ Jesus neither circumcision nor uncircumcision avails anything, but a new creation.

Blessing and a Plea

[16]And as many as walk according to this rule, peace and mercy *be* upon them, and upon the Israel of God.

[17]From now on let no one trouble me, for I bear in my body the marks of the Lord Jesus.

[18]Brethren, the grace of our Lord Jesus Christ *be* with your spirit. Amen.

5:14 [a]Leviticus 19:18   **5:19** [a]NU-Text omits *adultery.*   **5:21** [a]NU-Text omits *murders.*
6:14 [a]Or *by which* (the cross)

EPHESIANS

Author: Paul

When Written: Around A.D. 60

Theme: Building the Body of Christ

Key Verses: Ephesians 2:8–10—For by grace you have been saved through faith, and that not of yourselves; it is the gift of God, not of works, lest anyone should boast. For we are His workmanship, created in Christ Jesus for good works, which God prepared beforehand that we should walk in them.

Key Chapter: Ephesians 6—Even though the Christian is blessed with all spiritual blessings in Christ, spiritual warfare is still the daily experience of believers in the world. The chapter captures the essence of how that warfare is waged.

The believers in Ephesus were rich beyond measure in Christ, yet were living as beggars, simply because they were ignorant of their wealth. Paul begins in chapters 1–3 to describe the vast spiritual blessings they have received in Christ. Having demonstrated that huge spiritual endowment, he continues in chapter 4–6 to describe how the Christian learns a spiritual walk rooted in his spiritual wealth.

The same is true regarding the "inalienable rights" described in the Declaration of Independence. John Dickinson, a Pennsylvania Quaker and signer of the U.S. Constitution, wrote in the same year of the Constitution's adoption: "Kings or parliaments could not give the rights essential to happiness—we claim them from a higher source—from the King of kings and the Lord of all the Earth. They are not annexed to us by parchments or seals. They are created in us by the decrees of Providence, which establish the laws of our nature. They are born with us; and cannot be taken from us by any human power."

EPHESIANS

Greeting

1 Paul, an apostle of Jesus Christ by the will of God,

To the saints who are in Ephesus, and faithful in Christ Jesus:

[2]Grace to you and peace from God our Father and the Lord Jesus Christ.

Redemption in Christ

[3]Blessed *be* the God and Father of our Lord Jesus Christ, who has blessed us with every spiritual blessing in the heavenly *places* in Christ, [4]just as He chose us in Him before the foundation of the world, that we should be holy and without blame before Him in love, [5]having predestined us to adoption as sons by Jesus Christ to Himself, according to the good pleasure of His will, [6]to the praise of the glory of His grace, by which He made us accepted in the Beloved.

[7]In Him we have redemption through His blood, the forgiveness of sins, according to the riches of His grace [8]which He made to abound toward us in all wisdom and prudence, [9]having made known to us the mystery of His will, according to His good pleasure which He purposed in Himself, [10]that in the dispensation of the fullness of the times He might gather together in one all things in Christ, both[a] which are in heaven and which are on earth—in Him. [11]In Him also we have obtained an inheritance, being predestined according to the purpose of Him who works all things according to the counsel of His will, [12]that we who first trusted in Christ should be to the praise of His glory.

[13]In Him you also *trusted,* after you heard the word of truth, the gospel of your salvation; in whom also, having believed, you were sealed with the Holy Spirit of promise, [14]who[a] is the guarantee of our inheritance until the redemption of the purchased possession, to the praise of His glory.

Prayer for Spiritual Wisdom

[15]Therefore I also, after I heard of your faith in the Lord Jesus and your love for all the saints, [16]do not cease to give thanks for you, making mention of you in my prayers: [17]that the God of our Lord Jesus Christ, the Father of glory, may give to you the spirit of wisdom and revelation in the knowledge of Him, [18]the eyes of your understanding[a] being enlightened; that you may know what is the hope of His calling, what are the riches of the glory of His inheritance in the saints, [19]and what *is* the exceeding greatness of His power toward us who believe, according to the working of His mighty power [20]which He worked in Christ when He raised Him from the dead and seated *Him* at His right hand in the heavenly *places,* [21]far above all principality and power and might and dominion, and every name that is named, not only in this age but also in that which is to come. [22]And He put all *things* under His feet, and gave Him *to be* head over all *things* to the church, [23]which is His body, the fullness of Him who fills all in all.

By Grace Through Faith

2 And you *He made alive,* who were dead in trespasses and sins, [2]in which you once walked according to the course of this world, according to the prince of the power of the air, the spirit who now works in the sons of disobedience, [3]among whom also we all once conducted ourselves in the lusts of our flesh, fulfilling the desires of the flesh and of the mind, and were by nature children of wrath, just as the others.

[4]But God, who is rich in mercy, because of His great love with which He loved us, [5]even when we were dead in trespasses, made us alive together with Christ (by

---

1:10 [a]NU-Text and M-Text omit *both.*   **1:14** [a]NU-Text reads *which.*   **1:18** [a]NU-Text and M-Text read *hearts.*

grace you have been saved), [6]and raised *us* up together, and made *us* sit together in the heavenly *places* in Christ Jesus, [7]that in the ages to come He might show the exceeding riches of His grace in *His* kindness toward us in Christ Jesus. [8]For by grace you have been saved through faith, and that not of yourselves; *it is* the gift of God, [9]not of works, lest anyone should boast. [10]For we are His workmanship, created in Christ Jesus for good works, which God prepared beforehand that we should walk in them.

Brought Near by His Blood

[11]Therefore remember that you, once Gentiles in the flesh—who are called Uncircumcision by what is called the Circumcision made in the flesh by hands— [12]that at that time you were without Christ, being aliens from the commonwealth of Israel and strangers from the covenants of promise, having no hope and without God in the world. [13]But now in Christ Jesus you who once were far off have been brought near by the blood of Christ.

Christ Our Peace

[14]For He Himself is our peace, who has made both one, and has broken down the middle wall of separation, [15]having abolished in His flesh the enmity, *that is,* the law of commandments *contained* in ordinances, so as to create in Himself one new man *from* the two, *thus* making peace, [16]and that He might reconcile them both to God in one body through the cross, thereby putting to death the enmity. [17]And He came and preached peace to you who were afar off and to those who were near. [18]For through Him we both have access by one Spirit to the Father.

Christ Our Cornerstone

[19]Now, therefore, you are no longer strangers and foreigners, but fellow citizens with the saints and members of the household of God, [20]having been built on the foundation of the apostles and prophets, Jesus Christ Himself being the chief cornerstone, [21]in whom the whole building, being fitted together, grows into a holy temple in

---

FAITH

. . . having no hope and without God in the world.

EPHESIANS 2:12

Ronald Reagan

"WITHOUT GOD"

In August 1984, Ronald Reagan spoke to an ecumenical prayer breakfast in Dallas, Texas, and stated:

> *We establish no religion in this country, nor will we ever. We command no worship. We mandate no belief. But we poison our society when we remove its theological underpinnings. We court corruption when we leave it bereft of belief. All are free to believe or not believe; all are free to practice a faith or not. But those who believe must be free to speak of and act on their belief, to apply moral teaching to public questions.*
>
> *I submit to you that the tolerant society is open to and encouraging of all religions. And this does not weaken us; it strengthens us. . . .*
>
> *Without God, there is no virtue, because there's no prompting of the conscience. Without God, we're mired in the material, that flat world that tells us only what the senses perceive. Without God, there is a coarsening of the society. And without God, democracy will not and cannot long endure. If we ever forget that we're One Nation Under God, then we will be a nation gone under.*

the Lord, [22]in whom you also are being built together for a dwelling place of God in the Spirit.

The Mystery Revealed

3 For this reason I, Paul, the prisoner of Christ Jesus for you Gentiles— [2]if indeed you have heard of the dispensation of the grace of God which was given to me for you, [3]how that by revelation He made known to me the mystery (as I have briefly written already, [4]by which, when you read, you may understand my knowledge in the mystery of Christ), [5]which in other ages was not made known to the sons of men, as it has now been revealed by the Spirit to His holy apostles and prophets: [6]that the Gentiles should be fellow heirs, of the same body, and partakers of His promise in Christ through the gospel, [7]of which I became a minister according to the gift of the grace of God given to me by the effective working of His power.

Purpose of the Mystery

[8]To me, who am less than the least of all the saints, this grace was given, that I should preach among the Gentiles the unsearchable riches of Christ, [9]and to make all see what *is* the fellowship[a] of the mystery, which from the beginning of the ages has been hidden in God who created all things through Jesus Christ;[b] [10]to the intent that now the manifold wisdom of God might be made known by the church to the principalities and powers in the heavenly *places,* [11]according to the eternal purpose which He accomplished in Christ Jesus our Lord, [12]in whom we have boldness and access with confidence through faith in Him. [13]Therefore I ask that you do not lose heart at my tribulations for you, which is your glory.

Appreciation of the Mystery

[14]For this reason I bow my knees to the Father of our Lord Jesus Christ,[a] [15]from whom the whole family in heaven and earth is named, [16]that He would grant you, according to the riches of His glory, to be strengthened with might through His Spirit in the inner man, [17]that Christ may dwell in your hearts through faith; that you,

being rooted and grounded in love, [18]may be able to comprehend with all the saints what *is* the width and length and depth and height— [19]to know the love of Christ which passes knowledge; that you may be filled with all the fullness of God.

[20]Now to Him who is able to do exceedingly abundantly above all that we ask or think, according to the power that works in us, [21]to Him *be* glory in the church by Christ Jesus to all generations, forever and ever. Amen.

Walk in Unity

4 I, therefore, the prisoner of the Lord, beseech you to walk worthy of the calling with which you were called, [2]with all lowliness and gentleness, with longsuffering, bearing with one another in love, [3]endeavoring to keep the unity of the Spirit in the bond of peace. [4]*There is* one body and one Spirit, just as you were called in one hope of your calling; [5]one Lord, one faith, one baptism; [6]one God and Father of all, who *is* above all, and through all, and in you[a] all.

Spiritual Gifts

[7]But to each one of us grace was given according to the measure of Christ's gift. [8]Therefore He says:

> "When He ascended on high,
>   He led captivity captive,
>   And gave gifts to men."[a]

[9](Now this, "He ascended"—what does it mean but that He also first[a] descended into the lower parts of the earth? [10]He who descended is also the One who ascended far above all the heavens, that He might fill all things.) [11]And He Himself gave some *to be* apostles, some prophets, some evangelists, and some pastors and teachers, [12]for the equipping of the saints for the work of ministry, for the edifying of the body of Christ, [13]till

---

3:9 [a]NU-Text and M-Text read *stewardship* (dispensation). [b]NU-Text omits *through Jesus Christ.*
3:14 [a]NU-Text omits *of our Lord Jesus Christ.*
4:6 [a]NU-Text omits *you;* M-Text reads *us.*
4:8 [a]Psalm 68:18   **4:9** [a]NU-Text omits *first.*

we all come to the unity of the faith and of the knowledge of the Son of God, to a perfect man, to the measure of the stature of the fullness of Christ; [14]that we should no longer be children, tossed to and fro and carried about with every wind of doctrine, by the trickery of men, in the cunning craftiness of deceitful plotting, [15]but, speaking the truth in love, may grow up in all things into Him who is the head—Christ— [16]from whom the whole body, joined and knit together by what every joint supplies, according to the effective working by which every part does its share, causes growth of the body for the edifying of itself in love.

The New Man

[17]This I say, therefore, and testify in the Lord, that you should no longer walk as the rest of[a] the Gentiles walk, in the futility of their mind, [18]having their understanding darkened, being alienated from the life of God, because of the ignorance that is in them, because of the blindness of their heart; [19]who, being past feeling, have given themselves over to lewdness, to work all uncleanness with greediness.

[20]But you have not so learned Christ, [21]if indeed you have heard Him and have been taught by Him, as the truth is in Jesus: [22]that you put off, concerning your former conduct, the old man which grows corrupt according to the deceitful lusts, [23]and be renewed in the spirit of your mind, [24]and that you put on the new man which was created according to God, in true righteousness and holiness.

Do Not Grieve the Spirit

[25]Therefore, putting away lying, *"Let each one of you speak truth with his neighbor,"*[a] for we are members of one another. [26]*"Be angry, and do not sin":*[a] do not let the sun go down on your wrath, [27]nor give place to the devil. [28]Let him who stole steal no longer, but rather let him labor, working with *his* hands what is good, that he may have something to give him who has need. [29]Let no corrupt word proceed out of your mouth, but what is good for necessary edification, that it may impart grace to the hearers. [30]And do not grieve the Holy Spirit of God, by whom you were sealed for the day of redemption. [31]Let all bitterness, wrath, anger, clamor, and evil speaking be put away from you, with all malice. [32]And be kind to one another, tenderhearted, forgiving one another, even as God in Christ forgave you.

Walk in Love

5 Therefore be imitators of God as dear children. [2]And walk in love, as Christ also has loved us and given Himself for us, an offering and a sacrifice to God for a sweet-smelling aroma.

[3]But fornication and all uncleanness or covetousness, let it not even be named among you, as is fitting for saints; [4]neither filthiness, nor foolish talking, nor coarse jesting, which are not fitting, but rather giving of thanks. [5]For this you know,[a] that no fornicator, unclean person, nor covetous man, who is an idolater, has any inheritance in the kingdom of Christ and God. [6]Let no one deceive you with empty words, for because of these things the wrath of God comes upon the sons of disobedience. [7]Therefore do not be partakers with them.

Walk in Light

[8]For you were once darkness, but now *you are* light in the Lord. Walk as children of light [9](for the fruit of the Spirit[a] *is* in all goodness, righteousness, and truth), [10]finding out what is acceptable to the Lord. [11]And have no fellowship with the unfruitful works of darkness, but rather expose *them.* [12]For it is shameful even to speak of those things which are done by them in secret. [13]But all things that are exposed are made manifest by the light, for whatever makes manifest is light. [14]Therefore He says:

> "Awake, you who sleep,
>   Arise from the dead,
>   And Christ will give you light."

4:17 [a]NU-Text omits *the rest of.* 4:25 [a]Zechariah 8:16 4:26 [a]Psalm 4:4 5:5 [a]NU-Text reads *For know this.* 5:9 [a]NU-Text reads *light.*

Walk in Wisdom

¹⁵See then that you walk circumspectly, not as fools but as wise, ¹⁶redeeming the time, because the days are evil.

¹⁷Therefore do not be unwise, but understand what the will of the Lord *is.* ¹⁸And do not be drunk with wine, in which is dissipation; but be filled with the Spirit, ¹⁹speaking to one another in psalms and hymns and spiritual songs, singing and making melody in your heart to the Lord, ²⁰giving thanks always for all things to God the Father in the name of our Lord Jesus Christ, ²¹submitting to one another in the fear of God.ᵃ

Marriage—Christ and the Church

²²Wives, submit to your own husbands, as to the Lord. ²³For the husband is head of the wife, as also Christ is head of the church; and He is the Savior of the body. ²⁴Therefore, just as the church is subject to Christ, so *let* the wives *be* to their own husbands in everything.

²⁵Husbands, love your wives, just as Christ also loved the church and gave Himself for her, ²⁶that He might sanctify and cleanse her with the washing of water by the word, ²⁷that He might present her to Himself a glorious church, not having spot or wrinkle or any such thing, but that she should be holy and without blemish. ²⁸So husbands ought to love their own wives as their own bodies; he who loves his wife loves himself. ²⁹For no one ever hated his own flesh, but nourishes and cherishes it, just as the Lord *does* the church. ³⁰For we are members of His body,ᵃ of His flesh and of His bones. ³¹*"For this reason a man shall leave his father and mother and be joined to his wife, and the two shall become one flesh."*ᵃ ³²This is a great mystery, but I

5:21 ᵃNU-Text reads *Christ.*   **5:30** ᵃNU-Text omits the rest of this verse.   **5:31** ᵃGenesis 2:24

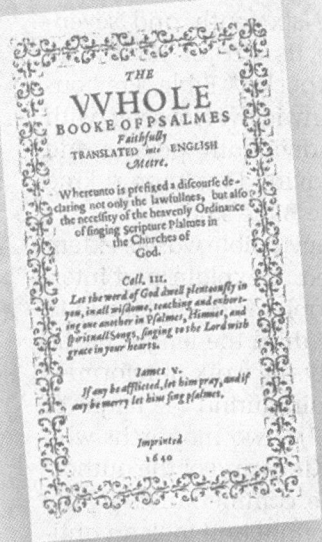

The Bay Psalm Book

THE FIRST BOOK PUBLISHED IN THE AMERICAN COLONIES

When the Pilgrim Fathers arrived at Plymouth, Massachusetts, the influence of the Bible and their Christian faith over their lives and literature came with them. A mere 20 years later, *The Bay Psalm Book* (originally titled *The Whole Booke of Psalmes Faithfully Translated into English Metre*) was printed in 1640 in Cambridge, Massachusetts. It was the first book printed in the colonies as well as the first book entirely written in the colonies. The first printing press in New England was purchased and imported specifically to print this volume.

The early residents of the Massachusetts Bay Colony brought with them several books of Psalms in metrical translations into English, but they were dissatisfied with the translations from Hebrew and hired "thirty pious and learned Ministers" to undertake a new translation. It represented a sacred value held by the Puritans—a faithful translation of God's Word, to be sung in worship by the entire congregation. Given the harsh living condition of those early years, it was a remarkable achievement.

The Bay Psalm Book went through several editions and remained in use for well over a century. This psalter and *The New England Primer* were, next to the Bible, the most commonly owned books in seventeenth-century New England.

speak concerning Christ and the church. [33]Nevertheless let each one of you in particular so love his own wife as himself, and let the wife *see* that she respects *her* husband.

Children and Parents

6 Children, obey your parents in the Lord, for this is right. [2]"Honor your *father and mother,*" which is the first commandment with promise: [3]"*that it may be well with you and you may live long on the earth.*"[a]

[4]And you, fathers, do not provoke your children to wrath, but bring them up in the training and admonition of the Lord.

Bondservants and Masters

[5]Bondservants, be obedient to those who are your masters according to the flesh, with fear and trembling, in sincerity of heart, as to Christ; [6]not with eyeservice, as men-pleasers, but as bondservants of Christ, doing the will of God from the heart, [7]with goodwill doing service, as to the Lord, and not to men, [8]knowing that whatever good anyone does, he will receive the same from the Lord, whether *he is* a slave or free.

[9]And you, masters, do the same things to them, giving up threatening, knowing that your own Master also[a] is in heaven, and there is no partiality with Him.

The Whole Armor of God

[10]Finally, my brethren, be strong in the Lord and in the power of His might. [11]Put on the whole armor of God, that you may be able to stand against the wiles of the devil. [12]For we do not wrestle against flesh and blood, but against principalities, against powers, against the rulers of the darkness of this age,[a] against spiritual *hosts* of wickedness in the heavenly *places.* [13]Therefore take up the whole armor of God, that you may be able to withstand in the evil day, and having done all, to stand.

6:3 [a]Deuteronomy 5:16   **6:9** [a]NU-Text reads *He who is both their Master and yours.*   **6:12** [a]NU-Text reads *rulers of this darkness.*

TRUTH

. . . and the sword of the Spirit, which is the word of God. . . .

EPHESIANS 6:17

The Geneva Bible

THE BIBLE OF THE EARLY COLONISTS

The Geneva Bible (over 140 editions were printed from 1560 to 1644) was the Bible that the early religious colonists brought to America's shores and was the most widely read and influential English Bible of the sixteenth and seventeenth centuries. This Bible, despite its size of nearly six inches by eight inches, was called a "pocket" Bible. Previous editions of the Bible were huge and unwieldy. However, with the Geneva Bible, a person could individually possess and also read the Word of God without having to rely on a king or church official to interpret what the Bible said.

The most unique feature of the Geneva Bible was its extensive marginal notes that were included to explain and interpret the scriptures for the common people. These notes run to approximately 300,000 words, or one-third the length of the text of the Bible itself, and were largely the work of reformers who had been driven from Great Britain during the reigns of Bloody Mary (1553) and James I (1603)—two monarchs who were advocates of the Divine Right of Kings and of the authority of the State over the Church. The commentaries in the Geneva Bible reflected reformation thought and took an anti-autocratic tone toward both church leaders and state leaders.

[14]Stand therefore, having girded your waist with truth, having put on the breastplate of righteousness, [15]and having shod your feet with the preparation of the gospel of peace; [16]above all, taking the shield of faith with which you will be able to quench all the fiery darts of the wicked one. [17]And take the helmet of salvation, and the sword of the Spirit, which is the word of God; [18]praying always with all prayer and supplication in the Spirit, being watchful to this end with all perseverance and supplication for all the saints— [19]and for me, that utterance may be given to me, that I may open my mouth boldly to make known the mystery of the gospel, [20]for which I am an ambassador in chains; that in it I may speak boldly, as I ought to speak.

A Gracious Greeting

[21]But that you also may know my affairs *and* how I am doing, Tychicus, a beloved brother and faithful minister in the Lord, will make all things known to you; [22]whom I have sent to you for this very purpose, that you may know our affairs, and *that* he may comfort your hearts.

[23]Peace to the brethren, and love with faith, from God the Father and the Lord Jesus Christ. [24]Grace *be* with all those who love our Lord Jesus Christ in sincerity. Amen.

PHILIPPIANS

Author: Paul

When Written: Around A.D. 60

Theme: To Live Is Christ

Key Verse: Philippians 1:21—For to me, to live is Christ, and to die is gain.

Key Chapter: Philippians 2—Jesus Christ, whose humility is revealed in what it meant to leave heaven to become a servant of man, is clearly set forth as the Christian's example.

Philippians is the epistle of joy and encouragement in the midst of adverse circumstances. Paul writes a letter of thank you to the believers in Philippi for their help in his time of need, and he lovingly urges them to center their actions and thoughts on the pursuit of the person and power of Christ. His central thought is simple: only in Christ are real unity and joy possible. With Christ as our model of humility and service, we can enjoy a oneness of purpose, attitude, goal, and labor.

Paul reminds the Philippians that their citizenship is in heaven. Adlai Stevenson, who served as the ambassador to the United Nations from 1961 to 1965, reminds us of the privilege of being an American citizen today: "When an American says that he loves his country, he means not only that he loves the New England hills, the prairies glistening in the sun, the wide and rising plains, the great mountains, and the sea. He means that he loves an inner air, an inner light in which freedom lives and in which a man can draw the breath of self-respect."

PHILIPPIANS

Greeting

1 Paul and Timothy, bondservants of Jesus Christ,

To all the saints in Christ Jesus who are in Philippi, with the bishops[a] and deacons:

2Grace to you and peace from God our Father and the Lord Jesus Christ.

Thankfulness and Prayer

3I thank my God upon every remembrance of you, 4always in every prayer of mine making request for you all with joy, 5for your fellowship in the gospel from the first day until now, 6being confident of this very thing, that He who has begun a good work in you will complete *it* until the day of Jesus Christ; 7just as it is right for me to think this of you all, because I have you in my heart, inasmuch as both in my chains and in the defense and confirmation of the gospel, you all are partakers with me of grace. 8For God is my witness, how greatly I long for you all with the affection of Jesus Christ.

9And this I pray, that your love may abound still more and more in knowledge and all discernment, 10that you may approve the things that are excellent, that you may be sincere and without offense till the day of Christ, 11being filled with the fruits of righteousness which *are* by Jesus Christ, to the glory and praise of God.

Christ Is Preached

12But I want you to know, brethren, that the things *which happened* to me have actually turned out for the furtherance of the gospel, 13so that it has become evident to the whole palace guard, and to all the rest, that my chains are in Christ; 14and most of the brethren in the Lord, having become confident by my chains, are much more bold to speak the word without fear.

15Some indeed preach Christ even from envy and strife, and some also from goodwill: 16The former[a] preach Christ from selfish ambition, not sincerely, supposing to add affliction to my chains; 17but the latter out of love, knowing that I am appointed for the defense of the gospel. 18What then? Only *that* in every way, whether in pretense or in truth, Christ is preached; and in this I rejoice, yes, and will rejoice.

To Live Is Christ

19For I know that this will turn out for my deliverance through your prayer and the supply of the Spirit of Jesus Christ, 20according to my earnest expectation and hope that in nothing I shall be ashamed, but with all boldness, as always, so now also Christ will be magnified in my body, whether by life or by death. 21For to me, to live *is* Christ, and to die *is* gain. 22But if *I* live on in the flesh, this *will mean* fruit from *my* labor; yet what I shall choose I cannot tell. 23For[a] I am hard-pressed between the two, having a desire to depart and be with Christ, *which is* far better. 24Nevertheless to remain in the flesh *is* more needful for you. 25And being confident of this, I know that I shall remain and continue with you all for your progress and joy of faith, 26that your rejoicing for me may be more abundant in Jesus Christ by my coming to you again.

Striving and Suffering for Christ

27Only let your conduct be worthy of the gospel of Christ, so that whether I come and see you or am absent, I may hear of your affairs, that you stand fast in one spirit, with one mind striving together for the faith of the gospel, 28and not in any way terrified by your adversaries, which is to them a proof of perdition, but to you of salvation,[a]

1:1 [a]Literally *overseers* **1:16** [a]NU-Text reverses the contents of verses 16 and 17. **1:23** [a]NU-Text and M-Text read *But*. **1:28** [a]NU-Text reads *of your salvation*.

FREEDOM REQUIRES BRAVERY

RICHARD ALLEN

According to a popular legend surrounding the Declaration of Independence, John Hancock signed his name largely and distinctly so King George could read it without his spectacles. While that may not be true, it is true that one of colonial America's most ardent revolutionaries and rich merchants put his life on the line with his signature. If the revolution was lost or he was caught, he would be hanged by the British.

Certainly, all 56 patriots who signed the Declaration of Independence made the same solemn declaration "with a firm reliance on the protection of Divine Providence, we mutually pledge to each other our lives, our fortunes, and our sacred honor." Even in victory, many of the signers endured hardships and losses, as did thousands of other Americans.

John Adams wrote to his wife regarding the meaning of his signature on the document of freedom: "I am well aware of the toil, and blood, and treasure, that it will cost us to maintain this declaration. . . . I can see that the end is more than worth all the means, and that posterity will triumph in that day's transaction."

A few months before signing the Declaration, Patrick Henry addressed the Virginia Convention and declared: "We are not weak if we make a proper use of those means which the God of nature hath placed in our power. Three millions of people, armed in the holy cause of liberty, and in such a country as that which we possess, are invincible by any force which our enemy can send against us. Besides, sir, we shall not fight our battles alone. There is a just God who presides over the destinies of nations, and who will raise up friends to fight our battles for us. The battle, sir, is not to the strong alone; it is to the vigilant, the active, the brave."

When the authors of *The Day America Told the Truth* took polls in the early 1990s asking people which beliefs they would die for, 48 percent said "none." Only 30 percent would die for God and their faith under any circumstance, and fewer would die for their country. The question is, "Can America restore courage to its soul?"

and that from God. [29]For to you it has been granted on behalf of Christ, not only to believe in Him, but also to suffer for His sake, [30]having the same conflict which you saw in me and now hear *is* in me.

Unity Through Humility

2 Therefore if *there is* any consolation in Christ, if any comfort of love, if any fellowship of the Spirit, if any affection and mercy, [2]fulfill my joy by being like-minded, having the same love, *being* of one accord, of one mind. [3]*Let* nothing *be done* through selfish ambition or conceit, but in lowliness of mind let each esteem others better than himself. [4]Let each of you look out not only for his own interests, but also for the interests of others.

The Humbled and Exalted Christ

[5]Let this mind be in you which was also in Christ Jesus, [6]who, being in the form of God, did not consider it robbery to be equal with God, [7]but made Himself of no reputation, taking the form of a bondservant, *and* coming in the likeness of men. [8]And being found in appearance as a man, He humbled Himself and became obedient to *the point of* death, even the death of the cross. [9]Therefore God also has highly exalted Him and given Him the name which is above every name, [10]that at the name of Jesus every knee should bow, of those in heaven, and of those on earth, and of those under the earth, [11]and *that* every tongue should confess that Jesus Christ *is* Lord, to the glory of God the Father.

Light Bearers

[12]Therefore, my beloved, as you have always obeyed, not as in my presence only, but now much more in my absence, work out your own salvation with fear and trembling; [13]for it is God who works in you both to will and to do for *His* good pleasure.

[14]Do all things without complaining and disputing, [15]that you may become blameless and harmless, children of God without fault in the midst of a crooked and perverse generation, among whom you shine as lights in the world, [16]holding fast the word of life, so that I may rejoice in the day of Christ that I have not run in vain or labored in vain.

[17]Yes, and if I am being poured out *as a drink offering* on the sacrifice and service of your faith, I am glad and rejoice with you all. [18]For the same reason you also be glad and rejoice with me.

Timothy Commended

[19]But I trust in the Lord Jesus to send Timothy to you shortly, that I also may be encouraged when I know your state. [20]For I have no one like-minded, who will sincerely care for your state. [21]For all seek their own, not the things which are of Christ Jesus. [22]But you know his proven character, that as a son with *his* father he served with me in the gospel. [23]Therefore I hope to send him at once, as soon as I see how it goes with me. [24]But I trust in the Lord that I myself shall also come shortly.

Epaphroditus Praised

[25]Yet I considered it necessary to send to you Epaphroditus, my brother, fellow worker, and fellow soldier, but your messenger and the one who ministered to my need; [26]since he was longing for you all, and was distressed because you had heard that he was sick. [27]For indeed he was sick almost unto death; but God had mercy on him, and not only on him but on me also, lest I should have sorrow upon sorrow. [28]Therefore I sent him the more eagerly, that when you see him again you may rejoice, and I may be less sorrowful. [29]Receive him therefore in the Lord with all gladness, and hold such men in esteem; [30]because for the work of Christ he came close to death, not regarding his life, to supply what was lacking in your service toward me.

All for Christ

3 Finally, my brethren, rejoice in the Lord. For me to write the same things to you *is* not tedious, but for you *it is* safe.

[2]Beware of dogs, beware of evil workers, beware of the mutilation! [3]For we are the circumcision, who worship God in the Spirit,[a]

3:3 [a]NU-Text and M-Text read *who worship in the Spirit of God.*

rejoice in Christ Jesus, and have no confidence in the flesh, [4]though I also might have confidence in the flesh. If anyone else thinks he may have confidence in the flesh, I more so: [5]circumcised the eighth day, of the stock of Israel, *of* the tribe of Benjamin, a Hebrew of the Hebrews; concerning the law, a Pharisee; [6]concerning zeal, persecuting the church; concerning the righteousness which is in the law, blameless.

[7]But what things were gain to me, these I have counted loss for Christ. [8]Yet indeed I also count all things loss for the excellence of the knowledge of Christ Jesus my Lord, for whom I have suffered the loss of all things, and count them as rubbish, that I may gain Christ [9]and be found in Him, not having my own righteousness, which *is* from the law, but that which *is* through faith in Christ, the righteousness which is from God by faith; [10]that I may know Him and the power of His resurrection, and the fellowship of His sufferings, being conformed to His death, [11]if, by any means, I may attain to the resurrection from the dead.

Pressing Toward the Goal

[12]Not that I have already attained, or am already perfected; but I press on, that I may lay hold of that for which Christ Jesus has also laid hold of me. [13]Brethren, I do not count myself to have apprehended; but one thing *I do,* forgetting those things which are behind and reaching forward to those things which are ahead, [14]I press toward the goal for the prize of the upward call of God in Christ Jesus. [15]Therefore let us, as many as are mature, have this mind; and if in anything you think otherwise, God will reveal even this to you. [16]Nevertheless, to *the degree* that we have already attained, let us walk by the same rule,[a] let us be of the same mind.

Our Citizenship in Heaven

[17]Brethren, join in following my example, and note those who so walk, as you have us for a pattern. [18]For many walk, of whom I have told you often, and now tell you even weeping, *that they are* the enemies of the cross of Christ: [19]whose end is destruction, whose god *is their* belly, and *whose* glory *is* in their shame—who set their mind on earthly things. [20]For our citizenship is in heaven, from which we also eagerly wait for the Savior, the Lord Jesus Christ, [21]who will transform our lowly body that it may be conformed to His glorious body, according to the working by which He is able even to subdue all things to Himself.

PRAYER

. . . in everything by prayer and supplication. . . .

PHILIPPIANS 4:6

The Power of Prayer

General Robert E. Lee (1807–1870), Commander of the Confederate Army of Northern Virginia, wrote:

Knowing that intercessory prayer is our mightiest weapon and supreme call for Christians today, I pleadingly urge our people everywhere to pray. . . . Let there be prayer at sunup, at noonday, at sundown, at midnight, all through the day. Let us all pray for our children, our youth, our aged, our pastors, our homes. Let us pray for our churches.

Let us pray for ourselves, that we may not lose the word "concern" for those who have never known Jesus Christ and redeeming love, for moral forces everywhere, for our national leaders. Let prayer be our passion. Let prayer be our practice.

4 Therefore, my beloved and longed-for brethren, my joy and crown, so stand fast in the Lord, beloved.

Be United, Joyful, and in Prayer

[2]I implore Euodia and I implore Syntyche to be of the same mind in the Lord. [3]And[a] I urge you also, true companion, help these women who labored with me in the gospel, with Clement also, and the rest of my fellow workers, whose names *are* in the Book of Life.

[4]Rejoice in the Lord always. Again I will say, rejoice!

3:16 [a]NU-Text omits *rule* and the rest of the verse.
4:3 [a]NU-Text and M-Text read *Yes.*

[5]Let your gentleness be known to all men. The Lord *is* at hand.

[6]Be anxious for nothing, but in everything by prayer and supplication, with thanksgiving, let your requests be made known to God; [7]and the peace of God, which surpasses all understanding, will guard your hearts and minds through Christ Jesus.

Meditate on These Things

[8]Finally, brethren, whatever things are true, whatever things *are* noble, whatever things *are* just, whatever things *are* pure, whatever things *are* lovely, whatever things *are* of good report, if *there is* any virtue and if *there is* anything praiseworthy—meditate on these things. [9]The things which you learned and received and heard and saw in me, these do, and the God of peace will be with you.

Philippian Generosity

[10]But I rejoiced in the Lord greatly that now at last your care for me has flourished again; though you surely did care, but you lacked opportunity. [11]Not that I speak in regard to need, for I have learned in whatever state I am, to be content: [12]I know how to be abased, and I know how to abound. Everywhere and in all things I have learned both to be full and to be hungry, both to abound and to suffer need. [13]I can do all things through Christ[a] who strengthens me.

[14]Nevertheless you have done well that you shared in my distress. [15]Now you Philippians know also that in the beginning of the gospel, when I departed from Macedonia, no church shared with me concerning giving and receiving but you only. [16]For even in Thessalonica you sent *aid* once and again for my necessities. [17]Not that I seek the gift, but I seek the fruit that abounds to your account. [18]Indeed I have all and abound. I am full, having received from Epaphroditus the things *sent* from you, a sweet-smelling aroma, an acceptable sacrifice, well pleasing to God. [19]And my God shall supply all your need according to His riches in glory by Christ Jesus. [20]Now to our God and Father *be* glory forever and ever. Amen.

Greeting and Blessing

[21]Greet every saint in Christ Jesus. The brethren who are with me greet you. [22]All the saints greet you, but especially those who are of Caesar's household.

[23]The grace of our Lord Jesus Christ be with you all.[a] Amen.

4:13 [a]NU-Text reads *Him who.*   **4:23** [a]NU-Text reads *your spirit.*

COLOSSIANS

Author: Paul

When Written: Around A.D. 60

Theme: The Preeminence of Christ

Key Verses: Colossians 2:9, 10—For in Him dwells all the fullness of the Godhead bodily; and you are complete in Him, who is the head of all principality and power.

Key Chapter: Colossians 3—In refuting a threatening heresy that is devaluing Christ, Paul shows that the believer is risen with Christ, is to put off the old man and is to put on the new, which will result in holiness in all relationships.

Colossians is perhaps the most Christ-centered book in the Bible. Paul stresses the preeminence of Christ and the completeness of the salvation He provides, in order to combat a growing heresy that is devaluing Christ. This false teaching is countered by Paul's positive presentation of His true attributes and accomplishments. A proper view of Christ is always the most powerful antidote to heresy.

Just as the Colossians needed to guard the truth of the Gospel, so we need to guard the welfare our country. President Calvin Coolidge said, "The issues of the world must be met and met squarely. The forces of evil do not distain preparation, they are always prepared and always preparing. . . . The welfare of America, the cause of civilization will forever require the contribution, of some part of the life, of all our citizens, to the natural, the necessary, and the inevitable demand for the defense of the right and the truth."

Greeting

1 Paul, an apostle of Jesus Christ by the will of God, and Timothy our brother,

2To the saints and faithful brethren in Christ *who are* in Colosse:

Grace to you and peace from God our Father and the Lord Jesus Christ.ᵃ

Their Faith in Christ

3We give thanks to the God and Father of our Lord Jesus Christ, praying always for you, 4since we heard of your faith in Christ Jesus and of your love for all the saints; 5because of the hope which is laid up for you in heaven, of which you heard before in the word of the truth of the gospel, 6which has come to you, as *it has* also in all the world, and is bringing forth fruit,ᵃ as *it is* also among you since the day you heard and knew the grace of God in truth; 7as you also learned from Epaphras, our dear fellow servant, who is a faithful minister of Christ on your behalf, 8who also declared to us your love in the Spirit.

Preeminence of Christ

9For this reason we also, since the day we heard it, do not cease to pray for you, and to ask that you may be filled with the knowledge of His will in all wisdom and spiritual understanding; 10that you may walk worthy of the Lord, fully pleasing *Him,* being fruitful in every good work and increasing in the knowledge of God; 11strengthened with all might, according to His glorious power, for all patience and longsuffering with joy; 12giving thanks to the Father who has qualified us to be partakers of the inheritance of the saints in the light. 13He has delivered us from the power of darkness and conveyed *us* into the kingdom of the Son of His love, 14in whom we have redemption through His blood,ᵃ the forgiveness of sins.

15He is the image of the invisible God, the firstborn over all creation. 16For by Him all things were created that are in heaven and that are on earth, visible and invisible, whether thrones or dominions or principalities or powers. All things were created through Him and for Him. 17And He is before all things, and in Him all things consist. 18And He is the head of the body, the church, who is the beginning, the firstborn from the dead, that in all things He may have the preeminence.

Reconciled in Christ

19For it pleased *the Father that* in Him all the fullness should dwell, 20and by Him to reconcile all things to Himself, by Him, whether things on earth or things in heaven, having made peace through the blood of His cross.
21And you, who once were alienated and enemies in your mind by wicked works, yet now He has reconciled 22in the body of His flesh through death, to present you holy, and blameless, and above reproach in His sight— 23if indeed you continue in the faith, grounded and steadfast, and are not moved away from the hope of the gospel which you heard, which was preached to every creature under heaven, of which I, Paul, became a minister.

Sacrificial Service for Christ

24I now rejoice in my sufferings for you, and fill up in my flesh what is lacking in the afflictions of Christ, for the sake of His body, which is the church, 25of which I became a minister according to the stewardship from God which was given to me for you, to fulfill the word of God, 26the mystery which has been hidden from ages and from generations, but now has been revealed to His saints. 27To them God willed to make known

---

1:2 ᵃNU-Text omits *and the Lord Jesus Christ.*
1:6 ᵃNU-Text and M-Text add *and growing.*
1:14 ᵃNU-Text and M-Text omit *through His blood.*

what are the riches of the glory of this mystery among the Gentiles: which[a] is Christ in you, the hope of glory. [28]Him we preach, warning every man and teaching every man in all wisdom, that we may present every man perfect in Christ Jesus. [29]To this *end* I also labor, striving according to His working which works in me mightily.

Not Philosophy but Christ

2 For I want you to know what a great conflict I have for you and those in Laodicea, and *for* as many as have not seen my face in the flesh, [2]that their hearts may be encouraged, being knit together in love, and *attaining* to all riches of the full assurance of understanding, to the knowledge of the mystery of God, both of the Father and[a] of Christ, [3]in whom are hidden all the treasures of wisdom and knowledge.

[4]Now this I say lest anyone should deceive you with persuasive words. [5]For though I am absent in the flesh, yet I am with you in spirit, rejoicing to see your *good* order and the steadfastness of your faith in Christ.

[6]As you therefore have received Christ Jesus the Lord, so walk in Him, [7]rooted and built up in Him and established in the faith, as you have been taught, abounding in it[a] with thanksgiving.

[8]Beware lest anyone cheat you through philosophy and empty deceit, according to the tradition of men, according to the basic principles of the world, and not according to Christ. [9]For in Him dwells all the fullness of the Godhead bodily; [10]and you are complete in Him, who is the head of all principality and power.

Not Legalism but Christ

[11]In Him you were also circumcised with the circumcision made without hands, by putting off the body of the sins[a] of the flesh, by the circumcision of Christ, [12]buried with Him in baptism, in which you also were raised with *Him* through faith in the working of God, who raised Him from the dead. [13]And you, being dead in your trespasses and the uncircumcision of your flesh, He has made alive together with Him, having forgiven you all trespasses, [14]having wiped out the handwriting of requirements that was against us,

---

1:27 [a]M-Text reads *who.*   **2:2** [a]NU-Text omits *both of the Father and.*   **2:7** [a]NU-Text omits *in it.*
2:11 [a]NU-Text omits *of the sins.*

INSPIRING

. . . rooted and built up in Him and established in the faith. . . .

COLOSSIANS 2:7

John Quincy Adams

THE CHRISTMAS/JULY 4 LINK

On the 61st anniversary of the Declaration of Independence, John Quincy Adams, the sixth president of the United States, proclaimed:

Why is it that, next to the birthday of the Savior of the world, your most joyous and most venerated festival returns on this day? Is it not that, in the chain of human events, the birthday of the nation is indissolubly linked with the birthday of the Savior? That it forms a leading event in the progress of the Gospel dispensation? Is it not that the Declaration of Independence first organized the social compact on the foundation of the Redeemer's mission upon earth? That it laid the cornerstone of human government upon the first precepts of Christianity and gave to the world the first irrevocable pledge of the fulfillment of the prophecies announced directly from heaven at the birth of the Savior and predicted by the greatest of the Hebrew prophets 600 years before.

which was contrary to us. And He has taken it out of the way, having nailed it to the cross. [15]Having disarmed principalities and powers, He made a public spectacle of them, triumphing over them in it.

[16]So let no one judge you in food or in drink, or regarding a festival or a new moon or sabbaths, [17]which are a shadow of things to come, but the substance is of Christ. [18]Let no one cheat you of your reward, taking delight in *false* humility and worship of angels, intruding into those things which he has not[a] seen, vainly puffed up by his fleshly mind, [19]and not holding fast to the Head, from whom all the body, nourished and knit together by joints and ligaments, grows with the increase *that is* from God.

[20]Therefore,[a] if you died with Christ from the basic principles of the world, why, as *though* living in the world, do you subject yourselves to regulations— [21]"Do not touch, do not taste, do not handle," [22]which all concern things which perish with the using—according to the commandments and doctrines of men? [23]These things indeed have an appearance of wisdom in self-imposed religion, *false* humility, and neglect of the body, *but are* of no value against the indulgence of the flesh.

Not Carnality but Christ

3 If then you were raised with Christ, seek those things which are above, where Christ is, sitting at the right hand of God. [2]Set your mind on things above, not on things on the earth. [3]For you died, and your life is hidden with Christ in God. [4]When Christ *who is* our life appears, then you also will appear with Him in glory.

[5]Therefore put to death your members which are on the earth: fornication, uncleanness, passion, evil desire, and covetousness, which is idolatry. [6]Because of these things the wrath of God is coming upon the sons of disobedience, [7]in which you yourselves once walked when you lived in them.

[8]But now you yourselves are to put off all these: anger, wrath, malice, blasphemy, filthy language out of your mouth. [9]Do not lie to one another, since you have put off the old man with his deeds, [10]and have put on the new *man* who is renewed in knowledge according to the image of Him who created him, [11]where there is neither Greek nor Jew, circumcised nor uncircumcised, barbarian, Scythian, slave *nor* free, but Christ *is* all and in all.

Character of the New Man

[12]Therefore, as *the* elect of God, holy and beloved, put on tender mercies, kindness, humility, meekness, longsuffering; [13]bearing with one another, and forgiving one another, if anyone has a complaint against another; even as Christ forgave you, so you also *must do.* [14]But above all these things put on love, which is the bond of perfection. [15]And let the peace of God rule in your hearts, to which also you were called in one body; and be thankful. [16]Let the word of Christ dwell in you richly in all wisdom, teaching and admonishing one another in psalms and hymns and spiritual songs, singing with grace in your hearts to the Lord. [17]And whatever you do in word or deed, *do* all in the name of the Lord Jesus, giving thanks to God the Father through Him.

The Christian Home

[18]Wives, submit to your own husbands, as is fitting in the Lord.

[19]Husbands, love your wives and do not be bitter toward them.

[20]Children, obey your parents in all things, for this is well pleasing to the Lord.

[21]Fathers, do not provoke your children, lest they become discouraged.

[22]Bondservants, obey in all things your masters according to the flesh, not with eyeservice, as men-pleasers, but in sincerity of heart, fearing God. [23]And whatever you do, do it heartily, as to the Lord and not to men, [24]knowing that from the Lord you will receive the reward of the inheritance; for[a] you serve the Lord Christ. [25]But he who does wrong will be repaid for what he has done, and there is no partiality.

4 Masters, give your bondservants what is just and fair, knowing that you also have a Master in heaven.

2:18 [a]NU-Text omits *not.*   **2:20** [a]NU-Text and M-Text omit *Therefore.*   **3:24** [a]NU-Text omits *for.*

INTEGRITY

And whatever you do in word or deed. . . .

COLOSSIANS 3:17

THE PRINCIPLE OF THE WORK ETHIC

Engrained deep within the American spirit is the Puritan work ethic, which places a high moral value on doing a good job because work has intrinsic value for its own sake. To the Puritan, all of life was to be lived in relation to God, a principle which gave sacred significance to every activity. Work was valued as a vital part of their service and worship to God, and they took the Bible seriously when it said, "And whatever you do in word or deed, do all in the name of the Lord Jesus, giving thanks to God the Father through Him" (Col. 3:17). Just as the Israelites were instructed to work six days and then rest on the seventh (Ex. 20:9, 10), the Puritans regarded work and worship as a lifestyle of obedience to Christ.

God Himself taught us this by example as He created this universe and all that is in it. He could have merely thought creation into being, but He took six days and rested on the seventh. Man was created in God's image with a purpose, to work by creating a desirable habitat (Gen. 1:28). Man was created to work toward the betterment of both himself and others for six days, and then the Sabbath rest offers opportunities for worship that renew the spirit.

When God completed His creation, He declared it "very good"—the quality was a reflection of His character. Similarly, the quality of our work reflects our personal character. Whatever our trade or craft, we should do all to the glory of God and in the service of mankind. God is worthy of the best we can offer, for He has endowed us with gifts to be used for the good of all. God has designed our labor to have dignity and consequence.

This spiritual heritage has led America to be the strongest economic powerhouse in the history of the world. There is no desire in this independent spirit to simply exist on handouts from a government agency or siphon off a living from benevolence or friendships. And it flies in the face of a pleasure-oriented society that exalts leisure above all else. The object of life is not to see how much work can be avoided or how much fun we can have, but to give our very best "with goodwill doing service, as to the Lord, and not to men" (Eph. 6:7).

Christian Graces

2Continue earnestly in prayer, being vigilant in it with thanksgiving; 3meanwhile praying also for us, that God would open to us a door for the word, to speak the mystery of Christ, for which I am also in chains, 4that I may make it manifest, as I ought to speak.

5Walk in wisdom toward those *who are* outside, redeeming the time. 6*Let* your speech always *be* with grace, seasoned with salt, that you may know how you ought to answer each one.

Final Greetings

7Tychicus, a beloved brother, faithful minister, and fellow servant in the Lord, will tell you all the news about me. 8I am sending him to you for this very purpose, that hea may know your circumstances and comfort your hearts, 9with Onesimus, a faithful and beloved brother, who is *one* of you. They will make known to you all things which *are happening* here.

10Aristarchus my fellow prisoner greets you, with Mark the cousin of Barnabas (about whom you received instructions: if he comes to you, welcome him), 11and Jesus who is called Justus. These *are my* only fellow workers for the kingdom of God who are of the circumcision; they have proved to be a comfort to me.

12Epaphras, who is *one* of you, a bondservant of Christ, greets you, always laboring fervently for you in prayers, that you may stand perfect and completea in all the will of God. 13For I bear him witness that he has a great zeala for you, and those who are in Laodicea, and those in Hierapolis. 14Luke the beloved physician and Demas greet you. 15Greet the brethren who are in Laodicea, and Nymphas and the church that *is* in hisa house.

Closing Exhortations and Blessing

16Now when this epistle is read among you, see that it is read also in the church of the Laodiceans, and that you likewise read the *epistle* from Laodicea. 17And say to Archippus, "Take heed to the ministry which you have received in the Lord, that you may fulfill it."

18This salutation by my own hand—Paul. Remember my chains. Grace *be* with you. Amen.

4:8 aNU-Text reads *you may know our circumstances and he may.*   **4:12** aNU-Text reads *fully assured.* **4:13** aNU-Text reads *concern.*   **4:15** aNU-Text reads *Nympha . . . her house.*

1 THESSALONIANS

Author: Paul

When Written: Around A.D. 51

Theme: Holiness in Light of Christ's Return

Key Verses: 1 Thessalonians 3:12, 13—And may the Lord make you increase and abound in love to one another and to all, just as we do to you, so that He may establish your hearts blameless in holiness before our God and Father at the coming of our Lord Jesus Christ with all His saints.

Key Chapter: 1 Thessalonians 4—This chapter includes a definitive passage on the coming of the Lord when the dead in Christ shall rise first, and those who remain are caught up together with them in the clouds.

Paul had been forced to leave the Thessalonians prematurely, and his concern for them caused him to send Timothy to check on their progress in the faith. His great relief upon hearing Timothy's positive report prompts Paul to write this warm epistle of commendation, exhortation, and consolation. He closes the letter with instruction regarding the return of the Lord, whose advent signifies hope and comfort for believers both living and dead.

As president, Ronald Reagan frequently invoked the words of George Washington, who said that religion and morality were "indispensable supports" to the prosperity of our political system. During a radio address in December 1983, he described one of his favorite paintings, which shows George Washington praying at Valley Forge. He said the painting "personified a people who knew it was not enough to depend on their own courage and goodness; they must also seek help from God, their Father and their Preserver." Similarly, Paul exhorts the Thessalonian believers to be diligent to put on "the breastplate of faith and love, and as a helmet the hope of salvation" (5:8) as they stand for Christ.

1 THESSALONIANS

Greeting

1 Paul, Silvanus, and Timothy,

To the church of the Thessalonians in God the Father and the Lord Jesus Christ:

Grace to you and peace from God our Father and the Lord Jesus Christ.[a]

Their Good Example

[2]We give thanks to God always for you all, making mention of you in our prayers, [3]remembering without ceasing your work of faith, labor of love, and patience of hope in our Lord Jesus Christ in the sight of our God and Father, [4]knowing, beloved brethren, your election by God. [5]For our gospel did not come to you in word only, but also in power, and in the Holy Spirit and in much assurance, as you know what kind of men we were among you for your sake.

[6]And you became followers of us and of the Lord, having received the word in much affliction, with joy of the Holy Spirit, [7]so that you became examples to all in Macedonia and Achaia who believe. [8]For from you the word of the Lord has sounded forth, not only in Macedonia and Achaia, but also in every place. Your faith toward God has gone out, so that we do not need to say anything. [9]For they themselves declare concerning us what manner of entry we had to you, and how you turned to God from idols to serve the living and true God, [10]and to wait for His Son from heaven, whom He raised from the dead, *even* Jesus who delivers us from the wrath to come.

Paul's Conduct

2 For you yourselves know, brethren, that our coming to you was not in vain. [2]But even[a] after we had suffered before and were spitefully treated at Philippi, as you know, we were bold in our God to speak to you the gospel of God in much conflict.

[3]For our exhortation *did* not *come* from error or uncleanness, nor *was it* in deceit. [4]But as we have been approved by God to be entrusted with the gospel, even so we speak, not as pleasing men, but God who tests our hearts. [5]For neither at any time did we use flattering words, as you know, nor a cloak for covetousness—God *is* witness. [6]Nor did we seek glory from men, either from you or from others, when we might have made demands as apostles of Christ. [7]But we were gentle among you, just as a nursing *mother* cherishes her own children. [8]So, affectionately longing for you, we were well pleased to impart to you not only the gospel of God, but also our own lives, because you had become dear to us. [9]For you remember, brethren, our labor and toil; for laboring night and day, that we might not be a burden to any of you, we preached to you the gospel of God.

[10]You *are* witnesses, and God *also*, how devoutly and justly and blamelessly we behaved ourselves among you who believe; [11]as you know how we exhorted, and comforted, and charged[a] every one of you, as a father *does* his own children, [12]that you would walk worthy of God who calls you into His own kingdom and glory.

Their Conversion

[13]For this reason we also thank God without ceasing, because when you received the word of God which you heard from us, you welcomed *it* not *as* the word of men, but as it is in truth, the word of God, which also effectively works in you who believe. [14]For you, brethren, became imitators of the churches of God which are in Judea in Christ Jesus. For you also suffered the same things from your own countrymen, just as they *did* from the Judeans, [15]who killed both the Lord Jesus and their own

---

1:1 [a]NU-Text omits *from God our Father and the Lord Jesus Christ.* **2:2** [a]NU-Text and M-Text omit *even.* **2:11** [a]NU-Text and M-Text read *implored.*

prophets, and have persecuted us; and they do not please God and are contrary to all men, [16]forbidding us to speak to the Gentiles that they may be saved, so as always to fill up *the measure of* their sins; but wrath has come upon them to the uttermost.

Longing to See Them

[17]But we, brethren, having been taken away from you for a short time in presence, not in heart, endeavored more eagerly to see your face with great desire. [18]Therefore we wanted to come to you— even I, Paul, time and again—but Satan hindered us. [19]For what *is* our hope, or joy, or crown of rejoicing? *Is it* not even you in the presence of our Lord Jesus Christ at His coming? [20]For you are our glory and joy.

Concern for Their Faith

3 Therefore, when we could no longer endure it, we thought it good to be left in Athens alone, [2]and sent Timothy, our brother and minister of God, and our fellow laborer in the gospel of Christ, to establish you and encourage you concerning your faith, [3]that no one should be shaken by these afflictions; for you yourselves know that we are appointed to this. [4]For, in fact, we told you before when we were with you that we would suffer tribulation, just as it happened, and you know. [5]For this reason, when I could no longer endure it, I sent to know your faith, lest by some means the tempter had tempted you, and our labor might be in vain.

Encouraged by Timothy

[6]But now that Timothy has come to us from you, and brought us good news of your faith and love, and that you always have good remembrance of us, greatly desiring to see us, as we also *to see* you— [7]therefore, brethren, in all our affliction and distress we were comforted concerning you by your faith. [8]For now we live, if you stand fast in the Lord.

[9]For what thanks can we render to God for you, for all the joy with which we rejoice

CHARITY

But concerning brotherly love . . . you yourselves are taught by God to love one another. . . .

1 THESSALONIANS 4:9

William Penn

THE "HOLY EXPERIMENT"

William Penn (1644–1718), the founder of Pennsylvania, had been imprisoned in England more than three times for his faith as a Quaker. While imprisoned in the Tower of London for eight months, he wrote the classic book, *No Cross, No Crown*, in which he stated:

> *No pain, no palm; no thorns, no throne; no gall, no glory; no cross, no crown.*

In 1682, Penn established the Pennsylvania colony as a land of religious freedom, granting toleration to every denomination. He printed advertisements in six different languages and sent them across Europe. Soon Quakers, Mennonites, Lutherans, Dunkards (Church of the Brethren), Amish, Moravians, Huguenots (French Protestants), Catholics, and Jews from England, Sweden, Wales, Germany, Scotland, Ireland, and Holland began arriving in his "holy experiment." To emphasize his plan for Christians working together, he planned and named their city "Philadelphia," which is Greek for "City of Brotherly Love." His concept was that religion is not to be limited to a Sunday ceremonial ritual, but should be an integral aspect of every day life, demonstrated by working with others.

for your sake before our God, ¹⁰night and day praying exceedingly that we may see your face and perfect what is lacking in your faith?

Prayer for the Church

¹¹Now may our God and Father Himself, and our Lord Jesus Christ, direct our way to you. ¹²And may the Lord make you increase and abound in love to one another and to all, just as we *do* to you, ¹³so that He may establish your hearts blameless in holiness before our God and Father at the coming of our Lord Jesus Christ with all His saints.

Plea for Purity

4 Finally then, brethren, we urge and exhort in the Lord Jesus that you should abound more and more, just as you received from us how you ought to walk and to please God; ²for you know what commandments we gave you through the Lord Jesus.

³For this is the will of God, your sanctification: that you should abstain from sexual immorality; ⁴that each of you should know how to possess his own vessel in sanctification and honor, ⁵not in passion of lust, like the Gentiles who do not know God; ⁶that no one should take advantage of and defraud his brother in this matter, because the Lord *is* the avenger of all such, as we also forewarned you and testified. ⁷For God did not call us to uncleanness, but in holiness. ⁸Therefore he who rejects *this* does not reject man, but God, who has also given[a] us His Holy Spirit.

A Brotherly and Orderly Life

⁹But concerning brotherly love you have no need that I should write to you, for you yourselves are taught by God to love one another; ¹⁰and indeed you do so toward all the brethren who are in all Macedonia. But we urge you, brethren, that you increase more and more; ¹¹that you also aspire to lead a quiet life, to mind your own business, and to work with your own hands, as we commanded you, ¹²that you may walk properly toward those who are outside, and *that* you may lack nothing.

The Comfort of Christ's Coming

¹³But I do not want you to be ignorant, brethren, concerning those who have fallen asleep, lest you sorrow as others who have no hope. ¹⁴For if we believe that Jesus died and rose again, even so God will bring with Him those who sleep in Jesus.[a]

¹⁵For this we say to you by the word of the Lord, that we who are alive *and* remain until the coming of the Lord will by no means precede those who are asleep. ¹⁶For the Lord Himself will descend from heaven with a shout, with the voice of an archangel, and with the trumpet of God. And the dead in Christ will rise first. ¹⁷Then we who are alive *and* remain shall be caught up together with them in the clouds to meet the Lord in the air. And thus we shall always be with the Lord. ¹⁸Therefore comfort one another with these words.

The Day of the Lord

5 But concerning the times and the seasons, brethren, you have no need that I should write to you. ²For you yourselves know perfectly that the day of the Lord so comes as a thief in the night. ³For when they say, "Peace and safety!" then sudden destruction comes upon them, as labor pains upon a pregnant woman. And they shall not escape. ⁴But you, brethren, are not in darkness, so that this Day should overtake you as a thief. ⁵You are all sons of light and sons of the day. We are not of the night nor of darkness. ⁶Therefore let us not sleep, as others *do,* but let us watch and be sober. ⁷For those who sleep, sleep at night, and those who get drunk are drunk at night. ⁸But let us who are of the day be sober, putting on the breastplate of faith and love, and *as* a helmet the hope of salvation. ⁹For God did not appoint us to wrath, but to obtain salvation through our Lord Jesus Christ, ¹⁰who died for us, that whether we wake or sleep, we should live together with Him.

¹¹Therefore comfort each other and edify one another, just as you also are doing.

4:8 [a]NU-Text reads *who also gives.*   **4:14** [a]Or *those who through Jesus sleep*

Various Exhortations

¹²And we urge you, brethren, to recognize those who labor among you, and are over you in the Lord and admonish you, ¹³and to esteem them very highly in love for their work's sake. Be at peace among yourselves.

¹⁴Now we exhort you, brethren, warn those who are unruly, comfort the fainthearted, uphold the weak, be patient with all. ¹⁵See that no one renders evil for evil to anyone, but always pursue what is good both for yourselves and for all.

¹⁶Rejoice always, ¹⁷pray without ceasing, ¹⁸in everything give thanks; for this is the will of God in Christ Jesus for you.

¹⁹Do not quench the Spirit. ²⁰Do not despise prophecies. ²¹Test all things; hold fast what is good. ²²Abstain from every form of evil.

Blessing and Admonition

²³Now may the God of peace Himself sanctify you completely; and may your whole spirit, soul, and body be preserved blameless at the coming of our Lord Jesus Christ. ²⁴He who calls you *is* faithful, who also will do *it.*

²⁵Brethren, pray for us.

²⁶Greet all the brethren with a holy kiss.

²⁷I charge you by the Lord that this epistle be read to all the holyᵃ brethren.

²⁸The grace of our Lord Jesus Christ *be* with you. Amen.

5:27 ᵃNU-Text omits *holy.*

PRAYER

. . . pray without ceasing. . . .

1 THESSALONIANS 5:17

Daily Prayer

Thomas "Stonewall" Jackson (1824–1863), probably the most revered Confederate commander after General Robert E. Lee, said:

When we take our meals, there is the grace. When I take a draught of water, I always pause . . . to lift up my heart to God in thanks and prayer for the water of life. . . . When I break the seal of a letter just received, I stop to pray to God that He may prepare me for its contents and make it a messenger of good. When I go to my classroom and await the arrangement of the cadets in their places, that is my time to intercede with God for them.

2 THESSALONIANS

Author: Paul

When Written: Around A.D. 51

Theme: Understanding the Day of the Lord

Key Verses: 2 Thessalonians 2:2, 3—. . . not to be soon shaken in mind or troubled, either by spirit or by word or by letter, as if from us, as though the day of Christ had come. Let no one deceive you by any means; for that Day will not come unless the falling away comes first, and the man of sin is revealed, the son of perdition. . . .

Key Chapter: 2 Thessalonians 2—To correct the false teaching that the day of the Lord had already come, Paul makes it clear that certain identifiable events will precede that day and that those events have not yet occurred.

Since Paul's first letter, which developed the theme of the coming day of the Lord, the Thessalonians have fallen prey to false teaching or outright deception, thinking the day of the Lord had already begun. It is possible that the false teachers were actually twisting Paul's previous instructions to them regarding the coming of the Lord. Paul writes this epistle to correct the error and also to encourage those believers whose faith is being tested by the difficulties presented by persecution.

The apostle Paul always moved quickly to deal with heresy before it could damage the churches. Using the authority of his apostleship, he did not ask anyone's permission to be straightforward about the truth of the Gospel. Similarly, after the terrorist attacks of September 11, 2001, President George W. Bush said, "America will never seek a permission slip to defend the security of our country." He immediately announced a Global War on Terrorism, which commenced with the invasion of Afghanistan and the overthrow of the Taliban regime.

2 THESSALONIANS

Greeting

1 Paul, Silvanus, and Timothy,

To the church of the Thessalonians in God our Father and the Lord Jesus Christ:

²Grace to you and peace from God our Father and the Lord Jesus Christ.

HUMILITY
. . . may be counted worthy of the kingdom. . . .
2 THESSALONIANS 1:5

Worthy of the Name
Francis Scott Key (1779–1843), the American lawyer and poet who wrote the "Star-Spangled Banner," stated:

The patriot who feels himself in the service of God, who acknowledges Him in all his ways, has the promise of Almighty direction, and will find His Word in his greatest darkness, "a lantern to his feet and a lamp unto his paths." . . . He will therefore seek to establish for his country in the eyes of the world, such a character as shall make her not unworthy of the name of a Christian nation.

God's Final Judgment and Glory

³We are bound to thank God always for you, brethren, as it is fitting, because your faith grows exceedingly, and the love of every one of you all abounds toward each other, ⁴so that we ourselves boast of you among the churches of God for your patience and faith in all your persecutions and tribulations that you endure, ⁵*which is* manifest evidence of the righteous judgment of God, that you may be counted worthy of the kingdom of God, for which you also suffer; ⁶since *it is* a righteous thing with God to repay with tribulation those who trouble you, ⁷and to *give* you who are troubled rest with us when the Lord Jesus is revealed from heaven with His mighty angels, ⁸in flaming fire taking vengeance on those who do not know God, and on those who do not obey the gospel of our Lord Jesus Christ. ⁹These shall be punished with everlasting destruction from the presence of the Lord and from the glory of His power, ¹⁰when He comes, in that Day, to be glorified in His saints and to be admired among all those who believe,ᵃ because our testimony among you was believed.

¹¹Therefore we also pray always for you that our God would count you worthy of *this* calling, and fulfill all the good pleasure of *His* goodness and the work of faith with power, ¹²that the name of our Lord Jesus Christ may be glorified in you, and you in Him, according to the grace of our God and the Lord Jesus Christ.

The Great Apostasy

2 Now, brethren, concerning the coming of our Lord Jesus Christ and our gathering together to Him, we ask you, ²not to be soon shaken in mind or troubled, either by spirit or by word or by letter, as if from us, as though the day of Christᵃ had come. ³Let no one deceive you by any means; for *that Day will not come* unless the falling away comes first, and the man of sinᵃ is revealed, the son of perdition, ⁴who opposes and exalts himself above all that is called God or that is worshiped, so that he sits as Godᵃ in the temple of God, showing himself that he is God.

⁵Do you not remember that when I was still with you I told you these things? ⁶And now you know what is restraining, that he may be revealed in his own time. ⁷For the mystery of lawlessness is already at work; only Heᵃ who now restrains *will do so* until Heᵇ is taken out of the way. ⁸And then the lawless one will be revealed, whom the

---

1:10 ᵃNU-Text and M-Text read *have believed.*
2:2 ᵃNU-Text reads *the Lord.*   **2:3** ᵃNU-Text reads *lawlessness.*   **2:4** ᵃNU-Text omits *as God.*   **2:7** ᵃOr *he* ᵇOr *he*

Lord will consume with the breath of His mouth and destroy with the brightness of His coming. [9]The coming of the *lawless one* is according to the working of Satan, with all power, signs, and lying wonders, [10]and with all unrighteous deception among those who perish, because they did not receive the love of the truth, that they might be saved. [11]And for this reason God will send them strong delusion, that they should believe the lie, [12]that they all may be condemned who did not believe the truth but had pleasure in unrighteousness.

FREEDOM
. . . stand fast and hold the traditions which you were taught. . . .　　　2 THESSALONIANS 2:15

The Groundwork of Human Freedom
Horace Greeley (1811–1872), the editor of America's most influential newspaper from the 1840s to the 1870s, the *New York Tribune*, wrote:

> It is impossible to mentally or socially enslave a Bible-reading people. The principles of the Bible are the groundwork of human freedom.

Stand Fast
[13]But we are bound to give thanks to God always for you, brethren beloved by the Lord, because God from the beginning chose you for salvation through sanctification by the Spirit and belief in the truth, [14]to which He called you by our gospel, for the obtaining of the glory of our Lord Jesus Christ. [15]Therefore, brethren, stand fast and hold the traditions which you were taught, whether by word or our epistle.

[16]Now may our Lord Jesus Christ Himself, and our God and Father, who has loved us and given *us* everlasting consolation and good hope by grace, [17]comfort your hearts and establish you in every good word and work.

Pray for Us
3 Finally, brethren, pray for us, that the word of the Lord may run *swiftly* and be glorified, just as *it is* with you, [2]and that we may be delivered from unreasonable and wicked men; for not all have faith.

[3]But the Lord is faithful, who will establish you and guard *you* from the evil one. [4]And we have confidence in the Lord concerning you, both that you do and will do the things we command you.

[5]Now may the Lord direct your hearts into the love of God and into the patience of Christ.

Warning Against Idleness
[6]But we command you, brethren, in the name of our Lord Jesus Christ, that you withdraw from every brother who walks disorderly and not according to the tradition which he[a] received from us. [7]For you yourselves know how you ought to follow us, for we were not disorderly among you; [8]nor did we eat anyone's bread free of charge, but worked with labor and toil night and day, that we might not be a burden to any of you, [9]not because we do not have authority, but to make ourselves an example of how you should follow us.

[10]For even when we were with you, we commanded you this: If anyone will not work, neither shall he eat. [11]For we hear that there are some who walk among you in a disorderly manner, not working at all, but are busybodies. [12]Now those who are such we command and exhort through our Lord Jesus Christ that they work in quietness and eat their own bread.

[13]But *as for* you, brethren, do not grow weary *in* doing good. [14]And if anyone does not obey our word in this epistle, note that person and do not keep company with him, that he may be ashamed. [15]Yet do not count *him* as an enemy, but admonish *him* as a brother.

Benediction
[16]Now may the Lord of peace Himself give you peace always in every way. The Lord *be* with you all.

[17]The salutation of Paul with my own hand, which is a sign in every epistle; so I write.

[18]The grace of our Lord Jesus Christ *be* with you all. Amen.

3:6 [a]NU-Text and M-Text read *they*.

1 TIMOTHY

Author: Paul

When Written: Around A.D. 62

Theme: Leadership within the Church

Key Verses: 1 Timothy 3:15, 16—. . . I write so that you may know how you ought to conduct yourself in the house of God, which is the church of the living God, the pillar and ground of the truth. And without controversy great is the mystery of godliness. . . .

Key Chapter: 1 Timothy 3—Paul enumerates the qualifications for the leaders of God's church, the elders and deacons. True leadership emanates from our walk with God rather than from achievements or vocational success.

Paul, the aged and experienced apostle, writes to the young pastor Timothy, who is facing a heavy burden of responsibility in the church at Ephesus. There are false teachings that must be erased, public worship safeguarded, and mature leadership developed. Paul talks pointedly about the conduct of the minister and counsels Timothy on the qualities that make for a man of God. He must be careful to avoid false teachers and greedy motives, pursuing instead righteousness, godliness, faith, love, perseverance, and the gentleness that befits a servant of God.

Taking over responsibility for the church that Paul had founded at Ephesus, it would have been a great mistake for Timothy to try to fill the apostle's shoes. Timothy could never be the apostle Paul, but he could still use all his gifts and strengths to help the church. Likewise, Charles F. Browne said, "We can't all be Washingtons, but we can all be patriots." We will never be the father of our country, but we can serve our country to the best of our abilities.

1 TIMOTHY

Greeting

1 Paul, an apostle of Jesus Christ, by the commandment of God our Savior and the Lord Jesus Christ, our hope,

2 To Timothy, a true son in the faith:

Grace, mercy, *and* peace from God our Father and Jesus Christ our Lord.

No Other Doctrine

3 As I urged you when I went into Macedonia—remain in Ephesus that you may charge some that they teach no other doctrine, 4 nor give heed to fables and endless genealogies, which cause disputes rather than godly edification which is in faith. 5 Now the purpose of the commandment is love from a pure heart, *from* a good conscience, and *from* sincere faith, 6 from which some, having strayed, have turned aside to idle talk, 7 desiring to be teachers of the law, understanding neither what they say nor the things which they affirm.

8 But we know that the law *is* good if one uses it lawfully, 9 knowing this: that the law is not made for a righteous person, but for *the* lawless and insubordinate, for *the* ungodly and for sinners, for *the* unholy and profane, for murderers of fathers and murderers of mothers, for manslayers, 10 for fornicators, for sodomites, for kidnappers, for liars, for perjurers, and if there is any other thing that is contrary to sound doctrine, 11 according to the glorious gospel of the blessed God which was committed to my trust.

Glory to God for His Grace

12 And I thank Christ Jesus our Lord who has enabled me, because He counted me faithful, putting *me* into the ministry, 13 although I was formerly a blasphemer, a persecutor, and an insolent man; but I obtained mercy because I did *it* ignorantly in unbelief. 14 And the grace of our Lord was exceedingly abundant, with faith and love which are in Christ Jesus. 15 This *is* a faithful saying and worthy of all acceptance, that Christ Jesus came into the world to save sinners, of whom I am chief. 16 However, for this reason I obtained mercy, that in me first Jesus Christ might show all longsuffering, as a pattern to those who are going to believe on Him for everlasting life. 17 Now to the King eternal, immortal, invisible, to God who alone is wise,[a] *be* honor and glory forever and ever. Amen.

Fight the Good Fight

18 This charge I commit to you, son Timothy, according to the prophecies previously made concerning you, that by them you may wage the good warfare, 19 having faith and a good conscience, which some having rejected, concerning the faith have suffered shipwreck, 20 of whom are Hymenaeus and Alexander, whom I delivered to Satan that they may learn not to blaspheme.

Pray for All Men

2 Therefore I exhort first of all that supplications, prayers, intercessions, *and* giving of thanks be made for all men, 2 for kings and all who are in authority, that we may lead a quiet and peaceable life in all godliness and reverence. 3 For this *is* good and acceptable in the sight of God our Savior, 4 who desires all men to be saved and to come to the knowledge of the truth. 5 For *there is* one God and one Mediator between God and men, *the* Man Christ Jesus, 6 who gave Himself a ransom for all, to be testified in due time, 7 for which I was appointed a preacher and an apostle—I am speaking the truth in Christ[a] *and* not lying—a teacher of the Gentiles in faith and truth.

1:17 [a]NU-Text reads *to the only God.*   **2:7** [a]NU-Text omits *in Christ.*

PRAY FOR AMERICA

As believers, it is our responsibility to pray for America—always, not just in times of national crisis. Without diminishing the importance of the Supreme Court or the Congress or the president, they are not the source of our future or our hope. Only God and the power of the Holy Spirit working in the lives of citizens can sustain the strength and the future of this nation.

James 5:16 encourages us that "the effective, fervent prayer of a righteous man avails much," and throughout the Bible we see how true these words are. Prayers moved the hand of God and changes came to nations, leaders, laws, and individuals. S. D. Gordon said, "The greatest thing anyone can do for God and man is pray. It is not the only thing, but it is the chief thing."

First, as God's people, we must humble ourselves and confess to God the sins of our nation as well as our own lives—our self-centeredness, lusts, addictions, the love of the world, and any area in which we are disobeying His Word. God has said, "If My people who are called by My name will humble themselves, and pray and seek My face, and turn from their wicked ways, then I will hear from heaven, and will forgive their sin and heal their land" (2 Chr. 7:14). John Wesley adds, "Storm the throne of grace and persevere therein, and mercy will come down."

Second, we must pray for our leaders and authorities. Ask the Lord to give godly wisdom, protection, and direction to the president, Congress, state and local officials, judges, as well as all those whom God has raised up to lead His people (Ezra 6:10; Rom. 13:1–5; 1 Tim. 2:1–3). If we see nonbelievers taking control of the government, passing laws that violate the laws of God, and jeopardizing our God-given freedoms, our mandate is to intercede and trust God to restore godliness to our nation and communities.

Third, we must pray that the Lord will work in a powerful way in the hearts of believers and people from all walks of life (Ps. 85; Hos. 6:1–3; Hab. 3:2). Only God has the power to free people from the sins that destroy their lives as well as the foundations of righteousness.

Fourth, we must pray for families, for school systems, for the military, for the economy, and for the vital aspects of our society. Be aware of what is going on, and pray.

Men and Women in the Church

8I desire therefore that the men pray everywhere, lifting up holy hands, without wrath and doubting; 9in like manner also, that the women adorn themselves in modest apparel, with propriety and moderation, not with braided hair or gold or pearls or costly clothing, 10but, which is proper for women professing godliness, with good works. 11Let a woman learn in silence with all submission. 12And I do not permit a woman to teach or to have authority over a man, but to be in silence. 13For Adam was formed first, then Eve. 14And Adam was not deceived, but the woman being deceived, fell into transgression. 15Nevertheless she will be saved in childbearing if they continue in faith, love, and holiness, with self-control.

Qualifications of Overseers

3 This *is* a faithful saying: If a man desires the position of a bishop,a he desires a good work. 2A bishop then must be blameless, the husband of one wife, temperate, sober-minded, of good behavior, hospitable, able to teach; 3not given to wine, not violent, not greedy for money,a but gentle, not quarrelsome, not covetous; 4one who rules his own house well, having *his* children in submission with all reverence 5(for if a man does not know how to rule his own house, how will he take care of the church of God?); 6not a novice, lest being puffed up with pride he fall into the *same* condemnation as the devil. 7Moreover he must have a good testimony among those who are outside, lest he fall into reproach and the snare of the devil.

Qualifications of Deacons

8Likewise deacons *must be* reverent, not double-tongued, not given to much wine, not greedy for money, 9holding the mystery of the faith with a pure conscience. 10But let these also first be tested; then let them serve as deacons, being *found* blameless. 11Likewise, *their* wives *must be* reverent,

---

3:1 aLiterally *overseer* **3:3** aNU-Text omits *not greedy for money.*

FAMILY VALUES

. . . husbands of one wife, ruling their children and their own houses well.

1 TIMOTHY 3:12

Ronald and Nancy Reagan and family

THE CORNERSTONE OF AMERICAN SOCIETY

Ronald Reagan, the 40th President of the United States (1981–1989), wrote:

The family has always been the cornerstone of American society. Our families nurture, preserve, and pass on to each succeeding generation the values we share and cherish, values that are the foundation for our freedoms. In the family, we learn our first lessons of God and man, love and discipline, rights and responsibilities, human dignity and human frailty.

Our families give us daily examples of these lessons being put into practice. In raising and instructing our children, in providing personal and compassionate care for the elderly, in maintaining the spiritual strength of religious commitment among our people—in these and other ways, America's families make immeasurable contributions to America's well-being.

Today more than ever, it is essential that these contributions not be taken for granted and that each of us remember that the strength of our families is vital to the strength of our nation.

not slanderers, temperate, faithful in all things. ¹²Let deacons be the husbands of one wife, ruling *their* children and their own houses well. ¹³For those who have served well as deacons obtain for themselves a good standing and great boldness in the faith which is in Christ Jesus.

The Great Mystery

¹⁴These things I write to you, though I hope to come to you shortly; ¹⁵but if I am delayed, *I write* so that you may know how you ought to conduct yourself in the house of God, which is the church of the living God, the pillar and ground of the truth. ¹⁶And without controversy great is the mystery of godliness:

Godª was manifested in the flesh,
Justified in the Spirit,
Seen by angels,
Preached among the Gentiles,
Believed on in the world,
Received up in glory.

The Great Apostasy

4 Now the Spirit expressly says that in latter times some will depart from the faith, giving heed to deceiving spirits and doctrines of demons, ²speaking lies in hypocrisy, having their own conscience seared with a hot iron, ³forbidding to marry, *and commanding* to abstain from foods which God created to be received with thanksgiving by those who believe and know the truth. ⁴For every creature of God *is* good, and nothing is to be refused if it is received with thanksgiving; ⁵for it is sanctified by the word of God and prayer.

A Good Servant of Jesus Christ

⁶If you instruct the brethren in these things, you will be a good minister of Jesus Christ, nourished in the words of faith and of the good doctrine which you have carefully followed. ⁷But reject profane and old wives' fables, and exercise yourself toward godliness. ⁸For bodily exercise profits a little, but godliness is profitable for all things, having promise of the life that now is and of that which is to come. ⁹This *is* a faithful saying and worthy of all acceptance. ¹⁰For to this *end* we both labor and

suffer reproach,ª because we trust in the living God, who is *the* Savior of all men, especially of those who believe. ¹¹These things command and teach.

> **MORAL STRENGTH**
> . . . in word, in conduct, in love, in spirit, in faith, in purity.   1 TIMOTHY 4:12
>
> ### Virtue and a Free Constitution
> On June 21, 1776, John Adams, the future second President of the United States, wrote:
>
> > Statesmen . . . may plan and speculate for liberty, but it is religion and morality alone which can establish the principles upon which freedom can securely stand.
> >
> > The only foundation of a free constitution is pure virtue, and if this cannot be inspired into our people in a greater measure, than they have it now, they may change their rulers and the forms of government, but they will not obtain a lasting liberty.

Take Heed to Your Ministry

¹²Let no one despise your youth, but be an example to the believers in word, in conduct, in love, in spirit,ª in faith, in purity. ¹³Till I come, give attention to reading, to exhortation, to doctrine. ¹⁴Do not neglect the gift that is in you, which was given to you by prophecy with the laying on of the hands of the eldership. ¹⁵Meditate on these things; give yourself entirely to them, that your progress may be evident to all. ¹⁶Take heed to yourself and to the doctrine. Continue in them, for in doing this you will save both yourself and those who hear you.

Treatment of Church Members

5 Do not rebuke an older man, but exhort *him* as a father, younger men as brothers, ²older women as mothers, younger women as sisters, with all purity.

Honor True Widows

³Honor widows who are really widows. ⁴But if any widow has children or grandchildren, let them first learn to show piety

---

3:16 ªNU-Text reads *Who*.   **4:10** ªNU-Text reads *we labor and strive*.   **4:12** ªNU-Text omits *in spirit*.

at home and to repay their parents; for this is good and[a] acceptable before God. [5]Now she who is really a widow, and left alone, trusts in God and continues in supplications and prayers night and day. [6]But she who lives in pleasure is dead while she lives. [7]And these things command, that they may be blameless. [8]But if anyone does not provide for his own, and especially for those of his household, he has denied the faith and is worse than an unbeliever.

[9]Do not let a widow under sixty years old be taken into the number, *and not unless* she has been the wife of one man, [10]well reported for good works: if she has brought up children, if she has lodged strangers, if she has washed the saints' feet, if she has relieved the afflicted, if she has diligently followed every good work.

[11]But refuse *the* younger widows; for when they have begun to grow wanton against Christ, they desire to marry, [12]having condemnation because they have cast off their first faith. [13]And besides they learn *to be* idle, wandering about from house to house, and not only idle but also gossips and busybodies, saying things which they ought not. [14]Therefore I desire that *the* younger *widows* marry, bear children, manage the house, give no opportunity to the adversary to speak reproachfully. [15]For some have already turned aside after Satan. [16]If any believing man or[a] woman has widows, let them relieve them, and do not let the church be burdened, that it may relieve those who are really widows.

Honor the Elders

[17]Let the elders who rule well be counted worthy of double honor, especially those who labor in the word and doctrine. [18]For the Scripture says, *"You shall not muzzle an ox while it treads out the grain,"*[a] and, *"The laborer is worthy of his wages."*[b] [19]Do not receive an accusation against an elder except from two or three witnesses. [20]Those who are sinning rebuke in the presence of all, that the rest also may fear.

[21]I charge *you* before God and the Lord Jesus Christ and the elect angels that you observe these things without prejudice, doing nothing with partiality. [22]Do not lay hands on anyone hastily, nor share in other people's sins; keep yourself pure.

[23]No longer drink only water, but use a little wine for your stomach's sake and your frequent infirmities.

[24]Some men's sins are clearly evident, preceding *them* to judgment, but those of some *men* follow later. [25]Likewise, the good works *of some* are clearly evident, and those that are otherwise cannot be hidden.

Honor Masters

6 Let as many bondservants as are under the yoke count their own masters worthy of all honor, so that the name of God and *His* doctrine may not be blasphemed. [2]And those who have believing masters, let them not despise *them* because they are brethren, but rather serve *them* because those who are benefited are believers and beloved. Teach and exhort these things.

Error and Greed

[3]If anyone teaches otherwise and does not consent to wholesome words, *even* the words of our Lord Jesus Christ, and to the doctrine which accords with godliness, [4]he is proud, knowing nothing, but is obsessed with disputes and arguments over words, from which come envy, strife, reviling, evil suspicions, [5]useless wranglings[a] of men of corrupt minds and destitute of the truth, who suppose that godliness is a *means of* gain. From such withdraw yourself.[b]

[6]Now godliness with contentment is great gain. [7]For we brought nothing into *this* world, *and it is* certain[a] we can carry nothing out. [8]And having food and clothing, with these we shall be content. [9]But those who desire to be rich fall into temptation and a snare, and *into* many foolish and harmful lusts which drown men in destruction and perdition. [10]For the love of money is a root of all *kinds of* evil, for which some have strayed from the faith in their greediness, and pierced themselves through with many sorrows.

5:4 [a]NU-Text and M-Text omit *good and.*
5:16 [a]NU-Text omits *man or.*   **5:18** [a]Deuteronomy 25:4 [b]Luke 10:7   **6:5** [a]NU-Text and M-Text read *constant friction.* [b]NU-Text omits this sentence.
6:7 [a]NU-Text omits *and it is certain.*

PROTECTOR

. . . God who gives life to all things. . . .

1 TIMOTHY 6:13

The Transcendent Right to Life

Ronald Reagan, the 40th president of the United States (1981–1989), stated:

> Abraham Lincoln recognized that we could not survive as a free land when some men could decide that others were not fit to be free and should therefore be slaves. Likewise, we cannot survive as a free nation when some men decide that others are not fit to live and should be abandoned to abortion or infanticide.
>
> My administration is dedicated to the preservation of America as a free land, and there is no cause more important for preserving that freedom than affirming the transcendent right to life of all human beings, the right without which no other rights have any meaning.

The Good Confession

¹¹But you, O man of God, flee these things and pursue righteousness, godliness, faith, love, patience, gentleness. ¹²Fight the good fight of faith, lay hold on eternal life, to which you were also called and have confessed the good confession in the presence of many witnesses. ¹³I urge you in the sight of God who gives life to all things, and before Christ Jesus who witnessed the good confession before Pontius Pilate, ¹⁴that you keep this commandment without spot, blameless until our Lord Jesus Christ's appearing, ¹⁵which He will manifest in His own time, He who is the blessed and only Potentate, the King of kings and Lord of lords, ¹⁶who alone has immortality, dwelling in unapproachable light, whom no man has seen or can see, to whom be honor and everlasting power. Amen.

Instructions to the Rich

¹⁷Command those who are rich in this present age not to be haughty, nor to trust in uncertain riches but in the living God, who gives us richly all things to enjoy. ¹⁸Let them do good, that they be rich in good works, ready to give, willing to share, ¹⁹storing up for themselves a good foundation for the time to come, that they may lay hold on eternal life.

Guard the Faith

²⁰O Timothy! Guard what was committed to your trust, avoiding the profane and idle babblings and contradictions of what is falsely called knowledge— ²¹by professing it some have strayed concerning the faith.

Grace be with you. Amen.

AMERICA

2 TIMOTHY

Author: Paul

When Written: Around A.D. 67

Theme: Endurance in the Pastoral Ministry

Key Verses: 2 Timothy 2:3, 4—You therefore must endure hardship as a good soldier of Jesus Christ. No one engaged in warfare entangles himself with the affairs of this life, that he may please him who enlisted him as a soldier.

Key Chapter: 2 Timothy 2—Paul lists the keys to a successful ministry: a reproducing ministry, an enduring ministry, a studying ministry, and a holy ministry. This epistle should be required daily reading for every pastor and full-time Christian worker.

Paul knows as he writes this final epistle that his days on earth are quickly drawing to a close. He seeks to challenge and strengthen his somewhat timid but faithful associate, Timothy, in his difficult ministry in Ephesus. In spite of his bleak circumstances, this is a fantastic letter of encouragement that urges Timothy to remain steadfast in the fulfillment of his divinely appointed task.

Paul's poignant words to Timothy, ". . . the time of my departure is at hand," (4:6) were echoed by Ronald Reagan in his letter to the American people revealing his Alzheimer's diagnosis in November 1994: "In closing, let me thank you, the American people, for giving me the great honor of allowing me to serve as your president. When the Lord calls me home, whenever that day may be, I will leave with the greatest love for this country of ours and eternal optimism for its future. I now begin the journey that will lead me into the sunset of my life. I know that for America there will always be a bright dawn ahead."

2 TIMOTHY

Greeting

1 Paul, an apostle of Jesus Christ[a] by the will of God, according to the promise of life which is in Christ Jesus,

²To Timothy, a beloved son:

Grace, mercy, *and* peace from God the Father and Christ Jesus our Lord.

Timothy's Faith and Heritage

³I thank God, whom I serve with a pure conscience, as *my* forefathers *did,* as without ceasing I remember you in my prayers night and day, ⁴greatly desiring to see you, being mindful of your tears, that I may be filled with joy, ⁵when I call to remembrance the genuine faith that is in you, which dwelt first in your grandmother Lois and your mother Eunice, and I am persuaded is in you also. ⁶Therefore I remind you to stir up the gift of God which is in you through the laying on of my hands. ⁷For God has not given us a spirit of fear, but of power and of love and of a sound mind.

Not Ashamed of the Gospel

⁸Therefore do not be ashamed of the testimony of our Lord, nor of me His prisoner, but share with me in the sufferings for the gospel according to the power of God, ⁹who has saved us and called *us* with a holy calling, not according to our works, but according to His own purpose and grace which was given to us in Christ Jesus before time began, ¹⁰but has now been revealed by the appearing of our Savior Jesus Christ, *who* has abolished death and brought life and immortality to light through the gospel, ¹¹to which I was appointed a preacher, an apostle, and a teacher of the Gentiles.[a] ¹²For this reason I also suffer these things; nevertheless I am not ashamed, for I know whom I have believed and am persuaded that He is able to keep what I have committed to Him until that Day.

Be Loyal to the Faith

¹³Hold fast the pattern of sound words which you have heard from me, in faith and love which are in Christ Jesus. ¹⁴That good thing which was committed to you, keep by the Holy Spirit who dwells in us.

¹⁵This you know, that all those in Asia have turned away from me, among whom are Phygellus and Hermogenes. ¹⁶The Lord grant mercy to the household of Onesiphorus, for he often refreshed me, and was not ashamed of my chain; ¹⁷but when he arrived in Rome, he sought me out very zealously and found *me.* ¹⁸The Lord grant to him that he may find mercy from the Lord in that Day—and you know very well how many ways he ministered *to me*[a] at Ephesus.

Be Strong in Grace

2 You therefore, my son, be strong in the grace that is in Christ Jesus. ²And the things that you have heard from me among many witnesses, commit these to faithful men who will be able to teach others also. ³You therefore must endure[a] hardship as a good soldier of Jesus Christ. ⁴No one engaged in warfare entangles himself with the affairs of *this* life, that he may please him who enlisted him as a soldier. ⁵And also if anyone competes in athletics, he is not crowned unless he competes according to the rules. ⁶The hardworking farmer must be first to partake of the crops. ⁷Consider what I say, and may[a] the Lord give you understanding in all things.

⁸Remember that Jesus Christ, of the seed of David, was raised from the dead according to my gospel, ⁹for which I suffer trouble

---

1:1 [a]NU-Text and M-Text read *Christ Jesus.*
1:11 [a]NU-Text omits *of the Gentiles.*   **1:18** [a]*To me* is from the Vulgate and a few Greek manuscripts.
2:3 [a]NU-Text reads *You must share.*   **2:7** [a]NU-Text reads *the Lord will give you.*

as an evildoer, *even* to the point of chains; but the word of God is not chained. [10]Therefore I endure all things for the sake of the elect, that they also may obtain the salvation which is in Christ Jesus with eternal glory. [11]*This is* a faithful saying:

> For if we died with *Him,*
> We shall also live with *Him.*
> [12] If we endure,
> We shall also reign with *Him.*
> If we deny *Him,*
> He also will deny us.
> [13] If we are faithless,
> He remains faithful;
> He cannot deny Himself.

Approved and Disapproved Workers

[14]Remind *them* of these things, charging *them* before the Lord not to strive about words to no profit, to the ruin of the hearers. [15]Be diligent to present yourself approved to God, a worker who does not need to be ashamed, rightly dividing the word of truth. [16]But shun profane *and* idle babblings, for they will increase to more ungodliness. [17]And their message will spread like cancer. Hymenaeus and Philetus are of this sort, [18]who have strayed concerning the truth, saying that the resurrection is already past; and they overthrow the faith of some. [19]Nevertheless the solid foundation of God stands, having this seal: "The Lord knows those who are His," and, "Let everyone who names the name of Christ[a] depart from iniquity."

[20]But in a great house there are not only vessels of gold and silver, but also of wood and clay, some for honor and some for dishonor. [21]Therefore if anyone cleanses himself from the latter, he will be a vessel for honor, sanctified and useful for the Master, prepared for every good work. [22]Flee also youthful lusts; but pursue righteousness, faith, love, peace with those who call on the Lord out of a pure heart. [23]But avoid foolish and ignorant disputes, knowing that they generate strife. [24]And a servant of the Lord must not quarrel but be gentle to all, able to teach, patient, [25]in humility correcting those who are in opposition, if God perhaps will grant them repentance, so that they may know the truth, [26]and *that* they may come to their senses *and escape* the snare of the devil, having been taken captive by him to *do* his will.

Perilous Times and Perilous Men

3 But know this, that in the last days perilous times will come: [2]For men will be lovers of themselves, lovers of money, boasters, proud, blasphemers, disobedient to parents, unthankful, unholy, [3]unloving, unforgiving, slanderers, without self-control, brutal, despisers of good, [4]traitors, headstrong, haughty, lovers of pleasure rather than lovers of God, [5]having a form of godliness but denying its power. And from such people turn away! [6]For of this sort are those who creep into households and make captives of gullible women loaded down with sins, led away by various lusts, [7]always learning and never able to come to the knowledge of the truth. [8]Now as Jannes and Jambres resisted Moses, so do these also resist the truth: men of corrupt minds, disapproved concerning the faith; [9]but they will progress no further, for their folly will be manifest to all, as theirs also was.

The Man of God and the Word of God

[10]But you have carefully followed my doctrine, manner of life, purpose, faith, longsuffering, love, perseverance, [11]persecutions, afflictions, which happened to me at Antioch, at Iconium, at Lystra—what persecutions I endured. And out of *them* all the Lord delivered me. [12]Yes, and all who desire to live godly in Christ Jesus will suffer persecution. [13]But evil men and impostors will grow worse and worse, deceiving and being deceived. [14]But you must continue in the things which you have learned and been assured of, knowing from whom you have learned *them,* [15]and that from childhood you have known the Holy Scriptures, which are able to make you wise for salvation through faith which is in Christ Jesus.

[16]All Scripture *is* given by inspiration of God, and *is* profitable for doctrine, for

---

2:19 [a]NU-Text and M-Text read *the Lord.*

RELIGION in PUBLIC SCHOOLS

JOSEPH STORY

In 1844, Justice Joseph Story decided *Vidal v. Girard's Executors*, one of the Supreme Court's first religion cases with implications for our nation's approach to the role of religion in public schools. In *Vidal*, Joseph Story decided that religion played a vital role in public education and upheld the use of the Bible and the teaching of Christian moral principles in a city-run school.

Story wrote:"[W]e are compelled to admit that although Christianity be a part of the common law of [Pennsylvania], yet it is so in this qualified sense, that its divine origin and truth are admitted, and therefore it is not to be maliciously and openly reviled and blasphemed against, to the annoyance of believers or the injury of the public."

In this case, Girard's will permitted the teaching of the Christian religion, just not by members of the clergy. Story's opinion that Girard's will was not derogatory to the Christian religion rested on two determinations. First, a layman was capable of teaching the general principles of Christianity. "Why may not laymen instruct in the general principles of Christianity as well as ecclesiastics[?] There is no restriction as to the religious opinion of the instructors and officers."

And second, Girard's will actually permitted the teaching of the Bible in the school:"Why may not the Bible, and especially the New Testament, without note or comment be read and taught as a divine revelation in the college—its general precepts expounded, its evidences explained, and its glorious principles of morality inculcated? What is there to prevent a work, not sectarian, upon the general evidences of Christianity, from being read and taught in the college by lay teachers? Certainly there is nothing in the will, that proscribes such studies. . . . Now, it may well be asked, what is there in all this, which is positively enjoined, inconsistent with the spirit or truths of Christianity? Are not these truths all taught by Christianity, although it teaches much more? Where can the purest principles of morality be learned so clearly or so perfectly as from the New Testament? Where are benevolence, the love of truth, sobriety, and industry, so powerfully and irresistibly inculcated as in the sacred volume?"

The Court's decision held that Girard's will did not attack or revile Christianity, because it permitted the teaching of Christian values and moral principles in a nonsectarian way.

reproof, for correction, for instruction in righteousness, [17]that the man of God may be complete, thoroughly equipped for every good work.

Preach the Word

4 I charge *you* therefore before God and the Lord Jesus Christ, who will judge the living and the dead at[a] His appearing and His kingdom: [2]Preach the word! Be ready in season *and* out of season. Convince, rebuke, exhort, with all longsuffering and teaching. [3]For the time will come when they will not endure sound doctrine, but according to their own desires, *because* they have itching ears, they will heap up for themselves teachers; [4]and they will turn *their* ears away from the truth, and be turned aside to fables. [5]But you be watchful in all things, endure afflictions, do the work of an evangelist, fulfill your ministry.

SERVICE
I have fought the good fight. . . .
　　　　　　　　　　　　　　　2 TIMOTHY 4:7

What We Owe This Land

"Eddie" Rickenbacker (1890–1973), an American fighter ace in France during World War I and Congressional Medal of Honor recipient and later a pioneer in air transportation, stated:

> I pray to God every night of my life to be given the strength and power to continue my efforts to inspire in others the interest, the obligation, and the responsibilities that we owe to this land for the sake of future generations—for my boys and girls—so that we can always look back when the candle of life burns low and say, "Thank God, I have contributed my best to the land that contributed so much to me."

Paul's Valedictory

[6]For I am already being poured out as a drink offering, and the time of my departure is at hand. [7]I have fought the good fight, I have finished the race, I have kept the faith. [8]Finally, there is laid up for me the crown of righteousness, which the Lord, the righteous Judge, will give to me on that Day, and not to me only but also to all who have loved His appearing.

The Abandoned Apostle

[9]Be diligent to come to me quickly; [10]for Demas has forsaken me, having loved this present world, and has departed for Thessalonica—Crescens for Galatia, Titus for Dalmatia. [11]Only Luke is with me. Get Mark and bring him with you, for he is useful to me for ministry. [12]And Tychicus I have sent to Ephesus. [13]Bring the cloak that I left with Carpus at Troas when you come—and the books, especially the parchments.

[14]Alexander the coppersmith did me much harm. May the Lord repay him according to his works. [15]You also must beware of him, for he has greatly resisted our words.

[16]At my first defense no one stood with me, but all forsook me. May it not be charged against them.

The Lord Is Faithful

[17]But the Lord stood with me and strengthened me, so that the message might be preached fully through me, and *that* all the Gentiles might hear. Also I was delivered out of the mouth of the lion. [18]And the Lord will deliver me from every evil work and preserve *me* for His heavenly kingdom. To Him *be* glory forever and ever. Amen!

Come Before Winter

[19]Greet Prisca and Aquila, and the household of Onesiphorus. [20]Erastus stayed in Corinth, but Trophimus I have left in Miletus sick.

[21]Do your utmost to come before winter. Eubulus greets you, as well as Pudens, Linus, Claudia, and all the brethren.

Farewell

[22]The Lord Jesus Christ[a] be with your spirit. Grace be with you. Amen.

4:1 [a]NU-Text omits *therefore* and reads *and by* for *at*.
4:22 [a]NU-Text omits *Jesus Christ*.

TITUS

Author: Paul

When Written: Around A.D. 63

Theme: Conduct Manual for Church

Key Verse: Titus 1:5—For this reason I left you in Crete, that you should set in order the things that are lacking, and appoint elders in every city as I commanded you. . . .

Key Chapter: Titus 2—This chapter summarizes the key commands to be obeyed which insure godly relationships within the church.

Titus, a young pastor, faces the difficult assignment of setting in order the church at Crete. Paul writes advising him to appoint elders, men of proven spiritual character in their homes and businesses, to oversee the work of the church. In addition, men and women, young and old, each are shown to have vital functions to fulfill in the church if they are to be living examples of the doctrine they profess to believe.

President John F. Kennedy said, "Few will have the greatness to bend history itself; but each of us can work to change a small portion of events, and in the total of all those acts will be written the history of this generation." Titus may not bring the greatness that accompanied the apostle Paul, but he was a remarkably reliable and gifted associate whom Paul could trust with the most difficult of missions.

TITUS

Greeting

1 Paul, a bondservant of God and an apostle of Jesus Christ, according to the faith of God's elect and the acknowledgment of the truth which accords with godliness, ²in hope of eternal life which God, who cannot lie, promised before time began, ³but has in due time manifested His word through preaching, which was committed to me according to the commandment of God our Savior;

⁴To Titus, a true son in *our* common faith:

Grace, mercy, *and* peace from God the Father and the Lord Jesus Christᵃ our Savior.

Qualified Elders

⁵For this reason I left you in Crete, that you should set in order the things that are lacking, and appoint elders in every city as I commanded you— ⁶if a man is blameless, the husband of one wife, having faithful children not accused of dissipation or insubordination. ⁷For a bishopᵃ must be blameless, as a steward of God, not self-willed, not quick-tempered, not given to wine, not violent, not greedy for money, ⁸but hospitable, a lover of what is good, sober-minded, just, holy, self-controlled, ⁹holding fast the faithful word as he has been taught, that he may be able, by sound doctrine, both to exhort and convict those who contradict.

The Elders' Task

¹⁰For there are many insubordinate, both idle talkers and deceivers, especially those of the circumcision, ¹¹whose mouths must be stopped, who subvert whole households, teaching things which they ought not, for the sake of dishonest gain. ¹²One of them, a prophet of their own, said, "Cretans *are* always liars, evil beasts, lazy gluttons." ¹³This testimony is true. Therefore rebuke them sharply, that they may be sound in the faith, ¹⁴not giving heed to Jewish fables and commandments of men who turn from the truth. ¹⁵To the pure all things are pure, but to those who are defiled and unbelieving nothing is pure; but even their mind and conscience are defiled. ¹⁶They profess to know God, but in works they deny *Him,* being abominable, disobedient, and disqualified for every good work.

MORAL STRENGTH

. . . but even their mind and conscience are defiled. TITUS 1:15

Brilliance Without Conscience

General Omar Bradley was one of the main U.S. Army field commanders in North Africa and Europe during World War II and the first officer assigned to the post of Chairman of the Joint Chiefs of Staff. In 1948, he stated:

> We have grasped the mystery of the atom and rejected the Sermon on the Mount. . . . The world has achieved brilliance without conscience. Ours is a world of nuclear giants and ethical infants.

Qualities of a Sound Church

2 But as for you, speak the things which are proper for sound doctrine: ²that the older men be sober, reverent, temperate, sound in faith, in love, in patience; ³the older women likewise, that they be reverent in behavior, not slanderers, not given to much wine, teachers of good things— ⁴that they admonish the young women to love their husbands, to love their children, ⁵to be discreet, chaste, homemakers, good, obedient to their own husbands, that the word of God may not be blasphemed.

⁶Likewise, exhort the young men to be sober-minded, ⁷in all things showing yourself

---

1:4 ᵃNU-Text reads *and Christ Jesus.*   **1:7** ᵃLiterally *overseer*

to be a pattern of good works; in doctrine *showing* integrity, reverence, incorruptibility,[a] [8]sound speech that cannot be condemned, that one who is an opponent may be ashamed, having nothing evil to say of you.[a]

[9]*Exhort* bondservants to be obedient to their own masters, to be well pleasing in all *things,* not answering back, [10]not pilfering, but showing all good fidelity, that they may adorn the doctrine of God our Savior in all things.

Trained by Saving Grace

[11]For the grace of God that brings salvation has appeared to all men, [12]teaching us that, denying ungodliness and worldly lusts, we should live soberly, righteously, and godly in the present age, [13]looking for the blessed hope and glorious appearing of our great God and Savior Jesus Christ, [14]who gave Himself for us, that He might redeem us from every lawless deed and purify for Himself *His* own special people, zealous for good works.

[15]Speak these things, exhort, and rebuke with all authority. Let no one despise you.

Graces of the Heirs of Grace

3 Remind them to be subject to rulers and authorities, to obey, to be ready for every good work, [2]to speak evil of no one, to be peaceable, gentle, showing all humility to all men. [3]For we ourselves were also once foolish, disobedient, deceived, serving various lusts and pleasures, living in malice

---

2:7 [a]NU-Text omits *incorruptibility.*   **2:8** [a]NU-Text and M-Text read *us.*

MORAL STRENGTH

. . . and purify for Himself His own special people, zealous for good works.

TITUS 2:14

Samuel Sullivan Cox

THE PURIFYING INFLUENCE OF CHRISTIANITY

Samuel Sullivan Cox (1824–1889) was a Congressman and U.S. Ambassador to the Ottoman Empire who stated in a Memorial address to Congress:

> I believe in the religion which was taught and exemplified in the life of the Nazarene, and I never fail to bear testimony to the ennobling and purifying influence of the Christian religion. . . .
>
> There was a poignancy in my heart when I saw the old church, where I so often worshipped, razed to the ground. Was it not there I attended my first Sunday school? There it was that I learned my Bible verses. . . .
>
> Those early memories were cut in durable stone. Tarnished by worldliness, dusted with the activities of life, they have pursued me through the various vicissitudes of professional, literary, and political life. They became the nucleus of studies in college; the very coat of mail in the struggles against selfishness and skepticism; in fine, they prefigured and preordained my choice of spiritual belief against the delusive sophistries of new philosophies and mere material science.
>
> They have enabled me, in following and studying the physical advancement of the past century, to perceive in all the atoms, forms, and forces of nature and the phenomena of mind, the truth and benignity of the great scheme of human redemption, which is founded on the veracity of Christ, and becomes, with lapsing years, more beautiful with the white radiance of an ennobling spirituality.

and envy, hateful and hating one another. ⁴But when the kindness and the love of God our Savior toward man appeared, ⁵not by works of righteousness which we have done, but according to His mercy He saved us, through the washing of regeneration and renewing of the Holy Spirit, ⁶whom He poured out on us abundantly through Jesus Christ our Savior, ⁷that having been justified by His grace we should become heirs according to the hope of eternal life.

⁸This is a faithful saying, and these things I want you to affirm constantly, that those who have believed in God should be careful to maintain good works. These things are good and profitable to men.

Avoid Dissension

⁹But avoid foolish disputes, genealogies, contentions, and strivings about the law; for they are unprofitable and useless. ¹⁰Reject a divisive man after the first and second admonition, ¹¹knowing that such a person is warped and sinning, being self-condemned.

Final Messages

¹²When I send Artemas to you, or Tychicus, be diligent to come to me at Nicopolis, for I have decided to spend the winter there. ¹³Send Zenas the lawyer and Apollos on their journey with haste, that they may lack nothing. ¹⁴And let our *people* also learn to maintain good works, to *meet* urgent needs, that they may not be unfruitful.

Farewell

¹⁵All who *are* with me greet you. Greet those who love us in the faith.

Grace *be* with you all. Amen.

PHILEMON

Author: Paul

When Written: Around A.D. 60

Theme: Forgiveness

Key Verses: Philemon 16, 17—. . . no longer as a slave but more than a slave—a beloved brother, especially to me but how much more to you, both in the flesh and in the Lord. If then you count me as a partner, receive him as you would me.

This briefest of Paul's epistles is a model of courtesy, discretion, and loving concern for the forgiveness of a slave who would otherwise face the sentence of death for running away from his master. With much tact and tenderness, Paul asks Philemon to receive Onesimus back with the same gentleness he would receive Paul himself. He is confident that brotherly love and forgiveness will carry the day.

Paul never suggests that Philemon had committed a sin in owning Onesimus. Pro-slavery advocates used this fact in defending the moral propriety of slavery before the Civil War. Abolitionists, on the other hand, said that referring to slaves as "brothers" undercut the social distinctions inherent in slavery. Abolitionists were correct when they argued that although Paul did not directly condemn slavery, the spirit of his words embodies the principle of love, which motivates Christian action against the oppression of slavery and its violation of the concept of justice and the dignity and value and equality of every human person.

PHILEMON

Greeting

Paul, a prisoner of Christ Jesus, and Timothy *our* brother,

To Philemon our beloved *friend* and fellow laborer, [2]to the beloved[a] Apphia, Archippus our fellow soldier, and to the church in your house:

[3]Grace to you and peace from God our Father and the Lord Jesus Christ.

Philemon's Love and Faith

[4]I thank my God, making mention of you always in my prayers, [5]hearing of your love and faith which you have toward the Lord Jesus and toward all the saints, [6]that the sharing of your faith may become effective by the acknowledgment of every good thing which is in you[a] in Christ Jesus. [7]For we have[a] great joy[b] and consolation in your love, because the hearts of the saints have been refreshed by you, brother.

The Plea for Onesimus

[8]Therefore, though I might be very bold in Christ to command you what is fitting, [9]yet for love's sake I rather appeal *to you*— being such a one as Paul, the aged, and now also a prisoner of Jesus Christ— [10]I appeal to you for my son Onesimus, whom I have begotten *while* in my chains, [11]who once was unprofitable to you, but now is profitable to you and to me.

[12]I am sending him back.[a] You therefore receive him, that is, my own heart, [13]whom I wished to keep with me, that on your behalf he might minister to me in my chains for the gospel. [14]But without your consent I wanted to do nothing, that your good deed might not be by compulsion, as it were, but voluntary.

[15]For perhaps he departed for a while for this *purpose,* that you might receive him forever, [16]no longer as a slave but more than a slave—a beloved brother, especially to me but how much more to you, both in the flesh and in the Lord.

Philemon's Obedience Encouraged

[17]If then you count me as a partner, receive him as *you would* me. [18]But if he has wronged you or owes anything, put that on my account. [19]I, Paul, am writing with my own hand. I will repay—not to mention to you that you owe me even your own self besides. [20]Yes, brother, let me have joy from you in the Lord; refresh my heart in the Lord.

[21]Having confidence in your obedience, I write to you, knowing that you will do even more than I say. [22]But, meanwhile, also prepare a guest room for me, for I trust that through your prayers I shall be granted to you.

Farewell

[23]Epaphras, my fellow prisoner in Christ Jesus, greets you, [24]*as do* Mark, Aristarchus, Demas, Luke, my fellow laborers.

[25]The grace of our Lord Jesus Christ *be* with your spirit. Amen.

---

2 [a]NU-Text reads *to our sister Apphia.*   **6** [a]NU-Text and M-Text read *us.*   **7** [a]NU-Text reads *had.* [b]M-Text reads *thanksgiving.*   **12** [a]NU-Text reads *back to you in person, that is, my own heart.*

HEBREWS

Author: Unknown

When Written: Before A.D. 64

Theme: The Superiority of Christ

Key Verses: Hebrews 4:14–16—Seeing then that we have a great High Priest who has passed through the heavens, Jesus the Son of God, let us hold fast our confession. For we do not have a High Priest who cannot sympathize with our weaknesses, but was in all points tempted as we are, yet without sin. Let us therefore come boldly to the throne of grace, that we may obtain mercy and find grace to help in time of need.

Key Chapter: Hebrews 11—The "Faith Hall of Fame" of the Scriptures is located in this chapter and records those who willingly took God at His word even when there was nothing to cling to but His promise.

For the Jewish believers who, having stepped out of Judaism into Christianity, want to reverse their course in order to escape persecution, this epistle directs them to the superiority of Christ over the Judaic system. Christ is better than angels, better than the Aaronic priesthood, and better than the Law. In short, there is infinitely more to be gained in Christ than to be lost by yielding up their faith.

Just as the recipients of the Book of Hebrews faced persecution, even death, for their Christian confession, it is worth noting that the marching song of the Union Army during the Civil War included the line "as Christ died to make men holy let us die to make men free." Although that phrase was later changed to "let us live to make men free," for the soldiers who were placing their lives on the line to end slavery and preserve the Union, the original line was the right one.

HEBREWS

God's Supreme Revelation

1 God, who at various times and in various ways spoke in time past to the fathers by the prophets, ²has in these last days spoken to us by *His* Son, whom He has appointed heir of all things, through whom also He made the worlds; ³who being the brightness of *His* glory and the express image of His person, and upholding all things by the word of His power, when He had by Himself[a] purged our[b] sins, sat down at the right hand of the Majesty on high, ⁴having become so much better than the angels, as He has by inheritance obtained a more excellent name than they.

The Son Exalted Above Angels

⁵For to which of the angels did He ever say:

"You are My Son,
Today I have begotten You"?[a]

And again:

"I will be to Him a Father,
And He shall be to Me a Son"?[b]

⁶But when He again brings the firstborn into the world, He says:

"Let all the angels of God worship Him."[a]

⁷And of the angels He says:

"Who makes His angels spirits
And His ministers a flame of fire."[a]

⁸But to the Son *He* says:

"Your throne, O God, is forever and ever;
A scepter of righteousness is the scepter
of Your kingdom.
⁹ You have loved righteousness and
hated lawlessness;

Therefore God, Your God, has
anointed You
With the oil of gladness more than
Your companions."[a]

¹⁰And:

"You, LORD, in the beginning laid the
foundation of the earth,
And the heavens are the work of Your
hands.
¹¹ They will perish, but You remain;
And they will all grow old like a
garment;
¹² Like a cloak You will fold them up,
And they will be changed.
But You are the same,
And Your years will not fail."[a]

¹³But to which of the angels has He ever said:

"Sit at My right hand,
Till I make Your enemies Your
footstool"?[a]

¹⁴Are they not all ministering spirits sent forth to minister for those who will inherit salvation?

Do Not Neglect Salvation

2 Therefore we must give the more earnest heed to the things we have heard, lest we drift away. ²For if the word spoken through angels proved steadfast, and every transgression and disobedience received a just reward, ³how shall we escape if we neglect so great a salvation, which at the first began to be spoken by the Lord, and was confirmed to us by those who heard *Him*, ⁴God also bearing witness both with signs and

---

1:3 aNU-Text omits *by Himself.* bNU-Text omits *our.*
1:5 aPsalm 2:7 b2 Samuel 7:14 **1:6** aDeuteronomy 32:43 (Septuagint, Dead Sea Scrolls); Psalm 97:7
1:7 aPsalm 104:4 **1:9** aPsalm 45:6, 7
1:12 aPsalm 102:25–27 **1:13** aPsalm 110:1

wonders, with various miracles, and gifts of the Holy Spirit, according to His own will?

The Son Made Lower than Angels

[5]For He has not put the world to come, of which we speak, in subjection to angels. [6]But one testified in a certain place, saying:

> "What is man that You are mindful of him,
> Or the son of man that You take care of him?
> [7] You have made him a little lower than the angels;
> You have crowned him with glory and honor,[a]
> And set him over the works of Your hands.
> [8] You have put all things in subjection under his feet."[a]

For in that He put all in subjection under him, He left nothing *that is* not put under him. But now we do not yet see all things put under him. [9]But we see Jesus, who was made a little lower than the angels, for the suffering of death crowned with glory and honor, that He, by the grace of God, might taste death for everyone.

Bringing Many Sons to Glory

[10]For it was fitting for Him, for whom *are* all things and by whom *are* all things, in bringing many sons to glory, to make the captain of their salvation perfect through sufferings. [11]For both He who sanctifies and those who are being sanctified *are* all of one, for which reason He is not ashamed to call them brethren, [12]saying:

> "I will declare Your name to My brethren;
> In the midst of the assembly I will sing praise to You."[a]

[13]And again:

> "I will put My trust in Him."[a]

And again:

> "Here am I and the children whom God has given Me."[b]

[14]Inasmuch then as the children have partaken of flesh and blood, He Himself likewise shared in the same, that through death He might destroy him who had the power of death, that is, the devil, [15]and release those who through fear of death were all their lifetime subject to bondage. [16]For indeed He does not give aid to angels, but He does give aid to the seed of Abraham. [17]Therefore, in all things He had to be made like *His* brethren, that He might be a merciful and faithful High Priest in things *pertaining* to God, to make propitiation for the sins of the people. [18]For in that He Himself has suffered, being tempted, He is able to aid those who are tempted.

The Son Was Faithful

3 Therefore, holy brethren, partakers of the heavenly calling, consider the Apostle and High Priest of our confession, Christ Jesus, [2]who was faithful to Him who appointed Him, as Moses also *was faithful* in all His house. [3]For this One has been counted worthy of more glory than Moses, inasmuch as He who built the house has more honor than the house. [4]For every house is built by someone, but He who built all things *is* God. [5]And Moses indeed *was* faithful in all His house as a servant, for a testimony of those things which would be spoken *afterward,* [6]but Christ as a Son over His own house, whose house we are if we hold fast the confidence and the rejoicing of the hope firm to the end.[a]

Be Faithful

[7]Therefore, as the Holy Spirit says:

> "Today, if you will hear His voice,
> [8] Do not harden your hearts as in the rebellion,
> In the day of trial in the wilderness,
> [9] Where your fathers tested Me, tried Me,
> And saw My works forty years.
> [10] Therefore I was angry with that generation,

2:7 [a]NU-Text and M-Text omit the rest of verse 7.
2:8 [a]Psalm 8:4–6   **2:12** [a]Psalm 22:22
2:13 [a]2 Samuel 22:3; Isaiah 8:17 [b]Isaiah 8:18
3:6 [a]NU-Text omits *firm to the end.*

And said, 'They always go astray in
   their heart,
And they have not known My ways.'
11   So I swore in My wrath,
   'They shall not enter My rest.' "ᵃ

¹²Beware, brethren, lest there be in any
of you an evil heart of unbelief in departing from the living God; ¹³but exhort one
another daily, while it is called "Today," lest
any of you be hardened through the deceitfulness of sin. ¹⁴For we have become partakers of Christ if we hold the beginning of
our confidence steadfast to the end, ¹⁵while
it is said:

"Today, if you will hear His voice,
   Do not harden your hearts as in the
   rebellion."ᵃ

Failure of the Wilderness Wanderers

¹⁶For who, having heard, rebelled?
Indeed, was it not all who came out of
Egypt, led by Moses? ¹⁷Now with whom was
He angry forty years? Was it not with those
who sinned, whose corpses fell in the
wilderness? ¹⁸And to whom did He swear
that they would not enter His rest, but to
those who did not obey? ¹⁹So we see that
they could not enter in because of unbelief.

The Promise of Rest

4 Therefore, since a promise remains of
   entering His rest, let us fear lest any of
you seem to have come short of it. ²For
indeed the gospel was preached to us as
well as to them; but the word which they
heard did not profit them,ᵃ not being
mixed with faith in those who heard it.
³For we who have believed do enter that
rest, as He has said:

"So I swore in My wrath,
   'They shall not enter My rest,' "ᵃ

although the works were finished from the
foundation of the world. ⁴For He has spoken in a certain place of the seventh day in
this way: "And God rested on the seventh
day from all His works";ᵃ ⁵and again in
this place: "They shall not enter My rest."ᵃ

⁶Since therefore it remains that some
must enter it, and those to whom it was
first preached did not enter because of
disobedience, ⁷again He designates a certain day, saying in David, "Today," after
such a long time, as it has been said:

"Today, if you will hear His voice,
   Do not harden your hearts."ᵃ

⁸For if Joshua had given them rest, then
He would not afterward have spoken of
another day. ⁹There remains therefore a
rest for the people of God. ¹⁰For he who has
entered His rest has himself also ceased
from his works as God did from His.

The Word Discovers Our Condition

¹¹Let us therefore be diligent to enter that
rest, lest anyone fall according to the same
example of disobedience. ¹²For the word of
God is living and powerful, and sharper
than any two-edged sword, piercing even
to the division of soul and spirit, and of
joints and marrow, and is a discerner of the
thoughts and intents of the heart. ¹³And
there is no creature hidden from His sight,
but all things are naked and open to the
eyes of Him to whom we must give account.

Our Compassionate High Priest

¹⁴Seeing then that we have a great High
Priest who has passed through the heavens, Jesus the Son of God, let us hold fast
our confession. ¹⁵For we do not have a High
Priest who cannot sympathize with our
weaknesses, but was in all points tempted
as we are, yet without sin. ¹⁶Let us therefore
come boldly to the throne of grace, that we
may obtain mercy and find grace to help
in time of need.

Qualifications for High Priesthood

5 For every high priest taken from among
   men is appointed for men in things pertaining to God, that he may offer both gifts

---

3:11 ᵃPsalm 95:7–11   **3:15** ᵃPsalm 95:7, 8
4:2 ᵃNU-Text and M-Text read profit them, since they
were not united by faith with those who heeded it.
4:3 ᵃPsalm 95:11   **4:4** ᵃGenesis 2:2   **4:5** ᵃPsalm
95:11   **4:7** ᵃPsalm 95:7, 8

"SUPREME CONFIDENCE
IN THE BIBLE"

HOWARD A. KELLY

DEVOTION

*For the word of God
is . . . a discerner of the
thoughts and intents
of the heart.*

HEBREWS 4:12

Dr. Howard A. Kelly was considered by many to be the most famous medical practitioner in this country in the first half of the twentieth century. He was a pioneer in the field of gynecology and radium therapy, a professor of gynecology and obstetrics at Johns Hopkins University, and a surgeon of gynecology at John Hopkins Hospital. His published works were unsurpassed in his day, writing some twenty scientific books and five hundred medical and scientific articles.

When asked what the secret of his greatness was, Dr. Kelly said:

I rise regularly at six, and after dressing, give all of my time until our eight o'clock breakfast to the study of God's Word. I find time for brief studies during the day and again in the evening. I make it a general rule to touch nothing but the Bible after the evening meal.

And what difference did the Bible make in this busy surgeon's life?

One of the most cogent reasons for my supreme confidence in the Bible is that it reveals to me, as does no other book in the world, that which appeals to a physician—a clear diagnosis of my spiritual condition, showing me clearly what I am by nature, one lost in sin and alienated from life that is in God. I find it to be a consistent and wonderful revelation, from Genesis to Revelation, of the character of God, far removed from any man's natural imaginings. It also reveals a tenderness and nearness of God in Christ that satisfies the heart's yearnings and presents the infinite God, Creator of the world, as taking our very nature upon Him in infinite love to become one of His people in order to redeem them.

Another great American, George Washington, rose regularly and spent the time from five until six in the morning on his knees before a chair on which lay an open Bible. He retired every evening at nine o'clock to the same study, to the same chair, to the same open Bible.

and sacrifices for sins. [2]He can have compassion on those who are ignorant and going astray, since he himself is also subject to weakness. [3]Because of this he is required as for the people, so also for himself, to offer *sacrifices* for sins. [4]And no man takes this honor to himself, but he who is called by God, just as Aaron *was.*

A Priest Forever

[5]So also Christ did not glorify Himself to become High Priest, but *it was* He who said to Him:

"*You are My Son,*
   Today I have begotten You."[a]

[6]As *He* also says in another *place:*

"*You are a priest forever*
   According to the order of Melchizedek";[a]

[7]who, in the days of His flesh, when He had offered up prayers and supplications, with vehement cries and tears to Him who was able to save Him from death, and was heard because of His godly fear, [8]though He was a Son, *yet* He learned obedience by the things which He suffered. [9]And having been perfected, He became the author of eternal salvation to all who obey Him, [10]called by God as High Priest "*according to the order of Melchizedek,*" [11]of whom we have much to say, and hard to explain, since you have become dull of hearing.

Spiritual Immaturity

[12]For though by this time you ought to be teachers, you need *someone* to teach you again the first principles of the oracles of God; and you have come to need milk and not solid food. [13]For everyone who partakes *only* of milk *is* unskilled in the word of righteousness, for he is a babe. [14]But solid food belongs to those who are of full age, *that is,* those who by reason of use have their senses exercised to discern both good and evil.

The Peril of Not Progressing

6 Therefore, leaving the discussion of the elementary *principles* of Christ, let us go on to perfection, not laying again the foundation of repentance from dead works and of faith toward God, [2]of the doctrine of baptisms, of laying on of hands, of resurrection of the dead, and of eternal judgment. [3]And this we will[a] do if God permits.

[4]For *it is* impossible for those who were once enlightened, and have tasted the heavenly gift, and have become partakers of the Holy Spirit, [5]and have tasted the good word of God and the powers of the age to come, [6]if they fall away,[a] to renew them again to repentance, since they crucify again for themselves the Son of God, and put *Him* to an open shame.

[7]For the earth which drinks in the rain that often comes upon it, and bears herbs useful for those by whom it is cultivated, receives blessing from God; [8]but if it bears thorns and briers, *it is* rejected and near to being cursed, whose end *is* to be burned.

A Better Estimate

[9]But, beloved, we are confident of better things concerning you, yes, things that accompany salvation, though we speak in this manner. [10]For God *is* not unjust to forget your work and labor of[a] love which you have shown toward His name, *in that* you have ministered to the saints, and do minister. [11]And we desire that each one of you show the same diligence to the full assurance of hope until the end, [12]that you do not become sluggish, but imitate those who through faith and patience inherit the promises.

God's Infallible Purpose in Christ

[13]For when God made a promise to Abraham, because He could swear by no one greater, He swore by Himself, [14]saying, "*Surely blessing I will bless you, and multiplying I will multiply you.*"[a] [15]And so, after he had patiently endured, he obtained the promise. [16]For men indeed swear by the greater, and an oath for confirmation *is* for them an end of all dispute. [17]Thus God, determining to show more abundantly to

---

5:5 [a]Psalm 2:7   **5:6** [a]Psalm 110:4   **6:3** [a]M-Text reads *let us do.*   **6:6** [a]Or *and have fallen away*   **6:10** [a]NU-Text omits *labor of.*   **6:14** [a]Genesis 22:17

the heirs of promise the immutability of His counsel, confirmed *it* by an oath, ¹⁸that by two immutable things, in which it *is* impossible for God to lie, we might[a] have strong consolation, who have fled for refuge to lay hold of the hope set before *us.*

¹⁹This *hope* we have as an anchor of the soul, both sure and steadfast, and which enters the *Presence* behind the veil, ²⁰where the forerunner has entered for us, *even* Jesus, having become High Priest forever according to the order of Melchizedek.

The King of Righteousness

7 For this Melchizedek, king of Salem, priest of the Most High God, who met Abraham returning from the slaughter of the kings and blessed him, ²to whom also Abraham gave a tenth part of all, first being translated "king of righteousness," and then also king of Salem, meaning "king of peace," ³without father, without mother, without genealogy, having neither beginning of days nor end of life, but made like the Son of God, remains a priest continually.

⁴Now consider how great this man *was,* to whom even the patriarch Abraham gave a tenth of the spoils. ⁵And indeed those who are of the sons of Levi, who receive the priesthood, have a commandment to receive tithes from the people according to the law, that is, from their brethren, though they have come from the loins of Abraham; ⁶but he whose genealogy is not derived from them received tithes from Abraham and blessed him who had the promises. ⁷Now beyond all contradiction the lesser is blessed by the better. ⁸Here mortal men receive tithes, but there he *receives them,* of whom it is witnessed that he lives. ⁹Even Levi, who receives tithes, paid tithes through Abraham, so to speak, ¹⁰for he was still in the loins of his father when Melchizedek met him.

Need for a New Priesthood

¹¹Therefore, if perfection were through the Levitical priesthood (for under it the people received the law), what further need *was there* that another priest should rise according to the order of Melchizedek, and not be called according to the order of Aaron? ¹²For the priesthood being changed, of necessity there is also a change of the law. ¹³For He of whom these things are spoken belongs to another tribe, from which no man has officiated at the altar.

¹⁴For *it is* evident that our Lord arose from Judah, of which tribe Moses spoke nothing concerning priesthood.[a] ¹⁵And it is yet far more evident if, in the likeness of Melchizedek, there arises another priest ¹⁶who has come, not according to the law of a fleshly commandment, but according to the power of an endless life. ¹⁷For He testifies:[a]

> *"You are a priest forever*
> *According to the order of Melchizedek."*[b]

¹⁸For on the one hand there is an annulling of the former commandment because of its weakness and unprofitableness, ¹⁹for the law made nothing perfect; on the other hand, *there is the* bringing in of a better hope, through which we draw near to God.

Greatness of the New Priest

²⁰And inasmuch as *He was* not *made priest* without an oath ²¹(for they have become priests without an oath, but He with an oath by Him who said to Him:

> *"The Lord has sworn*
> *And will not relent,*
> *'You are a priest forever*[a]
> *According to the order of*
> *Melchizedek' "*),[b]

²²by so much more Jesus has become a surety of a better covenant.

²³Also there were many priests, because they were prevented by death from continuing. ²⁴But He, because He continues forever, has an unchangeable priesthood. ²⁵Therefore He is also able to save to the uttermost those who come to God through Him, since He always lives to make intercession for them.

6:18 [a]M-Text omits *might.*   7:14 [a]NU-Text reads *priests.*   7:17 [a]NU-Text reads *it is testified.* [b]Psalm 110:4   7:21 [a]NU-Text ends the quotation here. [b]Psalm 110:4

26For such a High Priest was fitting for us, *who is* holy, harmless, undefiled, separate from sinners, and has become higher than the heavens; 27who does not need daily, as those high priests, to offer up sacrifices, first for His own sins and then for the people's, for this He did once for all when He offered up Himself. 28For the law appoints as high priests men who have weakness, but the word of the oath, which came after the law, *appoints* the Son who has been perfected forever.

The New Priestly Service

8 Now *this is* the main point of the things we are saying: We have such a High Priest, who is seated at the right hand of the throne of the Majesty in the heavens, 2a Minister of the sanctuary and of the true tabernacle which the Lord erected, and not man.

3For every high priest is appointed to offer both gifts and sacrifices. Therefore *it is* necessary that this One also have something to offer. 4For if He were on earth, He would not be a priest, since there are priests who offer the gifts according to the law; 5who serve the copy and shadow of the heavenly things, as Moses was divinely instructed when he was about to make the tabernacle. For He said, *"See that you make all things according to the pattern shown you on the mountain."*ᵃ 6But now He has obtained a more excellent ministry, inasmuch as He is also Mediator of a better covenant, which was established on better promises.

A New Covenant

7For if that first *covenant* had been faultless, then no place would have been sought for a second. 8Because finding fault with them, He says: *"Behold, the days are coming, says the LORD, when I will make a new covenant with the house of Israel and with the house of Judah— 9not according to the covenant that I made with their fathers in the day when I took them by the hand to lead them out of the land of Egypt; because they did not continue in My covenant, and I disregarded them, says the LORD. 10For this is the covenant that I will make with the house of Israel after those days, says the LORD: I will put My laws in their mind and write them on their hearts; and I will be their God, and they shall be My people. 11None of them shall teach his neighbor, and none his brother, saying, 'Know the LORD,' for all shall know Me, from the least of them to the greatest of them. 12For I will be merciful to their unrighteousness, and their sins and their lawless deeds*ᵃ *I will remember no more."*ᵇ

13In that He says, *"A new covenant,"* He has made the first obsolete. Now what is becoming obsolete and growing old is ready to vanish away.

The Earthly Sanctuary

9 Then indeed, even the first *covenant* had ordinances of divine service and the earthly sanctuary. 2For a tabernacle was prepared: the first *part,* in which *was* the lampstand, the table, and the showbread, which is called the sanctuary; 3and behind the second veil, the part of the tabernacle which is called the Holiest of All, 4which had the golden censer and the ark of the covenant overlaid on all sides with gold, in which *were* the golden pot that had the manna, Aaron's rod that budded, and the tablets of the covenant; 5and above it were the cherubim of glory overshadowing the mercy seat. Of these things we cannot now speak in detail.

Limitations of the Earthly Service

6Now when these things had been thus prepared, the priests always went into the first part of the tabernacle, performing the services. 7But into the second part the high priest *went* alone once a year, not without blood, which he offered for himself and *for* the people's sins *committed* in ignorance; 8the Holy Spirit indicating this, that the way into the Holiest of All was not yet made manifest while the first tabernacle was still standing. 9It *was* symbolic for the present time in which both gifts and sacrifices are offered which cannot make him who performed the service perfect in regard to the conscience— 10concerned only

with foods and drinks, various washings, and fleshly ordinances imposed until the time of reformation.

The Heavenly Sanctuary

[11]But Christ came *as* High Priest of the good things to come,[a] with the greater and more perfect tabernacle not made with hands, that is, not of this creation. [12]Not with the blood of goats and calves, but with His own blood He entered the Most Holy Place once for all, having obtained eternal redemption. [13]For if the blood of bulls and goats and the ashes of a heifer, sprinkling the unclean, sanctifies for the purifying of the flesh, [14]how much more shall the blood of Christ, who through the eternal Spirit offered Himself without spot to God, cleanse your conscience from dead works to serve the living God? [15]And for this reason He is the Mediator of the new covenant, by means of death, for the redemption of the transgressions under the first covenant, that those who are called may receive the promise of the eternal inheritance.

The Mediator's Death Necessary

[16]For where there *is* a testament, there must also of necessity be the death of the testator. [17]For a testament *is* in force after men are dead, since it has no power at all while the testator lives. [18]Therefore not even the first *covenant* was dedicated without blood. [19]For when Moses had spoken every precept to all the people according to the law, he took the blood of calves and goats, with water, scarlet wool, and hyssop, and sprinkled both the book itself and all the people, [20]saying, "This is the blood of the covenant which God has commanded you."[a] [21]Then likewise he sprinkled with blood both the tabernacle and all the vessels of the ministry. [22]And according to the law almost all things are purified with blood, and without shedding of blood there is no remission.

Greatness of Christ's Sacrifice

[23]Therefore *it was* necessary that the copies of the things in the heavens should be purified with these, but the heavenly things themselves with better sacrifices than these. [24]For Christ has not entered the holy places made with hands, *which are* copies of the true, but into heaven itself, now to appear in the presence of God for us; [25]not that He should offer Himself often, as the high priest enters the Most Holy Place every year with blood of another— [26]He then would have had to suffer often since the foundation of the world; but now, once at the end of the ages, He has appeared to put away sin by the sacrifice of Himself. [27]And as it is appointed for men to die once, but after this the judgment, [28]so Christ was offered once to bear the sins of many. To those who eagerly wait for Him He will appear a second time, apart from sin, for salvation.

Animal Sacrifices Insufficient

10 For the law, having a shadow of the good things to come, *and* not the very image of the things, can never with these same sacrifices, which they offer continually year by year, make those who approach perfect. [2]For then would they not have ceased to be offered? For the worshipers, once purified, would have had no more consciousness of sins. [3]But in those *sacrifices there is* a reminder of sins every year. [4]For *it is* not possible that the blood of bulls and goats could take away sins.

Christ's Death Fulfills God's Will

[5]Therefore, when He came into the world, He said:

> "Sacrifice and offering You did not desire,
> But a body You have prepared for Me.
> [6] In burnt offerings and sacrifices for sin
> You had no pleasure.
> [7] Then I said, 'Behold, I have come—
> In the volume of the book it is written
>   of Me—
> To do Your will, O God.' "[a]

[8]Previously saying, "Sacrifice and offering, burnt offerings, and offerings for sin You did not desire, nor had pleasure in them" (which are offered according to the law), [9]then He

---

9:11 [a]NU-Text reads *that have come.*
9:20 [a]Exodus 24:8   **10:7** [a]Psalm 40:6–8

RELIGIOUS SERVICES AND FEDERAL BUILDINGS

THE DOME OF THE
U.S. CAPITOL

It may come as a surprise that on December 4, 1800, Congress approved the use of the Capitol building for religious services even before it officially moved into the building, and this practice lasted until well after the Civil War and Reconstruction. While it is true that there were no churches in the city at that time, even after dozens of churches were established in the city, religious services still continued at the Capitol.

Even more fascinating is the fact that within a year of his inauguration, Thomas Jefferson, who recommended that there exist "a wall of separation between church and state," began attending church services in the House of Representatives. Throughout his presidency (1801–1809), he permitted church services in executive branch buildings, because they were nondiscriminatory and voluntary. Apparently, Jefferson's concern for "separation" regarded the opposition to an official state-sponsored church rather than excluding religion from government. Preachers of every Protestant denomination appeared, and Catholic priests began officiating in 1826.

Jefferson's successor, James Madison, also attended church at the Capitol, as did many more presidents through Abraham Lincoln. It was also a common practice for many members of Congress to attend those services, and often the floor of the House was filled. From 1807 to 1857, services were held in what is now Statuary Hall. The services were interdenominational and overseen by the chaplains appointed by the House and Senate.

In addition to this service held in the Hall of the House, several individual churches met in the Capitol each week for their own services; there could be up to four different church services at the Capitol each Sunday. In 1867, the First Congregational Church in Washington was holding services for nearly 2,000 every Sunday in the Hall of Representatives while they raised funds to build their own sanctuary. At the time, that made it not only the largest church in the city, but the largest Protestant church in the United States. Church services were also held in the Supreme Court Chamber as well as in the Senate Chamber.

said, *"Behold, I have come to do Your will, O God."*[a] He takes away the first that He may establish the second. [10]By that will we have been sanctified through the offering of the body of Jesus Christ once *for all.*

Christ's Death Perfects the Sanctified

[11]And every priest stands ministering daily and offering repeatedly the same sacrifices, which can never take away sins. [12]But this Man, after He had offered one sacrifice for sins forever, sat down at the right hand of God, [13]from that time waiting till His enemies are made His footstool. [14]For by one offering He has perfected forever those who are being sanctified.

[15]But the Holy Spirit also witnesses to us; for after He had said before,

[16]*"This is the covenant that I will make with them after those days, says the LORD: I will put My laws into their hearts, and in their minds I will write them,"*[a] [17]then He adds, *"Their sins and their lawless deeds I will remember no more."*[a] [18]Now where there is remission of these, *there is* no longer an offering for sin.

Hold Fast Your Confession

[19]Therefore, brethren, having boldness to enter the Holiest by the blood of Jesus, [20]by a new and living way which He consecrated for us, through the veil, that is, His flesh, [21]and *having* a High Priest over the house of God, [22]let us draw near with a true heart in full assurance of faith, having our hearts sprinkled from an evil conscience and our bodies washed with pure water. [23]Let us hold fast the confession of *our* hope without wavering, for He who promised *is* faithful. [24]And let us consider one another in order to stir up love and good works, [25]not forsaking the assembling of ourselves together, as *is* the manner of some, but exhorting *one another,* and so much the more as you see the Day approaching.

The Just Live by Faith

[26]For if we sin willfully after we have received the knowledge of the truth, there no longer remains a sacrifice for sins, [27]but a certain fearful expectation of judgment, and fiery indignation which will devour the adversaries. [28]Anyone who has rejected Moses' law dies without mercy on *the testimony of* two or three witnesses. [29]Of how much worse punishment, do you suppose, will he be thought worthy who has trampled the Son of God underfoot, counted the blood of the covenant by which he was sanctified a common thing, and insulted the Spirit of grace? [30]For we know Him who said, *"Vengeance is Mine, I will repay,"*[a] says the Lord.[b] And again, *"The LORD will judge His people."*[c] [31]It is a fearful thing to fall into the hands of the living God.

[32]But recall the former days in which, after you were illuminated, you endured a great struggle with sufferings: [33]partly while you were made a spectacle both by reproaches and tribulations, and partly while you became companions of those who were so treated; [34]for you had compassion on me[a] in my chains, and joyfully accepted the plundering of your goods, knowing that you have a better and an enduring possession for yourselves in heaven.[b] [35]Therefore do not cast away your confidence, which has great reward. [36]For you have need of endurance, so that after you have done the will of God, you may receive the promise:

[37] *"For yet a little while,*
     And He[a] *who is coming will come and*
        will not tarry.
[38]   *Now the*[a] *just shall live by faith;*
     But if anyone draws back,
     My soul has no pleasure in him."[b]

[39]But we are not of those who draw back to perdition, but of those who believe to the saving of the soul.

By Faith We Understand

11 Now faith is the substance of things hoped for, the evidence of things not seen. [2]For by it the elders obtained a *good* testimony.

10:9 [a]NU-Text and M-Text omit *O God.*
10:16 [a]Jeremiah 31:33   **10:17** [a]Jeremiah 31:34
10:30 [a]Deuteronomy 32:35 [b]NU-Text omits *says the Lord.* [c]Deuteronomy 32:36   **10:34** [a]NU-Text reads *the prisoners* instead of *me in my chains.*
[b]NU-Text omits *in heaven.*   **10:37** [a]Or *that which*
10:38 [a]NU-Text reads *My just one.* [b]Habakkuk 2:3, 4

[3]By faith we understand that the worlds were framed by the word of God, so that the things which are seen were not made of things which are visible.

Faith at the Dawn of History

[4]By faith Abel offered to God a more excellent sacrifice than Cain, through which he obtained witness that he was righteous, God testifying of his gifts; and through it he being dead still speaks. [5]By faith Enoch was taken away so that he did not see death, *"and was not found, because God had taken him"*;[a] for before he was taken he had this testimony, that he pleased God. [6]But without faith *it is* impossible to please *Him,* for he who comes to God must believe that He is, and *that* He is a rewarder of those who diligently seek Him. [7]By faith Noah, being divinely warned of things not yet seen, moved with godly fear, prepared an ark for the saving of his household, by which he condemned the world and became heir of the righteousness which is according to faith.

Faithful Abraham

[8]By faith Abraham obeyed when he was called to go out to the place which he would receive as an inheritance. And he went out, not knowing where he was going. [9]By faith he dwelt in the land of promise as *in* a foreign country, dwelling in tents with Isaac and Jacob, the heirs with him of the same promise; [10]for he waited for the city which has foundations, whose builder and maker *is* God. [11]By faith Sarah herself also received strength to conceive seed, and she bore a child[a] when she was past the age, because she judged Him faithful who had promised. [12]Therefore from one man, and him as good as dead, were born *as many* as the stars of the sky in multitude—innumerable as the sand which is by the seashore.

The Heavenly Hope

[13]These all died in faith, not having received the promises, but having seen them afar off were assured of them,[a] embraced *them* and confessed that they were strangers and pilgrims on the earth. [14]For those who

say such things declare plainly that they seek a homeland. [15]And truly if they had called to mind that *country* from which they had come out, they would have had opportunity to return. [16]But now they desire a better, that is, a heavenly *country.* Therefore God is not ashamed to be called their God, for He has prepared a city for them.

The Faith of the Patriarchs

[17]By faith Abraham, when he was tested, offered up Isaac, and he who had received the promises offered up his only begotten *son,* [18]of whom it was said, *"In Isaac your seed shall be called,"*[a] [19]concluding that God *was* able to raise *him* up, even from the dead, from which he also received him in a figurative sense. [20]By faith Isaac blessed Jacob and Esau concerning things to come. [21]By faith Jacob, when he was dying, blessed each of the sons of Joseph, and worshiped, *leaning* on the top of his staff. [22]By faith Joseph, when he was dying, made mention of the departure of the children of Israel, and gave instructions concerning his bones.

The Faith of Moses

[23]By faith Moses, when he was born, was hidden three months by his parents, because they saw *he was* a beautiful child; and they were not afraid of the king's command. [24]By faith Moses, when he became of age, refused to be called the son of Pharaoh's daughter, [25]choosing rather to suffer affliction with the people of God than to enjoy the passing pleasures of sin, [26]esteeming the reproach of Christ greater riches than the treasures in[a] Egypt; for he looked to the reward. [27]By faith he forsook Egypt, not fearing the wrath of the king; for he endured as seeing Him who is invisible. [28]By faith he kept the Passover and the sprinkling of blood, lest he who destroyed the firstborn should touch them.

11:5 [a]Genesis 5:24   **11:11** [a]NU-Text omits *she bore a child.*   **11:13** [a]NU-Text and M-Text omit *were assured of them.*   **11:18** [a]Genesis 21:12   **11:26** [a]NU-Text and M-Text read *of.*

29By faith they passed through the Red Sea as by dry *land, whereas* the Egyptians, attempting to do so, were drowned.

By Faith They Overcame

30By faith the walls of Jericho fell down after they were encircled for seven days. 31By faith the harlot Rahab did not perish with those who did not believe, when she had received the spies with peace.

32And what more shall I say? For the time would fail me to tell of Gideon and Barak and Samson and Jephthah, also *of* David and Samuel and the prophets: 33who through faith subdued kingdoms, worked righteousness, obtained promises, stopped the mouths of lions, 34quenched the violence of fire, escaped the edge of the sword, out of weakness were made strong, became valiant in battle, turned to flight the armies of the aliens. 35Women received their dead raised to life again.

Others were tortured, not accepting deliverance, that they might obtain a better resurrection. 36Still others had trial of mockings and scourgings, yes, and of chains and imprisonment. 37They were stoned, they were sawn in two, were tempted,a were slain with the sword. They wandered about in sheepskins and goatskins, being destitute, afflicted, tormented— 38of whom the world was not worthy. They wandered in deserts and mountains, *in* dens and caves of the earth.

39And all these, having obtained a good testimony through faith, did not receive the promise, 40God having provided something better for us, that they should not be made perfect apart from us.

The Race of Faith

12 Therefore we also, since we are surrounded by so great a cloud of witnesses, let us lay aside every weight, and the sin which so easily ensnares *us,* and let us run with endurance the race that is set before us, 2looking unto Jesus, the author and finisher of *our* faith, who for the joy that was set before Him endured the cross, despising the shame, and has sat down at the right hand of the throne of God.

The Discipline of God

3For consider Him who endured such hostility from sinners against Himself, lest you become weary and discouraged in your souls. 4You have not yet resisted to bloodshed, striving against sin. 5And you have forgotten the exhortation which speaks to you as to sons:

> "My son, do not despise the chastening
>   of the LORD,
>   Nor be discouraged when you are
>   rebuked by Him;
> 6   For whom the LORD loves He chastens,
>   And scourges every son whom He
>   receives."a

7Ifa you endure chastening, God deals with you as with sons; for what son is there whom a father does not chasten? 8But if you are without chastening, of which all have become partakers, then you are illegitimate and not sons. 9Furthermore, we have had human fathers who corrected *us,* and we paid *them* respect. Shall we not much more readily be in subjection to the Father of spirits and live? 10For they indeed for a few days chastened *us* as seemed *best* to them, but He for *our* profit, that *we* may be partakers of His holiness. 11Now no chastening seems to be joyful for the present, but painful; nevertheless, afterward it yields the peaceable fruit of righteousness to those who have been trained by it.

Renew Your Spiritual Vitality

12Therefore strengthen the hands which hang down, and the feeble knees, 13and make straight paths for your feet, so that what is lame may not be dislocated, but rather be healed.

14Pursue peace with all *people,* and holiness, without which no one will see the Lord: 15looking carefully lest anyone fall short of the grace of God; lest any root of bitterness springing up cause trouble, and by this many become defiled; 16lest there *be* any fornicator or profane person like Esau, who for

---

11:37 aNU-Text omits *were tempted.*
12:6 aProverbs 3:11, 12   **12:7** aNU-Text and M-Text read *It is for discipline that you endure; God . . . .*

WASHINGTON
AT VALLEY FORGE

*. . . of whom the world
was not worthy.*

HEBREWS 11:38

VALLEY FORGE,
DECEMBER 1777

After defeats to the British in the Battles of Brandywine and German-town in the fall of 1777, the Continental Army was encamped at Valley Forge, struggling to survive the winter. Nine out of ten soldiers had no shoes, and for a month in the bitter cold and snow, 12,000 American troops lived in tents while building huts. There was not enough food or firewood, and many people wouldn't sell to the army because the paper money wasn't worth anything. Many soldiers subsisted on "firecake," a tasteless mixture of flour and water while Washington pleaded with Congress for supplies. More than 2,000 soldiers died that winter from diseases such as pneumonia, typhoid, and dysentery.

Over one hundred years later, Henry Armitt Brown vividly described the experience of the soldiers at Valley Forge:

> *. . . Trials that rarely have failed to break the fortitude of men await them here. False friends shall endeavor to undermine their virtue and secret enemies to shake their faith; the Congress whom they serve shall prove helpless to protect them, and their country herself seem unmindful of their suffering. . . .*

Nevertheless, Brown added these words of tribute to the sacrifices and sufferings of so many who served to secure for us the freedoms we enjoy:

> *. . . Danger shall not frighten nor temptation have power to seduce them. Doubt shall not shake their love of country nor suffering over-come their fortitude. The powers of evil shall not prevail against them, for they are the Continental Army, and these are the hills of Valley Forge!*

> *The heroic dead who have suffered here are beyond our reach. No human eulogy can make their glory greater, no failure to do them justice can make it less. . . . Their trials here secured the happiness of a continent; their labors have born fruit in the free institutions of a powerful nation; their examples give hope to every race and clime; their names live on the lips of a grateful people; their memory is cherished in their children's hearts, and shall endure forever.*

one morsel of food sold his birthright. [17]For you know that afterward, when he wanted to inherit the blessing, he was rejected, for he found no place for repentance, though he sought it diligently with tears.

The Glorious Company

[18]For you have not come to the mountain that[a] may be touched and that burned with fire, and to blackness and darkness[b] and tempest, [19]and the sound of a trumpet and the voice of words, so that those who heard *it* begged that the word should not be spoken to them anymore. [20](For they could not endure what was commanded: "*And if so much as a beast touches the mountain, it shall be stoned[a] or shot with an arrow.*"[b] [21]And so terrifying was the sight *that* Moses said, "*I am exceedingly afraid and trembling.*"[a])

[22]But you have come to Mount Zion and to the city of the living God, the heavenly Jerusalem, to an innumerable company of angels, [23]to the general assembly and church of the firstborn *who are* registered in heaven, to God the Judge of all, to the spirits of just men made perfect, [24]to Jesus the Mediator of the new covenant, and to the blood of sprinkling that speaks better things than *that of* Abel.

Hear the Heavenly Voice

[25]See that you do not refuse Him who speaks. For if they did not escape who refused Him who spoke on earth, much more *shall we not escape* if we turn away from Him who *speaks* from heaven, [26]whose voice then shook the earth; but now He has promised, saying, "*Yet once more I shake[a] not only the earth, but also heaven.*"[b] [27]Now this, "*Yet once more,*" indicates the removal of those things that are being shaken, as of things that are made, that the things which cannot be shaken may remain.

[28]Therefore, since we are receiving a kingdom which cannot be shaken, let us have grace, by which we may[a] serve God acceptably with reverence and godly fear. [29]For our God *is* a consuming fire.

Concluding Moral Directions

13 Let brotherly love continue. [2]Do not forget to entertain strangers, for by

so *doing* some have unwittingly entertained angels. [3]Remember the prisoners as if chained with them—those who are mistreated—since you yourselves are in the body also.

[4]Marriage *is* honorable among all, and the bed undefiled; but fornicators and adulterers God will judge.

[5]*Let your* conduct *be* without covetousness; *be* content with such things as you have. For He Himself has said, "*I will never leave you nor forsake you.*"[a] [6]So we may boldly say:

> "The LORD *is my helper;*
> *I will not fear.*
> *What can man do to me?*"[a]

Concluding Religious Directions

[7]Remember those who rule over you, who have spoken the word of God to you, whose faith follow, considering the outcome of *their* conduct. [8]Jesus Christ *is* the same yesterday, today, and forever. [9]Do not be carried about[a] with various and strange doctrines. For *it is* good that the heart be established by grace, not with foods which have not profited those who have been occupied with them.

[10]We have an altar from which those who serve the tabernacle have no right to eat. [11]For the bodies of those animals, whose blood is brought into the sanctuary by the high priest for sin, are burned outside the camp. [12]Therefore Jesus also, that He might sanctify the people with His own blood, suffered outside the gate. [13]Therefore let us go forth to Him, outside the camp, bearing His reproach. [14]For here we have no continuing city, but we seek the one to come. [15]Therefore by Him let us continually offer the sacrifice of praise to God, that is, the fruit of *our* lips, giving thanks to His name. [16]But do not forget to do good and to share, for with such sacrifices God is well pleased.

[17]Obey those who rule over you, and be submissive, for they watch out for your

---

12:18 [a]NU-Text reads *to that which.* [b]NU-Text reads *gloom.*   **12:20** [a]NU-Text and M-Text omit the rest of this verse. [b]Exodus 19:12, 13   **12:21** [a]Deuteronomy 9:19   **12:26** [a]NU-Text reads *will shake.* [b]Haggai 2:6   **12:28** [a]M-Text omits *may.*   **13:5** [a]Deuteronomy 31:6, 8; Joshua 1:5   **13:6** [a]Psalm 118:6   **13:9** [a]NU-Text and M-Text read *away.*

The NATION'S GUIDING PRINCIPLE

JOHN F. KENNEDY

In a speech given in February 1961, President John F. Kennedy stated:

This country was founded by men and women who were dedicated or came to be dedicated to two propositions: first, a strong religious conviction, and secondly a recognition that this conviction could flourish only under a system of freedom.

I think it is appropriate that we pay tribute to this great constitutional principle which is enshrined in the First Amendment of the Constitution: the principle of religious independence, of religious liberty, of religious freedom. But I think it is also important that we pay tribute and acknowledge another great principle, and that is the principle of religious conviction. Religious freedom has no significance unless it is accompanied by conviction. And therefore the Puritans and the Pilgrims of my own section of New England, the Quakers of Pennsylvania, the Catholics of Maryland, the Presbyterians of North Carolina, the Methodists and the Baptists who came later, all shared these two great traditions which, like silver threads, have run through the warp and the woof of American history.

No man who enters upon the office to which I have succeeded can fail to recognize how every president of the United States has placed special reliance upon his faith in God. Every president has taken comfort and courage when told . . . that the Lord "will be with thee. He will not fail thee nor forsake thee. Fear not—neither be thou dismayed." While they came from a wide variety of religious backgrounds and held a wide variety of religious beliefs, each of our presidents in his own way has placed a special trust in God. Those who were strongest intellectually were also strongest spiritually.

. . . [L]et us go forth to lead this land that we love, joining in the prayer of General George Washington in 1783, "that God would have you in His holy protection, that He would incline the hearts of the citizens . . . to entertain a brotherly love and affection one for another . . . and finally that He would most graciously be pleased to dispose us all to do justice, to love mercy, and to demean ourselves with . . . the characteristics of the Divine Author of our blessed religion, without an humble imitation of whose example we can never hope to be a happy nation."

The guiding principle and prayer of this nation has been, is now, and shall ever be "In God We Trust."

souls, as those who must give account. Let them do so with joy and not with grief, for that would be unprofitable for you.

Prayer Requested

[18]Pray for us; for we are confident that we have a good conscience, in all things desiring to live honorably. [19]But I especially urge *you* to do this, that I may be restored to you the sooner.

Benediction, Final Exhortation, Farewell

[20]Now may the God of peace who brought up our Lord Jesus from the dead, that great Shepherd of the sheep, through the blood of the everlasting covenant, [21]make you complete in every good work to do His will, working in you[a] what is well pleasing in His sight, through Jesus Christ, to whom *be* glory forever and ever. Amen.

[22]And I appeal to you, brethren, bear with the word of exhortation, for I have written to you in few words. [23]Know that *our* brother Timothy has been set free, with whom I shall see you if he comes shortly.

[24]Greet all those who rule over you, and all the saints. Those from Italy greet you.

[25]Grace *be* with you all. Amen.

13:21 [a]NU-Text and M-Text read *us*.

JAMES

Author: James, the half brother of Jesus

When Written: Around A.D. 46

Theme: Faith That Works

Key Verses: James 2:14–17—What does it profit, my brethren, if someone says he has faith but does not have works? Can faith save him? If a brother or sister is naked and destitute of daily food, and one of you says to them, "Depart in peace, be warmed and filled," but you do not give them the things which are needed for the body, what does it profit? Thus also faith by itself, if it does not have works, is dead.

Key Chapter: James 1—This chapter reveals the Christian's correct response to one of the most difficult areas of life—testings and temptations.

The Book of James is "the Proverbs of the New Testament" because it is written in the terse moralistic style of wisdom literature. But James's impassioned preaching against inequity and social injustice also earns him the title of "the Amos of the New Testament." Throughout this epistle to Jewish believers, James integrates true faith and everyday practical experience by stressing that true faith must manifest itself in works of faith.

Nathan Hale was a man of action whom James would have commended. When he heard about the British Siege of Boston in 1775, he declared, "Let us march immediately, and never lay down our arms until we obtain our independence." Later in the Revolutionary War, Hale volunteered as a spy, but was captured by the British and hanged on September 22, 1776. He is the great American hero who reportedly said to his captors, "I only regret that I have but one life to give my country."

JAMES

Greeting to the Twelve Tribes

1 James, a bondservant of God and of the Lord Jesus Christ,

To the twelve tribes which are scattered abroad:

Greetings.

Profiting from Trials

2My brethren, count it all joy when you fall into various trials, 3knowing that the testing of your faith produces patience. 4But let patience have *its* perfect work, that you may be perfect and complete, lacking nothing. 5If any of you lacks wisdom, let him ask of God, who gives to all liberally and without reproach, and it will be given to him. 6But let him ask in faith, with no doubting, for he who doubts is like a wave of the sea driven and tossed by the wind. 7For let not that man suppose that he will receive anything from the Lord; 8*he is* a double-minded man, unstable in all his ways.

The Perspective of Rich and Poor

9Let the lowly brother glory in his exaltation, 10but the rich in his humiliation, because as a flower of the field he will pass away. 11For no sooner has the sun risen with a burning heat than it withers the grass; its flower falls, and its beautiful appearance perishes. So the rich man also will fade away in his pursuits.

Loving God Under Trials

12Blessed *is* the man who endures temptation; for when he has been approved, he will receive the crown of life which the Lord has promised to those who love Him. 13Let no one say when he is tempted, "I am tempted by God"; for God cannot be tempted by evil, nor does He Himself tempt anyone. 14But each one is tempted when he is drawn away by his own desires and enticed. 15Then, when desire has conceived, it gives birth to sin; and sin, when it is full-grown, brings forth death.

16Do not be deceived, my beloved brethren. 17Every good gift and every perfect gift is from above, and comes down from the Father of lights, with whom there is no variation or shadow of turning. 18Of His own will He brought us forth by the word of truth, that we might be a kind of firstfruits of His creatures.

HUMILITY
Every good gift and every perfect gift. . . .

JAMES 1:17

A Thankful Nation
In his 1815 Thanksgiving Day proclamation, President James Madison stated:

> No people ought to feel greater obligations to celebrate the goodness of the Great Disposer of Events of the destiny of Nations than the people of the United States. . . . And to the same Divine Author of Every Good and Perfect Gift we are indebted for all those privileges and advantages, religious as well as civil, which are so richly enjoyed in this favored land.

Qualities Needed in Trials

19So then,a my beloved brethren, let every man be swift to hear, slow to speak, slow to wrath; 20for the wrath of man does not produce the righteousness of God.

Doers—Not Hearers Only

21Therefore lay aside all filthiness and overflow of wickedness, and receive with meekness the implanted word, which is able to save your souls.

Theodore Roosevelt placed his hand on James 1:22, 23 as he took the presidential oath of office in 1905.

1:19 aNU-Text reads *Know this* or *This you know.*

ABRAHAM LINCOLN
ON SKEPTICISM

ABRAHAM LINCOLN

Joshua Speed was a close friend of Abraham Lincoln, a skeptic when both were young men. He later published a small volume called *Reminiscences of Abraham Lincoln*, which includes a story from 1864 when he visited Lincoln in Washington:

I have often been asked what were Mr. Lincoln's religious opinions. When I knew him, in early life, he was a skeptic. He had tried hard to be a believer, but his reason could not grasp and solve the great problem of redemption as taught. He was very cautious never to give expression to any thought or sentiment that would grate harshly upon a Christian's ear. For a sincere Christian, he had great respect. He often said that the most ambitious man might live to see every hope fail; but, no Christian could live to see his fail, because fulfillment could only come when life ended. But this was a subject we never discussed.

The only evidence I have of any change, was in the summer before he was killed. I was invited out to the Soldier's Home to spend the night. As I entered the room, near night, he was sitting near a window intently reading his Bible.

Approaching him I said, "I am glad to see you so profitably engaged."

"Yes," said he, "I am profitably engaged."

"Well," said I, "if you have recovered from your skepticism, I am sorry to say that I have not."

Looking me earnestly in the face and placing his hand on my shoulder, he said, "You are wrong, Speed. Take all of this book upon reason that you can, and the balance on faith, and you will live and die a happier and better man."

²²But be doers of the word, and not hearers only, deceiving yourselves. ²³For if anyone is a hearer of the word and not a doer, he is like a man observing his natural face in a mirror; ²⁴for he observes himself, goes away, and immediately forgets what kind of man he was. ²⁵But he who looks into the perfect law of liberty and continues *in it,* and is not a forgetful hearer but a doer of the work, this one will be blessed in what he does.

²⁶If anyone among you[a] thinks he is religious, and does not bridle his tongue but deceives his own heart, this one's religion *is* useless. ²⁷Pure and undefiled religion before God and the Father is this: to visit orphans and widows in their trouble, *and* to keep oneself unspotted from the world.

Beware of Personal Favoritism

2 My brethren, do not hold the faith of our Lord Jesus Christ, *the Lord* of glory, with partiality. ²For if there should come into your assembly a man with gold rings, in fine apparel, and there should also come in a poor man in filthy clothes, ³and you pay attention to the one wearing the fine clothes and say to him, "You sit here in a good place," and say to the poor man, "You stand there," or, "Sit here at my footstool," ⁴have you not shown partiality among yourselves, and become judges with evil thoughts?

⁵Listen, my beloved brethren: Has God not chosen the poor of this world *to be* rich in faith and heirs of the kingdom which He promised to those who love Him? ⁶But you have dishonored the poor man. Do not the rich oppress you and drag you into the courts? ⁷Do they not blaspheme that noble name by which you are called?

⁸If you really fulfill *the* royal law according to the Scripture, *"You shall love your neighbor as yourself,"*[a] you do well; ⁹but if you show partiality, you commit sin, and are convicted by the law as transgressors. ¹⁰For whoever shall keep the whole law, and yet stumble in one *point,* is guilty of all. ¹¹For He who said, *"Do not commit adultery,"*[a] also said, *"Do not murder."*[b] Now if you do not commit adultery, but you do murder, you have become a transgressor of

the law. ¹²So speak and so do as those who will be judged by the law of liberty. ¹³For judgment is without mercy to the one who has shown no mercy. Mercy triumphs over judgment.

Faith Without Works Is Dead

¹⁴What *does it* profit, my brethren, if someone says he has faith but does not have works? Can faith save him? ¹⁵If a brother or sister is naked and destitute of daily food, ¹⁶and one of you says to them, "Depart in peace, be warmed and filled," but you do not give them the things which are needed for the body, what *does it* profit? ¹⁷Thus also faith by itself, if it does not have works, is dead.

¹⁸But someone will say, "You have faith, and I have works." Show me your faith without your[a] works, and I will show you my faith by my[b] works. ¹⁹You believe that there is one God. You do well. Even the demons believe—and tremble! ²⁰But do you want to know, O foolish man, that faith without works is dead?[a] ²¹Was not Abraham our father justified by works when he offered Isaac his son on the altar? ²²Do you see that faith was working together with his works, and by works faith was made perfect? ²³And the Scripture was fulfilled which says, *"Abraham believed God, and it was accounted to him for righteousness."*[a] And he was called the friend of God. ²⁴You see then that a man is justified by works, and not by faith only.

²⁵Likewise, was not Rahab the harlot also justified by works when she received the messengers and sent *them* out another way? ²⁶For as the body without the spirit is dead, so faith without works is dead also.

The Untamable Tongue

3 My brethren, let not many of you become teachers, knowing that we shall receive a stricter judgment. ²For we all stumble in many things. If anyone does not stumble in word, he *is* a perfect man,

1:26 [a]NU-Text omits *among you.*   **2:8** [a]Leviticus 19:18   **2:11** [a]Exodus 20:14; Deuteronomy 5:18 [b]Exodus 20:13; Deuteronomy 5:17   **2:18** [a]NU-Text omits *your.* [b]NU-Text omits *my.*   **2:20** [a]NU-Text reads *useless.*   **2:23** [a]Genesis 15:6

RELIGION
AND DEMOCRACY—1835

ALEXIS DE TOCQUEVILLE

ALEXIS DE TOCQUEVILLE

FREEDOM

*But he who looks
into the perfect law
of liberty. . . .*

JAMES 1:25

In 1831, Alexis de Tocqueville, a young French nobleman, spent nine months traveling America, venturing as far west as the unspoiled wilderness of Michigan and then south to New Orleans. But the majority of his time was spent in Boston, New York, and Philadelphia. He interviewed people from every walk of life, then wrote down these amazing observations in *Democracy in America.*

Upon my arrival in the United States, the religious aspect of the country was the first thing that struck my attention; and the longer I stayed there the more did I perceive the great political consequences resulting from this state of things, to which I was unaccustomed. In France I had almost always seen the spirit of religion and the spirit of freedom pursuing courses diametrically opposed to each other; but in America I found that they were intimately united, and that they reigned in common over the same country.

. . . they brought with them into the New World a form of Christianity which I cannot better describe than by styling it a democratic and republican religion. This sect contributed powerfully to the establishment of a democracy and a republic, and from the earliest settlement of the emigrants politics and religion contracted an alliance which has never been dissolved.

. . . there is no country in the whole world in which the Christian religion retains a greater influence over the souls of men than in America; and there can be no greater proof of its utility, and of its conformity to human nature, than that its influence is most powerfully felt over the most enlightened and free nation of the earth.

Religion in America takes no direct part in the government of society, but it must nevertheless be regarded as the foremost of the political institutions of that country; for if it does not impart a taste for freedom, it facilitates the use of free institutions. . . . I am certain that they hold it to be indispensable to the maintenance of republican institutions. This opinion is not peculiar to a class of citizens or to a party, but it belongs to the whole nation, and to every rank of society.

The Americans combine the notions of Christianity and of liberty so intimately in their minds, that it is impossible to make them conceive the one without the other.

able also to bridle the whole body. ³Indeed,ᵃ we put bits in horses' mouths that they may obey us, and we turn their whole body. ⁴Look also at ships: although they are so large and are driven by fierce winds, they are turned by a very small rudder wherever the pilot desires. ⁵Even so the tongue is a little member and boasts great things.

See how great a forest a little fire kindles! ⁶And the tongue *is* a fire, a world of iniquity. The tongue is so set among our members that it defiles the whole body, and sets on fire the course of nature; and it is set on fire by hell. ⁷For every kind of beast and bird, of reptile and creature of the sea, is tamed and has been tamed by mankind. ⁸But no man can tame the tongue. *It is* an unruly evil, full of deadly poison. ⁹With it we bless our God and Father, and with it we curse men, who have been made in the similitude of God. ¹⁰Out of the same mouth proceed blessing and cursing. My brethren, these things ought not to be so. ¹¹Does a spring send forth fresh *water* and bitter from the same opening? ¹²Can a fig tree, my brethren, bear olives, or a grapevine bear figs? Thus no spring yields both salt water and fresh.ᵃ

Heavenly Versus Demonic Wisdom

¹³Who *is* wise and understanding among you? Let him show by good conduct *that* his works *are done* in the meekness of wisdom. ¹⁴But if you have bitter envy and self-seeking in your hearts, do not boast and lie against the truth. ¹⁵This wisdom does not descend from above, but *is* earthly, sensual, demonic. ¹⁶For where envy and self-seeking *exist,* confusion and every evil thing *are* there. ¹⁷But the wisdom that is from above is first pure, then peaceable, gentle, willing to yield, full of mercy and good fruits, without partiality and without hypocrisy. ¹⁸Now the fruit of righteousness is sown in peace by those who make peace.

Pride Promotes Strife

4 Where do wars and fights *come* from among you? Do *they* not *come* from your *desires for* pleasure that war in your members? ²You lust and do not have. You murder and covet and cannot obtain. You

fight and war. Yetᵃ you do not have because you do not ask. ³You ask and do not receive, because you ask amiss, that you may spend *it* on your pleasures. ⁴Adulterers andᵃ adulteresses! Do you not know that friendship with the world is enmity with God? Whoever therefore wants to be a friend of the world makes himself an enemy of God. ⁵Or do you think that the Scripture says in vain, "The Spirit who dwells in us yearns jealously"?

⁶But He gives more grace. Therefore He says:

"God resists the proud,
* But gives grace to the humble."ᵃ*

Humility Cures Worldliness

⁷Therefore submit to God. Resist the devil and he will flee from you. ⁸Draw near to God and He will draw near to you. Cleanse *your* hands, *you* sinners; and purify *your* hearts, *you* double-minded. ⁹Lament and mourn and weep! Let your laughter be turned to mourning and *your* joy to gloom. ¹⁰Humble yourselves in the sight of the Lord, and He will lift you up.

Do Not Judge a Brother

¹¹Do not speak evil of one another, brethren. He who speaks evil of a brother and judges his brother, speaks evil of the law and judges the law. But if you judge the law, you are not a doer of the law but a judge. ¹²There is one Lawgiver,ᵃ who is able to save and to destroy. Whoᵇ are you to judge another?ᶜ

Do Not Boast About Tomorrow

¹³Come now, you who say, "Today or tomorrow we willᵃ go to such and such a city, spend a year there, buy and sell, and make a profit"; ¹⁴whereas you do not know what *will happen* tomorrow. For what *is*

3:3 ᵃNU-Text reads *Now if.*   **3:12** ᵃNU-Text reads *Neither can a salty spring produce fresh water.*
4:2 ᵃNU-Text and M-Text omit *Yet.*   **4:4** ᵃNU-Text omits *Adulterers and.*   **4:6** ᵃProverbs 3:34
4:12 ᵃNU-Text adds *and Judge.* ᵇNU-Text and M-Text read *But who.* ᶜNU-Text reads *a neighbor.*   **4:13** ᵃM-Text reads *let us.*

your life? It is even a vapor that appears for a little time and then vanishes away. [15]Instead you *ought* to say, "If the Lord wills, we shall live and do this or that." [16]But now you boast in your arrogance. All such boasting is evil.

[17]Therefore, to him who knows to do good and does not do *it,* to him it is sin.

Rich Oppressors Will Be Judged

5 Come now, *you* rich, weep and howl for your miseries that are coming upon *you!* [2]Your riches are corrupted, and your garments are moth-eaten. [3]Your gold and silver are corroded, and their corrosion will be a witness against you and will eat your flesh like fire. You have heaped up treasure in the last days. [4]Indeed the wages of the laborers who mowed your fields, which you kept back by fraud, cry out; and the cries of the reapers have reached the ears of the Lord of Sabaoth.[a] [5]You have lived on the earth in pleasure and luxury; you have fattened your hearts as[a] in a day of slaughter. [6]You have condemned, you have murdered the just; he does not resist you.

Be Patient and Persevering

[7]Therefore be patient, brethren, until the coming of the Lord. See *how* the farmer waits for the precious fruit of the earth, waiting patiently for it until it receives the early and latter rain. [8]You also be patient. Establish your hearts, for the coming of the Lord is at hand.

[9]Do not grumble against one another, brethren, lest you be condemned.[a] Behold, the Judge is standing at the door! [10]My brethren, take the prophets, who spoke in the name of the Lord, as an example of suffering and patience. [11]Indeed we count them blessed who endure. You have heard of the perseverance of Job and seen the end *intended by* the Lord—that the Lord is very compassionate and merciful.

[12]But above all, my brethren, do not swear, either by heaven or by earth or with any other oath. But let your "Yes" be "Yes," and *your* "No," "No," lest you fall into judgment.[a]

5:4 [a]Literally, in Hebrew, *Hosts*   **5:5** [a]NU-Text omits *as.*   **5:9** [a]NU-Text and M-Text read *judged.* **5:12** [a]M-Text reads *hypocrisy.*

PRAYER

Elijah was a man with a nature like ours, and he prayed earnestly. . . .

JAMES 5:17

George Washington

GEORGE WASHINGTON'S "EARNEST PRAYER"

The prayer below was written by Washington at Newburgh, New York, at the close of the Revolutionary War on June 14, 1783. It was sent to the 13 governors of the newly freed states in a "Circular Letter Addressed to the Governors of all the States on the Disbanding of the Army."

I now make it my earnest prayer that God would have you, and the State over which you preside, in His holy protection; that He would incline the hearts of the citizens to cultivate a spirit of subordination and obedience to government, to entertain a brotherly affection and love for one another, for their fellow-citizens of the United States at large, and particularly for brethren who have served in the field; and finally that He would most graciously be pleased to dispose us all to do justice, to love mercy, and to demean ourselves with that charity, humility, and pacific temper of mind, which were the characteristics of the Divine Author of our blessed religion, and without an humble imitation of whose example in these things, we can never hope to be a happy nation.

Meeting Specific Needs

[13]Is anyone among you suffering? Let him pray. Is anyone cheerful? Let him sing psalms. [14]Is anyone among you sick? Let him call for the elders of the church, and let them pray over him, anointing him with oil in the name of the Lord. [15]And the prayer of faith will save the sick, and the Lord will raise him up. And if he has committed sins, he will be forgiven. [16]Confess *your* trespasses[a] to one another, and pray for one another, that you may be healed. The effective, fervent prayer of a righteous man avails much. [17]Elijah was a man with a nature like ours, and he prayed earnestly that it would not rain; and it did not rain on the land for three years and six months. [18]And he prayed again, and the heaven gave rain, and the earth produced its fruit.

Bring Back the Erring One

[19]Brethren, if anyone among you wanders from the truth, and someone turns him back, [20]let him know that he who turns a sinner from the error of his way will save a soul[a] from death and cover a multitude of sins.

5:16 [a]NU-Text reads *Therefore confess your sins.*
5:20 [a]NU-Text reads *his soul.*

1 PETER

Author: Peter

When Written: Around A.D. 64

Theme: Suffering for the Cause of Christ

Key Verses: 1 Peter 4:12, 13—Beloved, do not think it strange concerning the fiery trial which is to try you, as though some strange thing happened to you; but rejoice to the extent that you partake of Christ's sufferings, that when His glory is revealed, you may also be glad with exceeding joy.

Key Chapter: 1 Peter 4—The apostle Peter reveals how to handle persecution and suffering caused by one's Christian testimony. Not only is Christ's suffering our model, but also we are to rejoice in that we share in His suffering.

In writing to Jewish believers struggling in the midst of persecution, Peter encourages them to conduct themselves courageously for the person and message of Christ. He provides them with a divine perspective on these trials so that they will be able to endure them without wavering in their faith. Having been born again to a living hope, they are to imitate the Holy One who has called them.

As the Supreme Commander of the Allied forces in Europe during World War II and later president of the United States, Dwight D. Eisenhower also knew a great deal about the strength of men and women in difficult times. He said, "The spirit of man is more important than mere physical strength, and the spiritual fiber of a nation than its wealth. The Bible is endorsed by the ages. Our civilization is built upon its words. In no other book is there such a collection of inspired wisdom, reality, and hope."

1 PETER

Greeting to the Elect Pilgrims

1 Peter, an apostle of Jesus Christ,

To the pilgrims of the Dispersion in Pontus, Galatia, Cappadocia, Asia, and Bithynia, [2]elect according to the foreknowledge of God the Father, in sanctification of the Spirit, for obedience and sprinkling of the blood of Jesus Christ:

Grace to you and peace be multiplied.

A Heavenly Inheritance

[3]Blessed *be* the God and Father of our Lord Jesus Christ, who according to His abundant mercy has begotten us again to a living hope through the resurrection of Jesus Christ from the dead, [4]to an inheritance incorruptible and undefiled and that does not fade away, reserved in heaven for you, [5]who are kept by the power of God through faith for salvation ready to be revealed in the last time.

[6]In this you greatly rejoice, though now for a little while, if need be, you have been grieved by various trials, [7]that the genuineness of your faith, *being* much more precious than gold that perishes, though it is tested by fire, may be found to praise, honor, and glory at the revelation of Jesus Christ, [8]whom having not seen[a] you love. Though now you do not see *Him,* yet believing, you rejoice with joy inexpressible and full of glory, [9]receiving the end of your faith—the salvation of *your* souls.

[10]Of this salvation the prophets have inquired and searched carefully, who prophesied of the grace *that would come* to you, [11]searching what, or what manner of time, the Spirit of Christ who was in them was indicating when He testified beforehand the sufferings of Christ and the glories that would follow. [12]To them it was revealed that, not to themselves, but to us[a] they were ministering the things which now have been reported to you through those who have preached the gospel to you by the Holy Spirit sent from heaven—things which angels desire to look into.

Living Before God Our Father

[13]Therefore gird up the loins of your mind, be sober, and rest *your* hope fully upon the grace that is to be brought to you at the revelation of Jesus Christ; [14]as obedient children, not conforming yourselves to the former lusts, *as* in your ignorance; [15]but as He who called you *is* holy, you also be holy in all *your* conduct, [16]because it is written, *"Be holy, for I am holy."*[a]

[17]And if you call on the Father, who without partiality judges according to each one's work, conduct yourselves throughout the time of your stay *here* in fear; [18]knowing that you were not redeemed with corruptible things, *like* silver or gold, from your aimless conduct *received* by tradition from your fathers, [19]but with the precious blood of Christ, as of a lamb without blemish and without spot. [20]He indeed was foreordained before the foundation of the world, but was manifest in these last times for you [21]who through Him believe in God, who raised Him from the dead and gave Him glory, so that your faith and hope are in God.

The Enduring Word

[22]Since you have purified your souls in obeying the truth through the Spirit[a] in sincere love of the brethren, love one another fervently with a pure heart, [23]having been born again, not of corruptible seed but incorruptible, through the word of God which lives and abides forever,[a] [24]because

"All flesh is as grass,

1:8 [a]M-Text reads *known.*   **1:12** [a]NU-Text and M-Text read *you.*   **1:16** [a]Leviticus 11:44, 45; 19:2; 20:7   **1:22** [a]NU-Text omits *through the Spirit.* **1:23** [a]NU-Text omits *forever.*

And all the glory of man[a] as the
   flower of the grass.
The grass withers,
And its flower falls away,
25 But the word of the LORD endures
   forever."[a]

Now this is the word which by the gospel was preached to you.

EQUIPPER

. . . through the word of God which lives and abides forever. . . .
           1 PETER 1:23

The Bible Came with Them

Daniel Webster (1782–1852) was a leading American statesman during the nation's Antebellum Period. In 1843, he spoke of the Founding Fathers' regard for the Bible in an address celebrating the completion of the Bunker Hill Monument:

> The Bible came with them. And it is not to be doubted, that to free and universal reading of the Bible, in that age, men were much indebted for right views of civil liberty.

> The Bible is a book of faith, and a book of doctrine, and a book of morals, and a book of religion, of special revelation from God; but it is also a book which teaches man his own individual responsibility, his own dignity, and his equality with his fellowman.

---

2 Therefore, laying aside all malice, all deceit, hypocrisy, envy, and all evil speaking, [2]as newborn babes, desire the pure milk of the word, that you may grow thereby,[a] [3]if indeed you have tasted that the Lord *is* gracious.

The Chosen Stone and His Chosen People

[4]Coming to Him *as to* a living stone, rejected indeed by men, but chosen by God *and* precious, [5]you also, as living stones, are being built up a spiritual house, a holy priesthood, to offer up spiritual sacrifices acceptable to God through Jesus Christ. [6]Therefore it is also contained in the Scripture,

"Behold, I lay in Zion
   A chief cornerstone, elect, precious,

And he who believes on Him will by
   no means be put to shame."[a]

[7]Therefore, to you who believe, *He is* precious; but to those who are disobedient,[a]

"The stone which the builders rejected
   Has become the chief cornerstone,"[b]

[8]and

"A stone of stumbling
   And a rock of offense."[a]

They stumble, being disobedient to the word, to which they also were appointed. [9]But you *are* a chosen generation, a royal priesthood, a holy nation, His own special people, that you may proclaim the praises of Him who called you out of darkness into His marvelous light; [10]who once *were* not a people but *are* now the people of God, who had not obtained mercy but now have obtained mercy.

Living Before the World

[11]Beloved, I beg *you* as sojourners and pilgrims, abstain from fleshly lusts which war against the soul, [12]having your conduct honorable among the Gentiles, that when they speak against you as evildoers, they may, by *your* good works which they observe, glorify God in the day of visitation.

Submission to Government

[13]Therefore submit yourselves to every ordinance of man for the Lord's sake, whether to the king as supreme, [14]or to governors, as to those who are sent by him for the punishment of evildoers and *for the* praise of those who do good. [15]For this is the will of God, that by doing good you may put to silence the ignorance of foolish men— [16]as free, yet not using liberty as a cloak for vice, but as bondservants of God. [17]Honor all *people.* Love the brotherhood. Fear God. Honor the king.

1:24 [a]NU-Text reads *all its glory.*
1:25 [a]Isaiah 40:6–8   **2:2** [a]NU-Text adds *up to salvation.*   **2:6** [a]Isaiah 28:16   **2:7** [a]NU-Text reads *to those who disbelieve.* [b]Psalm 118:22
2:8 [a]Isaiah 8:14

Submission to Masters

18Servants, *be* submissive to *your* masters with all fear, not only to the good and gentle, but also to the harsh. 19For this *is* commendable, if because of conscience toward God one endures grief, suffering wrongfully. 20For what credit *is it* if, when you are beaten for your faults, you take it patiently? But when you do good and suffer, if you take it patiently, this *is* commendable before God. 21For to this you were called, because Christ also suffered for us,a leaving usb an example, that you should follow His steps:

22 *"Who committed no sin,*
Nor was deceit found in His mouth";a

23who, when He was reviled, did not revile in return; when He suffered, He did not threaten, but committed *Himself* to Him who judges righteously; 24who Himself bore our sins in His own body on the tree, that we, having died to sins, might live for righteousness—by whose stripes you were healed. 25For you were like sheep going astray, but have now returned to the Shepherd and Overseera of your souls.

Submission to Husbands

3 Wives, likewise, *be* submissive to your own husbands, that even if some do not obey the word, they, without a word, may be won by the conduct of their wives, 2when they observe your chaste conduct *accompanied* by fear. 3Do not let your adornment be *merely* outward—arranging the hair, wearing gold, or putting on *fine* apparel— 4rather *let it be* the hidden person of the heart, with the incorruptible *beauty* of a gentle and quiet spirit, which is very precious in the sight of God. 5For in this manner, in former times, the holy women who trusted in God also adorned themselves, being submissive to their own husbands, 6as Sarah obeyed Abraham, calling him lord, whose daughters you are if you do good and are not afraid with any terror.

2:21 aNU-Text reads *you.* bNU-Text and M-Text read *you.* **2:22** aIsaiah 53:9 **2:25** aGreek *Episkopos*

FREEDOM

. . . as free, yet not using liberty as a cloak for vice, but as bondservants of God.

1 PETER 2:16

Will Durant

FREEDOM MUST BE PRACTICED

We must be free not because we claim freedom, but because we practice it.   WILLIAM FAULKNER

Have we too much freedom? Have we so long ridiculed authority in the family, discipline in education, rules in art, decency in conduct, and law in the state that our liberation has brought us close to chaos in the family and the school, in morals, arts, ideas, and government? We forgot to make ourselves intelligent when we made ourselves free.
                                                                    WILL DURANT

We proclaim ourselves as indeed we are: the defenders of freedom, wherever it continues to exist in the world. But we cannot defend freedom abroad by deserting it at home.
                                                            EDWARD R. MURROW

Injustice anywhere is a threat to justice everywhere.
                                                        MARTIN LUTHER KING JR.

No one is free when others are oppressed.
                                                                    UNKNOWN

A Word to Husbands

[7]Husbands, likewise, dwell with *them* with understanding, giving honor to the wife, as to the weaker vessel, and as *being* heirs together of the grace of life, that your prayers may not be hindered.

Called to Blessing

[8]Finally, all *of you be* of one mind, having compassion for one another; love as brothers, *be* tenderhearted, *be* courteous;[a] [9]not returning evil for evil or reviling for reviling, but on the contrary blessing, knowing that you were called to this, that you may inherit a blessing. [10]For

> "He who would love life
> And see good days,
> Let him refrain his tongue from evil,
> And his lips from speaking deceit.
> [11] Let him turn away from evil and do
>   good;
> Let him seek peace and pursue it.
> [12] For the eyes of the LORD are on the
>   righteous,
> And His ears are open to their prayers;
> But the face of the LORD is against
>   those who do evil."[a]

Suffering for Right and Wrong

[13]And who *is* he who will harm you if you become followers of what is good? [14]But even if you should suffer for righteousness' sake, *you are* blessed. *"And do not be afraid of their threats, nor be troubled."*[a] [15]But sanctify the Lord God[a] in your hearts, and always *be* ready to *give* a defense to everyone who asks you a reason for the hope that is in you, with meekness and fear; [16]having a good conscience, that when they defame you as evildoers, those who revile your good conduct in Christ may be ashamed. [17]For *it is* better, if it is the will of God, to suffer for doing good than for doing evil.

Christ's Suffering and Ours

[18]For Christ also suffered once for sins, the just for the unjust, that He might bring us[a] to God, being put to death in the flesh but made alive by the Spirit, [19]by whom also He went and preached to the spirits in prison, [20]who formerly were disobedient,

---

3:8 [a]NU-Text reads *humble.*   **3:12** [a]Psalm 34:12–16
3:14 [a]Isaiah 8:12   **3:15** [a]NU-Text reads *Christ as Lord.*   **3:18** [a]NU-Text and M-Text read *you.*

MORAL STRENGTH

. . . leaving us an example, that you should follow His steps. . . .

1 PETER 2:21

Major General Wesley Merritt

RULES OF MORAL ACTION

Wesley Merritt, a Major General in the Union Army during the Civil War and the superintendent of the U.S. Military Academy at West Point (1882–1887), stated:

The principles of life as taught in the Bible, the inspired Word, and exemplified in the matchless life of Him "who spake as never man spake," are the rules of moral action which have resulted in civilizing the world.

The testimony of great men, like Gladstone and his fellow statesmen; like Havelock and his fellow soldiers, who have made the teachings of the Scriptures their rule of conduct in life, are wonderful helps to men of lesser note and smaller intellectual and moral powers. One example, even of the smallest of these, more than offsets the efforts of an hundred unbelievers in active opposition.

They are the worthy followers of the religion of the Bible, and in their daily lives interpret the inimitable example and Divine precepts of the Son of God, our Savior.

when once the Divine longsuffering wait-ed[a] in the days of Noah, while *the* ark was being prepared, in which a few, that is, eight souls, were saved through water. [21]There is also an antitype which now saves us—baptism (not the removal of the filth of the flesh, but the answer of a good conscience toward God), through the resurrection of Jesus Christ, [22]who has gone into heaven and is at the right hand of God, angels and authorities and powers having been made subject to Him.

4 Therefore, since Christ suffered for us[a] in the flesh, arm yourselves also with the same mind, for he who has suffered in the flesh has ceased from sin, [2]that he no longer should live the rest of *his* time in the flesh for the lusts of men, but for the will of God. [3]For we *have spent* enough of our past lifetime[a] in doing the will of the Gentiles—when we walked in lewdness, lusts, drunkenness, revelries, drinking parties, and abominable idolatries. [4]In regard to these, they think it strange that you do not run with *them* in the same flood of dissipation, speaking evil of *you.* [5]They will give an account to Him who is ready to judge the living and the dead. [6]For this reason the gospel was preached also to those who are dead, that they might be judged according to men in the flesh, but live according to God in the spirit.

Serving for God's Glory

[7]But the end of all things is at hand; therefore be serious and watchful in your prayers. [8]And above all things have fervent love for one another, for *"love will cover a multitude of sins."*[a] [9]*Be* hospitable to one another without grumbling. [10]As each one has received a gift, minister it to one another, as good stewards of the manifold grace of God. [11]If anyone speaks, *let him speak* as the oracles of God. If anyone ministers, *let him do it* as with the ability which God supplies, that in all things God may be glorified through Jesus Christ, to whom belong the glory and the dominion forever and ever. Amen.

Suffering for God's Glory

[12]Beloved, do not think it strange concerning the fiery trial which is to try you,

as though some strange thing happened to you; [13]but rejoice to the extent that you partake of Christ's sufferings, that when His glory is revealed, you may also be glad with exceeding joy. [14]If you are reproached for the name of Christ, blessed *are you,* for the Spirit of glory and of God rests upon you.[a] On their part He is blasphemed, but on your part He is glorified. [15]But let none of you suffer as a murderer, a thief, an evildoer, or as a busybody in other people's matters. [16]Yet if *anyone suffers* as a Christian, let him not be ashamed, but let him glorify God in this matter.[a]

[17]For the time *has come* for judgment to begin at the house of God; and if *it begins* with us first, what will *be* the end of those who do not obey the gospel of God? [18]Now

"If the righteous one is scarcely saved,
Where will the ungodly and the sinner
appear?"[a]

[19]Therefore let those who suffer according to the will of God commit their souls *to Him* in doing good, as to a faithful Creator.

Shepherd the Flock

5 The elders who are among you I exhort, I who am a fellow elder and a witness of the sufferings of Christ, and also a partaker of the glory that will be revealed: [2]Shepherd the flock of God which is among you, serving as overseers, not by compulsion but willingly,[a] not for dishonest gain but eagerly; [3]nor as being lords over those entrusted to you, but being examples to the flock; [4]and when the Chief Shepherd appears, you will receive the crown of glory that does not fade away.

Submit to God, Resist the Devil

[5]Likewise you younger people, submit yourselves to *your* elders. Yes, all of *you* be submissive to one another, and be clothed with humility, for

---

3:20 [a]NU-Text and M-Text read *when the longsuffering of God waited patiently.*   **4:1** [a]NU-Text omits *for us.*   **4:3** [a]NU-Text reads *time.*   **4:8** [a]Proverbs 10:12   **4:14** [a]NU-Text omits the rest of this verse.   **4:16** [a]NU-Text reads *name.*   **4:18** [a]Proverbs 11:31   **5:2** [a]NU-Text adds *according to God.*

"God resists the proud,
*But gives grace to the humble."*ᵃ

⁶Therefore humble yourselves under the mighty hand of God, that He may exalt you in due time, ⁷casting all your care upon Him, for He cares for you.

⁸Be sober, be vigilant; becauseᵃ your adversary the devil walks about like a roaring lion, seeking whom he may devour. ⁹Resist him, steadfast in the faith, knowing that the same sufferings are experienced by your brotherhood in the world. ¹⁰But mayᵃ the God of all grace, who called usᵇ to His eternal glory by Christ Jesus, after you have suffered a while, perfect, establish, strengthen, and settle *you.* ¹¹To Him *be* the glory and the dominion forever and ever. Amen.

Farewell and Peace

¹²By Silvanus, our faithful brother as I consider him, I have written to you briefly, exhorting and testifying that this is the true grace of God in which you stand.

¹³She who is in Babylon, elect together with *you,* greets you; and *so does* Mark my son. ¹⁴Greet one another with a kiss of love.

Peace to you all who are in Christ Jesus. Amen.

5:5 ᵃProverbs 3:34   **5:8** ᵃNU-Text and M-Text omit *because.*   **5:10** ᵃNU-Text reads *But the God of all grace . . . will perfect, establish, strengthen, and settle you.* ᵇNU-Text and M-Text read *you.*

2 PETER

Author: Peter

When Written: Around A.D. 66

Theme: Guard Against False Teachers

Key Verses: 2 Peter 1:20, 21—. . . knowing this first, that no prophecy of Scripture is of any private interpretation, for prophecy never came by the will of man, but holy men of God spoke as they were moved by the Holy Spirit.

Key Chapter: 2 Peter 1—This chapter clearly defines the relationship between God and man on the issue of inspiration and the interpretation of Scriptures.

Peter wrote his first epistle to deal with problems associated with persecution. His second epistle warns the believers about the false teachers whose heresies can seduce believers into error and immorality. Peter stresses the need for diligence and growth in the grace and knowledge of Christ as the antidote for error.

The apostle begins by urging his readers to keep a close watch over their personal lives. The false teachers are sensual, arrogant, greedy, and covetous, whereas the Christian life demands pursuing godliness, virtue, knowledge, patience, and brotherly kindness. Benjamin Franklin had a similar warning for his fellow citizens: "A great empire, like a great cake, is most easily diminished from its edges."

2 PETER

Greeting the Faithful

1 Simon Peter, a bondservant and apostle of Jesus Christ,

To those who have obtained like precious faith with us by the righteousness of our God and Savior Jesus Christ:

²Grace and peace be multiplied to you in the knowledge of God and of Jesus our Lord, ³as His divine power has given to us all things that *pertain* to life and godliness, through the knowledge of Him who called us by glory and virtue, ⁴by which have been given to us exceedingly great and precious promises, that through these you may be partakers of the divine nature, having escaped the corruption *that is* in the world through lust.

Fruitful Growth in the Faith

⁵But also for this very reason, giving all diligence, add to your faith virtue, to virtue knowledge, ⁶to knowledge self-control, to self-control perseverance, to perseverance godliness, ⁷to godliness brotherly kindness, and to brotherly kindness love. ⁸For if these things are yours and abound, *you* will be neither barren nor unfruitful in the knowledge of our Lord Jesus Christ. ⁹For he who lacks these things is shortsighted, even to blindness, and has forgotten that he was cleansed from his old sins.

¹⁰Therefore, brethren, be even more diligent to make your call and election sure, for if you do these things you will never stumble; ¹¹for so an entrance will be supplied to you abundantly into the everlasting kingdom of our Lord and Savior Jesus Christ.

Peter's Approaching Death

¹²For this reason I will not be negligent to remind you always of these things, though you know and are established in the present truth. ¹³Yes, I think it is right, as long as I am in this tent, to stir you up by reminding *you,* ¹⁴knowing that shortly I *must* put off my tent, just as our Lord Jesus Christ showed me. ¹⁵Moreover I will be careful to ensure that you always have a reminder of these things after my decease.

The Trustworthy Prophetic Word

¹⁶For we did not follow cunningly devised fables when we made known to you the power and coming of our Lord Jesus Christ, but were eyewitnesses of His majesty. ¹⁷For He received from God the Father honor and glory when such a voice came to Him from the Excellent Glory: "This is My beloved Son, in whom I am well pleased." ¹⁸And we heard this voice which came from heaven when we were with Him on the holy mountain.

¹⁹And so we have the prophetic word confirmed,ᵃ which you do well to heed as a light that shines in a dark place, until the day dawns and the morning star rises in your hearts; ²⁰knowing this first, that no prophecy of Scripture is of any private interpretation,ᵃ ²¹for prophecy never came by the will of man, but holy men of Godᵃ spoke *as they were* moved by the Holy Spirit.

Destructive Doctrines

2 But there were also false prophets among the people, even as there will be false teachers among you, who will secretly bring in destructive heresies, even denying the Lord who bought them, *and* bring on themselves swift destruction. ²And many will follow their destructive ways, because of whom the way of truth will be blasphemed. ³By covetousness they will exploit you with deceptive words; for a long time their judgment has not been idle, and their destruction doesᵃ not slumber.

1:19 ᵃOr *We also have the more sure prophetic word.*
1:20 ᵃOr *origin*   **1:21** ᵃNU-Text reads *but men spoke from God.*   **2:3** ᵃM-Text reads *will not.*

Doom of False Teachers

⁴For if God did not spare the angels who sinned, but cast *them* down to hell and delivered *them* into chains of darkness, to be reserved for judgment; ⁵and did not spare the ancient world, but saved Noah, *one of eight people,* a preacher of righteousness, bringing in the flood on the world of the ungodly; ⁶and turning the cities of Sodom and Gomorrah into ashes, condemned *them* to destruction, making *them* an example to those who afterward would live ungodly; ⁷and delivered righteous Lot, *who was* oppressed by the filthy conduct of the wicked ⁸(for that righteous man, dwelling among them, tormented *his* righteous soul from day to day by seeing and hearing *their* lawless deeds)— ⁹*then* the Lord knows how to deliver the godly out of temptations and to reserve the unjust under punishment for the day of judgment, ¹⁰and especially those who walk according to the flesh in the lust of uncleanness and despise authority. *They are* presumptuous, self-willed. They are not afraid to speak evil of dignitaries, ¹¹whereas angels, who are greater in power and might, do not bring a reviling accusation against them before the Lord.

Depravity of False Teachers

¹²But these, like natural brute beasts made to be caught and destroyed, speak evil of the things they do not understand, and will utterly perish in their own corruption, ¹³*and* will receive the wages of unrighteousness, *as* those who count it pleasure to carouse in the daytime. *They are* spots and blemishes, carousing in their own deceptions while they feast with you, ¹⁴having

Charles Anderson Dana

EQUIPPER

For we did not follow cunningly devised fables. . . .

2 PETER 1:16

NO BOOK LIKE THE BIBLE

Charles Anderson Dana (1819–1897) was the editor-in-chief of the *New York Sun*, one of the largest newspapers in the country, and considered by many the most brilliant journalist in the country at that time. He wrote:

> *I believe in Christianity; that it is the religion taught to men by God Himself in person on earth. I also believe the Bible to be a Divine revelation. Christianity is not comparable with any other religion. It is the religion which came from God's own lips, and therefore the only true religion. The incarnation is a fact, and Christianity is based on revealed truth.*
>
> *There are some books that are absolutely indispensable to the kind of education that we are contemplating, and to the profession that we are now considering; and of all these, the most indispensable, the most useful, the one whose knowledge is most effective, is the Bible. There is no book from which more valuable lessons can be learned. I am considering it now as a manual of utility, or professional preparation, and professional use for a journalist.*
>
> *There is no book whose style is more suggestive and more instructive, from which you learn more directly that sublime simplicity which never exaggerates, which recounts the greatest event with solemnity, of course, but without sentimentality or affection, none which you open with such confidence and lay down with such reverence; there is no book like the Bible.*

eyes full of adultery and that cannot cease from sin, enticing unstable souls. They have a heart trained in covetous practices, *and are* accursed children. 15They have forsaken the right way and gone astray, following the way of Balaam the *son* of Beor, who loved the wages of unrighteousness; 16but he was rebuked for his iniquity: a dumb donkey speaking with a man's voice restrained the madness of the prophet.

17These are wells without water, clouds[a] carried by a tempest, for whom is reserved the blackness of darkness forever.[b]

DEFENDER

. . . they themselves are slaves of corruption. . . .

2 PETER 2:19

Christianity and Republicanism

Benjamin Rush, a signer of the Declaration of Independence, wrote in a letter to Thomas Jefferson:

I have always considered Christianity as the strong ground of republicanism. The spirit is opposed, not only to the splendor, but even to the very forms of monarchy, and many of its precepts have for their objects republican liberty and equality as well as simplicity, integrity, and economy in government. It is only necessary for republicanism to ally itself to the Christian religion to overturn all the corrupted political and religious institutions in the world.

Deceptions of False Teachers

18For when they speak great swelling *words* of emptiness, they allure through the lusts of the flesh, through lewdness, the ones who have actually escaped[a] from those who live in error. 19While they promise them liberty, they themselves are slaves of corruption; for by whom a person is overcome, by him also he is brought into bondage. 20For if, after they have escaped the pollutions of the world through the knowledge of the Lord and Savior Jesus Christ, they are again entangled in them and overcome, the latter end is worse for them than the beginning. 21For it would have been better for them not to have known the way of righteousness, than having known *it,* to turn from the holy commandment delivered to them. 22But it has

happened to them according to the true proverb: *"A dog returns to his own vomit,"*[a] and, "a sow, having washed, to her wallowing in the mire."

God's Promise Is Not Slack

3 Beloved, I now write to you this second epistle (in *both of* which I stir up your pure minds by way of reminder), 2that you may be mindful of the words which were spoken before by the holy prophets, and of the commandment of us,[a] the apostles of the Lord and Savior, 3knowing this first: that scoffers will come in the last days, walking according to their own lusts, 4and saying, "Where is the promise of His coming? For since the fathers fell asleep, all things continue as *they were* from the beginning of creation." 5For this they willfully forget: that by the word of God the heavens were of old, and the earth standing out of water and in the water, 6by which the world *that* then existed perished, being flooded with water. 7But the heavens and the earth *which* are now preserved by the same word, are reserved for fire until the day of judgment and perdition of ungodly men.

8But, beloved, do not forget this one thing, that with the Lord one day *is* as a thousand years, and a thousand years as one day. 9The Lord is not slack concerning *His* promise, as some count slackness, but is longsuffering toward us,[a] not willing that any should perish but that all should come to repentance.

The Day of the Lord

10But the day of the Lord will come as a thief in the night, in which the heavens will pass away with a great noise, and the elements will melt with fervent heat; both the earth and the works that are in it will be burned up.[a] 11Therefore, since all these things will be dissolved, what manner *of*

2:17 aNU-Text reads *and mists.* bNU-Text omits *forever.*
2:18 aNU-Text reads *are barely escaping.*
2:22 aProverbs 26:11　　**3:2** aNU-Text and M-Text read *commandment of the apostles of your Lord and Savior* or *commandment of your apostles of the Lord and Savior.*　　**3:9** aNU-Text reads *you.*　　**3:10** aNU-Text reads *laid bare* (literally *found*).

persons ought you to be in holy conduct and godliness, [12]looking for and hastening the coming of the day of God, because of which the heavens will be dissolved, being on fire, and the elements will melt with fervent heat? [13]Nevertheless we, according to His promise, look for new heavens and a new earth in which righteousness dwells.

Be Steadfast

[14]Therefore, beloved, looking forward to these things, be diligent to be found by Him in peace, without spot and blameless; [15]and consider *that* the longsuffering of our Lord *is* salvation—as also our beloved brother Paul, according to the wisdom given to him, has written to you, [16]as also in all his epistles, speaking in them of these things, in which are some things hard to understand, which untaught and unstable *people* twist to their own destruction, *as they do* also the rest of the Scriptures.

[17]You therefore, beloved, since you know *this* beforehand, beware lest you also fall from your own steadfastness, being led away with the error of the wicked; [18]but grow in the grace and knowledge of our Lord and Savior Jesus Christ.

To Him *be* the glory both now and forever. Amen.

1 JOHN

Author: John

When Written: Around A.D. 90

Theme: Fellowship with God

Key Verses: 1 John 1:3, 4—...that which we have seen and heard we declare to you, that you also may have fellowship with us; and truly our fellowship is with the Father and with His Son Jesus Christ. And these things we write to you that your joy may be full.

Key Chapter: 1 John 1—The apostle John points out that when Christians do not abide in Christ, they break fellowship with God and must seek forgiveness before fellowship can be restored.

John writes his epistle at a time when apostolic doctrine is being challenged by a proliferation of false teachings. He writes to refute erroneous doctrine and to encourage its readers to walk in the knowledge of the truth. John lists the criteria and characteristics of fellowship with God and shows that those who abide in Christ can have confidence and assurance before Him.

Just as the apostle reminded his readers of the divinity of Jesus and the marvelous fact of being children of God, President Woodrow Wilson reminds us that "a nation that does not remember what it was yesterday, does not know what it is today, nor what it is trying to do. We are trying to do a futile thing if we do not know where we came from or what we have been about."

1 JOHN

What Was Heard, Seen, and Touched

1 That which was from the beginning, which we have heard, which we have seen with our eyes, which we have looked upon, and our hands have handled, concerning the Word of life— ²the life was manifested, and we have seen, and bear witness, and declare to you that eternal life which was with the Father and was manifested to us— ³that which we have seen and heard we declare to you, that you also may have fellowship with us; and truly our fellowship *is* with the Father and with His Son Jesus Christ. ⁴And these things we write to you that your[a] joy may be full.

Fellowship with Him and One Another

⁵This is the message which we have heard from Him and declare to you, that God is light and in Him is no darkness at all. ⁶If we say that we have fellowship with Him, and walk in darkness, we lie and do not practice the truth. ⁷But if we walk in the light as He is in the light, we have fellowship with one another, and the blood of Jesus Christ His Son cleanses us from all sin.

⁸If we say that we have no sin, we deceive ourselves, and the truth is not in us. ⁹If we confess our sins, He is faithful and just to forgive us *our* sins and to cleanse us from all unrighteousness. ¹⁰If we say that we have not sinned, we make Him a liar, and His word is not in us.

2 My little children, these things I write to you, so that you may not sin. And if anyone sins, we have an Advocate with the Father, Jesus Christ the righteous. ²And He Himself is the propitiation for our sins, and not for ours only but also for the whole world.

The Test of Knowing Him

³Now by this we know that we know Him, if we keep His commandments. ⁴He who says, "I know Him," and does not keep His commandments, is a liar, and the truth is not in him. ⁵But whoever keeps His word, truly the love of God is perfected in him. By this we know that we are in Him. ⁶He who says he abides in Him ought himself also to walk just as He walked.

⁷Brethren,[a] I write no new commandment to you, but an old commandment which you have had from the beginning. The old commandment is the word which you heard from the beginning.[b] ⁸Again, a new commandment I write to you, which thing is true in Him and in you, because the darkness is passing away, and the true light is already shining.

⁹He who says he is in the light, and hates his brother, is in darkness until now. ¹⁰He who loves his brother abides in the light, and there is no cause for stumbling in him. ¹¹But he who hates his brother is in darkness and walks in darkness, and does not know where he is going, because the darkness has blinded his eyes.

Their Spiritual State

12 I write to you, little children,
　　Because your sins are forgiven you
　　　　for His name's sake.
13 I write to you, fathers,
　　Because you have known Him *who
　　　　is* from the beginning.
I write to you, young men,
　　Because you have overcome the
　　　　wicked one.
I write to you, little children,
　　Because you have known the Father.
14 I have written to you, fathers,
　　Because you have known Him *who
　　　　is* from the beginning.
I have written to you, young men,
　　Because you are strong, and the
　　　　word of God abides in you,
　　And you have overcome the wicked
　　　　one.

1:4 ᵃNU-Text and M-Text read *our.* 2:7 ᵃNU-Text reads *Beloved.* ᵇNU-Text omits *from the beginning.*

A CHURCHLESS NATION

THEODORE ROOSEVELT

In 1917, Theodore Roosevelt, 26th president of the United States, stated:

The most perfect machinery of government will not keep us as a nation from destruction if there is not within us a soul. No abounding material prosperity shall avail us if our spiritual senses atrophy. The foes of our own household shall surely prevail against us unless there be in our people an inner life which finds its outward expression in a morality not very widely different from that preached by the seers and prophets of Judea when the grandeur that was Greece and the glory that was Rome still lay in the future.

In his Farewell Address to his countryman, Washington said: "Morality is a necessary spring of popular government . . . and let us with caution indulge the supposition that morality can be maintained without religion. Whatever may be conceded to the influence of refined education on minds of peculiar structure, reason and experience both forbid us to expect that national morality can prevail in exclusion of religious principle."

. . . [His words were] given expression when the European movement with which the American people were in most complete sympathy— the French Revolution—had endeavored to destroy the abuses of priestcraft and bigotry by abolishing not only Christianity but religion, . . . The result was a cynical disregard of morality and a carnival of cruelty and bigotry, committed in the name of reason and liberty, which equaled anything ever done by Torquemada and the fanatics of the Inquisition in the name of religion and order. Washington wished his fellow countrymen to walk clear of such folly and iniquity. As in all cases where he dealt with continuing causes, his words are as well worth pondering now as when they were written. . . .

In this actual world, a churchless community, a community where men have abandoned and scoff at or ignore their Christian duties, is a community on the rapid downgrade. It is perfectly true that occasional individuals or families may have nothing to do with church or with religious practices and observances and yet maintain the highest standard of spirituality and of ethical obligation. But this does not affect the case in the world as it now is, any more than that exceptional men and women under exceptional conditions have disregarded the marriage tie without moral harm to themselves interferes with the larger fact that such disregard if at all common means the complete moral disintegration of the body politic.

Do Not Love the World

¹⁵Do not love the world or the things in the world. If anyone loves the world, the love of the Father is not in him. ¹⁶For all that *is* in the world—the lust of the flesh, the lust of the eyes, and the pride of life—is not of the Father but is of the world. ¹⁷And the world is passing away, and the lust of it; but he who does the will of God abides forever.

Deceptions of the Last Hour

¹⁸Little children, it is the last hour; and as you have heard that theᵃ Antichrist is coming, even now many antichrists have come, by which we know that it is the last hour. ¹⁹They went out from us, but they were not of us; for if they had been of us, they would have continued with us; but *they went out* that they might be made manifest, that none of them were of us. ²⁰But you have an anointing from the Holy One, and you know all things.ᵃ ²¹I have not written to you because you do not know the truth, but because you know it, and that no lie is of the truth.

²²Who is a liar but he who denies that Jesus is the Christ? He is antichrist who denies the Father and the Son. ²³Whoever denies the Son does not have the Father either; he who acknowledges the Son has the Father also.

Let Truth Abide in You

²⁴Therefore let that abide in you which you heard from the beginning. If what you heard from the beginning abides in you, you also will abide in the Son and in the Father. ²⁵And this is the promise that He has promised us—eternal life.

²⁶These things I have written to you concerning those who *try to* deceive you. ²⁷But the anointing which you have received from Him abides in you, and you do not

---

2:18 ᵃNU-Text omits *the*.   **2:20** ᵃNU-Text reads *you all know*.

MORAL STRENGTH

Behold what manner of love the Father has bestowed on us. . . .

1 JOHN 3:1

Benjamin Franklin Butler

THE PUREST MORALITY

Benjamin Franklin Butler (1795–1858), a lawyer who served as the U.S. Attorney General under President Andrew Jackson (1833–1838), stated:

He is truly happy, whatever may be his temporal condition, who can call God his Father in the full assurance of faith and hope. And amid all his trials, conflicts, and doubts, the feeblest Christian is still comparatively happy; because cheered by the hope . . . that the hour is coming when he shall be delivered from "this body of sin and death" and in the vision of his Redeemer . . . approximate to the . . . felicity of angels.

Not only does the Bible inculcate, with sanctions of the highest import, a system of the purest morality, but in the person and character of our Blessed Savior it exhibits a tangible illustration of that system.

In Him we have set before us—what, till the publication of the Gospel, the world had never seen—a model of feeling and action, adapted to all times, places, and circumstances; and combining so much of wisdom, benevolence, and holiness, that none can fathom its sublimity; and yet, presented in a form so simple, that even a child may be made to understand and taught to love it.

need that anyone teach you; but as the same anointing teaches you concerning all things, and is true, and is not a lie, and just as it has taught you, you will[a] abide in Him.

The Children of God

28And now, little children, abide in Him, that when[a] He appears, we may have confidence and not be ashamed before Him at His coming. 29If you know that He is righteous, you know that everyone who practices righteousness is born of Him.

3 Behold what manner of love the Father has bestowed on us, that we should be called children of God![a] Therefore the world does not know us,[b] because it did not know Him. 2Beloved, now we are children of God; and it has not yet been revealed what we shall be, but we know that when He is revealed, we shall be like Him, for we shall see Him as He is. 3And everyone who has this hope in Him purifies himself, just as He is pure.

Sin and the Child of God

4Whoever commits sin also commits lawlessness, and sin is lawlessness. 5And you know that He was manifested to take away our sins, and in Him there is no sin. 6Whoever abides in Him does not sin. Whoever sins has neither seen Him nor known Him.

7Little children, let no one deceive you. He who practices righteousness is righteous, just as He is righteous. 8He who sins is of the devil, for the devil has sinned from the beginning. For this purpose the Son of God was manifested, that He might destroy the works of the devil. 9Whoever has been born of God does not sin, for His seed remains in him; and he cannot sin, because he has been born of God.

The Imperative of Love

10In this the children of God and the children of the devil are manifest: Whoever does not practice righteousness is not of God, nor is he who does not love his brother. 11For this is the message that you heard from the beginning, that we should love one another, 12not as Cain who was of the wicked one and murdered his brother. And

why did he murder him? Because his works were evil and his brother's righteous.

13Do not marvel, my brethren, if the world hates you. 14We know that we have passed from death to life, because we love the brethren. He who does not love his brother[a] abides in death. 15Whoever hates his brother is a murderer, and you know that no murderer has eternal life abiding in him.

The Outworking of Love

16By this we know love, because He laid down His life for us. And we also ought to lay down our lives for the brethren. 17But whoever has this world's goods, and sees his brother in need, and shuts up his heart from him, how does the love of God abide in him? 18My little children, let us not love in word or in tongue, but in deed and in truth. 19And by this we know[a] that we are of the truth, and shall assure our hearts before Him. 20For if our heart condemns us, God is greater than our heart, and knows all things. 21Beloved, if our heart does not condemn us, we have confidence toward God. 22And whatever we ask we receive from Him, because we keep His commandments and do those things that are pleasing in His sight. 23And this is His commandment: that we should believe on the name of His Son Jesus Christ and love one another, as He gave us[a] commandment.

The Spirit of Truth and the Spirit of Error

24Now he who keeps His commandments abides in Him, and He in him. And by this we know that He abides in us, by the Spirit whom He has given us.

4 Beloved, do not believe every spirit, but test the spirits, whether they are of God; because many false prophets have gone out into the world. 2By this you know the Spirit of God: Every spirit that confesses that Jesus Christ has come in the flesh is of God, 3and every spirit that does not confess that[a] Jesus Christ has come in the flesh is

---

2:27 [a]NU-Text reads you abide.   **2:28** [a]NU-Text reads if.   **3:1** [a]NU-Text adds And we are. [b]M-Text reads you.   **3:14** [a]NU-Text omits his brother.   **3:19** [a]NU-Text reads we shall know.   **3:23** [a]M-Text omits us.   **4:3** [a]NU-Text omits that and Christ has come in the flesh.

not of God. And this is the *spirit* of the Antichrist, which you have heard was coming, and is now already in the world.

[4]You are of God, little children, and have overcome them, because He who is in you is greater than he who is in the world. [5]They are of the world. Therefore they speak *as* of the world, and the world hears them. [6]We are of God. He who knows God hears us; he who is not of God does not hear us. By this we know the spirit of truth and the spirit of error.

Knowing God Through Love

[7]Beloved, let us love one another, for love is of God; and everyone who loves is born of God and knows God. [8]He who does not love does not know God, for God is love. [9]In this the love of God was manifested toward us, that God has sent His only begotten Son into the world, that we might live through Him. [10]In this is love, not that we loved God, but that He loved us and sent His Son *to be* the propitiation for our sins. [11]Beloved, if God so loved us, we also ought to love one another.

Seeing God Through Love

[12]No one has seen God at any time. If we love one another, God abides in us, and His love has been perfected in us. [13]By this we know that we abide in Him, and He in us, because He has given us of His Spirit. [14]And we have seen and testify that the Father has sent the Son *as* Savior of the world. [15]Whoever confesses that Jesus is the Son of God, God abides in him, and he in God. [16]And we have known and believed the love that God has for us. God is love, and he who abides in love abides in God, and God in him.

The Consummation of Love

[17]Love has been perfected among us in this: that we may have boldness in the day of judgment; because as He is, so are we in this world. [18]There is no fear in love; but perfect love casts out fear, because fear involves torment. But he who fears has not been made perfect in love. [19]We love Him[a] because He first loved us.

Obedience by Faith

[20]If someone says, "I love God," and hates his brother, he is a liar; for he who does not love his brother whom he has seen, how can[a] he love God whom he has not seen? [21]And this commandment we have from Him: that he who loves God *must* love his brother also.

5 Whoever believes that Jesus is the Christ is born of God, and everyone who loves Him who begot also loves him who is begotten of Him. [2]By this we know that we love the children of God, when we love God and keep His commandments. [3]For this is the love of God, that we keep His commandments. And His commandments are not burdensome. [4]For whatever is born of God overcomes the world. And this is the victory that has overcome the world—our[a] faith. [5]Who is he who overcomes the world, but he who believes that Jesus is the Son of God?

The Certainty of God's Witness

[6]This is He who came by water and blood—Jesus Christ; not only by water, but by water and blood. And it is the Spirit who bears witness, because the Spirit is truth. [7]For there are three that bear witness in heaven: the Father, the Word, and the Holy Spirit; and these three are one. [8]And there are three that bear witness on earth:[a] the Spirit, the water, and the blood; and these three agree as one.

[9]If we receive the witness of men, the witness of God is greater; for this is the witness of God which[a] He has testified of His Son. [10]He who believes in the Son of God has the witness in himself; he who does not believe God has made Him a liar, because he has not believed the testimony that God has given of His Son. [11]And this is the testimony: that God has given us eternal life, and this life is in His Son. [12]He who has the Son has life; he who does not have the Son of God does not have life. [13]These things I have written

---

4:19 [a]NU-Text omits *Him.*   **4:20** [a]NU-Text reads *he cannot.*   **5:4** [a]M-Text reads *your.*   **5:8** [a]NU-Text and M-Text omit the words from *in heaven* (verse 7) through *on earth* (verse 8). Only four or five very late manuscripts contain these words in Greek.
5:9 [a]NU-Text reads *God, that.*

to you who believe in the name of the Son of God, that you may know that you have eternal life,[a] and that you may *continue to* believe in the name of the Son of God.

Confidence and Compassion in Prayer

[14]Now this is the confidence that we have in Him, that if we ask anything according to His will, He hears us. [15]And if we know that He hears us, whatever we ask, we know that we have the petitions that we have asked of Him.

[16]If anyone sees his brother sinning a sin *which does* not *lead* to death, he will ask, and He will give him life for those who commit sin not *leading* to death. There is sin *leading* to death. I do not say that he should pray about that. [17]All unrighteousness is sin, and there is sin not *leading* to death.

Knowing the True—Rejecting the False

[18]We know that whoever is born of God does not sin; but he who has been born of God keeps himself,[a] and the wicked one does not touch him.

[19]We know that we are of God, and the whole world lies *under the sway of* the wicked one.

[20]And we know that the Son of God has come and has given us an understanding, that we may know Him who is true; and we are in Him who is true, in His Son Jesus Christ. This is the true God and eternal life.

[21]Little children, keep yourselves from idols. Amen.

5:13 [a]NU-Text omits the rest of this verse.
5:18 [a]NU-Text reads *him.*

2 JOHN

Author: John

When Written: Around A.D. 90

Theme: Avoid Fellowship with False Teachers

Key Verses: 2 John 9, 10—Whoever transgresses and does not abide in the doctrine of Christ does not have God. He who abides in the doctrine of Christ has both the Father and the Son. If anyone comes to you and does not bring this doctrine, do not receive him into your house nor greet him. . . .

Having much in common with 1 John, this epistle includes a warning about the danger of false teachers who deny the incarnation of Christ. Christian love must be discerning, and false charity opens the door to false teaching. We must have fellowship with Christians, but not with false teachers. John is insistent that "the elect lady and her children" deny even the slightest assistance to itinerant teachers who promote an erroneous view of Christ.

The apostle would have concurred with Elias Boudinot, a Founding Father and the president of the Continental Congress (1782–1783), who said, "Good government generally begins in the family, and if the moral character of a people once degenerate, their political character must soon follow." If you allow a bit of heresy or evil into the home, it will spread out into the church and into the world.

2 JOHN

Greeting the Elect Lady

The Elder,

To the elect lady and her children, whom I love in truth, and not only I, but also all those who have known the truth, [2]because of the truth which abides in us and will be with us forever:

[3]Grace, mercy, *and* peace will be with you[a] from God the Father and from the Lord Jesus Christ, the Son of the Father, in truth and love.

Walk in Christ's Commandments

[4]I rejoiced greatly that I have found *some* of your children walking in truth, as we received commandment from the Father. [5]And now I plead with you, lady, not as though I wrote a new commandment to you, but that which we have had from the beginning: that we love one another. [6]This is love, that we walk according to His commandments. This is the commandment, that as you have heard from the beginning, you should walk in it.

Beware of Antichrist Deceivers

[7]For many deceivers have gone out into the world who do not confess Jesus Christ *as* coming in the flesh. This is a deceiver and an antichrist. [8]Look to yourselves, that we[a] do not lose those things we worked for, but *that* we[b] may receive a full reward. [9]Whoever transgresses[a] and does not abide in the doctrine of Christ does not have God. He who abides in the doctrine of Christ has both the Father and the Son. [10]If anyone comes to you and does not bring this doctrine, do not receive him into your house nor greet him; [11]for he who greets him shares in his evil deeds.

Guardians of Freedom
In his Farewell Address, Andrew Jackson, the seventh president of the United States (1829–1837), stated:

> You have the highest of human trusts committed to your care. Providence has showered on this favored land blessings without number, and has chosen you as the guardians of freedom, to preserve it for the benefit of the human race. May He who holds in His hands the destinies of nations make you worthy of the favors He has bestowed, and enable you, with pure hearts and hands and sleepless vigilance, to guard and defend to the end of time, the great charge He has committed to your keeping.

John's Farewell Greeting

[12]Having many things to write to you, I did not wish *to do so* with paper and ink; but I hope to come to you and speak face to face, that our joy may be full.
[13]The children of your elect sister greet you. Amen.

---

3 [a]NU-Text and M-Text read *us.*   **8** [a]NU-Text reads *you.* [b]NU-Text reads *you.*   **9** [a]NU-Text reads *goes ahead.*

3 JOHN

Author: John

When Written: Around A.D. 70

Theme: Enjoy Fellowship with the Brethren

Key Verse: 3 John 11—Beloved, do not imitate what is evil, but what is good. He who does good is of God, but he who does evil has not seen God.

This may be the shortest book in the Bible, but it is personal and vivid. John strongly encourages the showing of hospitality and support for missionaries and fellow Christian workers. He commends Gaius who has responded positively and is walking in the truth, but the faithless Diotrephes stands condemned by his actions and is walking in error.

During the Revolutionary War, there were far more Loyalists (American colonists who remained loyal to the British monarchy) than one might think. Historian Robert Calhoun writes that "best estimates put the proportion of adult white male Loyalists somewhere between 15 and 20 percent [approximately 500,000 men]. Approximately half the colonists of European ancestry tried to avoid involvement in the struggle. The Patriots received active support from perhaps 40 to 45 percent of the white populace, and at most no more than a bare majority." One can imagine the divisiveness that resulted. Many Loyalists, having endured hardships at the hands of the Patriots, fled the country, resettling in Britain or Canada or the British West Indies.

3 JOHN

Greeting to Gaius

The Elder,

To the beloved Gaius, whom I love in truth:

[2]Beloved, I pray that you may prosper in all things and be in health, just as your soul prospers. [3]For I rejoiced greatly when brethren came and testified of the truth *that is* in you, just as you walk in the truth. [4]I have no greater joy than to hear that my children walk in truth.[a]

Gaius Commended for Generosity

[5]Beloved, you do faithfully whatever you do for the brethren and[a] for strangers, [6]who have borne witness of your love before the church. If you send them forward on their journey in a manner worthy of God, you will do well, [7]because they went forth for His name's sake, taking nothing from the Gentiles. [8]We therefore ought to receive[a] such, that we may become fellow workers for the truth.

4 [a]NU-Text reads *the truth.*   **5** [a]NU-Text adds *especially.*   **8** [a]NU-Text reads *support.*

HOPE

. . . that you may prosper in all things. . . .

3 JOHN 2

Daniel Webster

STAYING TRUE TO THE CHRISTIAN RELIGION

Daniel Webster (1782–1852) was a leading American statesman and considered one of the greatest orators in American history. He served as a U.S. congressman, senator, and as the Secretary of State for three different presidents.

In a speech given before the Historical Society of New York, February 23, 1852, he said:

> If we and our posterity shall be true to the Christian religion, if we and they shall live always in the fear of God, and shall respect His commandments, if we and they shall maintain just moral sentiments and such conscientious convictions of duty as shall control the heart and life, we may have the highest hopes of the future fortunes of our country; and if we maintain those institutions of government and that political union, exceeding all praise as much as it exceeds all former examples of political associations, we may be sure of one thing, that while our country furnishes material for a thousand masters of the historic art, it will afford no topic for a Gibbon. It will have no decline and fall. It will go on prospering and to prosper.
>
> But if we and our posterity reject religious institutions and authority, violate the rules of eternal justice, trifle with the injunctions of morality, and recklessly destroy the political constitution which holds us together, no man can tell how sudden a catastrophe may overwhelm us that shall bury all our glory in profound obscurity.

Diotrephes and Demetrius

9I wrote to the church, but Diotrephes, who loves to have the preeminence among them, does not receive us. 10Therefore, if I come, I will call to mind his deeds which he does, prating against us with malicious words. And not content with that, he himself does not receive the brethren, and forbids those who wish to, putting *them* out of the church.

11Beloved, do not imitate what is evil, but what is good. He who does good is of God, buta he who does evil has not seen God.

12Demetrius has a *good* testimony from all, and from the truth itself. And we also bear witness, and you know that our testimony is true.

Farewell Greeting

13I had many things to write, but I do not wish to write to you with pen and ink; 14but I hope to see you shortly, and we shall speak face to face.

Peace to you. Our friends greet you. Greet the friends by name.

---

11 aNU-Text and M-Text omit *but.*

JUDE

Author: Jude

When Written: Around A.D. 64

Theme: Contend for the Faith

Key Verse: Jude 3—Beloved, while I was very diligent to write to you concerning our common salvation, I found it necessary to write to you exhorting you to contend earnestly for the faith which was once for all delivered to the saints.

While several epistles confront the problem of false teachers, Jude goes beyond all other New Testament epistles in its relentless and passionate denunciation of the apostate teachers who have crept into the church. Believers are challenged to contend for the faith and to expose those who are turning God's grace into unbounded license to do as they please. The danger is very real and not to be minimized. Combining the theme of 2 Peter with the style of James, the Book of Jude is potent in spite of its brevity.

Vigilance in guarding our freedom is also vital to every citizen. General Douglas MacArthur officially accepted the Japanese surrender at the end of World War II and oversaw the Occupation of Japan from 1945 to 1951, being credited with implementing far-ranging democratic changes in that country. Well aware of the constant dangers in the world to freedom, he stated: "No man is entitled to the blessings of freedom unless he be vigilant in its preservation."

JUDE

Greeting to the Called

Jude, a bondservant of Jesus Christ, and brother of James,

To those who are called, sanctified[a] by God the Father, and preserved in Jesus Christ:

[2]Mercy, peace, and love be multiplied to you.

Contend for the Faith

[3]Beloved, while I was very diligent to write to you concerning our common salvation, I found it necessary to write to you exhorting you to contend earnestly for the faith which was once for all delivered to the saints. [4]For certain men have crept in unnoticed, who long ago were marked out for this condemnation, ungodly men, who turn the grace of our God into lewdness and deny the only Lord God[a] and our Lord Jesus Christ.

Old and New Apostates

[5]But I want to remind you, though you once knew this, that the Lord, having saved the people out of the land of Egypt, afterward destroyed those who did not believe. [6]And the angels who did not keep their proper domain, but left their own abode, He has reserved in everlasting chains under darkness for the judgment of the great day; [7]as Sodom and Gomorrah, and the cities around them in a similar manner to these, having given themselves over to sexual immorality and gone after strange flesh, are set forth as an example, suffering the vengeance of eternal fire.

[8]Likewise also these dreamers defile the flesh, reject authority, and speak evil of dignitaries. [9]Yet Michael the archangel, in contending with the devil, when he disputed about the body of Moses, dared not bring against him a reviling accusation, but said, "The Lord rebuke you!" [10]But these speak evil of whatever they do not know; and whatever they know naturally, like brute beasts, in these things they corrupt themselves. [11]Woe to them! For they have gone in the way of Cain, have run greedily in the error of Balaam for profit, and perished in the rebellion of Korah.

Apostates Depraved and Doomed

[12]These are spots in your love feasts, while they feast with you without fear, serving *only* themselves. *They are* clouds without water, carried about[a] by the winds; late autumn trees without fruit, twice dead, pulled up by the roots; [13]raging waves of the sea, foaming up their own shame; wandering stars for whom is reserved the blackness of darkness forever.

[14]Now Enoch, the seventh from Adam, prophesied about these men also, saying, "Behold, the Lord comes with ten thousands of His saints, [15]to execute judgment on all, to convict all who are ungodly among them of all their ungodly deeds which they have committed in an ungodly way, and of all the harsh things which ungodly sinners have spoken against Him."

Apostates Predicted

[16]These are grumblers, complainers, walking according to their own lusts; and they mouth great swelling *words,* flattering people to gain advantage. [17]But you, beloved, remember the words which were spoken before by the apostles of our Lord Jesus Christ: [18]how they told you that there would be mockers in the last time who would walk according to their own ungodly lusts. [19]These are sensual persons, who cause divisions, not having the Spirit.

Maintain Your Life with God

[20]But you, beloved, building yourselves up on your most holy faith, praying in the

---

1 [a]NU-Text reads *beloved.*   **4** [a]NU-Text omits *God.*
12 [a]NU-Text and M-Text read *along.*

Holy Spirit, [21]keep yourselves in the love of God, looking for the mercy of our Lord Jesus Christ unto eternal life.

[22]And on some have compassion, making a distinction;[a] [23]but others save with fear, pulling *them* out of the fire,[a] hating even the garment defiled by the flesh.

Glory to God

[24] Now to Him who is able to keep you[a]
    from stumbling,
And to present *you* faultless
Before the presence of His glory with
    exceeding joy,

[25] To God our Savior,[a]
    Who alone is wise,[b]
    Be glory and majesty,
    Dominion and power,[c]
    Both now and forever.
    Amen.

---

22 [a]NU-Text reads *who are doubting* (or *making distinctions*).   **23** [a]NU-Text adds *and on some have mercy with fear* and omits *with fear* in first clause.   **24** [a]M-Text reads *them*.   **25** [a]NU-Text reads *To the only God our Savior.* [b]NU-Text omits *Who . . . is wise* and adds *Through Jesus Christ our Lord.* [c]NU-Text adds *Before all time.*

SERVICE

To God our Savior,
Who alone is wise,
be glory and majesty. . . .

JUDE 25

The signing of
the Mayflower Compact

THE MAYFLOWER COMPACT

This was America's first great governmental document, signed on November 11, 1620, by the 41 adult male members of the Pilgrims on the *Mayflower*. This established the powerful idea of self-government through laws made by the people, which lies at the heart of democracy. John Adams and many historians have referred to the Mayflower Compact as the foundation of the U.S. Constitution written more than 150 years later.

In the name of God, Amen. We, whose names are underwritten, the Loyal Subjects of our dread Sovereign Lord, King James, by the Grace of God, of England, France, and Ireland, King, Defender of the Faith, &c. Having undertaken for the Glory of God, and Advancement of the Christian Faith, and the Honour of our King and Country, a voyage to plant the first colony in the northern parts of Virginia; do by these presents, solemnly and mutually in the Presence of God and one of another, covenant and combine ourselves together into a civil Body Politick, for our better Ordering and Preservation, and Furtherance of the Ends aforesaid; And by Virtue hereof to enact, constitute, and frame, such just and equal Laws, Ordinances, Acts, Constitutions and Offices, from time to time, as shall be thought most meet and convenient for the General good of the Colony; unto which we promise all due submission and obedience. In Witness whereof we have hereunto subscribed our names at Cape Cod the eleventh of November, in the Reign of our Sovereign Lord, King James of England, France, and Ireland, the eighteenth, and of Scotland the fifty-fourth. Anno Domini, 1620.

REVELATION

Author: John

When Written: Around A.D. 95

Theme: The Revelation of the Coming of Christ

Key Verse: Revelation 1:19—Write the things which you have seen, and the things which are, and the things which will take place after this.

Key Chapters: Revelation 19–22—The apostle John describes in explicit terms the plans of God for the last days and for all of eternity.

Just as Genesis is the book of beginnings, Revelation is the book of consummation. The book is an unveiling of the character and message of God. Penned by John during his exile on the island of Patmos, Revelation centers around visions and symbols of the resurrected Christ, who alone has the authority to judge the earth, to remake it, and to rule it in righteousness. In it, the divine program of redemption is brought to fruition.

In the last chapter, Jesus Christ says to the apostle John, "I am the Alpha and the Omega, the Beginning and the End, the First and the Last." There is no doubt regarding His worthiness to be praised and worshiped throughout eternity. It is interesting that in our nation's capital, the first and last rays of sunlight fall every day upon its tallest building—the 555-foot Washington Monument. And there on its top, inscribed on the four-sided aluminum capstone are the Latin words *Laus Deo*, which means "Praise to God." This simple expression of praise reflects America's abiding belief that God has blessed our country with liberty and divine favor, for which we all should humbly give thanks.

REVELATION

Introduction and Benediction

1 The Revelation of Jesus Christ, which God gave Him to show His servants—things which must shortly take place. And He sent and signified *it* by His angel to His servant John, ²who bore witness to the word of God, and to the testimony of Jesus Christ, to all things that he saw. ³Blessed *is* he who reads and those who hear the words of this prophecy, and keep those things which are written in it; for the time *is* near.

Greeting the Seven Churches

⁴John, to the seven churches which are in Asia:

Grace to you and peace from Him who is and who was and who is to come, and from the seven Spirits who are before His throne, ⁵and from Jesus Christ, the faithful witness, the firstborn from the dead, and the ruler over the kings of the earth.

To Him who loved us and washedᵃ us from our sins in His own blood, ⁶and has made us kingsᵃ and priests to His God and Father, to Him *be* glory and dominion forever and ever. Amen.

⁷Behold, He is coming with clouds, and every eye will see Him, even they who pierced Him. And all the tribes of the earth will mourn because of Him. Even so, Amen.

⁸"I am the Alpha and the Omega, *the* Beginning and *the* End,"ᵃ says the Lord,ᵇ "who is and who was and who is to come, the Almighty."

Vision of the Son of Man

⁹I, John, bothᵃ your brother and companion in the tribulation and kingdom and patience of Jesus Christ, was on the island that is called Patmos for the word of God and for the testimony of Jesus Christ. ¹⁰I was in the Spirit on the Lord's Day, and I heard behind me a loud voice, as of a trumpet, ¹¹saying, "I am the Alpha and the Omega, the First and the Last,"ᵃ and, "What you see, write in a book and send *it* to the seven churches which are in Asia:ᵇ to Ephesus, to Smyrna, to Pergamos, to Thyatira, to Sardis, to Philadelphia, and to Laodicea."

¹²Then I turned to see the voice that spoke with me. And having turned I saw seven golden lampstands, ¹³and in the midst of the seven lampstands *One* like the Son of Man, clothed with a garment down to the feet and girded about the chest with a golden band. ¹⁴His head and hair *were* white like wool, as white as snow, and His eyes like a flame of fire; ¹⁵His feet *were* like fine brass, as if refined in a furnace, and His voice as the sound of many waters; ¹⁶He had in His right hand seven stars, out of His mouth went a sharp two-edged sword, and His countenance *was* like the sun shining in its strength. ¹⁷And when I saw Him, I fell at His feet as dead. But He laid His right hand on me, saying to me,ᵃ "Do not be afraid; I am the First and the Last. ¹⁸I *am* He who lives, and was dead, and behold, I am alive forevermore. Amen. And I have the keys of Hades and of Death. ¹⁹Writeᵃ the things which you have seen, and the things which are, and the things which will take place after this. ²⁰The mystery of the seven stars which you saw in My right hand, and the seven golden lampstands: The seven stars are the angels of the seven churches, and the seven lampstands which you sawᵃ are the seven churches.

1:5 ᵃNU-Text reads *loves us and freed;* M-Text reads *loves us and washed.* **1:6** ᵃNU-Text and M-Text read *a kingdom.* **1:8** ᵃNU-Text and M-Text omit *the Beginning and the End.* ᵇNU-Text and M-Text add *God.* **1:9** ᵃNU-Text and M-Text omit *both.* **1:11** ᵃNU-Text and M-Text omit *I am* through third *and.* ᵇNU-Text and M-Text omit *which are in Asia.* **1:17** ᵃNU-Text and M-Text omit *to me.* **1:19** ᵃNU-Text and M-Text read *Therefore, write.* **1:20** ᵃNU-Text and M-Text omit *which you saw.*

The Loveless Church

2 "To the angel of the church of Ephesus write,

'These things says He who holds the seven stars in His right hand, who walks in the midst of the seven golden lampstands: 2"I know your works, your labor, your patience, and that you cannot bear those who are evil. And you have tested those who say they are apostles and are not, and have found them liars; 3and you have persevered and have patience, and have labored for My name's sake and have not become weary. 4Nevertheless I have *this* against you, that you have left your first love. 5Remember therefore from where you have fallen; repent and do the first works, or else I will come to you quickly and remove your lampstand from its place—unless you repent. 6But this you have, that you hate the deeds of the Nicolaitans, which I also hate.

7"He who has an ear, let him hear what the Spirit says to the churches. To him who overcomes I will give to eat from the tree of life, which is in the midst of the Paradise of God."'

The Persecuted Church

8"And to the angel of the church in Smyrna write,

'These things says the First and the Last, who was dead, and came to life: 9"I know your works, tribulation, and poverty (but you are rich); and *I know* the blasphemy of those who say they are Jews and are not, but *are* a synagogue of Satan. 10Do not fear any of those things which you are about to suffer. Indeed, the devil is about to throw *some* of you into prison, that you may be tested, and you will have tribulation ten days. Be faithful until death, and I will give you the crown of life.

11"He who has an ear, let him hear what the Spirit says to the churches. He who overcomes shall not be hurt by the second death."'

The Compromising Church

12"And to the angel of the church in Pergamos write,

'These things says He who has the sharp two-edged sword: 13"I know your works, and where you dwell, where Satan's throne *is.* And you hold fast to My name, and did not deny My faith even in the days in which Antipas *was* My faithful martyr, who was killed among you, where Satan dwells. 14But I have a few things against you, because you have there those who hold the doctrine of Balaam, who taught Balak to put a stumbling block before the children of Israel, to eat things sacrificed to idols, and to commit sexual immorality. 15Thus you also have those who hold the doctrine of the Nicolaitans, which thing I hate.[a] 16Repent, or else I will come to you quickly and will fight against them with the sword of My mouth.

17"He who has an ear, let him hear what the Spirit says to the churches. To him who overcomes I will give some of the hidden manna to eat. And I will give him a white stone, and on the stone a new name written which no one knows except him who receives *it.*"'

The Corrupt Church

18"And to the angel of the church in Thyatira write,

'These things says the Son of God, who has eyes like a flame of fire, and His feet like fine brass: 19"I know your works, love, service, faith,[a] and your patience; and *as* for your works, the last *are* more than the first. 20Nevertheless I have a few things against you, because you allow[a] that woman[b] Jezebel, who calls herself a prophetess, to teach and seduce[c] My servants to commit sexual immorality and eat things sacrificed to idols. 21And I gave her time to repent of her sexual immorality, and she did not repent.[a] 22Indeed I will cast her into a sickbed, and those who commit adultery with her into great tribulation, unless they repent of their[a] deeds. 23I will kill her chil-

---

2:15 [a]NU-Text and M-Text read *likewise* for *which thing I hate.*   **2:19** [a]NU-Text and M-Text read *faith, service.*   **2:20** [a]NU-Text and M-Text read *I have against you that you tolerate.* [b]M-Text reads *your wife Jezebel.* [c]NU-Text and M-Text read *and teaches and seduces.*   **2:21** [a]NU-Text and M-Text read *time to repent, and she does not want to repent of her sexual immorality.*   **2:22** [a]NU-Text and M-Text read *her.*

dren with death, and all the churches shall know that I am He who searches the minds and hearts. And I will give to each one of you according to your works.

[24]"Now to you I say, and[a] to the rest in Thyatira, as many as do not have this doctrine, who have not known the depths of Satan, as they say, I will[b] put on you no other burden. [25]But hold fast what you have till I come. [26]And he who overcomes, and keeps My works until the end, to him I will give power over the nations—

[27] 'He shall rule them with a rod of iron;
    They shall be dashed to pieces like the
      potter's vessels'[a]—

as I also have received from My Father; [28]and I will give him the morning star.

[29]"He who has an ear, let him hear what the Spirit says to the churches." '

The Dead Church

3 "And to the angel of the church in Sardis write,

'These things says He who has the seven Spirits of God and the seven stars: "I know your works, that you have a name that you are alive, but you are dead. [2]Be watchful, and strengthen the things which remain, that are ready to die, for I have not found your works perfect before God.[a] [3]Remember therefore how you have received and heard; hold fast and repent. Therefore if you will not watch, I will come upon you as a thief, and you will not know what hour I will come upon you. [4]You[a] have a few names even in Sardis who have not defiled their garments; and they shall walk with Me in white, for they are worthy. [5]He who overcomes shall be clothed in white garments, and I will not blot out his name from the Book of Life; but I will confess his name before My Father and before His angels.

[6]"He who has an ear, let him hear what the Spirit says to the churches." '

The Faithful Church

[7]"And to the angel of the church in Philadelphia write,

'These things says He who is holy, He who is true, *"He who has the key of David,*

He who opens and no one shuts, and shuts and no one opens":[a] [8]"I know your works. See, I have set before you an open door, and no one can shut it;[a] for you have a little strength, have kept My word, and have not denied My name. [9]Indeed I will make *those* of the synagogue of Satan, who say they are Jews and are not, but lie—indeed I will make them come and worship before your feet, and to know that I have loved you. [10]Because you have kept My command to persevere, I also will keep you from the hour of trial which shall come upon the whole world, to test those who dwell on the earth. [11]Behold,[a] I am coming quickly! Hold fast what you have, that no one may take your crown. [12]He who overcomes, I will make him a pillar in the temple of My God, and he shall go out no more. I will write on him the name of My God and the name of the city of My God, the New Jerusalem, which comes down out of heaven from My God. And *I will write on him* My new name.

[13]"He who has an ear, let him hear what the Spirit says to the churches." '

The Lukewarm Church

[14]"And to the angel of the church of the Laodiceans[a] write,

'These things says the Amen, the Faithful and True Witness, the Beginning of the creation of God: [15]"I know your works, that you are neither cold nor hot. I could wish you were cold or hot. [16]So then, because you are lukewarm, and neither cold nor hot,[a] I will vomit you out of My mouth. [17]Because you say, 'I am rich, have become wealthy, and have need of nothing'—and do not know that you are wretched, miserable, poor, blind, and naked— [18]I counsel you to buy from Me gold refined in the fire, that you may be rich; and white garments, that you may be clothed, *that* the shame of your

---

2:24 [a]NU-Text and M-Text omit *and.* [b]NU-Text and M-Text omit *will.* **2:27** [a]Psalm 2:9 **3:2** [a]NU-Text and M-Text read *My God.* **3:4** [a]NU-Text and M-Text read *Nevertheless you have a few names in Sardis.* **3:7** [a]Isaiah 22:22 **3:8** [a]NU-Text and M-Text read *which no one can shut.* **3:11** [a]NU-Text and M-Text omit *Behold.* **3:14** [a]NU-Text and M-Text read *in Laodicea.* **3:16** [a]NU-Text and M-Text read *hot nor cold.*

nakedness may not be revealed; and anoint your eyes with eye salve, that you may see. [19]As many as I love, I rebuke and chasten. Therefore be zealous and repent. [20]Behold, I stand at the door and knock. If anyone hears My voice and opens the door, I will come in to him and dine with him, and he with Me. [21]To him who overcomes I will grant to sit with Me on My throne, as I also overcame and sat down with My Father on His throne.

[22]"He who has an ear, let him hear what the Spirit says to the churches." ' "

INTEGRITY

"Because you say, 'I am rich. . . .'"

REVELATION 3:17

When Prosperity Devours Religion

Cotton Mather (1663–1728), an American colonial clergyman and educator, wrote the most detailed history of the first fifty years of New England, *The Great Achievement of Christ in America*. Observing the rising trend toward materialism in the colonies, he wrote:

> *Religion begat prosperity, and the daughter devoured the mother.*

The Throne Room of Heaven

4 After these things I looked, and behold, a door *standing* open in heaven. And the first voice which I heard *was* like a trumpet speaking with me, saying, "Come up here, and I will show you things which must take place after this." [2]Immediately I was in the Spirit; and behold, a throne set in heaven, and *One* sat on the throne. [3]And He who sat there was[a] like a jasper and a sardius stone in appearance; and *there was* a rainbow around the throne, in appearance like an emerald. [4]Around the throne *were* twenty-four thrones, and on the thrones I saw twenty-four elders sitting, clothed in white robes; and they had crowns[a] of gold on their heads. [5]And from the throne proceeded lightnings, thunderings, and voices.[a] Seven lamps of fire *were* burning before the throne, which are the[b] seven Spirits of God. [6]Before the throne *there was*[a] a sea of glass, like crystal. And in the midst of the

throne, and around the throne, *were* four living creatures full of eyes in front and in back. [7]The first living creature *was* like a lion, the second living creature like a calf, the third living creature had a face like a man, and the fourth living creature *was* like a flying eagle. [8]*The* four living creatures, each having six wings, were full of eyes around and within. And they do not rest day or night, saying:

> "Holy, holy, holy,[a]
> Lord God Almighty,
> Who was and is and is to come!"

[9]Whenever the living creatures give glory and honor and thanks to Him who sits on the throne, who lives forever and ever, [10]the twenty-four elders fall down before Him who sits on the throne and worship Him who lives forever and ever, and cast their crowns before the throne, saying:

> [11] "You are worthy, O Lord,[a]
> To receive glory and honor and
>   power;
> For You created all things,
> And by Your will they exist[b] and were
>   created."

The Lamb Takes the Scroll

5 And I saw in the right *hand* of Him who sat on the throne a scroll written inside and on the back, sealed with seven seals. [2]Then I saw a strong angel proclaiming with a loud voice, "Who is worthy to open the scroll and to loose its seals?" [3]And no one in heaven or on the earth or under the earth was able to open the scroll, or to look at it. [4]So I wept much, because no one was found worthy to open and read[a] the scroll, or to look at it. [5]But one of the elders said to me, "Do not weep. Behold, the Lion of

---

4:3 [a]M-Text omits *And He who sat there was* (which makes the description in verse 3 modify the throne rather than God).   **4:4** [a]NU-Text and M-Text read *robes, with crowns.*   **4:5** [a]NU-Text and M-Text read *voices, and thunderings.* [b]M-Text omits *the.*
4:6 [a]NU-Text and M-Text add *something like.*
4:8 [a]M-Text has *holy* nine times.   **4:11** [a]NU-Text and M-Text read *our Lord and God.* [b]NU-Text and M-Text read *existed.*   **5:4** [a]NU-Text and M-Text omit *and read.*

the tribe of Judah, the Root of David, has prevailed to open the scroll and to loose[a] its seven seals."

[6]And I looked, and behold,[a] in the midst of the throne and of the four living creatures, and in the midst of the elders, stood a Lamb as though it had been slain, having seven horns and seven eyes, which are the seven Spirits of God sent out into all the earth. [7]Then He came and took the scroll out of the right hand of Him who sat on the throne.

Worthy Is the Lamb

[8]Now when He had taken the scroll, the four living creatures and the twenty-four elders fell down before the Lamb, each having a harp, and golden bowls full of incense, which are the prayers of the saints. [9]And they sang a new song, saying:

"You are worthy to take the scroll,
  And to open its seals;
  For You were slain,
  And have redeemed us to God by Your
    blood
  Out of every tribe and tongue and
    people and nation,
[10] And have made us[a] kings[b] and priests
    to our God;
  And we[c] shall reign on the earth."

[11]Then I looked, and I heard the voice of many angels around the throne, the living creatures, and the elders; and the number of them was ten thousand times ten thousand, and thousands of thousands, [12]saying with a loud voice:

"Worthy is the Lamb who was slain
  To receive power and riches and
    wisdom,
  And strength and honor and glory
    and blessing!"

[13]And every creature which is in heaven and on the earth and under the earth and such as are in the sea, and all that are in them, I heard saying:

"Blessing and honor and glory and
  power

Be to Him who sits on the throne,
  And to the Lamb, forever and ever!"[a]

[14]Then the four living creatures said, "Amen!" And the twenty-four[a] elders fell down and worshiped Him who lives forever and ever.[b]

First Seal: The Conqueror

6 Now I saw when the Lamb opened one of the seals;[a] and I heard one of the four living creatures saying with a voice like thunder, "Come and see." [2]And I looked, and behold, a white horse. He who sat on it had a bow; and a crown was given to him, and he went out conquering and to conquer.

Second Seal: Conflict on Earth

[3]When He opened the second seal, I heard the second living creature saying, "Come and see."[a] [4]Another horse, fiery red, went out. And it was granted to the one who sat on it to take peace from the earth, and that *people* should kill one another; and there was given to him a great sword.

Third Seal: Scarcity on Earth

[5]When He opened the third seal, I heard the third living creature say, "Come and see." So I looked, and behold, a black horse, and he who sat on it had a pair of scales in his hand. [6]And I heard a voice in the midst of the four living creatures saying, "A quart[a] of wheat for a denarius,[b] and three quarts of barley for a denarius; and do not harm the oil and the wine."

Fourth Seal: Widespread Death on Earth

[7]When He opened the fourth seal, I heard the voice of the fourth living creature saying, "Come and see." [8]So I looked, and behold, a pale horse. And the name of

---

5:5 [a]NU-Text and M-Text omit *to loose.*
5:6 [a]NU-Text and M-Text read *I saw in the midst . . . a Lamb standing.*   **5:10** [a]NU-Text and M-Text read *them.* [b]NU-Text reads *a kingdom.* [c]NU-Text and M-Text read *they.*   **5:13** [a]M-Text adds *Amen.*
5:14 [a]NU-Text and M-Text omit *twenty-four.* [b]NU-Text and M-Text omit *Him who lives forever and ever.*
6:1 [a]NU-Text and M-Text read *seven seals.*
6:3 [a]NU-Text and M-Text omit *and see.*   **6:6** [a]Greek *choinix;* that is, approximately one quart [b]This was approximately one day's wage for a worker.

him who sat on it was Death, and Hades followed with him. And power was given to them over a fourth of the earth, to kill with sword, with hunger, with death, and by the beasts of the earth.

Fifth Seal: The Cry of the Martyrs

⁹When He opened the fifth seal, I saw under the altar the souls of those who had been slain for the word of God and for the testimony which they held. ¹⁰And they cried with a loud voice, saying, "How long, O Lord, holy and true, until You judge and avenge our blood on those who dwell on the earth?" ¹¹Then a white robe was given to each of them; and it was said to them that they should rest a little while longer, until both *the number of* their fellow servants and their brethren, who would be killed as they *were,* was completed.

Sixth Seal: Cosmic Disturbances

¹²I looked when He opened the sixth seal, and behold,ᵃ there was a great earthquake; and the sun became black as sackcloth of hair, and the moonᵇ became like blood. ¹³And the stars of heaven fell to the earth, as a fig tree drops its late figs when it is shaken by a mighty wind. ¹⁴Then the sky receded as a scroll when it is rolled up, and every mountain and island was moved out of its place. ¹⁵And the kings of the earth, the great men, the rich men, the commanders,ᵃ the mighty men, every slave and every free man, hid themselves in the caves and in the rocks of the mountains, ¹⁶and said to the mountains and rocks, "Fall on us and hide us from the face of Him who sits on the throne and from the wrath of the Lamb! ¹⁷For the great day of His wrath has come, and who is able to stand?"

The Sealed of Israel

7 After these things I saw four angels standing at the four corners of the earth, holding the four winds of the earth, that the wind should not blow on the earth, on the sea, or on any tree. ²Then I saw another angel ascending from the east, having the seal of the living God. And he cried with a loud voice to the four angels to whom it was granted to harm the earth and the sea, ³saying, "Do not harm the earth, the sea, or the trees till we have sealed the servants of our God on their foreheads." ⁴And I heard the number of those who were sealed. One hundred *and* forty-four thousand of all the tribes of the children of Israel *were* sealed:

5   of the tribe of Judah twelve thousand *were* sealed;ᵃ
of the tribe of Reuben twelve thousand *were* sealed;
of the tribe of Gad twelve thousand *were* sealed;

6   of the tribe of Asher twelve thousand *were* sealed;
of the tribe of Naphtali twelve thousand *were* sealed;
of the tribe of Manasseh twelve thousand *were* sealed;

7   of the tribe of Simeon twelve thousand *were* sealed;
of the tribe of Levi twelve thousand *were* sealed;
of the tribe of Issachar twelve thousand *were* sealed;

8   of the tribe of Zebulun twelve thousand *were* sealed;
of the tribe of Joseph twelve thousand *were* sealed;
of the tribe of Benjamin twelve thousand *were* sealed.

A Multitude from the Great Tribulation

⁹After these things I looked, and behold, a great multitude which no one could number, of all nations, tribes, peoples, and tongues, standing before the throne and before the Lamb, clothed with white robes, with palm branches in their hands, ¹⁰and crying out with a loud voice, saying, "Salvation *belongs* to our God who sits on the throne, and to the Lamb!" ¹¹All the angels stood around the throne and the elders and the four living creatures, and fell on

---

6:12 ᵃNU-Text and M-Text omit *behold.* ᵇNU-Text and M-Text read *the whole moon.*   **6:15** ᵃNU-Text and M-Text read *the commanders, the rich men.*   **7:5** ᵃIn NU-Text and M-Text *were sealed* is stated only in verses 5a and 8c; the words are understood in the remainder of the passage.

their faces before the throne and worshiped God, [12]saying:

"Amen! Blessing and glory and
  wisdom,
Thanksgiving and honor and power
  and might,
Be to our God forever and ever.
Amen."

[13]Then one of the elders answered, saying to me, "Who are these arrayed in white robes, and where did they come from?" [14]And I said to him, "Sir,[a] you know."

So he said to me, "These are the ones who come out of the great tribulation, and washed their robes and made them white in the blood of the Lamb. [15]Therefore they are before the throne of God, and serve Him day and night in His temple. And He who sits on the throne will dwell among them. [16]They shall neither hunger anymore nor thirst anymore; the sun shall not strike them, nor any heat; [17]for the Lamb who is in the midst of the throne will shepherd them and lead them to living fountains of waters.[a] And God will wipe away every tear from their eyes."

Seventh Seal: Prelude to the Seven Trumpets

8 When He opened the seventh seal, there was silence in heaven for about half an hour. [2]And I saw the seven angels who stand before God, and to them were given seven trumpets. [3]Then another angel, having a golden censer, came and stood at the altar. He was given much incense, that he should offer *it* with the prayers of all the saints upon the golden altar which was before the throne. [4]And the smoke of the incense, with the prayers of the saints, ascended before God from the angel's hand. [5]Then the angel took the censer, filled it with fire from the altar, and threw *it* to the earth. And there were noises, thunderings, lightnings, and an earthquake.

[6]So the seven angels who had the seven trumpets prepared themselves to sound.

First Trumpet: Vegetation Struck

[7]The first angel sounded: And hail and fire followed, mingled with blood, and they were thrown to the earth.[a] And a third of the trees were burned up, and all green grass was burned up.

Second Trumpet: The Seas Struck

[8]Then the second angel sounded: And *something* like a great mountain burning with fire was thrown into the sea, and a third of the sea became blood. [9]And a third of the living creatures in the sea died, and a third of the ships were destroyed.

Third Trumpet: The Waters Struck

[10]Then the third angel sounded: And a great star fell from heaven, burning like a torch, and it fell on a third of the rivers and on the springs of water. [11]The name of the star is Wormwood. A third of the waters became wormwood, and many men died from the water, because it was made bitter.

Fourth Trumpet: The Heavens Struck

[12]Then the fourth angel sounded: And a third of the sun was struck, a third of the moon, and a third of the stars, so that a third of them were darkened. A third of the day did not shine, and likewise the night.

[13]And I looked, and I heard an angel[a] flying through the midst of heaven, saying with a loud voice, "Woe, woe, woe to the inhabitants of the earth, because of the remaining blasts of the trumpet of the three angels who are about to sound!"

Fifth Trumpet: The Locusts from the Bottomless Pit

9 Then the fifth angel sounded: And I saw a star fallen from heaven to the earth. To him was given the key to the bottomless pit. [2]And he opened the bottomless pit, and smoke arose out of the pit like the smoke of a great furnace. So the sun and the air were darkened because of the smoke of the pit. [3]Then out of the smoke locusts came upon the earth. And to them was given power, as the scorpions of the earth have power. [4]They were commanded

---

7:14 [a]NU-Text and M-Text read *My lord.*
7:17 [a]NU-Text and M-Text read *to fountains of the waters of life.*   **8:7** [a]NU-Text and M-Text add *and a third of the earth was burned up.*   **8:13** [a]NU-Text and M-Text read *eagle.*

not to harm the grass of the earth, or any green thing, or any tree, but only those men who do not have the seal of God on their foreheads. ⁵And they were not given *authority* to kill them, but to torment them *for* five months. Their torment *was* like the torment of a scorpion when it strikes a man. ⁶In those days men will seek death and will not find it; they will desire to die, and death will flee from them.

⁷The shape of the locusts was like horses prepared for battle. On their heads were crowns of something like gold, and their faces *were* like the faces of men. ⁸They had hair like women's hair, and their teeth were like lions' *teeth*. ⁹And they had breastplates like breastplates of iron, and the sound of their wings *was* like the sound of chariots with many horses running into battle. ¹⁰They had tails like scorpions, and there were stings in their tails. Their power *was* to hurt men five months. ¹¹And they had as king over them the angel of the bottomless pit, whose name in Hebrew *is* Abaddon, but in Greek he has the name Apollyon.

¹²One woe is past. Behold, still two more woes are coming after these things.

Sixth Trumpet: The Angels from the Euphrates

¹³Then the sixth angel sounded: And I heard a voice from the four horns of the golden altar which is before God, ¹⁴saying to the sixth angel who had the trumpet, "Release the four angels who are bound at the great river Euphrates." ¹⁵So the four angels, who had been prepared for the hour and day and month and year, were released to kill a third of mankind. ¹⁶Now the number of the army of the horsemen *was* two hundred million; I heard the number of them. ¹⁷And thus I saw the horses in the vision: those who sat on them had breastplates of fiery red, hyacinth blue, and sulfur yellow; and the heads of the horses *were* like the heads of lions; and out of their mouths came fire, smoke, and brimstone. ¹⁸By these three *plagues* a third of mankind was killed—by the fire and the smoke and the brimstone which came out of their mouths. ¹⁹For their power[a] is in their mouth and in their tails; for their tails

are like serpents, having heads; and with them they do harm.

²⁰But the rest of mankind, who were not killed by these plagues, did not repent of the works of their hands, that they should not worship demons, and idols of gold, silver, brass, stone, and wood, which can neither see nor hear nor walk. ²¹And they did not repent of their murders or their sorceries[a] or their sexual immorality or their thefts.

The Mighty Angel with the Little Book

10 I saw still another mighty angel coming down from heaven, clothed with a cloud. And a rainbow *was* on his head, his face *was* like the sun, and his feet like pillars of fire. ²He had a little book open in his hand. And he set his right foot on the sea and *his* left *foot* on the land, ³and cried with a loud voice, as *when* a lion roars. When he cried out, seven thunders uttered their voices. ⁴Now when the seven thunders uttered their voices,[a] I was about to write; but I heard a voice from heaven saying to me,[b] "Seal up the things which the seven thunders uttered, and do not write them."

⁵The angel whom I saw standing on the sea and on the land raised up his hand[a] to heaven ⁶and swore by Him who lives forever and ever, who created heaven and the things that are in it, the earth and the things that are in it, and the sea and the things that are in it, that there should be delay no longer, ⁷but in the days of the sounding of the seventh angel, when he is about to sound, the mystery of God would be finished, as He declared to His servants the prophets.

John Eats the Little Book

⁸Then the voice which I heard from heaven spoke to me again and said, "Go, take the little book which is open in the hand of the angel who stands on the sea and on the earth."

⁹So I went to the angel and said to him, "Give me the little book."

9:19 [a]NU-Text and M-Text read *the power of the horses.* **9:21** [a]NU-Text and M-Text read *drugs.* **10:4** [a]NU-Text and M-Text read *sounded.* [b]NU-Text and M-Text omit *to me.* **10:5** [a]NU-Text and M-Text read *right hand.*

And he said to me, "Take and eat it; and it will make your stomach bitter, but it will be as sweet as honey in your mouth."

¹⁰Then I took the little book out of the angel's hand and ate it, and it was as sweet as honey in my mouth. But when I had eaten it, my stomach became bitter. ¹¹And heᵃ said to me, "You must prophesy again about many peoples, nations, tongues, and kings."

The Two Witnesses

11 Then I was given a reed like a measuring rod. And the angel stood,ᵃ saying, "Rise and measure the temple of God, the altar, and those who worship there. ²But leave out the court which is outside the temple, and do not measure it, for it has been given to the Gentiles. And they will tread the holy city underfoot *for* forty-two months. ³And I will give *power* to my two witnesses, and they will prophesy one thousand two hundred and sixty days, clothed in sackcloth."

⁴These are the two olive trees and the two lampstands standing before the Godᵃ of the earth. ⁵And if anyone wants to harm them, fire proceeds from their mouth and devours their enemies. And if anyone wants to harm them, he must be killed in this manner. ⁶These have power to shut heaven, so that no rain falls in the days of their prophecy; and they have power over waters to turn them to blood, and to strike the earth with all plagues, as often as they desire.

The Witnesses Killed

⁷When they finish their testimony, the beast that ascends out of the bottomless pit will make war against them, overcome them, and kill them. ⁸And their dead bodies *will lie* in the street of the great city which spiritually is called Sodom and Egypt, where also ourᵃ Lord was crucified. ⁹Then *those* from the peoples, tribes, tongues, and nations will see their dead bodies three-and-a-half days, and not allowᵃ their dead bodies to be put into graves. ¹⁰And those who dwell on the earth will rejoice over them, make merry, and send gifts to one another, because these two prophets tormented those who dwell on the earth.

The Witnesses Resurrected

¹¹Now after the three-and-a-half days the breath of life from God entered them, and they stood on their feet, and great fear fell on those who saw them. ¹²And theyᵃ heard a loud voice from heaven saying to them, "Come up here." And they ascended to heaven in a cloud, and their enemies saw them. ¹³In the same hour there was a great earthquake, and a tenth of the city fell. In the earthquake seven thousand people were killed, and the rest were afraid and gave glory to the God of heaven.

¹⁴The second woe is past. Behold, the third woe is coming quickly.

FAITH

"We give You thanks, O Lord God Almighty. . . ."
REVELATION 11:17

State Constitutions

Dr. James Kennedy, influential pastor of Coral Ridge Presbyterian Church in Florida, stated:

In reading over the Constitutions of all fifty of our states, I discovered . . . there is in all fifty, without exception, an appeal or a prayer to the Almighty God of the universe. . . . Through all fifty state Constitutions, without exception, there runs this same appeal and reference to God who is the Creator of our liberties and the preserver of our freedoms.

Seventh Trumpet: The Kingdom Proclaimed

¹⁵Then the seventh angel sounded: And there were loud voices in heaven, saying, "The kingdomsᵃ of this world have become *the kingdoms* of our Lord and of His Christ, and He shall reign forever and ever!" ¹⁶And the twenty-four elders who sat before God on their thrones fell on their faces and worshiped God, ¹⁷saying:

10:11 ᵃNU-Text and M-Text read *they*.
11:1 ᵃNU-Text and M-Text omit *And the angel stood*.
11:4 ᵃNU-Text and M-Text read *Lord*.
11:8 ᵃNU-Text and M-Text read *their*.
11:9 ᵃNU-Text and M-Text read *nations see . . . and will not allow*.   **11:12** ᵃM-Text reads *I*.
11:15 ᵃNU-Text and M-Text read *kingdom . . . has become*.

"We give You thanks, O Lord God
Almighty,
The One who is and who was and
who is to come,ª
Because You have taken Your great
power and reigned.

18 The nations were angry, and Your
wrath has come,
And the time of the dead, that they
should be judged,
And that You should reward Your
servants the prophets and the
saints,
And those who fear Your name, small
and great,
And should destroy those who destroy
the earth."

¹⁹Then the temple of God was opened
in heaven, and the ark of His covenantª
was seen in His temple. And there were
lightnings, noises, thunderings, an earthquake, and great hail.

The Woman, the Child, and the Dragon

12 Now a great sign appeared in heav-
en: a woman clothed with the sun,
with the moon under her feet, and on her
head a garland of twelve stars. ²Then being
with child, she cried out in labor and in
pain to give birth.

³And another sign appeared in heaven:
behold, a great, fiery red dragon having
seven heads and ten horns, and seven
diadems on his heads. ⁴His tail drew a third
of the stars of heaven and threw them to
the earth. And the dragon stood before the
woman who was ready to give birth, to
devour her Child as soon as it was born.

11:17 ªNU-Text and M-Text omit *and who is to come.*
11:19 ªM-Text reads *the covenant of the Lord.*

COURAGE

*. . . and they did not love
their lives to the death.*

REVELATION 12:11

United Flight 93 Memorial

"LET'S ROLL!"

On the morning of September 11, 2001, United Flight 93
from Newark to San Francisco was hijacked by terrorists who
claimed to have a bomb. With telephone confirmation that
other planes had hit the Twin Towers of the World Trade
Center, the passengers understood the hijackers' intent.

Todd Beamer, a 32-year-old businessman picked up a
seat-back phone and reached Lisa Jefferson, a GTE supervi-
sor. He told her that he and others were going to "jump on"
a hijacker who was guarding the passengers in the rear.
Beamer asked her to pray the Lord's Prayer with him. He
also made her promise to call his wife, Lisa, and tell her that
he loved her and their two little boys.

Dropping the phone after talking with Jefferson, Beamer
said, "Jesus help me." Then after reciting Psalm 23, he said,
"Are you guys ready? Okay, let's roll." Those were the unforgettable last words Beamer said before he and others rushed
the hijackers of United Airlines Flight 93. There were screams,
then silence.

Brave American civilians, complete strangers, rose
against impossible odds and tried to save the 757-200 air-
craft. In doing so, they made the ultimate patriotic sacrifice.
United Flight 93 crashed into a large field near Shanksville,
Pennsylvania, killing all 44 aboard. Of the four hijacked
planes that morning, United 93 was the only one that failed
to hit a targeted site.

⁵She bore a male Child who was to rule all nations with a rod of iron. And her Child was caught up to God and His throne. ⁶Then the woman fled into the wilderness, where she has a place prepared by God, that they should feed her there one thousand two hundred and sixty days.

Satan Thrown Out of Heaven

⁷And war broke out in heaven: Michael and his angels fought with the dragon; and the dragon and his angels fought, ⁸but they did not prevail, nor was a place found for themᵃ in heaven any longer. ⁹So the great dragon was cast out, that serpent of old, called the Devil and Satan, who deceives the whole world; he was cast to the earth, and his angels were cast out with him. ¹⁰Then I heard a loud voice saying in heaven, "Now salvation, and strength, and the kingdom of our God, and the power of His Christ have come, for the accuser of our brethren, who accused them before our God day and night, has been cast down. ¹¹And they overcame him by the blood of the Lamb and by the word of their testimony, and they did not love their lives to the death. ¹²Therefore rejoice, O heavens, and you who dwell in them! Woe to the inhabitants of the earth and the sea! For the devil has come down to you, having great wrath, because he knows that he has a short time."

The Woman Persecuted

¹³Now when the dragon saw that he had been cast to the earth, he persecuted the woman who gave birth to the male *Child*. ¹⁴But the woman was given two wings of a great eagle, that she might fly into the wilderness to her place, where she is nourished for a time and times and half a time, from the presence of the serpent. ¹⁵So the serpent spewed water out of his mouth like a flood after the woman, that he might cause her to be carried away by the flood. ¹⁶But the earth helped the woman, and the earth opened its mouth and swallowed up the flood which the dragon had spewed out of his mouth. ¹⁷And the dragon was enraged with the woman, and he went to make war with the rest of her offspring, who keep the commandments of God and have the testimony of Jesus Christ.ᵃ

The Beast from the Sea

13 Then Iᵃ stood on the sand of the sea. And I saw a beast rising up out of the sea, having seven heads and ten horns,ᵇ and on his horns ten crowns, and on his heads a blasphemous name. ²Now the beast which I saw was like a leopard, his feet were like *the feet of* a bear, and his mouth like the mouth of a lion. The dragon gave him his power, his throne, and great authority. ³And I saw one of his heads as if it had been mortally wounded, and his deadly wound was healed. And all the world marveled and followed the beast. ⁴So they worshiped the dragon who gave authority to the beast; and they worshiped the beast, saying, "Who *is* like the beast? Who is able to make war with him?"

⁵And he was given a mouth speaking great things and blasphemies, and he was given authority to continueᵃ for forty-two months. ⁶Then he opened his mouth in blasphemy against God, to blaspheme His name, His tabernacle, and those who dwell in heaven. ⁷It was granted to him to make war with the saints and to overcome them. And authority was given him over every tribe,ᵃ tongue, and nation. ⁸All who dwell on the earth will worship him, whose names have not been written in the Book of Life of the Lamb slain from the foundation of the world.

⁹If anyone has an ear, let him hear. ¹⁰He who leads into captivity shall go into captivity; he who kills with the sword must be killed with the sword. Here is the patience and the faith of the saints.

The Beast from the Earth

¹¹Then I saw another beast coming up out of the earth, and he had two horns like a lamb and spoke like a dragon. ¹²And he exercises all the authority of the first beast in his presence, and causes the earth and

---

12:8 ᵃM-Text reads *him*.   **12:17** ᵃNU-Text and M-Text omit *Christ*.   **13:1** ᵃNU-Text reads *he*. ᵇNU-Text and M-Text read *ten horns and seven heads*. **13:5** ᵃM-Text reads *make war*.   **13:7** ᵃNU-Text and M-Text add *and people*.

those who dwell in it to worship the first beast, whose deadly wound was healed. [13]He performs great signs, so that he even makes fire come down from heaven on the earth in the sight of men. [14]And he deceives those[a] who dwell on the earth by those signs which he was granted to do in the sight of the beast, telling those who dwell on the earth to make an image to the beast who was wounded by the sword and lived. [15]He was granted *power* to give breath to the image of the beast, that the image of the beast should both speak and cause as many as would not worship the image of the beast to be killed. [16]He causes all, both small and great, rich and poor, free and slave, to receive a mark on their right hand or on their foreheads, [17]and that no one may buy or sell except one who has the mark or[a] the name of the beast, or the number of his name.

[18]Here is wisdom. Let him who has understanding calculate the number of the beast, for it is the number of a man: His number *is* 666.

The Lamb and the 144,000

14 Then I looked, and behold, a[a] Lamb standing on Mount Zion, and with Him one hundred *and* forty-four thousand, having[b] His Father's name written on their foreheads. [2]And I heard a voice from heaven, like the voice of many waters, and like the voice of loud thunder. And I heard the sound of harpists playing their harps. [3]They sang as it were a new song before the throne, before the four living creatures, and the elders; and no one could learn that song except the hundred *and* forty-four thousand who were redeemed from the earth. [4]These are the ones who were not defiled with women, for they are virgins. These are the ones who follow the Lamb wherever He goes. These were redeemed[a] from *among* men, *being* firstfruits to God and to the Lamb. [5]And in their mouth was found no deceit,[a] for they are without fault before the throne of God.[b]

The Proclamations of Three Angels

[6]Then I saw another angel flying in the midst of heaven, having the everlasting gospel to preach to those who dwell on the earth—to every nation, tribe, tongue, and people— [7]saying with a loud voice, "Fear God and give glory to Him, for the hour of His judgment has come; and worship Him who made heaven and earth, the sea and springs of water."

[8]And another angel followed, saying, "Babylon[a] is fallen, is fallen, that great city, because she has made all nations drink of the wine of the wrath of her fornication."

[9]Then a third angel followed them, saying with a loud voice, "If anyone worships the beast and his image, and receives *his* mark on his forehead or on his hand, [10]he himself shall also drink of the wine of the wrath of God, which is poured out full strength into the cup of His indignation. He shall be tormented with fire and brimstone in the presence of the holy angels and in the presence of the Lamb. [11]And the smoke of their torment ascends forever and ever; and they have no rest day or night, who worship the beast and his

---

DEVOTION

. . . who follow the Lamb wherever He goes.

REVELATION 14:4

Christ-ocrat

Benjamin Rush, a signer of the Declaration of Independence who worked with the Rev. Richard Allen to found the AME church, served in the administrations of three different presidents, each of whom was from a different political party. Asked for his own party affiliation, he once explained:

I have been alternately called an Aristocrat and a Democrat. I am now neither. I am a Christ-ocrat. I believe all power . . . will always fail of producing order and happiness in the hands of man. He alone who created and redeemed man is qualified to govern him.

13:14 [a]M-Text reads *my own people.* **13:17** [a]NU-Text and M-Text omit *or.* **14:1** [a]NU-Text and M-Text read *the.* [b]NU-Text and M-Text add *His name and.* **14:4** [a]M-Text adds *by Jesus.* **14:5** [a]NU-Text and M-Text read *falsehood.* [b]NU-Text and M-Text omit *before the throne of God.* **14:8** [a]NU-Text reads *Babylon the great is fallen, is fallen, which has made;* M-Text reads *Babylon the great is fallen. She has made.*

image, and whoever receives the mark of his name."

[12]Here is the patience of the saints; here *are* those[a] who keep the commandments of God and the faith of Jesus.

[13]Then I heard a voice from heaven saying to me,[a] "Write: 'Blessed *are* the dead who die in the Lord from now on.'"

"Yes," says the Spirit, "that they may rest from their labors, and their works follow them."

Reaping the Earth's Harvest

[14]Then I looked, and behold, a white cloud, and on the cloud sat *One* like the Son of Man, having on His head a golden crown, and in His hand a sharp sickle. [15]And another angel came out of the temple, crying with a loud voice to Him who sat on the cloud, "Thrust in Your sickle and reap, for the time has come for You[a] to reap, for the harvest of the earth is ripe." [16]So He who sat on the cloud thrust in His sickle on the earth, and the earth was reaped.

Reaping the Grapes of Wrath

[17]Then another angel came out of the temple which is in heaven, he also having a sharp sickle. [18]And another angel came out from the altar, who had power over fire, and he cried with a loud cry to him who had the sharp sickle, saying, "Thrust in your sharp sickle and gather the clusters of the vine of the earth, for her grapes are fully ripe." [19]So the angel thrust his sickle into the earth and gathered the vine of the earth, and threw *it* into the great winepress of the wrath of God. [20]And the winepress was trampled outside the city, and blood came out of the winepress, up to the horses' bridles, for one thousand six hundred furlongs.

Prelude to the Bowl Judgments

15 Then I saw another sign in heaven, great and marvelous: seven angels having the seven last plagues, for in them the wrath of God is complete.

[2]And I saw *something* like a sea of glass mingled with fire, and those who have the victory over the beast, over his image and over his mark[a] *and* over the number of his name, standing on the sea of glass, having harps of God. [3]They sing the song of Moses, the servant of God, and the song of the Lamb, saying:

TRUTH

"Great and marvelous are Your works,
Lord God Almighty!"   REVELATION 15:3

The Word and the Works of God

Benjamin Silliman (1779–1864), an American physicist, chemist, and geologist who founded and edited the *American Journal of Science and Arts*, stated:

> The relation of geology, as well as astronomy, to the Bible, when both are well understood, is that of perfect harmony. The Bible nowhere limits the age of the globe, while its chronology assigns a recent origin to the human race; and geology not only confirms that Genesis presents a true statement of the progress of the terrestrial arrangements and of the introduction of living beings in the order in which their fossil remains are found entombed in the strata.

> The Word and the works of God cannot conflict, and the more they are studied the more perfect will their harmony appear.

"Great and marvelous *are* Your works,
    Lord God Almighty!
    Just and true *are* Your ways,
    O King of the saints![a]
[4] Who shall not fear You, O Lord, and
        glorify Your name?
    For *You* alone *are* holy.
    For all nations shall come and
        worship before You,
    For Your judgments have been
        manifested."

[5]After these things I looked, and behold,[a] the temple of the tabernacle of the testimony in heaven was opened. [6]And out of the temple came the seven angels having

---

14:12 [a]NU-Text and M-Text omit *here are those.*
14:13 [a]NU-Text and M-Text omit *to me.*
14:15 [a]NU-Text and M-Text omit *for You.*
15:2 [a]NU-Text and M-Text omit *over his mark.*
15:3 [a]NU-Text and M-Text read *nations.*
15:5 [a]NU-Text and M-Text omit *behold.*

the seven plagues, clothed in pure bright linen, and having their chests girded with golden bands. 7Then one of the four living creatures gave to the seven angels seven golden bowls full of the wrath of God who lives forever and ever. 8The temple was filled with smoke from the glory of God and from His power, and no one was able to enter the temple till the seven plagues of the seven angels were completed.

16 Then I heard a loud voice from the temple saying to the seven angels, "Go and pour out the bowlsᵃ of the wrath of God on the earth."

First Bowl: Loathsome Sores

2So the first went and poured out his bowl upon the earth, and a foul and loathsome sore came upon the men who had the mark of the beast and those who worshiped his image.

Second Bowl: The Sea Turns to Blood

3Then the second angel poured out his bowl on the sea, and it became blood as of a dead *man;* and every living creature in the sea died.

Third Bowl: The Waters Turn to Blood

4Then the third angel poured out his bowl on the rivers and springs of water, and they became blood. 5And I heard the angel of the waters saying:

"You are righteous, O Lord,ᵃ
  The One who is and who was and
    who is to be,ᵇ
  Because You have judged these things.
6   For they have shed the blood of saints
    and prophets,
  And You have given them blood to
    drink.
  Forᵃ it is their just due."

7And I heard another fromᵃ the altar saying, "Even so, Lord God Almighty, true and righteous *are* Your judgments."

Abraham Lincoln placed his hand on Matthew 7:1, 18:7, and Revelation 16:7 as he took the presidential oath of office in 1865.

Fourth Bowl: Men Are Scorched

8Then the fourth angel poured out his bowl on the sun, and power was given to him to scorch men with fire. 9And men were scorched with great heat, and they blasphemed the name of God who has power over these plagues; and they did not repent and give Him glory.

Fifth Bowl: Darkness and Pain

10Then the fifth angel poured out his bowl on the throne of the beast, and his kingdom became full of darkness; and they gnawed their tongues because of the pain. 11They blasphemed the God of heaven because of their pains and their sores, and did not repent of their deeds.

Sixth Bowl: Euphrates Dried Up

12Then the sixth angel poured out his bowl on the great river Euphrates, and its water was dried up, so that the way of the kings from the east might be prepared. 13And I saw three unclean spirits like frogs *coming* out of the mouth of the dragon, out of the mouth of the beast, and out of the mouth of the false prophet. 14For they are spirits of demons, performing signs, *which* go out to the kings of the earth andᵃ of the whole world, to gather them to the battle of that great day of God Almighty.

15"Behold, I am coming as a thief. Blessed *is* he who watches, and keeps his garments, lest he walk naked and they see his shame."

16And they gathered them together to the place called in Hebrew, Armageddon.ᵃ

Seventh Bowl: The Earth Utterly Shaken

17Then the seventh angel poured out his bowl into the air, and a loud voice came out of the temple of heaven, from the throne, saying, "It is done!" 18And there were noises and thunderings and lightnings; and there was a great earthquake,

---

16:1 ᵃNU-Text and M-Text read *seven bowls.*
16:5 ᵃNU-Text and M-Text omit *O Lord.* ᵇNU-Text and M-Text read *who was, the Holy One.*   16:6 ᵃNU-Text and M-Text omit *For.*   16:7 ᵃNU-Text and M-Text omit *another from.*   16:14 ᵃNU-Text and M-Text omit *of the earth and.*   16:16 ᵃM-Text reads *Megiddo.*

such a mighty and great earthquake as had not occurred since men were on the earth. ¹⁹Now the great city was divided into three parts, and the cities of the nations fell. And great Babylon was remembered before God, to give her the cup of the wine of the fierceness of His wrath. ²⁰Then every island fled away, and the mountains were not found. ²¹And great hail from heaven fell upon men, *each hailstone* about the weight of a talent. Men blasphemed God because of the plague of the hail, since that plague was exceedingly great.

The Scarlet Woman and the Scarlet Beast

17 Then one of the seven angels who had the seven bowls came and talked with me, saying to me,ᵃ "Come, I will show you the judgment of the great harlot who sits on many waters, ²with whom the kings of the earth committed fornication, and the inhabitants of the earth were made drunk with the wine of her fornication."

³So he carried me away in the Spirit into the wilderness. And I saw a woman sitting on a scarlet beast *which was* full of names of blasphemy, having seven heads and ten horns. ⁴The woman was arrayed in purple and scarlet, and adorned with gold and precious stones and pearls, having in her hand a golden cup full of abominations and the filthiness of her fornication.ᵃ ⁵And on her forehead a name *was* written:

MYSTERY, BABYLON THE GREAT, THE MOTHER OF HARLOTS AND OF THE ABOMINATIONS OF THE EARTH.

⁶I saw the woman, drunk with the blood of the saints and with the blood of the martyrs of Jesus. And when I saw her, I marveled with great amazement.

The Meaning of the Woman and the Beast

⁷But the angel said to me, "Why did you marvel? I will tell you the mystery of the woman and of the beast that carries her, which has the seven heads and the ten horns. ⁸The beast that you saw was, and is not, and will ascend out of the bottomless pit and go to perdition. And those who dwell on the earth will marvel, whose names are not written in the Book of Life from the

foundation of the world, when they see the beast that was, and is not, and yet is.ᵃ

⁹"Here *is* the mind which has wisdom: The seven heads are seven mountains on which the woman sits. ¹⁰There are also seven kings. Five have fallen, one is, *and* the other has not yet come. And when he comes, he must continue a short time. ¹¹The beast that was, and is not, is himself also the eighth, and is of the seven, and is going to perdition.

¹²"The ten horns which you saw are ten kings who have received no kingdom as yet, but they receive authority for one hour as kings with the beast. ¹³These are of one mind, and they will give their power and authority to the beast. ¹⁴These will make war with the Lamb, and the Lamb will overcome them, for He is Lord of lords and King of kings; and those *who are* with Him *are* called, chosen, and faithful."

¹⁵Then he said to me, "The waters which you saw, where the harlot sits, are peoples, multitudes, nations, and tongues. ¹⁶And the ten horns which you saw onᵃ the beast, these will hate the harlot, make her desolate and naked, eat her flesh and burn her with fire. ¹⁷For God has put it into their hearts to fulfill His purpose, to be of one mind, and to give their kingdom to the beast, until the words of God are fulfilled. ¹⁸And the woman whom you saw is that great city which reigns over the kings of the earth."

The Fall of Babylon the Great

18 After these things I saw another angel coming down from heaven, having great authority, and the earth was illuminated with his glory. ²And he cried mightilyᵃ with a loud voice, saying, "Babylon the great is fallen, is fallen, and has become a dwelling place of demons, a prison for every foul spirit, and a cage for every unclean and hated bird! ³For all the nations have drunk of the wine of the wrath of her fornication, the kings of the earth have

---

17:1 ᵃNU-Text and M-Text omit *to me.*
17:4 ᵃM-Text reads *the filthiness of the fornication of the earth.*   **17:8** ᵃNU-Text and M-Text read *and shall be present.*   **17:16** ᵃNU-Text and M-Text read *saw, and the beast.*   **18:2** ᵃNU-Text and M-Text omit *mightily.*

committed fornication with her, and the merchants of the earth have become rich through the abundance of her luxury."

[4]And I heard another voice from heaven saying, "Come out of her, my people, lest you share in her sins, and lest you receive of her plagues. [5]For her sins have reached[a] to heaven, and God has remembered her iniquities. [6]Render to her just as she rendered to you,[a] and repay her double according to her works; in the cup which she has mixed, mix double for her. [7]In the measure that she glorified herself and lived luxuriously, in the same measure give her torment and sorrow; for she says in her heart, 'I sit *as* queen, and am no widow, and will not see sorrow.' [8]Therefore her plagues will come in one day—death and mourning and famine. And she will be utterly burned with fire, for strong *is* the Lord God who judges[a] her.

The World Mourns Babylon's Fall

[9]"The kings of the earth who committed fornication and lived luxuriously with her will weep and lament for her, when they see the smoke of her burning, [10]standing at a distance for fear of her torment, saying, 'Alas, alas, that great city Babylon, that mighty city! For in one hour your judgment has come.'

[11]"And the merchants of the earth will weep and mourn over her, for no one buys their merchandise anymore: [12]merchandise of gold and silver, precious stones and pearls, fine linen and purple, silk and scarlet, every kind of citron wood, every kind of object of ivory, every kind of object of most precious wood, bronze, iron, and marble; [13]and cinnamon and incense, fragrant oil and frankincense, wine and oil, fine flour and wheat, cattle and sheep, horses and chariots, and bodies and souls of men. [14]The fruit that your soul longed for has gone from you, and all the things which are rich and splendid have gone from you,[a] and you shall find them no more at all. [15]The merchants of these things, who became rich by her, will stand at a distance for fear of her torment, weeping and wailing, [16]and saying, 'Alas, alas, that great city that was clothed in fine linen, purple,

and scarlet, and adorned with gold and precious stones and pearls! [17]For in one hour such great riches came to nothing.' Every shipmaster, all who travel by ship, sailors, and as many as trade on the sea, stood at a distance [18]and cried out when they saw the smoke of her burning, saying, 'What *is* like this great city?'

[19]"They threw dust on their heads and cried out, weeping and wailing, and saying, 'Alas, alas, that great city, in which all who had ships on the sea became rich by her wealth! For in one hour she is made desolate.'

[20]"Rejoice over her, O heaven, and *you* holy apostles[a] and prophets, for God has avenged you on her!"

Finality of Babylon's Fall

[21]Then a mighty angel took up a stone like a great millstone and threw *it* into the sea, saying, "Thus with violence the great city Babylon shall be thrown down, and shall not be found anymore. [22]The sound of harpists, musicians, flutists, and trumpeters shall not be heard in you anymore. No craftsman of any craft shall be found in you anymore, and the sound of a millstone shall not be heard in you anymore. [23]The light of a lamp shall not shine in you anymore, and the voice of bridegroom and bride shall not be heard in you anymore. For your merchants were the great men of the earth, for by your sorcery all the nations were deceived. [24]And in her was found the blood of prophets and saints, and of all who were slain on the earth."

Heaven Exults over Babylon

19 After these things I heard[a] a loud voice of a great multitude in heaven, saying, "Alleluia! Salvation and glory and honor and power *belong* to the Lord[b] our God! [2]For true and righteous *are* His judgments, because He has judged the great

---

18:5 [a]NU-Text and M-Text read *have been heaped up.*
18:6 [a]NU-Text and M-Text omit *to you.*
18:8 [a]NU-Text and M-Text read *has judged.*
18:14 [a]NU-Text and M-Text read *been lost to you.*
18:20 [a]NU-Text and M-Text read *saints and apostles.*
19:1 [a]NU-Text and M-Text add *something like.*
[b]NU-Text and M-Text omit *the Lord.*

harlot who corrupted the earth with her fornication; and He has avenged on her the blood of His servants *shed* by her." ³Again they said, "Alleluia! Her smoke rises up forever and ever!" ⁴And the twenty-four elders and the four living creatures fell down and worshiped God who sat on the throne, saying, "Amen! Alleluia!" ⁵Then a voice came from the throne, saying, "Praise our God, all you His servants and those who fear Him, bothᵃ small and great!"

⁶And I heard, as it were, the voice of a great multitude, as the sound of many waters and as the sound of mighty thunderings, saying, "Alleluia! For theᵃ Lord God Omnipotent reigns! ⁷Let us be glad and rejoice and give Him glory, for the marriage of the Lamb has come, and His wife has made herself ready." ⁸And to her it was granted to be arrayed in fine linen, clean and bright, for the fine linen is the righteous acts of the saints.

⁹Then he said to me, "Write: 'Blessed *are* those who are called to the marriage supper of the Lamb!'" And he said to me, "These are the true sayings of God." ¹⁰And I fell at his feet to worship him. But he said to me, "See *that you do* not *do that!* I am your fellow servant, and of your brethren who have the testimony of Jesus. Worship God! For the testimony of Jesus is the spirit of prophecy."

Christ on a White Horse

¹¹Now I saw heaven opened, and behold, a white horse. And He who sat on him *was* called Faithful and True, and in righteousness He judges and makes war. ¹²His eyes *were* like a flame of fire, and on His head *were* many crowns. He hadᵃ a name written that no one knew except Himself. ¹³He *was* clothed with a robe dipped in blood, and His name is called The Word of God. ¹⁴And the armies in heaven, clothed in fine linen, white and clean,ᵃ followed Him on white horses. ¹⁵Now out of His mouth goes a sharpᵃ sword, that with it He should strike the nations. And He Himself will rule them with a rod of iron. He Himself treads the winepress of the fierceness and wrath of Almighty God. ¹⁶And He has on *His* robe and on His thigh a name written:

KING OF KINGS AND LORD OF LORDS.

The Beast and His Armies Defeated

¹⁷Then I saw an angel standing in the sun; and he cried with a loud voice, saying to all the birds that fly in the midst of heaven, "Come and gather together for the supper of the great God,ᵃ ¹⁸that you may eat the flesh of kings, the flesh of captains, the flesh of mighty men, the flesh of horses and of those who sit on them, and the flesh of all *people,* freeᵃ and slave, both small and great."

¹⁹And I saw the beast, the kings of the earth, and their armies, gathered together to make war against Him who sat on the horse and against His army. ²⁰Then the beast was captured, and with him the false prophet who worked signs in his presence, by which he deceived those who received the mark of the beast and those who worshiped his image. These two were cast alive into the lake of fire burning with brimstone. ²¹And the rest were killed with the sword which proceeded from the mouth of Him who sat on the horse. And all the birds were filled with their flesh.

Satan Bound 1,000 Years

20 Then I saw an angel coming down from heaven, having the key to the bottomless pit and a great chain in his hand. ²He laid hold of the dragon, that serpent of old, who is *the* Devil and Satan, and bound him for a thousand years; ³and he cast him into the bottomless pit, and shut him up, and set a seal on him, so that he should deceive the nations no more till the thousand years were finished. But after these things he must be released for a little while.

The Saints Reign with Christ 1,000 Years

⁴And I saw thrones, and they sat on them, and judgment was committed to them. Then *I saw* the souls of those who had been beheaded for their witness to

---

19:5 ᵃNU-Text and M-Text omit *both.*
19:6 ᵃNU-Text and M-Text read *our.*
19:12 ᵃM-Text adds *names written, and.*
19:14 ᵃNU-Text and M-Text read *pure white linen.*
19:15 ᵃM-Text adds *two-edged.*
19:17 ᵃNU-Text and M-Text read *the great supper of God.* **19:18** ᵃNU-Text and M-Text read *both free.*

Jesus and for the word of God, who had not worshiped the beast or his image, and had not received *his* mark on their foreheads or on their hands. And they lived and reigned with Christ for a[a] thousand years. [5]But the rest of the dead did not live again until the thousand years were finished. This *is* the first resurrection. [6]Blessed and holy *is* he who has part in the first resurrection. Over such the second death has no power, but they shall be priests of God and of Christ, and shall reign with Him a thousand years.

Satanic Rebellion Crushed

[7]Now when the thousand years have expired, Satan will be released from his prison [8]and will go out to deceive the nations which are in the four corners of the earth, Gog and Magog, to gather them together to battle, whose number *is* as the sand of the sea. [9]They went up on the breadth of the earth and surrounded the camp of the saints and the beloved city. And fire came down from God out of heaven and devoured them. [10]The devil, who deceived them, was cast into the lake of fire and brimstone where[a] the beast and the false prophet *are*. And they will be tormented day and night forever and ever.

The Great White Throne Judgment

[11]Then I saw a great white throne and Him who sat on it, from whose face the earth and the heaven fled away. And there was found no place for them. [12]And I saw the dead, small and great, standing before God,[a] and books were opened. And another book was opened, which is *the Book* of Life. And the dead were judged according to their works, by the things which were written in the books. [13]The sea gave up the dead who were in it, and Death and Hades delivered up the dead who were in them. And they were judged, each one according to his works. [14]Then Death and Hades were cast into the lake of fire. This is the second death.[a] [15]And anyone not found written in the Book of Life was cast into the lake of fire.

All Things Made New

21 Now I saw a new heaven and a new earth, for the first heaven and the first earth had passed away. Also there was no more sea. [2]Then I, John,[a] saw the holy city, New Jerusalem, coming down out of heaven from God, prepared as a bride adorned for her husband. [3]And I heard a loud voice from heaven saying, "Behold, the tabernacle of God *is* with men, and He will dwell with them, and they shall be His people. God Himself will be with them *and be* their God. [4]And God will wipe away every tear from their eyes; there shall be no more death, nor sorrow, nor crying. There shall be no more pain, for the former things have passed away."

[5]Then He who sat on the throne said, "Behold, I make all things new." And He said to me,[a] "Write, for these words are true and faithful."

MORAL STRENGTH

". . . and all liars shall have their part in the lake which burns with fire. . . ."   REVELATION 21:8

Lying

Thomas Jefferson, a Founding Father and the third President of the United States (1801–1809), wrote:

> *He who permits himself to tell a lie once, finds it much easier to do it a second and third time, till at length it becomes habitual; he tells lies without attending to it, and truths without the world's believing him. This falsehood of the tongue leads to that of the heart, and in time depraves all its good dispositions.*

---

[6]And He said to me, "It is done![a] I am the Alpha and the Omega, the Beginning and the End. I will give of the fountain of the water of life freely to him who thirsts. [7]He who overcomes shall inherit all things,[a] and I will be his God and he shall be My son. [8]But the cowardly, unbelieving,[a] abominable, murderers, sexually immoral, sorcerers, idolaters, and all liars shall have their part in the lake which

---

20:4 [a]M-Text reads *the*.   **20:10** [a]NU-Text and M-Text add *also*.   **20:12** [a]NU-Text and M-Text read *the throne*.   **20:14** [a]NU-Text and M-Text add *the lake of fire*.   **21:2** [a]NU-Text and M-Text omit *John*. **21:5** [a]NU-Text and M-Text omit *to me*. **21:6** [a]M-Text omits *It is done*.   **21:7** [a]M-Text reads *overcomes, I shall give him these things*. **21:8** [a]M-Text adds *and sinners*.

burns with fire and brimstone, which is the second death."

The New Jerusalem

9Then one of the seven angels who had the seven bowls filled with the seven last plagues came to mea and talked with me, saying, "Come, I will show you the bride, the Lamb's wife."b 10And he carried me away in the Spirit to a great and high mountain, and showed me the great city, the holya Jerusalem, descending out of heaven from God, 11having the glory of God. Her light *was* like a most precious stone, like a jasper stone, clear as crystal. 12Also she had a great and high wall with twelve gates, and twelve angels at the gates, and names written on them, which are *the names* of the twelve tribes of the children of Israel: 13three gates on the east, three gates on the north, three gates on the south, and three gates on the west.

14Now the wall of the city had twelve foundations, and on them were the namesa of the twelve apostles of the Lamb. 15And he who talked with me had a gold reed to measure the city, its gates, and its wall. 16The city is laid out as a square; its length is as great as its breadth. And he measured the city with the reed: twelve thousand furlongs. Its length, breadth, and height are equal. 17Then he measured its wall: one hundred *and* forty-four cubits, *according* to the measure of a man, that is, of an angel. 18The construction of its wall was *of* jasper; and the city *was* pure gold, like clear glass. 19The foundations of the wall of the city *were* adorned with all kinds of precious stones: the first foundation *was* jasper, the second sapphire, the third chalcedony, the fourth emerald, 20the fifth sardonyx, the sixth sardius, the seventh chrysolite, the eighth beryl, the ninth topaz, the tenth chrysoprase, the eleventh jacinth, and the twelfth amethyst. 21The twelve gates *were* twelve pearls: each individual gate was of one pearl. And the street of the city *was* pure gold, like transparent glass.

The Glory of the New Jerusalem

22But I saw no temple in it, for the Lord God Almighty and the Lamb are its temple.

23The city had no need of the sun or of the moon to shine in it,a for the gloryb of God illuminated it. The Lamb *is* its light. 24And the nations of those who are saveda shall walk in its light, and the kings of the earth bring their glory and honor into it.b 25Its gates shall not be shut at all by day (there shall be no night there). 26And they shall bring the glory and the honor of the nations into it.a 27But there shall by no means enter it anything that defiles, or causesa an abomination or a lie, but only those who are written in the Lamb's Book of Life.

The River of Life

22 And he showed me a purea river of water of life, clear as crystal, proceeding from the throne of God and of the Lamb. 2In the middle of its street, and on either side of the river, *was* the tree of life, which bore twelve fruits, each *tree* yielding its fruit every month. The leaves of the tree *were* for the healing of the nations. 3And there shall be no more curse, but the throne of God and of the Lamb shall be in it, and His servants shall serve Him. 4They shall see His face, and His name *shall be* on their foreheads. 5There shall be no night there: They need no lamp nor light of the sun, for the Lord God gives them light. And they shall reign forever and ever.

The Time Is Near

6Then he said to me, "These words *are* faithful and true." And the Lord God of the holya prophets sent His angel to show His servants the things which must shortly take place.

7"Behold, I am coming quickly! Blessed *is* he who keeps the words of the prophecy of this book."

21:9 aNU-Text and M-Text omit *to me.* bM-Text reads *I will show you the woman, the Lamb's bride.* **21:10** aNU-Text and M-Text omit *the great* and read *the holy city, Jerusalem.* **21:14** aNU-Text and M-Text read *twelve names.* **21:23** aNU-Text and M-Text omit *in it.* bM-Text reads *the very glory.* **21:24** aNU-Text and M-Text omit *of those who are saved.* bM-Text reads *the glory and honor of the nations to Him.* **21:26** aM-Text adds *that they may enter in.* **21:27** aNU-Text and M-Text read *anything profane, nor one who causes.* **22:1** aNU-Text and M-Text omit *pure.* **22:6** aNU-Text and M-Text read *spirits of the prophets.*

⁸Now I, John, saw and heard[a] these things. And when I heard and saw, I fell down to worship before the feet of the angel who showed me these things. ⁹Then he said to me, "See *that you do* not *do that.* For[a] I am your fellow servant, and of your brethren the prophets, and of those who keep the words of this book. Worship God." ¹⁰And he said to me, "Do not seal the words of the prophecy of this book, for the time is at hand. ¹¹He who is unjust, let him be unjust still; he who is filthy, let him be filthy still; he who is righteous, let him be righteous[a] still; he who is holy, let him be holy still."

Jesus Testifies to the Churches

¹²"And behold, I am coming quickly, and My reward *is* with Me, to give to every one according to his work. ¹³I am the Alpha and the Omega, *the* Beginning and *the* End, the First and the Last."[a]

¹⁴Blessed *are* those who do His commandments,[a] that they may have the right to the tree of life, and may enter through the gates into the city. ¹⁵But[a] outside *are* dogs and sorcerers and sexually immoral and murderers and idolaters, and whoever loves and practices a lie. ¹⁶"I, Jesus, have sent My angel to testify to you these things in the churches. I am the Root and the Offspring of David, the Bright and Morning Star." ¹⁷And the Spirit and the bride say, "Come!" And let him who hears say, "Come!" And let him who thirsts come. Whoever desires, let him take the water of life freely.

22:8 [a]NU-Text and M-Text read *am the one who heard and saw.* 22:9 [a]NU-Text and M-Text omit *For.*
22:11 [a]NU-Text and M-Text read *do right.*
22:13 [a]NU-Text and M-Text read *the First and the Last, the Beginning and the End.* 22:14 [a]NU-Text reads *wash their robes.* 22:15 [a]NU-Text and M-Text omit *But.*

HOPE

"And behold, I am coming quickly, and My reward is with Me, to give to every one according to his work."

REVELATION 22:12

Dr. Billy Graham

YES, THERE IS HOPE

On September 14, 2001, in the aftermath of the September 11 attacks, Dr. Billy Graham led a national prayer and remembrance service at Washington National Cathedral in which he reminded every American:

This event reminds us of the brevity and the uncertainty of life. We never know when we too will be called into eternity. I doubt if even one of those people who got on those planes or walked into the World Trade Center or the Pentagon last Tuesday morning thought it would be the last day of their lives. It didn't occur to them. And that's why each of us needs to face our own spiritual need and commit ourselves to God and His will now.

Here in this majestic National Cathedral we see all around us symbols of the Cross. For the Christian, I'm speaking for the Christian now, the Cross tells us that God understands our sin and our suffering, for He took upon Himself in the person of Jesus Christ our sins and our suffering. And from the Cross, God declares, "I love you. I know the heartaches and the sorrows and the pains that you feel. But I love you."

The story does not end with the Cross, for Easter points us beyond the tragedy of the Cross to the empty tomb. It tells us that there is hope for eternal life, for Christ has conquered evil and death, and hell. Yes, there is hope.

A Warning

[18]For[a] I testify to everyone who hears the words of the prophecy of this book: If anyone adds to these things, God will add[b] to him the plagues that are written in this book; [19]and if anyone takes away from the words of the book of this prophecy, God shall take away[a] his part from the Book[b] of Life, from the holy city, and *from* the things which are written in this book.

I Am Coming Quickly

[20]He who testifies to these things says, "Surely I am coming quickly."

Amen. Even so, come, Lord Jesus!

[21]The grace of our Lord Jesus Christ *be* with you all.[a] Amen.

22:18 [a]NU-Text and M-Text omit *For.* [b]M-Text reads *may God add.* **22:19** [a]M-Text reads *may God take away.* [b]NU-Text and M-Text read *tree of life.* **22:21** [a]NU-Text reads *with all;* M-Text reads *with all the saints.*

PRESIDENTS OF THE UNITED STATES OF AMERICA

1. George Washington	1789–1797	25. William McKinley	1897–1901
2. John Adams	1797–1801	26. Theodore Roosevelt	1901–1909
3. Thomas Jefferson	1801–1809	27. William H. Taft	1909–1913
4. James Madison	1809–1817	28. Woodrow Wilson	1913–1921
5. James Monroe	1817–1825	29. Warren G. Harding	1921–1923
6. John Q. Adams	1825–1829	30. Calvin Coolidge	1923–1929
7. Andrew Jackson	1829–1837	31. Herbert C. Hoover	1929–1933
8. Martin Van Buren	1837–1841	32. Franklin D. Roosevelt	1933–1945
9. William H. Harrison	1841	33. Harry S. Truman	1945–1953
10. John Tyler	1841–1845	34. Dwight D. Eisenhower	1953–1961
11. James K. Polk	1845–1849	35. John F. Kennedy	1961–1963
12. Zachary Taylor	1849–1850	36. Lyndon B. Johnson	1963–1969
13. Millard Fillmore	1850–1853	37. Richard M. Nixon	1969–1974
14. Franklin Pierce	1853–1857	38. Gerald R. Ford	1974–1977
15. James Buchanan	1857–1861	39. James E. Carter Jr.	1977–1981
16. Abraham Lincoln	1861–1865	40. Ronald W. Reagan	1981–1989
17. Andrew Johnson	1865–1869	41. George H.W. Bush	1989–1993
18. Ulysses S. Grant	1869–1877	42. William J. Clinton	1993–2001
19. Rutherford B. Hayes	1877–1881	43. George W. Bush	2001–2009
20. James A. Garfield	1881	44. Barack H. Obama	2009–
21. Chester A. Arthur	1881–1885		
22. Grover Cleveland	1885–1889		
23. Benjamin Harrison	1889–1893		
24. Grover Cleveland	1893–1897		

SUBJECT INDEX

In the following index, entries that begin with CAPITAL LETTERS lead to articles that deal with outstanding characteristics of the American patriot. Entries that include *Italic Titles* refer to the four-page, full-color inserts that are interspersed throughout the Bible and numbered consecutively, starting with I-1 and ending with I-48. An entry that includes "Introduction to . . ." refers to the introduction to a specific book of the Bible or to the general Introduction to the Bible. The last number in each entry represents the page number in the Bible where this article is found. Note: Several presidential inaugurations do not have an inaugural passage. In some cases that information was unavailable, or a closed Bible was used.

CONCORDANCE

The Concordance includes proper names and significant topics, defined by phrases and scripture references. Occasionally, a keyword applies to more than one Bible person, place, or topic. This is the case with "Abijah," for whom the Concordance lists four different persons by that name. The second, third, and following occurrences are distinguished by the dash ("————").

AARON
Ancestry and family of, Ex 6:16–20, 23
Helper and prophet to Moses, Ex 4:13–31; 7:1, 2
Appears before Pharaoh, Ex 5:1–4
Performs miracles, Ex 7:9, 10, 19, 20
Supports Moses' hands, Ex 17:10–12
Ascends Mt. Sinai; sees God's glory, Ex 19:24; 24:1, 9, 10
Judges Israel in Moses' absence, Ex 24:14
Chosen by God as priest, Ex 28:1
Consecrated, Ex 29; Lev 8
Duties prescribed, Ex 30:7–10
Tolerates Israel's idolatry, Ex 32
Priestly ministry begins, Lev 9
Sons offer profane fire; Aaron's humble response, Lev 10
Conspires against Moses, Num 12:1–16
Rebelled against by Korah, Num 16
Intercedes to stop plague, Num 16:45–48
Rod buds to confirm his authority, Num 17:1–10
With Moses, fails at Meribah, Num 20:1–13
Dies; son succeeds him as priest, Num 20:23–29
His priesthood compared:
with Melchizedek's, Heb 7:11–19
with Christ's, Heb 9:6–15, 23–28

ABADDON
Angel of the bottomless pit, Rev 9:11

ABASED
I know how to be a . . . . Phil 4:12

ABBA
And He said, "A . . . . Mark 14:36
by whom we cry out, "A . . . Rom 8:15
crying out, "A . . . . Gal 4:6

ABED-NEGO
Name given to Azariah, a Hebrew captive, Dan 1:7
Appointed by Nebuchadnezzar, Dan 2:49
Refuses to serve idols; cast into furnace but delivered, Dan 3:12–30

ABEL
Adam's second son, Gen 4:2
His offering accepted, Gen 4:4
Murdered by Cain, Gen 4:8
His sacrifice offered by faith, Heb 11:4

ABHOR
My soul shall not a . . . . . . Lev 26:11
Therefore I a myself . . . . Job 42:6
nations will a him . . . . . . Prov 24:24
a the pride of Jacob . . . . Amos 6:8
A what is evil . . . . Rom 12:9

ABHORRED
a His own inheritance . . . . . Ps 106:40
he who is a by the . . . . . . Prov 22:14
and their soul also a . . . . . . Zech 11:8

ABHORRENCE
They shall be an a . . . . Is 66:24

ABHORRENT
you have made us a . . . . Ex 5:21

ABIATHAR
A priest who escapes Saul at Nob, 1 Sam 22:20–23
Becomes high priest under David, 1 Sam 23:6, 9–12
Remains faithful to David, 2 Sam 15:24–29
Informs David about Ahithophel, 2 Sam 15:34–36
Supports Adonijah's usurpation, 1 Kin 1:7, 9, 25
Deposed by Solomon, 1 Kin 2:26, 27, 35

ABIDE
nor a in its paths . . . . Job 24:13
LORD, who may a . . . . Ps 15:1
He shall a before God . . . . Ps 61:7
the Most High shall a . . . . Ps 91:1
"If you a in My word . . . . . John 8:31
And a slave does not a . . . . John 8:35
Helper, that He may a . . . . John 14:16
A in Me and I in you . . . . . John 15:4
If you a in Me . . . . John 15:7
a in My love . . . . John 15:9
And now a faith . . . . 1 Cor 13:13
does the love of God a . . . 1 John 3:17
by this we know that we a . . 1 John 4:13

ABIDES
even He who a from of old . . Ps 55:19
He who a in Me . . . . John 15:5
lives and a forever . . . . 1 Pet 1:23
will of God a forever . . . . 1 John 2:17

ABIDING
not have His word a . . . . . John 5:38
has eternal life a . . . . 1 John 3:15

ABIGAIL
Wise wife of foolish Nabal, 1 Sam 25:3
Appeases David and becomes his wife, 1 Sam 25:14–42
Mother of Chileab, 2 Sam 3:3

ABIHU
Second son of Aaron, Ex 6:23
Offers profane fire and dies, Lev 10:1–7

ABIJAH
Samuel's second son; follows corrupt ways, 1 Sam 8:2, 3
———— Descendant of Aaron; head of an office of priests, 1 Chr 24:3, 10
Zechariah belongs to division of, Luke 1:5

———— Son of Jeroboam I, 1 Kin 14:1–18
———— Another name for King Abijam, 2 Chr 11:20

ABIJAM (or Abijah)
King of Judah, 1 Kin 14:31
Follows the sins of his father, 1 Kin 15:1–7
Defeats Jeroboam and takes cities, 2 Chr 13:13–20

ABILITY
who had a to serve . . . . Dan 1:4
according to his own a . . . Matt 25:15
and beyond their a . . . . 2 Cor 8:3
a which God supplies . . . . . 1 Pet 4:11

ABIMELECH
King of Gerar; takes Sarah in ignorance, Gen 20:1–18
Makes treaty with Abraham, Gen 21:22–34
———— A second king of Gerar; sends Isaac away, Gen 26:1–16
Makes treaty with Isaac, Gen 26:17–33
———— Gideon's son by a concubine, Judg 8:31
Conspires to become king, Judg 9

ABINADAB
A man of Kirjath Jearim in whose house the ark was kept, 1 Sam 7:1, 2
———— The second of Jesse's eight sons, 1 Sam 16:8
Serves in Saul's army, 1 Sam 17:13
———— A son of Saul slain at Mt. Gilboa, 1 Sam 31:1–8
Bones of, buried by men of Jabesh, 1 Chr 10:1–12

ABIRAM
Reubenite who conspired against Moses, Num 16:1–50

ABISHAG
A Shunammite employed as David's nurse, 1 Kin 1:1–4, 15
Witnessed David's choice of Solomon as successor, 1 Kin 1:15–31
Adonijah slain for desiring to marry her, 1 Kin 2:13–25

ABISHAI
David's nephew; joins Joab in blood revenge against Abner, 2 Sam 2:18–24
Loyal to David during Absalom's and Sheba's rebellion, 2 Sam 16:9–12; 20:1–6, 10
Rebuked by David, 2 Sam 16:9–12; 19:21–23
His exploits, 2 Sam 21:16, 17; 23:18; 1 Chr 18:12, 13

ABLE

you are *a* to number . . . . . Gen 15:5
shall give as he is *a* . . . . . . Deut 16:17
For who is *a* to judge . . . . . . 1 Kin 3:9
"The LORD is *a* . . . . 2 Chr 25:9
Who then is *a* to stand . . . . Job 41:10
God whom we serve is *a* . . . Dan 3:17
God is *a* to raise up . . . . . . Matt 3:9
believe that I am *a* . . . . . . Matt 9:28
fear Him who is *a* . . . . Matt 10:28
Are you *a* to drink the . . . Matt 20:22
beyond what you are *a* . 1 Cor 10:13
And God is *a* to make . . . . . 2 Cor 9:8
may be *a* to comprehend . . . Eph 3:18
persuaded that He is *a* . . 2 Tim 1:12
learning and never *a* . . . . . 2 Tim 3:7
being tempted, He is *a* . . . . Heb 2:18
that God was *a* to . . . . Heb 11:19
to Him who is *a* . . . . Jude 24
has come, and who is *a* . . . . Rev 6:17

ABNER

Saul's cousin; commander of his
    army, 1 Sam 14:50, 51
Rebuked by David, 1 Sam 26:5, 14–16
Supports Ishbosheth; defeated by
    David's men; kills Asahel, 2 Sam
    2:8–32
Makes covenant with David, 2 Sam
    3:6–21
Killed by Joab; mourned by David,
    2 Sam 3:22–39

ABODE

but left their own *a* . . . . Jude 6

ABOLISHED

your works may be *a* . . . . . Ezek 6:6
having *a* in His flesh . . . . . . Eph 2:15
Christ, who has *a* . . . . 2 Tim 1:10

ABOMINABLE

not make yourselves *a* . . . . Lev 11:43
They have done *a* . . . . Ps 14:1
your grave like an *a* . . . . Is 14:19
Oh, do not do this *a* . . . . . . Jer 44:4
they deny Him, being *a* . . . Titus 1:16
and *a* idolatries . . . . 1 Pet 4:3
unbelieving, *a* . . . . Rev 21:8

ABOMINATION

every shepherd is an *a* . . . . Gen 46:34
If we sacrifice the *a* . . . . Ex 8:26
You have made me an *a* . . . . . Ps 88:8
yes, seven are an *a* . . . . Prov 6:16
wickedness is an *a* . . . . Prov 8:7
Dishonest scales are an *a* . . Prov 11:1
the scoffer is an *a* . . . . Prov 24:9
prayer is an *a* . . . . Prov 28:9
An unjust man is an *a* . . . . Prov 29:27
incense is an *a* . . . . Is 1:13
and place there the *a* . . . . . Dan 11:31
the *a* of desolation . . . . . . Dan 12:11
the '*a* of desolation,' . . . . Matt 24:15
among men is an *a* . . . . . Luke 16:15

ABOMINATIONS

to follow the *a* . . . . Deut 18:9
delights in their *a* . . . . Is 66:3
will put away your *a* . . . . Jer 4:1
your harlotry, your *a* . . . . . Jer 13:27
will see greater *a* . . . . Ezek 8:6
a which they commit . . . . Ezek 8:17
you, throw away the *a* . . . . Ezek 20:7
show her all her *a* . . . . . . Ezek 22:2
a golden cup full of *a* . . . . . Rev 17:4
of the *a* of the earth . . . . . . Rev 17:5

ABOUND

lawlessness will *a* . . . . . . Matt 24:12
the offense might *a* . . . . . . Rom 5:20
sin that grace may *a* . . . . . . Rom 6:1

thanksgiving to *a* . . . . 2 Cor 4:15
to make all grace *a* . . . . 2 Cor 9:8
and I know how to *a* . . . . . . Phil 4:12
that you should *a* . . . . . . 1 Thess 4:1
things are yours and *a* . . . . 2 Pet 1:8

ABOUNDED

But where sin *a* . . . . Rom 5:20

ABOUNDING

and *a* in mercy . . . . Ps 103:8
immovable, always *a* . . . 1 Cor 15:58

ABOVE

that is in heaven *a* . . . . Ex 20:4
"He sent from *a* . . . . . . 2 Sam 22:17
A it stood seraphim . . . . Is 6:2
nor a servant *a* his master Matt 10:24
He who comes from *a* . . . . . John 3:31
I am from *a* . . . . John 8:23
been given you from *a* . . . John 19:11
who is *a* all . . . . Eph 4:6
the name which is *a* . . . . . . Phil 2:9
things which are *a* . . . . Col 3:1
perfect gift is from *a* . . . . James 1:17

ABRAHAM

Ancestry and family, Gen 11:26–31
Receives God's call; enters Canaan,
    Gen 12:1–6
Promised Canaan by God; pitched
    tent near Bethel, Gen 12:7, 8
Deceives Egyptians concerning Sarai,
    Gen 12:11–20
Separates from Lot; inherits Canaan,
    Gen 13
Rescues Lot from captivity,
    Gen 14:11–16
Gives a tithe to Melchizedek; refuses
    spoil, Gen 14:18–24
Covenant renewed; promised a son,
    Gen 15
Takes Hagar as concubine; Ishmael
    born, Gen 16
Name changed from Abram; circum-
    cision commanded, Gen 17
Entertains Lord and angels, Gen
    18:1–15
Intercedes for Sodom, Gen 18:16–33
Deceives Abimelech concerning
    Sarah, Gen 20
Birth of Isaac, Gen 21:1–7
Sends Hagar and Ishmael away,
    Gen 21:9–14
Offers Isaac in obedience to God,
    Gen 22:1–19
Finds wife for Isaac, Gen 24
Marries Keturah; fathers other chil-
    dren; dies, Gen 25:1–10
Friend of God, 2 Chr 20:7
Justified by faith, Rom 4:1–12
Father of true believers, Rom 4:11–25
In the line of faith, Heb 11:8–10
Eternal home of, in heaven, Luke
    16:19–25

ABRAM

See ABRAHAM

ABSALOM

Son of David, 2 Sam 3:3
Kills Amnon for raping Tamar; flees
    from David, 2 Sam 13:20–39
Returns through Joab's intrigue; rec-
    onciled to David, 2 Sam 14
Attempts to usurp throne, 2 Sam
    15:1—18:8
Caught and killed by Joab, 2 Sam
    18:9–18
Mourned by David, 2 Sam 18:19—
    19:8

ABSENT

For I indeed, as *a* . . . . 1 Cor 5:3
in the body we are *a* . . . . . 2 Cor 5:6

ABSTAIN

we write to them to *a* . . . . Acts 15:20
A from every form . . . . 1 Thess 5:22
and commanding to *a* . . . 1 Tim 4:3
a from fleshly lusts . . . . . . 1 Pet 2:11

ABUNDANCE

is the sound of *a* . . . . 1 Kin 18:41
workmen with you in *a* . 1 Chr 22:15
and *a* of peace . . . . Ps 72:7
nor he who loves *a* . . . . . . Eccl 5:10
delight itself in *a* . . . . Is 55:2
For out of the *a* . . . . Matt 12:34
put in out of their *a* . . . . . Mark 12:44
not consist in the *a* . . . . . Luke 12:15
of affliction the *a* . . . . 2 Cor 8:2
above measure by the *a* . 2 Cor 12:7
rich through the *a* . . . . Rev 18:3

ABUNDANT

Longsuffering and *a* . . . . . . Ps 86:15
slow to anger and *a* . . . . . . Jon 4:2
in labors more *a* . . . . 2 Cor 11:23
Lord was exceedingly *a* . . 1 Tim 1:14
a mercy has begotten . . . . . 1 Pet 1:3

ABUNDANTLY

a satisfied with the . . . . Ps 36:8
may have it more *a* . . . . . . John 10:10
to do exceedingly *a* . . . . . . Eph 3:20
to show more *a* to the . . . . . Heb 6:17

ACACIA GROVE

Spies sent from, Josh 2:1
Israel's last camp before crossing the
    Jordan, Josh 3:1

ACCEPT

For I will *a* him . . . . Job 42:8
a your burnt sacrifice . . . . . . Ps 20:3
offering, I will not *a* . . . . . Jer 14:12
Should I *a* this from . . . . . . Mal 1:13

ACCEPTABLE

sought to find *a* . . . . Eccl 12:10
a time I have heard . . . . Is 49:8
proclaim the *a* year . . . . Is 61:2
proclaim the *a* year . . . . . Luke 4:19
is that good and *a* . . . . Rom 12:2
finding out what is *a* . . . . . Eph 5:10
For this is good and *a* . . . . 1 Tim 2:3
spiritual sacrifices *a* . . . . . . 1 Pet 2:5

ACCEPTABLY

we may serve God *a* . . . . . Heb 12:28

ACCEPTED

Behold, now is the *a* . . . . . 2 Cor 6:2
by which He made us *a* . . . . Eph 1:6

ACCESS

we have *a* by faith . . . . Rom 5:2
we have boldness and *a* . . . . Eph 3:12

ACCOMPLISHED

today the LORD has *a* . . . 1 Sam 11:13
A desire *a* is sweet to . . . . Prov 13:19
must still be *a* . . . . Luke 22:37
all things were now *a* . . . . John 19:28

ACCORD

and Israel with one *a* . . . . . Josh 9:2
serve Him with one *a* . . . . . Zeph 3:9
continued with one *a* . . . . . Acts 1:14
daily with one *a* . . . . Acts 2:46
what *a* has Christ with . . . 2 Cor 6:15
love, being of one *a* . . . . Phil 2:2

ACCOUNT

they will give *a* . . . . Matt 12:36
The former *a* I made . . . . . . Acts 1:1

each of us shall give *a*.... Rom 14:12
put that on my *a* .... Philem 18
those who must give *a* .... Heb 13:17

ACCOUNTED
and He *a* it to him .... Gen 15:6
And that was *a* to him .... Ps 106:31
his faith is *a* .... Rom 4:5
a as sheep for the .... Rom 8:36
and it was *a* to him .... Gal 3:6
and it was *a* to him ..... James 2:23

ACCURSED
he who is hanged is *a*.... Deut 21:23
regarding the *a* things...... Josh 7:1
years old shall be *a* .... Is 65:20
not know the law is *a*..... John 7:49
that I myself were *a* .... Rom 9:3
calls Jesus *a*, and no one.. 1 Cor 12:3
let him be *a* .... Gal 1:8

ACCUSATION
they wrote an *a* against .... Ezra 4:6
over His head the *a* .... Matt 27:37
they might find an *a* ...... Luke 6:7
Do not receive an *a*...... 1 Tim 5:19
not bring a reviling *a*..... 2 Pet 2:11

ACCUSE
anyone or *a* falsely....... Luke 3:14
they began to *a* Him ..... Luke 23:2
think that I shall *a*...... John 5:45

ACCUSED
forward and *a* the Jews..... Dan 3:8
while He was being *a* .... Matt 27:12

ACCUSER
a of our brethren........ Rev 12:10

ACCUSING
their thoughts *a* or else.... Rom 2:15

ACHAIA
Visited by Paul, Acts 18:1, 12
Apollos preaches in, Acts 18:24–28
Gospel proclaimed throughout,
1 Thess 1:7, 8

ACHAN (or Achar)
Sin of, caused Israel's defeat, Josh
7:1–15
Stoned to death, Josh 7:16–25
Sin of, recalled, Josh 22:20
Also called Achar, 1 Chr 2:7

ACHISH
A king of Gath, 1 Sam 21:10–15
David seeks refuge with, 1 Sam
27:1–12
Forced by Philistine lords to expel
David, 1 Sam 29:1–11
Receives Shimei's servants, 1 Kin
2:39, 40

ACHOR, VALLEY OF
Site of Achan's stoning, Josh 7:24–26
On Judah's boundary, Josh 15:7
Promises concerning, Is 65:10

ACHSAH
A daughter of Caleb, 1 Chr 2:49
Given to Othniel, Josh 15:16–19
Given springs of water, Judg 1:12–15

ACKNOWLEDGE
did he *a* his brothers...... Deut 33:9
a my transgressions .... Ps 51:3
in all your ways *a*....... Prov 3:6
and Israel does not *a* ..... Is 63:16
a your iniquity .... Jer 3:13
let him *a* that the things . 1 Cor 14:37

ACKNOWLEDGED
of Israel, and God *a* them ... Ex 2:25
a my sin to You........... Ps 32:5

ACKNOWLEDGES
there is no one who *a* ...... Ps 142:4
he who *a* the Son has ... 1 John 2:23

ACQUAINT
a yourself with Him....... Job 22:21

ACQUAINTANCES
All my *a* watched for ..... Jer 20:10
But all His *a* .... Luke 23:49

ACQUAINTED
and are *a* with all my ways . Ps 139:3
a Man of sorrows and *a*..... Is 53:3

ACQUIT
at all *a* the wicked......... Nah 1:3

ACT
seen every great *a*....... Deut 11:7
is time for You to *a*...... Ps 119:126
His *a*, His unusual *a*....... Is 28:21
in the very *a*............ John 8:4

ACTIONS
by Him *a* are weighed .... 1 Sam 2:3

ACTS
LORD, the righteous *a*..... Judg 5:11
His *a* to the children ...... Ps 103:7
declare Your mighty *a*..... Ps 145:4
of Your awesome *a* .... Ps 145:6

ADAM
Creation of, Gen 1:26, 27; 2:7
Given dominion over the earth, Gen
1:28–30
Given a wife, Gen 2:18–25
Temptation, fall, and exile from
Eden, Gen 3
Children of, Gen 4:1, 2; 5:3, 4
Transgression results in sin and
death, Rom 5:12–14
——— Last or second Adam, an appel-
lation of Christ, Rom 5:14, 15;
1 Cor 15:20–24, 45–48

ADD
You shall not *a* .... Deut 4:2
Do not *a* to His words ..... Prov 30:6

ADDED
things shall be *a*........ Matt 6:33
And the Lord *a* to the ..... Acts 2:47
many people were *a*...... Acts 11:24
It was *a* because of .... Gal 3:19

ADMINISTERS
a justice for the .... Deut 10:18

ADMONISH
also to *a* one another ..... Rom 15:14
a him as a brother ..... 2 Thess 3:15

ADMONISHED
further, my son, be *a* ..... Eccl 12:12
Angel of the LORD *a* .... Zech 3:6

ADMONISHING
a one another in .... Col 3:16

ADMONITION
were written for our *a* ... 1 Cor 10:11
in the training and *a*....... Eph 6:4

ADONIJAH
David's fourth son, 2 Sam 3:2, 4
Attempts to usurp throne, 1 Kin 1:5–53
Desires Abishag as wife, 1 Kin 2:13–18
Executed by Solomon, 1 Kin 2:19–25

ADONIRAM (or Adoram)
Official under David, Solomon, and
Rehoboam, 2 Sam 20:24; 1 Kin
5:14; 12:18
Stoned by angry Israelites, 1 Kin
12:18
Called Hadoram, 2 Chr 10:18

ADOPTION
the Spirit of *a*............ Rom 8:15
waiting for the *a*........ Rom 8:23
to whom pertain the *a* ..... Rom 9:4
we might receive the *a*..... Gal 4:5
a as sons by Jesus......... Eph 1:5

ADORN
a the monuments .... Matt 23:29
also, that the women *a*.... 1 Tim 2:9

ADORNED
By His Spirit He *a* .... Job 26:13
You shall again be *a* ...... Jer 31:4
temple, how it was *a*..... Luke 21:5
also *a* themselves .... 1 Pet 3:5
prepared as a bride *a* ..... Rev 21:2

ADRIFT
A among the dead......... Ps 88:5

ADULTERER
the *a* and the adulteress ... Lev 20:10
The eye of the *a*......... Job 24:15

ADULTERERS
the land is full of *a*....... Jer 23:10
nor idolaters, nor *a* ...... 1 Cor 6:9
a God will judge......... Heb 13:4
A and adulteresses .... James 4:4

ADULTERIES
I have seen your *a* .... Jer 13:27
her sight, and her *a*........ Hos 2:2
evil thoughts, *a* .... Mark 7:21

ADULTEROUS
evil and *a* generation .... Matt 12:39

ADULTERY
You shall not commit *a* .... Ex 20:14
Whoever commits *a* ...... Prov 6:32
Israel had committed *a* ..... Jer 3:8
already committed *a* .... Matt 5:28
is divorced commits *a* .... Matt 5:32
another commits *a* ..... Mark 10:11
a woman caught in *a* ..... John 8:3
those who commit *a*....... Rev 2:22

ADVANTAGE
a will it be to You .... Job 35:3
man has no *a* over....... Eccl 3:19
a that I go away .... John 16:7
What *a* then has the....... Rom 3:1
Satan should take *a*...... 2 Cor 2:11
no one should take *a* .... 1 Thess 4:6
people to gain *a* .... Jude 16

ADVERSARIES
The *a* of the LORD .... 1 Sam 2:10
rid Myself of My *a* .... Is 1:24
a will not be able .... Luke 21:15
and there are many *a* .... 1 Cor 16:9
terrified by your *a* .... Phil 1:28
will devour the *a* .... Heb 10:27

ADVERSARY
in the way as an *a* ..... Num 22:22
battle he become our *a* .. 1 Sam 29:4
how long will the *a* .... Ps 74:10
a has spread his hand..... Lam 1:10
Agree with your *a*........ Matt 5:25
justice for me from my *a* .. Luke 18:3
opportunity to the *a* ..... 1 Tim 5:14
your *a* the devil walks ..... 1 Pet 5:8

ADVERSITIES
you from all your *a* .... 1 Sam 10:19
known my soul in *a* .... Ps 31:7

ADVERSITY
them with every *a* ...... 2 Chr 15:6
I shall never be in *a* .... Ps 10:6
from the days of *a*........ Ps 94:13
brother is born for *a* ..... Prov 17:17

faint in the day of *a* . . . . . Prov 24:10
the day of *a* consider . . . . . . Eccl 7:14
you the bread of *a* . . . . Is 30:20

ADVICE
And blessed is your *a* . . . 1 Sam 25:33
in this I give my *a* . . . . 2 Cor 8:10

ADVOCATE
we have an *A* with the . . . 1 John 2:1

AFAR
and worship from *a* . . . . Ex 24:1
sons shall come from *a* . . . . . Is 60:4
and not a God *a* . . . . Jer 23:23
and saw Abraham *a* . . . . Luke 16:23
to all who are *a* . . . . Acts 2:39
to you who were *a* . . . . Eph 2:17
but having seen them *a* . . Heb 11:13

AFFAIRS
he will guide his *a* . . . . Ps 112:5
I may hear of your *a* . . . . . . Phil 1:27
himself with the *a* . . . . 2 Tim 2:4

AFFECTION
to his wife the *a* . . . . 1 Cor 7:3
for you all with the *a* . . . . . . Phil 1:8
if any *a* and mercy . . . . Phil 2:1

AFFECTIONATE
Be kindly *a* to one . . . . . . Rom 12:10

AFFIRM
you to *a* constantly. . . . . . . Titus 3:8

AFFLICT
a them with their . . . . Ex 1:11
oath to *a* her soul . . . . . . Num 30:13
may be bound to *a* you . . . Judg 16:6
a the descendants. . . . . . . 1 Kin 11:39
will hear, and *a* them . . . . . Ps 55:19
a Your heritage . . . . Ps 94:5
a man to *a* his soul . . . . Is 58:5
to destroy, and to *a* . . . . . Jer 31:28
For He does not *a* . . . . Lam 3:33
deal with all who *a* . . . . . Zeph 3:19

AFFLICTED
"Why have You *a* . . . . . . Num 11:11
and the Almighty has *a* . . . Ruth 1:21
To him who is *a* . . . . Job 6:14
hears the cry of the *a* . . . . . Job 34:28
You *a* the peoples . . . . Ps 44:2
Before I was *a* . . . . Ps 119:67
I am *a* very much . . . . Ps 119:107
Many a time they have *a* . . . Ps 129:1
the cause of the *a* . . . . Ps 140:12
days of the *a* are evil. . . . . Prov 15:15
Smitten by God, and *a* . . . . . . Is 53:4
oppressed and He was *a* . . . . . Is 53:7
"O you *a* one . . . . Is 54:11
Why have we *a* our . . . . Is 58:3
and satisfy the *a* . . . . Is 58:10
her virgins are *a* . . . . Lam 1:4
she has relieved the *a* . . . . 1 Tim 5:10
being destitute, *a* . . . . Heb 11:37

AFFLICTING
A the just and taking . . . . Amos 5:12

AFFLICTION
in the land of my *a* . . . . . . Gen 41:52
the bread of *a* . . . . Deut 16:3
indeed look on the *a* . . . . 1 Sam 1:11
L<small>ORD</small> saw that the *a* . . . . 2 Kin 14:26
a take hold of me . . . . Job 30:16
days of *a* confront me . . . . Job 30:27
held in the cords of *a* . . . . . Job 36:8
of death, bound in *a* . . . . . Ps 107:10
is my comfort in my *a* . . . . Ps 119:50
and it is an evil *a* . . . . Eccl 6:2
a He was afflicted . . . . Is 63:9
refuge in the day of *a* . . . . Jer 16:19

"O L<small>ORD</small>, behold my *a* . . . . . Lam 1:9
not grieved for the *a* . . . . . Amos 6:6
For our light *a* . . . . 2 Cor 4:17
supposing to add *a*. . . . . . . Phil 1:16
the word in much *a* . . . . 1 Thess 1:6

AFRAID
garden, and I was *a* . . . . . . Gen 3:10
saying, "Do not be *a* . . . . . Gen 15:1
his face, for he was *a* . . . . Ex 3:6
none will make you *a* . . . . . Lev 26:6
of whom you are *a* . . . . . . Deut 7:19
I will not be *a* . . . . Ps 3:6
ungodliness made me *a* . . . Ps 18:4
Do not be *a* when one. . . . . Ps 49:16
Whenever I am *a* . . . . Ps 56:3
farthest parts are *a* . . . . Ps 65:8
nor be *a* of their threats. . . . . Is 8:12
no one will make them *a* . . . Is 17:2
that you should be *a* . . . . . . Is 51:12
dream which made me *a* . . . Dan 4:5
do not be *a* . . . . Matt 14:27
if you do evil, be *a* . . . . . . Rom 13:4
do good and are not *a* . . . . 1 Pet 3:6

AFTERWARD
A he will let you go. . . . . . . Ex 11:1
a we will speak . . . . Job 18:2
a receive me to glory. . . . . . Ps 73:24
you shall follow Me *a* . . . . John 13:36
the firstfruits, *a*. . . . . 1 Cor 15:23

AGAG
A king of Amalek in Balaam's
    prophecy, Num 24:7
——— Amalekite king spared by Saul,
    but slain by Samuel, 1 Sam 15:8,
    9, 20–24, 32, 33

AGAIN
day He will rise *a* . . . . . . Matt 20:19
'You must be born *a* . . . . . . John 3:7
to renew them *a*. . . . . Heb 6:6
having been born *a* . . . . . . 1 Pet 1:23

AGAINST
his hand shall be *a*. . . . . . Gen 16:12
I will set My face *a* . . . . Lev 20:3
come to 'set a man *a* . . . . Matt 10:35
or house divided *a* . . . . . . Matt 12:25
not with Me is *a* Me . . . . . Matt 12:30
blasphemy *a* the Spirit . . . Matt 12:31
For nation will rise *a* . . . . . Matt 24:7
out, as *a* a robber . . . . . . Matt 26:55
I have sinned *a* . . . . Luke 15:18
lifted up his heel *a* . . . . . . John 13:18
L<small>ORD</small> and *a* His Christ . . . . Acts 4:26
to kick *a* the goads . . . . Acts 9:5
all men everywhere *a* . . . . Acts 21:28
let us not fight *a* . . . . Acts 23:9
a the promises of God. . . . . Gal 3:21
we do not wrestle *a*. . . . . . . Eph 6:12
I have a few things *a* . . . . . . Rev 2:20

AGE
well advanced in *a*. . . . . . . Gen 18:11
Israel were dim with *a* . . . . Gen 48:10
the flower of their *a* . . . . . 1 Sam 2:33
the grave at a full *a* . . . . Job 5:26
a is as nothing. . . . . Ps 39:5
and in the *a* to come . . . . Mark 10:30
"The sons of this *a* . . . . . . Luke 20:34
He is of *a* . . . . John 9:21
who are of full *a*. . . . . Heb 5:14
the powers of the *a* . . . . Heb 6:5

AGED
Wisdom is with *a* . . . . Job 12:12
a one as Paul, the . . . . Philem 9

AGES
ordained before the *a* . . . . 1 Cor 2:7

in other *a* was not . . . . Eph 3:5
at the end of the *a*. . . . . Heb 9:26

AGONY
And being in *a* . . . . Luke 22:44

AGREE
A with your adversary . . . . Matt 5:25
that if two of you *a* . . . . . . Matt 18:19
testimonies did not *a* . . . . Mark 14:56
and these three *a*. . . . . 1 John 5:8

AGREED
unless they are *a*. . . . . Amos 3:3
they were glad, and *a*. . . . . Luke 22:5

AGREEMENT
with Sheol we are in *a* . . . . . Is 28:15
the North to make an *a* . . . Dan 11:6
what *a* has the temple. . . . 2 Cor 6:16

AHAB
A wicked king of Israel, 1 Kin 16:29
Marries Jezebel; promotes Baal wor-
    ship, 1 Kin 16:31–33; 18:17–46
Denounced by Elijah, 1 Kin 17:1
Wars against Ben-Hadad, 1 Kin 20:1–43
Covets Naboth's vineyard, 1 Kin
    21:1–16
Death predicted; repentance delays
    judgment, 1 Kin 21:17–29
Goes to war in spite of Micaiah's
    warning; killed in battle, 1 Kin.
    22:1–37
Prophecy concerning, fulfilled,
    1 Kin 22:38
——— Lying prophet, Jer 29:21–23

AHASUERUS
The father of Darius the Mede, Dan
    9:1
——— Persian king, probably Xerxes I,
    486–465 B.C., Ezra 4:6; Esth 1:1
Makes Esther queen, Esth 2:16, 17
Orders Jews annihilated, by Haman's
    advice, Esth 3:8–15
Reverses decree at Esther's request,
    Esth 7; 8
Exalts Mordecai, Esth 10:1–3

AHAZ
King of Judah; pursues idolatry; sub-
    mits to Assyrian rule; desecrates
    the temple, 2 Kin 16
Defeated by Syria and Israel, 2 Chr
    28:5–15
Comforted by Isaiah; refuses to ask a
    sign, Is 7:1–17

AHAZIAH
King of Israel; son of Ahab and
    Jezebel; worships Baal, 1 Kin
    22:51–53
Falls through lattice; calls on Baal-
    Zebub; dies according to Elijah's
    word, 2 Kin 1:2–18
——— King of Judah; Ahab's son-in-law;
    reigns wickedly, 2 Kin 8:25–29;
    2 Chr 22:1–6
Killed by Jehu, 2 Kin 9:27–29; 2 Chr
    22:7–9

AHIJAH
A prophet of Shiloh who foretells
    division of Solomon's kingdom,
    1 Kin 11:29–39
Foretells elimination of Jeroboam's
    line, 1 Kin 14:1–18
A writer of prophecy, 2 Chr 9:29

AHIKAM
Sent in Josiah's mission to Huldah,
    2 Kin 22:12–14

Protects Jeremiah, Jer 26:24
The father of Gedaliah, governor
under Nebuchadnezzar, 2 Kin
25:22; Jer 39:14

AHIMAAZ
A son of Zadok the high priest,
1 Chr 6:8, 9
Warns David of Absalom's plans,
2 Sam 15:27, 36
First to tell David of Absalom's
defeat, 2 Sam 18:19–30

AHIMELECH
High priest in Saul's reign; helps
David, 1 Sam 21:1–9
Betrayed and killed by Doeg; son
Abiathar escapes, 1 Sam 22:9–20
David writes concerning, Ps 52:title

AHINOAM
Wife of David, 1 Sam 25:43; 27:3;
30:5, 18
Mother of Amnon, 2 Sam 3:2

AHITHOPHEL
David's counselor, 2 Sam 15:12
Joins Absalom's insurrection; coun-
sels him, 2 Sam 15:31; 16:20–23
His counsel rejected; commits suicide,
2 Sam 17:1–23

AI
Israel defeated at, Josh 7:2–5
Israel destroys completely, Josh 8:1–28

AIDE
the king's personal *a* . . . . . Acts 12:20

AIJALON
Amorites not driven from, Judg 1:35
Miracle there, Josh 10:12, 13
City of refuge, 1 Chr 6:66–69
Fortified by Rehoboam, 2 Chr 11:5, 10
Captured by Philistines, 2 Chr 28:18

AIR
the birds of the *a* . . . . Gen 1:26
of the *a* have nests . . . . . . Luke 9:58
as one who beats the *a* . . 1 Cor 9:26
be speaking into the *a* . . . 1 Cor 14:9
of the power of the *a* . . . . Eph 2:2
meet the Lord in the *a* . . 1 Thess 4:17
his bowl into the *a* . . . . Rev 16:17

AKEL DAMA
Field called "Field of Blood," Acts 1:19

ALARM
to sound the *a* against. . . 2 Chr 13:12
A day of trumpet and *a* . . . Zeph 1:16

ALEXANDER
A member of the high-priestly
family, Acts 4:6
——— A Jew in Ephesus, Acts 19:33, 34
——— An apostate condemned by Paul,
1 Tim 1:19, 20

ALEXANDRIA
Men of, persecute Stephen, Acts 6:9
Paul sails in ship of, Acts 27:6

ALIEN
because you were an *a* . . . . Deut 23:7
I am an *a* in their . . . . Job 19:15
who turn away an *a* . . . . Mal 3:5

ALIENATED
a herself from them . . . . . . Ezek 23:17
darkened, being *a*. . . . . Eph 4:18
you, who once were *a* . . . . . . Col 1:21

ALIENS
For we are *a* and . . . . . . 1 Chr 29:15

For I have loved *a* . . . . Jer 2:25
A have devoured his. . . . . . . Hos 7:9
without Christ, being *a* . . . . Eph 2:12
the armies of the *a* . . . . . . Heb 11:34

ALIKE
All things come *a*. . . . . Eccl 9:2
esteems every day *a* . . . . . Rom 14:5

ALIVE
in the ark remained *a* . . . . Gen 7:23
with them went down *a* . . Num 16:33
LORD your God are *a* . . . . . . Deut 4:4
I kill and I make *a* . . . . . . Deut 32:39
Let them go down *a*. . . . . . . Ps 55:15
he preserves himself *a* . . . Ezek 18:27
heard that He was *a* . . . . Mark 16:11
son was dead and is *a*. . . . Luke 15:24
presented Himself *a* . . . . Acts 1:3
dead indeed to sin, but *a* . . Rom 6:11
I was *a* once without . . . . . . Rom 7:9
all shall be made *a* . . . . . 1 Cor 15:22
trespasses, made us *a*. . . . . . Eph 2:5
flesh, He has made *a* . . . . . . Col 2:13
that we who are *a*. . . . . 1 Thess 4:15
the flesh but made *a* . . . . . 1 Pet 3:18
and behold, I am *a*. . . . . Rev 1:18
a name that you are *a*. . . . . Rev 3:1
These two were cast *a*. . . . Rev 19:20

ALL
for this is man's *a*. . . . . . . Eccl 12:13

ALLELUIA
Again they said, "*A*. . . . . . . Rev 19:3

ALLOW
a Your Holy One . . . . Ps 16:10
a My faithfulness. . . . . Ps 89:33
nor do you *a* those . . . . . . Matt 23:13
a Your Holy One . . . . Acts 2:27
who will not *a* . . . . 1 Cor 10:13

ALLOWED
bygone generations *a*. . . . . Acts 14:16

ALLURE
behold, I will *a* . . . . Hos 2:14
they *a* through the lusts . . . 2 Pet 2:18

ALMOND
a blossoms on one . . . . Ex 25:33
a tree blossoms . . . . Eccl 12:5

ALMOST
for me, my feet had *a* . . . . . . Ps 73:2
a persuade me to. . . . . Acts 26:28
a all things are. . . . . Heb 9:22

ALMS
But rather give *a* . . . . Luke 11:41
you have and give *a* . . . . Luke 12:33
I came to bring *a* . . . . Acts 24:17

ALOES
with myrrh and *a* . . . . Ps 45:8
my bed with myrrh, *a* . . . . . Prov 7:17
mixture of myrrh and *a* . . John 19:39

ALPHA
I am the *A* and the . . . . Rev 1:8
I am the *A* and the . . . . . . Rev 22:13

ALTAR
Then Noah built an *a* . . . . . Gen 8:20
An *a* of earth you. . . . . Ex 20:24
a shall be kept . . . . Lev 6:9
it to you upon the *a* . . . . . . Lev 17:11
offering for the *a* . . . . Num 7:84
called the *a* Witness. . . . . . Josh 22:34
and tear down the *a*. . . . . . Judg 6:25
"Go up, erect an *a* . . . . . 2 Sam 24:18
cried out against the *a*. . . . 1 Kin 13:2
I will go to the *a* . . . . Ps 43:4
there will be an *a*. . . . . Is 19:19

Lord has spurned His *a*. . . . . Lam 2:7
you cover the *a*. . . . . Mal 2:13
your gift to the *a*. . . . . Matt 5:23
swears by the *a* . . . . Matt 23:18
I even found an *a* . . . . . . Acts 17:23
the offerings of the *a* . . . . 1 Cor 9:13
partakers of the *a*. . . . . . 1 Cor 10:18
We have an *a* from. . . . . . . Heb 13:10
Isaac his son on the *a* . . . James 2:21
and stood at the *a* . . . . Rev 8:3

ALTARS
a Hezekiah has taken . . . 2 Kin 18:22
Even Your *a*, O LORD . . . . . . Ps 84:3
on the horns of your *a*. . . . . Jer 17:1
a shall be broken. . . . . Ezek 6:4
has made many *a* . . . . Hos 8:11
a shall be heaps . . . . Hos 12:11
destruction on the *a* . . . . . Amos 3:14
and torn down Your *a*. . . . . Rom 11:3

ALTERED
of His face was *a*. . . . . Luke 9:29

ALWAYS
delight, rejoicing *a* . . . . Prov 8:30
the poor with you *a* . . . . . Matt 26:11
Me you do not have *a*. . . . . Matt 26:11
lo, I am with you *a*. . . . . . Matt 28:20
'Son, you are *a* . . . . Luke 15:31
men *a* ought to pray. . . . . . Luke 18:1
immovable, *a* abounding 1 Cor 15:58
Rejoice in the Lord *a* . . . . . . Phil 4:4
thus we shall *a* . . . . 1 Thess 4:17
a be ready to give *a* . . . . . 1 Pet 3:15

AM
to Moses, "I *A* WHO I *A* . . . . . Ex 3:14
First and I *a* the Last . . . . Is 44:6
in My name, I *a* there. . . . Matt 18:20
I *a* the bread of life . . . . . . John 6:35
I *a* the light of the. . . . . . . John 8:12
I *a* from above . . . . John 8:23
Abraham was, I *A*. . . . . John 8:58
I *a* the door. . . . . John 10:9
I *a* the good shepherd . . . . John 10:11
I *a* the resurrection . . . . . . John 11:25
to him, "I *a* the way . . . . . . John 14:6
of God I *a* what I *a*. . . . . 1 Cor 15:10

AMALEK
Grandson of Esau, Gen 36:11, 12
A chief of Edom, Gen 36:16
First among nations, Num 24:20

AMALEKITES
Destruction predicted, Ex 17:14; Deut
25:17–19
Defeated by Israel, Ex 17:8–13; Judg
7:12–25; 1 Sam 14:47, 48; 27:8, 9;
1 Chr 4:42, 43
Overcome Israel, Num 14:39–45;
Judg 3:13

AMASA
Commands Absalom's rebels, 2 Sam
17:25
Made David's commander, 2 Sam
19:13
Treacherously killed by Joab, 2 Sam
20:9–12
Death avenged, 1 Kin 2:28–34

AMAZED
trembled and were *a* . . . . . Mark 16:8

AMAZIAH
King of Judah; kills his father's assas-
sinators, 2 Kin 14:1–6; 2 Chr 25:1–4
Hires troops from Israel; is rebuked
by a man of God; sends troops
home, 2 Chr 25:5–10

Defeats Edomites; worships their
   gods, 2 Chr 25:11–16
Wars with Israel, 2 Kin 14:8–14;
   2 Chr 25:17–24
Killed by conspirators, 2 Chr 25:25–28

AMBASSADOR
but a faithful *a* . . . . Prov 13:17
for which I am an *a* . . . . . . Eph 6:20

AMBASSADORS
cry outside, the *a* . . . . Is 33:7
we are *a* for Christ. . . . . . 2 Cor 5:20

AMBITION
Christ from selfish *a* . . . . . . Phil 1:16
through selfish *a* . . . . Phil 2:3

AMEN
uninformed say "A. . . . . 1 Cor 14:16
are Yes, and in Him *A* . . . . 2 Cor 1:20
creatures said, "A . . . . Rev 5:14

AMEND
A your ways and your . . . . Jer 7:3
from his evil way, *a* . . . . Jer 35:15

AMMON
A nation fathered by Lot, Gen 19:36, 38

AMMONITES
Excluded from assembly for hostility
   to Israel, Deut 23:3–6
Propose cruel treaty; conquered by
   Saul, 1 Sam 11:1–3, 11
Abuse David's ambassadors; con-
   quered by his army, 2 Sam 10:1–14
Harass postexilic Jews, Neh 4:3, 7, 8
Defeated by Israel and Judah, Judg
   11:4–33; 2 Chr 20:1–25; 27:5, 6
Prophecies concerning, Ps 83:1–18;
   Jer 25:9–21; Ezek 25:1–7; Amos
   1:13–15; Zeph 2:9–11

AMNON
A son of David, 2 Sam 3:2
Rapes his half sister, 2 Sam 13:1–18
Killed by Absalom, 2 Sam 13:19–29

AMON
King of Judah, 2 Kin 21:18, 19
Follows evil, 2 Chr 33:22, 23
Killed by conspiracy, 2 Kin 21:23, 24
—— A governor of Samaria, 1 Kin
   22:10, 26

AMORITES
Defeated by Joshua, Josh 10:1–43
Not driven out of Canaan, Judg
   1:34–36
Put to forced labor under Solomon,
   1 Kin 9:20, 21

AMOS
A prophet of Israel, Amos 1:1
Pronounces judgment against
   nations, Amos 1:1–3, 15
Denounces Israel's sins, Amos 4:1—
   7:9
Condemns Amaziah, the priest of
   Bethel, Amos 7:10–17
Predicts Israel's downfall, Amos 9:1–10
Foretells great blessings, Amos 9:11–15

AMRAM
Son of Kohath, Num 3:17–19
The father of Aaron, Moses, and
   Miriam, Ex 6:18–20; 1 Chr 6:3

ANAKIM
A race of giants; very strong, Num
   13:28–33; Deut 2:10, 11, 21
Defeated
   by Joshua, Josh 10:36–39; 11:21
   by Caleb, Josh 14:6–15

ANANIAS
Disciple at Jerusalem; slain for lying
   to God, Acts 5:1–11
—— A Christian disciple at Damas-
   cus, Acts 9:10–19; 22:12–16
—— A Jewish high priest, Acts 23:1–5

ANATHOTH
A Levitical city in Benjamin, Josh 21:18
Jeremiah's birthplace; he buys prop-
   erty there, Jer 1:1; 32:6–15
To be invaded by Assyria, Is 10:30

ANCHOR
hope we have as an *a* . . . . . Heb 6:19

ANCIENT
Do not remove the *a* . . . . . Prov 23:10
a times that I . . . . Is 37:26
until the *A* of Days . . . . Dan 7:22

ANDREW
A disciple of John the Baptist, then
   of Christ, Matt 4:18, 19; John
   1:40–42
Enrolled among the Twelve, Matt
   10:2
Mentioned, Mark 13:3, 4; John 6:8, 9;
   12:20–22; Acts 1:13

ANGEL
Now the *A* of the LORD . . . . . Gen 16:7
A who has redeemed me . . Gen 48:16
"Behold, I send an *A* . . . . . . Ex 23:20
the donkey saw the *A*. . . . Num 22:23
For I have seen the *A* . . . . Judg 6:22
Manoah said to the *A* . . . . Judg 13:17
in my sight as an *a* . . . . . 1 Sam 29:9
a who was destroying. . . 2 Sam 24:16
night that the *a* . . . . 2 Kin 19:35
the *A* of His Presence . . . . Is 63:9
struggled with the *A* . . . . . . Hos 12:4
standing before the *A* . . . . . Zech 3:3
like God, like the *A* . . . . . . Zech 12:8
things, behold, an *a* . . . . . . Matt 1:20
for an *a* of the Lord . . . . . Matt 28:2
Then an *a* of the Lord. . . . . Luke 1:11
And behold, an *a* . . . . Luke 2:9
a appeared to Him from. . Luke 22:43
For an *a* went down at . . . . John 5:4
a has spoken to Him. . . . . John 12:29
But at night an *a* . . . . Acts 5:19
A who appeared to him. . . . Acts 7:35
Then immediately an *a*. . . Acts 12:23
and no *a* or spirit. . . . . Acts 23:8
a has spoken to him . . . . . Acts 23:9
by me this night an *a* . . . Acts 27:23
himself into an *a* . . . . 2 Cor 11:14
even if we, or an *a* . . . . Gal 1:8
Then I saw a strong *a*. . . . . . Rev 5:2
over them the *a*. . . . . Rev 9:11
Then I saw an *a* . . . . Rev 19:17
Jesus, have sent My *a* . . . . Rev 22:16

ANGELS
If He charges His *a* . . . . . . Job 4:18
lower than the *a* . . . . Ps 8:5
He shall give His *a*. . . . . . . Ps 91:11
Praise Him, all His *a* . . . . . Ps 148:2
He shall give His *a* . . . . Matt 4:6
a will come forth. . . . . . . Matt 13:49
a always see the face. . . . Matt 18:10
but are like *a*. . . . . Matt 22:30
not even the *a*. . . . . Matt 24:36
and all the holy *a* . . . . . . Matt 25:31
twelve legions of *a* . . . . . Matt 26:53
the presence of the *a* . . . . Luke 15:10
was carried by the *a* . . . . Luke 16:22
are equal to the *a*. . . . . . . Luke 20:36
And she saw two *a* . . . . . . John 20:12
that we shall judge *a*. . . . . 1 Cor 6:3

head, because of the *a* . . . 1 Cor 11:10
and worship of *a* . . . . Col 2:18
with His mighty *a* . . . . 2 Thess 1:7
the Spirit, seen by *a* . . . . . 1 Tim 3:16
much better than the *a* . . . . . Heb 1:4
does not give aid to *a*. . . . . Heb 2:16
company of *a* . . . . Heb 12:22
entertained *a* . . . . Heb 13:2
things which *a* desire . . . . 1 Pet 1:12
did not spare the *a* . . . . 2 Pet 2:4
a who did not keep . . . . Jude 6
Michael and his *a* . . . . Rev 12:7

ANGER
Cursed be their *a* . . . . Gen 49:7
sun, that the fierce *a* . . . . Num 25:4
fierceness of His *a* . . . . . Deut 13:17
of this great *a* . . . . Deut 29:24
So the *a* of the LORD . . . . . Judg 10:7
to provoke Me to *a*. . . . . . . 1 Kin 16:2
For His *a* is but for *a* . . . . . . Ps 30:5
a time He turned His *a* . . . . Ps 78:38
made a path for His *a* . . . . . Ps 78:50
You prolong Your *a* . . . . Ps 85:5
the power of Your *a* . . . . . . Ps 90:11
gracious, slow to *a*. . . . . . . Ps 103:8
Nor will He keep His *a* . . . . Ps 103:9
harsh word stirs up *a* . . . . Prov 15:1
a sins against his own . . . . Prov 20:2
a rests in the bosom. . . . . . . Eccl 7:9
a the Holy One of . . . . Is 1:4
a is not turned away . . . . Is 5:25
a is turned away . . . . Is 12:1
'I will not cause My *a*. . . . . . Jer 3:12
For great is the *a* . . . . Jer 36:7
and I will send My *a* . . . . . . Ezek 7:3
does not retain His *a* . . . . . Mic 7:18
fierceness of His *a* . . . . Nah 1:6
a is kindled against. . . . . . Zech 10:3
around at them with *a* . . . . Mark 3:5
bitterness, wrath, *a*. . . . . . . Eph 4:31

ANGRY
Cain, "Why are you *a* . . . . . Gen 4:6
"Let not the Lord be *a* . . . Gen 18:30
the Son, lest He be *a* . . . . Ps 2:12
judge, and God is *a*. . . . . Ps 7:11
When once You are *a* . . . . . . Ps 76:7
Will you be *a* forever. . . . . . . Ps 79:5
friendship with an *a* . . . . Prov 22:24
backbiting tongue an *a*. . . Prov 25:23
a man stirs up strife . . . . Prov 29:22
in your spirit to be *a* . . . . . . Eccl 7:9
I was *a* with My people . . . . . Is 47:6
nor will I always be *a*. . . . . . Is 57:16
covetousness I was *a*. . . . . . Is 57:17
right for you to be *a* . . . . Jon 4:4
LORD has been very *a* . . . . . Zech 1:2
I am exceedingly *a* . . . . . . Zech 1:15
you that whoever is *a*. . . . . Matt 5:22
"Be *a*, and do not sin". . . . . Eph 4:26
Therefore I was *a* . . . . Heb 3:10
with whom was He *a* . . . . . Heb 3:17
The nations were *a* . . . . . . Rev 11:18

ANGUISH
a has come upon me . . . . 2 Sam 1:9
I will be in *a* over my . . . . . Ps 38:18
trouble and *a* have
   overtaken . . . . Ps 119:143
longer remembers the *a* . . John 16:21
tribulation and *a* . . . . Rom 2:9
much affliction and *a*. . . . 2 Cor 2:4

ANIMAL
of every clean *a*. . . . . Gen 7:2
Whoever kills an *a* . . . . . . Lev 24:18
the life of his *a* . . . . Prov 12:10
set him on his own *a* . . . . Luke 10:34

ANIMALS
of *a* after their kind . . . . . . Gen 6:20
sacrifices of fat *a* . . . . Ps 66:15
of four-footed *a* . . . . Acts 10:12
and four-footed *a* . . . . Rom 1:23

ANISE
tithe of mint and *a* . . . . . . Matt 23:23

ANNA
Aged prophetess, Luke 2:36–38

ANNAS
A Jewish high priest, Luke 3:2
Christ appeared before, John 18:12–24
Peter and John appeared before,
   Acts 4:6

ANNUL
and who will *a* . . . . Is 14:27
years later, cannot *a* . . . . . . Gal 3:17

ANNULLING
one hand there is an *a*. . . . . Heb 7:18

ANNULS
is confirmed, no one *a* . . . . . Gal 3:15

ANOINT
You shall *a* them. . . . . Ex 28:41
but you shall not *a* . . . . . Deut 28:40
you shall *a* for Me the . . . 1 Sam 16:3
a yourself with oil. . . . . . 2 Sam 14:2
a my head with oil . . . . Ps 23:5
Arise, you princes, *a*. . . . . Is 21:5
a the Most Holy . . . . Dan 9:24
when you fast, *a* . . . . Matt 6:17
a My body for burial . . . . Mark 14:8
they might come and *a* . . . Mark 16:1
a your eyes with eye . . . . . . Rev 3:18

ANOINTED
the priest, who is *a* . . . . . . Lev 16:32
"Surely the LORD's *a* . . . . . 1 Sam 16:6
destroy the LORD's *a* . . . . . 1 Sam 1:14
he cursed the LORD's *a*. . . 2 Sam 19:21
shows mercy to His *a* . . . 2 Sam 22:51
"Do not touch My *a* . . . . 1 Chr 16:22
the LORD saves His *a* . . . . . . Ps 20:6
because the LORD has *a* . . . . . Is 61:1
"These are the two *a*. . . . . Zech 4:14
Because He has *a* . . . . Luke 4:18
but this woman has *a*. . . . . Luke 7:46
a the eyes of the . . . . John 9:6
It was that Mary who *a* . . . John 11:2
Jesus, whom You *a*. . . . . . . Acts 4:27
and has *a* us is God . . . . . . 2 Cor 1:21

ANOINTING
also made the holy *a* . . . . . Ex 37:29
a oil on Aaron's head . . . . . . Lev 8:12
destroyed because of the *a*. . . Is 10:27
pray over him, *a* him . . . . James 5:14
But you have an *a*. . . . . . 1 John 2:20
but as the same *a* . . . . . . 1 John 2:27

ANOTHER
that you love one *a* . . . . . John 13:34
and He will give you *a* . . . John 14:16
'Let *a* take his . . . . Acts 1:20

ANSWER
will give Pharaoh an *a*. . . . Gen 41:16
a I should take back. . . . 2 Sam 24:13
Him, he could not *a* . . . . Job 9:3
Call, and I will *a* . . . . Job 13:22
how shall I *a* Him . . . . Job 31:14
and you shall *a*. . . . . Job 40:7
the day that I call, *a* . . . . . . Ps 102:2
In Your faithfulness *a* . . . . . Ps 143:1
a turns away wrath. . . . . . Prov 15:1
A man has joy by the *a*. . Prov 15:23
He who gives a right *a* . . Prov 24:26
a a fool according . . . . Prov 26:4

was there none to *a* . . . . Is 50:2
for there is no *a* . . . . Mic 3:7
or what you should *a* . . . Luke 12:11
you may have an *a* . . . . . . 2 Cor 5:12
ought to *a* each one . . . . . . Col 4:6

ANSWERS
a a matter before he . . . . Prov 18:13
but the rich *a* . . . . Prov 18:23
money *a* everything . . . . . . Eccl 10:19

ANT
Go to the *a* . . . . Prov 6:6

ANTICHRIST
heard that the *A*. . . . . 1 John 2:18
a who denies the . . . . 1 John 2:22
is the spirit of the *A* . . . . . . 1 John 4:3
is a deceiver and an *a* . . . . . 2 John 7

ANTIOCH
——— In Syria:
First Gentile church established, Acts
   11:19–21
Disciples first called "Christians" in,
   Acts 11:26
Church commissions Paul, Acts 13:1–
   4; 15:35–41
Church troubled by Judaizers, Acts
   15:1–4; Gal 2:11–21
——— In Pisidia:
Paul visits; Jews reject the gospel,
   Acts 13:14, 42–51

ANTITYPE
a which now saves us. . . . . 1 Pet 3:21

ANXIETIES
the multitude of my *a* . . . . . Ps 94:19
Try me, and know my *a* . . . Ps 139:23

ANXIETY
A in the heart of man . . . . Prov 12:25
eat their bread with *a* . . . . Ezek 12:19

ANXIOUS
drink, nor have an *a*. . . . . Luke 12:29
Be *a* for nothing. . . . . Phil 4:6

APART
that you shall set *a* . . . . Ex 13:12
she shall be set *a* . . . . Lev 15:19
the LORD has set *a* . . . . Ps 4:3
justified by faith *a* . . . . Rom 3:28

APOLLOS
An Alexandrian Jew; instructed by
   Aquila and Priscilla and sent to
   Achaia, Acts 18:24–28
Referred to as having ministered in
   Corinth, 1 Cor 1:12; 3:4, 22; 4:6;
   16:12

APOLLYON
Angel of the bottomless pit, Rev 9:11

APOSTLE
called to be an *a*. . . . . Rom 1:1
inasmuch as I am an *a*. . . Rom 11:13
Am I not an *a* . . . . 1 Cor 9:1
the signs of an *a* were . . . 2 Cor 12:12
a preacher and an *a*. . . . . . 1 Tim 2:7
consider the *A* . . . . Heb 3:1

APOSTLES
of the twelve *a*. . . . . Matt 10:2
whom He also named *a* . . . Luke 6:13
of note among the *a* . . . . . Rom 16:7
displayed us, the *a*. . . . . . . 1 Cor 4:9
first *a*, second prophets . . 1 Cor 12:28
am the least of the *a* . . . . . 1 Cor 15:9
to the most eminent *a* . . . . 2 Cor 11:5
themselves into *a* . . . . 2 Cor 11:13
none of the other *a*. . . . . Gal 1:19
gave some to be *a* . . . . Eph 4:11

who say they are *a* . . . . Rev 2:2
heaven, and you holy *a* . . . Rev 18:20

APOSTLESHIP
in this ministry and *a* . . . . Acts 1:25
received grace and *a* . . . . . . Rom 1:5
are the seal of my *a*. . . . . . 1 Cor 9:2
in Peter for the *a*. . . . . Gal 2:8

APPAREL
is glorious in His *a*. . . . . Is 63:1
clothed with foreign *a* . . . . . Zeph 1:8
by them in white *a* . . . . Acts 1:10
themselves in modest *a* . . . 1 Tim 2:9
gold rings, in fine *a* . . . . . . James 2:2
or putting on fine *a* . . . . . . 1 Pet 3:3

APPEAL
I *a* to Caesar. . . . . Acts 25:11
love's sake I rather *a* . . . . . Philem 9

APPEAR
and let the dry land *a* . . . . . Gen 1:9
all your males shall *a* . . . . . Ex 23:17
all Israel comes to *a* . . . . . Deut 31:11
shall I come and *a* . . . . Ps 42:2
Let Your work *a* . . . . Ps 90:16
He shall *a* in His . . . . Ps 102:16
doings your sins *a* . . . . . . Ezek 21:24
faces that they may *a* . . . . . Matt 6:16
also outwardly *a*. . . . . Matt 23:28
kingdom of God would *a* . Luke 19:11
For we must all *a* . . . . 2 Cor 5:10
for Him He will *a* . . . . Heb 9:28
and the sinner *a* . . . . 1 Pet 4:18

APPEARANCE
Do not look at his *a* . . . . . 1 Sam 16:7
a is blacker than soot . . . . . Lam 4:8
As He prayed, the *a* . . . . . Luke 9:29
judge according to *a*. . . . . . John 7:24
those who boast in *a* . . . . . 2 Cor 5:12
to the outward *a* . . . . 2 Cor 10:7
found in *a* as a man . . . . . . Phil 2:8
indeed have an *a* . . . . Col 2:23

APPEARED
an angel of the Lord *a* . . . Luke 1:11
who *a* in glory and . . . . . . Luke 9:31
brings salvation has *a* . . . . Titus 2:11
of the ages, He has *a*. . . . . Heb 9:26

APPEARING
Lord Jesus Christ's *a* . . . . 1 Tim 6:14
been revealed by the *a* . . . 2 Tim 1:10
and the dead at His *a*. . . . 2 Tim 4:1
who have loved His *a*. . . . . 2 Tim 4:8
hope and glorious *a* . . . . . Titus 2:13

APPEARS
can stand when He *a*. . . . . . Mal 3:2
who is our life *a* . . . . Col 3:4
the Chief Shepherd *a* . . . . . 1 Pet 5:4
in Him, that when He *a* . 1 John 2:28

APPETITE
or satisfy the *a*. . . . . Job 38:39
are a man given to *a* . . . . . Prov 23:2

APPLE
He kept him as the *a* . . . . Deut 32:10
And my law as the *a*. . . . . . Prov 7:2
Like an *a* tree among. . . . . . Song 2:3
touches the *a* of His eye . . . Zech 2:8

APPLES
fitly spoken is like *a*. . . . . Prov 25:11
refresh me with *a* . . . . Song 2:5

APPLIED
a my heart to know . . . . . . Eccl 7:25

APPOINT
I will even *a* terror. . . . . . . Lev 26:16
a each of them to his . . . . . Num 4:19

APPOINTED
a me ruler over the. . . . . . 2 Sam 6:21
a salvation for walls . . . . Is 26:1
For God did not *a* . . . . . . 1 Thess 5:9
a elders in every city. . . . . . Titus 1:5

APPOINTED
You have *a* his limits. . . . . . . Job 14:5
To release those *a* . . . . Ps 102:20
And as it is *a* for men . . . . . Heb 9:27

APPROACH
a anyone who is near. . . . . . Lev 18:6
And cause to *a* You . . . . Ps 65:4
year, make those who *a*. . . . Heb 10:1

APPROACHING
take delight in *a* God. . . . . . . Is 58:2
as you see the Day *a* . . . . . Heb 10:25

APPROVE
their posterity who *a* . . . . . . Ps 49:13
do the same but also *a* . . . . Rom 1:32
a the things that . . . . Rom 2:18
a the things that are . . . . . Phil 1:10

APPROVED
to God and *a* by men . . . . Rom 14:18
to present yourself *a* . . . . . 2 Tim 2:15
when he has been *a* . . . . . James 1:12

AQUILA
Paul's host in Corinth, Acts 18:2, 3
Travels to Syria and Ephesus with
     Paul, Acts 18:18, 19
Instructs Apollos, Acts 18:24–26
Esteemed by Paul, Rom 16:3, 4

AR
A chief Moabite city, Num 21:15
On Israel's route, Deut 2:18
Destroyed by Sihon, Num 21:28
Destroyed by God, Is 15:1

ARABIA
Pays tribute to Solomon,
     1 Kin 10:14, 15
Plunders Jerusalem, 2 Chr 21:16, 17
Defeated by Uzziah, 2 Chr 26:1, 7
Denounced by prophets, Is 21:13–17

ARARAT
Site of ark's landing, Gen 8:4
Assassins flee to, 2 Kin 19:37; Is 37:38

ARAUNAH (or Ornan)
A Jebusite, 2 Sam 24:15–25
His threshing floor bought by David,
     2 Sam 24:18–25
     becomes site of temple, 2 Chr 3:1
Also called Ornan, 1 Chr 21:18–28

ARBITRATOR
a judge or an *a* over . . . . . Luke 12:14

ARCHANGEL
with the voice of an *a*. . . 1 Thess 4:16
Yet Michael the *a*. . . . . Jude 9

ARCHELAUS
Son of Herod the Great, Matt 2:22

AREOPAGUS
Paul preaches at, Acts 17:18–34

ARGUMENTS
fill my mouth with *a*. . . . . . . Job 23:4
casting down *a* and. . . . . 2 Cor 10:5

ARIEL
Ezra's friend, Ezra 8:15–17
—— Name applied to Jerusalem, Is
     29:1, 2, 7

ARISE
needy, now I will *a* . . . . Ps 12:5
A for our help . . . . Ps 44:26
Let God *a*. . . . . Ps 68:1
A, shine; for your light. . . . . . Is 60:1

But the LORD will *a*. . . . . Is 60:2
Righteousness shall *a*. . . . . . Mal 4:2
I will *a* and go to. . . . . Luke 15:18
you who sleep, *a*. . . . . Eph 5:14

ARISTARCHUS
A Macedonian Christian, Acts 19:29
Accompanies Paul, Acts 20:1, 4
Imprisoned with Paul, Col 4:10

ARK
Make yourself an *a* . . . . Gen 6:14
she took an *a* of bulrushes. . . . Ex 2:3
Bezalel made the *a*. . . . . Ex 37:1
seat which is on the *a*. . . . . . Lev 16:2
Let us bring the *a*. . . . . 1 Sam 4:3
golden censer and the *a* . . . . Heb 9:4
of Noah, while the *a* . . . . . 1 Pet 3:20
in heaven, and the *a*. . . . . . Rev 11:19

ARM
with an outstretched *a*. . . . . . Ex 6:6
"Has the LORD's *a* . . . . . . Num 11:23
With him is an *a* . . . . 2 Chr 32:8
a that has no strength . . . . . Job 26:2
Have you an *a* like God . . . . Job 40:9
Break the *a* of the . . . . Ps 10:15
You have a mighty *a*. . . . . . Ps 89:13
a have gained Him the. . . . . . Ps 98:1
a shall rule for Him . . . . Is 40:10
therefore His own *a* . . . . Is 59:16
strength with His *a*. . . . . . . Luke 1:51
with an uplifted *a*. . . . . . . Acts 13:17
a yourselves also with . . . . . 1 Pet 4:1

ARMAGEDDON
See MEGIDDO
Possible site of final battle, Rev 16:16

ARMED
You have *a* me with . . . . 2 Sam 22:40
a strong man, fully *a* . . . . Luke 11:21

ARMIES
make captains of the *a* . . . Deut 20:9
"I defy the *a* . . . . 1 Sam 17:10
any number to His *a*. . . . . . Job 25:3
not go out with our *a* . . . . . Ps 60:10
And he sent out his *a*. . . . Matt 22:7
surrounded by *a* . . . . Luke 21:20
And the *a* in heaven. . . . . . Rev 19:14
the earth, and their *a* . . . . Rev 19:19

ARMOR
but he put his *a* . . . . . . 1 Sam 17:54
spears, put on the *a*. . . . . . . Jer 46:4
let us put on the *a*. . . . . . Rom 13:12
Put on the whole *a*. . . . . . . Eph 6:11

ARMS
are the everlasting *a*. . . . Deut 33:27
into the clash of *a* . . . . Job 39:21
It is God who *a* . . . . Ps 18:32
My *a* will judge the . . . . Is 51:5
wounds between your *a* . . . Zech 13:6
took them up in His *a* . . . Mark 10:16
took Him up in his *a* . . . . . Luke 2:28

ARMY
went out before the *a* . . . 2 Chr 20:21
the multitude of an *a* . . . . . Ps 33:16
an exceedingly great *a*. . . Ezek 37:10
the number of the *a* . . . . . . Rev 9:16

ARNON
Boundary between Moab and
     Ammon, Num 21:13, 26
Border of Reuben, Deut 3:12, 16
Ammonites reminded of, Judg
     11:18–26

AROMA
smelled a soothing *a* . . . . . Gen 8:21
To the one we are the *a* . . . 2 Cor 2:16

---

for a sweet-smelling *a* . . . . . Eph 5:2
a sweet-smelling *a* . . . . Phil 4:18

AROUSED
the LORD was greatly *a* . . . Num 11:10
his wrath was *a*. . . . . Job 32:2
Then Joseph, being *a* . . . . Matt 1:24

ARPHAXAD
A son of Shem, Gen 10:22, 24
Born two years after the flood,
     Gen 11:10–13
An ancestor of Christ, Luke 3:36

ARRAYED
his glory was not *a*. . . . . . Matt 6:29
"Who are these *a* . . . . Rev 7:13
The woman was *a*. . . . . Rev 17:4

ARREST
when they *a* you. . . . . . . Mark 13:11

ARROGANCE
Pride and *a* and the. . . . . . Prov 8:13
I will halt the *a*. . . . . Is 13:11

ARROGANT
the fruit of the *a*. . . . . Is 10:12
My sanctuary, your *a* boast . . Ezek 24:21

ARROW
deliverance and the *a*. . . . 2 Kin 13:17
a cannot make him flee . . . Job 41:28
make ready their *a* . . . . Ps 11:2
a that flies by day . . . . Ps 91:5
a sword, and a sharp *a* . . . Prov 25:18
Their tongue is an *a*. . . . . . . Jer 9:8
as a target for the *a*. . . . . . Lam 3:12

ARROWS
He sent out *a* and. . . . . . 2 Sam 22:15
a pierce me deeply . . . . Ps 38:2
There He broke the *a*. . . . . . Ps 76:3
Like *a* in the hand of. . . . . Ps 127:4
He has caused the *a* . . . . . Lam 3:13
were sworn over Your *a*. . . . Hab 3:9

ARTAXERXES
Artaxerxes I, king of Persia (465–
     425 B.C.), authorizes Ezra's mission
     to Jerusalem, Ezra 7:1–28
Temporarily halts rebuilding pro-
     gram at Jerusalem, Ezra 4:7–23
Authorizes Nehemiah's mission, Neh
     2:1–10
Permits Nehemiah to return, Neh 13:6

ARTEMIS
Worship of, at Ephesus, creates
     uproar, Acts 19:23–41

ASA
Third king of Judah; restores true
     worship, 1 Kin 15:8–15; 2 Chr
     14—15
Hires Ben-Hadad against Baasha;
     rebuked by a prophet, 1 Kin
     15:16–22; 2 Chr 16:1–10
Diseased, seeks physicians rather
     than the Lord, 2 Chr 16:12
Death and burial, 2 Chr 16:13, 14

ASAHEL
David's nephew; captain in his
     army; noted for valor, 2 Sam 2:18;
     23:24; 1 Chr 2:16; 27:7
Killed by Abner, 2 Sam 2:19–23
Avenged by Joab, 2 Sam 3:27, 30

ASAPH
A Levite choir leader under David
     and Solomon, 1 Chr 15:16–19;
     16:1–7; 2 Chr 5:6, 12
Twelve Psalms assigned to, 2 Chr
     29:30; Ps 50; 73—83

ASCEND
Who may *a* into the . . . . Ps 24:3
If I *a* into heaven. . . . . Ps 139:8
'I will *a* into heaven . . . . Is 14:13
a as high as the eagle . . . . . . Obad 4
see the Son of Man *a* . . . . . John 6:62

ASCENDED
You have *a* on high . . . . Ps 68:18
Who has *a* into heaven . . . Prov 30:4
No one has *a* . . . . John 3:13
"When He *a* on high . . . . . . Eph 4:8
also the One who *a* . . . . . . Eph 4:10
And they *a* to heaven . . . . . Rev 11:12

ASCENDING
angels of God were *a* . . . . Gen 28:12
the angels of God *a* . . . . . . John 1:51

ASCRIBE
a greatness to our God . . . . Deut 32:3
a righteousness . . . . Job 36:3
A strength to God . . . . Ps 68:34

ASENATH
Daughter of Poti-Pherah and wife of
Joseph, Gen 41:45
Mother of Manasseh and Ephraim,
Gen 41:50–52; 46:20

ASHAMED
I am too *a* and . . . . Ezra 9:6
all my enemies be *a* . . . . Ps 6:10
Let me not be *a* . . . . Ps 25:2
who waits on You be *a* . . . . . Ps 25:3
The wise men are *a* . . . . Jer 8:9
forsake You shall be *a* . . . . . Jer 17:13
And Israel shall be *a* . . . . . . Hos 10:6
For whoever is *a* . . . . Mark 8:38
am not *a* of the gospel . . . . Rom 1:16
nothing I shall be *a* . . . . Phil 1:20
Therefore God is not *a* . . . . Heb 11:16
in Christ may be *a* . . . . 1 Pet 3:16
let him not be *a* . . . . 1 Pet 4:16
and not be *a* before . . . . . 1 John 2:28

ASHDOD
One of five Philistine cities, Josh 13:3
Seat of Dagon worship, 1 Sam 5:1–8
Opposes Nehemiah, Neh 4:7
Women of, marry Jews, Neh 13:23, 24
Called Azotus, Acts 8:40

ASHER
Jacob's second son by Zilpah, Gen
30:12, 13
Goes to Egypt with Jacob, Gen 46:8, 17
Blessed by Jacob, Gen 49:20
—— Tribe of:
Census of, Num 1:41; 26:47
Slow to fight against Canaanites,
Judg 1:31, 32; 5:17
Among Gideon's army, Judg 6:35;
7:23
A godly remnant among, 2 Chr
30:11

ASHERAH
The female counterpart of Baal, Judg
3:7; 1 Kin 18:19
Image of, erected by Manasseh in
the temple, 2 Kin 21:7
Vessels of, destroyed by Josiah, 2 Kin
23:4
—— Translated "wooden images,"
idols used in the worship of
Asherah, Ex 34:13; Deut 12:3;
16:21; 1 Kin 16:32, 33; 2 Kin 23:6, 7

ASHES
are proverbs of *a* . . . . Job 13:12
become like dust and *a* . . . . Job 30:19
For I have eaten *a* . . . . Ps 102:9

He feeds on *a* . . . . Is 44:20
sackcloth and sat in *a* . . . . . . Jon 3:6
in sackcloth and *a* . . . . . . Luke 10:13
and the *a* of a heifer . . . . . Heb 9:13

ASHKELON
One of five Philistine cities, Josh 13:3;
Jer 47:5, 7
Captured by Judah, Judg 1:18
Men of, killed by Samson,
Judg 14:19, 20
Repossessed by Philistines, 1 Sam
6:17; 2 Sam 1:20
Doom of, pronounced by the
prophets, Jer 47:5, 7; Amos 1:8;
Zeph 2:4, 7; Zech 9:5

ASHTAROTH
A city in Bashan; residence of King
Og, Deut 1:4; Josh 12:4
Captured by Israel, Josh 9:10
—— A general designation of the
Canaanite female deities, 1 Sam
7:3, 4; 31:10

ASHTORETH
A mother-goddess worshiped by the
Philistines, 1 Sam 31:10
Israel ensnared by, Judg 2:13; 10:6
Worshiped by Solomon, 1 Kin 11:5, 33
Destroyed by Josiah, 2 Kin 23:13

ASIA
Paul forbidden to preach in, Acts 16:6
Paul's later ministry in, Acts 19:1–26
Seven churches of, Rev 1:4, 11

ASIDE
lay something *a*, storing . . 1 Cor 16:2
lay *a* all filthiness . . . . James 1:21
Therefore, laying *a* . . . . 1 Pet 2:1

ASK
"Why is it that you *a* . . . . Gen 32:29
when your children *a* . . . . . . Josh 4:6
A of Me, and I will give . . . . . . Ps 2:8
"A a sign for yourself . . . . Is 7:11
They shall *a* the way . . . . . . Jer 50:5
the young children *a* . . . . . . Lam 4:4
A the LORD for rain in . . . . . Zech 10:1
whatever things you *a* . . . Matt 21:22
a, and it will be . . . . Luke 11:9
that whatever You *a* . . . . . John 11:22
a anything in My . . . . John 14:14
in that day you will *a* . . . . John 16:23
something, let them *a* . . . 1 Cor 14:35
above all that we *a* . . . . Eph 3:20
wisdom, let him *a* . . . . James 1:5
But let him *a* in faith . . . . . James 1:6
because you do not *a* . . . . James 4:2
hears us, whatever we *a* . 1 John 5:15

ASKS
For everyone who *a* . . . . . . Matt 7:8
if his son *a* for bread . . . . . . Matt 7:9
Or if he *a* for a fish . . . . . Luke 11:11

ASLEEP
down, and was fast *a* . . . . . . Jon 1:5
But He was *a* . . . . Matt 8:24
but some have fallen *a* . . . 1 Cor 15:6
those who are *a* . . . . 1 Thess 4:15
the fathers fell *a* . . . . 2 Pet 3:4

ASSEMBLED
of the God of Israel *a* . . . . . Ezra 9:4
behold, the kings *a* . . . . Ps 48:4

ASSEMBLING
not forsaking the *a* . . . . . . Heb 10:25

ASSEMBLY
to kill this whole *a* . . . . Ex 16:3
It is a sacred *a* . . . . Lev 23:36

a I will praise You . . . . Ps 22:22
I have hated the *a* . . . . Ps 26:5
also in the *a* of the . . . . Ps 89:5
to be feared in the *a* . . . . . . Ps 89:7
will rest in the *a* of the . . . Prov 21:16
fast, call a sacred *a* . . . . Joel 1:14
people, sanctify the *a* . . . . . Joel 2:16
a I will sing praise . . . . Heb 2:12
to the general *a* . . . . Heb 12:23
come into your *a* . . . . James 2:2

ASSHUR
One of the sons of Shem; progenitor
of the Assyrians, Gen 10:22;
1 Chr 1:17
—— The chief god of the Assyrians;
seen in names like Ashurbanipal
(Osnapper), Ezra 4:10
—— A city in Assyria or the nation of
Assyria, Num 24:22, 24

ASSURANCE
night, and have no *a* . . . . Deut 28:66
riches of the full *a* . . . . Col 2:2
Spirit and in much *a* . . . . 1 Thess 1:5
to the full *a* of hope . . . . . . Heb 6:11
a true heart in full *a* . . . . . Heb 10:22

ASSURE
a our hearts before . . . . . . 1 John 3:19

ASSURED
I will give you *a* peace . . . . . Jer 14:13
learned and been *a* . . . . . . 2 Tim 3:14

ASSYRIA (or Asshur)
Founded by Nimrod, Gen 10:8–12;
Mic 5:6
Agent of God's purposes, Is 7:17–20;
10:5, 6
Attacks and finally conquers Israel,
2 Kin 15:19, 20; 17:3–41
Invades and threatens Judah,
2 Kin 18:13–37
Hezekiah prays for help against;
army miraculously slain,
2 Kin 19:1–35
Prophecies concerning, Num 24:22–
24; Is 10:12–19; 14:24, 25; 19:23–
25; Hos 10:6; 11:5; Nah 3:1–19

ASTONISHED
Just as many were *a* . . . . Is 52:14
that the people were *a* . . . . Matt 7:28
who heard Him were *a* . . . . Luke 2:47

ASTONISHMENT
you shall become an *a* . . . Deut 28:37
a has taken hold . . . . Jer 8:21

ASTRAY
is a people who go *a* . . . . . . Ps 95:10
a fool, shall not go *a* . . . . . . Is 35:8
Their lies lead them *a* . . . . . Amos 2:4
and one of them goes *a* . . Matt 18:12
'They always go *a* . . . . Heb 3:10
like sheep going *a* . . . . 1 Pet 2:25

ATHALIAH
Daughter of Ahab and Jezebel, 2 Kin
8:18, 26; 2 Chr 22:2, 3
Kills royal children; usurps throne,
2 Kin 11:1–3; 2 Chr 22:10, 11
Killed in priestly uprising, 2 Kin 11:4–
16; 2 Chr 23:1–21

ATHENS
Paul preaches in, Acts 17:15–34
Paul resides in, 1 Thess 3:1

ATONEMENT
a year he shall make *a* . . . . Ex 30:10
priest shall make *a* . . . . Lev 16:30
the blood that makes *a* . . . . Lev 17:11

for it is the Day of *A* . . . . . Lev 23:28
what shall I make *a* . . . . . 2 Sam 21:3
offerings to make *a* . . . . . . Neh 10:33
a is provided for. . . . . Prov 16:6
there will be no *a* . . . . Is 22:14
I provide you an *a* . . . . Ezek 16:63

ATTAIN
It is high, I cannot *a* . . . . Ps 139:6
understanding will *a* . . . . Prov 1:5
How long until they *a* . . . . . . Hos 8:5
worthy to *a* that age . . . . . Luke 20:35
by any means, I may *a* . . . . Phil 3:11

ATTEND
just cause, O LORD, *a* . . . . Ps 17:1
And *a* to the voice of. . . . . . . Ps 86:6
behold, I will *a* . . . . Jer 23:2

ATTENTION
My son, give *a* to my . . . . . Prov 4:20
Till I come, give *a* . . . . 1 Tim 4:13
and you pay *a* to the . . . . . James 2:3

ATTENTIVE
Let Your ears be *a* . . . . Ps 130:2
the people were very *a* . . . Luke 19:48

ATTESTED
a Man *a* by God to you . . . . Acts 2:22

AUSTERE
because you are an *a* . . . . Luke 19:21

AUTHOR
For God is not the *a* . . . . . 1 Cor 14:33
He became the *a* . . . . Heb 5:9
unto Jesus, the *a* . . . . Heb 12:2

AUTHORITIES
a that exist are . . . . Rom 13:1
of God, angels and *a* . . . . 1 Pet 3:22

AUTHORITY
give some of your *a* . . . . . Num 27:20
Jew, wrote with full *a* . . . . . Esth 9:29
the righteous are in *a* . . . . . Prov 29:2
them as one having *a* . . . . Matt 7:29
who are great exercise *a*. . Matt 20:25
"All *a* has been given . . . . Matt 28:18
a I will give You . . . . Luke 4:6
and has given Him *a* . . . . . John 5:27
You have given Him *a* . . . . John 17:2
has put in His own *a* . . . . Acts 1:7
For there is no *a* . . . . Rom 13:1
to have a symbol of *a* . . . 1 Cor 11:10
and all who are in *a* . . . . . . 1 Tim 2:2
and rebuke with all *a* . . . . . Titus 2:15
defile the flesh, reject *a* . . . . . Jude 8

AUTUMN
a trees without fruit . . . . Jude 12

AVAILS
nor uncircumcision *a* . . . . . . Gal 5:6
of a righteous man *a* . . . . James 5:16

AVEN
The city of On in Egypt near Cairo;
known as Heliopolis, Gen 41:45;
Ezek 30:17
——— A name contemptuously applied
to Bethel, Hos 10:5, 8
——— Valley in Syria, Amos 1:5

AVENGE
for He will *a* the . . . . Deut 32:43
you that He will *a* . . . . Luke 18:8
Beloved, do not *a* . . . . Rom 12:19
a our blood on those . . . . . . Rev 6:10

AVENGER
The *a* of blood . . . . Num 35:19
the enemy and the *a* . . . . Ps 8:2
God's minister, an *a* . . . . . . Rom 13:4
the Lord is the *a* . . . . 1 Thess 4:6

AVENGES
It is God who *a* . . . . 2 Sam 22:48
When He *a* blood . . . . Ps 9:12

AWAKE
be satisfied when I *a* . . . . . . Ps 17:15
I lie *a* . . . . Ps 102:7
A, lute and harp . . . . Ps 108:2
My eyes are *a* through . . . . Ps 119:148
A, O north wind . . . . Song 4:16
but my heart is *a* . . . . Song 5:2
of the earth shall *a* . . . . Dan 12:2
it is high time to *a* . . . . Rom 13:11
A to righteousness . . . . . . 1 Cor 15:34
"*A*, you who sleep. . . . . Eph 5:14

AWAY
the wind drives *a* . . . . Ps 1:4
Do not cast me *a* . . . . Ps 51:11
A time to cast *a* . . . . Eccl 3:5
fair one, and come *a* . . . . . Song 2:10
and the shadows flee *a* . . . . Song 2:17
minded to put her *a* . . . . . . Matt 1:19
and earth will pass *a* . . . . Matt 24:35
and steal Him *a* . . . . Matt 27:64
the rich He has sent *a* . . . . Luke 1:53
of God who takes *a* . . . . . . John 1:29
"I am going *a* . . . . John 8:21
they cried out, "*A* . . . . John 19:15
"They have taken *a* . . . . . . John 20:2
crying out, "*A* . . . . Acts 21:36
the veil is taken *a* . . . . 2 Cor 3:14
Barnabas was carried *a* . . . . Gal 2:13
unless the falling *a* . . . . . 2 Thess 2:3
in Asia have turned *a* . . . . 2 Tim 1:15
heard, lest we drift *a* . . . . . . Heb 2:1
if they fall *a* . . . . Heb 6:6
which can never take *a* . . Heb 10:11
that does not fade *a* . . . . . . 1 Pet 5:4
the world is passing *a* . . . 1 John 2:17
and the heaven fled *a* . . . . Rev 20:11
if anyone takes *a* . . . . Rev 22:19
God shall take *a* . . . . Rev 22:19

AWE
the world stand in *a* . . . . Ps 33:8
my heart stands in *a* . . . . . Ps 119:161

AWESOME
a is this place . . . . Gen 28:17
a thing that I will do . . . . . Ex 34:10
God, the great and *a* . . . . . Deut 7:21
God, mighty and *a* . . . . . . Deut 10:17
Angel of God, very *a* . . . . . Judg 13:6
a deeds for Your land . . . . 2 Sam 7:23
heaven, O great and *a* . . . . . Neh 1:5
hand shall teach You *a* . . . . . Ps 45:4
By *a* deeds in . . . . Ps 65:5
a are Your works . . . . Ps 66:3
He is *a* in His doing. . . . . Ps 66:5
O God, You are more *a* . . . . Ps 68:35
He is *a* to the kings . . . . Ps 76:12
Your great and *a* name. . . . . Ps 99:3
of the might of Your *a* . . . . Ps 145:6
When You did *a* things . . . . . Is 64:3
with me as a mighty, *a* . . . . Jer 20:11
her collapse was *a*. . . . . Lam 1:9
"O Lord, great and *a* . . . . . . Dan 9:4

AWL
his ear with an *a* . . . . Ex 21:6
you shall take an *a* . . . . . . Deut 15:17

AX
a stroke with the *a* . . . . . . Deut 19:5
Abimelech took an *a*. . . . . . Judg 9:48
a tree, the iron *a* . . . . 2 Kin 6:5
If the *a* is dull . . . . Eccl 10:10
a boast itself against . . . . . . Is 10:15
And even now the *a* . . . . . . Matt 3:10

AZARIAH
A prophet who encourages King Asa,
2 Chr 15:1–8
——— Son of King Jehoshaphat, 2 Chr
21:2
——— King of Judah, 2 Kin 15:1
——— A high priest who rebukes King
Uzziah, 2 Chr 26:16–20
——— Chief priest in the time of Hezeki-
ah, 2 Chr 31:9, 10
——— The Hebrew name of Abed-Nego,
Dan 1:7

AZEKAH
Camp of Goliath, 1 Sam 17:1, 4, 17
Besieged by Nebuchadnezzar, Jer 34:7

BAAL (or Baals)
Deities of Canaanite polytheism,
Judg 10:10–14
The male god of the Phoenicians and
Canaanites; the counterpart of
the female Ashtaroth, 2 Kin 23:5
Nature of the worship of, 1 Kin
18:26, 28; 19:18; Ps 106:28; Jer 7:9;
19:5; Hos 9:10; 13:1, 2
Worshiped by Israelites, Num 25:1–5;
Judg 2:11–14; 3:7; 6:28–32; 1 Kin
16:31, 32; 2 Kin 21:3; Jer 11:13;
Hos 2:8
Ahaz makes images to, 2 Chr 28:1–4
Overthrown by Elijah, 1 Kin 18:17–40
by Josiah, 2 Kin 23:4, 5
Denounced by prophets, Jer 19:4–6;
Ezek 16:1, 2, 20, 21
Historic retrospect, Rom 11:4

BAAL PEOR (or Baal of Peor)
A Moabite god; worshiped by
Israelites, Num 25:1–9

BAAL PERAZIM
Site of David's victory over the
Philistines, 2 Sam 5:18–20
Same as Perazim, Is 28:21

BAAL-ZEBUB
A Philistine god at Ekron, 2 Kin 1:2
Ahaziah inquires of, 2 Kin 1:2, 6, 16
Also called Beelzebub, Matt 10:25;
12:24

BAALAH
A town also known as Kirjath
Jearim, Josh 15:9, 10

BAALS
Deities of Canaanite polytheism,
Judg 10:10–14
Ensnare Israelites, Judg 2:11–14; 3:7
Ahaz makes images to, 2 Chr 28:1–4

BAANAH
A murderer of Ishbosheth, 2 Sam
4:1–12

BAASHA
Usurps throne of Israel; his evil reign;
wars with Judah, 1 Kin 15:16—16:7

BABBLER
b is no different. . . . . Eccl 10:11
"What does this *b*. . . . . Acts 17:18

BABBLINGS
the profane and idle *b* . . . 1 Tim 6:20

BABE
the *b* leaped in my . . . . Luke 1:44
You will place a *B* . . . . Luke 2:12
for he is a *b* . . . . Heb 5:13

BABEL, TOWER OF
A huge brick structure intended to

magnify man and preserve the unity of the race, Gen 11:1–4
Objectives of, thwarted by God, Gen 11:5–9

BABES
Out of the mouth of *b* . . . . Ps 8:2
b shall rule over them . . . . Is 3:4
revealed them to *b* . . . . . Matt 11:25
'Out of the mouth of *b* . . . Matt 21:16
a teacher of *b* . . . . Rom 2:20
as to carnal, as to *b* . . . . . . 1 Cor 3:1
as newborn *b* . . . . 1 Pet 2:2

BABYLON
Built by Nimrod; Tower of Babel, Gen 10:8–10; 11:1–9
Descriptions of, Is 13:19; 14:4; Jer 51:44; Dan 4:30
Jews carried captive to, 2 Kin 25:1–21; 2 Chr 36:5–21
Inhabitants of, described, Is 47:1, 9–13; Jer 50:35–38; Dan 5:1–3
Prophecies concerning, Is 13:1–22; Jer 21:1–7; 25:9–12; 27:5–8; 29:10; Jer 50:1–46; Dan 2:31–38; 7:2–4
The prophetic city, Rev 14:8; 16:19; 17:1—18:24

BACK
Jordan turned *b* . . . . Ps 114:3
but a rod is for the *b* . . . . . Prov 10:13
for the fool's *b* . . . . Prov 26:3
I gave My *b* to those . . . . Is 50:6
cast Me behind your *b* . . . . Ezek 23:35
found Him, bring *b* word . . . Matt 2:8
plow, and looking *b* . . . . . Luke 9:62
they drew *b* and fell . . . . . John 18:6
I am sending him *b* . . . . . . Philem 12
of those who draw *b* . . . . . Heb 10:39
someone turns him *b* . . . . James 5:19
inside and on the *b* . . . . Rev 5:1

BACKBITERS
b, haters of God . . . . Rom 1:30

BACKBITING
b tongue an angry . . . . . . Prov 25:23

BACKSLIDER
The *b* in heart will be . . . . Prov 14:14

BACKSLIDINGS
b will rebuke you . . . . Jer 2:19
And I will heal your *b* . . . . . . Jer 3:22
b have increased . . . . Jer 5:6
for our *b* are many . . . . Jer 14:7

BACKWARD
fell off the seat *b* . . . . 1 Sam 4:18
shadow ten degrees *b* . . . . 2 Kin 20:11

BAD
speak to you either *b* . . . . . Gen 24:50
good for *b* or *b* for good . . . Lev 27:10
b tree bears *b* fruit . . . . Matt 7:17

BAG
is sealed up in a *b* . . . . Job 14:17
wages to put into a *b* . . . . . . Hag 1:6
nor *b* for your . . . . Matt 10:10

BAKE
b twelve cakes with it . . . . . Lev 24:5

BAKED
b unleavened cakes . . . . Ex 12:39
b unleavened bread . . . . 1 Sam 28:24

BAKER
the butler and the *b* . . . . . . Gen 40:1

BAKERS
of bread from the *b* . . . . . . Jer 37:21

BAKES
kindles it and *b* bread . . . . . Is 44:15

BALAAM
Sent by Balak to curse Israel, Num 22:5–7; Josh 24:9
Hindered by talking donkey, Num 22:22–35; 2 Pet 2:16
Curse becomes a blessing, Deut 23:4, 5; Josh 24:10
Prophecies of, Num 23:7–10, 18–24; 24:3–9, 15–24
NT references to, 2 Pet 2:15, 16; Jude 11; Rev 2:14

BALAK
A Moabite king, Num 22:4
Hires Balaam to curse Israel, Num 22–24

BALANCE
b is an abomination . . . . . . Prov 11:1
small dust on the *b* . . . . Is 40:15

BALANCES
falsifying the *b* . . . . Amos 8:5

BALD
shall not make any *b* . . . . . Lev 21:5
every head shall be *b* . . . . . Jer 48:37
completely *b* because . . . . Ezek 27:31

BALDHEAD
Go up, you *b* . . . . 2 Kin 2:23

BALM
a little *b* and a . . . . Gen 43:11
no *b* in Gilead . . . . Jer 8:22

BAND
A *b* of robbers takes . . . . Hos 7:1
with a golden *b* . . . . Rev 1:13

BANDAGED
him, and *b* his wounds . . . Luke 10:34

BANKERS
my money with the *b* . . . . Matt 25:27

BANNERS
we will set up our *b* . . . . . . Ps 20:5
They set up their *b* . . . . Ps 74:4
as an army with *b* . . . . . . Song 6:4

BANQUET
b that I have prepared . . . . Esth 5:4
companions make a *b* . . . . Job 41:6
lords, came to the *b* . . . . . Dan 5:10

BANQUETING
He brought me to the *b* . . . Song 2:4

BANQUETS
b shall be removed . . . . . . Amos 6:7

BAPTISM
coming to his *b* . . . . Matt 3:7
b that I am baptized . . . . Matt 20:22
The *b* of John . . . . Matt 21:25
But I have a *b* . . . . Luke 12:50
said, "Into John's *b* . . . . . Acts 19:3
with Him through *b* . . . . . Rom 6:4
Lord, one faith, one *b* . . . . Eph 4:5
buried with Him in *b* . . . . . Col 2:12
now saves us—*b* . . . . 1 Pet 3:21

BAPTISMS
of the doctrine of *b* . . . . . . Heb 6:2

BAPTIZE
I indeed *b* you with . . . . . . Matt 3:11
"Why then do you *b* . . . . . John 1:25
Himself did not *b* . . . . John 4:2
did not send me to *b* . . . . 1 Cor 1:17

BAPTIZED
"I need to be *b* . . . . Matt 3:14
b will be saved . . . . Mark 16:16

b more disciples . . . . John 4:1
be *b* with the Holy Spirit . . . . Acts 1:5
every one of you be *b* . . . . Acts 2:38
all his family were *b* . . . . . Acts 16:33
believed and were *b* . . . . . Acts 18:8
Arise and be *b* . . . . Acts 22:16
were *b* into Christ . . . . Rom 6:3
I thank God that I *b* . . . . . 1 Cor 1:14
b the household . . . . 1 Cor 1:16
all were *b* into Moses . . . . . 1 Cor 10:2
Spirit we were all *b* . . . . . 1 Cor 12:13
who are *b* for the dead . . 1 Cor 15:29
as many of you as were *b* . . Gal 3:27

BAPTIZING
b them in the name of . . . Matt 28:19
therefore I came *b* . . . . John 1:31

BAR-JESUS (or Elymas)
A Jewish false prophet, Acts 13:6–12

BAR-JONAH
Surname of Simon (Peter), Matt 16:17

BARABBAS
A murderer released in place of Jesus, Matt 27:16–26; Acts 3:14, 15

BARAK
Defeats Jabin, Judg 4:1–24
A man of faith, Heb 11:32

BARBARIAN
nor uncircumcised, *b* . . . . . . Col 3:11

BARE
make yourselves *b* . . . . Is 32:11
The LORD has made *b* . . . . . . Is 52:10

BARLEY
a land of wheat and *b* . . . . Deut 8:8
loaf of *b* bread tumbled . . . Judg 7:13
beginning of *b* harvest . . . . Ruth 1:22
who has five *b* loaves . . . . . John 6:9
and three quarts of *b* . . . . . Rev 6:6

BARN
seed still in the *b* . . . . Hag 2:19
the wheat into my *b* . . . . . Matt 13:30
storehouse nor *b* . . . . Luke 12:24

BARNABAS
A disciple from Cyprus; gives property, Acts 4:36, 37
Supports Paul, Acts 9:27
Ministers in Antioch, Acts 11:22–30
Travels with Paul, Acts 12:25; 13—15
Breaks with Paul over John Mark, Acts 15:36–39

BARNS
b will be filled . . . . Prov 3:10
b are broken down . . . . Joel 1:17
reap nor gather into *b* . . . . Matt 6:26
I will pull down my *b* . . . . Luke 12:18

BARREN
But Sarai was *b* . . . . Gen 11:30
b has borne seven . . . . . . 1 Sam 2:5
He grants the *b* . . . . Ps 113:9
"Sing, O *b* . . . . Is 54:1
'Blessed are the *b* . . . . . Luke 23:29
"Rejoice, O *b* . . . . Gal 4:27
you will be neither *b* . . . . . 2 Pet 1:8

BARRENNESS
A fruitful land into *b* . . . . . Ps 107:34

BARS
has strengthened the *b* . . . Ps 147:13
bronze and cut the *b* . . . . . . Is 45:2
the earth with its *b* . . . . . . Jon 2:6

BARSABAS
Nominated to replace Judas, Acts 1:23
Sent to Antioch, Acts 15:22

BARTHOLOMEW
Called Nathanael, John 1:45, 46
One of the twelve apostles, Matt 10:3; Acts 1:13

BARTIMAEUS
Blind beggar healed by Jesus, Mark 10:46–52

BARUCH
Son of Neriah, Jer 32:12, 13
Jeremiah's faithful friend and scribe, Jer 36:4–32

BARZILLAI
Supplies David with food, 2 Sam 17:27–29
Age restrains him from following David, 2 Sam 19:31–39

BASE
the elder, and the *b* . . . . Is 3:5
and the *b* things of . . . . . . 1 Cor 1:28

BASHAN
Conquered by Israel, Num 21:33–35
Assigned to Manasseh, Deut 3:13
Conquered by Hazael, king of Syria, 2 Kin 10:32, 33

BASIN
poured water into a *b* . . . . . John 13:5

BASKET
Cursed shall be your *b* . . . Deut 28:17
b had very good figs . . . . . . Jer 24:2
and put it under a *b* . . . . . Matt 5:15
I was let down in a *b* . . . . 2 Cor 11:33

BASKETS
there were three white *b* . . . Gen 40:16
and there were two *b* . . . . Jer 24:1
they took up twelve *b* . . . . Matt 14:20
took up seven large *b* . . . . Matt 15:37

BATHED
My sword shall be *b* . . . . Is 34:5
to him, "He who is *b* . . . . . John 13:10

BATHSHEBA
Wife of Uriah, taken by David, 2 Sam 11
Her first child dies, 2 Sam 12:14–19
Bears Solomon, 2 Sam 12:24
Secures throne for Solomon, 1 Kin 1:15–31
Deceived by Adonijah, 1 Kin 2:13–25

BATS
To the moles and *b* . . . . Is 2:20

BATTLE
b is the Lord's . . . . 1 Sam 17:47
out to God in the *b* . . . . . 1 Chr 5:20
strength for the *b* . . . . Ps 18:39
The Lord mighty in *b* . . . . Ps 24:8
for the day of *b* . . . . Prov 21:31
the *b* to the strong . . . . Eccl 9:11
who turn back the *b* . . . . Is 28:6
A sound of *b* is in the . . . . . Jer 50:22
prepare for *b* . . . . 1 Cor 14:8
became valiant in *b* . . . . Heb 11:34
gather them to the *b* . . . . . Rev 16:14

BEAR
greater than I can *b* . . . . . . Gen 4:13
whom Sarah shall *b* . . . . . . Gen 17:21
not *b* false witness . . . . Ex 20:16
from the paw of the *b* . . . 1 Sam 17:37
they shall *b* you up in . . . . . . Ps 91:12
b a broken spirit . . . . Prov 18:14
be clean, you who *b* . . . . Is 52:11
b their iniquities . . . . Is 53:11
Lord could no longer *b* . . . . Jer 44:22
b deprived of her cubs . . . . . Hos 13:8

lion, and a *b* met him. . . . Amos 5:19
He shall *b* the glory . . . . . . Zech 6:13
child, and *b* a Son . . . . Matt 1:23
A good tree cannot *b* . . . . . Matt 7:18
how long shall I *b* . . . . . . Matt 17:17
by, to *b* His cross. . . . . Mark 15:21
wife Elizabeth will *b* . . . . . . Luke 1:13
And whoever does not *b* . . Luke 14:27
in Me that does not *b* . . . . . John 15:2
for he does not *b* . . . . Rom 13:4
are strong ought to *b* . . . . . Rom 15:1
you may be able to *b* . . . . 1 Cor 10:13
B one another's. . . . . Gal 6:2
I *b* in my body the . . . . Gal 6:17
b the sins of many . . . . Heb 9:28
like the feet of a *b* . . . . Rev 13:2

BEARD
the edges of your *b* . . . . . . Lev 19:27
I caught it by its *b* . . . . 1 Sam 17:35
took Amasa by the *b* . . . . 2 Sam 20:9
Running down on the *b* . . . . Ps 133:2

BEARING
goes forth weeping, *b* . . . . . Ps 126:6
And He, *b* His cross . . . . . John 19:17
b with one another . . . . Col 3:13
the camp, *b* His reproach. . Heb 13:13

BEARS
Every branch that *b* . . . . . John 15:2
b all things. . . . . 1 Cor 13:7
it is the Spirit who *b* . . . . . 1 John 5:6

BEAST
b has devoured him. . . . . . Gen 37:20
You preserve man and *b* . . . . Ps 36:6
I was like a *b* before . . . . . . Ps 73:22
to the *b* its food . . . . Ps 147:9
b touches the mountain. . . Heb 12:20
And I saw a *b* rising . . . . . . Rev 13:1
Then I saw another *b* . . . . . Rev 13:11
the mark of the *b* . . . . Rev 19:20

BEASTS
are we counted as *b*. . . . . . . Job 18:3
The *b* go into dens. . . . . Job 37:8
like the *b* that perish . . . . . . Ps 49:12
I have fought with *b* . . . . 1 Cor 15:32
like brute *b* . . . . Jude 10

BEAT
I will *b* down his foes . . . . . Ps 89:23
You shall *b* him with a . . . Prov 23:14
b their swords into. . . . . Is 2:4
you shall *b* in pieces. . . . . . . Mic 4:13
spat in His face and *b*. . . . Matt 26:67
but *b* his breast . . . . Luke 18:13

BEATEN
and you will be *b*. . . . . Mark 13:9
his will, shall be *b*. . . . . . . Luke 12:47
Three times I was *b* . . . . . 2 Cor 11:25
when you are *b* for your . . 1 Pet 2:20

BEAUTIFUL
but Rachel was *b* . . . . Gen 29:17
B in elevation . . . . Ps 48:2
has made everything *b*. . . . . Eccl 3:11
my love, you are as *b*. . . . . Song 6:4
of the Lord shall be *b* . . . . . . Is 4:2
How *b* upon the. . . . . Is 52:7
indeed appear *b* . . . . Matt 23:27
begging alms at the *B* . . . . . Acts 3:10
they saw he was a *b* . . . . . Heb 11:23

BEAUTIFY
b the humble with. . . . . Ps 149:4
b the place of My . . . . Is 60:13

BEAUTY
for glory and for *b* . . . . Ex 28:2
"The *b* of Israel is . . . . . . 2 Sam 1:19

To behold the *b* . . . . Ps 27:4
and *b* is passing. . . . . Prov 31:30
see the King in His *b* . . . . . . Is 33:17
no *b* that we should. . . . . Is 53:2
the one I called *B* . . . . Zech 11:7
Do not let your *b* . . . . 1 Pet 3:3
the incorruptible *b* . . . . 1 Pet 3:4

BECAME
b a living being . . . . Gen 2:7
to the Jews I *b* . . . . 1 Cor 9:20
for I *b* like you. . . . . Gal 4:12

BED
house, if I make my *b* . . . . . Job 17:13
I remember You on my *b* . . . . Ps 63:6
if I make my *b* in hell . . . . . Ps 139:8
Also too short is *b* is green . . . . . . Song 1:16
b is too short to stretch . . . . Is 28:20
you have set your *b* . . . . Is 57:7
"Arise, take up your *b* . . . . . Matt 9:6
be two men in one *b* . . . . . Luke 17:34
and the *b* undefiled . . . . . . Heb 13:4

BEDS
sing aloud on their *b*. . . . . . Ps 149:5
shall rest in their *b*. . . . . Is 57:2
who lie on *b* of ivory. . . . . . Amos 6:4

BEE
Egypt, and for the *b*. . . . . . . Is 7:18

BEELZEBUB
Jesus accused of serving, Matt 10:25; 12:24–27

BEER LAHAI ROI
Angel meets Hagar there, Gen 16:7–14
Isaac dwells in, Gen 24:62

BEERSHEBA
God appears there to Hagar, Gen 21:14–19
to Isaac, Gen 26:23–25
to Jacob, Gen 46:1–5
to Elijah, 1 Kin 19:3–7
Oaths sworn there by Abraham, Gen 21:31–33
by Isaac, Gen 26:26–33

BEFOREHAND
do not worry *b* . . . . Mark 13:11
told you all things *b*. . . . . Mark 13:23
not to meditate *b*. . . . . . . Luke 21:14
when He testified *b* . . . . . . 1 Pet 1:11

BEG
I would *b* mercy of my . . . . . Job 9:15
I am ashamed to *b* . . . . . . Luke 16:3
b you as sojourners. . . . . . . 1 Pet 2:11

BEGAN
Then men *b* to call on. . . . . Gen 4:26
since the world *b*. . . . . Luke 1:70

BEGETS
b a scoffer does . . . . Prov 17:21
b a wise child will . . . . . . Prov 23:24
b a hundred children. . . . . . Eccl 6:3

BEGGAR
and lifts the *b*. . . . . 1 Sam 2:8
there was a certain *b* . . . . Luke 16:20

BEGGARLY
weak and *b* elements . . . . . . Gal 4:9

BEGINNING
b God created the . . . . Gen 1:1
Though your *b* was. . . . . Job 8:7
of the Lord is the *b*. . . . . . . Ps 111:10
that God does from *b* . . . . . Eccl 3:11
who made them at the *b* . . Matt 19:4
In the *b* was the Word . . . . John 1:1
This *b* of signs Jesus . . . . . . John 2:11
a murderer from the *b* . . . . John 8:44

with Me from the *b* . . . . . . John 15:27
the *b*, the firstborn . . . . Col 1:18
having neither *b* . . . . Heb 7:3
True Witness, the *B* . . . . Rev 3:14
and the Omega, the *B* . . . . . Rev 21:6

BEGOTTEN
I have *b* You . . . . Ps 2:7
heart, 'Who has *b* . . . . Is 49:21
glory of the only *b* . . . . . John 1:14
Christ Jesus I have *b* . . . . . 1 Cor 4:15
abundant mercy has *b* . . . . . 1 Pet 1:3
loves him who is *b* . . . . . . 1 John 5:1

BEGUILING
b unstable souls . . . . 2 Pet 2:14

BEGUN
Having *b* in the Spirit . . . . . . Gal 3:3
that He who has *b* . . . . Phil 1:6

BEHALF
to speak on God's *b* . . . . Job 36:2
you on Christ's *b* . . . . 2 Cor 5:20
has been granted on *b* . . . Phil 1:29

BEHAVE
I will *b* wisely in a . . . . Ps 101:2
does not *b* rudely . . . . 1 Cor 13:5

BEHAVED
sent him, and *b* wisely . . . 1 Sam 18:5
and blamelessly we *b* . . . 1 Thess 2:10

BEHAVIOR
of good *b*, hospitable . . . . . 1 Tim 3:2
they be reverent in *b* . . . . . . Titus 2:3

BEHEADED
he sent and had John *b* . . Matt 14:10
those who had been *b* . . . . . Rev 20:4

BEHEMOTH
Described, Job 40:15–24

BEHOLD
the eyes to *b* the sun . . . . . . Eccl 11:7
B, you are fair . . . . Song 1:15
B, the virgin shall . . . . Is 7:14
Judah, "*B* your God . . . . Is 40:9
B the Lamb of God . . . . . . John 1:36
I am, that they may *b* . . . John 17:24
to them, "*B* the Man . . . . . John 19:5
B what manner of love . . . 1 John 3:1

BEHOLDING
with unveiled face, *b* . . . . . 2 Cor 3:18

BEING
man became a living *b* . . . . . Gen 2:7
God while I have my *b* . . . . Ps 104:33
move and have our *b* . . . . Acts 17:28
who, *b* in the form of . . . . . . Phil 2:6

BEL
Patron god of Babylon, Is 46:1;
   Jer 50:2; 51:44

BELIEF
by the Spirit and *b* . . . . . 2 Thess 2:13

BELIEVE
B in the LORD your God . . 2 Chr 20:20
tears, "Lord, I *b* . . . . Mark 9:24
b that you receive . . . . . . Mark 11:24
because they did not *b* . . . Mark 16:14
have no root, who *b* . . . . . . Luke 8:13
and slow of heart to *b* . . . Luke 24:25
to those who *b* . . . . John 1:12
how will you *b* . . . . John 3:12
sent, Him you do not *b* . . . . John 5:38
we may see it and *b* . . . . . . John 6:30
to him, "Do you *b* . . . . John 9:35
this, that they may *b* . . . . John 11:42
you *b* in God . . . . John 14:1
written that you may *b* . . . John 20:31

King Agrippa, do you *b* . . . Acts 26:27
the Lord Jesus and *b* . . . . . Rom 10:9
And how shall they *b* . . . . Rom 10:14
a wife who does not *b* . . . . 1 Cor 7:12
I spoke," we also *b* . . . . . . 2 Cor 4:13
given to those who *b* . . . . . Gal 3:22
Christ, not only to *b* . . . . . . Phil 1:29
comes to God must *b* . . . . . Heb 11:6
b that there is one . . . . . . James 2:19
Even the demons *b* . . . . . James 2:19
Beloved, do not *b* . . . . 1 John 4:1

BELIEVED
And he *b* in the LORD . . . . . . Gen 15:6
b that I would see the . . . . . Ps 27:13
Who has *b* our report . . . . . . Is 53:1
of that city *b* in Him . . . . . John 4:39
seen Me, you have *b* . . . . John 20:29
who heard the word *b* . . . . . Acts 4:4
of those who *b* were of . . . . Acts 4:32
Holy Spirit when you *b* . . . Acts 19:2
"Abraham *b* God . . . . Rom 4:3
I know whom I have *b* . . . 2 Tim 1:12

BELIEVERS
be an example to the *b* . . . 1 Tim 4:12
are benefited are *b* . . . . . . 1 Tim 6:2

BELIEVES
The simple *b* every . . . . . . Prov 14:15
He who *b* and is . . . . Mark 16:16
that whoever *b* in Him . . . . John 3:16
He who *b* in the Son . . . . . John 3:36
with the heart one *b* . . . . Rom 10:10
b all things . . . . 1 Cor 13:7

BELIEVING
you ask in prayer, *b* . . . . . Matt 21:22
blessed with *b* Abraham . . . . Gal 3:9

BELLY
On your *b* you shall go . . . Gen 3:14
And Jonah was in the *b* . . . . Jon 1:17
three nights in the *b* . . . . Matt 12:40
whose god is their *b* . . . . . . Phil 3:19

BELONG
To the Lord our God *b* . . . . . Dan 9:9
My name, because you *b* . . Mark 9:41

BELOVED
"The *b* of the LORD . . . . . . Deut 33:12
so He gives His *b* . . . . Ps 127:2
of myrrh is my *b* . . . . Song 1:13
My *b* is mine . . . . Song 2:16
b more than another . . . . . . Song 5:9
Where has your *b* . . . . Song 6:1
leaning upon her *b* . . . . . . Song 8:5
a song of my *B* . . . . Is 5:1
for you are greatly *b* . . . . . Dan 9:23
"This is My *b* . . . . Matt 3:17
election they are *b* . . . . . . Rom 11:28
us accepted in the *B* . . . . . . Eph 1:6
Luke the *b* physician . . . . . . Col 4:14
than a slave as a *b* . . . . . . Philem 16
"This is My *b* . . . . 2 Pet 1:17
our *b* brother Paul . . . . . . 2 Pet 3:15
the saints and the *b* . . . . . . Rev 20:9

BELSHAZZAR
King of Babylon; Daniel interprets
   his dream, Dan 5

BELT
with a leather *b* . . . . Matt 3:4
us, he took Paul's *b* . . . . . Acts 21:11

BELTESHAZZAR
Daniel's Babylonian name, Dan 1:7

BEMOAN
Or who will *b* you . . . . Jer 15:5
for the dead, nor *b* . . . . . . Jer 22:10

BEN-AMMI
Son of Lot; father of the Ammonites,
   Gen 19:38

BEN-HADAD
Ben-Hadad I, king of Damascus;
   hired by Asa, king of Judah, to
   attack Baasha, king of Israel,
   1 Kin 15:18–21
—— Ben-Hadad II, king of Damascus;
   makes war on Ahab, king of
   Israel, 1 Kin 20
Falls in siege against Samaria, 2 Kin
   6:24–33; 7:6–20
Killed by Hazael, 2 Kin 8:7–15
—— Ben-Hadad III, king of Damascus; loses all Israelite conquests
   made by Hazael, his father, 2 Kin
   13:3–25

BEN-ONI
Rachel's name for Benjamin, Gen
   35:16–18

BENAIAH
The son of Jehoiada; a mighty man,
   2 Sam 23:20–23
Faithful to David, 2 Sam 15:18; 20:23
Escorts Solomon to the throne, 1 Kin
   1:38–40
Executes Adonijah, Joab and Shimei,
   1 Kin 2:25, 29–34, 46
—— A Pirathonite; another of David's
   mighty men, 2 Sam 23:30
Divisional commander, 1 Chr 27:14

BEND
The wicked *b* their bow . . . . . Ps 11:2

BENEATH
and on the earth *b* . . . . Deut 4:39
"You are from *b* . . . . John 8:23

BENEFACTORS
them are called '*b* . . . . . . Luke 22:25

BENEFIT
That I may see the *b* . . . . . . Ps 106:5
people who could not *b* . . . . . Is 30:5
might have a second *b* . . . . 2 Cor 1:15

BENJAMIN
Jacob's youngest son, Gen 35:16–20
Taken to Egypt against Jacob's wishes,
   Gen 42–45
Jacob's prophecy concerning, Gen
   49:27
—— Tribe of:
Families of, Num 26:38–41
Territory allotted to, Josh 18:11–28
Attacked by remaining tribes for
   condoning sin of Gibeah, Judg
   20:12–48
Wives provided for remnant of, Judg
   21:1–23
Tribe of Saul, 1 Sam 9:1, 2
of Paul, Phil 3:5

BENT
behold, this vine *b* . . . . Ezek 17:7

BEREA
A city of Macedonia; visited by Paul,
   Acts 17:10–15

BEREAVE
I will *b* them of . . . . Jer 15:7
no more shall you *b* . . . . . Ezek 36:12
children, yet I will *b* . . . . . . Hos 9:12

BERNICE
Sister of Herod Agrippa II, Acts
   25:13, 23
Hears Paul's defense, Acts 26:1–30

BERODACH-BALADAN
See MERODACH-BALADAN
A king of Babylon, 2 Kin 20:12–19

BESEECH
Return, we *b* You . . . . Ps 80:14
b you therefore . . . . Rom 12:1
of the Lord, *b* you to . . . . Eph 4:1

BESIDE
He leads me *b* the . . . . Ps 23:2
"Paul, you are *b*. . . . . Acts 26:24
For if we are *b* . . . . 2 Cor 5:13

BEST
with the *b* ointments. . . . . . Amos 6:6
'Bring out the *b*. . . . . Luke 15:22
earnestly desire the *b*. . . . 1 Cor 12:31

BESTOW
LORD, that He may *b*. . . . . . Ex 32:29
b greater honor . . . . 1 Cor 12:23

BESTOWED
love the Father has *b*. . . . . 1 John 3:1

BETH HORON
Twin towns of Ephraim, Josh 16:3, 5
Fortified by Solomon, 2 Chr 8:3–5
Prominent in battles, Josh 10:10–14;
1 Sam 13:18

BETH PEOR
Town near Pisgah, Deut 3:29
Moses buried near, Deut 34:6
Assigned to Reubenites, Josh 13:15, 20

BETH SHAN (or Beth Shean)
A town in Issachar, Josh 17:11–16
Saul's corpse hung up at, 1 Sam
31:10–13; 2 Sam 21:12–14

BETH SHEMESH
Ark brought to, 1 Sam 6:12–19
Joash defeats Amaziah at, 2 Kin
14:11
Taken by Philistines, 2 Chr 28:18

BETHABARA
A place beyond the Jordan where
John baptized, John 1:28

BETHANY
A town on the Mt. of Olives, Luke 19:29
Home of Lazarus, John 11:1
Home of Simon, the leper, Matt 26:6
Jesus visits there, Mark 11:1, 11, 12
Scene of the Ascension, Luke 24:50, 51

BETHEL
Abram settles near, Gen 12:7, 8
Site of Abram's altar, Gen 13:3, 4
Site of Jacob's vision of the ladder,
Gen 28:10–19
Jacob returns to, Gen 35:1–15
Samuel judges there, 1 Sam 7:15, 16
Site of worship and sacrifice, 1 Sam
10:3
Center of idolatry, 1 Kin 12:28–33
Josiah destroys altars of, 2 Kin 23:4,
15–20
Denounced by prophets, 1 Kin 13:1–
10; Amos 7:10–13; Jer 48:13; Hos
10:15

BETHESDA
Jerusalem pool, John 5:2–4

BETHLEHEM
Originally called Ephrath, Gen 35:16
Rachel buried there, Gen 35:19
Home of Naomi and Boaz, Ruth 1:1,
19; 4:9–11
Home of David, 1 Sam 16:1–18
Predicted place of Messiah's birth,
Mic 5:2

Christ born there, Matt 2:1; Luke
2:4–7; John 7:42
Infants of, killed by Herod, Matt
2:16–18

BETHPHAGE
Village near Bethany, Mark 11:1
Near Mt. of Olives, Matt 21:1

BETHSAIDA
A city of Galilee, Mark 6:45
Home of Andrew, Peter and Philip,
John 1:44; 12:21
Blind man healed there, Mark 8:22,
23
5,000 fed nearby, Luke 9:10–17
Unbelief of, denounced, Matt 11:21;
Luke 10:13

BETRAY
the outcasts, do not *b*. . . . . Is 16:3
you, one of you will *b*. . . . Matt 26:21
Now brother will *b* . . . . . . Mark 13:12

BETRAYED
Man is about to be *b*. . . . . Matt 17:22
in which He was *b* . . . . . . 1 Cor 11:23

BETRAYER
See, My *b* is at. . . . . Matt 26:46

BETRAYING
"Judas, are you *b* . . . . Luke 22:48

BETRAYS
who is the one who *b* . . . . John 21:20

BETROTH
"You shall *b* a wife . . . . . . Deut 28:30
"I will *b* you to Me . . . . Hos 2:19

BETROTHED
to a virgin *b* to a man . . . . Luke 1:27
For I have *b* you to . . . . . . 2 Cor 11:2

BETTER
b than sacrifice. . . . . 1 Sam 15:22
It is *b* to trust in . . . . Ps 118:8
B is a little with the . . . . . Prov 15:16
B is a dry morsel . . . . Prov 17:1
B is the poor who. . . . . Prov 19:1
B to dwell in. . . . . Prov 21:19
b is a neighbor. . . . . Prov 27:10
B a handful with . . . . Eccl 4:6
Two are *b* than one . . . . Eccl 4:9
B a poor and wise. . . . . Eccl 4:13
were the former days *b*. . . . . Eccl 7:10
features appeared *b*. . . . . . . Dan 1:15
For it is *b* to marry. . . . . . . 1 Cor 7:9
Christ, which is far *b* . . . . . Phil 1:23
b than the angels. . . . . Heb 1:4
b things concerning. . . . . . . Heb 6:9
b things than that . . . . Heb 12:24

BEULAH
A symbol of true Israel, Is 62:4, 5

BEWARE
"*B* of false prophets. . . . . . Matt 7:15
b of evil workers. . . . . Phil 3:2
B lest anyone cheat . . . . Col 2:8

BEWITCHED
b you that you should . . . . . Gal 3:1

BEYOND
b what is written . . . . 1 Cor 4:6
b their ability. . . . . 2 Cor 8:3
advanced in Judaism *b*. . . . . Gal 1:14

BEZALEL
Hur's grandson, 1 Chr 2:20
Tabernacle builder, Ex 31:1–11;
35:30–35

BILDAD
One of Job's friends, Job 2:11

Makes three speeches, Job 8:1–22;
18:1–21; 25:1–6

BILHAH
Rachel's maid, Gen 29:29
The mother of Dan and Naphtali,
Gen 30:1–8
Commits incest with Reuben,
Gen 35:22

BILLOWS
b have gone over me . . . . Ps 42:7
all Your *b* and Your. . . . . Jon 2:3

BIND
b the cluster of the. . . . . . . Job 38:31
b the wild ox in the . . . . . . Job 39:10
b them around your . . . . . . Prov 3:3
B them on your fingers. . . . . Prov 7:3
B up the testimony. . . . . Is 8:16
but He will *b* us up. . . . . Hos 6:1
and whatever you *b* . . . . Matt 16:19
'*B* him hand and foot. . . . Matt 22:13
b heavy burdens. . . . . Matt 23:4

BIRD
the blood of the *b* . . . . Lev 14:52
with him as with a *b*. . . . . . Job 41:5
soul, "Flee as a *b* . . . . Ps 11:1
has escaped as a *b*. . . . . Ps 124:7
b hastens to the snare. . . . . Prov 7:23
for a *b* of the air may. . . . . Eccl 10:20
fly away like a *b*. . . . . Hos 9:11
unclean and hated *b* . . . . . Rev 18:2

BIRDS
b will eat your flesh . . . . . Gen 40:19
b make their nests . . . . . . Ps 104:17
b caught in a snare . . . . . . Eccl 9:12
Look at the *b*. . . . . Matt 6:26
"Foxes have holes and *b* . . Matt 8:20

BIRTH
heaven, who gives it *b* . . . . Job 38:29
makes the deer give *b*. . . . . . Ps 29:9
the day of one's *b*. . . . . Eccl 7:1
bring to the time of *b*. . . . . . Is 66:9
the deer also gave *b*. . . . . . Jer 14:5
Now the *b* of Jesus . . . . . . Matt 1:18
will rejoice at his *b* . . . . . . Luke 1:14
who was blind from *b* . . . . John 9:1
conceived, it gives *b* . . . . James 1:15

BIRTHDAY
which was Pharaoh's *b* . . . Gen 40:20
b gave a feast for his . . . . Mark 6:21

BIRTHRIGHT
"Sell me your *b*. . . . . Gen 25:31
Esau despised his *b* . . . . . Gen 25:34
according to his *b*. . . . . . . Gen 43:33
of food sold his *b* . . . . Heb 12:16

BISHOP
the position of a *b*. . . . . . . 1 Tim 3:1
b must be blameless. . . . . . Titus 1:7

BIT
and they *b* the people . . . . Num 21:6
be harnessed with *b* . . . . . . Ps 32:9

BITE
A serpent may *b* . . . . Eccl 10:11
But if you *b* and. . . . . Gal 5:15

BITHYNIA
The Spirit keeps Paul from, Acts 16:7
Peter writes to Christians of, 1 Pet 1:1

BITS
the great house into *b*. . . . Amos 6:11
Indeed, we put *b*. . . . . James 3:3

BITTER
made their lives *b*. . . . . Ex 1:14
b herbs they . . . . Ex 12:8

to those who are *b*........ Prov 31:6
who put *b* for sweet......... Is 5:20
and do not be *b*........... Col 3:19
But if you have *b* .... James 3:14
make your stomach *b*..... Rev 10:9

BITTERLY
has dealt very *b*........ Ruth 1:20
And Hezekiah wept *b* .... 2 Kin 20:3
he went out and wept *b* .. Matt 26:75

BITTERNESS
man dies in the *b* .... Job 21:25
heart knows its own *b* .... Prov 14:10
all my years in the *b* ...... Is 38:15
you are poisoned by *b*.... Acts 8:23
b springing up cause ..... Heb 12:15

BLACK
My skin grows *b* .... Job 30:30
wavy, and *b* as a raven ... Song 5:11
one hair white or *b*...... Matt 5:36
a *b* horse .... Rev 6:5
and the sun became *b* .... Rev 6:12

BLACKNESS
the heavens with *b* .... Is 50:3
whom is reserved the *b* ..... Jude 13

BLACKSMITH
The *b* with the tongs ..... Is 44:12
I have created the *b*....... Is 54:16

BLADE
went in after the *b* ...... Judg 3:22
first the *b* .... Mark 4:28

BLAME
that anyone should *b* .... 2 Cor 8:20
be holy and without *b*..... Eph 1:4

BLAMELESS
You shall be *b* .... Deut 18:13
and that man was *b*....... Job 1:1
when You speak, and *b*..... Ps 51:4
Let my heart be *b*..... Ps 119:80
end, that you may be *b*... 1 Cor 1:8
which is in the law, *b*..... Phil 3:6
you holy, and *b*......... Col 1:22
your hearts *b* in ..... 1 Thess 3:13
body be preserved *b* .... 1 Thess 5:23
bishop then must be *b* .... 1 Tim 3:2
deacons, being found *b*... 1 Tim 3:10
without spot and *b* ..... 2 Pet 3:14

BLAMELESSLY
b we behaved .... 1 Thess 2:10

BLASPHEME
b Your name forever ...... Ps 74:10
compelled them to *b* ..... Acts 26:11
may learn not to *b* ...... 1 Tim 1:20
b that noble name ...... James 2:7
God, to *b* His name........ Rev 13:6

BLASPHEMED
a foolish people has *b* ..... Ps 74:18
b continually every .... Is 52:5
who passed by *b* Him .... Matt 27:39
who were hanged *b* .... Luke 23:39
The name of God is *b*..... Rom 2:24
doctrine may not be *b* .... 1 Tim 6:1
On their part He is *b* .... 1 Pet 4:14
great heat, and they *b* ..... Rev 16:9

BLASPHEMER
I was formerly a *b*...... 1 Tim 1:13

BLASPHEMERS
boasters, proud, *b*........ 2 Tim 3:2

BLASPHEMES
b the name of the LORD.... Lev 24:16
"This Man *b* .... Matt 9:3

BLASPHEMIES
false witness, *b*....... Matt 15:19

is this who speaks *b* ..... Luke 5:21
great things and *b* .... Rev 13:5

BLASPHEMY
but the *b* against........ Matt 12:31
"He has spoken *b* ...... Matt 26:65
was full of names of *b* ..... Rev 17:3

BLAST
By the *b* of God they........ Job 4:9
for the *b* of the............. Is 25:4

BLASTED
"I *b* you with blight ...... Amos 4:9

BLEATING
"What then is this *b* .... 1 Sam 15:14

BLEMISH
shall be without *b*........ Ex 12:5
LORD, a ram without *b* ..... Lev 6:6
be holy and without *b* ..... Eph 5:27
as of a lamb without *b*.... 1 Pet 1:19

BLEMISHED
to the Lord what is *b* ..... Mal 1:14

BLESS
b those who *b* you .... Gen 12:3
You go unless You *b*...... Gen 32:26
"The LORD *b* you and ..... Num 6:24
b the LORD at all .... Ps 34:1
b You while I live........... Ps 63:4
b His holy name .... Ps 103:1
b the house of Israel...... Ps 115:12
b those who fear the ..... Ps 115:13
b you in the name of ...... Ps 129:8
I will abundantly *b* .... Ps 132:15
b those who curse...... Luke 6:28
B those who persecute.... Rom 12:14
Being reviled, we *b*....... 1 Cor 4:12
With it we *b* our God ..... James 3:9

BLESSED
And God *b* them .... Gen 1:22
the earth shall be *b* ...... Gen 12:3
b be those who.......... Gen 27:29
indeed he shall be *b*..... Gen 27:33
B is he who............ Num 24:9
B shall be the .... Deut 28:4
You have *b* the work of.... Job 1:10
B is the man who walks .... Ps 1:1
B is the man to whom ...... Ps 32:2
B is the nation whose ...... Ps 33:12
B is he who considers ...... Ps 41:1
B are those who keep ..... Ps 106:3
B is he who comes........ Ps 118:26
b who fears the LORD....... Ps 128:4
rise up and call her *b* .... Prov 31:28
will call you *b*............ Mal 3:12
B are the poor in.......... Matt 5:3
B are those who mourn .... Matt 5:4
B are the meek .... Matt 5:5
B are those who hunger.... Matt 5:6
B are the merciful......... Matt 5:7
B are the pure in......... Matt 5:8
B are the peacemakers..... Matt 5:9
B are those who are ..... Matt 5:10
B are you when they..... Matt 5:11
b is he who is .... Matt 11:6
b are your eyes .... Matt 13:16
B is He who comes ..... Matt 21:9
hand, 'Come, you *b* .... Matt 25:34
Jesus took bread, *b* ...... Matt 26:26
b are you among women.. Luke 1:28
know these things, *b*..... John 13:17
B are those who have .... John 20:29
'It is more *b* to give ...... Acts 20:35
the Creator, who is *b*..... Rom 1:25
all, the eternally *b* .... Rom 9:5
B be the God and......... Eph 1:3
b God which was........ 1 Tim 1:11

the lesser is *b* .... Heb 7:7
this one will be *b* .... James 1:25
B is he who reads .... Rev 1:3
'*B* are the dead who ...... Rev 14:13
B is he who watches ...... Rev 16:15
B are those who are .... Rev 19:9
B and holy is he who ...... Rev 20:6
B is he who keeps the..... Rev 22:7
B are those who do His.... Rev 22:14

BLESSING
and you shall be a *b* ..... Gen 12:2
I will command My *b*.... Lev 25:21
before you today a *b*.... Deut 11:26
The *b* of a perishing ...... Job 29:13
Your *b* is upon Your ...... Ps 3:8
The *b* of the LORD......... Prov 10:22
shall be showers of *b*.... Ezek 34:26
relent, and leave a *b*..... Joel 2:14
and you shall be a *b* ..... Zech 8:13
the fullness of the *b*..... Rom 15:29
b which we bless........ 1 Cor 10:16
that the *b* of Abraham.... Gal 3:14
with every spiritual *b*...... Eph 1:3
cultivated, receives *b* ...... Heb 6:7
to inherit the *b*......... Heb 12:17
honor and glory and *b*...... Rev 5:12

BLESSINGS
of the law, the *b*......... Josh 8:34
B are on the head of ...... Prov 10:6

BLIGHT
"I blasted you with *b* ..... Amos 4:9
I struck you with *b*........ Hag 2:17

BLIND
I was eyes to the *b*........ Job 29:15
B yourselves and be......... Is 29:9
To open *b* eyes .... Is 42:7
I will bring the *b*.......... Is 42:16
b people who have eyes..... Is 43:8
His watchmen are *b*....... Is 56:10
They wandered *b*....... Lam 4:14
when you offer the *b* ...... Mal 1:8
The *b* see .... Matt 11:5
b leads the *b* .... Matt 15:14
of sight to the *b*.......... Luke 4:18
to Him, "Are we *b*....... John 9:40
miserable, poor, *b*........ Rev 3:17

BLINDED
b their eyes and......... John 12:40
and the rest were *b* .... Rom 11:7
of this age has *b* .... 2 Cor 4:4
the darkness has *b*...... 1 John 2:11

BLINDS
a bribe, for a bribe *b*..... Deut 16:19

BLOOD
of your brother's *b*...... Gen 4:10
b shall be shed............ Gen 9:6
you are a husband of *b* ..... Ex 4:25
b that makes atonement... Lev 17:11
b sustains its life .... Lev 17:14
do not cover my *b*....... Job 16:18
is there in my *b*............ Ps 30:9
And condemn innocent *b*... Ps 94:21
hands are full of *b*....... Is 1:15
also disclose her *b* .... Is 26:21
And the moon into *b* ...... Joel 2:31
For this is My *b*......... Matt 26:28
called the Field of *B* ...... Matt 27:8
"His *b* be on us and ..... Matt 27:25
new covenant in My *b* .... Luke 22:20
were born, not of *b*...... John 1:13
b has eternal life........ John 6:54
b every nation of men.... Acts 17:26
with His own *b*........ Acts 20:28
propitiation by His *b*..... Rom 3:25
justified by His *b*......... Rom 5:9

BLOODSHED *(continued)*
through His *b* . . . . Eph 1:7
brought near by the *b* . . . . . Eph 2:13
against flesh and *b* . . . . Eph 6:12
peace through the *b* . . . . Col 1:20
"This is the *b* . . . . Heb 9:20
are purified with *b* . . . . Heb 9:22
of *b* there is no . . . . Heb 9:22
the Holiest by the *b* . . . . Heb 10:19
sprinkling of the *b* . . . . 1 Pet 1:2
with the precious *b* . . . . . 1 Pet 1:19
b of Jesus Christ His . . . . . . 1 John 1:7
our sins in His own *b* . . . . . . Rev 1:5
us to God by Your *b* . . . . Rev 5:9
them white in the *b* . . . . . Rev 7:14
overcame him by the *b* . . . . Rev 12:11
a robe dipped in *b* . . . . Rev 19:13

BLOODSHED
me from the guilt of *b* . . . . . Ps 51:14
the land is full of *b* . . . . Ezek 9:9
build up Zion with *b* . . . . . . Mic 3:10

BLOODTHIRSTY
The LORD abhors the *b* . . . . Ps 5:6
B and deceitful men . . . . . . Ps 55:23

BLOSSOM
Israel shall *b* and bud . . . . Is 27:6
and *b* as the rose . . . . Is 35:1
the fig tree may not *b* . . . . . Hab 3:17

BLOT
say that He would *b* . . . . 2 Kin 14:27
from my sins, and *b* . . . . Ps 51:9
and I will not *b* . . . . Rev 3:5

BLOTTED
Let them be *b* out of . . . . . . Ps 69:28
I have *b* out . . . . Is 44:22
your sins may be *b* . . . . Acts 3:19

BLOW
an east wind to *b* . . . . Ps 78:26
B upon my garden . . . . Song 4:16
with a very severe *b* . . . . Jer 14:17

BLOWS
B that hurt cleanse . . . . . Prov 20:30
breath of the LORD *b* . . . . Is 40:7
The wind *b* where it . . . . John 3:8

BOANERGES
Surname of James and John, Mark
3:17

BOAST
puts on his armor *b* . . . . . 1 Kin 20:11
soul shall make its *b* . . . . Ps 34:2
God we *b* all day long . . . . . . Ps 44:8
and make your *b* . . . . Rom 2:17
that we are your *b* . . . . 2 Cor 1:14
you, and not to *b* . . . . . . 2 Cor 10:16
that I also may *b* . . . . . . 2 Cor 11:16
lest anyone should *b* . . . . Eph 2:9
your hearts, do not *b* . . . . James 3:14

BOASTERS
God, violent, proud, *b* . . . . Rom 1:30
lovers of money, *b* . . . . 2 Tim 3:2

BOASTFUL
b shall not stand . . . . Ps 5:5
I was envious of the *b* . . . . . . Ps 73:3

BOASTING
Where is *b* then . . . . Rom 3:27
should make my *b* . . . . 1 Cor 9:15
you, great is my *b* . . . . 2 Cor 7:4
All such *b* is evil . . . . James 4:16

BOASTS
Whoever falsely *b* . . . . Prov 25:14

BOAZ
A wealthy Bethlehemite, Ruth 2:1,
4–18
Husband of Ruth, Ruth 4:10–13
Ancestor of Christ, Matt 1:5
——— Pillar of the temple, 1 Kin
7:21

BODIES
valley of the dead *b* . . . . Jer 31:40
b a living sacrifice . . . . Rom 12:1
not know that your *b* . . . . 1 Cor 6:15
also celestial *b* . . . . 1 Cor 15:40
wives as their own *b* . . . . . . Eph 5:28
and chariots, and *b* . . . . Rev 18:13

BODILY
b form like a dove . . . . Luke 3:22
b presence is weak . . . . . . 2 Cor 10:10
of the Godhead *b* . . . . Col 2:9
b exercise . . . . 1 Tim 4:8

BODY
b clings to the ground . . . . . . Ps 44:25
b is carved ivory . . . . Song 5:14
b was wet with the dew . . . . Dan 4:33
of the *b* is the eye . . . . Matt 6:22
those who kill the *b* . . . . . Matt 10:28
this is My *b* . . . . Matt 26:26
and asked for the *b* . . . . . . Matt 27:58
around his naked *b* . . . . . Mark 14:51
of the temple of His *b* . . . . . John 2:21
deliver me from this *b* . . . . . Rom 7:24
redemption of our *b* . . . . . . Rom 8:23
members in one *b* . . . . Rom 12:4
and the Lord for the *b* . . . . 1 Cor 6:13
against his own *b* . . . . 1 Cor 6:18
not know that your *b* . . . . . 1 Cor 6:19
glorify God in your *b* . . . . . 1 Cor 6:20
But I discipline my *b* . . . . . 1 Cor 9:27
one bread and one *b* . . . . 1 Cor 10:17
b which is broken . . . . 1 Cor 11:24
be guilty of the *b* . . . . 1 Cor 11:27
For as the *b* is one . . . . . . 1 Cor 12:12
baptized into one *b* . . . . . 1 Cor 12:13
b is not one member . . . . 1 Cor 12:14
are the *b* of Christ . . . . . . 1 Cor 12:27
though I give my *b* . . . . 1 Cor 13:3
It is sown a natural *b* . . . . 1 Cor 15:44
both to God in one *b* . . . . . . Eph 2:16
be magnified in my *b* . . . . . Phil 1:20
in the *b* of His flesh . . . . . . Col 1:22
by putting off the *b* . . . . Col 2:11
and neglect of the *b* . . . . . . Col 2:23
were called in one *b* . . . . . . Col 3:15
b You have prepared . . . . . . Heb 10:5
the offering of the *b* . . . . . . Heb 10:10
For as the *b* without . . . . . James 2:26
our sins in His own *b* . . . . . 1 Pet 2:24

BOILS
Job with painful *b* . . . . Job 2:7

BOLD
the righteous are *b* . . . . . . Prov 28:1
whatever anyone is *b* . . . . 2 Cor 11:21
are much more *b* . . . . Phil 1:14

BOLDLY
I may open my mouth *b* . . . Eph 6:19
therefore come *b* . . . . Heb 4:16
So we may *b* say . . . . Heb 13:6

BOLDNESS
Great is my *b* of . . . . 2 Cor 7:4
in whom we have *b* . . . . Eph 3:12
but with all *b* . . . . Phil 1:20
standing and great *b* . . . . . 1 Tim 3:13
brethren, having *b* . . . . Heb 10:19
that we may have *b* . . . . . 1 John 4:17

BOND
bring you into the *b* . . . . . Ezek 20:37
of the Spirit in the *b* . . . . Eph 4:3
love, which is the *b* . . . . Col 3:14

BONDAGE
because of the *b* . . . . Ex 2:23
out of the house of *b* . . . . . . Ex 13:14
the spirit of *b* . . . . Rom 8:15
might bring us into *b* . . . . . . Gal 2:4
which gives birth to *b* . . . . . Gal 4:24
again with a yoke of *b* . . . . . Gal 5:1
lifetime subject to *b* . . . . . . Heb 2:15
he is brought into *b* . . . . . 2 Pet 2:19

BONDS
"Let us break Their *b* . . . . Ps 2:3

BONDSERVANTS
B, be obedient to . . . . Eph 6:5
Masters, give your *b* . . . . Col 4:1
for vice, but as *b* . . . . 1 Pet 2:16

BONDWOMAN
"Cast out this *b* . . . . Gen 21:10
the one by a *b* . . . . Gal 4:22

BONE
"This is now *b* . . . . Gen 2:23
b clings to my skin . . . . Job 19:20
bonds came together, *b* . . . . Ezek 37:7

BONES
shall carry up my *b* . . . . . Gen 50:25
which made all my *b* . . . . . . Job 4:14
His *b* are like beams . . . . . . Job 40:18
I can count all My *b* . . . . Ps 22:17
and my *b* waste away . . . . . . Ps 31:10
I kept silent, my *b* . . . . Ps 32:3
the wind, or how the *b* . . . . Eccl 11:5
say to them, 'O dry *b* . . . . . Ezek 37:4
b are the whole house . . . . Ezek 37:11
of dead men's *b* . . . . Matt 23:27
b shall be broken . . . . John 19:36
concerning his *b* . . . . Heb 11:22

BOOK
you will find in the *b* . . . . . Ezra 4:15
distinctly from the *b* . . . . . . Neh 8:8
were inscribed in a *b* . . . . . Job 19:23
"Search from the *b* . . . . Is 34:16
'Write in a *b* for . . . . Jer 30:2
found written in the *b* . . . . . Dan 12:1
so a *b* of remembrance . . . . Mal 3:16
are written in the *b* . . . . Gal 3:10
sprinkled both the *b* . . . . . . Heb 9:19
in the Lamb's *B* . . . . Rev 21:27
the prophecy of this *b* . . . . Rev 22:18
the words of the *b* . . . . Rev 22:19

BOOKS
b there is no end . . . . Eccl 12:12
not contain the *b* . . . . John 21:25
magic brought their *b* . . . . Acts 19:19
God, and *b* were opened . . . Rev 20:12

BOOTH
b which a watchman . . . . . . Job 27:18
of Zion is left as a *b* . . . . Is 1:8

BORDERS
and enlarge your *b* . . . . Ex 34:24
makes peace in your *b* . . . . Ps 147:14
and enlarge the *b* . . . . Matt 23:5

BORE
conceived and *b* Cain . . . . . Gen 4:1
And to Sarah who *b* . . . . Is 51:2
b the sin of many . . . . Is 53:12
and He *b* them and . . . . Is 63:9
b our sicknesses . . . . Matt 8:17
who Himself *b* our sins . . . . 1 Pet 2:24
b a male Child who was . . . . Rev 12:5

BORN
"Every son who is *b* . . . . Ex 1:22
yet man is *b* to . . . . Job 5:7
"Man who is *b* . . . . Job 14:1
'This one was *b* . . . . Ps 87:4

A time to be *b*. . . . . Eccl 3:2
unto us a Child is *b* . . . . Is 9:6
Or shall a nation be *b* . . . . Is 66:8
b Jesus who is called . . . . . Matt 1:16
For there is *b* . . . . Luke 2:11
unless one is *b* again . . . . . . John 3:3
That which is *b*. . . . . John 3:6
For this cause I was *b* . . . . John 18:37
me also, as by one *b* . . . . . 1 Cor 15:8
of the bondwoman was *b*. . . Gal 4:23
having been *b* again . . . . . 1 Pet 1:23
who loves is *b* of God . . . . 1 John 4:7
is the Christ is *b* . . . . 1 John 5:1
know that whoever is *b*. . 1 John 5:18

BORNE
And as we have *b*. . . . . . . 1 Cor 15:49

BORROWER
b is servant to the . . . . Prov 22:7
lender, so with the *b* . . . . Is 24:2

BORROWS
The wicked *b* and does . . . . . Ps 37:21

BOSOM
man take fire to his *b* . . . . Prov 6:27
consolation of her *b* . . . . . . Is 66:11
angels to Abraham's *b* . . . Luke 16:22
Son, who is in the *b* . . . . . . John 1:18
leaning on Jesus' *b* . . . . . . John 13:23

BOTTLE
b shall be filled . . . . Jer 13:12

BOTTOMLESS
given the key to the *b*. . . . . . Rev 9:1
ascend out of the *b* . . . . Rev 17:8
the key to the *b*. . . . . Rev 20:1

BOUGHS
She sent out her *b* . . . . Ps 80:11

BOUGHT
the hand of him who *b* . . . Lev 25:28
not your Father, who *b*. . . . Deut 32:6
b the threshing floor . . . 2 Sam 24:24
b the field from. . . . . Jer 32:9
all that he had and *b* . . . . Matt 13:46
For you were *b* at a . . . . . . 1 Cor 6:20
denying the Lord who *b*. . . . 2 Pet 2:1

BOUND
of the wicked have *b* . . . . . Ps 119:61
b the waters in a . . . . Prov 30:4
not been closed or *b*. . . . . Is 1:6
on earth will be *b* . . . . . . Matt 16:19
b hand and foot with . . . . John 11:44
And see, now I go *b*. . . . . Acts 20:22
of Israel I am *b* . . . . Acts 28:20
who has a husband is *b*. . . . Rom 7:2
Are you *b* to a wife . . . . . . 1 Cor 7:27
Devil and Satan, and *b* . . . . Rev 20:2

BOUNDARY
b that they may not . . . . . . Ps 104:9

BOUNTIFUL
the miser said to be *b* . . . . . Is 32:5
you into a *b* country . . . . Jer 2:7

BOUNTIFULLY
Because He has dealt *b*. . . . . Ps 13:6
and he who sows *b* . . . . . . 2 Cor 9:6

BOW
b remained in strength . . . Gen 49:24
You shall not *b* . . . . Ex 23:24
to serve them and *b* . . . . . Judg 2:19
b is renewed in my . . . . . . Job 29:20
will not trust in my *b* . . . . . Ps 44:6
He breaks the *b*. . . . . Ps 46:9
like a deceitful *b* . . . . Ps 78:57
let us worship and *b*. . . . . . Ps 95:6
B down Your heavens . . . . . Ps 144:5

not save them by *b* . . . . Hos 1:7
who sat on it had a *b* . . . . . Rev 6:2

BOWED
stood all around and *b* . . . . Gen 37:7
b the heavens also . . . . . 2 Sam 22:10
whose knees have not *b*. . 1 Kin 19:18
They have *b* down and. . . . . Ps 20:8
And they *b* the knee . . . . Matt 27:29
men who have not *b*. . . . . Rom 11:4

BOWL
his hand in the *b*. . . . . Prov 19:24
or the golden *b* . . . . Eccl 12:6
and poured out his *b* . . . . . Rev 16:2

BOWLS
who drink wine from *b*. . . . Amos 6:6
a harp, and golden *b* . . . . . . Rev 5:8
Go and pour out the *b* . . . . Rev 16:1
who had the seven *b* . . . . . Rev 21:9

BOWS
"The *b* of the mighty . . . . . 1 Sam 2:4

BOX
Judas had the money *b*. . . John 13:29

BOYS
Shall be full of *b*. . . . . Zech 8:5

BOZRAH
City of Edom, Gen 36:33
Destruction of, foretold, Amos 1:12
Figurative of Messiah's victory, Is 63:1

BRAIDED
not with *b* hair or . . . . 1 Tim 2:9

BRAMBLE
gather grapes from a *b* . . . Luke 6:44

BRANCH
blossoms on one *b* . . . . Ex 25:33
b will not be green. . . . . . . Job 15:32
from Israel, palm *b* . . . . Is 9:14
B shall grow out of. . . . . Is 11:1
raise to David a *B*. . . . . Jer 23:5
grow up to David a *B*. . . . . Jer 33:15
forth My Servant the *B*. . . . Zech 3:8
whose name is the *B*. . . . . Zech 6:12
b has already become. . . . Matt 24:32
b that bears fruit He . . . . . John 15:2
b cannot bear fruit . . . . John 15:4
he is cast out as a *b* . . . . . John 15:6

BRANCHES
in the sun, and his *b*. . . . . . Job 8:16
and bring forth *b*. . . . . Job 14:9
and cut down the *b* . . . . Is 18:5
and its *b* are broken . . . . . Jer 11:16
His *b* shall spread. . . . . Hos 14:6
vine, you are the *b* . . . . . . John 15:5
b were broken off. . . . . . . Rom 11:17

BRASS
become sounding *b* . . . . . 1 Cor 13:1
feet were like fine *b*. . . . . . . Rev 1:15

BRAVE
in the faith, be *b* . . . . 1 Cor 16:13

BREACHES
Heal its *b* . . . . Ps 60:2

BREAD
face you shall eat *b* . . . . . . Gen 3:19
of Salem brought out *b* . . . Gen 14:18
"Behold, I will rain *b* . . . . . Ex 16:4
shall eat unleavened *b* . . . Ex 23:15
not live by *b* alone . . . . . . Deut 8:3
lives, I do not have *b* . . . 1 Kin 17:12
new wine, a land of *b* . . 2 Kin 18:32
that his life abhors *b*. . . . . Job 33:20
people as they eat *b* . . . . . . Ps 14:4
Can He give *b* also . . . . . . Ps 78:20

up late, to eat the *b*. . . . . . Ps 127:2
her poor with *b* . . . . Ps 132:15
For they eat the *b* . . . . Prov 4:17
b eaten in secret is. . . . . . . Prov 9:17
B gained by deceit is . . . . Prov 20:17
Go, eat your *b* with . . . . Eccl 9:7
Cast your *b* upon the . . . . . Eccl 11:1
b will be given him . . . . Is 33:16
for what is not *b*. . . . . Is 55:2
to share your *b* . . . . Is 58:7
We get our *b* at the . . . . . . Lam 5:9
who give me my *b* . . . . Hos 2:5
For their *b* shall be. . . . . Hos 9:4
And lack of *b* in all . . . . . . Amos 4:6
these stones become *b* . . . . Matt 4:3
not live by *b* alone . . . . Matt 4:4
this day our daily *b*. . . . . . . Matt 6:11
eating, Jesus took *b*. . . . . Matt 26:26
no bag, no *b* . . . . Mark 6:8
is he who shall eat *b*. . . . . Luke 14:15
gives you the true *b* . . . . . . John 6:32
I am the *b* of life. . . . . John 6:48
having dipped the *b*. . . . . John 13:26
b which we break. . . . . . . 1 Cor 10:16
He was betrayed took *b*. . 1 Cor 11:23
as you eat this *b*. . . . . 1 Cor 11:26
did we eat anyone's *b*. . . . 2 Thess 3:8
and eat their own *b* . . . . 2 Thess 3:12

BREADTH
is as great as its *b* . . . . Rev 21:16

BREAK
b their bones and. . . . . Num 24:6
torment my soul, and *b* . . . . Job 19:2
They *b* up my path . . . . . . Job 30:13
B their teeth in their . . . . . . Ps 58:6
And now they *b* down. . . . . . Ps 74:6
b My statutes and do. . . . . . Ps 89:31
covenant I will not *b*. . . . . . Ps 89:34
Remember, do not *b* . . . . . Jer 14:21
together to *b* bread . . . . . . Acts 20:7

BREAKING
in the *b* of bread . . . . Acts 2:42
b bread from house to . . . . . Acts 2:46
weeping and *b* my heart . . Acts 21:13
dishonor God through *b*. . . Rom 2:23

BREAKS
He *b* in pieces mighty . . . . Job 34:24
My soul *b* with longing . . . . Ps 119:20
Until the day *b* . . . . Song 2:17
Whoever therefore *b* . . . . . Matt 5:19

BREAST
back on Jesus' *b* . . . . John 13:25

BREASTPLATE
a *b*, an ephod . . . . Ex 28:4
righteousness as a *b* . . . . . . Is 59:17
having put on the *b*. . . . . . Eph 6:14

BREASTS
blessings of the *b* . . . . Gen 49:25
on My mother's *b* . . . . Ps 22:9
doe, let her *b* satisfy . . . . . Prov 5:19
Your two *b* are like . . . . . . Song 4:5
b which nursed You. . . . . . Luke 11:27
done, beat their *b*. . . . . . . Luke 23:48

BREATH
nostrils the *b* of life . . . . Gen 2:7
at the blast of the *b* . . . . 2 Sam 22:16
that there was no *b* . . . . . 1 Kin 17:17
perish, and by the *b* . . . . . . Job 4:9
as long as my *b*. . . . . Job 27:3
has made me, and the *b*. . . Job 33:4
You take away their *b*. . . . Ps 104:29
Man is like a *b*. . . . . Ps 144:4
everything that has *b* . . . . Ps 150:6
they all have one *b* . . . . . Eccl 3:19

BREATHE
from it, who gives *b* . . . . Is 42:5
"Surely I will cause *b*. . . . . Ezek 37:5
God who holds your *b*. . . . . Dan 5:23
gives to all life, *b* . . . . Acts 17:25
consume with the *b* . . . . 2 Thess 2:8
power to give *b* . . . . Rev 13:15

BREATHE
me, and such as *b*. . . . . Ps 27:12
winds, O breath, and *b*. . . . Ezek 37:9

BREATHED
He *b* on them . . . . John 20:22

BREATHES
indeed he *b* his last . . . . Job 14:10

BRETHREN
presence of all his *b* . . . . . Gen 16:12
be lifted above his *b* . . . . . Deut 17:20
and you are all *b* . . . . Matt 23:8
least of these My *b*. . . . . . Matt 25:40
Go and tell My *b*. . . . . . . Matt 28:10
firstborn among many *b* . . Rom 8:29
to judge between his *b* . . . . 1 Cor 6:5
thus sin against the *b* . . . . 1 Cor 8:12
over five hundred *b* . . . . . 1 Cor 15:6
perils among false *b* . . . . 2 Cor 11:26
b secretly brought. . . . . Gal 2:4
to be made like His *b*. . . . . Heb 2:17
sincere love of the *b* . . . . . 1 Pet 1:22
because we love the *b* . . . 1 John 3:14
our lives for the *b*. . . . . . 1 John 3:16
does not receive the *b*. . . . 3 John 10
of your *b* the prophets . . . . Rev 22:9

BRIBE
you shall take no *b*. . . . . Ex 23:8
b blinds the eyes . . . . Deut 16:19
b debases the heart . . . . Eccl 7:7

BRIBERY
consume the tents of *b* . . . . Job 15:34

BRIBES
hand is full of *b*. . . . . Ps 26:10
but he who hates *b* . . . . . Prov 15:27
but he who receives *b* . . . . Prov 29:4
everyone loves *b* . . . . Is 1:23
the just and taking *b*. . . . Amos 5:12

BRICK
people straw to make *b* . . . . . . Ex 5:7
incense on altars of *b* . . . . . . Is 65:3
Make strong the *b* . . . . Nah 3:14

BRICKS
"Come, let us make *b* . . . . . Gen 11:3
b which they made. . . . . Ex 5:8
deliver the quota of *b*. . . . . . Ex 5:18
b have fallen down . . . . Is 9:10

BRIDE
them on you as a *b* . . . . Is 49:18
He who has the *b* . . . . John 3:29
I will show you the *b* . . . . . Rev 21:9
the Spirit and the *b*. . . . . . Rev 22:17

BRIDEGROOM
righteousness, as a *b* . . . . . . Is 61:10
and as the *b* rejoices . . . . Is 62:5
mourn as long as the *b* . . . Matt 9:15
b will be taken away. . . . . Matt 9:15
went out to meet the *b*. . . . Matt 25:1
b fast while the . . . . Mark 2:19
the friend of the *b*. . . . . . . John 3:29

BRIDLE
with bit and *b* . . . . Ps 32:9
b the whole body . . . . James 3:2

BRIER
b shall come up the . . . . Is 55:13
longer be a pricking *b*. . . . Ezek 28:24
of them is like a *b*. . . . . Mic 7:4

BRIERS
there shall come up *b* . . . . Is 5:6
their words, though *b* . . . . . Ezek 2:6

BRIGHTER
Her Nazirites were *b* . . . . . . Lam 4:7
a light from heaven, *b*. . . . Acts 26:13

BRIGHTNESS
From the *b* before Him . . 2 Sam 22:13
and kings to the *b* . . . . Is 60:3
goes forth as *b* . . . . Is 62:1
very dark, with no *b* . . . . . Amos 5:20
who being the *b*. . . . . Heb 1:3

BRIMSTONE
Then the LORD rained *b* . . . Gen 19:24
b is scattered on his . . . . Job 18:15
fire, smoke, and *b*. . . . . Rev 9:17
the lake of fire and *b* . . . . Rev 20:10

BRING
LORD your God will *b* . . . . . Deut 30:3
b back his soul. . . . . Job 33:30
for they *b* down. . . . . Ps 50:5
Lord said, "I will *b*. . . . . Ps 68:22
B forth your . . . . Is 41:21
b forth justice. . . . . Is 42:3
b My righteousness. . . . . Is 46:13
Though they *b* up their . . . . Hos 9:12
And she will *b*. . . . . Matt 1:21
b no fruit to maturity . . . . Luke 8:14
b this Man's blood. . . . . Acts 5:28
Who shall *b* a charge . . . . . Rom 8:33
b Christ down from . . . . . . Rom 10:6
b Christ up from the . . . . . . Rom 10:7
even so God will *b* . . . . 1 Thess 4:14

BROAD
set me in a *b* place . . . . Ps 118:5
b is the way that. . . . . Matt 7:13
their phylacteries *b*. . . . . . Matt 23:5

BROKE
b them at the foot of. . . . . . Ex 32:19
b open the fountain. . . . . Ps 74:15
covenant which they *b*. . . . . Jer 31:32
He blessed and *b*. . . . . Matt 14:19
b the flask and poured. . . . Mark 14:3
b the legs of the. . . . . John 19:32

BROKEN
he has *b* My covenant . . . . Gen 17:14
I am like a *b* vessel . . . . Ps 31:12
their bows shall be *b* . . . . . . Ps 37:15
He has *b* his covenant. . . . . . Ps 55:20
heart the spirit is *b*. . . . . . Prov 15:13
b spirit dries the. . . . . Prov 17:22
but who can bear a *b* . . . . Prov 18:14
in the staff of this *b* . . . . Is 36:6
heart within me is *b*. . . . . . . Jer 23:9
is oppressed and *b* . . . . Hos 5:11
this stone will be *b* . . . . . Matt 21:44
Scripture cannot be *b* . . . . John 10:35
is My body which is *b* . . . 1 Cor 11:24

BROKENHEARTED
He heals the *b* and . . . . Ps 147:3

BRONZE
So Moses made a *b* . . . . . . Num 21:9
your head shall be *b*. . . . . Deut 28:23
b serpent that Moses . . . . 2 Kin 18:4
Or is my flesh *b*. . . . . Job 6:12
b as rotten wood . . . . Job 41:27
broken the gates of *b* . . . . Ps 107:16
b I will bring. . . . . Is 60:17
b walls against the. . . . . Jer 1:18
people a fortified *b*. . . . . . . Jer 15:20
a third kingdom of *b* . . . . . Dan 2:39
make your hooves *b*. . . . . . . Mic 4:13
were mountains of *b*. . . . . . Zech 6:1

BROOD
The *b* of evildoers. . . . . Is 14:20
B of vipers. . . . . Matt 12:34
hen gathers her *b* . . . . . . Luke 13:34

BROOK
stones from the *b* . . . . . 1 Sam 17:40
shall drink of the *b* . . . . Ps 110:7
disciples over the *B* . . . . . . John 18:1

BROOKS
good land, a land of *b* . . . . Deut 8:7
b that pass away . . . . Job 6:15
for the water *b*. . . . . Ps 42:1

BROTHER
"Where is Abel your *b* . . . . . Gen 4:9
he were my friend or *b* . . . . Ps 35:14
speak against your *b*. . . . . . Ps 50:20
and a *b* is born for. . . . . . Prov 17:17
b offended is harder. . . . . . Prov 18:19
has neither son nor *b*. . . . . . Eccl 4:8
and do not trust any *b*. . . . . Jer 9:4
he pursued his *b* . . . . Amos 1:11
Was not Esau Jacob's *b* . . . . Mal 1:2
b will deliver up . . . . Matt 10:21
how often shall my *b* . . . . Matt 18:21
"Teacher, tell my *b* . . . . . Luke 12:13
b will rise again. . . . . John 11:23
do you judge your *b* . . . . Rom 14:10
b goes to law against . . . . 1 Cor 6:6
shall the weak *b*. . . . . 1 Cor 8:11
slave—a beloved *b*. . . . . . Philem 16
He who loves his *b*. . . . . 1 John 2:10
and murdered his *b* . . . . 1 John 3:12
Whoever hates his *b* . . . . 1 John 3:15
b sinning a sin which . . . 1 John 5:16
I, John, both your *b* . . . . Rev 1:9

BROTHERHOOD
the covenant of *b* . . . . Amos 1:9
I might break the *b*. . . . . Zech 11:14
Love the *b*. . . . . 1 Pet 2:17
experienced by your *b* . . . . 1 Pet 5:9

BROTHERLY
to one another with *b* . . . . Rom 12:10
b love continue. . . . . Heb 13:1

BROTHER'S
Am I my *b* keeper . . . . Gen 4:9
at the speck in your *b*. . . . . Matt 7:3

BROTHERS
My *b* have dealt. . . . . Job 6:15
a stranger to my *b*. . . . . Ps 69:8
is My mother, or My *b*. . . . Mark 3:33
b are these who hear . . . . Luke 8:21
b did not believe. . . . . John 7:5
love as *b* . . . . 1 Pet 3:8

BROUGHT
He *b* out His people. . . . . . Ps 105:48
The king has *b* me into . . . . Song 1:4
to heaven, will be *b*. . . . . Luke 10:15

BRUISE
He shall *b* your head . . . . . Gen 3:15
LORD binds up the *b*. . . . . . Is 30:26
the LORD to *b* Him . . . . Is 53:10

BRUISED
b reed He will not. . . . . Is 42:3
He was *b* for our. . . . . Is 53:5
b reed He will not . . . . . Matt 12:20

BRUTAL
b men who are. . . . . Ezek 21:31

BUCKLER
be your shield and *b*. . . . . . Ps 91:4

BUD
it bring forth and *b* . . . . Is 55:10

BUFFET
of Satan to *b* me . . . . . . 2 Cor 12:7

BUILD
b ourselves a city . . . . Gen 11:4
"Would you a house . . . 2 Sam 7:5
b a temple for the name . . 1 Kin 8:17
that the LORD will *b* . . . . . 1 Chr 17:10
Solomon who shall *b* . . . 1 Chr 28:6
able to *b* Him a temple . . . . 2 Chr 2:6
labor in vain who *b* . . . . Ps 127:1
down, and a time to *b* . . . . . Eccl 3:3
house that you will *b* . . . . Is 66:1
I will *b* them and not . . . . . . Jer 24:6
Who *b* up Zion with . . . . Mic 3:10
b the desolate. . . . . Mal 1:4
'This man began to *b* . . . . Luke 14:30
What house will you *b* . . . . Acts 7:49
b you up and give you . . . Acts 20:32
named, lest I should *b* . . . Rom 15:20
For if I *b* again . . . . Gal 2:18

BUILDER
me, as a wise master *b* . . 1 Cor 3:10
foundations, whose *b* . . . . Heb 11:10

BUILDING
field, you are God's *b* . . . . . . 1 Cor 3:9
destroyed, we have a *b* . . . . 2 Cor 5:1
in whom the whole *b* . . . . . . Eph 2:21
But you, beloved, *b* . . . . Jude 20

BUILDS
The LORD *b* up . . . . Ps 147:2
The wise woman *b* . . . . Prov 14:1
one take heed how he *b* . . 1 Cor 3:10

BUILT
Wisdom has *b* her house . . . Prov 9:1
my works great, I *b* . . . . Eccl 2:4
Babylon, that I have *b* . . . . Dan 4:30
to a wise man who *b* . . . . . Matt 7:24
a foolish man who *b* . . . . . Matt 7:26
work which he has *b* . . . . . 1 Cor 3:14
having been *b* on the. . . . . . Eph 2:20
rooted and *b* up in Him . . . . . Col 2:7
For every house is *b* . . . . Heb 3:4
stones, are being *b* . . . . 1 Pet 2:5

BULL
I will not take a *b* . . . . Ps 50:9
like an untrained *b* . . . . Jer 31:18

BULLS
in the blood of *b*. . . . . Is 1:11
For if the blood of *b* . . . . . . Heb 9:13

BULWARKS
Mark well her *b* . . . . Ps 48:13
for walls and *b*. . . . . Is 26:1

BUNDLE
each man's *b* of money . . . Gen 42:35
A *b* of myrrh is my . . . . Song 1:13

BURDEN
You have laid the *b* . . . . . Num 11:11
one knows his own *b* . . . . 2 Chr 6:29
so that I am a *b* . . . . Job 7:20
Cast your *b* on the. . . . . . . Ps 55:22
the grasshopper is a *b* . . . . Eccl 12:5
in that day that his *b* . . . . . . Is 10:27
its reproach is a *b* . . . . Zeph 3:18
easy and My *b* is light . . . Matt 11:30
as it may, I did not *b* . . . . 2 Cor 12:16
we might not be a *b* . . . . . 1 Thess 2:9
on you no other *b*. . . . . Rev 2:24

BURDENED
but you have *b* Me with. . . . . Is 43:24

BURDENS
and looked at their *b* . . . . . . Ex 2:11
For they bind heavy *b* . . . . Matt 23:4
Bear one another's *b* . . . . . . Gal 6:2

BURDENSOME
b task God has given . . . . . . Eccl 1:13

his life will be *b* . . . . Is 15:4
I myself was not *b* . . . . . . 2 Cor 12:13
commandments are not *b*. 1 John 5:3

BURIAL
indeed he has no *b*. . . . . Eccl 6:3
she did it for My *b*. . . . . . . Matt 26:12
for the day of My *b*. . . . . . . John 12:7
Stephen to his *b*. . . . . Acts 8:2

BURIED
and there will I be *b* . . . . . . Ruth 1:17
I saw the wicked *b* . . . . Eccl 8:10
away the body and *b* . . . . Matt 14:12
also died and was *b* . . . . . Luke 16:22
Therefore we were *b* . . . . . . Rom 6:4
and that He was *b* . . . . . . 1 Cor 15:4
b with Him in baptism . . . . . Col 2:12

BURN
the bush does not *b* . . . . Ex 3:3
that My wrath may *b* . . . . . . Ex 32:10
b their chariots. . . . . Josh 11:6
both will *b* together . . . . Is 1:31
"Did not our heart *b* . . . . Luke 24:32
eat her flesh and *b* . . . . Rev 17:16

BURNED
If anyone's work is *b* . . . . . 1 Cor 3:15
my body to be *b*. . . . . 1 Cor 13:3
whose end is to be *b* . . . . . . Heb 6:8
be touched and that *b* . . . . Heb 12:18
are *b* outside the camp. . . . Heb 13:11
in it will be *b*. . . . . 2 Pet 3:10
all green grass was *b* . . . . . . Rev 8:7

BURNING
b torch that passed. . . . . . . Gen 15:17
with severe *b* fever . . . . . . Deut 28:22
on his lips like a *b*. . . . . . . Prov 16:27
b fire shut up in my. . . . . . . Jer 20:9
b jealousy against the. . . . . Ezek 36:5
plucked from the *b* . . . . . . Amos 4:11
a great mountain *b* . . . . Rev 8:8
fell from heaven, *b* . . . . Rev 8:10

BURNT
lamb for a *b* offering . . . . . Gen 22:7
delight in *b* offering . . . . . . Ps 51:16
b offerings are not . . . . Jer 6:20
Though you offer Me *b* . . . Amos 5:22

BURST
it is ready to *b* . . . . Job 32:19
with doors, when it *b* . . . . . Job 38:8
the new wine will *b*. . . . . . Luke 5:37
falling headlong, he *b* . . . . Acts 1:18

BURY
b your dead in the . . . . Gen 23:6
was no one to *b* them . . . . . . Ps 79:3
go and *b* my father. . . . . . . Matt 8:21
and let the dead *b* . . . . Matt 8:22

BUSH
from the midst of a *b* . . . . Ex 3:2
Him who dwelt in the *b* . . Deut 33:16
to him in the *b*. . . . . Acts 7:35

BUSINESS
in ships, who do *b*. . . . . Ps 107:23
farm, another to his *b* . . . . Matt 22:5
about My Father's *b* . . . . . Luke 2:49

BUSYBODIES
at all, but are *b*. . . . . 2 Thess 3:11
but also gossips and *b*. . . . 1 Tim 5:13

BUTLER
b did not remember . . . . . . Gen 40:23

BUTTER
So he took *b* and milk . . . . Gen 18:8
were smoother than *b* . . . . Ps 55:21
of milk produces *b*. . . . . . . Prov 30:33

BUY
in Egypt to *b* grain . . . . . . Gen 41:57
B the truth . . . . Prov 23:23
Yes, come, *b* wine and . . . . . . Is 55:1
that we may *b* the poor . . . Amos 8:6
b food for all these . . . . . . Luke 9:18
"*B* those things we . . . . . . John 13:29
rejoice, those who *b*. . . . . . 1 Cor 7:30
spend a year there, *b* . . . . James 4:13
I counsel you to *b*. . . . . Rev 3:18
and that no one may *b*. . . . Rev 13:17

BUYER
nothing," cries the *b* . . . . . Prov 20:14
as with the *b* . . . . Is 24:2
'Let not the *b* . . . . Ezek 7:12

BUYS
a field and *b* it . . . . Prov 31:16
has and *b* that field . . . . . Matt 13:44
b their merchandise . . . . . . Rev 18:11

BYGONE
b generations . . . . Acts 14:16

BYWORD
But He has made me a *b* . . . Job 17:6
You made us a *b* . . . . Ps 44:14

CAESAR
—— Augustus Caesar (31 B.C.–A.D. 14):
  Decree of brings Joseph and Mary
    to Bethlehem, Luke 2:1–5
—— Tiberius Caesar (A.D. 14–37):
  Christ's ministry dated by, Luke 3:1–23
  Tribute paid to, Matt 22:17–21
  Jews side with, John 19:12
—— Claudius Caesar (A.D. 41–54):
  Famine in time of, Acts 11:28
  Banished Jews from Rome, Acts 18:2
—— Nero Caesar (A.D. 54–68):
  Paul appealed to, Acts 25:8–12
  Christian converts in household of,
    Phil 4:22
  Paul tried before, 2 Tim 4:16–18
  Called Augustus, Acts 25:21

CAESAREA
  Roman capital of Palestine, Acts
    12:19; 23:33
  Paul escorted to, Acts 23:23–33
  Paul imprisoned at; appeals to Caesar,
    Acts 25:4, 8–13
  Peter preaches at, Acts 10:34–43
  Paul preaches at, Acts 9:26–30; 18:22;
    21:8

CAESAREA PHILIPPI
  A city in northern Palestine; scene of
    Peter's great confession, Matt
    16:13–20
  Probable site of the Transfiguration,
    Matt 17:1–3

CAGE
c is full of birds. . . . . Jer 5:27
foul spirit, and a *c* . . . . Rev 18:2

CAIAPHAS
  Son-in-law of Annas; high priest,
    John 18:13
  Makes prophecy, John 11:49–52
  Jesus appears before, John 18:23, 24
  Apostles appear before, Acts 4:1–22

CAIN
  Adam's first son, Gen 4:1
  His offering rejected, Gen 4:2–7; Heb
    11:4
  Murders Abel; is exiled; settles in
    Nod, Gen 4:8–17
  A type of evil, Jude 11

CAKE
Ephraim is a *c* . . . . Hos 7:8

CAKES
Sustain me with *c*. . . . . Song 2:5
and love the raisin *c* . . . . . . Hos 3:1

CALAMITIES
refuge, until these *c*. . . . . Ps 57:1

CALAMITY
for the day of their *c*. . . . . Deut 32:35
will laugh at your *c* . . . . . Prov 1:26
c shall come suddenly. . . . . Prov 6:15
If there is *c* in a. . . . . Amos 3:6

CALCULATED
c the dust of the . . . . Is 40:12

CALDRON
this city is the *c* . . . . Ezek 11:3

CALEB
Sent as spy; gives good report;
rewarded, Num 13:2, 6, 27, 30;
14:5–9, 24–38
Inherits Hebron, Josh 14:6–15
Conquers his territory with Othniel's
help, Josh 15:13–19

CALF
and made a molded *c* . . . . . . Ex 32:4
They made a *c* in Horeb . . . Ps 106:19
is, than a fatted *c*. . . . . Prov 15:17
like a stubborn *c*. . . . . Hos 4:16
Your *c* is rejected. . . . . Hos 8:5
And bring the fatted *c* . . . . Luke 15:23
creature like a *c* . . . . Rev 4:7

CALL
I will *c* to the LORD . . . . . 1 Sam 12:17
c their lands after . . . . Ps 49:11
To you, O men, I *c* . . . . Prov 8:4
c upon Him while He. . . . . . . Is 55:6
'*C* to Me . . . . Jer 33:3
Arise, *c* on your God. . . . . . . Jon 1:6
They will *c* on My name. . . Zech 13:9
c His name JESUS . . . . Matt 1:21
c the righteous . . . . Matt 9:13
Lord our God will *c* . . . . . . Acts 2:39
c them My people. . . . . Rom 9:25
then shall they *c* . . . . Rom 10:14
For God did not *c* . . . . . . 1 Thess 4:7
c and election sure . . . . . . 2 Pet 1:10

CALLED
c the light Day. . . . . Gen 1:5
c his wife's name Eve. . . . . . Gen 3:20
"I, the LORD, have *c* . . . . Is 42:6
I have *c* you by your . . . . Is 43:1
The LORD has *c* Me from . . . . . Is 49:1
and out of Egypt I *c* . . . . . . Hos 11:1
"Out of Egypt I *c* . . . . Matt 2:15
a city *c* Nazareth . . . . Matt 2:23
For many are *c* . . . . Matt 20:16
to those who are the *c* . . . . Rom 8:28
these He also *c* . . . . Rom 8:30
But God has *c* us to . . . . . . 1 Cor 7:15
praises of Him who *c*. . . . . . 1 Pet 2:9
knowledge of Him who *c*. . . 2 Pet 1:3
c children of God. . . . . 1 John 3:1

CALLING
the gifts and the *c* . . . . . . Rom 11:29
For you see your *c* . . . . . . 1 Cor 1:26
remain in the same *c* . . . . 1 Cor 7:20
to walk worthy of the *c* . . . . Eph 4:1
in one hope of your *c*. . . . . . Eph 4:4
us with a holy *c* . . . . 2 Tim 1:9
of the heavenly *c*. . . . . Heb 3:1

CALLS
c them all by name. . . . . . . Ps 147:4
there is no one who *c* . . . . . . Is 64:7

David himself *c* . . . . Mark 12:37
c his own sheep. . . . . John 10:3
For "whoever *c*. . . . . Rom 10:13

CALM
the sea will become *c* . . . . . Jon 1:12
there was a great *c* . . . . . . Matt 8:26

CALMED
Surely I have *c*. . . . . Ps 131:2

CALVARY
Christ crucified there, Luke 23:33
Same as "Golgotha" in Hebrew, John
19:17

CALVES
made two *c* of gold. . . . . . 1 Kin 12:28
their cow *c* without . . . . Job 21:10
like stall-fed *c*. . . . . Mal 4:2
blood of goats and *c* . . . . . Heb 9:12
he took the blood of *c* . . . . Heb 9:19

CAMEL
it is easier for a *c*. . . . . . . Matt 19:24
and swallow a *c* . . . . Matt 23:24

CAMP
"This is God's *c*. . . . . Gen 32:2
who went before the *c*. . . . . Ex 14:19
to Him, outside the *c* . . . . . Heb 13:13

CAN
I *c* do all things . . . . Phil 4:13

CANA
A village of upper Galilee; home of
Nathanael, John 21:2
Site of Christ's first miracle,
John 2:1–11
Healing at, John 4:46–54

CANAAN
A son of Ham, Gen 10:6
Cursed by Noah, Gen 9:20–25
—— Promised Land, Gen 12:5
Boundaries of, Gen 10:19
God's promises concerning, given to
Abraham, Gen 12:1–3
to Isaac, Gen 26:2, 3
to Jacob, Gen 28:10–13
to Israel, Ex 3:8
Conquest of, announced, Gen 15:7–21
preceded by spying expedition,
Num 13:1–33
delayed by unbelief, Num 14:1–35
accomplished by the Lord,
Josh 23:1–16
achieved only in part, Judg 1:21,
27–36

CANAANITES
Israelites commanded to:
drive them out; not serve their
gods, Ex 23:23–33
shun their abominations,
Lev 18:24–30
not make covenants or intermarry
with them, Deut 7:1–3

CANCER
will spread like *c*. . . . . . . 2 Tim 2:17

CANE
bought Me no sweet *c* . . . . . Is 43:24
Sheba, and sweet *c*. . . . . . . Jer 6:20

CANOPIES
He made darkness *c* . . . . 2 Sam 22:12

CANOPY
His *c* around Him was. . . . . . Ps 18:11

CAPERNAUM
Simon Peter's home, Mark 1:21, 29

Christ performs healings there, Matt
8:5–17; 9:1–8; Mark 1:21–28; John
4:46–54
preaches there, Mark 9:33–50; John
6:24–71
uses as headquarters, Matt 4:13–17
pronounces judgment upon, Matt
11:23, 24

CAPPADOCIA
Jews from, at Pentecost, Acts 2:1, 9
Christians of, addressed by Peter,
1 Pet 1:1

CAPSTONE
bring forth the *c* . . . . Zech 4:7

CAPTAIN
which, having no *c*. . . . . Prov 6:7

CAPTIVE
have led captivity *c*. . . . . . . Ps 68:18
of your neck, O *c* . . . . Is 52:2
they shall now go *c*. . . . . . . Amos 6:7
and be led away *c*. . . . . . . Luke 21:24
He led captivity *c* . . . . Eph 4:8

CAPTIVES
will bring back the *c* . . . . . Amos 9:14
and return their *c*. . . . . Zeph 2:7
make *c* of gullible women . 2 Tim 3:6

CAPTIVITY
bring you back from *c* . . . . Deut 30:3
high, You have led *c* . . . . . . Ps 68:18
Judah has gone into *c*. . . . . . Lam 1:3
from David until the *c* . . . . Matt 1:17
and bringing me into *c*. . . . Rom 7:23
every thought into *c* . . . . . 2 Cor 10:5
on high, He led *c*. . . . . Eph 4:8
shall go into *c* . . . . Rev 13:10

CARCASS
honey were in the *c*. . . . . . . Judg 14:8
For wherever the *c*. . . . . . Matt 24:28

CARE
"Lord, do You not *c*. . . . . . Luke 10:40
you to be without *c* . . . . . . 1 Cor 7:32
who will sincerely *c* . . . . . . Phil 2:20
how will he take *c*. . . . . 1 Tim 3:5
casting all your *c* . . . . 1 Pet 5:7

CARED
he said, not that he *c* . . . . . John 12:6

CAREFULLY
c keep all these . . . . Deut 11:22
I shall walk *c* all my . . . . . . Is 38:15

CARELESS
but he who is *c*. . . . . Prov 19:16

CARES
no one *c* for my soul . . . . . . Ps 142:4
and are choked with *c* . . . . Luke 8:14
He who is unmarried *c* . . . 1 Cor 7:32
for He *c* for you . . . . 1 Pet 5:7

CARMEL
City of Judah, Josh 15:55
Site of Saul's victory, 1 Sam 15:12
—— A mountain of Palestine, Josh
19:26
Scene of Elijah's triumph, 1 Kin
18:19–45
Elisha visits, 2 Kin 2:25

CARNAL
spiritual, but I am *c* . . . . . . Rom 7:14
c mind is enmity . . . . Rom 8:7
for you are still *c* . . . . 1 Cor 3:3
our warfare are not *c*. . . . . 2 Cor 10:4

CARNALLY
we may know them *c*. . . . . . Gen 19:5
that we may know him *c* . Judg 19:22
c minded is death . . . . Rom 8:6

CAROUSE
count it pleasure to *c* . . . . . 2 Pet 2:13

CAROUSING
be weighed down with *c* . . Luke 21:34

CARPENTER
Is this not the *c* . . . . Mark 6:3

CARRIED
the LORD your God *c* . . . . . Deut 1:31
and *c* our sorrows. . . . . Is 53:4
parted from them and *c* . . Luke 24:51
c me away in the . . . . Rev 17:3

CARRY
their hands cannot *c* . . . . . . Job 5:12
c them away like a . . . . Ps 90:5
I am not worthy to *c* . . . . . Matt 3:11
for you to *c* your bed . . . . . John 5:10
it is certain we can *c* . . . . . . 1 Tim 6:7

CARRYING
a man will meet you *c* . . Mark 14:13
always *c* about in the . . . . 2 Cor 4:10

CASE
c that is too hard . . . . Deut 1:17
I have prepared my *c* . . . . . Job 13:18
I would present my *c* . . . . . . Job 23:4
"Present your *c* . . . . Is 41:21
Festus laid Paul's *c* . . . . . . Acts 25:14

CASSIA
myrrh and aloes and *c* . . . . . Ps 45:8

CAST
When they *c* you down . . . . Job 22:29
c away Their . . . . Ps 2:3
Why are you *c* down . . . . . . Ps 42:5
But You have *c* us off . . . . . . Ps 44:9
c me away from Your . . . . . . Ps 51:11
He *c* on them the . . . . Ps 78:49
the LORD will not *c* . . . . Ps 94:14
me up and *c* me away. . . . . Ps 102:10
and the earth shall *c* . . . . . . Is 26:19
My sight, as I have *c* . . . . . . Jer 7:15
C away from you all . . . . Ezek 18:31
brought Daniel and *c* . . . . Dan 6:16
c all our sins into . . . . Mic 7:19
whole body to be *c* . . . . . . Matt 5:29
the kingdom will be *c* . . . . Matt 8:12
spirits, to *c* them out . . . . . Matt 10:1
In My name they will *c* . . Mark 16:17
by no means *c* out . . . . John 6:37
c away His people . . . . Rom 11:1
c away your confidence . . . Heb 10:35
c their crowns before. . . . . . Rev 4:10
the great dragon was *c* . . . . . Rev 12:9

CASTING
nation which I am *c* . . . . . Lev 20:23
Andrew his brother, *c* . . . . . Matt 4:18
c down arguments . . . . . . 2 Cor 10:5
c all your care. . . . . 1 Pet 5:7

CASTS
If Satan *c* . . . . Matt 12:26
perfect love *c* out . . . . . . 1 John 4:18

CATCH
in wait to *c* the poor . . . . Ps 10:9
c Him in His words. . . . Mark 12:13
down your nets for a *c* . . . Luke 5:4
From now on you will *c* . . Luke 5:10

CATCHES
and the wolf *c* the . . . . . . John 10:12
c the wise in their . . . . . 1 Cor 3:19

CATERPILLAR
their crops to the *c*. . . . . . . Ps 78:46

CATTLE
c you shall take as. . . . . . . Josh 8:2
does not let their *c*. . . . . Ps 107:38

CAUGHT
behind him was a ram *c* . . Gen 22:13
and that night they *c* . . . . John 21:3
Spirit of the Lord *c* . . . . Acts 8:39
her Child was *c* up . . . . Rev 12:5

CAUSE
I would commit my *c* . . . . . . Job 5:8
my enemy without *c*. . . . . Ps 7:4
hate me without a *c* . . . . . . Ps 35:19
c His face to shine . . . . Ps 67:1
C me to know the way . . . . Ps 143:8
one to plead his *c*. . . . . . . Prov 18:17
God, Who pleads the *c* . . . . Is 51:22
He judged the *c*. . . . . Jer 22:16
brother without a *c*. . . . . . Matt 5:22
hated Me without a *c* . . . . John 15:25
For this *c* I was born . . . . . John 18:37

CAVES
the people hid in *c*. . . . . . 1 Sam 13:6
rocks, and into the *c* . . . . Is 2:19
in dens and *c* of the . . . . . Heb 11:38

CEASE
and night shall not *c*. . . . . . Gen 8:22
Why should the work *c* . . . . Neh 6:3
There the wicked *c*. . . . . Job 3:17
He makes wars *c* . . . . Ps 46:9
C listening to . . . . Prov 19:27
C to do evil. . . . . Is 1:16
tongues, they will *c* . . . . . 1 Cor 13:8
do not *c* to give. . . . . Eph 1:16
do not *c* to pray for. . . . . Col 1:9

CEASED
c building the city . . . . Gen 11:8
the sea, and the sea *c* . . . . . Jon 1:15

CEASES
for the godly man *c*. . . . . Ps 12:1

CEASING
c your work of faith . . . . . 1 Thess 1:3
thank God without *c* . . . 1 Thess 2:13
pray without *c*. . . . . 1 Thess 5:17

CEDAR
dwell in a house of *c* . . . . 2 Sam 7:2
He shall grow like a *c* . . . . . Ps 92:12
of our houses are *c* . . . . . Song 1:17
it, paneling it with *c* . . . . . . Jer 22:14
Indeed Assyria was a *c* . . . Ezek 31:3

CEDARS
the LORD breaks the *c* . . . . . Ps 29:5
c of Lebanon which He . . . . Ps 104:16

CELESTIAL
but the glory of the *c* . . . 1 Cor 15:40

CENCHREA
A harbor of Corinth, Acts 18:18
Home of Phoebe, Rom 16:1

CENSER
Aaron, each took his *c* . . . . Lev 10:1
Each man had a *c* . . . . Ezek 8:11
which had the golden *c* . . . . Heb 9:4
the angel took the *c* . . . . . . Rev 8:5

CEPHAS
Aramaic for Peter, John 1:42

CERTAINTY
make you know the *c* . . . . Prov 22:21
you may know the *c*. . . . . . Luke 1:4

CERTIFICATE
a man to write a *c* . . . . . . Mark 10:4

CERTIFIED
His testimony has *c*. . . . . . John 3:33

CHAFF
c that a storm . . . . Job 21:18
c which the wind. . . . . Ps 1:4

Let them be like *c* . . . . Ps 35:5
be chased like the *c* . . . . Is 17:13
You shall conceive *c* . . . . . . Is 33:11
the day passes like *c* . . . . . Zeph 2:2
He will burn up the *c* . . . . Matt 3:12

CHAIN
He has made my *c* . . . . Lam 3:7
pit and a great *c* . . . . Rev 20:1

CHAINED
of God is not *c*. . . . . 2 Tim 2:9
the prisoners as if *c* . . . . . Heb 13:3

CHAINS
their kings with *c* . . . . Ps 149:8
your neck with *c* . . . . Song 1:10
And his *c* fell off. . . . . Acts 12:7
am, except for these *c* . . Acts 26:29
Remember my *c* . . . . Col 4:18
minister to me in my *c*. . . . Philem 13
delivered them into *c* . . . . 2 Pet 2:4

CHALDEA
Originally, the southern portion of
   Babylonia, Gen 11:31
Applied later to all Babylonia,
   Dan 3:8
Abram came from, Gen 11:28–31

CHALDEANS
Attack Job, Job 1:17
Nebuchadnezzar, king of, 2 Kin 24:1
Jerusalem defeated by, 2 Kin 25:1–21
Babylon, "the glory of," Is 13:19
Predicted captivity of Jews among,
   Jer 25:1–26
God's agent, Hab 1:6

CHAMBERS
and the *c* of the south. . . . . . Job 9:9
brought me into his *c*. . . . . Song 1:4
and his *c* by injustice . . . . . Jer 22:13

CHAMPION
And a *c* went out from . . . 1 Sam 17:4

CHANGE
c his countenance . . . . Job 14:20
c the night into day. . . . . . Job 17:12
and who can make Him *c*. . Job 23:13
Because they do not *c* . . . . Ps 55:19
a cloak You will *c* . . . . Ps 102:26
with those given to *c* . . . . Prov 24:21
Can the Ethiopian *c* . . . . . Jer 13:23
c times and law. . . . . Dan 7:25
c their glory into . . . . Hos 4:7
the LORD, I do not *c* . . . . . . Mal 3:6
now and to *c* my tone . . . . . Gal 4:20
there is also a *c* . . . . Heb 7:12

CHANGED
But My people have *c* . . . . . Jer 2:11
c the glory of the. . . . . Rom 1:23
but we shall all be *c*. . . . . 1 Cor 15:51
the priesthood being *c* . . . . Heb 7:12

CHANGERS'
and poured out the *c* . . . . John 2:15

CHANGES
c the times and the . . . . . . Dan 2:21

CHANNELS
c of the sea were seen . . . . Ps 18:15

CHARACTER
and *c*, hope. . . . . Rom 5:4

CHARGED
May it not be *c* . . . . 2 Tim 4:16

CHARIOT
He took off their *c*. . . . . . . Ex 14:25
that suddenly a *c* . . . . 2 Kin 2:11
makes the clouds His *c* . . . Ps 104:3
and overtake this *c* . . . . . . Acts 8:29

CHARIOTS
the clatter of his *c* . . . . Judg 5:28
Some trust in *c* . . . . Ps 20:7
The *c* of God are . . . . Ps 68:17

CHARITABLE
you do not do your *c* . . . . . . Matt 6:1
that your *c* deed . . . . Matt 6:4
c deeds which she . . . . Acts 9:36

CHARM
C is deceitful and. . . . . Prov 31:30

CHARMERS
heed the voice of *c* . . . . Ps 58:5

CHARMS
women who sew magic *c*. . Ezek 13:18

CHASE
Five of you shall *c* . . . . Lev 26:8
How could one *c* . . . . Deut 32:30
angel of the LORD *c* . . . . Ps 35:5

CHASTE
may present you as a *c* . . . 2 Cor 11:2
to be discreet, *c* . . . . Titus 2:5
c conduct accompanied . . . . 1 Pet 3:2

CHASTEN
C your son while there . . . Prov 19:18
is My desire, I will *c* . . . . . . Hos 10:10
a father does not *c* . . . . Heb 12:7
I love, I rebuke and *c* . . . . . . Rev 3:19

CHASTENED
c my soul with fasting . . . . . . Ps 69:10
c every morning. . . . . Ps 73:14
The LORD has *c* me . . . . Ps 118:18
In vain I have *c* . . . . Jer 2:30
c us as seemed best. . . . . . Heb 12:10

CHASTENING
have not seen the *c*. . . . . . Deut 11:2
do not despise the *c*. . . . . . . Job 5:17
'I have borne *c*. . . . . Job 34:31
a prayer when Your *c* . . . . . Is 26:16
if you are without *c* . . . . Heb 12:8
Now no *c* seems to be. . . . Heb 12:11

CHASTENS
the LORD loves He *c* . . . . . . Heb 12:6

CHASTISE
and I, even I, will *c* . . . . . . Lev 26:28
c them according . . . . Hos 7:12
I will therefore *c* . . . . Luke 23:22

CHASTISEMENT
the *c* for our peace . . . . Is 53:5

CHATTER
c leads only to . . . . Prov 14:23

CHEAT
'You shall not *c* . . . . Lev 19:13
Beware lest anyone *c* . . . . . . Col 2:8

CHEATED
let yourselves be *c* . . . . 1 Cor 6:7
we have *c* no one . . . . 2 Cor 7:2

CHEBAR
River in Babylonia, Ezek 1:3
Site of Ezekiel's visions, Ezek 10:15, 20

CHEDORLAOMER
A king of Elam; invaded Canaan,
  Gen 14:1–16

CHEEK
Let him give his *c* . . . . Lam 3:30
with a rod on the *c*. . . . . Mic 5:1
on your right *c* . . . . Matt 5:39

CHEEKBONE
my enemies on the *c*. . . . . . . Ps 3:7

CHEEKS
c are lovely with . . . . Song 1:10

His *c* are like a bed . . . . . . Song 5:13
struck Me, and My *c* . . . . Is 50:6

CHEER
and let your heart *c* . . . . . . Eccl 11:9
"Son, be of good *c*. . . . . . . Matt 9:2

CHEERFUL
for God loves a *c* . . . . 2 Cor 9:7
Is anyone *c* . . . . James 5:13

CHEERFULNESS
shows mercy, with *c* . . . . . Rom 12:8

CHEESE
and curdle me like *c* . . . . . . Job 10:10

CHEMOSH
The god of the Moabites, Num 21:29
Children sacrificed to, 2 Kin 3:26, 27
Solomon builds altars to, 1 Kin 11:7
Josiah destroys altars of, 2 Kin 23:13

CHERISHES
but nourishes and *c* . . . . . . Eph 5:29
as a nursing mother *c* . . . 1 Thess 2:7

CHERUB
He rode upon a *c* . . . . . . 2 Sam 22:11

CHERUBIM
and He placed *c*. . . . . Gen 3:24
dwell between the *c*. . . . . Ps 80:1
fire from among the *c*. . . . . Ezek 10:2
above it were the *c*. . . . . Heb 9:5

CHIEF
is white and ruddy, *c* . . . . . Song 5:10
of whom I am *c*. . . . . 1 Tim 1:15
Zion a *c* cornerstone. . . . . . . 1 Pet 2:6
has become the *c*. . . . . 1 Pet 2:7
C Shepherd appears . . . . 1 Pet 5:4

CHILD
Like a weaned *c*. . . . . Ps 131:2
c is known by his. . . . . . . Prov 20:11
Train up a *c* in the . . . . . . Prov 22:6
For unto us a C . . . . Is 9:6
c shall lead them . . . . Is 11:6
When Israel was a *c*. . . . . . . Hos 11:1
virgin shall be with *c* . . . . Matt 1:23
He took a little *c* . . . . Mark 9:36
of God as a little *c* . . . . . Mark 10:15
kind of *c* will this be . . . . . Luke 1:66
So the *c* grew and. . . . . . . Luke 1:80
When I was a *c*. . . . . 1 Cor 13:11
She bore a male C. . . . . Rev 12:5

CHILDBEARING
she will be saved in *c* . . . . 1 Tim 2:15

CHILDBIRTH
pain as a woman in *c* . . . . . . Is 13:8

CHILDHOOD
from your flesh, for *c* . . . . Eccl 11:10
And he said, "From *c* . . . . Mark 9:21
c you have known. . . . . . . 2 Tim 3:15

CHILDLESS
give me, seeing I go *c* . . . . Gen 15:2
this man down as *c* . . . . . . Jer 22:30

CHILDREN
she bore Jacob no *c* . . . . . . Gen 30:1
and all of you are *c*. . . . . Ps 82:6
c are a heritage . . . . Ps 127:3
He has blessed your *c* . . . . Ps 147:13
let the *c* of Zion be. . . . . . . Ps 149:2
c are blessed after . . . . . . Prov 20:7
c rise up and call her. . . . . Prov 31:28
c are their oppressors . . . . Is 3:12
c whom the LORD has. . . . . . Is 8:18
be the peace of your *c* . . . . Is 54:13
they are My people, *c* . . . . . Is 63:8
the hearts of the *c* . . . . . . Mal 4:6

c will rise up against. . . . . Matt 10:21
and become as little *c*. . . . . Matt 18:3
c were brought to Him . . . Matt 19:13
"Let the little *c*. . . . . Matt 19:14
the right to become *c* . . . . . John 1:12
you were Abraham's *c* . . . . John 8:39
spirit that we are *c* . . . . . . Rom 8:16
but as my beloved *c*. . . . . 1 Cor 4:14
Brethren, do not be *c* . . . 1 Cor 14:20
c ought not to lay up . . . . 2 Cor 12:14
and were by nature *c*. . . . . . Eph 2:3
should no longer be *c*. . . . . . Eph 4:14
Walk as *c* of light. . . . . Eph 5:8
and harmless, *c* . . . . Phil 2:15
now we are *c* of God . . . . . 1 John 3:2
that we love the *c* . . . . 1 John 5:2
to hear that my *c*. . . . . 3 John 4

CHILION
Elimelech's son, Ruth 1:2
Orpah's deceased husband, Ruth 1:4, 5
Boaz redeems his estate, Ruth 4:9

CHINNERETH (or Chinneroth)
Fortified city in Naphtali, Deut 3:17
A region bordering the Sea of
  Galilee, 1 Kin 15:20
Same as the plain of Gennesaret,
  Matt 14:34
———— The OT name for the Sea of
  Galilee, Num 34:11
Also called Lake of Gennesaret,
  Luke 5:1

CHOICE
rather than *c* gold . . . . Prov 8:10

CHOOSE
therefore *c* life . . . . Deut 30:19
c none of his ways. . . . . . . Prov 3:31
evil and *c* the good . . . . Is 7:15
will still *c* Israel . . . . Is 14:1
will again *c* Jerusalem . . . . Zech 1:17
You did not *c* . . . . John 15:16
yet what I shall *c* . . . . Phil 1:22

CHOOSES
in the way He *c* . . . . Ps 25:12

CHOSE
a good while ago God *c*. . . . Acts 15:7
just as He *c* us in Him . . . . . Eph 1:4
from the beginning *c* . . . 2 Thess 2:13

CHOSEN
of Jacob, His *c* . . . . 1 Chr 16:13
people He has *c*. . . . . Ps 33:12
a covenant with My *c*. . . . . . Ps 89:3
c the way of truth . . . . . . Ps 119:30
servant whom I have *c* . . . . . Is 43:10
c that good part . . . . Luke 10:42
I know whom I have *c* . . . . John 13:18
c you that you should . . . . Acts 22:14
c the foolish things . . . . . . 1 Cor 1:27
Has God not *c* the poor . . . James 2:5
But you are a *c*. . . . . 1 Pet 2:9

CHRIST
genealogy of Jesus C. . . . . . . Matt 1:1
Jesus who is called C. . . . . . Matt 1:16
"You are the C. . . . . Matt 16:16
if You are the C. . . . . Matt 26:63
a Savior, who is C . . . . Luke 2:11
that He Himself is C . . . . . . Luke 23:2
the law that the C . . . . John 12:34
he preached the C . . . . Acts 9:20
have the Spirit of C . . . . Rom 8:9
It is C who died . . . . Rom 8:34
C did not please . . . . Rom 15:3
Is C divided . . . . 1 Cor 1:13
Him you are in C Jesus . . . 1 Cor 1:30
to be justified by C . . . . Gal 2:17

been crucified with *C* . . . . . . Gal 2:20
but *C* lives in me . . . . Gal 2:20
your Seed," who is *C* . . . . . . Gal 3:16
before by God in *C* . . . . Gal 3:17
C may dwell in your . . . . . . Eph 3:17
C will give you . . . . Eph 5:14
C is head of the . . . . Eph 5:23
to me, to live is *C* . . . . Phil 1:21
confess that Jesus *C* . . . . . . Phil 2:11
C who strengthens . . . . Phil 4:13
which is *C* in you . . . . Col 1:27
C who is our . . . . Col 3:4
C is all and in all . . . . Col 3:11
and men, the Man *C* . . . . . 1 Tim 2:5
Jesus *C* is the same . . . . Heb 13:8
C His Son cleanses us . . . . 1 John 1:7
that Jesus is the *C* . . . . . . 1 John 5:1
of His *C* have come . . . . . . Rev 12:10
and reigned with *C* . . . . . . Rev 20:4

CHRISTIAN
me to become a *C* . . . . . . Acts 26:28
anyone suffers as a *C* . . . . 1 Pet 4:16

CHRISTIANS
were first called *C* . . . . . . Acts 11:26

CHRISTS
For false *c* and . . . . Matt 24:24

CHURCH
rock I will build My *c* . . . . Matt 16:18
them, tell it to the *c* . . . . . Matt 18:17
c daily those who were . . . . Acts 2:47
elders in every *c* . . . . Acts 14:23
do you despise the *c* . . . 1 Cor 11:22
be made known by the *c* . . . Eph 3:10
also loved the *c* . . . . Eph 5:25
Himself a glorious *c* . . . . . Eph 5:27
as the Lord does the *c* . . . . Eph 5:29
body, which is the *c* . . . . . . Col 1:24
and do not let the *c* . . . . . 1 Tim 5:16
general assembly and *c* . . Heb 12:23
To the angel of the *c* . . . . . . Rev 2:1

CHURCHES
strengthening the *c* . . . . . Acts 15:41
The *c* of Christ greet . . . . . Rom 16:16
imitators of the *c* . . . . . . 1 Thess 2:14
John, to the seven *c* . . . . . . Rev 1:4
angels of the seven *c* . . . . . Rev 1:20
these things in the *c* . . . . . Rev 22:16

CHURNING
For as the *c* of milk . . . . . . Prov 30:33

CHURNS
My heart *c* within Me . . . . . Hos 11:8

CILICIA
Paul's homeland, Acts 21:39
Students from, argued with Stephen,
Acts 6:9
Paul labors in, Gal 1:21

CIRCLE
He walks above the *c* . . . . . Job 22:14
when He drew a *c* . . . . Prov 8:27
who sits above the *c* . . . . . . Is 40:22

CIRCUIT
of heaven, and its *c* . . . . Ps 19:6
comes again on its *c* . . . . . . Eccl 1:6

CIRCUMCISE
c the foreskin of your . . . . Deut 10:16
Lord your God will *c* . . . . . Deut 30:6
C yourselves to the . . . . Jer 4:4
is necessary to *c* them . . . . Acts 15:5

CIRCUMCISED
among you shall be *c* . . . . Gen 17:10
who will justify the *c* . . . . . Rom 3:30
While he was *c* . . . . Rom 4:10
the gospel for the *c* . . . . Gal 2:7

if you become *c* . . . . Gal 5:2
c the eighth day . . . . Phil 3:5
In Him you were also *c* . . . . Col 2:11

CIRCUMCISION
him the covenant of *c* . . . . . Acts 7:8
c that which is outward . . . Rom 2:28
c is that of the heart . . . . . Rom 2:29
a servant to the *c* . . . . Rom 15:8
C is nothing and . . . . 1 Cor 7:19
Christ Jesus neither *c* . . . . . Gal 5:6
For we are the *c* . . . . Phil 3:3
circumcised with the *c* . . . . Col 2:11
those of the *c* . . . . Titus 1:10

CIRCUMSPECTLY
then that you walk *c* . . . . . Eph 5:15

CISTERN
waters of his own *c* . . . . 2 Kin 18:31
from your own *c* . . . . Prov 5:15

CITIES
He overthrew those *c* . . . . Gen 19:25
repair the ruined *c* . . . . Is 61:4
c are a wilderness . . . . Is 64:10
c will be laid waste . . . . Jer 4:7
three parts, and the *c* . . . . Rev 16:19

CITIZEN
But I was born a *c* . . . . . . Acts 22:28

CITIZENS
But his *c* hated him . . . . . . Luke 19:14
but fellow *c* with the . . . . . . Eph 2:19

CITIZENSHIP
sum I obtained this *c* . . . . Acts 22:28
For our *c* is in heaven . . . . . Phil 3:20

CITY
And he built a *c* . . . . Gen 4:17
shall make glad the *c* . . . . . . Ps 46:4
c shall flourish . . . . Ps 72:16
They found no *c* . . . . Ps 107:4
c that is compact . . . . Ps 122:3
the Lord guards the *c* . . . . . Ps 127:1
at the entry of the *c* . . . . . . Prov 8:3
c has become a harlot . . . . . . Is 1:21
upon Zion, the *c* . . . . Is 33:20
after the holy *c* . . . . Is 48:2
How lonely sits the *c* . . . . . Lam 1:1
Nineveh, that great *c* . . . . . Jon 4:11
c that dwelt securely . . . . . Zeph 2:15
to the oppressing *c* . . . . . . Zeph 3:1
c called Nazareth . . . . Matt 2:23
c that is set on a . . . . Matt 5:14
He has prepared a *c* . . . . . Heb 11:16
Zion and to the *c* . . . . Heb 12:22
have no continuing *c* . . . . Heb 13:14
will tread the holy *c* . . . . . . Rev 11:2
fallen, that great *c* . . . . Rev 14:8
and the beloved *c* . . . . Rev 20:9
John, saw the holy *c* . . . . . . Rev 21:2
c was pure gold . . . . Rev 21:18
c had no need of the . . . . . Rev 21:23
the gates into the *c* . . . . . . Rev 22:14

CLAP
c their hands at him . . . . . Job 27:23
Oh, *c* your hands . . . . Ps 47:1
let the rivers *c* . . . . Ps 98:8
of the field shall *c* . . . . Is 55:12

CLAUDIUS LYSIAS
Roman commander who protected
Paul, Acts 24:22–24, 26

CLAY
dwell in houses of *c* . . . . Job 4:19
have made me like *c* . . . . . . Job 10:9
are defenses of *c* . . . . Job 13:12
been formed out of *c* . . . . . . Job 33:6
takes on form like *c* . . . . . . Job 38:14

pit, out of the miry *c* . . . . . . Ps 40:2
be esteemed as the *c* . . . . . . Is 29:16
Shall the *c* say to him . . . . . Is 45:9
We are the *c* . . . . Is 64:8
"Look, as the *c* . . . . Jer 18:6
iron and partly of *c* . . . . . Dan 2:33
blind man with the *c* . . . . John 9:6
have power over the *c* . . . . Rom 9:21

CLEAN
seven each of every *c* . . . . . Gen 7:2
between unclean and *c* . . . Lev 10:10
wash in them and be *c* . . . 2 Kin 5:12
Who can bring a *c* . . . . Job 14:4
He who has *c* hands and . . . . Ps 24:4
make yourselves . . . . Is 1:16
Then I will sprinkle *c* . . . . Ezek 36:25
c out His threshing . . . . . . Matt 3:12
You can make me *c* . . . . Matt 8:2
all things are *c* . . . . Luke 11:41
but is completely *c* . . . . . . John 13:10
"You are not all *c* . . . . John 13:11
You are already *c* . . . . John 15:3
in fine linen, *c* . . . . Rev 19:8

CLEANSE
You shall *c* the altar . . . . . . Ex 29:36
C me from secret . . . . Ps 19:12
and *c* me from my sin . . . . . Ps 51:2
How can a young man *c* . . . Ps 119:9
I will *c* you from all . . . . . Ezek 36:25
c the lepers, raise . . . . Matt 10:8
might sanctify and *c* . . . . . Eph 5:26
c your conscience . . . . Heb 9:14
C your hands . . . . James 4:8
us our sins and to *c* . . . . . 1 John 1:9

CLEANSED
Surely I have *c* . . . . Ps 73:13
and you were not *c* . . . . . Ezek 24:13
the lepers are *c* . . . . Matt 11:5
"Were there not ten *c* . . . . Luke 17:17

CLEANSES
Therefore if anyone *c* . . . . 2 Tim 2:21
Jesus Christ His Son *c* . . . . 1 John 1:7

CLEAR
c shining after rain . . . . . 2 Sam 23:4
fair as the moon, *c* . . . . . . Song 6:10
yourselves to be *c* . . . . 2 Cor 7:11
like a jasper stone, *c* . . . . . Rev 21:11
of life, *c* as crystal . . . . Rev 22:1

CLEFTS
to go into the *c* . . . . Is 2:21
valleys and in the *c* . . . . Is 7:19
you who dwell in the *c* . . . Jer 49:16

CLERK
c had quieted the . . . . Acts 19:35

CLIFF
secret places of the *c* . . . . . Song 2:14

CLIMB
go into thickets and *c* . . . . . Jer 4:29
mighty men, they *c* . . . . . . Joel 2:7
though they *c* up to . . . . . . Amos 9:2

CLIMBS
c up some other way . . . . . John 10:1

CLING
and that you may *c* . . . . Deut 30:20
to her, "Do not *c* . . . . John 20:17
C to what is good . . . . Rom 12:9

CLINGS
and My tongue *c* . . . . Ps 22:15
My soul *c* to the dust . . . . Ps 119:25

CLOAK
c You will change them . . . . Ps 102:26
let him have your *c* . . . . . . Matt 5:40

c You will fold them . . . . . . Heb 1:12
using liberty as a *c* . . . . . . 1 Pet 2:16

CLOSE
c friends abhor me . . . . Job 19:19
of Christ he came *c* . . . . . . Phil 2:30

CLOSED
and has *c* your eyes . . . . Is 29:10
for the words are *c* . . . . . . Dan 12:9
the deep *c* around me . . . . . . Jon 2:5

CLOTH
a piece of unshrunk *c* . . . . . Matt 9:16
in a clean linen *c* . . . . . . Matt 27:59

CLOTHE
c them with tunics . . . . Ex 40:14
c me with skin and . . . . Job 10:11
c her priests with . . . . Ps 132:16
His enemies I will *c* . . . . . . Ps 132:18
Though you *c* yourself . . . . . . Jer 4:30
He not much more *c* . . . . . . Matt 6:30

CLOTHED
of skin, and *c* them . . . . Gen 3:21
Have you *c* his neck . . . . Job 39:19
off my sackcloth and *c* . . . . Ps 30:11
The pastures are *c* . . . . Ps 65:13
the LORD is *c* . . . . Ps 93:1
You are *c* with honor . . . . . . Ps 104:1
c himself with cursing . . . . . Ps 109:18
Let Your priests be *c* . . . . . . Ps 132:9
all her household is *c* . . . . Prov 31:21
c you with fine linen . . . . Ezek 16:10
A man *c* in soft . . . . Matt 11:8
I was naked and you *c* . . . . Matt 25:36
legion, sitting and *c* . . . . . Mark 5:15
And they *c* Him with . . . . Mark 15:17
rich man who was *c* . . . . Luke 16:19
desiring to be *c* . . . . 2 Cor 5:2
that you may be *c* . . . . Rev 3:18
a woman *c* with the sun . . . . Rev 12:1
He was *c* with a robe . . . . . Rev 19:13

CLOTHES
c will abhor me . . . . Job 9:31
c became shining . . . . Mark 9:3
many spread their *c* . . . . Luke 19:36
laid down their *c* . . . . Acts 7:58
and tore off their *c* . . . . . Acts 22:23
a poor man in filthy *c* . . . . James 2:2

CLOTHING
c they cast lots . . . . Ps 22:18
c is woven with gold . . . . . . Ps 45:13
will provide your *c* . . . . . . Prov 27:26
and honor are her *c* . . . . . Prov 31:25
of vengeance for *c* . . . . Is 59:17
the body more than *c* . . . . . Matt 6:25
do you worry about *c* . . . . . Matt 6:28
to you in sheep's *c* . . . . . . Matt 7:15
those who wear soft *c* . . . . Matt 11:8
c as white as snow . . . . . . Matt 28:3
c they cast lots . . . . John 19:24
before me in bright *c* . . . . Acts 10:30

CLOTHS
wrapped in swaddling *c* . . . Luke 2:12
in, saw the linen *c* . . . . . . John 20:5

CLOUD
My rainbow in the *c* . . . . . . Gen 9:13
day in a pillar of *c* . . . . . . Ex 13:21
c covered the mountain . . . . Ex 24:15
c descended and stood . . . . . Ex 33:9
camp; as long as the *c* . . . . Num 9:18
c did not depart . . . . Neh 9:19
He led them with the *c* . . . . Ps 78:14
his favor is like a *c* . . . . . Prov 16:15
these who fly like a *c* . . . . . Is 60:8
like a morning *c* . . . . Hos 6:4
behold, a bright *c* . . . . . . Matt 17:5

of Man coming in a *c* . . . . Luke 21:27
c received Him out of . . . . . . Acts 1:9
were under the *c* . . . . 1 Cor 10:1
by so great a *c* . . . . Heb 12:1

CLOUDS
a morning without *c* . . . . 2 Sam 23:3
c poured out water . . . . Ps 77:17
and hail, snow and *c* . . . . . . Ps 148:8
c drop down the dew . . . . . Prov 3:20
he who regards the *c* . . . . . Eccl 11:4
of Man coming on the *c* . . Matt 24:30
with them in the *c* . . . . . 1 Thess 4:17
are *c* without water . . . . Jude 12
He is coming with *c* . . . . . . Rev 1:7

CLOUDY
them by day with a *c* . . . . . Neh 9:12
spoke to them in the *c* . . . . . Ps 99:7

CLOVEN
the hoof, having *c* . . . . Lev 11:3
chew the cud or have *c* . . . . Deut 14:7

CLUSTER
beloved is to me a *c* . . . . . Song 1:14
wine is found in the *c* . . . . . Is 65:8

COAL
in his hand a live *c* . . . . Is 6:6
it shall not be a *c* . . . . Is 47:14

COALS
wicked He will rain *c* . . . . . . Ps 11:6
c were kindled by it . . . . . . Ps 18:8
let burning *c* fall . . . . Ps 140:10
Can one walk on hot *c* . . . . Prov 6:28
so you will heap *c* . . . . . . Prov 25:22
doing you will heap *c* . . . . Rom 12:20

COBRA
it becomes *c* venom . . . . . . Job 20:14
c that stops its ear . . . . Ps 58:4
the lion and the *c* . . . . Ps 91:13

COBRA'S
shall play by the *c* . . . . Is 11:8

COFFIN
and he was put in a *c* . . . . Gen 50:26
David followed the *c* . . . . 2 Sam 3:31
touched the open *c* . . . . . . Luke 7:14

COIN
sold for a copper *c* . . . . . Matt 10:29
if she loses one *c* . . . . Luke 15:8

COLD
and harvest, C and . . . . . . Gen 8:22
can stand before His *c* . . . . Ps 147:17
Like the *c* of snow in . . . . . Prov 25:13
c water to a weary . . . . . . Prov 25:25
c water in the name of . . . . Matt 10:42
of many will grow *c* . . . . Matt 24:12
that you are neither *c* . . . . . Rev 3:15

COLLECTED
coming I might have *c* . . . Luke 19:23

COLLECTION
from Jerusalem the *c* . . . . 2 Chr 24:6
concerning the *c* . . . . 1 Cor 16:1

COLOSSE
A city in Asia Minor, Col 1:2
Evangelized by Epaphras, Col 1:7
Not visited by Paul, Col 2:1
Paul writes against errors of, Col
2:16–23

COLT
and his donkey's *c* . . . . . . Gen 49:11
on a donkey, a *c* . . . . Zech 9:9
on a donkey, a *c* . . . . Matt 21:5
own clothes on the *c* . . . . Luke 19:35

COME
then does wisdom *c* . . . . . . Job 28:20

of glory shall *c* . . . . Ps 24:7
Our God shall *c* . . . . Ps 50:3
You all flesh will *c* . . . . Ps 65:2
C with me from Lebanon . . . Song 4:8
He will *c* and save you . . . . . Is 35:4
who have no money, C . . . . . Is 55:1
Your kingdom *c* . . . . Matt 6:10
C to Me . . . . Matt 11:28
For many will *c* . . . . Matt 24:5
Israel, let Him now *c* . . . . . Matt 27:42
If anyone desires to *c* . . . . Luke 9:23
kingdom of God has *c* . . . . Luke 10:9
I have *c* in My . . . . John 5:43
and I have not *c* . . . . John 7:28
thirsts, let him *c* . . . . John 7:37
c that they may have . . . . . John 10:10
c as a light into the . . . . . . John 12:46
I will *c* to you . . . . John 14:18
If I had not *c* . . . . John 15:22
savage wolves will *c* . . . . . Acts 20:29
O Lord, *c* . . . . 1 Cor 16:22
the door, I will *c* . . . . Rev 3:20
the bride say, "C . . . . Rev 22:17

COMELINESS
He has no form or *c* . . . . Is 53:2

COMES
Who is this who *c* . . . . Is 63:1
'Come,' and he *c* . . . . Matt 8:9
Lord's death till He *c* . . . . 1 Cor 11:26
Then *c* the end . . . . 1 Cor 15:24

COMFORT
with him, and to *c* him . . . . . Job 2:11
and Your staff, they *c* . . . . . . Ps 23:4
When will you *c* . . . . Ps 119:82
yes, *c* My people . . . . Is 40:1
For the LORD will *c* . . . . Is 51:3
c all who mourn . . . . Is 61:2
she has none to *c* her . . . . . Lam 1:2
the LORD will again *c* . . . . . Zech 1:17
and God of all *c* . . . . 2 Cor 1:3
trouble, with the *c* . . . . . . 2 Cor 1:4
in Christ, if any *c* . . . . Phil 2:1
c each other and edify . . 1 Thess 5:11

COMFORTED
So Isaac was *c* after . . . . . Gen 24:67
soul refused to be *c* . . . . . . Ps 77:2
For the LORD has *c* . . . . Is 49:13
refusing to be *c* . . . . Jer 31:15
but now he is *c* . . . . Luke 16:25

COMFORTER
She had no *c* . . . . Lam 1:9

COMFORTS
the army, as one who *c* . . . . Job 29:25
I, even I, am He who *c* . . . . . Is 51:12
him, and restore *c* . . . . Is 57:18
one whom his mother *c* . . . . Is 66:13
who *c* us in all our . . . . . . 2 Cor 1:4
who *c* the downcast . . . . . 2 Cor 7:6

COMING
your salvation is *c* . . . . Is 62:11
behold, the day is *c* . . . . . . Mal 4:1
but He who is *c* . . . . Matt 3:11
"Are You the C . . . . Matt 11:3
be the sign of Your *c* . . . . . Matt 24:3
is delaying his *c* . . . . Matt 24:48
see the Son of Man *c* . . . . Mark 13:26
mightier than I is *c* . . . . . . Luke 3:16
are Christ's at His *c* . . . . . 1 Cor 15:23
to you the power and *c* . . . . 2 Pet 1:16
the promise of His *c* . . . . . 2 Pet 3:4
Behold, I am *c* . . . . Rev 3:11
"Behold, I am *c* . . . . Rev 22:7
"Surely I am *c* . . . . Rev 22:20

COMMAND
in order that he may *c* . . . Gen 18:19

"The Lord will *c* . . . . Deut 28:8
in that I *c* you . . . . Deut 30:16
c His lovingkindness . . . . Ps 42:8
c victories for Jacob . . . . Ps 44:4
to all that I *c* . . . . Jer 11:4
if it is You, *c* . . . . Matt 14:28
c fire to come down . . . . . Luke 9:54
c I have received . . . . John 10:18
And I know that His *c* . . . . . John 12:50
if you do whatever I *c* . . . . John 15:14
do the things we *c* . . . . . . 2 Thess 3:4

COMMANDED
"Have you *c* the . . . . Job 38:12
c His covenant forever . . . . . . Ps 111:9
For there the Lord *c* . . . . Ps 133:3
it is the God who *c* . . . . . . 2 Cor 4:6
not endure what was *c* . . . . Heb 12:20

COMMANDMENT
c of the Lord is pure . . . . Ps 19:8
c is exceedingly broad . . . . . Ps 119:96
For the *c* is a lamp . . . . Prov 6:23
Me is taught by the . . . . Is 29:13
which is the great *c* . . . . . Matt 22:36
A new *c* I give to . . . . John 13:34
the Father gave Me *c* . . . . . John 14:31
law, but when the *c* . . . . . . Rom 7:9
the *c* might become . . . . . . Rom 7:13
which is the first *c* . . . . Eph 6:2
c is the word which . . . . . . 1 John 2:7
And this is His *c* . . . . 1 John 3:23
as we received *c* . . . . 2 John 4
This is the *c* . . . . 2 John 6

COMMANDMENTS
covenant, the Ten C . . . . Ex 34:28
to observe all these *c* . . . . . Deut 6:25
who remember His *c* . . . . . Ps 103:18
do not hide Your *c* . . . . . . Ps 119:19
myself in Your *c* . . . . Ps 119:47
for I believe Your *c* . . . . . . Ps 119:66
Your *c* are faithful . . . . Ps 119:86
c more than gold . . . . Ps 119:127
as doctrines the *c* . . . . Matt 15:9
c hang all the Law . . . . . Matt 22:40
He who has My *c* . . . . John 14:21
according to the *c* . . . . Col 2:22
Now he who keeps His *c* . 1 John 3:24

COMMANDS
with authority He *c* . . . . . . Mark 1:27

COMMEND
But food does not *c* . . . . . . 1 Cor 8:8

COMMENDABLE
For this is *c* . . . . 1 Pet 2:19
patiently, this is *c* . . . . 1 Pet 2:20

COMMENDED
A man will be *c* . . . . Prov 12:8
c the unjust steward . . . . . . Luke 16:8
where they had been *c* . . . Acts 14:26

COMMENDING
of the truth *c* . . . . 2 Cor 4:2

COMMENDS
but whom the Lord *c* . . . . 2 Cor 10:18

COMMIT
"You shall not *c* . . . . Ex 20:14
C your works to the . . . . . . Prov 16:3
mammon, who will *c* . . . . Luke 16:11
into Your hands I *c* . . . . . Luke 23:46
But Jesus did not *c* . . . . . . John 2:24
c sexual immorality . . . . . . 1 Cor 10:8
c these to faithful . . . . 2 Tim 2:2
c their souls to Him . . . . . 1 Pet 4:19
c sin not leading . . . . 1 John 5:16

COMMITS
to you, whoever *c* . . . . John 8:34
sin also *c* lawlessness . . . . . 1 John 3:4

COMMITTED
For My people have *c* . . . . . . Jer 2:13
c things deserving . . . . . . Luke 12:48
For God has *c* them all . . . Rom 11:32
Guard what was *c* . . . . . . 1 Tim 6:20
"Who *c* no sin . . . . 1 Pet 2:22
c Himself to Him who . . . 1 Pet 2:23

COMMON
of the *c* people sins . . . . Lev 4:27
poor have this in *c* . . . . Prov 22:2
c people heard Him . . . . Mark 12:37
had all things in *c* . . . . Acts 2:44
never eaten anything *c* . . . Acts 10:14
not call any man *c* . . . . . . Acts 10:28
a true son in our *c* . . . . Titus 1:4
concerning our *c* . . . . Jude 3

COMMOTION
there arose a great *c* . . . . . Acts 19:23

COMMUNED
I *c* with my heart . . . . Eccl 1:16

COMMUNION
bless, is it not the *c* . . . . . 1 Cor 10:16
c has light with . . . . 2 Cor 6:14
c of the Holy Spirit . . . . . 2 Cor 13:14

COMPANION
a man my equal, My *c* . . . Ps 55:13
I am a *c* of all who . . . . Ps 119:63
the Man who is My C . . . . Zech 13:7
urge you also, true *c* . . . . . . Phil 4:3
your brother and *c* . . . . Rev 1:9

COMPANIONS
are rebellious, and *c* . . . . Is 1:23
and calling to their *c* . . . . Matt 11:16
more than Your *c* . . . . Heb 1:9
while you became *c* . . . . . Heb 10:33

COMPANY
great was the *c* . . . . Ps 68:11
epistle not to keep *c* . . . . . . 1 Cor 5:9
c corrupts good habits . . . 1 Cor 15:33
and do not keep *c* . . . . . . 2 Thess 3:14
to an innumerable *c* . . . . . Heb 12:22

COMPARE
may desire cannot *c* . . . . . Prov 3:15
c ourselves with those . . . 2 Cor 10:12

COMPARED
the heavens can be *c* . . . . . . Ps 89:6
may desire cannot be *c* . . . Prov 8:11
are not worthy to be *c* . . . . Rom 8:18

COMPASSION
show you mercy, have *c* . . Deut 13:17
His people and have *c* . . . Deut 32:36
He, being full of *c* . . . . Ps 78:38
are a God full of *c* . . . . Ps 86:15
will return and have *c* . . . . Jer 12:15
yet He will show *c* . . . . Lam 3:32
c everyone to his . . . . Zech 7:9
He was moved with *c* . . . . Matt 9:36
also have had *c* . . . . Matt 18:33
"I have *c* on the . . . . Mark 8:2
whomever I will have *c* . . . Rom 9:15
He can have *c* on those . . . . Heb 5:2
of one mind, having *c* . . . 1 Pet 3:8
And on some have *c* . . . . . . Jude 22

COMPASSIONATE
c women have cooked . . . . . Lam 4:10
the Lord is very *c* . . . . . . James 5:11

COMPASSIONS
because His *c* fail not . . . . . Lam 3:22

COMPEL
c them to come in . . . . . . Luke 14:23

COMPELLED
Macedonia, Paul was *c* . . . . Acts 18:5

COMPELS
the spirit within me *c* . . . . Job 32:18
And whoever *c* . . . . Matt 5:41
the love of Christ *c* . . . . . . 2 Cor 5:14

COMPLACENCY
slay them, and the *c* . . . . . Prov 1:32
who are settled in *c* . . . . . . Zeph 1:12

COMPLAIN
should a living man *c* . . . . . Lam 3:39

COMPLAINED
and you *c* in your . . . . Deut 1:27
but *c* in their tents . . . . Ps 106:25
some of them also *c* . . . . . 1 Cor 10:10

COMPLAINERS
These are grumblers, *c* . . . . . Jude 16

COMPLAINING
all things without *c* . . . . . . Phil 2:14

COMPLAINT
"Even today my *c* . . . . Job 23:2
I pour out my *c* . . . . Ps 142:2
for the Lord has a *c* . . . . Mic 6:2
if anyone has a *c* . . . . Col 3:13

COMPLAINTS
Who has *c* . . . . Prov 23:29
laid many serious *c* . . . . . . Acts 25:7

COMPLETE
that you may be made *c* . . 2 Cor 13:9
work in you will *c* . . . . Phil 1:6
and you are *c* in Him . . . . . Col 2:10
of God may be *c* . . . . 2 Tim 3:17
make you *c* in every . . . . . Heb 13:21
the wrath of God is *c* . . . . . . Rev 15:1

COMPLETELY
I made a man *c* well . . . . . . John 7:23
Himself sanctify you *c* . . 1 Thess 5:23

COMPOSED
But God *c* the body . . . . . 1 Cor 12:24

COMPREHEND
which we cannot *c* . . . . Job 37:5
c my path and my lying . . . . Ps 139:3
the darkness did not *c* . . . . . John 1:5
may be able to *c* . . . . Eph 3:18

CONCEAL
Almighty I will not *c* . . . . . Job 27:11
c pride from man . . . . Job 33:17
of God to *c* a matter . . . . . . Prov 25:2

CONCEALED
c Your lovingkindness . . . . . Ps 40:10
than love carefully *c* . . . . . Prov 27:5

CONCEIT
selfish ambition or *c* . . . . . . Phil 2:3

CONCEITED
Let us not become *c* . . . . . . Gal 5:26

CONCEIVE
the virgin shall *c* . . . . Is 7:14
And behold, you will *c* . . . . Luke 1:31

CONCEIVED
in sin my mother *c* . . . . Ps 51:5
when desire has *c* . . . . . . James 1:15

CONCERN
Neither do I *c* myself . . . . . Ps 131:1
the things which *c* . . . . Acts 28:31
my deep *c* for all the . . . . 2 Cor 11:28

CONCERNED
Is it oxen God is *c* . . . . 1 Cor 9:9

CONCESSION
But I say this as a *c* . . . . . . 1 Cor 7:6

CONCILIATION
c pacifies great . . . . Eccl 10:4

CONCLUSION
Let us hear the *c* . . . . Eccl 12:13

CONDEMN
say to God, 'Do not *c* . . . . . . Job 10:2
world to *c* the world . . . . . . John 3:17
her, "Neither do I *c* . . . . . . John 8:11
judge another you *c* . . . . . . Rom 2:1
our heart does not *c* . . . . . 1 John 3:21

CONDEMNATION
will receive greater *c* . . . . . Matt 23:14
can you escape the *c* . . . . . Matt 23:33
subject to eternal *c* . . . . . . Mark 3:29
And this is the *c* . . . . John 3:19
the resurrection of *c* . . . . . John 5:29
Their *c* is just. . . . . Rom 3:8
therefore now no *c* . . . . . . Rom 8:1
of *c* had glory . . . . 2 Cor 3:9
having *c* because they . . . 1 Tim 5:12
marked out for this *c* . . . . Jude 4

CONDEMNED
words you will be *c* . . . . . Matt 12:37
does not believe is *c* . . . . . John 3:18
c sin in the flesh . . . . Rom 8:3

CONDEMNS
Who is he who *c* . . . . Rom 8:34
For if our heart *c* . . . . . 1 John 3:20

CONDUCT
c yourselves like men. . . . . 1 Sam 4:9
who are of upright *c* . . . . . . Ps 37:14
c yourself in the. . . . . 1 Tim 3:15
c that his works are . . . . . James 3:13
to each one's work, *c* . . . . 1 Pet 1:17
from your aimless *c* . . . . . 1 Pet 1:18
may be won by the *c* . . . . . 1 Pet 3:1

CONFESS
c my transgressions. . . . . Ps 32:5
that if you *c* with. . . . . Rom 10:9
every tongue shall *c* . . . . . Rom 14:11
C your trespasses. . . . . . . James 5:16
If we *c* our sins. . . . . 1 John 1:9
but I will *c* his name . . . . . . Rev 3:5

CONFESSED
c that He was Christ . . . . . . John 9:22
c the good confession . . . . 1 Tim 6:12

CONFESSES
prosper, but whoever *c* . . . . Prov 28:13
c that Jesus is the. . . . . . 1 John 4:15

CONFESSION
of Israel, and make *c* . . . . . Josh 7:19
with the mouth *c*. . . . . . . Rom 10:10
confessed the good *c* . . . . 1 Tim 6:12
witnessed the good *c* . . . . 1 Tim 6:13
High Priest of our *c* . . . . Heb 3:1
let us hold fast our *c* . . . . . Heb 4:14

CONFIDENCE
You who are the *c* . . . . Ps 65:5
the LORD than to put *c* . . . . . Ps 118:8
c shall be your . . . . Is 30:15
Jesus, and have no *c* . . . . . . Phil 3:3
if we hold fast the *c* . . . . . . Heb 3:6
appears, we may have *c* . 1 John 2:28

CONFINED
saying, "I am *c*. . . . . Jer 36:5
the Scripture has *c* . . . . . . Gal 3:22

CONFIRM
c the promises . . . . Rom 15:8
who will also *c*. . . . . 1 Cor 1:8

CONFIRMED
covenant that was *c* . . . . . . Gal 3:17
by the Lord, and was *c* . . . . Heb 2:3
c it by an oath . . . . Heb 6:17
prophetic word *c*. . . . . . . 2 Pet 1:19

CONFIRMING
c the word through the . . Mark 16:20

CONFLICT
having the same *c* . . . . Phil 1:30
to know what a great *c* . . . . . Col 2:1

CONFLICTS
Outside were *c*. . . . . 2 Cor 7:5

CONFORMED
predestined to be *c* . . . . . Rom 8:29
And do not be *c*. . . . . Rom 12:2
sufferings, being *c* . . . . Phil 3:10
body that it may be *c*. . . . . Phil 3:21

CONFOUNDED
who seek You be *c* . . . . Ps 69:6

CONFUSE
c their language. . . . . Gen 11:7

CONFUSED
there the LORD *c* . . . . Gen 11:9
the assembly was *c* . . . . . . Acts 19:32

CONFUSION
c who plot my hurt. . . . . Ps 35:4
us drink the wine of *c*. . . . . Ps 60:3

CONGREGATION
Nor sinners in the *c* . . . . Ps 1:5
the *c* of the wicked . . . . Ps 22:16
God stands in the *c* . . . . . . Ps 82:1

CONIAH
King of Judah, Jer 22:24, 28
Same as Jehoiachin, 2 Kin 24:8

CONQUER
conquering and to *c* . . . . . . Rev 6:2

CONQUERORS
we are more than *c* . . . . . Rom 8:37

CONSCIENCE
convicted by their *c* . . . . . . John 8:9
strive to have a *c* . . . . . . Acts 24:16
I am not lying, my *c* . . . . . Rom 9:1
wrath but also for *c* . . . . . Rom 13:5
no questions for *c*. . . . . . 1 Cor 10:25
faith with a pure *c* . . . . . . 1 Tim 3:9
having their own *c* . . . . . . 1 Tim 4:2
to God, cleanse your *c* . . . . Heb 9:14
from an evil *c* and our. . . . Heb 10:22
having a good *c* . . . . 1 Pet 3:16

CONSECRATE
"*C* to Me all the . . . . Ex 13:2
c himself this day . . . . . . 1 Chr 29:5
the trumpet in Zion, *c* . . . . . Joel 2:15
c their gain to the. . . . . Mic 4:13

CONSECRATED
c this house which you . . . . 1 Kin 9:3

CONSENT
entice you, do not *c*. . . . . . Prov 1:10
and does not *c* to . . . . 1 Tim 6:3

CONSENTED
you saw a thief, you *c*. . . . . Ps 50:18
He had not *c* to their . . . . Luke 23:51

CONSENTING
Now Saul was *c* to his . . . . . Acts 8:1

CONSIDER
When I *c* Your heavens. . . . . . Ps 8:3
c her palaces . . . . Ps 48:13
c carefully what is. . . . . . . Prov 23:1
C the work of God . . . . . . Eccl 7:13
My people do not *c* . . . . Is 1:3
c the operation. . . . . Is 5:12
your God will *c* . . . . Jon 1:6
"*C* your ways . . . . Hag 1:5
C the lilies of the. . . . . . . Matt 6:28
C the ravens . . . . Luke 12:24

Let a man so *c* us . . . . 1 Cor 4:1
c how great this man. . . . . . Heb 7:4
c one another in order . . . . Heb 10:24
c Him who endured . . . . . . Heb 12:3

CONSIDERS
c all their works. . . . . Ps 33:15

CONSIST
in Him all things *c* . . . . Col 1:17

CONSOLATION
waiting for the *C* . . . . Luke 2:25
have received your *c*. . . . . Luke 6:24
abound in us, so our *c* . . . . 2 Cor 1:5
if there is any *c* . . . . Phil 2:1
given us everlasting *c* . . . 2 Thess 2:16
we might have strong *c* . . . . Heb 6:18

CONSOLATIONS
Are the *c* of God too. . . . . . Job 15:11

CONSOLE
c those who mourn . . . . Is 61:3

CONSPIRE
What do you *c* against . . . . . Nah 1:9

CONSTANT
c prayer was. . . . . Acts 12:5

CONSULT
They only *c* to cast . . . . Ps 62:4

CONSULTED
c together against . . . . Ps 83:3

CONSUME
your midst, lest I *c* . . . . Ex 33:3
this great fire will *c*. . . . . . Deut 5:25
C them in wrath . . . . Ps 59:13
whom the Lord will *c* . . . . 2 Thess 2:8

CONSUMED
but the bush was not *c*. . . . . . Ex 3:2
c the burnt . . . . 1 Kin 18:38
For we have been *c* . . . . Ps 90:7
mercies we are not *c* . . . . . Lam 3:22
beware lest you be *c* . . . . . Gal 5:15

CONSUMING
the LORD was like a *c* . . . . . Ex 24:17
before you as a *c* . . . . Deut 9:3
our God is a *c* fire. . . . . . . Heb 12:29

CONSUMMATION
I have seen the *c* . . . . Ps 119:96

CONSUMPTION
will strike you with *c*. . . . . Deut 28:22

CONTAIN
of heavens cannot *c* . . . . . 2 Chr 2:6
c the books that . . . . John 21:25

CONTEMPT
He pours *c* on princes . . . . . Job 12:21
wicked comes, *c* comes . . . . Prov 18:3
and everlasting *c* . . . . Dan 12:2
and be treated with *c*. . . . . Mark 9:12

CONTEMPTIBLE
of the LORD is *c*. . . . . Mal 1:7
also have made you *c* . . . . . Mal 2:9
and his speech *c*. . . . . . . 2 Cor 10:10

CONTEND
show me why You *c*. . . . . . . Job 10:2
Will you *c* for God . . . . . . Job 13:8
let us *c* together . . . . Is 43:26
for I will *c* with him. . . . . . . Is 49:25
then how can you *c* . . . . . . Jer 12:5
c earnestly for the . . . . Jude 3

CONTENDED
Therefore the people *c* . . . . . Ex 17:2

CONTENT
state I am, to be *c*. . . . . . . Phil 4:11

these we shall be *c* . . . . 1 Tim 6:8
covetousness; be *c* . . . . Heb 13:5

CONTENTION
lips enter into *c* . . . . Prov 18:6
and *c* will leave . . . . Prov 22:10
strife and a man of *c* . . . . . Jer 15:10

CONTENTIONS
Casting lots causes *c* . . . . . Prov 18:18
sorcery, hatred, *c*. . . . . Gal 5:20
genealogies, *c* . . . . Titus 3:9

CONTENTIOUS
than with a *c* and . . . . Prov 21:19
shared with a *c* woman . . Prov 25:24
anyone seems to be *c*. . . . 1 Cor 11:16

CONTENTMENT
c is great gain . . . . 1 Tim 6:6

CONTINUAL
a merry heart has a *c* . . . . Prov 15:15
in wrath with a *c* . . . . Is 14:6
c coming she weary me . . . Luke 18:5
c grief in my heart . . . . Rom 9:2

CONTINUALLY
heart was only evil *c* . . . . . . Gen 6:5
His praise shall *c*. . . . . Ps 34:1
and Your truth *c* . . . . Ps 40:11
of God endures *c* . . . . Ps 52:1
I keep Your law *c* . . . . Ps 119:44
Before Me *c* are grief . . . . Jer 6:7
and wait on your God *c* . . . . Hos 12:6
will give ourselves *c*. . . . . . . Acts 6:4
remains a priest *c* . . . . Heb 7:3
c offer the sacrifice . . . . . . Heb 13:15

CONTINUE
tells lies shall not *c* . . . . Ps 101:7
persuaded them to *c*. . . . . Acts 13:43
Shall we *c* in sin that . . . . . Rom 6:1
who does not *c* in all . . . . . . Gal 3:10
C earnestly in prayer . . . . . . Col 4:2
because they did not *c*. . . . . Heb 8:9
Let brotherly love *c* . . . . . . Heb 13:1
asleep, all things *c* . . . . 2 Pet 3:4

CONTINUED
c steadfastly in the. . . . . . . Acts 2:42
us, they would have *c* . . . 1 John 2:19

CONTINUES
But He, because He *c*. . . . . . Heb 7:24
law of liberty and *c* . . . . . James 1:25

CONTRADICTIONS
idle babblings and *c*. . . . . 1 Tim 6:20

CONTRARY
to worship God *c* . . . . Acts 18:13
and these are *c* . . . . Gal 5:17
please God and are *c* . . . 1 Thess 2:15
other thing that is *c* . . . . . 1 Tim 1:10

CONTRIBUTION
to make a certain *c*. . . . . . Rom 15:26

CONTRITE
saves such as have a *c* . . . . . Ps 34:18
a broken and a *c*. . . . . Ps 51:17
with him who has a *c* . . . . . Is 57:15
poor and of a *c* spirit. . . . . . . Is 66:2

CONTROVERSY
another, matters of *c*. . . . . Deut 17:8
For the LORD has a *c*. . . . . . Jer 25:31
c great is . . . . 1 Tim 3:16

CONVERSION
describing the *c* . . . . Acts 15:3

CONVERTED
unless you are *c* . . . . Matt 18:3

CONVEYED
of darkness and *c* . . . . Col 1:13

CONVICT
He has come, He will *c*. . . . John 16:8
c those who. . . . . Titus 1:9
c all who are ungodly . . . . . . Jude 15

CONVICTS
Which of you *c* . . . . John 8:46

CONVINCED
Let each be fully *c*. . . . . Rom 14:5

COOKED
c their own children . . . . . . Lam 4:10

COOL
in the garden in the *c* . . . . . Gen 3:8
and *c* my tongue. . . . . Luke 16:24

COPIES
necessary that the *c*. . . . . . Heb 9:23
hands, which are *c*. . . . . . . Heb 9:24

COPPER
hills you can dig *c* . . . . Deut 8:9
of cups, pitchers, *c* . . . . Mark 7:4
sold for two *c* coins . . . . . . Luke 12:6

COPPERSMITH
c did me much harm . . . . 2 Tim 4:14

COPY
who serve the *c* . . . . Heb 8:5

CORD
this line of scarlet *c* . . . . . . Josh 2:18
And a threefold *c* . . . . Eccl 4:12
before the silver *c* . . . . Eccl 12:6

CORDS
in pieces the *c* . . . . Ps 129:4
he is caught in the *c* . . . . . . Prov 5:22
draw iniquity with *c* . . . . Is 5:18
them with gentle *c* . . . . Hos 11:4
had made a whip of *c*. . . . . John 2:15

CORINTH
Paul labors at, Acts 18:1–18
Site of church, 1 Cor 1:2
Visited by Apollos, Acts 19:1

CORNELIUS
A religious Gentile, Acts 10:1–48

CORNER
was not done in a *c*. . . . . . Acts 26:26

CORNERSTONE
Or who laid its *c* . . . . Job 38:6
has become the chief *c* . . . Ps 118:22
stone, a precious *c* . . . . Is 28:16
become the chief *c* . . . . . . Matt 21:42
in Zion a chief *c*. . . . . 1 Pet 2:6

CORPSE
c was thrown on the . . . . 1 Kin 13:24
c trodden underfoot . . . . Is 14:19

CORRECT
with rebukes You *c*. . . . . . . Ps 39:11
C your son . . . . Prov 29:17
But I will *c* you in. . . . . Jer 30:11

CORRECTED
human fathers who *c*. . . . . Heb 12:9

CORRECTION
nor detest His *c* . . . . Prov 3:11
but he who refuses *c* . . . . Prov 10:17
but he who hates *c* . . . . Prov 12:1
c will drive it . . . . Prov 22:15
Do not withhold *c* . . . . Prov 23:13
they received no *c* . . . . Jer 2:30
for reproof, for *c* . . . . 2 Tim 3:16

CORRECTS
is the man whom God *c* . . . Job 5:17
the LORD loves He *c*. . . . . . . Prov 3:12

CORRODED
and silver are *c*. . . . . James 5:3

CORRUPT
have together become *c* . . . . Ps 14:3
have together become *c* . . . . Ps 53:3
old man which grows *c* . . . . Eph 4:22
men of *c* minds. . . . . 2 Tim 3:8
in these things they *c* . . . . . . Jude 10

CORRUPTED
for all flesh had *c*. . . . . Gen 6:12
we have *c* no one . . . . 2 Cor 7:2
so your minds may be *c* . . 2 Cor 11:3
Your riches are *c* . . . . James 5:2
the great harlot who *c* . . . . Rev 19:2

CORRUPTIBLE
For this *c* must put on . . . 1 Cor 15:53
redeemed with *c* things . . . 1 Pet 1:18

CORRUPTION
Your Holy One to see *c* . . . . Ps 16:10
God raised up saw no *c* . . . Acts 13:37
from the bondage of *c* . . . . Rom 8:21
The body is sown in *c* . . . 1 Cor 15:42
c inherit incorruption . . . 1 Cor 15:50
of the flesh reap *c*. . . . . Gal 6:8
having escaped the *c* . . . . . 2 Pet 1:4
perish in their own *c* . . . . . 2 Pet 2:12

COST
and count the *c*. . . . . Luke 14:28

COULD
has done what she *c* . . . . . Mark 14:8
c remove mountains . . . . . 1 Cor 13:2
which no one *c* number. . . . . Rev 7:9

COUNCILS
deliver you up to *c*. . . . . . . Mark 13:9

COUNSEL
and strength, He has *c* . . . . Job 12:13
the *c* of the wicked is . . . . . Job 21:16
when the friendly *c*. . . . . . . Job 29:4
is this who darkens *c*. . . . . . Job 38:2
who walks not in the *c* . . . . . . Ps 1:1
We took sweet *c* . . . . Ps 55:14
guide me with Your *c* . . . . . Ps 73:24
you disdained all my *c* . . . . Prov 1:25
have none of my *c* . . . . Prov 1:30
Where there is no *c* . . . . . . Prov 11:14
C in the heart of man. . . . . Prov 20:5
by wise *c* wage war . . . . . Prov 20:18
whom did He take *c*. . . . . . . Is 40:14
You are great in *c* . . . . Jer 32:19
according to the *c* . . . . Eph 1:11
immutability of His *c*. . . . . . Heb 6:17
I *c* you to buy from . . . . Rev 3:18

COUNSELOR
be called Wonderful, *C* . . . . . . Is 9:6
but there was no *c* . . . . Is 41:28
Has your *c* perished . . . . . . Mic 4:9
who has become His *c*. . . . Rom 11:34

COUNSELORS
c there is safety . . . . Prov 11:14

COUNT
c the people of Israel . . . . 2 Sam 24:4
c my life dear to. . . . . Acts 20:24
c me as a partner. . . . . Philem 17
His promise, as some *c*. . . . 2 Pet 3:9

COUNTED
Even a fool is *c*. . . . . Prov 17:28
c as the small dust . . . . Is 40:15
the wages are not *c*. . . . . . . Rom 4:4
He *c* me faithful . . . . 1 Tim 1:12
who rule well be *c*. . . . . . . 1 Tim 5:17

COUNTENANCE
The LORD lift up His *c*. . . . . Num 6:26
c they did not cast. . . . . . . Job 29:24
up the light of Your *c* . . . . . . Ps 4:6
His *c* is like Lebanon. . . . . . Song 5:15

with a sad *c*. . . . . Matt 6:16
His *c* was like . . . . Matt 28:3
of the glory of his *c*. . . . . . . 2 Cor 3:7
sword, and His *c*. . . . . Rev 1:16

COUNTRY
"Get out of your *c* . . . . Gen 12:1
good news from a far *c*. . . . . Prov 25:25
and went into a far *c* . . . . . Matt 21:33
as in a foreign *c*. . . . . Heb 11:9
that is, a heavenly *c*. . . . . . Heb 11:16

COUNTRYMEN
for my brethren, my *c*. . . . . Rom 9:3

COURAGE
strong and of good *c*. . . . . Deut 31:6
thanked God and took *c* . . Acts 28:15

COURSE
and sets on fire the *c* . . . . James 3:6

COURT
appoint my day in *c*. . . . . . Job 9:19
by you or by a human *c*. . . 1 Cor 4:3
They zealously *c* . . . . Gal 4:17

COURTEOUS
be tenderhearted, be *c* . . . 1 Pet 3:8

COURTS
he may dwell in Your *c*. . . . Ps 65:4
even faints for the *c* . . . . . . Ps 84:2
flourish in the *c*. . . . . Ps 92:13
and into His *c*. . . . . Ps 100:4
drink it in My holy *c* . . . . . . Is 62:9

COVENANT
I will establish My *c*. . . . . . Gen 6:18
the LORD made a *c* . . . . . . Gen 15:18
for Me, behold, My *c* . . . . . Gen 17:4
as a perpetual *c*. . . . . Ex 31:16
it is a *c* of salt . . . . Num 18:19
Remember His *c* forever. . 1 Chr 16:15
"I have made a *c*. . . . . Job 31:1
will show them His *c*. . . . . . Ps 25:14
c shall stand firm . . . . Ps 89:28
sons will keep My *c* . . . . . Ps 132:12
and give You as a *C*. . . . . . Is 42:6
the words of this *c* . . . . Jer 11:2
I will make a new *c*. . . . . . Jer 31:31
'I made a *c* with your. . . . . Jer 34:13
I might break the *c* . . . . . Zech 11:10
the Messenger of the *c*. . . . Mal 3:1
cup is the new *c* . . . . Luke 22:20
c that was confirmed . . . . . Gal 3:17
Mediator of a better *c*. . . . . Heb 8:6
c had been faultless. . . . . . . Heb 8:7
He says, "A new *c*. . . . . . . Heb 8:13
Mediator of the new *c* . . . Heb 12:24
of the everlasting *c*. . . . . . Heb 13:20

COVENANTED
your kingdom, as I *c*. . . . . 2 Chr 7:18
to the word that I *c* . . . . . . Hag 2:5

COVENANTS
the glory, the *c* . . . . Rom 9:4
these are the two *c*. . . . . . . Gal 4:24

COVER
the rock, and will *c*. . . . . . Ex 33:22
He shall *c* you with. . . . . . . Ps 91:4
c Yourself with light. . . . . . Ps 104:2
LORD as the waters *c*. . . . . . Is 11:9
and will no more *c*. . . . . . . Is 26:21
from the wind and a *c*. . . . . Is 32:2
not to *c* his head . . . . 1 Cor 11:7
c a multitude of sins. . . . . James 5:20

COVERED
The depths have *c*. . . . . . . Ex 15:5
c my transgressions as. . . . Job 31:33
Whose sin is *c* . . . . Ps 32:1
the wings of a dove *c*. . . . . Ps 68:13

c all their sin . . . . Ps 85:2
You *c* me in my . . . . Ps 139:13
with two he *c* his face . . . . . . Is 6:2
of Jacob will be *c* . . . . Is 27:9
You have *c* Yourself. . . . . . Lam 3:44
For there is nothing *c* . . . Matt 10:26

COVERING
spread a cloud for a *c* . . . . Ps 105:39
make sackcloth their *c*. . . . . Is 50:3
given to her for a *c*. . . . . 1 Cor 11:15

COVERINGS
and made themselves *c*. . . . Gen 3:7

COVET
"You shall not *c* . . . . Ex 20:17
c fields and take them . . . . . Mic 2:2
You murder and *c*. . . . . . . James 4:2

COVETED
c no one's silver . . . . Acts 20:33

COVETOUS
nor thieves, nor *c*. . . . . . . 1 Cor 6:10
trained in *c* practices . . . . . 2 Pet 2:14

COVETOUSNESS
but he who hates *c* . . . . . Prov 28:16
for nothing but your *c* . . . . Jer 22:17
heed and beware of *c* . . . Luke 12:15
would not have known *c* . . . Rom 7:7
all uncleanness or *c*. . . . . . Eph 5:3
conduct be without *c* . . . . Heb 13:5

COWARDLY
the *c*, unbelieving. . . . . Rev 21:8

CRAFTINESS
wise in their own *c* . . . . . . Job 5:13
not walking in *c* . . . . 2 Cor 4:2
deceived Eve by his *c*. . . . 2 Cor 11:3
in the cunning *c*. . . . . Eph 4:14

CRAFTSMAN
instructor of every *c*. . . . . . Gen 4:22
c encouraged the . . . . Is 41:7
c stretches out his. . . . . Is 44:13

CRAFTY
Jonadab was a very *c*. . . . 2 Sam 13:3
the devices of the *c* . . . . . . Job 5:12
They have taken . . . . Ps 83:3
of a harlot, and a *c* . . . . . . Prov 7:10
Nevertheless, being *c* . . . . 2 Cor 12:16

CRANE
Like a *c* or a swallow . . . . . . Is 38:14

CRAVES
and his soul still *c* . . . . Is 29:8

CREAM
she brought out *c* . . . . Judg 5:25
were bathed with *c* . . . . . . Job 29:6

CREATE
peace and *c* calamity. . . . . . Is 45:7
For behold, I *c*. . . . . Is 65:17

CREATED
So God *c* man in His . . . . . Gen 1:27
Spirit, they are *c* . . . . Ps 104:30
and they were *c*. . . . . Ps 148:5
and see who has *c* . . . . . . Is 40:26
of Israel has *c*. . . . . Is 41:20
For the LORD has *c* . . . . . . Jer 31:22
Has not one God *c* . . . . . Mal 2:10
Nor was man *c* for the. . . . 1 Cor 11:9
c in Christ Jesus . . . . Eph 2:10
hidden in God who *c*. . . . . Eph 3:9
new man which was *c*. . . . Eph 4:24
Him all things were *c* . . . . Col 1:16
from foods which God *c* . . 1 Tim 4:3
for You *c* all things . . . . . . Rev 4:11

CREATION
c which God . . . . Mark 13:19

c was subjected . . . . Rom 8:20
know that the whole *c* . . . . Rom 8:22
Christ, he is a new *c* . . . . 2 Cor 5:17
anything, but a new *c* . . . . Gal 6:15
firstborn over all *c*. . . . . . . Col 1:15

CREATOR
Remember now your *C*. . . . Eccl 12:1
God, the LORD, the *C* . . . . . Is 40:28
rather than the *C* . . . . Rom 1:25
to a faithful *C*. . . . . 1 Pet 4:19

CREATURE
the gospel to every *c*. . . . Mark 16:15
For every *c* of God is . . . . . 1 Tim 4:4
And there is no *c* . . . . Heb 4:13
And every *c* which is. . . . . . Rev 5:13
and every living *c* . . . . Rev 16:3

CREATURES
created great sea *c*. . . . . . . Gen 1:21
firstfruits of His *c*. . . . . . James 1:18
were four living *c* . . . . Rev 4:6

CREDIT
who love you, what *c*. . . . . Luke 6:32
For what *c* is it if. . . . . . . 1 Pet 2:20

CREDITOR
Every *c* who has lent. . . . . Deut 15:2
c is coming to take my . . . . 2 Kin 4:1
c seize all that he. . . . . Ps 109:11
There was a certain *c* . . . . Luke 7:41

CREEP
of the forest *c*. . . . . Ps 104:20
sort are those who *c* . . . . . 2 Tim 3:6

CREEPING
c thing and beast of. . . . . . Gen 1:24
every sort of *c* thing. . . . . . Ezek 8:10

CREPT
For certain men have *c* . . . . . Jude 4

CRETE
Paul visits, Acts 27:7–21
Titus dispatched to, Titus 1:5
Inhabitants of, evil and lazy,
Titus 1:12

CRIED
the poor who *c* out . . . . . . Job 29:12
They *c* to You. . . . . Ps 22:5
of the depths I have *c*. . . . . Ps 130:1

CRIES
your brother's blood *c* . . . . Gen 4:10
with vehement *c* . . . . Heb 5:7

CRIMES
land is filled with *c* . . . . . . Ezek 7:23

CRIMINALS
also two others, *c* . . . . . . Luke 23:32

CRISPUS
Chief ruler of synagogue of Corinth,
Acts 18:8
Baptized by Paul, 1 Cor 1:14

CROOKED
turn aside to their *c*. . . . . . Ps 125:5
whose ways are *c*. . . . . . . Prov 2:15
c places shall be made. . . . . Is 40:4
c places straight . . . . Is 45:2
c places shall be made. . . . Luke 3:5
in the midst of a *c* . . . . . . Phil 2:15

CROSS
does not take his *c* . . . . . Matt 10:38
to bear His *c* . . . . Matt 27:32
down from the *c* . . . . . . Matt 27:40
lest the *c* of Christ . . . . . . 1 Cor 1:17
persecution for the *c*. . . . . Gal 6:12
boast except in the *c*. . . . . Gal 6:14
one body through the *c* . . . . Eph 2:16

the enemies of the *c* . . . . . . Phil 3:18
Him endured the *c* . . . . Heb 12:2

CROWD
shall not follow a *c* . . . . Ex 23:2

CROWN
You set a *c* of pure . . . . Ps 21:3
c the year with Your . . . . . . Ps 65:11
have profaned his *c* . . . . Ps 89:39
upon Himself His *c* . . . . . . Ps 132:18
The *c* of the wise is . . . . . . Prov 14:24
head is a *c* of glory . . . . Prov 16:31
Woe to the *c* of pride . . . . Is 28:1
hosts will be for a *c* . . . . Is 28:5
c has fallen from our . . . . . Lam 5:16
they had twisted a *c* . . . . Matt 27:29
obtain a perishable *c* . . . . 1 Cor 9:25
brethren, my joy and *c* . . . . Phil 4:1
laid up for me the *c* . . . . 2 Tim 4:8
he will receive the *c* . . . . . James 1:12
no one may take your *c* . . . Rev 3:11
on His head a golden *c* . . . . Rev 14:14

CROWNED
angels, and You have *c* . . . . . . Ps 8:5
but the prudent are *c* . . . . . Prov 14:18
athletics, he is not *c* . . . . . 2 Tim 2:5
You have *c* him with glory . . Heb 2:7

CROWNS
and they had *c* of gold . . . . . Rev 4:4
on his horns ten *c* . . . . Rev 13:1
His head were many *c* . . . . Rev 19:12

CRUCIFIED
"Let Him be *c* . . . . Matt 27:22
Calvary, there they *c* . . . . Luke 23:33
lawless hands, have *c* . . . . Acts 2:23
that our old man was *c* . . . . Rom 6:6
Was Paul *c* for you . . . . . . 1 Cor 1:13
Jesus Christ and Him *c* . . . . 1 Cor 2:2
they would not have *c* . . . . 1 Cor 2:8
though He was *c* . . . . . . 2 Cor 13:4
I have been *c* . . . . Gal 2:20

CRUCIFY
out again, "C Him . . . . . . Mark 15:13
I have power to *c* You . . . . John 19:10
since they *c* again . . . . Heb 6:6

CRUEL
wrath, for it is *c* . . . . Gen 49:7
spirit and *c* bondage . . . . Ex 6:9
hate me with *c* hatred . . . . . Ps 25:19
of the wicked are *c* . . . . . Prov 12:10

CRUELTY
of *c* are in their . . . . Gen 49:5
the haunts of *c* . . . . Ps 74:20
c you have ruled . . . . Ezek 34:4

CRUSH
that a foot may *c* . . . . Job 39:15
that your foot may *c* . . . . . . Ps 68:23
the poor, who *c* . . . . Amos 4:1
of peace will *c* . . . . Rom 16:20

CRUSHED
in the dust, who are *c* . . . . . Job 4:19
c my life to the . . . . Ps 143:3
every side, yet not *c* . . . . . 2 Cor 4:8

CRUST
man is reduced to a *c* . . . . . Prov 6:26

CRY
and their *c* came up to . . . . . . Ex 2:23
of oppressions they *c* . . . . . . Job 35:9
heart and my flesh *c* . . . . . . Ps 84:2
I *c* out with my whole . . . . Ps 119:145
Does not wisdom *c* . . . . Prov 8:1
"What shall I *c* . . . . Is 40:6
nor lift up a *c* . . . . Jer 7:16

c mightily to God . . . . Jon 3:8
at midnight a *c* . . . . Matt 25:6
His own elect who *c* . . . . . Luke 18:7

CRYING
"The voice of one *c* . . . . Matt 3:3
nor sorrow, nor *c* . . . . Rev 21:4

CRYSTAL
nor *c* can equal it . . . . Job 28:17
your gates of *c* . . . . Is 54:12
of an awesome *c* . . . . Ezek 1:22
a sea of glass, like *c* . . . . . . Rev 4:6

CUBIT
shall finish it to a *c* . . . . . . Gen 6:16
can add one *c* . . . . Matt 6:27

CUCUMBERS
in Egypt, the *c* . . . . Num 11:5
a hut in a garden of *c* . . . . . . Is 1:8

CUNNING
the serpent was more *c* . . . . . Gen 3:1
c comes quickly . . . . Job 5:13
c craftiness of deceitful . . . . . Eph 4:14

CUP
My *c* runs over . . . . Ps 23:5
waters of a full *c* are . . . . . Ps 73:10
the LORD there is a *c* . . . . . . Ps 75:8
I will take up the *c* . . . . Ps 116:13
the dregs of the *c* . . . . Is 51:17
men give them the *c* . . . . . . Jer 16:7
"Take this wine *c* . . . . Jer 25:15
The *c* of the LORD's . . . . Hab 2:16
make Jerusalem a *c* . . . . . Zech 12:2
little ones only a *c* . . . . . . Matt 10:42
Then He took the *c* . . . . . Matt 26:27
possible, let this *c* . . . . . . Matt 26:39
c is the new covenant . . . . Luke 22:20
cannot drink the *c* . . . . . . 1 Cor 10:21
c is the new . . . . 1 Cor 11:25
to give her the *c* . . . . Rev 16:19

CURE
but they could not *c* . . . . . Matt 17:16
and to *c* diseases . . . . Luke 9:1

CURES
and perform *c* . . . . Luke 13:32

CURSE
c the ground for man's . . . . Gen 8:21
c a ruler of your . . . . Ex 22:28
You shall not *c* . . . . Lev 19:14
c this people for me . . . . . Num 22:6
Balaam, "Neither *c* . . . . . Num 23:25
your God turned the *c* . . . . Deut 23:5
said to him, 'C David . . . 2 Sam 16:10
C God and die . . . . Job 2:9
mouth, but they *c* . . . . Ps 62:4
The *c* of the LORD is . . . . . Prov 3:33
a *c* without cause . . . . . . Prov 26:2
Do not *c* the king . . . . . . Eccl 10:20
do not *c* the rich . . . . Eccl 10:20
"I will send a *c* . . . . Mal 2:2
are cursed with a *c* . . . . Mal 3:9
law are under the *c* . . . . . . Gal 3:10

CURSED
c more than all cattle . . . . . Gen 3:14
C is the man who . . . . Jer 17:5
c is he who keeps . . . . Jer 48:10
'Depart from Me, you *c* . . Matt 25:41
and near to being *c* . . . . . . Heb 6:8

CURSES
I will curse him who *c* . . . . Gen 12:3
'For everyone who *c* . . . . . . Lev 20:9
c his father or his . . . . . . Prov 20:20

CURSINGS
by the sword for the *c* . . . . . Hos 7:16

CURTAIN
of each *c* shall be . . . . Ex 26:2
the heavens like a *c* . . . . . . Ps 104:2

CUSH
Ham's oldest son, 1 Chr 1:8–10
—— Another name for Ethiopia, Is
18:1

CUSTOM
to me, as Your *c* . . . . Ps 119:132
according to the *c* . . . . . . Acts 15:1
we have no such *c* . . . . . 1 Cor 11:16

CUT
confidence shall be *c* . . . . . . Job 8:14
evildoers shall be *c* . . . . Ps 37:9
the wicked will be *c* . . . . . Prov 2:22
causes you to sin, *c* . . . . . Matt 5:30
and will *c* him in . . . . Matt 24:51
him whose ear Peter *c* . . . . John 18:26
He had his hair *c* . . . . Acts 18:18

CYMBAL
or a clanging *c* . . . . 1 Cor 13:1

CYPRUS
Mentioned in prophecies, Num
24:24; Is 23:1–12; Jer 2:10
Christians preach to Jews of, Acts
11:19, 20
Paul and Barnabas visit, Acts 13:4–
13; 15:39

CYRENE
A Greek colonial city in North Africa;
home of Simon the cross-bearer,
Matt 27:32
Synagogue of, Acts 6:9
Christians from, become missionar-
ies, Acts 11:20

CYRUS
King of Persia, referred to as God's
anointed, Is 44:28—45:1

DAGON
The national god of the Philistines,
Judg 16:23
Falls before ark, 1 Sam 5:1–5

DAILY
much as they gather *d* . . . . . . Ex 16:5
d He shall be . . . . Ps 72:15
to me, watching *d* . . . . Prov 8:34
Yet they seek Me *d* . . . . Is 58:2
Give us this day our *d* . . . . Matt 6:11
I sat *d* with you . . . . Matt 26:55
take up his cross *d* . . . . . . Luke 9:23
the Scriptures *d* . . . . Acts 17:11
our Lord, I die *d* . . . . 1 Cor 15:31
stands ministering *d* . . . . . Heb 10:11

DALMATIA
A region east of the Adriatic Sea;
Titus departs for, 2 Tim 4:10

DAMASCUS
Capital of Syria; captured by David;
ruled by enemy kings, 2 Sam 8:5,
6; 1 Kin 11:23, 24; 15:18
Elisha's prophecy in, 2 Kin 8:7–15
Taken by Assyrians, 2 Kin 16:9
Prophecy concerning, Is 8:3, 4
Paul converted on road to; first
preaches there, Acts 9:1–22
escapes from, 2 Cor 11:32, 33
revisits, Gal 1:17

DAN
Jacob's son by Bilhah, Gen 30:5, 6
Prophecy concerning, Gen 49:16, 17
—— Tribe of:
Numbered, Num 1:38, 39

and tested them ten *d* . . . . . Dan 1:14
had shortened those *d* . . . Mark 13:20
raise it up in three *d* . . . . . . John 2:20
You observe *d* and. . . . . Gal 4:10
life and see good *d* . . . . . . 1 Pet 3:10

DAYSPRING
with which the *D* . . . . Luke 1:78

DEACONS
with the bishops and *d* . . . . . Phil 1:1
d must be reverent . . . . 1 Tim 3:8
d be the husbands. . . . . . . 1 Tim 3:12

DEAD
"We shall all be *d* . . . . Ex 12:33
he stood between the *d* . . Num 16:48
work wonders for the *d* . . . . Ps 88:10
who have long been *d* . . . . . Ps 143:3
But the *d* know nothing. . . . . Eccl 9:5
shall cast out the *d* . . . . Is 26:19
d bury their own *d* . . . . . . Matt 8:22
d are raised up and. . . . . . Matt 11:5
not the God of the *d* . . . . . Matt 22:32
became like *d* men . . . . . . Matt 28:4
for this my son was *d* . . . . Luke 15:24
d will hear the voice. . . . . . John 5:25
was raised from the *d* . . . . . Rom 6:4
yourselves to be *d* . . . . Rom 6:11
from the law sin was *d* . . . . Rom 7:8
be Lord of both the *d* . . . . . Rom 14:9
resurrection of the *d* . . . . 1 Cor 15:12
baptized for the *d* . . . . . . 1 Cor 15:29
made alive, who were *d* . . . . Eph 2:1
And the *d* in Christ. . . . . 1 Thess 4:16
d while she lives . . . . 1 Tim 5:6
without works is *d* . . . . . . James 2:26
fell at His feet as *d* . . . . Rev 1:17
d did not live again . . . . . . Rev 20:5
And the *d* were judged . . . . Rev 20:12

DEAD SEA
Called the:
    Salt Sea, Gen 14:3
    Sea of the Arabah, Deut 3:17

DEADLY
they drink anything *d* . . . Mark 16:18
evil, full of *d* poison . . . . . James 3:8
d wound was healed. . . . . . . Rev 13:3

DEADNESS
the *d* of Sarah's womb . . . . Rom 4:19

DEAF
makes the mute, the *d* . . . . . Ex 4:11
d shall hear the words . . . . . Is 29:18
d shall be unstopped . . . . Is 35:5
d as My messenger. . . . . Is 42:19
d who have ears. . . . . Is 43:8
their ears shall be *d* . . . . . . Mic 7:16
are cleansed and the *d* . . . . Matt 11:5

DEAL
Do you thus *d* with the. . . . Deut 32:6
My Servant shall *d* . . . . Is 52:13

DEATH
Let me die the *d* . . . . Num 23:10
d parts you and me . . . . . . Ruth 1:17
and the shadow of *d* . . . . . . Job 10:21
You will bring me to *d*. . . . . Job 30:23
For in *d* there is no . . . . Ps 6:5
I sleep the sleep of *d* . . . . . . Ps 13:3
of the shadow of *d* . . . . Ps 23:4
my soul from *d* . . . . Ps 56:13
can live and not see *d*. . . . . Ps 89:48
house leads down to *d*. . . . . Prov 2:18
who hate me love *d* . . . . . . Prov 8:36
D and life are in the . . . . . Prov 18:21
swallow up *d* forever . . . . Is 25:8
no pleasure in the *d*. . . . . Ezek 18:32
redeem them from *d* . . . . . Hos 13:14

turns the shadow of *d*. . . . . Amos 5:8
who shall not taste *d* . . . . Matt 16:28
but has passed from *d* . . . . John 5:24
he shall never see *d* . . . . . . John 8:51
Nevertheless *d* reigned . . . . Rom 5:14
as sin reigned in *d*. . . . . . . Rom 5:21
D no longer has . . . . Rom 6:9
the wages of sin is *d* . . . . . Rom 6:23
to bear fruit to *d* . . . . Rom 7:5
proclaim the Lord's *d*. . . . 1 Cor 11:26
since by man came *d* . . . . 1 Cor 15:21
D is swallowed up in . . . . 1 Cor 15:54
The sting of *d* is sin . . . . . 1 Cor 15:56
we are the aroma of *d*. . . . 2 Cor 2:16
d is working in us . . . . 2 Cor 4:12
the world produces *d* . . . . . 2 Cor 7:10
to the point of *d*. . . . . Phil 2:8
d crowned with glory. . . . . . Heb 2:9
who had the power of *d*. . . . Heb 2:14
that he did not see *d* . . . . . Heb 11:5
brings forth *d* . . . . James 1:15
to God, being put to *d* . . . 1 Pet 3:18
is sin leading to *d* . . . . . . 1 John 5:16
Be faithful until *d*. . . . . Rev 2:10
Over such the second *d* . . . . Rev 20:6
shall be no more *d* . . . . Rev 21:4
which is the second *d* . . . . . Rev 21:8

DEBIR
City of Judah; captured by Joshua,
    Josh 10:38, 39
Recaptured by Othniel; formerly
    called Kirjath Sepher, Josh 15:15–
    17; Judg 1:11–13

DEBORAH
A prophetess and judge, Judg 4:4–14
Composed song of triumph,
    Judg 5:1–31

DEBTOR
I am a *d* both to . . . . Rom 1:14
that he is a *d* to keep . . . . . . Gal 5:3

DEBTORS
as we forgive our *d* . . . . . . Matt 6:12
of his master's *d* . . . . Luke 16:5
brethren, we are *d*. . . . . Rom 8:12
and they are their *d* . . . . . Rom 15:27

DECEIT
spirit there is no *d* . . . . Ps 32:2
from speaking *d* . . . . Ps 34:13
d shall not dwell . . . . Ps 101:7
D is in the heart of . . . . . . Prov 12:20
Nor any *d* in His. . . . . Is 53:9
They hold fast to *d* . . . . Jer 8:5
in whom is no *d* . . . . John 1:47
"O full of all *d* . . . . Acts 13:10
philosophy and empty *d* . . . . Col 2:8
no sin, nor was *d* . . . . 1 Pet 2:22
mouth was found no *d*. . . . . Rev 14:5

DECEITFUL
deliver me from the *d* . . . . . . Ps 43:1
d men shall not. . . . . Ps 55:23
of the wicked are *d* . . . . . . Prov 12:5
of an enemy are *d*. . . . . . . Prov 27:6
"The heart is *d* . . . . Jer 17:9
are false apostles, *d* . . . . 2 Cor 11:13

DECEITFULLY
an idol, nor sworn *d* . . . . . . Ps 24:4
the word of God *d* . . . . . . 2 Cor 4:2

DECEITFULNESS
this world and the *d* . . . . Matt 13:22
hardened through the *d* . . . . Heb 3:13

DECEIVE
'Do not *d* yourselves. . . . . . Jer 37:9
rise up and *d* many. . . . . . Matt 24:11
wonders to *d* . . . . Matt 24:24

Let no one *d* himself . . . . . 1 Cor 3:18
Let no one *d* you with . . . . . . Eph 5:6
we have no sin, we *d*. . . . . 1 John 1:8

DECEIVED
"The serpent *d* . . . . Gen 3:13
d heart has turned him . . . . . Is 44:20
by the commandment, *d* . . Rom 7:11
as the serpent *d* . . . . 2 Cor 11:3
but the woman being *d* . . 1 Tim 2:14
deceiving and being *d* . . . . 2 Tim 3:13

DECEIVER
"But cursed be the *d* . . . . . . Mal 1:14
how that *d* said. . . . . Matt 27:63
This is a *d* and an. . . . . 2 John 7

DECEIVES
heed that no one *d* . . . . . . Matt 24:4
d his own heart. . . . . James 1:26

DECENTLY
all things be done *d* . . . . 1 Cor 14:40

DECEPTION
d all the day long . . . . Ps 38:12

DECEPTIVE
you with *d* words . . . . 2 Pet 2:3

DECISION
but its every *d* . . . . Prov 16:33
in the valley of *d* . . . . Joel 3:14

DECLARE
The heavens *d* the. . . . . Ps 19:1
d Your name to My . . . . Ps 22:22
d what He had done . . . . . . Ps 66:16
d that the LORD is. . . . . Ps 92:15
d His generation. . . . . Is 53:8
"I will *d* Your name . . . . . . Heb 2:12
seen and heard we *d*. . . . . 1 John 1:3

DECLARED
the Father, He has *d* . . . . . John 1:18
and *d* to be the Son of . . . . . Rom 1:4

DECREE
"I will declare the *d* . . . . Ps 2:7
d which shall not pass. . . . . Ps 148:6
in those days that a *d* . . . . . Luke 2:1

DEDICATED
house and has not *d*. . . . . Deut 20:5
every *d* thing in. . . . . Ezek 44:29
first covenant was *d*. . . . . . Heb 9:18

DEDICATION
sacrifices at the *d*. . . . . . . Ezra 6:17
it was the Feast of *D* . . . . John 10:22

DEED
d has been done . . . . Judg 19:30
you do a charitable *d*. . . . . . Matt 6:2
you do in word or *d* . . . . . . Col 3:17

DEEDS
Declare His *d* among. . . . . . . Ps 9:11
vengeance on their *d* . . . . . . Ps 99:8
harlot by their own *d* . . . . Ps 106:39
declare His *d* among . . . . Is 12:4
they surpass the *d* . . . . Jer 5:28
because their *d* . . . . John 3:19
You do the *d* . . . . John 8:41
one according to his *d* . . . . . Rom 2:6
you put to death the *d* . . . . Rom 8:13
shares in his evil *d* . . . . . . 2 John 11

DEEP
LORD God caused a *d* . . . . . . Gen 2:21
He lays up the *d* . . . . Ps 33:7
D calls unto *d* . . . . Ps 42:7
In His hand are the *d* . . . . . . Ps 95:4
His wonders in the *d* . . . . . Ps 107:24
put out in *d* darkness . . . . Prov 20:20
led them through the *d* . . . . Is 63:13

d closed around me . . . . Jon 2:5
d uttered its voice. . . . . Hab 3:10
"Launch out into the *d*. . . . . Luke 5:4
I have been in the *d* . . . . 2 Cor 11:25

DEEPER
D than Sheol . . . . Job 11:8

DEEPLY
Drink, yes, drink *d* . . . . Song 5:1
But He sighed *d* . . . . Mark 8:12

DEER
like the feet of *d*. . . . . Ps 18:33
As the *d* pants for the water . . Ps 42:1
lame shall leap like a *d*. . . . . Is 35:6

DEFEATED
and Israel was *d* . . . . 1 Sam 4:10

DEFECT
who has any *d*. . . . . Lev 21:17

DEFEND
'For I will *d* this . . . . 2 Kin 19:34
d my own ways before. . . . . Job 13:15
D the poor and . . . . Ps 82:3
d the fatherless. . . . . Is 1:17
of hosts *d* Jerusalem. . . . . Is 31:5

DEFENDER
a *d* of widows . . . . Ps 68:5

DEFENSE
For wisdom is a *d* . . . . Eccl 7:12
d will be the . . . . Is 33:16
am appointed for the *d* . . . . Phil 1:17
d no one stood with me . . 2 Tim 4:16
be ready to give a *d* . . . . . 1 Pet 3:15

DEFILE
the heart, and they *d* . . . . Matt 15:18
also these dreamers *d*. . . . . . . Jude 8

DEFILED
d the dwelling place . . . . Ps 74:7
For your hands are *d* . . . . Is 59:3
lest they should be *d*. . . . . John 18:28
to those who are *d* . . . . Titus 1:15
and conscience are *d* . . . . . Titus 1:15
even the garment *d* . . . . Jude 23

DEFILES
mouth, this *d* a man. . . . . . Matt 15:11
d the temple of God. . . . . . 1 Cor 3:17
it anything that *d* . . . . Rev 21:27

DEFRAUD
d his brother in this . . . . . 1 Thess 4:6

DEGENERATE
before Me into the *d*. . . . . . . Jer 2:21
d is your heart . . . . Ezek 16:30

DEGREES
go forward ten *d* . . . . 2 Kin 20:9

DELICACIES
let me eat of their *d*. . . . . . Ps 141:4
Do not desire his *d* . . . . . . Prov 23:3
of the king's *d* . . . . Dan 1:5

DELICATE
be called tender and *d*. . . . . . Is 47:1
a lovely and *d* woman. . . . . . Jer 6:2

DELIGHT
the LORD as great *d*. . . . . 1 Sam 15:22
And his heart took *d*. . . . . 2 Chr 17:6
Will He *d* himself in. . . . . . Job 27:10
But his *d* is in the . . . . Ps 1:2
D yourself also in the . . . . . . Ps 37:4
I *d* to do Your will . . . . Ps 40:8
Your law had been my *d* . . Ps 119:92
d ourselves with love . . . . . Prov 7:18
And I was daily His *d* . . . . Prov 8:30
truthfully are His *d* . . . . . Prov 12:22
And let your soul *d* . . . . Is 55:2

call the Sabbath a *d*. . . . . . Is 58:13
For I *d* in the law of . . . . . . Rom 7:22

DELIGHTED
The LORD *d* only in . . . . . . Deut 10:15

DELIGHTS
O love, with your *d* . . . . . . Song 7:6
For the LORD *d* in you. . . . . . Is 62:4
forever, because He *d* . . . . . Mic 7:18

DELILAH
Deceives Samson, Judg 16:4–22

DELIVER
d them out of the hand . . . . . Ex 3:8
He shall *d* you in six . . . . . . Job 5:19
is no one who can *d* . . . . . . Job 10:7
'*D* him from going down . . Job 33:24
Let Him *d* Him . . . . Ps 22:8
d their soul from . . . . Ps 33:19
I will *d* him and honor . . . . . Ps 91:15
d you from the immoral . . . Prov 2:16
wickedness will not *d* . . . . . . Eccl 8:8
have I no power to *d* . . . . Is 50:2
we serve is able to *d*. . . . . . Dan 3:17
into temptation, but . . . . . . Matt 6:13
let Him *d* Him now if . . . . Matt 27:43
d such a one to Satan . . . . . 1 Cor 5:5
And the Lord will *d* . . . . . . 2 Tim 4:18
d the godly out of. . . . . 2 Pet 2:9

DELIVERANCE
d He gives to His king . . . . . Ps 18:50
but *d* is of the LORD . . . . . . Prov 21:31
not accepting *d*. . . . . Heb 11:35

DELIVERED
d the poor who cried . . . . . Job 29:12
for You have *d* my soul . . . . Ps 56:13
For He has *d* the life. . . . . . Jer 20:13
All things have been *d* . . . Matt 11:27
who was *d* up because . . . . Rom 4:25
But now we have been *d* . . . Rom 7:6
who *d* us from so great . . . 2 Cor 1:10
was once for all *d*. . . . . Jude 3

DELIVERER
the LORD raised up a *d* . . . . . Judg 3:9
LORD gave Israel a *d*. . . . . 2 Kin 13:5
D will come out of. . . . . . . Rom 11:26

DELIVERERS
d who saved them . . . . Neh 9:27

DELIVERS
d the kingdom to God . . . 1 Cor 15:24
even Jesus who *d* . . . . . . 1 Thess 1:10

DELUSION
send them strong *d*. . . . 2 Thess 2:11

DEMAS
Follows Paul, Col 4:14
Forsakes Paul, 2 Tim 4:10

DEMETRIUS
A silversmith at Ephesus,
    Acts 19:24–31
——— A good Christian, 3 John 12

DEMON
Jesus rebuked the *d* . . . . . Matt 17:18
you say, 'He has a *d* . . . . . Luke 7:33
and have a *d*. . . . . John 8:48

DEMONIC
is earthly, sensual, *d*. . . . . James 3:15

DEMONS
They sacrificed to *d*. . . . . . Deut 32:17
their daughters to *d* . . . . . Ps 106:37
authority over all *d* . . . . . . Luke 9:1
the *d* are subject . . . . Luke 10:17
Lord and the cup of *d* . . . 1 Cor 10:21
Even the *d* believe. . . . . . James 2:19

a dwelling place of *d* . . . . . Rev 18:2

DEMONSTRATE
faith, to *d* His . . . . Rom 3:25

DEMONSTRATES
d His own love toward . . . . . Rom 5:8

DEN
in the viper's *d* . . . . Is 11:8
by My name, become a *d* . . . Jer 7:11
cast him into the *d* . . . . . . Dan 6:16
it a '*d* of thieves. . . . . Matt 21:13

DENARIUS
the laborers for a *d* . . . . . . Matt 20:2
they brought Him a *d* . . . . Matt 22:19
quart of wheat for a *d* . . . . . Rev 6:6

DENIED
before men will be *d*. . . . . . Luke 12:9
Peter then *d* again. . . . . . . John 18:27
d the Holy One and the. . . . Acts 3:14
things cannot be *d*. . . . . . . Acts 19:36
household, he has *d* . . . . . . 1 Tim 5:8
word, and have not *d* . . . . . . Rev 3:8

DENIES
But whoever *d* . . . . Matt 10:33
d that Jesus is the. . . . . . . 1 John 2:22

DENS
lie down in their *d*. . . . . . . Ps 104:22
and mountains, in *d* . . . . . Heb 11:38

DENY
lest I be full and *d*. . . . . . . Prov 30:9
let him *d* himself. . . . . Matt 16:24
He cannot *d* Himself. . . . . 2 Tim 2:13
in works they *d*. . . . . Titus 1:16
d the only Lord. . . . . Jude 4
d My faith even. . . . . Rev 2:13

DENYING
but *d* its power . . . . 2 Tim 3:5
d ungodliness and . . . . Titus 2:12
d the Lord who bought . . . . 2 Pet 2:1

DEPART
scepter shall not *d* . . . . . . Gen 49:10
they say to God, '*D* . . . . . . Job 21:14
D from evil. . . . . Ps 34:14
fear the LORD and *d*. . . . . . Prov 3:7
the mountains, shall *d*. . . . . Is 54:10
on the left hand, '*D* . . . . . Matt 25:41
will *d* from the faith . . . . . . 1 Tim 4:1

DEPARTED
the day that you *d* . . . . Deut 9:7

DEPARTING
heart of unbelief in *d*. . . . . . Heb 3:12

DEPARTURE
d savage wolves will . . . . . Acts 20:29
and the time of my *d* . . . . . 2 Tim 4:6

DEPRESSION
of man causes *d*. . . . . Prov 12:25

DEPRIVE
d myself of good. . . . . Eccl 4:8
d one another except . . . . . 1 Cor 7:5

DEPTH
because they had no *d* . . . . Matt 13:5
nor height nor *d* . . . . Rom 8:39
Oh, the *d* of the . . . . Rom 11:33
width and length and *d*. . . . Eph 3:18

DEPTHS
d have covered them . . . . . . Ex 15:5
The *d* also trembled. . . . . . . Ps 77:16
my soul from the *d* . . . . Ps 86:13
led them through the *d*. . . . Ps 106:9
go down again to the *d*. . . . Ps 107:26
d I was brought forth . . . . . Prov 8:24
our sins into the *d*. . . . . Mic 7:19

have not known the *d* . . . . . Rev 2:24

DERANGED
the nations are *d* . . . . Jer 51:7

DERBE
Paul visits, Acts 14:6, 20
Paul meets Timothy at, Acts 16:1

DERISION
shall hold them in *d* . . . . Ps 2:4
I am in *d* daily . . . . Jer 20:7

DESCEND
His glory shall not *d* . . . . . . Ps 49:17
d now from the cross . . . . Mark 15:32
Lord Himself will *d* . . . . 1 Thess 4:16
This wisdom does not *d* . . James 3:15

DESCENDANTS
All you *d* of Jacob . . . . Ps 22:23
d shall inherit the . . . . Ps 25:13
In the LORD all the *d* . . . . . . Is 45:25
"We are Abraham's *d* . . . . John 8:33

DESCENDED
because the LORD *d* . . . . Ex 19:18
that He also first *d* . . . . Eph 4:9
He who *d* is also the . . . . . . Eph 4:10

DESCENDING
were ascending and *d* . . . . Gen 28:12
"I saw the Spirit *d* . . . . John 1:32
God ascending and *d* . . . . John 1:51
the holy Jerusalem, *d* . . . . Rev 21:10

DESERT
d shall rejoice . . . . Is 35:1
and rivers in the *d* . . . . Is 43:19
'Look, He is in the *d* . . . . Matt 24:26

DESERTED
d place by Himself . . . . . . Matt 14:13

DESERTS
led them through the *d* . . . . . Is 48:21
They wandered in *d* . . . . . Heb 11:38

DESERVE
to them what they *d* . . . . Ps 28:4
d I will judge them . . . . Ezek 7:27

DESIGN
with an artistic *d* . . . . Ex 26:31
may keep its whole *d* . . . . Ezek 43:11

DESIRABLE
the eyes, and a tree *d* . . . . . . Gen 3:6
d that we should leave . . . . . Acts 6:2

DESIRE
d shall be for your . . . . Gen 3:16
for we do not *d* . . . . Job 21:14
him his heart's *d* . . . . Ps 21:2
Behold, You *d* truth in . . . . . . Ps 51:6
upon earth that I *d* . . . . Ps 73:25
the *d* of the wicked . . . . Ps 112:10
and satisfy the *d* . . . . Ps 145:16
The *d* of the lazy . . . . Prov 21:25
a burden, and *d* fails . . . . . . Eccl 12:5
the *d* of our soul is . . . . Is 26:8
d I have desired . . . . Luke 22:15
"Father, I *d* that . . . . John 17:24
all manner of evil *d* . . . . . . Rom 7:8
Brethren, my heart's *d* . . . . Rom 10:1
d the best gifts . . . . 1 Cor 12:31
d spiritual gifts . . . . 1 Cor 14:1
the two, having a *d* . . . . . . Phil 1:23
passion, evil *d* . . . . Col 3:5
d has conceived . . . . James 1:15

DESIRED
d are they than gold . . . . . . Ps 19:10
One thing I have *d* . . . . Ps 27:4
guides them to their *d* . . . Ps 107:30
What is *d* in a man is . . . . Prov 19:22

Whatever my eyes *d* . . . . . . Eccl 2:10
desire I have *d* . . . . Luke 22:15

DESIRES
Who is the man who *d* . . . . . Ps 34:12
shall give you the *d* . . . . Ps 37:4
the devil, and the *d* . . . . . John 8:44
fulfilling the *d* . . . . Eph 2:3
not come from your *d* . . . . James 4:1

DESOLATE
on me, for I am *d* . . . . Ps 25:16
the wilderness in a *d* . . . . . . Ps 107:4
my children and am *d* . . . . . Is 49:21
any more be termed *D* . . . . . Is 62:4
to make your land *d* . . . . Jer 4:7
house is left to you *d* . . . . Matt 23:38
one hour she is made *d* . . . . Rev 18:19

DESOLATION
the 'abomination of *d* . . . . Matt 24:15
then know that its *d* . . . . . Luke 21:20

DESOLATIONS
LORD, who has made *d* . . . . . Ps 46:8

DESPAIRED
turned my heart and *d* . . . . Eccl 2:20
strength, so that we *d* . . . . 2 Cor 1:8

DESPERATELY
he flees *d* from its . . . . Job 27:22

DESPISE
if you *d* My statutes . . . . . Lev 26:15
d Me shall be lightly . . . . 1 Sam 2:30
d your mother when she . . Prov 23:22
d your feast days . . . . Amos 5:21
to you priests who *d* . . . . . . Mal 1:6
one and *d* the other . . . . . . Matt 6:24
d the riches of His . . . . Rom 2:4
d the church of God . . . . 1 Cor 11:22
and *d* authority . . . . 2 Pet 2:10

DESPISED
poor man's wisdom is *d* . . . . Eccl 9:16
d the word of the Holy . . . . . . Is 5:24
He is *d* and rejected . . . . Is 53:3
the things which are *d* . . . 1 Cor 1:28

DESPISES
wisdom *d* his neighbor . . . Prov 11:12
d the word will be . . . . . . Prov 13:13
d his neighbor sins . . . . . . Prov 14:21
but a foolish man *d* . . . . . . Prov 15:20
d the scepter of My . . . . . . Ezek 21:10

DESPISING
the cross, *d* the shame . . . . . Heb 12:2

DESTINY
did not consider her *d* . . . . . Lam 1:9

DESTITUTE
the prayer of the *d* . . . . . . Ps 102:17
of corrupt minds and *d* . . . . 1 Tim 6:5
sister is naked and *d* . . . . James 2:15

DESTROY
d the righteous . . . . Gen 18:23
d all the wicked . . . . Ps 101:8
of the LORD I will *d* . . . . . . Ps 118:10
the wicked He will *d* . . . . . Ps 145:20
Why should you *d* . . . . Eccl 7:16
shall not hurt nor *d* . . . . Is 11:9
have mercy, but will *d* . . . . Jer 13:14
d them with double . . . . . . Jer 17:18
I did not come to *d* . . . . . . Matt 5:17
Him who is able to *d* . . . . Matt 10:28
Barabbas and *d* Jesus . . . . Matt 27:20
d this temple . . . . Mark 14:58
to save life or to *d* . . . . Luke 6:9
d men's lives but to . . . . . . Luke 9:56
d the work of God for . . . . Rom 14:20
d the wisdom of the . . . . . 1 Cor 1:19

foods, but God will *d* . . . . 1 Cor 6:13
able to save and to *d* . . . . James 4:12

DESTROYED
d all living things . . . . Gen 7:23
d those who hated me . . 2 Sam 22:41
My people are *d* . . . . Hos 4:6
"O Israel, you are *d* . . . . . . Hos 13:9
house, this tent, is *d* . . . . . 2 Cor 5:1

DESTROYER
the paths of the *d* . . . . Ps 17:4
him who is a great *d* . . . . . Prov 18:9
destroyed by the *d* . . . . . 1 Cor 10:10

DESTRUCTION
not be afraid of *d* . . . . Job 5:21
D has no covering . . . . Job 26:6
d come upon him . . . . Ps 35:8
cast them down to *d* . . . . . . Ps 73:18
You turn man to *d* . . . . Ps 90:3
d that lays waste . . . . Ps 91:6
your life from *d* . . . . Ps 103:4
d will come to the . . . . . . Prov 10:29
Pride goes before a *d* . . . . Prov 16:18
d the heart of a man . . . . Prov 18:12
called the City of *D* . . . . . . Is 19:18
neither wasting nor *d* . . . . . Is 60:18
heifer, but *d* comes . . . . . . Jer 46:20
wrath prepared for *d* . . . . . Rom 9:22
one to Satan for the *d* . . . . 1 Cor 5:5
whose end is *d* . . . . Phil 3:19
then sudden *d* . . . . 1 Thess 5:3
with everlasting *d* . . . . . . 2 Thess 1:9
which drown men in *d* . . . 1 Tim 6:9
twist to their own *d* . . . . . 2 Pet 3:16

DESTRUCTIVE
bring in *d* heresies . . . . 2 Pet 2:1

DETERMINED
Since his days are *d* . . . . . . Job 14:5
of hosts will make a *d* . . . . Is 10:23
"Seventy weeks are *d* . . . . . Dan 9:24
d their preappointed . . . . Acts 17:26
For I *d* not to know . . . . . . 1 Cor 2:2

DETESTABLE
shall not eat any *d* . . . . . . Deut 14:3

DEVICE
there is no work or *d* . . . . . Eccl 9:10

DEVICES
not ignorant of his *d* . . . . 2 Cor 2:11

DEVIL
to be tempted by the *d* . . . . Matt 4:1
prepared for the *d* . . . . . . Matt 25:41
forty days by the *d* . . . . . . Luke 4:2
then the *d* comes and . . . . Luke 8:12
and one of you is a *d* . . . . . John 6:70
of your father the *d* . . . . . John 8:44
d having already put . . . . John 13:2
give place to the *d* . . . . . . Eph 4:27
the wiles of the *d* . . . . Eph 6:11
the snare of the *d* . . . . . . 2 Tim 2:26
Resist the *d* and he . . . . . James 4:7
the works of the *d* . . . . . . 1 John 3:8
contending with the *d* . . . . . Jude 9
Indeed, the *d* is about . . . . Rev 2:10

DEVIOUS
crooked, and who are *d* . . . Prov 2:15

DEVISE
Do not *d* evil against . . . . Prov 3:29
Woe to those who *d* . . . . . . Mic 2:1

DEVISES
d wickedness on his . . . . Ps 36:4
he *d* evil continually . . . . . Prov 6:14
d wicked plans to . . . . Is 32:7
But a generous man *d* . . . . . Is 32:8

DEVOID
He who is *d* of wisdom . . . Prov 11:12

DEVOTED
d offering is most . . . . Lev 27:28
"Every *d* thing in . . . . . . Num 18:14
Your servant, who is *d* . . . . . Ps 119:38

DEVOUR
A fire shall *d* before. . . . . Ps 50:3
For you *d* widows' . . . . . . Matt 23:14
bite and *d* one another. . . . Gal 5:15
seeking whom he may *d* . . . 1 Pet 5:8
d her Child as . . . . Rev 12:4

DEVOURED
Some wild beast has *d*. . . . Gen 37:20
rebel, you shall be *d* . . . . Is 1:20
the curse has *d*. . . . . Is 24:6
Your sword has *d* . . . . Jer 2:30
For shame has *d* . . . . Jer 3:24
have *d* their judges. . . . . Hos 7:7
trees, the locust *d* . . . . Amos 4:9
birds came and *d* them. . . . Matt 13:4
of heaven and *d* them . . . . . Rev 20:9

DEVOURER
I will rebuke the *d* . . . . Mal 3:11

DEVOURING
You love all *d* words . . . . Ps 52:4
the flame of *d* fire . . . . Is 29:6

DEVOUT
man was just and *d* . . . . . Luke 2:25
d men carried . . . . Acts 8:2
d soldier from among . . . . Acts 10:7
d proselytes. . . . . Acts 13:43

DEW
God give you of the *d* . . . . Gen 27:28
shall also drop *d* . . . . Deut 33:28
his favor is like a . . . . Prov 19:12
your *d* is like the *d* . . . . Is 26:19
like the early *d* . . . . Hos 6:4
many peoples, like *d* . . . . . . Mic 5:7

DIADEM
LORD, and a royal *d* . . . . Is 62:3

DIADEMS
ten horns, and seven *d* . . . . Rev 12:3

DIAMOND
d it is engraved. . . . . Jer 17:1

DIBON
Amorite town, Num 21:30
Taken by Israel, Num 32:2–5
Destruction of, foretold, Jer 48:18, 22

DICTATES
according to the *d*. . . . . Jer 23:17

DIE
it you shall surely *d* . . . . Gen 2:17
but a person shall *d* . . . . . 2 Chr 25:4
sees wise men *d*. . . . . Ps 49:10
I shall not *d* . . . . Ps 118:17
who are appointed to *d*. . . . Prov 31:8
how does a wise man *d* . . . . Eccl 2:16
born, and a time to *d*. . . . . . Eccl 3:2
why should you *d* . . . . Eccl 7:17
wicked way, he shall *d* . . . . Ezek 3:19
"Even if I have to *d*. . . . . Matt 26:35
nor can they *d* . . . . Luke 20:36
eat of it and not *d*. . . . . . . John 6:50
to you that you will *d*. . . . . John 8:24
though he may *d* . . . . John 11:25
that one man should *d*. . . . John 11:50
that Jesus would *d*. . . . . . John 11:51
our law He ought to *d* . . . . John 19:7
the flesh you will *d* . . . . . . Rom 8:13
For as in Adam all *d* . . . . 1 Cor 15:22
and to *d* is gain . . . . Phil 1:21

for men to *d* once. . . . . Heb 9:27
are the dead who *d* . . . . . . Rev 14:13

DIED
And all flesh *d* . . . . Gen 7:21
"Oh, that we had *d*. . . . . Ex 16:3
was that the beggar *d*. . . . Luke 16:22
in due time Christ *d* . . . . . . Rom 5:6
Christ *d* for us . . . . Rom 5:8
For he who has *d* . . . . Rom 6:7
Now if we *d* with. . . . . Rom 6:8
sin revived and I *d* . . . . Rom 7:9
that if One *d* for all . . . . 2 Cor 5:14
and He *d* for all . . . . 2 Cor 5:15
through the law *d*. . . . . Gal 2:19
who *d* for us . . . . 1 Thess 5:10
for if we *d* with Him . . . . . 2 Tim 2:11
These all *d* in faith . . . . . . Heb 11:13
having *d* to sins . . . . 1 Pet 2:24

DIES
made alive unless it *d* . . . 1 Cor 15:36

DIFFERS
for one star *d* from . . . . . . 1 Cor 15:41

DIFFUSED
By what way is light *d* . . . . Job 38:24

DILIGENCE
d is man's. . . . . Prov 12:27
d it produced in you . . . . . 2 Cor 7:11
of your love by the *d*. . . . . . 2 Cor 8:8

DILIGENT
and my spirit makes *d* . . . . . Ps 77:6
d makes rich . . . . Prov 10:4
of the *d* will rule . . . . Prov 12:24
d shall be made rich . . . . . . Prov 13:4
Let us therefore be *d*. . . . . . Heb 4:11

DILIGENTLY
d followed every good. . . . 1 Tim 5:10
d lest anyone fall . . . . Heb 12:15

DIM
His eyes were not *d*. . . . . . Deut 34:7
the windows grow *d* . . . . . . Eccl 12:3
the gold has become *d* . . . . . Lam 4:1

DIMLY
we see in a mirror, *d* . . . . 1 Cor 13:12

DINAH
Daughter of Leah, Gen 30:20, 21
Defiled by Shechem, Gen 34:1–24
Avenged by brothers, Gen 34:25–31

DINE
asked Him to *d* with . . . . . Luke 11:37
come in to him and *d* . . . . . Rev 3:20

DINNER
I have prepared my *d*. . . . . Matt 22:4
invites you to *d* . . . . 1 Cor 10:27

DIOTREPHES
Unruly church member, 3 John 9, 10

DIP
d your piece of bread . . . . . Ruth 2:14

DIPPED
d his finger in the. . . . . Lev 9:9
of bread when I have *d* . . John 13:26
clothed with a robe *d* . . . . . Rev 19:13

DIRECT
the morning I will *d* . . . . Ps 5:3
d their work in truth . . . . Is 61:8
Now may the Lord *d* . . . . 2 Thess 3:5

DIRT
I cast them out like *d* . . . . . Ps 18:42
cast up mire and *d*. . . . . Is 57:20

DISAPPEARS
As water *d* from the . . . . . . Job 14:11

DISARMED
d principalities. . . . . Col 2:15

DISARMS
and *d* the mighty. . . . . Job 12:21

DISASTER
D will come upon . . . . Ezek 7:26
you shall see *d* . . . . Zeph 3:15
voyage will end with *d*. . . . Acts 27:10

DISCERN
Can I *d* between the . . . . 2 Sam 19:35
Then you shall again *d* . . . . Mal 3:18
d the face of the sky . . . . . . Matt 16:3
senses exercised to *d*. . . . . . Heb 5:14

DISCERNED
they are spiritually *d* . . . . 1 Cor 2:14

DISCERNER
d of the thoughts . . . . Heb 4:12

DISCERNMENT
and takes away the *d* . . . . Job 12:20

DISCERNS
a wise man's heart *d* . . . . . . Eccl 8:5

DISCIPLE
d is not above his . . . . . . Matt 10:24
in the name of a *d* . . . . . Matt 10:42
he cannot be My *d* . . . . . Luke 14:26
d whom Jesus loved . . . . . John 21:7

DISCIPLES
but Your *d* do not fast. . . . Matt 9:14
d transgress the. . . . . Matt 15:2
took the twelve *d* . . . . . . Matt 20:17
My word, you are My *d* . . . John 8:31
to become His *d* . . . . John 9:27
but we are Moses' *d* . . . . . John 9:28
so you will be My *d*. . . . . . John 15:8

DISCIPLINE
Harsh *d* is for him who . . . Prov 15:10

DISCIPLINES
but he who loves him *d*. . . Prov 13:24

DISCLOSE
d my dark saying . . . . Ps 49:4

DISCORD
and one who sows *d* . . . . . . Prov 6:19

DISCOURAGED
will not fail nor be *d* . . . . Is 42:4
lest they become *d*. . . . . Col 3:21
you become weary and *d*. . . Heb 12:3

DISCRETION
D will preserve you . . . . Prov 2:11
out knowledge and *d*. . . . . . Prov 8:12
woman who lacks *d*. . . . . . Prov 11:22
The *d* of a man makes. . . . Prov 19:11
the heavens at His *d*. . . . . . Jer 10:12

DISFIGURE
d their faces that. . . . . Matt 6:16

DISGUISES
and he *d* his face . . . . Job 24:15
He who hates, *d*. . . . . Prov 26:24

DISHONOR
d who wish me evil . . . . Ps 40:14
d the pride of all . . . . Is 23:9
My Father, and you *d* Me . . John 8:49
d their bodies among . . . . . Rom 1:24
and another for *d* . . . . Rom 9:21
It is sown in *d*. . . . . 1 Cor 15:43
honor and some for *d* . . . . 2 Tim 2:20

DISHONORED
But you have *d* the. . . . . . James 2:6

DISHONORS
For son *d* father . . . . Mic 7:6
covered, *d* his head . . . . . 1 Cor 11:4

DISOBEDIENCE
d many were made . . . . Rom 5:19
works in the sons of *d* . . . . . Eph 2:2
d received a just . . . . Heb 2:2

DISOBEDIENT
out My hands to a *d* . . . . Rom 10:21
d, deceived, serving . . . . . . Titus 3:3
They stumble, being *d* . . . . 1 Pet 2:8
who formerly were *d* . . . . 1 Pet 3:20

DISORDERLY
for this *d* gathering . . . . . . Acts 19:40
brother who walks *d*. . . . . 2 Thess 3:6

DISPENSATION
d of the fullness of . . . . Eph 1:10
d of the grace of God . . . . . . Eph 3:2

DISPERSE
d them throughout the . . . Ezek 20:23

DISPERSION
intend to go to the *D* . . . . . John 7:35
the pilgrims of the *D* . . . . . . 1 Pet 1:1

DISPLEASE
LORD see it, and it *d*. . . . . Prov 24:18

DISPLEASED
that David had done *d*. . 2 Sam 11:27
You have been *d* . . . . Ps 60:1
they were greatly *d* . . . . . Matt 20:24
it, He was greatly *d* . . . . . Mark 10:14

DISPUTE
Now there was also a *d* . . Luke 22:24

DISPUTER
Where is the *d* of this . . . . 1 Cor 1:20

DISPUTES
d rather than godly . . . . . 1 Tim 1:4
but is obsessed with *d*. . . . 1 Tim 6:4
foolish and ignorant *d* . . . 2 Tim 2:23
But avoid foolish *d* . . . . Titus 3:9

DISQUALIFIED
myself should become *d* . 1 Cor 9:27
indeed you are *d* . . . . 2 Cor 13:5
though we may seem *d*. . . 2 Cor 13:7

DISQUIETED
And why are you *d* . . . . Ps 42:5

DISSENSION
had no small *d* and . . . . Acts 15:2

DISSENSIONS
selfish ambitions, *d* . . . . Gal 5:20

DISSIPATION
not accused of *d* . . . . Titus 1:6
in the same flood of *d* . . . . . 1 Pet 4:4

DISSOLVED
of heaven shall be *d* . . . . Is 34:4
the heavens will be *d* . . . . 2 Pet 3:12

DISTINCTION
and made no *d* . . . . Acts 15:9
For there is no *d*. . . . . Rom 10:12
compassion, making a *d* . . . . Jude 22

DISTRESS
me in the day of my *d* . . . . Gen 35:3
When you are in *d* . . . . Deut 4:30
my life from every *d* . . . . . 1 Kin 1:29
you out of dire *d* . . . . Job 36:16
keep you from *d* . . . . Job 36:19
d them in His deep . . . . Ps 2:5
on the LORD in *d*. . . . . Ps 118:5
a whirlwind, when *d*. . . . . . Prov 1:27
and on the earth *d* . . . . . . Luke 21:25
tribulation, or *d*. . . . . Rom 8:35
of the present *d* . . . . 1 Cor 7:26

DISTRESSED
heart within me is *d* . . . . . . Ps 143:4
troubled and deeply *d* . . . Mark 14:33

DISTRESSES
bring me out of my *d* . . . . . . Ps 25:17

DISTRIBUTE
that you have and *d*. . . . . Luke 18:22

DISTRIBUTED
and they *d* to each as . . . . . Acts 4:35
But as God has *d* . . . . 1 Cor 7:17

DISTRIBUTING
d to the needs of the . . . . . Rom 12:13

DITCH
will fall into a *d*. . . . . Matt 15:14

DIVERSITIES
There are *d*. . . . . 1 Cor 12:4

DIVIDE
D the living child. . . . . 1 Kin 3:25
d their tongues . . . . Ps 55:9
d the spoil with the . . . . . . Prov 16:19
d the inheritance. . . . . Luke 12:13
"Take this and *d* . . . . Luke 22:17

DIVIDED
and the waters were *d*. . . . . . Ex 14:21
death they were not *d* . . . 2 Sam 1:23
And You *d* the sea . . . . Neh 9:11
"Who has *d* a channel . . . . Job 38:25
shall they ever be *d* . . . . . Ezek 37:22
kingdom has been *d* . . . . . Dan 5:28
your land shall be *d* . . . . . Amos 7:17
"Every kingdom *d* . . . . . . Matt 12:25
and a house *d* against . . . Luke 11:17
in one house will be *d*. . . . Luke 12:52
So he *d* to them his . . . . . . Luke 15:12
appeared to them *d*. . . . . . . Acts 2:3
d them among all . . . . Acts 2:45
Is Christ *d*. . . . . 1 Cor 1:13
the great city was *d*. . . . . . Rev 16:19

DIVIDES
at home *d* the spoil . . . . Ps 68:12

DIVIDING
rightly *d* the word of . . . . 2 Tim 2:15

DIVINATION
shall you practice *d*. . . . . . Lev 19:26
D is on . . . . Prov 16:10
darkness without *d*. . . . . Mic 3:6
a spirit of *d* met us . . . . . . Acts 16:16

DIVINE
futility and who *d* . . . . Ezek 13:9
and her prophets *d* . . . . Mic 3:11
d service and the . . . . Heb 9:1
d power has given . . . . 2 Pet 1:3

DIVINERS
your prophets, your *d* . . . . . Jer 27:9

DIVISION
So there was a *d* . . . . John 7:43
piercing even to the *d* . . . . . Heb 4:12

DIVISIONS
note those who cause *d* . . . Rom 16:17
and that there be no *d*. . . . 1 Cor 1:10
envy, strife, and *d* . . . . 1 Cor 3:3
hear that there are *d* . . . . 1 Cor 11:18
persons, who cause *d* . . . . . . Jude 19

DIVISIVE
Reject a *d* man after . . . . . . Titus 3:10

DIVORCE
her a certificate of *d* . . . . . Deut 24:1
of your mother's *d* . . . . Is 50:1
a certificate of *d* . . . . Mark 10:4

DO
set in them to *d* evil . . . . . . Eccl 8:11
I will also *d* it . . . . Is 46:11
men to *d* to you, *d* . . . . . . Matt 7:12
d this and you will . . . . . . Luke 10:28

He sees the Father *d* . . . . . . John 5:19
without Me you can *d*. . . . . John 15:5
"Sirs, what must I *d* . . . . . Acts 16:30
d evil that good may . . . . . . Rom 3:8
For what I will to *d* . . . . . . Rom 7:15
good that I will to *d* . . . . . . Rom 7:19
or whatever you *d*, *d* . . . . 1 Cor 10:31
d all things through . . . . . . Phil 4:13
d in word or deed, ... Col 3:17
d good and to share . . . . . Heb 13:16
and *d* this or that . . . . James 4:15

DOCTRINE
said, 'My *d* is pure. . . . . Job 11:4
for I give you good *d* . . . . . Prov 4:2
idol is a worthless *d* . . . . . . Jer 10:8
of bread, but of the *d* . . . . Matt 16:12
What new *d* is this. . . . . . . Mark 1:27
"My *d* is not Mine . . . . John 7:16
Jerusalem with your *d*. . . . Acts 5:28
heart that form of *d* . . . . . . Rom 6:17
with every wind of *d*. . . . . . Eph 4:14
is contrary to sound *d*. . . . 1 Tim 1:10
followed my *d* . . . . 2 Tim 3:10
is profitable for *d*. . . . . 2 Tim 3:16
not endure sound *d*. . . . . . 2 Tim 4:3
in *d* showing. . . . . Titus 2:7
they may adorn the *d* . . . . Titus 2:10
not abide in the *d*. . . . . 2 John 9

DOCTRINES
the commandments and *d* . . Col 2:22
spirits and of *d* . . . . 1 Tim 4:1
various and strange *d* . . . . Heb 13:9

DOEG
An Edomite; chief of Saul's herds-
    men, 1 Sam 21:7
Betrays David, 1 Sam 22:9, 10
Kills 85 priests, 1 Sam 22:18, 19

DOERS
of God, but the *d*. . . . . Rom 2:13
But be *d* of the word . . . . . James 1:22

DOG
to David, "Am I a *d* . . . . 1 Sam 17:43
they growl like a *d* . . . . Ps 59:6
d returns to his own . . . . . Prov 26:11
d is better than a . . . . Eccl 9:4
d returns to his own . . . . . . 2 Pet 2:22

DOGS
Yes, they are greedy *d*. . . . . . Is 56:11
what is holy to the *d* . . . . . Matt 7:6
d eat the crumbs which . . Matt 15:27
Moreover the *d* came . . . . Luke 16:21
But outside are *d*. . . . . Rev 22:15

DOMINION
let them have *d* . . . . Gen 1:26
"*D* and fear belong . . . . Job 25:2
made him to have *d* . . . . Ps 8:6
let them not have *d* . . . . . . Ps 19:13
besides You have had *d*. . . . . Is 26:13
d is an everlasting . . . . Dan 4:34
sin shall not have *d* . . . . . . Rom 6:14
Not that we have *d* . . . . . . 2 Cor 1:24
glory and majesty, *d* . . . . . . Jude 25

DONKEY
d saw the Angel . . . . Num 22:23
Does the wild *d* . . . . Job 6:5
d its master's crib. . . . . Is 1:3
and riding on a *d* . . . . Zech 9:9
colt, the foal of a *d* . . . . . . Matt 21:5
He had found a young *d*. . . John 12:14
d speaking with a . . . . 2 Pet 2:16

DONKEY'S
d colt is born a man . . . . . . Job 11:12

DONKEYS
d quench their thirst . . . . . . Ps 104:11

a chariot of *d* . . . . Is 21:7
And the wild *d* stood . . . . Jer 14:6

DOOM
for the day of *d* . . . . Prov 16:4

DOOR
sin lies at the *d* . . . . Gen 4:7
keep watch over the *d* . . . . . Ps 141:3
d turns on its hinges . . . . . Prov 26:14
stone against the *d* . . . . . Matt 27:60
to you, I am the *d* . . . . John 10:7
and effective *d* . . . . 1 Cor 16:9
d was opened to me by . . . 2 Cor 2:12
would open to us a *d* . . . . Col 4:3
is standing at the *d* . . . . . . James 5:9
before you an open *d* . . . . . . Rev 3:8
I stand at the *d* . . . . Rev 3:20
and behold, a *d* . . . . Rev 4:1

DOORKEEPER
I would rather be a *d* . . . . . . Ps 84:10
To him the *d* . . . . John 10:3

DOORPOSTS
write them on the *d* . . . . . . Deut 6:9
"Strike the *d* . . . . Amos 9:1

DOORS
up, you everlasting *d* . . . . . . Ps 24:7
the entrance of the *d* . . . . . Prov 8:3
when the *d* are shut in . . . . Eccl 12:4
who would shut the *d* . . . . . Mal 1:10

DORCAS
Disciple at Joppa, also called
Tabitha; raised to life, Acts
9:36–42

DOUBLE
d portion of your spirit . . . . 2 Kin 2:9
from the Lord's hand *d* . . . . . Is 40:2
you shall have *d* honor . . . . . . Is 61:7
first I will repay *d* . . . . Jer 16:18
worthy of *d* honor . . . . 1 Tim 5:17
and repay her *d* . . . . Rev 18:6

DOUBLE-MINDED
I hate the *d* . . . . Ps 119:113
he is a *d* man . . . . James 1:8
your hearts, you *d* . . . . . . James 4:8

DOUBT
life shall hang in *d* . . . . . Deut 28:66
faith, why did you *d* . . . . Matt 14:31

DOUBTING
without wrath and *d* . . . . . 1 Tim 2:8
in faith, with no *d* . . . . . . James 1:6

DOUBTS
And why do *d* arise in . . . Luke 24:38
for I have *d* about you . . . . . Gal 4:20
doubting, for he who *d* . . . . James 1:6

DOVE
d found no resting . . . . Gen 8:9
I had wings like a *d* . . . . . . Ps 55:6
I mourned like a *d* . . . . Is 38:14
also is like a silly *d* . . . . . . Hos 7:11
descending like a *d* . . . . . . Matt 3:16

DOVES
and moan sadly like *d* . . . . . Is 59:11
and harmless as *d* . . . . . Matt 10:16
of those who sold *d* . . . . . Matt 21:12

DOWNCAST
who comforts the *d* . . . . . . 2 Cor 7:6

DRAGNET
gather them in their *d* . . . . Hab 1:15
d that was cast . . . . Matt 13:47

DRAGON
a great, fiery red *d* . . . . . . Rev 12:3
fought with the *d* . . . . Rev 12:7

they worshiped the *d* . . . . . Rev 13:4
He laid hold of the *d* . . . . . Rev 20:2

DRAIN
wicked of the earth *d* . . . . . . Ps 75:8

DRAINED
all faces are *d* . . . . Joel 2:6

DRANK
them, and they all *d* . . . . Mark 14:23
d the same spiritual . . . . . . 1 Cor 10:4

DRAW
d honey from the rock . . . Deut 32:13
me to *d* near to God . . . . Ps 73:28
and the years *d* . . . . Eccl 12:1
D me away . . . . Song 1:4
Woe to those who *d* . . . . Is 5:18
with joy you will *d* . . . . Is 12:3
"*D* some out now . . . . John 2:8
You have nothing to *d* . . . . John 4:11
will *d* all peoples . . . . John 12:32
let us *d* near with a . . . . . Heb 10:22
D near to God and He . . . . James 4:8

DRAWN
The wicked have *d* . . . . Ps 37:14
tempted when he is *d* . . . . James 1:14

DRAWS
and my life *d* near to . . . . Ps 88:3
your redemption *d* . . . . . . Luke 21:28

DREAD
fear of you and the *d* . . . . . . Gen 9:2
begin to put the *d* . . . . Deut 2:25

DREADFUL
of the great and *d* . . . . Mal 4:5

DREAM
Now Joseph had a *d* . . . . . . Gen 37:5
I speak to him in a *d* . . . . . Num 12:6
will fly away like a *d* . . . . . . Job 20:8
As a *d* when one awakes . . . Ps 73:20
like those who *d* . . . . Ps 126:1
For a *d* comes through . . . . . Eccl 5:3
her, shall be as a *d* . . . . Is 29:7
prophet who has a *d* . . . . . Jer 23:28
do not let the *d* . . . . Dan 4:19
your old men shall *d* . . . . . . Joel 2:28
to Joseph in a *d* . . . . Matt 2:13
things today in a *d* . . . . . . Matt 27:19
your old men shall *d* . . . . . . Acts 2:17

DREAMERS
d defile the flesh . . . . Jude 8

DREAMS
in the multitude of *d* . . . . . . Eccl 5:7
when a hungry man *d* . . . . . Is 29:8
Nebuchadnezzar had *d* . . . . Dan 2:1

DREGS
d shall all the wicked . . . . . . Ps 75:8
has settled on his *d* . . . . . . Jer 48:11

DRIED
My strength is *d* . . . . Ps 22:15
of her blood was *d* . . . . . . Mark 5:29
saw the fig tree *d* . . . . . . Mark 11:20
and its water was *d* . . . . . . Rev 16:12

DRIFT
have heard, lest we *d* . . . . . . Heb 2:1

DRINK
"What shall we *d* . . . . Ex 15:24
"Do not *d* wine or . . . . Lev 10:9
and let him *d* of the . . . . . . Job 21:20
gave me vinegar to *d* . . . . . Ps 69:21
D water from your own . . . . Prov 5:15
mocker, strong *d* . . . . Prov 20:1
lest they *d* and forget . . . . Prov 31:5
Give strong *d* to him . . . . . Prov 31:6

Let him *d* and forget . . . . . Prov 31:7
d your wine with a . . . . Eccl 9:7
follow intoxicating *d* . . . . Is 5:11
mixing intoxicating *d* . . . . . . Is 5:22
d the milk of the . . . . Is 60:16
My servants shall *d* . . . . . . Is 65:13
bosom, that you may *d* . . . . Is 66:11
d water by measure . . . . . Ezek 4:11
"Bring wine, let us *d* . . . . . Amos 4:1
to you of wine and *d* . . . . . . Mic 2:11
and you gave Me no *d* . . . Matt 25:42
that day when I *d* . . . . . . Matt 26:29
mingled with gall to *d* . . . Matt 27:34
with myrrh to *d* . . . . Mark 15:23
to her, "Give Me a *d* . . . . . . John 4:7
him come to Me and *d* . . . . John 7:37
d wine nor do anything . . Rom 14:21
do, as often as you *d* . . . . 1 Cor 11:25
all been made to *d* . . . . . . 1 Cor 12:13
No longer *d* only water . . . 1 Tim 5:23
has made all nations *d* . . . . Rev 14:8

DRINKS
to her, "Whoever *d* . . . . . . John 4:13
d My blood has . . . . John 6:54
For he who eats and *d* . . . 1 Cor 11:29
For the earth which *d* . . . . . Heb 6:7

DRIPPING
wife are a continual *d* . . . . Prov 19:13
His lips are lilies, *d* . . . . . . Song 5:13

DRIVE
of the wicked *d* . . . . Ps 36:11
They shall *d* you from . . . . . Dan 4:25
temple and began to *d* . . . Mark 11:15

DRIVEN
They were *d* out from . . . . . Job 30:5
Let them be *d* backward . . . . Ps 40:14
sail and so were *d* . . . . . . Acts 27:17
a wave of the sea *d* . . . . . . James 1:6

DROP
They *d* on the pastures . . . . Ps 65:12
the nations are as a *d* . . . . . Is 40:15

DROSS
of the earth like *d* . . . . . . Ps 119:119
Take away the *d* . . . . Prov 25:4
purge away your *d* . . . . Is 1:25
of Israel has become *d* . . . Ezek 22:18

DROUGHT
through a land of *d* . . . . Jer 2:6
in the year of *d* . . . . Jer 17:8
For I called for a *d* . . . . Hag 1:11

DROVE
So He *d* out the man . . . . . Gen 3:24
temple of God and *d* . . . . Matt 21:12
a whip of cords, He *d* . . . . John 2:15

DROWN
nor can the floods *d* . . . . . Song 8:7
harmful lusts which *d* . . . . 1 Tim 6:9

DROWSINESS
d will clothe a . . . . Prov 23:21

DRUNK
of the wine and was *d* . . . . Gen 9:21
d my wine with my milk . . . Song 5:1
you afflicted, and *d* . . . . Is 51:21
My anger, made them *d* . . . . Is 63:6
be satiated and made *d* . . . Jer 46:10
the guests have well *d* . . . . John 2:10
For these are not *d* . . . . . . Acts 2:15
and another is *d* . . . . 1 Cor 11:21
And do not be *d* . . . . Eph 5:18
and those who get *d* . . . . 1 Thess 5:7
the earth were made *d* . . . . Rev 17:2
I saw the woman, *d* . . . . . . Rev 17:6

DRUNKARD
d could be included. . . . . . Deut 29:19
d is a proverb in the . . . . . . Prov 26:9
to and fro like a *d* . . . . Is 24:20
or a reviler, or a *d* . . . . . . 1 Cor 5:11

DRUNKEN
I am like a *d* man . . . . Jer 23:9

DRUNKENNESS
will be filled with *d* . . . . . . Ezek 23:33
Jerusalem a cup of *d* . . . . . Zech 12:2
with carousing, *d* . . . . . . Luke 21:34
not in revelry and *d* . . . . . Rom 13:13
envy, murders, *d* . . . . Gal 5:21
lusts, *d*. . . . . 1 Pet 4:3

DRY
place, and let the *d* . . . . Gen 1:9
made the sea into *d* . . . . . . Ex 14:21
It was *d* on the fleece . . . . . Judg 6:40
I will *d* up her sea . . . . . . Jer 51:36
d tree flourish. . . . . Ezek 17:24
will make the rivers *d* . . . . Ezek 30:12
will be done in the *d*. . . . Luke 23:31

DUE
because it is your *d* . . . . . . Lev 10:13
their food in *d* season . . . . . Ps 104:27
pay all that was *d* . . . . . . Matt 18:34
d time Christ died. . . . . Rom 5:6
to whom taxes are *d* . . . . . . Rom 13:7
d season we shall . . . . Gal 6:9
exalt you in *d* time. . . . . . . 1 Pet 5:6

DULL
heart of this people *d*. . . . . . . Is 6:10
people have grown *d*. . . . . Matt 13:15
you have become *d* . . . . . . Heb 5:11

DUMB
the tongue of the *d* . . . . Is 35:6
"Deaf and *d* spirit . . . . . . Mark 9:25

DUNGHILL
the land nor for the *d* . . . . Luke 14:35

DUST
formed man of the *d* . . . . . . Gen 2:7
d you shall return . . . . Gen 3:19
descendants as the *d* . . . . . Gen 13:16
now, I who am but *d* . . . . . Gen 18:27
"Who can count the *d* . . . . . Num 23:10
lay your gold in the *d* . . . . . Job 22:24
and repent in *d* . . . . Job 42:6
Will the *d* praise You. . . . . . . Ps 30:9
like the whirling *d* . . . . Ps 83:13
show favor to her *d* . . . . . . Ps 102:14
that we are *d* . . . . Ps 103:14
or the primal *d* . . . . Prov 8:26
all are from the *d*. . . . . . . Eccl 3:20
counted as the small *d*. . . . . Is 40:15
They shall lick the *d* . . . . . . Mic 7:17
city, shake off the *d* . . . . . Matt 10:14
image of the man of *d*. . . 1 Cor 15:49

DUTY
done what was our *d*. . . . Luke 17:10

DWELL
O LORD, make me *d* . . . . Ps 4:8
Who may *d* in Your holy . . . Ps 15:1
He himself shall *d*. . . . . Ps 25:13
d in the land . . . . Ps 37:3
the LORD God might *d* . . . . . Ps 68:18
of my God than *d* . . . . Ps 84:10
Him, that glory may *d* . . . . . Ps 85:9
Woe is me, that I *d* . . . . . . Ps 120:5
he will *d* on high . . . . Is 33:16
into Egypt to *d* there . . . . . . Is 52:4
"I *d* in the high and. . . . . . . Is 57:15
"They shall no longer *d* . . . Lam 4:15
they enter and *d* there . . . Matt 12:45

of Judea and all who *d* . . . . Acts 2:14
"I will *d* in them . . . . 2 Cor 6:16
that Christ may *d*. . . . . Eph 3:17
the fullness should *d*. . . . . . Col 1:19
the word of Christ *d* . . . . . . Col 3:16
men, and He will *d*. . . . . . . Rev 21:3

DWELLER
fled and became a *d* . . . . . Acts 7:29

DWELLING
A people *d* alone . . . . Num 23:9
is the way to the *d*. . . . . . . Job 38:19
built together for a *d* . . . . . Eph 2:22
a foreign country, *d* . . . . . . Heb 11:9

DWELLS
He who *d* in the secret. . . . . . Ps 91:1
but the Father who *d*. . . . . John 14:10
do it, but sin that *d*. . . . . . Rom 7:17
the Spirit of God *d*. . . . . Rom 8:9
from the dead *d*. . . . . Rom 8:11
the Spirit of God *d* . . . . . . 1 Cor 3:16
d all the fullness . . . . Col 2:9
which righteousness *d* . . . . 2 Pet 3:13
you, where Satan *d*. . . . . . . Rev 2:13

DWELT
Egypt, and Jacob *d* . . . . . . Ps 105:23
became flesh and *d*. . . . . . . John 1:14
By faith he *d* in the . . . . Heb 11:9

DYING
I do not object to *d*. . . . . . Acts 25:11
in the body the *d*. . . . . 2 Cor 4:10
Jacob, when he was *d*. . . . . Heb 11:21

EAGLE
As an *e* stirs up its. . . . . . . Deut 32:11
e swooping on its prey . . . . . Job 9:26
fly away like an *e*. . . . . Prov 23:5
The way of an *e*. . . . . Prov 30:19
nest as high as the *e*. . . . . . Jer 49:16
had the face of an *e* . . . . . Ezek 1:10
like a flying *e*. . . . . Rev 4:7
two wings of a great *e*. . . . Rev 12:14

EAGLES
up with wings like *e*. . . . . . . Is 40:31
are swifter than *e* . . . . Jer 4:13
e will be gathered . . . . . . Matt 24:28

EAGLES'
how I bore you on *e* . . . . . . Ex 19:4

EAR
shall pierce his *e*. . . . . Ex 21:6
Does not the *e* test . . . . . . Job 12:11
Bow down Your *e*. . . . . Ps 31:2
And the *e* of the wise. . . . . Prov 18:15
He awakens My *e*. . . . . Is 50:4
e is uncircumcised . . . . Jer 6:10
what you hear in the *e* . . . Matt 10:27
cut off his right *e* . . . . John 18:10
not seen, nor *e* heard . . . . . 1 Cor 2:9
if the *e* should say . . . . . . 1 Cor 12:16
He who has an *e*. . . . . Rev 2:7

EARLY
Very *e* in the morning . . . . Mark 16:2
arrived at the tomb *e* . . . . Luke 24:22

EARNEST
must give the more *e*. . . . . . Heb 2:1

EARNESTLY
if you *e* obey My . . . . Deut 11:13
He prayed more *e*. . . . . . . Luke 22:44
in this we groan, *e*. . . . . . . 2 Cor 5:2
e that it would not . . . . . . James 5:17
you to contend *e* . . . . Jude 3

EARS
both his *e* will tingle . . . . 2 Kin 21:12

Whoever shuts his *e*. . . . . . Prov 21:13
And hear with their *e* . . . . . . Is 6:10
He who has *e*. . . . . Matt 11:15
e are hard of hearing . . . . Matt 13:15
they have itching *e*. . . . . . 2 Tim 4:3
e are open to their . . . . . . 1 Pet 3:12

EARTH
e which is under you . . . . Deut 28:23
e are the LORD's . . . . 1 Sam 2:8
coming to judge the *e* . . 1 Chr 16:33
service for man on *e* . . . . . . Job 7:1
He hangs the *e* on. . . . . Job 26:7
foundations of the *e* . . . . . . Job 38:4
e is the LORD's . . . . Ps 24:1
the shields of the *e* . . . . Ps 47:9
You visit the *e* . . . . Ps 65:9
You had formed the *e* . . . . . Ps 90:2
let the *e* be moved. . . . . Ps 99:1
glory is above the *e* . . . . . Ps 148:13
wisdom founded the *e*. . . . Prov 3:19
there was ever an *e* . . . . . Prov 8:23
For three things the *e* . . . . Prov 30:21
e abides forever . . . . Eccl 1:4
for the meek of the *e* . . . . . . Is 11:4
e is My footstool. . . . . Is 66:1
and the *e* shone with. . . . . Ezek 43:2
I will darken the *e* . . . . Amos 8:9
e will be filled. . . . . Hab 2:14
shall inherit the *e*. . . . . Matt 5:5
heaven and *e* pass away . . Matt 5:18
e as it is in heaven . . . . Matt 6:10
treasures on *e* . . . . Matt 6:19
then shook the *e*. . . . . Heb 12:26
"Do not harm the *e* . . . . Rev 7:3
from whose face the *e*. . . . Rev 20:11
new heaven and a new *e* . . . Rev 21:1

EARTHLY
If I have told you *e* . . . . . . John 3:12
that if our *e* house. . . . . . . 2 Cor 5:1
their mind on *e* things . . . . Phil 3:19
from above, but is *e* . . . . James 3:15

EARTHQUAKE
after the wind an *e*. . . . . . 1 Kin 19:11
as you fled from the *e* . . . . Zech 14:5
there was a great *e* . . . . . . Matt 28:2
there was a great *e* . . . . Rev 6:12

EARTHQUAKES
And there will be *e*. . . . . . Mark 13:8

EASE
I was at *e* . . . . Job 16:12
you women who are at *e*. . . . Is 32:9
to you who are at *e*. . . . . . Amos 6:1
take your *e*. . . . . Luke 12:19

EASIER
Which is *e*, to say . . . . Mark 2:9
It is *e* for a camel. . . . . . . Mark 10:25

EAST
goes toward the *e*. . . . . Gen 2:14
the LORD brought an *e* . . . . Ex 10:13
e wind scattered. . . . . Job 38:24
As far as the *e* . . . . Ps 103:12
descendants from the *e* . . . . Is 43:5
wise men from the *E*. . . . . . Matt 2:1
many will come from *e*. . . . Matt 8:11
will come from the *e* . . . . Luke 13:29
e might be prepared . . . . . Rev 16:12

EAT
you may freely *e* . . . . Gen 2:16
'You shall not *e* . . . . Gen 3:17
my people as they *e* . . . . . . Ps 53:4
good to *e* much honey . . . Prov 25:27
e this scroll. . . . . Ezek 3:1
on your couches, *e* . . . . . . Amos 6:4
e the flesh of My. . . . . Mic 3:3

life, what you will *e* . . . . . Matt 6:25
You to *e* the Passover . . . . Matt 26:17
give us His flesh to *e* . . . . . John 6:52
one believes he may *e* . . . . . Rom 14:2
e meat nor drink wine . . . . Rom 14:21
I will never again *e* . . . . . 1 Cor 8:13
neither shall he *e* . . . . . 2 Thess 3:10
e your flesh like fire . . . . . James 5:3

EATEN
Have you *e* from the . . . . . . Gen 3:11
e my honeycomb with my . . Song 5:1
e the fruit of lies . . . . Hos 10:13
And he was *e* by worms . . . Acts 12:23

EATS
The righteous *e* . . . . Prov 13:25
receives sinners and *e* . . . . . Luke 15:2
Whoever *e* My flesh . . . . . John 6:54
e this bread will live . . . . . . John 6:58
e despise him who does . . . Rom 14:3
He who *e*, *e* to the . . . . Rom 14:6
an unworthy manner *e* . . 1 Cor 11:29

EBAL
Mountain in Samaria, Deut 27:12, 13
Stones of the law erected upon, Deut
27:1–8; Josh 8:30–35

EBENEZER
Site of Israel's defeat, 1 Sam 4:1–10
Ark transferred from, 1 Sam 5:1
Site of memorial stone,
1 Sam 7:10, 12

EBER
Great-grandson of Shem, Gen 10:21–
24; 1 Chr 1:25
Progenitor of the:
Hebrews, Gen 11:16–26
Arabians and Arameans,
Gen 10:25–30
Ancestor of Christ, Luke 3:35

EDEN
First home of mankind, Gen 2:8–15
Zion becomes like, Is 51:3
Called the "garden of God,"
Ezek 28:13

EDIFICATION
his good, leading to *e* . . . . . Rom 15:2
prophesies speaks *e* . . . . . 1 Cor 14:3
things be done for *e* . . . . . 1 Cor 14:26
the Lord gave us for *e* . . . . 2 Cor 10:8
has given me for *e* . . . . . 2 Cor 13:10
rather than godly *e* . . . . . . 1 Tim 1:4

EDIFIES
puffs up, but love *e* . . . . . . 1 Cor 8:1
he who prophesies *e* . . . . 1 Cor 14:4

EDIFY
but not all things *e* . . . . 1 Cor 10:23
and *e* one another . . . . . 1 Thess 5:11

EDIFYING
of the body for the *e* . . . . . . Eph 4:16

EDOM
Name given to Esau, Gen 25:30
—— Land of Esau; called Seir,
Gen 32:3
Called Edom and Idumea, Mark 3:8
People of, cursed, Is 34:5, 6

EDOMITES
Descendants of Esau, Gen 36:9
Refuse passage to Israel, Num
20:18–20
Hostile to Israel, Gen 27:40; 1 Sam
14:47; 2 Chr 20:10; Ps 137:7
Prophecies concerning, Gen 27:37; Is
34:5–17; Ezek 25:12–14; 35:5–7;
Amos 9:11, 12

EFFECTIVELY
for He who worked *e* . . . . . . Gal 2:8
e works in you who . . . . . 1 Thess 2:13

EGG
in the white of an *e* . . . . Job 6:6
Or if he asks for an *e* . . . . . Luke 11:12

EGYPT
Abram visits, Gen 12:10
Joseph sold into, Gen 37:28, 36
Joseph becomes leader in, Gen 39:1–4
Hebrews move to, Gen 46:5–7
Hebrews persecuted in, Ex 1:15–22
Plagues on, Ex 7—11
Israel leaves, Ex 12:31–33
Army of, perishes, Ex 14:26–28
Prophecies concerning, Gen 15:13;
Is 19:18–25; Ezek 29:14, 15; 30:24,
25; Matt 2:15

EHUD
Son of Gera, Judg 3:15
Slays Eglon, Judg 3:16–26

EIGHT
a few, that is, *e* . . . . 1 Pet 3:20

EKRON
Philistine city, Josh 13:3
Captured by Judah, Judg 1:18
Assigned to Dan, Josh 19:40, 43
Ark sent to, 1 Sam 5:10
Denounced by the prophets,
Jer 25:9, 20

ELAH
King of Israel, 1 Kin 16:6, 8–10

ELAMITES
Descendants of Shem, Gen 10:22
Destruction of, Jer 49:34–39
In Persian Empire, Ezra 4:9
Jews from, at Pentecost, Acts 2:9

ELATH
Seaport on Red Sea, 1 Kin 9:26
Built by Azariah, 2 Kin 14:21, 22
Captured by Syrians, 2 Kin 16:6
Same as Ezion Geber, 2 Chr 8:17

EL BETHEL
Site of Jacob's altar, Gen 35:6, 7

ELDER
The *e* and honorable . . . . Is 9:15
against an *e* except . . . . . . 1 Tim 5:19
I who am a fellow *e* . . . . 1 Pet 5:1

ELDERS
and seventy of the *e* . . . . . . Ex 24:1
And teach his *e* . . . . Ps 105:22
and counsel from the *e* . . . . Ezek 7:26
the tradition of the *e* . . . . . Matt 15:2
be rejected by the *e* . . . . . . Luke 9:22
they had appointed *e* . . . . Acts 14:23
and called for the *e* . . . . . Acts 20:17
e who rule well be . . . . . . 1 Tim 5:17
lacking, and appoint *e* . . . . Titus 1:5
e obtained a good . . . . Heb 11:2
Let him call for the *e* . . . . James 5:14
e who are among you I . . . . 1 Pet 5:1
I saw twenty-four *e* . . . . Rev 4:4

ELDERSHIP
of the hands of the *e* . . . . . 1 Tim 4:14

ELEAZAR
Son of Aaron; succeeds him as high
priest, Ex 6:23, 25; 28:1; Lev 10:6,
7; Num 3:32; 20:25–28; Josh 14:1;
24:33

ELECT
whom I uphold, My *E* . . . . . . Is 42:1
and Israel My *e* . . . . Is 45:4

e shall long enjoy the . . . . . Is 65:22
gather together His *e* . . . Matt 24:31
e have obtained it . . . . Rom 11:7
e according to the . . . . 1 Pet 1:2
a chief cornerstone, *e* . . . . 1 Pet 2:6
e sister greet you . . . . 2 John 13

ELECTION
e they are beloved . . . . . . Rom 11:28
call and *e* sure . . . . 2 Pet 1:10

ELEMENTS
weak and beggarly *e* . . . . . . Gal 4:9
e will melt with . . . . 2 Pet 3:10

ELEVEN
and his *e* sons . . . . Gen 32:22
e disciples went away . . . . Matt 28:16
numbered with the *e* . . . . . Acts 1:26

ELI
Officiates in Shiloh, 1 Sam 1:3
Blesses Hannah, 1 Sam 1:12–19
Becomes Samuel's guardian, 1 Sam
1:20–28
Samuel ministers before, 1 Sam 2:11
Sons of, 1 Sam 2:12–17
Rebukes sons, 1 Sam 2:22–25
Rebuked by a man of God, 1 Sam
2:27–36
Instructs Samuel, 1 Sam 3:1–18
Death of, 1 Sam 4:15–18

ELIAB
Brother of David, 1 Sam 16:5–13
Fights in Saul's army, 1 Sam 17:13
Discounts David's worth, 1 Sam
17:28, 29

ELIAKIM
Son of Hilkiah, 2 Kin 18:18
Confers with Rabshakeh, Is 36:4,
11–22
Sent to Isaiah, Is 37:2–5
Becomes type of the Messiah, Is
22:20–25
—— Son of King Josiah, 2 Kin 23:34
Name changed to Jehoiakim, 2 Chr
36:4

ELIASHIB
High priest, Neh 12:10
Rebuilds Sheep Gate, Neh 3:1, 20, 21
Allies with foreigners, Neh 13:4, 5, 28

ELIHU
David's brother, 1 Chr 27:18
Called Eliab, 1 Sam 16:6
—— One who reproved Job and his
friends, Job 32:2, 4–6

ELIJAH
Denounces Ahab; goes into hiding;
fed by ravens, 1 Kin 17:1–7
Dwells with widow; performs mira-
cles for her, 1 Kin 17:8–24
Sends message to Ahab; overthrows
prophets of Baal, 1 Kin 18:1–40
Brings rain, 1 Kin 18:41–45
Flees from Jezebel; fed by angels,
1 Kin 19:1–8
Receives revelation from God, 1 Kin
19:9–18
Condemns Ahab, 1 Kin 21:15–29
Condemns Ahaziah; fire consumes
troops sent against him, 2 Kin
1:1–16
Taken up to heaven, 2 Kin 2:1–15
Appears with Christ in Transfigura-
tion, Matt 17:1–4
Type of John the Baptist, Mal 4:5, 6;
Luke 1:17

ELIMELECH
Naomi's husband, Ruth 1:1–3; 2:1, 3; 4:3–9

ELIPHAZ
One of Job's friends, Job 2:11
Rebukes Job, Job 4:1, 5
Is forgiven, Job 42:7–9

ELISHA
Chosen as Elijah's successor; follows him, 1 Kin 19:16–21
Witnesses Elijah's translation; receives his spirit and mantle, 2 Kin 2:1–18
Performs miracles, 2 Kin 2:19–25; 4:1—6:23
Prophesies victory over Moab; fulfilled, 2 Kin 3:11–27
Prophesies end of siege; fulfilled, 2 Kin 7
Prophesies death of Ben-Hadad, 2 Kin 8:7–15
Sends servant to anoint Jehu, 2 Kin 9:1–3
Last words and death; miracle performed by his bones, 2 Kin 13:14–21

ELIZABETH
Barren wife of Zacharias, Luke 1:5–7
Conceives a son, Luke 1:13, 24, 25
Salutation to Mary, Luke 1:36–45
Mother of John the Baptist, Luke 1:57–60

ELIZAPHAN
Chief of Kohathites, Num 3:30
Heads family, 1 Chr 15:5, 8
Family consecrated, 2 Chr 29:12–16

ELKANAH
Father of Samuel, 1 Sam 1:1–23
—— Son of Korah, Ex 6:24
Escapes judgment, Num 26:11

ELNATHAN
Father of Nehushta, 2 Kin 24:8
Goes to Egypt, Jer 26:22
Entreats with king, Jer 36:25

ELOQUENT
"O my Lord, I am not *e* ..... Ex 4:10
an *e* man and mighty .... Acts 18:24

ELYMAS
Arabic name of Bar-Jesus, a false prophet, Acts 13:6–12

EMBALM
to *e* his father............ Gen 50:2

EMBANKMENT
will build an *e*.......... Luke 19:43

EMERALDS
for your wares *e*........ Ezek 27:16

EMMAUS
Town near Jerusalem, Luke 24:13–18

EMPTY
appear before Me *e*........ Ex 23:15
e things which .... 1 Sam 12:21
not listen to *e* talk .... Job 35:13
LORD makes the earth *e*...... Is 24:1
comes, he finds it *e*...... Matt 12:44
He has sent away *e*....... Luke 1:53
you with *e* words .... Eph 5:6

EMPTY-HEADED
e man will be wise........ Job 11:12

EN GEDI
Occupied by the Amorites, Gen 14:7
Assigned to Judah, Josh 15:62, 63

David's hiding place, 1 Sam 23:29
Noted for vineyards, Song 1:14

EN HAKKORE
Miraculous spring, Judg 15:14–19

EN ROGEL
Fountain outside Jerusalem, 2 Sam 17:17
Seat of Adonijah's plot, 1 Kin 1:5–9

ENABLED
our Lord who has *e*...... 1 Tim 1:12

ENCHANTER
and the expert *e*............ Is 3:3

ENCOURAGED
is, that I may be *e*....... Rom 1:12
and all may be *e* .... 1 Cor 14:31
their hearts may be *e*....... Col 2:2

END
yet your latter *e*........... Job 8:7
make me to know my *e* ..... Ps 39:4
shall keep it to the *e* ..... Ps 119:33
e is the way of death ..... Prov 14:12
There was no *e* of all ..... Eccl 4:16
Declaring the *e*........... Is 46:10
Our *e* was near .... Lam 4:18
whose iniquity shall *e*..... Ezek 21:25
what shall be the *e*...... Dan 12:8
e has come upon my ..... Amos 8:2
the harvest is the *e*...... Matt 13:39
to pass, but the *e* ...... Matt 24:6
always, even to the *e* .... Matt 28:20
He loved them to the *e*.... John 13:1
For Christ is the *e* ...... Rom 10:4
the hope firm to the *e*..... Heb 3:6
but now, once at the *e*..... Heb 9:26
of Job and seen the *e* .... James 5:11
But the *e* of all .... 1 Pet 4:7
what will be the *e*....... 1 Pet 4:17
the latter *e* is worse ..... 2 Pet 2:20
My works until the *e*...... Rev 2:26
Beginning and the *E*...... Rev 22:13

ENDEAVORING
e to keep the unity........ Eph 4:3

ENDLESS
and *e* genealogies........ 1 Tim 1:4
to the power of an *e*...... Heb 7:16

ENDS
All the *e* of the world ...... Ps 22:27
established all the *e* ...... Prov 30:4
she came from the *e*.... Matt 12:42
to the *e* of the.......... Acts 13:47
their words to the *e*...... Rom 10:18

ENDURANCE
For you have need of *e*.... Heb 10:36
e the race that .... Heb 12:1

ENDURE
But the LORD shall *e*........ Ps 9:7
as the sun and moon *e*...... Ps 72:5
His name shall *e*......... Ps 72:17
nor does a crown *e* ...... Prov 27:24
Can your heart *e*....... Ezek 22:14
persecuted, we *e*....... 1 Cor 4:12
Therefore I *e* all........ 2 Tim 2:10
them blessed who *e*..... James 5:11

ENDURED
what persecutions I *e* .... 2 Tim 3:11
he had patiently *e*........ Heb 6:15
e as seeing Him who .... Heb 11:27
For consider Him who *e*.... Heb 12:3

ENDURES
And His truth *e*.......... Ps 100:5
For His mercy *e* .... Ps 136:1
But he who *e* to the...... Matt 10:22

e only for a while .... Matt 13:21
for the food which *e* ...... John 6:27
he has built on it *e* ...... 1 Cor 3:14
hopes all things, *e* .... 1 Cor 13:7
is the man who *e* .... James 1:12
word of the LORD *e* ...... 1 Pet 1:25

ENDURING
the LORD is clean, *e*........ Ps 19:9
e possession for.......... Heb 10:34

ENEMIES
Your *e* be scattered ..... Num 10:35
delivers me from my *e*..... Ps 18:48
the presence of my *e*....... Ps 23:5
Let not my *e* triumph ...... Ps 25:2
But my *e* are vigorous...... Ps 38:19
e will lick the dust.......... Ps 72:9
me wiser than my *e*...... Ps 119:98
I count them my *e*....... Ps 139:22
e are the men of his .... Mic 7:6
to you, love your *e* .... Matt 5:44
e will be those .... Matt 10:36
be saved from our *e* ...... Luke 1:71
e we were reconciled ..... Rom 5:10
the gospel they are *e*....... Rom 11:28
till He has put all *e* ...... 1 Cor 15:25
were alienated and *e*...... Col 1:21
His *e* are made His .... Heb 10:13
and devours their *e*....... Rev 11:5

ENEMY
then I will be an *e* .... Ex 23:22
regard me as Your *e*...... Job 13:24
He counts me as His *e*.... Job 33:10
or have plundered my *e* ...... Ps 7:4
You may silence the *e*....... Ps 8:2
e does not triumph .... Ps 41:11
e who reproaches me....... Ps 55:12
e has persecuted my ...... Ps 143:3
If your *e* is hungry...... Prov 25:21
e are deceitful .... Prov 27:6
with the wound of an *e* .... Jer 30:14
rejoice over me, my *e*...... Mic 7:8
and hate your *e* .... Matt 5:43
last *e* that will be ...... 1 Cor 15:26
become your *e* because..... Gal 4:16
not count him as an *e* .. 2 Thess 3:15
makes himself an *e* ...... James 4:4

ENGRAVE
two onyx stones and *e*..... Ex 28:9
e its inscription........... Zech 3:9

ENJOY
e its sabbaths as long ..... Lev 26:34
therefore *e* pleasure .... Eccl 2:1
richly all things to *e*..... 1 Tim 6:17
than to *e* the passing ..... Heb 11:25

ENJOYMENT
So I commended *e* .... Eccl 8:15

ENLARGES
He *e* nations............. Job 12:23
e his desire as hell........ Hab 2:5

ENLIGHTEN
E my eyes................. Ps 13:3
the LORD my God will *e*..... Ps 18:28

ENLIGHTENED
those who were once *e*..... Heb 6:4

ENMITY
And I will put *e*.......... Gen 3:15
the carnal mind is *e*...... Rom 8:7
in His flesh the *e*........ Eph 2:15
putting to death the *e*..... Eph 2:16
with the world is *e* ...... James 4:4

ENOCH
Father of Methuselah, Gen 5:21
Walks with God, Gen 5:22

Taken up to heaven, Gen 5:24
Prophecy of, cited, Jude 14, 15

ENOUGH
never say, "E . . . . Prov 30:15
It is e . . . . Mark 14:41
servants have bread e . . . . Luke 15:17

ENRAGED
being exceedingly e . . . . . Acts 26:11
And the dragon was e . . . . . Rev 12:17

ENRAPTURED
And always be e . . . . Prov 5:19

ENRICHED
that you were e . . . . 1 Cor 1:5
while you are e . . . . 2 Cor 9:11

ENSNARED
The wicked is e . . . . Prov 12:13

ENSNARES
sin which so easily e . . . . . Heb 12:1

ENTANGLE
how they might e . . . . . . Matt 22:15

ENTANGLES
engaged in warfare e . . . . . 2 Tim 2:4

ENTER
E into His gates . . . . Ps 100:4
Do not e into judgment . . . . . Ps 143:2
E into the rock . . . . Is 2:10
He shall e into peace . . . . Is 57:2
you will by no means e . . . Matt 5:20
"E by the narrow . . . . Matt 7:13
e the kingdom of God . . . . Matt 19:24
E into the joy of your . . . . Matt 25:21
and pray, lest you e . . . . . Matt 26:41
"Strive to e through . . . . . Luke 13:24
you, he who does not e . . . . John 10:1
who have believed do e . . . . . Heb 4:3
e the Holiest by the . . . . . . Heb 10:19
e the temple till the . . . . . . Rev 15:8
e through the gates . . . . . . Rev 22:14

ENTERED
Then Satan e Judas . . . . . . Luke 22:3
through one man sin e . . . . Rom 5:12
ear heard, nor have e . . . . 1 Cor 2:9
the forerunner has e . . . . . Heb 6:20
e the Most Holy Place . . . . . Heb 9:12

ENTERS
If anyone e by Me . . . . . . John 10:9
e the Presence behind . . . . . Heb 6:19

ENTHRONED
You are holy, e in . . . . Ps 22:3

ENTICED
his own desires and e . . . . James 1:14

ENTICING
e speech she caused . . . . . . Prov 7:21

ENTIRELY
give yourself e . . . . 1 Tim 4:15

ENTRANCE
The e of Your words . . . . . Ps 119:130
e will be supplied . . . . 2 Pet 1:11

ENTREAT
"E me not to leave you . . . . Ruth 1:16
"But now e God's favor . . . . . Mal 1:9
being defamed, we e . . . . . 1 Cor 4:13

ENTREATED
man of God e the LORD . . . 1 Kin 13:6
e our God for this . . . . Ezra 8:23

ENVIOUS
For I was e of the . . . . Ps 73:3
Do not be e of evil . . . . Prov 24:1
patriarchs, becoming e . . . . Acts 7:9

ENVY
e slays a simple . . . . Job 5:2
e the oppressor . . . . Prov 3:31
e is rottenness . . . . Prov 14:30
not let your heart e . . . . . Prov 23:17
e have now perished . . . . Eccl 9:6
full of e . . . . Rom 1:29
not in strife and e . . . . . . Rom 13:13
love does not e . . . . 1 Cor 13:4
e, murders . . . . Gal 5:21
living in malice and e . . . . . Titus 3:3
For where e and . . . . James 3:16
deceit, hypocrisy, e . . . . 1 Pet 2:1

EPAPHRAS
Leader of the Colossian church, Col
1:7, 8
Suffers as a prisoner in Rome,
Philem 23

EPAPHRODITUS
Messenger from Philippi, Phil
2:25–27
Brings a gift to Paul, Phil 4:18

EPHESUS
Paul visits, Acts 18:18–21
Miracles done here, Acts 19:11–21
Demetrius stirs up riot in, Acts
19:24–29
Elders of, addressed by Paul at Mile-
tus, Acts 20:17–38
Letter sent to, Eph 1:1
Site of one of seven churches, Rev
1:11

EPHRAIM
Joseph's younger son, Gen 41:52
Obtains Jacob's blessing,
Gen 48:8–20
——— Tribe of:
Predictions concerning, Gen 48:20
Territory assigned to, Josh 16:1–10
Assist Deborah, Judg 5:14, 15
Assist Gideon, Judg 7:24, 25
Quarrel with Gideon, Judg 8:1–3
Quarrel with Jephthah, Judg 12:1–4
Leading tribe of kingdom of Israel,
Is 7:2–17
Provoke God by sin, Hos 12:7–14
Many of, join Judah, 2 Chr 15:8, 9
Captivity of, predicted, Hos 9:3–17
Messiah promised to, Zech 9:9–13

EPHRATHAH
Ancient name of Bethlehem, Ruth
4:11
Prophecy concerning, Mic 5:2

EPHRON
Hittite who sold Machpelah to Abraham, Gen 23:8–20

EPICUREANS
Sect of pleasure-loving philosophers,
Acts 17:18

EPISTLE
You are our e written . . . . . 2 Cor 3:2
you are an e . . . . 2 Cor 3:3
by word or our e . . . . 2 Thess 2:15
our word in this e . . . . . . 2 Thess 3:14
is a sign in every e . . . . . 2 Thess 3:17

EPISTLES
e of commendation to . . . . . 2 Cor 3:1
as also in all his e . . . . 2 Pet 3:16

EQUAL
it was you, a man my e . . . . Ps 55:13
and you made them e . . . Matt 20:12
making Himself e . . . . John 5:18
it robbery to be e . . . . Phil 2:6

EQUALITY
that there may be e . . . . . . 2 Cor 8:14

EQUITY
You have established e . . . . . Ps 99:4
judgment, and e . . . . Prov 1:3
and e cannot enter . . . . Is 59:14
and pervert all e . . . . Mic 3:9
with Me in peace and e . . . . Mal 2:6

ER
Son of Judah, Gen 38:1–7; 46:12

ERASTUS
Paul's friend at Ephesus, Acts 19:21,
22; 2 Tim 4:20
Treasurer of Corinth, Rom 16:23

ERR
you cause you to e . . . . Is 3:12
My people Israel to e . . . . . Jer 23:13

ERROR
God that it was an e . . . . . . Eccl 5:6
e which was due . . . . Rom 1:27
a sinner from the e . . . . . . James 5:20
led away with the e . . . . . 2 Pet 3:17
and the spirit of e . . . . 1 John 4:6
run greedily in the e . . . . Jude 11

ERRORS
can understand his e . . . . . . Ps 19:12

ESARHADDON
Son of Sennacherib; king of Assyria
(681–669 B.C.), 2 Kin 19:36, 37

ESAU
Isaac's favorite son, Gen 25:25–28
Sells his birthright, Gen 25:29–34
Deprived of blessing; seeks to kill
Jacob, Gen 27
Reconciled to Jacob, Gen 33:1–17
Descendants of, Gen 36

ESCAPE
E to the mountains . . . . . . Gen 19:17
and they shall not e . . . . . . Job 11:20
Shall they e by . . . . Ps 56:7
speaks lies will not e . . . . . Prov 19:5
and how shall we e . . . . Is 20:6
e all these things . . . . . . Luke 21:36
same, that you will e . . . . . . Rom 2:3
also make the way of e . . 1 Cor 10:13
how shall we e if we . . . . Heb 2:3
e who refused Him who . . . Heb 12:25

ESCAPED
my flesh, and I have e . . . . Job 19:20
Our soul has e as a . . . . Ps 124:7
after they have e . . . . 2 Pet 2:20

ESHCOL
Valley near Hebron, Num 13:22–27;
Deut 1:24

ESTABLISH
to e them forever . . . . 2 Chr 9:8
'Your seed I will e . . . . Ps 89:4
e the work of our . . . . Ps 90:17
E Your word to Your . . . . . . Ps 119:38
e an everlasting . . . . Ezek 16:60
e justice in the gate . . . . . Amos 5:15
seeking to e their own . . . . Rom 10:3
faithful, who will e . . . . . 2 Thess 3:3
E your hearts . . . . James 5:8
a while, perfect, e . . . . 1 Pet 5:10

ESTABLISHED
also is firmly e . . . . 1 Chr 16:30
David my father be e . . . . . 2 Chr 1:9
a rock, and e my steps . . . . . Ps 40:2
e a testimony in Jacob . . . . . Ps 78:5
Your throne is e . . . . Ps 93:2
let all your ways be e . . . . . Prov 4:26

e the clouds above . . . . Prov 8:28
lip shall be *e* forever . . . . . Prov 12:19
house shall be *e* . . . . Is 2:2
by His power, He has *e* . . . . Jer 10:12
built up in Him and *e* . . . . . . Col 2:7
covenant, which was *e* . . . . . Heb 8:6
that the heart be *e* . . . . Heb 13:9

ESTABLISHES
The king *e* the land by . . . . Prov 29:4
Now He who *e* us with. . . . 2 Cor 1:21

ESTEEM
high wall in his own *e* . . . . Prov 18:11
and we did not *e* . . . . Is 53:3
e others better than . . . . Phil 2:3
and hold such men in *e* . . . . Phil 2:29
e them very highly . . . . . 1 Thess 5:13

ESTEEMED
For what is highly *e* . . . . . Luke 16:15
those who are least *e* . . . . . 1 Cor 6:4

ESTEEMS
One person *e* one day . . . . Rom 14:5

ESTHER
Selected for harem, Esth 2:7–16
Chosen to be queen, Esth 2:17, 18
Agrees to intercede for her people,
Esth 4
Invites king to banquet, Esth 5:1–8
Denounces Haman; obtains reversal
of decree, Esth 7:1—8:8
Establishes Purim, Esth 9:29–32

ESTRANGED
The wicked are *e* . . . . Ps 58:3
because they are all *e* . . . . . Ezek 14:5
You have become *e* . . . . Gal 5:4

ETAM
Rock where Samson took refuge,
Judg 15:8–19

ETERNAL
e God is your refuge . . . . . Deut 33:27
For man goes to his *e* . . . . . . Eccl 12:5
I do that I may have *e* . . . Matt 19:16
and inherit *e* life . . . . Matt 19:29
in the age to come, *e* . . . . Mark 10:30
not perish but have *e* . . . . . John 3:15
you think you have *e* . . . . . John 5:39
And I give them *e* life . . . . John 10:28
that He should give *e* . . . . . John 17:2
And this is *e* life . . . . John 17:3
e life to those who by . . . . . . Rom 2:7
the gift of God is *e* . . . . Rom 6:23
e weight of glory . . . . 2 Cor 4:17
are not seen are *e* . . . . 2 Cor 4:18
not made with hands, *e* . . . 2 Cor 5:1
lay hold on *e* life . . . . 1 Tim 6:12
e life which God . . . . Titus 1:2
and of *e* judgment . . . . Heb 6:2
e life which was . . . . 1 John 1:2
that no murderer has *e* . . 1 John 3:15
God has given us *e* . . . . . 1 John 5:11
that you have *e* life . . . . . 1 John 5:13
Jesus Christ unto *e* . . . . Jude 21

ETERNITY
Also He has put *e* . . . . Eccl 3:11
One who inhabits *e* . . . . Is 57:15

ETHIOPIA
See CUSH
Hostile to Israel and Judah, 2 Chr
12:2, 3; 14:9–15; Is 43:3; Dan 11:43
Prophecies against, Is 20:1–6; Ezek
30:4–9

ETHIOPIANS
Skin of, unchangeable, Jer 13:23

EUNICE
Mother of Timothy, 2 Tim 1:5

EUNUCH
of Ethiopia, a *e* . . . . Acts 8:27

EUNUCHS
have made themselves *e* . . Matt 19:12

EUPHRATES
River of Eden, Gen 2:14
Boundary of Promised Land, Gen
15:18; 1 Kin 4:21, 24
Scene of battle, Jer 46:2, 6, 10
Angels bound there, Rev 9:14

EUTYCHUS
Sleeps during Paul's sermon, Acts
20:9
Restored to life, Acts 20:12

EVANGELIST
of Philip the *e* . . . . Acts 21:8
do the work of an *e* . . . . 2 Tim 4:5

EVANGELISTS
some prophets, some *e* . . . . . Eph 4:11

EVEN
E in laughter the . . . . Prov 14:13
E a child is known . . . . Prov 20:11
e nature itself teach . . . . . 1 Cor 11:14
e denying the Lord who . . . . 2 Pet 2:1

EVENING
At *e* they return . . . . Ps 59:6
e it is cut down and . . . . Ps 90:6
of my hands as the *e* . . . . . . Ps 141:2
e do not withhold your . . . . . Eccl 11:6
and more fierce than *e* . . . . . Hab 1:8

EVERLASTING
God of Israel from *e* . . . . 1 Chr 16:36
of the LORD is from *e* . . . . . . Ps 103:17
righteousness is an *e* . . . . . Ps 119:142
Your kingdom is an *e* . . . . . Ps 145:13
in YAH, the LORD, is *e* . . . . Is 26:4
will be to you an *e* . . . . Is 60:19
from *E* is Your name . . . . Is 63:16
awake, some to *e* life . . . . . Dan 12:2
not perish but have *e* . . . . . John 3:16
Him who sent Me has *e* . . . John 5:24
endures to *e* life . . . . John 6:27
in Him may have *e* . . . . John 6:40
believes in Me has *e* . . . . . . John 6:47
unworthy of *e* life . . . . Acts 13:46
of the Spirit reap *e* . . . . Gal 6:8
e destruction from the . . . 2 Thess 1:9

EVERYONE
said, 'Repent now *e* . . . . Jer 25:5
e who is born of the . . . . John 3:8
E who is of the truth . . . . . John 18:37

EVIDENCE
e of things not seen . . . . Heb 11:1

EVIDENT
the sight of God is *e* . . . . Gal 3:11
of some are clearly *e* . . . . . 1 Tim 5:25
e that our Lord arose . . . . . Heb 7:14

EVIL
of good and *e* . . . . Gen 2:9
knowing good and *e* . . . . Gen 3:5
his heart was only *e* . . . . . . Gen 6:5
e have been the . . . . Gen 47:9
rebellious and *e* city . . . . . . Ezra 4:12
e shall touch you . . . . Job 5:19
I looked for good, *e* . . . . . . Job 30:26
nor shall *e* dwell . . . . Ps 5:4
I will fear no *e* . . . . Ps 23:4
E shall slay the . . . . Ps 34:21
he does not abhor *e* . . . . Ps 36:4
e more than good . . . . Ps 52:3
e shall befall you . . . . Ps 91:10
To do *e* is like sport . . . . . . Prov 10:23
shall be filled with *e* . . . . . Prov 12:21

e will bow before the . . . . Prov 14:19
Keeping watch on the *e* . . . Prov 15:3
Whoever rewards *e* . . . . . Prov 17:13
E will not depart . . . . Prov 17:13
e all the days of her . . . . Prov 31:12
There is a severe *e* . . . . Eccl 5:13
of men are full of *e* . . . . Eccl 9:3
to those who call *e* . . . . Is 5:20
is taken away from *e* . . . . Is 57:1
of peace and not of *e* . . . . . Jer 29:11
commit this great *e* . . . . Jer 44:7
Seek good and not *e* . . . . . Amos 5:14
deliver us from the *e* . . . . . Matt 6:13
If you then, being *e* . . . . . . Matt 7:11
"Why do you think *e* . . . . . Matt 9:4
e treasure brings . . . . Matt 12:35
everyone practicing *e* . . . . . John 3:20
bear witness of the *e* . . . . John 18:23
e I will not to do . . . . Rom 7:19
then a law, that *e* . . . . Rom 7:21
done any good or *e* . . . . Rom 9:11
Abhor what is *e* . . . . Rom 12:9
Repay no one *e* for . . . . . . Rom 12:17
not be overcome by *e* . . . . Rom 12:21
simple concerning *e* . . . . . Rom 16:19
provoked, thinks no *e* . . . . 1 Cor 13:5
from every form of *e* . . . 1 Thess 5:22

EVIL-MERODACH
Babylonian king (562–560 B.C.), 2 Kin
25:27–30

EVIL-MINDEDNESS
strife, deceit, *e* . . . . Rom 1:29

EVILDOER
"If He were not an *e* . . . . . John 18:30
suffer trouble as an *e* . . . . . 2 Tim 2:9
a thief, an *e* . . . . 1 Pet 4:15

EVILDOERS
e shall be cut off . . . . Ps 37:9
Depart from me, you *e* . . . Ps 119:115
iniquity, a brood of *e* . . . . Is 1:4
e shall never be . . . . Is 14:20
against you as *e* . . . . 1 Pet 2:12

EVILS
e have surrounded me . . . . . Ps 40:12
have committed two *e* . . . . . Jer 2:13

EXALT
God, and I will *e* . . . . Ex 15:2
e the horn of His . . . . 1 Sam 2:10
e His name together . . . . Ps 34:3
E the LORD our God . . . . Ps 99:5
are my God, I will *e* . . . . . . Ps 118:28
if I do not *e* . . . . Ps 137:6
into heaven, I will *e* . . . . . . Is 14:13
E the humble . . . . Ezek 21:26
and he shall *e* himself . . . . . Dan 8:25

EXALTATION
e comes neither from . . . . . . Ps 75:6
who rejoice in My *e* . . . . Is 13:3
brother glory in his *e* . . . . James 1:9

EXALTED
Let God be *e* . . . . 2 Sam 22:47
built You an *e* . . . . 2 Chr 6:2
name, which is *e* . . . . Neh 9:5
when vileness is *e* . . . . Ps 12:8
I will be *e* among the . . . . . Ps 46:10
righteous shall be *e* . . . . . . Ps 75:10
favor our horn is *e* . . . . Ps 89:17
You are *e* far above . . . . Ps 97:9
His name alone is *e* . . . . . . Ps 148:13
upright the city is *e* . . . . . Prov 11:11
LORD alone shall be *e* . . . . Is 2:11
valley shall be *e* . . . . Is 40:4
Him God has *e* . . . . Acts 5:31
And lest I should be *e* . . . 2 Cor 12:7
also has highly *e* . . . . Phil 2:9

EXALTS
Righteousness *e* . . . . Prov 14:34
high thing that *e* . . . . 2 Cor 10:5
e himself above all . . . . . . 2 Thess 2:4

EXAMINE
E me, O LORD. . . . . Ps 26:2
But let a man *e* . . . . 1 Cor 11:28
But let each one *e* . . . . Gal 6:4

EXAMPLE
to make her a public *e* . . . . Matt 1:19
I have given you an *e* . . . . John 13:15
in following my *e* . . . . Phil 3:17
to make ourselves an *e* . 2 Thess 3:9
youth, but be an *e* . . . . 1 Tim 4:12
us, leaving us an *e* . . . . 1 Pet 2:21
making them an *e* . . . . 2 Pet 2:6
are set forth as an *e* . . . . Jude 7

EXAMPLES
happened to them as *e* . 1 Cor 10:11
so that you became *e* . . . . 1 Thess 1:7
to you, but being *e* . . . . 1 Pet 5:3

EXCEEDING
He might show the *e* . . . . . . Eph 2:7

EXCEEDINGLY
for the LORD must be *e* . . 1 Chr 22:5
You have made him *e* . . . . . . Ps 21:6
is far off and *e* deep . . . . . . Eccl 7:24
e high mountain . . . . Matt 4:8
Rejoice and be *e* . . . . Matt 5:12

EXCEEDS
your righteousness *e* . . . . . Matt 5:20

EXCEL
you His angels, who *e* . . . . Ps 103:20
but you *e* them all . . . . Prov 31:29
that you seek to *e* . . . . . . 1 Cor 14:12

EXCELLENCE
e You have overthrown . . . . . . Ex 15:7
did not come with *e* . . . . . 1 Cor 2:1

EXCELLENT
He is *e* in power . . . . Job 37:23
It shall be as *e* . . . . Ps 141:5
will speak of *e* things . . . . . . Prov 8:6
like Lebanon, *e* . . . . Song 5:15
for He has done *e* . . . . Is 12:5
in counsel and *e* . . . . Is 28:29
Inasmuch as an *e* . . . . Dan 5:12
the things that are *e* . . . . . . Rom 2:18
the things that are *e* . . . . . . Phil 1:10
e sacrifice than Cain . . . . . Heb 11:4
came to Him from the *E* . . . 2 Pet 1:17

EXCELS
Do you see a man who *e* . Prov 22:29
I saw that wisdom *e* . . . . . . Eccl 2:13
of the glory that *e* . . . . . . 2 Cor 3:10

EXCHANGE
man give in *e* for his soul. Matt 16:26

EXCHANGED
Nor can it be *e* . . . . Job 28:17
e the truth of God for . . . . . Rom 1:25
For even their women *e* . . . Rom 1:26

EXCLUDE
you, and when they *e* . . . . . Luke 6:22
they want to *e* you . . . . Gal 4:17

EXCUSE
God be angry at your *e* . . . . Eccl 5:6
but now they have no *e* . . John 15:22
they are without *e* . . . . Rom 1:20
do you think that we *e* . . 2 Cor 12:19

EXCUSES
began to make *e* . . . . Luke 14:18

EXECUTE
e vengeance on the . . . . Ps 149:7
if you thoroughly *e* . . . . Jer 7:5
e the fierceness . . . . Hos 11:9
e judgment also . . . . John 5:27
e wrath on him who . . . . . . Rom 13:4

EXECUTES
by the judgment He *e* . . . . . . Ps 9:16
e righteousness . . . . Ps 103:6
e justice for the . . . . Ps 146:7
e justice for me . . . . Mic 7:9

EXERCISE
those who are great *e* . . . . Matt 20:25
e yourself toward . . . . 1 Tim 4:7
e profits a little . . . . 1 Tim 4:8

EXERCISED
have their senses *e* . . . . Heb 5:14

EXHORT
we command and *e* . . . . 2 Thess 3:12
e him as a father . . . . 1 Tim 5:1
and *e* these things . . . . 1 Tim 6:2
doctrine, both to *e* . . . . Titus 1:9
Speak these things, *e* . . . . . Titus 2:15
e one another . . . . Heb 3:13

EXHORTATION
you have any word of *e* . . . Acts 13:15
he who exhorts, in *e* . . . . . . Rom 12:8
to reading, to *e* . . . . 1 Tim 4:13
with the word of *e* . . . . Heb 13:22

EXHORTED
For I earnestly *e* . . . . Jer 11:7
e and strengthened . . . . . . Acts 15:32
as you know how we *e* . . 1 Thess 2:11

EXILE
and also an *e* from . . . . . 2 Sam 15:19
The captive *e* hastens . . . . . . Is 51:14

EXIST
things which do not *e* . . . . . Rom 4:17
by Your will they *e* . . . . Rev 4:11

EXPECT
an hour you do not *e* . . . . Luke 12:40

EXPECTATION
The *e* of the poor . . . . Ps 9:18
God alone, for my *e* . . . . Ps 62:5
the people were in *e* . . . . . . Luke 3:15
a certain fearful *e* . . . . Heb 10:27

EXPERT
and the *e* enchanter . . . . Is 3:3
those of an *e* warrior . . . . . Jer 50:9
because you are *e* . . . . Acts 26:3

EXPLAIN
was no one who could *e* . . Gen 41:24
days they could not *e* . . . . Judg 14:14
"*E* this parable to us . . . . . Matt 15:15
to say, and hard to *e* . . . . . . Heb 5:11

EXPLAINED
He *e* all things to His . . . . . Mark 4:34

EXPLOIT
e all your . . . . Is 58:3
against those who *e* . . . . Mal 3:5
they will *e* you with . . . . . . 2 Pet 2:3

EXPOSED
his deeds should be *e* . . . . John 3:20
all things that are *e* . . . . . . Eph 5:13

EXPOUNDED
He *e* to them in all . . . . . Luke 24:27

EXPRESS
man cannot *e* it . . . . Eccl 1:8
of His glory and the *e* . . . . . . Heb 1:3

EXPRESSLY
of the LORD came *e* . . . . . . Ezek 1:3
Now the Spirit *e* . . . . 1 Tim 4:1

EXTEND
none to *e* mercy to him . . . . Ps 109:12
"Behold, I will *e* . . . . Is 66:12
did not *e* to you . . . . 2 Cor 10:14

EXTINGUISHED
broken, my days are *e* . . . . . Job 17:1
They are *e* . . . . Is 43:17

EXTOL
I will *e* You . . . . Ps 30:1
e Him who rides . . . . Ps 68:4

EXTOLLED
shall be exalted and *e* . . . . . Is 52:13

EXTORTION
e gathers it for him . . . . . . Prov 28:8
your neighbors by *e* . . . . . Ezek 22:12
they are full of *e* . . . . Matt 23:25

EXTORTIONERS
e will inherit . . . . 1 Cor 6:10

EXULT
in anguish I would *e* . . . . . . Job 6:10

EYE
e for *e* . . . . Ex 21:24
the ear, but now my *e* . . . . . Job 42:5
guide you with My *e* . . . . Ps 32:8
Behold, the *e* of the . . . . Ps 33:18
He who formed the *e* . . . . Ps 94:9
and the seeing *e* . . . . Prov 20:12
who has a generous *e* . . . . Prov 22:9
A man with an evil *e* . . . . . Prov 28:22
e that mocks his . . . . Prov 30:17
e is not satisfied . . . . Eccl 1:8
labors, nor is his *e* . . . . Eccl 4:8
for they shall see . . . . Is 52:8
e seen any God besides . . . . . Is 64:4
the apple of His *e* . . . . Zech 2:8
if your right *e* . . . . Matt 5:29
it was said, 'An *e* . . . . Matt 5:38
plank in your own *e* . . . . . . Matt 7:3
e causes you to sin . . . . . . Matt 18:9
Or is your *e* evil . . . . Matt 20:15
e causes you to sin . . . . . . Mark 9:47
the *e* of a needle . . . . Luke 18:25
"Because I am not an *e* . . 1 Cor 12:16
whole body were an *e* . . . 1 Cor 12:17
the twinkling of an *e* . . . . 1 Cor 15:52
every *e* will see Him . . . . Rev 1:7
your eyes with *e* salve . . . . . Rev 3:18

EYELIDS
His eyes behold, His *e* . . . . . Ps 11:4
e look right before . . . . Prov 4:25

EYES
e will be opened . . . . Gen 3:5
and you can be our *e* . . . . Num 10:31
she put paint on her *e* . . . 2 Kin 9:30
For the *e* of the . . . . 2 Chr 16:9
Do You have *e* of flesh . . . . . Job 10:4
And my *e* shall behold . . . . Job 19:27
I was *e* to the blind . . . . . . Job 29:15
e observe from afar . . . . . . Job 39:29
e are secretly fixed . . . . Ps 10:8
e are ever toward the . . . . . Ps 25:15
The *e* of the LORD are . . . . . . Ps 34:15
e fail while I wait . . . . Ps 69:3
e shall you look . . . . Ps 91:8
I will lift up my *e* . . . . Ps 121:1
not give sleep to my *e* . . . . Ps 132:4
e saw my substance . . . . . Ps 139:16
e look straight ahead . . . . . Prov 4:25
but the *e* of a fool . . . . . . Prov 17:24
Will you set your *e* . . . . . . Prov 23:5
Who has redness of *e* . . . . Prov 23:29
be wise in his own *e* . . . . . Prov 26:5
so the *e* of man are . . . . . Prov 27:20
The wise man's *e* . . . . Eccl 2:14

e than the wandering . . . . . . Eccl 6:9
You have dove's *e* . . . . Song 1:15
e have seen the King . . . . Is 6:5
of the book, and the *e* . . . . . Is 29:18
e fail from looking . . . . Is 38:14
O LORD, are not Your *e* . . . . . . Jer 5:3
Who have *e* and see . . . . Jer 5:21
e will weep bitterly . . . . Jer 13:17
For I will set My *e* . . . . Jer 24:6
rims were full of *e* . . . . Ezek 1:18
full of *e* all around . . . . . . Ezek 10:12
that horn which had *e* . . . . Dan 7:20
horn between his *e* . . . . Dan 8:5
You are of purer *e* . . . . Hab 1:13
But blessed are your *e* . . . . Matt 13:16
"He put clay on my *e* . . . . . John 9:15
e they have closed . . . . Acts 28:27
e that they should not . . . . Rom 11:8
plucked out your own *e* . . . . Gal 4:15
have seen with our *e* . . . . 1 John 1:1
the lust of the *e* . . . . 1 John 2:16
as snow, and His *e* . . . . Rev 1:14
and anoint your *e* . . . . Rev 3:18
creatures full of *e* . . . . Rev 4:6
horns and seven *e* . . . . Rev 5:6
tear from their *e* . . . . Rev 21:4

EYESERVICE
not with *e* . . . . Eph 6:6
the flesh, not with *e* . . . . . . Col 3:22

EYEWITNESSES
the beginning were *e* . . . . . Luke 1:2
e of His majesty . . . . 2 Pet 1:16

EZEKIEL
Sent to rebellious Israel, Ezek 2; 3
Prophesies by symbolic action:
    siege of Jerusalem, Ezek 4
    destruction of Jerusalem, Ezek 5
    captivity of Judah, Ezek 12:1–20
    destruction of the temple,
        Ezek 24:15–27
Visions of:
    God's glory, Ezek 1:4–28
    abominations, Ezek 8:5–18
    valley of dry bones, Ezek 37:1–14
    messianic times, Ezek 40—48
    river of life, Ezek 47:1–5
Parables, allegories, dirges of, Ezek
    15; 16; 17; 19; 23; 24

EZION GEBER
See ELATH
Town on the Red Sea, 1 Kin 9:26
Israelite encampment, Num 33:35
Seaport of Israel's navy, 1 Kin 22:48

EZRA
Scribe, priest and reformer of postex-
    ilic times; commissioned by
    Artaxerxes, Ezra 7
Returns with exiles to Jerusalem,
    Ezra 8
Institutes reforms, Ezra 9
Reads the Law, Neh 8
Assists in dedication of wall, Neh
    12:27–43

FABLES
nor give heed to *f* . . . . 1 Tim 1:4
be turned aside to *f* . . . . . . 2 Tim 4:4
cunningly devised *f* . . . . . 2 Pet 1:16

FACE
"For I have seen God *f* . . . . Gen 32:30
f shone while he . . . . Ex 34:29
he put a veil on his *f* . . . . . Ex 34:33
the LORD make His *f* . . . . . Num 6:25
Then he turned his *f* . . . . 2 Kin 20:2
curse You to Your *f* . . . . Job 1:11

me, I will see Your *f* . . . . . . Ps 17:15
Why do You hide Your *f* . . . Ps 44:24
and cause His *f* . . . . Ps 67:1
of his *f* is changed . . . . Eccl 8:1
sins have hidden His *f* . . . . . . Is 59:2
I have made your *f* . . . . . . Ezek 3:8
but to us shame of *f* . . . . . . Dan 9:7
deep sleep on my *f* . . . . Dan 10:9
before Your *f* who . . . . . . Matt 11:10
f shone like the sun . . . . . . Matt 17:2
always before my *f* . . . . . . Acts 2:25
dimly, but then *f* . . . . . . 1 Cor 13:12
look steadily at the *f* . . . . . 2 Cor 3:7
with unveiled *f* . . . . 2 Cor 3:18
withstood him to his *f* . . . . Gal 2:11
his natural *f* in a . . . . James 1:23
but the *f* of the LORD . . . . . 1 Pet 3:12
They shall see His *f* . . . . . . Rev 22:4

FACES
f were not ashamed . . . . Ps 34:5
hid, as it were, our *f* . . . . Is 53:3
be afraid of their *f* . . . . Jer 1:8
and all *f* turned pale . . . . . . Jer 30:6
they disfigure their *f* . . . . . Matt 6:16

FACTIONS
there must also be *f* . . . . 1 Cor 11:19

FADE
we all *f* as a leaf . . . . Is 64:6
and the leaf shall *f* . . . . Jer 8:13
rich man also will *f* . . . . James 1:11
and that does not *f* . . . . 1 Pet 1:4

FADES
withers, the flower *f* . . . . Is 40:7

FAIL
eyes shall look and *f* . . . . Deut 28:32
flesh and my heart *f* . . . . . . Ps 73:26
of the thirsty to *f* . . . . Is 32:6
their tongues *f* . . . . Is 41:17
whose waters do not *f* . . . . . Is 58:11
have caused wine to *f* . . . . Jer 48:33
of the olive may *f* . . . . Hab 3:17
nor shall the vine *f* . . . . Mal 3:11
that when you *f* . . . . Luke 16:9
tittle of the law to *f* . . . . . Luke 16:17
faith should not *f* . . . . . . Luke 22:32
they will *f* . . . . 1 Cor 13:8
Your years will not *f* . . . . . . Heb 1:12
For the time would *f* . . . . . Heb 11:32

FAILED
Not a word *f* of any . . . . . Josh 21:45
My relatives have *f* . . . . . . Job 19:14
refuge has *f* me . . . . Ps 142:4

FAILING
men's hearts *f* . . . . Luke 21:26

FAILS
my strength *f* because . . . . . Ps 31:10
my spirit *f* . . . . Ps 143:7
and every vision *f* . . . . . Ezek 12:22
Love never *f* . . . . 1 Cor 13:8

FAINT
the youths shall *f* . . . . Is 40:30
shall walk and not *f* . . . . . . Is 40:31
my heart is *f* in me . . . . Jer 8:18
and the infants *f* . . . . Lam 2:11

FAINTED
thirsty, their soul *f* . . . . . . Ps 107:5

FAINTHEARTED
unruly, comfort the *f* . . . 1 Thess 5:14

FAINTS
longs, yes, even *f* . . . . Ps 84:2
My soul *f* for Your . . . . Ps 119:81
And the whole heart *f* . . . . . . Is 1:5
the earth, neither *f* . . . . Is 40:28

FAIR
Behold, you are *f* . . . . Song 1:15
of the Lord is not *f* . . . . . . Ezek 18:25
to a place called *F* . . . . Acts 27:8
what is just and *f* . . . . Col 4:1

FAIR-MINDED
These were more *f* . . . . . . Acts 17:11

FAIRER
f than the sons . . . . Ps 45:2

FAIREST
another beloved, O *f* . . . . . Song 5:9
your beloved gone, O *f* . . . . Song 6:1

FAITH
in whom is no *f* . . . . Deut 32:20
shall live by his *f* . . . . Hab 2:4
you, O you of little *f* . . . . . Matt 6:30
not found such great *f* . . . . Matt 8:10
f as a mustard seed . . . . . Matt 17:20
that you have no *f* . . . . Mark 4:40
to them, "Have *f* . . . . Mark 11:22
"Increase our *f* . . . . Luke 17:5
will He really find *f* . . . . . Luke 18:8
a man full of *f* . . . . Acts 6:5
are sanctified by *f* . . . . . . Acts 26:18
for obedience to the *f* . . . . . Rom 1:5
God is revealed from *f* . . . . Rom 1:17
God, through *f* . . . . Rom 3:22
f apart from the deeds . . . . Rom 3:28
his *f* is accounted for . . . . . . Rom 4:5
f is made void and the . . . . Rom 4:14
those who are of the *f* . . . . Rom 4:16
f which we preach . . . . Rom 10:8
f comes by hearing . . . . . . Rom 10:17
and you stand by *f* . . . . . . Rom 11:20
in proportion to our *f* . . . . Rom 12:6
Do you have *f* . . . . Rom 14:22
he does not eat from *f* . . . . Rom 14:23
though I have all *f* . . . . . . 1 Cor 13:2
And now abide *f* . . . . 1 Cor 13:13
For we walk by *f* . . . . 2 Cor 5:7
the flesh I live by *f* . . . . . . Gal 2:20
or by the hearing of *f* . . . . . Gal 3:2
f are sons of Abraham . . . . . Gal 3:7
the law is not of *f* . . . . Gal 3:12
But after *f* has come . . . . . . Gal 3:25
f working through love . . . . . Gal 5:6
of the household of *f* . . . . . Gal 6:10
been saved through *f* . . . . . Eph 2:8
one Lord, one *f* . . . . Eph 4:5
to the unity of the *f* . . . . . . Eph 4:13
taking the shield of *f* . . . . . Eph 6:16
your work of *f* . . . . 1 Thess 1:3
for not all have *f* . . . . . . 2 Thess 3:2
having *f* and a good . . . . . 1 Tim 1:19
the mystery of the *f* . . . . . . 1 Tim 3:9
he has denied the *f* . . . . . . 1 Tim 5:8
I have kept the *f* . . . . 2 Tim 4:7
in our common *f* . . . . Titus 1:4
not being mixed with *f* . . . . Heb 4:2
f is the substance . . . . Heb 11:1
without *f* it is . . . . Heb 11:6
someone says he has *f* . . . . James 2:14
Show me your *f* . . . . James 2:18
and not by *f* only . . . . . . James 2:24
f will save the sick . . . . . . James 5:15
add to your *f* virtue . . . . . . 2 Pet 1:5
on your most holy *f* . . . . . . Jude 20
the patience and the *f* . . . . Rev 13:10
of God and the *f* . . . . Rev 14:12

FAITHFUL
God, He is God, the *f* . . . . . Deut 7:9
f disappear from among . . . . . Ps 12:1
LORD preserves the *f* . . . . . . Ps 31:23
whose spirit was not *f* . . . . . Ps 78:8
eyes shall be on the *f* . . . . . Ps 101:6

f spirit conceals a . . . . Prov 11:13
But who can find a *f* . . . . . Prov 20:6
f witness between us. . . . . . . Jer 42:5
the Holy One who is *f* . . . . Hos 11:12
"Who then is a *f* . . . . Matt 24:45
good and *f* servant . . . . . Matt 25:23
He who is *f* in what . . . . . Luke 16:10
if you have not been *f* . . . . Luke 16:12
have judged me to be *f* . . . Acts 16:15
God is *f*. . . . . 1 Cor 1:9
is my beloved and *f* . . . . . 1 Cor 4:17
But as God is *f* . . . . 2 Cor 1:18
f brethren in Christ. . . . . Col 1:2
He who calls you is *f* . . . 1 Thess 5:24
This is a *f* saying and . . . . 1 Tim 1:15
f High Priest in . . . . Heb 2:17
as Moses also was *f* . . . . . . Heb 3:2
He who promised is *f* . . . . Heb 10:23
He is *f* and just to . . . . . . 1 John 1:9
Be *f* until death. . . . . Rev 2:10
words are true and *f* . . . . . . Rev 21:5

FAITHFULNESS
I have declared Your *f* . . . . Ps 40:10
f You shall establish . . . . Ps 89:2
Your *f* also surrounds . . . . . . Ps 89:8
and Your *f* every night . . . . . Ps 92:2
f endures to all . . . . Ps 119:90
In Your *f* answer me . . . . . . Ps 143:1
counsels of old are *f*. . . . . . . Is 25:1
great is Your *f* . . . . Lam 3:23
unbelief make the *f* . . . . Rom 3:3

FAITHLESS
"O *f* generation . . . . Mark 9:19
If we are *f* . . . . 2 Tim 2:13

FALL
a deep sleep to *f* . . . . Gen 2:21
but do not let me *f* . . . . 2 Sam 24:14
Let them *f* by their . . . . Ps 5:10
For I am ready to *f* . . . . Ps 38:17
Yes, all kings shall *f* . . . . . . Ps 72:11
righteous man may *f* . . . . Prov 24:16
but the wicked shall *f* . . . . Prov 24:16
digs a pit will *f*. . . . . Prov 26:27
all their host shall *f* . . . . Is 34:4
men shall utterly *f* . . . . Is 40:30
of music, you shall *f* . . . . . Dan 3:5
And great was its *f* . . . . . . Matt 7:27
the blind, both will *f* . . . . Matt 15:14
the stars shall *f* . . . . Matt 24:29
"I saw Satan . . . . Luke 10:18
that they should *f* . . . . . . Rom 11:11
take heed lest he *f* . . . . . 1 Cor 10:12
with pride he *f*. . . . . 1 Tim 3:6
if they *f* away. . . . . Heb 6:6
lest anyone *f* short of . . . . . Heb 12:15
it all joy when you *f*. . . . . . James 1:2
and rocks, "F on us. . . . . . . Rev 6:16

FALLEN
"Babylon is *f*. . . . . Is 21:9
you have *f* from grace . . . . . Gal 5:4
And I saw a star *f*. . . . . Rev 9:1
"Babylon is *f*. . . . . Rev 14:8

FALLING
great drops of blood *f*. . . . Luke 22:44
f away comes first . . . . . 2 Thess 2:3

FALLS
who is alone when he *f* . . . . Eccl 4:10
And whoever *f*. . . . . Matt 21:44
master he stands or *f*. . . . . . Rom 14:4
its flower *f*. . . . . James 1:11
so that no rain *f* . . . . Rev 11:6

FALSE
"You shall not bear *f* . . . . . . Ex 20:16
I hate every *f* way . . . . . Ps 119:104
gives heed to *f* lips. . . . . . . Prov 17:4

f witness shall perish. . . . . Prov 21:28
and do not love a *f* . . . . . . Zech 8:17
"Beware of *f* prophets . . . . Matt 7:15
f christs and *f* . . . . Matt 24:24
and we are found *f*. . . . . . 1 Cor 15:15
among *f* brethren. . . . . . . 2 Cor 11:26
of *f* brethren . . . . Gal 2:4
f prophets have gone. . . . . 1 John 4:1
mouth of the *f* prophet . . . . Rev 16:13

FALSEHOOD
those who speak *f*. . . . . Ps 5:6
and brings forth *f* . . . . Ps 7:14
For their deceit is *f* . . . . . . Ps 119:118
remove *f* and lies far. . . . . . Prov 30:8
under *f* we have hidden. . . . . Is 28:15
offspring of *f*. . . . . Is 57:4

FALSELY
it, and swears *f* . . . . Lev 6:3
nor have we dealt *f* . . . . . . Ps 44:17
surely they swear *f*. . . . . Jer 5:2
words, swearing *f*. . . . . Hos 10:4
of evil against you *f* . . . . . Matt 5:11
f called knowledge . . . . . . 1 Tim 6:20

FAME
Sheba heard of the *f* . . . . 1 Kin 10:1
Your *f* went out. . . . . Ezek 16:14
them for praise and *f* . . . . . Zeph 3:19
Then His *f* went. . . . . Matt 4:24

FAMILIES
in you all the *f*. . . . . Gen 12:3
and makes their *f* . . . . Ps 107:41
the God of all the *f*. . . . . . . Jer 31:1
f which the LORD has . . . . . Jer 33:24
in your seed all the *f*. . . . . . Acts 3:25

FAMILY
shall mourn, every *f* . . . . . Zech 12:12
f were baptized. . . . . Acts 16:33
from whom the whole *f*. . . . . Eph 3:15

FAMINE
Now there was a *f* . . . . Gen 12:10
keep them alive in *f* . . . . . . Ps 33:19
He called for a *f*. . . . . Ps 105:16
send the sword, the *f* . . . . . Jer 24:10
of the fever of *f* . . . . Lam 5:10
I will increase the *f* . . . . . . Ezek 5:16
there arose a severe *f* . . . . . Luke 15:14

FAMINES
And there will be *f* . . . . . . Matt 24:7

FAMISH
righteous soul to *f* . . . . Prov 10:3

FAMISHED
honorable men are *f* . . . . Is 5:13

FAMOUS
and may his name be *f* . . . Ruth 4:14

FAN
not to *f* or to cleanse . . . . . Jer 4:11
His winnowing *f* . . . . Matt 3:12

FANCIES
with their own *f*. . . . . Prov 1:31

FAR
removed my brothers *f* . . . . Job 19:13
Your judgments are *f*. . . . . . . Ps 10:5
Be not *f* from Me . . . . Ps 22:11
those who are *f* . . . . Ps 73:27
The LORD is *f* from the . . . . Prov 15:29
but it was *f* from me. . . . . . . Eccl 7:23
removed their hearts *f* . . . . . . Is 29:13
Those near and those *f* . . . . Ezek 22:5
their heart is *f* from . . . . . Matt 15:8
going to a *f* country . . . . . Mark 13:34
though He is not *f* . . . . Acts 17:27
you who once were *f* . . . . . . Eph 2:13

FARMER
The hardworking *f* . . . . 2 Tim 2:6
See how the *f* waits. . . . . . . James 5:7

FASHIONED
have made me and *f* . . . . . . Job 10:8

FASHIONS
He *f* their hearts. . . . . Ps 33:15

FAST
f for me. . . . . Esth 4:16
f as you do this day . . . . Is 58:4
f that I have chosen. . . . . Is 58:5
Consecrate a *f* . . . . Joel 1:14
"Moreover, when you *f* . . . . Matt 6:16
disciples do not *f* . . . . Matt 9:14
I *f* twice a week . . . . Luke 18:12

FASTED
'Why have we *f* . . . . Is 58:3
'When you *f* and. . . . . Zech 7:5
And when He had *f* . . . . . . Matt 4:2

FASTENED
were its foundations *f*. . . . . . Job 38:6
'the peg that is *f*. . . . . Is 22:25

FASTING
I was *f* and praying. . . . . . . Neh 1:4
humbled myself with *f* . . . . Ps 35:13
are weak through *f* . . . . . . Ps 109:24
house on the day of *f*. . . . . . Jer 36:6
prayer and supplications,
    with *f* . . . . Dan 9:3
except by prayer and *f* . . . Matt 17:21
Four days ago I was *f*. . . . . Acts 10:30
give yourselves to *f* . . . . . . 1 Cor 7:5

FASTINGS
served God with *f* and
    prayers. . . . . Luke 2:37
in sleeplessness, in *f* . . . . . 2 Cor 6:5
in *f* often. . . . . 2 Cor 11:27

FAT
and you will eat the *f* . . . . Gen 45:18
f is the LORD's. . . . . Lev 3:16
Now Eglon was a very *f* . . . Judg 3:17
have closed up their *f* . . . . . Ps 17:10

FATHER
man shall leave his *f* . . . . . Gen 2:24
and you shall be a *f* . . . . . . Gen 17:4
'You are my *f* . . . . Job 17:14
I was a *f* to the poor . . . . . Job 29:16
A *f* of the fatherless. . . . . . . Ps 68:5
f pities his children . . . . . . Ps 103:13
the instruction of a *f* . . . . . Prov 4:1
God, Everlasting *F* . . . . Is 9:6
You, O LORD, are our *F* . . . . . Is 63:16
time cry to Me, My *F* . . . . . . Jer 3:4
for I am a *F* to Israel . . . . . . Jer 31:9
"A son honors his *f* . . . . . . Mal 1:6
Have we not all one *F* . . . . Mal 2:10
Our *F* in heaven. . . . . Matt 6:9
He who loves *f*. . . . . Matt 10:37
does anyone know the *F*. . Matt 11:27
'He who curses *f* . . . . Matt 15:4
for One is your *F* . . . . Matt 23:9
F will be divided . . . . Luke 12:53
F loves the Son . . . . John 3:35
F has been working. . . . . . . John 5:17
F raises the dead . . . . John 5:21
F judges no one. . . . . John 5:22
He has seen the *F* . . . . John 6:46
F who sent Me bears . . . . . John 8:18
we have one *F* . . . . John 8:41
of your *F* the devil. . . . . . . John 8:44
I and My *F* are one . . . . . John 10:30
and believe that the *F*. . . . John 10:38
'I am going to the *F* . . . . . John 14:28
F is the vinedresser. . . . . . . John 15:1

came forth from the *F* . . . . John 16:28
that he might be the *f* . . . Rom 4:11
"I have made you a *f* . . . . . Rom 4:17
"I will be a *F* . . . . 2 Cor 6:18
one God and *F* of all . . . . . . Eph 4:6
but exhort him as a *f* . . . . . 1 Tim 5:1
"I will be to Him a *F* . . . . Heb 1:5
without *f*, without mother . . . Heb 7:3
comes down from the *F* . . James 1:17
if you call on the *F* . . . . 1 Pet 1:17
and testify that the *F* . . . . 1 John 4:14

FATHER'S
you in My *F* kingdom . . . . Matt 26:29
I must be about My *F* . . . . . Luke 2:49
F house are many . . . . John 14:2
that a man has his *f* . . . . . . 1 Cor 5:1

FATHERLESS
my hand against the *f* . . . . Job 31:21
the helper of the *f* . . . . Ps 10:14
to do justice to the *f* . . . . . . Ps 10:18
He relieves the *f* . . . . Ps 146:9
the fields of the *f* . . . . Prov 23:10
do not defend the *f* . . . . Is 1:23
they may rob the *f* . . . . Is 10:2
You the *f* finds mercy . . . . . . Hos 14:3

FATHERS
the LORD God of our *f* . . . . . Ezra 7:27
f trusted in You . . . . Ps 22:4
our ears, O God, our *f* . . . . . . Ps 44:1
have sinned with our *f* . . . . Ps 106:6
f ate the manna . . . . John 6:31
of whom are the *f* . . . . Rom 9:5
you do not have many *f* . 1 Cor 4:15
unaware that all our *f* . . . . 1 Cor 10:1

FATLING
and the *f* together . . . . Is 11:6

FATNESS
as with marrow and *f* . . . . . . Ps 63:5
of the root and *f* . . . . Rom 11:17

FATTED
f cattle are . . . . Matt 22:4
has killed the *f* . . . . Luke 15:27

FATTENED
f your hearts as . . . . James 5:5

FAULT
find no charge or *f* . . . . Dan 6:4
I have found no *f* . . . . Luke 23:14
does He still find *f* . . . . . . Rom 9:19
of God without *f* . . . . Phil 2:15
for they are without *f* . . . . . Rev 14:5

FAULTLESS
covenant had been *f* . . . . . . Heb 8:7
to present you *f* . . . . Jude 24

FAULTS
"I remember my *f* . . . . Gen 41:9
me from secret *f* . . . . Ps 19:12
are beaten for your *f* . . . . . 1 Pet 2:20

FAVOR
granted me life and *f* . . . . . Job 10:12
f You will . . . . Ps 5:12
His *f* is for life . . . . Ps 30:5
A good man obtains *f* . . . . Prov 12:2
but his *f* is like dew . . . . Prov 19:12
and seek the LORD's *f* . . . . Jer 26:19
and stature, and in *f* . . . . . Luke 2:52
God and having *f* . . . . Acts 2:47
to do the Jews a *f* . . . . . . Acts 24:27

FAVORABLE
And will He be *f* . . . . Ps 77:7
LORD, You have been *f* . . . . . Ps 85:1

FAVORED
because You *f* them . . . . Ps 44:3
"Rejoice, highly *f* . . . . Luke 1:28

FAVORITISM
do not show personal *f* . . . Luke 20:21
God shows personal *f* . . . . . . Gal 2:6

FEAR
this and live, for I *f* God . . . Gen 42:18
f the people of the . . . . Num 14:9
to put the dread and *f* . . . . Deut 2:25
f Me all the days . . . . Deut 4:10
the LORD your God . . . . . . Deut 6:2
book, that you may *f* . . . . Deut 28:58
said, "Does Job *f* . . . . Job 1:9
Yes, you cast off *f* . . . . Job 15:4
Surely no *f* of me will . . . . . . Job 33:7
He mocks at *f* . . . . Job 39:22
they are in great *f* . . . . Ps 14:5
The *f* of the LORD is . . . . Ps 19:9
of death, I will *f* . . . . Ps 23:4
whom shall I *f* . . . . Ps 27:1
Let all the earth *f* . . . . Ps 33:8
Oh, *f* the LORD . . . . Ps 34:9
there is no *f* of God . . . . Ps 36:1
they are in great *f* . . . . Ps 53:5
hear, all you who *f* . . . . Ps 66:16
f You as long as the . . . . Ps 72:5
heart to *f* Your name . . . . . . Ps 86:11
The *f* of the LORD is . . . . Ps 111:10
f You will be glad . . . . Ps 119:74
f the LORD and depart . . . . . Prov 3:7
The *f* of man brings a . . . . Prov 29:25
it, that men should *f* . . . . . . Eccl 3:14
F God and keep His . . . . . . Eccl 12:13
let Him be your *f* . . . . Is 8:13
"Be strong, do not *f* . . . . Is 35:4
Do you not *f* Me . . . . Jer 5:22
who would not *f* . . . . Jer 10:7
but I will put My *f* . . . . Jer 32:40
who *f* My name the Sun . . . . Mal 4:2
f Him who is able . . . . Matt 10:28
"Do not *f* . . . . Luke 12:32
a judge who did not *f* . . . . Luke 18:2
"Do you not even *f* . . . . . . Luke 23:40
And walking in the *f* . . . . . . Acts 9:31
the rest also may *f* . . . . . . 1 Tim 5:20
given us a spirit of *f* . . . . . . 2 Tim 1:7
those who through *f* . . . . Heb 2:15
His rest, let us *f* . . . . Heb 4:1
because of His godly *f* . . . . . Heb 5:7
F God . . . . 1 Pet 2:17
love casts out *f* . . . . 1 John 4:18
Do not *f* any of . . . . Rev 2:10

FEARED
But the midwives *f* . . . . Ex 1:17
He is also to be *f* . . . . 1 Chr 16:25
f God more than . . . . Neh 7:2
Yourself, are to be *f* . . . . Ps 76:7
Then those who *f* . . . . Mal 3:16

FEARFUL
f in praises, doing . . . . Ex 15:11
them, "Why are you *f* . . . . Matt 8:26
It is a *f* thing to . . . . Heb 10:31

FEARFUL-HEARTED
to those who are *f* . . . . Is 35:4

FEARFULLY
f and wonderfully made . . . Ps 139:14

FEARFULNESS
F and trembling have . . . . . . Ps 55:5
f has seized the . . . . Is 33:14

FEARING
is devoted to *f* You . . . . Ps 119:38
sincerity of heart, *f* . . . . . . Col 3:22
forsook Egypt, not *f* . . . . . . Heb 11:27

FEARS
upright man, one who *f* . . . . Job 1:8
Who is the man that *f* . . . . . Ps 25:12

me from all my *f* . . . . Ps 34:4
an oath as he who *f* . . . . Eccl 9:2
every nation whoever *f* . . . Acts 10:35
f has not been made . . . . 1 John 4:18

FEAST
Then he made them a *f* . . . Gen 19:3
and you shall keep a *f* . . . Num 29:12
f is made for laughter . . . . Eccl 10:19
f day the terrors that . . . . . Lam 2:22
hate, I despise your *f* . . . . Amos 5:21
every year at the *F* . . . . . . Luke 2:41
when you give a *f* . . . . . . Luke 14:13
Now the Passover, a *f* . . . . . John 6:4
great day of the *f* . . . . John 7:37
let us keep the *f* . . . . 1 Cor 5:8

FEASTING
go to the house of *f* . . . . . . Eccl 7:2

FEASTS
I will turn your *f* . . . . Amos 8:10
the best places at *f* . . . . . Luke 20:46
spots in your love *f* . . . . Jude 12

FED
f me all my life long . . . . Gen 48:15
and *f* you with manna . . . . Deut 8:3
but the shepherds *f* . . . . . Ezek 34:8
f you with milk and . . . . . 1 Cor 3:2

FEEBLE
strengthened the *f* . . . . Job 4:4
And there was none *f* . . . . Ps 105:37
And my flesh is *f* . . . . Ps 109:24
Every hand will be *f* . . . . . Ezek 7:17
hang down, and the *f* . . . . Heb 12:12

FEED
ravens to *f* you there . . . . 1 Kin 17:4
death shall *f* on them . . . . . Ps 49:14
of the righteous *f* . . . . . . Prov 10:21
and *f* your flocks . . . . Is 61:5
to him, "*F* My lambs . . . . . John 21:15
to him, "*F* My sheep . . . . . John 21:17
your enemy hungers, *f* . . . Rom 12:20
my goods to *f* the poor . . . 1 Cor 13:3

FEEDS
"Ephraim *f* on the wind . . . . Hos 12:1
your heavenly Father *f* . . . Matt 6:26

FEET
So she lay at his *f* . . . . Ruth 3:14
so my *f* did not slip . . . . 2 Sam 22:37
f they hang far . . . . Job 28:4
I was *f* to the lame . . . . . . Job 29:15
all things under his *f* . . . . . . Ps 8:6
He makes my *f* like the . . . . Ps 18:33
You have set my *f* . . . . Ps 31:8
does not allow our *f* . . . . . . Ps 66:9
f had almost stumbled . . . . . Ps 73:2
f have been standing . . . . . Ps 122:2
For their *f* run to . . . . Prov 1:16
Her *f* go down to death . . . . Prov 5:5
sandals off your *f* . . . . Is 20:2
called him to His *f* . . . . Is 41:2
up the dust of your *f* . . . . . Is 49:23
mountains are the *f* . . . . . . Is 52:7
place of My *f* glorious . . . . Is 60:13
are the dust of His *f* . . . . . Nah 1:3
my *f* like deer's *f* . . . . . . Hab 3:19
in that day His *f* . . . . Zech 14:4
two hands or two *f* . . . . . . Matt 18:8
began to wash His *f* . . . . . Luke 7:38
also sat at Jesus' *f* . . . . . Luke 10:39
wash the disciples' *f* . . . . . John 13:5
at the apostles' *f* . . . . Acts 4:35
f are swift to shed . . . . . . Rom 3:15
beautiful are the *f* . . . . . . Rom 10:15
all things under His *f* . . . 1 Cor 15:27
and having shod your *f* . . . Eph 6:15

fell at His *f* as dead . . . . Rev 1:17
And I fell at his *f* . . . . Rev 19:10

FELIX
Governor of Judea; letter addressed
to, Acts 23:24–30
Paul's defense before, Acts 24:1–27

FELLOW
f servants who owed . . . . . Matt 18:28
begins to beat his *f* . . . . . . Matt 24:49
f worker concerning . . . . . 2 Cor 8:23
f citizens with the . . . . Eph 2:19
Gentiles should be *f* . . . . . . Eph 3:6
rest of my *f* workers . . . . Phil 4:3
These are my only *f* . . . . . Col 4:11
that we may become *f* . . . . 3 John 8
I am your *f* servant . . . . . . Rev 19:10

FELLOWSHIP
doctrine and *f* . . . . Acts 2:42
were called into the *f* . . . . 1 Cor 1:9
not want you to have *f* . 1 Cor 10:20
f has righteousness . . . . . . 2 Cor 6:14
the right hand of *f* . . . . Gal 2:9
And have no *f* with the . . . . Eph 5:11
for your *f* in the . . . . Phil 1:5
of love, if any *f* . . . . Phil 2:1
and the *f* of His . . . . Phil 3:10
also may have *f* . . . . 1 John 1:3
we say that we have *f* . . . 1 John 1:6
the light, we have *f* . . . . . 1 John 1:7

FENCE
and a tottering *f* . . . . Ps 62:3

FENCED
He has *f* up my way . . . . . . Job 19:8

FERTILIZE
I dig around it and *f* . . . . . Luke 13:8

FERVENT
and being *f* in spirit . . . . . . Acts 18:25
f prayer of a . . . . James 5:16
all things have *f* . . . . 1 Pet 4:8
will melt with *f* . . . . 2 Pet 3:10

FERVENTLY
you, always laboring *f* . . . . . Col 4:12
love one another *f* . . . . . . 1 Pet 1:22

FESTIVAL
night when a holy *f* . . . . Is 30:29
or regarding a *f* . . . . Col 2:16

FESTUS
Governor of Judea, Acts 24:27
Paul's defense made to, Acts 25:1–22

FETCH
f my knowledge from . . . . . . Job 36:3

FETTERS
hurt his feet with *f* . . . . . . Ps 105:18
their nobles with *f* . . . . Ps 149:8

FEVER
f which shall . . . . Lev 26:16
my bones burn with *f* . . . . . Job 30:30
and rebuked the *f* . . . . Luke 4:39

FEW
f and evil have been . . . . . Gen 47:9
f days and full of . . . . Job 14:1
Let his days be *f* . . . . Ps 109:8
let your words be *f* . . . . Eccl 5:2
and there are *f* . . . . Matt 7:14
but the laborers are *f* . . . . . Matt 9:37
called, but *f* chosen . . . . . . Matt 20:16
"Lord, are there *f* . . . . Luke 13:23
prepared, in which a *f* . . . 1 Pet 3:20
I have a *f* things . . . . Rev 2:20

FIDELITY
but showing all good *f* . . . . Titus 2:10

FIELD
Let the *f* be joyful . . . . Ps 96:12
to house; they add *f* . . . . Is 5:8
becomes a fruitful *f* . . . . Is 32:15
The *f* is the world . . . . . . Matt 13:38
and buys that *f* . . . . Matt 13:44
f has been called the . . . . Matt 27:8
you are God's *f* . . . . 1 Cor 3:9

FIELD OF BLOOD
A field bought as a cemetery for
Judas's burial, Matt 27:1–10
Predicted in the OT, Zech 11:12, 13

FIELDS
f yield no food . . . . Hab 3:17
living out in the *f* . . . . Luke 2:8
eyes and look at the *f* . . . . John 4:35

FIERCENESS
f has deceived you . . . . Jer 49:16
the winepress of the *f* . . . . Rev 19:15

FIERY
the LORD sent *f* serpents . . . Num 21:6
right hand came a *f* . . . . . . Deut 33:2
shall make them as a *f* . . . . Ps 21:9
offspring will be a *f* . . . . Is 14:29
burning *f* furnace . . . . Dan 3:6
concerning the *f* . . . . 1 Pet 4:12
f red dragon having . . . . . . Rev 12:3

FIG
f leaves together . . . . Gen 3:7
his vine and his *f* . . . . 1 Kin 4:25
fruit falling from a *f* . . . . Is 34:4
f tree may not blossom . . . . Hab 3:17
fruit on this *f* . . . . Luke 13:7
"Look at the *f* . . . . Luke 21:29
'I saw you under the *f* . . . . John 1:50
Can a *f* tree . . . . James 3:12
f tree drops its late . . . . Rev 6:13

FIGHT
The LORD will *f* . . . . Ex 14:14
you go with me to *f* . . . . . 1 Kin 22:4
Our God will *f* for us . . . . . Neh 4:20
My servants would *f* . . . . . John 18:36
to him, let us not *f* . . . . . . Acts 23:9
F the good *f* . . . . 1 Tim 6:12
have fought the good *f* . . . 2 Tim 4:7
You *f* and war . . . . James 4:2

FIGHTS
your God is He who *f* . . . . Josh 23:10
because my lord *f* . . . . . . 1 Sam 25:28
f come from among . . . . . . James 4:1

FIGS
puts forth her green *f* . . . . Song 2:13
f set before the . . . . Jer 24:1
from thornbushes or *f* . . . . Matt 7:16
men do not gather *f* . . . . . Luke 6:44
or a grapevine bear *f* . . . . James 3:12

FIGURATIVELY
brethren, I have *f* . . . . 1 Cor 4:6

FIGURE
and using no *f* . . . . John 16:29

FILL
f the earth and subdue . . . . Gen 1:28
wealth, that I may *f* . . . . . . Prov 8:21
"Do I not *f* heaven . . . . Jer 23:24
f this temple with . . . . Hag 2:7
"*F* the waterpots . . . . John 2:7
that He might *f* . . . . Eph 4:10
so as always to *f* . . . . 1 Thess 2:16

FILLED
the whole earth be *f* . . . . . . Ps 72:19
Then our mouth was *f* . . . . Ps 126:2
for they shall be *f* . . . . Matt 5:6
"Let the children be *f* . . . . Mark 7:27

he would gladly have *f* . . . Luke 15:16
all *f* with the Holy Spirit . . . . Acts 2:4
all *f* with the Holy Spirit . . . Acts 4:31
being *f* with all . . . . Rom 1:29
full of goodness, *f* . . . . . . Rom 15:14
that you may be *f* . . . . Eph 3:19
but be *f* with the . . . . Eph 5:18
being *f* with the . . . . Phil 1:11
peace, be warmed and *f* . . James 2:16

FILTH
has washed away the *f* . . . . . Is 4:4
been made as the *f* . . . . . 1 Cor 4:13
the removal of the *f* . . . . . 1 Pet 3:21

FILTHINESS
from all your *f* . . . . Ezek 36:25
ourselves from all *f* . . . . . . 2 Cor 7:1
lay aside all *f* . . . . James 1:21
abominations and the *f* . . . Rev 17:4

FILTHY
is abominable and *f* . . . . . . Job 15:16
with *f* garments . . . . Zech 3:3
malice, blasphemy, *f* . . . . . . Col 3:8
poor man in *f* clothes . . . . James 2:2
oppressed by the *f* . . . . . . 2 Pet 2:7
let him be *f* . . . . Rev 22:11

FIND
sure your sin will *f* . . . . . Num 32:23
Almighty, we cannot *f* . . . . Job 37:23
life to those who *f* . . . . Prov 4:22
that no one can *f* . . . . Eccl 3:11
waters, for you will *f* . . . . . Eccl 11:1
seek, and you will *f* . . . . . . Matt 7:7
for My sake will *f* . . . . . . Matt 10:39
when he comes, will *f* . . . . Matt 24:46
f a Babe wrapped . . . . Luke 2:12
f no fault in this Man . . . . Luke 23:4
If *f* then a law . . . . Rom 7:21
f grace to help in . . . . Heb 4:16

FINDING
great things past *f* . . . . Job 9:10
and *f* none . . . . Luke 11:24
and His ways past *f* . . . . . Rom 11:33

FINDS
f me *f* life . . . . Prov 8:35
f a wife *f* a good . . . . Prov 18:22
Whatever your hand *f* . . . . Eccl 9:10
and he who seeks *f* . . . . . . Matt 7:8
f his life will lose . . . . . . Matt 10:39
and he who seeks *f* . . . . . Luke 11:10

FINE
Then I beat them as *f* . . . 2 Sam 22:43
gold, yea, than much *f* . . . . Ps 19:10
f gold is a wise . . . . Prov 25:12
set on bases of *f* gold . . . . Song 5:15
more rare than *f* . . . . Is 13:12
and for *f* clothing . . . . Is 23:18
how changed the *f* . . . . Lam 4:1
rings, in *f* apparel . . . . James 2:2
for the *f* linen is the . . . . . . Rev 19:8

FINGER
written with the *f* . . . . Ex 31:18
f shall be thicker . . . . 1 Kin 12:10
the pointing of the *f* . . . . Is 58:9
dip the tip of his *f* . . . . . . Luke 16:24
the ground with His *f* . . . . . John 8:6
"Reach your *f* . . . . John 20:27

FINGERS
the work of Your *f* . . . . Ps 8:3
he points with his *f* . . . . . . Prov 6:13
that which their own *f* . . . . . . Is 2:8
with one of their *f* . . . . . . Matt 23:4

FINISH
city, to the *f* . . . . Dan 9:24

he has enough to *f* . . . . . . Luke 14:28
has given Me to *f* . . . . John 5:36
so that I may *f* . . . . Acts 20:24

FINISHED
f the work which You . . . . . John 17:4
He said, "It is *f* . . . . John 19:30
I have *f* the race . . . . 2 Tim 4:7
thousand years were *f* . . . . . Rev 20:3

FIRE
rained brimstone and *f* . . . Gen 19:24
to him in a flame of *f* . . . . . Ex 3:2
by day, and *f* was over . . . . . Ex 40:38
God, who answers by *f* . . . 1 Kin 18:24
LORD was not in the *f* . . . . 1 Kin 19:12
I was musing, the *f* . . . . Ps 39:3
we went through *f* . . . . Ps 66:12
they have set *f* . . . . Ps 74:7
f goes before Him . . . . Ps 97:3
f and hail. . . . . Ps 148:8
burns as the *f* . . . . Is 9:18
says the LORD, whose *f* . . . . . Is 31:9
you walk through the *f* . . . . . Is 43:2
f that burns all the. . . . . Is 65:5
on whose bodies the *f* . . . . Dan 3:27
He break out like *f* . . . . . . Amos 5:6
for conflict by *f* . . . . Amos 7:4
like a refiner's *f* . . . . Mal 3:2
the Holy Spirit and *f* . . . . . Matt 3:11
f is not quenched . . . . Mark 9:44
"I came to send *f* . . . . Luke 12:49
tongues, as of *f* . . . . Acts 2:3
f taking vengeance. . . . . . 2 Thess 1:8
and that burned with *f* . . . Heb 12:18
And the tongue is a *f* . . . . James 3:6
vengeance of eternal *f* . . . . . Jude 7
f came down from God . . . Rev 20:9
into the lake of *f* . . . . Rev 20:14

FIREBRAND
f plucked from the. . . . . . Amos 4:11

FIREBRANDS
a madman who throws *f* . . Prov 26:18
two stubs of smoking *f* . . . . . Is 7:4

FIRM
their strength is *f* . . . . Ps 73:4
f the feeble knees . . . . Is 35:3
of the hope *f* to the . . . . Heb 3:6

FIRMAMENT
Thus God made the *f* . . . . . . Gen 1:7
f shows His handiwork . . . . . Ps 19:1
in His mighty *f* . . . . Ps 150:1
brightness of the *f* . . . . Dan 12:3

FIRST
The *f* one to plead his . . . . Prov 18:17
f father sinned . . . . Is 43:27
desires to be *f* . . . . Matt 20:27
f shall be slave . . . . Mark 10:44
And the gospel must *f* . . . Mark 13:10
evil, of the Jew *f* . . . . Rom 2:9
"Or who has *f* . . . . Rom 11:35
f man Adam became a . . 1 Cor 15:45
f a willing mind. . . . . 2 Cor 8:12
that we who *f* trusted . . . . . Eph 1:12
For Adam was formed *f* . 1 Tim 2:13
f covenant had been . . . . . . Heb 8:7
love Him because He *f* . . 1 John 4:19
I am the F and the . . . . Rev 1:17
you have left your *f* . . . . . . Rev 2:4
is the *f* resurrection. . . . . . . Rev 20:5

FIRSTBORN
LORD struck all the *f* . . . . . Ex 12:29
I will make him My *f* . . . . . Ps 89:27
Shall I give my *f*. . . . . Mic 6:7
brought forth her *f* . . . . . . Matt 1:25
that He might be the *f* . . . Rom 8:29

invisible God, the *f* . . . . Col 1:15
the beginning, the *f* . . . . . . Col 1:18
witness, the *f* from . . . . Rev 1:5

FIRSTFRUIT
For if the *f* is holy . . . . . . Rom 11:16

FIRSTFRUITS
and with the *f*. . . . . Prov 3:9
also who have the *f* . . . . . Rom 8:23
and has become the *f* . . 1 Cor 15:20
Christ the *f* . . . . 1 Cor 15:23
might be a kind of *f* . . . . James 1:18
among men, being *f*. . . . . Rev 14:4

FISH
f taken in a cruel net . . . . . . Eccl 9:12
had prepared a great *f* . . . . . Jon 1:17
do You make men like *f*. . . Hab 1:14
Or if he asks for a *f* . . . . . . Matt 7:10
belly of the great *f*. . . . . . Matt 12:40
five loaves and two *f* . . . . Matt 14:17
and likewise the *f* . . . . . . John 21:13

FISHERMEN
The *f* also will mourn . . . . . . Is 19:8
I will send for many *f*. . . . . Jer 16:16

FISHERS
and I will make you *f* . . . . Matt 4:19

FIT
and looking back, is *f*. . . . Luke 9:62

FITTING
Is it *f* to say to a. . . . . Job 34:18
Luxury is not *f*. . . . . Prov 19:10
so honor is not *f* . . . . Prov 26:1
things which are not *f* . . . . Rom 1:28
a High Priest was *f*. . . . . . . Heb 7:26

FIVE
f smooth stones. . . . . . . 1 Sam 17:40
about *f* thousand men . . . Matt 14:21
and *f* were foolish. . . . . . . Matt 25:2

FIXED
f My limit for it . . . . Job 38:10
is a great gulf *f* . . . . Luke 16:26

FLAME
appeared to him in a *f* . . . . . Ex 3:2
f will dry out his . . . . Job 15:30
f consumes the chaff . . . . Is 5:24
and tempest and the *f*. . . . . . Is 29:6
nor shall the *f*. . . . . Is 43:2
behind them a *f*. . . . . Joel 2:3
am tormented in this *f* . . . Luke 16:24
and His ministers a *f* . . . . . Heb 1:7
and His eyes like a *f* . . . . . . Rev 1:14

FLAMES
the LORD divides the *f* . . . . . Ps 29:7

FLAMING
f sword which turned. . . . . Gen 3:24
f fire in their land . . . . Ps 105:32
in *f* fire taking . . . . 2 Thess 1:8

FLATTER
I do not know how to *f* . . . Job 32:22
They *f* with their . . . . Ps 5:9

FLATTERED
Nevertheless they *f* . . . . . . Ps 78:36

FLATTERING
f mouth works ruin . . . . . Prov 26:28
f speech deceive . . . . Rom 16:18
any did we use *f*. . . . 1 Thess 2:5
swelling words, *f*. . . . . Jude 16

FLATTERS
with one who *f* with . . . . . Prov 20:19
f his neighbor spreads. . . . . Prov 29:5

FLATTERY
shall corrupt with *f* . . . . . Dan 11:32

FLAVOR
the salt loses its *f* . . . . Matt 5:13

FLAVORLESS
f food be eaten . . . . Job 6:6

FLAX
f He will not quench . . . . Is 42:3
f He will not quench. . . . . Matt 12:20

FLED
The sea saw it and *f*. . . . . . Ps 114:3
who have *f* for refuge. . . . . Heb 6:18

FLEE
f away secretly . . . . Gen 31:27
those who hate You *f* . . . . Num 10:35
such a man as I *f* . . . . Neh 6:11
who see me outside *f*. . . . . . Ps 31:11
Or where can I *f* . . . . Ps 139:7
And the shadows *f* . . . . . . Song 2:17
who are in Judea *f* . . . . . Matt 24:16
F sexual immorality . . . . 1 Cor 6:18
f these things and . . . . 1 Tim 6:11
devil and he will *f* . . . . James 4:7

FLESH
bone of my bones and *f* . . . Gen 2:23
shall become one *f*. . . . . . . Gen 2:24
f had corrupted their . . . . . Gen 6:12
f I shall see God. . . . . Job 19:26
My *f* also will rest in . . . . . . Ps 16:9
that they were but *f*. . . . . . . Ps 78:39
my heart and my *f* . . . . Ps 84:2
f shall bless His holy . . . . . Ps 145:21
is wearisome to the *f*. . . . . Eccl 12:12
And all *f* shall see it. . . . . . . Is 40:5
"All *f* is grass . . . . Is 40:6
out My Spirit on all *f* . . . . . Joel 2:28
Simon Bar-Jonah, for *f*. . . Matt 16:17
two shall become one *f*. . . Matt 19:5
were shortened, no *f*. . . . Matt 24:22
shall become one *f*. . . . . . Mark 10:8
f shall see the . . . . Luke 3:6
And the Word became *f*. . . John 1:14
I shall give is My *f* . . . . . . John 6:51
unless you eat the *f*. . . . . . John 6:53
f profits nothing . . . . John 6:63
according to the *f* . . . . John 8:15
when we were in the *f* . . . . Rom 7:5
of God, but with the *f* . . . . Rom 7:25
on the things of the *f* . . . . . Rom 8:5
you are not in the *f*. . . . . . . Rom 8:9
to the *f* you will die. . . . . . . Rom 8:13
f should glory in His . . . . . 1 Cor 1:29
"shall become one *f*. . . . . . 1 Cor 6:16
there is one kind of *f* . . . . 1 Cor 15:39
For the *f* lusts. . . . . Gal 5:17
have crucified the *f*. . . . . . . Gal 5:24
good showing in the *f*. . . . . Gal 6:12
may boast in your *f* . . . . . . Gal 6:13
f has ceased from sin . . . . . 1 Pet 4:1
of his time in the *f* . . . . 1 Pet 4:2
the lust of the *f* . . . . 1 John 2:16
has come in the *f*. . . . . . . 1 John 4:2
dreamers defile the *f* . . . . . . Jude 8

FLESHLY
f wisdom but by the. . . . . . 2 Cor 1:12
law of a *f* commandment . . Heb 7:16
f lusts which . . . . 1 Pet 2:11

FLIES
will send swarms of *f* . . . . . Ex 8:21
He sent swarms of *f*. . . . . . Ps 78:45
Dead *f* putrefy the . . . . Eccl 10:1

FLIGHT
put ten thousand to *f*. . . . . Lev 26:8
f shall perish from. . . . . . . Amos 2:14
And pray that your *f* . . . . Matt 24:20

FLINT
will seem like *f*. . . . . Is 5:28
set My face like a *f*. . . . . Is 50:7

FLINTY
out of the *f* rock . . . . Deut 8:15

FLOAT
and he made the iron *f*. . . . 2 Kin 6:6

FLOCK
Your people like a *f* . . . . Ps 77:20
wilderness like a *f* . . . . Ps 78:52
lead Joseph like a *f*. . . . . . . Ps 80:1
the footsteps of the *f*. . . . . Song 1:8
He will feed His *f* . . . . Is 40:11
you do not feed the *f*. . . . Ezek 34:3
are My *f*, the *f* . . . . Ezek 34:31
though the *f* be cut . . . . . . Hab 3:17
my God, "Feed the *f* . . . . . Zech 11:4
sheep of the *f* . . . . Matt 26:31
"Do not fear, little *f*. . . . . Luke 12:32
there will be one *f*. . . . . . John 10:16
of the milk of the *f* . . . . . . 1 Cor 9:7
Shepherd the *f* of God . . . . 1 Pet 5:2
examples to the *f*. . . . . 1 Pet 5:3

FLOCKS
are clothed with *f* . . . . Ps 65:13

FLOOD
the waters of the *f* . . . . Gen 7:10
sat enthroned at the F. . . . . Ps 29:10
them away like a *f* . . . . Ps 90:5
will you do in the *f*. . . . . . . Jer 12:5
the days before the *f*. . . . Matt 24:38
bringing in the *f*. . . . . 2 Pet 2:5
of his mouth like a *f*. . . . . Rev 12:15

FLOODS
me, and the *f* of. . . . . Ps 18:4
f on the dry ground . . . . Is 44:3
rain descended, the *f* . . . . Matt 7:25

FLOURISH
the righteous shall *f* . . . . . . Ps 72:7

FLOURISHED
your care for me has *f*. . . . Phil 4:10

FLOURISHES
In the morning it *f* . . . . Ps 90:6

FLOW
f away as waters which. . . . . Ps 58:7
and the waters *f*. . . . . Ps 147:18
that its spices may *f*. . . . . Song 4:16
all nations shall *f* . . . . Is 2:2
of his heart will *f* . . . . John 7:38

FLOWER
comes forth like a *f*. . . . . . Job 14:2
as a *f* of the field . . . . Ps 103:15
beauty is a fading *f*. . . . . . . Is 28:4
is like the *f* of the. . . . . Is 40:6
grass withers, the *f*. . . . . . . Is 40:7
if she is past the *f* . . . . . . 1 Cor 7:36
of man as the *f*. . . . . 1 Pet 1:24

FLOWERS
f appear on the earth . . . . Song 2:12

FLOWING
'a land *f* with milk . . . . Deut 6:3
of wisdom is a *f*. . . . . Prov 18:4
the Gentiles like a *f* . . . . . . Is 66:12

FLUTE
play the harp and *f*. . . . . . Gen 4:21
sound of the horn, *f*. . . . . . Dan 3:5

FLUTES
instruments and *f* . . . . Ps 150:4

FLUTISTS
harpists, musicians, *f* . . . . Rev 18:22

FLY
I would *f* . . . . Ps 55:6
soon cut off, and we *f*. . . . Ps 90:10
they *f* away like an . . . . . . Prov 23:5

FOE
and scattered the *f*. . . . . . . Ps 18:14

FOES
my enemies and *f* . . . . Ps 27:2
I will beat down his *f* . . . . . Ps 89:23

FOLD
are not of this *f*. . . . . John 10:16
a cloak You will *f*. . . . . Heb 1:12

FOLDING
slumber, a little *f*. . . . . Prov 6:10

FOLLOW
f what is altogether. . . . . . Deut 16:20
to Me, you who *f*. . . . . Is 51:1
f You wherever You go . . . . Matt 8:19
He said to him, "F . . . . Matt 9:9
up his cross, and *f* . . . . Mark 8:34
someone who does not *f* . . Mark 9:38
will by no means *f*. . . . . . . John 10:5
serves Me, let him *f*. . . . . . John 12:26
those of some men *f* . . . . . 1 Tim 5:24
that you should *f* . . . . 1 Pet 2:21
f the Lamb wherever He . . . . Rev 14:4
and their works *f*. . . . . Rev 14:13

FOLLOWED
f the Lord my God. . . . . Josh 14:8
Lord took me as I *f* . . . . . . Amos 7:15
we have left all and *f*. . . . Mark 10:28

FOLLOWS
My soul *f* close behind . . . . . Ps 63:8
f Me shall not walk. . . . . . . John 8:12

FOLLY
taken much notice of *f* . . . . Job 35:15
not turn back to *f*. . . . . Ps 85:8
F is joy to him who is . . . . Prov 15:21
of fools is *f*. . . . . Prov 16:22
F is set in great . . . . Eccl 10:6

FOOD
you it shall be for *f* . . . . . . Gen 1:29
that lives shall be *f* . . . . . . Gen 9:3
stranger, giving him *f*. . . . Deut 10:18
He gives *f* in. . . . . Job 36:31
he may bring forth *f* . . . . . Ps 104:14
Who gives *f* to all . . . . Ps 136:25
Much *f* is in the . . . . Prov 13:23
night, and provides *f*. . . . Prov 31:15
f which you eat shall. . . . . . Ezek 4:10
the fields yield no *f* . . . . . . Hab 3:17
that there may be *f* . . . . . . Mal 3:10
to give them *f*. . . . . Matt 24:45
and you gave Me *f* . . . . . . Matt 25:35
and he who has *f*. . . . . Luke 3:11
have you any *f*. . . . . John 21:5
they ate their *f*. . . . . Acts 2:46
our hearts with *f*. . . . . Acts 14:17
destroy with your *f*. . . . . . Rom 14:15
f makes my brother . . . . . . 1 Cor 8:13
the same spiritual *f*. . . . . . 1 Cor 10:3
sower, and bread for *f*. . . . 2 Cor 9:10
And having *f* and. . . . . 1 Tim 6:8
and not solid *f* . . . . Heb 5:12
But solid *f* belongs to . . . . . Heb 5:14
of *f* sold his . . . . Heb 12:16
destitute of daily *f*. . . . . . James 2:15

FOODS
F for the stomach. . . . . 1 Cor 6:13
f which God. . . . . 1 Tim 4:3

FOOL
f has said in his. . . . . Ps 14:1
is like sport to a *f*. . . . . . . Prov 10:23

f will be servant. . . . . Prov 11:29
f is right in his own . . . . . Prov 12:15
f lays open his folly . . . . . Prov 13:16
is too lofty for a *f*. . . . . . . Prov 24:7
whoever says, 'You *f*. . . . . Matt 5:22
I speak as a *f* . . . . 2 Cor 11:23
I have become a *f*. . . . . . . 2 Cor 12:11

FOOLISH
of the *f* women speaks . . . . . Job 2:10
I was so *f* and . . . . Ps 73:22
f pulls it down with . . . . . . Prov 14:1
f man squanders it . . . . . . Prov 21:20
"For My people are *f* . . . . . . Jer 4:22
Has not God made *f* . . . . . 1 Cor 1:20
O *f* Galatians . . . . Gal 3:1
were also once *f* . . . . Titus 3:3
But avoid *f* disputes . . . . . . Titus 3:9

FOOLISHLY
I speak *f* . . . . 2 Cor 11:21

FOOLISHNESS
O God, You know my *f* . . . . . Ps 69:5
Forsake *f* and live . . . . Prov 9:6
of fools proclaims *f* . . . . . Prov 12:23
The *f* of a man twists . . . . . Prov 19:3
F is bound up in the . . . . . Prov 22:15
devising of *f* is sin . . . . . . Prov 24:9
person will speak *f*. . . . . . . Is 32:6
of the cross is *f* . . . . 1 Cor 1:18
Because the *f* of God . . . . 1 Cor 1:25

FOOLS
f despise wisdom . . . . Prov 1:7
folly of *f* is deceit. . . . . . . Prov 14:8
F mock at sin. . . . . Prov 14:9
has no pleasure in *f* . . . . . . Eccl 5:4
We are *f* for Christ's . . . . . 1 Cor 4:10

FOOT
will not allow your *f* . . . . . . Ps 121:3
f will not stumble . . . . Prov 3:23
From the sole of the *f*. . . . . . Is 1:6
you turn away your *f* . . . . . Is 58:13
f causes you to sin. . . . . . Matt 18:8
you dash your *f*. . . . . Luke 4:11
If the *f* should say . . . . . 1 Cor 12:15

FOOTMEN
have run with the *f* . . . . . . Jer 12:5

FOOTSTEPS
f were not known. . . . . Ps 77:19
and shall make His *f*. . . . . Ps 85:13

FOOTSTOOL
Your enemies Your *f*. . . . . . Ps 110:1
Your enemies Your *f* . . . . Matt 22:44
"Sit here at my *f*. . . . . . . James 2:3

FORBID
said, "Do not *f*. . . . . Mark 9:39
"Can anyone *f*. . . . . Acts 10:47
prophesy, and do not *f*. . . 1 Cor 14:39
f that I should boast. . . . . . Gal 6:14

FORBIDDING
confidence, no one *f* . . . . Acts 28:31
f us to speak to the . . . . . 1 Thess 2:16
f to marry . . . . 1 Tim 4:3

FORCE
violent take it by *f*. . . . . . Matt 11:12
come and take Him by *f*. . . John 6:15
a testament is in *f* . . . . . . Heb 9:17

FORCEFUL
f are right words . . . . Job 6:25

FORCES
Though they join *f*. . . . . . Prov 11:21

FOREFATHERS
f who refused to hear . . . . . Jer 11:10
and oppressed our *f*. . . . . Acts 7:19
conscience, as my *f*. . . . . . 2 Tim 1:3

FOREHEADS

against their *f* . . . . Ezek 3:8
put a mark on the *f* . . . . Ezek 9:4
seal of God on their *f* . . . . Rev 9:4
his mark on their *f* . . . . Rev 20:4

FOREIGNER

"I am a *f* and a . . . . Gen 23:4
of me, since I am a *f* . . . . . Ruth 2:10
to God except this *f* . . . . Luke 17:18
who speaks will be a *f* . . . 1 Cor 14:11

FOREIGNERS

with the children of *f* . . . . Is 2:6
f shall build up your . . . . Is 60:10
f who were there . . . . Acts 17:21
longer strangers and *f* . . . . . Eph 2:19

FOREKNEW

For whom He *f* . . . . Rom 8:29
His people whom He *f* . . . . . Rom 11:2

FOREKNOWLEDGE

purpose and *f* of God . . . . . Acts 2:23
according to the *f* . . . . 1 Pet 1:2

FOREORDAINED

He indeed was *f* . . . . 1 Pet 1:20

FORERUNNER

f has entered for us . . . . Heb 6:20

FORESAW

'I *f* the LORD . . . . Acts 2:25

FORESEEING

f that God would . . . . Gal 3:8

FORESEES

A prudent man *f* . . . . Prov 22:3

FOREST

beast of the *f* is Mine . . . . . . Ps 50:10
See how great a *f* . . . . James 3:5

FORESTS

and strips the *f* . . . . Ps 29:9

FORETOLD

have also *f* these days . . . . . Acts 3:24
killed those who *f* . . . . Acts 7:52

FOREVER

and eat, and live *f* . . . . Gen 3:22
to our children *f* . . . . Deut 29:29
has loved Israel *f* . . . . 1 Kin 10:9
I would not live *f* . . . . Job 7:16
from this generation *f* . . . . Ps 12:7
LORD sits as King *f* . . . . Ps 29:10
Do not cast us off *f* . . . . Ps 44:23
throne, O God, is *f* . . . . Ps 45:6
"You are a priest *f* . . . . Ps 110:4
His mercy endures *f* . . . . . . Ps 136:1
will bless Your name *f* . . . . . Ps 145:1
who keeps truth *f* . . . . Ps 146:6
The LORD shall reign *f* . . . . Ps 146:10
for riches are not *f* . . . . . . Prov 27:24
Trust in the LORD *f* . . . . Is 26:4
of our God stands *f* . . . . Is 40:8
My salvation will be *f* . . . . . . Is 51:6
will not cast off *f* . . . . Lam 3:31
be the name of God *f* . . . . . Dan 2:20
Like the stars *f* . . . . Dan 12:3
of the LORD our God *f* . . . . . . Mic 4:5
and the glory *f* . . . . Matt 6:13
the Christ remains *f* . . . . John 12:34
who is blessed *f* . . . . 2 Cor 11:31
to whom be glory *f* . . . . Gal 1:5
generation, *f* and ever . . . . . Eph 3:21
and Father be glory *f* . . . . . Phil 4:20
throne, O God, is *f* . . . . Heb 1:8
has been perfected *f* . . . . . . Heb 7:28
lives and abides *f* . . . . 1 Pet 1:23
of darkness *f* . . . . Jude 13
power, both now and *f* . . . . . Jude 25
And they shall reign *f* . . . . Rev 22:5

FOREVERMORE

Blessed be the LORD *f* . . . . . . Ps 89:52
this time forth and *f* . . . . . . Ps 113:2
behold, I am alive *f* . . . . . . Rev 1:18

FOREWARNED

all such, as we also *f* . . . . 1 Thess 4:6

FORGAVE

f the iniquity of my . . . . Ps 32:5
to repay, he freely *f* . . . . . . Luke 7:42
God in Christ *f* . . . . Eph 4:32
even as Christ *f* . . . . Col 3:13

FORGED

The proud have *f* . . . . Ps 119:69

FORGERS

But you *f* of lies . . . . Job 13:4

FORGET

"For God has made me *f* . . Gen 41:51
yourselves, lest you *f* . . . . . . Deut 4:23
f the covenant of your . . . . Deut 4:31
the LORD who brought . . . Deut 6:12
the paths of all who *f* . . . . Job 8:13
all the nations that *f* . . . . Ps 9:17
this, you who *f* . . . . Ps 50:22
f the works of God . . . . Ps 78:7
I will not *f* Your word . . . . . Ps 119:16
If I *f* you . . . . Ps 137:5
My son, do not *f* . . . . Prov 3:1
f her nursing child . . . . Is 49:15
f the LORD your Maker . . . . . . Is 51:13
f her ornaments . . . . Jer 2:32
f your work and labor . . . . . Heb 6:10

FORGETFULNESS

in the land of *f* . . . . Ps 88:12

FORGETS

f the covenant of her . . . . . Prov 2:17
and immediately *f* . . . . . James 1:24

FORGETTING

f those things which . . . . . . Phil 3:13

FORGIVE

dwelling place, and *f* . . . . 1 Kin 8:39
f their sin and heal . . . . . 2 Chr 7:14
good, and ready to *f* . . . . . . Ps 86:5
And *f* us our debts . . . . . . Matt 6:12
Father will also *f* . . . . Matt 6:14
f men their trespasses . . . . Matt 6:15
his heart, does not *f* . . . . Matt 18:35
Who can *f* sins but God . . . Mark 2:7
f the sins of any . . . . John 20:23
you ought rather to *f* . . . . . 2 Cor 2:7
anything, I also *f* . . . . 2 Cor 2:10
F me this wrong . . . . 2 Cor 12:13
f us our sins and to . . . . . 1 John 1:9

FORGIVEN

transgression is *f* . . . . Ps 32:1
sins be *f* them . . . . Mark 4:12
to whom little is *f* . . . . Luke 7:47
indeed have a *f* . . . . 2 Cor 2:10
f you all trespasses . . . . . . Col 2:13
sins, he will be *f* . . . . James 5:15
your sins are *f* . . . . 1 John 2:12

FORGIVENESS

But there is *f* with . . . . Ps 130:4
God belong mercy and *f* . . . Dan 9:9
preached to you the *f* . . . . Acts 13:38
they may receive *f* . . . . . . Acts 26:18
His blood, the *f* . . . . Eph 1:7

FORGIVES

f all your iniquities . . . . Ps 103:3
"Who is this who even *f* . . . Luke 7:49

FORGIVING

tenderhearted, *f* . . . . Eph 4:32
and *f* one another . . . . Col 3:13

FORGOT

remember Joseph, but *f* . . . Gen 40:23
f the LORD their God . . . . . . Judg 3:7
f His works and His . . . . . . Ps 78:11
They soon *f* His works . . . . Ps 106:13

FORGOTTEN

f the God who fathered . . . Deut 32:18
"Why have You *f* . . . . Ps 42:9
If we had *f* the name . . . . . . Ps 44:20
memory of them is *f* . . . . . . Eccl 9:5
you will not be *f* . . . . Is 44:21
And my Lord has *f* . . . . Is 49:14
I have *f* prosperity . . . . Lam 3:17
not one of them is *f* . . . . . Luke 12:6
f the exhortation . . . . Heb 12:5
f that he was cleansed . . . . 2 Pet 1:9

FORM

earth was without *f* . . . . Gen 1:2
Who would *f* a god or . . . . . . Is 44:10
f the light and create . . . . Is 45:7
descended in bodily *f* . . . . Luke 3:22
time, nor seen His *f* . . . . . . John 5:37
For the *f* of this . . . . 1 Cor 7:31
who, being in the *f* . . . . Phil 2:6
Abstain from every *f* . . . 1 Thess 5:22
having a *f* of . . . . 2 Tim 3:5

FORMED

And the LORD God *f* . . . . Gen 2:7
And His hands *f* . . . . Ps 95:5
f my inward parts . . . . Ps 139:13
f everything gives the . . . . Prov 26:10
say of him who *f* . . . . Is 29:16
Me there was no God *f* . . . . . Is 43:10
This people I have *f* . . . . . . Is 43:21
"Before I *f* you in . . . . Jer 1:5
Will the thing *f* . . . . Rom 9:20
say to him who *f* . . . . Rom 9:20
until Christ is *f* . . . . Gal 4:19
For Adam was *f* first . . . . . 1 Tim 2:13

FORMER

f lovingkindness . . . . Ps 89:49
f days better than . . . . Eccl 7:10
f rain to the earth . . . . Hos 6:3
f prophets preached . . . . . . Zech 1:4
f conduct in Judaism . . . . . . Gal 1:13
your *f* conduct . . . . Eph 4:22
f things have passed . . . . . . Rev 21:4

FORMS

clay say to him who *f* . . . . . . Is 45:9
f the spirit of man . . . . Zech 12:1

FORNICATION

"We were not born of *f* . . . . John 8:41
of the wrath of her *f* . . . . . . Rev 14:8

FORNICATOR

you know, that no *f* . . . . Eph 5:5
lest there be any *f* . . . . Heb 12:16

FORNICATORS

but *f* and adulterers . . . . . . Heb 13:4

FORSAKE

but if you *f* Him . . . . 2 Chr 15:2
"If his sons *f* . . . . Ps 89:30
f His inheritance . . . . Ps 94:14
But I did not *f* . . . . Ps 119:87
father, and do not *f* . . . . Prov 1:8
worthless idols *f* . . . . Jon 2:8
of you does not *f* . . . . Luke 14:33
never leave you nor *f* . . . . . Heb 13:5

FORSAKEN

My God, why have You *f* . . . Ps 22:1
seen the righteous *f* . . . . . . Ps 37:25
you dread will be *f* . . . . Is 7:16
cities will be as a *f* . . . . Is 17:9
a mere moment I have *f* . . . . Is 54:7

no longer be termed *F* . . . . Is 62:4
they have *f* Me . . . . Jer 2:13
My God, why have You *f* . Matt 27:46
persecuted, but not *f* . . . . . 2 Cor 4:9
for Demas has *f* . . . . 2 Tim 4:10
f the right way . . . . 2 Pet 2:15

FORSAKING
f the assembling . . . . Heb 10:25

FORSOOK
f God who made him . . . . Deut 32:15
all the disciples *f* . . . . Matt 26:56
with me, but all *f* . . . . . . 2 Tim 4:16
By faith he *f* Egypt . . . . Heb 11:27

FORTRESS
Lord is my rock, my *f* . . . . 2 Sam 22:2
my rock of refuge, a *f* . . . . . . Ps 31:2

FOUL
My wounds are *f* . . . . Ps 38:5
f weather today . . . . Matt 16:3
a prison for every *f* . . . . . . Rev 18:2

FOUND
f a helper comparable . . . . . Gen 2:20
where can wisdom be *f* . . . . Job 28:12
when You may be *f* . . . . Ps 32:6
f My servant David . . . . Ps 89:20
a thousand I have *f* . . . . Eccl 7:28
this only I have *f* . . . . Eccl 7:29
f the one I love . . . . Song 3:4
Lord while He may be *f* . . . . . Is 55:6
your fruit is *f* . . . . Hos 14:8
fruit on it and *f* none . . . . Luke 13:6
he was lost and is *f* . . . . . Luke 15:24
f the Messiah" (which . . . . . John 1:41
I *f* to bring death . . . . Rom 7:10
and be *f* in Him . . . . Phil 3:9
be diligent to be *f* . . . . . . 2 Pet 3:14

FOUNDATION
he shall lay its *f* . . . . Josh 6:26
His *f* is in the holy . . . . Ps 87:1
and justice are the *f* . . . . . . Ps 89:14
Of old You laid the *f* . . . . . Ps 102:25
has an everlasting *f* . . . . . Prov 10:25
deep and laid the *f* . . . . . . Luke 6:48
the earth without a *f* . . . . Luke 6:49
loved Me before the *f* . . . . John 17:24
I have laid the *f* . . . . 1 Cor 3:10
f can anyone lay than . . . . 1 Cor 3:11
us in Him before the *f* . . . . . Eph 1:4
the solid *f* of God . . . . 2 Tim 2:19
not laying again the *f* . . . . . Heb 6:1
Lamb slain from the *f* . . . . Rev 13:8
the first *f* was jasper . . . . . Rev 21:19

FOUNDATIONS
when I laid the *f* . . . . Job 38:4
f are destroyed . . . . Ps 11:3
You who laid the *f* . . . . Ps 104:5
shall raise up the *f* . . . . Is 58:12
The *f* of the wall . . . . Rev 21:19

FOUNDED
For He has *f* it upon . . . . Ps 24:2
shake it, for it was *f* . . . . . Luke 6:48

FOUNTAIN
will become in him a *f* . . . . John 4:14

FOUNTAINS
on that day all the *f* . . . . . . Gen 7:11
f be dispersed abroad . . . . . Prov 5:16
when there were no *f* . . . . . Prov 8:24
lead them to living *f* . . . . . Rev 7:17

FOX
build, if even a *f* . . . . Neh 4:3
"Go, tell that *f* . . . . Luke 13:32

FOXES
caught three hundred *f* . . . . Judg 15:4

f that spoil the vines . . . . . . Song 2:15
F have holes and birds . . . . Luke 9:58

FRAGMENTS
f that remained . . . . Matt 14:20
of the leftover *f* . . . . Luke 9:17
baskets with the *f* . . . . John 6:13

FRAGRANCE
garments is like the *f* . . . . Song 4:11
was filled with the *f* . . . . . John 12:3
we are to God the *f* . . . . . 2 Cor 2:15

FRAIL
that I may know how *f* . . . . . Ps 39:4

FRAME
For He knows our *f* . . . . . . Ps 103:14
f was not hidden . . . . Ps 139:15

FRAMED
that the worlds were *f* . . . . . Heb 11:3

FREE
and the servant is *f* . . . . Job 3:19
let the oppressed go *f* . . . . . . Is 58:6
'You will be made *f* . . . . . . John 8:33
if the Son makes you *f* . . . . John 8:36
And having been set *f* . . . . Rom 6:18
now having been set *f* . . . . Rom 6:22
Jesus has made me *f* . . . . . . Rom 8:2
Am I not *f* . . . . 1 Cor 9:1
is neither slave nor *f* . . . . . . Gal 3:28
Jerusalem above is *f* . . . . . . Gal 4:26
Christ has made us *f* . . . . Gal 5:1
he is a slave or *f* . . . . Eph 6:8
poor, *f* and slave . . . . Rev 13:16

FREED
has died has been *f* . . . . Rom 6:7

FREEDMAN
slave is the Lord's *f* . . . . . . 1 Cor 7:22

FREELY
the garden you may *f* . . . . . Gen 2:16
I will love them *f* . . . . Hos 14:4
F you have received . . . . . . Matt 10:8
f give us all . . . . Rom 8:32
that have been *f* . . . . 1 Cor 2:12
the water of life *f* . . . . Rev 22:17

FREEWOMAN
the other by a *f* . . . . Gal 4:22
with the son of the *f* . . . . . . Gal 4:30

FRESH
My glory is *f* within . . . . . . Job 29:20
They shall be *f* . . . . Ps 92:14
both salt water and *f* . . . . James 3:12

FRETS
and his heart *f* . . . . Prov 19:3

FRIEND
a man speaks to his *f* . . . . . Ex 33:11
of Abraham Your *f* . . . . . . 2 Chr 20:7
though he were my *f* . . . . . . Ps 35:14
f You have put . . . . Ps 88:18
f loves at all times . . . . . . Prov 17:17
f who sticks closer . . . . . . Prov 18:24
not forsake your own *f* . . . . Prov 27:10
a *f* of tax collectors . . . . . Matt 11:19
of you shall have a *f* . . . . . Luke 11:5
f Lazarus sleeps . . . . John 11:11
you are not Caesar's *f* . . . . John 19:12
Philemon our beloved *f* . . . . Philem 1
he was called the *f* . . . . . . James 2:23
wants to be a *f* . . . . James 4:4

FRIENDS
and hate your *f* . . . . 2 Sam 19:6
My *f* scorn me . . . . Job 16:20
f have forgotten me . . . . . . Job 19:14
the rich has many *f* . . . . . . Prov 14:20
one's life for his *f* . . . . John 15:13

You are My *f* . . . . John 15:14
I have called you *f* . . . . . . John 15:15
to forbid any of his *f* . . . . Acts 24:23

FROGS
your territory with *f* . . . . Ex 8:2
f coming out of the . . . . . . Rev 16:13

FRONTLETS
on your hand and as *f* . . . . Ex 13:16
and they shall be as *f* . . . . . Deut 6:8

FROZEN
the broad waters are *f* . . . . Job 37:10

FRUIT
and showed them the *f* . . Num 13:26
Blessed shall be the *f* . . . . Deut 28:4
brings forth its *f* . . . . Ps 1:3
f is better than gold . . . . . Prov 8:19
The *f* of the righteous . . . . Prov 11:30
with good by the *f* . . . . . . Prov 12:14
f was sweet to my . . . . Song 2:3
they shall eat the *f* . . . . Is 3:10
like the first *f* . . . . Is 28:4
"I create the *f* . . . . Is 57:19
f is found in Me . . . . Hos 14:8
does not bear good *f* . . . . Matt 3:10
good tree bears good *f* . . . Matt 7:17
not drink of this *f* . . . . . . Matt 26:29
and blessed is the *f* . . . . . . Luke 1:42
life, and bring no *f* . . . . . . Luke 8:14
and he came seeking *f* . . . . Luke 13:6
And if it bears *f* . . . . Luke 13:9
branch that bears *f* . . . . . . John 15:2
that you bear much *f* . . . . . John 15:8
should go and bear *f* . . . . John 15:16
f did you have then in . . . . Rom 6:21
God, you have your *f* . . . . . Rom 6:22
that we should bear *f* . . . . . Rom 7:4
But the *f* of the . . . . Gal 5:22
but I seek the *f* . . . . Phil 4:17
yields the peaceable *f* . . . . Heb 12:11
Now the *f* of . . . . James 3:18
autumn trees without *f* . . . . Jude 12
tree yielding its *f* . . . . Rev 22:2

FRUITFUL
them, saying, "Be *f* . . . . . . Gen 1:22
a *f* bough, a *f* . . . . Gen 49:22
wife shall be like a *f* . . . . . Ps 128:3
heaven and *f* seasons . . . . Acts 14:17
pleasing Him, being *f* . . . . . Col 1:10

FRUITS
Therefore bear *f* . . . . Matt 3:8
know them by their *f* . . . . . Matt 7:16
and increase the *f* . . . . . . 2 Cor 9:10
of mercy and good *f* . . . . James 3:17
which bore twelve *f* . . . . . . Rev 22:2

FUEL
people shall be as *f* . . . . Is 9:19
into the fire for *f* . . . . Ezek 15:4

FULFILL
the Lord, to *f* his vow . . . . Lev 22:21
And you shall *f* . . . . 1 Kin 5:9
f all your petitions . . . . Ps 20:5
f the desire of those . . . . . Ps 145:19
for us to *f* all . . . . Matt 3:15
f the law of Christ . . . . Gal 6:2
f my joy by being . . . . Phil 2:2
and *f* all the good . . . . . . 2 Thess 1:11
If you really *f* . . . . James 2:8

FULFILLED
the law till all is *f* . . . . Matt 5:18
of the Gentiles are *f* . . . . . Luke 21:24
all things must be *f* . . . . . . Luke 24:44
of the law might be *f* . . . . . Rom 8:4
loves another has *f* . . . . . . Rom 13:8
For all the law is *f* . . . . Gal 5:14

FULFILLMENT
for there will be a *f*...... Luke 1:45
love is the *f* of the ...... Rom 13:10

FULL
I went out *f*........... Ruth 1:21
For I am *f* of words .... Job 32:18
of the LORD is *f*............ Ps 29:4
who has his quiver *f*...... Ps 127:5
Lest I be *f* and deny....... Prov 30:9
yet the sea is not *f*........ Eccl 1:7
the whole earth is *f*......... Is 6:3
and it was *f* of bones...... Ezek 37:1
But truly I am *f*........... Mic 3:8
whole body will be *f*..... Matt 6:22
of the Father, *f*........... John 1:14
your joy may be *f*....... John 15:11
chose Stephen, a man *f*..... Acts 6:5
You are already *f*......... 1 Cor 4:8
learned both to be *f*...... Phil 4:12
I am *f*, having received .... Phil 4:18

FULL-GROWN
and sin, when it is *f*..... James 1:15

FULLNESS
satisfied with the *f*......... Ps 36:8
f we have all received.... John 1:16
to Israel until the *f*...... Rom 11:25
But when the *f* of the ...... Gal 4:4
dispensation of the *f*...... Eph 1:10
filled with all the *f*...... Eph 3:19
Him dwells all the *f*....... Col 2:9

FUNCTION
do not have the same *f*.... Rom 12:4

FURIOUS
You have been *f*.......... Ps 89:38
f man do not go .... Prov 22:24
fury and in *f* rebukes...... Ezek 5:15
LORD avenges and is *f*..... Nah 1:2
this, they were *f*......... Acts 5:33

FURIOUSLY
for he drives *f*.......... 2 Kin 9:20

FURNACE
you out of the iron *f*..... Deut 4:20
tested you in the *f*...... Is 48:10
of a burning fiery *f*........ Dan 3:6
cast them into the *f*..... Matt 13:42
the smoke of a great *f*...... Rev 9:2

FURNISHED
also *f* her table .... Prov 9:2
a large upper room, *f*.... Mark 14:15

FURY
F is not in Me............. Is 27:4
they are full of the *f*...... Is 51:20
f to His adversaries......... Is 59:18
and My own *f*............. Is 63:5
even in anger and *f*....... Jer 21:5
and I will cause My *f*..... Ezek 5:13
Thus will I spend My *f*..... Ezek 6:12
in anger and *f* on the...... Mic 5:15

FUTILE
For it is not a *f*...... Deut 32:47
of the peoples are *f*..... Jer 10:3
wise, that they are *f*..... 1 Cor 3:20
risen, your faith is *f*.... 1 Cor 15:17

FUTILITY
allotted months of *f*...... Job 7:3
f have You created all .... Ps 89:47
was subjected to *f*....... Rom 8:20

FUTURE
for the *f* of that man....... Ps 37:37
the *f* of the wicked......... Ps 37:38
to give you a *f*....... Jer 29:11

GAAL
Son of Ebed; vilifies Abimelech, Judg 9:26–41

GAASH
Hill of Ephraim, Judg 2:9
Joshua buried near, Josh 24:30

GABBATHA
Place of Pilate's court, John 19:13

GABRIEL
Messenger archangel; interprets Daniel's vision, Dan 8:16–27
Reveals the prophecy of 70 weeks, Dan 9:21–27
Announces John's birth, Luke 1:11–22
Announces Christ's birth, Luke 1:26–38
Stands in God's presence, Luke 1:19

GAD
Son of Jacob by Zilpah, Gen 30:10, 11
Blessed by Jacob, Gen 49:19
——— Tribe of:
Census of, Num 1:24, 25
Territory of, Num 32:20–36
Captivity of, 1 Chr 5:26
Later references to, Rev 7:5
——— Prophet in David's reign, 1 Sam 22:5
Message of, to David, 2 Sam 24:10–16

GADARENES (or Gergesenes)
People east of the Sea of Galilee, Mark 5:1
Healing of demon-possessed in territory of, Matt 8:28–34

GAIN
g than fine gold........ Prov 3:14
will have no lack of *g* .... Prov 31:11
a time to *g* .... Eccl 3:6
to get dishonest *g* .... Ezek 22:27
him who covets evil *g*...... Hab 2:9
and to die is *g*......... Phil 1:21
rubbish, that I may *g*...... Phil 3:8
is a means of *g* .... 1 Tim 6:5
contentment is great *g* .... 1 Tim 6:6
for dishonest *g* .... 1 Pet 5:2

GAINED
g more wisdom than all.... Eccl 1:16
g five more talents ...... Matt 25:20

GAINS
g the whole world....... Matt 16:26

GAIUS
Companion of Paul, Acts 19:29
——— Convert at Derbe, Acts 20:4
——— Paul's host at Corinth, Rom 16:23; 1 Cor 1:14

GALATIA
Paul visits, Acts 16:6; 18:23
Paul writes to Christians in, Gal 1:1
Peter writes to Christians in, 1 Pet 1:1

GALILEANS
Speech of, Mark 14:70
Faith of, John 4:45
Pilate's cruelty toward, Luke 13:1, 2

GALILEE
Prophecies concerning, Deut 33:18–23; Is 9:1, 2
Dialect of, distinctive, Matt 26:73
Herod's jurisdiction over, Luke 3:1
Christ's contacts with, Matt 2:22; 4:12–25; 26:32; 27:55; John 4:1, 3

GALILEE, SEA OF
Scene of many events in Christ's life, Mark 7:31

Called Chinnereth, Num 34:11
Later called Gennesaret, Luke 5:1

GALL
They also gave me *g* .... Ps 69:21
the wormwood and the *g* .. Lam 3:19
turned justice into *g* ..... Amos 6:12
wine mingled with *g* .... Matt 27:34

GALLIO
Roman proconsul of Achaia, dismisses charges against Paul, Acts 18:12–17

GAMALIEL
Famous Jewish teacher, Acts 22:3
Respected by people, Acts 5:34–39

GAP
and stand in the *g*...... Ezek 22:30

GARDEN
LORD God planted a *g* ...... Gen 2:8
g enclosed is my .... Song 4:12
like a watered *g*........... Is 58:11
Eden, the *g* of God....... Ezek 28:13
raise up for them a *g*..... Ezek 34:29
where there was a *g*...... John 18:1
in the *g* a new tomb .... John 19:41

GARDENER
Him to be the *g*........ John 20:15

GARDENS
I made myself *g*........... Eccl 2:5
plant *g* and eat their ...... Jer 29:5

GARLANDS
brought oxen and *g*...... Acts 14:13

GARMENT
beautiful Babylonian *g* .... Josh 7:21
g that is moth-eaten ...... Job 13:28
made sackcloth my *g*...... Ps 69:11
with light as with a *g* ...... Ps 104:2
one who takes away a *g*.. Prov 25:20
the hem of His *g*........ Matt 9:20
have on a wedding *g*.... Matt 22:11
cloth on an old *g*........ Mark 2:21
all grow old like a *g*...... Heb 1:11
hating even the *g*........ Jude 23

GARMENTS
g did not wear out on...... Deut 8:4
Why are your *g* hot....... Job 37:17
They divide My *g*......... Ps 22:18
g always be white......... Eccl 9:8
g rolled in blood .... Is 9:5
from Edom, with dyed *g* ..... Is 63:1
Take away the filthy *g* ..... Zech 3:4
man clothed in soft *g* ..... Matt 11:8
spread their *g* on the ..... Matt 21:8
and divided His *g* .... Matt 27:35
by them in shining *g* ..... Luke 24:4
g are moth-eaten .... James 5:2
be clothed in white *g* .... Rev 3:5

GARRISON
gathered the whole *g* .... Matt 27:27
Damascenes with a *g*.... 2 Cor 11:32

GATE
This is the *g* of the........ Ps 118:20
by the narrow *g* .... Matt 7:13
by the Sheep *G* a pool .... John 5:2
laid daily at the *g*........ Acts 3:2
suffered outside the *g*..... Heb 13:12
each individual *g* .... Rev 21:21

GATES
possess the *g* of those..... Gen 24:60
g are burned with fire ...... Neh 1:3
they go down to the *g* ..... Job 17:16
up your heads, O you *g* ..... Ps 24:7
The LORD loves the *g* .... Ps 87:2

Open to me the *g* . . . . Ps 118:19
is known in the *g* . . . . Prov 31:23
go through the *g* . . . . Is 62:10
and the *g* of Hades . . . . . . Matt 16:18
wall with twelve *g* . . . . Rev 21:12
g were twelve pearls . . . . . Rev 21:21
g shall not be shut . . . . . . Rev 21:25

GATH
Philistine city, 1 Sam 6:17
Ark carried to, 1 Sam 5:8
David takes refuge in, 1 Sam 21:10–15
David's second flight to, 1 Sam 27:3–12
Captured by David, 1 Chr 18:1
Destruction of, prophetic, Amos 6:1–3
Name becomes proverbial, Mic 1:10

GATHER
g my soul with sinners . . . . . . Ps 26:9
G My saints . . . . Ps 50:5
and a time to *g* stones . . . . . . Eccl 3:5
g the lambs with His . . . . Is 40:11
g His wheat into the . . . . . Matt 3:12
sow nor reap nor *g* . . . . . . Matt 6:26
Do men *g* grapes from . . . . Matt 7:16
g where I have not . . . . . . Matt 25:26
g together His . . . . Mark 13:27

GATHERED
g little had no lack . . . . Ex 16:18
And *g* out of the lands . . . . . Ps 107:3
g some of every kind . . . . . Matt 13:47
the nations will be *g* . . . . . Matt 25:32

GATHERING
g together of the . . . . Gen 1:10
g together to Him . . . . 2 Thess 2:1

GATHERS
g the waters of the . . . . Ps 33:7
His heart of iniquity . . . . Ps 41:6
g her food in the . . . . Prov 6:8
The Lord GOD, who *g* . . . . Is 56:8
together, as a hen *g* . . . . Matt 23:37

GAVE
to be with me, she *g* . . . . . Gen 3:12
g You this authority . . . . . Matt 21:23
that He *g* His only . . . . John 3:16
Those whom You *g* . . . . . . John 17:12
but God *g* the increase . . . . 1 Cor 3:6
g Himself for our sins . . . . . . Gal 1:4
g Himself for me . . . . Gal 2:20
g Himself for it . . . . Eph 5:25
The sea *g* up the dead . . . . Rev 20:13

GAZA
Philistine city, Josh 13:3
Samson removes the gates of, Judg 16:1–3
Samson taken there as prisoner; his revenge, Judg 16:21–31
Sin of, condemned, Amos 1:6, 7
Philip journeys to, Acts 8:26

GAZED
g into heaven and saw . . . . Acts 7:55

GAZING
why do you stand *g* . . . . . . Acts 1:11

GEDALIAH
Made governor of Judah, 2 Kin 25:22–26
Befriends Jeremiah, Jer 40:5, 6
Murdered by Ishmael, Jer 41:2, 18

GEHAZI
Elisha's servant; seeks reward from Naaman, 2 Kin 5:20–24
Afflicted with leprosy, 2 Kin 5:25–27
Relates Elisha's deeds to Jehoram, 2 Kin 8:4–6

GENEALOGIES
fables and endless *g* . . . . . . 1 Tim 1:4

GENEALOGY
The book of the *g* . . . . Matt 1:1
mother, without *g* . . . . Heb 7:3

GENERATION
perverse and crooked *g* . . . . Deut 32:5
The *g* of the upright . . . . Ps 112:2
g shall praise Your . . . . Ps 145:4
g that curses its . . . . Prov 30:11
g that is pure in its . . . . . . Prov 30:12
One *g* passes away . . . . Eccl 1:4
g it shall lie . . . . Is 34:10
who will declare His *g* . . . . . . Is 53:8
and adulterous *g* . . . . Matt 12:39
this *g* will by no . . . . Matt 24:34
from this perverse *g* . . . . . . Acts 2:40
But you are a chosen *g* . . . . 1 Pet 2:9

GENERATIONS
be remembered in all *g* . . . . . Ps 45:17
Your praise to all *g* . . . . Ps 79:13
for a thousand *g* . . . . Ps 105:8
g will call me blessed . . . . Luke 1:48

GENEROUS
g soul will be made . . . . . . Prov 11:25
g eye will be blessed . . . . . Prov 22:9
no longer be called *g* . . . . Is 32:5
g man devises . . . . Is 32:8

GENTILES
G were separated . . . . Gen 10:5
as a light to the G . . . . Is 42:6
G shall come to your . . . . Is 60:3
the riches of the G . . . . Is 61:6
all these things the G . . . . . Matt 6:32
into the way of the G . . . . . Matt 10:5
revelation to the G . . . . Luke 2:32
G are fulfilled . . . . Luke 21:24
bear My name before G . . . . Acts 9:15
poured out on the G . . . . . . Acts 10:45
a light to the G . . . . Acts 13:47
blasphemed among the G . Rom 2:24
also the God of the G . . . . . Rom 3:29
even named among the G . 1 Cor 5:1
mystery among the G . . . . . . Col 1:27
a teacher of the G . . . . 1 Tim 2:7
nothing from the G . . . . 3 John 7

GENTLE
g tongue breaks a bone . . . Prov 25:15
from Me, for I am *g* . . . . . Matt 11:29
But we were *g* among . . . 1 Thess 2:7
to be peaceable, *g* . . . . Titus 3:2
only to the good and *g* . . . . 1 Pet 2:18
ornament of a *g* . . . . 1 Pet 3:4

GENTLENESS
g has made me great . . . . . . Ps 18:35
love and a spirit of *g* . . . . . 1 Cor 4:21
g, self-control . . . . Gal 5:23
all lowliness and *g* . . . . Eph 4:2
Let your *g* be known to . . . . . Phil 4:5
love, patience, *g* . . . . 1 Tim 6:11

GERAR
Town of Philistia, Gen 10:19
Visited by Abraham, Gen 20:1–18
Visited by Isaac, Gen 26:1–17
Abimelech, king of, Gen 26:1, 26

GERIZIM
See MOUNT GERIZIM

GERSHOM (or Gershon)
Son of Moses, Ex 2:21, 22
Circumcised, Ex 4:25
Founder of Levite family, 1 Chr 23:14–16

GESHUR
Inhabitants of, not expelled by Israel, Josh 13:13
Talmai, king of, grandfather of Absalom, 2 Sam 3:3
Absalom flees to, 2 Sam 13:37, 38

GETHSEMANE
Garden near Jerusalem, Matt 26:30, 36
Often visited by Christ, Luke 22:39
Scene of Christ's agony and betrayal, Matt 26:36–56; John 18:1–12

GEZER
Canaanite city, Josh 10:33
Inhabitants not expelled, Josh 16:10
Given as dowry of Pharaoh's daughter, 1 Kin 9:15–17

GHOST
supposed it was a *g* . . . . . . Mark 6:49

GIBEAH
Town of Benjamin; known for wickedness, Judg 19:12–30
Destruction of, Judg 20:1–48
Saul's birthplace, 1 Sam 10:26
Saul's political capital, 1 Sam 15:34
Wickedness of, long remembered, Hos 9:9

GIBEON
Sun stands still at, Josh 10:12
Location of tabernacle, 1 Chr 16:39
Joab struck Amasa at, 2 Sam 20:8–10
Joab killed at, 1 Kin 2:28–34
Site of Solomon's sacrifice and dream, 1 Kin 3:5–15

GIBEONITES
Trick Joshua into making treaty; subjected to forced labor, Josh 9:3–27
Rescued by Joshua, Josh 10
Massacred by Saul; avenged by David, 2 Sam 21:1–9

GIDEON
Called by an angel, Judg 6:11–24
Destroys Baal's altar, Judg 6:25–32
Fleece confirms call from God, Judg 6:36–40
Miraculous victory over the Midianites, Judg 7
Takes revenge on Succoth and Penuel, Judg 8:4–21
Refuses kingship; makes an ephod, Judg 8:22–28
Fathers seventy-one sons; dies, Judg 8:29–35

GIFT
g makes room for him . . . . Prov 18:16
A *g* in secret pacifies . . . . . Prov 21:14
it is the *g* of God . . . . Eccl 3:13
is Corban"—'(that is, a *g* . . Mark 7:11
"If you knew the *g* . . . . John 4:10
But the free *g* is not . . . . . . Rom 5:15
but the *g* of God is . . . . Rom 6:23
each one has his own *g* . . . . 1 Cor 7:7
though I have the *g* . . . . . . 1 Cor 13:2
it is the *g* of God . . . . Eph 2:8
Not that I seek the *g* . . . . Phil 4:17
Do not neglect the *g* . . . . . 1 Tim 4:14
you to stir up the *g* . . . . 2 Tim 1:6
tasted the heavenly *g* . . . . . . Heb 6:4
Every good *g* and every . . James 1:17
one has received a *g* . . . . . . 1 Pet 4:10

GIFTED
the women who were *g* . . . . Ex 35:25
but good-looking, *g* . . . . Dan 1:4

GIFTS

g you shall offer . . . . Num 18:29
You have received *g*. . . . . . . Ps 68:18
and Seba will offer *g* . . . . . . Ps 72:10
though you give many *g* . . Prov 6:35
to one who gives *g*. . . . . Prov 19:6
how to give good *g* . . . . . . Matt 7:11
rich putting their *g*. . . . . . . Luke 21:1
g differing . . . . Rom 12:6
are diversities of *g* . . . . 1 Cor 12:4
and desire spiritual *g*. . . . . 1 Cor 14:1
captive, and gave *g* . . . . Eph 4:8

GIHON

River of Eden, Gen 2:13
—— Spring outside Jerusalem,
    1 Kin 1:33–45
Source of water supply, 2 Chr 32:30

GILBOA

Range of limestone hills in Issachar,
    1 Sam 28:4
Scene of Saul's death, 1 Sam 31:1–9
Under David's curse, 2 Sam 1:17, 21

GILEAD

Plain east of the Jordan; taken from
    the Amorites and assigned to
    Gad, Reuben, and Manasseh,
    Num 21:21–31; 32:33–40; Deut
    3:12, 13; Josh 13:24–31
Ishbosheth rules over, 2 Sam 2:8, 9
David takes refuge in, 2 Sam
    17:21–26
Conquered by Hazael, 2 Kin 10:32, 33
Balm of, figurative of national heal-
    ing, Jer 8:22

GILGAL

Site of memorial stones, circumci-
    sion, first Passover in the Prom-
    ised Land, Josh 4:19–5:12
Site of Gibeonite covenant, Josh
    9:3–15
One location on Samuel's circuit,
    1 Sam 7:15, 16
Saul made king and later rejected,
    1 Sam 11:15; 13:4–15
Denounced for idolatry, Hos 9:15

GIRD

G Your sword upon Your. . . . . Ps 45:3
of wrath You shall *g* . . . . Ps 76:10
I will *g* you. . . . . Is 45:5
and another will *g*. . . . . . . John 21:18
Therefore *g* up the . . . . 1 Pet 1:13

GIRDED

a towel and *g* Himself. . . . . John 13:4
down to the feet and *g* . . . . . Rev 1:13

GIRGASHITES

Descendants of Canaan, Gen
    10:15, 16
Land of, given to Abraham's descen-
    dants, Gen 15:18, 21
Delivered to Israel, Josh 24:11

GITTITES

600 follow David, 2 Sam 15:18–23

GIVE

g thanks to the LORD . . . . . 1 Chr 16:8
g me wisdom and . . . . 2 Chr 1:10
G ear to my prayer . . . . Ps 17:1
G to them according. . . . . . . Ps 28:4
g you the desires . . . . Ps 37:4
Yes, the LORD will *g* . . . . Ps 85:12
G me understanding . . . . . . Ps 119:34
g me your heart. . . . . Prov 23:26
You will *g* truth to . . . . . . Mic 7:20
G to him who asks . . . . Matt 5:42
G us this day our. . . . . Matt 6:11

what you have and *g* . . . . Matt 19:21
authority I will *g*. . . . . Luke 4:6
g them eternal life . . . . . . John 10:28
A new commandment I *g*. John 13:34
but what I do have I *g* . . . . . Acts 3:6
g us all things . . . . Rom 8:32
G no offense. . . . . 1 Cor 10:32
So let each one *g* . . . . 2 Cor 9:7
g him who has need . . . . . . Eph 4:28
g thanks to God always . 2 Thess 2:13
g yourself entirely . . . . 1 Tim 4:15
good works, ready to *g* . . . . 1 Tim 6:18

GIVEN

to him more will be *g* . . . . Matt 13:12
has, more will be *g*. . . . . . Matt 25:29
to whom much is *g*. . . . . . Luke 12:48
g Me I should lose. . . . . John 6:39
Spirit was not yet *g* . . . . . . John 7:39
have been freely *g* . . . . 1 Cor 2:12
not *g* to wine. . . . . 1 Tim 3:3

GIVES

He who *g* to the poor . . . . Prov 28:27
For God *g* wisdom and. . . . . Eccl 2:26
g life to the world . . . . John 6:33
All that the Father *g*. . . . . . John 6:37
The good shepherd *g*. . . . . John 10:11
not as the world *g* . . . . John 14:27
g us richly all things . . . . . 1 Tim 6:17
who *g* to all liberally . . . . James 1:5
But He *g* more grace. . . . . . James 4:6
g grace to the humble . . . . James 4:6

GLAD

I will be *g* and. . . . . Ps 9:2
my heart is *g* . . . . Ps 16:9
Be *g* in the LORD and. . . . . . Ps 32:11
streams shall make *g* . . . . . . Ps 46:4
And wine that makes *g*. . . . Ps 104:15
I was *g* when they said . . . . Ps 122:1
make merry and be *g* . . . . Luke 15:32
he saw it and was *g* . . . . . . John 8:56

GLADNESS

in the day of your *g* . . . . . Num 10:10
day of feasting and *g* . . . . . Esth 9:17
You have put *g* in my. . . . . . . Ps 4:7
me hear joy and *g* . . . . Ps 51:8
Serve the LORD with *g* . . . . . Ps 100:2
shall obtain joy and *g* . . . . . Is 35:10
over you with *g* . . . . Zeph 3:17
receive it with *g* . . . . Mark 4:16

GLASS

there was a sea of *g* . . . . Rev 4:6
like transparent *g* . . . . Rev 21:21

GLORIFIED

the people I must be *g* . . . . . Lev 10:3
and they *g* the God of. . . . Matt 15:31
Jesus was not yet *g* . . . . . . John 7:39
when Jesus was *g*. . . . . . . John 12:16
By this My Father is *g*. . . . . John 15:8
I have *g* You on the. . . . . . . John 17:4
g His servant Jesus. . . . . Acts 3:13
these He also *g* . . . . Rom 8:30
things God may be *g* . . . . . 1 Pet 4:11

GLORIFY

My altar, and I will *g*. . . . . . . Is 60:7
g your Father in . . . . Matt 5:16
"Father, *g* Your name . . . John 12:28
He will *g* Me . . . . John 16:14
And now, O Father, *g*. . . . . John 17:5
what death he would *g*. . . John 21:19
God, they did not *g* . . . . Rom 1:21
therefore *g* God in . . . . . . 1 Cor 6:20
also Christ did not *g* . . . . . . Heb 5:5
ashamed, but let him *g* . . . 1 Pet 4:16

GLORIOUS

daughter is all *g* . . . . Ps 45:13
And blessed be His *g* . . . . . . Ps 72:19
G things are spoken . . . . Ps 87:3
is honorable and *g* . . . . Ps 111:3
g splendor of Your . . . . Ps 145:5
habitation, holy and *g*. . . . . Is 63:15
it to Himself a *g* . . . . Eph 5:27
be conformed to His *g* . . . . Phil 3:21
g appearing of our . . . . . . Titus 2:13

GLORY

"Please, show me Your *g*. . . . Ex 33:18
g has departed from. . . . . 1 Sam 4:21
G in His holy name . . . . 1 Chr 16:10
g of the LORD filled
    the house . . . . 2 Chr 5:14
g of the LORD on the temple 2 Chr 7:3
a shield for me, my *g* . . . . Ps 3:3
who have set Your *g* . . . . Ps 8:1
Who is this King of *g* . . . . . . Ps 24:8
the place where Your *g* . . . . Ps 26:8
Your power and Your *g* . . . . Ps 63:2
shall speak of the *g* . . . . . . Ps 145:11
wise shall inherit *g* . . . . . Prov 3:35
The *g* of young men is . . . Prov 20:29
It is the *g* of God to . . . . . . Prov 25:2
the *g* there will be a covering. . . Is 4:5
"*G* to the righteous. . . . . Is 24:16
g I will not give . . . . Is 42:8
g will be seen upon . . . . Is 60:2
then be likened in *g* . . . . . Ezek 31:18
I will change their *g*. . . . . . . Hos 4:7
g of this latter temple . . . . . Hag 2:9
and I will be the *g* . . . . Zech 2:5
He shall bear the *g* . . . . . . Zech 6:13
that they may have *g*. . . . . . Matt 6:2
the power and the *g* . . . . . Matt 6:13
g was not arrayed. . . . . . . Matt 6:29
Man will come in the *g*. . . . Matt 16:27
with power and great *g* . . Matt 24:30
"*G* to God in the . . . . Luke 2:14
and we beheld His *g* . . . . . . John 1:14
and manifested His *g* . . . . . John 2:11
I do not seek My own *g* . . . John 8:50
"Give God the *g* . . . . John 9:24
g which I had with You . . . John 17:5
g which You gave Me I . . . John 17:22
he did not give *g* . . . . Acts 12:23
doing good seek for *g* . . . . . Rom 2:7
fall short of the *g* . . . . Rom 3:23
in faith, giving *g* . . . . Rom 4:20
the adoption, the *g*. . . . . . . Rom 9:4
the riches of His *g* . . . . Rom 9:23
God, alone wise, be *g* . . . . Rom 16:27
who glories, let him *g* . . . . 1 Cor 1:31
but woman is the *g* . . . . . . 1 Cor 11:7
of the *g* that excels . . . . 2 Cor 3:10
of the gospel of the *g*. . . . . . 2 Cor 4:4
eternal weight of *g*. . . . . . . 2 Cor 4:17
who glories, let him *g* . . . 2 Cor 10:17
to His riches in *g* . . . . Phil 4:19
appear with Him in *g*. . . . . . Col 3:4
For you are our *g* . . . . . . 1 Thess 2:20
many sons to *g*. . . . . Heb 2:10
grass, and all the *g*. . . . . . . 1 Pet 1:24
to whom belong the *g* . . . . 1 Pet 4:11
for the Spirit of *g*. . . . . 1 Pet 4:14
the presence of His *g* . . . . . . Jude 24
O Lord, to receive *g*. . . . . . . Rev 4:11
g of God illuminated . . . . . Rev 21:23

GLORYING

Your *g* is not good . . . . 1 Cor 5:6

GLUTTON

g will come to poverty. . . . Prov 23:21
you say, 'Look, a *g* . . . . Luke 7:34

GLUTTONS
g shames his . . . . Prov 28:7
evil beasts, lazy *g* . . . . Titus 1:12

GNASHING
will be weeping and *g*. . . . . Matt 8:12

GO
He said, "Let Me *g* . . . . . Gen 32:26
'Let My people *g*. . . . . Ex 5:1
Presence does not *g*. . . . . . . Ex 33:15
for wherever you *g* . . . . Ruth 1:16
"Look, I *g* forward. . . . . Job 23:8
For I used to *g* . . . . Ps 42:4
g astray as soon as . . . . Ps 58:3
I will *g* in the . . . . Ps 71:16
Those who *g* down to . . . . Ps 107:23
Where can I *g* from . . . . Ps 139:7
G to the ant. . . . . Prov 6:6
All *g* to one place . . . . Eccl 3:20
of mourning than to *g*. . . . . Eccl 7:2
of Zion shall *g* . . . . Is 2:3
You wherever You *g*. . . . . . Matt 8:19
do not *g* out . . . . Matt 24:26
He said to them, "*G* . . . . Mark 16:15
And I say to one, '*G* . . . . . . Luke 7:8
also want to *g* away . . . . . . John 6:67
to whom shall we *g* . . . . . . John 6:68
g you cannot come . . . . John 8:21
I *g* to prepare a place . . . . . John 14:2
will do, because I *g* . . . . . . John 14:12
seek Me, let these *g*. . . . . . John 18:8
and he shall *g* out no more . Rev 3:12

GOADS
of the wise are like *g*. . . . . Eccl 12:11
to kick against the *g* . . . . . . Acts 9:5

GOAL
I press toward the *g* . . . . . . Phil 3:14

GOATS
drink the blood of *g*. . . . . . Ps 50:13
his sheep from the *g*. . . . Matt 25:32
with the blood of *g*. . . . . . . Heb 9:12
g could take away . . . . Heb 10:4

GOD
G created the heavens. . . . . . Gen 1:1
Abram of *G* Most High. . . . Gen 14:19
and I will be their *G*. . . . . . Gen 17:8
of the Mighty *G*. . . . . Gen 49:24
the *G* of Abraham . . . . Ex 3:6
He is my *G* . . . . Ex 15:2
Stand before *G* for the. . . . . Ex 18:19
"I am the LORD your *G*. . . . . Ex 20:2
"This is your *g*. . . . . Ex 32:4
G is not a man . . . . Num 23:19
G is a consuming fire . . . . . Deut 4:24
great and awesome *G*. . . . . Deut 7:21
my people, and your *G*. . . . Ruth 1:16
know that there is a *G* . . 1 Sam 17:46
a rock, except our *G*. . . . 2 Sam 22:32
If the LORD is *G*. . . . . 1 Kin 18:21
G is greater than all . . . . . . 2 Chr 2:5
G is greater than . . . . Job 33:12
"Behold, *G* is mighty. . . . . . Job 36:5
"Behold, *G* is great . . . . . . Job 36:26
You have been My *G*. . . . . . Ps 22:10
"Where is your *G*. . . . . Ps 42:3
G is our refuge. . . . . Ps 46:1
G is in the midst of . . . . Ps 46:5
G is the King of all . . . . Ps 47:7
The Mighty One, *G*. . . . . Ps 50:1
I am *G*. . . . . Ps 50:7
me a clean heart, O *G*. . . . . Ps 51:10
Our *G* is the *G* . . . . Ps 68:20
Who is so great a *G*. . . . . . . Ps 77:13
Restore us, O *G* . . . . Ps 80:7
You alone are *G*. . . . . Ps 86:10
Exalt the LORD our *G*. . . . . . . Ps 99:9

Yes, our *G* is merciful. . . . . . Ps 116:5
give thanks to the *G* . . . . . Ps 136:26
For *G* is in heaven . . . . Eccl 5:2
Counselor, Mighty *G* . . . . Is 9:6
G is my salvation. . . . . Is 12:2
Behold, this is our *G* . . . . Is 25:9
"Behold your *G* . . . . Is 40:9
Is there a *G* besides . . . . Is 44:8
to Zion, "Your *G*. . . . . Is 52:7
stricken, smitten by *G* . . . . . . Is 53:4
and I will be their *G*. . . . . . . Jer 31:33
and I saw visions of *G*. . . . . Ezek 1:1
Who is a *G* like You . . . . . . Mic 7:18
"*G* with us. . . . . Matt 1:23
in *G* my Savior . . . . Luke 1:47
the Word was with *G* . . . . . . John 1:1
enter the kingdom of *G* . . . . John 3:5
For *G* so loved the . . . . John 3:16
has certified that *G*. . . . . . . John 3:33
G is Spirit. . . . . John 4:24
"My Lord and my *G*. . . . . John 20:28
Christ is the Son of *G*. . . . . . Acts 8:37
To the Unknown *G*. . . . . . . Acts 17:23
Indeed, let *G* be true. . . . . . Rom 3:4
If *G* is for us. . . . . Rom 8:31
G is faithful . . . . 1 Cor 1:9
us there is one *G* . . . . 1 Cor 8:6
G shall supply all. . . . . Phil 4:19
and I will be their *G*. . . . . . . Heb 8:10
G is a consuming fire. . . . . Heb 12:29
G is greater than our. . . . 1 John 3:20
for *G* is love . . . . 1 John 4:8
No one has seen *G*. . . . . . 1 John 4:12
in the temple of My *G* . . . . Rev 3:12
gave glory to the *G* . . . . . . Rev 11:13
G Himself will be . . . . Rev 21:3
and I will be his *G* . . . . Rev 21:7

GODDESS
after Ashtoreth the *g* . . . . . 1 Kin 11:5
of the great *g* Diana . . . . . Acts 19:35

GODHEAD
eternal power and *G*. . . . . . Rom 1:20
the fullness of the *G* . . . . Col 2:9

GODLINESS
is the mystery of *g*. . . . . . . 1 Tim 3:16
g is profitable . . . . 1 Tim 4:8
Now *g* with contentment . . 1 Tim 6:6
having a form of *g* . . . . 2 Tim 3:5
pertain to life and *g*. . . . . . 2 Pet 1:3
to perseverance *g* . . . . 2 Pet 1:6

GODLY
Himself him who is *g* . . . . Ps 4:3
everyone who is *g* . . . . Ps 32:6
who desire to live *g* . . . . . . 2 Tim 3:12
righteously, and *g* . . . . Titus 2:12
reverence and *g* fear. . . . . . Heb 12:28
to deliver the *g* . . . . 2 Pet 2:9

GODS
your God is God of *g*. . . . . Deut 10:17
the household *g* . . . . 2 Kin 23:24
He judges among the *g*. . . . . Ps 82:1
I said, "You are *g*. . . . . Ps 82:6
yourselves with *g*. . . . . Is 57:5
If He called them *g* . . . . . . John 10:35
g have come down to. . . . . Acts 14:11

GOG
Prince of Rosh, Meshech, and Tubal,
  Ezek 38:2, 3
——— Leader of the final battle, Rev
  20:8–15

GOLD
And the *g* of that land. . . . . Gen 2:12
a mercy seat of pure *g* . . . . . Ex 25:17
multiply silver and *g*. . . . . Deut 17:17
"If I have made *g* . . . . Job 31:24

yea, than much fine *g*. . . . . Ps 19:10
is like apples of *g*. . . . . . . Prov 25:11
is Mine, and the *g* . . . . Hag 2:8
g I do not have . . . . Acts 3:6
with braided hair or *g* . . . . 1 Tim 2:9
a man with *g* rings. . . . . . James 2:2
Your *g* and silver are . . . . James 5:3
more precious than *g*. . . . . 1 Pet 1:7
like silver or *g* . . . . 1 Pet 1:18
of the city was pure *g* . . . . Rev 21:21

GOLGOTHA
Where Jesus died, Matt 27:33–35

GOLIATH
Giant of Gath, 1 Sam 17:4
Killed by David, 1 Sam 17:50
——— Brother of above; killed by
  Elhanan, 2 Sam 21:19

GOMER
Son of Japheth, Gen 10:2, 3; 1 Chr
  1:5, 6
Northern nation, Ezek 38:6
——— Wife of Hosea, Hos 1:2, 3

GOMORRAH
With Sodom, defeated by Chedor-
  laomer; Lot captured, Gen 14:8–12
Destroyed by God, Gen 19:23–29
Later references to, Is 1:10; Amos
  4:11; Matt 10:15

GONE
I am *g* like a shadow. . . . . . Ps 109:23
I have *g* astray like a . . . . . Ps 119:176
the word has *g* out of. . . . . . Is 45:23
like sheep have *g*. . . . . Is 53:6

GOOD
God saw that it was *g* . . . . . Gen 1:10
but God meant it for *g*. . . . Gen 50:20
LORD has promised *g* . . . . Num 10:29
you have spoken is *g*. . . . 2 Kin 20:19
seeking the good of his . . . . . . Esth 10:3
indeed accept *g*. . . . . Job 2:10
"Who will show us any *g* . . . . Ps 4:6
is none who does *g* . . . . Ps 14:1
G and upright is the . . . . . . Ps 25:8
that he may see *g* . . . . Ps 34:12
Truly God is *g* to . . . . Ps 73:1
g man deals graciously. . . . . Ps 112:5
Your Spirit is *g* . . . . Ps 143:10
g man obtains favor . . . . . Prov 12:2
g word makes it glad. . . . . Prov 12:25
on the evil and the *g*. . . . . Prov 15:3
A merry heart does *g*. . . . . Prov 17:22
who knows what is *g* . . . . . Eccl 6:12
learn to do *g*. . . . . Is 1:17
Zion, you who bring *g*. . . . . . Is 40:9
tidings of *g* things . . . . Is 52:7
talked to me, with *g* . . . . . . Zech 1:13
they may see your *g* . . . . . Matt 5:16
said, "Be of *g* cheer. . . . . . Matt 9:22
A *g* man out of the . . . . . Matt 12:35
"*G* Teacher, what *g* . . . . . Matt 19:16
No one is *g* but One . . . . . Matt 19:17
For she has done a *g* . . . . Matt 26:10
behold, I bring you *g* . . . . Luke 2:10
love your enemies, do *g* . . Luke 6:35
"Can anything *g*. . . . . John 1:46
Some said, "He is *g*. . . . . . . John 7:12
g works I have shown. . . . . John 10:32
who went about doing *g* . . Acts 10:38
For he was a *g* man . . . . . Acts 11:24
in that He did *g* . . . . Acts 14:17
g man someone would. . . . . Rom 5:7
in my flesh) nothing *g* . . . . Rom 7:18
overcome evil with *g*. . . . . Rom 12:21
Jesus for *g* works. . . . . Eph 2:10
fruitful in every *g* . . . . Col 1:10

know that the law is *g* . . . . 1 Tim 1:8
For this is *g* and . . . . 1 Tim 2:3
bishop, he desires a *g* . . . . 1 Tim 3:1
for this is *g* and. . . . . 1 Tim 5:4
be rich in *g* works . . . . 1 Tim 6:18
prepared for every *g* . . . . 2 Tim 2:21
and have tasted the *g* . . . . . Heb 6:5
Every *g* gift and every. . . James 1:17
g works which they. . . . . . 1 Pet 2:12
to suffer for doing *g* . . . . . 1 Pet 3:17

GOODNESS
"I will make all My *g* . . . . Ex 33:19
and abounding in *g* . . . . Ex 34:6
"You are my Lord, my *g* . . . . Ps 16:2
Surely *g* and mercy. . . . . Ps 23:6
that I would see the *g* . . . . Ps 27:13
how great is Your *g* . . . . . . Ps 31:19
The *g* of God endures . . . . . . Ps 52:1
how great is its *g*. . . . . . . Zech 9:17
the riches of His *g*. . . . . . . Rom 2:4
consider the *g* and. . . . . . Rom 11:22
kindness, *g* . . . . Gal 5:22

GOODS
When *g* increase. . . . . Eccl 5:11
and plunder his *g*. . . . . . Matt 12:29
ruler over all his *g*. . . Matt 24:47
"Soul, you have many *g*. . Luke 12:19
man was wasting his *g*. . . . Luke 16:1
I give half of my *g* . . . . . . Luke 19:8
has this world's *g*. . . . . . 1 John 3:17

GOSHEN
District of Egypt where Israel lived;
   the best of the land, Gen 45:10;
   46:28, 29; 47:1–11

GOSPEL
The beginning of the *g* . . . . Mark 1:1
and believe in the *g*. . . . . Mark 1:15
g must first be. . . . . Mark 13:10
to testify to the *g* . . . . . . Acts 20:24
separated to the *g*. . . . . Rom 1:1
not ashamed of the *g* . . . . Rom 1:16
should live from the *g* . . . 1 Cor 9:14
if our *g* is veiled. . . . . 2 Cor 4:3
to a different *g* . . . . Gal 1:6
of truth, the *g*. . . . . Eph 1:13
the mystery of the *g* . . . . . Eph 6:19
g which you heard . . . . Col 1:23
the everlasting *g* . . . . Rev 14:6

GOSSIPS
only idle but also *g* . . . . . 1 Tim 5:13

GOVERNMENT
and the *g* will be upon . . . . . . Is 9:6

GRACE
But Noah found *g* . . . . Gen 6:8
G is poured upon Your . . . . . Ps 45:2
The LORD will give *g* . . . . . . Ps 84:11
the Spirit of *g*. . . . . Zech 12:10
and the *g* of God was . . . . Luke 2:40
g and truth came . . . . John 1:17
And great *g* was upon. . . . . Acts 4:33
G to you and peace. . . . . . . Rom 1:7
receive abundance of *g* . . . Rom 5:17
g is no longer *g* . . . . Rom 11:6
The *g* of our Lord . . . . . . Rom 16:20
For you know the *g* . . . . . . 2 Cor 8:9
g is sufficient . . . . 2 Cor 12:9
The *g* of the Lord . . . . . . 2 Cor 13:14
you have fallen from *g*. . . . . Gal 5:4
to the riches of His *g* . . . . . Eph 1:7
g you have been. . . . . Eph 2:8
dispensation of the *g* . . . . . Eph 3:2
g was given according . . . . . Eph 4:7
G be with all those. . . . . . Eph 6:24
shaken, let us have *g* . . . . Heb 12:28
But He gives more *g* . . . . . James 4:6

this is the true *g* . . . . 1 Pet 5:12
but grow in the *g* . . . . 2 Pet 3:18

GRACIOUS
he said, "God be *g* . . . . . . Gen 43:29
I will be *g* to whom I . . . . . Ex 33:19
then He is *g* to him . . . . . . Job 33:24
wise man's mouth are *g* . . . Eccl 10:12
of hosts will be *g* . . . . Amos 5:15
know that You are a *g* . . . . . Jon 4:2
that He may be *g*. . . . . Mal 1:9
at the *g* words which . . . . . Luke 4:22
that the Lord is *g* . . . . 1 Pet 2:3

GRAFTED
in unbelief, will be *g* . . . . Rom 11:23

GRAIN
Israel went to buy *g*. . . . . . Gen 42:5
it treads out the *g*. . . . . . . Deut 25:4
You provide their *g* . . . . . . Ps 65:9
be an abundance of *g* . . . . . Ps 72:16
him who withholds *g* . . . . Prov 11:26
be revived like *g* . . . . Hos 14:7
G shall make the young. . . Zech 9:17
to pluck heads of *g* . . . . . . Matt 12:1
unless a *g* of wheat. . . . . . John 12:24
it treads out the *g* . . . . . . 1 Cor 9:9

GRANT
and *g* us Your . . . . Ps 85:7
G that these two . . . . Matt 20:21
who overcomes I will *g*. . . . Rev 3:21

GRAPES
in the blood of *g*. . . . . Gen 49:11
their *g* are *g* of gall. . . . . Deut 32:32
g give a good smell. . . . . . Song 2:13
vines have tender *g*. . . . . . Song 2:15
brought forth wild *g* . . . . Is 5:2
Yet gleaning *g* will be. . . . . . . Is 17:6
"No *g* shall be. . . . . Jer 8:13
have eaten sour *g* . . . . Ezek 18:2
Do men gather *g*. . . . . Matt 7:16
g are fully ripe. . . . . Rev 14:18

GRASPING
all is vanity and *g* . . . . Eccl 1:14

GRASS
they were as the *g* . . . . . . 2 Kin 19:26
offspring like the *g* . . . . Job 5:25
g which grows up . . . . Ps 90:5
his days are like *g* . . . . . . Ps 103:15
The *g* withers . . . . Is 40:7
so clothes the *g*. . . . . Matt 6:30
to sit down on the *g* . . . . Matt 14:19
"All flesh is as *g* . . . . 1 Pet 1:24

GRASSHOPPERS
inhabitants are like *g* . . . . . Is 40:22
generals like great *g* . . . . . Nah 3:17

GRAVE
g does not come . . . . Job 7:9
for the *g* as my house . . . . Job 17:13
my soul up from the *g* . . . . . Ps 30:3
the power of the *g* . . . . Ps 49:15
or wisdom in the *g* . . . . . . Eccl 9:10
And they made His *g* . . . . . . Is 53:9
the power of the *g*. . . . . . . Hos 13:14

GRAVES
there were no *g* . . . . Ex 14:11
and the *g* were opened. . . Matt 27:52
g which are not. . . . . Luke 11:44
g will hear His voice. . . . . John 5:28

GRAY
would bring down my *g* . . Gen 42:38
the man of *g* hairs . . . . . Deut 32:25
of old men is their *g* . . . . Prov 20:29

GREAT
and make your name *g*. . . . Gen 12:2

He has done us this *g*. . . . 1 Sam 6:9
For the LORD is *g* . . . . . . 1 Chr 16:25
I build will be *g*. . . . . 2 Chr 2:5
"The work is *g* . . . . Neh 4:19
Who does *g* things . . . . Job 5:9
G men are not always. . . . . Job 32:9
in the *g* assembly . . . . Ps 22:25
g are Your works . . . . Ps 92:5
my God, You are very *g* . . . Ps 104:1
"The LORD has done *g* . . . . . Ps 126:2
g is the sum of them . . . . Ps 139:17
in the place of the *g* . . . . Prov 25:6
g is the Holy One . . . . Is 12:6
And do you seek *g* . . . . Jer 45:5
g is Your faithfulness. . . . . Lam 3:23
The *g* day of the LORD . . . . Zeph 1:14
he shall be called *g*. . . . . . Matt 5:19
one pearl of *g* price. . . . . Matt 13:46
desires to become *g*. . . . . Matt 20:26
g drops of blood . . . . Luke 22:44
that he was someone *g* . . . . Acts 8:9
"*G* is Diana of the . . . . Acts 19:28
that I have *g* sorrow . . . . . . Rom 9:2
without controversy *g* . . . . 1 Tim 3:16
with contentment is *g*. . . . . 1 Tim 6:6
But in a *g* house . . . . 2 Tim 2:20
appearing of our *g* . . . . Titus 2:13
See how a *g* forest. . . . . . . James 3:5
g men, the rich men. . . . . . Rev 6:15
Babylon the *G*. . . . . Rev 17:5
Then I saw a *g* white . . . . . Rev 20:11
the dead, small and *g*. . . . . Rev 20:12

GREATER
the throne will I be *g* . . . Gen 41:40
g than all the gods . . . . . . Ex 18:11
whose appearance was *g* . . Dan 7:20
latter temple shall be *g* . . . Hag 2:9
kingdom of heaven is *g*. . . Matt 11:11
place there is One *g* . . . . . Matt 12:6
g than Jonah is here . . . . Matt 12:41
g than Solomon is here. . . Matt 12:42
g things than these. . . . . . John 1:50
g than our father . . . . John 4:12
a servant is not *g*. . . . . . . John 13:16
g than he who sent him . . John 13:16
g works than these . . . . . . John 14:12
G love has no one . . . . John 15:13
'A servant is not *g*. . . . . . John 15:20
parts have *g* modesty. . . . 1 Cor 12:23
he who prophesies is *g* . . . 1 Cor 14:5
swear by no one *g* . . . . Heb 6:13
condemns us, God is *g* . . . 1 John 3:20
witness of God is *g*. . . . . . 1 John 5:9

GREATEST
little child is the *g* . . . . . . Matt 18:4
be considered the *g*. . . . . . Luke 22:24
but the *g* of these is . . . . . 1 Cor 13:13

GREATNESS
And in the *g* of Your. . . . . . Ex 15:7
According to the *g*. . . . . . . Ps 79:11
g is unsearchable. . . . . Ps 145:3
I will declare Your *g*. . . . . . Ps 145:6
I have attained *g* . . . . Eccl 1:16
traveling in the *g* . . . . Is 63:1
is the exceeding *g* . . . . Eph 1:19

GREECE
Paul preaches in, Acts 17:16–31
Daniel's vision of, Dan 8:21

GREED
part is full of *g*. . . . . Luke 11:39

GREEDINESS
all uncleanness with *g* . . . . Eph 4:19
the faith in their *g*. . . . . . . 1 Tim 6:10

GREEDY
of everyone who is *g* . . . . . Prov 1:19

GREEK
not violent, not *g* . . . . 1 Tim 3:3
not violent, not *g* . . . . Titus 1:7

GREEK
written in Hebrew, *G*. . . . . John 19:20
and also for the *G*. . . . . . Rom 1:16
with me, being a *G*. . . . . . . Gal 2:3
is neither Jew nor *G* . . . . . . Gal 3:28

GREEKS
Natives of Greece, Joel 3:6; Acts 16:1
Spiritual state of, Rom 10:12
Some believe, Acts 14:1

GREEN
lie down in *g* pastures. . . . . . Ps 23:2

GREET
g your brethren only. . . . . . Matt 5:47
G one another with a . . 1 Cor 16:20
into your house nor *g*. . . . . 2 John 10
G the friends by name . . . . 3 John 14

GREETED
and *g* Elizabeth. . . . . Luke 1:40

GREW
And the Child *g* . . . . Luke 2:40
But the word of God *g* . . . . Acts 12:24
the word of the Lord *g* . . . . Acts 19:20

GRIEF
burden and his own *g*. . . 2 Chr 6:29
g were fully weighed. . . . . . . Job 6:2
Though I speak, my *g* . . . . . Job 16:6
observe trouble and *g* . . . . . Ps 10:14
of mirth may be *g* . . . . . . Prov 14:13
much wisdom is much *g* . . . Eccl 1:18
and acquainted with *g* . . . . . Is 53:3
joy and not with *g* . . . . . . Heb 13:17

GRIEVE
g the children of men . . . . Lam 3:33
g the Holy Spirit. . . . . Eph 4:30

GRIEVED
earth, and He was *g* . . . . . . Gen 6:6
Has not my soul *g*. . . . . . . Job 30:25
forty years I was *g*. . . . . . . Ps 95:10
a woman forsaken and *g* . . . . Is 54:6
g His Holy Spirit . . . . Is 63:10
with anger, being *g* . . . . . Mark 3:5
Peter was *g* because. . . . . John 21:17

GRINDING
the sound of *g* is low . . . . . Eccl 12:4
g the faces of the . . . . Is 3:15
Two women will be *g* . . . Matt 24:41

GROAN
The dying *g* in the. . . . . Job 24:12
even we ourselves *g* . . . . . . Rom 8:23
who are in this tent *g* . . . . . 2 Cor 5:4

GROANING
So God heard their *g* . . . . . . Ex 2:24
I am weary with my *g* . . . . . . Ps 6:6
Then Jesus, again *g*. . . . . . John 11:38

GROANINGS
g which cannot. . . . . Rom 8:26

GROPE
And you shall *g* . . . . Deut 28:29
They *g* in the dark. . . . . . . Job 12:25
We *g* for the wall like. . . . . . Is 59:10
hope that they might *g* . . . Acts 17:27

GROUND
"Cursed is the *g* . . . . Gen 3:17
you stand is holy *g*. . . . . Ex 3:5
up your fallow *g* . . . . Jer 4:3
give its fruit, the *g*. . . . . . . Zech 8:12
others fell on good *g*. . . . . Matt 13:8
bought a piece of *g*. . . . . . Luke 14:18
God, the pillar and *g* . . . . 1 Tim 3:15

GROUNDED
being rooted and *g*. . . . . . . Eph 3:17

GROW
they will all *g* . . . . Ps 102:26
the horn of David *g*. . . . . . Ps 132:17
the earth will *g* . . . . Is 51:6
you shall go out and *g* . . . . Mal 4:2
truth in love, may *g* . . . . . . Eph 4:15
and they will all *g* . . . . Heb 1:11
but *g* in the grace and . . . . 2 Pet 3:18

GRUDGINGLY
in his heart, not *g* . . . . 2 Cor 9:7

GRUMBLERS
These are *g* . . . . Jude 16

GUARANTEE
in our hearts as a *g* . . . . . . 2 Cor 1:22
us the Spirit as a *g*. . . . . . . 2 Cor 5:5
who is the *g* of our . . . . Eph 1:14

GUARD
g the way to the tree . . . . . Gen 3:24
will be your rear *g* . . . . Is 52:12
g the doors of your. . . . . Mic 7:5
we were kept under *g* . . . . . Gal 3:23
G what was committed. . . 1 Tim 6:20

GUARDIANS
but is under *g* and . . . . Gal 4:2

GUARDS
Unless the LORD *g*. . . . . Ps 127:1
And the *g* shook for . . . . . Matt 28:4

GUIDANCE
and excellent in *g* . . . . Is 28:29

GUIDE
He will be our *g*. . . . . Ps 48:14
Father, You are the *g* . . . . . . Jer 3:4
g our feet into the. . . . . . . Luke 1:79
has come, He will *g*. . . . . . John 16:13
Judas, who became a *g* . . . . Acts 1:16
you yourself are a *g* . . . . . . Rom 2:19

GUIDES
to you, blind *g*. . . . . Matt 23:16
unless someone *g*. . . . . Acts 8:31

GUILT
they accept their *g* . . . . . . Lev 26:41
g has grown up to the. . . . . . Ezra 9:6
of your fathers' *g*. . . . . . . Matt 23:32

GUILTLESS
g who takes His name . . . . . Ex 20:7
have condemned the *g* . . . . Matt 12:7

GUILTY
"We are truly *g*. . . . . Gen 42:21
we have been very *g* . . . . . . Ezra 9:7
the world may become *g* . . Rom 3:19
in one point, he is *g* . . . . . James 2:10

GULF
you there is a great *g* . . . . Luke 16:26

HABAKKUK
Prophet in Judah just prior to Bab
ylonian invasion, Hab 1:1
Prayer of, in praise of God, Hab
3:1–19

HABITATION
to Your holy *h* . . . . Ex 15:13
your rightful *h*. . . . . Job 8:6
Is God in His holy *h* . . . . . . Ps 68:5
their *h* be desolate. . . . . . . Ps 69:25
the Most High, your *h*. . . . . Ps 91:9
go to a city for *h* . . . . Ps 107:7
establish a city for *h* . . . . Ps 107:36
but He blesses the *h*. . . . . . Prov 3:33
in a peaceful *h* . . . . Is 32:18

Jerusalem, a quiet *h*. . . . . . Is 33:20
from His holy *h*. . . . . Zech 2:13
'Let his *h* be . . . . Acts 1:20
be clothed with our *h* . . . . 2 Cor 5:2

HADASSAH
Esther's Jewish name, Esth 2:7

HADES
be brought down to *H*. . . . Matt 11:23
H shall not. . . . . Matt 16:18
being in torments in *H* . . . Luke 16:23
not leave my soul in *H* . . . . Acts 2:27
I have the keys of *H* . . . . . . Rev 1:18
H were cast into the . . . . . Rev 20:14

HAGAR
Sarah's servant; bears Ishmael to
Abraham, Gen 16
Abraham sends her away; God com-
forts her, Gen 21:9–21
Paul explains symbolic meaning of,
Gal 4:22–31

HAGGAI
Postexilic prophet; contemporary
of Zechariah, Ezra 5:1, 2; 6:14;
Hag 1:1

HAGGITH
One of David's wives, 2 Sam 3:4
Mother of Adonijah, 1 Kin 1:5

HAIL
cause very heavy *h*. . . . . Ex 9:18
seen the treasury of *h* . . . . Job 38:22
He casts out His *h* . . . . . . Ps 147:17
h will sweep away the . . . . . Is 28:17
of the plague of the *h* . . . . Rev 16:21

HAILSTONES
clouds passed with *h* . . . . . Ps 18:12

HAIR
bring down my gray *h*. . . . Gen 42:38
the *h* on my body stood . . . . Job 4:15
Your *h* is like a flock. . . . . . Song 4:1
you cannot make one *h*. . . Matt 5:36
But not a *h* of your . . . . . Luke 21:18
if a woman has long *h*. . . 1 Cor 11:15
not with braided *h* . . . . . . 1 Tim 2:9
h like women's *h*. . . . . Rev 9:8

HAIRS
are more than the *h* . . . . . . Ps 40:12
h I will carry you . . . . Is 46:4
yes, gray *h* are here . . . . . . Hos 7:9
But the very *h* . . . . Matt 10:30

HAIRY
h garment all over. . . . . . . Gen 25:25
him, "A *h* man . . . . 2 Kin 1:8

HAKKOZ
Descendant of Aaron, 1 Chr 24:1, 10
Called Koz, Ezra 2:61, 62
Descendants of, kept from priest-
hood, Neh 7:63, 64

HALLOW
hosts, Him you shall *h*. . . . . . Is 8:13
h the Holy One of . . . . Is 29:23
h the Sabbath day . . . . Jer 17:24

HALLOWED
the Sabbath day and *h*. . . . . Ex 20:11
but I will be *h* . . . . Lev 22:32
who is holy shall be *h* . . . . . Is 5:16
heaven, *h* be Your name . . . Matt 6:9

HAM
Noah's youngest son, Gen 5:32
Enters ark, Gen 7:7
His immoral behavior merits Noah's
curse, Gen 9:22–25
Father of descendants of repopulated
earth, Gen 10:6–20

HAMAN
Plots to destroy Jews, Esth 3:3–15
Invited to Esther's banquet, Esth 5:1–14
Forced to honor Mordecai, Esth 6:5–14
Hanged on his own gallows, Esth 7:1–10

HAMATH
Israel's northern boundary, Num 34:8; 1 Kin 8:65; Ezek 47:16–20
Conquered, 2 Kin 18:34; Jer 49:23
Israelites exiled there, Is 11:11

HAMMER
h that breaks the rock . . . . . Jer 23:29
How the *h* of the whole . . . . Jer 50:23

HAMOR
Sells land to Jacob, Gen 33:18–20; Acts 7:16
Killed by Jacob's sons, Gen 34:1–31

HANANI
Father of Jehu the prophet, 1 Kin 16:1, 7
Rebukes Asa; confined to prison, 2 Chr 16:7–10
—— Nehemiah's brother; brings news concerning the Jews, Neh 1:2
Becomes a governor of Jerusalem, Neh 7:2

HANANIAH
False prophet who contradicts Jeremiah, Jer 28:1–17
—— Hebrew name of Shadrach, Dan 1:6, 7, 11

HAND
h shall be against . . . . Gen 16:12
tooth for tooth, *h* . . . . Ex 21:24
lay your *h* on him . . . . . Num 27:18
the *h* of God was . . . . . . 1 Sam 5:11
and strengthened his *h*. . 1 Sam 23:16
Uzzah put out his *h* . . . . 2 Sam 6:6
let us fall into the *h* . . . . 2 Sam 24:14
Then, by the good *h*. . . . . . Ezra 8:18
He would loose His *h* . . . . . . Job 6:9
he stretches out his *h*. . . . . . Job 15:25
that your own right *h* . . . . Job 40:14
h has held me up . . . . Ps 18:35
My times are in Your *h* . . . . . Ps 31:15
and night Your *h*. . . . . Ps 32:4
Your right *h* is full . . . . Ps 48:10
Let Your *h* be upon the . . . . . Ps 80:17
h shall be established . . . . . Ps 89:21
"Sit at My right *h*. . . . . Ps 110:1
And laid Your *h* upon me . . . Ps 139:5
days is in her right *h*. . . . . Prov 3:16
heart is in the *h*. . . . . Prov 21:1
Whatever your *h*. . . . . Eccl 9:10
is at his right *h* . . . . Eccl 10:2
do not withhold your *h* . . . . Eccl 11:6
His left *h* is under my. . . . . . Song 8:3
My *h* has laid the. . . . . Is 48:13
Behold, the LORD's *h*. . . . . Is 59:1
are the work of Your *h*. . . . . . Is 64:8
Am I a God near at *h*. . . . . Jer 23:23
of heaven is at *h*. . . . . Matt 3:2
if your right *h* . . . . Matt 5:30
do not let your left *h*. . . . . . Matt 6:3
lay Your *h* on her . . . . Matt 9:18
h causes you to sin. . . . . . . Mark 9:43
sitting at the right *h*. . . . Mark 14:62
delivered from the *h* . . . . . Luke 1:74
at the right *h* of God . . . . . Acts 7:55
is even at the right *h*. . . . . Rom 8:34
with my own *h*. . . . . 1 Cor 16:21
to you with my own *h* . . . . Gal 6:11
The Lord is at *h* . . . . Phil 4:5
"Sit at My right *h*. . . . . Heb 1:13
down at the right *h* . . . . . . Heb 10:12
stars in His right *h* . . . . Rev 2:1

HANDIWORK
firmament shows His *h*. . . . . . Ps 19:1

HANDLE
h the law did not know . . . . . Jer 2:8
H Me and see . . . . Luke 24:39
do not taste, do not *h* . . . . . Col 2:21

HANDLED
and our hands have *h*. . . . 1 John 1:1

HANDS
the *h* are the *h* . . . . Gen 27:22
Aaron and Hur supported his *h* . . . . Ex 17:12
here we are, in your *h*. . . . . Josh 9:25
took his life in his *h* . . . . 1 Sam 19:5
put my life in my *h* . . . . 1 Sam 28:21
but His *h* make whole . . . . . Job 5:18
and cleanse my *h* . . . . Job 9:30
h have made me and . . . . . . Job 10:8
They pierced My *h*. . . . . Ps 22:16
h formed the dry land. . . . . . Ps 95:5
trains my *h* for war . . . . . . Ps 144:1
stretches out her *h* . . . . . . Prov 31:19
say, 'He has no *h* . . . . Is 45:9
than having two *h* . . . . . . Matt 18:8
Behold My *h* and My . . . . Luke 24:39
only, but also my *h*. . . . . . . John 13:9
h the print of the . . . . John 20:25
know that these *h* . . . . . . Acts 20:34
his *h* what is good . . . . Eph 4:28
lifting up holy *h* . . . . 1 Tim 2:8
the laying on of the *h*. . . . 1 Tim 4:14
to fall into the *h* . . . . Heb 10:31

HANDWRITING
having wiped out the *h*. . . . . Col 2:14

HANGED
for he who is *h* . . . . Deut 21:23
went and *h* himself. . . . . . Matt 27:5

HANGS
h the earth on nothing . . . . Job 26:7
is everyone who *h*. . . . . Gal 3:13

HANNAH
Barren wife of Elkanah; prays for a son, 1 Sam 1:1–18
Bears Samuel and dedicates him to the Lord, 1 Sam 1:19–28
Magnifies God, 1 Sam 2:1–10

HANUN
King of Ammon; disgraces David's ambassadors and is defeated by him, 2 Sam 10:1–14

HAPPEN
show us what will *h* . . . . Is 41:22
understand what will *h* . . . Dan 10:14
not know what will *h* . . . . James 4:14

HAPPINESS
one year, and bring *h*. . . . . Deut 24:5

HAPPY
H is the man who has. . . . . . Ps 127:5
H are the people who . . . . . Ps 144:15
H is the man who finds. . . . Prov 3:13
mercy on the poor, *h*. . . . . Prov 14:21
trusts in the LORD, *h*. . . . . . Prov 16:20
h is he who keeps . . . . Prov 29:18
H is he who does not. . . . . . Rom 14:22

HARAN
Abraham's younger brother, Gen 11:26–31
City of Mesopotamia, Gen 11:31
Abraham leaves, Gen 12:4, 5
Jacob dwells at, Gen 29:4–35

HARASS
and Judah shall not *h* . . . . . . Is 11:13
h some from the church . . . Acts 12:1

HARD
Is anything too *h* . . . . Gen 18:14
His heart is as *h*. . . . . Job 41:24
shown Your people *h*. . . . . . . Ps 60:3
I knew you to be a *h*. . . . . Matt 25:24
"This is a *h* saying . . . . John 6:60
are some things *h*. . . . . . . 2 Pet 3:16

HARDEN
But I will *h* his heart. . . . . . . Ex 4:21
Do not *h* your hearts. . . . . . . Ps 95:8
h your hearts as . . . . Heb 3:8

HARDENED
But Pharaoh *h* his . . . . Ex 8:32
Who has *h* himself . . . . Job 9:4
their heart was *h* . . . . Mark 6:52
eyes and *h* their hearts . . . John 12:40
lest any of you be *h* . . . . . . Heb 3:13

HARDENS
A wicked man *h* his. . . . . . Prov 21:29
h his heart will fall . . . . . Prov 28:14
whom He wills He *h* . . . . . Rom 9:18

HARDSHIP
h that has befallen us . . . Num 20:14
h as a good soldier . . . . . . 2 Tim 2:3

HARLOT
of a *h* named Rahab. . . . . . Josh 2:1
h is a deep pit . . . . Prov 23:27
h is one body with . . . . . . 1 Cor 6:16
h Rahab did not perish . . . Heb 11:31
of the great *h* who . . . . Rev 17:1

HARLOTRIES
the land with your *h* . . . . . . Jer 3:2
Let her put away her *h* . . . . Hos 2:2

HARLOTRY
through her casual *h* . . . . . . Jer 3:9
the lewdness of your *h* . . . . Jer 13:27
let them put their *h* . . . . . Ezek 43:9
are the children of *h*. . . . . . Hos 2:4
Ephraim, you commit *h*. . . . . Hos 5:3
for the spirit of *h* . . . . Hos 5:4

HARLOTS
his blood while the *h* . . . . 1 Kin 22:38
h enter the. . . . . Matt 21:31
Great, The Mother of *H* . . . . Rev 17:5

HARM
do My prophets no *h*. . . . 1 Chr 16:22
and I will not *h* . . . . Jer 25:6
and do not *h* the oil . . . . . . Rev 6:6

HARMLESS
become blameless and *h* . . . Phil 2:15
for us, who is holy, *h* . . . . . Heb 7:26

HARMONIOUS
the harp, with *h* sound . . . . . Ps 92:3

HARP
those who play the *h*. . . . . . Gen 4:21
with the lute and *h* . . . . . . Ps 150:3
Lamb, each having a *h* . . . . . Rev 5:8

HARPS
We hung our *h* upon the. . . . Ps 137:2
playing their *h* . . . . Rev 14:2

HARSH
"Your words have been *h*. . . Mal 3:13
but also to the *h* . . . . 1 Pet 2:18

HARVEST
seedtime and *h*. . . . . Gen 8:22
to the joy of *h* . . . . Is 9:3
shall eat up your *h*. . . . . . . Jer 5:17
"The *h* is past. . . . . Jer 8:20

HASTE

of her *h* will come . . . . Jer 51:33
h truly is plentiful . . . . Matt 9:37
pray the Lord of the *h.* . . . . Matt 9:38
sickle, because the *h* . . . . . Mark 4:29
already white for *h* . . . . . . John 4:35
the *h* of the earth is . . . . . . Rev 14:15

HASTE

you shall eat it in *h.* . . . . . . Ex 12:11
For I said in my *h* . . . . Ps 31:22
And they came with *h* . . . . Luke 2:16
"Zacchaeus, make *h* . . . . . . Luke 19:5

HASTEN

be multiplied who *h* . . . . Ps 16:4
Do not *h* in your . . . . Eccl 7:9
I, the LORD, will *h* . . . . Is 60:22

HASTENING

h the coming of the . . . . . 2 Pet 3:12

HASTENS

and he sins who *h* . . . . Prov 19:2
with an evil eye *h* . . . . . . Prov 28:22
is near and *h* quickly . . . . . Zeph 1:14

HASTILY

utter anything *h.* . . . . Eccl 5:2
lay hands on anyone *h.* . . 1 Tim 5:22

HASTY

Do you see a man *h* . . . . Prov 29:20

HATE

'You shall not *h* . . . . Lev 19:17
h all workers of . . . . Ps 5:5
h the righteous shall . . . . . Ps 34:21
love the LORD, *h* evil . . . . . . Ps 97:10
h every false way . . . . Ps 119:104
h the double-minded . . . . . Ps 119:113
I *h* and abhor lying . . . . . Ps 119:163
love, and a time to *h* . . . . . . Eccl 3:8
h robbery for burnt . . . . Is 61:8
You who *h* good and . . . . . . Mic 3:2
either he will *h* . . . . Matt 6:24

HATED

Therefore I *h* life . . . . Eccl 2:17
h all my labor in . . . . Eccl 2:18
but Esau I have *h.* . . . . Mal 1:3
And you will be *h* . . . . . . Matt 10:22
have seen and also *h* . . . . John 15:24
but Esau I have *h* . . . . Rom 9:13
For no one ever *h* . . . . Eph 5:29
and *h* lawlessness. . . . . Heb 1:9

HATEFUL

h woman when she is . . . . Prov 30:23
in malice and envy, *h* . . . . . Titus 3:3

HATERS

The *h* of the LORD. . . . . Ps 81:15
backbiters, *h* of God . . . . . Rom 1:30

HATES

six things the LORD *h.* . . . . Prov 6:16
lose it, and he who *h* . . . . John 12:25
"If the world *h* . . . . John 15:18
h his brother is . . . . 1 John 2:11

HAUGHTY

Your eyes are on the *h* . . 2 Sam 22:28
bring down *h* looks . . . . . . Ps 18:27
my heart is not *h.* . . . . Ps 131:1
h spirit before a fall . . . . . Prov 16:18
A proud and *h* man . . . . Prov 21:24
Do not be *h* . . . . Rom 11:20
age not to be *h* . . . . 1 Tim 6:17

HAUNTS

are full of the *h* . . . . Ps 74:20

HAVEN

shall dwell by the *h* . . . . . Gen 49:13
to their desired *h* . . . . Ps 107:30

HAVOC

for Saul, he made *h.* . . . . . . Acts 8:3

HAZAEL

Anointed king of Syria by Elijah,
1 Kin 19:15–17
Elisha predicts his taking the throne,
2 Kin 8:7–15
Oppresses Israel, 2 Kin 8:28, 29;
10:32, 33; 12:17, 18; 13:3–7, 22

HAZEROTH

Scene of sedition of Miriam and
Aaron, Num 11:35—12:16

HAZOR

Royal Canaanite city destroyed by
Joshua, Josh 11:1–13
Rebuilt and assigned to Naphtali,
Josh 19:32, 36
Army of, defeated by Deborah and
Barak, Judg 4:1–24

HEAD

He shall bruise your *h* . . . . Gen 3:15
my skin, and laid my *h* . . . . Job 16:15
return upon his own *h* . . . . . Ps 7:16
h is covered with dew . . . . . Song 5:2
The whole *h* is sick. . . . . Is 1:5
it to bow down his *h* . . . . . . Is 58:5
could lift up his *h* . . . . Zech 1:21
you swear by your *h* . . . . . Matt 5:36
having his *h* covered . . . . 1 Cor 11:4
and gave Him to be *h* . . . . . Eph 1:22
For the husband is *h* . . . . . Eph 5:23
His *h* and his hair. . . . . Rev 1:14

HEADS

men to ride over our *h* . . . . Ps 66:12
Him, wagging their *h* . . . . Matt 27:39
dragon having seven *h.* . . . . Rev 12:3

HEAL

I wound and I *h* . . . . Deut 32:39
O LORD, *h* me. . . . . Ps 6:2
sent Me to *h* the . . . . Is 61:1
h your backslidings . . . . . . Jer 3:22
who can *h* you. . . . . Lam 2:13
torn, but He will *h* . . . . Hos 6:1
H the sick . . . . Matt 10:8
so that I should *h* . . . . . . Matt 13:15
sent Me to *h* the . . . . Luke 4:18
Physician, *h* yourself. . . . . Luke 4:23

HEALED

His word and *h* them . . . . Ps 107:20
And return and be *h* . . . . . . Is 6:10
His stripes we are *h* . . . . . . Is 53:5
h the hurt of My . . . . Jer 6:14
When I would have *h* . . . . . Hos 7:1
and He *h* them . . . . Matt 4:24
he had faith to be *h.* . . . . . Acts 14:9
that you may be *h* . . . . . . James 5:16
his deadly wound was *h.* . . Rev 13:3

HEALING

h shall spring forth . . . . Is 58:8
so that there is no *h* . . . . . . Jer 14:19
Your malady has no *h* . . . . Nah 3:19
shall arise with *h* . . . . Mal 4:2
and *h* all kinds of . . . . Matt 4:23
tree were for the *h.* . . . . . . Rev 22:2

HEALINGS

to another gifts of *h.* . . . . 1 Cor 12:9
Do all have gifts of *h* . . . . 1 Cor 12:30

HEALS

h all your diseases. . . . . . . Ps 103:3
h the stroke of their . . . . . . Is 30:26
Jesus the Christ *h.* . . . . Acts 9:34

HEALTH

to the soul and *h.* . . . . Prov 16:24

and for a time of *h.* . . . . . . Jer 8:15
no recovery for the *h* . . . . . Jer 8:22
all things and be in *h.* . . . 3 John 2

HEAP

I could *h* up words. . . . . Job 16:4
sea together as a *h* . . . . Ps 33:7
ears, they will *h.* . . . . 2 Tim 4:3

HEAPS

Though he *h* up silver . . . . . Job 27:16

HEAR

"*H,* O Israel. . . . . Deut 6:4
Him you shall *h* . . . . Deut 18:15
H me when I call . . . . Ps 4:1
O You who *h* prayer . . . . . . Ps 65:2
h what God the LORD . . . . . . Ps 85:8
ear, shall He not *h.* . . . . Ps 94:9
h the words of the . . . . . . Prov 22:17
h rather than to give . . . . . . Eccl 5:1
H, O heavens . . . . Is 1:2
H, you who are afar. . . . . . . Is 33:13
Let the earth *h* . . . . Is 34:1
I spoke, you did not *h* . . . . . Is 65:12
'Hearing you will *h* . . . . . Matt 13:14
if he will not *h.* . . . . Matt 18:16
"Take heed what you *h* . . . Mark 4:24
ears, do you not *h* . . . . . . Mark 8:18
h the sound of it . . . . John 3:8
that God does not *h* . . . . . . John 9:31
And how shall they *h* . . . . Rom 10:14
man be swift to *h* . . . . . . James 1:19
h what the Spirit says. . . . . . Rev 2:7

HEARD

h the sound of the . . . . Gen 3:8
h their cry because of . . . . . Ex 3:7
you only *h* a voice . . . . . . Deut 4:12
certainly God has *h.* . . . . . Ps 66:19
quietly, should be *h* . . . . . Eccl 9:17
Have you not *h.* . . . . Is 40:21
world men have not *h* . . . . . Is 64:4
Who has *h* such a thing . . . Is 66:8
h Ephraim bemoaning . . . . Jer 31:18
that they will be *h* . . . . . . Matt 6:7
h the word believed . . . . . . Acts 4:4
I say, have they not *h* . . . . Rom 10:18
not seen, nor ear *h* . . . . . . 1 Cor 2:9
h inexpressible . . . . 2 Cor 12:4
things that you have *h.* . . . 2 Tim 2:2
the things we have *h* . . . . . Heb 2:1
the word which they *h.* . . . . Heb 4:2
from death, and was *h* . . . . Heb 5:7
which we have *h* . . . . 1 John 1:1
Lord's Day, and I *h.* . . . . . . Rev 1:10

HEARER

if anyone is a *h.* . . . . James 1:23
is not a forgetful *h* . . . . . . James 1:25

HEARERS

for not the *h* of the . . . . . . Rom 2:13
impart grace to the *h.* . . . . Eph 4:29
of the word, and not *h* . . . James 1:22

HEARING

and read in the *h* . . . . Ex 24:7
Book of Moses in the *h* . . . . Neh 13:1
Do not speak in the *h* . . . . Prov 23:9
'Keep on *h* . . . . Is 6:9
h they do not. . . . . Matt 13:13
h they may hear . . . . Mark 4:12
If the whole were *h.* . . . . 1 Cor 12:17
or by the *h* of faith . . . . Gal 3:2
have become dull of *h.* . . . . Heb 5:11

HEARS

for Your servant *h* . . . . . . 1 Sam 3:9
out, and the LORD *h.* . . . . . . Ps 34:17
He who *h* you *h* Me. . . . . Luke 10:16
of God *h* God's words . . . . John 8:47

And if anyone *h* . . . . John 12:47
who is of the truth *h* . . . . . John 18:37
He who knows God *h* . . . . 1 John 4:6
And let him who *h* . . . . Rev 22:17

HEART

h was only evil. . . . . Gen 6:5
for you know the *h* . . . . Ex 23:9
not let your *h* faint . . . . . . Deut 20:3
great searchings of *h*. . . . . . Judg 5:16
h rejoices in the LORD . . . . . 1 Sam 2:1
God gave him another *h* . 1 Sam 10:9
LORD looks at the *h* . . . . . 1 Sam 16:7
his wives turned his *h* . . . 1 Kin 11:4
prepared his *h* to seek . . . . . Ezra 7:10
He pierces my *h* . . . . Job 16:13
How my *h* yearns within. . . Job 19:27
For God made my *h*. . . . . . Job 23:16
My *h* is in turmoil and . . . . Job 30:27
My *h* also instructs me . . . . . . Ps 16:7
your *h* live forever. . . . . Ps 22:26
h is overflowing. . . . . Ps 45:1
My *h* is steadfast . . . . Ps 57:7
Thus my *h* was grieved . . . . Ps 73:21
my *h* and my flesh cry . . . . . Ps 84:2
h shall depart from me . . . . . Ps 101:4
look and a proud *h* . . . . Ps 101:5
with my whole *h* . . . . Ps 111:1
h is not haughty . . . . Ps 131:1
h makes a cheerful . . . . . . Prov 15:13
The king's *h* is in the . . . . . Prov 21:1
as he thinks in his *h* . . . . . Prov 23:7
with a wicked *h*. . . . . Prov 26:23
h reveals the man . . . . Prov 27:19
trusts in his own *h*. . . . . . . Prov 28:26
The *h* of the wise is . . . . Eccl 7:4
and a wise man's *h* . . . . Eccl 8:5
h yearned for him . . . . Song 5:4
and the whole *h*. . . . . Is 1:5
h shall resound. . . . . Is 16:11
the yearning of Your *h* . . . . . . Is 63:15
the mind and the *h* . . . . . . Jer 11:20
h is deceitful above. . . . . Jer 17:9
I will give them a *h* . . . . Jer 24:7
therefore My *h* yearns . . . . Jer 31:20
and take the stony *h* . . . Ezek 11:19
get yourselves a new *h*. . . Ezek 18:31
uncircumcised in *h* . . . . . . Ezek 44:7
are the pure in *h*. . . . . Matt 5:8
is, there your *h* . . . . Matt 6:21
of the *h* proceed evil . . . . Matt 15:19
pondered them in her *h* . . . Luke 2:19
h will flow rivers . . . . John 7:38
"Let not your *h* . . . . John 14:1
believed were of one *h*. . . . Acts 4:32
Satan filled your *h*. . . . . . . Acts 5:3
h is not right in the . . . . . . Acts 8:21
h that God has raised . . . . Rom 10:9
in sincerity of *h* . . . . Eph 6:5
refresh my *h* in the . . . . . . Philem 20
and shuts up his *h*. . . . . . 1 John 3:17
if our *h* condemns us. . . . 1 John 3:20

HEARTILY

you do, do it *h*. . . . . Col 3:23

HEARTS

God tests the *h* . . . . Ps 7:9
who seek God, your *h* . . . . Ps 69:32
let the *h* of those . . . . Ps 105:3
And he will turn the *h*. . . . . Mal 4:6
h failing them from . . . . . Luke 21:26
purifying their *h*. . . . . Acts 15:9
will guard your *h*. . . . . Phil 4:7
of God rule in your *h* . . . . . Col 3:15

HEATHEN

repetitions as the *h*. . . . . . Matt 6:7
him be to you like a *h*. . . . Matt 18:17

HEAVEN

called the firmament *H*. . . . . Gen 1:8
precious things of *h*. . . . . Deut 33:13
LORD looks down from *h* . . . . Ps 14:2
word is settled in *h*. . . . . . Ps 119:89
For God is in *h* . . . . Eccl 5:2
"*H* is My throne . . . . Is 66:1
"If *h* above can be . . . . Jer 31:37
and the birds of the *h* . . . . Dan 2:38
come to know that *H* . . . . . Dan 4:26
for the kingdom of *h* . . . . . . Matt 3:2
your Father in *h* . . . . Matt 5:16
on earth as it is in *h*. . . . . Matt 6:10
H and earth will . . . . Matt 24:35
from Him a sign from *h*. . . . Mark 8:11
have sinned against *h*. . . . Luke 15:18
you shall see *h* . . . . John 1:51
one has ascended to *h* . . . . John 3:13
the true bread from *h*. . . . . John 6:32
a voice came from *h* . . . . . John 12:28
sheet, let down from *h* . . . . Acts 11:5
the whole family in *h*. . . . . . Eph 3:15
laid up for you in *h* . . . . Col 1:5
and the *h* gave rain . . . . James 5:18
there was silence in *h*. . . . . . . Rev 8:1
sign appeared in *h* . . . . Rev 12:1
Now I saw a new *h* . . . . Rev 21:1

HEAVENLY

your *h* Father will . . . . Matt 6:14
h host praising God . . . . . . Luke 2:13
if I tell you *h* things . . . . . . John 3:12
are those who are *h*. . . . . 1 Cor 15:48
blessing in the *h*. . . . . Eph 1:3
and have tasted the *h* . . . . . Heb 6:4
h things themselves . . . . . . Heb 9:23
a better, that is, a *h* . . . . . Heb 11:16
the living God, the *h* . . . . Heb 12:22

HEAVENS

I will make your *h*. . . . . . . Lev 26:19
and the highest *h* . . . . Deut 10:14
h cannot contain . . . . 1 Kin 8:27
the LORD made the *h* . . . 1 Chr 16:26
Till the *h* are no more . . . . . Job 14:12
in the *h* shall laugh . . . . Ps 2:4
h declare the glory . . . . Ps 19:1
Let the *h* declare His . . . . Ps 50:6
h can be compared . . . . Ps 89:6
The *h* are Yours . . . . Ps 89:11
For as the *h* are high . . . . . Ps 103:11
When He prepared the *h* . . Prov 8:27
h are higher than the . . . . . . Is 55:9
behold, I create new *h* . . . . . Is 65:17
and behold, the *h*. . . . . Matt 3:16
h will be shaken . . . . Matt 24:29
h are the work of Your . . . . . Heb 1:10
h will pass away. . . . . 2 Pet 3:10

HEAVINESS

and I am full of *h* . . . . Ps 69:20
My soul melts from *h*. . . . . Ps 119:28

HEAVY

the bondage was *h*. . . . . . . Neh 5:18

HEBREW

Term applied to:
    Abram, Gen 14:13
    Israelites, 1 Sam 4:6, 9
    Jews, Acts 6:1
    Paul, Phil 3:5

HEBRON

Abram, Isaac, and Jacob dwell there,
    Gen 13:18; 23:2–20; 35:27
Visited by spies, Num 13:21, 22
Defeated by Joshua, Josh 10:1–37
Caleb's inheritance, Josh 14:12–15
David's original capital; sons born
    there, 2 Sam 2:1–3, 11; 3:2–5

Site of Absalom's rebellion, 2 Sam
    15:7–10

HEDGE

behold, I will *h* . . . . Hos 2:6
sharper than a thorn *h* . . . . . Mic 7:4
a vineyard and set a *h*. . . . Mark 12:1

HEDGED

and whom God has *h* . . . . . . Job 3:23
You have *h* me behind . . . . . Ps 139:5
He has *h* me in so that . . . . Lam 3:7

HEED

By taking *h* according . . . . . . Ps 119:9
if you *h* Me . . . . Jer 17:24
and let us not give *h*. . . . . . Jer 18:18
nor give *h* to fables. . . . . . . 1 Tim 1:4
the more earnest *h*. . . . . Heb 2:1

HEEDS

h counsel is wise . . . . Prov 12:15

HEEL

you shall bruise His *h* . . . . . Gen 3:15
took hold of Esau's *h* . . . . . Gen 25:26
has lifted up his *h*. . . . . Ps 41:9
Me has lifted up his *h* . . . . John 13:18

HEIGHT

"Is not God in the *h*. . . . . . . Job 22:12
looked down from the *h* . . . Ps 102:19
nor *h* nor depth. . . . . Rom 8:39
length and depth and *h*. . . . . Eph 3:18

HEIR

Has he no *h* . . . . Jer 49:1
Now I say that the *h*. . . . . Gal 4:1
if a son, then an *h* . . . . Gal 4:7
He has appointed *h*. . . . . Heb 1:2
the world and became *h* . . . Heb 11:7

HEIRS

if children, then *h* . . . . Rom 8:17
of God and joint *h*. . . . . Rom 8:17
should be fellow *h* . . . . Eph 3:6
be rich in faith and *h*. . . . . James 2:5
vessel, and as being *h* . . . . 1 Pet 3:7

HELL

shall be turned into *h* . . . . Ps 9:17
go down alive into *h* . . . . . . Ps 55:15
house is the way to *h* . . . . . Prov 7:27
his soul from *h*. . . . . Prov 23:14
H and Destruction are. . . . Prov 27:20
"*H* from beneath is . . . . Is 14:9
be in danger of *h* fire . . . . . Matt 5:22
to be cast into *h* . . . . Matt 18:9
the condemnation of *h*. . . . Matt 23:33
power to cast into *h* . . . . . . Luke 12:5
it is set on fire by *h*. . . . . . James 3:6

HELLENISTS

Greek-speaking Jews, Acts 6:1
Hostile to Paul, Acts 9:29
Gospel preached to, Acts 11:20

HELMET

a breastplate, and a *h* . . . . . . Is 59:17
And take the *h* of . . . . Eph 6:17
and love, and as a *h* . . . . 1 Thess 5:8

HELP

the shield of your *h*. . . . . . Deut 33:29
Is my *h* not within me. . . . . Job 6:13
"There is no *h* . . . . Ps 3:2
May He send you *h*. . . . . Ps 20:2
He is our *h* and our. . . . . . . Ps 33:20
yet praise Him, the *h*. . . . . . Ps 42:11
A very present *h* . . . . Ps 46:1
Give us *h* from trouble . . . . . Ps 60:11
God, make haste to *h* . . . . . Ps 71:12
"I have given *h* . . . . Ps 89:19
the LORD had been my *h*. . . . Ps 94:17
there was none to *h*. . . . . . Ps 107:12

He is their *h* and . . . . Ps 115:9
Our *h* is in the name. . . . . . . Ps 124:8
let no one *h* him . . . . Prov 28:17
h my unbelief. . . . . Mark 9:24
tell her to *h* me . . . . Luke 10:40
and find grace to *h*. . . . . . . Heb 4:16

HELPED
far the LORD has *h* . . . . . . 1 Sam 7:12
fall, but the LORD *h*. . . . . . Ps 118:13
of salvation I have *h* . . . . Is 49:8
h His servant Israel. . . . . . Luke 1:54

HELPER
I will make him a *h*. . . . . . . Gen 2:18
Behold, God is my *h* . . . . Ps 54:4
give you another *H* . . . . . John 14:16
"But when the *H*. . . . . . . John 15:26
she has been a *h* . . . . Rom 16:2
"The LORD is my *h* . . . . Heb 13:6

HELPFUL
all things are not *h* . . . . . 1 Cor 6:12

HELPS
the Spirit also *h*. . . . . Rom 8:26
gifts of healings, *h* . . . . . 1 Cor 12:28

HEM
and touched the *h* . . . . . . Matt 9:20
might only touch the *h*. . . Matt 14:36

HEMAN
Composer of a Psalm, Ps 88:title

HERE
Then I said, "*H* am I . . . . Is 6:8

HERESIES
dissensions, *h* . . . . Gal 5:20
in destructive *h*. . . . . 2 Pet 2:1

HERITAGE
give it to you as a *h* . . . . Ex 6:8
have given me the *h* . . . . . . Ps 61:5
for that is his *h*. . . . . Eccl 3:22
for it is his *h* . . . . Eccl 5:18
This is the *h* of the . . . . Is 54:17
of My people, My *h* . . . . . . Joel 3:2
The flock of Your *h* . . . . . . Mic 7:14

HERMES
Paul acclaimed as, Acts 14:12

HERMON
Highest mountain (9,166 ft.) in Syria;
also called Sirion, Shenir, Deut
3:8, 9

HEROD
——— Herod the Great, procurator of
Judea (37–4 B.C.), Luke 1:5
Inquires about Jesus' birth, Matt
2:3–8
Slays infants of Bethlehem, Matt
2:12–18
——— Herod Antipas, the tetrarch, ruler
of Galilee and Perea (4 B.C.–A.D.
39), Luke 3:1
Imprisons John the Baptist, Luke
3:18–21
Has John the Baptist beheaded, Matt
14:1–12
Disturbed about Jesus, Luke 9:7–9
Jesus sent to him, Luke 23:7–11
——— Herod Agrippa I (A.D. 37–44), Acts
12:1, 19
Kills James, Acts 12:1, 2
Imprisons Peter, Acts 12:3–11, 19
Slain by an angel, Acts 12:20–23
——— Herod Agrippa II (A.D. 53–70);
called Agrippa and King Agrippa,
Acts 25:22–24, 26
Festus tells him about Paul, Acts
25:13–27

Paul makes a defense before, Acts
26:1–32

HERODIANS
Join Pharisees against Jesus, Mark
3:6
Seek to trap Jesus, Matt 22:15–22
Jesus warns against, Mark 8:15

HERODIAS
Granddaughter of Herod the Great;
plots John's death, Matt 14:3–12
Married her uncle, Mark 6:17, 18

HESHBON
Ancient Moabite city; taken by
Moses, Num 21:23–34
Assigned to Reubenites, Num 32:1–37
Prophecies concerning, Is 15:1–4;
16:8–14; Jer 48:2, 34, 35

HETH
Son of Canaan, Gen 10:15
Abraham buys field from sons of,
Gen 23:3–20
Esau marries daughters of, Gen 27:46

HEWN
in a tomb that was *h* . . . . Luke 23:53

HEZEKIAH
Righteous king of Judah; reforms
temple and worship, 2 Chr 29–31
Wars with Assyria; prayer for deliverance is answered, 2 Kin 18:7—
19:37
His sickness and recovery; thanksgiving, 2 Kin 20:1–11; Is 38:9–22
Boasts to Babylonian ambassadors,
2 Kin 20:12–19
Death, 2 Kin 20:20, 21

HID
and I *h* myself . . . . Gen 3:10

HIDDEKEL
Hebrew name of the river Tigris, Gen
2:14; Dan 10:4

HIDDEN
and the LORD has *h* . . . . . . 2 Kin 4:27
It is *h* from the eyes. . . . . . . Job 28:21
h Your righteousness . . . . Ps 40:10
and my sins are not *h*. . . . . . Ps 69:5
Your word I have *h*. . . . . . . Ps 119:11
h riches of secret. . . . . Is 45:3
there His power was *h*. . . . . Hab 3:4
h that will not. . . . . Matt 10:26
the *h* wisdom which God . . 1 Cor 2:7
bring to light the *h* . . . . . . 1 Cor 4:5
have renounced the *h* . . . . . 2 Cor 4:2
rather let it be the *h*. . . . . . . 1 Pet 3:4
give some of the *h*. . . . . Rev 2:17

HIDE
H me under the shadow . . . . . Ps 17:8
You shall *h* them in. . . . . . . Ps 31:20
O God, and do not *h*. . . . . . . Ps 55:1
You *h* Your face . . . . Ps 104:29
darkness shall not *h*. . . . . . Ps 139:12
You are God, who *h* . . . . . . Is 45:15
h yourself from your . . . . Is 58:7
"Fall on us and *h* . . . . Rev 6:16

HIDES
He *h* His face . . . . Ps 10:11

HIDING
You are my *h* place . . . . Ps 32:7
A man will be as a *h* . . . . Is 32:2

HIEL
Native of Bethel; rebuilds Jericho,
1 Kin 16:34
Fulfills Joshua's curse, Josh 6:26

HIGH
priest of God Most *H* . . . . . Gen 14:18
For the LORD Most *H* . . . . Ps 47:2
h is Your right . . . . Ps 89:13
are on *h* forevermore . . . . . . Ps 92:8
the LORD is on *h*. . . . . Ps 138:6
"I dwell in the *h* . . . . Is 57:15
know that the Most *H* . . . . Dan 4:17
whose habitation is *h*. . . . . . Obad 3
up on a *h* mountain by . . . Matt 17:1
your mind on *h* things . . . Rom 12:16
h thing that exalts. . . . . 2 Cor 10:5
and faithful *H* Priest. . . . . . . Heb 2:17

HIGHER
They are *h* than heaven . . . . Job 11:8
you, 'Friend, go up *h*. . . . . Luke 14:10
h than the heavens . . . . . . Heb 7:26

HIGHWAY
of the upright is a *h*. . . . . . Prov 15:19
in the desert a *h*. . . . . Is 40:3
up, build up the *H* . . . . Is 62:10

HIGHWAYS
h shall be elevated . . . . Is 49:11
go into the *h*. . . . . Matt 22:9

HILKIAH
Shallum's son, 1 Chr 6:13
High priest in Josiah's reign, 2 Chr
34:9–22
Oversees temple work, 2 Kin 22:4–7
Finds the Book of the Law, 2 Kin
22:8–14
Aids in reformation, 2 Kin 23:4

HILL
My King on My holy *h* . . . . . . Ps 2:6
h cannot be hidden. . . . . . . Matt 5:14
and *h* brought low . . . . Luke 3:5
to the brow of the *h* . . . . . . Luke 4:29

HILLS
of the everlasting *h* . . . . . . Gen 49:26
possess is a land of *h*. . . . . Deut 11:11
of the *h* are His also . . . . Ps 95:4
up my eyes to the *h*. . . . . . . Ps 121:1
settled, before the *h*. . . . . . Prov 8:25

HINDER
takes away, who can *h* . . . . . Job 9:12
all things lest we *h*. . . . . . . 1 Cor 9:12

HINDERED
come to you (but was *h* . . . Rom 1:13
Who *h* you from obeying. . . . Gal 5:7
prayers may not be *h*. . . . . . 1 Pet 3:7

HINNOM, VALLEY OF THE SON OF
See TOPHET
Place near Jerusalem used for
human sacrifice, 2 Kin 23:10;
2 Chr 28:3; Jer 7:31, 32; 19:1–15

HIP
socket of Jacob's *h* . . . . Gen 32:25

HIRAM
King of Tyre; provided for David's
palace and Solomon's temple,
2 Sam 5:11; 1 Kin 5:1–12; 9:10–14,
26–28; 10:11; 1 Chr 14:1

HIRE
h laborers for his. . . . . Matt 20:1

HIRED
h man who eagerly. . . . . Job 7:2
h servants have bread. . . . Luke 15:17

HIRELING
The *h* flees because . . . . . . John 10:13

HITTITES
One of seven Canaanite nations,
Deut 7:1

Israelites intermarry with, Judg 3:5, 6; 1 Kin 11:1; Ezra 9:1, 2

HIVITES
One of seven Canaanite nations, Deut 7:1
Esau intermarries with, Gen 36:2
Gibeonites belong to, Josh 9:3, 7

HOLD
h my eyelids open . . . . Ps 77:4
right hand shall *h* . . . . Ps 139:10
LORD your God, will *h* . . . . Is 41:13
I cannot *h* my peace . . . . Jer 4:19
h fast that word . . . . 1 Cor 15:2
h fast our confession . . . . . . Heb 4:14
h fast and repent . . . . Rev 3:3

HOLES
"Foxes have *h* . . . . Matt 8:20

HOLIER
near me, for I am *h* . . . . Is 65:5

HOLIEST
the way into the *H* . . . . Heb 9:8
to enter the *H* by the . . . . . Heb 10:19

HOLINESS
You, glorious in *h* . . . . Ex 15:11
has spoken in His *h* . . . . Ps 60:6
I have sworn by My *h* . . . . . Ps 89:35
h adorns Your house . . . . Ps 93:5
the Highway of *H* . . . . Is 35:8
to the Spirit of *h* . . . . Rom 1:4
spirit, perfecting *h* . . . . 2 Cor 7:1
uncleanness, but in *h* . . . . 1 Thess 4:7
be partakers of His *h* . . . . . Heb 12:10

HOLY
where you stand is *h* . . . . Ex 3:5
priests and a *h* nation . . . . . . Ex 19:6
day, to keep it *h* . . . . Ex 20:8
distinguish between *h* . . . . . Lev 10:10
the LORD your God am *h* . . . Lev 19:2
"No one is *h* . . . . 1 Sam 2:2
to the Most *H* Place . . . . 1 Kin 8:6
h seed is mixed . . . . Ezra 9:2
h ones will you turn . . . . Job 5:1
God sits on His *h* . . . . Ps 47:8
God, in His *h* mountain . . . . . Ps 48:1
my life, for I am *h* . . . . Ps 86:2
"*H*, *h*, *h* is the LORD . . . . Is 6:3
child of the *H* Spirit. . . . . . . Matt 1:18
baptize you with the *H* . . . . . Mark 1:8
who speak, but the *H* . . . . Mark 13:11
H Spirit will come . . . . Luke 1:35
H Spirit descended . . . . Luke 3:22
Father give the *H* . . . . Luke 11:13
H Spirit will teach . . . . Luke 12:12
H Spirit was not . . . . John 7:39
H Spirit has come . . . . Acts 1:8
all filled with the *H* . . . . Acts 2:4
apostles' hands the *H* . . . . . Acts 8:18
to speak, the *H* Spirit . . . . . Acts 11:15
good to the *H* Spirit . . . . . Acts 15:28
receive the *H* Spirit. . . . . . . Acts 19:2
if the firstfruit is *h* . . . . . . Rom 11:16
peace and joy in the *H* . . . . Rom 14:17
one another with a *h* . . . . . Rom 16:16
H Spirit teaches . . . . 1 Cor 2:13
that we should be *h* . . . . Eph 1:4
were sealed with the *H*. . . . . Eph 1:13
partakers of the *H* . . . . Heb 6:4
Most *H* Place once for all. . . Heb 9:12
has not entered the *h*. . . . . . Heb 9:24
H Spirit sent from . . . . 1 Pet 1:12
He who called you is *h* . . . . 1 Pet 1:15
it is written, "Be *h* . . . . 1 Pet 1:16
moved by the *H* Spirit . . . . 2 Pet 1:21
anointing from the *H* . . . 1 John 2:20
says He who is *h*. . . . . Rev 3:7

For You alone are *h*. . . . . . . Rev 15:4
is *h*, let him be *h* . . . . Rev 22:11

HOME
LORD has brought me *h* . . . Ruth 1:21
sparrow has found a *h* . . . . . Ps 84:3
the stork has her *h*. . . . . . . Ps 104:17
to his eternal *h* . . . . Eccl 12:5
said to him, "Go *h* . . . . Mark 5:19
into an everlasting *h*. . . . . Luke 16:9
to him and make Our *h* . . John 14:23
took her to his own *h* . . . . John 19:27
let him eat at *h* . . . . 1 Cor 11:34
own husbands at *h* . . . . . 1 Cor 14:35
that while we are at *h*. . . . . 2 Cor 5:6
to show piety at *h*. . . . . 1 Tim 5:4

HOMELESS
and beaten, and *h*. . . . . . . 1 Cor 4:11

HOMEMAKERS
be discreet, chaste, *h*. . . . . . Titus 2:5

HONEST
we are *h* men . . . . Gen 42:11

HONEY
"What is sweeter than *h* . . Judg 14:18
and with *h* from the . . . . . . Ps 81:16
My son, eat *h* because. . . . Prov 24:13
not good to eat much *h* . . Prov 25:27
h and milk are under . . . . Song 4:11
was locusts and wild *h*. . . . Matt 3:4

HONEYCOMB
than honey and the *h*. . . . . Ps 19:10
words are like a *h* . . . . . . Prov 16:24
fish and some *h* . . . . Luke 24:42

HONOR
H your father and your . . . . Ex 20:12
both riches and *h*. . . . . 1 Kin 3:13
the king delights to *h* . . . . . Esth 6:6
earth, and lay my *h* . . . . Ps 7:5
A man who is in *h* . . . . Ps 49:20
Sing out the *h* of His . . . . . . Ps 66:2
will deliver him and *h*. . . . . Ps 91:15
H and majesty are . . . . Ps 96:6
h have all His saints . . . . . . Ps 149:9
H the LORD with your . . . . . . Prov 3:9
before *h* is humility . . . . . . Prov 15:33
h is not fitting . . . . Prov 26:1
spirit will retain *h* . . . . . . Prov 29:23
Father, where is My *h* . . . . . Mal 1:6
is not without *h*. . . . . Matt 13:57
'*H* your father and your . . Matt 15:4
h the Son just as they . . . . John 5:23
"I do not receive *h*. . . . . . . John 5:41
but I My Father . . . . John 8:49
"If I *h* Myself . . . . John 8:54
him My Father will *h* . . . John 12:26
make one vessel for *h* . . . . Rom 9:21
to whom fear, *h* . . . . Rom 13:7
we bestow greater *h*. . . . . 1 Cor 12:23
sanctification and *h* . . . . 1 Thess 4:4
alone is wise, be *h*. . . . . . . 1 Tim 1:17
worthy of double *h* . . . . . . 1 Tim 5:17
and clay, some for *h* . . . . . 2 Tim 2:20
no man takes this *h*. . . . . . . Heb 5:4
H the king. . . . . 1 Pet 2:17
from God the Father *h* . . . 2 Pet 1:17
give glory and *h*. . . . . Rev 4:9

HONORABLE
of God, and he is an *h*. . . . 1 Sam 9:6
His work is *h* and. . . . . Ps 111:3
It is *h* for a man to . . . . . . Prov 20:3
traders are the *h*. . . . . Is 23:8
holy day of the LORD *h*. . . . . Is 58:13
providing *h* things. . . . . . . 2 Cor 8:21
Marriage is *h* among . . . . . Heb 13:4
having your conduct *h*. . . . 1 Pet 2:12

HONORABLY
desiring to live *h*. . . . . Heb 13:18

HONORS
h those who fear the . . . . . . Ps 15:4
'This people *h* Me . . . . . . Mark 7:6
It is My Father who *h* . . . . John 8:54

HOOKS
will lament who cast *h* . . . . . Is 19:8
spears into pruning *h*. . . . . Mic 4:3

HOPE
I should say I have *h* . . . . Ruth 1:12
are spent without *h*. . . . . . . Job 7:6
so You destroy the *h*. . . . . Job 14:19
where then is my *h* . . . . . Job 17:15
h He has uprooted . . . . . . Job 19:10
also will rest in *h* . . . . Ps 16:9
heart, all you who *h* . . . . . Ps 31:24
My *h* is in You . . . . Ps 39:7
For You are my *h*. . . . . Ps 71:5
I *h* in Your word . . . . Ps 119:147
O Israel, *h* in the . . . . . . Ps 130:7
h will not be cut. . . . . . . Prov 23:18
There is more *h* . . . . Prov 26:12
the living there is *h* . . . . . . Eccl 9:4
O the *H* of Israel. . . . . Jer 14:8
good that one should *h* . . Lam 3:26
Achor as a door of *h*. . . . . Hos 2:15
you prisoners of *h*. . . . . . Zech 9:12
I have *h* in God . . . . Acts 24:15
to *h*, in *h* believed . . . . . . Rom 4:18
and rejoice in *h* . . . . Rom 5:2
h does not disappoint. . . . . Rom 5:5
were saved in this *h* . . . . . Rom 8:24
h that is seen is . . . . Rom 8:24
But if we *h* for what . . . . . Rom 8:25
And now abide faith, *h* . . 1 Cor 13:13
life only we have *h*. . . . . . 1 Cor 15:19
may know what is the *h* . . . Eph 1:18
were called in one *h*. . . . . . Eph 4:4
h which is laid . . . . Col 1:5
Christ in you, the *h*. . . . . . . Col 1:27
For what is our *h*. . . . . . . 1 Thess 2:19
others who have no *h*. . . 1 Thess 4:13
and as a helmet the *h* . . . 1 Thess 5:8
Jesus Christ, our *h*. . . . . . . 1 Tim 1:1
in *h* of eternal life. . . . . . . Titus 1:2
for the blessed *h* . . . . Titus 2:13
to lay hold of the *h* . . . . . . Heb 6:18
of a better *h* . . . . Heb 7:19
us again to a living *h*. . . . . 1 Pet 1:3
you a reason for the *h* . . . . 1 Pet 3:15
who has this *h* in Him. . . . 1 John 3:3

HOPED
substance of things *h* . . . . . Heb 11:1

HOPHNI
Wicked son of Eli, 1 Sam 1:3; 2:12–17, 22–25
Prophecy against, 1 Sam 2:27–36; 3:11–14
Carries ark into battle; killed, 1 Sam 4:1–11

HOR
Mountain of Edom; scene of Aaron's death, Num 20:22–29; 33:37–39

HOREB
See SINAI
God appears to Moses at, Ex 3:1–22
Water flows from, Ex 17:6
Elijah lodged here 40 days, 1 Kin 19:8, 9

HORITES
Inhabitants of Mt. Seir, Gen 36:20
Defeated by Chedorlaomer, Gen 14:5, 6

Driven out by Esau's descendants,
Gen 36:20–29; Deut 2:12, 22

HORN
my shield and the *h* . . . . Ps 18:2
h will be exalted . . . . Ps 112:9
goat had a notable *h* . . . . . . Dan 8:5
and has raised up a *h*. . . . Luke 1:69

HORRIBLE
h thing has been . . . . Jer 5:30
I have seen a *h*. . . . . Hos 6:10

HORROR
and behold, *h* and . . . . Gen 15:12
sorrow, the cup of *h*. . . . . Ezek 23:33
you will become a *h* . . . . Ezek 27:36

HORSE
The *h* and its rider He. . . . . . Ex 15:1
Have you given the *h* . . . . . Job 39:19
h is a vain hope. . . . . Ps 33:17
the strength of the *h* . . . . . Ps 147:10
h is prepared for the . . . . . Prov 21:31
and behold, a white *h* . . . . . Rev 6:2
and behold, a black *h* . . . . . Rev 6:5
and behold, a pale *h* . . . . . . Rev 6:8
and behold, a white *h*. . . . Rev 19:11

HORSES
seen servants on *h* . . . . Eccl 10:7
h are swifter than. . . . . Jer 4:13
Do *h* run on rocks . . . . . . Amos 6:12
we put bits in *h*. . . . . James 3:3

HOSANNA
H in the highest . . . . Matt 21:9

HOSEA
Son of Beeri, prophet of the northern
kingdom, Hos 1:1

HOSHEA
Original name of Joshua, the son of
Nun, Deut 32:44; Num 13:8, 16
——— Israel's last king; usurps throne,
2 Kin 15:30
Reigns wickedly; Israel taken to Assyr-
ia during reign, 2 Kin 17:1–23

HOSPITABLE
of good behavior, *h*. . . . . . . 1 Tim 3:2
Be *h* to one another . . . . 1 Pet 4:9

HOST
who brings out their *h*. . . . . . Is 40:26
of the heavenly *h* . . . . Luke 2:13

HOSTILITY
Him who endured such *h*. . . Heb 12:3

HOSTS
name of the LORD of *h* . . 1 Sam 17:45
As the LORD of *h* lives . . . . 1 Kin 18:15
The LORD of *h* is with. . . . . . . Ps 46:7
LORD, all you His *h*. . . . . . . Ps 103:21
praise Him, all His *h* . . . . . . Ps 148:2
word of the LORD of *h*. . . . . . . Is 39:5
LORD of *h* is His name . . . . . . Is 47:4
against spiritual *h* . . . . Eph 6:12

HOT
of the LORD was *h* . . . . Judg 2:14
My heart was *h* within . . . . . Ps 39:3
are neither cold nor *h*. . . . . . Rev 3:15

HOUND
My enemies would *h*. . . . . . . Ps 56:2

HOUR
h what you should . . . . . Matt 10:19
day and *h* no one knows . Matt 24:36
Man is coming at an *h*. . . Matt 24:44
Behold, the *h* is at. . . . . . Matt 26:45
But this is your *h*. . . . . . . Luke 22:53
h has not yet come. . . . . John 2:4

But the *h* is coming . . . . . John 4:23
h has come that the . . . . . John 12:23
save Me from this *h* . . . . John 12:27
"Father, the *h* . . . . John 17:1
will not know what *h*. . . . . . Rev 3:3
keep you from the *h* . . . . . . Rev 3:10

HOURS
Are there not twelve *h* . . . . John 11:9

HOUSE
from your father's *h*. . . . . . Gen 12:1
But as for me and my *h*. . . . Josh 24:15
h appointed for all . . . . Job 30:23
with them to the *h* . . . . Ps 42:4
the goodness of Your *h* . . . . . Ps 65:4
For her *h* leads down. . . . . . Prov 2:18
Through wisdom a *h*. . . . . . Prov 24:3
better to go to the *h* . . . . Eccl 7:2
of the *h* tremble . . . . Eccl 12:3
to the *h* of the God of . . . . Is 2:3
to those who join the *h* . . . . . . Is 5:8
h was filled with . . . . Is 6:4
'Set your *h* in order . . . . Is 38:1
h shall be called a . . . . Is 56:7
and beat on that *h*. . . . . . Matt 7:25
h divided against . . . . . . Matt 12:25
h shall be called a. . . . . . Matt 21:13
h may be filled . . . . Luke 14:23
make My Father's *h* . . . . . . John 2:16
h are many mansions. . . . John 14:2
publicly and from *h*. . . . . . Acts 20:20
in his own rented *h* . . . . . Acts 28:30
who rules his own *h* . . . . . 1 Tim 3:4
the church in your *h* . . . . . Philem 2
For every *h* is built. . . . . Heb 3:4
His own *h*, whose *h* . . . . Heb 3:6
him into your *h* . . . . 2 John 1:10

HOUSEHOLD
over the ways of her *h*. . . . Prov 31:27
If the *h* is worthy. . . . . . . Matt 10:13
be those of his own *h* . . . . Matt 10:36
h were baptized . . . . Acts 16:15
saved, you and your *h*. . . . Acts 16:31
also baptized the *h* . . . . . . 1 Cor 1:16
those who are of the *h* . . . . . Gal 6:10
who are of Caesar's *h*. . . . . Phil 4:22

HOUSEHOLDER
h who brings out of. . . . . . Matt 13:52

HOUSES
h are safe from fear. . . . . Job 21:9
Yet He filled their *h* . . . . . . Job 22:18
is that their *h*. . . . . Ps 49:11
H and riches are an. . . . . . Prov 19:14
who has left *h* or. . . . . . . Matt 19:29
you devour widows' *h*. . . . Matt 23:14
Do you not have *h*. . . . . . 1 Cor 11:22

HOVERING
Spirit of God was *h* . . . . Gen 1:2

HOW
"*H* can this be. . . . . Luke 1:34
H long do You keep. . . . . . John 10:24
h you turned to God. . . . 1 Thess 1:9

HULDAH
Wife of Shallum, 2 Kin 22:14
Foretells Jerusalem's ruin, 2 Kin
22:15–17; 2 Chr 34:22–25
Exempts Josiah from trouble, 2 Kin
22:18–20

HUMAN
we have had *h* fathers . . . . . Heb 12:9

HUMBLE
man Moses was very *h*. . . . Num 12:3
h you and test you . . . . Deut 8:2
h themselves, and pray. . . 2 Chr 7:14

who is proud, and *h* . . . . . Job 40:11
the cry of the *h* . . . . Ps 9:12
Do not forget the *h* . . . . Ps 10:12
the desire of the *h* . . . . Ps 10:17
h He guides in justice . . . . . . Ps 25:9
h shall hear of it and . . . . . . Ps 34:2
LORD lifts up the *h*. . . . . Ps 147:6
h spirit with the . . . . Prov 16:19
contrite and *h* spirit . . . . Is 57:15
a meek and *h* people . . . . Zeph 3:12
associate with the *h*. . . . . . Rom 12:16
gives grace to the *h* . . . . . James 4:6
H yourselves in the . . . . . . James 4:10
gives grace to the *h* . . . . . 1 Pet 5:5
h yourselves under the. . . . 1 Pet 5:6

HUMBLED
h himself greatly . . . . . . 2 Chr 33:12
as a man, He *h* Himself. . . . Phil 2:8

HUMBLES
h Himself to behold. . . . . . . Ps 113:6

HUMILIATION
to plunder, and to *h* . . . . . . Ezra 9:7
h His justice was . . . . Acts 8:33
but the rich in his *h* . . . . James 1:10

HUMILITY
By *h* and the fear of . . . . . Prov 22:4
righteousness, seek *h* . . . . . Zeph 2:3
the Lord with all *h*. . . . . . Acts 20:19
delight in false *h*. . . . . Col 2:18
mercies, kindness, *h* . . . . . . Col 3:12
h correcting those . . . . . . 2 Tim 2:25
gentle, showing all *h* . . . . . Titus 3:2
and be clothed with *h* . . . . 1 Pet 5:5

HUNGER
you, allowed you to *h*. . . . . Deut 8:3
lack and suffer *h* . . . . Ps 34:10
They shall neither *h*. . . . . . . Is 49:10
likely to die from *h*. . . . . . . Jer 38:9
are those who *h* . . . . Matt 5:6
for you shall *h* . . . . Luke 6:25
to Me shall never *h*. . . . . . John 6:35
present hour we both *h* . . . 1 Cor 4:11
They shall neither *h* . . . . Rev 7:16

HUNGRY
bread from the *h*. . . . . Job 22:7
and fills the *h* . . . . Ps 107:9
gives food to the *h*. . . . . . . Ps 146:7
h soul every bitter . . . . . . Prov 27:7
your soul to the *h*. . . . . Is 58:10
for I was *h* and you . . . . Matt 25:35
when did we see You *h* . . . Matt 25:37
and one is *h* and . . . . . . 1 Cor 11:21
But if anyone is *h*. . . . . . . 1 Cor 11:34
to be full and to be *h* . . . . . Phil 4:12

HUNT
Yet you *h* my life to . . . . 1 Sam 24:11
h the violent man . . . . Ps 140:11
h the souls of My . . . . Ezek 13:18

HUNTER
Nimrod the mighty *h*. . . . . . Gen 10:9
Esau was a skillful *h* . . . . . Gen 25:27

HUR
Man of Judah; of Caleb's house,
1 Chr 2:18–20
Supports Moses' hands, Ex 17:10–12
Aids Aaron, Ex 24:14

HURAM
Master craftsman of Solomon's temple,
1 Kin 7:13–40, 45; 2 Chr 2:13, 14

HURT
h a woman with child . . . . . Ex 21:22
who plot my *h*. . . . . Ps 35:4
but I was not *h* . . . . Prov 23:35

another to his own *h* . . . . . . Eccl 8:9
They shall not *h* . . . . Is 11:9
of my people I am *h*. . . . . . . Jer 8:21
Woe is me for my *h*. . . . . . . Jer 10:19
it will by no means *h* . . . . Mark 16:18
shall not be *h* by the. . . . . . . Rev 2:11

HUSBAND
She also gave to her *h* . . . . . . Gen 3:6
"Surely you are a *h* . . . . Ex 4:25
h safely trusts her. . . . . Prov 31:11
your Maker is your *h* . . . . Is 54:5
though I was a *h* . . . . Jer 31:32
now have is not your *h*. . . . John 4:18
woman have her own *h* . . . . 1 Cor 7:2
For the unbelieving *h* . . . . 1 Cor 7:14
you will save your *h* . . . . 1 Cor 7:16
betrothed you to one *h* . . . . 2 Cor 11:2
For the *h* is head of . . . . Eph 5:23
the *h* of one wife. . . . . 1 Tim 3:2

HUSBANDS
them ask their own *h*. . . . 1 Cor 14:35
H, love your wives . . . . . . Eph 5:25
Let deacons be the *h* . . . . . 1 Tim 3:12

HUSHAI
Archite; David's friend, 2 Sam
15:32–37
Feigns sympathy with Absalom,
2 Sam 16:16–19
Defeats Ahithophel's advice, 2 Sam
17:5–23

HYMENAEUS
False teacher excommunicated by
Paul, 1 Tim 1:19, 20

HYMN
they had sung a *h* . . . . . . Matt 26:30

HYMNS
praying and singing *h*. . . . Acts 16:25
in psalms and *h* . . . . Eph 5:19

HYPOCRISY
you are full of *h* . . . . Matt 23:28
Pharisees, which is *h*. . . . . Luke 12:1
Let love be without *h* . . . . . Rom 12:9
away with the *h* . . . . Gal 2:13
and without *h* . . . . James 3:17
malice, all deceit, *h* . . . . 1 Pet 2:1

HYPOCRITE
of the *h* shall perish . . . . Job 8:13
and the joy of the *h* . . . . . . Job 20:5
is the hope of the *h*. . . . . . . Job 27:8
for everyone is a *h*. . . . . Is 9:17
also played the *h* . . . . Gal 2:13

HYPOCRITES
"But the *h* in heart . . . . Job 36:13
will I go in with *h*. . . . . Ps 26:4
For you were *h* . . . . Jer 42:20
not be like the *h* . . . . Matt 6:5
do you test Me, you *h*. . . . Matt 22:18
and Pharisees, *h* . . . . Matt 23:13

HYSSOP
Purge me with *h* . . . . Ps 51:7
sour wine, put it on *h* . . . . John 19:29

IBZAN
Judge of Israel; father of 60 children,
Judg 12:8, 9

ICE
dark because of the *i*. . . . . . . Job 6:16

ICHABOD
Son of Phinehas, 1 Sam 4:19–22

ICONIUM
City of Asia Minor; visited by Paul,
Acts 13:51
Many converts in, Acts 14:1–6

IDDO
Leader of Jews at Casiphia, Ezra
8:17–20
—— Seer whose writings are cited,
2 Chr 9:29

IDLE
For they are *i* . . . . Ex 5:8
i person will suffer . . . . . . Prov 19:15
i word men may speak . . . Matt 12:36
saw others standing *i* . . . . Matt 20:3
they learn to be *i*. . . . . 1 Tim 5:13
both *i* talkers and . . . . Titus 1:10

IDOL
if he blesses an *i*. . . . . Is 66:3
thing offered to an *i* . . . . . . 1 Cor 8:7
That an *i* is anything. . . . 1 Cor 10:19

IDOLATER
or covetous, or an *i* . . . . . 1 Cor 5:11
man, who is an *i* . . . . Eph 5:5

IDOLATERS
fornicators, nor *i* . . . . 1 Cor 6:9
immoral, sorcerers, *i*. . . . . . Rev 21:8
and murderers and *i*. . . . . . Rev 22:15

IDOLATRIES
and abominable *i*. . . . . 1 Pet 4:3

IDOLATRY
beloved, flee from *i* . . . . . 1 Cor 10:14
i, sorcery . . . . Gal 5:20

IDOLS
stolen the household *i* . . . . Gen 31:19
of the peoples are *i* . . . . Ps 96:5
i are silver and gold. . . . . . . Ps 115:4
land is also full of *i* . . . . Is 2:8
insane with their *i* . . . . Jer 50:38
in the room of his *i* . . . . . Ezek 8:12
from their wooden *i* . . . . . . Hos 4:12
who regard worthless *i* . . . . . Jon 2:8
i speak delusion . . . . Zech 10:2
things polluted by *i* . . . . . Acts 15:20
You who abhor *i* . . . . Rom 2:22
This was offered to *i*. . . . 1 Cor 10:28
keep yourselves from *i* . . . 1 John 5:21
worship demons, and *i*. . . . Rev 9:20

IDUMEA
Name used by Greeks and Romans
to designate Edom, Mark 3:8

IGNORANCE
that you did it in *i* . . . . . . Acts 3:17
i God overlooked . . . . Acts 17:30
sins committed in *i* . . . . Heb 9:7
to silence the *i*. . . . . 1 Pet 2:15

IGNORANT
I was so foolish and *i* . . . . . Ps 73:22
though Abraham was *i* . . . . . Is 63:16
not want you to be *i* . . . . 1 Cor 12:1
But if anyone is *i* . . . . . . 1 Cor 14:38
on those who are *i*. . . . . Heb 5:2

IGNORANTLY
because I did it *i* . . . . 1 Tim 1:13

ILLEGITIMATE
then you are *i*. . . . . Heb 12:8

ILLUMINATED
after you were *i*. . . . . Heb 10:32
and the earth was *i*. . . . . . . Rev 18:1
for the glory of God *i* . . . . Rev 21:23

ILLYRICUM
Paul preaches in, Roman 15:19

IMAGE
Us make man in Our *i* . . . . Gen 1:26
yourselves a carved *i*. . . . . Deut 4:16
shall despise their *i* . . . . Ps 73:20

the king made an *i* . . . . Dan 3:1
to them, "Whose *i*. . . . . . . Matt 22:20
since he is the *i* . . . . 1 Cor 11:7
He is the *i* of the . . . . Col 1:15
and not the very *i* . . . . Heb 10:1
the beast and his *i* . . . . Rev 14:9
who worshiped his *i* . . . . . Rev 19:20

IMAGINATION
the proud in the *i* . . . . Luke 1:51

IMITATE
I urge you, *i* me . . . . 1 Cor 4:16
as I also *i* Christ. . . . . 1 Cor 11:1
i those who through. . . . . . . Heb 6:12

IMMANUEL
shall call His name *I* . . . . Is 7:14
shall call His name *I* . . . . Matt 1:23

IMMEDIATELY
i the Spirit. . . . . Mark 1:12
hear, Satan comes *i* . . . . . . Mark 4:15
i forgets what . . . . James 1:24
I I was in the Spirit. . . . . Rev 4:2

IMMORAL
i woman is a deep pit . . . . Prov 22:14
murderers, sexually *i* . . . . . . Rev 21:8

IMMORALITY
except sexual *i* . . . . Matt 5:32
i as is not even named . . . . 1 Cor 5:1
abstain from sexual *i*. . . . 1 Thess 4:3

IMMORTAL
to the King eternal, *i*. . . . . 1 Tim 1:17

IMMORTALITY
glory, honor, and *i* . . . . Rom 2:7
mortal must put on *i*. . . . 1 Cor 15:53
who alone has *i*. . . . . 1 Tim 6:16
and brought life and *i*. . . . 2 Tim 1:10

IMMOVABLE
be steadfast, *i*. . . . . 1 Cor 15:58

IMMUTABLE
that by two *i* things . . . . Heb 6:18

IMPART
see you, that I may *i*. . . . . . Rom 1:11
that it may *i* grace . . . . Eph 4:29

IMPENITENT
i heart you are . . . . Rom 2:5

IMPLANTED
with meekness the *i* . . . . . James 1:21

IMPOSSIBLE
and nothing will be *i* . . . . Matt 17:20
"With men this is *i* . . . . . . Matt 19:26
God nothing will be *i* . . . . Luke 1:37
without faith it is *i* . . . . Heb 11:6

IMPOSTORS
i will grow worse . . . . 2 Tim 3:13

IMPRISONMENT
and of chains and *i* . . . . . . Heb 11:36

IMPRISONMENTS
in stripes, in *i*. . . . . 2 Cor 6:5

IMPULSIVE
but he who is *i*. . . . . Prov 14:29

IMPURITY
a woman during her *i* . . . . Ezek 18:6

IMPUTE
"Do not let my lord *i* . . . . 2 Sam 19:19
the LORD does not *i* . . . . Ps 32:2
the LORD shall not *i*. . . . . . . Rom 4:8

IMPUTED
bloodshed shall be *i* . . . . . . Lev 17:4
might be *i* to them . . . . . . Rom 4:11
alone that it was *i*. . . . . . . Rom 4:23
but sin is not *i*. . . . . Rom 5:13

IMPUTES
i righteousness apart . . . . . . Rom 4:6

INCENSE
golden bowls full of *i* . . . . Rev 5:8

INCLINE
i your heart to the . . . . Josh 24:23
i my heart to any evil . . . . . . Ps 141:4

INCORRUPTIBLE
the glory of the *i* . . . . Rom 1:23
dead will be raised *i* . . . . . 1 Cor 15:52
to an inheritance *i* . . . . 1 Pet 1:4
corruptible seed but *i* . . . . . 1 Pet 1:23

INCORRUPTION
it is raised in *i* . . . . 1 Cor 15:42
corruption inherit *i* . . . . . 1 Cor 15:50
must put on *i* . . . . 1 Cor 15:53

INCREASE
if riches *i* . . . . Ps 62:10
the LORD give you *i* . . . . Ps 115:14
hear and *i* learning. . . . . Prov 1:5
When goods *i* . . . . Eccl 5:11
Of the *i* of His . . . . Is 9:7
and knowledge shall *i* . . . . . Dan 12:4
Lord, "*I* our faith. . . . . Luke 17:5
He must *i* . . . . John 3:30
but God gave the *i* . . . . 1 Cor 3:6
grows with the *i* . . . . Col 2:19
for they will *i* . . . . 2 Tim 2:16

INCREASED
The waters *i* and. . . . . Gen 7:17
i your mercy which you . . . Gen 19:19
nation and *i* its joy . . . . Is 9:3
And Jesus *i* in wisdom . . . . Luke 2:52

INCREASES
i knowledge *i*. . . . . Eccl 1:18
who have no might He *i* . . . . Is 40:29

INCREDIBLE
should it be thought *i* . . . . . Acts 26:8

INCURABLE
My wound is *i* . . . . Job 34:6
'Your affliction is *i* . . . . Jer 30:12
Your sorrow is *i*. . . . . Jer 30:15

INDEBTED
everyone who is *i* . . . . Luke 11:4

INDEED
i it was very . . . . Gen 1:31
"But will God *i*. . . . . 1 Kin 8:27
"Behold, an Israelite *i*. . . . . John 1:47

INDIA
Eastern limit of Persian Empire,
Esth 1:1

INDICATING
the Holy Spirit *i* . . . . Heb 9:8
who was in them was *i*. . . . 1 Pet 1:11

INDIGNANT
saw it, they were *i*. . . . . . . Matt 26:8

INDIGNATION
of His anger, wrath, *i*. . . . . . Ps 78:49
I has taken hold. . . . . Ps 119:53
in whose hand is My *i*. . . . . . Is 10:5
For the *i* of the LORD. . . . . Is 34:2
have filled me with *i*. . . . . . Jer 15:17
can stand before His *i* . . . . . Nah 1:6
i which will devour . . . . . . Heb 10:27
into the cup of His *i* . . . . . Rev 14:10

INDUCED
O LORD, You *i* me . . . . Jer 20:7
if the prophet is *i* . . . . Ezek 14:9
I the LORD have *i* . . . . Ezek 14:9

INDULGENCE
no value against the. *i*. . . . . Col 2:23

INEXCUSABLE
Therefore you are *i*. . . . . Rom 2:1

INEXPRESSIBLE
Paradise and heard *i*. . . . . 2 Cor 12:4
you rejoice with joy *i* . . . . . 1 Pet 1:8

INFALLIBLE
suffering by many *i*. . . . . Acts 1:3

INFANTS
i who never saw. . . . . Job 3:16
they also brought *i* . . . . . Luke 18:15

INFERIOR
another kingdom *i*. . . . . Dan 2:39
that I am not at all *i* . . . . . 2 Cor 11:5

INFIRMITIES
"He Himself took our *i* . . . . Matt 8:17
boast, except in my *i* . . . . 2 Cor 12:5
and your frequent *i*. . . . . . 1 Tim 5:23

INFLAMING
i yourselves with gods . . . . . . Is 57:5

INHABIT
the wicked will not *i* . . . . . Prov 10:30
cities and *i* them . . . . Amos 9:14

INHABITANT
Cry out and shout, O *i*. . . . . . Is 12:6
And the *i* will not say . . . . . Is 33:24

INHABITANTS
He looks on all the *i* . . . . . . Ps 33:14
give ear, all *i* . . . . Ps 49:1
Let the *i* of Sela sing. . . . . . Is 42:11
Woe to the *i* of the. . . . . . . Rev 12:12

INHABITED
rejoicing in His *i* . . . . Prov 8:31
'You shall be *i*. . . . . Is 44:26
who formed it to be *i* . . . . . . Is 45:18

INHERIT
i the iniquities . . . . Job 13:26
descendants shall *i* . . . . . . Ps 25:13
The righteous shall *i* . . . . . . Ps 37:29
The wise shall *i* . . . . Prov 3:35
love me to *i* wealth . . . . . . Prov 8:21
The simple *i* folly . . . . Prov 14:18
the blameless will *i* . . . . . . Prov 28:10
i the kingdom prepared . . Matt 25:34
I do that I may *i*. . . . . Mark 10:17
unrighteous will not *i* . . . . . 1 Cor 6:9
you may *i* a blessing . . . . . . 1 Pet 3:9
who overcomes shall *i* . . . . . Rev 21:7

INHERITANCE
"You shall have no *i*. . . . . Num 18:20
is the place of His *i* . . . . . . Deut 32:9
the portion of my *i* . . . . Ps 16:5
yes, I have a good *i*. . . . . Ps 16:6
i shall be forever . . . . Ps 37:18
He will choose our *i*. . . . . . . Ps 47:4
You confirmed Your *i*. . . . . . Ps 68:9
the tribe of Your *i*. . . . . Ps 74:2
i gained hastily . . . . Prov 20:21
right of *i* is yours . . . . Jer 32:8
i has been turned . . . . Lam 5:2
will arise to your *i* . . . . Dan 12:13
And God gave him no *i*. . . . . Acts 7:5
and give you an *i* . . . . Acts 20:32
For if the *i* is of the . . . . Gal 3:18
we have obtained an *i* . . . . . Eph 1:11
be partakers of the *i* . . . . . . Col 1:12
receive as an *i*. . . . . Heb 11:8
i incorruptible. . . . . 1 Pet 1:4

INIQUITIES
How many are my *i* . . . . . . Job 13:23
i have overtaken me . . . . . . Ps 40:12
I prevail against me . . . . Ps 65:3
forgives all your *i* . . . . Ps 103:3

LORD, should mark *i* . . . . . . Ps 130:3
was bruised for our *i* . . . . Is 53:5
He shall bear their *i* . . . . Is 53:11
i have separated you . . . . Is 59:2

INIQUITY
God, visiting the *i* of the . . . . Ex 20:5
He has not observed *i*. . . . Num 23:21
wicked brings forth *i* . . . . . . Ps 7:14
O LORD, pardon my *i*. . . . . . Ps 25:11
i I have not hidden . . . . Ps 32:5
was brought forth in *i*. . . . . Ps 51:5
If I regard *i* in my . . . . Ps 66:18
Add *i* to their . . . . Ps 69:27
workers of *i* flourish. . . . . . . Ps 92:7
i boast in themselves. . . . . . . Ps 94:4
Shall the throne of *i* . . . . . . Ps 94:20
i have dominion. . . . . Ps 119:133
i will reap sorrow. . . . . Prov 22:8
a people laden with *i*. . . . . . . Is 1:4
i is taken away. . . . . Is 6:7
has laid on Him the *i* . . . . . . Is 53:6
will remember their *i* . . . . . Hos 9:9
to those who devise *i* . . . . . . Mic 2:1
like You, pardoning *i* . . . . . . Mic 7:18
all you workers of *i* . . . . . Luke 13:27
a fire, a world of *i*. . . . . . . James 3:6

INJUSTICE
of truth and without *i* . . . . Deut 32:4
i shuts her mouth . . . . Job 5:16
i have your fathers. . . . . Jer 2:5

INK
us, written not with *i*. . . . . 2 Cor 3:3
do so with paper and *i* . . . . 2 John 12

INN
room for them in the *i* . . . . Luke 2:7
brought him to an *i* . . . . . Luke 10:34

INNOCENCE
of my heart and *i*. . . . . Gen 20:5
washed my hands in *i*. . . . . . Ps 73:13

INNOCENT
do not kill the *i*. . . . . Ex 23:7
a bribe to slay an *i* . . . . . Deut 27:25
i will divide the . . . . Job 27:17
a bribe against the *i* . . . . . . Ps 15:5
because I was found *i* . . . . . Dan 6:22
saying, "I am *i* . . . . Matt 27:24
this day that I am *i* . . . . . Acts 20:26

INNUMERABLE
i as the sand which is. . . . . Heb 11:12
i company of angels. . . . . . Heb 12:22

INQUIRED
children of Israel *i*. . . . . . . Judg 20:27
Therefore David *i*. . . . . . 1 Sam 23:2
the LORD, nor *i* of Him . . . . . Zeph 1:6
the prophets have *i*. . . . . . . 1 Pet 1:10

INQUIRY
shall make careful *i* . . . . . Deut 19:18

INSANE
images, and they are *i* . . . . Jer 50:38
the spiritual man is *i* . . . . . . Hos 9:7

INSCRIBED
Oh, that they were *i* . . . . . . Job 19:23
See, I have *i* you on . . . . Is 49:16

INSPIRATION
is given by *i* of God . . . . . 2 Tim 3:16

INSTRUCT
good Spirit to *i* them . . . . . Neh 9:20
I will *i* you and teach . . . . . . Ps 32:8
the LORD that he may *i* . . . 1 Cor 2:16

INSTRUCTED
Surely you have *i* . . . . Job 4:3
counsel, and who *i*. . . . . Is 40:14

This man had been *i* . . . . . Acts 18:25
are excellent, being *i* . . . . . . Rom 2:18
Moses was divinely *i* . . . . Heb 8:5

INSTRUCTION
seeing you hate *i* . . . . Ps 50:17
despise wisdom and *i* . . . . . Prov 1:7
Take firm hold of *i* . . . . Prov 4:13
Hear *i* and be wise. . . . . . . Prov 8:33
Give *i* to a wise man . . . . . . Prov 9:9
i loves knowledge . . . . Prov 12:1
Cease listening to *i* . . . . . Prov 19:27
Apply your heart to *i* . . . . . Prov 23:12
for correction, for *i* . . . . . . 2 Tim 3:16

INSTRUCTORS
have ten thousand *i* . . . . . 1 Cor 4:15

INSTRUCTS
My heart also *i* . . . . Ps 16:7
He who *i* the nations . . . . . . Ps 94:10

INSTRUMENT
to Him with an *i* . . . . Ps 33:2
on an *i* of ten strings . . . . Ps 92:3

INSTRUMENTS
i of cruelty are in . . . . Gen 49:5
with stringed *i* . . . . Ps 150:4
i of unrighteousness . . . . . Rom 6:13
i of righteousness. . . . . Rom 6:13

INSUBORDINATE
for the lawless and *i* . . . . . 1 Tim 1:9
For there are many *i* . . . . . Titus 1:10

INSUBORDINATION
of dissipation or *i* . . . . Titus 1:6

INSULTED
will be mocked and *i* . . . . Luke 18:32
i the Spirit of grace . . . . . . Heb 10:29

INSULTS
nor be afraid of their *i* . . . . . . Is 51:7

INTEGRITY
In the *i* of my heart . . . . . . Gen 20:5
he holds fast to his *i* . . . . Job 2:3
that God may know my *i* . . . Job 31:6
I have walked in my *i* . . . . . . Ps 26:1
You uphold me in my *i* . . . . . Ps 41:12
The *i* of the upright . . . . Prov 11:3
in doctrine showing *i* . . . . . . Titus 2:7

INTERCEDE
the Lord, who will *i* . . . . . 1 Sam 2:25

INTERCESSION
of many, and made *i* . . . . Is 53:12
Spirit Himself makes *i* . . . . . Rom 8:26
always lives to make *i* . . . . . Heb 7:25

INTERCESSOR
that there was no *i* . . . . Is 59:16

INTEREST
shall not charge him *i* . . . . . Ex 22:25
men lent to me for *i* . . . . Jer 15:10
collected it with *i* . . . . Luke 19:23

INTERPRET
Do all *i* . . . . 1 Cor 12:30
pray that he may *i* . . . . 1 Cor 14:13
in turn, and let one *i* . . . . . 1 Cor 14:27

INTERPRETATION
"This is the *i* . . . . Gen 40:12
to another the *i* . . . . 1 Cor 12:10
a revelation, has an *i* . . . . . 1 Cor 14:26
of any private *i* . . . . 2 Pet 1:20

INTERPRETATIONS
Do not *i* belong to God . . . . Gen 40:8
that you can give *i* . . . . Dan 5:16

INTRIGUE
seize the kingdom by *i* . . . . Dan 11:21
join with them by *i* . . . . . . Dan 11:34

INVISIBLE
of the world His *i* . . . . Rom 1:20
is the image of the *i* . . . . Col 1:15
eternal, immortal, *i* . . . . . 1 Tim 1:17
as seeing Him who is *i* . . . . Heb 11:27

INWARD
i part is destruction . . . . Ps 5:9
Both the *i* thought. . . . . Ps 64:6
You have formed my *i* . . . . . Ps 139:13
God according to the *i* . . . . Rom 7:22
i man is being renewed . . . 2 Cor 4:16

INWARDLY
i they are . . . . Matt 7:15
is a Jew who is one *i* . . . . . . Rom 2:29

IRON
He regards *i* as straw . . . . . Job 41:27
i sharpens *i*. . . . . Prov 27:17
and your neck was an *i* . . . . . . Is 48:4
its feet partly of *i* . . . . Dan 2:33

ISAAC
Promised heir of the covenant, Gen
17:16–21
Born and circumcised, Gen 21:1–7
Offered up as a sacrifice, Gen
22:1–19
Marries Rebekah, Gen 24:62–67
Prays for children; prefers Esau, Gen
25:21–28
Dealings with Abimelech, king of
Gerar, Gen 26:1–31
Mistakenly blesses Jacob, Gen 27:1—
28:5
Dies in his old age, Gen 35:28, 29
NT references to, Luke 3:34; Gal
4:21–31; Heb 11:9, 20

ISAIAH
Prophet during reigns of Uzziah,
Jotham, Ahaz, and Hezekiah,
Is 1:1
Responds to prophetic call, Is 6:1–13
Prophesies to Hezekiah, 2 Kin 19; 20
Writes Uzziah's biography, 2 Chr
26:22
Writes Hezekiah's biography, 2 Chr
32:32
Quoted in NT, Matt 1:22, 23; 3:3;
8:17; 12:17–21; Luke 4:17–19; Acts
13:34; Rom 9:27, 29; 10:16, 20, 21;
11:26, 27; 15:12; 1 Pet 2:22

ISCARIOT, JUDAS
Listed among the Twelve, Mark 3:14,
19; Luke 6:16
Criticizes Mary, John 12:3–6
Identified as betrayer, John 13:21–30
Takes money to betray Christ, Matt
26:14–16
Betrays Christ with a kiss, Mark
14:43–45
Repents and commits suicide, Matt
27:3–10
His place filled, Acts 1:15–26

ISHBOSHETH
One of Saul's sons; made king,
2 Sam 2:8–10
Offends Abner, 2 Sam 3:7–11
Slain; his assassins executed, 2 Sam
4:1–12

ISHMAEL
Abram's son by Hagar, Gen 16:3, 4,
11–16
Circumcised, Gen 17:25
Scoffs at Isaac's feast; exiled with his
mother, Gen 21:8–21
His sons; his death, Gen 25:12–18

——— Son of Nethaniah; kills Gedaliah,
2 Kin 25:22–26

ISHMAELITES
Settle at Havilah, Gen 25:17, 18
Joseph sold to, Gen 37:25–28
Sell Joseph to Potiphar, Gen 39:1

ISRAEL
Used to refer to:
Jacob, Gen 32:28
descendants of Jacob, Gen 49:16, 28
ten northern tribes (in contrast to
Judah), 1 Kin 11:8
restored nation after exile, Ezra 9:1
true church, Gal 6:16

ISRAEL
be called Jacob, but *I* . . . . . Gen 32:28
"Hear, O *I* . . . . Deut 6:4
shepherd My people *I* . . . . 2 Sam 7:7
Truly God is good to *I* . . . . . . Ps 73:1
helped His servant *I* . . . . . . Luke 1:54
For they are not all *I*. . . . . . . Rom 9:6
and upon the *I* of God . . . . . Gal 6:16

ISRAELITES
Afflicted in Egypt, Ex 1:12–22
Escape from Egypt, Ex 12:29–42, 50;
13:17–22
Receive law at Sinai, Ex 19
Idolatry and rebellion of, Ex 32;
Num 13; 14
Wander in the wilderness,
Num 14:26–39
Cross Jordan; conquer Canaan,
Josh 4; 12
Ruled by judges, Judg 2
Saul chosen as king, 1 Sam 10
Kingdom divided, 1 Kin 12
Northern kingdom carried captive,
2 Kin 17
Southern kingdom carried captive,
2 Kin 24
70 years in exile, 2 Chr 36:20, 21
Return after exile, Ezra 1:1–5
Nation rejects Christ, Matt 27:20–27
Nation destroyed, Luke 21:20–24

ISSACHAR
Jacob's fifth son, Gen 30:17, 18
——— Tribe of:
Genealogy of, 1 Chr 7:1–5
Prophecy concerning, Gen 49:14, 15
Census at Sinai, Num 1:28, 29
Inheritance of, Josh 19:17–23

ITALY
Jews expelled from, Acts 18:2
Paul sails for, Acts 27:1, 6
Christians in, Acts 28:14

ITCHING
they have *i* ears. . . . . 2 Tim 4:3

ITHAMAR
Youngest son of Aaron, Ex 6:23
Consecrated as priest, Ex 28:1
Duty entrusted to, Ex 38:21
Jurisdiction over Gershonites and
Merarites, Num 4:21–33

ITINERANT
i Jewish exorcists . . . . Acts 19:13

JABBOK
River entering the Jordan about 20
miles north of the Dead Sea,
Num 21:24
Scene of Jacob's conflict, Gen
32:22–32
Boundary marker, Deut 3:16

JABESH GILEAD
Consigned to destruction, Judg 21:8–15
Saul defeats the Ammonites at, 1 Sam 11:1–11
Citizens of, rescue Saul's body, 1 Sam 31:11–13
David thanks citizens of, 2 Sam 2:4–7

JABEZ
J called on the God . . . . . . 1 Chr 4:10

JABIN
Canaanite king of Hazor; leads confederacy against Joshua, Josh 11:1–14
—— Another king of Hazor; oppresses Israelites, Judg 4:2
Defeated by Deborah and Barak, Judg 4:3–24
Immortalized in poetry, Judg 5:1–31

JACHIN
One of two pillars in front of Solomon's temple, 1 Kin 7:21, 22

JACOB
Son of Isaac and Rebekah; Rebekah's favorite, Gen 25:21–28
Obtains birthright, Gen 25:29–34
Obtains blessing meant for Esau; flees, Gen 27:1—28:5
Sees vision of ladder, Gen 28:10–22
Serves Laban for Rachel and Leah, Gen 29:1–30
Fathers children, Gen 29:31—30:24
Flees from, makes covenant with Laban, Gen 30:25—31:55
Makes peace with Esau, Gen 32:1–21; 33:1–17
Wrestles with God, Gen 32:22–32
Returns to Bethel; renamed Israel, Gen 35:1–15
Shows preference for Joseph, Gen 37:3
Mourns Joseph's disappearance, Gen 37:32–35
Sends sons to Egypt for food, Gen 42:1–5
Reluctantly allows Benjamin to go, Gen 43:1–15
Moves his household to Egypt, Gen 45:25—47:12
Blesses his sons and grandsons; dies, Gen 48; 49
Buried in Canaan, Gen 50:1–14

JACOB'S WELL
Christ teaches a Samaritan woman at, John 4:5–26

JAEL
Wife of Heber the Kenite; kills Sisera, Judg 4:17–22
Praised by Deborah, Judg 5:24–27

JAIR
Manassite warrior; conquers towns in Gilead, Num 32:41; Deut 3:14
—— Eighth judge of Israel, Judg 10:3–5

JAIRUS
Ruler of the synagogue; Jesus raises his daughter, Mark 5:22–24, 35–43

JAMES
Son of Zebedee, called as disciple, Matt 4:21, 22; Luke 5:10, 11
One of the Twelve, Matt 10:2; Mark 3:17
Zealous for the Lord, Luke 9:52–54
Ambitious for honor, Mark 10:35–45
Witnesses Transfiguration, Matt 17:1–9
Martyred by Herod Agrippa, Acts 12:2
—— Son of Alphaeus; one of the Twelve, Matt 10:3, 4
Called "the Less," Mark 15:40
—— Jesus' half brother, Matt 13:55, 56; Gal 1:19
Becomes leader of Jerusalem Council and Jerusalem church, Acts 15:13–22; Gal 2:9
Author of an epistle, James 1:1

JANNES AND JAMBRES
Two Egyptian magicians; oppose Moses, Ex 7:11–22; 2 Tim 3:8

JAPHETH
One of Noah's three sons, Gen 5:32
Receives blessing, Gen 9:20–27
His descendants occupy Asia Minor and Europe, Gen 10:2–5

JARED
Father of Enoch, Gen 5:15–20
Ancestor of Noah, 1 Chr 1:2
Ancestor of Christ, Luke 3:37

JASHER
Book of, quoted, Josh 10:13

JASON
Welcomes Paul at Thessalonica, Acts 17:5–9
Described as Paul's kinsman, Rom 16:21

JAVAN
Son of Japheth, Gen 10:2, 4
Descendants of, to receive good news, Is 66:19, 20

JEALOUS
your God, am a *j* God . . . . . . Ex 20:5
LORD, whose name is *J* . . . . . Ex 34:14
a consuming fire, a *j* . . . . . Deut 4:24
For I am *j* for you. . . . . 2 Cor 11:2

JEALOUSY
They provoked Him to *j* . . Deut 32:16
Will Your *j* burn like . . . . Ps 79:5
j is a husband's . . . . Prov 6:34
as strong as death, *j* . . . . . . Song 8:6
will provoke you to *j* . . . . . Rom 10:19
for you with godly *j* . . . . . . 2 Cor 11:2

JEBUS
Canaanite name of Jerusalem before captured by David, 1 Chr 11:4–8

JEBUSITES
Descendants of Canaan, Gen 15:18–21; Num 13:29
Defeated by Joshua, Josh 11:1–12
Not driven from Jerusalem; later conquered by David, Judg 1:21; 2 Sam 5:6–8
Put to forced labor under Solomon, 1 Kin 9:20, 21

JECONIAH
See JEHOIACHIN
Variant form of Jehoiachin, 1 Chr 3:16, 17
Abbreviated to Coniah, Jer 22:24, 28

JEDIDIAH
Name given to Solomon by Nathan, 2 Sam 12:24, 25

JEDUTHUN
Levite musician appointed by David, 1 Chr 16:41, 42
Heads a family of musicians, 2 Chr 5:12
Name appears in Psalm titles, Ps 39; 62; 77

JEGAR SAHADUTHA
Name given by Laban to memorial stones, Gen 31:46, 47

JEHOAHAZ
Son and successor of Jehu, king of Israel, 2 Kin 10:35
Seeks the Lord in defeat, 2 Kin 13:2–9
—— Son and successor of Josiah, king of Judah, 2 Kin 23:30–34
Called Shallum, 1 Chr 3:15
—— Another form of Ahaziah, youngest son of King Joram, 2 Chr 21:17

JEHOASH
See JOASH

JEHOIACHIN
Son of Jehoiakim; next to the last king of Judah, 2 Kin 24:8
Deported to Babylon, 2 Kin 24:8–16
Liberated by Evil-Merodach, Jer 52:31–34

JEHOIADA
High priest during reign of Joash, 2 Kin 11:4—12:16
Instructs Joash, 2 Kin 12:2

JEHOIAKIM
Wicked king of Judah; son of Josiah; serves Pharaoh and Nebuchadnezzar, 2 Kin 23:34—24:7
Taken captive to Babylon, 2 Chr 36:6–8
Kills prophet Urijah, Jer 26:20–23
Destroys Jeremiah's scroll; cursed by God, Jer 36

JEHORAM (or Joram)
Wicked king of Judah; son of Jehoshaphat, 2 Kin 8:16–24
Marries Athaliah, 2 Kin 8:18, 19
Kills his brothers, 2 Chr 21:2, 4
Elijah prophesies against him; prophecy fulfilled, 2 Chr 21:12–20
—— Wicked king of Israel; son of Ahab, 2 Kin 3:1–3
Counseled by Elisha, 2 Kin 3; 5:8; 6:8–12
Wounded in battle, 2 Kin 8:28, 29
Killed by Jehu, 2 Kin 9:14–26

JEHOSHAPHAT
Righteous king of Judah; son of Asa, 1 Kin 22:41–50
Goes to war with Ahab against Syria, 1 Kin 22:1–36
Institutes reforms; sends out teachers of the Law, 2 Chr 17:6–9; 19
His enemies defeated through his faith, 2 Chr 20:1–30

JEHOZABAD
Son of a Moabitess; assassinates Joash, 2 Kin 12:20, 21
Put to death, 2 Chr 25:3

JEHU
Prophet; denounces Baasha, 1 Kin 16:1–7
Rebukes Jehoshaphat, 2 Chr 19:2, 3
—— Commander under Ahab; anointed king, 1 Kin 19:16; 2 Kin 9:1–13
Destroys the house of Ahab, 2 Kin 9:14—10:30

Turns away from the Lord; dies,
2 Kin 10:31–36

JEHUDI
Reads Jeremiah's scroll, Jer 36:14,
21, 23

JEOPARDY
stand in *j* every hour . . . . 1 Cor 15:30

JEPHTHAH
Gilead's son by a harlot, Judg 11:1
Driven out, then brought back to
command army against
Ammonites, Judg 11:2–28
Sacrifices his daughter to fulfill a
vow, Judg 11:29–40
Chastises Ephraim, Judg 12:1–7

JEREMIAH
Prophet under Josiah, Jehoiakim,
and Zedekiah, Jer 1:1–3
Called by God, Jer 1:4–9
Forbidden to marry, Jer 16:2
Imprisoned by Pashhur, Jer 20:1–6
Prophecy written, destroyed, rewrit-
ten, Jer 36
Accused of defection and imprisoned;
released by Zedekiah, Jer 37
Cast into dungeon; rescued; prophe-
sies to Zedekiah, Jer 38
Set free by Nebuchadnezzar, Jer
39:11—40:6
Forcibly taken to Egypt, Jer 43:5–7

JERICHO
City near the Jordan, Num 22:1
Called the city of palm trees, Deut
34:3; 2 Chr 28:15
Miraculously defeated by Joshua,
Josh 6
Rebuilt by Hiel, 1 Kin 16:34
Visited by Jesus, Matt 20:29–34; Luke
19:1–10

JEROBOAM
Son of Nebat; receives prophecy that
he will be king, 1 Kin 11:26–40
Made king; leads revolt against
Rehoboam, 1 Kin 12:1–24
Sets up idols, 1 Kin 12:25–33
Rebuked by a man of God, 1 Kin
13:1–10
Judgment on house of, 1 Kin 13:33—
14:20
——— Wicked king of Israel; son of
Joash; successful in war, 2 Kin
14:23–29
Prophecy concerning, by Amos,
Amos 7:7–13

JERUBBAAL
Name given to Gideon for destroying
Baal's altar, Judg 6:32

JERUSALEM
Originally called Salem, Gen 14:18
Jebusite city, Josh 15:8; Judg 1:8, 21
King of, defeated by Joshua, Josh
10:5–23
Conquered by David; made capital,
2 Sam 5:6–9
Ark brought to, 2 Sam 6:12–17; 1 Kin
8:1–13
Saved from plague, 2 Sam 24:16
Temple built and dedicated here,
1 Kin 6; 8:14–66
Suffers in war, 1 Kin 14:25–27; 2 Kin
14:13, 14; Is 7:1
Miraculously saved, 2 Kin 19:31–36
Captured by Babylon, 2 Kin 24:10—
25:21; Jer 39:1–8

Exiles return and rebuild temple,
Ezra 1:1–4; 2:1
Walls of, dedicated, Neh 12:27–47
Christ enters as king, Matt 21:4–11
Christ laments for, Matt 23:37; Luke
19:41–44
Church born in, Acts 2
Christians of, persecuted, Acts 4

JESHUA (or Joshua)
Postexilic high priest; returns with
Zerubbabel, Ezra 2:2
Aids in rebuilding temple, Ezra 3:2–8
Also called Joshua; seen in vision,
Zech 3:1–10

JESHURUN
Poetic name of endearment for
Israel, Deut 32:15

JESSE
Grandson of Ruth and Boaz, Ruth
4:17–22
Father of David, 1 Sam 16:1–13
Mentioned in prophecy, Is 11:1, 10

JESTING
talking, nor coarse *j* . . . . Eph 5:4

JESUS
J Christ was as. . . . . Matt 1:18
shall call His name *J*. . . . . . Matt 1:21
J was led up by the . . . . Matt 4:1
These twelve *J* sent . . . . . . Matt 10:5
and laid hands on *J* . . . . . Matt 26:50
Barabbas and destroy *J* . . Matt 27:20
we to do with You, *J*. . . . . Mark 1:24
J withdrew with His . . . . Mark 3:7
J went into Jerusalem . . . . Mark 11:11
as they were eating, *J*. . . . Mark 14:22
and he delivered *J* . . . . . Mark 15:15
J rebuked the. . . . . Luke 9:42
truth came through *J* . . . . . John 1:17
J lifted up His eyes . . . . John 6:5
J wept. . . . . John 11:35
J was crucified . . . . John 19:20
This *J* God has raised. . . . . . Acts 2:32
of Your holy Servant *J* . . . . . Acts 4:30
believed on the Lord *J* . . . . Acts 11:17
baptized into Christ *J* . . . . . Rom 6:3
your mouth the Lord *J* . . . . Rom 10:9
among you except *J* . . . . . . 1 Cor 2:2
the day of the Lord *J* . . . . . . 1 Cor 5:5
perfect in Christ *J* . . . . Col 1:28
J who is called . . . . Col 4:11
exhort in the Lord *J* . . . . . 1 Thess 4:1
But we see *J* . . . . Heb 2:9
looking unto *J*. . . . . Heb 12:2
J Christ the righteous. . . . . 1 John 2:1
Revelation of *J* Christ . . . . Rev 1:1
so, come, Lord *J* . . . . Rev 22:20

JETHER
Gideon's oldest son, Judg 8:20, 21

JETHRO
Priest of Midian; becomes Moses'
father-in-law, Ex 2:16–22
Blesses Moses' departure, Ex 4:18
Visits and counsels Moses, Ex 18
Also called Reuel, Num 10:29

JEWELS
your thighs are like *j*. . . . . . Songs 7:1
that I make them My *j*. . . . . Mal 3:17

JEWS
Jesus born King of the, Matt 2:2
Salvation comes through the, John
4:22; Acts 11:19; Rom 1:16; 2:9, 10
Reject Christ, Matt 27:21–25
Reject the gospel, Acts 13:42–46

JEZEBEL
Ahab's idolatrous wife, 1 Kin 16:31
Her abominable acts, 1 Kin 18:4, 13;
19:1, 2; 21:1–16
Death prophesied; prophecy fulfilled,
1 Kin 21:23; 2 Kin 9:7, 30–37
——— Type of paganism in the church,
Rev 2:20

JEZREEL
Ahab's capital, 1 Kin 18:45; 21:1
Ahab's family destroyed at, 1 Kin
21:23; 2 Kin 9:30–37; 10:1–11

JOAB
David's nephew; commands his
army, 2 Sam 2:10–32; 8:16; 10:1–
14; 11:1, 14–25; 20:1–23
Kills Abner, 2 Sam 3:26, 27
Intercedes for Absalom, 2 Sam 14:1–
33
Remains loyal to David; kills Absalom, 2 Sam 18:1–5, 9–17
Demoted; kills Amasa, 2 Sam 19:13;
20:8–10
Opposes census, 2 Sam 24:1–9; 1 Chr
21:1–6
Supports Adonijah, 1 Kin 1:7
Solomon orders his death in obedience to David's command, 1 Kin
2:1–6, 28–34

JOANNA
Wife of Chuza, Herod's steward, Luke
8:1–3
With others, heralds Christ's resurrection, Luke 23:55, 56

JOASH (or Jehoash)
Son of Ahaziah; saved from Atha-
liah's massacre and crowned
by Jehoiada, 2 Kin 11:1–12
Repairs the temple, 2 Kin 12:1–16
Turns away from the Lord and is
killed, 2 Chr 24:17–25
——— Wicked king of Israel; son of
Jehoahaz, 2 Kin 13:10–25
Defeats Amaziah in battle, 2 Kin
14:8–15; 2 Chr 25:17–24

JOB
Model of righteousness, Job 1:1–5
His faith tested, Job 1:6—2:10
Debates with his three friends; com-
plains to God, Job 3–33
Elihu intervenes, Job 34—37
God's answer, Job 38—41
Humbles himself and repents, Job
42:1–6
Restored to prosperity, Job 42:10–17

JOCHEBED
Daughter of Levi; mother of Miriam,
Aaron, and Moses, Ex 6:20

JOEL
Preexilic prophet, Joel 1:1
Quoted in NT, Acts 2:16

JOHANAN
Military leader of Judah; warns
Gedaliah of Ishmael's plot, Jer
40:13–16
Avenges Gedaliah; takes the people
to Egypt, Jer 41:11–18

JOHN
The apostle, son of Zebedee; called as
disciple, Matt 4:21, 22; Luke 5:1–11
Chosen as one of the Twelve,
Matt 10:2
Especially close to Christ, Matt 17:1–9;
Mark 13:3; John 13:23–25; 19:26,
27; 20:2–8; 21:7, 20

Ambitious and overzealous, Mark 10:35–41; Luke 9:54–56

Sent to prepare the Passover, Luke 22:8–13

With Peter, heals a man and is arrested, Acts 3:1—4:22

Goes on missionary trip with Peter, Acts 8:14–25

Exiled on Patmos, Rev 1:9

Author of Gospel, three epistles, and the Revelation, John 21:23–25; 1 John; 2 John; 3 John; Rev 1:1

—— The Baptist; OT prophecy concerning, Is 40:3–5; Mal 4:5

His birth announced and accomplished, Luke 1:11–20, 57–80

Preaches repentance, Luke 3:1–20

Bears witness to Christ, John 1:19–36; 3:25–36

Baptizes Jesus, Matt 3:13–17

Jesus speaks about, Matt 11:7–19

Identified with Elijah, Matt 11:13, 14

Herod imprisons and kills, Matt 14:3–12

—— Surnamed Mark: see MARK

JOIN
Woe to those who *j* . . . . Is 5:8
'Come and let us *j* . . . . Jer 50:5
of the rest dared *j* . . . . Acts 5:13

JOINED
and mother and be *j* . . . . . . Gen 2:24
for him who is *j* . . . . Eccl 9:4
"Ephraim is *j* . . . . Hos 4:17
what God has *j* . . . . Matt 19:6
you be perfectly *j* . . . . 1 Cor 1:10
But he who is *j* . . . . 1 Cor 6:17
the whole body, *j* . . . . Eph 4:16

JOINT
j as He wrestled . . . . Gen 32:25
My bones are out of *j* . . . . . Ps 22:14
j heirs with Christ . . . . Rom 8:17
by what every *j* . . . . Eph 4:16

JOINTS
and knit together by *j* . . . . . Col 2:19
and spirit, and of *j* . . . . Heb 4:12

JONADAB (or Jehonadab)
David's nephew; encourages Amnon in sin, 2 Sam 13:3–5, 32–36

—— Son of Rechab; father of the Rechabites, Jer 35:5–19

Helps Jehu overthrow Baal, 2 Kin 10:15–28

JONAH
Prophet sent to Nineveh; rebels and is punished, Jon 1

Repents and is saved, Jon 2

Preaches in Nineveh, Jon 3

Becomes angry at God's mercy, Jon 4

Type of Christ's resurrection, Matt 12:39, 40

JONATHAN
King Saul's eldest son; his exploits in battle, 1 Sam 13:2, 3; 14:1–14, 49

Saved from his father's wrath, 1 Sam 14:24–45

Makes covenant with David; protects him from Saul, 1 Sam 18:1–4; 19:1–7; 20:1–42; 23:15–18

Killed by Philistines, 1 Sam 31:2, 8

Mourned by David; his son provided for, 2 Sam 1:17–27; 9:1–8

—— Son of high priest Abiathar; faithful to David, 2 Sam 15:26–36; 17:15–22

Informs Adonijah of Solomon's coronation, 1 Kin 1:41–49

JOPPA
Scene of Peter's vision, Acts 10:5–23, 32

JORAM
See JEHORAM

JORDAN RIVER
Lot dwells near, Gen 13:8–13

Canaan's eastern boundary, Num 34:12

Moses forbidden to cross, Deut 3:27

Miraculous dividing of, for Israel, Josh 3:1–17

by Elijah, 2 Kin 2:5–8

by Elisha, 2 Kin 2:13,14

Naaman healed in, 2 Kin 5:10–14

John baptizes in, Matt 3:6, 13–17

JOSEPH
Son of Jacob by Rachel, Gen 30:22–24

Loved by Jacob; hated by his brothers, Gen 37:3–11

Sold into slavery, Gen 37:12–36

Unjustly imprisoned in Egypt, Gen 39:1–23

Interprets dreams in prison, Gen 40:1–23

Wins Pharaoh's favor, Gen 41:1–44

Prepares Egypt for famine, Gen 41:45–57

Sells grain to his brothers, Gen 42—44

Reveals identity and reconciles with brothers; sends for Jacob, Gen 45:1–28

Settles family in Egypt, Gen 47:1–12

His sons blessed by Jacob, Gen 48:1–22

Blessed by Jacob, Gen 49:22–26

Buries his father; reassures his brothers, Gen 50:1–21

His death, Gen 50:22–26

—— Husband of Mary, Jesus' mother, Matt 1:16

Visited by angel, Matt 1:19–25

Takes Mary to Bethlehem, Luke 2:3–7

Protects Jesus from Herod, Matt 2:13–23

Jesus subject to, Luke 2:51

—— Secret disciple from Arimathea; donates tomb and assists in Christ's burial, Mark 15:42–46; Luke 23:50–53; John 19:38–42

JOSES
One of Jesus' half brothers, Matt 13:55

—— The name of Barnabas, Acts 4:36

JOSHUA
See JESHUA

—— Leader of Israel succeeding Moses, Num 27:18–23

Leads battle against Amalek, Ex 17:8–16

Sent as spy into Canaan; reports favorably, Num 13:16–25; 14:6–9

Assumes command, Josh 1:1–18

Sends spies to Jericho, Josh 2:1

Leads Israel across Jordan, Josh 3:1–17

Sets up commemorative stones, Josh 4:1–24

Circumcises the people, Josh 5:2–9

Conquers Jericho, Josh 5:13—6:27

Punishes Achan, Josh 7:10–26

Conquers Canaan, Josh 8—12

Divides the land, Josh 13—19

Addresses rulers, Josh 23:1–16

Addresses the people, Josh 24:1–28

His death, Josh 24:29, 30

JOSIAH
Righteous king of Judah; son of Amon, 2 Kin 22:1, 2

Repairs the temple, 2 Kin 22:3–9

Hears the Law; spared for his humility, 2 Kin 22:10–20

Institutes reforms, 2 Kin 23:1–25

Killed in battle, 2 Chr 35:20–25

JOT
one *j* or one tittle . . . . Matt 5:18

JOTHAM
Gideon's youngest son; escapes Abimelech's massacre, Judg 9:5

Utters prophetic parable, Judg 9:7–21

—— Righteous king of Judah; son of Azariah, 2 Kin 15:32–38; 2 Chr 27:1–9

JOURNEY
us go three days' *j* . . . . Ex 3:18
busy, or he is on a *j* . . . . 1 Kin 18:27
Nevertheless I must *j* . . . . Luke 13:33
wearied from His *j* . . . . John 4:6

JOY
LORD your God with *j* . . . . Deut 28:47
heart to sing for *j* . . . . Job 29:13
is fullness of *j* . . . . Ps 16:11
j comes in the morning . . . . . Ps 30:5
To God my exceeding *j* . . . . . Ps 43:4
You according to the *j* . . . . . . Is 9:3
j you will draw . . . . Is 12:3
ashes, the oil of *j* . . . . Is 61:3
j shall be theirs. . . . . Is 61:7
shall sing for *j* . . . . Is 65:14
word was to me the *j* . . . . . Jer 15:16
receives it with *j* . . . . Matt 13:20
Enter into the *j* . . . . Matt 25:21
in my womb for *j* . . . . Luke 1:44
there will be more *j* . . . . . . Luke 15:7
did not believe for *j* . . . . . Luke 24:41
My *j* may remain in . . . . . John 15:11
they may have My *j* . . . . . John 17:13
fill you with all *j* . . . . Rom 15:13
that my *j* is the . . . . 2 Cor 2:3
the Spirit is love, *j* . . . . Gal 5:22
brethren, my *j* and. . . . . . . Phil 4:1
longsuffering with *j* . . . . Col 1:11
are our glory and *j* . . . . 1 Thess 2:20
j that was set before . . . . . . Heb 12:2
count it all *j* . . . . James 1:2
j inexpressible. . . . . 1 Pet 1:8
with exceeding *j* . . . . 1 Pet 4:13
I have no greater *j* . . . . 3 John 4

JOYFUL
And my soul shall be *j* . . . . . . Ps 35:9
Make a *j* shout to the . . . . . Ps 100:1
of prosperity be *j*. . . . . Eccl 7:14
and make them *j* . . . . Is 56:7
I am exceedingly *j*. . . . . . . 2 Cor 7:4

JOZACHAR
Assassin of Joash, 2 Kin 12:19–21

Called Zabad, 2 Chr 24:26

JUBAL
Son of Lamech, Gen 4:21

JUBILEE
fiftieth year shall be a *J* . . . Lev 25:11

JUDAH
Son of Jacob and Leah, Gen 29:30–35

Intercedes for Joseph, Gen 37:26, 27

Fails in duty to Tamar, Gen 38:1–30

Offers himself as Benjamin's ransom, Gen 44:18–34

Jacob bestows birthright on, Gen 49:3–10

Ancestor of Christ, Matt 1:3, 16
—— Tribe of:
Prophecy concerning, Gen 49:8–12
Numbered at Sinai, Num 1:26, 27
Territory assigned to, Josh 15:1–63
Leads in conquest of Canaan, Judg
1:1–19
Makes David king, 2 Sam 2:1–11
Loyal to David and his house, 2 Sam
20:1, 2; 1 Kin 12:20
Becomes leader of southern king-
dom, 1 Kin 14:21, 22
Taken to Babylon, 2 Kin 24:1–16
Returns after exile, 2 Chr 36:20–23

JUDAISM
And I advanced in *J* . . . . Gal 1:14

JUDAS
Judas Lebbaeus, surnamed Thad-
daeus, Matt 10:3
One of Christ's apostles, Luke
6:13, 16
Offers a question, John 14:22
—— Judas Barsabas, a chief deputy,
Acts 15:22–32
—— Betrayer of Christ: *see* ISCARIOT

JUDE (or Judas)
Half brother of Christ, Matt 13:55
Does not believe in Christ, John 7:5
Becomes Christ's disciple, Acts 1:14
Writes an epistle, Jude 1

JUDEA
Christ born in, Matt 2:1, 5, 6
Hostile toward Christ, John 7:1
Gospel preached in, Acts 8:1, 4
Churches established in, Acts 9:31

JUDGE
The LORD *j* between . . . . Gen 16:5
For the LORD will *j* . . . . . . Deut 32:36
coming to *j* the earth. . . . 1 Chr 16:33
Rise up, O *J* of the . . . . Ps 94:2
sword the LORD will *j* . . . . Is 66:16
deliver you to the *j* . . . . . . Matt 5:25
"*J* not, that you be not . . . . . Matt 7:1
"Man, who made Me a *j* . . Luke 12:14
j who did not fear God . . . . Luke 18:2
As I hear, I *j* . . . . John 5:30
Do not *j* according . . . . . . John 7:24
I *j* no one. . . . . John 8:15
j the world but to. . . . . John 12:47
this, O man, you who *j* . . . . Rom 2:3
then how will God *j* . . . . . . Rom 3:6
Therefore let us not *j* . . . . Rom 14:13
Christ, who will *j*. . . . . 2 Tim 4:1
Lord, the righteous *J* . . . . . 2 Tim 4:8
heaven, to God the *J* . . . . Heb 12:23
But if you *j* the law . . . . . James 4:11
are you to *j* another . . . . . James 4:12

JUDGES
j who delivered . . . . Judg 2:16
in the days when the *j* . . . . . Ruth 1:1
Surely He is God who *j* . . . . Ps 58:11
He *j* among the gods. . . . . . . Ps 82:1
He makes the *j* of the. . . . . . Is 40:23
j are evening wolves . . . . . Zeph 3:3
For the Father . . . . John 5:22
he who is spiritual *j*. . . . . 1 Cor 2:15
j me is the Lord . . . . 1 Cor 4:4
Him who *j* righteously . . . . 1 Pet 2:23

JUDGMENT
show partiality in *j* . . . . . . Deut 1:17
Teach me good *j*. . . . . Ps 119:66
him in righteous . . . . Is 28:26
from prison and from *j* . . . . . Is 53:8
I will also speak *j* . . . . Jer 4:12

j was made in favor of . . . . Dan 7:22
be in danger of the *j* . . . . . Matt 5:21
will rise up in the *j* . . . . . Matt 12:42
shall not come into *j* . . . . . John 5:24
and My *j* is righteous . . . . John 5:30
if I do judge, My *j* . . . . John 8:16
Now is the *j* . . . . John 12:31
the righteous *j*. . . . . Rom 1:32
j which came from one. . . . Rom 5:16
all stand before the *j* . . . . Rom 14:10
eats and drinks *j* . . . . . . 1 Cor 11:29
appear before the *j* . . . . . 2 Cor 5:10
after this the *j*. . . . . Heb 9:27
For *j* is without mercy. . . . James 2:13
receive a stricter *j* . . . . . . James 3:1
time has come for *j*. . . . . . 1 Pet 4:17
a long time their *j* . . . . . . 2 Pet 2:3
darkness for the *j* . . . . Jude 6

JUDGMENTS
The *j* of the LORD are. . . . . . . Ps 19:9
j are a great deep . . . . Ps 36:6
I dread, for Your *j*. . . . . . . Ps 119:39
unsearchable are His *j*. . . . Rom 11:33
righteous are His *j*. . . . . . . Rev 19:2

JULIUS
Roman centurion assigned to guard
Paul, Acts 27:1–44

JUST
Noah was a *j* man. . . . . Gen 6:9
Hear a *j* cause . . . . Ps 17:1
It is a joy for the *j* . . . . . . Prov 21:15
j man who perishes . . . . . . Eccl 7:15
For there is not a *j* . . . . . . Eccl 7:20
j is uprightness. . . . . Is 26:7
the blood of the *j*. . . . . . . Lam 4:13
j shall live by his . . . . Hab 2:4
He is *j* and having . . . . . . Zech 9:9
her husband, being a *j*. . . . Matt 1:19
resurrection of the *j*. . . . . Luke 14:14
j persons who need no . . . Luke 15:7
the Holy One and the *J* . . . . Acts 3:14
dead, both of the *j* . . . . . . Acts 24:15
j shall live by faith . . . . . . Rom 1:17
that He might be *j* . . . . Rom 3:26
whatever things are *j*. . . . . . Phil 4:8
j men made perfect . . . . . Heb 12:23
have murdered the *j*. . . . . James 5:6
He is faithful and *j* . . . . . 1 John 1:9
J and true are Your . . . . . . Rev 15:3

JUSTICE
for all His ways are *j*. . . . . Deut 32:4
the Almighty pervert *j* . . . . . Job 8:3
j as the noonday . . . . Ps 37:6
and Your poor with *j*. . . . . . Ps 72:2
He will bring *j* . . . . Ps 72:4
Do *j* to the afflicted. . . . . . . Ps 82:3
and *j* are the . . . . Ps 89:14
revenues without *j*. . . . . . Prov 16:8
do not understand *j* . . . . Prov 28:5
j the measuring line. . . . . . Is 28:17
the LORD is a God of *j*. . . . . Is 30:18
He will bring forth *j*. . . . . . Is 42:1
No one calls for *j* . . . . Is 59:4
J is turned back. . . . . Is 59:14
I, the LORD, love *j* . . . . Is 61:8
you, O home of *j* . . . . . . Jer 31:23
plundering, execute *j* . . . . Ezek 45:9
truth, and His ways *j* . . . . Dan 4:37
observe mercy and *j* . . . . Hos 12:6
'Execute true *j*. . . . . Zech 7:9
"Where is the God of *j* . . . . Mal 2:17
And He will declare *j*. . . . Matt 12:18
His humiliation His *j* . . . . Acts 8:33

JUSTIFICATION
because of our *j*. . . . . Rom 4:25
offenses resulted in *j* . . . . Rom 5:16
men, resulting in *j*. . . . . . . Rom 5:18

JUSTIFIED
Me that you may be *j* . . . . Job 40:8
of Israel shall be *j* . . . . Is 45:25
words you will be *j* . . . . . Matt 12:37
But wisdom is *j*. . . . . Luke 7:35
j rather than the . . . . Luke 18:14
who believes is *j* . . . . Acts 13:39
"That You may be *j*. . . . . . . Rom 3:4
law no flesh will be *j*. . . . . Rom 3:20
j freely by His grace . . . . . Rom 3:24
having been *j* by. . . . . Rom 5:1
these He also *j*. . . . . Rom 8:30
but you were *j* . . . . 1 Cor 6:11
that we might be *j* . . . . . . Gal 2:16
no flesh shall be *j* . . . . . . Gal 2:16
who attempt to be *j* . . . . . . Gal 5:4
j in the Spirit . . . . 1 Tim 3:16
then that a man is *j* . . . . James 2:24
the harlot also *j* . . . . . . James 2:25

JUSTIFIER
be just and the *j* . . . . Rom 3:26

JUSTIFIES
He who *j* the wicked . . . . Prov 17:15
It is God who *j*. . . . . Rom 8:33

JUSTIFY
j the wicked for a . . . . Is 5:23
wanting to *j* himself . . . . Luke 10:29
"You are those who *j*. . . . Luke 16:15
is one God who will *j* . . . . Rom 3:30
that God would *j* . . . . Gal 3:8

JUSTLY
of you but to do *j*. . . . . Mic 6:8
And we indeed *j* . . . . . . Luke 23:41
how devoutly and *j*. . . . 1 Thess 2:10

JUSTUS
Surname of Joseph, a disciple,
Acts 1:23
—— Man of Corinth; befriends Paul,
Acts 18:7

KADESH
Spies sent from, Num 13:3, 26
Moses strikes rock at, Num 20:1–13
Boundary in the new Israel, Ezek
47:19

KADESH BARNEA
Boundary of Promised Land, Num
34:1–4
Limit of Joshua's military campaign,
Josh 10:41

KEEP
k you wherever you . . . . . . Gen 28:15
day, to *k* it holy . . . . Ex 20:8
and *k* My judgments. . . . . Lev 25:18
k all My commandments. . 1 Kin 6:12
that You would *k* . . . . . . 1 Chr 4:10
Even he who cannot *k*. . . . Ps 22:29
K my soul . . . . Ps 25:20
do not *k* silence . . . . Ps 35:22
k Your righteous . . . . Ps 119:106
k them in the midst of. . . . . Prov 4:21
K your heart with all. . . . . . Prov 4:23
a time to *k* silence . . . . Eccl 3:7
Let all the earth *k* . . . . Hab 2:20
k the commandments . . . . Matt 19:17
If you love Me, *k* . . . . John 14:15
k through Your name . . . . John 17:11
orderly and *k* the law. . . . . Acts 21:24
Let your women *k* . . . . . . 1 Cor 14:34
k the unity of the . . . . Eph 4:3
k yourself pure . . . . 1 Tim 5:22
k His commandments . . . . 1 John 2:3
k yourselves in the . . . . Jude 21
k you from stumbling . . . . . Jude 24
k those things . . . . Rev 1:3

KEEPER
Am I my brother's *k*. . . . . . . Gen 4:9
The LORD is your *k* . . . . Ps 121:5

KEEPERS
in the day when the *k* . . . . . Eccl 12:3

KEEPS
the faithful God who *k* . . . . . Deut 7:9
k truth forever . . . . Ps 146:6
k his way preserves . . . . . . Prov 16:17
k the commandment . . . . . Prov 19:16
Whoever *k* the law is a . . . . Prov 28:7
none of you *k* the law . . . . . John 7:19
born of God *k* himself . . . 1 John 5:18
and *k* his garments . . . . Rev 16:15

KEILAH
Town of Judah; rescued from
 Philistines by David, 1 Sam 23:1–5
Prepares to betray David; he escapes,
 1 Sam 23:6–13

KENITES
Canaanite tribe whose land is prom-
 ised to Abraham's seed, Gen 15:19
Subjects of Balaam's prophecy, Num
 24:20–22
Settle with Judahites, Judg 1:16
Spared by Saul in war with
 Amalekites, 1 Sam 15:6

KEPT
For I have *k* the ways. . . 2 Sam 22:22
vineyard I have not *k* . . . . . Song 1:6
these things I have *k* . . . . . Matt 19:20
all these things I have *k* . Mark 10:20
k all these things. . . . . Luke 2:19
love, just as I have *k* . . . . . John 15:10
k back part of the . . . . Acts 5:2
I have *k* the faith . . . . 2 Tim 4:7
who are *k* by the power . . . . 1 Pet 1:5
which now exist are *k* . . . . . 2 Pet 3:7

KETURAH
Abraham's second wife, Gen 25:1
Sons of:
 Listed, Gen 25:1, 2
 Given gifts and sent away, Gen 25:6

KEY
The *k* of the house of . . . . Is 22:22
have taken away the *k* . . . Luke 11:52
"He who has the *k* . . . . Rev 3:7
heaven, having the *k* . . . . . . Rev 20:1

KEYS
I will give you the *k* . . . . . Matt 16:19
And I have the *k* . . . . Rev 1:18

KIBROTH HATTAAVAH
Burial site of Israelites slain by God,
 Num 11:33–35

KICK
is hard for you to *k* . . . . Acts 9:5

KIDNAPPERS
for sodomites, for *k* . . . . . 1 Tim 1:10

KIDNAPS
"He who *k* a man and . . . . . Ex 21:16

KIDRON
Valley near Jerusalem; crossed by
 David and Christ, 2 Sam 15:23;
 John 18:1
Idols dumped there, 2 Chr 29:16

KILL
who finds me will *k* . . . . . . Gen 4:14
k the Passover . . . . Ex 12:21
I *k* and I make alive . . . . . Deut 32:39
"Am I God, to *k* . . . . 2 Kin 5:7
a time to *k* . . . . Eccl 3:3
to save life or to *k* . . . . Mark 3:4

of them they will *k* . . . . . . Luke 11:49
afraid of those who *k* . . . . . Luke 12:4
Why do you seek to *k* . . . . . John 7:19
"Rise, Peter; *k* and eat . . . . Acts 10:13

KILLED
Abel his brother and *k* . . . . . Gen 4:8
For I have *k* a man for. . . . . Gen 4:23
LORD *k* all the. . . . . Ex 13:15
Your servant has *k* . . . . . 1 Sam 17:36
for Your sake we are *k* . . . . . Ps 44:22
and scribes, and be *k* . . . . . Matt 16:21
Siloam fell and *k* them . . . . Luke 13:4
k the Prince of life . . . . Acts 3:15
me, and by it *k* . . . . Rom 7:11
"For Your sake we are *k* . . . Rom 8:36
who *k* both the Lord . . . . 1 Thess 2:15
martyr, who was *k* . . . . Rev 2:13

KILLS
"The LORD *k* and. . . . . 1 Sam 2:6
the one who *k* the . . . . Matt 23:37
for the letter *k* . . . . 2 Cor 3:6

KIND
animals after their *k* . . . . . Gen 6:20
k can come out by . . . . Mark 9:29
For He is *k* to the. . . . . Luke 6:35
suffers long and is *k* . . . . . 1 Cor 13:4
And be *k* to one . . . . Eph 4:32

KINDLED
When His wrath is *k* . . . . Ps 2:12
I, the LORD, have *k* . . . . . . Ezek 20:48
wish it were already *k* . . . . Luke 12:49

KINDLY
The LORD deal *k* . . . . Ruth 1:8
Julius treated Paul *k* . . . . . Acts 27:3
k affectionate to one . . . . . Rom 12:10

KINDNESS
may the LORD show *k* . . . . . 2 Sam 2:6
anger, abundant in *k* . . . . . Neh 9:17
me His marvelous *k* . . . . . . Ps 31:21
For His merciful *k* . . . . Ps 117:2
tongue is the law of *k* . . . . Prov 31:26
k shall not depart. . . . . Is 54:10
I remember you, the *k* . . . . . Jer 2:2
by longsuffering, by *k* . . . . 2 Cor 6:6
longsuffering, *k* . . . . Gal 5:22
But when the *k* and the . . . . Titus 3:4
and to brotherly *k* . . . . 2 Pet 1:7

KING
Then Melchizedek *k* . . . . . Gen 14:18
days there was no *k* . . . . . . Judg 17:6
said, "Give us a *k* . . . . 1 Sam 8:6
"Long live the *k* . . . . 1 Sam 10:24
they anointed David *k*. . . . 2 Sam 2:4
Yet I have set My *K* . . . . Ps 2:6
The LORD is *K* forever . . . . . . Ps 10:16
K answer us when we . . . . . . Ps 20:9
And the *K* of glory. . . . . Ps 24:7
k is saved by the . . . . Ps 33:16
k Your judgments. . . . . Ps 72:1
For God is my *K*. . . . . Ps 74:12
do who succeeds the *k* . . . . Eccl 2:12
out of prison to be *k* . . . . . . Eccl 4:14
when your *k* is a child . . . . Eccl 10:16
In the year that *K* . . . . Is 6:1
k will reign in. . . . . Is 32:1
the LORD is our *K* . . . . Is 33:22
Is not her *K* in her . . . . Jer 8:19
and the everlasting *K* . . . . . Jer 10:10
k of Babylon, *k* . . . . Ezek 26:7
I gave you a *k* in My . . . . . . Hos 13:11
the LORD shall be *K* . . . . Zech 14:9
He who has been born *K* . . . Matt 2:2
This Is Jesus the *K* . . . . Matt 27:37
by force to make Him *k* . . . . John 6:15
"Behold your *K* . . . . John 19:14

there is another *k*. . . . . Acts 17:7
Now to the *K* eternal. . . . . . 1 Tim 1:17
only Potentate, the *K*. . . . . . 1 Tim 6:15
this Melchizedek, *k*. . . . . Heb 7:1
Honor the *k*. . . . . 1 Pet 2:17
K of kings and Lord of. . . . . Rev 19:16

KINGDOM
you shall be to Me a *k* . . . . . Ex 19:6
LORD has torn the *k*. . . . . 1 Sam 15:28
Yours is the *k* . . . . 1 Chr 29:11
k is the LORD's . . . . Ps 22:28
the scepter of Your *k* . . . . . . Ps 45:6
in heaven, and His *k*. . . . . . Ps 103:19
is an everlasting *k* . . . . Ps 145:13
k which shall never be . . . . Dan 2:44
High rules in the *k*. . . . . Dan 4:17
k shall be the LORD's . . . . . . Obad 21
"Repent, for the *k* . . . . Matt 3:2
for Yours is the *k* . . . . Matt 6:13
But seek first the *k*. . . . . Matt 6:33
the mysteries of the *k* . . . . Matt 13:11
are the sons of the *k* . . . . . Matt 13:38
of such is the *k*. . . . . Matt 19:14
up to half of my *k* . . . . Mark 6:23
are not far from the *k* . . . . Mark 12:34
back, is fit for the *k*. . . . . . . Luke 9:62
against nation, and *k* . . . . Luke 21:10
he cannot see the *k*. . . . . John 3:3
he cannot enter the *k* . . . . . . John 3:5
If My *k* were of this . . . . . . John 18:36
for the *k* of God is . . . . Rom 14:17
when He delivers the *k*. . . 1 Cor 15:24
will not inherit the *k*. . . . . . . Gal 5:21
the scepter of Your *k*. . . . . . . Heb 1:8
we are receiving a *k* . . . . . . Heb 12:28
into the everlasting *k* . . . . . 2 Pet 1:11

KINGDOMS
the *k* were moved . . . . Ps 46:6
tremble, who shook *k* . . . . . . Is 14:16
showed Him all the *k* . . . . . Matt 4:8
have become the *k* . . . . Rev 11:15

KINGS
The *k* of the earth set . . . . . . Ps 2:2
k shall fall down . . . . Ps 72:11
He is awesome to the *k* . . . . Ps 76:12
By me *k* reign. . . . . Prov 8:15
He will stand before *k* . . . . Prov 22:29
k is unsearchable . . . . Prov 25:3
that which destroys *k* . . . . . Prov 31:3
it is not for *k* . . . . Prov 31:4
K shall be your foster. . . . . . . Is 49:23
"They set up *k* . . . . Hos 8:4
before governors and *k* . . . Matt 10:18
k have desired to see. . . . . . Luke 10:24
You have reigned as *k* . . . . . 1 Cor 4:8
and has made us *k*. . . . . Rev 1:6
that the way of the *k*. . . . . . Rev 16:12
may eat the flesh of *k* . . . . . Rev 19:18

KIRJATH ARBA
Ancient name of Hebron, Gen 23:2
Possessed by Judah, Judg 1:10

KIRJATH JEARIM
Gibeonite town, Josh 9:17
Ark taken from, 1 Chr 13:5

KISH
Benjamite of Gibeah; father of King
 Saul, 1 Sam 9:1–3

KISHON
River of north Palestine; Sisera's
 army swept away by, Judg 4:7, 13
Elijah executes prophets of Baal at,
 1 Kin 18:40

KISS
K the Son . . . . Ps 2:12
Let him *k* me with the . . . . . Song 1:2

You gave Me no *k* . . . . Luke 7:45
another with a holy *k* . . . . Rom 16:16
one another with a *k* . . . . 1 Pet 5:14

KISSED
And they *k* one another . 1 Sam 20:41
and *k* Him . . . . Matt 26:49
and she *k* His feet and . . . . Luke 7:38

KNEE
that to Me every *k* . . . . Is 45:23
And they bowed the *k*. . . . Matt 27:29
have not bowed the *k* . . . . Rom 11:4
every *k* shall bow to. . . . . Rom 14:11
of Jesus every *k* . . . . Phil 2:10

KNEES
make firm the feeble *k*. . . . . . Is 35:3
be dandled on her *k*. . . . . . Is 66:12
this reason I bow my *k*. . . . Eph 3:14
and the feeble *k* . . . . Heb 12:12

KNEW
Adam *k* Eve his wife . . . . . . Gen 4:1
in the womb I *k* . . . . Jer 1:5
to them, 'I never *k* . . . . . Matt 7:23
k what was in man. . . . . . John 2:25
For He made Him who *k* . . 2 Cor 5:21

KNIT
of Jonathan was *k* . . . . . 1 Sam 18:1
k me together with. . . . . . . Job 10:11
be encouraged, being *k*. . . . . Col 2:2

KNOCK
k, and it will be. . . . . Matt 7:7
at the door and *k* . . . . Rev 3:20

KNOW
k good and evil . . . . Gen 3:22
and I did not *k* . . . . Gen 28:16
k that I am the LORD . . . . Ex 6:7
k that there is no God . . . . 2 Kin 5:15
you, my son Solomon, *k* . . 1 Chr 28:9
Hear it, and *k* for. . . . . Job 5:27
and *k* nothing. . . . . Job 8:9
k that my Redeemer . . . . . . Job 19:25
'What does God *k* . . . . Job 22:13
k Your name will put. . . . . . . Ps 9:10
k that I am God. . . . . Ps 46:10
make me to *k* wisdom. . . . . . Ps 51:6
Who can it . . . . Jer 17:9
saying, 'K the LORD. . . . . . . Jer 31:34
for you to *k* justice . . . . Mic 3:1
k what hour your Lord . . . Matt 24:42
an oath, "I do not *k* . . . . . Matt 26:72
the world did not *k* . . . . . . John 1:10
We speak what We *k*. . . . . . John 3:11
k what we worship . . . . . . John 4:22
k that You are . . . . John 6:69
hear My voice, and I *k* . . . John 10:27
If you *k* these things . . . . John 13:17
k whom I have chosen . . . John 13:18
we are sure that You *k* . . . John 16:30
k that I love You . . . . John 21:15
k times or seasons . . . . Acts 1:7
and said, "Jesus I *k*. . . . . . Acts 19:15
wisdom did not *k*. . . . . 1 Cor 1:21
nor can *k* them . . . . 1 Cor 2:14
For we *k* in part and . . . . . 1 Cor 13:9
k a man in Christ who . . . 2 Cor 12:2
k the love of Christ. . . . . . . Eph 3:19
k whom I have believed . . 2 Tim 1:12
so that they may *k* . . . . . . 2 Tim 2:25
this we *k* that we *k* Him. . . 1 John 2:3
He who says, "I *k*. . . . . 1 John 2:4
and you *k* all things . . . . 1 John 2:20
By this we *k* love . . . . . . 1 John 3:16
k that we are of the . . . . . 1 John 3:19
k that He abides. . . . . 1 John 3:24
k that we are of God . . . . 1 John 5:19
"I *k* your works. . . . . Rev 2:2

KNOWLEDGE
and the tree of the *k* . . . . . . Gen 2:9
LORD is the God of *k* . . . . . 1 Sam 2:3
Can anyone teach God *k* . . Job 21:22
who is perfect in *k*. . . . . Job 36:4
unto night reveals *k* . . . . Ps 19:2
k is too wonderful . . . . Ps 139:6
k the depths were . . . . Prov 3:20
k rather than . . . . Prov 8:10
Wise men store up *k*. . . . . Prov 10:14
k is easy to him who . . . . . Prov 14:6
k spares his words . . . . . . Prov 17:27
a soul to be without *k* . . . . Prov 19:2
and he who increases *k* . . . . Eccl 1:18
k is that wisdom . . . . Eccl 7:12
no work or device or *k* . . . . Eccl 9:10
Whom will he teach *k* . . . . . . Is 28:9
k shall increase . . . . Dan 12:4
you have rejected *k* . . . . Hos 4:6
having more accurate *k*. . Acts 24:22
having the form of *k*. . . . . . Rom 2:20
by the law is the *k* of sin . . Rom 3:20
K puffs up . . . . 1 Cor 8:1
whether there is *k* . . . . . . 1 Cor 13:8
Christ which passes *k*. . . . . Eph 3:19
is falsely called *k*. . . . . 1 Tim 6:20
in the grace and *k*. . . . . . . 2 Pet 3:18

KNOWN
In Judah God is *k* . . . . Ps 76:1
my mouth will I make *k*. . . . . Ps 89:1
If you had *k* Me. . . . . John 8:19
My sheep, and am *k* . . . . . John 10:14
The world has not *k* . . . . . John 17:25
peace they have not *k*. . . . . Rom 3:17
I would not have *k* . . . . Rom 7:7
"For who has *k* . . . . Rom 11:34
after you have *k* . . . . Gal 4:9
requests be made *k* . . . . Phil 4:6
k the Holy Scriptures . . . . . 2 Tim 3:15

KNOWS
For God *k* that in . . . . Gen 3:5
k the secrets of the . . . . Ps 44:21
he understands and *k* . . . . . . Jer 9:24
k what is in the . . . . Dan 2:22
k those who trust. . . . . Nah 1:7
k the things you have. . . . . . Matt 6:8
and hour no one *k* . . . . . . Matt 24:36
k who the Son is . . . . Luke 10:22
but God *k* your hearts. . . . Luke 16:15
searches the hearts *k*. . . . . . Rom 8:27
k the things of God . . . . . . 1 Cor 2:11
k those who are His. . . . . . 2 Tim 2:19
to him who *k* to do . . . . . James 4:17
and *k* all things . . . . 1 John 3:20
written which no one *k*. . . . . Rev 2:17

KOHATH
Second son of Levi, Gen 46:8, 11
Brother of Jochebed, mother of
    Aaron and Moses, Ex 6:16–20

KOHATHITES
Numbered, Num 3:27, 28
Duties assigned to, Num 4:15–20
Leaders of temple music, 1 Chr 6:31–
    38; 2 Chr 20:19

KORAH
Leads rebellion against Moses and
    Aaron; supernaturally destroyed,
    Num 16:1–35
Sons of, not destroyed, Num 26:9–11

LABAN
Son of Bethuel; brother of Rebekah;
    father of Leah and Rachel, Gen
    24:15, 24, 29; 29:16
Agrees to Rebekah's marriage to
    Isaac, Gen 24:50, 51

Entertains Jacob, Gen 29:1–14
Substitutes Leah for Rachel, Gen
    29:15–30
Agrees to division of cattle; grows
    resentful of Jacob, Gen 30:25—
    31:2
Pursues Jacob and makes covenant
    with him, Gen 31:21–55

LABOR
Six days you shall *l* . . . . Ex 20:9
why then do I *l* . . . . Job 9:29
their boast is only *l* . . . . Ps 90:10
The *l* of the righteous. . . . . Prov 10:16
l will increase. . . . . Prov 13:11
l there is profit . . . . Prov 14:23
things are full of *l* . . . . Eccl 1:8
has man for all his *l*. . . . . . . Eccl 2:22
He shall see the *l* . . . . Is 53:11
"Before she was in *l* . . . . Is 66:7
from the womb to see *l* . . . . Jer 20:18
to Me, all you who *l* . . . . Matt 11:28
Do not *l* for the. . . . . John 6:27
knowing that your *l*. . . . . . 1 Cor 15:58
but rather let him *l* . . . . Eph 4:28
mean fruit from my *l* . . . . . . Phil 1:22
your work of faith, *l*. . . . . 1 Thess 1:3
forget your work and *l* . . . . . Heb 6:10
your works, your *l*. . . . . Rev 2:2

LABORED
l more abundantly than . 1 Cor 15:10
for you, lest I have *l* . . . . Gal 4:11

LABORERS
but the *l* are few . . . . Matt 9:37

LABORING
of a *l* man is sweet . . . . Eccl 5:12
l night and day. . . . . 1 Thess 2:9

LABORS
The person who *l*. . . . . Prov 16:26
is no end to all his *l*. . . . . . . Eccl 4:8
entered into their *l* . . . . . . John 4:38
creation groans and *l* . . . . . Rom 8:22
l more abundant . . . . 2 Cor 11:23
may rest from their *l*. . . . . . Rev 14:13

LACHISH
Defeated by Joshua, Josh 10:3–33
Taken by Sennacherib, 2 Kin 18:13–
    17; Is 36:1, 2; 37:8

LACK
anyone perish for *l* . . . . Job 31:19
the LORD shall not *l*. . . . . Ps 34:10
to the poor will not *l* . . . . . Prov 28:27
What do I still *l*. . . . . Matt 19:20
"One thing you *l* . . . . Mark 10:21

LACKED
among them who *l* . . . . . . Acts 4:34

LACKING
the things that are *l* . . . . . . Titus 1:5

LADDER
and behold, a *l*. . . . . Gen 28:12

LADEN
nation, a people *l* . . . . Is 1:4
and are heavy *l*. . . . . Matt 11:28

LADIES
wisest *l* answered her . . . . . Judg 5:29
very day the noble *l*. . . . . . . Esth 1:18

LADY
'I shall be a *l* . . . . Is 47:7
To the elect *l* . . . . 2 John 1

LAGGING
not *l* in diligence . . . . Rom 12:11

LAHAI ROI
Name of a well, Gen 16:7, 14
Same as Beer Lahai Roi, Gen 24:62

LAID
But man dies and is *l*...... Job 14:10
the place where they *l*.... Mark 16:6
"Where have you *l*...... John 11:34

LAISH
Called Leshem, Josh 19:47;
   Judg 18:29
Taken by Danites, Judg 18:7, 14, 27

LAKE
cast alive into the *l*...... Rev 19:20

LAMB
but where is the *l*........ Gen 22:7
took the poor man's *l*.... 2 Sam 12:4
shall dwell with the *l*........ Is 11:6
He was led as a *l*...... Is 53:7
l shall feed together....... Is 65:25
The *L* of God who takes... John 1:29
of Christ, as of a *l*..... 1 Pet 1:19
the elders, stood a *L*..... Rev 5:6
"Worthy is the *L*......... Rev 5:12
by the blood of the *L*..... Rev 12:11
Book of Life of the *L*...... Rev 13:8
supper of the *L*.......... Rev 19:9

LAME
l take the prey............ Is 33:23
l shall leap like a........ Is 35:6
when you offer the *l*....... Mal 1:8
blind see and the *l*...... Matt 11:5
And a certain man *l*...... Acts 3:2
so that what is *l*........ Heb 12:13

LAMECH
Son of Methushael, of Cain's race,
   Gen 4:17, 18
—— Son of Methuselah; father of
   Noah, Gen 5:25–31

LAMENTATION
was heard in Ramah, *l*..... Jer 31:15
was heard in Ramah, *l*.... Matt 2:18
and made great *l*......... Acts 8:2

LAMP
For You are my *l*....... 2 Sam 22:29
"How often is the *l*....... Job 21:17
You will light my *l*........ Ps 18:28
Your word is a *l*........ Ps 119:105
the *l* of the wicked....... Prov 13:9
his *l* will be put out..... Prov 20:20
Nor do they light a *l*.... Matt 5:15
"The *l* of the body....... Matt 6:22
when he has lit a *l*...... Luke 8:16
l gives you light........ Luke 11:36
does not light a *l*....... Luke 15:8
burning and shining *l*.... John 5:35
l shall not shine......... Rev 18:23
They need no *l* nor....... Rev 22:5

LAMPS
he made its seven *l*....... Ex 37:23
Jerusalem with *l*........ Zeph 1:12
and trimmed their *l*..... Matt 25:7
Seven *l* of fire............ Rev 4:5

LAMPSTAND
branches of the *l*........ Ex 25:32
and there is a *l*........... Zech 4:2
a basket, but on a *l*..... Matt 5:15
in which was the *l*...... Heb 9:2
and remove your *l*........ Rev 2:5

LAND
l that I will show you..... Gen 12:1
l flowing with milk...... Ex 3:8
l which I am giving........ Josh 1:2
is heard in our *l*........ Song 2:12

they will see the *l*.......... Is 33:17
Bethlehem, in the *l*....... Matt 2:6

LANDMARK
your neighbor's *l*....... Deut 19:14
remove the ancient *l*.... Prov 22:28
those who remove a *l*..... Hos 5:10

LANGUAGE
whole earth had one *l*..... Gen 11:1
is no speech nor *l*....... Ps 19:3
a people of strange *l*...... Ps 114:1
the peoples a pure *l*...... Zeph 3:9
speak in his own *l*........ Acts 2:6
blasphemy, filthy *l*....... Col 3:8

LANGUAGES
according to their *l*...... Gen 10:20
be, so many kinds of *l*... 1 Cor 14:10

LAODICEA
Paul's concern for, Col 2:1; 4:12–16
Letter to church of, Rev 3:14–22

LAST
He shall stand at *l*........ Job 19:25
First and I am the *L*........ Is 44:6
l man the same as...... Matt 20:14
l will be first............ Matt 20:16
children, it is the *l*..... 1 John 2:18
the First and the *L*........ Rev 1:11

LATTER
former rain, and the *l*..... Joel 2:23
l times some will........ 1 Tim 4:1

LATTICE
I looked through my *l*...... Prov 7:6
gazing through the *l*..... Song 2:9

LAUGH
Why did Sarah *l*........ Gen 18:13
"God has made me *l*...... Gen 21:6
You, O LORD, shall *l*........ Ps 59:8
Woe to you who *l*....... Luke 6:25

LAUGHS
he *l* at the threat of...... Job 41:29
The Lord *l* at him........ Ps 37:13

LAUGHTER
was filled with *l*.......... Ps 126:2
your *l* be turned to....... James 4:9

LAW
stones a copy of the *l*..... Josh 8:32
When He made a *l*...... Job 28:26
The *l* of the LORD is........ Ps 19:7
The *l* of his God is in...... Ps 37:31
I delight in Your *l*....... Ps 119:70
The *l* of Your mouth is..... Ps 119:72
l is my delight........... Ps 119:77
Oh, how I love Your *l*..... Ps 119:97
And Your *l* is truth....... Ps 119:142
and the *l* a light........ Prov 6:23
shall go forth the *l*......... Is 2:3
l will proceed from Me...... Is 51:4
in whose heart is My *l*...... Is 51:7
the *L* is no more......... Lam 2:9
The *l* of truth was in...... Mal 2:6
to destroy the *L*......... Matt 5:17
for this is the *L*........ Matt 7:12
hang all the *L* and the... Matt 22:40
"The *l* and the......... Luke 16:16
l was given through...... John 1:17
"Does our *l* judge a...... John 7:51
l is the knowledge........ Rom 3:20
because the *l* brings...... Rom 4:15
when there is no *l*....... Rom 5:13
you are not under *l*...... Rom 6:14
Is the *l* sin............. Rom 7:7
For we know that the *l*.... Rom 7:14
warring against the *l*..... Rom 7:23
For what the *l* could...... Rom 8:3

who are without *l*....... 1 Cor 9:21
l that I might live........ Gal 2:19
under guard by the *l*..... Gal 3:23
born under the *l*.......... Gal 4:4
l is fulfilled in one........ Gal 5:14
l is not made for a....... 1 Tim 1:9
into the perfect *l*....... James 1:25
fulfill the royal *l*........ James 2:8

LAWFUL
doing what is not *l*...... Matt 12:2
Is it *l* to pay taxes...... Matt 22:17
All things are *l*......... 1 Cor 6:12

LAWGIVER
Judah is My *l*............. Ps 60:7
the LORD is our *L*.......... Is 33:22
There is one *L*......... James 4:12

LAWLESS
l one will be revealed.... 2 Thess 2:8
and hearing their *l*....... 2 Pet 2:8

LAWLESSNESS
Me, you who practice *l*.... Matt 7:23
l is already at work...... 2 Thess 2:7
and hated *l*............. Heb 1:9
and sin is *l*............ 1 John 3:4

LAWYERS
l rejected the will of..... Luke 7:30
Woe to you also, *l*....... Luke 11:46

LAY
nowhere to *l* His head.... Matt 8:20
l hands may receive..... Acts 8:19
Do not *l* hands on...... 1 Tim 5:22
l aside all............ James 1:21

LAZARUS
Beggar described in a parable, Luke
   16:20–25
—— Brother of Mary and Martha;
   raised from the dead, John 11:1–44
Attends a supper, John 12:1, 2
Jews seek to kill, John 12:9–11

LAZINESS
L casts one into a........ Prov 19:15
l the building decays...... Eccl 10:18

LAZY
l man will be put to...... Prov 12:24
l man does not roast..... Prov 12:27
soul of a *l* man desires.... Prov 13:4
l man buries his hand.... Prov 19:24
by the field of the *l*...... Prov 24:30
l man is wiser in his..... Prov 26:16
wicked and *l* servant.... Matt 25:26
liars, evil beasts, *l*........ Titus 1:12

LEAD
they sank like *l*.......... Ex 15:10
L me in Your truth and...... Ps 25:5
L me and guide me........ Ps 31:3
Your hand shall *l*....... Ps 139:10
And do not *l* us into...... Matt 6:13
"Can the blind *l*........ Luke 6:39

LEADS
He *l* me beside the......... Ps 23:2
He *l* me in the paths........ Ps 23:3
And if the blind *l*....... Matt 15:14
by name and *l* them out... John 10:3
the goodness of God *l*...... Rom 2:4

LEAF
plucked olive *l*........... Gen 8:11
Will You frighten a *l*...... Job 13:25
l will be green............ Jer 17:8

LEAH
Laban's eldest daughter; given to
   Jacob deceitfully, Gen 29:16–27
Unloved by Jacob, but bears children,
   Gen 29:30–35; 30:16–21

LEAN
all your heart, and *l* . . . . Prov 3:5
Yet they *l* on the LORD . . . . . . Mic 3:11

LEANING
Then, *l* back on Jesus' . . . . John 13:25
l on the top of his . . . . Heb 11:21

LEANNESS
request, but sent *l* . . . . Ps 106:15
of hosts, will send *l* . . . . Is 10:16

LEAP
by my God I can *l* . . . . Ps 18:29
Then the lame shall *l* . . . . Is 35:6

LEARN
it, may hear and *l* . . . . . . Deut 31:13
l Your statutes . . . . Ps 119:71
lest you *l* his ways . . . . . . Prov 22:25
l to do good . . . . Is 1:17
neither shall they *l* . . . . Is 2:4
My yoke upon you and *l* . Matt 11:29
Let a woman *l* in . . . . 1 Tim 2:11
let our people also *l* . . . . . Titus 3:14

LEARNED
Me the tongue of the *l* . . . . . . Is 50:4
who has heard and *l* . . . . . John 6:45
have not so *l* Christ . . . . . . Eph 4:20
in all things I have *l* . . . . Phil 4:12
l obedience by the . . . . Heb 5:8

LEARNING
hear and increase *l* . . . . Prov 1:5
l is driving you mad . . . . . Acts 26:24
were written for our *l* . . . . . Rom 15:4

LEAST
Judah, are not the *l* . . . . . . Matt 2:6
so, shall be called *l* . . . . . . Matt 5:19
For I am the *l* of the . . . . . 1 Cor 15:9

LEAVE
a man shall *l* his . . . . Gen 2:24
He will not *l* you nor . . . . . Deut 31:6
For You will not *l* . . . . Ps 16:10
do not *l* me nor . . . . Ps 27:9
"I will never *l* . . . . Heb 13:5

LEAVEN
day you shall remove *l* . . . . Ex 12:15
of heaven is like *l* . . . . . . Matt 13:33
and beware of the *l* . . . . . Matt 16:6
know that a little *l* . . . . . . 1 Cor 5:6
l leavens the whole . . . . Gal 5:9

LEAVES
and they sewed fig *l* . . . . . . Gen 3:7
nothing on it but *l* . . . . . . Matt 21:19
l the sheep and flees . . . . . John 10:12
The *l* of the tree . . . . Rev 22:2

LEBANON
Part of Israel's inheritance,
   Josh 13:5–7
Not completely conquered,
   Judg 3:1–3
Source of materials for temple,
   1 Kin 5:2–18; Ezra 3:7
Mentioned in prophecy, Is 10:34;
   29:17; 35:2; Ezek 17:3; Hos 14:5–7

LEBBAEUS
See JUDAS
Surname of Judas (Jude), Matt 10:3

LED
l the people around by . . . . . Ex 13:18
so the LORD alone *l* . . . . . Deut 32:12
l them forth by the . . . . Ps 107:7
l them by the right . . . . Is 63:12
For as many as are *l* . . . . . . Rom 8:14
l captivity captive . . . . Eph 4:8
l away by various . . . . 2 Tim 3:6

LEFT
l hand know what your . . . . Matt 6:3
"See, we have *l* . . . . Matt 19:27
And everyone who has *l* . . Matt 19:29

LEGACY
shame shall be the *l* . . . . . . Prov 3:35

LEGS
Like the *l* of the lame . . . . Prov 26:7
l are pillars of . . . . Song 5:15
did not break His *l* . . . . . . John 19:33

LEHI
Samson kills Philistines at, Judg
   15:9–19

LEMUEL
King taught by his mother, Prov
   31:1–31

LEND
"If you *l* money to . . . . Ex 22:25
l him sufficient . . . . Deut 15:8
And if you *l* . . . . Luke 6:34
l me three loaves . . . . Luke 11:5

LENDER
is servant to the *l* . . . . Prov 22:7
as with the *l* . . . . Is 24:2

LENDING
and my servants, am *l* . . . . Neh 5:10

LENDS
ever merciful, and *l* . . . . Ps 37:26
deals graciously and *l* . . . . . Ps 112:5
has pity on the poor *l* . . . . Prov 19:17

LENGTH
The *l* of the ark shall . . . . . Gen 6:15
is your life, and the *l* . . . . Deut 30:20
L of days is in her . . . . Prov 3:16
l is as great as its . . . . Rev 21:16

LENGTHENS
a shadow when it *l* . . . . . . Ps 109:23

LEOPARD
the *l* shall lie down . . . . Is 11:6
or the *l* its spots . . . . Jer 13:23

LEPERS
And when these *l* . . . . 2 Kin 7:8
And many *l* were in . . . . . Luke 4:27

LET
"*L* there be light" . . . . Gen 1:3
L the little . . . . Matt 19:14

LETTER
the oldness of the *l* . . . . Rom 7:6
for the *l* kills . . . . 2 Cor 3:6
you sorry with my *l* . . . . . . 2 Cor 7:8
or by word or by *l* . . . . . . 2 Thess 2:2

LETTERS
does this Man know *l* . . . . . John 7:15
or *l* of commendation . . . . . 2 Cor 3:1
"For his *l*," they say . . . . . 2 Cor 10:10
with what large *l* . . . . Gal 6:11

LEVI
Third son of Jacob and Leah,
   Gen 29:34
Avenges rape of Dinah,
   Gen 34:25–31
Jacob's prophecy concerning,
   Gen 49:5–7
Ancestor of Moses and Aaron,
   Ex 6:16–27

LEVIATHAN
"Can you draw out *L* . . . . . . Job 41:1
L which You have made . . . Ps 104:26

LEVITE
"Is not Aaron the *L* . . . . Ex 4:14

Likewise a *L* . . . . Luke 10:32
a *L* of the country of . . . . . Acts 4:36

LEVITES
Rewarded for dedication, Ex 32:26–29
Appointed over tabernacle, Num
   1:47–54
Substituted for Israel's firstborn, Num
   3:12–45
Consecrated to the Lord's service,
   Num 8:5–26
Cities assigned to, Num 35:2–8; Josh
   14:3, 4; 1 Chr 6:54–81
Organized for temple service, 1 Chr
   9:14–34; 23:1—26:28

LEVITICAL
were through the *L* . . . . Heb 7:11

LEWDNESS
wickedness, deceit, *l* . . . . . Mark 7:22
drunkenness, not in *l* . . . . . Rom 13:13
themselves over to *l* . . . . . . Eph 4:19
when we walked in *l* . . . . . 1 Pet 4:3

LIAR
for he is a *l* and the . . . . . . John 8:44
but every man a *l* . . . . Rom 3:4
we make Him a *l* . . . . 1 John 1:10
Who is a *l* but he who . . . 1 John 2:22
his brother, he is a *l* . . . . . 1 John 4:20
God has made Him a *l* . . 1 John 5:10

LIARS
"All men are *l* . . . . Ps 116:11
Cretans are always *l* . . . . . Titus 1:12
and have found them *l* . . . . . Rev 2:2
l shall have their . . . . Rev 21:8

LIBERALITY
he who gives, with *l* . . . . . Rom 12:8
the riches of their *l* . . . . . . 2 Cor 8:2

LIBERALLY
who gives to all *l* . . . . James 1:5

LIBERTY
year, and proclaim *l* . . . . . Lev 25:10
And I will walk at *l* . . . . . Ps 119:45
to proclaim *l* to the . . . . Is 61:1
to proclaim *l* to the . . . . . . Luke 4:18
into the glorious *l* . . . . Rom 8:21
For why is my *l* . . . . 1 Cor 10:29
Lord is, there is *l* . . . . 2 Cor 3:17
therefore in the *l* . . . . Gal 5:1
l as an opportunity . . . . Gal 5:13
the perfect law of *l* . . . . . James 1:25
yet not using *l* . . . . 1 Pet 2:16

LIBNAH
Canaanite city, captured by Joshua,
   Josh 10:29, 30
Given to Aaron's descendants, Josh
   21:13

LIBYA
Mentioned in prophecy, Ezek 30:5;
   Dan 11:43
Jews from, present at Pentecost, Acts
   2:1–10

LIE
man, that He should *l* . . . Num 23:19
For now I will *l* . . . . Job 7:21
I will not *l* to David . . . . . . Ps 89:35
Do not *l* to one . . . . Col 3:9
God, who cannot *l* . . . . Titus 1:2
do not boast and *l* . . . . . James 3:14
know it, and that no *l* . . . 1 John 2:21
an abomination or a *l* . . . . Rev 21:27

LIED
They have *l* about the . . . . . Jer 5:12
You have not *l* to men . . . . Acts 5:4

LIES

sin *l* at the door . . . . Gen 4:7
and he who speaks *l* . . . . . . Prov 19:5
speaking *l* in . . . . 1 Tim 4:2
and the whole world *l* . . . 1 John 5:19

LIFE

the breath of *l* . . . . Gen 2:7
l was also in the . . . . Gen 2:9
then you shall give *l* . . . . . . Ex 21:23
For the *l* of the . . . . Lev 17:11
before you today *l* . . . . . . Deut 30:15
You have granted me *l* . . . . Job 10:12
in whose hand is the *l* . . . . . Job 12:10
God takes away his *l* . . . . . . Job 27:8
with the light of *l* . . . . Job 33:30
He will redeem their *l* . . . . . . Ps 72:14
word has given me *l* . . . . . Ps 119:50
regain the paths of *l* . . . . . . Prov 2:19
She is a tree of *l* . . . . Prov 3:18
so they will be *l* . . . . Prov 3:22
finds me finds *l* . . . . Prov 8:35
l winds upward for the . . . Prov 15:24
thief hates his own *l* . . . . Prov 29:24
is that wisdom gives *l* . . . . . Eccl 7:12
I have cut off my *l* . . . . Is 38:12
you the way of *l* . . . . Jer 21:8
l shall be as a prize . . . . Jer 39:18
not worry about your *l* . . . . Matt 6:25
l does not consist . . . . Luke 12:15
L is more than . . . . Luke 12:23
l was the light . . . . John 1:4
so the Son gives *l* . . . . John 5:21
as the Father has *l* . . . . John 5:26
spirit, and they are *l* . . . . . . John 6:63
have the light of *l* . . . . John 8:12
and I lay down My *l* . . . . . John 10:15
resurrection and the *l* . . . . John 11:25
you lay down your *l* . . . . . John 13:38
God, who gives *l* . . . . Rom 4:17
that pertain to this *l* . . . . . . 1 Cor 6:3
Lord Jesus, that the *l* . . . . . 2 Cor 4:10
l which I now live . . . . Gal 2:20
l is hidden with . . . . Col 3:3
of God who gives *l* . . . . . . 1 Tim 6:13
For what is your *l* . . . . . . James 4:14
that pertain to *l* . . . . 2 Pet 1:3
l was manifested . . . . 1 John 1:2
and the pride of *l* . . . . . . 1 John 2:16
has given us eternal *l* . . . 1 John 5:11
who has the Son has *l* . . . 1 John 5:12
the Lamb's Book of *L* . . . . Rev 21:27
right to the tree of *l* . . . . . . Rev 22:14
the water of *l* freely . . . . . . Rev 22:17
from the Book of *L* . . . . . . Rev 22:19

LIFT

I will *l* up my hands . . . . Ps 63:4
I will *l* up my eyes to . . . . . . Ps 121:1
l up your voice like a . . . . Is 58:1
l our hearts and hands . . . . Lam 3:41
Lord, and He will *l* . . . . . . James 4:10

LIFTED

O Lord, for You have *l* . . . . . . Ps 30:1
your heart is *l* . . . . Ezek 28:2
in Hades, he *l* up his . . . . . Luke 16:23
the Son of Man be *l* . . . . . . John 3:14
And I, if I am *l* . . . . John 12:32
of Man must be *l* . . . . John 12:34

LIGHT

"Let there be *l* . . . . Gen 1:3
"The *l* of the wicked . . . . . . Job 18:5
l will shine on your . . . . . . Job 22:28
the wicked their *l* . . . . Job 38:15
to the dwelling of *l* . . . . . . Job 38:19
Lord, lift up the *l* . . . . Ps 4:6
The Lord is my *l* . . . . Ps 27:1
Oh, send out Your *l* . . . . Ps 43:3

L is sown for the . . . . Ps 97:11
and He has given us *l* . . . . Ps 118:27
and a *l* to my path . . . . Ps 119:105
The *l* of the righteous . . . . . Prov 13:9
The *l* of the eyes . . . . Prov 15:30
The Lord gives *l* . . . . Prov 29:13
Truly the *l* is sweet . . . . Eccl 11:7
let us walk in the *l* . . . . Is 2:5
l is darkened by the . . . . Is 5:30
because there is no *l* . . . . Is 8:20
moon will be as the *l* . . . . . . Is 30:26
l shall break forth . . . . Is 58:8
for your *l* has come . . . . Is 60:1
be your everlasting *l* . . . . . . Is 60:20
gives the sun for a *l* . . . . . . Jer 31:35
l that goes . . . . Hos 6:5
"You are the *l* . . . . Matt 5:14
Let your *l* so shine . . . . . . Matt 5:16
body will be full of *l* . . . . . Matt 6:22
than the sons of *l* . . . . Luke 16:8
and the life was the *l* . . . . . . John 1:4
That was the true *L* . . . . John 1:9
darkness rather than *l* . . . . John 3:19
evil hates the *l* . . . . John 3:20
truth comes to the *l* . . . . . . John 3:21
saying, "I am the *l* . . . . John 8:12
believe in the *l* . . . . John 12:36
I have come as a *l* . . . . . . John 12:46
l the hidden . . . . 1 Cor 4:5
God who commanded *l* . . . . 2 Cor 4:6
Walk as children of *l* . . . . . . Eph 5:8
You are all sons of *l* . . . . . 1 Thess 5:5
and immortality to *l* . . . . . 2 Tim 1:10
into His marvelous *l* . . . . 1 Pet 2:9
do well to heed as a *l* . . . . . 2 Pet 1:19
to you, that God is *l* . . . . . . 1 John 1:5
l as He is in the . . . . 1 John 1:7
says he is in the *l* . . . . 1 John 2:9
The Lamb is its *l* . . . . Rev 21:23
Lord God gives them *l* . . . . . Rev 22:5

LIGHTEN

L the yoke which . . . . 1 Kin 12:9
the sea, to *l* the load . . . . Jon 1:5

LIGHTLY

this, did I do it *l* . . . . 2 Cor 1:17

LIGHTNING

For as the *l* . . . . Matt 24:27
countenance was like *l* . . . . Matt 28:3
saw Satan fall like *l* . . . . . Luke 10:18

LIGHTNINGS

were thunderings and *l* . . . . Ex 19:16
the *l* lit up the world . . . . . . Ps 77:18
l light the world . . . . Ps 97:4
the throne proceeded *l* . . . . . Rev 4:5

LIGHTS

"Let there be *l* . . . . Gen 1:14
Him who made great *l* . . . . Ps 136:7
whom you shine as *l* . . . . . . Phil 2:15
from the Father of *l* . . . . . . James 1:17

LIKE

"Who is *l* You . . . . Ex 15:11
A lily among thorns . . . . Song 2:2
be made *l* His brethren . . . . Heb 2:17

LIKE-MINDED

grant you to be *l* . . . . Rom 15:5
For I have no one *l* . . . . . . Phil 2:20

LIKENESS

according to Our *l* . . . . Gen 1:26
carved image—any *l* . . . . . . Ex 20:4
when I awake in Your *l* . . . . Ps 17:15
His own Son in the *l* . . . . . . Rom 8:3
and coming in the *l* . . . . Phil 2:7

LILY

the *l* of the valleys . . . . Song 2:1

Like *a l* among thorns . . . . . Song 2:2
shall grow like the *l* . . . . . . Hos 14:5

LIMIT

Do you *l* wisdom to . . . . Job 15:8
to the sea its *l* . . . . Prov 8:29

LIMITED

l the Holy One of . . . . Ps 78:41

LINE

l has gone out through . . . . . Ps 19:4
upon precept, *l* upon *l* . . . . Is 28:10
I am setting a plumb *l* . . . . Amos 7:8

LINEAGE

was of the house and *l* . . . . Luke 2:4

LINEN

her clothing is fine *l* . . . . . Prov 31:22
wrapped Him in the *l* . . . . Mark 15:46
l is the righteous . . . . Rev 19:8

LINGER

Those who *l* long at . . . . . Prov 23:30
salvation shall not *l* . . . . Is 46:13

LION

he lies down as a *l* . . . . Gen 49:9
like a fierce *l* . . . . Job 10:16
l shall eat straw . . . . Is 11:7
For I will be like a *l* . . . . . . Hos 5:14

LIONS

My soul is among *l* . . . . Ps 57:4
the mouths of *l* . . . . Heb 11:33

LIPS

of uncircumcised *l* . . . . Ex 6:12
off all flattering *l* . . . . Ps 12:3
Let the lying *l* . . . . Ps 31:18
The *l* of the righteous . . . . Prov 10:21
but the *l* of knowledge . . . Prov 20:15
am a man of unclean *l* . . . . . . Is 6:5
asps is under their *l* . . . . . . Rom 3:13
other *l* I will speak . . . . . . 1 Cor 14:21
from evil, and his *l* . . . . 1 Pet 3:10

LISTEN

L carefully to Me . . . . Is 55:2
O Lord, *l* and act . . . . Dan 9:19
you are not able to *l* . . . . . . John 8:43
Why do you *l* to Him . . . . John 10:20
you who fear God, *l* . . . . . Acts 13:16

LISTENS

but whoever *l* to me . . . . . . Prov 1:33

LITTLE

l foxes that spoil the . . . . . Song 2:15
We have a *l* sister . . . . Song 8:8
upon line, here a *l* . . . . Is 28:10
though you are *l* . . . . Mic 5:2
indeed it came to *l* . . . . Hag 1:9
for I was a *l* angry . . . . . . Zech 1:15
l ones only a cup . . . . Matt 10:42
"O you of *l* faith . . . . Matt 14:31
Whoever receives one *l* . . . . Matt 18:5
to whom *l* is forgiven . . . . . Luke 7:47
faithful in a very *l* . . . . . . Luke 19:17
exercise profits in a *l* . . . . . 1 Tim 4:8

LIVE

eat, and *l* forever . . . . Gen 3:22
a man does, he shall *l* . . . . Lev 18:5
I would not *l* forever . . . . . . Job 7:16
L joyfully with the . . . . Eccl 9:9
by these things men *l* . . . . . Is 38:16
sin, that man surely *l* . . . . . Ezek 3:21
"Seek Me and *l* . . . . Amos 5:4
but the just shall *l* . . . . Hab 2:4
l by bread alone . . . . Matt 4:4
who feeds on Me will *l* . . . . John 6:57
for in Him we *l* . . . . Acts 17:28
l peaceably with all . . . . . . Rom 12:18

the life which I now *l* . . . . . . Gal 2:20
If we *l* **in the Spirit** . . . . Gal 5:25
to me, to *l* **is Christ.** . . . . Phil 1:21
l **godly in Christ.** . . . . 2 Tim 3:12
to *l* **honorably.** . . . . Heb 13:18
l **according to God in** . . . . . . 1 Pet 4:6

LIVED
   died and rose and *l* . . . . Rom 14:9
   And they *l* **and reigned** . . . . Rev 20:4

LIVES
   but man *l* **by every** . . . . Deut 8:3
   have risked their *l* . . . . Acts 15:26
   He *l* **to God** . . . . Rom 6:10
   For none of us *l* . . . . Rom 14:7
   but Christ *l* **in me** . . . . Gal 2:20
   to lay down our *l* . . . . . . 1 John 3:16
   I am He who *l* . . . . Rev 1:18

LIVING
   and man became a *l* . . . . Gen 2:7
   in the light of the *l* . . . . Ps 56:13
   l **will take it to** . . . . Eccl 7:2
   l **know that they will** . . . . . . Eccl 9:5
   Why should a *l* **man** . . . . . . Lam 3:39
   the dead, but of the *l* . . . . Matt 22:32
   Why do you seek the *l* . . . . Luke 24:5
   to be Judge of the *l* . . . . . . Acts 10:42
   who will judge the *l* . . . . . . 2 Tim 4:1
   the word of God is *l* . . . . . . Heb 4:12
   ready to judge the *l* . . . . . . 1 Pet 4:5
   l **creature was like a** . . . . Rev 4:7

LO-AMMI
   Symbolic name of Hosea's son,
      Hos 1:8, 9

LO-RUHAMAH
   Symbolic name of Hosea's daughter,
      Hos 1:6

LOAD
   shall bear his own *l* . . . . Gal 6:5

LOATHE
   I *l* **my life** . . . . Job 7:16
   l **themselves for the** . . . . Ezek 6:9

LOATHSOME
   but a wicked man is *l* . . . . Prov 13:5

LOAVES
   have here only five *l* . . . . Matt 14:17
   He took the seven *l* . . . . . Matt 15:36
   lend me three *l* . . . . Luke 11:5
   you ate of the *l* . . . . John 6:26

LOCUST
   What the chewing *l* . . . . Joel 1:4
   left, the swarming *l* . . . . . . Joel 1:4

LOCUSTS
   as numerous as *l* . . . . Judg 7:12
   He spoke, and *l* **came** . . . . Ps 105:34
   the *l* **have no king.** . . . . . . Prov 30:27
   and his food was *l* . . . . Matt 3:4
   waist, and he ate *l* . . . . . . Mark 1:6
   out of the smoke *l* . . . . Rev 9:3

LODGED
   them in and *l* **them** . . . . . Acts 10:23
   children, if she has *l* . . . . 1 Tim 5:10

LOFTILY
   they speak *l* . . . . Ps 73:8

LOFTY
   haughty, nor my eyes *l* . . . . Ps 131:1
   Wisdom is too *l* . . . . Prov 24:7
   l **are their eyes** . . . . Prov 30:13
   and *L* **One who** . . . . Is 57:15

LOINS
   gird up the *l* **of your** . . . . . 1 Pet 1:13

LONG
   your days may be *l* . . . . . . Deut 5:16

---

who *l* **for death** . . . . Job 3:21
me the thing that I *l* . . . . Job 6:8
I *l* **for Your salvation.** . . . . . Ps 119:174
go around in *l* **robes.** . . . . . Mark 12:38
how greatly I *l* . . . . Phil 1:8

LONGSUFFERING
   and gracious, *l* . . . . Ps 86:15
   is love, joy, peace, *l* . . . . . . Gal 5:22
   and gentleness, with *l* . . . . . Eph 4:2
   for all patience and *l* . . . . . . Col 1:11
   might show all *l* . . . . 1 Tim 1:16
   when once the Divine *l* . . . 1 Pet 3:20
   and consider that the *l* . . . . 2 Pet 3:15

LOOK
   Do not *l* **behind you** . . . . . . Gen 19:17
   who has a haughty *l* . . . . . . Ps 101:5
   A proud *l* . . . . Prov 6:17
   that day a man will *l* . . . . Is 17:7
   L **upon Zion** . . . . Is 33:20
   "L to Me . . . . Is 45:22
   we *l* **for light.** . . . . Is 59:9
   we *l* **for justice.** . . . . Is 59:11
   l **on Me whom they** . . . . . . Zech 12:10
   say to you, 'L here. . . . . . . Luke 17:23
   of Israel could not *l* . . . . . . 2 Cor 3:7
   while we do not *l* . . . . 2 Cor 4:18
   Let each of you *l* . . . . Phil 2:4
   L **to yourselves** . . . . 2 John 8

LOOKED
   But when I *l* **for good** . . . . . Job 30:26
   They *l* **to Him and were** . . . . . Ps 34:5
   For He *l* **down from the** . . . . Ps 102:19
   He *l* **for justice** . . . . Is 5:7
   "We *l* **for peace** . . . . Jer 8:15
   "You *l* **for much** . . . . Hag 1:9
   the Lord turned and *l* . . . . Luke 22:61
   for he *l* **to the reward** . . . . . Heb 11:26

LOOKING
   the plow, and *l* **back** . . . . . . Luke 9:62
   l **for the blessed hope** . . . . . Titus 2:13
   l **unto Jesus** . . . . Heb 12:2
   l **carefully lest** . . . . Heb 12:15
   l **for the mercy of** . . . . Jude 21

LOOKS
   Absalom for his good *l*. . 2 Sam 14:25
   Then he *l* **at men and** . . . . . Job 33:27
   God *l* **down from heaven** . . . . Ps 53:2
   The lofty *l* **of man** . . . . Is 2:11
   to you that whoever *l* . . . . Matt 5:28

LOOM
   and the web from the *l* . . . Judg 16:14
   cuts me off from the *l* . . . . . Is 38:12

LOOSE
   l **the armor of kings** . . . . Is 45:1
   and whatever you *l* . . . . . . Matt 16:19
   said to them, "L him . . . . . John 11:44

LOOSED
   You have *l* **my bonds** . . . . . . Ps 116:16
   the silver cord is *l* . . . . Eccl 12:6

LORD
   L **is my strength** . . . . Ex 15:2
   L **is a man of war** . . . . Ex 15:3
   L **our God, the** *L* . . . . Deut 6:4
   sacrifice to the *L* **your God** . Deut 17:1
   may know that the *L*. . . . . 1 Kin 8:60
   If the *L* **is God** . . . . 1 Kin 18:21
   You alone are the *L* . . . . Neh 9:6
   The *L* **of hosts** . . . . Ps 24:10
   belongs to the *L* . . . . Ps 89:18
   let us sing to the *L* . . . . Ps 95:1
   L **is the great God** . . . . Ps 95:3
   Gracious is the *L* . . . . Ps 116:5
   L **surrounds His people** . . . . . Ps 125:2
   The *L* **is righteous** . . . . Ps 129:4

L **is near to all who** . . . . . . Ps 145:18
L **is a God of justice** . . . . Is 30:18
L **Our Righteousness.** . . . . . . Jer 23:6
L **has done marvelous** . . . . . Joel 2:21
L **God is my strength** . . . . . Hab 3:19
"The *L* **is one** . . . . Zech 14:9
shall not tempt the *L* . . . . . Matt 4:7
shall worship the *L* . . . . . . Matt 4:10
Son of Man is also *L* . . . . . Mark 2:28
who is Christ the *L* . . . . Luke 2:11
why do you call Me 'L . . . . Luke 6:46
L **is risen indeed** . . . . Luke 24:34
call Me Teacher and *L*. . . . John 13:13
He is *L* **of all** . . . . Acts 10:36
'Who are You, *L* . . . . Acts 26:15
with your mouth the *L* . . . . Rom 10:9
Greek, for the same *L* . . . . Rom 10:12
say that Jesus is *L* . . . . 1 Cor 12:3
second Man is the *L* . . . . . 1 Cor 15:47
the Spirit of the *L*. . . . . 2 Cor 3:17
that Jesus Christ is *L* . . . . . . Phil 2:11
and deny the only *L*. . . . . Jude 4
L **God Omnipotent** . . . . Rev 19:6

LORDS
   many gods and many *l*. . . . 1 Cor 8:5
   nor as being *l* **over** . . . . 1 Pet 5:3
   for He is Lord of *l*. . . . . Rev 17:14

LORDSHIP
   Gentiles exercise *l* . . . . . . Luke 22:25

LOSE
   gain, and a time to *l* . . . . . . Eccl 3:6
   save his life will *l* . . . . Matt 16:25
   reap if we do not *l* . . . . Gal 6:9
   that we do not *l* . . . . 2 John 8

LOSES
   but if the salt *l*. . . . . Matt 5:13
   and *l* **his own soul** . . . . Matt 16:26
   if she *l* **one coin.** . . . . Luke 15:8
   l **his life will.** . . . . Luke 17:33

LOSS
   he will suffer *l* . . . . 1 Cor 3:15
   count all things *l* . . . . Phil 3:8

LOST
   are dry, our hope is *l* . . . . . Ezek 37:11
   save that which was *l* . . . . Matt 18:11
   the one which is *l* . . . . Luke 15:4
   my sheep which was *l*. . . . . Luke 15:6
   the piece which I *l*. . . . . . . Luke 15:9
   and none of them is *l* . . . . John 17:12
   You gave Me I have *l* . . . . . John 18:9

LOT
   Abram's nephew; accompanies him,
      Gen 11:27—12:5; 13:1
   Separates from Abram, Gen 13:5–12
   Rescued by Abram, Gen 14:12–16
   Saved from Sodom for his hospitality,
      Gen 19:1–29
   Tricked into committing incest, Gen
      19:30–38

LOT
   shall be divided by *l*. . . . . Num 26:55
   You maintain my *l* . . . . Ps 16:5
   cast in your *l* **among** . . . . . . Prov 1:14
   l **is cast into the lap** . . . . . . Prov 16:33

LOT'S WIFE
   Disobedient, becomes pillar of salt,
      Gen 19:26
   Event to be remembered, Luke 17:32

LOTS
   l **causes contentions** . . . . . . Prov 18:18
   garments, casting *l*. . . . . . Mark 15:24
   And they cast their *l* . . . . . . Acts 1:26

LOUD
   I cried out with a *l* . . . . Gen 39:14

Him with *l* cymbals . . . . Ps 150:5
cried out with a *l*. . . . . . . Matt 27:46
I heard behind me a *l*. . . . . Rev 1:10

LOVE
l your neighbor as . . . . Lev 19:18
l the LORD your God . . . . . . Deut 6:5
your *l* to me was . . . . . . 2 Sam 1:26
How long will you *l*. . . . . Ps 4:2
Oh, *l* the LORD . . . . Ps 31:23
l righteousness. . . . . Ps 45:7
he has set his *l* . . . . Ps 91:14
Oh, how I *l* Your law . . . . . Ps 119:97
peace have those who *l* . . . Ps 119:165
preserves all who *l*. . . . . . . Ps 145:20
us take our fill of *l*. . . . . . . Prov 7:18
l covers all sins. . . . . Prov 10:12
a time to *l*. . . . . Eccl 3:8
People know neither *l* . . . . . Eccl 9:1
l is better than wine . . . . . . Song 1:2
banner over me was *l*. . . . . Song 2:4
stir up nor awaken *l*. . . . . . . Song 3:5
I will give you my *l* . . . . . . Song 7:12
l is as strong as. . . . . Song 8:6
waters cannot quench *l* . . . . Song 8:7
time was the time of *l* . . . . Ezek 16:8
backsliding, I will *l*. . . . . . . Hos 14:4
do justly, to *l* mercy . . . . . . Mic 6:8
to you, *l* your enemies . . . Matt 5:44
l those who *l* you. . . . . . . Matt 5:46
which of them will *l*. . . . . . Luke 7:42
you do not have the *l*. . . . . John 5:42
if you have *l* for one . . . . John 13:35
"If you *l* Me . . . . John 14:15
and My Father will *l*. . . . . John 14:23
l one another as I . . . . . . John 15:12
l has no one than this. . . . John 15:13
l Me more than these . . . John 21:16
of Jonah, do you *l* . . . . . . John 21:16
You know that I *l*. . . . . . . John 21:16
because the *l* of God . . . . . Rom 5:5
Let *l* be without . . . . Rom 12:9
to *l* one another. . . . . Rom 13:8
l does no harm to a . . . . . Rom 13:10
up, but *l* edifies . . . . 1 Cor 8:1
l suffers long and is. . . . . 1 Cor 13:4
l does not envy. . . . . 1 Cor 13:4
l does not parade . . . . . . 1 Cor 13:4
l never fails . . . . 1 Cor 13:8
greatest of these is *l* . . . . 1 Cor 13:13
For the *l* of Christ. . . . . . . 2 Cor 5:14
and the God of *l*. . . . . . . 2 Cor 13:11
of the Spirit is *l* . . . . Gal 5:22
Husbands, *l* your wives . . . . Eph 5:25
of the Son of His *l* . . . . . . Col 1:13
l your wives and do. . . . . . Col 3:19
the commandment is *l*. . . . 1 Tim 1:5
continue in faith, *l* . . . . . 1 Tim 2:15
word, in conduct, in *l* . . . 1 Tim 4:12
For the *l* of money is . . . . 1 Tim 6:10
l their husbands . . . . Titus 2:4
Let brotherly *l*. . . . . Heb 13:1
having not seen you *l* . . . . 1 Pet 1:8
l the brotherhood. . . . . . . 1 Pet 2:17
for "*l* will cover a . . . . 1 Pet 4:8
with a kiss of *l*. . . . . 1 Pet 5:14
brotherly kindness *l* . . . . . 2 Pet 1:7
loves the world, the *l*. . . . 1 John 2:15
we *l* the brethren . . . . . . 1 John 3:14
By this we know *l*. . . . . . 1 John 3:16
him, how does the *l*. . . . . 1 John 3:17
Beloved, let us *l* . . . . 1 John 4:7
know God, for God is *l* . . 1 John 4:8
In this is *l*. . . . . 1 John 4:10
If we *l* one another . . . . . 1 John 4:12
l has been perfected . . . . 1 John 4:17
There is no fear in *l* . . . . . 1 John 4:18
l Him because He first . . . 1 John 4:19

who loves God must *l* . . . 1 John 4:21
For this is the *l*. . . . . 1 John 5:3
have left your first *l* . . . . . . Rev 2:4
and they did not *l*. . . . . . . Rev 12:11

LOVED
Because the LORD has *l*. . . 1 Kin 10:9
L one and friend You . . . . . . Ps 88:18
"I have *l* you . . . . Mal 1:2
Yet Jacob I have *l*. . . . . Mal 1:2
forgiven, for she *l* . . . . Luke 7:47
so *l* the world that. . . . . John 3:16
"See how He *l* . . . . John 11:36
whom Jesus *l*. . . . . John 13:23
"As the Father *l*. . . . . John 15:9
l them as You have . . . . . John 17:23
"Jacob I have *l*. . . . . Rom 9:13
the Son of God, who *l*. . . . . Gal 2:20
l the church and gave . . . . Eph 5:25
l righteousness . . . . Heb 1:9
God, but that He *l* . . . . . 1 John 4:10
Beloved, if God so *l* . . . . 1 John 4:11
To Him who *l* us and . . . . . . Rev 1:5

LOVELY
l is Your tabernacle . . . . Ps 84:1
l woman who lacks . . . . . Prov 11:22
he is altogether *l*. . . . . Song 5:16
whatever things are *l*. . . . . . Phil 4:8

LOVER
a *l* of what is good . . . . Titus 1:8

LOVERS
For men will be *l*. . . . . 2 Tim 3:2

LOVES
l righteousness. . . . . Ps 33:5
life, and *l* many days . . . . . Ps 34:12
A friend *l* at all . . . . Prov 17:17
He who *l* father or. . . . . . Matt 10:37
l his life will lose . . . . John 12:25
l Me will be loved . . . . . . John 14:21
l a cheerful giver . . . . 2 Cor 9:7
who *l* his wife . . . . Eph 5:28
If anyone *l* the world . . . . 1 John 2:15
l God must love his . . . . . 1 John 4:21
l him who is. . . . . 1 John 5:1

LOVESICK
apples, for I am *l*. . . . . Song 2:5
you tell him I am *l*. . . . . . . Song 5:8

LOVINGKINDNESS
not concealed Your *l* . . . . . Ps 40:10
l is better than life . . . . Ps 63:3
to declare Your *l* . . . . Ps 92:2
l I have drawn . . . . Jer 31:3

LOW
He brings *l* and lifts . . . . . 1 Sam 2:7
both *l* and high . . . . Ps 49:2
it *l*, He lays it *l*. . . . . Is 26:5
and hill brought *l*. . . . . Luke 3:5

LOWER
made him a little *l* . . . . Ps 8:5
shall go into the *l* . . . . Ps 63:9
made him a little *l*. . . . . Heb 2:7

LOWEST
and sets over it the *l* . . . . . Dan 4:17

LOWLINESS
with all *l* and . . . . Eph 4:2
or conceit, but in *l* . . . . Phil 2:3

LOWLY
yet He regards the *l*. . . . . . Ps 138:6
for I am gentle and *l*. . . . . Matt 11:29
He has regarded the *l*. . . . . Luke 1:48
and exalted the *l*. . . . . Luke 1:52
in presence am I . . . . 2 Cor 10:1
l body that it may be . . . . . Phil 3:21
l brother glory. . . . . James 1:9

LOYAL
or else he will be *l*. . . . . . Matt 6:24

LUCIFER
Name applied to Satan, Is 14:12

LUKE
"The beloved physician," Col 4:14
Paul's last companion, 2 Tim 4:11

LUKEWARM
because you are *l* . . . . Rev 3:16

LUMP
from the same *l*. . . . . Rom 9:21
you may be a new *l*. . . . . . 1 Cor 5:7

LUST
Do not *l* after her . . . . Prov 6:25
caught by their *l* . . . . Prov 11:6
looks at a woman to *l*. . . . Matt 5:28
not fulfill the *l*. . . . . Gal 5:16
not in passion of *l* . . . . . . 1 Thess 4:5
You *l* and do not have . . . James 4:2
the *l* of the flesh. . . . . . . 1 John 2:16

LUSTS
to fulfill its *l*. . . . . Rom 13:14
l which drown men. . . . . . 1 Tim 6:9
also youthful *l*. . . . . 2 Tim 2:22
and worldly *l*. . . . . Titus 2:12
to the former *l*. . . . . 1 Pet 1:14
abstain from fleshly *l* . . . . 1 Pet 2:11
to their own ungodly *l* . . . . . Jude 18

LUTE
Awake, *l* and harp. . . . . Ps 57:8
l I will praise You. . . . . Ps 71:22
harp with the *l* . . . . Ps 81:2
ten strings, on the *l*. . . . . . . Ps 92:3
Awake, *l* and harp. . . . . . . Ps 108:2
Praise Him with the *l*. . . . . . Ps 150:3

LUXURY
L is not fitting . . . . Prov 19:10
l are in kings' courts. . . . . . Luke 7:25
in pleasure and *l* . . . . James 5:5
the abundance of her *l* . . . . Rev 18:3

LYDDA
Aeneas healed at, Acts 9:32–35

LYDIA
Woman of Thyatira; Paul's first European convert, Acts 16:14, 15, 40
——— District of Asia Minor containing Ephesus, Smyrna, Thyatira, and Sardis, Rev 1:11

LYING
I hate and abhor *l* . . . . . . Ps 119:163
righteous man hates *l*. . . . Prov 13:5
not trust in these *l* . . . . Jer 7:4
in swaddling cloths, *l* . . . . Luke 2:12
saw the linen cloths *l* . . . . John 20:5
putting away *l* . . . . Eph 4:25
signs, and *l* wonders. . . . 2 Thess 2:9

LYSIAS, CLAUDIUS
See CLAUDIUS LYSIAS

LYSTRA
Paul visits; is worshiped by people of and stoned by Jews, Acts 14:6–20
Home of Timothy, Acts 16:1, 2

MAACAH (or Maachah)
Small Syrian kingdom near Mt. Hermon, Deut 3:14
Not possessed by Israel, Josh 13:13
——— David's wife; mother of Absalom, 2 Sam 3:3
——— Wife of Rehoboam; mother of King Abijah, 2 Chr 11:18–21
Makes idol; is deposed as queen mother, 1 Kin 15:13

MACEDONIA
Paul preaches in, Acts 16:9—17:14
Paul's troubles in, 2 Cor 7:5
Churches of, generous, Rom 15:26; 2 Cor 8:1–5

MACHIR
Manasseh's only son, Gen 50:23
Founder of the family of Machirites, Num 26:29
Conqueror of Gilead, Num 32:39, 40

MACHPELAH
Field containing a cave; bought by Abraham, Gen 23:9–18
Sarah and Abraham buried here, Gen 23:19; 25:9, 10
Isaac, Rebekah, Leah, and Jacob buried here, Gen 49:29–31

MAD
has a demon and is *m* . . . John 10:20
he said, "I am not *m* . . . . . Acts 26:25

MADE
m the stars also . . . . Gen 1:16
wife the LORD God *m* . . . . . Gen 3:21
hear long ago how I *m* . . . . . Is 37:26
things My hand has *m* . . . . . . Is 66:2
All things were *m* . . . . John 1:3

MADNESS
before them, *m* . . . . 1 Sam 21:13
wisdom and to know *m* . . . . Eccl 1:17
m is in their hearts . . . . Eccl 9:3

MAGDALENE
See MARY

MAGIC
women who sew *m* . . . . . . Ezek 13:18
m brought their books . . . . Acts 19:19

MAGNIFICENCE
m I cannot endure . . . . Job 31:23

MAGNIFIED
So let Your name be *m* . . . 2 Sam 7:26
"Let the LORD be *m* . . . . Ps 35:27
for You have *m* Your . . . . . . Ps 138:2
the Lord Jesus was *m* . . . . . Acts 19:17
also Christ will be *m* . . . . . Phil 1:20

MAGNIFIES
"My soul *m* the Lord . . . . . Luke 1:46

MAGNIFY
m the LORD with me . . . . Ps 34:3
m himself above every . . . . Dan 11:36

MAGOG
People among Japheth's descendants, Gen 10:2
Associated with Gog, Ezek 38:2
Representatives of final enemies, Rev 20:8

MAHANAIM
Name given by Jacob to a sacred site, Gen 32:2
Becomes Ishbosheth's capital, 2 Sam 2:8–29
David flees to, during Absalom's rebellion, 2 Sam 17:24, 27

MAHER-SHALAL-HASH-BAZ
Symbolic name of Isaiah's second son; prophetic of the fall of Damascus and Samaria, Is 8:1–4

MAHLON
Husband of Ruth; without child, Ruth 1:2–5

MAIDENS
Both young men and *m* . . . Ps 148:12
She has sent out her *m* . . . . . Prov 9:3

MAIDSERVANT
"I am Ruth, your *m* . . . . Ruth 3:9
save the son of Your *m* . . . . . Ps 86:16
"Behold the *m* . . . . Luke 1:38
lowly state of His *m* . . . . . Luke 1:48

MAIDSERVANTS
m shall lead her as . . . . Nah 2:7
m I will pour out My . . . . . . Acts 2:18

MAIMED
to enter into life *m* . . . . . . Mark 9:43
the poor and the *m* . . . . . Luke 14:21

MAINTAIN
and *m* their cause . . . . . . 1 Kin 8:45

MAINTAINED
For You have *m* my . . . . Ps 9:4

MAJESTY
with God is awesome *m* . . . Job 37:22
splendor of Your *m* . . . . Ps 145:5
right hand of the *M* . . . . Heb 1:3
eyewitnesses of His *m* . . . . . 2 Pet 1:16
wise, be glory and *m* . . . . Jude 25

MAKE
"Let Us *m* man in Our . . . . . Gen 1:26
let us *m* a name for . . . . . . Gen 11:4
m you a great nation . . . . . . Gen 12:2
"You shall not *m* . . . . Ex 20:4
m Our home with him . . . John 14:23

MAKER
where is God my *M* . . . . . . Job 35:10
man will look to his *M* . . . . . Is 17:7
who strives with his *M* . . . . . Is 45:9
M is your husband . . . . Is 54:5
has forgotten his *M* . . . . . . Hos 8:14
builder and *m* is God . . . . . Heb 11:10

MALACHI
Prophet and writer, Mal 1:1

MALCHISHUA
Son of King Saul, 1 Sam 14:49
Killed at Gilboa, 1 Sam 31:2

MALCHUS
Servant of the high priest, John 18:10

MALICE
in *m* be babes . . . . 1 Cor 14:20
pleasures, living in *m* . . . . . . Titus 3:3
laying aside all *m* . . . . 1 Pet 2:1

MALICIOUSNESS
covetousness, *m* . . . . Rom 1:29

MALIGN
m a servant to his . . . . Prov 30:10

MALTA
Paul's shipwreck, Acts 28:1–8

MAMRE
Town or district near Hebron, Gen 23:19
Abram dwells by the oaks of, Gen 13:18

MAN
"Let Us make *m* . . . . Gen 1:26
"You are the *m* . . . . 2 Sam 12:7
"What is *m* . . . . Job 7:17
For an empty-headed *m* . . . Job 11:12
"Are you the first *m* . . . . Job 15:7
m that You are mindful . . . . . . Ps 8:4
What can *m* do to me . . . . . . Ps 118:6
coming of the Son of *M* . . Matt 24:27
"Behold the *M* . . . . John 19:5
m is not from woman . . . . 1 Cor 11:8
since by *m* came death . . 1 Cor 15:21
though our outward *m* . . . . 2 Cor 4:16
in Himself one new *m* . . . . Eph 2:15
that the *m* of God may . . . 2 Tim 3:17
is the number of a *m* . . . . . Rev 13:18

MANASSEH
Joseph's firstborn son, Gen 41:50, 51
Adopted by Jacob, Gen 48:5, 6
Loses his birthright to Ephraim, Gen 48:13–20
—— Tribe of:
Numbered, Num 1:34, 35
Half-tribe of, settle east of Jordan, Num 32:33–42; Deut 3:12–15
Help Joshua against Canaanites, Josh 1:12–18
Land assigned to western half-tribe, Josh 17:1–13
Eastern half-tribe builds altar, Josh 22:9–34
Some of, help David, 1 Chr 12:19–31
—— Wicked king of Judah; son of Hezekiah, 2 Kin 21:1–18; 2 Chr 33:1–9
Captured and taken to Babylon; repents and is restored, 2 Chr 33:10–13
Removes idols and altars, 2 Chr 33:14–20

MANGER
Will he bed by your *m* . . . . . Job 39:9
and laid Him in a *m* . . . . . . Luke 2:7
the Babe lying in a *m* . . . . . Luke 2:16

MANIFEST
m Myself to him . . . . John 14:21
is it that You will *m* . . . . . . John 14:22

MANIFESTATION
But the *m* of the . . . . 1 Cor 12:7
deceitfully, but by *m* . . . . . 2 Cor 4:2

MANIFESTED
"I have *m* Your name . . . . . John 17:6
God was *m* in the flesh . . . 1 Tim 3:16
the life was *m* . . . . 1 John 1:2
the love of God was *m* . . . . 1 John 4:9

MANIFOLD
m are Your works . . . . Ps 104:24
the *m* wisdom of God . . . . . . Eph 3:10
good stewards of the *m* . . . . 1 Pet 4:10

MANNA
of Israel ate *m* . . . . Ex 16:35
had rained down *m* . . . . Ps 78:24
Our fathers ate the *m* . . . . . John 6:31
of the hidden *m* . . . . Rev 2:17

MANNER
Is this the *m* of man . . . . . 2 Sam 7:19
in an unworthy *m* . . . . . . 1 Cor 11:27
sorrowed in a godly *m* . . . . 2 Cor 7:11
as is the *m* of some . . . . . . Heb 10:25
what *m* of persons . . . . 2 Pet 3:11
Behold what *m* of love . . . 1 John 3:1
m worthy of God . . . . 3 John 6

MANOAH
Danite; father of Samson, Judg 13:1–25

MANSIONS
house are many *m* . . . . John 14:2

MANTLE
Then he took the *m* . . . . . . 2 Kin 2:14

MARA
Name chosen by Naomi, Ruth 1:20

MARAH
First Israelite camp after passing through the Red Sea, Num 33:8, 9

MARCHED
people, when You *m* . . . . Ps 68:7

MARK (John)
Son of Mary of Jerusalem; travels

with Barnabas and Saul, Acts
12:12, 25
Leaves Paul at Perga, Acts 13:13
Barnabas and Paul separate because
of him, Acts 15:37–40
Later approved by Paul, Col 4:10;
2 Tim 4:11
Companion of Peter, 1 Pet 5:13
Author of the second Gospel, Mark 1:1

MARK
And the LORD set a *m* ...... Gen 4:15
M the blameless man ...... Ps 37:37
slave, to receive a *m* ...... Rev 13:16
whoever receives the *m* .... Rev 14:11

MARKET
is sold in the meat *m* .... 1 Cor 10:25

MARRED
so His visage was *m* .... Is 52:14
he made of clay was *m* ..... Jer 18:4

MARRIAGE
nor are given in *m* ...... Matt 22:30
her in *m* does well .... 1 Cor 7:38
M is honorable among..... Heb 13:4
the *m* of the Lamb has ..... Rev 19:7

MARRIED
"for I am *m* to you .... Jer 3:14
But he who is *m* .... 1 Cor 7:33
But she who is *m* .... 1 Cor 7:34

MARROW
and of joints and *m* .... Heb 4:12

MARRY
it is better not to *m* ...... Matt 19:10
they neither *m* nor are ... Matt 22:30
let them *m* .... 1 Cor 7:9
forbidding to *m*.......... 1 Tim 4:3
the younger widows *m* ... 1 Tim 5:14

MARRYING
and drinking, *m* .... Matt 24:38

MARTHA
Sister of Mary and Lazarus; loved by
Jesus, John 11:1–5
Affirms her faith, John 11:19–28
Offers hospitality to Jesus, Luke
10:38; John 12:1, 2
Gently rebuked by Christ, Luke
10:39–42

MARTYR
m Stephen was shed ..... Acts 22:20
was My faithful *m*........ Rev 2:13

MARTYRS
the blood of the *m* .... Rev 17:6

MARVEL
Do not *m* at this .... John 5:28

MARVELED
Jesus heard it, He *m* ..... Matt 8:10
And the multitudes *m*..... Matt 9:33
so that Pilate *m* .... Mark 15:5
And all the world *m* .... Rev 13:3
when I saw her, I *m* ...... Rev 17:6

MARVELOUS
m things He did........... Ps 78:12
It is *m* in our eyes .... Ps 118:23
M are Your works .... Ps 139:14
of darkness into His *m* .... 1 Pet 2:9

MARVELS
people I will do *m*......... Ex 34:10

MARY
Mother of Christ, Matt 1:16
Visited by angel, Luke 1:26–38
Visits Elizabeth and offers praise,
Luke 1:39–56

Gives birth to Jesus, Luke 2:6–20
Flees to Egypt, Matt 2:13–18
Visits Jerusalem with Jesus, Luke
2:41–52
Entrusted to John's care, John
19:25–27
——— Mother of James and Joses; pres-
ent at crucifixion and burial,
Matt 27:55–61
Sees the risen Lord; informs disciples,
Matt 28:1–10
——— Magdalene; delivered from seven
demons; supports Christ's min-
istry, Luke 8:2, 3
Present at crucifixion and burial,
Matt 27:55–61
First to see the risen Lord, Mark 16:1–
10; John 20:1–18
——— Sister of Martha and Lazarus;
loved by Jesus, John 11:1–5
Grieves for Lazarus, John 11:19, 20,
28–33
Anoints Jesus, Matt 26:6–13; John
12:1–8
Commended by Jesus, Luke 10:38–42
——— Mark's mother, Acts 12:12–17

MASSAH AND MERIBAH
First, at Rephidim, Israel just out of
Egypt, Ex 17:1–7
Second, at Kadesh Barnea, 40 years
later, Num 20:1–13

MASTER
of Abraham his *m* .... Gen 24:9
a servant like his *m* ..... Matt 10:25
greater than his *m* ...... John 15:20
m builder I have laid .... 1 Cor 3:10
and useful for the *M* ..... 2 Tim 2:21

MASTERS
m besides You have .... Is 26:13
can serve two *m*......... Luke 16:13
M, give your bondservants... Col 4:1
who have believing *m* .... 1 Tim 6:2

MATTANIAH
King Zedekiah's original name, 2 Kin
24:17

MATTER
m is found in me .... Job 19:28
He who answers a *m* ..... Prov 18:13

MATTERS
the weightier *m*......... Matt 23:23
judge the smallest *m*...... 1 Cor 6:2

MATTHEW
Becomes Christ's follower, Matt 9:9
Chosen as one of the Twelve, Matt
10:2, 3
Called Levi, the son of Alphaeus,
Mark 2:14
Author of the first Gospel, Matt (title)

MATTHIAS
Chosen by lot to replace Judas, Acts
1:15–26

MATURE
among those who are *m* ... 1 Cor 2:6
understanding be *m*..... 1 Cor 14:20
us, as many as are *m*...... Phil 3:15

MEAN
What do you *m*........... Ex 12:26

MEANING
'What is the *m* .... Deut 6:20
if I do not know the *m* ... 1 Cor 14:11

MEANT
but God *m* it for good .... Gen 50:20

MEASURE
a perfect and just *m* ..... Deut 25:15
apportion the waters by *m* . Job 28:25
and the short *m* .... Mic 6:10
give the Spirit by *m*....... John 3:34
to each one a *m* .... Rom 12:3
m the temple of God...... Rev 11:1

MEASURED
m the waters in the .... Is 40:12
you use, it will be *m*....... Matt 7:2
Then he *m* its wall .... Rev 21:17

MEASURES
your house differing *m* ... Deut 25:14
weights and diverse *m*.... Prov 20:10

MEASURING
the man's hand was a *m* .. Ezek 40:5
behold, a man with a *m* .... Zech 2:1
m themselves by........ 2 Cor 10:12
given a reed like a *m* ..... Rev 11:1

MEAT
Can He provide *m*......... Ps 78:20
He also rained *m*.......... Ps 78:27
good neither to eat *m* .... Rom 14:21
will never again eat *m*.... 1 Cor 8:13
is sold in the *m*........ 1 Cor 10:25

MEDDLE
why should you *m* ...... 2 Kin 14:10

MEDES, MEDIA
Part of Medo-Persian Empire, Esth
1:19
Israel deported to, 2 Kin 17:6
Babylon falls to, Dan 5:30, 31
Daniel rises high in kingdom of,
Dan 6:1–28
Cyrus, king of, allows Jews to return,
2 Chr 36:22, 23
Agents in Babylon's fall, Is 13:17–19

MEDIATE
a mediator does not *m* ..... Gal 3:20

MEDIATOR
Nor is there any *m* .... Job 9:33
by the hand of a *m*........ Gal 3:19
is one God and one *M* .... 1 Tim 2:5
as He is also *M* .... Heb 8:6
to Jesus the *M* of the...... Heb 12:24

MEDICINE
does good, like *m*....... Prov 17:22
their leaves for *m*........ Ezek 47:12

MEDITATE
Isaac went out to *m* ...... Gen 24:63
but you shall *m*........... Josh 1:8
M within your heart on ...... Ps 4:4
I *m* within my heart .... Ps 77:6
I will *m* on Your .... Ps 119:15
Your heart will *m* .... Is 33:18
m beforehand on what ... Luke 21:14
m on these things.......... Phil 4:8

MEDITATES
in His law he *m*............. Ps 1:2

MEDITATION
of my mouth and the *m* .... Ps 19:14
m be sweet to Him........ Ps 104:34
It is my *m* all the day...... Ps 119:97

MEDITERRANEAN SEA
Described as:
Sea, Gen 49:13
Great Sea, Josh 1:4; 9:1
Sea of the Philistines, Ex 23:31
Western Sea, Deut 11:24; Joel 2:20;
Zech 14:8

MEDIUM
a woman who is a *m* ..... Lev 20:27
a woman who is a *m* .... 1 Sam 28:7

MEDIUM'S
shall be like a *m* . . . . Is 29:4

MEDIUMS
"Seek those who are *m*. . . . . . Is 8:19

MEEK
with equity for the *m* . . . . Is 11:4
Blessed are the *m* . . . . Matt 5:5

MEEKNESS
with you by the *m* . . . . . . 2 Cor 10:1
are done in the *m* . . . . . . James 3:13

MEET
For You *m* him with the . . . . . Ps 21:3
prepare to *m* your God . . . Amos 4:12
go out to *m* him . . . . Matt 25:6
m the Lord in the air . . . 1 Thess 4:17

MEETING
In the tabernacle of *m* . . . . . Ex 27:21
burned up all the *m* . . . . Ps 74:8

MEGIDDO
City of Canaan; scene of battles,
    Judg 5:19–21; 2 Kin 23:29, 30
Fortified by Solomon, 1 Kin 9:15
Possible site of Armageddon,
    Rev 16:16

MELCHIZEDEK
Priest and king of Salem, Gen
    14:18–20
Type of Christ's eternal priesthood,
    Heb 7:1–22

MELODY
make sweet *m*. . . . . Is 23:16
singing and making *m*. . . . . Eph 5:19

MELT
You make his beauty *m*. . . . . Ps 39:11
man's heart will *m*. . . . . Is 13:7
the elements will *m* . . . . . . 2 Pet 3:10

MEMBER
body is not one *m*. . . . . . . 1 Cor 12:14
tongue is a little *m* . . . . James 3:5

MEMBERS
you that one of your *m* . . . Matt 5:29
do not present your *m*. . . . . . Rom 6:13
that your bodies are *m* . . . 1 Cor 6:15
neighbor, for we are *m*. . . . . Eph 4:25

MEMORIAL
and this is My *m*. . . . . Ex 3:15
also be told as a *m* . . . . . . Matt 26:13
be told of as a *m* . . . . Mark 14:9

MEMORY
The *m* of him perishes . . . . . Job 18:17
He may cut off the *m*. . . . . . Ps 109:15
The *m* of the righteous . . . . Prov 10:7

MEMPHIS (or Noph)
Ancient capital of Egypt, Hos 9:6
Prophesied against by Isaiah, Is 19:13
Jews flee to, Jer 44:1
Denounced by the prophets, Jer 46:19

MEN
m began to call on the . . . . Gen 4:26
saw the daughters of *m* . . . . . Gen 6:2
you shall die like *m*. . . . . Ps 82:7
the Egyptians are *m*. . . . . Is 31:3
make you fishers of *m* . . . . Matt 4:19
goodwill toward *m* . . . . Luke 2:14
from heaven or from *m* . . . Luke 20:4
Likewise also the *m*. . . . . . . Rom 1:27
let no one boast in *m* . . . . 1 Cor 3:21
the Lord, and not to *m*. . . . . . Eph 6:7
between God and *m* . . . . . 1 Tim 2:5

MENAHEM
Cruel king of Israel, 2 Kin 15:14–18

MENSERVANTS
And also on My *m* . . . . Joel 2:29
And on My *m* and on My . . Acts 2:18

MENTION
I will make *m* of Your . . . . . . Ps 71:16
by You only we make *m* . . . . Is 26:13
You who make *m* of the. . . . . . Is 62:6
he was dying, made *m*. . . . Heb 11:22

MEPHIBOSHETH
Son of King Saul, 2 Sam 21:8
—— Grandson of King Saul; crippled
    son of Jonathan, 2 Sam
    4:4–6
Sought out and honored by David,
    2 Sam 9:1–13
Accused by Ziba, 2 Sam 16:1–4
Later explains himself to David,
    2 Sam 19:24–30
Spared by David, 2 Sam 21:7

MERAB
King Saul's eldest daughter, 1 Sam
    14:49
Saul promises her to David, but gives
    her to Adriel, 1 Sam 18:17–19

MERARI
Third son of Levi, Gen 46:11
—— Descendants of, called Merarites:
Duties in the tabernacle, Num
    3:35–37
Cities assigned to, Josh 21:7, 34–40
Duties in the temple, 1 Chr 26:10–19
Assist Ezra after exile, Ezra 8:18, 19

MERCHANDISE
perceives that her *m* . . . . . Prov 31:18
house a house of *m*. . . . . . . John 2:16

MERCHANTS
set it in a city of *m*. . . . . . . Ezek 17:4
have multiplied your *m* . . . . Nah 3:16
m were the great men. . . . . Rev 18:23

MERCIES
for His *m* are great . . . . . 2 Sam 24:14
and His tender *m*. . . . . Ps 145:9
give you the sure *m* . . . . . Acts 13:34
the Father of *m* . . . . 2 Cor 1:3

MERCIFUL
Lord, the Lord God, *m* . . . . . . Ex 34:6
He is ever *m*. . . . . Ps 37:26
God be *m* to us and. . . . . Ps 67:1
Blessed are the *m* . . . . Matt 5:7
saying, 'God be *m*. . . . . . . Luke 18:13
For I will be *m* . . . . Heb 8:12
compassionate and *m*. . . . James 5:11

MERCY
but showing *m* to . . . . Ex 20:6
and abundant in *m* . . . . . . Num 14:18
m endures forever . . . . . . 1 Chr 16:34
to Your *m* remember me. . . . . Ps 25:7
I trust in the *m* . . . . Ps 52:8
shall send forth His *m* . . . . . Ps 57:3
You, O Lord, belongs *m*. . . . . Ps 62:12
m ceased forever . . . . Ps 77:8
M and truth have met. . . . . Ps 85:10
M shall be built. . . . . Ps 89:2
m and truth go before . . . . . Ps 89:14
m is everlasting . . . . Ps 100:5
I will sing of . . . . Ps 101:1
For Your *m* is great . . . . Ps 108:4
is full of Your *m* . . . . Ps 119:64
the Lord there is *m* . . . . . . Ps 130:7
Let not *m* and truth . . . . . . Prov 3:3
who honors Him has *m*. . . . Prov 14:31
cruel and have no *m* . . . . . . Jer 6:23
Lord our God belong *m*. . . . Dan 9:9

MENSERVANTS
For I desire *m* and not . . . . . . Hos 6:6
do justly, to love *m*. . . . . Mic 6:8
'I desire *m* and not . . . . . . Matt 9:13
And His *m* is on those. . . . . Luke 1:50
"I will have *m* . . . . Rom 9:15
of God who shows *m*. . . . . . Rom 9:16
that He might have *m*. . . . Rom 11:32
m has made trustworthy. . 1 Cor 7:25
as we have received *m*. . . . . 2 Cor 4:1
God, who is rich in *m*. . . . . . Eph 2:4
but I obtained *m* . . . . 1 Tim 1:13
that he may find *m*. . . . . . . 2 Tim 1:18
to His *m* He saved us . . . . . Titus 3:5
that we may obtain *m* . . . . . Heb 4:16
judgment is without *m* . . . James 2:13
God, looking for the *m*. . . . . . Jude 21

MERIB-BAAL
Another name for Mephibosheth,
    1 Chr 8:34

MERODACH
Supreme deity of the Babylonians,
    Jer 50:2
Otherwise called Bel, Is 46:1

MERODACH-BALADAN
Sends ambassadors to Hezekiah, Is
    39:1–8
Also called Berodach-Baladan, 2 Kin
    20:12

MERRY
m heart makes a . . . . Prov 15:13
eat, drink, and be *m*. . . . . . . Eccl 8:15
we should make *m* . . . . . . Luke 15:32

MESHACH
Name given to Mishael, Dan 1:7
Advanced to high position, Dan 2:49
Remains faithful in testing, Dan
    3:13–30

MESHECH
Son of Japheth, Gen 10:2
His descendants, mentioned in
    prophecy, Ezek 27:13; 32:26;
    38:2, 3

MESOPOTAMIA
Home of Abraham's relatives, Gen
    24:4, 10, 15
Called Padan Aram and Syria, Gen
    25:20; 31:20, 24
Israel enslaved to, Judg 3:8–10
Jews from, present at Pentecost,
    Acts 2:9

MESSAGE
I have heard a *m* . . . . Jer 49:14
For the *m* of the cross. . . . . 1 Cor 1:18

MESSENGER
is a faithful *m* . . . . Prov 25:13
"Behold, I send My *m* . . . . . . Mal 3:1
'Behold, I send My *m* . . . . Matt 11:10

MESSIAH
until *M* the Prince . . . . Dan 9:25
"We have found the *M* . . . . John 1:41

METHUSELAH
Oldest man on record, Gen 5:27

MICAH
Prophet, contemporary of Isaiah, Is
    1:1; Mic 1:1

MICAIAH (or Michaiah)
Prophet who predicts Ahab's death,
    1 Kin 22:8–28
—— Contemporary of Jeremiah, Jer
    36:11–13

MICHAEL
Chief prince, Dan 10:13, 21

Disputes with Satan, Jude 9
Fights the dragon, Rev 12:7–9

MICHAL
Daughter of King Saul, 1 Sam 14:49
Loves and marries David, 1 Sam 18:20–28
Saves David from Saul, 1 Sam 19:9–17
Given to Palti, 1 Sam 25:44
David demands her from Abner, 2 Sam 3:13–16
Ridicules David; becomes barren, 2 Sam 6:16–23

MICHMASH
Site of battle with Philistines, 1 Sam 13:5, 11, 16, 23
Scene of Jonathan's victory, 1 Sam 14:1–16

MIDIAN
Son of Abraham by Keturah, Gen 25:1–4
——— Region in the Arabian desert occupied by the Midianites, Gen 25:6; Ex 2:15

MIDIANITES
Descendants of Abraham by Keturah, Gen 25:1, 2
Moses flees to, Ex 2:15
Join Moab in cursing Israel, Num 22:4–7
Intermarriage with incurs God's wrath, Num 25:1–18
Defeated by Israel, Num 31:1–10
Oppress Israel; defeated by Gideon, Judg 6; 7

MIDST
God is in the *m* . . . . Ps 46:5
that I am in the *m* . . . . Joel 2:27
I am there in the *m*. . . . . . Matt 18:20

MIGHT
'My power and the *m* . . . . . Deut 8:17
shall speak of the *m* . . . . . . Ps 145:6
the greatness of His *m* . . . . . . Is 40:26
man glory in his *m* . . . . Jer 9:23
their *m* has failed . . . . Jer 51:30
'Not by *m* nor by . . . . Zech 4:6
in the power of His *m*. . . . . . Eph 6:10
greater in power and *m* . . . 2 Pet 2:11
honor and power and *m*. . . . Rev 7:12

MIGHTIER
coming after me is *m* . . . . . Matt 3:11

MIGHTILY
to shake the earth *m* . . . . Is 2:19
which works in me *m* . . . . . . Col 1:29

MIGHTY
He was a *m* hunter. . . . . . . Gen 10:9
for they are too *m* . . . . . . Num 22:6
How the *m* have fallen. . . 2 Sam 1:19
is wise in heart and *m* . . . . . . Job 9:4
The LORD *m* in battle. . . . . . . Ps 24:8
their Redeemer is *m*. . . . . Prov 23:11
Woe to men *m* at . . . . Is 5:22
great in counsel and *m* . . . . Jer 32:19
m men are made red. . . . . . Nah 2:3
m has done great . . . . Luke 1:49
He has put down the *m* . . . Luke 1:52
the flesh, not many *m*. . . . 1 Cor 1:26
the working of His *m* . . . . . Eph 1:19
from heaven with His *m* . 2 Thess 1:7

MILCOM
Solomon went after, 1 Kin 11:5
Altar destroyed by Josiah, 2 Kin 23:12, 13

MILETUS
Paul meets Ephesian elders here, Acts 20:15–38
Paul leaves Trophimus here, 2 Tim 4:20

MILK
for water, she gave *m* . . . . . Judg 5:25
honey and *m* are under . . . Song 4:11
come, buy wine and *m* . . . . . . Is 55:1
and whiter than *m* . . . . Lam 4:7
shall flow with *m* . . . . Joel 3:18
have come to need *m*. . . . . Heb 5:12
m is unskilled in the. . . . . . Heb 5:13
desire the pure *m* . . . . 1 Pet 2:2

MILL
be grinding at the *m*. . . . . Matt 24:41

MILLO
Fort at Jerusalem, 2 Sam 5:9
Prepared by Solomon, 1 Kin 9:15
Strengthened by Hezekiah, 2 Chr 32:5
Scene of Joash's death, 2 Kin 12:20, 21

MILLSTONE
m were hung around his . . Matt 18:6
a stone like a great *m* . . . . . Rev 18:21

MIND
put wisdom in the *m* . . . . . . Job 38:36
perfect peace, whose *m* . . . . . Is 26:3
nor have an anxious *m* . . Luke 12:29
m I myself serve the . . . . . Rom 7:25
who has known the *m*. . . . Rom 11:34
Be of the same *m*. . . . . . . Rom 12:16
convinced in his own *m* . . . Rom 14:5
"who has known the *m* . . . 1 Cor 2:16
you are out of your *m* . . . 1 Cor 14:23
Let this *m* be in you. . . . . . . Phil 2:5
to *m* your own. . . . . 1 Thess 4:11
love and of a sound *m* . . . . 2 Tim 1:7

MINDFUL
is man that You are *m* . . . . . . Ps 8:4
The LORD has been *m*. . . . . Ps 115:12
for you are not *m* . . . . . . Matt 16:23
is man that You are *m* . . . . . Heb 2:6

MINDS
people change their *m* . . . . Ex 13:17
put My law in their *m* . . . . Jer 31:33
I stir up your pure *m* . . . . . 2 Pet 3:1
He who searches the *m*. . . . Rev 2:23

MINISTER
to make you a *m* . . . . Acts 26:16
for he is God's *m* . . . . Rom 13:4
you will be a good *m* . . . . . 1 Tim 4:6
a *M* of the sanctuary . . . . . . Heb 8:2

MINISTERED
But the child *m*. . . . . 1 Sam 2:11
a thousand thousands *m*. . . Dan 7:10
As they *m* to the Lord . . . . Acts 13:2

MINISTERS
angels spirits, His *m* . . . . . . Ps 104:4
for they are God's *m* . . . . . Rom 13:6
commend ourselves as *m* . . 2 Cor 6:4
Are they *m* of Christ. . . . . 2 Cor 11:23
If anyone *m*. . . . . 1 Pet 4:11

MINISTRIES
are differences of *m* . . . . . 1 Cor 12:5

MINISTRY
I magnify my *m*. . . . . Rom 11:13
But if the *m* of death . . . . . 2 Cor 3:7
since we have this *m*. . . . . . 2 Cor 4:1
and has given us the *m*. . . . 2 Cor 5:18
for the work of *m* . . . . Eph 4:12
m which you have. . . . . Col 4:17

MINT
For you pay tithe of *m* . . . Matt 23:23

MIRACLE
saying, 'Show a *m* . . . . Ex 7:9
no one who works a *m* . . . Mark 9:39
that a notable *m* . . . . Acts 4:16

MIRACLES
God worked unusual *m* . . . Acts 19:11
the working of *m* . . . . 1 Cor 12:10
Are all workers of *m* . . . . . 1 Cor 12:29
with various *m* . . . . Heb 2:4

MIRIAM
Sister of Aaron and Moses, Num 26:59
Chosen by God; called a prophetess, Ex 15:20
Punished for rebellion, Num 12:1–16
Buried at Kadesh, Num 20:1

MIRTH
I will test you with *m* . . . . . . Eccl 2:1
is in the house of *m* . . . . Eccl 7:4
joy is darkened, the *m* . . . . . Is 24:11

MISER
eat the bread of a *m* . . . . . Prov 23:6

MISERIES
m that are coming . . . . James 5:1

MISERY
would forget your *m* . . . . . . Job 11:16
and remember his *m* . . . . . Prov 31:7

MISTREATED
But the Egyptians *m*. . . . . Deut 26:6
those who are *m*. . . . . Heb 13:3

MISTREATS
m his father and . . . . Prov 19:26

MITES
widow putting in two *m* . . Luke 21:2

MIZPAH
Site of covenant between Jacob and Laban, Gen 31:44–53
——— Town of Benjamin; outraged Israelites gather here, Josh 18:21, 26; Judg 20:1, 3
Samuel gathers Israel, 1 Sam 7:5–16; 10:17–25
Residence of Gedaliah, 2 Kin 25:23, 25

MOAB
Son of Lot, Gen 19:33–37
——— Country of the Moabites, Deut 1:5

MOABITES
Descendants of Lot, Gen 19:36, 37
Join Midian in cursing Israel, Num 22:4
Excluded from Israel, Deut 23:3–6
Kindred of Ruth, Ruth 1:4
Subdued by Israel, 1 Sam 14:47; 2 Sam 8:2; 2 Kin 3:4–27
Women of, lead Solomon astray, 1 Kin 11:1–8
Prophecies concerning, Is 11:14; 15:1–9; Jer 48:1–47; Amos 2:1–3

MOAN
m sadly like doves . . . . Is 59:11

MOCK
I will *m* when your . . . . . . Prov 1:26
Fools *m* at sin. . . . . Prov 14:9
to the Gentiles to *m*. . . . . Matt 20:19

MOCKED
at noon, that Elijah *m* . . . 1 Kin 18:27

"I am one *m* by his . . . . Job 12:4
knee before Him and *m* . . Matt 27:29
deceived, God is not *m* . . . . . . Gal 6:7

MOCKER
Wine is a *m* . . . . Prov 20:1

MOCKERS
that there would be *m* . . . . . . Jude 18

MOCKINGS
others had trial of *m* . . . . . Heb 11:36

MOCKS
He who *m* the poor . . . . Prov 17:5

MODERATION
with propriety and *m* . . . . . 1 Tim 2:9

MOLECH
God of the Ammonites; worshiped by
    Solomon, 1 Kin 11:7
Human sacrifice made to, Lev 18:21;
    2 Kin 23:10

MOMENT
consume them in a *m* . . . . Num 16:21
In a *m* they die . . . . Job 34:20
face from you for a *m* . . . . Is 54:8
in a *m*, in the . . . . 1 Cor 15:52
which is but for a *m* . . . . . 2 Cor 4:17

MONEY
does not put out his *m* . . . . . . Ps 15:5
m answers every . . . . Eccl 10:19
be redeemed without *m* . . . . . Is 52:3
and you who have no *m* . . . . . Is 55:1
of the *m* changers . . . . . . Matt 21:12
and hid his lord's *m* . . . . Matt 25:18
promised to give him *m* . . Mark 14:11
Carry neither *m*. . . . . Luke 10:4
I sent you without *m* . . . . Luke 22:35
the *m* changers doing . . . . John 2:14
be purchased with *m* . . . . . Acts 8:20
not greedy for *m* . . . . 1 Tim 3:3
m is a root of all . . . . 1 Tim 6:10
not greedy for *m* . . . . Titus 1:7

MONSTER
me up like a *m* . . . . Jer 51:34
of Egypt, O great *m* . . . . . . Ezek 29:3

MOON
until the *m* is no more . . . . . Ps 72:7
morning, fair as the *m* . . . . Song 6:10
sun and *m* grow dark . . . . . . Joel 2:10
m will not give its. . . . . . . Mark 13:24

MORDECAI
Esther's guardian; advises her, Esth
    2:5–20
Reveals plot to kill the king, Esth
    2:21–23
Refuses homage to Haman, Esth
    3:1–6
Honored by the king, Esth 6:1–12
Exalted highly, Esth 8:15; 9:4
Institutes feast of Purim, Esth 9:20–31

MORIAH
God commands Abraham to sacrifice
    Isaac here, Gen 22:1–13
Site of Solomon's temple, 2 Chr 3:1

MORNING
the eyelids of the *m* . . . . . . Job 41:18
Evening and *m* and at. . . . . . Ps 55:17
the wings of the *m*. . . . . Ps 139:9
looks forth as the *m* . . . . . Song 6:10
Lucifer, son of the *m*. . . . . . . Is 14:12
established as the *m*. . . . . . . Hos 6:3
very early in the *m*. . . . . . . Luke 24:1
the Bright and *M* Star . . . . . Rev 22:16

MORSEL
or eaten my *m* by . . . . Job 31:17

Better is a dry *m* . . . . Prov 17:1
Esau, who for one *m*. . . . . . Heb 12:16

MORTAL
sin reign in your *m* . . . . Rom 6:12
and this *m* must put . . . . 1 Cor 15:53

MORTALITY
m may be swallowed. . . . . . 2 Cor 5:4

MORTALS
with idolatrous *m* . . . . Ps 26:4

MOSES
Born; hidden by mother; adopted by
    Pharaoh's daughter, Ex 2:1–10
Kills Egyptian and flees to Midian, Ex
    2:11–22
Receives call from God, Ex 3:1—4:17
Returns to Israelites in Egypt, Ex
    4:18–31
Wins Israel's deliverance with
    plagues, Ex 5:1—6:13; 6:28—
    11:10; 12:29–42
Leads Israel out of Egypt and
    through the Red Sea, Ex 13:17—
    14:31
His song of praise, Ex 15:1–18
Provides miraculously for the people,
    Ex 15:22—17:7
Appoints judges, Ex 18
Receives the law on Mount Sinai, Ex
    19—23
Receives instructions for tabernacle,
    Ex 25—31
Intercedes for Israel's sin, Ex 32
Recommissioned and encouraged, Ex
    33; 34
Further instructions and building of
    the tabernacle, Ex 35—40
Consecrates Aaron, Lev 8:1–36
Takes census, Num 1:1–54
Resumes journey to Canaan, Num
    10:11–36
Complains; 70 elders appointed,
    Num 11:1–35
Intercedes for people when they
    refuse to enter Canaan, Num
    14:11–25
Puts down Korah's rebellion, Num 16
Sins in anger, Num 20:1–13
Makes bronze serpent, Num 21:4–9
Travels toward Canaan, Num
    21:10–20
Takes second census, Num 26
Commissions Joshua as his successor,
    Num 27:12–23
Receives further laws, Num 28—30
Commands conquest of Midian,
    Num 31
Final instructions, Num 32—36
Forbidden to enter Promised Land,
    Deut 3:23–28
Gives farewell messages, Deut 32; 33
Sees Promised Land; dies, Deut
    34:1–7
Is mourned and extolled, Deut
    34:8–12
Appears with Christ at Transfigura-
    tion, Matt 17:1–3

MOST
His mouth is *m* sweet . . . . . Song 5:16
on your *m* holy faith . . . . . . Jude 20

MOTH
m will eat them . . . . Is 50:9
where *m* and rust . . . . Matt 6:19

MOTHER
because she was the *m* . . . . Gen 3:20
like a joyful *m* . . . . Ps 113:9

the only one of her *m*. . . . . Song 6:9
m might have been my . . . . Jer 20:17
leave his father and *m* . . . . Matt 19:5
"Behold your *m*. . . . . John 19:27
free, which is the *m* . . . . . . Gal 4:26
The *M* of Harlots. . . . . Rev 17:5

MOUNT
come up to *M* Sinai. . . . . . . Ex 19:23
you like *M* Carmel . . . . Song 7:5
they shall *m* up with . . . . . . Is 40:31
for this Hagar is *M* . . . . Gal 4:25

MOUNT CARMEL
Prophets gather at, 1 Kin 18:19, 20
Elisha journeys to, 2 Kin 2:25
Shunammite woman comes to Elisha
    at, 2 Kin 4:25

MOUNT EBAL
Cursed by God, Deut 11:29
Joshua builds an altar on, Josh 8:30

MOUNT GERIZIM
Mount of blessing, Deut 11:29; 27:12
Jotham speaks to people of Shechem
    here, Judg 9:7
Samaritans' sacred mountain, John
    4:20, 21

MOUNT GILBOA
Men of Israel slain at, 1 Sam 31:1
Saul and his sons slain at, 1 Sam
    31:8

MOUNT GILEAD
Gideon divides the people for battle
    at, Judg 7:3

MOUNT HOR
Lord speaks to Moses and Aaron on,
    Num 20:23
Aaron dies on, Num 20:25–28

MOUNT HOREB
Sons of Israel stripped of ornaments
    at, Ex 33:6
The same as Sinai, Ex 3:1

MOUNT OF OLIVES
See OLIVES, MOUNT OF

MOUNT SINAI
Lord descends upon, in fire, Ex 19:18
Lord calls Moses to the top of,
    Ex 19:20
The glory of the Lord rests on, for six
    days, Ex 24:16

MOUNT TABOR
Deborah sends Barak there to defeat
    Canaanites, Judg 4:6–14

MOUNT ZION
Survivors shall go out from, 2 Kin
    19:31

MOUNTAIN
to Horeb, the *m*. . . . . Ex 3:1
"But as a *m* falls . . . . Job 14:18
You have made my *m* . . . . . Ps 30:7
of many peaks is the *m* . . . . Ps 68:15
let us go up to the *m* . . . . Is 2:3
image became a great *m* . . Dan 2:35
Who are you, O great *m* . . . Zech 4:7
you will say to this *m* . . . . Matt 17:20
with Him on the holy *m*. . . 2 Pet 1:18

MOUNTAINS
He removes the *m* . . . . Job 9:5
Surely the *m* yield . . . . Job 40:20
m will bring peace. . . . . Ps 72:3
excellent than the *m* . . . . . . Ps 76:4
m were brought forth . . . . . Ps 90:2
m melt like wax at the . . . . . Ps 97:5
m skipped like rams. . . . . . . Ps 114:4

MOURN (continued)

m surround Jerusalem...... Ps 125:2
m shall depart and the .... Is 54:10
in Judea flee to the *m*.. Matt 24:16
that I could remove *m*.... 1 Cor 13:2
m were not found .... Rev 16:20

MOURN
and you *m* at last .... Prov 5:11
a time to *m*............. Eccl 3:4
are those who *m*......... Matt 5:4
Lament and *m* and weep.. James 4:9
of the earth will *m* .... Rev 1:7

MOURNED
we *m* to you............ Matt 11:17
and have not rather *m* .... 1 Cor 5:2

MOURNING
This is a deep *m*....... Gen 50:11
m all the day long........ Ps 38:6
m shall be ended .... Is 60:20
men break bread in *m*..... Jer 16:7
I will turn their *m*....... Jer 31:13
shall be a great *m* ...... Zech 12:11
be turned to *m* and...... James 4:9

MOURNS
heavily, as one who *m* .... Ps 35:14
The earth *m* and fades....... Is 24:4
for Him as one *m* .... Zech 12:10

MOUTH
"Who has made man's *m*.... Ex 4:11
Out of the *m* of babes........ Ps 8:2
The *m* of the righteous ..... Ps 37:30
m shall speak wisdom...... Ps 49:3
iniquity stops its *m* .... Ps 107:42
knowledge, but the *m* ..... Prov 10:14
m preserves his life ...... Prov 13:3
The *m* of an immoral ..... Prov 22:14
and a flattering *m*....... Prov 26:28
m speaking pompous ...... Dan 7:8
the doors of your *m* .... Mic 7:5
m defiles a man......... Matt 15:11
m I will judge you...... Luke 19:22
I will give you a *m* ..... Luke 21:15
m confession is made .... Rom 10:10
m great swelling words...... Jude 16
vomit you out of My *m*..... Rev 3:16

MOVE
and the earth will *m*....... Is 13:13
the mountain shall *m*..... Zech 14:4
in Him we live and *m* .... Acts 17:28

MOVED
shall never be *m* .... Ps 15:5
she shall not be *m*....... Ps 46:5
spoke as they were *m* ..... 2 Pet 1:21

MUCH
m study is .... Eccl 12:12
m better than wine is ..... Song 4:10
to whom *m* is given...... Luke 12:48
M more then........... Rom 5:9

MULTIPLIED
sorrows shall be *m*......... Ps 16:4
of the disciples *m*......... Acts 6:7
word of God grew and *m*.. Acts 12:24

MULTIPLY
"Be fruitful and *m* .... Gen 1:22
m your descendants ...... Gen 16:10
m my days as the .... Job 29:18
m the descendants .... Jer 33:22

MULTITUDE
stars of heaven in *m*...... Deut 1:10
Your house in the *m*....... Ps 5:7
m that kept a pilgrim ..... Ps 42:4
In the *m* of words sin..... Prov 10:19
In a *m* of people is a .... Prov 14:28
compassion on the *m* .... Matt 15:32

with the angel a *m*....... Luke 2:13
"love will cover a *m*....... 1 Pet 4:8
and behold, a great *m* ...... Rev 7:9

MURDER
"You shall not *m*......... Ex 20:13
'You shall not *m* .... Matt 5:21
threats and *m* against...... Acts 9:1
You *m* and covet and .... James 4:2

MURDERED
sons of those who *m* ..... Matt 23:31
Jesus whom you *m*....... Acts 5:30
one and *m* his brother... 1 John 3:12

MURDERER
He was a *m* from the ..... John 8:44
and asked for a *m* .... Acts 3:14
of you suffer as a *m* ..... 1 Pet 4:15
his brother is a *m*....... 1 John 3:15

MURDERERS
in it, but now *m*........... Is 1:21
and profane, for *m* .... 1 Tim 1:9
abominable, *m*........... Rev 21:8

MURDERS
evil thoughts, *m*........ Matt 15:19
envy, *m*, drunkenness...... Gal 5:21

MUSIC
So David played *m* .... 1 Sam 18:10
m are brought low .... Eccl 12:4
the house, he heard *m* ... Luke 15:25

MUSING
while I was *m* .... Ps 39:3

MUTE
Or who makes the *m* .... Ex 4:11
m who does not open ...... Ps 38:13
I was *m* with silence ...... Ps 39:2
I was *m* .... Ps 39:9

MUTILATION
beware of the *m*.......... Phil 3:2

MUTUAL
by the *m* faith both....... Rom 1:12

MUZZLE
"You shall not *m*........ Deut 25:4
"You shall not *m* .... 1 Tim 5:18

MYSTERIES
to you to know the *m* .... Matt 13:11
and understand all *m* .... 1 Cor 13:2
the spirit he speaks *m* .... 1 Cor 14:2

MYSTERIOUS
today is not too *m*...... Deut 30:11

MYSTERY
given to know the *m* ..... Mark 4:11
wisdom of God in a *m*..... 1 Cor 2:7
Behold, I tell you a *m* .... 1 Cor 15:51
made known to us the *m*.... Eph 1:9
This is a great *m*.......... Eph 5:32
m which has been......... Col 1:26
the *m* of godliness .... 1 Tim 3:16

NAAMAN
Captain in the Syrian army, 2 Kin 5:1–11
Healed of his leprosy, 2 Kin 5:14–17
Referred to by Christ, Luke 4:27

NABAL
Refuses David's request, 1 Sam 25:2–12
Escapes David's wrath but dies of a stroke, 1 Sam 25:13–39

NABOTH
Murdered for his vineyard by King Ahab, 1 Kin 21:1–16
His murder avenged, 1 Kin 21:17–25

NADAB
Eldest of Aaron's four sons, Ex 6:23
Takes part in affirming covenant, Ex 24:1, 9–12
Becomes priest, Ex 28:1
Consumed by fire, Lev 10:1–7
——— King of Israel, 1 Kin 14:20
Killed by Baasha, 1 Kin 15:25–31

NAHASH
King of Ammon; makes impossible demands, 1 Sam 11:1–15

NAHOR
Grandfather of Abraham, Gen 11:24–26
——— Son of Terah, brother of Abraham, Gen 11:17

NAHUM
Inspired prophet to Judah concerning Nineveh, Nah 1:1

NAILED
n it to the cross .... Col 2:14

NAIN
Village south of Nazareth; Jesus raises widow's son here, Luke 7:11–17

NAIOTH
Prophets' school in Ramah, 1 Sam 19:18, 19, 22, 23

NAKED
And they were both *n* ..... Gen 2:25
knew that they were *n*...... Gen 3:7
"*N* I came from my .... Job 1:21
Isaiah has walked *n* .... Is 20:3
I was *n* and you .... Matt 25:36
and fled from them *n*...... Mark 14:52
shall not be found *n* ...... 2 Cor 5:3
but all things are *n* .... Heb 4:13
brother or sister is *n* ..... James 2:15
poor, blind, and *n*....... Rev 3:17

NAKEDNESS
of Canaan, saw the *n* ..... Gen 9:22
or famine, or *n* .... Rom 8:35
often, in cold and ..... 2 Cor 11:27
n may not be revealed ..... Rev 3:18

NAME
Abram called on the *n*..... Gen 13:4
Israel shall be your *n*..... Gen 35:10
This is My *n* forever .... Ex 3:15
shall not take the *n* .... Ex 20:7
are called by the *n* ...... Deut 28:10
glorious and awesome *n*.. Deut 28:58
by My *n* will humble ..... 2 Chr 7:14
and he has no *n*......... Job 18:17
excellent is Your *n*........ Ps 8:1
n will put their trust .... Ps 9:10
be His glorious *n* .... Ps 72:19
n is great in Israel .... Ps 76:1
do not call on Your *n* ...... Ps 79:6
to Your *n* give glory........ Ps 115:1
above all Your *n* .... Ps 138:2
He calls them all by *n*...... Ps 147:4
The *n* of the LORD is a .... Prov 18:10
A good *n* is to be .... Prov 22:1
what is His Son's *n* ...... Prov 30:4
make mention of Your *n* .... Is 26:13
the LORD, that is My *n* .... Is 42:8
be to the LORD for a *n*....... Is 55:13
be called by a new *n* ...... Is 62:2
Everlasting is Your *n*....... Is 63:16
who calls on Your *n*....... Is 64:7
it shall be to Me a *n*....... Jer 33:9
and made Yourself a *n* .... Dan 9:15
we will walk in the *n* ..... Mic 4:5
They will call on My *n* .... Zech 13:9
n shall be great.......... Mal 1:11

NEIGHBOR

Participates with Ezra in restored
worship, Neh 8—10
Registers the people and the priests
and Levites, Neh 11:1—12:26
Dedicates the wall, Neh 12:27–43
Returns to Jerusalem after absence
and institutes reforms, Neh
13:4–31

NEIGHBOR
you shall love your *n*..... Lev 19:18
for better is a *n*.......... Prov 27:10
every man teach his *n*..... Jer 31:34
gives drink to his *n*...... Hab 2:15
'You shall love your *n*..... Matt 5:43
"And who is my *n*....... Luke 10:29
"You shall love your *n*..... Rom 13:9

NEST
and make its *n*.......... Job 39:27
n is a man who wanders... Prov 27:8
though you set your *n*...... Obad 4
that he may set his *n*...... Hab 2:9

NET
me with His *n*............ Job 19:6
have hidden their *n*....... Ps 35:7
They have prepared a *n*..... Ps 57:6
an antelope in a *n*....... Is 51:20
catch in their *n*.......... Hab 1:15
I will let down the *n*...... Luke 5:5
to them, "Cast the *n*...... John 21:6

NETHINIM
Servants of the Levites, Ezra 8:20
Possible origins of:
Gibeonites, Josh 9:23–27
Solomon's forced laborers, 1 Kin
9:20, 21
Mentioned, 1 Chr 9:2; Ezra 2:43–54;
7:24; 8:17; Neh 3:31; 7:46–60, 73;
10:28, 29; 11:21

NEVER
in Me shall *n* thirst....... John 6:35
in Me shall *n* die........ John 11:26
Love *n* fails............ 1 Cor 13:8
n take away sins........ Heb 10:11
"I will *n* leave you .... Heb 13:5
prophecy *n* came by...... 2 Pet 1:21

NEW
Now there arose a *n*........ Ex 1:8
the LORD creates a *n*..... Num 16:30
They chose *n* gods........ Judg 5:8
and there is nothing *n*...... Eccl 1:9
Behold, I will do a *n*....... Is 43:19
For behold, I create *n*...... Is 65:17
when I will make a *n*..... Jer 31:31
n every morning....... Lam 3:23
wine into *n* wineskins..... Matt 9:17
of the *n* covenant .... Matt 26:28
n commandment I give ... John 13:34
tell or to hear some *n*..... Acts 17:21
he is a *n* creation........ 2 Cor 5:17
n man who is renewed ..... Col 3:10
when I will make a *n*..... Heb 8:8
n heavens and a *n* ..... 2 Pet 3:13
n name written which ..... Rev 2:17
And they sang a *n*....... Rev 5:9
And I saw a *n* heaven ..... Rev 21:1
I make all things *n*....... Rev 21:5

NEWNESS
also should walk in *n*..... Rom 6:4
should serve in the *n* ...... Rom 7:6

NEWS
heard this bad *n*.......... Ex 33:4
soul, so is good *n*....... Prov 25:25
him who brings good *n*..... Is 52:7

NICANOR
One of the first seven deacons, Acts
6:1–5

NICODEMUS
Pharisee; converses with Jesus, John
3:1–12
Protests unfairness of Christ's trial,
John 7:50–52
Brings gifts to anoint Christ's body,
John 19:39, 40

NICOLAITANS
Group teaching moral laxity, Rev
2:6–15

NICOLAS
One of the first seven deacons,
Acts 6:5

NIGHT
darkness He called *N*....... Gen 1:5
It is a *n* of solemn........ Ex 12:42
pillar of fire by *n*........ Ex 13:22
and the *n* be ended........ Job 7:4
gives songs in the *n*...... Job 35:10
n reveals knowledge .... Ps 19:2
awake through the *n*..... Ps 119:148
and stars to rule by *n*..... Ps 136:9
desired You in the *n*........ Is 26:9
and perished in a *n*....... Jon 4:10
and continued all *n* ...... Luke 6:12
man came to Jesus by *n*.... John 3:2
n is coming when no ..... John 9:4
came to Jesus by *n*....... John 19:39
The *n* is far spent....... Rom 13:12
as a thief in the *n*...... 1 Thess 5:2
We are not of the *n* ..... 1 Thess 5:5
there shall be no *n*...... Rev 21:25
there shall be no *n*....... Rev 22:5

NILE
Hebrew children drowned in, Ex 1:22
Moses hidden in, Ex 2:3–10
Water of, turned to blood, Ex 7:14–21
Mentioned in prophecies, Is 19:5–8;
23:3; 27:12; Jer 46:7–9; Amos 9:5

NIMROD
Ham's grandson, Gen 10:6–12

NINE
where are the *n*........ Luke 17:17

NINETY-NINE
he not leave the *n*...... Matt 18:12
n just persons .... Luke 15:7

NINEVEH
Capital of Assyria, 2 Kin 19:36
Jonah preaches to; people repent, Jon
3:1–10; Matt 12:41
Prophecy against, Nah 2:13—3:19;
Zeph 2:13–15

NOAH
Son of Lamech, Gen 5:28–32
Finds favor with God; commissioned
to build the ark, Gen 6:8–22
Fills ark and survives flood, Gen 7
Leaves ark; builds altar; receives
God's promise, Gen 8
God's covenant with, Gen 9:1–17
Blesses and curses his sons; dies, Gen
9:18–29

NOB
City of priests; David flees to, 1 Sam
21:1–9
Priests of, killed by Saul, 1 Sam
22:9–23

NOBLE
whatever things are *n* ...... Phil 4:8
not blaspheme that *n*..... James 2:7

NOBLES
voice of *n* was hushed..... Job 29:10
king is the son of *n*...... Eccl 10:17
n have sent their lads...... Jer 14:3
your *n* rest in the........ Nah 3:18

NOD
Place (east of Eden) of Cain's exile,
Gen 4:16, 17

NOISE
The *n* of a multitude .... Is 13:4
people who make a *n*...... Is 17:12
of Egypt, is but a *n*...... Jer 46:17
They have made a *n*...... Lam 2:7
away with a great *n*..... 2 Pet 3:10

NOSTRILS
n the breath of life......... Gen 2:7
breath of God in my *n* ... Job 27:3
breath is in his *n*.......... Is 2:22

NOTE
urge you, brethren, *n*..... Rom 16:17
n those who so walk...... Phil 3:17

NOTHING
For now you are *n*........ Job 6:21
rich, yet has *n*.......... Prov 13:7
"It is good for *n*....... Prov 20:14
before Him are as *n*........ Is 40:17
their works are *n*.......... Is 41:29
I can of Myself do *n*..... John 5:30
Me you can do *n*....... John 15:5
men, it will come to *n*..... Acts 5:38
bring to *n* the things ..... 1 Cor 1:28
For I know of *n* against.... 1 Cor 4:4
have not love, I am *n* ..... 1 Cor 13:2
love, it profits me *n* ..... 1 Cor 13:3
Be anxious for *n*.......... Phil 4:6
For we brought *n*....... 1 Tim 6:7
complete, lacking *n* ...... James 1:4
name's sake, taking *n* ..... 3 John 7

NOTORIOUS
n prisoner called .... Matt 27:16

NOURISHED
"I have *n* and............. Is 1:2
n and knit together....... Col 2:19
n in the words of........ 1 Tim 4:6

NOURISHES
n and cherishes it....... Eph 5:29

NOVICE
not a *n*, lest being....... 1 Tim 3:6

NUMBER
if a man could *n*........ Gen 13:16
that I may know the *n*... 2 Sam 24:2
things without *n* .... Job 5:9
For now You *n* my steps..... Job 14:16
n the clouds by wisdom..... Job 38:37
teach us to *n* our days...... Ps 90:12
He counts the *n*.......... Ps 147:4
which no one could *n*...... Rev 7:9
His *n* is 666 .... Rev 13:18

NUMBERED
are more than can be *n* ..... Ps 40:5
God has *n* your kingdom .. Dan 5:26
'And He was *n* with ..... Luke 22:37

OAKS
Wail, O *o* of Bashan ...... Zech 11:2

OATH
people feared the *o*..... 1 Sam 14:26
for the sake of your *o*...... Eccl 8:2
I may establish the *o* ...... Jer 11:5
And you shall be an *o* ..... Jer 42:18
he denied with an *o*..... Matt 26:72
o which He swore .... Luke 1:73
themselves under an *o*.... Acts 23:12

OATHS
shall perform your o..... Matt 5:33
because of the o........ Matt 14:9

OBADIAH
King Ahab's steward, 1 Kin 18:3–16
—— Prophet of Judah, Obad 1

OBED
Son of Boaz and Ruth, Ruth 4:17–22

OBED-EDOM
Philistine from Gath; ark of the Lord left in his house, 2 Sam 6:10–12; 1 Chr 13:13, 14

OBEDIENCE
and apostleship for o...... Rom 1:5
o many will be made..... Rom 5:19
captivity to the o........ 2 Cor 10:5
confidence in your o..... Philem 21
yet He learned o.......... Heb 5:8
for o and sprinkling....... 1 Pet 1:2

OBEDIENT
you are willing and o....... Is 1:19
of the priests were o....... Acts 6:7
make the Gentiles o...... Rom 15:18
bondservants, be o to..... Eph 6:5
Himself and became o..... Phil 2:8
homemakers, good, o..... Titus 2:5
as o children............ 1 Pet 1:14

OBEY
Lord, that I should o....... Ex 5:2
God and o His voice..... Deut 4:30
o the commandments.... Deut 11:27
His voice we will o....... Josh 24:24
o is better than........ 1 Sam 15:22
they hear of me they o..... Ps 18:44
if you diligently o....... Zech 6:15
o God rather than men.... Acts 5:29
and do not o the truth..... Rom 2:8
yourselves slaves to o..... Rom 6:16
o your parents in all...... Col 3:20
Bondservants, o in all...... Col 3:22
on those who do not o.... 2 Thess 1:8
O those who rule....... Heb 13:17
if some do not o.......... 1 Pet 3:1

OBEYED
of sin, yet you o.......... Rom 6:17
they have not all o..... Rom 10:16
By faith Abraham o....... Heb 11:8
as Sarah o Abraham...... 1 Pet 3:6

OBEYING
o the truth through...... 1 Pet 1:22

OBSCURITY
shall see out of o.......... Is 29:18

OBSERVANCE
the Lord, a solemn o...... Ex 12:42

OBSERVATION
does not come with o.... Luke 17:20

OBSERVE
man, and o the upright.... Ps 37:37
and let your eyes o...... Prov 23:26
o mercy and justice....... Hos 12:6
teaching them to o all... Matt 28:20
o days and months and.... Gal 4:10
o your chaste conduct..... 1 Pet 3:2

OBSERVES
o the wind will not....... Eccl 11:4
He who o the day....... Rom 14:6

OBSERVING
o his natural face...... James 1:23

OBSESSED
nothing, but is o........ 1 Tim 6:4

OBSOLETE
Now what is becoming o... Heb 8:13

OBSTINATE
and made his heart o..... Deut 2:30
I knew that you were o...... Is 48:4

OBTAIN
They shall o joy and....... Is 35:10
they also may o mercy... Rom 11:31
o salvation through.... 1 Thess 5:9
and covet and cannot o... James 4:2

OBTAINED
o a part in this.......... Acts 1:17
yet have now o mercy.... Rom 11:30
endured, he o the...... Heb 6:15
To those who have o...... 2 Pet 1:1

OBTAINS
o favor from the Lord..... Prov 8:35

ODED
Prophet of Samaria, 2 Chr 28:9–15

OFFEND
I will o no more.......... Job 34:31
that devour him will o...... Jer 2:3
lest we o them.......... Matt 17:27
than that he should o.... Luke 17:2
them, "Does this o...... John 6:61

OFFENDED
So they were o at Him.... Matt 13:57
stumbles or is o........ Rom 14:21

OFFENDER
who make a man an o..... Is 29:21
For if I am an o........ Acts 25:11

OFFENSE
and a rock of o............ Is 8:14
You are an o to Me...... Matt 16:23
by the one man's o..... Rom 5:17
Give no o............. 1 Cor 10:32
the o of the cross......... Gal 5:11
sincere and without o..... Phil 1:10
and a rock of o......... 1 Pet 2:8

OFFENSES
For o must come........ Matt 18:7
impossible that no o..... Luke 17:1
up because of our o...... Rom 4:25

OFFER
o the blind as a.......... Mal 1:8
come and o your gift..... Matt 5:24
let us continually o....... Heb 13:15

OFFERED
to eat those things o..... 1 Cor 8:10
the eternal Spirit o....... Heb 9:14
so Christ was o.......... Heb 9:28
o one sacrifice.......... Heb 10:12
By faith Abel o......... Heb 11:4

OFFERING
you shall bring your o...... Lev 1:2
o You did not require....... Ps 40:6
You made His soul an o..... Is 53:10
to the Lord an o........ Mal 3:3
Himself for us, an o...... Eph 5:2
out as a drink o.......... Phil 2:17
o You did not.......... Heb 10:5
o He has perfected...... Heb 10:14
is no longer an o........ Heb 10:18

OFFERINGS
and offered burnt o....... Gen 8:20
He remember all your o..... Ps 20:3
In burnt o and........ Heb 10:6

OFFICE
let another take his o...... Ps 109:8
sitting at the tax o....... Matt 9:9

OFFICERS
also make your o......... Is 60:17

OFFSCOURING
You have made us an o... Lam 3:45
the o of all things....... 1 Cor 4:13

OFFSPRING
My blessing on your o...... Is 44:3
He seeks godly o....... Mal 2:15
wife and raise up o..... Matt 22:24
For we are also His o..... Acts 17:28
am the Root and the O.... Rev 22:16

OFTEN
o I wanted to gather..... Luke 13:34
as o as you eat this..... 1 Cor 11:26
in sleeplessness o....... 2 Cor 11:27
should offer Himself o..... Heb 9:25

OG
Amorite king of Bashan, Deut 3:1–13
Defeated and killed by Israel, Num 21:32–35

OHOLAH
Symbolic name of Samaria, Ezek 23:4, 5, 36

OIL
for the anointing o......... Ex 25:6
I cease giving my o...... Judg 9:9
a bin, and a little o..... 1 Kin 17:12
poured out rivers of o..... Job 29:6
anointed with fresh o..... Ps 92:10
the heart of man, o....... Ps 104:15
like the precious o....... Ps 133:2
be as excellent o....... Ps 141:5
thousand rivers of o...... Mic 6:7
very costly fragrant o..... Matt 26:7
o might have been sold... Matt 26:9
anointing him with o..... James 5:14
and do not harm the o..... Rev 6:6

OINTMENT
O and perfume delight.... Prov 27:9
your name is o.......... Song 1:3

OLD
young, and now am o...... Ps 37:25
all manner, new and o.... Song 7:13
was said to those of o..... Matt 5:21
yet fifty years o......... John 8:57
but when you are o...... John 21:18
Your o men shall dream... Acts 2:17
o man was crucified..... Rom 6:6
of the O Testament...... 2 Cor 3:14
o things have passed..... 2 Cor 5:17
have put off the o man.... Col 3:9
obsolete and growing o.... Heb 8:13
that serpent of o....... Rev 20:2

OLDER
o shall serve the........ Gen 25:23
o than your father........ Job 15:10
"Now his o son was..... Luke 15:25
not rebuke an o man.... 1 Tim 5:1
o women as mothers...... 1 Tim 5:2

OLDEST
beginning with the o...... John 8:9

OLIVE
a freshly plucked o........ Gen 8:11
I am like a green o..... Ps 52:8
of the o may fail........ Hab 3:17
o tree which is wild..... Rom 11:24

OLIVES, MOUNT OF
David flees to, 2 Sam 15:30
Prophecy concerning, Zech 14:4
Christ's triumphal entry from, Matt 21:1
Prophetic discourse delivered from, Matt 24:3
Christ's ascension from, Acts 1:9–12

OMNIPOTENT
For the Lord God O....... Rev 19:6

OMRI
Made king of Israel by army, 1 Kin 16:16, 21, 22
Builds Samaria; reigns wickedly, 1 Kin 16:23–27

ON
City of Lower Egypt; center of sun worship, Gen 41:45, 50
Called Beth Shemesh, Jer 43:13

ONAN
Second son of Judah; slain for failure to give his brother an heir, Gen 38:8–10

ONCE
died, He died to sin *o* ..... Rom 6:10
for men to die *o* .... Heb 9:27
also suffered *o* .... 1 Pet 3:18

ONE
God may speak in *o* way ... Job 33:14
Two are better than *o* ..... Eccl 4:9
"*O* thing you lack ...... Mark 10:21
o thing is needed .... Luke 10:42
I and My Father are *o* .... John 10:30
Me, that they may be *o* ... John 17:11
o accord in the temple ..... Acts 2:46
for you are all *o* .... Gal 3:28
to create in Himself *o* ...... Eph 2:15
o body and *o* Spirit .... Eph 4:4
o hope of your calling ..... Eph 4:4
o Lord, *o* faith, *o* .... Eph 4:5
o God and Father of .... Eph 4:6
For there is *o* God and .... 1 Tim 2:5
o Mediator between God .. 1 Tim 2:5
the husband of *o* wife..... 1 Tim 3:2
a thousand years as *o* ..... 2 Pet 3:8
and these three are *o* ..... 1 John 5:7

ONESIMUS
Slave of Philemon converted by Paul in Rome, Philem 10–17
With Tychicus, carries Paul's letters to Colosse and to Philemon, Col 4:7–9

ONESIPHORUS
Ephesian Christian commended for his service, 2 Tim 1:16–18

OPEN
o His lips against you ..... Job 11:5
You *o* Your hand .... Ps 104:28
O your mouth for the ..... Prov 31:8
and no one shall *o* .... Is 22:22
a lamb in *o* country ...... Hos 4:16
Can a demon the eyes .. John 10:21
our heart is wide *o* ...... 2 Cor 6:11
things are naked and *o* .... Heb 4:13
o the scroll and to .... Rev 5:2

OPENED
o not His mouth .... Is 53:7
Then their eyes were *o* ... Luke 24:31
o the Scriptures .... Luke 24:32
o their understanding .... Luke 24:45
effective door has *o* ...... 1 Cor 16:9
when the Lamb *o* .... Rev 6:1
Now I saw heaven *o* ..... Rev 19:11

OPENS
o the ears of men .... Job 33:16
The LORD *o* the eyes of ..... Ps 146:8
him the doorkeeper *o* ..... John 10:3
and shuts and no one *o* .... Rev 3:7

OPHIR
Famous for gold, 1 Chr 29:4

OPHRAH
Town in Manasseh; home of Gideon, Judg 6:11, 15
Site of Gideon's burial, Judg 8:32

OPINION
dared not declare my *o* ..... Job 32:6
be wise in your own *o* .... Rom 11:25

OPINIONS
falter between two *o* ..... 1 Kin 18:21

OPPORTUNITY
But sin, taking *o* .... Rom 7:8
as we have *o* .... Gal 6:10
but you lacked *o* .... Phil 4:10
they would have had *o* ... Heb 11:15

OPPOSES
who *o* and exalts .... 2 Thess 2:4

OPPRESS
you shall not *o* .... Lev 25:17
You that You should *o* ..... Job 10:3
He does not *o* .... Job 37:23
he loves to *o* .... Hos 12:7
o the widow or the .... Zech 7:10
Do not the rich *o* .... James 2:6

OPPRESSED
Whom have I *o* .... 1 Sam 12:3
For he has *o* and .... Job 20:19
fatherless and the *o* ...... Ps 10:18
for all who are *o* .... Ps 103:6
The tears of the *o* .... Eccl 4:1
He was *o* and He was .... Is 53:7
her midst, and the *o* ...... Amos 3:9
healing all who were *o* ... Acts 10:38
Lot, who was *o* by .... 2 Pet 2:7

OPPRESSES
o the poor reproaches .... Prov 14:31
o the poor to increase ... Prov 22:16
A poor man who *o* ...... Prov 28:3

OPPRESSION
have surely seen the *o* ...... Ex 3:7
"For the *o* of the .... Ps 12:5
Do not trust in *o* .... Ps 62:10
their life from *o* .... Ps 72:14
brought low through *o* .... Ps 107:39
Redeem me from the *o* .... Ps 119:134
considered all the *o* .... Eccl 4:1
o destroys a wise .... Eccl 7:7
justice, but behold, *o* .... Is 5:7
surely seen the *o* .... Acts 7:34

OPPRESSIONS
of *o* they cry out .... Job 35:9

OPPRESSOR
the voice of the *o* .... Job 3:18
Do not envy the *o* .... Prov 3:31
is a great *o* .... Prov 28:16
of the fury of the *o* .... Is 51:13
No more shall an *o* .... Zech 9:8

OPPRESSORS
not leave me to my *o* ..... Ps 119:121
o there is power .... Eccl 4:1

ORACLES
received the living *o* ..... Acts 7:38
were committed the *o* ..... Rom 3:2
principles of the *o* .... Heb 5:12
let him speak as the *o* .... 1 Pet 4:11

ORDAINED
infants You have *o* .... Ps 8:2
o you a prophet .... Jer 1:5
the Man whom He has *o* .. Acts 17:31

ORDER
'Set your house in *o* ..... 2 Kin 20:1
set your words in *o* .... Job 33:5
you, and set them in *o* ..... Ps 50:21
swept, and put in *o* ..... Matt 12:44
done decently and in *o* .. 1 Cor 14:40
each one in his own *o* ... 1 Cor 15:23
to see your good *o* .... Col 2:5
according to the *o* .... Heb 5:6

ORDERS
o his conduct aright I ...... Ps 50:23

ORDINANCE
resists the *o* of God ...... Rom 13:2
yourselves to every *o* .... 1 Pet 2:13

ORDINANCES
Do you know the *o* .... Job 38:33
"If those *o* depart .... Jer 31:36
not appointed the *o* ...... Jer 33:25
gone away from My *o* ...... Mal 3:7
and fleshly imposed ..... Heb 9:10

ORION
Brilliant constellation, Job 9:9

ORNAMENT
will be a graceful *o* .... Prov 1:9
of gold and an *o* .... Prov 25:12
with them all as an *o* ...... Is 49:18

ORNAMENTS
a virgin forget her *o* .... Jer 2:32

ORPAH
Ruth's sister-in-law, Ruth 1:4, 14

ORPHANS
We have become *o* .... Lam 5:3
I will not leave you *o* .... John 14:18
to visit *o* and widows .... James 1:27

OSNAPPER
Called "the great and noble," Ezra 4:10

OSTRICHES
o will dwell there .... Is 13:21
is cruel, like *o* .... Lam 4:3
a mourning like the *o* ...... Mic 1:8

OTHNIEL
Son of Kenaz, Caleb's youngest brother, Judg 1:13
Captures Kirjath Sepher; receives Caleb's daughter as wife, Josh 15:15–17
First judge of Israel, Judg 3:9–11

OUGHT
what Israel *o* to do ...... 1 Chr 12:32
These you *o* to have ..... Matt 23:23
pray for as we *o* .... Rom 8:26
how you *o* to conduct .... 1 Tim 3:15
which they *o* not .... 1 Tim 5:13
persons *o* you to be .... 2 Pet 3:11

OUTCAST
they called you an *o* ...... Jer 30:17

OUTCASTS
gathers together the *o* ..... Ps 147:2
will assemble the *o* .... Is 11:12
hide the *o* .... Is 16:3
Let My *o* dwell with .... Is 16:4

OUTCRY
that there be no *o* .... Ps 144:14

OUTRAGE
lewdness and *o* in .... Judg 20:6

OUTRAN
the other disciple *o* ...... John 20:4

OUTSIDE
and dish, that the *o* ..... Matt 23:26
Pharisees make the *o* ... Luke 11:39
toward those who are *o* ..... Col 4:5
to Him, *o* the camp ...... Heb 13:13
But *o* are dogs and .... Rev 22:15

OUTSTRETCHED
and with an *o* arm ...... Deut 26:8
against you with an *o* .... Jer 21:5

OUTWARD
at the *o* appearance ..... 1 Sam 16:7
adornment be merely *o* ... 1 Pet 3:3

OUTWARDLY
appear beautiful o . . . . . Matt 23:27
not a Jew who is one o . . . . Rom 2:28

OUTWIT
The enemy shall not o . . . . . Ps 89:22

OVEN
make them as a fiery o . . . . . Ps 21:9
burning like an o . . . . Mal 4:1
is thrown into the o . . . . . . Matt 6:30

OVERCAME
My throne, as I also o . . . . . Rev 3:21
And they o him by . . . . Rev 12:11

OVERCOME
good cheer, I have o . . . . . John 16:33
o evil with good . . . . Rom 12:21
because you have o . . . . 1 John 2:13
and the Lamb will o . . . . . . Rev 17:14

OVERCOMES
of God o the world . . . . . . 1 John 5:4
o I will give to eat . . . . Rev 2:7
o shall not be hurt . . . . Rev 2:11
o shall inherit all . . . . Rev 21:7

OVERFLOWING
My heart is o with a . . . . Ps 45:1

OVERSEER
Then he made him o . . . . . Gen 39:4
having no captain, o . . . . . . Prov 6:7
to the Shepherd and O . . . . 1 Pet 2:25

OVERSEERS
Spirit has made you o . . . . Acts 20:28
you, serving as o . . . . 1 Pet 5:2

OVERSHADOW
of the Highest will o . . . . . . Luke 1:35

OVERTAKE
does righteousness o . . . . Is 59:9
you feared shall o . . . . Jer 42:16
and o this chariot . . . . Acts 8:29
that this Day should o . . . 1 Thess 5:4

OVERTAKEN
No temptation has o . . . . 1 Cor 10:13
if a man is o in any . . . . Gal 6:1

OVERTHREW
So He o those cities . . . . . . Gen 19:25
will be as when God o . . . . . Is 13:19
As God o Sodom and . . . . . Jer 50:40
"I o some of you . . . . Amos 4:11

OVERTHROW
you shall utterly o . . . . Ex 23:24
o the righteous in . . . . Prov 18:5
o the throne of . . . . Hag 2:22
o the faith of some . . . . . 2 Tim 2:18

OVERTHROWN
Their judges are o . . . . Ps 141:6
of Sodom, which was o . . . . Lam 4:6
I will make it o . . . . Ezek 21:27
and Nineveh shall be o . . . . . Jon 3:4

OVERTHROWS
and o the mighty . . . . Job 12:19
o them in the night . . . . . . Job 34:25
o the words of the . . . . . . Prov 22:12

OVERTURNED
my heart is o within . . . . . Lam 1:20
o the tables of the . . . . . . Matt 21:12
money and o the tables . . . John 2:15

OVERWHELM
o the fatherless . . . . Job 6:27
sends them out, they o . . . . Job 12:15

OVERWHELMED
when my heart is o . . . . Ps 61:2
and my spirit was o . . . . Ps 77:3

o their enemies . . . . Ps 78:53
waters would have o . . . . . . Ps 124:4
my spirit is o within . . . . . . Ps 143:4

OVERWORK
Do not o to be rich . . . . . . Prov 23:4

OWE
'How much do you o . . . . Luke 16:5
O no one anything . . . . . . Rom 13:8
o me even your own . . . . . Philem 19

OWED
o him ten thousand . . . . Matt 18:24
fellow servants who o . . . . Matt 18:28
o five hundred denarii . . . . Luke 7:41

OWN
He came to His o . . . . John 1:11
having loved His o . . . . John 13:1
world would love its o . . . John 15:19
and you are not your o . . . 1 Cor 6:19
But each one has his o . . . 1 Cor 7:7
For all seek their o . . . . Phil 2:21
from our sins in His o . . . . . . Rev 1:5

OX
shall not muzzle an o . . . . Deut 25:4
"Will the wild o . . . . Job 39:9
you bind the wild o . . . . . . Job 39:10
like a young wild o . . . . Ps 29:6
exalted like a wild o . . . . . . Ps 92:10
o knows its owner . . . . Is 1:3
had the face of an o . . . . . Ezek 1:10
Sabbath loose his o . . . . . Luke 13:15
shall not muzzle an o . . . . 1 Cor 9:9

PACE
are majestic in p . . . . Prov 30:29

PACIFIES
A gift in secret p . . . . Prov 21:14
for conciliation p . . . . Eccl 10:4

PADAN ARAM
Same as Mesopotamia, Gen 24:10;
    see MESOPOTAMIA
Home of Isaac's wife, Gen 25:20
Jacob flees to, Gen 28:2–7
Jacob returns from, Gen 31:17, 18
People of, called Syrians, Gen 31:24
Language of, called Aramaic,
    2 Kin 18:26

PAIN
p you shall bring . . . . Gen 3:16
p as a woman in . . . . Is 13:8
are filled with p . . . . Is 21:3
before him p came . . . . Is 66:7
Why is my p perpetual . . . . Jer 15:18
shall be no more p . . . . Rev 21:4

PAINED
My heart is severely p . . . . . . Ps 55:4
I am p in my very . . . . Jer 4:19

PAINFUL
this, it was too p . . . . Ps 73:16
for the present, but p . . . . . Heb 12:11

PAINS
The p of death . . . . Ps 116:3
having loosed the p . . . . . . Acts 2:24
upon them, as labor p . . . 1 Thess 5:3

PAINT
and she put p on her . . . . . 2 Kin 9:30
your eyes with p . . . . Jer 4:30

PAINTING
it with cedar and p . . . . . . Jer 22:14

PALACE
enter the King's p . . . . Ps 45:15
a p of foreigners . . . . Is 25:2

guards his own p . . . . Luke 11:21
evident to the whole p . . . . Phil 1:13

PALACES
out of the ivory p . . . . Ps 45:8
God is in her p . . . . Ps 48:3
has entered our p . . . . Jer 9:21

PALE
his face now grow p . . . . . . Is 29:22
and all faces turned p . . . . Jer 30:6
behold, a p horse . . . . Rev 6:8

PALM
of water and seventy p . . . . Ex 15:27
p trees and went out . . . . John 12:13
p branches in their . . . . Rev 7:9

PALMS
struck Him with the p . . . . Matt 26:67

PALTI (or Paltiel)
Man to whom Saul gives Michal,
    David's wife, in marriage, 1 Sam
    25:44; 2 Sam 3:15

PAMPERS
p his servant from . . . . . . Prov 29:21

PAMPHYLIA
People from, at Pentecost, Acts 2:10
Paul visits; John Mark returns home
    from, Acts 13:13; 15:38
Paul preaches in cities of, Acts
    14:24, 25

PANGS
The p of death . . . . Ps 18:4
P and sorrows will . . . . Is 13:8
labors with birth p . . . . . . Rom 8:22

PANICKED
the men of Benjamin p . . . Judg 20:41

PANT
They p after the dust . . . . . Amos 2:7

PANTS
As the deer p for the . . . . . . Ps 42:1

PAPHOS
Paul blinds Elymas at, Acts 13:6–13

PAPYRUS
"Can the p grow up . . . . . . Job 8:11

PARABLE
open my mouth in a p . . . . . Ps 78:2
p He did not speak . . . . . Matt 13:34
do You speak this p . . . . . Luke 12:41

PARABLES
'Does he not speak p . . . . Ezek 20:49
understand all the p . . . . Mark 4:13
rest it is given in p . . . . . . Luke 8:10

PARADE
love does not p . . . . 1 Cor 13:4

PARADISE
will be with Me in P . . . . . Luke 23:43
was caught up into P . . . . 2 Cor 12:4
in the midst of the P . . . . Rev 2:7

PARAN
Residence of exiled Ishmael,
    Gen 21:21
Israelites camp in, Num 10:12
Headquarters of spies, Num 13:3, 26
Site of David's refuge, 1 Sam 25:1

PARCHMENTS
especially the p . . . . 2 Tim 4:13

PARDON
p your transgressions . . . . . Ex 23:21
O LORD, p my iniquity . . . . . Ps 25:11
He will abundantly p . . . . . . Is 55:7
p all their iniquities . . . . . . Jer 33:8

PARDONING
is a God like You, *p* . . . . Mic 7:18

PARENTS
will rise up against *p* . . . . Matt 10:21
has left house or *p* . . . . . . Luke 18:29
disobedient to *p* . . . . Rom 1:30
to lay up for the *p* . . . . . 2 Cor 12:14

PARMENAS
One of the first seven deacons, Acts 6:5

PART
You have no *p* in the . . . . . Josh 22:25
has chosen that good *p*. . . Luke 10:42
you, you have no *p* . . . . . . John 13:8
For we know in *p* . . . . 1 Cor 13:9
p has a believer . . . . 2 Cor 6:15
shall take away his *p* . . . . . Rev 22:19

PARTAKE
for we all *p* of that . . . . . . 1 Cor 10:17
you cannot *p* of the . . . . . 1 Cor 10:21

PARTAKER
and have been a *p* . . . . Ps 50:18
in hope should be *p*. . . . . . 1 Cor 9:10
Christ, and also a *p* . . . . . . 1 Pet 5:1

PARTAKERS
Gentiles have been *p*. . . . . Rom 15:27
of the sacrifices *p* . . . . . . 1 Cor 10:18
know that as you are *p*. . . . 2 Cor 1:7
gospel, you all are *p* . . . . . . Phil 1:7
qualified us to be *p* . . . . . . Col 1:12
For we have become *p* . . . . . Heb 3:14

PARTED
them, that He was *p*. . . . . Luke 24:51
so sharp that they *p*. . . . . . Acts 15:39

PARTIAL
You shall not be *p* . . . . Lev 19:15

PARTIALITY
You shall not show *p* . . . . . Deut 1:17
unjustly, and show *p*. . . . . . Ps 82:2
is not good to show *p* . . . . Prov 18:5
but have shown *p* . . . . Mal 2:9
that God shows no *p* . . . . . Acts 10:34
For there is no *p* . . . . Rom 2:11
doing nothing with *p* . . . . . 1 Tim 5:21
but if you show *p* . . . . James 2:9
good fruits, without *p* . . . . James 3:17

PARTIES
revelries, drinking *p* . . . . . . 1 Pet 4:3

PARTITION
the Testimony, and *p* . . . . . . Ex 40:3

PARTNER
Whoever is a *p* with a . . . . Prov 29:24
you count me as a *p* . . . . . Philem 17

PARTRIDGE
when one hunts a *p*. . . . 1 Sam 26:20

PARTS
anything but death *p* . . . . . Ruth 1:17
in the inward *p* . . . . Ps 51:6
Shout, you lower *p* . . . . Is 44:23
but our presentable *p*. . . . 1 Cor 12:24
into the lower *p* . . . . Eph 4:9

PASHHUR
Official opposing Jeremiah, Jer 21:1; 38:1–13
——— Priest who puts Jeremiah in jail, Jer 20:1–6

PASS
I will *p* over you . . . . Ex 12:13
All have come to *p*. . . . . . Josh 23:14
of the sea that *p* . . . . Ps 8:8
When you *p* through the. . . . . Is 43:2

PASSED
"I will make you *p*. . . . . . Ezek 20:37
I will not *p* by them . . . . . . Amos 7:8
and earth will *p* . . . . Matt 24:35

PASSED
And behold, the LORD *p* . . 1 Kin 19:11
forbearance God had *p*. . . . . Rom 3:25
High Priest who has *p* . . . . . Heb 4:14
know that we have *p*. . . . 1 John 3:14

PASSES
For the wind *p* over it . . . . Ps 103:16
of Christ which *p* . . . . Eph 3:19

PASSION
than to burn with *p*. . . . . . 1 Cor 7:9
uncleanness, *p*, evil. . . . . Col 3:5

PASSIONS
gave them up to vile *p* . . . . Rom 1:26

PASSOVER
It is the LORD's *P* . . . . Ex 12:11
of King Josiah this *P*. . . . 2 Kin 23:23
I will keep the *P* . . . . Matt 26:18
indeed Christ, our *P*. . . . . . 1 Cor 5:7
By faith he kept the *P*. . . . . Heb 11:28

PAST
My days are *p* . . . . Job 17:11
lo, the winter is *p* . . . . Song 2:11
and His ways *p* finding . . . . Rom 11:33
ways spoke in time *p*. . . . . . Heb 1:1
p lifetime in doing . . . . 1 Pet 4:3

PASTORS
and some *p* and . . . . Eph 4:11

PASTURE
the sheep of Your *p* . . . . Ps 74:1
the people of His *p* . . . . Ps 95:7
feed them in good *p* . . . . Ezek 34:14
in and out and find *p*. . . . . John 10:9

PASTURES
to lie down in green *p*. . . . . Ps 23:2

PATH
p no bird knows. . . . . Job 28:7
You will show me the *p* . . . . Ps 16:11
lead me in a smooth *p* . . . . Ps 27:11
But the *p* of the just. . . . . . Prov 4:18
way in the sea and a *p* . . . . Is 43:16

PATHROS
Described as a lowly kingdom, Ezek 29:14–16
Refuge for dispersed Jews, Jer 44:1–15
Jews to be regathered from, Is 11:11

PATHS
He leads me in the *p*. . . . . . Ps 23:3
Teach me Your *p* . . . . Ps 25:4
and all her *p* are . . . . Prov 3:17
p they have not . . . . Is 42:16
themselves crooked *p*. . . . . . Is 59:8
Make His *p* straight . . . . . . Matt 3:3
and make straight *p*. . . . . . Heb 12:13

PATIENCE
'Master, have *p* . . . Matt 18:26
and bear fruit with *p* . . . . Luke 8:15
Now may the God of *p* . . . . Rom 15:5
labor of love, and *p* . . . . . 1 Thess 1:3
faith, love, *p* . . . . 1 Tim 6:11
your faith produces *p* . . . . James 1:3
p have its perfect . . . . James 1:4
in the kingdom and *p* . . . . . Rev 1:9
Here is the *p* and the. . . . . Rev 13:10

PATIENT
rejoicing in hope, *p* . . . . . Rom 12:12
uphold the weak, be *p* . . 1 Thess 5:14

PATIENTLY
the LORD, and wait *p*. . . . . . Ps 37:7
if you take it *p* . . . . 1 Pet 2:20

PATMOS
John, banished here, receives the Revelation, Rev 1:9

PATRIARCHS
begot the twelve *p* . . . . Acts 7:8

PATTERN
p which you were . . . . Ex 26:30
as you have us for a *p* . . . . Phil 3:17
Hold fast the *p*. . . . . 2 Tim 1:13
p shown you on the. . . . . . . Heb 8:5

PAUL
Roman citizen from Tarsus; studied under Gamaliel, Acts 22:3, 25–28
Originally called Saul; persecutes the church, Acts 7:58; 8:1, 3; 9:1, 2
Converted on road to Damascus, Acts 9:3–19
Preaches in Damascus; escapes to Jerusalem and then to Tarsus, Acts 9:20–30
Ministers in Antioch; sent to Jerusalem, Acts 11:25–30
First missionary journey, Acts 13; 14
Speaks for Gentiles at Jerusalem Council, Acts 15:1–5, 12
Second missionary journey, Acts 15:36—18:22
Third missionary journey, Acts 18:23—21:14
Arrested in Jerusalem; defense before Roman authorities, Acts 21:15—26:32
Sent to Rome, Acts 27:1—28:31
His epistles, Rom; 1 and 2 Cor; Gal; Eph; Phil; Col; 1 and 2 Thess; 1 and 2 Tim; Titus; Philem

PAULUS, SERGIUS
Roman proconsul of Cyprus, Acts 13:4, 7

PAVILION
shall hide me in His *p*. . . . . . Ps 27:5
them secretly in a *p*. . . . . . Ps 31:20

PAWS
He *p* in the valley . . . . Job 39:21

PAY
with which to *p* . . . . Prov 22:27
priests teach for *p* . . . . Mic 3:11
with me, and I will *p* . . . . Matt 18:26
p taxes to Caesar . . . . Matt 22:17
For you *p* tithe of . . . . Matt 23:23

PEACE
"These men are at *p* . . . . . Gen 34:21
I will give *p* in the. . . . . . . Lev 26:6
you, and give you *p* . . . . . Num 6:26
'Make *p* with me by a . . . 2 Kin 18:31
field shall be at *p* . . . . Job 5:23
both lie down in *p* . . . . Ps 4:8
seek *p* and pursue it . . . . . Ps 34:14
for He will speak *p* . . . . Ps 85:8
p have those who . . . . Ps 119:165
I am for *p* . . . . Ps 120:7
for the *p* of Jerusalem . . . . . Ps 122:6
P be within your walls. . . . . Ps 122:7
P be upon Israel . . . . Ps 125:5
war, and a time of *p*. . . . . . Eccl 3:8
Father, Prince of *P* . . . . Is 9:6
keep him in perfect *p*. . . . . Is 26:3
p they have not . . . . Is 59:8
slightly, saying, '*P* . . . . Jer 6:14
"We looked for *p*. . . . . Jer 8:15
give you assured *p* . . . . . . Jer 14:13
they will seek *p* . . . . Ezek 7:25
P be multiplied . . . . Dan 4:1
this One shall be *p*. . . . . . . Mic 5:5

place I will give *p* . . . . Hag 2:9
is worthy, let your *p*. . . . . Matt 10:13
that I came to bring *p*. . . . Matt 10:34
and on earth *p* . . . . Luke 2:14
if a son of *p* is there . . . . . . Luke 10:6
that make for your *p* . . . . Luke 19:42
I leave with you, My *p* . . . John 14:27
in Me you may have *p* . . . John 16:33
Grace to you and *p*. . . . . . . Rom 1:7
by faith, we have *p*. . . . . . . Rom 5:1
God has called us to *p* . . . . 1 Cor 7:15
p will be with you. . . . . . . 2 Cor 13:11
Spirit is love, joy, *p* . . . . . . Gal 5:22
He Himself is our *p*. . . . . . . Eph 2:14
and the *p* of God . . . . Phil 4:7
heaven, having made *p* . . . . Col 1:20
And let the *p* of God . . . . . . Col 3:15
Be at *p* among . . . . 1 Thess 5:13
faith, love, *p* . . . . 2 Tim 2:22
meaning "king of *p*," . . . . . . Heb 7:2
is sown in *p* by those . . . . James 3:18
p be multiplied. . . . . 2 Pet 1:2

PEACEABLE
and *p* life in all . . . . 1 Tim 2:2
is first pure, then *p* . . . . . James 3:17

PEACEABLY
on you, live *p*. . . . . Rom 12:18

PEACEFUL
in a *p* habitation . . . . Is 32:18

PEACEMAKERS
Blessed are the *p*. . . . . Matt 5:9

PEARL
had found one *p* . . . . Matt 13:46
gate was of one *p* . . . . . . Rev 21:21

PEARLS
nor cast your *p* . . . . Matt 7:6
hair or gold or *p* . . . . 1 Tim 2:9
gates were twelve *p* . . . . . . Rev 21:21

PEG
wife, took a tent *p* . . . . Judg 4:21
will fasten him as a *p* . . . . . . Is 22:23

PEKAH
Son of Remaliah; usurps Israel's
  throne, 2 Kin 15:25–28
Forms alliance with Rezin of Syria
  against Ahaz, Is 7:1–9
Alliance defeated; captives returned,
  2 Kin 16:5–9
Territory of, overrun by Tiglath-
  Pileser, 2 Kin 15:29
Assassinated by Hoshea, 2 Kin 15:30

PEKAHIAH
Son of Menahem; king of Israel,
  2 Kin 15:22–26
Assassinated by Pekah, 2 Kin
  15:23–25

PEN
My tongue is the *p* . . . . Ps 45:1
on it with a man's *p* . . . . Is 8:1
to write to you with *p* . . . . . 3 John 13

PENNY
have paid the last *p* . . . . . Matt 5:26

PENTECOST
P had fully come . . . . Acts 2:1

PENUEL
Place east of Jordan; site of Jacob's
  wrestling with angel, Gen 32:24–31
Inhabitants of, slain by Gideon, Judg
  8:8, 9, 17

PEOPLE
will take you as My *p*. . . . . . . Ex 6:7
Who is like you, a *p* . . . . . Deut 33:29

p shall be my *p* . . . . Ruth 1:16
if My *p* who are called. . . . 2 Chr 7:14
p who know the joyful. . . . . Ps 89:15
We are His *p* and the. . . . . . Ps 100:3
Happy are the *p*. . . . . Ps 144:15
"Blessed is Egypt My *p*. . . . . Is 19:25
this is a rebellious *p*. . . . . . . Is 30:9
p who provoke Me. . . . . Is 65:3
and they shall be My *p* . . . . Jer 24:7
for you are not My *p*. . . . . . . Hos 1:9
like *p*, like priest. . . . . Hos 4:9
to make ready a *p*. . . . . Luke 1:17
take out of them a *p* . . . . . Acts 15:14
who were not My *p*. . . . . . . Rom 9:25
and they shall be My *p* . . . 2 Cor 6:16
His own special *p* . . . . Titus 2:14
LORD will judge His *p* . . . . Heb 10:30
but are now the *p*. . . . . 1 Pet 2:10
tribe and tongue and *p* . . . . . Rev 5:9
they shall be His *p* . . . . Rev 21:3

PEOR
Mountain of Moab opposite Jericho,
  Num 23:28
Israel's camp seen from, Num 24:2
—— Moabite god called Baal of Peor,
  Num 25:3, 5, 18
Israelites punished for worship of,
  Num 31:16

PERCEIVE
given you a heart to *p* . . . . Deut 29:4
but I cannot *p* . . . . Job 23:8
seeing, but do not *p*. . . . . Is 6:9
may see and not *p*. . . . . . . Mark 4:12

PERDITION
except the son of *p* . . . . . John 17:12
to them a proof of *p*. . . . . . Phil 1:28
revealed, the son of *p*. . . . 2 Thess 2:3
who draw back to *p* . . . . . Heb 10:39
day of judgment and *p* . . . . 2 Pet 3:7

PEREZ
One of Judah's twin sons by Tamar,
  Gen 38:24–30

PERFECT
Noah was a just man, *p* . . . . Gen 6:9
one who is *p* in . . . . Job 36:4
for God, His way is *p*. . . . . . Ps 18:30
You were *p* in your. . . . . . . Ezek 28:15
Father in heaven is *p*. . . . . Matt 5:48
"If you want to be *p* . . . . . Matt 19:21
they may be made *p*. . . . . John 17:23
and *p* will of God . . . . Rom 12:2
when that which is *p*. . . . . 1 Cor 13:10
present every man *p*. . . . . . Col 1:28
the law made nothing *p* . . . . Heb 7:19
of just men made *p* . . . . . . Heb 12:23
good gift and every *p* . . . . James 1:17
in word, he is a *p* . . . . James 3:2
p love casts out fear. . . . . 1 John 4:18

PERFECTED
third day I shall be *p* . . . . Luke 13:32
or am already *p* . . . . Phil 3:12
the Son who has been *p* . . . . Heb 7:28
the love of God is *p* . . . . . 1 John 2:5

PERFECTION
the *p* of beauty . . . . Ps 50:2
consummation of all *p* . . . . Ps 119:96
let us go on to *p*. . . . . Heb 6:1

PERFORM
p Your statutes . . . . Ps 119:112
am ready to *p* My word . . . . Jer 1:12
how to *p* what is good. . . . . Rom 7:18

PERGA
Visited by Paul, Acts 13:13, 14; 14:25

PERGAMOS
Site of one of the seven churches,
  Rev 1:11
Special message to, Rev 2:12–17

PERIL
or nakedness, or *p*. . . . . . . Rom 8:35

PERILOUS
from the *p* pestilence. . . . . . . Ps 91:3
in the last days *p* . . . . 2 Tim 3:1

PERILS
journeys often, in *p* . . . . . 2 Cor 11:26

PERISH
"Surely we die, we *p* . . . . Num 17:12
All flesh would *p* . . . . Job 34:15
they *p* at the rebuke . . . . . . Ps 80:16
very day his plans *p* . . . . . Ps 146:4
so that we may not *p* . . . . . . Jon 1:6
little ones should *p* . . . . . Matt 18:14
will all likewise *p* . . . . Luke 13:3
in Him should not *p* . . . . . John 3:16
they shall never *p* . . . . . . John 10:28
concern things which *p* . . . . Col 2:22
among those who *p* . . . . . 2 Thess 2:10
that any should *p*. . . . . 2 Pet 3:9

PERISHABLE
do it to obtain a *p* . . . . . . 1 Cor 9:25

PERISHED
p being innocent. . . . . Job 4:7
Truth has *p* and has. . . . . . . Jer 7:28
The faithful man has *p* . . . . . Mic 7:2

PERISHING
We are *p* . . . . Matt 8:25
to those who are *p*. . . . . . . 2 Cor 4:3

PERIZZITES
One of seven Canaanite nations,
  Deut 7:1
Possessed Palestine in Abraham's
  time, Gen 13:7
Jacob's fear of, Gen 34:30
Many of, slain by Judah, Judg 1:4, 5

PERJURER
p shall be expelled . . . . Zech 5:3

PERMIT
the Spirit did not *p*. . . . . . . Acts 16:7
I do not *p* a woman . . . . . 1 Tim 2:12

PERMITS
you, if the Lord *p* . . . . . . 1 Cor 16:7
we will do if God *p*. . . . . . . Heb 6:3

PERMITTED
p no one to do them . . . . . . Ps 105:14

PERPETUATED
Your name shall be *p* . . . . . Nah 1:14

PERPLEXED
at one another, *p*. . . . . John 13:22
we are *p*. . . . . 2 Cor 4:8

PERSECUTE
p me as God does . . . . Job 19:22
p me wrongfully. . . . . Ps 119:86
when they revile and *p*. . . . Matt 5:11
Bless those who *p*. . . . . . . Rom 12:14

PERSECUTED
p the poor and needy . . . . . Ps 109:16
p the prophets who . . . . . . Matt 5:12
If they *p* Me. . . . . John 15:20
p the church of God. . . . . . 1 Cor 15:9
p, but not forsaken . . . . . . 2 Cor 4:9
p us now preaches the . . . . Gal 1:23

PERSECUTES
wicked in his pride *p*. . . . . . Ps 10:2

PERSECUTION
p arises because of. . . . . . Matt 13:21

At that time a great *p* . . . . . . Acts 8:1
do I still suffer *p* . . . . Gal 5:11

PERSECUTOR
a blasphemer, a *p* . . . . 1 Tim 1:13

PERSEVERANCE
tribulation produces *p* . . . . . Rom 5:3
to this end will all *p* . . . . . . Eph 6:18
longsuffering, love, *p* . . . . . 2 Tim 3:10
to self-control *p* . . . . 2 Pet 1:6

PERSEVERE
kept My command to *p* . . . . Rev 3:10

PERSISTENCE
p he will rise and . . . . Luke 11:8

PERSON
In whose eyes a vile *p* . . . . Ps 15:4
p will suffer hunger . . . . . . Prov 19:15
do not regard the *p* . . . . . . Matt 22:16
express image of His *p* . . . . Heb 1:3
let it be the hidden *p* . . . . . 1 Pet 3:4

PERSUADE
"You almost *p* me . . . . Acts 26:28
the Lord, we *p* men . . . . . 2 Cor 5:11
For do I now *p* men . . . . . . Gal 1:10

PERSUADED
a ruler is *p* . . . . Prov 25:15
neither will they be *p* . . . . Luke 16:31
p that He is able . . . . 2 Tim 1:12

PERSUASIVE
p words of human . . . . 1 Cor 2:4
you with *p* words . . . . Col 2:4

PERTAINING
Priest in things *p* . . . . Heb 2:17
for men in things *p* . . . . Heb 5:1

PERTURBED
things the earth is *p* . . . . . Prov 30:21

PERVERSE
your way is *p* . . . . Num 22:32
for the *p* person is an . . . . . Prov 3:32
p lips far from you . . . . Prov 4:24
p heart will be . . . . Prov 12:8
p man sows strife . . . . Prov 16:28
but he who is *p* . . . . Prov 28:18
from this *p* generation . . . . . Acts 2:40

PERVERSITY
in oppression and *p* . . . . Is 30:12

PERVERT
You shall not *p* . . . . Deut 16:19
and *p* all equity . . . . Mic 3:9
p the gospel of Christ . . . . . . Gal 1:7

PERVERTING
We found this fellow *p* . . . . Luke 23:2
will you not cease *p* . . . . . . Acts 13:10

PERVERTS
p the words of the . . . . Ex 23:8
p his ways will become . . . . Prov 10:9

PESTILENCE
from the perilous *p* . . . . Ps 91:3
p that walks in . . . . Ps 91:6
Before Him went *p* . . . . Hab 3:5

PESTILENCES
will be famines, *p* . . . . Matt 24:7

PETER
Fisherman; called to discipleship,
Matt 4:18–20; John 1:40–42
Called as apostle, Matt 10:2–4
Walks on water, Matt 14:28–33
Confesses Christ's deity, Matt
16:13–19
Rebuked by Christ, Matt 16:21–23
Witnesses Transfiguration, Matt
17:1–8; 2 Pet 1:16–18

Denies Christ three times, Matt
26:69–75
Commissioned to feed Christ's sheep,
John 21:15–17
Leads disciples, Acts 1:15–26
Preaches at Pentecost, Acts 2:1–41
Performs miracles, Acts 3:1–11; 5:14–
16; 9:32–43
Called to minister to Gentiles, Acts 10
Defends his visit to Gentiles, Acts
11:1–18
Imprisoned and delivered, Acts
12:3–19
Speaks at Jerusalem Council, Acts
15:7–14
Writes epistles, 1 Pet 1:1; 2 Pet 1:1

PETITION
of Israel grant your *p* . . . . 1 Sam 1:17

PETITIONS
fulfill all your *p* . . . . Ps 20:5
p that we have asked . . . . 1 John 5:15

PHARAOH
Kings of Egypt, contemporaries of:
Abraham, Gen 12:15–20
Joseph, Gen 40; 41
Moses in youth, Ex 1:8–11
the Exodus, Ex 5—14
Solomon, 1 Kin 3:1; 11:17–20
Other Pharaohs, 1 Kin 14:25, 26;
2 Kin 17:4; 18:21; 19:9; 23:29;
Jer 44:30

PHARISEE
to pray, one a *P* . . . . Luke 18:10
and brethren, I am a *P* . . . . Acts 23:6

PHILADELPHIA
City of Lydia in Asia Minor; church
established here, Rev 1:11

PHILEMON
Christian at Colosse to whom Paul
writes, Philem 1
Paul appeals to him to receive Onesimus, Philem 9–21

PHILETUS
False teacher, 2 Tim 2:17, 18

PHILIP
Son of Herod the Great, Matt 14:3
——— One of the twelve apostles, Matt
10:3
Brings Nathanael to Christ, John
1:43–48
Tested by Christ, John 6:5–7
Introduces Greeks to Christ, John
12:20–22
Gently rebuked by Christ, John
14:8–12
——— One of the first seven deacons,
Acts 6:5
Called an evangelist, Acts 21:8
Preaches in Samaria, Acts 8:5–13
Leads the Ethiopian eunuch to
Christ, Acts 8:26–40

PHILIPPI
City of Macedonia (named after
Philip of Macedon); visited by
Paul, Acts 16:12; 20:6
Paul writes letter to church of,
Phil 1:1

PHILISTIA
The land of the Philistines, Gen
21:32, 34; Josh 13:2; Ps 60:8

PHILISTINES
Not attacked by Joshua, Josh 13:1–3
Left to test Israel, Judg 3:1–4

God delivers Israel to, as punish-
ment, Judg 10:6, 7
Israel delivered from, by Samson,
Judg 13—16
Capture, then return the ark of the
Lord, 1 Sam 4—6
Wars and dealings with Saul and
David, 1 Sam 13:15—14:23; 17:1–
52; 18:25–27; 21:10–15; 27:1—28:6;
29:1–11; 31:1–13; 2 Sam 5:17–25
Originally on the island of Caphtor,
Jer 47:4
Prophecies concerning, Is 9:11, 12; Jer
25:15–20; 47:1–7; Ezek 25:15–17;
Zeph 2:4–6

PHILOSOPHERS
p encountered him . . . . Acts 17:18

PHILOSOPHY
cheat you through *p* . . . . Col 2:8

PHINEHAS
Aaron's grandson; executes God's
judgment, Num 25:1–18; Ps
106:30, 31
Settles dispute over memorial altar,
Josh 22:11–32
——— Younger son of Eli; abuses his
office, 1 Sam 1:3; 2:12–17, 22–36
Killed by Philistines, 1 Sam 4:11, 17

PHOENICIA
Mediterranean coastal region including the cities of Ptolemais, Tyre,
Zarephath and Sidon; evangelized by early Christians, Acts
11:19
Jesus preaches here, Matt 15:21

PHRYGIA
Jews from, at Pentecost, Acts 2:1, 10
Visited twice by Paul, Acts 16:6

PHYLACTERIES
They make their *p* . . . . . . Matt 23:5

PHYSICIAN
Gilead, is there no *p* . . . . Jer 8:22
have no need of a *p* . . . . . . Matt 9:12
Luke the beloved *p* . . . . Col 4:14

PHYSICIANS
are all worthless *p* . . . . Job 13:4
her livelihood on *p* . . . . Luke 8:43

PIECES
for my wages thirty *p* . . . . Zech 11:12
they took the thirty *p* . . . . . Matt 27:9
shall be dashed to *p* . . . . Rev 2:17

PIERCE
and his master shall *p* . . . . . . Ex 21:6
a sword will *p* . . . . Luke 2:35

PIERCED
p My hands and My feet . . . . Ps 22:16
on Me whom they have *p* . Zech 12:10
of the soldiers *p* . . . . John 19:34
p themselves through . . . . 1 Tim 6:10
and they also who *p* . . . . Rev 1:7

PIERCING
p even to the division . . . . . . Heb 4:12

PIETY
first learn to show *p* . . . . . . 1 Tim 5:4

PI HAHIROTH
Israel camps there before crossing
the Red Sea, Ex 14:2, 9;
Num 33:7, 8

PILATE, PONTIUS
Governor of Judea (A.D. 26–36),
Luke 3:1

Questions Jesus and delivers Him to Jews, Matt 27:2, 11–26; John 18:28—19:16

PILGRIMAGE
heart is set on *p*. . . . . Ps 84:5
In the house of my *p* . . . . . . Ps 119:54

PILGRIMS
we are aliens and *p* . . . . . 1 Chr 29:15
were strangers and *p* . . . . . Heb 11:13

PILLAR
and she became a *p* . . . . . Gen 19:26
and by night in a *p* . . . . Ex 13:21
the living God, the *p* . . . . 1 Tim 3:15

PILLARS
break their sacred *p* . . . . . . Ex 34:13
I set up its *p* firmly . . . . Ps 75:3
out her seven *p* . . . . Prov 9:1
blood and fire and *p* . . . . . . Joel 2:30
and his feet like *p* . . . . Rev 10:1

PILOT
rudder wherever the *p* . . . . James 3:4

PINE
cypress tree and the *p*. . . . . . Is 41:19
for these *p* away . . . . Lam 4:9

PINNACLE
set Him on the *p*. . . . . Luke 4:9

PISGAH
Balaam offers sacrifice upon, Num 23:14
Moses views Promised Land from, Deut 3:27
Site of Moses' death, Deut 34:1–7

PISHON
One of Eden's four rivers, Gen 2:10, 11

PISIDIA
Twice visited by Paul, Acts 13:13, 14; 14:24

PIT
cast him into some *p* . . . . . Gen 37:20
soul draws near the *P* . . . . . Job 33:22
who go down to the *p* . . . . . . Ps 28:1
woman is a deep *p* . . . . . . Prov 22:14
a harlot is a deep *p* . . . . . Prov 23:27
fall into his own *p* . . . . . . Prov 28:10
my life in the *p* . . . . Lam 3:53
who descend into the *P* . . . Ezek 31:16
up my life from the *p* . . . . . . Jon 2:6
from the waterless *p* . . . . . Zech 9:11
if it falls into a *p* . . . . Matt 12:11
into the bottomless *p* . . . . . Rev 20:3

PITCHERS
hand, with empty *p*. . . . . . Judg 7:16

PITIABLE
of all men the most *p*. . . . 1 Cor 15:19

PITS
The proud have dug *p* . . . . . Ps 119:85

PITY
eye shall have no *p*. . . . . . Deut 7:16
"Have *p* on me. . . . . Job 19:21
for someone to take *p* . . . . . Ps 69:20
He who has *p* on the . . . . . Prov 19:17
p He redeemed them . . . . Is 63:9
land, and *p* His people. . . . . Joel 2:18
And should I not *p* . . . . Jon 4:11
just as I had *p* . . . . Matt 18:33

PLACE
p know him anymore . . . . . . Job 7:10
All go to one *p* . . . . Eccl 3:20
return again to My *p* . . . . . . Hos 5:15
Come, see the *p*. . . . . Matt 28:6

My word has no *p*. . . . . . . John 8:37
I go to prepare a *p* . . . . . . John 14:2
might go to his own *p*. . . . . Acts 1:25

PLACES
set them in slippery *p* . . . . . Ps 73:18
dark *p* of the earth . . . . Ps 74:20
and the rough *p* . . . . Is 40:4
They love the best *p* . . . . . Matt 23:6
in the heavenly *p*. . . . . Eph 1:3

PLAGUE
bring yet one more *p* . . . . . . Ex 11:1
p come near your . . . . Ps 91:10
and the *p* was stopped . . . . Ps 106:30

PLAGUES
I will send all My *p*. . . . . . . Ex 9:14
I will be your *p* . . . . Hos 13:14
p that are written . . . . Rev 22:18

PLAINLY
the Christ, tell us *p* . . . . . John 10:24
now You are speaking *p* . . . John 16:29
such things declare *p* . . . . Heb 11:14

PLAN
p evil things in their . . . . . . Ps 140:2
Let none of you *p* . . . . Zech 7:10

PLANK
First remove the *p*. . . . . . . Matt 7:5

PLANS
He makes the *p* of the . . . . . Ps 33:10
in that very day his *p* . . . . . Ps 146:4
that devises wicked *p*. . . . . Prov 6:18
A man's heart *p*. . . . . Prov 16:9
P are established . . . . Prov 20:18

PLANT
A time to *p* . . . . Eccl 3:2
Him as a tender *p* . . . . Is 53:2
they shall *p* vineyards . . . . . Is 65:21
p of an alien vine. . . . . Jer 2:21
p which My heavenly . . . . Matt 15:13

PLANTED
shall be like a tree *p* . . . . Ps 1:3
Your right hand has *p*. . . . . Ps 80:15
shall they be *p* . . . . Is 40:24
by the roots and be *p* . . . . Luke 17:6
I *p*, Apollos watered. . . . . . 1 Cor 3:6

PLANTS
our sons may be as *p*. . . . . Ps 144:12
down its choice *p* . . . . Is 16:8
neither he who *p* . . . . 1 Cor 3:7

PLATFORM
scribe stood on a *p*. . . . . . . Neh 8:4

PLATTER
head here on a *p*. . . . . Matt 14:8

PLAY
and rose up to *p* . . . . Ex 32:6
p skillfully with a . . . . Ps 33:3
nursing child shall *p* . . . . . . Is 11:8
and rose up to *p*. . . . . 1 Cor 10:7

PLEAD
the one who would *p* . . . . . Judg 6:31
Oh, that one might *p* . . . . . Job 16:21
p my cause against an . . . . . Ps 43:1
p with your friend. . . . . . . Prov 6:3
Behold, I will *p*. . . . . Jer 2:35
p His case with all . . . . Jer 25:31

PLEADED
Then Moses *p* with the . . . . Ex 32:11
this thing I *p* with . . . . . . 2 Cor 12:8

PLEADING
though God were *p* . . . . . 2 Cor 5:20

PLEASANT
food, that it was *p* . . . . Gen 3:6

they despised the *p* . . . . . Ps 106:24
how good and how *p*. . . . . . Ps 133:1
and knowledge is *p* . . . . . Prov 2:10
P words are like a . . . . . . Prov 16:24
p places of the. . . . . Jer 23:10
Is he a *p* child. . . . . Jer 31:20
I ate no *p* food . . . . Dan 10:3

PLEASANTNESS
Her ways are ways of *p* . . . . Prov 3:17

PLEASE
When a man's ways *p*. . . . . Prov 16:7
do those things that *p* . . . . John 8:29
in the flesh cannot *p*. . . . . . Rom 8:8
p his neighbor for his . . . . Rom 15:2
how he may *p* the Lord. . . 1 Cor 7:32
Or do I seek to *p* men. . . . . Gal 1:10
is impossible to *p* Him . . . . Heb 11:6

PLEASED
Then You shall be *p*. . . . . . Ps 51:19
The LORD is well *p*. . . . . . . Is 42:21
Would he be *p* with you . . . . Mal 1:8
in whom I am well *p* . . . . . Matt 3:17
God was not well *p* . . . . . 1 Cor 10:5
testimony, that he *p*. . . . . . Heb 11:5
in whom I am well *p* . . . . . 2 Pet 1:17

PLEASES
He does whatever He *p* . . . . Ps 115:3
Whatever the LORD *p*. . . . . . Ps 135:6

PLEASING
sacrifice, well *p*. . . . . Phil 4:18
for this is well *p*. . . . . Col 3:20
in you what is well *p* . . . . . Heb 13:21

PLEASURE
not a God who takes *p* . . . . . Ps 5:4
Do good in Your good *p* . . . . Ps 51:18
Your servants take *p* . . . . . Ps 102:14
p will be a poor man. . . . . Prov 21:17
for He has no *p*. . . . . Eccl 5:4
shall perform all My *p*. . . . . Is 44:28
your fast you find *p*. . . . . . . Is 58:3
nor finding your own *p* . . . . Is 58:13
Do I have any *p*. . . . . . . Ezek 18:23
I have no *p* in you . . . . Mal 1:10
your Father's good *p* . . . . . Luke 12:32
to the good *p* of His . . . . . . Eph 1:5
fulfill all the good *p* . . . . 2 Thess 1:11
p is dead while . . . . 1 Tim 5:6
for sin You had no *p* . . . . . . Heb 10:6
back, My soul has no *p* . . . . Heb 10:38
p that war in your . . . . James 4:1
on the earth in *p* . . . . James 5:5

PLEASURES
Your right hand are *p* . . . . . Ps 16:11
cares, riches, and *p*. . . . . . Luke 8:14
to enjoy the passing *p* . . . . Heb 11:25

PLEIADES
Part of God's creation, Job 9:9; Amos 5:8

PLENTIFUL
You, O God, sent a *p*. . . . . . Ps 68:9
The harvest truly is *p* . . . . . Matt 9:37

PLENTIFULLY
rich man yielded *p* . . . . . Luke 12:16

PLENTY
p which were in the . . . . . Gen 41:53
LORD will grant you *p* . . . . Deut 28:11
his land will have *p*. . . . . . Prov 28:19

PLIGHT
He laughs at the *p*. . . . . . . Job 9:23

PLOT
and the people *p*. . . . . Ps 2:1
p became known to Saul. . . Acts 9:24

PLOTS
The wicked *p* against....... Ps 37:12

PLOTTED
and *p* to take Jesus by .... Matt 26:4
chief priests *p*.......... John 12:10

PLOW
lazy man will not *p*...... Prov 20:4
Does one *p* there with.... Amos 6:12
put his hand to the *p*.... Luke 9:62
he who plows should *p* ... 1 Cor 9:10

PLOWED
"Zion shall be *p*........ Jer 26:18
You have *p* wickedness.... Hos 10:13
of you Zion shall be *p*...... Mic 3:12

PLOWMAN
p shall overtake the...... Amos 9:13

PLUCK
grain, you may *p*...... Deut 23:25
who pass by the way *p*...... Ps 80:12
obey, I will utterly *p*...... Jer 12:17
p the heads of grain .... Mark 2:23

PLUCKED
p the victim from his...... Job 29:17
cheeks to those who *p*...... Is 50:6
And His disciples *p*....... Luke 6:1
you would have *p*......... Gal 4:15

PLUMB
a *p* line, with a *p*......... Amos 7:7
rejoice to see the *p*...... Zech 4:10

PLUNDER
p the Egyptians............ Ex 3:22
who pass by the way *p*..... Ps 89:41
The *p* of the poor is...... Is 3:14
p you shall become...... Jer 30:16
house and *p* his goods ... Matt 12:29

PLUNDERED
stouthearted were *p*....... Ps 76:5
a people robbed and *p*...... Is 42:22
"And when you are *p*...... Jer 4:30
Because you have *p*....... Hab 2:8

PLUNDERING
me because of the *p*........ Is 22:4
accepted the *p* of your .... Heb 10:34

POETS
some of your own *p*...... Acts 17:28

POISON
the *p* of asps is under .... Ps 140:3
"The *p* of asps is .... Rom 3:13
evil, full of deadly *p*...... James 3:8

POISONED
p by bitterness .... Acts 8:23
p their minds against ..... Acts 14:2

POLLUTIONS
have escaped the *p*....... 2 Pet 2:20

POMP
multitude and their *p*...... Is 5:14
p is brought down to .... Is 14:11
had come with great *p* .... Acts 25:23

POMPOUS
and a mouth speaking *p*.... Dan 7:8

PONDER
P the path of your....... Prov 4:26

PONDERED
p them in her heart ..... Luke 2:19

PONDERS
p all his paths .... Prov 5:21

PONTUS
Jews from, at Pentecost, Acts 2:5, 9
Home of Aquila, Acts 18:2

Christians of, addressed by Peter,
  1 Pet 1:1

POOL
the wilderness a *p*......... Is 41:18
by the Sheep Gate a *p* ..... John 5:2

POOLS
also covers it with *p* .... Ps 84:6
a wilderness into *p* ...... Ps 107:35
your eyes like the *p* ...... Song 7:4

POOR
p shall not give less ...... Ex 30:15
be partial to the *p*....... Lev 19:15
p will never cease .... Deut 15:11
So the *p* have hope .... Job 5:16
and forsaken the *p* .... Job 20:19
I delivered the *p*....... Job 29:12
soul grieved for the *p* ..... Job 30:25
p shall eat and be......... Ps 22:26
p man cried out....... Ps 34:6
But I am *p* and needy...... Ps 40:17
goodness for the *p*........ Ps 68:10
Let the *p* and needy....... Ps 74:21
yet He sets the *p*........ Ps 107:41
He raises the *p*........... Ps 113:7
a slack hand becomes *p* .... Prov 10:4
p man is hated even .... Prov 14:20
has mercy on the *p* ..... Prov 14:21
who oppresses the *p*..... Prov 14:31
p reproaches his Maker.... Prov 17:5
p man is better than a ... Prov 19:22
p have this in common.... Prov 22:2
Do not rob the *p* .... Prov 22:22
p man who oppresses ..... Prov 28:3
remembered that same *p*... Eccl 9:15
for silver, and the *p*...... Amos 2:6
the alien or the *p* .... Zech 7:10
in particular the *p*....... Zech 11:7
"Blessed are the *p*........ Matt 5:3
p have the gospel ...... Matt 11:5
For you have the *p* ...... Matt 26:11
your sakes He became *p* ... 2 Cor 8:9
should remember the *p*..... Gal 2:10
God not chosen the *p*..... James 2:5
have dishonored the *p* .... James 2:6
wretched, miserable, *p* ..... Rev 3:17

PORCIUS FESTUS
Paul stands trial before, Acts 25:1–22

PORTION
For the Lord's *p*.......... Deut 32:9
double *p* of your spirit..... 2 Kin 2:9
This is the *p* from God .... Job 20:29
O Lord, You are the *p*...... Ps 16:5
heart and my *p* forever..... Ps 73:26
You are my *p*........... Ps 119:57
I will divide Him a *p* ...... Is 53:12
rejoice in their *p*............ Is 61:7
The *P* of Jacob is not...... Jer 10:16
they have trodden My *p*.... Jer 12:10
"The Lord is my *p*....... Lam 3:24
and appoint him his *p*... Matt 24:51
to give them their *p* .... Luke 12:42
give me the *p*........... Luke 15:12

PORTRAYED
Christ was clearly *p* .... Gal 3:1

POSITION
If a man desires the *p*..... 1 Tim 3:1

POSSESS
descendants shall *p* ...... Gen 22:17
p the land which .... Josh 1:11
By your patience *p* ...... Luke 21:19
p his own vessel .... 1 Thess 4:4

POSSESSED
much land yet to be *p*..... Josh 13:1
"The Lord *p* me at....... Prov 8:22
of the things he *p*....... Acts 4:32

POSSESSING
and yet *p* all things ...... 2 Cor 6:10

POSSESSION
as an everlasting *p*....... Gen 17:8
the rest of their *p*....... Ps 17:14
they did not gain *p*........ Ps 44:3
of the purchased *p* ...... Eph 1:14
and an enduring *p*...... Heb 10:34

POSSESSIONS
is full of Your *p* .... Ps 104:24
kinds of precious *p* .... Prov 1:13
Yes, I had greater *p* .... Eccl 2:7
for he had great *p* ...... Mark 10:22
and there wasted his *p* ... Luke 15:13
and sold their *p* .... Acts 2:45

POSSIBLE
God all things are *p* ..... Matt 19:26
p that the blood .... Heb 10:4

POSTERITY
to preserve a *p*........... Gen 45:7
p shall serve Him .... Ps 22:30
p who approve their .... Ps 49:13

POT
to Aaron, "Take a *p* ...... Ex 16:33
from a boiling *p* .... Job 41:20
The refining *p* is for....... Prov 17:3
p that had the manna...... Heb 9:4

POTENTATE
the blessed and only *P* ... 1 Tim 6:15

POTIPHAR
High Egyptian officer, Gen 39:1
Puts Joseph in jail, Gen 39:20

POTS
when we sat by the *p* .... Ex 16:3
also took away the *p* ..... Jer 52:18
are regarded as clay *p*..... Lam 4:2

POTSHERD
for himself a *p*............. Job 2:8
is dried up like a *p*......... Ps 22:15
Let the *p* strive with .... Is 45:9

POTTER'S FIELD
Judas's money used for purchase of,
  Matt 27:7, 8

POUR
p out your heart .... Ps 62:8
P out Your wrath .... Ps 79:6
p My Spirit on your .... Is 44:3
and let the skies *p* .... Is 45:8
P out Your fury .... Jer 10:25
that I will *p* out My .... Joel 2:28
"And I will *p* .... Zech 12:10
angels, "Go and *p*........ Rev 16:1

POURED
And now my soul is *p* ..... Job 30:16
I am *p* out like water....... Ps 22:14
grace is *p* upon Your....... Ps 45:2
name is ointment *p* ...... Song 1:3
visited You, they *p*....... Is 26:16
strong, because He *p* .... Is 53:12
and My fury will be *p*..... Jer 7:20
His fury is *p* out like .... Nah 1:6
broke the flask and *p*..... Mark 14:3
of God has been *p*........ Rom 5:5
if I am being *p*........... Phil 2:17
I am already being *p* ..... 2 Tim 4:6
whom He *p* out on us...... Titus 3:6

POVERTY
of the poor is their *p* ..... Prov 10:15
but it leads to *p* .... Prov 11:24
P and shame will come ... Prov 13:18
leads only to *p*.......... Prov 14:23
lest you come to *p* ...... Prov 20:13

give me neither *p* . . . . Prov 30:8
p put in all the . . . . Luke 21:4
and their deep *p* . . . . 2 Cor 8:2
p might become rich . . . . . 2 Cor 8:9
tribulation, and *p* . . . . Rev 2:9

POWER
that I may show My *p* . . . . . . Ex 9:16
become glorious in *p* . . . . . . Ex 15:6
for God who is to help . . . . 2 Chr 25:8
him who is without *p* . . . . . . Job 26:2
p who can understand . . . . Job 26:14
p belongs to God . . . . Ps 62:11
p Your enemies shall . . . . . . Ps 66:3
gives strength and *p* . . . . . . Ps 68:35
a king is, there is *p* . . . . Eccl 8:4
No one has *p* over the . . . . . Eccl 8:8
the strength of His *p* . . . . . . Is 40:26
truly I am full of *p* . . . . Mic 3:8
anger and great in *p* . . . . . . Nah 1:3
'Not by might nor by *p* . . . . Zech 4:6
the kingdom and the *p* . . . . Matt 6:13
the Son of Man has *p* . . . . . Matt 9:6
who had given such *p* . . . . . Matt 9:8
p over unclean spirits . . . . . Matt 10:1
Scriptures nor the *p* . . . . . Matt 22:29
p to heal sicknesses . . . . . . Mark 3:15
p had gone out of Him . . . Mark 5:30
Jesus returned in the *p* . . . Luke 4:14
And the *p* of the Lord . . . . Luke 5:17
p went out from Him . . . . Luke 6:19
you are endued with *p* . . . Luke 24:49
I have *p* to lay it . . . . John 10:18
not know that I have *p* . . . John 19:10
"You could have no *p* . . . . John 19:11
you shall receive *p* . . . . Acts 1:8
as though by our own *p* . . . Acts 3:12
man is the great *p* . . . . Acts 8:10
"Give me this *p* . . . . Acts 8:19
for it is the *p* . . . . Rom 1:16
even His eternal *p* . . . . Rom 1:20
saved it is the *p* . . . . 1 Cor 1:18
Greeks, Christ the *p* . . . . 1 Cor 1:24
not in word but in *p* . . . . 1 Cor 4:20
be brought under the *p* . . 1 Cor 6:12
that the *p* of Christ . . . . . . 2 Cor 12:9
greatness of His *p* . . . . Eph 1:19
working of His *p* . . . . Eph 3:7
the Lord and in the *p* . . . . . Eph 6:10
to His glorious *p* . . . . Col 1:11
the glory of His *p* . . . . . . 2 Thess 1:9
of fear, but of *p* . . . . 2 Tim 1:7
by the word of His *p* . . . . . . Heb 1:3
p of death, that . . . . Heb 2:14
but according to the *p* . . . . Heb 7:16
as His divine *p* . . . . 2 Pet 1:3
dominion and *p* . . . . Jude 25
to him I will give *p* . . . . . . Rev 2:26
glory and honor and *p* . . . . Rev 4:11
honor and glory and *p* . . . . Rev 5:13

POWERFUL
of the Lord is *p* . . . . Ps 29:4
of God is living and *p* . . . . Heb 4:12

POWERS
principalities and *p* . . . . Col 2:15
word of God and the *p* . . . . Heb 6:5

PRAETORIUM
Pilate's, in Jerusalem, Mark 15:16;
　　John 18:28; Matt 27:27
———— Herod's palace at Caesarea, Acts
　　23:35

PRAISE
your brothers shall *p* . . . . . . Gen 49:8
He is your *p* . . . . Deut 10:21
I will sing *p* to the . . . . Judg 5:3
p shall be of You in . . . . Ps 22:25

For *p* from the upright . . . . . . Ps 33:1
p shall continually be . . . . . . Ps 34:1
the people shall *p* . . . . Ps 45:17
Whoever offers *p* . . . . Ps 50:23
P is awaiting You. . . . . Ps 65:1
make His *p* glorious . . . . Ps 66:2
let all the peoples *p* . . . . Ps 67:3
Let heaven and earth *p* . . . . Ps 69:34
p shall be continually . . . . . . Ps 71:6
And the heavens will *p* . . . . . Ps 89:5
silent, O God of my *p* . . . . Ps 109:1
Seven times a day I *p* . . . . Ps 119:164
All Your works shall *p* . . . . Ps 145:10
shall speak the *p* . . . . Ps 145:21
P the Lord . . . . Ps 148:1
that has breath *p* . . . . Ps 150:6
Let another man *p* . . . . Prov 27:2
let her own works *p* . . . . . . Prov 31:31
And your gates *P* . . . . Is 60:18
He makes Jerusalem a *p* . . . . Is 62:7
For You are my *p* . . . . Jer 17:14
Me a name of joy, a *p* . . . . . Jer 33:9
give you fame and *p* . . . . . . Zeph 3:20
You have perfected *p* . . . . Matt 21:16
of men more than the *p* . . John 12:43
p is not from men but . . . . . Rom 2:29
Then each one's *p* . . . . 1 Cor 4:5
the brother whose *p* . . . . . . 2 Cor 8:18
should be to the *p* . . . . Eph 1:12
to the glory and *p* . . . . Phil 1:11
I will sing *p* to You . . . . Heb 2:12
the sacrifice of *p* . . . . Heb 13:15
and for the *p* of those . . . . 1 Pet 2:14
saying, "*P* our God . . . . Rev 19:5

PRAISED
who is worthy to be *p* . . . . 2 Sam 22:4
daily He shall be *p* . . . . Ps 72:15
Lord's name is to be *p* . . . . Ps 113:3
and greatly to be *p* . . . . Ps 145:3
where our fathers *p* . . . . Is 64:11
the Most High and *p* . . . . . Dan 4:34

PRAISES
enthroned in the *p* . . . . Ps 22:3
it is good to sing *p* . . . . Ps 147:1
and he *p* her . . . . Prov 31:28
shall proclaim the *p* . . . . Is 60:6
you may proclaim the *p* . . . 1 Pet 2:9

PRAISEWORTHY
if there is anything *p* . . . . . . Phil 4:8

PRAISING
they will still be *p* . . . . Ps 84:4
of the heavenly host *p* . . . . Luke 2:13
in the temple *p* . . . . Luke 24:53

PRAY
Lord in ceasing to *p* . . . . 1 Sam 12:23
humble themselves,
　　and *p* . . . . 2 Chr 7:14
at noon I will *p* . . . . Ps 55:17
who hate you, and *p* . . . . . Matt 5:44
"And when you *p* . . . . Matt 6:5
But you, when you *p* . . . . . . Matt 6:6
manner, therefore, *p* . . . . . . Matt 6:9
Watch and *p* . . . . Matt 26:41
to the mountain to *p* . . . . . Mark 6:46
"Lord, teach us to *p* . . . . . . Luke 11:1
men always ought to *p* . . . . Luke 18:1
And I will *p* . . . . John 14:16
I do not *p* for the . . . . John 17:9
"I do not *p* for . . . . John 17:20
know what we should *p* . . . Rom 8:26
I will *p* with the . . . . 1 Cor 14:15
p without ceasing . . . . . . 1 Thess 5:17
Brethren, *p* for us . . . . . . 1 Thess 5:25
therefore that the men *p* . . 1 Tim 2:8
Let him *p* . . . . James 5:13

to one another, and *p* . . . James 5:16
say that he should *p* . . . . 1 John 5:16
p that you may prosper . . . . 3 John 2

PRAYED
Pharisee stood and *p* . . . . Luke 18:11
p more earnestly . . . . Luke 22:44
p earnestly that it . . . . . . James 5:17

PRAYER
in heaven their *p* . . . . 1 Kin 8:45
p made in this place . . . . . 2 Chr 7:15
fear, and restrain *p* . . . . Job 15:4
And my *p* is pure . . . . Job 16:17
p would return to my . . . . . Ps 35:13
A *p* to the God of my . . . . . . Ps 42:8
P also will be made . . . . Ps 72:15
Let my *p* come before . . . . . Ps 88:2
He shall regard the *p* . . . . . Ps 102:17
but I give myself to *p* . . . . . Ps 109:4
to the Lord, but the *p* . . . . Prov 15:8
not go out except by *p* . . . Matt 17:21
all night in *p* to God . . . . . Luke 6:12
continually to *p* . . . . Acts 6:4
where *p* was . . . . Acts 16:13
steadfastly in *p* . . . . Rom 12:12
to fasting and *p* . . . . 1 Cor 7:5
always with all *p* . . . . Eph 6:18
but in everything by *p* . . . . . Phil 4:6
the word of God and *p* . . . 1 Tim 4:5
And the *p* of faith . . . . James 5:15

PRAYERS
though you make many *p* . . . . Is 1:15
pretense make long *p* . . . . Matt 23:14
fervently for you in *p* . . . . . . Col 4:12
that supplications, *p* . . . . . . 1 Tim 2:1
p may not be hindered . . . . 1 Pet 3:7
are open to their *p* . . . . . . 1 Pet 3:12
and watchful in your *p* . . . . 1 Pet 4:7
which are the *p* . . . . Rev 5:8
with the *p* of the saints . . . . Rev 8:4

PREACH
that great city, and *p* . . . . . . Jon 3:2
time Jesus began to *p* . . . . Matt 4:17
you hear in the ear, *p* . . . Matt 10:27
P the gospel to the . . . . . . Luke 4:18
p the kingdom of God . . . Luke 9:60
And how shall they *p* . . . . Rom 10:15
p Christ crucified . . . . 1 Cor 1:23
is me if I do not *p* . . . . 1 Cor 9:16
I or they, so we *p* . . . . . . 1 Cor 15:11
For we do not *p* . . . . 2 Cor 4:5
p Christ even from . . . . Phil 1:15
P the word . . . . 2 Tim 4:2

PREACHED
p that people . . . . Mark 6:12
out and everywhere . . . Mark 16:20
of sins should be *p* . . . . . Luke 24:47
p Christ to them . . . . Acts 8:5
through this Man is *p* . . . . Acts 13:38
lest, when I have *p* . . . . . . 1 Cor 9:27
whom we have not *p* . . . . . 2 Cor 11:4
than what we have *p* . . . . . . Gal 1:8
in truth, Christ is *p* . . . . . . Phil 1:18
the gospel was *p* . . . . Heb 4:2
also He went and *p* . . . . . . 1 Pet 3:19

PREACHER
The words of the *P* . . . . Eccl 1:1
they hear without a *p* . . . . Rom 10:14
I was appointed a *p* . . . . . . 1 Tim 2:7
of eight people, a *p* . . . . . . 2 Pet 2:5

PREACHES
the Jesus whom Paul *p* . . . Acts 19:13
p another Jesus whom . . . . 2 Cor 11:4
p any other gospel . . . . Gal 1:9
p the faith which he . . . . . . Gal 1:23

PREACHING
p Jesus as the . . . . Acts 5:42

to my gospel and the *p*... Rom 16:25
not risen, then our *p*.... 1 Cor 15:14

PRECEDE
p those who are asleep.. 1 Thess 4:15

PRECEPT
p must be upon *p*......... Is 28:10

PRECEPTS
and commanded them *p*... Neh 9:14
all His *p* are sure .... Ps 111:7
us to keep Your *p*......... Ps 119:4
how I love Your *p*...... Ps 119:159
and kept all his *p*........ Jer 35:18

PRECIOUS
because my life was *p*.. 1 Sam 26:21
P in the sight of .... Ps 116:15
How *p* also are Your....... Ps 139:17
She is more *p* than ...... Prov 3:15
Since you were *p* .... Is 43:4
p things shall not........ Is 44:9
if you take out the *p*...... Jer 15:19
The *p* sons of Zion........ Lam 4:2
farmer waits for the *p*... James 5:7
more *p* than gold .... 1 Pet 1:7
who believe, He is *p*...... 1 Pet 2:7
p in the sight of .... 1 Pet 3:4

PREDESTINED
He foreknew, He also *p*.... Rom 8:29
having *p* us to .... Eph 1:5
inheritance, being *p*...... Eph 1:11

PREEMINENCE
He may have the *p*....... Col 1:18
loves to have the *p*....... 3 John 9

PREFERENCE
in honor giving *p*....... Rom 12:10

PREFERRED
comes after me is *p*...... John 1:15

PREJUDICE
these things without *p*.... 1 Tim 5:21

PREMEDITATE
p what you will........ Mark 13:11

PREPARATION
Now it was the *P*........ John 19:14
your feet with the *p* ...... Eph 6:15

PREPARE
p your hearts for the .... 1 Sam 7:3
p a table before me in....... Ps 23:5
p mercy and truth.......... Ps 61:7
P the way of the LORD .... Is 40:3
P the way for the .... Is 62:10
P the way of the LORD .... Mark 1:3
will, and did not *p*...... Luke 12:47
p a place for you......... John 14:2

PREPARED
place which I have *p* ..... Ex 23:20
You *p* room for it.......... Ps 80:9
When He *p* the heavens ... Prov 8:27
for the LORD has *p* .... Zeph 1:7
for whom it is *p*........ Matt 20:23
which You have *p*...... Luke 2:31
mercy, which He had *p*... Rom 9:23
things which God has *p* ... 1 Cor 2:9
Now He who has *p* ...... 2 Cor 5:5
p beforehand that we...... Eph 2:10
God, for He has *p*....... Heb 11:16

PRESENCE
themselves from the *p*..... Gen 3:8
went out from the *p*...... Gen 4:16
we die in your *p*...... Gen 47:15
P will go with you......... Ex 33:14
and honor the *p* .... Lev 19:32
afraid in any man's *p*.... Deut 1:17
am terrified at His *p* ...... Job 23:15

p is fullness of joy .... Ps 16:11
shall dwell in Your *p* ...... Ps 140:13
not tremble at My *p*....... Jer 5:22
shall shake at My *p*..... Ezek 38:20
Be silent in the *p* .... Zeph 1:7
and drank in Your *p*..... Luke 13:26
full of joy in Your *p*...... Acts 2:28
but his bodily .... 2 Cor 10:10
obeyed, not as in my *p*.... Phil 2:12

PRESENT
we are all *p* before .... Acts 10:33
evil is *p* with me .... Rom 7:21
p your bodies a living..... Rom 12:1
or death, or things *p*..... 1 Cor 3:22
absent in body but *p*...... 1 Cor 5:3
not only when I am *p*...... Gal 4:18
that He might *p* .... Eph 5:27
to *p* yourself............. 2 Tim 2:15
p you faultless .... Jude 24

PRESENTED
treasures, they *p* .... Matt 2:11
For just as you *p* .... Rom 6:19

PRESENTS
kings will bring *p* .... Ps 68:29

PRESERVE
before you to *p* life........ Gen 45:5
You shall *p* me from .... Ps 32:7
O LORD, You *p* man and ... Ps 36:6
He shall *p* your soul .... Ps 121:7
The LORD shall *p* .... Ps 121:8
children, I will *p* .... Jer 49:11
pardon those whom I *p*.... Jer 50:20
loses his life will *p*...... Luke 17:33
every evil work and *p*.... 2 Tim 4:18

PRESERVED
and my life is *p* .... Gen 32:30
soul, and body be *p* .... 1 Thess 5:23

PRESERVES
For the LORD *p* the ...... Ps 31:23
p the souls of His.......... Ps 97:10
The LORD *p* the simple ..... Ps 116:6
who guards his mouth *p*... Prov 13:3
he who keeps his way *p*... Prov 16:17

PRESS
I *p* toward the goal........ Phil 3:14

PRESSED
p her virgin bosom ...... Ezek 23:8
We are hard *p* on every.... 2 Cor 4:8
For I am hard *p* .... Phil 1:23

PRESUMPTUOUS
servant also from *p* .... Ps 19:13

PRETENDED
before them, *p* madness . 1 Sam 21:13

PRETENSE
whole heart, but in *p*....... Jer 3:10
p make long prayers..... Matt 23:14

PREVAIL
no man shall *p*.......... 1 Sam 2:9
our tongue we will *p*...... Ps 12:4
but they shall not *p*...... Jer 1:19
of Hades shall not *p* .... Matt 16:18

PREVAILED
hand, that Israel *p* ...... Ex 17:11
with the Angel and *p*...... Hos 12:4
grew mightily and *p* ..... Acts 19:20

PREY
the mountains of *p* .... Ps 76:4
has not given us as *p* ..... Ps 124:6
Shall the *p* be taken........ Is 49:24
evil makes himself a *p*.... Is 59:15
shall no longer be a *p*... Ezek 34:22
when he has no *p* .... Amos 3:4

PRICE
be weighed for its *p*....... Job 28:15
a fool the purchase *p*..... Prov 17:16
one pearl of great *p*..... Matt 13:46
back part of the *p* .... Acts 5:3
you were bought at a *p*... 1 Cor 6:20

PRIDE
p come against me .... Ps 36:11
p serves as .... Ps 73:6
p and arrogance and...... Prov 8:13
By *p* comes nothing...... Prov 13:10
P goes before .... Prov 16:18
p will bring him low ..... Prov 29:23
and her daughter had *p* .. Ezek 16:49
p He is able to put down.. Dan 4:37
was hardened in *p*....... Dan 5:20
has sworn by the *p* ...... Amos 8:7
For the *p* of the .... Zech 11:3
evil eye, blasphemy, *p*.... Mark 7:22
p he fall into the......... 1 Tim 3:6
eyes, and the *p* of life.... 1 John 2:16

PRIEST
he was the *p* of God ..... Gen 14:18
Myself a faithful *p* ...... 1 Sam 2:35
p forever according .... Ps 110:4
the *p* and the prophet .... Is 28:7
So He shall be a *p*....... Zech 6:13
of a *p* should keep .... Mal 2:17
and faithful High *P* ...... Heb 2:17
we have a great High *P* ... Heb 4:14
p forever according ...... Heb 5:6
Christ came as High *P*..... Heb 9:11

PRIESTHOOD
be an everlasting *p*........ Ex 40:15
have defiled the *p* ...... Neh 13:29
p being changed.......... Heb 7:12
has an unchangeable *p*.... Heb 7:24
house, a holy *p*........... 1 Pet 2:5
generation, a royal *p* ...... 1 Pet 2:9

PRIESTS
to Me a kingdom of *p*...... Ex 19:6
her *p* teach for pay .... Mic 3:11
made us kings and *p*...... Rev 1:6
but they shall be *p*........ Rev 20:6

PRINCE
"Who made you a *p*........ Ex 2:14
is the house of the *p* ..... Job 21:28
is the downfall of a *p* .... Prov 14:28
Everlasting Father, *P* .... Is 9:6
until Messiah the *P* ...... Dan 9:25
except Michael your *p*.... Dan 10:21
days without king or *p*..... Hos 3:4
p asks for gifts............. Mic 7:3
and killed the *P* .... Acts 3:15
His right hand to be *P*..... Acts 5:31
the *p* of the power .... Eph 2:2

PRINCES
He is not partial to *p*...... Job 34:19
to bind his *p* at his .... Ps 105:22
He may seat him with *p* .... Ps 113:8
to put confidence in *p* ...... Ps 118:9
P also sit and speak...... Ps 119:23
p and all judges of........ Ps 148:11
good, nor to strike *p* ..... Prov 17:26
is a child, and your *p* ..... Eccl 10:16
of nobles, and your *p*.... Eccl 10:17
children to be their *p*...... Is 3:4
p will rule with.............. Is 32:1
He brings the *p*............ Is 40:23

PRINCIPAL
Wisdom is the *p* .... Prov 4:7

PRINCIPALITIES
nor *p* nor powers......... Rom 8:38
p and powers in the
  heavenly places......... Eph 3:10

against *p*, against powers . . Eph 6:12
Having disarmed *p* and
  powers . . . . Col 2:15

PRINCIPALITY
far above all *p* . . . . Eph 1:21
is the head of all *p* . . . . Col 2:10

PRINCIPLES
from the basic *p* . . . . Col 2:20
again the first *p* . . . . Heb 5:12

PRISCILLA (or Prisca)
Wife of Aquila, Acts 18:1–3
With Aquila, instructs Apollos, Acts
  18:26
Mentioned by Paul, Rom 16:3; 1 Cor
  16:19; 2 Tim 4:19

PRISON
and put him into the *p* . . . Gen 39:20
Bring my soul out of *p* . . . . . Ps 142:7
in darkness from the *p*. . . . . . Is 42:7
the opening of the *p*. . . . . . . Is 61:1
should put him in *p*. . . . . . . Jer 29:26
John had heard in *p* . . . . . Matt 11:2
I was in *p* and you . . . . . . Matt 25:36
to the spirits in *p*. . . . . 1 Pet 3:19

PRISONER
the groaning of the *p*. . . . . . Ps 79:11
reason I, Paul, the *p*. . . . . . . Eph 3:1
Lord, nor of me His *p* . . . . . 2 Tim 1:8

PRISONERS
p rest together . . . . Job 3:18
does not despise His *p* . . . . Ps 69:33
gives freedom to the *p*. . . . . Ps 146:7
the stronghold, you *p* . . . . Zech 9:12
Remember the *p* as if . . . . . Heb 13:3

PRISONS
the synagogues and *p*. . . . Luke 21:12
p more frequently . . . . . . 2 Cor 11:23

PRIZE
life shall be as a *p* . . . . Jer 21:9
but one receives the *p* . . . . 1 Cor 9:24
the goal for the *p* . . . . Phil 3:14

PROCEED
For they *p* from evil . . . . Jer 9:3
of the same mouth *p* . . . . James 3:10

PROCEEDED
for I *p* forth . . . . John 8:42

PROCEEDS
by every word that *p* . . . . . Deut 8:3
by every word that *p* . . . . . Matt 4:4
Spirit of truth who *p* . . . . John 15:26
back part of the *p* . . . . Acts 5:2

PROCESSION
They have seen Your *p* . . . . . Ps 68:24

PROCHORUS
One of the first seven deacons,
  Acts 6:5

PROCLAIM
you, and I will *p* . . . . Ex 33:19
p the name of the Lord . . . Deut 32:3
p it not in the. . . . . 2 Sam 1:20
and they shall *p*. . . . . Is 60:6
began to *p* it freely. . . . . . Mark 1:45
knowing, Him I *p*. . . . . . . Acts 17:23
drink this cup, you *p* . . . . 1 Cor 11:26

PROCLAIMED
p the good news . . . . Ps 40:9
company of those who *p*. . . . Ps 68:11
he went his way and *p*. . . . Luke 8:39
inner rooms will be *p* . . . . Luke 12:3

PROCLAIMER
"He seems to be a *p* . . . . . Acts 17:18

PROCLAIMS
good news, who *p* . . . . Is 52:7

PROCONSUL
seeking to turn the *p* . . . . . Acts 13:8
When Gallio was *p*. . . . . . Acts 18:12

PRODIGAL
with *p* living . . . . Luke 15:13

PRODUCE
land shall yield its *p*. . . . . . Lev 26:4
all kinds of *p* . . . . Ps 144:13

PROFANE
and offered *p* fire. . . . . Lev 10:1
and priest are *p*. . . . . Jer 23:11
"But you *p* it. . . . . Mal 1:12
tried to *p* the temple . . . . . Acts 24:6
But reject *p* and old . . . . . . 1 Tim 4:7
p person like Esau. . . . . . . Heb 12:16

PROFANED
p his crown by casting. . . . . Ps 89:39
and *p* My Sabbaths. . . . . . . Ezek 22:8
p the Lord's holy . . . . Mal 2:11

PROFANENESS
of Jerusalem *p* has . . . . . . Jer 23:15

PROFANING
p the covenant of the. . . . . Mal 2:10

PROFESS
They *p* to know God . . . . . Titus 1:16

PROFESSING
P to be wise . . . . Rom 1:22
is proper for women *p*. . . . 1 Tim 2:10

PROFIT
p is there in my blood. . . . . . Ps 30:9
p has a man from all. . . . . . Eccl 1:3
There was no *p* under. . . . . Eccl 2:11
for they will not *p*. . . . . Is 57:12
words that cannot *p*. . . . . . . Jer 7:8
p which you have made . . Ezek 22:13
p is it that we have. . . . . . . Mal 3:14
For what *p* is it to . . . . . . Matt 16:26
For what will it *p* . . . . Mark 8:36
For what *p* is it to . . . . Luke 9:25
her masters much *p* . . . . . Acts 16:16
hope of *p* was gone . . . . . Acts 16:19
brought no small *p* . . . . . Acts 19:24
what is the *p* of. . . . . Rom 3:1
not seeking my own *p* . . . 1 Cor 10:33
Christ will *p* you . . . . Gal 5:2
about words to no *p* . . . . . 2 Tim 2:14
them, but He for our *p* . . . . Heb 12:10
What does it *p*. . . . . James 2:14
and sell, and make a *p*. . . James 4:13

PROFITABLE
"Can a man be *p* . . . . Job 22:2
It is doubtless not *p* . . . . . 2 Cor 12:1
of God, and is *p*. . . . . 2 Tim 3:16
things are good and *p* . . . . Titus 3:8
to you, but now is *p*. . . . . . Philem 11

PROFITS
p a man nothing that. . . . . . Job 34:9
have not love, it *p*. . . . . . . 1 Cor 13:3
exercise *p* a little. . . . . 1 Tim 4:8

PROFOUND
with things too *p* . . . . Ps 131:1

PROLONG
you will not *p* your. . . . . . . Deut 4:26
p Your anger to all . . . . Ps 85:5
nor will he *p* his days. . . . . Eccl 8:13

PROLONGED
and his days are *p* . . . . Eccl 8:12

PROLONGS
The fear of the Lord *p* . . . . Prov 10:27

PROMISE
of all His good *p*. . . . . 1 Kin 8:56
Behold, I send the *P* . . . . Luke 24:49
but to wait for the *P* . . . . . . Acts 1:4
For the *p* is to you . . . . . . Acts 2:39
p drew near which God . . . . Acts 7:17
for the hope of the *p* . . . . . Acts 26:6
is made void and the *p*. . . . Rom 4:14
p might be sure . . . . Rom 4:16
it is no longer of *p*. . . . . . . Gal 3:18
Therefore, since a *p* . . . . . . Heb 4:1
to the heirs of *p* . . . . Heb 6:17
did not receive the *p*. . . . . Heb 11:39
they *p* them liberty. . . . . . 2 Pet 2:19
p that He has promised. . 1 John 2:25

PROMISED
bless you as He has *p* . . . . Deut 1:11
He who *p* is faithful . . . . . Heb 10:23
Him faithful who had *p* . . . Heb 11:11

PROMISES
For all the *p* of God . . . . . 2 Cor 1:20
his Seed were the *p*. . . . . . . Gal 3:16
patience inherit the *p*. . . . . Heb 6:12
having received the *p*. . . . . Heb 11:13
great and precious *p* . . . . . 2 Pet 1:4

PROMPTLY
him disciplines him *p* . . . . Prov 13:24

PROOF
which is to them a *p* . . . . . Phil 1:28

PROOFS
by many infallible *p* . . . . . . Acts 1:3

PROPER
you, but for what is *p* . . . . 1 Cor 7:35
Is it *p* for a woman to . . . 1 Cor 11:13
but, which is *p*. . . . . 1 Tim 2:10

PROPERLY
Let us walk *p* . . . . Rom 13:13

PROPHECY
miracles, to another *p* . . . 1 Cor 12:10
for *p* never came by . . . . . 2 Pet 1:21
is the spirit of *p* . . . . Rev 19:10
of the book of this *p* . . . . . Rev 22:19

PROPHESIED
upon them, that they *p* . . Num 11:25
to them, yet they *p* . . . . . . Jer 23:21
Lord, have we not *p* . . . . . Matt 7:22
prophets and the law *p*. . . Matt 11:13
virgin daughters who *p* . . . Acts 21:9
even more that you *p* . . . . 1 Cor 14:5

PROPHESIES
for the prophet who *p* . . . . Jer 28:9
woman who prays or *p* . . . 1 Cor 11:5
p edifies the church . . . . . 1 Cor 14:4

PROPHESY
prophets, "Do not *p* . . . . . . Is 30:10
The prophets *p* falsely . . . . Jer 5:31
your daughters shall *p*. . . . Joel 2:28
Who can but *p* . . . . Amos 3:8
saying, "*P* to us. . . . . Matt 26:68
your daughters shall *p*. . . . Acts 2:17
if prophecy, let us *p* . . . . . Rom 12:6
know in part and we *p* . . . 1 Cor 13:9
that you may *p* . . . . 1 Cor 14:1
desire earnestly to *p*. . . . . 1 Cor 14:39

PROPHET
shall be your *p*. . . . . Ex 7:1
raise up for you a *P*. . . . . Deut 18:15
arisen in Israel a *p* . . . . . Deut 34:10
"I alone am left a *p* . . . . . 1 Kin 18:22
is no longer any *p* . . . . . . Ps 74:9
I ordained you a *p*. . . . . . . Jer 1:5
p is induced to speak. . . . Ezek 14:9
The *p* is a fool. . . . . Hos 9:7

nor was I a son of a *p* .... Amos 7:14
send you Elijah the *p* ...... Mal 4:5
p shall receive a. .... Matt 10:41
p is not without honor .... Matt 13:57
by Daniel the *p.* .... Mark 13:14
is not a greater *p.* .... Luke 7:28
it cannot be that a *p* .... Luke 13:33
Nazareth, who was a *P.* .. Luke 24:19
"Are you the *P.* .... John 1:21
"This is truly the *P* ...... John 6:14
with him the false *p* ..... Rev 19:20

PROPHETESS
Miriam the *p.* .... Ex 15:20
Deborah, a *p.* .... Judg 4:4
Huldah the *p* .... 2 Kin 22:14
Anna, a *p* .... Luke 2:36

PROPHETIC
p word confirmed .... 2 Pet 1:19

PROPHETS
LORD's people were *p.* .... Num 11:29
Saul also among the *p* .. 1 Sam 10:12
the mouth of all his *p* ... 1 Kin 22:22
believe His *p* .... 2 Chr 20:20
Where now are your *p* .... Jer 37:19
prophesy against the *p* .. Ezek 13:2
His servants the *p* .... Amos 3:7
Her *p* are insolent. .... Zeph 3:4
the Law or the *P* .... Matt 5:17
is the Law and the *P.* ..... Matt 7:12
or one of the *p.* .... Matt 16:14
the tombs of the *p.* ...... Matt 23:29
indeed, I send you *p* .... Matt 23:34
one who kills the *p* ..... Matt 23:37
Then many false *p* ...... Matt 24:11
have Moses and the *p.* ... Luke 16:29
You are sons of the *p.* .... Acts 3:25
p did your fathers not .... Acts 7:52
To Him all the *p* .... Acts 10:43
do you believe the *p* .... Acts 26:27
before through His *p* ...... Rom 1:2
by the Law and the *P* ..... Rom 3:21
have killed Your *p* .... Rom 11:3
p are subject to the. ..... 1 Cor 14:32
to be apostles, some *p* .... Eph 4:11
brethren, take the *p* .... James 5:10
this salvation the *p* ...... 1 Pet 1:10
were also false *p* .... 2 Pet 2:1
because many false *p* .... 1 John 4:1
blood of saints and *p* ..... Rev 16:6
found the blood of *p* ..... Rev 18:24
of your brethren the *p* ... Rev 22:9

PROPITIATION
set forth as a *p* .... Rom 3:25
to God, to make *p* .... Heb 2:17
He Himself is the *p* ..... 1 John 2:2
His Son to be the *p* ..... 1 John 4:10

PROPORTION
let us prophesy in *p.* ...... Rom 12:6

PROPRIETY
modest apparel, with *p.* .... 1 Tim 2:9

PROSECUTOR
answer me, that my *P.* ... Job 31:35

PROSELYTE
and sea to win one *p* .... Matt 23:15

PROSELYTES
Rome, both Jews and *p* .... Acts 2:10

PROSPER
made all he did to *p* ...... Gen 39:3
you shall not *p* .... Deut 28:29
and you shall *p.* .... 2 Chr 20:20
LORD, God made him *p.* .. 2 Chr 26:5
they *p* who love you ...... Ps 122:6
his sins will not *p.* .... Prov 28:13

of the LORD shall *p* .... Is 53:10
against you shall *p.* .... Is 54:17
please, and it shall *p* ...... Is 55:11
of the wicked *p.* .... Jer 12:1
King shall reign and *p.* ..... Jer 23:5
storing up as he may *p* ... 1 Cor 16:2
I pray that you may *p* ..... 3 John 2

PROSPERED
since the LORD has *p.* ..... Gen 24:56

PROSPERING
His ways are always *p.* ...... Ps 10:5

PROSPERITY
p all your days .... Deut 23:6
p exceed the fame .... 1 Kin 10:7
p the destroyer .... Job 15:21
spend their days in *p.* ..... Job 36:11
Now in my *p* I said .... Ps 30:6
has pleasure in the *p.* ...... Ps 35:27
When I saw the *p* .... Ps 73:3
I pray, send now *p* .... Ps 118:25
the day of *p* be joyful ..... Eccl 7:14
that we have our *p.* ...... Acts 19:25

PROSPEROUS
had made his journey *p.* .. Gen 24:21
will make your way *p* ..... Josh 1:8

PROSPERS
he turns, he *p* .... Prov 17:8
just as your soul *p* .... 3 John 2

PROSTRATE
of the proud lie *p.* .... Job 9:13

PROUD
p waves must stop .... Job 38:11
tongue that speaks *p.* .... Ps 12:3
and fully repays the *p.* ..... Ps 31:23
does not respect the *p.* ..... Ps 40:4
a haughty look and a *p.* ..... Ps 101:5
p He knows from afar ..... Ps 138:6
the house of the *p.* ...... Prov 15:25
Everyone *p* .... Prov 16:5
p heart stirs up .... Prov 28:25
is better than the *p.* ...... Eccl 7:8
by wine, he is a *p.* .... Hab 2:5
He has scattered the *p* .... Luke 1:51
"God resists the *p* .... 1 Pet 5:5

PROVE
p yourself a man .... 1 Kin 2:2
does your arguing *p* ...... Job 6:25
mind, that you may *p.* .... Rom 12:2

PROVERB
an astonishment, a *p* .... Deut 28:37
incline my ear to a *p* ...... Ps 49:4
that hang limp is a *p* ..... Prov 26:7
of a drunkard is a *p* ...... Prov 26:9
one shall take up a *p* ...... Mic 2:4
to the true *p* .... 2 Pet 2:22

PROVERBS
spoke three thousand *p* ... 1 Kin 4:32
in order many *p* .... Eccl 12:9

PROVIDE
"My son, God will *p.* ...... Gen 22:8
Can He *p* meat for His ..... Ps 78:20
prosperity that I *p* .... Jer 33:9
P neither gold nor .... Matt 10:9
if anyone does not *p.* ..... 1 Tim 5:8

PROVIDED
these hands have *p* ...... Acts 20:34
p something better .... Heb 11:40

PROVIDES
p food for the raven. ..... Job 38:41
p her supplies in the ...... Prov 6:8

PROVISION
abundantly bless her *p* .... Ps 132:15
no *p* for the flesh .... Rom 13:14

PROVOKE
do not *p* Him. .... Ex 23:21
p God are secure .... Job 12:6
Do they *p* Me to .... Jer 7:19
p them to jealousy. ...... Rom 11:11
you, fathers, do not *p.* ..... Eph 6:4

PROVOKED
How often they *p.* .... Ps 78:40
p the Most High. .... Ps 78:56
Thus they *p* Him to ...... Ps 106:29
his spirit was *p* .... Acts 17:16
seek its own, is not *p* .... 1 Cor 13:5

PRUDENCE
To give *p* to the .... Prov 1:4
wisdom, dwell with *p.* ..... Prov 8:12
us in all wisdom and *p* .... Eph 1:8

PRUDENT
p man covers shame ..... Prov 12:16
A *p* man conceals .... Prov 12:23
The wisdom of the *p* ..... Prov 14:8
p considers well .... Prov 14:15
heart will be called *p.* ..... Prov 16:21
p acquires knowledge ..... Prov 18:15
p wife is from the. .... Prov 19:14
p man foresees evil ...... Prov 22:3
perished from the *p.* ...... Jer 49:7
Therefore the *p* .... Amos 5:13
from the wise and *p* .... Matt 11:25

PRUDENTLY
Servant shall deal *p* .... Is 52:13

PRUNES
that bears fruit He *p* ...... John 15:2

PSALM
and the sound of a *p.* .... Ps 98:5
in the second *P.* .... Acts 13:33
each of you has a *p.* .... 1 Cor 14:26

PSALMIST
And the sweet *p* .... 2 Sam 23:1

PSALMS
Sing to Him, sing *p* ..... 1 Chr 16:9
to one another in *p* ...... Eph 5:19
Let him sing *p.* .... James 5:13

PSALTERY
harp, lyre, and *p* .... Dan 3:10

PUBLISHED
to be proclaimed and *p* ..... Jon 3:7

PUFFED
Now some are *p* up ...... 1 Cor 4:18
itself, is not *p* .... 1 Cor 13:4
a novice, lest being *p* ..... 1 Tim 3:6

PUFFS
Knowledge *p* up. .... 1 Cor 8:1

PUL
King of Assyria; same as Tiglath-
Pileser, 2 Kin 15:19
—— Country and people in Africa, Is
66:19

PULL
P me out of the net .... Ps 31:4
I will *p* down my barns... Luke 12:18

PUNISH
take that man and *p.* ..... Deut 22:18
p the righteous is. .... Prov 17:26
"I will *p* the world. .... Is 13:11
Shall I not *p* them for ...... Jer 5:9
p all who oppress them ... Jer 30:20
p your iniquity .... Lam 4:22
So I will *p* them for .... Hos 4:9

PUNISHED
You our God have *p.* ..... Ezra 9:13
because He has not *p* .... Job 35:15

p them often in every .... Acts 26:11
These shall be *p* .... 2 Thess 1:9

PUNISHES
will you say when He *p* .... Jer 13:21

PUNISHMENT
p is greater than I .... Gen 4:13
you do in the day of *p* .... Is 10:3
p they shall be cast. .... Jer 8:12
p they shall perish .... Jer 10:15
a man for the *p* .... Lam 3:39
The *p* of the iniquity ...... Lam 4:6
days of *p* have come .... Hos 9:7
not turn away its *p* ...... Amos 1:3
into everlasting *p* .... Matt 25:46
p which was inflicted. .... 2 Cor 2:6
Of how much worse *p* .... Heb 10:29
sent by him for the *p* .... 1 Pet 2:14
the unjust under *p* .... 2 Pet 2:9

PURCHASED
of God could be *p* .... Acts 8:20
of the *p* possession .... Eph 1:14

PURE
a mercy seat of *p* gold .... Ex 25:17
Can a man be more *p*..... Job 4:17
if you were *p* and .... Job 8:6
'My doctrine is *p* .... Job 11:4
that he could be *p* .... Job 15:14
the heavens are not *p* .... Job 15:15
the stars are not *p*........ Job 25:5
of the LORD are *p*......... Ps 12:6
will show Yourself *p*...... Ps 18:26
To such as are *p*.......... Ps 73:1
of the *p* are pleasant .... Prov 15:26
ways of a man are *p*...... Prov 16:2
my heart clean, I am *p*.... Prov 20:9
but as for the *p* .... Prov 21:8
a generation that is *p* .... Prov 30:12
Shall I count *p* .... Mic 6:11
things indeed are *p*...... Rom 14:20
whatever things are *p* ..... Phil 4:8
keep yourself *p* .... 1 Tim 5:22
p all things are *p*........ Titus 1:15
above is first *p*.......... James 3:17
babes, desire the *p* .... 1 Pet 2:2
just as He is *p*.......... 1 John 3:3

PURER
p eyes than to behold ..... Hab 1:13

PURGE
P me with hyssop .... Ps 51:7
p them as gold and .... Mal 3:3

PURGED
away, and your sin *p*........ Is 6:7
He had by Himself *p* .... Heb 1:3

PURIFICATION
for the water of *p* .... Num 19:9
with the water of *p*...... Num 31:23

PURIFIED
earth, *p* seven times .... Ps 12:6
all things are *p*........... Heb 9:22
Since you have *p* .... 1 Pet 1:22

PURIFIES
hope in Him *p* himself ... 1 John 3:3

PURIFY
p the sons of Levi.......... Mal 3:3
and *p* your hearts........ James 4:8

PURIFYING
thus *p* all foods......... Mark 7:19
p their hearts by......... Acts 15:9
sanctifies for the *p* ...... Heb 9:13

PURIM
called these days *P*....... Esth 9:26

PURITY
be delivered by the *p*..... Job 22:30
He who loves *p* of .... Prov 22:11
by *p*, by knowledge .... 2 Cor 6:6
spirit, in faith, in *p* ..... 1 Tim 4:12

PURPLE
who was clothed in *p* .... Luke 16:19
they put on Him a *p*...... John 19:2
She was a seller of *p*..... Acts 16:14

PURPOSE
and fulfill all your *p*........ Ps 20:4
A time for every *p* .... Eccl 3:1
p that is purposed .... Is 14:26
But for this *p* I came .... John 12:27
by the determined *p* ..... Acts 2:23
them all that with *p*..... Acts 11:23
to the eternal *p* .... Eph 3:11
Now the *p* of the........ 1 Tim 1:5
to fulfill His *p*........... Rev 17:17

PURPOSED
For the LORD had *p* .... 2 Sam 17:14
LORD of hosts has *p* .... Is 23:9
But Daniel *p* in his ...... Dan 1:8
pleasure which He *p* .... Eph 1:9

PURPOSES
each one give as he *p* ..... 2 Cor 9:7

PURSE
let us all have one *p* ...... Prov 1:14

PURSES
p his lips and brings ..... Prov 16:30

PURSUE
And will You *p* dry........ Job 13:25
p my honor as the wind ... Job 30:15
The sword shall *p*......... Jer 48:2
but their hearts *p*........ Ezek 33:31
Let us know, let us *p*........ Hos 6:3
p righteousness .... Rom 9:30
P love, and desire........ 1 Cor 14:1
p righteousness .... 1 Tim 6:11
him seek peace and *p*..... 1 Pet 3:11

PURSUES
Evil *p* sinners .... Prov 13:21
flee when no one *p* ...... Prov 28:1

PURSUING
but Israel, *p* the law ..... Rom 9:31

PUT
Also He has *p* eternity ..... Eccl 3:11
pride He is able to *p* down . Dan 4:37
what you will *p* on........ Matt 6:25
p my hand into His ..... John 20:25
But *p* on the Lord....... Rom 13:14

QUAIL
and it brought *q* .... Num 11:31
and He brought *q* .... Ps 105:40

QUAKED
the whole mountain *q* ..... Ex 19:18
and the earth *q*........ Matt 27:51

QUAKES
The earth *q* before .... Joel 2:10

QUALIFIED
the Father who has *q* ..... Col 1:12

QUARREL
see how he seeks a *q* .... 2 Kin 5:7
any fool can start a *q* .... Prov 20:3
He will not *q* nor cry..... Matt 12:19
of the Lord must not *q* ... 2 Tim 2:24

QUARRELSOME
but gentle, not *q*........ 1 Tim 3:3

QUARTZ
be made of coral or *q* ..... Job 28:18

QUEEN
Q Vashti also made a ...... Esth 1:9
stands the *q* in gold .... Ps 45:9
burn incense to the *q*..... Jer 44:17
The *q* of the South..... Matt 12:42
under Candace the *q*..... Acts 8:27
heart, 'I sit as *q*.......... Rev 18:7

QUEENS
There are sixty *q*........ Song 6:8
q your nursing mothers..... Is 49:23

QUENCH
Many waters cannot *q*..... Song 8:7
so that no one can *q* ...... Jer 4:4
flax He will not *q* ...... Matt 12:20
q all the fiery .... Eph 6:16
Do not *q* the Spirit ..... 1 Thess 5:19

QUENCHED
LORD, the fire was *q* ..... Num 11:2
they were *q* like a......... Ps 118:12
their fire is not *q*.......... Is 66:24
that shall never be *q* ..... Mark 9:43
and the fire is not *q*..... Mark 9:44
q the violence of fire...... Heb 11:34

QUESTIONS
test him with hard *q* ..... 1 Kin 10:1
and asking them *q* .... Luke 2:46
market, asking no *q*.... 1 Cor 10:25

QUICKLY
have turned aside *q* .... Ex 32:8
with your adversary *q* .... Matt 5:25
"What you do, do *q* ..... John 13:27
Behold, I am coming *q*..... Rev 3:11
"Surely I am coming *q* .... Rev 22:20

QUICK-TEMPERED
q man acts foolishly ..... Prov 14:17
not self-willed, not *q*...... Titus 1:7

QUIET
lain still and been *q* ...... Job 3:13
'Take heed, and be *q* .... Is 7:4
earth is at rest and *q* ...... Is 14:7
gladness, He will *q* ...... Zeph 3:17
warned him to be *q* ..... Mark 10:48
aspire to lead a *q* ...... 1 Thess 4:11
we may lead a *q* and ..... 1 Tim 2:2
a gentle and *q* spirit...... 1 Pet 3:4

QUIETED
calmed and *q* my soul...... Ps 131:2
the city clerk had *q* ...... Acts 19:35

QUIETNESS
will give peace and *q* .... 1 Chr 22:9
When He gives *q*........ Job 34:29
a handful with *q* .... Eccl 4:6
in *q* and confidence ...... Is 30:15
of righteousness, *q* .... Is 32:17
that they work in *q*.... 2 Thess 3:12

QUIETS
q the earth by the .... Job 37:17

QUIVER
q rattles against him...... Job 39:23
the man who has his *q* ..... Ps 127:5
q He has hidden Me........ Is 49:2
Their *q* is like an........... Jer 5:16

RAAMSES
Treasure city built by Hebrew slaves,
    Ex 1:11

RABBAH
Capital of Ammon, Amos 1:14
Besieged by Joab; defeated and
    enslaved by David, 2 Sam
    12:26–31
Destruction of, foretold, Jer 49:2, 3

RABBI
be called by men, 'R . . . . . . Matt 23:7
do not be called 'R . . . . Matt 23:8

RABBONI
Mary addresses Christ as, John 20:16

RABSARIS
Title applied to:
Assyrian officials sent by Sennacherib, 2 Kin 18:17
Babylonian prince, Jer 39:3, 13

RABSHAKEH
Sent by king of Assyria to threaten Hezekiah, 2 Kin 18:17–37; Is 36:2–22
The Lord sends rumor to take him away, 2 Kin 19:6–8; Is 37:6–8

RACA
to his brother, 'R . . . . Matt 5:22

RACE
man to run its r . . . . Ps 19:5
r is not to the swift . . . . Eccl 9:11
who run in a r all run . . . . 1 Cor 9:24
I have finished the r . . . . . . 2 Tim 4:7
with endurance the r . . . . . . Heb 12:1

RACHEL
Laban's younger daughter; Jacob's favorite wife, Gen 29:28–30
Supports her husband's position, Gen 31:14–16
Mother of Joseph and Benjamin, Gen 30:22–25
Prophecy concerning; quoted, Jer 31:15; Matt 2:18

RADIANT
to Him and were r . . . . Ps 34:5

RAGE
Disperse the r of your . . . . . Job 40:11
Why do the nations r . . . . Ps 2:1
'Why did the nations r . . . . Acts 4:25

RAGES
he r against all wise . . . . . . Prov 18:1

RAGS
clothe a man with r . . . . . Prov 23:21

RAHAB
Prostitute in Jericho; helps Joshua's spies, Josh 2:1–21
Spared in battle, Josh 6:17–25
Mentioned in the NT, Matt 1:5; Heb 11:31; James 2:25
———— Used figuratively of Egypt, Ps 87:4

RAIN
had not caused it to r . . . . . . Gen 2:5
And the r was on the . . . . . Gen 7:12
He gives r on the . . . . Job 5:10
to the gentle r . . . . Job 37:6
sent a plentiful r . . . . Ps 68:9
clouds, who prepares r . . . . . Ps 147:8
snow in summer and r . . . . Prov 26:1
r which leaves no food . . . . Prov 28:3
not return after the r . . . . . Eccl 12:2
the r is over and gone . . . . . Song 2:11
our God, who gives r . . . . . . Jer 5:24
I will r down on him . . . . . Ezek 38:22
given you the former r . . . . . Joel 2:23
there will be no r . . . . Zech 14:17
the good, and sends r . . . . . Matt 5:45
and the r descended . . . . . . Matt 7:25
He did good, gave us r . . . . Acts 14:17
r that often comes . . . . Heb 6:7
that it would not r . . . . . . James 5:17
and the heaven gave r . . . James 5:18

RAINBOW

I set My r in the . . . . Gen 9:13
and there was a r . . . . Rev 4:3

RAINED
had r down manna on . . . . . Ps 78:24
r fire and brimstone . . . . . Luke 17:29

RAINS
r righteousness . . . . Hos 10:12

RAISE
third day He will r . . . . Hos 6:2
that God is able to r . . . . . . Matt 3:9
in three days I will r . . . . . . John 2:19
and I will r him up at . . . . . John 6:40
Lord and will also r . . . . . 1 Cor 6:14
and the Lord will r . . . . . James 5:15

RAISED
this purpose I have r . . . . . . Ex 9:16
be killed, and be r . . . . . . Matt 16:21
whom God r up . . . . Acts 2:24
just as Christ was r . . . . . . Rom 6:4
Spirit of Him who r . . . . . Rom 8:11
And God both r up the . . . 1 Cor 6:14
"How are the dead r . . . 1 Cor 15:35
and the dead will be r . . . 1 Cor 15:52
and r us up together . . . . Eph 2:6
then you were r . . . . Col 3:1

RAISES
r the poor out of the . . . . . . Ps 113:7
r those who are bowed . . . . . Ps 146:8
For as the Father r . . . . John 5:21
but in God who r . . . . 2 Cor 1:9

RAM
r which had two horns . . . . . Dan 8:3

RAMAH
Fortress built, 1 Kin 15:17–22
Samuel's headquarters, 1 Sam 7:15, 17
David flees to, 1 Sam 19:18–23

RAMOTH GILEAD
City of refuge east of Jordan, Deut 4:43; Josh 20:8; 1 Chr 6:80
Site of Ahab's fatal conflict with Syrians, 1 Kin 22:1–39

RAMS
the sweet aroma of r . . . . . . Ps 66:15
r of Nebaioth shall . . . . Is 60:7

RAN
they both r together . . . . . . John 20:4
You r well . . . . Gal 5:7

RANSOM
r would not help you . . . . . Job 36:18
nor give to God a r . . . . Ps 49:7
The r of a man's life . . . . . . Prov 13:8
"I will r them from . . . . . . Hos 13:14
to give His life a r . . . . . . Mark 10:45
who gave Himself a r . . . . . 1 Tim 2:6

RANSOMED
and the r of the LORD . . . . . . Is 35:10
redeemed Jacob, and r . . . . . Jer 31:11

RARE
of the LORD was r . . . . 1 Sam 3:1
make a mortal more r . . . . . Is 13:12

RASH
Do not be r with your . . . . . Eccl 5:2

RASHLY
so that he spoke r . . . . Ps 106:33
and do nothing r . . . . Acts 19:36

RAVEN
food for the r . . . . Job 38:41
and black as a r . . . . Song 5:11

RAVENOUS
inwardly they are r . . . . . . Matt 7:15

RAVENS
and to the young r . . . . Ps 147:9
Consider the r . . . . Luke 12:24

RAVISHED
You have r my heart . . . . . . Song 4:9
r the women in Zion . . . . . . Lam 5:11

RAZOR
like a sharp r . . . . Ps 52:2

REACHED
earth, and its top r . . . . . . Gen 28:12
For her sins have r . . . . Rev 18:5

REACHING
r forward to those . . . . Phil 3:13

READ
"Have you never r . . . . . . Matt 21:42
day, and stood up to r . . . . Luke 4:16
hearts, known and r . . . . . 2 Cor 3:2
when Moses is r . . . . 2 Cor 3:15
when this epistle is r . . . . . Col 4:16

READER
let the r understand . . . . . Mark 13:14

READINESS
the word with all r . . . . . . Acts 17:11
that as there was a r . . . . . 2 Cor 8:11

READING
r the prophet Isaiah . . . . . . Acts 8:30
give attention to r . . . . 1 Tim 4:13

READS
that he may run who r . . . . . Hab 2:2
Blessed is he who r . . . . Rev 1:3

READY
"The LORD was r . . . . Is 38:20
and those who were r . . . . Matt 25:10
"Lord, I am r . . . . Luke 22:33
and being r to punish . . . . 2 Cor 10:6
Be r in season and out . . . . 2 Tim 4:2
and always be r . . . . 1 Pet 3:15

REAFFIRM
r your love to him . . . . 2 Cor 2:8

REAP
in tears shall r . . . . Ps 126:5
r the whirlwind . . . . Hos 8:7
they neither sow nor r . . . . Matt 6:26
you knew that I r . . . . Matt 25:26
that he will also r . . . . Gal 6:7
due season we shall r . . . . . . Gal 6:9

REAPED
wheat but r thorns . . . . Jer 12:13
you have r iniquity . . . . . . Hos 10:13

REAPER
r does not fill his . . . . Ps 129:7

REAPERS
I will say to the r . . . . Matt 13:30
r are the angels . . . . Matt 13:39

REAPING
r what I did not . . . . Luke 19:22

REAPS
One sows and another r . . . John 4:37

REASON
out wisdom and the r . . . . . . Eccl 7:25
Come now, and let us r . . . . . Is 1:18
faith, why do you r . . . . . . Matt 16:8
words of truth and r . . . . . Acts 26:25
who asks you a r . . . . 1 Pet 3:15

REASONED
for three Sabbaths r . . . . . . Acts 17:2
r about righteousness . . . . Acts 24:25

REBEKAH
Great-niece of Abraham, Gen 22:20–23

Becomes Isaac's wife, Gen 24:15–67
Mother of Esau and Jacob, Gen
25:21–28
Encourages Jacob to deceive Isaac,
then to flee, Gen 27:1–29, 42–46

REBEL
Only do not *r* . . . . Num 14:9
Will you *r* against the . . . . . Neh 2:19
There are those who *r* . . . . . Job 24:13
and they did not *r* . . . . Ps 105:28
if you refuse and *r* . . . . Is 1:20

REBELLING
more against Him by *r* . . . . . Ps 78:17

REBELLION
r is as the sin . . . . 1 Sam 15:23
For he adds *r* to his . . . . . . Job 34:37
evil man seeks only *r* . . . . . Prov 17:11
you have taught *r* . . . . Jer 28:16
hearts as in the *r* . . . . Heb 3:8
and perished in the *r* . . . . . . Jude 11

REBELLIOUS
r exalt themselves . . . . Ps 66:7
but the *r* dwell in a . . . . Ps 68:6
day long to a *r* people . . . . . . Is 65:2
a defiant and *r* heart . . . . . . Jer 5:23
their princes are *r* . . . . Hos 9:15

REBELS
are all stubborn *r* . . . . Jer 6:28

REBUILD
God, to *r* its ruins . . . . Ezra 9:9
tombs, that I may *r* . . . . Neh 2:5
r it as in the days of . . . . . Amos 9:11

REBUKE
He will surely *r* . . . . Job 13:10
astonished at His *r* . . . . Job 26:11
they perish at the *r* . . . . Ps 80:16
At Your *r* they fled . . . . Ps 104:7
And let him *r* me . . . . Ps 141:5
Turn at my *r* . . . . Prov 1:23
r a wise man . . . . Prov 9:8
R is more effective . . . . Prov 17:10
r is better than love . . . . . . Prov 27:5
better to hear the *r* . . . . Eccl 7:5
r the oppressor . . . . Is 1:17
sake I have suffered *r* . . . . . Jer 15:15
r strong nations . . . . Mic 4:3
sins against you, *r* . . . . Luke 17:3
r Your disciples . . . . Luke 19:39
Do not *r* an older man . . . 1 Tim 5:1
who are sinning *r* . . . . . . 1 Tim 5:20
r them sharply . . . . Titus 1:13
"The Lord *r* you . . . . Jude 9
As many as I love, I *r* . . . . . Rev 3:19

REBUKED
r the winds and the . . . . . Matt 8:26
r their unbelief . . . . . Mark 16:14
when you are *r* by Him . . . Heb 12:5
but he was *r* for his . . . . . 2 Pet 2:16

REBUKES
with *r* You correct . . . . Ps 39:11
r a wicked man . . . . Prov 9:7
ear that hears the *r* . . . . . Prov 15:31
r a man will find more . . . Prov 28:23

RECALL
r the former days . . . . Heb 10:32

RECEIVE
He shall *r* blessing . . . . Ps 24:5
r us graciously . . . . Hos 14:2
you are willing to *r* . . . . . Matt 11:14
believing, you will *r* . . . . . Matt 21:22
and His own did not *r* . . . . John 1:11
"I do not *r* honor . . . . John 5:41
will come again and *r* . . . . John 14:3

the world cannot *r* . . . . . . John 14:17
Ask, and you will *r* . . . . . John 16:24
"*R* the Holy Spirit . . . . . . John 20:22
"Lord Jesus, *r* . . . . Acts 7:59
r the Holy Spirit . . . . Acts 8:15
r the Holy Spirit . . . . Acts 19:2
R one who is weak . . . . . . Rom 14:1
that each one may *r* . . . . 2 Cor 5:10
r the grace of God in . . . . . 2 Cor 6:1
r the Spirit by the . . . . Gal 3:2
R him therefore in the . . . . Phil 2:29
suppose that he will *r* . . . . James 1:7
whatever we ask we *r* . . . 1 John 3:22

RECEIVED
r your consolation . . . . . . Luke 6:24
in your lifetime you *r* . . . . Luke 16:25
But as many as *r* . . . . John 1:12
for God has *r* him . . . . Rom 14:3
For I *r* from the Lord . . . . 1 Cor 11:23
have *r* Christ Jesus . . . . Col 2:6
r up in glory . . . . 1 Tim 3:16
For He *r* from God the . . . . 2 Pet 1:17

RECEIVES
r correction is prudent . . . . . Prov 15:5
r you *r* Me . . . . Matt 10:40
r one little child . . . . Matt 18:5
and whoever *r* Me . . . . . . Mark 9:37

RECEIVING
r a kingdom which . . . . . . Heb 12:28

RECHAB
Assassin of Ishbosheth, 2 Sam 4:2, 6
—— Father of Jehonadab, founder of
the Rechabites, 2 Kin 10:15–23
Related to the Kenites, 1 Chr 2:55

RECHABITES
Kenite clan fathered by Rechab, committed to nomadic life, Jer 35:1–19

RECOMPENSE
He will accept no *r* . . . . . . Prov 6:35
not say, "I will *r* . . . . Prov 20:22
days of *r* have come . . . . Hos 9:7

RECOMPENSED
of my hands He has *r* . . . 2 Sam 22:21
the LORD has *r* me . . . . . 2 Sam 22:25

RECONCILE
and that He might *r* . . . . . . Eph 2:16
r all things to . . . . Col 1:20

RECONCILED
First be *r* to your . . . . Matt 5:24
were enemies we were *r* . . . Rom 5:10
Christ's behalf, be *r* . . . . . 2 Cor 5:20

RECONCILIATION
now received the *r* . . . . . . Rom 5:11
to us the word of *r* . . . . . . 2 Cor 5:19

RECONCILING
cast away is the *r* . . . . Rom 11:15
God was in Christ *r* . . . . . 2 Cor 5:19

RECORD
r My name I will come . . . . Ex 20:24

RED
the first came out *r* . . . . . . Gen 25:25
though they are *r* . . . . Is 1:18
Why is Your apparel *r* . . . . . Is 63:2
for the sky is *r* . . . . Matt 16:2

REDEEM
man you shall surely *r* . . . Num 18:15
in our power to *r* them . . . . Neh 5:5
In famine He shall *r* . . . . . . Job 5:20
R me from the hand of . . . . Job 6:23
can by any means *r* . . . . Ps 49:7
But God will *r* my soul . . . . Ps 49:15

r their life from . . . . Ps 72:14
And He shall *r* Israel . . . . . Ps 130:8
all that it cannot *r* . . . . Is 50:2
I will *r* them from . . . . Hos 13:14
was going to *r* Israel . . . . Luke 24:21
r those who were . . . . Gal 4:5
us, that He might *r* . . . . . . Titus 2:14

REDEEMED
people whom You have *r* . . . Ex 15:13
r them from the hand . . . . . Ps 106:10
Let the *r* of the LORD . . . . . Ps 107:2
r shall walk there . . . . Is 35:9
sea a road for the *r* . . . . Is 51:10
and you shall be *r* . . . . Is 52:3
and *r* His people . . . . Luke 1:68
Christ has *r* us from . . . . . . Gal 3:13
that you were not *r* . . . . . . 1 Pet 1:18
were slain, and have *r* . . . . . Rev 5:9
These were *r* from . . . . Rev 14:4

REDEEMER
For I know that my *R* . . . . Job 19:25
Most High God their *R* . . . . Ps 78:35
for their *R* is mighty . . . . . Prov 23:11
the LORD and your *R* . . . . . . Is 41:14
R will come to Zion . . . . Is 59:20
our *R* from Everlasting . . . . . Is 63:16
Their *R* is strong . . . . Jer 50:34

REDEEMING
r the time . . . . Eph 5:16

REDEMPTION
For the *r* of their . . . . Ps 49:8
with Him is abundant *r* . . . . Ps 130:7
r is yours to buy it . . . . Jer 32:7
those who looked for *r* . . . . Luke 2:38
your *r* draws near . . . . . . Luke 21:28
grace through the *r* . . . . Rom 3:24
the adoption, the *r* . . . . Rom 8:23
sanctification and *r* . . . . . 1 Cor 1:30
In Him we have *r* . . . . Eph 1:7
for the day of *r* . . . . Eph 4:30
obtained eternal *r* . . . . Heb 9:12

RED SEA
Divided for Israelites, Ex 14:15–31
Boundary of Promised Land, Ex
23:31

REED
r He will not break . . . . Is 42:3
r shaken by the wind . . . . . Matt 11:7
on the head with a *r* . . . . Mark 15:19

REEDS
r flourish without . . . . Job 8:11
the beasts of the *r* . . . . Ps 68:30

REFINED
where gold is *r* . . . . Job 28:1
us as silver is *r* . . . . Ps 66:10

REFINER
He will sit as a *r* . . . . Mal 3:3

REFORMATION
until the time of *r* . . . . Heb 9:10

REFRAIN
R from meddling with . . . 2 Chr 35:21
who have no right to *r* . . . . 1 Cor 9:6
good days, let him *r* . . . . . 1 Pet 3:10

REFRESH
bread, that you may *r* . . . . Gen 18:5
r my heart in the Lord . . . . Philem 20

REFRESHED
of God, and may be *r* . . . . Rom 15:32
r my spirit and yours . . . . 1 Cor 16:18
his spirit has been *r* . . . . . 2 Cor 7:13
for he often *r* . . . . 2 Tim 1:16

REFRESHES
r the soul of his . . . . Prov 25:13

REFRESHING
r may come from the . . . . . . Acts 3:19

REFUGE
six cities of *r* . . . . Num 35:6
eternal God is your *r* . . . . Deut 33:27
you have come for *r* . . . . . Ruth 2:12
My stronghold and my *r* . 2 Sam 22:3
but the Lord is his *r* . . . . Ps 14:6
God is our *r* and . . . . Ps 46:1
wings I will make my *r* . . . . Ps 57:1
God is *a r* for us . . . . Ps 62:8
You are my strong *r* . . . . Ps 71:7
my *r* and my fortress . . . . Ps 91:2
who have fled for *r* . . . . Heb 6:18

REFUSE
r the evil and choose . . . . Is 7:15
through deceit they *r* . . . . Jer 9:6
hear or whether they *r* . . . . Ezek 2:5
See that you do not *r* . . . . . Heb 12:25

REFUSED
They *r* to obey . . . . Neh 9:17

REFUSES
My soul *r* to touch . . . . Job 6:7
And if he *r* to hear . . . . . . Matt 18:17

REGARD
r the rich more than . . . . . . Job 34:19
r iniquity in my heart . . . . . . Ps 66:18
r the prayer of the . . . . . . Ps 102:17
did not fear God nor *r* . . . . . Luke 18:2

REGARDED
my hand and no one *r* . . . . Prov 1:24
r the lowly state . . . . Luke 1:48

REGARDS
r a rebuke will be . . . . Prov 13:18
He no longer *r* them . . . . . Lam 4:16

REGENERATION
to you, that in the *r* . . . . . Matt 19:28
the washing of *r* . . . . Titus 3:5

REGISTERED
So all went to be *r* . . . . Luke 2:3
firstborn who are *r* . . . . . . Heb 12:23

REGRETTED
but afterward he *r* . . . . . . Matt 21:29

REGULATIONS
yourselves to *r* . . . . Col 2:20

REHOBOAM
Son and successor of Solomon; refuses reform, 1 Kin 11:43—12:15
Ten tribes revolt against, 1 Kin 12:16–24
Reigns over Judah 17 years, 1 Kin 14:21–31; 2 Chr 11:5–23
Apostasizes, then repents, 2 Chr 12:1–16

REHOBOTH
Name of a well dug by Isaac, Gen 26:22

REIGN
but a king shall *r* . . . . . . 1 Sam 12:12
hypocrite should not *r* . . . . Job 34:30
so the Lord will *r* . . . . Mic 4:7
And He will *r* . . . . Luke 1:33
not have this man to *r* . . . . Luke 19:14
righteousness will *r* . . . . . . Rom 5:17
so grace might *r* . . . . Rom 5:21
do not let sin *r* . . . . Rom 6:12
For He must *r* till He . . . . 1 Cor 15:25
and we shall *r* on the . . . . . Rev 5:10
of Christ, and shall *r* . . . . . . Rev 20:6

REIGNED
so that as sin *r* . . . . Rom 5:21
You have *r* as kings . . . . . . 1 Cor 4:8
And they lived and *r* . . . . . . Rev 20:4

REIGNS
God *r* over the nations . . . . . . Ps 47:8
The Lord *r* . . . . Ps 93:1
to Zion, "Your God *r* . . . . Is 52:7
Lord God Omnipotent *r* . . . . Rev 19:6

REJECT
will these people *r* . . . . Num 14:11
r all those who stray . . . . . Ps 119:118
"All too well you *r* . . . . Mark 7:9
R a divisive man . . . . Titus 3:10

REJECTED
r has become the chief . . . . . Ps 118:22
He is despised and *r* . . . . Is 53:3
Israel has *r* the . . . . Hos 8:3
r has become the chief . . . Matt 21:42
many things and be *r* . . . . Luke 17:25
This Moses whom they *r* . . . . Acts 7:35
to a living stone, *r* . . . . 1 Pet 2:4
r has become the chief . . . . . 1 Pet 2:7

REJECTION
you shall know My *r* . . . . Num 14:34

REJECTS
he who *r* Me *r* . . . . Luke 10:16
r this does not reject . . . . . 1 Thess 4:8

REJOICE
so the Lord will *r* . . . . Deut 28:63
let the field *r* . . . . 1 Chr 16:32
and let Your saints *r* . . . . . 2 Chr 6:41
r who put their trust . . . . Ps 5:11
people, let Jacob . . . . Ps 14:7
R in the Lord . . . . Ps 33:1
mutual confusion who *r* . . . . Ps 35:26
The righteous shall *r* . . . . . . Ps 58:10
of Your wings I will *r* . . . . . . Ps 63:7
But the king shall *r* . . . . . . Ps 63:11
Let them *r* before God . . . . . . Ps 68:3
In Your name they *r* . . . . . . Ps 89:16
Let the heavens . . . . Ps 96:11
Let the earth *r* . . . . Ps 97:1
righteous see it and *r* . . . . . Ps 107:42
we will *r* and be glad . . . . . Ps 118:24
who *r* in doing evil . . . . Prov 2:14
be blessed, and *r* . . . . Prov 5:18
she shall *r* in time to . . . . . Prov 31:25
R, O young man . . . . Eccl 11:9
We will be glad and *r* . . . . . Song 1:4
among men shall *r* . . . . Is 29:19
I will greatly *r* . . . . Is 61:10
My servants shall *r* . . . . Is 65:13
your heart shall *r* . . . . Is 66:14
Yes, I will . . . . Jer 32:41
Do not *r* over me . . . . Mic 7:8
He will *r* over you . . . . Zeph 3:17
do not *r* in this . . . . Luke 10:20
loved Me, you would *r* . . . John 14:28
but the world will *r* . . . . . John 16:20
and your heart will *r* . . . . . John 16:22
R with those who . . . . Rom 12:15
and in this I *r* . . . . Phil 1:18
faith, I am glad and *r* . . . . . Phil 2:17
R in the Lord always . . . . . . Phil 4:4
R always . . . . 1 Thess 5:16
yet believing, you *r* . . . . 1 Pet 1:8

REJOICED
for good as He *r* . . . . Deut 30:9
for my heart *r* . . . . Eccl 2:10
and my spirit has *r* . . . . . . Luke 1:47
In that hour Jesus *r* . . . . . Luke 10:21
Your father Abraham *r* . . . . John 8:56
But I *r* in the Lord . . . . Phil 4:10

REJOICES
glad, and my glory *r* . . . . . . Ps 16:9
but *r* in the truth . . . . 1 Cor 13:6

REJOICING
His works with *r* . . . . Ps 107:22
The voice of *r* and . . . . Ps 118:15
for they are the *r* . . . . Ps 119:111
come again with *r* . . . . Ps 126:6
r in His inhabited . . . . Prov 8:31
he went on his way *r* . . . . . Acts 8:39
yet always *r* . . . . 2 Cor 6:10
or joy, or crown of *r* . . . . 1 Thess 2:19
confidence and the *r* . . . . . . Heb 3:6

RELATIVES
r stand afar off . . . . Ps 38:11

RELEASE
do you want me to *r* . . . . . Matt 27:17
and power to *r* You . . . . . . John 19:10
"*R* the four angels . . . . Rev 9:14

RELENT
sworn and will not *r* . . . . . . Ps 110:4
and will not *r* . . . . Jer 4:28
then the Lord will *r* . . . . . . Jer 26:13
if He will turn and *r* . . . . . . Joel 2:14
sworn and will not *r* . . . . . . Heb 7:21

RELENTED
So the Lord *r* from the . . . . . Ex 32:14
the Lord looked and *r* . . . 1 Chr 21:15
and God *r* from the . . . . Jon 3:10

RELENTING
I am weary of *r* . . . . Jer 15:6

RELIEF
saw that there was *r* . . . . . . Ex 8:15
that I may find *r* . . . . Job 32:20

RELIEVE
of my lips would *r* . . . . Job 16:5
r those who are really . . . . 1 Tim 5:16

RELIEVED
You have *r* me when I . . . . . . Ps 4:1

RELIEVES
r the fatherless . . . . Ps 146:9

RELIGION
about their own *r* . . . . Acts 25:19
in self-imposed *r* . . . . Col 2:23
heart, this one's *r* . . . . . . James 1:26
and undefiled *r* . . . . James 1:27

RELIGIOUS
things you are very *r* . . . . . Acts 17:22
you thinks he is *r* . . . . James 1:26

RELY
name of the Lord and *r* . . . . . Is 50:10
You *r* on your sword . . . . . Ezek 33:26

REMAIN
shall let none of it *r* . . . . . . Ex 12:10
r angry forever . . . . Jer 3:5
and this city shall *r* . . . . . . Jer 17:25
that if ten men *r* . . . . Amos 6:9
you, that My joy may *r* . . . . John 15:11
your fruit should *r* . . . . . . John 15:16
"If I will that he *r* . . . . John 21:22
the greater part *r* . . . . 1 Cor 15:6
Nevertheless to *r* . . . . Phil 1:24
we who are alive and *r* . . 1 Thess 4:15
the things which *r* . . . . Rev 3:2

REMAINDER
with the *r* of wrath . . . . Ps 76:10
I am deprived of the *r* . . . . . Is 38:10

REMAINED
Also my wisdom *r* . . . . Eccl 2:9
And Mary *r* with her . . . . . Luke 1:56
like a dove, and He *r* . . . . . John 1:32

REMAINS
"While the earth *r* . . . . Gen 8:22
Therefore your sin *r* . . . . . . John 9:41
There *r* therefore a . . . . Heb 4:9
sin, for His seed *r* . . . . 1 John 3:9

REMEMBER
But *r* me when it is . . . . . . Gen 40:14
R the Sabbath day . . . . Ex 20:8
r that you were a . . . . Deut 15:15
R His marvelous works . . 1 Chr 16:12
but we will *r* the name . . . . . . Ps 20:7
r the sins of my youth . . . . . . Ps 25:7
r Your name in the . . . . Ps 119:55
R now your Creator . . . . Eccl 12:1
r your love more than . . . . . Song 1:4
r the former things . . . . Is 43:18
"I *r* you, the kindness . . . . . . Jer 2:2
and their sin I will *r* . . . . . . Jer 31:34
r the covenant of . . . . Amos 1:9
in wrath *r* mercy . . . . Hab 3:2
and to *r* His holy . . . . Luke 1:72
R Lot's wife . . . . Luke 17:32
r the words of the . . . . Acts 20:35
R my chains . . . . Col 4:18
R that Jesus Christ . . . . . . 2 Tim 2:8
R those who rule . . . . Heb 13:7

REMEMBERED
Then God *r* Noah . . . . Gen 8:1
r His covenant with . . . . Ex 2:24
I *r* God . . . . Ps 77:3
r His covenant forever . . . . . Ps 105:8
r Your judgments . . . . Ps 119:52
Who *r* us in our lowly . . . . . Ps 136:23
yea, we wept when we *r* . . . . . Ps 137:1
r that same poor man . . . . . Eccl 9:15
r the days of old . . . . Is 63:11
And Peter *r* the word . . . . Matt 26:75
r the word of the Lord . . . . Acts 11:16

REMEMBERS
My soul still *r* . . . . Lam 3:20

REMEMBRANCE
in death there is no *r* . . . . Ps 6:5
I call to *r* my song . . . . Ps 77:6
There is no *r* of . . . . Eccl 1:11
Put Me in *r* . . . . Is 43:26
do this in *r* of Me . . . . . . Luke 22:19
do this in *r* of Me . . . . . . 1 Cor 11:24

REMIND
r you always of these . . . . . 2 Pet 1:12
But I want to *r* you . . . . Jude 5

REMINDER
there is a *r* of sins . . . . Heb 10:3
you always have a *r* . . . . . 2 Pet 1:15
pure minds by way of *r* . . . . 2 Pet 3:1

REMISSION
repentance for the *r* . . . . . . Mark 1:4
Jesus Christ for the *r* . . . . . Acts 2:38
where there is *r* . . . . Heb 10:18

REMNANT
to us a very small *r* . . . . Is 1:9
The *r* will return . . . . Is 10:21
be well with your *r* . . . . Jer 15:11
I will gather the *r* . . . . Jer 23:3
and all the *r* of Judah . . . . . Jer 44:28
Yet I will leave a *r* . . . . Ezek 6:8
r whom the LORD calls . . . . Joel 2:32
I will not treat the *r* . . . . . . Zech 8:11
time there is a *r* . . . . Rom 11:5

REMORSEFUL
been condemned, was *r* . . Matt 27:3

REMOVE
R Your plague from me . . . . . Ps 39:10
R Your gaze from me . . . . . . Ps 39:13

r your foot from evil . . . . . Prov 4:27
r falsehood and lies . . . . . . Prov 30:8
Therefore *r* sorrow . . . . Eccl 11:10
r this cup from Me . . . . . Luke 22:42
r your lampstand . . . . Rev 2:5

REMOVED
Though the earth be *r* . . . . . . Ps 46:2
r our transgressions . . . . . Ps 103:12
will never be *r* . . . . Prov 10:30
and the hills be *r* . . . . Is 54:10
this mountain, 'Be *r* . . . . . Matt 21:21

REMOVES
r the mountains . . . . Job 9:5

REND
So *r* your heart . . . . Joel 2:13

RENDER
What shall I *r* to the . . . . . Ps 116:12
who will *r* to him the . . . . Matt 21:41
"*R* therefore to Caesar . . . . Matt 22:21

RENEW
r a steadfast . . . . Ps 51:10
r the face of the . . . . Ps 104:30
on the LORD shall *r* . . . . Is 40:31

RENEWED
that your youth is *r* . . . . . . Ps 103:5
inward man is being *r* . . . . 2 Cor 4:16
and be *r* in the spirit . . . . . . Eph 4:23
the new man who is *r* . . . . . . Col 3:10

RENEWING
transformed by the *r* . . . . . Rom 12:2
of regeneration and *r* . . . . . Titus 3:5

RENOUNCE
Why do the wicked *r* . . . . . Ps 10:13

RENOUNCED
r the covenant of Your . . . . . Ps 89:39
r the hidden things . . . . . . 2 Cor 4:2

RENOUNCES
greedy and *r* the LORD . . . . . . Ps 10:3

RENOWN
were of old, men of *r* . . . . . . Gen 6:4

REPAID
done, so God has *r* . . . . Judg 1:7
And he has *r* me evil . . . 1 Sam 25:21
good shall be *r* . . . . Prov 13:21
Shall evil be *r* . . . . Jer 18:20

REPAIR
r the house of your . . . . . 2 Chr 24:5
r the ruined cities . . . . Is 61:4

REPAY
He will *r* him to his . . . . . . Deut 7:10
silence, but will *r* . . . . Is 65:6
He will surely *r* . . . . Jer 51:56
again, I will *r* . . . . Luke 10:35
because they cannot *r* . . . . Luke 14:14
R no one evil for evil . . . . Rom 12:17
is Mine, I will *r* . . . . Rom 12:19
r their parents . . . . 1 Tim 5:4
I will *r* . . . . Philem 19

REPAYS
and who *r* him for what . . . Job 21:31
r the proud person . . . . Ps 31:23
shall he be who *r* . . . . Ps 137:8
the LORD, who fully *r* . . . . . . Is 66:6

REPEATS
r a matter separates . . . . . Prov 17:9

REPENT
I abhor myself, and *r* . . . . . Job 42:6
"*R*, for the kingdom . . . . . . Matt 3:2
you *r* you will all . . . . Luke 13:3
said to them, "*R* . . . . Acts 2:38
men everywhere to *r* . . . . Acts 17:30
be zealous and *r* . . . . Rev 3:19

REPENTANCE
you with water unto *r* . . . . Matt 3:11
a baptism of *r* for the . . . . Mark 1:4
persons who need no *r* . . . Luke 15:7
sorrow produces *r* . . . . . . 2 Cor 7:10
will grant them *r* . . . . 2 Tim 2:25
renew them again to *r* . . . . . Heb 6:6
found no place for *r* . . . . . Heb 12:17
all should come to *r* . . . . . 2 Pet 3:9

REPENTED
No man *r* of his . . . . Jer 8:6
after my turning, I *r* . . . . . . Jer 31:19
it, because they *r* . . . . Matt 12:41

REPETITIONS
r as the heathen do . . . . . . Matt 6:7

REPHAIM
Valley near Jerusalem, 2 Sam 23:13, 14
Scene of Philistine defeats, 2 Sam
  5:18–22

REPHIDIM
Israelite camp, Num 33:12–15
Moses strikes rock at, Ex 17:1–7
Amalek defeated at, Ex 17:8–16

REPORT
circulate a false *r* . . . . Ex 23:1
For it is not a good *r* . . . . 1 Sam 2:24
r makes the bones . . . . . . Prov 15:30
Who has believed our *r* . . . . . Is 53:1
who has believed our *r* . . . Rom 10:16
things are of good *r* . . . . . . Phil 4:8

REPRIMANDED
And they *r* him sharply . . . . Judg 8:1

REPROACH
r me as long as I live . . . . . . Job 27:6
does he take up a *r* . . . . Ps 15:3
You make us a *r* . . . . Ps 44:13
sake I have borne . . . . Ps 69:7
R has broken my heart . . . . . Ps 69:20
nation, but sin is a *r* . . . . . Prov 14:34
with dishonor comes . . . . . Prov 18:3
do not fear the *r* . . . . Is 51:7
not remember the *r* . . . . Is 54:4
bring an everlasting *r* . . . . . Jer 23:40
because I bore the *r* . . . . . . Jer 31:19
you shall bear the *r* . . . . . . Mic 6:16
these things You *r* . . . . . . Luke 11:45
lest he fall into *r* . . . . 1 Tim 3:7
esteeming the *r* . . . . Heb 11:26
and without *r* . . . . James 1:5

REPROACHED
If you are *r* for the . . . . . . 1 Pet 4:14

REPROACHES
is not an enemy who *r* . . . . . Ps 55:12
oppresses the poor *r* . . . . Prov 14:31
curse, and Israel to *r* . . . . . . Is 43:28
in infirmities, in *r* . . . . . . 2 Cor 12:10

REPROACHFULLY
they strike me *r* . . . . Job 16:10

REPROOF
for doctrine, for *r* . . . . . . 2 Tim 3:16

REPROOFS
R of instruction are . . . . . . Prov 6:23

REPUTATION
seven men of good *r* . . . . . . Acts 6:3
to those who were of *r* . . . . . Gal 2:2
made Himself of no *r* . . . . . Phil 2:7

REQUEST
not withheld the *r* . . . . Ps 21:2
He gave them their *r* . . . . . Ps 106:15
the Lord God to make *r* . . . . Dan 9:3
For Jews *r* a sign . . . . 1 Cor 1:22
of mine making *r* . . . . Phil 1:4

r deep and secret . . . . Dan 2:22
r secrets has made . . . . Dan 2:29
He *r* His secret to . . . . Amos 3:7

REVELATION
Where there is no *r* . . . . . Prov 29:18
the day of wrath and *r* . . . . . Rom 2:5
has a tongue, has a *r* . . 1 Cor 14:26
it came through the *r* . . . . . Gal 1:12
spirit of wisdom and *r* . . . . Eph 1:17
r He made known to . . . . . Eph 3:3
and glory at the *r* . . . . 1 Pet 1:7

REVELATIONS
come to visions and *r* . . . . 2 Cor 12:1

REVELRIES
drunkenness, *r* . . . . Gal 5:21
lusts, drunkenness, *r*. . . . . . 1 Pet 4:3

REVENGE
and we will take our *r* . . . . . Jer 20:10

REVENUES
than vast *r* without . . . . . . Prov 16:8

REVERENCE
and *r* My sanctuary. . . . . . . Lev 19:30
and to be held in *r* . . . . Ps 89:7
Master, where is My *r*. . . . . . Mal 1:6
submission with all *r* . . . . 1 Tim 3:4
God acceptably with *r* . . . . Heb 12:28

REVERENT
man who is always *r*. . . . . Prov 28:14
their wives must be *r*. . . . . 1 Tim 3:11
older men be sober, *r* . . . . . . Titus 2:2

REVILE
are you when they *r* . . . . . . Matt 5:11
r God's high priest . . . . Acts 23:4
evildoers, those who *r* . . . . 1 Pet 3:16

REVILED
crucified with Him *r*. . . . . Mark 15:32
who, when He was *r* . . . . . . 1 Pet 2:23

REVILER
or an idolater, or a *r* . . . . . 1 Cor 5:11

REVILERS
nor drunkards, nor *r* . . . . . 1 Cor 6:10

REVILING
come envy, strife, *r* . . . . 1 Tim 6:4

REVIVAL
give us a measure of *r*. . . . . Ezra 9:8

REVIVE
troubles, shall *r*. . . . . Ps 71:20
Will You not *r* us . . . . Ps 85:6
r me according to Your . . . . Ps 119:25
r the spirit of the. . . . . Is 57:15
two days He will *r*. . . . . Hos 6:2
r Your work in the . . . . . . Hab 3:2

REVIVED
they shall be *r*. . . . . Hos 14:7
came, sin *r* and I died. . . . . Rom 7:9

REVOLT
You will *r* more and. . . . . Is 1:5

REVOLTED
Israel have deeply *r* . . . . Is 31:6
they have *r* and . . . . Jer 5:23

REVOLTERS
r are deeply involved . . . . . . Hos 5:2

REWARD
exceedingly great *r*. . . . . . Gen 15:1
them there is great *r* . . . . . . Ps 19:11
r me evil for good . . . . Ps 35:12
"Surely there is a *r* . . . . Ps 58:11
look, and see the *r*. . . . . Ps 91:8
will a sure *r* . . . . Prov 11:18
and the LORD will *r* . . . . . Prov 25:22

and this was my *r*. . . . . Eccl 2:10
behold, His *r* is with . . . . Is 40:10
r them for their deeds. . . . . . Hos 4:9
You have loved for *r*. . . . . . . Hos 9:1
for great is your *r* . . . . Matt 5:12
you have no *r* from . . . . . . Matt 6:1
you, they have their *r*. . . . . Matt 6:2
receive a prophet's *r* . . . . Matt 10:41
by no means lose his *r* . . . Matt 10:42
r will be great . . . . Luke 6:35
we receive the due *r* . . . . Luke 23:41
will receive his own *r* . . . . . 1 Cor 3:8
cheat you of your *r* . . . . Col 2:18
for he looked to the *r*. . . . . Heb 11:26
may receive a full *r* . . . . . . 2 John 8
quickly, and My *r* . . . . Rev 22:12

REWARDED
Thus they have *r*. . . . . Ps 109:5

REWARDER
and that He is a *r*. . . . . Heb 11:6

REWARDS
Whoever *r* evil for . . . . . . Prov 17:13
and follows after *r* . . . . Is 1:23
and give your *r* . . . . Dan 5:17

REZIN
King of Damascus; joins Pekah
   against Ahaz, 2 Kin 15:37
Confederacy of, inspires Isaiah's
   great messianic prophecy,
   Is 7:1—9:12

REZON
Son of Eliadah; establishes Syrian
   kingdom, 1 Kin 11:23–25

RHODA
Servant girl, Acts 12:13–16

RIBLAH
Headquarters of:
   Pharaoh Necho, 2 Kin 23:31–35
   Nebuchadnezzar, 2 Kin 25:6, 20, 21
   Zedekiah blinded here, Jer 39:5–7

RICH
Abram was very *r*. . . . . Gen 13:2
makes poor and makes *r*. . 1 Sam 2:7
r man will lie down . . . . Job 27:19
the *r* among the people. . . . . Ps 45:12
when one becomes *r* . . . . . . Ps 49:16
soul will be made *r* . . . . . Prov 11:25
who makes himself *r* . . . . . Prov 13:7
r has many friends . . . . . . Prov 14:20
The *r* and the poor . . . . . . Prov 22:2
r rules over the poor . . . . . Prov 22:7
r man is wise in his . . . . . Prov 28:11
do not curse the *r* . . . . Eccl 10:20
it is hard for a *r* . . . . Matt 19:23
to you who are *r* . . . . Luke 6:24
from the *r* man's table . . . Luke 16:21
for he was very *r* . . . . Luke 18:23
Lord over all is *r* . . . . Rom 10:12
You are already *r*. . . . . 1 Cor 4:8
though He was *r* . . . . 2 Cor 8:9
who desire to be *r* . . . . 1 Tim 6:9
but the *r* in his . . . . James 1:9
So the *r* man also will. . . . James 1:11
of this world to be *r* . . . . . James 2:5
you say, 'I am *r*. . . . . Rev 3:17

RICHES
Both *r* and honor come . . 1 Chr 29:12
He swallows down *r*. . . . . . Job 20:15
he heaps up *r* . . . . Ps 39:6
the abundance of his *r* . . . . . Ps 52:7
if *r* increase . . . . Ps 62:10
r will be in his house . . . . . . Ps 112:3
in her left hand *r*. . . . . Prov 3:16
R and honor are . . . . Prov 8:18

R do not profit . . . . Prov 11:4
in his *r* will fall . . . . Prov 11:28
yet has great *r* . . . . Prov 13:7
of the wise is their *r*. . . . . Prov 14:24
and *r* are an. . . . . Prov 19:14
of the LORD are *r* . . . . Prov 22:4
r are not forever. . . . . Prov 27:24
r kept for their owner . . . . . Eccl 5:13
darkness and hidden *r*. . . . . Is 45:3
you shall eat the *r* . . . . Is 61:6
so is he who gets *r*. . . . . . . Jer 17:11
have increased your *r* . . . . Ezek 28:5
for those who have *r* . . . . Mark 10:23
do you despise the *r* . . . . . . Rom 2:4
might make known the *r* . . Rom 9:23
what are the *r*. . . . . Eph 1:18
show the exceeding *r*. . . . . Eph 2:7
the unsearchable *r*. . . . . . . Eph 3:8
trust in uncertain *r* . . . . . 1 Tim 6:17
r than the treasures . . . . . Heb 11:26
r are corrupted . . . . James 5:2
to receive power and *r* . . . . Rev 5:12

RICHLY
Christ dwell in you *r*. . . . . . Col 3:16
God, who gives us *r*. . . . . 1 Tim 6:17

RIDDLE
"Let me pose a *r*. . . . . Judg 14:12

RIDDLES
the wise and their *r*. . . . . . . Prov 1:6

RIDE
wind and cause me to *r* . . . Job 30:22
in Your majesty *r*. . . . . Ps 45:4
have caused men to *r* . . . . . Ps 66:12

RIDER
r He has thrown . . . . Ex 15:1
the horse and its *r* . . . . Job 39:18

RIDES
Behold, the LORD *r* . . . . Is 19:1

RIDGES
You water its *r* . . . . Ps 65:10

RIDICULE
those who see Me *r* Me . . . . . Ps 22:7
Whom do you *r* . . . . Is 57:4

RIDICULED
they *r* Him. . . . . Matt 9:24

RIGHT
you shall do what is *r*. . . . . Deut 6:18
the *r* of the firstborn . . . . . Deut 21:17
did what was *r* in his . . . . Judg 21:25
"Is your heart *r*. . . . . 2 Kin 10:15
them forth by the *r* . . . . . . Ps 107:7
Lord, "Sit at My *r*. . . . . Ps 110:1
is a way which seems *r* . . . Prov 14:12
way of a man is *r* . . . . Prov 21:2
things that are *r* . . . . Is 45:19
until He comes whose *r* . . . Ezek 21:27
of the LORD are *r* . . . . Hos 14:9
do not know to do *r* . . . . . Amos 3:10
and whatever is *r* . . . . Matt 20:4
clothed and in his *r* . . . . . Mark 5:15
not judge what is *r* . . . . . . Luke 12:57
to them He gave the *r*. . . . . John 1:12
your heart is not *r* . . . . Acts 8:21
Do we have no *r* . . . . 1 Cor 9:4
seven stars in His *r* . . . . Rev 2:1

RIGHTEOUS
also destroy the *r* . . . . Gen 18:23
and they justify the *r* . . . . . Deut 25:1
"You are more *r* . . . . 1 Sam 24:17
that he could be *r* . . . . Job 15:14
r will hold to his way . . . . . Job 17:9
"The *r* see it and . . . . Job 22:19
knows the way of the *r*. . . . . Ps 1:6

LORD, will bless the *r* . . . . Ps 5:12
r God tests the hearts . . . . Ps 7:9
what can the *r* . . . . Ps 11:3
The *r* cry out . . . . Ps 34:17
the LORD upholds the *r* . . . . . Ps 37:17
r shows mercy and . . . . Ps 37:21
I have not seen the *r* . . . . . . Ps 37:25
the *r* will be in . . . . Ps 112:6
The LORD is *r* in all . . . . Ps 145:17
the LORD loves the *r* . . . . Ps 146:8
will not allow the *r* . . . . Prov 10:3
r is a well of life . . . . Prov 10:11
The labor of the *r* . . . . Prov 10:16
r will be gladness . . . . Prov 10:28
r is delivered from . . . . Prov 11:8
r will be delivered . . . . Prov 11:21
r will flourish . . . . Prov 11:28
r will be recompensed . . . . Prov 11:31
r man regards the life . . . . . Prov 12:10
r should choose his . . . . . . Prov 12:26
r there is much . . . . Prov 15:6
the prayer of the *r* . . . . Prov 15:29
the *r* run to it and . . . . Prov 18:10
r are bold as a lion . . . . . . Prov 28:1
When the *r* are in . . . . Prov 29:2
r considers the cause . . . . . Prov 29:7
Do not be overly *r* . . . . Eccl 7:16
event happens to the *r* . . . . Eccl 9:2
r that it shall be . . . . Is 3:10
the gates, that the *r* . . . . . . Is 26:2
with My *r* right hand . . . . . . Is 41:10
By His knowledge My *r* . . . . Is 53:11
The *r* perishes . . . . Is 57:1
people shall all be *r* . . . . . . Is 60:21
R are You . . . . Jer 12:1
your sins by being *r* . . . . . Dan 4:27
they sell the *r* . . . . Amos 2:6
not come to call the *r* . . . . Matt 9:13
r men desired to see . . . . . Matt 13:17
r will shine forth as . . . . . Matt 13:43
And they were both *r* . . . . . Luke 1:6
that they were *r* . . . . Luke 18:9
"Certainly this was a *r* . . Luke 23:47
"There is none *r* . . . . Rom 3:10
r man will one die . . . . Rom 5:7
witness that he was *r* . . . . . Heb 11:4
Jesus Christ the *r* . . . . . . 1 John 2:1
just as He is *r* . . . . 1 John 3:7
r are Your . . . . Rev 16:7
fine linen is the *r* . . . . Rev 19:8

RIGHTEOUSLY
judge the people *r* . . . . Ps 67:4
He who walks *r* and . . . . Is 33:15
should live soberly, *r* . . . . . Titus 2:12
to Him who judges *r* . . . . . 1 Pet 2:23

RIGHTEOUSNESS
it to him for *r* . . . . Gen 15:6
My *r* I hold fast . . . . Job 27:6
I put on *r* . . . . Job 29:14
I will ascribe *r* . . . . Job 36:3
I call, O God of my *r* . . . . . . Ps 4:1
righteous, He loves *r* . . . . . . Ps 11:7
from the LORD, and *r* . . . . . . Ps 24:5
shall speak of Your *r* . . . . . Ps 35:28
the good news of *r* . . . . Ps 40:9
You love *r* and hate . . . . Ps 45:7
heavens declare His *r* . . . . . Ps 50:6
sing aloud of Your *r* . . . . . Ps 51:14
r and peace have . . . . Ps 85:10
R will go before Him . . . . . Ps 85:13
r they are exalted . . . . Ps 89:16
will return to *r* . . . . Ps 94:15
r and justice are the . . . . . . Ps 97:2
and he who does *r* . . . . . . Ps 106:3
r endures forever . . . . Ps 111:3
r is an everlasting . . . . . . Ps 119:142
r delivers from death . . . . Prov 10:2

The *r* of the blameless . . . . Prov 11:5
The *r* of the upright . . . . . . Prov 11:6
r leads to life . . . . Prov 11:19
the way of *r* is life . . . . . . Prov 12:28
R guards him whose way . . Prov 13:6
R exalts a nation . . . . Prov 14:34
found in the way of *r* . . . . Prov 16:31
He who follows *r* . . . . Prov 21:21
r lodged in it . . . . Is 1:21
r He shall judge . . . . Is 11:4
R shall be the belt . . . . Is 11:5
he will not learn *r* . . . . Is 26:10
and *r* the plummet . . . . Is 28:17
r will be peace . . . . Is 32:17
in the LORD I have *r* . . . . Is 45:24
who are far from *r* . . . . Is 46:12
r will be forever . . . . Is 51:8
I will declare your *r* . . . . . . Is 57:12
and His own *r* . . . . Is 59:16
r as a breastplate . . . . Is 59:17
be called trees of *r* . . . . Is 61:3
r goes forth as . . . . Is 62:1
THE LORD OUR *R* . . . . Jer 23:6
to David a Branch of *r* . . . . Jer 33:15
has revealed our *r* . . . . Jer 51:10
The *r* of the righteous . . . . Ezek 18:20
O Lord, *r* belongs . . . . Dan 9:7
in everlasting *r* . . . . Dan 9:24
who turn many to *r* . . . . . . Dan 12:3
for yourselves *r* . . . . Hos 10:12
to fulfill all *r* . . . . Matt 3:15
exceeds the *r* of the . . . . . . Matt 5:20
to you in the way of *r* . . . . Matt 21:32
in holiness and *r* . . . . Luke 1:75
For in it the *r* . . . . Rom 1:17
even the *r* of God . . . . Rom 3:22
a seal of the *r* . . . . Rom 4:11
accounted to him for *r* . . . . Rom 4:22
r will reign in life . . . . Rom 5:17
might reign through *r* . . . . . Rom 5:21
is life because of *r* . . . . Rom 8:10
who did not pursue *r* . . . . . Rom 9:30
pursuing the law of *r* . . . . . Rom 9:31
ignorant of God's *r* . . . . . . Rom 10:3
we might become the *r* . . . 2 Cor 5:21
r comes through the . . . . . . Gal 2:21
the breastplate of *r* . . . . . . Eph 6:14
not having my own *r* . . . . . . Phil 3:9
things and pursue *r* . . . . . . 1 Tim 6:11
r which we have . . . . Titus 3:5
r which is according . . . . . . Heb 11:7
does not produce the *r* . . . James 1:20
should suffer for *r* . . . . 1 Pet 3:14
a preacher of *r* . . . . 2 Pet 2:5
a new earth in which *r* . . . . 2 Pet 3:13
who practices *r* . . . . 1 John 2:29
He who practices *r* . . . . . . 1 John 3:7
does not practice *r* . . . . . . 1 John 3:10

RIGHTLY
wise uses knowledge *r* . . . . Prov 15:2
R do they love you . . . . . Song 1:4
"You have answered *r* . . . Luke 10:28
r dividing the word . . . . . 2 Tim 2:15

RIGHTS
and her marriage *r* . . . . Ex 21:10

RING
the king's signet *r* . . . . . . Esth 8:8
make you like a signet *r* . . . Hag 2:23

RINGLEADER
the world, and a *r* . . . . . . Acts 24:5

RINGS
a man with gold *r* . . . . . . James 2:2

RIPE
figs that are first *r* . . . . Jer 24:2

RISE
is vain for you to *r* . . . . . . Ps 127:2
"Now I will *r* . . . . Is 33:10
for He makes His sun *r* . . . Matt 5:45
of Nineveh will *r* . . . . Matt 12:41
third day He will *r* . . . . . . Matt 20:19
false prophets will *r* . . . . . Matt 24:24
persuaded though one *r* . . . Luke 16:31
third day He will *r* . . . . . . Luke 18:33
had to suffer and *r* . . . . . . Acts 17:3
be the first to *r* . . . . Acts 26:23
fact the dead do not *r* . . . 1 Cor 15:15
in Christ will *r* . . . . 1 Thess 4:16

RISEN
of the LORD is *r* . . . . Is 60:1
women there has not *r* . . . Matt 11:11
disciples that He is *r* . . . . . Matt 28:7
"The Lord is *r* . . . . Luke 24:34
furthermore is also *r* . . . . . Rom 8:34
then Christ is not *r* . . . . . 1 Cor 15:13
if Christ is not *r* . . . . 1 Cor 15:17
But now Christ is *r* . . . . . 1 Cor 15:20

RISES
shall I do when God *r* . . . . Job 31:14
every tongue which *r* . . . . . . Is 54:17

RISING
may know from the *r* . . . . . . Is 45:6
questioning what the *r* . . . Mark 9:10
for the fall and *r* . . . . Luke 2:34

RIVER
Indeed the *r* may rage . . . . . Job 40:23
them drink from the *r* . . . . . Ps 36:8
r whose streams shall . . . . . . Ps 46:4
the *r* of God is full . . . . Ps 65:9
went through the *r* . . . . Ps 66:6
peace to her like a *r* . . . . . . Is 66:12
r that I could not cross . . . . Ezek 47:5
in the Jordan *R* . . . . Mark 1:5
the great *r* Euphrates . . . . . Rev 16:12
he showed me a pure *r* . . . . . Rev 22:1

RIVERS
He turns *r* into a . . . . Ps 107:33
R of water run down . . . . . Ps 119:136
By the *r* of Babylon . . . . . . Ps 137:1
Like the *r* of water . . . . . . Prov 21:1
All the *r* run into the . . . . . . Eccl 1:7
us a place of broad *r* . . . . . . Is 33:21
the wilderness and *r* . . . . . . Is 43:19
the sea, I make the *r* . . . . Is 50:2
his heart will flow *r* . . . . . . John 7:38

RIZPAH
Saul's concubine taken by Abner,
  2 Sam 3:6–8
Sons of, killed, 2 Sam 21:8, 9
Grief-stricken, cares for corpses,
  2 Sam 21:10–14

ROAD
I will even make a *r* . . . . Is 43:19
depths of the sea a *r* . . . . . . Is 51:10
seen the Lord on the *r* . . . . Acts 9:27

ROAR
Let the sea *r* . . . . 1 Chr 16:32
though its waters *r* . . . . Ps 46:3
The young lions *r* . . . . Ps 104:21
'The LORD will *r* . . . . Jer 25:30
He will *r* like a lion . . . . . . Hos 11:10
The LORD also will *r* . . . . . . Joel 3:16
Will a lion *r* in the . . . . . . Amos 3:4

ROARING
wrath is like the *r* . . . . Prov 19:12
Like a *r* lion and a . . . . . . Prov 28:15
and the waves *r* . . . . Luke 21:25
walks about like a *r* . . . . . 1 Pet 5:8

ROARS

their voice *r* like the . . . . Jer 6:23
"The Lord *r* from . . . . Amos 1:2
as when a lion *r* . . . . Rev 10:3

ROB

r the poor because he . . . . Prov 22:22
r the needy of justice . . . . Is 10:2
"Will a man *r* God . . . . Mal 3:8
do you *r* temples . . . . Rom 2:22

ROBBED

r their treasuries . . . . Is 10:13
But this is a people *r* . . . . . . Is 42:22
Yet you have *r* Me . . . . Mal 3:8
r other churches . . . . 2 Cor 11:8

ROBBER

a son who is a *r* . . . . Ezek 18:10
is a thief and a *r* . . . . John 10:1
Barabbas was a *r* . . . . John 18:40

ROBBERS

and Israel to the *r* . . . . Is 42:24
also crucified two *r* . . . . . Mark 15:27
Me are thieves and *r* . . . . . John 10:8
here who are neither *r* . . . . Acts 19:37
waters, in perils of *r* . . . . . 2 Cor 11:26

ROBBERY

nor vainly hope in *r* . . . . Ps 62:10
I hate *r* for burnt . . . . Is 61:8
did not consider it *r* . . . . Phil 2:6

ROBE

justice was like a *r* . . . . Job 29:14
instead of a rich *r* . . . . Is 3:24
covered me with the *r* . . . . . . Is 61:10
'Bring out the best *r* . . . . Luke 15:22
on Him a purple *r* . . . . John 19:2
Then a white *r* was . . . . Rev 6:11

ROBES

to the King in *r* . . . . Ps 45:14
have stained all My *r* . . . . . . Is 63:3
clothe you with rich *r* . . . . . Zech 3:4
go around in long *r* . . . . Luke 20:46
clothed with white *r* . . . . Rev 7:9

ROCK

you shall strike the *r* . . . . Ex 17:6
and struck the *r* . . . . Num 20:11
R who begot you . . . . Deut 32:18
For their *r* is not . . . . Deut 32:31
nor is there any *r* . . . . 1 Sam 2:2
"The Lord is my *r* . . . . . . 2 Sam 22:2
And who is a *r* . . . . 2 Sam 22:32
Blessed be my *R* . . . . . . 2 Sam 22:47
away, and as a *r* . . . . Job 14:18
set me high upon a *r* . . . . . . Ps 27:5
For You are my *r* . . . . Ps 31:3
r that is higher than . . . . Ps 61:2
and my God the *r* . . . . Ps 94:22
who turned the *r* . . . . Ps 114:8
been mindful of the *R* . . . . . Is 17:10
shadow of a great *r* . . . . Is 32:2
his house on the *r* . . . . Matt 7:24
r I will build My . . . . Matt 16:18
Some fell on *r* . . . . Luke 8:6
stumbling stone and *r* . . . . . Rom 9:33
R that followed them . . . . . 1 Cor 10:4

ROCKS

and the *r* were split . . . . . . Matt 27:51
to the mountains and *r* . . . . Rev 6:16

ROD

And Moses took the *r* . . . . Ex 4:20
chasten him with the *r* . . . . 2 Sam 7:14
Your *r* and Your staff . . . . . . Ps 23:4
The *r* and rebuke give . . . . Prov 29:15
shall come forth a *R* . . . . Is 11:1
you pass under the *r* . . . . . Ezek 20:37

I come to you with a *r* . . . . 1 Cor 4:21
rule them with a *r* . . . . Rev 2:27

ROLL

ruinous storm they *r* . . . . . Job 30:14
r away the stone . . . . Mark 16:3

ROLLED

the heavens shall be *r* . . . . . . Is 34:4
the stone had been *r* . . . . Mark 16:4

ROME

Jews expelled from, Acts 18:2
Paul:
   Writes to Christians of, Rom 1:7
   Desires to go to, Acts 19:21
   Comes to, Acts 28:14
   Imprisoned in, Acts 28:16

ROOM

You prepared *r* for it . . . . Ps 80:9
until no more *r* . . . . Zech 10:10
you a large upper *r* . . . . . Mark 14:15
no *r* for them in the . . . . Luke 2:7
still there is *r* . . . . Luke 14:22
into the upper *r* . . . . Acts 1:13

ROOMS

make *r* in the ark . . . . Gen 6:14
He is in the inner *r* . . . . . . Matt 24:26

ROOSTER

him, "Before the *r* . . . . Matt 26:75

ROOT

r bearing bitterness . . . . . . Deut 29:18
the foolish taking *r* . . . . Job 5:3
r may grow old in the . . . . . . Job 14:8
day there shall be a *R* . . . . . . Is 11:10
shall again take *r* . . . . Is 37:31
because they had no *r* . . . . Matt 13:6
and if the *r* is holy . . . . . . Rom 11:16
of money is a *r* . . . . 1 Tim 6:10
lest any *r* of . . . . Heb 12:15
I am the *R* and the . . . . . . Rev 22:16

ROOTED

that you, being *r* . . . . Eph 3:17
r and built up in Him . . . . . . Col 2:7

ROOTS

because its *r* reached . . . . . Ezek 31:7
and lengthen his *r* . . . . Hos 14:5
dried up from the *r* . . . . Mark 11:20
pulled up by the *r* . . . . Jude 12

ROSE

I am the *r* of Sharon . . . . . . Song 2:1
and blossom as the *r* . . . . . . Is 35:1
end Christ died and *r* . . . . Rom 14:9
buried, and that He *r* . . . . 1 Cor 15:4
that Jesus died and *r* . . . 1 Thess 4:14

RUBIES

of wisdom is above *r* . . . . . Job 28:18
more precious than *r* . . . . . Prov 3:15
is better than *r* . . . . Prov 8:11
worth is far above *r* . . . . . Prov 31:10
your pinnacles of *r* . . . . Is 54:12
ruddy in body than *r* . . . . . Lam 4:7

RUDDY

Now he was *r* . . . . 1 Sam 16:12
beloved is white and *r* . . . . Song 5:10

RUIN

r those two can bring . . . . Prov 24:22
have made a city a *r* . . . . Is 25:2
will not be your *r* . . . . Ezek 18:30
And the *r* of that . . . . Luke 6:49
to no profit, to the *r* . . . . . 2 Tim 2:14

RUINED

shall be utterly *r* . . . . Is 60:12
the mighty trees are *r* . . . . Zech 11:2
wineskins will be *r* . . . . . . Luke 5:37

RUINS

rebuild the old *r* . . . . Is 61:4

RULE

and he shall *r* . . . . Gen 3:16
r the raging of the . . . . Ps 89:9
A wise servant will *r* . . . . . Prov 17:2
Yet he will *r* over all . . . . . . Eccl 2:19
puts an end to all *r* . . . . . 1 Cor 15:24
us walk by the same *r* . . . . Phil 3:16
let the peace of God *r* . . . . . Col 3:15
Let the elders who *r* . . . . . 1 Tim 5:17
Remember those who *r* . . . . Heb 13:7

RULER

the sheep, to be *r* . . . . 2 Sam 7:8
down to eat with a *r* . . . . . Prov 23:1
bear is a wicked *r* . . . . Prov 28:15
r pays attention . . . . Prov 29:12
to Me the One to be *r* . . . . . Mic 5:2
by Beelzebub, the *r* . . . . . Matt 12:24
I will make you *r* . . . . Matt 25:21
the *r* of this world . . . . . . John 12:31
because the *r* of this . . . . . John 16:11
'Who made you a *r* . . . . . . Acts 7:27
speak evil of a *r* . . . . Acts 23:5

RULERS

and the *r* take counsel . . . . . . Ps 2:2
r decree justice . . . . Prov 8:15
"You know that the *r* . . . . Matt 20:25
Have any of the *r* . . . . John 7:48
r are not a . . . . Rom 13:3
which none of the *r* . . . . . . 1 Cor 2:8
powers, against the *r* . . . . . . Eph 6:12
to be subject to *r* . . . . Titus 3:1

RULES

'He who *r* over men . . . . . 2 Sam 23:3
them know that God *r* . . . . . Ps 59:13
He *r* by His power . . . . Ps 66:7
r his spirit than he . . . . . . Prov 16:32
that the Most High *r* . . . . . Dan 4:17
that the Most High *r* . . . . . Dan 4:32
r his own house well . . . . . 1 Tim 3:4
according to the *r* . . . . 2 Tim 2:5

RULING

r their children . . . . 1 Tim 3:12

RUMOR

r will be upon *r* . . . . Ezek 7:26

RUMORS

hear of wars and *r* . . . . . . Matt 24:6
you hear of wars and *r* . . . Mark 13:7

RUN

I will *r* the course of . . . . . . Ps 119:32
r and not be weary . . . . Is 40:31
many shall *r* to and . . . . . . Dan 12:4
Therefore I *r* thus . . . . 1 Cor 9:26
I might *r*, or had *r* . . . . Gal 2:2
that I have not *r* . . . . Phil 2:16
us, and let us *r* . . . . Heb 12:1
that you do not *r* . . . . 1 Pet 4:4

RUNNER

are swifter than a *r* . . . . Job 9:25
r will run to meet . . . . Jer 51:31

RUNS

word *r* very swiftly . . . . . . Ps 147:15
nor of him who *r* . . . . Rom 9:16

RUSH

The nations will *r* . . . . Is 17:13

RUTH

Moabitess, Ruth 1:4
Follows Naomi, Ruth 1:6–18
Marries Boaz, Ruth 4:9–13
Ancestress of Christ, Ruth 4:13, 21, 22

SABAOTH
S had left us a . . . . Rom 9:29
ears of the Lord of *S* . . . . . James 5:4

SABBATH
'Tomorrow is a *S* . . . . Ex 16:23
"Remember the *S* . . . . Ex 20:8
S was made for man . . . . . Mark 2:27
is also Lord of the *S* . . . . . Mark 2:28
not only broke the *S* . . . . . John 5:18

SABBATHS
S you shall keep . . . . Ex 31:13
The New Moons, the *S* . . . . . . Is 1:13
also gave them My *S* . . . . . Ezek 20:12

SACKCLOTH
You have put off my *s* . . . . Ps 30:11
and remove the *s* . . . . Is 20:2

SACRED
iniquity and the *s* . . . . Is 1:13

SACRIFICE
do you kick at My *s* . . . 1 Sam 2:29
S and offering You did . . . . . . Ps 40:6
offer to You the *s* . . . . Ps 116:17
to the LORD than *s* . . . . Prov 21:3
For the LORD has a *s* . . . . Is 34:6
who will bring the *s* . . . . Jer 33:11
of My offerings they *s* . . . . . Hos 8:13
But I will *s* to You . . . . Jon 2:9
LORD has prepared a *s* . . . . . Zeph 1:7
offer the blind as a *s* . . . . Mal 1:8
desire mercy and not *s* . . . . Matt 9:13
s will be seasoned . . . . Mark 9:49
an offering and a *s* . . . . Eph 5:2
aroma, an acceptable *s* . . . . Phil 4:18
put away sin by the *s* . . . . . Heb 9:26
He had offered one *s* . . . . . Heb 10:12
no longer remains a *s* . . . . Heb 10:26
God a more excellent *s* . . . . Heb 11:4
offer the *s* of praise . . . . Heb 13:15

SACRIFICED
s their sons and their . . . . . . Ps 106:37
to eat things *s* . . . . Rev 2:14

SACRIFICES
The *s* of God are a . . . . Ps 51:17
multitude of your *s* . . . . Is 1:11
Bring no more futile *s* . . . . . . Is 1:13
he who *s* a lamb . . . . Is 66:3
acceptable, nor your *s* . . . . . Jer 6:20
by him the daily *s* . . . . Dan 8:11
burnt offerings and *s* . . . . Mark 12:33
priests, to offer up *s* . . . . . . Heb 7:27
s God is well pleased . . . . . Heb 13:16
offer up spiritual *s* . . . . 1 Pet 2:5

SAD
"Why is your face *s* . . . . Neh 2:2
s countenance the . . . . Eccl 7:3
whom I have not made *s* . Ezek 13:22
as you walk and are *s* . . . . Luke 24:17

SADDUCEES
Rejected by John, Matt 3:7
Test Jesus, Matt 16:1–12
Silenced by Jesus, Matt 22:23–34
Disturbed by teaching of resurrec-
tion, Acts 4:1, 2
Oppose apostles, Acts 5:17–40

SAFE
and I shall be *s* . . . . Ps 119:117
in the LORD shall be *s* . . . . Prov 29:25
he has received him *s* . . . . Luke 15:27

SAFELY
And He led them on *s* . . . . . Ps 78:53
make them lie down *s* . . . . . Hos 2:18

SAFETY
sons are far from *s* . . . . Job 5:4

take your rest in *s* . . . . Job 11:18
will set him in the *s* . . . . Ps 12:5
say, "Peace and *s* . . . . . . 1 Thess 5:3

SAFETY'S
by you for *s* sake . . . . Prov 3:29

SAINTS
ten thousands of *s* . . . . . . Deut 33:2
the feet of His *s* . . . . 1 Sam 2:9
puts no trust in His *s* . . . . . Job 15:15
s who are on the earth . . . . . Ps 16:3
does not forsake His *s* . . . . . Ps 37:28
"Gather My *s* . . . . Ps 50:5
the souls of His *s* . . . . Ps 97:10
is the death of His *s* . . . . . Ps 116:15
the way of His *s* . . . . Prov 2:8
war against the *s* . . . . Dan 7:21
shall persecute the *s* . . . . . Dan 7:25
Jesus, called to be *s* . . . . . 1 Cor 1:2
the least of all the *s* . . . . Eph 3:8
Christ with all His *s* . . . . 1 Thess 3:13
be glorified in His *s* . . . . 2 Thess 1:10
all delivered to the *s* . . . . Jude 3
ways, O King of the *s* . . . . . Rev 15:3
shed the blood of *s* . . . . Rev 16:6
the camp of the *s* . . . . Rev 20:9

SALEM
Jerusalem's original name, Gen 14:18
Used poetically, Ps 76:2

SALOME
One of the ministering women, Mark
15:40, 41
Visits empty tomb, Mark 16:1
—— Herodias' daughter (not named
in the Bible), Matt 14:6–11

SALT
shall season with *s* . . . . Lev 2:13
"You are the *s* . . . . Matt 5:13
s loses its flavor . . . . Mark 9:50

SALT SEA
OT name for the Dead Sea, Gen 14:3;
Num 34:3, 12

SALVATION
still, and see the *s* . . . . Ex 14:13
For this is all my *s* . . . . . 2 Sam 23:5
the good news of His *s* . . . 1 Chr 16:23
S belongs to the LORD . . . . Ps 3:8
is my light and my *s* . . . . Ps 27:1
on earth, Your *s* . . . . Ps 67:2
God is the God of *s* . . . . Ps 68:20
and Your *s* all the day . . . . . Ps 71:15
Surely His *s* is near . . . . Ps 85:9
and He has become my *s* . . Ps 118:14
S is far from the . . . . Ps 119:155
God will appoint *s* . . . . Is 26:1
with an everlasting *s* . . . . . . Is 45:17
for My *s* is about to . . . . Is 56:1
call your walls *S* . . . . Is 60:18
s as a lamp that burns . . . . . . Is 62:1
LORD our God is the *s* . . . . . Jer 3:23
joy in the God of my *s* . . . . Hab 3:18
is just and having *s* . . . . . . Zech 9:9
raised up a horn of *s* . . . . . Luke 1:69
eyes have seen Your *s* . . . . Luke 2:30
to him, "Today *s* . . . . Luke 19:9
what we worship, for *s* . . . John 4:22
Nor is there *s* . . . . Acts 4:12
you should be for *s* . . . . . . Acts 13:47
the power of God to *s* . . . . Rom 1:16
s is nearer than . . . . Rom 13:11
now is the day of *s* . . . . . . 2 Cor 6:2
work out your own *s* . . . . . . Phil 2:12
wrath, but to obtain *s* . . . 1 Thess 5:9
chose you for *s* . . . . 2 Thess 2:13
also may obtain the *s* . . . . 2 Tim 2:10
of God that brings *s* . . . . . . Titus 2:11

neglect so great a *s* . . . . Heb 2:3
s the prophets have . . . . . . 1 Pet 1:10

SAMARIA
Capital of Israel, 1 Kin 16:24–29
Besieged by Ben-Hadad, 1 Kin
20:1–21
Besieged again; miraculously deliv-
ered, 2 Kin 6:24—7:20
Inhabitants deported by Assyria;
repopulated with foreigners, 2 Kin
17:5, 6, 24–41
—— District of Palestine in Christ's
time, Luke 17:11–19
Disciples forbidden to preach in,
Matt 10:5
Gospel preached there after the
Ascension, Acts 1:8; 9:31; 15:3

SAMARITAN
But a certain *S* . . . . Luke 10:33
a drink from me, a *S* . . . . . . John 4:9

SAMARITANS
People of mixed heredity, 2 Kin
17:24–41
Christ preaches to, John 4:5–42
Story of "the Good Samaritan," Luke
10:30–37
Converts among, Acts 8:5–25

SAMSON
Birth predicted and accomplished,
Judg 13:2–25
Marries Philistine; avenges betrayal,
Judg 14
Defeats Philistines single-handedly,
Judg 15
Betrayed by Delilah; loses strength,
Judg 16:4–22
Destroys many in his death, Judg
16:23–31

SAMUEL
Born in answer to prayer; dedicated
to God, 1 Sam 1:1–28
Receives revelation; recognized as
prophet, 1 Sam 3:1–21
Judges Israel, 1 Sam 7:15–17
Warns Israel against a king, 1 Sam
8:10–18
Anoints Saul, 1 Sam 9:15—10:1
Rebukes Saul, 1 Sam 15:10–35
Anoints David, 1 Sam 16:1–13
Death of, 1 Sam 25:1

SANBALLAT
Influential Samaritan; attempts to
thwart Nehemiah's plans, Neh
2:10; 4:7, 8; 6:1–14

SANCTIFICATION
righteousness and *s* . . . . . . 1 Cor 1:30
will of God, your *s* . . . . . . 1 Thess 4:3
salvation through *s* . . . . 2 Thess 2:13

SANCTIFIED
I have commanded My *s* . . . . . Is 13:3
you were born I *s* . . . . Jer 1:5
Him whom the Father *s* . . John 10:36
they also may be *s* . . . . . . John 17:19
might be acceptable, *s* . . . . Rom 15:16
to those who are *s* . . . . 1 Cor 1:2
washed, but you were *s* . . . 1 Cor 6:11
husband is *s* by the . . . . . . 1 Cor 7:14
for it is *s* by the . . . . 1 Tim 4:5
those who are being *s* . . . . . Heb 2:11
will we have been *s* . . . . . . Heb 10:10
who are called, *s* . . . . Jude 1

SANCTIFIES
or the temple that *s* . . . . . Matt 23:17
For both He who *s* . . . . Heb 2:11

SANCTIFY

SANCTIFY
would send and *s* them .... Job 1:5
s My great name .... Ezek 36:23
that I, the LORD, *s* ...... Ezek 37:28
Myself and *s* Myself..... Ezek 38:23
S them by Your........ John 17:17
for their sakes I *s*...... John 17:19
that He might *s* .... Eph 5:26

SANCTUARY
let them make Me a *s* ..... Ex 25:8
I went into the *s*........ Ps 73:17
set fire to Your *s*......... Ps 74:7
O God, is in the *s*....... Ps 77:13
He will be as a *s*........ Is 8:14
He has abandoned His *s*.... Lam 2:7
I shall be a little *s* ...... Ezek 11:16
to shine on Your *s* ...... Dan 9:17
and the earthly *s*........ Heb 9:1

SAND
descendants as the *s*..... Gen 32:12
be heavier than the *s* ..... Job 6:3
in number than the *s* .... Ps 139:18
O Israel, be as the *s*..... Is 10:22
innumerable as the *s* .... Heb 11:12

SAPPHIRA
Wife of Ananias; struck dead for
lying, Acts 5:1–11

SAPPHIRES
are the source of *s*........ Job 28:6

SARAH (or Sarai)
Barren wife of Abram, Gen 11:29–31
Represented as Abram's sister, Gen
12:10–20
Gives Abram her maid, Gen 16:1–3
Receives promise of a son, Gen
17:15–21
Gives birth to Isaac, Gen 21:1–8

SARDIS
Site of one of the seven churches,
Rev 1:11

SAT
of Babylon, there we *s*..... Ps 137:1
I *s* down in his shade...... Song 2:3
s alone because of .... Jer 15:17
into heaven, and *s*...... Mark 16:19
And He who *s* there was .... Rev 4:3

SATAN
S stood up against....... 1 Chr 21:1
before the LORD, and *S* ..... Job 1:6
And the LORD said to *S* ..... Zech 3:2
"Away with you, *S* ...... Matt 4:10
"Get behind Me, *S*...... Matt 16:23
"How can *S* cast out..... Mark 3:23
to them, "I saw *S*...... Luke 10:18
S has asked for you...... Luke 22:31
S filled your heart .... Acts 5:3
such a one to *S* .... 1 Cor 5:5
For *S* himself........... 2 Cor 11:14
to the working of *S*...... 2 Thess 2:9
are a synagogue of *S* ...... Rev 2:9
you, where *S* dwells..... Rev 2:13
known the depths of *S* ..... Rev 2:24
called the Devil and *S*..... Rev 12:9
years have expired, *S* ..... Rev 20:7

SATIATED
s the weary soul .... Jer 31:25
It shall be *s* and made ..... Jer 46:10

SATISFIED
I shall be *s* when I........ Ps 17:15
his land will be *s* .... Prov 12:11
a good man will be *s* ..... Prov 14:14
s soul loathes the........ Prov 27:7
that are never *s* .... Prov 30:15

silver will not be *s*........ Eccl 5:10
left hand and not be *s*..... Is 9:20
of His soul, and be *s*....... Is 53:11
My people shall be *s*...... Jer 31:14
still were not *s* .... Ezek 16:28
but they were not *s* ...... Amos 4:8
and cannot be *s*.......... Hab 2:5

SATISFIES
s your mouth with good .... Ps 103:5
s the longing soul .... Ps 107:9

SATISFY
s us early with Your....... Ps 90:14
long life I will *s* .... Ps 91:16
s her poor with bread ..... Ps 132:15
for what does not *s* .... Is 55:2

SATISFYING
eats to the *s* of his ...... Prov 13:25

SAUL
Becomes first king of Israel, 1 Sam
9—11
Sacrifices unlawfully, 1 Sam 13:1–14
Wars with Philistines, 1 Sam 13:15—
14:52
Disregards the Lord's command;
rejected by God, 1 Sam 15
Suffers from distressing spirits, 1 Sam
16:14–23
Becomes jealous of David; attempts
to kill him, 1 Sam 18:5—19:22
Pursues David; twice spared by him,
1 Sam 22—24; 26
Consults medium, 1 Sam 28:7–25
Defeated, commits suicide; buried,
1 Sam 31
——— of Tarsus, apostle to the Gentiles:
see PAUL

SAVE
the LORD does not *s*..... 1 Sam 17:47
there was none to *s* ..... 2 Sam 22:42
s the humble person ...... Job 22:29
Oh, *s* me for Your .... Ps 6:4
S Your people.............. Ps 28:9
send from heaven and *s*..... Ps 57:3
s the children of the .... Ps 72:4
s the souls of the .... Ps 72:13
LORD, and He will *s* ..... Prov 20:22
He will come and *s* .... Is 35:4
LORD was ready to *s* .... Is 38:20
s your children............. Is 49:25
that it cannot *s*........... Is 59:1
mighty to *s* .... Is 63:1
one who cannot *s*.......... Jer 14:9
s you and deliver you...... Jer 15:20
s me, and I shall be ...... Jer 17:14
O LORD, *s* Your people ...... Jer 31:7
other, That he may *s*...... Hos 13:10
Assyria shall not *s* .... Hos 14:3
the Mighty One, will *s* ..... Zeph 3:17
JESUS, for He will *s* .... Matt 1:21
s his life would .... Matt 16:25
s that which was .... Matt 18:11
s life or to kill......... Mark 3:4
let Him *s* Himself if..... Luke 23:35
You are the Christ, *s*...... Luke 23:39
'Father, *s* Me from ...... John 12:27
but to *s* the world ...... John 12:47
and *s* some of them...... Rom 11:14
the world to *s* sinners .... 1 Tim 1:15
doing this you will *s* ..... 1 Tim 4:16
able to *s* your souls...... James 1:21
Can faith *s* him......... James 2:14

SAVED
like you, a people *s*...... Deut 33:29
But You have *s* us from...... Ps 44:7
and we are not *s* .... Jer 8:20

"Who then can be *s* ..... Matt 19:25
"He *s* others............ Matt 27:42
That we should be *s* ..... Luke 1:71
"Your faith has *s*........ Luke 7:50
through Him might be *s*.... John 3:17
them, saying, "Be *s* ...... Acts 2:40
what must I do to be *s*.... Acts 16:30
For we were *s* in this ..... Rom 8:24
is that they may be *s* ..... Rom 10:1
all Israel will be *s* ...... Rom 11:26
his spirit may be *s*....... 1 Cor 5:5
which also you are *s* ..... 1 Cor 15:2
those who are being *s* ..... 2 Cor 2:15
grace you have been *s*...... Eph 2:8
all men to be *s* .... 1 Tim 2:4
she will be *s* in.......... 1 Tim 2:15
to His mercy He *s*....... Titus 3:5
eight souls, were *s* ...... 1 Pet 3:20
of those who are *s*....... Rev 21:24

SAVES
s the needy from the ...... Job 5:15
s such as have a .... Ps 34:18
antitype which now *s*..... 1 Pet 3:21

SAVIOR
forgot God their *S* .... Ps 106:21
He will send them a *S* ..... Is 19:20
of Israel, your *S* .... Is 43:3
Me, a just God and a *S* ..... Is 45:21
I, the LORD, am your *S* ..... Is 60:16
So He became their *S*....... Is 63:8
for there is no *s*........... Hos 13:4
rejoiced in God my *S*..... Luke 1:47
the city of David a *S*..... Luke 2:11
the Christ, the *S* .... John 4:42
to be Prince and *S* ...... Acts 5:31
up for Israel a *S* .... Acts 13:23
and He is the *S*.......... Eph 5:23
of God our *S* and the ..... 1 Tim 1:1
God, who is the *S* .... 1 Tim 4:10
of our *S* Jesus Christ ..... 2 Tim 1:10
God and *S* Jesus Christ .... Titus 2:13

SAVIORS
s shall come to Mount ..... Obad 21

SAWN
stoned, they were *s*...... Heb 11:37

SAY
But I *s* to you that....... Matt 5:22
"But who do you *s*...... Matt 16:15
s that we have no sin .... 1 John 1:8

SAYING
disclose my dark *s* .... Ps 49:4
cannot accept this *s* ..... Matt 19:11
"This is a hard *s* .... John 6:60
This is a faithful *s* ...... 1 Tim 1:15

SAYINGS
I will utter dark *s*.......... Ps 78:2
whoever hears these *s*..... Matt 7:24

SCALES
You shall have honest *s* ... Lev 19:36
be weighed on honest *s*.... Job 31:6
on it had a pair of *s* ...... Rev 6:5

SCARLET
s cord in the window ..... Josh 2:18
are like a strand of *s* ..... Song 4:3
your sins are like *s*....... Is 1:18
s beast which was full...... Rev 17:3

SCATTER
I will *s* you among the .... Lev 26:33
S the peoples who ...... Ps 68:30
s the sheep of My......... Jer 23:1
I will *s* to all winds....... Jer 49:32

SCATTERED
lest we be *s* abroad........ Gen 11:4

SCATTERS (cont.)
of iniquity shall be *s* . . . . Ps 92:9
"You have *s* My flock . . . . . . Jer 23:2
s Israel will gather . . . . Jer 31:10
"Israel is like *s* sheep . . . . . . Jer 50:17
they were weary and *s* . . . . Mark 9:36
the sheep will be *s* . . . . . Mark 14:27
that you will be *s* . . . . . . John 16:32

SCATTERS
s the frost like ashes . . . . . . Ps 147:16
There is one who *s* . . . . . . Prov 11:24
throne of judgment *s* . . . . . Prov 20:8
not gather with Me *s* . . . . Matt 12:30

SCEPTER
s shall not depart . . . . Gen 49:10
S shall rise out of . . . . . . Num 24:17
a *s* of righteousness . . . . Ps 45:6
a *s* of righteousness . . . . Heb 1:8

SCHEME
perfected a shrewd *s* . . . . Ps 64:6

SCHEMER
will be called a *s* . . . . Prov 24:8

SCHEMES
who brings wicked *s* . . . . Ps 37:7
sought out many *s* . . . . . . Eccl 7:29

SCHISM
there should be no *s* . . . 1 Cor 12:25

SCHOOL
daily in the *s* of . . . . Acts 19:9

SCOFF
They *s* and speak . . . . Ps 73:8
They *s* at kings . . . . Hab 1:10

SCOFFER
"He who corrects a *s* . . . . . . Prov 9:7
s does not listen . . . . Prov 13:1
s seeks wisdom and . . . . . . Prov 14:6
s is an abomination . . . . . . Prov 24:9

SCOFFERS
S ensnare a city . . . . Prov 29:8
s will come in the . . . . 2 Pet 3:3

SCORCHED
sun was up they were *s* . . . Matt 13:6
And men were *s* with . . . . . . Rev 16:9

SCORN
My friends *s* me . . . . Job 16:20
to our neighbors, a *s* . . . . . . Ps 44:13

SCORNED
consider, for I am *s* . . . . Lam 1:11
and princes are *s* . . . . Hab 1:10

SCORNS
He *s* the scornful . . . . Prov 3:34
s obedience to his . . . . . . Prov 30:17

SCORPIONS
and you dwell among *s* . . . . Ezek 2:6
on serpents and *s* . . . . . . Luke 10:19
They had tails like *s* . . . . . . Rev 9:10

SCOURGE
hosts will stir up a *s* . . . . . . Is 10:26
up to councils and *s* . . . . Matt 10:17
will mock Him, and *s* . . . . Mark 10:34

SCOURGES
s every son whom . . . . . . Heb 12:6

SCRIBE
"Where is the *s* . . . . Is 33:18

SCRIBES
and not as the *s* . . . . Matt 7:29
"But woe to you, *s* . . . . . Matt 23:13
"Beware of the *s* . . . . . . Mark 12:38

SCRIPTURE
what is noted in the *S* . . . . Dan 10:21

S was fulfilled which . . . . Mark 15:28
"Today this *S* . . . . Luke 4:21
S cannot be broken . . . . . . John 10:35
For what does the *S* . . . . Rom 4:3
S has confined all . . . . Gal 3:22
All *S* is given by . . . . 2 Tim 3:16
that no prophecy of *S* . . . . 2 Pet 1:20

SCRIPTURES
not knowing the *S* . . . . . . Matt 22:29
S must be fulfilled . . . . . Mark 14:49
and mighty in the *S* . . . . . Acts 18:24
have known the Holy *S* . . 2 Tim 3:15
also the rest of the *S* . . . . . 2 Pet 3:16

SCROLL
in the *s* of the book . . . . Ps 40:7
and note it on a *s* . . . . Is 30:8
eat this *s* . . . . Ezek 3:1
saw there a flying *s* . . . . . . Zech 5:1
on the throne a *s* . . . . Rev 5:1
was able to open the *s* . . . . . Rev 5:3
the sky receded as a *s* . . . . . Rev 6:14

SEA
drowned in the Red *S* . . . . . . Ex 15:4
this great and wide *s* . . . . . Ps 104:25
who go down to the *s* . . . . Ps 107:23
to the *s* its limit . . . . Prov 8:29
rebuke I dry up the *s* . . . . Is 50:2
the waters cover the *s* . . . . . Hab 2:14
and the *s* obey Him . . . . . . Matt 8:27
throne there was a *s* . . . . Rev 4:6
standing on the *s* . . . . Rev 15:2
there was no more *s* . . . . . . Rev 21:1

SEAL
Set me as a *s* upon . . . . Song 8:6
of circumcision, a *s* . . . . . . Rom 4:11
stands, having this *s* . . . . . 2 Tim 2:19
He opened the second *s* . . . . Rev 6:3

SEALED
My transgression is *s* . . . . . Job 14:17
who also has *s* us and . . . . 2 Cor 1:22
by whom you were *s* . . . . . . Eph 4:30
of those who were *s* . . . . Rev 7:4

SEAM
tunic was without *s* . . . . . John 19:23

SÉANCE
"Please conduct a *s* . . . . . 1 Sam 28:8

SEARCH
"Can you *s* out the . . . . Job 11:7
would not God *s* . . . . Ps 44:21
glory of kings is to *s* . . . . . Prov 25:2
found it by secret *s* . . . . Jer 2:34
I, the LORD, *s* the . . . . Jer 17:10
s the Scriptures . . . . John 5:39

SEARCHED
O LORD, You have *s* . . . . Ps 139:1
s the Scriptures . . . . Acts 17:11
and *s* carefully . . . . 1 Pet 1:10

SEARCHES
for the LORD *s* all . . . . 1 Chr 28:9
s the hearts knows . . . . . . Rom 8:27
For the Spirit *s* . . . . 1 Cor 2:10
that I am He who *s* . . . . Rev 2:23

SEASON
there is a *s* . . . . Eccl 3:1
Be ready in *s* and out . . . . . 2 Tim 4:2

SEASONED
how shall it be *s* . . . . Matt 5:13
"For everyone will be *s* . . . Mark 9:49

SEASONS
days and months and *s* . . . . Gal 4:10
the times and the *s* . . . . . . 1 Thess 5:1

SEAT
shall make a mercy *s* . . . . . Ex 25:17
I might come to His *s* . . . . . . Job 23:3
that He may *s* him with . . . . Ps 113:8
sit in Moses' *s* . . . . Matt 23:2
before the judgment *s* . . . . 2 Cor 5:10
the mercy *s* . . . . Heb 9:5

SEATS
at feasts, the best *s* . . . . . . Matt 23:6
you love the best *s* . . . . . . Luke 11:43

SECRET
s things belong . . . . Deut 29:29
darkness His *s* place . . . . Ps 18:11
The *s* of the LORD is . . . . Ps 25:14
in the *s* place of His . . . . Ps 27:5
s place of Your presence . . . . Ps 31:20
s place of the Most High . . . . . Ps 91:1
when I was made in *s* . . . . . Ps 139:15
do not disclose the *s* . . . . . Prov 25:9
s places of the cliff . . . . . . Song 2:14
I have not spoken in *s* . . . . . . Is 45:19
He reveals His *s* to . . . . . . Amos 3:7
Father who is in the *s* . . . . . Matt 6:6
are done by them in *s* . . . . . Eph 5:12

SECRETLY
"Now a word was *s* . . . . Job 4:12
He lies in wait *s* . . . . Ps 10:9

SECRETS
would show you the *s* . . . . . Job 11:6
For He knows the *s* . . . . Ps 44:21
A talebearer reveals *s* . . . . Prov 11:13
heaven who reveals *s* . . . . . Dan 2:28
God will judge the *s* . . . . . . Rom 2:16
And thus the *s* of his . . . . 1 Cor 14:25

SECT
him (which is the *s* . . . . . . Acts 5:17
to the strictest *s* . . . . Acts 26:5

SECURELY
pleasures, who dwell *s* . . . . . Is 47:8
nation that dwells *s* . . . . . . Jer 49:31

SEDUCED
flattering lips she *s* . . . . . . Prov 7:21
because they have *s* . . . . . Ezek 13:10

SEE
for no man shall *s* . . . . Ex 33:20
the LORD does not *s* . . . . . 1 Sam 16:7
in my flesh I shall *s* . . . . . . Job 19:26
s the works of God . . . . Ps 66:5
lest they *s* with their . . . . Is 6:10
for sin, He shall *s* . . . . Is 53:10
for they shall *s* God . . . . . . Matt 5:8
seeing they do not *s* . . . . . Matt 13:13
s greater things than . . . . . John 1:50
rejoiced to *s* My day . . . . . John 8:56
we wish to *s* Jesus . . . . . . John 12:21
and the world will *s* . . . . . John 14:19
Him, for we shall *s* . . . . . . 1 John 3:2
They shall *s* His face . . . . . . Rev 22:4

SEED
s shall be called . . . . Gen 21:12
s shall be its stump . . . . Is 6:13
He shall see His *s* . . . . Is 53:10
you a noble vine, a *s* . . . . . . Jer 2:21
s is the word of God . . . . . Luke 8:11
had left us a *s* . . . . Rom 9:29
to each *s* its own body . . . 1 Cor 15:38
S were the promises . . . . . . Gal 3:16
you are Abraham's *s* . . . . . . Gal 3:29
Jesus Christ, of the *s* . . . . . 2 Tim 2:8
of corruptible *s* . . . . 1 Pet 1:23
not sin, for His *s* . . . . 1 John 3:9

SEEDS
the good *s* are the . . . . . . Matt 13:38
not say, "And to *s* . . . . Gal 3:16

SEEK

will find Him if you s . . . . Deut 4:29
pray and s My face . . . . . . 2 Chr 7:14
your heart to s God . . . . . . 2 Chr 19:3
s your God as you do . . . . . Ezra 4:2
may God above not s . . . . . . Job 3:4
countenance does not s . . . . . . Ps 10:4
LORD, that will I s . . . . Ps 27:4
You said, "S My face . . . . Ps 27:8
early will I s You . . . . Ps 63:1
s me diligently will . . . . . . Prov 8:17
s one's own glory . . . . Prov 25:27
s justice, rebuke . . . . Is 1:17
Should they s the dead . . . Is 8:19
the Gentiles shall s . . . . Is 11:10
Jacob, 'S Me in vain . . . . Is 45:19
S the LORD while He . . . . . . Is 55:6
Yet they s Me daily . . . . Is 58:2
s great things for . . . . Jer 45:5
s what was lost . . . . Ezek 34:16
"S Me and live . . . . Amos 5:4
and people should s . . . . . . Mal 2:7
things the Gentiles s . . . . . Matt 6:32
s, and you will find . . . . . . Matt 7:7
of Man has come to s . . . . Luke 19:10
because I do not s . . . . John 5:30
You will s Me and . . . . John 7:34
in doing good s . . . . Rom 2:7
Because they did not s . . . . Rom 9:32
Let no one s his own . . . . 1 Cor 10:24
for I do not s yours . . . . . . 2 Cor 12:14
For all s their own . . . . Phil 2:21
s those things which . . . . Col 3:1
s the one to come . . . . Heb 13:14

SEEKING

run to and fro, s . . . . Amos 8:12
and he came s fruit . . . . . . Luke 13:6
for the Father is s . . . . John 4:23
like a roaring lion, s . . . . . . 1 Pet 5:8

SEEKS

no one s her . . . . Jer 30:17
receives, and he who s . . . . Matt 7:8
There is none who s . . . . . . Rom 3:11

SEEMS

There is a way which s . . . Prov 14:12
have, even what he s . . . . . Luke 8:18
If anyone among you s . . . 1 Cor 3:18

SEEN

s God face to face . . . . Gen 32:30
All this I have s . . . . Eccl 8:9
s the one I love . . . . Song 3:3
Who has s such things . . . . . . Is 66:8
s strange things today . . . . Luke 5:26
No one has s God at . . . . . . John 1:18
time, nor s His form . . . . . . John 5:37
I speak what I have s . . . . John 8:38
s Me has s the . . . . John 14:9
things which we have s . . . Acts 4:20
s Jesus Christ our . . . . 1 Cor 9:1
things which are not s . . . . 2 Cor 4:18
whom no man has s . . . . . 1 Tim 6:16
heard, which we have s . . 1 John 1:1

SEES

here seen Him who s . . . . . Gen 16:13
s all the sons of men . . . . . . Ps 33:13
s his brother in need . . . . 1 John 3:17
s his brother sinning . . . . 1 John 5:16

SEIR

Home of Esau, Gen 32:3
Horites of, dispossessed by Esau's
   descendants, Deut 2:12
Desolation of, Ezek 35:15

SELF-CONFIDENT

a fool rages and is s . . . . . Prov 14:16

SELF-CONTROL

about righteousness, s . . . . Acts 24:25
they cannot exercise s . . . . . 1 Cor 7:9
gentleness, s . . . . Gal 5:23
slanderers, without s . . . . . 2 Tim 3:3
to knowledge s . . . . 2 Pet 1:6

SELF-CONTROLLED

just, holy, s . . . . Titus 1:8

SELF-SEEKING

envy and s exist . . . . James 3:16

SELL

said, "S me your . . . . Gen 25:31
s Your people for . . . . Ps 44:12
s the righteous . . . . Amos 2:6
s whatever you have . . . . Mark 10:21
no sword, let him s . . . . . Luke 22:36
no one may buy or s . . . . . Rev 13:17

SEND

He shall s from heaven . . . . . Ps 57:3
"Whom shall I s . . . . Is 6:8
s them a Savior . . . . Is 19:20
"Behold, I s you out . . . . Matt 10:16
The Son of Man will s . . . . Matt 13:41
s Lazarus that he . . . . Luke 16:24
whom the Father will s . . . John 14:26
has sent Me, I also s . . . . . John 20:21

SENNACHERIB

Assyrian king (705–681 B.C.); son and
   successor of Sargon II, 2 Kin 18:13
Death of, by assassination, 2 Kin
   19:36, 37

SENSELESS

Understand, you s . . . . Ps 94:8

SENSES

of use have their s . . . . Heb 5:14

SENSIBLY

who can answer s . . . . . . Prov 26:16

SENSUAL

but is earthly, s . . . . James 3:15
These are s persons . . . . Jude 19

SENT

and His Spirit have s . . . . . . Is 48:16
s these prophets . . . . Jer 23:21
As the Father has s . . . . . . John 20:21
unless they are s . . . . Rom 10:15
s His Son to be the . . . . . . 1 John 4:10

SEPARATE

he shall s himself . . . . Num 6:3
s yourselves from the . . . . Ezra 10:11
let not man s . . . . Matt 19:6
Who shall s us from . . . . . Rom 8:35
harmless, undefiled, s . . . . Heb 7:26

SEPARATED

but the poor is s . . . . Prov 19:4
"The LORD has utterly s . . . . . Is 56:3
to be an apostle, s . . . . Rom 1:1
it pleased God, who s . . . . . Gal 1:15

SEPARATES

who repeats a matter s . . . . Prov 17:9

SEPARATION

the middle wall of s . . . . . . Eph 2:14

SERAPHIM

Above it stood s . . . . Is 6:2

SERGIUS PAULUS

Roman proconsul of Cyprus, converted by Paul, Acts 13:7–12

SERIOUS

therefore be s and . . . . 1 Pet 4:7

SERPENT

s was more cunning . . . . Gen 3:1

"The s deceived me . . . . . . Gen 3:13
"Make a fiery s . . . . Num 21:8
like the poison of a s . . . . . . Ps 58:4
s you shall trample . . . . . . Ps 91:13
their tongues like a s . . . . . Ps 140:3
air, the way of a s . . . . . . Prov 30:19
s may bite when it is . . . . . Eccl 10:11
be a fiery flying s . . . . Is 14:29
and wounded the s . . . . Is 51:9
will he give him a s . . . . . Matt 7:10
Moses lifted up the s . . . . . John 3:14
was cast out, that s . . . . . . Rev 12:9

SERPENTS

is the poison of s . . . . Deut 32:33
be wise as s . . . . Matt 10:16
to trample on s . . . . Luke 10:19

SERVANT

a s of servants he . . . . Gen 9:25
s who earnestly . . . . Job 7:2
and the fool will be s . . . . Prov 11:29
s will rule over a son . . . . . Prov 17:2
A s will not be . . . . Prov 29:19
Who is blind but My s . . . . . Is 42:19
You are My s . . . . Is 49:3
"Is Israel a s . . . . Jer 2:14
and a s his master . . . . Mal 1:6
you, let him be your s . . . Matt 20:26
good and faithful s . . . . . . Matt 25:21
'You wicked and lazy s . . . Matt 25:26
the unprofitable s . . . . . . Matt 25:30
that s who knew his . . . . . Luke 12:47
s does not know what . . . . John 15:15
against Your holy S . . . . . . Acts 4:27

SERVANTS

puts no trust in His s . . . . . . Job 4:18
for all your s . . . . Ps 119:91
on the ground like s . . . . . Eccl 10:7
shall call you the s . . . . Is 61:6
S rule over us . . . . Lam 5:8
are unprofitable s . . . . . . Luke 17:10
longer do I call you s . . . . John 15:15
so consider us, as s . . . . . . 1 Cor 4:1

SERVE

LORD your God and s . . . . . Deut 6:13
land, so you shall s aliens . . . Jer 5:19
s Him with one accord . . . . Zeph 3:9
You cannot s God and . . . . Matt 6:24
to be served, but to s . . . . Matt 20:28
the mind I myself s . . . . . . Rom 7:25
but through love s . . . . Gal 5:13
s the Lord Christ . . . . Col 3:24
s the living God . . . . Heb 9:14
s Him day and night in . . . . Rev 7:15

SERVES

If anyone s Me . . . . John 12:26

SERVICE

do you mean by this s . . . . . Ex 12:26
that he offers God s . . . . . . John 16:2
is your reasonable s . . . . . . Rom 12:1
with goodwill doing s . . . . . Eph 6:7
your works, love, s . . . . Rev 2:19

SERVING

years I have been s . . . . . Luke 15:29
s the Lord with all . . . . . . Acts 20:19
fervent in spirit, s . . . . . . Rom 12:11
you, s as overseers . . . . . . 1 Pet 5:2

SET

"See, I have s . . . . Deut 30:15
s the LORD always . . . . Ps 16:8
I will s him on high . . . . . . Ps 91:14
s aside the grace . . . . Gal 2:21

SETH

Third son of Adam, Gen 4:25
In Christ's ancestry, Luke 3:38

SETTLE
Therefore *s* it in . . . . Luke 21:14

SETTLED
and my speech *s* . . . . Job 29:22
O Lord, Your word is *s* . . . . . Ps 119:89
the mountains were *s* . . . . Prov 8:25
s accounts with them . . . . Matt 25:19

SEVEN
S times a day I praise . . . . . Ps 119:164
s other spirits more . . . . . . Luke 11:26
s times in a day . . . . Luke 17:4
out from among you *s* . . . . . Acts 6:3
s churches which are . . . . Rev 1:4

SEVENTY
S weeks are . . . . Dan 9:24
up to *s* times seven . . . . . . Matt 18:22
Then the *s* returned . . . . . . Luke 10:17

SEVERE
My wound is *s* . . . . Jer 10:19
not to be too *s* . . . . 2 Cor 2:5

SEVERITY
the goodness and *s* . . . . . . Rom 11:22

SHADE
I sat down in his *s* . . . . Song 2:3
be a tabernacle for *s* . . . . Is 4:6
may nest under its *s* . . . . . Mark 4:32

SHADOW
May darkness and the *s* . . . . Job 3:5
He flees like a *s* . . . . Job 14:2
hide me under the *s* . . . . . . Ps 17:8
walks about like a *s* . . . . . Ps 39:6
like a passing *s* . . . . Ps 144:4
he passes like a *s* . . . . Eccl 6:12
and to trust in the *s* . . . . Is 30:2
In the *s* of His hand . . . . Is 49:2
which are a *s* of . . . . Col 2:17
the law, having a *s* . . . . . . Heb 10:1
is no variation or *s* . . . . . James 1:17

SHADOWS
my members are like *s* . . . Job 17:7
and the *s* flee away . . . . . . Song 2:17

SHADRACH
Hananiah's Babylonian name,
Dan 1:3, 7
Cast into the fiery furnace, Dan
3:1–28

SHAKE
Who is he who will *s* . . . . . . Job 17:3
s the earth . . . . Is 2:19
S yourself from the . . . . Is 52:2
s their heads at the . . . . . . Lam 2:15
and the knees *s* . . . . Nah 2:10
hiss and *s* his fist . . . . Zeph 2:15
I will *s* all nations . . . . Hag 2:7
s not only the earth . . . . . Heb 12:26

SHAKEN
he will never be *s* . . . . Ps 112:6
together was *s* . . . . Acts 4:31
not to be soon *s* . . . . 2 Thess 2:2

SHAKES
s the earth out of its . . . . . . Job 9:6
s the Wilderness . . . . Ps 29:8

SHALLUM
King of Israel, 2 Kin 15:10–15

SHALMANESER
Assyrian king, 2 Kin 17:3

SHAME
you turn my glory to *s* . . . . . Ps 4:2
let them be put to *s* . . . . . . Ps 83:17
s who serve carved . . . . . . Ps 97:7
hate Zion be put to *s* . . . . . . Ps 129:5

s shall be the . . . . Prov 3:35
is a son who causes *s* . . . . Prov 10:5
hide My face from *s* . . . . Is 50:6
S has covered our . . . . Jer 51:51
their glory into *s* . . . . Hos 4:7
never be put to *s* . . . . Joel 2:26
the unjust knows no *s* . . . . Zeph 3:5
worthy to suffer *s* . . . . Acts 5:41
will not be put to *s* . . . . . . Rom 9:33
to put to *s* the wise . . . . . 1 Cor 1:27
I say this to your *s* . . . . . . 1 Cor 6:5
glory is in their *s* . . . . Phil 3:19
put Him to an open *s* . . . . . . Heb 6:6

SHAMEFUL
committing what is *s* . . . . . Rom 1:27
for it is *s* for women . . . . . 1 Cor 14:35
For it is *s* even to . . . . Eph 5:12

SHAMGAR
Judge of Israel; strikes down 600
Philistines, Judg 3:31

SHAMMAH
Son of Jesse, 1 Sam 16:9
Called Shimea, 1 Chr 2:13
—— One of David's mighty men,
2 Sam 23:11
Also called Shammoth the Harorite,
1 Chr 11:27

SHAPHAN
Scribe under Josiah, 2 Kin 22:3–14

SHARE
a stranger does not *s* . . . . Prov 14:10
s your bread with the . . . . Is 58:7
is taught the word *s* . . . . Gal 6:6
to give, willing to *s* . . . . . . 1 Tim 6:18
to do good and to *s* . . . . . . Heb 13:16

SHARING
for your liberal *s* . . . . 2 Cor 9:13

SHARON
Coastal plain between Joppa and Mt.
Carmel, 1 Chr 27:29
Famed for roses, Song 2:1
Inhabitants of, turn to the Lord, Acts
9:35

SHARP
S as a two-edged sword . . . . . Prov 5:4

SHARPEN
s their tongue like a . . . . . . Ps 64:3
and one does not *s* . . . . . . Eccl 10:10

SHARPNESS
I should use *s* . . . . 2 Cor 13:10

SHATTERED
at ease, but He has *s* . . . . . Job 16:12

SHEALTIEL
Son of King Jeconiah and father of
Zerubbabel, 1 Chr 3:17

SHEAR-JASHUB
Symbolic name given to Isaiah's son,
Is 7:3

SHEATH
'Return it to its *s* . . . . Ezek 21:30
your sword into the *s* . . . . . John 18:11

SHEAVES
bringing his *s* . . . . Ps 126:6
nor he who binds *s* . . . . . . Ps 129:7
gather them like *s* . . . . Mic 4:12

SHEBA
Land of, occupied by Sabeans,
famous traders, Job 1:15; Ps 72:10
Queen of, visits Solomon; marvels at
his wisdom, 1 Kin 10:1–13
Mentioned by Christ, Matt 12:42

SHEBAH
Name given to a well and town
(Beersheba), Gen 26:31–33

SHEBNA
Treasurer under Hezekiah, Is 22:15
Demoted to position of scribe, 2 Kin
19:2
Man of pride and luxury, replaced
by Eliakim, Is 22:19–21

SHECHEM
Son of Hamor; rapes Dinah, Jacob's
daughter, Gen 34:1–31
—— Ancient city of Ephraim,
Gen 33:18
Joshua's farewell address delivered
at, Josh 24:1–25
Supports Abimelech; destroyed,
Judg 9
Rebuilt by Jeroboam I, 1 Kin 12:25

SHED
which is *s* for many . . . . . Matt 26:28

SHEDDING
blood, and without *s* . . . . . . Heb 9:22

SHEEP
astray like a lost *s* . . . . . . Ps 119:176
slaughter, and as a *s* . . . . Is 53:7
Pull them out like *s* . . . . . . Jer 12:3
have been lost *s* . . . . Jer 50:6
will search for My *s* . . . . . Ezek 34:11
shall judge between *s* . . . . Ezek 34:17
s will be scattered . . . . Zech 13:7
rather to the lost *s* . . . . . . Matt 10:6
I send you out as *s* . . . . . . Matt 10:16
And He will set the *s* . . . . . Matt 25:33
having a hundred *s* . . . . Luke 15:4
and he calls his own *s* . . . . John 10:3
and I know My *s* . . . . John 10:14
s I have which are not . . . John 10:16
"He was led as a *s* . . . . Acts 8:32
like *s* going astray . . . . 1 Pet 2:25

SHEEPFOLDS
lie down among the *s* . . . . . Ps 68:13

SHEET
object like a great *s* . . . . . Acts 10:11

SHELTER
I will trust in the *s* . . . . Ps 61:4
in You I take *s* . . . . Ps 143:9
the Lord will be a *s* . . . . . . Joel 3:16

SHELTERS
s him all the day long . . . Deut 33:12
be pastures, with *s* . . . . . . Zeph 2:6

SHEM
Oldest son of Noah, Gen 5:32
Escapes the Flood, Gen 7:13
Receives a blessing, Gen 9:23, 26
Ancestor of Semitic people, Gen
10:22–32

SHEMAIAH
Prophet of Judah, 1 Kin 12:22–24
Explains Shishak's invasion as divine
punishment, 2 Chr 12:5–8
Records Rehoboam's reign, 2 Chr
12:15

SHEMER
Sells Omri the hill on which Samaria
is built, 1 Kin 16:23, 24

SHEOL
down to the gates of *S* . . . . . Job 17:16
not leave my soul in *S* . . . . Ps 16:10
S laid hold of me . . . . Ps 116:3
S cannot thank . . . . Is 38:18
the belly of *S* I cried . . . . . . Jon 2:2

SHEPHERD
s is an abomination...... Gen 46:34
s My people Israel .... 2 Sam 5:2
The Lord is my *s* .... Ps 23:1
s Jacob His people .... Ps 78:71
His flock like a *s* .... Is 40:11
of Cyrus, 'He is My *s* .... Is 44:28
s who follows You .... Jer 17:16
because there was no *s* ... Ezek 34:5
I will establish one *s* .... Ezek 34:23
"As a *s* takes from ...... Amos 3:12
to the worthless *s*....... Zech 11:17
'I will strike the *S* ...... Matt 26:31
"I am the good *s* .... John 10:11
s the church of God...... Acts 20:28
the dead, that great *S*.... Heb 13:20
S the flock of God...... 1 Pet 5:2
when the Chief *S* .... 1 Pet 5:4
of the throne will *s* .... Rev 7:17

SHEPHERDS
your sons shall be *s* .... Num 14:33
And they are *s* who ...... Is 56:11
And I will give you *s* ..... Jer 3:15
s who destroy and .... Jer 23:1
s who feed My people ...... Jer 23:2
s have led them astray.... Jer 50:6
s fed themselves......... Ezek 34:8
in the same country *s*..... Luke 2:8

SHESHACH
Symbolic of Babylon, Jer 25:26

SHESHBAZZAR
Prince of Judah, Ezra 1:8, 11

SHIELD
I am your *s*............. Gen 15:1
He is a *s* to all who..... 2 Sam 22:31
my *s* and the horn of .... Ps 18:2
God is a sun and *s*........ Ps 84:11
truth shall be your *s* .... Ps 91:4
all, taking the *s* .... Eph 6:16

SHIHOR
Name given to the Nile, Is 23:3
Israel's southwestern border, Josh 13:3

SHILOH
Center of worship, Judg 18:31
Headquarters for division of Promised Land, Josh 18:1, 10
Benjamites seize women of, Judg 21:19–23
Ark of the covenant taken from, 1 Sam 4:3–11
Punishment given to, Jer 7:12–15
——— Messianic title, Gen 49:10

SHIMEI
Benjamite; insults David, 2 Sam 16:5–13
Pardoned, but confined, 2 Sam 19:16–23
Breaks agreement; executed by Solomon, 1 Kin 2:39–46

SHIMSHAI
Scribe opposing the Jews, Ezra 4:8–24

SHINAR
Tower built at, Gen 11:2–9

SHINE
Lord make His face *s* ..... Num 6:25
cause His face to *s*.......... Ps 67:1
the cherubim, *s*........... Ps 80:1
Make Your face *s* ...... Ps 119:135
who are wise shall *s* ...... Dan 12:3
the righteous will *s* ..... Matt 13:43
among whom you *s*....... Phil 2:15

SHINED
them a light has *s* .... Is 9:2

SHINES
And the light *s* .... John 1:5

SHINING
the earth, by clear *s* .... 2 Sam 23:4
His clothes became *s* ..... Mark 9:3
light is already *s* ...... 1 John 2:8
was like the sun *s* .... Rev 1:16

SHIPS
pass by like swift *s*........ Job 9:26
down to the sea in *s* ..... Ps 107:23
like the merchant *s* ..... Prov 31:14
Look also at *s* .... James 3:4

SHIPWRECK
faith have suffered *s* ..... 1 Tim 1:19

SHOOT
they *s* out the lip........... Ps 22:7
But God shall *s* .... Ps 64:7

SHORT
have sinned and fall *s* .... Rom 3:23
the work and cut it *s*..... Rom 9:28

SHORTENED
his youth You have *s*...... Ps 89:45
the wicked will be *s*...... Prov 10:27
those days were *s* ...... Matt 24:22

SHOT
shall be stoned or *s* ...... Heb 12:20

SHOUT
s joyfully to the Rock........ Ps 95:1
S joyfully to the Lord .... Ps 98:4
Make a joyful *s* .... Ps 100:1
from heaven with a *s* ... 1 Thess 4:16

SHOW
a land that I will *s*...... Gen 12:1
S me Your ways........... Ps 25:4
s yourselves men .... Is 46:8
s Him greater works ...... John 5:20
s us the Father.......... John 14:8

SHOWBREAD
you shall set the *s*........ Ex 25:30
s which had been taken.. 1 Sam 21:6
s which was not lawful.... Matt 12:4

SHOWERS
make it soft with *s* ...... Ps 65:10
s have been withheld........ Jer 3:3
can the heavens give *s*..... Jer 14:22
from the Lord, like *s*....... Mic 5:7

SHREWDLY
because he had dealt *s*.... Luke 16:8

SHRINES
who made silver *s* ...... Acts 19:24

SHUFFLES
with his eyes, he *s*........ Prov 6:13

SHULAMITE
Beloved of the bridegroom king, Song 6:13

SHUNAMMITE
Abishag, David's nurse, 1 Kin 1:3, 15
——— Woman who cared for Elisha, 2 Kin 4:8–12

SHUNNED
feared God and *s* evil .... Job 1:1

SHUSHAN
Residence of Persian monarchs, Esth 1:2

SHUT
"Or who *s* in the sea .... Job 38:8

Has He in anger *s* .... Ps 77:9
For you *s* up the .... Matt 23:13

SHUTS
s his ears to the cry ..... Prov 21:13
s his eyes from seeing....... Is 33:15
brother in need, and *s* ... 1 John 3:17
who opens and no one *s* .... Rev 3:7

SICK
have made him *s*.......... Hos 7:5
I was *s* and you......... Matt 25:36
he whom You love is *s* .... John 11:3
many are weak and *s* ... 1 Cor 11:30
have left in Miletus *s* .... 2 Tim 4:20
faith will save the *s*...... James 5:15

SICKLE
Put in the *s*.............. Joel 3:13
"Thrust in Your *s* ...... Rev 14:15

SICKNESS
will sustain him in *s* ..... Prov 18:14
"This *s* is not unto........ John 11:4

SICKNESSES
And bore our *s* .... Matt 8:17

SIDE
The Lord is on my *s*....... Ps 118:6
the net on the right *s* ..... John 21:6

SIDON
Canaanite city; inhabitants not expelled, Judg 1:31
Hostile relations with Israel, Judg 10:12; Is 23:12; Joel 3:4–6
Jesus preaches to, Matt 15:21; Luke 6:17

SIFT
s the nations with the ...... Is 30:28
s the house of Israel ...... Amos 9:9
for you, that he may *s* ... Luke 22:31

SIFTS
A wise king *s* out the .... Prov 20:26

SIGH
our years like a *s*........ Ps 90:9
the merry-hearted *s*........ Is 24:7
of the men who *s* .... Ezek 9:4

SIGHING
For my *s* comes before...... Job 3:24
s is not hidden............. Ps 38:9

SIGHT
and see this great *s*......... Ex 3:3
seemed good in Your *s* ... Matt 11:26
by faith, not by *s*......... 2 Cor 5:7

SIGN
Show me a *s* for good ...... Ps 86:17
will give you a *s*............ Is 7:14
for an everlasting *s*......... Is 55:13
we want to see a *s*....... Matt 12:38
seeks after a *s* .... Matt 12:39
And what will be the *s*.... Matt 24:3
s which will be spoken .... Luke 2:34
again is the second *s* ..... John 4:54
For Jews request a *s* .... 1 Cor 1:22
Now a great *s* appeared .... Rev 12:1

SIGNET
the king's *s* ring.......... Esth 8:8
make you like a *s* ring..... Hag 2:23

SIGNS
and let them be for *s* ..... Gen 1:14
you not know their *s*...... Job 21:29
They performed His *s* ..... Ps 105:27
We are for *s* and........... Is 8:18
How great are His *s*........ Dan 4:3
cannot discern the *s*...... Matt 16:3
the accompanying *s*..... Mark 16:20

s Jesus did in Cana of . . . . . John 2:11
no one can do these s . . . . . . John 3:2
you people see s . . . . John 4:48
because you saw the s . . . . John 6:26
is a sinner do such s . . . . . . John 9:16
this Man works many s . . . John 11:47
Jesus did many other s . . . John 20:30
demons, performing s . . . . . Rev 16:14

SIHON
Amorite king; defeated by Israel,
   Num 21:21–32
Territory of, assigned to Reuben and
   Gad, Num 32:1–38

SILAS (or Silvanus)
Leader in Jerusalem church; sent to
   Antioch, Acts 15:22–35
Travels with Paul, Acts 15:40, 41
Jailed and released, Acts 16:25–40
Mentioned in epistles, 2 Cor 1:19;
   1 Thess 1:1; 2 Thess 1:1; 1 Pet 5:12

SILENCE
that You may s . . . . Ps 8:2
I was mute with s . . . . Ps 39:2
soon have settled in s . . . . . . Ps 94:17
"Sit in s . . . . Is 47:5
seal, there was s . . . . Rev 8:1

SILENT
the wicked shall be s . . . 1 Sam 2:9
season, and am not s . . . . . . Ps 22:2
Do not be s to me . . . . Ps 28:1
Let them be s in the. . . . . Ps 31:17
Be s in the presence . . . . Zeph 1:7
Let your women keep s . . 1 Cor 14:34

SILK
and covered you with s . . Ezek 16:10

SILOAM
Tower of, falls and kills 18 people,
   Luke 13:4
Blind man washes in pool of, John
   9:1–11

SILVER
and your precious s . . . . . . Job 22:25
Though he heaps up s . . . . . Job 27:16
s tried in a furnace . . . . Ps 12:6
have refined us as s . . . . Ps 66:10
than the profits of s . . . . Prov 3:14
chosen rather than s . . . . Prov 16:16
refining pot is for s . . . . Prov 17:3
He who loves s will. . . . . . . Eccl 5:10
s has become dross . . . . Is 1:22
call them rejected s . . . . Jer 6:30
may buy the poor for s . . . . Amos 8:6
him thirty pieces of s . . . . Matt 26:15

SIMEON
Son of Jacob by Leah, Gen 29:32, 33
Avenged his sister's dishonor, Gen
   34:25–31
Held hostage by Joseph, Gen 42:18–
   20, 24
Rebuked by Jacob, Gen 49:5–7
—— Tribe of:
   Numbered, Num 1:23; 26:12–14
   Receive inheritance, Josh 19:1–9
   Fight Canaanites with Judah, Judg
      1:1–3, 17–20
—— Just man; blesses infant Jesus,
   Luke 2:25–35

SIMILITUDE
been made in the s . . . . . . James 3:9

SIMON
Simon Peter: *see* PETER
—— One of the Twelve; called "the
   Cananite," Matt 10:4

—— One of Jesus' half brothers, Matt
   13:55
—— Pharisee, Luke 7:36–40
—— Man of Cyrene, Matt 27:32
—— Sorcerer, Acts 8:9–24
—— Tanner in Joppa, Acts 9:43

SIMPLE
making wise the s . . . . Ps 19:7
LORD preserves the s. . . . . . . Ps 116:6
understanding to the s. . . . Ps 119:130
s believes every word. . . . . Prov 14:15
the hearts of the s . . . . . . Rom 16:18

SIMPLICITY
ones, will you love s . . . . . Prov 1:22
in the world in s. . . . . 2 Cor 1:12
corrupted from the s . . . . . 2 Cor 11:3

SIN
committed a great s . . . . . . Ex 32:20
he died in his own s . . . . . Num 27:3
and be sure your s . . . . . . Num 32:23
to death for his own s . . . . Deut 24:16
all this Job did not s . . . . . . Job 2:10
and search out my s . . . . . . Job 10:6
Be angry, and do not s . . . . . Ps 4:4
my ways, lest I s . . . . Ps 39:1
s is always before me . . . . . . Ps 51:3
in s my mother . . . . Ps 51:5
s is a reproach . . . . Prov 14:34
good and does not s . . . . . . Eccl 7:20
soul an offering for s . . . . . . Is 53:10
And He bore the s. . . . . Is 53:12
s I will remember no . . . . . Jer 31:34
They eat up the s . . . . Hos 4:8
Now they s more and. . . . . . Hos 13:2
who believe in Me to s . . . . Matt 18:6
who takes away the s. . . . . John 1:29
S no more . . . . John 5:14
"He who is without s . . . . . . John 8:7
convict the world of s . . . . John 16:8
they are all under s . . . . . . Rom 3:9
s entered the world . . . . . . Rom 5:12
s is not imputed . . . . Rom 5:13
s that grace may. . . . . Rom 6:1
died to s once for all . . . . . Rom 6:10
s shall not have. . . . . Rom 6:14
Shall we s because we. . . . Rom 6:15
s that dwells in me . . . . . . Rom 7:17
Him who knew no s . . . . . 2 Cor 5:21
man of s is revealed . . . . . 2 Thess 2:3
we are, yet without s . . . . . Heb 4:15
appeared to put away s. . . . Heb 9:26
s willfully after we . . . . . . Heb 10:26
it gives birth to s. . . . . James 1:15
do it, to him it is s. . . . . . . James 4:17
"Who committed no s . . . . 1 Pet 2:22
say that we have no s . . . . 1 John 1:8
that you may not s . . . . . . 1 John 2:1
s is lawlessness. . . . . 1 John 3:4
in Him there is no s. . . . . . 1 John 3:5
and he cannot s . . . . 1 John 3:9
for those who commit s . . 1 John 5:16
unrighteousness is s. . . . . 1 John 5:17

SINAI
Mountain (same as Horeb) where the
   law was given, Ex 19:1–25
Used allegorically by Paul, Gal
   4:24, 25

SINCERE
Holy Spirit, by s love . . . . 2 Cor 6:6
and from s faith . . . . 1 Tim 1:5
s love of the brethren . . . . 1 Pet 1:22

SINCERITY
LORD, serve Him in s . . . . . Josh 24:14
unleavened bread of s. . . . . 1 Cor 5:8

simplicity and godly s . . . . 2 Cor 1:12
men-pleasers, but in s . . . . . Col 3:22

SINFUL
Alas, s nation. . . . . Is 1:4
and s generation . . . . Mark 8:38
from me, for I am a s . . . . . . Luke 5:8
the hands of s men . . . . . . Luke 24:7
become exceedingly s . . . . Rom 7:13
likeness of s flesh . . . . Rom 8:3

SING
"S to the LORD . . . . Ex 15:21
the widow's heart to s . . . . Job 29:13
S out the honor. . . . . Ps 66:2
I will s of mercy and . . . . . . Ps 101:1
"S us one of the songs . . . . Ps 137:3
My servants shall s. . . . . Is 65:14
I will s with the . . . . 1 Cor 14:15
assembly I will s . . . . Heb 2:12
Let him s psalms. . . . . James 5:13

SINGERS
The s went before . . . . Ps 68:25
male and female s . . . . Eccl 2:8

SINGING
His presence with s . . . . . . Ps 100:2
and our tongue with s. . . . . Ps 126:2
the time of s has come . . . . Song 2:12
break forth into s . . . . Is 14:7
even with joy and s . . . . Is 35:2
come to Zion with s . . . . Is 35:10
and spiritual songs, s . . . . Eph 5:19

SINISTER
who understands s . . . . . . Dan 8:23

SINK
I s in deep mire . . . . Ps 69:2
to s he cried out. . . . . Matt 14:30

SINNED
You only, have I s . . . . Ps 51:4
Jerusalem has s . . . . Lam 1:8
Our fathers s and are . . . . . Lam 5:7
"Father, I have s . . . . Luke 15:18
"Rabbi, who s . . . . John 9:2
For as many as have s . . . . Rom 2:12
for all have s and . . . . Rom 3:23
marries, she has not s . . . . 1 Cor 7:28
say that we have not s. . . . 1 John 1:10
for the devil has s . . . . 1 John 3:8

SINNER
s He gives the work . . . . Eccl 2:26
s does evil a hundred . . . . . Eccl 8:12
s destroys much good. . . . . Eccl 9:18
the city who was a s . . . . . Luke 7:37
s who repents than . . . . . . Luke 15:7
can a man who is a s . . . . . John 9:16
the ungodly and the s . . . 1 Pet 4:18

SINNERS
in the path of s . . . . Ps 1:1
therefore He teaches s. . . . . Ps 25:8
soul with s . . . . Ps 26:9
s be consumed from the . . . Ps 104:35
son, if s entice you. . . . . . . Prov 1:10
The s in Zion are . . . . Is 33:14
the righteous, but s . . . . . . Matt 9:13
tax collectors and s . . . . . Matt 11:19
s love those who love . . . . Luke 6:32
Galileans were worse s . . . Luke 13:2
God does not hear s . . . . . John 9:31
while we were still s . . . . . Rom 5:8
many were made s . . . . Rom 5:19
the ungodly and for s . . . . 1 Tim 1:9
the world to save s . . . . . . 1 Tim 1:15
separate from s . . . . Heb 7:26
such hostility from s. . . . . . Heb 12:3
things which ungodly s . . . . . Jude 15

SINS
my iniquities and *s* . . . . Job 13:23
from presumptuous *s* . . . . . . Ps 19:13
You, our secret *s* . . . . Ps 90:8
but he who *s* against. . . . . Prov 8:36
s have hidden His face. . . . . . Is 59:2
the soul who *s* shall. . . . . . Ezek 18:4
to make an end of *s* . . . . . . Dan 9:24
if your brother *s*. . . . . . Matt 18:15
I take away their *s*. . . . . . Rom 11:27
s according to the . . . . . . 1 Cor 15:3
are still in your *s* . . . . . . 1 Cor 15:17
the forgiveness of *s*. . . . . . . Eph 1:7
s are clearly evident . . . . . 1 Tim 5:24
once to bear the *s*. . . . . Heb 9:28
If we confess our *s* . . . . . . 1 John 1:9
propitiation for our *s*. . . . . 1 John 2:2
s are forgiven you . . . . . 1 John 2:12
Whoever *s* has neither . . . 1 John 3:6
you share in her *s*. . . . . Rev 18:4

SION
See ZION
Name given to all or part of Mt. Hermon, Deut 4:48

SISERA
Canaanite commander of Jabin's
army; slain by Jael, Judg 4:2–22

SISTER
are my mother and my *s*. . . Job 17:14
We have a little *s* . . . . Song 8:8
is My brother and *s*. . . . . Matt 12:50
to you Phoebe our *s* . . . . . . Rom 16:1
s is not under bondage . . . 1 Cor 7:15

SIT
Those who *s* in the . . . . Ps 69:12
"Come down and *s* . . . . Is 47:1
"Why do we *s* still . . . . Jer 8:14
but to *s* on My right . . . . Matt 20:23
and the Pharisees *s*. . . . . . Matt 23:2
"*S* at My right hand. . . . . . . Heb 1:13
say to him, "You *s* . . . . . . James 2:3
I will grant to *s*. . . . . Rev 3:21
heart, 'I *s* as queen . . . . Rev 18:7

SITS
God *s* on His holy . . . . Ps 47:8
It is He who *s* above. . . . . . . Is 40:22
so that he *s* as God. . . . . 2 Thess 2:4
where the harlot *s*. . . . . . . Rev 17:15

SITTING
You know my *s* down and. . . Ps 139:2
see the Son of Man *s* . . . . Mark 14:62
where Christ is, *s*. . . . . Col 3:1

SKILL
hand forget its *s*. . . . . Ps 137:5
nor favor to men of *s* . . . . . Eccl 9:11
them knowledge and *s* . . . . Dan 1:17
forth to give you *s* . . . . Dan 9:22

SKILLFULNESS
guided them by the *s*. . . . . . Ps 78:72

SKIN
God made tunics of *s*. . . . . Gen 3:21
LORD and said, "*S* . . . . Job 2:4
have escaped by the *s*. . . . Job 19:20
Ethiopian change his *s* . . . Jer 13:23
s is hot as an oven . . . . . . Lam 5:10

SKIP
He makes them also *s*. . . . . . Ps 29:6

SKIPPING
upon the mountains, *s*. . . . Song 2:8

SKULL
to say, Place of a *S* . . . . . Matt 27:33

SKY
s receded as a scroll . . . . . . Rev 6:14

SLACK
He will not be *s*. . . . . Deut 7:10
s hand becomes poor . . . . . Prov 10:4
The Lord is not *s*. . . . . 2 Pet 3:9

SLAIN
s his thousands. . . . . 1 Sam 18:7
beauty of Israel is *s*. . . . . 2 Sam 1:19
the dead, like the *s* . . . . Ps 88:5
and all who were *s*. . . . . . . Prov 7:26
I shall be *s* in the. . . . . . . Prov 22:13
s men are not *s* . . . . Is 22:2
no more cover her *s*. . . . . . . Is 26:21
and the *s* of the LORD. . . . . . Is 66:16
and night for the *s*. . . . . Jer 9:1
Those *s* by the sword. . . . . . Lam 4:9
the prophets, I have *s*. . . . . Hos 6:5
is the Lamb who was *s*. . . . Rev 5:12

SLANDER
s your own mother's . . . . . . Ps 50:20
and whoever spreads *s* . . . Prov 10:18

SLANDERERS
be reverent, not *s*. . . . . . . 1 Tim 3:11
unforgiving, *s* . . . . 2 Tim 3:3
in behavior, not *s* . . . . Titus 2:3

SLANDEROUSLY
as we are *s* reported . . . . . . Rom 3:8

SLAUGHTER
as sheep for the *s*. . . . . Ps 44:22
led as a lamb to the *s* . . . . . Is 53:7
but the Valley of *S* . . . . Jer 7:32
"Feed the flock for *s* . . . . . Zech 11:4
as sheep for the *s* . . . . Rom 8:36

SLAVE
that you were a *s*. . . . . . . Deut 15:15
commits sin is a *s*. . . . . . . John 8:34
you called while a *s*. . . . . . 1 Cor 7:21
you are no longer a *s*. . . . . . Gal 4:7

SLAVES
should no longer be *s*. . . . . Rom 6:6
though you were *s*. . . . . . . Rom 6:17
your members as *s* . . . . . . Rom 6:19
do not become *s*. . . . . 1 Cor 7:23

SLAY
s the righteous . . . . Gen 18:25
s a righteous nation . . . . . Gen 20:4
Evil shall *s* the. . . . . Ps 34:21
Oh, that You would *s*. . . . . Ps 139:19
s them before me . . . . Luke 19:27

SLEEP
God caused a deep *s* . . . . . Gen 2:21
the night, when deep *s* . . . . Job 4:13
my eyes, lest I *s* . . . . Ps 13:3
Why do You *s* . . . . Ps 44:23
have sunk into their *s*. . . . . . Ps 76:5
they are like a *s*. . . . . Ps 90:5
neither slumber nor *s* . . . . Ps 121:4
He gives His beloved *s*. . . . Ps 127:2
I will not give *s* . . . . Ps 132:4
s will be sweet . . . . Prov 3:24
For they do not *s* . . . . Prov 4:16
A little *s* . . . . Prov 6:10
Do not love *s*. . . . . Prov 20:13
The *s* of a laboring. . . . . Eccl 5:12
the spirit of deep *s* . . . . Is 29:10
Also his *s* went from . . . . . . Dan 6:18
I was in a deep *s* . . . . Dan 8:18
deep *s* on my face. . . . . Dan 10:9
them, "Why do you *s* . . . . Luke 22:46
among you, and many *s*. 1 Cor 11:30
We shall not all *s*. . . . . . . 1 Cor 15:51
"Awake, you who *s*. . . . . . . Eph 5:14

SKY
with Him those who *s* . . . 1 Thess 4:14
Therefore let us not *s* . . . . 1 Thess 5:6

SLEEPERS
gently the lips of *s* . . . . Song 7:9

SLEEPING
is not dead, but *s* . . . . . . Matt 9:24
"Are you still *s* . . . . Matt 26:45
that night Peter was *s* . . . . Acts 12:6

SLEEPLESSNESS
in labors, in *s* . . . . 2 Cor 6:5
and toil, in *s* often . . . . . 2 Cor 11:27

SLEEPS
wise son; he who *s*. . . . . . Prov 10:5
"Our friend Lazarus *s* . . . . John 11:11

SLEPT
I lay down and *s*. . . . . Ps 3:5
but while men *s* . . . . Matt 13:25

SLIGHTED
is the one who is *s*. . . . . . . Prov 12:9

SLING
he had, and his *s* . . . . . . 1 Sam 17:40
a stone in a *s* is he . . . . . . Prov 26:8

SLIP
their foot shall *s* . . . . Deut 32:35
my footsteps may not *s*. . . . . Ps 17:5

SLIPPERY
way be dark and *s*. . . . . Ps 35:6
set them in *s* places . . . . . . Ps 73:18
be to them like *s*. . . . . Jer 23:12

SLOOPS
all the beautiful *s*. . . . . Is 2:16

SLOW
but I am *s* of speech . . . . . . Ex 4:10
He who is *s* to wrath . . . . Prov 14:29
hear, *s* to speak, *s* . . . . . . James 1:19

SLUGGARD
will you slumber, O *s* . . . . . Prov 6:9

SLUMBERED
delayed, they all *s* . . . . . . Matt 25:5

SLUMBERING
upon men, while *s*. . . . . . . Job 33:15

SMALL
'The place is too *s* . . . . Is 49:20
I will make you *s* . . . . Jer 49:15
may stand, for he is *s*. . . . . Amos 7:2
I will make you *s* . . . . Obad 2
the day of *s* things . . . . . . Zech 4:10
And I saw the dead, *s*. . . . . Rev 20:12

SMELL
and he smelled the *s* . . . . Gen 27:27
s there will be a . . . . Is 3:24

SMELLS
s the battle from afar . . . . . Job 39:25

SMITTEN
Him stricken, *s*. . . . . Is 53:4

SMOKE
went up like the *s*. . . . . . . Gen 19:28
s, because the LORD
   descended. . . . . Ex 19:18
s is driven away . . . . Ps 68:2
are consumed like *s*. . . . . . Ps 102:3
like a wineskin in *s*. . . . . . Ps 119:83
like pillars of *s* . . . . Song 3:6
a cloud and *s* by day. . . . . . . Is 4:5
house was filled with *s* . . . . . Is 6:4
s shall ascend forever. . . . . Is 34:10
vanish away like *s* . . . . Is 51:6
fire and vapor of *s* . . . . . . Acts 2:19
s arose out of the pit . . . . . Rev 9:2

was filled with *s* . . . . Rev 15:8
Her *s* rises up. . . . . Rev 19:3

SMOOTH
speak to us *s* things . . . . Is 30:10
And the rough places *s* . . . . . . Is 40:4
though they speak *s* . . . . Jer 12:6
the rough ways *s* . . . . Luke 3:5

SMOOTH-SKINNED
man, and I am a *s* . . . . Gen 27:11

SMYRNA
Site of one of the seven churches, Rev
1:11

SNARE
it will surely be a *s* . . . . Ex 23:33
It became a *s* to. . . . . Judg 8:27
that she may be a *s* . . . . 1 Sam 18:21
s snatches their . . . . Job 5:5
and he walks into a *s* . . . . . . Job 18:8
their table become a *s*. . . . . Ps 69:22
as a bird from the *s*. . . . . . . Ps 124:7
birds caught in a *s* . . . . Eccl 9:12
and the pit and the *s*. . . . . . Is 24:17
I have laid a *s*. . . . . Jer 50:23
s have come upon us . . . . . Lam 3:47
is a fowler's *s* . . . . Hos 9:8
a bird fall into a *s*. . . . . Amos 3:5
it will come as a *s*. . . . . . . Luke 21:35
temptation and a *s*. . . . . . . 1 Tim 6:9
and escape the *s* . . . . 2 Tim 2:26

SNARED
The wicked is *s*. . . . . Ps 9:16
and be broken, be *s* . . . . Is 8:15
all of them are *s*. . . . . Is 42:22

SNARES
the *s* of death. . . . . Ps 18:5
who seek my life lay *s*. . . . . Ps 38:12
and built great *s*. . . . . Eccl 9:14
wait as one who sets *s* . . . . . Jer 5:26

SNATCH
s the fatherless. . . . . Job 24:9
neither shall anyone *s* . . . John 10:28

SNATCHES
s away what was. . . . . . . Matt 13:19

SNEER
and you *s* at it . . . . Mal 1:13

SNIFFED
they *s* at the wind. . . . . Jer 14:6

SNORTING
s strikes terror . . . . Job 39:20

SNOW
and heat consume the *s* . . . Job 24:19
For He says to the *s*. . . . . . . Job 37:6
the treasury of *s*. . . . . Job 38:22
shall be whiter than *s*. . . . . . Ps 51:7
He gives *s* like wool . . . . . Ps 147:16
As *s* in summer and . . . . . . Prov 26:1
She is not afraid of *s* . . . . Prov 31:21
shall be as white as *s*. . . . . . . Is 1:18
garment was white as *s* . . . . Dan 7:9
clothing as white as *s*. . . . . Matt 28:3
wool, as white as *s* . . . . . . Rev 1:14

SOAKED
their land shall be *s*. . . . . Is 34:7

SOAP
lye, and use much *s*. . . . . . . Jer 2:22

SOBER
of the day be *s* . . . . 1 Thess 5:8
the older men be *s* . . . . . . Titus 2:2

SOBERLY
think, but to think *s*. . . . . . Rom 12:3
we should live *s*. . . . . Titus 2:12

SOCKET
touched the *s* of his hip. . . Gen 32:25

SODA
and like vinegar on *s* . . . . Prov 25:20

SODOM
Lot chooses to live there, Gen
13:10–13
Plundered by Chedorlaomer, Gen
14:8–24
Abraham intercedes for, Gen
18:16–33
Destroyed by God, Gen 19:1–29
Cited as example of sin and destruction, Deut 29:23; 32:32; Is 1:9, 10;
3:9; Jer 23:14; 49:18; Lam 4:6;
Ezek 16:46–63; Matt 11:23, 24;
2 Pet 2:6; Jude 7

SODOMITES
nor homosexuals, nor *s*. . . . 1 Cor 6:9
for fornicators, for *s*. . . . . . 1 Tim 1:10

SOFTER
his words were *s*. . . . . Ps 55:21

SOJOURNER
But no *s* had to lodge . . . . . Job 31:32

SOJOURNERS
are strangers and *s*. . . . . . . Lev 25:23
I beg you as *s* . . . . 1 Pet 2:11

SOLD
s his birthright . . . . Gen 25:33
the house that was *s*. . . . . . Lev 25:33
their Rock had *s* . . . . Deut 32:30
and He *s* them into the. . . . Judg 2:14
s themselves to do . . . . . . 2 Kin 17:17
Had we been *s* as male . . . . . Esth 7:4
who was *s* as a slave . . . . . Ps 105:17
s all that he had . . . . Matt 13:46
they bought, they *s*. . . . . . Luke 17:28
s their possessions . . . . Acts 2:45
but I am carnal, *s*. . . . . . . Rom 7:14
Eat whatever is *s* . . . . . . 1 Cor 10:25

SOLDIER
hardship as a good *s* . . . . . 2 Tim 2:3
enlisted him as a *s* . . . . . . 2 Tim 2:4

SOLDIERS
sum of money to the *s* . . . Matt 28:12
The *s* also mocked . . . . . . Luke 23:36
s twisted a crown. . . . . John 19:2

SOLEMNLY
saying, "The man *s* . . . . . . Gen 43:3
s testified of the . . . . Acts 28:23

SOLITARILY
heritage, who dwell *s* . . . . . Mic 7:14

SOLITARY
God sets the *s* in . . . . Ps 68:6

SOLOMON
David's son by Bathsheba, 2 Sam
12:24
Becomes king, 1 Kin 1:5–53
Receives and carries out David's
instructions, 1 Kin 2
Prays for and demonstrates wisdom,
1 Kin 3:3–28; 4:29–34
Builds and dedicates temple; builds
palace, 1 Kin 5—8
Lord appears to, 1 Kin 9:1–9
His fame and glory, 1 Kin 9:10—
10:29
Falls into idolatry; warned by God,
1 Kin 11:1–13
Adversaries arise, 1 Kin 11:14–40
Death of, 1 Kin 11:41–43

Writings credited to him, Ps 72; 127;
Prov 1:1; 10:1; 25:1; Eccl 1:1;
Song 1:1

SOMEBODY
up, claiming to be *s*. . . . . . . Acts 5:36

SOMETHING
"Simon, I have *s* . . . . Luke 7:40
thinks himself to be *s* . . . . . . Gal 6:3

SON
Me, 'You are My *S* . . . . Ps 2:7
I was my father's *s* . . . . Prov 4:3
s makes a glad father . . . . Prov 10:1
s is a grief to his . . . . Prov 17:25
And what, *s* of my womb . . Prov 31:2
is born, unto us a *S* . . . . Is 9:6
heaven, O Lucifer, *s* . . . . . . Is 14:12
fourth is like the *S*. . . . . . . Dan 3:25
He is an unwise *s* . . . . Hos 13:13
prophet, nor was I a *s* . . . . Amos 7:14
s honors his father. . . . . Mal 1:6
will bring forth a *S* . . . . . . Matt 1:21
"This is My beloved *S* . . . . Matt 3:17
Jesus, You *S* of God . . . . . Matt 8:29
not the carpenter's *s* . . . . Matt 13:55
You are the *S* of God . . . . Matt 14:33
are the Christ, the *S*. . . . . Matt 16:16
of all he sent his *s* . . . . . . Matt 21:37
Whose *S* is He . . . . Matt 22:42
'Lord,' how is He his *S* . . . Matt 22:45
as much a *s* of hell . . . . . Matt 23:15
of the *S* of Man . . . . Matt 24:37
'I am the *S* of God'. . . . . . Matt 27:43
"Truly this was the *S*. . . . . Matt 27:54
of Jesus Christ, the *S* . . . . . Mark 1:1
called the *S* of the. . . . . . . Luke 1:32
out, the only *s*. . . . . Luke 7:12
And if a *s* of peace . . . . . Luke 10:6
to be called your *s* . . . . . . Luke 15:19
because he also is a *s* . . . . Luke 19:9
The only begotten *S* . . . . . John 1:18
that this is the *S* . . . . John 1:34
of the only begotten *S*. . . . John 3:18
S can do nothing. . . . . John 5:19
s abides forever. . . . . John 8:35
you believe in the *S* . . . . . John 9:35
I said, 'I am the *S* . . . . . . John 10:36
"Woman, behold your *s* . . John 19:26
Jesus Christ is the *S* . . . . . . Acts 8:37
declared to be the *S* . . . . . . Rom 1:4
in the gospel of His *S* . . . . . Rom 1:9
by sending His own *S* . . . . . Rom 8:3
not spare His own *S* . . . . . Rom 8:32
S Himself will also be. . . . 1 Cor 15:28
live by faith in the *S*. . . . . . Gal 2:20
God sent forth His *S* . . . . . . Gal 4:4
longer a slave but a *s* . . . . . . Gal 4:7
the knowledge of the *S*. . . . Eph 4:13
you for my *s* Onesimus . . . Philem 10
"You are My *S* . . . . Heb 1:5
but Christ as a *S* over His . . . Heb 3:6
though He was a *S* . . . . Heb 5:8
but made like the *S* . . . . . . Heb 7:3
to be called the *s* . . . . Heb 11:24
"This is My beloved *S* . . . . 2 Pet 1:17
Whoever denies the *S* . . . 1 John 2:23
God has given of His *S*. . . 1 John 5:10
One like the *S* of Man. . . . . Rev 1:13

SONG
is my strength and *s*. . . . . . Ex 15:2
Sing to Him a new *s* . . . . . . Ps 33:3
He has put a new *s* . . . . . . Ps 40:3
in the night His *s* . . . . Ps 42:8
me, and I am the *s* . . . . . . Ps 69:12
asked of us a *s*. . . . . Ps 137:3
I will sing a new *s* . . . . Ps 144:9
to my Well-beloved a *s* . . . . . Is 5:1

their taunting s . . . . Lam 3:14
I am their taunting s . . . . . Lam 3:63
as a very lovely s . . . . Ezek 33:32
They sang a new s . . . . Rev 5:9
And they sing the s . . . . Rev 15:3

SONGS
my Maker, who gives s . . . . Job 35:10
surround me with s . . . . Ps 32:7
have been my s in the . . . . . Ps 119:54
Sing us one of the s . . . . Ps 137:3
is one who sings s . . . . . . Prov 25:20
and spiritual s . . . . Eph 5:19

SONS
s come to honor . . . . Job 14:21
shall be Your s . . . . Ps 45:16
my beloved among the s . . Song 2:3
s shall come from afar . . . . . . Is 60:4
"Has Israel no s . . . . Jer 49:1
The precious s of Zion . . . . . Lam 4:2
'You are the s . . . . Hos 1:10
He will purify the s . . . . Mal 3:3
to him, "Then the s . . . . . Matt 17:26
and you will be s . . . . Luke 6:35
that you may become s . . John 12:36
You are s of the . . . . Acts 3:25
of God, these are s . . . . . . Rom 8:14
who are of faith are s . . . . . . Gal 3:7
the adoption as s . . . . Gal 4:5
because you are s . . . . Gal 4:6
You are all s of light . . . . . 1 Thess 5:5
in bringing many s . . . . Heb 2:10
speaks to you as to s . . . . . Heb 12:5
illegitimate and not s . . . . . Heb 12:8

SOON
for it is s cut off . . . . Ps 90:10
s forgot His works . . . . Ps 106:13

SOOTHED
or bound up, or s . . . . Is 1:6

SORCERER
omens, or a s . . . . Deut 18:10
But Elymas the s . . . . Acts 13:8

SORCERERS
soothsayers, or your s . . . . . . Jer 27:9
outside are dogs and s . . . . Rev 22:15

SORCERESS
shall not permit a s . . . . . . Ex 22:18

SORCERY
For there is no s . . . . Num 23:23
idolatry, s . . . . Gal 5:20

SORES
and putrefying s . . . . Is 1:6
Lazarus, full of s . . . . Luke 16:20

SORROW
multiply your s . . . . Gen 3:16
s dances before him . . . . . . Job 41:22
in my soul, having s . . . . Ps 13:2
s is continually . . . . Ps 38:17
I found trouble and s . . . . . . Ps 116:3
And He adds no s . . . . Prov 10:22
the heart may s . . . . Prov 14:13
S is better than . . . . Eccl 7:3
Therefore remove s . . . . . . Eccl 11:10
and desperate s . . . . Is 17:11
you shall cry for s . . . . Is 65:14
to see labor and s . . . . Jer 20:18
Your s is incurable . . . . Jer 30:15
added grief to my s . . . . Jer 45:3
gather those who s . . . . . . Zeph 3:18
them sleeping from s . . . . Luke 22:45
s has filled your . . . . John 16:6
s will be turned . . . . John 16:20
that I have great s . . . . Rom 9:2
s produces repentance . . . . 2 Cor 7:10

lest I should have s . . . . . . Phil 2:27
s as others who have . . . 1 Thess 4:13
no more death, nor s . . . . . Rev 21:4

SORROWFUL
am a woman of s spirit . . 1 Sam 1:15
But I am poor and s . . . . . . Ps 69:29
For all his days are s . . . . . Eccl 2:23
replenished every s . . . . . . Jer 31:25
were exceedingly s . . . . . Matt 17:23
saying, he went away s . . Matt 19:22
soul is exceedingly s . . . . Matt 26:38
and went away s . . . . Mark 10:22
and you will be s . . . . John 16:20
if I make you s . . . . 2 Cor 2:2
and I may be less s . . . . . . Phil 2:28

SORROWS
the s of Sheol . . . . 2 Sam 22:6
s God distributes . . . . Job 21:17
s shall be multiplied . . . . Ps 16:4
by men, a Man of s . . . . Is 53:3
are the beginning of s . . . Matt 24:8
through with many s . . . . 1 Tim 6:10

SORRY
s that He had made man . . . Gen 6:6
who will be s for you . . . . . . Is 51:19
And the king was s . . . . . . Matt 14:9
For you were made s . . . . . 2 Cor 7:9

SOSTHENES
Ruler of the synagogue at Corinth,
    Acts 18:17
—— Paul's Christian brother,
    1 Cor 1:1

SOUGHT
I s the LORD . . . . Ps 34:4
whole heart I have s . . . . . Ps 119:10
s the one I love . . . . Song 3:1
shall be called S Out . . . . . . Is 62:12
So I s for a man . . . . Ezek 22:30
s what was lost . . . . Ezek 34:4
s favor from Him . . . . Hos 12:4
LORD, and have not s . . . . . Zeph 1:6
s it diligently . . . . Heb 12:17

SOUL
s enter their council . . . . . . Gen 49:6
with all your s . . . . Deut 6:5
was knit to the s . . . . 1 Sam 18:1
your heart and your s . . . 1 Chr 22:19
"My s loathes my life . . . . . . Job 10:1
as you do, if your s . . . . Job 16:4
s draws near the Pit . . . . . . Job 33:22
will not leave my s . . . . Ps 16:10
converting the s . . . . Ps 19:7
He restores my s . . . . Ps 23:3
s shall make its boast . . . . . . Ps 34:2
s shall be joyful . . . . Ps 35:9
you cast down, O my s . . . . . Ps 42:5
s silently waits . . . . Ps 62:1
He has done for my s . . . . . . Ps 66:16
Let my s live . . . . Ps 119:175
s knows you well . . . . Ps 139:14
No one cares for my s . . . . . Ps 142:4
so destroys his own s . . . . . Prov 6:32
me wrongs his own s . . . . . Prov 8:36
it is not good for a s . . . . . . Prov 19:2
A satisfied s loathes . . . . . . Prov 27:7
When You make His s . . . . . Is 53:10
s delight itself . . . . Is 55:2
and your s shall live . . . . Is 55:3
you have heard, O my s . . . . Jer 4:19
the s of the father as . . . . . Ezek 18:4
the proud, his s . . . . Hab 2:4
able to destroy both s . . . . Matt 10:28
and loses his own s . . . . . Matt 16:26
with all your s . . . . Matt 22:37
Now My s is troubled . . . . John 12:27

of one heart and one s . . . Acts 4:32
your whole spirit, s . . . . . 1 Thess 5:23
to the saving of the s . . . . Heb 10:39
his way will save a s . . . . James 5:20
his righteous . . . . 2 Pet 2:8
health, just as your s . . . . . 3 John 2

SOULS
and will save the s . . . . Ps 72:13
and he who wins s . . . . . . Prov 11:30
s shall be like a . . . . Jer 31:12
who made our very s . . . . Jer 38:16
unsettling your s . . . . Acts 15:24
is able to save your s . . . . James 1:21

SOUND
s heart is life . . . . Prov 14:30
one rises up at the s . . . . . . Eccl 12:4
voice was like the s . . . . . Ezek 43:2
s an alarm in My holy . . . . . . Joel 2:1
do not s a trumpet . . . . Matt 6:2
s words which you . . . . . . 2 Tim 1:13
that they may be s . . . . . . Titus 1:13

SOUNDNESS
There is no s in my . . . . Ps 38:3
him this perfect s . . . . Acts 3:16

SOUNDS
Dreadful s are in his . . . . . Job 15:21
a distinction in the s . . . . 1 Cor 14:7

SOW
s trouble reap . . . . Job 4:8
then let me s . . . . Job 31:8
s fields and plant . . . . Ps 107:37
Those who s in tears . . . . . Ps 126:5
the wind will not s . . . . . . Eccl 11:4
Blessed are you who s . . . . . Is 32:20
ground, and do not s . . . . . . Jer 4:3
"They s the wind . . . . Hos 8:7
S for yourselves . . . . Hos 10:12
s is not made alive . . . . . 1 Cor 15:36

SOWER
may give seed to the s . . . . Is 55:10
"Behold, a s went . . . . . . Matt 13:3

SOWN
shall they be s . . . . Is 40:24
a land not s . . . . Jer 2:2
"You have s much . . . . Hag 1:6
s spiritual things . . . . 1 Cor 9:11
It is s in weakness . . . . . 1 Cor 15:43
of righteousness is s . . . . James 3:18

SOWS
s righteousness will . . . . . Prov 11:18
s the good seed is the . . . . Matt 13:37
'One s and another . . . . . . John 4:37
s sparingly will . . . . 2 Cor 9:6
for whatever a man s . . . . . . Gal 6:7

SPARE
The LORD would not s . . . . Deut 29:20
hand, but s his life . . . . Job 2:6
S the poor and needy . . . . . Ps 72:13
I will not pity nor s . . . . . . Jer 13:14
say, "S Your people . . . . . . Joel 2:17
s them as a man spares . . . . Mal 3:17
He who did not s . . . . Rom 8:32
s the natural branches . . . Rom 11:21
branches, He may not s . . Rom 11:21
flesh, but I would . . . . 1 Cor 7:28
if God did not s . . . . 2 Pet 2:4

SPARES
s his rod hates his . . . . . . Prov 13:24

SPARK
the work of it as a s . . . . Is 1:31

SPARKLES
it is red, when it s . . . . . . Prov 23:31

SPARKS
to trouble, as the *s* . . . . Job 5:7
s you have kindled. . . . . Is 50:11

SPARROW
s has found a home . . . . Ps 84:3
awake, and am like a *s*. . . . Ps 102:7

SPARROWS
more value than many *s* . Matt 10:31

SPAT
Then they *s* on Him . . . . . Matt 27:30
in his ears, and He *s* . . . . Mark 7:33

SPEAK
S to the rock . . . . Num 20:8
only the word that I *s*. . . . Num 22:35
s just once more . . . . Judg 6:39
s good words to them. . . . . 1 Kin 12:7
oh, that God would *s*. . . . . . Job 11:5
Will you *s* wickedly . . . . Job 13:7
For God may *s* in one . . . . Job 33:14
Will he *s* softly to. . . . . Job 41:3
Do not *s* in the . . . . Prov 23:9
and a time to *s*. . . . . Eccl 3:7
If they do not *s*. . . . . Is 8:20
tongue He will *s* . . . . Is 28:11
s anymore in His name. . . . Jer 20:9
at the end it will *s*. . . . . Hab 2:3
s each man the truth . . . . Zech 8:16
or what you should *s* . . . . Matt 10:19
it is not you who *s* . . . . . Matt 10:20
to you when all men *s*. . . . Luke 6:26
s what We know and . . . . . John 3:11
s what I have seen . . . . . . John 8:38
He hears He will *s*. . . . . . John 16:13
Spirit and began to *s*. . . . . . Acts 2:4
Do all *s* with tongues. . . . 1 Cor 12:30
I would rather *s* . . . . 1 Cor 14:19
So *s* and so do as . . . . . . James 2:12

SPEAKING
s your own words. . . . . Is 58:13
while they are still *s*. . . . . . . Is 65:24
a proof of Christ *s* . . . . . 2 Cor 13:3
envy, and all evil *s*. . . . . . . 1 Pet 2:1

SPEAKS
to face, as a man *s* . . . . Ex 33:11
this day that God *s*. . . . . . Deut 5:24
day that I am He who *s*. . . . . Is 52:6
He whom God has sent *s* . . John 3:34
When he *s* a lie. . . . . John 8:44
he being dead still *s*. . . . . . Heb 11:4
of sprinkling that *s*. . . . . . Heb 12:24

SPEAR
lay hold on bow and *s*. . . . . Jer 6:23
His side with a *s* . . . . John 19:34

SPEARS
whose teeth are *s*. . . . . Ps 57:4
and their *s* into . . . . Is 2:4
pruning hooks into *s* . . . . . Joel 3:10

SPECK
do you look at the *s* . . . . . . Matt 7:3

SPECTACLE
and make you a *s*. . . . . Nah 3:6
we have been made a *s*. . . . 1 Cor 4:9
He made a public *s*. . . . . . . Col 2:15
you were made a *s*. . . . . . . Heb 10:33

SPEECH
one language and one *s* . . . Gen 11:1
drop as the rain, my *s* . . . Deut 32:2
s settled on them as . . . . . Job 29:22
There is no *s* nor . . . . Ps 19:3
s is not becoming . . . . Prov 17:7
your *s* shall be low. . . . . Is 29:4
a people of obscure *s* . . . . . Is 33:19
not understand My *s*. . . . . . John 8:43

s deceive the hearts . . . . . Rom 16:18
and his *s* contemptible. . 2 Cor 10:10
I am untrained in *s*. . . . . . 2 Cor 11:6
s always be with grace . . . . . Col 4:6

SPEECHLESS
your mouth for the *s*. . . . . Prov 31:8
And he was *s*. . . . . Matt 22:12

SPEED
they shall come with *s*. . . . . . Is 5:26

SPEEDILY
judgment be executed *s* . . . Ezra 7:26
to me, deliver me *s* . . . . Ps 31:2
I call, answer me *s* . . . . . . Ps 102:2

SPEND
Why do you *s* money for. . . . . Is 55:2
whatever more you *s* . . . . Luke 10:35
I will very gladly *s* . . . . . 2 Cor 12:15
amiss, that you may *s* . . . . James 4:3

SPENT
strength shall be *s*. . . . . . . Lev 26:20
For my life is *s*. . . . . Ps 31:10
in vain, I have *s*. . . . . Is 49:4
"But when he had *s* . . . . Luke 15:14

SPEW
nor hot, I will *s*. . . . . Rev 3:16

SPIDER
s skillfully grasps. . . . . . . Prov 30:28

SPIES
to them, "You are *s* . . . . . . Gen 42:9
men who had been *s*. . . . . Josh 6:23
s who pretended . . . . Luke 20:20

SPIKENARD
very costly oil of *s*. . . . . . . John 12:3

SPIN
neither toil nor *s*. . . . . Matt 6:28

SPINDLE
her hand holds the *s* . . . . Prov 31:19

SPIRIT
And the *S* of God was . . . . . . Gen 1:2
S shall not strive . . . . Gen 6:3
in whom is the *S*. . . . . Gen 41:38
and everyone whose *s* . . . . Ex 35:21
S that is upon you. . . . . . . Num 11:17
And the *S* rested upon . . . Num 11:26
LORD would put His *S* . . . Num 11:29
he has a different *s*. . . . . . Num 14:24
in whom is the *S*. . . . . . . Num 27:18
portion of your *s* . . . . 2 Kin 2:9
there was no more *s* . . . . . 2 Chr 9:4
s came forward and . . . . 2 Chr 18:20
also gave Your good *S*. . . . Neh 9:20
against them by Your *S* . . . Neh 9:30
Then a *s* passed before . . . . Job 4:15
And whose *s* came from . . . Job 26:4
The *S* of God has made. . . . Job 33:4
hand I commit my *s* . . . . . . Ps 31:5
s was not faithful . . . . Ps 78:8
You send forth Your *S* . . . . Ps 104:30
Your *S* is good. . . . . Ps 143:10
The *s* of a man is the . . . . Prov 20:27
Who knows the *s* . . . . Eccl 3:21
s will return to God . . . . Eccl 12:7
night, yes, by my *s* . . . . Is 26:9
out on you the *s*. . . . . Is 29:10
are flesh, and not *s* . . . . Is 31:3
S has gathered them . . . . . Is 34:16
is the life of my *s* . . . . Is 38:16
I have put My *S* . . . . Is 42:1
and His *S* have sent Me . . . . Is 48:16
s would fail before Me . . . . . Is 57:16
"The *S* of the Lord . . . . Is 61:1
S entered me when He . . . . Ezek 2:2
the *S* lifted me up . . . . Ezek 3:12

who follow their own *s* . . . . Ezek 13:3
new heart and a new *s* . . . Ezek 18:31
be feeble, every *s*. . . . . Ezek 21:7
I will put My *S* . . . . Ezek 36:27
in him is the *S*. . . . . Dan 4:8
as an excellent *s* . . . . Dan 5:12
walk in a false *s* . . . . Mic 2:11
and forms the *s* . . . . Zech 12:1
and He saw the *S* . . . . Matt 3:16
I will put My *S*. . . . . Matt 12:18
S descending upon Him. . . Mark 1:10
Immediately the *S* . . . . . . Mark 1:12
s indeed is willing. . . . . . Mark 14:38
go before Him in the *s* . . . . Luke 1:17
in the power of the *S*. . . . . Luke 4:14
manner of *s* you are of. . . . Luke 9:55
hands I commit My *s* . . . . Luke 23:46
they had seen a *s* . . . . . . Luke 24:37
s does not have flesh . . . Luke 24:39
God is *S*. . . . . John 4:24
I speak to you are *s*. . . . . . John 6:63
He was troubled in *s*. . . . . John 13:21
the *S* of truth . . . . John 14:17
when He, the *S* . . . . John 16:13
but if a *s* or an angel. . . . . Acts 23:9
whom I serve with my *s*. . . . Rom 1:9
according to the *S*. . . . . . . Rom 8:5
the flesh but in the *S*. . . . . Rom 8:9
does not have the *S*. . . . . . Rom 8:9
s that we are children . . . . . Rom 8:16
what the mind of the *S*. . . . Rom 8:27
to us through His *S* . . . . . 1 Cor 2:10
also have the *S* . . . . 1 Cor 7:40
gifts, but the same *S* . . . . 1 Cor 12:4
in a tongue, my *s*. . . . . . . 1 Cor 14:14
but the *S* gives life. . . . . . 2 Cor 3:6
Now the Lord is the *S*. . . . 2 Cor 3:17
we have the same *s* . . . . . 2 Cor 4:13
Having begun in the *S* . . . . Gal 3:3
has sent forth the *S* . . . . . . Gal 4:6
he who sows to the *S* . . . . . Gal 6:8
with the Holy *S*. . . . . Eph 1:13
may give to you the *s*. . . . . Eph 1:17
the unity of the *S* . . . . Eph 4:3
is one body and one *S* . . . . . Eph 4:4
stand fast in one *s* . . . . Phil 1:27
yet I am with you in *s* . . . . . . Col 2:5
and may your whole *s* . . 1 Thess 5:23
S expressly says that. . . . . . 1 Tim 4:1
division of soul and *s*. . . . . Heb 4:12
through the eternal *S* . . . . . Heb 9:14
S who dwells in us . . . . . . James 4:5
made alive by the *S* . . . . . 1 Pet 3:18
S whom He has given . . . 1 John 3:24
do not believe every *s* . . . . 1 John 4:1
By this you know the *S* . . . 1 John 4:2
By this we know the *s* . . . 1 John 4:6
has given us of His *S* . . . 1 John 4:13
S who bears witness. . . . . 1 John 5:6
not having the *S*. . . . . Jude 19
I was in the *S* on the. . . . . . Rev 1:10
him hear what the *S*. . . . . . Rev 2:7
And the *S* and the. . . . . . . Rev 22:17

SPIRITS
God, the God of the *s*. . . . Num 16:22
who makes His angels *s* . . . Ps 104:4
the LORD weighs the *s* . . . . Prov 16:2
power over unclean *s* . . . . Matt 10:1
heed to deceiving *s* . . . . . . 1 Tim 4:1
not all ministering *s*. . . . . . Heb 1:14
to the Father of *s* . . . . Heb 12:9
and preached to the *s*. . . . 1 Pet 3:19
spirit, but test the *s* . . . . . 1 John 4:1

SPIRITUAL
s judges all things . . . . . . 1 Cor 2:15
s people but as to . . . . 1 Cor 3:1
to be a prophet or *s*. . . . . 1 Cor 14:37

However, the s is not . . . . 1 Cor 15:46
s restore such a one . . . . Gal 6:1

SPIRITUALLY
s minded is life . . . . Rom 8:6
because they are s . . . . . . 1 Cor 2:14

SPITEFULLY
for those who s . . . . Matt 5:44

SPITTING
face from shame and s . . . . . Is 50:6

SPLENDOR
on the glorious s . . . . Ps 145:5
of Zion all her s. . . . . Lam 1:6

SPOIL
hate us have taken s . . . . . . Ps 44:10
when they divide the s . . . . . . Is 9:3
He shall divide the s. . . . . . . Is 53:12
Take s of silver. . . . . Nah 2:9
s will be divided . . . . Zech 14:1

SPOILER
I have created the s . . . . Is 54:16

SPOKE
s they did not hear. . . . . Is 66:4
who feared the LORD s . . . . . Mal 3:16
"No man ever s. . . . . John 7:46
We know that God s. . . . . John 9:29
I was a child, I s . . . . 1 Cor 13:11
in various ways s . . . . Heb 1:1
s as they were moved . . . . 2 Pet 1:21

SPOKEN
'just as you have s . . . . . Num 14:28
God has s once. . . . . Ps 62:11
I have not s in secret . . . . . . Is 45:19
'What have we s. . . . . Mal 3:13
why am I evil s . . . . 1 Cor 10:30

SPOKESMAN
So he shall be your s. . . . . . . Ex 4:16

SPONGE
them ran and took a s . . . Matt 27:48

SPOT
and there is no s. . . . . Song 4:7
church, not having s . . . . . . Eph 5:27
commandment without s . 1 Tim 6:14
Himself without s. . . . . Heb 9:14

SPOTS
They are s and . . . . 2 Pet 2:13
These are s in your. . . . . Jude 12

SPREAD
fell on my knees and s . . . . Ezra 9:5
they have s a net by . . . . . . Ps 140:5
Then He s it before me . . . Ezek 2:10
Then the word of God s. . . . . Acts 6:7
the Lord was being s . . . . Acts 13:49
their message will s . . . . . . 2 Tim 2:17

SPREADS
He alone s out the. . . . . Job 9:8
s them out like a tent. . . . . . Is 40:22
Zion s out her hands. . . . . . Lam 1:17

SPRING
Truth shall s out of . . . . Ps 85:11
is like a murky s . . . . Prov 25:26
sister, my spouse, a s . . . . . Song 4:12
s forth I tell you . . . . Is 42:9
of Israel to s forth . . . . . . Ezek 29:21
s shall become dry . . . . . . Hos 13:15
s send forth fresh. . . . . . . James 3:11

SPRINGING
a fountain of water s . . . . . John 4:14
of bitterness s . . . . Heb 12:15

SPRINGS
"Have you entered the s . . Job 38:16
He sends the s into . . . . . . Ps 104:10

and the thirsty land s . . . . Is 35:7
and the dry land s . . . . Is 41:18

SPRINKLE
He s many nations. . . . . Is 52:15
Then I will s. . . . . Ezek 36:25

SPRINKLED
s dust on his head . . . . Job 2:12
and hyssop, and s . . . . Heb 9:19
having our hearts s . . . . . . Heb 10:22

SPRINKLING
s that speaks. . . . . Heb 12:24
for obedience and s . . . . . . 1 Pet 1:2

SPROUT
down, that it will s . . . . Job 14:7
and the seed should s . . . Mark 4:27

SPY
s out the land of Canaan. . Num 13:2
sent to s out the land . . . Num 14:36

SQUARES
voice in the open s . . . . . . Prov 1:20
s I will seek the one . . . . . . Song 3:2

STABILITY
will be the s of your. . . . . Is 33:6

STAFF
this Jordan with my s. . . . . Gen 32:10
your feet, and your s. . . . . . Ex 12:11
Your rod and Your s . . . . . . Ps 23:4
LORD has broken the s . . . . . . Is 14:5
'How the strong s . . . . Jer 48:17
they have been a s . . . . . . Ezek 29:6
on the top of his s. . . . . . . Heb 11:21

STAGGER
and He makes them s . . . . Job 12:25
they will drink and s . . . . . . Jer 25:16

STAGGERS
as a drunken man s. . . . . . . Is 19:14

STAKES
s will ever be removed. . . . . Is 33:20

STALLS
be no herd in the s. . . . . . . Hab 3:17

STAMMERERS
s will be ready . . . . Is 32:4

STAMMERING
For with s lips and . . . . Is 28:11
s tongue that you. . . . . Is 33:19

STAMPING
At the noise of the s . . . . . . Jer 47:3

STAND
S still, and see the salvation . Ex 14:13
one shall be able to s . . . . . Deut 7:24
"Who is able to s . . . . 1 Sam 6:20
s still and see the
salvation. . . . . 2 Chr 20:17
but it does not s. . . . . Job 8:15
lives, and He shall s . . . . . Job 19:25
ungodly shall not s. . . . . Ps 1:5
Why do You s afar off. . . . . . Ps 10:1
Or who may s in His. . . . . . . Ps 24:3
Who will s up for me. . . . . . Ps 94:16
and let an accuser s . . . . . Ps 109:6
he will not s before . . . . . Prov 22:29
Do not take your s . . . . Eccl 8:3
"It shall not s. . . . . Is 7:7
"S in the ways and . . . . Jer 6:16
not lack a man to s . . . . . . Jer 35:19
whose words will s . . . . . . Jer 44:28
and it shall s . . . . Dan 2:44
but she shall not s . . . . Dan 11:17
Who can s before His . . . . . . Nah 1:6
And who can s when He . . . . Mal 3:2
that kingdom cannot s . . . Mark 3:24

he will be made to s . . . . . Rom 14:4
Watch, s fast in the . . . . . 1 Cor 16:13
for by faith you s . . . . 2 Cor 1:24
having done all, to s . . . . . Eph 6:13
S therefore. . . . . Eph 6:14
s fast in the Lord . . . . Phil 4:1
now we live, if you s . . . . 1 Thess 3:8
of God in which you s . . . 1 Pet 5:12
Behold, I s at the . . . . Rev 3:20

STANDARD
LORD will lift up a s. . . . . Is 59:19
Set up the s toward . . . . Jer 4:6

STANDING
the LORD, and Satan s. . . . . Zech 3:1
they love to pray s . . . . Matt 6:5
and the Son of Man s . . . . Acts 7:56
Then I saw an angel s . . . . Rev 19:17

STANDS
The LORD s up to plead . . . . . Is 3:13
him who thinks he s . . . . 1 Cor 10:12

STAR
S shall come out of. . . . . Num 24:17
For we have seen His s . . . . Matt 2:2
for one s differs from . . . . 1 Cor 15:41
give him the morning s . . . . Rev 2:28
And a great s fell . . . . Rev 8:10
Bright and Morning S. . . . . Rev 22:16

STARS
He made the s also . . . . Gen 1:16
s are not pure in His . . . . . . Job 25:5
when the morning s . . . . . . Job 38:7
the moon and the s . . . . Ps 8:3
praise Him, all you s . . . . . . Ps 148:3
born as many as the s . . . . Heb 11:12
wandering s for whom . . . . . Jude 13
a garland of twelve s . . . . . . Rev 12:1

STARVED
His strength is s . . . . Job 18:12

STATE
man at his best s . . . . Ps 39:5
us in our lowly s . . . . Ps 136:23
and the last s of that. . . . . Matt 12:45
learned in whatever s . . . . . Phil 4:11

STATURE
add one cubit to his s . . . . Matt 6:27
in wisdom and s . . . . Luke 2:52
the measure of the s . . . . . . Eph 4:13

STATUTE
shall be a perpetual s . . . . . Lev 3:17

STATUTES
the s of the LORD are . . . . Ps 19:8
Teach me Your s . . . . Ps 119:12
s have been my songs . . . . Ps 119:54
not walked in My s . . . . Ezek 5:6

STAY
her feet would not s . . . . . . Prov 7:11
S here and watch with . . . Matt 26:38
for today I must s . . . . Luke 19:5
the time of your s . . . . 1 Pet 1:17

STEADFAST
yes, you could be s. . . . . . . Job 11:15
O God, my heart is s . . . . . . Ps 57:7
their heart was not s . . . . . . Ps 78:37
his heart is s . . . . Ps 112:7
God, and s forever. . . . . . . Dan 6:26
brethren, be s. . . . . 1 Cor 15:58
faith, grounded and s. . . . . . Col 1:23
angels proved s . . . . Heb 2:2
of our confidence s . . . . . . Heb 3:14
soul, both sure and s . . . . . Heb 6:19
Resist him, s in the. . . . . . . 1 Pet 5:9

STEADFASTLY
s set His face to go . . . . Luke 9:51
And they continued *s* . . . . . Acts 2:42
continuing *s* in . . . . Rom 12:12

STEADFASTNESS
good order and the *s*. . . . . . Col 2:5
from your own *s* . . . . 2 Pet 3:17

STEADILY
could not look *s* . . . . 2 Cor 3:13

STEADY
and his hands were *s* . . . . . . Ex 17:12

STEAL
"You shall not *s*. . . . . Ex 20:15
Will you *s* . . . . Jer 7:9
s My words every one. . . . . Jer 23:30
thieves break in and *s*. . . . . Matt 6:19
night and *s* Him away . . . Matt 27:64
murder, 'Do not *s* . . . . . . Mark 10:19
not come except to *s* . . . . . John 10:10
a man should not *s* . . . . . . Rom 2:21
Let him who stole *s* . . . . . . Eph 4:28

STEEP
s places shall fall. . . . . . . Ezek 38:20
waters poured down a *s* . . . . . Mic 1:4
violently down the *s* . . . . . Matt 8:32

STEM
forth a Rod from the *s* . . . . . . Is 11:1

STENCH
there will be a *s* . . . . Is 3:24
this time there is a *s* . . . . John 11:39

STEP
there is but a *s* . . . . 1 Sam 20:3
s has turned from the . . . . . . Job 31:7

STEPHEN
One of the first seven deacons, Acts 6:1–8
Falsely accused by Jews; gives defense, Acts 6:9—7:53
Becomes first Christian martyr, Acts 7:54–60

STEPS
has held fast to His *s* . . . . . Job 23:11
and count all my *s* . . . . . . Job 31:4
and He sees all his *s* . . . . Job 34:21
Uphold my *s* in Your . . . . . . Ps 17:5
The *s* of a good man . . . . . Ps 37:23
of his *s* shall slide . . . . . . Ps 37:31
and established my *s* . . . . . . Ps 40:2
hide, they mark my *s* . . . . . Ps 56:6
s had nearly slipped . . . . . . Ps 73:2
Direct my *s* by Your . . . . Ps 119:133
s will not be hindered . . . . Prov 4:12
the LORD directs his *s*. . . . Prov 16:9
A man's *s* are of the . . . . Prov 20:24
to direct his own *s* . . . . . . Jer 10:23
should follow His *s* . . . . . . 1 Pet 2:21

STEWARD
faithful and wise *s* . . . . . Luke 12:42
you can no longer be *s*. . . . Luke 16:2
commended the unjust *s* . . Luke 16:8
be blameless, as a *s* . . . . . . Titus 1:7

STEWARDS
of Christ and *s*. . . . . 1 Cor 4:1
one another, as good *s* . . . . 1 Pet 4:10

STEWARDSHIP
entrusted with a *s* . . . . . . 1 Cor 9:17

STICK
and his bones *s* . . . . Job 33:21
'For Joseph, the *s* . . . . . . Ezek 37:16

STICKS
a man gathering *s* . . . . . Num 15:32
And the *s* on which. . . . . Ezek 37:20

STIFF
rebellion and your *s* . . . . . Deut 31:27
do not speak with a *s* . . . . . . Ps 75:5

STIFF-NECKED
Now do not be *s* . . . . 2 Chr 30:8
"You *s* and uncircumcised. . Acts 7:51

STILL
Stand *s*, and see the salvation . . . . Ex 14:13
a *s* small voice . . . . 1 Kin 19:12
stand *s* and see the salvation. . . . . 2 Chr 20:17
on your bed, and be *s* . . . . Ps 4:4
s the noise of the. . . . . Ps 65:7
earth feared and was *s* . . . . . . Ps 76:8
that its waves are *s* . . . . . . Ps 107:29
When I awake, I am *s* . . . . . Ps 139:18
time, I have been *s* . . . . Is 42:14
rest and be *s* . . . . Jer 47:6
sea, "Peace, be *s* . . . . Mark 4:39
let him be holy *s* . . . . Rev 22:11

STILLBORN
hidden like a *s* child . . . . Job 3:16
as it goes, like a *s* . . . . Ps 58:8
burial, I say that a *s*. . . . . . . Eccl 6:3

STINGS
like a serpent, and *s* . . . . . Prov 23:32

STIR
that he would dare *s* . . . . . Job 41:10
S up Yourself . . . . Ps 35:23
I remind you to *s* . . . . 2 Tim 1:6
another in order to *s* . . . . . Heb 10:24

STIRRED
fulfilled, the LORD *s* . . . . . 2 Chr 36:22
and my sorrow was *s* . . . . . . Ps 39:2
So the LORD *s* up the . . . . . Hag 1:14

STIRS
and the innocent *s* . . . . Job 17:8
it *s* up the dead for. . . . . Is 14:9
on Your name, who *s*. . . . . . . Is 64:7

STOCKS
put my feet in the *s* . . . . . Job 13:27
s that were in the. . . . . Jer 20:2

STOIC
and *S* philosophers. . . . . . Acts 17:18

STOMACH
mouth goes into the *s* . . . . Matt 15:17
his heart but his *s* . . . . . . Mark 7:19
Foods for the *s* . . . . 1 Cor 6:13

STOMACH'S
little wine for your *s* . . . . . 1 Tim 5:23

STONE
him, a pillar of *s* . . . . Gen 35:14
to the bottom like a *s* . . . . . . Ex 15:5
s shall be a witness . . . . Josh 24:27
heart is as hard as *s* . . . . . Job 41:24
s which the builders. . . . . . Ps 118:22
s is heavy and sand is. . . . . Prov 27:3
I lay in Zion a *s* . . . . Is 28:16
foundation, a tried *s* . . . . . . Is 28:16
take the heart of *s*. . . . . . Ezek 36:26
You watched while a *s*. . . . . Dan 2:34
s will cry out from . . . . Hab 2:11
to silent *s* . . . . Hab 2:19
will give him a *s*. . . . . Matt 7:9
s will be broken. . . . . Matt 21:44
secure, sealing the *s* . . . . Matt 27:66
s which the builders . . . . . Luke 20:17
you, let him throw a *s* . . . . . John 8:7
those works do you *s*. . . . . John 10:32
Jews sought to *s* You . . . . . John 11:8
not on tablets of *s*. . . . . . . 2 Cor 3:3

Him as to a living *s* . . . . . . 1 Pet 2:4
give him a white *s* . . . . Rev 2:17
angel took up a *s* . . . . Rev 18:21
like a jasper *s* . . . . Rev 21:11

STONED
s Stephen as he was. . . . . . Acts 7:59
once I was *s* . . . . 2 Cor 11:25
They were *s*. . . . . Heb 11:37

STONES
I will lay your *s* . . . . Is 54:11
Among the smooth *s* . . . . Is 57:6
Abraham from these *s* . . . . Matt 3:9
command that these *s* . . . . Matt 4:3
see what manner of *s* . . . . Mark 13:1
also, as living *s*. . . . . 1 Pet 2:5
kinds of precious *s*. . . . . . Rev 21:19

STONY
them, and take the *s* . . . . Ezek 11:19
Some fell on *s* ground . . . . Mark 4:5

STOOPED
And again He *s* down. . . . . . John 8:8

STOPPED
speak lies shall be *s*. . . . . . Ps 63:11
her flow of blood *s* . . . . . . Luke 8:44

STORE
no room to *s* my crops . . . Luke 12:17
exist are kept in *s*. . . . . . . 2 Pet 3:7

STORK
s has her home in the . . . . . Ps 104:17
"Even the *s* in the. . . . . Jer 8:7

STORM
from the windy *s*. . . . . Ps 55:8
He calms the *s* . . . . Ps 107:29
terror comes like a *s* . . . . . Prov 1:27
for a shelter from *s* . . . . Is 4:6
a refuge from the *s* . . . . Is 25:4
and a destroying *s* . . . . Is 28:2
coming like a *s* . . . . Ezek 38:9
whirlwind and in the *s* . . . . Nah 1:3

STOUTHEARTED
s were plundered . . . . Ps 76:5

STRAIGHT
make Your way *s*. . . . . Ps 5:8
for who can make *s* . . . . . . Eccl 7:13
make *s* in the desert a . . . . . . Is 40:3
Their legs were *s* . . . . Ezek 1:7
LORD; make His paths *s* . . . Luke 3:4
to the street called *S*. . . . . Acts 9:11
and make *s* paths for. . . . . Heb 12:13

STRAIGHTFORWARD
that they were not *s* . . . . . . Gal 2:14

STRAIN
Blind guides, who *s*. . . . . . Matt 23:24

STRAITS
and desperate *s*. . . . . Deut 28:53

STRANGE
were considered a *s*. . . . . . Hos 8:12
"We have seen *s* . . . . Luke 5:26
are bringing some *s*. . . . . Acts 17:20
these, they think it *s*. . . . . 1 Pet 4:4
s thing happened . . . . 1 Pet 4:12

STRANGER
but he acted as a *s* . . . . . . Gen 42:7
"I have been a *s* . . . . Ex 2:22
neither mistreat a *s* . . . . . . Ex 22:21
and loves the *s* . . . . Deut 10:18
I have become a *s* . . . . Ps 69:8
s will suffer for it . . . . . . Prov 11:15
s does not share its . . . . . Prov 14:10
should You be like a *s* . . . . . Jer 14:8

I was a *s* and you took . . . Matt 25:35
"Are You the only *s* . . . . . Luke 24:18

STRANGERS
descendants will be *s* . . . . Gen 15:13
s plunder his labor. . . . . . . Ps 109:11
watches over the *s*. . . . . . . Ps 146:9
s devour your land . . . . Is 1:7
S shall stand and feed . . . . . . Is 61:5
know the voice of *s* . . . . . . John 10:5
of Israel and *s*. . . . . Eph 2:12
you are no longer *s* . . . . . . Eph 2:19
if she has lodged *s*. . . . . . 1 Tim 5:10
that they were *s* . . . . Heb 11:13
forget to entertain *s* . . . . . . Heb 13:2
the brethren and for *s* . . . . 3 John 5

STRANGLING
that my soul chooses *s* . . . . Job 7:15

STRAP
than I, whose sandal *s* . . . . Mark 1:7

STRAW
They are like *s* . . . . Job 21:18
stones, wood, hay, *s*. . . . . . 1 Cor 3:12

STRAY
the cursed, who *s* . . . . Ps 119:21
who make my people *s* . . . . Mic 3:5

STRAYED
yet I have not *s*. . . . . Ps 119:110
for which some have *s* . . . . 1 Tim 6:10
who have *s* concerning. . . 2 Tim 2:18

STREAM
like an overflowing *s* . . . . . . Is 30:28
of the LORD, like a *s* . . . . Is 30:33
like a flowing *s* . . . . Is 66:12

STREAMS
He dams up the *s*. . . . . Job 28:11
He also brought *s*. . . . . Ps 78:16
O LORD, as the *s*. . . . . Ps 126:4

STREET
to be heard in the *s* . . . . Is 42:2
s called Straight . . . . Acts 9:11
And the *s* of the city . . . . . Rev 21:21
In the middle of its *s*. . . . . . Rev 22:2

STREETS
the corners of the *s*. . . . . . . Matt 6:5
You taught in our *s* . . . . . . Luke 13:26
out quickly into the *s* . . . . Luke 14:21

STRENGTH
for by *s* of hand the . . . . Ex 13:3
just as my *s* was then. . . . . Josh 14:11
my soul, march on in *s*. . . . Judg 5:21
a man is, so is his *s*. . . . . . . Judg 8:21
s no man shall . . . . 1 Sam 2:9
the God of my *s* . . . . 2 Sam 22:3
have armed me with *s* . . 2 Sam 22:40
the LORD glory and *s* . . . . 1 Chr 16:28
Is my *s* the . . . . Job 6:12
Him are wisdom and *s* . . . Job 12:13
him because his *s* . . . . Job 39:11
You have ordained *s* . . . . Ps 8:2
love You, O LORD, my *s* . . . . . Ps 18:1
The LORD is the *s* . . . . Ps 27:1
The LORD is their *s*. . . . . Ps 28:8
The LORD will give *s*. . . . . . . Ps 29:11
delivered by great *s* . . . . . . Ps 33:16
He is their *s* in the. . . . . Ps 37:39
are the God of my *s* . . . . Ps 43:2
is our refuge and *s* . . . . Ps 46:1
is He who gives *s* . . . . Ps 68:35
I will go in the *s* . . . . Ps 71:16
but God is the *s*. . . . . Ps 73:26
They go from *s* to . . . . Ps 84:7
the glory of their *s* . . . . Ps 89:17
s and beauty are in. . . . . Ps 96:6

made me bold with *s*. . . . . . . Ps 138:3
of the LORD is *s*. . . . . Prov 10:29
knowledge increases *s*. . . . Prov 24:5
S and honor are her . . . . . Prov 31:25
is better than *s* . . . . Eccl 9:16
for *s* and not for . . . . Eccl 10:17
For You have been a *s* . . . . . . Is 25:4
him because of My *s* . . . . Is 27:5
of His might and the *s*. . . . . . Is 40:26
might He increases *s* . . . . . . Is 40:29
works it with the *s* . . . . Is 44:12
righteousness and *s* . . . . Is 45:24
Put on your *s* . . . . Is 52:1
O LORD, my *s* and my . . . . . Jer 16:19
I will destroy the *s* . . . . Hag 2:22
He has shown *s* with . . . . . Luke 1:51
were still without *s* . . . . Rom 5:6
s is made perfect . . . . 2 Cor 12:9
you have a little *s*. . . . . Rev 3:8

STRENGTHEN
and He shall *s* . . . . Ps 27:14
S the weak hands. . . . . Is 35:3
"So I will *s* them in . . . . . Zech 10:12
s your brethren . . . . Luke 22:32
s the hands . . . . Heb 12:12
s the things. . . . . Rev 3:2

STRENGTHENED
weak you have not *s*. . . . . Ezek 34:4
unbelief, but was *s* . . . . . . Rom 4:20
of His glory, to be *s*. . . . . . . Eph 3:16
stood with me and *s* . . . . 2 Tim 4:17

STRENGTHENING
s the souls of the . . . . Acts 14:22

STRENGTHENS
s the wise more than . . . . . . Eccl 7:19
through Christ who *s* . . . . . Phil 4:13

STRETCH
will quickly *s* out her. . . . . . Ps 68:31
said to the man, "S . . . . . Matt 12:13
are old, you will *s* . . . . . . John 21:18

STRETCHED
I have *s* out my hands . . . . . Ps 88:9
His wisdom, and has *s* . . . . Jer 10:12
"All day long I have *s* . . . . Rom 10:21

STRETCHES
For he *s* out his hand . . . . . Job 15:25

STRICKEN
My heart is *s* and . . . . Ps 102:4
yet we esteemed Him *s* . . . . . Is 53:4
of My people He was *s*. . . . . . Is 53:8
You have *s* them . . . . Jer 5:3
He has *s*, but He will . . . . . . Hos 6:1

STRIFE
let there be no *s* . . . . Gen 13:8
You have made us a *s* . . . . . . Ps 80:6
at the waters of *s*. . . . . Ps 106:32
Hatred stirs up *s* . . . . Prov 10:12
comes nothing but *s* . . . . . Prov 13:10
man stirs up *s* . . . . Prov 15:18
transgression loves *s* . . . . Prov 17:19
borne me, a man of *s*. . . . . . Jer 15:10
and lust, not in *s*. . . . . Rom 13:13
even from envy and *s* . . . . . Phil 1:15
which come envy, *s*. . . . . . . 1 Tim 6:4

STRIKE
said, "S this people. . . . . . 2 Kin 6:18
The sun shall not *s* . . . . . . Ps 121:6
Let the righteous *s* . . . . . . Ps 141:5
S a scoffer. . . . . Prov 19:25
s your hands . . . . Ezek 21:14
s the waves of the sea . . . . Zech 10:11
"S the Shepherd. . . . . Zech 13:7
s the earth with a. . . . . Mal 4:6

'I will *s* the Shepherd . . . . Matt 26:31
if well, why do you *s* . . . . John 18:23
the sun shall not *s* . . . . Rev 7:16
s the earth with all . . . . Rev 11:6

STRINGED
of your *s* instruments . . . . . . Is 14:11
of your *s* instruments . . . . Amos 5:23

STRIP
S yourselves . . . . Is 32:11
s her naked and expose. . . . . Hos 2:3

STRIPES
their iniquity with *s*. . . . . . Ps 89:32
s we are healed . . . . Is 53:5
be beaten with many *s* . . . Luke 12:47
I received forty *s*. . . . . 2 Cor 11:24
s you were healed. . . . . 1 Pet 2:24

STRIVE
"My Spirit shall not *s* . . . . . . Gen 6:3
He will not always *s* . . . . . . Ps 103:9
Do not *s* with a man. . . . . . Prov 3:30
Let the potsherd *s* . . . . Is 45:9
"S to enter through . . . . . Luke 13:24
the Lord not to *s* . . . . 2 Tim 2:14

STRIVING
for a man to stop *s* . . . . . . Prov 20:3

STROKE
with a mighty *s*. . . . . Jer 14:17

STRONG
Be *s* and conduct . . . . 1 Sam 4:9
indeed He is *s* . . . . Job 9:19
The LORD *s* and mighty. . . . . . Ps 24:8
bring me to the *s*. . . . . Ps 60:9
s is Your hand . . . . Ps 89:13
A wise man is *s* . . . . Prov 24:5
s shall be as tinder. . . . . Is 1:31
"We have a *s* city. . . . . Is 26:1
the weak say, 'I am *s* . . . . . Joel 3:10
When a *s* man. . . . . Luke 11:21
We then who are *s* . . . . . . Rom 15:1
I am weak, then I am *s* . . 2 Cor 12:10
are weak and you are *s*. . . 2 Cor 13:9
my brethren, be *s* . . . . Eph 6:10
weakness were made *s*. . . Heb 11:34
s is the Lord God. . . . . Rev 18:8

STRONGHOLD
of my salvation, my *s* . . . . . Ps 18:2
down the trusted *s*. . . . . . Prov 21:22

STRONGHOLDS
pulling down *s*. . . . . 2 Cor 10:4

STRUCK
s the rock twice. . . . . Num 20:11
the hand of God has *s*. . . . . Job 19:21
s all my enemies . . . . Ps 3:7
Behold, He *s* the rock . . . . . Ps 78:20
I was angry and *s*. . . . . Is 57:17
in My wrath I *s*. . . . . Is 60:10
s the head from the . . . . Hab 3:13
I *s* you with blight . . . . Hag 2:17
took the reed and *s*. . . . . . Matt 27:30
Him, they *s* Him on the . . Luke 22:64

STUBBLE
shall bring forth *s*. . . . . Is 33:11
his sword, as driven *s*. . . . . . Is 41:2
they shall be as *s* . . . . Is 47:14
s that passes . . . . Jer 13:24
do wickedly will be *s* . . . . . Mal 4:1

STUBBORN
If a man has a *s* . . . . Deut 21:18
and *s* children . . . . Ezek 2:4

STUBBORN-HEARTED
"Listen to Me, you *s* . . . . . . Is 46:12

STUBBORNNESS
do not look on the s . . . . . Deut 9:27

STUDIED
having never s . . . . John 7:15

STUMBLE
causes them to s . . . . Ps 119:165
to make my steps s . . . . . . Ps 140:4
your foot will not s . . . . . . Prov 3:23
know what makes them s . . Prov 4:19
one will be weary or s . . . . . . Is 5:27
among them shall s . . . . . . Is 8:15
we s at noonday as at . . . . . . Is 59:10
that they might not s . . . . . . Is 63:13
before your feet s . . . . Jer 13:16
they will s and fall . . . . Jer 46:6
have caused many to s . . . . Mal 2:8
you will be made to s . . . . Matt 26:31
if all are made to s . . . . . Matt 26:33
immediately they s . . . . . . Mark 4:17
who believe in Me to s . . . . Mark 9:42
the day, he does not s . . . . . John 11:9
Who is made to s . . . . 2 Cor 11:29
whole law, and yet s . . . . . James 2:10
For we all s in many . . . . . James 3:2

STUMBLED
and those who s . . . . 1 Sam 2:4
God, for you have s . . . . . . Hos 14:1
s that they should . . . . . . Rom 11:11

STUMBLES
word, immediately he s . . Matt 13:21

STUMBLING
the deaf, nor put a s . . . . Lev 19:14
but a stone of s . . . . Is 8:14
Behold, I will lay s . . . . Jer 6:21
watched for my s . . . . Jer 20:10
it became their s . . . . Ezek 7:19
stumbled at that s . . . . Rom 9:32
I lay in Zion a s . . . . Rom 9:33
this, not to put a s . . . . . . Rom 14:13
to the Jews a s . . . . 1 Cor 1:23
of yours become a s . . . . . . 1 Cor 8:9
and "A stone of s . . . . 1 Pet 2:8
is no cause for s . . . . 1 John 2:10
to keep you from s . . . . Jude 24

STUPID
and regarded as s . . . . Job 18:3
who hates correction is s . . Prov 12:1
Surely I am more s . . . . . . Prov 30:2

SUBDUE
s the peoples under us . . . . . . Ps 47:3
shall s three kings . . . . . . Dan 7:24
s our iniquities . . . . Mic 7:19
s all things to . . . . Phil 3:21

SUBJECT
for it is not s . . . . Rom 8:7
Let every soul be s . . . . . . Rom 13:1
all things are made s . . . . 1 Cor 15:28
Himself will also be s . . . . 1 Cor 15:28
Remind them to be s . . . . . Titus 3:1
all their lifetime s . . . . Heb 2:15
having been made s . . . . . 1 Pet 3:22

SUBJECTED
because of Him who s . . . . Rom 8:20

SUBJECTION
put all things in s . . . . Heb 2:8
more readily be in s . . . . . Heb 12:9

SUBMISSION
in silence with all s . . . . . 1 Tim 2:11
his children in s . . . . 1 Tim 3:4

SUBMISSIVE
Wives, likewise, be s . . . . . 1 Pet 3:1
Yes, all of you be s . . . . . . 1 Pet 5:5

SUBMIT
Your enemies shall s . . . . Ps 66:3
Wives, s to your own . . . . . Eph 5:22
Therefore s to God . . . . . . James 4:7
s yourselves to every . . . . 1 Pet 2:13
you younger people, s . . . . 1 Pet 5:5

SUBMITTING
s to one another . . . . Eph 5:21

SUBSIDED
and the waters s . . . . Gen 8:1
the king's wrath s . . . . Esth 7:10

SUBSTANCE
Bless his s . . . . Deut 33:11
the LORD, and their s . . . . . . Mic 4:13

SUCCEED
For this will not s . . . . . . Num 14:41
you shall not s . . . . Jer 32:5

SUCCESS
please give me s . . . . Gen 24:12
You shall my s . . . . Job 30:22
but wisdom brings s . . . . . Eccl 10:10

SUCCESSFUL
Joseph, and he was a s . . . . Gen 39:2

SUCCOTH
Place east of the Jordan, Judg 8:4, 5
Jacob's residence here, Gen 33:17
—— Israel's first camp, Ex 12:37

SUDDENLY
whom you seek, will s . . . . . Mal 3:1
s there was with the . . . . . Luke 2:13

SUE
s you and take away . . . . Matt 5:40

SUFFER
for a stranger will s . . . . . Prov 11:15
for the Christ to s . . . . . . Luke 24:46
Christ, if indeed we s . . . . . Rom 8:17
all the members s . . . . . 1 Cor 12:26
that they may not s . . . . . . Gal 6:12
in Him, but also to s . . . . . Phil 1:29
s trouble as an . . . . 2 Tim 2:9
when you do good and s . . 1 Pet 2:20
the will of God, to s . . . . . 1 Pet 3:17
s as a murderer . . . . 1 Pet 4:15
you are about to s . . . . Rev 2:10

SUFFERED
s these things and to . . . . Luke 24:26
Have you s so many . . . . . . Gal 3:4
for whom I have s . . . . Phil 3:8
with His own blood, s . . . . Heb 13:12
because Christ also s . . . . . 1 Pet 2:21
For Christ also s . . . . 1 Pet 3:18
since Christ s . . . . 1 Pet 4:1
after you have s . . . . 1 Pet 5:10

SUFFERING
My eyes bring s . . . . Lam 3:51
Is anyone among you s . . James 5:13
forth as an example, s . . . . . . Jude 7

SUFFERINGS
I consider that the s . . . . . Rom 8:18
share with me in the s . . . 2 Tim 1:8
perfect through s . . . . Heb 2:10
great struggle with s . . . . Heb 10:32
beforehand the s . . . . 1 Pet 1:11

SUFFERS
Love s long and is . . . . . . 1 Cor 13:4

SUFFICIENCY
but our s is from God . . . . 2 Cor 3:5
always having all s . . . . . . 2 Cor 9:8

SUFFICIENT
S for the day is its . . . . . . Matt 6:34
by the majority is s . . . . . 2 Cor 2:6
Not that we are s . . . . 2 Cor 3:5

SUITABLE
by the hand of a s . . . . . . Lev 16:21

SUM
How great is the s . . . . . . Ps 139:17
s I obtained this . . . . Acts 22:28

SUMMED
commandment, are all s . . Rom 13:9

SUMMER
and heat, winter and s . . . . Gen 8:22
into the drought of s . . . . . . Ps 32:4
You have made s . . . . Ps 74:17
you know that s . . . . Matt 24:32

SUMPTUOUSLY
fine linen and fared s . . . . Luke 16:19

SUN
So the s stood still . . . . . . Josh 10:13
grows green in the s . . . . . Job 8:16
a tabernacle for the s . . . . . Ps 19:4
the LORD God is a s . . . . . . Ps 84:11
s shall not strike you . . . . . Ps 121:6
the s to rule by day . . . . . Ps 136:8
to behold the s . . . . Eccl 11:7
while the s and the . . . . . . Eccl 12:2
moon, clear as the s . . . . . Song 6:10
s will be sevenfold . . . . Is 30:26
s returned ten degrees . . . . Is 38:8
s shall no longer be . . . . Is 60:19
LORD, who gives the s . . . . Jer 31:35
the s and moon grow . . . . . Joel 2:10
s shall be turned . . . . Joel 2:31
s shall go down on the . . . . Mic 3:6
The s and moon stood . . . . Hab 3:11
S of Righteousness shall arise Mal 4:2
for He makes His s . . . . . . Matt 5:45
the s was darkened . . . . . Luke 23:45
is one glory of the s . . . . 1 Cor 15:41
do not let the s . . . . Eph 4:26
s became black as . . . . Rev 6:12
s shall not strike . . . . Rev 7:16
had no need of the s . . . . . Rev 21:23

SUPPER
man gave a great s . . . . . Luke 14:16
to eat the Lord's S . . . . . . 1 Cor 11:20
took the cup after s . . . . . 1 Cor 11:25
together for the s . . . . Rev 19:17

SUPPLICATION
s that you have made . . . . . 1 Kin 9:3
and make your s . . . . Job 8:5
LORD has heard my s . . . . . . Ps 6:9
to the LORD I made s . . . . . . Ps 30:8
Yourself from my s . . . . Ps 55:1
Let my s come before . . . . Ps 119:170
They will make s . . . . Is 45:14
with all prayer and s . . . . . Eph 6:18
by prayer and s . . . . Phil 4:6

SUPPLIES
Now may He who s . . . . . 2 Cor 9:10
Therefore He who s . . . . Gal 3:5
by what every joint s . . . . . Eph 4:16

SUPPLY
s what was lacking . . . . . . Phil 2:30
And my God shall s . . . . . . Phil 4:19

SUPPORT
but the LORD was my s . . 2 Sam 22:19
this, that you must s . . . . Acts 20:35

SUPREME
to the king as s . . . . 1 Pet 2:13

SURE
s your sin will find . . . . . Num 32:23
but no man is s . . . . Job 24:22
call and election s . . . . . . 2 Pet 1:10

SURETY
Be *s* for Your servant . . . . . Ps 119:122
one who hates being *s*. . . . Prov 11:15
Jesus has become a *s* . . . . . . Heb 7:22

SURROUND
But you shall *s* . . . . 2 Kin 11:8
LORD, mercy shall *s* . . . . Ps 32:10

SURROUNDED
the waves of death *s* . . . . 2 Sam 22:5
The pangs of death *s*. . . . . . . Ps 18:4
The pains of death *s* . . . . . . Ps 116:3
All nations *s* me. . . . . Ps 118:10
their own deeds have *s* . . . . . Hos 7:2
and the floods *s*. . . . . Jon 2:3
also, since we are *s*. . . . . . . Heb 12:1

SURVIVOR
was no refugee or *s* . . . . . . Lam 2:22

SUSANNA
Believing woman ministering to
Christ, Luke 8:2, 3

SUSPICIONS
reviling, evil *s* . . . . 1 Tim 6:4

SUSTAIN
You will *s* him on his . . . . Ps 41:3
of a man will *s*. . . . . Prov 18:14
S me with cakes of . . . . Song 2:5

SWADDLING
thick darkness its *s* . . . . Job 38:9
Him in *s* cloths . . . . Luke 2:7

SWALLOW
like a flying *s*. . . . . Prov 26:2
Like a crane or a *s* . . . . Is 38:14
s observe the time . . . . Jer 8:7
great fish to *s* Jonah . . . . . . Jon 1:17
a gnat and *s* a camel . . . . Matt 23:24

SWEAR
shall I make you *s* . . . . . . 1 Kin 22:16
in the earth shall *s*. . . . . Is 65:16
s oaths by the LORD . . . . . . Zeph 1:5
'You shall not *s*. . . . . Matt 5:33
began to curse and *s*. . . . Matt 26:74
because He could *s*. . . . . . . Heb 6:13
my brethren, do not *s*. . . . James 5:12

SWEARING
By *s* and lying . . . . Hos 4:2

SWEARS
he who *s* to his own . . . . Ps 15:4
everyone who *s* by Him. . . . . Ps 63:11
but whoever *s* by the. . . . Matt 23:18

SWEAT
In the *s* of your face. . . . . . Gen 3:19
Then His *s* became like. . . Luke 22:44

SWEET
Though evil is *s*. . . . . Job 20:12
s are Your words. . . . . . . Ps 119:103
His mouth is most *s* . . . . . Song 5:16
but it will be as *s*. . . . . Rev 10:9

SWEETNESS
'Should I cease my *s* . . . . . Judg 9:11
called prudent, and *s*. . . . Prov 16:21
mouth like honey in *s*. . . . . Ezek 3:3

SWELLING
they speak great *s*. . . . . . . 2 Pet 2:18

SWIFT
s as the eagle flies. . . . . . Deut 28:49
pass by like *s* ships . . . . . . Job 9:26
handles the bow, the *s* . . . Amos 2:15
let every man be *s* . . . . . James 1:19

SWIFTLY
His word runs very *s* . . . . . Ps 147:15

SWIM
night I make my bed *s* . . . . . . Ps 6:6

SWOON
as they *s* like the . . . . Lam 2:12

SWORD
s which turned every . . . . . Gen 3:24
but not with your *s* . . . . . . Josh 24:12
the wicked with Your *s*. . . . . Ps 17:13
land by their own *s*. . . . . Ps 44:3
my bow, nor shall my *s* . . . . Ps 44:6
their tongue a sharp *s*. . . . . . Ps 57:4
shall not lift up *s* . . . . Is 2:4
s shall be bathed . . . . Is 34:5
The *s* of the LORD is . . . . Is 34:6
And I will send a *s* . . . . . . Jer 9:16
will die by the *s* . . . . Ezek 7:15
'A *s*, a *s* is sharpened. . . . . Ezek 21:9
'A *s*, a *s* is drawn . . . . . . Ezek 21:28
Bow and *s* of battle I . . . . . Hos 2:18
"Awake, O *s* . . . . Zech 13:7
to bring peace but a *s*. . . . Matt 10:34
for all who take the *s* . . . Matt 26:52
s will pierce through. . . . . . Luke 2:35
he does not bear the *s*. . . . . Rom 13:4
the *s* of the Spirit . . . . Eph 6:17
than any two-edged *s* . . . . . Heb 4:12
a sharp two-edged *s* . . . . . . Rev 1:16
mouth goes a sharp *s* . . . . Rev 19:15

SWORDS
yet they were drawn *s* . . . . . Ps 55:21
shall beat their *s* . . . . Is 2:4
look, here are two *s*. . . . . Luke 22:38

SWORE
So I *s* in My wrath. . . . . Ps 95:11
So I *s* in My wrath . . . . Heb 3:11
and *s* by Him who lives . . . . Rev 10:6

SWORN
"By Myself I have *s* . . . . . . Gen 22:16
The LORD has *s* in. . . . . Ps 132:11
I have *s* by Myself . . . . Is 45:23
"The LORD has *s* . . . . Heb 7:21

SYMBOLIC
which things are *s* . . . . Gal 4:24
It was *s* for the . . . . Heb 9:9

SYMBOLS
I have given *s* through . . . . Hos 12:10

SYMPATHIZE
Priest who cannot *s* . . . . . . Heb 4:15

SYMPATHY
My *s* is stirred . . . . Hos 11:8

SYNAGOGUE
He went into the *s*. . . . . . . Luke 4:16
but are a *s* of Satan . . . . Rev 2:9

SYRIANS
Abraham's kindred, Gen 22:20–23;
25:20
Hostile to Israel, 2 Sam 8:11–13; 10:6–
19; 1 Kin 20:1–34; 22:1–38; 2 Kin
6:8—7:7
Defeated by Assyria, 2 Kin 16:9
Destruction of, foretold, Is 17:1–3
Gospel preached to, Acts 15:23, 41

SYRO-PHOENICIAN
Daughter of, freed of demon, Mark
7:25–31

TABERAH
Israelite camp; fire destroys many
there, Num 11:1–3

TABERNACLE
you shall make the *t* . . . . . . Ex 26:1
t He shall hide me. . . . . Ps 27:5

I will abide in Your *t* . . . . Ps 61:4
In Salem also is His *t*. . . . . . . Ps 76:2
How lovely is Your *t* . . . . Ps 84:1
quiet home, a *t* . . . . Is 33:20
You also took up the *t* . . . . . Acts 7:43
and will rebuild the *t*. . . . Acts 15:16
and more perfect *t* . . . . Heb 9:11
Behold, the *t* . . . . Rev 21:3

TABERNACLES
us make here three *t*. . . . . Matt 17:4
Feast of *T* was at hand . . . . . John 7:2

TABITHA
See DORCAS

TABLE
shall also make a *t*. . . . . . . Ex 25:23
prepare a *t* before me . . . . . . Ps 23:5
t become a snare. . . . . Ps 69:22
dogs under the *t*. . . . . Mark 7:28
t become a snare. . . . . Rom 11:9
of the Lord's *t* . . . . 1 Cor 10:21

TABLES
t are full of vomit. . . . . Is 28:8
and overturned the *t*. . . . . Matt 21:12
of God and serve *t* . . . . Acts 6:2

TABLET
write them on the *t* . . . . . . Prov 3:3
is engraved on the *t* . . . . . . Jer 17:1

TABOR
Scene of rally against Sisera, Judg
4:6, 12, 14

TAHPANHES (or Tehaphnehes)
City of Egypt; refuge of fleeing Jews,
Jer 2:16; 44:1; Ezek 30:18

TAIL
the head and not the *t* . . . Deut 28:13
t drew a third of the . . . . . . Rev 12:4

TAKE
T your sandal off your. . . . . Josh 5:15
t Your Holy Spirit. . . . . Ps 51:11
t not the word of . . . . Ps 119:43
in You I *t* shelter . . . . Ps 143:9
t words with you. . . . . Hos 14:2
T My yoke upon . . . . Matt 11:29
T what is yours and . . . . . Matt 20:14
and *t* up his cross. . . . . . . Mark 8:34
T this cup away . . . . Mark 14:36
My life that I may *t*. . . . . . John 10:17
I urge you to *t* heart . . . . . Acts 27:22

TAKEN
you are *t* by the words . . . . . Prov 6:2
He was *t* from prison . . . . Is 53:8
one will be *t* and the. . . . . Matt 24:40
what he has will be *t*. . . . . Mark 4:25
He was *t* up . . . . Acts 1:9
until He is *t* out of . . . . . 2 Thess 2:7
By faith Enoch was *t* away . Heb 11:5

TALEBEARER
not go about as a *t* . . . . . . Lev 19:16
t reveals secrets . . . . Prov 11:13

TALENT
went and hid your *t* . . . . . Matt 25:25

TALK
shall *t* of them when . . . . . . Deut 6:7
t be vindicated. . . . . Job 11:2
with unprofitable *t* . . . . Job 15:3
My tongue also shall *t* . . . . . Ps 71:24
entangle Him in His *t*. . . . Matt 22:15
I will no longer *t* . . . . John 14:30
turned aside to idle *t*. . . . . 1 Tim 1:6

TALKED
within us while He *t* . . . . . Luke 24:32

TALKERS
both idle t and . . . . Titus 1:10

TALL
to a nation t and . . . . Is 18:2

TAMAR
Wife of Er and mother of Perez and
Zerah, Gen 38:6–30
—— Absalom's sister, 2 Sam 13:1–32

TAMBOURINE
They sing to the t. . . . . Job 21:12
The mirth of the t . . . . Is 24:8

TARES
the t also appeared. . . . . Matt 13:26

TARGET
You set me as Your t . . . . . . Job 7:20
and set me up as a t . . . . . Lam 3:12

TARRY
who turns aside to t . . . . Jer 14:8
come and will not t . . . . . . Heb 10:37

TARSHISH
City at a great distance from Pales-
tine, Jon 1:3
Ships of, noted in commerce, Ps 48:7

TARSUS
Paul's birthplace, Acts 21:39
Saul sent to, Acts 9:30
Visited by Barnabas, Acts 11:25

TARTAN
Sent to fight against Jerusalem, 2 Kin
18:17

TASK
this burdensome t. . . . . Eccl 1:13

TASTE
and its t was like the . . . . . Num 11:8
Oh, t and see that the. . . . . . Ps 34:8
are Your words to my t. . . . Ps 119:103
was sweet to my t . . . . Song 2:3
Do not touch, do not t . . . . . Col 2:21
might t death for . . . . Heb 2:9

TASTED
But when He had t . . . . . . Matt 27:34
t the heavenly gift . . . . Heb 6:4
t the good word . . . . Heb 6:5
t that the Lord is. . . . . 1 Pet 2:3

TAUGHT
O God, You have t. . . . . Ps 71:17
as His counselor has t . . . . . . Is 40:13
presence, and You t. . . . . Luke 13:26
they shall all be t . . . . John 6:45
but as My Father t . . . . . . John 8:28
from man, nor was I t . . . . . Gal 1:12

TAUNT
and a byword, a t. . . . . Jer 24:9

TAX
t collectors do the . . . . Matt 5:46
received the temple t. . . . . Matt 17:24
I say to you that t . . . . . . Matt 21:31
Show Me the t . . . . Matt 22:19

TAXES
take customs or t. . . . . . . Matt 17:25
Is it lawful to pay t . . . . . Matt 22:17
forbidding to pay t . . . . . . Luke 23:2
t to whom t . . . . Rom 13:7

TEACH
t them diligently. . . . . Deut 6:7
t Jacob Your judgments. . . Deut 33:10
t you the good and the. . 1 Sam 12:23
"Can anyone t. . . . . Job 21:22
"I will t you about. . . . . . . Job 27:11
t me what I do not see . . . . Job 34:32
t me Your paths. . . . . Ps 25:4

T me Your way. . . . . Ps 27:11
t you the fear of the . . . . Ps 34:11
t You awesome things. . . . . . Ps 45:4
t transgressors Your . . . . . . Ps 51:13
So t us to number our . . . . . Ps 90:12
He will t us His ways . . . . Is 2:3
"Whom will he t . . . . Is 28:9
a bribe, her priests t . . . . . . Mic 3:11
t the way of God in . . . . Matt 22:16
in My name, He will t. . . . John 14:26
even nature itself t . . . . . 1 Cor 11:14
permit a woman to t . . . . . 1 Tim 2:12
things command and t . . . . 1 Tim 4:11
T and exhort these . . . . 1 Tim 6:2
t you again the first . . . . . . Heb 5:12

TEACHER
for One is your T. . . . . Matt 23:8
asked Him, "Good T. . . . . Mark 10:17
know that You are a t. . . . . John 3:2
You call Me T. . . . . John 13:13
named Gamaliel, a t. . . . . . Acts 5:34
a t of babes, having . . . . . . Rom 2:20
a t of the Gentiles in. . . . . . 1 Tim 2:7

TEACHERS
than all my t . . . . Ps 119:99
t will not be moved . . . . Is 30:20
prophets, third t. . . . . . . 1 Cor 12:28
and some pastors and t . . . . Eph 4:11
desiring to be t . . . . 1 Tim 1:7
time you ought to be t. . . . . Heb 5:12
of you become t . . . . James 3:1
there will be false t. . . . . . . 2 Pet 2:1

TEACHES
therefore He t sinners . . . . . Ps 25:8
the Holy Spirit t . . . . 1 Cor 2:13
If anyone t otherwise . . . . . 1 Tim 6:3
the same anointing t. . . . 1 John 2:27

TEACHING
t them to observe all. . . . Matt 28:20
they did not cease t . . . . . . Acts 5:42
he who teaches, in t . . . . . . Rom 12:7
t every man in all. . . . . Col 1:28
t things which they. . . . . . Titus 1:11
t us that. . . . . Titus 2:12

TEAR
lest they t me like a . . . . Ps 7:2
I, even I, will t. . . . . Hos 5:14
feet, and turn and t . . . . Matt 7:6
will wipe away every t . . . . . Rev 21:4

TEARS
I have seen your t . . . . 2 Kin 20:5
my couch with my t . . . . Ps 6:6
t have been my food. . . . . . . Ps 42:3
with the bread of t . . . . Ps 80:5
drench you with my t . . . . . . Is 16:9
God will wipe away. . . . . . . Is 25:8
eyes may run with t . . . . Jer 9:18
My eyes fail with t. . . . . Lam 2:11
His feet with her t . . . . Luke 7:38
night and day with t . . . . . Acts 20:31
mindful of your t . . . . 2 Tim 1:4
vehement cries and t. . . . . . Heb 5:7
it diligently with t. . . . . . . Heb 12:17

TEETH
t whiter than milk . . . . Gen 49:12
by the skin of my t . . . . Job 19:20
You have broken the t . . . . . . Ps 3:7
As vinegar to the t. . . . . . . Prov 10:26
you cleanness of t . . . . Amos 4:6

TEKOA
Home of a wise woman, 2 Sam
14:2, 4, 9
Home of Amos, Amos 1:1

TELL
that you may t it to. . . . . . . Ps 48:13
the message that I t . . . . Jon 3:2
Who can t if God . . . . Jon 3:9
t him his fault. . . . . Matt 18:15
whatever they t. . . . . Matt 23:3
He comes, He will t. . . . . . John 4:25

TEMAN
Tribe in northeast Edom, Gen 36:34
Judgment pronounced against,
Amos 1:12
God appears from, Hab 3:3

TEMPERATE
for the prize is t in all . . . . 1 Cor 9:25
husband of one wife, t . . . . 1 Tim 3:2

TEMPEST
the windy storm and t . . . . . . Ps 55:8
one, tossed with t . . . . Is 54:11
And suddenly a great t. . . . Matt 8:24

TEMPLE
So Solomon built the t. . . . 1 Kin 6:14
Lord is in His holy t . . . . Ps 11:4
to inquire in His t . . . . Ps 27:4
suddenly come to His t . . . . . Mal 3:1
One greater than the t . . . . Matt 12:6
murdered between the t . . Matt 23:35
found Him in the t . . . . Luke 2:46
"Destroy this t. . . . . John 2:19
was speaking of the t . . . . . John 2:21
one accord in the t . . . . Acts 2:46
that you are the t. . . . . 1 Cor 3:16
your body is the t. . . . . 1 Cor 6:19
grows into a holy t . . . . Eph 2:21
sits as God in the t . . . . . . 2 Thess 2:4
Then the t of God was. . . . . Rev 11:19
But I saw no t in it . . . . Rev 21:22
and the Lamb are its t . . . . Rev 21:22

TEMPLES
t made with hands . . . . Acts 7:48

TEMPORARY
which are seen are t . . . . . 2 Cor 4:18

TEMPT
Why do you t the Lord. . . . . Ex 17:2
they even t God . . . . Mal 3:15
t the Lord your God . . . . . . Matt 4:7
that Satan does not t. . . . . 1 Cor 7:5
nor let us t Christ. . . . . . . 1 Cor 10:9
nor does He Himself t . . . . James 1:13

TEMPTATION
do not lead us into t . . . . . . Matt 6:13
lest you enter into t. . . . . . Matt 26:41
in time of t fall away. . . . . Luke 8:13
t has overtaken you. . . . . 1 Cor 10:13
to be rich fall into t. . . . . . . 1 Tim 6:9
the man who endures t . . James 1:12

TEMPTED
forty days, t by Satan. . . . . Mark 1:13
not allow you to be t . . . . 1 Cor 10:13
lest you also be t. . . . . Gal 6:1
has suffered, being t. . . . . . Heb 2:18
in all points t . . . . Heb 4:15
But each one is t. . . . . . . James 1:14

TEMPTER
Now when the t came . . . . . Matt 4:3

TENDER
your heart was t. . . . . 2 Kin 22:19
t shoots will not. . . . . Job 14:7
no more be called t . . . . Is 47:1
through the t mercy of . . . . Luke 1:78
put on t mercies . . . . Col 3:12

TENDERHEARTED
to one another, t. . . . . Eph 4:32
love as brothers, be t . . . . . 1 Pet 3:8

TENDS
t a flock and does not . . . . . 1 Cor 9:7

TENT
shall know that your *t* . . . . . Job 5:24
like a shepherd's *t* . . . . Is 38:12
the place of your *t* . . . . Is 54:2
My *t* is plundered . . . . Jer 10:20
earthly house, this *t* . . . . . 2 Cor 5:1
long as I am in this *t* . . . . 2 Pet 1:13
I must put off my *t* . . . . . . 2 Pet 1:14

TENTMAKERS
occupation they were *t* . . . . Acts 18:3

TENTS
those who dwell in *t* . . . . . . Gen 4:20
"How lovely are your *t*. . . . Num 24:5
The *t* of robbers . . . . Job 12:6
than dwell in the *t* . . . . Ps 84:10
I dwell among the *t* . . . . . . Ps 120:5
Lord will save the *t* . . . . . . Zech 12:7

TERAH
Father of Abram, Gen 11:26
Idolater, Josh 24:2
Dies in Haran, Gen 11:25–32

TERRESTRIAL
bodies and *t* bodies . . . . . 1 Cor 15:40

TERRIBLE
t wilderness . . . . Deut 1:19
haughtiness of the *t* . . . . Is 13:11
is great and very *t*. . . . . Joel 2:11

TERRIFIED
to you, 'Do not be *t* . . . . . . Deut 1:29
But they were *t* . . . . Luke 24:37
and not in any way *t*. . . . . Phil 1:28

TERRIFIES
and the Almighty *t* . . . . Job 23:16

TERRIFY
me with dreams and *t*. . . . . . Job 7:14
not let dread of Him *t* . . . . . Job 9:34
are coming to *t* them . . . . . Zech 1:21

TERRIFYING
t was the sight . . . . Heb 12:21

TERROR
there shall be *t* . . . . Deut 32:25
are nothing, you see *t* . . . . . . Job 6:21
not be afraid of the *t* . . . . . . Ps 91:5
I will make you a *t* . . . . Jer 20:4
but a great *t* fell . . . . Dan 10:7

TERRORS
the *t* of God are . . . . Job 6:4
T frighten him on . . . . Job 18:11
before the king of *t* . . . . . . Job 18:14
T overtake him like a . . . . . Job 27:20
consumed with *t* . . . . Ps 73:19

TERTULLUS
Orator who accuses Paul, Acts 24:1–8

TEST
God has come to *t* you . . . . . Ex 20:20
t him with hard . . . . 1 Kin 10:1
behold, His eyelids *t* . . . . Ps 11:4
t them as gold is . . . . Zech 13:9
said, "Why do you *t* . . . . Matt 22:18
t the Spirit of the . . . . Acts 5:9
why do you *t* God by . . . . Acts 15:10
and the fire will *t* . . . . 1 Cor 3:13
T yourselves . . . . 2 Cor 13:5
T all things . . . . 1 Thess 5:21
but *t* the spirits . . . . 1 John 4:1

TESTAMENT
where there is a *t* . . . . Heb 9:16
For a *t* is in force . . . . Heb 9:17

TESTATOR
be the death of the *t*. . . . . . Heb 9:16

TESTED
that God *t* Abraham . . . . . . Gen 22:1
You have *t* my heart . . . . Ps 17:3
And they *t* God in . . . . Ps 78:18
t you at the waters of . . . . . . Ps 81:7
When your fathers *t* . . . . Ps 95:9
t them ten days . . . . Dan 1:14
also first be *t* . . . . 1 Tim 3:10
Where your fathers *t* . . . . . . Heb 3:9
though it is *t* by fire . . . . . . 1 Pet 1:7
t those who say they . . . . . . Rev 2:2

TESTIFIED
Yet the Lord *t* against. . . . 2 Kin 17:13
he who has seen has *t* . . . John 19:35
for as you have *t* . . . . Acts 23:11
t beforehand the . . . . 1 Pet 1:11
of God which He has *t*. . . . 1 John 5:9

TESTIFIES
and heard, that He *t* . . . . . John 3:32
that the Holy Spirit *t* . . . . Acts 20:23

TESTIFY
yes, your own lips *t* . . . . Job 15:6
You, and our sins *t* . . . . Is 59:12
T against Me . . . . Mic 6:3
t what We have . . . . John 3:11
these are they which *t* . . . . John 5:39
t that the Father . . . . 1 John 4:14
sent My angel to *t* . . . . Rev 22:16

TESTIFYING
was righteous, God *t* . . . . . Heb 11:4
t that this is . . . . 1 Pet 5:12

TESTIMONIES
those who keep His *t* . . . . . . Ps 119:2
for I have kept Your *t* . . . . . Ps 119:22
t are my meditation . . . . . . Ps 119:99
I love Your *t* . . . . Ps 119:119
t are wonderful . . . . Ps 119:129

TESTIMONY
two tablets of the *T* . . . . Ex 31:18
For He established a *t* . . . . . . Ps 78:5
that I may keep the *t* . . . . . Ps 119:88
Bind up the *t* . . . . Is 8:16
under your feet as a *t* . . . . Mark 6:11
Now this is the *t* . . . . John 1:19
no one receives His *t* . . . . . John 3:32
who has received His *t* . . . . John 3:33
in your law that the *t* . . . . . John 8:17
and we know that his *t* . . . John 21:24
declaring to you the *t* . . . . 1 Cor 2:1
obtained a good *t* . . . . Heb 11:2
he had this *t* . . . . Heb 11:5
not believed the *t* . . . . 1 John 5:10
And this is the *t* . . . . 1 John 5:11
For the *t* of Jesus is . . . . . . Rev 19:10

TESTING
came to Him, *t* Him . . . . . Matt 19:3
knowing that the *t* . . . . James 1:3

TESTS
the righteous God *t* . . . . Ps 7:9
gold, but the Lord *t* . . . . . Prov 17:3
men, but God who *t* . . . . 1 Thess 2:4

THADDAEUS
One of the Twelve, Mark 3:18

THANK
"I *t* You and praise . . . . . . Dan 2:23
"I *t* You, Father . . . . Matt 11:25
t that servant because . . . . Luke 17:9
t You that I am not . . . . . . Luke 18:11
First, I *t* my God . . . . Rom 1:8
t Christ Jesus our . . . . 1 Tim 1:12

THANKFUL
Be *t* to Him . . . . Ps 100:4
Him as God, nor were *t*. . . . Rom 1:21

THANKFULNESS
Felix, with all *t*. . . . . Acts 24:3

THANKS
the cup, and gave *t*. . . . . Matt 26:27
t He distributed them . . . . John 6:11
for he gives God *t* . . . . . . Rom 14:6
T be to God for His. . . . . 2 Cor 9:15
giving *t* always for . . . . . . Eph 5:20
t can we render . . . . 1 Thess 3:9

THANKSGIVING
with the voice of *t* . . . . Ps 26:7
Offer to God *t*. . . . . Ps 50:14
His presence with *t* . . . . . . Ps 95:2
into His gates with *t* . . . . . Ps 100:4
the sacrifices of *t* . . . . . . Ps 107:22
supplication, with *t* . . . . . . Phil 4:6
vigilant in it with *t* . . . . Col 4:2
to be received with *t* . . . . . 1 Tim 4:3

THEATER
and rushed into the *t*. . . . Acts 19:29

THEOPHILUS
Luke addresses his writings to, Luke
1:3; Acts 1:1

THESSALONICA
Paul preaches in, Acts 17:1–13
Paul writes letters to churches of,
1 Thess 1:1

THIEF
When you saw a *t* . . . . Ps 50:18
do not despise a *t* . . . . . . Prov 6:30
t hates his own life . . . . . Prov 29:24
t is ashamed when he . . . . . Jer 2:26
the windows like a *t* . . . . . . Joel 2:9
t shall be expelled . . . . . . Zech 5:3
known what hour the *t*. . . Matt 24:43
t approaches nor moth. . . Luke 12:33
way, the same is a *t* . . . . . John 10:1
because he was a *t* . . . . . . John 12:6
Lord will come as a *t* . . . . 2 Pet 3:10
upon you as a *t* . . . . Rev 3:3

THIEVES
And companions of *t*. . . . . . . Is 1:23
destroy and where *t* . . . . . Matt 6:19
before Me and *t*. . . . . John 10:8

THIGH
them hip and *t* with a. . . . Judg 15:8
good piece, the *t* . . . . Ezek 24:4

THINGS
in heaven give good *t* . . . . Matt 7:11
evil, speak good *t* . . . . . . Matt 12:34
kept all these *t* . . . . Luke 2:51
Lazarus evil *t*. . . . . Luke 16:25
the Scriptures the *t* . . . . . Luke 24:27
share in all good *t* . . . . Gal 6:6

THINK
nor does his heart *t* . . . . Is 10:7
t that they will be . . . . Matt 6:7
t you have eternal . . . . . . John 5:39
not to *t* of himself . . . . . . Rom 12:3
of ourselves to *t* . . . . 2 Cor 3:5
all that we ask or *t* . . . . . . Eph 3:20

THINKS
yet the Lord *t* upon me. . . . Ps 40:17
for as he is in his . . . . Prov 23:7
t that he knows . . . . 1 Cor 8:2
t he stands take heed. . . . 1 Cor 10:12
For if anyone *t* . . . . Gal 6:3
t he is religious . . . . James 1:26

THIRST
tongues fail for *t*. . . . . Is 41:17
those who hunger and *t*. . . . Matt 5:6
in Me shall never *t* . . . . . . John 6:35
said, "I *t*!" . . . . John 19:28

THIRSTS
we both hunger and *t* .... 1 Cor 4:11
anymore nor *t* anymore.... Rev 7:16

THIRSTS
My soul *t* for God .... Ps 42:2
saying, "If anyone *t* ...... John 7:37
if he *t*. .... Rom 12:20
freely to him who *t*....... Rev 21:6
And let him who *t*....... Rev 22:17

THIRSTY
and if he is *t* .... Prov 25:21
as when a *t* man dreams..... Is 29:8
the drink of the *t* .... Is 32:6
t land springs of........... Is 35:7
on him who is *t*........... Is 44:3
but you shall be *t*......... Is 65:13
I was *t* and you gave .... Matt 25:35
we see You hungry or *t*... Matt 25:44

THISTLES
t grow instead of .... Job 31:40
or figs from *t*........... Matt 7:16

THOMAS
Apostle of Christ, Matt 10:3
Ready to die with Christ, John 11:16
Doubts Christ's resurrection, John
20:24–29

THORN
t that goes into the ...... Prov 26:9
t shall come up the ...... Is 55:13
a *t* in the flesh was ..... 2 Cor 12:7

THORNBUSHES
gather grapes from *t*...... Matt 7:16

THORNS
Both *t* and thistles it...... Gen 3:18
T and snares are .... Prov 22:5
all overgrown with *t* .... Prov 24:31
the crackling of *t* .... Eccl 7:6
Like a lily among *t*...... Song 2:2
and do not sow among *t*.... Jer 4:3
wheat but reaped *t*....... Jer 12:13
And some fell among *t*.... Matt 13:7
wearing the crown of *t*.... John 19:5

THOUGHT
t is that their houses ...... Ps 49:11
You *t* that I was........... Ps 50:21
Both the inward *t*........ Ps 64:6
I *t* about my ways .... Ps 119:59
You understand my *t*..... Ps 139:2
"Surely, as I have *t*........ Is 14:24
to man what his *t* ...... Amos 4:13
perceiving the *t*......... Luke 9:47
And he *t* within........ Luke 12:17
I *t* as a child........... 1 Cor 13:11

THOUGHTS
the intent of the *t* ...... 1 Chr 28:9
is in none of his *t* .... Ps 10:4
t toward us .... Ps 40:5
t are very deep........... Ps 92:5
The LORD knows the *t* ...... Ps 94:11
t will be established....... Prov 16:3
unrighteous man his *t*....... Is 55:7
For My *t* are not your..... Is 55:8
long shall your evil *t*..... Jer 4:14
they do not know the *t*.... Mic 4:12
Jesus, knowing their *t*..... Matt 9:4
heart proceed evil *t*...... Matt 15:19
futile in their *t*.......... Rom 1:21
The LORD knows the *t* .... 1 Cor 3:20

THOUSAND
put ten *t* to flight .... Lev 26:8
you shall chase a *t*....... Josh 23:10
cattle on a *t* hills .... Ps 50:10
Your courts is better than a *t* Ps 84:10
A *t* may fall at your side..... Ps 91:7

one day is as a *t* years ..... 2 Pet 3:8
bound him for a *t* years.... Rev 20:2

THREAT
shall flee at the *t* .... Is 30:17

THREATEN
suffered, He did not *t* ..... 1 Pet 2:23

THREATENING
to them, giving up *t*........ Eph 6:9

THREATS
Lord, look on their *t*...... Acts 4:29
still breathing *t* .... Acts 9:1

THREE
you will deny Me *t* ...... Matt 26:34
hope, love, these *t* ...... 1 Cor 13:13
and these *t* are one ..... 1 John 5:7

THRESH
he does not *t* it........... Is 28:28
t the mountains .... Is 41:15
it is time to *t* her......... Jer 51:33
"Arise and *t*............. Mic 4:13

THRESHING
t shall last till the ...... Lev 26:5
like the dust at *t*........ 2 Kin 13:7
Oh, my *t* and the grain ..... Is 21:10

THROAT
t is an open tomb .... Ps 5:9
put a knife to your *t* ...... Prov 23:2
unshod, and your *t* ...... Jer 2:25
t is an open tomb .... Rom 3:13

THRONE
LORD sitting on His *t*..... 1 Kin 22:19
He has prepared His *t*...... Ps 9:7
temple, the LORD's *t*........ Ps 11:4
Your *t*, O God, is .... Ps 45:6
has established His *t* ...... Ps 103:19
he upholds his *t*......... Prov 20:28
Lord sitting on a *t* .... Is 6:1
"Heaven is My *t*........... Is 66:1
shall be called The *T* ...... Jer 3:17
do not disgrace the *t*...... Jer 14:21
A glorious high *t*......... Jer 17:12
t was a fiery flame .... Dan 7:9
sit and rule on His *t* ...... Zech 6:13
for it is God's *t*........ Matt 5:34
will give Him the *t* ..... Luke 1:32
"Your *t*, O God, is........... Heb 1:8
come boldly to the *t*...... Heb 4:16
where Satan's *t* .... Rev 2:13
My Father on His *t* ...... Rev 3:21
I saw a great white *t*..... Rev 20:11

THRONES
t are set there............. Ps 122:5
also sit on twelve *t* ..... Matt 19:28
mighty from their *t*...... Luke 1:52
invisible, whether *t* ...... Col 1:16
t I saw twenty-four .... Rev 4:4

THRONG
house of God in the *t*...... Ps 55:14

THROW
of your land and *t* ...... Mic 5:11
t Yourself down .... Matt 4:6
children's bread and *t*.... Matt 15:26

THROWN
their slain shall be *t*........ Is 34:3
neck, and he were *t* ..... Mark 9:42

THRUST
and rose up and *t*...... Luke 4:29

THUNDER
But the *t* of His power ..... Job 26:14
The voice of Your *t*........ Ps 77:18
the secret place of *t* ...... Ps 81:7

t they hastened away ...... Ps 104:7
that is, "Sons of *T*"...... Mark 3:17
the voice of loud *t*........ Rev 14:2

THUNDERED
"The LORD *t* from ...... 2 Sam 22:14
The LORD *t* .... Ps 18:13

THUNDERINGS
people witnessed the *t* ..... Ex 20:18
the sound of mighty *t*...... Rev 19:6

THUNDERS
t marvelously with His ..... Job 37:5
The God of glory *t*......... Ps 29:3

THYATIRA
Residence of Lydia, Acts 16:14
Site of one of the seven churches, Rev
2:18–24

TIBERIAS
Sea of Galilee called, John 6:1, 23

TIDINGS
be afraid of evil *t*......... Ps 112:7
I bring you good *t*........ Luke 2:10
who bring glad *t* .... Rom 10:15

TIGLATH-PILESER
Powerful Assyrian king who invades
Samaria, 2 Kin 15:29

TILL
no man to *t* the ground..... Gen 2:5

TILLER
but Cain was a *t* .... Gen 4:2

TILLS
t his land will be .... Prov 12:11
t his land will have ..... Prov 28:19

TIME
pray to You in a *t* .... Ps 32:6
ashamed in the evil *t* ...... Ps 37:19
how short my *t* is.......... Ps 89:47
A *t* to be born............. Eccl 3:2
but *t* and chance .... Eccl 9:11
your *t* was the *t*.......... Ezek 16:8
you did not know the *t*.... Luke 19:44
t has not yet come ...... John 7:6
I have a convenient *t* .... Acts 24:25
for the *t* is near........... Rev 1:3

TIMES
understanding of the *t*... 1 Chr 12:32
t are not hidden .... Job 24:1
t are in Your hand......... Ps 31:15
the signs of the *t* .... Matt 16:3
Gentiles until the *t* ..... Luke 21:24
not for you to know *t* ...... Acts 1:7
their preappointed *t*..... Acts 17:26
last days perilous *t* .... 2 Tim 3:1
God, who at various *t* ..... Heb 1:1

TIMON
One of the first seven deacons, Acts
6:1–5

TIMOTHY
Paul's companion, Acts 16:1–3; 18:5;
20:4, 5; 2 Cor 1:19; Phil 1:1; 2 Tim
4:9, 21
Ministers independently, Acts 17:14,
15; 19:22; 1 Cor 4:17; Phil 2:19, 23;
1 Thess 3:1–6; 1 Tim 1:1–3; 4:14

TIRZAH
Seat of Jeroboam's rule, 1 Kin 14:17
Capital of Israel until Omri's reign,
1 Kin 16:6–23

TITHE
And he gave him a *t*..... Gen 14:20
LORD, a tenth of the *t* .... Num 18:26
"You shall truly *t*........ Deut 14:22

shall bring out the *t* . . . . . Deut 14:28
laying aside all the *t*. . . . . Deut 26:12
in abundantly the *t*. . . . . . 2 Chr 31:5
Judah brought the *t*. . . . . . Neh 13:12
For you pay *t* of mint . . . . Matt 23:23

TITHES
to redeem any of his *t*. . . . . Lev 27:31
t which you receive. . . . . . Num 18:28
and to bring the *t*. . . . . . . Neh 10:37
firstfruits, and the *t* . . . . . Neh 12:44
the articles, the *t* . . . . . . Neh 13:5
Bring all the *t*. . . . . Mal 3:10
I give *t* of all that I . . . . . Luke 18:12
to receive *t* from the. . . . . . Heb 7:5
mortal men receive *t* . . . . . Heb 7:8
Levi, who receives *t* . . . . . . Heb 7:9

TITHING
the year of *t*. . . . . Deut 26:12

TITLE
Now Pilate wrote a *t* . . . . . John 19:19

TITTLE
away, one jot or one *t*. . . . . Matt 5:18

TITUS
Ministers in Crete, Titus 1:4, 5
Paul's representative in Corinth,
2 Cor 7:6, 7, 13, 14; 8:6–23

TOBIAH
Ammonite servant; ridicules the
Jews, Neh 2:10

TODAY
t I have begotten You . . . . Ps 2:7
of the field, which *t* . . . . . Matt 6:30
the grass, which *t* . . . . . . Luke 12:28
t you will be with Me . . . . Luke 23:43
t I have begotten You . . . . . . Heb 1:5
"*T*, if you will hear. . . . . Heb 3:7
the same yesterday, *t* . . . . . Heb 13:8

TOIL
t you shall eat of . . . . Gen 3:17
they neither *t* nor . . . . Matt 6:28
our labor and *t*. . . . . 1 Thess 2:9

TOILED
"Master, we have *t* . . . . Luke 5:5

TOLD
Behold, I have *t* . . . . Matt 28:7
things which were *t* . . . . . . Luke 2:18
t me all things that I . . . . . John 4:29
t you the truth which . . . . . John 8:40
so, I would have *t* . . . . John 14:2
"And now I have *t* . . . . . John 14:29

TOLERABLE
you, it will be more *t*. . . . . Matt 10:15

TOMB
throat is an open *t* . . . . Ps 5:9
in the garden a new *t* . . . . John 19:41
throat is an open *t* . . . . . . Rom 3:13

TOMBS
like whitewashed *t* . . . . . . Matt 23:27
you build the *t* . . . . Matt 23:29
For you build the *t* . . . . . Luke 11:47

TOMORROW
drink, for *t* we die. . . . . Is 22:13
t will be as today . . . . Is 56:12
t is thrown into the. . . . . . Matt 6:30
do not worry about *t* . . . . . Matt 6:34
drink, for *t* we die. . . . . . . 1 Cor 15:32
what will happen *t* . . . . . . James 4:14

TONGUE
the scourge of the *t* . . . . Job 5:21
hides it under his *t* . . . . . . Job 20:12
Keep your *t* from evil. . . . . . Ps 34:13

t shall speak of Your . . . . Ps 35:28
lest I sin with my *t* . . . . Ps 39:1
to you, you false *t* . . . . Ps 120:3
laughter, and our *t* . . . . . . Ps 126:2
remember you, let my *t*. . . . . Ps 137:6
is not a word on my *t* . . . . . Ps 139:4
but the perverse *t*. . . . . . . Prov 10:31
forever, but a lying *t* . . . . Prov 12:19
A wholesome *t* is a . . . . . . Prov 15:4
t keeps his soul . . . . Prov 21:23
t breaks a bone . . . . Prov 25:15
t shall take an oath . . . . Is 45:23
GOD has given Me the *t*. . . . . . Is 50:4
t should confess that . . . . . Phil 2:11
does not bridle his *t* . . . . . James 1:26
t is a little member. . . . . . . James 3:5
And the *t* is a fire . . . . James 3:6
no man can tame the *t* . . . James 3:8
love in word or in *t* . . . . . 1 John 3:18
every nation, tribe, *t*. . . . . . Rev 14:6

TONGUES
From the strife of *t*. . . . . . . Ps 31:20
speak with new *t* . . . . . . Mark 16:17
to them divided *t*, as of fire. . Acts 2:3
speak with *t* and magnify . Acts 10:46
and they spoke with *t* . . . . . Acts 19:6
I speak with the *t*. . . . . . . 1 Cor 13:1
Therefore *t* are for a. . . . . 1 Cor 14:22
do not forbid to speak
    with *t*. . . . . 1 Cor 14:39

TOOTH
eye for eye, *t* . . . . Ex 21:24
is like a bad *t* . . . . Prov 25:19
eye for an eye and a *t*. . . . . Matt 5:38

TOPHET
See HINNOM, VALLEY OF THE SON OF
T was established. . . . . Is 30:33
the high places of *T* . . . . . . Jer 7:31
make this city like *T* . . . . . Jer 19:12
like the place of *T*. . . . . . . Jer 19:13

TORCH
and like a fiery *t* . . . . Zech 12:6

TORCHES
When he had set the *t* . . . . Judg 15:5
his eyes like *t* . . . . Dan 10:6
come with flaming *t* . . . . . . Nah 2:3

TORMENT
"How long will you *t*. . . . . . . Job 19:2
shall lie down in *t* . . . . Is 50:11
You come here to *t* . . . . . . Matt 8:29
to this place of *t* . . . . Luke 16:28
fear involves *t* . . . . 1 John 4:18
t ascends forever . . . . Rev 14:11

TORMENTED
for I am *t* in this . . . . Luke 16:24
And they will be *t*. . . . . . . Rev 20:10

TORMENTS
And being in *t*. . . . . Luke 16:23

TORN
aside my ways and *t*. . . . . . Lam 3:11
for He will. . . . . Hos 6:1
of the temple was *t*. . . . . . Matt 27:51

TORTURED
Others were *t* . . . . Heb 11:35

TOSSED
t with tempest. . . . . Is 54:11
t to and fro and . . . . Eph 4:14

TOTTER
drunkard, and shall *t* . . . . . Is 24:20

TOUCH
seven no evil shall *t* . . . . . . Job 5:19
t no unclean thing . . . . Is 52:11

"If only I may *t*. . . . . Matt 9:21
that they might only *t* . . . Matt 14:36
a man not to *t* a woman . . 1 Cor 7:1
wicked one does not *t* . . . 1 John 5:18

TOUCHED
whose hearts God had *t*. 1 Sam 10:26
t my mouth with it . . . . Is 6:7
hand and *t* my mouth. . . . . . Jer 1:9
mountain that may be *t* . . Heb 12:18

TOUCHES
He *t* the hills . . . . Ps 104:32
t you *t* the. . . . . Zech 2:8

TOWER
t whose top is in the. . . . . . Gen 11:4
for me, a strong *t*. . . . . Ps 61:3
my fortress, my high *t*. . . . . Ps 144:2
like an ivory *t*. . . . . Song 7:4
a watchman in the *t* . . . . Is 21:5
in it and built a *t* . . . . . . Matt 21:33

TRACKED
t our steps so that we . . . . . Lam 4:18

TRADERS
are princes, whose *t*. . . . . . . Is 23:8

TRADITION
transgress the *t* . . . . Matt 15:2
of no effect by your *t* . . . . Matt 15:6
according to the *t* . . . . Col 2:8
t which he received . . . . 2 Thess 3:6
conduct received by *t* . . . . 1 Pet 1:18

TRADITIONS
zealous for the *t* . . . . Gal 1:14
t which you were . . . . . . 2 Thess 2:15

TRAIN
T up a child in the . . . . . . Prov 22:6
t of His robe filled . . . . Is 6:1

TRAINED
who is perfectly *t*. . . . . . . Luke 6:40
those who have been *t*. . . . Heb 12:11

TRAINING
bring them up in the *t*. . . . . Eph 6:4

TRAINS
t my hands for war . . . . . . Ps 144:1

TRAITOR
also became a *t*. . . . . Luke 6:16

TRAITORS
t, headstrong. . . . . 2 Tim 3:4

TRAMPLE
Your name we will *t* . . . . . . Ps 44:5
serpent you shall *t*. . . . . . . Ps 91:13
hand, to *t* My courts . . . . . . Is 1:12
You shall *t* the wicked . . . . . Mal 4:3
swine, lest they *t*. . . . . . . Matt 7:6
you the authority to *t* . . . . . Lk 10:19

TRAMPLED
t them in My fury . . . . Is 63:3
now she will be *t*. . . . . Mic 7:10
t the nations in anger . . . . Hab 3:12
Jerusalem will be *t* . . . . . . Luke 21:24
t the Son of God. . . . . Heb 10:29
the winepress was *t*. . . . . . Rev 14:20

TRANCE
he fell into a *t*. . . . . Acts 10:10
t I saw a vision. . . . . Acts 11:5

TRANSFIGURED
and was *t* before them . . . . Matt 17:2

TRANSFORMED
this world, but be *t* . . . . . . Rom 12:2
the Lord, are being *t* . . . . . 2 Cor 3:18

TRANSGRESS
t the command of the. . . . Num 14:41

the LORD's people t ...... 1 Sam 2:24
my mouth shall not t .... Ps 17:3
his mouth must not t ...... Prov 16:10
of bread a man will t .... Prov 28:21
do Your disciples t .... Matt 15:2

TRANSGRESSED
t My covenant .... Josh 7:11
your mediators have t ...... Is 43:27
the rulers also t .... Jer 2:8
their fathers have t .... Ezek 2:3
Yes, all Israel has t .... Dan 9:11
t your commandment .... Luke 15:29

TRANSGRESSES
"Indeed, because he t ...... Hab 2:5
Whoever t and does not .... 2 John 9

TRANSGRESSION
iniquity and t and sin ...... Ex 34:7
Make me know my t .... Job 13:23
t is sealed up in a .... Job 14:17
be innocent of great t ...... Ps 19:13
because of their t .... Ps 107:17
He who covers a t .... Prov 17:9
He who loves t loves ...... Prov 17:19
tell My people their t .... Is 58:1
at Gilgal multiply t .... Amos 4:4
my firstborn for my t ...... Mic 6:7
and passing over the t .... Mic 7:18
no law there is no t .... Rom 4:15
deceived, fell into t ...... 1 Tim 2:14
steadfast, and every t ...... Heb 2:2

TRANSGRESSIONS
if I have covered my t ..... Job 31:33
"I will confess my t .... Ps 32:5
me from all my t .... Ps 39:8
mercies, blot out my t ...... Ps 51:1
For I acknowledge my t ..... Ps 51:3
has He removed our t ..... Ps 103:12
who blots out your t ...... Is 43:25
was wounded for our t ...... Is 53:5
for the t of My people .... Is 53:8
from you all the t ...... Ezek 18:31
was added because of t ..... Gal 3:19
redemption of the t ...... Heb 9:15

TRANSGRESSOR
and were called a t .... Is 48:8
I make myself a t .... Gal 2:18

TRANSGRESSORS
Then I will teach t .... Ps 51:13
to any wicked t .... Ps 59:5
numbered with the t ...... Is 53:12
numbered with the t .... Mark 15:28

TRAP
of Israel, as a t .... Is 8:14
where there is no t .... Amos 3:5

TRAPS
they have set t .... Ps 140:5
for me, and from the t ..... Ps 141:9

TRAVEL
For you t land and sea ... Matt 23:15

TRAVELER
t who turns aside .... Jer 14:8

TREACHEROUS
the t dealer deals .... Is 21:2
an assembly of t men ...... Jer 9:2
are insolent, t .... Zeph 3:4

TREACHEROUSLY
and you who deal t .... Is 33:1
happy who deal so t ...... Jer 12:1
even they have dealt t ..... Jer 12:6
They have dealt t .... Hos 5:7
Why do we deal t .... Mal 2:10
that you do not deal t ..... Mal 2:16
This man dealt t .... Acts 7:19

TREAD
t down the wicked in ..... Job 40:12
it is He who shall t .... Ps 60:12
You shall t upon the ...... Ps 91:13
shout, as those who t ..... Jer 25:30
will come down and t ..... Mic 1:3
And they will t .... Rev 11:2

TREADS
like one who t in the .... Is 63:2
t the high places .... Amos 4:13
an ox while it t .... 1 Tim 5:18
t the winepress .... Rev 19:15

TREASURE
to you His good t .... Deut 28:12
one who finds great t ..... Ps 119:162
for His special t .... Ps 135:4
there is much t .... Prov 15:6
There is desirable t ..... Prov 21:20
of the LORD is His t .... Is 33:6
For where your t .... Matt 6:21
t brings forth evil ...... Matt 12:35
t things new and old .... Matt 13:52
and you will have t ...... Matt 19:21
So is he who lays up t .... Luke 12:21
But we have this t .... 2 Cor 4:7
You have heaped up t .... James 5:3

TREASURED
t the words of His .... Job 23:12

TREASURER
Erastus, the t of the ..... Rom 16:23

TREASURES
sealed up among My t ... Deut 32:34
it more than hidden t ..... Job 3:21
her as for hidden t .... Prov 2:4
t of wickedness profit ..... Prov 10:2
Getting t by a lying ...... Prov 21:6
is no end to their t .... Is 2:7
I will give you the t .... Is 45:3
Are there yet the t .... Mic 6:10
for yourselves t .... Matt 6:19
are hidden all the t .... Col 2:3
riches than the t .... Heb 11:26

TREATY
Now Solomon made a t .... 1 Kin 3:1

TREE
but of the t .... Gen 2:17
you eaten from the t ..... Gen 3:11
there is hope for a t ...... Job 14:7
t planted by the .... Ps 1:3
like a native green t ...... Ps 37:35
t falls to the south .... Eccl 11:3
Like an apple t .... Song 2:3
for as the days of a t ...... Is 65:22
t planted by the .... Jer 17:8
t bears good fruit ...... Matt 7:17
His own body on the t .... 1 Pet 2:24
give to eat from the t ...... Rev 2:7
the river, was the t ...... Rev 22:2

TREES
t once went forth .... Judg 9:8
Also he spoke of t ...... 1 Kin 4:33
Then all the t of the ...... Ps 96:12
The t of the LORD are ..... Ps 104:16
all kinds of fruit t .... Eccl 2:5
they may be called t ...... Is 61:3
and on beast, on the t ..... Jer 7:20
so that all the t ...... Ezek 31:9
"I see men like t .... Mark 8:24
late autumn t without ..... Jude 12
the sea, or the t .... Rev 7:3

TREMBLE
T before Him .... 1 Chr 16:30
have made the earth t ...... Ps 60:2
let the peoples t .... Ps 99:1

who made the earth t .... Is 14:16
That the nations may t ...... Is 64:2
'Will you not t .... Jer 5:22
wrath the earth will t ..... Jer 10:10
they shall fear and t .... Jer 33:9
my kingdom men must t .. Dan 6:26
made me t on my knees .. Dan 10:10

TREMBLED
of Edom, the earth t .... Judg 5:4
for his heart t .... 1 Sam 4:13
Then everyone who t ...... Ezra 9:4
the earth shook and t ...... Ps 18:7
and indeed they t .... Jer 4:24

TREMBLES
the earth sees and t .... Ps 97:4

TREMBLING
it was a very great t .... 1 Sam 14:15
your water with t .... Ezek 12:18
in fear, and in much t .... 1 Cor 2:3
t you received .... 2 Cor 7:15
flesh, with fear and t ...... Eph 6:5
with fear and t .... Phil 2:12

TRENCH
and he made a t .... 1 Kin 18:32

TRESPASSES
still goes on in his t .... Ps 68:21
forgive men their t .... Matt 6:14
not imputing their t ...... 2 Cor 5:19
who were dead in t .... Eph 2:1
forgiven you all t .... Col 2:13

TRIAL
as in the day of t .... Ps 95:8
in the day of t .... Heb 3:8
concerning the fiery t .... 1 Pet 4:12
t which shall come .... Rev 3:10

TRIBE
of old, the t of Your .... Ps 74:2
belongs to another t ...... Heb 7:13
the Lion of the t .... Rev 5:5
blood out of every t .... Rev 5:9

TRIBES
where the t go up .... Ps 122:4
to raise up the t .... Is 49:6
promise our twelve t ..... Acts 26:7
t which are scattered ..... James 1:1

TRIBULATION
there will be great t ...... Matt 24:21
world you will have t ..... John 16:33
in hope, patient in t ..... Rom 12:12
joyful in all our t .... 2 Cor 7:4
that we would suffer t ... 1 Thess 3:4
t those who .... 2 Thess 1:6
and you will have t ...... Rev 2:10
with her into great t ...... Rev 2:22
out of the great t .... Rev 7:14

TRIBULATIONS
t enter the kingdom ...... Acts 14:22
but we also glory in t ...... Rom 5:3
not lose heart at my t ..... Eph 3:13
t that you endure ...... 2 Thess 1:4

TRIED
You have t me and have .... Ps 17:3
a t stone, a precious .... Is 28:16

TRIMMED
and t their lamps .... Matt 25:7

TRIUMPH
Let not my enemies t ...... Ps 25:2
I will t in the works .... Ps 92:4
always leads us in t ..... 2 Cor 2:14

TRIUMPHED
the LORD, for He has t ...... Ex 15:1

TROAS
Paul receives vision at, Acts 16:8–11

TRODDEN
t the winepress alone . . . . Is 63:3

TROUBLE
that they were in *t* . . . . Ex 5:19
no rest, for *t* comes . . . . Job 3:26
few days and full of *t* . . . . . . Job 14:1
for the time of *t* . . . . Job 38:23
have increased who *t* . . . . . . Ps 3:1
under his tongue is *t* . . . . . . Ps 10:7
from Me, for *t* is near . . . . . . Ps 22:11
t He shall hide me. . . . . Ps 27:5
O LORD, for I am in *t* . . . . Ps 31:9
not in *t* as other men . . . . . . Ps 73:5
will be with him in *t* . . . . . . Ps 91:15
walk in the midst of *t* . . . . . Ps 138:7
is delivered from *t* . . . . Prov 11:8
of the wicked is *t* . . . . Prov 15:6
t they have . . . . Is 26:16
also in the time of *t* . . . . Is 33:2
and there was *t*. . . . . Jer 8:15
Savior in time of *t*. . . . . Jer 14:8
such will have *t* . . . . 1 Cor 7:28
there are some who *t* . . . . . . Gal 1:7

TROUBLED
Your face, and I was *t* . . . . . . Ps 30:7
Your face, they are *t* . . . . . Ps 104:29
wicked are like the *t* . . . . . . Is 57:20
You are worried and *t* . . . . Luke 10:41
to give you who are *t* . . . . 2 Thess 1:7
shaken in mind or *t* . . . . . 2 Thess 2:2

TROUBLES
"What *t* the people. . . . . . 1 Sam 11:5
deliver you in six *t*. . . . . Job 5:19
The *t* of my heart have . . . . . Ps 25:17
out of all their *t*. . . . . Ps 25:22
my soul is full of *t* . . . . Ps 88:3
because the former *t* . . . . . . Is 65:16
will be famines and *t*. . . . . Mark 13:8
him out of all his *t*. . . . . Acts 7:10

TROUBLING
spirit from God is *t* . . . . . 1 Sam 16:15
wicked cease from *t*. . . . . . . Job 3:17

TRUE
and Your words are *t* . . . . 2 Sam 7:28
But the LORD is the *t* . . . . . . Jer 10:10
"Let the LORD be a *t* . . . . Jer 42:5
we know that You are *t*. . . . Matt 22:16
He who sent Me is *t* . . . . . . John 7:28
about this Man were *t*. . . . John 10:41
Indeed, let God be *t* . . . . . . Rom 3:4
whatever things are *t*. . . . . Phil 4:8
may know Him who is *t* . 1 John 5:20
is holy, He who is *t*. . . . . Rev 3:7
"These are the *t*. . . . . Rev 19:9
for these words are *t* . . . . . . Rev 21:5

TRUMPET
Blow the *t* at the time . . . . . . Ps 81:3
"Blow the *t* in the. . . . . Jer 4:5
deed, do not sound a *t* . . . . Matt 6:2
t makes an uncertain . . . . 1 Cor 14:8
For the *t* will sound . . . . 1 Cor 15:52
loud voice, as of a *t* . . . . . . Rev 1:10

TRUST
If God puts no *t* . . . . Job 15:15
T in the LORD . . . . Ps 37:3
You are my *t* from my. . . . . . Ps 71:5
T in the LORD with all . . . . . Prov 3:5
my salvation, I will *t* . . . . . . Is 12:2
Let him *t* in the name . . . . Is 50:10
Do not *t* in these . . . . Jer 7:4
Do not *t* in a friend . . . . . . Mic 7:5
those who *t* in riches . . . Mark 10:24
committed to your *t* . . . . . 1 Tim 6:20

TRUSTED
"He *t* in the LORD. . . . . Ps 22:8
He *t* in God . . . . Matt 27:43
that we who first *t* . . . . Eph 1:12
the holy women who *t*. . . . . 1 Pet 3:5

TRUSTS
But he who *t* in the . . . . Ps 32:10
He who *t* in his own . . . . . Prov 28:26

TRUTH
led me in the way of *t* . . . . Gen 24:48
justice, a God of *t* . . . . Deut 32:4
and speaks the *t* . . . . Ps 15:2
t continually preserve . . . . . . Ps 40:11
Behold, You desire *t* . . . . Ps 51:6
T shall spring out of . . . . . . Ps 85:11
t shall be your shield. . . . . . . Ps 91:4
t utterly out of my . . . . Ps 119:43
and Your law is *t* . . . . Ps 119:142
of Your word is *t* . . . . Ps 119:160
t is fallen in the . . . . Is 59:14
not valiant for the *t* . . . . Jer 9:3
"There is no *t* . . . . Hos 4:1
called the City of *T*. . . . . . . Zech 8:3
speak each man the *t* . . . . . Zech 8:16
t was in his mouth. . . . . Mal 2:6
you shall know the *t* . . . . . John 8:32
"I am the way, the *t* . . . . . John 14:6
He, the Spirit of *t*. . . . . . . John 16:13
to Him, "What is *t* . . . . . . John 18:38
speak the words of *t* . . . . Acts 26:25
who suppress the *t* . . . . . . Rom 1:18
of sincerity and *t* . . . . 1 Cor 5:8
but, speaking the *t* . . . . Eph 4:15
your waist with *t* . . . . Eph 6:14
in the word of the *t*. . . . . Col 1:5
the love of the *t*. . . . . 2 Thess 2:10
I am speaking the *t* . . . . . . 1 Tim 2:7
they may know the *t* . . . . 2 Tim 2:25
the knowledge of the *t* . . . . 2 Tim 3:7
in the present *t* . . . . 2 Pet 1:12
way of *t* will be. . . . . 2 Pet 2:2
that we are of the *t* . . . . . 1 John 3:19
the Spirit is *t* . . . . 1 John 5:6
t that is in you . . . . 3 John 3

TRY
t my mind and my heart . . . . Ps 26:2
refine them and *t* them . . . . . Jer 9:7
t Me now in this. . . . . Mal 3:10
which is to *t* you. . . . . 1 Pet 4:12

TUBAL
Son of Japheth, Gen 10:2
——— Tribe associated with Javan and
Meshech, Is 66:19
In Gog's army, Ezek 38:2, 3
Punishment of, Ezek 32:26, 27

TUBAL-CAIN
Son of Lamech, Gen 4:19–22

TUMULT
their waves, and the *t*. . . . . . Ps 65:7
Your enemies make a *t* . . . . . Ps 83:2

TUNIC
Also he made him a *t* . . . . Gen 37:3
and take away your *t*. . . . . Matt 5:40

TUNICS
the LORD God made *t*. . . . . . Gen 3:21
not to put on two *t* . . . . . . Mark 6:9
weeping, showing the *t* . . . . Acts 9:39

TURBAN
like a robe and a *t*. . . . . . . Job 29:14
"Remove the *t* . . . . Ezek 21:26

TURN
you shall not *t*. . . . . Deut 17:11
Then we will not *t* . . . . Ps 80:18

but let them not *t* . . . . Ps 85:8
yet I do not *t* . . . . Ps 119:51
T at my rebuke . . . . Prov 1:23
not let your heart *t* . . . . . . Prov 7:25
'*T* now everyone from . . . . . Jer 35:15
"Repent, *t* away from . . . . Ezek 14:6
yes, let every one *t* . . . . Jon 3:8
"*T* now from your evil . . . . Zech 1:4
on your right cheek, *t*. . . . . Matt 5:39
t the hearts of the . . . . Luke 1:17
you that you should *t* . . . . Acts 14:15
t them from darkness . . . . Acts 26:18
Let him *t* away from. . . . . . 1 Pet 3:11

TURNED
kept His way and not *t* . . . . Job 23:11
The wicked shall be *t*. . . . . . . Ps 9:17
let them be *t* back and . . . . . Ps 70:2
t my feet to Your. . . . . Ps 119:59
of Israel, they have *t* . . . . Is 1:4
number believed and *t*. . . . Acts 11:21
and how you *t* to God . . . 1 Thess 1:9

TURNING
marvel that you are *t*. . . . . . Gal 1:6
or shadow of *t*. . . . . James 1:17

TURNS
of the wicked He *t* . . . . Ps 146:9
A soft answer *t*. . . . . Prov 15:1
but no one *t* back . . . . Nah 2:8
that he who *t* . . . . James 5:20

TURTLEDOVE
the life of Your *t*. . . . . Ps 74:19
t is heard in our land . . . . Song 2:12

TUTOR
the law was our *t* . . . . Gal 3:24
no longer under a *t* . . . . . . Gal 3:25

TWIST
All day they *t* my . . . . Ps 56:5
unstable people *t* to . . . . . 2 Pet 3:16

TWO
the ark to Noah, *t* . . . . Gen 7:15
t young pigeons . . . . Lev 12:8
T are better than one. . . . . . Eccl 4:9
t he covered his . . . . Is 6:2
t shall become one . . . . . . Matt 19:5
t young pigeons . . . . Luke 2:24
new man from the *t*. . . . . . Eph 2:15

TYCHICUS
Paul's companion, Acts 20:1, 4
Paul's messenger, Eph 6:21, 22; Col
4:7–9; 2 Tim 4:12

TYPE
of Adam, who is a *t* . . . . . . Rom 5:14

ULAI
Scene of Daniel's visions, Dan 8:2–16

UNAFRAID
Do you want to be *u* . . . . . Rom 13:3

UNBELIEF
because of their *u* . . . . . . Matt 13:58
help my *u*. . . . . Mark 9:24
and He rebuked their *u* . . Mark 16:14
did it ignorantly in *u*. . . . . 1 Tim 1:13
you an evil heart of *u* . . . . Heb 3:12
enter in because of *u* . . . . . Heb 3:19

UNBELIEVERS
who believe but to *u* . . . . 1 Cor 14:22
are uninformed or *u* . . . . 1 Cor 14:23
yoked together with *u* . . . . 2 Cor 6:14

UNBELIEVING
Do not be *u*. . . . . John 20:27
u Jews stirred up the . . . . . Acts 14:2
For the *u* husband is . . . . . 1 Cor 7:14

u nothing is pure . . . . Titus 1:15
But the cowardly, *u*. . . . . Rev 21:8

UNCIRCUMCISED
You stiff-necked and *u*. . . . . Acts 7:51
not the physically *u* . . . . . . Rom 2:27
by faith and the *u*. . . . . Rom 3:30
u had been committed. . . . . . Gal 2:7

UNCLEAN
of animals that are *u*. . . . . . Gen 7:2
who touches any *u* . . . . Lev 7:21
I am a man of *u* lips . . . . Is 6:5
u shall no longer come . . . . . . Is 52:1
He commands even the *u* . Mark 1:27
He rebuked the *u*. . . . . . . Mark 9:25
any man common or *u*. . . Acts 10:28
there is nothing *u* . . . . Rom 14:14
Do not touch what is *u* . . . 2 Cor 6:17
that no fornicator, *u*. . . . . . . Eph 5:5

UNCLEANNESS
men's bones and all *u*. . . . Matt 23:27
members as slaves of *u*. . . . Rom 6:19
did not call us to *u* . . . . . . 1 Thess 4:7
flesh in the lust of *u* . . . . . . 2 Pet 2:10

UNCLEANNESSES
from all your *u* . . . . Ezek 36:29

UNCLOTHED
we want to be *u*. . . . . 2 Cor 5:4

UNCOVER
skirt, *u* the thigh . . . . Is 47:2

UNCOVERS
u deep things out of. . . . . . Job 12:22

UNDEFILED
Blessed are the *u* . . . . Ps 119:1
all, and the bed *u*. . . . . Heb 13:4
incorruptible and *u* . . . . 1 Pet 1:4

UNDERMINE
And you *u* your friend. . . . . . Job 6:27

UNDERSTAND
u one another's speech. . . . . Gen 11:7
if there are any who *u*. . . . . . . Ps 14:2
in Egypt did not *u* . . . . Ps 106:7
is to *u* his way . . . . Prov 14:8
Evil men do not *u* . . . . Prov 28:5
hearing, but do not *u* . . . . Dan 1:4
set your heart to *u* . . . . . . Dan 10:12
u shall instruct many. . . . Dan 11:33
of the wicked shall . . . . . . Dan 12:10
people who do not *u*. . . . . . Hos 4:14
Let him *u* these things . . . . Hos 14:9
Why do you not *u*. . . . . . . John 8:43
u what you are reading. . . . Acts 8:30
lest they should *u*. . . . . . . Acts 28:27
u all mysteries . . . . 1 Cor 13:2
some things hard to *u* . . . . 2 Pet 3:16

UNDERSTANDING
asked for yourself *u* . . . . . . 1 Kin 3:11
He has counsel and *u* . . . . . Job 12:13
is the place of *u* . . . . Job 28:12
depart from evil is *u* . . . . . . Job 28:28
Almighty gives him *u* . . . . . . Job 32:8
not endow her with *u* . . . . . Job 39:17
my heart shall give *u* . . . . . . Ps 49:3
Give me *u*. . . . . Ps 119:34
Your precepts I get *u* . . . . Ps 119:104
His *u* is infinite. . . . . Ps 147:5
apply your heart to *u* . . . . . Prov 2:2
lean not on your own *u* . . . . Prov 3:5
u He established . . . . Prov 3:19
and go in the way of . . . . . . Prov 9:6
of the Holy One is *u* . . . . . . Prov 9:10
a man of *u* has wisdom. . . Prov 10:23
U is a wellspring . . . . Prov 16:22

u will find good . . . . Prov 19:8
and instruction and *u* . . . . . Prov 23:23
but the poor who has *u* . . . Prov 28:11
Spirit of wisdom and *u* . . . . . . Is 11:2
His *u* is unsearchable. . . . . . Is 40:28
the heaven by His *u* . . . . . . Jer 51:15
also still without *u* . . . . . . Matt 15:16
And He opened their *u* . . . Luke 24:45
also pray with the *u* . . . . . 1 Cor 14:15
five words with my *u* . . . . 1 Cor 14:19
and spiritual *u* . . . . Col 1:9
the Lord give you *u*. . . . . . . 2 Tim 2:7
Who is wise and *u*. . . . . . . James 3:13
and has given us an *u*. . . 1 John 5:20

UNDERSTANDS
all plain to him who *u* . . . . . Prov 8:9
is easy to him who *u*. . . . . . Prov 14:6
there is none who *u*. . . . . . . Rom 3:11

UNDERSTOOD
Then I *u* their end . . . . Ps 73:17
My heart has *u* great . . . . . Eccl 1:16
Have you not *u* from . . . . . . Is 40:21
u all these things. . . . . . . Matt 13:51
clearly seen, being *u*. . . . . Rom 1:20

UNDESIRABLE
gather together, O *u*. . . . . . Zeph 2:1

UNDIGNIFIED
I will be even more *u* . . . . 2 Sam 6:22

UNDISCERNING
u, untrustworthy . . . . Rom 1:31

UNDONE
"Woe is me, for I am *u* . . . . . . Is 6:5
leaving the others *u* . . . . . Matt 23:23

UNEDUCATED
that they were *u*. . . . . Acts 4:13

UNFAITHFUL
u will be uprooted . . . . Prov 2:22
way of the *u* is hard. . . . . . Prov 13:15

UNFAITHFULLY
back and acted *u*. . . . . Ps 78:57

UNFORGIVING
unloving, *u* . . . . Rom 1:31

UNFORMED
substance, being yet *u* . . . . Ps 139:16

UNFRUITFUL
and it becomes *u* . . . . Mark 4:19
that they may not be *u*. . . . Titus 3:14

UNGODLINESS
u made me afraid . . . . Ps 18:4
heaven against all *u* . . . . . Rom 1:18
He will turn away *u* . . . . . Rom 11:26

UNGODLY
delivered me to the *u*. . . . . Job 16:11
u shall not stand. . . . . Ps 1:5
of the *u* shall perish . . . . Ps 1:6
my cause against an *u* . . . . . Ps 43:1
u man digs up evil. . . . . . . Prov 16:27
who justifies the *u*. . . . . Rom 4:5
Christ died for the *u* . . . . . . Rom 5:6
and perdition of *u* men . . . . 2 Pet 3:7
convict all who are *u* . . . . . . Jude 15

UNHOLY
the holy and *u*. . . . . Ezek 22:26
for sinners, for the *u*. . . . . . 1 Tim 1:9

UNINFORMED
the place of the *u*. . . . . . . 1 Cor 14:16

UNINTENTIONALLY
kills his neighbor *u*. . . . . . . Deut 4:42

UNITE
U my heart to fear. . . . . Ps 86:11

UNITY
to dwell together in *u* . . . . . Ps 133:1
to keep the *u* of the . . . . Eph 4:3
we all come to the *u*. . . . . . . Eph 4:13

UNJUST
hope of the *u* perishes. . . . . Prov 11:7
u knows no shame. . . . . Zeph 3:5
commended the *u* . . . . Luke 16:8
extortioners, *u* . . . . Luke 18:11
of the just and the *u*. . . . . . Acts 24:15
u who inflicts wrath . . . . . . Rom 3:5
For God is not *u* . . . . Heb 6:10
the just for the *u* . . . . 1 Pet 3:18
let him be *u* still . . . . Rev 22:11

UNJUSTLY
long will you judge *u* . . . . . . Ps 82:2
he will deal *u*. . . . . Is 26:10

UNKNOWN
not stand before *u* . . . . . . Prov 22:29
To The *U* God . . . . Acts 17:23
And I was *u* by face to . . . . Gal 1:22

UNLEAVENED
the Feast of *U* Bread . . . . . . Ex 12:17
the Feast of *U* Bread. . . . . Mark 14:1
since you truly are *u* . . . . . 1 Cor 5:7

UNLOVING
untrustworthy, *u* . . . . Rom 1:31

UNMERCIFUL
unforgiving, *u*. . . . . Rom 1:31

UNPREPARED
with me and find you *u* . . . 2 Cor 9:4

UNPRESENTABLE
u parts have greater. . . . . 1 Cor 12:23

UNPROFITABLE
And cast the *u*. . . . . Matt 25:30
'We are *u* servants. . . . . . Luke 17:10
have together become *u* . . . Rom 3:12
who once was *u* to you . . . Philem 11
for that would be *u*. . . . . . Heb 13:17

UNPROFITABLENESS
of its weakness and *u* . . . . . Heb 7:18

UNPUNISHED
wicked will not go *u*. . . . . Prov 11:21
be rich will not go *u* . . . . . Prov 28:20

UNQUENCHABLE
up the chaff with *u*. . . . . . Matt 3:12
He will burn with *u*. . . . . . Luke 3:17

UNRESTRAINED
that the people were *u* . . . . Ex 32:25

UNRIGHTEOUS
u man his thoughts. . . . . Is 55:7
been faithful in the *u* . . . . Luke 16:11
u will not inherit the. . . . . 1 Cor 6:9

UNRIGHTEOUSNESS
and there is no *u*. . . . . Ps 92:15
builds his house by *u* . . . . . Jer 22:13
Him is true, and no *u*. . . . . John 7:18
all ungodliness and *u*. . . . . Rom 1:18
the truth, but obey *u*. . . . . . Rom 2:8
Is there a with God . . . . Rom 9:14
cleanse us from all *u*. . . . . 1 John 1:9
All *u* is sin . . . . 1 John 5:17

UNRULY
those who are *u* . . . . 1 Thess 5:14
It is an *u* evil. . . . . James 3:8

UNSEARCHABLE
heart of kings is *u* . . . . Prov 25:3
u are His judgments . . . . . Rom 11:33

UNSKILLED
only of milk is *u*. . . . . Heb 5:13

UNSPOTTED
to keep oneself *u* . . . . . . James 1:27

UNSTABLE
U as water . . . . Gen 49:4

UNSTOPPED
of the deaf shall be *u* . . . . Is 35:5

UNTAUGHT
which *u* and unstable. . . . . 2 Pet 3:16

UNTRUSTWORTHY
undiscerning, *u* . . . . Rom 1:31

UNWASHED
eat bread with *u* hands . . . . Mark 7:5

UNWISE
He is an *u* son . . . . Hos 13:13
Therefore do not be *u* . . . . . . Eph 5:17

UNWORTHY
and judge yourselves *u* . . . Acts 13:46
u manner will be . . . . 1 Cor 11:27

UPHOLD
u the evildoers. . . . . Job 8:20
U me according to . . . . Ps 119:116
My Servant whom I *u* . . . . Is 42:1
there was no one to *u* . . . . . . Is 63:5

UPHOLDING
u all things by the . . . . Heb 1:3

UPHOLDS
Your right hand *u* . . . . Ps 63:8
Lord *u* all who fall. . . . . . . Ps 145:14

UPPER
show you a large *u*. . . . . Mark 14:15
went up into the *u*. . . . . . . Acts 1:13
many lamps in the *u*. . . . . Acts 20:8

UPRIGHT
righteous and *u* is He . . . . . Deut 32:4
where were the *u*. . . . . Job 4:7
Good and *u* is the Lord. . . . . Ps 25:8
u shall have dominion . . . . . Ps 49:14
u will be blessed. . . . . Ps 112:2
u there arises light. . . . . Ps 112:4
is strength for the *u*. . . . . . Prov 10:29
u will guide them . . . . Prov 11:3
u will deliver them. . . . . Prov 11:6
u will flourish. . . . . Prov 14:11
u is His delight. . . . . Prov 15:8
of the *u* is a highway. . . . . Prov 15:19
that God made man *u* . . . . . Eccl 7:29
and there is no one *u* . . . . . . Mic 7:2
his soul is not *u* . . . . Hab 2:4

UPRIGHTNESS
to show man His *u* . . . . Job 33:23
me in the land of *u* . . . . . . Ps 143:10
princes for their *u* . . . . Prov 17:26
of the just is *u* . . . . Is 26:7
land of *u* he will deal. . . . . . Is 26:10

UPROOT
then I will *u*. . . . . 2 Chr 7:20
u you from the land . . . . Ps 52:5
u the wheat with. . . . . Matt 13:29

UR OF THE CHALDEANS
City of Abram's early life, Gen 11:28–
31; 15:7
Located in Mesopotamia by Stephen,
Acts 7:2, 4

URIAH
Hittite; one of David's warriors,
2 Sam 23:39
Husband of Bathsheba; condemned
to death by David, 2 Sam 11:1–27

URIJAH
High priest in Ahaz's time, 2 Kin
16:10–16

——— Prophet in Jeremiah's time, Jer
26:20–23

URIM
of judgment of *U* . . . . Ex 28:30
Thummim and Your *U* . . . . Deut 33:8

US
"God with *u*. . . . . Matt 1:23
who is not against *u* . . . . . Mark 9:40
If God is for *u* . . . . Rom 8:31
They went out from *u* . . . 1 John 2:19
of them were of *u*. . . . . . . 1 John 2:19

USE
who spitefully *u* you . . . . . Matt 5:44
leaving the natural *u* . . . . . Rom 1:27
u this world as not. . . . . . . 1 Cor 7:31
u liberty as an . . . . Gal 5:13
u a little wine . . . . 1 Tim 5:23
reason of *u* have their . . . . . Heb 5:14

USELESS
all of them are *u* . . . . Is 44:9
are unprofitable and *u*. . . . . Titus 3:9
one's religion is *u* . . . . James 1:26

USES
if one *u* it lawfully . . . . 1 Tim 1:8

USING
u no figure of speech. . . . . John 16:29
perish with the *u*. . . . . Col 2:22
u liberty as a. . . . . 1 Pet 2:16

USURY
Take no *u* or . . . . Lev 25:36
put out his money at *u*. . . . . Ps 15:5

UTTER
u pure knowledge . . . . Job 33:3
u dark sayings of old. . . . . . . Ps 78:2
let not your heart *u* . . . . Eccl 5:2
lawful for a man to *u* . . . . 2 Cor 12:4

UTTERANCE
the Spirit gave them *u* . . . . . Acts 2:4
u may be given to me . . . . . Eph 6:19

UTTERED
The deep *u* its voice . . . . . . Hab 3:10
which cannot be *u* . . . . Rom 8:26
the seven thunders *u*. . . . . . Rev 10:4

UTTERMOST
upon them to the *u*. . . . . 1 Thess 2:16
u those who come . . . . Heb 7:25

UTTERS
Day unto day *u* speech . . . . . Ps 19:2
u His voice from . . . . Amos 1:2
and the great man *u* . . . . Mic 7:3

UZZAH
Son of Abinadab, struck down for
touching the ark of the covenant,
2 Sam 6:3–11

UZZIAH
King of Judah, called Azariah, 2 Kin
14:21; 15:1–7
Reigns righteously, 2 Chr 26:1–15
Usurps priestly function; stricken
with leprosy, 2 Chr 26:16–21
Life of, written by Isaiah, 2 Chr
26:22, 23

VAGABOND
v you shall be on the . . . . . . Gen 4:12

VAIN
the people plot a *v* . . . . Ps 2:1
v life which he passes. . . . . . Eccl 6:12
'I have labored in *v* . . . . Is 49:4
you believed in *v* . . . . 1 Cor 15:2

VALIANT
Only be *v* for me. . . . . . . 1 Sam 18:17

They are not *v* for the . . . . . . Jer 9:3
v men swept away . . . . Jer 46:15

VALIANTLY
while Israel does *v* . . . . . Num 24:18
God we will do *v* . . . . Ps 60:12
of the Lord does *v*. . . . . . . Ps 118:15

VALLEY
I walk through the *v*. . . . . . . Ps 23:4
pass through the *V* . . . . Ps 84:6
the verdure of the *v*. . . . . . Song 6:11
v shall be exalted. . . . . Is 40:4
in the midst of the *v* . . . . . . Ezek 37:1
v shall be filled . . . . Luke 3:5

VALOR
a mighty man of *v* . . . . . 1 Sam 16:18

VALUE
does not know its *v* . . . . Job 28:13
of more *v* than they . . . . . . Matt 6:26
they counted up the *v* . . . . Acts 19:19

VALUED
It cannot be *v* in the . . . . . . Job 28:16

VANISH
when it is hot, they *v*. . . . . . Job 6:17
For the heavens will *v*. . . . . . Is 51:6
knowledge, it will *v* . . . . . 1 Cor 13:8
old is ready to *v* away . . . . . Heb 8:13

VANISHED
and He *v* from their . . . . . Luke 24:31

VANITY
of vanities, all is *v* . . . . Eccl 1:2

VAPOR
best state is but *v*. . . . . Ps 39:5
surely every man is *v*. . . . . . Ps 39:11
It is even a *v* that . . . . James 4:14

VARIATION
whom there is no *v* . . . . . . James 1:17

VASHTI
Queen of Ahasuerus, deposed and
divorced, Esth 1:9–22

VEGETABLES
and let them give us *v*. . . . . Dan 1:12
is weak eats only *v* . . . . Rom 14:2

VEHEMENT
of fire, a most *v*. . . . . Song 8:6

VEIL
he put a *v* on his face. . . . . . Ex 34:33
v of the temple was. . . . . . Matt 27:51
Moses, who put a *v* . . . . . . 2 Cor 3:13
Presence behind the *v*. . . . . . Heb 6:19

VENGEANCE
You shall not take *v*. . . . . . Lev 19:18
V is Mine. . . . . Deut 32:35
spare in the day of *v*. . . . . . Prov 6:34
God will come with *v*. . . . . . . Is 35:4
on the garments of *v* . . . . . . Is 59:17
let me see Your *v* . . . . Jer 11:20
are the days of *v* . . . . Luke 21:22
written, "*V* is Mine. . . . . . Rom 12:19
flaming fire taking *v* . . . . 2 Thess 1:8
suffering the *v*. . . . . Jude 7

VENOM
It becomes cobra *v*. . . . . . . Job 20:14

VESSEL
like a potter's *v* . . . . Ps 2:9
v that he made of clay . . . . . Jer 18:4
like a precious *v* . . . . Jer 25:34
been emptied from *v*. . . . . . Jer 48:11
for he is a chosen *v* . . . . . . Acts 9:15
lump to make one *v* . . . . . . Rom 9:21

VESSELS (cont.)
to possess his own *v* . . . . . 1 Thess 4:4
to the weaker *v* . . . . 1 Pet 3:7

VESSELS
longsuffering the *v* . . . . Rom 9:22
treasure in earthen *v* . . . . . 2 Cor 4:7
like the potter's *v* . . . . Rev 2:27

VEXED
grieved, and I was *v* . . . . Ps 73:21

VICE
as a cloak for *v* . . . . 1 Pet 2:16

VICTIM
and plucked the *v* . . . . Job 29:17

VICTORY
who gives us the *v* . . . . . 1 Cor 15:57
v that has overcome . . . . . 1 John 5:4

VIEW
"Go, *v* the land . . . . Josh 2:1

VIGILANT
in prayer, being *v* . . . . Col 4:2
Be sober, be *v* . . . . 1 Pet 5:8

VIGOR
nor his natural *v* . . . . Deut 34:7

VILE
sons made themselves *v* . . 1 Sam 3:13
"Behold, I am *v* . . . . Job 40:4
them up to *v* passions. . . . . Rom 1:26

VINDICATED
know that I shall be *v* . . . . . Job 13:18

VINDICATION
Let my *v* come from . . . . Ps 17:2

VINE
to the choice *v* . . . . Gen 49:11
their *v* is of the *v* . . . . Deut 32:32
You have brought a *v* . . . . . . Ps 80:8
planted you a noble *v* . . . . . Jer 2:21
grapes shall be on the *v* . . . . Jer 8:13
Israel empties his *v* . . . . Hos 10:1
shall sit under his *v* . . . . Mic 4:4
of this fruit of the *v* . . . . . Matt 26:29
"I am the true *v* . . . . John 15:1

VINEDRESSER
and My Father is the *v* . . . . John 15:1

VINEGAR
As *v* to the teeth and . . . . Prov 10:26
weather, and like *v* . . . . . . Prov 25:20

VINES
foxes that spoil the *v* . . . . Song 2:15
nor fruit be on the *v* . . . . . . Hab 3:17

VINEYARD
v which Your right . . . . Ps 80:15
laborers for his *v* . . . . Matt 20:1
Who plants a *v* and . . . . . . 1 Cor 9:7

VIOLENCE
was filled with *v* . . . . Gen 6:11
You save me from *v* . . . . . 2 Sam 22:3
the one who loves *v* . . . . Ps 11:5
such as breathe out *v* . . . . . Ps 27:12
from oppression and *v* . . . . . Ps 72:14
v covers the . . . . Prov 10:6
He had done no *v* . . . . Is 53:9
and *v* in the land . . . . Jer 51:46
cause the seat of *v* . . . . Amos 6:3
way and from the *v* . . . . Jon 3:8
rich men are full of *v* . . . . . Mic 6:12
For plundering and *v* . . . . . . Hab 1:3
one's garment with *v* . . . . . Mal 2:16
of heaven suffers *v* . . . . . . Matt 11:12

VIOLENT
me from the *v* man . . . . Ps 18:48
let evil hunt the *v* . . . . Ps 140:11

violence, and the *v* . . . . . . Matt 11:12
haters of God, *v* . . . . Rom 1:30
given to wine, not *v* . . . . . . 1 Tim 3:3

VIPER
and stings like a *v* . . . . . . Prov 23:32
will come forth a *v* . . . . Is 14:29
which is crushed a *v* . . . . Is 59:5

VIPERS
to them, "Brood of *v* . . . . . . Matt 3:7

VIRGIN
v shall conceive . . . . Is 7:14
O you oppressed *v* . . . . Is 23:12
v daughter of my . . . . Jer 14:17
The *v* of Israel has. . . . . Amos 5:2
"Behold, the *v* shall . . . . . . Matt 1:23
between a wife and a *v* . . . 1 Cor 7:34
you as a chaste *v* . . . . 2 Cor 11:2

VIRGINS
v who took their lamps. . . . Matt 25:1
women, for they are *v* . . . . . Rev 14:4

VIRTUE
if there is any *v* . . . . Phil 4:8
us by glory and *v* . . . . 2 Pet 1:3
to your faith *v* . . . . 2 Pet 1:5

VIRTUOUS
you are a *v* woman. . . . . . . Ruth 3:11
a *v* wife. . . . . Prov 31:10

VISAGE
v was marred more than . . . . Is 52:14

VISIBLE
that are on earth, *v* . . . . . . Col 1:16
of things which are *v* . . . . . Heb 11:3

VISION
chased away like a *v* . . . . . . Job 20:8
Then You spoke in a *v* . . . . . Ps 89:19
the Valley of V . . . . Is 22:1
a dream of a night *v* . . . . . . Is 29:7
her prophets find no *v* . . . . Lam 2:9
Daniel, had seen the *v* . . . . Dan 8:15
have night without *v* . . . . . . Mic 3:6
Write the *v* . . . . Hab 2:2
they had also seen a *v* . . . Luke 24:23
in a trance I saw a *v* . . . . . . Acts 11:5
v appeared to Paul in . . . . . Acts 16:9
to the heavenly *v* . . . . Acts 26:19

VISIONS
thoughts from the *v* . . . . Job 4:13
young men shall see *v* . . . . . Joel 2:28
I will come to *v* . . . . 2 Cor 12:1

VISIT
but God will surely *v* . . . . . Gen 50:24
in the day when I *v* . . . . . . Ex 32:34
v the earth and water . . . . . . Ps 65:9
Oh, *v* me with Your . . . . . . Ps 106:4
v orphans and widows . . . James 1:27

VISITATION
the time of your *v* . . . . . . Luke 19:44
God in the day of *v* . . . . . . 1 Pet 2:12

VISITED
he will not be *v* . . . . Prov 19:23
Israel, for He has *v* . . . . . . Luke 1:68
how God at the first *v* . . . . Acts 15:14

VISITING
v the iniquity of the fathers . . Ex 20:5

VISITOR
am a foreigner and a *v* . . . Gen 23:4

VITALITY
v was turned into the . . . . . . Ps 32:4

VOICE
"I heard Your *v* . . . . Gen 3:10
v is Jacob's *v* . . . . Gen 27:22

I should obey His *v* . . . . Ex 5:2
fire a still small *v* . . . . 1 Kin 19:12
and my flute to the *v* . . . . . Job 30:31
you thunder with a *v* . . . . . Job 40:9
He uttered His *v* . . . . Ps 46:6
He sends out His *v* . . . . Ps 68:33
have lifted up their *v*. . . . . . . Ps 93:3
if you will hear His *v* . . . . . . Ps 95:7
word, heeding the *v* . . . . . . Ps 103:20
for your *v* is sweet. . . . . . . Song 2:14
The *v* of one crying in . . . . . . Is 40:3
the *v* of weeping shall . . . . . Is 65:19
A *v* from the temple. . . . . Is 66:6
v was heard in Ramah . . . . Jer 31:15
who has a pleasant *v* . . . . Ezek 33:32
v was heard in Ramah . . . Matt 2:18
"The *v* of one crying . . . . . Matt 3:3
And suddenly a *v* . . . . Matt 3:17
will anyone hear His *v* . . . Matt 12:19
and suddenly a *v* . . . . Matt 17:5
for they know his *v* . . . . . John 10:4
v did not come because. . . John 12:30
the truth hears My *v* . . . . John 18:37
the *v* of an archangel . . . 1 Thess 4:16
whose *v* then shook the . . . Heb 12:26
glory when such a *v* . . . . . 2 Pet 1:17
If anyone hears My *v* . . . . . Rev 3:20

VOICES
shall lift up their *v* . . . . Is 52:8
And there were loud *v* . . . . Rev 11:15

VOID
they are a nation *v* . . . . . . Deut 32:28
the LORD had made a *v* . . . Judg 21:15
regarded Your law as *v* . . . Ps 119:126
Do we then make *v* . . . . . . Rom 3:31
heirs, faith is made *v* . . . . . Rom 4:14
make my boasting *v* . . . . . 1 Cor 9:15

VOLUME
in the *v* of the book . . . . . . Heb 10:7

VOLUNTEERS
Your people shall be *v* . . . . Ps 110:3

VOMIT
lest the land *v* . . . . Lev 18:28
man staggers in his *v* . . . . . . Is 19:14
returns to his own *v* . . . . . 2 Pet 2:22

VOW
Then Jacob made a *v* . . . . Gen 28:20
And Jephthah made a *v* . . Judg 11:30
he carried out his *v* . . . . . Judg 11:39
v shall be performed . . . . . . Ps 65:1
When you make a *v* . . . . . . Eccl 5:4
not to than to *v* . . . . Eccl 5:5
for he had taken a *v* . . . . . Acts 18:18
men who have taken a *v*. . . Acts 21:23

VOWS
you will pay your *v* . . . . . . Job 22:27
I will pay My *v* . . . . Ps 22:25
V made to You are. . . . . Ps 56:12
Make *v* to the LORD . . . . . . Ps 76:11
today I have paid my *v*. . . . Prov 7:14
to reconsider his *v* . . . . . Prov 20:25
And what, son of my *v* . . . Prov 31:2
to the LORD and took *v* . . . . Jon 1:16

WAGE
those who exploit *w* . . . . . . Mal 3:5
w the good warfare . . . . . . 1 Tim 1:18

WAGES
I will give you your *w*. . . . . . . Ex 2:9
the *w* of the wicked . . . . . Prov 10:16
w will be troubled. . . . . Is 19:10
and he who earns *w* . . . . . . Hag 1:6
to you, give me my *w* . . . . Zech 11:12

and give them their *w* .... Matt 20:8
be content with your *w* .... Luke 3:14
is worthy of his *w* .... Luke 10:7
him who works, the *w* ..... Rom 4:4
For the *w* of sin is .... Rom 6:23
is worthy of his *w* .... 1 Tim 5:18
Indeed the *w* of the .... James 5:4

WAIL
My heart shall *w*. .... Jer 48:36
"Son of man, *w* .... Ezek 32:18

WAILING
w is heard from Zion .... Jer 9:19
of heart and bitter *w* ..... Ezek 27:31
There will be *w* .... Matt 13:42

WAIT
hard service I will *w*. ...... Job 14:14
If I *w* for the grave .... Job 17:13
W on the LORD .... Ps 27:14
w patiently for Him........ Ps 37:7
my eyes fail while I *w* ...... Ps 69:3
These all *w* for You .... Ps 104:27
And I will *w* on the .... Is 8:17
the LORD will *w* on the .... Is 30:18
those who *w* on the .... Is 40:31
not be ashamed who *w* .... Is 49:23
w quietly for the .... Lam 3:26
I will *w* for the God........ Mic 7:7
be like men who *w* ...... Luke 12:36
see, we eagerly *w*........ Rom 8:25
w for one another. ...... 1 Cor 11:33
the Spirit eagerly *w*........ Gal 5:5
we also eagerly *w*........ Phil 3:20
and to *w* for His Son. ... 1 Thess 1:10
To those who eagerly *w* .... Heb 9:28

WAITED
and when I *w* for light .... Job 30:26
w patiently for the.......... Ps 40:1
we have *w* for Him .... Is 25:9
And the people *w* .... Luke 1:21
day you have *w* and ..... Acts 27:33
Divine longsuffering *w*.... 1 Pet 3:20

WAITING
w at the posts of my ...... Prov 8:34
w for the Consolation..... Luke 2:25
who himself was also *w*... Luke 23:51
ourselves, eagerly ...... Rom 8:23
from that time *w*......... Heb 10:13

WAITS
of the adulterer *w* .... Job 24:15
my soul silently *w*......... Ps 62:1
My soul *w* for the Lord .... Ps 130:6
for the one who *w* .... Is 64:4
the creation eagerly *w*.... Rom 8:19

WAKE
us, that whether we *w*... 1 Thess 5:10

WALK
w before Me and be .... Gen 17:1
in which they must *w*...... Ex 18:20
You shall *w* in all .... Deut 5:33
Yea, though I *w* .... Ps 23:4
W about Zion............. Ps 48:12
that Israel would *w* .... Ps 81:13
I will *w* within my......... Ps 101:2
I will *w* before the .... Ps 116:9
Though I *w* in the .... Ps 138:7
W prudently when you .... Eccl 5:1
w in the ways of your..... Eccl 11:9
come and let us *w* .... Is 2:5
"This is the way, *w*....... Is 30:21
be weary, they shall *w* .... Is 40:31
w in the light of your...... Is 50:11
people, who *w* in a way...... Is 65:2
commit adultery and *w* .... Jer 23:14
the righteous *w*.......... Hos 14:9

w humbly with your God.... Mic 6:8
take up your bed and *w* .... John 5:8
W while you have the.... John 12:35
so we also should *w* ...... Rom 6:4
Let us *w* properly......... Rom 13:13
For we *w* by faith........ 2 Cor 5:7
W in the Spirit............. Gal 5:16
that we should *w* .... Eph 2:10
And *w* in love........... Eph 5:2
W as children of light ...... Eph 5:8
attained, let us *w* .... Phil 3:16
note those who *w* so...... Phil 3:17
that you may *w* worthy ... Col 1:10
Jesus the Lord, so *w*........ Col 2:6
us how you ought to *w*. .. 1 Thess 4:1
w just as He .... 1 John 2:6
and they shall *w*.......... Rev 3:4

WALKED
Enoch *w* with God .... Gen 5:22
by His light I *w* .... Job 29:3
The people who *w* .... Is 9:2
He *w* with Me in peace ..... Mal 2:6
Jesus no longer *w*........ John 11:54
w according to the....... 2 Cor 10:2
in which you once *w* ...... Eph 2:2
to walk just as He *w* .... 1 John 2:6

WALKING
of the LORD God *w* .... Gen 3:8
see four men loose, *w* ..... Dan 3:25
before God, *w* in all .... Luke 1:6
they saw Jesus *w* .... John 6:19
And *w* in the fear of..... Acts 9:31
you are no longer *w* ..... Rom 14:15
not *w* in craftiness........ 2 Cor 4:2
of your children *w* .... 2 John 4

WALKS
the LORD your God *w* ..... Deut 23:14
is the man who *w*.......... Ps 1:1
He who *w* uprightly........ Ps 15:2
He who *w* with........... Prov 10:9
He who *w* with wise men . Prov 13:20
w blamelessly will be...... Prov 28:18
a wisely will be .... Prov 28:26
Whoever *w* the road........ Is 35:8
Who *w* in darkness and .... Is 50:10
it is not in man who *w*..... Jer 10:23
do good to him who *w*..... Mic 2:7
If anyone *w* in the day .... John 11:9
he who *w* in darkness.... John 12:35
adversary the devil *w*...... 1 Pet 5:8
is in darkness and *w* .... 1 John 2:11

WALL
then the *w* of the city ..... Josh 6:5
his face toward the *w*.... 2 Kin 20:2
like a leaning *w*........... Ps 62:3
and like a high *w*........ Prov 18:11
If she is a *w*.............. Song 8:9
We broke the *w*.......... Is 59:10
you, you whitewashed *w*... Acts 23:3
a window in the *w* ...... 2 Cor 11:33
down the middle *w*........ Eph 2:14
Now the *w* of the city .... Rev 21:14

WALLS
broken down, without *w*.. Prov 25:28
salvation for *w*............ Is 26:1
you shall call your *w* ...... Is 60:18
By faith the *w* of......... Heb 11:30

WANDER
and makes them *w* .... Job 12:24
ones cry to God, and *w* .... Job 38:41
Indeed, I would *w* .... Ps 55:7
Oh, let me not *w* .... Ps 119:10
they have loved to *w*...... Jer 14:10

WANDERED
w blind in the streets..... Lam 4:14

My sheep *w* through ...... Ezek 34:6
They *w* in deserts and..... Heb 11:38

WANDERERS
And they shall be *w* .... Hos 9:17

WANDERING
learn to be idle, *w* .... 1 Tim 5:13
w stars for whom is......... Jude 13

WANDERS
He *w* about for bread...... Job 15:23
Like a bird that *w* .... Prov 27:8
if anyone among you *w* .. James 5:19

WANT
I shall not *w* .... Ps 23:1
he began to be in *w*..... Luke 15:14

WANTING
balances, and found *w* .... Dan 5:27

WANTON
necks and *w* eyes .... Is 3:16
have begun to grow *w*.... 1 Tim 5:11

WAR
"There is a noise of *w* ...... Ex 32:17
the LORD for the *w* .... Num 32:20
my hands to make *w* .... 2 Sam 22:35
day of battle and *w*....... Job 38:23
w may rise against .... Ps 27:3
speak, they are for *w*...... Ps 120:7
trains my hands for *w* .... Ps 144:1
by wise counsel wage *w*.. Prov 20:18
will wage your own *w*.... Prov 24:6
shall they learn *w* .... Is 2:4
from the distress of *w*..... Is 21:15
we shall see no *w* .... Jer 42:14
same horn was making *w*.. Dan 7:21
men returned from *w*...... Mic 2:8
king, going to make *w* .... Luke 14:31
Who ever goes to *w*....... 1 Cor 9:7
for pleasure that *w*...... James 4:1
You fight and *w* .... James 4:2
fleshly lusts which *w*..... 1 Pet 2:11
w broke out in heaven..... Rev 12:7
He judges and makes *w* ... Rev 19:11

WARFARE
to her, that her *w*........... Is 40:2
w are not carnal......... 2 Cor 10:4
may wage the good *w*.... 1 Tim 1:18
w entangles............... 2 Tim 2:4

WARM
they will keep *w* .... Eccl 4:11
but no one is *w* .... Hag 1:6

WARMED
w himself at the fire..... Mark 14:54
Depart in peace, be *w*.... James 2:16

WARMING
when she saw Peter *w*.... Mark 14:67

WARMS
He even *w* himself and...... Is 44:16

WARN
w the wicked from his ..... Ezek 3:18
w everyone night........ Acts 20:31
beloved children I *w*...... 1 Cor 4:14
w those who are .... 1 Thess 5:14

WARNED
"The man solemnly *w* ..... Gen 43:3
them Your servant is *w* ..... Ps 19:11
Then, being divinely *w*.... Matt 2:12
Who *w* you to flee......... Matt 3:7
Noah, being divinely *w* .... Heb 11:7

WARNING
w every man and .... Col 1:28

WARPED
such a person is *w*....... Titus 3:11

WARRING
w against the law of . . . . . Rom 7:23

WARRIOR
He runs at me like a *w*. . . . Job 16:14

WARS
He makes *w* cease to . . . . Ps 46:9
And you will hear of *w*. . . . Matt 24:6
Where do *w* and fights . . . . James 4:1

WASH
w myself with snow. . . . . . . Job 9:30
I will *w* my hands in. . . . . . . Ps 26:6
W me thoroughly . . . . Ps 51:2
he shall *w* his feet in . . . . . Ps 58:10
"*W* yourselves. . . . . Is 1:16
O Jerusalem, *w* your. . . . . . . Jer 4:14
head and *w* your face. . . . Matt 6:17
For they do not *w* . . . . . . Matt 15:2
not eat unless they *w*. . . . . Mark 7:3
w His feet with her . . . . Luke 7:38
said to him, "Go, *w*. . . . . . . John 9:7
w the disciples' . . . . John 13:5
"You shall never *w* . . . . . . John 13:8
w one another's . . . . John 13:14
w away your sins . . . . Acts 22:16

WASHED
and *w* my hands in . . . . Ps 73:13
When the Lord has *w* . . . . Is 4:4
cut, nor were you *w*. . . . . . Ezek 16:4
w his hands before the . . . Matt 27:24
My feet, but she has *w* . . . . Luke 7:44
So when He had *w*. . . . . . John 13:12
w their stripes . . . . Acts 16:33
But you were *w*. . . . . 1 Cor 6:11
if she has *w* the . . . . 1 Tim 5:10
Him who loved us and *w*. . . . Rev 1:5
w their robes and made . . . . Rev 7:14

WASHING
cleanse her with the *w*. . . . . Eph 5:26
us, through the *w* . . . . Titus 3:5

WASHINGS
and drinks, various . . . . . . Heb 9:10

WASTE
who are left shall *w*. . . . . . Lev 26:39
the cities are laid *w* . . . . Is 6:11
empty and makes it *w*. . . . . . Is 24:1
w the mountains . . . . Is 42:15
"Why this *w* . . . . Matt 26:8

WASTED
The field is *w*. . . . . Joel 1:10
this fragrant oil *w* . . . . . . Mark 14:4
w his possessions . . . . Luke 15:13

WASTELAND
w shall be glad. . . . . Is 35:1

WASTING
w and destruction are . . . . Is 59:7
that this man was *w*. . . . . Luke 16:1

WATCH
w between you and me . . . Gen 31:49
keep the *w* of the Lord . . . 2 Chr 23:6
of them we set a *w*. . . . . Neh 4:9
my steps, but do not *w*. . . . Job 14:16
is past, and like a *w*. . . . . . . Ps 90:4
keep *w* over the door. . . . . . Ps 141:3
and all who *w* for. . . . . Is 29:20
W the road. . . . . Nah 2:1
Look among the nations
    and *w* . . . . Hab 1:5
W therefore, for you . . . . Matt 24:42
"What! Could you not *w*. . . Matt 26:40
W and pray, lest you. . . . Matt 26:41
W, stand fast in the . . . . 1 Cor 16:13
submissive, for they *w* . . . . Heb 13:17

WATCHED
in the days when God *w* . . . . Job 29:2
come, he would have *w* . . Matt 24:43

WATCHES
w the righteous . . . . Ps 37:32
She *w* over the ways of . . . Prov 31:27
Blessed is he who *w*. . . . . . Rev 16:15

WATCHFUL
But you be *w* in all . . . . 2 Tim 4:5
be serious and *w*. . . . . 1 Pet 4:7

WATCHING
who listens to me, *w* . . . . Prov 8:34
the flock, who were *w* . . . . Zech 11:11
he comes, will find *w*. . . . . Luke 12:37

WATCHMAN
guards the city, the *w* . . . . . Ps 127:1
W, what of the night . . . . . . Is 21:11
I have made you a *w*. . . . . Ezek 3:17
I have made you a *w* . . . . Ezek 33:7
the day of your *w* . . . . Mic 7:4

WATCHMEN
w who go about the . . . . . . Song 3:3
w shall lift up their . . . . Is 52:8
His *w* are blind. . . . . Is 56:10
I have set *w* on your. . . . . . . Is 62:6
Also, I set *w* over you . . . . . Jer 6:17
strong, set up the *w* . . . . . Jer 51:12

WATER
Eden to *w* the garden. . . . . Gen 2:10
Unstable as *w*. . . . . Gen 49:4
and *w* will come out. . . . . . . Ex 17:6
your bread and your *w*. . . . Ex 23:25
w for them out of the rock. Num 20:8
of affliction and *w* . . . . . 1 Kin 22:27
w wears away stones . . . . . Job 14:19
drinks iniquity like *w*. . . . . Job 15:16
not given the weary *w*. . . . . Job 22:7
He binds up the *w*. . . . . Job 26:8
I am poured out like *w* . . . . Ps 22:14
where there is no *w*. . . . . Ps 63:1
they have shed like *w* . . . . . . Ps 79:3
Drink *w* from your own. . . . Prov 5:15
"Stolen *w* is sweet . . . . . . Prov 9:17
the whole supply of *w* . . . . . . Is 3:1
and needy seek *w* . . . . Is 41:17
For I will pour *w*. . . . . Is 44:3
silence and given us *w*. . . . . Jer 8:14
eye overflows with *w*. . . . . Lam 1:16
will be as weak as *w* . . . . . Ezek 7:17
w the land from the . . . . . Ezek 32:6
w came up to my ankles. . . Ezek 47:3
justice run down like *w*. . . Amos 5:24
walked on the *w* . . . . Matt 14:29
you gave Me no *w* . . . . Luke 7:44
there was much *w*. . . . . John 3:23
given you living *w*. . . . . John 4:10
rivers of living *w*. . . . . John 7:38
blood and *w* came out . . . John 19:34
"Can anyone forbid *w* . . . Acts 10:47
with the washing of *w* . . . . Eph 5:26
can yield both salt *w*. . . . . James 3:12
were saved through *w* . . . . 1 Pet 3:20
is He who came by *w*. . . . . 1 John 5:6
the Spirit, the *w* . . . . 1 John 5:8
are clouds without *w* . . . . . . Jude 12
its *w* was dried up . . . . Rev 16:12
let him take the *w*. . . . . . . Rev 22:17

WATERED
w the whole face . . . . Gen 2:6
that it was well *w* . . . . Gen 13:10
I planted, Apollos *w* . . . . . . 1 Cor 3:6

WATERS
and struck the *w*. . . . . Ex 7:20
If He withholds the *w*. . . . . Job 12:15

me beside the still *w* . . . . Ps 23:2
though its *w* roar and. . . . . . . Ps 46:3
w have come up to my . . . . . Ps 69:1
then the *w* would have . . . . Ps 124:4
rich, and he who *w* . . . . . . Prov 11:25
Who has bound the *w*. . . . . Prov 30:4
your bread upon the *w*. . . . . Eccl 11:1
a well of living *w* . . . . Song 4:15
w cannot quench love . . . . Song 8:7
of the Lord as the *w* . . . . Is 11:9
w will fail from the. . . . . Is 19:5
because I give *w*. . . . . Is 43:20
have sworn that the *w*. . . . . . Is 54:9
thirsts, come to the *w*. . . . . . Is 55:1
fountain of living *w* . . . . Jer 2:13
w flowed over my head. . . . Lam 3:54
the sound of many *w* . . . . Ezek 43:2
w surrounded me . . . . Jon 2:5
shall be that living *w* . . . . . Zech 14:8
often, in perils of *w* . . . . . 2 Cor 11:26
living fountains of *w*. . . . . . Rev 7:17
w became wormwood. . . . . Rev 8:11

WAVE
Its fruit shall *w*. . . . . Ps 72:16

WAVER
He did not *w* at the. . . . . . Rom 4:20

WAVERING
of our hope without *w* . . . . Heb 10:23

WAVES
and here your proud *w* . . . . Job 38:11
all Your *w* and billows. . . . . . Ps 42:7
the noise of their *w* . . . . Ps 65:7
the multitude of its *w*. . . . . Jer 51:42
was covered with the *w*. . . . Matt 8:24
sea, tossed by the *w*. . . . . . Matt 14:24
raging *w* of the sea. . . . . Jude 13

WAX
My heart is like *w* . . . . Ps 22:14
w melts before the. . . . . Ps 68:2
mountains melt like *w* . . . . . Ps 97:5

WAY
and show them the *w*. . . . . Ex 18:20
day I am going the *w*. . . . . Josh 23:14
and the right *w*. . . . . 1 Sam 12:23
As for God, His *w* . . . . . . 2 Sam 22:31
to a man whose *w*. . . . . Job 3:23
But He knows the *w*. . . . . . Job 23:10
"Where is the *w* . . . . Job 38:19
the Lord knows the *w* . . . . . . Ps 1:6
you perish in the *w* . . . . Ps 2:12
Teach me Your *w* . . . . Ps 27:11
This is the *w* of those. . . . . . Ps 49:13
w may be known on . . . . Ps 67:2
Your *w* was in the sea . . . . . Ps 77:19
where there is no *w* . . . . . . Ps 107:40
I have chosen the *w* . . . . . Ps 119:30
I hate every false *w* . . . . . Ps 119:104
in the *w* everlasting. . . . . . Ps 139:24
and preserves the *w* . . . . . . Prov 2:8
The *w* of the wicked is. . . . . Prov 4:19
instruction are the *w* . . . . . Prov 6:23
w that seems right . . . . . . Prov 14:12
not know what is the *w* . . . . Eccl 11:5
of terrors in the *w* . . . . Eccl 12:5
The *w* of the just is. . . . . Is 26:7
"This is the *w* . . . . Is 30:21
Lord, who makes a *w*. . . . . . Is 43:16
wicked forsake his *w* . . . . . . Is 55:7
O Lord, I know the *w*. . . . . Jer 10:23
one heart and one *w* . . . . . Jer 32:39
Israel, is it not My *w* . . . . Ezek 18:25
w which is not fair. . . . . . Ezek 33:17
and pervert the *w* . . . . Amos 2:7
the Lord has His *w* . . . . Nah 1:3

he will prepare the *w* . . . . . . Mal 3:1
and broad is the *w* . . . . . . Matt 7:13
and difficult is the *w* . . . . . Matt 7:14
will prepare Your *w* . . . . . Matt 11:10
and teach the *w*. . . . . Matt 22:16
and the *w* you know . . . . . . John 14:4
to him, "I am the *w* . . . . . . John 14:6
proclaim to us the *w* . . . . . Acts 16:17
explained to him the *w* . . . Acts 18:26
you a more excellent *w* . . 1 Cor 12:31
w which He consecrated. . . Heb 10:20
forsaken the right *w* . . . . . . 2 Pet 2:15
to have known the *w* . . . . . 2 Pet 2:21
have gone in the *w* . . . . Jude 11

WAYS
for all His *w* are . . . . Deut 32:4
they do not know its *w* . . . . Job 24:13
is the first of the *w* . . . . . . Job 40:19
Show me Your *w* . . . . Ps 25:4
transgressors Your *w* . . . . . Ps 51:13
would walk in My *w* . . . . . . Ps 81:13
w were directed . . . . Ps 119:5
I thought about my *w* . . . . . Ps 119:59
righteous in all His *w* . . Ps 145:17
For the *w* of man are. . . . . Prov 5:21
w please the LORD . . . . Prov 16:7
He will teach us His *w* . . . . . . Is 2:3
nor are your *w* . . . . Is 55:8
"Stand in the *w* . . . . Jer 6:16
"Amend your *w* . . . . Jer 7:3
and examine our *w*. . . . . . Lam 3:40
and owns all your *w* . . . . . Dan 5:23
w are everlasting . . . . Hab 3:6
misery are in their *w* . . . . . Rom 3:16
judgments and His *w*. . . . Rom 11:33
unstable in all his *w* . . . . James 1:8
their destructive *w* . . . . . . 2 Pet 2:2
and true are Your *w* . . . . . Rev 15:3

WEAK
then I shall become *w*. . . . Judg 16:7
And I am *w* today . . . . . . 2 Sam 3:39
me, O LORD, for I am *w*. . . . . . Ps 6:2
gives power to the *w*. . . . . . Is 40:29
knee will be as *w* . . . . Ezek 7:17
let the *w* say . . . . Joel 3:10
not your hands be *w*. . . . . Zeph 3:16
but the flesh is *w*. . . . . . . Matt 26:41
And not being *w* . . . . Rom 4:19
Receive one who is *w*. . . . . Rom 14:1
God has chosen the *w* . . . . 1 Cor 1:27
We are *w*, but you are . . . 1 Cor 4:10
to the *w* I became as *w* . . 1 Cor 9:22
this reason many are *w* . . 1 Cor 11:30
For when I am *w* . . . . 2 Cor 12:10

WEAKENED
w my strength in the . . . . . Ps 102:23
the ground, you who *w* . . . . Is 14:12

WEAKENS
w the hands of the men . . . . Jer 38:4

WEAKER
house of Saul grew *w* . . . . 2 Sam 3:1
the wife, as to the *w* . . . . . 1 Pet 3:7

WEAKNESS
than men, and the *w* . . . . 1 Cor 1:25
I was with you in *w* . . . . . . 1 Cor 2:3
It is sown in *w* . . . . 1 Cor 15:43
is also subject to *w*. . . . . . . Heb 5:2
w were made strong . . . . . Heb 11:34

WEAKNESSES
also helps in our *w* . . . . . . Rom 8:26
sympathize with our *w*. . . . Heb 4:15

WEALTH
have gained me this *w* . . . . Deut 8:17
a man of great *w* . . . . Ruth 2:1

not asked riches or *w*. . . . 2 Chr 1:11
who trust in their *w*. . . . . . . Ps 49:6
w is his strong city . . . . . Prov 10:15
W gained by dishonesty . . Prov 13:11
W makes many friends . . . . Prov 19:4
may bring to you the *w* . . . . . Is 60:11

WEALTHY
w nation that dwells. . . . . . Jer 49:31
rich, have become *w* . . . . . . Rev 3:17

WEANED
w child shall put his. . . . . . . Is 11:8
Those just *w* from milk . . . . . Is 28:9

WEAPON
w formed against you . . . . . Is 54:17
with a deadly *w*. . . . . Ezek 9:1

WEAPONS
is better than *w*. . . . . Eccl 9:18
the LORD and His *w* . . . . . . Is 13:5
For the *w* of our . . . . 2 Cor 10:4

WEAR
but the just will *w* . . . . Job 27:17
'What shall we *w* . . . . Matt 6:31

WEARIED
you have *w* Me with. . . . . . Is 43:24
You are *w* in the . . . . Is 57:10
and they have *w* . . . . Jer 12:5
You have *w* the LORD . . . . . Mal 2:17
therefore, being *w*. . . . . . . John 4:6

WEARINESS
say, 'Oh, what a *w* . . . . . . Mal 1:13
in *w* and toil. . . . . 2 Cor 11:27

WEARISOME
and much study is *w*. . . . . Eccl 12:12

WEARY
to Isaac, "I am *w* . . . . Gen 27:46
lest he become *w* . . . . Prov 25:17
As cold water to a *w* . . . . Prov 25:25
No one will be *w* . . . . Is 5:27
you may cause the *w*. . . . . . Is 28:12
shall run and not be *w*. . . . . Is 40:31
to him who is *w*. . . . . Is 50:4
I am *w* of holding it . . . . . . Jer 6:11
w themselves to commit . . . . Jer 9:5
I was *w* of holding it . . . . Jer 20:9
continual coming she *w* . . . Luke 18:5
And let us not grow *w* . . . . . Gal 6:9
do not grow *w* in. . . . . . 2 Thess 3:13
lest you become *w* . . . . Heb 12:3

WEATHER
a garment in cold *w* . . . . Prov 25:20
'It will be fair *w*. . . . . Matt 16:2

WEDDING
were invited to the *w* . . . . Matt 22:3
Come to the *w*. . . . . Matt 22:4
find, invite to the *w* . . . . . Matt 22:9
in with him to the *w*. . . . Matt 25:10
day there was a *w*. . . . . John 2:1

WEEK
with many for one *w*. . . . . . Dan 9:27
the first day of the *w*. . . . . Matt 28:1
the first day of the *w* . . . . . Acts 20:7
the first day of the *w* . . . . . 1 Cor 16:2

WEEKS
w are determined. . . . . Dan 9:24
w Messiah shall be cut . . . . Dan 9:26

WEEP
"Hannah, why do you *w* . . 1 Sam 1:8
a time to *w* . . . . Eccl 3:4
you shall *w* no more . . . . . . Is 30:19
it, my soul will *w* . . . . Jer 13:17
W not for the dead. . . . . . . Jer 22:10
to the LORD, *w* between . . . . Joel 2:17

this commotion and *w*. . . . Mark 5:39
Blessed are you who *w* . . . . Luke 6:21
to her, "Do not *w* . . . . Luke 7:13
and you did not *w* . . . . Luke 7:32
of Jerusalem, do not *w* . . . Luke 23:28
to the tomb to *w* there. . . . John 11:31
w with those who *w*. . . . . Rom 12:15
those who *w* as though . . . 1 Cor 7:30

WEEPING
of Israel, who were *w* . . . . Num 25:6
w as they went up. . . . . . 2 Sam 15:30
the noise of the *w*. . . . . . . Ezra 3:13
face is flushed from *w* . . . . Job 16:16
the voice of my *w* . . . . Ps 6:8
my drink with *w* . . . . Ps 102:9
of hosts called for *w* . . . . . . Is 22:12
w shall no longer . . . . Is 65:19
They shall come with *w* . . . . Jer 31:9
w they shall come . . . . Jer 50:4
were sitting there *w* . . . . . Ezek 8:14
with fasting, with *w* . . . . . . Joel 2:12
with tears, with *w*. . . . . . . Mal 2:13
There will be *w* . . . . Matt 8:12
outside by the tomb *w*. . . . John 20:11
"Woman, why are you *w* . . John 20:13
"What do you mean by *w* . Acts 21:13

WEIGH
You *w* out the violence . . . . . Ps 58:2
O Most Upright, You *w* . . . . . Is 26:7

WEIGHED
nor can silver be *w* . . . . . . Job 28:15
W the mountains . . . . Is 40:12
You have been *w* . . . . Dan 5:27
lest your hearts be *w*. . . . . Luke 21:34

WEIGHS
eyes, but the LORD *w* . . . . . Prov 16:2
Where is he who *w*. . . . . Is 33:18

WEIGHT
a perfect and just *w* . . . . . Deut 25:15
a just *w* is His delight . . . . Prov 11:1
and eternal *w* of glory. . . . 2 Cor 4:17
us lay aside every *w*. . . . . . Heb 12:1

WEIGHTIER
have neglected the *w* . . . . Matt 23:23

WELFARE
does not seek the *w* . . . . . . Jer 38:4

WELL
If you do *w*. . . . . Gen 4:7
that it may go *w* . . . . Deut 4:40
you when you do *w*. . . . . . . Ps 49:18
daughters have done *w*. . . Prov 31:29
know that it will be *w* . . . . Eccl 8:12
wheel broken at the *w* . . . . Eccl 12:6
that it shall be *w* . . . . Is 3:10
"Those who are *w* . . . . Matt 9:12
said to him, 'W done . . . . Matt 25:21
faith has made you *w* . . . . Mark 5:34
Now Jacob's *w* was . . . . John 4:6
the elders who rule *w* . . . . 1 Tim 5:17

WELL-BEING
them, and their *w* . . . . Ps 69:22
each one the other's *w*. . . 1 Cor 10:24

WELLS
draw water from the *w*. . . . . Is 12:3
These are *w* without . . . . . 2 Pet 2:17

WENT
They *w* out from us . . . . . 1 John 2:19

WEPT
and the man of God *w*. . . 2 Kin 8:11
for the people *w*. . . . . Ezra 10:1
that I sat down and *w*. . . . . Neh 1:4
Have I not *w* for him. . . . . Job 30:25
down, yea, we *w* . . . . Ps 137:1

out and *w* bitterly . . . . Matt 26:75
He saw the city and *w*. . . . Luke 19:41
Jesus *w*. . . . . John 11:35
So I *w* much . . . . Rev 5:4

WET
They are *w* with the . . . . . . Job 24:8
his body was *w* with . . . . . . Dan 4:33

WHEAT
with the finest of *w* . . . . Ps 81:16
we may trade *w*. . . . . Amos 8:5
even sell the bad *w* . . . . . . Amos 8:6
but gather the *w* . . . . Matt 13:30
w falls into the. . . . . John 12:24
perhaps *w* or some. . . . . . 1 Cor 15:37
oil, fine flour and *w*. . . . . . Rev 18:13

WHEEL
brings the threshing *w* . . . Prov 20:26
the fountain, or the *w* . . . . . Eccl 12:6
in the middle of a *w* . . . . . Ezek 1:16

WHEELS
off their chariot *w*. . . . . . . Ex 14:25
the rumbling of his *w*. . . . . . Jer 47:3
appearance of the *w* . . . . . Ezek 1:16
noise of rattling *w* . . . . Nah 3:2

WHERE
not knowing *w* he was . . . . Heb 11:8

WHIP
A *w* for the horse. . . . . Prov 26:3
The noise of a *w* . . . . Nah 3:2

WHIRLWIND
Elijah went up by a *w* . . . . 2 Kin 2:11
Job out of the *w* . . . . Job 38:1
them away as with a *w*. . . . . Ps 58:9
w will take them away. . . . . Is 40:24
w shall scatter them . . . . Is 41:16
w shall be raised. . . . . Jer 25:32
has His way in the *w*. . . . . . Nah 1:3

WHISPER
my ear received a *w*. . . . . . . Job 4:12
and wizards, who *w*. . . . . Is 8:19

WHISPERER
w separates the best. . . . . Prov 16:28

WHISPERERS
they are *w* . . . . Rom 1:29

WHISPERINGS
backbitings, *w* . . . . 2 Cor 12:20

WHITE
My beloved is *w* . . . . Song 5:10
and make them *w* . . . . . . Dan 11:35
be purified, made *w*. . . . . . Dan 12:10
for they are already *w* . . . . John 4:35
walk with Me in *w*. . . . . Rev 3:4
clothed in *w* garments . . . . . Rev 3:5
behold, a *w* horse . . . . Rev 6:2
and made them *w* . . . . Rev 7:14
Then I saw a great *w* . . . . . Rev 20:11

WHOLE
w body were an eye . . . . . 1 Cor 12:17

WHOLESOME
w tongue is a tree . . . . Prov 15:4
not consent to *w* words . . . . 1 Tim 6:3

WHOLLY
w followed the Lord . . . . . . Deut 1:36
I will not leave you *w*. . . . . . Jer 46:28

WICKED
w shall be silent . . . . 1 Sam 2:9
Should you help the *w*. . . . 2 Chr 19:2
Why do the *w* live and . . . . . Job 21:7
w are reserved for the . . . . . Job 21:30
to nobles, 'You are *w*. . . . . Job 34:18
with the *w* every day. . . . . . . Ps 7:11

w is snared in the . . . . Ps 9:16
w shall be turned. . . . . Ps 9:17
do the *w* renounce God . . . . . Ps 10:13
w bend their bow. . . . . Ps 11:2
w He will rain coals. . . . . Ps 11:6
Evil shall slay the *w*. . . . . . . Ps 34:21
w shall be no more . . . . Ps 37:10
The *w* watches the. . . . . Ps 37:32
how long will the *w*. . . . . Ps 94:3
and the *w* be no more . . . . Ps 104:35
is far from the *w*. . . . . Ps 119:155
if there is any *w*. . . . . Ps 139:24
w will be cut off from . . . . . Prov 2:22
w will fall by his own . . . . . Prov 11:5
Lord is far from the *w* . . . . Prov 15:29
w flee when no one . . . . Prov 28:1
Do not be overly *w* . . . . Eccl 7:17
not be well with the *w* . . . . Eccl 8:13
w forsake his way. . . . . Is 55:7
But the *w* are like the. . . . . . Is 57:20
and desperately *w*. . . . . Jer 17:9
w shall do wickedly . . . . . Dan 12:10
at all acquit the *w*. . . . . Nah 1:3
w one does not touch. . . . 1 John 5:18
the sway of the *w*. . . . . . . 1 John 5:19

WICKEDLY
Will you speak *w*. . . . . Job 13:7
God will never do *w*. . . . . . . Job 34:12
Those who do *w* . . . . Dan 11:32
yes, all who do *w*. . . . . Mal 4:1

WICKEDNESS
Lord saw that the *w*. . . . . . Gen 6:5
can I do this great *w* . . . . . . Gen 39:9
'W proceeds from the . . . 1 Sam 24:13
w oppress them. . . . . 2 Sam 7:10
Is not your *w* great . . . . Job 22:5
Oh, let the *w* of the. . . . . Ps 7:9
alive into hell, for *w* . . . . . . Ps 55:15
in the tents of *w*. . . . . Ps 84:10
I will not know *w*. . . . . Ps 101:4
eat the bread of *w* . . . . Prov 4:17
w is an abomination. . . . . . Prov 8:7
w will not deliver . . . . Eccl 8:8
w burns as the . . . . Is 9:18
have trusted in your *w*. . . . . Is 47:10
w will correct you . . . . Jer 2:19
wells up with her *w* . . . . Jer 6:7
man repented of his *w*. . . . . . Jer 8:6
not turn from his *w*. . . . . . . Ezek 3:19
You have plowed *w*. . . . . . Hos 10:13
and cannot look on *w* . . . . . Hab 1:13
for those who do *w* . . . . Mal 3:15
is full of greed and *w* . . . . Luke 11:39
sexual immorality, *w* . . . . . Rom 1:29
spiritual hosts of *w*. . . . . Eph 6:12
and overflow of *w*. . . . . . . James 1:21

WIDE
shall open your hand *w* . . . Deut 15:8
opened their mouth *w*. . . . . Job 29:23
w his lips shall have . . . . . . Prov 13:3
will build myself a *w* . . . . . . Jer 22:14
w is the gate and. . . . . Matt 7:13
to you, our heart is *w* . . . . . 2 Cor 6:11

WIDOW
does no good for the *w* . . . Job 24:21
They slay the *w*. . . . . Ps 94:6
and his wife a *w* . . . . Ps 109:9
the fatherless and *w* . . . . . Ps 146:9
plead for the *w*. . . . . Is 1:17
How like a *w* is she . . . . . . Lam 1:1
Then one poor *w* . . . . Mark 12:42
w has children or . . . . 1 Tim 5:4
Do not let a *w* under. . . . . . 1 Tim 5:9

WIDOW'S
and I caused the *w* . . . . . . Job 29:13

WIDOWS
a defender of *w* . . . . Ps 68:5
and let your *w* trust . . . . . . Jer 49:11
w were neglected . . . . Acts 6:1
that the younger *w* . . . . . 1 Tim 5:14
to visit orphans and *w* . . . James 1:27

WIFE
and be joined to his *w* . . . . Gen 2:24
an excellent *w* is the . . . . . Prov 12:4
w finds a good thing . . . . Prov 18:22
but a prudent *w*. . . . . Prov 19:14
w whom you love all . . . . . . Eccl 9:9
like a youthful *w* . . . . Is 54:6
"Go, take yourself a *w* . . . . . Hos 1:2
for a *w* he tended sheep . . . Hos 12:12
with the *w* of his. . . . . Mal 2:15
"Whoever divorces his *w* . Mark 10:11
'I have married a *w* . . . . . Luke 14:20
Remember Lot's *w*. . . . . . Luke 17:32
all seven had her as *w* . . . Luke 20:33
so love his own *w* . . . . Eph 5:33
the husband of one *w*. . . . . . Titus 1:6
giving honor to the *w*. . . . . 1 Pet 3:7
bride, the Lamb's *w*. . . . . . . Rev 21:9

WILD
locusts and *w* honey. . . . . . Matt 3:4
olive tree which is *w* . . . . . Rom 11:24

WILDERNESS
wasteland, a howling *w* . Deut 32:10
w yields food for them. . . . . Job 24:5
coming out of the *w*. . . . . . Song 3:6
made the world as a *w*. . . . . Is 14:17
I will make the *w* . . . . Is 41:18
Let the *w* and its. . . . . Is 42:11
Have I been a *w* . . . . Jer 2:31
of one crying in the *w* . . . . Matt 3:3
the serpent in the *w* . . . . . John 3:14
congregation in the *w* . . . . Acts 7:38

WILES
to stand against the *w* . . . . Eph 6:11

WILL
w be done on earth as . . . . Matt 6:10
but he who does the *w* . . . . Matt 7:21
of the two did the *w* . . . . . Matt 21:31
nevertheless not My *w* . . . Luke 22:42
flesh, nor of the *w*. . . . . John 1:13
I do not seek My own *w* . . . John 5:30
not to do My own *w* . . . . . . John 6:38
This is the *w* . . . . John 6:39
wills to do His *w* . . . . John 7:17
w is present with me . . . . . . Rom 7:18
and perfect *w* of God. . . . . . Rom 12:2
works in you both to *w*. . . . . Phil 2:13
the knowledge of His *w*. . . . . Col 1:9
according to His own *w*. . . . . Heb 2:4
come to do Your *w* . . . . Heb 10:9
good work to do His *w* . . . . Heb 13:21
but he who does the *w*. . . 1 John 2:17

WILLFULLY
For if we sin *w*. . . . . Heb 10:26
For this they *w* . . . . 2 Pet 3:5

WILLING
is of a *w* heart. . . . . Ex 35:5
If you are *w* and. . . . . Is 1:19
him, saying, "I am *w* . . . . . . Matt 8:3
The spirit indeed is *w* . . . . Matt 26:41
The spirit indeed is *w*. . . . Mark 14:38
if there is first a *w* . . . . . . 2 Cor 8:12
w that any should . . . . 2 Pet 3:9

WILLINGLY
to futility, not *w*. . . . . Rom 8:20
For if I do this *w*. . . . . 1 Cor 9:17
by compulsion but *w* . . . . . 1 Pet 5:2

WILLOWS
our harps upon the *w* . . . . . Ps 137:2

WILLS
to whom the Son *w* . . . . . Matt 11:27
it is not of him who *w* . . . . Rom 9:16
say, "If the Lord *w* . . . . . James 4:15

WIN
w one proselyte . . . . Matt 23:15
to all, that I might *w* . . . . 1 Cor 9:19

WIND
LORD was not in the *w* . . . 1 Kin 19:11
w carries him away . . . . Job 27:21
the chaff which the *w* . . . . . . Ps 1:4
He causes His *w* . . . . Ps 147:18
will inherit the *w* . . . . Prov 11:29
He who observes the *w* . . . . Eccl 11:4
is the way of the *w* . . . . . . Eccl 11:5
Awake, O north *w* . . . . Song 4:16
the prophets become *w* . . . . Jer 5:13
He brings the *w* . . . . Jer 51:16
Ephraim feeds on the *w* . . . Hos 12:1
and creates the *w* . . . . Amos 4:13
A reed shaken by the *w* . . . Matt 11:7
And the *w* ceased and . . . . Mark 4:39
and rebuked the *w* . . . . . . Luke 8:24
The *w* blows where . . . . John 3:8
of a rushing mighty *w* . . . . . Acts 2:2
about with every *w* . . . . Eph 4:14

WINDOWS
looking through the *w* . . . . Song 2:9
has come through our *w* . . . Jer 9:21
upper room, with his *w* . . . Dan 6:10
not open for you the *w* . . . . Mal 3:10

WINDS
from the four *w* . . . . Ezek 37:9
be, that even the *w* . . . . . Matt 8:27
holding the four *w* . . . . Rev 7:1

WINDSTORM
And a great *w* arose . . . . . . Mark 4:37

WINE
Noah awoke from his *w* . . . Gen 9:24
w that makes glad . . . . Ps 104:15
W is a mocker . . . . Prov 20:1
Do not look on the *w* . . . . Prov 23:31
love is better than *w* . . . . . Song 1:2
w inflames them. . . . . Is 5:11
Yes, come, buy *w* . . . . Is 55:1
they gave Him sour *w* . . . . Matt 27:34
when they ran out of *w* . . . . John 2:3
do not be drunk with *w* . . . . Eph 5:18
but use a little *w* . . . . 1 Tim 5:23
not given to much *w* . . . . . . Titus 2:3
her the cup of the *w* . . . . . Rev 16:19

WINEBIBBERS
Do not mix with *w* . . . . . Prov 23:20

WINEPRESS
"I have trodden the *w* . . . . . . Is 63:3
for the *w* is full . . . . Joel 3:13
into the great *w* . . . . Rev 14:19
Himself treads the *w* . . . . . Rev 19:15

WINESKIN
I have become like a *w* . . . Ps 119:83

WINESKINS
new wine into old *w* . . . . . Matt 9:17

WING
One *w* of the cherub . . . . 1 Kin 6:24
so I spread My *w* . . . . Ezek 16:8

WINGS
w you have come . . . . Ruth 2:12
He flew upon the *w* . . . . . . Ps 18:10
the shadow of Your *w* . . . . . Ps 36:7
If I take the *w* . . . . Ps 139:9

WINNOW
You shall *w* them . . . . Is 41:16

WINS
w souls is wise . . . . Prov 11:30

WINTER
have made summer and *w* . . Ps 74:17
For lo, the *w* is past . . . . . Song 2:11
w it shall occur . . . . Zech 14:8
flight may not be in *w* . . . Matt 24:20

WIPE
the Lord GOD will *w* . . . . . . Is 25:8
w them with the towel . . . John 13:5
w away every tear . . . . Rev 21:4

WISDOM
for this is your *w* . . . . Deut 4:6
w will die with you . . . . . . Job 12:2
will make me to know *w* . . . Ps 51:6
is the man who finds *w* . . . Prov 3:13
Get *w*! Get understanding! . . Prov 4:5
W is the principal . . . . Prov 4:7
is the beginning of *w* . . . . Prov 9:10
to get *w* than gold . . . . . . Prov 16:16
w loves his own soul . . . . . Prov 19:8
W is too lofty for a . . . . . . Prov 24:7
w is much grief . . . . Eccl 1:18
W is better than . . . . Eccl 9:16
w is justified by her . . . . . Matt 11:19
Jesus increased in *w* . . . . . Luke 2:52
riches both of the *w* . . . . . Rom 11:33
the gospel, not with *w* . . . . 1 Cor 1:17
Greeks seek after *w* . . . . . 1 Cor 1:22
For the *w* of this world . . . 1 Cor 3:19
not with fleshly *w* . . . . 2 Cor 1:12
now the manifold *w* . . . . . . Eph 3:10
all the treasures of *w* . . . . . Col 2:3
Walk in *w* toward those . . . . Col 4:5
If any of you lacks *w* . . . . James 1:5
power and riches and *w* . . . Rev 5:12
and glory and *w* . . . . Rev 7:12

WISE
great nation is a *w* . . . . . . Deut 4:6
He catches the *w* . . . . Job 5:13
God is *w* in heart and . . . . . Job 9:4
men are not always *w* . . . . Job 32:9
when will you be *w* . . . . . . Ps 94:8
w will observe these . . . . . Ps 107:43
Do not be *w* in your . . . . . Prov 3:7
he who wins souls is *w* . . . Prov 11:30
The *w* in heart will be . . . . Prov 16:21
folly, but he be *w* . . . . . . Prov 26:5
they are exceedingly *w* . . . Prov 30:24
The words of the *w* . . . . . Eccl 12:11
They are *w* to do evil . . . . . Jer 4:22
Therefore be *w* as . . . . . . Matt 10:16
five of them were *w* . . . . . Matt 25:2
barbarians, both to *w* . . . . Rom 1:14
to God, alone *w* . . . . Rom 16:27
Where is the *w* . . . . 1 Cor 1:20
sake, but you are *w* . . . . . 1 Cor 4:10
not as fools but as *w* . . . . . Eph 5:15
are able to make you *w* . . 2 Tim 3:15

WISELY
I will behave *w* . . . . Ps 101:2
who heeds the word *w* . . . Prov 16:20
you do not inquire *w* . . . . . Eccl 7:10

WISER
he was *w* than all men . . . 1 Kin 4:31
w than the birds . . . . Job 35:11
w than my enemies . . . . . Ps 119:98
of God is *w* than men . . . . 1 Cor 1:25

WISH
for me to do what I *w* . . . Matt 20:15
w it were already . . . . Luke 12:49

WISHED
Then he *w* death for . . . . . . Jon 4:8

WITCHCRAFT
is as the sin of *w* . . . . . . 1 Sam 15:23

WITHDRAW
God will not *w* His . . . . Job 9:13
He does not *w* His eyes . . . . Job 36:7
From such *w* yourself . . . . . 1 Tim 6:5

WITHER
also shall not *w* . . . . Ps 1:3
w as the green . . . . Ps 37:2
leaves will not *w* . . . . Ezek 47:12
How did the fig tree *w* . . . Matt 21:20

WITHERS
The grass *w* . . . . Is 40:7
burning heat than it *w* . . . James 1:11
The grass *w* . . . . 1 Pet 1:24

WITHHELD
and your sins have *w* . . . . . Jer 5:25

WITHHOLD
w Your tender mercies . . . . . Ps 40:11
good thing will He *w* . . . . . Ps 84:11
Do not *w* good from . . . . . Prov 3:27
your cloak, do not *w* . . . . Luke 6:29

WITHOUT
having no hope and *w* . . . . Eph 2:12
pray *w* ceasing . . . . 1 Thess 5:17
w controversy . . . . 1 Tim 3:16
w works is dead . . . . James 2:26

WITHSTAND
was I that I could *w* . . . . . Acts 11:17
you may be able to *w* . . . . Eph 6:13

WITHSTOOD
I *w* him to his face . . . . Gal 2:11

WITNESS
see, God is *w* between . . . . Gen 31:50
Surely even now my *w* . . . . Job 16:19
like the faithful *w* . . . . Ps 89:37
w does not lie . . . . Prov 14:5
have given him as a *w* . . . . . Is 55:4
a true and faithful *w* . . . . . Jer 42:5
I will be a swift *w* . . . . Mal 3:5
all the world as a *w* . . . . . Matt 24:14
This man came for a *w* . . . . John 1:7
do not receive Our *w* . . . . John 3:11
"If I bear *w* of . . . . John 5:31
is another who bears *w* . . . John 5:32
But I have a greater *w* . . . . John 5:36
who was bearing *w* . . . . . . Acts 14:3
For you will be His *w* . . . . . Acts 22:15
For God is my *w* . . . . Phil 1:8
are three who bear *w* . . . . 1 John 5:7
If we receive the *w* . . . . . . 1 John 5:9
who bore *w* to the word . . . . Rev 1:2
Christ, the faithful *w* . . . . . Rev 1:5
beheaded for their *w* . . . . . Rev 20:4

WITNESSED
is revealed, being *w* . . . . . Rom 3:21
w the good confession . . . 1 Tim 6:13

WITNESSES
of two or three *w* . . . . Deut 17:6
for Myself faithful *w* . . . . . . Is 8:2
"You are My *w* . . . . Is 43:10
the presence of many *w* . . 1 Tim 6:12
the Holy Spirit also *w* . . . . Heb 10:15
so great a cloud of *w* . . . . . Heb 12:1
give power to my two *w* . . . Rev 11:3

WIVES
Husbands, love your *w* . . . . Eph 5:25
w must be reverent . . . . . 1 Tim 3:11

WIZARDS
who are mediums and *w* . . . . . Is 8:19

WOLF
The *w* and the lamb. . . . . . . Is 65:25
the sheep, sees the *w* . . . . . John 10:12

WOLVES
they are ravenous *w* . . . . . . Matt 7:15
out as lambs among *w* . . . . Luke 10:3
savage *w* will come in . . . . Acts 20:29

WOMAN
she shall be called *W* . . . . . . Gen 2:23
w builds her house. . . . . Prov 14:1
w who fears the Lord. . . . . Prov 31:30
w shall encompass a . . . . . . Jer 31:22
whoever looks at a *w* . . . . . Matt 5:28
"Do you see this *w* . . . . Luke 7:44
Then the *w* of Samaria. . . . . John 4:9
brought to Him a *w* . . . . . . John 8:3
"*W*, behold your . . . . John 19:26
w was full of good . . . . . . Acts 9:36
natural use of the *w* . . . . . . Rom 1:27
a man not to touch a *w* . . . 1 Cor 7:1
w is the glory of man. . . . . 1 Cor 11:7
His Son, born of a *w* . . . . . . Gal 4:4
Let a *w* learn in . . . . 1 Tim 2:11
I do not permit a *w* . . . . 1 Tim 2:12
w being deceived . . . . 1 Tim 2:14
w clothed with the sun . . . . Rev 12:1
the earth helped the *w* . . . . Rev 12:16

WOMB
nations are in your *w* . . . . Gen 25:23
Lord had closed her *w* . . . . 1 Sam 1:5
took Me out of the *w* . . . . . . Ps 22:9
in my mother's *w* . . . . Ps 139:13
formed you from the *w* . . . . Is 44:2
called Me from the *w* . . . . . . Is 49:1
in the *w* I knew you . . . . Jer 1:5
is the fruit of your *w* . . . . . Luke 1:42
"Blessed is the *w* . . . . . . Luke 11:27
from my mother's *w* . . . . . . Gal 1:15

WOMEN
blessed is she among *w* . . . . Judg 5:24
among Your honorable *w* . . . . Ps 45:9
O fairest among *w* . . . . Song 1:8
w rule over them . . . . Is 3:12
new wine the young *w* . . . . Zech 9:17
w will be grinding . . . . . . Matt 24:41
are you among *w* . . . . Luke 1:28
w keep silent in the . . . . . 1 Cor 14:34
admonish the young *w* . . . . Titus 2:4
times, the holy *w* . . . . 1 Pet 3:5
not defiled with *w* . . . . Rev 14:4

WONDER
I have become as a *w* . . . . . . Ps 71:7
marvelous work and a *w* . . . . Is 29:14

WONDERFUL
name, seeing it is *w* . . . . Judg 13:18
Your love to me was *w* . . 2 Sam 1:26
things too *w* for me . . . . . . Job 42:3
Your testimonies are *w* . . . . Ps 119:129
name will be called *W*. . . . . . . Is 9:6
of hosts, who is *w* . . . . Is 28:29
and scribes saw the *w* . . . . Matt 21:15
our own tongues the *w* . . . . Acts 2:11

WONDERFULLY
fearfully and *w* made . . . . . Ps 139:14

WONDERS
w which I will do . . . . Ex 3:20
are the God who does *w* . . . . Ps 77:14
Shall Your *w* be known . . . . . Ps 88:12
who alone does great *w* . . . . Ps 136:4
Egypt with signs and *w* . . . . Jer 32:21
and how mighty His *w* . . . . . Dan 4:3
He works signs and *w* . . . . Dan 6:27

"And I will show *w* . . . . Joel 2:30
and done many *w* . . . . Matt 7:22
signs, and lying *w* . . . . . . 2 Thess 2:9
both with signs and *w* . . . . . Heb 2:4

WONDROUS
and tell of all Your *w* . . . . . . Ps 26:7
w works declare that . . . . Ps 75:1
w works in the land of. . . . . Ps 106:22
for they are a *w*. . . . . Zech 3:8

WONDROUSLY
God, who has dealt *w*. . . . . Joel 2:26

WOOD
precious stones, *w* . . . . 1 Cor 3:12

WOODCUTTERS
but let them be *w*. . . . . Josh 9:21

WOOL
they shall be as *w*. . . . . Is 1:18
head was like pure *w*. . . . . . Dan 7:9
hair were white like *w*. . . . . . Rev 1:14

WORD
w that proceeds. . . . . Deut 8:3
w is very near you. . . . . . . Deut 30:14
w I have hidden . . . . Ps 119:11
w has given me life . . . . . . Ps 119:50
w is a lamp to my feet . . . Ps 119:105
w makes it glad . . . . Prov 12:25
w spoken in due season. . . Prov 15:23
w fitly spoken is. . . . . Prov 25:11
Every *w* of God is pure . . . . Prov 30:5
The Lord sent a *w* . . . . Is 9:8
the *w* of our God . . . . Is 40:8
w has gone out of My . . . . . . Is 45:23
w be that goes forth . . . . Is 55:11
But His *w* was in my . . . . . . Jer 20:9
w will be his oracle . . . . Jer 23:36
w which I speak will . . . . . Ezek 12:28
But only speak a *w* . . . . . . Matt 8:8
for every idle *w* . . . . Matt 12:36
The seed is the *w*. . . . . Luke 8:11
mighty in deed and *w* . . . . Luke 24:19
beginning was the *W* . . . . . . John 1:1
W became flesh and . . . . . John 1:14
if anyone keeps My *w* . . . . . John 8:51
w which you hear is . . . . . John 14:24
Your *w* is truth . . . . John 17:17
and glorified the *w*. . . . . . Acts 13:48
to one is given the *w* . . . . . 1 Cor 12:8
of water by the *w* . . . . Eph 5:26
holding fast the *w*. . . . . Phil 2:16
Let the *w* of Christ. . . . . . . Col 3:16
come to you in *w* only . . . 1 Thess 1:5
in every good *w*. . . . . . . 2 Thess 2:17
by the *w* of His power . . . . . Heb 1:3
w which they heard did. . . . . Heb 4:2
For the *w* of God is . . . . . . Heb 4:12
the implanted *w* . . . . James 1:21
does not stumble in *w* . . . . . James 3:2
through the *w* of God. . . . . 1 Pet 1:23
that by the *w* of God . . . . . 2 Pet 3:5
whoever keeps His *w* . . . . . 1 John 2:5
let us not love in *w* . . . . . . 1 John 3:18
the Father, the *W*. . . . . . . 1 John 5:7
name is called The *W* . . . . . Rev 19:13

WORDS
Give ear to my *W* . . . . Ps 5:1
Let the *w* of my mouth . . . . . Ps 19:14
How sweet are Your *w* . . . Ps 119:103
pay attention to the *w*. . . . . Prov 7:24
The *w* of the wise are . . . . . Eccl 12:11
And I have put My *w*. . . . . . . Is 51:16
Take *w* with you . . . . Hos 14:2
Do not My *w* do good to . . . . Mic 2:7
pass away, but My *w* . . . . Matt 24:35
at the gracious *w* . . . . Luke 4:22
w that I speak to you . . . . . John 6:63

You have the *w* of . . . . John 6:68
And remember the *w*. . . . Acts 20:35
not with wisdom of *w* . . . . . 1 Cor 1:17
those who hear the *w*. . . . . . Rev 1:3
is he who keeps the *w*. . . . . Rev 22:7

WORK
day God ended His *w*. . . . . . Gen 2:2
Moses finished the *w*. . . . . . Ex 40:33
people had a mind to *w* . . . . Neh 4:6
You shall desire the *w* . . . . Job 14:15
for they are all the *w* . . . . Job 34:19
the *w* of Your fingers . . . . Ps 8:3
I hate the *w* of those . . . . . . Ps 101:3
the heavens are the *w* . . . . Ps 102:25
Man goes out to his *w*. . . . Ps 104:23
w is honorable and . . . . Ps 111:3
man deceptive *w* . . . . Prov 11:18
then I saw all the *w* . . . . . . Eccl 8:17
for there is no *w* . . . . Eccl 9:10
God will bring every *w* . . . . Eccl 12:14
that He may do His *w* . . . . . Is 28:21
and all we are the *w* . . . . Is 64:8
him nothing for his *w* . . . . Jer 22:13
and mighty in *w*. . . . . Jer 32:19
For I will *w* a *w*. . . . . Hab 1:5
and said, 'Son, go, *w*. . . . . Matt 21:28
could do no mighty *w* . . . . Mark 6:5
we do, that we may *w* . . . . John 6:28
"This is the *w* of God . . . . . John 6:29
I must *w* the works . . . . John 9:4
w which You have given. . . John 17:4
know that all things *w* . . . . Rom 8:28
He will finish the *w*. . . . . . Rom 9:28
w is no longer *w*. . . . . . . Rom 11:6
Do not destroy the *w* . . . . Rom 14:20
w will become manifest. . . 1 Cor 3:13
Are you not my *w* . . . . 1 Cor 9:1
abounding in the *w* . . . . . 1 Cor 15:58
without ceasing your *w* . . 1 Thess 1:3
every good word and *w* . 2 Thess 2:17
If anyone will not *w* . . . . 2 Thess 3:10
but a doer of the *w* . . . . . James 1:25

WORKED
with one hand they *w* . . . . . Neh 4:17
and wonders God had *w* . . Acts 15:12
which He *w* in Christ . . . . . . Eph 1:20

WORKER
w is worthy of his . . . . . . Matt 10:10
Timothy, my fellow *w* . . . . Rom 16:21
w who does not need. . . . . 2 Tim 2:15

WORKERS
You hate all *w* of. . . . . Ps 5:5
we are God's fellow *w* . . . . 1 Cor 3:9
dogs, beware of evil *w* . . . . . Phil 3:2

WORKING
everywhere, the Lord *w* . . Mark 16:20
My Father has been *w*. . . . John 5:17
according to the *w* . . . . Eph 1:19
through faith in the *w*. . . . . . Col 2:12
manner, not *w* at all. . . . 2 Thess 3:11

WORKMANSHIP
For we are His *w*. . . . . Eph 2:10

WORKS
the wondrous *w* of God . . . . Job 37:14
are Your wonderful *w* . . . . . . Ps 40:5
Come and see the *w* . . . . . . Ps 66:5
how great are Your *w* . . . . . Ps 92:5
manifold are Your *w* . . . . . Ps 104:24
The *w* of the Lord are . . . . . Ps 111:2
w shall praise You . . . . Ps 145:10
and let her own *w* . . . . . . Prov 31:31
"For I know their *w*. . . . . Is 66:18
of whose *w* are truth . . . . . Dan 4:37
show Him greater *w* . . . . . John 5:20
w that I do in My . . . . John 10:25

w that I do he will do . . . . John 14:12
w righteousness . . . . Acts 10:35
might stand, not of w . . . . . Rom 9:11
let us cast off the w . . . . . Rom 13:12
is the same God who w . . 1 Cor 12:6
not justified by the w . . . . . Gal 2:16
Now the w of the flesh . . . . Gal 5:19
the spirit who now w . . . . . . Eph 2:2
not of w, lest anyone . . . . . . Eph 2:9
with the unfruitful w . . . . . Eph 5:11
for it is God who w . . . . Phil 2:13
w they deny Him. . . . . Titus 1:16
zealous for good w . . . . Titus 2:14
repentance from dead w . . . . Heb 6:1
but does not have w . . . . . James 2:14
also justified by w . . . . . . James 2:25
He might destroy the w . . . 1 John 3:8
"I know your w . . . . Rev 2:2
their w follow them . . . . . . Rev 14:13
according to their w . . . . . . Rev 20:12

WORLD
He shall judge the w . . . . Ps 9:8
For the w is Mine . . . . Ps 50:12
w is established . . . . Ps 93:1
The field is the w . . . . . . Matt 13:38
w are more shrewd . . . . . . Luke 16:8
He was in the w. . . . . John 1:10
For God so loved the w . . . John 3:16
His Son into the w . . . . . . John 3:17
the Savior of the w . . . . . John 4:42
w cannot hate you . . . . John 7:7
You are of this w . . . . John 8:23
Look, the w has gone . . . . John 12:19
w will see Me no more. . . . John 14:19
"If the w hates you . . . . . . John 15:18
If you were of the w. . . . . John 15:19
I have overcome the w . . . John 16:33
do not pray for the w . . . . . John 17:9
w has not known You . . . . John 17:25
w may become guilty . . . . . Rom 3:19
be conformed to this w . . . Rom 12:2
things of the w. . . . . 1 Cor 1:27
w is foolishness. . . . . 1 Cor 3:19
w has been crucified . . . . . . Gal 6:14
without God in the w . . . . . Eph 2:12
loved this present w . . . . . 2 Tim 4:10
He has not put the w . . . . . . Heb 2:5
unspotted from the w . . . . James 1:27
w is enmity with God . . . . James 4:4
Do not love the w. . . . . . 1 John 2:15
all that is in the w . . . . . . 1 John 2:16
w is passing away . . . . . . 1 John 2:17
w does not know us . . . . . 1 John 3:1
They are of the w. . . . . . . 1 John 4:5
so are we in this w . . . . . 1 John 4:17
And all the w marveled . . . Rev 13:3

WORLDS
also He made the w. . . . . Heb 1:2

WORM
w should feed sweetly . . . . Job 24:20
But I am a w . . . . Ps 22:6
"Fear not, you w . . . . Is 41:14
their w does not die . . . . Is 66:24
w does not die and the. . . . Mark 9:44

WORMS
flesh is caked with w . . . . . . Job 7:5
you, and w cover you . . . . . Is 14:11
And he was eaten by w . . . Acts 12:23

WORMWOOD
end she is bitter as w . . . . . . Prov 5:4
who turn justice to w . . . . . Amos 5:7
of the star is W . . . . Rev 8:11

WORRY
to you, do not w . . . . Matt 6:25
Therefore do not w . . . . . . Matt 6:31

WORRYING
by w can add one cubit . . . Matt 6:27

WORSE
w than their fathers . . . . Jer 7:26

WORSHIP
I will go yonder and w. . . . . Gen 22:5
He is your Lord, w . . . . Ps 45:11
Oh come, let us w . . . . Ps 95:6
and have come to w Him. . . Matt 2:2
will fall down and w. . . . . . Matt 4:9
And in vain they w. . . . . . Matt 15:9
w what you do not know . . John 4:22
true worshipers will . . . . . John 4:23
the One whom you w . . . . Acts 17:23
w the God of my. . . . . Acts 24:14
false humility and w. . . . . . . Col 2:18
the angels of God w. . . . . . . Heb 1:6
make them come and w. . . . Rev 3:9
w Him who lives . . . . Rev 4:10
w Him who made . . . . Rev 14:7

WORSHIPED
Our fathers w . . . . John 4:20
w Him who lives . . . . Rev 5:14
on their faces and w . . . . . Rev 11:16
w God who sat on the. . . . . Rev 19:4

WORSHIPER
if anyone is a w. . . . . John 9:31

WORTH
and make my speech w . . . Job 24:25
of the wicked is w . . . . . . Prov 10:20

WORTHLESS
looking at w things . . . . . . Ps 119:37
A w person, a wicked man . Prov 6:12
Indeed they are all w . . . . . . Is 41:29

WORTHLESSNESS
long will you love w . . . . Ps 4:2

WORTHY
I am not w of the . . . . Gen 32:10
sandals I am not w . . . . . . Matt 3:11
inquire who in it is w . . . . Matt 10:11
invited were not w . . . . . . Matt 22:8
should do this was w . . . . . Luke 7:4
and I am no longer w . . . . Luke 15:19
present time are not w . . . . Rom 8:18
apostles, who am not w. . . 1 Cor 15:9
to walk w of the calling . . . Eph 4:1
"The laborer is w. . . . . . . 1 Tim 5:18
the world was not w . . . . . Heb 11:38
white, for they are w . . . . . Rev 3:4
"You are w, O Lord . . . . . . Rev 4:11
"W is the Lamb who. . . . . . Rev 5:12

WOUND
I w and I heal . . . . Deut 32:39
My w is incurable . . . . Job 34:6
But God will w the. . . . . . . Ps 68:21
and my w incurable . . . . . . Jer 15:18
and w their weak . . . . 1 Cor 8:12
and his deadly w. . . . . Rev 13:3

WOUNDED
and my heart is w . . . . . . Ps 109:22
and w the serpent . . . . Is 51:9
But He was w for our . . . . . . Is 53:5
there remained only w . . . . Jer 37:10
with which I was w . . . . . . Zech 13:6
to the beast who was w. . . . Rev 13:14

WOUNDING
killed a man for w . . . . Gen 4:23

WOUNDS
and binds up their w. . . . . Ps 147:3
Faithful are the w . . . . Prov 27:6
and bandaged his w . . . . . Luke 10:34

WRANGLINGS
useless w of men of. . . . . . 1 Tim 6:5

WRATH
w has gone out from. . . . . Num 16:46
provoked the LORD to w . . . Deut 9:22
Had I not feared the w . . . Deut 32:27
w kills a foolish . . . . Job 5:2
speak to them in His w . . . . . Ps 2:5
living and burning w . . . . . . Ps 58:9
Surely the w of man. . . . . . . Ps 76:10
Your fierce w has gone. . . . . Ps 88:16
Will Your w burn like . . . . . Ps 89:46
w we are terrified. . . . . Ps 90:7
So I swore in My w. . . . . . . Ps 95:11
in the day of His w. . . . . . Ps 110:5
death is the king's w . . . . Prov 16:14
The king's w is like. . . . . . Prov 19:12
of great w will suffer . . . . Prov 19:19
w is heavier than. . . . . Prov 27:3
W is cruel and anger a . . . . Prov 27:4
w I will give him . . . . Is 10:6
With a little w . . . . Is 54:8
in My w I struck you . . . . . . Is 60:10
I will pour out my w. . . . . . Hos 5:10
w remember mercy . . . . Hab 3:2
you to flee from the w . . . . Matt 3:7
see life, but the w . . . . . . John 3:36
For the w of God is . . . . . . Rom 1:18
up for yourself w. . . . . Rom 2:5
the law brings about w. . . . Rom 4:15
wanting to show His w . . . . Rom 9:22
rather give place to w . . . . Rom 12:19
not only because of w. . . . . Rom 13:5
outbursts of w. . . . . 2 Cor 12:20
nature children of w. . . . . . . Eph 2:3
sun go down on your w. . . . Eph 4:26
Let all bitterness, w. . . . . . . Eph 4:31
delivers us from the w. . . 1 Thess 1:10
w has come upon them . 1 Thess 2:16
holy hands, without w . . . . 1 Tim 2:8
So I swore in My w. . . . . . . Heb 3:11
not fearing the w . . . . Heb 11:27
for the w of man does. . . James 1:20
throne and from the w . . . . Rev 6:16
to you, having great w . . . Rev 12:12
of the wine of the w . . . . . Rev 14:8
winepress of the w. . . . . . . Rev 14:19
for in them the w . . . . Rev 15:1
fierceness of His w . . . . . . Rev 16:19

WRATHFUL
w man stirs up strife . . . . Prov 15:18

WRESTLE
For we do not w . . . . Eph 6:12

WRETCHED
w man that I am. . . . . Rom 7:24
know that you are w. . . . . . Rev 3:17

WRETCHEDNESS
do not let me see my w. . . Num 11:15

WRINKLE
not having spot or w . . . . . Eph 5:27

WRITE
"W these words. . . . . Ex 34:27
w bitter things . . . . Job 13:26
w them on the tablet. . . . . . Prov 7:3
'W this man down as. . . . . Jer 22:30
"W the vision. . . . . Hab 2:2
w them on their hearts. . . . Heb 8:10
their minds I will w. . . . . . Heb 10:16
I had many things to w . . . 3 John 13

WRITING
the w was the w. . . . . Ex 32:16

WRITINGS
do not believe his w . . . . . John 5:47

PHOTO & ILLUSTRATION CREDITS

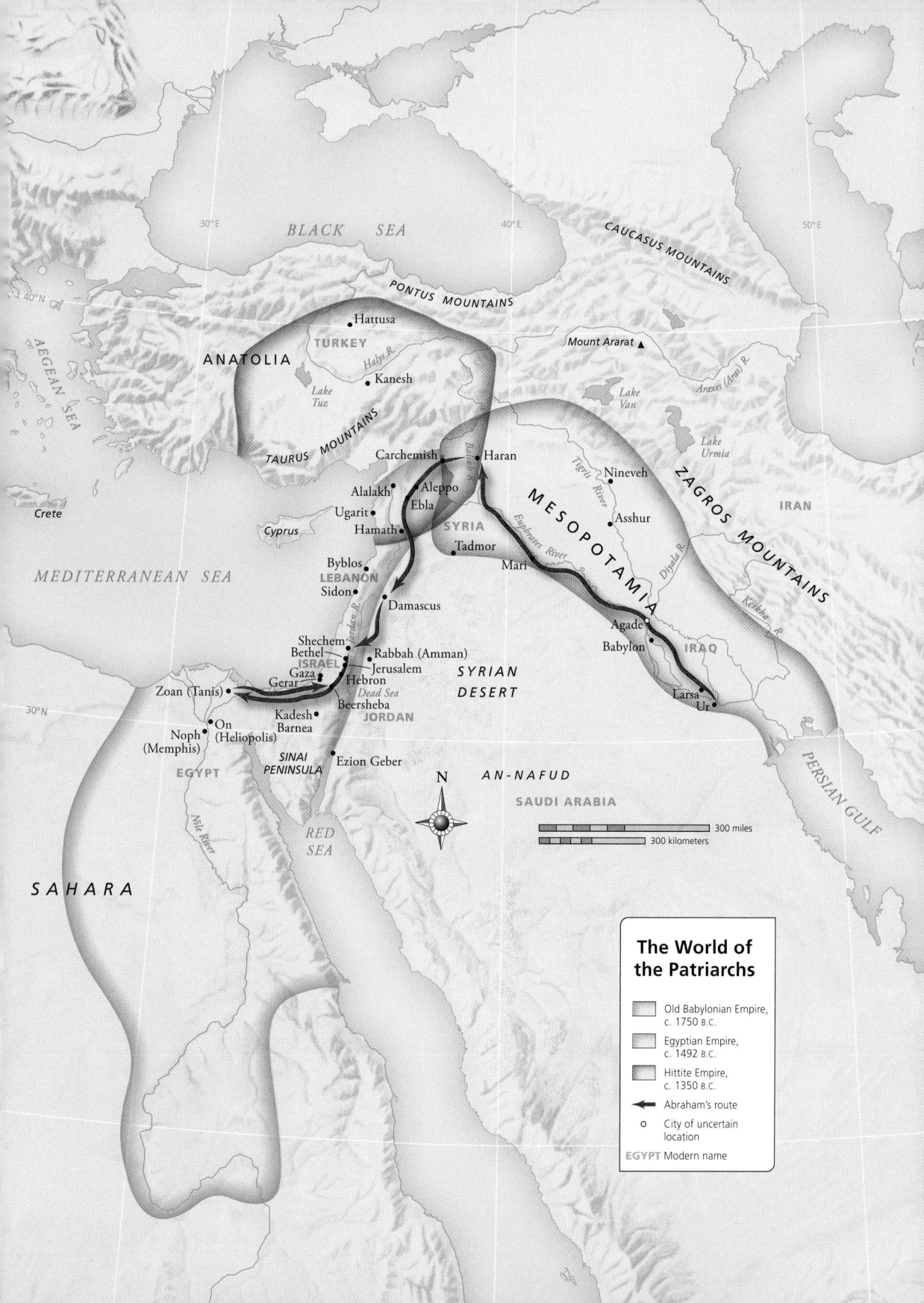

BLACK SEA

30°E   40°E   50°E

CAUCASUS MOUNTAINS

40°N

PONTUS MOUNTAINS

• Hattusa

TURKEY

ANATOLIA

Mount Ararat ▲

Halys R.

• Kanesh

Lake Van

Araxes (Aras) R.

Lake Tuz

TAURUS MOUNTAINS

AEGEAN SEA

Carchemish   • Haran

Balih R.

Nineveh •

ZAGROS MOUNTAINS

Tigris River

MESOPOTAMIA

IRAN

Lake Urmia

Crete

Cyprus

Alalakh   • Aleppo
Ugarit •   Ebla •
          Hamath •

SYRIA

Asshur •

Euphrates River

Diyala R.

Byblos •

Tadmor •

LEBANON
Sidon •

Mari •

Kerkha R.

MEDITERRANEAN SEA

• Damascus

Agade •

Jordan R.

Shechem •
Bethel •
      Gaza •   • Rabbah (Amman)
         • Jerusalem

SYRIAN DESERT

Babylon •

IRAQ

30°N

Zoan (Tanis) •

Gerar •   Hebron •
            Beersheba •

ISRAEL

Dead Sea

JORDAN

Larsa •
    • Ur

Noph
(Memphis)

• On
(Heliopolis)

Kadesh •
Barnea

EGYPT

SINAI
PENINSULA

• Ezion Geber

N

AN-NAFUD

SAUDI ARABIA

PERSIAN GULF

RED SEA

SAHARA

Nile River

300 miles
300 kilometers

The World of the Patriarchs

Old Babylonian Empire,
c. 1750 B.C.

Egyptian Empire,
c. 1492 B.C.

Hittite Empire,
c. 1350 B.C.

← Abraham's route

○ City of uncertain
location

EGYPT Modern name

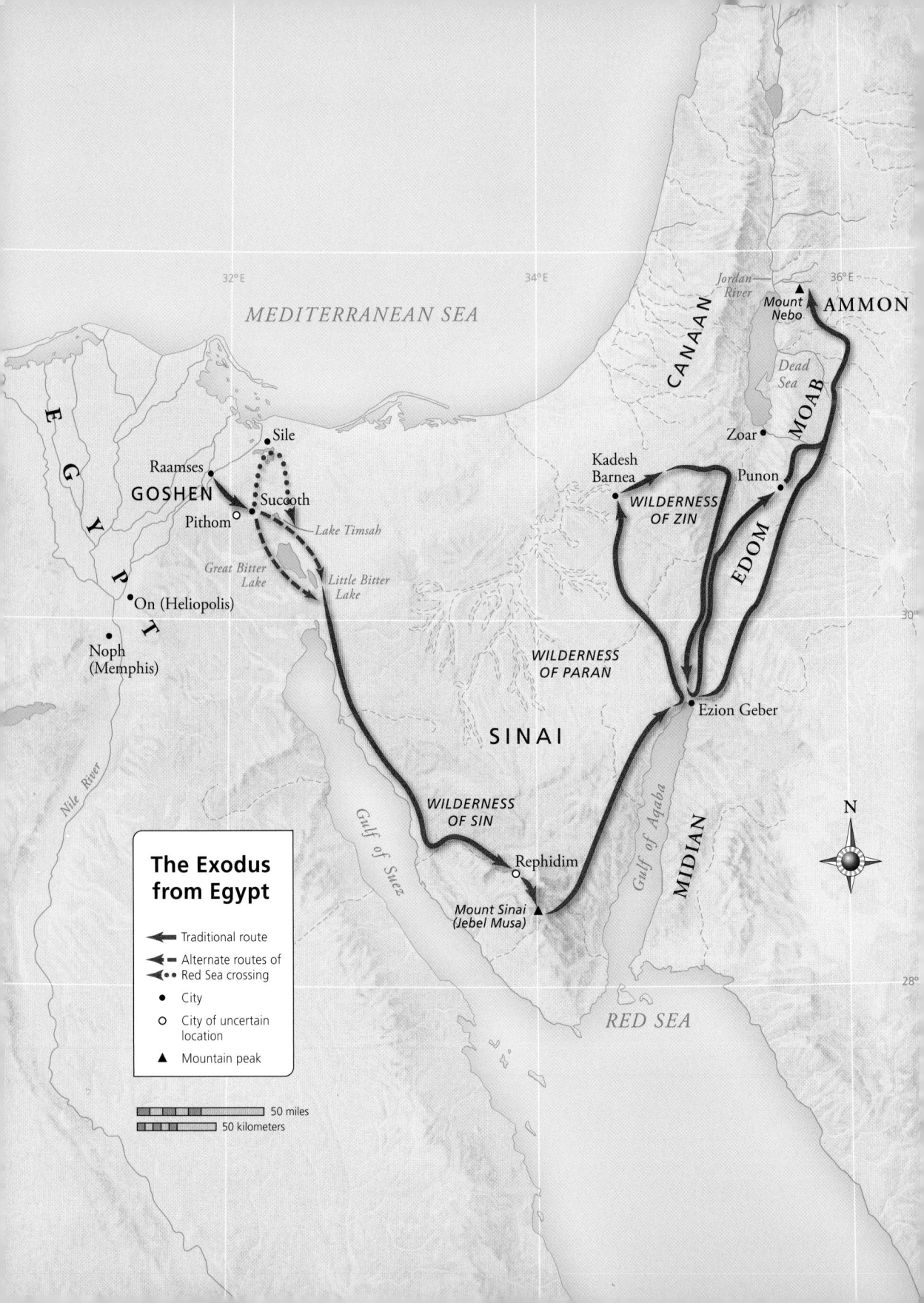

MEDITERRANEAN SEA

32°E   34°E   36°E

Jordan River
Mount Nebo ▲   AMMON

CANAAN

Dead Sea

EGYPT

GOSHEN
Sile
Raamses
Pithom
Succoth

Lake Timsah

Great Bitter Lake   *Little Bitter Lake*

On (Heliopolis)

Noph (Memphis)

Nile River

Gulf of Suez

Kadesh Barnea

WILDERNESS OF ZIN

Zoar

MOAB

Punon

EDOM

WILDERNESS OF PARAN

Ezion Geber

SINAI

WILDERNESS OF SIN

Rephidim

Mount Sinai (Jebel Musa) ▲

Gulf of Aqaba

MIDIAN

N

RED SEA

30°

28°

The Exodus from Egypt

⬅ Traditional route
⬅--- Alternate routes of
⬅••• Red Sea crossing
• City
○ City of uncertain location
▲ Mountain peak

50 miles
50 kilometers

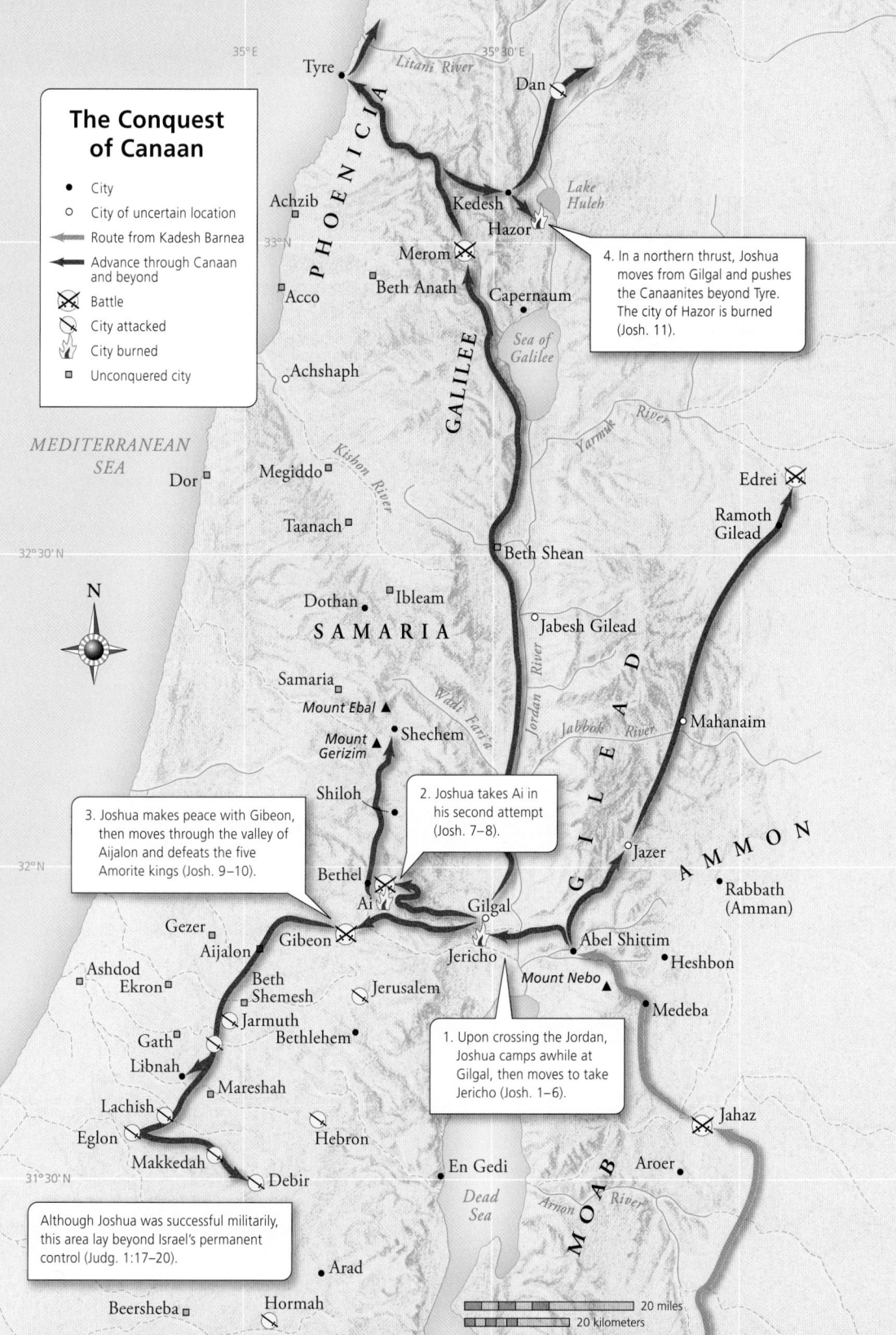

The Conquest of Canaan

- ● City
- ○ City of uncertain location
- ⬅ Route from Kadesh Barnea
- ⬅ Advance through Canaan and beyond
- ☒ Battle
- City attacked
- City burned
- ▪ Unconquered city

35°E

Tyre

Litani River

35°30'E

Dan

PHOENICIA

Achzib

Kedesh

Lake Huleh

Hazor

Merom ☒

4. In a northern thrust, Joshua moves from Gilgal and pushes the Canaanites beyond Tyre. The city of Hazor is burned (Josh. 11).

33°N

Acco

Beth Anath

Capernaum

Achshaph

GALILEE

Sea of Galilee

Yarmuk River

MEDITERRANEAN SEA

Dor

Megiddo

Kishon River

Taanach

Beth Shean

Edrei ☒

Ramoth Gilead

32°30'N

N

Dothan

Ibleam

SAMARIA

Jabesh Gilead

Samaria

Mount Ebal ▲

Wadi Fariʿa

Shechem

Mount Gerizim ▲

Shiloh

Jordan River

Jabbok River

Mahanaim

GILEAD

3. Joshua makes peace with Gibeon, then moves through the valley of Aijalon and defeats the five Amorite kings (Josh. 9–10).

2. Joshua takes Ai in his second attempt (Josh. 7–8).

Jazer

AMMON

Rabbath (Amman)

32°N

Bethel

Ai

Gilgal

Gibeon

Jericho

Abel Shittim

Heshbon

Gezer

Aijalon

Jerusalem

Mount Nebo ▲

Ashdod

Ekron

Beth Shemesh

Medeba

Jarmuth

Bethlehem

Gath

Libnah

Mareshah

1. Upon crossing the Jordan, Joshua camps awhile at Gilgal, then moves to take Jericho (Josh. 1–6).

Lachish

Eglon

Makkedah

Debir

Hebron

En Gedi

Jahaz ☒

Aroer

MOAB

Although Joshua was successful militarily, this area lay beyond Israel's permanent control (Judg. 1:17–20).

31°30'N

Arnon River

Dead Sea

Arad

Beersheba

Hormah

20 miles

20 kilometers

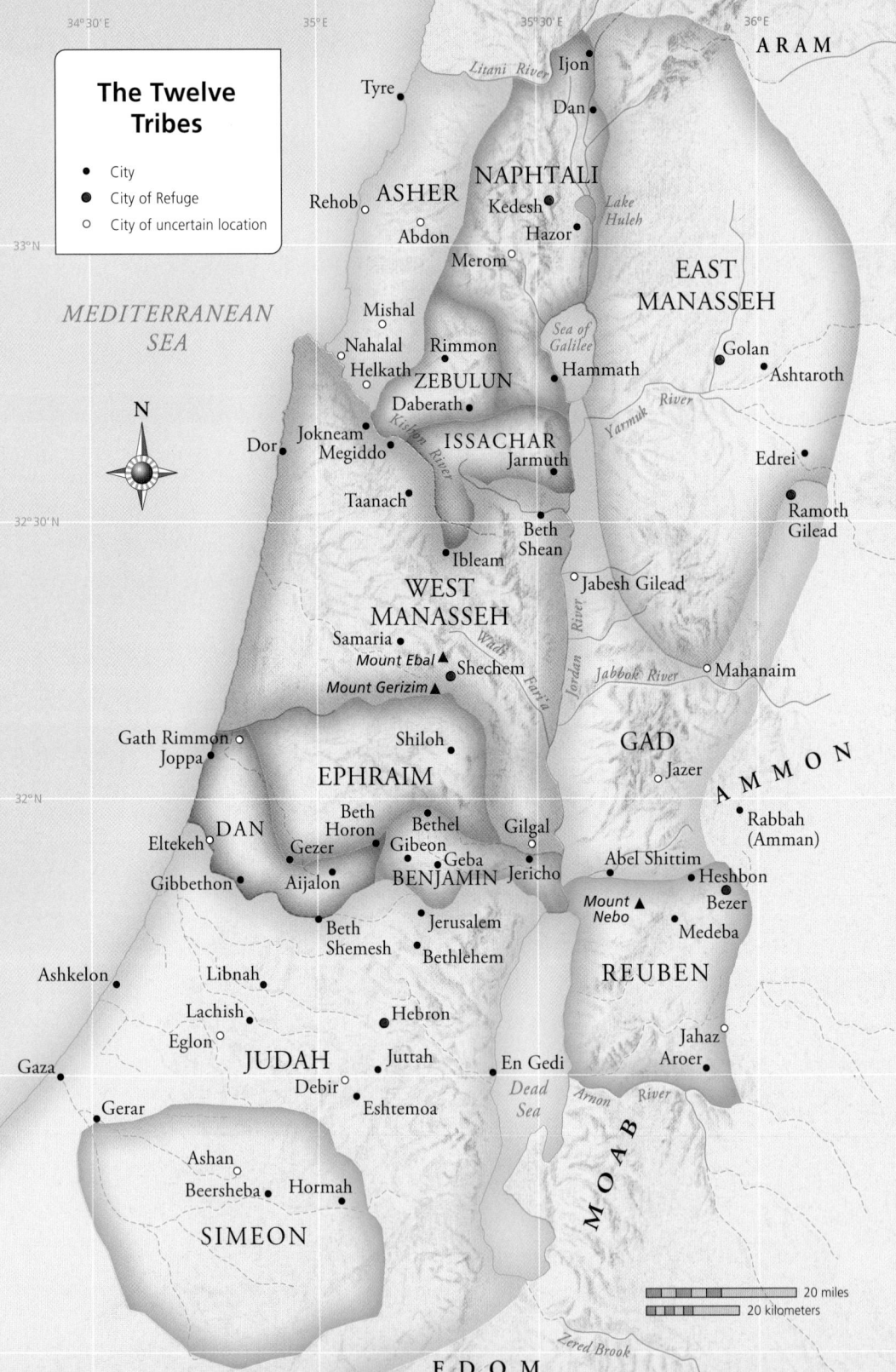

The Twelve Tribes

- ● City
- ⬤ City of Refuge
- ○ City of uncertain location

ARAM

Litani River

Tyre

Ijon

Dan

NAPHTALI

Rehob

ASHER

Kedesh

Abdon

Hazor

Merom

Lake Huleh

EAST MANASSEH

MEDITERRANEAN SEA

Mishal

Nahalal

Rimmon

Helkath

ZEBULUN

Daberath

Sea of Galilee

Hammath

Golan

Ashtaroth

Yarmuk River

N

Dor

Jokneam

Megiddo

Kishon River

ISSACHAR

Jarmuth

Edrei

Ramoth Gilead

Taanach

Beth Shean

Ibleam

WEST MANASSEH

Jabesh Gilead

Wadi Farah

Samaria

Mount Ebal ▲

Shechem

Mount Gerizim ▲

Jordan River

Jabbok River

Mahanaim

GAD

Gath Rimmon

Joppa

Shiloh

EPHRAIM

Jazer

AMMON

Rabbah (Amman)

Eltekeh

DAN

Beth Horon

Gezer

Bethel

Gibeon

Gilgal

Geba

Abel Shittim

Heshbon

Gibbethon

Aijalon

BENJAMIN

Jericho

Mount Nebo ▲

Bezer

Medeba

Beth Shemesh

Jerusalem

Bethlehem

REUBEN

Ashkelon

Libnah

Lachish

Hebron

Eglon

Juttah

En Gedi

Jahaz

Aroer

Gaza

JUDAH

Debir

Eshtemoa

Dead Sea

Arnon River

Gerar

M O A B

Ashan

Beersheba

Hormah

SIMEON

20 miles

20 kilometers

Zered Brook

E D O M

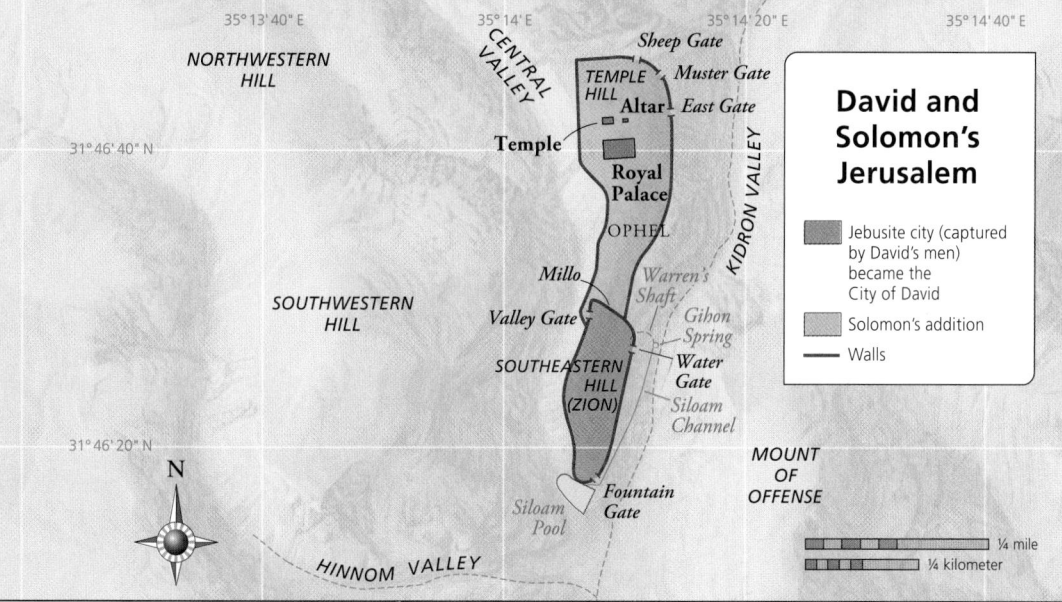

David and Solomon's Jerusalem

NORTHWESTERN HILL

CENTRAL VALLEY

35° 13' 40" E
35° 14' E
35° 14' 20" E
35° 14' 40" E

31° 46' 40" N
31° 46' 20" N

TEMPLE HILL

Sheep Gate
Muster Gate
East Gate

Altar

Temple

Royal Palace

OPHEL

KIDRON VALLEY

SOUTHWESTERN HILL

Millo

Warren's Shaft

Gihon Spring

Valley Gate

SOUTHEASTERN HILL (ZION)

Water Gate

Siloam Channel

Siloam Pool

Fountain Gate

MOUNT OF OFFENSE

N

HINNOM VALLEY

¼ mile
¼ kilometer

Legend:
- Jebusite city (captured by David's men) became the City of David
- Solomon's addition
- Walls

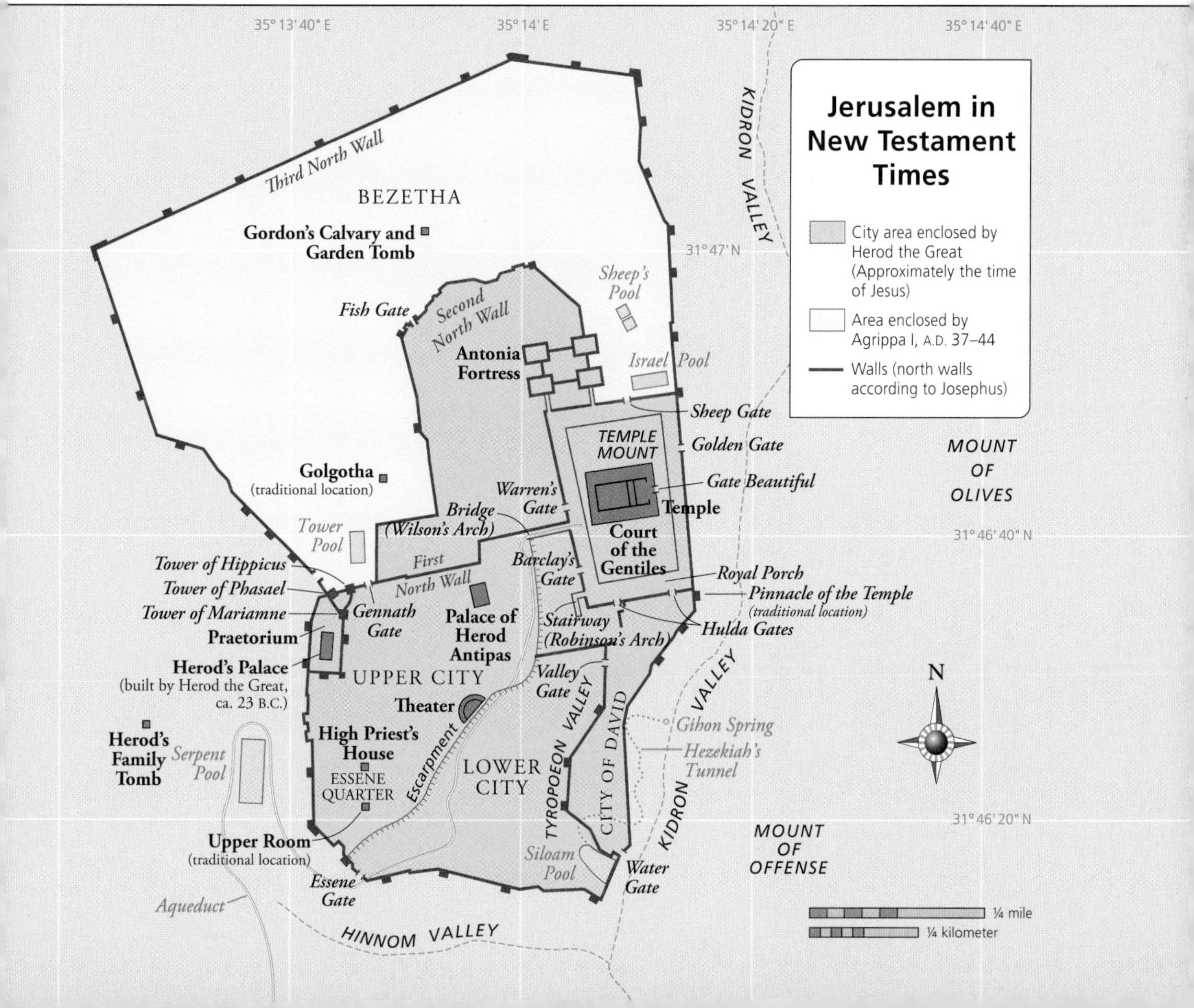

Jerusalem in New Testament Times

35° 13' 40" E
35° 14' E
35° 14' 20" E
35° 14' 40" E

31° 47' N
31° 46' 40" N
31° 46' 20" N

Third North Wall

BEZETHA

Gordon's Calvary and Garden Tomb

Fish Gate

Second North Wall

Sheep's Pool

Antonia Fortress

Israel Pool

Sheep Gate
Golden Gate

TEMPLE MOUNT

Golgotha (traditional location)

Warren's Gate

Gate Beautiful

Temple

Bridge (Wilson's Arch)

Tower Pool

First North Wall

Court of the Gentiles

Barclay's Gate

Royal Porch

Tower of Hippicus
Tower of Phasael
Tower of Mariamne
Praetorium

Gennath Gate

Palace of Herod Antipas

Stairway (Robinson's Arch)

Pinnacle of the Temple (traditional location)

Hulda Gates

Herod's Palace (built by Herod the Great, ca. 23 B.C.)

UPPER CITY

Valley Gate

Herod's Family Tomb

Serpent Pool

Theater

High Priest's House

ESSENE QUARTER

Escarpment

LOWER CITY

TYROPOEON VALLEY

CITY OF DAVID

Gihon Spring

Hezekiah's Tunnel

KIDRON VALLEY

MOUNT OF OLIVES

N

MOUNT OF OFFENSE

Upper Room (traditional location)

Aqueduct

Essene Gate

Siloam Pool

Water Gate

HINNOM VALLEY

¼ mile
¼ kilometer

Legend:
- City area enclosed by Herod the Great (Approximately the time of Jesus)
- Area enclosed by Agrippa I, A.D. 37–44
- Walls (north walls according to Josephus)

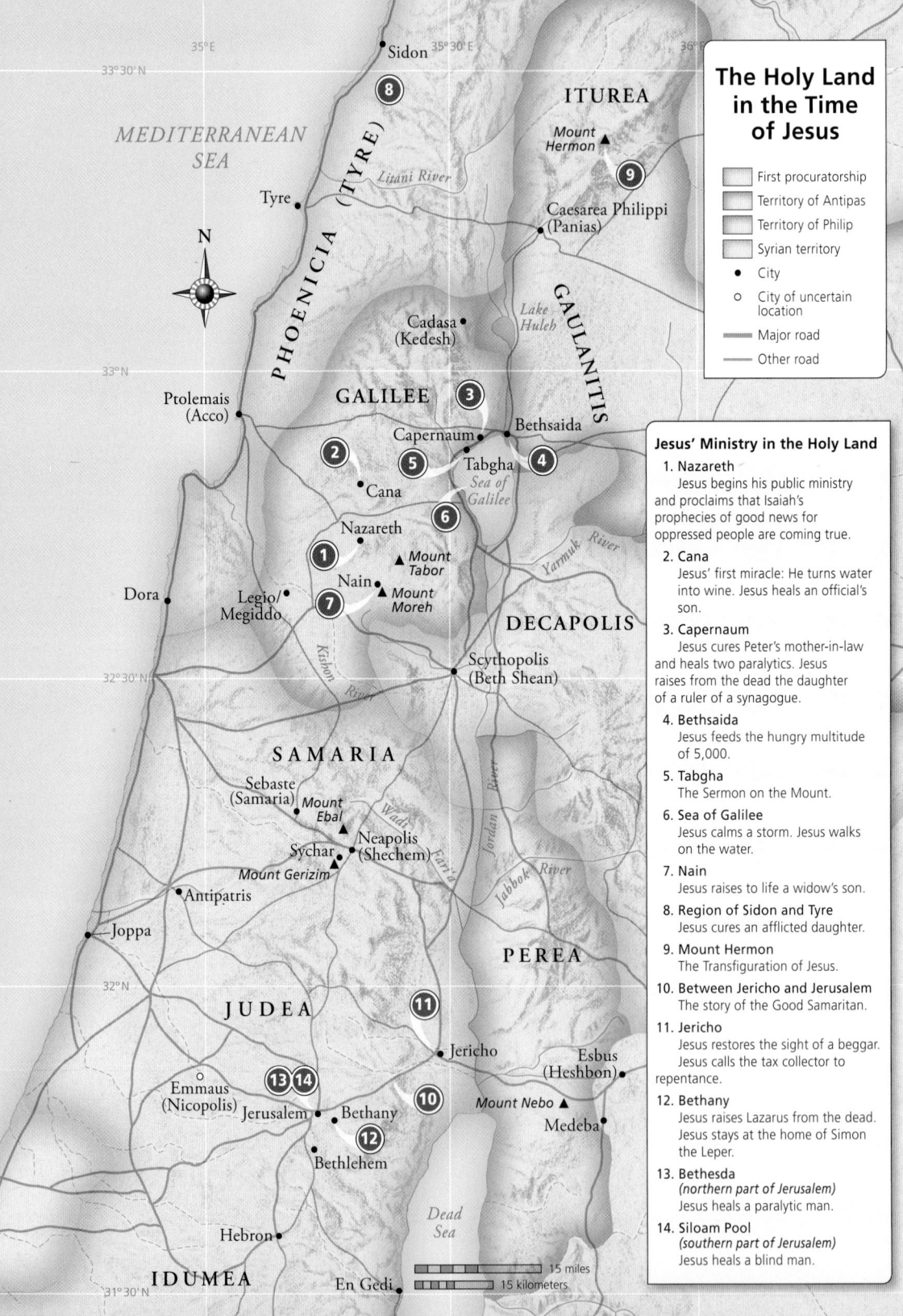

The Holy Land in the Time of Jesus

- First procuratorship
- Territory of Antipas
- Territory of Philip
- Syrian territory
- • City
- ○ City of uncertain location
- Major road
- Other road

Jesus' Ministry in the Holy Land

1. Nazareth
Jesus begins his public ministry and proclaims that Isaiah's prophecies of good news for oppressed people are coming true.

2. Cana
Jesus' first miracle: He turns water into wine. Jesus heals an official's son.

3. Capernaum
Jesus cures Peter's mother-in-law and heals two paralytics. Jesus raises from the dead the daughter of a ruler of a synagogue.

4. Bethsaida
Jesus feeds the hungry multitude of 5,000.

5. Tabgha
The Sermon on the Mount.

6. Sea of Galilee
Jesus calms a storm. Jesus walks on the water.

7. Nain
Jesus raises to life a widow's son.

8. Region of Sidon and Tyre
Jesus cures an afflicted daughter.

9. Mount Hermon
The Transfiguration of Jesus.

10. Between Jericho and Jerusalem
The story of the Good Samaritan.

11. Jericho
Jesus restores the sight of a beggar. Jesus calls the tax collector to repentance.

12. Bethany
Jesus raises Lazarus from the dead. Jesus stays at the home of Simon the Leper.

13. Bethesda
(northern part of Jerusalem)
Jesus heals a paralytic man.

14. Siloam Pool
(southern part of Jerusalem)
Jesus heals a blind man.

MEDITERRANEAN SEA

Sidon
Tyre
PHOENICIA (TYRE)
Litani River
ITUREA
Mount Hermon
Caesarea Philippi (Panias)
GAULANITIS
Ptolemais (Acco)
Cadasa (Kedesh)
Lake Huleh
GALILEE
Capernaum
Bethsaida
Cana
Tabgha
Sea of Galilee
Nazareth
Mount Tabor
Nain
Mount Moreh
Legio/ Megiddo
Dora
Yarmuk River
DECAPOLIS
Kishon River
Scythopolis (Beth Shean)
SAMARIA
Sebaste (Samaria)
Mount Ebal
Neapolis (Shechem)
Sychar
Mount Gerizim
Wadi Fari'a
Jordan River
Jabbok River
Antipatris
Joppa
PEREA
Esbus (Heshbon)
Jericho
Mount Nebo
Medeba
JUDEA
Emmaus (Nicopolis)
Jerusalem
Bethany
Bethlehem
Hebron
Dead Sea
IDUMEA
En Gedi

15 miles
15 kilometers

N

35°E   35°30'E   36°
33°30'N
33°N
32°30'N
32°N
31°30'N

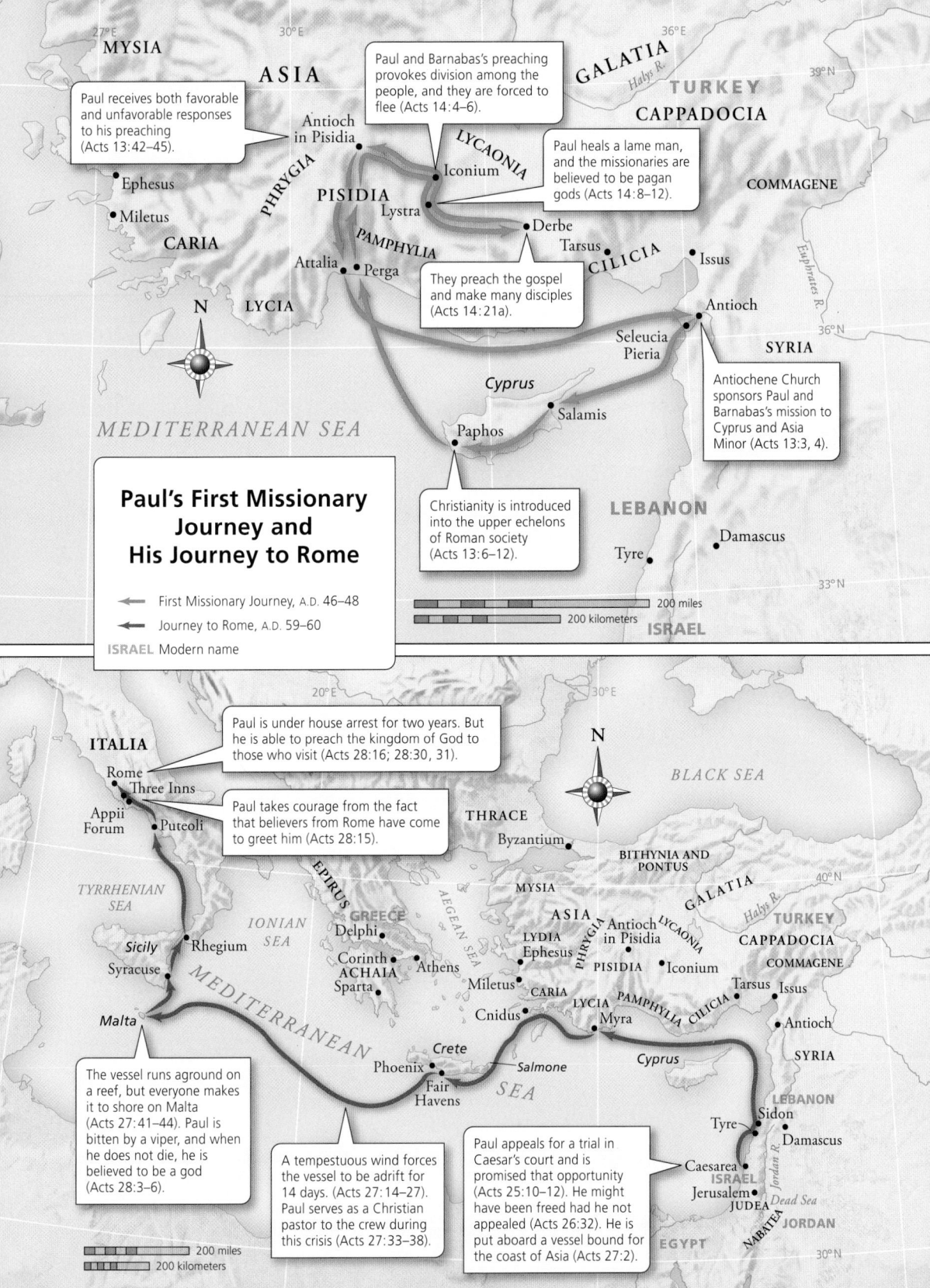

Paul's First Missionary Journey and His Journey to Rome

First Missionary Journey, A.D. 46–48
Journey to Rome, A.D. 59–60
ISRAEL Modern name

Paul receives both favorable and unfavorable responses to his preaching (Acts 13:42–45).

Paul and Barnabas's preaching provokes division among the people, and they are forced to flee (Acts 14:4–6).

Paul heals a lame man, and the missionaries are believed to be pagan gods (Acts 14:8–12).

They preach the gospel and make many disciples (Acts 14:21a).

Antiochene Church sponsors Paul and Barnabas's mission to Cyprus and Asia Minor (Acts 13:3, 4).

Christianity is introduced into the upper echelons of Roman society (Acts 13:6–12).

Paul is under house arrest for two years. But he is able to preach the kingdom of God to those who visit (Acts 28:16; 28:30, 31).

Paul takes courage from the fact that believers from Rome have come to greet him (Acts 28:15).

The vessel runs aground on a reef, but everyone makes it to shore on Malta (Acts 27:41–44). Paul is bitten by a viper, and when he does not die, he is believed to be a god (Acts 28:3–6).

A tempestuous wind forces the vessel to be adrift for 14 days. (Acts 27:14–27). Paul serves as a Christian pastor to the crew during this crisis (Acts 27:33–38).

Paul appeals for a trial in Caesar's court and is promised that opportunity (Acts 25:10–12). He might have been freed had he not appealed (Acts 26:32). He is put aboard a vessel bound for the coast of Asia (Acts 27:2).

200 miles
200 kilometers

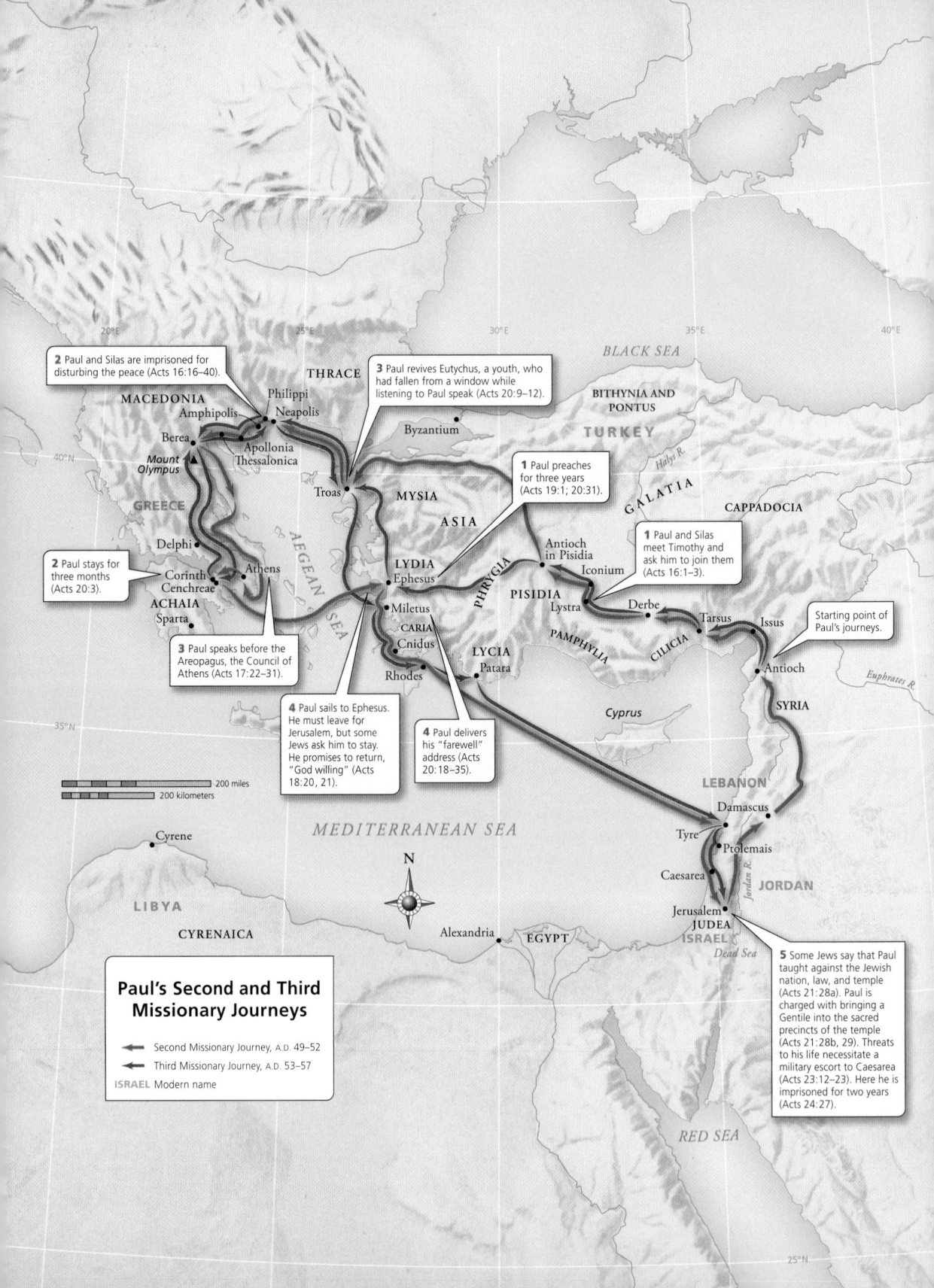

Paul's Second and Third Missionary Journeys

Second Missionary Journey, A.D. 49–52
Third Missionary Journey, A.D. 53–57
ISRAEL Modern name

200 miles
200 kilometers

2 Paul and Silas are imprisoned for disturbing the peace (Acts 16:16–40).

3 Paul revives Eutychus, a youth, who had fallen from a window while listening to Paul speak (Acts 20:9–12).

1 Paul preaches for three years (Acts 19:1; 20:31).

1 Paul and Silas meet Timothy and ask him to join them (Acts 16:1–3).

1 Paul and Silas meet Timothy and ask him to join them (Acts 16:1–3).

Starting point of Paul's journeys.

2 Paul stays for three months (Acts 20:3).

3 Paul speaks before the Areopagus, the Council of Athens (Acts 17:22–31).

4 Paul sails to Ephesus. He must leave for Jerusalem, but some Jews ask him to stay. He promises to return, "God willing" (Acts 18:20, 21).

4 Paul delivers his "farewell" address (Acts 20:18–35).

5 Some Jews say that Paul taught against the Jewish nation, law, and temple (Acts 21:28a). Paul is charged with bringing a Gentile into the sacred precincts of the temple (Acts 21:28b, 29). Threats to his life necessitate a military escort to Caesarea (Acts 23:12–23). Here he is imprisoned for two years (Acts 24:27).

BLACK SEA
THRACE
MACEDONIA
Philippi
Neapolis
Amphipolis
Berea
Mount Olympus
Apollonia
Thessalonica
Byzantium
BITHYNIA AND PONTUS
TURKEY
GALATIA
Holy R.
CAPPADOCIA
GREECE
Troas
MYSIA
ASIA
Delphi
AEGEAN SEA
LYDIA
Ephesus
PHRYGIA
Antioch in Pisidia
Iconium
PISIDIA
Lystra
Derbe
Tarsus
Issus
Corinth
Cenchreae
Athens
ACHAIA
Sparta
Miletus
CARIA
Cnidus
LYCIA
Patara
Rhodes
PAMPHYLIA
CILICIA
Antioch
SYRIA
Euphrates R.
Cyprus
MEDITERRANEAN SEA
LEBANON
Damascus
Tyre
Ptolemais
Caesarea
JORDAN
Jerusalem
JUDEA
ISRAEL
Jordan R.
Dead Sea
Cyrene
LIBYA
CYRENAICA
Alexandria
EGYPT
RED SEA

N